POPULATION ABSTRACT

of the

UNITED STATES

Compiled and Edited by

John L. Andriot

Volume 1. Tables

ANDRIOT ASSOCIATES
McLean, Virginia

ANDRIOT ASSOCIATES

Box 195

McLean, Virginia   22101

FOREWORD

Population Abstract of the United States is being published as a companion volume to the *Township Atlas of the United States* to provide, in a single source, all available historical totals for the 50 States, 3,064 counties, and 2,217 incorporated places with a 1980 population of 10,000 or more.

Each State section contains a brief history of the formation of the State; a map and index showing names and locations of counties; historical population totals for the State, counties, and cities from 1980 back to the earliest census; and a comparative table showing the 1970 and 1980 population for all minor civil divisions for each county.

Volume 1 of the *Population Abstract* contains the tables, while Volume 2 contains the index of over 70,000 entries. This is a complete index to the populated places published in the *1980 Census of Population, Volume 1, Characteristics of the Population, Chapters A, Number of Inhabitants*, plus over 20,000 names of Minor Civil Divisions not included in the Bureau of the Census 1980 reports.

A new feautre has been added to this enlarged and revised edition—a listing of all counties and cities shown historically in Volume 1, but this time by rank for each State and for the United States. This feature will provide relative comparisons for counties and cities of approximately the same size, either within the State or for the entire United States area.

Indexes and maps to counties, minor civil divisions, incorporated places, and unincorporated places with a 1970 population of 1,000 or more, can be found in the companion volume, *Township Atlas of the United States*, published in 1979 by Andriot Associates.

Note:—The tables showing 1970 and 1980 population for minor civil divisions were reproduced directly from the Bureau of the Census reports. The footnote references to county entries are not applicable in this volume since the voluminous notes have not been included. Please disregard the numbered references.

Volume 1. Tables

United States Totals 1790—1980

Year	Total
1790	3,929,214
1800	5,308,483
1810	7,239,881
1820	9,638,453
1830	12,866,020
1840	17,069,453
1850	23,191,876
1860	31,443,321
1870	38,558,371
1880	50,189,209
1890	62,979,766
1900	76,212,168
1910	92,228,496
1920	106,021,537
1930	123,202,624
1940	132,164,569
1950	151,325,798
1960	179,323,175
1970	203,211,926
1980	224,454,272*

(*) This 1980 total was taken from the individual State totals published in the Chapters A of the *1980 Census of Population* reports. Correction pages of minor changes have been included in each State section when applicable.

ALABAMA

Alabama takes its name from an Indian tribe which at one time lived in that region. The name probably means "glade" or "thicket cleared of trees."

The territory now constituting Alabama was first explored in 1540 by the Spaniard, De Soto, who passed through it on his way from Florida to the Mississippi. The first permanent settlement was made by the French on Mobile Bay in 1702, and was removed to the present site of Mobile in 1711.

Toward the close of the seventeenth century France asserted its title to this region, basing its claim on the discoveries of Marquette and Joliet, who descended the Mississippi to the Arkansas in 1673, and of La Salle, who sailed down the Mississippi to its mouth in 1682. England, too, claimed the region north of the Gulf of Mexico, and the territory now forming Alabama was included wholly or in part by the Carolina charters of 1663 and 1665 and by the Georgia charter of 1732.

In 1763 the territory now forming Alabama was ceded by France to Great Britain. In the same year the province of Florida was transferred to Great Britain by Spain and not long afterwards was divided into East and West Florida. West Florida was extended westward to the Mississippi and northward to the latitude of the mouth of the Yazoo (about 32°30'), and thus included the southern part of the Alabama region. At the close of the Revolution all the present area of Alabama except that portion lying south of the thirty-first parallel was ceded by Great Britain to the United States. The Floridas were transferred by Great Britain to Spain at the same time, and for more than a decade the title to what is now southern Alabama was in dispute between the United States and Spain. In 1795, however, the latter country relinquished its claims to the territory north of the thirty-first parallel, and three years later this territory was organized as Mississippi territory.

In 1787 a narrow strip in the northern part of the present state of Alabama was ceded by South Carolina to the United States and a few years later was organized as part of the southwest territory. The region between this territory and Mississippi territory continued in the possession of Georgia until 1802, when it was ceded to the National Government. Two years later the limits of Mississippi territory were extended so as to include all the present state of Alabama except the small area lying south of the thirty-first parallel. This area was in dispute between the United States and Spain after the Louisiana purchase in 1803, and during the War of 1812 was taken from Spain and added to Mississippi territory. Spain, however, did not formally relinquish its claim until the Florida cession in 1819.

Alabama, with boundaries as at present, was organized as a territory in March, 1817, and became a state in December, 1819.

COUNTY LOCATION INDEX

Autauga	D-4	Elmore	D-4	Montgomery	E-4
Baldwin	G-2	Escambia	F-3	Morgan	B-3
Barbour	E-5	Etowah	B-4	Perry	D-3
Bibb	D-3	Fayette	C-2	Pickens	C-2
Blount	C-4	Franklin	B-2	Pike	F-5
Bullock	E-5	Geneva	F-5	Randolph	C-5
Butler	F-4	Greene	D-2	Russell	E-5
Calhoun	C-5	Hale	D-3	St. Clair	C-4
Chambers	D-5	Henry	F-5	Shelby	D-4
Cherokee	B-5	Houston	F-5	Sumter	D-2
Chilton	D-4	Jackson	A-4	Talladega	C-4
Choctaw	E-2	Jefferson	C-3	Tallapoosa	D-5
Clarke	F-2	Lamar	C-2	Tuscaloosa	C-3
Clay	C-5	Lauderdale	A-3	Walker	C-3
Cleburne	C-5	Lawrence	B-3	Washington	F-2
Coffee	F-4	Lee	D-5	Wilcox	E-3
Colbert	B-2	Limestone	A-3	Winston	B-3
Conecuh	F-3	Lowndes	E-4		
Coosa	D-4	Macon	E-5		
Covington	F-4	Madison	A-4		
Crenshaw	F-4	Marengo	E-2		
Cullman	B-3	Marion	B-2		
Dale	F-5	Marshall	B-4		
Dallas	E-3	Mobile	G-2		
De Kalb	B-5	Monroe	F-3		

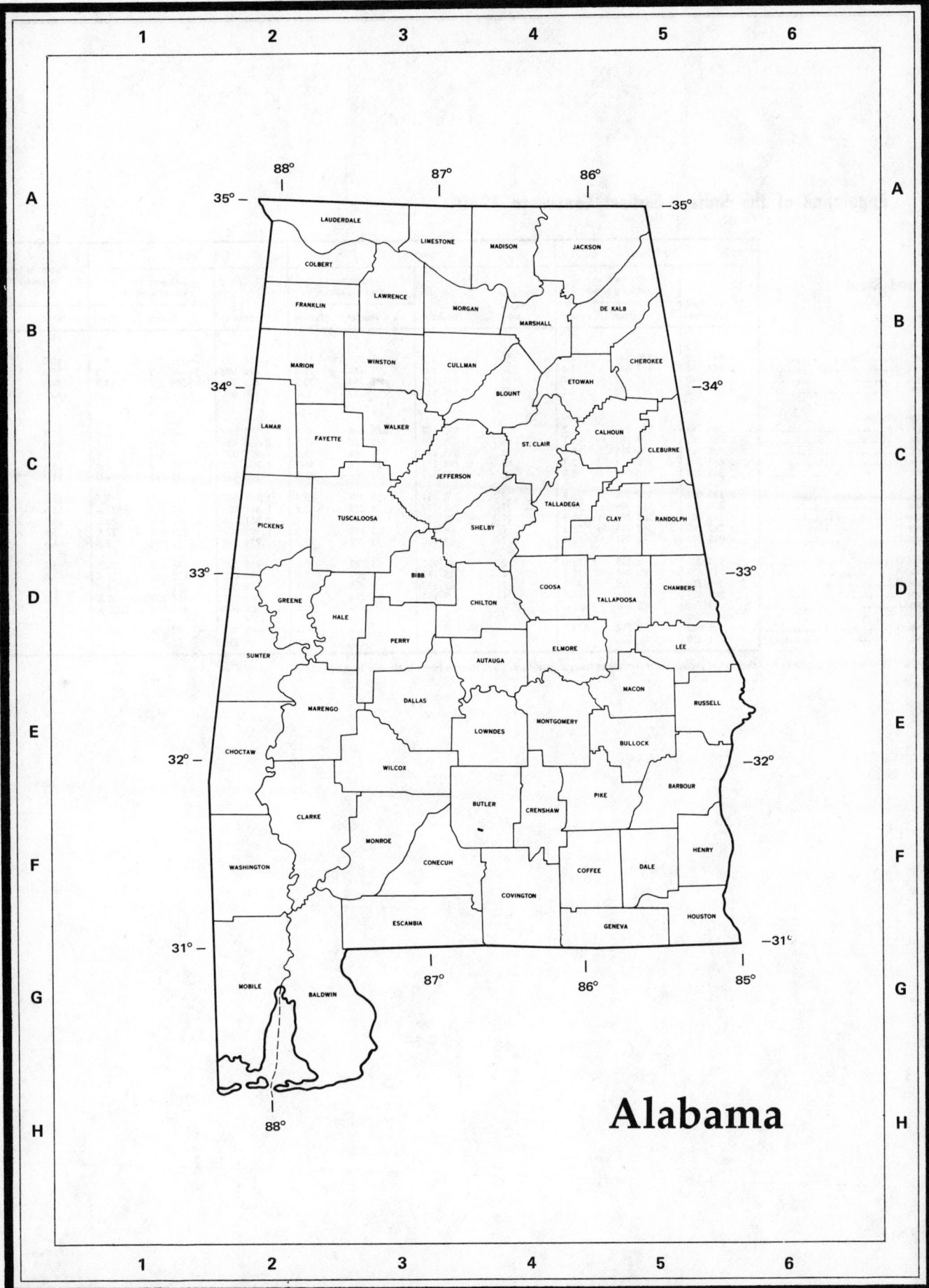

Alabama

Population of the State: Earliest Census to 1980

Urban and Rural

| | The State | | | Urban | | | | Rural | | | Percent of total population | |
	Total population	Change from preceding census Number	Percent	Places of 2,500 or more	Population	Change from preceding census Number	Percent	Population	Change from preceding census Number	Percent	Urban	Rural
Current urban definition:												
1980 (Apr. 1)	3 893 888	449 534	13.1	150	2 337 713	320 228	15.9	1 556 175	129 495	9.1	60.0	40.0
1970 (Apr. 1)	3 444 354	177 614	5.4	123	2 017 485	225 764	12.6	1 426 680	−48 339	−3.3	58.6	41.4
1960 (Apr. 1)	3 266 740	204 997	6.7	109	1 791 721	450 784	33.6	1 475 019	−245 787	−14.3	54.8	45.2
1950 (Apr. 1)	3 061 743	228 782	8.1	85	1 340 937	...	...	1 720 806	...	...	43.8	56.2
Previous urban definition:												
1960 (Apr. 1)	3 266 740	204 997	6.7	106	1 696 657	468 448	38.1	1 570 083	−263 451	−14.4	51.9	48.1
1950 (Apr. 1)	3 061 743	228 782	8.1	76	1 228 209	372 268	43.5	1 833 534	−143 486	−7.3	40.1	59.9
1940 (Apr. 1)	2 832 961	186 713	7.1	59	855 941	111 668	15.0	1 977 020	75 045	3.9	30.2	69.8
1930 (Apr. 1)	2 646 248	298 074	12.7	53	744 273	234 956	46.1	1 901 975	63 118	3.4	28.1	71.9
1920 (Jan. 1)	2 348 174	210 081	9.8	39	509 317	138 886	37.5	1 838 857	71 195	4.0	21.7	78.3
1910 (Apr. 15)	2 138 093	309 396	16.9	28	370 431	153 717	70.9	1 767 662	155 679	9.7	17.3	82.7
1900 (June 1)	1 828 697	315 296	20.8	27	216 714	64 479	42.4	1 611 983	250 817	18.4	11.9	88.1
1890 (June 1)	1 513 401	250 896	19.9	19	152 235	83 717	122.2	1 361 166	167 179	14.0	10.1	89.9
1880 (June 1)	1 262 505	265 513	26.6	7	68 518	5 818	9.3	1 193 987	259 695	27.8	5.4	94.6
1870 (June 1)	996 992	32 791	3.4	7	62 700	13 799	28.2	934 292	18 992	2.1	6.3	93.7
1860 (June 1)	964 201	192 578	25.0	5	48 901	13 722	39.0	915 300	178 856	24.3	5.1	94.9
1850 (June 1)	771 623	180 867	30.6	4	35 179	22 507	177.6	736 444	158 360	27.4	4.6	95.4
1840 (June 1)	590 756	281 229	90.9	1	12 672	9 478	296.7	578 084	271 751	88.7	2.1	97.9
1830 (June 1)	309 527	181 626	142.0	1	3 194	3 194	...	306 333	178 432	139.5	1.0	99.0
1820 (Aug. 7)	127 901	118 855	1000+	−	−	−	−	127 901	118 855	1000+	−	100.0
1810 (Aug. 6)	9 046	7 796	623.7	−	−	−	−	9 046	7 796	623.7	−	100.0
1800 (Aug. 4)	1 250	...	...	−	−	...	...	1 250	...	...	−	100.0

NOTE: 1810 and 1800 population is of that part of the Mississippi Territory as then constituted which was taken to form the Alabama Territory in 1817.

AUTAUGA

Year	Population
1820	3,853
1830	11,874
1840	14,342
1850	15,023
1860	16,739
1870	11,623
1880	13,108
1890	13,330
1900	17,915
1910	20,038
1920	18,908
1930	19,694
1940	20,997
1950	18,186
1960	18,739
1970	24,460
1980	32,259

BALDWIN

Year	Population
1810	1,427
1820	1,713
1830	2,324
1840	2,951
1850	4,414
1860	7,630
1870	6,004
1880	8,603
1890	8,941
1900	13,194
1910	18,178
1920	29,730
1930	28,289
1940	32,324
1950	40,997
1960	49,088
1970	59,382
1980	78,556

BARBOUR

Year	Population
1840	12,024
1850	23,632
1860	30,842
1870	29,309
1880	33,979
1890	34,898
1900	35,152
1910	32,728
1920	32,067
1930	32,454
1940	32,722
1950	28,892
1960	24,700
1970	22,543
1980	24,756

BIBB

Year	Population
1820	3,676
1830	6,306
1840	8,284
1850	9,969
1860	11,894
1870	7,469
1880	9,487
1890	13,824
1900	18,498
1910	22,791
1920	23,144
1930	20,780
1940	20,155
1950	17,987
1960	14,357

Year	Population
1970	13,812
1980	15,723

BLOUNT

Year	Population
1820	2,415
1830	4,233
1840	5,570
1850	7,367
1860	10,865
1870	9,945
1880	15,369
1890	21,927
1900	23,119
1910	21,456
1920	25,538
1930	28,020
1940	29,490
1950	28,975
1960	25,449
1970	26,853
1980	36,459

BULLOCK

Year	Population
1870	24,474
1880	29,066
1890	27,063
1900	31,944
1910	30,196
1920	25,333
1930	20,016
1940	19,810
1950	16,054
1960	13,462
1970	11,824
1980	10,596

BUTLER

Year	Population
1820	1,405
1830	5,650
1840	8,685
1850	10,836
1860	18,122
1870	14,981
1880	19,649
1890	21,641
1900	25,761
1910	29,030
1920	29,531
1930	30,195
1940	32,447
1950	29,228
1960	24,560
1970	22,007
1980	21,680

CALHOUN

Year	Population
1840	14,260
1850	17,163
1860	21,539
1870	13,980
1880	19,591
1890	33,835
1900	34,847
1910	39,115
1920	47,422
1930	55,611
1940	63,319
1950	79,539
1960	95,878
1970	103,092
1980	119,761

CHAMBERS

Year	Population
1840	17,333
1850	23,960
1860	23,214
1870	17,562
1880	23,440
1890	23,319
1900	32,554
1910	36,056
1920	41,201
1930	39,313
1940	42,146
1950	39,528
1960	37,828
1970	36,356
1980	39,191

CHEROKEE

Year	Population
1840	8,773
1850	13,884
1860	18,360
1870	11,132
1880	19,108
1890	20,459
1900	21,096
1910	20,226
1920	20,862
1930	20,219
1940	19,028
1950	17,634
1960	16,303
1970	15,606
1980	18,760

CHILTON

Year	Population
1870	6,194
1880	10,793
1890	14,549
1900	16,592
1910	23,187
1920	22,770
1930	24,579
1940	27,955
1950	26,992
1960	25,693
1970	25,180
1980	30,612

CHOCTAW

Year	Population
1850	8,389
1860	13,877
1870	12,676
1880	15,731
1890	17,526
1900	18,136
1910	18,483
1920	20,753
1930	20,513
1940	20,195
1950	19,152
1960	17,870
1970	16,589
1980	16,839

CLARKE

Year	Population
1820	5,839
1830	7,595
1840	8,640
1850	9,786
1860	15,049
1870	14,663

Year	Population
1880	17,806
1890	22,624
1900	27,790
1910	30,987
1920	26,409
1930	26,016
1940	27,636
1950	26,548
1960	25,738
1970	26,724
1980	27,702

CLAY

Year	Population
1870	9,560
1880	12,938
1890	15,765
1900	17,099
1910	21,006
1920	22,645
1930	17,768
1940	16,907
1950	13,929
1960	12,400
1970	12,636
1980	13,703

CLEBURNE

Year	Population
1870	8,017
1880	10,976
1890	13,218
1900	13,206
1910	13,385
1920	13,360
1930	12,877
1940	13,629
1950	11,904
1960	10,911
1970	10,996
1980	12,595

COFFEE

Year	Population
1850	5,940
1860	9,623
1870	6,171
1880	8,119
1890	12,170
1900	20,972
1910	26,119
1920	30,070
1930	32,556
1940	31,987
1950	30,720
1960	30,583
1970	34,872
1980	38,533

COLBERT

Year	Population
1870	12,537
1880	16,153
1890	20,189
1900	22,341
1910	24,802
1920	31,997
1930	29,860
1940	34,093
1950	39,561
1960	46,506
1970	49,632
1980	54,519

CONECUH

Year	Population
1820	5,713
1830	7,444
1840	8,197
1850	9,322
1860	11,311
1870	9,574
1880	12,605
1890	14,594
1900	17,514
1910	21,433
1920	24,593
1930	25,429
1940	25,489
1950	21,776
1960	17,762
1970	15,645
1980	15,884

COOSA

Year	Population
1840	6,995
1850	14,543
1860	19,273
1870	11,945
1880	15,113
1890	15,906
1900	16,144
1910	16,634
1920	14,839
1930	12,460
1940	13,460
1950	11,766
1960	10,726
1970	10,662
1980	11,377

COVINGTON

Year	Population
1830	1,522
1840	2,435
1850	3,645
1860	6,469
1870	4,868
1880	5,639
1890	7,536
1900	15,346
1910	32,124
1920	38,103
1930	41,356
1940	42,417
1950	40,373
1960	35,361
1970	34,079
1980	36,850

CRENSHAW

Year	Population
1870	11,156
1880	11,726
1890	15,425
1900	19,668
1910	23,313
1920	23,017
1930	23,656
1940	23,631
1950	18,981
1960	14,909
1970	13,188
1980	14,110

CULLMAN

Year	Population
1880	6,355
1890	13,439

Year	Population
1900	17,849
1910	28,321
1920	33,034
1930	41,051
1940	47,343
1950	49,046
1960	45,572
1970	52,445
1980	61,642

DALE

Year	Population
1830	2,031
1840	7,397
1850	6,382
1860	12,197
1870	11,325
1880	12,677
1890	17,225
1900	21,189
1910	21,608
1920	22,711
1930	23,175
1940	22,685
1950	29,828
1960	31,066
1970	52,995
1980	47,821

DALLAS

Year	Population
1820	6,003
1830	14,017
1840	25,199
1850	29,727
1860	33,625
1870	40,705
1880	48,433
1890	49,350
1900	54,657
1910	53,401
1920	54,697
1930	55,094
1940	55,245
1950	56,270
1960	56,667
1970	55,296
1980	53,981

DE KALB

Year	Population
1840	5,929
1850	8,245
1860	10,705
1870	7,126
1880	12,675
1890	21,106
1900	23,558
1910	28,261
1920	34,426
1930	40,104
1940	43,075
1950	45,048
1960	41,417
1970	41,981
1980	53,658

ELMORE

Year	Population
1870	14,477
1880	17,502
1890	21,732
1900	26,099
1910	28,245
1920	28,085
1930	34,280
1940	34,546
1950	31,649
1960	30,524
1970	33,535
1980	43,390

ESCAMBIA

Year	Population
1870	4,041
1880	5,719
1890	8,666
1900	11,320
1910	18,889
1920	22,464
1930	27,963
1940	30,671
1950	31,443
1960	33,511
1970	34,906
1980	38,440

ETOWAH

Year	Population
1870	10,109
1880	15,398
1890	21,926
1900	27,361
1910	39,109
1920	47,275
1930	63,399
1940	72,580
1950	93,892
1960	96,980
1970	94,144
1980	103,057

FAYETTE

Year	Population
1830	3,547
1840	6,942
1850	9,681
1860	12,850
1870	7,136
1880	10,135
1890	12,823
1900	14,132
1910	16,248
1920	18,365
1930	18,433
1940	21,651
1950	19,388
1960	16,148
1970	16,252
1980	18,809

FRANKLIN

Year	Population
1820	4,988
1830	11,078
1840	14,270
1850	19,610
1860	18,627
1870	8,006
1880	9,155
1890	10,681
1900	16,511
1910	19,369
1920	22,011
1930	25,372
1940	27,552
1950	25,705
1960	21,988
1970	23,933
1980	28,350

GENEVA

Year	Population
1870	2,959
1880	4,342
1890	10,690
1900	19,096
1910	26,230
1920	29,315
1930	30,104
1940	29,172
1950	25,899
1960	22,310
1970	21,924
1980	24,253

GREENE

Year	Population
1820	4,554
1830	15,026
1840	24,024
1850	31,441
1860	30,859
1870	18,399
1880	21,931
1890	22,007
1900	24,182
1910	22,717
1920	18,133
1930	19,745
1940	19,185
1950	16,482
1960	13,600
1970	10,650
1980	11,021

HALE

Year	Population
1870	21,792
1880	26,553
1890	27,501
1900	31,011
1910	17,883
1920	24,289
1930	26,265
1940	25,533
1950	20,832
1960	19,537
1970	15,888
1980	15,604

HENRY

Year	Population
1820	2,638
1830	4,020
1840	5,787
1850	9,019
1860	14,918
1870	14,191
1880	18,761
1890	24,847
1900	36,147
1910	20,943
1920	21,547
1930	22,820
1940	21,912
1950	18,674
1960	15,286
1970	13,254
1980	15,302

HOUSTON

Year	Population
1910	32,414
1920	37,334
1930	45,935
1940	45,665
1950	46,522
1960	50,718
1970	56,574
1980	74,632

JACKSON

Year	Population
1820	8,751
1830	12,700
1840	15,715
1850	14,088
1860	18,283
1870	19,410
1880	25,114
1890	28,026
1900	30,508
1910	32,918
1920	35,864
1930	36,881
1940	41,802
1950	38,998
1960	36,681
1970	39,202
1980	51,407

JEFFERSON

Year	Population
1830	6,855
1840	7,131
1850	8,989
1860	11,746
1870	12,345
1880	23,272
1890	88,501
1900	140,420
1910	226,476
1920	310,054
1930	431,493
1940	459,930
1950	558,928
1960	634,864
1970	644,991
1980	671,324

LAMAR

Year	Population
1870	8,893
1880	12,142
1890	14,187
1900	16,084
1910	17,487
1920	18,149
1930	18,001
1940	19,708
1950	16,441
1960	14,271
1970	14,335
1980	16,453

LAUDERDALE

Year	Population
1820	4,963
1830	11,781
1840	14,485
1850	17,172
1860	17,420
1870	15,091
1880	21,035
1890	23,739
1900	26,559
1910	30,936
1920	39,556
1930	41,130
1940	46,230
1950	54,179
1960	61,622
1970	68,111
1980	80,546

LAWRENCE

Year	Population
1830	14,984
1840	13,313
1850	15,258
1860	13,975
1870	16,658
1880	21,392
1890	20,725
1900	29,124
1910	21,984
1920	24,307
1930	26,942
1940	27,880
1950	17,128
1960	24,501
1970	27,281
1980	30,170

LEE

Year	Population
1870	21,750
1880	27,262
1890	28,694
1900	31,826
1910	32,867
1920	32,821
1930	36,063
1940	36,445
1950	45,073
1960	49,754
1970	61,268
1980	76,283

LIMESTONE

Year	Population
1820	9,871
1830	14,807
1840	14,374
1850	16,483
1860	15,306
1870	15,017
1880	21,006
1890	21,201
1900	22,387
1910	26,880
1920	31,341
1930	36,629
1940	35,642
1950	35,766
1960	36,513
1970	41,699
1980	46,005

LOWNDES

Year	Population
1830	9,410
1840	19,539
1850	21,915
1860	27,716
1870	25,719
1880	31,176
1890	31,550
1900	35,651
1910	31,894
1920	25,406
1930	22,878
1940	22,661
1950	18,018
1960	15,417
1970	12,897
1980	13,253

MACON

1840	11,247
1850	26,898
1860	26,802
1870	17,727
1880	17,371
1890	18,439
1900	23,126
1910	26,049
1920	23,561
1930	27,103
1940	27,654
1950	30,561
1960	26,717
1970	24,841
1980	26,829

MADISON

1810	4,699
1820	17,481
1830	27,990
1840	25,706
1850	26,427
1860	26,451
1870	31,267
1880	37,625
1890	38,119
1900	43,702
1910	47,401
1920	51,268
1930	64,623
1940	66,317
1950	72,903
1960	117,348
1970	186,540
1980	196,966

MARENGO

1820	2,933
1830	7,700
1840	17,264
1850	27,831
1860	31,171
1870	26,151
1880	30,890
1890	33,095
1900	38,315
1910	39,923
1920	36,065
1930	36,426
1940	35,736
1950	29,494
1960	27,098
1970	23,819
1980	25,047

MARION

1830	4,058
1840	5,847
1850	7,833
1860	11,182
1870	6,059
1880	9,364
1890	11,347
1900	14,494
1910	17,495
1920	22,008
1930	25,967
1940	28,776
1950	27,264
1960	21,837
1970	23,788
1980	30,041

MARSHALL

1840	7,553
1850	8,846
1860	11,472
1870	9,871
1880	14,585
1890	18,935
1900	23,289
1910	28,533
1920	32,669
1930	39,802
1940	42,395
1950	45,090
1960	48,018
1970	54,211
1980	65,622

MOBILE

1820	2,672
1830	6,267
1840	18,741
1850	27,600
1860	41,131
1870	49,311
1880	48,653
1890	51,587
1900	62,740
1910	80,854
1920	100,117
1930	118,363
1940	141,974
1950	231,105
1960	314,301
1970	317,308
1980	364,980

MONROE

1820	8,838
1830	8,782
1840	10,680
1850	12,013
1860	15,667
1870	14,214
1880	17,091
1890	18,990
1900	23,666
1910	27,155
1920	28,884
1930	30,070
1940	29,465
1950	25,732
1960	22,372
1970	20,883
1980	22,651

MONTGOMERY

1820	6,604
1830	12,695
1840	24,574
1850	29,711
1860	35,904
1870	43,704
1880	52,356
1890	56,172
1900	72,047
1910	82,178
1920	80,853
1930	98,671
1940	114,420
1950	138,965
1960	169,210
1970	167,790
1980	197,038

MORGAN

1820	5,263
1830	9,062
1840	9,841
1850	10,125
1860	11,335
1870	12,187
1880	16,428
1890	24,089
1900	28,820
1910	33,781
1920	40,196
1930	46,176
1940	48,148
1950	52,924
1960	60,454
1970	77,306
1980	90,231

PERRY

1830	11,490
1840	19,086
1850	22,285
1860	27,724
1870	24,975
1880	30,741
1890	29,332
1900	31,783
1910	31,222
1920	25,373
1930	26,285
1940	26,610
1950	20,439
1960	17,358
1970	15,388
1980	15,012

PICKENS

1830	6,622
1840	17,118
1850	21,512
1860	22,316
1870	17,690
1880	21,479
1890	22,470
1900	24,402
1910	25,055
1920	25,353
1930	24,902
1940	27,671
1950	24,349
1960	21,882
1970	20,326
1980	21,481

PIKE

1830	7,108
1840	10,108
1850	15,920
1860	24,435
1870	17,423
1880	20,640
1890	24,423
1900	29,172
1910	30,815
1920	31,631
1930	32,240
1940	32,493
1950	30,608
1960	25,987
1970	25,038
1980	28,050

RANDOLPH

1840	4,973
1850	11,581
1860	20,059
1870	12,006
1880	16,575
1890	17,219
1900	21,647
1910	24,659
1920	27,064
1930	26,861
1940	25,516
1950	22,513
1960	19,477
1970	18,331
1980	20,075

RUSSELL

1840	13,513
1850	19,548
1860	26,592
1870	21,636
1880	24,837
1890	24,093
1900	27,083
1910	25,937
1920	27,448
1930	27,377
1940	35,775
1950	40,364
1960	46,351
1970	45,394
1980	47,356

SAINT CLAIR

1820	4,166
1830	5,975
1840	5,638
1850	6,829
1860	11,013
1870	9,360
1880	14,462
1890	17,353
1900	19,425
1910	20,715
1920	23,383
1930	24,510
1940	27,336
1950	26,687
1960	25,388
1970	26,956
1980	41,205

SHELBY

1820	2,416
1830	5,704
1840	6,122
1850	9,536
1860	12,618
1870	12,218
1880	17,236
1890	20,886
1900	23,684
1910	26,949
1920	27,097
1930	27,576
1940	28,962
1950	30,362
1960	32,132
1970	38,037
1980	66,298

SUMTER

1840	29,937
1850	22,250
1860	24,035
1870	24,109
1880	28,728
1890	29,574
1900	32,710
1910	28,699
1920	25,569
1930	26,969
1940	27,321
1950	23,610
1960	20,041
1970	16,974
1980	16,908

TALLADEGA

1840	12,587
1850	18,624
1860	23,520
1870	18,064
1880	23,360
1890	29,346
1900	35,773
1910	37,921
1920	41,005
1930	45,241
1940	51,832
1950	63,639
1960	65,495
1970	65,280
1980	73,826

TALLAPOOSA

1840	6,444
1850	15,584
1860	23,827
1870	16,963
1880	23,401
1890	25,460
1900	29,675
1910	31,034
1920	29,744
1930	31,188
1940	35,270
1950	35,074
1960	35,007
1970	33,840
1980	38,676

TUSCALOOSA

1820	8,229
1830	13,646
1840	16,583
1850	18,056
1860	23,200
1870	20,081
1880	24,957
1890	30,352
1900	36,147
1910	47,559
1920	53,680
1930	64,153
1940	76,036
1950	94,092
1960	109,047
1970	116,029
1980	137,541

WALKER

Year	Population
1830	2,202
1840	4,032
1850	5,124
1860	7,980
1870	6,543
1880	9,479
1890	16,078
1900	25,162
1910	37,013
1920	50,593
1930	59,445
1940	64,201
1950	63,769
1960	54,211
1970	56,246
1980	68,660

WASHINGTON

Year	Population
1830	3,474
1840	5,300
1850	2,713
1860	4,669
1870	3,912
1880	4,538
1890	7,935
1900	11,134
1910	14,454
1920	14,279
1930	16,365
1940	16,118
1950	15,612
1960	15,372
1970	16,241
1980	16,821

WILCOX

Year	Population
1820	2,917
1830	9,548
1840	15,278
1850	17,352
1860	24,618
1870	28,377
1880	31,828
1890	30,816
1900	35,631
1910	33,810
1920	31,080
1930	24,880
1940	26,279
1950	23,467
1960	18,739
1970	16,303
1980	14,755

WINSTON

Year	Population
1850	1,542
1860	3,576
1870	4,155
1880	4,253
1890	6,552
1900	9,554
1910	12,855
1920	14,378
1930	15,596
1940	18,746
1950	18,250
1960	14,858
1970	16,654
1980	21,953

NOTES

BIBB

Name changed from Cahaba in 1820.

CALHOUN

Name changed from Benton in 1858.

CHILTON

Name changed from Baker in 1874.

COVINGTON

Period August 6 to October 10, 1868 named Jones County.

ETOWAH

Name changed from Blaine in 1868.

LAMAR

Formed 1867 as Jones county; re-established as Sanford county in 1868; name changed to Lamar in 1877.

MORGAN

Name changed from Cataco in 1821.

WINSTON

Name changed from Hancock in 1858.

ALBERTVILLE

1910	1,544
1920	1,666
1930	2,716
1940	3,651
1950	5,397
1960	8,250
1970	9,963
1980	12,039

ALEXANDER CITY

1880	796
1890	679
1900	1,061
1910	1,710
1920	2,293
1930	4,519
1940	6,640
1950	6,430
1960	13,140
1970	12,358
1980	13,807

ANDAULSIA

1880	596
1890	270
1900	551
1910	2,480
1920	4,023
1930	5,154
1940	6,886
1950	9,162
1960	10,263
1970	10,092
1980	10,415

ANNISTON

1880	942
1890	9,998
1900	9,695
1910	12,794
1920	17,734
1930	22,345
1940	25,523
1950	31,066
1960	33,657
1970	31,533
1980	29,523

ATHENS

1880	1,011
1890	940
1900	1,010
1910	1,715
1920	3,323
1930	4,238
1940	4,342
1950	6,309
1960	9,330
1970	14,360
1980	14,558

AUBURN

1870	1,018
1880	1,161
1890	1,440
1900	1,447
1910	1,408
1920	2,143
1930	2,800

1940	4,652
1950	12,939
1960	16,261
1970	22,767
1980	28,471

BESSEMER

1890	4,544
1900	6,358
1910	10,864
1920	18,674
1930	20,721
1940	22,826
1950	28,445
1960	33,054
1970	33,428
1980	31,729

BIRMINGHAM

1880	3,086
1890	26,178
1900	38,145
1910	132,685
1920	178,806
1930	259,678
1940	267,583
1950	326,037
1960	340,887
1970	300,910
1980	284,413

CULLMAN

1880	426
1890	1,017
1900	1,255
1910	2,130
1920	2,467
1930	2,786
1940	5,074
1950	7,523
1960	10,883
1970	12,601
1980	13,084

DECATUR

1850	606
1870	671
1880	1,063
1890	2,765
1900	3,114
1910	4,228
1920	4,752
1930	15,593
1940	16,604
1950	19,974
1960	29,217
1970	38,044
1980	42,002

DOTHAN

1890	247
1900	3,275
1910	7,016
1920	10,034
1930	16,046
1940	17,194
1950	21,584
1960	31,440
1970	36,733
1980	48,750

ENTERPRISE

1900	610
1910	2,322
1920	3,013
1930	3,702
1940	4,353
1950	7,288
1960	11,410
1970	15,591
1980	18,033

EUFAULA

1870	3,185
1880	3,836
1890	4,394
1900	4,532
1910	4,259
1920	4,939
1930	5,208
1940	6,269
1950	6,906
1960	8,357
1970	9,102
1980	12,097

FAIRFIELD

1920	5,003
1930	11,059
1940	11,703
1950	13,177
1960	15,816
1970	14,369
1980	13,040

FLORENCE

1850	802
1860	1,359
1870	2,003
1880	1,359
1890	6,012
1900	6,478
1910	6,689
1920	10,529
1930	11,729
1940	15,043
1950	23,879
1960	31,649
1970	34,031
1980	37,029

FORT PAYNE

1890	2,698
1900	1,037
1910	2,042
1920	2,837
1930	4,309
1940	3,375
1950	4,424
1960	6,226
1970	8,435
1980	11,485

GADSDEN

1880	1,697
1890	2,901
1900	4,282
1910	10,557
1920	14,737
1930	24,042
1940	36,975

1950	55,725
1960	58,088
1970	53,928
1980	47,565

HOMEWOOD

1930	6,103
1940	7,397
1950	12,866
1960	20,289
1970	21,245
1980	21,412

HOOVER

1970	688
1980	19,792

HUEYTOWN

1960	5,997
1970	11,640
1980	13,309

HUNTSVILLE

1850	2,863
1860	3,634
1870	4,907
1880	4,977
1890	7,955
1900	8,068
1910	7,611
1920	8,018
1930	11,554
1940	13,050
1950	16,437
1960	72,365
1970	137,802
1980	142,513

JASPER

1880	269
1890	780
1900	1,661
1910	2,509
1920	3,246
1930	5,313
1940	6,847
1950	8,589
1960	10,799
1970	10,798
1980	11,894

MOBILE

1830	3,194
1840	12,672
1850	20,515
1860	29,258
1870	32,034
1880	29,132
1890	31,076
1900	38,469
1910	51,521
1920	60,777
1930	68,202
1940	78,720
1950	129,009
1960	194,856
1970	190,026
1980	200,452

MONTGOMERY

1840	2,179
1850	8,728
1860	8,843
1870	10,588
1880	16,713
1890	21,183
1900	30,346
1910	38,136
1920	43,464
1930	66,079
1940	78,084
1950	106,525
1960	134,393
1970	133,386
1980	177,857

MOUNTAIN BROOK

1950	8,359
1960	12,680
1970	19,474
1980	19,718

NORTHPORT

1890	413
1900	424
1910	599
1920	1,606
1930	2,173
1940	3,187
1950	3,885
1960	5,245
1970	9,435
1980	14,291

OPELIKA

1880	3,245
1890	3,703
1900	4,245
1910	4,734
1920	4,960
1930	6,156
1940	8,487
1950	12,295
1960	15,678
1970	19,027
1980	21,896

OZARK

1880	426
1890	1,195
1900	1,570
1910	2,229
1920	2,518
1930	3,103
1940	3,601
1950	5,238
1960	9,534
1970	13,555
1980	13,188

PHOENIX CITY

1880	2,224
1890	3,700
1900	4,163
1910	4,555
1920	5,432
1930	13,862
1940	15,351
1950	23,305

1960	27,630
1970	25,281
1980	26,928

PRATTVILLE

1880	977
1890	724
1900	1,929
1910	2,222
1920	2,316
1930	2,331
1940	2,664
1950	4,385
1960	6,616
1970	13,779
1980	18,647

PRICHARD

1930	4,580
1940	6,084
1950	19,014
1960	47,371
1970	41,578
1980	39,541

SCOTTSBORO

1870	357
1880	722
1890	959
1900	1,014
1910	1,019
1920	1,417
1930	2,304
1940	2,834
1950	4,731
1960	6,449
1970	9,324
1980	14,758

SELMA

1850	3,033
1860	3,177
1870	6,484
1880	7,529
1890	7,622
1900	8,713
1910	13,649
1920	15,589
1930	18,012
1940	19,834
1950	22,840
1960	28,385
1970	27,379
1980	26,684

SHEFFIELD

1890	2,731
1900	3,333
1910	4,865
1920	6,682
1930	6,221
1940	7,933
1950	10,767
1960	13,491
1970	13,115
1980	11,903

SYLACAUGA

1890	464
1900	880

1910	1,456
1920	2,141
1930	4,115
1940	6,269
1950	9,606
1960	12,857
1970	12,255
1980	12,708

TALLADEGA

1850	1,320
1860	(NA)
1870	1,933
1880	1,233
1890	2,063
1900	5,056
1910	5,854
1920	6,546
1930	7,596
1940	9,298
1950	13,134
1960	17,742
1970	17,662
1980	19,128

TROY

1870	1,058
1880	2,294
1890	3,449
1900	4,097
1910	4,961
1920	5,696
1930	6,814
1940	7,055
1950	8,555
1960	10,234
1970	11,482
1980	12,945

TUSCALOOSA

1860	3,989
1870	1,689
1880	2,418
1890	4,215
1900	5,094
1910	8,407
1920	11,996
1930	20,659
1940	27,493
1950	46,396
1960	63,370
1970	65,773
1980	75,211

TUSKEGEE

1880	2,370
1890	1,803
1900	2,170
1910	2,803
1920	2,475
1930	3,314
1940	3,937
1950	6,712
1960	7,240
1970	11,028
1980	13,327

VESTAVIA HILLS

1960	4,029
1970	12,250
1980	15,722

CORRECTION NOTE

The official 1980 census counts of total population shown in
this report supersede counts issued previously. Corrections
to the figures were made after the counts were provided to
the State for redistricting purposes and released in Advance
Report PHC80-V for this State.

Shown below are corrections to the 1980 census counts of the
total population made after the tabulations for this report
were completed. Any additional corrections made after this
report is printed are available by writing to Data User
Services Division, Customer Service (Corrections), Bureau of
the Census, Washington, D.C. 20233.

The 1980, figures shown in this publication are subject to
change pending the outcome of the various lawsuits dealing
with the census counts.

	1980 population	
	As shown in the tables	Corrected
Etowah County:		
Gadsden division:		
Southside town (pt.)...........	4 806	5 099
Jefferson County:		
Birmingham division:		
Fairfield city................	13 040	13 242
Hueytown city (pt.)...........	13 304	13 376
Midfield city.................	6 536	6 203
Concord-Hopkins division:		
Hueytown city (pt.)...........	5	102
Marion County:		
Hamilton division:		
Weston town...................	344	350
Hueytown city (total).............	13 309	13 478
Southside town (total)............	4 848	5 141

County Subdivisions	1980	1970
The State	3 893 888	'3 444 354
Autauga County[1]	32 259	24 460
Autaugaville division	3 163	2 876
Autaugaville town	843	870
Billingsley division	2 172	1 952
Billingsley town	106	110
Marbury division	2 835	2 198
Prattville division	24 089	17 434
Prattville city (pt.)[1]	18 536	13 116
Baldwin County[2]	78 556	59 382
Bay Minette division	17 040	13 347
Bay Minette city[2]	7 455	6 727
Daphne division	13 563	8 461
Daphne city[2]	3 406	2 382
Lake Forest (CDP)	3 489	...
Spanish Fort (CDP)	3 415	2 364
Elberta division	4 230	3 076
Elberta town	491	395
Fairhope division	13 782	10 562
Fairhope city[2]	7 286	5 720
Point Clear (CDP)	1 812	...
Foley division	14 133	10 416
Foley city[2]	4 003	3 368
Gulf Shores town[2]	1 349	909
Robertsdale division	9 993	8 257
Loxley town	804	859
Robertsdale city	2 306	2 078
Silverhill town	624	552
Stockton division	3 704	3 470
Summerdale division	2 111	1 793
Summerdale town	546	550
Barbour County[3]	24 756	22 543
Bakerhill division	2 189	1 813
Eufaula city (pt.)[3]	255	...
Clayton division	3 144	3 250
Clayton town	1 589	1 626
Clio division	3 105	3 215
Blue Springs town[3]	112	137
Clio town[3]	1 224	1 065
Eufaula division	13 766	11 967
Eufaula city (pt.)[3]	11 842	9 102
Louisville division	2 552	2 298
Louisville town	791	785
Bibb County[4]	15 723	13 812
Centreville–Brent division	9 602	...
Brent city	2 862	2 093
Centreville city	2 504	2 233
Piper–Coleanor division	879	851
West Blocton division	5 242	4 224
West Blocton town	1 147	1 172
Blount County[5]	36 459	26 853
Blountsville division	5 212	4 165
Blountsville town (pt.)[5]	1 490	1 254
Nectar town[5]	367	...
Brooksville division	3 549	3 071
Blountsville town (pt.)[5]	19	...
Clarence division	3 928	3 374
Snead town[5]	667	347
Cleveland division	2 361	...
Cleveland town	487	413
Rosa town (pt.)[5]	63	...
Hayden division	5 812	3 056
Hayden town[5]	268	195
Locust Fork division	5 035	2 751
County Line town (pt.)	100	84
Locust Fork town[5]	488	...
Oneonta division	10 562	...
Allgood town[5]	387	272
Highland Lake town	210	108
Oneonta city	4 824	4 390
Rosa town (pt.)[5]	141	...
Bullock County	10 596	11 824
Fitzpatrick division	1 069	1 155
Inverness division	2 251	2 241
Midway division	1 290	2 441
Midway town	593	558
Union Springs division	5 986	5 987
Union Springs city	4 431	4 324
Butler County[6]	21 680	22 007
Chapman division	1 913	...
Forest Home division	1 786	2 052
Georgiana–McKenzie division	5 161	...
Georgiana town	1 993	2 148
McKenzie town[6]	605	491
Greenville division	12 820	...
Greenville city	7 807	8 033
Calhoun County[7]	119 761	103 092
Anniston division	83 265	...
Anniston city[7]	29 523	31 533
Blue Mountain town	284	446
Bynum (CDP)	2 235	...
Eulaton (CDP)	1 869	...
Fort McClellan (CDP)	7 605	5 334
Hobson City town[7]	1 268	1 124
Oxford city (pt.)[7]	8 463	4 361
Saks (CDP)	11 118	6 609

County Subdivisions	1980	1970
Calhoun County—Con.		
Anniston division—Con.		
Vinnette (CDP)	1 809	...
Weaver town[7]	2 765	2 091
West End–Cobb Town (CDP)	5 189	5 515
Choccolocco division	3 753	...
Jacksonville division	14 487	...
Jacksonville city[7]	9 735	7 715
Ohatchee division	2 857	2 021
Ohatchee town	860	445
Southside town (pt.)[7]	42	...
Piedmont division	8 089	7 492
Piedmont city[7]	5 544	5 063
Websters Chapel–Alexandria Valley division	7 310	...
Glencoe city (pt.)[7]	14	...
Chambers County[8]	39 191	36 356
Five Points division	2 464	...
Five Points town	197	247
Lafayette division	6 618	...
Lafayette city	3 647	3 530
Lanett division	12 203	...
Huguley (CDP) (pt.)	2 799	...
Lanett city[8]	6 897	6 908
Little Shawmut (CDP) (pt.)	1 199	1 394
Langdale division	15 358	13 377
Fairfax (CDP)	3 776	2 772
Huguley (CDP) (pt.)	148	...
Langdale (CDP)	2 034	2 235
Little Shawmut (CDP) (pt.)	1 594	1 288
River View (CDP)	1 314	1 109
Shawmut (CDP)	2 284	2 181
Milltown division	1 254	1 322
Waverly division	1 294	...
Waverly town	190	197
Cherokee County[9]	18 760	15 606
Cedar Bluff–Gaylesville division	4 988	3 842
Cedar Bluff town[9]	1 129	956
Gaylesville town	192	161
Centre division	6 659	6 018
Centre city[9]	2 351	2 418
Leesburg division	3 413	2 569
Collinsville (pt.)	11	29
Leesburg town	116	98
Mud Creek division	3 700	3 177
Chilton County[10]	30 612	25 180
Clanton division	11 702	...
Clanton city	5 832	5 868
Isabella–Pletcher division	2 163	1 841
Jemison division	8 643	...
Jemison town	1 828	1 423
Thorsby town[10]	1 422	944
Maplesville division	2 892	2 598
Maplesville town[10]	754	'704
Mineral Springs division	1 852	...
Verbena division	3 360	2 914
Choctaw County[11]	16 839	16 589
Butler division	5 217	5 381
Butler city[11]	1 882	2 064
Lisman town (pt.)	–	...
Gilbertown–Toxey division	4 289	...
Gilbertown town	218	207
Toxey town[11]	265	304
Lisman division	4 660	4 864
Lisman town (pt.)[11]	638	...
Pennington town[11]	355	'301
Silas division	2 673	...
Silas town	343	345
Clarke County[12]	27 702	26 724
Coffeeville division	1 482	1 623
Coffeeville town	448	441
Fulton division	2 188	...
Fulton town	606	628
Grove Hill division	6 527	6 300
Grove Hill town	1 912	1 825
Jackson Northwest division	8 060	...
Jackson city	6 073	5 957
Jackson Southeast division	2 740	...
Thomasville division	6 705	...
Thomasville city	4 387	3 769
Clay County[13]	13 703	12 636
Ashland division	6 167	5 852
Ashland town[13]	2 052	1 921
Lineville division	5 087	4 572
Lineville town[13]	2 257	1 984
Millerville–Hollins division	2 449	2 212
Cleburne County[14]	12 595	10 996
Fruithurst division	1 846	1 536
Fruithurst city	239	229
Heflin division	7 166	6 513
Edwardsville town[14]	207	146
Heflin city	3 014	2 872
Ranburne division	3 583	2 947
Ranburne town	417	371

County Subdivisions

County Subdivisions	1980	1970
Coffee County[15]	38 533	34 872
Elba division	7 429	7 350
Elba city	4 355	4 634
Enterprise division	24 412	...
Enterprise city (pt.)[15]	17 777	15 591
New Brockton town[15]	1 392	1 374
Goodman division	1 958	1 780
Jack division	1 484	1 262
Kinston division	1 453	1 406
Kinston town	604	540
Victoria division	1 797	1 692
Colbert County[16]	54 519	49 632
Cherokee division	4 851	4 529
Cherokee town	1 589	1 484
Leighton division	7 891	...
Leighton town	1 218	1 231
Littleville division	8 412	...
Littleville town	1 262	858
Tri-Cities division	33 365	...
Muscle Shoals city	8 911	6 907
Sheffield city[16]	11 903	13 115
Tuscumbia city[16]	9 137	8 828
Conecuh County[17]	15 884	15 645
Castleberry division	3 986	...
Castleberry town	847	666
Evergreen division	6 870	...
Evergreen city	4 171	3 924
Lyeffion division	2 260	2 462
Repton division	1 881	1 670
Repton town	313	277
Shreve division	887	938
Coosa County	11 377	10 662
Goodwater–Kellyton division	4 348	4 501
Goodwater city	1 895	2 172
Rockford division	3 529	3 207
Rockford town	494	603
Weogufka–Marble Valley division	3 500	2 954
Covington County[18]	36 850	34 079
Andalusia division	18 168	...
Andalusia city	10 415	10 092
Babbie town[18]	553	82
Heath town	354	229
Libertyville town	141	141
Red Level town	504	616
River Falls town	669	580
Sanford town	250	256
Falco division	1 449	1 334
Carolina town	203	192
Florala division	3 976	4 793
Florala city	2 165	2 701
Lockhart town	547	698
Opp division	9 912	8 223
County Line town[18]	124	...
Horn Hill town[18]	186	...
Onycha town[18]	147	...
Opp city[18]	7 204	6 493
Rosehill–Gantt division	3 345	...
Gantt town[18]	314	...
Crenshaw County[19]	14 110	13 188
Brantley division	3 677	3 364
Brantley town	1 151	1 066
Dozier town	494	304
Luverne division	6 818	...
Glenwood town	341	378
Luverne city	2 639	2 440
Rutledge town	496	353
Petrey–Highland Home division	3 615	3 278
Petrey town	93	122
Cullman County[20]	61 642	52 445
Baileyton–Joppa division	4 597	...
Baileyton town[20]	396	...
Bremen division	5 233	4 444
Crane Hill division	1 497	1 017
Cullman division	20 145	18 863
Cullman city[20]	13 084	12 601
Good Hope town[20]	1 442	840
West Point town (pt.)[20]	7	...
Hanceville division	6 127	5 064
Garden City town	655	745
Hanceville city	2 220	2 027
Holly Pond division	3 471	...
Holly Pond town	493	325
Jones Chapel division	3 588	3 050
Logan division	2 926	2 131
West Point town (pt.)[20]	71	...
Simcoe division	5 646	4 583
Fairview town	450	313
Vinemont division	6 807	4 943
South Vinemont town[20]	615	480
West Point town (pt.)[20]	170	...
Welti division	1 605	1 495
Dale County[21]	47 821	52 995
Daleville division	8 586	...
Clayhatchee town[21]	560	505
Daleville city (pt.)[21]	4 250	5 182
Enterprise city (pt.)[21]	256	...

County Subdivisions

County Subdivisions	1980	1970
Dale County—Con.		
Daleville division—Con.		
Level Plains town[21]	867	1 007
Echo division	1 880	2 058
Fort Rucker division	8 932	...
Daleville city (pt.)	–	...
Fort Rucker (CDP)	8 932	14 242
Newton town (pt.)[21]	–	(NA)
Newton–Midland City division	7 504	...
Dothan city (pt.)[21]	–	...
Grimes town[21]	298	191
Midland City town[21]	1 903	1 172
Napier Field town[21]	493	572
Newton town (pt.)[21]	1 357	(NA)
Pinckard town	771	609
Ozark division	20 919	...
Ariton town[21]	844	643
Newton town (pt.)[21]	183	(NA)
Ozark city[21]	13 188	13 555
Dallas County[22]	53 981	55 296
Carlowville division	1 309	1 941
Craig–Tyler division	8 045	9 943
Selmont–West Selmont (CDP)	5 255	2 270
Orrville division	4 246	4 655
Orrville town	349	362
Safford division	1 246	1 554
Sardis division	2 197	2 319
Selma division	36 938	...
Selma city[22]	26 684	27 379
De Kalb County[23]	53 658	41 981
Collinsville division	3 107	2 560
Collinsville town (pt.)	1 372	1 271
Crossville division	4 486	...
Crossville town	1 222	1 035
Fort Payne division	15 708	...
Fort Payne city[23]	11 485	8 435
Fyffe division	4 889	3 740
Fyffe town[23]	1 305	311
Lakeview town[23]	441	13
Shiloh town (pt.)[23]	121	105
Geraldine division	4 955	...
Geraldine town[23]	911	610
Henagar division	3 053	2 383
Henagar town[23]	1 188	812
Ider division	4 990	3 533
Ider town[23]	698	...
Rainsville–Sylvania division	9 397	7 149
Powell's Crossroads town[23]	636	474
Rainsville city[23]	3 907	2 099
Shiloh town (pt.)[23]	176	128
Sylvania town[23]	1 156	476
Valley Head–Mentone division	3 073	2 342
Hammondville town[23]	369	221
Mentone town	476	407
Valley Head town[23]	609	470
Elmore County[24]	43 390	33 661
Deatsville division	4 667	3 003
Eclectic division	6 217	4 970
Eclectic town	1 124	1 184
Elmore division	12 552	8 907
Coosada town[24]	980	...
Millbrook city[24]	3 101	...
Prattville city (pt.)[24]	111	...
Robinson Springs (CDP)	1 395	...
Tallassee division	6 306	5 758
Tallassee city (pt.)[24]	3 540	3 404
Titus division	2 118	1 680
Wetumpka division	11 530	9 343
Wetumpka city	4 341	3 912
Escambia County[25]	38 440	34 912
Atmore division	13 672	12 221
Atmore city[25]	8 789	8 293
Brewton division	11 301	10 221
Brewton city[25]	6 680	6 747
Pollard town	144	86
East Escambia division	6 309	5 433
East Brewton city[25]	3 012	2 336
Riverview town[25]	132	110
Flomaton division	3 593	3 153
Flomaton town[25]	1 882	1 584
McCullough–Huxford division	3 565	3 884
Etowah County[26]	103 057	94 144
Altoona division	3 976	3 401
Altoona town	928	781
Walnut Grove town[26]	510	224
Gadsden division	77 496	...
Attalla city[26]	7 737	7 510
Gadsden city (pt.)[26]	47 255	53 928
Glencoe city (pt.)[26]	4 184	2 901
Rainbow City city[26]	6 299	3 099
Reece City town (pt.)[26]	452	496
Ridgeville town[26]	182	177
Southside town (pt.)[26]	4 806	983
Hokes Bluff division	7 505	...
Gadsden city (pt.)[26]	19	...

County Subdivisions	1980	1970
Etowah County—Con.		
Hokes Bluff division—Con.		
Glencoe city (pt.)[26]	450	...
Hokes Bluff town[26]	3 216	2 133
Lookout Mountain division	2 640	...
Gadsden city (pt.)[26]	–	...
Mountainboro division	7 089	5 119
Boaz city (pt.)[26]	401	170
Mountainboro town[26]	266	311
Sardis city[26]	883	368
Turkeytown division	3 124	...
Gadsden city (pt.)[26]	291	...
Wills Valley division	1 227	...
Reece City town (pt.)[26]	266	...
Fayette County[27]	18 809	16 252
Berry division	3 964	3 183
Berry town	916	679
Fayette division	9 727	8 409
Belk town[27]	308	'64
Fayette city[27]	5 287	4 568
North River division	1 585	...
Russell division	3 533	...
Glen Allen town (pt.)	259	197
Winfield city (pt.)	127	139
Franklin County[28]	28 350	23 933
Phil Campbell division	5 605	4 492
Phil Campbell town	1 549	1 230
Red Bay division	5 280	4 251
Red Bay city[28]	3 232	2 464
Russellville division	15 669	13 537
Russellville city[28]	8 195	7 814
Vina division	1 796	1 653
Hodges town	250	207
Vina town[28]	346	366
Geneva County[29]	24 253	21 924
Bellwood–Coffee Springs division	2 296	2 242
Coffee Springs town	339	329
Geneva division	5 605	...
Geneva city (pt.)[29]	4 754	4 398
Hartford division	5 130	...
Black town	156	171
Eunola town[29]	169	141
Geneva city (pt.)[29]	112	...
Hartford city	2 647	2 648
Samson division	4 887	...
Samson city[29]	2 402	2 257
Slocomb division	6 335	5 416
Malvern town[29]	558	227
Slocomb town	2 153	1 883
Greene County[30]	11 021	10 650
Boligee division	1 119	...
Boligee town	164	225
Eutaw division	5 328	...
Eutaw city	2 444	2 805
Union town (pt.)[30]	151	...
Forkland–Tishabee division	2 281	2 402
Forkland town[30]	429	...
Mantua–West Greene division	2 293	2 252
Union town (pt.)[30]	207	...
Hale County[31]	15 604	15 888
Greensboro division	4 461	...
Greensboro city	3 248	3 371
Moundville division	2 321	2 146
Moundville town (pt.)[31]	1 269	981
Mount Herman Valley division	1 794	...
Prairie Eden–Newbern division	2 093	...
Newbern town	307	286
River Bend division	1 014	...
Sawyerville division	2 132	...
Stewart–Akron division	1 789	2 064
Akron town	604	535
Henry County[32]	15 302	13 254
Abbeville division	5 480	4 939
Abbeville city[32]	3 155	2 996
Haleburg division	1 409	1 412
Haleburg town	106	104
Headland–Newville division	6 372	...
Headland city	3 327	2 545
Newville town	814	465
Shorterville division	2 041	1 606
Houston County[33]	74 632	56 574
Columbia division	1 702	1 513
Columbia town	881	891
Cottonwood division	3 890	...
Cottonwood town	1 352	1 149
Dothan division	63 302	...
Ashford town	2 165	1 980
Avon town	433	374
Cowarts town	418	350
Dothan city (pt.)[33]	48 750	36 733
Kinsey town[33]	1 239	219
Taylor town (pt.)[33]	101	...
Webb town	448	354
Gordon division	2 381	1 956
Gordon town	362	312
Madrid division	3 357	...

County Subdivisions	1980	1970
Houston County—Con.		
Madrid division—Con.		
Dothan city (pt.)[33]	–	...
Madrid town	172	238
Taylor town (pt.)[33]	902	174
Jackson County[34]	51 407	39 202
Bridgeport division	4 390	3 721
Bridgeport city	2 974	2 908
Long Island division	5 422	4 125
Paint Rock division	2 617	2 203
Paint Rock town	221	226
Woodville town[34]	609	322
Pisgah division	4 165	3 238
Pisgah town	699	519
Princeton division	2 153	1 899
Scottsboro division	20 017	14 023
Hollywood town[34]	1 110	301
Scottsboro city[34]	14 758	9 324
Section division	6 036	4 646
Dutton town[34]	276	423
Section town	821	702
Stevenson division	6 607	5 347
Stevenson city[34]	2 568	2 390
Jefferson County[35]	671 324	644 991
Birmingham division	543 277	...
Bessemer city (pt.)[35]	29 623	(NA)
Birmingham city (pt.)[35]	284 388	(NA)
Brighton city[35]	5 308	2 277
Brookside city	339	...
Brownville city[35]	2 386	501
Center Point (CDP)	23 317	15 675
Fairfield city[35]	13 040	14 369
Forestdale (CDP) (pt.)	8 019	(NA)
Fultondale city (pt.)[35]	4 149	(NA)
Gardendale city (pt.)[35]	–	(NA)
Homewood city[35]	20 533	(NA)
Hoover city (pt.)[35]	8 520	(NA)
Hueytown city (pt.)[35]	13 304	(NA)
Irondale city[35]	6 510	3 166
Lipscomb city (pt.)[35]	3 741	(NA)
Maytown town (pt.)[35]	71	...
Midfield city[35]	6 536	'6 621
Mountain Brook city (pt.)[35]	19 718	(NA)
Mulga town	405	582
Pleasant Grove city (pt.)[35]	7 102	(NA)
Roosevelt City city[35]	3 352	3 663
Tarrant City city[35]	8 148	6 835
Trussville city (pt.)[35]	–	(NA)
Vestavia Hills city (pt.)[35]	13 053	(NA)
Brookside division	3 858	...
Brookside town (pt.)[35]	1 070	(NA)
Cardiff town	140	127
Clay division	5 168	...
Concord–Hopkins division	6 524	...
Hueytown city (pt.)[35]	5	(NA)
Gardendale division	17 118	...
Fultondale city (pt.)[35]	2 068	(NA)
Gardendale city (pt.)[35]	7 928	(NA)
Kimberly town (pt.)[35]	–	(NA)
Morris town (pt.)[35]	–	(NA)
Graysville–Adamsville division	14 496	...
Adamsville city[35]	2 498	2 412
Forestdale (CDP) (pt.)	2 795	(NA)
Graysville city	2 642	3 182
Maytown town (pt.)[35]	5	...
Greenwood division	6 241	...
Bessemer city (pt.)[35]	2 106	(NA)
Hoover division	26 519	...
Bessemer city (pt.)[35]	–	(NA)
Birmingham city (pt.)[35]	8	(NA)
Homewood city (pt.)[35]	879	(NA)
Hoover city (pt.)[35]	11 272	(NA)
Lipscomb city (pt.)[35]	–	(NA)
Vestavia Hills city (pt.)[35]	2 669	(NA)
Kimberly–Morris division	6 764	...
County Line town (pt.)[35]	99	115
Kimberly town (pt.)[35]	1 043	(NA)
Morris town (pt.)[35]	623	(NA)
Trafford town (pt.)[35]	673	(NA)
Leeds division	9 264	...
Leeds city (pt.)[35]	7 881	6 697
Mountain Brook city (pt.)[35]	–	(NA)
Maytown–Sylvan Springs division	3 751	...
Birmingham city (pt.)[35]	17	(NA)
Maytown town (pt.)[35]	462	667
Pleasant Grove city (pt.)[35]	–	(NA)
Sylvan Springs town[35]	450	344
North Johns division	3 863	...
North Johns town	243	241
Palmerdale division	3 260	...
Robbins Crossroads division	4 729	...
Sumiton town (pt.)[35]	–	...
Trussville division	8 654	...
Trussville city (pt.)[35]	3 507	(NA)
Warrior division	5 568	...
Trafford town (pt.)[35]	–	(NA)
Warrior city[35]	3 260	2 621
West Jefferson division	2 270	...

County Subdivisions

County Subdivisions	1980	1970
Jefferson County—Con.		
West Jefferson division—Con.		
West Jefferson town[35]	357	233
Lamar County[36]	16 453	14 335
Millport division	4 434	3 887
Kennedy town[36]	604	415
Millport town[36]	1 287	1 070
Sulligent division	5 755	5 064
Beaverton town	360	265
Detroit town[36]	326	191
Sulligent town[36]	2 130	1 762
Vernon division	6 264	5 384
Vernon city[36]	2 609	2 190
Lauderdale County[37]	80 546	68 111
Cloverdale division	5 418	4 205
Florence division	47 859	...
Florence city (pt.)[37]	37 001	34 031
St. Florian town[37]	305	...
Underwood–Petersville (CDP)	3 836	...
Killen division	10 609	7 436
Killen town[37]	747	683
Lexington division	3 936	2 996
Lexington town[37]	884	278
Oakland division	4 008	3 743
Florence city (pt.)[37]	28	...
Rogersville division	6 783	5 873
Anderson town[37]	405	...
Rogersville town	1 224	950
Waterloo division	1 933	1 504
Waterloo town	260	262
Lawrence County[38]	30 170	27 281
Hatton division	4 078	...
Hillsboro division	2 040	2 325
Hillsboro town	278	222
Morris Chapel division	7 775	6 291
Moulton division	6 740	6 020
Moulton city[38]	3 197	2 470
Mount Hope division	1 728	...
Speake–Oakville division	1 880	1 698
Town Creek–Courtland division	5 929	5 942
Courtland town	456	547
Town Creek town	1 201	1 203
Lee County[39]	76 283	61 268
Auburn–Opelika division	55 511	...
Auburn city (pt.)[39]	28 325	(NA)
Opelika city[39]	21 896	19 027
Beauregard–Marvyn division	5 017	...
Auburn city (pt.)[39]	146	(NA)
Beulah division	2 726	...
Loachapoka–Roxana division	2 854	...
Auburn city (pt.)[39]	–	(NA)
Loachapoka town[39]	335	...
Notasulga town (pt.)	15	11
Waverly town (pt.)	38	50
Smiths–Salem division	10 175	...
Phenix City city (pt.)[39]	545	...
Limestone County[40]	46 005	41 699
Athens division	40 056	...
Ardmore town	1 096	761
Athens city[40]	14 558	14 360
Elkmont town[40]	429	394
Mooresville division	3 029	3 511
Mooresville town	58	72
Salem division	2 920	2 321
Lester town	117	70
Lowndes County[41]	13 253	12 897
Benton–Collirene division	2 202	2 664
Benton town	74	115
Braggs–Prairie Hill division	2 300	2 317
Mosses town[41]	649	...
Fort Deposit division	4 109	3 620
Fort Deposit town	1 519	1 438
Hayneville division	3 519	...
Hayneville town	592	473
Lowndesboro division	1 123	...
Lowndesboro town[41]	207	219
White Hall town[41]	195	...
Macon County[42]	26 829	24 841
Fort Davis division	1 389	682
Little Texas–Society Hill division	1 681	1 724
Notasulga division	2 981	2 862
Notasulga town (pt.)	861	822
Tuskegee city (pt.)	–	...
Shorter–Hardaway division	2 386	2 266
Tuskegee–Milstead division	16 856	...
Franklin town[42]	133	...
Tuskegee city (pt.)[42]	13 240	11 028
Warrior–Creek Stand division	1 536	...
Tuskegee city (pt.)	87	...
Madison County[43]	196 966	186 540
Arsenal division	5 770	...
Huntsville city (pt.)[43]	–	...
Redstone Arsenal (CDP)	5 728	...
Gurley division	3 892	...
Gurley town	735	647
Huntsville city (pt.)[43]	29	...

County Subdivisions

County Subdivisions	1980	1970
Madison County—Con.		
Hazel Green division	4 666	3 930
Hazel Green (CDP)	1 503	...
Huntsville division	158 038	...
Huntsville city (pt.)[43]	142 227	'139 282
Madison city (pt.)	3	...
Meridianville (CDP)	1 403	...
Madison division	5 865	...
Madison city (pt.)	4 054	3 086
Madison Crossroads division	4 709	4 093
New Hope division	7 043	6 317
Huntsville city (pt.)[43]	92	...
New Hope town	1 546	1 300
Owens Crossroads town	804	767
New Market division	5 825	5 627
Triana–Blackwall division	1 158	...
Huntsville city (pt.)[43]	165	...
Triana town	285	228
Marengo County[44]	25 047	23 819
Demopolis division	10 282	9 040
Demopolis city[44]	7 678	7 651
Dixons Mill division	2 874	2 525
Faunsdale division	1 198	1 225
Dayton town	113	115
Faunsdale town	174	227
Linden division	5 774	6 001
Linden city	2 773	2 697
Myrtlewood town	252	334
Providence town[44]	363	...
Sweet Water division	2 764	2 646
Sweet Water town[44]	253	265
Thomaston division	2 155	2 382
Thomaston town	679	824
Marion County[45]	30 041	23 788
Bear Creek division	4 314	3 142
Bear Creek town	353	336
Bexar division	1 843	1 609
Brilliant division	2 926	2 493
Brilliant town	871	726
Guin division	3 482	...
Guin town	2 418	2 220
Gu-Win town (pt.)	266	231
Winfield city (pt.)[45]	–	...
Hackleburg division	2 849	2 215
Hackleburg town[45]	883	726
Hamilton division	9 401	6 664
Hamilton city[45]	5 093	3 088
Weston town	344	187
Winfield division	5 226	...
Glen Allen town (pt.)	53	79
Gu-Win town (pt.)	–	...
Winfield city (pt.)[45]	3 654	3 153
Marshall County[46]	65 622	54 211
Albertville–Boaz division	24 970	...
Albertville city (pt.)[46]	11 878	9 963
Boaz city (pt.)[46]	6 750	'5 465
Arab division	11 393	9 008
Arab city[46]	5 967	4 399
Douglas division	3 715	3 005
Douglas town[46]	116	...
Grant division	7 508	5 639
Grant town[46]	632	382
Guntersville division	11 995	10 400
Albertville city (pt.)[46]	161	...
Guntersville city[46]	7 041	6 491
Town Creek division	1 830	1 689
Union Grove division	4 211	3 576
Union Grove town	127	118
Mobile County[47]	364 980	317 308
Bayou La Batre division	8 276	7 766
Bayou La Batre city (pt.)[47]	1 999	2 664
Citronelle division	5 787	4 602
Citronelle city[47]	2 841	1 935
Grand Bay division	15 723	9 685
Bayou La Batre city (pt.)[47]	6	...
Grand Bay (CDP)	3 185	...
Mobile division	284 274	...
Chickasaw city[47]	7 402	8 447
Creola town[42]	1 652	...
Mobile city[47]	200 452	190 026
Prichard city[47]	39 541	41 578
Saraland city[47]	9 833	7 840
Satsuma city[47]	3 822	2 035
Tillmans Corner (CDP) (pt.)	5 752	...
Mount Vernon division	5 870	6 531
Mount Vernon town	1 038	1 079
Semmes division	10 760	...
Wilmer town[47]	581	...
Tanner–Williams division	12 974	5 860
Theodore division	21 316	...
Theodore (CDP)	6 392	...
Tillmans Corner (CDP) (pt.)	10 189	...
Monroe County	22 651	20 883
Beatrice division	1 945	1 932
Beatrice town	558	455
Frisco City division	5 062	4 505

County Subdivisions	1980	1970
Monroe County—Con.		
Frisco City division—Con.		
Excel town	385	422
Frisco City town	1 424	1 286
Monroeville division	9 334	7 778
Monroeville city	5 674	4 846
Peterman division	2 093	2 139
Uriah division	1 785	1 664
Vredenburgh division	2 432	2 865
Vredenburgh town	433	521
Montgomery County[48]	197 038	167 790
Hope Hull division	9 084	...
Montgomery city (pt.)[48]	5 511	...
Montgomery division	177 406	...
Montgomery city (pt.)[48]	171 887	133 386
Mount Meigs division	3 358	2 318
Pike Road division	3 142	...
Montgomery city (pt.)	459	...
Pine Level division	1 463	1 798
Ramer division	2 585	3 155
Morgan County[49]	90 231	77 306
Danville division	4 404	3 679
Decatur division	48 929	44 890
Decatur city (pt.)[49]	40 829	38 044
Flint City town[49]	673	404
Trinity town[49]	1 328	881
Eva division	4 200	3 540
Eva town	185	146
Falkville division	4 217	3 665
Falkville town[49]	1 310	946
Hartselle division	15 096	11 831
Decatur city (pt.)[49]	744	...
Hartselle city[49]	8 858	7 355
Priceville town (pt.)[49]	354	...
Laceys Spring division	6 594	5 383
Somerville division	6 791	4 318
Decatur city (pt.)[49]	429	...
Priceville town (pt.)[49]	612	...
Somerville town	140	185
Perry County[50]	15 012	15 388
Hamburg division	1 041	...
Heiberger division	1 305	...
Marion division	6 131	...
Marion city[50]	4 467	4 289
Sprott division	1 830	1 931
Uniontown division	4 705	4 892
Uniontown city[50]	2 112	2 133
Pickens County[51]	21 481	20 326
Aliceville division	5 456	5 739
Aliceville city	3 207	2 851
McMullen town[51]	164	...
Memphis town[51]	95	...
Carrollton division	4 108	3 318
Carrollton town	1 104	923
Pickensville town	132	132
Ethelsville division	2 257	2 090
Ethelsville town	95	98
Gordo division	4 409	4 111
Gordo town[51]	2 112	1 991
Raleigh division	967	891
Reform division	4 284	4 177
Reform city[51]	2 245	1 893
Pike County[52]	28 050	25 038
Banks—Josie division	2 123	2 447
Banks town	160	170
Brundidge division	5 419	4 825
Brundidge city[52]	3 213	2 709
Goshen—Shady Grove division	2 242	2 011
Goshen town[52]	365	279
Henderson—Spring Hill division	2 324	1 674
Troy city (pt.)	197	...
Needmore division	1 186	1 210
Troy city (pt.)	161	...
Troy division	14 756	12 871
Troy city (pt.)[52]	12 587	11 482
Randolph County[53]	20 075	18 331
Folsom division	2 573	2 601
Roanoke division	9 447	8 411
Roanoke city[53]	5 896	5 251
Wadley division	1 939	1 890
Wadley town	532	626
Wedowee division	3 372	3 079
Wedowee town[53]	908	842
Woodland division	2 744	2 350
Woodland town[53]	192	177
Russell County[54]	47 356	45 394
Cottonton—Seale division	4 015	4 293
Crawford division	2 905	2 347
Hurtsboro division	3 196	3 860
Hurtsboro town	752	937
Phenix City division	37 240	...
Phenix City city (pt.)	26 383	25 281

County Subdivisions	1980	1970
St. Clair County[55]	41 205	27 956
Ashville division	6 347	4 895
Ashville town (pt.)[55]	1 467	986
Steele town	795	798
Moody division	10 420	...
Branchville town (pt.)	137	...
Leeds city (pt.)[55]	643	257
Moody town[55]	1 840	504
Whites Chapel town	336	334
Pell City division	13 642	9 850
Pell City city[55]	6 616	'5 602
Riverside town	849	351
Vincent town (pt.)[55]	—	...
Ragland division	3 738	3 112
Ashville town (pt.)[55]	22	...
Ragland town[55]	1 860	1 239
Springville division	7 058	...
Branchville town (pt.)	228	225
Margaret town	757	685
Odenville town	724	533
Springville town[55]	1 476	1 153
Shelby County[56]	66 298	38 037
Alabaster—Helena division	33 674	...
Alabaster city[56]	7 079	2 642
Helena town[56]	2 130	1 110
Hoover city (pt.)	—	...
Pelham city[56]	6 759	931
Calera division	4 239	3 554
Calera town	2 035	1 655
Chelsea division	5 790	3 931
Leeds city (pt.)[56]	114	37
Columbiana division	6 311	4 727
Columbiana city[56]	2 655	2 248
Montevallo division	8 969	7 556
Montevallo city[56]	3 965	3 719
Wilton town[56]	642	573
Vincent division	4 999	4 300
Harpersville town	934	639
Vincent town (pt.)	1 652	1 419
Wilsonville division	2 316	1 718
Wilsonville town[56]	914	659
Sumter County[57]	16 908	16 974
Belmont division	853	977
Cuba division	1 550	1 548
Cuba town (pt.)[57]	486	386
Gainesville division	906	967
Gainesville town	207	255
Livingston division	5 829	5 785
Epes town	399	293
Livingston city[57]	3 187	2 358
Panola—Geiger division	1 517	1 838
Geiger town	200	120
York division	6 253	5 859
Cuba town (pt.)[57]	—	...
York city	3 392	3 044
Talladega County[58]	73 826	65 280
Childersburg division	8 095	7 198
Bon Air town	118	214
Childersburg city	5 084	4 831
Lincoln—Eastaboga division	4 366	3 664
Lincoln town[58]	2 081	1 127
Munford division	5 603	4 792
Oxford city (pt.)[58]	476	...
Renfroe—Lanier division	2 445	...
Vincent town (pt.)[58]	—	...
Sycamore—Winterboro division	5 040	4 424
Sylacauga city (pt.)[58]	—	...
Sylacauga division	22 343	...
Gantts Quarry town	71	63
Mignon (CDP)	2 054	1 726
Oak Grove town	638	482
Sylacauga city (pt.)[58]	12 708	12 255
Talladega Springs town	196	143
Talladega division	25 934	...
Talladega city[58]	19 128	17 662
Waldo town[58]	231	...
Tallapoosa County[59]	38 676	33 840
Alexander City division	18 637	...
Alexander City city[59]	13 807	12 358
Camp Hill division	2 498	2 337
Camp Hill town	1 628	1 554
Dadeville division	9 214	6 781
Dadeville city[59]	3 263	2 847
New Site division	2 474	2 446
Daviston town	334	247
Goldville town[59]	89	...
New Site town	340	'548
Tallassee division	5 853	5 715
Carrville town	820	895
Tallassee city (pt.)[59]	1 223	1 405
Tuscaloosa County[60]	137 541	116 029
Abernant division	3 064	1 958
Vance town (pt.)[60]	—	...
Big Sandy—Duncanville division	4 358	2 601
Moundville town (pt.)[60]	41	15
Brookwood division	3 338	2 611

County Subdivisions

County Subdivisions	1980	1970
Tuscaloosa County—Con.		
Brookwood division—Con.		
Brookwood town[60]	492	...
Tuscaloosa city (pt.)[60]	22	...
Coaling–Vance division	3 985	2 713
Vance town (pt.)[60]	254	...
Coker division	6 030	...
Northport city (pt.)[60]	2 225	(NA)
Tuscaloosa city (pt.)[60]	263	...
Elrod–Moores Bridge–Echola division	1 073	1 086
Fosters division	2 857	2 553
Samantha division	2 690	...
Tuscaloosa division	107 774	...
Northport city (pt.)[60]	12 066	(NA)
Tuscaloosa city (pt.)[60]	74 742	65 773
Windham Springs division	2 372	1 367
Tuscaloosa city (pt.)[60]	184	...
Walker County[61]	68 660	56 246
Carbon Hill division	4 449	3 969
Carbon Hill city (pt.)[61]	2 452	1 929
Eldridge town[61]	230	...
Kansas town	267	227
Cordova division	4 537	4 030
Cordova city[61]	3 123	2 750
Dora division	8 367	7 010
Dora town[61]	2 327	1 862
Sumiton town (pt.)[61]	2 815	2 374
Empire division	2 456	2 009
Flat Creek–Wegra division	2 093	1 735
Jasper division	22 496	...
Jasper city[61]	11 894	10 798
Manchester division	3 737	2 521
Nauvoo division	3 504	3 014
Carbon Hill city (pt.)	–	...
Nauvoo town	259	265
Oakman division	3 484	3 224
Oakman town	770	853
Parrish division	5 107	4 634
Parrish town[61]	1 583	1 742
Sipsey division	4 680	3 256
Sipsey town	678	608
Townley division	3 750	2 848
Carbon Hill city (pt.)[61]	–	...
Washington County[62]	16 821	16 241
Chatom division	3 816	...
Chatom town	1 122	1 059
Fruitdale division	2 196	2 285
McIntosh division	4 180	4 067
McIntosh town[62]	319	...
Millry division	3 139	...
Millry town	956	911
Wagarville division	3 490	...
Wilcox County[63]	14 755	16 303
Alberta division	2 039	2 424
Camden division	5 176	5 020
Camden town[63]	2 406	1 742
Coy–Fatama division	1 442	1 737
Pine Apple division	1 861	2 467
Oak Hill town	63	86
Pine Apple town[63]	298	347
Pine Hill division	4 237	4 655
Pine Hill town	510	697
Winston County[64]	21 953	16 654
Addison division	5 744	4 585
Addison town[64]	746	692
Arley town[64]	276	164
Double Springs division	4 489	3 213
Double Springs town[64]	1 057	957
Haleyville division	9 657	7 152
Haleyville city[64]	5 306	4 190
Lynn division	2 063	1 704
Lynn town[64]	554	286

ALASKA

Alaska derives its name from an English corruption of the native word *Al-ay-ek-sa*, probably meaning "The great land" or "Mainland."

The region now known as Alaska was first explored by the Russian offices Bering and Chirikov in 1741. Russian traders and trappers soon entered the country and through their activity other nations became interested in this region. Spanish expeditions in 1774 and 1775 visited the southeastern shore, and in 1778 the English explorer, Capt. James Cook, made extensive surveys of the coast for the British Government.

The first settlement was made by the Russians at Three Saints on Kodiak Island in 1784, and in 1804 the Russian-American Company founded Sitka, making it the seat of government in the following year.

In 1799 the trade and regulation of the Russian possessions in America were given over to the Russian-American Company for a term of 20 years, which was afterwards twice renewed for similar periods.

In 1821 Russia attempted by *ukase* to exclude foreign navigators from Bering Sea and the Pacific coast of her possessions, which caused a controversy with the United States and Great Britain. The question was settled by a treaty with the United States in 1824 and one with Great Britain in 1825, by which the boundaries of the Russian possessions in America were permanently fixed.

In March, 1867, Alaska was purchased by the United States for the sum of $7,200,000 in gold, and in October of the same year the formal transfer was made at Sitka. From 1867 to 1877 Alaska was governed by the War Department, although the customs were from the beginning collected by the Treasury Department, and with the latter the control rested from 1877 until the passage of the act of 1884. This act extended over Alaska the laws of the state of Oregon so far as they were applicable, created a judicial district and a land district, put in force the mining laws of the United States, and gave the country an admistrative system.

The influx of settlers after the discovery of gold in the Klondike in 1896 rendered more adequate laws necessary. In 1899 and 1900 Congress made provisions for a code of civil and criminal law, and in 1903 passed a homestead act. In the meantime a serious boundary dispute had arisen between the United States and Canada regarding the interpretation of the treaty of 1825. This was settled in 1903 by an agreement whereby the seacoast of Canada extended no farther north than 54°40'.

By an act of May 7, 1906, Alaska was authorized to elect a delegate to Congress.

Alaska was admitted as a state in 1959.

LOCATION INDEX

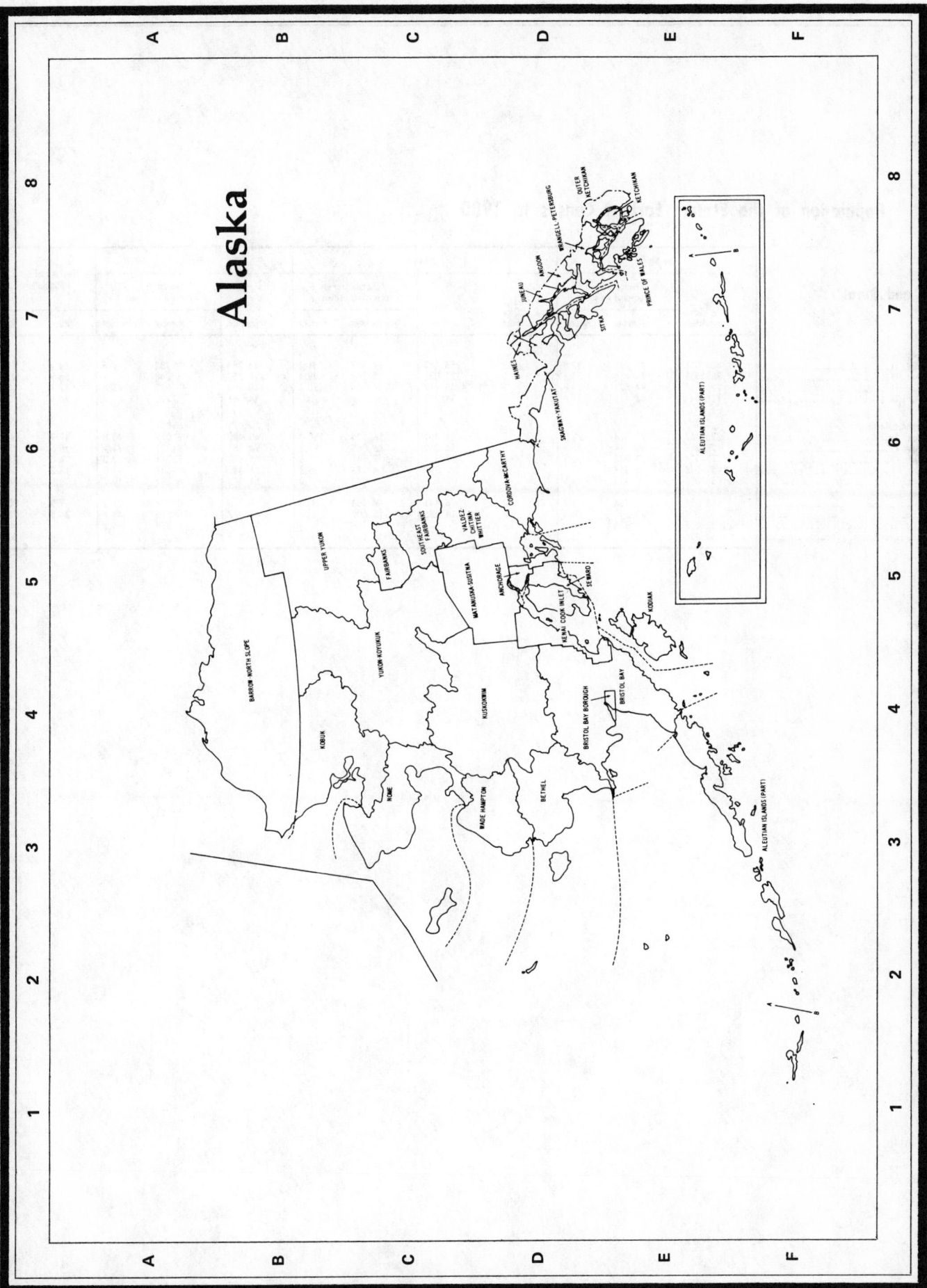

Alaska

21

Population of the State: Earliest Census to 1980

Urban and Rural

	The State			Urban					Rural			Percent of total population	
	Total population	Change from preceding census		Places of 2,500 or more	Population	Change from preceding census		Population	Change from preceding census			Urban	Rural
		Number	Percent			Number	Percent		Number	Percent			
Current urban definition:													
1980 (Apr. 1)	401 851	99 268	32.8	13	258 567	87 537	51.2	143 284	13 932	10.8		64.3	35.7
1970 (Apr. 1)	'302 583	76 416	33.8	15	171 030	85 263	99.4	129 352	−11 048	−7.9		56.9	43.1
1960 (Apr. 1)	226 167	97 524	75.8	7	85 767	51 505	150.3	140 400	46 019	48.8		37.9	62.1
1950 (Apr. 1)	128 643	56 119	77.4	6	34 262	...	...	94 381	...	...		26.6	73.4
Previous urban definition:													
1960 (Apr. 1)	226 167	97 524	75.8	7	85 767	51 505	150.3	140 400	46 019	48.8		37.9	62.1
1950 (Apr. 1)	128 643	56 119	77.4	6	34 262	16 888	97.2	94 381	39 231	71.1		26.6	73.4
1939 (Oct. 1)	72 524	13 246	22.3	4	17 374	9 535	121.6	55 150	3 711	7.2		24.0	76.0
1929 (Oct. 1)	59 278	4 242	7.7	2	7 839	4 781	156.3	51 439	−539	−1.0		13.2	86.8
1920 (Jan. 1)	55 036	−9 320	−14.5	1	3 058	−3 083	−50.2	51 978	−6 237	−10.7		5.6	94.4
1910	64 356	764	1.2	2	6 141	−9 464	−60.6	58 215	10 228	21.3		9.5	90.5
1900	63 592	31 540	98.4	2	15 605	15 605	...	47 987	15 935	49.7		24.5	75.5
1890	32 052	−1 374	−4.1	−	−	−	−	32 052	−1 374	−4.1		−	100.0
1880	33 426	...	...	−	−	...	...	33 426	...	...		−	100.0

ANCHORAGE

1920	1,856
1929	2,277
1939	3,495
1950	11,254
1960	44,237
1970	48,029
1980	174,431

FAIRBANKS

1910	3,541
1920	1,155
1929	2,101
1939	3,455
1950	5,771
1960	13,311
1970	14,771
1980	22,645

JUNEAU

1890	1,253
1900	1,864
1910	1,644
1920	3,058
1929	4,043
1939	5,729
1950	5,956
1960	6,797
1970	13,556
1980	19,528

Note:—Historical tables for the boroughs of Alaska are not included in this edition.

Subdivisions

Subdivisions	1980	1970
The State[1]	401 851	r302 583
Aleutian Islands Census Area[2]	7 768	...
Aleutian Islands census subarea	7 768	...
Adak Station (CDP)	3 315	2 249
Akutan city[2]	169	...
Atka (CDP)	93	88
Attu (CDP)	29	...
Cold Bay (CDP)	228	256
False Pass (CDP)	70	62
King Cove city	460	283
Nelson Lagoon (CDP)	59	43
Nikolski (CDP)	50	57
St. George (CDP)	158	163
St. Paul city[2]	551	...
Sand Point city	625	360
Shemya Station (CDP)	600	1 131
Unalaska city	1 322	r342
Anchorage Borough[3]	174 431	r126 385
Anchorage census subarea	174 431	...
Anchorage city[3]	174 431	r48 081
Bethel Census Area[4]	10 999	...
Aniak census subarea	1 301	...
Aniak city[4]	341	...
Chuathbaluk city[4]	105	...
Crooked Creek (CDP)	108	59
Lime Village (CDP)	48	25
Lower Kalskag city	246	183
Red Devil (CDP)	39	81
Sleetmute (CDP)	107	109
Sparrevohn Station (CDP)	26	...
Stony River (CDP)	62	74
Upper Kalskag city[4]	129	...
Lower Kuskokwim census subarea	9 698	...
Akiachak city[4]	438	...
Akiak city[4]	198	...
Akolmiut city[4]	641	526
Atmautluak city[4]	219	...
Bethel city	3 576	2 416
Cape Newenham (CDP)	43	...
Chefornak city[4]	230	...
Eek city[4]	228	...
Goodnews Bay city[4]	168	...
Kipnuk (CDP)	371	325
Kongiganak (CDP)	239	190
Kwethluk city[4]	454	...
Kwigillingok (CDP)	354	148
Mekoryuk city	160	249
Napakiak city[4]	262	...
Napaskiak city[4]	244	...
Newtok city (pt.)[4]	131	...
Nightmute city[4]	119	...
Oscarville (CDP)	56	41
Platinum city[4]	55	...
Quinhagak city[4]	412	...
Toksook Bay city[4]	333	...
Tuluksak city[4]	236	...
Tuntutuliak (CDP)	216	158
Tununak city[4]	298	...
Bristol Bay Borough	1 094	1 147
Bristol Bay census subarea	1 094	...
King Salmon (CDP)	545	202
Naknek (CDP)	318	r318
South Naknek (CDP)	145	154
Dillingham Census Area[5]	4 616	...
Dillingham census subarea	4 616	...
Aleknagik city[5]	154	...
Chignik (CDP)	178	83
Chignik Lagoon (CDP)	48	...
Chignik Lake (CDP)	138	117
Clark's Point city[5]	79	...
Dillingham city	1 563	914
Egegik (CDP)	75	148
Ekwok city[5]	77	...
Igiugig (CDP)	33	36
Iliamna (CDP)	94	58
Ivanof Bay (CDP)	40	48
Kokhanok (CDP)	83	88
Koliganek (CDP)	117	142
Levelock (CDP)	79	74
Manokotak city[5]	294	...
Newhalen city[5]	87	...
New Stuyahok city[5]	331	...
Nondalton city[5]	173	...
Pedro Bay (CDP)	33	65
Perryville (CDP)	111	94
Pilot Point (CDP)	66	68
Portage Creek (CDP)	48	...
Port Heiden city[5]	92	...
Togiak city	470	383
Twin Hills (CDP)	70	67
Fairbanks North Star Borough[6]	53 983	45 864
Eielson Reservation census subarea	5 320	...
Eielson AFB (CDP)	5 232	6 149
Fairbanks North Star census subarea[6]	48 663	...
Big Horn (CDP)	360	...
College (CDP)	4 043	3 434
Ester (CDP)	149	264
Fairbanks[6]	22 645	14 771
Fox (CDP)	123	...

Subdivisions

Subdivisions	1980	1970
Fairbanks North Star Borough—Con.		
Fairbanks North Star census subarea—Con.		
Harding Lake (CDP)	38	...
Moose Creek (CDP)	510	...
Murphy Dome (CDP)	72	...
North Pole city[6]	724	265
Salcha (CDP)	319	...
Two Rivers (CDP)	359	...
Haines Borough[7]	1 680	...
Haines census subarea	1 680	...
Haines city[7]	993	463
Juneau Borough[8]	19 528	13 556
Juneau census subarea	19 528	...
Juneau city[8]	19 528	6 050
Kenai Peninsula Borough[9]	25 282	...
Kenai—Cook Inlet census subarea	22 473	...
Anchor Point (CDP)	226	102
Clam Gulch (CDP)	50	47
Cooper Landing (CDP)	116	31
Fritz Creek (CDP)	302	27
Halibut Cove (CDP)	47	44
Homer city	2 209	1 083
Hope (CDP)	103	51
Jakolof Bay (CDP)	36	...
Kachemak city	403	76
Kalifonsky (CDP)	92	...
Kasilof (CDP)	201	71
Kenai city	4 324	3 533
Moose Pass (CDP)	76	53
Nikishka (CDP)	1 109	...
Ninilchik (CDP)	341	134
Salamatof (CDP)	334	...
Seldovia city	479	437
Soldotna city[9]	2 320	1 202
Sterling (CDP)	919	30
Tyonek (CDP)	239	232
Seward census subarea	2 809	...
English Bay (CDP)	124	58
Port Graham (CDP)	161	107
Portlock (CDP)	31	...
Seward city[9]	1 843	1 587
Ketchikan Gateway Borough[10]	11 316	10 041
Ketchikan census subarea	11 316	...
Clover Pass (CDP)	451	261
Herring Cove (CDP)	99	114
Ketchikan city[10]	7 198	6 994
Ketchikan East (CDP)	387	...
Mountain Point (CDP)	396	459
North Tongass Highway (CDP)	1 722	...
Pennock Island (CDP)	90	78
Saxman city	273	135
Saxman East (CDP)	411	...
Kobuk Census Area[11]	4 831	...
Kobuk census subarea	4 831	...
Ambler city[11]	192	...
Buckland city	177	104
Deering city[11]	150	...
Kiana city	345	278
Kivalina city	241	188
Kobuk city[11]	62	...
Kotzebue city[11]	2 054	1 696
Noatak (CDP)	273	293
Noorvik city	492	462
Selawik city	361	429
Shungnak city	202	165
Kodiak Island Borough[12]	9 939	9 409
Kodiak Island census subarea[12]	8 569	...
Akhiok city[12]	105	...
Karluk (CDP)	96	98
Kodiak city[12]	4 756	3 798
Larsen Bay city[12]	168	...
Old Harbor city	340	290
Ouzinkie city	173	160
Port Lions city	215	227
Kodiak Station census subarea	1 370	...
Kodiak Station (CDP)	1 370	3 052
Matanuska—Susitna Borough[13]	17 816	6 509
Matanuska—Susitna census subarea	17 816	...
Big Lake (CDP)	410	36
Bodenburg Butte (CDP)	988	...
Houston city[13]	370	69
Montana (CDP)	40	33
Palmer city[13]	2 141	1 140
Sutton (CDP)	182	76
Talkeetna (CDP)	264	182
Wasilla city[13]	1 559	...
Willow (CDP)	139	38
Nome Census Area[14]	6 537	5 749
Nome census subarea	6 537	...
Brevig Mission city	138	123
Diomede city[14]	139	...
Elim city[14]	211	...
Gambell city	445	372
Golovin city[14]	87	...
Koyuk city[14]	188	...
Nome city	2 301	r2 357
Perkinsville (CDP)	33	...

Subdivisions

Subdivisions	1980	1970
Nome Census Area—Con.		
Nome census subarea—Con.		
Port Clarence (CDP)	29	...
St. Michael city	239	207
Savoonga city	491	364
Shaktoolik city[14]	164	151
Shishmaref city[14]	394	267
Stebbins city	331	231
Teller city	212	220
Unalakleet city[14]	623	...
Wales city	133	131
White Mountain city	125	87
North Slope Borough[15]	4 199	...
Barrow–Point Hope census subarea	3 784	...
Anaktuvuk Pass city	203	99
Atkasook (CDP)	107	...
Barrow city	2 207	2 104
Cape Lisburne (CDP)	36	83
Nuiqsut city[15]	208	...
Point Hope city	464	386
Point Lay (CDP)	68	...
Wainwright city	405	315
Prudhoe Bay–Kaktovik census subarea	415	...
Deadhorse (CDP)	64	163
Kaktovik city[15]	165	...
Prudhoe Bay (CDP)	50	49
Prince of Wales–Outer Ketchikan Census Area[16]	3 822	...
Outer Ketchikan census subarea	1 333	...
Annette (CDP)	139	195
Hyder (CDP)	77	49
Metlakatla (CDP)	1 056	1 050
Meyers Chuck (CDP)	50	37
Prince of Wales census subarea	2 489	...
Cape Pole (CDP)	29	123
Coffman Cove (CDP)	193	...
Craig city[16]	527	272
Hydaburg city	298	214
Kasaan city[16]	25	...
Klawock city	318	213
North Whale Pass (CDP)	90	...
Point Baker (CDP)	90	...
Thorne Bay (CDP)	320	443
Sitka Borough[17]	7 803	...
Sitka census subarea	7 803	...
Sitka city[17]	7 803	3 370
Skagway–Yakutat–Angoon Census Area[18]	3 478	...
Angoon census subarea	712	...
Angoon city[18]	465	400
Tenakee Springs city[18]	138	...
Hoonah–Yakutat census subarea	1 817	...
Elfin Cove (CDP)	28	49
Gustavus (CDP)	98	64
Hoonah city	680	748
Pelican city	180	133
Yakutat city[18]	449	190
Klukwan census subarea	135	...
Klukwan (CDP)	135	103
Skagway census subarea	814	...
Skagway city[18]	768	675
Southeast Fairbanks Census Area[19]	5 676	...
Southeast Fairbanks census subarea	5 676	...
Big Delta (CDP)	285	...
Chicken (CDP)	37	...
Delta Junction city[19]	945	703
Dot Lake (CDP)	67	42
Eagle city	110	36
Eagle Village (CDP)	54	...
Fort Greely (CDP)	1 635	1 820
Healy Lake (CDP)	33	...
Northway (CDP)	73	40
Northway Village (CDP)	112	...
Tanacross (CDP)	117	84
Tetlin (CDP)	107	114
Tok (CDP)	589	214
Valdez–Cordova Census Area[20]	8 348	...
Copper River census subarea	2 721	...
Chistochina (CDP)	55	33
Chitina (CDP)	42	38
Copper Center (CDP)	213	206
Gakona (CDP)	87	88
Glennallen (CDP)	511	363
Gulkana (CDP)	104	53
Lower Tonsina (CDP)	40	...
Mentasta Lake (CDP)	59	68
Paxson (CDP)	30	...
Slana (CDP)	49	...
Tazlina (CDP)	31	...
Tonsina (CDP)	135	...
Cordova census subarea	2 241	...
Cordova city[20]	1 879	1 164
Eyak (CDP)	47	...
Prince William Sound census subarea	3 386	...
Tatitlek (CDP)	68	111
Valdez city[20]	3 079	1 005
Whittier city[20]	198	130

Subdivisions

Subdivisions	1980	1970
Wade Hampton Census Area[21]	4 665	3 917
Wade Hampton census subarea	4 665	
Alakanuk city[21]	522	'414
Chevak city	466	387
Emmonak city[21]	567	439
Fortuna Ledge city[21]	262	...
Hooper Bay city	627	490
Kotlik city[21]	293	...
Mountain Village city	583	419
Newtok city (pt.)[21]	–	...
Pilot Station city	325	290
Pitkas Point (CDP)	88	70
Russian Mission city[21]	169	...
St. Mary's city	382	384
Scammon Bay city	250	166
Sheldon Point city[21]	103	...
Wrangell–Petersburg Census Area[22]	6 167	...
Petersburg census subarea	3 804	...
Kake city[22]	555	448
Kupreanof city[22]	47	...
Petersburg[22]	2 821	2 042
Port Alexander city[22]	86	36
Wrangell census subarea	2 363	...
Wrangell city[22]	2 184	2 029
Yukon–Koyukuk Census Area[23]	7 873	...
Koyukuk–Middle Yukon census subarea	5 323	...
Allakaket[23]	163	...
Anderson city[23]	517	362
Campion Station (CDP)	62	...
Cantwell (CDP)	89	62
Dunbar (CDP)	50	...
Evansville (CDP)	94	57
Galena city[23]	765	...
Healy (CDP)	334	79
Hughes city[23]	73	...
Huslia city	188	159
Indian Mountain (CDP)	27	...
Kaltag city	247	206
Koyukuk city[23]	98	...
McKinley Park (CDP)	32	...
Manley Hot Springs (CDP)	61	34
Minto (CDP)	153	168
Nenana city	470	'382
Nulato city	350	308
Rampart (CDP)	50	36
Ruby city[23]	197	...
Stevens Village (CDP)	96	74
Suntrana (CDP)	56	67
Tanana city	388	'406
Usibelli Mine (CDP)	53	65
McGrath–Holy Cross census subarea	1 343	...
Anvik city	114	83
Grayling city	209	139
Holy Cross city	241	199
McGrath city[23]	355	...
Nikolai city[23]	91	...
Shageluk city[23]	131	...
Takotna (CDP)	48	...
Tatalina Station (CDP)	46	...
Telida (CDP)	33	...
Yukon Flats census subarea	1 207	...
Arctic Village (CDP)	111	85
Beaver (CDP)	66	101
Birch Creek (CDP)	32	...
Central (CDP)	36	26
Chalkyitsik (CDP)	100	130
Circle (CDP)	81	54
Fort Yukon city	619	448
Venetie (CDP)	132	112

ARIZONA

The name Arizona is of Spanish-Indian origin and is variously stated to signify "small or few springs," "little creek," and "silver bearing."

The first recorded exploration of the region now constituting Arizona was made in 1539 by the Spaniard, Marcos de Niza, who was sent out from Mexico to confirm the rumors of great wealth which de Vaca had heard of in his wanderings. In 1540 the Coronado traversed the region in his journey northward. The earliest settlements were made by Spanish missionaries toward the close of the seventeenth century.

This region formed a part of Mexico, which was under the dominion of Spain until by the Mexican Revolution of 1821 it achieved its independence. In February, 1848, at the close of the Mexican War, Mexico ceded to the United States her claims to territory north of the Rio Grande and Gila River and extending westward to the Pacific Ocean, and in December, 1853, by the Gadsden purchase, the United States acquired from Mexico a strip of territory bounded on the north principally by the Gila River and on the south by the present Mexican line.

In 1850 a territorial form of government had been established for New Mexico, which at that time extended westward to the California boundary, and in 1854 the territory acquired by the Gadsden purchase was added to New Mexico. In 1863, by authority of an act of Congress passed in February of that year, the territory of Arizona was organized, with boundaries as at present, except that the northern line extended westward to California. The boundary between Arizona and Nevada was established at its present location in 1866.

In June, 1910, Congress passed an act to enable Arizona and New Mexico to form state constitutions and governments and to be admitted to the Union. In December of that year, a proposed state constitution for Arizona was adopted by a convention held at Phoenix and was ratified by the people in February, 1911. This constitution received the conditional approval of the Federal Government in August, 1911, and was referred to the people of the territory for amendment. February 14, 1912, the territory became a state of the Union.

COUNTY LOCATION INDEX

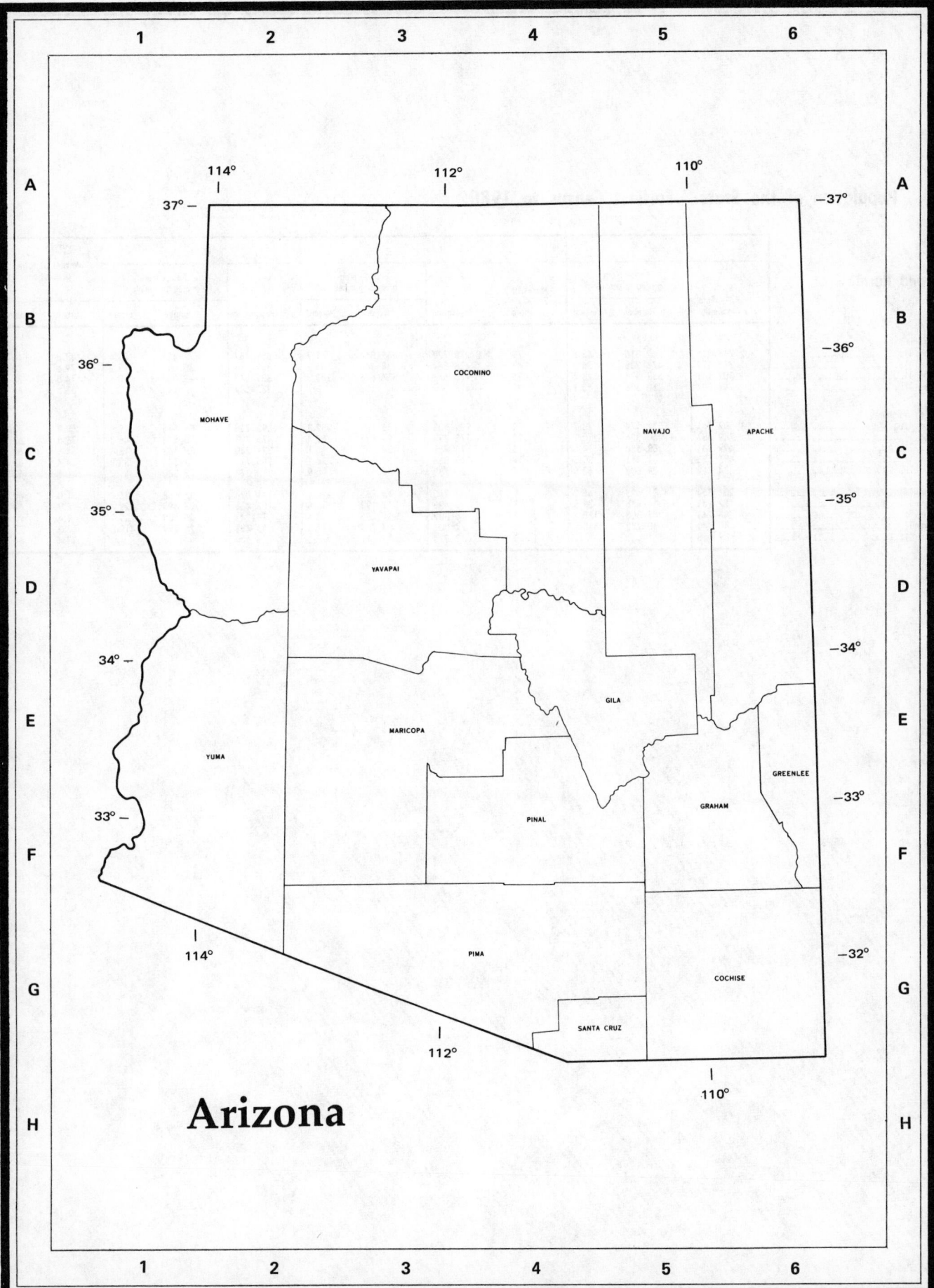

Arizona

Population of the State: Earliest Census to 1980

Urban and Rural

	The State			Urban				Rural			Percent of total population	
	Total population	Change from preceding census		Places of 2,500 or more	Population	Change from preceding census		Population	Change from preceding census		Urban	Rural
		Number	Percent			Number	Percent		Number	Percent		
Current urban definition:												
1980 (Apr. 1)	2 718 215	942 816	53.1	77	2 278 728	869 864	61.7	439 487	77 451	21.4	83.8	16.2
1970 (Apr. 1)	'1 775 399	473 238	36.3	47	1 408 864	438 248	45.2	362 036	30 491	9.2	79.6	20.4
1960 (Apr. 1)	1 302 161	552 574	73.7	35	970 616	554 616	133.3	331 545	-2 042	-0.6	74.5	25.5
1950 (Apr. 1)	749 587	250 326	50.1	32	416 000	...	...	333 587	...	...	55.5	44.5
Previous urban definition:												
1960 (Apr. 1)	1 302 161	552 574	73.7	29	909 903	636 109	232.3	392 258	-83 535	-17.6	69.9	30.1
1950 (Apr. 1)	749 587	250 326	50.1	22	273 794	99 813	57.4	475 793	150 513	46.3	36.5	63.5
1940 (Apr. 1)	499 261	63 688	14.6	16	173 981	24 125	16.1	325 280	39 563	13.8	34.8	65.2
1930 (Apr. 1)	435 573	101 411	30.3	14	149 856	29 068	24.1	285 717	72 343	33.9	34.4	65.6
1920 (Jan. 1)	334 162	129 808	63.5	15	120 788	57 528	90.9	213 374	72 280	51.2	36.1	63.9
1910 (Apr. 15)	204 354	81 423	66.2	9	63 260	43 765	224.5	141 094	37 658	36.4	31.0	69.0
1900 (June 1)	122 931	34 688	39.3	4	19 495	11 193	134.8	103 436	23 495	29.4	15.9	84.1
1890 (June 1)	88 243	47 803	118.2	2	8 302	1 295	18.5	79 941	46 508	139.1	9.4	90.6
1880 (June 1)	40 440	30 782	318.7	1	7 007	3 783	117.3	33 433	26 999	419.6	17.3	82.7
1870 (June 1)	9 658	...	...	1	3 224	...	...	6 434	...	...	33.4	66.6

APACHE

1880	5,283
1890	4,281
1900	8,297
1910	9,196
1920	13,196
1930	17,765
1940	24,095
1950	27,767
1960	30,438
1970	32,298
1980	52,108

COCHISE

1890	6,938
1900	9,251
1910	34,591
1920	46,465
1930	40,998
1940	34,627
1950	31,448
1960	55,039
1970	61,918
1980	85,686

COCONINO

1900	5,514
1910	8,130
1920	9,982
1930	14,064
1940	18,770
1950	23,910
1960	41,857
1970	48,326
1980	75,008

GILA

1890	2,021
1900	4,973
1910	16,348
1920	25,678
1930	31,016
1940	23,867
1950	24,158
1960	25,745
1970	29,255
1980	37,080

GRAHAM

1890	5,670
1900	14,162
1910	23,999
1920	10,148
1930	10,373
1940	12,113
1950	12,985
1960	14,045
1970	16,578
1980	22,862

GREENLEE

1920	15,362
1930	9,886
1940	8,698
1950	12,805
1960	11,509
1970	10,330
1980	11,406

MARICOPA

1880	5,689
1890	10,986
1900	20,457
1910	34,488
1920	89,576
1930	150,970
1940	186,193
1950	331,770
1960	663,510
1970	971,228
1980	1,509,052

MAHAVE

1870	179
1880	1,190
1890	1,444
1900	3,426
1910	3,773
1920	5,259
1930	5,572
1940	8,591
1950	8,510
1960	7,736
1970	25,857
1980	55,865

NAVAJO

1900	8,829
1910	11,471
1920	16,077
1930	21,202
1940	25,309
1950	29,446
1960	37,994
1970	47,715
1980	67,629

PIMA

1870	5,716
1880	17,006
1890	12,673
1900	14,689
1910	22,818
1920	34,680
1930	55,676
1940	72,838
1950	141,216
1960	265,660
1970	351,667
1980	531,443

PINAL

1880	3,044
1890	4,251
1900	7,779
1910	9,045
1920	16,130
1930	22,081
1940	28,841
1950	43,191
1960	62,673
1970	68,579
1980	90,918

SANTA CRUZ

1900	4,545
1910	6,766
1920	12,689
1930	9,684

1940	9,482
1950	9,344
1960	10,808
1970	13,966
1980	20,459

YAVAPAI

1870	2,142
1880	5,013
1890	8,685
1900	13,799
1910	15,996
1920	24,016
1930	28,470
1940	26,511
1950	24,991
1960	28,912
1970	37,005
1980	68,145

YUMA

1870	1,621
1880	3,215
1890	2,671
1900	4,145
1910	7,733
1920	14,904
1930	17,816
1940	19,326
1950	28,006
1960	46,235
1970	60,827
1980	90,554

NOTES

PIMA

Name changed from Ewell in (?).

YUMA

Name changed from Castle Dome in (?).

CASA GRANDE

1920	948
1930	1,351
1940	1,545
1950	4,181
1960	8,311
1970	10,536
1980	14,971

CHANDLER

1930	1,378
1940	1,239
1950	3,799
1960	9,531
1970	13,763
1980	29,673

DOUGLAS

1910	6,437
1920	9,916
1930	9,828
1940	8,623
1950	9,442
1960	11,925
1970	12,462
1980	13,058

FLAGSTAFF

1890	963
1900	1,271
1910	1,633
1920	3,186
1930	3,891
1940	5,080
1950	7,663
1960	18,214
1970	26,117
1980	34,743

GLENDALE

1920	2,737
1930	3,665
1940	4,855
1950	8,179
1960	15,893
1970	36,228
1980	97,172

LAKE HAVASU CITY

1980	15,909

MESA

1900	722
1910	1,692
1920	3,036
1930	3,711
1940	7,224
1950	16,790
1960	33,772
1970	63,049
1980	152,453

NOGALES

1940	5,135
1950	6,153
1960	7,286
1970	8,946
1980	15,683

PARADISE VALLEY

1970	6,637
1980	11,085

PEORIA

1960	2,593
1970	4,792
1980	12,251

PHOENIX

1890	3,152
1900	5,544
1910	11,134
1920	29,053
1930	48,118
1940	65,114
1950	106,818
1960	439,170
1970	584,303
1980	789,704

PRESCOTT

1870	668
1880	1,836
1890	1,759
1900	3,559
1910	5,092
1920	5,010
1930	5,517
1940	6,018
1950	6,764
1960	12,861
1970	13,030
1980	20,055

SCOTTSDALE

1960	10,026
1970	67,823
1980	88,412

SIERRA VISTA

1970	17,394
1980	24,937

TEMPE

1900	885
1910	1,473
1920	1,963
1930	2,495
1940	2,906
1950	7,684
1960	24,897
1970	63,550
1980	106,743

TUCSON

1870	3,224
1880	7,007
1890	5,150
1900	7,531
1910	13,193
1920	20,292
1930	32,506
1940	35,752
1950	45,454
1960	212,892
1970	262,933
1980	330,537

YUMA

1880	1,200
1890	1,773
1900	1,519
1910	2,914
1920	4,237
1930	4,892
1940	5,325
1950	9,145
1960	23,974
1970	29,007
1980	42,433

CORRECTION NOTE

The official 1980 census counts of total population shown in this report supersede counts issued previously. Corrections to the figures were made after the counts were provided to the State for redistricting purposes and released in Advance Report PHC80-V for this State.

Shown below are corrections to the 1980 census counts of the total population made after the tabulations for this report were completed. Any additional corrections made after this report is printed are available by writing to Data User Services Division, Customer Services (Corrections), Bureau of the Census, Washington, D.C. 20233.

The 1980 figures shown in this publication are subject to change pending the outcome of the various lawsuits dealing with the census counts.

	1980 population	
	As shown in the tables	Corrected
The State.....................	2 718 215	2 718 425
Apache County:		
Fort Apache division:		
McNary (CDP)(pt.)..............	318	(1)
Gila County:		
Globe division:		
Globe city....................	6 708	6 886
Maricopa County...................	1 509 052	1 509 262
Deer Valley division:		
Peoria city (pt.).............	3	66
Phoenix division................	1 421 448	1 421 658
Peoria city (pt.).............	12 248	12 241
Scottsdale city...............	88 412	88 622
Navajo County:		
Apache division:		
McNary (CDP)(pt.)..............	1 002	(1)
Yuma County:		
Somerton division:		
Yuma city (pt.)...............	-	21
Yuma division:		
Yuma city (pt.)...............	42 433	42 460
McNary (CDP)(total)...............	1 320	(1)
Peoria city (total)..............	12 251	12 307
Yuma city (total)................	42 433	42 481

[1]Delete.

County Subdivisions	1980	1970
The State	2 718 215	'1 775 399
Apache County[1]	52 108	'32 304
Chinle division	14 337	...
Chinle (CDP)	2 815	...
Lukachukai (CDP)	1 049	...
Many Farms (CDP)	1 364	...
Dennehotso division	1 631	...
Eagar–Springerville division	5 389	'3 101
Eagar town[1]	2 791	1 279
Springerville town[1]	1 452	'1 151
Fort Apache division	368	810
McNary (CDP) (pt.)	318	
Fort Defiance division	20 071	...
Fort Defiance (CDP)	3 431	...
Window Rock (CDP)	2 230	...
Puerco division	774	632
St. Johns division	4 767	1 589
St. Johns city[1]	3 368	1 320
Sweetwater division	4 771	...
Cochise County[2]	85 686	'61 918
Benson division	9 459	...
Benson town	4 190	2 839
Bisbee division	14 571	...
Bisbee city[2]	7 154	8 328
Bowie division	1 469	1 273
Douglas division	17 703	15 830
Douglas city[2]	13 058	12 462
Pirtleville (CDP)	1 425	...
Elfrida division	1 608	1 298
Tombstone division	33 939	...
Huachuca City town[2]	1 661	'1 241
Sierra Vista city[2]	24 937	6 689
Tombstone city[2]	1 632	1 241
Willcox division	6 937	4 957
Willcox city[2]	3 243	2 568
Coconino County[3]	75 008	48 326
Coconino division	45 922	30 990
Flagstaff city[3]	34 743	26 117
Sedona (pt.)	1 778	792
Havasupai division	282	...
Hopi division	1 306	...
Hualapai division	8	...
Kaibab division	1 417	967
Fredonia town[3]	1 040	798
Tuba City division	21 248	...
Page city[3]	4 907	...
Tuba City (CDP)	5 045	...
Williams division	4 825	...
Grand Canyon Village (CDP)	1 348	1 011
Williams city[3]	2 266	2 386
Gila County[4]	37 080	29 255
Globe division	14 328	...
Central Heights–Midland City (CDP)	2 791	2 289
Globe city[4]	6 708	7 333
Miami division	6 038	6 532
Claypool (CDP)	2 362	2 245
Miami town	2 716	3 394
Reservation division	4 927	4 668
San Carlos (CDP)	2 668	2 542
Tonto division	9 193	3 208
Payson town[4]	5 068	...
Winkelman division	2 594	...
Hayden town (pt.)	1 205	1 283
Winkelman town[4]	1 060	974
Graham County[5]	22 862	16 578
Bonita–Klondyke division	1 674	...
Pima division	2 783	...
Pima town	1 599	1 184
Safford division	15 986	...
Safford city[5]	7 010	'5 493
Thatcher town[5]	3 374	2 320
San Carlos division	2 419	...
Bylas (CDP)	1 175	1 125
Greenlee County[6]	11 406	10 330
Clifton division	8 872	8 298
Clifton town	4 245	5 087
Morenci (CDP)	2 736	
Stargo (CDP)	1 038	1 194
Duncan division	2 534	2 032
Duncan town[6]	603	773
Maricopa County[7]	1 509 052	'971 228
Buckeye division	11 223	7 807
Buckeye town[7]	3 434	2 599
Chandler division	39 387	23 142
Chandler city (pt.)[7]	23 889	13 763
Gilbert town (pt.)[7]	50	...
Sun Lakes (CDP)	1 925	...
Tempe city (pt.)[7]	292	...
Williams AFB (CDP)	3 435	3 443
Deer Valley division	12 693	...
Cave Creek (CDP)	1 589	...
Glendale city (pt.)[7]	3 899	...
Peoria city (pt.)[7]	3	...
Phoenix city (pt.)[7]	15	...

County Subdivisions	1980	1970
Maricopa County—Con.		
Gila Bend division[7]	4 902	3 469
Gila Bend town[7]	1 585	1 795
Goodyear town (pt.)[7]		...
Phoenix division[7]	1 421 448	...
Avondale city[7]	8 168	'6 626
Cashion (CDP)	3 014	2 705
Chandler city (pt.)[7]	5 784	...
Dreamland–Velda Rose (CDP)	5 969	...
El Mirage town[7]	4 307	3 258
Fountain Hills (CDP)	2 771	...
Gilbert town (pt.)[7]	5 667	1 971
Glendale city (pt.)[7]	93 273	36 228
Goodyear town (pt.)[7]	2 747	2 140
Guadalupe town[7]	4 506	...
Litchfield Park (CDP)	3 657	1 664
Luke AFB (CDP)	3 515	5 047
Mesa city[7]	152 453	'63 049
Paradise Valley town[7]	11 085	'6 637
Peoria city (pt.)[7]	12 248	4 792
Phoenix city (pt.)[7]	789 685	'584 303
Scottsdale city[7]	88 412	67 823
Sun City (CDP)	40 505	13 670
Surprise town[7]	3 723	2 427
Tempe city (pt.)[7]	106 451	'63 550
Tolleson city[7]	4 433	3 881
Youngtown town[7]	2 254	1 886
St. Johns division	2 265	814
Phoenix city (pt.)[7]	4	
Salt River division	4 438	994
Tonto division	428	204
Wickenburg division	12 268	
Sun City West (CDP)	3 772	...
Wickenburg town[7]	3 535	2 698
Mohave County[8]	55 865	25 857
Kingman North division	20 311	
Kingman city[8]	9 257	7 312
Kingman South division	33 768	
Bullhead City–Riviera (CDP)	10 364	...
Lake Havasu City city[8]	15 909	...
Mohave North division	1 786	950
Navajo County[9]	67 629	'47 559
Apache division	6 164	5 158
McNary (CDP) (pt.)	1 002	...
Whiteriver (CDP)	2 256	...
Hopi division	5 590	...
Indian Wells division	4 767	...
Little Colorado division	16 778	14 609
Holbrook city[9]	5 785	4 759
Winslow city	7 921	8 066
Pinon division	5 914	...
Snowflake division	20 196	'10 328
Lakeside (CDP)	1 333	...
Pinetop (CDP)	1 527	...
Show Low city[9]	4 298	'2 129
Snowflake town[9]	3 510	'1 977
Taylor town[9]	1 915	888
Western division	8 220	...
Kayenta (CDP)	3 343	...
Pima County[10]	531 443	351 667
Ajo division	5 978	6 705
Ajo (CDP)	5 189	5 881
Arivaca division	22 266	...
Green Valley (CDP)	7 999	...
Marana division	9 320	...
Marana town (pt.)[10]	1 574	...
Papago division	6 436	4 447
Sells (CDP)	1 864	...
Tucson division	487 443	...
Catalina (CDP)	2 749	...
Davis–Monthan AFB (CDP)	6 279	...
Marana town (pt.)[10]	100	...
Oro Valley town[10]	1 489	...
South Tucson city	6 554	6 220
Tucson city[10]	330 537	262 933
Tucson Estates (CDP)	2 814	...
Pinal County[11]	90 918	'68 579
Casa Grande division	19 129	...
Casa Grande city[11]	14 971	10 536
Coolidge division	9 967	'9 891
Coolidge city[11]	6 851	'5 314
Eloy division	8 867	...
Eloy city[11]	6 240	5 381
Florence division	7 478	...
Florence town	3 391	2 173
Gila River division	5 250	...
Sacaton (CDP)	1 951	...
Maricopa–Stanfield division	3 940	...
North Pinal division	22 195	...
Apache Junction city[11]	9 935	...
Hayden town (pt.)[11]	—	...
Kearny town	2 646	2 829
Superior town[11]	4 600	...
Papago division	611	...
San Manuel division	13 481	...
Dudleyville (CDP)	1 205	...
Mammoth town	1 906	1 953
Oracle (CDP)	2 484	...
San Manuel (CDP)	5 443	4 332

County Subdivisions

County Subdivisions	1980	1970
Santa Cruz County[12]	20 459	13 966
Nogales division	18 813	...
Nogales city[12]	15 683	8 946
Patagonia division	1 646	...
Patagonia town[12]	980	630
Yavapai County[13]	68 145	'37 005
Ashfork division	1 382	1 392
Congress division	3 195	1 788
Humboldt division	1 891	1 189
Mingus Mountain division	8 431	...
Clarkdale town[13]	1 512	892
Cottonwood town (pt.)[13]	4 510	'2 610
Jerome town	420	290
Prescott Valley town (pt.)[13]	165	...
Prescott division	39 308	'23 235
Bagdad (CDP)	2 331	2 079
Chino Valley town[13]	2 858	...
Prescott city[13]	20 055	'13 631
Prescott Valley town (pt.)[13]	2 119	...
Verde division	13 938	...
Camp Verde (CDP)	1 125	...
Cottonwood town (pt.)[13]	40	...
Sedona (CDP) (pt.)	3 590	1 230
Yuma County[14]	90 554	60 827
Parker division	11 467	...
Parker town	2 542	1 948
Somerton division	11 065	...
San Luis town[14]	1 946	...
Somerton town[14]	5 761	2 225
Yuma city (pt.)[14]	–	...
Wellton division	6 508	...
Wellton town[14]	911	...
Yuma Proving Ground (CDP)	1 098	1 349
Yuma division	61 514	...
Yuma city (pt.)	42 433	29 007

ARKANSAS

Arkansas takes its name from the Akansa tribe of Indians which once inhabited part of the territory now constituting this state.

The Arkansas country was first visited by white men in 1541, when the Spanish explorer, De Soto, crossed the Mississippi near the present site of Memphis and penetrated to the northern part of the present state. The first white settlement was made at Arkansas Post by the French in 1686.

Arkansas was formed from a portion of the territory originally known as Louisiana. This region was claimed by the French by virtue of the discoveries of Marquette and Joliet, who descended the Mississippi as far as the mouth of the Arkansas in 1673, and of La Salle, who sailed down the Mississippi to its mouth in 1682. The Louisiana region was ceded by France to Spain in 1762, retroceded to France in 1800, and purchased from France by the United States in 1803. It then included practically all the western watershed of the Mississippi, but its western boundaries were not definitely fixed until 1819.

In 1804 the region was divided by the thirty-third parallel, the present southern boundary of Arkansas, into the territory of Orleans on the south and the district of Louisiana on the north. In the following year the district of Louisiana was named the territory of Lousiana, and in 1812 it was renamed the territory of Missouri.

Arkansas was erected successively into a territory of the first and second class by the acts of Congress of March, 1819, and of April, 1820; it then included, in addition to the area of the present state, that portion of the territory now forming Oklahoma which lay south of 36°30' north latitude. In 1824 the western boundary, north of the Red River, was placed about 40 miles west of where it now stands, and in 1828 it was fixed at its present location. In January, 1836, a convention met at Little Rock, drew up a state constitution, and applied for admission into the Union. On June 15 of the same year Arkansas became a state of the Union.

COUNTY LOCATION INDEX

Arkansas	D-6	Garland	D-3	Newton	B-3
Ashley	F-5	Grant	D-4	Ouachita	E-4
Baxter	A-4	Greene	A-6	Perry	C-4
Benton	A-2	Hempstead	E-3	Phillips	D-6
Boone	A-3	Hot Spring	D-4	Pike	D-3
Bradley	E-5	Howard	D-2	Poinsett	B-6
Calhoun	E-4	Independence	B-5	Polk	D-2
Carroll	A-3	Izard	B-5	Pope	B-3
Chicot	E-7	Jackson	B-6	Prairie	C-5
Clark	D-3	Jefferson	D-5	Pulaski	C-4
Clay	A-7	Johnson	B-3	Randolph	A-6
Cleburne	B-5	Lafayette	F-3	St. Francis	C-3
Cleveland	E-5	Lawrence	B-6	Saline	D-4
Columbia	F-3	Lee	C-6	Scott	C-2
Conway	C-4	Lincoln	E-5	Searcy	B-4
Craighead	B-6	Little River	E-2	Sebastian	C-2
Crawford	B-2	Logan	C-3	Sevier	D-2
Crittenden	C-7	Lonoke	C-5	Sharp	A-5
Cross	C-6	Madison	B-3	Stone	B-5
Dallas	E-4	Marion	A-4	Union	F-4
Desha	E-6	Miller	E-2	Van Buren	B-4
Drew	E-5	Mississippi	B-7	Washington	B-2
Faulkner	C-4	Monroe	C-6	White	C-5
Franklin	B-2	Montgomery	D-3	Woodruff	C-6
Fulton	A-5	Nevada	E-3	Yell	C-3

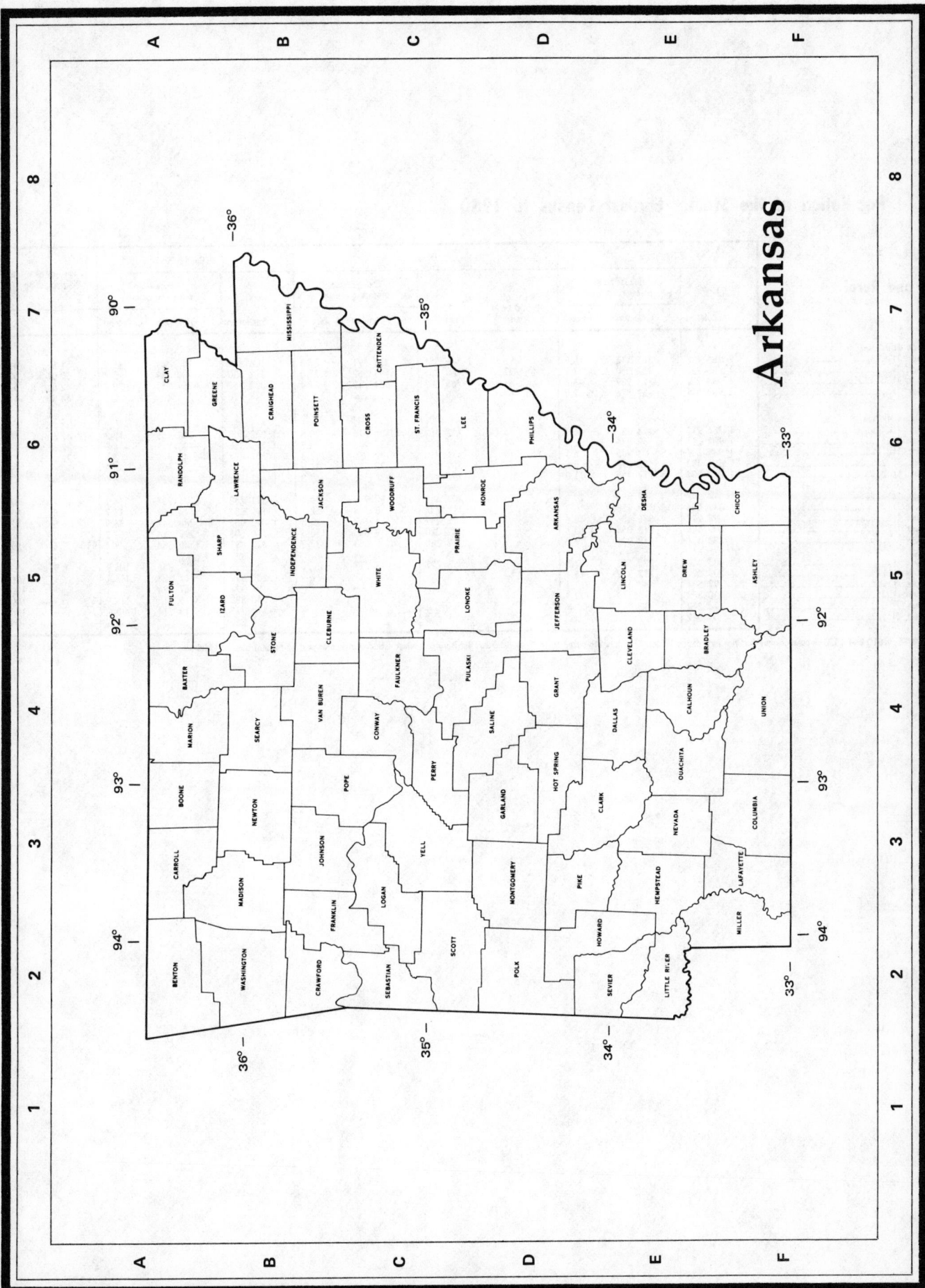

Arkansas

Population of the State: Earliest Census to 1980

Urban and Rural

	The State			Urban				Rural				Percent of total population	
	Total population	Change from preceding census		Places of 2,500 or more	Population	Change from preceding census		Population	Change from preceding census			Urban	Rural
		Number	Percent			Number	Percent		Number	Percent			
Current urban definition:													
1980 (Apr. 1)	2 286 435	363 113	18.9	96	1 179 556	218 691	22.8	1 106 879	144 449	15.0		51.6	48.4
1970 (Apr. 1)	1 923 322	137 050	7.7	77	960 865	195 562	25.6	962 430	−58 539	−5.7		50.0	50.0
1960 (Apr. 1)	1 786 272	−123 239	−6.5	66	765 303	134 712	21.4	1 020 969	−257 951	−20.2		42.8	57.2
1950 (Apr. 1)	1 909 511	−39 876	−2.0	64	630 591	...	...	1 278 920	...	...		33.0	67.0
Previous urban definition:													
1960 (Apr. 1)	1 786 272	−123 239	−6.5	65	742 869	125 716	20.4	1 043 403	−248 955	−19.3		41.6	58.4
1950 (Apr. 1)	1 909 511	−39 876	−2.0	62	617 153	185 243	42.9	1 292 358	−225 119	−14.8		32.3	67.7
1940 (Apr. 1)	1 949 387	94 905	5.1	53	431 910	49 032	12.8	1 517 477	45 873	3.1		22.2	77.8
1930 (Apr. 1)	1 854 482	102 278	5.8	49	382 878	92 381	31.8	1 471 604	9 897	0.7		20.6	79.4
1920 (Jan. 1)	1 752 204	177 755	11.3	41	290 497	87 816	43.3	1 461 707	89 939	6.6		16.6	83.4
1910 (Apr. 15)	1 574 449	262 885	20.0	28	202 681	90 948	81.4	1 371 768	171 937	14.3		12.9	87.1
1900 (June 1)	1 311 564	183 353	16.3	15	111 733	38 574	52.7	1 199 831	144 779	13.7		8.5	91.5
1890 (June 1)	1 128 211	325 686	40.6	9	73 159	41 139	128.5	1 055 052	284 547	36.9		6.5	93.5
1880 (June 1)	802 525	318 054	65.6	7	32 020	19 640	158.6	770 505	298 414	63.2		4.0	96.0
1870 (June 1)	484 471	49 021	11.3	1	12 380	8 653	232.2	472 091	40 368	9.4		2.6	97.4
1860 (June 1)	435 450	225 553	107.5	1	3 727	3 727	...	431 723	221 826	105.7		0.9	99.1
1850 (June 1)	209 897	112 323	115.1	–	–	–	–	209 897	112 323	115.1		–	100.0
1840 (June 1)	97 574	67 186	221.1	–	–	–	–	97 574	67 186	221.1		–	100.0
1830 (June 1)	30 388	16 115	112.9	–	–	–	–	30 388	16 115	112.9		–	100.0
1820 (Aug. 7)	14 273	13 211	1000+	–	–	–	–	14 273	13 211	1000+		–	100.0
1810 (Aug. 6)	1 062	...	...	–	–	...	...	1 062	...	...		–	100.0

NOTE: 1810 and 1820 populations are for that part of the Missouri Territory organized in 1819 as Arkansas Territory and which included a greater part of present area of Oklahoma.

ARKANSAS	
1810	1,062
1820	1,260
1830	1,426
1840	1,346
1850	3,245
1860	8,844
1870	8,268
1880	8,038
1890	11,432
1900	12,973
1910	16,103
1920	21,483
1930	22,300
1940	24,437
1950	23,665
1960	23,355
1970	23,347
1980	24,175

ASHLEY

1850	2,058
1860	8,590
1870	8,042
1880	10,156
1890	13,295
1900	19,734
1910	25,268
1920	23,410
1930	25,151
1940	26,785
1950	25,660
1960	24,220
1970	24,976
1980	26,538

BAXTER

1880	6,004
1890	8,527
1900	9,298
1910	10,389
1920	10,216
1930	9,519
1940	10,281
1950	11,683
1960	9,943
1970	15,319
1980	27,409

BENTON

1840	2,228
1850	3,710
1860	9,306
1870	13,831
1880	20,328
1890	27,716
1900	31,611
1910	33,389
1920	36,253
1930	35,253
1940	36,148
1950	38,076
1960	36,272
1970	50,476
1980	78,115

BOONE

1870	7,032
1880	12,146
1890	15,816
1900	16,396
1910	14,318
1920	16,098
1930	14,937
1940	15,860
1950	16,260
1960	16,116
1970	19,073
1980	26,067

BRADLEY

1850	3,829
1860	8,388
1870	8,646
1880	6,285
1890	7,972
1900	9,651
1910	14,518
1920	15,970
1930	17,497
1940	18,097
1950	15,987
1960	14,029
1970	12,778
1980	13,803

CALHOUN

1860	4,103
1870	3,853
1880	5,671
1890	7,267
1900	8,539
1910	9,804
1920	11,807
1930	7,562
1940	9,636
1950	7,132
1960	5,991
1970	5,573
1980	6,079

CARROLL

1840	2,844
1850	4,614
1860	9,383
1870	5,780
1880	13,337
1890	17,288
1900	18,848
1910	16,829
1920	17,786
1930	15,820
1940	14,737
1950	13,244
1960	11,284
1970	12,301
1980	16,203

CHICOT

1830	1,165
1840	3,806
1850	5,115
1860	9,234
1870	7,214
1880	10,117
1890	11,419
1900	14,528
1910	21,987
1920	21,749
1930	22,646
1940	27,452
1950	22,306
1960	18,990
1970	18,164
1980	17,793

CLARK

1820	1,040
1830	1,369
1840	2,309
1850	4,070
1860	9,735
1870	11,953
1880	15,771
1890	20,997
1900	21,289
1910	23,686
1920	25,632
1930	24,932
1940	24,402
1950	22,998
1960	20,950
1970	21,537
1980	23,326

CLAY

1880	7,213
1890	12,200
1900	15,886
1910	23,690
1920	27,276
1930	27,278
1940	28,386
1950	26,674
1960	21,258
1970	18,771
1980	20,616

CLEBURNE

1890	7,884
1900	9,628
1910	11,903
1920	12,696
1930	11,373
1940	13,134
1950	11,487
1960	9,059
1970	10,349
1980	16,909

CLEVELAND

1880	8,370
1890	11,362
1900	11,620
1910	13,481
1920	12,260
1930	12,744
1940	12,520
1950	8,956
1960	6,944
1970	6,605
1980	7,868

COLUMBIA

1860	12,449
1870	11,397
1880	14,090
1890	19,893
1900	22,077
1910	23,820
1920	27,670
1930	27,320
1940	29,822
1950	28,770
1960	27,400
1970	25,952
1980	26,644

CONWAY

1830	982
1840	2,892
1850	3,583
1860	6,697
1870	8,112
1880	12,755
1890	19,459
1900	19,772
1910	22,729
1920	22,578
1930	21,949
1940	21,536
1950	18,137
1960	15,430
1970	16,805
1980	19,505

CRAIGHEAD

1860	3,066
1870	4,577
1880	7,037
1890	12,025
1900	19,505
1910	27,627
1920	37,541
1930	44,740
1940	47,200
1950	50,613
1960	47,303
1970	52,068
1980	63,239

CRAWFORD

1830	2,440
1840	4,266
1850	7,960
1860	7,850
1870	8,957
1880	14,740
1890	21,714
1900	21,270
1910	23,942
1920	25,739
1930	22,549
1940	23,920
1950	22,727
1960	21,318
1970	25,677
1980	36,892

CRITTENDEN

1830	1,272
1840	1,561
1850	2,648
1860	4,920
1870	3,831
1880	9,415
1890	13,940
1900	14,529
1910	22,447
1920	29,309
1930	39,717
1940	42,473
1950	47,184
1960	47,564
1970	48,106
1980	49,499

CROSS

1870	3,915

DALLAS

1850	6,877
1860	8,283
1870	5,707
1880	6,505
1890	9,296
1900	11,518
1910	12,621
1920	14,424
1930	14,671
1940	14,471
1950	12,416
1960	10,522
1970	10,022
1980	10,515

DESHA

1840	1,598
1850	2,911
1860	6,459
1870	6,125
1880	8,973
1890	10,324
1900	11,511
1910	15,274
1920	20,297
1930	21,814
1940	27,160
1950	25,155
1960	20,770
1970	18,761
1980	19,760

DREW

1850	3,276
1860	9,078
1870	9,960
1880	12,231
1890	17,352
1900	19,451
1910	21,960
1920	21,822
1930	19,928
1940	19,831
1950	17,959
1960	15,213
1970	15,157
1980	17,910

FAULKNER

1880	12,786
1890	18,342
1900	20,780
1910	23,708
1920	27,681
1930	28,381
1940	25,880
1950	25,289
1960	24,303
1970	31,578
1980	46,192

CONWAY (top right column continued)

1880	5,050
1890	7,693
1900	11,051
1910	14,042
1920	18,579
1930	25,723
1940	26,046
1950	24,757
1960	19,551
1970	19,783
1980	20,434

FRANKLIN

1840	2,665
1850	3,972
1860	7,298
1870	9,627
1880	14,951
1890	19,934
1900	17,395
1910	20,638
1920	19,364
1930	15,762
1940	15,683
1950	12,358
1960	10,213
1970	11,301
1980	14,705

FULTON

1850	1,819
1860	4,024
1870	4,843
1880	6,720
1890	10,984
1900	12,917
1910	12,193
1920	11,182
1930	10,834
1940	10,253
1950	9,187
1960	6,657
1970	7,699
1980	9,975

GARLAND

1880	9,023
1890	15,328
1900	18,773
1910	27,271
1920	25,785
1930	36,031
1940	41,664
1950	47,102
1960	46,697
1970	54,131
1980	70,531

GRANT

1870	3,943
1880	6,185
1890	7,786
1900	7,671
1910	9,425
1920	10,710
1930	9,834
1940	10,477
1950	9,024
1960	8,294
1970	9,711
1980	13,008

GREENE

1840	1,586
1850	2,593
1860	5,843
1870	7,573
1880	7,480
1890	12,908
1900	16,979
1910	23,852
1920	26,105
1930	26,127

1940	30,204
1950	29,149
1960	25,198
1970	24,765
1980	30,744

HEMPSTEAD

1820	2,248
1830	2,512
1840	4,921
1850	7,672
1860	13,989
1870	13,768
1880	19,015
1890	22,796
1900	24,101
1910	28,285
1920	31,602
1930	30,847
1940	32,770
1950	25,080
1960	19,661
1970	19,308
1980	23,635

HOT SPRING

1830	458
1840	1,907
1850	3,609
1860	5,635
1870	5,877
1880	7,775
1890	11,603
1900	12,748
1910	15,022
1920	17,784
1930	18,105
1940	18,916
1950	22,181
1960	21,893
1970	21,963
1980	26,819

HOWARD

1880	9,917
1890	13,789
1900	14,076
1910	16,898
1920	18,565
1930	17,489
1940	16,621
1950	13,342
1960	10,878
1970	11,412
1980	13,459

INDEPENDENCE

1830	2,031
1840	3,669
1850	7,767
1860	14,307
1870	14,566
1880	18,086
1890	21,961
1900	22,557
1910	24,776
1920	23,967
1930	24,225
1940	25,643
1950	23,448
1960	20,048
1970	22,723
1980	30,147

IZARD

1830	1,266
1840	2,240
1850	3,213
1860	7,215
1870	6,806
1880	10,857
1890	13,038
1900	13,506
1910	14,561
1920	13,871
1930	12,872
1940	12,834
1950	9,953
1960	6,677
1970	7,381
1980	10,768

JACKSON

1830	333
1840	1,540
1850	3,086
1860	10,493
1870	7,268
1880	10,877
1890	15,197
1900	18,383
1910	23,501
1920	25,446
1930	27,943
1940	26,427
1950	25,912
1960	22,843
1970	20,452
1980	21,646

JEFFERSON

1830	772
1840	2,566
1850	5,834
1860	14,971
1870	15,733
1880	22,386
1890	40,881
1900	40,972
1910	52,734
1920	60,330
1930	64,154
1940	65,101
1950	76,075
1960	81,373
1970	85,329
1980	90,718

JOHNSON

1840	3,433
1850	5,227
1860	7,612
1870	9,152
1880	11,565
1890	16,758
1900	17,448
1910	19,698
1920	21,062
1930	19,289
1940	18,795
1950	16,138
1960	12,421
1970	13,630
1980	17,423

LAFAYETTE

1830	748
1840	2,200
1850	5,220
1860	8,464
1870	9,139
1880	5,730
1890	7,700
1900	10,594
1910	13,741
1920	15,552
1930	16,934
1940	16,851
1950	13,203
1960	11,030
1970	10,018
1980	10,213

LAWRENCE

1820	5,602
1830	2,806
1840	2,835
1850	5,274
1860	9,372
1870	5,981
1880	8,782
1890	12,984
1900	16,491
1910	20,001
1920	22,098
1930	21,663
1940	22,651
1950	21,303
1960	17,267
1970	16,320
1980	18,447

LEE

1880	13,288
1890	18,886
1900	19,409
1910	24,252
1920	28,852
1930	26,637
1940	26,810
1950	24,322
1960	21,001
1970	18,884
1980	15,539

LINCOLN

1880	9,255
1890	10,255
1900	13,389
1910	15,118
1920	18,774
1930	20,250
1940	19,709
1950	17,079
1960	14,447
1970	12,913
1980	13,369

LITTLE RIVER

1870	3,236
1880	6,404
1890	8,903
1900	13,731
1910	13,597
1920	16,301
1930	15,515

1940	15,932
1950	11,690
1960	9,211
1970	11,194
1980	13,952

LOGAN

1880	14,885
1890	20,774
1900	20,563
1910	26,350
1920	25,866
1930	24,110
1940	25,967
1950	20,260
1960	15,957
1970	16,789
1980	20,144

LONOKE

1880	12,146
1890	19,263
1900	22,544
1910	27,983
1920	33,400
1930	33,759
1940	29,862
1950	27,278
1960	24,551
1970	26,249
1980	34,518

MADISON

1840	2,775
1850	4,823
1860	7,740
1870	8,231
1880	11,455
1890	17,402
1900	19,864
1910	16,056
1920	14,918
1930	13,334
1940	14,531
1950	11,734
1960	9,068
1970	9,453
1980	11,373

MARION

1840	1,325
1850	2,308
1860	6,192
1870	3,979
1880	7,907
1890	10,390
1900	11,377
1910	10,203
1920	10,154
1930	8,876
1940	9,464
1950	8,609
1960	6,041
1970	7,000
1980	11,334

MILLER

1820	999
1830	356
1880	9,919
1890	14,714

1900	17,558
1910	19,555
1920	24,021
1930	30,586
1940	31,874
1950	32,614
1960	31,686
1970	33,385
1980	37,766

MISSISSIPPI

1840	1,410
1850	2,368
1860	3,895
1870	3,633
1880	7,332
1890	11,635
1900	16,384
1910	30,468
1920	47,320
1930	69,289
1940	80,217
1950	82,375
1960	70,174
1970	62,060
1980	59,517

MONROE

1830	461
1840	936
1850	2,049
1860	5,657
1870	8,336
1880	9,574
1890	15,336
1900	16,816
1910	19,907
1920	21,601
1930	20,651
1940	21,133
1950	19,540
1960	17,327
1970	15,657
1980	14,052

MONTGOMERY

1850	1,958
1860	3,633
1870	2,984
1880	5,729
1890	7,923
1900	9,444
1910	12,455
1920	11,112
1930	10,768
1940	8,876
1950	6,680
1960	5,370
1970	5,821
1980	7,771

NEVADA

1880	12,959
1890	14,832
1900	16,609
1910	19,334
1920	21,934
1930	20,407
1940	19,869
1950	14,781
1960	10,700
1970	10,111
1980	11,097

NEWTON

1850	1,758
1860	3,393
1870	4,374
1880	6,120
1890	9,950
1900	12,538
1910	10,621
1920	11,199
1930	10,564
1940	10,881
1950	8,685
1960	5,963
1970	5,844
1980	7,756

OUACHITA

1850	9,951
1860	12,936
1870	12,975
1880	11,758
1890	17,033
1900	20,892
1910	21,774
1920	20,636
1930	29,890
1940	31,151
1950	33,051
1960	31,641
1970	30,896
1980	30,541

PERRY

1850	978
1860	2,465
1870	2,685
1880	3,872
1890	5,538
1900	7,294
1910	9,402
1920	9,905
1930	7,695
1940	8,392
1950	5,978
1960	4,927
1970	5,634
1980	7,266

PHILLIPS

1820	1,201
1830	1,152
1840	3,547
1850	6,935
1860	14,877
1870	15,372
1880	21,262
1890	25,341
1900	26,561
1910	33,535
1920	44,530
1930	40,683
1940	45,970
1950	46,254
1960	43,997
1970	40,046
1980	34,772

PIKE

1840	969
1850	1,861
1860	4,025
1870	3,788
1880	6,345
1890	8,537
1900	10,301
1910	12,565
1920	12,397
1930	11,792
1940	11,786
1950	10,032
1960	7,864
1970	8,711
1980	10,373

POINSETT

1840	1,320
1850	2,308
1860	3,621
1870	1,720
1880	2,192
1890	4,272
1900	7,025
1910	12,791
1920	20,848
1930	29,695
1940	37,670
1950	39,311
1960	30,834
1970	26,843
1980	27,032

POLK

1850	1,263
1860	4,262
1870	3,376
1880	5,857
1890	9,283
1900	18,352
1910	17,216
1920	16,412
1930	14,857
1940	15,832
1950	14,182
1960	11,981
1970	13,297
1980	17,007

POPE

1830	1,483
1840	2,850
1850	4,710
1860	7,883
1870	8,386
1880	14,322
1890	19,458
1900	21,715
1910	24,527
1920	27,153
1930	26,547
1940	25,682
1950	23,291
1960	21,177
1970	28,607
1980	39,021

PRAIRIE

1850	2,097
1860	8,854
1870	5,604
1880	8,435
1890	11,374
1900	11,875
1910	13,853
1920	17,447
1930	15,187

1940	15,304
1950	13,768
1960	10,515
1970	10,495
1980	10,140

PULASKI

1820	1,923
1830	2,395
1840	5,350
1850	5,657
1860	11,699
1870	32,066
1880	32,616
1890	47,329
1900	63,179
1910	86,751
1920	109,464
1930	137,727
1940	156,085
1950	196,685
1960	242,980
1970	287,189
1980	340,613

RANDOLPH

1840	2,196
1850	3,275
1860	6,261
1870	7,466
1880	11,724
1890	14,485
1900	17,156
1910	18,987
1920	17,713
1930	16,871
1940	18,319
1950	15,982
1960	12,520
1970	12,645
1980	16,834

SAINT FRANCIS

1830	1,505
1840	2,499
1850	4,479
1860	8,672
1870	6,714
1880	8,389
1890	13,543
1900	17,157
1910	22,548
1920	28,385
1930	33,394
1940	36,043
1950	36,841
1960	33,303
1970	30,799
1980	30,858

SALINE

1840	2,061
1850	3,903
1860	6,640
1870	3,911
1880	8,953
1890	11,311
1900	13,122
1910	16,657
1920	16,781
1930	15,660
1940	19,163
1950	23,816
1960	28,956

1970	36,107
1980	53,161

SCOTT

1840	1,694
1850	3,083
1860	5,145
1870	7,483
1880	9,174
1890	12,635
1900	13,183
1910	14,302
1920	13,232
1930	11,803
1940	13,300
1950	10,057
1960	7,297
1970	8,207
1980	9,685

SEARCY

1840	936
1850	1,979
1860	5,271
1870	5,614
1880	7,278
1890	9,664
1900	11,988
1910	14,825
1920	14,590
1930	11,056
1940	11,942
1950	10,424
1960	8,124
1970	7,731
1980	8,847

SEBASTIAN

1860	9,238
1870	12,940
1880	19,560
1890	33,200
1900	36,935
1910	52,278
1920	56,739
1930	54,426
1940	62,809
1950	64,202
1960	66,685
1970	79,237
1980	95,172

SEVIER

1830	634
1840	2,810
1850	4,240
1860	10,516
1870	4,492
1880	6,192
1890	10,072
1900	16,339
1910	16,616
1920	18,301
1930	16,364
1940	15,248
1950	12,293
1960	10,156
1970	11,272
1980	14,060

SHARP

1870	5,400
1880	9,047
1890	10,418
1900	12,199
1910	11,688
1920	11,132
1930	10,715
1940	11,497
1950	8,999
1960	6,319
1970	8,233
1980	14,607

STONE

1880	5,089
1890	7,043
1900	8,100
1910	8,946
1920	8,779
1930	7,993
1940	8,603
1950	7,662
1960	6,294
1970	6,838
1980	9,022

UNION

1830	640
1840	2,889
1850	10,298
1860	12,288
1870	10,571
1880	13,419
1890	14,997
1900	22,495
1910	30,723
1920	29,691
1930	55,800
1940	50,461
1950	49,686
1960	49,518
1970	45,428
1980	48,573

VAN BUREN

1840	1,518
1850	2,864
1860	5,357
1870	5,107
1880	9,565
1890	8,567
1900	11,220
1910	13,509
1920	13,666
1930	11,962
1940	12,518
1950	9,687
1960	7,228
1970	8,275
1980	13,357

WASHINGTON

1830	2,182
1840	7,148
1850	9,970
1860	14,683
1870	17,266
1880	23,844
1890	32,024
1900	34,256
1910	33,889

1920	25,468
1930	39,255
1940	41,114
1950	49,979
1960	55,797
1970	77,370
1980	100,494

WHITE

1840	929
1850	2,619
1860	8,316
1870	10,347
1880	17,794
1890	22,946
1900	24,864
1910	28,574
1920	34,603
1930	38,269
1940	37,176
1950	38,040
1960	32,745
1970	39,253
1980	50,835

WOODRUFF

1870	6,891
1880	8,646
1890	14,009
1900	16,304
1910	20,049
1920	21,547
1930	22,682
1940	22,133
1950	18,957
1960	13,954
1970	11,566
1980	11,222

YELL

1850	3,341
1860	6,333
1870	8,048
1880	13,852
1890	18,015
1900	22,750
1910	26,323
1920	25,655
1930	21,313
1940	20,790
1950	14,057
1960	11,940
1970	14,208
1980	17,026

NOTES

CLAY

Name changed from Claton in 1875.

CLEVELAND

Name changed from Dorsey in 1885.

LOGAN

Name changed from Sarber in 1875.

MARION

Name changed from Searcy in 1835.

ARKADELPHIA	
1850	248
1860	825
1870	948
1880	1,506
1890	2,455
1900	2,739
1910	2,745
1920	3,311
1930	3,380
1940	5,078
1950	6,819
1960	8,069
1970	9,841
1980	10,005

BENTON	
1880	452
1890	647
1900	1,025
1910	1,708
1920	2,933
1930	3,445
1940	3,502
1950	6,277
1960	10,399
1970	16,499
1980	17,717

BLYTHEVILLE	
1900	302
1910	3,849
1920	6,447
1930	10,098
1940	10,652
1950	16,234
1960	20,797
1970	24,752
1980	23,844

CAMDEN	
1850	894
1860	1,343
1870	1,612
1880	1,503
1890	2,571
1900	2,840
1910	3,995
1920	3,238
1930	7,273
1940	8,975
1950	11,372
1960	15,823
1970	15,147
1980	15,356

CONWAY	
1880	1,208
1890	1,207
1900	2,003
1910	2,794
1920	4,564
1930	5,534
1940	5,782
1950	8,610
1960	9,791
1970	15,510
1980	20,375

EL DORADO	
1880	443
1890	455
1900	1,069
1910	4,202
1920	3,887
1930	16,421
1940	15,858
1950	23,076
1960	25,292
1970	25,283
1980	25,270

FAYETTEVILLE	
1840	425
1850	598
1860	972
1870	955
1880	1,788
1890	2,942
1900	4,061
1910	4,471
1920	5,362
1930	7,394
1940	8,212
1950	17,071
1960	20,274
1970	30,729
1980	36,608

FORREST CITY	
1880	903
1890	1,021
1900	1,361
1910	2,484
1920	3,377
1930	4,594
1940	5,699
1950	7,607
1960	10,544
1970	12,521
1980	13,803

FORT SMITH	
1850	964
1860	1,532
1870	2,227
1880	3,099
1890	11,311
1900	11,587
1910	23,975
1920	28,870
1930	31,429
1940	36,584
1950	47,942
1960	52,991
1970	62,802
1980	71,626

HOPE	
1880	1,233
1890	1,937
1900	1,644
1910	3,690
1920	4,790
1930	6,008
1940	7,475
1950	8,605
1960	8,399
1970	8,830
1980	10,290

HOT SPRINGS	
1860	201
1870	964
1880	1,276
1890	8,086
1900	9,973
1910	14,434
1920	11,695
1930	20,238
1940	21,370
1950	29,307
1960	28,337
1970	35,631
1980	35,781

JACKSONVILLE	
1950	2,474
1960	14,488
1970	19,832
1980	27,589

JONESBORO	
1870	155
1880	(NA)
1890	2,065
1900	4,508
1910	7,123
1920	9,384
1930	10,326
1940	11,729
1950	16,310
1960	21,418
1970	27,050
1980	31,530

LITTLE ROCK	
1850	2,167
1860	3,727
1870	12,380
1880	13,138
1890	25,874
1900	38,307
1910	45,941
1920	65,142
1930	81,679
1940	88,039
1950	102,213
1960	107,813
1970	132,483
1980	158,461

MAGNOLIA	
1860	424
1870	259
1880	536
1890	1,486
1900	1,614
1910	2,045
1920	2,158
1930	3,008
1940	4,236
1950	6,918
1960	10,651
1970	11,303
1980	11,909

MALVERN	
1890	1,520
1900	1,582
1910	2,778

1920	3,864
1930	5,115
1940	5,290
1950	8,072
1960	9,566
1970	9,739
1980	10,163

NORTH LITTLE ROCK	
1910	11,138
1920	14,048
1930	19,418
1940	21,137
1950	44,097
1960	58,032
1970	60,040
1980	64,288

PARAGOULD	
1890	1,666
1900	3,324
1910	5,248
1920	6,306
1930	5,966
1940	7,709
1950	9,668
1960	9,947
1970	10,639
1980	15,248

PINE BLUFF	
1850	460
1860	1,396
1870	2,081
1880	3,203
1890	9,952
1900	11,496
1910	15,102
1920	19,280
1930	20,760
1940	21,290
1950	37,162
1960	44,037
1970	57,389
1980	56,636

ROGERS	
1890	1,265
1900	2,158
1910	2,820
1920	3,318
1930	3,554
1940	3,550
1950	4,962
1960	5,700
1970	11,050
1980	17,429

RUSSELLVILLE	
1880	825
1890	1,321
1900	1,832
1910	2,936
1920	4,505
1930	5,628
1940	5,927
1950	8,166
1960	8,921
1970	11,750
1980	14,031

SEARCY	
1860	621
1870	874
1880	840
1890	1,203
1900	1,995
1910	2,331
1920	2,836
1930	3,387
1940	3,670
1950	6,024
1960	6,272
1970	9,040
1980	13,612

SHERWOOD	
1950	717
1960	1,222
1970	2,754
1980	10,586

SPRINGDALE	
1880	198
1890	906
1900	1,251
1910	1,755
1920	2,263
1930	2,763
1940	3,319
1950	5,835
1960	10,076
1970	16,783
1980	23,458

STUTTGART	
1890	1,165
1900	1,258
1910	2,740
1920	4,522
1930	4,927
1940	5,628
1950	7,276
1960	9,661
1970	10,477
1980	10,941

TEXARKANA	
1880	1,390
1890	3,528
1900	4,914
1910	5,655
1920	8,257
1930	10,764
1940	11,821
1950	15,875
1960	19,788
1970	21,682
1980	21,459

VAN BUREN	
1850	1,382
1860	2,397
1870	985
1880	1,029
1890	2,291
1900	2,573
1910	3,878
1920	5,224
1930	5,182
1940	5,422

1950	6,413
1960	6,787
1970	8,373
1980	12,020

WEST HELENA

1920	6,226
1930	4,489
1940	4,717
1950	6,107
1960	8,385
1970	11,007
1980	11,367

WEST MEMPHIS

1930	895
1940	3,369
1950	9,112
1960	19,374
1970	26,070
1980	28,138

CORRECTION NOTE

The official 1980 census counts of total population shown in this report supersede counts issued previously. Corrections to the figures were made after the counts were provided to the State for redistricting purposes and released in Advance Report PHC80-V for this State.

Shown below are corrections to the 1980 census counts of the total population made after the tabulations for this report were completed. Any additional corrections made after this report is printed are available by writing to Data User Services Division, Customer Services (Corrections), Bureau of the Census, Washington, D.C. 20233.

The 1980 figures shown in this publication are subject to change pending the outcome of the various lawsuits dealing with the census counts.

	1980 population	
	As shown in the tables	Corrected
Carroll County:		
North Yocum township............	443	347
Oak Grove town (pt.)..........	181	85
South Yocum township............	404	500
Oak Grove town (pt.).........	84	180
Poinsett County:		
Willis township:		
Trumann city.................	6 044	6 405
Pulaski County:		
Hill township:		
Sherwood city................	10 586	10 406
St. Francis County:		
Madison township:		
Madison city (pt.)...........	1 227	1 238
Madison city (total).............	1 227	1 238
Oak Grove town (total)...........	265	(1)

[1]No change.

County Subdivisions	1980	1970
The State	2 286 435	1 923 322
Arkansas County[1]	24 175	23 347
Arkansas township	152	163
Barton township	275	232
Bayou Meto township	382	450
Brewer township	97	113
Chester township	438	430
Crockett township	219	257
Garland township	335	328
Gum Pond township	11 176	10 940
Stuttgart city (pt.)[1]	10 771	10 473
Henton township	669	695
Humphrey town (pt.)	454	434
Keaton township	1 083	1 021
La Grue township	5 511	5 080
De Witt city	3 928	3 728
McFall township	179	238
Mill Bayou township	686	623
Almyra town	294	220
Morris township	528	369
Stuttgart city (pt.)[1]	170	4
Point Deluce township	422	269
Prairie township	1 001	1 147
St. Charles town	199	201
Stanley township	1 022	992
Gillett city	927	860
Ashley County[2]	26 538	24 976
Banner township	139	185
Bayou township	81	84
Bearhouse township	66	50
Beech Creek township	123	148
Carter township	4 801	4 177
Hamburg city[2]	3 394	3 102
De Bastrop township	646	807
Parkdale city	471	459
Egypt township	13 065	11 991
Crossett city[2]	6 706	6 191
North Crossett (CDP) (pt.)	3 455	2 891
West Crossett (CDP)	1 466	...
Elon township	553	431
Extra township	120	201
Longview township	846	588
Marie Saline township	240	153
Mill Creek township	1 295	1 073
North Crossett (CDP) (pt.)	58	–
Montrose township	751	744
Montrose city[2]	641	558
Portland township	971	1 368
Portland city[2]	701	662
Prairie township	337	284
Union township	132	253
White township	877	735
Fountain Hill town	352	266
Wilmot township	1 495	1 704
Wilmot city	1 227	1 132
Baxter County[3]	27 409	15 319
Bayou township	301	192
Big Flat township	294	290
Big Flat town	150	189
Buckhorn township	602	393
Norfork city (pt.)[3]	8	4
Salesville town[3]	406	156
Buford township	747	432
Greenwood township	219	170
Grover township	1 711	920
Lakeview town[3]	512	...
Independence township	1 232	676
Logan township	736	509
Lone Rock township	260	100
Matney township	76	96
Mill township	1 929	1 221
Mountain Home township	13 395	6 612
Mountain Home city[3]	8 066	3 936
North Fork township	1 029	857
Norfork city (pt.)[3]	391	266
Pigeon township	839	298
Union township	1 165	498
Whiteville township	2 874	2 055
Cotter city[3]	920	858
Gassville city[3]	859	434
Benton County[4]	78 115	50 476
Anderson township	705	656
Cave Springs city (pt.)[4]	6	...
Apple Glenn township	521	425
Ball township	446	328
Beatie township	442	291
Big Spring township	1 962	946
Brightwater township	1 951	1 088
Avoca town	256	173
Cherokee township	284	317
Colville township	2 038	1 763
Cave Springs city (pt.)	423	469
Decatur township	1 710	1 379
Decatur town[4]	1 013	847
Dickson township	1 759	909

County Subdivisions	1980	1970
Benton County—Con.		
Dickson township—Con.		
Bella Vista (CDP) (pt.)	530	...
Eldorado township	548	350
Esculapia township	21 958	12 714
Little Flock city (pt.)[4]	645	...
Rogers city (pt.)[4]	17 212	10 829
Felker township	283	203
Flint township	593	394
Garfield township	742	481
Garfield town (pt.)[4]	157	130
Garland township	1 430	987
Centerton city[4]	425	312
Gentry township	2 562	2 157
Gentry city[4]	1 468	1 022
Hico township	9 835	7 270
Siloam Springs city[4]	7 940	6 009
Hoover township	379	385
Highfill town	92	80
Logan township	313	239
Mason Valley township	667	519
Mount Vernon township	2 442	1 681
Little Flock city (pt.)[4]	–	...
Pea Ridge city[4]	1 488	1 088
Osage township	14 229	7 414
Bella Vista (CDP) (pt.)	2 059	...
Bentonville city[4]	8 756	5 508
Little Flock city (pt.)[4]	18	...
Rogers city (pt.)[4]	11	15
Pine Log township	303	35
Roller Ridge township	393	309
Garfield town (pt.)	30	33
Gateway town	75	83
Round Prairie township	452	455
Sugar Creek township	471	313
Sulphur Springs township	893	817
Sulphur Springs city	496	503
Wager township	461	323
Wallace township	2 142	1 732
Gravette city[4]	1 218	1 154
Walnut township	888	327
War Eagle township	366	323
Washington township	3 685	2 730
Bethel Heights town[4]	296	284
Lowell city[4]	1 078	653
Rogers city (pt.)	206	206
Springdale city (pt.)[4]	681	377
Yell township	262	216
Boone County[5]	26 067	19 073
Batavia township	272	171
Bellefonte township	1 860	1 283
Bellefonte town	393	300
Harrison city (pt.)[5]	293	210
Blythe township	235	112
Bryan township	903	573
Harrison city (pt.)[5]	–	...
Carrollton township	753	648
Alpena town	344	309
Elixir township	1 573	924
Bergman town	320	249
Ewing township[5]	270	...
Gaither township[5]	592	...
Jackson township	703	526
Harrison city (pt.)[5]	13	...
Jefferson township	858	526
Valley Springs town[5]	190	...
Lee township	978	658
Long Creek township	520	419
North Harrison township	7 117	5 471
Harrison city (pt.)[5]	5 956	4 092
Olvey township	367	274
Omaha township	1 077	774
Omaha town	191	160
Prairie township	433	367
Everton town	134	124
South Harrison township	5 174	4 161
Harrison city (pt.)[5]	3 305	2 937
Sugar Loaf township	1 632	1 016
Diamond City city[5]	650	282
Lead Hill town[5]	247	143
South Lead Hill town[5]	85	...
Summit township	288	257
Zinc township	462	278
Zinc town	113	58
Bradley County[6]	13 803	12 778
Clay township	864	818
Banks town	216	189
Eagle township	190	185
Marion township	290	190
Moro township	76	62
Ouachita township	297	218
Palestine township	432	425
Pennington township	10 114	9 356
Warren city[6]	7 646	6 433
River township	143	115
Sumpter township	240	280

County Subdivisions	1980	1970
Bradley County—Con.		
Washington township	1 157	1 129
Hermitage town	378	399
Calhoun County[7]	6 079	5 573
Caswell township	834	823
Thornton town (pt.)	603	'619
Champagnolle township	319	288
Dallas township	151	148
Fayette township	48	34
Franklin township	2 017	1 636
Hampton city[7]	1 627	1 252
Huey township	89	83
Jackson township	694	557
Harrell town	302	269
Jefferson township	218	195
Tinsman city	112	113
Locust Bayou township	—	—
Moro township	591	679
Thornton town (pt.)	108	127
Polk township	345	327
River township	607	740
Shumaker (unorg.)[7]	166	...
Carroll County[8]	16 203	12 301
Beaver township	528	236
Cabanal township	274	187
Carrollton township	473	328
Cedar township	2 778	2 082
Eureka Springs city[8]	1 989	1 670
Clifty township	165	53
Coin township	378	321
Cross township	111	122
Delmar township	94	90
Dry Fork township	173	152
Franklin township	269	40
Hickory township	2 880	2 296
Green Forest city[8]	1 609	1 354
Kings River township	371	291
Liberty township	115	95
Long Creek township	486	399
North Yocum township[8]	443	...
Blue Eye town (pt.)	41	(NA)
Oak Grove town (pt.)	181	(NA)
Omega township	356	243
Osage township	202	181
Packard Springs township	106	103
Piney township	187	205
Polo township	818	592
Prairie township	4 335	3 401
Berryville city[8]	2 966	2 271
South Yocum township[8]	404	...
Blue Eye town (pt.)	2	(NA)
Oak Grove town (pt.)	84	(NA)
Winona township	257	162
Chicot County[9]	17 793	18 164
Bowie township	5 409	5 249
Dermott city[9]	4 731	4 250
Carlton township	6 123	6 388
Lake Village city[9]	3 088	3 310
Planters township	6 261	6 527
Eudora city[9]	3 840	3 687
Clark County[10]	23 326	21 537
Amity township	1 917	1 600
Amity city[10]	859	614
Caddo township	14 990	14 109
Arkadelphia city[10]	10 005	9 841
Caddo Valley town[10]	388	...
Gum Springs town	255	269
Missouri township	5 356	4 699
Gurdon city	2 707	2 075
Okolona town (pt.)[10]	77	(NA)
Whelen Springs town	156	126
Terre Noire township	1 063	1 129
Okolona town (pt.)	123	(NA)
Clay County[11]	20 616	18 771
Bennett township	901	799
McDougal town[11]	239	328
Blue Cane township	333	472
Bradshaw township[11]	193	226
Brown township	350	346
Cache township	749	687
Knobel town	503	375
Carpenter township	346	363
Success town[11]	223	201
Chalk Bluff township	273	247
Clark township	370	423
Peach Orchard town	243	256
Cleveland township	778	598
Gleghorn township	237	277
Haywood township	625	705
Greenway town	317	240
Johnson township	320	395
Kilgore township	4 666	3 898
Corning city[11]	3 650	2 705
Knob township	282	271
Lemmons township	171	236

County Subdivisions	1980	1970
Clay County—Con.		
Liddell township	390	406
St. Francis city	266	297
Nelson township	356	370
Datto town	112	142
Oak Bluff township	3 136	2 881
Rector city[11]	2 336	1 990
Payne township	411	403
Nimmons town	112	135
Pollard township	741	765
Pollard town	298	253
St. Francis township	4 591	3 512
Piggott city[11]	3 762	3 087
Swain township	169	256
Wilson township	228	235
Cleburne County[12]	16 909	10 349
Big Creek township	50	38
Cadron township	1 291	881
Quitman town[12]	556	354
California township	309	191
Center Post township	323	197
Clayton township	604	398
Francis township	480	257
Giles township	955	560
Greers Ferry city	558	389
Grassy township	942	696
Concord town	234	163
Healing Springs township	885	635
Heber township	6 305	3 648
Heber Springs city[12]	4 589	2 497
McJester township	233	86
Morgan township	236	87
Mountain township	391	215
Peter Creek township	1 021	730
Pickens township	332	217
Pine township	93	77
Piney township	887	564
Poff township	52	66
Saline township	308	158
Higden town	45	46
Sugar Camp township	242	221
Sugar Loaf township	262	156
Valley township	495	121
Wilburn township	213	150
Cleveland County	7 868	6 605
Bowman township	415	243
Harper township	495	411
Hudgin township	116	110
Hurricane township	451	419
Jackson township	29	42
Kingsland township	1 159	925
Kingsland city	320	304
Lee township	411	343
Miller township	410	310
Niven township	368	328
Redland township	754	798
Rison township	1 566	1 533
Rison town	1 325	1 214
Rowell township	295	199
Saline township	83	104
Smith township	430	310
White Oak township	267	197
Whiteville township	619	333
Columbia County[13]	26 644	25 952
Emerson township	2 169	2 252
Emerson town	444	393
McNeil township	1 855	1 934
McNeil city[13]	725	684
Magnolia township	17 037	15 837
Magnolia city[13]	11 909	11 303
Taylor township	1 818	2 014
Taylor city	657	671
Village township	963	943
Waldo township	2 802	2 972
Waldo city	1 685	1 658
Conway County[14]	19 505	16 805
Austin township	298	265
Bentley township	1 152	611
Oppelo city[14]	486	147
Bird township	580	490
Catholic Point township	277	234
Cedar Falls township	251	246
Gregory township	351	251
Griffin township	497	468
Higgins township	188	217
Howard township	1 864	1 771
Menifee city[14]	368	251
Plumerville city[14]	785	724
Lick Mountain township	668	555
McLaren township	143	155
Martin township	73	92
Nichols township	668	594
Old Hickory township	138	94
Petit Jean township	74	74
St. Vincent township	489	350
Steele township	471	377
Union township	762	722

County Subdivisions	1980	1970
Conway County—Con.		
Washington township	1 430	930
Welborn township	9 076	8 272
Morrilton city[14]	7 355	6 814
White Eagle township	55	37
Craighead County[15]	63 239	52 068
Big Creek township	2 195	1 731
Bono town[15]	967	428
Black Oak township	2 751	2 825
Black Oak town	309	272
Caraway town[15]	1 165	952
Brookland township	1 864	1 374
Brookland town[15]	840	465
Buffalo township	2 160	2 251
Monette city[15]	1 165	1 076
Gilkerson township	1 683	1 251
Jonesboro city (pt.)[15]	92	...
Greenfield township	1 055	722
Herndon township	637	449
Jonesboro township	35 806	28 235
Jonesboro city (pt.)[15]	25 882	22 355
Lake City township	2 164	1 487
Lake City town[15]	1 842	948
Lester township	586	741
Little Texas township	454	525
Cash town (pt.)	42	34
Maumelle township	2 406	1 778
Bay city[15]	1 605	751
Nettleton township	7 390	6 545
Jonesboro city (pt.)[15]	5 556	4 695
Powell township	848	573
Prairie township	161	182
Promised Land township	311	475
Taylor township	330	425
Texas township	438	499
Cash town (pt.)[15]	243	231
Crawford County[16]	36 892	25 677
Alma township	4 409	2 783
Alma city (pt.)[16]	2 742	1 613
Cedar Creek township	379	165
Cedarville township	1 004	629
Chester township	550	411
Chester town[16]	139	82
Mountainburg town (pt.)	17	31
Cove City township	146	146
Dora township	361	238
Van Buren city (pt.)[16]	41	...
Dyer township	1 178	779
Dyer town	608	486
Jasper township	1 166	831
Lafayette township	1 393	804
Alma city (pt.)[16]	8	...
Lancaster township	517	440
Lees Creek township	496	374
Maxey township	1 660	1 427
Mulberry city (pt.)	1 266	1 211
Mountain township	1 428	1 022
Mountainburg town (pt.)[16]	578	493
Oliver Springs township	927	664
Porter township	179	149
Richland township	923	693
Kibler town (pt.)	416	383
Rudy township	821	538
Alma city (pt.)[16]	5	...
Rudy town	79	103
Sand Point township	213	148
Shepherd township	51	50
Union township	469	394
Upper township	118	79
Van Buren township	17 141	11 943
Kibler town (pt.)	382	228
Van Buren city (pt.)[16]	11 979	8 373
Vine Prairie township	452	428
Mulberry city (pt.)[16]	178	129
Whitley township	840	484
Winfrey township	71	58
Crittenden County[17]	49 499	48 106
Black Oak township	840	939
Bob Ward township	1 532	1 980
Edmondson town	344	412
Fogleman township	2 330	2 289
Gilmore town	503	461
Turrell city	1 041	783
Jackson township	2 020	2 848
Crawfordsville town	685	831
Jasper township	5 554	4 089
Marion city[17]	2 996	'1 431
Sunset town[17]	582	...
Lucas township	1 417	1 152
Mississippi township	28 700	26 985
West Memphis city (pt.)[17]	28 135	'25 860
Mound City township	367	212
Proctor township	830	993
West Memphis city (pt.)[17]	3	210
Tyronza township	4 549	4 730
Earle city[17]	3 517	3 146
Wappanocca township	1 360	1 889

County Subdivisions	1980	1970
Cross County[18]	20 434	19 783
Bedford township	589	665
Brushy Lake township	618	700
Coldwater township	589	681
Ellis township	557	583
Fair Oaks township	382	485
Hickory Ridge township	905	898
Hickory Ridge city[18]	478	410
Mitchell township	1 328	1 148
Cherry Valley city[18]	729	556
Searcy township	1 389	1 402
Smith township	1 565	1 459
Twist township	87	160
Tyronza township	2 965	3 260
Parkin city[18]	2 035	1 731
Wynne township	9 460	8 342
Wynne city[18]	7 805	6 696
Dallas County[19]	10 515	10 022
Bunn township	16	25
Chester township	741	782
Carthage city	568	566
Dry Run township	330	409
Fordyce city (pt.)[19]	220	147
Fordyce township	5 692	5 215
Fordyce city (pt.)	4 955	4 690
Holly Springs township	438	345
Jackson township	246	207
Liberty township	52	46
Manchester township	487	469
Nix township	199	224
Owen township	1 331	1 361
Sparkman town	622	663
Princeton township	252	268
Smith township	242	256
Southall township	368	323
Willow township	121	92
Desha County[20]	19 760	18 761
Bowie township	5 940	5 412
McGehee city (pt.)[20]	5 620	4 683
Clayton township	1 250	1 293
Reed town[20]	395	403
Tillar city (pt.)	71	57
Franklin township	809	760
Arkansas City city[20]	668	615
Halley township	458	604
McGehee city (pt.)[20]	51	...
Jefferson township	466	553
Mississippi township	418	600
Randolph township	7 263	5 713
Dumas city (pt.)[20]	6 091	4 600
Mitchellville city	618	494
Red Fork township	1 458	1 716
Watson city[20]	433	371
Richland township	564	696
Silver Lake township	555	628
Walnut Lake township	579	786
Dumas city (pt.)[20]	–	...
Drew County[21]	17 910	15 157
Bartholomew township	439	743
Jerome city	54	76
Bearhouse township	56	46
Clear Creek township	400	359
Collins township	309	199
Cominto township	299	201
Crook township	261	314
Franklin township	754	906
Tillar city (pt.)	209	236
Live Oak township	812	683
Winchester city	279	234
Marion township	11 699	9 060
Monticello city[21]	8 259	5 085
Saline township	1 390	1 255
Wilmar city	747	653
Spring Hill township	623	564
Veasey township	868	827
Faulkner County[22]	46 192	'31 578
Benedict township	175	136
Benton township	497	431
Bristol township	185	149
Cadron township	27 468	19 520
Conway city[22]	20 375	15 510
Mayflower city (pt.)[22]	35	...
California township	990	703
Guy town	209	179
Clifton township	950	625
Wooster town	398	307
Cypress township	1 918	1 108
Vilonia town (pt.)[22]	666	405
Danley township	2 604	1 622
Mayflower city (pt.)[22]	1 302	469
Eagle township	878	559
East Fork township	1 066	527
Enola township	520	'418
Enola town	186	'173
Hardin township	2 106	1 234
Greenbrier city[22]	1 423	582

County Subdivisions

County Subdivisions	1980	1970
Faulkner County—Con.		
Harve township	405	302
Matthews township	309	233
Mountain township	173	194
Mount Vernon township	396	343
Mount Vernon town[22]	157	...
Newton township	423	239
Palarm township	1 048	677
Vilonia town (pt.)[22]	70	18
Pine Mountain township	2 165	1 193
Mayflower city (pt.)[22]	44	...
Union township	716	495
Walker township	754	664
Damascus town (pt.)	135	99
Wilson township	446	206
Franklin County[23]	14 705	11 301
Alix township	538	399
Wiederkehr Village city (pt.)[23]	9	...
Barham township	121	109
Black Oak township	194	122
Boston township	402	214
Cobb township	–	–
Cravens township	156	133
Donald township	534	513
Branch city[23]	353	325
Grover township	264	201
Hogan township	1 258	1 055
Altus city[23]	441	418
Denning city	238	203
Wiederkehr Village city (pt.)[23]	45	...
Hurricane township	170	146
Ivy township	536	390
Limestone township	36	10
McIlroy township	14	44
Middle township	649	484
Mill Creek township	194	143
Miller township	69	52
Morgan township	31	34
Mountain township	227	152
Mulberry township	232	188
Prairie township	2 458	2 001
Charleston city[23]	1 748	1 497
Shores township	7	–
Six Mile township	96	88
Walker township	266	189
Wallace township	217	156
Watalula township	357	208
Weaver township	214	149
White Oak township	4 854	3 660
Ozark city[23]	3 597	2 592
Wiederkehr Village city (pt.)[23]	17	...
White Rock township	92	94
Wittich township	519	367
Fulton County[24]	9 975	7 699
Afton township	509	237
Bennett Bayou township	140	107
Benton township	2 127	1 860
Salem city[24]	1 424	1 277
Big Creek township	356	268
Cleveland township	316	264
Fulton township	854	712
Viola town	362	360
Mammoth Spring township	2 011	1 656
Mammoth Spring city[24]	1 158	1 072
Mount Calm township	160	142
Myatt township	165	178
Pleasant Ridge township	1 180	597
Cherokee Village–Hidden Valley (CDP) (pt.)	269	40
South Fork township	497	409
Strawberry township	473	275
Horseshoe Bend city (pt.)[24]	8	...
Union township	297	263
Vidette township	159	156
Washington township	362	299
Wild Cherry township	69	68
Wilson township	300	208
Garland County[25]	70 531	54 131
Antioch township	2 917	1 779
Lake Hamilton (CDP) (pt.)	936	...
Bain township	5 085	2 378
Piney (CDP) (pt.)	2 270	...
Baxter township	409	258
Hale township	1 906	1 827
Mountain Pine city[25]	1 068	1 127
Hot Springs township	40 747	39 010
Hot Springs city[25]	35 781	35 631
Lake Hamilton (CDP) (pt.)	118	...
Piney (CDP) (pt.)	13	...
Rockwell (CDP) (pt.)	–	...
Jessieville township	3 380	733
Hot Springs Village (CDP)	2 083	...
Lake Hamilton township	3 434	1 774
Rockwell (CDP) (pt.)	2 610	...
Lee township	1 217	519
Rockwell (CDP) (pt.)	65	...
Mazarn township	963	539

County Subdivisions	1980	1970
Garland County—Con.		
Mill township	3 655	1 100
Phillips township	343	241
Lonsdale town	117	104
Sulphur township	1 805	1 039
Union township	3 202	2 007
Valley township	751	520
Whittington township	717	407
Grant County[26]	13 008	9 711
Calvert township	996	704
Darysaw township	497	459
Davis township	207	167
Dekalb township	488	330
Tull town	281	179
Fenter township	791	666
Poyen town[26]	329	265
Franklin township	231	153
Madison township	540	373
Merry Green township	5 175	4 175
Sheridan city[26]	3 042	2 480
River township	1 184	936
Prattsville town	317	299
Simpson township	1 187	822
Tennessee township	713	597
Leola town[26]	481	390
Washington township	999	329
Greene County[27]	30 744	24 765
Blue Cane township	223	273
Breckenridge township	1 000	818
Lafe town[27]	215	...
Bryan township	387	428
Cache township	971	729
Clark township	14 403	12 196
Paragould city (pt.)[27]	13 082	10 614
Collier township	367	323
Paragould city (pt.)[27]	...	...
Crowley township	390	510
Evening Shade township	173	187
Friendship township	716	530
Hays township	285	254
Hopewell township	397	365
Hurricane township	1 512	1 034
Marmaduke city[27]	1 168	821
Jones township	828	857
Delaplaine town	161	145
Lake township	394	460
Main Shore township	438	522
Poland township	530	341
Reynolds township	232	324
St. Francis township	894	658
Paragould city (pt.)[27]	–	...
Salem township	521	398
Shady Grove township	217	341
Spring Grove township	3 427	1 779
Paragould city (pt.)[27]	2 166	25
Sugar Creek township	553	459
Union township	1 679	770
Oak Grove Heights town[27]	486	...
Paragould city (pt.)[27]	–	...
Walnut Corner township	207	209
Hempstead County[28]	23 635	19 308
Bodcaw township	512	414
Patmos town	88	77
Bois d'Arc township	1 246	1 056
Fulton city	326	323
De Roan township	13 621	10 874
Hope city[28]	10 290	8 830
Perrytown city	282	148
Garland township	319	243
Mine Creek township	1 436	997
Ozan city (pt.)[28]	49	...
Noland township	372	353
Emmet city (pt.)[28]	21	...
Ozan township	1 614	1 508
Oakhaven city	72	83
Ozan city (pt.)	62	134
Washington city	265	290
Redland township	742	587
McCaskill city	87	58
Saline township	845	779
Springhill township	1 445	1 142
Wallaceburg township	926	909
Blevins city	314	265
Water Creek township	557	446
Hot Spring County[29]	26 819	21 963
Antioch township[29]	351	...
Big Creek township[29]	301	...
Bismarck township[29]	1 157	...
Brown Springs township[29]	176	...
Butterfield township[29]	1 128	...
Clear Creek township[29]	312	...
De Roche township[29]	838	...
Dover township	355	260
Fenter township[29]	12 976	...
Malvern city[29]	10 163	8 739
Perla town	149	227

County Subdivisions	1980	1970
Hot Spring County—Con.		
Fenter township—Con.		
Rockport town[29]	231	158
Gifford township[29]	1 074	...
Harrison township[29]	235	...
Henderson township[29]	625	...
Lone Hill township[29]	673	...
Magnet township[29]	2 069	...
Midway township[29]	899	...
Montgomery township[29]	729	...
Ouachita township[29]	691	...
Prairie township[29]	813	...
Friendship town	163	150
Saline township [29]	1 002	...
Valley township[29]	415	...
Howard County[30]	13 459	11 412
Blackland township[30]	158	567
Blue Bayou township	73	95
Blue Ridge township	182	150
Brewer township	183	140
Buck Range township	240	227
Burg township	87	48
Center Point township	716	535
Clay township	178	124
County Line township	464	341
Dillard township	367	259
Duckett township	43	49
Franklin township	211	213
Holly Creek township	210	166
Madison township	1 771	1 544
Dierks city[30]	1 249	1 159
Mineral Springs township	1 052	835
Mineral Springs city	936	761
Mountain township	324	336
Muddy Fork township	141	116
Nashville township	5 974	5 029
Nashville city[30]	4 554	4 016
Saline township	90	85
Saratoga township	255	286
Tollette township[30]	407	...
Tollette town[30]	407	...
Umpire township[30]	333	...
Independence County[31]	30 147	22 723
Ashley township	1 197	657
Barren township	824	690
Cave City city (pt.)[31]	89	105
Big Bottom township	1 228	944
Newark city (pt.)[31]	1 109	849
Black River township	249	201
Christian township	513	625
Oil Trough city (pt.)	280	524
Cushman township	1 018	820
Cushman town (pt.)	340	266
Departee township	222	197
Dota township	517	417
Fairview township	1 127	873
Pleasant Plains town[31]	267	162
Gainsboro township	814	513
Greenbrier township	1 571	985
Hill township	380	322
Huff township	385	234
Jefferson township	168	171
Liberty township	618	630
Logan township	94	63
McHue township	3 044	1 705
Magness township	438	287
Magness town	196	139
Marshall township	174	188
Moorefield township	1 301	739
Batesville city (pt.)[31]	49	–
Moorefield town	129	127
Oil Trough township	190	194
Oil Trough city (pt.)[31]	–	...
Relief township	398	258
Rosie township	483	256
Ruddell township	10 207	8 609
Batesville city (pt.)[31]	8 214	7 209
Salado township	818	449
Union township	321	256
Cushman town (pt.)	29	27
Vaughn township	216	161
Washington township	844	608
White River township	686	582
Sulphur Rock town	316	290
Wycough township[31]	289	223
Newark city (pt.)[31]	19	...
Izard County[32]	10 768	7 381
Athens township	105	111
Baker township	173	169
Horseshoe Bend city (pt.)[32]	24	...
Barren Fork township	456	297
Mount Pleasant town (pt.)	316	231
Big Spring township	169	98
Bryan township	414	297
Claiborne township	92	68
Drytown township	240	204

County Subdivisions	1980	1970
Izard County—Con.		
Drytown township—Con.		
Mount Pleasant town (pt.)	122	115
Franklin township	394	279
Franklin town (pt.)[32]	253	117
Horseshoe Bend city (pt.)[32]	13	...
Gid township	239	197
Guion township	219	256
Guion town	177	213
Guthrie township	122	129
Jefferson township	2 022	478
Franklin town (pt.)[32]	–	...
Horseshoe Bend city (pt.)[32]	1 864	321
Lacrosse township	175	165
Lafferty township	76	98
Lunenburg township	128	86
Mill Creek township	1 778	1 379
Melbourne city (pt.)[32]	1 589	1 043
Mount Olive township	66	25
Newburg township	418	367
New Hope township	650	495
Oxford town[32]	520	271
Pleasant Hill township	226	151
Sage township	231	191
Melbourne city (pt.)[32]	30	...
Strawberry township	148	124
Union township	1 893	1 459
Calico Rock city[32]	1 046	723
Pineville town[32]	163	...
Violet Hill township	249	201
White River township	85	57
Jackson County[33]	21 646	20 452
Barren township	742	574
Bateman township	144	176
Newport city (pt.)[33]	5	...
Bird township	2 982	2 745
Tuckerman city	2 078	1 731
Breckenridge township	871	989
Tupelo town[33]	248	246
Weldon town	161	133
Bryan township	202	310
Cache township	477	517
Cow Lake township	703	824
Beedeville town[33]	183	144
Glaize township	969	766
Glass township	1 343	1 343
Swifton city[33]	859	703
Grubbs township	965	931
Grubbs town[33]	546	442
Jefferson township	1 159	915
Campbell Station town	297	218
Diaz city (pt.)[33]	141	...
Jacksonport town	288	306
Richwoods township	617	720
Amagon town	126	136
Union township	10 273	9 013
Diaz city (pt.)[33]	1 051	283
Newport city (pt.)[33]	8 289	7 725
Village township	199	629
Newport city (pt.)[33]	45	...
Jefferson County[34]	90 718	85 329
Barraque township	1 415	731
Redfield town[34]	745	277
Bogy township	428	604
Bolivar township	377	389
Dudley Lake township	1 759	1 817
Dunnington township	763	1 360
Wabbaseka city	428	644
Jefferson township	1 990	850
Melton township	886	664
Niven township[34]	5 263	...
Old River township	193	330
Pastoria township	455	673
Plum Bayou township[34]	2 794	...
Altheimer city[34]	1 231	1 037
Sherrill town	161	208
Richland township	880	1 101
Roberts township	547	525
Humphrey town (pt.)	418	384
Spring township	2 175	1 140
Talladega township	763	379
Vaugine township[34]	59 180	...
Pine Bluff city	56 636	57 389
Victoria township	991	1 005
Villemont township	178	231
Washington township	8 214	5 443
White Hall city[34]	2 214	1 300
Whiteville township	1 467	908
Johnson County[35]	17 423	13 630
Batson township	232	190
Dickerson township	44	26
Grant township	1 281	1 006
Coal Hill city	859	733
Hickey township[35]	361	218
Hill township	86	59
Horsehead township	421	350
Howell township	694	468

County Subdivisions

County Subdivisions	1980	1970
Johnson County—Con.		
Howell township—Con.		
Knoxville city	264	202
King township	810	531
Lee township	150	116
Low Gap township	110	176
McKennon township[35]	589	229
Mulberry township	255	67
Perry township[35]	628	570
Pilot Rock township	25	79
Piney township	67	73
Pittsburg township[35]	1 669	1 423
Lamar city[35]	708	589
Prairie township	761	561
Clarksville city (pt.)	66	37
Red Lick township	795	528
Sherman township	333	241
Spadra township	7 031	5 832
Clarksville city (pt.)[35]	5 171	4 579
Stonewall township	310	265
Ward township	771	622
Hartman town[35]	517	400
Lafayette County[36]	10 213	10 018
Baker township	3 214	2 916
Stamps city (pt.)[36]	2 828	2 448
French township	205	147
Hadley township	1 255	994
Buckner city	436	392
Stamps city (pt.)[36]	31	...
La Grange township	491	555
Lewisville city (pt.)	130	138
Mars Hill township	151	145
Roane township	2 172	2 330
Bradley city	790	706
Russell township	176	208
Steel township	1 895	2 138
Lewisville city (pt.)	1 346	1 515
Walker Creek township	654	585
Lawrence County[37]	18 447	16 320
Annieville township	289	166
Ashland township	397	362
Minturn town	169	97
Black River township	415	236
Powhatan town	49	84
Black Rock township	1 237	1 023
Black Rock city (pt.)[37]	848	498
Boas township	3 350	2 701
Hoxie city	2 961	2 265
Cache township	474	919
College City town (pt.)	76	454
Campbell township	5 303	4 540
College City town (pt.)[37]	356	191
Walnut Ridge city[37]	4 152	3 800
Dent township	924	669
Imboden town[37]	661	496
Dowell township	537	572
Duty township	611	521
Black Rock city (pt.)	—	—
Portia town	480	381
Eaton township	350	254
Flat Creek township	105	94
Jesup township	118	93
Lawrence township	315	383
Marion township	603	686
Alicia town	246	246
Morgan township	615	524
Lynn town[37]	345	274
Promised Land township	650	690
Sedgwick town	205	168
Reeds Creek township	874	744
Strawberry town	280	218
Richwoods township	199	267
Spring River township	282	228
Ravenden town (pt.)[37]	—	...
Strawberry township	364	352
Smithville town[37]	113	89
Thacker township	435	296
Ravenden town (pt.)	338	219
Lee County[38]	15 539	18 884
Bear Creek township	68	91
Big Creek township	218	411
Council township	166	344
Fleener township	507	585
Hampton township	1 504	1 858
Moro town	327	489
Hardy township	14	26
Independence township	7 946	7 908
Marianna city[38]	6 220	6 196
Liberty township	191	502
Oak Forest township	797	1 280
Richland township	1 132	1 504
Rondo town	330	379
St. Francis township	511	916
Spring Creek township	1 077	1 497
Aubrey town	267	351
Texas township	664	990
Union township	721	912
Lee County—Con.		
Union township—Con.		
Haynes town[38]	359	...
Walnut township	23	60
Lincoln County[39]	13 369	12 913
Auburn township	1 923	1 390
Bartholomew township	1 113	1 244
Cane Creek township	3 537	3 355
Star City city[39]	2 066	2 032
Choctaw township	1 129	1 431
Grady city	488	688
Gould township	1 883	2 041
Gould city	1 671	1 683
Kimbrough township	241	343
Lone Pine township	458	303
Mill Creek township	310	257
Owen township	837	555
Smith township	429	387
Spring township	789	602
Wells Bayou township	720	1 005
Little River County[40]	13 952	11 194
Arden township	392	362
Arkinda township	81	109
Burke township[40]	321	...
Caney township	169	146
Cleveland township[40]	946	...
Wilton town	495	427
Franklin township	596	156
Jackson township	1 997	1 776
Foreman city[40]	1 377	1 173
Jeff Davis township[40]	277	...
Jefferson township[40]	5 129	...
Ashdown city (pt.)[40]	3 962	3 522
Jewell township	243	195
Johnson township	986	944
Ogden town	334	286
Lick Creek township[40]	1 065	...
Ashdown city (pt.)	256	...
Little River township[40]	482	...
Winthrop city	238	240
Red River township[40]	582	...
Richland township	95	194
Wallace township[40]	591	...
Logan County[41]	20 144	16 789
Barber township	198	126
Bear Wallow township	63	72
Blue Mountain township	176	156
Blue Mountain town	112	108
Boone township	5 276	4 493
Booneville city[41]	3 718	3 239
Cane Creek township	313	262
Cauthron township	303	253
Clark township	1 401	977
Subiaco town	744	375
Delaware township	534	392
Driggs township	254	225
Ellsworth township	591	476
Johnson township	237	192
Logan township	409	366
Mountain township	103	64
Petit Jean township	315	235
Revilee township	1 303	1 034
Magazine city	799	677
River township	623	593
Morrison Bluff town[41]	69	49
Scranton city	244	222
Roseville township	152	129
Shoal Creek township	478	323
Short Mountain township	5 325	4 817
Paris city[41]	3 991	3 646
Six Mile township	931	760
Caulksville town	234	208
Ratcliff city	197	184
Sugar Creek township	333	229
Titsworth township	2	6
Tomlinson township	266	239
Washburn township	558	370
Lonoke County[42]	34 518	26 249
Butler township	982	753
Carlisle township	3 070	2 614
Carlisle city[42]	2 567	2 048
Caroline township	1 607	910
Austin town	269	236
Cleveland township	227	170
Crooked Creek township	1 156	1 227
Allport town	295	307
Humnoke city[42]	442	398
Dortch township	150	266
Eagle township	440	230
Fletcher township	306	378
Furlow township	566	371
Goodrum township	1 102	688
Gray township	2 142	792
Gum Woods township	3 451	3 422
England city[42]	3 081	3 075

County Subdivisions	1980	1970
Lonoke County—Con.		
Hamilton township	292	349
Indian Bayou township	550	836
Coy town	183	240
Isbell township	195	216
Lafayette township	406	457
Keo town[42]	208	226
Lonoke township	4 979	4 042
Lonoke city[42]	4 128	3 140
Magness township	899	561
Oak Grove township	1 721	580
Pettus township	379	676
Prairie township	301	244
Pulaski township	436	617
Richwoods township	307	414
Scott township	111	145
Totten township	373	314
Walls township	53	115
Ward township	1 652	1 066
Ward city[42]	981	619
Williams township	255	276
York township	6 410	3 520
Cabot city[42]	4 806	2 903
Madison County[43]	11 373	9 453
Alabam township	914	662
Bohannon township	348	313
Boston township	257	182
Bowen township	357	318
California township	812	663
Hilburn township	372	366
St. Paul town	198	145
Japton township	325	298
Kentucky township	252	186
Kings River township	624	529
Lamar township	612	509
Lincoln township	197	136
Marble township	347	245
Mill Creek township	554	454
Prairie township	981	854
Purdy township	242	183
Richland township	365	243
Valley township	430	357
Venus township	157	129
War Eagle township	2 595	2 327
Huntsville city[43]	1 394	1 287
Wharton Creek township	308	247
White River township	324	252
Marion County[44]	11 334	7 000
Bearden township	44	41
Big Creek township	14	4
Big Springs township	143	71
Blythe township	615	388
Pyatt town	217	137
Buffalo township	30	14
Cedar Creek township	35	26
Crockett township	82	59
Crooked Creek township	244	110
De Soto township	203	120
Dodd City township	183	115
Franklin township	327	220
Hampton township	264	233
Independence township	189	160
James Creek township	1 691	821
Bull Shoals city[44]	1 312	430
Jefferson township	59	34
Joe Burleson township	248	199
Keesee township	176	76
Keeter township	149	88
Liberty township	161	79
North Fork township	541	292
Prairie township	359	267
Sugarloaf township	309	204
Summit township	1 045	592
Summit town[44]	506	321
Yellville city (pt.)[44]	284	69
Union township	1 385	1 047
Yellville city (pt.)	760	791
Water Creek township	578	374
White River township	2 260	1 366
Flippin city[44]	1 072	626
Miller County[45]	37 766	33 385
Beech township	2 763	1 993
Fouke city	614	506
Cleveland township	1 760	737
Cut Off township	198	299
Days Creek township	807	444
Garland township	29 670	27 575
Texarkana city[45]	21 459	21 682
Homan township	298	286
Red River township	811	717
Garland town[45]	660	321
Sulphur township	1 459	1 334

County Subdivisions	1980	1970
Mississippi County[46]	59 517	62 060
Big Lake township	3 608	3 803
Manila city[46]	2 553	1 961
Bowen township	7 558	6 172
Blytheville city (pt.)	3 715	4 273
Gosnell city (pt.)[46]	3 210	1 383
Burdette township	498	573
Burdette town[46]	328	173
Canadian township	281	511
Carson Lake township	791	882
Marie town	287	72
Chickasawba township	21 916	22 811
Blytheville city (pt.)[46]	20 129	20 479
Clear Lake township	1 044	1 137
Dyess township	1 158	1 364
Dyess town	446	433
Fletcher township	2 152	2 280
Luxora town	1 739	1 566
Victoria town	175	198
Golden Lake township	1 295	1 431
Wilson town	1 115	1 009
Half Moon Lake township	519	433
Gosnell city (pt.)	5	3
Hector township	1 001	1 275
Dell town[46]	310	358
Hickman township	372	663
Little River township	1 497	2 083
McGavock township	1 060	1 343
Joiner city[46]	725	839
Monroe township	10 323	9 648
Keiser town[46]	962	688
Osceola city[46]	8 881	7 892
Neal township	2 401	2 550
Leachville city	1 882	1 582
Pecan Point township[46]	95	232
Scott township	890	1 305
Bassett town	243	265
Swayne township	208	335
Troy township	205	430
Whitton township	645	799
Monroe County[47]	14 052	15 657
Brinkley township[47]	5 445	...
Brinkley city (pt.)[47]	4 907	5 275
Brown township[47]	4	...
Cache township[47]	2 718	...
Clarendon city	2 361	2 563
Cleburne township[47]	220	...
Cypress Ridge township	638	716
Dixon township[47]	486	...
Brinkley city (pt.)	2	...
Duncan township[47]	1 542	...
Holly Grove town	754	840
Greenfield township[47]	421	...
Hindman township[47]	238	...
Jackson township	344	413
Keevil township[47]	341	...
Montgomery township	237	258
Pine Ridge township	206	217
Raymond township[47]	188	...
Richland township[47]	327	...
Roc Roe township	493	412
Roe town	136	127
Smalley township	204	302
Montgomery County[48]	7 771	5 821
Big Fork township	151	114
Caddo township[48]	329	...
Black Springs town[48]	92	'72
Caney township	464	391
Center township[48]	647	...
Gap township	570	415
Leverney township	186	188
Mazarn township	143	149
Ouachita township	448	278
Parks township[48]	267	...
Pencil Bluff township	314	193
Polk township[48]	749	...
Oden town	186	141
South Fork township[48]	1 843	...
Mount Ida city	1 023	819
Sulphur township[48]	407	312
Walnut township	381	224
Womble township	872	766
Norman town	539	'505
Nevada County[49]	11 097	10 111
Alabama township	350	394
Albany township	603	470
Boughton township	455	395
Caney township	568	560
Cale town[49]	110	...
Rosston town[49]	274	...
Emmet township	638	599
Emmet city (pt.)	454	433
Georgia township	218	227
Jackson township	266	196
Leake township	191	202
Missouri township	5 333	4 873

County Subdivisions	1980	1970
Nevada County—Con.		
Missouri township—Con.		
Prescott city[49]	4 103	3 921
Parker township	670	501
Bodcaw town	197	158
Redland township	565	452
Taylor township	792	760
Willisville town[49]	209	...
Union township	448	482
Bluff City town	292	244
Reader town (pt.)	36	22
Newton County[50]	7 756	5 844
Big Creek township	478	322
Boston township	87	121
Grove township[50]	695	...
Western Grove town[50]	378	179
Hasty township	217	261
Hickory Grove township	142	121
Hudson township	328	219
Jackson township	1 394	1 029
Jasper city	519	394
Jefferson township	226	154
Jones township	56	63
Kentucky township	72	54
Lincoln township	224	127
Low Gap township	262	151
Marble City township[50]	574	...
Murray township	156	106
Osage township	170	125
Pleasant Hill township	400	280
Plumlee township	229	219
Polk township	201	203
Ponca township	200	192
Prairie township	176	87
Richland township	296	266
Union township	156	120
Van Buren township	137	92
Walnut township	86	52
White township	794	714
Ouachita County[51]	30 541	30 896
Behestian township	278	325
Bradley township	1 530	1 598
Camden city (pt.)	–	–
East Camden town[51]	632	589
Bragg township	448	474
Bridge Creek township	690	655
Carroll township	303	323
Cleveland township	257	201
Ecore Fabre township	11 983	13 015
Camden city (pt.)[51]	10 846	11 595
Freeo township	450	406
Jefferson township	250	291
Lafayette township	6 720	5 820
Camden city (pt.)[51]	4 510	3 552
Liberty township	163	205
Marion township	628	636
Red Hill township	796	856
Chidester city[51]	342	232
Reader town (pt.)	91	121
River township	118	109
Smackover township	1 964	2 016
Stephens city[51]	1 366	1 184
Union township	1 780	1 875
Bearden city[51]	1 191	1 272
Valley township	1 273	1 089
Washington township	910	1 002
Louann town	282	245
Perry County[52]	7 266	5 634
Aplin township	283	163
Casa township	498	413
Casa town	179	208
Cherry Hill township	264	163
Fourche Lafave township	1 303	1 073
Perryville city	1 058	815
Houston township	508	404
Houston town	183	200
Kenney township	108	107
Lake township	441	455
Perry town	254	218
Maumelle township	436	290
New Tennessee township	198	147
Perry township	660	546
Bigelow town[52]	373	258
Fourche town[52]	51	46
Petit Jean township	457	281
Adona town	230	204
Rankin township	759	532
Rose Creek township	223	211
Tyler township	254	235
Union township	404	280
Union Valley township	250	232
Wye township	220	102
Phillips County[53]	34 772	40 046
Big Creek township	692	820
Cleburne township	534	455
Cleveland township	439	623

County Subdivisions	1980	1970
Phillips County—Con.		
Cypress township	189	449
Hickory Ridge township	2 363	2 955
Marvell city[53]	1 724	1 980
Hicksville township	424	613
Hornor township	12 699	13 252
Helena city (pt.)[53]	155	53
West Helena city (pt.)[53]	11 367	11 005
James R. Bush township	349	782
Lake View town (pt.)[53]	1	...
Lake township	181	349
L'Anguille township	29	34
Marion township	1 029	1 309
Mooney township	778	938
St. Francis township	9 854	11 062
Helena city (pt.)	9 443	10 362
West Helena city (pt.)	–	2
Searcy township	1 364	1 539
Lake View town (pt.)[53]	608	...
Spring Creek township	1 803	2 251
Tappan township	2 045	2 615
Elaine city	991	1 210
Pike County[54]	10 373	8 711
Antoine township[54]	587	...
Brewer township	281	184
Clark township[54]	2 633	...
Glenwood town	1 402	1 212
Eagle township	271	138
Missouri township	846	889
Delight city	431	439
Mountain township	264	246
Muddy Fork township	216	163
Pike City township	253	221
Saline township	407	381
Self Creek township	662	496
Daisy town	177	100
Thompson township	2 589	2 225
Murfreesboro city[54]	1 883	1 350
White township	650	568
Wolf Creek township	714	666
Antoine town	194	182
Poinsett County[55]	27 032	26 843
Bolivar township	4 087	3 685
Harrisburg city[55]	1 921	1 931
Dobson township	337	377
Greenfield township	1 215	1 105
Greenwood township	2 913	3 205
Lepanto city	1 964	1 846
Little River township	4 895	4 367
Marked Tree city[55]	3 201	3 229
Lunsford township	845	1 153
Owen township	1 073	1 287
Fisher town	302	361
Waldenburg town	124	164
Scott township	969	822
Tyronza township	1 298	2 088
Tyronza town	777	510
West Prairie township	1 194	1 110
Weiner city	750	715
Willis township	8 206	7 644
Trumann city	6 044	6 023
Polk County[56]	17 007	13 297
Acorn township	977	691
Big Fork township	196	102
Cedar township	81	69
Center township	6 448	5 387
Mena city[56]	5 154	4 530
Cove township	1 134	950
Hatfield town[56]	410	377
Eagle township	496	328
Faulkner township	10	–
Freedom township	386	257
Fulton township	538	405
Gap Springs township	129	76
Mill Creek township	165	118
Mountain township	559	344
Ouachita township	688	451
Ozark township	2 101	1 638
Grannis town[56]	349	177
Wickes town[56]	464	409
Potter township	1 208	875
Rich Mountain township	107	86
White township	1 784	1 520
Cove town	391	334
Vandervoort town	98	108
Pope County[57]	39 021	28 607
Bayliss township[57]	427	244
Burnett township[57]	264	153
Center township[57]	355	214
Clark township[57]	1 969	1 369
London town[57]	859	539
Convenience township[57]	742	594
Dover township	3 000	1 788
Dover city[57]	948	662
Freeman township[57]	156	...
Galla township[57]	1 765	1 082
Pottsville town	564	411

County Subdivisions	1980	1970
Pope County—Con.		
Griffin township	749	529
Gum Log township[57]	511	408
Illinois township[57]	19 511	15 488
Norristown town[57]	625	170
Russellville city[57]	14 031	11 750
Jackson township[57]	1 002	...
Hector town[57]	449	387
Liberty township[57]	676	...
Martin township[57]	1 078	...
Moreland township	612	424
Phoenix township[57]	201	130
Smyrna township[57]	197	...
Valley township[57]	1 732	833
Wilson township[57]	4 074	...
Atkins city	3 002	2 015
Prairie County[58]	10 140	10 249
Belcher township	115	134
Bullard township	159	221
Calhoun township	405	415
Center township	414	303
Des Arc township	268	333
Hazen township	2 165	2 246
Hazen city	1 636	1 605
Hickory Plain township	557	626
Lower Surrounded Hill township	829	1 008
Fredonia (Biscoe) town[58]	486	340
Roc Roe township	530	608
Ulm town	201	185
Tyler township	362	386
Union township	85	73
Upper Surrounded Hill township	191	230
Watensaw township	1 484	1 241
De Valls Bluff town	738	622
White River township	2 576	2 425
Des Arc city	2 001	1 714
Pulaski County[59]	340 613	287 189
Big Rock township	204 143	177 003
Alexander town	223	272
Cammack Village city	920	1 165
Little Rock city[59]	158 461	132 483
Parkers–Iron Springs (CDP)	3 643	...
Tafton–Wrightsville (CDP)	1 434	...
Hill township	136 470	110 186
Jacksonville city[59]	27 589	19 832
North Little Rock city[59]	64 288	60 040
Sherwood city[59]	10 586	2 754
Randolph County[60]	16 834	12 645
Baker township	82	54
Bristow township	441	316
Butler township	33	22
Columbia township	732	540
Current River township	573	599
Biggers town	363	372
Davidson township	187	124
Demun township	7 147	5 408
Pocahontas city[60]	5 995	4 544
Eleven Points township	225	144
Elm Store township	74	69
Foster township	382	254
Ingram township	227	148
Jackson township	170	131
Janes Creek township	592	431
Ravenden Springs town[60]	230	107
Little Black township	533	437
O'Kean township	582	553
O'Kean town	291	244
Reyno township	644	482
Reyno town	521	356
Richardson township	723	523
Maynard town (pt.)[60]	361	224
Roanoke township	1 114	818
Running Lake township	202	118
Shiloh township	675	269
Siloam township	359	326
Maynard town (pt.)[60]	20	...
Spring River township	265	182
Union township	146	152
Warm Springs township	250	160
Water Valley township	246	106
Wiley township	230	279
St. Francis County[61]	30 858	30 799
Black Fish township	285	626
Franks township	1 141	1 379
Garland township	2 651	2 857
Hughes city	1 919	1 872
Goodwin township	753	824
Griggs township	1 706	2 376
Madison city (pt.)	–	–
Widener town	316	292
Heth township	1 026	1 405
Johnson township	1 597	1 375
L'Anguille township	845	593
Madison township	16 615	15 362
Forrest City city[61]	13 803	12 521
Madison city (pt.)[61]	1 227	984

County Subdivisions	1980	1970
St. Francis County—Con.		
Prairie township	1 566	1 690
Palestine city[61]	976	755
Telico township	1 995	1 569
Caldwell town	283	292
Colt city[61]	378	301
Wheatley township	678	743
Wheatley city[61]	523	507
Saline County[62]	53 161	36 107
Banner township	2 495	1 465
Bauxite township[62]	838	...
Bauxite town[62]	433	...
Benton city (pt.)[62]	35	...
Beaver township	1 369	731
Bryant township[62]	5 174	...
Bryant city[62]	2 682	1 199
Dyer township	669	556
Fairplay township	1 282	990
Haskell township	2 786	2 377
Haskell city[62]	1 074	239
Holland township	370	301
Hurricane township	1 371	709
Jefferson township	210	150
Kentucky township	498	334
Liberty township	422	308
Marble township	88	44
Newcomb township	578	332
Otter township	5 328	2 240
Shannon Hills town[62]	1 656	...
Owen township[62]	4 741	...
Salem township	4 878	1 876
Benton city (pt.)[62]	166	...
Saline township[62]	18 141	...
Benton city (pt.)[62]	17 516	16 499
Shaw township	627	337
Smith township	481	289
Traskwood township	566	437
Traskwood town	459	358
Union township	249	135
Scott County[63]	9 685	8 207
Black Fork township	75	71
Blansett township	152	123
Brawley township	62	56
Cauthron township	131	132
Cedar township	129	118
Coal township	255	219
Denton township	259	194
Hickman township	3 983	3 459
Waldron city[63]	2 642	2 132
Hon township	351	251
Hunt township	223	215
James township	136	134
Jones township	126	81
La Fave township	117	110
Lafayette township	87	86
Lamb township	385	237
Lewis township	1 082	932
Mansfield city (pt.)[63]	340	327
Little Texas township	22	23
Mill Creek township[63]	327	...
Mountain township[63]	568	...
Mount Pleasant township	406	294
Oliver township	49	46
Parks township[63]	401	...
Tate township	86	52
Tomlinson township	273	188
Searcy County[64]	8 847	7 731
Bear Creek township	2 654	2 337
Marshall city[64]	1 595	1 397
Beaver township	130	105
Big Creek township	671	602
Calf Creek township	368	374
Campbell township	378	253
Clark township	73	91
Long Creek township	122	84
Maumee township	42	26
Mount Pleasant township	270	246
Mount Vernon township	213	111
Prairie township	600	439
Red River township	177	143
Richland township	105	111
Rock Creek township	350	400
St. Joe township	602	556
Shady Grove township	140	126
Spring township	443	379
Sulphur Springs township	195	130
Tomahawk township	300	284
Gilbert town	43	45
Wileys Cove township	1 014	934
Leslie city	501	563
Sebastian County[65]	95 172	79 237
Bass Little township	855	477
Beverly township	420	386
Big Creek township	2 084	1 324
Lavaca city[65]	1 092	532
Bloomer township	528	474

County Subdivisions

	1980	1970
Sebastian County—Con.		
Center township	4 329	2 444
Greenwood city[65]	3 317	2 032
Cole township	1 285	908
Hackett city[65]	505	462
Dayton township	457	369
Diamond township	1 029	932
Huntington city[65]	662	627
Mansfield city (pt.)	22	29
Fort Chaffee (unorg.)[65]	176	...
Hartford township	873	860
Hartford city[65]	613	616
Island township	288	255
Jim Fork township	620	562
Midland town	286	294
Lon Norris township	2 295	985
Fort Smith city (pt.)[65]	1 714	...
Marion township	2 041	1 141
Bonanza town[65]	553	342
Mississippi township	521	348
Mont Sandels township[65]	4 100	2 044
Barling city[65]	3 761	1 739
Central City town[65]	339	...
Prairie township	557	358
Rogers township	889	618
Sugarloaf township	1 240	1 057
Mansfield city (pt.)	638	625
Upper township	69 912	63 312
Fort Smith city (pt.)[65]	69 912	62 802
Washburn township	337	229
White Oak township	336	154
Sevier County[66]	14 060	11 272
Bear Creek township	6 157	4 851
De Queen city (pt.)[66]	4 484	3 759
Ben Lomond township	235	235
Ben Lomond town	155	155
Buckhorn township	137	139
Clear Creek township	2 836	2 178
Horatio city[66]	989	852
Jefferson township	110	116
Mill Creek township	80	73
Mineral township	999	773
Gillham town	252	200
Monroe township	991	756
De Queen city (pt.)[66]	110	104
Paraclifta township	406	295
Red Colony township	1 276	1 146
Lockesburg town	616	620
Saline township	338	260
Washington township	495	450
Sharp County[67]	14 607	8 233
Big Creek township	315	197
Cave township	2 134	1 077
Cave City city (pt.)[67]	1 545	702
Cherokee township	3 486	1 107
Cherokee Village–Hidden Valley (CDP) (pt.)	3 462	1 107
Davidson township	157	103
East Sullivan township	319	216
Hardy township[67]	1 075	...
Cherokee Village–Hidden Valley (CDP) (pt.)	29	6
Hardy city	643	692
Highland township	750	354
Cherokee Village–Hidden Valley (CDP) (pt.)	298	147
Jackson township[67]	384	...
Williford town	169	175
Johnson township	106	67
Lave Creek township	253	87
Lower North township	493	267
Morgan township	167	104
North Big Rock township	212	166
North Lebanon township	77	78
North Union township	226	192
Ozark township[67]	577	...
Piney Fork township	796	611
Evening Shade town[67]	397	309
Richwoods township	1 181	628
Ash Flat town[67]	524	211
Horseshoe Bend city (pt.)[67]	–	...
Scott township	355	221
South Big Rock township	118	85
South Lebanon township	120	126
South Union township	317	286
Strawberry township	173	118
Upper North township	239	219
Washington township	213	99
West Sullivan township	364	249
Sidney town[67]	270	109
Stone County[68]	9 022	6 838
Bellmore township	108	101
Blue Mountain township	2 889	2 317
Mountain View city (pt.)[68]	2 147	1 866
Bryan township	206	160
Chalybeate Springs township	79	16
Cove township	202	116
Farris township	353	312
Flag township	108	111
Franklin township	408	326

County Subdivisions

	1980	1970
Stone County—Con.		
Harris township	555	296
Mountain View city (pt.)[68]	–	...
Herd township	119	105
Hixson township	76	81
Jones township	72	49
Liberty township	240	162
Locust Grove township	190	163
Northwest township	262	209
Fifty-Six city[68]	157	...
Red River township	158	72
Redstripe township	268	188
Richwoods township	296	256
Roasting Ear township	125	104
Smart township	162	65
Sylamore township	606	417
Timbo township	371	298
Turkey Creek township	270	217
Union township	415	286
Wallace township	159	213
Washington township	142	114
Wilson township	183	84
Union County[69]	48 573	45 428
Boone township[69]	575	...
Cornie township[69]	435	...
El Dorado township[69]	31 026	...
El Dorado city[69]	25 270	25 283
Franklin township[69]	2 263	...
Calion city[69]	638	535
Garner township[69]	406	...
Harrison township[69]	772	...
Henderson township[69]	1 013	...
Junction City city	813	763
Jackson township[69]	688	...
Johnson township[69]	1 363	...
Lapile township[69]	3 339	...
Felsenthal town[69]	220	158
Huttig town	976	822
Strong city	785	965
Norphlet township	1 666	1 694
Norphlet city[69]	756	755
Smackover township[69]	3 238	...
Smackover city[69]	2 453	2 058
Tubal township[69]	347	...
Van Buren township[69]	556	...
Wesson township[69]	310	...
Wilmington township[69]	576	...
Van Buren County[70]	13 357	8 275
Archey Valley township	201	183
Barnett township	552	442
Damascus town (pt.)	172	156
Bradley township	785	520
Cadron township	151	133
Cargile township	397	356
Choctaw township	983	385
Craig township	687	481
Culpepper township	459	321
Davis township	723	438
Griggs township	3 112	2 299
Clinton city[70]	1 284	1 029
Hartsugg township	126	131
Holley township[70]	233	213
Indian Rock township[70]	1 419	...
Liberty township	209	161
Linn Creek township	294	201
Mountain township	183	130
Red River township[70]	612	...
Union township[70]	1 250	...
Shirley town[70]	354	269
Washington township	537	443
Wheeler township	444	292
Washington County[71]	100 494	77 370
Boston township	302	190
Brush Creek township	1 250	1 103
Cane Hill township	970	651
Center township	4 580	3 157
Farmington city[71]	1 283	908
Fayetteville city (pt.)[71]	145	207
Cove Creek township	510	402
Crawford township	680	387
Durham township	584	480
Dutch Mills township	316	262
Elm Springs township	2 060	1 680
Elm Springs town[71]	781	260
Springdale city (pt.)[71]	7	...
Goshen township	897	699
Greenland township	1 582	1 462
Fayetteville city (pt.)[71]	143	185
Greenland town[71]	622	650
Harmon township	855	719
Tontitown town (pt.)[71]	100	...
Illinois township	544	503
Johnson township	4 510	1 920
Fayetteville city (pt.)[71]	47	99
Johnson city	519	274

County Subdivisions	1980	1970
Washington County—Con.		
Johnson township—Con.		
Springdale city (pt.)[71]	2 717	634
Tontitown town (pt.)	2	
Lees Creek township	413	220
Litteral township	1 760	1 021
Marrs Hill township	658	443
Morrow township	403	352
Prairie township	38 461	31 898
Fayetteville city (pt.)[71]	35 865	30 098
Prairie Grove township	2 661	2 322
Prairie Grove city[71]	1 708	1 582
Price township	436	363
Reed township	301	252
Rheas Mill township	387	305
Richland township	1 318	1 050
Elkins town[71]	579	418
Fayetteville city (pt.)[71]	12	–
Springdale township	23 907	18 369
Fayetteville city (pt.)[71]	–	5
Springdale city (pt.)[71]	20 053	15 772
Starr Hill township	2 449	1 955
Lincoln city[71]	1 422	1 023
Tontitown township	1 274	953
Tontitown town (pt.)[71]	513	426
Valley township	729	450
Vineyard township	290	248
Wedington township	221	279
West Fork township	2 610	1 485
West Fork city[71]	1 526	919
White River township	589	386
Winslow township	1 030	883
Winslow town	247	227
Wyman township	957	521
Fayetteville city (pt.)[71]	396	135
White County[72]	50 835	39 253
Albion township[72]	213	200
Antioch township	307	188
Bald Knob township	4 291	3 272
Bald Knob city[72]	2 756	2 094
Big Creek township	1 200	1 019
Pangburn city	673	654
Cadron township	236	204
Cane township	709	393
Chrisp township	398	210
Clay township	406	289
Cleveland township	54	41
Coffey township	433	335
Coldwell township	316	242
Crosby township	336	187
Cypert township	347	387
Denmark township	527	393
Des Arc township	400	300
Dogwood township	645	669
Griffithville town	254	227
El Paso township	483	313
Francure township	278	310
Garner township	441	430
Garner town[72]	216	...
Gravel Hill township	133	121
Gray township	15 476	11 201
Searcy city (pt.)[72]	12 754	8 956
Gum Springs township	1 653	845
Searcy city (pt.)[72]	847	84
Guthrie township	698	628
Harrison township	4 354	3 403
Judsonia city (pt.)	2 025	1 667
Hartsell township	588	496
Higginson township	793	776
Higginson town[72]	333	343
Jackson township	341	296
Jefferson township	224	102
Joy township	376	261
Kensett township	2 203	1 816
Kensett city	1 751	1 444
Searcy city (pt.)[72]	11	...
Kentucky township	822	677
Rose Bud town	202	157
Liberty township	1 687	1 534
Bradford city[72]	950	826
McRae township	1 213	1 113
McRae city	641	643
Marion township	405	292
Letona town[72]	231	191
Marshall township	298	237
Mount Pisgah township	94	81
Red River township	567	537
Judsonia city (pt.)[72]	–	...
West Point town[72]	226	184
Royal township	297	195
Russell township	617	679
Russell town[72]	232	231
Union township	4 919	3 713
Beebe city[72]	3 599	2 805
Velvet Ridge township	788	586
Walker township	269	282

County Subdivisions	1980	1970
Woodruff County[73]	11 222	11 566
Augusta township	4 135	3 846
Augusta city[73]	3 496	2 777
Patterson town (pt.)	–	–
Barnes township	299	408
McCrory city (pt.)	6	31
Cache township	186	398
Caney township	544	525
Hunter town	170	131
Cotton Plant township	1 599	2 101
Cotton Plant city	1 323	1 657
Dent township	355	247
De View township	2 939	2 222
McCrory city (pt.)[73]	1 936	1 347
Patterson town (pt.)[73]	567	417
Franks township	198	244
Freeman township	114	294
Garden township	75	187
Point township	239	446
Pumpkin Bend township	359	283
White River township	180	365
Yell County[74]	17 026	14 208
Bluffton township	231	169
Briggsville township	174	144
Centerville township	875	740
Compton township	78	69
Crawford township	47	118
Danville township	2 207	1 821
Belleville city (pt.)[74]	49	...
Corinth town[74]	38	...
Danville city[74]	1 698	1 362
Dardanelle township	5 626	4 132
Dardanelle city[74]	3 621	3 297
Dutch Creek township	88	101
Ferguson township	1 018	929
Belleville city (pt.)[74]	522	379
Galla Rock township	252	204
Gilkey township	1 038	194
Plainview city[74]	752	677
Gravelly Hill township	171	226
Herring township	194	148
Ions Creek township	132	14
Lamar township[74]	121	895
Magazine township	714	626
Mason township	207	223
Mountain township	151	125
Prairie township	323	291
Reed Keathly township	89	77
Richland township	193	184
Riley township	732	688
Havana city	352	308
Rover township	281	169
Sulphur Springs township	236	219
Ward township	1 454	1 301
Ola city	1 121	1 029
Waveland township	302	287
Wilson township	92	114

CALIFORNIA

California was named by Spanish discoverers from a fabulous island described in a Spanish romance as "on the right hand of the Indies * * * very near to the Terrestrial Paradise."

The territory now constituting the state of California was first visited by white men in 1542, when Juan Cabrillo, a Portuguese navigator in the service of Spain, explored the coast and islands in the Santa Barbara region and probably sailed as far north as Monterey Bay. In 1579 Sir Francis Drake sailed along the coast and landed, supposedly at Drake's Bay, a few miles northwest of San Francisco. He named the country New Albion and took possession in the name of Elizabeth of England. The English did not occupy the region, however, and the first settlement was made by the Spaniards, in 1769, when the Franciscan Fathers founded a mission at San Diego. In 1776 the Mission Dolores was established where San Francisco now stands.

California was under Spanish rule until 1822, when, on the successful termination of the Mexican Revolution, it declared its independence of Spain and its allegiance to the newly established Mexican Government.

For several years prior to 1846 large numbers of immigrants from the United States had been arriving in California, and in June of that year a revolt against Mexico was begun by the American settlers. The Mexican War was already in progress, and during July and August, 1846, the American flag was raised at Monterey, San Francisco, Sonoma, Sacramento, San Jose, San Juan Bautista, San Diego, Santa Barbara, San Pedro, and Los Angeles. The final surrender of the Mexican forces to those of the United States took place in January, 1847. In February, 1848, by the treaty of Guadalupe Hidalgo, the Mexican claims to California and to territory north of the Gila and Rio Grande were ceded to the United States.

From 1846 to 1849 California was under military and provisional rule by the United States. In October, 1849, a state constitution was adopted by a convention held at Monterey; in the following month it was ratified by the people, and state officers were elected. On September 9, 1850, California became a state of the Union.

COUNTY LOCATION INDEX

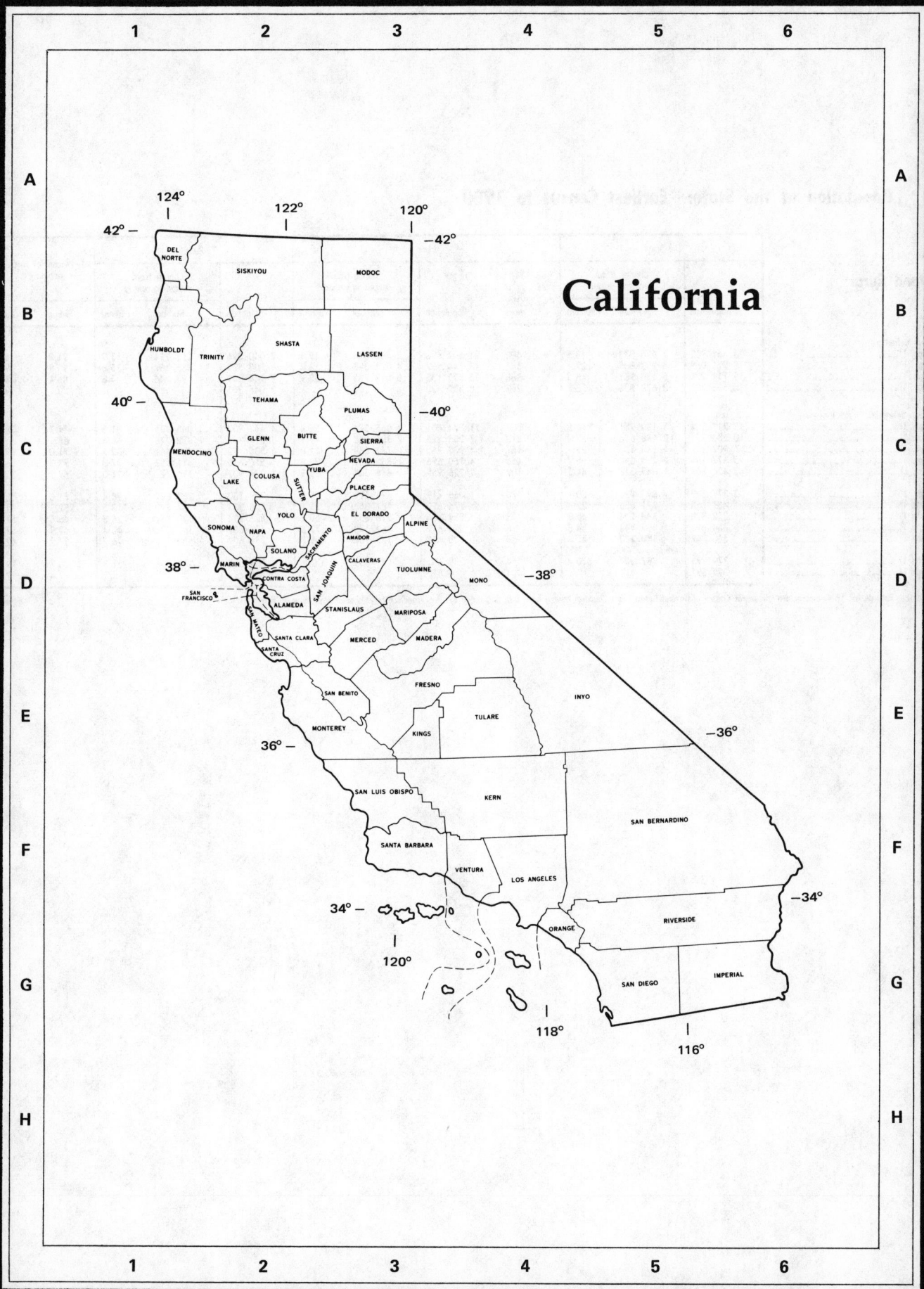

California

Population of the State: Earliest Census to 1980

Urban and Rural

	The State			Urban				Rural				Percent of total population	
	Total population	Change from preceding census		Places of 2,500 or more	Population	Change from preceding census		Population	Change from preceding census			Urban	Rural
		Number	Percent			Number	Percent		Number	Percent			
Current urban definition:													
1980 (Apr. 1)	23 667 902	3 696 833	18.5	600	21 607 606	3 463 054	19.1	2 060 296	251 714	13.9		91.3	8.7
1970 (Apr. 1)	'19 971 069	4 253 865	27.1	541	18 144 552	4 571 397	33.7	1 808 582	−335 467	−15.6		90.9	9.1
1960 (Apr. 1)	15 717 204	5 130 981	48.5	388	13 573 155	5 033 735	58.9	2 144 049	97 246	4.8		86.4	13.6
1950 (Apr. 1)	10 586 223	3 678 836	53.3	253	8 539 420	...	...	2 046 803	...	...		80.7	19.3
Previous urban definition:													
1960 (Apr. 1)	15 717 204	5 130 981	48.5	301	11 274 401	4 065 576	56.4	4 442 803	1 065 405	31.5		71.7	28.3
1950 (Apr. 1)	10 586 223	3 678 836	53.3	212	7 208 825	2 306 560	47.1	3 377 398	1 372 276	68.4		68.1	31.9
1940 (Apr. 1)	6 907 387	1 230 136	21.7	167	4 902 265	741 669	17.8	2 005 122	488 467	32.2		71.0	29.0
1930 (Apr. 1)	5 677 251	2 250 390	65.7	155	4 160 596	1 833 637	78.8	1 516 655	416 753	37.9		73.3	26.7
1920 (Jan. 1)	3 426 861	1 049 312	44.1	107	2 326 959	858 540	58.5	1 099 902	190 772	21.0		67.9	32.1
1910 (Apr. 15)	2 377 549	892 496	60.1	70	1 468 419	691 599	89.0	909 130	200 897	28.4		61.8	38.2
1900 (June 1)	1 485 053	271 655	22.4	40	776 820	187 356	31.8	708 233	84 299	13.5		52.3	47.7
1890 (June 1)	1 213 398	348 704	40.3	33	589 464	218 853	59.1	623 934	129 851	26.3		48.6	51.4
1880 (June 1)	864 694	304 447	54.3	18	370 611	162 173	77.8	494 083	142 274	40.4		42.9	57.1
1870 (June 1)	560 247	180 253	47.4	8	208 438	129 787	165.0	351 809	50 466	16.7		37.2	62.8
1860 (June 1)	379 994	287 397	310.4	4	78 651	71 831	1000+	301 343	215 566	251.3		20.7	79.3
1850 (June 1)	92 597	...	...	1	6 820	...	...	85 777	...	...		7.4	92.6

NOTE: Returns for 1850 incomplete, those for Contra Costa and Santa Clara Counties having been lost and those for San Francisco having been destroyed by fire.

ALAMEDA

1860	8,927
1870	24,237
1880	62,976
1890	93,864
1900	130,197
1910	246,131
1920	344,177
1930	464,883
1940	513,011
1950	740,315
1960	908,209
1970	1,071,446
1980	1,105,379

ALPINE

1870	685
1880	539
1890	667
1900	509
1910	309
1920	243
1930	241
1940	323
1950	241
1960	397
1970	484
1980	1,097

AMADOR

1860	10,930
1870	9,582
1880	11,384
1890	10,320
1900	11,116
1910	9,086
1920	7,793
1930	8,494
1940	8,973
1950	9,151
1960	9,990
1970	11,821
1980	19,314

BUTTE

1850	3,574
1860	12,106
1870	11,403
1880	18,721
1890	17,939
1900	17,117
1910	27,301
1920	30,030
1930	34,093
1940	42,840
1950	64,930
1960	82,030
1970	101,969
1980	143,851

CALAVERAS

1850	16,884
1860	16,299
1870	8,895
1880	9,094
1890	8,882
1900	11,200
1910	9,171
1920	6,183
1930	6,008
1940	8,221
1950	9,902
1960	10,289
1970	13,585
1980	20,710

COLUSA

1850	115
1860	2,274
1870	6,165
1880	13,118
1890	14,640
1900	7,364
1910	7,732
1920	9,290
1930	10,258
1940	9,788
1950	11,651
1960	12,075
1970	12,430
1980	12,791

CONTRA COSTA

1860	5,328
1870	8,461
1880	12,525
1890	13,515
1900	18,046
1910	31,674
1920	53,889
1930	78,608
1940	100,450
1950	289,984
1960	409,030
1970	556,116
1980	656,380

DEL NORTE

1860	1,993
1870	2,022
1880	2,584
1890	2,592
1900	2,408
1910	2,417
1920	2,759
1930	4,739
1940	4,745
1950	8,078
1960	17,771
1970	14,580
1980	18,217

EL DORADO

1850	20,057
1860	20,562
1870	10,309
1880	10,683
1890	9,232
1900	8,986
1910	7,492
1920	6,426
1930	8,325
1940	13,229
1950	16,207
1960	29,390
1970	43,833
1980	85,812

FRESNO

1860	4,605
1870	6,336
1880	9,478
1890	32,026
1900	37,862
1910	75,657
1920	128,779
1930	144,379
1940	178,565
1950	276,515
1960	365,945
1970	413,329
1980	514,621

GLENN

900	5,150
1910	7,172
1920	11,853
1930	10,935
1940	12,195
1950	15,448
1960	17,245
1970	17,521
1980	21,350

HUMBOLDT

1860	2,694
1870	6,140
1880	15,512
1890	23,469
1900	27,104
1910	33,857
1920	37,413
1930	43,233
1940	45,812
1950	69,241
1960	104,892
1970	99,692
1980	108,514

IMPERIAL

1910	13,591
1920	43,453
1930	60,903
1940	59,740
1950	62,975
1960	72,105
1970	74,492
1980	92,110

INYO

1870	1,956
1880	2,928
1890	3,544
1900	4,377
1910	6,974
1920	7,031
1930	6,555
1940	7,625
1950	11,658
1960	11,684
1970	15,571
1980	17,895

KERN

1870	2,925
1880	5,601
1890	9,808
1900	16,480
1910	37,715
1920	54,843
1930	82,570
1940	135,124
1950	228,309
1960	291,984
1970	330,234
1980	403,089

KINGS

1900	9,871
1910	16,230
1920	22,031
1930	25,385
1940	35,168
1950	46,786
1960	49,954
1970	66,717
1980	73,738

KLAMATH

1860	1,803
1870	1,686

LAKE

1870	2,969
1880	6,596
1890	7,101
1900	6,017
1910	5,526
1920	5,402
1930	7,166
1940	8,069
1950	11,481
1960	13,786
1970	19,548
1980	36,366

LASSEN

1870	1,327
1880	3,340
1890	4,239
1900	4,511
1910	4,802
1920	8,507
1930	12,589
1940	14,479
1950	18,474
1960	13,597
1970	16,796
1980	21,661

LOS ANGELES

1850	3,530
1860	11,333
1870	15,309
1880	33,381
1890	101,454
1900	170,298
1910	504,131
1920	936,455
1930	2,208,492
1940	2,785,643
1950	4,151,687
1960	6,038,771
1970	7,041,980
1980	7,477,503

MADERA

1900	6,364
1910	8,368
1920	12,203
1930	17,164
1940	23,314

MARIN

1850	323
1860	3,334
1870	6,903
1880	11,324
1890	13,072
1900	15,702
1910	25,114
1920	27,342
1930	41,648
1940	52,907
1950	85,619
1960	146,820
1970	208,652
1980	222,568

MARIPOSA

1850	4,379
1860	6,243
1870	4,572
1880	4,339
1890	3,787
1900	4,720
1910	3,956
1920	2,775
1930	3,233
1940	5,605
1950	5,145
1960	5,064
1970	6,015
1980	11,108

MENDOCINO

1850	55
1860	3,976
1870	7,545
1880	12,800
1890	17,612
1900	20,465
1910	23,929
1920	24,116
1930	23,505
1940	27,864
1950	40,854
1960	51,059
1970	51,101
1980	66,738

MERCED

1860	1,141
1870	2,807
1880	5,656
1890	8,085
1900	9,215
1910	15,148
1920	24,579
1930	36,748
1940	46,998
1950	59,780
1960	90,446
1970	104,629
1980	134,560

MODOC

1880	4,399
1890	4,986

MARIN

1950	36,964
1960	40,468
1970	41,519
1980	63,116

1900	5,076
1910	6,191
1920	5,425
1930	8,038
1940	8,713
1950	9,678
1960	8,308
1970	7,469
1980	8,610

MONO

1870	430
1880	7,499
1890	2,002
1900	2,167
1910	2,042
1920	960
1930	1,360
1940	2,299
1950	2,115
1960	2,213
1970	4,016
1980	8,577

MONTEREY

1850	1,872
1860	4,739
1870	9,876
1880	11,302
1890	18,637
1900	19,380
1910	24,146
1920	27,980
1930	53,705
1940	73,032
1950	130,498
1960	198,351
1970	247,450
1980	290,444

NAPA

1850	405
1860	5,521
1870	7,163
1880	13,235
1890	16,411
1900	16,451
1910	19,800
1920	20,678
1930	22,879
1940	28,503
1950	46,603
1960	65,890
1970	79,140
1980	99,199

NEVADA

1860	16,446
1870	19,134
1880	20,823
1890	17,369
1900	17,789
1910	14,955
1920	10,850
1930	10,596
1940	19,283
1950	19,888
1960	20,911
1970	26,346
1980	51,645

ORANGE

1890	13,589
1900	19,696
1910	34,436
1920	61,375
1930	118,674
1940	130,760
1950	216,244
1960	703,925
1970	1,421,233
1980	1,932,709

PLACER

1860	13,270
1870	11,357
1880	14,232
1890	15,101
1900	15,786
1910	18,237
1920	18,584
1930	24,468
1940	28,108
1950	41,649
1960	56,998
1970	77,632
1980	117,247

PLUMAS

1860	4,363
1870	4,489
1880	6,180
1890	4,933
1900	4,657
1910	5,259
1920	5,681
1930	7,913
1940	11,548
1950	13,519
1960	11,620
1970	11,707
1980	17,340

RIVERSIDE

1900	17,897
1910	34,696
1920	50,279
1930	81,024
1940	105,524
1950	170,046
1960	306,191
1970	456,916
1980	663,166

SACRAMENTO

1850	9,087
1860	24,142
1870	26,830
1880	34,390
1890	40,339
1900	45,915
1910	67,806
1920	91,029
1930	141,999
1940	170,333
1950	277,140
1960	502,778
1970	531,498
1980	783,381

SAN BENITO

1880	5,584
1890	6,412
1900	6,633
1910	8,041
1920	8,995
1930	11,311
1940	11,392
1950	14,370
1960	15,396
1970	18,226
1980	25,005

SAN BERNARDINO

1860	5,551
1870	3,988
1880	7,786
1890	25,497
1900	27,929
1910	56,706
1920	73,401
1930	133,900
1940	161,108
1950	281,642
1960	503,591
1970	584,072
1980	895,016

SAN DIEGO

1850	793
1860	4,324
1870	4,951
1880	8,618
1890	34,987
1900	35,090
1910	61,655
1920	112,248
1930	209,659
1940	289,348
1950	556,808
1960	1,033,011
1970	1,357,854
1980	1,861,846

SAN FRANCISCO

1860	56,802
1870	149,473
1880	233,959
1890	298,997
1900	342,782
1910	416,912
1920	506,676
1930	634,394
1940	634,536
1950	775,357
1960	740,316
1970	715,674
1980	678,974

SAN JOAQUIN

1850	3,647
1860	9,435
1870	21,050
1880	24,349
1890	28,629
1900	35,452
1910	50,731
1920	79,905
1930	102,940
1940	134,207
1950	200,750

1960	249,989
1970	290,208
1980	347,342

SAN LUIS OBISPO

1850	336
1860	1,782
1870	4,772
1880	9,142
1890	16,072
1900	16,637
1910	19,383
1920	21,893
1930	29,613
1940	33,246
1950	51,417
1960	81,044
1970	105,690
1980	155,435

SAN MATEO

1860	3,214
1870	6,635
1880	8,669
1890	10,087
1900	12,094
1910	26,585
1920	36,781
1930	77,405
1940	111,782
1950	235,659
1960	444,387
1970	557,361
1980	587,329

SANTA BARBARA

1850	1,185
1860	3,543
1870	7,784
1880	9,513
1890	15,754
1900	18,934
1910	27,738
1920	41,097
1930	65,167
1940	70,555
1950	98,220
1960	168,962
1970	264,324
1980	298,694

SANTA CLARA

1860	11,912
1870	26,246
1880	35,039
1890	48,005
1900	60,216
1910	83,539
1920	100,687
1930	145,118
1940	174,949
1950	290,547
1960	642,315
1970	1,065,313
1980	1,295,071

SANTA CRUZ

1850	643
1860	4,944
1870	8,743
1880	12,802

1890	19,270
1900	21,512
1910	26,140
1920	26,269
1930	36,433
1940	45,057
1950	66,534
1960	84,219
1970	123,170
1980	188,141

SHASTA

1850	378
1860	4,360
1870	4,173
1880	9,492
1890	12,133
1900	17,318
1910	18,920
1920	13,361
1930	13,927
1940	28,800
1950	36,413
1960	59,468
1970	77,640
1980	115,715

SIERRA

1860	11,387
1870	5,619
1880	6,623
1890	5,051
1900	4,017
1910	4,098
1920	1,783
1930	2,422
1940	3,025
1950	2,410
1960	2,247
1970	2,365
1980	3,073

SISKIYOU

1860	7,629
1870	6,848
1880	8,610
1890	12,163
1900	16,962
1910	18,801
1920	18,545
1930	25,480
1940	28,598
1950	30,733
1960	32,885
1970	33,225
1980	39,732

SOLANO

1850	580
1860	7,169
1870	16,861
1880	18,475
1890	20,946
1900	24,143
1910	27,559
1920	40,602
1930	40,834
1940	49,118
1950	104,833
1960	134,597
1970	171,989
1980	235,203

SONOMA

1850	560
1860	11,867
1870	19,817
1880	25,926
1890	32,721
1900	38,480
1910	48,394
1920	52,090
1930	62,222
1940	69,052
1950	103,405
1960	147,375
1970	204,885
1980	299,681

STANISLAUS

1860	2,245
1870	6,499
1880	8,751
1890	10,040
1900	9,550
1910	22,522
1920	43,557
1930	56,641
1940	74,866
1950	127,231
1960	157,294
1970	194,506
1980	265,900

SUTTER

1850	3,444
1860	3,390
1870	5,030
1880	5,159
1890	5,469
1900	5,886
1910	6,328
1920	10,115
1930	14,618
1940	18,680
1950	26,239
1960	33,380
1970	41,935
1980	52,246

TEHAMA

1860	4,044
1870	3,587
1880	9,301
1890	9,961
1900	10,996
1910	11,401
1920	12,882
1930	13,866
1940	14,316
1950	19,276
1960	25,305
1970	29,517
1980	38,888

TRINITY

1850	1,635
1860	5,125
1870	3,213
1880	4,999
1890	3,719
1900	4,383
1910	3,301
1920	2,551

1930	2,809
1940	3,970
1950	5,087
1960	9,706
1970	7,615
1980	11,858

TULARE

1860	4,638
1870	4,533
1880	11,281
1890	24,574
1900	18,375
1910	35,440
1920	59,031
1930	77,442
1940	107,152
1950	149,264
1960	168,403
1970	188,322
1980	245,738

TUOLUMNE

1880	7,848
1890	6,082
1900	11,166
1910	9,979
1920	7,768
1930	9,271
1940	10,887
1950	12,584
1960	14,404
1970	22,169
1980	33,928

VENTURA

1880	5,073
1890	10,071
1900	14,367
1910	18,347
1920	28,724
1930	54,976
1940	69,685
1950	114,647
1960	199,138
1970	378,497
1980	529,174

YOLO

1850	1,086
1860	4,716
1870	9,899
1880	11,772
1890	12,684
1900	13,618
1910	13,926
1920	17,105
1930	23,644
1940	27,243
1950	40,640
1960	65,727
1970	91,778
1980	113,374

YUBA

1850	9,673
1860	13,668
1870	10,851
1880	11,284
1890	9,636
1900	8,620

1910	10,042
1920	10,375
1930	11,331
1940	17,034
1950	24,420
1960	33,859
1970	44,736
1980	49,733

NOTES

KLAMATH

Annexed to Humboldt and Siskiyou in 1874.

SANTA CRUZ

Name changed from Branciforte in 1850.

ALAMEDA

1860	460
1870	1,577
1880	5,708
1890	11,165
1900	16,464
1910	23,383
1920	28,806
1930	35,033
1940	36,256
1950	64,430
1960	63,855
1970	70,968
1980	63,852

ALBANY

1910	808
1920	2,462
1930	8,569
1940	11,493
1950	17,590
1960	14,804
1970	14,674
1980	15,130

ALHAMBRA

1910	5,021
1920	9,096
1930	29,472
1940	38,935
1950	51,359
1960	54,807
1970	62,125
1980	64,615

ANAHEIM

1870	881
1880	883
1890	1,273
1900	1,456
1910	2,628
1920	5,526
1930	10,995
1940	11,031
1950	14,556
1960	104,184
1970	166,408
1980	219,311

ANTIOCH

1880	626
1890	535
1900	674
1910	1,124
1920	1,936
1930	3,563
1940	5,106
1950	11,051
1960	17,305
1970	28,060
1980	42,683

ARCADIA

1910	696
1920	2,239
1930	5,216
1940	9,122
1950	23,066
1960	41,005
1970	45,138
1980	45,994

ARCATA

1910	696
1920	2,239
1930	1,709
1940	1,855
1950	3,729
1960	5,235
1970	8,985
1980	12,340

ARROYO GRANDE

1920	760
1930	892
1940	1,090
1950	1,723
1960	3,291
1970	7,454
1980	11,290

ARTESIA

1960	9,993
1970	14,757
1980	14,301

ATASCADERO

1950	3,443
1960	(NA)
1970	(NA)
1980	16,232

ATWATER

1930	917
1940	1,235
1950	2,856
1960	7,318
1970	11,640
1980	17,530

AZUSA

1860	315
1870	320
1900	863
1910	1,477
1920	2,460
1930	4,808
1940	5,209
1950	11,042
1960	20,497
1970	25,217
1980	29,380

BAKERSFIELD

1890	2,626
1900	4,836
1910	12,727
1920	18,638
1930	26,015
1940	29,252
1950	34,784
1960	56,848
1970	69,515
1980	105,611

BALDWIN PARK

1960	33,951
1970	47,285
1980	50,554

BANNING

1930	2,752
1940	3,874
1950	7,034
1960	10,250
1970	12,034
1980	14,020

BARSTOW

1950	6,135
1960	11,644
1970	17,442
1980	17,690

BELL

1930	7,884
1940	11,264
1950	15,430
1960	19,450
1970	21,836
1980	25,450

BELLFLOWER

1960	45,909
1970	52,334
1980	53,441

BELL GARDENS

1960	26,467
1970	29,308
1980	34,117

BELMONT

1930	984
1940	1,229
1950	5,567
1960	15,996
1970	23,538
1980	24,505

BENICIA

1860	1,470
1870	1,656
1880	1,794
1890	2,361
1900	2,751
1910	2,360
1920	2,693
1930	2,913
1940	2,419
1950	7,284
1960	6,070
1970	7,349
1980	15,376

BERKELEY

1890	5,101
1900	13,214
1910	40,534
1920	56,036
1930	82,109
1940	85,547
1950	113,805
1960	111,268
1970	114,091
1980	103,328

BEVERLY HILLS

1920	674
1930	17,429
1940	26,823
1950	29,032
1960	30,817
1970	33,416
1980	32,367

BRAWLEY

1910	881
1920	5,389
1930	10,439
1940	11,718
1950	11,922
1960	12,703
1970	13,746
1980	14,946

BREA

1920	1,037
1930	2,435
1940	2,567
1950	3,208
1960	8,487
1970	18,447
1980	27,913

BUENA PARK

1960	46,401
1970	63,646
1980	64,165

BURBANK

1920	2,913
1930	16,662
1940	34,337
1950	78,577
1960	90,155
1970	88,871
1980	84,625

BURLINGAME

1910	1,565
1920	4,107
1930	13,270
1940	15,940
1950	19,886
1960	24,036
1970	27,320
1980	26,173

CALEXICO

1910	797
1920	6,223
1930	6,299
1940	5,415
1950	6,433
1960	7,992
1970	10,625
1980	14,412

CAMARILLO

1960	2,359
1970	19,219
1980	37,797

CAMPBELL

1960	11,863
1970	23,797
1980	27,067

CARLSBAD

1960	9,253
1970	14,944
1980	35,490

CARPINTERIA

1950	2,864
1960	4,998
1970	6,982
1980	10,835

CARSON

1960	38,059
1970	71,750
1980	81,221

CERES

1920	637
1930	981
1940	1,332
1950	2,351
1960	4,406
1970	6,029
1980	13,281

CERRITOS

1960	3,508
1970	15,856
1980	53,020

CHICO

1880	3,300
1890	2,894
1900	2,640
1910	3,750
1920	9,339
1930	7,961
1940	9,287
1950	12,272
1960	14,757
1970	19,580
1980	40,165

CHINO

1930	3,118
1940	4,204
1950	5,784
1960	10,305
1970	20,411
1980	40,165

CHULA VISTA

1920	1,718
1930	3,869
1940	5,138
1950	15,927
1960	42,034
1970	67,901
1980	83,937

CLAREMONT

1930	2,719
1940	3,057
1950	6,327
1960	12,633
1970	24,776
1980	30,950

CLOVIS

1920	1,157
1930	1,316
1940	1,626
1950	2,766
1960	5,546
1970	13,856
1980	33,021

COLTON

1890	1,315
1900	1,285
1910	3,980
1920	4,282
1930	8,014
1940	9,686
1950	14,465
1960	18,666
1970	20,016
1980	21,310

COMMERCE

1960	9,555
1970	10,635
1980	10,509

COMPTON

1910	922
1920	1,478
1930	12,516
1940	16,198
1950	47,991
1960	71,812
1970	78,547
1980	81,286

CONCORD

1910	703
1920	912
1930	1,125
1940	1,373
1950	6,953
1960	36,000
1970	85,164
1980	103,255

CORONA

1900	1,434
1910	3,540
1920	4,129
1930	7,018
1940	8,764
1950	10,223
1960	13,336
1970	20,020
1980	37,791

CORONADO

1900	935
1910	1,477
1920	3,289
1930	5,425
1940	6,932
1950	12,700
1960	18,039
1970	20,910
1980	16,859

COSTA MESA

1960	37,550
1970	72,660
1980	82,562

COVINA

1930	2,774
1940	3,049
1950	3,956
1960	20,124
1970	30,395
1980	33,751

CUDAHY

1970	16,998
1980	17,984

CULVER CITY

1920	503
1930	5,669
1940	8,976
1950	19,720
1960	32,163
1970	34,451
1980	38,139

CUPERTINO

1960	3,664
1970	17,895
1980	34,015

CYPRESS

1960	1,753
1970	31,569
1980	40,391

DALY CITY

1920	3,779
1930	7,838
1940	9,625
1950	15,191
1960	44,791
1970	66,922
1980	78,519

DAVIS

1920	939
1930	1,243
1940	1,672
1950	3,554
1960	8,910
1970	23,488
1980	36,640

DELANO

1930	2,632
1940	4,573
1950	8,717
1960	11,913
1970	14,559
1980	16,491

DOWNEY

1960	82,505
1970	88,573
1980	82,602

DUARTE

1960	13,962
1970	14,981
1980	16,766

EL CAJON

1920	469
1930	1,050
1940	1,471
1950	5,600
1960	37,618
1970	52,273
1980	73,892

EL CENTRO

1910	1,610
1920	5,464
1930	8,434
1940	10,017
1950	12,590
1960	16,811
1970	19,272
1980	23,996

EL CERRITO

1920	1,505
1930	3,870
1940	6,137
1950	18,011
1960	25,437
1970	25,190
1980	22,731

EL MONTE

1930	3,479
1940	4,746
1950	8,101
1960	13,163
1970	69,892
1980	79,494

EL SEGUNDO

1930	3,503
1940	3,738
1950	8,011
1960	14,219
1970	15,620
1980	13,752

ESCONDIDO

1930	3,421
1940	4,560
1950	6,544
1960	16,377
1970	36,792
1980	64,355

EUREKA

1860	281
1870	2,049
1880	2,639
1890	4,858
1900	7,327
1910	11,845
1920	12,923
1930	15,752
1940	17,055
1950	23,058
1960	28,137
1970	24,377
1980	24,153

FAIRFIELD

1910	834
1920	1,008
1930	1,131
1940	1,312
1950	3,118
1960	14,968
1970	44,146
1980	58,099

FONTANA

1960	14,659
1970	20,673
1980	37,111

FOLSOM

1950	1,690
1960	3,925
1970	5,810
1980	11,003

FOSTER CITY

1980	23,287

FOUNTAIN VALLEY

1960	2,068
1970	31,886
1980	55,080

FREMONT

1960	43,790
1970	100,869
1980	131,945

FRENSO

1880	1,112
1890	10,818
1900	12,470
1910	24,892
1920	45,086
1930	52,513
1940	60,685
1950	91,669
1960	133,929
1970	165,655
1980	218,202

FULLERTON

1910	1,725
1920	4,415
1930	10,860
1940	10,442
1950	13,958
1960	56,180
1970	85,987
1980	102,034

GARDENA

1940	5,909
1950	14,405
1960	35,943
1970	41,021
1980	45,165

GARDEN GROVE

1960	84,238
1970	121,155
1980	123,307

GILROY

1900	1,820
1910	2,437
1920	2,862
1930	3,502
1940	3,615
1950	4,951
1960	7,348
1970	12,684
1980	21,641

GLENDALE

1910	2,746
1920	13,536
1930	62,736
1940	82,582
1950	95,702
1960	119,442
1970	132,664
1980	139,060

GLENDORA

1930	2,761
1940	2,822
1950	3,988
1960	20,752
1970	31,380
1980	38,654

HANFORD

1900	2,929
1910	4,829
1920	5,888
1930	7,028
1940	8,234
1950	10,028
1960	10,133
1970	15,179
1980	20,958

HAWAIIAN GARDENS

1970	9,052
1980	10,548

HAWTHORNE

1930	6,596
1940	8,263
1950	16,316
1960	33,035
1970	53,304
1980	56,447

HAYWARD

1870	504
1880	1,231
1890	1,419
1900	1,965
1910	2,746
1920	3,487
1930	5,530
1940	6,736
1950	14,272
1960	72,700
1970	93,058
1980	94,167

HEMET

1910	992
1920	1,480
1930	2,235
1940	2,595
1950	3,386
1960	5,416
1970	12,252
1980	22,454

HERMOSA BEACH

1910	679
1920	2,327
1930	4,796
1940	7,197
1950	11,826
1960	16,115
1970	17,412
1980	18,070

HILLSBOROUGH

1950	3,547
1960	7,554
1970	8,753
1980	10,451

HOLLISTER

1880	1,034
1890	1,234
1900	1,315
1910	2,308
1920	2,781
1930	3,757
1940	3,881
1950	4,903
1960	6,071
1970	7,663
1980	11,488

HUNTINGTON BEACH

1930	3,690
1940	3,738
1950	5,237
1960	11,492
1970	115,960
1980	170,505

HUNTINGTON PARK

1910	1,299
1920	4,513
1930	24,591
1940	28,648
1950	29,450
1960	29,920
1970	33,744
1980	46,233

IMPERIAL BEACH

1960	17,773
1970	20,244
1980	22,689

INDIO

1940	2,296
1950	5,300
1960	9,745
1970	14,459
1980	21,611

INGLEWOOD

1910	1,536
1920	3,286
1930	19,480
1940	30,114
1950	46,185
1960	63,390
1970	89,985
1980	94,245

IRVINE

1980	62,134

LA CANADA-FLINTRIDGE

1960	18,338
1970	20,652
1980	20,153

LAFAYETTE

1960	7,114
1970	20,484
1980	20,879

LAGUNA BEACH

1930	1,981
1940	4,460
1950	6,661
1960	9,288
1970	14,550
1980	17,901

LA HABRA

1930	2,273
1940	2,499
1950	4,961
1960	25,136
1970	41,350
1980	45,232

LAKEWOOD

1960	67,126
1970	83,025
1980	74,654

LA MESA

1920	1,004
1930	2,513
1940	3,925
1950	10,946
1960	30,441
1970	39,178
1980	50,308

LA MIRADA

1960	22,444
1970	30,808
1980	40,986

LANCASTER

1960	26,012
1970	30,948
1980	48,027

LA PALMA

1960	662
1970	9,687
1980	15,399

LA PUENTE

1960	24,723
1970	31,092
1980	30,882

LARKSPUR

1910	594
1920	612
1930	1,241
1940	1,558
1950	2,905
1960	5,710
1970	10,487
1980	11,064

LA VERNE

1910	954
1920	1,698
1930	2,860
1940	3,092
1950	4,198
1960	6,516
1970	12,965
1980	23,508

LAWNDALE

1960	21,740
1970	24,825
1980	23,460

LEMON GROVE

1960	19,348
1970	19,690
1980	20,780

LIVERMORE

1930	3,119
1940	2,885
1950	4,364
1960	16,058
1970	37,703
1980	48,349

LODI

1910	2,697
1920	4,850
1930	6,788
1940	11,079
1950	13,798
1960	22,229
1970	28,691
1980	35,221

LOMA LINDA

1980	10,694

LOMITA

1970	19,784
1980	18,807

LOMPOC

1880	226
1890	1,015
1900	972
1910	1,482
1920	1,876
1930	2,845
1940	3,379
1950	5,520
1960	14,415
1970	25,284
1980	26,267

LONG BEACH

1890	564
1900	2,252
1910	17,809
1920	55,593
1930	142,032
1940	164,271
1950	250,767
1960	344,168
1970	358,879
1980	361,334

LOS ANAMITOS

1960	4,312
1970	11,346
1980	11,529

LOS ALTOS

1960	19,696
1970	25,062
1980	25,769

LOS ANGELES

1850	1,610
1860	4,385
1870	5,728
1880	11,183
1890	50,395
1900	102,479
1910	319,198
1920	576,673
1930	1,238,048
1940	1,504,277
1950	1,970,358
1960	2,479,015
1970	2,811,801
1980	2,966,850

LOS BANOS

1910	745
1920	1,276
1930	1,875
1940	3,214
1950	3,868
1960	5,272
1970	9,188
1980	10,341

LOS GATOS

1880	555
1890	1,652
1900	1,915
1910	2,232
1920	2,317
1930	3,168
1940	3,597
1950	4,907
1960	9,036
1970	22,613
1980	26,907

LYNWOOD

1930	7,323
1940	10,982
1950	25,823
1960	31,614
1970	43,354
1980	48,548

MADERA

1890	950
1900	(NA)
1910	2,404
1920	3,444
1930	4,665
1940	6,457
1950	10,497
1960	14,430
1970	16,044
1980	21,732

MANHATTAN BEACH

1920	859
1930	1,891
1940	6,398
1950	17,330
1960	33,934
1970	35,352
1980	31,542

MANTECA

1920	1,286
1930	1,614
1940	1,981
1950	3,804
1960	8,242
1970	13,845
1980	24,925

MARINA

1980	20,647

MARTINEZ

1890	1,600
1900	1,380
1910	2,115
1920	3,858
1930	6,569
1940	7,381
1950	8,268
1960	9,604
1970	16,506
1980	22,582

MAYWOOD

1930	6,794
1940	10,731
1950	13,292
1960	14,588
1970	16,996
1980	21,810

MENLO PARK

1930	2,254
1940	3,258
1950	13,587
1960	26,957
1970	26,826
1980	26,369

MERCED

1880	1,446
1890	2,009
1900	1,969
1910	3,102
1920	3,974
1930	7,066
1940	10,135
1950	15,278
1960	20,068
1970	22,670
1980	36,499

MILLBREA

1950	8,972
1960	15,873
1970	20,920
1980	20,058

MILL VALLEY

1910	2,551
1920	2,554
1930	4,164
1940	4,847
1950	7,331
1960	10,411
1970	12,942
1980	12,967

MILPITAS

1960	6,572
1970	26,561
1980	37,280

MODESTO

1890	2,402
1900	2,024
1910	4,034
1920	9,241
1930	13,842
1940	16,379
1950	17,389
1960	36,585
1970	61,712
1980	106,602

MONROVIA

1890	907
1900	1,205
1910	3,576
1920	5,480
1930	10,890
1940	12,807
1950	20,186
1960	27,079
1970	30,562
1980	30,531

MONTCLAIR

1960	13,546
1970	22,546
1980	22,628

MONTEBELLO

1930	5,498
1940	8,016
1950	21,735
1960	32,097
1970	42,807
1980	52,929

MONTEREY

1850	1,092
1860	...
1870	1,112
1880	1,396
1890	1,662
1900	1,748
1910	4,923
1920	5,479
1930	9,141
1940	10,084
1950	16,205
1960	22,618
1970	26,302
1980	27,558

MONTEREY PARK

1920	4,108
1930	6,406
1940	8,531
1950	20,395
1960	37,821
1970	49,166
1980	54,338

MORAGA

1970	14,205
1980	15,014

MORGAN HILL

1910	607
1920	646
1930	908
1940	1,014
1950	1,627
1960	3,151
1970	5,579
1980	17,060

MOUNTAIN VIEW

1930	3,308
1940	3,946
1950	6,563
1960	30,889
1970	54,132
1980	58,655

NAPA

1850	159
1860	(NA)
1870	1,879
1880	3,731
1890	4,395
1900	4,036
1910	5,791
1920	6,757
1930	6,437
1940	7,740
1950	13,579
1960	22,170
1970	36,103
1980	50,879

NATIONAL CITY

1880	248
1890	1,353
1900	1,086
1910	1,733
1920	3,116
1930	7,301
1940	10,344
1950	21,199
1960	32,771
1970	43,184
1980	48,772

NEWARK

1960	9,884
1970	27,153
1980	32,126

NEWPORT BEACH

1910	445
1920	894
1930	2,203
1940	4,438
1950	12,120
1960	26,564
1970	49,582
1980	62,556

NORCO

1950	1,584
1960	4,964
1970	14,511
1980	21,126

NORWALK

1960	88,739
1970	90,164
1980	85,286

NOVATO

1960	17,881
1970	31,006
1980	43,916

OAKLAND

1860	1,543
1870	10,500
1880	34,555
1890	48,682
1900	66,960
1910	150,174
1920	216,261
1930	284,063
1940	302,163
1950	384,575
1960	367,548
1970	361,561
1980	339,337

OCEANSIDE

1900	330
1910	673
1920	1,161
1930	3,508
1940	4,651
1950	12,881
1960	24,971
1970	40,494
1980	76,698

ONTARIO

1890	683
1900	722
1910	4,274
1920	7,280
1930	13,583
1940	14,197
1950	22,872
1960	46,617
1970	64,118
1980	88,820

ORANGE

1880	679
1890	866
1900	1,216
1910	2,920
1920	4,884
1930	8,066
1940	7,901
1950	10,027
1960	26,444
1970	77,365
1980	91,788

OXNARD

1910	2,555
1920	4,417
1930	6,285
1940	8,519
1950	21,567
1960	40,265
1970	71,225
1980	108,195

PACIFICA

1960	20,995
1970	36,020
1980	36,866

PACIFIC GROVE

1910	2,384
1920	2,974
1930	5,558
1940	6,249
1950	9,623
1960	12,121
1970	13,505
1980	15,755

PALM DESERT

1980	11,801

PALM SPRINGS

1940	3,434
1950	7,660
1960	13,468
1970	20,936
1980	32,271

PALMDALE

1960	11,522
1970	8,511
1980	12,277

PALO ALTO

1900	1,658
1910	4,486
1920	5,900
1930	13,652
1940	16,774
1950	25,475
1960	52,287
1970	56,040
1980	55,225

PALOS VERDES ESTATES

1940	987
1950	1,963
1960	9,564
1970	13,631
1980	14,376

PARADISE

1980	22,571

PARAMOUNT

1960	27,249
1970	34,734
1980	36,407

PASADENA

1890	4,882
1900	9,117
1910	30,291
1920	45,354
1930	76,086
1940	81,864
1950	104,577
1960	116,407
1970	112,951
1980	118,550

PETALUMA

1880	3,326
1890	3,692
1900	3,871
1910	5,880
1920	6,226
1930	8,245
1940	8,034
1950	10,315
1960	14,035
1970	24,870
1980	33,834

PICO RIVERA

1960	49,150
1970	54,170
1980	53,459

PIEDMONT

1890	634
1910	1,719
1920	4,282
1930	9,333
1940	9,866
1950	10,132
1960	11,117
1970	10,917
1980	10,498

PINOLE

1910	798
1920	967
1930	781
1940	934
1950	1,147
1960	6,064
1970	13,266
1980	14,253

PITTSBURG

1910	2,372
1920	4,715
1930	9,610
1940	9,520
1950	12,763
1960	19,062
1970	21,423
1980	33,034

PLACENTIA

1930	1,606
1940	1,472
1950	1,682
1960	5,861
1970	21,948
1980	35,041

PLEASANT HILL

1950	5,686
1960	23,844
1970	24,610
1980	25,124

PLEASANTON

1900	1,100
1910	1,254
1920	991
1930	1,237
1940	1,278
1950	2,244
1960	4,203
1970	18,328
1980	35,160

POMONA

1890	3,634
1900	5,526
1910	10,207
1920	13,505
1930	20,804
1940	23,539
1950	35,405
1960	67,157
1970	87,384
1980	92,742

PORTERVILLE

1910	2,696
1920	4,097
1930	5,303
1940	6,270
1950	6,904
1960	7,991
1970	12,602
1980	19,707

PORT HUENEME

1950	3,024
1960	11,067
1970	14,295
1980	17,803

RANCHO PALOS VERDES

1970	33,385
1980	36,577

REDDING

1880	600
1890	1,821
1900	2,946
1910	3,572
1920	2,962
1930	4,188
1940	8,109
1950	10,256
1960	12,773
1970	16,659
1980	41,995

REDLANDS

1890	1,904
1900	4,797
1910	10,449
1920	9,571
1930	14,177
1940	14,324
1950	18,429
1960	26,829
1970	36,355
1980	43,619

REDONDO BEACH

1890	603
1900	855
1910	2,935
1920	4,913
1930	9,347
1940	13,092
1950	25,226
1960	46,986
1970	57,451
1980	57,102

REDWOOD CITY

1870	727
1880	1,383
1890	1,572
1900	1,653
1910	2,442
1920	4,020
1930	8,962
1940	12,453
1950	25,544
1960	46,290
1970	55,686
1980	54,951

REEDLEY

1920	2,447
1930	2,589
1940	3,170
1950	4,135
1960	5,850
1970	8,131
1980	11,071

RIALTO

1920	961
1930	1,642
1940	1,770
1950	3,156
1960	18,567
1970	28,370
1980	37,474

RICHMOND

1910	6,802
1920	16,843
1930	20,093
1940	23,642
1950	99,545
1960	71,854
1970	79,043
1980	74,676

RIDGECREST

1970	7,629
1980	15,929

RIVERSIDE

1890	4,686
1900	7,973
1910	15,212
1920	19,341
1930	29,696
1940	34,696
1950	46,764
1960	84,332
1970	140,089
1980	170,876

ROHNERT PARK

1970	6,133
1980	22,965

ROSEMEAD

1960	15,476
1970	40,972
1980	42,604

ROSEVILLE

1910	2,608
1920	4,477
1930	6,425
1940	6,653
1950	8,723
1960	13,421
1970	17,895
1980	24,247

SACRAMENTO

1850	6,820
1860	13,785
1870	16,283
1880	21,420
1890	26,386
1900	29,282
1910	44,696
1920	65,908
1930	93,750
1940	105,958
1950	137,572
1960	191,667
1970	257,105
1980	275,741

SALINAS

1890	2,339
1900	3,304
1910	3,736
1920	4,308
1930	10,263
1940	11,586
1950	13,917
1960	28,957
1970	58,896
1980	80,497

SAN ANSELMO

1910	1,531
1920	2,475
1930	4,650
1940	5,790
1950	9,188
1960	11,584
1970	13,031
1980	12,053

SAN BERNARDINO

1880	1,673
1890	4,012
1900	6,150
1910	12,779
1920	18,721
1930	37,481
1940	43,646
1950	63,058
1960	91,922
1970	106,869
1980	117,490

SAN BRUNO

1920	1,562
1930	3,610
1940	6,519
1950	12,478
1960	29,063
1970	36,254
1980	35,417

SAN CARLOS

1930	1,132
1940	3,520
1950	14,371
1960	21,370
1970	26,053
1980	24,710

SAN CLEMENTE

1930	667
1940	479
1950	2,008
1960	8,527
1970	17,063
1980	27,325

SAN DIEGO

1860	731
1870	2,300
1880	2,637
1890	16,159
1900	17,700
1910	39,578
1920	74,361
1930	147,995
1940	203,341
1950	334,387
1960	573,224
1970	697,471
1980	875,538

SAN DIMAS

1970	15,692
1980	24,014

SAN FERNANDO

1920	3,204
1930	7,567
1940	9,094
1950	12,992
1960	16,093
1970	16,571
1980	17,731

SAN FRANCISCO

1850	34,776
1860	56,802
1870	149,473
1880	233,959
1890	298,997
1900	342,782
1910	416,912
1920	506,676
1930	634,394
1940	634,536
1950	775,357
1960	740,316
1970	715,674
1980	678,974

SAN GABRIEL

1920	2,640
1930	7,224
1940	11,867
1950	20,343
1960	22,561
1970	29,176
1980	30,072

SANGER

1920	2,578
1930	2,967
1940	4,017
1950	6,400
1960	8,072
1970	10,088
1980	12,542

SAN JOSE

1870	9,089
1880	12,567
1890	18,060
1900	21,500
1910	28,946
1920	39,642
1930	57,651
1940	68,457
1950	95,280
1960	204,196
1970	459,913
1980	629,442

SAN JUAN CAPISTRANO

1960	1,120
1970	3,781
1980	18,959

SAN LEANDRO

1870	426
1880	1,369
1900	2,253
1910	3,471
1920	5,703
1930	11,455
1940	14,601
1950	27,542
1960	65,962
1970	68,698
1980	63,952

SAN LUIS OBISPO

1880	2,243
1890	2,995
1900	3,021
1910	5,157
1920	5,895
1930	8,276
1940	8,881
1950	14,180
1960	20,437
1970	28,036
1980	34,252

SAN MARCOS

1970	3,896
1980	17,479

SAN MARINO

1920	584
1930	3,730
1940	8,175
1950	11,230
1960	13,658
1970	14,177
1980	13,307

SAN MATEO

1900	1,832
1910	4,384
1920	5,979
1930	13,444
1940	19,403
1950	41,782
1960	69,870
1970	78,991
1980	77,561

SAN PABLO

1950	14,476
1960	19,687
1970	21,461
1980	19,750

SAN RAFAEL

1870	841
1880	2,276
1890	3,290
1900	3,879
1910	5,934
1920	5,512
1930	8,022
1940	8,573
1950	13,848
1960	20,460
1970	38,977
1980	44,700

SANTA ANA

1890	3,628
1900	4,933
1910	8,429
1920	15,485
1930	30,322
1940	31,921
1950	45,533
1960	100,350
1970	155,710
1980	203,713

SANTA BARBARA

1880	3,460
1890	5,864
1900	6,587
1910	11,659
1920	19,441
1930	33,613
1940	34,958
1950	44,854
1960	58,768
1970	70,215
1980	74,414

SANTA CLARA

1880	2,916
1890	2,891
1900	3,650
1910	4,348
1920	5,220
1930	6,302
1940	6,650
1950	11,702
1960	58,880
1970	86,118
1980	87,746

SANTA CRUZ

1850	950
1860	2,561
1870	3,898
1880	5,596
1890	5,659
1900	5,659
1910	11,146
1920	10,917
1930	14,395
1940	16,896
1950	21,970
1960	25,596
1970	32,076
1980	41,483

SANTA FE SPRINGS

1960	16,342
1970	14,750
1980	14,520

SANTA MARIA

1910	2,260
1920	3,943
1930	7,057
1940	8,522
1950	10,440
1960	20,027
1970	32,749
1980	39,685

SANTA MONICA

1890	1,580
1900	3,057
1910	7,847
1920	15,252
1930	37,146
1940	53,500
1950	71,595
1960	83,249
1970	88,289
1980	88,314

SANTA PAULA

1910	2,216
1920	3,967
1930	7,452
1940	8,986
1950	11,049
1960	13,279
1970	18,001
1980	20,552

SANTA ROSA

1860	425
1880	3,616
1890	5,220
1900	6,673
1910	7,817
1920	8,758
1930	10,636
1940	12,605
1950	17,902
1960	31,027
1970	50,006
1980	83,320

SARATOGA

1960	14,861
1970	26,810
1980	29,261

SEAL BEACH

1920	669
1930	1,156
1940	1,553
1950	3,553
1960	6,994
1970	24,441
1980	25,795

SEASIDE

1960	19,353
1970	36,883
1980	36,567

SELMA

1890	1,150
1900	1,080
1910	1,750
1920	3,158
1930	3,047
1940	3,667
1950	5,964
1960	6,934
1970	7,459
1980	10,942

SIERRA MADRE

1910	1,303
1920	2,026
1930	3,550
1940	4,581
1950	7,273
1960	9,732
1970	12,140
1980	10,837

SIMI VALLEY

1970	59,832
1980	77,500

SOUTH EL MONTE

1960	4,850
1970	13,443
1980	16,623

SOUTH GATE

1930	19,632
1940	26,945
1950	51,116
1960	53,831
1970	56,909
1980	66,784

SOUTH LAKE TAHOE

1970	12,921
1980	20,681

SOUTH PASADENA

1880	623
1890	1,001
1900	1,001
1910	4,649
1920	7,652
1930	13,730
1940	14,356
1950	16,935
1960	19,706
1970	22,979
1980	22,681

SOUTH SAN FRANCISCO

1910	1,989
1920	4,411
1930	6,193
1940	6,629
1950	19,351
1960	39,418
1970	46,646
1980	49,393

STANTON

1960	11,163
1970	17,947
1980	23,723

STOCKTON

1860	3,679
1870	10,066
1880	10,282
1890	14,424
1900	17,506
1910	23,253
1920	40,296
1930	47,963
1940	54,714
1950	70,853
1960	86,321
1970	109,963
1980	149,779

SUISUN CITY

1860	1,394
1870	462
1880	554
1890	499
1900	625
1910	641
1920	769
1930	905
1940	706
1950	946
1960	2,470
1970	2,917
1980	11,087

SUNNYVALE

1930	3,094
1940	4,373
1950	9,829
1960	52,898
1970	95,976
1980	106,618

TEMPLE CITY

1970	31,034
1980	28,972

THOUSAND OAKS

1950	1,243
1960	2,934
1970	35,873
1980	77,072

TORRANCE

1930	7,271
1940	9,950
1950	22,241
1960	100,991
1970	134,968
1980	129,881

TRACY

1930	3,829
1940	4,056
1950	8,410
1960	11,289
1970	14,724
1980	18,428

TULARE

1880	447
1890	2,697
1900	2,216
1910	2,758
1920	3,539
1930	6,207
1940	8,259
1950	12,445
1960	13,824
1970	16,235
1980	22,526

TURLOCK

1910	1,573
1920	3,394
1930	4,276
1940	4,839

1950	6,235
1960	9,116
1970	13,992
1980	26,287

TUSTIN

1930	926
1940	953
1950	1,143
1960	2,006
1970	22,190
1980	32,317

UKIAH

1890	1,627
1900	1,850
1910	2,136
1920	2,305
1930	3,124
1940	3,731
1950	6,120
1960	9,900
1970	10,095
1980	12,035

UNION CITY

1960	6,618
1970	14,724
1980	39,406

UPLAND

1910	2,384
1920	2,912
1930	4,713
1940	6,316
1950	9,203
1960	15,918
1970	32,551
1980	47,647

VACAVILLE

1880	361
1890	725
1900	1,220
1910	1,177
1920	1,254
1930	1,556
1940	1,614
1950	3,169
1960	10,898
1970	21,690
1980	43,367

VALLEJO

1880	5,987
1890	6,323
1900	7,965
1910	11,340
1920	21,107
1930	16,072
1940	20,072
1950	26,038
1960	60,877
1970	71,710
1980	80,303

VENTURA

1880	1,370
1890	2,320
1900	2,470
1910	2,901
1920	4,156
1930	11,603
1940	13,264
1950	16,534
1960	29,114
1970	55,797
1980	74,393

VICTORVILLE

1970	10,845
1980	14,220

VISALIA

1860	548
1870	913
1880	1,412
1890	2,885
1900	3,085
1910	4,550
1920	5,753
1930	7,263
1940	8,904
1950	11,749
1960	15,791
1970	27,130
1980	49,729

VISTA

1970	24,688
1980	35,834

WALNUT

1960	934
1970	5,992
1980	12,478

WALNUT CREEK

1920	538
1930	1,014
1940	1,578
1950	2,420
1960	9,903
1970	39,844
1980	53,643

WATSONVILLE

1860	398
1870	1,151
1880	1,799
1890	2,149
1900	3,528
1910	4,446
1920	5,013
1930	8,344
1940	8,937
1950	11,572
1960	13,293
1970	14,719
1980	23,543

WEST COVINA

1930	769
1940	1,072
1950	4,499
1960	50,645
1970	68,034
1980	80,291

WESTMINSTER

1960	25,750
1970	59,865
1980	71,133

WHITTIER

1890	585
1900	1,590
1910	4,550
1920	7,997
1930	14,822
1940	16,115
1950	23,433
1960	33,663
1970	72,863
1980	69,717

WOODLAND

1880	2,257
1890	3,069
1900	2,886
1910	3,187
1920	4,147
1930	5,542
1940	6,637
1950	9,386
1960	13,524
1970	20,677
1980	30,235

YORBA LINDA

1960	1,198
1970	11,856
1980	28,254

YUBA CITY

1910	1,160
1920	1,708
1930	3,605
1940	4,968
1950	7,861
1960	11,507
1970	13,986
1980	18,736

CORRECTION NOTE

The official 1980 census counts of total population shown in this report supersede counts issued previously. Corrections to the figures were made after the counts were provided to the State for redistricting purposes and released in Advance Report PHC80-V for this State.

Shown below are corrections to the 1980 census counts of the total population made after the tabulations for this report were completed. Any additional corrections made after this report is printed are available by writing to Data User Services Division, Customer Services (Corrections), Bureau of the Census, Washington, D.C. 20233.

The 1980 figures shown in this publication are subject to change pending the outcome of the various lawsuits dealing with the census counts.

	1980 population	
	As shown in the tables	Corrected
The State....................	23 667 902	23 667 565
Alameda County:		
Hayword divison:		
Hayward city (pt.)...........	94 165	94 340
Fresno County...................	514 621	514 229
Fresno division:		
Fresno city................	218 202	217 289
Sierra division...............	11 885	11 493
Humboldt County:		
Arcata division:		
Arcata city..................	12 340	12 850
Kern County:		
Bakersfield division:		
Bakersfield city (pt.)........	105 599	105 723
Los Angeles County:		
East San Gabriel Valley division:		
Glendora city (pt.)...........	38 649	38 495
Pasadena division:		
Altadena (CDP)................	40 510	40 983
Pasadena city................	118 550	118 072
Whittier division:		
Pico Rivera city (pt.).......	53 459	53 387
Marin County....................	222 568	222 592
Ross Valley division...........	54 843	54 867
San Anselmo town............	12 053	12 067
Merced County...................	134 560	134 558
Dos Palos division............	6 411	6 409
Dos Palos city..............	3 123	3 121
Orange County:		
Anaheim-Santa Ana-		
Garden Grove division:		
Anaheim city..................	219 311	219 494
Orange city..................	91 788	91 450
Santa Ana city (pt.).........	203 713	204 023
Riverside County................	663 166	663 199
Cathedral City-Palm Desert division:		
Palm Springs city (pt.).......	869	862
Jurupa division:		
Riverside city (pt.)..........	285	-
Rubidoux (CDP) (pt.)..........	16 763	17 048
Palm Springs division.........	34 298	34 331
Palm Springs city (pt.).......	31 391	31 486
San Bernardino County:		
San Bernardino division:		
Bloomington (CDP).............	12 781	18 888
Colton city..................	21 310	15 201
Fontana city (pt.)...........	37 111	37 107
San Bernardino city (pt.).....	116 374	117 678
San Diego County:		
San Diego division:		
Coronado city................	16 859	18 790

	1980 population	
	As shown in the tables	Corrected
San Mateo County:		
San Mateo division:		
Hillsborough city............	10 451	10 372
San Mateo city................	77 561	77 640
Santa Clara County:		
San Jose division:		
Campbell city.................	27 067	26 910
Cupertino city...............	34 015	34 265
San Jose city (pt.)..........	629 288	629 392
Santa Clara city.............	87 746	87 700
Santa Cruz County:		
Watsonville division:		
Watsonville city.............	23 543	23 663
Sonoma County:		
Petaluma division:		
Cotati city..................	3 475	3 346
Bakersfield city (total)..........	105 611	105 735
Fontana city (total)..............	37 111	37 107
Glendora city (total).............	38 654	38 500
Hayward city (total)..............	94 167	94 342
Palm Springs city (total).........	32 271	32 366
Pico Rivera city (total)..........	53 459	53 387
Riverside city (total)............	170 876	170 591
Rubidoux (CDP) (total)............	16 763	17 048
San Bernardino city (total).......	117 490	118 794
San Jose city (total).............	629 442	629 546
Santa Ana city (total)............	203 713	204 023

County Subdivisions	1980	1970
The State	23 667 902	ʳ19 971 069
Alameda County[1]	1 105 379	ʳ1 071 446
Alameda division	63 852	70 968
Alameda city[1]	63 852	70 968
Berkeley division	118 458	
Albany city	15 130	ʳ15 561
Berkeley city[1]	103 328	ʳ114 091
Fremont division	203 025	
Fremont city[1]	131 945	100 869
Newark city[1]	32 126	27 153
Union City city (pt.)[1]	38 914	14 724
Hayward division	262 079	
Ashland (CDP)	13 893	14 810
Castro Valley (CDP)	44 011	44 760
Cherryland (CDP)	9 425	9 969
Hayward city (pt.)[1]	94 165	93 058
San Leandro city[1]	63 952	68 698
San Lorenzo (CDP)	20 545	24 633
Union City city (pt.)[1]	492	...
Livermore—Pleasanton division	104 406	
Dublin (CDP)	13 496	13 641
Hayward city (pt.)[1]	2	...
Livermore city[1]	48 349	37 703
Pleasanton city[1]	35 160	18 328
Oakland division	353 559	
Emeryville city[1]	3 714	2 681
Oakland city[1]	339 337	361 561
Piedmont city	10 498	10 917
Alpine County	1 097	484
Markleeville division	1 097	484
Amador County[2]	19 314	11 821
Ione division	3 427	...
Ione city[2]	2 207	2 369
Jackson division	4 683	...
Jackson city[2]	2 331	1 924
Sutter Creek city (pt.)[2]	–	...
Pine Grove—Silver Lake division	5 953	
Sutter Creek—Plymouth division	5 251	
Amador City[2]	136	156
Plymouth city[2]	699	501
Sutter Creek city (pt.)[2]	1 705	1 508
Butte County[3]	143 851	101 969
Biggs division	3 014	...
Biggs city[3]	1 413	1 115
Chico division	58 319	
Chico city (pt.)[3]	26 603	19 580
Chico North (CDP)	11 733	6 656
Chico West (CDP)	6 378	4 787
Mulberry (CDP)	1 946	1 795
Durham division	3 858	...
Feather Falls division	3 477	939
Gridley division	8 836	7 808
Gridley city[3]	3 982	3 534
Oroville division	28 450	
Oroville city[3]	8 683	7 536
South Oroville (CDP)	7 246	4 111
Thermalito (CDP)	4 961	4 217
Palermo division	6 250	
Palermo (CDP)	2 572	1 966
Paradise division	31 647	...
Chico city (pt.)[3]	–	...
Paradise city[3]	22 571	...
Calaveras County[4]	20 710	13 585
Angels division	5 637	4 520
Angels city[4]	2 302	1 710
Murphys (CDP)	1 183	...
San Andreas division	7 964	5 064
San Andreas (CDP)	1 912	1 564
West Point—Wilseyville division	7 109	4 001
Arnold (CDP)	2 385	...
Colusa County[5]	12 791	12 430
Central Colusa division	5 577	5 502
Arbuckle (CDP)	1 306	1 037
Williams city[5]	1 655	1 571
East Colusa division	6 609	6 381
Colusa city[5]	4 075	3 842
West Colusa division	605	547
Contra Costa County[6]	656 380	ʳ556 116
Antioch—Pittsburg division	87 469	...
Antioch city[6]	42 683	28 060
Pittsburg city (pt.)[6]	33 034	ʳ21 423
West Pittsburg (CDP)	8 773	5 969
Briones division	1 306	...
Martinez city (pt.)[6]	51	...
Pinole city (pt.)[6]	140	...
Central Contra Costa division	361 392	...
Alamo (CDP)	8 505	...
Clayton city[6]	4 325	1 385
Concord city[6]	103 255	85 164
Danville (CDP)	26 446	...
Lafayette city[6]	20 879	20 484
Martinez city (pt.)[6]	22 531	16 506
Moraga Town city[6]	15 014	...
Orinda (CDP)	16 825	6 790
Pittsburg city (pt.)[6]	–	...
Pleasant Hill city[6]	25 124	24 610
San Ramon (CDP)	22 356	4 084

County Subdivisions	1980	1970
Contra Costa County—Con.		
Central Contra Costa division—Con.		
Vine Hill—Pacheco (CDP)	6 129	...
Walnut Creek city[6]	53 643	39 844
Walnut Creek West (CDP)	5 893	8 330
East Contra Costa division	20 841	...
Bethel Island (CDP)	1 774	1 398
Brentwood city[6]	4 434	2 649
Discovery Bay (CDP)	1 326	...
Oakley (CDP)	2 816	1 306
Sand Hill (CDP)	2 606	...
Tassajara division	2 527	...
West Contra Costa division	182 845	...
El Cerrito city[6]	22 731	25 190
El Sobrante (CDP)	10 535	252
Hercules city	5 963	...
Kensington (CDP)	5 342	5 823
Pinole city (pt.)[6]	14 113	ʳ13 266
Richmond city[6]	74 676	79 043
Rodeo (CDP)	8 286	5 356
San Pablo city[6]	19 750	21 461
Tara Hills—Montalvin Manor (CDP)	9 471	...
Del Norte County[7]	18 217	14 580
Crescent City division	13 729	...
Crescent City city[7]	3 075	2 586
Crescent North (CDP)	2 846	3 053
Klamath division	1 420	...
Smith River—Gasquet division	3 068	2 158
El Dorado County[8]	85 812	43 833
North El Dorado division	15 495	...
Pollock Pines (CDP)	1 941	...
Placerville division	11 281	8 608
Placerville city[8]	6 739	5 416
South El Dorado division	31 565	...
Cameron Park (CDP)	5 607	...
Diamond Springs (CDP)	2 287	...
El Dorado Hills (CDP)	3 453	...
Shingle Springs (CDP)	1 268	...
South Lake Tahoe division	27 471	...
South Lake Tahoe city[8]	20 681	12 921
Fresno County[9]	514 621	ʳ413 329
Caruthers—Raisin City division	8 280	6 831
Caruthers (CDP)	1 514	...
Coalinga division	7 855	7 357
Coalinga city[9]	6 593	6 161
Firebaugh division	6 760	6 400
Firebaugh city[9]	3 740	2 517
Fowler division	7 403	6 689
Fowler city[9]	2 496	2 239
Fresno division	358 823	
Calwa (CDP)	6 640	5 191
Clovis city[9]	33 021	13 856
Easton (CDP)	1 710	1 065
Fresno city[9]	218 202	ʳ165 655
Huron division	5 053	3 524
Huron city[9]	2 768	1 525
Kerman division	12 308	10 339
Kerman city[9]	4 002	2 667
Kingsburg division	6 736	5 292
Kingsburg city[9]	5 115	3 843
Laton division	2 511	2 338
Laton (CDP)	1 100	1 071
Mendota division	7 140	5 632
Mendota city[9]	5 038	2 705
Orange Cove division	4 963	4 320
Orange Cove city[9]	4 026	3 392
Parlier—Del Rey division	10 973	9 074
Del Rey (CDP)	1 126	...
Parlier city[9]	2 902	1 993
Reedley city (pt.)[9]	–	...
West Parlier (CDP)	2 811	...
Reedley division	16 370	ʳ12 928
Reedley city (pt.)[9]	11 071	8 131
Riverdale division	3 735	3 565
Riverdale (CDP)	1 866	1 722
Sanger division	19 764	...
Sanger city[9]	12 542	10 088
San Joaquin—Tranquillity division	5 138	4 530
San Joaquin city	1 930	1 506
Selma division	18 924	15 022
Selma city[9]	10 942	7 459
Sierra division	11 885	4 965
Glenn County[10]	21 350	17 521
Orland division	12 098	...
Hamilton City (CDP)	1 337	...
Orland city[10]	4 031	2 884
Willows division	9 252	...
Willows city[10]	4 777	4 085
Humboldt County[11]	108 514	99 692
Arcata division	19 378	...
Arcata city[11]	12 340	8 985
Blue Lake city (pt.)[11]	–	...
Eureka city (pt.)[11]	–	...
Eureka division	42 373	...
Cutten (CDP)	2 375	2 228
Eureka city (pt.)[11]	24 153	24 337
Myrtletown (CDP)	3 959	3 922

County Subdivisions	1980	1970
Humboldt County—Con.		
Eureka division—Con.		
Pine Hills (CDP)	2 686	...
Ferndale division	3 296	3 156
Ferndale city	1 367	1 352
Fortuna division	12 809	...
Fortuna city[11]	7 591	4 203
Garberville division	10 962	...
Redway (CDP)	1 094	...
Rio Dell city	2 687	2 817
North Coastal division	15 141	13 912
Blue Lake city (pt.)[11]	1 201	1 112
McKinleyville (CDP)	7 772	...
Trinidad city[11]	379	300
Trinity—Klamath division	4 555	3 857
Imperial County[12]	92 110	74 492
Brawley division	17 911	...
Brawley city[12]	14 946	13 746
Calexico division	15 907	12 020
Calexico city[12]	14 412	10 625
Calipatria—Westmorland division	6 954	...
Calipatria city[12]	2 636	1 824
Niland (CDP)	1 042	...
Westmorland city	1 590	1 175
East Imperial division	1 529	...
El Centro division	33 691	...
El Centro city[12]	23 996	19 272
Heber (CDP)	2 221	...
Imperial city (pt.)[12]	35	...
Seeley (CDP)	1 058	...
Holtville division	6 670	5 485
Holtville city[12]	4 399	3 496
Imperial division	4 994	4 072
Imperial city (pt.)[12]	3 416	3 094
West Imperial division	2 026	1 174
Winterhaven—Bard division	2 428	2 316
Inyo County[13]	17 895	15 571
Bishop division	11 655	9 817
Big Pine (CDP) (pt.)	469	...
Bishop city[13]	3 333	3 498
Death Valley division	1 433	1 092
Independence division	2 017	1 990
Big Pine (CDP) (pt.)	1 041	...
Lone Pine division	2 790	2 672
Lone Pine (CDP)	1 684	1 241
Kern County[14]	403 089	330 234
Arvin—Lamont division	22 836	18 089
Arvin city (pt.)[14]	6 863	5 199
Bakersfield city (pt.)[14]	1	...
Lamont (CDP)	9 616	7 007
Weed Patch (CDP)	1 553	...
Bakersfield division	219 870	...
Bakersfield city (pt.)[14]	105 599	69 515
Oildale (CDP)	23 382	20 879
Buttonwillow division	2 480	2 335
Bakersfield city (pt.)[14]	—	...
Buttonwillow (CDP)	1 350	1 193
East Kern division	50 314	44 988
Boron (CDP)	2 040	1 999
California City city[14]	2 743	1 309
China Lake (CDP)	4 275	11 105
Edwards AFB (CDP)	8 554	10 331
Mojave (CDP)	2 886	2 573
North Edwards (CDP)	1 107	...
Ridgecrest city[14]	15 929	7 629
Rosamond (CDP)	2 869	2 281
Greenfield—Panama division	5 190	4 774
Bakersfield city (pt.)[14]	—	...
Lake Isabella division	14 476	...
Bakersfield city (pt.)[14]	11	...
Bodfish (CDP)	1 379	...
Kernville (CDP)	1 660	...
Lake Isabella (CDP)	3 428	...
Tehachapi city (pt.)[14]	38	...
Wofford Heights (CDP)	2 112	...
McFarland—Delano division	23 943	...
Delano city[14]	16 491	14 559
McFarland city[14]	5 151	4 177
Rosedale division	8 032	4 844
Bakersfield city (pt.)[14]	—	...
Greenacres (CDP)	5 381	2 116
Shafter division	12 641	10 975
Shafter city[14]	7 010	5 327
Tehachapi division	8 872	...
Arvin city (pt.)[14]	—	...
Tehachapi city (pt.)[14]	4 088	4 211
Wasco division	12 945	10 605
Wasco city[14]	9 613	8 269
Westside division	21 490	18 838
Ford City (CDP)	3 392	3 503
Frazier Park (CDP)	1 444	1 167
Maricopa city	946	740
South Taft (CDP)	2 073	2 214
Taft city[14]	5 316	4 285
Taft Heights (CDP)	2 111	2 108

County Subdivisions	1980	1970
Kings County[15]	73 738	66 717
Avenal division	4 475	3 320
Avenal city (pt.)[15]	4 101	...
Corcoran division	9 182	9 550
Corcoran city[15]	6 454	5 249
Hanford division	33 815	...
Armona (CDP)	2 644	1 392
Hanford city[15]	20 958	15 179
Home Garden (CDP)	1 495	2 494
Short Acres (CDP)	1 266	1 476
Hanford Northeast division	3 369	3 412
Lemoore division	19 558	19 090
Lemoore city[15]	8 832	4 219
Lemoore Station (CDP)	5 888	9 210
Stratford division	3 339	2 813
Avenal city (pt.)[15]	36	...
Kettleman City (CDP)	1 051	...
Lake County[16]	36 366	19 548
Lakeport division	14 533	7 963
Kelseyville (CDP)	1 567	...
Lakeport city[16]	3 675	3 005
Lower Lake—Middletown division	13 614	6 614
Clearlake Highlands—Clearlake Park (CDP)	4 983	2 836
Lower Lake (CDP)	1 043	...
Upper Lake—Clearlake Oaks division	8 219	4 971
Clearlake Oaks (CDP)	1 610	...
Lucerne (CDP)	1 767	1 300
Lassen County[17]	21 661	16 796
Big Valley division	1 481	1 078
Honey Lake division	2 874	...
Herlong (CDP)	1 188	...
Madeline Plains division	321	...
Susanville division	14 087	10 707
Susanville city[17]	6 520	6 608
Westwood division	2 898	1 934
Westwood (CDP)	2 081	1 862
Los Angeles County[18]	7 477 503	7 041 980
Burbank division	84 625	88 871
Burbank city[18]	84 625	88 871
Calabasas division	52 795	30 644
Hidden Hills city[18]	1 760	1 529
Los Angeles city (pt.)[18]	22	...
Point Dume (CDP)	2 438	...
Compton division	280 365	...
Carson city[18]	81 221	71 150
Compton city[18]	81 286	78 547
East Compton (CDP)	6 435	5 853
Long Beach city (pt.)[18]	50	...
Lynwood city (pt.)[18]	48 513	43 354
Paramount city (pt.)[18]	5	...
West Carson (CDP)	17 997	15 918
West Compton (CDP)	5 907	5 605
Willowbrook (CDP)	30 845	32 328
Downey—Norwalk division	325 767	...
Artesia city	14 301	14 757
Bellflower city	53 441	52 334
Cerritos city	53 020	15 856
Downey city[18]	82 602	88 573
Lakewood city (pt.)[18]	715	...
Norwalk city (pt.)[18]	85 286	90 164
Paramount city (pt.)[18]	36 402	34 734
East San Gabriel Valley division	688 305	...
Avocado Heights (CDP)	11 721	9 810
Azusa city[18]	29 380	25 217
Baldwin Park city (pt.)[18]	50 554	47 285
Charter Oak (CDP)	6 840	...
Citrus (CDP)	12 450	...
Claremont city[18]	30 950	24 776
Covina city[18]	33 751	30 395
Diamond Bar (CDP)	28 045	10 576
Glendora city[18]	38 649	31 380
Hacienda Heights (CDP)	49 422	35 969
Industry city[18]	646	712
Irwindale city[18]	1 030	784
La Habra Heights city (pt.)[18]	266	...
La Puente city[18]	30 882	31 092
La Verne city (pt.)[18]	23 508	12 965
Pomona city[18]	92 742	87 384
Rowland Heights (CDP)	28 252	16 881
San Dimas city[18]	24 014	15 692
South San Jose Hills (CDP)	16 049	12 386
Valinda (CDP)	18 700	18 837
Walnut city[18]	12 478	5 992
West Covina city[18]	80 291	68 034
West Puente Valley (CDP)	20 445	20 733
Glendale division	156 224	...
Glendale city[18]	139 060	132 664
La Canada Flintridge city (pt.)[18]	633	...
La Crescenta—Montrose (CDP)	16 531	19 620
Inglewood division	296 401	295 435
Alondra Park (CDP)	12 096	12 193
Del Aire (CDP)	8 487	11 930
Gardena city[18]	45 165	41 021
Hawthorne city[18]	56 447	53 304
Inglewood city (pt.)[18]	94 245	89 985
Lawndale city	23 460	24 825
Lennox (CDP)	18 445	16 121
West Athens (CDP)	8 531	13 311
Westmont (CDP)	27 916	29 310

County Subdivisions	1980	1970
Los Angeles County—Con.		
Long Beach–Lakewood division	453 088	...
Hawaiian Gardens city[18]	10 548	ʳ9 052
Lakewood city[18]	73 939	ʳ83 025
Long Beach city (pt.)[18]	361 284	ʳ358 879
Signal Hill city	5 734	ʳ5 588
Los Angeles division	3 122 307	...
Beverly Hills city[18]	32 367	33 416
Culver City[18]	38 139	ʳ34 451
Inglewood city (pt.)[18]	–	...
Ladera Heights (CDP)	6 647	ʳ6 535
Los Angeles city (pt.)[18]	2 966 525	ʳ2 811 801
Marina Del Rey (CDP)	8 065	...
San Fernando city	17 731	16 571
View Park–Windsor Hills (CDP)	12 101	12 268
West Hollywood (CDP)	35 703	ʳ34 622
Newhall division	73 160	...
Canyon Country (CDP)	15 728	...
Los Angeles city (pt.)[18]	–	...
Newhall (CDP)	12 029	9 651
Saugus–Bouquet Canyon (CDP)	16 283	4 860
Valencia (CDP)	12 163	4 243
North Antelope Valley division	65 263	ʳ50 152
Lancaster city (pt.)[18]	48 027	...
Palmdale city (pt.)[18]	64	...
Quartz Hill (CDP) (pt.)	5 522	3 705
Palos Verdes division	91 949	...
Avalon city[18]	2 022	1 520
Lomita city[18]	18 807	19 784
Palos Verdes Estates city	14 376	ʳ13 631
Rancho Palos Verdes city[18]	36 577	...
Rolling Hills city[18]	2 049	2 050
Rolling Hills Estates city[18]	7 701	ʳ6 735
Pasadena division	223 159	...
Altadena (CDP)	40 510	ʳ42 415
La Canada Flintridge city (pt.)[18]	19 520	...
Pasadena city[18]	118 550	ʳ112 951
San Marino city[18]	13 307	14 177
South Pasadena city	22 681	22 979
Santa Monica division	88 314	88 289
Santa Monica city[18]	88 314	88 289
South Antelope Valley division	48 427	...
Desert View Highlands (CDP)	2 175	2 172
Glendora city (pt.)[18]	5	...
Lancaster city (pt.)[18]	–	...
La Verne city (pt.)[18]	–	...
Los Angeles city (pt.)[18]	303	...
Palmdale city (pt.)[18]	12 213	8 511
Palmdale East (CDP)	2 920	3 560
Quartz Hill (CDP) (pt.)	1 899	1 230
South Bay Cities division	123 219	ʳ128 741
El Segundo city[18]	13 752	15 620
Hermosa Beach city	18 070	17 412
Manhattan Beach city	31 542	35 352
Redondo Beach city	57 102	ʳ57 451
Southeast division	395 259	...
Bell city	25 450	21 836
Bell Gardens city[18]	34 117	29 308
Commerce city[18]	10 509	ʳ10 635
Cudahy city	17 984	16 998
East Los Angeles (CDP) (pt.)	109 594	ʳ104 881
Florence–Graham (CDP)	48 662	ʳ42 900
Huntington Park city[18]	46 223	33 744
Lynwood city (pt.)[18]	35	...
Maywood city	21 810	16 996
Montebello city (pt.)[18]	205	...
Monterey Park city (pt.)[18]	1 735	...
South Gate city[18]	66 784	56 909
Vernon city[18]	90	261
Walnut Park (CDP)	11 811	8 925
Southwest San Gabriel Valley division	260 598	...
Alhambra city[18]	64 615	62 125
East Los Angeles (CDP) (pt.)	423	...
Montebello city (pt.)[18]	52 724	42 807
Monterey Park city (pt.)[18]	52 603	49 166
Rosemead city[18]	42 604	40 972
San Gabriel city[18]	30 072	ʳ29 336
South San Gabriel (CDP)	5 421	5 051
Torrance division	129 881	...
Torrance city	129 881	ʳ134 968
Upper San Gabriel Valley division	256 806	...
Arcadia city[18]	45 994	ʳ45 138
Baldwin Park city (pt.)[18]	–	...
Bradbury city	846	ʳ838
Duarte city[18]	16 766	14 981
El Monte city[18]	79 494	ʳ69 892
Industry city (pt.)[18]	15	...
Mayflower Village (CDP)	5 017	...
Monrovia city	30 531	ʳ30 562
Pico Rivera city (pt.)	–	...
Sierra Madre city	10 837	12 140
South El Monte city[18]	16 623	13 443
Temple City city[18]	28 972	ʳ31 034
Whittier division	261 591	...
East La Mirada (CDP)	9 688	12 339
Industry city (pt.)[18]	3	...
La Habra Heights city (pt.)[18]	4 520	...
La Mirada city[18]	40 986	30 808
Norwalk city (pt.)[18]		...

County Subdivisions	1980	1970
Los Angeles County—Con.		
Whittier division—Con.		
Pico Rivera city (pt.)	53 459	54 170
Santa Fe Springs city[18]	14 520	14 750
South Whittier (CDP)	43 815	46 641
West Whittier–Los Nietos (CDP)	21 001	20 845
Whittier city[18]	69 717	72 863
Madera County[19]	63 116	41 519
Chowchilla division	8 798	...
Chowchilla city[19]	5 122	4 349
Madera division	34 937	...
Bonadelle Ranchos–Madera Ranchos (CDP) (pt.)	2 836	...
Madera city[19]	21 732	16 044
Madera Acres (CDP)	2 173	...
Parksdale (CDP)	1 267	...
Parkwood (CDP)	1 146	...
Madera Southeast division	5 311	...
Bonadelle Ranchos–Madera Ranchos (CDP) (pt.)	436	...
Madera West division	1 565	1 479
Oakhurst–North Fork division	12 505	5 852
Oakhurst	1 959	...
Marin County[20]	222 568	ʳ208 652
Northeast Marin division	49 985	...
Novato city (pt.)[20]	42 966	31 006
Northwest Marin division	8 142	...
Lagunitas–Forest Knolls (CDP)	1 465	–
Novato city (pt.)[20]	1 300	...
Woodacre (CDP)	1 300	...
Ross Valley division	54 843	...
Corte Madera town[20]	8 074	8 464
Fairfax town[20]	7 391	7 661
Larkspur city (pt.)[20]	11 064	10 487
Mill Valley city (pt.)[20]	–	...
Ross town[20]	2 801	2 742
San Anselmo town[20]	12 053	13 031
San Rafael city (pt.)[20]	–	...
San Rafael division	58 401	...
Larkspur city (pt.)[20]	–	...
Lucas Valley–Marinwood (CDP)	6 409	...
Novato city (pt.)[20]	950	...
San Rafael city (pt.)[20]	44 700	38 977
Southeast Marin division	47 983	...
Belvedere city	2 401	2 599
Larkspur city (pt.)[20]	–	...
Mill Valley city (pt.)[20]	12 967	12 942
Sausalito city (pt.)[20]	7 337	(NA)
Tamalpais–Homestead Valley (CDP) (pt.)	8 511	...
Tiburon town[20]	6 685	6 209
Southwest Marin division	3 214	...
Bolinas (CDP)	1 225	...
Sausalito city (pt.)[20]	1	(NA)
Tamalpais–Homestead Valley (CDP) (pt.)	–	...
Mariposa County	11 108	6 015
Coulterville division	1 531	719
Mariposa division	8 243	3 876
Mariposa (CDP)	1 150	...
Yosemite division	1 334	1 420
Yosemite Valley (CDP)	1 073	...
Mendocino County[21]	66 738	51 101
Covelo division	2 143	...
Covelo (CDP)	1 448	...
Fort Bragg division	9 294	7 796
Fort Bragg city (pt.)[21]	5 011	4 455
Hopland division	2 221	...
Laytonville–Leggett division	3 515	2 615
Laytonville (CDP)	1 096	...
Mendocino–Anderson division	8 987	5 623
Fort Bragg city (pt.)[21]	8	...
Mendocino (CDP)	1 008	...
Point Arena division	2 838	...
Point Arena city	425	424
Redwood–Potter division	8 761	5 922
Ukiah division	19 440	...
Talmage (CDP)	1 514	...
Ukiah city[21]	12 035	10 095
Willits division	9 539	...
Willits city[21]	4 008	3 091
Merced County[22]	134 560	104 629
Atwater division	29 048	...
Atwater city[22]	17 530	11 640
Winton (CDP)	4 995	3 393
Dos Palos division	6 411	5 358
Dos Palos city[22]	3 123	2 496
Gustine division	5 253	4 733
Gustine city[22]	3 142	2 793
Hilmar–Irwin division	6 266	...
Hilmar–Irwin (CDP)	1 706	...
Livingston–Delhi division	14 324	...
Delhi (CDP)	2 832	2 063
Livingston city[22]	5 326	2 588
Los Banos division	13 667	11 777
Los Banos city[22]	10 341	9 188
Merced division	52 908	...
Merced city[22]	36 499	22 670
Planada–Le Grand division	5 479	4 666
Planada (CDP)	2 406	2 056

County Subdivisions	1980	1970
Merced County—Con.		
Snelling division	1 204	769
Modoc County[23]	8 610	7 469
Adin—Lookout division	1 494	1 071
Alturas division	4 810	...
Alturas city[23]	3 025	2 799
Surprise Valley division	1 454	...
Tule Lake division	852	1 325
Mono County	8 577	4 016
Mono North division	1 760	1 127
Mono South division	6 817	2 889
Mammoth Lakes (CDP)	3 929	...
Monterey County[24]	290 444	'247 450
Carmel division	15 798	...
Carmel-by-the-Sea city[24]	4 707	4 525
Carmel Valley division	4 725	3 608
Carmel Valley (CDP)	4 013	3 026
Castroville division	14 564	9 342
Castroville (CDP)	4 396	3 235
Marina city (pt.)[24]	—	...
Coastal division	1 271	898
Gonzales division	9 459	7 567
Gonzales city[24]	2 891	2 575
Greenfield division	5 854	...
Greenfield city[24]	4 181	2 608
King City division	8 188	...
King City city[24]	5 495	3 717
Pajaro division	11 771	7 615
Las Lomas (CDP)	1 740	...
Pajaro (CDP)	1 426	1 407
Salinas division	92 345	...
Marina city (pt.)[24]	—	...
Salinas city[24]	80 479	58 896
San Ardo division	3 597	2 966
Seaside—Monterey division	108 858	...
Del Rey Oaks city	1 557	1 823
Marina city (pt.)[24]	20 647	...
Monterey city[24]	27 558	26 302
Pacific Grove city[24]	15 755	13 505
Sand City city	182	212
Seaside city[24]	36 567	'36 883
Soledad division	7 591	'5 771
Soledad city[24]	5 928	'4 222
Toro division	6 423	3 858
Napa County[25]	99 199	79 140
Angwin division	6 142	...
Angwin (CDP)	3 526	2 690
Deer Park (CDP)	1 454	...
Berryessa division	736	563
Calistoga division	5 131	2 836
Calistoga city[25]	3 879	1 882
Napa division	79 499	...
American Canyon (CDP)	5 712	...
Napa city[25]	50 879	'36 103
Yountville city	2 893	2 332
St. Helena division	7 691	...
St. Helena city	4 898	3 173
Nevada County[26]	51 645	26 346
Donner division	5 696	2 528
Truckee (CDP)	2 389	1 392
Grass Valley division	36 871	...
Alta Hill (CDP)	1 229	1 185
Alta Sierra (CDP)	2 168	...
Grass Valley city[26]	6 697	5 149
Penn Valley (CDP)	1 032	...
Nevada City division	9 078	...
Nevada City city[26]	2 431	2 314
Orange County[27]	1 932 709	'1 421 233
Anaheim—Santa Ana—Garden Grove division	1 153 646	...
Anaheim city[27]	219 311	'166 408
Brea city[27]	27 913	18 447
Buena Park city[27]	64 165	63 646
Cypress city[27]	40 391	'31 569
Fountain Valley city (pt.)[27]	1 600	...
Fullerton city[27]	102 034	'85 987
Garden Grove city (pt.)[27]	122 797	'121 155
Irvine city (pt.)[27]	—	...
La Habra city[27]	45 232	41 350
La Palma city[27]	15 399	9 687
Los Alamitos city[27]	11 529	11 346
Orange city[27]	91 788	'77 365
Placentia city[27]	35 041	21 948
Rossmoor (CDP)	10 457	12 922
Santa Ana city (pt.)[27]	203 713	'155 710
Seal Beach city (pt.)[27]	1 662	(NA)
Stanton city[27]	23 723	'18 186
Tustin city (pt.)[27]	32 301	(NA)
Tustin Foothills (CDP)	26 174	'26 699
Villa Park city	7 137	2 723
Westminster city (pt.)[27]	143	...
Yorba Linda city[27]	28 254	11 856
Central Coast division	170 644	...
Costa Mesa city (pt.)[27]	82 562	72 660
Irvine city (pt.)[27]	20 078	...
Newport Beach city[27]	62 556	'49 582

County Subdivisions	1980	1970
Orange County—Con.		
Central Coast division—Con.		
Santa Ana city (pt.)[27]	76 627	—	...
El Toro division	76 627	...
El Toro (CDP) (pt.)	25 300	8 596
El Toro Station (CDP)	7 632	6 970
Irvine city (pt.)[27]	42 056	...
Tustin city (pt.)[27]	16	(NA)
North Coast division	326 875	...
Costa Mesa city (pt.)[27]	—	...
Fountain Valley city (pt.)[27]	53 480	'31 886
Garden Grove city (pt.)[27]	510	...
Huntington Beach city[27]	170 505	115 960
Santa Ana city (pt.)[27]	—	...
Seal Beach city (pt.)[27]	24 313	(NA)
Westminster city (pt.)[27]	70 990	'60 076
South Coast division	134 696	...
Capistrano Beach (CDP)	6 168	4 149
Dana Point (CDP)	10 602	4 745
Irvine city (pt.)[27]	—	...
Laguna Beach city[27]	17 901	14 550
Laguna Hills (CDP)	33 600	13 676
Laguna Niguel (CDP)	12 237	4 644
San Clemente city[27]	27 325	17 063
San Juan Capistrano city (pt.)[27]	14 892	3 781
South Laguna (CDP)	6 013	2 566
Trabuco division	70 221	...
El Toro (CDP) (pt.)	12 853	58
Mission Viejo (CDP)	50 666	11 933
San Clemente city (pt.)[27]	—	...
San Juan Capistrano city (pt.)[27]	4 067	...
Placer County[28]	117 247	'77 632
Auburn division	28 463	20 083
Auburn city[28]	7 540	6 570
North Auburn (CDP)	7 619	2 089
Colfax—Summit division	11 414	...
Colfax city[28]	981	798
Meadow Vista (CDP)	2 683	...
Foresthill—Back Country division	2 844	...
Foresthill (CDP)	1 304	...
Lake Tahoe division	8 418	...
Kings Beach (CDP)	1 942	...
Sunnyside—Tahoe City (CDP)	1 836	1 394
Loomis Basin—Folsom Lake division	30 034	15 645
Loomis (CDP)	1 284	1 108
Rocklin city[28]	7 344	3 039
Roseville city (pt.)[28]	137	...
Roseville division	26 386	'20 215
Roseville city (pt.)[28]	24 210	'18 221
West Valley division	9 688	6 713
Lincoln city[28]	4 132	3 176
Plumas County[29]	17 340	11 707
Chester division	3 504	2 104
Chester (CDP)	1 756	1 531
Greenville division	3 166	...
Greenville (CDP)	1 537	1 073
Portola division	4 141	2 759
Portola city[29]	1 885	1 625
Quincy division	6 529	...
Quincy—East Quincy (CDP)	4 451	3 343
Riverside County[30]	663 166	'456 916
Cathedral City—Palm Desert division	37 932	...
Cathedral City (CDP)	4 130	3 640
Indian Wells city[30]	1 394	760
La Quinta (CDP)	3 328	...
Palm Desert city[30]	11 801	...
Palm Springs city (pt.)[30]	869	...
Rancho Mirage city[30]	6 281	...
Chuckwalla division	4 424	...
Eagle Mountain (CDP)	1 890	2 453
Coachella Valley division	47 625	...
Coachella city[30]	9 129	8 353
Indio city[30]	21 611	14 459
Mecca (CDP)	1 698	...
Corona division	48 591	...
Corona city (pt.)[30]	37 791	27 519
Home Gardens (CDP)	5 783	5 116
Norco city[30]	864	...
Riverside city (pt.)[30]	728	...
Desert Hot Springs division	13 174	...
Desert Hot Springs city[30]	5 941	2 738
Palm Springs city (pt.)[30]	—	...
Thousand Palms (CDP)	1 718	...
Elsinore Valley division	20 154	...
Lake Elsinore city[30]	5 982	3 530
Lakeland Village (CDP)	2 796	1 724
Sedco Hills (CDP)	2 678	...
Hemet—San Jacinto division	62 563	...
East Hemet (CDP)	14 712	8 598
Hemet city (pt.)[30]	22 448	12 252
San Jacinto city[30]	7 098	4 385
Valle Vista (CDP)	5 474	...
Idyllwild division	5 953	3 048
Idyllwild—Pine Cove (CDP)	2 959	...
Palm Springs city (pt.)[30]	11	...
Jurupa division	49 892	37 095
Corona city (pt.)[30]	—	...
Glen Avon (CDP)	8 444	5 759

County Subdivisions	1980	1970
Riverside County—Con.		
Jurupa division—Con.		
Mira Loma (CDP)	8 707	8 482
Norco city (pt.)[30]	1 394	...
Riverside city (pt.)[30]	285	...
Rubidoux (CDP) (pt.)	16 763	13 969
Lake Mathews division	7 064	...
Murrieta division	11 530	...
Murrieta Hot Springs (CDP)	1 091	...
Temecula (CDP)	1 783	...
Norco division	18 868	...
Norco city (pt.)[30]	18 868	14 511
Palm Springs division	34 298	...
Palm Springs city (pt.)[30]	31 391	20 936
Palo Verde division	12 758	12 250
Blythe city[30]	6 805	7 047
East Blythe (CDP)	1 660	1 252
Perris Valley division	43 896	...
Canyon Lake (CDP)	2 039	...
Hemet city (pt.)[30]	6	...
Homeland (CDP)	2 616	1 187
Moreno (CDP)	1 175	...
Nuevo (CDP)	1 628	...
Perris city (pt.)[30]	6 827	4 228
Romoland (CDP)	1 349	...
Sun City (CDP)	8 460	5 519
Riverside division	209 713	...
Edgemont (CDP)	5 215	...
March AFB (CDP)	3 607	2 002
Norco city (pt.)[30]	–	...
Perris city (pt.)[30]	–	...
Riverside city (pt.)[30]	169 863	140 089
Rubidoux (CDP) (pt.)	–	...
Sunnymead (CDP)	11 554	6 708
San Gorgonio Pass division	34 731	...
Banning city[30]	14 020	12 034
Beaumont city[30]	6 818	5 484
Cherry Valley (CDP)	5 012	3 165
Sacramento County[31]	783 381	'634 373
Delta division	4 800	4 653
Isleton city[31]	914	909
Elk Grove division	17 327	...
Elk Grove (CDP)	10 959	3 721
Folsom division	11 015	'8 372
Folsom city (pt.)[31]	11 003	5 810
Galt division	12 847	8 003
Galt city[31]	5 514	3 200
Mather division	78 968	...
La Riviera (CDP)	10 906	...
Mather AFB (CDP)	5 245	7 027
Rancho Cordova (CDP)	42 881	30 451
Rosemont (CDP)	18 888	...
Sacramento division	657 030	...
Arden–Arcade (CDP)	87 570	82 492
Carmichael (CDP)	43 108	37 625
Citrus Heights (CDP)	85 911	21 760
Fair Oaks (CDP)	22 602	11 256
Florin (CDP)	16 523	9 640
Folsom city (pt.)	–	...
Foothill Farms (CDP)	13 700	...
North Highlands (CDP)	37 825	31 854
Orangevale (CDP)	20 585	16 493
Parkway–Sacramento South (CDP)	26 815	28 574
Rio Linda (CDP)	7 359	7 524
Sacramento city[31]	275 741	'257 105
Sloughhouse division	1 394	653
San Benito County[32]	25 005	18 226
Hollister division	20 148	...
Hollister city (pt.)[32]	11 488	7 663
San Benito–Bitterwater division	525	580
San Juan Bautista division	4 332	...
Hollister city (pt.)[32]	–	...
San Juan Bautista city[32]	1 276	1 164
San Bernardino County[33]	895 016	'682 233
Arrowhead division	19 568	...
Crestline (CDP)	6 715	3 509
Lake Arrowhead (CDP)	6 272	2 682
San Bernardino city (pt.)[33]	1 116	...
Barstow–Victorville division	107 417	...
Adelanto city[33]	2 164	...
Apple Valley (CDP)	14 305	6 702
Barstow city[33]	17 690	17 442
George AFB (CDP)	7 061	7 404
Hesperia (CDP)	13 540	4 592
Lenwood (CDP)	2 974	3 834
Mountain View Acres (CDP)	1 686	...
Nebo Center (CDP)	1 749	1 828
Victorville city[33]	14 220	10 845
Yermo (CDP)	1 092	1 304
Big Bear division	13 426	7 830
Big Bear (CDP)	11 151	5 268
San Bernardino city (pt.)[33]	–	...
Mount Baldy–Wrightwood division	3 760	2 107
Rancho Cucamonga city (pt.)[33]	6	...
Wrightwood (CDP)	2 511	...
Needles division	6 679	5 872
Needles city[33]	4 120	4 051
Newberry–Baker division	3 061	'2 615

County Subdivisions	1980	1970
San Bernardino County—Con.		
Ontario division	281 935	...
Chino city[33]	40 165	20 411
Fontana city (pt.)[33]	–	–
Montclair city[33]	22 628	22 546
Ontario city (pt.)[33]	85 808	64 118
Rancho Cucamonga city (pt.)[33]	54 650	...
Upland city[33]	47 647	32 551
Red Mountain–Trona division	4 285	'7 085
Searles Valley (CDP)	3 439	3 828
San Bernardino division	386 521	...
Bloomington (CDP)	12 781	11 957
Colton city[33]	21 310	'20 016
Fontana city (pt.)[33]	37 111	20 673
Grand Terrace city[33]	8 498	...
Highland (CDP)	10 908	12 669
Loma Linda city[33]	10 694	...
Muscoy (CDP)	6 188	7 091
Ontario city (pt.)[33]	3 012	...
Rancho Cucamonga city (pt.)[33]	594	...
Redlands city (pt.)[33]	43 619	36 355
Rialto city[33]	37 474	28 370
San Bernardino city (pt.)[33]	116 374	'106 869
Twentynine Palms–Morongo Valley division	40 475	24 103
Joshua Tree (CDP)	2 083	1 211
Morongo Valley (CDP)	1 137	...
Twentynine Palms (CDP)	7 465	5 667
Twentynine Palms Base (CDP)	7 079	5 647
Yucca Valley (CDP)	8 294	3 893
Yucaipa division	27 889	...
Redlands city (pt.)[33]	–	...
Yucaipa (CDP)	23 345	19 284
San Diego County[34]	1 861 846	1 357 854
Alpine division	6 476	...
Alpine (CDP)	5 368	1 570
Anza–Borrego Springs division	2 191	1 087
Borrego Springs (CDP)	1 405	...
Fallbrook division	23 504	12 038
Fallbrook (CDP)	14 041	6 945
Rainbow (CDP)	1 092	...
Jamul division	6 202	2 842
Jamul (CDP)	1 826	...
Laguna–Pine Valley division	3 825	...
Mountain Empire division	3 705	2 492
Oceanside–Escondido division	271 728	...
Carlsbad city (pt.)[34]	35 490	14 944
Escondido city[34]	64 355	36 792
Oceanside city[34]	76 698	40 494
San Diego city (pt.)[34]	312	(NA)
San Marcos city (pt.)[34]	17 479	3 896
Vista city[34]	35 834	24 688
Palomar–Julian division	4 388	...
Julian (CDP)	1 320	...
Pauma Valley division	3 568	...
Pendleton division	26 705	32 861
Camp Pendleton North (CDP)	2 065	11 803
Camp Pendleton South (CDP)	7 952	13 692
Ramona division	14 949	...
Ramona (CDP)	8 173	3 554
San Diego city (pt.)[34]	59	...
San Diego division	1 485 749	...
Bonita (CDP)	6 257	...
Cardiff-by-the-Sea (CDP)	10 054	5 724
Carlsbad city (pt.)[34]	–	...
Casa de Oro–Mount Helix (CDP)	19 651	8 723
Castle Park–Otay (CDP)	21 049	15 445
Chula Vista city[34]	83 927	67 901
Coronado city	16 859	'20 020
Del Mar city	5 017	3 956
El Cajon city[34]	73 892	52 273
Encinitas (CDP)	10 796	5 375
Escondido city (pt.)[34]	–	...
Imperial Beach city	22 689	20 244
Lakeside (CDP)	23 921	11 991
La Mesa city[34]	50 308	39 178
Lemon Grove city[34]	20 780	...
Leucadia (CDP)	9 478	...
National City city[34]	48 772	43 184
Poway (CDP)	32 263	9 422
Rancho Santa Fe (CDP)	4 014	...
San Diego city (pt.)[34]	875 167	(NA)
San Marcos city (pt.)[34]	–	...
Santee (CDP)	47 080	21 107
Solana Beach (CDP)	13 047	5 023
Spring Valley (CDP)	40 191	'29 666
Valley Center division	8 856	...
Valley Center (CDP)	1 242	...
San Francisco County	678 974	715 674
San Francisco division	678 974	715 674
San Francisco city	678 974	715 674
San Joaquin County[35]	347 342	'291 073
Escalon division	8 116	6 986
Escalon city[35]	3 127	2 366
Linden–Farmington division	3 410	3 017
Lockeford division	7 507	5 139
Lockeford (CDP)	1 852	...
Lodi division	46 774	...
Lodi city[35]	35 221	28 691
Woodbridge (CDP)	1 672	1 397

County Subdivisions

County Subdivisions	1980	1970
San Joaquin County—Con.		
Manteca division	39 240	26 559
Lathrop (CDP)	3 717	2 137
Manteca city[35]	24 925	13 845
Stockton city (pt.)[35]	–	...
Ripon division	6 173	5 362
Ripon city[35]	3 509	2 679
Stockton division	207 296	...
August (CDP)	5 445	r6 735
Country Club (CDP)	9 585	...
Garden Acres (CDP)	7 361	7 870
Lincoln Village (CDP)	6 476	r6 112
Stockton city (pt.)[35]	149 779	r109 963
Thornton division	1 993	2 121
Tracy division	26 798	...
Tracy city[35]	18 428	14 724
San Luis Obispo County[36]	155 435	105 690
Arroyo Grande division	43 571	...
Arroyo Grande city[36]	11 290	7 454
Grover City city[36]	8 827	5 939
Nipomo (CDP)	5 247	3 642
Oceano (CDP)	4 478	2 564
Pismo Beach city[36]	5 364	4 043
Atascadero division	24 229	...
Atascadero city (pt.)[36]	16 232	...
North Coast division	27 939	15 152
Atascadero city (pt.)[36]	–	...
Baywood–Los Osos (CDP)	10 933	3 487
Cambria (CDP)	3 061	1 716
Cayucos (CDP)	2 301	1 772
Morro Bay city[36]	9 064	7 109
San Luis Obispo city (pt.)[36]	568	...
Paso Robles division	17 205	...
El Paso de Robles city[36]	9 163	7 168
San Luis Obispo division	42 491	...
San Luis Obispo city (pt.)[36]	33 684	28 036
San Mateo County[37]	587 329	r557 361
San Mateo division	310 337	...
Atherton town	7 797	8 085
Belmont city[37]	24 505	r23 538
East Palo Alto (CDP)	18 191	r18 727
Foster City city[37]	23 287	...
Hillsborough city	10 451	8 753
Menlo Park city[37]	26 369	r26 826
North Fair Oaks (CDP)	10 308	9 740
Portola Valley town	3 939	r4 996
Redwood City city[37]	54 951	55 686
San Carlos city[37]	24 710	r26 053
San Mateo city[37]	77 561	78 991
Woodside town[37]	5 291	r4 734
South Coastside division	19 948	...
El Granada (CDP)	3 582	1 473
Half Moon Bay city[37]	7 282	4 023
Millbrae city (pt.)	–	...
Montara (CDP)	1 972	1 459
Moss Beach (CDP)	1 868	...
South San Francisco division	257 044	...
Brisbane city[37]	2 969	3 003
Burlingame city[37]	26 173	27 320
Colma town[37]	395	537
Daly City city[37]	78 519	66 922
Millbrae city (pt.)	20 058	r20 920
Pacifica city	36 866	36 020
San Bruno city[37]	35 417	36 254
South San Francisco city[37]	49 393	46 646
Santa Barbara County[38]	298 694	264 324
Carpinteria Valley division	15 408	9 959
Carpinteria city[38]	10 835	6 982
Cuyama division	1 180	1 212
Guadalupe division	4 322	3 858
Guadalupe city[38]	3 629	3 145
Lompoc Valley division	44 779	...
Lompoc city[38]	26 267	25 284
Mission Hills (CDP)	2 797	2 699
Vandenberg AFB (CDP)	8 136	13 193
Vandenberg Village (CDP)	5 839	4 874
Santa Barbara division	155 448	...
Santa Barbara city[38]	74 414	70 215
Santa Maria Valley division	63 460	...
Santa Maria city[38]	39 685	32 749
Santa Ynez Valley division	14 097	8 328
Buellton (CDP)	2 364	1 402
Santa Ynez (CDP)	3 335	...
Solvang (CDP)	3 091	2 004
Santa Clara County[39]	1 295 071	r1 065 313
Diablo Range division	830	...
Morgan Hill city (pt.)[39]	–	...
San Jose city (pt.)[39]	–	...
Gilroy division	24 748	r15 708
Gilroy city (pt.)[39]	21 622	r12 684
Lexington division	3 874	r2 838
Chemeketa Park–Redwood Estates (CDP)	1 847	r1 427
Llagas–Uvas division	2 112	...
Gilroy city (pt.)[39]	10	...
San Jose city (pt.)[39]	154	...
San Jose division	1 262 972	...
Alum Rock (CDP)	16 890	r18 127

County Subdivisions	1980	1970
Santa Clara County—Con.		
San Jose division—Con.		
Campbell city[39]	27 067	r23 797
Cupertino city[39]	34 015	r17 895
Gilroy city (pt.)[39]	9	...
Los Altos city[39]	25 769	r25 062
Los Altos Hills city[39]	7 421	r6 871
Los Gatos town[39]	26 906	r22 613
Milpitas city[39]	37 820	r26 561
Monte Sereno city[39]	3 434	r2 847
Morgan Hill city (pt.)[39]	17 060	r5 579
Mountain View city[39]	58 655	r54 132
Palo Alto city (pt.)[39]	55 142	r56 040
San Jose city (pt.)[39]	629 288	r459 913
San Martin (CDP)	1 731	r1 429
Santa Clara city[39]	87 746	r86 118
Saratoga city[39]	29 261	r26 810
Stanford (CDP)	11 045	8 691
Sunnyvale city[39]	106 618	r95 976
West Santa Clara division	535	...
Palo Alto city (pt.)[39]	83	...
Santa Cruz County[40]	188 141	123 790
San Lorenzo Valley division	22 175	...
Ben Lomond (CDP)	7 238	2 793
Boulder Creek (CDP)	5 662	1 806
Santa Cruz division	114 923	...
Aptos (CDP)	7 039	8 704
Capitola city[40]	9 095	5 080
Felton (CDP)	4 564	2 062
Live Oak (CDP)	11 482	6 443
Opal Cliffs (CDP)	5 041	5 425
Rio del Mar (CDP)	7 067	...
Santa Cruz city[40]	41 483	32 076
Scotts Valley city[40]	6 891	3 621
Soquel (CDP)	6 212	5 795
Twin Lakes (CDP)	4 502	3 012
Seaside division	2 946	...
Watsonville division	48 097	...
Freedom (CDP)	6 416	5 563
La Selva Beach (CDP)	1 603	1 171
Watsonville city[40]	23 543	r14 719
Shasta County[41]	115 715	77 640
Central Shasta division	6 784	...
East Shasta division	7 863	5 280
Burney (CDP)	3 187	2 190
Johnson Park (CDP)	1 008	...
Redding–Anderson division	96 298	...
Anderson city[41]	7 381	5 492
Central Valley (CDP)	3 424	2 361
Cottonwood (CDP)	1 553	1 288
Pine Grove (CDP)	1 049	...
Project City (CDP)	1 657	1 431
Redding city[41]	41 995	16 659
Summit City (CDP)	1 136	...
Sacramento Canyon division	1 669	1 164
Southwest Shasta division	3 101	...
Sierra County[42]	3 073	2 365
East Sierra division	1 810	1 404
Loyalton city[42]	1 030	945
West Sierra division	1 263	961
Siskiyou County[43]	39 732	33 225
Butte Valley division	1 802	...
Dorris city[43]	836	840
Dunsmuir division	2 858	2 819
Dunsmuir city[43]	2 253	2 214
Etna division	3 169	2 211
Etna city[43]	754	667
Fort Jones division	1 454	...
Fort Jones town[43]	544	515
Happy Camp division	3 194	2 782
Happy Camp (CDP)	1 110	...
Hornbrook division	805	978
McCloud–Medicine Lake division	1 973	2 046
McCloud (CDP) (pt.)	1 656	1 643
Montague division	3 014	...
Montague city[43]	1 285	890
Mount Shasta division	5 577	...
McCloud (CDP) (pt.)	–	...
Mount Shasta city[43]	2 837	r2 256
Tule Lake division	1 310	1 535
Tulelake city[43]	783	857
Weed division	4 909	...
Weed city[43]	2 879	2 983
Yreka division	9 667	...
Yreka city[43]	5 916	5 394
Solano County[44]	235 203	r171 989
Dixon division	10 194	7 780
Dixon city[44]	7 541	4 432
Vacaville city (pt.)[44]	–	...
Fairfield–Suisun division	73 049	...
Fairfield city[44]	58 099	44 146
Suisun City city[44]	11 087	2 917
Vallejo city (pt.)[44]	–	...
Rio Vista division	4 310	4 136
Rio Vista city[44]	3 142	3 135
Vacaville division	49 164	25 224

County Subdivisions

County Subdivisions	1980	1970
Solano County—Con.		
Vacaville division—Con.		
Vacaville city (pt.)[44]	43 367	21 690
Vallejo division	98 486	...
Benicia city[44]	15 376	'7 349
Vallejo city (pt.)[44]	80 303	'71 710
Sonoma County[45]	299 681	204 885
Cloverdale—Geyserville division	8 980	...
Cloverdale city[45]	3 989	3 251
Healdsburg division	19 499	...
Healdsburg city[45]	7 217	5 438
Petaluma division	76 710	...
Cotati city[45]	3 475	1 368
Petaluma city[45]	33 834	24 870
Rohnert Park city[45]	22 965	6 133
Russian River—Coastal division	18 419	10 077
Graton (CDP) (pt.)	324	...
Guerneville (CDP)	1 525	...
Monte Rio (CDP)	1 137	...
Santa Rosa division	122 862	...
Rohnert Park city (pt.)[45]	–	...
Roseland (CDP)	7 915	5 105
Santa Rosa city[45]	83 320	50 006
Sebastopol city (pt.)[45]	49	...
Sebastopol division	23 680	17 206
Graton (CDP) (pt.)	962	...
Sebastopol city (pt.)[45]	5 546	3 993
Sonoma division	29 531	...
Boyes Hot Springs (CDP)	4 177	3 558
El Verano (CDP)	2 384	1 753
Fetters Hot Springs—Agua Caliente (CDP)	1 675	...
Glen Ellen (CDP)	1 014	...
Sonoma city[45]	6 054	'4 259
Stanislaus County[46]	265 900	194 506
Hughson division	8 223	6 495
Hughson city[46]	2 943	...
Modesto division	172 431	...
Ceres city[46]	13 281	6 029
Modesto city (pt.)[46]	106 600	61 712
Riverbank city[46]	5 695	3 949
South Modesto (CDP)	12 492	7 889
Newman division	4 881	4 680
Newman city[46]	2 785	2 505
Oakdale division	15 413	12 152
Oakdale city[46]	8 474	6 594
Patterson division	7 983	...
Patterson city[46]	3 908	3 147
Salida division	6 760	...
Turlock division	40 560	26 618
Denair (CDP)	2 892	1 128
South Turlock (CDP)	1 700	1 762
Turlock city[46]	26 287	13 992
Waterford division	6 477	5 400
Modesto city (pt.)[46]	2	...
Waterford city	2 683	2 243
Westport division	3 172	...
Sutter County[47]	52 246	41 935
Live Oak division	5 523	...
Live Oak city[47]	3 103	2 645
Meridian—Robbins division	1 381	1 615
South Sutter division	2 797	2 298
Sutter division	2 674	2 160
Sutter (CDP)	2 225	1 488
Yuba City division	37 850	...
South Yuba City (CDP)	7 530	5 352
Tierra Buena (CDP)	2 374	...
Yuba City city[47]	18 736	13 986
Yuba Rural division	2 021	...
Tehama County[48]	38 888	29 517
Corning division	8 838	6 508
Corning city[48]	4 745	3 573
East Tehama division	3 419	...
Los Molinos (CDP)	1 241	...
Red Bluff division	25 607	...
Red Bluff city[48]	9 490	7 676
Tehama city	365	317
West Tehama division	1 024	605
Trinity County[49]	11 858	7 615
Hayfork division	3 138	...
Hayfork (CDP)	1 788	...
Lower Trinity division	1 856	...
Mad River division	914	593
Weaverville division	5 950	...
Weaverville (CDP)	2 787	1 489
Tulare County[50]	245 738	188 322
Dinuba division	19 478	16 076
Dinuba city[50]	9 907	7 917
London (CDP)	1 257	...
Earlimart division	8 995	7 180
Earlimart (CDP)	4 578	3 080
Richgrove (CDP)	1 398	1 023
Exeter division	17 099	...
Exeter city[50]	5 606	4 475
Farmersville city[50]	5 544	3 456
Ivanhoe division	5 460	...
Ivanhoe (CDP)	2 684	1 595

County Subdivisions	1980	1970
Tulare County—Con.		
Lindsay division	11 019	8 600
Lindsay city[50]	6 924	5 206
Orosi—Cutler division	10 415	8 319
Cutler (CDP)	3 149	2 503
Orosi (CDP)	4 076	2 757
Pixley division	4 171	3 651
Pixley (CDP)	2 488	1 584
Porterville division	40 888	...
East Porterville (CDP)	5 218	4 042
Poplar—Cotton Center (CDP) (pt.)	1 289	1 205
Porterville city (pt.)[50]	19 692	12 602
Springville—Johnsondale division	4 160	2 877
Strathmore division	5 437	4 353
Porterville city (pt.)	15	...
Strathmore (CDP)	1 955	1 221
Terra Bella division	4 211	2 651
Terra Bella (CDP)	1 807	1 037
Tipton division	5 033	4 193
Poplar—Cotton Center (CDP) (pt.)	6	34
Tipton (CDP)	1 185	...
Woodville (CDP)	1 507	1 031
Tulare division	35 595	...
Tulare city[50]	22 526	16 235
Tulare East (CDP)	2 168	2 361
Tulare Northwest (CDP)	1 936	1 950
Visalia division	65 047	...
Goshen (CDP)	1 809	1 324
Visalia city[50]	49 729	'27 130
Woodlake—Three Rivers division	8 730	6 709
Woodlake city[50]	4 343	3 371
Tuolumne County[51]	33 928	22 169
Groveland division	2 050	884
Sonora division	17 004	12 498
Jamestown (CDP)	2 206	...
Sonora city[51]	3 247	3 100
Stanislaus—Yosemite division	890	786
Twain Harte—Tuolumne division	13 984	8 001
Mono Vista (CDP)	1 154	...
Tuolumne City (CDP)	1 708	1 365
Twain Harte (CDP)	1 369	1 484
Ventura County[52]	529 174	'378 497
Camarillo division	43 058	...
Camarillo city (pt.)[52]	33 523	19 219
Camarillo Heights (CDP)	6 341	5 892
Thousand Oaks city (pt.)[52]	111	...
Fillmore—Piru division	13 350	10 229
Fillmore city[52]	9 602	6 285
Piru (CDP)	1 284	...
Las Posas division	3 027	...
Oxnard city (pt.)[52]	594	...
Los Padres division	487	375
Meiners Oaks—Ojai division	25 783	...
Casitas Springs (CDP) (pt.)	947	1 090
Meiners Oaks—Mira Monte (CDP)	9 512	7 025
Oak View (CDP)	4 671	4 872
Ojai city[52]	6 816	5 591
San Buenaventura (Ventura) city (pt.)[52]	–	...
Moorpark division	8 724	4 800
Moorpark (CDP)	4 030	3 380
Simi Valley city (pt.)[52]	–	...
Oxnard division	143 443	...
El Rio (CDP)	5 674	6 173
Oxnard city (pt.)[52]	107 601	71 225
Point Mugu (CDP)	2 701	3 351
Port Hueneme city[52]	17 803	14 295
Santa Paula division	23 847	...
Santa Paula city[52]	20 552	18 001
Simi Valley division	81 381	...
Simi Valley city (pt.)[52]	77 500	'59 832
Thousand Oaks division	101 541	...
Camarillo city (pt.)[52]	4 274	...
Simi Valley city (pt.)[52]	–	...
Thousand Oaks city (pt.)[52]	76 961	'35 873
Triunfo Pass—Coastal division	1 058	760
Thousand Oaks city (pt.)[52]		
Ventura division	83 475	...
Casitas Springs (CDP) (pt.)	91	23
San Buenaventura (Ventura) city (pt.)[52]	74 393	'57 964
Yolo County[53]	113 374	91 788
Clarksburg division	1 581	1 585
Davis division	43 894	29 824
Davis city[53]	36 640	23 488
East Yolo division	24 720	27 392
Broderick—Bryte (CDP)	10 194	12 782
West Sacramento (CDP)	10 875	12 002
Esparto division	3 339	2 671
Esparto (CDP)	1 303	1 088
Knights Landing division	2 902	2 646
Winters division	3 949	3 561
Winters city[53]	2 652	2 419
Woodland division	32 989	24 109
Woodland city[53]	30 235	20 677

County Subdivisions

	1980	1970
Yuba County[54]	49 733	44 736
Linda division	10 682	...
Linda (CDP)	10 225	7 731
Marysville city (pt.)[54]	–	...
Linda Rural division	8 185	...
Beale AFB East (CDP)	6 329	7 029
Marysville city (pt.)[54]	–	...
Marysville division	10 370	...
Marysville city (pt.)[54]	9 898	9 353
Marysville Rural division	4 523	...
Marysville city (pt.)[54]	–	...
Olivehurst division	9 935	...
Olivehurst (CDP)	8 929	8 100
Wheatland division	2 096	1 943
Wheatland city[54]	1 474	1 280
Yuba Foothills division	3 942	1 784

COLORADO

The name Colorado, which was first applied to the river and later to the territory and state, is derived from the Spanish *colorado*, meaning colored of red.

The first explorers of the region now forming the state of Colorado were probably Spaniards. Claims have been made that Coronado's expedition of 1540 led through this country, but the first well-authenticated exploration was made in 1776 by Padre Francisco Escalante, who visited the region of the Dolores and Gunnison Rivers. The Spanish, however, made no attempts at settlement, and very few white men came to the Colorado country until long after the United States in 1803. That part not originally comprised within the Louisiana region belonged to Spain until the Mexican revolution of 1821, after which it formed a part of Mexico. The eastern part of this Mexican territory became a part of Texas, which achieved its independence in 1836, and in 1845 was annexed to the United State; the western part was included in the lands ceded by Mexico to the United States in 1848 at the close of the Mexican War.

The section of Colorado included in the Louisiana Purchase belonged successively to the district of Louisiana (1804-5), the territory of Louisiana (1805-12), the territory of Missouri (1812-34), and the "Indian Country" (1834-54). When the territories of Utah and New Mexico were organized, in 1850, the western portion of what is now Colorado was included in Utah; the region east of the Rocky Mountains, south of the Arkansas, and west of the one hundred and third meridian and south of the Arkansas was left without organized government, as was the Indian Country to the north of it. In 1854, when Kansas and Nebraska were organized, all the Colorado region not included in Utah or New Mexico became a part of Kansas if south of the fortieth parallel and a part of Nebraska if north of that line.

In February, 1861, the region lying between the thirty-seventh and forty-first parallels and extending from the twenty-fifth to the thirty-second meridian from Washington (approximately the one hundred and second and one hundred and ninth meridians from Greenwich) was organized as the territory of Colorado; and in August, 1876, the territory, without change of boundaries, became a state of the Union.

COUNTY LOCATION INDEX

Adams	B-5	El Paso	D-5	Moffat	B-2
Alamosa	E-4	Fremont	D-5	Montezuma	E-2
Arapahoe	C-5	Garfield	C-2	Montrose	D-2
Archuleta	E-3	Gilpin	B-5	Morgan	B-6
Baca	E-7	Grand	B-4	Otero	E-6
Bent	D-7	Gunnison	D-3	Ouray	D-3
Boulder	B-5	Hinsdale	E-3	Park	C-4
Chaffee	D-4	Huerfano	E-5	Phillips	B-7
Cheyenne	D-7	Jackson	B-4	Pitkin	C-3
Clear Creek	C-4	Jefferson	C-5	Prowers	D-7
Conejos	E-4	Kiowa	D-7	Pueblo	D-5
Costilla	E-5	Kit Carson	C-7	Rio Blanco	B-2
Crowley	D-6	Lake	C-4	Rio Grande	E-4
Custer	D-5	La Plata	E-3	Routt	B-3
Delta	D-3	Larimer	B-5	Saguache	D-4
Denver	C-5	Las Animas	E-6	San Juan	E-3
Dolores	E-2	Lincoln	C-6	San Miguel	D-2
Douglas	C-5	Logan	B-6	Sedgwick	A-7
Eagle	C-4	Mesa	C-2	Summit	C-4
Elbert	C-6	Mineral	E-3	Teller	C-5
				Washington	B-6
				Weld	B-5
				Yuma	B-7

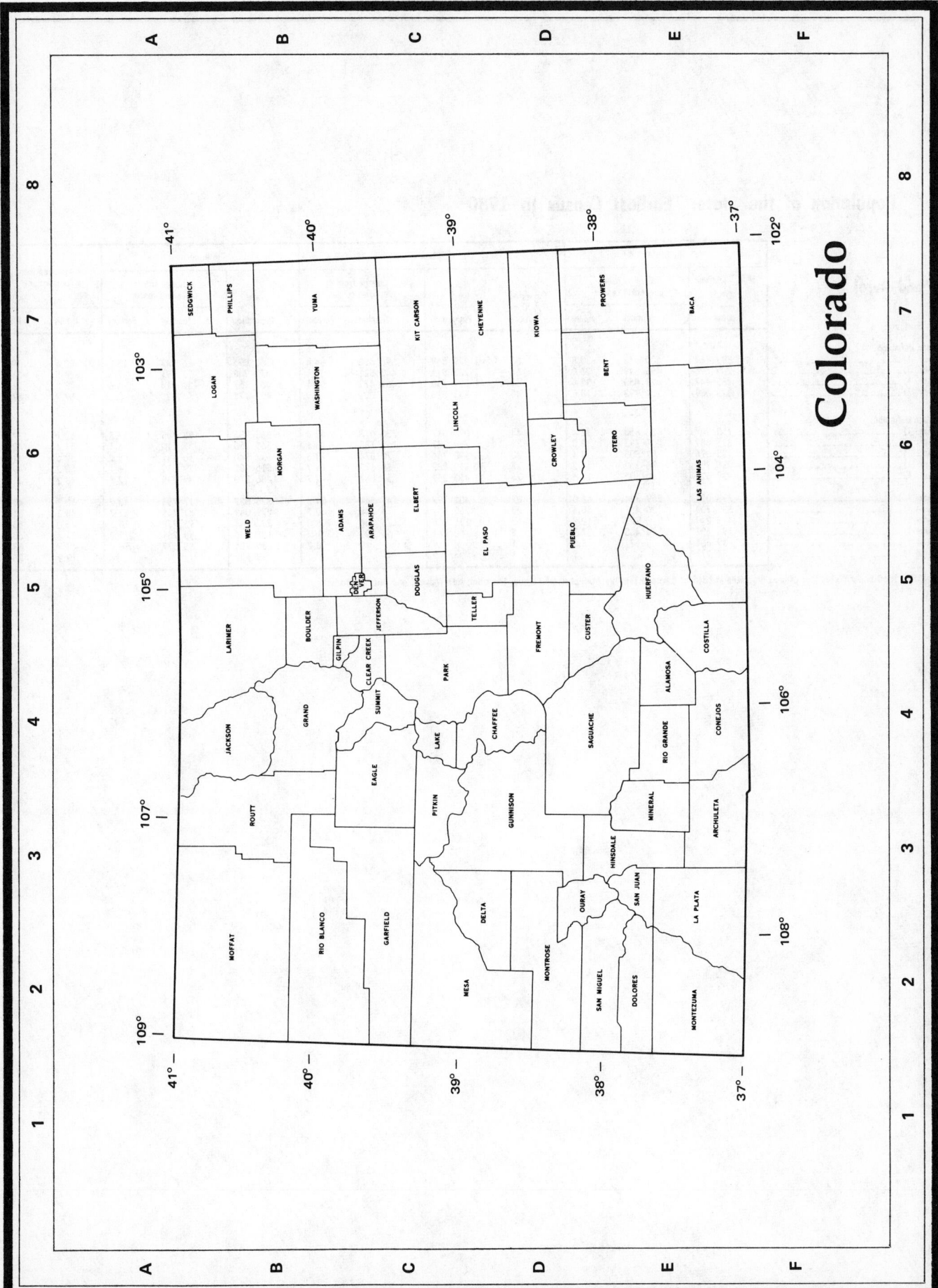

Colorado

Population of the State: Earliest Census to 1980

Urban and Rural

	The State			Urban				Rural				Percent of total population	
	Total population	Change from preceding census		Places of 2,500 or more	Population	Change from preceding census		Population	Change from preceding census			Urban	Rural
		Number	Percent			Number	Percent		Number	Percent			
Current urban definition:													
1980 (Apr. 1)	2 889 964	680 368	30.8	85	2 329 869	596 558	34.4	560 095	86 147	18.2		80.6	19.4
1970 (Apr. 1)	'2 209 596	455 649	26.0	64	1 733 311	440 521	34.1	473 948	12 791	2.8		78.5	21.5
1960 (Apr. 1)	1 753 947	428 858	32.4	51	1 292 790	461 472	55.5	461 157	-32 614	-6.6		73.7	26.3
1950 (Apr. 1)	1 325 089	201 793	18.0	40	831 318	...	...	493 771	...	...		62.7	37.3
Previous urban definition:													
1960 (Apr. 1)	1 753 947	428 858	32.4	44	1 090 012	330 073	43.4	663 935	98 785	17.5		62.1	37.9
1950 (Apr. 1)	1 325 089	201 793	18.0	36	759 939	169 183	28.6	565 150	32 610	6.1		57.4	42.6
1940 (Apr. 1)	1 123 296	87 505	8.4	30	590 756	70 874	13.6	532 540	16 631	3.2		52.6	47.4
1930 (Apr. 1)	1 035 791	96 162	10.2	27	519 882	66 623	14.7	515 909	29 539	6.1		50.2	49.8
1920 (Jan. 1)	939 629	140 605	17.6	26	453 259	51 067	12.7	486 370	89 538	22.6		48.2	51.8
1910 (Apr. 15)	799 024	259 324	48.0	27	402 192	141 541	54.3	396 832	117 783	42.2		50.3	49.7
1900 (June 1)	539 700	126 451	30.6	20	260 651	74 746	40.2	279 049	51 705	22.7		48.3	51.7
1890 (June 1)	413 249	218 922	112.7	13	185 905	124 944	205.0	227 344	93 978	70.5		45.0	55.0
1880 (June 1)	194 327	154 463	387.5	5	60 961	56 202	1000+	133 366	98 261	279.9		31.4	68.6
1870 (June 1)	39 864	5 587	16.3	1	4 759	10	0.2	35 105	5 577	18.9		11.9	88.1
1860 (June 1)	34 277	...	...	1	4 749	...	...	29 528	...	...		13.9	86.1

NOTE: 1860 population is that of area organized in 1861 as Colorado Territory from parts of Kansas, Nebraska, New Mexico, and Utah Territories.

ADAMS

1910	8,892
1920	14,430
1930	20,245
1940	22,481
1950	40,234
1960	120,296
1970	185,789
1980	245,944

ALAMOSA

1920	5,148
1930	8,602
1940	10,484
1950	10,531
1960	10,000
1970	11,422
1980	11,799

ARAPAHOE

1870	6,829
1880	38,644
1890	132,135
1900	153,017
1910	10,263
1920	13,766
1930	22,627
1940	32,150
1950	52,125
1960	113,426
1970	162,142
1980	293,621

ARCHULETA

1890	826
1900	2,177
1910	3,302
1920	3,590
1930	3,204
1940	3,806
1950	3,030
1960	2,629
1970	2,733
1980	3,664

BACA

1890	1,479
1900	759
1910	2,516
1920	8,721
1930	10,570
1940	6,207
1950	7,964
1960	6,310
1970	5,674
1980	5,419

BENT

1870	592
1880	1,654
1890	1,313
1900	3,049
1910	5,043
1920	9,705
1930	9,134
1940	9,653
1950	8,775
1960	7,419
1970	6,493
1980	5,945

BOULDER

1870	1,939
1880	9,723
1890	14,082
1900	21,544
1910	30,330
1920	31,861
1930	32,456
1940	37,438
1950	48,296
1960	74,254
1970	131,889
1980	189,625

CHAFFEE

1880	6,512
1890	6,612
1900	7,085
1910	7,622
1920	7,753
1930	8,126
1940	8,109
1950	7,168
1960	8,298
1970	10,162
1980	13,227

CHEYENNE

1890	534
1900	501
1910	3,687
1920	3,746
1930	3,723
1940	2,964
1950	3,453
1960	7,789
1970	2,396
1980	2,153

CLEAR CREEK

1870	1,596
1880	7,823
1890	7,184
1900	7,082
1910	5,001
1920	2,891
1930	2,155
1940	3,784
1950	3,289
1960	2,793
1970	4,819
1980	7,308

CONEJOS

1870	2,504
1880	5,605
1890	7,193
1900	8,794
1910	11,285
1920	8,416
1930	9,803
1940	11,648
1950	10,171
1960	8,428
1970	7,846
1980	7,794

COSTILLA

1870	1,779
1880	2,879
1890	3,491
1900	4,632
1910	5,498
1920	5,032
1930	5,779
1940	7,533
1950	6,067
1960	4,219
1970	3,091
1980	3,071

CROWLEY

1920	6,383
1930	5,934
1940	5,398
1950	5,222
1960	3,978
1970	3,086
1980	2,988

CUSTER

1880	8,080
1890	2,970
1900	2,937
1910	1,947
1920	2,172
1930	2,124
1940	2,270
1950	1,573
1960	1,305
1970	1,120
1980	1,528

DELTA

1890	2,534
1900	5,487
1910	13,688
1920	13,688
1930	14,204
1940	16,470
1950	17,365
1960	15,602
1970	15,286
1980	21,225

DENVER

1910	213,381
1920	256,491
1930	287,861
1940	322,412
1950	415,786
1960	493,887
1970	514,678
1980	492,365

DOLORES

1890	1,498
1900	1,134
1910	642
1920	1,243
1930	1,412
1940	1,958
1950	1,966
1960	2,196
1970	1,641
1980	1,658

DOUGLAS

1870	1,388
1880	2,486

1890	3,006
1900	3,120
1910	3,192
1920	3,517
1930	3,498
1940	3,496
1950	3,507
1960	4,816
1970	8,407
1980	25,153

EAGLE

1890	3,725
1900	3,008
1910	2,985
1920	3,385
1930	3,924
1940	5,361
1950	4,488
1960	4,677
1970	7,498
1980	13,320

ELBERT

1890	1,708
1900	1,856
1910	3,101
1920	5,331
1930	6,980
1940	5,460
1950	4,477
1960	3,708
1970	3,903
1980	6,850

EL PASO

1870	987
1880	7,949
1890	21,239
1900	31,602
1910	43,321
1920	44,027
1930	49,570
1940	54,025
1950	74,523
1960	143,742
1970	235,972
1980	309,424

FREMONT

1870	1,064
1880	4,735
1890	9,156
1900	15,636
1910	18,181
1920	17,883
1930	18,896
1940	19,742
1950	18,366
1960	20,196
1970	21,942
1980	28,676

GARFIELD

1890	4,478
1900	5,835
1910	10,144
1920	9,304
1930	9,975
1940	10,560
1950	11,625

1960	12,017
1970	14,812
1980	22,514

GILPIN

1870	5,490
1880	6,489
1890	5,876
1900	6,690
1910	4,131
1920	1,364
1930	1,212
1940	1,625
1950	850
1960	685
1970	1,272
1980	2,441

GRAND

1880	417
1890	604
1900	741
1910	1,862
1920	2,659
1930	2,108
1940	3,587
1950	3,963
1960	3,557
1970	4,107
1980	7,475

GREENWOOD

1870	510

GUNNISON

1880	8,235
1890	4,359
1900	5,331
1910	5,897
1920	5,590
1930	5,527
1940	6,192
1950	5,716
1960	5,477
1970	7,578
1980	10,689

HINSDALE

1880	1,487
1890	862
1900	1,609
1910	643
1920	538
1930	449
1940	349
1950	263
1960	208
1970	202
1980	408

HUERFANO

1870	2,250
1880	4,124
1890	6,882
1900	8,395
1910	13,320
1920	16,879
1930	17,602
1940	16,088
1950	10,549

1960	7,867
1970	6,590
1980	6,440

JACKSON

1910	1,013
1920	1,340
1930	1,386
1940	1,798
1950	1,976
1960	1,758
1970	1,811
1980	1,863

JEFFERSON

1870	2,390
1880	6,804
1890	8,450
1900	9,360
1910	14,231
1920	14,400
1930	21,810
1940	30,725
1950	55,687
1960	127,520
1970	235,368
1980	371,753

KIOWA

1890	1,243
1900	701
1910	2,899
1920	3,755
1930	3,786
1940	2,793
1950	3,003
1960	2,425
1970	2,029
1980	1,936

KIT CARSON

1890	2,472
1900	1,580
1910	7,483
1920	8,915
1930	9,725
1940	7,512
1950	8,600
1960	6,957
1970	7,530
1980	7,599

LAKE

1870	522
1880	23,563
1890	14,663
1900	18,054
1910	10,600
1920	6,630
1930	4,899
1940	6,883
1950	6,150
1960	7,101
1970	8,282
1980	8,830

LA PLATA

1880	1,110
1890	5,509

1900	7,016
1910	10,812
1920	11,218
1930	12,975
1940	15,494
1950	14,880
1960	19,225
1970	19,199
1980	27,424

LARIMER

1870	838
1880	4,892
1890	9,712
1900	12,168
1910	25,270
1920	27,872
1930	33,137
1940	35,539
1950	43,554
1960	53,343
1970	89,900
1980	149,184

LAS ANIMAS

1870	4,276
1880	8,903
1890	17,208
1900	21,842
1910	33,643
1920	38,975
1930	36,008
1940	32,369
1950	25,902
1960	19,983
1970	15,744
1980	14,897

LINCOLN

1890	689
1900	926
1910	5,917
1920	8,273
1930	7,850
1940	5,882
1950	5,909
1960	5,310
1970	4,836
1980	4,663

LOGAN

1890	3,070
1900	3,292
1910	9,549
1920	18,427
1930	19,946
1940	18,370
1950	17,187
1960	20,302
1970	18,852
1980	19,800

MESA

1890	4,260
1900	9,267
1910	22,197
1920	22,281
1930	25,908
1940	33,791
1950	33,974
1960	50,715

1970	54,374
1980	81,530

MINERAL

1900	1,913
1910	1,239
1920	779
1930	640
1940	975
1950	698
1960	424
1970	786
1980	804

MOFFAT

1920	5,129
1930	4,861
1940	5,086
1950	5,946
1960	7,061
1970	6,525
1980	13,133

MONTEZUMA

1890	1,529
1900	3,058
1910	5,029
1920	6,260
1930	7,789
1940	10,463
1950	9,991
1960	14,024
1970	12,952
1980	16,510

MONTROSE

1890	3,980
1900	4,535
1910	10,291
1920	11,852
1930	11,742
1940	15,418
1950	15,220
1960	18,286
1970	18,366
1980	24,352

MORGAN

1890	1,601
1900	3,268
1910	9,577
1920	16,124
1930	18,284
1940	17,214
1950	18,074
1960	21,192
1970	20,105
1980	22,513

OTERO

1890	4,192
1900	11,522
1910	20,201
1920	22,623
1930	24,390
1940	23,571
1950	25,275
1960	24,128
1970	23,523
1980	22,567

OURAY

1880	2,669
1890	6,510
1900	4,731
1910	3,514
1920	2,620
1930	1,784
1940	2,089
1950	2,103
1960	1,601
1970	1,546
1980	1,925

PARK

1870	447
1880	3,970
1890	3,548
1900	2,998
1910	2,492
1920	1,977
1930	2,052
1940	3,272
1950	1,870
1960	1,822
1970	2,185
1980	5,333

PHILLIPS

1890	2,642
1900	1,583
1910	3,179
1920	5,499
1930	5,797
1940	4,948
1950	4,924
1960	4,440
1970	4,131
1980	4,542

PITKIN

1890	8,929
1900	7,020
1910	4,566
1920	2,707
1930	1,770
1940	1,836
1950	1,646
1960	13,296
1970	6,185
1980	10,338

PROWERS

1890	1,969
1900	3,766
1910	9,520
1920	13,845
1930	14,762
1940	12,304
1950	14,836
1960	13,296
1970	13,258
1980	13,070

PUEBLO

1870	2,265
1880	7,617
1890	31,491
1900	34,448
1910	52,223
1920	57,638

1930	66,038
1940	68,870
1950	90,188
1960	118,707
1970	118,238
1980	125,972

RIO BLANCO

1890	1,200
1900	1,690
1910	2,332
1920	3,135
1930	2,980
1940	2,943
1950	4,719
1960	5,150
1970	4,842
1980	6,255

RIO GRANDE

1880	1,944
1890	3,451
1900	4,080
1910	6,563
1920	7,855
1930	9,953
1940	12,404
1950	12,832
1960	11,160
1970	10,494
1980	10,511

ROUTT

1880	140
1890	2,369
1900	3,661
1910	7,561
1920	8,948
1930	9,352
1940	10,525
1950	8,940
1960	5,900
1970	6,592
1980	13,404

SAGUACHE

1870	304
1880	1,973
1890	3,313
1900	3,853
1910	4,160
1920	4,638
1930	6,250
1940	6,173
1950	5,664
1960	4,473
1970	3,827
1980	3,935

SAN JUAN

1880	1,087
1890	1,572
1900	2,342
1910	3,063
1920	1,700
1930	1,935
1940	1,439
1950	1,471
1960	849
1970	831
1980	833

SAN MIGUEL

1890	2,909
1900	5,379
1910	4,700
1920	5,281
1930	2,184
1940	3,664
1950	2,693
1960	2,944
1970	1,949
1980	3,192

SEDGWICK

1890	2,909
1900	5,379
1910	3,061
1920	4,207
1930	5,580
1940	5,294
1950	5,095
1960	4,242
1970	3,405
1980	3,266

SUMMIT

1870	258
1880	5,459
1890	1,906
1900	2,744
1910	2,003
1920	1,724
1930	987
1940	1,754
1950	1,135
1960	2,073
1970	2,665
1980	8,848

TELLER

1900	29,002
1910	14,351
1920	6,696
1930	4,141
1940	6,463
1950	2,754
1960	2,495
1970	3,316
1980	8,034

WASHINGTON

1890	2,301
1900	1,241
1910	6,002
1920	11,208
1930	9,591
1940	8,336
1950	7,520
1960	6,625
1970	5,550
1980	5,304

WELD

1870	1,636
1880	5,646
1890	11,736
1900	16,808
1910	39,177
1920	54,059
1930	65,097

1940	63,747
1950	67,504
1960	72,344
1970	89,297
1980	123,438

YUMA

1890	2,596
1900	1,729
1910	8,499
1920	13,897
1930	13,613
1940	12,102
1950	10,827
1960	8,912
1970	8,544
1980	9,682

NOTES

CHAFFEE

Name changed from Lake in 1879.

CONEJOS

Name changed from Guadalupe in 1861.

GREENWOOD

Taken to form Bent and part of Elbert in 1874.

LAKE

Name changed from Carbonate in 1879.

OURAY

Name changed from Uncompahgre in 1883.

SAN MIGUEL

Name changed from Ouray in 1883.

ARVADA

1910	840
1920	915
1930	1,276
1940	1,482
1950	2,359
1960	19,242
1970	49,844
1980	84,576

AURORA

1900	202
1910	679
1920	983
1930	2,295
1940	3,437
1950	11,421
1960	48,548
1970	74,974
1980	158,588

BOULDER

1870	343
1880	3,069
1890	3,330
1900	6,150
1910	9,539
1920	11,006
1930	11,223
1940	12,958
1950	19,999
1960	37,718
1970	66,870
1980	76,685

BRIGHTON

1890	306
1900	366
1910	850
1920	2,715
1930	3,394
1940	4,024
1950	4,336
1960	7,055
1970	8,309
1980	12,773

BROOMFIELD

1970	7,261
1980	20,730

CANON CITY

1940	6,690
1950	6,345
1960	8,973
1970	9,206
1980	13,037

COLORADO SPRINGS

1880	4,226
1890	11,140
1900	21,085
1910	29,078
1920	30,105
1930	33,237
1940	36,789
1950	45,472
1960	70,194
1970	135,517
1980	215,150

COMMERCE CITY

1960	8,970
1970	17,407
1980	16,234

DENVER

1860	4,749
1870	4,759
1880	35,629
1890	105,713
1900	133,859
1910	213,381
1920	256,941
1930	287,861
1940	322,412
1950	415,786
1960	493,887
1970	514,678
1980	492,365

DURANGO

1890	2,726
1900	3,317
1910	4,686
1920	4,116
1930	5,400
1940	5,887
1950	7,459
1960	10,530
1970	10,333
1980	11,426

ENGLEWOOD

1910	2,983
1920	4,356
1930	7,980
1940	9,680
1950	16,869
1960	33,398
1970	33,695
1980	30,021

FORT COLLINS

1880	1,356
1890	2,011
1900	3,053
1910	8,210
1920	8,755
1930	11,489
1940	12,251
1950	14,937
1960	25,027
1970	43,337
1980	65,092

GOLDEN

1860	1,014
1870	587
1880	2,730
1890	2,383
1900	2,152
1910	2,477
1920	2,135
1930	2,426
1940	3,175
1950	5,238
1960	7,118
1970	9,817
1980	12,237

GRAND JUNCTION

1890	2,030
1900	3,503
1910	7,754
1920	8,665
1930	10,247
1940	12,479
1950	14,504
1960	18,694
1970	20,170
1980	28,144

GREELY

1870	480
1880	1,297
1890	2,395
1900	3,023
1910	8,179
1920	10,958
1930	12,203
1940	15,995
1950	20,354
1960	26,314
1970	38,902
1980	53,006

LAKEWOOD

1960	19,338
1970	92,787
1980	112,860

LITTLETON

1900	738
1910	1,373
1920	1,636
1930	2,019
1940	2,244
1950	3,378
1960	13,670
1970	26,466
1980	28,631

LONGMONT

1880	773
1890	1,543
1900	2,201
1910	4,256
1920	5,848
1930	6,029
1940	7,406
1950	8,099
1960	11,489
1970	23,209
1980	42,942

LOVELAND

1880	236
1890	698
1900	1,091
1910	3,651
1920	5,065
1930	5,506
1940	6,145
1950	6,773
1960	9,734
1970	16,220
1980	30,244

NORTHGLENN

1970	27,785
1980	29,847

PUEBLO

1880	3,217
1890	24,558
1900	28,157
1910	41,747
1920	43,050
1930	50,096
1940	52,162
1950	63,685
1960	91,181
1970	97,774
1980	101,686

STERLING

1890	540
1900	998
1910	3,044
1920	6,415
1930	7,195
1940	7,411
1950	7,534
1960	10,751
1970	10,636
1980	11,385

THORNTON

1960	11,353
1970	13,326
1980	40,343

WESTMINSTER

1920	235
1930	436
1940	534
1950	1,686
1960	13,850
1970	19,512
1980	50,211

WHEAT RIDGE

1960	21,619
1970	29,795
1980	30,293

CORRECTION NOTE

The official 1980 census counts of total population shown in
this report supersede counts issued previously. Corrections
to the figures were made after the counts were provided to
the State for redistricting purposes and released in Advance
Report PHC80-V for this State.

Shown below are corrections to the 1980 census counts of the
total population made after the tabulations for this report
were completed. Any additional corrections made after this
report is printed are available by writing to Data User
Services Division, Customer Services (Corrections), Bureau of
the Census, Washington, D.C. 20233.

The 1980 figures shown in this publication are subject to
change pending the outcome of the various lawsuits dealing
with the census counts.

	1980 population	
	As shown in the tables	Corrected
The State...................	2 889 964	2 889 735
El Paso County:		
Colorado Springs division:		
Colorado Springs city (pt.)...	214 914	214 585
Jefferson County:		
Northeast Jefferson division:		
Edgewater city...............	5 714	4 766
Lakewood city................	112 860	113 808
La Plata County.................	27 424	27 195
Durango division...............	19 084	18 855
Durango city.................	11 426	11 649
Mesa County:		
Grand Junction division:		
Grand Junction city (pt.).....	28 134	27 946
Colorado Springs city (total).....	215 150	214 821
Grand Junction city (total).......	28 144	27 956

Population of County Subdivisions

County Subdivisions	1980	1970
The State	2 889 964	²2 209 596
Adams County¹	245 944	185 789
Brighton division	18 428	...
Brighton city (pt.)¹	12 773	8 309
Thornton city (pt.)¹	—	...
Commerce City division	26 062	
Commerce City city¹	16 234	17 407
Derby (CDP)	8 578	10 206
Thornton city (pt.)¹	8	
East Adams division	3 218	2 233
Bennett town¹	942	613
Strasburg (CDP) (pt.)	670	...
North Aurora division	30 642	
Aurora city (pt.)¹	29 193	27 159
West Adams division	167 594	
Arvada city (pt.)¹	1 229	¹1 663
Broomfield city (pt.)¹	5 467	
Federal Heights city¹	7 846	1 502
Northglenn city¹	29 847	²27 785
Sherrelwood (CDP)	17 629	18 868
Thornton city (pt.)¹	40 335	13 326
Welby (CDP)	9 668	6 875
Westminster city (pt.)¹	32 046	¹9 512
Westminster East (CDP)	6 002	7 576
Alamosa County²	11 799	11 422
Alamosa division	10 836	...
Alamosa city²	6 830	6 985
Alamosa East (CDP)	1 175	1 040
Mosca–Hooper division	963	...
Hooper town	71	80
Arapahoe County³	293 621	162 142
East Arapahoe division	4 737	...
Aurora city (pt.)³	55	
Deer Trail town³	463	374
Strasburg (CDP) (pt.)	335	...
South Aurora division	144 326	...
Aurora city (pt.)³	129 340	47 815
Glendale city³	2 496	765
Southwest Arapahoe division	144 558	...
Bow Mar town (pt.)³	690	659
Castlewood (CDP)	16 413	...
Cherry Hills Village city³	5 127	4 605
Columbine (CDP) (pt.)	1 801	...
Columbine Valley town³	923	481
Englewood city³	30 021	33 695
Greenwood Village city³	5 729	³3 095
Littleton city (pt.)³	28 503	26 466
Sheridan city³	5 377	4 787
Southglenn (CDP)	37 787	22 899
Archuleta County⁴	3 664	2 733
Arboles division	449	342
Pagosa Springs division	3 215	2 391
Pagosa Springs town⁴	1 331	1 360
Baca County⁵	5 419	5 674
Campo division	651	724
Campo town	185	206
Pritchett division	483	...
Pritchett town	183	170
Springfield division	2 383	...
Springfield town⁵	1 657	1 660
Vilas town⁵	118	83
Walsh division	1 902	2 137
Two Buttes town	84	138
Walsh town⁵	884	989
Bent County⁶	5 945	6 493
Las Animas division	4 730	...
Las Animas city⁶	2 818	3 148
McClave division	851	
Purgatoire Valley division	364	388
Boulder County⁷	189 625	131 889
Bald Mountain division	7 500	4 008
Boulder city (pt.)⁷	8	
Jamestown town⁷	223	185
Nederland town⁷	1 212	492
Ward town⁷	129	32
Boulder division	94 305	...
Boulder city (pt.)⁷	76 677	66 870
Gunbarrel (CDP) (pt.)	4 181	...
Louisville city (pt.)⁷	14	...
Superior town (pt.)⁷	208	171
Lafayette–Louisville division	33 455	...
Broomfield city (pt.)⁷	14 514	7 261
Erie town (pt.)⁷	23	7
Lafayette city⁷	8 985	3 498
Louisville city (pt.)⁷	5 579	2 409
Superior town (pt.)⁷	—	...
Longmont division	53 791	31 218
Boulder city (pt.)⁷		...
Gunbarrel (CDP) (pt.)	991	
Longmont city⁷	42 942	23 209
Lyons town⁷	1 137	958
Upper St. Vrain division	574	387

County Subdivisions	1980	1970
Chaffee County⁸	13 227	10 162
Buena Vista division	5 514	3 776
Buena Vista town⁸	2 075	1 962
Salida division	7 713	6 386
Poncha Springs town	321	198
Salida city⁸	4 870	4 355
Cheyenne County⁹	2 153	2 396
Cheyenne Wells division	1 478	1 630
Cheyenne Wells town⁹	950	982
Kit Carson division	675	766
Kit Carson town⁹	278	220
Clear Creek County¹⁰	7 308	4 819
Georgetown division	2 287	1 464
Empire town	423	249
Georgetown town	830	542
Silver Plume town	140	164
Idaho Springs division	5 021	3 355
Idaho Springs city¹⁰	2 077	2 003
Conejos County¹¹	7 794	7 846
Antonito division	2 119	...
Antonito town¹¹	1 103	1 113
Conejos West division	542	...
La Jara division	3 349	...
La Jara town¹¹	858	768
Sanford town	687	638
Manassa division	1 784	...
Manassa town	945	814
Romeo town	308	352
Costilla County¹²	3 071	3 091
Blanca division	900	868
Blanca town	252	212
San Luis division	2 171	2 223
San Luis town¹²	842	781
Crowley County¹³	2 988	3 086
Ordway division	2 538	2 587
Crowley town	192	216
Olney Springs town	253	264
Ordway town¹³	1 135	1 017
Sugar City division	450	499
Sugar City town	306	307
Custer County¹⁴	1 528	1 120
Westcliffe division	1 528	1 120
Silver Cliff town¹⁴	280	126
Westcliffe town¹⁴	324	243
Delta County¹⁵	21 225	15 286
Cedaredge division	5 074	2 992
Cedaredge town¹⁵	1 184	581
Orchard City town¹⁵	1 914	1 163
Delta division	8 897	7 201
Delta city¹⁵	3 931	3 694
Hotchkiss division	4 073	2 684
Crawford town¹⁵	268	171
Hotchkiss town¹⁵	849	507
Paonia division	3 181	2 409
Paonia town¹⁵	1 425	1 161
Denver County¹⁶	492 365	514 678
Denver division	492 365	...
Denver city¹⁶	492 365	514 678
Dolores County¹⁷	1 658	1 641
Dove Creek division	1 565	1 336
Dove Creek town¹⁷	826	619
Rico division	93	305
Rico town¹⁷	76	275
Douglas County¹⁸	25 153	8 407
Castle Rock division	6 829	3 543
Castle Rock town¹⁸	3 921	1 531
Larkspur town¹⁸	141	
Parker division	11 234	3 008
Sedalia division	7 090	1 856
Littleton city (pt.)¹⁸	128	...
Eagle County¹⁹	13 320	7 498
Basalt division	2 571	...
Basalt town (pt.)¹⁹	529	419
Eagle–Gypsum division	3 441	...
Eagle town¹⁹	950	790
Gypsum town¹⁹	743	420
Minturn–Red Cliff division	7 308	...
Avon town¹⁹	640	...
Minturn town¹⁹	1 060	706
Red Cliff town	409	621
Vail town¹⁹	2 261	484
Elbert County²⁰	6 850	3 903
Agate division	369	385
Kiowa division	5 202	2 226
Elizabeth town²⁰	789	493
Kiowa town²⁰	206	235
Simla division	1 279	1 292
Simla town²⁰	494	460
El Paso County²¹	309 424	235 972
Black Forest–Peyton division	10 669	...
Black Forest (CDP)	3 372	...
Calhan town²¹	541	465
Ramah town	119	101

County Subdivisions	1980	1970
El Paso County—Con.		
Black Forest—Peyton division—Con.		
Woodmoor (CDP)	1 490	...
Cheyenne Mountain division	1 122	...
Colorado Springs city (pt.)[21]	180	...
Colorado Springs division	231 242	...
Colorado Springs city (pt.)[21]	214 914	'135 517
Fountain city (pt.)[21]	501	...
Manitou Springs city (pt.)[21]	4 475	4 278
Stratmoor (CDP)	5 519	...
Elsmere division	7 989	...
Cimarron Hills (CDP)	6 597	...
Colorado Springs city (pt.)[21]	–	...
Fountain division	41 991	...
Colorado Springs city (pt.)[21]	4	...
Fort Carson (CDP)	13 219	19 399
Fountain city (pt.)[21]	7 823	3 515
Security–Widefield (CDP)	18 768	15 297
Monument division	11 245	...
Air Force Academy (CDP)	8 655	...
Colorado Springs city (pt.)[21]	5	...
Monument town[21]	690	393
Palmer Lake town[21]	1 130	947
Pikes Peak division	2 534	...
Colorado Springs city (pt.)[21]	47	...
Green Mountain Falls town (pt.)	589	349
Manitou Springs city (pt.)[21]	–	...
Southeastern El Paso division	2 632	...
Colorado Springs city (pt.)[21]	–	...
Fremont County[22]	28 676	21 942
Canon City division	20 651	...
Brookside town[22]	178	173
Canon City city[22]	13 037	9 206
Lincoln Park (CDP)	3 426	2 984
Prospect Heights town	34	38
Williamsburg town (pt.)	–	...
Cotopaxi division	1 334	723
Florence division	4 346	4 117
Coal Creek town	190	225
Florence city[22]	2 987	2 846
Rockvale town	338	359
Williamsburg town (pt.)	72	75
Penrose–Portland division	2 345	1 347
Garfield County[23]	22 514	14 821
Glenwood Springs division	12 394	8 729
Carbondale town[23]	2 084	726
Glenwood Springs city[23]	4 637	4 106
Grand Valley division	956	819
Grand Valley town[23]	338	270
New Castle division	3 943	1 976
New Castle town[23]	563	499
Silt town[23]	923	434
Rifle division	5 221	3 297
Rifle city[23]	3 215	2 150
Gilpin County	2 441	1 272
Central City division	2 441	1 272
Black Hawk town	232	217
Central City town	329	228
Grand County[24]	7 475	4 107
Granby division	5 325	2 902
Fraser town[24]	470	221
Granby town[24]	963	554
Grand Lake town[24]	382	189
Hot Sulphur Springs town[24]	405	220
Winter Park town[24]	480	...
Kremmling division	2 150	1 205
Kremmling town[24]	1 296	764
Gunnison County[25]	10 689	7 578
Crested Butte division	1 562	463
Crested Butte town	959	372
Mount Crested Butte town[25]	272	...
Gunnison division	8 608	6 735
Gunnison city[25]	5 785	4 613
Pitkin town	59	44
Sapinero division	206	116
Somerset division	313	264
Marble town[25]	30	'13
Hinsdale County[26]	408	202
Lake City division	408	202
Lake City town[26]	206	91
Huerfano County[27]	6 440	6 590
Gardner division	587	453
La Veta division	1 132	1 015
La Veta town[27]	611	589
Walsenburg division	4 721	5 122
Walsenburg city[27]	3 945	4 329
Jackson County[28]	1 863	1 811
Walden division	1 863	1 811
Walden town[28]	947	907
Jefferson County[29]	371 753	'235 368
Central Jefferson division	15 818	...
Evergreen (CDP)	6 376	2 321
Morrison town (pt.)	405	...
Golden division	20 171	...

County Subdivisions	1980	1970
Jefferson County—Con.		
Golden division—Con.		
Applewood (CDP) (pt.)	319	8 214
Golden city (pt.)[29]	11 314	9 817
Morrison town (pt.)	73	439
Northeast Jefferson division	326 674	...
Applewood (CDP) (pt.)	11 721	...
Arvada city (pt.)[29]	83 347	'48 181
Bow Mar town (pt.)	240	286
Broomfield city (pt.)[29]	749	–
Columbine (CDP) (pt.)	21 609	...
Edgewater city	5 714	'4 910
Golden city (pt.)[29]	923	...
Ken Caryl (CDP)	10 661	'17
Lakeside town	19	'17
Lakewood city[29]	112 860	'92 743
Mountain View town	584	706
Westminster city (pt.)[29]	18 165	...
Wheat Ridge[29]	30 293	'29 778
South Jefferson division	9 090	...
Columbine (CDP) (pt.)	113	...
Kiowa County[30]	1 936	2 029
Eads division	1 197	1 128
Eads town[30]	878	795
Haswell division	198	269
Haswell town	126	135
Sheridan Lake division	541	632
Sheridan Lake town	87	86
Kit Carson County[31]	7 599	7 530
Burlington division	4 585	...
Bethune town	149	99
Burlington city[31]	3 107	2 828
Flagler division	1 379	...
Flagler town	550	615
Seibert town	180	192
Stratton division	1 635	...
Stratton town[31]	705	790
Vona town	94	114
Lake County[32]	8 830	8 282
Leadville division	7 705	...
Leadville city	3 879	4 314
Leadville North (CDP)	1 851	1 717
Leadville North division	1 125	...
La Plata County[33]	27 424	19 199
Bayfield division	3 009	...
Bayfield town[33]	724	320
Durango division	19 084	...
Durango city[33]	11 426	10 333
Durango Southwest division	2 228	...
Ignacio division	3 103	2 362
Ignacio town[33]	667	613
Larimer County[34]	149 184	89 900
Berthoud division	6 397	3 144
Berthoud town[34]	2 362	1 446
Estes Park division	6 733	3 554
Estes Park town[34]	2 703	1 616
Fort Collins division	86 299	...
Fort Collins city[34]	65 092	43 337
Livermore division	1 342	764
Loveland division	42 627	23 039
Loveland city[34]	30 244	16 220
Timnath–Wellington division	5 786	...
Timnath town[34]	185	177
Wellington town[34]	1 215	691
Las Animas County[35]	14 897	15 744
Aguilar division	1 016	1 089
Aguilar town	624	699
Branson division	239	234
Branson town	73	70
Kim division	461	582
Kim town[35]	100	...
Model division	191	...
Trinidad division	11 869	...
Cokedale town	90	101
Starkville town	127	166
Trinidad city[35]	9 663	9 901
Weston division	1 121	1 033
Lincoln County[36]	4 663	4 836
Arriba division	492	...
Arriba town (pt.)[36]	236	254
Hugo division	1 127	...
Arriba town (pt.)[36]	–	...
Hugo town	776	759
Karval division	648	692
Limon division	2 396	...
Genoa town	165	161
Limon town[36]	1 805	1 814
Logan County[37]	19 800	18 852
Crook division	702	806
Crook town	177	199
Fleming division	1 839	1 485
Fleming town[37]	388	349
Sterling city (pt.)[37]	129	...
Merino division	1 082	1 007
Merino town[37]	255	260
Peetz division	575	590

County Subdivisions	1980	1970
Logan County—Con.		
Peetz division—Con.		
Peetz town[37]	220	186
Sterling division	15 602	14 964
Iliff town	218	193
Sterling city (pt.)[37]	11 256	10 636
Mesa County[38]	81 530	54 374
Clifton division	13 682	...
Clifton (CDP)	5 223	...
Orchard Mesa (CDP) (pt.)	191	(NA)
Palisade town[38]	1 551	874
Collbran division	1 862	1 428
Collbran town[38]	344	225
De Beque division	449	306
De Beque town[38]	279	155
Fruita division	8 892	5 837
Fruita town[38]	2 810	1 822
Grand Junction city (pt.)[38]	10	...
Glade Park—Gateway division	1 250	817
Grand Junction division	54 212	...
Grand Junction city (pt.)[38]	28 134	20 170
Orchard Mesa (CDP) (pt.)	4 685	(NA)
Whitewater—Kahnah Creek division	1 183	605
Mineral County	804	786
Creede division	804	786
Creede town	610	653
Moffat County[39]	13 133	6 525
Artesia division	410	360
Dinosaur town	313	247
Craig division	12 257	5 732
Craig city[39]	8 133	4 205
Maybell—Powder Wash division	466	433
Montezuma County[40]	16 510	12 952
Cortez division	11 227	...
Cortez city[40]	7 095	6 032
Dolores division	1 865	1 701
Dolores town[40]	802	820
Mancos division	1 785	...
Mancos town	870	709
Pleasant View division	495	...
Ute Mountain division	1 138	...
Montrose County[41]	24 352	18 366
Montrose division	16 116	11 353
Montrose city[41]	8 722	6 496
Nucla division	3 952	3 960
Naturita town[41]	819	820
Nucla town	1 027	949
Olathe division	4 284	3 053
Olathe town[41]	1 262	756
Morgan County[42]	22 513	20 105
Brush division	6 790	...
Brush city[42]	4 082	3 377
Hillrose town[42]	213	121
Fort Morgan division	13 280	...
Fort Morgan city[42]	8 768	7 594
Log Lane Village town[42]	709	329
Weldona division	587	...
Wiggins division	1 856	1 778
Wiggins town[42]	531	...
Otero County[43]	22 567	23 523
Cheraw division	2 333	2 585
Cheraw town[43]	233	129
North La Junta (CDP)	1 076	1 249
Fowler division	1 807	1 951
Fowler town[43]	1 227	1 241
La Junta division	10 475	10 603
La Junta city[43]	8 338	8 205
Swink town[43]	668	381
Manzanola division	1 173	1 115
Manzanola town	459	451
Rocky Ford division	6 610	7 075
Rocky Ford city[43]	4 804	4 859
Timpas division	169	194
Ouray County[44]	1 925	1 546
Ouray division	1 925	1 546
Ouray city	684	741
Ridgway town[44]	369	262
Park County[45]	5 333	2 185
Fairplay division	4 799	1 859
Alma town	132	73
Fairplay town[45]	421	419
Lake George division	534	326
Phillips County[46]	4 542	4 131
Haxtun division	1 645	1 610
Haxtun town[46]	1 014	899
Paoli town[46]	81	52
Holyoke division	2 897	2 521
Holyoke town[46]	2 092	1 640
Pitkin County[47]	10 338	6 185
Aspen division	6 457	...
Aspen city[47]	3 678	2 437
Snowmass division	3 881	...
Basalt town (pt.)[47]	-	...

County Subdivisions	1980	1970
Pitkin County—Con.		
Snowmass division—Con.		
Snowmass Village town[47]	999	...
Prowers County[48]	13 070	13 258
Granada division	1 174	...
Granada town	557	551
Holly division	1 609	...
Hartman town	122	129
Holly town	969	993
Lamar division	9 793	...
Lamar city[48]	7 713	7 797
Wiley town[48]	425	357
Two Butte Creek division	494	...
Pueblo County[49]	125 972	118 238
Avondale division	2 655	2 688
Colorado City—Rye division	2 702	...
Rye town[49]	232	207
Huerfano Valley division	750	624
Northeast Pueblo division	949	1 115
Boone town[49]	431	448
Pueblo division	106 998	...
Pueblo city (pt.)[49]	101 686	97 774
Pueblo West division	2 821	...
St. Charles Mesa division	9 097	...
Pueblo city (pt.)[49]	-	...
Rio Blanco County[50]	6 255	4 842
Meeker division	3 642	2 472
Meeker town[50]	2 356	1 597
Rangely division	2 613	2 370
Rangely town[50]	2 113	1 591
Rio Grande County[51]	10 511	10 494
Del Norte division	3 320	2 897
Del Norte town[51]	1 709	1 569
Monte Vista division	5 913	6 102
Monte Vista city[51]	3 902	3 909
Sargent division	1 278	1 495
Center town (pt.)[51]	-	-
Routt County[52]	13 404	6 592
Hayden division	2 386	...
Hayden town[52]	1 720	763
Oak Creek division	2 005	1 010
Oak Creek town[52]	929	492
Steamboat Springs division	8 175	...
Steamboat Springs city[52]	5 098	2 340
Yampa division	838	644
Yampa town	472	286
Saguache County[53]	3 935	3 827
Center division	2 349	...
Center town (pt.)[53]	1 630	1 470
Cochetopa division	88	111
Saguache division	1 498	...
Bonanza City town[53]	8	10
Crestone town	54	34
Moffat town	105	98
Saguache town	656	642
San Juan County[54]	833	831
Silverton division	833	831
Silverton town[54]	794	797
San Miguel County[55]	3 192	1 949
Gladel division	330	328
Norwood division	1 145	767
Norwood town[55]	478	408
Telluride division	1 717	854
Ophir town	38	6
Sawpit town	41	26
Telluride town[55]	1 047	553
Sedgwick County[56]	3 266	3 405
Julesburg division	2 681	2 810
Julesburg town	1 528	1 578
Ovid town	439	463
Sedgwick town[56]	258	208
Table Land division	585	595
Summit County[57]	8 848	2 665
Breckenridge division	4 979	...
Blue River town[57]	230	8
Breckenridge town[57]	818	548
Frisco town (pt.)[57]	1 221	471
Silverthorne division	3 869	...
Dillon town[57]	337	182
Frisco town (pt.)[57]	-	...
Silverthorne town[57]	989	400
Teller County[58]	8 034	3 316
Cripple Creek division	1 221	791
Cripple Creek city	655	425
Victor city[58]	265	258
Divide division	6 813	2 525
Green Mountain Falls town (pt.)	18	10
Woodland Park city[58]	2 634	1 022
Washington County[59]	5 304	5 550
Akron division	2 729	2 808
Akron town[59]	1 716	1 775
Cope division	723	816
Linden division	660	770
Otis division	1 192	1 156

County Subdivisions

County Subdivisions	1980	1970
Washington County—Con.		
Otis division—Con.		
Otis town[59]	534	521
Weld County[60]	123 438	89 297
Ault division	4 291	3 747
Ault town[60]	1 056	841
Nunn town	295	269
Pierce town[60]	878	452
Erie—Frederick division	9 701	...
Dacono town	2 321	360
Erie town (pt.)[60]	1 231	1 083
Firestone town[60]	1 204	570
Frederick town[60]	855	696
Fort Lupton division	7 813	...
Brighton city (pt.)[60]	—	...
Fort Lupton city[60]	4 251	2 489
Greeley division	69 726	...
Eaton town[60]	1 932	1 389
Evans city[60]	5 063	2 570
Garden City town[60]	85	142
Greeley city[60]	53 006	38 902
Rosedale town	38	66
Grover division	590	555
Grover town	158	121
Johnstown—Milliken division	7 025	...
Johnstown town[60]	1 535	1 191
Mead town	356	195
Milliken town[60]	1 506	702
Keenesburg—Hudson division	5 803	...
Hudson town	698	518
Keenesburg town[60]	541	427
Lochbuie town[60]	895	...
Kersey—Gill division	3 822	...
Kersey town[60]	913	474
La Salle—Gilcrest division	4 622	...
Gilcrest town[60]	1 025	382
La Salle town[60]	1 929	1 227
Platteville division	3 123	...
Platteville town[60]	1 662	683
Raymer division	725	...
Keota town	4	6
Raymer town	80	68
Windsor division	6 197	...
Severance town	102	59
Windsor town[60]	4 277	1 564
Yuma County[61]	9 682	8 544
South Divide division	1 271	1 273
Wray division	4 010	...
Wray city[61]	2 131	1 953
Yuma division	4 401	...
Eckley town	262	193
Yuma town	2 824	2 259

CONNECTICUT

Connecticut derives its name from that of the Connecticut River, the pure Indian form of the name, *Quinnitukut,* meaning "long river."

The first European to visit the region now constituting Connecticut was probably Adrian Block, a Dutch navigator, who in 1614 discovered and explored the Connecticut River. The English claimed it by virtue of the discoveries of the Cabots of 1497 and more particularly of 1498. The present area of Connecticut was included in the grants conveyed by James I of England to the Plymouth Company in 1606 and 1620.

In 1633 some English settlers from the Plymouth colony sailed up the Connecticut River and erected a trading house on the present site of Windsor. They found that the Dutch had already constructed a rude earthwork at a point where Hartford now stands, a post which men of the nation named held for the next 20 years. The first permanent settlements, however, were made during the period 1634-1636 at Wethersfield, Windsor, and Hartford by the migration of a large majority of the inhabitants of three Massachusetts towns, Dorchester, Watertown, and Newtown, who moved to Connecticut on account of their dissatisfaction with the theocratic government of Massachusetts. A constitution for the government of these colonies was approved by general vote of the people in 1639.

In July, 1635, John Winthrop, Jr., was made governor of the "River Connecticut." In 1635 a party of 20 men was sent out by Winthrop and took possession of the region at the mouth of the Connecticut River. This tract, of between 60 and 80 square miles, which they called Saybrook, remained independent of the other colonies until 1644, when it was sold to Connecticut by its agent, Col. Fenwick, on his own authority.

New Haven was settled in 1638 by a group mainly composed of Londoners who had the previous year come to Boston under the leadership of John Davenport.

In 1662 the colony of Connecticut obtained from the King a charter, which was really a royal confirmation of the constitution of 1639. By this charter Connecticut was defined as bounded on the north by Massachusetts and as extending from Narragansett Bay to the Pacific Ocean. Accordingly the colony of New Haven, in spite of its vehement opposition, was incorporated into the colony of Connecticut.

With the exception of the brief period of the Andros regime, the charter of 1662 remained the fundamental law of the colony and later of the state until 1818, when the present constitution was adopted. Boundary disputes with Rhode Island on the east and New York on the west were finally adjusted by the adoption of what are practically the present boundary lines, the former in 1727-28, the latter in 1683.

In 1786 Connecticut ceded to the Federal Government her claims to western lands which were based on the charter of 1662, but the state was given title to the region in northeastern Ohio known as the Western Reserve. In 1792 part of this tract was devoted to the relief of persons burned out or plundered by the British; the rest of it was sold—the last of it being disposed of in 1825.

Connecticut was one of the original thirteen states.

COUNTY LOCATION INDEX

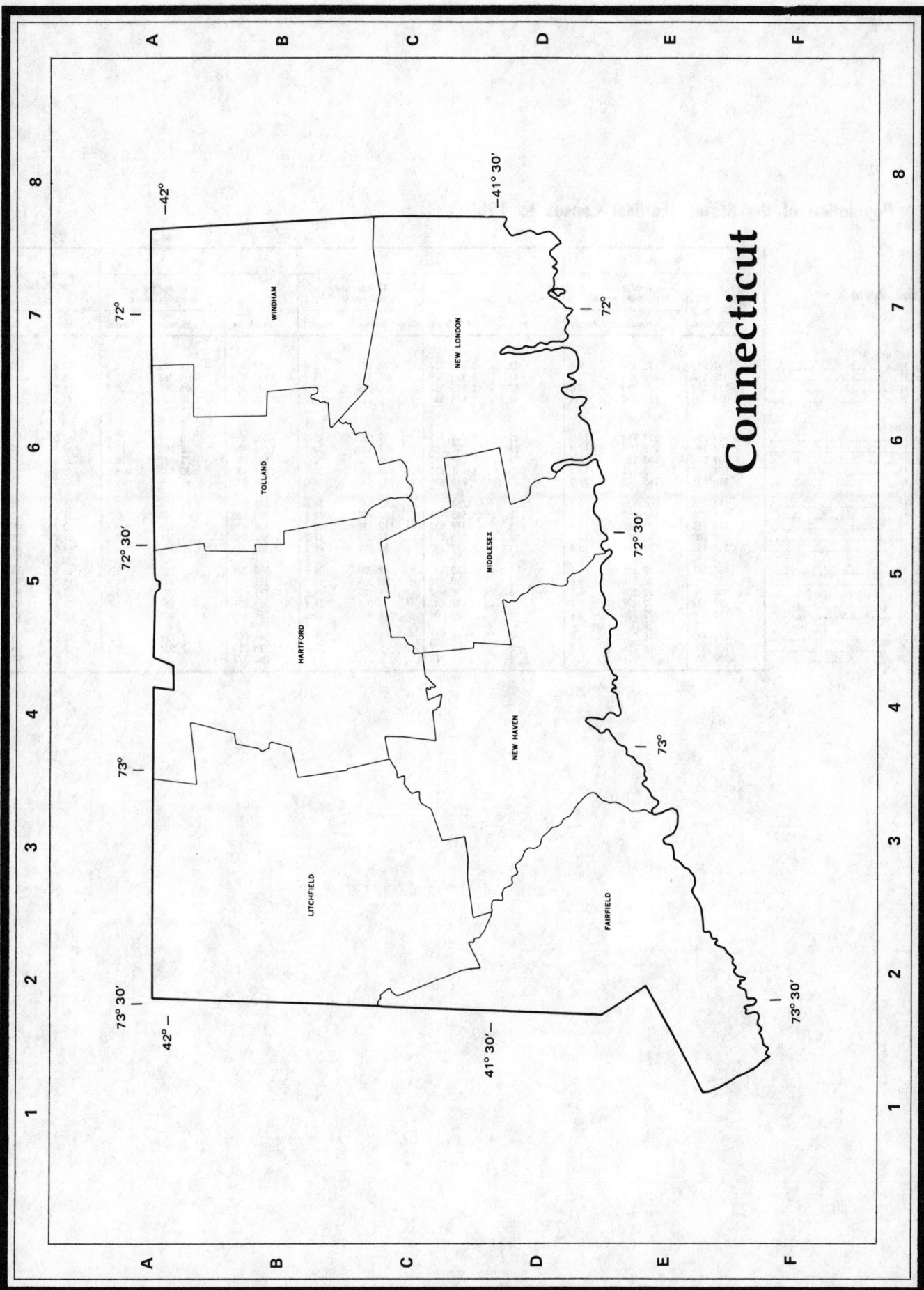

Connecticut

Population of the State: Earliest Census to 1980

Urban and Rural

	The State			Urban				Rural				Percent of total population	
	Total population	Change from preceding census		Places of 2,500 or more	Population	Change from preceding census		Population	Change from preceding census			Urban	Rural
		Number	Percent			Number	Percent		Number	Percent			
Current urban definition:													
1980 (Apr. 1)	3 107 576	75 359	2.5	75	2 449 774	73 695	3.1	657 802	2 172	0.3		78.8	21.2
1970 (Apr. 1)	'3 032 217	496 983	19.6	46	2 376 079	390 512	19.7	655 630	105 963	19.3		78.4	21.6
1960 (Apr. 1)	2 535 234	527 954	26.3	62	1 985 567	426 925	27.4	549 667	101 029	22.5		78.3	21.7
1950 (Apr. 1)	2 007 280	298 038	17.4	41	1 558 642	...	...	448 638	...	...		77.6	22.4
Previous urban definition:													
1960 (Apr. 1)	2 535 234	527 954	26.3	42	1 749 569	359 065	25.8	785 665	168 889	27.4		69.0	31.0
1950 (Apr. 1)	2 007 280	298 038	17.4	36	1 390 504	232 342	20.1	616 776	65 696	11.9		69.3	30.7
1940 (Apr. 1)	1 709 242	102 339	6.4	32	1 158 162	26 392	2.3	551 080	75 947	16.0		67.8	32.2
1930 (Apr. 1)	1 606 903	226 272	16.4	33	1 131 770	195 431	20.9	475 133	30 841	6.9		70.4	29.6
1920 (Jan. 1)	1 380 631	265 875	23.9	30	936 339	204 542	28.0	444 292	61 333	16.0		67.8	32.2
1910 (Apr. 15)	1 114 756	206 336	22.7	32	731 797	188 042	34.6	382 959	18 294	5.0		65.6	34.4
1900 (June 1)	908 420	162 162	21.7	28	543 755	163 902	43.1	364 665	-1 740	-0.5		59.9	40.1
1890 (June 1)	746 258	123 558	19.8	21	379 853	119 135	45.7	366 405	4 423	1.2		50.9	49.1
1880 (June 1)	622 700	85 246	15.9	20	260 718	83 565	47.2	361 982	1 681	0.5		41.9	58.1
1870 (June 1)	537 454	77 307	16.8	11	177 153	55 032	45.1	360 301	22 275	6.6		33.0	67.0
1860 (June 1)	460 147	89 355	24.1	8	122 121	62 800	105.9	338 026	26 555	8.5		26.5	73.5
1850 (June 1)	370 792	60 814	19.6	6	59 321	20 369	52.3	311 471	40 445	14.9		16.0	84.0
1840 (June 1)	309 978	12 303	4.1	6	38 952	11 105	39.9	271 026	1 198	0.4		12.6	87.4
1830 (June 1)	297 675	22 427	8.1	5	27 847	7 043	33.9	269 828	15 384	6.0		9.4	90.6
1820 (Aug. 7)	275 248	13 306	5.1	5	20 804	4 863	30.5	254 444	8 443	3.4		7.6	92.4
1810 (Aug. 6)	261 942	10 940	4.4	4	15 941	3 219	25.3	246 001	7 721	3.2		6.1	93.9
1800 (Aug. 4)	251 002	13 056	5.5	3	12 722	5 552	77.4	238 280	7 504	3.3		5.1	94.9
1790 (Aug. 2)	237 946	...	...	2	7 170	...	...	230 776	...	...		3.0	97.0

FAIRFIELD

1790	36,250
1800	38,208
1810	40,950
1820	42,739
1830	47,010
1840	49,917
1850	59,775
1860	77,476
1870	95,276
1880	112,042
1890	150,081
1900	184,203
1910	245,322
1920	320,936
1930	386,702
1940	418,384
1950	504,342
1960	653,589
1970	792,814
1980	807,143

HARTFORD

1790	38,029
1800	42,147
1810	44,733
1820	47,264
1830	51,131
1840	55,629
1850	69,967
1860	89,962
1870	109,007
1880	125,382
1890	147,180
1900	195,480
1910	250,182
1920	336,027
1930	421,097
1940	450,189
1950	539,661
1960	689,555
1970	816,737
1980	807,766

LITCHFIELD

1790	38,755
1800	41,214
1810	41,375
1820	41,267
1830	42,858
1840	40,448
1850	45,253
1860	47,318
1870	48,727
1880	52,044
1890	53,542
1900	63,672
1910	70,260
1920	76,262
1930	82,556
1940	87,041
1950	98,872
1960	119,856
1970	144,091
1980	156,769

MIDDLESEX

1790	18,855
1800	19,847
1810	20,723
1820	22,405
1830	24,844
1840	24,879
1850	27,216
1860	30,859
1870	36,099
1880	35,589
1890	39,524
1900	41,760
1910	45,637
1920	47,550
1930	51,388
1940	55,999
1950	67,332
1960	88,865
1970	115,018
1980	129,017

NEW HAVEN

1790	30,830
1800	32,162
1810	37,064
1820	39,616
1830	43,847
1840	48,582
1850	65,588
1860	97,345
1870	121,257
1880	156,523
1890	209,058
1900	269,163
1910	337,282
1920	415,214
1930	463,449
1940	484,316
1950	545,784
1960	660,315
1970	744,948
1980	761,337

NEW LONDON

1790	33,200
1800	34,883
1810	34,707
1820	35,943
1830	42,201
1840	44,463
1850	51,821
1860	61,731
1870	66,570
1880	73,152
1890	76,634
1900	82,758
1910	91,253
1920	104,611
1930	118,966
1940	125,224
1950	144,821
1960	185,745
1970	230,654
1980	238,409

TOLLAND

1790	13,106
1800	14,319
1810	13,779
1820	14,330
1830	18,702
1840	17,980
1850	20,091
1860	21,177
1870	22,000
1880	24,112
1890	25,081
1900	24,523
1910	26,459
1920	27,216
1930	28,659
1940	31,866
1950	44,709
1960	68,737
1970	103,440
1980	114,823

WINDHAM

1790	28,921
1800	28,222
1810	28,611
1820	31,684
1830	27,082
1840	28,080
1850	31,081
1860	34,279
1870	38,518
1880	43,856
1890	45,158
1900	46,861
1910	48,361
1920	52,815
1930	54,086
1940	56,223
1950	61,759
1960	68,572
1970	84,515
1980	92,312

ANSONIA

1870	2,749
1880	3,855
1900	12,681
1910	15,152
1920	17,643
1930	19,898
1940	19,210
1950	18,706
1960	19,819
1970	21,160
1980	19,039

BRIDGEPORT

1840	3,294
1850	7,560
1860	13,299
1870	18,969
1880	27,643
1890	48,866
1900	70,966
1910	102,054
1920	143,555
1930	146,716
1940	147,121
1950	158,709
1960	156,748
1970	156,542
1980	142,546

BRISTOL

1900	6,268
1910	9,527
1920	20,620
1930	28,451
1940	30,167
1950	35,961
1960	45,499
1970	55,487
1980	57,370

DANBURY

1860	4,482
1870	6,542
1890	16,552
1900	16,537
1910	20,234
1920	18,943
1930	22,261
1940	22,339
1950	22,067
1960	22,928
1970	50,781
1980	60,470

DERBY

1880	3,026
1890	4,413
1900	7,930
1910	8,991
1920	11,238
1930	10,788
1940	10,287
1950	10,259
1960	12,132
1970	12,599
1980	12,346

GROTON

1850	2,001
1860	2,174
1870	5,124
1880	5,128
1890	5,539
1900	(NA)
1910	1,895
1920	4,236
1930	4,122
1940	4,719
1950	7,036
1960	10,111
1970	8,933
1980	10,086

HARTFORD

1790	2,683
1800	3,523
1810	3,955
1820	4,726
1830	7,074
1840	9,468
1850	17,966
1860	29,152
1870	37,180
1880	42,015
1890	53,230
1900	79,850
1910	98,915
1920	138,036
1930	164,072
1940	166,267
1950	177,397
1960	162,178
1970	158,017
1980	136,392

MERIDEN

1870	8,893
1880	15,540
1890	21,652
1900	24,296
1910	27,265
1920	29,867
1930	38,481
1940	39,494
1950	44,088
1960	51,850
1970	55,959
1980	57,118

MIDDLETOWN

1810	2,014
1820	2,618
1840	3,511
1850	4,211
1860	5,182
1870	6,923
1880	6,826
1890	9,013
1900	9,589
1910	11,851
1920	13,638
1930	24,554
1940	26,495
1950	29,711
1960	33,250
1970	36,924
1980	39,040

MILFORD

1790	2,098
1800	2,417
1810	2,674
1820	2,785
1830	2,256
1840	2,455
1850	2,465
1860	2,828
1870	3,405
1880	3,347
1890	3,811
1900	3,783
1910	4,366
1920	10,193
1930	12,660
1940	16,439
1950	26,870
1960	41,662
1970	50,858
1980	49,101

NAUGATUCK

1900	10,541
1910	12,722
1920	15,051
1930	14,315
1940	15,388
1950	17,455
1960	19,511
1970	23,034
1980	26,456

NEW BRITAIN

1870	8,002
1880	11,800
1890	16,519
1900	25,998
1910	43,916
1920	59,316
1930	68,128
1940	68,685
1950	73,726
1960	82,201
1970	83,411
1980	73,840

NEW HAVEN

1790	4,487
1800	4,049
1810	5,772
1820	7,147
1830	10,180
1840	12,960
1850	20,345
1860	39,267
1870	50,840
1880	62,882
1890	81,298
1900	108,027
1910	133,605
1920	162,537
1930	162,655
1940	160,605
1950	164,443
1960	152,048
1970	137,707
1980	126,109

NEW LONDON

1800	5,150
1810	3,238
1820	3,330
1830	4,335
1840	5,519
1850	8,991
1860	10,115
1870	9,576
1880	10,537
1890	13,757
1900	17,548
1910	19,659
1920	25,668
1930	29,640
1940	30,456
1950	30,551
1960	34,182
1970	31,630
1980	28,842

NORWALK

1870	5,308
1900	6,125
1910	6,954
1920	27,743
1930	36,019
1940	39,849
1950	49,460
1960	67,775
1970	79,288
1980	77,767

NORWICH

1810	2,976
1820	2,983
1830	3,135
1840	4,200
1850	6,139
1860	14,048
1870	16,653
1880	15,122
1890	16,156
1900	17,251
1910	20,367
1920	22,304
1930	23,021
1940	23,652
1950	23,429
1960	38,506
1970	41,739
1980	38,074

SHELTON

1890	1,952
1900	2,837
1910	4,807
1920	9,475
1930	10,133
1940	10,971
1950	12,694
1960	18,190
1970	27,165
1980	31,314

STAMFORD

1880	2,540
1900	15,997
1910	25,138
1920	35,096
1930	46,346
1940	47,938
1950	74,293
1960	92,713
1970	108,798
1980	102,453

TORRINGTON

1890	4,283
1900	8,360
1910	15,483
1920	20,623
1930	26,040
1940	26,988
1950	27,820
1960	30,045
1970	31,952
1980	30,987

WATERBURY

1860	10,004
1870	10,826
1880	17,806
1890	28,646
1900	45,859
1910	73,141
1920	91,175
1930	99,902
1940	99,314
1950	104,477
1960	107,310
1970	108,033
1980	103,266

WEST HAVEN

1940	30,021
1950	32,010
1960	43,002
1970	52,851
1980	53,184

WILLIMANTIC

1880	6,608
1890	8,648
1900	8,937
1910	11,230
1920	12,330
1930	12,102
1940	12,101
1950	13,586
1960	13,881
1970	14,402
1980	14,652

County Subdivisions	1980	1970
The State	3 107 576	ʳ3 032 217
Fairfield County[1]	807 143	792 814
Bethel town	16 004	10 945
Bethel (CDP)	8 755	...
Bridgeport town	142 546	156 542
Bridgeport city	142 546	156 542
Brookfield town	12 872	9 688
Danbury town	60 470	50 781
Danbury city	60 470	50 781
Darien town	18 892	ʳ20 336
Darien (CDP)	18 892	...
Easton town	5 962	4 885
Fairfield town	54 849	56 487
Stratfield–Brooklawn (CDP)	8 890	...
Greenwich town	59 578	59 755
Monroe town	14 010	12 047
New Canaan town	17 931	ʳ17 451
New Fairfield town	11 260	6 991
Newtown town	19 107	16 942
Newtown borough[1]	2 022	1 963
Norwalk town	77 767	ʳ79 288
Norwalk city	77 767	ʳ79 288
Redding town	7 272	5 590
Georgetown (CDP) (pt.)	362	...
Ridgefield town	20 120	18 188
Ridgefield (CDP)	6 066	5 878
Shelton town	31 314	27 165
Shelton city	31 314	27 165
Sherman town	2 281	1 459
Stamford town	102 453	108 798
Stamford city	102 453	108 798
Stratford town	50 541	49 775
Stratford (CDP)	50 541	...
Trumbull town	32 989	31 394
Trumbull (CDP)	32 989	...
Weston town	8 284	7 417
Georgetown (CDP) (pt.)	194	154
Westport town	25 290	ʳ27 318
Westport (CDP)	25 290	...
Wilton town	15 351	13 572
Georgetown (CDP) (pt.)	1 278	947
Hartford County[2]	807 766	816 737
Avon town	11 201	8 352
Avon (CDP)	1 434	...
Berlin town	15 121	14 149
Kensington (CDP)	7 502	...
Bloomfield town	18 608	18 301
Bristol town	57 370	55 487
Bristol city	57 370	55 487
Burlington town	5 660	4 070
Canton town	7 635	6 868
Canton (CDP)	1 680	...
Collinsville (CDP)	2 555	2 897
East Granby town	4 102	3 532
East Hartford town[2]	52 563	57 583
East Hartford (CDP)	52 563	...
East Windsor town	8 925	8 513
Enfield town	42 695	46 189
Enfield (CDP)	8 151	...
Hazardville (CDP)	5 436	...
Sherwood Manor (CDP)	6 303	...
Southwood Acres (CDP)	9 779	...
Farmington town	16 407	14 390
Glastonbury town	24 327	20 651
Glastonbury (CDP)	7 049	...
Granby town	7 956	6 150
Granby (CDP)	1 912	...
Hartford town[2]	136 392	158 017
Hartford city[2]	136 392	158 017
Hartland town	1 416	1 303
Manchester town	49 761	47 994
Manchester (CDP)	31 058	...
Marlborough town	4 746	2 991
Marlborough (CDP)	1 039	...
New Britain town	73 840	83 441
New Britain city	73 840	83 441
Newington town	28 841	26 037
Newington (CDP)	28 841	...
Plainville town	16 401	16 733
Rocky Hill town	14 559	11 103
Simsbury town	21 161	17 475
Simsbury (CDP)	5 488	4 994
Tariffville (CDP)	1 324	1 337
Weatogue (CDP)	2 249	2 396
West Simsbury (CDP)	2 140	1 419
Southington town	36 879	30 946
South Windsor town[2]	17 198	15 553
Suffield town	9 294	8 634
Suffield (CDP)	1 122	...
West Hartford town	61 301	68 031
West Hartford (CDP)	61 301	...
Wethersfield town	26 013	26 662
Wethersfield (CDP)	26 013	...
Windsor town	25 204	22 502
Windsor (CDP)	17 517	...
Windsor Locks town	12 190	15 080

County Subdivisions	1980	1970
Hartford County—Con.		
Windsor Locks town—Con.		
Windsor Locks (CDP)	12 190	...
Litchfield County[3]	156 769	144 091
Barkhamsted town	2 935	2 066
Bethlehem town	2 573	1 923
Bethlehem (CDP)	1 762	...
Bridgewater town	1 563	1 277
Canaan town	1 002	931
Colebrook town	1 221	1 020
Cornwall town	1 288	1 177
Goshen town	1 706	1 351
Harwinton town	4 889	4 318
Harwinton (CDP)	3 293	...
Kent town	2 505	1 990
Litchfield town	7 605	7 399
Bantam borough	860	881
Litchfield borough	1 489	1 559
Morris town	1 899	1 609
New Hartford town	4 884	3 970
New Hartford (CDP)	1 310	1 076
New Milford town	19 420	14 601
New Milford (CDP)	5 186	4 606
Norfolk town	2 156	2 073
North Canaan town	3 185	3 045
Canaan (CDP)	1 160	1 083
Plymouth town	10 732	10 321
Terryville (CDP)	5 234	...
Roxbury town	1 468	1 238
Salisbury town	3 896	3 573
Sharon town	2 623	2 491
Thomaston town	6 276	6 233
Torrington town	30 987	31 952
Torrington city	30 987	31 952
Warren town	1 027	827
Washington town	3 657	3 121
New Preston (CDP)	1 209	...
Watertown town	19 489	18 610
Oakville (CDP)	8 737	...
Winchester town[3]	10 841	11 106
Winsted (CDP)	8 092	...
Woodbury town	6 942	5 869
Woodbury (CDP)	1 290	1 342
Middlesex County	129 017	ʳ115 018
Chester town	3 068	2 982
Chester (CDP)	1 388	1 569
Clinton town	11 195	10 267
Clinton (CDP)	3 168	5 957
Cromwell town	10 265	7 400
Deep River town	3 994	3 690
Deep River (CDP)	2 495	2 333
Durham town	5 143	4 489
Durham (CDP)	2 641	...
East Haddam town	5 621	ʳ4 676
Moodus (CDP)	1 179	1 352
East Hampton town	8 572	7 078
East Hampton (CDP)	2 152	1 982
Lake Pocotopaug (CDP)	2 137	1 515
Essex town	5 078	4 911
Essex (CDP)	2 501	2 473
Haddam town	6 383	4 934
Higganum (CDP)	1 660	...
Killingworth town	3 976	2 435
Middlefield town	3 796	4 132
Middletown town	39 040	36 924
Middletown city	39 040	36 924
Old Saybrook town	9 287	8 468
Fenwick borough	41	45
Old Saybrook (CDP)	1 857	2 281
Saybrook Manor (CDP)	1 140	...
Portland town	8 383	8 812
Portland (CDP)	5 914	...
Westbrook town	5 216	3 820
Westbrook (CDP)	2 035	1 509
New Haven County[4]	761 337	744 948
Ansonia town	19 039	21 160
Ansonia city	19 039	21 160
Beacon Falls town	3 995	3 546
Bethany town	4 330	3 857
Branford town[4]	23 363	20 444
Branford (CDP)	5 438	2 080
Cheshire town	21 788	19 051
Cheshire (CDP)	5 722	...
Derby town	12 346	12 599
Derby city	12 346	12 599
East Haven town	25 028	25 120
East Haven (CDP)	25 028	...
Guilford town	17 375	12 033
Guilford (CDP)	2 555	3 632
Hamden town	51 071	49 357
Madison town	14 031	9 768
Madison (CDP)	2 069	4 310
Meriden town	57 118	55 959
Meriden city	57 118	55 959
Middlebury town	5 995	5 542
Milford town[4]	50 898	50 858

County Subdivisions	1980	1970
New Haven County—Con.		
Milford town—Con.		
Milford city*	49 101	50 858
Woodmont borough⁴	1 797	¹2 114
Naugatuck town	26 456	23 034
Naugatuck borough	26 456	23 034
New Haven town	126 109	137 707
New Haven city	126 109	137 707
North Branford town	11 554	10 778
North Haven town	22 080	22 194
North Haven (CDP)	22 080	...
Orange town	13 237	13 524
Orange (CDP)	13 237	...
Oxford town	6 634	4 480
Prospect town	6 807	6 543
Seymour town	13 434	12 776
Southbury town	14 156	7 852
Wallingford town	37 274	35 714
Wallingford (CDP)	17 821	...
Waterbury town	103 266	108 033
Waterbury city	103 266	108 033
West Haven town	53 184	52 851
West Haven city	53 184	52 851
Wolcott town	13 008	12 495
Woodbridge town	7 761	7 673
New London County	238 409	¹230 654
Bozrah town	2 135	2 036
Colchester town	7 761	6 603
Colchester borough	3 190	3 529
East Lyme town	13 870	11 399
Niantic (CDP)	3 151	3 422
Franklin town	1 592	1 356
Griswold town	8 967	7 763
Jewett City borough	3 294	3 372
Groton town	41 062	¹38 244
Conning Towers—Nautilus Park (CDP)	9 665	9 791
Groton city	10 086	8 933
Noank (CDP)	1 406	¹1 371
Poquonock Bridge (CDP)	2 549	3 165
West Mystic (CDP)	3 364	¹3 415
Lebanon town	4 762	3 804
Ledyard town	13 735	¹14 837
Gales Ferry (CDP)	1 191	...
Lisbon town	3 279	2 808
Lyme town	1 822	1 484
Montville town	16 455	15 662
Montville (CDP)	1 711	1 688
Uncasville (CDP) (pt.)	1 240	1 342
New London town	28 842	31 630
New London city	28 842	31 630
North Stonington town	4 219	3 748
Norwich town	38 074	¹41 739
Norwich city	38 074	¹41 739
Old Lyme town	6 159	4 964
Preston town	4 644	3 593
Salem town	2 335	1 453
Sprague town	2 996	2 912
Stonington town	16 220	15 940
Mystic (CDP)	2 333	2 568
Pawcatuck (CDP)	5 216	5 255
Stonington borough	1 228	1 413
Voluntown town	1 637	1 452
Waterford town	17 843	17 227
Pleasure Beach (CDP)	1 356	1 394
Quaker Hill (CDP)	2 052	¹2 155
Uncasville (CDP) (pt.)	357	408
Waterford (CDP)	2 736	...
Tolland County	114 823	103 440
Andover town	2 144	2 099
Bolton town	3 951	3 691
Columbia town	3 386	3 129
Coventry town	8 895	8 140
South Coventry (CDP)	3 769	3 735
Ellington town	9 711	7 707
Hebron town	5 453	3 815
Mansfield town	20 634	19 994
Mansfield Center (CDP)	1 043	...
Storrs (CDP)	11 394	10 691
Somers town	8 473	6 893
Somers (CDP)	1 643	1 274
Stafford town	9 268	8 680
Stafford Springs borough	3 392	3 339
Tolland town	9 694	7 857
Union town	546	443
Vernon town	27 974	27 237
Willington town	4 694	3 755
Windham County	92 312	84 515
Ashford town	3 221	2 156
Brooklyn town	5 691	4 965
East Brooklyn (CDP)	1 251	1 377
Canterbury town	3 426	2 673
Chaplin town	1 793	1 621
Eastford town	1 028	922
Hampton town	1 322	1 129
Killingly town	14 519	13 573
Danielson borough	4 553	4 580
Plainfield town	12 774	11 957

County Subdivisions	1980	1970
Windham County—Con.		
Plainfield town—Con.		
Moosup (CDP)	3 308	3 376
Plainfield (CDP)	2 799	2 923
Pomfret town	2 775	2 529
Putnam town	8 580	8 598
Putnam city	6 855	6 918
Scotland town	1 072	1 022
Sterling town	1 791	1 853
Thompson town	8 141	7 580
North Grosvenor Dale (CDP)	1 856	2 156
Quinebaug (CDP)	1 088	...
Windham town	21 062	19 626
South Windham (CDP)	1 399	...
Willimantic city	14 652	14 402
Woodstock town	5 117	4 311
South Woodstock (CDP)	1 319	...

DELAWARE

Delaware takes its name from the river and bay which form a part of its eastern boundary, and which were named in honor of Lord de la Warr, governor of Virginia, by Samuel Argall, one of his associates, who explored the bay in 1611.

The region now constituting Delaware was included in the several Virginia charters (1606-1612), but the first explorer to visit it was Henry Hudson, sailing under the Dutch flag, who discovered the bay and river in 1609. In 1631 a Dutch settlement was made near the present site of Lewes, but it was destroyed by the Indians shortly afterwards. The first permanent settlement within the present limits of the state was made in 1638 by a colony of Swedes under Peter Minuit, who built Fort Christiana near the present site of Wilmington and named the country New Sweden. The Swedes were conquered by the Dutch of New Netherland in 1655, and from that time until 1664 the Dutch claimed and controlled the territory.

In 1664 New Netherland was taken by the English under the Duke of York. The counties now forming Delaware were surrendered by the Dutch at the same time, and from 1664 to 1673 were under the jurisdiction of New York. In the latter year the Dutch retook New York and a Dutch governor was appointed for the Delaware counties. In the following year, however, these counties reverted to the English and again passed under the jurisdiction of New York.

In 1682 William Penn, who in the preceding year had been granted the province of Pennsylvania, acquired the Delaware counties (then called "The Territories"), from the Duke of York. Lord Baltimore disputed the possession of this territory, but the crown ruled against his claim. For about 20 years The Territories were governed as a part of Pennsylvania; then they were given a separate legislature, but remained under the governor of Pennsylvania until the outbreak of the Revolution.

In 1776 The Territories, under the name of Delaware and with substantially the present boundaries of the state, adopted a state constitution. The new commonwealth took part in the Revolution, and in December, 1787, ratified the Federal Constitution.

Delaware was one of the original thirteen states.

COUNTY LOCATION INDEX

A   1   2   3   4   5   6

75° 30'

Delaware

NEW CASTLE

−39° 30'

KENT

−39°

SUSSEX

−38° 30'

75° 30'

Population of the State: Earliest Census to 1980

Urban and Rural

	The State			Urban				Rural			Percent of total population	
	Total population	Change from preceding census		Places of 2,500 or more	Population	Change from preceding census		Population	Change from preceding census		Urban	Rural
		Number	Percent			Number	Percent		Number	Percent		
Current urban definition:												
1980 (Apr. 1)	594 338	46 234	8.4	18	419 819	24 250	6.1	174 519	21 984	14.4	70.6	29.4
1970 (Apr. 1)	548 104	101 812	22.8	14	395 569	102 781	35.1	152 535	-969	-0.6	72.2	27.8
1960 (Apr. 1)	446 292	128 207	40.3	10	292 788	93 666	47.0	153 504	34 541	29.0	65.6	34.4
1950 (Apr. 1)	318 085	51 580	19.4	9	199 122	...	...	118 963	...	...	62.6	37.4
Previous urban definition:												
1960 (Apr. 1)	446 292	128 207	40.3	10	145 469	-2 421	-1.6	300 823	130 628	76.8	32.6	67.4
1950 (Apr. 1)	318 085	51 580	19.4	9	147 890	8 458	6.1	170 195	43 122	33.9	46.5	53.5
1940 (Apr. 1)	266 505	28 125	11.8	8	139 432	16 286	13.2	127 073	11 839	10.3	52.3	47.7
1930 (Apr. 1)	238 380	15 377	6.9	5	123 146	2 379	2.0	115 234	12 998	12.7	51.7	48.3
1920 (Jan. 1)	223 003	20 681	10.2	4	120 767	23 682	24.4	102 236	-3 001	-2.9	54.2	45.8
1910 (Apr. 15)	202 322	17 587	9.5	4	97 085	11 368	13.3	105 237	6 219	6.3	48.0	52.0
1900 (June 1)	184 735	16 242	9.6	4	85 717	14 650	20.6	99 018	1 592	1.6	46.4	53.6
1890 (June 1)	168 493	21 885	14.9	4	71 067	22 078	45.1	97 426	-193	-0.2	42.2	57.8
1880 (June 1)	146 608	21 593	17.3	3	48 989	18 148	58.8	97 619	3 445	3.7	33.4	66.6
1870 (June 1)	125 015	12 799	11.4	1	30 841	9 583	45.1	94 174	3 216	3.5	24.7	75.3
1860 (June 1)	112 216	20 684	22.6	1	21 258	7 279	52.1	90 958	13 405	17.3	18.9	81.1
1850 (June 1)	91 532	13 447	17.2	1	13 979	5 612	67.1	77 553	7 835	11.2	15.3	84.7
1840 (June 1)	78 085	1 337	1.7	1	8 367	8 367	...	69 718	-7 030	-9.2	10.7	89.3
1830 (June 1)	76 748	3 999	5.5	-	-	-	-	76 748	3 999	5.5	-	100.0
1820 (Aug. 7)	72 749	75	0.1	-	-	-	-	72 749	75	0.1	-	100.0
1810 (Aug. 6)	72 674	8 401	13.1	-	-	-	-	72 674	8 401	13.1	-	100.0
1800 (Aug. 4)	64 273	5 177	8.8	-	-	-	-	64 273	5 177	8.8	-	100.0
1790 (Aug. 2)	59 096	...	...	-	-	...	...	59 096	...	...	-	100.0

KENT

1790	18,920
1800	29,554
1810	20,495
1820	20,793
1830	19,913
1840	19,872
1850	22,816
1860	27,804
1870	29,804
1880	32,874
1890	32,664
1900	32,762
1910	32,721
1920	31,023
1930	31,841
1940	34,441
1950	37,870
1960	65,651
1970	81,892
1980	98,219

NEW CASTLE

1790	19,688
1800	25,361
1810	24,429
1820	27,899
1830	29,720
1840	33,120
1850	42,780
1860	54,797
1870	63,515
1880	77,716
1890	97,182
1900	109,697
1910	123,188
1920	148,239
1930	161,032
1940	179,562
1950	218,879
1960	307,446
1970	385,856
1980	398,115

SUSSEX

1790	20,488
1800	19,358
1810	27,750
1820	24,057
1830	27,115
1840	25,093
1850	25,936
1860	29,615
1870	31,696
1880	36,018
1890	38,647
1900	42,276
1910	46,413
1920	43,741
1930	45,507
1940	52,502
1950	61,336
1960	73,195
1970	80,356
1980	98,004

NOTES

KENT

Name changed from Saint Jones in 1683.

SUSSEX

Name changed from Deale in 1683.

DOVER

1870	1,906
1880	2,811
1890	3,061
1900	3,329
1910	3,720
1920	4,042
1930	4,800
1940	5,517
1950	6,223
1960	7,250
1970	17,488
1980	23,512

NEWARK

1860	693
1870	915
1880	1,148
1890	1,191
1900	1,213
1910	1,913
1920	2,183
1930	3,899
1940	4,502
1950	6,731
1960	11,404
1970	20,757
1980	25,247

WILMINGTON

1840	8,367
1850	13,979
1860	21,258
1870	30,841
1880	42,478
1890	61,431
1900	76,508
1910	87,411
1920	110,168
1930	106,597
1940	112,504
1950	110,356
1960	95,827
1970	80,386
1980	70,195

CORRECTION NOTE

The official 1980 census counts of total population shown in
this report supersede counts issued previously. Corrections
to the figures were made after the counts were provided to
the State for redistricting purposes and released in Advance
Report PHC80-V for this State.

Shown below are corrections to the 1980 census counts of the
total population made after the tabulations for this report
were completed. Any additional corrections made after this
report is printed are available by writing to Data User
Services Division, Customer Services (Corrections), Bureau of
the Census, Washington, D.C. 20233.

The 1980 figures shown in this publication are subject to
change pending the outcome of the various lawsuits dealing
with the census counts.

	1980 population	
	As shown in the tables	Corrected
The State.................	594 338	594 317
Kent County:		
Dover division:		
Dover city...................	23 512	23 507
Milford North division:		
Milford city (pt.)...........	2 147	2 157
New Castle County:		
Central Pencader division.......	8 605	8 610
Greater Newark division.........	57 475	57 470
Sussex County....................	98 004	97 983
Georgetown division..............	6 470	6 449
Selbyville-Frankford division:		
Frankford town................	686	828
Milford city (total).............	5 356	5 366

County Subdivisions	1980	1970
The State	594 338	548 104
Kent County[1]	98 219	81 892
Central Kent division	14 152	...
Bowers town	198	268
Magnolia town	197	319
Rising Sun–Lebanon (CDP) (pt.)	1 980	...
Viola town	167	154
Woodside town	248	223
Woodside East (CDP)	1 490	...
Dover division	53 315	...
Camden town[1]	1 757	1 241
Cheswold town[1]	269	286
Dover city[1]	23 512	17 488
Dover Base Housing (CDP)	4 391	8 106
Dupont Manor (CDP)	1 059	1 256
Hartly town	106	180
Highland Acres (CDP)	2 994	1 471
Kent Acres (CDP)	1 590	1 573
Leipsic town	228	247
Little Creek town	230	215
Rising Sun–Lebanon (CDP) (pt.)	196	...
Rodney Village (CDP)	1 753	2 127
Star Hill–Briar Park (CDP)	1 114	...
Wyoming town	960	1 062
Felton division	4 152	...
Felton town[1]	547	495
Harrington division	7 436	...
Farmington town	141	109
Harrington city[1]	2 405	2 407
Houston town	357	317
Kenton division	3 738	...
Kenton town	243	205
Milford North division	6 304	...
Frederica town	864	878
Milford city (pt.)[1]	2 147	2 029
Smyrna division	9 122	...
Clayton town[1]	1 216	1 015
Smyrna town (pt.)[1]	4 750	4 243
New Castle County[2]	398 115	385 856
Brandywine division	84 766	87 753
Arden village	516	'555
Ardencroft village[2]	267	...
Ardentown village[2]	307	...
Bellefonte town	1 279	1 442
Claymont (CDP)	10 022	6 584
Edgemoor (CDP)	7 397	...
Talleyville (CDP)	6 880	...
Central Pencader division	8 605	...
Newark city (pt.)[2]	6	...
Greater Newark division	57 475	...
Brookside (CDP)	15 255	7 856
Newark city (pt.)[2]	25 241	'21 298
Lower Christiana division	39 280	46 741
Elsmere town	6 493	8 415
Newport town[2]	1 167	1 366
Middletown–Odessa division	13 187	10 040
Middletown town[2]	2 946	2 644
Odessa town	384	547
Smyrna town (pt.)[2]	–	–
Townsend town[2]	386	505
New Castle division	56 139	...
New Castle city	4 907	4 814
Wilmington Manor (CDP)	9 233	10 134
Piedmont division	17 295	14 163
Pike Creek–Central Kirkwood division	31 519	30 791
Stanton (CDP)	5 495	...
Red Lion division	3 930	3 623
Delaware City city[2]	1 858	2 024
Upper Christiana division	15 724	9 906
Wilmington division	70 195	80 386
Wilmington city[2]	70 195	80 386
Sussex County[3]	98 004	80 356
Bridgeville–Greenwood division	6 285	...
Bridgeville town	1 238	1 317
Greenwood town	578	654
Georgetown division	6 470	5 615
Georgetown town	1 710	1 844
Laurel–Delmar division	13 856	...
Bethel town[3]	197	219
Delmar town	948	943
Laurel town[3]	3 052	2 408
Lewes division	11 530	...
Henlopen Acres town[3]	176	...
Lewes city[3]	2 197	2 563
Rehoboth Beach city[3]	1 730	'1 495
Milford South division	12 323	...
Ellendale town	361	399
Milford city (pt.)	3 209	3 285
Slaughter Beach town[3]	121	84
Millsboro division	9 971	...
Millsboro town[3]	1 233	1 073
Milton division	5 902	...
Milton town	1 359	1 490
Seaford division	17 153	...
Blades town	664	632
Seaford city[3]	5 256	5 537
Selbyville–Frankford division	14 514	...

County Subdivisions	1980	1970
Sussex County—Con.		
Selbyville–Frankford division—Con.		
Bethany Beach town[3]	330	189
Dagsboro town	344	375
Fenwick Island town	114	56
Frankford town	686	635
Millville town[3]	178	224
Ocean View town[3]	495	411
Selbyville town[3]	1 251	1 099
South Bethany town[3]	115	'24

District of Columbia

ALEXANDRIA

1800	5,949
1810	8,552
1820	9,703
1830	9,573
1840	9,967

WASHINGTON

1800	8,144
1810	15,471
1820	23,336
1830	30,261
1840	33,745
1850	51,687
1860	75,080
1870	313,700
1880	177,624
1890	230,392
1900	278,718
1910	331,069
1920	437,571
1930	486,869
1940	663,091
1950	802,178
1960	763,956
1970	756,668
1980	638,333

FLORIDA

Florida was given this name by its discoverer, Ponce de Leon, a Spaniard, who sighted the coast near the present site of St. Augustine on Easter Sunday (Pascua Florida, The Feast of Flowers) of the year 1513.

Ponce de Leon and other Spanish explorers made attempts at settlement in Florida, but it remained for the French to found the first colony at the mouth of the St. Johns in 1564. The next year Spaniards destroyed this colony and founded St. Augustine, which was the first permanent settlement. In 1586 this city was burned by Sir Francis Drake; in 1665 it was plundered by English buccaneers. Rivalry between the English colonies and the Spanish settlements continued and St. Augustine was attacked at the beginning of the eighteenth century by the English in the Carolinas, and later by the Georgians under Oglethorpe.

In 1763, under the terms of the Treaty of Paris, Spain transferred Florida to Great Britain in exchange for Cuba, which had been recently conquered by England. Later in the same year the province was divided into east and west Florida, with the Apalachicola River as the boundary between the two, the British claiming the Mississippi as the western limit. In 1783 Great Britain retroceded the Floridas to Spain. The region south of the thirty-first parallel and between the Mississippi and Perdido Rivers, which had been claimed by both France and Spain, was in dispute between the United States and Spain from 1803, the year in which the United States acquired Louisiana from France, until 1819, when Florida was purchased by the United States from Spain. In July, 1821, the transfer was made, and in 1822 a territorial government was established for east and west Florida, which together comprised the same area as the present state; in the following year east and west Florida were united.

In 1839 Florida adopted a state constitution, but was not admitted to the Union until March, 1845.

COUNTY LOCATION INDEX

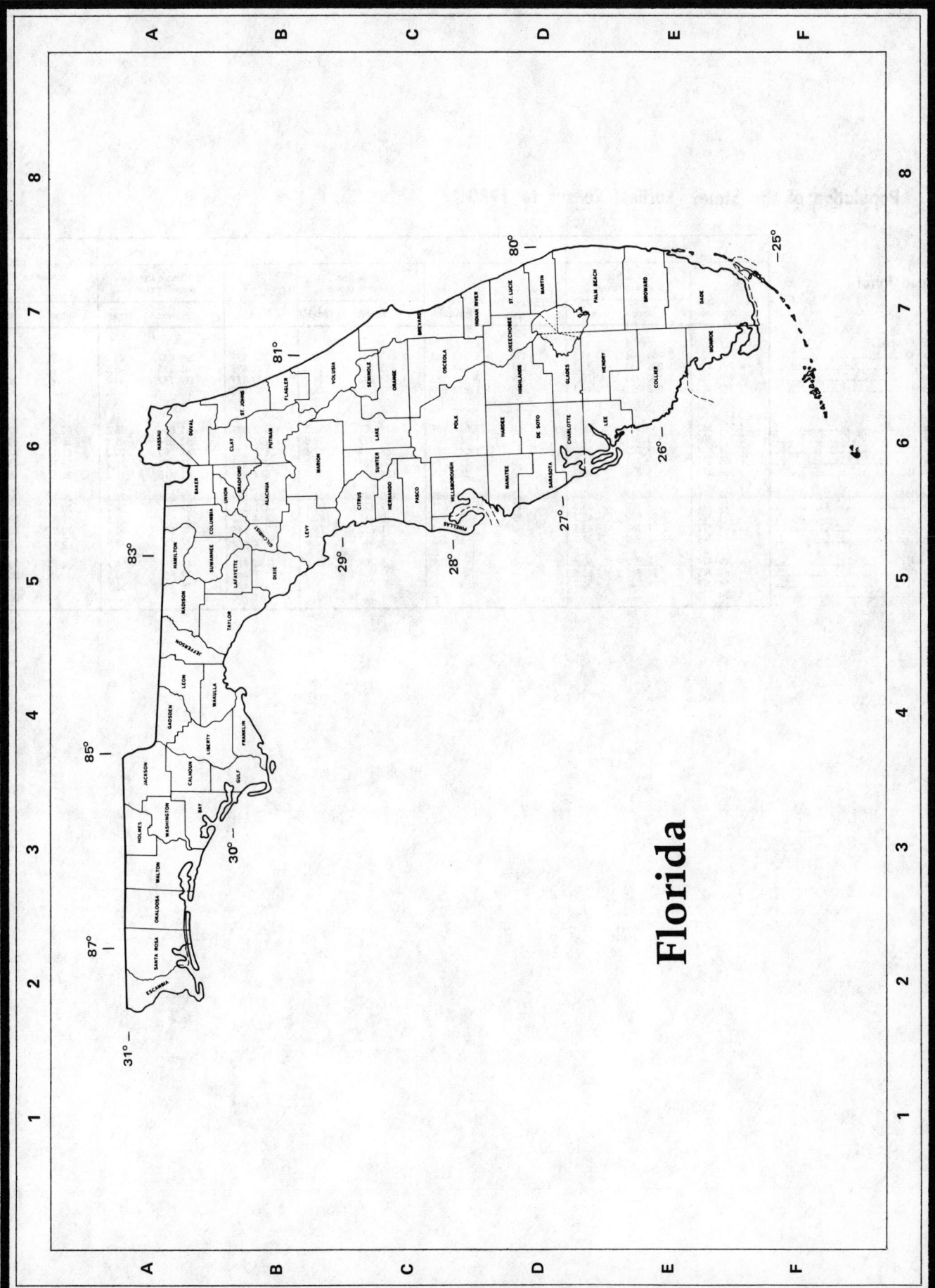

Florida

Population of the State: Earliest Census to 1980

Urban and Rural

	The State			Urban					Rural			Percent of total population	
	Total population	Change from preceding census		Places of 2,500 or more	Population	Change from preceding census		Population	Change from preceding census			Urban	Rural
		Number	Percent			Number	Percent			Number	Percent		
Current urban definition:													
1980 (Apr. 1)_____	9 746 324	2 954 906	43.5	430	8 212 385	2 667 834	48.1	1 533 939	289 047	23.2		84.3	15.7
1970 (Apr. 1)_____	'6 791 418	1 839 858	37.2	285	5 544 551	1 883 168	51.4	1 244 892	−45 285	−3.5		81.7	18.3
1960 (Apr. 1)_____	4 951 560	2 180 255	78.7	179	3 661 383	1 847 493	101.9	1 290 177	332 762	34.8		73.9	26.1
1950 (Apr. 1)_____	2 771 305	873 891	46.1	98	1 813 890	...	...	957 415	...	...		65.5	34.5
Previous urban definition:													
1960 (Apr. 1)_____	4 951 560	2 180 255	78.7	160	3 077 989	1 511 201	96.5	1 873 571	669 054	55.5		62.2	37.8
1950 (Apr. 1)_____	2 771 305	873 891	46.1	94	1 566 788	520 997	49.8	1 204 517	352 894	41.4		56.5	43.5
1940 (Apr. 1)_____	1 897 414	429 203	29.2	70	1 045 791	286 013	37.6	851 623	143 190	20.2		55.1	44.9
1930 (Apr. 1)_____	1 468 211	499 741	51.6	58	759 778	406 263	114.9	708 433	93 478	15.2		51.7	48.3
1920 (Jan. 1)_____	968 470	215 851	28.7	30	353 515	134 435	61.4	614 955	81 416	15.3		36.5	63.5
1910 (Apr. 15)_____	752 619	224 077	42.4	23	219 080	112 049	104.7	533 539	112 028	26.6		29.1	70.9
1900 (June 1)_____	528 542	137 120	35.0	12	107 031	29 673	38.4	421 511	107 447	34.2		20.3	79.7
1890 (June 1)_____	391 422	121 929	45.2	12	77 358	50 411	187.1	314 064	71 518	29.5		19.8	80.2
1880 (June 1)_____	269 493	81 745	43.5	4	26 947	11 672	76.4	242 546	70 073	40.6		10.0	90.0
1870 (June 1)_____	187 748	47 324	33.7	3	15 275	9 567	167.6	172 473	37 757	28.0		8.1	91.9
1860 (June 1)_____	140 424	52 979	60.6	2	5 708	5 708	–	134 716	47 271	54.1		4.1	95.9
1850 (June 1)_____	87 445	32 968	60.5	–	–	–	–	87 445	32 968	60.5		–	100.0
1840 (June 1)_____	54 477	19 747	56.9	–	–	–	–	54 477	19 747	56.9		–	100.0
1830 (June 1)_____	34 730	...	...	–	–	...	...	34 730	...	...		–	100.0

ALACHUA

Year	Population
1830	2,204
1840	2,282
1850	2,524
1860	8,232
1870	17,328
1880	16,462
1890	22,934
1900	32,245
1910	34,305
1920	31,689
1930	34,365
1940	38,607
1950	57,026
1960	74,074
1970	104,764
1980	151,348

BAKER

Year	Population
1870	1,325
1880	2,303
1890	3,333
1900	4,516
1910	4,805
1920	4,622
1930	6,273
1940	6,510
1950	6,313
1960	7,363
1970	9,242
1980	15,289

BAY

Year	Population
1920	11,407
1930	12,091
1940	20,686
1950	42,689
1960	67,131
1970	75,283
1980	97,740

BRADFORD

Year	Population
1870	3,671
1880	6,112
1890	7,516
1900	10,295
1910	14,090
1920	12,503
1930	9,405
1940	8,717
1950	11,457
1960	12,446
1970	14,625
1980	20,023

BREVARD

Year	Population
1860	246
1870	1,216
1880	1,478
1890	3,401
1900	5,158
1910	4,717
1920	8,505
1930	13,283
1940	16,142
1950	23,653
1960	111,435
1970	230,006
1980	272,959

BROWARD

Year	Population
1920	5,135
1930	20,094
1940	39,794
1950	83,933
1960	333,946
1970	620,100
1980	1,018,200

CALHOUN

Year	Population
1840	1,142
1850	1,377
1860	1,446
1870	998
1880	1,580
1890	1,681
1900	5,132
1910	7,465
1920	8,775
1930	7,298
1940	8,218
1950	7,922
1960	7,422
1970	7,624
1980	9,294

CHARLOTTE

Year	Population
1930	4,013
1940	3,663
1950	4,286
1960	12,594
1970	27,559
1980	58,460

CITRUS

Year	Population
1890	2,394
1900	5,391
1910	6,731
1920	5,220
1930	5,516
1940	5,846
1950	6,111
1960	9,628
1970	19,196
1980	54,703

CLAY

Year	Population
1860	1,914
1870	2,098
1880	2,838
1890	5,154
1900	5,635
1910	6,116
1920	5,621
1930	6,859
1940	6,468
1950	14,323
1960	19,535
1970	32,059
1980	67,052

COLLIER

Year	Population
1930	2,883
1940	5,102
1950	6,488
1960	15,753
1970	38,040
1980	85,971

COLUMBIA

Year	Population
1840	2,102
1850	4,808
1860	4,646
1870	7,335
1880	9,589
1890	12,877
1900	17,094
1910	17,689
1920	14,290
1930	14,638
1940	16,859
1950	18,216
1960	20,077
1970	25,250
1980	35,399

DADE

Year	Population
1840	446
1850	159
1860	83
1870	85
1880	257
1890	861
1900	4,955
1910	11,933
1920	42,753
1930	142,955
1940	267,739
1950	495,084
1960	935,047
1970	1,267,792
1980	1,625,781

DE SOTO

Year	Population
1890	4,944
1900	8,047
1910	14,200
1920	25,434
1930	7,745
1940	7,792
1950	9,242
1960	11,683
1970	13,060
1980	19,039

DIXIE

Year	Population
1930	6,419
1940	7,018
1950	3,928
1960	4,479
1970	5,480
1980	7,751

DUVAL

Year	Population
1830	1,970
1840	4,156
1850	4,539
1860	5,044
1870	11,921
1880	19,431
1890	26,800
1900	39,733
1910	75,163
1920	113,540
1930	115,503
1940	210,143
1950	304,029
1960	455,411
1970	528,865
1980	571,003

ESCAMBIA

Year	Population
1830	2,518
1840	3,993
1850	4,351
1860	5,768
1870	7,817
1880	12,156
1890	20,188
1900	28,313
1910	38,029
1920	49,386
1930	53,594
1940	74,667
1950	112,706
1960	173,829
1970	205,334
1980	233,794

FLAGLER

Year	Population
1920	2,442
1930	2,466
1940	3,008
1950	3,367
1960	4,566
1970	4,454
1980	10,913

FRANKLIN

Year	Population
1840	1,030
1850	1,561
1860	1,904
1870	1,256
1880	1,791
1890	3,308
1900	4,890
1910	5,201
1920	5,318
1930	6,283
1940	5,991
1950	5,814
1960	6,576
1970	7,065
1980	7,661

GADSDEN

Year	Population
1830	4,895
1840	5,992
1850	8,784
1860	9,396
1870	9,802
1880	12,169
1890	11,894
1900	15,294
1910	22,198
1920	23,539
1930	29,890
1940	31,450
1950	36,457
1960	41,989
1970	39,184
1980	41,565

GILCHRIST

Year	Population
1930	4,137
1940	4,250
1950	3,499
1960	2,868
1970	3,551
1980	5,767

GLADES

Year	Population
1930	2,762
1940	2,745
1950	2,199
1960	2,950
1970	3,669
1980	5,992

GULF

Year	Population
1930	3,182
1940	6,951
1950	7,460
1960	9,937
1970	10,096
1980	10,658

HAMILTON

Year	Population
1830	553
1840	1,464
1850	2,511
1860	4,154
1870	5,749
1880	6,790
1890	8,507
1900	11,881
1910	11,825
1920	9,873
1930	9,454
1940	9,778
1950	8,981
1960	7,705
1970	7,787
1980	8,761

HARDEE

Year	Population
1930	10,348
1940	10,158
1950	10,073
1960	12,370
1970	14,889
1980	19,379

HENDRY

Year	Population
1930	3,492
1940	5,237
1950	6,051
1960	8,119
1970	11,859
1980	18,599

HERNANDO

Year	Population
1850	926
1860	1,200
1870	2,938
1880	4,248
1890	2,476
1900	3,638
1910	4,997
1920	4,548
1930	4,948
1940	5,641
1950	6,693
1960	11,205
1970	17,004
1980	44,469

HIGHLANDS

Year	Population
1930	9,192
1940	9,246

1950	13,636	1890	15,757	1870	2,018	1950	38,187		
1960	21,338	1900	16,195	1880	5,767	1960	51,616		
1970	29,507	1910	17,210	1890	6,586	1970	69,030		
1980	47,526	1920	14,502	1900	8,603	1980	122,488		

HILLSBOROUGH

1840	452
1850	2,377
1860	2,981
1870	3,216
1880	5,814
1890	14,941
1900	36,013
1910	78,374
1920	88,257
1930	153,519
1940	180,148
1950	249,894
1960	397,788
1970	490,265
1980	646,960

HOLMES

1850	1,205
1860	1,386
1870	1,572
1880	2,170
1890	4,336
1900	7,762
1910	11,557
1920	12,850
1930	12,924
1940	15,447
1950	13,988
1960	10,844
1970	10,720
1980	14,723

INDIAN RIVER

1930	6,724
1940	8,957
1950	11,872
1960	25,309
1970	35,992
1980	59,896

JACKSON

1830	3,907
1840	4,681
1850	6,639
1860	10,209
1870	9,528
1880	14,372
1890	17,514
1900	23,377
1910	29,821
1920	31,224
1930	31,969
1940	34,428
1950	34,645
1960	36,208
1970	34,434
1980	39,154

JEFFERSON

1830	3,312
1840	5,713
1850	7,713
1860	9,876
1870	13,398
1880	16,065

LAFAYETTE

1860	2,068
1870	1,783
1880	2,441
1890	3,686
1900	4,987
1910	6,710
1920	6,242
1930	4,361
1940	4,405
1950	3,440
1960	2,889
1970	2,892
1980	4,035

LAKE

1890	8,034
1900	7,467
1910	9,509
1920	12,744
1930	23,161
1940	27,255
1950	36,340
1960	57,383
1970	69,305
1980	104,870

LEE

1890	1,414
1900	3,071
1910	6,294
1920	9,540
1930	14,990
1940	17,488
1950	23,404
1960	54,539
1970	105,216
1980	205,266

LEON

1830	6,494
1840	10,713
1850	11,442
1860	12,343
1870	15,236
1880	19,662
1890	17,752
1900	19,887
1910	19,437
1920	18,059
1930	23,476
1940	31,646
1950	51,590
1960	74,225
1970	103,047
1980	148,655

LEVY

1850	465
1860	1,781

LIBERTY

1860	1,457
1870	1,050
1880	1,362
1890	1,452
1900	2,956
1910	4,700
1920	5,006
1930	4,067
1940	3,752
1950	3,182
1960	3,138
1970	3,379
1980	4,260

MADISON

1830	525
1840	2,644
1850	5,490
1860	7,779
1870	11,121
1880	14,798
1890	14,316
1900	15,446
1910	16,919
1920	16,516
1930	15,614
1940	16,190
1950	14,197
1960	14,154
1970	13,481
1980	14,894

MANATEE

1860	854
1870	1,931
1880	3,544
1890	2,895
1900	4,663
1910	9,550
1920	18,712
1930	22,502
1940	26,098
1950	34,704
1960	69,168
1970	97,115
1980	148,442

MARION

1850	3,338
1860	8,609
1870	10,804
1880	13,046
1890	20,796
1900	24,403
1910	26,941
1920	23,968
1930	29,578
1940	31,243

MARTIN

1930	5,111
1940	6,295
1950	7,807
1960	16,932
1970	28,035
1980	64,014

MONROE

1830	517
1840	688
1850	2,645
1860	2,913
1870	5,657
1880	10,940
1890	18,786
1900	18,006
1910	21,563
1920	19,550
1930	13,624
1940	14,078
1950	29,957
1960	47,921
1970	52,586
1980	63,188

NASSAU

1830	1,511
1840	1,892
1850	2,164
1860	3,644
1870	4,247
1880	6,635
1890	8,294
1900	9,654
1910	10,525
1920	11,340
1930	9,375
1940	10,826
1950	12,811
1960	17,189
1970	20,626
1980	32,894

NEW RIVER

1860	3,820

OKALOOSA

1920	9,360
1930	9,897
1940	12,900
1950	27,533
1960	61,175
1970	88,187
1980	109,920

OKEECHOBEE

1920	2,132
1930	4,129
1940	3,000
1950	3,454
1960	6,434
1970	11,233
1980	20,264

ORANGE

1830	733
1840	73
1850	466
1860	987
1870	2,195
1880	6,618
1890	12,584
1900	11,374
1910	19,107
1920	19,890
1930	49,737
1940	70,074
1950	114,950
1960	263,540
1970	344,311
1980	471,016

OSCEOLA

1890	3,133
1900	3,444
1910	5,507
1920	7,195
1930	10,699
1940	10,119
1950	11,406
1960	19,029
1970	25,267
1980	49,287

PALM BEACH

1910	5,577
1920	18,654
1930	51,781
1940	79,989
1950	114,688
1960	228,106
1970	348,993
1980	576,863

PASCO

1890	4,249
1900	6,054
1910	7,502
1920	8,802
1930	10,574
1940	13,981
1950	20,529
1960	36,785
1970	75,955
1980	193,643

PINELLAS

1920	28,265
1930	62,149
1940	91,852
1950	159,249
1960	374,665
1970	522,239
1980	728,531

POLK

1870	3,169
1880	3,181
1890	7,905
1900	12,472
1910	24,148
1920	38,661
1930	72,291
1940	86,665

1950	123,997
1960	195,139
1970	228,515
1980	321,652

PUTNAM

1850	687
1860	2,712
1870	3,821
1880	6,261
1890	11,186
1900	11,641
1910	13,096
1920	14,568
1930	18,096
1940	18,698
1950	23,615
1960	32,212
1970	36,424
1980	50,549

SAINT JOHNS

1830	2,538
1840	2,694
1850	2,525
1860	3,038
1870	2,618
1880	4,535
1890	8,172
1900	9,165
1910	13,208
1920	13,061
1930	18,676
1940	20,012
1950	24,998
1960	30,034
1970	31,035
1980	51,303

SAINT LUCIE

1850	139
1910	4,075
1920	7,886
1930	7,057
1940	11,871
1950	20,180
1960	39,294
1970	50,836
1980	87,182

SANTA ROSA

1830	868
1850	2,883
1860	5,480
1870	3,312
1880	6,645
1890	7,961
1900	10,293
1910	14,897
1920	13,670
1930	14,083
1940	16,085
1950	18,554
1960	29,547
1970	37,741
1980	55,988

SARASOTA

1930	12,440
1940	16,160
1950	28,827

1960	76,895
1970	120,413
1980	202,251

SEMINOLE

1920	10,986
1930	18,735
1940	22,304
1950	26,883
1960	54,947
1970	83,692
1980	179,752

SUMTER

1860	1,549
1870	2,952
1880	4,686
1890	5,363
1900	6,187
1910	6,696
1920	7,851
1930	10,644
1940	11,041
1950	11,330
1960	11,869
1970	14,839
1980	24,272

SUWANNEE

1860	2,303
1870	3,556
1880	7,161
1890	10,524
1900	14,554
1910	18,603
1920	19,789
1930	15,731
1940	17,073
1950	16,986
1960	14,961
1970	14,839
1980	22,287

TAYLOR

1860	1,384
1870	1,453
1880	2,297
1890	2,122
1900	3,999
1910	7,103
1920	11,219
1930	13,136
1940	11,565
1950	10,416
1960	13,168
1970	13,641
1980	16,532

UNION

1930	7,428
1940	7,094
1950	8,906
1960	6,043
1970	8,112
1980	10,166

VOLUSIA

1860	1,158
1870	1,723
1880	3,294

1890	8,467
1900	10,003
1910	16,510
1920	23,374
1930	42,757
1940	52,710
1950	74,229
1960	125,319
1970	169,487
1980	258,762

WAKULLA

1850	1,955
1860	2,839
1870	2,506
1880	2,723
1890	3,117
1900	5,149
1910	4,802
1920	5,129
1930	5,468
1940	5,463
1950	5,258
1960	5,257
1970	6,308
1980	10,887

WALTON

1830	1,207
1840	1,461
1850	1,817
1860	3,037
1870	3,041
1880	4,201
1890	4,816
1900	9,346
1910	16,460
1920	12,119
1930	14,576
1940	14,246
1950	14,725
1960	15,576
1970	16,087
1980	21,300

WASHINGTON

1830	987
1840	859
1850	1,950
1860	2,154
1870	2,302
1880	4,089
1890	6,426
1900	10,154
1910	16,403
1920	11,828
1930	12,180
1940	12,302
1950	11,888
1960	11,249
1970	11,453
1980	14,509

NOTES

HERNANDO

Name changed from Benton prior to 1860.

NEW RIVER

Taken to form Baker and Bradford prior to 1870.

ORANGE

Name changed from Mosquito prior to 1850.

SAINT LUCIE

Part taken to form Brevard, and parts annexed to Dade, Polk, and Volusia prior to 1860. Re-established in 1905.

ALTAMONTE

1930	281
1940	551
1950	858
1960	1,212
1970	4,391
1980	22,028

BARTOW

1880	77
1890	1,386
1900	1,983
1910	2,662
1920	4,203
1930	5,269
1940	6,158
1950	8,694
1960	12,849
1970	12,891
1980	14,780

BELLE GLADE

1930	926
1940	3,806
1950	7,219
1960	11,273
1970	15,949
1980	16,535

BOCA RATON

1930	447
1940	723
1950	992
1960	6,961
1970	28,506
1980	49,505

BOYNTON BEACH

1930	1,053
1940	1,326
1950	2,542
1960	10,467
1970	18,115
1980	35,624

BRADENTON

1910	1,866
1920	3,868
1930	5,986
1940	7,444
1950	13,604
1960	19,380
1970	21,040
1980	30,170

CAPE CORAL

1970	10,192
1980	32,103

CASSELBERRY

1950	407
1960	2,463
1970	9,438
1980	15,247

CLEARWATER

1900	343
1910	1,171
1920	2,427
1930	7,607
1940	10,136
1950	15,581
1960	34,653
1970	52,072
1980	85,528

COCOA

1890	312
1900	382
1910	613
1920	1,445
1930	2,164
1940	3,098
1950	4,245
1960	12,294
1970	16,110
1980	16,096

COCOA BEACH

1930	31
1940	49
1950	246
1960	3,475
1970	9,952
1980	10,926

COOPER CITY

1960	550
1970	2,535
1980	10,140

CORAL GABLES

1930	5,697
1940	8,294
1950	19,837
1960	34,793
1970	42,494
1980	

CORAL SPRINGS

1970	1,489
1980	37,349

DANIA

1910	269
1920	762
1960	7,065
1970	9,013
1980	11,811

DAVIE

1970	5,859
1980	20,877

DAYTONA BEACH

1910	331
1920	825
1930	16,598
1940	22,584
1950	30,187
1960	37,395
1970	45,327
1980	54,176

DEERFIELD BEACH

1930	1,483
1940	1,850
1950	2,088
1960	9,573
1970	17,130
1980	39,193

DE LAND

1890	1,113
1900	1,449
1910	2,812
1920	3,324
1930	5,246
1940	7,041
1950	8,652
1960	10,775
1970	11,641
1980	15,354

DELRAY BEACH

1920	1,051
1930	2,333
1940	3,737
1950	6,312
1960	12,230
1970	19,366
1980	34,325

DUNEDIN

1900	113
1910	256
1920	642
1930	1,435
1940	1,758
1950	3,202
1960	8,444
1970	17,639
1980	30,203

FORT LAUDERDALE

1920	2,065
1930	8,666
1940	17,996
1950	36,328
1960	83,648
1970	139,590
1980	153,279

FORT MYERS

1900	943
1910	2,463
1920	3,678
1930	9,082
1940	10,604
1950	13,195
1960	22,523
1970	27,351
1980	36,638

FORT PIERCE

1910	1,333
1920	2,115
1930	4,803
1940	8,040

1950	13,502
1960	25,256
1970	29,721
1980	33,802

FORT WALTON BEACH

1950	2,463
1960	12,147
1970	19,994
1980	20,829

GAINESVILLE

1890	2,790
1900	3,633
1910	6,183
1920	6,860
1930	10,465
1940	13,757
1950	26,861
1960	29,701
1970	64,510
1980	81,371

GULFPORT

1930	851
1940	1,581
1950	3,702
1960	9,730
1970	9,976
1980	11,180

HAINES CITY

1920	651
1930	3,037
1940	3,890
1950	5,630
1960	9,135
1970	8,956
1980	10,799

HALLANDALE

1930	1,012
1940	1,827
1950	3,886
1960	10,483
1970	23,849
1980	36,517

HIALEAH

1930	2,600
1940	3,958
1950	19,676
1960	66,972
1970	102,452
1980	145,254

HOLLYWOOD

1930	2,869
1940	6,239
1950	14,351
1960	35,237
1970	106,873
1980	121,323

HOMESTEAD

1920	1,307
1930	2,319
1940	3,154
1950	4,573
1960	9,152
1970	13,674
1980	20,668

JACKSONVILLE

1850	1,045
1860	2,118
1870	6,912
1880	7,650
1890	17,201
1900	28,429
1910	57,699
1920	91,558
1930	129,549
1940	173,065
1950	204,517
1960	201,030
1970	528,865
1980	540,920

JACKSONVILLE BEACH

1910	249
1920	357
1930	409
1940	3,566
1950	6,430
1960	12,049
1970	13,326
1980	15,462

KEY WEST

1840	688
1860	2,832
1880	9,890
1890	18,080
1900	17,114
1910	19,945
1920	18,749
1930	12,831
1940	12,927
1950	26,433
1960	33,956
1970	27,563
1980	24,382

KISSIMMEE

1950	4,310
1960	6,845
1970	7,119
1980	15,487

LAKELAND

1890	552
1900	1,180
1910	3,719
1920	7,062
1930	18,554
1940	22,068
1950	30,851
1960	41,350
1970	41,550
1980	47,406

LAKE WORTH

1920	1,106
1930	5,940
1940	7,408
1950	11,777
1960	20,758
1970	23,714
1980	27,048

LARGO

1910	291
1920	599
1930	1,429
1940	1,031
1950	1,547
1960	5,302
1970	22,031
1980	58,977

LAUDERDALE LAKES

1970	10,577
1980	

LAUDERHILL

1960	132
1970	8,465
1980	37,271

LEESBURG

1880	200
1890	772
1900	765
1910	991
1920	1,835
1930	4,113
1940	4,687
1950	7,395
1960	11,172
1970	11,869
1980	13,191

LIGHTHOUSE POINT

1960	2,453
1970	9,071
1980	11,488

LONGWOOD

1920	106
1930	318
1940	406
1950	717
1960	1,689
1970	3,203
1980	10,029

MARGATE

1960	2,646
1970	8,867
1980	36,044

MELBOURNE

1890	99
1900	131
1910	137
1920	533
1930	2,677

1940	2,622
1950	4,223
1960	11,982
1970	40,236
1980	46,536

MIAMI

1900	1,681
1910	5,471
1920	29,571
1930	110,637
1940	172,172
1950	249,276
1960	291,688
1970	334,859
1980	346,865

MIAMI BEACH

1920	644
1930	6,494
1940	28,012
1950	46,282
1960	63,145
1970	87,072
1980	96,298

MIAMI SPRINGS

1930	402
1940	898
1950	5,108
1960	11,229
1970	13,279
1980	12,350

MIRAMAR

1960	5,485
1970	23,973
1980	32,813

NAPLES

1930	390
1940	1,253
1950	1,465
1960	4,655
1970	12,042
1980	17,581

NEW PORT RICHEY

1930	758
1940	920
1950	1,512
1960	3,520
1970	6,098
1980	11,196

NEW SMYRNA BEACH

1900	543
1910	1,121
1920	2,007
1930	4,149
1940	4,402
1950	5,775
1960	8,781
1970	10,580
1980	13,557

NORTH LAUDERDALE

1970	1,213
1980	18,479

NORTH MIAMI

1940	1,973
1950	10,734
1960	28,708
1970	34,767
1980	42,566

NORTH MIAMI BEACH

1940	871
1950	2,129
1960	21,405
1970	30,723
1980	36,553

NORTH PALM BEACH

1960	2,684
1970	9,035
1980	11,344

OAKLAND PARK

1930	463
1940	815
1950	1,295
1960	5,331
1970	16,261
1980	23,035

OCALA

1870	600
1880	803
1890	2,904
1900	3,380
1910	4,370
1920	4,914
1930	7,281
1940	8,986
1950	11,741
1960	13,598
1970	22,583
1980	37,170

OPA-LOCKA

1930	339
1940	497
1950	5,271
1960	9,810
1970	11,902
1980	14,460

ORLANDO

1890	2,856
1900	2,481
1910	3,894
1920	9,292
1930	27,330
1940	36,736
1950	52,367
1960	88,135
1970	99,006
1980	128,291

ORMOND BEACH

1890	239
1900	595
1910	780
1920	1,292
1930	1,517
1940	1,914
1950	3,418
1960	8,658
1970	14,063
1980	21,378

PALATKA

1860	613
1870	720
1880	1,616
1890	3,039
1900	3,301
1910	3,779
1920	5,102
1930	6,500
1940	7,140
1950	9,176
1960	11,028
1970	9,444
1980	10,175

PALM BAY

1960	2,808
1970	7,176
1980	18,560

PALM BEACH GARDENS

1960	1
1970	6,102
1980	14,407

PEMBROKE PINES

1960	1,429
1970	15,520
1980	35,776

PANAMA CITY

1910	422
1920	1,722
1930	5,402
1940	11,610
1950	25,814
1960	33,275
1970	32,096
1980	33,346

PENSACOLA

1850	2,164
1860	2,876
1870	3,347
1880	6,845
1890	11,750
1900	17,747
1910	22,982
1920	31,035
1930	31,579
1940	37,449
1950	43,479
1960	56,752
1970	59,507
1980	57,619

PINELLAS PARK

1920	134
1930	465
1940	691
1950	2,924
1960	10,848
1970	22,287
1980	32,811

PLANTATION

1960	4,772
1970	23,523
1980	48,501

PLANT CITY

1890	349
1900	720
1910	2,481
1920	3,729
1930	6,800
1940	7,491
1950	9,230
1960	15,711
1970	15,451
1980	19,270

POMPANO BEACH

1910	269
1920	636
1930	2,614
1940	4,427
1950	5,682
1960	15,992
1970	37,724
1980	52,618

PORT ORANGE

1920	380
1930	678
1940	662
1950	1,201
1960	1,801
1970	3,781
1980	18,756

PORT SAINT LUCIE

1970	330
1980	14,690

RIVIERA BEACH

1930	811
1940	1,981
1950	4,065
1960	13,046
1970	21,401
1980	26,489

ROCKLEDGE

1920	453
1930	551
1940	725
1950	1,347
1960	3,481
1970	10,523
1980	11,877

SAINT AUGUSTINE

1830	1,708
1840	2,450
1850	1,934
1860	1,914
1870	1,717
1880	2,293
1890	4,742
1900	4,272
1910	5,494
1920	6,192
1930	12,111
1940	12,090
1950	13,555
1960	14,734
1970	12,352
1980	11,985

SAINT PETERSBURG

1890	278
1900	1,575
1910	4,127
1920	14,237
1930	40,425
1940	60,812
1950	96,738
1960	181,298
1970	216,232
1980	238,647

SANFORD

1890	2,016
1900	1,450
1910	3,570
1920	5,588
1930	10,100
1940	10,217
1950	11,935
1960	19,175
1970	17,393
1980	23,176

SARASOTA

1910	840
1920	2,149
1930	8,398
1940	11,141
1950	18,896
1960	34,083
1970	40,237
1980	48,868

SOUTH DAYTONA

1940	571
1950	692
1960	1,954
1970	4,979
1980	11,252

SOUTH MIAMI

1930	1,160
1940	2,408
1950	4,809
1960	9,846
1970	19,571
1980	10,944

SUNRISE

1970	7,403
1980	39,681

TALLAHASSEE

1840	1,616
1850	(NA)
1860	1,932
1870	2,023
1880	2,494
1890	2,934
1900	2,981
1910	5,018
1920	5,637
1930	10,700
1940	16,240
1950	27,237
1960	48,174
1970	71,897
1980	81,548

TAMARAC

1970	5,193
1980	29,376

TAMPA

1870	796
1880	720
1890	5,534
1900	15,839
1910	37,782
1920	51,608
1930	101,161
1940	108,391
1950	124,681
1960	274,970
1970	277,767
1980	271,523

TARPON SPRINGS

1900	514
1910	2,212
1920	2,105
1930	3,414
1940	3,402
1950	4,323
1960	6,768
1970	7,118
1980	13,251

TEMPLE TERRACE

1940	215
1950	433
1960	3,812
1970	7,347
1980	11,097

TITUSVILLE

1890	746
1900	756
1910	868
1920	1,361
1930	2,089
1940	2,220
1950	2,604
1960	6,410
1970	30,515
1980	31,910

VENICE

1930	309
1940	507
1950	727
1960	3,444
1970	6,648
1980	12,153

VERO BEACH

1920	793
1930	2,268
1940	3,050
1950	4,746
1960	8,849
1970	11,908
1980	16,176

WEST PALM BEACH

1900	564
1910	1,743
1920	8,659
1930	26,610
1940	33,693
1950	43,162
1960	56,208
1970	57,375
1980	63,305

WILTON MANORS

1950	883
1960	8,257
1970	10,948
1980	12,742

WINTER HAVEN

1920	1,597
1930	7,130
1940	6,199
1950	8,605
1960	16,277
1970	16,136
1980	21,119

WINTER PARK

1890	270
1900	366
1910	570
1920	1,078
1930	3,686
1940	4,715
1950	8,250
1960	17,162
1970	21,895
1980	22,239

WINTER SPRINGS

1960	609
1970	1,161
1980	10,475

CORRECTION NOTE

The official 1980 census counts of total population shown in
this report supersede counts issued previously. Corrections
to the figures were made after the counts were provided to
the State for redistricting purposes and released in Advance
Report PHC80-V for this State.

Shown below are corrections to the 1980 census counts of the
total population made after the tabulations for this report
were completed. Any additional corrections made after this
report is printed are available by writing to Data User
Services Division, Customer Services (Corrections), Bureau of
the Census, Washington, D.C. 20233.

The 1980 figures shown in this publication are subject to
change pending the outcome of the various lawsuits dealing
with the census counts.

	1980 population	
	As shown in the tables	Corrected
The State......................	9 746 324	9 746 342
Broward County:		
Fort Lauderdale division:		
Browardale (CDP)................	7 571	7 409
Melrose Park (CDP)..............	5 662	5 672
Plantation city (pt.)..........	68	220
Margate division:		
Broadview-Pompano		
Park (CDP)(pt.)...............	3 886	3 853
Margate city...................	36 044	35 900
North Lauderdale city (pt.)......	16 594	16 768
Hillsborough County:		
Plant City division:		
Plant City city................	19 270	17 064
Pasco County........................	193 643	193 661
Central Pasco division.............	17 602	17 620
St. Leo town...................	899	917
Sarasota County:		
Englewood division:		
Englewood (CDP)(pt.)............	6 744	6 148
Broadview-Pompano Park (CDP)(total)..	5 256	5 223
Englewood (CDP)(total)..............	10 229	9 633
North Lauderdale city (total)........	18 479	18 653
Plantation city (total).............	48 501	48 653

County Subdivisions	1980	1970
The State	9 746 324	r6 791 418
Alachua County[1]	151 348	104 764
Gainesville division	112 522	...
Gainesville city (pt.)[1]	79 143	64 510
Hawthorne division	4 683	3 628
Hawthorne city[1]	1 303	1 126
High Springs—Alachua division	16 523	9 079
Alachua city[1]	3 561	2 252
Gainesville city (pt.)[1]	2 228	...
High Springs city[1]	2 491	2 787
La Crosse town	170	365
Micanopy division	2 259	...
Micanopy town[1]	737	759
Newberry—Archer division	9 965	...
Archer city[1]	1 230	898
Newberry city[1]	1 826	1 247
Waldo division	5 396	...
Waldo city[1]	993	800
Baker County[2]	15 289	9 242
Macclenny division	9 436	...
Macclenny town[2]	3 851	2 733
Sanderson division	5 853	...
Glen St. Mary town	462	357
Bay County[3]	97 740	75 283
Lynn Haven division	10 386	...
Lynn Haven city (pt.)[3]	5 918	4 044
Mexico Beach division	5 178	4 839
Mexico Beach city[3]	632	588
Tyndall AFB (CDP)	4 542	4 248
Panama City division	67 691	...
Callaway city[3]	7 154	3 240
Cedar Grove town[3]	1 104	689
Hiland Park (CDP)	4 763	3 691
Lynn Haven city (pt.)[3]	321	...
Panama City city[3]	33 346	32 096
Parker city	4 298	4 212
Pretty Bayou (CDP)	3 340	...
Springfield city[3]	7 220	5 949
Panama City Beaches division	8 252	...
Lower Grand Lagoon (CDP)	1 619	...
Panama City Beach city[3]	2 148	67
Upper Grand Lagoon (CDP)	3 314	...
Southport division	3 810	...
Southport (CDP)	1 992	1 560
Youngstown division	2 423	...
Bradford County[4]	20 023	14 625
Brooker division	1 012	767
Brooker city	429	340
Hampton division	4 118	2 288
Hampton city	466	386
Lawtey division	3 600	2 484
Lawtey city	692	636
Starke division	11 293	9 086
Starke city[4]	5 306	4 848
Brevard County[5]	272 959	230 006
Cocoa Beach—Cape Canaveral division	18 690	...
Cape Canaveral city[5]	5 733	4 258
Cocoa Beach city[5]	10 926	9 952
Cocoa—Rockledge division	47 550	...
Cocoa city[5]	16 096	16 110
Cocoa West (CDP)	6 432	5 779
Port St. John (CDP)	1 837	...
Rockledge city[5]	11 877	10 523
Sharpes (CDP)	4 149	...
Indialantic—Melbourne Beach division	41 253	...
Indialantic town[5]	2 883	2 685
Indian Harbour Beach city[5]	5 967	5 371
Melbourne city (pt.)[5]	999	...
Melbourne Beach town[5]	2 713	2 262
Patrick AFB North (CDP)	1 638	1 652
Patrick AFB South (CDP)	1 205	1 583
Satellite Beach city	9 163	6 558
South Patrick Shores (CDP)	9 816	10 313
Malabar division	5 857	...
Malabar town	1 118	634
Micco (CDP)	3 585	...
Palm Bay city (pt.)[5]		...
Melbourne division	61 542	...
June Park (CDP) (pt.)	3 733	(NA)
Melbourne city (pt.)[5]	45 534	40 236
Melbourne Village town	1 004	597
Palm Bay city (pt.)[5]	3	...
Palm Shores town	77	202
West Eau Gallie (CDP)	2 591	2 705
West Melbourne city[5]	5 078	3 050
Melbourne Shores—Floridana Beach division	2 073	...
Merritt Island division	32 514	...
Merritt Island (CDP)	30 708	29 233
Palm Bay division	18 801	...
Melbourne city (pt.)[5]	3	...
Palm Bay city (pt.)[5]	18 557	r7 176
Space Center division	21	...
Titusville division	43 632	...
Mims (CDP)	7 583	8 309
Titusville city[5]	31 910	30 515
West Brevard division	1 026	...

County Subdivisions	1980	1970
Brevard County—Con.		
West Brevard division—Con.		
June Park (CDP) (pt.)	318	(NA)
Melbourne city (pt.)[5]	3	...
Palm Bay city (pt.)[5]		(NA)
Broward County[6]	1 018 200	r620 100
Conservation division	–	–
Davie division	55 411	...
Cooper City[6]	10 140	2 535
Davie town[6]	20 877	r5 859
Hacienda Village city (pt.)[6]	21	r35
Sunrise city (pt.)	–	...
Deerfield Beach division	75 068	40 665
Coconut Creek city (pt.)[6]	360	...
Coral Springs city (pt.)[6]	–	...
Deerfield Beach city[6]	39 193	r16 662
Hillsboro Beach town	1 554	r1 181
Lighthouse Point city[6]	11 488	9 071
Parkland city[6]	545	165
Pompano Beach Highlands (CDP)	16 154	5 014
Fort Lauderdale division	273 727	...
Broadview—Pompano Park (CDP) (pt.)	545	...
Browardale (CDP)	7 571	17 444
Dania city (pt.)[6]	–	...
Fort Lauderdale city (pt.)[6]	153 266	r139 590
Lauderdale-by-the-Sea town	2 639	2 879
Lauderdale Lakes city	25 426	10 577
Lauderhill city (pt.)[6]	571	...
Lazy Lake village	31	48
Melrose Park (CDP)	5 662	6 111
North Andrews Gardens (CDP)	8 967	7 082
North Lauderdale city (pt.)[6]	–	...
Oakland Park city[6]	23 035	16 261
Plantation city (pt.)[6]	68	...
Pompano Beach city (pt.)[6]	1 379	...
Riverland (CDP)	5 919	5 512
Sea Ranch Lakes village	584	660
Tamarac city (pt.)[6]	3 970	(NA)
Washington Park (CDP)	7 240	...
Wilton Manors city	12 742	10 948
Hallandale division	50 277	...
Hallandale city (pt.)	36 460	23 849
Miami Gardens—Utopia—Carver (CDP) (pt.)	5 618	...
Pembroke Park town (pt.)[6]	3 744	2 949
Hollywood division	150 636	...
Dania city (pt.)[6]	11 811	9 013
Fort Lauderdale city (pt.)[6]	13	...
Hacienda Village city (pt.)[6]	105	...
Hollywood city	121 323	106 873
Margate division	105 472	...
Broadview—Pompano Park (CDP) (pt.)	3 886	...
Coconut Creek city (pt.)[6]	238	...
Coral Springs city (pt.)[6]	37 349	1 489
Margate city[6]	36 044	8 867
North Lauderdale city (pt.)[6]	16 594	1 213
Tamarac city (pt.)[6]	10 422	(NA)
Miramar—Pembroke Pines division	74 438	...
Miami Gardens—Utopia—Carver (CDP) (pt.)	3 407	...
Miramar city[6]	32 813	r23 997
Pembroke Park town (pt.)[6]	1 039	...
Pembroke Pines city[6]	35 776	r15 496
Plantation division	150 155	...
Broadview Park (CDP)	6 022	6 049
Broadview—Pompano Park (CDP) (pt.)	825	...
Lauderhill city (pt.)[6]	36 700	8 465
North Lauderdale city (pt.)[6]	1 885	...
Plantation city (pt.)[6]	48 433	23 523
Sunrise city (pt.)[6]	39 681	7 403
Tamarac city (pt.)[6]	14 984	(NA)
Pompano Beach division	83 016	60 124
Coconut Creek city (pt.)[6]	5 690	1 359
Collier City (CDP)	7 135	...
Collier Manor—Cresthaven (CDP)	7 045	7 202
Kendall Green (CDP)	6 768	...
Pompano Beach city (pt.)[6]	51 239	r38 587
Calhoun County	9 294	7 624
Altha division	1 679	1 338
Altha town	478	423
Blountstown division	5 674	4 949
Blountstown city	2 632	2 384
Calhoun West division	1 941	1 337
Charlotte County[7]	58 460	27 559
Grove City—Rotonda division	10 015	...
Englewood (CDP) (pt.)	3 485	r1 769
Grove City (CDP)	1 932	r1 252
Manasota Key (CDP) (pt.)	838	...
Rotonda (CDP)	1 432	...
Port Charlotte division	30 870	...
Charlotte Harbor (CDP)	2 084	...
Port Charlotte (CDP)	25 770	10 769
Punta Gorda division	17 575	9 634
Charlotte Park (CDP)	1 605	...
Cleveland (CDP)	2 417	...
Punta Gorda city[7]	6 797	3 879
Solana (CDP)	1 408	1 286

County Subdivisions	1980	1970
Citrus County[8]	54 703	19 196
Crystal River division	23 275	8 063
Citrus Springs (CDP)	1 360	...
Crystal River city[8]	2 778	1 696
Homosassa (CDP)	1 426	...
Inverness division	31 428	11 133
Beverly Hills (CDP)	5 024	...
Floral City (CDP)	1 181	...
Hernando (CDP)	1 653	...
Inverness city[8]	4 095	2 299
Clay County[9]	67 052	32 059
Green Cove Springs division	9 275	
Green Cove Springs city[9]	4 154	3 857
Keystone Heights division	6 145	2 996
Keystone Heights city[9]	1 056	800
Middleburg–Clay Hill division	8 218	...
Orange Park division	39 645	...
Bellair–Meadowbrook Terrace (CDP)	12 144	...
Lakeside (CDP)	10 534	...
Orange Park town[9]	8 766	5 019
Penney Farms division	3 769	...
Asbury Lake (CDP)	1 605	...
Penney Farms town	630	561
Collier County[10]	85 971	38 040
Everglades division	9 877	...
Everglades city	524	462
Henderson Creek (CDP) (pt.)	1 039	...
Marco (CDP)	4 679	...
Immokalee division	13 723	...
Immokalee (CDP)	11 038	3 764
Naples division	62 371	...
Bonita Shores (CDP) (pt.)	651	...
East Naples (CDP)	12 127	6 152
Golden Gate (CDP)	4 327	...
Henderson Creek (CDP) (pt.)	10	...
Lely (CDP)	1 376	...
Naples city[10]	17 581	12 042
Naples Manor (CDP)	3 161	...
Naples Park (CDP)	5 438	1 522
North Naples (CDP)	7 950	3 201
Columbia County[11]	35 399	25 250
Fort White division	4 377	2 494
Fort White town	386	365
Lake City division	30 210	...
Five Points (CDP)	1 691	1 214
Lake City city[11]	9 257	10 575
Watertown (CDP)	3 804	3 624
North Columbia division	812	...
Dade County[12]	1 625 781	1 267 792
Everglades division	3 180	...
Hialeah division	166 331	...
Hialeah city (pt.)	141 356	102 452
Hialeah Gardens city	2 700	492
Miami Lakes (CDP)	9 809	...
Palm Springs North (CDP)	5 838	...
Pennsuco town (pt.)	9	74
Homestead division	51 865	28 857
Florida City city	6 174	5 133
Homestead city[12]	20 668	13 674
Islandia city	12	8
Leisure City (CDP) (pt.)	14 960	...
Kendale Lakes–Lindgren Acres division	77 623	...
Kendale Lakes (CDP)	32 769	...
Kendall (CDP) (pt.)	3 811	...
Lindgren Acres (CDP)	11 986	...
Medley town (pt.)	3	...
Pennsuco town (pt.)	6	...
South Miami Heights (CDP) (pt.)	4 577	2 613
Tamiami (CDP) (pt.)	17 607	...
Kendall–Perrine division	135 869	...
Coral Gables city (pt.)	7 352	(NA)
Cutler (CDP)	15 593	...
Kendall (CDP) (pt.)	68 994	35 497
Palmetto Estates (CDP)	11 116	...
Perrine (CDP) (pt.)	15 683	10 257
Richmond Heights (CDP)	8 577	6 663
Sunset (CDP)	4 376	...
Key Biscayne division	6 337	4 563
Key Biscayne (CDP)	6 313	...
Miami city (pt.)	–	...
Miami division	771 794	...
Aventura (CDP)	9 698	...
Biscayne Park village	3 088	2 717
Brownsville (CDP)	18 058	23 442
Coral Gables city (pt.)	35 889	(NA)
Coral Terrace (CDP)	22 702	...
El Portal village	2 055	2 068
Gladeview (CDP)	18 919	...
Glenvar Heights (CDP)	13 216	...
Golden Glades (CDP)	23 154	...
Hialeah city (pt.)	3 898	...
Ives Estates (CDP) (pt.)	10 613	...
Kendall (CDP) (pt.)	953	...
Miami city (pt.)	346 865	334 859
Miami Shores village	9 244	9 425
Miami Springs city	12 350	13 279
Norland (CDP) (pt.)	4 666	...
North Miami city[12]	42 566	34 767
North Miami Beach city[12]	36 553	30 544

County Subdivisions	1980	1970
Dade County—Con.		
Miami division—Con.		
Ojus (CDP)	17 344	...
Olympia Heights (CDP) (pt.)	3 009	...
Opa-locka city	14 460	11 902
Opa-locka North (CDP)	5 721	...
Pinewood (CDP)	16 252	...
South Miami city[12]	10 944	11 780
Virginia Gardens village	2 098	2 524
West Little River (CDP)	32 492	...
West Miami city	6 076	5 494
Westview (CDP)	9 102	...
Miami Beach division	126 450	...
Bal Harbour village	2 973	2 038
Bay Harbor Islands town	4 869	4 619
Golden Beach town	612	849
Indian Creek village	103	82
Miami city (pt.)	–	...
Miami Beach city	96 298	87 072
North Bay Village city[12]	4 920	4 831
Sunny Isles (CDP)	12 564	...
Surfside town	3 763	3 614
Northwest Dade division	88 080	61 166
Carol City (CDP)	47 349	27 361
Ives Estates (CDP) (pt.)	2 010	...
Lake Lucerne (CDP)	9 762	...
Norland (CDP) (pt.)	14 805	14 973
Scott Lake (CDP)	14 154	...
North Westside division	35 352	...
Medley town (pt.)	534	351
Miami city (pt.)	–	...
Sweetwater city[12]	8 251	3 357
Tamiami (CDP) (pt.)	–	...
Princeton–Goulds division	82 892	53 451
Cutler Ridge (CDP)	20 886	17 441
Goulds (CDP)	7 078	6 690
Homestead AFB (CDP)	7 594	8 257
Leisure City (CDP) (pt.)	2 945	...
Naranja–Princeton (CDP)	10 381	...
Perrine (CDP) (pt.)	446	...
South Miami Heights (CDP) (pt.)	18 982	7 782
South Westside division	80 008	...
Olympia Heights (CDP) (pt.)	30 103	...
Sunset (CDP) (pt.)	9 155	...
Tamiami (CDP) (pt.)	–	...
Westchester (CDP)	29 272	...
Westwood Lakes (CDP)	11 478	12 811
De Soto County[13]	19 039	13 060
Arcadia East division	12 585	...
Arcadia city (pt.)[13]	6 002	5 658
Arcadia West division	6 454	...
Arcadia city (pt.)[13]	–	...
Dixie County[14]	7 751	5 480
Cross City North division	5 375	...
Cross City town[14]	2 154	2 268
Cross City South division	2 376	...
Horseshoe Beach town	304	124
Duval County[15]	571 003	528 865
Jacksonville division	571 003	528 865
Atlantic Beach city	7 847	6 132
Baldwin town	1 526	1 408
Jacksonville city	540 920	504 265
Jacksonville Beach city	15 462	12 779
Neptune Beach city	5 248	4 281
Escambia County[16]	233 794	205 334
Cantonment division	23 389	13 433
Ensley (CDP) (pt.)	3 549	...
Ferry Pass (CDP) (pt.)	2 493	...
Gonzalez (CDP)	6 084	...
Century division	8 333	8 015
Century town[16]	495	329
Century (CDP)	1 805	2 679
Molino (CDP) (pt.)	1 027	...
Northwest Escambia division	2 985	2 879
Molino (CDP) (pt.)	429	...
Pensacola division	199 087	...
Bellview (CDP)	15 439	...
Brent (CDP)	21 872	...
Ensley (CDP) (pt.)	10 873	...
Ferry Pass (CDP) (pt.)	14 417	...
Goulding (CDP)	5 352	...
Myrtle Grove (CDP)	14 238	16 186
Pensacola city[16]	57 619	59 507
Warrington (CDP)	15 792	15 848
West Pensacola (CDP)	24 371	20 924
Flagler County[17]	10 913	4 454
Bunnell division	4 166	...
Bunnell city	1 816	1 687
Flagler Beach division	6 747	...
Beverly Beach town	217	21
Flagler Beach city[17]	2 208	1 042
Marineland town (pt.)	8	2
Painters Hill town	40	14
Palm Coast (CDP)	2 837	...

County Subdivisions	1980	1970
Franklin County	7 661	7 065
Apalachicola division	3 917	3 959
Apalachicola city	2 565	3 102
Carrabelle division	2 075	1 732
Carrabelle city	1 304	1 044
Eastpoint division	1 669	1 374
Eastpoint (CDP)	1 246	1 188
Gadsden County[18]	41 565	39 184
Chattahoochee division	7 179	9 485
Chattahoochee city[18]	5 332	7 944
Greensboro division	2 574	2 975
Greensboro town	562	716
Havana division	9 063	6 670
Havana town	2 782	2 022
Quincy division	22 749	...
Gretna town[18]	1 448	883
Quincy city	8 591	8 334
Gilchrist County[19]	5 767	3 551
Bell division	2 240	...
Bell town	227	227
Trenton division	3 527	...
Fanning Springs city (pt.)[19]	164	80
Trenton city[19]	1 131	1 074
Glades County	5 992	3 669
Northeast Glades division	2 054	860
Southwest Glades division	3 938	2 809
Moore Haven city	1 250	974
Gulf County	10 658	10 096
Port St. Joe division	6 832	6 934
Port St. Joe city	4 027	4 401
Ward Ridge city	104	8
Wewahitchka division	3 826	3 162
Wewahitchka town	1 742	1 733
Hamilton County[20]	8 761	7 787
Jasper division	4 841	...
Jasper city[20]	2 093	2 221
Jennings division	2 232	1 866
Jennings town	749	582
White Springs division	1 688	...
White Springs town	781	767
Hardee County[21]	19 379	14 889
Bowling Green division	4 378	3 410
Bowling Green city[21]	2 310	1 357
Wauchula division	9 696	7 762
Wauchula city[21]	2 986	3 007
Zolfo Springs division	5 305	3 717
Zolfo Springs town	1 495	1 117
Hendry County[22]	18 599	11 859
Clewiston division	11 135	7 520
Clewiston city	5 219	3 896
Harlem (CDP)	2 669	2 006
La Belle division	7 464	4 339
La Belle city[22]	2 287	1 823
Hernando County[23]	44 469	17 004
Brooksville division	18 900	...
Brooksville city[23]	5 582	4 060
Mountain Park (CDP)	1 007	...
North Brooksville (CDP)	1 014	...
South Brooksville (CDP)	1 218	...
Ridge Manor division	2 552	...
Ridge Manor (CDP)	1 074	...
Weeki Wachee division	23 017	...
Brookridge (CDP)	1 268	...
High Point (CDP)	1 727	...
South Weeki Wachee (CDP)	1 701	...
Spring Hill (CDP)	6 468	...
Weeki Wachee city	8	76
Weeki Wachee Acres (CDP)	1 037	...
Highlands County[24]	47 526	29 507
Avon Park division	14 401	10 929
Avon Park city[24]	8 026	6 712
Lake Placid division	11 282	6 129
Hiway Park (CDP)	1 578	...
Lake Placid town[24]	963	656
Sylvan Shores (CDP)	1 402	...
Sebring division	21 843	12 449
Sebring city[24]	8 736	7 223
Hillsborough County[25]	646 960	490 265
Brandon division	69 271	...
Brandon (CDP)	41 826	12 749
Mango–Seffner (CDP)	6 493	...
Citrus Park–Fern Lake division	22 775	7 907
Lake Carroll (CDP) (pt.)	2 950	...
Gibsonton division	7 219	4 450
Palm River–East Tampa division	21 717	...
Palm River–Clair Mel (CDP)	14 447	8 536
Tampa city (pt.)	8	...
Plant City division	47 717	...
Dover (CDP)	2 354	2 094
Plant City city[25]	19 270	15 451
Ruskin division	18 807	8 510
Apollo Beach (CDP)	4 014	1 042
Ruskin (CDP)	5 117	2 414
Sun City Center (CDP)	5 605	2 143
Tampa division	430 771	...

County Subdivisions	1980	1970
Hillsborough County—Con.		
Tampa division—Con.		
Bay Crest (CDP)	5 927	...
Del Rio (CDP)	7 409	...
East Lake–Orient Park (CDP)	5 612	'5 711
Egypt Lake (CDP)	11 932	7 556
Lake Carroll (CDP) (pt.)	10 062	5 577
Lake Magdalene (CDP)	13 331	9 266
Leto (CDP)	9 003	8 458
Lutz (CDP)	5 555	...
Tampa city (pt.)	271 515	'277 714
Temple Terrace city	11 097	7 347
Town 'n' Country (CDP)	37 834	...
University (CDP)	24 514	10 039
Thonotosassa division	14 529	...
Wimauma–Lithia division	14 154	5 534
Wimauma (CDP)	1 477	...
Holmes County[26]	14 723	10 720
Bonifay division	7 118	4 947
Bonifay city[26]	2 534	2 068
Esto–Noma division	3 289	2 339
Esto town	304	210
Noma town[26]	113	...
Holmes West division	4 316	3 434
Ponce de Leon town[26]	454	288
Westville town[26]	343	...
Indian River County[27]	59 896	35 992
Fellsmere division	4 422	1 827
Fellsmere city	1 161	813
Vero Beach division	55 474	...
Florida Ridge (CDP)	4 988	1 338
Gifford (CDP)	6 240	5 772
Indian River Shores town[27]	1 254	76
Orchid town	42	8
Roseland (CDP)	1 607	...
Sebastian city[27]	2 831	825
Vero Beach city[27]	16 176	11 908
Vero Beach South (CDP)	12 636	7 330
Wabasso (CDP)	2 157	...
Jackson County[28]	39 154	34 434
Alford division	2 468	1 928
Alford town	548	402
Campbellton division	1 811	1 836
Campbellton town	336	304
Cottondale division	3 106	2 573
Cottondale town[28]	1 056	765
Cypress division	3 880	3 107
Grand Ridge town	591	512
Graceville division	4 869	4 264
Graceville city[28]	2 918	2 560
Greenwood division	2 878	2 589
Greenwood town	577	'449
Malone division	2 578	2 349
Bascom town[28]	134	'87
Malone town[28]	897	667
Marianna division	12 781	11 837
Marianna city[28]	7 006	'7 282
Sneads division	4 783	3 951
Sneads town	1 690	1 550
Jefferson County[29]	10 703	8 778
Monticello division	7 253	...
Monticello city[29]	2 994	2 473
Wacissa division	3 450	...
Lafayette County[30]	4 035	2 892
Day division	644	...
Mayo division	3 391	...
Mayo town	891	793
Lake County[31]	104 870	69 305
Clermont division	9 947	...
Clermont city[31]	5 461	3 661
Minneola city[31]	851	878
Montverde town[31]	397	308
Eustis division	12 329	...
Eustis city (pt.)[31]	9 202	6 722
Fruitland Park–Lady Lake division	8 563	...
Fruitland Park city (pt.)[31]	2 247	1 '359
Lady Lake town[31]	1 193	382
Groveland–Mascotte division	7 453	...
Groveland city[31]	1 992	1 928
Mascotte city[31]	1 112	966
Howey-in-the-Hills–Okahumpka division	4 974	...
Hawthorne (CDP)	1 874	...
Howey-in-the-Hills town	626	466
Leesburg division	17 333	...
Fruitland Park city (pt.)[31]	12	...
Leesburg city (pt.)[31]	13 062	11 869
Leesburg East division	9 603	...
Bassville Park (CDP)	3 064	...
Leesburg city (pt.)[31]	129	...
Mount Dora division	13 229	...
Eustis city (pt.)[31]	99	...
Mount Dora city[31]	5 883	'4 646
Oakland Park (CDP)	2 063	...
Sylvan Shores (CDP)	1 104	...
Tavares division	9 063	...
Astatula town[31]	755	388

County Subdivisions	1980	1970
Lake County—Con.		
Tavares division—Con.		
Eustis city (pt.)[31]	3	...
Tavares city[31]	4 103	3 261
Umatilla division	12 376	...
Eustis city (pt.)[31]	149	...
Umatilla city[31]	1 872	1 600
Lee County[32]	205 266	105 216
Boca Grande division	642	...
Bonita Springs division	13 818	...
Bonita Shores (CDP) (pt.)	1 145	...
Bonita Springs (CDP)	5 435	1 932
San Carlos Park (CDP)	3 590	...
Cape Coral division	38 303	...
Cape Coral city[32]	32 103	...
North Fort Myers (CDP) (pt.)	4 656	(NA)
Estero Island division	6 308	...
Bonita Shores (CDP) (pt.)	555	...
Fort Myers Beach (CDP)	5 753	4 305
Fort Myers division	86 828	...
Cypress Lake (CDP)	8 721	...
Fort Myers city[32]	36 638	27 351
Franklin Park (CDP)	2 792	...
Tanglewood (CDP)	8 229	...
Tice (CDP)	6 645	7 254
Villas (CDP)	8 724	3 408
Fort Myers Shores division	9 022	...
Fort Myers Shores (CDP)	4 426	...
Lehigh Acres division	15 572	...
Lehigh Acres (CDP)	9 604	4 394
North Fort Myers division	27 040	...
North Fort Myers (CDP) (pt.)	18 152	(NA)
Suncoast Estates (CDP)	4 399	...
Pine Island division	3 841	...
St. James City (CDP)	1 298	...
Sanibel Island division	3 892	...
Sanibel city[32]	3 363	...
Leon County[33]	148 655	103 047
Tallahassee division	108 132	86 017
Tallahassee city[33]	81 548	72 624
Tallahassee East division	11 080	6 380
Tallahassee Northeast division	12 853	3 217
Killearn (CDP)	8 700	...
Tallahassee Northwest division	5 747	2 078
Tallahassee Southeast division	5 502	2 748
Woodville (CDP)	1 768	...
Tallahassee Southwest division	5 341	2 607
Levy County[34]	19 870	12 756
Cedar Key—Yankeetown division	4 212	2 710
Cedar Key city[34]	700	714
Inglis town	1 173	449
Otter Creek town (pt.)[34]	167	230
Yankeetown town	600	490
Chiefland division	6 051	4 109
Chiefland city	1 986	1 965
Fanning Springs city (pt.)[34]	150	35
Otter Creek town (pt.)[34]	—	...
Williston—Bronson division	9 607	5 937
Bronson town	853	698
Williston city	2 240	1 939
Liberty County	4 260	3 379
East Liberty division	1 333	1 213
West Liberty division	2 927	2 166
Bristol city	1 044	626
Madison County[35]	14 894	13 481
Greenville division	3 548	3 466
Greenville town	1 096	1 141
Madison division	11 346	...
Lee town	297	240
Madison city[35]	3 487	3 737
Manatee County[36]	148 442	97 115
Bradenton division	121 182	...
Anna Maria city	1 537	1 137
Bayshore Gardens (CDP)	14 945	9 255
Bradenton city (pt.)[36]	29 642	21 040
Bradenton Beach city	1 595	1 370
Cortez (CDP)	3 821	...
Ellenton (CDP)	1 561	1 421
El Ranchero Village (CDP)	1 760	1 859
Holmes Beach city	4 023	2 699
Longboat Key town (pt.)	2 460	1 397
Oneco (CDP)	6 417	3 246
Palma Sola (CDP)	5 297	1 745
Samoset (CDP)	5 747	4 070
South Bradenton (CDP)	14 297	10 820
Trailer Estates (CDP)	2 243	1 759
West Bradenton (CDP)	4 065	6 162
Whitfield Estates (CDP)	4 328	1 362
Myakka division	5 831	...
Bradenton city (pt.)[36]	528	...
Palmetto division	18 603	...
Memphis (CDP)	5 501	3 207
Palmetto city[36]	8 637	7 422
Parrish division	2 826	...

County Subdivisions	1980	1970
Marion County[37]	122 488	69 030
Belleview division	19 776	...
Belleview city[37]	1 913	916
Silver Springs Shores (CDP) (pt.)	—	...
Dunnellon division	4 822	...
Dunnellon city	1 427	1 146
East Marion division	10 592	3 907
Fellowship division	3 783	...
Fort McCoy—Anthony division	9 171	...
Ocala division	66 142	...
Ocala city[37]	37 170	22 583
Silver Springs (CDP)	1 082	...
Silver Springs Shores (CDP) (pt.)	3 983	...
Reddick—McIntosh division	8 202	...
McIntosh town	404	287
Reddick town	657	305
Martin County[38]	64 014	28 035
Indiantown division	8 470	...
Indiantown (CDP)	3 383	2 283
Port Salerno—Hobe Sound division	23 542	...
Hobe Sound (CDP)	6 822	2 029
Jupiter Island town	364	295
Port Salerno (CDP)	4 511	1 161
Stuart division	32 002	...
Jensen Beach (CDP)	6 639	...
North River Shores (CDP)	2 867	...
Ocean Breeze Park town[38]	469	714
Palm City (CDP)	2 177	...
Rio (CDP)	1 205	...
Sewall's Point town	1 187	298
Stuart city[38]	9 467	4 820
Monroe County[39]	63 188	52 586
Cape Sable division	—	154
Key West division	31 727	...
Big Coppitt Key (CDP)	1 856	...
Key West city	24 382	29 312
Stock Island (CDP)	4 446	...
Lower Keys division	6 353	...
Big Pine Key (CDP)	2 350	...
Middle Keys division	10 221	5 756
Key Colony Beach city	977	371
Layton city[39]	88	100
Marathon (CDP)	7 568	4 397
Upper Keys division	14 887	7 012
Islamorada (CDP)	1 441	1 251
Key Largo (CDP)	7 447	2 866
Plantation (CDP)	2 887	...
Tavernier (CDP)	1 834	...
Nassau County[40]	32 894	20 626
Callahan—Hilliard division	14 471	...
Callahan town[40]	869	772
Hilliard town[40]	1 869	1 205
Nassau Village—Ratliff (CDP)	2 165	...
Fernandina Beach division	10 841	9 140
Fernandina Beach city[40]	7 224	6 955
Yulee division	7 582	...
Yulee (CDP)	3 168	...
Okaloosa County[41]	109 920	88 187
Baker division	4 376	3 764
Crestview division	14 940	12 162
Crestview city[41]	7 617	7 952
Eglin division	9 956	10 349
Eglin AFB (CDP)	7 574	7 769
Fort Walton Beach city (pt.)[41]	—	...
Mary Esther town (pt.)[41]	—	...
Niceville city (pt.)[41]	—	...
Fort Walton Beach division	60 575	46 626
Cinco Bayou town	202	362
Destin (CDP)	3 672	1 536
Fort Walton Beach city (pt.)[41]	20 829	19 994
Lake Lorraine (CDP)	5 427	...
Longwood (CDP)	2 040	...
Mary Esther town (pt.)[41]	3 530	3 192
Ocean City (CDP)	5 582	5 267
Okaloosa Island (CDP)	1 554	...
Shalimar town[41]	390	578
Wright (CDP)	13 011	...
Laurel Hill division	1 482	1 030
Laurel Hill city[41]	610	418
Niceville—Valparaiso division	18 591	14 256
Niceville city (pt.)[41]	8 543	4 155
Valparaiso city	6 142	6 504
Okeechobee County[42]	20 264	11 233
North Okeechobee division	3 650	...
Okeechobee division	16 614	...
Cypress Quarters (CDP)	1 479	1 310
Okeechobee city	4 225	3 715
Taylor Creek (CDP)	2 479	...
Orange County[43]	471 016	344 311
Apopka division	31 674	...
Apopka city[43]	6 019	4 045
South Apopka (CDP)	5 687	2 293
Zellwood (CDP)	1 760	...
East Orange division	5 860	...
Bithlo (CDP)	3 143	...
Orlando division	349 718	...
Azalea Park (CDP)	8 301	7 367

County Subdivisions

County Subdivisions	1980	1970
Orange County—Con.		
Orlando division—Con.		
Belle Isle city	2 848	2 705
Conway (CDP)	24 027	8 642
Eatonville town[43]	2 185	2 024
Edgewood city[43]	1 034	392
Fairview Shores (CDP)	10 174	...
Goldenrod (CDP) (pt.)	5 563	...
Holden Heights (CDP)	13 864	6 206
Lockhart (CDP)	10 569	5 809
Maitland city[43]	8 763	7 157
Oak Ridge (CDP) (pt.)	12 450	...
Orlando city (pt.)[43]	127 622	99 006
Orlovista (CDP)	6 474	...
Pine Castle (CDP)	9 992	...
Pine Hills (CDP) (pt.)	31 029	13 882
Sky Lake (CDP)	6 692	...
Winter Park city[43]	22 339	21 895
Southwest Orange division	18 798	...
Bay Lake city[43]	74	'24
Lake Buena Vista city[43]	98	'12
Oak Ridge (CDP) (pt.)	3 027	...
Orlando city (pt.)[43]	669	...
Windermere town[43]	1 302	894
Union Park division	36 792	...
Goldenrod (CDP) (pt.)	2 528	...
Orlando city (pt.)[43]	−	...
Union Park (CDP)	19 175	'2 827
Winter Garden—Ocoee division	28 174	...
Oakland city	658	672
Ocoee city[43]	7 803	3 937
Pine Hills (CDP) (pt.)	4 742	...
Winter Garden city[43]	6 789	5 153
Osceola County[44]	49 287	25 267
Kissimmee division	27 316	...
Campbell (CDP)	2 941	...
Kissimmee city (pt.)[44]	14 495	7 119
St. Cloud division	19 952	...
Kissimmee city (pt.)[44]	992	...
St. Cloud city[44]	7 840	5 041
South and East Osceola division	2 019	1 337
Palm Beach County[45]	576 863	'348 993
Belle Glade—Pahokee division	35 571	...
Belle Glade city[45]	16 535	15 949
Belle Glade Camp (CDP)	1 645	1 892
Pahokee city	6 346	5 663
South Bay city[45]	3 886	2 958
Boca Raton division	58 129	...
Boca Raton city[45]	49 505	28 506
Highland Beach town	2 030	'624
Boynton Beach—Delray Beach division	120 627	...
Boynton Beach city[45]	35 624	18 115
Briny Breezes town	387	481
Delray Beach city[45]	34 325	'19 915
Golf village[45]	110	50
Gulf Stream town	475	408
Hypoluxo town	573	336
Kings Point (CDP)	8 724	...
Lantana town (pt.)	8 048	7 126
Manalapan town	329	205
Ocean Ridge town[45]	1 355	1 074
Glades division	2 515	...
Jupiter division	22 134	...
Juno Beach town (pt.)[45]	175	(NA)
Jupiter town (pt.)[45]	9 868	(NA)
Jupiter Inlet Colony town[45]	378	396
Palm Beach Gardens city (pt.)[45]	2 214	(NA)
Tequesta village[45]	3 685	2 642
Lake Worth division	114 880	...
Atlantis city[45]	1 325	425
Cloud Lake town	160	136
Glen Ridge town	235	216
Greenacres City town[45]	8 843	1 731
Lake Clarke Shores town	3 174	2 328
Lake Worth city[45]	27 048	23 714
Lantana town (pt.)	−	...
Palm Beach town (pt.)	845	...
Palm Springs village[45]	8 166	4 340
South Palm Beach town	1 304	188
Riviera Beach division	78 476	...
Juno Beach town (pt.)[45]	967	(NA)
Lake Park town[45]	6 909	6 993
North Palm Beach village[45]	11 344	9 035
Palm Beach Gardens city (pt.)	12 152	(NA)
Palm Beach Shores town	1 232	1 214
Riviera Beach city[45]	26 489	21 401
West Palm Beach city (pt.)[45]	−	...
Royal Palm Beach—West Jupiter division	14 136	...
Jupiter town (pt.)[45]	−	(NA)
Palm Beach Gardens city (pt.)	41	(NA)
Royal Palm Beach village[45]	3 423	475
West Palm Beach city (pt.)[45]	−	...
Sunshine Parkway division	23 266	...
Sandalfoot Cove (CDP)	5 299	...
Wellington (CDP)	4 622	...
West Palm Beach division	107 129	...
Century Village (CDP)	10 619	...
Golfview town	210	201
Haverhill town	1 249	1 034

County Subdivisions

County Subdivisions	1980	1970
Palm Beach County—Con.		
West Palm Beach division—Con.		
Mangonia Park town	1 419	827
Palm Beach town (pt.)	8 884	9 086
West Palm Beach city (pt.)[45]	63 305	57 375
Pasco County[46]	193 643	75 955
Central Pasco division	17 602	...
Land O' Lakes (CDP) (pt.)	4 327	...
St. Leo town[46]	899	1 145
San Antonio city	529	473
Dade City division	12 483	...
Dade City city[46]	4 923	4 241
Dade City North (CDP) (pt.)	2 619	1 837
Lacoochee division	5 443	...
Dade City North (CDP) (pt.)	538	...
Lacoochee (CDP)	1 720	1 380
New Port Richey division	74 437	...
Beacon Square (CDP)	6 513	2 927
Elfers (CDP)	11 396	...
Holiday (CDP)	18 392	...
Land O' Lakes (CDP) (pt.)	188	...
New Port Richey city[46]	11 196	6 098
New Port Richey East (CDP)	6 147	2 758
Port Richey city (pt.)[46]	336	...
Port Richey division	59 582	...
Bayonet Point (CDP)	16 455	...
Hudson (CDP)	5 799	2 278
Jasmine Estates (CDP)	11 995	2 967
Port Richey city (pt.)[46]	1 829	1 259
Zephyrhills division	24 096	...
Zephyrhills city[46]	5 742	3 369
Zephyrhills North (CDP)	1 710	...
Zephyrhills South (CDP)	1 986	...
Zephyrhills West (CDP)	3 698	...
Pinellas County[47]	728 531	522 329
Boca Ciega division	62 848	'41 816
Bay Pines (CDP)	5 757	...
Indian Shores town[47]	984	791
Largo city (pt.)[47]	879	...
Madeira Beach city[47]	4 520	'4 177
North Redington Beach town	1 156	768
Redington Beach town	1 708	1 583
Redington Shores town	2 142	1 733
Seminole city[47]	4 586	...
Clearwater division	262 607	...
Belleair town	3 673	2 962
Belleair Beach city	1 643	952
Belleair Bluffs city	2 522	1 910
Belleair Shore town	80	124
Clearwater city[47]	85 528	52 074
Dunedin city (pt.)[47]	28 714	(NA)
Indian Rocks Beach city	3 717	2 666
Largo city (pt.)[47]	58 098	'24 230
Oldsmar city (pt.)[47]	997	...
Safety Harbor city[47]	6 461	3 103
St. Petersburg division	348 797	...
Gulfport city[47]	11 180	'9 976
Kenneth City town[47]	4 344	3 862
Lealman (CDP)	19 873	...
Pinellas Park city[47]	32 811	22 287
St. Petersburg city[47]	238 647	'216 159
St. Petersburg Beach city (pt.)	−	...
Seminole city (pt.)[47]	−	...
South Pasadena city	4 188	'2 465
St. Petersburg Beach division	15 670	...
St. Petersburg Beach city (pt.)	9 354	8 024
Treasure Island city	6 316	6 120
Tarpon Springs division	38 609	...
Dunedin city (pt.)[47]	1 489	(NA)
Oldsmar city (pt.)[47]	1 611	1 538
Palm Harbor (CDP)	5 215	...
Tarpon Springs city[47]	13 251	7 118
Polk County[48]	321 652	'228 515
Bartow division	41 091	...
Bartow city[48]	14 780	12 891
Bradley Junction (CDP)	1 108	1 276
Fort Meade city[48]	5 546	4 374
Gordonville (CDP) (pt.)	1 201	...
Mulberry city[48]	2 932	2 701
Willow Oak (CDP) (pt.)	2 111	...
Frostproof division	7 787	...
Frostproof city[48]	2 995	2 814
Haines City division	32 443	...
Davenport town	1 509	'1 303
Dundee town	2 227	1 660
Haines City city (pt.)[48]	10 799	8 956
Lake Hamilton town	1 552	'1 165
Polk City town[48]	119	(NA)
Waverly (CDP)	1 208	1 172
Winter Haven city (pt.)[48]	−	...
Lakeland division	136 445	...
Auburndale city (pt.)[48]	88	...
Combee Settlement (CDP)	5 400	4 963
Crystal Lake (CDP)	6 827	6 227
Eaton Park (CDP)	1 385	...
Gibsonia (CDP)	5 011	...
Highland City (CDP)	1 555	...
Kathleen (CDP)	1 866	...

County Subdivisions

County Subdivisions	1980	1970
Polk County—Con.		
Lakeland division—Con.		
Lakeland city[48]	47 406	ʳ42 803
Lakeland Highlands (CDP)	10 426	...
Medulla (CDP)	2 258	...
Polk City town[48]	457	(NA)
Willow Oak (CDP) (pt.)	4	
Winston (CDP)	9 315	4 505
Lake Wales division	25 012	...
Highland Park village[48]	184	88
Hillcrest Heights town	177	154
Lake Wales city[48]	8 466	8 240
Winter Haven—Auburndale division	78 874	...
Auburndale city (pt.)[48]	6 413	5 386
Cypress Gardens (CDP)	8 043	3 757
Eagle Lake city[48]	1 678	1 373
East Auburndale (CDP)	2 402	2 621
East Winter Haven (CDP)	1 001	1 148
Eloise (CDP)	1 408	1 504
Gordonville (CDP) (pt.)	1 433	...
Haines City city (pt.)[48]	–	...
Inwood (CDP)	6 668	7 716
Jan Phyl Village (CDP)	2 785	1 340
Lake Alfred city[48]	3 134	2 847
Lake Shipp Heights (CDP)	1 250	1 114
North Winter Haven (CDP)	1 140	1 659
Wahneta (CDP)	3 329	2 733
Winter Haven city (pt.)[48]	21 119	16 136
Putnam County[49]	50 549	ʳ36 424
Crescent City division	9 058	6 153
Crescent City city	1 722	1 734
Pomona Park town	791	578
Welaka town	492	496
East Palatka division	6 814	5 299
East Palatka (CDP)	1 613	1 446
Interlachen—Florahome division	12 553	...
Interlachen town[49]	848	478
Palatka division	22 124	...
Palatka city[49]	10 175	ʳ9 444
St. Johns County[50]	51 303	ʳ31 035
Fruit Cove division	4 142	...
Fruit Cove—Switzerland (CDP)	3 906	...
Hastings division	4 753	ʳ3 469
Hastings town	636	ʳ628
Matanzas division	3 040	...
Marineland town (pt.)	23	11
St. Augustine Shores (CDP)	2 105	...
Ponte Vedra division	5 498	...
St. Augustine division	33 870	...
St. Augustine city	11 985	12 352
St. Augustine Beach city	1 289	632
St. Augustine South (CDP)	2 581	...
St. Lucie County[51]	87 182	50 836
Fort Pierce division	65 733	...
Fort Pierce city (pt.)[51]	31 465	29 721
Fort Pierce Northwest (CDP)	5 929	3 269
Fort Pierce South (CDP)	3 324	...
Lakewood Park (CDP)	3 411	...
Port St. Lucie city (pt.)[51]	2 817	(NA)
St. Lucie village[51]	593	428
White City (CDP)	4 110	...
Hutchinson Island division	3 718	...
Fort Pierce city (pt.)[51]	2 337	...
Port St. Lucie division	15 285	...
Port St. Lucie city (pt.)[51]	11 873	(NA)
West St. Lucie division	2 446	...
Santa Rosa County[52]	55 988	37 741
Gulf Breeze—Harold division	17 400	9 447
Gulf Breeze city	5 478	4 190
Jay division	3 983	3 399
Jay town	633	646
Milton division	16 564	14 525
Milton city[52]	7 206	5 360
Munson—McLellen division	2 712	2 194
Pace division	15 329	8 176
Bagdad (CDP)	1 479	...
Pace (CDP)	5 006	1 776
Sarasota County[53]	202 251	120 413
Englewood division	7 657	...
Englewood (CDP) (pt.)	6 744	3 339
Manasota Key (CDP) (pt.)	317	...
South Venice (CDP) (pt.)	–	...
Gulf Gate—Osprey division	14 498	8 324
Coral Cove (CDP)	2 042	1 520
Gulf Gate Estates (CDP) (pt.)	7 422	4 391
Osprey (CDP)	1 660	1 115
Vamo (CDP)	2 574	...
Interior County division	8 686	...
Fruitville (CDP) (pt.)	519	...
Nokomis (CDP) (pt.)	979	...
North Port city (pt.)[53]	46	(NA)
South Venice (CDP) (pt.)	103	...
Venice city (pt.)[53]	120	...
Longboat Key division	2 383	...
Longboat Key town (pt.)	2 383	1 453
North Port division	7 857	...
North Port city (pt.)[53]	6 159	(NA)
Sarasota division	122 216	...

County Subdivisions	1980	1970
Sarasota County—Con.		
Sarasota division—Con.		
Bee Ridge (CDP)	3 313	...
Desoto Lakes (CDP)	1 981	...
Fruitville (CDP) (pt.)	2 551	1 531
Gulf Gate Estates (CDP) (pt.)	1 826	1 483
Kensington Park (CDP)	2 887	3 138
North Sarasota (CDP)	4 997	1 737
Phillippi Gardens (CDP)	2 525	...
Pinecraft (CDP)	1 170	1 208
Pine Shores (CDP)	1 591	1 115
Point O' Rocks (CDP)	1 777	...
Ridge Wood Heights (CDP)	3 951	2 528
Sarasota city[53]	48 868	40 237
Sarasota Springs (CDP)	13 860	4 405
Siesta Key (CDP)	7 010	4 460
Southgate (CDP)	7 322	6 885
South Gate Ridge (CDP)	4 259	2 043
South Sarasota (CDP)	4 267	3 730
Tri Par Estates (CDP)	1 397	1 080
Venice division	38 954	...
Laurel (CDP)	6 368	...
Nokomis (CDP) (pt.)	2 129	3 238
South Venice (CDP) (pt.)	7 972	4 680
Venice city (pt.)[53]	12 033	6 648
Venice East (CDP)	1 675	...
Venice Gardens (CDP)	6 568	...
Seminole County[54]	179 752	83 692
Casselberry—Altamonte Springs division	122 387	...
Altamonte Springs city[54]	22 028	4 391
Casselberry city[54]	15 247	9 438
Fern Park (CDP)	8 890	...
Forest City (CDP)	6 819	...
Goldenrod (CDP) (pt.)	5 586	...
Longwood city (pt.)[54]	9 445	3 203
Wekiva Springs (CDP)	13 386	(NA)
Winter Springs city (pt.)[54]	8 114	(NA)
Oviedo division	13 197	...
Chuluota (CDP)	1 394	...
Geneva (CDP)	1 120	...
Goldenrod (CDP) (pt.)	5	...
Oviedo city[54]	3 074	1 870
Winter Springs city (pt.)[54]	2 361	(NA)
Sanford division	44 168	...
Lake Mary city[54]	2 853	...
Longwood city (pt.)[54]	584	...
Sanford city[54]	23 176	17 393
Sumter County[55]	24 272	14 839
Sumter South division	13 511	7 944
Bushnell city[55]	983	700
Center Hill city	751	371
Lake Panasoffkee (CDP) (pt.)	2 035	...
Webster city[55]	856	739
Wildwood division	10 761	6 895
Coleman city	1 022	614
Lake Panasoffkee (CDP) (pt.)	333	...
Wildwood city[55]	2 665	2 082
Suwannee County[56]	22 287	15 559
Branford division	3 126	2 104
Branford town[56]	622	820
Dowling Park division	3 537	2 055
Live Oak division	12 283	9 118
Live Oak city	6 732	6 830
McAlpin—Wellborn division	3 341	2 282
Taylor County[57]	16 532	13 641
Perry North division	13 689	...
Perry city	8 254	7 701
Perry South division	2 843	...
Union County[58]	10 166	8 112
Lake Butler division	4 661	3 118
Lake Butler city[58]	1 830	1 598
Raiford division	3 836	3 729
Raiford town[58]	259	...
Worthington division	1 669	1 265
Worthington Springs town	220	214
Volusia County[59]	258 762	169 487
Central Volusia division	5 564	...
Daytona Beach city (pt.)[59]	–	...
Ormond Beach city (pt.)[59]	–	...
Port Orange city (pt.)[59]	176	...
Samsula—Spruce Creek (CDP)	1 971	...
Daytona Beach division	40 405	...
Daytona Beach city (pt.)[59]	38 010	(NA)
De Bary—Orange City division	13 001	...
De Bary (CDP)	4 980	3 154
Orange City city[59]	2 795	1 777
De Land division	38 205	...
De Land city[59]	15 354	11 641
De Land Southwest (CDP)	1 481	...
De Leon Springs (CDP)	1 669	1 134
Lake Helen city (pt.)[59]	24	(NA)
North De Land (CDP)	1 557	...
West De Land (CDP)	3 055	...
Deltona division	19 379	...
Deltona (CDP)	15 710	4 868
Lake Helen city (pt.)[59]	2 023	(NA)

County Subdivisions

	1980	1970
Volusia County—Con.		
New Smyrna division[59]	29 876	...
Edgewater city[59]	6 726	3 348
Glencoe (CDP)	1 640	...
New Smyrna Beach city[59]	13 557	10 580
Oak Hill city[59]	938	747
Ponce Inlet town (pt.)	–	...
Port Orange city (pt.)[59]	–	...
North Peninsula division	29 065	...
Daytona Beach city (pt.)[59]	13 997	(NA)
Ormond Beach city (pt.)[59]	6 892	(NA)
Ormond-By-The-Sea (CDP)	7 665	6 002
Ormond Beach division	35 620	...
Holly Hill city	9 953	8 191
Ormond Beach city (pt.)[59]	14 486	(NA)
Pierson—Seville division	4 934	3 246
Pierson town	1 085	654
Port Orange division	35 600	...
Daytona Beach city (pt.)[59]	2 169	(NA)
Ponce Inlet town (pt.)	–	...
Port Orange city (pt.)[59]	18 247	3 781
South Daytona city (pt.)[59]	11 181	4 979
South Peninsula division	7 113	5 317
Daytona Beach Shores city[59]	1 324	768
Ponce Inlet town (pt.)[59]	1 003	328
Port Orange city (pt.)[59]	333	...
South Daytona city (pt.)[59]	71	...
Wakulla County[60]	10 887	6 308
East Wakulla division	7 346	3 732
Crawfordville (CDP)	1 110	...
St. Marks town	286	366
West Wakulla division	3 541	2 576
Sopchoppy city[60]	444	460
Walton County[61]	21 300	16 087
De Funiak Springs division	8 219	6 797
De Funiak Springs city[61]	5 563	4 966
Freeport division[61]	5 494	3 198
Freeport town[61]	669	518
Paxton—Darlington division	5 371	4 282
Paxton town[61]	659	243
Redbay division	2 216	1 810
Washington County[62]	14 509	11 453
Caryville division	2 616	2 161
Caryville town	633	724
Chipley division	6 350	5 595
Chipley city[62]	3 330	3 347
Vernon division	5 543	3 697
Ebro town	233	125
Vernon city	885	691
Wausau town	347	288

GEORGIA

Georgia, the last of the thirteen original colonies in order of settlement, was named in honor of George II of England.

The region now forming this state was first explored in 1540, when De Soto, a Spaniard, traversed it on his way from Florida to the Mississippi. French explorers also visited this region within the next 25 years, but no permanent settlements were made by either the French or the Spanish. Mining operations, however, were begun by the Spanish in 1560 and continued during a period of more than a hundred years.

The greater part of what is now Georgia was included in the Carolina grant of 1663 and all was included in the Carolina grant of 1665 made by King Charles II to the proprietors of Carolina. No settlements within the present limits of the state were made under these grants, and in 1729 seven of the eight proprietors sold their shares of the territory to the English Crown. In June, 1732, the "Trustees for Establishing the Colony of Georgia in America" obtained a royal charter granting them all the lands between the Savannah and the Altamaha, and from the heads of these rivers to the Pacific Ocean. Twelve years later Lord Carteret sold to the trustees the remaining eighth of the Carolina grant.

The first settlement within the limits of what is now Georgia was made at Savannah in February, 1733, by colonists under James Oglethorpe, one of the trustees. One of the objects of the colony was to provide a refuge for the oppressed and the destitute, especially poor debtors, orphans, friendless children and youth, and sufferers from religious persecution in Germany and other continental countries.

In 1763 the charter of the trustees expired and Georgia became a royal province, with the St. Marys River as the southern boundary. South Carolina, however, did not relinquish its claim to the tract between the Altamaha and St. Marys Rivers until 1787.

At the close of the Revolution the territory claimed by Georgia extended westward to the Mississippi. In 1798 the area now in Alabama and Mississippi north of the thirty-first parallel and south of the latitude of the mouth of the Yazoo (about 32°30') was organized as the territory of Mississippi. In 1802 Georgia ceded to the United States all its claims to the region between its present western boundary and the Mississippi; and at the same time the northern boundary of the state, which had been a few miles south of the thirty-fifth parallel, was fixed at that line. Since 1802 the boundaries of the state have remained unchanged.

The Indian claims to lands in Georgia were relinquished at various times between the close of the Revolution and the year 1835.

Georgia was one of the thirteen original colonies. It adopted a state constitution in 1777, and ratified the Federal Constitution in 1788.

COUNTY LOCATION INDEX

Appling	F-4	Columbia	C-5	Hancock	D-4
Atkinson	F-4	Columbus	E-2	Haralson	C-1
Bacon	F-4	Cook	G-3	Harris	D-2
Baker	F-2	Coweta	D-2	Hart	B-4
Baldwin	D-3	Crawford	D-3	Heard	D-1
Banks	B-3	Crisp	F-3	Henry	D-2
Barrow	C-3	Dade	B-1	Houston	E-3
Bartow	B-2	Dawson	B-2	Irwin	F-3
Ben Hill	F-4	Decatur	G-2	Jackson	C-3
Berrien	F-3	De Kalb	C-2	Jasper	D-3
Bibb	D-3	Dodge	E-4	Jeff Davis	F-4
Bleckley	E-3	Dooly	E-3	Jefferson	D-4
Brantley	F-5	Dougherty	F-2	Jenkins	D-5
Brooks	G-3	Douglas	C-2	Johnson	D-4
Bryan	E-5	Early	F-2	Jones	D-3
Bulloch	E-5	Echols	G-4	Lamar	D-2
Burke	D-5	Effingham	E-6	Lanier	G-4
Butts	D-3	Elbert	C-4	Laurens	E-4
Calhoun	F-2	Emanuel	E-4	Lee	F-2
Camden	G-5	Evans	E-5	Liberty	F-5
Candler	E-5	Fannin	B-2	Lincoln	C-4
Carroll	C-1	Fayette	D-2	Long	F-5
Catoosa	B-1	Floyd	B-1	Lowndes	G-3
Charlton	G-5	Forsyth	B-2	Lumpkin	B-3
Chatham	E-6	Franklin	B-3	McDuffie	D-4
Chattahoochee	E-2	Fulton	C-2	McIntosh	F-5
Chattooga	B-1	Gilmer	B-2	Macon	E-3
Cherokee	B-2	Glascock	D-4	Madison	C-3
Clarke	C-3	Glynn	F-5	Marion	E-2
Clay	F-1	Gordon	B-2	Meriwether	D-2
Clayton	C-2	Grady	G-2	Miller	G-2
Clinch	G-4	Greene	C-4	Mitchell	F-2
Cobb	C-2	Gwinnett	C-3	Monroe	D-3
Coffee	F-4	Habersham	B-3	Montgomery	E-4
Colquitt	F-3	Hall	B-3	Morgan	C-3

Murray	B-2	Spalding	D-2	Walker	B-1
Newton	C-3	Stephens	B-3	Walton	C-3
Oconee	C-3	Stewart	E-2	Ware	G-4
Oglethorpe	C-4	Sumter	E-2	Warren	D-4
Paulding	C-2	Talbot	E-2	Washington	D-4
Peach	E-3	Taliaferro	C-4	Wayne	F-5
Pickens	B-2	Tattnall	E-5	Webster	E-2
Pierce	F-5	Taylor	E-2	Wheeler	E-4
Pike	D-2	Telfair	E-4	White	B-3
Polk	C-1	Terrell	F-2	Whitfield	B-2
Pulaski	E-3	Thomas	G-3	Wilcox	E-3
Putnam	D-3	Tift	F-3	Wilkes	C-4
Quitman	F-1	Toombs	E-4	Wilkinson	D-4
Rabun	B-3	Towns	B-3	Worth	F-3
Randolph	F-2	Treutlen	E-4		
Richmond	D-5	Troup	D-1		
Rockdale	C-3	Turner	F-3		
Schley	E-2	Twiggs	E-3		
Screven	D-5	Union	B-3		
Seminole	G-2	Upson	D-2		

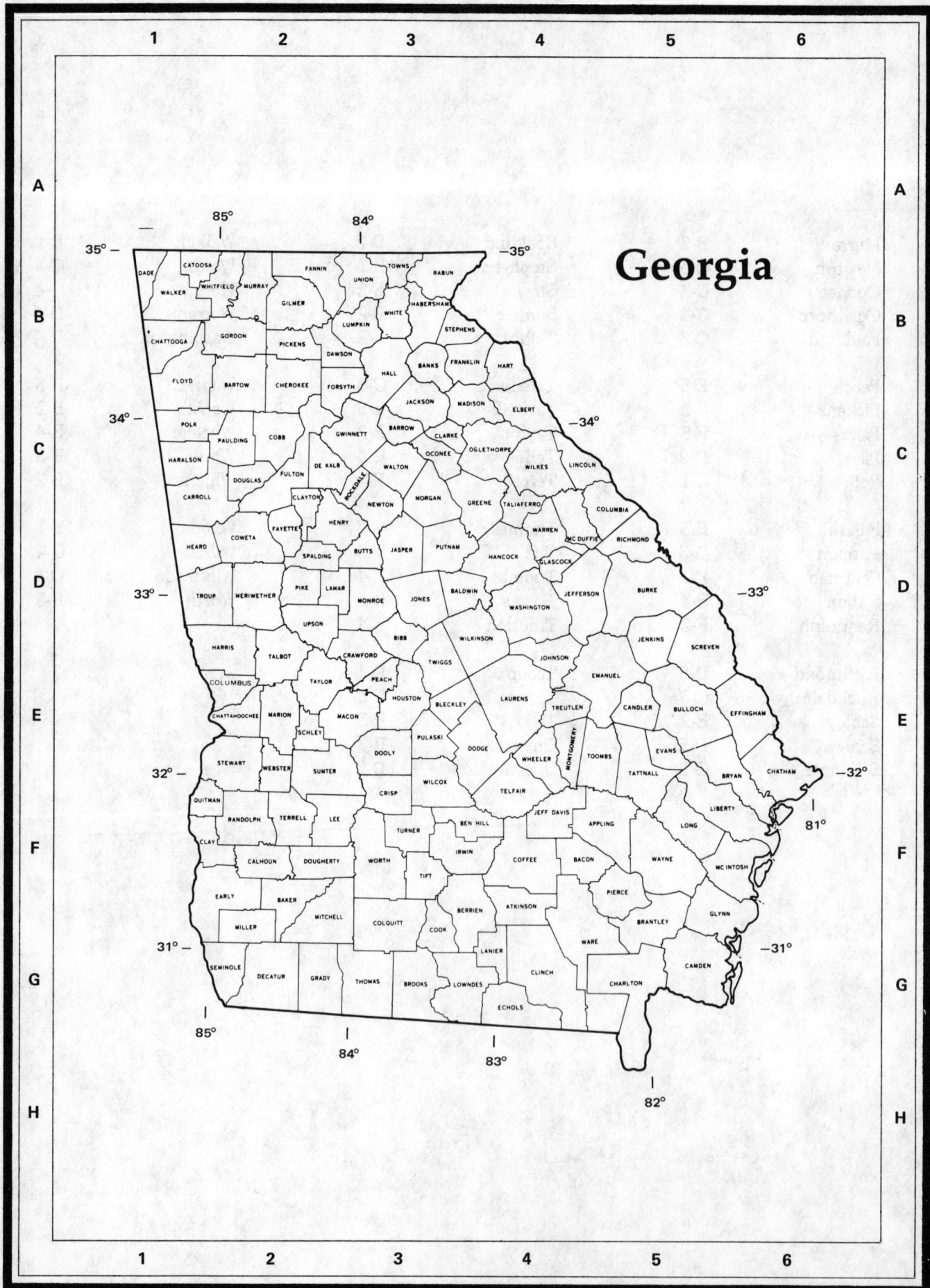

Georgia

Population of the State: Earliest Census to 1980

Urban and Rural

	The State			Urban				Rural			Percent of total population	
		Change from preceding census				Change from preceding census				Change from preceding census		
	Total population	Number	Percent	Places of 2,500 or more	Population	Number	Percent	Population	Number	Percent	Urban	Rural
Current urban definition:												
1980 (Apr. 1)	5 463 105	875 175	19.1	188	3 409 081	641 007	23.2	2 054 024	232 523	12.8	62.4	37.6
1970 (Apr. 1)	'4 587 930	644 814	16.4	147	2 768 074	587 838	27.0	1 821 501	58 621	3.3	60.3	39.7
1960 (Apr. 1)	3 943 116	498 538	14.5	124	2 180 236	620 789	39.8	1 762 880	-122 251	-6.5	55.3	44.7
1950 (Apr. 1)	3 444 578	320 855	10.3	106	1 559 447	...	...	1 885 131	...	...	45.3	54.7
Previous urban definition:												
1960 (Apr. 1)	3 943 116	498 538	14.5	120	1 963 012	536 806	37.6	1 980 104	-38 268	-1.9	49.8	50.2
1950 (Apr. 1)	3 444 578	320 855	10.3	103	1 426 206	352 398	32.8	2 018 372	-31 543	-1.5	41.4	58.6
1940 (Apr. 1)	3 123 723	215 217	7.4	78	1 073 808	178 316	19.9	2 049 915	36 901	1.8	34.4	65.6
1930 (Apr. 1)	2 908 506	12 674	0.4	64	895 492	167 633	23.0	2 013 014	-154 959	-7.1	30.8	69.2
1920 (Jan. 1)	2 895 832	286 711	11.0	59	727 859	189 209	35.1	2 167 973	97 502	4.7	25.1	74.9
1910 (Apr. 15)	2 609 121	392 790	17.7	45	538 650	192 268	55.5	2 070 471	200 522	10.7	20.6	79.4
1900 (June 1)	2 216 331	378 978	20.6	31	346 382	88 910	34.5	1 869 949	290 068	18.4	15.6	84.4
1890 (June 1)	1 837 353	295 173	19.1	22	257 472	112 382	77.5	1 579 881	182 791	13.1	14.0	86.0
1880 (June 1)	1 542 180	358 071	30.2	14	145 090	45 037	45.0	1 397 090	313 034	28.9	9.4	90.6
1870 (June 1)	1 184 109	126 823	12.0	10	100 053	24 587	32.6	1 084 056	102 236	10.4	8.4	91.6
1860 (June 1)	1 057 286	151 101	16.7	9	75 466	36 472	93.5	981 820	114 629	13.2	7.1	92.9
1850 (June 1)	906 185	214 793	31.1	5	38 994	14 336	58.1	867 191	200 457	30.1	4.3	95.7
1840 (June 1)	691 392	174 569	33.8	4	24 658	10 645	76.0	666 734	163 924	32.6	3.6	96.4
1830 (June 1)	516 823	175 834	51.6	2	14 013	6 490	86.3	502 810	169 344	50.8	2.7	97.3
1820 (Aug. 7)	340 989	88 556	35.1	1	7 523	2 308	44.3	333 466	86 248	34.9	2.2	97.8
1810 (Aug. 6)	252 433	89 747	55.2	1	5 215	69	1.3	247 218	89 678	56.9	2.1	97.9
1800 (Aug. 4)	162 686	80 138	97.1	1	5 146	5 146	...	157 540	74 992	90.8	3.2	96.8
1790 (Aug. 2)	82 548	...	...	-	-	...	...	82 548	...	...	-	100.0

NOTE: 1800 population includes that of areas now in Alabama and Mississippi. No population returned in 1790 for that part of Georgia now in Alabama and Mississippi.

APPLING

1820	1,264
1830	1,468
1840	2,052
1850	2,949
1860	4,190
1870	5,086
1880	5,276
1890	8,676
1900	12,336
1910	12,318
1920	10,594
1930	13,314
1940	14,497
1950	14,003
1960	13,246
1970	12,726
1980	15,565

ATKINSON

1920	7,656
1930	6,894
1940	7,093
1950	7,362
1960	6,188
1970	5,879
1980	6,141

BACON

1920	6,460
1930	7,055
1940	8,096
1950	8,940
1960	8,359
1970	8,233
1980	9,379

BAKER

1830	1,253
1840	4,226
1850	8,120
1860	4,985
1870	6,843
1880	7,307
1890	6,144
1900	6,704
1910	7,973
1920	8,293
1930	7,818
1940	7,344
1950	5,952
1960	4,453
1970	3,875
1980	3,808

BALDWIN

1810	6,356
1820	7,734
1830	7,295
1840	7,250
1850	8,148
1860	9,078
1870	10,618
1880	13,806
1890	14,608
1900	17,768
1910	18,354
1920	19,791
1930	22,878
1940	24,190
1950	29,706
1960	34,064
1970	34,240
1980	34,686

BANKS

1860	4,707
1870	4,973
1880	7,337
1890	8,562
1900	10,545
1910	11,244
1920	11,814
1930	9,703
1940	8,733
1950	6,935
1960	6,497
1970	6,833
1980	8,702

BARROW

1920	13,188
1930	12,401
1940	13,064
1950	13,115
1960	14,485
1970	16,859
1980	21,354

BARTOW

1840	9,390
1850	13,300
1860	15,724
1870	16,566
1880	18,690
1890	20,616
1900	20,823
1910	25,388
1920	24,527
1930	25,364
1940	25,283
1950	27,370
1960	28,267
1970	32,911
1980	40,760

BEN HILL

1910	11,863
1920	14,599
1930	13,047
1940	14,523
1950	14,879
1960	13,633
1970	13,171
1980	16,000

BERRIEN

1860	3,475
1870	4,518
1880	6,619
1890	10,694
1900	19,440
1910	22,772
1920	15,573
1930	14,646
1940	15,370
1950	13,966
1960	12,038
1970	11,556
1980	13,525

BIBB

1830	7,154
1840	9,802
1850	12,699
1860	16,291
1870	21,255
1880	27,147
1890	42,370
1900	50,473
1910	56,646
1920	71,304
1930	77,042
1940	83,783
1950	114,079
1960	141,249
1970	143,366
1980	150,256

BLECKLEY

1920	10,532
1930	9,133
1940	9,655
1950	9,218
1960	9,642
1970	10,291
1980	10,767

BRANTLEY

1930	6,895
1940	6,871
1950	6,387
1960	5,891
1970	5,940
1980	8,701

BROOKS

1860	6,356
1870	8,342
1880	11,727
1890	13,979
1900	18,606
1910	23,832
1920	24,538
1930	21,330
1940	20,497
1950	18,169
1960	15,292
1970	13,743
1980	15,255

BRYAN

1800	2,836
1810	2,827
1820	3,021
1830	3,139
1840	3,182
1850	3,424
1860	4,015
1870	4,929
1880	4,252
1890	5,520
1900	6,122
1910	6,702
1920	6,343
1930	5,952
1940	6,288
1950	5,965
1960	6,226
1970	6,539
1980	10,175

BULLOCH

1800	1,913
1810	2,305
1820	2,578
1830	2,597
1840	3,102
1850	4,300
1860	5,668
1870	5,610
1880	8,053
1890	13,712
1900	21,377
1910	26,464
1920	26,133
1930	26,509
1940	26,010
1950	24,740
1960	24,263
1970	31,585
1980	35,785

BURKE

1790	9,467
1800	9,504
1810	10,858
1820	11,577
1830	11,833
1840	13,176
1850	16,100
1860	17,165
1870	17,679
1880	27,128
1890	28,501
1900	30,165
1910	27,268
1920	30,836
1930	29,244
1940	26,520
1950	23,458
1960	20,596
1970	18,255
1980	19,349

BUTTS

1830	4,944
1840	5,308
1850	6,488
1860	6,455
1870	6,941
1880	8,311
1890	10,565
1900	12,805
1910	13,624
1920	12,237
1930	9,345
1940	9,182
1950	9,097
1960	8,976
1970	10,560
1980	13,665

CALHOUN

1860	4,913
1870	5,503
1880	7,024
1890	8,438
1900	9,274
1910	11,334
1920	10,225
1930	10,576
1940	10,438
1950	8,578
1960	7,341

1970	6,606
1980	5,717

CAMDEN

1790	305
1800	1,681
1810	3,941
1820	4,342
1830	4,578
1840	6,075
1850	6,319
1860	5,420
1870	4,615
1880	6,183
1890	6,178
1900	7,669
1910	7,690
1920	6,969
1930	6,338
1940	5,910
1950	7,322
1960	9,975
1970	11,334
1980	13,371

CAMPBELL

1830	3,323
1840	5,370
1850	7,232
1860	8,301
1870	9,176
1880	9,970
1890	9,115
1900	9,518
1910	10,874
1920	11,709
1930	9,903

CANDLER

1920	9,228
1930	8,991
1940	9,103
1950	8,063
1960	6,672
1970	6,412
1980	7,518

CARROLL

1830	3,419
1840	5,252
1850	9,357
1860	11,991
1870	11,782
1880	16,901
1890	22,301
1900	26,576
1910	30,855
1920	34,752
1930	34,272
1940	24,156
1950	34,112
1960	36,451
1970	45,404
1980	56,346

CATOOSA

1860	5,082
1870	4,409
1880	4,739
1890	5,431
1900	5,823

1910	7,184								
1920	6,677								
1930	9,421								
1940	12,199								
1950	15,146								
1960	21,101								
1970	28,271								
1980	36,991								

Column 1		Column 2		Column 3		Column 4		Column 5	

CHARLTON

1860	1,780
1870	1,897
1880	2,154
1890	3,335
1900	3,592
1910	4,722
1920	4,536
1930	4,381
1940	5,256
1950	4,821
1960	5,313
1970	5,680
1980	7,343

CHATHAM

1790	10,749
1800	12,946
1810	13,540
1820	14,737
1830	14,127
1840	18,801
1850	23,901
1860	31,043
1870	41,279
1880	45,023
1890	57,740
1900	71,239
1910	79,690
1920	100,032
1930	105,431
1940	117,970
1950	151,481
1960	188,299
1970	187,816
1980	202,226

CHATTAHOOCHEE

1860	5,797
1870	6,059
1880	5,670
1890	4,902
1900	5,790
1910	5,586
1920	5,266
1930	8,894
1940	15,138
1950	12,149
1960	13,011
1970	25,813
1980	21,732

CHATTOOGA

1840	3,438
1850	6,815
1860	7,165
1870	6,902
1880	10,021
1890	11,202
1900	12,952
1910	13,608
1920	14,312
1930	15,407

1940	18,532
1950	21,197
1960	19,954
1970	20,541
1980	21,856

CHEROKEE

1840	5,895
1850	12,800
1860	11,291
1870	10,399
1880	14,325
1890	15,412
1900	15,243
1910	16,661
1920	18,569
1930	20,003
1940	20,126
1950	20,750
1960	23,001
1970	31,059
1980	51,699

CLARKE

1810	7,628
1820	8,767
1830	10,176
1840	10,522
1850	11,119
1860	11,218
1870	12,941
1880	11,702
1890	15,186
1900	17,708
1910	23,273
1920	26,111
1930	25,613
1940	28,398
1950	36,550
1960	45,363
1970	65,177
1980	74,498

CLAY

1860	4,893
1870	5,493
1880	6,650
1890	7,817
1900	8,568
1910	8,960
1920	7,557
1930	6,943
1940	7,064
1950	5,844
1960	4,551
1970	3,636
1980	3,553

CLAYTON

1860	4,466
1870	5,477
1880	8,027
1890	8,295
1900	9,598
1910	10,453
1920	11,159
1930	10,260
1940	11,655
1950	22,872
1960	46,365
1970	98,126
1980	150,357

CLINCH

1850	637
1860	3,063
1870	3,945
1880	4,138
1890	6,652
1900	8,732
1910	8,424
1920	7,984
1930	7,015
1940	6,437
1950	6,007
1960	6,545
1970	6,405
1980	6,660

COBB

1840	7,539
1850	13,843
1860	14,242
1870	13,814
1880	20,748
1890	22,286
1900	24,664
1910	28,397
1920	30,437
1930	35,408
1940	38,272
1950	61,830
1960	114,174
1970	196,793
1980	297,718

COFFEE

1860	2,879
1870	3,192
1880	5,070
1890	10,483
1900	16,169
1910	21,953
1920	18,653
1930	19,739
1940	21,541
1950	23,961
1960	21,953
1970	22,828
1980	26,894

COLQUITT

1860	1,316
1870	1,654
1880	2,527
1890	4,794
1900	13,636
1910	19,789
1920	29,332
1930	30,622
1940	33,012
1950	33,999
1960	34,048
1970	32,298
1980	35,376

COLUMBIA

1800	8,345
1810	11,242
1820	12,695
1830	12,606
1840	11,356
1850	11,961
1860	11,860

1870	13,529
1880	10,465
1890	11,281
1900	10,653
1910	12,328
1920	11,718
1930	8,793
1940	9,433
1950	9,525
1960	13,423
1970	22,327
1980	40,118

COOK

1920	11,180
1930	11,311
1940	11,919
1950	12,201
1960	11,822
1970	12,129
1980	13,490

COWETA

1830	5,003
1840	10,364
1850	13,635
1860	14,703
1870	15,875
1880	21,109
1890	22,354
1900	24,980
1910	28,800
1920	29,047
1930	25,127
1940	26,972
1950	27,786
1960	28,893
1970	32,310
1980	39,268

CRAWFORD

1830	5,313
1840	7,981
1850	8,984
1860	7,693
1870	7,557
1880	8,656
1890	9,315
1900	10,368
1910	8,310
1920	8,893
1930	7,020
1940	7,128
1950	6,080
1960	5,816
1970	5,748
1980	7,684

CRISP

1910	16,423
1920	18,914
1930	17,343
1940	17,540
1950	17,663
1960	17,768
1970	18,087
1980	19,489

DADE

1840	1,364
1850	2,680

1860	3,069
1870	3,033
1880	4,702
1890	5,707
1900	4,578
1910	4,139
1920	3,918
1930	4,146
1940	5,894
1950	7,364
1960	8,666
1970	9,910
1980	12,318

DAWSON

1860	3,856
1870	4,369
1880	5,837
1890	5,612
1900	5,442
1910	4,686
1920	4,204
1930	3,502
1940	4,479
1950	3,712
1960	3,590
1970	3,639
1980	4,774

DECATUR

1830	4,854
1840	5,872
1850	8,262
1860	11,922
1870	15,183
1880	19,072
1890	19,949
1900	29,454
1910	29,045
1920	31,785
1930	23,662
1940	22,234
1950	23,620
1960	25,203
1970	22,310
1980	25,495

DE KALB

1830	10,042
1840	10,467
1850	14,328
1860	7,806
1870	10,014
1880	14,497
1890	17,189
1900	21,112
1910	27,881
1920	44,051
1930	70,278
1940	86,942
1950	136,395
1960	256,782
1970	415,387
1980	483,024

DODGE

1880	5,358
1890	11,452
1900	13,975
1910	20,127
1920	22,540
1930	21,599

1940	21,022
1950	17,865
1960	16,483
1970	15,658
1980	16,955

DOOLY

1830	2,135
1840	4,427
1850	8,361
1860	8,917
1870	9,790
1880	12,420
1890	18,146
1900	26,527
1910	20,544
1920	20,522
1930	18,025
1940	16,886
1950	14,159
1960	11,474
1970	10,404
1980	10,826

DOUGHERTY

1860	8,295
1870	11,517
1880	12,622
1890	12,206
1900	13,679
1910	16,035
1920	20,063
1930	22,306
1940	28,565
1950	43,617
1960	75,680
1970	89,639
1980	100,718

DOUGLAS

1880	6,934
1890	7,794
1900	8,745
1910	8,593
1920	10,477
1930	9,461
1940	10,053
1950	12,173
1960	16,741
1970	28,659
1980	54,573

EARLY

1820	768
1830	2,051
1840	5,444
1850	7,246
1860	6,149
1870	6,998
1880	7,611
1890	9,792
1900	14,828
1910	18,122
1920	18,983
1930	18,273
1940	18,679
1950	17,413
1960	13,151
1970	12,682
1980	13,158

ECHOLS

1860	1,491
1870	1,978
1880	2,553
1890	3,079
1900	3,209
1910	3,309
1920	3,313
1930	2,744
1940	2,964
1950	2,494
1960	1,876
1970	1,924
1980	2,297

EFFINGHAM

1790	2,424
1800	2,072
1810	2,585
1820	3,018
1830	2,924
1840	3,075
1850	3,864
1860	4,755
1870	4,214
1880	5,979
1890	5,599
1900	8,334
1910	9,971
1920	9,985
1930	10,164
1940	9,646
1950	9,133
1960	10,144
1970	13,632
1980	18,327

ELBERT

1800	10,094
1810	12,156
1820	11,788
1830	12,354
1840	11,125
1850	12,959
1860	10,433
1870	9,249
1880	12,957
1890	15,376
1900	19,729
1910	24,125
1920	23,905
1930	18,485
1940	19,618
1950	18,585
1960	17,835
1970	17,262
1980	18,758

EMANUEL

1820	2,928
1830	2,673
1840	3,129
1850	4,577
1860	5,081
1870	6,134
1880	9,754
1890	14,703
1900	21,279
1910	25,140
1920	25,862
1930	24,101
1940	23,517
1950	19,789

1960	17,815
1970	18,357
1980	20,795

EVANS

1920	6,594
1930	7,102
1940	7,401
1950	6,653
1960	6,952
1970	7,290
1980	8,428

FANNIN

1860	5,139
1870	5,429
1880	7,245
1890	8,724
1900	11,214
1910	12,574
1920	12,103
1930	12,969
1940	14,752
1950	15,192
1960	13,620
1970	13,357
1980	14,748

FAYETTE

1830	5,504
1840	6,191
1850	8,709
1860	7,047
1870	8,221
1880	8,605
1890	8,728
1900	10,114
1910	10,966
1920	11,396
1930	8,655
1940	8,170
1950	7,978
1960	8,199
1970	11,364
1980	29,043

FLOYD

1840	4,411
1850	8,205
1860	15,195
1870	17,230
1880	24,418
1890	28,391
1900	33,113
1910	36,736
1920	39,841
1930	48,667
1940	56,141
1950	62,899
1960	69,130
1970	73,742
1980	79,800

FORSYTH

1840	5,619
1850	8,850
1860	7,749
1870	7,983
1880	10,599
1890	11,155
1900	11,550

1910	11,940
1920	11,755
1930	10,624
1940	11,322
1950	11,005
1960	12,170
1970	17,928
1980	27,958

FRANKLIN

1790	1,041
1800	6,859
1810	10,815
1820	9,040
1830	10,107
1840	9,886
1850	11,513
1860	7,393
1870	7,893
1880	11,453
1890	14,670
1900	17,700
1910	17,894
1920	19,957
1930	15,902
1940	15,612
1950	14,446
1960	13,274
1970	12,784
1980	15,185

FULTON

1860	14,427
1870	33,446
1880	49,137
1890	84,655
1900	117,363
1910	117,733
1920	232,606
1930	318,587
1940	392,886
1950	473,572
1960	556,326
1970	605,210
1980	589,904

GILMER

1840	2,536
1850	8,440
1860	6,724
1870	6,664
1880	8,386
1890	9,074
1900	10,198
1910	9,237
1920	8,406
1930	7,344
1940	9,001
1950	9,963
1960	8,922
1970	8,956
1980	11,110

GLASCOCK

1860	2,437
1870	2,736
1880	3,577
1890	3,720
1900	4,516
1910	4,699
1920	4,192
1930	4,388

1940	4,547
1950	3,579
1960	2,672
1970	2,280
1980	2,382

GLYNN

1790	413
1800	1,874
1810	3,417
1820	3,418
1830	4,567
1840	5,302
1850	4,933
1860	3,889
1870	5,376
1880	6,497
1890	13,420
1900	14,317
1910	15,720
1920	19,370
1930	19,400
1940	21,920
1950	29,046
1960	41,954
1970	50,528
1980	54,981

GORDON

1850	5,984
1860	10,146
1870	9,268
1880	11,171
1890	12,758
1900	14,119
1910	15,861
1920	17,736
1930	16,846
1940	18,445
1950	18,922
1960	19,228
1970	23,570
1980	30,070

GRADY

1910	18,457
1920	20,306
1930	19,200
1940	19,654
1950	18,928
1960	18,015
1970	17,826
1980	19,845

GREENE

1790	5,405
1800	10,761
1810	11,679
1820	13,589
1830	12,549
1840	11,690
1850	13,068
1860	12,652
1870	12,454
1880	17,547
1890	17,051
1900	16,542
1910	18,512
1920	18,972
1930	12,616
1940	13,709
1950	12,843
1960	11,193

1970	10,212	1910	19,189	**HENRY**		1970	21,093	1920	13,546
1980	11,391	1920	28,357			1980	25,343	1930	12,681
		1930	13,070	1830	10,566			1940	12,953
GWINNETT		1940	12,764	1840	11,756	**JASPER**		1950	9,893
		1950	11,052	1850	14,726			1960	8,048
1820	4,589	1960	9,979	1860	10,702	1810	7,753	1970	7,727
1830	13,289	1970	9,019	1870	10,102	1820	14,614	1980	8,660
1840	10,804	1980	9,466	1880	14,193	1830	13,131		
1850	11,257			1890	16,220	1840	11,111	**JONES**	
1860	12,940	**HARALSON**		1900	18,602	1850	11,486		
1870	12,431			1910	19,927	1860	10,743	1810	8,587
1880	19,531	1860	3,039	1920	20,420	1870	10,439	1820	16,570
1890	19,899	1870	4,004	1930	15,924	1880	11,851	1830	13,345
1900	25,585	1880	5,974	1940	15,119	1890	13,879	1840	10,065
1910	28,824	1890	11,316	1950	15,857	1900	15,033	1850	10,224
1920	30,327	1900	11,922	1960	17,619	1910	16,552	1860	9,107
1930	27,853	1910	13,514	1970	23,724	1920	16,362	1870	9,436
1940	29,087	1920	14,440	1980	36,309	1930	8,594	1880	11,613
1950	32,320	1930	13,263			1940	8,772	1890	12,709
1960	43,541	1940	14,377	**HOUSTON**		1950	7,473	1900	13,358
1970	72,349	1950	14,663			1960	6,135	1910	13,103
1980	166,903	1960	14,543	1830	7,369	1970	5,760	1920	13,269
		1970	15,927	1840	9,711	1980	7,553	1930	8,992
HABERSHAM		1980	18,422	1850	16,450			1940	8,331
				1860	15,611	**JEFF DAVIS**		1950	7,538
1820	3,145	**HARRIS**		1870	20,406			1960	8,468
1830	10,671			1880	22,414	1910	6,050	1970	12,270
1840	7,961	1830	5,105	1890	21,613	1920	7,322	1980	16,579
1850	8,895	1840	13,933	1900	22,641	1930	8,118		
1860	5,966	1850	14,721	1910	23,609	1940	8,841	**LAMAR**	
1870	6,322	1860	13,736	1920	21,964	1950	9,299		
1880	8,718	1870	13,284	1930	11,280	1960	8,914	1930	9,745
1890	11,573	1880	15,758	1940	11,303	1970	9,425	1940	10,091
1900	13,604	1890	16,797	1950	20,964	1980	11,473	1950	10,242
1910	10,134	1900	18,009	1960	39,154			1960	10,240
1920	10,730	1910	17,886	1970	62,924	**JEFFERSON**		1970	10,688
1930	12,748	1920	15,775	1980	77,605			1980	12,215
1940	14,771	1930	11,140			1800	5,684		
1950	16,553	1940	11,428	**IRWIN**		1810	6,111	**LANIER**	
1960	18,116	1950	11,265			1820	7,056		
1970	20,691	1960	11,167	1820	411	1830	7,309	1930	5,190
1980	25,020	1970	11,520	1830	1,180	1840	7,254	1940	5,632
		1980	15,464	1840	2,038	1850	9,131	1950	5,151
HALL				1850	3,334	1860	10,219	1960	5,097
		HART		1860	1,699	1870	12,190	1970	5,031
1820	5,086			1870	1,837	1880	15,671	1980	5,654
1830	11,748	1860	6,137	1880	2,696	1890	17,213		
1840	7,875	1870	6,783	1890	6,316	1900	18,212	**LAURENS**	
1850	8,713	1880	9,094	1900	13,645	1910	21,379		
1860	9,366	1890	10,887	1910	10,461	1920	22,602	1810	2,210
1870	9,607	1900	14,492	1920	12,670	1930	20,727	1820	5,436
1880	15,298	1910	16,216	1930	12,199	1940	20,040	1830	5,589
1890	18,047	1920	17,944	1940	12,936	1950	18,885	1840	5,585
1900	20,752	1930	15,714	1950	11,973	1960	17,468	1850	6,442
1910	25,730	1940	15,512	1960	9,211	1970	17,174	1860	6,998
1920	26,822	1950	14,495	1970	8,036	1980	18,403	1870	7,834
1930	30,313	1960	15,229	1980	8,988			1880	10,053
1940	34,822	1970	15,814			**JENKINS**		1890	13,747
1950	40,113	1980	18,585	**JACKSON**				1900	25,908
1960	49,739					1910	11,520	1910	35,501
1970	59,405	**HEARD**		1800	7,736	1920	14,328	1920	39,605
1980	75,649			1810	10,569	1930	11,908	1930	32,693
		1840	5,329	1820	8,355	1940	11,843	1940	33,606
HANCOCK		1850	6,923	1830	9,004	1950	10,264	1950	33,123
		1860	7,805	1840	8,522	1960	9,148	1960	32,313
1800	14,456	1870	7,886	1850	9,768	1970	8,332	1970	32,738
1810	13,330	1880	8,769	1860	10,605	1980	8,841	1980	36,990
1820	12,734	1890	9,557	1870	11,181				
1830	11,820	1900	11,177	1880	16,297	**JOHNSON**		**LEE**	
1840	9,659	1910	11,180	1890	19,176				
1850	11,578	1920	11,126	1900	24,039	1860	2,919	1830	1,680
1860	12,044	1930	9,102	1910	30,169	1870	2,964	1840	4,520
1870	11,317	1940	8,160	1920	24,654	1880	4,800	1850	6,660
1880	16,989	1950	6,975	1930	21,609	1890	6,129	1860	7,196
1890	17,149	1960	5,333	1940	20,089	1900	11,409	1870	9,567
1900	18,277	1970	5,354	1950	18,897	1910	12,897	1880	10,577
		1980	6,520	1960	18,499				

1890	9,074
1900	10,344
1910	11,697
1920	10,904
1930	8,328
1940	7,837
1950	6,674
1960	6,204
1970	7,044
1980	11,684

LIBERTY

1790	5,355
1800	5,313
1810	6,228
1820	6,695
1830	7,233
1840	7,241
1850	6,926
1860	8,367
1870	7,688
1880	10,649
1890	12,887
1900	13,093
1910	12,924
1920	12,707
1930	8,153
1940	8,595
1950	8,444
1960	14,487
1970	17,569
1980	37,583

LINCOLN

1800	4,766
1810	4,555
1820	6,458
1830	6,145
1840	5,895
1850	5,998
1860	5,466
1870	5,413
1880	6,412
1890	6,146
1900	7,156
1910	8,714
1920	9,739
1930	7,847
1940	7,042
1950	6,462
1960	5,906
1970	5,895
1980	6,716

LONG

1930	4,180
1940	4,086
1950	3,598
1960	3,874
1970	3,746
1980	4,524

LOWNDES

1830	2,453
1840	5,574
1850	7,714
1860	5,249
1870	8,321
1880	11,049
1890	15,102
1900	20,036
1910	24,436
1920	26,521
1930	29,994
1940	31,860
1950	35,211
1960	49,270
1970	55,112
1980	67,972

LUMPKIN

1840	5,671
1850	8,955
1860	4,626
1870	5,161
1880	6,526
1890	6,867
1900	7,433
1910	5,444
1920	5,240
1930	4,927
1940	5,233
1950	6,574
1960	7,241
1970	8,728
1980	10,762

MACON

1840	5,045
1850	7,052
1860	8,449
1870	11,458
1880	11,675
1890	13,183
1900	14,093
1910	15,016
1920	17,667
1930	16,643
1940	15,947
1950	14,213
1960	13,170
1970	12,933
1980	14,003

MADISON

1820	3,735
1830	4,646
1840	4,510
1850	5,703
1860	5,933
1870	5,227
1880	7,978
1890	11,024
1900	13,224
1910	16,851
1920	18,803
1930	14,921
1940	13,431
1950	12,238
1960	11,246
1970	13,517
1980	17,747

MARION

1830	1,436
1840	4,812
1850	10,280
1860	7,390
1870	8,000
1880	8,598
1890	7,728
1900	10,080
1910	9,147
1920	7,604
1930	6,968
1940	6,954
1950	6,521
1960	5,477
1970	5,099
1980	5,297

McDUFFIE

1880	9,449
1890	8,789
1900	9,804
1910	10,325
1920	11,509
1930	9,014
1940	10,878
1950	11,443
1960	12,627
1970	15,276
1980	18,546

McINTOSH

1800	2,660
1810	3,739
1820	5,129
1830	4,998
1840	5,360
1850	6,027
1860	5,546
1870	4,491
1880	6,241
1890	6,471
1900	6,537
1910	6,442
1920	5,119
1930	5,763
1940	5,292
1950	6,008
1960	6,364
1970	7,371
1980	8,046

MERIWETHER

1830	4,422
1840	14,132
1850	16,476
1860	15,330
1870	13,756
1880	17,651
1890	20,740
1900	23,339
1910	25,180
1920	26,168
1930	22,437
1940	22,055
1950	21,055
1960	19,756
1970	19,461
1980	21,229

MILLER

1860	1,791
1870	3,091
1880	3,720
1890	4,275
1900	6,319
1910	7,986
1920	9,565
1930	9,076
1940	9,998
1950	9,023
1960	6,908
1970	6,424
1980	7,038

MILTON

1860	4,602
1870	4,284
1880	6,261
1890	6,208
1900	6,763
1910	7,239
1920	6,886
1930	6,730

MITCHELL

1860	4,308
1870	6,633
1880	9,392
1890	10,906
1900	14,767
1910	22,114
1920	25,588
1930	23,620
1940	23,261
1950	22,528
1960	19,652
1970	18,956
1980	21,114

MONROE

1830	16,202
1840	16,275
1850	16,985
1860	15,953
1870	17,213
1880	18,808
1890	19,137
1900	20,682
1910	20,450
1920	20,138
1930	11,606
1940	10,749
1950	10,532
1960	10,495
1970	10,991
1980	14,610

MONTGOMERY

1800	3,180
1810	2,954
1820	1,869
1830	1,269
1840	1,616
1850	2,154
1860	2,997
1870	3,586
1880	5,381
1890	9,248
1900	16,359
1910	19,638
1920	9,167
1930	10,020
1940	9,668
1950	7,901
1960	6,284
1970	6,099
1980	7,011

MORGAN

1810	8,369
1820	13,520
1830	12,046
1840	9,121
1850	10,744
1860	9,997
1870	10,696
1880	14,032
1890	16,041
1900	15,813
1910	19,717
1920	20,143
1930	12,488
1940	12,713
1950	11,899
1960	10,280
1970	9,904
1980	11,572

MURRAY

1840	4,695
1850	14,433
1860	7,083
1870	6,500
1880	8,269
1890	8,461
1900	8,263
1910	9,763
1920	9,490
1930	9,215
1940	11,137
1950	10,676
1960	10,447
1970	12,986
1980	19,685

MUSCOGEE

1830	3,508
1840	11,699
1850	18,578
1860	16,584
1870	16,663
1880	19,322
1890	27,761
1900	29,836
1910	36,227
1920	44,195
1930	57,558
1940	75,494
1950	118,028
1960	158,623
1970	167,377
1980	170,108

NEWTON

1830	11,155
1840	11,628
1850	13,296
1860	14,320
1870	14,615
1880	13,623
1890	14,310
1900	16,734
1910	18,449
1920	21,680
1930	17,290
1940	18,576
1950	20,185
1960	20,999
1970	26,282
1980	34,489

OCONEE

1880	6,351
1890	7,713
1900	8,602
1910	11,104
1920	11,067

1930	8,082
1940	7,576
1950	7,009
1960	6,304
1970	7,915
1980	12,427

OGLETHORPE

1800	9,780
1810	12,279
1820	14,046
1830	13,618
1840	10,868
1850	12,259
1860	11,549
1870	11,782
1880	15,400
1890	16,951
1900	17,881
1910	18,680
1920	20,278
1930	12,927
1940	12,430
1950	9,958
1960	7,926
1970	7,598
1980	8,929

PAULDING

1840	2,556
1850	7,039
1860	7,038
1870	7,369
1880	10,887
1890	11,948
1900	12,969
1910	14,124
1920	14,025
1930	12,327
1940	12,832
1950	11,752
1960	13,101
1970	17,520
1980	26,110

PEACH

1930	10,268
1940	10,378
1950	11,705
1960	13,846
1970	15,990
1980	19,151

PICKENS

1860	4,951
1870	5,317
1880	6,970
1890	8,182
1900	8,641
1910	9,041
1920	8,222
1930	9,687
1940	9,136
1950	8,855
1960	8,903
1970	9,260
1980	11,652

PIERCE

1860	1,973
1870	2,778

1880	4,538
1890	6,379
1900	8,100
1910	10,749
1920	11,934
1930	12,522
1940	11,800
1950	11,112
1960	9,678
1970	9,281
1980	11,897

PIKE

1830	6,149
1840	9,176
1850	14,306
1860	10,078
1870	10,905
1880	15,849
1890	16,300
1900	18,761
1910	19,495
1920	21,212
1930	10,853
1940	10,375
1950	8,459
1960	7,138
1970	7,316
1980	8,937

POLK

1860	6,295
1870	7,822
1880	11,952
1890	14,945
1900	17,856
1910	20,203
1920	20,357
1930	25,141
1940	28,467
1950	30,976
1960	28,015
1970	29,656
1980	32,386

PULASKI

1810	2,093
1820	5,283
1830	4,906
1840	5,389
1850	6,627
1860	8,744
1870	11,940
1880	14,058
1890	16,559
1900	18,489
1910	22,835
1920	11,587
1930	9,005
1940	9,829
1950	8,808
1960	8,204
1970	8,066
1980	8,950

PUTNAM

1810	10,029
1820	15,475
1830	13,261
1840	10,260
1850	10,794
1860	10,125

1870	10,461
1880	14,539
1890	14,842
1900	13,436
1910	13,876
1920	15,151
1930	8,367
1940	8,514
1950	7,731
1960	7,798
1970	8,394
1980	10,295

QUITMAN

1860	3,499
1870	4,150
1880	4,392
1890	4,471
1900	4,701
1910	4,594
1920	3,417
1930	3,820
1940	3,435
1950	3,015
1960	2,432
1970	2,180
1980	2,357

RABUN

1820	524
1830	2,176
1840	1,912
1850	2,448
1860	3,271
1870	3,256
1880	4,634
1890	5,606
1900	6,285
1910	5,562
1920	5,746
1930	6,331
1940	7,821
1950	7,424
1960	7,456
1970	8,327
1980	10,466

RANDOLPH

1830	2,191
1840	8,276
1850	12,868
1860	9,571
1870	10,561
1880	13,341
1890	15,267
1900	16,847
1910	18,841
1920	16,721
1930	17,174
1940	16,609
1950	13,804
1960	11,078
1970	8,734
1980	9,599

RICHMOND

1790	11,317
1800	5,475
1810	6,189
1820	8,608
1830	11,644
1840	11,932

1850	16,246
1860	21,284
1870	25,724
1880	34,665
1890	45,194
1900	53,735
1910	58,886
1920	63,692
1930	72,990
1940	81,863
1950	108,876
1960	135,601
1970	162,437
1980	181,629

ROCKDALE

1880	6,838
1890	6,813
1900	7,515
1910	8,916
1920	9,521
1930	7,247
1940	7,724
1950	8,464
1960	10,572
1970	18,152
1980	36,747

SCHLEY

1860	4,633
1870	5,129
1880	5,302
1890	5,443
1900	5,499
1910	5,213
1920	5,248
1930	5,347
1940	5,033
1950	4,036
1960	3,256
1970	3,079
1980	3,433

SCREVEN

1800	3,019
1810	4,477
1820	3,941
1830	4,776
1840	4,794
1850	6,274
1860	8,274
1870	9,175
1880	12,876
1890	14,424
1900	19,252
1910	20,202
1920	23,552
1930	20,503
1940	20,353
1950	18,000
1960	14,919
1970	12,591
1980	14,043

SEMINOLE

1930	7,389
1950	7,904
1960	6,802
1970	7,059
1980	9,057

SPALDING

1860	8,699
1870	10,205
1880	12,585
1890	13,117
1900	17,619
1910	19,741
1920	21,908
1930	23,495
1940	28,427
1950	31,045
1960	35,404
1970	39,514
1980	47,899

STEPHENS

1910	9,728
1920	11,215
1930	11,740
1940	12,972
1950	16,647
1960	18,391
1970	20,331
1980	21,763

STEWART

1840	12,933
1850	16,027
1860	13,422
1870	14,204
1880	13,998
1890	15,682
1900	15,856
1910	13,437
1920	12,089
1930	11,114
1940	10,603
1950	9,194
1960	7,371
1970	6,511
1980	5,896

SUMTER

1840	5,759
1850	10,322
1860	9,428
1870	16,559
1880	18,239
1890	22,107
1900	26,212
1910	29,092
1920	29,640
1930	26,800
1940	24,502
1950	24,208
1960	24,652
1970	26,931
1980	29,360

TALBOT

1830	5,940
1840	15,627
1850	16,534
1860	13,616
1870	11,913
1880	14,115
1890	13,258
1900	12,197
1910	11,696
1920	11,158
1930	8,458

1940	8,141		1930	14,997		1960	4,538		1930	6,340		1920	28,361
1950	7,687		1940	15,145		1970	4,565		1940	7,680		1930	26,558
1960	7,127		1950	13,221		1980	5,638		1950	7,138		1940	27,929
1970	6,625		1960	11,715					1960	6,510		1950	30,289
1980	6,536		1970	11,394		TREUTLEN			1970	6,811		1960	34,219
			1980	11,445					1980	9,390		1970	33,525
TALIAFERRO						1920	7,664					1980	37,180
			TERRELL			1930	7,488		UPSON				
1830	4,934					1940	7,632					WARREN	
1840	5,190		1860	6,232		1950	6,522		1830	7,013			
1850	5,146		1870	9,053		1960	5,874		1840	9,408		1800	8,329
1860	4,583		1880	10,451		1970	5,647		1850	9,424		1810	8,725
1870	4,796		1890	14, 03		1980	6,087		1860	9,910		1820	10,630
1880	7,034		1900	19,023					1870	9,430		1830	10,946
1890	7,291		1910	22,003		TROUP			1880	12,400		1840	9,789
1900	7,912		1920	19,601					1890	12,188		1850	12,425
1910	8,766		1930	18,290		1830	5,799		1900	13,670		1860	9,820
1920	8,841		1940	16,675		1840	15,733		1910	12,757		1870	10,545
1930	6,172		1950	14,314		1850	16,879		1920	14,786		1880	10,885
1940	6,287		1960	12,742		1860	16,262		1930	19,509		1890	10,957
1950	4,515		1970	11,416		1870	17,632		1940	25,064		1900	11,463
1960	3,370		1980	12,017		1880	20,565		1950	25,078		1910	11,860
1970	2,423					1890	20,723		1960	23,800		1920	11,828
1980	2,032		THOMAS			1900	24,002		1970	23,505		1930	11,181
						1910	26,228		1980	25,998		1940	10,236
TATTNALL			1830	3,299		1920	36,097					1950	8,779
			1840	6,766		1930	36,752		WALKER			1960	7,360
1810	2,206		1850	10,103		1940	43,879					1970	6,669
1820	2,644		1860	10,766		1950	49,841		1840	6,572		1980	6,583
1830	2,040		1870	14,523		1960	47,189		1850	13,109			
1840	2,724		1880	20,597		1970	44,466		1860	10,082		WASHINGTON	
1850	3,227		1890	26,154		1980	50,003		1870	9,925			
1860	4,352		1900	31,076					1880	11,056		1790	4,552
1870	4,860		1910	29,071		TURNER			1890	13,282		1800	10,300
1880	6,988		1920	33,044					1900	15,661		1810	9,940
1890	10,253		1930	32,612		1910	10,075		1910	18,692		1820	10,627
1900	20,419		1940	31,289		1920	12,466		1920	23,370		1830	9,820
1910	18,569		1950	33,932		1930	11,196		1930	26,206		1840	10,565
1920	14,502		1960	34,319		1940	10,846		1940	31,024		1850	11,766
1930	15,411		1970	34,562		1950	10,479		1950	38,198		1860	12,698
1940	16,243		1980	38,098		1960	8,439		1960	45,264		1870	15,842
1950	15,939					1970	8,790		1970	50,691		1880	21,964
1960	15,837		TIFT			1980	9,510		1980	56,470		1890	25,237
1970	16,557											1900	28,277
1980	18,134		1910	11,487		TWIGGS			WALTON			1910	28,174
			1920	14,493								1920	28,147
TAYLOR			1930	16,068		1810	3,405		1810	1,026		1930	25,030
			1940	18,599		1820	10,640		1820	4,192		1940	24,230
1860	5,998		1950	22,645		1830	8,031		1830	10,929		1950	21,012
1870	7,143		1960	23,487		1840	8,422		1840	10,209		1960	18,903
1880	8,597		1970	27,288		1850	8,179		1850	10,821		1970	17,480
1890	8,666		1980	32,862		1860	8,320		1860	11,074		1980	18,842
1900	9,846					1870	8,545		1870	11,038			
1910	10,839		TOOMBS			1880	8,918		1880	15,622		WAYNE	
1920	11,473					1890	8,195		1890	17,467			
1930	10,617		1910	11,206		1900	8,716		1900	20,942		1810	676
1940	10,768		1920	13,897		1910	10,736		1910	25,393		1820	1,010
1950	9,113		1930	17,165		1920	10,407		1920	24,216		1830	963
1960	8,311		1940	16,952		1930	8,372		1930	21,118		1840	1,258
1970	7,865		1950	17,382		1940	9,117		1940	20,777		1850	1,499
1980	7,902		1960	16,837		1950	8,308		1950	29,230		1860	2,268
			1970	19,151		1960	7,935		1960	20,481		1870	2,177
TELFAIR			1980	22,592		1970	8,222		1970	23,404		1880	5,980
						1980	9,354		1980	31,211		1890	7,485
1810	744		TOWNS									1900	9,449
1820	2,104					UNION			WARE			1910	13,069
1830	2,136		1860	2,459								1920	14,381
1840	2,763		1870	2,780		1840	3,152		1830	1,205		1930	12,647
1850	3,026		1880	3,261		1850	7,234		1840	2,323		1940	13,122
1860	2,713		1890	4,064		1860	4,413		1850	3,888		1950	14,248
1870	3,245		1900	4,748		1870	5,267		1860	2,200		1960	17,921
1880	4,828		1910	3,932		1880	6,431		1870	2,286		1970	17,858
1890	5,477		1920	3,937		1890	7,749		1880	4,139		1980	20,750
1900	10,083		1930	4,346		1900	8,481		1890	8,811			
1910	13,288		1940	4,925		1910	6,918		1900	13,761			
1920	15,291		1950	4,803		1920	5,455		1910	22,957			

WEBSTER

1860	5,030
1870	4,677
1880	5,237
1890	5,695
1900	6,618
1910	6,151
1920	5,342
1930	5,032
1940	4,726
1950	4,081
1960	3,247
1970	2,362
1980	2,341

WHEELER

1920	9,817
1930	9,149
1940	8,535
1950	6,712
1960	5,342
1970	4,596
1980	5,155

WHITE

1860	3,315
1870	4,606
1880	5,341
1890	6,151
1900	5,912
1910	5,110
1920	6,105
1930	6,056
1940	6,417
1950	5,951
1960	5,935
1970	7,742
1980	10,120

WHITFIELD

1860	10,047
1870	10,117
1880	11,900
1890	12,916
1900	14,509
1910	15,934
1920	16,897
1930	20,808
1940	26,105
1950	34,432
1960	42,109
1970	55,108
1980	65,789

WILCOX

1860	2,115
1870	2,439
1880	3,109
1890	7,980
1900	11,097
1910	13,486
1920	15,511
1930	13,439
1940	12,755
1950	10,167
1960	7,905
1970	6,998
1980	7,682

WILKES

1790	31,500
1800	13,103
1810	14,887
1820	17,607
1830	14,237
1840	10,148
1850	12,107
1860	11,420
1870	11,796
1880	15,985
1890	18,081
1900	20,866
1910	23,441
1920	24,210
1930	15,944
1940	15,084
1950	12,388
1960	10,961
1970	10,184
1980	10,951

WILKINSON

1810	2,154
1820	6,992
1830	6,513
1840	6,842
1850	8,296
1860	9,376
1870	9,383
1880	12,061
1890	10,781
1900	11,440
1910	10,078
1920	11,376
1930	10,844
1940	11,025
1950	9,781
1960	9,250
1970	9,393
1980	10,368

WORTH

1860	2,763
1870	3,778
1880	5,892
1890	10,048
1900	18,664
1910	18,147
1920	23,863
1930	21,094
1940	21,374
1950	19,357
1960	16,682
1970	14,770
1980	18,064

NOTES

BARTOW

Name changed from Cass in 1861.

CAMPBELL

Annexed to Fulton prior to 1940.

JASPER

Name changed from Randolph in 1812.

MILTON

Annexed to Fulton prior to 1940.

MUSCOGEE

Subsequent to the 1970 census, Muscogee County was replaced by a consolidated government of Columbus City and Muscogee County as a primary division of the State of Georgia. The new unit is called Columbus [Not Columbus County or Columbus City].

WEBSTER

Name changed from Kinchafoonee in 1856.

ALBANY

1860	1,618
1870	2,101
1880	3,216
1890	4,008
1900	4,606
1910	8,190
1920	11,555
1930	14,507
1940	19,055
1950	31,155
1960	55,890
1970	72,623
1980	74,059

AMERICUS

1870	3,259
1880	3,635
1890	6,398
1900	7,674
1910	8,063
1920	9,010
1930	8,760
1940	9,281
1950	11,389
1960	13,472
1970	16,091
1980	16,120

ATHENS

1850	1,661
1860	3,848
1870	4,251
1880	6,099
1890	8,369
1900	10,245
1910	14,913
1920	16,748
1930	18,192
1940	20,650
1950	28,180
1960	31,355
1970	44,342
1980	42,549

ATLANTA

1850	2,572
1860	9,554
1870	21,789
1880	37,409
1890	65,533
1900	89,872
1910	154,839
1920	200,616
1930	270,366
1940	302,288
1950	331,314
1960	487,455
1970	495,039
1980	425,022

AUGUSTA

1800	2,215
1810	2,476
1820	6,403
1840	12,493
1860	12,493
1870	15,389
1880	21,891
1890	33,300
1900	39,441
1910	41,040
1920	52,548
1930	60,342
1940	65,919
1950	71,508
1960	70,626
1970	59,864
1980	47,532

BAINBRIDGE

1860	1,869
1870	1,351
1880	1,436
1890	1,668
1900	2,641
1910	4,217
1920	4,792
1930	6,141
1940	6,352
1950	7,562
1960	12,714
1970	19,887
1980	10,553

BRUNSWICK

1860	825
1870	2,348
1880	2,891
1890	8,459
1900	9,081
1910	10,182
1920	14,413
1930	14,022
1940	15,035
1950	17,954
1960	21,703
1970	19,585
1980	17,605

CARROLLTON

1880	926
1890	1,451
1900	1,998
1910	3,297
1920	4,363
1930	5,052
1940	6,214
1950	7,753
1960	10,973
1970	13,520
1980	14,078

COLLEGE PARK

1900	517
1910	2,173
1920	3,622
1930	6,604
1940	8,213
1950	14,535
1960	23,469
1970	18,203
1980	24,632

COLUMBUS

1830	3,144
1840	5,942
1850	9,621
1860	7,401
1870	10,123
1880	17,303
1890	17,614
1900	17,614
1910	20,554
1920	31,125
1930	43,131
1940	53,280
1950	79,611
1960	116,779
1970	155,028
1980	169,441

CORDELE

1890	1,578
1900	3,473
1910	5,883
1920	6,538
1930	6,880
1940	7,929
1950	9,462
1960	10,609
1970	10,733
1980	10,914

COVINGTON

1870	1,121
1880	1,415
1890	1,823
1900	2,062
1910	2,697
1920	3,203
1930	3,203
1940	3,900
1950	5,192
1960	8,167
1970	10,267
1980	10,586

DALTON

1860	1,649
1870	1,809
1880	2,516
1890	3,046
1900	4,315
1910	5,324
1920	5,222
1930	8,160
1940	10,448
1950	15,968
1960	17,868
1970	18,872
1980	20,939

DECATUR

1870	401
1880	639
1890	1,013
1900	1,418
1910	2,466
1920	6,150
1930	13,276
1940	16,561
1950	21,635
1960	22,026
1970	21,943
1980	18,404

DOUGLAS

1900	617
1910	3,550
1920	3,401
1930	4,206
1940	5,175
1950	7,428
1960	8,736
1970	10,195
1980	10,980

DUBLIN

1880	572
1890	862
1900	2,987
1910	5,795
1920	7,707
1930	6,681
1940	7,814
1950	10,232
1960	13,814
1970	15,143
1980	16,083

EAST POINT

1880	195
1890	738
1900	1,315
1910	3,682
1920	5,241
1930	9,512
1940	12,403
1950	21,080
1960	35,633
1970	39,315
1980	32,486

FITZGERALD

1930	6,412
1940	7,338
1950	8,130
1960	8,781
1970	8,187
1980	10,187

FOREST PARK

1910	173
1920	308
1930	388
1940	577
1950	2,653
1960	14,201
1970	19,994
1980	18,782

GAINESVILLE

1860	344
1870	472
1880	1,919
1890	3,202
1900	4,382
1910	5,925
1920	6,272
1930	8,624
1940	10,243
1950	11,936
1960	16,523
1970	15,459
1980	15,280

GRIFFIN

1850	2,855
1860	3,421
1870	3,620
1880	4,503
1890	6,857
1900	6,857

1910	7,478
1920	8,240
1930	10,321
1940	13,222
1950	13,982
1960	21,735
1970	22,734
1980	20,728

HINESVILLE

1930	416
1940	630
1950	1,217
1960	3,174
1970	4,115
1980	11,309

LA GRANGE

1850	1,523
1860	(NA)
1870	2,053
1880	2,295
1890	3,090
1900	4,274
1910	5,587
1920	17,038
1930	20,131
1940	21,983
1950	25,025
1960	23,632
1970	23,301
1980	24,204

MACON

1840	3,927
1850	5,720
1860	8,247
1870	10,810
1880	12,749
1890	22,746
1900	23,272
1910	40,665
1920	52,995
1930	53,829
1940	57,865
1950	70,252
1960	69,764
1970	122,423
1980	116,896

MARIETTA

1870	1,888
1880	2,227
1890	3,384
1900	4,446
1910	5,949
1920	6,190
1930	7,638
1940	8,667
1950	20,687
1960	25,565
1970	27,216
1980	30,829

MILLEDGEVILLE

1840	2,095
1850	2,216
1860	2,480
1870	2,750
1880	3,800
1890	3,322
1900	4,219

1910	4,385
1920	4,619
1930	5,534
1940	6,778
1950	8,835
1960	11,117
1970	11,601
1980	12,176

MOULTRIE

1900	2,221
1910	3,349
1920	6,789
1930	8,027
1940	10,147
1950	11,639
1960	15,764
1970	14,400
1980	15,708

NEWNAN

1870	2,546
1880	1,917
1880	2,006
1890	2,859
1900	3,654
1910	5,548
1920	7,037
1930	6,386
1940	7,182
1950	8,218
1960	12,169
1970	11,205
1980	11,449

ROME

1860	4,010
1870	2,748
1880	3,877
1890	6,957
1900	7,291
1910	12,099
1920	13,252
1930	21,843
1940	26,282
1950	29,615
1960	32,226
1970	30,759
1980	29,654

ROSWELL

1930	1,432
1940	1,622
1950	2,123
1960	2,983
1970	5,430
1980	23,337

SAVANNAH

1800	5,146
1810	5,215
1820	7,523
1850	11,214
1850	15,312
1860	22,292
1870	28,235
1880	30,709
1890	43,189
1900	54,244
1910	65,064
1920	83,252
1930	85,024

1940	95,996
1950	119,638
1960	149,245
1970	118,349
1980	141,390

SMYRNA

1880	250
1890	416
1900	238
1910	599
1920	791
1930	1,178
1940	1,440
1950	2,005
1960	10,157
1970	19,157
1980	20,312

STATESBORO

1900	1,197
1910	2,529
1920	3,807
1930	3,996
1940	5,028
1950	6,097
1960	8,356
1970	14,616
1980	14,866

THOMASVILLE

1870	1,651
1880	2,555
1890	5,514
1900	5,322
1910	6,727
1920	8,196
1930	11,733
1940	12,683
1950	14,424
1960	18,246
1970	18,155
1980	18,463

TIFTON

1900	1,384
1910	2,381
1920	3,005
1930	3,390
1940	5,228
1950	6,831
1960	9,903
1970	12,179
1980	13,749

VALDOSTA

1860	166
1870	1,199
1880	1,515
1890	2,854
1900	5,613
1910	7,656
1920	10,783
1930	13,482
1940	15,595
1950	20,046
1960	30,652
1970	32,303
1980	37,596

VIDALIA

1930	513
1940	592
1950	620
1960	7,569
1970	9,507
1980	10,393

WARNER ROBINS

1950	7,986
1960	18,633
1970	33,491
1980	39,893

WAYCROSS

1890	3,364
1900	5,919
1910	14,485
1920	18,068
1930	15,510
1940	16,763
1950	18,899
1960	20,944
1970	18,996
1980	19,371

CORRECTION NOTE

The official 1980 census counts of total population shown in this report supersede counts issued previously. Corrections to the figures were made after the counts were provided to the State for redistricting purposes and released in Advance Report PHC80-V for this State.

Shown below are corrections to the 1980 census counts of the total population made after the tabulations for this report were completed. Any additional corrections made after this report is printed are available by writing to Data User Services Division, Customer Services (Corrections), Bureau of the Census, Washington, D.C. 20233.

The 1980 figures shown in this publication are subject to change pending the outcome of the various lawsuits dealing with the census counts.

	1980 population	
	As shown in the tables	Corrected
Bartow County:		
Cartersville division:		
Cartersville city (pt.).......	9 508	9 247
Crisp County:		
Cordele division:		
Cordele city.................	10 914	11 184
Dougherty County:		
West Dougherty division:		
Albany city (pt.).............	52 444	52 935
Gwinnett County:		
Buford division:		
Buford city (pt.).............	6 463	6 344
Sugar Hill city..............	2 340	2 473
Lowndes County:		
Lake Park division:		
Dasher town..................	659	(1)
Walker County:		
Chattanooga Valley division:		
Rossville city (pt.)..........	73	175
Albany city (total)..............	74 059	74 550
Buford city (total)..............	6 697	6 578
Cartersville city (total)........	9 508	9 247
Rossville city (total)...........	3 749	3 851

[1]Delete--never incorporated.

County Subdivisions	1980	1970
The State	5 463 105	ʳ4 587 930
Appling County[1]	15 565	12 726
Altamaha River division	2 152	1 583
Baxley division	8 626	6 650
Baxley city[1]	3 586	3 503
Satilla Creek division	2 965	2 725
Surrency–Thornton division	1 822	1 768
Surrency town	368	352
Atkinson County	6 141	5 879
Axson division	974	861
Pearson division	3 494	3 410
Pearson city	1 827	1 700
Willacoochee division	1 673	1 608
Willacoochee town	1 166	1 120
Bacon County[2]	9 379	8 233
Alma division	6 948	...
Alma city[2]	3 819	3 756
Rockingham division	2 431	...
Baker County	3 808	3 875
Milford division	1 534	1 724
Newton division	2 274	2 151
Newton city	711	624
Baldwin County[3]	34 686	34 240
Coopers division	4 192	...
Milledgeville–Midway–Hardwick division	27 619	...
Midway–Hardwick (CDP)	8 977	14 047
Milledgeville city (pt.)[3]	12 176	(NA)
Union Point division	2 875	1 756
Milledgeville city (pt.)[3]	–	(NA)
Banks County	8 702	6 833
Baldwin division	2 749	2 038
Alto town (pt.)	162	125
Baldwin town (pt.)	325	264
Davis Academy division	1 322	984
Homer division	2 628	2 213
Homer town	734	365
Maysville division	2 003	1 598
Gillsville town (pt.)	35	27
Lula city (pt.)	104	103
Maysville town (pt.)	368	305
Barrow County[4]	21 354	16 859
Auburn division	4 030	...
Auburn town[4]	692	361
Carl town	239	234
Bethlehem division	2 298	1 697
Bethlehem town	281	304
Statham division	3 869	2 790
Statham city	1 101	817
Winder division	11 157	...
Russell city	378	378
Winder city[4]	6 705	6 605
Bartow County[5]	40 760	ʳ32 911
Adairsville division	5 215	4 061
Adairsville city	1 739	1 676
Cartersville division	23 085	...
Cartersville city (pt.)[5]	9 508	ʳ10 138
Euharlee town (pt.)[5]	348	...
Emerson division	4 626	...
Emerson city[5]	1 110	813
Euharlee–Taylorsville division	1 880	1 734
Euharlee town (pt.)[5]	129	...
Taylorsville town (pt.)	222	212
Kingston division	2 470	1 737
Kingston city	733	714
White–Pine Log division	3 484	2 930
Cartersville city (pt.)[5]	–	...
White town	501	462
Ben Hill County[6]	16 000	13 171
Fitzgerald division	14 791	...
Fitzgerald city (pt.)[6]	10 187	ʳ8 187
Little House Creek division	1 209	...
Berrien County[7]	13 525	11 556
Alapaha division	1 629	1 441
Alapaha town[7]	771	633
Enigma division	2 132	1 877
Enigma town	574	505
Nashville division	7 951	6 732
Nashville city[7]	4 831	4 323
Ray City division	1 813	1 506
Ray City[7]	658	617
Bibb County[8]	150 256	ʳ143 366
Lizella division	8 510	4 209
Macon city (pt.)[8]	1	...
Macon division	126 381	...
Macon city (pt.)[8]	116 500	ʳ122 371
Payne city[8]	196	236
Rutland division	8 469	5 707
Swift Creek division	6 896	...
Bleckley County[9]	10 767	10 291
Cochran division	9 719	9 030
Cochran city[9]	5 121	5 161
Salem division	1 048	1 261
Allentown town (pt.)		

County Subdivisions	1980	1970
Brantley County	8 701	5 940
Hoboken division	3 191	1 916
Hoboken city	514	424
Nahunta division	3 592	2 962
Nahunta city	951	974
Waynesville division	1 918	1 062
Brooks County[10]	15 255	ʳ13 743
Barney division	854	808
Barney town[10]	146	...
Barwick–Pavo division	1 818	ʳ1 734
Barwick town (pt.)	141	ʳ163
Pavo city (pt.)	316	278
Dixie division	1 802	1 677
Dixie town[10]	259	...
Empress division	1 038	889
Morven division	2 405	1 925
Morven city	471	449
Quitman division	7 338	6 710
Quitman city[10]	5 188	4 818
Bryan County[11]	10 175	6 539
Fort Stewart division	–	ʳ–
Pembroke division	6 371	4 654
Pembroke city	1 400	1 361
Richmond Hill division	3 804	ʳ1 885
Richmond Hill city[11]	1 177	826
Bulloch County[12]	35 785	31 585
Brooklet division	3 559	3 587
Brooklet town[12]	1 035	683
Nevils–Stilson division	2 790	2 587
Portal division	3 091	2 603
Portal town	694	643
Register division	1 538	1 622
Statesboro division	24 807	...
Statesboro city	14 866	14 616
Burke County[13]	19 349	18 255
Girard division	1 109	1 095
Girard town	225	241
Greens Cut division	3 005	2 090
Keysville division	1 520	1 244
Blythe town (pt.)	2	3
Midville division	1 883	1 974
Midville city	670	665
Sardis division	1 983	2 047
Sardis town[13]	1 180	643
Vidette division	1 287	1 427
Waynesboro division	8 562	...
Waynesboro city[13]	5 760	5 530
Butts County[14]	13 665	10 560
Flovilla division	1 837	...
Flovilla city[14]	458	289
Jackson division	6 325	...
Jackson city[14]	4 133	3 778
Jenkinsburg division	1 607	...
Jenkinsburg town[14]	360	382
Towaliga division	2 313	1 159
Worthville division	1 583	...
Calhoun County[15]	5 717	6 606
Arlington division	1 448	1 685
Arlington city (pt.)	1 135	1 299
Edison division	1 823	2 178
Edison city	1 128	1 210
Leary division	1 252	1 486
Leary city	783	907
Morgan division	1 194	1 257
Morgan city	364	280
Camden County[16]	13 371	11 334
Kingsland division	4 166	3 154
Kingsland city	2 008	1 831
St. Marys division	5 208	4 373
St. Marys city[16]	3 596	3 408
Woodbine division	3 997	3 807
Woodbine city	910	1 002
Candler County[17]	7 518	6 412
Aline division	1 034	957
Metter division	5 025	4 211
Metter city[17]	3 531	2 912
Pulaski division	1 459	1 244
Pulaski town	257	230
Carroll County[18]	56 346	45 404
Bowdon division	7 948	7 180
Bowdon city[18]	1 743	1 753
Carrollton division	28 672	...
Carrollton city[18]	14 078	13 520
Mount Zion division	4 068	2 786
Bremen city (pt.)[18]	24	12
Mount Zion city[18]	445	264
Roopville division	2 243	1 676
Roopville town[18]	229	221
Temple division	3 891	...
Temple city[18]	1 520	864
Villa Rica division	7 449	...
Villa Rica city (pt.)[18]	3 389	3 837
Whitesburg division	2 075	1 758
Whitesburg town	775	720

County Subdivisions	1980	1970
Catoosa County[19]	36 991	28 271
Boynton Ridge division	7 664	...
Graysville town (pt.)	137	80
Catoosa Springs division	3 909	2 702
Ringgold city (pt.)[19]	102	...
Fort Oglethorpe–Lakeview division	15 237	...
Fort Oglethorpe city (pt.)[19]	5 287	3 810
Lakeview (CDP) (pt.)	4 422	...
Ringgold division	10 181	...
Graysville town (pt.)	56	...
Ringgold city (pt.)[19]	1 780	1 381
Charlton County[20]	7 343	5 680
Folkston division	5 764	4 736
Folkston city[20]	2 243	2 112
Homeland city	683	595
St. George division	1 579	944
Chatham County[21]	202 226	187 816
Montgomery division	10 378	7 156
Skidaway Island (CDP)	1 264	...
Pooler–Burroughs division	12 918	8 144
Bloomingdale city[21]	1 855	...
Georgetown (CDP)	2 785	...
Pooler town (pt.)[21]	2 543	1 517
Savannah city (pt.)[21]	–	...
Port Wentworth division	4 962	...
Garden City city (pt.)[21]	–	...
Pooler town (pt.)[21]	–	...
Port Wentworth city[21]	3 947	3 905
Savannah city (pt.)[21]	245	...
Savannah division	160 809	...
Garden City city (pt.)[21]	6 895	5 790
Savannah city (pt.)[21]	141 145	118 349
Thunderbolt town	2 165	2 750
Vernonburg town	178	136
Tybee Island–Wilmington division	13 159	6 618
Tybee Island city[21]	2 240	1 786
Wilmington Island (CDP)	7 546	3 284
Chattahoochee County	21 732	25 813
Cusseta division	2 247	2 185
Cusseta city	1 218	1 251
Fort Benning division	19 485	23 628
Fort Benning South (CDP)	15 074	18 787
Chattooga County[22]	21 856	20 541
Little Sand Mountain division	1 488	...
Lyerly division	2 273	...
Lyerly town	482	426
Menlo division	2 476	2 228
Menlo town[22]	611	593
Summerville division	9 610	9 246
Summerville city	4 878	5 043
Trion division	6 009	5 782
Trion town	1 732	1 965
Cherokee County[23]	51 699	31 059
Ball Ground division	3 428	2 918
Ball Ground city[23]	640	617
Nelson city (pt.)	128	101
Canton division	11 223	...
Canton city[23]	3 601	3 654
Holly Springs division	8 850	5 463
Holly Springs city[23]	687	575
Lathemtown division	4 687	...
Waleska division	2 487	1 950
Waleska city[23]	450	487
Woodstock division	21 024	6 993
Mountain Park city (pt.)	2	–
Woodstock city[23]	2 699	870
Clarke County[24]	74 498	65 177
Athens division	60 045	...
Athens city (pt.)[24]	42 458	44 342
Oconee Heights (CDP)	1 115	...
Bogart division	4 927	...
Bogart town (pt.)	105	146
Winterville division	9 526	...
Athens city (pt.)[24]	91	...
Winterville city	621	551
Clay County	3 553	3 636
Bluffton division	997	1 064
Bluffton town	132	105
Fort Gaines division	2 556	2 572
Fort Gaines city	1 260	1 255
Clayton County[25]	150 357	98 126
College Park division	10 289	...
College Park city (pt.)[25]	3 489	2 119
Forest Park–Morrow division	70 313	...
Conley (CDP)	6 033	...
Forest Park city[25]	18 782	19 994
Lake City city[25]	2 963	2 306
Morrow city[25]	3 791	3 708
Jonesboro division	27 751	14 892
Jonesboro city[25]	4 132	4 105
Lovejoy town[25]	205	...
Riverdale division	42 004	15 111
Riverdale city[25]	7 121	2 521

County Subdivisions	1980	1970
Clinch County[26]	6 660	6 405
Fargo division	699	985
Homerville division	5 961	5 420
Argyle town	206	206
Du Pont town	267	252
Homerville city[26]	3 112	3 025
Cobb County[27]	297 718	196 793
Acworth–Kennesaw division	29 481	...
Acworth[27]	3 648	3 929
Kennesaw[27]	5 095	3 548
Marietta city (pt.)[27]	51	...
Austell division	16 420	...
Austell city (pt.)[27]	3 542	2 632
Mableton (CDP) (pt.)	630	...
Fair Oaks division	21 710	...
Fair Oaks (CDP) (pt.)	6 363	...
Marietta city (pt.)[27]	526	...
Smyrna city (pt.)[27]	40	...
Mableton division	30 201	...
Austell city (pt.)[27]	389	...
Mableton (CDP) (pt.)	24 264	...
Marietta division	68 421	...
Fair Oaks (CDP) (pt.)	1 926	...
Marietta city (pt.)[27]	29 485	27 216
Northeast Cobb division	71 025	15 123
Marietta city (pt.)[27]	–	...
Smyrna city (pt.)[27]	708	...
Powder Springs division	11 501	7 720
Powder Springs city[27]	3 381	2 559
Smyrna division	37 390	...
Fair Oaks (CDP) (pt.)	197	...
Mableton (CDP) (pt.)	217	...
Marietta city (pt.)[27]	767	...
Smyrna city (pt.)[27]	19 117	19 157
Vinings division	11 569	...
Smyrna city (pt.)[27]	447	...
Coffee County[28]	26 894	22 828
Ambrose division	2 924	...
Ambrose city	360	253
Broxton division	2 860	...
Broxton city	1 117	957
Douglas division	17 007	14 407
Douglas city[28]	10 980	10 195
Nicholls division	2 242	2 034
Nicholls city	1 114	1 150
West Green division	1 861	1 544
Colquitt County[29]	35 376	32 298
Berlin–Ellenton division	2 488	2 229
Berlin town	538	422
Ellenton town	277	337
Doerun division	2 877	2 920
Doerun city	1 062	1 157
Funston division	4 250	...
Funston town	337	293
Moultrie city (pt.)[29]	248	...
Moultrie division	22 671	...
Moultrie city[29]	15 460	14 400
Riverside town	99	114
Norman Park division	3 090	2 800
Norman Park city	757	912
Omega city (pt.)[29]	8	4
Columbia County[30]	40 118	22 327
Appling division	3 618	2 724
Evans division	25 675	10 688
Martinez (CDP) (pt.)	10 104	...
Harlem division	10 825	8 915
Grovetown[30]	3 384	3 169
Harlem city	1 485	1 540
Cook County[31]	13 490	12 129
Adel–Sparks division	11 337	...
Adel city[31]	5 592	4 972
Cecil town	280	265
Sparks town	1 353	1 337
Lenox division	2 153	1 894
Lenox town[31]	965	860
Coweta County[32]	39 268	32 310
Grantville division	2 207	2 273
Corinth town	24	14
Grantville city[32]	1 110	1 128
Moreland division	1 847	1 452
Moreland town[32]	358	363
Newnan division	30 504	...
East Newnan (CDP)	1 495	1 634
Newnan city[32]	11 449	11 205
Palmetto city (pt.)[32]	145	136
Sharpsburg town (pt.)	–	...
Senoia division	4 710	3 740
Haralson town (pt.)	117	114
Senoia city[32]	900	910
Sharpsburg town (pt.)	194	161
Turin town	260	242
Crawford County	7 684	5 748
Roberta division	3 666	3 267
Roberta city	859	746
Zenith division	4 018	2 481

County Subdivisions	1980	1970
Crisp County[33]	19 489	18 087
Arabi division	1 256	998
Arabi town[33]	376	305
Cordele division	18 233	...
Cordele city[33]	10 914	10 733
Dade County[34]	12 318	9 910
Sand Mountain division	3 273	2 452
Trenton division	9 045	...
Trenton city[34]	1 636	1 523
Dawson County[35]	4 774	3 639
Dawsonville division	1 844	...
Dawsonville town	342	288
Juno division	2 930	...
Decatur County[36]	25 495	22 310
Attapulgus division	3 423	3 493
Attapulgus town	623	513
Bainbridge division	13 648	...
Bainbridge city[36]	10 553	10 887
Brinson division	2 915	...
Brinson town	274	231
Climax division	1 789	...
Climax town	407	275
Faceville division	2 400	...
Parkers division	1 320	...
De Kalb County[37]	483 024	415 387
Atlanta–Decatur division	291 409	...
Atlanta city (pt.)[37]	37 283	46 687
Avondale Estates city[37]	1 313	1 735
Belvedere Park (CDP)	17 766	...
Candler–McAfee (CDP)	27 306	...
Clarkston city[37]	4 539	3 127
Decatur city[37]	18 404	21 943
Druid Hills (CDP)	12 700	...
Gresham Park (CDP)	6 232	...
North Decatur (CDP)	11 830	...
North Druid Hills (CDP)	12 438	...
Panthersville (CDP)	11 366	...
Pine Lake city (pt.)	–	...
Scottdale (CDP)	8 770	...
Tucker (CDP) (pt.)	1 688	...
Chamblee–Doraville division	98 005	88 736
Chamblee city	7 137	9 127
Doraville city	7 414	'9 157
Dunwoody (CDP)	17 768	...
North Atlanta (CDP)	30 521	...
Lithonia division	22 793	...
Lithonia city[37]	2 637	2 270
Stone Mountain division	22 611	9 464
Pine Lake city (pt.)	901	866
Stone Mountain city[37]	4 867	1 899
Tucker division	48 206	44 504
Tucker (CDP) (pt.)	23 711	...
Dodge County[38]	16 955	15 658
Chauncey division	1 982	...
Chauncey town	350	308
Milan town (pt.)	637	496
Chester division	1 908	1 899
Chester town	409	409
Eastman division	11 431	...
Eastman city[38]	5 330	5 416
Plainfield town	128	77
Rhine division	1 634	...
Abbeville city (pt.)[38]	–	...
Rhine town	590	471
Dooly County[39]	10 826	10 404
Byromville division	2 232	2 139
Byromville town[39]	567	419
Lilly town	202	155
Unadilla division	3 621	3 646
Pinehurst city	431	405
Unadilla city	1 566	1 457
Vienna division	4 973	4 619
Vienna city	2 886	2 341
Dougherty County[40]	100 718	89 639
East Dougherty division	36 048	...
Albany city (pt.)[40]	21 615	(NA)
West Dougherty division	64 670	...
Albany city (pt.)[40]	52 444	(NA)
Douglas County[41]	54 573	28 659
Bill Arp division	18 565	3 308
Douglasville city (pt.)[41]	1 287	...
Fairplay division	2 574	1 554
Lithia Springs–Douglasville division	29 643	...
Austell city (pt.)	8	–
Douglasville city (pt.)[41]	6 326	5 472
Lithia Springs (CDP)	9 145	...
Winston division	3 791	2 232
Douglasville city (pt.)[41]	28	...
Villa Rica city (pt.)	31	85
Early County[42]	13 158	12 682
Blakely division	8 962	...
Blakely city[42]	5 880	5 267
Damascus division	1 973	2 171
Arlington city (pt.)	437	399
Damascus town	403	272

County Subdivisions	1980	1970
Early County—Con.		
Jakin division	2 223	2 132
Jakin town	194	172
Echols County[43]	2 297	1 924
East Echols division	1 379	...
West Echols division	918	...
Effingham County[44]	18 327	13 632
Guyton–Springfield division	6 731	5 630
Guyton city[44]	749	742
Pineora city	387	266
Springfield city	1 075	1 001
Rincon division	9 522	6 193
Rincon town	1 988	1 854
Shawnee division	2 074	1 809
Elbert County[45]	18 758	17 262
Bowman division	2 631	2 131
Bowman city	890	724
Coldwater Creek division	2 196	...
Elberton division	13 931	...
Elberton city[45]	5 686	6 438
Emanuel County[46]	20 795	'18 357
Adrian division	1 474	1 373
Adrian city (pt.)	376	332
Oak Park division	909	820
Oak Park town	256	226
Summertown division	2 191	1 860
Summertown town[46]	215	'159
Swainsboro division	12 078	10 571
Nunez town	168	117
Swainsboro city[46]	7 602	7 325
Twin City division	4 143	'3 733
Garfield town	222	214
Stillmore town	527	'522
Twin City city	1 402	1 119
Evans County[47]	8 428	7 290
Canoochee division	1 357	1 054
Claxton division	7 071	6 236
Bellville city	173	234
Claxton city[47]	2 694	2 669
Daisy city	174	150
Hagan city[47]	880	572
Fannin County[48]	14 748	13 357
Blue Ridge division	4 050	...
Blue Ridge city[48]	1 376	1 602
Higdon–Mobile division	1 521	1 380
McCaysville division	4 935	...
McCaysville city	1 219	1 619
Mineral Bluff division	1 906	1 411
Mineral Bluff town	130	119
Morganton division	2 336	1 902
Morganton town[48]	263	205
Fayette County[49]	29 043	11 364
Brooks division	3 087	1 757
Brooks town[49]	199	172
Woolsey town	99	91
Fayetteville division	14 344	6 435
Fayetteville city[49]	2 715	2 160
Tyrone division	11 612	3 172
Peachtree City city[49]	6 429	793
Tyrone town[49]	1 038	131
Floyd County[50]	79 800	73 742
Armuchee division	5 871	4 661
Glenwood (CDP)	1 610	...
Cave Spring division	3 678	3 672
Cave Spring city[50]	883	1 305
Rome division	66 500	...
Garden Lakes (CDP)	4 053	2 963
Lindale (CDP)	2 958	2 768
Rome city[50]	29 654	30 759
Rosemont Park (CDP)	1 906	...
Sherwood Forest (CDP)	1 992	...
Shannon division	3 751	3 529
Shannon (CDP)	2 040	1 563
Forsyth County[51]	27 958	16 928
Big Creek division	5 081	2 890
Chestatee division	3 503	...
Cumming division	15 856	...
Cumming city[51]	2 094	2 031
Silver City division	3 518	2 804
Franklin County[52]	15 185	12 784
Carnesville division	3 818	3 411
Carnesville city[52]	465	510
Lavonia division	4 931	4 062
Lavonia city	2 024	2 044
Martin town (pt.)[52]		
Royston division	4 556	4 014
Canon city (pt.)	636	653
Franklin Springs city	797	501
Royston city (pt.)[52]	1 767	1 959
Sandy Cross division	1 880	1 297
Fulton County[53]	589 904	'605 210
Atlanta division	453 060	...
Atlanta city (pt.)[53]	387 739	'448 352
Hapeville city	6 166	9 567

County Subdivisions	1980	1970
Fulton County—Con.		
Atlanta division—Con.		
Sandy Springs (CDP)	46 877	...
College Park division	20 592	16 592
College Park city (pt.)[53]	19 884	16 084
East Point division	40 422	
College Park city (pt.)	–	
East Point city[53]	37 486	39 315
Fairburn—Union City division	32 132	...
College Park city (pt.)[53]	1 259	
Fairburn city[53]	3 466	3 143
Union City city[53]	4 780	3 031
Palmetto division	3 998	4 170
Palmetto city (pt.)[53]	1 941	1 909
Roswell—Alpharetta division	39 700	...
Alpharetta city[53]	3 128	2 455
Mountain Park city (pt.)	376	268
Roswell city[53]	23 337	5 430
Gilmer County[54]	11 110	8 956
Cartecay division	2 096	
Cherry Log division	1 731	
Ellijay division	7 283	...
East Ellijay town[54]	469	488
Ellijay city[54]	1 507	1 326
Glascock County	2 382	2 280
Gibson division	1 615	1 565
Gibson city	730	701
Mitchell division	767	715
Edge Hill city	53	46
Mitchell town	214	187
Glynn County[55]	54 981	50 528
Brunswick division	33 381	...
Brunswick city[55]	17 605	19 585
Dock Junction (CDP)	6 189	6 009
Everett division	7 896	6 645
St. Simons division	9 406	6 818
St. Simons (CDP)	6 566	5 346
Thalmann division	4 298	3 558
Gordon County[56]	30 070	23 570
Calhoun division	19 268	...
Calhoun city (pt.)[56]	5 563	4 748
Plainville city	281	192
Fairmount division	3 256	2 437
Fairmount city[56]	842	623
Red Bud division	2 850	2 108
Oakman town	150	178
Ranger town	171	140
Sugar Valley—Resaca division	4 696	3 362
Calhoun city (pt.)[56]	–	
Industrial City city (pt.)[56]	615	...
Grady County[57]	19 845	17 826
Cairo division	13 443	11 820
Cairo city[57]	8 777	8 061
Calvary—Reno division	1 572	1 911
Duncanville division	548	511
Lime Sink division	558	583
Spence division	1 369	1 111
Whigham division	2 355	1 890
Whigham city[57]	507	381
Greene County[58]	11 391	10 212
Greensboro division	4 998	4 493
Greensboro city[58]	2 985	2 583
Greshamville division	503	448
Siloam division	1 198	1 056
Siloam town	446	319
Union Point division	2 578	2 387
Union Point city[58]	1 750	1 624
White Plains division	1 036	928
White Plains town	231	236
Woodville division	1 078	900
Woodville city	455	379
Gwinnett County[59]	166 903	72 349
Buford division	12 138	9 221
Buford city (pt.)[59]	6 463	4 545
Rest Haven town (pt.)	204	188
Sugar Hill city[59]	2 340	1 745
Suwanee city (pt.)[59]	–	
Dacula—Rocky Creek division	7 975	5 312
Buford city (pt.)[59]	225	...
Dacula city[59]	1 577	782
Lawrenceville division	30 230	13 892
Lawrenceville city (pt.)[59]	8 593	'5 207
Lilburn division	53 795	17 904
Lilburn city[59]	3 765	1 668
Mountain Park (CDP)	9 425	...
Norcross division	22 109	11 457
Berkeley Lake city[59]	503	219
Norcross city[59]	3 317	2 755
Snellville—Grayson division	30 552	8 284
Grayson city[59]	464	366
Lawrenceville city (pt.)[59]	335	
Loganville city (pt.)[59]	217	200
Snellville city[59]	8 514	1 990
Suwanee—Duluth division	10 104	6 279
Duluth city[59]	2 956	1 810
Suwanee city (pt.)[59]	1 026	615

County Subdivisions	1980	1970
Habersham County[60]	25 020	20 691
Clarkesville division	7 664	6 457
Clarkesville city[60]	1 348	1 294
Cornelia division	15 216	...
Alto town (pt.)[60]	456	247
Baldwin town (pt.)[60]	755	508
Cornelia city[60]	3 203	3 014
Demorest city	1 130	1 070
Mount Airy town[60]	670	463
Turnerville division	2 140	1 984
Tallulah Falls town (pt.)	90	187
Hall County[61]	75 649	59 405
Clermont division	6 739	...
Clermont town	300	290
Flowery Branch division	6 343	...
Buford city (pt.)[61]	9	95
Flowery Branch town[61]	755	779
Rest Haven town (pt.)[61]	27	...
Gainesville division	43 646	...
Gainesville city (pt.)[61]	15 280	15 459
Gainesville Mills (CDP)	1 281	2 060
Oakwood city (pt.)[61]	11	...
Westside (CDP)	2 769	...
Lula division	4 644	
Gillsville town (pt.)	107	73
Lula city (pt.)[61]	753	633
Murrayville division	7 411	...
Gainesville city (pt.)[61]	–	...
Oakwood division	6 866	...
Oakwood town (pt.)[61]	712	250
Hancock County	9 466	9 019
Devereux division	1 368	1 426
Linton division	1 095	1 109
Mayfield division	1 669	1 146
Sparta division	5 334	5 338
Sparta city	1 754	2 172
Haralson County[62]	18 422	15 927
Bremen division	7 758	...
Bremen city (pt.)[62]	3 942	3 472
Waco city[62]	471	431
Buchanan division	4 985	...
Buchanan city[62]	1 019	800
Tallapoosa division	5 679	5 404
Tallapoosa city[62]	2 647	2 896
Harris County[63]	15 464	11 520
Hamilton division	3 348	1 942
Hamilton city (pt.)[63]	495	357
Pine Mountain division	4 172	3 545
Hamilton city (pt.)[63]	11	...
Pine Mountain town[63]	984	862
West Point city (pt.)[63]	982	713
Shiloh division	2 214	1 894
Hamilton city (pt.)[63]	–	
Shiloh city[63]	392	298
Waverly Hall division	5 730	4 139
Waverly Hall town[63]	913	671
Hart County[64]	18 585	15 814
Bowersville division	2 224	1 885
Bowersville town	318	301
Hartwell division	10 713	...
Hartwell city[64]	4 855	4 865
Reed Creek division	3 303	...
Royston division	2 345	1 933
Canon city (pt.)	68	56
Royston city (pt.)	633	425
Heard County[65]	6 520	5 354
Centralhatchee division	2 657	...
Centralhatchee town[65]	240	186
Ephesus town	184	212
Franklin city (pt.)[65]	–	
Franklin division	2 198	...
Corinth town (pt.)	51	93
Franklin city (pt.)[65]	711	749
Texas division	1 665	...
Henry County[66]	36 309	23 724
Hampton division	4 479	3 985
Hampton city[66]	2 059	1 551
Locust Grove division	4 365	2 983
Locust Grove city[66]	1 479	642
McDonough division	13 316	9 884
Blacksville (CDP)	1 521	...
McDonough city[66]	2 778	2 675
Stockbridge division	14 149	6 922
Stockbridge city[66]	2 103	1 561
Houston County[67]	77 605	62 924
Elko division	3 227	3 007
Perry division	12 226	10 336
Perry city[67]	9 453	7 771
Warner Robins division	62 152	...
Centerville city[67]	2 622	1 725
Elberta (CDP)	1 559	...
Robins AFB (CDP)	3 571	...
Warner Robins city[67]	39 893	33 491

County Subdivisions

County Subdivisions	1980	1970
Irwin County[68]	8 988	8 036
Holt division	1 173	1 163
Irwinville division	1 950	1 348
Ocilla division	5 865	5 525
Fitzgerald city (pt.)[68]	–	...
Ocilla city[68]	3 436	3 185
Jackson County[69]	25 343	21 093
Commerce division	7 100	6 495
Commerce city[69]	4 092	3 702
Jefferson division	8 548	...
Arcade city	223	229
Jefferson city[69]	1 820	1 647
Maysville division	2 064	1 577
Maysville town (pt.)	251	248
Nicholson division	2 911	2 273
Center town	330	213
Nicholson town[69]	491	397
West Jackson division[66]	4 720	3 734
Braselton town[66]	308	386
Hoschton city	490	509
Pendergrass city	302	267
Jasper County[70]	7 553	5 760
Eudora division	1 025	493
Hillsboro division	627	...
Monticello division	4 785	...
Monticello city[70]	2 382	2 132
Shady Dale division	1 116	872
Newborn town (pt.)	4	25
Shady Dale town	155	190
Jeff Davis County[71]	11 473	9 425
Denton division	1 468	1 455
Denton city	286	244
Hazlehurst division	10 005	7 970
Hazlehurst city[71]	4 249	4 065
Jefferson County[72]	18 403	17 174
Louisville division	6 571	6 412
Louisville city[72]	2 823	2 691
Stapleton division	1 815	1 842
Avera town	248	217
Stapleton town	388	390
Wadley division	4 794	4 399
Bartow town	357	333
Wadley city	2 438	1 989
Wrens division	5 223	4 521
Wrens city[72]	2 415	2 204
Jenkins County[73]	8 841	8 332
North Ogeechee division	6 676	6 467
Millen city[73]	3 988	3 713
South Ogeechee division	2 165	1 865
Johnson County[74]	8 660	7 727
Adrian division	1 582	1 307
Adrian city (pt.)	380	373
Scott town (pt.)	137	215
Balls Ferry division	1 636	...
Kite division	1 316	1 252
Kite town	328	336
Wrightsville division	4 126	...
Wrightsville city	2 526	2 106
Jones County[75]	16 579	12 270
Gray–Griswold division	13 929	9 938
Gray city	2 145	2 014
Macon city (pt.)	395	52
Round Oak division	2 650	2 332
Lamar County[76]	12 215	10 688
Barnesville division	9 073	8 467
Aldora town	139	322
Barnesville city[76]	4 887	4 935
Milner division	3 142	2 221
Milner city[76]	320	270
Lanier County	5 654	5 031
East River division	1 177	1 101
Lakeland division	4 477	3 930
Lakeland city	2 647	2 569
Laurens County[27]	36 990	32 738
Brewton division	2 018	...
Scott town (pt.)[77]	2	'–
Cadwell division	1 286	1 317
Cadwell town	353	354
Cedar Grove division	897	1 072
Dexter division	1 575	1 355
Dexter town	527	438
Dublin division	21 122	...
Dublin city[77]	16 083	15 143
Dudley division	1 802	1 732
Allentown town (pt.)	2	6
Dudley city	425	423
Montrose town	170	199
East Dublin division	6 392	...
East Dublin town	2 916	'2 000
Scott town (pt.)	–	...
Rentz division	1 898	1 771
Rentz town	337	392

County Subdivisions	1980	1970
Lee County[78]	11 684	7 044
Leesburg division	7 185	3 692
Leesburg city[78]	1 301	996
Philema division	2 830	1 882
Smithville division	1 669	1 470
Smithville city (pt.)	867	711
Liberty County[79]	37 583	17 569
Hinesville division	31 528	13 419
Allenhurst town	606	230
Flemington city[79]	440	265
Fort Stewart (CDP)	15 031	4 467
Gumbranch city[79]	272	...
Hinesville city[79]	11 309	4 115
Walthourville city[79]	905	...
Midway division	4 088	2 280
Midway city[79]	457	167
Riceboro division	1 967	1 870
Riceboro city	216	252
Lincoln County	6 716	5 895
Lincolnton division	3 478	3 376
Lincolnton city	1 406	1 442
South Lincolnton division	3 238	2 519
Long County[80]	4 524	3 746
Ludowici North division	1 991	...
Ludowici South division	2 533	...
Ludowici city[80]	1 286	1 419
Lowndes County[81]	67 972	55 112
Barretts division	5 561	...
Moody AFB (CDP)	1 297	1 424
Hahira division	5 305	3 782
Hahira city	1 534	1 326
Lake Park division	4 471	...
Dasher town	659	452
Lake Park town[81]	448	361
Naylor division	2 187	...
Naylor town	228	244
Valdosta division	50 448	...
Remerton city	443	523
Valdosta city[81]	37 596	32 303
Lumpkin County[82]	10 762	8 728
Dahlonega division	6 357	...
Dahlonega city (pt.)[82]	2 844	2 658
Three Sisters Mountains division	4 405	...
Dahlonega city (pt.)[82]	–	...
McDuffie County[83]	18 546	15 276
Dearing division	3 700	2 509
Dearing town	539	555
Thomson division	14 846	...
Thomson city[83]	7 001	6 503
McIntosh County	8 046	7 371
Darien division	5 706	5 128
Darien city	1 731	1 826
Townsend division	2 340	2 243
Macon County[84]	14 003	12 933
Ideal division	2 119	2 346
Ideal town	619	543
Marshallville division	2 360	2 261
Marshallville town	1 540	1 376
Montezuma division	6 526	5 831
Montezuma city[84]	4 830	4 125
Oglethorpe division	2 998	2 495
Oglethorpe city	1 305	1 286
Madison County[85]	17 747	13 517
Broad River division	1 589	1 479
Royston city (pt.)	4	44
Colbert division	7 164	...
Colbert city	498	532
Hull town	188	222
Comer division	3 143	2 603
Carlton town	291	294
Comer town	930	828
Danielsville division	2 704	...
Danielsville city[85]	354	378
Ila division	3 147	2 332
Ila city[85]	287	202
Marion County[86]	5 297	5 099
Buena Vista division	3 255	...
Buena Vista city[86]	1 544	1 486
North Buena Vista division	2 042	...
Meriwether County[87]	21 229	19 461
Gay division	2 042	2 135
Alvaton town	91	114
Gay town	175	200
Haralson town (pt.)[87]	6	48
Rocky Mount town	56	53
Greenville division	2 829	2 556
Greenville city	1 213	1 085
Odessadale town	142	70
Luthersville division	3 194	2 596
Lone Oak town	119	129
Luthersville town	597	400
Primrose town	30	28
St. Marks town	36	25

County Subdivisions

County Subdivisions	1980	1970
Meriwether County—Con.		
Manchester division	6 519	6 297
Chalybeate Springs town	265	266
Manchester city (pt.)[87]	4 626	4 636
Warm Springs division	3 687	3 189
Durand town	206	192
Warm Springs city	425	523
White Sulphur Springs town	118	38
Woodbury division	2 958	2 688
Woodbury town	1 738	1 422
Miller County[88]	7 038	6 424
Bellview division	1 392	...
Colquitt division	4 018	...
Colquitt city	2 065	2 026
Mayhaw division	1 628	1 511
Mitchell County[89]	21 114	18 956
Baconton division	2 383	1 677
Baconton city	763	710
Branchville division	1 377	1 357
Camilla division	8 499	7 216
Camilla city[89]	5 414	4 987
Pelham division	7 374	7 074
Cotton town	122	102
Meigs city (pt.)	64	44
Pelham city[89]	4 306	4 539
Sale City division	1 481	1 632
Sale City town[89]	336	323
Monroe County[90]	14 610	10 991
Culloden—Bolingbroke division	4 473	3 322
Culloden city	281	272
Forsyth division	10 137	7 669
Forsyth city[90]	4 624	3 736
Montgomery County[91]	7 011	6 099
Mount Vernon—Ailey division	4 039	3 163
Ailey town[91]	579	487
Higgston town	152	175
Mount Vernon city	1 737	1 579
Vidalia city (pt.)	2	6
Tarrytown division	1 179	1 237
Tarrytown village	145	188
Uvalda division	1 793	1 699
Alston town[91]	111	104
Uvalda town	646	663
Morgan County[92]	11 572	9 904
Bostwick division	1 645	1 294
Bostwick town	357	289
Buckhead division	1 298	1 054
Buckhead town	219	177
Godfrey division	1 043	988
Madison division	5 649	4 965
Madison city[92]	2 954	2 890
Rutledge division	1 937	1 603
Rutledge city	694	628
Murray County[93]	19 685	12 986
Casey Springs division	1 770	897
Industrial City (pt.)[93]	297	...
Chatsworth division	12 320	7 961
Chatsworth city (pt.)[93]	2 493	2 706
Spring Place town	246	241
Cisco division	2 284	1 749
Crandall—Eton division	3 311	2 379
Chatsworth city (pt.)[93]	–	...
Eton town	301	286
Muscogee County[94]	170 108	167 377
Columbus division	170 108	...
Bibb City town[94]	667	812
Columbus city[94]	169 441	155 028
Newton County[95]	34 489	26 282
Covington—Porterdale division	27 636	...
Covington city	10 586	10 267
Oxford town[95]	1 750	1 373
Porterdale town	1 451	1 773
Mansfield division	4 339	2 759
Mansfield town	435	340
Newborn town (pt.)	387	269
Yellow River division	2 514	1 518
Oconee County[96]	12 427	7 915
Bogart division	3 016	2 209
Bogart town (pt.)	714	521
Elder division	913	641
Watkinsville division	8 498	5 065
Bishop town	172	235
North High Shoals town	256	165
Watkinsville town	1 240	986
Oglethorpe County[97]	8 929	7 598
Lexington—Crawford division	5 966	4 936
Arnoldsville city	187	181
Crawford city	498	624
Lexington city[97]	278	322
Maxeys division	1 211	1 174
Maxeys town	205	229
Vesta—Enterprise division	1 752	1 488

County Subdivisions	1980	1970
Paulding County[98]	26 110	17 520
Dallas division	9 971	...
Dallas city[98]	2 508	2 133
Hiram city (pt.)[98]	7	...
Hiram division	9 214	...
Hiram city (pt.)[98]	1 023	441
Huntsville division	3 251	2 114
Braswell city (pt.)[98]	88	22
Yorkville division	3 674	3 185
Braswell city (pt.)	2	...
Peach County[99]	19 151	15 990
Byron division	5 073	2 962
Byron city[99]	1 661	1 368
Fort Valley division	14 078	13 028
Fort Valley city[99]	9 000	9 251
Pickens County[100]	11 652	9 620
Jasper division	4 694	...
Jasper city	1 556	1 202
Ludville division	1 720	1 324
Talking Rock division	1 600	1 362
Talking Rock town	72	76
Tate division	3 638	...
Nelson city (pt.)	434	512
Pierce County[101]	11 897	9 281
Blackshear division	8 216	5 979
Blackshear city[101]	3 222	2 624
Bristol division	1 199	1 136
Patterson division	2 482	2 166
Patterson city[101]	763	788
Pike County[102]	8 937	7 316
Concord—Molena division	2 235	2 061
Concord town	317	312
Molena city	379	389
Meansville division	1 943	1 777
Meansville city	303	313
Williamson division	1 199	969
Williamson town[102]	250	284
Zebulon division	3 560	2 509
Zebulon city	995	776
Polk County[103]	32 386	29 656
Aragon division	4 168	3 491
Aragon city (pt.)[103]	855	...
Braswell city (pt.)[103]	92	...
Taylorsville town (pt.)	44	41
Cedartown division	19 050	...
Cedartown city[103]	8 619	9 253
Rockmart division	9 168	8 451
Aragon city (pt.)[103]	–	8
Braswell city (pt.)[103]	100	...
Rockmart city[103]	3 645	3 857
Van Wert town[103]	303	360
Pulaski County[104]	8 950	8 066
Finleyson division	1 376	1 468
Finleyson town[104]	101	...
Hartford division	1 450	1 351
Hawkinsville division	6 124	5 247
Hawkinsville city[104]	4 372	4 077
Putnam County[105]	10 295	8 394
Eatonton division	7 230	...
Eatonton city[105]	4 833	4 125
Little River division	1 574	...
Phoenix division	1 491	...
Quitman County[106]	2 357	2 180
Georgetown North division	1 485	...
Georgetown town	935	860
Georgetown South division	872	...
Rabun County[107]	10 466	8 327
Clayton division	5 277	4 084
Clayton city	1 838	1 569
Tiger division	2 658	1 966
Tallulah Falls town (pt.)	72	68
Tiger town	299	312
Valley division	2 531	2 277
Dillard town	238	186
Mountain City town	701	594
Sky Valley city[107]	65	...
Randolph County[108]	9 599	8 734
Benevolence division	440	1 101
Benevolence town	138	...
Cuthbert division	6 856	...
Coleman city	164	168
Cuthbert city	4 340	3 972
Shellman division	2 303	2 304
Shellman city	1 254	1 166
Richmond County[109]	181 629	162 437
Augusta division	144 126	...
Augusta city[109]	47 532	59 864
East Boundary (CDP)	4 699	...
Martinez (CDP) (pt.)	6 368	...
South Augusta (CDP)	51 072	...
West Augusta (CDP)	24 242	...
Fort Gordon division	14 069	15 589
Fort Gordon (CDP)	14 069	15 589
Gracewood division	14 461	5 753
Hephzibah division	8 973	5 026

County Subdivisions

County Subdivisions	1980	1970
Richmond County—Con.		
Hephzibah division—Con.		
Blythe town (pt.)	365	330
Hephzibah town	1 452	987
Rockdale County[110]	36 747	18 152
Conyers division	21 544	12 322
Conyers city[110]	6 567	4 890
Lakeview Estates (CDP)	1 576	...
North Rockdale division	5 113	2 892
South Rockdale division	10 090	2 938
Schley County[111]	3 433	3 097
Ellaville North division	2 619	...
Ellaville city[111]	1 684	1 391
Ellaville South division	814	...
Screven County[112]	14 043	12 591
Hilltonia division	1 386	1 054
Hilltonia city	515	294
Millhaven division	931	1 117
Newington division	2 340	2 203
Newington town	402	402
Oliver city	239	217
Rocky Ford division	1 783	1 695
Rocky Ford town	223	252
Sylvania division	7 603	6 522
Sylvania city[112]	3 352	3 199
Seminole County[113]	9 057	7 059
Donalsonville division	6 379	...
Donalsonville city (pt.)	3 320	2 907
Iron City town	367	351
Steam Mill division	2 678	...
Donalsonville city (pt.)	–	...
Spalding County[114]	47 899	39 514
Blantons Mill division	708	...
Digbey division	620	...
Griffin division	34 924	...
East Griffin (CDP)	1 570	1 479
Experiment (CDP)	3 731	2 256
Griffin city[114]	20 728	22 734
Orchard Hill division	3 356	...
Orchard Hill village[114]	162	...
Ringgold division	2 935	...
Sunny Side division	3 886	...
Sunny Side village	338	209
Vaughn division	1 470	...
Stephens County[115]	21 763	20 331
Broad River division	4 269	...
Avalon town	200	204
Martin town (pt.)[115]	305	201
Rock Creek division	3 188	...
Toccoa division	14 306	...
Toccoa city[115]	9 104	6 971
Stewart County[116]	5 896	6 511
Lumpkin division	2 346	...
Lumpkin city[116]	1 335	1 431
Omaha division	1 010	...
Omaha city	169	188
Richland division	2 540	2 680
Richland city	1 802	1 823
Sumter County[117]	29 360	26 931
Americus division	22 326	...
Americus city[117]	16 120	16 091
Smithville city (pt.)	–	2
Andersonville division	1 212	1 229
Andersonville village	267	274
Leslie–De Soto division	2 696	2 813
De Soto village	248	321
Leslie village	470	562
Plains division	3 126	2 937
Plains city	651	683
Talbot County[118]	6 536	6 625
Junction City division	1 842	1 843
Geneva town	232	250
Junction City town	254	269
Talbotton division	2 390	2 333
Talbotton city	1 140	1 045
Woodland division	2 304	2 449
Manchester city (pt.)[118]	170	143
Woodland city	664	689
Taliaferro County	2 032	2 423
Crawfordville division	1 407	1 753
Crawfordville city	594	735
Sharon division	625	670
Sharon city	140	160
Tattnall County[119]	18 134	16 557
Collins division	3 237	2 969
Cobbtown city[119]	494	321
Collins city	639	574
Glennville division	8 058	6 731
Glennville city[119]	4 144	2 965
Reidsville division	6 839	6 857
Manassas city	116	144
Reidsville city[119]	2 296	1 806

County Subdivisions

County Subdivisions	1980	1970
Taylor County	7 902	7 865
Butler division	3 496	3 200
Butler town	1 959	1 589
Carsonville–Panhandle division	1 217	1 489
Reynolds division	2 532	2 392
Reynolds town	1 298	1 253
Rupert division	657	784
Telfair County[120]	11 445	11 394
Jacksonville division	1 011	1 152
Jacksonville town	206	227
Lumber City division	2 089	1 981
Lumber City city (pt.)	1 426	1 377
McRae–Helena division	6 604	...
Helena town	1 390	1 230
McRae city[120]	3 409	3 151
Scotland city (pt.)	196	239
Milan division	1 741	1 916
Milan town (pt.)	478	588
Terrell County	12 017	11 416
Bronwood division	1 400	1 432
Bronwood town	524	500
Dawson division	8 172	7 684
Dawson city	5 699	5 383
Parrott division	1 151	1 131
Parrott town	222	222
Sasser division	1 294	1 169
Sasser town	407	339
Thomas County[121]	38 098	34 562
Boston division	2 896	2 758
Boston city	1 424	1 443
Coolidge division	2 159	2 000
Coolidge city	736	717
Meigs division	1 673	1 676
Meigs city (pt.)	1 167	1 182
Ochlocknee division	2 232	1 987
Ochlocknee town[121]	627	611
Pavo–Barwick division	2 152	2 096
Barwick town (pt.)	272	269
Pavo city (pt.)	514	497
Thomasville division	26 986	...
Thomasville city[121]	18 463	18 155
Tift County[122]	32 862	27 288
Brookfield division	2 368	1 840
Chula division	2 224	1 734
Oak Ridge division	2 820	...
Unionville (CDP) (pt.)	439	...
Omega division	1 947	1 668
Omega city (pt.)	988	831
Tifton division	21 249	...
Phillipsburg (CDP)	2 450	2 335
Tifton city[122]	13 749	12 179
Unionville (CDP) (pt.)	1 503	1 646
Ty Ty division	2 254	1 864
Ty Ty town	618	447
Toombs County[123]	22 592	19 151
Toombs Central division	2 931	2 408
Vidalia–Lyons division	19 661	...
Lyons city	4 203	3 739
Santa Claus city	167	118
Vidalia city (pt.)[123]	10 391	9 501
Towns County	5 638	4 565
Hiawassee division	2 055	1 665
Hiawassee town (pt.)	477	415
Macedonia division	1 416	1 146
Hiawassee town (pt.)	14	...
Young Harris division	2 167	1 754
Young Harris town	687	544
Treutlen County	6 087	5 647
Gillis Springs division	890	791
Soperton division	5 197	4 856
Soperton city	2 981	2 596
Troup County[124]	50 003	44 466
Abbottsford division	535	409
Hillcrest division	1 131	...
Hogansville division	5 227	4 936
Hogansville city[124]	3 362	3 075
La Grange division	36 307	...
La Grange city[124]	24 204	23 301
Lees Crossing (CDP)	1 117	...
Mountville town	168	218
Oak Grove division	1 479	1 079
West Point division	5 324	5 428
West Point city (pt.)[124]	3 312	3 519
Turner County[125]	9 510	8 790
Ashburn division	6 322	...
Ashburn city[125]	4 766	4 209
Rebecca division	777	790
Rebecca town	272	266
Sycamore division	2 411	...
Sycamore city	474	547
Twiggs County	9 354	8 222
Twiggs North division	5 109	4 378
Jeffersonville city	1 473	1 302
Twiggs South division	4 245	3 844

County Subdivisions

County Subdivisions	1980	1970
Twiggs County—Con.		
Twiggs South division—Con.		
Allentown town (pt.)	25	–
Danville town (pt.)	296	390
Union County[126]	9 390	6 811
Blairsville division	6 122	...
Blairsville city[126]	530	491
Ivylog division	2 666	...
Suches division	602	557
Upson County[127]	25 998	23 505
Gordon division	1 432	...
The Rock–Yatesville division	2 547	...
The Rock town	78	136
Yatesville town	390	423
Thomaston division	19 357	...
Hannahs Mill (CDP)	2 616	...
Lincoln Park (CDP)	1 755	1 852
Thomaston city[127]	9 682	10 024
Thurston division	2 662	1 941
Walker County[128]	56 470	50 691
Chattanooga Valley division	9 239	...
Fairview (CDP) (pt.)	1 475	...
Rossville city (pt.)[128]	73	(NA)
Chickamauga division	11 456	8 360
Chickamauga city[128]	2 232	1 842
Fairview (CDP) (pt.)	1 254	...
Fairyland division	2 837	2 490
Lookout Mountain city	1 505	1 538
Kensington division	2 550	...
La Fayette division	14 146	...
La Fayette city[128]	6 517	6 044
Linwood town	417	588
Rock Spring division	3 629	2 843
Rossville–Beverly Hills division	11 389	...
Fairview (CDP) (pt.)	3 829	...
Fort Oglethorpe city (pt.)	156	59
Lakeview (CDP) (pt.)	981	...
Rossville city (pt.)[128]	3 676	(NA)
Villanow division	1 224	1 128
Walton County[129]	31 211	23 404
Campton division	2 451	...
Good Hope division	2 614	...
Good Hope town	200	202
Jersey division	4 696	2 316
Jersey town	201	180
Walnut Grove town	387	175
Loganville division	5 903	3 268
Between town	87	94
Loganville city (pt.)[129]	1 624	1 118
Monroe division	11 862	...
Monroe city[129]	8 854	8 071
Social Circle division	3 685	3 297
Social Circle city[129]	2 591	1 961
Ware County[130]	37 180	33 525
Dixie Union division	1 429	1 422
Manor division	967	970
Waresboro division	4 375	3 266
Waycross division	30 409	...
Deenwood (CDP)	3 580	3 015
Sunnyside (CDP)	1 658	...
Waycross city[130]	19 371	18 996
Warren County[131]	6 583	6 669
Camak division	1 074	...
Camak town	283	224
Norris division	1 393	1 200
Norwood division	926	...
Norwood town	306	272
Panhandle division	367	470
Warrenton division	2 823	...
Warrenton city[131]	2 172	2 073
Washington County[132]	18 842	17 480
Davisboro division	2 488	...
Davisboro city	433	476
Riddleville town	154	143
Deepstep division	963	1 069
Deepstep town	120	107
Harrison division	1 472	1 290
Harrison town	456	329
Sandersville division	9 023	...
Sandersville city	6 137	5 546
Tennille division	3 734	...
Oconee town	306	262
Tennille city	1 709	1 753
Warthen division	1 162	...
Wayne County[133]	20 750	17 858
Jesup division	15 396	13 264
Jesup city[133]	9 418	9 091
Odum division	2 857	2 282
Odum town	401	379
Screven division	2 497	2 312
Screven city	872	936

County Subdivisions

County Subdivisions	1980	1970
Webster County[134]	2 341	2 362
Preston division	1 055	1 138
Preston city (pt.)[134]	422	226
Weston division	1 286	1 224
Preston city (pt.)[134]	7	...
Weston town	109	73
Wheeler County[135]	5 155	4 596
Alamo division	2 589	2 409
Alamo city	993	833
Scotland city (pt.)	26	22
Glenwood division	2 566	2 187
Glenwood city[135]	824	670
Lumber City city (pt.)	–	–
White County[136]	10 120	7 742
Cleveland division	5 829	...
Cleveland city	1 578	1 353
Helen division	1 542	1 256
Helen city[136]	265	252
Mossy Creek division	2 749	...
Whitfield County[137]	65 789	55 108
Dalton division	51 445	...
Dalton city (pt.)[137]	20 906	18 872
Industrial City city (pt.)[137]	142	...
North Whitfield division	5 219	3 366
Cohutta town[137]	407	393
Varnell city[137]	282	314
Westside division	9 125	6 063
Dalton city (pt.)[137]	33	...
Tunnel Hill city[137]	936	1 146
Wilcox County[138]	7 682	6 998
Abbeville division	1 910	1 744
Abbeville city (pt.)	985	781
Pineview division	1 269	1 232
Pineview town	564	528
Pitts division	1 591	1 568
Pitts city	384	345
Seville town[138]	209	...
Rochelle division	2 912	2 454
Rochelle city	1 626	1 380
Wilkes County[139]	10 951	10 184
Rayle division	1 666	1 691
Rayle town[139]	177	110
Tignall division	2 000	2 065
Tignall town	733	756
Washington–Metasville division	7 285	6 428
Washington city[139]	4 662	4 094
Wilkinson County[140]	10 368	9 393
Allentown division	1 339	1 303
Allentown town (pt.)	294	289
Danville town (pt.)	233	125
Gordon division	4 341	3 699
Gordon town	2 768	2 553
Ivey town	455	245
Irwinton division	3 561	...
Irwinton town	841	757
McIntyre town	386	471
Toomsboro division	1 127	...
Toomsboro town	673	682
Worth County[141]	18 064	14 770
Bridgeboro division	2 185	1 745
Poulan division	2 778	2 381
Poulan city	818	766
Sylvester city (pt.)	–	...
Sumner division	1 222	1 183
Sumner town	213	207
Sylvester division	9 578	6 994
Sylvester city (pt.)[141]	5 860	4 226
Warwick division	2 301	2 467
Oakfield town	113	171
Warwick city	488	466

HAWAII

The territory of Hawaii is an archipelago of nine inhabited islands, Hawaii, Maui, Oahu, Kauai, Molokai, Lanai, Niihau, Kahoolawe, and Midway, besides a number of small uninhabited islands. The island first named is the largest, and was formerly the most important, and has thus given its name to the archipelago and to the territory.

It is probable that the first white men to reach the archipelago were the survivors of the crews of two Spanish vessels which were wrecked on the coast of one of the islands about the year 1527. Juan Gaetano, a Spanish navigator, seems to have visited the islands in 1542 or 1555. In 1778 they were definitely discovered by the English navigator, Capt. James Cook.

At the time of Cook's visit, the archipelago seems to have been divided into three distinct kingdoms as follows: (1) Hawaii; (2) Oahu and Maui; and (3) Lanai and Molokai. On the death of the King of Hawaii in 1782 a period of civil war followed, which was brought to a close in 1791, when Kamehameha, the leader of one of the parties, had his rival assassinated. In 1795 he succeeded in establishing his sovereignty over the entire archipelago and founded a dynasty which governed the Hawaiian Islands until 1872.

Idolatry was overthrown by the king in 1819, and in the following year American missionaries began the work of educating the natives. In 1839 the King granted civil rights to the people and in 1840 promulgated a constitution. In 1846 the hitherto prevailing system of feudalism was abolished by the Land Act, under which the crown lands were yielded up and provision was made for the people to become owners of the soil.

About 1840 French and British officers attempted to gain a foothold in the islands, but their acts were disowned by their respective governments. In 1842 the independence of the islands was recognized by the United States and two years later by France and Great Britain.

The dynasty established by Kamehameha I became extinct with the death of Kamehameha V in December, 1872, whereupon the legislature elected as king Lunailo, who had received the unanimous nomination of the people. He died childless about a year later, and the legislature again elected a king, Kalakaua, who reigned until his death in January, 1891, when his sister, Liliuokalani, became queen. Her governmental policies were distasteful to the progressive element of the population, and in January, 1893, she was dethroned and a provisional government established. Negotiations for annexation to the United States were begun, but proved unsuccessful, whereupon the Republic of Hawaii was organized in July, 1894. Negotiations for annexation were renewed in 1897, and in August of the next year the archipelago passed into the possession of the United States. In June, 1900, the territory of Hawaii was organized, with its capital at Honolulu.

Hawaii was admitted as a state in 1959.

HAWAII

COUNTY LOCATION INDEX

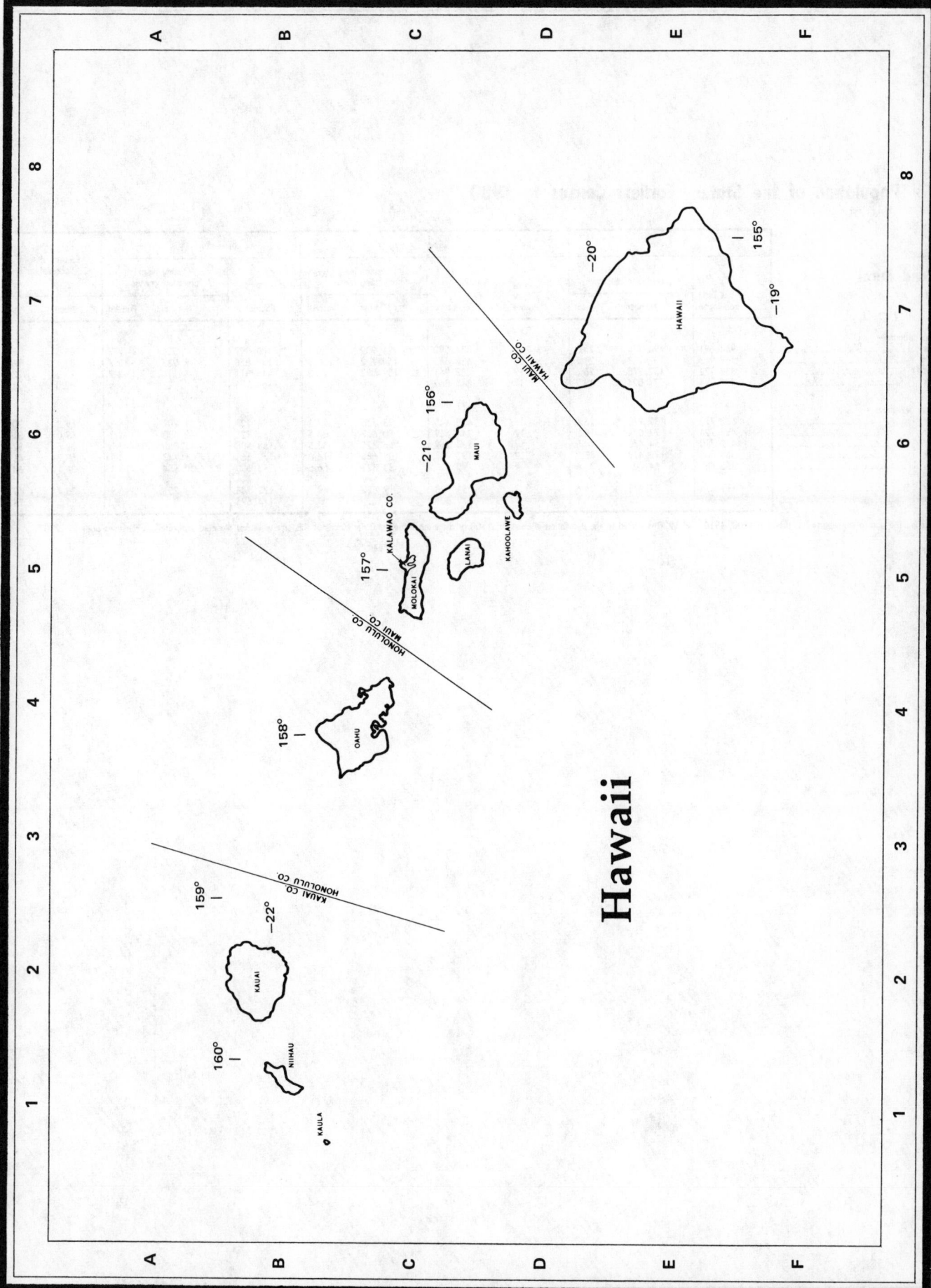

Hawaii

Population of the State: Earliest Census to 1980

Urban and Rural

	The State			Urban					Rural				Percent of total population	
	Total population	Change from preceding census		Places of 2,500 or more	Population	Change from preceding census		Population	Change from preceding census			Percent of total population		
		Number	Percent			Number	Percent			Number	Percent	Urban	Rural
Current urban definition:													
1980 (Apr. 1)_____	964 691	194 778	25.3	42	834 592	195 909	30.7	130 099	221	0.2		86.5	13.5
1970 (Apr. 1)_____	ʼ769 913	137 141	21.7	33	638 683	154 722	32.0	129 878	−18 933	−12.7		83.1	16.9
1960 (Apr. 1)_____	632 772	132 978	26.6	19	483 961	139 092	40.3	148 811	−6 114	−3.9		76.5	23.5
1950 (Apr. 1)_____	499 794	77 024	18.2	17	344 869	...	...	154 925	...	...		69.0	31.0
Previous urban definition:													
1960 (Apr. 1)_____	632 772	132 978	26.6	19	438 645	93 776	27.2	194 127	39 202	25.3		69.3	30.7
1950 (Apr. 1)_____	499 794	77 024	18.2	17	344 869	80 607	30.5	154 925	−3 583	−2.3		69.0	31.0
1940 (Apr. 1)_____	422 770	54 470	14.8	17	264 262	66 325	33.5	158 508	−11 855	−7.0		62.5	37.5
1930 (Apr. 1)_____	368 300	112 419	43.9	12	197 937	105 686	114.6	170 363	6 733	4.1		53.7	46.3
1920 (Jan. 1)_____	255 881	64 007	33.4	2	92 251	33 323	56.5	163 630	30 684	23.1		36.1	63.9
1910 (Apr. 15)_____	191 874	37 873	24.6	2	58 928	19 622	49.9	132 946	18 251	15.9		30.7	69.3
1900 (June 1)_____	154 001	...	...	1	39 306	...	...	114 695	...	...		25.5	74.5

NOTE: The population reported as urban in 1900, 1910, and 1920 is limited to the population in cities of 2,500 or more inhabitants. Other places of this size were not reported separately in censuses prior to 1930.

HAWAII

1960	61,322
1970	63,468
1980	92,053

HONOLULU

1960	500,409
1970	630,528
1980	762,565

KALAWAO

1970	(NA)
1980	144

KAUAI

1960	28,176
1970	29,761
1980	39,082

MAUI

1960	42,576
1970	46,156
1980	70,847

AIEA

1930	3,021
1940	3,553
1950	3,714
1960	11,826
1970	12,560
1980	32,879

EWA BEACH

1930	4,739
1940	3,570
1950	3,429
1960	4,627
1970	7,765
1980	14,369

KAHULUI

1940	3,579
1950	2,746
1960	4,223
1970	8,280
1980	12,978

HILO

1910	6,745
1920	10,431
1930	19,468
1950	27,198
1960	25,966
1970	26,353
1980	35,269

HONOLULU

1890	22,907
1900	39,306
1910	52,183
1920	81,820
1930	137,582
1940	179,326
1950	248,034
1960	294,194
1970	324,871
1980	365,048

KAILUA

1960	25,622
1970	33,783
1980	35,812

KANEOHE

1940	1,762
1950	3,208
1960	14,414
1970	29,903
1980	29,919

MILILANI TOWN

1970	2,035
1980	21,365

MOKAPU

1970	7,860
1980	11,615

PEARL CITY

1960	(NA)
1970	19,552
1980	42,575

SCHOLFIELD BARRACKS

1960	(NA)
1970	13,516
1980	18,851

WAHIAWA

1930	3,370
1940	5,420
1950	8,369
1960	15,512
1970	17,598
1980	16,911

WAILUKU

1930	6,998
1940	7,319
1950	7,424
1960	6,969
1970	7,979
1980	10,260

WAIPAHU

1960	(NA)
1970	24,150
1980	29,139

County Subdivisions

County Subdivisions	1980	1970
The State [1]	964 691	'769 913
Hawaii County	92 053	63 468
Hilo division	37 017	28 412
Hilo (CDP)	35 269	26 353
Wainaku (CDP)	1 045	...
Honokaa–Kukuihaele division	3 287	2 829
Honokaa (CDP) (pt.)	1 936	1 555
Kukuihaele (CDP)	332	310
Kau division	3 699	3 398
Naalehu (CDP)	1 168	1 014
Pahala (CDP)	1 619	1 507
Keaau–Mountain View division	7 055	3 802
Keaau	775	951
Mountain View (CDP)	540	419
North Hilo division	1 679	1 881
Laupahoehoe (CDP)	500	452
Ookala	401	486
North Kohala division	3 249	3 326
Hawi (CDP)	795	797
Kapaau (CDP)	612	237
North Kona division	13 748	4 832
Holualoa (CDP)	1 243	...
Kailua (CDP)	4 751	365
Kainaliu (CDP) (pt.)	408	...
Paauhau–Paauilo division	1 841	1 819
Honokaa (CDP) (pt.)	–	...
Paauilo (CDP)	755	710
Pahoa–Kalapana division	4 696	1 352
Pahoa	923	924
Papaikou–Wailea division	5 261	5 503
Honomu	559	737
Papaikou (CDP)	1 567	1 888
Paukaa	544	...
South Kohala division	4 607	2 310
Waimea (CDP)	1 179	756
South Kona division	5 914	4 004
Captain Cook (CDP)	2 008	1 263
Kainaliu (CDP) (pt.)	104	...
Kealakekua (CDP)	1 033	740
Honolulu County [2]	762 565	'630 528
Ewa division	191 051	'132 299
Aiea (CDP)	32 879	12 560
Barbers Point Housing (CDP)	1 373	1 947
Ewa (CDP)	2 637	2 906
Ewa Beach (CDP)	14 369	7 765
Hickam Housing (CDP)	4 425	7 352
Iroquois Point (CDP)	3 915	4 572
Makakilo City (CDP)	7 691	3 499
Mililani Town (CDP)	21 365	2 035
Pearl City (CDP)	42 575	19 552
Waipahu (CDP)	29 139	'24 150
Waipio Acres (CDP)	4 091	2 146
Honolulu division	365 048	324 871
Honolulu (CDP)	365 048	324 871
Koolauloa division	14 195	10 562
Hauula (CDP)	2 997	2 048
Kaaawa (CDP)	959	848
Kahuku (CDP)	935	917
Laie (CDP)	4 643	3 009
Koolaupoko division	109 373	92 219
Ahuimanu (CDP)	6 238	...
Heeia (CDP)	5 432	...
Kahaluu (CDP)	2 925	1 657
Kailua (CDP)	35 812	33 783
Kaneohe (CDP)	29 919	29 903
Maunawili (CDP)	5 239	5 303
Mokapu (CDP)	11 615	7 860
Waimanalo (CDP)	3 562	2 081·
Waimanalo Beach (CDP)	4 161	3 045
Wahiawa division	41 562	37 329
Schofield Barracks (CDP)	18 851	13 516
Wahiawa (CDP)	16 911	17 598
Whitmore Village (CDP)	2 318	2 015
Waialua division	9 849	9 171
Haleiwa (CDP)	2 412	2 626
Waialua (CDP)	4 051	4 047
Waianae division	31 487	24 077
Maili (CDP)	5 026	4 397
Makaha (CDP)	6 582	4 644
Nanakuli (CDP)	8 185	6 506
Waianae (CDP)	7 941	3 302
Kalawao County [3]	144	...
Kalawao division	144	172
Kauai County	39 082	29 761
Eleele–Kalaheo division	4 855	3 710
Eleele (CDP)	580	758
Kalaheo (CDP)	2 500	1 514
Hanalei division	2 668	1 182
Hanalei (CDP)	483	153
Kilauea (CDP)	895	671
Princeville (CDP)	500	...
Kapaa division	4 467	3 794
Kapaa (CDP)	4 467	3 794
Kaumakani–Hanapepe division	3 111	3 173
Hanapepe (CDP)	1 417	1 388
Kaumakani (CDP)	888	1 014

County Subdivisions

County Subdivisions	1980	1970
Kauai County—Con.		
Kekaha–Waimea division	5 256	4 159
Kekaha (CDP)	3 260	2 404
Waimea (CDP)	1 569	1 569
Koloa–Poipu division	3 879	3 141
Koloa (CDP)	1 457	1 368
Poipu	685	466
Lihue division	4 000	3 124
Lihue (CDP)	4 000	3 124
Niihau division	226	237
Puhi–Hanamaulu division	4 590	3 642
Hanamaulu (CDP)	3 227	2 461
Puhi (CDP)	991	772
Wailua–Anahola division	6 030	3 599
Anahola (CDP)	915	638
Wailua (CDP)	1 587	1 379
Maui County [4]	70 847	46 156
East Molokai division	3 574	2 574
Kaunakakai (CDP)	2 231	1 070
Haiku–Pauwela division	3 567	2 067
Haiku	619	464
Pauwela	468	355
Hana division	1 423	969
Hana (CDP)	643	459
Kahului division	13 026	8 287
Kahului (CDP)	12 978	8 280
Kihei division	6 035	1 636
Kihei (CDP)	5 644	...
Kula division	5 077	2 124
Wailea (CDP)	1 124	...
Lahaina division	10 284	5 524
Honokahua (CDP)	309	431
Kaanapali (CDP)	541	...
Lahaina (CDP)	6 095	3 718
Napili–Honokowai (CDP)	2 446	...
Lanai division	2 119	2 204
Lanai City (CDP)	2 092	2 122
Makawao–Paia division	10 361	5 788
Haliimaile (CDP)	741	638
Lower Paia (CDP)	1 500	1 105
Makawao (CDP)	2 900	1 066
Pukalani (CDP)	3 950	1 629
Puunene division	572	1 132
Puunene (CDP)	572	1 132
Spreckelsville division	220	781
Waihee–Waikapu division	1 584	1 299
Waihee (CDP)	413	346
Waikapu (CDP)	698	598
Wailuku division	10 674	9 084
Wailuku (CDP)	10 260	7 979
West Molokai division	2 331	2 515
Kualapuu (CDP)	502	441
Maunaloa (CDP)	633	872

IDAHO

The name Idaho is of Indian derivation and signifies "gem of the mountains."

The area now constituting this state was first visited by white men when an exploring expedition sent out by the United States Government under Lewis and Clark traversed it in 1805-6. The first permanent settlement was made in 1834, when a trading-post was established at Fort Hall, in what is now the southeastern part of the state. Few white men came to this region, however, until 1860 when the discovery of gold on Oro Fino Creek attracted prospectors and miners in large numbers.

The Oregon country, of which Idaho originally formed a part, was, at the beginning of the nineteenth century, claimed by the United States, Great Britain, Spain, and Russia, each nation basing its right to possession on discoveries and explorations. Spanish and English navigators had visited the Oregon coast at various times during the sixteenth and succeeding centuries. Russia had made settlements in Alaska in the early part of the eighteenth century and for this reason laid claim to territory as far south as the present state of California. Americans from ships sent out by Boston merchants late in the eighteenth century were the first white men to explore the interior of the Oregon country.

All that remained of the Spanish claim after the cession of Louisiana to France in 1800 was relinquished at the time of the Florida Purchase in 1819, when Spain transferred to the United States "all rights, claims, and pretensions to any country north of the forty-second parallel." In 1824 Russia surrendered to the United States all claims south of latitude 54°40'. In 1818 a treaty had been concluded between the United States and England, under which the United States and Great Britain jointly occupied the Oregon region, but in 1846 this joint occupation was terminated by a treaty fixing the present boundary between the United States and Canada.

The territory of Oregon, which included the area now constituting the state of Idaho, was organized in 1848. In 1853 the territory of Washington was organized, and included what is now northern Idaho, but left southern Idaho still a part of Oregon territory. In 1859, when Oregon, with its present boundaries became a state, the remainder of the region now forming Idaho was added to Washington territory. In March, 1863, Idaho territory was organized from parts of the territories of Washington, Dakota, and Nebraska; it then included the area now comprising Idaho; Montana, and part of Wyoming. The organization of Montana and Wyoming as territories in 1864 and 1868, respectively, left Idaho with its present boundaries.

In 1889 a state constitution was adopted, under authority of an act of Congress, and in 1890 Idaho was admitted to the Union.

COUNTY LOCATION INDEX

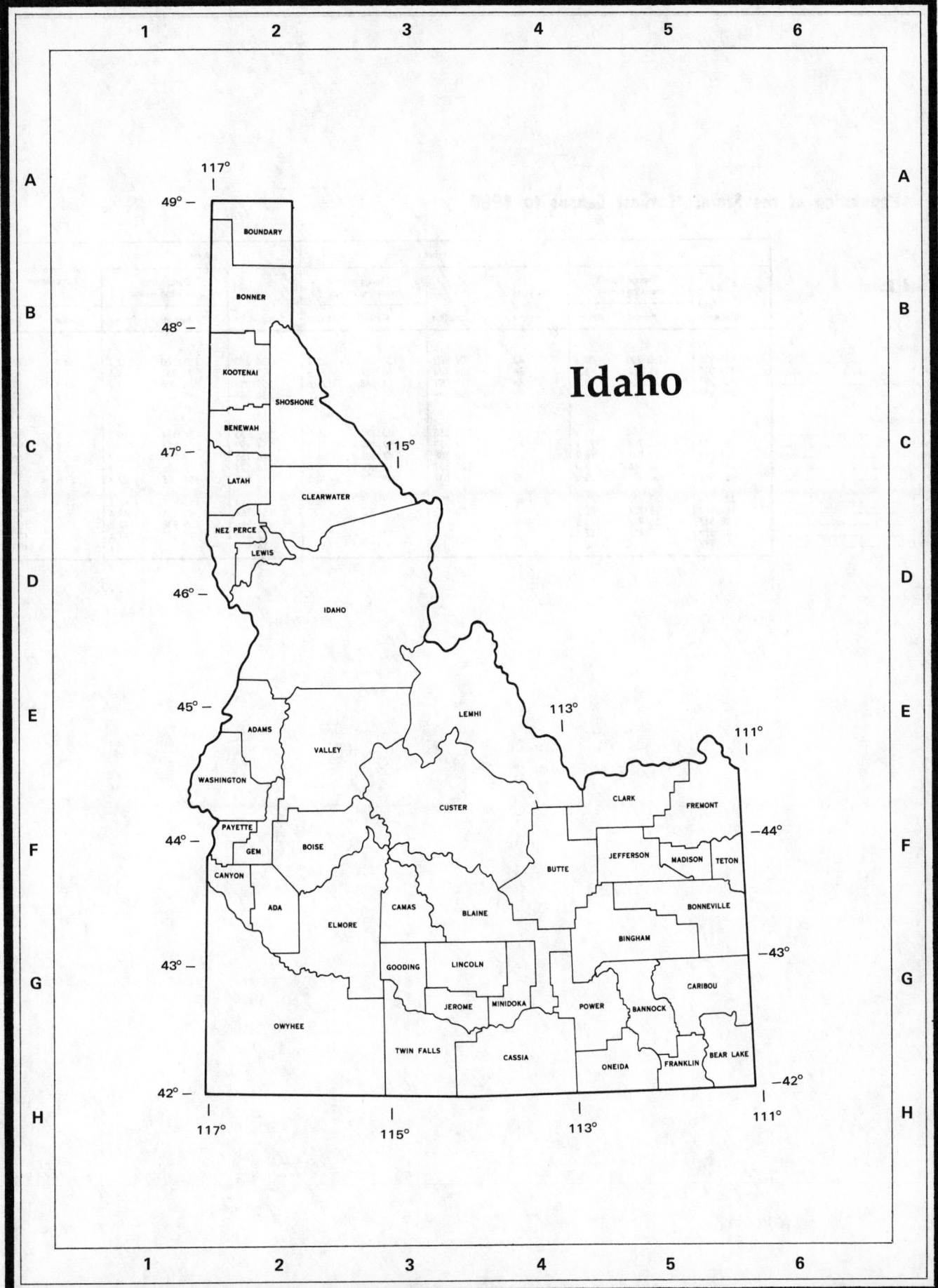

Idaho

A
B
C
D
E
F
G
H

1 2 3 4 5 6

117°
49°
48°
47°
46°
45°
44°
43°
42°

115°
113°
111°

44°
43°
42°

BOUNDARY
BONNER
KOOTENAI
SHOSHONE
BENEWAH
LATAH
CLEARWATER
NEZ PERCE
LEWIS
IDAHO
ADAMS
VALLEY
WASHINGTON
PAYETTE
GEM
BOISE
CANYON
ADA
ELMORE
CAMAS
BLAINE
LEMHI
CUSTER
BUTTE
CLARK
FREMONT
JEFFERSON
MADISON
TETON
BONNEVILLE
BINGHAM
GOODING
LINCOLN
JEROME
MINIDOKA
OWYHEE
TWIN FALLS
CASSIA
POWER
BANNOCK
CARIBOU
ONEIDA
FRANKLIN
BEAR LAKE

Population of the State: Earliest Census to 1980

Urban and Rural

	The State			Urban				Rural			Percent of total population	
	Total population	Change from preceding census		Places of 2,500 or more	Population	Change from preceding census		Population	Change from preceding census		Urban	Rural
		Number	Percent			Number	Percent		Number	Percent		
Current urban definition:												
1980 (Apr. 1)	943 935	**230 920**	**32.4**	42	509 702	124 268	32.2	434 233	107 100	32.7	54.0	46.0
1970 (Apr. 1)	'713 015	45 824	6.9	36	385 434	68 337	21.6	327 133	-22 961	-6.6	54.1	45.9
1960 (Apr. 1)	667 191	78 554	13.3	34	317 097	64 548	25.6	350 094	14 006	4.2	47.5	52.5
1950 (Apr. 1)	588 637	63 764	12.1	33	252 549	...	...	336 088	...	...	42.9	57.1
Previous urban definition:												
1960 (Apr. 1)	667 191	78 554	13.3	29	276 258	42 120	18.0	390 933	36 434	10.3	41.4	58.6
1950 (Apr. 1)	588 637	63 764	12.1	29	234 138	57 430	32.5	354 499	6 334	1.8	39.8	60.2
1940 (Apr. 1)	524 873	79 841	17.9	26	176 708	47 201	36.4	348 165	32 640	10.3	33.7	66.3
1930 (Apr. 1)	445 032	13 166	3.0	21	129 507	10 470	8.8	315 525	2 696	0.9	29.1	70.9
1920 (Jan. 1)	431 866	106 272	32.6	20	119 037	49 139	70.3	312 829	57 133	22.3	27.6	72.4
1910 (Apr. 15)	325 594	163 822	101.3	12	69 898	59 895	598.8	255 696	103 927	68.5	21.5	78.5
1900 (June 1)	161 772	73 224	82.7	2	10 003	10 003	...	151 769	63 221	71.4	6.2	93.8
1890 (June 1)	88 548	55 938	171.5	–	–	–	–	88 548	55 938	171.5	–	100.0
1880 (June 1)	32 610	17 611	117.4	–	–	–	–	32 610	17 611	117.4	–	100.0
1870 (June 1)	14 999	...	...	–	–	...	...	14 999	...	...	–	100.0

ADA

1870	2,675
1880	4,647
1890	8,368
1900	11,559
1910	29,088
1920	35,213
1930	37,925
1940	50,401
1950	70,649
1960	93,460
1970	112,230
1980	173,036

ADAMS

1920	2,966
1930	2,867
1940	3,407
1950	3,347
1960	2,978
1970	2,877
1980	3,347

ALTURAS

1870	689
1880	1,693
1890	2,629

BANNOCK

1900	11,702
1910	19,242
1920	27,532
1930	31,266
1940	34,759
1950	41,745
1960	49,342
1970	52,200
1980	65,421

BEAR LAKE

1880	3,235
1890	6,057
1900	7,051
1910	7,729
1920	8,783
1930	7,872
1940	7,911
1950	6,834
1960	7,148
1970	5,801
1980	6,931

BENEWAH

1920	6,997
1930	6,371
1940	7,332
1950	6,173
1960	6,036
1970	6,230
1980	8,292

BINGHAM

1890	13,575
1900	10,447
1910	23,306
1920	18,310
1930	18,561
1940	21,044
1950	23,271
1960	28,218
1970	29,617
1980	36,489

BLAINE

1900	4,900
1910	8,387
1920	4,473
1930	3,768
1940	5,295
1950	5,384
1960	4,598
1970	5,749
1980	9,841

BOISE

1870	3,834
1880	3,214
1890	3,342
1900	4,174
1910	5,250
1920	1,822
1930	1,847
1940	2,333
1950	1,776
1960	1,646
1970	1,763
1980	2,999

BONNER

1910	13,588
1920	12,957
1930	13,152
1940	15,667
1950	14,853
1960	15,587
1970	15,560
1980	24,163

BONNEVILLE

1920	17,501
1930	19,664
1940	25,697
1950	30,210
1960	46,906
1970	52,457
1980	65,980

BOUNDARY

1920	4,474
1930	4,555
1940	5,987
1950	5,908
1960	5,809
1970	5,484
1980	7,289

BUTTE

1920	2,940
1930	1,934
1940	1,877
1950	2,722
1960	3,498
1970	2,925
1980	3,342

CAMAS

1920	1,730
1930	1,411
1940	1,360
1950	1,079
1960	917
1970	728
1980	818

CANYON

1900	7,497
1910	25,323
1920	26,932
1930	20,930
1940	40,987
1950	53,597
1960	57,662
1970	61,288
1980	83,756

CARIBOU

1920	2,191
1930	2,121
1940	2,284
1950	5,576
1960	5,976
1970	6,534
1980	8,695

CASSIA

1880	1,312
1890	3,143
1900	3,951
1910	7,197
1920	15,659
1930	13,116
1940	14,430
1950	14,629
1960	16,121
1970	17,017
1980	19,427

CLARK

1920	1,886
1930	1,122
1940	1,005
1950	918
1960	915
1970	741
1980	798

CLEARWATER

1920	4,993
1930	6,599
1940	8,243
1950	8,217
1960	8,548
1970	10,871
1980	10,390

CUSTER

1890	2,176
1900	2,049
1910	3,001
1920	3,550
1930	3,162
1940	3,549
1950	3,318
1960	2,996
1970	2,967
1980	3,385

ELMORE

1890	1,870
1900	2,286
1910	4,785
1920	5,087
1930	4,491
1940	5,518
1950	6,687
1960	16,719
1970	17,479
1980	21,565

FRANKLIN

1920	8,650
1930	9,379
1940	10,229
1950	9,867
1960	8,457
1970	7,373
1980	8,895

FREMONT

1900	12,821
1910	24,606
1920	10,380
1930	9,924
1940	10,304
1950	9,351
1960	8,679
1970	8,710
1980	10,813

GEM

1920	6,427
1930	7,419
1940	9,544
1950	8,730
1960	9,127
1970	9,387
1980	11,972

GOODING

1920	7,548
1930	7,580
1940	9,257
1950	11,101
1960	9,544
1970	8,645
1980	11,874

IDAHO

1870	849
1880	2,031
1890	2,955
1900	9,121
1910	12,384
1920	11,749
1930	10,107
1940	12,691
1950	11,423
1960	13,524
1970	12,891
1980	14,769

JEFFERSON

1920	9,441
1930	9,171
1940	10,762
1950	10,495
1960	11,672
1970	11,740
1980	15,304

JEROME

1920	5,729
1930	9,358
1940	9,900
1950	12,080
1960	11,712
1970	10,253
1980	14,840

KOOTENAI

1880	518
1890	4,108
1900	10,216
1910	22,747
1920	17,878
1930	19,469
1940	22,283
1950	24,947
1960	29,556
1970	36,332
1980	59,770

LATAH

1890	9,173
1900	13,451
1910	18,818
1920	18,092
1930	17,798
1940	18,804
1950	20,971
1960	21,170
1970	24,898
1980	28,749

LEMHI

1870	988
1880	2,230
1890	1,915
1900	3,446
1910	4,786
1920	5,164
1930	4,643
1940	6,521
1950	6,278
1960	5,816
1970	5,566
1980	7,460

LEWIS

1920	5,851
1930	5,238
1940	4,666
1950	4,208
1960	4,423
1970	3,867
1980	4,118

LINCOLN

1900	1,784

1910	12,676
1920	3,446
1930	3,242
1940	4,230
1950	4,256
1960	3,686
1970	3,057
1980	3,436

LOGAN

1890	4,169

MADISON

1920	9,167
1930	8,316
1940	9,186
1950	9,156
1960	9,417
1970	13,452
1980	19,480

MINIDOKA

1920	9,035
1930	8,043
1940	9,870
1950	9,785
1960	14,394
1970	15,731
1980	19,718

NEZ PERCE

1870	1,607
1880	3,965
1890	2,847
1900	13,748
1910	24,860
1920	15,253
1930	17,591
1940	18,873
1950	22,658
1960	27,066
1970	30,376
1980	33,220

ONEIDA

1870	1,922
1880	6,964
1890	6,819
1900	8,933
1910	15,170
1920	6,723
1930	5,870
1940	5,417
1950	4,387
1960	3,603
1970	2,864
1980	3,258

OWYHEE

1870	1,713
1880	1,426
1890	2,021
1900	3,804
1910	4,044
1920	4,694
1930	4,103
1940	5,652
1950	6,307
1960	6,375
1970	6,422

1980	8,272

PAYETTE

1920	7,021
1930	7,318
1940	9,511
1950	11,921
1960	12,363
1970	12,401
1980	15,722

POWER

1920	5,105
1930	4,457
1940	3,965
1950	3,998
1960	4,111
1970	4,864
1980	6,844

SHOSHONE

1870	722
1880	469
1890	5,382
1900	11,950
1910	13,963
1920	14,250
1930	19,060
1940	21,230
1950	22,806
1960	20,876
1970	19,718
1980	19,226

TETON

1920	3,921
1930	3,573
1940	3,601
1950	3,204
1960	2,639
1970	2,351
1980	2,897

TWIN FALLS

1910	13,543
1920	28,398
1930	20,828
1940	36,403
1950	40,979
1960	41,842
1970	41,807
1980	52,927

VALLEY

1920	2,524
1930	3,448
1940	4,035
1950	4,270
1960	3,663
1970	3,609
1980	5,604

WASHINGTON

1880	879
1890	3,836
1900	6,882
1910	11,101
1920	9,424

1930	7,962
1940	8,853
1950	8,576
1960	8,378
1970	7,633
1980	8,803

NOTES

ALTURAS

Parts to form part of Custer in 1881, Elmore and Logan in 1889, and the remainder taken to form part of Blaine in 1895.

LOGAN

Organized from part of Alturas in 1889; taken to form Lincoln and part of Blaine in 1895.

BLACKFOOT

1910	2,202
1920	3,937
1930	2,466
1940	2,874
1950	4,078
1960	7,378
1970	8,716
1980	10,065

BOISE CITY

1870	995
1880	1,899
1890	2,311
1900	5,957
1910	17,358
1920	21,393
1930	21,544
1940	26,130
1950	34,393
1960	34,481
1970	74,990
1980	102,451

CALDWELL

1890	779
1900	997
1910	3,543
1920	5,601
1930	4,974
1940	7,272
1950	10,487
1960	12,230
1970	14,219
1980	17,699

COEUR D'ALENE

1890	491
1900	508
1910	7,291
1920	6,447
1930	8,297
1940	10,049
1950	12,198
1960	14,291
1970	16,228
1980	20,054

IDAHO FALLS

1900	1,262
1910	4,827
1920	8,064
1930	9,429
1940	15,024
1950	19,218
1960	33,161
1970	35,776
1980	39,590

LEWISTON

1880	739
1890	849
1900	2,425
1910	6,043
1920	6,574
1930	9,403
1940	10,548
1950	12,985
1960	12,691
1970	26,068
1980	27,986

MOSCOW

1900	2,484
1910	3,670
1920	3,956
1930	4,476
1940	6,014
1950	10,593
1960	11,183
1970	14,146
1980	16,513

NAMPA

1890	347
1900	799
1910	4,205
1920	7,621
1930	8,206
1940	12,149
1950	16,185
1960	18,897
1970	20,768
1980	25,112

POCATELLO

1900	4,046
1910	9,110
1920	15,001
1930	16,471
1940	18,131
1950	26,131
1960	28,534
1970	40,036
1980	46,340

REXBURG

1900	1,081
1910	1,893
1920	3,569
1930	3,048
1940	3,337
1950	4,253
1960	4,767
1970	8,272
1980	11,559

TWIN FALLS

1910	5,258
1920	8,324
1930	8,787
1940	11,851
1950	17,600
1960	20,126
1970	21,914
1980	26,209

CORRECTION NOTE

Shown below are corrections to the 1980 census counts of
the total population made after the tabulations for this
report were completed. Any additional corrections made
after this report is printed are available by writing to
Data User Services Division, Customer Services (Corrections),
Bureau of the Census, Washington, D.C. 20233.

The 1980 figures shown in this publication are subject
to change pending the outcome of the various lawsuits
dealing with the census counts.

	1980 population	
	As shown in the tables	Corrected
The State................	943 935	944 038
Ada County:		
Boise City division:		
Boise City city (pt.)......	102 451	102 160
Payette County.................	15 722	15 825
Fruitland division............	4 735	4 921
Fruitland city (pt.)........	2 373	2 559
Payette division.............	7 738	7 655
Fruitland city (pt.)........	83	(1)
Boise City city (total)........	102 451	102 160
Fruitland city (total).........	2 456	2 559

[1]Delete, not in Payette division.

County Subdivisions	1980	1970
The State	943 935	713 015
Ada County[1]	173 036	112 230
Boise City division	154 735	...
Boise City city (pt.)[1]	102 451	74 990
Garden City city (pt.)[1]	4 568	2 368
Meridian city[1]	6 658	2 616
Boise Hills division	1 184	360
Eagle division	8 631	4 128
Eagle city[1]	2 620	...
Garden City city (pt.)[1]	3	...
Kuna division	4 048	...
Kuna city[1]	1 767	593
Orchard division	4 438	411
Boise City city (pt.)[1]	–	...
Adams County[2]	3 347	2 877
Council division	2 235	...
Council city	917	899
New Meadows division	1 112	...
New Meadows city[2]	576	605
Bannock County[3]	65 421	52 200
Fort Hall division	1 622	954
Inkom division	2 825	...
Inkom city[3]	830	522
Pocatello city (pt.)[3]	12	...
Pocatello division	56 185	...
Chubbuck city[3]	7 052	2 924
Pocatello city (pt.)[3]	46 274	40 036
South Bannock division	4 789	...
Arimo city[3]	338	252
Downey city[3]	645	586
Lava Hot Springs city	467	516
McCammon city	770	623
Pocatello city (pt.)[3]	54	...
Bear Lake County[4]	6 931	5 801
Georgetown division	831	...
Georgetown city	544	421
Montpelier division	4 146	3 470
Montpelier city[4]	3 107	2 604
Paris division	1 954	...
Bloomington city	212	186
Paris city	707	615
St. Charles city	211	200
Benewah County[5]	8 292	6 230
Plummer division	2 309	...
Chatcolet city	181	95
Plummer city[5]	634	443
St. Maries division	5 352	...
St. Maries city	2 794	2 571
Tensed division	631	...
Tensed city	113	151
Bingham County[6]	36 489	29 167
Aberdeen division	2 848	3 107
Aberdeen city[6]	1 528	1 542
Alridge division	359	89
Atomic City division	2 266	...
Atomic City city[6]	34	24
Blackfoot division	12 173	...
Blackfoot city[6]	10 065	8 716
Firth division	3 023	...
Basalt city	414	349
Firth city[6]	460	362
Fort Hall division	2 262	1 728
Moreland division	7 765	...
Shelley division	5 793	...
Shelley city[6]	3 300	2 614
Blaine County[7]	9 841	5 749
Carey division	802	...
Hailey–Bellevue division	4 772	...
Bellevue city	1 016	537
Hailey city[7]	2 109	1 425
Ketchum division	4 267	2 273
Ketchum city[7]	2 200	1 454
Sun Valley city[7]	545	180
Boise County[8]	2 999	1 763
Garden Valley division	767	426
Crouch city	69	71
Horseshoe Bend division	1 264	...
Horseshoe Bend city	700	511
Placerville city	20	14
Idaho City division	968	...
Idaho City city[8]	300	164
Bonner County[9]	24 163	15 560
Blanchard–Glengary division	7 065	3 161
Oldtown city (pt.)	230	144
Ponderay city (pt.)[9]	3	–
Clark Fork division	1 672	1 000
Clark Fork city[9]	449	367
East Hope city	258	175
Hope city	106	63
Priest River division	4 314	3 137
Oldtown city (pt.)	27	17
Priest River city[9]	1 639	1 493

County Subdivisions	1980	1970
Bonner County—Con.		
Sandpoint division	11 112	8 262
Kootenai city[9]	280	168
Ponderay city (pt.)[9]	396	275
Sandpoint city[9]	4 460	4 144
Bonneville County[10]	65 980	52 457
Idaho Falls division	57 515	...
Ammon city[10]	4 669	2 545
Idaho Falls city[10]	39 590	35 776
Iona city	1 072	890
Idaho Falls West division	1 656	...
Swan Valley division	1 794	...
Irwin city	113	228
Swan Valley city[10]	135	235
Ucon division	5 015	...
Ririe city (pt.)[10]	60	47
Ucon city[10]	833	664
Boundary County[11]	7 289	5 484
Bonners Ferry division	4 908	...
Bonners Ferry city[11]	1 906	1 909
Moyie Springs division	1 326	...
Moyie Springs city[11]	386	203
Naples division	1 055	651
Butte County[12]	3 342	2 925
Arco division	2 903	2 532
Arco city[12]	1 241	1 244
Butte City city	93	42
Moore city	210	156
Howe division	439	393
Camas County	818	728
East Camas division	139	153
West Camas division	679	575
Fairfield city	404	336
Canyon County[13]	83 756	61 288
Caldwell division	23 286	...
Caldwell city[13]	17 699	14 219
Greenleaf city (pt.)[13]	613	...
Huston division	2 253	...
Melba division	1 247	1 105
Melba city[13]	276	197
Middleton division	6 062	...
Caldwell city (pt.)[13]	–	...
Middleton city[13]	1 901	739
Nampa division	41 783	...
Caldwell city (pt.)[13]		
Nampa city[13]	25 112	20 768
Notus division	1 493	...
Notus city	437	304
Parma division	3 991	...
Parma city[13]	1 820	1 228
Wilder division	3 641	...
Greenleaf city (pt.)[13]	50	...
Wilder city[13]	1 260	564
Caribou County[14]	8 695	6 534
Bancroft division	976	...
Bancroft city[14]	505	366
Fort Hall division	–	–
Grace division	2 434	...
Grace city	1 216	826
Soda Springs division	4 993	...
Soda Springs city[14]	4 051	2 977
Wayan division	292	250
Cassia County[15]	19 427	17 017
Albion division	2 470	...
Albion city	286	229
Malta city	196	196
Burley division	12 355	11 258
Burley city (pt.)[15]	8 525	8 079
Declo division	2 422	2 058
Declo city	276	251
Oakley division	2 180	...
Oakley city	663	656
Clark County[16]	798	741
East Clark division	130	...
Spencer city	29	45
West Clark division	668	...
Dubois city	413	400
Clearwater County[17]	10 390	10 871
Elk River division	1 086	...
Elk River city	265	383
Nez Perce division	6 079	...
Orofino city[17]	3 711	3 883
Pierce–Headquarters division	1 610	...
Pierce city	1 060	1 218
Weippe division	1 615	...
Weippe city[17]	828	713
Custer County[18]	3 385	2 967
Challis division	1 746	...
Challis city[18]	758	784
Clayton city	43	36
Mackay division	1 269	...
Lost River city	28	40
Mackay city[18]	541	539
Stanley division	370	...
Stanley city[18]	99	47

County Subdivisions

County Subdivisions	1980	1970
Elmore County[19]	21 565	17 479
Atlanta division	175	...
Glenns Ferry division	2 787	2 251
Glenns Ferry city[19]	1 374	1 386
Mountain Home division	18 603	15 060
Mountain Home city[19]	7 540	6 451
Mountain Home AFB (CDP)	6 403	6 038
Franklin County[20]	8 895	7 373
Dayton division	1 771	1 397
Clifton city[20]	208	137
Dayton city[20]	368	198
Oxford city	66	75
Weston city	310	230
Mink Creek division	780	658
Preston division	6 344	5 318
Franklin city	423	402
Preston city[20]	3 759	3 310
Fremont County[21]	10 813	8 710
Ashton division	2 547	...
Ashton city	1 219	1 187
Drummond city	25	13
Island Park division	765	...
Island Park city	154	136
Warm River city[21]	2	10
St. Anthony division	6 492	5 340
Parker city	262	266
St. Anthony city[21]	3 212	2 877
Teton—Newdale division	1 009	774
Newdale city	329	267
Teton city	559	390
Yellowstone National Park division	–	–
Gem County[22]	11 972	9 387
Emmett Bench division	2 548	1 876
Emmett Valley division	8 760	6 853
Emmett city[22]	4 605	3 945
Sweet division	664	658
Gooding County[23]	11 874	8 645
Bliss division	823	...
Bliss city	208	114
Gooding division	5 219	...
Gooding city[23]	2 949	2 599
Hagerman division	1 615	...
Hagerman city[23]	602	436
Wendell division	4 217	...
Wendell city[23]	1 974	1 122
Idaho County[24]	14 769	12 891
Cottonwood division	1 921	...
Cottonwood city[24]	941	867
Elk City division	1 795	...
Grangeville division	5 687	...
Grangeville city[24]	3 666	3 636
White Bird city	154	185
Nez Perce division	3 918	...
Ferdinand city	144	157
Kooskia city	784	809
Stites city[24]	253	263
Riggins division	1 448	...
Riggins city[24]	527	533
Jefferson County[25]	15 304	11 740
Hamer division	2 331	1 900
Hamer city	93	81
Mud Lake city[25]	243	194
Lewisville—Menan division	3 180	...
Lewisville city	502	468
Menan city	605	545
Rigby division	7 316	...
Rigby city[25]	2 624	2 324
Ririe division	1 157	1 041
Ririe city (pt.)[25]	495	528
Roberts division	1 320	910
Roberts city[25]	466	393
Jerome County[26]	14 840	10 253
Eden—Hazelton division	2 434	...
Eden city	355	343
Hazelton city[26]	496	396
Hunt division	474	491
Jerome division	11 932	...
Jerome city[26]	6 891	4 183
Kootenai County[27]	59 770	35 332
Coeur d'Alene division	35 550	...
Coeur d'Alene city[27]	20 054	16 228
Dalton Gardens city	1 795	1 559
Fernan Lake city[27]	178	179
Hayden city[27]	2 586	1 285
Hayden Lake city[27]	273	260
Harrison division	2 452	...
Harrison city[27]	260	249
Post Falls—Rathdrum division	15 605	...
Hauser city[27]	305	349
Huetter city	65	49
Post Falls city[27]	5 736	2 371
Rathdrum city[27]	1 369	741
State Line city[27]	26	22

County Subdivisions

County Subdivisions	1980	1970
Kootenai County—Con.		
Spirit Lake—Athol division	4 966	...
Athol city[27]	312	190
Spirit Lake city[27]	834	622
Worley division	1 197	...
Worley city	206	235
Latah County[28]	28 749	24 898
Deary—Bovill division	1 514	...
Bovill city	289	350
Deary city	539	411
Genesee division	1 392	1 165
Genesee city	791	619
Moscow division	19 464	...
Moscow city[28]	16 513	14 146
Potlatch division	3 417	...
Onaway city[28]	254	166
Potlatch city	819	871
Troy—Juliaetta—Kendrick division	2 962	...
Juliaetta city[28]	522	423
Kendrick city	395	426
Troy city[28]	820	541
Lemhi County[29]	7 460	5 566
Forney division	119	70
Leadore division	623	593
Leadore city	114	111
Patterson division	357	...
Salmon division	6 361	...
Salmon city[29]	3 308	2 910
Lewis County[30]	4 118	3 867
Craigmont division	863	...
Craigmont city[30]	617	554
Kamiah division	1 805	...
Kamiah city[30]	1 478	1 307
Lewis South division	28	...
Nezperce division	777	...
Nezperce city	517	555
Winchester division	645	...
Reubens city	87	81
Winchester city[30]	343	274
Lincoln County[31]	3 436	3 057
Richfield division	823	...
Richfield city	357	290
Shoshone division	2 613	2 427
Dietrich city	101	84
Shoshone city[31]	1 242	1 233
Madison County[32]	19 480	13 452
Moody Creek division	208	...
Sugar City division	3 869	...
Sugar City city[32]	1 022	617
Thornton division	15 403	...
Rexburg city[32]	11 559	8 272
Minidoka County[33]	19 718	15 731
Heyburn division	4 826	3 308
Burley city (pt.)	236	200
Heyburn city	2 889	1 637
Minidoka division	1 486	1 501
Minidoka city	101	131
Paul division	3 592	2 709
Paul city[33]	940	911
Rupert division	9 814	8 213
Acequia city	100	107
Rupert city[33]	5 476	4 563
Nez Perce County[34]	33 220	30 376
Leland division	380	...
Lewiston division	29 066	...
Lewiston city[34]	27 986	26 068
Nez Perce division	3 774	...
Culdesac city[34]	261	211
Lapwai city[34]	1 043	400
Peck city[34]	209	238
Oneida County[35]	3 258	2 864
Holbrook division	333	226
Malad division	2 925	2 638
Malad City city[35]	1 915	1 848
Owyhee County[36]	8 272	6 422
Bruneau division	682	571
Grand View division	1 285	954
Grand View city[36]	366	...
Homedale division	3 185	2 408
Homedale city[36]	2 078	1 411
Marsing division	2 095	1 739
Marsing city[36]	786	610
Murphy division	830	614
Western Shoshone division	195	136
Payette County[37]	15 722	12 401
Fruitland division	4 735	3 235
Fruitland city (pt.)[37]	2 373	1 576
New Plymouth division	3 249	2 629
New Plymouth city[37]	1 186	986
Payette division	7 738	...
Fruitland city (pt.)[37]	83	...
Payette city[37]	5 448	4 521
Power County[38]	6 844	4 864
American Falls division	5 094	3 747
American Falls city[38]	3 626	2 769

County Subdivisions

County Subdivisions	1980	1970
Power County—Con.		
Arbon division	167	...
Fort Hall division	899	...
Rockland division	684	547
Rockland city[38]	283	209
Shoshone County[39]	19 226	19 718
Avery–Clarkia division	560	506
Kellogg division	10 290	
Kellogg city[39]	3 417	3 811
Pinehurst city[39]	2 183	...
Smelterville city[39]	776	967
Wardner city[39]	423	492
Mullan division	1 517	1 517
Mullan city	1 269	1 279
Murray division	721	...
Wallace division	6 138	6 875
Osburn city	2 220	2 248
Wallace city	1 736	2 206
Teton County[40]	2 897	2 351
Driggs division	1 307	1 121
Driggs city[40]	727	727
Tetonia division	768	552
Tetonia city	191	176
Victor division	822	678
Victor city	323	241
Twin Falls County[41]	52 927	41 807
Buhl division	8 470	...
Buhl city[41]	3 629	2 975
Castleford city[41]	191	174
Filer division	4 204	...
Filer city[41]	1 645	1 173
Hollister division	915	...
Hollister city	167	57
Kimberly division	5 439	...
Hansen city[41]	1 078	415
Kimberly city[41]	2 307	1 557
Murtaugh division	1 097	1 086
Murtaugh city	114	124
Twin Falls division	32 161	...
Twin Falls city[41]	26 209	21 914
West Salmon Falls division	641	257
Valley County[42]	5 604	3 609
Cascade division	1 498	1 059
Cascade city[42]	945	833
McCall division	4 027	2 519
Donnelly city	139	114
McCall city[42]	2 188	1 758
Stibnite division	79	31
Washington County[43]	8 803	7 633
Cambridge division	967	901
Cambridge city[43]	428	383
Midvale division	745	767
Midvale city	205	176
Weiser division	7 091	5 965
Weiser city	4 771	4 108

ILLINOIS

This state takes its name from an Indian tribe which, at the time of the early French exploration, inhabitated the area now comprising Illinois and adjacent parts of Wisconsin, Iowa, and Missouri. The word is the gallicized plural of the Indian *illini*, meaning "man."

The region now constituting Illinois was first visited by white men in 1673, when Joliet and Marquette ascended the Illinois River and reached Lake Michigan by way of the Des Plaines and Chicago portage. Further explorations were made by La Salle and other Frenchmen a few years later. The first permanent settlement was made by the French at Kaskaskia about the year 1700, although mission stations and trading posts had been established some years earlier.

This region continued in the possession of the French, who made a number of other settlements, until the close of the French and Indian War, when, by the treaty of 1763, the "Illinois country" as it was then called, was ceded to Great Britain, together with the rest of the former French territory east of the Mississippi and south of the Great Lakes. Owing to the hostility of the Indians, however, the English did not take actual possession until October, 1765, when the British flag was raised at Fort Chartres, then the capital. In 1772 the seat of government was removed to Kaskaskia.

In 1778, during the Revolution, the region northwest of the Ohio River was conquered by a force of Virginians under George Rogers Clark, and later in the same year it was made a county of Virginia. In 1783, at the close of the Revolution, the British claims to all territory east of the Mississippi, north of Florida, and extending as far north as the present northern boundary of the United States, were relinquished in favor of the latter nation. The states which claimed title to lands northwest of the Ohio and east of the Mississippi later ceded their rights to the United States, and in 1787 a territorial government was established for this region, then called the Northwest Territory.

In 1800 the territory of Indiana, including the area now constituting Illinois, was organized from a part of the Northwest Territory. In 1809 the territory of Illinois, including all the region lying between the Mississippi and the present western boundary of Indiana, prolonged northward to the Canadian line, was organized from a part of Indiana. In 1812 the right of suffrage was greatly extended and the form of territorial government was changed from the first to the second grade, thus giving the people of Illinois the power to elect a legislature and a delegate in Congress.

In 1818, under authority of an enabling act passed by Congress in the same year, Illinois, with boundaries as at present, adopted a state constitution and was admitted to the Union.

COUNTY LOCATION INDEX

Adams	D-2	Henderson	C-2	Ogle	B-4
Alexander	G-4	Henry	C-3	Peoria	C-3
Bond	E-4	Iroquois	C-5	Perry	F-4
Boone	A-4	Jackson	G-4	Piatt	D-4
Brown	D-2	Jasper	E-5	Pike	E-2
Bureau	C-3	Jefferson	F-4	Pope	G-4
Calhoun	E-2	Jersey	E-3	Pulaski	G-4
Carroll	B-3	Jo Daviess	A-3	Putnam	C-4
Cass	D-3	Johnson	G-4	Randolph	F-3
Champaign	D-5	Kane	B-4	Richland	F-5
Christian	E-4	Kankakee	C-5	Rock Island	C-2
Clark	E-5	Kendall	B-4	St. Clair	F-3
Clay	F-4	Knox	C-3	Saline	G-4
Clinton	F-4	Lake	A-5	Sangamon	D-3
Coles	E-5	La Salle	C-4	Schuyler	D-2
Cook	B-5	Lawrence	F-5	Scott	E-3
Crawford	E-5	Lee	B-4	Shelby	E-4
Cumberland	E-5	Livingston	C-4	Stark	C-3
De Kalb	B-4	Logan	D-4	Stephenson	A-3
De Witt	D-4	McDonough	D-2	Tazewell	D-3
Douglas	D-5	McHenry	A-4	Union	G-4
Du Page	B-5	McLean	D-4	Vermilion	D-5
Edgar	E-5	Macon	D-4	Wabash	F-5
Edwards	F-5	Macoupin	E-3	Warren	C-2
Effingham	E-4	Madison	F-3	Washington	F-4
Fayette	E-4	Marion	F-4	Wayne	F-4
Ford	D-5	Marshall	C-4	White	F-5
Franklin	G-4	Mason	D-3	Whiteside	B-3
Fulton	D-3	Massac	G-4	Will	B-5
Gallatin	G-5	Menard	D-3	Williamson	G-4
Greene	E-3	Mercer	C-2	Winnebago	A-4
Grundy	C-4	Monroe	F-3	Woodford	C-4
Hamilton	F-4	Montgomery	E-3		
Hancock	D-2	Morgan	E-3		
Hardin	G-5	Moultrie	E-4		

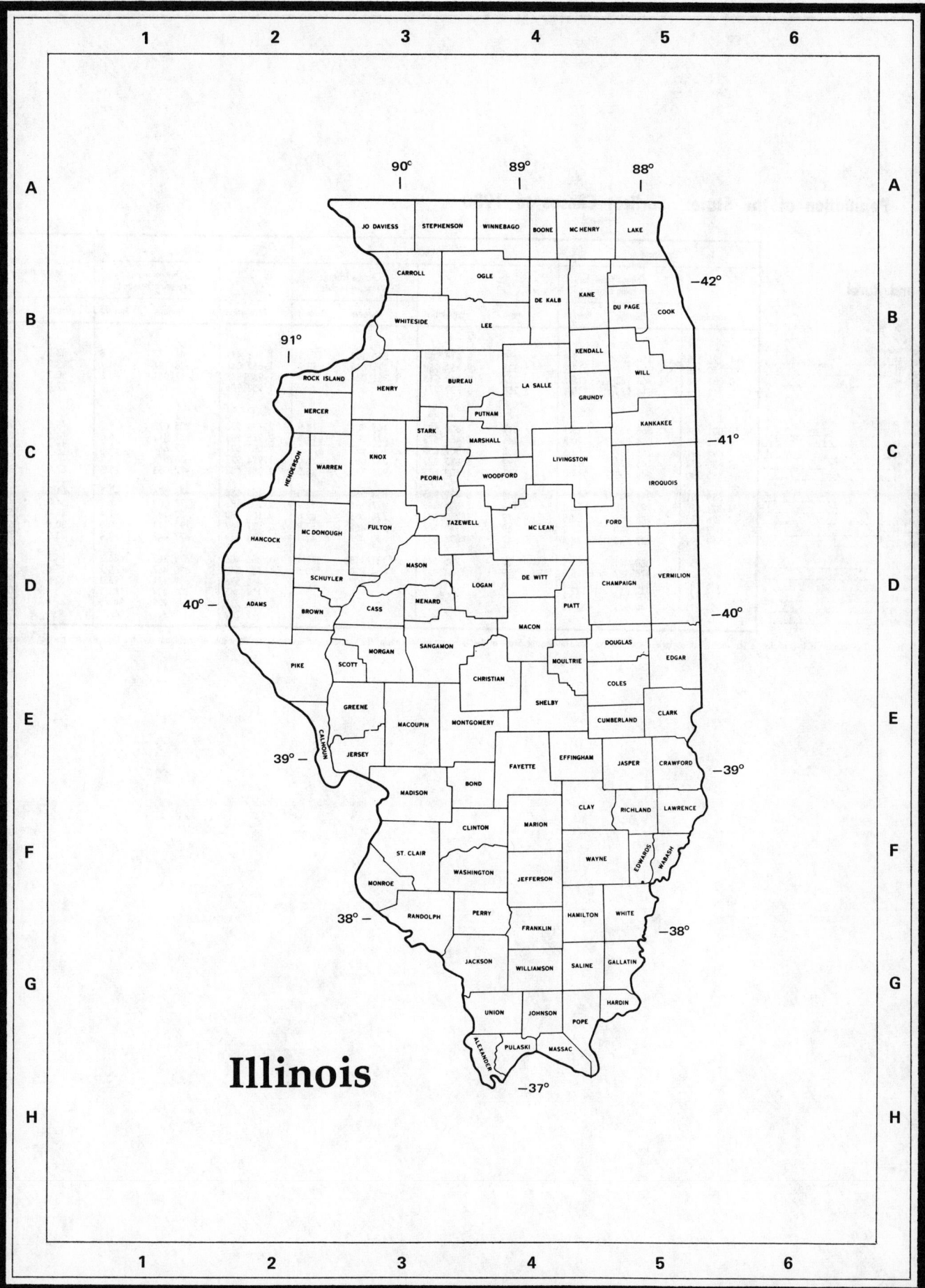

Illinois

Population of the State: Earliest Census to 1980

Urban and Rural

	The State			Urban				Rural				Percent of total population	
	Total population	Change from preceding census		Places of 2,500 or more	Population	Change from preceding census		Population	Change from preceding census			Urban	Rural
		Number	Percent			Number	Percent		Number	Percent			
Current urban definition:													
1980 (Apr. 1)	11 426 518	316 233	2.8	410	9 518 039	266 109	2.9	1 908 479	46 433	2.5		83.3	16.7
1970 (Apr. 1)	11 110 285	1 029 127	10.2	383	9 251 930	1 111 615	13.7	1 862 046	−78 797	−4.1		83.2	16.8
1960 (Apr. 1)	10 081 158	1 368 982	15.7	327	8 140 315	1 381 044	20.4	1 940 843	−12 062	−0.6		80.7	19.3
1950 (Apr. 1)	8 712 176	814 935	10.3	258	6 759 271	...	...	1 952 905	...	...		77.6	22.4
Previous urban definition:													
1960 (Apr. 1)	10 081 158	1 368 982	15.7	319	7 650 582	1 163 909	17.9	2 430 576	205 073	9.2		75.9	24.1
1950 (Apr. 1)	8 712 176	814 935	10.3	245	6 486 673	677 023	11.7	2 225 503	137 912	6.6		74.5	25.5
1940 (Apr. 1)	7 897 241	266 587	3.5	208	5 809 650	173 923	3.1	2 087 591	92 664	4.6		73.6	26.4
1930 (Apr. 1)	7 630 654	1 145 374	17.7	192	5 635 727	1 232 050	28.0	1 994 927	−86 676	−4.2		73.9	26.1
1920 (Jan. 1)	6 485 280	846 689	15.0	171	4 403 677	923 742	26.5	2 081 603	−77 053	−3.6		67.9	32.1
1910 (Apr. 15)	5 638 591	817 041	16.9	145	3 479 935	863 567	33.0	2 158 656	−46 526	−2.1		61.7	38.3
1900 (June 1)	4 821 550	995 198	26.0	114	2 616 368	897 196	52.2	2 205 182	98 002	4.7		54.3	45.7
1890 (June 1)	3 826 352	748 481	24.3	79	1 719 172	778 668	82.8	2 107 180	−30 187	−1.4		44.9	55.1
1880 (June 1)	3 077 871	537 980	21.2	69	940 504	344 462	57.8	2 137 367	193 518	10.0		30.6	69.4
1870 (June 1)	2 539 891	827 940	48.4	47	596 042	350 497	142.7	1 943 849	477 443	32.6		23.5	76.5
1860 (June 1)	1 711 951	860 481	101.1	23	245 545	181 118	281.1	1 466 406	679 363	86.3		14.3	85.7
1850 (June 1)	851 470	375 287	78.8	9	64 427	54 820	570.6	787 043	320 467	68.7		7.6	92.4
1840 (June 1)	476 183	318 738	202.4	3	9 607	9 607	...	466 576	309 131	196.3		2.0	98.0
1830 (June 1)	157 445	102 234	185.2	−	−	−	−	157 445	102 234	185.2		−	100.0
1820 (Aug. 7)	55 211	42 929	349.5	−	−	−	−	55 211	42 929	349.5		−	100.0
1810 (Aug. 6)	12 282	...	...	−	−	...	...	12 282	...	...		−	100.0

NOTE: 1810 population is that of Illinois Territory which comprised the area now constituting the State of Illinois, most of Wisconsin, the western part of the Upper Peninsula of Michigan, and the northeastern part of Minnesota.

ADAMS

1830	2,186
1840	14,476
1850	26,508
1860	41,323
1870	56,362
1880	59,135
1890	61,888
1900	67,058
1910	64,588
1920	61,188
1930	62,784
1940	65,229
1950	64,690
1960	68,467
1970	70,861
1980	71,622

ALEXANDER

1820	626
1830	1,390
1840	3,313
1850	2,484
1860	4,707
1870	10,564
1880	14,808
1890	16,563
1900	19,384
1910	22,741
1920	23,980
1930	22,542
1940	25,496
1950	20,316
1960	16,061
1970	12,015
1980	12,264

BOND

1820	2,931
1830	3,124
1840	5,060
1850	6,144
1860	9,815
1870	13,152
1880	14,866
1890	14,550
1900	16,078
1910	17,075
1920	16,045
1930	14,406
1940	14,540
1950	14,157
1960	14,060
1970	14,012
1980	16,224

BOONE

1840	1,705
1850	7,624
1860	11,678
1870	12,942
1880	11,508
1890	12,203
1900	15,791
1910	15,481
1920	15,322
1930	15,078
1940	15,202
1950	17,070
1960	20,326
1970	25,440
1980	28,630

BROWN

1840	4,183
1850	7,198
1860	9,938
1870	12,205
1880	13,041
1890	11,951
1900	11,557
1910	10,397
1920	9,336
1930	7,892
1940	8,053
1950	7,132
1960	6,210
1970	5,586
1980	5,411

BUREAU

1840	3,067
1850	8,841
1860	26,426
1870	32,415
1880	33,172
1890	35,014
1900	41,112
1910	43,975
1920	42,648
1930	38,845
1940	27,600
1950	37,711
1960	37,594
1970	38,541
1980	39,114

CALHOUN

1830	1,090
1840	1,741
1850	3,231
1860	5,144
1870	6,562
1880	7,467
1890	7,652
1900	8,917
1910	8,610
1920	8,245
1930	8,034
1940	8,207
1950	6,898
1960	5,933
1970	5,675
1980	5,867

CARROLL

1840	1,023
1850	4,586
1860	11,733
1870	16,705
1880	16,976
1890	18,320
1900	18,963
1910	18,035
1920	19,345
1930	18,433
1940	17,987
1950	18,976
1960	19,507
1970	19,276
1980	18,779

CASS

1840	2,981
1850	7,253
1860	11,235
1870	11,580
1880	14,493
1890	15,963
1900	17,222
1910	17,372
1920	17,896
1930	16,537
1940	16,435
1950	15,097
1960	14,539
1970	14,219
1980	15,084

CHAMPAIGN

1840	1,475
1850	2,649
1860	14,629
1870	32,737
1880	40,863
1890	43,159
1900	47,622
1910	51,829
1920	56,959
1930	64,273
1940	70,587
1950	106,100
1960	132,436
1970	163,281
1980	168,392

CHRISTIAN

1840	1,897
1850	3,203
1860	10,492
1870	20,363
1880	28,227
1890	30,531
1900	32,790
1910	34,594
1920	38,458
1930	37,538
1940	38,564
1950	38,816
1960	37,207
1970	35,948
1980	36,446

CLARK

1820	931
1830	3,940
1840	7,453
1850	9,532
1860	14,987
1870	18,719
1880	21,894
1890	21,899
1900	24,033
1910	23,517
1920	21,165
1930	17,872
1940	18,842
1950	17,362
1960	16,546
1970	16,216
1980	16,913

CLAY

1830	755
1840	3,228
1850	4,289
1860	9,336
1870	15,875
1880	16,192
1890	16,662
1900	19,553
1910	18,661
1920	17,684
1930	16,155
1940	18,947
1950	17,445
1960	15,815
1970	14,735
1980	15,283

CLINTON

1830	2,330
1840	3,718
1850	5,139
1860	10,941
1870	16,285
1880	18,714
1890	17,411
1900	19,824
1910	22,832
1920	22,947
1930	21,369
1940	22,912
1950	22,594
1960	24,029
1970	28,315
1980	32,617

COLES

1840	9,616
1850	9,335
1860	14,203
1870	25,235
1880	27,042
1890	30,093
1900	34,146
1910	34,517
1920	35,108
1930	37,315
1940	38,470
1950	40,328
1960	42,860
1970	47,815
1980	52,260

COOK

1840	10,201
1850	43,385
1860	144,954
1870	349,966
1880	607,524
1890	1,191,922
1900	1,838,735
1910	2,405,233
1920	3,053,017
1930	3,982,123
1940	4,063,342
1950	4,508,792
1960	5,129,725
1970	5,493,766
1980	5,253,655

CRAWFORD

1820	3,022
1830	3,117
1840	4,422
1850	7,135
1860	11,551
1870	13,889
1880	16,197
1890	17,283
1900	19,240
1910	26,281
1920	22,771
1930	21,085
1940	21,294
1950	21,137
1960	20,751
1970	19,824
1980	20,818

CUMBERLAND

1850	3,718
1860	8,311
1870	12,223
1880	13,759
1890	15,443
1900	16,124
1910	14,281
1920	12,858
1930	10,419
1940	11,698
1950	10,496
1960	9,936
1970	9,772
1980	11,062

DE KALB

1840	1,697
1850	7,540
1860	19,086
1870	23,265
1880	26,768
1890	27,066
1900	31,756
1910	33,457
1920	31,339
1930	32,644
1940	34,388
1950	40,781
1960	51,714
1970	71,654
1980	74,624

DE WITT

1840	3,247
1850	5,002
1860	10,820
1870	14,768
1880	17,010
1890	17,011
1900	18,972
1910	18,906
1920	19,252
1930	18,598
1940	18,244
1950	16,894
1960	17,253
1970	16,975
1980	18,108

DOUGLAS

1860	7,140
1870	13,484
1880	15,853
1890	17,669
1900	19,097
1910	19,591
1920	19,604
1930	17,914
1940	17,590
1950	16,706

1960	19,243
1970	18,997
1980	19,774

DU PAGE

1840	3,535
1850	9,290
1860	14,701
1870	16,685
1880	19,161
1890	22,551
1900	28,196
1910	33,432
1920	42,120
1930	91,998
1940	103,480
1950	154,599
1960	313,459
1970	487,966
1980	658,835

EDGAR

1830	4,071
1840	8,225
1850	10,692
1860	16,925
1870	21,450
1880	25,499
1890	26,787
1900	28,273
1910	27,336
1920	25,769
1930	24,966
1940	24,430
1950	23,407
1960	22,550
1970	21,591
1980	21,725

EDWARDS

1820	3,444
1830	1,649
1840	3,070
1850	3,524
1860	5,454
1870	7,565
1880	8,597
1890	9,444
1900	10,345
1910	10,049
1920	9,431
1930	8,303
1940	8,974
1950	9,056
1960	7,940
1970	7,090
1980	7,961

EFFINGHAM

1840	1,675
1850	3,799
1860	7,816
1870	15,653
1880	18,920
1890	19,358
1900	20,465
1910	20,055
1920	19,556
1930	19,013
1940	22,034
1950	21,675
1960	23,107

1970	24,608
1980	30,944

FAYETTE

1830	2,704
1840	6,328
1850	8,075
1860	11,189
1870	19,638
1880	23,241
1890	23,367
1900	28,065
1910	28,075
1920	28,187
1930	23,487
1940	29,159
1950	24,582
1960	21,946
1970	20,752
1980	22,167

FORD

1860	1,979
1870	9,103
1880	15,099
1890	17,035
1900	18,359
1910	17,096
1920	16,466
1930	15,489
1940	15,007
1950	15,901
1960	16,606
1970	16,382
1980	15,265

FRANKLIN

1820	1,763
1830	4,083
1840	3,682
1850	5,681
1860	9,393
1870	12,652
1880	16,129
1890	17,138
1900	19,675
1910	25,943
1920	57,293
1930	59,442
1940	53,137
1950	48,685
1960	39,281
1970	38,329
1980	43,201

FULTON

1830	1,841
1840	13,142
1850	22,508
1860	33,338
1870	38,291
1880	41,240
1890	43,110
1900	46,201
1910	49,549
1920	48,163
1930	43,983
1940	44,627
1950	43,716
1960	41,954
1970	41,900
1980	43,687

GALLATIN

1820	3,155
1830	7,405
1840	10,760
1850	5,448
1860	8,055
1870	11,134
1880	12,861
1890	14,935
1900	15,836
1910	14,628
1920	12,856
1930	10,091
1940	11,414
1950	9,818
1960	7,638
1970	7,418
1980	7,590

GREENE

1830	7,674
1840	11,951
1850	12,429
1860	16,093
1870	20,277
1880	23,010
1890	23,791
1900	23,402
1910	22,363
1920	22,883
1930	20,417
1940	20,292
1950	18,852
1960	17,460
1970	17,014
1980	16,661

GRUNDY

1850	3,023
1860	10,379
1870	14,938
1880	16,732
1890	21,024
1900	24,136
1910	24,162
1920	18,580
1930	18,678
1940	18,398
1950	19,217
1960	22,350
1970	26,535
1980	30,582

HAMILTON

1830	2,616
1840	3,945
1850	6,362
1860	9,915
1870	13,014
1880	16,712
1890	17,800
1900	20,197
1910	18,227
1920	15,920
1930	12,995
1940	13,454
1950	12,256
1960	10,010
1970	8,665
1980	9,172

IROQUOIS

1840	1,695
1850	4,149

HANCOCK

1830	483
1840	9,946
1850	14,652
1860	29,061
1870	35,935
1880	35,337
1890	31,907
1900	32,215
1910	30,638
1920	28,523
1930	26,420
1940	26,297
1950	25,790
1960	24,574
1970	23,664
1980	23,877

HARDIN

1840	1,378
1850	2,887
1860	3,759
1870	5,113
1880	6,024
1890	7,234
1900	7,448
1910	7,015
1920	7,533
1930	6,955
1940	7,759
1950	7,530
1960	5,879
1970	4,914
1980	5,383

HENDERSON

1850	4,612
1860	9,501
1870	12,582
1880	10,722
1890	9,876
1900	10,836
1910	9,724
1920	9,770
1930	9,778
1940	8,949
1950	8,416
1960	8,237
1970	8,451
1980	9,114

HENRY

1830	41
1840	1,260
1850	3,807
1860	20,660
1870	35,506
1880	36,597
1890	33,338
1900	40,049
1910	41,736
1920	45,162
1930	43,851
1940	43,798
1950	46,492
1960	49,317
1970	53,217
1980	57,968

1860	12,325
1870	25,782
1880	35,451
1890	35,167
1900	38,014
1910	35,543
1920	34,841
1930	32,913
1940	32,496
1950	32,348
1960	33,562
1970	33,532
1980	32,976

JACKSON

1820	1,542
1830	1,828
1840	3,566
1850	5,862
1860	9,589
1870	19,634
1880	22,505
1890	27,809
1900	33,871
1910	35,143
1920	37,091
1930	35,680
1940	37,920
1950	38,124
1960	42,151
1970	55,008
1970	61,522

JASPER

1840	1,472
1850	3,220
1860	8,364
1870	11,234
1880	14,515
1890	18,188
1900	20,160
1910	18,157
1920	16,064
1930	12,809
1940	13,431
1950	12,266
1960	11,346
1970	10,741
1980	11,318

JEFFERSON

1820	691
1830	2,555
1840	5,762
1850	8,109
1860	12,965
1870	17,864
1880	20,686
1890	22,590
1900	28,133
1910	29,111
1920	28,480
1930	31,034
1940	34,375
1950	35,892
1960	32,315
1970	31,848
1980	36,552

JERSEY

1800	100
1840	4,535
1850	7,354

1860	12,051	1890	28,732	1930	97,695	1960	33,656
1870	15,054	1900	37,154	1940	97,801	1970	33,538
1880	15,542	1910	40,752	1950	100,610	1980	31,802
1890	14,810	1920	44,940	1960	110,800		
1900	14,612	1930	50,095	1970	111,409		
1910	13,954	1940	60,877	1980	112,033		

MACOUPIN

1830	1,990
1840	7,826
1850	12,355
1860	24,602
1870	32,726
1880	37,692
1890	40,380
1900	42,256
1910	50,685
1920	57,274
1930	48,703
1940	46,304
1950	44,210
1960	43,524
1970	44,557
1980	49,384

JO DAVIESS

1830	2,111
1840	6,180
1850	18,604
1860	27,325
1870	27,820
1880	27,528
1890	25,101
1900	24,533
1910	22,657
1920	21,917
1930	20,235
1940	19,989
1950	21,459
1960	21,821
1970	21,766
1980	23,520

JOHNSON

1820	843
1830	1,596
1840	3,626
1850	4,114
1860	9,342
1870	11,248
1880	13,078
1890	15,013
1900	15,667
1910	14,311
1920	12,022
1930	10,203
1940	10,727
1950	8,729
1960	6,928
1970	7,550
1980	9,624

KANE

1840	6,501
1850	16,703
1860	30,062
1870	39,091
1880	44,939
1890	65,061
1900	78,792
1910	91,862
1920	99,499
1930	125,327
1940	130,206
1950	150,388
1960	208,246
1970	251,005
1980	278,405

KANKAKEE

1860	15,412
1870	24,352
1880	25,047

KENDALL

1850	7,730
1860	13,074
1870	12,399
1880	13,083
1890	12,106
1900	11,467
1910	10,777
1920	10,074
1930	10,555
1940	11,105
1950	12,115
1960	17,540
1970	26,374
1980	37,202

KNOX

1830	274
1840	7,060
1850	13,279
1860	28,663
1870	39,522
1880	38,344
1890	38,752
1900	43,612
1910	46,159
1920	46,727
1930	51,336
1940	52,250
1950	54,366
1960	61,280
1970	60,939
1980	61,607

LAKE

1840	2,634
1850	14,226
1860	18,257
1870	21,014
1880	21,296
1890	24,235
1900	34,504
1910	55,058
1920	74,285
1930	104,387
1940	121,094
1950	179,097
1960	293,656
1970	382,638
1980	440,372

LA SALLE

1840	9,348
1850	17,815
1860	48,332
1870	60,792
1880	70,403
1890	80,798
1900	87,776
1910	90,132
1920	92,925

LAWRENCE

1830	3,668
1840	7,092
1850	6,121
1860	9,214
1870	12,533
1880	13,663
1890	14,693
1900	16,523
1910	22,661
1920	21,380
1930	21,885
1940	21,075
1950	20,539
1960	18,540
1970	17,522
1980	17,807

LEE

1840	2,035
1850	5,292
1860	17,651
1870	27,171
1880	27,491
1890	26,187
1900	29,894
1910	27,750
1920	28,004
1930	32,329
1940	34,604
1950	36,451
1960	38,749
1970	37,947
1980	36,328

LIVINGSTON

1840	759
1850	1,552
1860	11,637
1870	31,471
1880	38,450
1890	38,455
1900	42,035
1910	40,445
1920	39,070
1930	39,092
1940	38,838
1950	37,809
1960	40,341
1970	40,690
1980	41,381

LOGAN

1840	2,333
1850	5,128
1860	14,272
1870	23,053
1880	25,037
1890	25,489
1900	28,680
1910	30,216
1920	29,562
1930	28,863
1940	29,438
1950	30,671

McDONOUGH

1840	5,308
1850	7,616
1860	20,069
1870	26,509
1880	27,970
1890	27,467
1900	28,412
1910	26,887
1920	27,074
1930	27,239
1940	26,944
1950	28,199
1960	28,928
1970	36,653
1980	37,467

McHENRY

1840	2,578
1850	14,978
1860	22,089
1870	23,762
1880	24,908
1890	26,114
1900	29,759
1910	32,509
1920	33,164
1930	35,079
1940	37,311
1950	50,656
1960	84,210
1970	111,555
1980	147,897

McLEAN

1840	6,565
1850	10,163
1860	28,772
1870	53,998
1880	60,100
1890	63,036
1900	67,843
1910	68,008
1920	70,107
1930	73,117
1940	73,930
1950	76,577
1960	83,877
1970	104,389
1980	119,149

MACON

1830	1,122
1840	3,039
1850	3,988
1860	13,738
1870	26,481
1880	30,665
1890	38,083
1900	44,003
1910	54,186
1920	65,175
1930	81,731
1940	84,693
1950	98,853
1960	118,257
1970	125,010
1980	131,375

MADISON

1820	13,550
1830	6,221
1840	14,433
1850	20,441
1860	31,251
1870	44,131
1880	50,126
1890	50,535
1900	64,694
1910	89,847
1920	106,895
1930	143,830
1940	149,349
1950	182,307
1960	224,689
1970	250,934
1980	247,691

MARION

1830	2,125
1840	4,742
1850	6,720
1860	12,739
1870	20,622
1880	23,686
1890	24,341
1900	30,446
1910	35,094
1920	37,497
1930	35,635
1940	47,989
1950	41,700
1960	39,349
1970	39,986
1980	43,523

MARSHALL

1840	1,849
1850	5,180
1860	13,437
1870	16,956
1880	15,055
1890	13,653
1900	16,370
1910	15,659
1920	14,760
1930	13,023
1940	13,179
1950	13,025
1960	13,334
1970	13,302
1980	14,479

MASON

1850	5,921
1860	10,931
1870	16,184
1880	16,242
1890	16,067
1900	17,491
1910	17,377
1920	16,634
1930	15,115
1940	15,358
1950	15,326
1960	15,193
1970	16,180
1980	19,492

MASSAC

1850	4,092
1860	6,213
1870	9,581
1880	10,443
1890	11,313
1900	13,110
1910	14,200
1920	13,559
1930	14,081
1940	14,937
1950	13,594
1960	14,341
1970	13,889
1980	14,990

MENARD

1840	4,431
1850	6,349
1860	9,584
1870	11,735
1880	13,024
1890	13,120
1900	14,336
1910	12,796
1920	11,694
1930	10,575
1940	10,663
1950	9,639
1960	9,248
1970	9,685
1980	11,700

MERCER

1830	26
1840	2,352
1850	5,246
1860	15,042
1870	18,769
1880	19,502
1890	18,545
1900	20,945
1910	19,723
1920	18,800
1930	16,641
1940	17,701
1950	17,374
1960	17,149
1970	17,294
1980	19,286

MONROE

1820	1,537
1830	2,000
1840	4,481
1850	7,679
1860	12,832
1870	12,982
1880	13,682
1890	12,948
1900	13,847
1910	13,508
1920	12,839
1930	12,369
1940	12,754
1950	13,282
1960	15,507
1970	18,831
1980	20,117

MONTGOMERY

1830	2,953
1840	4,490
1850	6,277
1860	13,979
1870	25,314
1880	28,078
1890	30,003
1900	30,836
1910	35,311
1920	41,403
1930	35,278
1940	34,499
1950	32,460
1960	31,244
1970	30,260
1980	31,686

MORGAN

1830	12,714
1840	19,547
1850	16,064
1860	22,122
1870	28,463
1880	31,514
1890	32,636
1900	35,006
1910	34,420
1920	33,567
1930	34,240
1940	36,378
1950	35,568
1960	36,571
1970	36,174
1980	37,502

MOULTRIE

1850	3,234
1860	6,385
1870	10,385
1880	13,699
1890	14,481
1900	15,224
1910	14,630
1920	14,839
1930	13,247
1940	13,477
1950	13,171
1960	13,635
1970	13,263
1980	14,546

OGLE

1840	3,479
1850	10,020
1860	22,888
1870	27,492
1880	29,937
1890	28,710
1900	29,129
1910	27,864
1920	26,830
1930	28,118
1940	29,869
1950	33,429
1960	38,106
1970	42,867
1980	46,338

PEORIA

1840	6,153
1850	17,547
1860	36,601
1870	47,540
1880	55,355
1890	70,378
1900	88,608
1910	100,255
1920	111,710
1930	141,344
1940	153,374
1950	174,347
1960	189,044
1970	195,318
1980	200,466

PERRY

1830	1,215
1840	3,222
1850	5,278
1860	9,552
1870	13,723
1880	16,007
1890	17,529
1900	19,830
1910	22,088
1920	22,901
1930	22,767
1940	23,438
1950	21,684
1960	19,184
1970	19,757
1980	21,714

PIATT

1850	1,606
1860	6,127
1870	10,953
1880	15,583
1890	17,062
1900	17,706
1910	16,376
1920	15,714
1930	15,588
1940	14,659
1950	13,970
1960	14,960
1970	15,509
1980	16,581

PIKE

1830	2,396
1840	11,728
1850	18,819
1860	27,249
1870	30,768
1880	33,751
1890	31,000
1900	31,595
1910	28,662
1920	26,866
1930	24,357
1940	25,340
1950	22,155
1960	20,552
1970	19,185
1980	18,896

POPE

1820	2,610
1830	3,316
1840	4,094
1850	3,975
1860	6,742
1870	11,437
1880	13,256
1890	14,016
1900	13,585
1910	11,215
1920	9,625
1930	7,996
1940	7,999
1950	5,779
1960	4,061
1970	3,857
1980	4,404

PULASKI

1850	2,265
1860	3,943
1870	8,752
1880	9,507
1890	11,355
1900	14,554
1910	15,650
1920	14,629
1930	14,834
1940	15,875
1950	13,639
1960	10,490
1970	8,741
1980	8,840

PUTNAM

1830	1,310
1840	2,131
1850	3,924
1860	5,587
1870	6,280
1880	5,554
1890	4,730
1900	4,746
1910	7,561
1920	7,579
1930	5,235
1940	5,289
1950	4,746
1960	4,570
1970	5,007
1980	6,085

RANDOLPH

1800	1,103
1810	7,275
1820	3,492
1830	4,429
1840	7,944
1850	11,079
1860	17,205
1870	20,859
1880	25,690
1890	25,049
1900	28,001
1910	29,120
1920	29,109
1930	29,313
1940	33,608
1950	31,673
1960	29,988
1970	31,379
1980	35,652

RICHLAND

1850	4,012
1860	9,711
1870	12,803
1880	15,545
1890	15,019
1900	16,391
1910	15,970
1920	14,044
1930	14,053
1940	17,137
1950	16,889
1960	16,299
1970	16,829
1980	17,587

ROCK ISLAND

1840	2,610
1850	6,937
1860	21,005
1870	29,783
1880	38,302
1890	41,917
1900	55,249
1910	70,404
1920	92,297
1930	98,191
1940	113,323
1950	133,558
1960	150,991
1970	166,734
1980	165,968

SAINT CLAIR

1800	1,255
1810	5,007
1820	5,253
1830	7,078
1840	13,631
1850	20,180
1860	37,694
1870	51,068
1880	61,806
1890	66,571
1900	86,685
1910	119,870
1920	136,520
1930	157,775
1940	166,899
1950	205,995
1960	262,509
1970	285,591
1980	267,531

SALINE

1850	5,588
1860	9,331
1870	12,714
1880	15,940
1890	19,342
1900	21,685

1910	30,204
1920	38,353
1930	37,100
1940	38,066
1950	33,420
1960	26,277
1970	25,721
1980	28,448

SANGAMON

1830	12,960
1840	14,716
1850	19,228
1860	32,274
1870	46,352
1880	52,894
1890	61,195
1900	71,593
1910	92,024
1920	100,262
1930	111,733
1940	117,912
1950	131,484
1960	146,539
1970	161,335
1980	176,089

SCHUYLER

1830	2,959
1840	6,972
1850	10,573
1860	14,684
1870	17,419
1880	16,249
1890	16,013
1900	16,129
1910	14,852
1920	13,285
1930	11,676
1940	11,430
1950	9,613
1960	8,746
1970	8,135
1980	8,365

SCOTT

1840	6,215
1850	7,914
1860	9,069
1870	10,530
1880	10,741
1890	10,304
1900	10,455
1910	10,067
1920	9,489
1930	8,539
1940	8,176
1950	7,245
1960	6,377
1970	6,096
1980	6,142

SHELBY

1830	2,972
1840	6,659
1850	7,807
1860	14,613
1870	25,476
1880	30,270
1890	31,191
1900	32,126
1910	31,693

STARK

1840	1,573
1850	3,710
1860	9,004
1870	10,751
1880	11,207
1890	9,982
1900	10,186
1910	10,098
1920	9,693
1930	9,184
1940	8,881
1950	8,721
1960	8,152
1970	7,510
1980	7,389

STEPHENSON

1840	2,800
1850	11,666
1860	25,112
1870	30,608
1880	31,963
1890	31,338
1900	34,933
1910	36,821
1920	37,743
1930	40,064
1940	40,646
1950	41,595
1960	47,207
1970	48,861
1980	49,536

TAZEWELL

1830	4,716
1840	7,221
1850	12,052
1860	21,470
1870	27,903
1880	29,666
1890	29,556
1900	33,221
1910	34,027
1920	38,540
1930	46,082
1940	58,362
1950	76,165
1960	99,789
1970	118,649
1980	132,078

UNION

1820	2,362
1830	3,239
1840	5,524
1850	7,615
1860	11,181
1870	16,518
1880	18,102
1890	21,549
1900	22,610
1910	21,856
1920	20,249

1920	20,601
1930	25,471
1940	26,290
1950	24,434
1960	23,404
1970	22,589
1980	23,923

VERMILION

1830	5,836
1840	9,303
1850	11,492
1860	19,800
1870	30,388
1880	41,588
1890	49,905
1900	65,635
1910	77,996
1920	86,162
1930	89,339
1940	86,791
1950	86,079
1960	96,176
1970	97,047
1980	95,222

WABASH

1830	2,710
1840	4,240
1850	4,690
1860	7,313
1870	8,841
1880	9,945
1890	11,886
1900	12,583
1910	14,913
1920	14,034
1930	13,197
1940	13,724
1950	14,651
1960	14,047
1970	12,841
1980	13,713

WARREN

1830	308
1840	6,739
1850	8,176
1860	18,336
1870	23,174
1880	22,933
1890	21,281
1900	23,163
1910	23,313
1920	21,488
1930	21,745
1940	21,286
1950	21,981
1960	21,587
1970	21,598
1980	21,943

WASHINGTON

1820	1,517
1830	1,675
1840	4,810
1850	6,953
1860	13,731
1870	17,599
1880	21,112
1890	19,262
1900	19,526
1910	18,759

1920	18,035
1930	16,286
1940	15,801
1950	14,460
1960	13,569
1970	13,780
1980	15,472

WAYNE

1820	1,114
1830	2,553
1840	5,133
1850	6,825
1860	12,223
1870	19,758
1880	21,291
1890	23,806
1900	27,626
1910	25,697
1920	22,772
1930	19,130
1940	22,092
1950	20,933
1960	19,008
1970	17,004
1980	18,059

WHITE

1820	4,828
1830	6,091
1840	7,919
1850	8,925
1860	12,403
1870	16,846
1880	23,087
1890	25,005
1900	25,386
1910	23,052
1920	20,081
1930	18,149
1940	20,027
1950	20,935
1960	19,373
1970	17,312
1980	17,864

WHITESIDE

1840	2,514
1850	5,361
1860	18,737
1870	27,503
1880	30,885
1890	30,854
1900	34,710
1910	34,507
1920	36,174
1930	39,019
1940	43,338
1950	49,336
1960	59,887
1970	62,877
1980	65,970

WILL

1840	10,167
1850	16,703
1860	29,321
1870	43,031
1880	53,422
1890	62,007
1900	74,764
1910	84,371

1920	92,911
1930	110,732
1940	114,210
1950	134,336
1960	191,617
1970	247,825
1980	324,460

WILLIAMSON

1840	4,457
1850	7,216
1860	12,205
1870	17,329
1880	19,324
1890	22,226
1900	27,796
1910	45,098
1920	61,092
1930	53,880
1940	51,424
1950	48,621
1960	46,117
1970	49,021
1980	56,538

WINNEBAGO

1840	4,609
1850	11,773
1860	24,491
1870	29,301
1880	30,505
1890	39,938
1900	47,845
1910	63,153
1920	90,929
1930	117,373
1940	121,178
1950	152,385
1960	209,765
1970	246,623
1980	250,884

WOODFORD

1850	4,415
1860	13,282
1870	18,956
1880	21,620
1890	21,429
1900	21,822
1910	20,506
1920	19,340
1930	18,792
1940	19,124
1950	21,335
1960	24,579
1970	39,012
1980	33,320

NOTE

CHRISTIAN

Name changed from Dane in 1840.

ADDISON

1890	485
1900	591
1910	579
1920	510
1930	916
1940	819
1950	813
1960	6,741
1970	24,482
1980	29,759

ALSIP

1930	327
1940	541
1950	1,228
1960	3,770
1970	11,141
1980	17,134

ALTON

1840	2,340
1850	3,585
1860	6,332
1870	8,665
1880	8,975
1890	10,294
1900	14,210
1910	17,528
1920	24,682
1930	30,151
1940	31,255
1950	32,550
1960	43,047
1970	39,700
1980	34,171

ARLINGTON HEIGHTS

1880	995
1890	1,424
1900	1,380
1910	1,943
1920	2,250
1930	4,997
1940	5,668
1950	8,768
1960	27,878
1970	65,058
1980	66,116

AURORA

1860	6,011
1870	11,162
1880	11,873
1890	19,688
1900	24,147
1910	29,807
1920	36,397
1930	46,589
1940	47,170
1950	50,576
1960	63,715
1970	74,389
1980	81,293

BARTLETT

1880	175
1890	263
1900	360
1910	408
1920	371
1930	504
1940	608
1950	716
1960	1,540
1970	3,501
1980	13,254

BATAVIA

1860	1,621
1870	3,018
1880	2,630
1890	3,543
1900	3,871
1910	4,436
1920	4,395
1930	7,548
1940	6,985
1950	5,353
1960	7,496
1970	9,060
1980	12,574

BELLEVILLE

1850	2,941
1860	7,520
1870	8,146
1880	10,683
1890	15,361
1900	17,484
1910	21,122
1920	24,823
1930	28,425
1940	28,405
1950	32,721
1960	37,264
1970	41,223
1980	41,580

BELLWOOD

1910	943
1920	1,881
1930	4,991
1940	5,220
1950	8,746
1960	20,729
1970	22,096
1980	19,811

BELVIDERE

1850	937
1860	2,446
1870	3,231
1880	2,951
1890	3,867
1900	6,937
1910	7,253
1920	7,804
1930	8,123
1940	8,094
1950	9,422
1960	11,223
1970	14,061
1980	15,176

BENSENVILLE

1880	136
1890	205
1900	374
1910	443
1920	650
1930	1,680

1940	1,869
1950	3,754
1960	9,141
1970	12,976
1980	16,124

BERWYN

1910	5,841
1920	14,150
1930	47,027
1940	28,451
1950	51,280
1960	54,224
1970	52,502
1980	46,849

BLOOMINGDALE

1930	337
1940	305
1950	339
1960	1,262
1970	2,974
1980	12,659

BLOOMINGTON

1850	1,594
1860	7,075
1870	14,590
1880	17,180
1890	20,484
1900	23,286
1910	25,768
1920	28,725
1930	30,930
1940	32,868
1950	34,163
1960	36,271
1970	39,992
1980	44,189

BLUE ISLAND

1880	1,542
1890	3,329
1900	6,114
1910	8,043
1920	11,424
1930	16,534
1940	16,638
1950	17,622
1960	19,618
1970	22,629
1980	21,855

BOLINGBROOK

1970	7,651
1980	37,261

BOURBONNAIS

1900	595
1910	611
1920	620
1930	685
1940	771
1950	1,598
1960	3,336
1970	5,909
1980	13,280

BRADLEY

1900	1,518
1910	1,942
1920	2,128
1930	3,408
1940	3,689
1950	5,699
1960	8,082
1970	9,881
1980	11,008

BRIDGEVIEW

1950	1,393
1960	7,334
1970	12,506
1980	14,155

BROOKFIELD

1900	1,111
1910	2,186
1920	3,589
1930	10,035
1940	10,817
1950	15,472
1960	20,429
1970	20,284
1980	19,395

BUFFALO GROVE

1960	1,492
1970	12,333
1980	22,230

BURBANK

1980	28,462

CAHOKIA

1930	286
1940	465
1950	794
1960	15,829
1970	20,649
1980	18,904

CALUMET CITY

1900	2,935
1910	4,948
1920	7,492
1930	12,298
1940	13,241
1950	15,799
1960	25,000
1970	33,107
1980	39,697

CANTON

1840	762
1850	1,568
1860	2,380
1870	3,308
1880	3,762
1890	5,604
1900	6,564
1910	10,453
1920	10,928
1930	11,718
1940	11,577

CARBONDALE

1880	2,213
1890	2,382
1900	3,318
1910	5,411
1920	6,267
1930	7,528
1940	8,550
1950	10,921
1960	14,670
1970	22,816
1980	26,287

CAROL STREAM

1960	836
1970	4,434
1980	15,472

CARPENTERSVILLE

1880	348
1890	754
1900	1,002
1910	1,128
1920	1,036
1930	1,461
1940	1,289
1950	1,523
1960	17,242
1970	24,059
1980	23,272

CENTRALIA

1870	3,190
1880	3,621
1890	4,763
1900	6,721
1910	9,680
1920	12,491
1930	12,583
1940	16,343
1950	12,863
1960	13,904
1970	15,217
1980	15,126

CHAMPAIGN

1860	1,727
1870	4,625
1880	5,103
1890	5,839
1900	9,098
1910	12,421
1920	15,873
1930	20,348
1940	23,302
1950	39,563
1960	49,583
1970	56,837
1980	58,133

CHARLESTON

1840	1,413
1850	849
1860	2,849
1870	2,867

1880	4,135
1890	5,488
1900	5,884
1910	5,884
1920	6,615
1930	8,012
1940	8,197
1950	9,164
1960	10,505
1970	16,421
1980	19,355

CHICAGO

1840	4,470
1850	29,963
1860	109,260
1870	298,977
1880	503,185
1890	1,099,850
1900	1,698,575
1910	2,185,283
1920	2,701,705
1930	3,376,438
1940	3,396,808
1950	3,620,962
1960	3,550,404
1970	3,369,357
1980	3,005,072

CHICAGO HEIGHTS

1900	5,100
1910	14,525
1920	19,653
1930	22,321
1940	22,461
1950	24,551
1960	34,331
1970	40,900
1980	37,026

CHICAGO RIDGE

1920	176
1930	269
1940	376
1950	888
1960	5,748
1970	9,187
1980	13,473

CICERO

1860	1,272
1870	1,545
1880	5,182
1890	10,204
1900	16,310
1910	14,557
1920	44,995
1930	66,602
1940	64,712
1950	67,544
1960	69,130
1970	67,058
1980	61,232

COLLINSVILLE

1880	2,887
1890	3,498
1900	4,021
1910	7,478
1920	9,753
1930	9,235

1940	9,767
1950	11,862
1960	14,217
1970	18,224
1980	19,613

COUNTRY CLUB HILLS

1960	3,421
1970	6,920
1980	14,676

CRESTWOOD

1950	33
1960	1,213
1970	5,770
1980	10,852

CRYSTAL LAKE

1880	546
1890	781
1900	950
1910	1,242
1920	2,249
1930	3,732
1940	3,917
1950	4,832
1960	8,314
1970	14,451
1980	18,590

DANVILLE

1840	503
1850	736
1860	1,632
1870	4,751
1880	7,733
1890	11,491
1900	16,354
1910	27,871
1920	33,776
1930	36,765
1940	36,919
1950	37,864
1960	41,856
1970	42,570
1980	38,985

DARIEN

1970	7,789
1980	14,536

DECATUR

1860	3,839
1870	7,161
1880	9,547
1890	16,841
1900	20,754
1910	31,140
1920	43,818
1930	57,510
1940	59,305
1950	66,269
1960	78,004
1970	90,397
1980	94,081

DEERFIELD

1910	476
1920	610
1930	1,852
1940	2,283
1950	3,288
1960	11,786
1970	18,949
1980	17,430

DE KALB

1880	1,598
1890	2,579
1900	5,904
1910	8,102
1920	7,871
1930	8,545
1940	9,146
1950	11,708
1960	18,486
1970	32,949
1980	33,099

DES PLAINES

1880	818
1890	986
1900	1,666
1910	2,348
1920	3,451
1930	8,798
1940	9,518
1950	14,994
1960	34,886
1970	57,239
1980	53,568

DIXON

1870	2,218
1880	4,055
1880	3,658
1890	5,161
1900	7,917
1910	7,216
1920	8,191
1930	9,908
1940	10,671
1950	11,523
1960	19,565
1970	18,147
1980	15,701

DOLTON

1880	448
1890	1,110
1900	1,229
1910	1,869
1920	2,076
1930	2,923
1940	3,068
1950	5,558
1960	18,746
1970	25,990
1980	24,766

DOWNERS GROVE

1880	586
1890	960
1900	2,103
1910	2,601
1920	3,543

1930	8,977
1940	9,526
1950	11,886
1960	21,154
1970	32,544
1980	42,572

EAST MOLINE

1910	2,665
1920	8,675
1930	10,107
1940	12,359
1950	13,913
1960	16,732
1970	20,936
1980	20,907

EAST PEORIA

1890	392
1900	899
1910	1,493
1920	2,214
1930	5,027
1940	6,806
1950	8,698
1960	12,310
1970	18,671
1980	22,385

EAST SAINT LOUIS

1870	5,644
1880	9,185
1890	15,169
1900	29,655
1910	58,547
1920	66,767
1930	74,347
1940	75,609
1950	82,295
1960	81,712
1970	70,169
1980	55,200

EDWARDSVILLE

1870	2,193
1880	2,887
1890	3,561
1900	4,157
1910	5,014
1920	5,336
1930	6,235
1940	8,008
1950	8,776
1960	9,996
1970	11,070
1980	12,480

EFFINGHAM

1870	2,383
1880	3,065
1890	3,260
1900	3,774
1910	3,898
1920	4,024
1930	4,798
1940	6,180
1950	6,892
1960	8,172
1970	9,458
1980	11,270

ELGIN

1860	2,797
1870	5,441
1880	8,787
1890	17,823
1900	22,433
1910	25,976
1920	27,454
1930	35,929
1940	38,333
1950	44,223
1960	49,447
1970	55,691
1980	62,798

ELK GROVE

1960	6,608
1970	20,346
1980	28,907

ELMHURST

1870	329
1880	723
1890	1,050
1900	1,728
1910	2,360
1920	4,594
1930	14,055
1940	15,458
1950	21,273
1960	36,991
1970	46,392
1980	44,276

ELMWOOD PARK

1920	1,380
1930	11,270
1940	13,689
1950	18,801
1960	23,866
1970	26,160
1980	24,016

EVANSTON

1880	4,400
1890	19,259
1900	19,259
1910	24,978
1920	37,234
1930	63,338
1940	65,389
1950	73,641
1960	79,283
1970	80,113
1980	73,706

EVERGREEN PARK

1900	445
1910	424
1920	705
1930	1,594
1940	3,313
1950	10,531
1960	24,178
1970	25,921
1980	22,260

FAIRVIEW HEIGHTS

1970	10,050
1980	12,414

FOREST PARK

1880	923
1900	4,085
1910	6,594
1920	10,768
1930	14,555
1940	14,840
1950	14,969
1960	14,452
1970	15,472
1980	15,177

FRANKLIN PARK

1900	483
1910	683
1920	914
1930	2,425
1940	3,007
1950	8,899
1960	18,322
1970	20,348
1980	17,507

FREEPORT

1840	491
1850	1,436
1860	5,376
1870	7,889
1880	8,516
1890	10,189
1900	13,258
1910	17,567
1920	19,669
1930	22,045
1940	22,366
1950	22,467
1960	26,628
1970	27,736
1980	26,266

GALESBURG

1850	323
1860	4,953
1870	10,158
1880	11,437
1890	15,264
1900	18,607
1910	22,089
1920	23,834
1930	28,830
1940	38,876
1950	31,425
1960	37,243
1970	36,290
1980	35,305

GLENDALE HEIGHTS

1960	173
1970	11,406
1980	23,163

GLEN ELLYN

1890	473
1900	793
1910	1,763
1920	2,851
1930	7,680
1940	8,055
1950	9,524
1960	15,972

1970	21,909
1980	23,649

GLENVIEW

1910	652
1920	760
1930	1,886
1940	2,500
1950	6,142
1960	18,132
1970	24,880
1980	32,060

GLENWOOD

1910	581
1920	738
1930	603
1940	643
1950	762
1960	882
1970	7,416
1980	10,538

GRANITE CITY

1900	3,122
1910	9,903
1920	14,757
1930	25,130
1940	22,974
1950	29,465
1960	40,073
1970	40,685
1980	36,815

HANOVER PARK

1960	451
1970	11,916
1980	28,850

HARRISBURG

1870	590
1880	934
1890	1,723
1900	2,202
1910	5,309
1920	7,125
1930	11,625
1940	11,453
1950	10,999
1960	9,171
1970	9,535
1980	10,410

HARVEY

1900	5,395
1910	7,227
1920	9,216
1930	16,374
1940	17,878
1950	20,683
1960	29,071
1970	34,636
1980	35,810

HAZEL CREST

1920	438
1930	1,162
1940	1,299

1950	2,129
1960	6,205
1970	10,329
1980	13,973

HERRIN

1900	1,559
1910	6,861
1920	10,986
1930	8,756
1940	8,463
1950	8,528
1960	9,474
1970	9,623
1980	10,549

HICKORY HILLS

1960	2,707
1970	13,176
1980	13,778

HIGHLAND PARK

1880	1,154
1890	2,163
1900	2,806
1910	4,209
1920	6,167
1930	12,203
1940	14,476
1950	16,808
1960	25,532
1970	32,263
1980	30,611

HINSDALE

1880	819
1890	1,584
1900	2,578
1910	2,451
1920	4,042
1930	6,923
1940	7,336
1950	8,676
1960	12,859
1970	15,918
1980	16,726

HOFFMAN ESTATES

1960	8,296
1970	22,238
1980	37,272

HOMEWOOD

1900	352
1910	713
1920	1,389
1930	3,227
1940	4,078
1950	5,887
1960	13,371
1970	18,871
1980	19,724

JACKSONVILLE

1850	2,745
1860	5,548
1870	9,203
1880	10,927

1890	12,935
1900	15,078
1910	15,326
1920	15,713
1930	17,747
1940	19,844
1950	20,387
1960	21,690
1970	20,553
1980	20,284

JOLIET

1840	2,558
1850	2,659
1860	7,104
1870	7,263
1880	11,657
1890	23,264
1900	29,353
1910	34,670
1920	38,442
1930	42,993
1940	42,365
1950	51,601
1960	66,780
1970	78,827
1980	77,956

JUSTICE

1920	183
1930	377
1940	499
1950	854
1960	2,803
1970	9,473
1980	10,552

KANKAKEE

1880	5,651
1890	9,025
1900	13,595
1910	13,986
1920	16,753
1930	20,620
1940	22,241
1950	26,856
1960	27,666
1970	30,944
1980	30,141

KEWANEE

1880	2,704
1890	4,569
1900	8,382
1910	9,307
1920	16,026
1930	17,093
1940	16,901
1950	16,821
1960	16,324
1970	15,762
1980	14,508

LA GRANGE

1880	531
1890	2,314
1900	3,969
1910	5,282
1920	6,525
1930	10,103
1940	10,479

1950	12,002
1960	15,285
1970	17,814
1980	15,445

LA GRANGE PARK

1900	730
1910	1,131
1920	1,684
1930	2,939
1940	3,406
1950	6,176
1960	13,793
1970	15,459
1980	13,359

LAKE FOREST

1880	877
1890	1,203
1900	2,215
1910	3,349
1920	3,657
1930	6,554
1940	6,885
1950	7,819
1960	10,678
1970	15,642
1980	15,245

LANSING

1900	830
1910	1,060
1920	1,409
1930	3,378
1940	4,462
1950	8,682
1960	18,098
1970	25,805
1980	29,039

LA SALLE

1860	4,016
1870	5,200
1880	7,847
1890	9,855
1900	10,446
1910	11,537
1920	13,050
1930	13,149
1940	12,812
1950	12,083
1960	11,897
1970	10,736
1980	10,347

LIBERTYVILLE

1880	695
1890	550
1900	864
1910	1,724
1920	2,125
1930	3,791
1940	3,930
1950	5,425
1960	8,560
1970	11,684
1980	16,520

LINCOLN

1880	5,639
1890	6,725
1900	8,962
1910	10,892
1920	11,882
1930	12,855
1940	12,752
1950	14,362
1960	16,890
1970	17,582
1980	16,327

LINCOLNWOOD

1910	359
1920	355
1930	473
1940	752
1950	3,072
1960	11,744
1970	12,929
1980	11,921

LISLE

1960	4,219
1970	5,329
1980	13,625

LOMBARD

1880	378
1890	515
1900	590
1910	883
1920	1,331
1930	6,197
1940	7,075
1950	9,817
1960	22,561
1970	34,043
1980	37,295

LOVES PARK

1950	5,366
1960	9,086
1970	12,390
1980	13,192

MACOMB

1850	756
1860	1,834
1870	2,748
1880	3,140
1890	4,052
1900	5,375
1910	5,744
1920	6,714
1930	8,509
1940	8,764
1950	10,592
1960	12,135
1970	19,643
1980	19,863

MARION

1880	881
1890	1,338
1900	2,510
1910	7,093
1920	9,582

1930	9,033
1940	9,251
1950	10,459
1960	11,274
1970	11,724
1980	14,031

MARKHAM

1930	349
1940	1,388
1950	2,753
1960	11,704
1970	15,987
1980	15,172

MATTESON

1930	736
1940	819
1950	1,211
1960	3,225
1970	4,741
1980	10,223

MATTOON

1880	5,737
1890	6,833
1900	9,622
1910	11,456
1920	13,552
1930	14,631
1940	15,827
1950	17,547
1960	19,088
1970	19,681
1980	19,055

MAYWOOD

1880	716
1900	4,532
1910	8,033
1920	12,072
1930	25,829
1940	26,648
1950	27,473
1960	27,330
1970	29,019
1980	27,998

McHENRY

1880	874
1890	979
1900	1,031
1910	1,031
1920	1,146
1930	1,354
1940	1,596
1950	2,080
1960	3,362
1970	6,772
1980	10,908

MELROSE PARK

1900	2,592
1910	4,806
1920	7,147
1930	10,741
1940	10,933
1950	13,366
1960	22,291
1970	22,716
1980	20,735

MIDLOTHIAN

1930	1,775
1940	2,430
1950	3,216
1960	6,605
1970	15,939
1980	14,274

MOLINE

1860	2,028
1870	4,166
1880	7,800
1890	12,000
1900	17,248
1910	24,199
1920	30,734
1930	32,236
1940	34,608
1950	37,397
1960	42,705
1970	46,237
1980	45,709

MONMOUTH

1850	797
1860	2,506
1870	4,662
1880	5,000
1890	5,936
1900	7,460
1910	9,128
1920	8,116
1930	8,666
1940	9,096
1950	10,193
1960	10,372
1970	11,022
1980	10,706

MORTON

1880	426
1890	657
1900	894
1910	1,004
1920	1,179
1930	1,501
1940	2,241
1950	3,693
1960	5,325
1970	10,811
1980	14,178

MORTON GROVE

1900	564
1910	836
1920	1,079
1930	1,974
1940	2,101
1950	3,926
1960	20,533
1970	26,369
1980	23,747

MOUNT PROSPECT

1920	349
1930	1,225
1940	1,720
1950	4,009
1960	18,906
1970	34,995
1980	52,634

MOUNT VERNON

1860	707
1870	1,167
1880	2,324
1890	3,233
1900	5,216
1910	8,007
1920	9,815
1930	12,375
1940	14,724
1950	15,600
1960	15,556
1970	15,980
1980	17,193

MUNDELEIN

1910	358
1920	420
1930	1,011
1940	1,328
1950	3,189
1960	10,526
1970	16,128
1980	17,053

NAPERVILLE

1870	1,713
1880	1,435
1890	1,481
1900	2,629
1910	3,449
1920	3,830
1930	5,118
1940	5,272
1950	7,013
1960	12,933
1970	22,794
1980	42,330

NILES

1900	514
1910	569
1920	1,258
1930	2,135
1940	2,168
1950	3,587
1960	20,393
1970	31,432
1980	30,363

NORMAL

1870	1,116
1880	2,470
1890	3,459
1900	3,795
1910	4,024
1920	5,143
1930	6,768
1940	6,983
1950	9,772
1960	13,357
1970	26,396
1980	35,672

NORRIDGE

1950	3,428
1960	14,087
1970	17,113
1980	16,483

NORTHBROOK

1910	441
1920	554
1930	1,193
1940	1,265
1950	3,348
1960	11,635
1970	25,422
1980	30,778

NORTH CHICAGO

1900	1,150
1910	3,306
1920	5,839
1930	8,466
1940	8,465
1950	8,628
1960	22,938
1970	47,275
1980	38,774

NORTHLAKE

1950	4,361
1960	12,318
1970	14,212
1980	12,166

OAK FOREST

1950	1,856
1960	3,724
1970	19,271
1980	26,096

OAK LAWN

1910	287
1920	489
1930	2,045
1940	3,483
1950	8,751
1960	27,471
1970	60,305
1980	60,590

OAK PARK

1880	1,888
1890	4,771
1910	19,444
1920	39,858
1930	63,982
1940	66,015
1950	63,529
1960	62,093
1970	62,511
1980	54,887

O'FALLON

1870	1,117
1880	923
1890	865
1900	1,267
1910	2,018
1920	2,379
1930	2,373
1940	2,407
1950	3,022
1960	4,018
1970	7,268
1980	12,241

ORLAND PARK

1900	366
1910	369
1920	843
1930	571
1940	631
1950	788
1960	2,592
1970	6,391
1980	23,045

OTTAWA

1870	7,736
1880	7,834
1890	9,985
1900	10,588
1910	9,535
1920	10,816
1930	15,094
1940	16,005
1950	16,957
1960	19,408
1970	18,716
1980	18,166

PALATINE

1880	731
1890	891
1900	1,020
1910	1,144
1920	1,210
1930	2,118
1940	2,222
1950	4,079
1960	11,504
1970	26,050
1980	32,166

PALOS HEIGHTS

1960	3,775
1970	8,544
1980	11,096

PALOS HILLS

1960	3,766
1970	6,629
1980	16,654

PARK FOREST

1950	8,138
1960	29,993
1970	30,638
1980	26,222

PARK RIDGE

1880	457
1890	987
1900	1,340
1910	2,009
1920	3,383
1930	10,417
1940	12,063
1950	16,602
1960	32,659
1970	42,614
1980	38,704

PEKIN

1850	1,678
1860	3,467
1870	5,696
1880	5,993
1890	6,347
1900	8,420
1910	9,897
1920	12,086
1930	16,129
1940	19,407
1950	21,858
1960	28,146
1970	31,375
1980	33,967

PEORIA

1840	1,467
1850	5,095
1860	14,045
1870	22,849
1880	29,259
1890	41,024
1900	56,100
1910	66,950
1920	76,121
1930	104,969
1940	105,087
1950	111,856
1960	103,162
1970	126,963
1980	124,160

PERU

1860	3,132
1870	3,650
1880	4,632
1890	5,550
1900	6,863
1910	7,984
1920	8,869
1930	9,121
1940	8,983
1950	8,653
1960	10,460
1970	11,772
1980	10,886

PONTIAC

1850	27
1860	1,264
1870	2,438
1880	2,245
1890	2,784
1900	4,266
1910	6,090
1920	6,664
1930	8,272
1940	9,585
1950	8,990
1960	8,435
1970	10,595
1980	11,227

PROSPECT HEIGHTS

1980	11,808

QUINCY

1840	2,319
1850	6,902
1860	13,718
1870	24,052
1880	27,268
1890	31,494
1900	36,252
1910	36,587
1920	35,978
1930	39,241
1940	40,469
1950	41,450
1960	43,793
1970	45,288
1980	42,554

RANTOUL

1880	850
1890	1,704
1900	1,207
1910	1,384
1920	1,551
1930	1,555
1940	2,367
1950	6,387
1960	22,116
1970	25,562
1980	20,161

RIVERDALE

1900	558
1910	917
1920	1,166
1930	2,504
1940	2,865
1950	5,840
1960	12,008
1970	15,806
1980	13,233

RIVER FOREST

1900	1,539
1910	2,456
1920	4,358
1930	8,829
1940	9,487
1950	10,823
1960	12,695
1970	13,402
1980	12,392

RIVER GROVE

1890	287
1900	333
1910	418
1920	484
1930	2,741
1940	3,301
1950	4,839
1960	8,464
1970	11,465
1980	10,368

ROCK FALLS

1870	471
1880	894
1890	1,900
1900	2,176
1910	2,657
1920	2,927
1930	3,893
1940	4,987
1950	7,983
1960	10,261
1970	10,287
1980	10,633

ROCKFORD

1860	6,979
1870	11,049
1880	13,129
1890	23,584
1900	31,051
1910	45,401
1920	65,651
1930	85,864
1940	84,637
1950	92,927
1960	126,706
1970	147,370
1980	139,712

ROCK ISLAND

1850	1,711
1860	5,130
1870	7,890
1880	11,659
1890	13,634
1900	19,493
1910	24,335
1920	35,117
1930	37,953
1940	42,775
1950	48,710
1960	51,863
1970	50,166
1980	47,036

ROLLING MEADOWS

1960	10,879
1970	19,178
1980	20,167

ROMEOVILLE

1900	113
1910	98
1920	74
1930	133
1940	170
1950	147
1960	3,574
1970	12,888
1980	15,519

ROSELLE

1960	3,581
1970	6,207
1980	16,948

ROUND LAKE BEACH

1940	410
1950	1,892
1960	5,011
1970	5,717
1980	12,921

SAINT CHARLES

1880	1,533
1890	1,690
1900	2,675
1910	4,046
1920	4,099
1930	5,377
1940	5,870
1950	6,709
1960	9,269
1970	12,945
1980	17,492

SAUK VILLAGE

1960	4,687
1970	7,479
1980	10,906

SCHAUMBURG

1960	986
1970	18,730
1980	53,305

SCHILLER PARK

1920	390
1930	709
1940	804
1950	1,384
1960	5,687
1970	12,712
1980	11,458

SKOKIE

1900	529
1910	568
1920	763
1930	5,007
1940	7,172
1950	14,832
1960	59,364
1970	68,322
1980	60,278

SOUTH HOLLAND

1890	1,005
1900	776
1910	1,065
1920	1,247
1930	1,873
1940	2,272
1950	3,247
1960	10,412
1970	23,931
1980	24,977

SPRINGFIELD

1840	2,579
1850	4,533
1860	9,320
1870	17,364
1880	19,743
1890	24,963
1900	34,159
1910	51,678
1920	59,183
1930	71,864
1940	75,503
1950	81,628
1960	83,721
1970	91,753
1980	99,637

STERLING

1860	2,428
1870	3,998
1880	5,087
1890	5,824
1900	6,309
1910	7,467
1920	8,182
1930	10,012
1940	11,363
1950	12,817
1960	15,668
1970	16,113
1980	16,281

STREAMWOOD

1960	4,821
1970	18,176
1980	23,456

STREATOR

1870	1,486
1880	5,157
1890	11,414
1900	14,079
1910	14,253
1920	14,779
1930	14,728
1940	14,930
1950	16,469
1960	16,868
1970	15,600
1980	14,791

SUMMIT

1900	547
1910	949
1920	4,019
1930	6,548
1940	7,043
1950	8,597
1960	10,374
1970	11,569
1980	10,110

TAYLORVILLE

1880	2,237
1890	2,829
1900	4,248
1910	5,446
1920	5,806
1930	7,316
1940	8,313
1950	9,188
1960	8,801
1970	10,644
1980	11,386

TINLEY PARK

1900	300
1910	309
1920	493
1930	823
1940	1,136
1950	2,326
1960	6,392
1970	12,572
1980	26,171

URBANA

1850	210
1860	1,370
1870	2,277
1880	2,942
1890	3,511
1900	5,728
1910	8,245
1920	10,244
1930	13,060
1940	14,064
1950	22,834
1960	27,294
1970	33,976
1980	35,978

VILLA PARK

1920	854
1930	6,220
1940	7,236
1950	8,821
1960	20,391
1970	25,891
1980	23,185

WASHINGTON

1850	712
1860	1,578
1870	1,607
1880	1,397
1890	1,301
1900	1,459
1910	1,530
1920	1,643
1930	1,741
1940	2,456
1950	4,285
1960	5,919
1970	6,790
1980	10,364

WAUKEGAN

1860	3,433
1870	4,507
1880	4,012
1890	4,915
1900	9,426
1910	16,069
1920	19,226
1930	33,499
1940	34,241
1950	38,946
1960	55,719
1970	65,134
1980	67,653

WESTCHESTER

1930	358
1940	621
1950	4,308
1960	18,902
1970	20,033
1980	17,730

WEST CHICAGO

1900	1,877
1910	2,378
1920	2,594
1930	3,477
1940	3,355

1950	3,973
1960	6,854
1970	10,111
1980	12,550

WESTERN SPRINGS

1880	172
1890	451
1900	662
1910	905
1920	1,258
1930	3,894
1940	4,856
1950	6,364
1960	10,838
1970	13,029
1980	12,876

WESTMONT

1930	2,733
1940	3,044
1950	3,402
1960	5,997
1970	8,832
1980	16,718

WHEATON

1860	645
1870	988
1900	2,345
1910	3,423
1920	4,137
1930	7,258
1940	7,389
1950	11,638
1960	24,312
1970	31,138
1980	43,043

WHEELING

1890	811
1900	331
1910	260
1920	313
1930	467
1940	550
1950	916
1960	7,169
1970	13,243
1980	23,266

WILMETTE

1880	419
1890	1,458
1900	2,300
1910	4,943
1920	7,184
1930	15,233
1940	17,226
1950	18,162
1960	28,268
1970	32,134
1980	28,229

WINNETKA

1880	584
1890	1,079
1900	1,833
1910	3,168
1920	6,694

1930	12,166
1940	12,430
1950	12,105
1960	13,368
1970	14,131
1980	12,772

WOOD DALE

1930	230
1940	738
1950	1,857
1960	3,071
1970	8,831
1980	11,251

WOODRIDGE

1960	542
1970	11,028
1980	22,322

WOOD RIVER

1910	84
1920	3,476
1930	8,136
1940	8,197
1950	10,190
1960	11,694
1970	13,186
1980	12,449

WOODSTOCK

1900	2,502
1910	4,331
1920	5,523
1930	5,471
1940	6,123
1950	7,192
1960	8,897
1970	10,226
1980	11,725

WORTH

1920	240
1930	411
1940	702
1950	1,472
1960	8,196
1970	11,999
1980	11,592

ZION

1910	4,789
1920	5,580
1930	5,991
1940	6,555
1950	8,950
1960	11,941
1970	17,268
1980	17,861

CORRECTION NOTE

The official 1980 census counts of total population shown in this report supersede counts issued previously. Corrections to the figures were made after the counts were provided to the State for redistricting purposes and released in Advance Report PHC80-V for this State.

Shown below are corrections to the 1980 census counts of the total population made after the tabulations for this report were completed. Any additional corrections made after this report is printed are available by writing to Data User Services Division, Customer Services (Corrections), Bureau of the Census, Washington, D.C. 20233.

The 1980 figures shown in this publication are subject to change pending the outcome of the various lawsuits dealing with the census counts.

	1980 population	
	As shown in the tables	Corrected
The State..................	11 426 518	11 426 596
Cook County:		
Thornton township:		
Thornton village............	3 022	3 024
Du Page County....................	658 835	658 829
Addison township................	82 937	82 868
Addison village (pt.)........	26 504	26 508
Lombard village (pt.)........	531	133
Bloomingdale township........	79 571	79 634
Addison village (pt.)........	3 255	3 318
Hanover Park village (pt.)...	5 272	5 141
Lisle township:		
Naperville city (pt.)........	26 221	26 492
Woodridge village (pt.)......	20 404	20 643
Milton township:		
Glen Ellyn village (pt.).....	23 103	23 171
Jackson County...................	61 522	61 649
Carbondale township............	31 670	31 797
Carbondale city..............	26 287	26 414
Jefferson County.................	36 552	36 558
Shiloh township.................	5 366	5 372
Johnson County:		
Goreville No. 1 precinct.......	1 043	1 075
Goreville village (pt.)......	697	729
Goreville No. 2 precinct.......	819	787
Goreville village (pt.)......	281	249
Kane County:		
Elgin township:		
Elgin city (pt.).............	52 234	52 417
South Elgin village (pt.)....	5 747	5 662
St. Charles township:		
South Elgin village (pt.)....	471	308
Lake County:		
Benton township:		
Winthrop Harbor village......	5 438	5 431
La Salle County:		
Otter Creek township:		
Streator city (pt.)..........	520	524
Livingston County:		
Dwight township.................	4 830	4 434
Nevada township.................	316	712
Madison County...................	247 691	247 661
Wood River township............	38 000	37 970
East Alton village............	7 123	7 096
Wood River city...............	12 449	12 446
Rock Island County:		
Blackhawk township:		
Rock Island city (pt.).......	2 992	2 968
South Moline township:		
Moline city (pt.)............	19 547	20 116

	1980 population	
	As shown in the tables	Corrected
Sangamon County..................	176 089	176 070
Ball township...................	3 283	3 280
Capital township................	99 637	100 054
Springfield city.............	99 637	100 054
Rochester township............	4 101	4 120
Springfield township..........	10 100	9 407
Woodside township..............	16 413	16 654
Leland Grove city............	1 692	1 864
Scott County:		
Winchester No. 1 precinct......	1 160	583
Winchester city (pt.)........	1 104	437
Winchester No. 2 precinct......	432	858
Winchester city (pt.)........	195	621
Winchester No. 3 precinct......	600	751
Winchester city (pt.)........	507	658
Williamson County:		
Herrin precinct:		
Herrin city (pt.)............	9 435	9 594
Addison village (total).........	29 759	29 826
Elgin city (total)..............	63 798	63 981
Glen Ellyn village (total)......	23 649	23 717
Goreville village (total).......	978	(1)
Hanover Park village (total)....	28 850	28 719
Herrin city (total).............	10 549	10 708
Lombard village (total).........	37 295	36 897
Moline city (total).............	45 709	46 278
Naperville city (total).........	42 330	42 601
Rock Island city (total)........	47 036	46 928
South Elgin village (total).....	6 218	5 970
Streator city (total)...........	14 791	14 795
Winchester city (total).........	1 716	(1)
Woodridge village (total).......	22 322	22 561

[1]No change.

County Subdivisions	1980	1970
The State	11 426 518	11 110 285
Adams County[1]	71 622	70 861
Beverly township	390	380
Burton township	959	842
Camp Point township	1 832	1 612
Camp Point village[1]	1 285	1 143
Clayton township	1 218	1 155
Clayton village	889	727
Golden village (pt.)[1]	3	...
Columbus township	531	448
Columbus village (pt.)	66	88
Concord township	294	274
Ellington township[1]	3 296	2 848
Fall Creek township	701	544
Gilmer township	1 005	789
Columbus village (pt.)	26	43
Honey Creek township	808	761
Coatsburg village	258	188
Houston township	288	371
Golden village (pt.)[1]	–	...
Keene township	772	752
Loraine village	382	372
Liberty township	1 261	952
Liberty village[1]	587	369
Lima township	677	623
Lima village	166	125
McKee township	239	274
Melrose township[1]	6 616	4 907
Mendon township	1 597	1 319
Mendon village	979	883
Northeast township	950	1 035
Golden village (pt.)[1]	555	571
La Prairie village	90	85
Payson township	1 911	1 432
Payson village[1]	1 065	589
Plainville village[1]	289	289
Quincy township	42 554	45 288
Quincy city[1]	42 554	45 288
Richfield township	471	513
Riverside township[1]	2 252	2 679
Ursa township	1 000	1 063
Ursa village[1]	454	423
Alexander County[2]	12 264	12 015
Cache precinct[2]	620	772
Cairo precinct	5 931	6 277
Cairo city[2]	5 931	6 277
East Cape precinct	730	...
East Cape Girardeau village[2]	539	...
Elco precinct	506	463
McClure precinct	654	...
Miller precinct	293	223
Olive Branch precinct	744	...
Sandusky precinct	909	...
Tamms precinct	966	789
Tamms village	826	645
Thebes precinct	911	...
Thebes village	455	442
Bond County[3]	16 224	14 012
Burgess township	2 052	1 716
Pierron village (pt.)[3]	524	432
Pocahontas village (pt.)	864	764
Central township	6 396	5 749
Greenville city[3]	5 271	4 631
Lagrange township[3]	768	591
Mills township	574	511
Mulberry Grove township	1 406	1 318
Mulberry Grove village	707	697
Old Ripley township	887	833
Old Ripley village	149	127
Pocahontas village (pt.)[3]	2	...
Pleasant Mound township	1 316	1 055
Smithboro village	236	203
Shoal Creek township	2 204	1 658
Donnellson village (pt.)[3]	25	12
Panama village (pt.)	394	149
Sorento village	677	625
Tamalco township	621	581
Keyesport village (pt.)[3]	188	154
Boone County[4]	28 630	25 440
Belvidere township	18 729	17 147
Belvidere city (pt.)[4]	15 094	14 053
Bonus township	1 848	1 563
Belvidere city (pt.)[4]	–	(NA)
Boone township	1 430	1 202
Capron village	678	654
Caledonia township	1 129	750
Flora township	1 451	1 002
Belvidere city (pt.)[4]	82	8
Le Roy township	509	570
Manchester township	901	859
Poplar Grove township	1 683	1 425
Poplar Grove village	818	607
Spring township	950	922

County Subdivisions	1980	1970
Brown County	5 411	5 586
Buckhorn township	120	137
Cooperstown township	376	412
Elkhorn township	371	308
Lee township	461	515
Mound Station village	175	203
Missouri township	204	261
Mount Sterling township	2 678	2 788
Mount Sterling city	2 186	2 182
Pea Ridge township	184	252
Ripley township	181	198
Ripley village	149	159
Versailles township	836	715
Versailles village	513	429
Bureau County[5]	39 114	38 541
Arispie township	989	948
Tiskilwa village (pt.)	508	503
Berlin township	843	825
Dover village (pt.)	33	32
Malden village	359	262
Bureau township	382	454
Clarion township	448	464
La Moille village (pt.)	11	–
Concord township	2 023	2 101
Buda village	668	675
Sheffield village (pt.)[5]	1 031	1 031
Dover township	649	676
Dover village (pt.)[5]	180	144
Princeton city (pt.)[5]	10	...
Fairfield township	457	515
Gold township	278	323
Greenville township	493	554
New Bedford village	152	152
Hall township	8 788	8 416
Dalzell village (pt.)[5]	679	579
De Pue village (pt.)[5]	–	–
Ladd village[5]	1 337	1 328
Seatonville village (pt.)[5]	348	293
Spring Valley city[5]	5 822	5 605
Indiantown township	905	931
Tiskilwa village (pt.)[5]	482	470
La Moille township	1 254	1 261
La Moille village (pt.)	723	669
Leepertown township	525	526
Bureau Junction village	455	466
De Pue village (pt.)[5]	–	...
Macon township	371	370
Manlius township	830	852
Manlius village	439	402
Milo township	336	410
Mineral township	673	757
Mineral village	325	286
Sheffield village (pt.)[5]	99	7
Neponset township	1 031	935
Neponset village	575	507
Ohio township	1 012	1 033
Ohio village	544	506
Princeton township	9 3?2	8 493
Princeton city (pt.)[5]	7 332	6 959
Selby township	2 683	2 828
De Pue village (pt.)[5]	1 873	1 919
Hollowayville village	92	94
Seatonville village (pt.)[5]	21	25
Walnut township	2 000	1 820
Walnut village[5]	1 513	1 295
Westfield township	1 131	1 218
Arlington village	236	250
Cherry village[5]	541	551
Wheatland township	185	170
Wyanet township	1 526	1 661
Wyanet village	1 069	1 005
Calhoun County[6]	5 867	5 675
Belleview precinct	452	449
Carlin precinct	236	196
Kampsville village (pt.)[6]	15	...
Crater precinct	642	727
Kampsville village (pt.)[6]	408	439
Gilead precinct	336	299
Hamburg precinct	669	643
Hamburg village	166	162
Hardin precinct	1 444	1 446
Hardin village	1 107	1 035
Point precinct	1 191	1 161
Brussels village	168	191
Richwood precinct	897	754
Batchtown village[6]	254	217
Carroll County[7]	18 779	19 276
Cherry Grove–Shannon township[7]	1 607	...
Shannon village[7]	938	848
Elkhorn Grove township	260	321
Fairhaven township	1 113	1 110
Chadwick village[7]	631	605
Freedom township	395	388
Mount Carroll township	2 693	2 857
Mount Carroll city (pt.)[7]	1 891	2 099
Rock Creek–Lima township[7]	2 199	...

County Subdivisions

County Subdivisions	1980	1970
Carroll County—Con.		
Rock Creek—Lima township—Con.		
Lanark city[7]	1 483	1 495
Salem township[7]	459	474
Mount Carroll city (pt.)[7]	45	44
Savanna township	5 247	5 525
Savanna city[7]	4 529	4 942
Washington township	473	763
Woodland township	382	394
Wysox township	1 679	1 727
Milledgeville village[7]	1 209	1 130
York township	2 272	1 852
Thomson village[7]	911	617
Cass County[8]	15 084	14 219
Arenzville township	1 020	834
Arenzville village	495	403
Ashland township	1 479	1 262
Ashland village	1 351	1 128
Beardstown township	7 232	6 923
Beardstown city[8]	6 338	6 222
Bluff Springs township	720	607
Chandlerville township	758	682
Chandlerville village (pt.)[8]	563	516
Hagener township	456	396
Newmansville township	123	143
Panther Creek township	457	471
Chandlerville village (pt.)[8]	279	246
Philadelphia township	296	372
Sangamon Valley township	380	361
Virginia city (pt.)	—	
Virginia township	2 163	2 168
Virginia city (pt.)[8]	1 825	1 814
Champaign County[9]	168 392	163 281
Ayers township	503	504
Allerton village (pt.)	8	6
Broadlands village	346	315
Brown township	1 616	1 837
Fisher village (pt.)	1 108	1 249
Foosland village	153	172
Champaign township[9]	8 184	'6 592
Savoy village (pt.)[9]	1 634	223
Champaign City township	58 133	'56 837
Champaign city[9]	58 133	'56 837
Colfax township	355	412
Compromise township	1 588	1 707
Gifford village (pt.)[9]	769	814
Condit township	477	407
Fisher village (pt.)[9]	98	—
Crittenden township	312	384
Cunningham township	35 978	'33 976
Urbana city[9]	35 978	'33 976
East Bend township	817	821
Fisher village (pt.)[9]	257	193
Harwood township	625	471
Gifford village (pt.)[9]	79	...
Hensley township[9]	1 254	629
Kerr township	177	225
Ludlow township	5 114	5 750
Ludlow village	397	531
Rantoul village (pt.)[9]	4 233	4 573
Mahomet township	6 909	3 862
Lake of the Woods (CDP)	2 443	...
Mahomet village[9]	1 986	1 296
Newcomb township	805	617
Fisher village (pt.)	109	83
Ogden township	1 574	1 373
Ogden village[9]	818	'703
Royal village[9]	274	197
Pesotum township	994	864
Pesotum village[9]	651	536
Philo township	1 483	1 453
Philo village[9]	973	1 022
Rantoul township	18 139	22 568
Rantoul village (pt.)[9]	15 928	20 989
Thomasboro village[9]	1 242	806
Raymond township	529	581
Longview village	207	224
Sadorus township	1 189	1 296
Ivesdale village (pt.)	337	353
Sadorus village	435	454
St. Joseph township	3 612	2 494
St. Joseph village[9]	1 900	1 554
Scott township	1 094	1 181
Bondville village[9]	442	...
Sidney township	1 358	1 378
Sidney village[9]	886	915
Somer township	1 238	1 321
South Homer township	1 617	1 722
Homer village[9]	1 279	1 354
Stanton township	513	546
Tolono township	3 410	2 853
Savoy village (pt.)[9]	492	369
Tolono village[9]	2 434	2 027
Urbana township[9]	8 795	'8 620

County Subdivisions	1980	1970
Christian County[10]	36 446	35 948
Assumption township	1 645	1 980
Assumption city[10]	1 283	1 487
Bear Creek township	675	679
Palmer village	278	244
Buckhart township	2 114	2 007
Edinburg village[10]	1 231	1 153
Greenwood township	279	381
Johnson township	607	426
Taylorville city (pt.)[10]	18	—
King township	322	360
Harvel village (pt.)	75	76
Locust township	745	678
Owaneco village	285	278
Taylorville city (pt.)[10]	91	1
May township	1 468	1 013
Taylorville city (pt.)[10]	95	...
Mosquito township	434	534
Mount Auburn township	1 215	1 159
Mount Auburn village	598	520
Pana township	7 019	7 350
Pana city[10]	6 040	6 326
Prairieton township	459	420
Moweaqua village (pt.)[10]	—	
Ricks township	1 449	1 528
Morrisonville village	1 208	1 178
Rosamond township	469	566
South Fork township	3 151	3 039
Bulpitt village	301	275
Jeiseyville village[10]	178	182
Kincaid village[10]	1 591	1 424
Tovey village	598	'620
Stonington township	1 462	1 488
Stonington village[10]	1 184	1 096
Taylorville township	12 933	12 340
Taylorville city (pt.)[10]	11 182	10 643
Clark County[11]	16 913	16 216
Anderson township	396	323
Auburn township	310	271
Casey township	4 219	3 954
Casey city (pt.)[11]	3 007	2 994
Darwin township	435	379
Dolson township	336	390
Douglas township	170	183
Johnson township	394	387
Marshall township	4 373	4 296
Marshall city (pt.)[11]	3 371	3 468
Martinsville township	1 815	1 876
Martinsville city[11]	1 298	1 374
Melrose township	396	391
Orange township	326	352
Parker township	248	235
Wabash township	1 903	1 608
Marshall city (pt.)[11]	284	...
Westfield township	882	827
Westfield village	733	678
York township	710	744
Clay County[12]	15 283	14 735
Bible Grove township	444	459
Blair township	620	586
Clay City township	1 494	1 484
Clay City village	1 038	1 049
Harter township	6 879	6 642
Flora city (pt.)[12]	5 342	5 272
Hoosier township	426	387
Sailor Springs village (pt.)	14	14
Larkinsburg township	650	586
Iola village	178	163
Louisville township	1 835	1 697
Louisville village[12]	1 166	1 020
Oskaloosa township	353	363
Pixley township	842	797
Sailor Springs village (pt.)	145	123
Songer township	342	358
Stanford township	690	673
Flora city (pt.)[12]	37	11
Xenia township	708	703
Xenia village[12]	475	464
Clinton County[13]	32 617	28 315
Breese township	4 677	4 134
Breese city[13]	3 516	2 885
Brookside township	4 557	4 123
Centralia city (pt.)[13]	2 773	'2 615
Wamac city (pt.)[13]	753	500
Carlyle township	3 805	3 414
Carlyle city[13]	3 388	3 139
Clement township	500	441
Huey village	215	205
East Fork township	442	325
Germantown township	1 904	1 759
Germantown village[13]	1 191	1 108
Irishtown township	838	550
Keyesport village (pt.)	311	198
Lake township	974	763
Hoffman village	467	346
Looking Glass township	4 882	3 868
Albers village	663	656

County Subdivisions

County Subdivisions	1980	1970
Clinton County—Con.		
Looking Glass township—Con.		
Damiansville village[13]	396	...
New Baden village (pt.)[13]	2 437	1 928
Meridian township	699	635
St. Rose township	1 256	1 134
Santa Fe township	1 101	916
Bartelso village[13]	389	439
Sugar Creek township	4 628	3 999
Aviston village[13]	846	828
Trenton city[13]	2 504	2 328
Wade township	1 771	1 693
Beckemeyer village[13]	1 119	1 069
Wheatfield township	583	561
Coles County[14]	52 260	47 815
Ashmore township	1 552	1 036
Ashmore village[14]	883	428
Charleston township	21 121	17 682
Charleston city (pt.)[14]	19 355	16 421
East Oakland township	1 564	1 538
Oakland city[14]	1 035	1 012
Humboldt township	1 482	1 017
Humboldt village	499	366
Hutton township	853	737
Lafayette township	3 889	3 178
Charleston city (pt.)	–	–
Mattoon city (pt.)[14]	2 553	1 797
Mattoon township	17 359	18 696
Mattoon city (pt.)[14]	16 254	17 884
Morgan township	425	446
North Okaw township	1 072	1 011
Paradise township	1 171	843
Mattoon city (pt.)[14]	248	–
Pleasant Grove township	1 342	1 155
Lerna village[14]	386	288
Seven Hickory township	430	476
Cook County[15]	5 253 655	5 493 766
Barrington township	9 600	7 607
Barrington village (pt.)[15]	4 215	4 715
Barrington Hills village (pt.)[15]	1 980	1 796
Hoffman Estates village (pt.)[15]	1 609	6
Inverness village (pt.)[15]	180	2
South Barrington village (pt.)[15]	983	177
Berwyn township	46 849	52 502
Berwyn city	46 849	52 502
Bloom township	101 424	94 757
Chicago Heights city[15]	37 026	40 900
East Chicago Heights village	5 347	5 000
Flossmoor village (pt.)[15]	2 098	2 013
Glenwood village (pt.)[15]	9 569	6 964
Homewood village (pt.)	9 640	10 081
Lansing village (pt.)[15]	5 466	2 889
Lynwood village[15]	4 195	1 042
Olympia Fields village (pt.)[15]	484	478
Park Forest village (pt.)	4 744	6 012
Sauk Village village[15]	10 906	7 479
South Chicago Heights village[15]	3 932	4 923
Steger village (pt.)	3 414	3 060
Bremen township	109 023	93 906
Blue Island city (pt.)	1 182	1 088
Country Club Hills city (pt.)[15]	9 377	4 437
Crestwood village (pt.)[15]	6 237	2 611
Harvey city (pt.)	1 687	1 170
Hazel Crest village (pt.)[15]	9 954	6 936
Homewood village (pt.)	2 357	1 259
Markham city (pt.)	9 692	10 814
Midlothian village[15]	14 274	14 422
Oak Forest city[15]	26 096	19 271
Orland Park village (pt.)[15]	–	...
Posen village (pt.)	4 350	5 183
Robbins village (pt.)	6 530	8 327
Tinley Park village (pt.)[15]	13 663	9 514
Calumet township	21 637	23 614
Blue Island city (pt.)[15]	10 203	10 443
Calumet Park village[15]	8 788	10 069
Riverdale village (pt.)	2 645	3 099
Chicago city (pt.)[15]	3 005 061	3 369 357
Cicero township	61 232	67 058
Cicero town	61 232	67 058
Elk Grove township	88 283	77 116
Arlington Heights village (pt.)[15]	10 724	8 845
Des Plaines city (pt.)[15]	11 915	11 974
Elk Grove Village village[15]	22 432	20 305
Mount Prospect village (pt.)[15]	30 268	23 255
Rolling Meadows city (pt.)[15]	4 759	4 344
Schaumburg village (pt.)[15]	–	–
Evanston township	73 706	80 113
Evanston city	73 706	80 113
Hanover township	47 717	33 696
Bartlett village (pt.)[15]	4 705	2 510
Elgin city (pt.)[15]	11 020	5 347
Hanover Park village (pt.)[15]	8 059	5 596
Hoffman Estates village (pt.)[15]	30	52
South Barrington village (pt.)	–	39
Streamwood village (pt.)[15]	22 313	18 176
Lemont township	8 850	8 314
Lemont village[15]	5 640	5 080
Leyden township[15]	91 572	100 013
Cook County—Con.		
Leyden township—Con.		
Bensenville village (pt.)[15]	3	2
Elmwood Park village	24 016	26 160
Franklin Park village[15]	17 507	20 348
Melrose Park village (pt.)[15]	1 965	1 488
Norridge village (pt.)[15]	2 186	2 180
Northlake city (pt.)[15]	8 730	9 990
Park Ridge city (pt.)[15]	2 298	2 408
River Grove village[15]	10 368	11 465
Rosemont village (pt.)[15]	2 722	2 971
Schiller Park village	11 458	12 712
Lyons township	105 317	102 076
Bedford Park village (pt.)[15]	986	573
Bridgeview village (pt.)[15]	9 764	8 756
Brookfield village (pt.)[15]	8 248	7 406
Burr Ridge village (pt.)[15]	1 548	795
Countryside city[15]	6 538	2 864
Hickory Hills city[15]	1 891	1 827
Hinsdale village (pt.)[15]	2 414	2 259
Hodgkins village[15]	2 005	2 270
Indian Head Park village[15]	2 915	473
Justice village[15]	10 552	9 473
La Grange village[15]	15 445	17 814
Lyons village (pt.)	9 726	10 736
McCook village[15]	303	333
Riverside village (pt.)	134	58
Summit village[15]	10 110	11 569
Western Springs village (pt.)[15]	12 379	12 366
Willow Springs village (pt.)[15]	3 992	3 196
Maine township	130 676	140 194
Des Plaines city (pt.)[15]	41 014	44 679
Glenview village (pt.)	3 991	4 538
Morton Grove village (pt.)	7 158	8 382
Mount Prospect village (pt.)[15]	–	...
Niles village (pt.)[15]	21 741	22 185
Park Ridge city (pt.)[15]	32 056	35 152
Rosemont village (pt.)	1 415	1 854
New Trier township	58 224	65 365
Glencoe village (pt.)	9 200	10 542
Glenview village (pt.)	3 100	3 584
Kenilworth village	2 708	2 980
Northfield village (pt.)[15]	1 410	1 259
Wilmette village (pt.)[15]	28 093	31 966
Winnetka village[15]	12 772	14 131
Niles township[15]	99 447	110 892
Glenview village (pt.)	1 555	1 903
Golf village	482	504
Lincolnwood village[15]	11 921	12 929
Morton Grove village (pt.)	16 589	17 987
Niles village (pt.)[15]	8 622	9 247
Skokie village[15]	60 278	68 322
Northfield township	74 243	65 557
Deerfield village (pt.)[15]	–	9
Glencoe village (pt.)	–	–
Glenview village (pt.)	23 414	14 855
Northbrook village (pt.)[15]	30 744	25 422
Northfield village (pt.)[15]	4 397	3 751
Prospect Heights city (pt.)[15]	9	...
Wilmette village (pt.)	136	168
Norwood Park township	28 070	30 947
Harwood Heights village	8 228	9 060
Norridge village (pt.)	14 297	14 933
Park Ridge city (pt.)	4 350	5 054
Oak Park township	54 887	62 511
Oak Park village	54 887	62 511
Orland township	42 607	15 028
Orland Park village (pt.)[15]	22 655	6 391
Tinley Park village (pt.)[15]	12 479	3 058
Westhaven village[15]	2 784	470
Palatine township	83 201	54 963
Arlington Heights village (pt.)[15]	466	13
Barrington village (pt.)[15]	740	416
Hoffman Estates village (pt.)[15]	7 457	815
Inverness village (pt.)[15]	3 866	1 672
Palatine village[15]	32 166	26 050
Rolling Meadows city (pt.)[15]	14 486	12 996
Schaumburg village (pt.)[15]	1 162	152
South Barrington village (pt.)[15]	185	132
Palos township	46 412	33 100
Bridgeview village (pt.)[15]	1 747	342
Hickory Hills village (pt.)[15]	11 887	11 349
Orland Park village (pt.)	390	–
Palos Heights city (pt.)[15]	5 697	3 940
Palos Hills city[15]	16 654	6 629
Palos Park village[15]	3 150	3 297
Willow Springs village (pt.)[15]	155	122
Worth village (pt.)	2 972	2 671
Proviso township	156 519	172 536
Bellwood village[15]	19 811	22 096
Berkeley village[15]	5 467	6 152
Broadview village	8 618	9 623
Brookfield village (pt.)	9 575	11 065
Forest Park village	15 177	15 472
Hillside village[15]	8 279	8 888
La Grange Park village[15]	13 359	15 459
Maywood village	27 998	29 019
Melrose Park village (pt.)[15]	18 770	21 228
Northlake city (pt.)	3 436	4 201
North Riverside village (pt.)[15]	1 842	2 197

County Subdivisions

County Subdivisions	1980	1970
Cook County—Con.		
Proviso township—Con.		
Oak Brook village (pt.)[15]	–	...
Stone Park village	4 273	ʹ4 429
Westchester village[15]	17 730	20 033
Western Springs village (pt.)[15]	497	ʹ663
Rich township	58 730	44 801
Country Club Hills city (pt.)[15]	5 299	2 483
Flossmoor village (pt.)[15]	6 325	5 833
Hazel Crest village (pt.)[15]	744	
Homewood village (pt.)	1 992	1 356
Matteson village[15]	10 223	4 741
Olympia Fields village (pt.)[15]	3 662	3 000
Park Forest village (pt.)[15]	18 167	21 959
Park Forest South village (pt.)[15]	2	...
Richton Park village[15]	9 403	2 558
Tinley Park village (pt.)	9	
River Forest township	12 392	13 402
River Forest village	12 392	13 402
Riverside township	15 930	18 475
Brookfield village (pt.)	1 572	1 813
Lyons village (pt.)	199	388
North Riverside village[15]	4 922	5 900
Riverside village (pt.)	9 102	ʹ10 299
Schaumburg township	103 920	ʹ50 995
Elk Grove Village village (pt.)[15]	6 475	30
Hanover Park village (pt.)[15]	10 099	6 139
Hoffman Estates village (pt.)[15]	28 176	ʹ21 365
Rolling Meadows city (pt.)	911	1 838
Roselle village (pt.)[15]	2 397	66
Schaumburg village (pt.)[15]	52 126	18 379
Streamwood village (pt.)[15]	1 143	...
Stickney township[15]	38 757	41 752
Bedford Park village (pt.)	2	10
Bridgeview village (pt.)[15]	346	ʹ607
Burbank city[15]	28 462	...
Forest View village	764	927
Stickney village	5 893	6 601
Thornton township	191 359	ʹ188 067
Blue Island city (pt.)	1 204	852
Burnham village	4 030	3 634
Calumet City city[15]	39 697	ʹ33 107
Dixmoor village	4 175	4 735
Dolton village[15]	24 766	ʹ25 990
East Hazel Crest village[15]	1 362	1 885
Glenwood village (pt.)	969	452
Harvey city (pt.)[15]	34 123	33 466
Hazel Crest village (pt.)	3 275	3 393
Homewood village (pt.)[15]	5 735	6 175
Lansing village[15]	23 573	22 916
Markham city (pt.)	5 480	5 173
Phoenix village	2 850	3 596
Posen village (pt.)	292	315
Riverdale village[15]	10 588	12 707
South Holland village[15]	24 977	23 931
Thornton village[15]	3 022	3 714
Wheeling township	129 853	119 218
Arlington Heights village (pt.)[15]	54 926	ʹ56 200
Buffalo Grove village (pt.)[15]	13 144	ʹ10 500
Des Plaines city[15]	639	586
Mount Prospect village (pt.)[15]	22 366	11 740
Northbrook village (pt.)[15]	34	...
Prospect Heights city (pt.)[15]	11 799	...
Rolling Meadows city (pt.)[15]	11	...
Wheeling village (pt.)[15]	23 242	ʹ13 243
Worth township[15]	158 157	155 834
Alsip village[15]	17 134	ʹ11 608
Blue Island city (pt.)[15]	9 266	ʹ10 246
Bridgeview village (pt.)	2 298	2 801
Chicago Ridge village[15]	13 473	9 187
Crestwood village (pt.)[15]	4 615	3 159
Evergreen Park village	22 260	ʹ25 921
Hometown city	5 324	6 729
Merrionette Park village	2 054	2 303
Oak Lawn village[15]	60 590	60 305
Palos Heights city (pt.)[15]	5 399	ʹ4 604
Robbins village (pt.)[15]	2 323	1 314
Worth village (pt.)[15]	8 620	9 328
Crawford County[16]	20 818	19 824
Honey Creek township	1 476	1 365
Flat Rock village (pt.)	405	425
Hutsonville township	1 438	1 195
Hutsonville village	705	544
Lamotte township	2 579	2 500
Palestine village[16]	1 718	1 640
Licking township	401	392
Martin township	669	685
Montgomery township	791	758
Flat Rock village (pt.)	88	79
Oblong township	3 222	3 124
Oblong village	1 840	1 860
Stoy village	167	199
Prairie township	782	678
Robinson township	9 349	9 026
Robinson city[16]	7 285	7 178
Southwest township	111	101
Cumberland County[17]	11 062	9 772
Cottonwood township	556	564
Crooked Creek township	545	505
Greenup township	2 587	2 412

County Subdivisions	1980	1970
Cumberland County—Con.		
Greenup township—Con.		
Greenup village[17]	1 655	1 618
Neoga township	2 958	2 308
Neoga city[17]	1 736	1 270
Spring Point township	1 092	956
Montrose village (pt.)[17]	–	(NA)
Sumpter township	1 970	1 745
Toledo village[17]	1 284	1 068
Union township	771	742
Casey city (pt.)[17]	19	...
Woodbury township	583	540
Jewett village	230	211
De Kalb County[18]	74 624	71 654
Afton township	605	708
Clinton township	1 451	1 591
Waterman village[18]	943	990
Cortland township	4 297	3 037
Cortland town[18]	1 019	541
De Kalb city (pt.)	–	
Maple Park village (pt.)[18]	–	
Sycamore city (pt.)[18]	2 306	1 387
De Kalb township	36 375	35 976
De Kalb city (pt.)[18]	33 099	32 949
Sycamore city (pt.)[18]	1 115	260
Franklin township	1 891	1 950
Kirkland village[18]	1 155	1 138
Genoa township	4 195	3 797
Genoa city (pt.)	3 276	3 003
Kingston township	1 809	1 347
Genoa city (pt.)[18]	–	
Kingston village[18]	618	481
Malta township	1 484	1 532
Malta village[18]	995	961
Mayfield township	769	766
Milan township	413	461
Paw Paw township	398	481
Pierce township	512	622
Sandwich township	5 739	ʹ5 250
Sandwich city (pt.)[18]	5 241	ʹ4 992
Shabbona township	1 372	1 354
Lee village (pt.)	145	121
Shabbona village[18]	851	730
Somonauk township	1 610	ʹ1 448
Sandwich city (pt.)[18]	–	ʹ54
Somonauk village[18]	1 107	1 012
South Grove township	532	605
Squaw Grove township	2 175	1 770
Hinckley village[18]	1 447	1 053
Sycamore township	8 549	8 522
Sycamore city (pt.)[18]	5 798	6 196
Victor township	448	437
De Witt County[19]	18 108	16 975
Barnett township	571	500
Clintonia township	8 524	8 089
Clinton city (pt.)[19]	7 830	7 570
Creek township	489	529
De Witt township	469	461
De Witt village	232	199
Harp township	270	440
Nixon township	720	774
Weldon village	531	553
Rutledge township	229	229
Santa Anna township	2 706	2 552
Farmer City city[19]	2 252	2 217
Texas township	1 012	589
Clinton city (pt.)[19]	ʹ84	ʹ11
Tunbridge township	872	856
Kenney village[19]	443	367
Wapella township	1 165	902
Wapella village	768	572
Waynesville township	884	802
Waynesville village[19]	569	522
Wilson township	197	252
Douglas County[20]	19 774	18 997
Arcola township	3 219	2 820
Arcola city[20]	2 714	2 276
Bourbon township	3 043	2 883
Arthur village (pt.)[20]	1 332	1 529
Bowdre township	872	968
Hindsboro village	407	418
Camargo township	3 591	3 333
Camargo village	428	241
Villa Grove city[20]	2 707	2 605
Garrett township	1 519	1 439
Atwood village (pt.)[20]	632	519
Garrett village	205	224
Murdock township	383	435
Newman township	1 391	1 353
Newman city[20]	1 079	1 018
Sargent township	399	371
Tuscola township	5 357	5 395
Tuscola city[20]	3 839	3 917

County Subdivisions	1980	1970
Du Page County[21]	658 835	'487 966
Addison township[21]	82 937	'72 542
Addison village (pt.)[21]	26 504	24 373
Bensenville village (pt.)[21]	16 121	'12 954
Elk Grove Village village (pt.)	–	11
Elmhurst city (pt.)[21]	11 582	'9 664
Itasca village (pt.)[21]	5 605	4 527
Lombard village (pt.)[21]	531	8
Villa Park village (pt.)[21]	534	271
Wood Dale city[21]	11 251	8 831
Bloomingdale township[21]	79 571	36 654
Addison village (pt.)[21]	3 255	109
Bloomingdale village[21]	12 659	2 974
Carol Stream village (pt.)[21]	7 806	3 485
Glendale Heights village (pt.)[21]	22 602	11 404
Hanover Park village (pt.)[21]	5 272	...
Itasca village (pt.)[21]	1 524	111
Roselle village (pt.)[21]	14 551	'6 141
Schaumburg village (pt.)[21]	17	'...
Chicago city (pt.)[21]	11	
Downers Grove township	122 865	'94 268
Burr Ridge village (pt.)[21]	2 285	842
Clarendon Hills village[21]	6 870	6 750
Darien city[21]	14 536	'7 789
Downers Grove village (pt.)[21]	34 740	'27 559
Hinsdale village (pt.)[21]	13 781	13 627
Oak Brook village (pt.)	84	'46
Westmont village (pt.)[21]	15 885	'8 832
Willowbrook village[21]	4 953	'1 457
Woodridge village (pt.)[21]	1 918	...
Lisle township	82 575	'47 818
Bolingbrook village (pt.)[21]	1 154	'8
Downers Grove village (pt.)[21]	4 760	'3 565
Lisle village (pt.)[21]	13 625	5 329
Naperville city (pt.)[21]	26 221	'13 651
Woodridge village (pt.)[21]	20 404	11 028
Milton township	97 167	'75 872
Carol Stream village (pt.)[21]	5 038	949
Downers Grove village (pt.)[21]	–	6
Glendale Heights village (pt.)[21]	561	2
Glen Ellyn village (pt.)[21]	23 103	21 551
Lisle village (pt.)[21]	–	...
Lombard village (pt.)[21]	608	'358
Naperville city (pt.)[21]	18	...
Wheaton city (pt.)[21]	43 043	31 138
Winfield village (pt.)[21]	1 048	1 000
Naperville township	21 053	13 028
Aurora city (pt.)[21]	1 657	...
Naperville city (pt.)[21]	15 190	'9 143
Warrenville city (pt.)[21]	384	'302
Wayne township	23 246	'5 492
Bartlett village (pt.)[21]	8 549	991
Carol Stream village (pt.)[21]	2 628	–
Hanover Park village (pt.)[21]	5 420	'...
St. Charles city (pt.)	21	'17
Wayne village (pt.)[21]	460	461
West Chicago city (pt.)[21]	880	28
Winfield township	28 940	23 001
Aurora city (pt.)[21]	26	...
Batavia city (pt.)[21]	–	...
Naperville city (pt.)	–	
Warrenville city (pt.)[21]	7 135	'2 979
West Chicago city (pt.)[21]	11 670	'9 960
Wheaton city (pt.)[21]	–	'...
Winfield village (pt.)[21]	3 374	3 285
York township	120 470	'119 291
Downers Grove village (pt.)[21]	3 072	1 414
Elmhurst city (pt.)[21]	32 694	'36 728
Glen Ellyn village (pt.)[21]	546	358
Hinsdale village (pt.)[21]	531	32
Lombard village (pt.)[21]	36 156	'33 677
Oak Brook village (pt.)[21]	6 557	4 118
Oakbrook Terrace city[21]	2 285	1 126
Villa Park village (pt.)[21]	22 651	25 620
Westmont village (pt.)[21]	833	...
Edgar County[22]	21 725	21 591
Brouillets Creek township	307	343
Buck township	293	394
Redmon village (pt.)	106	137
Edgar township	630	644
Elbridge township	733	689
Vermilion village (pt.)	23	19
Embarrass township	943	921
Brocton village	393	349
Redmon village (pt.)	118	114
Grandview township	650	667
Hunter township	330	376
Kansas township	1 097	1 098
Kansas village	791	779
Paris township	11 354	11 306
Paris city[22]	9 885	9 971
Prairie township	392	395
Ross township	1 747	1 576
Chrisman city[22]	1 413	1 285
Shiloh township	356	465
Hume village (pt.)[22]	21	19
Stratton township	671	699
Vermilion village (pt.)	276	314
Symmes township	1 206	860

County Subdivisions	1980	1970
Edgar County—Con.		
Young America township	1 016	1 158
Hume village (pt.)[22]	462	477
Metcalf village	278	269
Edwards County[23]	7 961	7 090
Albion precinct	2 921	2 543
Albion city[23]	2 285	1 791
Bone Gap precinct	559	521
Bone Gap village	350	308
Browns precinct	426	419
Browns village	213	198
Dixon precinct	262	222
Ellery precinct	182	171
French Creek precinct	1 361	1 186
Grayville city (pt.)[23]	1 064	799
Salem precinct	1 614	1 405
West Salem village	1 145	979
Shelby precinct	636	623
Effingham County[24]	30 944	24 608
Banner township	543	490
Shumway village	278	235
Bishop township	1 190	1 043
Dieterich village[24]	633	532
Douglas township	12 156	10 904
Effingham city (pt.)[24]	10 904	9 458
Jackson township	951	629
Liberty township	874	745
Beecher City village	492	466
Lucas township	517	507
Mason township	1 524	1 322
Edgewood village	574	495
Mason village	480	415
Moccasin township	496	435
Mound township	3 504	2 599
Altamont city[24]	2 389	1 929
St. Francis township	1 200	993
Montrose village (pt.)	321	312
Teutopolis village (pt.)	54	48
Summit township	2 289	1 030
Teutopolis township	2 276	1 798
Teutopolis village (pt.)[24]	1 360	1 201
Union township	588	431
Watson township	2 360	1 258
Effingham city (pt.)[24]	366	...
Watson village[24]	551	276
West township	476	424
Fayette County[25]	22 167	20 752
Avena township	2 335	2 292
St. Elmo city[25]	1 611	1 676
Bear Grove township	653	590
Bowling Green township	467	308
Carson township	208	183
Hurricane township	229	213
Kaskaskia township	676	588
La Clede township	1 055	1 103
Farina village[25]	594	634
Lone Grove township	752	871
St. Peter village[25]	372	380
Loudon township	871	758
Otego township	1 435	1 254
Brownstown village (pt.)[25]	696	674
Pope township	233	213
Ramsey township	1 918	1 899
Ramsey village	1 058	830
Sefton township	645	661
Brownstown village (pt.)	12	15
Seminary township	616	449
Shafter township	549	399
Sharon township	1 527	1 270
South Hurricane township	409	404
Bingham village	128	84
Vandalia township	6 636	6 469
Vandalia city[25]	5 338	5 160
Wheatland township	513	402
Wilberton township	440	426
Ford County[26]	15 265	16 382
Brenton township	1 073	1 124
Piper City village (pt.)[26]	849	817
Button township	335	385
Dix township	792	898
Elliott village[26]	370	365
Drummer township	4 071	4 580
Gibson city[26]	3 498	3 454
Lyman township	688	838
Roberts village	422	506
Mona township	479	510
Kempton village (pt.)[26]	192	201
Patton township	5 327	5 410
Paxton city[26]	4 258	4 373
Peach Orchard township	700	720
Melvin village[26]	519	492
Pella township	285	341
Piper City village (pt.)[26]	56	'25
Rogers township	569	457
Cabery village (pt.)	219	216
Kempton village (pt.)[26]	73	62

County Subdivisions

County Subdivisions	1980	1970
Ford County—Con.		
Sullivant township	692	827
Sibley village[26]	370	381
Wall township	254	292
Franklin County[27]	43 201	38 329
Barren township	503	332
Sesser city (pt.)[27]	4	...
Benton township	9 754	8 254
Benton city (pt.)[27]	7 716	6 474
Hanaford village[27]	328	289
Browning township	2 446	2 461
Benton city (pt.)[27]	62	359
Buckner village	520	489
Urbain village	28	49
Valier village (pt.)	186	122
West City village[27]	886	637
Cave township	1 587	1 096
Thompsonville village	610	449
Denning township	5 728	5 187
Freeman Spur village (pt.)	178	171
Orient city	480	502
West Frankfort city (pt.)[27]	3 355	3 230
Eastern township	602	468
Ewing township	1 350	964
Ewing village	321	220
Frankfort township	8 018	7 046
West Frankfort city (pt.)[27]	6 082	5 624
Goode township	3 063	2 714
Sesser city (pt.)[27]	2 234	2 125
Northern township	433	407
Macedonia village (pt.)	23	24
Six Mile township	4 088	3 957
Royalton village[27]	1 320	1 166
Zeigler city[27]	1 858	1 940
Tyrone township	5 629	5 443
Christopher city[27]	3 086	2 910
North City village	404	356
Valier village (pt.)	543	506
Fulton County[28]	43 687	41 900
Astoria township	1 844	1 738
Astoria town[28]	1 370	1 281
Banner township	580	694
Banner village	224	235
Bernadotte township	409	383
Buckheart township	1 885	1 770
Bryant village	333	326
Canton city (pt.)[28]	61	33
Dunfermline village	313	282
St. David village	786	773
Canton township	16 065	15 764
Canton city (pt.)[28]	14 565	14 184
Norris village (pt.)	126	145
Cass township	863	819
Smithfield village	340	318
Deerfield township	448	424
Ellisville township	309	230
Ellisville village	168	137
Fairview township	864	923
Fairview village	594	601
Farmers township	520	498
Table Grove village (pt.)[28]	345	330
Farmington township	4 184	3 998
Farmington city[28]	3 118	2 959
Norris village (pt.)	150	214
Harris township	545	520
Marietta village	192	169
Isabel township	299	300
Joshua township	601	641
Kerton township	176	178
Lee township	393	404
Lewistown township	3 547	3 252
Lewistown city[28]	2 758	2 706
Liverpool township	924	844
Liverpool village[28]	243	218
Orion township	1 313	898
Pleasant township	1 038	1 018
Ipava village[28]	661	608
Putman township	2 479	2 115
Cuba city[28]	1 648	1 581
Union township	1 332	1 387
Avon village	1 019	1 013
Vermont township	1 276	1 399
Table Grove village (pt.)[28]	144	139
Vermont village[28]	885	947
Waterford township	316	238
Woodland township	603	596
Young Hickory township	874	869
London Mills village (pt.)	569	585
Gallatin County[29]	7 590	7 418
Asbury township	174	164
Bowlesville township	211	222
Eagle Creek township	191	169
Equality township	1 137	977
Equality village	831	732
Gold Hill township	2 301	2 250
Junction village	192	199
Shawneetown city (pt.)[29]	1 760	1 739

County Subdivisions	1980	1970
Gallatin County—Con.		
New Haven township	654	707
New Haven village[29]	559	606
North Fork township	633	577
Ridgway village (pt.)[29]	348	243
Omaha township	504	540
Omaha village	295	304
Ridgway township	1 239	1 369
Ridgway village (pt.)[29]	897	917
Shawnee township	546	443
Old Shawneetown village	396	342
Shawneetown city (pt.)	81	3
Greene County[30]	16 661	17 014
Athensville township	445	388
Bluffdale township	742	757
Eldred village[30]	286	292
Carrollton township	3 375	3 394
Carrollton city[30]	2 816	2 866
Kane township	1 124	1 127
Kane village	445	432
Linder township	339	395
Patterson township	919	905
Hillview village	328	322
Wilmington village	185	141
Rockbridge township	1 833	1 861
Greenfield city[30]	1 090	1 179
Rockbridge village	258	256
Roodhouse township	2 827	2 894
Roodhouse city[30]	2 364	2 357
Rubicon township	414	422
Walkerville township	285	332
White Hall township	3 425	3 515
White Hall city	2 935	2 979
Woodville township	522	619
Wrights township	411	405
Grundy County[31]	30 582	26 535
Aux Sable township	2 767	2 401
Minooka village (pt.)[31]	1 427	768
Braceville township	3 637	3 540
Braceville village	721	668
Coal City village (pt.)[31]	1 865	2 034
Diamond village (pt.)[31]	158	169
Godley village (pt.)	51	47
Erienna township	609	330
Morris city (pt.)[31]	439	83
Seneca village (pt.)[31]	–	...
Felix township	3 721	2 192
Carbon Hill village	406	317
Coal City village (pt.)	1 163	1 006
Diamond village (pt.)[31]	1 012	283
Eileen village	569	371
Garfield township	1 520	1 409
Gardner village (pt.)[31]	1 314	1 212
Goodfarm township	408	447
Dwight village (pt.)[31]	29	...
Goose Lake township	1 236	439
Greenfield township	1 030	1 011
East Brooklyn village[31]	84	72
Gardner village (pt.)[31]	8	...
South Wilmington village	747	725
Highland township	431	529
Kinsman village	153	153
Maine township	216	196
Mazon township	1 406	1 284
Mazon village[31]	828	727
Morris township	7 337	7 529
Morris city (pt.)[31]	7 298	7 461
Nettle Creek township	366	391
Norman township	200	181
Saratoga township	2 695	1 965
Morris city (pt.)[31]	1 096	650
Vienna township	613	653
Verona village[31]	251	220
Wauponsee township	2 390	2 038
Morris city (pt.)	–	...
Hamilton County[32]	9 172	8 665
Beaver Creek township	346	380
Crook township	429	451
Crouch township	482	537
Belle Prairie City town	58	52
Dahlgren township	1 178	1 153
Dahlgren village	508	487
Flannigan township	254	250
Knight Prairie township	498	476
Macedonia village (pt.)	47	62
McLeansboro township	4 022	3 677
McLeansboro city[32]	2 960	2 630
Mayberry township	585	584
Broughton village	263	235
South Crouch township	328	232
South Flannigan township	158	129
South Twigg township	200	197
Twigg township	692	599

Population of County Subdivisions

County Subdivisions	1980	1970
Hancock County[33]	23 877	'23 664
Appanoose township	730	734
Augusta township	997	1 112
Augusta village	764	824
Bear Creek township	454	'516
Basco village	155	'193
Carthage township	3 495	3 890
Carthage city[33]	2 978	3 350
Chili township	773	779
Bowen village	525	489
Dallas City township	1 395	1 297
Dallas City city (pt.)	1 107	1 006
Durham township	420	453
Fountain Green township	414	444
Hancock township	302	303
Harmony township	485	576
Bently town	49	94
La Harpe township	1 821	1 701
La Harpe city	1 471	1 240
Montebello township	4 141	3 379
Elvaston village (pt.)	10	16
Hamilton city[33]	3 509	2 764
Nauvoo township	1 260	1 036
Nauvoo city (pt.)	1 101	1 018
Pilot Grove township	397	468
Pontoosuc township	556	428
Pontoosuc village	261	226
Prairie township	536	582
Elvaston village (pt.)	221	222
Ferris village (pt.)	—	—
Rock Creek township	525	610
Ferris village (pt.)	202	200
Rocky Run township	241	260
St. Albans township	575	575
West Point village	223	237
St. Mary township	902	1 050
Plymouth village[33]	649	740
Sonora township	626	576
Nauvoo city (pt.)	32	29
Walker township	481	565
Warsaw township	1 842	1 758
Warsaw city	1 842	1 758
Wilcox township	195	201
Wythe township	314	371
Hardin County	5 383	4 914
Battery Rock precinct	257	235
Cave-In-Rock precinct	1 036	875
Cave-In-Rock village	468	503
East Monroe precinct	306	311
East Rosiclare precinct	963	964
Rosiclare city (pt.)	941	964
McFarlan precinct	635	559
Elizabethtown village	478	436
Peters Creek precinct	298	248
Rock Creek precinct	275	257
Stone Church precinct	641	636
West Monroe precinct	398	304
West Rosiclare precinct	574	525
Rosiclare city (pt.)	500	457
Henderson County[34]	9 114	8 451
Bald Bluff township	434	437
Biggsville township	702	718
Biggsville village[34]	411	391
Carman township	473	325
Gulf Port village (pt.)	1	20
Gladstone township	1 423	1 149
Gladstone village	354	344
Gulf Port village (pt.)[34]	223	200
Lomax township	1 142	1 099
Dallas City city (pt.)	301	278
Lomax village	601	565
Media township	557	582
Media village	179	180
Stronghurst village (pt.)	123	110
Oquawka township	2 095	1 677
Oquawka village	1 533	1 352
Raritan township	403	484
Raritan village	177	206
Rozetta township	365	393
Stronghurst township	1 147	1 140
Stronghurst village (pt.)	742	726
Terre Haute township	373	447
Henry County[35]	57 968	53 217
Alba township	321	382
Andover township	1 180	982
Andover village	612	420
Annawan township	1 334	1 267
Annawan town	908	787
Atkinson township	1 603	1 476
Atkinson town (pt.)	1 135	1 053
Burns township	467	514
Cambridge township	2 926	2 596
Cambridge village[35]	2 217	2 095
Clover township	1 195	1 284
Woodhull village (pt.)	826	898

County Subdivisions	1980	1970
Henry County—Con.		
Colona township	7 616	6 027
Cleveland village (pt.)	23	261
Coal Valley village (pt.)[35]	30	...
Colona village[35]	2 172	1 293
Green Rock city[35]	3 324	2 744
Cornwall township	362	429
Atkinson town (pt.)[35]	3	...
Edford township	811	586
Galva township	3 683	3 562
Galva city[35]	3 185	3 061
Geneseo township	7 357	6 603
Geneseo city[35]	6 373	5 840
Hanna township	2 402	912
Cleveland village (pt.)	315	6
Kewanee township	11 951	12 949
Kewanee city (pt.)[35]	10 521	11 617
Loraine township	428	460
Lynn township	837	802
Munson township	626	665
Osco township	601	661
Oxford township	1 397	1 274
Alpha village[35]	815	771
Woodhull village (pt.)[35]	75	'7
Phenix township	1 704	951
Weller township	630	653
Bishop Hill village	166	191
Western township	3 411	2 686
Orion village[35]	2 013	1 801
Wethersfield township	4 484	4 805
Kewanee city (pt.)[35]	3 987	4 145
Yorktown township	642	691
Hooppole village	235	227
Iroquois County[36]	32 976	33 532
Artesia township	1 068	1 298
Buckley village[36]	604	680
Ash Grove township	853	959
Ashkum township	1 535	1 445
Ashkum village[36]	735	590
Beaver township	581	668
Donovan village[36]	301	343
Beaverville township	764	893
Beaverville village	377	442
Belmont township	2 682	2 729
Watseka city (pt.)[36]	1 571	1 650
Woodland village	333	350
Chebanse township	3 298	3 034
Chebanse village (pt.)[36]	730	756
Clifton village	1 390	1 339
Concord township	594	655
Iroquois village	227	226
Crescent township	714	672
Crescent City village (pt.)[36]	300	233
Danforth township	959	887
Danforth village[36]	554	404
Douglas township	2 334	2 207
Gilman city[36]	1 913	1 786
Fountain Creek township	481	565
Iroquois township	706	749
Crescent City village (pt.)[36]	341	364
Loda township	1 306	1 101
Loda village	486	525
Lovejoy township	629	747
Wellington village[36]	370	410
Martinton township	1 111	1 002
Martinton village	363	278
Middleport township	4 645	4 303
Watseka city (pt.)[36]	3 972	3 644
Milford township	2 192	2 214
Milford village[36]	1 716	1 656
Milks Grove township	305	405
Onarga township	1 661	1 929
Onarga village (pt.)[36]	1 269	1 436
Papineau township	585	605
Papineau village	179	219
Pigeon Grove township	1 212	1 177
Cissna Park village[36]	825	773
Prairie Green township	310	338
Ridgeland township	463	508
Onarga village (pt.)[36]	—	...
Thawville village	275	271
Sheldon township	1 542	1 869
Sheldon village	1 215	1 455
Stockland township	446	573
Jackson County[37]	61 522	55 008
Bradley township	1 808	1 562
Ava city	811	728
Campbell Hill village[37]	389	300
Carbondale township	31 670	30 029
Carbondale city[37]	26 287	22 816
Degognia township	218	220
De Soto township	2 011	1 273
De Soto city[37]	1 589	966
Elk township	2 003	1 742
Dowell village[37]	480	423
Elkville village[37]	973	850

County Subdivisions

County Subdivisions	1980	1970
Jackson County—Con.		
Fountain Bluff township	380	415
Grand Tower township	897	893
Grand Tower city[37]	748	664
Kinkaid township	340	232
Levan township	533	352
Makanda township	3 391	1 765
Makanda village[37]	402	176
Murphysboro township	11 712	11 258
Murphysboro city (pt.)	8 430	9 004
Ora township	434	436
Pomona township	634	574
Sand Ridge township	968	766
Gorham village	381	361
Somerset township	3 796	2 788
Murphysboro city (pt.)[37]	1 436	1 009
Vergennes township	727	703
Vergennes village[37]	360	323
Jasper County[38]	11 318	10 741
Crooked Creek township	914	895
Hidalgo village	161	171
Rose Hill village	121	103
Fox township	680	662
Grandville township	440	430
Yale village	129	108
Grove township	641	678
Hunt City township	418	411
North Muddy township	827	812
Wheeler village	166	173
Ste. Marie township	789	836
Ste. Marie village	312	335
Smallwood township	495	505
South Muddy township	337	419
Wade township	4 919	4 246
Newton city[38]	3 186	3 024
Willow Hill township	858	847
Willow Hill village	292	296
Jefferson County[39]	36 552	'31 848
Bald Hill township	769	654
Waltonville village (pt.)	216	190
Blissville township	356	354
Waltonville village (pt.)	3	5
Casner township	799	618
Woodlawn village (pt.)	165	104
Dodds township	2 564	1 581
Mount Vernon city (pt.)[39]	665	...
Elk Prairie township	838	716
Nason city	272	186
Waltonville village (pt.)	138	118
Farrington township	536	491
Field township	1 146	689
Grand Prairie township	738	692
McClellan township	1 105	830
Waltonville village (pt.)	57	68
Moores Prairie township	316	271
Mount Vernon township	16 282	'17 007
Mount Vernon city (pt.)[39]	12 878	'13 821
Pendleton township	1 064	778
Belle Rive village	401	279
Rome township	1 312	915
Dix village[39]	319	167
Shiloh township	5 366	3 619
Mount Vernon city (pt.)[39]	3 650	2 449
Woodlawn village (pt.)	306	204
Spring Garden township	1 430	1 152
Bonnie village	452	314
Ina village	460	333
Webber township	1 931	1 481
Bluford village[39]	728	465
Jersey County[40]	20 538	18 492
Elsah township	2 570	1 964
Elsah village[40]	990	'928
English township	461	532
Fidelity township	600	633
Fidelity village	98	132
Jersey township	8 835	8 452
Jerseyville city[40]	7 506	7 446
Mississippi township	1 609	1 323
Otter Creek township	728	667
Otterville town	146	142
Piasa township	2 737	2 010
Brighton village (pt.)	359	306
Quarry township	1 427	1 419
Grafton city[40]	1 024	1 018
Richwood township	711	621
Fieldon village	299	257
Rosedale township	510	549
Ruyle township	350	322
Jo Daviess County[41]	23 520	21 766
Apple River township	649	666
Apple River village	472	482
Berreman township	182	209
Council Hill township	202	192
Derinda township	368	376
Dunleith township	4 883	3 393
East Dubuque city	2 194	2 408
East Galena township	1 070	1 078

County Subdivisions	1980	1970
Jo Daviess County—Con.		
East Galena township—Con.		
Galena city (pt.)[41]	559	628
Elizabeth township	1 171	1 150
Elizabeth village (pt.)[41]	741	707
Guilford township	369	334
Hanover township	1 537	1 699
Hanover village	1 069	1 243
Menominee township	1 071	795
Menominee village[41]	231	217
Nora township	493	544
Nora village	185	175
Pleasant Valley township	352	422
Rawlins township	310	215
Rice township	256	231
Rush township	487	492
Scales Mound township	606	640
Scales Mound village	347	382
Stockton township	2 471	2 505
Stockton village[41]	1 872	1 930
Thompson township	464	380
Vinegar Hill township	249	228
Wards Grove township	299	277
Warren township	1 853	1 830
Warren village[41]	1 595	1 523
West Galena township	3 505	3 451
Galena city (pt.)	3 317	3 302
Woodbine township	673	659
Elizabeth village (pt.)[41]	31	...
Johnson County[42]	9 624	7 550
Bloomfield precinct	658	'467
Vienna city (pt.)[42]	17	...
Burnside precinct	538	...
New Burnside village	276	249
Cache precinct	1 043	1 026
Belknap village	172	193
Cypress village	271	261
Elvira precinct	749	604
Buncombe village	231	187
Goreville No. 1 precinct	1 043	...
Goreville village (pt.)	697	(NA)
Goreville No. 2 precinct	819	...
Goreville village (pt.)	281	(NA)
Grantsburg No. 1 precinct	927	'572
Grantsburg No. 2 precinct	242	...
Ozark precinct	454	...
Simpson precinct	543	429
Simpson village	67	82
Tunnel Hill precinct	733	304
Vienna No. 1 precinct	1 148	1 829
Vienna city (pt.)[42]	1 022	(NA)
Vienna No. 2 precinct	727	...
Vienna city (pt.)	381	(NA)
Kane County[43]	278 405	251 005
Aurora township	99 162	95 176
Aurora city (pt.)[43]	79 260	'74 389
Montgomery village (pt.)[43]	3 329	3 258
North Aurora village (pt.)[43]	3 236	3 194
Batavia township	16 200	'13 384
Aurora city (pt.)[43]	4	...
Batavia city (pt.)[43]	11 201	'8 305
North Aurora village (pt.)[43]	1 969	1 639
Big Rock township	1 924	1 349
Blackberry township	3 121	2 450
Elburn village (pt.)[43]	1 068	1 043
Burlington township	1 422	1 233
Burlington village	442	456
Campton township	5 928	2 152
Elburn village (pt.)[43]	156	79
Dundee township	35 662	34 575
Algonquin village (pt.)[43]	258	...
Barrington Hills village (pt.)[43]	105	91
Carpentersville village[43]	23 272	24 059
East Dundee village[43]	2 618	2 920
Elgin city (pt.)[43]	544	–
Gilberts village (pt.)[43]	–	...
Sleepy Hollow village[43]	2 000	1 729
West Dundee village[43]	3 551	3 295
Elgin township	61 576	58 972
Elgin city (pt.)[43]	52 234	50 344
South Elgin village (pt.)[43]	5 747	4 083
Geneva township	12 371	'10 721
Batavia city (pt.)[43]	1 373	755
Geneva city[43]	9 881	'9 049
St. Charles city (pt.)[43]	–	...
Hampshire township	2 991	2 517
Hampshire village	1 735	1 611
Kaneville township	1 259	870
Plato township	2 143	1 307
Pingree Grove village (pt.)	77	75
Rutland township	1 850	1 264
Gilberts village (pt.)[43]	405	336
Pingree Grove village (pt.)	106	99
St. Charles township	27 319	20 352
St. Charles city (pt.)[43]	17 471	12 928
South Elgin village (pt.)[43]	471	206
Valley View village[43]	2 112	1 723

County Subdivisions

County Subdivisions	1980	1970
Kane County—Con.		
St. Charles township—Con.		
Wayne village (pt.)[43]	480	111
Sugar Grove township	3 588	2 974
Aurora city (pt.)[43]	346	–
Sugar Grove village[43]	1 366	1 230
Virgil township	1 889	1 709
Maple Park village (pt.)[43]	637	660
Kankakee County[44]	102 926	97 250
Aroma township	6 107	5 847
Aroma Park village[44]	673	896
Kankakee city (pt.)	882	819
Bourbonnais township	29 316	20 987
Bourbonnais village[44]	13 280	5 909
Bradley village[44]	11 008	9 881
Kankakee city (pt.)[44]	552	761
Essex township[44]	995	802
Essex village	463	364
Ganeer township	3 490	3 404
Momence city (pt.)[44]	1 609	1 437
Kankakee township	31 081	33 819
Kankakee city (pt.)[44]	28 707	29 364
Limestone township	4 627	4 092
Kankakee city (pt.)[44]	—	r—
Manteno township	4 951	8 159
Manteno village[44]	3 155	2 864
Momence township	4 383	3 545
Momence city (pt.)[44]	1 688	1 399
Norton township	1 239	1 130
Buckingham village	330	198
Cabery village (pt.)	108	71
Reddick village (pt.)	203	214
Union Hill village[44]	82	r85
Otto township	2 714	2 649
Chebanse village (pt.)[44]	461	429
Irwin village[44]	112	87
Pembroke township	4 693	4 351
Pembroke village[44]	673	...
Pilot township[44]	1 868	1 665
Herscher village[44]	1 214	988
Rockville township	612	696
St. Anne township	2 547	2 408
St. Anne village[44]	1 421	1 271
Salina township[44]	1 218	1 004
Bonfield village[44]	294	241
Sumner township	815	772
Yellowhead township	2 270	1 920
Grant Park village[44]	1 038	r914
Kendall County[45]	37 202	26 374
Big Grove township	1 448	1 271
Lisbon village (pt.)	144	148
Newark village	798	590
Bristol township	5 209	3 521
Yorkville city (pt.)[45]	1 802	674
Fox township	1 056	1 166
Millington village (pt.)	219	209
Kendall township	3 321	2 381
Yorkville city (pt.)[45]	1 620	1 375
Lisbon township	759	789
Lisbon village (pt.)	115	113
Little Rock township	6 945	5 988
Plano city[45]	4 875	4 664
Sandwich city (pt.)	3	10
Naausay township	906	514
Oswego township	16 772	10 143
Boulder Hill (CDP)	9 333	...
Montgomery village (pt.)[45]	40	20
Oswego village[45]	3 021	1 862
Seward township	786	601
Knox County[46]	61 607	r60 939
Cedar township	4 098	3 824
Abingdon city (pt.)[46]	2 708	2 584
Chestnut township	438	476
London Mills village (pt.)	18	25
Copley township	441	r469
Victoria village (pt.)	143	r142
Elba township	373	409
Galesburg township	666	1 240
Galesburg City township	35 305	36 290
Galesburg city[46]	35 305	36 290
Haw Creek township	608	666
Henderson township[46]	1 914	1 681
Henderson village[46]	369	210
Indian Point township	2 204	2 079
Abingdon city (pt.)[46]	1 502	1 352
St. Augustine village	204	204
Knox township[46]	5 942	4 682
East Galesburg village[46]	928	706
Knoxville city[46]	3 432	2 930
Lynn township	433	436
Maquon township	705	780
Maquon village[46]	350	374
Ontario township	1 129	1 149
Oneida city[46]	765	728
Orange township	702	596
Persifer township	822	600
Rio township	693	631

County Subdivisions	1980	1970
Knox County—Con.		
Rio township—Con.		
Rio village	282	186
Salem township	1 268	1 277
Yates City village[46]	860	840
Sparta township	1 441	1 047
Wataga village[46]	996	570
Truro township	972	1 001
Williamsfield village[46]	585	552
Victoria township	482	619
Victoria village[46]	246	299
Walnut Grove township	971	987
Altona village[46]	610	542
Lake County[47]	440 372	382 638
Antioch township	15 118	11 639
Antioch village[47]	4 419	3 189
Channel Lake (CDP)	1 613	...
Fox Lake village (pt.)[47]	753	...
Grass Lake (CDP)	2 066	...
Lake Catherine (CDP)	1 335	1 219
Avon township	29 938	19 953
Grayslake village (pt.)[47]	5 260	4 907
Hainesville village	187	142
Long Lake (CDP) (pt.)	1 202	...
Round Lake village (pt.)[47]	2 642	1 531
Round Lake Beach village[47]	12 921	5 717
Round Lake Heights village[47]	1 192	1 144
Round Lake Park village (pt.)[47]	3 981	3 148
Third Lake village (pt.)[47]	185	199
Benton township[47]	14 538	13 598
Waukegan city (pt.)[47]	990	730
Winthrop Harbor village[47]	5 438	4 794
Cuba township	11 826	9 097
Barrington village (pt.)[47]	2 376	2 205
Barrington Hills village (pt.)[47]	524	368
Deer Park village (pt.)	14	4
Lake Barrington village (pt.)[47]	2 320	347
North Barrington village (pt.)[47]	1 470	1 411
Tower Lakes village[47]	1 177	r932
Deerfield township	35 220	37 190
Deerfield village (pt.)	1 213	1 390
Highland Park city (pt.)[47]	26 784	29 003
Highwood city	5 452	4 973
Lake Forest city (pt.)[47]	1 771	1 813
Ela township	19 969	12 208
Barrington village (pt.)[47]	1 698	1 245
Deer Park village (pt.)[47]	1 354	r722
Forest Lake (CDP)	1 148	...
Hawthorn Woods village (pt.)[47]	1 653	939
Kildeer village[47]	1 609	643
Lake Zurich village[47]	8 225	4 082
Long Grove village (pt.)[47]	1 329	866
North Barrington village (pt.)[47]	5	...
Fremont township	12 234	12 186
Grayslake village (pt.)[47]	—	...
Hawthorn Woods village (pt.)[47]	5	...
Libertyville village (pt.)	1	...
Mundelein village (pt.)[47]	7 984	8 167
Round Lake Park village (pt.)[47]	51	...
Wauconda village (pt.)[47]	30	...
Grant township	12 868	11 007
Fox Lake village (pt.)[47]	5 871	4 511
Ingleside (CDP)	1 676	1 621
Long Lake (CDP) (pt.)	999	...
Round Lake village (pt.)[47]	2	...
Lake Villa township	16 114	11 593
Fox Lake Hills (CDP)	2 199	1 869
Grass Lake (CDP) (pt.)	125	...
Lake Villa village[47]	1 462	1 090
Lindenhurst village[47]	6 220	3 141
Venetian Village (CDP)	2 817	2 554
Libertyville township	34 071	25 577
Green Oaks village[47]	1 415	659
Libertyville village (pt.)[47]	16 519	11 684
Mettawa village (pt.)[47]	192	182
Mundelein village (pt.)[47]	8 114	7 954
Vernon Hills village (pt.)[47]	2 608	...
Waukegan city (pt.)[47]	34	...
Newport township	3 042	2 660
Old Mill Creek village[47]	84	164
Wadsworth village[47]	961	756
Shields township	45 132	55 093
Lake Bluff village[47]	4 434	r5 008
Lake Forest city (pt.)	8 092	8 817
North Chicago city (pt.)[47]	30 583	39 675
Vernon township	32 285	12 835
Arlington Heights village (pt.)	—	—
Bannockburn village[47]		
Buffalo Grove village (pt.)[47]	9 086	1 833
Indian Creek village	236	270
Lake Forest city (pt.)	588	559
Lincolnshire village (pt.)[47]	4 151	2 531
Long Grove village (pt.)[47]	684	330
Mettawa village (pt.)	138	103
Mundelein village (pt.)[47]	955	7
Riverwoods village (pt.)[47]	2 123	1 442
Vernon Hills village (pt.)[47]	7 219	1 056
Wheeling village (pt.)[47]	24	r—
Warren township	22 591	16 291

County Subdivisions

County Subdivisions	1980	1970
Lake County—Con.		
Warren township—Con.		
Gages Lake (CDP)	3 814	...
Gurnee village (pt.)[47]	7 165	2 738
North Chicago city (pt.)[47]	–	...
Park City city (pt.)[47]	2 270	1 469
Third Lake village (pt.)[47]	37	...
Wadsworth village (pt.)[47]	143	...
Waukegan city (pt.)[47]	1 311	16
Wildwood (CDP)	2 034	...
Wauconda township	11 708	10 494
Island Lake village (pt.)[47]	1 569	1 395
Lake Barrington village (pt.)	–	–
Wauconda village (pt.)[47]	5 658	5 460
Waukegan township	78 471	76 680
Gurnee village (pt.)[47]	14	...
North Chicago city (pt.)[47]	8 191	7 600
Park City city (pt.)[47]	1 403	ʳ1 437
Waukegan city (pt.)[47]	65 318	ʳ64 388
West Deerfield township	27 386	27 269
Bannockburn village (pt.)[47]	1 316	ʳ1 359
Deerfield village (pt.)[47]	16 217	ʳ17 477
Highland Park city (pt.)[47]	3 827	3 260
Lake Forest city (pt.)	4 794	4 453
Lincolnshire village (pt.)[47]	–	...
Riverwoods village (pt.)[47]	681	129
Zion township	17 861	17 268
Zion city[47]	17 861	17 268
La Salle County[48]	112 033	111 409
Adams township	1 296	1 291
Leland village	775	743
Allen township	748	940
Ransom village	456	440
Brookfield township	797	600
Bruce township	15 639	16 747
Streator city (pt.)[48]	13 291	14 237
Dayton township	1 287	1 098
Ottawa city (pt.)[48]	279	52
Deer Park township	616	505
Dimmick township	654	668
La Salle city (pt.)[48]	6	...
Peru city (pt.)[48]	11	...
Eagle township	2 095	2 082
Kangley village	280	290
Streator city (pt.)[48]	903	893
Earl township	2 233	2 217
Earlville city[48]	1 382	1 410
Eden township	1 579	1 651
Cedar Point village	344	304
Tonica village	695	821
Fall River township	776	558
Farm Ridge township	1 097	1 138
Grand Ridge village	684	698
Freedom township	652	684
Grand Rapids township	400	335
Groveland township	978	896
Dana village	243	173
Rutland village	487	437
Hope township	818	818
Lostant village[48]	539	465
La Salle township	15 276	15 929
La Salle city (pt.)[48]	10 341	10 736
Oglesby city[48]	3 979	4 175
Manlius township	5 630	4 883
Marseilles city (pt.)[48]	2 921	2 494
Seneca village (pt.)[48]	2 098	1 781
Mendota township	7 372	7 323
Mendota city (pt.)[48]	6 640	6 606
Meriden township	385	417
Miller township	569	574
Mission township	2 431	1 618
Millington village (pt.)[48]	220	129
Sheridan village	719	724
Northville township	2 614	1 031
Somonauk village (pt.)[48]	237	100
Ophir township	659	616
Osage township	410	491
Ottawa township	13 301	14 834
Naplate village	581	686
Ottawa city (pt.)[48]	11 112	12 759
Otter Creek township	3 346	3 003
Streator city (pt.)[48]	520	427
Peru township	11 432	12 189
Dalzell village (pt.)[48]	145	...
La Salle city (pt.)[48]	–	(NA)
Peru city (pt.)[48]	10 875	11 772
Richland township	545	595
Leonore village	196	196
Rutland township	3 546	3 491
Marseilles city (pt.)[48]	1 845	1 826
Ottawa city (pt.)[48]	–	...
Serena township	862	1 140
South Ottawa township	7 698	7 067
Ottawa city (pt.)[48]	6 775	5 905
Troy Grove township	1 345	1 220
Mendota city (pt.)[48]	494	296
Troy Grove village	297	281

County Subdivisions

County Subdivisions	1980	1970
La Salle County—Con.		
Utica township	1 601	1 370
North Utica village	1 067	974
Vermillion township	351	346
Wallace township	420	479
Waltham township	575	565
Lawrence County[49]	17 807	17 522
Allison township	381	355
Bond township	951	933
Birds village	193	215
Bridgeport township	2 799	2 738
Bridgeport city[49]	2 281	2 262
Christy township	1 914	1 805
Sumner city	1 238	1 201
Denison township	2 054	1 973
St. Francisville city	1 040	997
Lawrence township	7 830	7 734
Lawrenceville city	5 652	5 863
Lukin township	466	485
Petty township	839	931
Russell township	573	568
Russellville village	171	174
Lee County[50]	36 328	37 947
Alto township	599	671
Steward village[50]	298	308
Amboy township	3 080	2 917
Amboy city[50]	2 377	2 184
Ashton township	1 375	1 321
Ashton village[50]	1 140	1 112
Bradford township	387	430
Brooklyn township	1 024	1 140
Compton village	376	399
West Brooklyn village	210	225
China township	1 466	1 404
Franklin Grove village[50]	965	968
Dixon township	17 903	19 894
Dixon city (pt.)[50]	15 682	18 147
East Grove township	330	380
Hamilton township	269	362
Harmon township	588	621
Harmon village[50]	193	205
Lee Center township	561	700
Marion township	396	382
May township	350	353
Nachusa township	619	560
Nelson township	884	763
Nelson village	215	263
Palmyra township	2 275	1 587
Reynolds township	359	375
South Dixon township	970	1 109
Dixon city (pt.)[50]	19	–
Sublette township	839	797
Sublette village[50]	442	361
Viola township	304	325
Willow Creek township	554	574
Lee village (pt.)[50]	159	131
Wyoming township	1 196	1 282
Paw Paw village[50]	839	846
Livingston County[51]	41 381	40 690
Amity township	1 039	985
Cornell village	603	532
Avoca township	388	417
Belle Prairie township	190	288
Broughton township	368	410
Campus village (pt.)	49	60
Emington village (pt.)	83	63
Charlotte township	209	283
Chatsworth township	1 431	1 534
Chatsworth town	1 187	1 255
Dwight township	4 830	4 420
Dwight village (pt.)[51]	4 117	3 841
Eppards Point township	539	612
Esmen township	424	481
Fayette township	335	388
Strawn village	143	144
Forrest township	1 756	1 721
Forrest village[51]	1 246	1 219
Germanville township	137	185
Indian Grove township	4 045	3 989
Fairbury city[51]	3 544	3 359
Long Point township	652	720
Long Point village	313	310
Nebraska township	1 343	1 477
Flanagan village[51]	978	ʳ976
Nevada township	316	358
Newtown township	897	1 001
Odell township	1 366	1 417
Odell village[51]	1 083	1 076
Owego township	386	342
Pike township	320	392
Pleasant Ridge township	386	414
Pontiac township	13 083	12 014
Pontiac city[51]	11 227	ʳ10 595
Reading township	3 039	2 975
South Streator (CDP)	2 334	1 869
Streator city (pt.)[51]	77	43

County Subdivisions	1980	1970
Livingston County—Con.		
Rooks Creek township	580	504
Round Grove township	597	568
Campus village (pt.)[51]	175	157
Reddick village (pt.)	40	33
Saunemin township	799	798
Saunemin village[51]	463	415
Sullivan township	877	862
Cullom village[51]	608	572
Sunbury township	332	391
Union township	302	351
Emington village (pt.)	36	38
Waldo township	415	393
Logan County[52]	31 802	33 538
Aetna township	579	624
Atlanta township	2 048	1 909
Atlanta city	1 807	1 640
Broadwell township	1 359	2 035
Broadwell village	183	159
Chester township	773	590
Lincoln city (pt.)[52]	—	—
Corwin township	747	951
Middletown village	503	626
East Lincoln township	9 302	9 306
Lincoln city (pt.)[52]	8 547	8 556
Elkhart township	703	805
Elkhart village (pt.)[52]	289	266
Eminence township	618	595
Hurlbut township	389	411
Elkhart village (pt.)[52]	204	169
Laenna township	870	740
Latham village[52]	564	361
Lake Fork township	187	202
Mount Pulaski township	2 404	2 376
Mount Pulaski city[52]	1 783	1 677
Oran township	508	535
Orvil township	1 294	1 320
Emden village[52]	527	552
Hartsburg village	379	363
Prairie Creek township	641	619
San Jose village (pt.)[52]	268	175
Sheridan township	592	706
New Holland village	295	321
West Lincoln township	8 788	9 814
Lincoln city (pt.)[52]	7 780	9 026
McDonough County[53]	37 467	36 653
Bethel township	363	372
Blandinsville township	1 149	1 209
Blandinsville village (pt.)[53]	832	874
Bushnell township	4 015	3 930
Bushnell city[53]	3 811	3 703
Chalmers township[53]	806	768
Colchester township	2 218	2 215
Colchester city	1 729	1 747
Eldorado township	326	361
Emmet township[53]	2 108	821
Hire township	369	442
Blandinsville village (pt.)	54	48
Industry township	984	982
Industry village	600	558
Lamoine township	334	365
Macomb township[53]	867	1 110
Bardolph village (pt.)	288	322
Macomb City township	19 863	19 643
Macomb city[53]	19 863	19 643
Mound township	396	430
Bardolph village (pt.)	6	9
New Salem township	530	609
Prairie City township	738	804
Prairie City village[53]	580	630
Sciota township	720	859
Good Hope village (pt.)[53]	304	325
Sciota village	81	101
Scotland township[53]	648	593
Tennessee township	465	534
Tennessee village	175	179
Walnut Grove township	568	606
Good Hope village (pt.)[53]	153	152
McHenry County[54]	147 897	111 555
Alden township	1 304	929
Algonquin township	44 287	31 948
Algonquin village (pt.)[54]	5 576	3 515
Barrington Hills village (pt.)	1 022	550
Cary village[54]	6 640	4 358
Crystal Lake city (pt.)[54]	13 168	9 792
Fox River Grove village[54]	2 515	2 245
Fox River Valley Gardens village (pt.)[54]	194	164
Lake in the Hills village[54]	5 651	3 240
Lakewood village (pt.)	228	231
Oakwood Hills village (pt.)	46	54
Burton township	1 768	1 072
Fox Lake village (pt.)[54]	207	...
Spring Grove village[54]	281	259
Chemung township	5 884	6 014
Harvard city (pt.)[54]	4 615	4 812
Coral township	2 303	1 576
Union village[54]	622	579

County Subdivisions	1980	1970
McHenry County—Con.		
Dorr township	12 199	10 765
Bull Valley village (pt.)[54]	265	...
Crystal Lake city (pt.)[54]	85	106
Woodstock city (pt.)[54]	9 122	8 315
Dunham township	1 755	1 536
Harvard city (pt.)[54]	511	365
Grafton township	6 837	5 018
Crystal Lake city (pt.)[54]	1 654	1 212
Huntley village[54]	1 646	1 432
Lakewood village (pt.)[54]	1 026	551
Greenwood township	6 965	4 777
Bull Valley village (pt.)[54]	148	...
Sunrise Ridge village[54]	752	...
Wonder Lake (CDP) (pt.)	1 726	1 541
Woodstock city (pt.)[54]	2 550	1 909
Hartland township	1 523	1 083
Hebron township	1 780	1 515
Hebron village[54]	786	781
McHenry township	31 611	22 989
Bull Valley village (pt.)[54]		
Lakemoor village (pt.)	458	475
McCullom Lake village	947	873
McHenry city (pt.)[54]	10 901	6 762
Pistakee Highlands (CDP)	3 623	...
Sunnyside village[54]	1 432	367
Wonder Lake (CDP) (pt.)	4 191	3 265
Marengo township	5 319	4 926
Marengo city (pt.)[54]	4 156	4 054
Nunda township	18 102	12 873
Bull Valley village (pt.)[54]	96	...
Crystal Lake city (pt.)[54]	3 683	3 431
Fox River Valley Gardens village (pt.)[54]	326	264
Holiday Hills village[54]	802	...
Island Lake village (pt.)[54]	724	578
Lakemoor village (pt.)	265	322
McHenry city (pt.)[54]	7	10
McHenry Shores village[54]	1 041	...
Oakwood Hills village (pt.)[54]	1 209	422
Prairie Grove village[54]	680	...
Richmond township	2 839	2 316
Richmond village[54]	1 068	1 153
Spring Grove village (pt.)[54]	290	89
Riley township	1 356	1 030
Marengo city (pt.)[54]	205	181
Seneca township	2 065	1 188
Marengo city (pt.)[54]	—	...
Woodstock city (pt.)[54]	53	2
McLean County[55]	119 149	104 389
Allin township	1 057	1 053
Stanford village[55]	720	657
Anchor township	441	528
Anchor village	192	200
Arrowsmith township	566	646
Arrowsmith village[55]	292	305
Bellflower township	794	952
Bellflower village[55]	421	400
Bloomington township[55]	4 939	4 896
Bloomington City township	44 189	39 992
Bloomington city[55]	44 189	39 992
Blue Mound township	616	685
Cooksville village[55]	259	241
Cheney's Grove township[55]	1 223	1 192
Saybrook village[55]	882	814
Chenoa township	2 368	2 440
Chenoa city[55]	1 847	1 860
Cropsey township	288	341
Dale township	1 018	953
Danvers township	1 595	1 486
Danvers village[55]	921	854
Dawson township	688	756
Ellsworth village	244	259
Downs township	1 014	1 170
Downs village (pt.)[55]	551	637
Dry Grove township	1 501	993
Empire township	3 473	2 957
Le Roy city[55]	2 870	2 435
Funks Grove township	358	425
Gridley township	1 805	1 628
Gridley village[55]	1 246	1 007
Hudson township	1 766	1 619
Hudson village	929	802
Lawndale township	273	357
Lexington township	2 441	2 206
Lexington city[55]	1 806	1 615
Martin township	1 180	1 287
Colfax village[55]	920	935
Money Creek township	780	780
Mount Hope township	1 170	1 276
McLean village[55]	836	820
Normal township[55]	36 163	27 532
Normal town[55]	35 672	26 396
Oldtown township	1 570	960
Downs village (pt.)[55]	10	14
Randolph township	3 010	2 700
Heyworth village[55]	1 598	1 441
Towanda township	1 375	1 031
Towanda village	630	578

County Subdivisions

County Subdivisions	1980	1970
McLean County—Con.		
West township	318	424
White Oak township	761	647
Carlock village	410	373
Yates township	409	477
Macon County[56]	131 375	125 010
Austin township	300	320
Blue Mound township	1 040	1 036
Decatur township	71 849	77 546
Decatur city (pt.)[56]	70 183	75 044
Friends Creek township	1 554	1 600
Argenta village[56]	994	1 034
Harristown township	2 209	2 209
Decatur city (pt.)[56]	–	...
Harristown village[56]	1 456	⌐1 253
Hickory Point township	16 596	12 303
Decatur city (pt.)[56]	11 893	7 393
Forsyth village[56]	1 072	⌐585
Illini township	1 656	1 162
Warrensburg village[56]	1 372	⌐811
Long Creek township	11 957	9 951
Decatur city (pt.)[56]	7 829	5 458
Maroa township	2 116	1 959
Maroa city[56]	1 760	1 467
Milam township	138	163
Mount Zion township	6 097	3 531
Mount Zion village[56]	4 563	2 343
Niantic township	1 019	988
Niantic village	761	705
Oakley township	1 023	869
Decatur city (pt.)	19	8
Pleasant View township	1 656	1 552
Blue Mound village[56]	1 338	1 181
South Macon township	1 697	1 713
Macon city	1 300	1 249
South Wheatland township	5 219	4 810
Decatur city (pt.)[56]	1 469	1 498
Whitmore township	5 249	3 298
Decatur city (pt.)[56]	2 688	996
Oreana village[56]	999	1 092
Macoupin County[57]	49 384	44 557
Barr township	437	466
Hettick village (pt.)	114	118
Bird township	363	347
Brighton township	3 830	2 694
Brighton village[57]	2 005	1 583
Brushy Mound township	544	478
Bunker Hill township	3 114	2 647
Bunker Hill city[57]	1 700	1 465
Cahokia township	3 515	3 148
Benld city (pt.)	1 638	1 736
Eagarville village[57]	148	116
East Gillespie village (pt.)	104	112
Gillespie city (pt.)[57]	665	625
Carlinville township	6 714	6 724
Carlinville city[57]	5 439	5 675
Chesterfield township	1 095	1 029
Chesterfield village	280	262
Medora village (pt.)	376	349
Dorchester township	1 551	1 312
Dorchester village (pt.)	78	74
Wilsonville village	608	691
Gillespie township	4 111	3 849
Benld city (pt.)	–	–
Dorchester village (pt.)	77	96
East Gillespie village (pt.)	93	75
Gillespie city (pt.)[57]	3 075	2 832
Mount Clare village	300	298
Girard township	2 557	2 206
Girard city[57]	2 246	1 881
Hillyard township	892	653
Royal Lakes village[57]	270	...
Honey Point township	308	308
Mount Olive township	3 561	3 361
Mount Olive city[57]	2 357	2 288
Sawyerville village	381	315
White City village[57]	214	196
Nilwood township	781	719
Nilwood town (pt.)	269	245
Standard City village (pt.)	116	101
North Otter township	852	493
North Palmyra township	1 060	961
Modesto village	260	221
Palmyra village (pt.)	382	362
Polk township	441	327
Scottville township	490	473
Scottville village	214	196
Shaws Point township	529	524
Standard City village (pt.)	32	38
Shipman township	1 437	1 370
Medora village (pt.)	156	156
Shipman town[57]	581	482
South Otter township	510	475
Nilwood town (pt.)	9	–
South Palmyra township	957	932
Hettick village (pt.)	148	140
Palmyra village (pt.)	482	414
Staunton township	5 223	5 036

County Subdivisions	1980	1970
Macoupin County—Con.		
Staunton township—Con.		
Staunton city[57]	4 744	4 396
Virden township	4 225	3 744
Virden city (pt.)[57]	3 885	3 504
Western Mound township	287	281
Madison County[58]	247 691	⌐250 911
Alhambra township	1 322	1 152
Alhambra village[58]	643	594
Alton township	34 171	39 700
Alton city[58]	34 171	39 700
Chouteau township[58]	8 627	8 521
Hartford village (pt.)[58]	1 054	1 198
Pontoon Beach village (pt.)[58]	89	–
Roxana village (pt.)	–	...
South Roxana village[58]	2 286	⌐2 241
Collinsville township	27 158	⌐26 373
Collinsville city (pt.)[58]	17 599	⌐17 794
Glen Carbon village (pt.)[58]	69	49
Maryville village[58]	1 937	⌐1 067
Edwardsville township	23 249	18 166
Edwardsville city (pt.)[58]	12 251	11 070
Glen Carbon village (pt.)[58]	5 128	1 848
Fort Russell township	5 912	5 487
Bethalto village (pt.)[58]	2 391	2 417
Meadowbrook (CDP)	1 082	1 295
Foster township[58]	3 502	2 760
Godfrey township[58]	15 860	16 168
Granite City township[58]	36 815	⌐40 685
Granite City city[58]	36 815	⌐40 685
Hamel township	1 744	1 470
Hamel village[58]	537	454
Helvetia township	6 898	5 902
Highland city[58]	5 616	4 871
Jarvis township	6 322	3 957
Troy city[58]	3 772	2 144
Leef township	524	486
Grantfork village (pt.)[58]	130	99
Marine township	1 871	1 475
Marine village	957	882
Moro township	2 135	1 704
Nameoki township[58]	13 606	⌐13 872
Collinsville city (pt.)[58]	20	...
Madison city (pt.)	409	577
Pontoon Beach village (pt.)[58]	3 247	2 448
New Douglas township	632	627
New Douglas village	389	378
Olive township	1 950	1 855
Livingston village[58]	949	916
Williamson village	319	324
Omphghent township	1 964	1 939
Worden village	953	1 091
Pin Oak township	1 593	1 366
Edwardsville city (pt.)[58]	229	...
St. Jacob township	1 735	1 394
St. Jacob village[58]	792	659
Saline township	2 979	2 448
Grantfork village (pt.)	138	63
Highland city (pt.)[58]	1 506	1 110
Pierron village (pt.)	53	35
Venice township[58]	9 122	12 925
Madison city (pt.)	5 506	6 465
Venice city	3 480	4 680
Wood River township[58]	38 000	40 479
Bethalto village (pt.)[58]	6 239	4 657
East Alton village[58]	7 123	7 309
Forest Homes (CDP)	1 701	1 998
Hartford village (pt.)	833	1 045
Rosewood Heights (CDP)	5 085	3 391
Roxana village (pt.)	1 587	1 882
Wood River city[58]	12 449	13 186
Marion County[59]	43 523	38 986
Alma township	893	775
Alma village	428	369
Carrigan township	442	394
Centralia township	17 954	17 560
Central City village[59]	1 505	1 377
Centralia city (pt.)[59]	12 353	13 351
Walnut Hill village	223	149
Wamac city (pt.)[59]	767	714
Foster township	350	315
Haines township	843	744
Kell village	283	173
Iuka township	884	827
Iuka village	353	343
Kinmundy township	1 379	1 139
Kinmundy city	945	759
Meacham township	421	420
Odin township	1 839	1 677
Odin village	1 285	1 263
Omega township	497	413
Patoka township	1 187	1 116
Patoka village[59]	662	562
Vernon village	199	203
Raccoon township	1 384	969
Romine township	489	450
Salem township	10 055	8 111

Population of County Subdivisions

County Subdivisions	1980	1970
Marion County—Con.		
Salem township—Con.		
Salem city (pt.)[59]	7 741	6 187
Sandoval township	2 861	2 529
Junction City village	456	305
Sandoval village[59]	1 734	1 332
Stevenson township	1 089	809
Tonti township	956	738
Salem city (pt.)[59]	72	–
Marshall County[60]	14 479	13 302
Bell Plain township	510	553
La Rose village	173	165
Bennington township	1 876	1 811
Toluca city (pt.)[60]	1 471	1 319
Evans township	1 376	1 508
Toluca city (pt.)[60]	–	...
Wenona city[60]	1 025	1 054
Henry township	3 242	2 917
Henry city[60]	2 740	2 610
Hopewell township	586	440
Lacon township	2 691	2 351
Lacon city[60]	2 135	2 147
La Prairie township	471	524
Richland township	553	528
Washburn village (pt.)[60]	84	94
Roberts township	961	727
Varna village[60]	441	417
Saratoga township	419	462
Steuben township	1 357	1 054
Sparland village[60]	624	585
Whitefield township	437	427
Mason County[61]	19 492	'16 180
Allen Grove township	859	825
San Jose village (pt.)	516	506
Bath township	1 076	947
Bath village[61]	475	422
Crane Creek township	219	230
Forest City township	828	602
Forest City village	298	301
Havana township	6 660	5 630
Havana city[61]	4 277	4 376
Kilbourne township	732	733
Kilbourne village	382	441
Lynchburg township	378	285
Manito township	3 099	1 946
Manito village[61]	1 869	1 334
Mason City township	3 003	2 999
Mason City city[61]	2 719	2 611
Pennsylvania township	322	306
Quiver township	1 342	'605
Topeka town	140	'74
Salt Creek township	281	373
Sherman township	693	699
Easton village[61]	392	386
Massac County[62]	14 990	13 889
Adkins precinct[62]	510	...
Metropolis city (pt.)[62]	510	(NA)
Benton precinct	481	490
East Brooklyn precinct	1 267	1 130
Brookport city (pt.)[62]	955	858
Franklin precinct[62]	1 234	...
Metropolis city (pt.)[62]	1 234	(NA)
Georges Creek precinct	311	291
Grant precinct	1 430	1 192
Hillerman precinct[62]	1 237	...
Joppa village	535	531
Jackson precinct	641	571
Jefferson precinct	1 586	723
Metropolis city (pt.)[62]	932	...
Lincoln precinct	889	844
Metropolis city (pt.)	889	844
Logan precinct	322	279
Metropolis No. 1 precinct	1 064	1 136
Metropolis city (pt.)	1 064	1 136
Metropolis No. 2 precinct	591	665
Metropolis city (pt.)	591	665
Metropolis No. 3 precinct	1 039	1 205
Metropolis city (pt.)	1 039	1 205
Metropolis No. 4 precinct	912	974
Metropolis city (pt.)	912	974
Washington precinct	802	551
West Brooklyn precinct	674	615
Brookport city (pt.)	173	188
Metropolis city (pt.)[62]	–	...
Menard County[63]	11 700	9 685
Athens precinct	2 385	1 699
Athens city[63]	1 371	1 158
Atterberry precinct	253	278
Fancy Prairie precinct	214	251
Greenview precinct	1 073	942
Greenview village[63]	830	740
Indian Creek precinct	286	258
Irish Grove precinct	243	267
Oakford precinct	524	410
Oakford village[63]	351	272
Petersburg precinct	4 616	3 896

County Subdivisions	1980	1970
Menard County—Con.		
Petersburg precinct—Con.		
Petersburg city	2 419	2 632
Rock Creek precinct	609	275
Sandridge precinct	193	206
Sugar Grove precinct	335	313
Tallula precinct	969	890
Tallula village	681	643
Mercer County[64]	19 286	17 294
Abington township	533	555
Seaton village	255	251
Duncan township	365	408
Eliza township	480	506
Greene township	1 944	1 717
Viola village[64]	1 144	946
Keithsburg township	1 058	952
Keithsburg city	936	836
Mercer township	4 458	3 957
Aledo city[64]	3 881	3 325
Millersburg township	972	1 005
Joy village	506	513
New Boston township	1 319	1 206
New Boston city	731	706
North Henderson township	595	594
Alexis village (pt.)[64]	43	24
North Henderson village[64]	234	246
Ohio Grove township	364	488
Perryton township	560	635
Reynolds village (pt.)[64]	22	17
Preemption township	1 997	1 562
Matherville village[64]	793	699
Reynolds village (pt.)[64]	13	10
Richland Grove township	2 410	1 674
Sherrard village	811	808
Rivoli township	1 350	1 188
Windsor village[64]	863	723
Suez township	881	847
Alexis village (pt.)[64]	407	384
Monroe County[65]	20 117	18 831
Precinct 1	531	...
Hecker village	531	380
Precinct 2	1 027	...
Columbia city (pt.)	1 027	(NA)
Precinct 3	820	...
Columbia city (pt.)	820	(NA)
Precinct 4	1 232	...
Columbia city (pt.)	1 232	(NA)
Precinct 5	1 190	...
Columbia city (pt.)	1 190	(NA)
Precinct 6	890	...
Precinct 7[65]	644	...
Precinct 8	1 065	...
Precinct 9	882	...
Precinct 10	811	...
Precinct 11	991	...
Precinct 12[65]	669	...
Precinct 13	627	...
Fults village	78	101
Maeystown village (pt.)[65]	–	(NA)
Precinct 14	371	...
Precinct 15[65]	671	...
Precinct 16	677	...
Waterloo city (pt.)	677	(NA)
Precinct 17	1 242	...
Waterloo city (pt.)	1 242	(NA)
Precinct 18	1 585	...
Waterloo city (pt.)[65]	1 585	(NA)
Precinct 19	1 142	...
Waterloo city (pt.)[65]	1 142	(NA)
Precinct 20	898	...
Valmeyer village[65]	898	733
Precinct 21	852	...
Precinct 22[65]	700	...
Precinct 23	600	...
Maeystown village (pt.)[65]	143	(NA)
Montgomery County[66]	31 686	30 260
Audubon township	718	696
Ohlman village	178	193
Bois D'Arc township	1 048	982
Farmersville village	686	495
Butler Grove township	801	684
Butler village	225	233
Hillsboro city (pt.)[66]	41	...
East Fork township	2 533	2 245
Coffeen city	842	641
Donnellson village (pt.)	106	139
Hillsboro city (pt.)[66]	77	...
Schram City village	708	657
Fillmore township	778	775
Fillmore village	350	397
Grisham township	744	754
Donnellson village (pt.)	125	160
Panama village (pt.)	243	274
Harvel township	337	359
Harvel village (pt.)	203	199
Hillsboro township	5 933	5 652
Hillsboro city (pt.)[66]	4 290	4 267

County Subdivisions	1980	1970
Montgomery County—Con.		
Hillsboro township—Con.		
Taylor Springs village[66]	671	620
Irving township	1 079	1 040
Hillsboro city (pt.)[66]	–	...
Irving village[66]	612	599
Nokomis township	3 695	3 460
Coalton village	406	304
Nokomis city[66]	2 656	2 532
Wenonah village	70	92
Witt city (pt.)[66]	9	8
North Litchfield township	5 436	5 247
Litchfield city (pt.)[66]	4 321	4 348
Pitman township	652	637
Waggoner village	277	257
Raymond township	1 295	1 233
Raymond village[66]	957	890
Rountree township	370	415
South Fillmore township	286	270
South Litchfield township	3 478	3 395
Litchfield city (pt.)[66]	2 883	2 842
Walshville township	412	485
Walshville village	106	100
Witt township	1 549	1 391
Witt city (pt.)	1 196	1 032
Zanesville township	542	540
Morgan County[67]	37 502	36 174
Alexander precinct	566	667
Arcadia precinct	305	266
Centerville precinct	144	148
Chapin precinct	948	835
Chapin village	648	552
Concord precinct	488	523
Concord village	205	207
Franklin precinct[67]	1 228	1 083
Franklin village[67]	645	565
Jacksonville precinct	25 614	25 106
Jacksonville city[67]	20 284	20 553
South Jacksonville village[67]	3 382	2 950
Literberry precinct	309	288
Lynnville precinct	528	434
Lynnville village	159	125
Markham precinct	482	255
Meredosia precinct	1 798	1 689
Meredosia village[67]	1 272	1 178
Murrayville precinct	1 144	1 005
Murrayville village	712	595
Nortonville precinct	332	346
Pisgah precinct	223	299
Prentice precinct	263	302
Sinclair precinct	239	267
Waverly precinct	1 898	1 805
Waverly city	1 537	1 442
Woodson precinct	993	856
Woodson village[67]	503	384
Moultrie County[68]	14 546	13 263
Dora township	932	855
Dalton City village	574	427
East Nelson township	1 013	'1 049
Allenville village	203	185
Jonathan Creek township	599	592
Lovington township	1 906	1 818
Lovington village[68]	1 313	1 303
Lowe township	1 590	1 483
Arthur village (pt.)[68]	790	685
Marrowbone township	1 973	1 668
Bethany village[68]	1 550	1 235
Sullivan township	5 777	'5 059
Sullivan city[68]	4 526	4 112
Whitley township	756	739
Gays village[68]	290	269
Ogle County[69]	46 338	42 867
Brookville township	317	359
Buffalo township	3 179	3 181
Polo city[69]	2 643	2 542
Byron township	3 541	2 690
Byron city[69]	2 035	1 749
Dement township	972	985
Creston village	527	595
Rochelle city (pt.)[69]	67	6
Eagle Point township	341	389
Flagg township	12 170	11 047
Hillcrest village[69]	818	630
Rochelle city (pt.)[69]	8 915	8 588
Forreston township	2 149	2 077
Forreston village[69]	1 384	1 227
Grand Detour township	781	668
Lafayette township	226	255
Leaf River township	1 420	1 404
Leaf River village	637	633
Lincoln township	558	629
Lynnville township	595	637
Marion township	2 793	2 144
Stillman Valley village (pt.)[69]	947	871
Maryland township	678	743
Adeline village	163	156

County Subdivisions	1980	1970
Ogle County—Con.		
Monroe township	1 355	1 152
Mount Morris township	4 043	4 200
Mount Morris village[69]	2 989	3 173
Nashua township	406	374
Oregon township	4 731	4 729
Oregon city[69]	3 559	3 539
Pine Creek township	732	766
Pine Rock township	1 002	937
Rockvale township	1 279	1 124
Scott township	1 414	936
Davis Junction village[69]	289	...
Stillman Valley village (pt.)[69]	14	...
Taylor township	512	244
White Rock township	769	843
Woosung township	375	354
Peoria County[70]	200 466	195 318
Akron township	986	896
Princeville village (pt.)[70]	487	349
Brimfield township	1 492	1 232
Brimfield village (pt.)[70]	836	729
Chillicothe township	9 283	8 151
Chillicothe city[70]	6 176	6 052
Rome (CDP)	2 744	1 919
Elmwood township	2 739	2 554
Elmwood city	2 117	2 014
Hallock township	1 308	1 054
Hollis township	1 985	1 481
Bartonville village (pt.)	18	27
Mapleton village[70]	255	281
Pekin city (pt.)[70]	4	4
Jubilee township	1 429	593
Brimfield village (pt.)[70]	54	...
Kickapoo township[70]	3 846	2 136
Limestone township[70]	20 925	20 321
Bartonville village (pt.)[70]	6 119	7 189
Bellevue village[70]	2 045	1 189
Norwood village	612	632
West Peoria (CDP) (pt.)	295	657
Logan township	3 389	2 635
Hanna City village[70]	1 361	1 282
Medina township[70]	5 972	4 388
Millbrook township	594	636
Peoria City township	124 160	126 963
Peoria city[70]	124 160	126 963
Princeville township	1 911	1 673
Princeville village (pt.)[70]	1 225	1 106
Radnor township	2 113	1 601
Dunlap village[70]	824	656
Richwoods township[70]	8 081	7 972
Peoria Heights village (pt.)[70]	7 453	7 943
Rosefield township	594	933
Timber township	2 731	2 509
Glasford village[70]	1 201	1 066
Kingston Mines village	340	380
Trivoli township	1 170	969
West Peoria township[70]	5 758	6 621
Bartonville village (pt.)	–	5
West Peoria (CDP) (pt.)	4 924	6 216
Perry County[71]	21 714	19 757
Beaucoup precinct	747	639
Cutler precinct	801	898
Cutler village	495	508
Du Quoin precinct	8 880	8 059
Du Quoin city[71]	6 594	6 691
St. Johns village (pt.)	284	220
Paradise precinct	391	304
Pinckneyville precinct	6 340	5 907
Pinckneyville city[71]	3 319	3 377
Sunfield precinct	865	634
St. Johns village (pt.)[71]	–	...
Swanwick precinct	830	736
Tamaroa precinct	1 898	1 691
Tamaroa village	885	799
Willisville precinct	962	889
Willisville village[71]	628	659
Piatt County[72]	16 581	15 509
Bement township	2 067	1 978
Bement village	1 770	1 638
Ivesdale village (pt.)	2	4
Blue Ridge township	1 418	1 473
Mansfield village[72]	921	870
Cerro Gordo township	2 474	2 355
Cerro Gordo village[72]	1 553	1 368
Goose Creek township	985	937
De Land village[72]	509	418
Monticello township	5 275	4 896
Monticello city[72]	4 753	4 130
Sangamon township	1 585	1 124
Unity township	1 906	1 793
Atwood village (pt.)[72]	832	745
Hammond village	556	502
Willow Branch township	871	953
Cisco village[72]	333	358

County Subdivisions

County Subdivisions	1980	1970
Pike County[73]	18 896	19 185
Atlas township	733	803
Barry township	1 931	1 891
Barry city (pt.)[73]	1 487	1 444
Chambersburg township	195	228
Cincinnati township	85	122
Derry township	296	321
El Dara village	87	82
Detroit township	441	407
Detroit village	156	124
Florence village	59	65
Fairmount township	279	300
Flint township	129	164
Valley City village	60	66
Griggsville township	1 603	1 543
Griggsville city[73]	1 301	1 245
Hadley township	304	329
Barry city (pt.)[73]	—	(NA)
Hardin township	274	288
Time village	27	39
Kinderhook township	1 084	1 191
Hull village	529	585
Kinderhook village	259	281
Levee township	181	222
Martinsburg township	397	421
Montezuma township	618	616
Milton village[73]	349	337
Newburg township	838	853
Pittsfield city (pt.)[73]	308	386
New Salem township	787	767
Baylis village	299	307
New Salem village	170	165
Pearl township	478	512
Pearl village	322	323
Perry township	806	760
Perry village[73]	487	451
Pittsfield township	4 344	4 241
Pittsfield city (pt.)[73]	3 862	3 858
Pleasant Hill township	1 467	1 463
Pleasant Hill village	1 112	1 064
Pleasant Vale township	698	812
New Canton town	420	486
Ross township	119	143
Spring Creek township	809	788
Nebo village	487	454
Pope County[74]	4 404	3 857
Eddyville No. 6 precinct	692	…
Eddyville village[74]	143	127
Golconda No. 1 precinct	590	…
Golconda No. 2 precinct	862	…
Golconda No. 3 precinct	960	…
Golconda city[74]	960	922
Jefferson No. 4 precinct	483	…
Hamletsburg village	93	79
Webster No. 5 precinct	817	…
Pulaski County[75]	8 840	8 741
America precinct	218	222
Grand Chain precinct	611	455
New Grand Chain village	232	215
Karnak precinct	798	786
Karnak village	646	641
Mound City precinct	1 124	1 222
Mound City city[75]	1 102	1 177
Mounds precinct	2 359	2 520
Mounds city	1 669	1 718
Olmsted precinct	760	794
Olmsted village	439	453
Perks precinct	309	297
Pulaski precinct	818	764
Pulaski village	477	471
Ullin precinct	969	851
Ullin village	550	546
Villa Ridge precinct	630	601
Wetaug precinct	244	229
Putnam County[76]	6 085	5 007
Granville township	3 070	2 565
Granville village	1 537	1 232
Mark village	424	379
Standard village	277	282
Hennepin township	1 166	875
Hennepin village[76]	716	535
Magnolia township	1 254	1 222
McNabb village	342	246
Magnolia village	308	328
Senachwine township	595	345
Randolph County[77]	35 652	31 379
Baldwin precinct	1 190	959
Baldwin village[77]	474	467
Blair precinct	273	278
Bremen precinct	465	446
Brewerville precinct	418	414
Central precinct	449	345
Chester precinct	9 253	8 157
Chester city[77]	8 401	5 310
Coulterville precinct	1 701	1 663
Coulterville village	1 118	1 186
Ellis Grove precinct	899	745

County Subdivisions	1980	1970
Randolph County—Con.		
Ellis Grove precinct—Con.		
Ellis Grove village[77]	296	277
Evansville precinct	1 269	1 244
Evansville village[77]	863	838
Kaskaskia precinct	150	293
Kaskaskia village	33	79
Palestine precinct	481	423
Percy precinct	1 361	1 129
Percy village[77]	1 053	967
Prairie du Rocher precinct	1 155	1 113
Prairie du Rocher village	701	658
Red Bud precinct	3 918	3 445
Red Bud city[77]	2 850	2 559
Rockwood precinct	325	234
Rockwood village	59	59
Ruma precinct	720	585
Ruma village[77]	254	154
Sparta precinct	6 343	5 371
Sparta city[77]	4 957	4 307
Steeleville precinct	2 887	2 406
Steeleville village[77]	2 240	1 957
Tilden precinct	1 289	1 154
Tilden village	1 025	909
Walsh precinct	688	577
Wine Hill precinct	418	398
Richland County[78]	17 587	16 829
Bonpas township	424	435
Claremont township	986	942
Claremont village	255	269
Decker township	426	437
Denver township	473	442
German township	471	468
Madison township	1 089	1 022
Calhoun village	267	238
Parkersburg village	268	262
Noble township	1 613	1 498
Noble village[78]	832	719
Olney township	10 702	10 581
Olney city[78]	9 026	8 974
Preston township	1 403	1 004
Rock Island County[79]	165 968	166 734
Andalusia township	2 261	1 577
Andalusia village[79]	1 238	950
Blackhawk township	12 520	9 531
Milan village (pt.)[79]	6 264	4 856
Oak Grove village (pt.)[79]	25	9
Rock Island city (pt.)[79]	2 992	1 296
Bowling township	3 655	2 893
Milan village (pt.)[79]	—	17
Oak Grove village (pt.)	670	609
Reynolds village (pt.)	—	—
Buffalo Prairie township	953	823
Canoe Creek township	962	784
Hillsdale village[79]	731	539
Coal Valley township	5 460	5 029
Coal Valley village (pt.)[79]	3 770	3 088
Moline city (pt.)[79]	11	…
Coe township	1 343	1 172
Port Byron village (pt.)[79]	—	…
Cordova township	1 050	1 003
Cordova village (pt.)	630	539
Drury township	836	816
Edgington township	1 900	1 620
Reynolds village (pt.)[79]	666	583
Hampton township	21 902	22 788
Carbon Cliff village[79]	1 578	1 369
East Moline city (pt.)[79]	4 909	5 805
Hampton village	1 873	1 612
Rapids City village (pt.)[79]	1 056	641
Silvis city[79]	7 130	5 907
Moline township	26 364	28 820
Moline city (pt.)[79]	26 151	28 789
Rock Island city (pt.)	8	31
Port Byron township	1 409	1 323
Cordova village (pt.)	67	50
Port Byron village (pt.)	1 289	1 222
Rapids City village (pt.)	2	15
Rock Island township	23 155	25 566
Moline city (pt.)	—	—
Rock Island city (pt.)	23 085	25 500
Rural township	1 276	1 143
South Moline township	39 003	37 598
East Moline city (pt.)[79]	15 998	15 151
Moline city (pt.)[79]	19 547	17 448
Rock Island city (pt.)[79]	84	—
South Rock Island township	21 111	23 480
Rock Island city (pt.)[79]	20 867	23 339
Zuma township	808	768
St. Clair County[80]	267 531	285 591
Belleville township	41 580	41 223
Belleville city[80]	41 580	41 223
Canteen township	16 593	20 521
Caseyville village (pt.)[80]	1 189	632
Fairmont City village	2 313	2 769
Fairview Heights city (pt.)[80]	1 229	…

County Subdivisions

County Subdivisions	1980	1970
St. Clair County—Con.		
Canteen township—Con.		
National City village (pt.)	−	−
Washington Park village	8 223	9 524
Caseyville township[80]	24 274	26 064
Caseyville village (pt.)[80]	3 119	2 779
Collinsville city (pt.)[80]	1 994	430
Fairview Heights city (pt.)[80]	11 185	10 050
O'Fallon city (pt.)	2 255	...
Centreville township[80]	35 568	40 500
Alorton village	2 237	3 573
Cahokia village[80]	18 904	20 649
Centreville city[80]	9 747	11 378
Sauget village[80]	205	220
East St. Louis township	55 200	70 169
East St. Louis city[80]	55 200	70 169
Englemann township	545	499
Fayetteville township	1 555	1 607
Fayetteville village[80]	385	379
St. Libory village[80]	549	448
Freeburg township	4 395	3 678
Freeburg village[80]	2 989	2 495
Lebanon township	4 179	4 244
Lebanon city (pt.)[80]	2 845	3 093
Summerfield village	487	443
Lenzburg township	888	654
Lenzburg village	435	437
New Athens village (pt.)	−	...
Marissa township	3 080	2 818
Marissa village[80]	2 568	2 004
Mascoutah township	5 698	5 967
Mascoutah city[80]	4 962	5 045
New Baden village (pt.)[80]	39	25
Scott AFB (CDP) (pt.)	−	...
Millstadt township	4 674	4 016
Millstadt village[80]	2 736	2 168
New Athens township	2 490	2 570
New Athens village (pt.)[80]	1 937	2 000
O'Fallon township	12 254	9 662
Lebanon city (pt.)[80]	400	471
O'Fallon city (pt.)[80]	9 986	7 268
Prairie Du Long township	853	838
St. Clair township[80]	21 774	18 914
Swansea village[80]	5 347	5 432
Shiloh Valley township[80]	11 245	10 767
Scott AFB (CDP) (pt.)	8 648	7 871
Shiloh village[80]	1 045	945
Smithton township	2 661	1 925
Smithton village[80]	1 447	847
Stites township	1 303	1 826
Brooklyn village	1 233	1 702
National City village (pt.)[80]	70	124
Stookey township[80]	9 726	9 955
Sugar Loaf township	6 996	7 174
Dupo village[80]	3 039	2 842
East Carondelet village[80]	628	542
Saline County[81]	28 448	25 721
Brushy township	928	870
Carriers Mills township[81]	2 950	2 582
Carriers Mills village[81]	2 268	2 013
Cottage township	243	258
East Eldorado township	7 155	6 285
Eldorado city[81]	5 198	3 876
Galatia township	1 398	1 063
Galatia village	1 042	792
Harrisburg township	12 418	11 880
Harrisburg city[81]	10 410	9 535
Muddy village[81]	88	109
Independence township	961	776
Long Branch township	256	212
Mountain township	284	239
Raleigh township	1 111	872
Raleigh village[81]	352	215
Rector township	100	147
Stonefort township	380	313
Stonefort village (pt.)	140	147
Tate township	264	224
Sangamon County[82]	176 089	161 335
Auburn township[82]	5 082	3 827
Auburn city[82]	3 616	2 594
Thayer village[82]	759	616
Virden city (pt.)[82]	14	...
Ball township[82]	3 283	1 717
Chatham village[82]	1 358	392
Buffalo Hart township	231	227
Capital township	99 637	91 753
Springfield city[82]	99 637	91 753
Cartwright township	1 414	1 511
Pleasant Plains village[82]	688	644
Chatham township	4 736	2 854
Chatham village (pt.)[82]	4 239	2 396
Clear Lake township[82]	7 587	4 593
Clear Lake village	236	228
Riverton village[82]	2 783	2 090
Spaulding village (pt.)[82]	428	220
Cooper township	748	547
Cotton Hill township	939	602
Curran township[82]	1 537	1 223

County Subdivisions

County Subdivisions	1980	1970
Sangamon County—Con.		
Divernon township	1 370	1 303
Divernon village[82]	1 081	1 010
Fancy Creek township	2 630	1 708
Cantrall village	141	138
Sherman village (pt.)	1 186	519
Gardner township[82]	3 037	1 747
Illiopolis township	1 629	1 678
Illiopolis village[82]	1 118	1 122
Island Grove township	565	542
Berlin village	210	175
Lanesville township	280	304
Loami township	1 095	798
Loami village[82]	770	537
Maxwell township	224	251
Mechanicsburg township	2 112	1 856
Buffalo village	514	462
Dawson village	532	427
Mechanicsburg village[82]	515	490
New Berlin township	1 069	1 045
New Berlin village[82]	834	754
Pawnee township	2 878	2 241
Pawnee village[82]	2 577	1 936
Rochester township[82]	4 101	2 912
Rochester village[82]	2 488	1 667
Salisbury township	591	392
Springfield township[82]	10 100	13 042
Grandview village	1 794	2 242
Sherman village (pt.)	12	−
Talkington township	319	316
Williams township	2 482	1 801
Sherman village (pt.)[82]	303	...
Spaulding village (pt.)[82]	−	...
Williamsville village[82]	996	923
Woodside township[82]	16 413	20 545
Jerome village[82]	1 374	1 673
Leland Grove city[82]	1 692	1 624
Southern View village	1 306	1 504
Schuyler County[83]	8 365	8 135
Bainbridge township	633	442
Birmingham township	210	268
Brooklyn township	272	309
Browning township	682	671
Browning village	246	276
Buena Vista township	1 479	1 474
Rushville city (pt.)[83]	1 100	1 090
Camden township	345	364
Camden village	120	121
Frederick township	248	237
Hickory township	224	228
Huntsville township	274	312
Littleton township	454	473
Littleton village	168	208
Oakland township	240	227
Rushville township	2 874	2 766
Rushville city (pt.)[83]	2 248	2 210
Woodstock township	430	364
Scott County[84]	6 142	6 096
Alsey precinct	713	...
Alsey village	318	242
Bloomfield precinct	355	...
Exeter–Bluffs precinct	955	...
Bluffs village (pt.)	561	(NA)
Exeter village	73	76
Glasgow precinct	442	...
Glasgow village	171	148
Manchester precinct	740	...
Manchester village	387	335
Merritt precinct	236	...
Naples–Bluffs precinct	509	...
Bluffs village (pt.)	260	(NA)
Naples town	128	100
Winchester No. 1 precinct	1 160	...
Winchester city (pt.)	1 014	(NA)
Winchester No. 2 precinct	432	...
Winchester city (pt.)[84]	195	(NA)
Winchester No. 3 precinct	600	...
Winchester city (pt.)[84]	507	(NA)
Shelby County[85]	23 923	22 589
Ash Grove township	519	558
Big Spring township	682	706
Clarksburg township	367	387
Cold Spring township	390	426
Dry Point township	1 130	974
Cowden village[85]	623	537
Flat Branch township	510	449
Herrick township	664	732
Herrick village	470	537
Holland township	453	412
Lakewood township	507	489
Moweaqua township	2 130	1 931
Moweaqua village (pt.)[85]	1 922	1 687
Oconee township	872	805
Oconee village	240	218
Okaw township	888	723
Findlay village (pt.)	442	422
Penn township	176	198

County Subdivisions

County Subdivisions	1980	1970
Shelby County—Con.		
Pickaway township	252	263
Prairie township	1 349	1 329
Stewardson village[85]	745	729
Strasburg village (pt.)[85]	22	...
Richland township	817	863
Strasburg village (pt.)[85]	466	456
Ridge township	542	597
Rose township	1 812	1 365
Shelbyville city (pt.)[85]	807	608
Rural township	363	384
Shelbyville township	5 152	5 075
Shelbyville city (pt.)[85]	4 452	4 279
Sigel township	781	737
Sigel town	360	337
Todds Point township	561	585
Findlay village (pt.)	426	387
Tower Hill township	1 449	1 140
Tower Hill village[85]	715	683
Windsor township	1 557	1 461
Windsor city	1 228	1 126
Stark County[86]	7 389	7 510
Elmira township	526	545
Essex township	802	901
Wyoming city (pt.)[86]	506	529
Goshen township	851	847
La Fayette village[86]	281	268
Toulon city (pt.)[86]	245	182
Osceola township	1 304	1 327
Bradford village	924	885
Penn township	391	478
Toulon township	2 632	2 444
Toulon city (pt.)[86]	1 145	1 025
Wyoming city (pt.)[86]	1 108	1 034
Valley township	493	520
West Jersey township	390	448
Stephenson County[87]	49 536	48 861
Buckeye township	1 646	1 563
Cedarville village (pt.)	506	432
Dakota township	932	876
Dakota town[87]	571	440
Erin township	524	513
Florence township[87]	1 556	1 359
Freeport township	26 406	27 736
Freeport city[87]	26 266	27 736
Harlem township[87]	2 920	2 173
Cedarville village (pt.)	183	66
Jefferson township	303	270
Kent township	799	741
Lena village (pt.)[87]	138	31
Lancaster township[87]	1 851	2 207
Cedarville village (pt.)	77	80
Loran township	1 338	1 207
Pearl City village[87]	661	535
Oneco township	1 325	1 267
Orangeville village	598	538
Ridott township	1 535	1 456
German Valley village[87]	414	206
Ridott village	194	244
Rock Grove township	957	659
Rock Run township	1 767	1 685
Davis village[87]	560	525
Rock City village[87]	293	251
Silver Creek township[87]	1 068	1 003
Waddams township	931	1 039
West Point township	2 881	2 348
Lena village (pt.)[87]	2 157	1 691
Winslow township	797	759
Winslow village	361	330
Tazewell County[88]	132 078	118 649
Boynton township	277	318
Cincinnati township	6 964	6 178
Pekin city (pt.)[88]	2 666	1 835
South Pekin village[88]	1 243	955
Deer Creek township	1 184	1 093
Deer Creek village (pt.)	683	647
Goodfield village (pt.)[88]	—	...
Delavan township	2 408	2 365
Delavan city[88]	1 973	1 844
Dillon township	980	626
Elm Grove township	2 946	2 084
Pekin city (pt.)[88]	617	75
Tremont village (pt.)	818	644
Fondulac township	13 574	13 681
East Peoria city (pt.)[88]	11 879	10 754
Peoria Heights village (pt.)	—	—
Groveland township	20 849	17 952
Creve Coeur village (pt.)[88]	6 101	5 551
East Peoria city (pt.)[88]	7 712	6 940
Marquette Heights city (pt.)	2 512	1 786
Morton village (pt.)[88]	221	303
Pekin city (pt.)[88]	784	335
Hittle township	680	728
Armington village[88]	297	368
Hopedale township	1 885	1 509
Hopedale village	913	923
Little Mackinaw township	1 689	1 453

County Subdivisions

County Subdivisions	1980	1970
Tazewell County—Con.		
Little Mackinaw township—Con.		
Minier village[88]	1 261	986
Mackinaw township	2 813	2 134
Mackinaw village[88]	1 354	1 293
Malone township	294	348
Morton township	15 725	11 815
Morton village (pt.)[88]	13 953	10 504
Pekin township	33 738	33 635
Creve Coeur village (pt.)[88]	750	889
Marquette Heights city (pt.)	874	972
North Pekin village[88]	1 824	1 886
Pekin city (pt.)[88]	29 896	29 126
Sand Prairie township	1 596	1 157
Green Valley village[88]	768	617
Spring Lake township	1 968	1 182
Tremont township	2 553	2 025
Morton village (pt.)	4	4
Tremont village (pt.)[88]	1 278	1 298
Washington township	19 955	18 366
East Peoria city (pt.)[88]	2 794	977
Morton village (pt.)[88]	—	...
Washington city[88]	10 364	6 790
Union County[89]	17 765	16 071
Alto Pass precinct	665	586
Alto Pass village	369	304
Anna District No. 1 precinct	236	...
Anna city (pt.)	—	(NA)
Anna District No. 2 precinct	1 761	...
Anna city (pt.)	1 621	(NA)
Anna District No. 3 precinct	781	...
Anna city (pt.)[89]	154	(NA)
Anna District No. 4 precinct	718	...
Anna city (pt.)[89]	256	(NA)
Anna District No. 5 precinct	1 137	...
Anna city (pt.)	1 137	(NA)
Anna District No. 6 precinct	2 264	...
Anna city (pt.)	2 235	(NA)
Balcom precinct	267	...
Cobden District No. 1 precinct	1 253	...
Cobden village (pt.)	571	(NA)
Cobden District No. 2 precinct	1 233	...
Cobden village (pt.)	639	(NA)
Dongola District No. 1 precinct	1 223	...
Dongola village (pt.)	611	(NA)
Dongola District No. 2 precinct	549	...
Dongola village (pt.)	275	(NA)
Jonesboro District No. 1 precinct	1 353	...
Anna city (pt.)	5	...
Jonesboro city (pt.)[89]	888	(NA)
Jonesboro District No. 2 precinct	1 620	...
Jonesboro city (pt.)[89]	954	(NA)
Lick Creek precinct	434	331
Mill Creek precinct	326	...
Mill Creek village	97	78
Saratoga precinct	438	360
Stokes precinct	476	355
Union District No. 2 precinct	517	...
Union District No. 1 precinct	514	...
Vermilion County[90]	95 222	97 047
Blount township	3 026	2 348
Danville city (pt.)[90]	1 041	633
Butler township	1 447	1 480
Rankin village	727	727
Carroll township	828	798
Indianola village	370	374
Catlin township	3 567	3 455
Catlin village[90]	2 226	2 093
Danville township	40 935	45 458
Belgium village (pt.)	339	315
Danville city (pt.)[90]	27 215	32 363
Hegeler (CDP)	1 853	1 595
Hillery—Batestown (CDP)	1 124	2 179
Tilton village[90]	2 405	2 544
Vermilion Heights (CDP)	1 448	...
Westville village (pt.)	266	244
Elwood township	2 012	1 848
Ridge Farm village[90]	1 096	1 015
Georgetown township	8 887	8 914
Belgium village (pt.)	229	263
Georgetown city[90]	4 220	3 984
Westville village (pt.)[90]	3 307	3 411
Grant township	7 387	7 430
Hoopeston city[90]	6 411	6 461
Rossville village (pt.)[90]	9	...
Jamaica township	281	306
Love township	333	445
McKendree township	772	718
Middlefork township	1 634	1 795
Potomac village[90]	874	909
Newell township	14 396	12 520
Danville city (pt.)[90]	10 729	9 574
Oakwood township	3 585	3 345
Fithian village	540	562
Muncie village	201	232
Oakwood village[90]	1 627	1 367
Pilot township	712	762

County Subdivisions	1980	1970
Vermilion County—Con.		
Ross township	1 649	1 784
Rossville village (pt.)	1 354	1 420
Sidell township	1 200	1 278
Allerton village (pt.)[90]	295	...
Sidell village	625	645
South Ross township	1 303	1 126
Alvin village[90]	378	318
Henning village	317	253
Vance township	1 268	1 237
Fairmount village[90]	851	785
Wabash County[91]	13 713	12 841
Bellmont precinct	820	728
Bellmont village	307	292
Coffee precinct	431	436
Keensburg village	244	242
Compton precinct	247	226
Friendsville precinct	541	478
Lancaster precinct	485	417
Lick Prairie precinct	228	245
Mount Carmel precinct	9 799	9 331
Mount Carmel city[91]	8 908	8 096
Wabash precinct	1 162	980
Allendale village[91]	613	425
Warren County[92]	21 943	21 595
Berwick township	583	559
Coldbrook township	650	703
Ellison township	470	505
Floyd township	646	598
Greenbush township	688	523
Hale township	455	382
Kelly township	580	489
Alexis village (pt.)[92]	17	7
Lenox township	418	453
Monmouth township	11 758	12 138
Monmouth city[92]	10 706	11 022
Point Pleasant township	250	356
Roseville township	1 617	1 441
Roseville village	1 254	1 111
Spring Grove township	1 312	1 128
Alexis village (pt.)[92]	609	531
Sumner township	726	729
Little York village	347	297
Swan township	431	384
Tompkins township	1 359	1 207
Kirkwood village	1 008	817
Washington County[93]	15 472	13 780
Ashley township	986	924
Ashley city	658	655
Beaucoup township	500	382
Nashville city (pt.)[93]	12	...
Bolo township	394	396
Covington township	425	440
New Minden village (pt.)	87	72
Du Bois township	830	770
Du Bois village	241	234
Radom village	174	172
Hoyleton township	1 212	1 103
Hoyleton village	542	457
New Minden village (pt.)	136	116
Irvington township	1 626	1 254
Irvington village[93]	789	489
Wamac city (pt.)	145	133
Johannisburg township	583	546
Venedy village (pt.)	2	5
Lively Grove township	741	674
Nashville township	3 697	3 508
Nashville city (pt.)[93]	3 174	3 027
Oakdale township	615	444
Oakdale village[93]	198	...
Okawville township	1 976	1 688
Addieville village (pt.)	147	140
Okawville village[93]	1 337	992
Pilot Knob township	431	348
Plum Hill township	548	487
Addieville village (pt.)	139	134
Richview township	465	408
Richview village	299	306
Venedy township	443	408
Venedy village (pt.)	145	150
Wayne County[94]	18 059	17 004
Arrington township	572	528
Sims village[94]	355	317
Barnhill township	410	411
Mill Shoals village (pt.)[94]	—	...
Bedford township	1 205	1 082
Cisne village	705	615
Berry township	413	401
Big Mound township	1 837	1 879
Fairfield city (pt.)[94]	1 127	1 256
Elm River township	351	381
Four Mile township	613	503
Keenes village	123	97
Garden Hill township	158	123
Grover township	4 654	4 300
Fairfield city (pt.)[94]	3 667	3 449

County Subdivisions	1980	1970
Wayne County—Con.		
Hickory Hill township	421	409
Indian Prairie township	555	544
Johnsonville village	71	72
Jasper township	1 510	1 568
Fairfield city (pt.)	719	964
Keith township	390	405
Lamard township	1 424	1 067
Fairfield city (pt.)[94]	441	228
Jeffersonville village[94]	340	294
Leech township	559	526
Golden Gate village[94]	126	99
Massilon township	197	242
Mount Erie township	486	495
Mount Erie village	135	149
Orchard township	584	531
Orel township	1 588	1 474
Wayne City village[94]	1 132	985
Zif township	132	135
White County[95]	17 864	17 312
Burnt Prairie township	565	542
Burnt Prairie village[95]	114	134
Carmi township	7 684	7 345
Carmi city (pt.)[95]	6 095	5 862
Emma township	575	652
Maunie village (pt.)	215	267
Enfield township	1 294	1 178
Enfield village	890	764
Gray township	1 484	1 445
Grayville city (pt.)[95]	1 249	1 236
Hawthorne township	630	651
Carmi city (pt.)	169	171
Maunie village (pt.)	10	8
Heralds Prairie township	646	586
Indian Creek township	2 502	2 196
Norris City village[95]	1 515	1 319
Mill Shoals township[95]	927	1 090
Mill Shoals village (pt.)[95]	333	292
Springerton village	154	228
Phillips township	1 557	1 627
Crossville village[95]	944	860
Phillipstown village	37	55
Whiteside County[96]	65 970	62 877
Albany township	1 254	1 119
Albany village	1 014	942
Clyde township	503	543
Coloma township	13 327	12 946
Rock Falls city[96]	10 633	10 287
Erie township	2 270	1 879
Erie village[96]	1 725	1 566
Fenton township	673	565
Fulton township	4 707	4 437
Fulton city (pt.)	3 936	3 630
Garden Plain township	1 119	978
Fulton city (pt.)[96]	—	...
Genesee township	1 005	952
Coleta village	219	208
Hahnaman township	468	454
Deer Grove village[96]	77	66
Hopkins township	2 527	2 207
Hume township	563	522
Jordan township	987	891
Lyndon township	1 254	1 140
Lyndon village[96]	777	673
Montmorency township	2 510	1 734
Mount Pleasant township	5 569	5 392
Morrison city (pt.)[96]	4 499	4 295
Newton township	545	523
Portland township	626	715
Prophetstown township	2 882	2 770
Prophetstown city[96]	2 141	1 915
Sterling township	19 827	20 087
Sterling city[96]	16 281	16 113
Tampico township	1 379	1 284
Tampico village[96]	966	838
Union Grove township	1 300	1 071
Morrison city (pt.)[96]	106	92
Ustick township	675	668
Will County[97]	324 460	247 825
Channahon township	4 420	2 712
Channahon village (pt.)[97]	2 718	1 505
Joliet city (pt.)[97]	18	...
Minooka village (pt.)[97]	138	...
Crete township	20 416	15 270
Crete village[97]	5 417	4 656
Park Forest village (pt.)[97]	941	...
Park Forest South village (pt.)[97]	129	...
Steger village (pt.)[97]	5 855	5 044
Custer township	1 101	949
Du Page township	47 088	20 037
Bolingbrook village (pt.)[97]	36 107	7 643
Naperville city (pt.)[97]	815	...
Romeoville village (pt.)[97]	9 122	9 945
Florence township	931	671
Symerton village	120	155
Wilmington city (pt.)[97]	4	...
Frankfort township	20 335	9 633

County Subdivisions

County Subdivisions	1980	1970
Will County—Con.		
Frankfort township—Con.		
Arbury Hills (CDP)	1 667	1 291
Frankfort village[97]	4 357	2 325
Mokena village[97]	4 578	1 643
Tinley Park village (pt.)	20	—
Green Garden township	1 420	791
Homer township	13 441	6 686
Lockport city (pt.)[97]	2	—
Jackson township	2 473	1 755
Elwood village	814	794
Joliet township	89 566	96 001
Crest Hill city (pt.)[97]	506	18
Joliet city (pt.)[97]	70 805	'75 022
New Lenox village (pt.)[97]	6	...
Rockdale village[97]	1 913	'2 015
Lockport township	34 641	33 354
Crest Hill city (pt.)[97]	7 524	7 391
Joliet city (pt.)	—	—
Lockport city (pt.)[97]	9 168	'9 861
Romeoville village[97]	6 397	'2 943
Manhattan township	3 386	2 374
Manhattan village[97]	1 944	1 530
Monee township	10 996	7 240
Monee village[97]	993	940
Park Forest village (pt.)[97]	2 370	2 667
Park Forest South village (pt.)[97]	6 114	1 748
New Lenox township	16 574	10 049
Joliet city (pt.)[97]	9	83
New Lenox village (pt.)[97]	5 786	2 855
Peotone township	3 319	2 914
Peotone village (pt.)[97]	2 708	2 336
Plainfield township	14 685	11 028
Crest Hill city (pt.)[97]	262	24
Joliet city (pt.)[97]	300	...
Plainfield village[97]	3 767	2 928
Reed township	3 944	2 646
Braidwood city[97]	3 429	2 323
Godley village (pt.)	322	195
Troy township	17 939	'9 895
Channahon village[97]	1 016	...
Crest Hill city (pt.)[97]	960	27
Joliet city (pt.)[97]	6 824	'3 722
Shorewood village[97]	4 714	1 749
Washington township	3 536	2 940
Beecher village[97]	2 024	1 770
Wesley township	2 397	2 331
Wheatland township	4 491	1 794
Naperville city (pt.)[97]	86	...
Will township	1 136	750
Peotone village (pt.)[97]	124	9
Wilmington township	5 538	5 296
Wilmington city (pt.)[97]	4 420	4 335
Wilton township	687	709
Williamson County[98]	56 538	49 021
Blairsville precinct	5 401	4 397
Bush village	368	357
Cambria village[98]	1 090	798
Carterville city (pt.)[98]	53	...
Colp village	278	271
Herrin city (pt.)[98]	1 114	737
Hurst city	938	934
Carterville precinct	6 634	5 536
Carterville city (pt.)[98]	3 392	3 061
Crainville village[98]	910	549
Corinth precinct	813	626
Crab Orchard precinct	1 187	986
Creal Springs precinct	2 088	1 513
Creal Springs city	845	830
East Marion precinct	7 717	6 806
Marion city (pt.)[98]	6 006	4 775
Pittsburg village (pt.)	82	62
Spillertown village	206	305
Grassy precinct	504	262
Herrin precinct	14 924	13 890
Energy village (pt.)	704	578
Freeman Spur village (pt.)	199	192
Herrin city (pt.)[98]	9 435	8 886
Johnston City city (pt.)	2 145	2 055
Whiteash village (pt.)	86	81
Lake Creek precinct	4 105	3 510
Johnston City city (pt.)	1 728	1 873
Pittsburg village (pt.)	523	447
Whiteash village (pt.)	182	100
Southern precinct	2 057	766
Stonefort precinct	901	751
Stonefort village (pt.)	176	178
West Marion precinct	10 207	9 978
Energy village (pt.)[98]	434	234
Marion city (pt.)[98]	8 025	6 949
Winnebago County[99]	250 884	246 623
Burritt township	956	800
Rockford city (pt.)[99]	—	...
Cherry Valley township	13 608	7 568
Cherry Valley village (pt.)[99]	829	942
Rockford city (pt.)[99]	4 148	2 536
Durand township	1 649	1 637
Durand village[99]	1 073	972

County Subdivisions

County Subdivisions	1980	1970
Winnebago County—Con.		
Harlem township	26 473	21 774
Loves Park city (pt.)[99]	4 339	2 766
North Park (CDP)	15 806	15 679
Rockford city (pt.)[99]	—	r—
Roscoe village (pt.)[99]	2	...
Harrison township	735	774
Laona township	825	460
Owen township	3 024	2 179
Rockford city (pt.)[99]	133	21
Pecatonica township	2 592	2 494
Pecatonica village[99]	1 732	1 781
Rockford township	178 858	191 671
Cherry Valley village (pt.)[99]	117	10
Loves Park city (pt.)[99]	8 853	9 624
Morristown village	687	669
Rockford city (pt.)[99]	135 431	144 813
Rockton township	9 163	8 554
Rockton village[99]	2 313	2 099
South Beloit city (pt.)[99]	3 346	2 916
Roscoe township	7 754	4 368
Roscoe village (pt.)[99]	1 386	'1 070
South Beloit city (pt.)[99]	742	888
Seward township	1 043	1 125
Shirland township	1 035	756
Winnebago township	3 169	2 463
Winnebago village[99]	1 644	1 285
Woodford County[100]	33 320	28 012
Cazenovia township	1 932	1 926
Washburn village (pt.)[100]	1 122	1 079
Clayton township	808	933
Benson village[100]	460	490
Minonk city (pt.)[100]	—	...
Cruger township	1 188	663
Eureka city (pt.)[100]	507	10
El Paso township	3 191	2 729
El Paso city	2 676	2 291
Kappa village	170	131
Greene township	367	451
Kansas township	329	189
Linn township	394	508
Metamora township	3 338	2 856
Metamora village[100]	2 482	2 176
Minonk township	2 406	2 616
Minonk city (pt.)[100]	2 039	2 267
Montgomery township	2 012	1 265
Congerville village	373	266
Deer Creek village (pt.)	5	—
Goodfield village (pt.)[100]	500	329
Olio township	4 416	3 897
Eureka city (pt.)[100]	3 799	3 018
Palestine township	979	984
Secor village[100]	488	508
Panola township	409	425
Panola village	31	30
Partridge township	503	434
Roanoke township	2 614	2 675
Roanoke village[100]	2 001	2 040
Spring Bay township	2 655	2 182
Bay View Gardens village	417	472
Peoria Heights village (pt.)	—	—
Spring Bay village[100]	496	427
Worth township	5 779	3 279
Germantown Hills village[100]	524	278

INDIANA

The name Indiana is of modern Latin derivation and signifies "land of Indians."

The region now constituting Indiana was first explored by La Salle in the latter part of the seventeenth century, probably about 1670, when he is said to have descended the Ohio as far as the Louisville rapids. His first well-authenticated exploration, however, took place late in 1679, when he traversed what is now the northwestern part of the state, by way of the St. Joseph and Kankakee Rivers. French trappers and fur traders also appeared at about the close of the seventeenth century. The first permanent settlement was made at Vincennes by a number of French families, probably in 1734 or 1735, although a fort and trading post had been established at this place some years earlier.

This region was in the possession of the French until the close of the French and Indian War, when, by the treaty of 1763, it was ceded to Great Britain.

In 1778, during the Revolution, Vincennes and Kaskaskia were captured from the British by a force of Virginians under George Rogers Clark, and later in the same year the region northwest of the Ohio was made the county of Illinois by the Virginia Legislature.

In 1783 the British claims to all territory east of the Mississippi and north of Florida were relinquished in favor of the United States. The states which claimed title to lands northwest of the Ohio and east of the Mississippi ceded their rights to the United States before 1787, and in that year this region was organized as the Northwest Territory.

In 1800 that part of the Northwest Territory lying between the Mississippi River and a line extending from a point on the Ohio River opposite the mouth of the Kentucky to Fort Recovery, and thence north to the Canadian line, was organized as the territory of Indiana. The new territory thus comprised nearly all of the present state of Indiana, together with the area now constituting Illinois, Wisconsin, northeastern Minnesota, and western Michigan. Two years later, by a clause in the enabling act for Ohio, the boundary between Indiana and Ohio was fixed at its present location, and by the same act the region north of Ohio was added to Indiana. In 1804, the form of territorial government was changed from the first to the second grade, thus giving Indiana a legislature and a Delegate in Congress. The organization of Michigan territory in 1805 and Illinois territory in 1809 left Indiana with its present boundaries, and in December, 1816, the state of Indiana was admitted to the Union.

COUNTY LOCATION INDEX

Adams	C-5	Harrison	G-4	Parke	D-2
Allen	B-5	Hendricks	D-3	Perry	G-3
Bartholomew	E-4	Henry	D-5	Pike	G-2
Benton	C-2	Howard	C-4	Porter	B-3
Blackford	C-5	Huntington	C-5	Posey	G-2
Boone	D-3	Jackson	F-4	Pulaski	B-3
Brown	E-4	Jasper	B-3	Putnam	E-3
Carroll	C-3	Jay	C-5	Randolph	D-5
Cass	C-4	Jefferson	F-5	Ripley	F-5
Clark	G-4	Jennings	F-4	Rush	E-5
Clay	E-3	Johnson	E-4	St. Joseph	A-4
Clinton	D-3	Knox	F-2	Scott	F-4
Crawford	G-3	Kosciusko	B-4	Shelby	E-4
Daviess	F-3	Lagrange	A-5	Spencer	G-3
Dearborn	E-5	Lake	B-2	Starke	B-3
Decatur	E-5	La Porte	B-3	Steuben	A-5
De Kalb	B-5	Lawrence	F-3	Sullivan	F-2
Delaware	D-5	Madison	D-4	Switzerland	F-5
Dubois	G-3	Marion	D-4	Tippecanoe	C-3
Elkhart	A-4	Marshall	B-4	Tipton	D-4
Fayette	E-5	Martin	F-3	Union	E-5
Floyd	G-4	Miami	C-4	Vanderburgh	G-2
Fountain	D-2	Monroe	E-3	Vermillion	D-2
Franklin	E-5	Montgomery	D-3	Vigo	E-2
Fulton	B-4	Morgan	E-3	Wabash	C-4
Gibson	G-2	Newton	B-2	Warren	C-2
Grant	C-4	Noble	B-5	Warrick	G-2
Greene	F-3	Ohio	F-5	Washington	F-4
Hamilton	D-4	Orange	F-3	Wayne	D-5
Hancock	D-4	Owen	E-3	Wells	C-5
				White	C-3
				Whitley	B-5

Indiana

Population of the State: Earliest Census to 1980

Urban and Rural

	The State			Urban				Rural			Percent of total population	
	Total population	Change from preceding census		Places of 2,500 or more	Population	Change from preceding census		Population	Change from preceding census		Urban	Rural
		Number	Percent			Number	Percent		Number	Percent		
Current urban definition:												
1980 (Apr. 1)	5 490 224	294 832	5.7	170	3 525 298	153 238	4.5	1 964 926	143 317	7.9	64.2	35.8
1970 (Apr. 1)	'5 195 392	532 894	11.4	151	3 372 060	461 911	15.9	1 821 609	69 260	4.0	64.9	35.1
1960 (Apr. 1)	4 662 498	728 274	18.5	137	2 910 149	552 953	23.5	1 752 349	175 321	11.1	62.4	37.6
1950 (Apr. 1)	3 934 224	506 428	14.8	119	2 357 196	...	...	1 577 028	...	...	59.9	40.1
Previous urban definition:												
1960 (Apr. 1)	4 662 498	728 274	18.5	133	2 650 378	432 910	19.5	2 012 120	295 364	17.2	56.8	43.2
1950 (Apr. 1)	3 934 224	506 428	14.8	116	2 217 468	329 756	17.5	1 716 756	176 672	11.5	56.4	43.6
1940 (Apr. 1)	3 427 796	189 293	5.8	98	1 887 712	91 820	5.1	1 540 084	97 473	6.8	55.1	44.9
1930 (Apr. 1)	3 238 503	308 113	10.5	95	1 795 892	313 037	21.1	1 442 611	−4 924	−0.3	55.5	44.5
1920 (Jan. 1)	2 930 390	229 514	8.5	93	1 482 855	339 020	29.6	1 447 535	−109 506	−7.0	50.6	49.4
1910 (Apr. 15)	2 700 876	184 414	7.3	88	1 143 835	281 146	32.6	1 557 041	−96 732	−5.8	42.4	57.6
1900 (June 1)	2 516 462	324 058	14.8	80	862 689	272 650	46.2	1 653 773	51 408	3.2	34.3	65.7
1890 (June 1)	2 192 404	214 103	10.8	63	590 039	203 828	52.8	1 602 365	10 275	0.6	26.9	73.1
1880 (June 1)	1 978 301	297 664	17.7	46	386 211	138 554	55.9	1 592 090	159 110	11.1	19.5	80.5
1870 (June 1)	1 680 637	330 209	24.5	32	247 657	131 753	113.7	1 432 980	198 456	16.1	14.7	85.3
1860 (June 1)	1 350 428	362 012	36.6	17	115 904	71 272	159.7	1 234 524	290 740	30.8	8.6	91.4
1850 (June 1)	988 416	302 550	44.1	8	44 632	33 916	316.5	943 784	268 634	39.8	4.5	95.5
1840 (June 1)	685 866	342 835	99.9	3	10 716	10 716	...	675 150	332 119	96.8	1.6	98.4
1830 (June 1)	343 031	195 853	133.1	−	−	−	−	343 031	195 853	133.1	−	100.0
1820 (Aug. 7)	147 178	122 658	500.2	−	−	−	−	147 178	122 658	500.2	−	100.0
1810 (Aug. 6)	24 520	18 879	334.7	−	−	−	−	24 520	18 879	334.7	−	100.0
1800 (Aug. 4)	5 641	...	...	−	−	...	...	5 641	...	...	−	100.0

NOTE: 1810 population includes that of area separated in 1816 and transferred to Michigan Territory in 1818. 1800 population includes that (3,124) of those portions of Indiana Territory taken to form Michigan and Illinois Territories in 1805 and 1809, respectively, and of that portion which was separated in 1816 and transferred to Michigan Territory in 1818.

ADAMS

1840	2,264
1850	5,797
1860	9,252
1870	11,382
1880	15,385
1890	20,181
1900	22,232
1910	21,840
1920	20,503
1930	19,957
1940	21,254
1950	22,393
1960	24,643
1970	26,871
1980	29,619

ALLEN

1830	996
1840	5,942
1850	16,919
1860	29,328
1870	43,494
1880	54,763
1890	66,689
1900	77,270
1910	93,386
1920	14,303
1930	146,743
1940	155,084
1950	183,722
1960	232,196
1970	280,455
1980	294,335

BARTHOLOMEW

1830	5,476
1840	10,042
1850	12,428
1860	17,865
1870	21,133
1880	22,777
1890	23,867
1900	24,594
1910	24,813
1920	23,887
1930	24,864
1940	28,276
1950	36,108
1960	48,198
1970	57,022
1980	65,088

BENTON

1850	1,144
1860	2,809
1870	5,615
1880	11,108
1890	11,903
1900	13,123
1910	12,688
1920	12,206
1930	11,886
1940	11,117
1950	11,462
1960	11,912
1970	11,262
1980	10,218

BLACKFORD

1840	1,226
1850	2,860

1860	4,122
1870	6,272
1880	8,020
1890	10,461
1900	17,213
1910	15,820
1920	14,084
1930	13,617
1940	13,783
1950	14,026
1960	14,792
1970	15,888
1980	15,570

BOONE

1830	621
1840	8,121
1850	11,631
1860	16,753
1870	22,593
1880	25,922
1890	26,572
1900	26,321
1910	24,673
1920	23,575
1930	22,290
1940	22,081
1950	23,993
1960	27,543
1970	30,870
1980	36,446

BROWN

1800	50
1840	2,364
1850	4,846
1860	6,507
1870	8,681
1880	10,264
1890	10,308
1900	9,727
1910	7,975
1920	7,019
1930	5,168
1940	6,189
1950	6,209
1960	7,024
1970	9,057
1980	12,377

CARROLL

1830	1,611
1840	7,819
1850	11,015
1860	13,489
1870	16,152
1880	18,345
1890	20,021
1900	19,958
1910	17,970
1920	16,315
1930	15,049
1940	15,410
1950	16,010
1960	16,934
1970	17,734
1980	19,722

CASS

1830	1,162
1840	5,480
1850	11,021

1860	16,843
1870	24,193
1880	27,611
1890	31,152
1900	34,545
1910	36,368
1920	38,333
1930	34,518
1940	36,908
1950	38,793
1960	40,931
1970	40,456
1980	40,936

CLARK

1810	5,670
1820	8,709
1830	10,686
1840	14,595
1850	15,828
1860	20,502
1870	24,770
1880	28,610
1890	30,259
1900	31,835
1910	30,260
1920	29,381
1930	30,764
1940	31,020
1950	48,330
1960	62,795
1970	75,876
1980	88,838

CLAY

1830	1,616
1840	5,567
1850	7,944
1860	12,161
1870	19,084
1880	25,854
1890	30,536
1900	34,285
1910	32,535
1920	29,447
1930	26,479
1940	25,365
1950	23,918
1960	24,207
1970	23,933
1980	24,862

CLINTON

1830	1,423
1840	7,508
1850	11,869
1860	14,505
1870	17,330
1880	23,472
1890	27,370
1900	28,202
1910	26,674
1920	27,737
1930	27,329
1940	28,411
1950	29,734
1960	30,765
1970	30,547
1980	31,545

CRAWFORD

1800	65
1820	2,583

1830	3,238
1840	5,282
1850	6,524
1860	8,226
1870	9,851
1880	12,356
1890	13,941
1900	13,476
1910	12,057
1920	11,201
1930	10,160
1940	10,171
1950	9,289
1960	8,379
1970	8,033
1980	9,820

DAVIESS

1820	3,432
1830	4,543
1840	6,720
1850	10,352
1860	13,323
1870	16,747
1880	21,552
1890	26,227
1900	29,914
1910	27,747
1920	26,856
1930	25,832
1940	26,163
1950	26,762
1960	26,636
1970	26,602
1980	27,836

DEARBORN

1810	7,310
1820	11,468
1830	13,974
1840	19,327
1850	20,166
1860	24,406
1870	24,116
1880	26,671
1890	23,364
1900	22,194
1910	21,396
1920	20,033
1930	21,056
1940	23,053
1950	25,141
1960	28,674
1970	29,430
1980	34,291

DECATUR

1830	5,887
1840	12,171
1850	15,107
1860	17,294
1870	19,053
1880	19,779
1890	19,277
1900	19,518
1910	18,793
1920	17,813
1930	17,308
1940	17,722
1950	18,218
1960	20,019
1970	22,738
1980	23,841

DE KALB

1840	1,968
1850	8,251
1860	13,880
1870	17,167
1880	20,225
1890	24,307
1900	25,711
1910	25,054
1920	25,600
1930	24,911
1940	24,756
1950	26,023
1960	28,271
1970	30,837
1980	33,606

DELAWARE

1820	3,677
1830	2,374
1840	8,843
1850	10,843
1860	15,753
1870	19,030
1880	22,926
1890	30,131
1900	49,624
1910	51,414
1920	56,377
1930	67,270
1940	74,963
1950	90,252
1960	110,938
1970	129,219
1980	128,587

DUBOIS

1820	1,168
1830	1,778
1840	3,632
1850	6,321
1860	10,394
1870	12,597
1880	15,992
1890	20,253
1900	20,357
1910	19,843
1920	19,915
1930	20,553
1940	22,579
1950	23,785
1960	27,463
1970	30,934
1980	34,238

ELKHART

1830	935
1840	6,660
1850	12,690
1860	20,968
1870	26,026
1880	33,454
1890	39,201
1900	45,052
1910	49,008
1920	56,348
1930	68,875
1940	72,634
1950	84,512
1960	106,790
1970	126,529
1980	137,330

FAYETTE

1820	5,950
1830	9,112
1840	9,837
1850	10,217
1860	10,225
1870	10,476
1880	11,394
1890	12,630
1900	13,495
1910	14,415
1920	17,142
1930	19,243
1940	19,411
1950	23,391
1960	24,454
1970	26,216
1980	28,272

FLOYD

1820	2,776
1830	6,361
1840	9,454
1850	14,875
1860	20,183
1870	23,300
1880	24,590
1890	29,458
1900	30,118
1910	30,293
1920	30,661
1930	34,665
1940	35,061
1950	43,995
1960	51,397
1970	55,622
1980	61,169

FOUNTAIN

1830	7,619
1840	11,218
1850	13,253
1860	15,566
1870	16,389
1880	20,228
1890	19,558
1900	21,446
1910	20,439
1920	18,832
1930	17,971
1940	18,299
1950	17,836
1960	18,207
1970	18,257
1980	19,033

FRANKLIN

1820	10,763
1830	10,190
1840	13,349
1850	17,968
1860	19,549
1870	20,223
1880	20,092
1890	18,366
1900	16,388
1910	15,335
1920	14,806
1930	14,498
1940	14,412
1950	16,034
1960	17,015

1970	16,943
1980	19,612

FULTON

1840	1,993
1850	5,982
1860	9,422
1870	12,726
1880	14,301
1890	16,746
1900	17,453
1910	16,879
1920	16,478
1930	15,038
1940	15,557
1950	16,565
1960	16,957
1970	16,984
1980	19,355

GIBSON

1820	3,876
1830	5,418
1840	8,977
1850	10,771
1860	14,532
1870	17,371
1880	22,742
1890	24,920
1900	30,099
1910	30,137
1920	29,201
1930	29,202
1940	30,709
1950	30,720
1960	29,949
1970	30,444
1980	33,156

GRANT

1840	4,875
1850	11,092
1860	15,797
1870	18,487
1880	23,618
1890	31,493
1900	54,693
1910	51,426
1920	51,353
1930	51,066
1940	55,813
1950	62,156
1960	75,741
1970	83,955
1980	80,934

GREENE

1830	4,242
1840	8,321
1850	12,313
1860	16,041
1870	19,514
1880	22,996
1890	24,379
1900	28,580
1910	36,878
1920	36,770
1930	31,481
1940	31,330
1950	27,886
1960	26,237
1970	26,894
1980	30,416

HAMILTON

1830	1,757
1840	9,855
1850	12,684
1860	17,310
1870	20,882
1880	24,801
1890	26,123
1900	29,914
1910	27,026
1920	24,222
1930	23,444
1940	24,614
1950	24,491
1960	40,132
1970	54,532
1980	82,027

HANCOCK

1830	1,436
1840	7,535
1850	9,698
1860	12,802
1870	15,123
1880	17,123
1890	17,829
1900	19,189
1910	19,030
1920	17,210
1930	16,605
1940	17,302
1950	20,332
1960	26,665
1970	35,096
1980	43,939

HARRISON

1810	3,595
1820	7,875
1830	10,273
1840	12,459
1850	15,286
1860	18,521
1870	19,913
1880	21,326
1890	20,786
1900	21,702
1910	20,232
1920	18,656
1930	17,254
1940	17,106
1950	17,858
1960	19,207
1970	20,423
1980	27,276

HENDRICKS

1830	3,975
1840	11,264
1850	14,083
1860	16,953
1870	20,277
1880	22,981
1890	21,498
1900	21,292
1910	20,840
1920	20,291
1930	19,725
1940	20,151
1950	24,594
1960	40,896
1970	53,974
1980	69,804

HENRY

1830	6,497
1840	15,128
1850	17,605
1860	20,119
1870	22,986
1880	24,016
1890	23,879
1900	25,088
1910	29,758
1920	34,682
1930	35,238
1940	40,208
1950	45,505
1960	48,899
1970	52,603
1980	53,336

HOWARD

1850	6,657
1860	12,524
1870	15,847
1880	19,584
1890	26,186
1900	28,575
1910	33,177
1920	43,965
1930	46,696
1940	47,752
1950	54,498
1960	69,509
1970	83,198
1980	86,896

HUNTINGTON

1840	1,579
1850	7,850
1860	14,867
1870	19,036
1880	21,805
1890	27,644
1900	28,901
1910	28,982
1920	31,671
1930	29,073
1940	29,931
1950	31,400
1960	33,814
1970	34,970
1980	35,596

JACKSON

1820	4,010
1830	4,870
1840	8,961
1850	11,047
1860	16,286
1870	18,974
1880	23,050
1890	24,139
1900	26,633
1910	24,727
1920	24,228
1930	23,731
1940	26,612
1950	28,237
1960	30,556
1970	33,187
1980	36,523

JASPER

1840	1,267
1850	3,540
1860	4,291
1870	6,354
1880	9,464
1890	11,185
1900	14,292
1910	13,044
1920	13,961
1930	13,338
1940	14,397
1950	17,031
1960	18,842
1970	20,429
1980	26,138

JAY

1840	3,863
1850	7,047
1860	11,399
1870	15,000
1880	19,282
1890	23,478
1900	26,818
1910	24,961
1920	23,318
1930	20,846
1940	22,601
1950	23,157
1960	22,572
1970	23,575
1980	23,239

JEFFERSON

1820	8,038
1830	11,465
1840	16,614
1850	23,916
1860	25,036
1870	29,741
1880	25,977
1890	24,507
1900	22,913
1910	20,483
1920	20,709
1930	19,182
1940	19,912
1950	21,613
1960	24,061
1970	27,006
1980	30,419

JENNINGS

1820	2,00
1830	3,974
1840	8,829
1850	12,096
1860	14,749
1870	16,218
1880	16,453
1890	14,608
1900	15,757
1910	14,203
1920	13,280
1930	11,800
1940	13,680
1950	15,250
1960	17,267
1970	19,454
1980	22,854

JERSEY	
1800	100

JOHNSON	
1830	4,019
1840	9,352
1850	12,101
1860	14,854
1870	18,366
1880	19,537
1890	19,561
1900	20,228
1910	20,394
1920	20,739
1930	21,706
1940	22,493
1950	26,183
1960	43,704
1970	61,138
1980	77,240

KNOX	
1800	2,517
1810	7,945
1820	5,437
1830	6,525
1840	10,657
1850	11,084
1860	16,056
1870	21,562
1880	25,324
1890	28,044
1900	32,746
1910	39,183
1920	46,195
1930	43,813
1940	43,973
1950	43,415
1960	41,561
1970	41,546
1980	41,838

KOSCIUSKO	
1840	4,170
1850	10,243
1860	17,418
1870	23,531
1880	26,494
1890	28,645
1900	29,109
1910	27,936
1920	27,120
1930	27,488
1940	39,561
1950	33,002
1960	40,373
1970	48,127
1980	59,555

LAGRANGE	
1840	3,664
1850	8,387
1860	11,366
1870	14,148
1880	15,630
1890	15,615
1900	15,284
1910	15,148
1920	14,009
1930	13,780
1940	14,352

1950	15,347
1960	17,380
1970	20,890
1980	25,550

LAKE	
1840	1,468
1850	3,991
1860	9,145
1870	12,339
1880	15,091
1890	23,886
1900	37,892
1910	82,864
1920	159,957
1930	261,310
1940	293,195
1950	368,152
1960	513,269
1970	546,253
1980	522,965

LA PORTE	
1840	8,184
1850	12,145
1860	22,919
1870	27,062
1880	30,985
1890	34,445
1900	38,386
1910	45,797
1920	50,443
1930	60,490
1940	63,660
1950	76,808
1960	95,111
1970	105,342
1980	108,632

LAWRENCE	
1820	4,116
1830	9,234
1840	11,782
1850	12,097
1860	13,692
1870	14,628
1880	18,543
1890	19,792
1900	25,729
1910	30,625
1920	28,228
1930	35,583
1940	35,045
1950	34,346
1960	36,564
1970	38,038
1980	42,472

MADISON	
1830	2,238
1840	8,874
1850	12,375
1860	16,518
1870	22,770
1880	27,527
1890	36,487
1900	70,470
1910	65,244
1920	69,151
1930	82,888
1940	88,575
1950	103.911

1960	125,819
1970	138,522
1980	139,336

MARION	
1830	7,192
1840	16,080
1850	24,103
1860	39,855
1870	71,939
1880	102,782
1890	141,156
1900	197,227
1910	263,661
1920	348,061
1930	422,666
1940	460,926
1950	551,777
1960	697,567
1970	793,769
1980	765,233

MARSHALL	
1840	1,651
1850	5,348
1860	12,722
1870	20,211
1880	23,414
1890	23,818
1900	25,119
1910	24,175
1920	23,744
1930	25,077
1940	25,935
1950	29,468
1960	32,443
1970	34,986
1980	39,155

MARTIN	
1820	1,032
1830	2,010
1840	3,875
1850	5,941
1860	8,975
1870	11,103
1880	13,475
1890	13,973
1900	14,711
1910	12,950
1920	11,865
1930	10,103
1940	10,300
1950	10,678
1960	10,608
1970	10,969
1980	11,001

MIAMI	
1840	3,048
1850	11,304
1860	16,851
1870	21,052
1880	24,083
1890	25,823
1900	28,344
1910	29,350
1920	29,668
1930	29,032
1940	27,926
1950	28,201
1960	38,000
1970	39,246
1980	39,820

MICHILIMACKINAC	
1800	551

MONROE	
1820	2,679
1830	6,577
1840	10,143
1850	11,286
1860	12,847
1870	14,168
1880	15,875
1890	17,673
1900	20,873
1910	23,426
1920	24,519
1930	35,974
1940	36,534
1950	50,080
1960	59,225
1970	85,221
1980	98,785

MONTGOMERY	
1830	7,317
1840	14,438
1850	18,084
1860	20,888
1870	23,765
1880	27,316
1890	28,025
1900	29,388
1910	29,296
1920	28,490
1930	26,980
1940	27,231
1950	29,122
1960	32,089
1970	33,930
1980	35,501

MORGAN	
1830	5,593
1840	10,741
1850	14,576
1860	16,110
1870	17,528
1880	18,900
1890	18,643
1900	20,457
1910	21,182
1920	20,010
1930	19,424
1940	19,801
1950	23,726
1960	33,875
1970	44,176
1980	51,999

NEWTON	
1860	2,360
1870	5,829
1880	8,167
1890	8,803
1900	10,448
1910	10,504
1920	10,144
1930	9,841
1940	10,775
1950	11,006
1960	11,502
1970	11,606
1980	14,844

NOBLE	
1840	2,702
1850	7,946
1860	14,915
1870	20,389
1880	22,956
1890	23,359
1900	23,533
1910	24,019
1920	22,470
1930	22,404
1940	22,776
1950	25,075
1960	28,162
1970	31,382
1980	35,443

OHIO	
1850	5,308
1860	5,462
1870	5,837
1880	5,563
1890	4,955
1900	4,742
1910	4,329
1920	4,024
1930	3,747
1940	3,782
1950	4,233
1960	4,165
1970	4,289
1980	5,114

ORANGE	
1820	5,368
1830	7,901
1840	9,602
1850	10,809
1860	12,076
1870	13,497
1880	14,363
1890	14,678
1900	16,854
1910	17,192
1920	16,974
1930	17,459
1940	17,311
1950	16,879
1960	16,877
1970	16,968
1980	18,677

OWEN	
1820	838
1830	4,017
1840	8,359
1850	12,106
1860	14,376
1870	16,137
1880	15,901
1890	15,040
1900	15,149
1910	14,053
1920	12,760
1930	11,351
1940	12,090
1950	11,763
1960	11,400
1970	12,163
1980	15,841

PARKE

1830	7,535
1840	13,499
1850	14,968
1860	15,538
1870	18,166
1880	19,460
1890	20,296
1900	23,000
1910	22,214
1920	18,875
1930	16,561
1940	17,358
1950	15,674
1960	14,804
1970	14,628
1980	16,372

PERRY

1820	2,330
1830	3,369
1840	4,655
1850	7,268
1860	11,847
1870	14,801
1880	16,997
1890	18,240
1900	18,778
1910	18,078
1920	16,692
1930	16,625
1940	17,770
1950	17,367
1960	17,232
1970	19,075
1980	19,346

PIKE

1820	1,472
1830	2,475
1840	4,769
1850	7,720
1860	10,078
1870	13,779
1880	16,383
1890	18,544
1900	20,486
1910	19,684
1920	18,684
1930	16,361
1940	17,045
1950	14,995
1960	12,797
1970	12,281
1980	13,465

PORTER

1840	2,162
1850	5,234
1860	10,313
1870	13,942
1880	17,227
1890	18,052
1900	19,175
1910	20,540
1920	20,256
1930	22,821
1940	27,836
1950	40,076
1960	60,279
1970	87,114
1980	119,816

POSEY

1820	4,061
1830	6,549
1840	9,683
1850	12,549
1860	16,167
1870	19,185
1880	20,857
1890	21,529
1900	22,333
1910	21,670
1920	19,334
1930	17,853
1940	19,183
1950	19,818
1960	19,214
1970	21,740
1980	26,414

PULASKI

1840	561
1850	2,595
1860	5,711
1870	7,801
1880	9,851
1890	11,233
1900	14,033
1910	13,312
1920	12,385
1930	11,195
1940	12,056
1950	12,493
1960	12,837
1970	12,534
1980	13,258

PUTNAM

1830	8,262
1840	16,843
1850	18,615
1860	20,681
1870	21,514
1880	22,501
1890	22,335
1900	21,478
1910	20,520
1920	19,880
1930	20,448
1940	20,839
1950	22,950
1960	24,927
1970	26,932
1980	29,163

RANDOLPH

1800	1,103
1820	1,808
1830	3,912
1840	10,684
1850	14,725
1860	18,997
1870	22,862
1880	26,435
1890	28,085
1900	28,653
1910	29,013
1920	26,484
1930	24,859
1940	26,766
1950	27,141
1960	28,434
1970	28,915
1980	29,997

RIPLEY

1820	1,822
1830	3,989
1840	10,392
1850	14,820
1860	19,054
1870	20,977
1880	21,627
1890	19,359
1900	19,881
1910	19,452
1920	18,694
1930	18,078
1940	18,898
1950	18,763
1960	20,641
1970	21,138
1980	24,398

RUSH

1830	9,707
1840	16,456
1850	16,455
1860	16,193
1870	17,626
1880	19,238
1890	19,034
1900	20,148
1910	19,394
1920	19,241
1930	19,412
1940	18,927
1950	19,799
1960	20,393
1970	20,352
1980	19,604

SAINT CLAIR

1800	1,255

SAINT JOSEPH

1830	287
1840	6,425
1850	10,924
1860	18,455
1870	25,322
1880	33,178
1890	42,457
1900	58,881
1910	84,312
1920	103,304
1930	160,033
1940	161,823
1950	205,058
1960	238,614
1970	244,827
1980	241,617

SCOTT

1820	2,334
1830	3,092
1840	4,242
1850	5,885
1860	7,303
1870	7,873
1880	8,343
1890	7,833
1900	8,307
1910	8,323
1920	7,424
1930	6,664
1940	8,978
1950	11,519
1960	14,643
1970	17,144
1980	20,422

SHELBY

1830	6,295
1840	12,005
1850	15,502
1860	19,569
1870	21,892
1880	25,257
1890	25,454
1900	26,491
1910	26,802
1920	25,982
1930	26,552
1940	25,953
1950	28,026
1960	34,093
1970	37,797
1980	39,887

SPENCER

1820	1,882
1830	3,196
1840	6,305
1850	8,616
1860	14,556
1870	17,998
1880	22,122
1890	22,060
1900	22,407
1910	20,676
1920	18,400
1930	16,713
1940	16,211
1950	16,174
1960	16,074
1970	17,134
1980	19,361

STARKE

1840	149
1850	557
1860	2,195
1870	3,888
1880	5,105
1890	7,339
1900	10,431
1910	10,567
1920	10,278
1930	10,620
1940	12,258
1950	15,282
1960	17,911
1970	19,280
1980	21,997

STEUBEN

1840	2,578
1850	6,104
1860	10,374
1870	12,854
1880	14,645
1890	14,478
1900	15,219
1910	14,274
1920	13,360
1930	13,386
1940	13,740
1950	17,087
1960	17,184
1970	20,159
1980	24,694

SULLIVAN

1820	3,498
1830	4,630
1840	8,315
1850	10,141
1860	15,064
1870	18,453
1880	20,336
1890	21,877
1900	26,005
1910	32,439
1920	31,630
1930	28,133
1940	27,014
1950	23,667
1960	21,721
1970	19,889
1980	21,107

SWITZERLAND

1820	3,934
1830	7,028
1840	9,920
1850	12,932
1860	12,698
1870	12,134
1880	13,336
1890	12,514
1900	11,840
1910	9,914
1920	9,311
1930	8,432
1940	8,167
1950	7,599
1960	7,092
1970	6,036
1980	7,153

TIPPECANOE

1830	7,187
1840	13,724
1850	19,377
1860	25,726
1870	33,515
1880	35,966
1890	35,078
1900	38,659
1910	40,063
1920	42,813
1930	47,535
1940	51,020
1950	74,473
1960	89,122
1970	109,378
1980	121,702

TIPON

1850	3,532
1860	8,170
1870	11,953
1880	14,407
1890	18,157
1900	19,116
1910	17,459
1920	16,152
1930	15,208
1940	15,135

1950	15,566	1930	98,861	1910	17,455	1930	15,931
1960	15,856	1940	99,709	1920	16,645	1940	17,001
1970	16,650	1950	105,160	1930	16,285	1950	18,828
1980	16,819	1960	108,458	1940	17,008	1960	20,954
		1970	114,528	1950	16,520	1970	23,395
		1980	112,385	1960	17,819	1980	26,215

UNION

1830	7,944
1840	8,017
1850	6,944
1860	7,109
1870	6,341
1880	7,673
1890	7,006
1900	6,748
1910	6,260
1920	6,021
1930	5,880
1940	6,017
1950	6,412
1960	6,457
1970	6,582
1980	6,860

VANDERBURGH

1820	1,798
1830	2,611
1840	6,250
1850	11,414
1860	20,552
1870	33,145
1880	42,193
1890	59,809
1900	71,769
1910	77,438
1920	92,393
1930	113,320
1940	130,783
1950	160,422
1960	165,794
1970	168,772
1980	167,515

VERMILLION

1830	5,692
1840	8,274
1850	8,661
1860	9,422
1870	10,840
1880	12,025
1890	13,154
1900	15,252
1910	18,865
1920	27,625
1930	23,238
1940	21,787
1950	19,723
1960	17,683
1970	17,793
1980	18,229

VIGO

1820	3,390
1830	5,776
1840	12,076
1850	15,289
1860	22,517
1870	33,549
1880	45,658
1890	50,195
1900	62,035
1910	87,930
1920	100,212

WABASH

1820	147
1840	2,756
1850	12,138
1860	17,547
1870	21,305
1880	25,241
1890	27,126
1900	28,235
1910	26,926
1920	27,321
1930	25,170
1940	26,601
1950	29,047
1960	32,605
1970	35,553
1980	36,640

WARREN

1830	2,861
1840	5,656
1850	7,387
1860	10,057
1870	10,204
1880	11,497
1890	10,955
1900	11,371
1910	10,899
1920	9,699
1930	9,167
1940	9,055
1950	8,535
1960	8,545
1970	8,705
1980	8,976

WARRICK

1820	1,749
1830	2,877
1840	6,321
1850	8,811
1860	13,261
1870	17,653
1880	20,162
1890	21,161
1900	22,329
1910	21,911
1920	19,862
1930	18,230
1940	19,435
1950	21,527
1960	23,577
1970	27,972
1980	41,474

WASHINGTON

1820	9,039
1830	13,064
1840	15,269
1850	17,040
1860	17,909
1870	18,495
1880	18,955
1890	18,619
1900	19,409

WAYNE

1820	12,119
1830	18,571
1840	23,290
1850	25,320
1860	29,588
1870	34,048
1880	38,613
1890	37,628
1900	38,970
1910	43,757
1920	49,136
1930	54,809
1940	59,229
1950	68,566
1960	74,039
1970	79,109
1980	76,058

WELLS

1840	1,822
1850	6,152
1860	10,844
1870	13,585
1880	18,442
1890	21,514
1900	23,449
1910	22,418
1920	20,509
1930	18,411
1940	19,099
1950	19,564
1960	21,220
1970	23,821
1980	25,401

WHITE

1840	1,832
1850	4,761
1860	8,258
1870	10,554
1880	13,795
1890	15,671
1900	19,138
1910	17,602
1920	17,351
1930	15,831
1940	17,037
1950	18,042
1960	19,709
1970	20,995
1980	23,867

WHITLEY

1840	1,237
1850	5,190
1860	10,730
1870	14,399
1880	16,941
1890	17,768
1900	17,328
1910	16,852
1920	15,660

ANDERSON

1850	383
1860	1,196
1870	3,126
1880	4,126
1890	10,741
1900	20,178
1910	22,476
1920	29,767
1930	39,084
1940	41,572
1950	46,820
1960	49,061
1970	70,787
1980	64,695

BEDFORD

1880	2,198
1890	3,351
1900	6,115
1910	8,716
1920	9,076
1930	13,208
1940	12,514
1950	12,562
1960	13,024
1970	13,087
1980	14,410

BEECH GROVE

1910	568
1920	1,459
1930	3,552
1940	3,907
1950	5,685
1960	10,973
1970	13,559
1980	13,196

BLOOMINGTON

1850	1,305
1860	2,419
1870	1,032
1880	2,756
1890	4,018
1900	6,460
1910	8,838
1920	11,595
1930	18,227
1940	20,870
1950	28,163
1960	31,357
1970	43,262
1980	52,044

CARMEL

1880	92
1890	471
1900	498
1910	626
1920	598
1930	316
1940	340
1950	432
1960	1,442
1970	6,691
1980	18,272

CLARKSVILLE

1880	1,037
1890	1,692
1900	2,370
1910	2,743
1920	2,322
1930	2,243
1940	2,386
1950	5,905
1960	8,088
1970	13,298
1980	15,164

COLUMBUS

1850	1,008
1860	1,840
1870	3,359
1880	4,813
1890	6,719
1900	8,130
1910	8,813
1920	8,990
1930	9,935
1940	11,738
1950	18,370
1960	20,770
1970	26,457
1980	30,614

CONNERSVILLE

1840	596
1850	1,396
1860	2,119
1870	2,496
1880	3,228
1890	4,548
1900	6,836
1910	7,738
1920	9,901
1930	12,795
1940	12,898
1950	15,550
1960	17,698
1970	17,604
1980	17,023

CRAWFORDSVILLE

1840	1,327
1850	1,513
1860	1,922
1870	3,701
1880	5,251
1890	6,089
1900	6,649
1910	9,371
1920	10,139
1930	10,355
1940	11,089
1950	12,851
1960	14,231
1970	13,842
1980	13,325

CROWN POINT

1880	1,708
1890	1,907
1900	2,336
1910	2,526
1920	3,232
1930	4,046
1940	4,646
1950	5,839

1960	8,443
1970	10,931
1980	16,455

EAST CHICAGO

1890	1,255
1900	3,411
1910	19,098
1920	35,967
1930	54,784
1940	54,637
1950	54,263
1960	57,669
1970	56,982
1980	39,786

ELKHART

1860	1,439
1870	3,265
1880	6,953
1890	11,360
1900	15,184
1910	19,282
1920	24,277
1930	32,949
1940	33,434
1950	35,646
1960	40,274
1970	43,152
1980	41,305

ELWOOD

1870	310
1880	751
1890	2,284
1900	12,950
1910	11,038
1920	10,790
1930	10,685
1940	10,913
1950	11,362
1960	11,793
1970	11,196
1980	10,867

EVANSVILLE

1850	3,234
1860	11,484
1870	21,830
1880	29,280
1890	50,756
1900	59,007
1910	69,647
1920	85,264
1930	102,249
1940	97,062
1950	128,636
1960	141,543
1970	138,764
1980	130,496

FORT WAYNE

1850	4,282
1860	4,282
1880	17,718
1890	26,880
1900	45,115
1910	63,933
1920	86,549
1930	114,946
1940	118,410

1950	133,607
1960	161,776
1970	178,269
1980	172,196

FRANKFORT

1850	582
1860	733
1870	1,300
1880	2,803
1890	5,919
1900	7,100
1910	8,634
1920	11,585
1930	12,196
1940	13,706
1950	15,028
1960	15,302
1970	14,956
1980	15,168

FRANKLIN

1850	882
1860	1,724
1870	2,707
1880	3,116
1890	3,781
1900	4,005
1910	4,502
1920	4,909
1930	5,682
1940	6,264
1950	7,316
1960	9,453
1970	11,477
1980	11,563

GARY

1910	16,802
1920	55,378
1930	100,426
1940	111,719
1950	133,911
1960	178,320
1970	175,415
1980	151,953

GOSHEN

1850	780
1860	2,053
1870	3,133
1880	4,123
1890	6,033
1900	7,810
1910	8,514
1920	9,525
1930	10,397
1940	11,375
1950	13,003
1960	13,718
1970	17,871
1980	19,665

GREENFIELD

1850	815
1860	744
1870	1,203
1880	2,013
1890	3,100
1900	4,489
1910	4,448

1920	4,168
1930	4,188
1940	4,821
1950	6,159
1960	9,049
1970	9,986
1980	11,439

GREENWOOD

1880	448
1890	862
1900	1,503
1910	1,608
1920	1,907
1930	2,377
1940	2,499
1950	3,066
1960	7,169
1970	11,869
1980	19,327

GRIFFITH

1910	523
1920	630
1930	1,176
1940	2,116
1950	4,470
1960	9,483
1970	18,168
1980	17,026

HAMMOND

1890	5,428
1900	12,376
1910	20,925
1920	36,004
1930	64,560
1940	70,184
1950	87,594
1960	111,698
1970	107,983
1980	93,714

HIGHLAND

1910	304
1920	542
1930	1,553
1940	2,723
1950	5,878
1960	16,284
1970	24,947
1980	25,935

HOBART

1880	600
1890	1,010
1900	1,390
1910	1,753
1920	3,450
1930	5,787
1940	7,166
1950	10,244
1960	18,680
1970	21,485
1980	22,987

HUNTINGTON

1850	594
1860	1,664
1870	2,925
1880	3,803
1890	7,328
1900	9,491
1910	10,272
1920	14,000
1930	13,420
1940	13,903
1950	15,079
1960	16,185
1970	16,217
1980	16,202

INDIANAPOLIS

1840	2,692
1850	8,091
1860	18,611
1870	48,244
1890	105,436
1900	169,164
1910	233,650
1920	314,194
1930	364,161
1940	386,972
1950	427,173
1960	476,258
1970	736,856
1980	700,807

JEFFERSONVILLE

1850	2,122
1860	4,020
1870	7,254
1880	9,357
1890	10,666
1900	10,774
1910	10,412
1920	10,098
1930	11,946
1940	11,493
1950	14,685
1960	19,522
1970	20,008
1980	21,220

KOKOMO

1860	1,040
1870	2,177
1880	4,042
1890	8,261
1900	10,609
1910	17,010
1920	30,067
1930	32,843
1940	33,795
1950	38,672
1960	47,197
1970	44,042
1980	47,808

LAFAYETTE

1850	6,129
1860	9,387
1870	13,506
1880	14,860
1890	16,243
1900	18,116
1910	20,081
1920	22,486

1930	26,240
1940	28,798
1950	35,568
1960	42,330
1970	44,955
1980	43,011

LA PORTE

1850	1,824
1860	5,028
1870	6,581
1880	6,195
1890	7,126
1900	7,113
1910	10,525
1920	15,158
1930	15,755
1940	16,180
1950	17,882
1960	21,157
1970	22,140
1980	21,796

LAWRENCE

1930	840
1940	1,087
1950	1,951
1960	10,103
1970	16,353
1980	25,591

LEBANON

1860	892
1870	1,572
1880	2,625
1890	3,682
1900	4,465
1910	5,474
1920	6,257
1930	6,445
1940	6,529
1950	7,631
1960	9,523
1970	9,766
1980	11,456

LOGANSPORT

1850	2,251
1860	2,979
1870	8,950
1880	11,198
1890	13,328
1900	16,204
1910	19,050
1920	21,626
1930	18,508
1940	20,177
1950	21,031
1960	21,106
1970	19,255
1980	17,899

MADISON

1850	8,012
1860	8,130
1870	10,709
1880	8,945
1890	8,936
1900	7,835
1910	6,934
1920	6,711

1930	6,530
1940	6,923
1950	7,506
1960	10,448
1970	13,081
1980	12,472

MARION

1850	703
1860	(NA)
1870	1,658
1880	3,182
1890	8,769
1900	17,337
1910	19,359
1920	23,747
1930	24,496
1940	26,767
1950	30,081
1960	37,854
1970	39,607
1980	35,874

MARTINSVILLE

1850	334
1860	640
1870	1,131
1880	1,943
1890	2,680
1900	4,038
1910	4,529
1920	4,895
1930	4,962
1940	5,091
1950	5,991
1960	7,525
1970	9,723
1980	11,311

MERRILLVILLE

1980	27,677

MICHIGAN CITY

1850	999
1860	3,320
1870	3,985
1880	7,366
1890	10,766
1900	14,850
1910	19,027
1920	19,457
1930	26,735
1940	26,476
1950	28,395
1960	36,653
1970	39,369
1980	36,850

MISHAWAKA

1850	1,412
1860	1,488
1870	2,617
1880	2,640
1890	3,371
1900	5,560
1910	11,886
1920	15,195
1930	28,630
1940	28,298
1950	32,913
1960	33,361

1970	36,060
1980	40,201

MUNCIE

1850	666
1860	1,782
1870	2,992
1880	5,219
1890	11,345
1900	20,942
1910	24,005
1920	36,524
1930	46,548
1940	49,720
1950	58,479
1960	68,603
1970	69,082
1980	77,216

MUNSTER

1910	543
1920	605
1930	975
1940	1,751
1950	4,753
1960	10,313
1970	16,514
1980	20,671

NEW ALBANY

1830	2,079
1840	4,226
1850	8,181
1860	12,647
1870	15,396
1880	16,423
1890	21,059
1900	20,628
1910	20,629
1920	22,992
1930	25,819
1940	25,414
1950	29,346
1960	37,812
1970	38,402
1980	37,103

NEW CASTLE

1850	666
1860	417
1870	1,556
1880	2,299
1890	2,697
1900	3,406
1910	9,446
1920	14,458
1930	14,027
1940	16,620
1950	18,271
1960	20,349
1970	21,215
1980	20,056

NOBLESVILLE

1850	664
1860	1,115
1870	1,435
1880	2,221
1890	3,054
1900	4,792
1910	5,073

1920	4,758
1930	4,811
1940	5,576
1950	6,567
1960	7,664
1970	7,548
1980	12,056

PERU

1850	1,266
1860	2,506
1870	3,617
1880	5,280
1890	7,028
1900	8,463
1910	10,910
1920	12,410
1930	12,730
1940	12,432
1950	13,308
1960	14,453
1970	14,139
1980	13,764

PORTAGE

1960	11,822
1970	19,127
1980	27,409

RICHMOND

1840	2,070
1850	1,443
1860	6,603
1870	9,445
1880	12,742
1890	16,608
1900	18,226
1910	22,324
1920	26,765
1930	32,493
1940	35,147
1950	39,539
1960	44,149
1970	43,999
1980	41,349

SCHERERVILLE

1920	483
1930	580
1940	998
1950	1,457
1960	2,875
1970	3,663
1980	13,209

SEYMOUR

1860	966
1870	2,372
1880	4,250
1890	5,337
1900	6,445
1910	6,305
1920	7,348
1930	7,508
1940	8,620
1950	9,629
1960	11,629
1970	13,352
1980	15,050

SHELBYVILLE

1840	446
1850	995
1860	1,960
1870	2,731
1880	3,745
1890	5,451
1900	7,169
1910	9,500
1920	9,701
1930	10,618
1940	10,791
1950	11,734
1960	14,317
1970	15,094
1980	14,989

SOUTH BEND

1850	1,652
1860	3,832
1870	7,206
1880	13,280
1890	21,819
1900	35,999
1910	53,684
1920	70,983
1930	104,193
1940	101,268
1950	115,911
1960	132,445
1970	125,580
1980	109,727

SPEEDWAY

1930	1,420
1940	2,325
1950	5,498
1960	9,624
1970	14,523
1980	12,641

TERRE HAUTE

1850	4,051
1860	8,594
1870	16,103
1880	26,042
1890	30,217
1900	36,673
1910	58,157
1920	66,083
1930	62,810
1940	62,693
1950	64,214
1960	72,500
1970	70,335
1980	61,125

VALPARAISO

1850	522
1860	1,698
1870	2,765
1880	4,461
1890	5,090
1900	6,280
1910	6,987
1920	6,518
1930	8,079
1940	8,736
1950	12,028
1960	15,227
1970	20,020
1980	22,247

VINCENNES

1850	2,070
1860	3,960
1870	5,440
1880	7,680
1890	8,853
1900	10,249
1910	14,895
1920	17,160
1930	17,564
1940	18,228
1950	18,831
1960	18,046
1970	19,867
1980	20,857

WABASH

1850	966
1860	1,520
1870	2,881
1880	3,800
1890	5,105
1900	8,618
1910	8,687
1920	9,872
1930	8,840
1940	9,653
1950	10,621
1960	12,621
1970	13,379
1980	12,985

WARSAW

1850	304
1860	(NA)
1870	2,206
1880	3,123
1890	3,574
1900	3,987
1910	4,430
1920	5,478
1930	5,730
1940	6,378
1950	6,625
1960	7,234
1970	7,506
1980	10,647

WASHINGTON

1870	2,901
1880	4,323
1890	6,064
1900	8,551
1910	7,854
1920	8,743
1930	9,070
1940	9,312
1950	10,987
1960	10,846
1970	11,358
1980	11,325

WEST LAFAYETTE

1880	717
1890	2,242
1900	2,302
1910	3,867
1920	3,830
1930	5,095
1940	6,270
1950	11,873
1960	12,680
1970	19,157
1980	21,247

CORRECTION NOTE

The official 1980 census counts of total population shown in this report supersede counts issued previously. Corrections to the figures were made after the counts were provided to the State for redistricting purposes and released in Advance Report PHC80-V for this State.

Shown below are corrections to the 1980 census counts of the total population made after the tabulations for this report were completed. Any additional corrections made after this report is printed are available by writing to Data User Services Division, Customer Services (Corrections), Bureau of the Census, Washington, D.C. 20233.

The 1980 figures shown in this publication are subject to change pending the outcome of the various lawsuits dealing with the census counts.

	1980 population	
	As shown in the tables	Corrected
The State....................	5 490 224	5 490 260
Allen County: St. Joseph township:		
Fort Wayne city (pt.)..........	20 244	20 069
Wayne township:		
Fort Wayne city (pt.)..........	123 620	123 627
Cass County: Eel township:		
Logansport city (pt.)..........	17 436	17 268
De Kalb County: Keyser township:		
Garrett city..................	4 874	4 751
Floyd County.....................	61 169	61 205
New Albany township..............	43 844	43 880
Hancock County: Center township:		
Greenfield city...............	11 439	11 299
Fort Wayne city (total).............	172 196	172 028
Logansport city (total).............	17 899	17 731

Population of County Subdivisions

County Subdivisions	1980	1970
The State	5 490 224	ʳ5 195 392
Adams County[1]	29 619	26 871
Blue Creek township	813	728
French township	834	733
Hartford township	775	784
Jefferson township	735	614
Kirkland township	814	755
Monroe township	3 902	3 595
Berne city (pt.)[1]	1 604	1 599
Monroe town (pt.)[1]	555	533
Preble township	1 026	1 016
Root township	3 365	2 391
Decatur city (pt.)[1]	785	507
St. Marys township	1 198	1 070
Union township	1 013	966
Wabash township	4 782	4 004
Berne city (pt.)[1]	1 696	1 389
Geneva town[1]	1 430	1 100
Washington township	10 362	10 215
Decatur city (pt.)[1]	7 864	7 938
Monroe town (pt.)[1]	184	89
Allen County[2]	294 335	280 455
Aboite township	11 663	6 132
Adams township	31 897	ʳ30 913
Fort Wayne city (pt.)[2]	13 660	ʳ10 873
New Haven city (pt.)[2]	6 684	ʳ5 346
Cedar Creek township	5 864	4 414
Grabill town[2]	658	570
Eel River township	2 423	1 622
Jackson township	602	651
Jefferson township	2 142	2 130
New Haven city (pt.)[2]	30	...
Lafayette township	2 389	2 035
Lake township	2 184	2 061
Madison township	1 729	1 711
Marion township	3 600	3 221
Maumee township	2 408	1 781
Woodburn city[2]	1 002	688
Milan township	3 178	2 335
Monroe township	2 174	2 153
Monroeville town[2]	1 372	1 353
Perry township	8 299	5 768
Huntertown town[2]	1 265	775
Pleasant township	3 472	2 474
Fort Wayne city (pt.)[2]	19	1
St. Joseph township	55 348	38 094
Fort Wayne city (pt.)[2]	20 244	ʳ12 327
Scipio township	396	409
Springfield township	2 987	2 608
Washington township	23 851	20 296
Fort Wayne city (pt.)[2]	14 653	ʳ11 687
Wayne township	127 729	ʳ149 637
Fort Wayne city (pt.)[2]	123 620	ʳ143 381
Bartholomew County[3]	65 088	57 022
Clay township	2 647	2 342
Columbus city (pt.)[3]	–	...
Clifty township	905	662
Columbus township	37 012	34 520
Columbus city (pt.)[3]	30 470	ʳ26 457
Flat Rock township	1 719	1 354
Clifford town	310	275
Columbus city (pt.)[3]	–	ʳ–
German township	5 631	4 033
Edinburgh town (pt.)[3]	461	ʳ623
Taylorsville (CDP)	1 247	...
Harrison township	2 520	2 294
Columbus city (pt.)[3]	97	...
Haw Creek township	4 517	3 238
Hartsville town	379	434
Hope town[3]	2 185	1 603
Jackson township	760	499
Ohio township	1 964	1 303
Rock Creek township	1 361	1 407
Sand Creek township	2 370	1 827
Elizabethtown town[3]	603	519
Wayne township	3 682	3 543
Columbus city (pt.)[3]	47	...
Jonesville town	213	202
Benton County[4]	10 218	11 262
Bolivar township	1 235	1 372
Otterbein town (pt.)[4]	818	899
Center township	3 062	3 418
Fowler town[4]	2 319	2 643
Gilboa township	311	363
Grant township	1 202	1 391
Boswell town[4]	810	998
Hickory Grove township	560	679
Ambia town	274	300
Oak Grove township	1 810	1 629
Oxford town[4]	1 327	1 098
Parish Grove township	395	510
Pine township	264	340
Richland township	767	867
Earl Park town	469	478
Union township	367	405
York township	245	288

County Subdivisions	1980	1970
Blackford County[5]	15 570	15 888
Harrison township	3 103	3 115
Montpelier city[5]	1 995	2 093
Jackson township	1 723	1 647
Dunkirk city (pt.)	163	202
Licking township	9 670	10 013
Hartford City[5]	7 622	8 207
Shamrock Lakes town[5]	206	...
Washington township	1 074	1 113
Boone County[6]	36 446	30 870
Center township	14 376	12 289
Lebanon city[6]	11 456	9 766
Ulen town	193	138
Clinton township	856	822
Eagle township	7 995	5 331
Zionsville town[6]	3 948	1 857
Harrison township	682	687
Jackson township	2 725	2 723
Advance town	559	561
Jamestown town (pt.)[6]	924	938
Jefferson township	1 090	1 087
Marion township	1 214	1 295
Perry township	1 144	847
Sugar Creek township	2 188	2 111
Thorntown town	1 468	1 399
Union township	1 634	984
Washington township	1 164	1 208
Worth township	1 378	1 486
Whitestown town[6]	497	569
Brown County[7]	12 377	9 057
Hamblen township	3 365	2 007
Jackson township	3 774	2 658
Van Buren township	1 207	950
Washington township	4 031	3 442
Nashville town[7]	705	527
Carroll County[8]	19 722	17 734
Adams township	567	453
Burlington township	1 933	1 469
Burlington town	680	685
Carrollton township	637	675
Clay township	787	667
Deer Creek township	4 458	4 258
Delphi city[8]	3 042	2 582
Democrat township	805	824
Jackson township	1 269	1 256
Camden town	618	577
Jefferson township	1 908	1 649
Yeoman town	154	145
Liberty township	523	502
Madison township	580	527
Monroe township	3 108	2 724
Flora town[8]	2 303	1 877
Rock Creek township	457	453
Tippecanoe township	1 982	1 469
Washington township	708	808
Cass County[9]	40 936	40 456
Adams township	969	892
Bethlehem township	941	935
Boone township	1 627	1 698
Royal Center town	908	987
Clay township	2 779	1 943
Logansport city (pt.)	288	87
Clinton township	1 249	2 244
Deer Creek township	1 069	1 061
Eel township	18 890	20 275
Logansport city (pt.)[9]	17 436	18 994
Harrison township	908	861
Jackson township	3 325	2 574
Galveston town[9]	1 822	1 284
Grissom AFB (CDP) (pt.)	–	...
Jefferson township	1 326	984
Miami township	1 306	1 059
Noble township	2 052	1 862
Logansport city (pt.)	175	174
Tipton township	2 684	2 390
Onward town	121	111
Walton town[9]	1 202	1 054
Washington township	1 811	1 678
Clark County[10]	88 838	75 876
Bethlehem township	359	499
Carr township	1 660	1 268
Charlestown township	9 196	8 441
Charlestown city[10]	5 596	ʳ5 933
Jeffersonville township	55 831	47 010
Clarksville town[10]	15 164	ʳ13 298
Jeffersonville city[10]	21 220	20 008
Oak Park (CDP) (pt.)	5 457	...
Monroe township	3 966	3 290
Henryville (CDP)	1 132	...
Oregon township	1 147	1 007
Owen township	690	629
Silver Creek township	7 887	6 267
Sellersburg town[10]	3 211	3 177
Union township	1 805	1 214
Utica township	2 704	2 728
Oak Park (CDP) (pt.)	414	...

County Subdivisions

County Subdivisions	1980	1970
Clark County—Con.		
Utica township—Con.		
Utica town[10]	501	r644
Washington township	1 566	1 463
Wood township	2 027	2 060
New Providence town[10]	384	337
Clay County[11]	24 862	23 933
Brazil township	8 422	8 568
Brazil city (pt.)[11]	7 751	8 053
Cass township	267	298
Dick Johnson township	1 125	1 136
Brazil city (pt.)	–	20
Harrison township	2 220	2 129
Clay City town	883	900
Jackson township	2 022	1 665
Brazil city (pt.)[11]	101	90
Lewis township	1 502	1 338
Perry township	971	939
Posey township	3 459	3 311
Staunton town	607	582
Sugar Ridge township	956	865
Center Point town	242	275
Van Buren township	3 168	2 990
Carbon town	307	344
Harmony town[11]	613	...
Knightsville town	763	788
Washington township	750	694
Clinton County[12]	31 545	30 547
Center township	16 338	16 210
Frankfort city (pt.)[12]	15 168	14 956
Forest township	935	953
Jackson township	1 200	1 231
Johnson township	679	765
Kirklin township	1 279	1 377
Kirklin town[12]	662	736
Madison township	1 847	1 837
Mulberry town	1 225	1 075
Michigan township	1 585	1 403
Michigantown town	453	457
Owen township	886	855
Perry township	1 462	1 312
Colfax town[12]	823	633
Ross township	2 182	1 779
Rossville town[12]	1 148	830
Sugar Creek township	508	535
Union township	850	643
Warren township	722	701
Washington township	1 072	946
Frankfort city (pt.)[12]	...	...
Crawford County[13]	9 820	8 033
Boone township	200	151
Alton town	64	56
Jennings township	1 285	952
Carefree town[13]	41	...
Leavenworth town	356	330
Johnson township	453	503
Liberty township	1 760	1 379
Marengo town[13]	892	767
Ohio township	508	467
Patoka township	1 185	992
Sterling township	1 799	1 560
English town	633	664
Union township	861	717
Whiskey Run township	1 769	1 312
Milltown town (pt.)	620	511
Daviess County[14]	27 836	26 602
Barr township	3 205	3 059
Cannelburg town	152	149
Montgomery town[14]	390	411
Bogard township	940	844
Elmore township	1 376	1 515
Elnora town[14]	756	873
Harrison township	600	485
Madison township	2 788	2 570
Odon town	1 463	1 433
Reeve township	723	641
Alfordsville town	132	105
Steele township	981	988
Plainville town	556	538
Van Buren township	1 333	1 125
Veale township	682	652
Washington township	15 208	14 723
Washington city[14]	11 325	11 358
Dearborn County[15]	34 291	29 430
Caesar Creek township	275	251
Center township	5 157	5 196
Aurora city (pt.)[15]	3 815	4 293
Clay township	2 444	2 027
Dillsboro town[15]	1 038	840
Harrison township	1 801	1 761
West Harrison town	328	395
Hogan township	932	682
Jackson township	1 124	928
Kelso township	1 706	1 452
St. Leon town	515	435
Lawrenceburg township	9 647	9 424

County Subdivisions	1980	1970
Dearborn County—Con.		
Lawrenceburg township—Con.		
Aurora city (pt.)[15]	1	–
Greendale town[15]	3 795	3 783
Lawrenceburg city[15]	4 403	4 636
Logan township	1 657	797
Manchester township	2 342	1 892
Miller township	2 903	1 676
Sparta township	2 314	1 684
Moores Hill town	566	616
Washington township	1 210	968
York township	779	692
Decatur County[16]	23 841	22 738
Adams township	1 903	1 657
St. Paul town (pt.)	650	545
Clay township	1 507	1 504
Milford town	177	187
Clinton township	497	583
Fugit township	1 520	1 156
Jackson township	1 092	1 153
Marion township	1 651	1 612
Millhousen town	214	252
Salt Creek township	1 119	1 192
Newpoint town	296	381
Sand Creek township	3 206	2 769
Westport town	1 450	1 170
Washington township	11 346	11 112
Greensburg city[16]	9 254	8 620
De Kalb County[17]	33 606	30 837
Butler township	1 612	1 274
Concord township	1 195	1 087
St. Joe town	546	564
Fairfield township	1 119	1 066
Franklin township	1 050	947
Hamilton town (pt.)	121	98
Grant township	2 769	2 514
Waterloo town (pt.)	1 916	1 876
Jackson township	1 899	1 624
Auburn city (pt.)[17]	127	34
Keyser township	6 148	6 156
Altona town	263	269
Auburn city (pt.)	–	r23
Garrett city[17]	4 874	4 715
Newville township	430	474
Richland township	1 201	1 132
Corunna town	304	359
Smithfield township	1 590	1 286
Ashley town (pt.)[17]	528	413
Waterloo town (pt.)	35	...
Spencer township	1 016	968
Stafford township	239	273
Troy township	311	329
Union township	9 293	8 345
Auburn city (pt.)[17]	7 995	r7 331
Wilmington township	3 734	3 362
Butler city[17]	2 509	2 394
Delaware County[18]	128 587	129 219
Center township	80 012	87 469
Muncie city (pt.)[18]	76 460	r69 082
Delaware township	4 267	4 201
Albany town (pt.)[18]	2 271	2 293
Hamilton township	7 525	4 803
Harrison township	3 585	2 983
Liberty township	5 487	5 620
Selma town[18]	1 056	890
Monroe township	3 839	3 425
Mount Pleasant township	10 812	9 008
Muncie city (pt.)[18]	756	...
Yorktown town[18]	3 945	1 673
Niles township	1 333	1 110
Albany town (pt.)	109	–
Perry township	1 528	1 334
Salem township	4 303	4 034
Union township	3 428	3 014
Eaton town[18]	1 804	1 594
Washington township	2 468	2 218
Gaston town[18]	1 150	928
Dubois County[19]	34 238	30 934
Bainbridge township	12 036	11 047
Jasper city[19]	9 097	8 641
Boone township	741	726
Cass township	1 911	1 504
Holland town[19]	683	662
Huntingburg city (pt.)[19]		r–
Columbia township	840	822
Ferdinand township	3 431	2 960
Ferdinand town[19]	2 192	1 432
Hall township	841	832
Harbison township	1 524	1 452
Jackson township	1 729	1 422
Jefferson township	1 377	1 205
Birdseye town	533	404
Madison township	1 492	1 476
Marion township	1 567	1 275
Patoka township	6 749	6 213
Huntingburg city (pt.)[19]	5 376	4 794

County Subdivisions

County Subdivisions	1980	1970
Elkhart County[20]	137 330	126 529
Baugo township	6 097	5 982
Elkhart city (pt.)[20]	—	
Benton township	1 479	1 354
Millersburg town (pt.)[20]	108	72
Cleveland township	6 547	5 207
Elkhart city (pt.)[20]	1 315	263
Clinton township	2 918	2 478
Millersburg town (pt.)[20]	701	546
Concord township	46 214	47 192
Dunlap (CDP)	5 397	...
Elkhart city (pt.)[20]	32 365	35 451
Goshen (pt.)[20]	218	...
Elkhart township	23 202	21 399
Goshen city (pt.)[20]	19 447	'17 871
Harrison township	2 421	2 175
Wakarusa town (pt.)[20]	21	...
Jackson township	2 642	2 416
New Paris (CDP)	1 062	1 080
Jefferson township	3 687	2 360
Locke township	3 137	2 834
Nappanee city (pt.)[20]	2 145	1 823
Middlebury township	4 604	3 453
Middlebury town[20]	1 665	1 055
Olive township	2 398	2 081
Wakarusa town (pt.)[20]	1 260	1 160
Osolo township	20 115	18 309
Elkhart city (pt.)[20]	7 625	7 438
Simonton Lake (CDP)	3 276	...
Union township	4 872	4 283
Nappanee city (pt.)[20]	2 549	2 288
Washington township	4 681	3 535
Bristol town[20]	1 203	1 100
York township	2 316	1 471
Fayette County[21]	28 272	26 216
Columbia township	1 078	851
Connersville township	14 479	13 584
Connersville city (pt.)[21]	11 007	11 413
Fairview township	397	499
Glenwood town (pt.)	34	37
Harrison township	7 797	7 385
Connersville city (pt.)[21]	6 016	6 191
Jackson township	1 582	1 208
Jennings township	803	681
Orange township	840	799
Glenwood town (pt.)	90	114
Posey township	607	668
Waterloo township	689	541
Floyd County[22]	61 169	55 622
Franklin township	1 213	986
Georgetown township	6 110	3 729
Georgetown town[22]	1 494	1 273
Greenville township	4 729	2 775
Galena (CDP)	1 186	...
Greenville town	537	611
Lafayette township	5 273	3 699
New Albany township	43 844	44 433
New Albany city[22]	37 103	38 402
Fountain County[23]	19 033	18 257
Cain township	1 242	1 023
Hillsboro town	561	505
Davis township	571	540
Fulton township	731	705
Jackson township	662	730
Wallace town	88	136
Logan township	4 456	4 831
Attica city[23]	3 841	4 262
Millcreek township	1 475	1 348
Kingman town	566	530
Richland township	1 149	1 307
Mellott town	294	325
Newtown town	277	286
Shawnee township	657	596
Troy township	4 019	3 458
Covington city[23]	2 883	2 641
Van Buren township	3 266	3 004
Veedersburg town	2 261	'2 198
Wabash township	805	715
Franklin County[24]	19 612	16 943
Bath township	453	455
Blooming Grove township	877	684
Brookville township	5 294	4 882
Brookville town	2 874	2 864
Butler township	942	846
Fairfield township	236	139
Highland township	1 273	1 083
Cedar Grove town	217	248
Laurel township	1 739	1 509
Laurel town[24]	819	753
Metamora township	977	997
Posey township	1 124	931
Ray township	2 999	2 420
Batesville city (pt.)[24]	683	330
Oldenburg town[24]	770	758
Salt Creek township	821	727
Springfield township	952	877
Mount Carmel town	151	128

County Subdivisions

County Subdivisions	1980	1970
Franklin County—Con.		
Whitewater township	1 925	1 393
Fulton County[25]	19 335	16 984
Aubbeenaubbee township	1 306	938
Henry township	2 698	2 587
Akron town[25]	1 045	1 019
Liberty township	1 827	1 567
Fulton town	393	372
Newcastle township	1 180	856
Richland township	945	847
Rochester township	9 057	8 107
Rochester city[25]	5 050	4 631
Union township	1 588	1 363
Kewanna town	711	614
Wayne township	734	719
Gibson County[26]	33 156	30 444
Barton township	1 921	1 736
Mackey town[26]	165	121
Somerville town	340	313
Center township	1 563	1 473
Francisco town[26]	612	621
Columbia township	4 717	4 603
Oakland City city[26]	3 301	3 289
Johnson township	2 882	2 649
Haubstadt town[26]	1 389	1 171
Montgomery township	3 112	2 760
Owensville town[26]	1 261	1 056
Patoka township	11 999	11 206
Princeton city[26]	8 976	7 431
Union township	4 197	3 788
Fort Branch town	2 504	2 535
Wabash township	88	139
Washington township	718	698
White River township	1 959	1 392
Hazleton town	368	416
Patoka town	832	529
Grant County[27]	80 934	83 955
Center township	28 703	32 606
Marion city (pt.)[27]	23 870	27 464
Fairmount township	4 868	4 832
Fairmount town[27]	3 286	3 427
Fowlerton town	300	337
Franklin township	9 405	9 976
Marion city (pt.)[27]	7 463	7 666
Sweetser town (pt.)	91	119
Green township	715	808
Jefferson township	5 516	5 077
Matthews town	745	728
Upland town[27]	3 335	3 202
Liberty township	1 418	1 192
Mill township	11 976	11 893
Gas City city[27]	6 370	5 742
Jonesboro town[27]	2 279	2 466
Marion city (pt.)[27]	12	—
Monroe township	1 520	972
Pleasant township	7 005	6 434
Marion city (pt.)[27]	2 828	2 414
Sweetser town (pt.)	853	957
Richland township	979	888
Converse town (pt.)[27]	124	...
Sims township	2 035	2 140
Swayzee town[27]	1 127	1 073
Van Buren township	2 055	2 134
Van Buren town[27]	935	1 057
Washington township	4 739	5 003
Marion city (pt.)[27]	1 701	2 063
Greene County[28]	30 416	26 894
Beech Creek township	1 464	1 274
Cass township	418	426
Newberry town	246	295
Center township	1 912	1 391
Fairplay township	645	651
Switz City town (pt.)	116	113
Grant township	764	668
Switz City town (pt.)	184	188
Highland township	581	513
Jackson township	1 328	1 182
Jefferson township	2 041	2 116
Worthington town	1 574	1 691
Richland township	4 882	4 336
Bloomfield town[28]	2 705	2 565
Smith township	440	419
Stafford township	590	535
Stockton township	8 658	7 383
Linton city[28]	6 315	5 450
Taylor township	1 107	938
Washington township	1 366	1 241
Lyons town	782	702
Wright township	4 220	3 821
Jasonville city	2 497	2 335
Hamilton County[29]	82 027	54 532
Adams township	4 307	4 009
Sheridan town[29]	2 200	2 137
Clay township	32 606	19 518
Carmel city[29]	18 272	'6 691

County Subdivisions	1980	1970
Hamilton County—Con.		
Delaware township	4 660	2 279
Fishers town[29]	2 008	628
Fall Creek township	2 757	2 046
Jackson township	7 435	5 411
Arcadia town[29]	1 801	1 338
Atlanta town	657	620
Cicero town[29]	2 557	1 378
Noblesville township	18 894	13 289
Noblesville city[29]	12 056	7 548
Washington township	7 425	4 789
Westfield town[29]	2 783	1 837
Wayne township	1 898	1 520
White River township	2 045	1 671
Hancock County[30]	43 939	35 096
Blue River township	1 201	977
Brandywine township	1 658	1 333
Brown township	2 703	2 552
Shirley town (pt.)	742	769
Wilkinson town	493	480
Buck Creek township	4 675	2 649
Cumberland town (pt.)[30]	633	224
Center township	16 135	13 559
Greenfield city[30]	11 439	9 986
Green township	1 686	1 333
Jackson township	1 884	1 756
Sugar Creek township	8 114	5 903
Cumberland town (pt.)[30]	496	255
New Palestine town	749	863
Spring Lake town[30]	236	263
Vernon township	5 883	5 034
Fortville town[30]	2 787	2 460
Harrison County[31]	27 276	20 423
Blue River township	1 471	1 218
Milltown town (pt.)	381	316
Boone township	1 065	985
Laconia town	58	64
Franklin township	2 872	1 952
Lanesville town	570	586
Harrison township	7 727	6 241
Corydon town[31]	2 724	2 719
Heth township	880	726
Mauckport town	109	119
Jackson township	3 977	2 331
Crandall town	176	188
Morgan township	2 965	1 958
Palmyra town	692	483
Posey township	2 203	1 833
Elizabeth town	178	195
Spencer township	1 625	1 033
Milltown town (pt.)[31]	5	2
Taylor township	611	537
Washington township	387	377
New Amsterdam town	31	32
Webster township	1 493	1 232
New Middletown town[31]	115	133
Hendricks County[32]	69 804	53 974
Brown township	4 176	2 113
Brownsburg town (pt.)[32]	–	...
Center township	7 057	5 819
Danville town[32]	4 220	3 771
Clay township	2 030	1 889
Amo town	444	422
Coatesville town	474	453
Eel River township	1 595	1 628
Jamestown town (pt.)[32]	–	...
North Salem town[32]	581	601
Franklin township	1 261	1 157
Stilesville town[32]	350	352
Guilford township	17 052	14 439
Plainfield town[32]	9 191	8 211
Liberty township	4 719	4 017
Clayton town[32]	703	736
Lincoln township	13 351	10 489
Brownsburg town (pt.)[32]	6 242	'5 751
Marion township	1 289	1 053
Middle township	3 189	2 345
Pittsboro town[32]	891	867
Union township	1 579	1 252
Lizton town[32]	456	397
Washington township	12 506	7 773
Henry County[33]	53 336	52 603
Blue River township	1 351	1 288
Mooreland town	479	495
Dudley township	1 401	1 468
Straughn town[33]	331	329
Fall Creek township	5 094	4 412
Middletown town[33]	2 978	2 046
Franklin township	1 457	1 250
Lewisville town	577	530
Greensboro township	1 503	1 738
Greensboro town	175	225
Kennard town[33]	441	518
Shirley town (pt.)	177	189
Harrison township	1 560	1 351

County Subdivisions	1980	1970
Henry County—Con.		
Harrison township—Con.	180	207
Cadiz town	180	207
Henry township	26 730	27 860
New Castle city[33]	20 056	21 215
Jefferson township	1 340	1 262
Sulphur Springs town	345	387
Liberty township	1 652	1 636
Prairie township	3 769	2 879
Mount Summit town	357	395
Springport town	221	236
Spiceland township	2 365	2 400
Dunreith town	184	200
Spiceland town	940	957
Stoney Creek township	989	958
Blountsville town	213	220
Wayne township	4 125	4 101
Knightstown town	2 325	2 456
Howard County[34]	86 896	83 198
Center township	52 504	53 282
Kokomo city (pt.)[34]	46 543	44 042
Clay township	3 970	3 572
Ervin township	1 966	1 678
Harrison township	6 960	4 965
Kokomo city (pt.)[34]	936	...
Honey Creek township	1 794	1 503
Russiaville town	973	844
Howard township	2 884	2 534
Jackson township	617	652
Liberty township	4 371	3 423
Greentown town[34]	2 265	1 870
Monroe township	1 241	973
Taylor township	9 628	9 744
Indian Heights (CDP)	4 277	...
Kokomo city (pt.)[34]	329	...
Union township	961	872
Huntington County[35]	35 596	34 970
Clear Creek township	1 286	1 316
Dallas township	2 072	1 859
Andrews town[35]	1 243	1 207
Huntington township	20 032	20 204
Huntington city[35]	16 202	16 217
Jackson township	3 325	2 530
Roanoke town[35]	891	858
Jefferson township	1 306	868
Mount Etna town (pt.)	33	49
Lancaster township	1 185	1 224
Mount Etna town (pt.)	72	102
Polk township	409	390
Mount Etna town (pt.)	15	13
Rock Creek township	1 463	1 564
Markle town (pt.)[35]	755	786
Salamonie township	2 018	2 513
Warren town	1 254	1 229
Union township	1 120	1 037
Warren township	759	806
Wayne township	621	659
Mount Etna town (pt.)	2	–
Jackson County[36]	36 523	33 187
Brownstown township	4 650	4 134
Brownstown town[36]	2 704	2 376
Carr township	1 554	1 457
Medora town	853	788
Driftwood township	937	980
Grassy Fork township	792	807
Hamilton township	1 509	1 415
Jackson township	15 784	13 920
Seymour city (pt.)[36]	13 901	12 198
Owen township	1 380	1 329
Pershing township	1 296	1 173
Redding township	3 786	3 557
Seymour city (pt.)[36]	1 149	1 154
Salt Creek township	314	279
Vernon township	3 613	3 213
Crothersville town	1 747	1 663
Washington township	908	923
Jasper County[37]	26 138	20 429
Barkley township	909	938
Carpenter township	2 038	1 765
Remington town	1 268	1 127
Gillam township	818	786
Hanging Grove township	313	324
Jordan township	374	420
Kankakee township	1 054	705
Keener township	6 578	3 511
De Motte town	2 559	1 697
Marion township	7 150	6 955
Collegeville (CDP)	1 059	...
Rensselaer city[37]	4 944	4 688
Milroy township	237	329
Newton township	715	498
Union township	1 260	1 137
Walker township	2 250	1 464
Wheatfield township	2 442	1 597
Wheatfield town	755	713

County Subdivisions	1980	1970
Jay County[38]	23 239	23 575
Bearcreek township	1 162	1 090
Bryant town	277	320
Greene township	1 066	1 077
Jackson township	829	715
Jefferson township	945	897
Knox township	602	575
Madison township	693	845
Salamonia town	147	162
Noble township	732	778
Penn township	1 362	1 401
Pennville town[38]	805	798
Pike township	955	957
Richland township	5 668	5 935
Dunkirk city (pt.)[38]	3 017	3 263
Redkey town	1 537	1 667
Wabash township	594	710
Wayne township	8 631	8 595
Portland city[38]	7 074	7 115
Jefferson County[39]	30 419	27 006
Graham township	1 446	1 262
Hanover township	5 162	3 738
Hanover town[39]	4 054	3 018
Lancaster township	1 484	1 345
Dupont town	392	357
Madison township	16 225	15 628
Madison city[39]	12 472	13 081
Milton township	1 204	818
Brooksburg town	132	104
Monroe township	357	398
Republican township	1 447	1 061
Saluda township	1 358	1 236
Shelby township	850	705
Smyrna township	886	815
Jennings County[40]	22 854	19 454
Bigger township	574	504
Campbell township	2 164	2 653
Center township	7 806	6 844
North Vernon city[40]	5 768	4 582
Columbia township	774	737
Geneva township	3 849	2 640
Lovett township	809	733
Marion township	984	802
Montgomery township	941	749
Sand Creek township	803	752
Spencer township	2 093	1 570
Vernon township	2 057	1 470
Vernon town	329	440
Johnson County[41]	77 240	61 138
Blue River township	5 319	7 254
Edinburgh town (pt.)[41]	4 395	4 456
Clark township	1 690	1 584
Franklin township	12 972	12 237
Franklin city (pt.)[41]	10 437	10 537
Whiteland town (pt.)[41]	-	...
Hensley township	2 265	2 054
Trafalgar town (pt.)[41]	466	453
Needham township	3 339	2 924
Franklin city (pt.)[41]	1 118	940
Nineveh township	2 999	1 864
Princes Lakes town	937	597
Trafalgar town (pt.)[41]	-	4
Pleasant township	26 106	20 684
Franklin city (pt.)[41]	8	...
Greenwood city (pt.)[41]	17 233	'11 869
New Whiteland town[41]	4 502	4 200
Whiteland town (pt.)[41]	1 956	1 492
Union township	2 023	1 797
Bargersville town (pt.)[41]	181	110
White River township	20 527	10 740
Bargersville town (pt.)[41]	1 466	763
Greenwood city (pt.)[41]	2 094	-
Knox County[42]	41 838	41 546
Busseron township	1 485	1 481
Oaktown town	776	726
Decker township	270	333
Harrison township	1 872	1 839
Monroe City town	569	603
Johnson township	1 501	1 544
Decker town	256	268
Palmyra township	1 578	1 188
Steen township	1 071	1 121
Wheatland town[42]	532	562
Vigo township	5 513	5 635
Bicknell city (pt.)[42]	3 502	3 312
Edwardsport town[42]	459	482
Sandborn town	576	528
Vincennes township	24 945	24 803
Vincennes city[42]	20 857	19 867
Washington township	2 316	2 324
Bicknell city (pt.)[42]	1 211	405
Bruceville town	646	627
Widner township	1 287	1 278
Kosciusko County[43]	59 555	48 127
Clay township	1 621	1 370
Claypool town	464	468
Etna township	1 150	1 037
Etna Green town[43]	522	516
Franklin township	1 019	940
Mentone town (pt.)[43]	226	180
Harrison township	3 226	2 523
Mentone town (pt.)[43]	747	650
Jackson township	1 251	1 151
Sidney town	194	179
Jefferson township	1 089	1 001
Nappanee city (pt.)	-	48
Lake township	1 661	1 548
Silver Lake town	576	588
Monroe township	932	734
Plain township	4 968	3 161
Leesburg town[43]	629	561
Prairie township	1 188	886
Scott township	1 190	957
Seward township	1 921	1 605
Burket town	260	210
Tippecanoe township	5 340	3 954
North Webster town[43]	709	456
Turkey Creek township	6 587	5 081
Syracuse town[43]	2 579	1 546
Van Buren township	3 118	2 665
Milford town[43]	1 153	1 264
Washington township	2 847	2 441
Pierceton town	1 086	1 175
Wayne township	20 447	17 073
Warsaw city[43]	10 647	7 506
Winona Lake town[43]	2 827	2 811
Lagrange County[44]	25 550	20 890
Bloomfield township	4 159	3 372
Lagrange town	2 164	2 053
Clay township	2 213	1 742
Clearspring township	2 778	2 162
Topeka town (pt.)	555	349
Eden township	2 067	1 794
Topeka town (pt.)[44]	321	328
Greenfield township	1 088	1 049
Johnson township	2 593	2 025
Wolcottville town (pt.)[44]	370	419
Lima township	1 889	1 664
Milford township	2 297	2 189
Newbury township	3 168	2 467
Shipshewana town[44]	466	448
Springfield township	1 094	851
Van Buren township	2 204	1 575
Lake County[45]	522 965	546 253
Calumet township	176 901	215 940
Gary city (pt.)[45]	151 651	175 022
Griffith town (pt.)	16 977	18 168
Lake Station city (pt.)[45]	1	5
Cedar Creek township	8 704	6 365
Lowell town (pt.)[45]	4 465	2 945
Center township	24 017	21 946
Cedar Lake town (pt.)[45]	4 275	3 637
Crown Point city (pt.)[45]	12 854	10 931
Eagle Creek township	1 421	786
Hanover township	7 101	6 515
Cedar Lake town (pt.)[45]	4 479	3 952
St. John town (pt.)[45]	405	...
Hobart township	42 548	40 825
Gary city (pt.)	302	393
Hobart city	22 987	21 485
Lake Station city (pt.)[45]	14 293	9 853
New Chicago town[45]	3 284	2 231
North township	185 736	203 480
East Chicago city	39 786	46 982
Hammond city	93 714	'107 983
Highland town	25 935	24 947
Munster town	20 671	16 514
Whiting city	5 630	'7 054
Ross township	34 842	28 845
Crown Point city (pt.)[45]	3 601	-
Merrillville town[45]	27 677	...
St. John township	33 718	16 829
Dyer town	9 555	4 906
Griffith town (pt.)[45]	49	...
St. John town (pt.)[45]	3 569	1 757
Schererville town[45]	13 209	3 663
West Creek township	4 316	3 391
Lowell town (pt.)[45]	1 362	894
Schneider town	364	426
Winfield township	3 661	1 331
La Porte County[46]	108 632	105 342
Cass township	1 772	1 473
Wanatah town (pt.)[46]	770	690
Center township	22 763	24 437
La Porte city (pt.)[46]	17 900	20 142
Pine Lake (CDP)	1 676	1 954
Clinton township	969	890
Wanatah town (pt.)	109	83
Cool Spring township	14 679	10 654
Michigan City city (pt.)[46]	7 026	4 929

County Subdivisions	1980	1970
La Porte County—Con.		
Cool Spring township—Con.		
Trail Creek town (pt.)	1 011	769
Dewey township	1 260	1 153
La Crosse town	713	696
Galena township	1 553	1 148
Hanna township	858	755
Hudson township	1 682	1 538
Hudson Lake (CDP)	1 347	1 134
Johnson township	228	233
Kankakee township	3 483	2 662
La Porte city (pt.)[46]	1 015	329
Lincoln township	1 739	1 596
Michigan township	34 653	40 135
Long Beach town	2 262	2 740
Michiana Shores town (pt.)	289	237
Michigan City city (pt.)	29 824	34 440
Pottawattomie Park town[46]	284	374
Trail Creek town (pt.)	1 570	1 928
New Durham township	4 413	4 234
Westville town[46]	2 887	2 614
Noble township	1 350	1 261
Pleasant township	3 770	2 330
La Porte city (pt.)	1 283	1 063
Prairie township	194	192
Scipio township	3 336	2 453
La Porte city (pt.)[46]	1 598	606
Springfield township	4 968	4 182
Michiana Shores town (pt.)	175	212
Union township	2 757	2 255
Kingsford Heights town[46]	1 618	1 200
Washington township	942	847
Kingsbury town	329	314
Wills township	1 263	914
Lawrence County[47]	42 472	38 038
Bono township	721	614
Guthrie township	1 275	1 160
Indian Creek township	2 296	1 836
Oolitic town (pt.)[47]	–	...
Marion township	8 913	7 390
Mitchell city[47]	4 641	4 092
Marshall township	3 509	2 380
Perry township	1 533	1 148
Pleasant Run township	1 579	1 601
Shawswick township	20 569	20 160
Bedford city[47]	14 410	13 087
Oolitic town (pt.)[47]	1 495	1 155
Spice Valley township	2 077	1 749
Madison County[48]	139 336	'138 522
Adams township	3 795	3 381
Markleville town[48]	427	457
Anderson township	65 134	71 004
Anderson city (pt.)	62 684	68 482
Country Club Heights town	97	118
Edgewood town	2 215	2 326
River Forest town	29	27
Woodlawn Heights town	109	51
Boone township	734	642
Duck Creek township	572	646
Elwood city (pt.)[48]	–	...
Fall Creek township	10 854	10 055
Pendleton town[48]	2 130	2 243
Green township	2 732	2 208
Ingalls town[48]	909	888
Jackson township	2 159	1 838
Lafayette township	6 166	5 952
Anderson city (pt.)[48]	1 686	1 825
Frankton town (pt.)	448	356
Monroe township	10 832	9 993
Alexandria city[48]	6 028	'5 600
Orestes town	539	519
Pipe Creek township	15 411	15 885
Elwood city (pt.)[48]	10 608	11 196
Frankton town (pt.)[48]	1 632	1 440
Richland township	5 634	4 304
Anderson city (pt.)[48]	289	480
Stony Creek township	3 890	'3 502
Lapel town[48]	1 881	'1 796
Union township	9 288	7 084
Anderson city (pt.)[48]	36	...
Chesterfield town[48]	2 701	3 001
Van Buren township	2 135	2 028
Summitville town[48]	1 085	1 104
Marion County[49]	765 233	'793 769
Center township	208 624	'273 634
Beech Grove city (pt.)	3 892	4 712
Indianapolis city (pt.)	204 732	'268 922
Decatur township	19 426	'15 285
Indianapolis city (pt.)	19 426	'15 285
Franklin township	16 477	'10 241
Beech Grove city (pt.)[49]	900	'428
Indianapolis city (pt.)[49]	15 577	'9 813
Lawrence township	75 860	66 296
Castleton town	80	'183
Indianapolis city (pt.)[49]	50 189	'49 760
Lawrence city[49]	25 591	'16 353

County Subdivisions	1980	1970
Marion County—Con.		
Perry township	78 485	'73 735
Beech Grove city (pt.)[49]	8 402	'8 419
Homecroft town	831	'964
Indianapolis city (pt.)[49]	66 986	'62 010
Southport city	2 266	'2 342
Pike township	25 336	'14 970
Clermont town (pt.)	401	...
Indianapolis city (pt.)	24 935	'14 970
Warren township	89 208	'87 238
Beech Grove city (pt.)	2	...
Cumberland town (pt.)	2 246	'999
Indianapolis city (pt.)	85 157	'84 352
Warren Park town	1 803	'1 887
Washington township	129 008	126 136
Crows Nest town	106	'100
Indianapolis city (pt.)	125 074	'121 657
Meridian Hills town	1 801	'1 850
North Crows Nest town	82	'50
Ravenswood town	424	'656
Rocky Ripple town	778	'1 192
Spring Hill town	27	'22
Williams Creek town	427	'485
Wynnedale town	289	'124
Wayne township	122 809	'126 234
Clermont town (pt.)	1 270	'1 423
Indianapolis city (pt.)	108 731	'110 093
Lynhurst town	167	'201
Speedway town[49]	12 641	'14 523
Marshall County[50]	39 155	34 986
Bourbon township	2 708	2 801
Bourbon town[50]	1 522	1 606
Center township	11 377	10 236
Plymouth city[50]	7 693	7 661
German township	7 166	6 484
Bremen town[50]	3 565	3 487
Green township	963	874
Argos town (pt.)[50]	38	21
North township	3 913	3 240
La Paz town	651	604
Polk township	2 527	2 171
Koontz Lake (CDP) (pt.)	166	...
Tippecanoe township	1 244	1 098
Union township	3 604	3 563
Culver town[50]	1 601	1 783
Walnut township	2 486	2 371
Argos town (pt.)[50]	1 509	1 372
West township	3 167	2 148
Martin County[51]	11 001	10 969
Center township	1 761	1 666
Shoals town (pt.)	616	631
Halbert township	1 646	1 673
Shoals town (pt.)	351	408
Lost River township	524	509
Mitcheltree township	792	714
Perry township	5 624	5 775
Crane town[51]	297	339
Loogootee city[51]	3 100	2 953
Rutherford township	654	632
Miami County[52]	39 820	39 246
Allen township	695	814
Macy town	282	273
Butler township	828	762
Clay township	811	857
Deer Creek township	1 809	1 518
Grissom AFB (CDP) (pt.)	–	...
Erie township	498	417
Harrison township	722	713
North Grove town	91	107
Jackson township	2 231	2 333
Amboy town	450	473
Converse town (pt.)[52]	1 155	1 163
Jefferson township	2 702	2 506
Denver town[52]	589	566
Perry township	905	882
Peru township	13 798	14 789
Peru city (pt.)[52]	11 356	12 345
Pipe Creek township	8 901	8 642
Bunker Hill town[52]	984	956
Grissom AFB (CDP) (pt.)	4 676	4 963
Richland township	1 115	1 079
Union township	967	819
Washington township	3 838	3 115
Peru city (pt.)	2 408	1 794
Monroe County[53]	98 785	'85 221
Bean Blossom township	2 168	1 709
Stinesville town	227	291
Benton township	2 892	1 976
Bloomington township	39 877	'37 545
Bloomington city (pt.)[53]	33 106	'29 274
Clear Creek township	3 089	2 474
Indian Creek township	1 281	876
Perry township	26 634	'24 605
Bloomington city (pt.)[53]	17 036	'13 711
Polk township	373	294
Richland township	9 765	6 826

County Subdivisions

	1980	1970
Monroe County—Con.		
Richland township—Con.		
Bloomington city (pt.)53	5	-
Ellettsville town53	3 328	1 627
Salt Creek township	1 157	798
Van Buren township	9 839	6 709
Bloomington city (pt.)53	1 897	277
Washington township	1 710	1 409
Montgomery County54	35 501	33 930
Brown township	1 764	1 603
New Market town (pt.)54	101	114
Waveland town	559	557
Clark township	1 972	1 751
Ladoga town	1 151	1 099
Coal Creek township	1 541	1 638
New Richmond town	403	381
Wingate town	373	437
Franklin township	1 700	1 592
Darlington town	811	802
Madison township	1 158	1 220
Linden town54	700	713
Ripley township	1 032	780
Alamo town	178	145
Scott township	826	807
New Market town (pt.)	189	193
Sugar Creek township	447	390
Union township	21 992	21 035
Crawfordsville city54	13 325	13 842
New Market town (pt.)54	318	333
Walnut township	1 475	1 448
New Ross town	306	318
Wayne township	1 594	1 666
Waynetown town	915	993
Morgan County55	51 999	44 176
Adams township	970	915
Ashland township	1 098	1 054
Baker township	549	455
Brown township	9 285	8 604
Brooklyn town (pt.)	1	6
Mooresville town55	5 349	5 800
Clay township	3 381	3 104
Bethany town	127	121
Brooklyn town (pt.)55	888	905
Green township55	1 968	1 706
Gregg township	2 315	1 918
Harrison township	1 501	1 242
Jackson township	2 668	2 264
Morgantown town	897	1 134
Jefferson township	2 617	2 047
Madison township	5 290	3 950
Monroe township	3 813	2 940
Lake Hart town55	231	...
Ray township	1 286	1 231
Paragon town55	538	538
Washington township	15 258	12 746
Martinsville city55	11 311	9 723
Newton County56	14 844	11 606
Beaver township	1 863	1 831
Morocco town56	1 348	1 285
Colfax township	213	256
Grant township	1 567	1 570
Goodland town56	1 200	1 176
Iroquois township	1 359	1 389
Brook town56	926	919
Jackson township	578	567
Mount Ayr town	207	194
Jefferson township	2 384	2 294
Kentland town56	1 936	1 864
Lake township	2 311	1 762
Lincoln township	3 753	1 191
McClellan township	280	244
Washington township	536	502
Noble County57	35 443	31 382
Albion township	1 732	1 597
Albion town57	1 637	1 498
Allen township	4 798	4 035
Avilla town57	1 272	881
Kendallville city (pt.)57	1 404	1 124
Elkhart township	1 501	1 245
Green township	1 301	1 064
Jefferson township	1 189	1 127
Noble township	2 490	2 291
Orange township	4 016	3 500
Rome City town57	1 319	1 354
Wolcottville town (pt.)57	520	496
Perry township	4 436	4 070
Ligonier city57	3 134	3 034
Sparta township	1 867	1 611
Cromwell town57	458	475
Swan township	1 861	1 529
Washington township	979	718
Wayne township	8 274	7 810
Kendallville city (pt.)57	5 895	5 714
York township	999	785

County Subdivisions

	1980	1970
Ohio County58	5 114	4 289
Cass township	481	398
Pike township	332	224
Randolph township	4 034	3 418
Rising Sun city58	2 478	2 305
Union township	267	249
Orange County59	18 677	16 968
French Lick township	5 184	4 896
French Lick town59	2 265	2 059
West Baden Springs town59	796	930
Greenfield township	469	338
Jackson township	346	474
Northeast township	594	626
Northwest township	343	326
Orangeville township	521	463
Orleans township	3 210	2 814
Orleans town59	2 161	1 834
Paoli township	5 780	5 151
Paoli town59	3 637	3 281
Southeast township	1 435	1 262
Stampers Creek township	795	618
Owen County60	15 841	12 163
Clay township	1 823	1 272
Franklin township	791	727
Harrison township	355	253
Jackson township	1 248	299
Jefferson township	853	751
Jennings township	640	370
Lafayette township	589	378
Marion township	723	730
Montgomery township	718	479
Morgan township	677	540
Taylor township	922	748
Washington township	5 070	4 400
Spencer town60	2 732	'2 553
Wayne township	1 432	1 216
Gosport town60	729	692
Parke County61	16 372	'14 628
Adams township	4 535	4 161
Rockville town61	2 785	2 820
Florida township	2 632	2 433
Rosedale town	744	817
Greene township	524	470
Howard township	226	204
Jackson township	669	549
Liberty township	889	852
Penn township	897	887
Bloomingdale town	409	391
Raccoon township	856	711
Reserve township	1 635	1 562
Montezuma town (pt.)61	1 325	1 157
Sugar Creek township	292	265
Union township	1 172	698
Wabash township	1 028	875
Mecca town61	482	...
Montezuma town (pt.)	27	35
Washington township	1 017	'961
Judson town	80	'63
Marshall town61	413	365
Perry County62	19 346	19 075
Anderson township	1 359	1 105
Clark township	1 111	1 126
Leopold township	619	566
Oil township	894	885
Tobin township	901	776
Troy township	13 921	14 077
Cannelton city62	2 373	2 280
Tell City city62	8 704	7 933
Troy town	550	575
Union township	541	540
Pike County63	13 465	12 281
Clay township	374	368
Jefferson township	1 657	1 653
Lockhart township	681	632
Logan township	380	514
Madison township	472	415
Marion township	587	516
Monroe township	839	842
Spurgeon town	250	285
Patoka township	3 213	2 898
Winslow town63	1 017	1 030
Washington township	5 262	4 443
Petersburg city63	2 987	2 697
Porter County64	119 816	87 114
Boone township	4 492	2 715
Hebron town64	2 696	1 624
Center township	29 392	25 191
Valparaiso city64	22 247	20 020
Jackson township	2 983	1 540
Liberty township	5 367	3 260
Chesterton town (pt.)	256	215
Morgan township	1 769	1 102
Pine township	3 311	3 098
Beverly Shores town	864	946
Town of Pines town	962	1 007

County Subdivisions	1980	1970
Porter County—Con.		
Pleasant township	3 172	2 462
Kouts town[64]	1 619	1 388
Portage township	39 765	28 371
Ogden Dunes town	1 489	1 361
Portage city (pt.)[64]	27 043	19 127
South Haven (CDP)	6 679	...
Porter township	6 493	2 420
Union township	5 337	2 077
Washington township	2 424	1 226
Westchester township	15 311	13 652
Burns Harbor town	920	1 284
Chesterton town (pt.)[64]	8 275	5 962
Dune Acres town	291	301
Portage city (pt.)	366	—
Porter town	2 988	3 058
Posey County[65]	26 414	21 740
Bethel township	386	359
Griffin town	192	178
Black township	10 429	9 268
Mount Vernon city[65]	7 656	6 770
Center township	1 151	938
Harmony township	1 536	1 618
New Harmony town[65]	945	971
Lynn township	891	649
Marrs township	4 182	2 931
Point township	443	415
Robb township	2 167	1 933
Poseyville town[65]	1 247	1 035
Robinson township	3 750	2 218
Smith township	1 479	1 411
Cynthiana town[65]	874	793
Pulaski County	13 258	12 534
Beaver township	439	426
Cass township	913	670
Franklin township	644	578
Harrison township	725	596
Indian Creek township	645	718
Jefferson township	482	491
Monroe township	3 833	3 664
Winamac town	2 370	2 341
Rich Grove township	811	852
Salem township	1 459	1 427
Francesville town	944	1 015
Tippecanoe township	1 041	920
Monterey town	236	268
Van Buren township	1 014	974
White Post township	1 252	1 218
Medaryville town	731	732
Putnam County[66]	29 163	26 932
Clinton township	1 144	829
Cloverdale township	2 584	2 049
Cloverdale town (pt.)[66]	1 352	870
Floyd township	1 487	734
Franklin township	1 699	1 712
Roachdale town	958	1 004
Greencastle township	10 986	11 498
Greencastle city[66]	8 403	8 852
Jackson township	797	706
Jefferson township	1 008	963
Madison township	1 040	953
Marion township	1 974	1 871
Monroe township	1 442	1 393
Bainbridge town[66]	644	703
Russell township	876	814
Russellville town	376	390
Warren township	2 174	1 884
Cloverdale town (pt.)[66]	5	...
Washington township	1 952	1 526
Randolph County[67]	29 997	28 915
Franklin township	1 578	1 539
Ridgeville town[67]	933	924
Green township	1 119	878
Albany town (pt.)[67]	245	...
Greensfork township	1 360	1 220
Jackson township	736	725
Monroe township	3 916	3 322
Farmland town[67]	1 560	1 262
Parker City town[67]	1 414	1 179
Stoney Creek township	1 113	997
Union township	2 628	2 555
Losantville town[67]	306	212
Modoc town	243	275
Ward township	1 370	1 454
Saratoga town[67]	338	406
Washington township	2 596	2 709
Lynn town[67]	1 250	1 360
Wayne township	5 160	5 339
Union City city[67]	3 908	3 995
White River township	8 421	8 177
Winchester city[67]	5 659	5 493
Ripley County[68]	24 398	21 138
Adams township	3 385	2 733
Batesville city (pt.)[68]	192	105
Sunman town	924	707
Brown township	1 461	1 313
Center township	2 498	2 248

County Subdivisions	1980	1970
Ripley County—Con.		
Center township—Con.		
Osgood town	1 554	1 346
Delaware township	1 181	1 027
Franklin township	3 434	2 907
Milan town (pt.)	1 100	1 046
Jackson township	1 033	945
Napoleon town	246	282
Johnson township	2 960	2 266
Versailles town[68]	1 560	1 080
Laughery township	4 357	4 231
Batesville city (pt.)[68]	3 277	3 364
Otter Creek township	1 377	1 337
Holton town[68]	487	...
Shelby township	901	830
Washington township	1 811	1 301
Milan town (pt.)[68]	466	214
Rush County[69]	19 604	20 352
Anderson township	1 487	1 463
Center township	1 177	1 440
Jackson township	435	466
Noble township	817	739
Orange township	828	810
Posey township	1 271	1 178
Richland township	460	516
Ripley township	1 988	1 998
Carthage town	886	946
Rushville township	8 596	8 894
Rushville city[69]	6 113	6 686
Union township	920	1 030
Glenwood town (pt.)	246	301
Walker township	1 057	1 100
Washington township	568	718
St. Joseph County[70]	241 617	244 827
Center township	12 402	11 474
South Bend city (pt.)[70]	6 309	4 398
Clay township	28 147	20 821
Indian Village town	151	86
Mishawaka city (pt.)[70]	1 780	—
Roseland town	832	895
South Bend city (pt.)[70]	2 059	1 900
German township	6 826	5 028
South Bend city (pt.)[70]	2 842	1 306
Greene township	3 036	2 799
Harris township	5 265	2 860
Liberty township	2 922	3 222
North Liberty town[70]	1 211	1 259
Lincoln township	2 875	2 907
Walkerton town[70]	2 051	2 006
Madison township	1 860	1 966
Olive township	3 418	3 383
New Carlisle town	1 439	1 434
Penn township	56 471	53 276
Mishawaka city (pt.)	38 421	36 060
Osceola town[70]	1 990	1 572
South Bend city (pt.)[70]	352	11
Portage township	109 694	129 273
South Bend city (pt.)[70]	98 165	117 965
Union township	3 374	3 039
Lakeville town	629	712
Warren township	5 327	4 779
Scott County[71]	20 422	17 144
Finley township	1 048	838
Jennings township	7 091	6 277
Austin town[71]	4 857	4 902
Johnson township	1 989	1 515
Lexington township	2 605	1 890
Vienna township	7 689	6 624
Scottsburg city[71]	5 068	4 791
Shelby County[72]	39 887	37 797
Addison township	17 334	17 790
Shelbyville city (pt.)[72]	14 989	15 094
Brandywine township	2 167	1 893
Shelbyville city (pt.)	—	—
Hanover township	2 134	2 048
Morristown town[72]	989	838
Hendricks township	1 244	1 266
Jackson township	1 196	1 030
Liberty township	1 844	1 778
Marion township	1 326	921
Moral township	4 565	3 511
Noble township	1 345	1 186
St. Paul town (pt.)[72]	326	240
Shelby township	2 122	1 981
Sugar Creek township	928	899
Union township	782	859
Van Buren township	1 488	1 280
Washington township	1 412	1 355
Spencer County[73]	19 361	17 134
Carter township	3 160	2 409
Dale town[73]	1 693	1 113
Santa Claus town (pt.)[73]	92	24
Clay township	996	596
Santa Claus town (pt.)[73]	420	39
Grass township	1 387	1 513
Chrisney town	537	550

County Subdivisions

County Subdivisions	1980	1970
Spencer County—Con.		
Hammond township	1 653	1 535
Grandview town	670	696
Harrison township	2 234	2 199
Santa Claus town (pt.)[73]	2	...
Huff township	1 034	1 022
Jackson township	848	630
Gentryville town	299	281
Luce township	2 981	2 718
Ohio township	5 068	4 512
Rockport city	2 590	2 565
Starke County[74]	21 997	19 280
California township	2 041	1 832
Center township	6 195	5 267
Knox city	3 674	3 519
Davis township	1 123	1 081
Hamlet town (pt.)	524	526
Jackson township	465	498
North Bend township	1 153	1 131
Oregon township	2 826	2 344
Hamlet town (pt.)	214	235
Koontz Lake (CDP) (pt.)	1 270	...
Railroad township	1 495	1 381
Washington township	2 112	1 606
Wayne township	4 587	4 140
North Judson town[74]	1 653	1 738
Steuben County[75]	24 694	20 159
Clear Lake township	576	501
Clear Lake town[75]	301	271
Fremont township	1 730	1 543
Fremont town[75]	1 180	1 043
Jackson township	1 157	973
Jamestown township	2 051	1 167
Millgrove township	1 295	1 083
Orland town	424	457
Otsego township	2 296	1 794
Hamilton town (pt.)	466	439
Pleasant township	9 387	7 804
Angola city[75]	5 486	5 117
Richland township	480	452
Salem township	1 945	1 567
Hudson town (pt.)	243	275
Scott township	831	745
Steuben township	2 352	1 986
Ashley town (pt.)	313	308
Hudson town (pt.)	204	189
York township	594	544
Sullivan County[76]	21 107	19 889
Cass township	2 454	2 263
Dugger town[76]	1 118	1 150
Curry township	3 988	3 778
Farmersburg town[76]	1 240	962
Shelburn town	1 259	1 281
Fairbanks township[76]	864	699
Gill township	1 089	1 083
Merom town[76]	360	305
Haddon township	1 817	1 972
Carlisle town	717	714
Hamilton township	6 945	6 555
Sullivan city	4 774	4 683
Jackson township	2 099	1 899
Hymera town	1 054	907
Jefferson township	887	800
Turman township	964	840
Switzerland County[77]	7 153	6 306
Cotton township	1 009	869
Craig township	761	709
Jefferson township	2 487	2 365
Vevay town[77]	1 343	1 463
Pleasant township	1 039	819
Posey township	1 149	921
Patriot town	265	216
York township	708	623
Tippecanoe County[78]	121 702	109 378
Fairfield township	44 533	45 439
Lafayette city (pt.)[78]	37 384	40 584
Jackson township	520	558
Lauramie township	2 125	2 245
Clarks Hill town	653	741
Perry township	2 720	2 257
Randolph township	754	787
Sheffield township	2 254	2 145
Dayton town[78]	781	...
Shelby township	1 855	1 580
Otterbein town (pt.)[78]	300	'17
Tippecanoe township	4 636	3 486
Battle Ground town[78]	812	818
Union township	1 713	1 577
Lafayette city (pt.)	-	...
Wabash township	44 267	37 853
West Lafayette city[78]	21 247	19 157
Washington township	2 394	2 245
Wayne township	1 233	1 034
Wea township	12 698	8 172
Lafayette city (pt.)[78]	5 627	4 371

County Subdivisions	1980	1970
Tipton County[79]	16 819	16 650
Cicero township	8 374	8 252
Tipton city	5 004	'5 313
Jefferson township	1 550	1 537
Kempton town	410	469
Liberty township	2 455	2 180
Sharpsville town[79]	617	672
Madison township	1 602	1 780
Elwood city (pt.)[79]	259	...
Prairie township	1 141	1 083
Wildcat township	1 697	1 818
Windfall City town	911	946
Union County[80]	6 860	6 582
Brownsville township	921	909
Center township	2 754	2 751
Liberty town[80]	1 844	1 831
Harmony township	377	335
Harrison township	538	554
Liberty township	873	712
Union township	1 397	1 321
West College Corner town	614	709
Vanderburgh County[81]	167 515	168 772
Armstrong township	1 665	1 587
Darmstadt town (pt.)[81]	101	...
Center township	23 839	21 695
Darmstadt town (pt.)[81]	26	...
Evansville city (pt.)[81]	13 516	13 328
German township	6 718	6 018
Darmstadt town (pt.)[81]	27	...
Evansville city (pt.)[81]	-	...
Knight township	63 515	61 850
Evansville city (pt.)	58 409	59 515
Perry township	19 455	19 094
Evansville city (pt.)	11 360	12 024
Pigeon township	47 226	53 899
Evansville city (pt.)	47 211	53 897
Scott township	4 674	4 175
Darmstadt town (pt.)[81]	1 126	...
Union township	423	454
Vermillion County[82]	18 229	16 793
Clinton township	9 781	9 084
Clinton city[82]	5 267	5 340
Fairview Park town	1 545	1 067
Universal town	428	462
Eugene township	2 407	2 127
Cayuga town[82]	1 258	1 090
Helt township	3 102	2 819
Dana town	803	720
Highland township	1 854	1 694
Perrysville town[82]	532	510
Vermillion township	1 085	1 069
Newport town	704	708
Vigo County[83]	112 385	114 528
Fayette township	3 095	2 734
Harrison township	60 462	'69 577
Terre Haute city (pt.)	60 462	'69 577
Honey Creek township	11 533	9 079
Terre Haute city (pt.)[83]	31	14
Linton township	1 451	1 435
Lost Creek township	7 753	'6 434
Seelyville town	1 374	1 195
Terre Haute city (pt.)	619	'681
Nevins township	2 306	2 200
Otter Creek township	9 485	7 801
Terre Haute city (pt.)	13	63
Pierson township	1 469	1 285
Prairie Creek township	1 339	1 216
Prairieton township	1 766	1 063
Riley township	2 224	1 976
Riley town	269	257
Sugar Creek township	9 502	9 728
West Terre Haute town[83]	2 806	2 704
Wabash County[84]	36 640	35 553
Chester township	8 334	8 015
North Manchester town[84]	5 998	5 791
Lagro township	2 990	2 981
Lagro town	549	552
Liberty township	2 506	1 946
La Fontaine town[84]	946	793
Noble township	17 314	17 574
Wabash city[84]	12 985	13 379
Paw Paw township	1 674	1 616
Roann town[84]	548	509
Pleasant township	2 456	2 164
Waltz township	1 366	1 257
Warren County[85]	8 976	8 705
Adams township	578	679
Pine Village town	257	291
Jordan township	364	428
Kent township	504	387
State Line City town	233	176
Liberty township	811	866
Medina township	381	403
Mound township	483	404
Pike township	1 480	1 266
West Lebanon town[85]	946	899

County Subdivisions

County Subdivisions	1980	1970
Warren County—Con.		
Pine township	442	489
Prairie township	396	397
Steuben township	575	555
Warren township	711	756
Washington township	2 251	2 075
Williamsport town[85]	1 747	1 661
Warrick County[86]	41 474	27 972
Anderson township	999	829
Boon township	11 420	9 497
Boonville city[86]	6 300	5 736
Chandler town (pt.)[86]	516	...
Campbell township	1 001	1 512
Greer township	1 935	1 588
Elberfeld town[86]	640	834
Hart township	1 360	1 102
Lynnville town	566	556
Lane township	302	237
Ohio township	21 318	10 696
Chandler town (pt.)[86]	2 527	2 032
Newburgh town[86]	2 906	2 302
Owen township	576	450
Pigeon township	992	818
Skelton township	1 571	1 243
Tennyson town	331	335
Washington County[87]	21 932	19 278
Brown township	1 336	1 305
Campbellsburg town	695	678
Saltillo town	134	134
Franklin township	1 290	1 066
Gibson township	917	911
Little York town	150	191
Howard township	1 079	834
Jackson township	972	602
Jefferson township	836	728
Madison township	555	513
Livonia town	120	120
Monroe township	460	462
Pierce township	1 738	1 536
New Pekin town (pt.)[87]	692	610
Polk township	1 682	1 384
New Pekin town (pt.)	433	302
Posey township	1 525	1 258
Fredericksburg town	233	207
Hardinsburg town	298	263
Vernon township	659	654
Washington township	8 883	8 025
Salem city[87]	5 290	5 041
Wayne County[88]	76 058	79 109
Abington township	793	727
Boston township	1 029	1 009
Boston town	189	210
Richmond city (pt.)	—	—
Center township	7 315	6 943
Centerville town[88]	2 284	2 380
Richmond city (pt.)[88]	3	...
Clay township	1 061	1 076
Greens Fork town	426	444
Dalton township	612	619
Franklin township	1 450	1 423
Whitewater town	107	111
Greene township	1 326	1 180
Harrison township	333	348
Jackson township	5 588	5 518
Cambridge City town[88]	2 407	2 481
Dublin town	979	1 021
East Germantown town	438	447
Mount Auburn town	192	157
Jefferson township	3 479	3 501
Hagerstown town[88]	1 950	2 059
New Garden township	1 924	1 889
Fountain City town	839	852
Perry township	762	775
Economy town[88]	237	285
Washington township	1 706	1 715
Milton town	729	694
Wayne township	47 236	51 104
Richmond city (pt.)[88]	41 346	43 999
Spring Grove town	469	437
Webster township	1 444	1 282
Wells County[89]	25 401	23 821
Chester township	1 085	1 072
Poneto town (pt.)	14	27
Harrison township	8 957	9 270
Bluffton city (pt.)[89]	6 673	7 249
Poneto town (pt.)	93	101
Vera Cruz town	117	140
Jackson township	864	991
Jefferson township	4 637	3 787
Ossian town[89]	1 945	1 538
Lancaster township	4 259	3 071
Bluffton city (pt.)[89]	2 032	1 048
Liberty township	1 264	1 361
Poneto town (pt.)	143	158
Nottingham township	1 132	1 238
Rock Creek township	1 323	1 369
Markle town (pt.)	141	106

County Subdivisions	1980	1970
Wells County—Con.		
Rock Creek township—Con.		
Uniondale town (pt.)	266	291
Union township	1 880	1 662
Markle town[89]	79	71
Uniondale town (pt.)	37	58
White County[90]	23 867	20 995
Big Creek township	911	975
Chalmers town[90]	554	544
Cass township	570	614
Honey Creek township	1 296	1 170
Reynolds town	632	641
Jackson township	862	742
Burnettsville town	496	510
Liberty township	1 733	1 371
Lincoln township	714	772
Monon township	3 389	2 998
Monon town[90]	1 540	1 548
Prairie township	2 788	2 180
Brookston town[90]	1 701	1 232
Princeton township	1 535	1 556
Wolcott town	923	894
Round Grove township	282	382
Union township	9 357	7 741
Monticello city[90]	5 162	4 869
West Point township	430	494
Whitley County[91]	26 215	23 395
Cleveland township	3 071	3 081
South Whitley town[91]	1 575	1 362
Columbia township	7 694	6 813
Columbia City city[91]	5 091	4 911
Etna—Troy township	1 453	1 369
Jefferson township	1 697	1 380
Richland township	1 452	1 431
Larwill town[91]	286	324
Smith township	4 821	4 130
Churubusco town[91]	1 638	1 528
Tri—Lakes (CDP) (pt.)	35	...
Thorncreek township	3 036	2 669
Tri—Lakes (CDP) (pt.)	1 321	1 193
Union township	1 801	1 434
Washington township	1 190	1 088

IOWA

Iowa takes its name from a tribe of Indians which formerly occupied the region now constituting the state. The meaning of the word is variously given as "this is the place," "the drowsy or sleepy ones," "the tribe beyond the river," and "beautiful region."

The eastern border of Iowa was visited by the French missionaries Marquette and Joliet in 1673. White settlers, however, did not come to the region for more than a century, and a century and a half elapsed before any permanent settlements were made.

In 1788 Julien Dubuque made a settlement on the site of the present city of Dubuque. At his death in 1810 this was abandoned and no permanent settlements were made within the present limits of the state until after 1830. Dubuque was permanently settled in 1833, and about the same time settlements were made at Burlington and Fort Madison.

Iowa originally formed a part of the vast Louisiana region claimed by the French on account of the discoveries of Marquette, Joliet, La Salle, and others. It was ceded to France by Spain in 1762, retroceded to France in 1800 and purchased by the United States in 1803. In 1804 the region was divided by the thirty-third parallel, the present northern boundary of Louisiana, into the territory of Orleans on the south and the district of Louisiana on the north, and the northern district was attached to the territory of Indiana. In the following year the district of Louisiana became the territory of Louisiana. In 1812 the state of Louisiana, formed in part from the territory of Orleans, was admitted to the union, and the territory of Louisiana became the territory of Missouri.

In 1834 the area now comprising the state of Iowa was added to the territory of Michigan. In 1836 it became a part of the territory of Wisconsin, organized in that year, and in 1838, a part of the area organized as the territory of Iowa. In 1845 Congress passed an act to enable Iowa to become a state. The northern and western boundaries were to be established about 45 miles north and about 90 miles east, respectively, of their present location. These boundaries were rejected by popular vote later in the same year. In 1846 a state constitution, providing for boundaries as they now exist, was adopted, and in December of the same year Iowa became one of the states of the Union.

COUNTY LOCATION INDEX

County	Loc	County	Loc	County	Loc
Adair	D-3	Fremont	E-2	O'Brien	B-2
Adams	D-3	Greene	C-3	Osceola	A-2
Allamakee	A-6	Grundy	C-5	Page	E-3
Appanoose	E-5	Guthrie	D-3	Palo Alto	B-3
Audubon	D-3	Hamilton	C-4	Plymouth	B-2
Benton	C-6	Hancock	B-4	Pocahontas	B-3
Black Hawk	C-5	Hardin	C-5	Polk	D-4
Boone	C-4	Harrison	D-2	Pottawattamie	D-2
Bremer	B-5	Henry	E-6	Poweshiek	D-5
Buchanan	B-6	Howard	A-5	Ringgold	E-3
Buena Vista	B-3	Humboldt	B-4	Sac	C-3
Butler	B-5	Ida	C-2	Scott	D-7
Calhoun	C-3	Iowa	D-6	Shelby	D-2
Carroll	C-3	Jackson	C-7	Sioux	B-2
Cass	D-3	Jasper	D-5	Story	C-4
Cedar	C-7	Jefferson	D-6	Tama	C-5
Cerro Gordo	B-4	Johnson	D-6	Taylor	E-3
Cherokee	B-2	Jones	C-7	Union	D-3
Chickasaw	B-5	Keokuk	D-6	Van Buren	E-6
Clarke	D-4	Kossuth	B-4	Wapello	D-5
Clay	B-3	Lee	E-6	Warren	D-4
Clayton	B-6	Linn	C-6	Washington	D-6
Clinton	C-7	Louisa	D-7	Wayne	E-4
Crawford	C-2	Lucas	D-4	Webster	C-4
Dallas	D-4	Lyon	A-2	Winnebago	A-4
Davis	E-5	Madison	D-4	Winneshiek	A-6
Decatur	E-4	Mahaska	D-5	Woodbury	C-2
Delaware	B-6	Marion	D-5	Worth	A-5
Des Moines	E-7	Marshall	C-5	Wright	B-4
Dickinson	A-3	Mills	D-2		
Dubuque	B-7	Mitchell	A-5		
Emmet	A-3	Monona	C-2		
Fayette	B-6	Monroe	D-5		
Floyd	B-5	Montgomery	D-3		
Franklin	B-5	Muscatine	D-7		

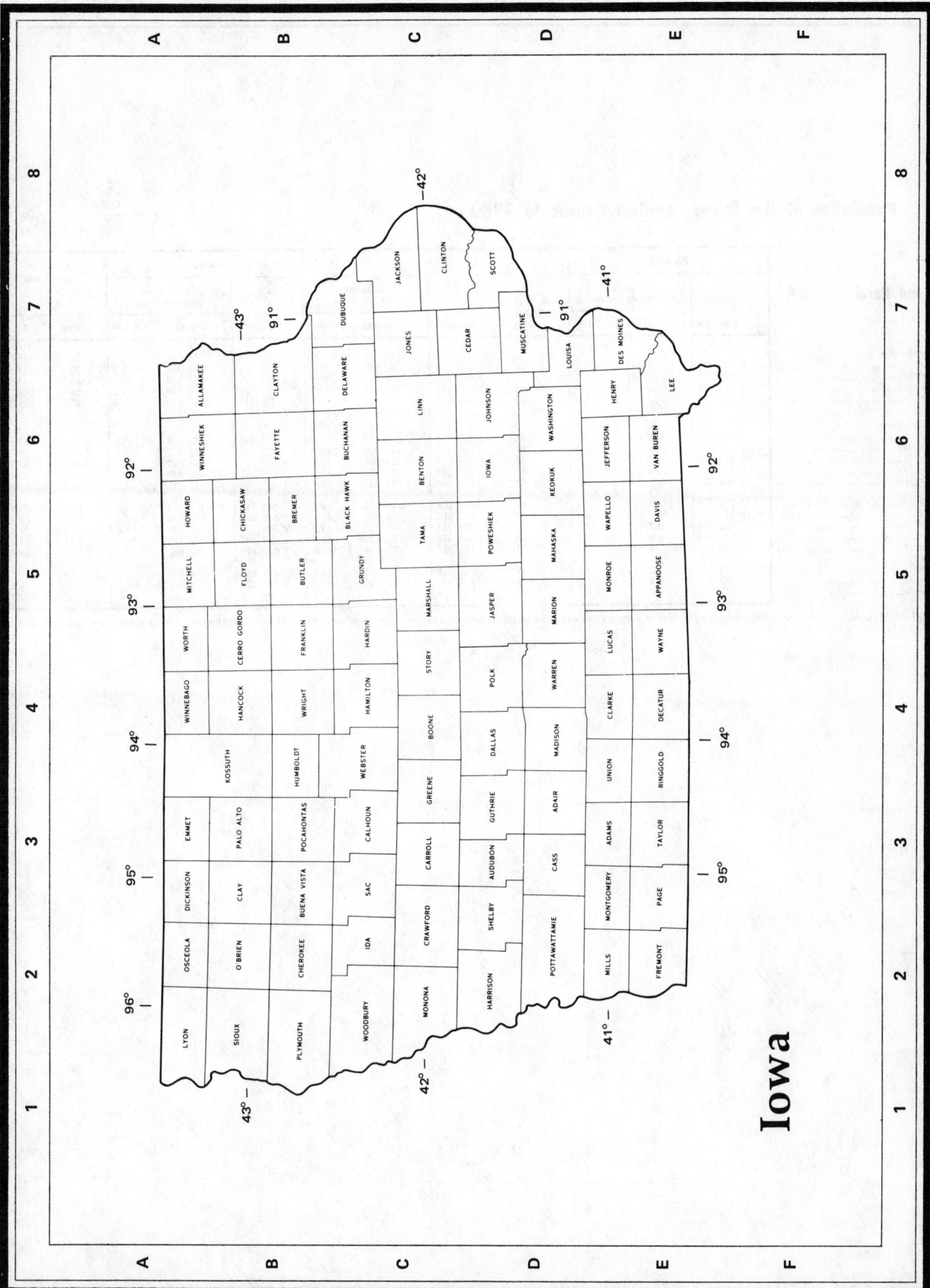

Iowa

Population of the State: Earliest Census to 1980

Urban and Rural

	The State			Urban				Rural			Percent of total population	
	Total population	Change from preceding census		Places of 2,500 or more	Population	Change from preceding census		Population	Change from preceding census		Urban	Rural
		Number	Percent			Number	Percent		Number	Percent		
Current urban definition:												
1980 (Apr. 1)_____	2 913 808	88 440	3.1	124	1 708 232	91 827	5.7	1 205 576	−2 395	−0.2	58.6	41.4
1970 (Apr. 1)_____	ʳ2 825 368	67 831	2.5	111	1 616 405	153 893	10.5	1 207 971	−87 054	−6.7	57.2	42.8
1960 (Apr. 1)_____	2 757 537	136 464	5.2	104	1 462 512	211 574	16.9	1 295 025	−75 110	−5.5	53.0	47.0
1950 (Apr. 1)_____	2 621 073	82 805	3.3	93	1 250 938	...	...	1 370 135	...	...	47.7	52.3
Previous urban definition:												
1960 (Apr. 1)_____	2 757 537	136 464	5.2	104	1 439 525	210 092	17.1	1 318 012	−73 628	−5.3	52.2	47.8
1950 (Apr. 1)_____	2 621 073	82 805	3.3	93	1 229 433	145 202	13.4	1 391 640	−62 397	−4.3	46.9	53.1
1940 (Apr. 1)_____	2 538 268	67 329	2.7	89	1 084 231	104 939	10.7	1 454 037	−37 610	−2.5	42.7	57.3
1930 (Apr. 1)_____	2 470 939	66 918	2.8	81	979 292	103 797	11.9	1 491 647	−36 879	−2.4	39.6	60.4
1920 (Jan. 1)_____	2 404 021	179 250	8.1	81	875 495	195 441	28.7	1 528 526	−16 191	−1.0	36.4	63.6
1910 (Apr. 15)_____	2 224 771	−7 082	−0.3	69	680 054	107 668	18.8	1 544 717	−114 750	−6.9	30.6	69.4
1900 (June 1)_____	2 231 853	319 556	16.7	70	572 386	166 622	41.1	1 659 467	152 934	10.2	25.6	74.4
1890 (June 1)_____	1 912 297	287 682	17.7	46	405 764	158 337	64.0	1 506 533	129 345	9.4	21.2	78.8
1880 (June 1)_____	1 624 615	430 595	36.1	34	247 427	91 100	58.3	1 377 188	339 495	32.7	15.2	84.8
1870 (June 1)_____	1 194 020	519 107	76.9	22	156 327	96 299	160.4	1 037 693	422 808	68.8	13.1	86.9
1860 (June 1)_____	674 913	482 699	251.1	9	60 028	50 298	516.9	614 885	432 401	237.0	8.9	91.1
1850 (June 1)_____	192 214	149 102	345.8	3	9 730	9 730	...	182 484	139 372	323.3	5.1	94.9
1840 (June 1)_____	43 112	...	...	−	−	...	...	43 112	...	...	−	100.0

NOTE: 1840 population includes that area now constituting that part of Minnesota lying west of the Mississippi River and a line drawn from its source northward to the Canadian boundary. This area formed part of Iowa Territory in 1840.

ADAIR

Year	Population
1860	984
1870	3,982
1880	11,667
1890	14,534
1900	16,192
1910	14,420
1920	14,259
1930	13,891
1940	13,196
1950	12,292
1960	10,893
1970	9,497
1980	9,509

ADAMS

Year	Population
1860	1,533
1870	4,614
1880	11,888
1890	12,292
1900	13,601
1910	10,998
1920	10,521
1930	10,437
1940	10,156
1950	8,753
1960	7,468
1970	6,322
1980	5,731

ALLAMAKEE

Year	Population
1850	777
1860	12,237
1870	17,868
1880	19,791
1890	17,907
1900	18,711
1910	17,328
1920	17,285
1930	16,328
1940	17,184
1950	16,351
1960	15,982
1970	14,968
1980	15,108

APPANOOSE

Year	Population
1850	3,131
1860	11,931
1870	16,456
1880	16,636
1890	18,961
1900	25,927
1910	28,701
1920	30,535
1930	24,835
1940	24,245
1950	19,683
1960	16,015
1970	15,007
1980	15,511

AUDUBON

Year	Population
1860	454
1870	1,212
1880	7,448
1890	12,412
1900	13,626
1910	12,671
1920	12,520
1930	12,264
1940	11,790
1950	11,579
1960	10,919
1970	9,595
1980	8,559

BENTON

Year	Population
1850	672
1860	8,496
1870	22,454
1880	24,888
1890	24,178
1900	25,177
1910	23,156
1920	24,080
1930	22,851
1940	22,879
1950	22,656
1960	23,422
1970	22,855
1980	23,649

BLACK HAWK

Year	Population
1850	135
1860	8,244
1870	21,706
1880	23,913
1890	24,219
1900	32,399
1910	44,865
1920	56,570
1930	69,146
1940	79,946
1950	100,448
1960	122,482
1970	132,916
1980	137,961

BOONE

Year	Population
1850	735
1860	4,232
1870	14,584
1880	20,838
1890	23,772
1900	28,200
1910	27,626
1920	29,892
1930	29,271
1940	29,782
1950	28,139
1960	28,037
1970	26,470
1980	26,184

BREMER

Year	Population
1860	4,915
1870	12,528
1880	14,081
1890	14,630
1900	16,035
1910	15,843
1920	16,728
1930	17,046
1940	17,932
1950	18,884
1960	21,108
1970	22,737
1980	24,820

BUCHANAN

Year	Population
1850	517
1860	7,906
1870	17,034
1880	18,546
1890	18,997
1900	21,427
1910	19,748
1920	19,890
1930	19,550
1940	20,991
1950	21,927
1960	22,293
1970	21,762
1980	22,900

BUENA VISTA

Year	Population
1860	57
1870	1,585
1880	7,537
1890	13,548
1900	16,975
1910	15,981
1920	18,556
1930	18,667
1940	19,838
1950	21,113
1960	21,189
1970	20,693
1980	20,774

BUTLER

Year	Population
1860	3,724
1870	9,951
1880	14,293
1890	15,463
1900	17,955
1910	17,119
1920	17,845
1930	17,617
1940	17,986
1950	17,394
1960	17,467
1970	16,953
1980	17,668

CALHOUN

Year	Population
1860	147
1870	1,602
1880	5,595
1890	13,107
1900	18,569
1910	17,090
1920	17,783
1930	17,605
1940	17,584
1950	16,925
1960	15,923
1970	14,292
1980	13,542

CARROLL

Year	Population
1860	281
1870	2,451
1880	12,351
1890	18,828
1900	20,319
1910	20,117
1920	21,549
1930	22,326
1940	22,770
1950	23,065
1960	23,431
1970	22,912
1980	22,951

CHICKASAW

Year	Population
1860	4,336
1870	10,180
1880	14,534
1890	15,019
1900	17,037
1910	15,375
1920	15,431
1930	14,637
1940	15,227
1950	15,228
1960	15,034
1970	14,969
1980	15,437

CASS

Year	Population
1860	1,612
1870	5,464
1880	16,943
1890	19,645
1900	21,274
1910	19,047
1920	19,421
1930	19,422
1940	18,647
1950	18,532
1960	17,919
1970	17,007
1980	16,932

CEDAR

Year	Population
1840	1,253
1850	3,941
1860	12,949
1870	19,731
1880	18,936
1890	18,253
1900	19,371
1910	17,765
1920	17,560
1930	16,760
1940	16,884
1950	16,910
1960	17,791
1970	17,665
1980	18,635

CERRO GORDO

Year	Population
1860	940
1870	4,722
1880	11,461
1890	14,864
1900	20,672
1910	25,011
1920	34,675
1930	38,476
1940	43,845
1950	46,053
1960	49,894
1970	49,223
1980	48,458

CHEROKEE

Year	Population
1860	58
1870	1,967
1880	8,240
1890	15,659
1900	16,570
1910	16,741
1920	17,760
1930	18,737
1940	19,258
1950	19,052
1960	18,598
1970	17,269
1980	16,238

CLARKE

Year	Population
1850	79
1860	5,427
1870	8,735
1880	11,513
1890	11,332
1900	12,400
1910	10,736
1920	10,506
1930	10,384
1940	10,233
1950	9,369
1960	8,222
1970	7,581
1980	8,612

CLAY

Year	Population
1860	52
1870	1,523
1880	4,248
1890	9,309
1900	13,401
1910	12,766
1920	15,660
1930	16,107
1940	17,762
1950	18,103
1960	18,504
1970	18,464
1980	19,576

CLAYTON

Year	Population
1840	1,101
1850	3,873
1860	20,728
1870	27,771
1880	28,829
1890	26,733
1900	27,750
1910	25,576
1920	25,032
1930	24,559
1940	24,334
1950	22,522
1960	21,962
1970	20,606
1980	21,098

CLINTON

Year	Population
1840	821
1850	2,822
1860	18,938
1870	35,357
1880	36,763
1890	41,199
1900	43,832
1910	45,394
1920	43,371
1930	44,377
1940	44,722
1950	49,664
1960	55,060
1970	56,749
1980	57,122

CRAWFORD

Year	Pop.
1860	383
1870	2,530
1880	12,413
1890	18,894
1900	21,685
1910	20,041
1920	20,614
1930	21,028
1940	20,538
1950	19,741
1960	18,569
1970	19,116
1980	18,935

DALLAS

Year	Pop.
1850	854
1860	5,244
1870	12,019
1880	18,746
1890	20,479
1900	23,058
1910	23,628
1920	25,120
1930	25,493
1940	24,649
1950	23,661
1960	24,123
1970	26,085
1980	29,513

DAVIS

Year	Pop.
1850	7,264
1860	13,764
1870	15,565
1880	16,468
1890	15,258
1900	15,620
1910	13,315
1920	12,574
1930	11,150
1940	11,136
1950	9,959
1960	9,199
1970	8,207
1980	9,104

DECATUR

Year	Pop.
1850	965
1860	8,677
1870	12,018
1880	15,336
1890	15,643
1900	18,115
1910	16,347
1920	16,566
1930	14,903
1940	14,012
1950	12,601
1960	10,539
1970	9,737
1980	9,794

DELAWARE

Year	Pop.
1840	168
1850	1,759
1860	11,024
1870	17,432
1880	17,950
1890	17,349
1900	19,185
1910	17,888
1920	18,183
1930	18,122
1940	18,487
1950	17,734
1960	18,483
1970	18,770
1980	18,933

DES MOINES

Year	Pop.
1840	5,577
1850	12,998
1860	19,611
1870	27,256
1880	33,099
1890	35,324
1900	35,989
1910	36,145
1920	35,520
1930	38,162
1940	36,804
1950	42,056
1960	44,605
1970	46,982
1980	46,203

DICKINSON

Year	Pop.
1860	180
1870	1,389
1880	1,901
1890	4,328
1900	7,995
1910	8,137
1920	10,241
1930	10,982
1940	12,185
1950	12,756
1960	12,574
1970	12,565
1980	15,629

DUBUQUE

Year	Pop.
1840	3,059
1850	10,841
1860	31,164
1870	38,969
1880	42,996
1890	49,848
1900	56,403
1910	57,450
1920	58,262
1930	61,214
1940	63,768
1950	71,337
1960	80,048
1970	90,609
1980	93,745

EMMET

Year	Pop.
1860	105
1870	1,392
1880	1,550
1890	4,274
1900	9,936
1910	9,816
1920	12,627
1930	12,856
1940	13,406
1950	14,102
1960	14,871
1970	14,009
1980	13,336

FAYETTE

Year	Pop.
1850	825
1860	12,073
1870	16,973
1880	22,258
1890	23,141
1900	29,845
1910	27,919
1920	29,251
1930	29,145
1940	29,151
1950	28,294
1960	28,581
1970	26,898
1980	25,448

FLOYD

Year	Pop.
1860	3,744
1870	10,768
1880	14,677
1890	15,424
1900	17,754
1910	17,119
1920	18,860
1930	19,524
1940	20,169
1950	21,505
1960	21,102
1970	19,860
1980	19,597

FRANKLIN

Year	Pop.
1860	1,309
1870	4,738
1880	10,249
1890	12,871
1900	14,996
1910	14,780
1920	15,807
1930	16,382
1940	16,379
1950	16,278
1960	15,472
1970	13,225
1980	13,036

FREMONT

Year	Pop.
1850	1,244
1860	5,074
1870	11,174
1880	17,652
1890	16,842
1900	18,546
1910	15,623
1920	15,447
1930	15,553
1940	14,645
1950	12,323
1960	10,282
1970	9,282
1980	9,401

GREENE

Year	Pop.
1860	1,374
1870	4,627
1880	12,727
1890	15,797
1900	17,820
1910	16,023
1920	16,467
1930	16,528
1940	16,599
1950	15,544
1960	14,379
1970	12,716
1980	12,119

GRUNDY

Year	Pop.
1860	793
1870	6,399
1880	12,639
1890	13,215
1900	13,757
1910	13,574
1920	14,420
1930	14,133
1940	13,518
1950	13,722
1960	14,132
1970	14,119
1980	14,366

GUTHRIE

Year	Pop.
1860	3,058
1870	7,061
1880	14,394
1890	17,380
1900	18,729
1910	17,374
1920	17,596
1930	17,324
1940	17,210
1950	15,710
1960	13,607
1970	12,243
1980	11,983

HAMILTON

Year	Pop.
1860	1,699
1870	6,055
1880	11,252
1890	15,319
1900	19,514
1910	19,242
1920	19,531
1930	20,978
1940	19,922
1950	19,660
1960	20,032
1970	18,383
1980	17,862

HANCOCK

Year	Pop.
1860	179
1870	999
1880	3,453
1890	7,621
1900	13,752
1910	12,731
1920	14,723
1930	14,802
1940	15,402
1950	15,077
1960	14,604
1970	13,506
1980	13,833

HARDIN

Year	Pop.
1860	5,440
1870	13,684
1880	17,807
1890	19,003
1900	22,724
1910	20,921
1920	23,337
1930	22,947
1940	22,530
1950	22,218
1960	22,533
1970	22,248
1980	21,776

HARRISON

Year	Pop.
1860	3,621
1870	8,931
1880	16,649
1890	21,356
1900	25,597
1910	23,162
1920	24,448
1930	24,897
1940	22,767
1950	19,560
1960	17,600
1970	16,240
1980	16,348

HENRY

Year	Pop.
1840	3,722
1850	8,707
1860	18,701
1870	21,463
1880	20,986
1890	18,895
1900	20,022
1910	18,640
1920	18,298
1930	17,660
1940	17,994
1950	18,708
1960	18,187
1970	18,114
1980	18,890

HOWARD

Year	Pop.
1860	3,168
1870	6,282
1880	10,837
1890	11,182
1900	14,512
1910	12,920
1920	13,750
1930	13,082
1940	13,531
1950	13,105
1960	12,734
1970	11,442
1980	11,114

HUMBOLDT

Year	Pop.
1860	332
1870	2,596
1880	5,341
1890	9,836
1900	12,667
1910	12,182
1920	12,951
1930	13,202
1940	13,459
1950	13,117
1960	13,156
1970	12,519
1980	12,246

IDA

1860	43
1870	226
1880	4,382
1890	10,705
1900	12,327
1910	11,296
1920	11,689
1930	11,933
1940	11,047
1950	10,697
1960	10,269
1970	9,283
1980	8,908

IOWA

1850	822
1860	8,029
1870	16,644
1880	19,221
1890	18,270
1900	19,544
1910	18,409
1920	18,600
1930	17,332
1940	17,016
1950	15,835
1960	16,396
1970	15,419
1980	15,429

JACKSON

1840	1,411
1850	7,210
1860	18,493
1870	22,619
1880	23,771
1890	22,771
1900	23,615
1910	21,258
1920	19,931
1930	18,481
1940	19,181
1950	18,622
1960	20,754
1970	20,839
1980	22,503

JASPER

1850	1,280
1860	9,883
1870	22,116
1880	25,963
1890	24,943
1900	26,976
1910	27,034
1920	27,855
1930	32,936
1940	31,496
1950	32,305
1960	35,282
1970	35,425
1980	36,425

JEFFERSON

1840	2,773
1850	9,904
1860	15,038
1870	17,839
1880	17,469
1890	15,184
1900	17,437
1910	15,951
1920	16,440
1930	16,241
1940	15,762
1950	15,696
1960	15,818
1970	15,774
1980	16,316

JOHNSON

1840	1,491
1850	4,472
1860	17,573
1870	24,898
1880	25,429
1890	23,082
1900	24,817
1910	25,914
1920	26,492
1930	30,276
1940	33,191
1950	45,756
1960	53,663
1970	72,127
1980	81,717

JONES

1840	471
1850	3,007
1860	13,306
1870	19,731
1880	21,052
1890	20,233
1900	21,954
1910	19,050
1920	18,607
1930	19,206
1940	19,950
1950	19,401
1960	20,693
1970	19,868
1980	20,401

KEOKUK

1850	4,822
1860	13,271
1870	19,434
1880	21,258
1890	23,862
1900	24,979
1910	21,160
1920	20,983
1930	19,148
1940	18,406
1950	16,797
1960	15,492
1970	13,943
1980	12,921

KOSSUTH

1860	416
1870	3,351
1880	6,178
1890	13,120
1900	22,720
1910	21,971
1920	25,082
1930	25,452
1940	26,630
1950	26,241
1960	25,314
1970	22,937
1980	21,891

LEE

1840	6,093
1850	18,861
1860	29,232
1870	37,210
1880	34,859
1890	37,715
1900	39,719
1910	36,702
1920	39,676
1930	41,268
1940	41,074
1950	43,102
1960	44,207
1970	42,996
1980	43,106

LINN

1840	1,373
1850	5,444
1860	18,947
1870	31,080
1880	37,237
1890	45,303
1900	55,392
1910	60,720
1920	74,004
1930	82,336
1940	89,142
1950	104,274
1960	136,889
1970	163,213
1980	169,775

LOUISA

1840	1,927
1850	4,939
1860	10,370
1870	12,877
1880	13,142
1890	11,873
1900	13,516
1910	12,855
1920	12,179
1930	11,575
1940	11,384
1950	11,101
1960	10,290
1970	10,683
1980	12,055

LUCAS

1850	471
1860	5,766
1870	10,388
1880	14,530
1890	14,563
1900	16,126
1910	13,462
1920	15,686
1930	15,114
1940	14,571
1950	12,069
1960	10,923
1970	10,163
1980	10,313

LYON

1870	221
1880	1,968
1890	8,680
1900	13,165
1910	14,624
1920	15,431
1930	15,293
1940	15,374
1950	14,697
1960	14,468
1970	13,340
1980	12,896

MADISON

1850	1,179
1860	7,339
1870	13,884
1880	17,224
1890	15,977
1900	17,710
1910	15,621
1920	15,020
1930	14,331
1940	14,525
1950	13,131
1960	12,295
1970	11,558
1980	12,597

MAHASKA

1850	5,989
1860	14,816
1870	22,508
1880	25,202
1890	28,805
1900	34,273
1910	29,860
1920	26,270
1930	25,804
1940	26,485
1950	24,672
1960	23,602
1970	22,177
1980	22,867

MARION

1850	5,482
1860	16,813
1870	24,236
1880	25,111
1890	23,058
1900	24,159
1910	22,295
1920	24,957
1930	25,727
1940	27,019
1950	25,930
1960	25,886
1970	26,352
1980	29,669

MARSHALL

1850	338
1860	6,015
1870	17,576
1880	23,752
1890	25,842
1900	29,991
1910	30,279
1920	32,630
1930	33,727
1940	35,406
1950	35,611
1960	37,984
1970	41,076
1980	41,652

MILLS

1860	4,481
1870	8,718
1880	14,137
1890	14,548
1900	16,764
1910	15,811
1920	15,422
1930	15,866
1940	15,064
1950	14,064
1960	13,050
1970	11,606
1980	13,406

MITCHELL

1860	3,409
1870	9,582
1880	14,363
1890	13,299
1900	14,916
1910	13,435
1920	13,921
1930	14,065
1940	14,121
1950	13,945
1960	14,043
1970	13,108
1980	12,329

MONONA

1860	832
1870	3,654
1880	9,055
1890	14,515
1900	17,980
1910	16,663
1920	17,125
1930	18,213
1940	18,238
1950	16,303
1960	13,916
1970	12,069
1980	11,692

MONROE

1850	2,884
1860	8,612
1870	12,724
1880	13,719
1890	13,666
1900	17,985
1910	25,429
1920	23,467
1930	15,010
1940	14,553
1950	11,814
1960	10,463
1970	9,357
1980	9,209

MONTGOMERY

1860	1,256
1870	5,934
1880	15,895
1890	15,848
1900	17,803
1910	16,604
1920	17,048
1930	16,752
1940	15,697

1950	15,685
1960	14,468
1970	12,781
1980	13,413

MUSCATINE

1840	1,942
1850	5,731
1860	16,444
1870	21,688
1880	23,170
1890	24,504
1900	28,242
1910	29,505
1920	29,042
1930	29,385
1940	31,296
1950	32,148
1960	33,840
1970	37,181
1980	40,436

O'BRIEN

1860	8
1870	715
1880	4,155
1890	13,060
1900	16,985
1910	17,262
1920	19,051
1930	18,409
1940	19,293
1950	18,970
1960	18,840
1970	17,522
1980	16,972

OSCEOLA

1880	2,219
1890	5,574
1900	8,725
1910	8,956
1920	10,223
1930	10,182
1940	10,607
1950	10,181
1960	10,064
1970	8,555
1980	8,371

PAGE

1850	551
1860	4,419
1870	9,975
1880	19,667
1890	21,341
1900	24,187
1910	24,002
1920	24,137
1930	25,904
1940	24,887
1950	23,921
1960	21,023
1970	18,537
1980	19,063

PALO ALTO

1860	132
1870	1,336
1880	4,131
1890	9,318

1900	14,354
1910	13,845
1920	15,486
1930	15,398
1940	16,170
1950	15,891
1960	14,736
1970	13,289
1980	12,721

PLYMOUTH

1860	148
1870	2,199
1880	8,566
1890	19,568
1900	22,209
1910	23,129
1920	23,584
1930	24,159
1940	23,502
1950	23,252
1960	23,906
1970	24,322
1980	24,743

POCAHONTAS

1860	103
1870	1,446
1880	3,713
1890	9,553
1900	15,339
1910	14,808
1920	15,602
1930	15,687
1940	16,266
1950	15,496
1960	14,234
1970	12,793
1980	11,369

POLK

1850	4,513
1860	11,625
1870	27,857
1880	42,395
1890	65,410
1900	82,624
1910	110,438
1920	154,029
1930	172,837
1940	195,835
1950	226,315
1960	266,315
1970	286,130
1980	303,170

POTTAWATTAMIE

1850	7,828
1860	4,968
1870	16,893
1880	39,850
1890	47,430
1900	54,336
1910	55,832
1920	61,550
1930	89,888
1940	55,756
1950	69,682
1960	83,102
1970	86,991
1980	86,561

POWESHIEK

1850	615
1860	5,668
1870	15,581
1880	18,936
1890	18,934
1900	19,414
1910	19,589
1920	19,910
1930	18,727
1940	18,758
1950	19,344
1960	19,300
1970	18,803
1980	19,306

RINGGOLD

1860	2,923
1870	5,691
1880	12,085
1890	13,556
1900	15,325
1910	12,904
1920	12,919
1930	11,966
1940	11,137
1950	9,528
1960	7,910
1970	6,373
1980	6,112

SAC

1860	246
1870	1,411
1880	8,774
1890	14,522
1900	17,639
1910	16,555
1920	17,500
1930	17,641
1940	17,639
1950	17,518
1960	17,007
1970	15,573
1980	14,118

SCOTT

1840	2,140
1850	5,986
1860	25,959
1870	38,599
1880	41,266
1890	43,164
1900	51,558
1910	60,000
1920	73,952
1930	77,332
1940	84,748
1950	100,698
1960	119,067
1970	142,687
1980	160,022

SHELBY

1860	818
1870	2,540
1880	12,696
1890	17,611
1900	17,932
1910	16,552
1920	16,065

1930	17,131
1940	16,720
1950	15,942
1960	15,825
1970	15,528
1980	15,043

SIOUX

1860	10
1870	576
1880	5,426
1890	18,370
1900	23,337
1910	25,248
1920	26,458
1930	26,806
1940	27,209
1950	26,381
1960	26,375
1970	27,996
1980	30,813

STORY

1860	4,051
1870	11,651
1880	16,906
1890	18,127
1900	23,159
1910	24,083
1920	26,185
1930	31,141
1940	33,434
1950	44,294
1960	49,327
1970	62,783
1980	72,326

TAMA

1850	8
1860	5,285
1870	16,131
1880	21,585
1890	21,651
1900	24,585
1910	22,156
1920	21,861
1930	21,987
1940	22,428
1950	21,688
1960	21,413
1970	20,147
1980	19,533

TAYLOR

1850	204
1860	3,590
1870	6,989
1880	15,635
1890	16,384
1900	18,784
1910	16,312
1920	15,514
1930	14,859
1940	14,258
1950	12,420
1960	10,288
1970	8,790
1980	8,353

UNION

1860	2,012
1870	5,986
1880	14,980
1890	16,900
1900	19,928
1910	16,616
1920	17,268
1930	17,435
1940	16,280
1950	15,651
1960	13,712
1970	13,557
1980	13,858

VAN BUREN

1840	6,146
1850	12,270
1860	17,081
1870	17,672
1880	17,043
1890	16,253
1900	17,354
1910	15,020
1920	14,060
1930	12,603
1940	12,053
1950	11,007
1960	9,778
1970	8,643
1980	8,626

WAPELLO

1850	8,471
1860	14,518
1870	22,346
1880	25,285
1890	30,426
1900	35,426
1910	37,743
1920	37,937
1930	40,480
1940	44,280
1950	47,397
1960	46,126
1970	42,149
1980	40,241

WARREN

1850	961
1860	10,281
1870	17,980
1880	19,578
1890	18,269
1900	20,376
1910	18,194
1920	18,047
1930	17,700
1940	17,695
1950	17,598
1960	20,829
1970	27,432
1980	34,878

WASHINGTON

1840	1,594
1850	4,957
1860	14,235
1870	18,952
1880	20,374
1890	18,468

1900	20,718	**WOODBURY**
1910	19,925	
1920	20,421	1860	1,119
1930	19,822	1870	6,172
1940	20,055	1880	14,996
1950	19,557	1890	55,632
1960	19,406	1900	54,610
1970	18,967	1910	67,617
1980	20,141	1920	92,171
		1930	101,669
		1940	103,627
WAYNE		1950	103,917
		1960	107,849
1850	340	1970	103,052
1860	6,409	1980	100,884

WAYNE

1850	340
1860	6,409
1870	11,287
1880	16,127
1890	15,670
1900	17,491
1910	16,184
1920	15,378
1930	13,787
1940	13,308
1950	11,737
1960	9,800
1970	8,405
1980	8,199

WEBSTER

1860	2,504
1870	10,484
1880	15,951
1890	21,582
1900	31,757
1910	34,629
1920	27,611
1930	40,425
1940	41,521
1950	44,241
1960	47,810
1970	48,391
1980	45,953

WINNEBAGO

1860	168
1870	1,582
1880	4,917
1890	7,325
1900	12,725
1910	11,914
1920	13,489
1930	13,143
1940	13,972
1950	13,450
1960	13,099
1970	12,990
1980	13,010

WINNESHIEK

1850	546
1860	13,942
1870	23,570
1880	23,938
1890	22,528
1900	23,731
1910	21,729
1920	22,091
1930	21,630
1940	22,263
1950	21,639
1960	21,651
1970	21,758
1980	21,876

WORTH

1860	756
1870	2,892
1880	7,953
1890	9,247
1900	10,887
1910	9,950
1920	11,630
1930	11,164
1940	11,449
1950	11,068
1960	10,259
1970	8,984
1980	9,075

WRIGHT

1860	653
1870	2,392
1880	5,062
1890	12,057
1900	18,227
1910	17,951
1920	20,348
1930	20,216
1940	20,038
1950	19,652
1960	19,447
1970	17,294
1980	16,319

NOTES

CALHOUN

Name changed from Fox in 1853.

LYON

Name changed from Buncombe in 1862.

MONROE

Name changed from Kishkekosh in 1846.

WASHINGTON

Name changed from Slaughter in 1839.

WEBSTER

Name changed from Risley in 1853.

WOODBURY

Name changed from Wahkaw in 1853.

AMES

1870	636
1880	1,153
1890	1,276
1900	2,422
1910	4,223
1920	6,270
1930	10,261
1940	12,555
1950	22,898
1960	27,003
1970	39,505
1980	45,775

ANKENY

1910	445
1920	648
1930	632
1940	779
1950	1,229
1960	2,964
1970	9,151
1980	15,429

BETTENDORF

1910	909
1920	2,178
1930	2,768
1940	3,143
1950	5,123
1960	11,534
1970	22,126
1980	27,381

BOONE

1880	3,330
1890	6,520
1900	8,880
1910	10,347
1920	10,451
1930	11,886
1940	12,373
1950	12,164
1960	12,468
1970	12,468
1980	12,602

BURLINGTON

1850	4,082
1860	6,706
1870	14,930
1880	19,450
1890	22,565
1900	23,201
1910	24,324
1920	24,057
1930	26,755
1940	25,832
1950	30,613
1960	32,430
1970	32,366
1980	29,529

CEDAR FALLS

1870	1,311
1880	3,020
1890	3,459
1900	5,319
1910	5,012
1920	6,316
1930	7,362
1940	9,349
1950	14,334
1960	21,195
1970	29,597
1980	36,322

CEDAR RAPIDS

1860	1,830
1870	5,940
1880	10,104
1890	18,020
1900	25,656
1910	32,811
1920	45,566
1930	56,097
1940	62,120
1950	72,296
1960	92,035
1970	110,642
1980	110,243

CLINTON

1870	6,129
1880	9,052
1890	13,619
1900	22,698
1910	25,577
1920	24,151
1930	25,726
1940	26,270
1950	30,379
1960	33,589
1970	34,719
1980	32,828

COUNCIL BLUFFS

1860	2,011
1870	10,020
1880	18,063
1890	21,474
1900	25,802
1910	29,292
1920	36,162
1930	42,048
1940	41,439
1950	45,429
1960	55,641
1970	60,348
1980	56,449

DAVENPORT

1850	1,848
1860	11,267
1870	20,038
1880	21,831
1890	26,872
1900	35,254
1910	43,028
1920	56,727
1930	60,751
1940	66,039
1950	74,549
1960	88,981
1970	98,469
1980	103,264

DES MOINES

1860	3,965
1870	12,035
1880	22,408
1890	50,093
1900	62,139
1910	86,368
1920	126,468
1930	142,559
1940	159,819
1950	177,965
1960	208,982
1970	200,587
1980	191,003

DUBUQUE

1850	3,108
1860	13,000
1870	18,434
1880	22,254
1890	30,311
1900	36,297
1910	38,494
1920	39,141
1930	41,679
1940	43,892
1950	49,671
1960	56,606
1970	62,309
1980	62,321

FORT DODGE

1860	672
1870	3,095
1880	3,586
1890	4,871
1900	12,162
1910	15,543
1920	19,347
1930	21,895
1940	22,904
1950	25,115
1960	28,399
1970	31,263
1980	29,423

FORT MADISON

1850	1,509
1860	2,886
1870	4,011
1880	4,679
1890	7,901
1900	9,278
1910	8,900
1920	12,066
1930	13,779
1940	14,063
1950	14,954
1960	15,247
1970	13,996
1980	13,520

INDIANOLA

1860	836
1870	1,428
1880	2,146
1890	2,254
1900	3,261
1910	3,283
1920	3,648
1930	3,488
1940	4,123
1950	5,145
1960	7,062
1970	8,852
1980	10,843

IOWA CITY

1850	1,250
1860	5,214
1870	5,914
1880	7,123
1890	7,016
1900	7,987
1910	10,091
1920	11,267
1930	15,340
1940	17,182
1950	27,212
1960	33,443
1970	46,850
1980	50,508

KEOKUK

1850	2,478
1860	8,136
1870	12,766
1880	12,117
1890	14,101
1900	14,641
1910	14,008
1920	14,423
1930	15,106
1940	15,076
1950	16,144
1960	16,316
1970	14,631
1980	13,536

MARION

1860	1,367
1870	1,822
1880	1,939
1890	3,094
1900	4,102
1910	4,400
1920	4,138
1930	4,348
1940	4,721
1950	5,916
1960	10,882
1970	18,028
1980	19,474

MARSHALLTOWN

1860	981
1870	3,218
1880	6,240
1890	8,914
1900	11,544
1910	13,374
1920	15,731
1930	17,373
1940	19,240
1950	19,821
1960	22,521
1970	26,219
1980	26,938

MASON CITY

1870	1,183
1880	2,510
1890	4,007
1900	6,746
1910	11,230
1920	20,065
1930	23,304
1940	27,080
1950	27,980
1960	30,642
1970	30,491
1980	30,144

MUSCATINE

1850	2,540
1860	5,324
1870	6,718
1880	8,295
1890	11,454
1900	14,073
1910	16,178
1920	16,068
1930	16,778
1940	18,286
1950	19,041
1960	20,997
1970	22,405
1980	23,467

NEWTON

1860	1,617
1870	1,983
1880	2,607
1890	2,564
1900	3,682
1910	4,616
1920	6,627
1930	11,560
1940	10,462
1950	11,723
1960	15,381
1970	15,619
1980	15,292

OSKALOOSA

1850	625
1860	4,393
1870	3,204
1880	4,598
1890	6,588
1900	9,212
1910	9,466
1920	9,427
1930	10,123
1940	11,024
1950	11,124
1960	11,053
1970	11,224
1980	10,989

OTTUMWA

1860	1,623
1870	5,214
1880	9,004
1890	14,001
1900	18,197
1910	22,012
1920	23,003
1930	38,075
1940	31,570
1950	33,631
1960	33,871
1970	29,610
1980	27,381

SIOUX CITY

1870	3,401
1880	7,366
1890	37,806
1900	33,111
1910	47,828
1920	71,227
1930	29,183
1940	82,364
1950	83,991
1960	19,159
1970	85,925
1980	82,003

SPENCER

1880	824
1890	1,813
1900	3,095
1910	3,005
1920	4,599
1930	5,019
1940	6,599
1950	7,446
1960	8,864
1970	10,278
1980	11,726

URBANDALE

1920	298
1930	596
1940	1,083
1950	1,777
1960	5,821
1970	14,434
1980	17,869

WATERLOO

1870	4,337
1880	5,630
1890	6,674
1900	12,580
1910	26,693
1920	36,230
1930	46,191
1940	51,743
1950	65,198
1960	71,755
1970	75,533
1980	75,985

WEST DES MOINES

1900	1,700
1910	2,573
1920	3,631
1930	4,280
1940	4,252
1950	5,615
1960	11,949
1970	16,441
1980	21,894

CORRECTION NOTE

The official 1980 census counts of total population shown in this report supersede counts issued previously. Corrections to the figures were made after the counts were provided to the State for redistricting purposes and released in Advance Report PHC80-V for this State.

Shown below are corrections to the 1980 census counts of the total population made after the tabulations for this report were completed. Any additional corrections made after this report is printed are available by writing to Data User Services Division, Customer Services (Corrections), Bureau of the Census, Washington, D.C. 20233.

The 1980 figures shown in this publication are subject to change pending the outcome of the various lawsuits dealing with the census counts.

	1980 population	
	As shown in the tables	Corrected
Polk County:		
Valley township.................	21 894	(1)
West Des Moines city.........	21 894	(1)
Walnut township.................	15 895	37 789
West Des Moines city.........	(2)	21 894
Scott County:		
Buffalo township:		
Buffalo city.................	1 441	1 569

 [1]Delete. West Des Moines city should be shown in Walnut township rather than coextensive with Valley township.
 [2]Not shown.

County Subdivisions	1980	1970
The State[1]	2 913 808	[2] 825 368
Adair County[2]	9 509	9 487
Bridgewater township	246	200
Bridgewater city (pt.)[2]	221	188
Eureka township	195	230
Grand River township	250	250
Greenfield township	2 310	2 273
Greenfield city (pt.)	2 240	2 212
Grove township	290	348
Harrison township	233	262
Jackson township	293	295
Bridgewater city (pt.)[2]	12	...
Jefferson township	273	320
Lee township	285	308
Greenfield city (pt.)[2]	3	...
Lincoln township	805	370
Stuart city (pt.)[2]	523	338
Orient township	664	589
Orient city	416	324
Prussia township	288	361
Richland township	293	354
Summerset township	1 198	1 182
Fontanelle city	805	752
Summit township	1 105	283
Adair city (pt.)	817	693
Union township	279	269
Walnut township	275	331
Casey city (pt.)	14	31
Washington township	227	231
Adams County[3]	5 731	6 322
Carl township	257	272
Colony township	242	278
Douglas township	354	400
Carbon township	110	135
Grant township	262	312
Lenox city (pt.)[3]	2	...
Jasper township	528	556
Corning city (pt.)	54	25
Lincoln township	197	266
Mercer township	233	268
Nodaway township	422	455
Nodaway city	185	176
Prescott township	571	564
Prescott city	349	305
Quincy township	2 177	2 355
Corning city (pt.)[3]	1 885	2 070
Union township	237	287
Washington township	251	309
Allamakee County[4]	15 108	14 968
Center township	339	383
Fairview township	134	156
Franklin township	510	471
French Creek township	191	212
Hanover township	240	262
Iowa township	839	873
New Albin city	609	644
Jefferson township	652	646
Lafayette township	419	436
Lansing township	1 692	1 625
Lansing city[4]	1 181	[1] 227
Linton township	287	342
Ludlow township	623	659
Makee township	4 623	4 351
Waukon city (pt.)[4]	3 775	3 684
Paint Creek township	505	518
Waterville city	157	158
Post township	2 015	2 075
Postville city (pt.)[4]	1 475	1 546
Taylor township	509	481
Harpers Ferry city	258	227
Union City township	277	341
Union Prairie township	798	731
Waukon city (pt.)	208	199
Waterloo township	455	406
Appanoose County[5]	15 511	15 007
Bellair township	697	710
Mystic city (pt.)	22	-
Numa city (pt.)	170	160
Caldwell township	537	484
Exline city	217	224
Centerville city[5]	6 558	6 531
Chariton township	154	92
Douglas township	220	206
Franklin township	210	195
Independence township	239	165
Johns township	449	430
Plano city	111	109
Lincoln township	337	245
Numa city (pt.)	35	5
Pleasant township	1 052	938
Cincinnati city	598	570
Sharon township	244	208
Taylor township	993	943
Moravia city	706	699
Udell township	411	453
Udell city	75	71

County Subdivisions	1980	1970
Appanoose County—Con.		
Udell township—Con.		
Unionville city	150	161
Union township	178	180
Vermilion township[5]	795	669
Walnut township	1 154	1 211
Mystic city (pt.)	643	696
Rathbun city	93	113
Washington township	923	998
Moulton city (pt.)	657	678
Wells township	360	349
Moulton city (pt.)	105	85
Audubon County[6]	8 559	9 595
Audubon township	342	465
Cameron township	272	335
Douglas township	401	446
Exira township	1 420	1 504
Brayton city (pt.)[6]	100	93
Exira city[6]	978	966
Greeley township	248	315
Hamlin township	401	490
Leroy township	3 347	3 482
Audubon city[6]	2 841	2 907
Lincoln township	467	584
Gray city	108	145
Melville township	226	288
Oakfield township	449	525
Brayton city (pt.)	70	58
Sharon township	707	782
Kimballton city	362	343
Viola township	279	379
Benton County[7]	23 649	22 885
Belle Plaine city[7]	2 903	2 810
Benton township	634	466
Big Grove township	317	387
Bruce township	390	406
Canton township	755	399
Cedar township	607	638
Mount Auburn city	188	200
Eden township	368	418
Eldorado township	1 308	1 150
Newhall city[7]	899	701
Florence township	1 349	1 266
Norway city[7]	633	554
Walford city (pt.)	266	285
Fremont township	1 346	1 130
Atkins city[7]	678	581
Harrison township	385	376
Homer township	321	362
Iowa township[7]	441	505
Luzerne city (pt.)	37	42
Jackson township	786	834
Garrison city	411	383
Kane township	942	986
Keystone city	618	549
Leroy township	1 153	1 140
Blairstown city	695	612
Luzerne city (pt.)	77	92
Monroe township	279	316
Polk township	1 298	1 332
Urbana city[7]	574	552
St. Clair township	506	641
Shellsburg city	771	740
Taylor township[7]	723	736
Union township	1 027	1 002
Van Horne city[7]	682	613
Vinton city[7]	5 040	4 845
Black Hawk County[8]	137 961	132 916
Barclay township	653	717
Bennington township	580	639
Big Creek township	2 699	2 595
La Porte City city	2 324	2 256
Black Hawk township	3 523	1 965
Cedar Falls city (pt.)[8]	854	...
Hudson city[8]	2 267	1 535
Cedar township[8]	2 209	2 261
Cedar Falls township	33 970	31 413
Cedar Falls city (pt.)[8]	33 608	29 597
Eagle township	599	605
East Waterloo township[8]	6 467	[6] 838
Elk Run Heights city (pt.)[8]	1 186	1 175
Evansdale city	4 798	5 038
Fox township	646	744
Lester township	1 602	1 208
Dunkerton city[8]	718	563
Lincoln township	470	504
Mount Vernon township	1 421	1 367
Cedar Falls city (pt.)[8]	142	...
Orange township[8]	450	384
Poyner township	2 920	2 802
Elk Run Heights city (pt.)[8]	-	...
Gilbertville city[8]	740	655
Raymond city	655	582
Spring Creek township	422	415
Union township	826	691
Cedar Falls city (pt.)[8]	2	...
Washington township	2 519	2 235

County Subdivisions

County Subdivisions	1980	1970
Black Hawk County—Con.		
Washington township—Con.		
Cedar Falls city (pt.)[8]	1 716	...
Janesville city (pt.)	112	45
Waterloo city[8]	75 985	75 533
Boone County[9]	26 184	26 470
Amaqua township	369	433
Beaver city	85	113
Beaver township	251	286
Berkley city (pt.)	6	10
Cass township	845	1 132
Colfax township	634	672
Luther city (pt.)	9	11
Des Moines township	13 663	13 707
Boone city (pt.)[9]	12 594	12 468
Dodge township	740	850
Fraser city (pt.)	129	136
Douglas township	2 224	2 202
Madrid city (pt.)	1 786	1 883
Garden township	1 081	1 116
Madrid city (pt.)[9]	495	565
Sheldahl city (pt.)	25	21
Grant township	543	581
Boxholm city	267	242
Harrison township	409	426
Jackson township	484	598
Marcy township	1 000	731
Ogden city (pt.)	241	147
Peoples township	392	408
Pilot Mound township	406	419
Fraser city (pt.)	4	7
Pilot Mound city	223	214
Union township	446	461
Berkley city (pt.)	43	46
Worth township	509	482
Boone city (pt.)[9]	8	(NA)
Luther city (pt.)	146	178
Yell township	2 188	1 966
Fraser city (pt.)	6	–
Ogden city (pt.)	1 712	1 514
Bremer County[10]	24 820	22 737
Dayton township	521	569
Douglas township	570	621
Franklin township	551	569
Frederika township	436	422
Frederika city	223	190
Fremont township	1 868	1 931
Tripoli city[10]	1 280	1 345
Jackson township	1 426	1 175
Janesville city (pt.)	728	696
Jefferson township	2 863	2 104
Denver city[10]	1 647	1 169
Lafayette township[10]	614	657
Le Roy township	285	316
Maxfield township	1 588	1 372
Readlyn city[10]	858	616
Polk township	1 194	1 208
Plainfield city	469	446
Sumner city	2 335	2 174
Sumner No. 2 township	485	518
Warren township	754	828
Washington township[10]	886	1 068
Waverly city[10]	8 444	7 205
Buchanan County[11]	22 900	'21 762
Buffalo township	729	724
Aurora city (pt.)	215	192
Stanley city	154	151
Byron township	1 194	1 221
Winthrop city[11]	767	750
Cono township	450	586
Fairbank township	1 663	1 610
Fairbank city (pt.)	837	761
Fremont township	400	485
Hazleton township	1 641	1 350
Hazleton city[11]	877	626
Homer township	693	684
Rowley city	275	241
Jefferson township	845	963
Brandon city	337	432
Liberty township	1 099	'1 059
Quasqueton city	599	'464
Madison township	969	992
Aurora city (pt.)	33	37
Lamont city[11]	554	498
Middlefield township	384	493
Newton township	488	528
Perry township	3 394	2 523
Jesup city	2 343	1 662
Sumner township	489	479
Independence city (pt.)[11]	12	...
Washington township	7 888	7 039
Independence city (pt.)[11]	6 380	5 910
Westburg township	574	1 026
Buena Vista County[12]	20 774	20 693
Barnes township	852	891
Linn Grove city	205	240
Rembrandt city	291	250

County Subdivisions	1980	1970
Buena Vista County—Con.		
Brooke township	245	285
Coon township	306	369
Elk township	280	361
Fairfield township	1 162	1 108
Albert City city[12]	818	683
Grant township	410	444
Hayes township[12]	1 225	857
Lakeside city[12]	589	353
Lee township[12]	330	349
Lincoln township	297	378
Maple Valley township	343	402
Newell township	1 280	1 304
Newell city	913	877
Nokomis township	2 155	2 193
Alta city[12]	1 720	1 717
Poland township	748	856
Marathon city	442	447
Providence township	426	477
Scott township	300	385
Sioux Rapids city[12]	897	813
Storm Lake city[12]	8 814	8 591
Washington township	704	630
Truesdale city	128	132
Butler County[13]	17 668	16 953
Albion township	2 258	1 836
Parkersburg city (pt.)[13]	1 716	1 379
Beaver township	1 550	1 296
New Hartford city	764	690
Bennezette township	361	473
Aredale city	88	126
Butler township	1 729	1 646
Clarksville city (pt.)[13]	1 151	1 114
Coldwater township	1 784	1 883
Greene city	1 332	1 363
Dayton township	387	465
Fremont township	464	495
Jackson township	828	820
Allison city (pt.)[13]	50	28
Clarksville city (pt.)	273	246
Jefferson township	385	429
Madison township	409	465
Monroe township	1 748	1 687
Aplington city[13]	1 027	936
Parkersburg city (pt.)	252	252
Pittsford township	1 223	1 185
Bristow city (pt.)	52	36
Dumont city	815	724
Ripley township	363	373
Shell Rock township	1 986	1 629
Shell Rock city[13]	1 478	1 159
Washington township	494	564
West Point township	1 699	1 707
Allison city (pt.)[13]	1 082	1 043
Bristow city (pt.)	200	194
Calhoun County[14]	13 542	'14 292
Butler township	1 258	1 226
Jolley city	91	112
Pomeroy city (pt.)	849	734
Calhoun township	224	321
Cedar township	592	597
Rinard city	97	88
Somers city	220	197
Center township	1 179	1 196
Rockwell City city (pt.)	747	734
Elm Grove township	299	'331
Yetter city	52	'52
Garfield township	327	345
Lytton city (pt.)	43	54
Greenfield township	495	531
Knierim city	125	131
Jackson township	354	371
Lake City city	2 006	1 910
Lake Creek township	246	324
Lincoln township	2 284	2 441
Manson city[14]	1 924	1 993
Logan township	245	322
Reading township	711	743
Farnhamville city (pt.)	461	393
Sherman township	501	445
Pomeroy city (pt.)	46	31
Twin Lakes township	1 760	1 974
Rockwell City city (pt.)	1 529	1 662
Union township	770	886
Lohrville city	521	553
Williams township	291	329
Carroll County[15]	22 951	22 912
Arcadia township	835	862
Arcadia city	454	414
Carroll[15]	9 705	8 716
Eden township	725	823
Templeton city	319	312
Ewoldt township[15]	395	509
Glidden township	1 497	1 449
Glidden city	1 076	964
Ralston city (pt.)	102	128
Grant township[15]	538	543

County Subdivisions	1980	1970
Carroll County—Con.		
Grant township—Con.		
Lidderdale city (pt.)	34	31
Jasper township	470	531
Lanesboro city	196	203
Kniest township	518	651
Breda city (pt.)	6	14
Manning city[15]	1 609	1 656
Maple River township[15]	710	702
Newton township	699	717
Dedham city	321	325
Pleasant Valley township	500	567
Willey city	94	72
Richland township	266	322
Roselle township	839	977
Halbur city[15]	229	235
Sheridan township	575	578
Lidderdale city (pt.)	163	142
Union township	1 816	1 859
Coon Rapids city[15]	1 448	1 381
Washington township	417	490
Wheatland township	837	960
Breda city (pt.)	496	504
Cass County[16]	16 932	17 007
Bear Grove township	327	349
Benton township	264	283
Brighton township	444	475
Marne city	162	187
Cass township	794	866
Lewis city	497	526
Edna township	223	216
Franklin township	492	498
Wiota city[16]	181	171
Grant township	1 486	1 455
Anita city	1 153	1 101
Grove township	8 217	641
Atlantic city (pt.)[16]	7 789	(NA)
Lincoln township	217	286
Massena township	809	760
Massena city	518	433
Noble township	499	523
Pleasant township	1 469	1 532
Griswold city[16]	1 176	1 181
Pymosa township	447	467
Union township	629	727
Cumberland city	351	385
Victoria township	256	283
Washington township	359	340
Atlantic city (pt.)[16]	—	(NA)
Cedar County[17]	18 635	17 655
Cass township	329	351
Center township	3 988	3 846
Tipton city[17]	3 055	2 877
Dayton township	1 347	1 339
Clarence city	1 001	915
Fairfield township	348	422
Farmington township	2 185	2 113
Durant city (pt.)[17]	1 579	1 463
Fremont township	1 086	1 066
Mechanicsville city (pt.)[17]	—	...
Stanwood city[17]	705	642
Gower township	486	518
Inland township	954	902
Bennett city[17]	458	385
Iowa township	408	425
Linn township	216	212
Massillon township	422	455
Pioneer township	1 669	1 361
Mechanicsville city (pt.)[17]	1 166	989
Red Oak township	263	330
Rochester township	550	458
Springdale township	2 825	2 256
West Branch city[17]	1 867	1 322
Springfield township	1 148	1 219
Lowden city	717	667
Sugar Creek township	411	382
Wilton city (pt.)[17]	9	...
Cerro Gordo County[18]	48 458	49 223
Bath township	465	529
Clear Lake township[18]	1 688	1 421
Ventura city	614	543
Clear Lake City city[18]	7 458	6 430
Dougherty township	376	464
Dougherty city	128	133
Falls township	1 261	1 261
Plymouth city	463	461
Rock Falls city	148	150
Geneseo township	1 337	1 249
Rockwell city	1 039	923
Grant township	420	442
Grimes township	1 034	1 094
Meservey city	324	354
Thornton city (pt.)	412	386
Lake township[18]	636	646
Lime Creek township[18]	728	749
Lincoln township	334	369
Mason township[18]	606	1 988

County Subdivisions	1980	1970
Cerro Gordo County—Con.		
Mason City city[18]	30 144	30 379
Mount Vernon township	395	401
Owen township	385	408
Pleasant Valley township	527	591
Swaledale city	186	222
Thornton city (pt.)	30	24
Portland township[18]	412	497
Union township	252	305
Cherokee County[19]	16 238	17 269
Afton township	377	437
Amherst township	336	415
Cedar township	491	511
Larrabee city	169	167
Cherokee township	7 678	7 820
Cherokee city (pt.)[19]	6 885	7 174
Diamond township	277	368
Grand Meadow township	307	414
Liberty township	316	350
Marcus township	1 478	1 638
Marcus city	1 206	1 272
Pilot township	469	473
Cherokee city (pt.)	119	98
Pitcher township	1 419	1 459
Aurelia city[19]	1 143	1 065
Rock township	317	396
Sheridan township	903	928
Cleghorn city[19]	275	274
Meriden city[19]	233	167
Silver township	350	373
Spring township	226	250
Tilden township	301	380
Willow township	993	1 017
Quimby city[19]	424	395
Washta city	320	319
Chickasaw County[20]	15 437	14 969
Bradford township	2 422	2 366
Nashua city	1 846	1 712
Chickasaw township	1 104	991
Bassett city	128	152
Ionia city	350	270
Dayton township	1 909	1 767
New Hampton city (pt.)[20]	1 287	1 163
Deerfield township	545	679
Dresden township	985	938
Fredericksburg city (pt.)	482	413
Fredericksburg township	1 077	1 006
Fredericksburg city (pt.)	593	499
Jacksonville township	681	712
New Hampton township	3 457	3 151
New Hampton city (pt.)[20]	2 653	2 458
Richland township	466	480
Stapleton township	1 020	1 037
Lawler city	534	513
Utica township	634	712
Washington township	1 137	1 130
Alta Vista city	314	283
North Washington city	142	134
Clarke County[21]	8 612	7 581
Doyle township	290	255
Franklin township	307	253
Fremont township	441	389
Green Bay township	282	300
Jackson township	496	486
Woodburn city	207	186
Knox township	250	234
Liberty township	356	315
Madison township	209	227
Osceola city[21]	3 750	3 124
Osceola township[21]	561	568
Troy township	975	890
Murray city	703	620
Ward township[21]	373	266
Washington township	322	274
Clay County[22]	19 576	18 464
Clay township	854	882
Royal city[22]	522	469
Douglas township	287	306
Freeman township	608	569
Dickens city	289	240
Garfield township	453	552
Webb city	222	234
Gillett Grove township	535	538
Gillett Grove city (pt.)[22]	80	...
Greenville city	122	117
Herdland township	259	316
Lake township	285	333
Lincoln township	392	466
Rossie city	72	91
Logan township	250	308
Gillett Grove city (pt.)[22]	13	...
Lone Tree township	1 078	1 084
Everly city	796	699
Meadow township[22]	457	435
Fostoria city (pt.)	—	6
Peterson township	787	822

County Subdivisions	1980	1970
Clay County—Con.		
Peterson township—Con.		
Peterson city	470	469
Riverton township[22]	379	391
Sioux township[22]	398	327
Spencer city[22]	11 726	10 278
Summit township[22]	580	548
Fostoria city (pt.)[22]	261	213
Waterford township	248	309
Clayton County[23]	21 098	20 606
Boardman township	2 167	2 091
Elkader city[23]	1 688	1 592
Buena Vista township	430	329
North Buena Vista city	155	118
Cass township	1 956	1 818
Strawberry Point city[23]	1 463	1 281
Clayton township	410	459
Clayton city	68	113
Cox Creek township	493	494
Littleport city (pt.)	64	64
Elk township	426	464
Farmersburg township	695	609
Farmersburg city (pt.)	267	128
Garnavillo township	1 075	1 026
Garnavillo city	723	634
Giard township	450	572
Grand Meadow township	530	557
Postville city (pt.)[23]	—	...
Highland township	315	300
Jefferson township	3 207	2 989
Guttenberg city	2 428	2 177
Osterdock city (pt.)	—	15
Lodomillo township	804	818
Edgewood city (pt.)	372	305
Mallory township	525	528
Osterdock city (pt.)	35	44
Marion township	439	465
Mendon township	1 956	1 959
McGregor city[23]	945	990
Marquette city	528	509
Millville township	572	508
Millville city	50	27
Monona township	2 359	2 255
Luana city	246	225
Monona city	1 530	1 395
Read township	353	372
Sperry township	651	645
Volga city[23]	310	305
Volga township	729	635
Elkport city	98	87
Garber city	140	148
Littleport city (pt.)	42	33
Wagner township	556	713
Farmersburg city (pt.)	9	104
St. Olaf city	138	140
Clinton County[24]	57 122	56 749
Bloomfield township	1 130	1 167
Delmar city	633	599
Brookfield township	566	565
Camanche township[24]	5 027	3 862
Camanche city[24]	4 725	3 470
Center township	718	733
Clinton city[24]	32 828	34 719
Deep Creek township	828	782
Goose Lake city	274	218
De Witt township	5 650	4 653
De Witt city[24]	4 512	3 647
Eden township	1 128	981
Low Moor city[24]	346	347
Elk River township	854	1 015
Andover city	107	90
Grant township	366	417
Hampshire township[24]	860	571
Liberty township	533	517
Toronto city	172	145
Olive township	959	903
Calamus city[24]	452	396
Orange township	1 284	1 052
Grand Mound city	674	627
Sharon township	956	988
Lost Nation city	524	547
Spring Rock township	1 305	1 281
Wheatland city	840	832
Washington township	554	608
Waterford township	936	1 017
Charlotte city	442	444
Welton township	640	659
Welton city	119	104
Crawford County[25]	18 935	'19 116
Boyer township	290	329
Charter Oak township	945	1 137
Charter Oak city	615	715
Denison township	7 219	'6 731
Denison city (pt.)	6 668	'6 213
East Boyer township	557	543
Denison city (pt.)	7	5
Goodrich township	412	374

County Subdivisions	1980	1970
Crawford County—Con.		
Hanover township	355	371
Hayes township	348	447
Iowa township	454	489
Aspinwall city	65	81
Jackson township	266	336
Milford township	688	711
Deloit city	345	279
Morgan township	346	387
Nishnabotny township	1 388	1 366
Manilla city	1 020	943
Otter Creek township	1 545	1 551
Kiron city	317	275
Schleswig city	868	875
Paradise township	411	428
Arion city (pt.)	83	66
Soldier township	418	499
Ricketts city	143	141
Stockholm township	361	422
Union township	1 087	1 038
Arion city (pt.)	124	133
Dow City city[25]	616	571
Washington township	416	405
Buck Grove city[25]	84	41
West Side township	1 155	1 212
Vail city	490	486
Westside city	387	389
Willow township	274	340
Dallas County[26]	29 513	26 085
Adams township	875	545
De Soto city (pt.)[26]	125	6
Adel township	4 743	4 119
Adel city	2 846	2 419
Dallas Center city (pt.)[26]	1 295	1 087
Beaver township	535	554
Bouton city	139	160
Boone township	1 477	800
Colfax township	425	448
Dallas township	513	583
Dawson city	229	232
Des Moines township	1 823	1 628
Woodward city[26]	1 212	1 010
Grant township	1 379	1 353
Granger city[26]	619	661
Lincoln township	329	423
Linn township	635	707
Linden city	264	278
Spring Valley township	7 637	7 474
Perry city[26]	7 053	6 906
Sugar Grove township	906	921
Dallas Center city (pt.)[26]	65	41
Minburn city	390	378
Union township	2 221	2 141
Dexter city	678	652
Redfield city[26]	959	921
Van Meter township	2 654	1 598
De Soto city (pt.)[26]	910	363
Van Meter city[26]	747	464
Walnut township	2 973	2 349
Waukee city[26]	2 227	1 577
Washington township	388	442
Davis County[27]	9 104	8 207
Bloomfield township[27]	2 849	2 718
Cleveland township[27]	554	505
Drakesville township	414	291
Drakesville city	212	163
Fabius township	211	254
Fox River township	325	254
Grove township	313	319
Lick Creek township	786	700
Floris city	187	145
Marion township	306	250
Perry township	309	267
Prairie township	519	401
Pulaski city	267	255
Roscoe township	265	183
Salt Creek township	429	384
Soap Creek township	558	451
Union township	385	414
West Grove township	402	385
Wyacondah township	479	431
Decatur County[28]	9 794	9 737
Bloomington township	194	206
Burrell township	438	403
Davis City city (pt.)	227	201
Center township[28]	430	365
Decatur township	431	416
Decatur City city	199	198
Eden township	286	288
Fayette township	198	203
Franklin township	444	471
Weldon city	187	155
Garden Grove township	550	587
Garden Grove city	297	285
Le Roy city	31	43
Grand River township	163	159
Hamilton township	242	219

County Subdivisions

County Subdivisions	1980	1970
Decatur County—Con.		
Hamilton township—Con.		
Pleasanton city	75	62
High Point township	189	243
Lamoni city	2 705	2 540
Leon city[28]	2 094	2 142
Long Creek township	464	483
Van Wert city	245	244
Morgan township	110	76
New Buda township	291	262
Davis City city (pt.)	100	100
Richland township	401	483
Grand River city	188	211
Woodland township	164	191
Delaware County[29]	18 933	18 770
Adams township	864	839
Ryan city (pt.)[29]	380	335
Bremen township	931	998
Dyersville city (pt.)[29]	45	73
Coffins Grove township	682	724
Masonville city	150	147
Colony township	1 123	1 060
Colesburg city[29]	463	379
Delaware township	6 074	5 549
Manchester city (pt.)[29]	4 942	4 641
Delhi township	1 078	1 120
Delaware city (pt.)[29]	–	–
Delhi city	511	527
Elk township	758	837
Greeley city	313	323
Hazel Green township	481	588
Ryan city (pt.)	10	8
Honey Creek township	1 057	1 097
Edgewood city (pt.)	528	481
Milo township	863	676
Manchester city (pt.)[29]	–	...
North Fork township	639	638
Oneida township	1 653	1 578
Delaware city (pt.)[29]	170	153
Earlville city	844	751
Oneida city	61	55
Prairie township	448	521
Richland township	621	661
Dundee city	164	166
South Fork township	1 327	1 491
Hopkinton city	774	800
Union township	334	393
Des Moines County[30]	46 203	46 982
Benton township	752	650
Burlington township	28 817	31 639
Burlington city (pt.)[30]	28 817	31 639
Concordia township	976	797
Burlington city (pt.)[30]	–	–
Danville township[30]	2 412	2 260
Danville city	994	948
Middletown city (pt.)	470	424
Flint River township	6 152	5 287
Burlington city (pt.)[30]	608	574
Middletown city (pt.)	17	19
West Burlington city (pt.)[30]	3 188	3 134
Franklin township	699	756
Huron township	418	453
Jackson township	181	203
Pleasant Grove township	442	436
Tama township	1 437	994
Burlington city (pt.)[30]	34	44
Union township[30]	1 250	774
Burlington city (pt.)[30]	70	109
West Burlington city (pt.)	183	5
Washington township	416	532
Yellow Springs township	2 251	1 971
Mediapolis city[30]	1 685	1 242
Dickinson County[31]	15 629	12 565
Center township	6 363	4 733
Arnolds Park city[31]	1 051	970
Okoboji city (pt.)[31]	493	320
Spirit Lake city (pt.)[31]	3 474	2 560
West Okoboji city (pt.)[31]	142	108
Diamond Lake township	290	322
Excelsior township	262	264
Lakeville township	1 495	801
Okoboji city (pt.)	66	41
Wahpeton city[31]	372	149
West Okoboji city (pt.)	293	102
Lloyd township	758	700
Terril city	420	397
Milford township[31]	853	751
Milford city (pt.)[31]	503	372
Okoboji township	1 929	1 625
Milford city (pt.)[31]	1 573	1 296
Richland township	306	356
Superior city (pt.)	22	23
Silver Lake township	1 306	1 215
Lake Park city[31]	1 123	918
Spirit Lake township	1 437	1 166

County Subdivisions	1980	1970
Dickinson County—Con.		
Spirit Lake township—Con.		
Orleans city[31]	546	396
Spirit Lake city (pt.)	502	454
Superior township	417	361
Superior city (pt.)	166	116
Westport township	213	271
Dubuque County[32]	93 745	90 609
Cascade township	1 265	1 182
Cascade city (pt.)[32]	777	704
Center township	1 603	1 172
Centralia city (pt.)	95	100
Graf city	98	70
Concord township	939	981
Holy Cross city	310	290
Dodge township	1 498	1 315
Dyersville city (pt.)[32]	74	...
Farley city (pt.)	81	37
Worthington city[32]	432	365
Dubuque city[32]	62 321	62 309
Dubuque township[32]	5 007	4 384
Asbury city[32]	2 017	410
Sageville city (pt.)	123	176
Iowa township	673	731
Bankston city	40	28
Jefferson township	1 614	1 493
Balltown city[32]	106	79
Rickardsville city	215	193
Sherrill city (pt.)[32]	191	190
Liberty township	841	813
Luxemburg city[32]	271	185
Mosalem township[32]	1 372	1 142
New Wine township	4 862	4 538
Dyersville city (pt.)[32]	3 706	3 364
New Vienna city[32]	430	392
Peru township	1 538	1 325
Durango city	41	55
Sageville city (pt.)	168	162
Sherrill city (pt.)[32]	17	...
Prairie Creek township	807	833
Bernard city[32]	130	148
Table Mound township[32]	3 128	2 843
Taylor township	3 326	2 950
Epworth city[32]	1 380	1 132
Farley city (pt.)	1 206	1 059
Vernon township	1 079	781
Centralia city (pt.)	11	5
Peosta city[32]	120	57
Washington township	651	698
Zwingle city (pt.)	89	82
Whitewater township	1 221	1 119
Cascade city (pt.)[32]	735	640
Emmet County[33]	13 336	14 009
Armstrong Grove township	1 497	1 439
Armstrong city[33]	1 153	1 061
Center township	470	499
Gruver city	145	135
Denmark township	810	833
Ringsted city	557	509
Ellsworth township	313	327
Emmet township	262	250
Estherville township	8 099	8 613
Estherville city[33]	7 518	8 108
High Lake township	589	546
Wallingford city (pt.)	227	204
Iowa Lake township	205	234
Jack Creek township	218	277
Lincoln township	319	317
Dolliver city	125	95
Swan Lake township	257	330
Twelve Mile Lake township	297	344
Wallingford city (pt.)	29	41
Fayette County[34]	25 488	26 898
Auburn township	786	805
St. Lucas city	194	194
Banks township	496	516
Bethel township	438	503
Center township	481	541
Donnan city	10	18
Randalia city	101	81
Clermont township	993	1 035
Clermont city	602	582
Dover township	645	685
Eden township	825	939
Waucoma city	308	357
Fairfield township	857	906
Arlington city	498	481
Fayette city	1 515	1 947
Fremont township	748	757
Westgate city	263	204
Harlan township	1 002	1 049
Maynard city	561	503
Illyria township	618	653
Wadena city	230	237
Jefferson township	8 498	8 692
Oelwein city[34]	7 564	7 735
Oran township	752	766

County Subdivisions

County Subdivisions	1980	1970
Fayette County—Con.		
Oran township—Con.		
Fairbank city (pt.)[34]	143	49
Pleasant Valley township	1 034	989
Elgin city[34]	702	613
Putnam township	478	527
Scott township	376	416
Smithfield township	373	483
Union township[34]	457	485
Westfield township	320	551
West Union city[34]	2 783	2 624
Windsor township	1 013	1 029
Hawkeye city	512	529
Floyd County[35]	19 597	19 860
Cedar township	369	376
Charles City city[35]	8 778	9 268
Floyd township	1 162	1 100
Floyd city	408	380
Niles township	614	620
Colwell city	91	100
Pleasant Grove township	359	399
Riverton township	645	718
Rockford township	1 447	1 359
Rockford city[35]	1 012	902
Rock Grove township	2 004	1 779
Nora Springs city	1 572	1 337
Rudd township	760	792
Rudd city	460	429
St. Charles township[35]	1 812	1 579
Scott township	307	415
Ulster township	475	471
Union township	865	984
Marble Rock city	419	461
Franklin County	13 036	13 255
Geneva township	463	495
Geneva city	218	201
Grant township	517	541
Hamilton township	271	310
Coulter city (pt.)	5	2
Hampton city	4 630	4 376
Ingham township	433	458
Hansell city	138	124
Lee township	287	358
Marion township	1 008	1 059
Coulter city (pt.)	257	259
Latimer city	441	393
Morgan township	469	526
Coulter city (pt.)	2	1
Dows city (pt.)	136	110
Mott township	619	556
Oakland township	383	464
Popejoy city	112	147
Osceola township	488	466
Ackley city (pt.)	69	49
Reeve township	417	445
Richland township	325	430
Ross township	474	485
Scott township	501	583
Alexander city	190	249
Coulter city (pt.)	—	...
Sheffield city	1 224	1 070
West Fork township	260	320
Wisner township	267	313
Fremont County[36]	9 401	9 282
Benton township	347	406
Fisher township	1 006	904
Farragut city	603	521
Shenandoah city (pt.)[36]	—	...
Green township	295	303
Hamburg city[36]	1 597	1 649
Locust Grove township	255	317
Madison township	255	300
Monroe township	456	469
Imogene city	188	192
Prairie township	215	214
Riverside township	441	452
Randolph city[36]	223	214
Riverton township	489	462
Riverton city	342	331
Scott township	539	548
Thurman city	221	230
Sidney township	1 996	1 727
Sidney city	1 308	1 061
Tabor city (pt.)	967	848
Walnut township	211	232
Washington township[36]	332	451
Greene County	12 119	12 716
Bristol township	355	397
Cedar township	292	329
Dawson township	267	317
Franklin township	235	324
Grant township	358	288
Greenbrier township	174	305
Hardin township	256	304
Highland township	757	825
Churdan city	540	598
Jackson township	394	348

County Subdivisions

County Subdivisions	1980	1970
Greene County—Con.		
Jefferson city	4 854	4 735
Junction township	1 458	1 567
Dana city	110	118
Grand Junction city	970	967
Kendrick township	278	356
Ralston city (pt.)	6	1
Paton township	529	630
Paton city	291	329
Scranton township	1 060	1 044
Scranton city	748	751
Washington township	643	671
Rippey city	304	270
Willow township	209	276
Grundy County[37]	14 366	14 119
Beaver township	702	729
Stout city[37]	190	196
Black Hawk township	2 145	2 107
Reinbeck city[37]	1 808	1 711
Clay township	1 689	1 552
Beaman city	219	222
Conrad city[37]	1 133	932
Colfax township	748	736
Holland city	278	258
Fairfield township	639	630
Felix township	361	456
German township	454	491
Grant township	1 671	1 271
Dike city[37]	987	794
Lincoln township	348	412
Melrose township	354	439
Palermo township	3 244	3 138
Grundy Center city	2 880	2 712
Pleasant Valley township	404	529
Shiloh township	1 200	1 197
Wellsburg city[37]	761	754
Washington township	407	432
Morrison city	146	136
Guthrie County[38]	11 983	12 243
Baker township	294	346
Guthrie Center city (pt.)[38]	2	...
Bear Grove township	306	326
Beaver township	736	794
Menlo city	410	391
Cass township	2 117	1 767
Panora city[38]	1 211	982
Yale city (pt.)	211	196
Dodge township	666	717
Bagley city	370	365
Grant township	376	422
Adair city (pt.)	66	57
Highland township	918	955
Bayard city	637	628
Jackson township	299	312
Orange township	302	338
Penn township	340	256
Richland township	662	741
Jamaica city	275	271
Yale city (pt.)	88	105
Seely township	280	339
Stuart township	1 237	1 133
Stuart city (pt.)[38]	1 127	1 016
Thompson township	737	897
Casey city (pt.)	459	530
Union township	178	248
Valley township	2 031	2 286
Guthrie Center city (pt.)[38]	1 711	1 834
Victory township	504	366
Guthrie Center city (pt.)[38]	—	...
Hamilton County[39]	17 862	18 383
Blairsburg township	562	592
Blairsburg city	288	287
Cass township[39]	497	512
Clear Lake township	838	895
Stanhope city	492	482
Ellsworth township	576	603
Randall city	171	179
Freedom township[39]	299	346
Fremont township	332	359
Hamilton township	257	342
Independence township[39]	571	650
Kamrar city	225	243
Liberty township	314	365
Lincoln township	766	871
Ellsworth city (pt.)	408	443
Lyon township	1 525	1 502
Ellsworth city (pt.)[39]	72	...
Jewell Junction city[39]	1 145	1 152
Marion township	1 127	1 044
Stratford city (pt.)	775	671
Rose Grove township	280	321
Scott township	371	441
Webster township	307	287
Webster City city[39]	8 572	8 488
Williams township	668	765
Williams city	410	456

County Subdivisions

County Subdivisions	1980	1970
Hancock County[40]	13 833	[1]13 506
Amsterdam township	1 027	[1]1 116
Kanawha city	756	[1]822
Avery township	513	589
Goodell city (pt.)	216	211
Bingham township	620	652
Woden city	287	265
Boone township	303	426
Corwith city (pt.)	52	77
Britt township	2 490	2 412
Britt city[40]	2 185	2 069
Concord township	3 289	[1]2 673
Garner city[40]	2 908	[1]2 257
Crystal township	631	643
Crystal Lake city	314	276
Ell township	963	[1]925
Klemme city	620	[1]554
Ellington township	595	561
Erin township	354	[1]413
Garfield township	552	589
Liberty township	362	[1]441
Madison township	844	652
Forest City city (pt.)	350	115
Magor township	656	[1]657
Corwith city (pt.)	428	[1]361
Orthel township	368	413
Twin Lake township	266	344
Goodell city (pt.)	4	7
Hardin County[41]	21 776	22 248
Alden township	1 494	1 461
Alden city[41]	953	876
Buckeye township	429	466
Buckeye city	154	143
Clay township	774	820
Steamboat Rock city	387	394
Concord township	434	471
Eldora city	3 063	3 223
Eldora township	381	389
Ellis township	380	413
Etna township	2 248	2 179
Ackley City (pt.)	1 831	1 745
Grant township	318	365
Hardin township	7 595	7 701
Iowa Falls city[41]	6 174	6 454
Jackson township	375	419
Owasa city	65	69
Pleasant township	635	446
Providence township	503	577
New Providence city	249	208
Sherman township	859	896
Radcliffe city	593	548
Tipton township	1 207	1 205
Hubbard city[41]	852	846
Union township	1 081	1 217
Union city	515	484
Whitten city	168	194
Harrison County[42]	16 348	16 240
Allen township	235	273
Boyer township	1 904	1 747
Woodbine city[42]	1 463	1 349
Calhoun township	297	250
Cass township	343	382
Cincinnati township	236	244
Clay township	148	186
Douglas township	310	411
Harrison township	1 743	1 680
Dunlap city[42]	1 374	1 292
Jackson township	612	570
Pisgah city	307	286
Jefferson township	2 115	2 018
Logan city[42]	1 540	1 526
La Grange township	346	303
Lincoln township	292	288
Little Sioux township	515	560
Little Sioux city	251	239
Magnolia township	661	766
Magnolia city	207	206
Morgan township	531	556
Mondamin city	423	420
Raglan township	248	218
St. Johns township	4 074	4 128
Missouri Valley city	3 107	3 519
Taylor township	567	516
Modale city[42]	373	297
Union township	335	391
Washington township	836	753
Persia city	355	316
Henry County[43]	18 890	18 114
Baltimore township	620	520
Canaan township	475	547
Mount Union city	145	173
Center township[43]	1 156	939
Jackson township	491	488
Jefferson township	1 278	1 304
Coppock city (pt.)	32	38
Wayland city	720	702
Marion township	380	458

County Subdivisions	1980	1970
Henry County—Con.		
Mount Pleasant city[43]	7 322	7 007
New London township	2 597	2 396
New London city[43]	2 043	1 900
Salem township	1 054	1 109
Hillsboro city[43]	208	252
Salem city	463	458
Scott township	1 387	1 319
Winfield city	1 042	897
Tippecanoe township	805	736
Rome city	113	135
Trenton township	566	506
Wayne township	759	785
Olds city[43]	225	206
Howard County[44]	11 114	11 442
Afton township	979	940
Elma city (pt.)	502	423
Albion township	372	335
Chester township	394	423
Chester city	175	185
Forest City township	767	795
Lime Springs city	476	497
Howard township	795	872
Elma city (pt.)	212	178
Howard Center township	356	411
Jamestown township	732	784
Riceville city (pt.)[44]	356	366
New Oregon township	992	1 063
Protivin city	368	333
Oak Dale township	274	294
Paris township	504	615
Saratoga township	373	367
Vernon Springs township	4 576	4 543
Cresco city[44]	3 860	3 927
Humboldt County[45]	12 246	12 519
Avery township	449	512
Bradgate city	151	130
Gilmore City city (pt.)	21	20
Beaver township	406	410
Corinth township[45]	449	381
Dakota City city	1 072	746
Delana township	699	760
Bode city	406	372
Grove township	344	362
Humboldt city[45]	4 794	4 665
Humboldt township	733	798
Livermore city	490	510
Lu Verne city (pt.)[45]	8	4
Lake township	365	426
Hardy city	72	73
Norway township	506	621
Thor city	200	212
Rutland township[45]	615	664
Rutland city	163	215
Vernon township	730	827
Lu Verne city (pt.)[45]	60	63
Renwick city	410	429
Wacousta township	381	443
Ottosen city	92	93
Weaver township	703	904
Gilmore City city (pt.)	345	457
Pioneer city	40	56
Ida County[46]	8 908	[1]9 283
Battle township	326	337
Blaine township	646	667
Arthur city	288	273
Corwin township	2 608	2 538
Ida Grove city[46]	2 285	2 261
Douglas township	314	392
Galva township	691	[1]735
Galva city	420	[1]412
Garfield township	248	304
Grant township	294	337
Griggs township	1 775	1 830
Holstein city[46]	1 477	1 445
Hayes township	272	329
Logan township	280	310
Maple township	1 230	1 152
Battle Creek city	919	837
Silver Creek township	224	352
Iowa County[47]	15 429	15 419
Dayton township	355	419
English township	1 588	1 632
Millersburg city	184	187
North English city (pt.)[47]	972	945
Fillmore township	569	587
Parnell city	234	175
Greene township	559	629
Hartford township	1 483	1 517
Ladora city (pt.)	252	293
Victor city (pt.)	897	843
Hilton township	710	631
Honey Creek township	396	375
Iowa township	620	597
Lenox township	1 503	1 493
Lincoln township	315	374

County Subdivisions	1980	1970
Iowa County—Con.		
Marengo township	2 413	2 413
Marengo city (pt.)	1 919	1 936
Pilot township	487	422
Sumner township	432	506
Ladora city (pt.)	37	28
Troy township	2 504	2 367
Williamsburg city[47]	2 033	1 544
Washington township	1 091	951
Marengo city (pt.)	389	299
York township	404	506
Jackson County[48]	22 503	20 839
Bellevue township	3 063	2 947
Bellevue city[48]	2 450	2 336
Brandon township	341	333
Butler township	444	490
Fairfield township	525	520
Spragueville city (pt.)	36	33
Farmers Creek township	518	556
Iowa township	824	847
Miles city (pt.)	344	358
Jackson township	637	697
Springbrook city	209	196
Maquoketa township	3 274	2 872
Maquoketa city (pt.)[48]	2 421	2 209
Monmouth township	840	870
Baldwin city	198	172
Monmouth city	210	257
Otter Creek township	604	488
Zwingle city (pt.)	30	14
Perry township	853	818
Andrew city	349	335
Prairie Springs township	678	643
La Motte city (pt.)[48]	203	175
Richland township	596	622
La Motte city (pt.)[48]	119	151
South Fork township	4 846	4 335
Hurstville city	57	88
Maquoketa city (pt.)[48]	3 892	3 468
Tete Des Morts township	904	631
St. Donatus city	197	164
Union township	1 091	1 022
Sabula city	824	845
Van Buren township	1 942	1 596
Miles city (pt.)	54	51
Preston city[48]	1 120	950
Spragueville city (pt.)	113	79
Washington township	523	552
Green Island city	103	112
Jasper County[49]	36 425	35 425
Buena Vista township	830	863
Clear Creek township	413	416
Des Moines township	1 896	1 757
Prairie City city (pt.)[49]	1 195	1 091
Elk Creek township	565	564
Fairview township	2 613	2 237
Monroe city[49]	1 875	1 389
Hickory Grove township	389	441
Independence township	1 464	1 274
Baxter city	951	788
Kellogg township	1 198	1 136
Kellogg city	654	607
Lynn Grove township	1 793	1 706
Lynnville city	406	381
Sully city	828	685
Malaka township	367	426
Mariposa township	318	371
Mound Prairie township	630	584
Colfax city (pt.)[49]	30	...
Prairie City city (pt.)	83	50
Newton township	17 061	17 047
Lambs Grove city	228	239
Newton city (pt.)[49]	15 080	15 535
Palo Alto township	1 363	1 143
Newton city (pt.)[49]	212	84
Reasnor city	277	284
Poweshiek township	1 004	977
Mingo city	303	260
Valeria city	80	96
Richland township	419	463
Rock Creek township	783	653
Oakland Acres city[49]	139	...
Sherman township	422	447
Washington township	2 897	2 920
Colfax city (pt.)[49]	2 204	2 293
Jefferson County[50]	16 316	15 774
Black Hawk township	371	409
Buchanan township[50]	562	641
Cedar township	440	365
Center township[50]	1 118	962
Des Moines township	327	386
Fairfield city[50]	9 428	8 715
Liberty township	675	672
Libertyville city	281	329
Lockridge township	723	717
Lockridge city	271	232

County Subdivisions	1980	1970
Jefferson County—Con.		
Locust Grove township	815	922
Batavia city	525	525
Penn township	568	618
Pleasant Plain city	144	121
Polk township	576	570
Packwood city	210	157
Round Prairie township	372	412
Walnut township	341	385
Coppock city (pt.)	7	7
Johnson County[51]	81 717	72 127
Big Grove township	2 213	1 795
Solon city[51]	969	837
Cedar township	465	425
Clear Creek township	1 643	1 273
Coralville city (pt.)[51]	905	661
North Liberty city (pt.)[51]	42	...
Tiffin city	413	299
East Lucas township[51]	459	348
Fremont township	1 542	1 422
Lone Tree city[51]	1 014	834
Graham township	452	552
Hardin township	536	586
Iowa City city[51]	50 508	46 850
Jefferson township	2 423	1 593
Shueyville city	287	'154
Swisher city[51]	654	417
Liberty township	925	948
Hills city	547	507
Lincoln township	297	317
Madison township	347	310
North Liberty city (pt.)[51]	10	...
Monroe township	538	484
Newport township	956	651
Oxford township	1 453	1 229
Oxford city[51]	676	666
Penn township	5 024	2 491
Coralville city (pt.)	1 458	509
North Liberty city (pt.)[51]	1 994	1 055
Pleasant Valley township	339	375
Scott township	1 404	1 045
Sharon township	1 217	1 067
Union township	567	632
Washington township	1 124	1 120
West Lucas township[51]	7 285	6 614
Coralville city (pt.)[51]	5 324	4 960
University Heights city	1 069	1 265
Jones County[52]	20 401	19 868
Cass township	709	574
Anamosa city (pt.)[52]	34	...
Castle Grove township	480	465
Clay township	271	300
Fairview township	6 053	5 456
Anamosa city (pt.)[52]	4 924	4 389
Greenfield township	716	779
Martelle city	316	'341
Morley city (pt.)	–	4
Hale township	412	444
Jackson township	472	461
Lovell township[52]	4 590	1 030
Monticello city[52]	3 641	3 509
Madison township	747	753
Center Junction city	182	172
Onslow city (pt.)	124	139
Oxford township	1 033	1 118
Oxford Junction city	600	666
Richland township	810	836
Cascade city (pt.)	395	394
Rome township	1 271	1 261
Morley city (pt.)	94	119
Olin city	735	710
Scotch Grove township	451	437
Washington township	388	392
Cascade city (pt.)	5	6
Wayne township	795	793
Wyoming township	1 203	1 260
Onslow city (pt.)	94	114
Wyoming city	702	746
Keokuk County[53]	12 921	13 943
Adams township	544	603
Keswick city	300	257
Benton township	1 170	1 117
Hedrick city	847	790
Clear Creek township	317	362
East Lancaster township	151	195
English River township	705	802
North English city (pt.)	18	20
South English city	211	218
Webster city	124	130
Jackson township	558	676
Ollie city	232	268
Lafayette township	1 526	1 706
Harper city	138	'173
Keota city	1 034	'1 112
Liberty township	394	522
Kinross city	79	98
Plank township	435	628

County Subdivisions

County Subdivisions	1980	1970
Keokuk County—Con.		
Prairie township	521	573
Gibson city	75	80
Thornburg city	103	98
Richland township	908	982
Richland city	600	595
Sigourney township	2 583	2 559
Sigourney city[53]	2 330	2 319
Steady Run township	451	412
Martinsburg city	174	140
Van Buren township	409	453
Warren township	731	760
Delta city	482	475
Washington township	1 214	1 273
What Cheer city	803	868
West Lancaster township	304	320
Hayesville city	93	93
Kossuth County[54]	21 891	22 937
Algona city[54]	6 289	6 032
Buffalo township	1 000	1 016
Titonka city[54]	607	599
Burt township	1 072	998
Burt city	689	608
Lone Rock city (pt.)	55	23
Cresco township[54]	1 241	762
Eagle township	171	209
Fenton township	795	940
Fenton city	394	403
Lone Rock city (pt.)	114	143
Garfield township	425	501
West Bend city (pt.)[54]	17	12
German township	356	461
Grant township	202	265
Greenwood township	1 416	1 474
Bancroft city	1 082	1 103
Harrison township	1 125	1 149
Swea City city	813	774
Hebron township	196	266
Irvington township[54]	419	508
Ledyard township	849	1 010
Lakota city	330	385
Ledyard city	215	240
Lincoln township	255	373
Lotts Creek township	373	461
Lu Verne township	580	615
Lu Verne city (pt.)[54]	350	313
Plum Creek township[54]	338	297
Portland township	311	370
Prairie township	372	518
Wesley city (pt.)[54]	10	...
Ramsey township	309	376
Riverdale township	400	471
Seneca township	295	359
Sherman township	340	397
Springfield township	194	268
Swea township	275	346
Union township[54]	349	447
Wesley township	880	898
Wesley city (pt.)	588	548
Whittemore township	1 064	1 150
Whittemore city[54]	647	658
Lee County[55]	43 106	42 996
Cedar township	489	515
Houghton city (pt.)[55]	115	101
Charleston township	785	755
Donnellson city (pt.)	105	129
Denmark township	909	701
Des Moines township	684	633
Franklin township	1 501	1 326
Donnellson city (pt.)[55]	867	669
Franklin city	142	111
Green Bay township	624	584
Harrison township	388	360
Jackson township[55]	1 865	1 977
Jefferson township	1 559	1 051
Fort Madison city (pt.)[55]	22	6
Keokuk city[55]	13 536	14 631
Madison township	13 426	14 000
Fort Madison city (pt.)[55]	13 413	13 980
Marion township	705	763
Houghton city (pt.)	9	18
St. Paul city	141	129
Montrose township	2 139	1 645
Montrose city	1 038	735
Pleasant Ridge township	493	518
West Point city (pt.)[55]	1	...
Van Buren township	400	345
Washington township	1 824	1 485
Fort Madison city (pt.)[55]	85	10
West Point township	1 779	1 707
West Point city (pt.)[55]	1 132	1 045
Linn County[56]	169 775	163 213
Bertram township[56]	2 327	2 141
Bertram city	216	177
Boulder township	733	774
Prairieburg city	197	182
Brown township	2 325	2 151

County Subdivisions

County Subdivisions	1980	1970
Linn County—Con.		
Brown township—Con.		
Springville city[56]	1 165	970
Buffalo township	582	683
Cedar Rapids city[56]	110 243	110 642
Clinton township[56]	1 867	1 581
College township[56]	854	844
Fairfax township[56]	2 072	1 732
Fairfax city[56]	683	635
Walford city (pt.)	19	1
Fayette township[56]	792	736
Palo city[56]	529	430
Franklin township	5 385	5 022
Lisbon city[56]	1 458	1 329
Mount Vernon city[56]	3 325	3 018
Grant township	1 286	1 148
Walker city[56]	733	622
Jackson township	1 456	1 381
Central City city (pt.)[56]	32	9
Coggon city[56]	639	656
Linn township	681	708
Maine township	1 744	1 867
Central City city (pt.)[56]	1 035	1 107
Marion township[56]	22 599	20 835
Marion city[56]	19 474	18 028
Robins city (pt.)[56]	133	116
Monroe township[56]	9 160	5 986
Hiawatha city[56]	4 825	2 416
Robins city (pt.)[56]	593	547
Otter Creek township	1 247	1 155
Alburnett city	411	418
Putnam township	1 139	918
Ely city[56]	425	275
Spring Grove township	844	848
Washington township	2 439	2 061
Center Point city[56]	1 591	1 456
Louisa County[57]	12 055	10 682
Columbus City township	2 466	2 228
Columbus City city	367	312
Columbus Junction city[57]	1 429	1 205
Cotter city[57]	60	55
Concord township	655	562
Fredonia city	224	168
Eliot township	758	690
Oakville city[57]	470	369
Elm Grove township	260	304
Grandview township	1 462	1 330
Grandview city	473	357
Letts city	473	434
Jefferson township	275	320
Marshall township	250	236
Morning Sun township	1 280	1 286
Morning Sun city	959	906
Oakland township	259	219
Port Louisa township	1 339	679
Union township	277	329
Wapello township	2 774	2 499
Wapello city[57]	2 011	1 873
Lucas County[58]	10 313	10 163
Benton township	322	348
Cedar township	287	320
Chariton city[58]	4 987	5 009
English township	617	643
Williamson city	210	216
Jackson township	526	477
Lucas city	292	247
Liberty township	312	311
Lincoln township[58]	710	467
Otter Creek township	250	299
Pleasant township	330	323
Union township	416	438
Derby city	171	161
Warren township	254	285
Washington township	816	836
Russell city	593	591
Whitebreast township	486	407
Lyon County[59]	12 896	13 340
Allison township	281	323
Lester city (pt.)	20	11
Centennial township	236	257
Cleveland township	427	445
Dale township	348	411
Doon township	1 177	1 121
Alvord city	246	204
Doon city	537	437
Elgin township	745	868
Little Rock city[59]	490	531
Garfield township	389	421
Grant township	417	509
Larchwood township	1 240	1 134
Larchwood city[59]	701	611
Lester city (pt.)	254	227
Liberal township	572	534
George city (pt.)	190	120
Logan township	380	493
Lyon township	305	310
Midland township	231	311

County Subdivisions	1980	1970
Lyon County—Con.		
Richland township	1 138	1 115
Inwood city	755	644
Riverside township	391	413
Rock Rapids city (pt.)	130	162
Rock township	2 853	2 812
Rock Rapids city (pt.)	2 563	2 470
Sioux township	331	371
Wheeler township	1 435	1 492
George city (pt.)	1 051	1 074
Madison County[60]	12 597	11 558
Crawford township	586	489
Bevington city (pt.)	55	47
Patterson city[60]	138	120
Douglas township[60]	415	445
Grand River township	375	381
Macksburg city	132	142
Jackson township	303	297
Jefferson township	346	333
Lee township	363	303
Lincoln township[60]	496	407
Madison township	1 140	1 102
Earlham city (pt.)	798	763
Monroe township	292	314
Ohio township	757	694
Truro city	407	359
Penn township	691	608
Earlham city (pt.)[60]	342	211
Scott township	559	433
South township	1 160	965
St. Charles city	507	443
Union township[60]	367	325
Walnut township	441	504
East Peru city	124	184
Webster township	285	304
Winterset city[60]	4 021	3 654
Mahaska County[61]	22 867	22 177
Adams township	324	378
Black Oak township	726	759
Leighton city	137	140
Cedar township[61]	1 172	1 030
Fremont city[61]	730	480
East Des Moines township	216	209
Eddyville city (pt.)[61]	2	...
Garfield township[61]	1 284	969
Beacon city	530	338
Harrison township	606	600
Eddyville city (pt.)[61]	189	157
Jefferson township	413	439
Lincoln township[61]	439	348
Madison township	466	463
Monroe township	316	385
Oskaloosa city[61]	10 989	11 224
Pleasant Grove township	469	506
Barnes City city (pt.)	244	218
Prairie township	1 694	1 395
New Sharon city	1 225	944
Richland township	557	641
Scott township	514	504
Spring Creek township[61]	1 543	1 177
Keomah city[61]	99	...
University Park city	645	534
Union township	351	344
West Des Moines township	219	206
White Oak township	569	600
Rose Hill city	214	192
Marion County[62]	29 669	26 352
Clay township	1 014	934
Harvey city	275	217
Dallas township	1 853	1 790
Dallas city	451	438
Melcher city[62]	953	913
Franklin township	391	489
Indiana township	813	862
Knoxville township	10 305	9 445
Knoxville city[62]	8 143	7 755
Lake Prairie township	9 705	7 949
Pella city[62]	8 349	6 668
Liberty township	1 210	1 127
Bussey city[62]	579	498
Hamilton city	163	186
Marysville city	84	91
Pleasant Grove township	2 492	2 058
Pleasantville city[62]	1 531	1 297
Swan city	102	56
Red Rock township	417	394
Summit township	677	585
Union township	279	217
Washington township	513	502
Marshall County[63]	41 652	41 076
Bangor township	215	293
Eden township	677	764
Rhodes city[63]	367	347
Greencastle township	1 357	1 274
Ferguson city	173	203
Gilman city	642	513

County Subdivisions	1980	1970
Marshall County—Con.		
Iowa township	942	993
Albion city	739	772
Jefferson township	919	951
Haverhill city	173	160
Laurel city	278	245
Le Grand township	1 657	1 269
Le Grand city	921	565
Marshalltown city (pt.)	6	10
Liberty township	405	477
St. Anthony city (pt.)	132	154
Liscomb township	602	715
Liscomb city	296	328
Logan township	1 080	1 140
Melbourne city	732	661
Marietta township	2 617	2 402
Marshalltown city (pt.)[63]	1 957	1 681
Marion township	1 030	1 023
Marshalltown city (pt.)	11	17
Marshall township	17 148	20 124
Marshalltown city (pt.)	17 148	20 124
Minerva township	567	658
Clemons city	175	178
St. Anthony city (pt.)	8	2
State Center township	1 722	1 732
State Center city	1 292	1 232
Taylor township	581	576
Timber Creek township	9 113	5 514
Marshalltown city (pt.)[63]	7 816	4 387
Vienna township	417	477
Washington township	603	694
Mills County[64]	13 406	'11 832
Anderson township	632	670
Henderson city[64]	236	211
Center township	449	360
Deer Creek township	282	291
Glenwood township	6 050	'4 930
Glenwood city[64]	5 280	'4 421
Indian Creek township	1 038	1 134
Emerson city	502	484
Hastings city	215	229
Ingraham township	545	573
Silver City city[64]	291	272
Lyons township	185	204
Malvern city[64]	1 244	1 158
Oak township	1 086	740
Plattville township	768	775
Pacific Junction city	511	505
Rawles township	352	458
St. Marys township	189	119
Silver Creek township[64]	217	169
Tabor city (pt.)	121	109
White Cloud township	248	251
Mitchell County[65]	12 329	13 108
Burr Oak township	321	418
Cedar township	627	670
Douglas township	481	591
East Lincoln township	213	188
Jenkins township	968	950
Riceville city (pt.)	563	511
Liberty township	365	424
Mitchell township	472	545
Mitchell city[65]	193	233
Newburg township	436	452
Carpenter city	109	122
Osage township	4 089	4 174
Osage city[65]	3 718	3 815
Otranto township	412	434
Rock township	381	441
St. Ansgar township	1 409	1 460
St. Ansgar city[65]	1 100	994
Stacyville township	968	1 037
Stacyville city[65]	538	598
Union township	359	417
Wayne township	493	574
McIntire city	197	234
West Lincoln township	335	333
Orchard city	95	115
Monona County[66]	11 692	12 069
Ashton township	661	648
Whiting city (pt.)	460	440
Belvidere township	302	350
Turin city	103	115
Center township	214	248
Castana city (pt.)	34	5
Cooper township	880	895
Mapleton city (pt.)	542	545
Fairview township	178	177
Franklin township[66]	337	319
Grant township	320	344
Rodney city	82	66
Jordan township	241	284
Kennebec township	430	450
Castana city (pt.)	194	206
Lake township	251	281
Whiting city (pt.)	2	3
Lincoln township	394	282

County Subdivisions

County Subdivisions	1980	1970
Monona County—Con.		
Lincoln township—Con.		
Whiting city (pt.)	120	12
Maple township	1 256	1 456
Mapleton city (pt.)	953	1 102
Onawa city[66]	3 283	3 154
St. Clair township	744	745
Ute city	479	512
Sherman township	424	457
Blencoe city	247	255
Sioux township	119	169
Soldier township	524	584
Soldier city[66]	257	242
Spring Valley township	534	604
Moorhead city	264	271
West Fork township	346	385
Whiting city (pt.)	152	135
Willow township	254	237
Monroe County[67]	9 209	9 357
Bluff Creek township	330	401
Cedar township	185	229
Franklin township	230	246
Guilford township	374	407
Jackson township	454	402
Melrose city	218	192
Mantua township	587	544
Monroe township	366	388
Pleasant township	422	360
Eddyville city (pt.)[67]	5	7
Troy township	4 711	4 784
Albia city	4 184	4 151
Union township	1 029	1 076
Lovilia city[67]	637	640
Urbana township	303	294
Wayne township	218	226
Montgomery County[68]	13 413	12 781
Douglas township	373	439
Grant city	143	152
East township[68]	1 706	335
Villisca city[68]	1 434	1 402
Frankfort township	376	327
Stanton city (pt.)	41	26
Garfield township	284	291
Grant township	415	385
Coburg city	52	36
Lincoln township	267	292
Pilot Grove township	328	309
Red Oak township	7 291	6 745
Red Oak city	6 810	6 210
Scott township	1 067	935
Stanton city (pt.)	706	548
Sherman township	768	723
Elliott city	493	423
Washington township	261	291
West township	277	307
Muscatine County[69]	40 436	37 181
Bloomington township	1 142	724
Muscatine city (pt.)[69]	353	...
Cedar township	290	282
Fruitland township	2 120	1 442
Fruitland city[69]	461	...
Muscatine city (pt.)[69]	805	...
Fulton township	947	921
Stockton city	240	222
Walcott city (pt.)	—	—
Goshen township	719	655
Atalissa city[69]	360	244
Lake township	531	490
Montpelier township	996	858
Moscow township	772	636
Wilton city (pt.)[69]	1	...
Muscatine township	22 309	22 405
Muscatine city (pt.)	22 309	22 405
Orono township	459	453
Conesville city	301	295
Pike township	891	954
Nichols city[69]	375	396
Seventy-Six township	426	438
Muscatine city (pt.)[69]	—	...
Sweetland township	2 419	1 484
Wapsinonoc township	3 394	2 971
West Liberty city[69]	2 723	2 296
Wilton township	3 021	2 468
Durant city (pt.)	—	4
Wilton city (pt.)[69]	2 492	1 873
O'Brien County[70]	16 972	17 522
Baker township	330	419
Caledonia township	444	561
Carroll township	555	586
Archer city (pt.)	129	134
Sheldon city (pt.)	36	54
Center township	523	589
Primghar city (pt.)	222	188
Dale township	558	634
Primghar city (pt.)	243	247
Floyd township	5 345	4 946
Sheldon city (pt.)[70]	4 952	4 481

County Subdivisions	1980	1970
O'Brien County—Con.		
Franklin township	1 781	1 854
Sanborn city	1 398	1 465
Grant township	292	323
Hartley township	2 019	2 070
Hartley city	1 700	1 694
Highland township	392	448
Primghar city (pt.)[70]	14	2
Liberty township	575	620
Calumet city	212	219
Sutherland city (pt.)	43	43
Lincoln township	294	390
Omega township	351	423
Moneta city	43	41
Summit township	874	917
Archer city (pt.)[70]	5	...
Primghar city (pt.)	571	558
Union township	1 556	1 640
Paullina city[70]	1 224	1 257
Waterman township	1 083	1 102
Sutherland city (pt.)[70]	854	832
Osceola County[71]	8 371	8 555
Allison township	251	325
Baker township	575	675
Melvin city	277	325
Fairview township	411	441
Harris city	228	195
Gilman township	818	863
Ashton city	441	483
Goewey township	341	395
Harrison township	386	442
Holman township	3 921	3 710
Sibley city[71]	3 051	2 749
Horton township	292	287
Ocheyedan township	918	880
Ocheyedan city[71]	599	545
Viola township	227	258
Wilson township	231	279
Page County[72]	19 063	18 537
Amity township	650	637
Braddyville city (pt.)	44	47
College Springs city	307	295
Buchanan township	387	422
Braddyville city (pt.)	155	160
Colfax township	376	393
Blanchard city	101	139
Coin city (pt.)	17	15
Douglas township	270	270
East River township	301	327
Clarinda city (pt.)[72]	7	59
Fremont township	349	365
Grant township	6 854	6 452
Shenandoah city (pt.)[72]	6 274	5 968
Harlan township	498	520
Clarinda city (pt.)	—	
Shambaugh city	197	178
Lincoln township	497	492
Coin city (pt.)	299	279
Morton township	272	247
Nebraska township	202	157
Nodaway township	6 146	6 159
Clarinda city (pt.)[72]	5 451	5 361
Yorktown city (pt.)	114	92
Pierce township	1 258	1 066
Essex city	1 001	770
Tarkio township	349	355
Yorktown city (pt.)	9	13
Valley township	318	303
Hepburn city	42	38
Washington township	336	372
Northboro city[72]	115	115
Palo Alto County[73]	12 721	13 289
Booth township	233	363
Ellington township	263	345
Emmetsburg township	3 381	3 006
Emmetsburg city (pt.)	3 006	2 540
Fairfield township	414	484
Cylinder city	119	133
Fern Valley township	340	473
Rodman city	86	104
Freedom township	1 877	1 910
Emmetsburg city (pt.)	1 615	1 610
Great Oak township	256	329
Highland township	1 126	1 132
Ruthven city[73]	769	708
Independence township	285	378
Lost Island township	310	328
Nevada township	188	284
Rush Lake township	740	817
Curlew city	85	95
Mallard city[73]	407	384
Silver Lake township	563	595
Ayrshire city[73]	243	243
Vernon township	215	318
Walnut township	1 294	1 292
Graettinger city[73]	923	907
West Bend township	1 236	1 235

County Subdivisions	1980	1970
Palo Alto County—Con.		
West Bend township—Con.		
West Bend city (pt.)[73]	924	853
Plymouth County[74]	24 743	'24 322
America township	8 853	8 686
Le Mars city[74]	8 276	8 159
Elgin township	520	584
Struble city	70	59
Elkhorn township	345	276
Kingsley city (pt.)[74]	–	...
Fredonia township	378	440
Garfield township	1 450	1 477
Kingsley city (pt.)	1 209	1 097
Grant township	516	'532
Craig city	105	'98
Hancock township	365	209
Henry township	346	390
Hungerford township	1 353	1 095
Hinton city[74]	659	488
Johnson township	325	403
Liberty township	382	462
Lincoln township	422	467
Marion township	687	741
Oyens city	146	145
Remsen city (pt.)[74]	103	41
Meadow township	427	518
Perry township	795	562
Plymouth township	1 098	1 130
Merrill city	737	790
Portland township	1 859	1 601
Akron city[74]	1 517	1 324
Preston township	387	403
Remsen township	1 928	1 857
Remsen city (pt.)[74]	1 489	1 326
Sioux township	380	384
Stanton township	424	493
Union township	362	419
Washington township	581	562
Brunsville city[74]	140	125
Westfield township	560	631
Westfield city	199	148
Pocahontas County[75]	11 369	'12 793
Bellville township	654	680
Palmer city	288	264
Cedar township	1 111	1 331
Fonda city	863	980
Center township	2 460	2 443
Pocahontas city[75]	2 352	2 338
Colfax township	345	433
Cummins township	586	'603
Havelock city	279	'248
Des Moines township	234	312
Dover township	359	455
Varina city[75]	122	140
Garfield township	375	444
Gilmore City city (pt.)	103	92
Grant township	279	313
Lake township	470	570
Gilmore City city (pt.)	157	197
Lincoln township	270	329
Lizard township	411	398
Marshall township	265	363
Powhatan township	389	429
Plover city	135	129
Rolfe city	796	767
Roosevelt township	207	314
Sherman township	229	368
Swan Lake township	1 929	'2 241
Laurens city[75]	1 606	'1 792
Polk County[76]	303 170	'286 130
Allen township	843	775
Carlisle city (pt.)[76]	–	...
Des Moines city (pt.)[76]	–	...
Beaver township	2 120	1 807
Mitchellville[76]	1 530	1 341
Bloomfield township	26 549	21 970
Des Moines city (pt.)[76]	23 469	19 919
Camp township	1 298	1 186
Runnells city[76]	377	354
Clay township	6 693	'3 675
Altoona city[76]	5 764	'2 883
Bondurant city (pt.)[76]	55	...
Pleasant Hill city (pt.)[76]	1	...
Crocker township	17 461	10 980
Ankeny city (pt.)[76]	15 398	9 128
Delaware township	5 277	5 228
Altoona city (pt.)[76]	–	...
Des Moines city (pt.)[76]	234	...
Pleasant Hill city (pt.)[76]	2	...
Des Moines township	103 566	116 970
Des Moines city (pt.)	103 566	116 970
Douglas township	1 129	636
Ankeny city (pt.)[76]	31	23
Bondurant city (pt.)	219	39
Elkhart township	865	862
Elkhart city[76]	256	269

County Subdivisions	1980	1970
Polk County—Con.		
Four Mile township	5 119	2 733
Pleasant Hill city (pt.)[76]	3 490	1 535
Franklin township	1 696	930
Bondurant city (pt.)	1 009	423
Jefferson township	2 496	1 110
Grimes city (pt.)[76]	1 215	355
Johnston city (pt.)[76]	315	222
Lee township	58 657	60 387
Des Moines city (pt.)	58 657	'60 387
Lincoln township	880	830
Alleman city[76]	307	...
Sheldahl city (pt.)	103	144
Madison township	1 800	1 160
Polk City city (pt.)[76]	1 653	715
Saylor township	5 454	6 300
Des Moines city (pt.)[76]	154	199
Saylorville Reservoir (unorg.)[76]	37	...
Johnston city (pt.)[76]	–	...
Polk City city (pt.)[76]	5	...
Union township	263	284
Sheldahl city (pt.)	29	22
Valley township	21 894	16 441
West Des Moines city	21 894	16 441
Walnut township	15 895	12 389
Clive city[76]	6 064	3 005
Des Moines city (pt.)	684	703
Urbandale city (pt.)	3 480	2 238
Windsor Heights city	5 474	6 303
Washington township	435	446
Webster township	22 743	19 031
Des Moines city (pt.)[76]	4 239	3 226
Grimes city (pt.)[76]	758	479
Johnston city (pt.)[76]	2 302	...
Urbandale city (pt.)[76]	14 389	12 196
Pottawattamie County[77]	86 561	86 991
Belknap township	1 733	1 815
Oakland city[77]	1 552	1 603
Boomer township	555	515
Carson township	923	978
Carson city	716	756
Center township	323	297
Crescent township	1 083	811
Crescent city	547	284
Garner township	3 590	2 261
Council Bluffs city (pt.)[77]	928	567
Grove township	286	276
Hardin township	739	655
McClelland city	177	146
Hazel Dell township	986	709
James township	298	329
Kane township	53 263	57 967
Carter Lake city	3 438	3 268
Council Bluffs city (pt.)	49 807	54 699
Keg Creek township	836	688
Treynor city (pt.)[77]	360	209
Knox township	1 954	1 853
Avoca city[77]	1 650	1 535
Lake township	1 070	981
Council Bluffs city (pt.)	–	...
Layton township	1 148	1 186
Walnut city[77]	897	870
Lewis township	10 027	8 140
Council Bluffs city (pt.)[77]	5 714	5 082
Lincoln township	243	304
Macedonia township	483	587
Macedonia city	279	330
Minden township	904	839
Minden city[77]	419	433
Neola city (pt.)	11	10
Neola township	1 276	1 480
Neola city (pt.)[77]	828	958
Norwalk township	933	871
Underwood city[77]	448	424
Pleasant township	369	343
Shelby city (pt.)	58	'6
Rockford township	843	574
Silver Creek township	946	620
Treynor city (pt.)[77]	621	263
Valley township	520	507
Hancock city	254	228
Washington township	392	414
Waveland township	272	333
Wright township	239	288
York township	327	370
Poweshiek County[78]	19 306	18 803
Bear Creek township	1 883	1 826
Brooklyn city[78]	1 509	1 410
Chester township	345	430
Deep River township	650	666
Deep River city	323	323
Grant township[78]	572	632
Grinnell city[78]	8 868	8 402
Jackson township	1 958	1 856
Barnes City city (pt.)	22	20
Montezuma city	1 485	1 353
Jefferson township	381	490

County Subdivisions

County Subdivisions	1980	1970
Poweshiek County—Con.		
Jefferson township—Con.		
Hartwick city	92	101
Lincoln township	375	430
Guernsey city	83	94
Madison township	551	522
Malcom township	785	788
Malcom city	418	388
Pleasant township	327	351
Scott township	350	354
Sheridan township	320	372
Sugar Creek township	498	483
Searsboro city	134	140
Union township	589	306
Warren township	468	493
Victor city (pt.)	149	106
Washington township	386	402
Ringgold County[79]	6 112	6 373
Athens township	488	545
Kellerton city	278	299
Benton township	139	193
Maloy city	38	45
Clinton township	247	273
Redding city	91	111
Grant township	201	217
Clearfield city (pt.)	15	13
Jefferson township	219	252
Diagonal city (pt.)	38	31
Shannon City city (pt.)	14	10
Liberty township[79]	193	263
Lincoln township	234	294
Lotts Creek township	108	137
Middle Fork township	170	181
Monroe township	243	291
Beaconsfield city (pt.)	39	48
Mount Ayr city[79]	1 938	1 762
Poe township	277	216
Rice township[79]	222	202
Delphos city	45	35
Riley township	112	139
Tingley township	409	498
Tingley city	210	244
Union township	289	267
Beaconsfield city (pt.)	–	–
Ellston city	60	76
Washington township[79]	508	521
Diagonal city (pt.)	324	296
Waubonsie township	115	122
Benton city	33	46
Sac County[80]	14 118	15 573
Boyer Valley township	1 037	1 136
Early city[80]	670	727
Cedar township	683	773
Lytton city (pt.)[80]	334	324
Clinton township	309	389
Cook township	293	368
Coon Valley township	321	425
Delaware township	432	489
Nemaha city	120	117
Douglas township	269	342
Eden township	304	371
Eureka township	1 128	1 219
Schaller city	832	835
Jackson township	3 378	3 732
Sac City city	3 000	3 268
Levey township	950	1 022
Wall Lake city (pt.)[80]	646	642
Richland township	1 596	1 659
Odebolt city[80]	1 299	1 323
Sac township	700	773
Auburn city	320	329
Viola township	703	847
Wall Lake city (pt.)	246	294
Wall Lake township	1 702	1 666
Lake View city[80]	1 291	1 249
Wheeler township	313	362
Scott County[81]	160 022	142 687
Allens Grove township	1 093	872
Dixon city (pt.)	148	140
Donahue city[81]	289	216
Blue Grass township	4 387	3 361
Blue Grass city (pt.)	926	696
Davenport city (pt.)	6	10
Walcott city (pt.)[81]	1 412	989
Buffalo township	4 424	3 023
Blue Grass city (pt.)	451	336
Buffalo city[81]	1 441	1 513
Butler township	3 244	1 361
McCausland city[81]	381	226
Park View (CDP)	2 140	...
Cleona township	509	554
Durant city (pt.)	4	5
Plain View city (pt.)	19	14
Walcott city (pt.)[81]	–	–
Davenport city (pt.)	103 153	98 322
Davenport city (pt.)	103 153	98 322
Hickory Grove township	835	816

County Subdivisions

County Subdivisions	1980	1970
Scott County—Con.		
Hickory Grove township—Con.		
Davenport city (pt.)	21	10
Maysville city	151	170
Plain View city (pt.)[81]	26	9
Walcott city (pt.)[81]	13	...
Le Claire township	4 495	3 691
Bettendorf city (pt.)[81]	33	...
Le Claire city	2 899	2 520
Liberty township	771	844
Dixon city (pt.)	164	136
New Liberty city	136	141
Lincoln township	693	695
Bettendorf city (pt.)[81]	39	...
Davenport city (pt.)	25	37
Pleasant Valley township	29 003	24 292
Bettendorf city (pt.)[81]	27 309	22 126
Panorama Park city	145	219
Riverdale city	462	684
Princeton township	1 615	1 243
Princeton city	965	633
Sheridan township	4 001	2 600
Davenport city (pt.)[81]	59	90
Eldridge city[81]	3 279	1 535
Winfield township	1 799	1 013
Long Grove city[81]	596	269
Shelby County[82]	15 043	15 528
Cass township	622	742
Portsmouth city	240	239
Center township[82]	455	476
Clay township	1 146	1 123
Elk Horn city[82]	746	667
Douglas township	435	468
Kirkman city	95	72
Fairview township	355	413
Greeley township	349	407
Irwin city (pt.)	39	43
Grove township	318	343
Harlan city[82]	5 357	5 049
Jackson township	450	506
Jefferson township	751	816
Irwin city (pt.)	388	403
Lincoln township	453	457
Monroe township	370	438
Polk township	273	331
Shelby township	1 018	990
Shelby city (pt.)	607	531
Tennant city	77	93
Union township	1 114	1 155
Defiance city	383	392
Earling city (pt.)	302	245
Washington township	652	732
Panama city	229	221
Westphalia township	925	1 082
Earling city (pt.)	218	328
Westphalia city	169	121
Sioux County[83]	30 813	27 996
Buncombe township	2 190	2 096
Hawarden city (pt.)	2 037	1 979
Capel township	562	539
Center township	452	513
Eagle township	368	425
East Orange township	690	789
Granville city	336	383
Floyd township	1 248	1 223
Hospers city	655	646
Garfield township	289	386
Grant township	572	555
Matlock city	109	89
Sheldon city (pt.)[83]	15	(NA)
Holland township	4 889	3 835
Orange City city (pt.)[83]	4 239	3 148
Lincoln township	2 324	2 164
Hull city[83]	1 714	1 523
Logan township	962	1 092
Chatsworth city	110	90
Hawarden city (pt.)[83]	685	810
Lynn township	503	479
Nassau township	1 748	1 921
Alton city	986	1 018
Orange City city (pt.)[83]	349	424
Plato township	664	658
Reading township	954	970
Ireton city[83]	588	582
Rock township	3 533	2 780
Rock Valley city[83]	2 706	2 205
Settlers township	152	132
Sheridan township	1 213	1 187
Boyden city[83]	708	670
Sherman township	692	706
Maurice city	288	266
Sioux township	383	410
Washington township	335	365
Welcome township	1 289	906
Sioux Center city[83]	504	273
West Branch township	4 801	3 865
Sioux Center city (pt.)[83]	4 084	3 177

County Subdivisions	1980	1970
Story County[84]	72 326	62 783
Collins township	779	816
Collins city	451	404
Franklin township	16 156	13 213
Ames city (pt.)[84]	13 687	11 653
Gilbert city[84]	805	521
Grant township	976	540
Ames city (pt.)[84]	171	26
Nevada city (pt.)[84]	272	15
Howard township	1 500	1 280
Roland city	1 005	803
Story City city (pt.)[84]	64	7
Indian Creek township	1 297	1 270
Maxwell city	783	758
Lafayette township	3 161	2 689
Story City city (pt.)[84]	2 698	2 097
Lincoln township	949	862
Zearing city	630	535
Milford township	518	589
Ames city (pt.)[84]	–	–
Nevada township	6 086	5 349
Nevada city (pt.)[84]	5 640	4 937
New Albany township	1 188	1 033
Colo city[84]	808	606
Palestine township	4 214	2 859
Huxley city[84]	1 884	937
Kelley city (pt.)[84]	96	125
Sheldahl city (pt.)	158	98
Slater city[84]	1 312	1 094
Richland township	470	556
Sherman township	299	372
Union township	1 172	1 062
Cambridge city	732	661
Warren township	573	656
McCallsburg city	304	307
Washington township	32 988	29 637
Ames city (pt.)[84]	31 917	27 826
Kelley city (pt.)	141	110
Tama County[85]	19 533	20 147
Buckingham township	384	425
Carlton township	1 024	1 003
Garwin city[85]	626	563
Carroll township	357	446
Clark township	1 711	1 669
Dysart city[85]	1 355	1 251
Columbia township	439	436
Crystal township	344	383
Geneseo township	383	341
Grant township	373	443
Highland township	321	385
Howard township	383	437
Indian Village township	894	902
Montour city	387	334
Lincoln township	505	593
Lincoln city	202	184
Oneida township	591	680
Clutier city	249	275
Otter Creek township	363	451
Perry township	2 080	2 093
Traer city	1 703	1 682
Richland township	285	335
Salt Creek township	670	717
Chelsea city	376	381
Spring Creek township	1 444	1 455
Gladbrook city[85]	970	961
Tama township	3 264	3 322
Tama city	2 968	3 000
Toledo township	3 085	2 998
Toledo city	2 445	2 361
York township	633	633
Elberon city	194	203
Vining city	96	71
Taylor County[86]	8 353	8 790
Bedford township	1 784	1 834
Bedford city	1 692	1 733
Benton township	206	227
Clayton township	184	219
Dallas township	859	827
New Market city	554	501
Gay township	152	177
Grant township	618	674
Clearfield city (pt.)	418	417
Grove township	271	279
Holt township	239	307
Jackson township	143	165
Jefferson township	465	507
Athelstan city	45	65
Blockton city	280	273
Marshall township	403	467
Conway city	93	91
Sharpsburg city	114	106
Mason township	246	242
Nodaway township	247	253
Platte township	1 596	1 498
Lenox city (pt.)[86]	1 336	1 215
Polk township	194	241
Ross township	223	258

County Subdivisions	1980	1970
Taylor County—Con.		
Washington township	523	615
Gravity city	245	286
Union County[87]	13 858	13 557
Creston city[87]	8 429	8 234
Dodge township	232	258
Douglas township[87]	702	578
Cromwell city	157	168
Grant township	375	375
Shannon City city (pt.)	79	90
Highland township	300	341
Jones township	350	399
Thayer city	87	100
Lincoln township	351	293
New Hope township	671	625
Lorimor city	405	346
Platte township	377	398
Kent city	70	86
Pleasant township	185	187
Sand Creek township	293	348
Arispe city	89	93
Spaulding township	295	353
Union township	1 298	1 168
Afton city	985	823
Van Buren County	8 626	8 643
Bonaparte township	699	697
Bonaparte city	489	517
Cedar township	437	487
Stockport city (pt.)	138	185
Chequest township	302	285
Des Moines township	263	289
Cantril city (pt.)	4	3
Farmington township	1 105	1 082
Farmington city	869	800
Harrisburg township	254	280
Henry township	191	180
Jackson township	1 302	1 250
Cantril city (pt.)	295	255
Milton city	567	567
Lick Creek township	531	529
Birmingham city (pt.)	90	102
Union township	785	837
Birmingham city (pt.)	320	350
Stockport city (pt.)	134	149
Van Buren township	1 508	1 399
Keosauqua city	1 003	1 018
Vernon township	338	374
Mount Sterling city	96	87
Village township	729	760
Washington township	182	194
Wapello County[88]	40 241	42 149
Adams township	897	850
Blakesburg city	404	403
Agency township	1 310	1 195
Agency city	657	610
Cass township	325	321
Chillicothe city	131	126
Center township	29 496	32 193
Ottumwa city (pt.)[88]	27 283	29 604
Columbia township	1 236	1 111
Eddyville city (pt.)[88]	920	781
Competine township	359	417
Dahlonega township	588	615
Ottumwa city (pt.)[88]	98	6
Green township	805	638
Highland township	371	423
Keokuk township	1 168	685
Pleasant township	354	397
Polk township	634	533
Richland township	789	912
Kirkville city	220	222
Ottumwa city (pt.)[88]	–	...
Washington township	1 909	1 859
Eldon city[88]	1 255	1 319
Warren County[89]	34 878	27 432
Allen township	3 472	2 559
Carlisle city (pt.)[89]	3 073	2 246
Belmont township	1 005	887
Milo city (pt.)	600	426
Greenfield township	3 896	3 510
Norwalk city (pt.)[89]	27	18
Spring Hill city	95	131
Indianola city[89]	10 843	8 852
Jackson township	671	648
St. Marys city[89]	111	105
Jefferson township	1 548	1 046
Bevington city (pt.)	5	7
Martensdale city	438	306
Liberty township	571	521
Lincoln township[89]	1 741	1 455
Ackworth city	83	111
Linn township	5 386	3 149
Cumming city	151	189
Norwalk city (pt.)[89]	2 649	1 727
Otter township[89]	647	519
Milo city (pt.)	178	135

County Subdivisions	1980	1970
Warren County—Con.		
Palmyra township	552	445
Richland township	1 137	965
Hartford city[88]	761	582
Squaw township	561	410
Union township	482	446
Sandyville city	86	89
Virginia township	992	851
New Virginia city	512	452
White Breast township	773	780
Lacona city	376	424
White Oak township[89]	601	389
Washington County[90]	20 141	18 967
Brighton township	1 024	861
Brighton city	804	632
Cedar township	341	381
Clay township	322	323
Crawford township	659	716
Crawfordsville city	290	288
Dutch Creek township	372	373
English River township	3 047	2 543
Kalona city[90]	1 862	1 488
Franklin township	550	602
West Chester city	191	199
Highland township	371	375
Iowa township	1 464	1 393
Riverside city	826	758
Jackson township	462	497
Lime Creek township	1 987	1 866
Wellman city[90]	1 125	977
Marion township	599	596
Coppock city (pt.)	8	13
Oregon township	1 019	916
Ainsworth city	547	455
Seventy-Six township	343	376
Washington township	7 581	7 149
Washington city[90]	6 584	6 317
Wayne County	8 199	8 405
Benton township	338	296
Corydon city (pt.)	52	30
Clay township	190	229
Clinton township	122	152
Corydon township	1 991	1 947
Corydon city (pt.)	1 766	1 715
Grand River township	557	648
Clio city (pt.)	95	108
Lineville city	319	385
Howard township	123	134
Jackson township	270	332
Jefferson township	181	208
Clio city (pt.)	11	5
Monroe township	121	144
Richman township	887	928
Humeston city	671	673
South Fork township	400	386
Promise City city	149	148
Union township	280	292
Millerton city	72	82
Walnut township	1 267	1 181
Seymour city	1 036	931
Warren township	910	905
Allerton city	670	643
Washington township	305	334
Wright township	257	289
Webster County[91]	45 953	48 391
Badger township	1 429	1 156
Badger city	653	465
Burnside township	399	454
Clay township	328	428
Colfax township	403	506
Duncombe city (pt.)	8	6
Cooper township[91]	718	970
Dayton township	1 381	1 406
Dayton city[91]	941	909
Deer Creek township	476	482
Douglas township[91]	1 002	887
Elkhorn township	1 053	1 170
Fort Dodge city[91]	29 423	31 263
Fulton township	678	739
Moorland city	257	269
Gowrie township	1 277	1 467
Farnhamville city (pt.)[91]	–	...
Gowrie city (pt.)[91]	1 031	1 199
Hardin township	173	190
Stratford city (pt.)	31	39
Jackson township	520	598
Clare city	229	249
Johnson township	628	545
Barnum city[91]	198	147
Lost Grove township	759	795
Gowrie city (pt.)[91]	58	26
Harcourt city	347	305
Newark township	476	626
Vincent city[91]	207	204
Otho township	1 158	1 059
Otho city	692	581

County Subdivisions	1980	1970
Webster County—Con.		
Pleasant Valley township	924	746
Roland township	772	807
Callender city	446	421
Sumner township	487	511
Lehigh city (pt.)	467	494
Washington township	975	962
Duncombe city (pt.)	496	412
Webster township	347	421
Lehigh city (pt.)	158	194
Yell township	167	203
Lehigh city (pt.)	29	51
Winnebago County[92]	13 010	12 990
Buffalo township	1 550	1 537
Buffalo Center city[92]	1 233	1 118
Center township	2 686	2 553
Lake Mills city	2 281	2 124
Eden township	224	298
Forest township	4 820	4 498
Forest City city (pt.)	3 920	3 726
Leland city	274	223
Grant township	276	429
King township	964	939
Thompson city	668	600
Lincoln township	522	618
Rake city	283	324
Linden township	264	362
Logan township	304	341
Scarville city (pt.)	51	44
Mount Valley township	618	559
Newton township	341	407
Norway township	441	449
Scarville city (pt.)	31	37
Winneshiek County[93]	21 876	21 758
Bloomfield township	652	709
Castalia city	188	210
Bluffton township	445	451
Burr Oak township	532	538
Calmar township	1 947	1 925
Calmar city (pt.)[93]	1 053	1 008
Spillville city	415	361
Canoe township	479	523
Decorah township	9 454	8 690
Decorah city[93]	7 991	7 237
Frankville township	588	629
Fremont township	319	304
Glenwood township	523	465
Hesper township	609	612
Highland township	350	372
Jackson township	441	569
Jackson Junction city	94	106
Lincoln township	708	699
Ridgeway city[93]	308	218
Madison township	462	537
Military township	1 415	1 457
Ossian city	829	847
Orleans township	379	443
Pleasant township	421	462
Springfield township	506	605
Sumner township	447	496
Washington township	1 199	1 272
Calmar city (pt.)[93]	–	–
Fort Atkinson city	374	339
Woodbury County[94]	100 884	103 052
Arlington township	1 667	1 639
Moville city[94]	1 273	1 198
Banner township	838	818
Lawton city	447	406
Concord township[94]	1 056	828
Floyd township	927	722
Bronson city	289	193
Grange township	297	302
Grant township	279	372
Kedron township	898	1 180
Anthon city (pt.)	558	711
Correctionville city (pt.)	67	73
Lakeport township	205	210
Liberty township	1 093	1 022
Salix city[94]	429	387
Sergeant Bluff city (pt.)	13	14
Liston township	792	895
Danbury city	492	527
Little Sioux township	589	661
Smithland city	282	293
Miller township	368	251
Anthon city (pt.)	129	–
Morgan township	278	330
Moville township	379	336
Oto township	481	541
Oto city	172	203
Rock 1 and Rock 2 township[94]	860	754
Correctionville city (pt.)[94]	279	238
Cushing city	270	204
Rutland township	752	858
Pierson city	408	421
Sioux City city[94]	82 003	85 925
Sloan township	1 165	1 086

County Subdivisions

	1980	1970
Woodbury County—Con.		
Sloan township—Con.		
Sloan city[94]	978	799
Union township	882	886
Correctionville city (pt.)	589	559
West Fork township	431	427
Willow township	553	600
Hornick city	239	250
Wolf Creek township	319	353
Woodbury township[94]	3 772	2 056
Sergeant Bluff city (pt.)[94]	2 403	'1 150
Worth County	9 075	'8 984
Barton township	285	334
Bristol township	526	559
Joice city	223	201
Brookfield township	347	379
Danville township	411	488
Hanlontown city (pt.)	102	106
Deer Creek township	262	272
Fertile township	891	897
Fertile city	372	394
Hanlontown city (pt.)	111	76
Grove township	2 448	2 211
Northwood city	2 193	1 950
Hartland township	311	318
Kensett township	658	'685
Kensett city	360	'361
Lincoln township	1 961	1 760
Manly city	1 496	1 294
Silver Lake township	324	387
Union township	651	694
Grafton city	255	254
Wright County[95]	16 319	17 294
Belmond township	531	519
Belmond city (pt.)	224	166
Blaine township	1 011	1 072
Dows city (pt.)	635	667
Galt city	60	50
Boone township	235	338
Dayton township	591	705
Clarion city (pt.)	315	329
Eagle Grove township	4 632	4 862
Eagle Grove city	4 324	4 489
Goldfield city (pt.)[95]	58	30
Grant township	1 726	1 724
Clarion city (pt.)	1 383	1 364
Iowa township	531	564
Rowan city	259	231
Lake township	465	501
Clarion city (pt.)	224	211
Liberty township	978	1 031
Goldfield city (pt.)	731	692
Lincoln township	1 377	1 429
Clarion city (pt.)	1 138	1 068
Norway township	241	327
Pleasant township	2 720	2 655
Belmond city (pt.)	2 281	2 192
Troy township	344	382
Vernon township	219	322
Wall Lake township	225	301
Woolstock township	493	562
Woolstock city	235	222

KANSAS

Kansas takes its name from the Kansa (Kaw) Indians, who once inhabited a large area about the Kansas or Kaw River, the meaning of the Indian word being "swift river."

This area was first visited by white men in 1541, when a Spanish expedition under the leadership of Coronado traversed it from southwest to northeast. Thereafter with the exception of explorations between 1719 and 1725, made by the French in an ineffectual attempt to gain possession of the territory, the Kansas region remained practically unknown until about the beginning of the nineteenth century. In 1804 Lewis and Clarke were sent out by the United States Government to explore the newly acquired territory of Louisiana and traversed that part of Kansas bordering on the Missouri River, but it remained for Pike in 1806 and Long in 1819 to give the first extensive information relating to the Kansas country.

Fort Leavenworth was established and United States troops stationed there in 1827. The Santa Fe Trail, the great overland route of commerce, led across Kansas, but no settlements had yet been made in 1834, when the territory was included in the immense Indian reservation known as the "Indian country." Twenty years later, when the territory of Kansas was organized, the few white civilian residents were either living at the military stations or engaged in missionary or educational work among the Indians. Immediately after the formation of the territory, however, settlers came in large numbers and within a few months Leavenworth, Atchison, Topeka, Lawrence, and other towns were founded.

With the exception of a small area in the southwestern part of the state, the territory now constituting Kansas was originally a portion of the vast Louisiana region claimed by the French on account of the discoveries of La Salle and others. This region was ceded by France to Spain in 1762, retroceded to France in 1800, and purchased by the United States in 1803. It belonged successively to the district of Louisiana (1804-5), the territory of Louisiana (1805-1812), the territory of Missouri (1812-1834), and the unorganized "Indian country" (1834-1854).

That part of Kansas lying south of the Arkansas River and west of the one hundredth meridian was a portion of the original Spanish possessions in America. In 1821 it became a part of Mexico at the time that country achieved its independence; and from 1836, when Texas became independent, until 1845, it was included in that republic. Texas was annexed to the United States in 1845. In 1850 its boundaries were fixed as they now stand, and from that time until the formation of the territory of Kansas the area south of the Arkansas River and west of the one hundredth meridian was without organized government.

In 1854 the territory of Kansas was organized. That part lying north of the thirty-eighth parallel then extended westward to the Rocky Mountains, while south of that parallel the territory was bounded on the west by the one hundred and third meridian, which is 1° west of the present western boundary.

The question whether Kansas should be admitted to the Union as a free or as a slave state led in 1856 to civil war in the territory. Four constitutions for the proposed state were framed during the period from 1855 to 1859, and in the latter year a constitution prohibiting slavery was adopted by a convention sitting at Wyandotte, and approved by popular vote, under which Kansas, with boundaries as at present, was admitted to the Union in January, 1861,

COUNTY LOCATION INDEX

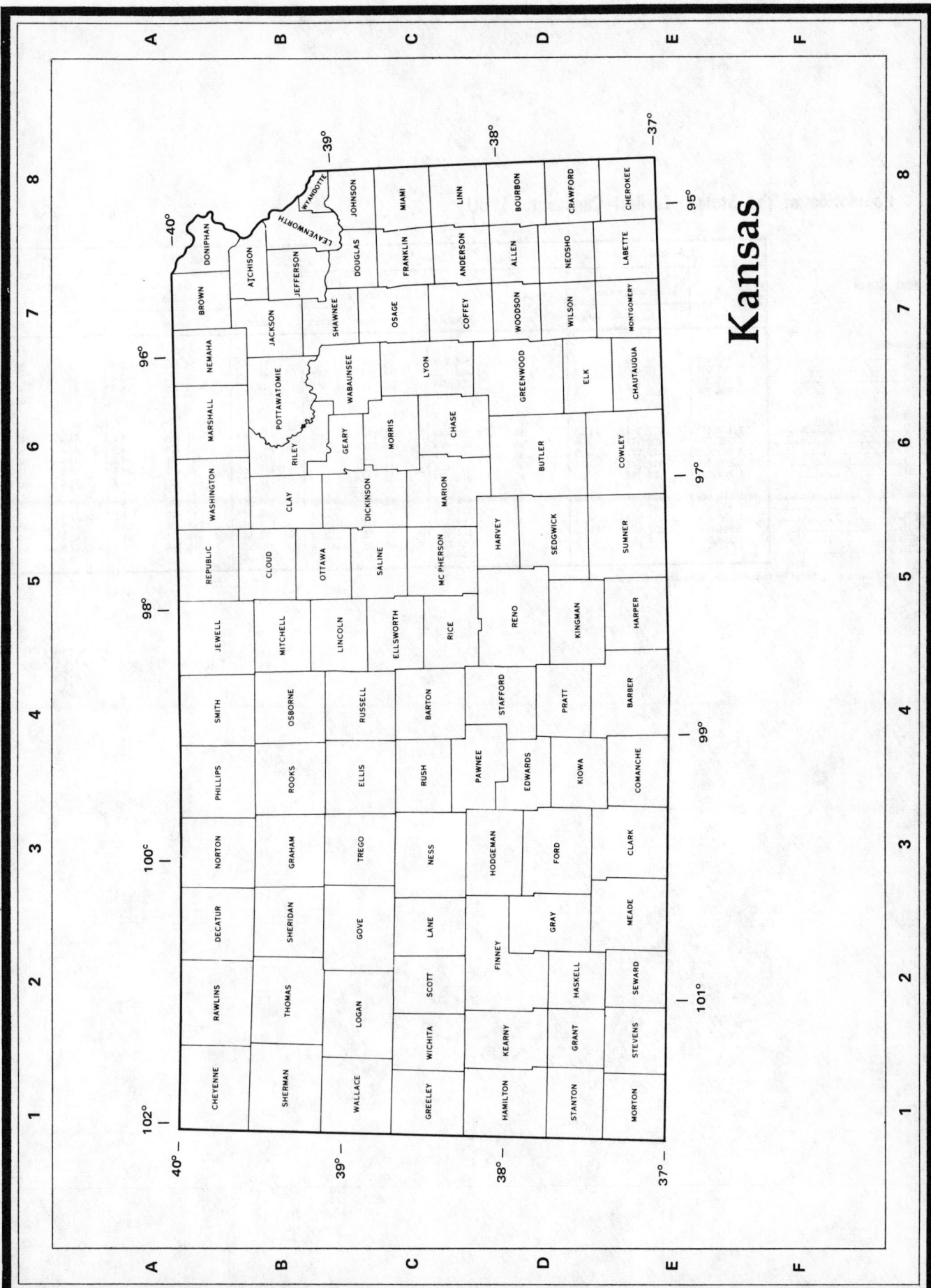

Kansas

Table 1. **Population of the State: Earliest Census to 1980**

Urban and Rural

	The State			Urban				Rural				Percent of total population	
	Total population	Change from preceding census		Places of 2,500 or more	Population	Change from preceding census		Population	Change from preceding census			Urban	Rural
		Number	Percent			Number	Percent		Number	Percent			
Current urban definition:													
1980 (Apr. 1) _____	2 363 679	114 608	5.1	96	1 575 899	91 029	6.1	787 780	26 072	3.4		66.7	33.3
1970 (Apr. 1) _____	'2 249 071	70 460	3.2	94	1 484 870	156 129	11.8	761 708	−88 162	−10.4		66.1	33.9
1960 (Apr. 1) _____	2 178 611	273 312	14.3	87	1 328 741	335 521	33.8	849 870	−62 209	−6.8		61.0	33.9
1950 (Apr. 1) _____	1 905 299	104 271	5.8	69	993 220	...	...	912 079	...	...		52.1	47.9
Previous urban definition:													
1960 (Apr. 1) _____	2 178 611	273 312	14.3	86	1 228 646	325 178	36.0	949 965	−51 866	−5.2		56.4	43.6
1950 (Apr. 1) _____	1 905 299	104 271	5.8	68	903 468	149 527	19.8	1 001 831	−45 256	−4.3		47.4	52.6
1940 (Apr. 1) _____	1 801 028	−79 971	−4.3	64	753 941	24 107	3.3	1 047 087	−104 078	−9.0		41.9	58.1
1930 (Apr. 1) _____	1 880 999	111 742	6.3	62	729 834	113 349	18.4	1 151 165	−1 607	−0.1		38.8	61.2
1920 (Jan. 1) _____	1 769 257	78 308	4.6	62	616 485	124 173	25.2	1 152 772	−45 865	−3.8		34.8	65.2
1910 (Apr. 15) _____	1 690 949	220 454	15.0	53	492 312	162 616	49.3	1 198 637	57 838	5.1		29.1	70.9
1900 (June 1) _____	1 470 495	42 387	3.0	40	329 696	60 157	22.3	1 140 799	−17 770	−1.5		22.4	77.6
1890 (June 1) _____	1 428 108	432 012	43.4	34	269 539	164 583	156.8	1 158 569	267 429	30.0		18.9	81.1
1880 (June 1) _____	996 096	631 697	173.4	17	104 956	53 086	102.3	891 140	578 611	185.1		10.5	89.5
1870 (June 1) _____	364 399	257 193	239.9	8	51 870	41 825	416.4	312 529	215 368	221.7		14.2	85.8
1860 (June 1) _____	107 206	...	...	2	10 045	...	...	97 161	...	...		9.4	90.6

NOTE: 1860 population is that of the part of Kansas Territory lying within present limits of State.

ALLEN

1860	3,082
1870	7,022
1880	11,303
1890	13,509
1900	19,507
1910	27,640
1920	23,509
1930	21,391
1940	19,879
1950	18,187
1960	16,369
1970	15,043
1980	15,654

ANDERSON

1860	2,400
1870	5,220
1880	9,057
1890	14,203
1900	13,938
1910	13,829
1920	12,986
1930	13,355
1940	11,658
1950	10,267
1960	9,035
1970	8,501
1980	8,749

ARAPAHOE

1880	3

ATCHISON

1860	7,729
1870	15,507
1880	26,668
1890	26,758
1900	28,606
1910	28,107
1920	23,411
1930	23,945
1940	22,222
1950	21,496
1960	20,898
1970	19,165
1980	18,397

BARBER

1880	2,661
1890	7,973
1900	6,594
1910	9,916
1920	9,739
1930	10,178
1940	9,073
1950	8,521
1960	8,713
1970	7,016
1980	6,548

BARTON

1870	2
1880	10,318
1890	13,172
1900	13,784
1910	17,876
1920	18,422
1930	19,776
1940	25,010
1950	29,909
1960	32,368
1970	30,663
1980	31,343

BOURBON

1860	6,101
1870	15,076
1880	19,591
1890	28,575
1900	24,712
1910	24,007
1920	23,198
1930	22,386
1940	20,944
1950	19,153
1960	16,090
1970	15,215
1980	15,969

BRECKENRIDGE

1860	3,197

BROWN

1860	2,607
1870	6,823
1880	12,817
1890	20,319
1900	22,369
1910	21,314
1920	20,949
1930	20,553
1940	17,395
1950	14,651
1960	13,229
1970	11,685
1980	11,955

BUFFALO

1880	191

BUTLER

1860	437
1870	3,035
1880	18,586
1890	24,055
1900	23,363
1910	23,059
1920	43,843
1930	35,904
1940	32,013
1950	31,001
1960	38,395
1970	38,658
1980	44,782

CHASE

1860	808
1870	1,975
1880	6,081
1890	8,233
1900	8,246
1910	7,527
1920	7,144
1930	6,952
1940	6,345
1950	4,831
1960	3,921
1970	3,408
1980	3,309

CHAUTAUQUA

1880	11,072
1890	12,297
1900	11,804
1910	11,429
1920	11,598
1930	10,352
1940	9,233
1950	7,376
1960	5,956
1970	4,642
1980	5,016

CHEROKEE

1860	1,501
1870	11,038
1880	21,905
1890	27,770
1900	42,694
1910	38,162
1920	33,609
1930	31,457
1940	29,817
1950	25,144
1960	22,279
1970	21,549
1980	22,304

CHEYENNE

1880	37
1890	4,401
1900	2,640
1910	4,248
1920	5,587
1930	6,948
1940	6,221
1950	5,668
1960	4,708
1970	4,256
1980	3,678

CLARK

1880	163
1890	2,357
1900	1,701
1910	4,093
1920	4,989
1930	4,796
1940	4,081
1950	3,946
1960	3,396
1970	2,896
1980	2,599

CLAY

1860	163
1870	2,942
1880	12,320
1890	16,146
1900	15,833
1910	15,251
1920	14,365
1930	14,556
1940	13,281
1950	11,697
1960	10,675
1970	9,890
1980	9,802

CLOUD

1870	2,323
1880	15,343
1890	19,295
1900	18,071
1910	18,388
1920	17,714
1930	18,006
1940	17,247
1950	16,104
1960	14,407
1970	13,466
1980	12,494

COFFEY

1860	2,942
1870	6,201
1880	11,438
1890	15,856
1900	16,643
1910	15,205
1920	14,254
1930	13,652
1940	12,278
1950	10,408
1960	8,403
1970	7,397
1980	9,370

COMANCHE

1880	372
1890	2,549
1900	1,619
1910	3,281
1920	5,302
1930	5,238
1940	4,412
1950	3,888
1960	3,271
1970	2,702
1980	2,554

COWLEY

1860	158
1870	1,175
1880	21,538
1890	34,478
1900	30,156
1910	31,790
1920	35,155
1930	40,903
1940	38,139
1950	36,905
1960	37,861
1970	35,012
1980	36,824

CRAWFORD

1870	8,160
1880	16,851
1890	30,286
1900	38,809
1910	51,178
1920	61,800
1930	49,329
1940	44,191
1950	40,231
1960	37,032
1970	37,850
1980	37,916

DECATUR

1880	4,180
1890	8,414
1900	9,234
1910	8,976
1920	8,121
1930	8,866
1940	7,434
1950	6,185
1960	5,778
1970	4,988
1980	4,509

DICKINSON

1860	378
1870	3,043
1880	15,251
1890	22,273
1900	21,816
1910	24,361
1920	25,777
1930	25,870
1940	22,929
1950	21,190
1960	21,572
1970	19,993
1980	20,175

DONIPHAN

1860	8,083
1870	13,969
1880	14,257
1890	13,535
1900	15,079
1910	14,422
1920	13,438
1930	14,063
1940	12,936
1950	10,499
1960	9,574
1970	9,107
1980	9,268

DOUGLAS

1860	8,637
1870	20,592
1880	21,700
1890	23,961
1900	25,096
1910	24,724
1920	23,998
1930	25,143
1940	25,171
1950	34,086
1960	43,720
1970	57,932
1980	67,640

EDWARDS

1880	2,409
1890	3,600
1900	3,682
1910	7,033
1920	7,057
1930	7,295
1940	6,377
1950	5,936
1960	5,118
1970	4,581
1980	4,271

ELK

1880	10,623
1890	12,216
1900	11,443
1910	10,128
1920	9,034
1930	9,210
1940	8,180
1950	6,679
1960	5,048
1970	3,858
1980	3,918

ELLIS

1870	1,336
1880	6,179
1890	7,942
1900	8,626
1910	12,170
1920	14,138
1930	15,907
1940	17,508
1950	19,043
1960	21,270
1970	24,730
1980	26,098

ELLSWORTH

1870	1,185
1880	8,494
1890	9,272
1900	9,626
1910	10,444
1920	10,379
1930	10,132
1940	9,855
1950	8,465
1960	7,677
1970	6,146
1980	6,640

FINNEY

1890	3,350
1900	3,469
1910	6,908
1920	7,674
1930	11,014
1940	10,092
1950	15,092
1960	16,093
1970	19,029
1980	23,825

FOOTE

1880	411

FORD

1870	427
1880	3,122
1890	5,308
1900	5,497
1910	11,393
1920	14,273
1930	20,647
1940	17,251
1950	19,670
1960	20,938
1970	22,587
1980	24,315

FRANKLIN

1860	3,030
1870	10,385
1880	16,797
1890	20,279
1900	21,354
1910	20,884
1920	21,946
1930	22,024
1940	20,889
1950	19,928
1960	19,548
1970	20,007
1980	22,062

GARFIELD

1890	881

GEARY

1860	1,163
1870	5,526
1880	6,994
1890	10,423
1900	10,744
1910	12,681
1920	13,452
1930	14,366
1940	15,222
1950	21,671
1960	28,779
1970	28,111
1980	29,852

GOVE

1880	1,196
1890	2,994
1900	2,441
1910	6,044
1920	4,748
1930	5,643
1940	4,793
1950	4,447
1960	4,107
1970	3,940
1980	3,726

GRAHAM

1880	4,258
1890	5,029
1900	5,173
1910	8,700
1920	7,624
1930	7,772
1940	6,071
1950	5,020
1960	5,586
1970	4,751
1980	3,995

GRANT

1880	9
1890	1,308
1900	422
1910	1,087
1920	1,087
1930	3,092
1940	1,946
1950	4,638
1960	5,269
1970	5,961

1980	6,977

GRAY

1890	2,415
1900	1,264
1910	3,121
1920	4,711
1930	6,211
1940	4,773
1950	4,894
1960	4,380
1970	4,516
1980	5,138

GREELEY

1880	3
1890	1,264
1900	493
1910	1,335
1920	1,028
1930	1,712
1940	1,638
1950	2,010
1960	2,087
1970	1,819
1980	1,764

GREENWOOD

1860	759
1870	3,484
1880	10,548
1890	16,309
1900	16,196
1910	16,060
1920	14,715
1930	19,235
1940	16,495
1950	13,574
1960	11,253
1970	9,141
1980	8,764

HAMILTON

1880	168
1890	2,027
1900	1,426
1910	3,360
1920	2,586
1930	3,328
1940	2,645
1950	3,696
1960	3,144
1970	2,747
1980	2,514

HARPER

1880	4,133
1890	13,266
1900	10,310
1910	14,748
1920	13,656
1930	12,823
1940	12,068
1950	10,263
1960	9,541
1970	7,871
1980	7,778

HARVEY

1880	11,451
1890	17,601
1900	17,591
1910	19,200
1920	20,744
1930	22,120
1940	21,712
1950	21,698
1960	25,865
1970	27,236
1980	30,531

HASKELL

1890	1,077
1900	457
1910	993
1920	1,455
1930	2,805
1940	2,088
1950	2,606
1960	2,900
1970	3,672
1980	3,814

HODGEMAN

1880	1,704
1890	2,395
1900	2,032
1910	2,930
1920	3,734
1930	4,157
1940	3,535
1950	3,310
1960	3,115
1970	2,662
1980	2,269

HOWARD

1860	19
1870	2,794

JACKSON

1860	1,936
1870	6,053
1880	10,718
1890	14,626
1900	17,117
1910	16,861
1920	15,495
1930	14,776
1940	13,382
1950	11,098
1960	10,309
1970	10,342
1980	11,644

JEFFERSON

1860	4,459
1870	12,526
1880	15,563
1890	16,620
1900	17,533
1910	15,826
1920	14,750
1930	14,129
1940	12,718
1950	11,084
1960	11,252
1970	11,945

1980	15,207

JEWELL

1870	207
1880	17,475
1890	19,349
1900	19,420
1910	18,148
1920	16,240
1930	14,462
1940	11,970
1950	9,698
1960	7,217
1970	6,099
1980	5,241

JOHNSON

1860	4,264
1870	13,684
1880	16,853
1890	17,385
1900	18,104
1910	18,288
1920	18,314
1930	27,179
1940	33,327
1950	62,783
1960	143,792
1970	220,073
1980	270,269

KEARNY

1880	159
1890	1,571
1900	1,107
1910	3,206
1920	2,617
1930	3,196
1940	2,525
1950	3,492
1960	3,108
1970	3,047
1980	3,435

KINGMAN

1880	3,713
1890	11,823
1900	10,663
1910	13,386
1920	12,119
1930	11,674
1940	12,001
1950	10,324
1960	9,958
1970	8,886
1980	8,960

KIOWA

1890	2,873
1900	2,365
1910	6,174
1920	6,164
1930	6,035
1940	5,122
1950	4,743
1960	4,626
1970	4,088
1980	4,046

LABETTE

1870	9,973
1880	22,735
1890	27,586
1900	27,387
1910	31,423
1920	34,047
1930	31,346
1940	30,352
1950	29,385
1960	26,805
1970	25,775
1980	25,682

LANE

1880	601
1890	2,060
1900	1,563
1910	2,603
1920	2,848
1930	3,372
1940	2,821
1950	2,808
1960	3,060
1970	2,707
1980	2,472

LEAVENWORTH

1860	12,606
1870	32,444
1880	32,355
1890	38,485
1900	40,940
1910	41,207
1920	38,402
1930	42,673
1940	41,122
1950	42,361
1960	48,524
1970	53,340
1980	54,809

LINCOLN

1870	516
1880	8,582
1890	9,709
1900	9,886
1910	10,142
1920	9,894
1930	9,707
1940	8,338
1950	6,643
1960	5,556
1970	4,582
1980	4,145

LINN

1860	6,336
1870	12,174
1880	15,298
1890	17,215
1900	16,689
1910	14,735
1920	13,815
1930	13,534
1940	11,969
1950	10,053
1960	8,274
1970	7,770
1980	8,234

LOGAN

1890	3,384
1900	1,962
1910	4,240
1920	3,223
1930	4,145
1940	3,688
1950	4,206
1960	4,036
1970	3,814
1980	3,478

LYON

1870	8,014
1880	17,236
1890	23,196
1900	25,074
1910	24,927
1920	26,154
1930	29,240
1940	26,424
1950	26,576
1960	26,928
1970	32,071
1980	35,108

McPHERSON

1870	738
1880	17,143
1890	21,614
1900	21,421
1910	21,521
1920	21,845
1930	23,588
1940	24,152
1950	23,670
1960	24,285
1970	24,778
1980	26,855

MADISON

1860	636

MARION

1860	74
1870	768
1880	12,453
1890	20,539
1900	20,676
1910	22,415
1920	22,923
1930	20,739
1940	18,951
1950	16,307
1960	15,143
1970	13,935
1980	13,522

MARSHALL

1860	2,280
1870	6,901
1880	16,136
1890	23,912
1900	24,355
1910	23,880
1920	22,730
1930	23,056
1940	20,986
1950	17,926
1960	15,598

1970	13,139
1980	12,787

MEADE

1880	296
1890	2,542
1900	1,581
1910	5,055
1920	5,542
1930	6,858
1940	5,522
1950	5,710
1960	5,505
1970	4,912
1980	4,788

MIAMI

1860	4,980
1870	11,725
1880	17,802
1890	19,614
1900	21,641
1910	20,030
1920	19,809
1930	21,243
1940	19,489
1950	19,698
1960	19,884
1970	19,254
1980	21,618

MITCHELL

1870	485
1880	14,911
1890	15,037
1900	14,647
1910	14,089
1920	13,886
1930	12,774
1940	11,339
1950	10,320
1960	8,866
1970	8,010
1980	8,117

MONTGOMERY

1870	7,564
1880	18,213
1890	23,104
1900	29,039
1910	49,474
1920	49,645
1930	51,411
1940	49,729
1950	46,487
1960	45,007
1970	39,949
1980	42,281

MORRIS

1860	770
1870	2,225
1880	9,265
1890	11,381
1900	11,967
1910	12,397
1920	12,005
1930	11,859
1940	10,363
1950	8,485
1960	7,392

1970	6,432
1980	6,419

MORTON

1880	9
1890	724
1900	304
1910	1,333
1920	3,177
1930	4,092
1940	2,186
1950	2,610
1960	3,354
1970	3,576
1980	3,454

NEMAHA

1860	2,436
1870	7,339
1880	12,462
1890	19,249
1900	20,376
1910	19,072
1920	18,487
1930	18,342
1940	16,761
1950	14,341
1960	12,897
1970	11,825
1980	11,211

NEOSHO

1860	88
1870	10,206
1880	15,121
1890	18,561
1900	19,254
1910	23,754
1920	24,000
1930	22,665
1940	22,210
1950	20,348
1960	19,445
1970	18,812
1980	18,967

NESS

1870	2
1880	3,722
1890	4,944
1900	4,535
1910	5,883
1920	7,490
1930	8,358
1940	6,864
1950	6,322
1960	5,470
1970	4,791
1980	4,498

NORTON

1880	6,998
1890	10,617
1900	11,325
1910	11,614
1920	11,423
1930	11,701
1940	9,831
1950	8,808
1960	8,035
1970	7,279

1980	6,689

OSAGE

1860	1,113
1870	7,648
1880	19,642
1890	25,062
1900	23,659
1910	19,905
1920	18,621
1930	17,538
1940	15,118
1950	12,811
1960	12,886
1970	13,352
1980	15,319

OSBORNE

1870	83
1880	12,517
1890	12,083
1900	11,844
1910	12,827
1920	12,441
1930	11,568
1940	9,835
1950	8,558
1960	7,506
1970	6,416
1980	5,959

OTOE

1860	238

OTTAWA

1870	2,127
1880	10,307
1890	12,581
1900	11,182
1910	11,811
1920	10,714
1930	9,819
1940	9,224
1950	7,265
1960	6,779
1970	6,183
1980	5,971

PAWNEE

1870	179
1880	5,396
1890	5,204
1900	5,084
1910	8,859
1920	9,323
1930	10,510
1940	10,300
1950	11,041
1960	10,254
1970	8,484
1980	8,065

PHILLIPS

1880	12,014
1890	13,661
1900	14,442
1910	14,150
1920	12,505
1930	12,159
1940	10,435

1950	9,273
1960	8,709
1970	7,888
1980	7,406

POTTAWATOMIE

1860	1,529
1870	7,848
1880	16,350
1890	17,722
1900	18,470
1910	17,522
1920	16,154
1930	15,862
1940	14,015
1950	12,344
1960	11,957
1970	11,755
1980	14,782

PRATT

1880	1,890
1890	8,118
1900	7,085
1910	11,156
1920	12,909
1930	13,312
1940	12,348
1950	12,156
1960	12,122
1970	10,056
1980	10,275

RAWLINS

1880	1,623
1890	6,756
1900	5,241
1910	6,380
1920	6,799
1930	7,362
1940	6,618
1950	5,728
1960	5,279
1970	5,393
1980	4,105

RENO

1880	12,826
1890	27,079
1900	29,027
1910	37,853
1920	44,423
1930	47,785
1940	52,165
1950	54,058
1960	59,055
1970	60,765
1980	64,983

REPUBLIC

1870	1,281
1880	14,913
1890	19,002
1900	18,248
1910	17,477
1920	15,855
1930	14,745
1940	13,124
1950	11,478
1960	9,768
1970	8,498
1980	7,569

RICE

1870	5
1880	9,292
1890	14,451
1900	14,745
1910	15,106
1920	14,832
1930	13,800
1940	17,213
1950	15,635
1960	13,909
1970	12,320
1980	11,900

RILEY

1860	1,224
1870	5,105
1880	10,430
1890	13,183
1900	13,828
1910	15,783
1920	20,650
1930	19,882
1940	20,617
1950	33,405
1960	41,914
1970	56,788
1980	63,505

ROOKS

1880	8,112
1890	8,018
1900	7,960
1910	11,282
1920	9,966
1930	9,534
1940	8,497
1950	9,043
1960	9,734
1970	7,628
1980	7,006

RUSH

1880	5,490
1890	5,204
1900	6,134
1910	7,826
1920	8,360
1930	9,093
1940	8,245
1950	7,231
1960	6,160
1970	5,117
1980	4,516

RUSSELL

1870	156
1880	7,351
1890	7,333
1900	8,489
1910	10,800
1920	10,748
1930	11,045
1940	13,464
1950	13,406
1960	11,348
1970	9,428
1980	8,868

SALINE

1870	4,246
1880	13,808
1890	17,442
1900	17,076
1910	20,338
1920	25,103
1930	29,337
1940	29,535
1950	33,409
1960	54,715
1970	46,592
1980	48,905

SCOTT

1880	43
1890	1,262
1900	1,098
1910	3,047
1920	3,121
1930	3,976
1940	3,773
1950	4,921
1960	5,228
1970	5,606
1980	5,782

SEDGWICK

1870	1,095
1880	18,753
1890	43,626
1900	44,037
1910	73,095
1920	92,234
1930	136,330
1940	143,311
1950	222,290
1960	343,231
1970	350,694
1980	366,531

SEQUOYAH

1880	568

SEWARD

1880	5
1890	1,503
1900	822
1910	4,091
1920	6,220
1930	8,075
1940	6,540
1950	9,972
1960	15,930
1970	15,744
1980	17,071

SHAWNEE

1860	3,513
1870	13,121
1880	29,093
1890	49,172
1900	53,727
1910	61,874
1920	69,159
1930	85,200
1940	91,247
1950	105,418
1960	141,286
1970	155,322
1980	154,916

SHERIDAN

1880	1,567
1890	3,733
1900	3,819
1910	5,651
1920	5,484
1930	6,038
1940	5,312
1950	5,607
1960	4,267
1970	3,859
1980	3,544

SHERMAN

1880	13
1890	5,261
1900	3,341
1910	4,549
1920	5,592
1930	7,400
1940	6,421
1950	7,373
1960	6,682
1970	7,792
1980	7,759

SMITH

1870	66
1880	13,883
1890	15,613
1900	16,384
1910	15,365
1920	14,985
1930	13,545
1940	10,582
1950	8,846
1960	7,776
1970	6,757
1980	5,947

STAFFORD

1880	4,755
1890	8,520
1900	9,829
1910	12,510
1920	11,559
1930	10,460
1940	10,487
1950	8,816
1960	7,451
1970	5,943
1980	5,694

STANTON

1880	5
1890	1,031
1900	327
1910	1,034
1920	908
1930	2,152
1940	1,443
1950	2,263
1960	2,108
1970	2,287
1980	2,339

STEVENS

1880	12
1890	1,418
1900	620
1910	2,453
1920	3,943
1930	4,655
1940	3,193
1950	4,516
1960	4,400
1970	4,198
1980	4,736

SUMNER

1870	22
1880	20,812
1890	30,271
1900	25,631
1910	30,654
1920	29,213
1930	28,960
1940	26,163
1950	23,646
1960	25,316
1970	23,553
1980	24,928

THOMAS

1880	161
1890	5,538
1900	4,112
1910	5,455
1920	5,517
1930	7,334
1940	6,425
1950	7,572
1960	7,358
1970	7,501
1980	8,451

TREGO

1870	166
1880	2,535
1890	2,535
1900	2,722
1910	5,398
1920	5,880
1930	6,470
1940	5,822
1950	5,868
1960	5,473
1970	4,436
1980	4,165

WABAUNSEE

1860	1,023
1870	3,362
1880	8,756
1890	11,720
1900	12,813
1910	12,712
1920	11,424
1930	10,830
1940	9,219
1950	7,212
1960	6,648
1970	6,397
1980	6,867

WALLACE

1870	538
1880	686
1890	2,468
1900	1,178
1910	2,759
1920	2,424
1930	2,882
1940	2,216
1950	2,508
1960	2,069
1970	2,215
1980	2,045

WASHINGTON

1860	383
1870	4,081
1880	14,910
1890	22,894
1900	21,963
1910	20,229
1920	17,984
1930	17,112
1940	15,921
1950	12,977
1960	10,739
1970	9,249
1980	8,543

WICHITA

1880	14
1890	1,827
1900	1,197
1910	2,006
1920	1,856
1930	2,579
1940	2,185
1950	2,640
1960	2,765
1970	3,274
1980	3,041

WILSON

1860	27
1870	6,694
1880	13,775
1890	15,286
1900	15,621
1910	19,810
1920	21,157
1930	18,646
1940	17,723
1950	14,815
1960	13,077
1970	11,317
1980	12,128

WOODSON

1860	1,488
1870	3,827
1880	6,535
1890	9,021
1900	10,022
1910	9,450
1920	8,984
1930	8,526
1940	8,014
1950	6,711
1960	5,423
1970	4,789
1980	4,600

WYANDOTTE

1860	2,609
1870	10,015
1880	19,143
1890	54,407
1900	73,277
1910	100,068
1920	122,218
1930	141,211
1940	145,071
1950	165,318
1960	185,495
1970	186,845
1980	172,335

NOTES

ARAPAHOE

Taken to form part of Finney in 1884.

BRECKENRIDGE

Taken to form part of Lyon prior to 1870.

BUFFALO

Part taken to form part of Finney and part annexed to Hodgeman in 1884.

CHEROKEE

Name changed from McGhee in 1860.

CLOUD

Name changed from Shirley in 1867.

COWLEY

Name changed from Hunter prior to 1870.

FINNEY

Name changed from Sequoyah in 1883.

FOOTE

Part taken to form part of Finney and parts annexed to Ford and Hodgeman in 1884.

GARFIELD

Organized from parts of Finney and Hodgeman in 1887; annexed to Finney in 1893.

GEARY

Name changed from Davis in 1889.

HOWARD

Name changed from Godfrey prior to 1870; taken to form Chautauqua and Elk in 1875.

JACKSON

Name changed from Calhoun in 1859.

LOGAN

Name changed from Saint John in 1887.

LYON

Name changed from Breckenridge in 1862.

MADISON

Part annexed to Greenwood and part taken to form part of Lyon prior to 1870.

MIAMI

Name changed from Lykins in 1861.

MORRIS

Name changed from Wise in 1859.

MORTON

Name changed from Kansas in 1886.

NEOSHO

Name changed from Dorn in 1861.

NORTON

Name changed from Billings in 1873; changed back to Norton in 1874.

OSAGE

Name changed from Weller in 1859.

OTOE

Annexed to Chase prior to 1870.

SEQUOYAH

Taken to form part of Finney in 1884.

SEWARD

Name changed from Godfrey in 1861; changed back to Seward in 1886.

WABAUNSEE

Name changed from Richardson in 1859.

ARKANSAS CITY

1880	1,012
1890	8,347
1900	6,140
1910	7,508
1920	11,253
1930	13,946
1940	12,752
1950	12,903
1960	14,262
1970	13,216
1980	13,201

ATCHISON

1860	2,616
1870	7,054
1880	15,105
1890	13,963
1900	15,722
1910	16,429
1920	12,630
1930	13,024
1940	12,648
1950	12,792
1960	12,529
1970	12,565
1980	11,407

CHANUTE

1880	887
1890	2,826
1900	4,208
1910	9,272
1920	10,286
1930	10,277
1940	10,142
1950	10,109
1960	10,849
1970	10,341
1980	10,506

COFFEYVILLE

1880	753
1890	2,282
1900	4,953
1910	12,687
1920	13,452
1930	16,198
1940	17,335
1950	17,113
1960	17,382
1970	15,116
1980	15,187

DODGE CITY

1880	996
1890	1,763
1900	1,942
1910	3,214
1920	5,061
1930	10,059
1940	8,487
1950	11,262
1960	13,520
1970	14,127
1980	18,001

EL DORADO

1880	1,411
1890	3,339
1900	3,466
1910	3,129
1920	10,995
1930	10,311
1940	10,045
1950	11,037
1960	12,523
1970	12,308
1980	10,510

EMPORIA

1870	2,168
1880	4,631
1890	7,551
1900	8,223
1910	9,058
1920	11,273
1930	14,067
1940	13,188
1950	15,669
1960	18,190
1970	23,327
1980	25,287

GARDEN CITY

1890	1,490
1900	1,590
1910	3,171
1920	3,848
1930	6,121
1940	6,285
1950	10,905
1960	11,811
1970	14,790
1980	18,256

GREAT BEND

1880	1,071
1890	2,450
1900	2,470
1910	4,622
1920	4,460
1930	5,548
1940	9,044
1950	12,665
1960	16,670
1970	16,133
1980	16,608

HAYS

1890	1,242
1900	1,136
1910	1,961
1920	3,165
1930	4,618
1940	6,385
1950	8,625
1960	11,947
1970	15,396
1980	16,301

HUTCHINSON

1880	1,540
1890	8,682
1900	9,379
1910	16,364
1920	23,298
1930	27,085
1940	30,013
1950	33,575
1960	37,574
1970	36,885
1980	40,284

INDEPENDENCE

1870	435
1880	2,915
1890	3,127
1900	4,851
1910	10,480
1920	11,920
1930	12,782
1940	11,565
1950	11,335
1960	11,222
1970	10,347
1980	10,598

JUNCTION CITY

1880	2,684
1890	4,502
1900	4,695
1910	5,598
1920	7,533
1930	7,407
1940	8,507
1950	13,462
1960	18,700
1970	19,018
1980	19,305

KANSAS CITY

1880	3,200
1890	38,316
1900	51,418
1910	82,331
1920	101,177
1930	121,857
1940	121,458
1950	129,553
1960	121,901
1970	168,213
1980	161,087

LAWRENCE

1860	1,645
1870	8,320
1880	8,510
1890	9,997
1900	10,862
1910	12,374
1920	12,456
1930	13,726
1940	14,390
1950	23,351
1960	32,858
1970	45,698
1980	52,738

LEAVENWORTH

1860	7,429
1870	17,873
1880	16,546
1890	19,768
1900	20,735
1910	19,363
1920	16,912
1930	17,466
1940	19,220
1950	20,579
1960	22,052
1970	25,147
1980	33,656

LEAWOOD

1950	1,167
1960	7,466
1970	10,645
1980	13,360

LENEXA

1960	2,487
1970	5,549
1980	18,639

LIBERAL

1900	426
1910	1,716
1920	3,613
1930	5,294
1940	4,410
1950	7,134
1960	13,813
1970	13,471
1980	14,911

McPHERSON

1880	1,590
1890	3,172
1900	2,996
1910	3,546
1920	4,595
1930	6,147
1940	7,194
1950	8,689
1960	9,996
1970	10,851
1980	11,753

MANHATTAN

1870	1,173
1880	2,105
1890	3,004
1900	3,438
1910	5,722
1920	7,989
1930	10,136
1940	11,659
1950	19,056
1960	22,993
1970	27,575
1980	32,644

MERRIAM

1960	5,084
1970	10,955
1980	10,794

NEWTON

1880	2,601
1890	5,605
1900	6,208
1910	7,862
1920	9,781
1930	11,034
1940	11,048
1950	11,590
1960	14,877
1970	15,439
1980	16,332

OLATHE

1870	1,817
1880	2,285
1890	3,294
1900	3,451
1910	3,272
1920	3,268
1930	3,656
1940	3,979
1950	5,593
1960	10,987
1970	17,917
1980	37,258

OTTAWA

1870	2,941
1880	4,032
1890	6,248
1900	6,934
1910	7,650
1920	9,018
1930	9,563
1940	10,193
1950	10,081
1960	10,673
1970	11,036
1980	11,016

OVERLAND PARK

1960	21,110
1970	77,934
1980	81,784

PARSONS

1880	4,199
1890	6,736
1900	7,682
1910	12,463
1920	16,028
1930	14,903
1940	14,294
1950	14,750
1960	13,929
1970	13,015
1980	12,898

PITTSBURG

1880	624
1890	6,697
1900	10,122
1910	14,755
1920	18,052
1930	18,145
1940	17,571
1950	19,341
1960	18,678
1970	20,171
1980	18,770

PRAIRIE VILLAGE

1960	25,356
1970	28,378
1980	24,657

SALINA

1870	918
1880	3,111
1890	6,149
1900	6,074
1910	9,688
1920	15,085
1930	20,155
1940	21,073
1950	26,176
1960	43,202
1970	37,714
1980	41,843

SHAWNEE

1930	553
1940	597
1950	845
1960	9,072
1970	20,946
1980	29,653

TOPEKA

1860	759
1870	5,790
1880	15,452
1890	31,007
1900	33,608
1910	43,684
1920	50,022
1930	64,120
1940	67,883
1950	78,791
1960	119,484
1970	125,011
1980	115,266

WICHITA

1880	4,911
1890	23,853
1900	24,671
1910	52,450
1920	72,217
1930	111,110
1940	114,966
1950	168,279
1960	254,698
1970	276,554
1980	279,272

WINFIELD

1870	472
1880	2,844
1890	5,184
1900	5,554
1910	6,700
1920	7,993
1930	9,398
1940	9,506
1950	10,264
1960	11,117
1970	11,405
1980	10,736

CORRECTION NOTE

The official 1980 census counts of total population shown in
this report supersede counts issued previously. Corrections
to the figures were made after the counts were provided to
the State for redistricting purposes and released in Advance
Report PHC80-V for this State.

Shown below are corrections to the 1980 census counts of the
total population made after the tabulations for this report
were completed. Any additional corrections made after this
report is printed are available by writing to Data User
Services Division, Customer Services (Corrections), Bureau of
the Census, Washington, D.C. 20233.

The 1980 figures shown in this publication are subject to
change pending the outcome of the various lawsuits dealing
with the census counts.

	1980 population	
	As shown in the tables	Corrected
The State...................	2 363 679	2 364 236
Cherokee County:		
Baxter Springs city.............	4 773	4 730
Garden township.................	2 470	2 462
Spring Valley township..........	825	876
Decatur County:		
Center township.................	67	63
Oberlin city (pt.).............	4	(1)
Liberty township................	75	62
Oberlin city (pt.).............	13	(1)
Oberlin township................	2 471	101
Oberlin city (pt.).............	2 370	(1)
Oberlin city....................	...	2 387
Rice County:		
Harrison township...............	214	232
Lyons city......................	4 152	4 134
Saline County:		
Eureka township.................	607	669
Gypsum township.................	280	218
Liberty township................	178	147
Smoky View township.............	899	857
Smolan township.................	675	717
Walnut township.................	472	503
Sedgwick County....................	366 531	367 088
Minneha township................	4 629	4 623
Wichita city....................	279 272	279 835
Wyandotte County:		
Kansas City city................	161 087	161 148
Shawnee township................	61	(2)

[1]Delete, Oberlin city is independent of any township.
[2]Delete, Shawnee township was annexed by Kansas City
city.

County Subdivisions

County Subdivisions	1980	1970
The State	2 363 679	r2 249 071
Allen County[1]	15 654	15 043
Carlyle township	279	281
Cottage Grove township	305	320
Deer Creek township	142	153
Elm township[1]	1 326	1 180
Gas city[1]	543	438
Elsmore township	535	593
Elsmore city[1]	104	116
Savonburg city	113	109
Geneva township	163	173
Humboldt city[1]	2 230	2 249
Humboldt township[1]	279	326
Iola city[1]	6 938	6 493
Iola township[1]	902	865
Bassett city[1]	31	62
La Harpe city[1]	687	509
Logan township	263	235
Marmaton township	956	924
Moran city[1]	643	550
Osage township	347	416
Mildred city	64	42
Salem township	302	326
Anderson County[2]	8 749	8 501
Garnett city[2]	3 310	3 169
Indian Creek township	175	207
Jackson township[2]	433	395
Lincoln township	239	183
Lone Elm township	269	313
Lone Elm city	55	66
Monroe township[2]	495	536
North Rich township	103	135
Ozark township	661	543
Colony city[2]	474	382
Putnam township	284	269
Reeder township	523	506
Harris city	80	41
Rich township	369	379
Kincaid city	192	189
Union township	189	180
Walker township	591	606
Greeley city[2]	405	368
Washington township	298	228
Welda township	330	334
Westphalia township	480	518
Westphalia city	204	185
Atchison County[3]	18 397	19 165
Atchison city[3]	11 407	12 565
Benton township	1 173	1 213
Effingham city	634	605
Center township	692	650
Grasshopper township	744	700
Muscotah city	248	206
Kapioma township	339	308
Lancaster township	878	937
Huron city	107	106
Lancaster city	274	279
Mount Pleasant township	778	696
Shannon township[3]	1 867	1 564
Walnut township	519	532
Barber County[4]	6 548	7 016
Aetna township	37	43
Deerhead township	30	40
Eagle township	97	102
Elm Mills township	100	106
Elwood township	446	458
Hardtner city[4]	336	300
Hazelton township[4]	251	247
Hazelton city	143	176
Kiowa township	1 532	1 538
Kiowa city[4]	1 409	1 414
Lake City township	94	106
McAdoo township	32	38
Medicine Lodge township	2 810	2 993
Medicine Lodge city[4]	2 384	2 545
Mingona township	89	106
Moore township	45	63
Nippawalla township	51	74
Ridge township	41	61
Sharon township	486	535
Sharon city[4]	283	265
Sun City township	131	174
Sun City city	85	119
Turkey Creek township	45	44
Valley township	231	233
Isabel city	137	147
Barton County[5]	31 343	30 663
Albion township	90	112
Beaver township	185	249
Buffalo township[5]	529	420
Cheyenne township	316	430
Clarence township	163	159
Cleveland township	91	141
Comanche township	362	401

County Subdivisions	1980	1970
Barton County—Con.		
Ellinwood city[5]	2 508	2 416
Eureka township	147	151
Fairview township	156	187
Galatia city	69	78
Grant township	119	142
Great Bend city[5]	16 608	16 133
Great Bend township[5]	1 918	1 523
Hoisington city[5]	3 678	3 710
Independent township	914	1 049
Claflin city	764	887
Lakin township[5]	346	426
Liberty township	316	291
Logan township	195	203
North Homestead township[5]	133	163
Pawnee Rock township	536	582
Pawnee Rock city	409	442
South Bend township	750	533
South Homestead township	480	312
Union township	161	217
Susank city	52	59
Walnut township	556	599
Albert city	236	235
Olmitz city	140	161
Wheatland township	86	114
Bourbon County[6]	15 969	15 215
Drywood township	406	388
Fort Scott city[6]	8 893	8 967
Franklin township	324	321
Freedom township	490	469
Fulton city	194	213
Marion township	1 301	1 179
Bronson city	414	397
Uniontown city[6]	371	286
Marmaton township	751	620
Redfield city	185	138
Mill Creek township	528	412
Osage township	374	357
Pawnee township	333	347
Scott township[6]	2 090	1 615
Timberhill township	302	302
Mapleton city	121	112
Walnut township	177	238
Brown County[7]	11 955	11 685
Hamlin township	419	529
Hamlin city	80	95
Reserve city (pt.)	100	106
Hiawatha city[7]	3 702	3 365
Hiawatha township[7]	859	885
Horton city[7]	2 130	2 177
Irving township	298	318
Mission township[7]	764	837
Willis city	85	82
Morrill township[7]	647	640
Morrill city	336	308
Padonia township	339	322
Reserve city (pt.)	5	11
Powhattan township	875	690
Powhattan city	95	111
Robinson township	589	581
Robinson city[7]	324	278
Sabetha city (pt.)[7]	4	...
Walnut township[7]	731	781
Fairview city	258	283
Washington township	598	560
Everest city	331	304
Butler County[8]	44 782	38 658
Augusta city[8]	6 968	5 977
Augusta township[8]	1 074	1 126
Benton township	1 404	963
Benton city[8]	609	517
Bloomington township	316	299
Bruno township	5 394	3 677
Andover city[8]	2 801	1 880
Chelsea township	99	225
Clay township	112	93
Clifford township	260	277
Douglass township	1 834	1 413
Douglass city[8]	1 450	1 126
El Dorado city[8]	10 510	12 308
El Dorado township[8]	2 456	1 268
Fairmount township	464	385
Elbing city	175	128
Fairview township	384	269
Glencoe township	254	248
Hickory township	101	137
Lincoln township	273	261
Little Walnut township	880	650
Leon city[8]	667	510
Logan township	96	119
Milton township	1 093	884
Whitewater city[8]	751	520
Murdock township	276	234
Pleasant township	2 938	1 307
Rose Hill city (pt.)[8]	1 176	80
Plum Grove township	763	692
Potwin city	563	497

County Subdivisions

County Subdivisions	1980	1970
Butler County—Con.		
Prospect township[8]	986	867
Richland township	963	833
Rose Hill city (pt.)[6]	381	307
Rock Creek township	228	218
Rosalia township	525	422
Spring township	1 055	922
Sycamore township	330	342
Cassoday city	122	123
Towanda township	2 040	1 669
Towanda city[8]	1 332	1 190
Union township	205	220
Latham city[8]	148	156
Walnut township	501	353
Chase County[9]	3 309	3 408
Bazaar township	95	137
Cedar township	167	158
Cottonwood township	235	251
Cedar Point city	66	73
Diamond Creek township	311	314
Elmdale city	109	102
Falls township	1 125	1 213
Cottonwood Falls city	954	987
Homestead township	108	117
Matfield township	175	226
Matfield Green city	71	77
Strong township	797	680
Strong City city[9]	675	545
Toledo township	296	312
Chautauqua County[10]	5 016	4 642
Belleville township	810	718
Chautauqua city	156	137
Peru city	286	289
Caneyville township	88	89
Center township	105	132
Harrison township	158	152
Hendricks township	241	193
Elgin city	139	115
Jefferson township	955	816
Cedar Vale city[10]	848	665
Lafayette township	86	65
Little Caney township	298	250
Niotaze city	104	83
Salt Creek township	139	132
Sedan township	1 878	1 859
Sedan city[10]	1 579	1 555
Summit township	126	122
Washington township	132	114
Cherokee County[11]	22 304	21 549
Baxter Springs city[11]	4 773	4 489
Cherokee township[11]	374	357
Columbus city[11]	3 426	3 356
Crawford township	559	498
Galena city[11]	3 587	3 712
Garden township[11]	2 470	1 973
Lola township	390	422
Lowell township	547	379
Lyon township	669	622
Treece city	194	225
Mineral township	291	318
Neosho township	349	340
Pleasant View township	576	546
Ross township	921	997
Roseland city	119	113
West Mineral city	229	232
Salamanca township[11]	559	597
Scammon city	501	457
Shawnee township	480	456
Sheridan township	302	334
Spring Valley township[11]	825	956
Weir city[11]	705	740
Cheyenne County[12]	3 678	4 256
Benkelman township	77	72
Bird City township[12]	947	747
Bird City city[12]	546	671
Calhoun township[12]	88	120
Cherry Creek township	114	130
Cleveland Run township	82	103
Jaqua township	75	88
Orlando township	91	105
Wano township[12]	2 204	1 999
St. Francis city	1 610	1 725
Clark County[13]	2 599	2 896
Appleton township[13]	908	822
Minneola city	712	630
Center township	1 238	1 451
Ashland city	1 096	1 244
Englewood township[13]	197	195
Englewood city	111	158
Lexington township	84	74
Liberty township	42	40
Sitka township	130	161

County Subdivisions	1980	1970
Clay County[14]	9 802	9 890
Athelstane township	194	208
Blaine township	293	249
Bloom township	122	163
Chapman township	264	275
Longford city	109	99
Clay Center city[14]	4 948	4 963
Clay Center township[14]	383	386
Exeter township	115	128
Five Creeks township	171	183
Garfield township	159	209
Gill township	150	167
Goshen township	110	145
Grant township	144	134
Hayes township[14]	221	233
Highland township	376	361
Green city[14]	155	163
Mulberry township	501	576
Clifton city (pt.)[14]	324	359
Vining city (pt.)	55	48
Oakland township	108	148
Oak Hill city[14]	35	41
Republican township	971	745
Wakefield city[14]	803	583
Sherman township	394	436
Morganville city[14]	261	257
Union township	178	181
Cloud County[15]	12 494	13 466
Arion township	137	166
Aurora township	230	280
Aurora city	130	120
Buffalo township	152	200
Center township	196	202
Colfax township	95	119
Concordia city[15]	6 847	7 221
Elk township	1 055	1 102
Clyde city	909	946
Grant township	551	604
Jamestown city	440	470
Lawrence township	230	202
Lincoln township[15]	356	286
Lyon township	148	180
Meredith township	104	116
Nelson township	172	193
Oakland township	70	85
Shirley township	226	274
Sibley township	239	212
Solomon township	855	963
Glasco city	710	767
Simpson city (pt.)	1	2
Starr township	757	948
Miltonvale city	588	718
Summit township	74	113
Coffey County[16]	9 370	7 397
Avon township	275	268
Burlington city[16]	2 901	2 099
Burlington township[16]	363	317
Hampden township[16]	105	138
Key West township	225	223
Le Roy township	792	649
Le Roy city	701	551
Liberty township	723	704
Gridley city	404	328
Lincoln township[16]	1 205	827
Lebo city[16]	966	589
Neosho township	173	188
Ottumwa township	742	288
New Strawn city[16]	457	...
Pleasant township[16]	270	184
Pottawatomie township	239	288
Rock Creek township	1 000	845
Waverly city[16]	671	510
Spring Creek township	160	152
Star township	197	172
Comanche County[17]	2 554	2 702
Avilla township	111	124
Coldwater township[17]	1 359	1 275
Coldwater city	989	1 016
Powell township	156	153
Wilmore city	97	96
Protection township[17]	928	896
Protection city[17]	684	673
Cowley County[18]	36 824	35 012
Arkansas City city[18]	13 201	13 216
Beaver township	225	232
Bolton township[18]	1 681	1 498
Geuda Springs city (pt.)	15	11
Cedar township	78	78
Creswell township[18]	2 290	1 522
Dexter township	570	469
Dexter city[18]	366	286
Fairview township	226	233
Grant township	93	95
Harvey township	118	125
Liberty township	199	148
Maple township	473	336

County Subdivisions	1980	1970
Cowley County—Con.		
Maple township—Con.		
Udall city (pt.)	86	45
Ninnescah township	1 142	883
Udall city (pt.)[18]	805	623
Omnia township	358	331
Atlanta city[18]	256	216
Otter township	73	80
Pleasant Valley township[18]	1 027	792
Richland township	170	166
Rock Creek township	233	248
Salem township[18]	273	245
Sheridan township	144	162
Silver Creek township	707	671
Burden city[18]	518	503
Silverdale township	376	296
Spring Creek township	89	122
Tisdale township	305	255
Vernon township	709	649
Walnut township[18]	1 105	520
Windsor township	223	235
Cambridge city	113	110
Winfield city[18]	10 736	11 405
Crawford County[19]	37 916	37 850
Baker township[19]	3 330	2 926
Crawford township[19]	761	827
Frontenac city[19]	2 586	2 223
Girard city[19]	2 888	2 591
Grant township	368	404
Lincoln township	1 048	920
Arcadia city	460	388
Mulberry city	647	622
Osage township	853	950
McCune city[19]	528	487
Pittsburg city[19]	18 770	20 171
Sheridan township	1 619	1 520
Cherokee city[19]	775	790
Sherman township	549	564
Walnut township	843	884
Hepler city	165	152
Walnut city	308	330
Washington township[19]	3 654	3 248
Arma city[19]	1 676	1 348
Decatur County[20]	4 509	4 988
Allison township	67	99
Altory township	36	44
Bassettville township	53	67
Beaver township	105	97
Center township	67	83
Oberlin city (pt.)	4	—
Cook township	55	62
Custer township	48	69
Dresden township	200	279
Dresden city	84	103
Finley township	91	111
Garfield township	46	83
Grant township	45	76
Harlan township	75	90
Jennings township	248	297
Jennings city (pt.)	171	214
Liberty township	75	87
Oberlin city (pt.)[20]	13	—
Lincoln township	268	360
Norcatur city	226	284
Logan township	65	81
Lyon township	34	53
Oberlin township	2 471	2 392
Oberlin city (pt.)[20]	2 370	2 291
Olive township	109	95
Pleasant Valley township	82	110
Clayton city (pt.)	9	7
Jennings city (pt.)	23	10
Prairie Dog township	72	90
Roosevelt township	42	71
Sappa township	55	68
Sherman township	58	75
Summit township	42	49
Dickinson County[21]	20 175	19 993
Abilene city[21]	6 572	6 661
Banner township	159	177
Buckeye township	411	407
Center township	1 298	1 305
Enterprise city[21]	839	868
Cheever township	149	198
Flora township	243	243
Manchester city	98	92
Fragrant Hill township	239	221
Garfield township	183	194
Grant township[21]	1 037	1 049
Hayes township	233	220
Herington city[21]	2 930	3 165
Holland township	144	126
Carlton city	49	40
Hope township	659	654
Hope city	468	438
Jefferson township	224	267
Liberty township	424	388

County Subdivisions	1980	1970
Dickinson County—Con.		
Liberty township—Con.		
Woodbine city	172	170
Lincoln township	1 618	1 394
Solomon city[21]	1 018	973
Logan township	246	276
Lyon township[21]	269	238
Newbern township	320	262
Noble township	1 719	1 419
Chapman city[21]	1 255	1 132
Ridge township	177	207
Rinehart township	208	224
Sherman township	140	190
Union township	212	174
Wheatland township	161	165
Willowdale township	200	169
Doniphan County[22]	9 268	9 107
Burr Oak township	232	266
Center township	1 944	1 904
Troy city[22]	1 240	1 047
Independence township	347	351
Iowa township	1 843	1 823
Highland city	954	899
White Cloud city	234	210
Marion township	264	300
Union township	390	443
Denton city[22]	156	162
Washington township	3 459	3 104
Elwood city	1 275	1 283
Wathena city	1 418	1 150
Wayne township	265	323
Wolf River township	524	593
Leona city	73	72
Severance city	134	128
Douglas County[23]	67 640	57 932
Clinton township	275	439
Eudora township	3 821	2 868
Eudora city[23]	2 934	2 071
Grant township[23]	430	490
Kanwaka township	704	646
Lawrence city[23]	52 738	45 698
Lecompton township	1 250	1 032
Lecompton city[23]	576	434
Marion township	600	557
Palmyra township	4 471	3 798
Baldwin City city[23]	2 829	2 520
Wakarusa township[23]	2 246	1 665
Willow Springs township	1 105	739
Edwards County[24]	4 271	4 581
Belpre township	277	326
Belpre city	154	191
Franklin township	137	167
Jackson township	118	176
Kinsley city[24]	2 074	2 212
Kinsley township[24]	201	228
Lincoln township	174	175
Logan township	62	101
North Brown township	97	98
South Brown township	110	121
Trenton township	333	333
Offerle city	244	212
Wayne township	688	644
Lewis city[24]	551	525
Elk County[25]	3 918	3 858
Elk Falls township	261	223
Elk Falls city	151	124
Greenfield township	423	415
Grenola city	335	290
Howard township	1 163	1 166
Howard city	965	918
Liberty township	132	157
Longton township	506	439
Longton city[25]	396	304
Oak Valley township	136	122
Painterhood township	94	76
Paw Paw township	191	232
Union Center township	199	218
Wild Cat township	813	810
Moline city[25]	553	555
Ellis County[26]	26 098	24 730
Big Creek township[26]	3 336	2 524
Buckeye township[26]	315	189
Catherine township[26]	292	306
Ellis city[26]	2 062	2 137
Ellis township[26]	482	352
Freedom township	208	213
Hays city[26]	16 301	15 396
Herzog township[26]	972	743
Victoria city (pt.)[26]	528	533
Lookout township[26]	591	489
Schoenchen city	209	182
Victoria township[26]	1 060	902
Victoria city (pt.)[26]	800	713
Wheatland township	479	469

County Subdivisions	1980	1970
Ellsworth County[27]	6 640	6 146
Ash Creek township	76	61
Black Wolf township	99	66
Carneiro township	65	78
Clear Creek township	110	85
Columbia township	92	130
Ellsworth city[27]	2 465	2 080
Ellsworth township[27]	979	899
Kanopolis city	729	626
Empire township	78	95
Garfield township	44	25
Green Garden township	250	254
Lorraine city	157	153
Langley township	81	85
Lincoln township	38	49
Mulberry township	36	21
Noble township	103	150
Palacky township	66	73
Sherman township	103	73
Thomas township	78	86
Trivoli township	80	57
Valley township	700	739
Holyrood city[27]	567	593
Wilson township	1 097	1 040
Wilson city[27]	978	870
Finney County[28]	23 825	19 029
Garden City city[28]	18 256	14 790
Garden City township[28]	2 724	1 940
Garfield township	342	479
Ivanhoe township	298	220
Pierceville township	422	334
Pleasant Valley township	118	112
Sherlock township	1 436	870
Holcomb[28]	816	272
Terry township	229	284
Ford County[29]	24 315	22 587
Bloom township	132	149
Bucklin township[29]	943	837
Bucklin city[29]	786	771
Concord township	99	124
Dodge township[29]	884	2 348
Dodge City city[29]	18 001	14 127
Enterprise township	633	545
Fairview township	320	189
Ford township	424	393
Ford city	272	246
Grandview township[29]	783	862
Richland township[29]	319	863
Royal township	107	97
Sodville township	129	135
Spearville township	1 172	1 340
Spearville city[29]	693	738
Wheatland township	235	342
Wilburn township	134	153
Franklin County[30]	22 062	20 007
Appanoose township	257	245
Centropolis township	758	616
Cutler township	714	537
Rantoul city	212	163
Franklin township	2 219	1 663
Wellsville city[30]	1 612	1 183
Greenwood township	347	260
Harrison township[30]	420	484
Hayes township	314	258
Homewood township	411	329
Lincoln township[30]	475	469
Ohio township	621	499
Princeton city[30]	244	159
Ottawa city[30]	11 016	11 036
Ottawa township[30]	923	665
Peoria township	514	374
Pomona township	1 080	718
Pomona city	868	541
Pottawatomie township	561	534
Lane city	249	254
Richmond township	780	722
Richmond city	510	464
Williamsburg township	652	598
Williamsburg city	362	286
Geary County[31]	29 852	28 111
Blakely township	94	100
Jackson township	100	84
Jefferson township[31]	1 740	1 113
Fort Riley—Camp Whiteside (CDP) (pt.)	34	–
Grandview Plaza city[31]	1 189	734
Junction City city[31]	19 305	19 018
Liberty township	286	252
Lyon township	272	193
Milford township	1 285	1 346
Milford city[31]	465	296
Smoky Hill township[31]	6 625	5 861
Camp Forsyth (CDP)	2 054	2 334
Fort Riley—Camp Whiteside (CDP) (pt.)	2 113	2 310
Fort Riley North (CDP) (pt.)	1 656	1 217
Wingfield township	145	144

County Subdivisions	1980	1970
Gove County[32]	3 726	3 940
Baker township	1 400	1 360
Quinter city[32]	951	930
Gaeland township	80	89
Gove township	293	365
Gove City city[32]	148	172
Grainfield township	585	615
Grainfield city	417	374
Grinnell township	678	723
Grinnell city	410	449
Jerome township	154	168
Larrabee township	102	111
Lewis township	26	26
Payne township	408	483
Park city	183	178
Graham County[33]	3 995	4 751
Allodium township	102	101
Bryant township	231	293
Gettysburg township	110	157
Morland city (pt.)	–	32
Graham township	76	101
Happy township	108	157
Hill City township	2 205	2 394
Hill City city[33]	2 028	2 071
Indiana township	65	89
Millbrook township	215	291
Morlan township	112	184
Nicodemus township	81	100
Pioneer township	67	106
Solomon township	317	386
Morland city (pt.)	223	268
Wild Horse township	306	392
Bogue city	197	257
Grant County[34]	6 977	5 961
Lincoln township	5 832	4 769
Ulysses city[34]	4 653	3 779
Sherman township	536	561
Sullivan township	609	631
Gray County[35]	5 138	4 516
Cimarron township	1 937	1 617
Cimarron city[35]	1 491	1 373
Copeland township	574	517
Copeland city[35]	323	267
East Hess township	396	422
Ensign city[35]	209	237
Foote township	152	160
Ingalls township	595	480
Ingalls city[35]	274	235
Logan township	197	205
Montezuma township[35]	1 287	922
Montezuma city[35]	730	606
Greeley County[36]	1 845	1 819
Colony township	235	220
Harrison township	185	144
Tribune township	1 425	1 455
Horace city	137	137
Tribune city[36]	955	1 013
Greenwood County[37]	8 764	9 141
Bachelor township	195	236
Eureka city[37]	3 425	3 576
Eureka township[37]	369	322
Fall River township	239	249
Climax city	81	64
Janesville township	665	693
Hamilton city[37]	363	349
Lane township	238	267
Virgil city	169	179
Madison township	1 431	1 447
Madison city[37]	1 099	1 061
Otter Creek township	238	300
Pleasant Grove township	66	101
Quincy township	195	222
Salem township	48	48
Salt Springs township	388	400
Fall River city	173	191
Shell Rock township	238	290
South Salem township	137	166
Spring Creek township	122	151
Twin Grove township	770	673
Severy city	447	384
Hamilton County[38]	2 514	2 747
Bear Creek township	81	119
Coolidge township	182	215
Coolidge city	82	102
Kendall township	103	138
Lamont township	108	144
Liberty township	32	65
Medway township	39	60
Richland township	40	55
Syracuse township	1 929	1 951
Syracuse city[38]	1 654	1 720
Harper County[39]	7 778	7 871
Anthony city	2 661	2 653
Harper city	1 823	1 665
Township No. 1[39]	1 206	...

County Subdivisions

County Subdivisions	1980	1970
Harper County—Con.		
Township No. 1—Con.		
Attica city	730	639
Township No. 2[39]	270	...
Waldron city	29	24
Township No. 3[39]	554	...
Township No. 4[39]	318	...
Bluff City city	95	109
Freeport city	12	21
Township No. 5[39]	551	...
Danville city	71	80
Township No. 6[39]	395	...
Harvey County[40]	30 531	27 236
Alta township	242	267
Burrton township	1 211	1 035
Burrton city[40]	976	808
Darlington township	527	409
Emma township	3 618	2 433
Hesston city[40]	3 013	1 926
Garden township	296	303
Halstead city[40]	1 994	1 716
Halstead township[40]	378	404
Highland township	386	342
Lake township	219	233
Lakin township[40]	346	306
Macon township[40]	632	456
Newton city[40]	16 332	15 439
Newton township[40]	1 708	1 499
North Newton city[40]	1 222	963
Pleasant township	323	258
Richland township	211	244
Sedgwick township	1 682	1 498
Sedgwick city (pt.)	1 343	1 083
Walton township	426	394
Walton city[40]	269	211
Haskell County[41]	3 814	3 672
Dudley township	1 541	1 579
Satanta city[41]	1 117	1 161
Haskell township	1 721	1 619
Sublette city	1 293	1 208
Lockport township	552	474
Hodgeman County[42]	2 269	2 662
Benton township	47	50
Center township	1 098	1 208
Jetmore city[42]	862	936
Hallet township	69	76
Marena township	500	568
Hanston city	257	282
North Roscoe township	76	115
Sawlog township	124	170
South Roscoe township	99	124
Sterling township	163	230
Valley township	93	121
Jackson County[43]	11 644	10 342
Adrian township	125	166
Banner township	329	264
Cedar township	1 164	828
Denison city (pt.)	12	4
Mayetta city[43]	287	246
Douglas township	1 711	1 243
Hoyt city[43]	536	420
Franklin township[43]	600	472
Garfield township	600	619
Denison city (pt.)	219	244
Grant township	211	178
Holton city[43]	3 132	3 063
Jefferson township	517	467
Circleville city	164	178
Liberty township	416	421
Lincoln township	756	528
Netawaka township	474	413
Netawaka city	218	192
Soldier township	493	479
Soldier city	165	173
Straight Creek township	193	236
Washington township	453	459
Delia city[43]	181	168
Whiting township	470	506
Whiting city[43]	270	256
Jefferson County[44]	15 207	11 945
Delaware township	1 981	1 889
Valley Falls city[44]	1 189	1 169
Fairview township	669	149
Jefferson township	1 241	1 045
Winchester city[44]	570	492
Kaw township	1 301	1 013
Kentucky township	1 453	1 129
Perry city[44]	907	664
Norton township	1 016	1 121
Nortonville city	692	727
Oskaloosa township	1 776	1 572
Oskaloosa city[44]	1 092	955
Ozawkie township	950	430
Ozawkie city	472	137
Rock Creek township	2 234	1 558

County Subdivisions

County Subdivisions	1980	1970
Jefferson County—Con.		
Rock Creek township—Con.		
Meriden city[44]	707	472
Rural township	588	476
Sarcoxie township	644	456
Union township[44]	1 354	1 107
McLouth city[44]	700	623
Jewell County[45]	5 241	6 099
Allen township	68	77
Athens township	105	141
Browns Creek township	71	90
Buffalo township	723	745
Jewell city[45]	589	569
Burr Oak township	473	568
Burr Oak city	366	426
Calvin township	73	78
Center township	1 366	1 477
Mankato city	1 205	1 287
Erving township	86	121
Esbon township	358	357
Esbon city[45]	234	206
Grant township	280	345
Formoso city	166	180
Harrison township	71	85
Highland township	67	98
Holmwood township	71	96
Ionia township	153	188
Jackson township	191	207
Webber city	53	49
Limestone township	103	131
Montana township	118	147
Odessa township	74	88
Prairie township	250	291
Randall city	154	195
Richland township	39	72
Sinclair township	111	148
Vicksburg township	60	95
Walnut township	113	178
Washington township	115	159
White Mound township	102	117
Johnson County[46]	270 269	[r]220 073
Aubry township	2 989	1 246
Countryside city	346	[r]411
De Soto city[46]	2 061	1 839
Edgerton city[46]	1 214	513
Fairway city	4 619	[r]5 227
Gardner city[46]	2 392	1 839
Gardner township[46]	2 595	[r]1 831
Lake Quivira city (pt.)[46]	1 029	...
Leawood city[46]	13 360	[r]10 645
Lenexa city[46]	18 639	[r]5 549
Lexington township[46]	1 978	2 854
McCamish township[46]	922	559
Merriam city	10 794	[r]10 955
Mission city	8 643	[r]8 125
Mission Hills city	3 904	[r]4 198
Mission Woods city	213	[r]237
Monticello township[46]	2 813	1 526
Olathe city[46]	37 258	17 917
Olathe township[46]	1 564	965
Overland Park city[46]	81 784	[r]77 934
Oxford township[46]	2 491	961
Prairie Village city	24 657	[r]28 378
Roeland Park city	7 962	[r]9 760
Shawnee city[46]	29 653	[r]20 946
Shawnee township	620	[r]1 177
Spring Hill city (pt.)[46]	1 963	1 186
Spring Hill township[46]	1 586	498
Westwood city	1 783	[r]2 383
Westwood Hills city	437	414
Kearny County[47]	3 435	3 047
Deerfield township	713	639
Deerfield city[47]	538	474
East Hibbard township	152	155
Hartland township	126	133
Kendall township	109	106
Lakin township	2 078	1 781
Lakin city[47]	1 823	1 570
Southside township	190	137
West Hibbard township	67	96
Kingman County[48]	8 960	8 886
Allen township	114	126
Belmont township	134	135
Bennett township	647	576
Norwich city[48]	476	414
Canton township	111	172
Chikaskia township	168	171
Spivey city	83	78
Dale township	217	258
Dresden township	402	454
Cunningham city (pt.)	287	308
Eagle township	159	162
Eureka township	147	174
Penalosa city	31	32
Evan township	425	264
Galesburg township	259	250

County Subdivisions	1980	1970
Kingman County—Con.		
Hoosier township	185	168
Kingman city[48]	3 563	3 622
Kingman township	184	241
Liberty township	220	211
Nashville city	127	107
Ninnescah township[48]	258	224
Peters township	229	286
Richland township	139	113
Rochester township	248	274
Zenda city	146	142
Rural township	374	317
Cunningham city (pt.)[48]	253	175
Union township	123	124
Valley township	130	145
Vinita township	208	222
White township[48]	316	197
Kiowa County[49]	4 046	4 088
East Kiowa (unorg.)[49]	579	98
Greensburg city[49]	1 885	1 907
Haviland city[49]	770	705
Mullinville city[49]	339	376
West Kiowa (unorg.)[49]	473	...
Labette County[50]	25 682	25 775
Canada township	281	320
Chetopa city[50]	1 751	1 596
Elm Grove township	947	825
Edna city[50]	537	418
Fairview township	281	285
Hackberry township	466	455
Bartlett city	163	138
Howard township	388	395
Labette township	323	311
Liberty township	485	387
Labette city	123	105
Montana township	240	212
Mound Valley township	862	912
Mound Valley city	381	467
Mount Pleasant township	1 342	1 163
Altamont city[50]	1 054	845
Neosho township	199	195
North township[50]	618	673
Osage township	689	646
Oswego city[50]	2 218	2 200
Oswego township[50]	326	306
Parsons city[50]	12 898	13 015
Richland township[50]	372	437
Walton township[50]	996	1 442
Lane County[51]	2 472	2 707
Alamota township	102	140
Blaine township[51]	138	129
Cheyenne township	333	359
Cleveland township	45	52
Dighton township	1 577	1 699
Dighton city	1 390	1 540
Spring Creek township	95	104
White Rock township	46	59
Wilson township	136	146
Leavenworth County[52]	54 809	53 340
Alexandria township	629	626
Delaware township[52]	6 031	6 357
Lansing city[52]	5 307	3 797
Easton township	1 178	1 020
Easton city[52]	460	435
Fairmount township	3 121	1 910
Basehor city[52]	1 483	724
High Prairie township[52]	1 312	1 002
Kickapoo township[52]	1 394	11 538
Leavenworth city[52]	33 656	25 147
Reno township	764	724
Sherman township	1 772	1 208
Linwood city	343	323
Stranger township	1 438	1 011
Tonganoxie city (pt.)[52]	84	–
Tonganoxie township[52]	3 514	2 797
Tonganoxie city (pt.)[52]	1 780	1 717
Lincoln County[53]	4 145	4 582
Battle Creek township	70	72
Beaver township	505	470
Lincoln Center city (pt.)	460	401
Cedron township	67	138
Colorado township	290	345
Beverly city[53]	171	193
Elkhorn township	1 123	1 213
Lincoln Center city (pt.)	942	1 007
Franklin township	105	119
Golden Belt township	78	90
Grant township	95	126
Hanover township	50	62
Highland township	59	76
Indiana township	263	262
Lincoln Center city (pt.)[53]	136	121
Logan township	70	74
Madison township	107	127
Marion township	123	127
Lincoln Center city (pt.)	61	53

County Subdivisions	1980	1970
Lincoln County—Con.		
Orange township	96	109
Pleasant township	549	565
Sylvan Grove city	376	403
Salt Creek township	99	123
Barnard city (pt.)	20	25
Scott township	205	249
Barnard city (pt.)	143	165
Valley township	67	88
Vesper township	124	147
Linn County[54]	8 234	7 770
Blue Mound township	584	628
Blue Mound city	319	308
Centerville township	448	514
Liberty township	813	780
Parker city[54]	270	255
Lincoln township	1 491	1 349
La Cygne city[54]	1 025	989
Mound City township	1 104	1 023
Mound City city[54]	755	714
Paris township	425	398
Potosi township	1 940	1 810
Pleasanton city[54]	1 303	1 216
Scott township	464	362
Sheridan township	552	492
Prescott city[54]	319	222
Stanton township	176	198
Valley township	237	216
Logan County[55]	3 478	3 814
Augustine township	28	52
Elkader township	36	49
Lees township	37	50
Logansport township	12	11
McAllaster township	40	47
Monument township	184	233
Oakley township	2 558	2 649
Oakley city (pt.)[55]	2 268	2 327
Paxton township	33	43
Russell Springs township	112	147
Russell Springs city	56	83
Western township	58	58
Winona township	380	475
Winona city	258	293
Lyon County[56]	35 108	32 071
Agnes City township	507	443
Allen city	205	175
Bushong city	62	39
Americus township	1 591	918
Americus city[56]	915	441
Center township	1 135	1 137
Olpe city[56]	477	453
Elmerdaro township	1 035	1 027
Hartford city	551	478
Emporia city[56]	25 287	23 327
Emporia township[56]	1 244	1 583
Fremont township	988	677
Ivy township	275	264
Admire city	158	144
Jackson township	1 013	862
Neosho Rapids city[56]	289	234
Pike township	1 212	972
Reading township	499	509
Reading city	244	247
Waterloo township	322	352
McPherson County[57]	26 855	24 778
Battle Hill township	120	119
Bonaville township	49	54
Canton township	1 187	1 144
Canton city	926	893
Castle township	250	288
Windom city	160	183
Delmore township	131	108
Empire township	1 079	864
Galva city	651	522
Groveland township	239	260
Gypsum Creek township	223	262
Harper township	167	156
Hayes township	287	285
Jackson township	290	259
King City township	404	365
Lindsborg city[57]	3 155	2 764
Little Valley township	472	411
Lone Tree township	422	450
McPherson city[57]	11 753	10 851
McPherson township[57]	607	433
Marquette township	877	775
Marquette city	639	578
Meridian township	346	379
Mound township	1 888	1 713
Moundridge city[57]	1 453	1 271
New Gottland township	269	246
Smoky Hill township[57]	297	265
South Sharps Creek township	124	116
Spring Valley township	437	411
Superior township	1 318	1 299
Inman city[57]	947	836

County Subdivisions

County Subdivisions	1980	1970
McPherson County—Con.		
Turkey Creek township	288	307
Union township	176	194
Marion County[58]	13 522	13 935
Blaine township	214	263
Tampa city	113	154
Catlin township	230	227
Peabody city (pt.)[58]	34	21
Center township	421	285
Clark township	217	247
Clear Creek township	668	648
Lincolnville city[58]	235	218
Colfax township	273	313
Ramona city	116	121
Doyle township[58]	95	96
Durham Park township	282	325
Durham city	130	143
East Branch township	202	196
Fairplay township[58]	162	180
Florence city[58]	729	777
Gale township	243	196
Grant township	159	169
Hillsboro city[58]	2 717	2 730
Lehigh township	334	351
Lehigh city	189	168
Liberty township[58]	297	356
Logan township	147	178
Lost Springs township	316	316
Lost Springs city	94	103
Marion city	1 951	2 052
Menno township	297	326
Milton township	339	382
Burns city[58]	224	268
Moore township	94	114
Peabody township	1 671	1 612
Peabody city (pt.)	1 440	1 347
Risley township[58]	233	294
Summit township	104	133
West Branch township	869	866
Goessel city[58]	421	386
Wilson township	258	303
Marshall County[59]	12 787	13 139
Balderson township	154	202
Bigelow township	113	94
Blue Rapids township	113	145
Blue Rapids City township	1 389	1 257
Blue Rapids city	1 280	1 148
Center township	164	191
Clear Fork township	52	96
Cleveland township	117	137
Cottage Hill township	166	187
Elm Creek township	229	219
Franklin township	332	303
Guittard township	505	499
Beattie city	316	288
Herkimer township	318	347
Lincoln township	181	239
Logan township	357	416
Marysville city[59]	3 670	3 588
Marysville township[59]	524	473
Murray township	737	755
Axtell city[59]	470	456
Noble township	302	422
Vermillion city[59]	191	191
Oketo township	316	377
Oketo city[59]	130	133
Richland township	247	342
Summerfield city (pt.)	100	118
Rock township	151	185
St. Bridget township	252	304
Summerfield city (pt.)	125	136
Vermillion township	1 218	1 174
Frankfort city	1 038	960
Walnut township	183	206
Waterville township	842	787
Waterville city	694	632
Wells township	155	194
Meade County[60]	4 788	4 912
Cimarron township	89	83
Crooked Creek township	79	104
Fowler township	794	843
Fowler city[60]	592	588
Logan township	149	161
Meade Center township	2 058	2 229
Meade city	1 777	1 899
Mertilla township	236	209
Odee township	79	99
Sand Creek township	76	104
West Plains township	1 228	1 080
West Plains city	1 044	857
Miami County[61]	21 618	19 254
Louisburg city[61]	1 744	1 033
Marysville township[61]	1 593	1 223
Miami township	415	407
Middle Creek township	1 002	769

County Subdivisions	1980	1970
Miami County—Con.		
Mound township	508	406
Osage township	592	544
Fontana city	173	160
Osawatomie city[61]	4 459	4 294
Osawatomie township[61]	697	1 246
Paola city[61]	4 557	4 622
Paola township[61]	738	514
Richland township	1 036	777
Spring Hill city (pt.)[61]	42	...
Stanton township	766	591
Sugar Creek township	322	323
Ten Mile township	798	649
Valley township[61]	1 262	804
Wea township[61]	1 087	2 085
Mitchell County[62]	8 117	8 010
Asherville township	152	150
Beloit city[62]	4 367	4 121
Beloit township[62]	443	368
Bloomfield township	117	112
Blue Hill township	44	73
Carr Creek township	33	40
Cawker township	706	817
Cawker City city	640	726
Center township	62	79
Custer township	208	232
Hunter city	135	150
Eureka township	45	57
Glen Elder township	599	540
Glen Elder city	491	422
Hayes township	38	58
Logan township	179	211
Simpson city (pt.)	122	129
Lulu township	121	126
Scottsville city	56	46
Pittsburg township	476	472
Tipton city	321	315
Plum Creek township	142	127
Round Springs township	47	31
Salt Creek township	54	69
Solomon Rapids township	84	95
Turkey Creek township	139	160
Walnut Creek township	61	72
Montgomery County[63]	42 281	39 949
Caney city[63]	2 284	2 192
Caney township[63]	1 289	1 207
Havana city	169	144
Tyro city (pt.)	190	132
Cherokee township[63]	580	581
Cherry township[63]	503	511
Cherryvale city[63]	2 769	2 609
Coffeyville city[63]	15 185	15 116
Drum Creek township	522	425
Fawn Creek township[63]	2 088	1 655
Dearing city[63]	475	338
Tyro city (pt.)	99	74
Independence city[63]	10 598	10 347
Independence township[63]	2 426	1 688
Liberty township	568	518
Liberty city	174	185
Louisburg township	791	737
Elk City city	404	432
Parker township[63]	1 194	1 136
Rutland township	282	293
Sycamore township[63]	994	733
West Cherry township	208	201
Morris County[64]	6 419	6 432
Council Grove city[64]	2 381	2 403
Highland township	133	143
Overland township	111	98
Township No. 1[64]	589	...
Dunlap city	82	102
Township No. 2[64]	627	...
Township No. 3[64]	510	...
Dwight city	320	322
Township No. 4[64]	234	...
Parkerville city	42	25
Township No. 5[64]	707	...
White City city	534	458
Township No. 6[64]	141	...
Latimer city	31	29
Township No. 7[64]	327	...
Township No. 8[64]	300	...
Township No. 9[64]	359	...
Wilsey city	179	169
Morton County[65]	3 454	3 576
Cimarron township	73	81
Jones township	16	24
Richfield township	316	332
Richfield city	81	82
Rolla township	561	561
Rolla city[65]	417	400
Taloga township	2 378	2 442
Elkhart city[65]	2 243	2 089
Westola township	110	136

County Subdivisions	1980	1970
Nemaha County[66]	11 211	11 825
Adams township	242	287
Berwick township	346	358
Capioma township	202	249
Center township	274	289
Clear Creek township	170	217
Gilman township	318	334
Oneida city	120	112
Granada township	127	167
Harrison township	424	503
Goff city	196	207
Home township	603	710
Centralia city (pt.)[66]	444	491
Illinois township	465	478
Centralia city (pt.)[66]	42	20
Corning city	158	162
Marion township	475	506
Mitchell township[66]	345	317
Nemaha township	196	223
Neuchatel township	165	143
Red Vermillion township	174	207
Reilly township	202	224
Richmond township[66]	460	652
Rock Creek township[66]	271	311
Sabetha city (pt.)[66]	2 282	2 376
Seneca city[66]	2 389	2 182
Washington township	539	498
Bern city[66]	220	191
Wetmore township	542	594
Wetmore city	376	392
Neosho County[67]	18 967	18 812
Big Creek township	558	482
Canville township[67]	527	533
Earlton city	79	102
Centerville township	526	493
Galesburg city	181	146
Chanute city[67]	10 506	10 341
Chetopa township[67]	934	804
Thayer city[67]	517	430
Erie township	1 821	1 767
Erie city[67]	1 415	1 414
Grant township	471	489
Stark city[67]	143	124
Ladore township	395	399
Lincoln township	381	370
Mission township	989	1 090
St. Paul city[67]	746	804
Shiloh township	286	312
Tioga township[67]	1 194	1 279
Walnut Grove township	379	453
Ness County[68]	4 498	4 791
Bazine township	611	636
Bazine city[68]	385	386
Center township	1 830	1 812
Ness City city	1 769	1 756
Eden township	124	139
Forrester township	108	124
Franklin township	203	241
Highpoint township	145	176
Johnson township	96	155
Nevada township	656	657
Ransom city	448	416
Ohio township	474	554
Utica city	275	297
Waring township	251	297
Brownell city	92	98
Norton County[69]	6 689	7 279
Almena–District 4 township[69]	762	...
Almena city	517	489
Center–District 1 township[69]	1 196	...
Harrison–District 6 township[69]	33	...
Highland–District 2 township[69]	1 016	...
Clayton city (pt.)	93	120
Lenora city	444	439
Norton city[69]	3 400	3 627
Solomon–District 3 township[69]	282	...
Edmond city	56	90
Osage County[70]	15 319	13 352
Agency township	565	590
Quenemo city	413	429
Arvonia township	116	181
Barclay township	203	214
Burlingame township	1 935	1 613
Burlingame city[70]	1 239	999
Dragoon township	277	273
Elk township	1 637	1 157
Overbrook city[70]	930	748
Fairfax township	302	252
Grant township[70]	342	297
Junction township	736	459
Lincoln township	138	145
Melvern township	842	797
Melvern city[70]	481	455
Olivet township	238	240
Olivet city	65	64
Osage City city[70]	2 667	2 600
Ridgeway township	2 353	1 776

County Subdivisions	1980	1970
Osage County—Con.		
Ridgeway township—Con.		
Carbondale city[70]	1 518	1 041
Scranton township	1 076	952
Scranton city[70]	664	575
Superior township[70]	356	334
Valley Brook township	1 536	1 472
Lyndon city[70]	1 132	958
Osborne County[71]	5 959	6 416
Bethany township	295	288
Portis city	172	178
Bloom township	148	195
Corinth township	66	91
Covert township	29	35
Delhi township	59	84
Grant township	54	76
Hancock township	36	65
Hawkeye township	35	52
Independence township	63	81
Jackson township	58	82
Kill Creek township	48	71
Lawrence township	56	79
Liberty township	27	25
Mount Ayr township	74	82
Natoma township	570	658
Natoma city	515	603
Osborne city[71]	2 120	1 980
Penn township[71]	176	205
Ross township	1 456	1 422
Downs city	1 324	1 268
Round Mound township	78	106
Sumner township	275	380
Alton city	135	214
Tilden township	134	197
Valley township	29	56
Victor township	42	51
Winfield township	31	55
Ottawa County[72]	5 971	6 183
Bennington township	781	843
Bennington city	579	561
Blaine township	111	93
Buckeye township	96	119
Center township	84	90
Chapman township	76	110
Concord township	177	143
Culver township	297	278
Culver city	167	148
Durham township	34	34
Fountain township	199	244
Garfield township	84	122
Grant township	94	106
Henry township	51	46
Lincoln township	161	164
Logan township	124	146
Minneapolis city	2 075	1 971
Morton township	483	552
Tescott city[72]	331	393
Ottawa township	46	59
Richland township	174	167
Sheridan township	699	728
Delphos city	570	599
Sherman township	81	105
Stanton township	44	63
Pawnee County[73]	8 065	8 484
Ash Valley township	66	79
Browns Grove township	336	366
Burdett city	275	285
Conkling township	33	69
Garfield township	326	338
Garfield city (pt.)	274	260
Grant township	293	320
Rozel city[73]	219	236
Keysville township	71	78
Larned city[73]	4 811	4 567
Larned township[73]	333	390
Lincoln township	54	57
Logan township	60	95
Morton township	89	124
Orange township	85	87
Garfield city (pt.)	3	1
Pawnee township	101	134
Pleasant Grove township	243	226
Pleasant Ridge township	83	106
Pleasant Valley township	134	187
River township	111	91
Santa Fe township	579	876
Sawmill township	36	54
Shiley township	33	46
Valley Center township	91	69
Walnut township	97	125
Phillips County[74]	7 406	7 888
Arcade township	106	121
Beaver township	94	103
Belmont township	114	164
Speed city	41	58
Bow Creek township	39	57

County Subdivisions	1980	1970
Phillips County—Con.		
Crystal township	82	85
Dayton township	64	89
Deer Creek township	105	99
Freedom township	109	118
Glenwood township	52	78
Granite township	68	99
Greenwood township	63	83
Kirwin township	329	375
Kirwin city	249	293
Logan township	802	875
Logan city	720	760
Long Island township	318	343
Long Island city	187	195
Mound township	192	255
Phillipsburg city[74]	3 229	3 241
Phillipsburg township[74]	433	343
Plainview township	21	45
Plum township	462	438
Agra city	321	294
Prairie View township	264	322
Prairie View city	145	201
Rushville township	36	62
Solomon township	258	307
Glade city[74]	131	180
Sumner township	55	76
Towanda township	23	35
Valley township	55	39
Walnut township	33	36
Pottawatomie County[75]	14 782	11 755
Belvue township	353	339
Belvue city[75]	212	161
Blue township	1 402	263
Blue Valley township	293	293
Olsburg city[75]	166	151
Center township	126	120
Clear Creek township	152	157
Emmett township	377	273
Emmett city[75]	223	156
Grant township	365	309
Havensville city	183	163
Green township	153	120
Lincoln township	122	134
Lone Tree township	231	262
Wheaton city	90	106
Louisville township	591	488
Louisville city	207	204
Manhattan city (pt.)	162	678
Mill Creek township	1 000	1 022
Onaga city[75]	752	761
Pottawatomie township	399	411
Westmoreland city (pt.)	52	30
Rock Creek township	701	616
Westmoreland city (pt.)[75]	546	455
St. Clere township	82	68
St. George township	1 697	1 001
St. George city[75]	309	241
St. Marys township	1 989	1 730
St. Marys city[75]	1 598	1 434
Shannon township	196	176
Sherman township	156	132
Spring Creek township	72	57
Union township	161	154
Vienna township	120	122
Wamego township	3 882	2 830
Wamego city[75]	3 159	2 507
Pratt County[76]	10 275	10 056
Pratt city[76]	6 885	6 736
Township No. 6	720	687
Preston city	227	239
Township No. 7	461	475
Iuka city	235	210
Township No. 8	246	246
Byers city	47	46
Township No. 9	425	435
Cullison city	154	117
Township No. 10	222	234
Coats city	153	152
Township No. 11	570	527
Sawyer city	213	164
Township No. 12[76]	746	716
Rawlins County[77]	4 105	4 393
Achilles township	94	105
Atwood township[77]	1 695	1 765
Atwood city	1 665	1 658
Center township[77]	461	...
Driftwood township	143	159
Herl township[77]	637	...
Herndon city	220	268
Jefferson township	64	79
Ludell township	187	208
Mirage township	70	83
Rocewood township[77]	680	...
McDonald city	239	269
Union township	74	81

County Subdivisions	1980	1970
Reno County[78]	64 983	60 765
Albion township	920	865
Pretty Prairie city[78]	655	561
Arlington township	798	652
Arlington city	631	503
Bell township	105	126
Castleton township	242	212
Center township	627	628
Partridge city	268	302
Clay township[78]	3 238	3 720
Enterprise township	146	184
Grant township[78]	1 263	789
Willowbrook city	109	100
Grove township	93	81
Haven township	1 539	1 633
Haven city[78]	1 125	1 146
Hayes township[78]	154	113
Huntsville township	176	207
Hutchinson[78]	40 284	36 885
Langdon township	246	240
Langdon city	84	93
Lincoln township	595	472
Little River township	1 824	1 483
Buhler city	1 188	1 019
Loda township	128	138
Medford township	185	179
Medora township	1 437	821
Miami township	575	571
Turon city	481	430
Nickerson city[78]	1 292	1 187
Ninnescah township	199	112
Plevna township	308	296
Plevna city	115	124
Reno township[78]	5 006	5 905
South Hutchinson city[78]	2 226	1 879
Roscoe township	128	114
Salt Creek township	453	446
Sumner township	397	368
Sylvia township	481	538
Sylvia city	353	390
Troy township	140	137
Valley township	878	553
Walnut township	138	195
Westminster township	246	270
Abbyville city	123	143
Yoder township	742	619
Republic County[79]	7 569	8 498
Albion township	256	283
Narka city[79]	120	130
Beaver township	149	172
Belleville city[79]	2 805	3 063
Belleville township[79]	254	260
Big Bend township	371	397
Republic city (pt.)	212	218
Courtland township	573	616
Courtland city[79]	377	403
Elk Creek township	234	278
Agenda city[79]	106	107
Fairview township	193	221
Munden city (pt.)[79]	75	70
Farmington township	147	179
Freedom township[79]	250	232
Grant township	127	155
Jefferson township	186	175
Liberty township	98	140
Lincoln township	147	155
Norway township	209	271
Richland township	416	508
Cuba city[79]	286	290
Rose Creek township	197	188
Munden city (pt.)[79]	77	53
Scandia township	612	726
Scandia city	480	567
Union township	80	102
Washington township	130	185
Republic city (pt.)	11	25
White Rock township	135	192
Rice County[80]	11 900	12 320
Atlanta township	258	258
Bell township	43	39
Center township	148	175
East Washington township	107	79
Eureka township	93	147
Frederick city	29	39
Farmer township	544	586
Bushton city	388	397
Galt township	74	113
Harrison township	214	232
Lincoln township	881	956
Chase city[80]	753	800
Lyons city	4 152	4 355
Mitchell township	170	163
Odessa township	76	89
Pioneer township	107	137
Raymond township	237	259
Raymond city	132	133
Rockville township	144	154

County Subdivisions	1980	1970
Rice County—Con.		
Sterling city[80]	2 312	2 312
Sterling township[80]	351	284
Union township	774	674
Little River city[80]	529	493
Valley township	311	363
Alden city[80]	214	238
Victoria township	614	587
Geneseo city	496	453
West Washington township	153	188
Wilson township	137	170
Riley County[81]	63 505	56 788
Ashland township	171	136
Bala township	762	793
Leonardville city[81]	437	412
Center township	102	141
Fancy Creek township	126	153
Fort Riley township[81]	15 192	...
Fort Riley North (CDP) (pt.)	14 430	11 252
Grant township	675	338
Jackson township	256	207
Randolph city	131	106
Madison township	991	916
Riley city[81]	779	668
Manhattan city (pt.)[81]	32 482	26 897
Manhattan township[81]	8 924	8 715
May Day township	125	146
Ogden township[81]	2 178	17 168
Ogden city	1 804	1 491
Sherman township	390	234
Swede Creek township	176	199
Wild Cat township	647	397
Zeandale township	308	348
Rooks County[82]	7 006	7 628
Township No. 1[82]	371	...
Woodston city	157	211
Township No. 2[82]	470	...
Stockton city (pt.)	267	214
Township No. 3[82]	1 711	...
Stockton city (pt.)	1 558	1 604
Township No. 4[82]	43	...
Township No. 5[82]	138	...
Township No. 6[82]	86	...
Township No. 7[82]	269	...
Damar city	204	245
Township No. 8[82]	424	...
Palco city	329	398
Township No. 9[82]	76	...
Township No. 10[82]	335	189
Zurich city	185	...
Township No. 11[82]	2 855	...
Plainville city[82]	2 458	2 627
Township No. 12[82]	228	...
Rush County[83]	4 516	5 117
Alexander—Belle Prairie township[83]	210	...
Alexander city[83]	116	129
Banner township	242	321
Timken city	99	123
Big Timber township	234	283
Liebenthal city[83]	163	169
Center township	336	387
Rush Center city	207	237
Garfield township	170	200
Hampton—Fairview township[83]	424	420
McCracken city	292	333
Illinois township	63	125
La Crosse—Brookdale township[83]	1 759	1 774
La Crosse city[83]	1 618	1 583
Lone Star township	370	414
Bison city	279	285
Pioneer township	535	550
Otis city[83]	410	387
Pleasantdale township	63	96
Union township	110	154
Russell County[84]	8 868	9 428
Big Creek township	508	572
Gorham city[84]	355	379
Center township	350	506
Bunker Hill city	124	181
Fairfield township	55	75
Fairview township	660	689
Lucas city[84]	524	524
Grant township	211	234
Lincoln township	146	205
Luray township	373	428
Luray city[84]	295	303
Paradise township	271	353
Paradise city	89	145
Plymouth township	373	430
Dorrance city[84]	220	234
Russell city[84]	5 427	5 371
Russell township[84]	217	204
Waldo township	177	232
Waldo city	75	123
Winterset township	100	129

County Subdivisions	1980	1970
Saline County[85]	48 905	46 592
Cambria township	463	380
New Cambria city	175	160
Dayton township	138	124
Elm Creek township[85]	675	472
Eureka township	607	645
Gypsum city[85]	423	391
Falun—Summit township[85]	223	238
Glendale township	83	83
Greeley township[85]	660	516
Gypsum township	280	188
Liberty township	178	129
Ohio township	402	375
Pleasant Valley township	273	114
Salina city[85]	41 843	37 714
Smoky Hill township[85]	362	2 257
Smoky View township	899	668
Assaria city[85]	414	303
Smolan township[85]	675	1 769
Smolan city[85]	169	175
Solomon township	241	212
Spring Creek township	359	324
Brookville city	259	238
Walnut township	472	308
Washington township	72	76
Scott County[86]	5 782	5 606
Beaver township	377	281
Isbel township	187	159
Keystone township	143	126
Lake township	124	170
Michigan township	161	153
Scott township	4 432	4 312
Scott City city[86]	4 154	4 001
Valley township	358	405
Sedgwick County[87]	366 531	350 694
Afton township	757	488
Attica township	5 019	2 621
Goddard city (pt.)[87]	1 427	955
Delano township[87]	2 148	2 366
Eagle township	738	619
Bentley city[87]	311	260
Erie township	119	79
Garden Plain township	1 449	1 189
Garden Plain city[87]	775	678
Goddard city (pt.)[87]	–	...
Grand River township	479	354
Grant township	2 538	2 071
Valley Center city (pt.)[87]	1 789	1 254
Greeley township	1 115	961
Mount Hope city[87]	791	665
Gypsum township[87]	5 432	5 196
Illinois township	1 297	753
Kechi township[87]	11 584	10 556
Kechi city	288	229
Park City (CDP)	3 778	2 529
Lincoln township	411	364
Minneha township[87]	4 629	'3 766
Eastborough city	854	'1 141
Morton township	1 668	1 443
Cheney city[87]	1 404	1 160
Ninnescah township	2 151	1 867
Clearwater city[87]	1 684	1 435
Ohio township	752	507
Haysville city (pt.)	–	–
Park township[87]	3 585	2 872
Maize city[87]	1 294	785
Payne township[87]	874	541
Riverside township[87]	11 725	10 539
Derby city (pt.)[87]	666	...
Haysville city (pt.)[87]	3 924	2 002
Rockford township	13 919	11 285
Derby city (pt.)[87]	9 120	7 947
Mulvane city (pt.)[87]	2 994	2 063
Salem township	7 697	7 380
Haysville city (pt.)[87]	4 079	'4 523
Sherman township	1 089	1 025
Andale city[87]	538	500
Union township	1 629	1 591
Colwich city[87]	935	879
Valley Center township	2 442	1 858
Sedgwick city (pt.)[87]	128	...
Valley Center city (pt.)[87]	1 511	1 297
Viola township	439	419
Viola city	199	193
Waco township[87]	1 574	1 430
Haysville city (pt.)	3	6
Wichita city[87]	279 272	276 554
Seward County[88]	17 071	15 744
Fargo township	961	652
Kismet city[88]	368	294
Liberal city[88]	14 911	'13 862
Liberal township[88]	803	'916
Seward township[88]	396	201

County Subdivisions	1980	1970
Shawnee County[89]	154 916	155 322
Auburn township	1 885	1 066
Auburn city[89]	890	261
Dover township	1 124	976
Willard city (pt.)[89]	123	124
Grove township	214	190
Menoken township	987	912
Mission township[89]	5 082	2 473
Monmouth township	1 645	1 113
Rossville township	1 596	1 376
Rossville city[89]	1 045	934
Silver Lake township	1 828	1 140
Silver Lake city[89]	1 350	811
Soldier township	11 017	7 225
Tecumseh township[89]	6 314	3 829
Topeka city[89]	115 266	125 011
Topeka township[89]	6 034	2 199
Williamsport township[89]	1 924	7 812
Sheridan County[90]	3 544	3 859
Adell township	46	135
Bloomfield township	56	52
Bow Creek township	71	92
East Saline township	106	135
Kenneth township	1 640	1 537
Hoxie city[90]	1 462	1 419
Logan township	213	197
Parnell township	124	136
Prairie Dog township	81	117
Sheridan township	386	406
Selden city	266	271
Solomon township	299	392
Spring Brook township	156	207
Union township	66	107
Valley township	162	177
West Saline township	138	169
Sherman County[91]	7 759	7 792
Goodland city[91]	5 708	5 510
Grant township	135	186
Iowa township	47	58
Itasca township[91]	327	266
Lincoln township	169	157
Llanos township	71	97
Logan township[91]	220	149
McPherson township	81	113
Shermanville township	41	86
Smoky township	113	119
State Line township	332	451
Kanorado city[91]	217	278
Union township	69	67
Voltaire township[91]	287	378
Washington township	159	155
Smith County[92]	5 947	6 757
Banner township	52	73
Beaver township	91	108
Blaine township	90	100
Cedar township	774	801
Kensington city[92]	681	653
Center township	2 413	2 549
Smith Center city[92]	2 240	2 389
Cora township	86	111
Crystal Plains township	64	72
Dor township	67	78
Garfield township	46	63
German township	40	65
Harlan township	145	183
Harvey township	167	191
Cedar city	53	46
Houston township	297	328
Gaylord city	203	211
Lane township	187	219
Athol city	90	108
Lincoln township	126	165
Logan township	89	109
Martin township	51	72
Oak township	565	700
Lebanon city	440	517
Pawnee township	82	112
Pleasant township	83	130
Swan township	72	75
Valley township	106	132
Washington township	93	103
Webster township	79	118
White Rock township	82	100
Stafford County[93]	5 694	5 943
Albano township	76	81
Byron township	106	115
Clear Creek township	60	62
Cleveland township	91	124
Douglas township	165	179
Radium city (pt.)	34	39
East Cooper township	77	94
Fairview township	122	154
Farmington township	614	563
Macksville city	546	484
Hayes township	275	306

County Subdivisions	1980	1970
Stafford County—Con.		
Hayes township—Con.		
Hudson city	157	181
Lincoln township	146	169
Radium city (pt.)	13	16
North Seward township	224	211
Seward city	88	66
Ohio township	453	498
St. John city (pt.)	357	395
Putnam township	39	33
Richland township	80	77
Rose Valley township	93	96
St. John township	1 221	1 185
St. John city (pt.)[93]	1 144	1 082
South Seward township	85	147
Stafford township	1 574	1 587
Stafford city	1 425	1 414
Union township	58	60
West Cooper township	74	106
York township	61	96
Stanton County[94]	2 339	2 287
Big Bow township	442	536
Manter township	426	479
Manter city[94]	205	219
Stanton township	1 471	1 272
Johnson City city	1 244	1 038
Stevens County[95]	4 736	4 198
Banner township	199	181
Center township	3 521	3 118
Hugoton city[95]	3 165	2 739
Harmony township	178	146
Moscow township	556	482
Moscow city	228	228
Voorhees township	128	148
West Center township	154	123
Sumner County[96]	24 928	23 553
Avon township	278	215
Belle Plaine township	2 926	2 182
Belle Plaine city[96]	1 706	1 553
Bluff township	136	196
Caldwell city	1 401	1 540
Caldwell township	313	329
Chikaskia township	112	121
Conway township	1 244	1 118
Conway Springs city (pt.)	953	849
Creek township	177	244
Dixon township	783	801
Argonia city[96]	587	591
Downs township	174	222
Eden township	324	285
Falls township	252	278
Gore township	2 229	1 789
Mulvane city (pt.)[96]	1 260	1 122
Greene township	92	107
Guelph township	171	196
Harmon township	237	185
Illinois township	130	134
Jackson township	175	171
London township	603	400
Morris township	48	63
Osborn township	278	303
Mayfield city	128	110
Oxford township	1 346	1 332
Oxford city	1 125	1 113
Palestine township	271	207
Ryan township	239	316
Milan city[96]	135	162
Seventy-Six township	248	271
South Haven township	733	726
Hunnewell city	86	77
South Haven city	439	413
Springdale township	565	526
Conway Springs city (pt.)[96]	360	304
Sumner township	180	184
Valverde township	140	147
Walton township	454	480
Geuda Springs city (pt.)	202	212
Wellington city[96]	8 212	8 072
Wellington township[96]	457	413
Thomas County[97]	8 451	7 501
Barrett township	178	160
Colby city[97]	5 544	4 658
East Hale township	146	197
Kingery township	113	148
Lacey township	158	143
Gem city	101	80
Menlo township	125	145
Menlo city	42	48
Morgan township[97]	568	455
North Randall township	117	121
Rovohl township	171	190
Smith township	280	304
Rexford city	204	231
South Randall township	315	276
Oakley city (pt.)[97]	75	...
Summers township	212	184

County Subdivisions

County Subdivisions	1980	1970
Thomas County—Con.		
Wendell township	114	118
West Hale township	410	402
Brewster city	327	320
Trego County[98]	4 165	4 436
Collyer township	523	596
Collyer city	151	182
Franklin township	130	182
Glencoe township	94	113
Ogallah township	288	326
Riverside township	196	265
Wa Keeney township	2 792	2 798
Wa Keeney city[98]	2 388	2 334
Wilcox township	142	156
Wabaunsee County[99]	6 867	6 397
Alma township	1 201	1 161
Alma city[99]	925	905
Farmer township	118	125
Garfield township	619	606
Alta Vista city[99]	430	402
Kaw township	257	225
Maple Hill township	777	607
Maple Hill city	381	327
Willard city (pt.)[99]	5	...
Mill Creek township	311	189
Mission Creek township	453	412
Newbury township	941	877
McFarland city[99]	242	209
Paxico city	168	216
Plumb township	654	599
Harveyville city[99]	280	279
Rock Creek township	113	155
Wabaunsee township	455	461
Washington township	114	145
Wilmington township	854	835
Eskridge city	603	589
Wallace County[100]	2 045	2 215
Harrison township	114	140
Morton township	73	78
North township	12	12
Sharon Springs township	1 264	1 321
Sharon Springs city[100]	982	1 012
Wallace township	218	280
Wallace city	86	112
Weskan township	364	384
Washington County[101]	8 543	9 249
Barnes township	394	351
Barnes city[101]	257	209
Brantford township	129	148
Charleston township	129	176
Clifton township	567	589
Clifton city (pt.)[101]	371	359
Vining city (pt.)	30	36
Coleman township	104	133
Farmington township	216	268
Franklin township	231	266
Hollenberg city[101]	57	47
Grant township	55	109
Greenleaf township	585	600
Greenleaf city[101]	462	448
Haddam township	385	477
Haddam city	239	289
Hanover township	1 071	1 073
Hanover city[101]	802	793
Highland township	80	92
Independence township	229	294
Kimeo township	124	138
Lincoln township	130	178
Linn township	686	643
Linn city[101]	483	388
Little Blue township	152	169
Logan township	168	171
Lowe township	120	132
Mill Creek township	333	397
Morrowville city[101]	180	201
Sheridan township	160	186
Sherman township	342	382
Palmer city	149	166
Strawberry township	227	230
Union township	192	208
Mahaska city[101]	119	122
Washington city[101]	1 488	1 584
Washington township[101]	246	255
Wichita County[102]	3 041	3 274
Leoti township[102]	3 041	2 360
Leoti city[102]	1 869	1 916
Wilson County[103]	12 128	11 317
Cedar township	862	717
Altoona city[103]	564	475
Center township[103]	684	649
Chetopa township	230	238
Clifton township	541	468
Buffalo city	386	321
Colfax township	525	402
Duck Creek township	131	126
Fall River township	392	384

County Subdivisions	1980	1970
Wilson County—Con.		
Fall River township—Con.		
New Albany city	78	59
Fredonia city[103]	3 047	3 080
Guilford township	236	218
Benedict city	111	91
Neodesha city[103]	3 414	3 295
Neodesha township[103]	700	587
Newark township	235	218
Pleasant Valley township	243	216
Prairie township	113	162
Talleyrand township	273	243
Verdigris township	427	256
Coyville city	98	93
Webster township	75	58
Woodson County[104]	4 600	4 789
Belmont township	135	124
Center township[104]	309	391
Eminence township	149	158
Everett township	174	178
Liberty township	205	223
Neosho Falls township	365	490
Neosho Falls city	157	184
North township	123	117
Owl Creek township	253	258
Perry township	147	150
Toronto township	742	733
Toronto city	466	431
Yates Center city[104]	1 998	1 967
Wyandotte County[105]	172 335	186 845
Bonner Springs city[105]	6 266	³3 884
Delaware township[105]	153	³3 550
Edwardsville city[105]	3 364	619
Kansas City city[105]	161 087	168 213
Lake Quivira city (pt.)[105]	58	...
Prairie township[105]	1 346	1 934
Shawnee township.[105]	61	1 810

KENTUCKY

The word "Kentucky" is of Indian origin and has been variously defined as signifying "prairie or meadow land," "the hunting ground," "at the head of a river," "river of blood," and "the dark and bloody ground." The last definition is the most generally accepted.

The region now constituting Kentucky was included within the limits of Virginia by the charters granted that colony by the English crown in 1609 and in 1612. The French also laid claim to this territory, together with the rest of the Mississippi Valley on account of the explorations made by Marquette, Joliet, La Salle, and others in the latter part of the seventeenth century. All French claims to land east of the Mississippi were, however, relinquished in favor of Great Britain in 1763, at the close of the French and Indian War. In 1768, by the treaty made at Fort Stanwix, N.Y., the Six Nations together with certain other dependent tribes of Indians ceded to Great Britain their rights to territory south of the Ohio River, including all but a small part of the area now known as Kentucky.

The first white man to visit what is now Kentucky was probably La Salle, a French explorer, who is said to have sailed down the Ohio to the Louisville Rapids in 1669. Capt. Thomas Batts, of Virginia, may also have reached Kentucky on his trip of exploration to the western wilderness in 1671. The first white men known to have discovered this region, however, were the French missionaries, Marquette and Joliet, who in 1673 passed along the western boundary of Kentucky on their trip down the Mississippi. The first extensive explorations within the state were made in 1750 by Dr. Thomas Walker, and in 1751 by Christopher Gist. They were followed within the next 20 years by a number of explorers and surveyors, the most prominent among whom was Daniel Boone. In 1774 settlement began at various points, notably at Harrodsburg, and in 1775 Boonesborough was founded and fortified.

In 1775 a code of laws for the newly settled region was drawn up by the settlers, but this was not authorized by the legislature of Virginia, and in the following year Kentucky County, with Harrodsburg as the county seat, was organized from a part of Fincastle County, Va. Eight years later the three counties then existing in this region were united into Kentucky district, with a district court of its own.

In spite of the hostility of the Indians the Kentucky settlements grew, and in 1786, 12 years after the period of settlement began, Virginia passed the first of four successive enabling acts giving conditional consent to the organization of Kentucky as a separate state. In 1792, under authority of an act passed by Congress in the preceding year, Kentucky adopted a constitution, and with its present boundaries was admitted to the Union.

COUNTY LOCATION INDEX

Adair	D-5	Grant	C-6	Mason	C-6
Allen	E-4	Graves	E-2	Meade	C-4
Anderson	C-5	Grayson	D-4	Menifee	C-7
Ballard	E-2	Green	D-5	Mercer	D-5
Barren	E-4	Greenup	C-7	Metcalfe	E-5
Bath	C-6	Hancock	D-4	Monroe	E-5
Bell	E-7	Hardin	D-4	Montgomery	C-6
Boone	B-5	Harlan	E-7	Morgan	C-7
Bourbon	C-6	Harrison	C-6	Muhlenberg	D-3
Boyd	C-7	Hart	D-4	Nelson	D-5
Boyle	D-5	Henderson	D-3	Nicholas	C-6
Bracken	C-6	Henry	C-5	Ohio	D-4
Breathitt	D-7	Hickman	E-2	Oldham	C-5
Breckinridge	D-4	Hopkins	D-3	Owen	C-5
Bullitt	C-5	Jackson	D-6	Owsley	D-6
Butler	D-4	Jefferson	C-5	Pendleton	C-6
Caldwell	D-3	Jessamine	C-6	Perry	D-7
Calloway	E-2	Johnson	C-7	Pike	D-8
Campbell	B-6	Kenton	B-6	Powell	D-6
Carlisle	E-2	Knott	D-7	Pulaski	D-6
Carroll	C-5	Knox	E-6	Robertson	C-6
Carter	C-7	Larue	D-5	Rockcastle	D-6
Casey	D-5	Laurel	D-6	Rowan	C-7
Christian	E-3	Lawrence	C-7	Russell	E-5
Clark	C-6	Lee	D-6	Scott	C-6
Clay	D-6	Leslie	D-7	Shelby	C-5
Clinton	E-5	Letcher	D-7	Simpson	E-4
Crittenden	D-3	Lewis	C-7	Spencer	C-5
Cumberland	E-5	Lincoln	D-6	Taylor	D-5
Daviess	D-3	Livingston	D-2	Todd	E-3
Edmonson	D-4	Logan	E-4	Trigg	E-3
Elliott	C-7	Lyon	E-3	Trimble	C-5
Estill	D-6	McCracken	E-2	Union	D-3
Fayette	C-6	McCreary	E-6	Warren	E-4
Fleming	C-6	McLean	D-3	Washington	D-5
Floyd	D-7	Madison	D-6	Wayne	E-6
Franklin	C-5	Magoffin	D-7	Webster	D-3
Fulton	E-2	Marion	D-5	Whitley	E-6
Gallatin	B-5	Marshall	E-2	Wolfe	D-7
Garrard	D-6	Martin	C-8	Woodford	C-6

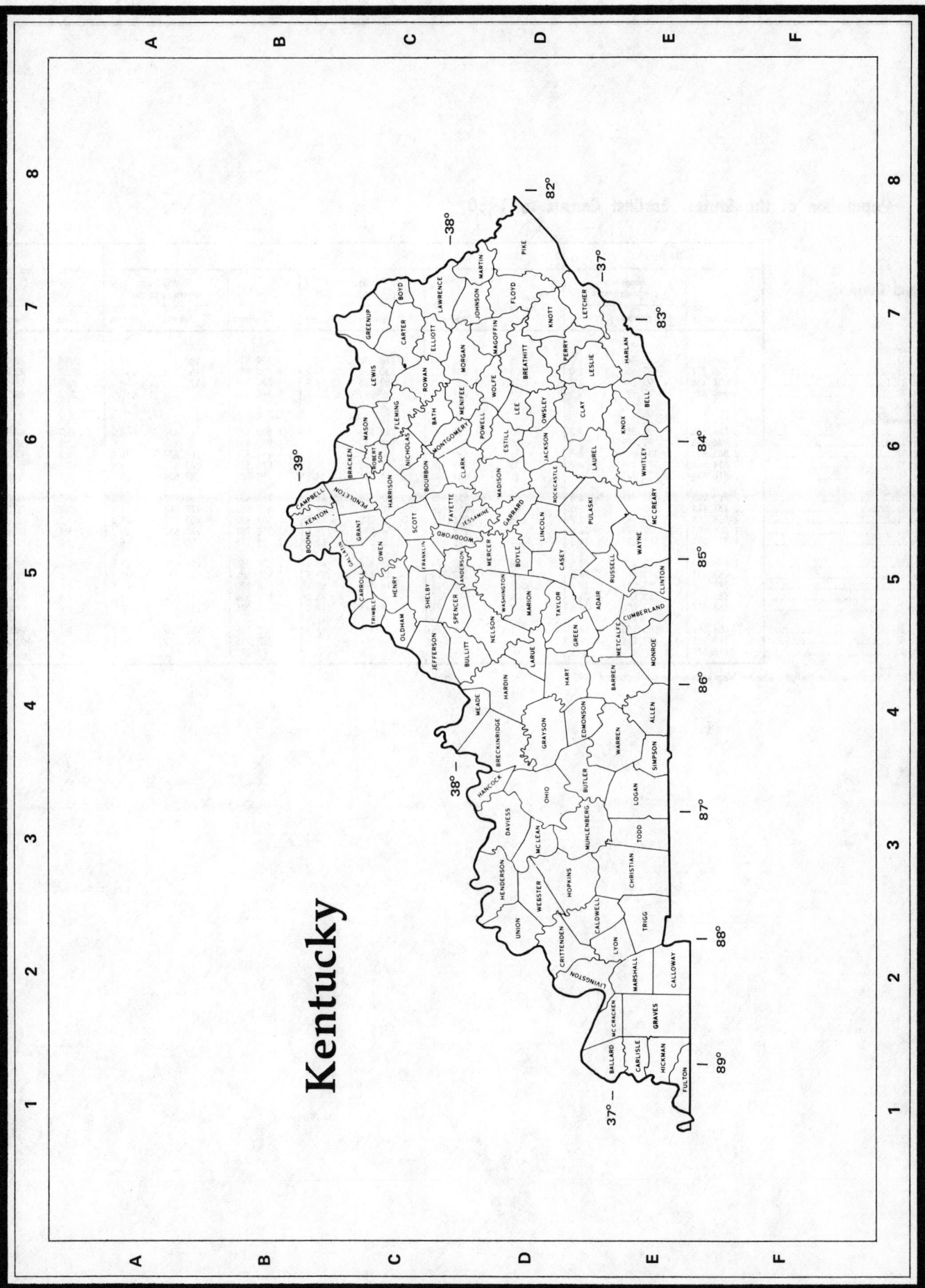

Kentucky

Population of the State: Earliest Census to 1980

Urban and Rural

	The State			Urban				Rural				Percent of total population	
	Total population	Change from preceding census		Places of 2,500 or more	Population	Change from preceding census		Population	Change from preceding census			Urban	Rural
		Number	Percent			Number	Percent		Number	Percent			
Current urban definition:													
1980 (Apr. 1)	3 660 777	440 066	13.7	125	1 862 183	178 130	10.6	1 798 594	263 941	17.2		50.9	49.1
1970 (Apr. 1)	¹3 220 711	182 555	6.0	103	1 684 053	330 838	24.4	1 534 653	−150 288	−8.9		52.3	47.7
1960 (Apr. 1)	3 038 156	93 350	3.2	88	1 353 215	269 145	24.8	1 684 941	−175 795	−9.4		44.5	55.5
1950 (Apr. 1)	2 944 806	99 179	3.5	74	1 084 070	...	...	1 860 736	...	...		36.8	63.2
Previous urban definition:													
1960 (Apr. 1)	3 038 156	93 350	3.2	83	1 144 583	158 844	16.1	1 893 573	−65 494	−3.3		37.7	62.3
1950 (Apr. 1)	2 944 806	99 179	3.5	68	985 739	136 412	16.1	1 959 067	−37 233	−1.9		33.5	66.5
1940 (Apr. 1)	2 845 627	231 038	8.8	56	849 327	50 301	6.3	1 996 300	180 737	10.0		29.8	70.2
1930 (Apr. 1)	2 614 589	197 959	8.2	53	799 026	165 483	26.1	1 815 563	32 476	1.8		30.6	69.4
1920 (Jan. 1)	2 416 630	126 725	5.5	51	633 543	78 101	14.1	1 783 087	48 624	2.8		26.2	73.8
1910 (Apr. 15)	2 289 905	142 731	6.6	40	555 442	87 774	18.8	1 734 463	54 957	3.3		24.3	75.7
1900 (June 1)	2 147 174	288 539	15.5	34	467 668	110 955	31.1	1 679 506	177 584	11.8		21.8	78.2
1890 (June 1)	1 858 635	209 945	12.7	26	356 713	106 790	42.7	1 501 922	103 155	7.4		19.2	80.8
1880 (June 1)	1 648 690	327 679	24.8	17	249 923	54 027	27.6	1 398 767	273 652	24.3		15.2	84.8
1870 (June 1)	1 321 011	165 327	14.3	14	195 896	75 272	62.4	1 125 115	90 055	8.7		14.8	85.2
1860 (June 1)	1 155 684	173 279	17.6	8	120 624	46 820	63.4	1 035 060	126 459	13.9		10.4	89.6
1850 (June 1)	982 405	202 577	26.0	6	73 804	42 856	138.5	908 601	159 721	21.3		7.5	92.5
1840 (June 1)	779 828	91 911	13.4	3	30 948	14 581	89.1	748 880	77 330	11.5		4.0	96.0
1830 (June 1)	687 917	123 600	21.9	2	16 367	7 076	76.2	671 550	116 524	21.0		2.4	97.6
1820 (Aug. 7)	564 317	157 806	38.8	2	9 291	4 965	114.8	555 026	152 841	38.0		1.6	98.4
1810 (Aug. 6)	406 511	185 556	84.0	1	4 326	4 326	...	402 185	181 230	82.0		1.1	98.9
1800 (Aug. 4)	220 955	147 278	199.9	–	–	–	–	220 955	147 278	199.9		–	100.0
1790 (Aug. 2)	73 677	...	...	–	–	...	...	73 677	...	...		–	100.0

NOTE: 1790 population is that of the part of Virginia taken to form Kentucky in 1792.

ADAIR

1810	6,011
1820	8,765
1830	8,217
1840	8,466
1850	9,898
1860	9,509
1870	11,065
1880	13,078
1890	13,721
1900	14,888
1910	16,503
1920	17,289
1930	16,401
1940	18,566
1950	17,603
1960	14,699
1970	13,037
1980	15,233

ALLEN

1820	5,327
1830	6,485
1840	7,329
1850	8,742
1860	9,187
1870	10,296
1880	12,089
1890	13,692
1900	14,657
1910	14,882
1920	16,761
1930	15,180
1940	15,496
1950	13,787
1960	12,269
1970	12,598
1980	14,128

ANDERSON

1830	4,520
1840	5,452
1850	6,260
1860	7,404
1870	5,449
1880	9,361
1890	10,610
1900	10,051
1910	10,146
1920	9,982
1930	8,494
1940	8,936
1950	8,984
1960	8,618
1970	9,358
1980	12,567

BALLARD

1850	5,496
1860	8,692
1870	12,576
1880	14,378
1890	8,390
1900	10,761
1910	12,690
1920	12,045
1930	9,910
1940	9,480
1950	8,545
1960	8,291
1970	8,276
1980	8,798

BARREN

1800	4,784
1810	11,286
1820	10,328
1830	15,079
1840	17,288
1850	20,240
1860	16,665
1870	17,780
1880	22,321
1890	21,490
1900	23,197
1910	25,293
1920	25,356
1930	25,844
1940	27,559
1950	28,461
1960	28,303
1970	28,677
1980	34,009

BATH

1820	7,961
1830	8,799
1840	9,763
1850	12,115
1860	12,113
1870	10,145
1880	11,982
1890	12,813
1900	14,734
1910	13,988
1920	11,996
1930	11,075
1940	11,451
1950	10,410
1960	9,114
1970	9,235
1980	10,025

BELL

1870	3,731
1880	6,055
1890	10,312
1900	15,701
1910	28,447
1920	33,988
1930	38,747
1940	43,812
1950	47,602
1960	35,336
1970	31,121
1980	34,330

BOONE

1800	1,534
1810	3,608
1820	6,542
1830	9,075
1840	10,034
1850	11,185
1860	11,196
1870	10,696
1880	11,996
1890	12,246
1900	11,170
1910	9,420
1920	9,572
1930	9,598
1940	10,820
1950	13,015
1960	21,940
1970	32,812

1980	45,842

BOURBON

1790	7,837
1800	12,825
1810	18,009
1820	17,664
1830	18,436
1840	14,478
1850	14,466
1860	14,860
1870	14,863
1880	15,956
1890	16,976
1900	18,069
1910	17,462
1920	18,418
1930	18,060
1940	17,932
1950	17,752
1960	18,178
1970	18,476
1980	19,405

BOYD

1860	6,044
1870	8,573
1880	12,165
1890	14,033
1900	18,834
1910	23,444
1920	29,281
1930	43,849
1940	45,938
1950	49,949
1960	52,163
1970	52,376
1980	55,513

BOYLE

1850	9,116
1860	9,304
1870	9,515
1880	11,930
1890	12,948
1900	13,817
1910	14,668
1920	14,998
1930	16,282
1940	17,075
1950	20,532
1960	21,257
1970	21,861
1980	25,066

BRACKEN

1800	2,606
1810	3,706
1820	5,280
1830	6,518
1840	7,053
1850	8,903
1860	11,021
1870	11,409
1880	13,509
1890	12,369
1900	12,137
1910	10,308
1920	10,210
1930	9,616
1940	9,389
1950	8,424

1960	7,422
1970	7,227
1980	7,738

BREATHITT

1840	2,195
1850	3,785
1860	4,980
1870	5,672
1880	7,742
1890	8,705
1900	14,322
1910	17,540
1920	20,614
1930	21,143
1940	23,946
1950	19,964
1960	15,490
1970	14,221
1980	17,004

BRECKINRIDGE

1800	807
1810	3,430
1820	7,485
1830	7,345
1840	8,944
1850	10,593
1860	13,236
1870	13,440
1880	17,486
1890	18,976
1900	20,534
1910	21,034
1920	19,652
1930	17,368
1940	17,744
1950	15,528
1960	14,734
1970	14,221
1980	16,861

BULLITT

1800	3,542
1810	4,311
1820	5,831
1830	5,652
1840	6,334
1850	6,774
1860	7,289
1870	7,781
1880	8,521
1890	8,291
1900	9,602
1910	9,487
1920	9,328
1930	8,868
1940	9,511
1950	11,349
1960	15,726
1970	26,090
1980	43,346

BUTLER

1810	2,181
1820	3,083
1830	3,058
1840	3,898
1850	5,755
1860	7,927
1870	9,404
1880	12,181

1890	13,956
1900	15,896
1910	15,805
1920	15,197
1930	12,620
1940	14,371
1950	11,309
1960	9,586
1970	9,723
1980	11,064

CALDWELL

1810	4,268
1820	9,022
1830	8,324
1840	10,365
1850	13,048
1860	9,318
1870	10,826
1880	11,282
1890	13,186
1900	14,510
1910	14,063
1920	13,975
1930	13,781
1940	14,499
1950	13,199
1960	13,073
1970	13,179
1980	13,473

CALLOWAY

1830	5,164
1840	9,794
1850	8,096
1860	9,915
1870	9,410
1880	13,295
1890	14,675
1900	17,633
1910	19,867
1920	20,802
1930	17,662
1940	19,041
1950	20,147
1960	20,972
1970	27,692
1980	30,031

CAMPBELL

1800	1,903
1810	3,473
1820	7,022
1830	9,883
1840	5,214
1850	13,127
1860	20,909
1870	27,406
1880	37,440
1890	44,208
1900	54,223
1910	59,369
1920	61,869
1930	73,391
1940	71,918
1950	76,196
1960	86,803
1970	88,704
1980	83,317

CARLISLE

1890	7,612

1900	10,195			
1910	9,048			
1920	8,231			
1930	7,363			
1940	7,650			
1950	6,206			
1960	5,608			
1970	5,354			
1980	5,487			

CARROLL

1840	3,966
1850	5,526
1860	6,578
1870	6,189
1880	8,953
1890	9,266
1900	9,825
1910	8,110
1920	8,346
1930	8,155
1940	8,657
1950	8,517
1960	7,978
1970	8,523
1980	9,270

CARTER

1840	2,905
1850	6,241
1860	8,516
1870	7,509
1880	12,345
1890	17,204
1900	20,228
1910	21,996
1920	22,474
1930	23,839
1940	25,545
1950	22,559
1960	20,817
1970	19,850
1980	25,060

CASEY

1810	3,285
1820	4,349
1830	4,342
1840	4,939
1850	6,556
1860	6,466
1870	8,884
1880	10,983
1890	11,848
1900	15,144
1910	15,479
1920	17,213
1930	16,747
1940	19,962
1950	17,446
1960	14,327
1970	12,930
1980	14,818

CHRISTIAN

1800	2,318
1810	11,020
1820	10,459
1830	12,684
1840	15,587
1850	19,580
1860	21,627

1870	23,227
1880	31,682
1890	34,118
1900	37,962
1910	38,845
1920	35,883
1930	34,283
1940	36,129
1950	42,359
1960	56,904
1970	56,224
1980	66,878

CLARK

1800	7,653
1810	11,519
1820	11,449
1830	13,051
1840	10,802
1850	12,683
1860	11,484
1870	10,882
1880	12,115
1890	15,434
1900	16,694
1910	17,987
1920	17,901
1930	17,640
1940	17,988
1950	18,898
1960	21,075
1970	24,090
1980	28,322

CLAY

1810	2,398
1820	4,393
1830	3,548
1840	4,607
1850	5,421
1860	6,652
1870	8,297
1880	10,222
1890	12,447
1900	15,364
1910	17,789
1920	19,795
1930	18,526
1940	23,901
1950	23,116
1960	20,748
1970	18,481
1980	22,752

CLINTON

1840	3,863
1850	4,889
1860	5,781
1870	6,497
1880	7,212
1890	7,047
1900	7,871
1910	9,153
1920	8,589
1930	9,004
1940	10,279
1950	10,605
1960	8,886
1970	8,174
1980	9,321

CRITTENDEN

1850	6,351
1860	8,796
1870	9,381
1880	11,688
1890	13,119
1900	15,191
1910	13,296
1920	13,125
1930	11,931
1940	12,115
1950	10,818
1960	8,648
1970	8,493
1980	9,207

CUMBERLAND

1800	3,284
1810	6,191
1820	8,058
1830	8,624
1840	6,090
1850	7,005
1860	7,340
1870	7,690
1880	8,894
1890	8,452
1900	8,962
1910	9,846
1920	10,648
1930	10,204
1940	11,923
1950	9,209
1960	7,835
1970	6,850
1980	7,289

DAVIESS

1820	3,876
1830	5,209
1840	8,331
1850	12,362
1860	15,549
1870	20,714
1880	27,730
1890	33,120
1900	38,667
1910	41,020
1920	40,733
1930	43,779
1940	52,335
1950	57,241
1960	70,588
1970	79,486
1980	85,949

EDMONSON

1830	2,642
1840	2,914
1850	4,088
1860	4,645
1870	4,459
1880	7,222
1890	8,005
1900	10,080
1910	10,469
1920	10,894
1930	11,475
1940	11,344
1950	9,376
1960	8,085
1970	8,751
1980	9,962

ELLIOTT

1870	4,433
1880	6,567
1890	9,214
1900	10,387
1910	9,814
1920	8,887
1930	7,571
1940	8,713
1950	7,085
1960	6,330
1970	5,993
1980	6,908

ESTILL

1810	2,082
1820	3,507
1830	4,618
1840	5,535
1850	5,985
1860	6,886
1870	9,198
1880	9,860
1890	10,836
1900	11,669
1910	12,273
1920	15,569
1930	17,079
1940	17,978
1950	14,677
1960	12,466
1970	12,752
1980	14,495

FAYETTE

1790	18,410
1800	14,028
1810	21,370
1820	23,250
1830	25,098
1840	22,194
1850	22,735
1860	22,599
1870	26,656
1880	29,023
1890	35,698
1900	42,071
1910	47,715
1920	54,664
1930	68,543
1940	78,899
1950	100,746
1960	131,906
1970	174,323
1980	204,165

FLEMING

1800	5,016
1810	8,947
1820	12,186
1830	13,499
1840	13,268
1850	13,914
1860	12,489
1870	13,398
1880	15,221
1890	16,078
1900	17,074
1910	16,066
1920	15,614
1930	12,931
1940	13,327
1950	11,962

1960	10,890
1970	11,366
1980	12,323

FLOYD

1800	478
1810	3,485
1820	8,207
1830	4,347
1840	6,302
1850	5,714
1860	6,388
1870	7,877
1880	10,176
1890	11,256
1900	15,522
1910	18,263
1920	27,427
1930	41,942
1940	52,986
1950	53,500
1960	41,642
1970	35,889
1980	48,764

FRANKLIN

1800	5,078
1810	8,013
1820	11,024
1830	9,254
1840	9,420
1850	12,462
1860	12,694
1870	15,300
1880	18,699
1890	21,267
1900	20,852
1910	21,125
1920	19,357
1930	21,064
1940	23,308
1950	25,933
1960	29,421
1970	34,481
1980	41,830

FULTON

1850	4,446
1860	5,317
1870	6,161
1880	7,977
1890	10,005
1900	11,546
1910	14,114
1920	15,197
1930	14,927
1940	15,413
1950	13,668
1960	11,256
1970	10,183
1980	8,971

GALLATIN

1800	1,291
1810	3,307
1820	7,075
1830	6,674
1840	4,003
1850	5,137
1860	5,056
1870	5,074
1880	4,832

1890	4,611
1900	5,163
1910	4,697
1920	4,664
1930	4,437
1940	4,307
1950	3,969
1960	3,867
1970	4,134
1980	4,842

GARRARD

1800	6,186
1810	9,186
1820	10,851
1830	11,871
1840	10,480
1850	10,237
1860	10,531
1870	10,376
1880	11,704
1890	11,138
1900	12,042
1910	11,894
1920	12,503
1930	11,562
1940	11,910
1950	11,029
1960	9,747
1970	9,457
1980	10,853

GRANT

1820	1,805
1830	2,986
1840	4,192
1850	6,531
1860	8,356
1870	9,529
1880	13,083
1890	12,671
1900	13,239
1910	10,581
1920	10,435
1930	9,876
1940	9,876
1950	9,809
1960	9,489
1970	9,999
1980	13,308

GRAVES

1830	2,504
1840	7,465
1850	11,397
1860	16,233
1870	19,398
1880	24,138
1890	28,534
1900	33,204
1910	33,539
1920	32,483
1930	30,778
1940	31,763
1950	31,364
1960	30,021
1970	30,939
1980	34,049

GRAYSON

1810	2,301
1820	4,055

1830	3,880
1840	4,461
1850	6,837
1860	7,982
1870	11,580
1880	15,784
1890	18,688
1900	19,878
1910	19,958
1920	19,927
1930	17,055
1940	17,562
1950	17,063
1960	15,834
1970	16,445
1980	20,854

GREEN

1800	6,096
1810	6,735
1820	11,943
1830	13,138
1840	14,212
1850	9,060
1860	8,806
1870	9,379
1880	11,871
1890	11,463
1900	12,255
1910	11,871
1920	11,391
1930	11,401
1940	12,321
1950	11,261
1960	11,249
1970	10,350
1980	11,043

GREENUP

1810	2,369
1820	4,311
1830	5,852
1840	6,297
1850	9,654
1860	8,760
1870	11,463
1880	13,371
1890	11,911
1900	15,432
1910	18,475
1920	20,062
1930	24,554
1940	24,917
1950	24,887
1960	29,238
1970	33,192
1980	39,132

HANCOCK

1830	1,515
1840	2,581
1850	3,853
1860	6,213
1870	6,591
1880	8,563
1890	9,214
1900	8,914
1910	8,512
1920	6,985
1930	6,147
1940	6,807
1950	6,009
1960	5,330
1970	7,080

1980	7,742

HARDIN

1800	3,653
1810	7,531
1820	10,498
1830	12,849
1840	16,357
1850	14,525
1860	15,189
1870	15,705
1880	22,564
1890	21,304
1900	22,937
1910	22,696
1920	24,287
1930	20,913
1940	29,108
1950	50,312
1960	67,789
1970	78,421
1980	88,917

HARLAN

1820	1,961
1830	2,929
1840	3,015
1850	4,268
1860	5,494
1870	4,415
1880	5,278
1890	6,197
1900	9,838
1910	10,566
1920	31,546
1930	64,557
1940	75,275
1950	71,751
1960	51,107
1970	37,370
1980	41,889

HARRISON

1800	4,350
1810	7,752
1820	12,278
1830	13,234
1840	12,472
1850	13,064
1860	13,779
1870	12,993
1880	16,504
1890	16,914
1900	18,570
1910	16,873
1920	15,798
1930	14,850
1940	15,124
1950	13,736
1960	13,704
1970	14,158
1980	15,166

HART

1820	4,184
1830	5,191
1840	7,031
1850	9,093
1860	10,348
1870	13,687
1880	17,133
1890	16,439

1900	18,390
1910	18,173
1920	18,544
1930	16,169
1940	17,239
1950	15,321
1960	14,119
1970	13,980
1980	15,402

HENDERSON

1800	1,468
1810	4,703
1820	5,714
1830	6,659
1840	9,548
1850	12,171
1860	14,262
1870	18,457
1880	24,515
1890	29,536
1900	32,907
1910	29,352
1920	27,609
1930	26,295
1940	27,020
1950	30,715
1960	33,519
1970	36,031
1980	40,849

HENRY

1800	3,258
1810	6,777
1820	10,816
1830	11,387
1840	10,015
1850	11,442
1860	11,949
1870	11,066
1880	14,492
1890	14,164
1900	14,620
1910	13,716
1920	13,411
1930	12,546
1940	12,220
1950	11,394
1960	10,978
1970	10,910
1980	12,740

HICKMAN

1830	5,198
1840	8,968
1850	4,791
1860	7,008
1870	8,453
1880	10,651
1890	11,637
1900	11,745
1910	11,750
1920	10,244
1930	8,725
1940	9,142
1950	7,778
1960	6,747
1970	6,264
1980	6,065

HOPKINS

1810	2,964

1820	5,322
1830	6,763
1840	9,171
1850	12,441
1860	11,875
1870	13,827
1880	19,122
1890	23,505
1900	30,995
1910	34,291
1920	34,133
1930	37,449
1940	37,789
1950	38,815
1960	38,458
1970	38,167
1980	46,174

JACKSON

1860	3,087
1870	4,547
1880	6,678
1890	8,261
1900	10,561
1910	10,734
1920	11,687
1930	10,467
1940	16,339
1950	13,101
1960	10,677
1970	10,005
1980	11,996

JEFFERSON

1790	4,765
1800	8,754
1810	13,399
1820	20,768
1830	23,979
1840	36,346
1850	59,831
1860	89,404
1870	118,953
1880	146,010
1890	188,598
1900	232,549
1910	262,920
1920	286,369
1930	355,350
1940	385,392
1950	484,615
1960	610,947
1970	695,055
1980	685,004

JESSAMINE

1800	5,461
1810	8,377
1820	9,297
1830	9,960
1840	9,396
1850	10,249
1860	9,465
1870	8,638
1880	10,864
1890	11,248
1900	11,925
1910	12,613
1920	12,205
1930	12,431
1940	12,174
1950	12,458
1960	13,625
1970	17,539

1980	26,146

JOHNSON

1850	3,873
1860	5,306
1870	7,494
1880	9,155
1890	11,027
1900	13,730
1910	17,482
1920	19,622
1930	22,968
1940	25,771
1950	23,846
1960	19,748
1970	17,539
1980	24,432

KENTON

1840	7,816
1850	17,038
1860	25,467
1870	36,096
1880	53,983
1890	54,161
1900	63,591
1910	70,355
1920	73,453
1930	93,534
1940	93,139
1950	104,254
1960	120,700
1970	129,440
1980	137,058

KNOTT

1890	5,438
1900	8,704
1910	10,791
1920	11,655
1930	15,230
1940	20,007
1950	20,320
1960	17,362
1970	14,698
1980	17,940

KNOX

1800	1,109
1810	5,875
1820	3,661
1830	4,315
1840	5,722
1850	7,050
1860	7,707
1870	8,294
1880	10,587
1890	13,762
1900	17,372
1910	22,116
1920	24,172
1930	26,266
1940	31,029
1950	30,409
1960	25,258
1970	23,689
1980	30,239

LARUE

1850	5,859
1860	6,891
1870	8,235
1880	9,793
1890	9,433
1900	10,764
1910	10,701
1920	10,004
1930	9,093
1940	9,622
1950	9,956
1960	10,346
1970	10,672
1980	11,922

LAUREL

1830	2,206
1840	3,079
1850	4,145
1860	5,488
1870	6,016
1880	9,131
1890	13,747
1900	17,592
1910	19,872
1920	19,814
1930	21,109
1940	25,640
1950	25,797
1960	24,901
1970	27,386
1980	38,982

LAWRENCE

1830	3,900
1840	4,730
1850	6,281
1860	7,601
1870	8,497
1880	13,262
1890	17,702
1900	19,612
1910	20,067
1920	17,643
1930	16,713
1940	17,275
1950	14,418
1960	12,134
1970	10,726
1980	14,121

LEE

1870	3,055
1880	4,254
1890	6,205
1900	7,988
1910	9,531
1920	11,918
1930	9,729
1940	10,860
1950	8,739
1960	7,420
1970	6,587
1980	7,754

LESLIE

1880	3,740
1890	3,964
1900	6,753
1910	8,976
1920	10,097
1930	10,765
1940	14,981
1950	15,537
1960	10,941
1970	11,623
1980	14,882

LETCHER

1850	2,512
1860	3,904
1870	4,608
1880	6,601
1890	6,920
1900	9,172
1910	10,623
1920	24,467
1930	35,702
1940	40,592
1950	39,522
1960	30,102
1970	23,165
1980	30,687

LEWIS

1810	2,357
1820	3,973
1830	5,229
1840	6,306
1850	7,202
1860	8,361
1870	9,115
1880	13,154
1890	14,803
1900	17,868
1910	16,887
1920	15,289
1930	14,315
1940	15,686
1950	13,520
1960	13,115
1970	12,355
1980	14,545

LINCOLN

1790	6,548
1800	8,621
1810	8,676
1820	9,979
1830	11,002
1840	10,187
1850	10,093
1860	10,647
1870	10,947
1880	15,080
1890	15,962
1900	17,059
1910	17,879
1920	16,481
1930	17,687
1940	19,859
1950	18,668
1960	16,503
1970	16,663
1980	19,053

LIVINGSTON

1800	2,856
1810	3,674
1820	5,824
1830	5,971
1840	9,025
1850	6,587
1860	7,213
1870	8,200
1880	9,165
1890	9,474
1900	11,354
1910	10,627
1920	9,732
1930	8,608
1940	9,127
1950	7,184
1960	7,029
1970	7,596
1980	9,219

LOGAN

1800	5,807
1810	12,123
1820	14,423
1830	13,012
1840	13,615
1850	16,581
1860	19,021
1870	20,429
1880	24,358
1890	23,812
1900	25,994
1910	24,977
1920	23,633
1930	21,875
1940	23,345
1950	22,335
1960	20,896
1970	21,793
1980	24,138

LYON

1860	5,307
1870	6,233
1880	6,768
1890	7,628
1900	9,319
1910	9,423
1920	8,795
1930	8,530
1940	9,067
1950	6,853
1960	5,924
1970	5,562
1980	6,490

MADISON

1790	5,772
1800	10,490
1810	15,540
1820	15,954
1830	18,751
1840	16,355
1850	15,727
1860	17,207
1870	19,543
1880	22,052
1890	24,348
1900	25,607
1910	26,951
1920	26,284
1930	27,621
1940	28,541
1950	31,179
1960	33,482
1970	42,730
1980	53,352

MAGOFFIN

1860	3,485
1870	4,684
1880	6,944
1890	9,196
1900	12,006
1910	13,654
1920	13,859
1930	15,719
1940	17,490
1950	13,839
1960	11,156
1970	10,443
1980	13,515

MARION

1840	11,032
1850	11,767
1860	12,593
1870	12,838
1880	14,693
1890	15,648
1900	16,290
1910	16,330
1920	15,527
1930	15,449
1940	16,913
1950	17,212
1960	16,887
1970	16,714
1980	17,910

MARSHALL

1850	5,269
1860	6,982
1870	9,455
1880	9,647
1890	11,287
1900	13,692
1910	15,771
1920	15,215
1930	12,889
1940	16,602
1950	13,387
1960	16,736
1970	20,381
1980	25,637

MARTIN

1880	3,057
1890	4,209
1900	5,780
1910	7,291
1920	7,654
1930	8,584
1940	10,970
1950	11,677
1960	10,201
1970	9,377
1980	13,925

MASON

1790	3,729
1800	12,182
1810	12,459
1820	13,588
1830	16,199
1840	15,719
1850	18,344
1860	18,222
1870	18,126
1880	20,469
1890	20,773
1900	20,446
1910	18,611

1920	17,760	1880	3,755	1830	10,240	1950	19,521	1880	17,401

1920 17,760
1930 18,862
1940 19,066
1950 18,486
1960 18,454
1970 17,273
1980 17,765

1880 3,755
1890 4,666
1900 6,818
1910 6,153
1920 5,779
1930 4,958
1940 5,691
1950 4,798
1960 4,276
1970 4,050
1980 5,177

1830 10,240
1840 9,332
1850 9,903
1860 7,859
1870 7,557
1880 10,566
1890 12,367
1900 12,834
1910 12,868
1920 12,245
1930 11,660
1940 12,280
1950 13,025
1960 13,461
1970 15,364
1980 20,046

1950 19,521
1960 22,168
1970 23,477
1980 27,584

NICHOLAS

1800 2,925
1810 4,898
1820 7,973
1830 8,834
1840 8,745
1850 10,361
1860 11,030
1870 9,129
1880 11,869
1890 10,764
1900 11,952
1910 10,601
1920 9,894
1930 8,561
1940 8,617
1950 7,532
1960 6,667
1970 6,508
1980 7,157

1880 17,401
1890 17,676
1900 17,553
1910 14,248
1920 12,554
1930 10,710
1940 10,924
1950 9,755
1960 8,237
1970 7,470
1980 8,924

McCRACKEN

1830 1,297
1840 4,745
1850 6,067
1860 10,360
1870 13,998
1880 16,262
1890 21,051
1900 28,733
1910 35,064
1920 37,246
1930 46,271
1940 48,534
1950 49,137
1960 57,306
1970 58,281
1980 61,310

MERCER

1790 7,091
1800 9,646
1810 12,630
1820 15,587
1830 17,694
1840 18,720
1850 14,067
1860 13,701
1870 13,144
1880 14,142
1890 15,034
1900 14,426
1910 14,063
1920 14,795
1930 14,471
1940 14,629
1950 14,643
1960 14,596
1970 15,960
1980 19,011

MORGAN

1830 2,857
1840 4,603
1850 7,620
1860 9,237
1870 5,975
1880 8,455
1890 11,249
1900 12,792
1910 16,259
1920 16,518
1930 15,130
1940 16,827
1950 13,624
1960 11,056
1970 10,019
1980 12,103

OWSLEY

1850 3,774
1860 5,335
1870 3,889
1880 4,942
1890 5,975
1900 6,874
1910 7,979
1920 7,820
1930 7,223
1940 8,957
1950 7,324
1960 5,369
1970 5,023
1980 5,709

OHIO

1800 1,223
1810 3,792
1820 3,897
1830 4,715
1840 6,592
1850 9,749
1860 12,209
1870 15,561
1880 19,669
1890 22,946
1900 27,287
1910 27,642
1920 26,473
1930 24,469
1940 24,421
1950 20,840
1960 17,725
1970 18,790
1980 21,765

PENDLETON

1800 1,613
1810 3,061
1820 3,086
1830 3,863
1840 4,455
1850 6,774
1860 10,443
1870 14,030
1880 16,702
1890 16,346
1900 14,947
1910 11,985
1920 11,719
1930 10,876
1940 10,392
1950 9,610
1960 9,968
1970 9,949
1980 10,989

McCREARY

1920 11,676
1930 14,627
1940 14,451
1950 16,660
1960 12,463
1970 12,548
1980 15,634

METCALFE

1860 6,745
1870 7,934
1880 9,423
1890 9,871
1900 9,988
1910 10,453
1920 10,075
1930 9,373
1940 10,853
1950 9,851
1960 8,367
1970 8,177
1980 9,484

MUHLENBERG

1800 1,443
1810 4,181
1820 4,979
1830 5,340
1840 6,964
1850 9,809
1860 10,725
1870 12,638
1880 15,098
1890 17,955
1900 20,741
1910 28,598
1920 33,353
1930 37,784
1940 37,554
1950 32,501
1960 27,791
1970 27,537
1980 32,238

OLDHAM

1830 9,588
1840 7,380
1850 7,629
1860 7,283
1870 9,027
1880 7,667
1890 6,754
1900 7,078
1910 7,248
1920 7,689
1930 7,402
1940 10,716
1950 11,018
1960 13,388
1970 14,687
1980 27,795

PERRY

1830 3,330
1840 3,089
1850 3,092
1860 3,950
1870 4,274
1880 5,607
1890 6,331
1900 8,276
1910 11,255
1920 26,042
1930 42,186
1940 47,828
1950 46,556
1960 34,961
1970 26,259
1980 33,763

McLEAN

1860 6,144
1870 7,614
1880 9,293
1890 9,887
1900 12,448
1910 13,241
1920 12,502
1930 11,072
1940 11,446
1950 10,021
1960 9,355
1970 9,062
1980 10,090

MONROE

1820 4,956
1830 5,340
1840 6,526
1850 7,756
1860 8,551
1870 9,231
1880 10,741
1890 10,989
1900 13,053
1910 13,663
1920 14,214
1930 13,077
1940 14,070
1950 13,770
1960 11,799
1970 11,642
1980 12,353

NELSON

1790 11,315
1800 9,866
1810 14,078
1820 16,273
1830 14,932
1840 13,637
1850 14,789
1860 15,799
1870 14,804
1880 16,609
1890 16,417
1900 16,587
1910 16,830
1920 16,137
1930 16,551
1940 18,004

OWEN

1820 2,031
1830 5,786
1840 8,232
1850 10,444
1860 12,719
1870 14,309

MEADE

1830 4,131
1840 5,780
1850 7,393
1860 8,858
1870 9,485
1880 10,323
1890 9,484
1900 10,533
1910 9,783
1920 9,442
1930 8,042
1940 8,827
1950 9,422
1960 18,938
1970 18,796
1980 22,854

MENIFEE

1870 1,986

MONTGOMERY

1800 7,082
1810 12,975
1820 9,587

PIKE

1830 2,677
1840 3,567
1850 5,365
1860 7,384

Year	Pop.	Year	Pop.	Year	Pop.	Year	Pop.	Year	Pop.
1870	9,562	1890	9,841	1860	16,433	1860	11,575	1820	11,776
1880	13,001	1900	12,416	1870	15,733	1870	12,612	1830	10,949
1890	17,378	1910	14,473	1880	16,813	1880	15,994	1840	15,446
1900	22,686	1920	15,406	1890	16,521	1890	16,814	1850	15,123
1910	31,679	1930	15,149	1900	18,340	1900	17,371	1860	17,320
1920	49,477	1940	17,165	1910	19,041	1910	16,488	1870	21,742
1930	63,267	1950	13,925	1920	18,532	1920	15,694	1880	27,531
1940	71,122	1960	12,334	1930	17,679	1930	13,520	1890	30,158
1950	81,154	1970	12,305	1940	17,759	1940	14,234	1900	29,970
1960	68,264	1980	13,973	1950	17,912	1950	12,890	1910	30,579
1970	61,059			1960	18,493	1960	11,364	1920	30,858
1980	81,123	**ROWAN**		1970	18,999	1970	10,823	1930	33,676
		1860	2,282	1980	23,328	1980	11,874	1940	36,631
POWELL		1870	2,991					1950	42,758
		1880	4,420	**SIMPSON**		**TRIGG**		1960	45,491
1860	2,257	1890	6,219					1970	57,884
1870	2,599	1900	8,277	1820	4,852	1820	3,874	1980	71,828
1880	3,639	1910	9,438	1830	5,815	1830	5,916		
1890	4,698	1920	9,467	1840	6,537	1840	7,716	**WASHINGTON**	
1900	6,443	1930	10,893	1850	7,733	1850	10,129		
1910	6,268	1940	12,734	1860	8,146	1860	11,051	1800	9,050
1920	6,745	1950	12,708	1870	9,573	1870	13,686	1810	13,248
1930	5,800	1960	12,808	1880	10,641	1880	14,489	1820	15,947
1940	7,671	1970	17,010	1890	10,878	1890	13,902	1830	19,017
1950	6,812	1980	19,049	1900	11,624	1900	14,073	1840	10,596
1960	6,674			1910	11,460	1910	14,539	1850	12,194
1970	7,704	**RUSSELL**		1920	11,150	1920	14,208	1860	11,575
1980	11,101	1830	3,879	1930	11,336	1930	12,531	1870	12,464
		1840	4,238	1940	11,752	1940	12,784	1880	14,419
PULASKI		1850	5,349	1950	11,678	1950	9,683	1890	13,622
1800	3,161	1860	6,024	1960	11,548	1960	8,870	1900	14,182
1810	6,897	1870	5,809	1970	13,054	1970	8,620	1910	13,940
1820	7,597	1880	7,591	1980	14,673	1980	9,384	1920	14,773
1830	9,500	1890	8,136					1930	12,623
1840	9,620	1900	9,965	**SPENCER**		**TRIMBLE**		1940	12,965
1850	14,195	1910	10,861					1950	12,777
1860	17,201	1920	11,854	1830	6,812	1840	4,480	1960	11,168
1870	17,670	1930	11,930	1840	6,581	1850	5,963	1970	10,728
1880	21,318	1940	13,615	1850	6,842	1860	5,880	1980	10,764
1890	25,731	1950	13,717	1860	6,188	1870	5,577		
1900	31,293	1960	11,076	1870	5,956	1880	7,171	**WAYNE**	
1910	35,986	1970	10,542	1880	7,040	1890	7,140		
1920	34,010	1980	13,708	1890	6,760	1900	7,272	1810	5,430
1930	35,640			1900	7,406	1910	6,512	1820	7,951
1940	39,863	**SCOTT**		1910	7,567	1920	6,011	1830	8,685
1950	38,452			1920	7,785	1930	5,348	1840	7,399
1960	34,403	1800	8,007	1930	6,606	1940	5,601	1850	8,692
1970	35,234	1810	12,419	1940	6,757	1950	5,148	1860	10,259
1980	45,803	1820	14,219	1950	6,157	1960	5,102	1870	10,602
		1830	14,677	1960	5,680	1970	5,349	1880	12,512
ROBERTSON		1840	13,668	1970	5,488	1980	6,253	1890	12,852
1870	5,399	1850	14,946	1980	5,929			1900	14,892
1880	5,814	1860	14,417			**UNION**		1910	17,518
1890	4,684	1870	11,607	**TAYLOR**		1820	3,470	1920	16,208
1900	4,900	1880	14,965			1830	4,764	1930	15,848
1910	4,121	1890	16,546	1850	7,250	1840	6,673	1940	17,204
1920	3,871	1900	18,076	1860	7,481	1850	9,012	1950	16,475
1930	3,344	1910	16,956	1870	8,226	1860	12,791	1960	14,700
1940	3,419	1920	15,318	1880	9,259	1870	13,640	1970	14,268
1950	2,881	1930	14,400	1890	9,353	1880	17,809	1980	17,022
1960	2,443	1940	14,314	1900	11,075	1890	18,299		
1970	2,163	1950	15,141	1910	11,961	1900	21,326	**WEBSTER**	
1980	2,265	1960	15,376	1920	12,236	1910	19,886		
		1970	17,948	1930	12,047	1920	18,046	1860	7,533
ROCKCASTLE		1980	21,813	1940	13,556	1930	17,053	1870	10,937
				1950	14,403	1940	17,411	1880	14,246
1810	1,731	**SHELBY**		1960	16,285	1950	14,893	1890	17,196
1820	2,249			1970	17,138	1960	14,537	1900	20,097
1830	2,865	1800	8,191	1980	21,178	1970	15,882	1910	20,974
1840	3,409	1810	14,877			1980	17,821	1920	20,762
1850	4,697	1820	21,047	**TODD**				1930	20,534
1860	5,343	1830	19,030			**WARREN**		1940	19,198
1870	7,145	1840	17,768	1820	5,089			1950	15,555
1880	9,670	1850	17,095	1830	8,680	1800	4,686	1960	14,244
				1840	9,991	1810	11,937	1970	13,282
				1850	12,268			1980	14,832

WHITLEY

1820	2,340
1830	3,806
1840	4,673
1850	7,447
1860	7,762
1870	8,278
1880	12,000
1890	17,590
1900	25,015
1910	31,982
1920	27,749
1930	29,730
1940	33,186
1950	31,940
1960	25,815
1970	24,145
1980	33,396

WOLFE

1870	3,603
1880	5,638
1890	7,180
1900	8,764
1910	9,864
1920	8,783
1930	8,425
1940	9,997
1950	7,615
1960	6,534
1970	5,669
1980	6,698

WOODFORD

1790	9,210
1800	6,624
1810	9,659
1820	12,207
1830	12,273
1840	11,740
1850	12,423
1860	11,219
1870	8,240
1880	11,800
1890	12,380
1900	13,134
1910	12,571
1920	11,784
1930	10,981
1940	11,847
1950	11,212
1960	11,913
1970	14,434
1980	17,778

NOTE

BELL

Name changed from Josh Bell prior to 1880.

ASHLAND

1870	1,459
1880	3,280
1890	4,195
1900	6,800
1910	8,688
1920	14,729
1930	29,074
1940	29,537
1950	31,131
1960	31,283
1970	29,245
1980	27,064

BOWLING GREEN

1870	4,574
1880	5,114
1890	7,803
1900	8,226
1910	9,173
1920	9,638
1930	12,348
1940	14,585
1950	18,347
1960	28,338
1970	36,705
1980	40,450

COVINGTON

1830	743
1840	2,026
1850	9,408
1860	16,471
1870	24,505
1880	29,270
1890	37,371
1900	42,938
1910	53,270
1920	57,121
1930	65,252
1940	62,018
1950	64,452
1960	60,376
1970	52,535
1980	49,563

DANVILLE

1860	4,962
1870	2,592
1880	3,074
1890	3,766
1900	4,285
1910	5,420
1920	5,099
1930	6,729
1940	6,734
1950	8,686
1960	9,101
1970	11,542
1980	12,942

ELIZABETHTOWN

1860	556
1870	1,743
1880	2,526
1890	2,260
1900	1,861
1910	1,970
1920	2,530
1930	2,590
1940	3,667

1950	5,807
1960	9,641
1970	11,748
1980	15,380

ERLANGER

1900	453
1910	700
1920	711
1930	1,853
1940	2,416
1950	3,694
1960	7,072
1970	12,676
1980	14,433

FLORENCE

1900	258
1910	250
1920	268
1930	450
1940	776
1950	1,325
1960	5,837
1970	11,661
1980	15,586

FORT THOMAS

1920	5,028
1930	10,008
1940	11,034
1950	10,870
1960	14,896
1970	16,338
1980	16,012

FRANKFORT

1800	628
1810	1,099
1820	1,679
1830	1,682
1840	1,917
1850	3,308
1860	3,702
1870	5,396
1880	5,958
1890	7,892
1900	9,487
1910	10,465
1920	9,805
1930	11,626
1940	11,492
1950	11,916
1960	18,365
1970	21,902
1980	25,973

GEORGETOWN

1900	3,823
1910	4,533
1920	3,903
1930	4,229
1940	4,420
1950	5,516
1960	6,986
1970	9,629
1980	10,972

GLASGOW

1830	617
1840	505
1850	933
1870	773
1880	1,510
1890	2,051
1900	2,019
1910	2,316
1920	2,559
1930	5,042
1940	5,815
1950	7,025
1960	10,069
1970	11,301
1980	12,958

HENDERSON

1850	1,775
1860	(NA)
1870	4,171
1880	5,365
1890	8,835
1900	10,272
1910	11,452
1920	12,169
1930	11,668
1940	13,160
1950	16,837
1960	16,892
1970	22,976
1980	24,834

HOPKINSVILLE

1860	2,289
1870	3,136
1880	4,229
1890	5,833
1900	7,280
1910	9,419
1920	9,696
1930	10,746
1940	11,724
1950	12,526
1960	19,465
1970	21,395
1980	27,318

JEFFERSONTOWN

1920	345
1930	350
1940	899
1950	1,246
1960	3,431
1970	9,701
1980	15,795

LEXINGTON

1790	834
1800	1,795
1810	4,326
1820	5,279
1830	6,026
1840	6,997
1860	9,321
1870	14,801
1880	16,656
1890	21,567
1900	26,369
1910	35,099
1920	41,534

1930	34,736
1940	49,304
1950	55,534
1960	62,810
1970	108,137
1980	204,165

LOUISVILLE

1790	200
1800	359
1810	1,357
1820	4,012
1830	10,341
1840	21,210
1850	43,194
1860	68,033
1870	100,753
1880	123,758
1890	161,129
1900	204,731
1910	223,928
1920	234,891
1930	307,745
1940	319,077
1950	369,129
1960	390,639
1970	361,706
1980	298,451

MADISONVILLE

1810	37
1820	(NA)
1830	112
1840	51
1850	(NA)
1860	602
1870	1,022
1880	1,544
1890	2,212
1900	3,628
1910	4,966
1920	5,030
1930	6,908
1940	8,209
1950	11,132
1960	13,110
1970	15,332
1980	16,979

MAYFIELD

1860	556
1870	779
1880	1,839
1890	2,909
1900	4,081
1910	5,916
1920	6,583
1930	8,177
1940	8,619
1950	8,990
1960	10,762
1970	10,724
1980	10,705

MIDDLESBOROUGH

1880	1,839
1890	3,271
1900	4,162
1910	7,305
1920	8,041
1930	10,351
1940	11,777

1950	14,482
1960	12,607
1970	11,878
1980	12,251

MURRAY

1860	218
1870	179
1880	636
1890	518
1900	1,822
1910	2,089
1920	2,415
1930	2,891
1940	3,773
1950	6,035
1960	9,303
1970	13,537
1980	14,248

NEWPORT

1800	106
1810	413
1820	(NA)
1830	715
1840	(NA)
1850	5,895
1860	10,046
1870	15,087
1880	20,433
1890	24,918
1900	28,301
1910	30,309
1920	29,317
1930	29,744
1940	30,631
1950	31,044
1960	30,070
1970	25,998
1980	21,587

NICHOLASVILLE

1860	800
1870	1,089
1880	2,303
1890	2,157
1900	2,393
1910	2,935
1920	2,786
1930	3,128
1940	3,192
1950	3,406
1960	4,275
1970	5,829
1980	10,400

OWENSBORO

1830	229
1840	(NA)
1850	1,215
1860	2,308
1870	3,437
1880	6,231
1890	9,837
1900	13,189
1910	16,011
1920	17,424
1930	22,765
1940	30,245
1950	33,651
1960	42,471
1970	50,329
1980	54,450

PADUCAH

1830	105
1840	(NA)
1850	2,428
1860	4,590
1870	6,866
1880	8,036
1890	12,797
1900	19,446
1910	22,760
1920	24,735
1930	33,541
1940	33,765
1950	32,828
1960	34,479
1970	31,627
1980	29,315

RADCLIFF

1960	3,384
1970	8,426
1980	14,519

RICHMOND

1800	110
1810	366
1820	(NA)
1830	947
1840	822
1850	411
1860	845
1870	1,629
1880	2,909
1890	5,073
1900	4,653
1910	5,340
1920	5,622
1930	6,495
1940	7,335
1950	10,268
1960	12,168
1970	16,861
1980	21,705

SAINT MATTHEWS

1960	8,738
1970	13,152
1980	13,354

SHIVELY

1940	1,273
1950	2,401
1960	15,155
1970	19,139
1980	16,819

SOMERSET

1850	412
1860	662
1870	587
1880	805
1890	2,625
1900	3,384
1910	4,491
1920	4,672
1930	5,506
1940	6,154
1950	7,097
1960	7,112
1970	10,436
1980	10,649

WINCHESTER

1860	1,142
1870	1,616
1880	2,277
1890	4,519
1900	5,964
1910	7,156
1920	8,333
1930	8,233
1940	8,594
1950	9,226
1960	10,187
1970	13,402
1980	15,216

CORRECTION NOTE

The official 1980 census counts of total population shown in
this report supersede counts issued previously. Corrections
to the figures were made after the counts were provided to
the State for redistricting purposes and released in Advance
Report PHC80-V for this State.

Shown below are corrections to the 1980 census counts of the
total population made after the tabulations for this report
were completed. Any additional corrections made after this
report is printed are available by writing to Data User
Services Division, Customer Services (Corrections), Bureau of
the Census, Washington, D.C. 20233.

The 1980 figures shown in this publication are subject to
change pending the outcome of the various lawsuits dealing
with the census counts.

	1980 population	
	As shown in the tables	Corrected
The State.....................	3 660 777	3 660 257
Hardin County:		
Radcliff division.................	24 794	24 786
West Point division...............	26 117	26 125
Jefferson County.....................	685 004	684 565
Louisville division...............	681 390	680 951
Buechel (CDP).....................	6 912	6 709
Devondale city...................	1 466	1 164
Louisville city..................	298 451	298 840
Meadowbrook Farm city...........	683	195
Rolling Hills city..............	1 067	1 122
St. Matthews city...............	13 354	13 519
Whipps Millgate city...........	227	720
Jessamine County.....................	26 146	26 065
Nicholasville division............	18 210	18 129
Nicholasville city..............	10 400	10 319
Lewis County:		
Tollesboro division:		
Concord city....................	(1)	67
Martin County:		
Martin West division:		
Inez city.......................	(1)	413

[1]Not shown.

County Subdivisions	1980	1970
The State	3 660 777	r3 220 711
Adair County[1]	15 233	13 037
Cane Valley division	1 186	1 067
Casey Creek division	1 420	1 189
Columbia division	6 661	...
Columbia city[1]	3 710	3 234
Glens Fork division	1 283	1 223
Gradyville division	2 071	1 849
White Oak division	2 612	...
Allen County[2]	14 128	12 598
Adolphus division	2 362	1 954
Halfway division	1 407	1 110
Holland division	1 362	1 319
Scottsville division	7 127	6 553
Scottsville city[2]	4 278	3 584
Settle division	1 870	1 662
Anderson County[3]	12 567	9 358
Anderson Northwest division	1 326	1 074
Anderson Southwest division	1 876	1 773
Lawrenceburg division	9 365	6 511
Lawrenceburg city[3]	5 167	3 579
Ballard County[4]	8 798	8 276
Barlow division	1 414	...
Barlow city	746	746
La Center division	4 421	...
Kevil city[4]	382	274
La Center city[4]	1 044	1 044
Wickliffe division	2 963	2 845
Wickliffe city[4]	1 034	1 211
Barren County[5]	34 009	28 677
Cave City division	5 440	...
Cave City city	2 098	1 818
Park City city[5]	614	567
Glasgow division	18 085	...
Glasgow city[5]	12 958	11 301
Hiseville division	2 915	2 538
Hiseville city[5]	349	152
Rocky Hill division	1 912	...
Temple Hill division	2 717	...
Tracy division	2 940	...
Bath County	10 025	9 235
Owingsville division	5 207	4 832
Owingsville city	1 419	1 381
Salt Lick division	2 797	2 433
Salt Lick city	347	441
Sharpsburg division	2 021	1 970
Sharpsburg city	339	307
Bell County[6]	34 330	r31 121
Kentucky Ridge division	1 930	1 397
Middlesborough division	15 726	...
Middlesborough city	12 251	r11 878
Pineville division	13 075	...
Pineville city[6]	2 599	2 817
Pruden—Fonde division	1 401	...
Tejay division	2 198	1 839
Boone County[7]	45 842	32 812
Burlington division	6 951	...
Florence division	26 435	...
Florence city[7]	15 586	r11 661
Union city (pt.)[7]	595	r175
Hebron division	4 750	...
Walton division	7 706	5 317
Union city (pt.)[7]	6	r58
Walton city[7]	1 651	1 801
Bourbon County[8]	19 405	18 476
Millersburg division	2 791	...
Millersburg city[8]	987	788
Paris city (pt.)[8]	154	...
North Middletown division	2 335	...
North Middletown city[8]	637	433
Paris division	14 279	...
Paris city (pt.)[8]	7 781	7 823
Boyd County[9]	55 513	52 376
Ashland division	33 998	...
Ashland city (pt.)[9]	26 913	29 245
Westwood (CDP)	5 973	...
Ashland Rural division	7 512	5 293
Ashland city (pt.)[9]	151	...
Cannonsburg division	6 923	3 809
Catlettsburg division	7 080	6 505
Catlettsburg city[9]	3 005	3 420
Boyle County[10]	25 066	r21 861
Danville division	17 612	r15 154
Danville city[10]	12 942	11 542
Junction City division	4 299	3 948
Junction City city (pt.)[10]	2 045	1 046
Perryville division	3 155	2 759
Perryville city	841	730
Bracken County[11]	7 738	7 227
Augusta division	2 632	2 596
Augusta city[11]	1 455	1 434
Brooksville division	3 483	...
Brooksville city[11]	680	609
Germantown city (pt.)[11]	161	160

County Subdivisions	1980	1970
Bracken County—Con.		
Foster division	1 623	...
Foster city	80	91
Breathitt County[12]	17 004	14 221
Canoe division	1 877	...
Haddix division	2 287	...
Hardshell division	2 555	...
Jackson division	4 917	...
Jackson city[12]	2 651	1 887
Oakdale division	2 158	...
Rousseau division	1 653	...
Taulbee division	1 557	...
Breckinridge County[13]	16 861	14 789
Breckinridge Southeast division	3 633	...
Breckinridge Southwest division	1 150	...
Cloverport division	3 375	...
Cloverport city[13]	1 585	1 388
Hardinsburg division	4 501	...
Hardinsburg city[13]	2 211	1 547
Irvington division	4 202	3 770
Irvington city	1 409	1 300
Bullitt County[14]	43 346	26 090
Fort Knox division	1	...
Lebanon Junction division	4 215	3 348
Lebanon Junction city	1 581	1 571
Mount Washington division	9 687	5 047
Mount Washington city[14]	3 997	2 020
Shepherdsville city (pt.)[14]	19	...
Shepherdsville Northwest division	25 169	14 846
Brooks (CDP)	1 344	...
Hillview city[14]	5 196	...
Hunters Hollow city[14]	260	...
Pioneer Village city[14]	390	...
Shepherdsville city (pt.)[14]	3 358	2 769
Shepherdsville Southeast division	4 274	2 849
Shepherdsville city (pt.)[14]	1 077	...
Butler County[15]	11 064	9 723
Jetson division	1 517	1 369
Morgantown division	3 616	3 199
Morgantown city[15]	2 000	1 394
Rochester division	1 640	1 489
Rochester city[15]	289	252
Sugar Grove division	1 384	1 271
Welchs Creek division	2 907	2 395
Caldwell County[16]	13 473	13 179
Fredonia division	2 247	...
Fredonia city[16]	535	450
Princeton division	11 226	...
Princeton city[16]	7 073	6 292
Calloway County[17]	30 031	27 692
Calloway Southwest division	2 900	...
Hazel city[17]	465	424
Kirksey division	3 326	...
Murray division	17 411	...
Murray city[17]	14 248	13 537
New Concord division	2 961	...
Shiloh division	3 433	...
Campbell County[18]	83 317	r88 704
Alexandria division	9 545	7 890
Alexandria city[18]	4 735	3 844
Grants Lick division	5 419	...
California city	135	90
Mentor city[18]	169	r138
Newport division	68 353	...
Bellevue city	7 678	8 847
Cold Spring city[18]	2 117	r1 406
Crestview city	528	r659
Dayton city[18]	6 979	r8 751
Fort Thomas city[18]	16 012	16 338
Highland Heights city[18]	4 435	r4 543
Melbourne city[18]	628	r275
Newport city[18]	21 587	25 998
Silver Grove city	1 260	1 365
Southgate city	2 833	3 212
Wilder city[18]	633	823
Woodlawn city	331	525
Carlisle County[19]	5 487	5 354
Arlington division	1 841	...
Arlington city[19]	511	549
Bardwell division	2 225	...
Bardwell city[19]	988	1 049
Cunningham division	1 421	...
Carroll County[20]	9 270	8 523
Carrollton division	7 442	6 746
Carrollton city	3 967	3 884
Ghent city	439	385
Sanders city	332	268
Worthville city	272	258
Prestonville division	1 828	1 777
Prestonville city	205	252
Carter County[21]	25 060	19 850
Carter division	1 640	1 335
Grahn division	2 847	...
Grayson division	8 613	...
Grayson city[21]	3 423	2 184

County Subdivisions

County Subdivisions	1980	1970
Carter County—Con.		
Olive Hill division	4 931	3 716
Olive Hill city[21]	2 539	1 197
Upper Tygarts division	3 185	2 505
Willard division	3 844	3 314
Casey County[22]	14 818	12 930
Clementsville division	2 270	2 002
Dunnville division	2 242	1 976
Liberty division	5 780	
Liberty city[22]	2 206	1 765
Middleburg division	3 220	
South Fork division	1 306	1 274
Christian County[23]	66 878	56 224
Crofton division	5 105	...
Crofton city	823	631
Fort Campbell division	17 800	13 619
Fort Campbell North (CDP)	17 211	13 616
Oak Grove city (pt.)[23]	–	...
Hopkinsville division	36 858	
Hopkinsville city[23]	27 318	'21 395
La Fayette division	2 285	2 362
La Fayette city	160	158
Oak Grove city (pt.)[23]	25	...
Pembroke division	4 830	3 376
Oak Grove city (pt.)[23]	2 063	...
Pembroke city[23]	636	634
Clark County[24]	28 322	24 090
Boonesboro division	1 935	...
Clark Southeast division	2 988	...
Winchester division	23 399	
Winchester city[24]	15 216	13 402
Clay County[25]	22 752	18 481
Ashers Fork division	1 948	...
Big Creek division	4 763	...
Burning Springs division	5 140	...
Manchester division	5 366	
Manchester city[25]	1 838	1 664
Oneida division	2 397	...
Sibert–Hima division	3 138	...
Clinton County[26]	9 321	8 174
Albany division	6 879	...
Albany city	2 083	1 891
Cumberland City division	2 442	2 332
Crittenden County[27]	9 207	8 493
Crittenden East division	1 617	...
Crittenden South division	1 788	...
Dycusburg city	64	**89**
Crittenden West division	1 196	...
Marion division	4 606	...
Marion city[27]	3 392	3 008
Cumberland County[28]	7 289	6 850
Burkesville division	4 677	4 306
Burkesville city (pt.)[28]	2 019	1 717
Cumberland South division	2 612	2 544
Burkesville city (pt.)[28]	32	...
Daviess County[29]	85 949	79 486
Daviess East division	17 562	...
Owensboro city (pt.)[29]	2	...
Whitesville city[29]	788	752
Daviess West division	18 697	...
Owensboro city (pt.)[29]	5 719	(NA)
Owensboro division	49 690	...
Owensboro city (pt.)[29]	48 729	(NA)
Edmonson County[30]	9 962	8 751
Brownsville division	4 300	3 702
Brownsville city (pt.)[30]	674	542
Brownsville North division	3 441	2 945
Lincoln division	1 185	1 120
Brownsville city (pt.)[30]	–	
Sunfish division	1 036	984
Elliott County[31]	6 908	5 933
Isonville division	2 346	2 091
Sandy Hook division	4 562	3 842
Sandy Hook city	627	'561
Estill County[32]	14 495	12 752
Irvine division	5 939	5 505
Irvine city[32]	2 889	2 918
Ravenna division	1 776	1 761
Ravenna city	793	784
Red Lick division	4 823	3 614
Station Camp division	1 957	1 872
Fayette County[33]	204 165	174 323
Fayette division	204 165	...
Lexington–Fayette[33]	204 165	108 137
Fleming County[34]	12 323	11 366
Ewing division	2 449	2 315
Ewing city[34]	144	...
Flemingsburg division	6 414	
Flemingsburg city[34]	2 835	2 483
Hillsboro division	3 460	...

County Subdivisions

County Subdivisions	1980	1970
Floyd County[35]	48 764	35 889
Allen–Martin division	6 909	...
Allen city	338	724
Martin city[35]	827	786
McDowell division	4 361	...
Mare Creek division	5 418	...
Mud Creek division	6 201	...
Prestonsburg division	14 160	...
Prestonsburg city[35]	4 011	3 422
Risner–Bull Creek division	2 116	...
Wayland division	4 529	...
Wayland city[35]	601	384
Wheelwright–Weeksbury division	5 070	4 074
Wheelwright city[35]	865	793
Franklin County[36]	41 830	34 481
Bald Knob division	1 243	...
Frankfort division	39 429	
Frankfort city[36]	25 973	'21 902
Peaks Mill division	1 158	...
Fulton County[37]	8 971	10 183
Fulton division	4 619	5 022
Fulton city[37]	3 137	3 250
Fulton West division	25	...
Hickman division	4 327	
Hickman city[37]	2 894	3 048
Gallatin County[38]	4 842	4 134
Warsaw division	4 842	4 134
Glencoe city[38]	354	'250
Sparta city (pt.)	146	168
Warsaw city	1 328	1 232
Garrard County[39]	10 853	9 457
Bryantsville division	2 268	1 736
Lancaster division	6 427	5 755
Lancaster city[39]	3 365	3 230
Paint Lick division	2 158	1 966
Grant County[40]	13 308	9 999
Corinth division	1 479	...
Corinth city (pt.)[40]	249	236
Crittenden division	3 226	
Crittenden city[40]	597	359
Williamstown–Dry Ridge division	8 603	
Dry Ridge city[40]	1 250	1 100
Williamstown city[40]	2 502	2 063
Graves County[41]	34 049	30 939
Fancy Farm division	1 935	...
Farmington division	2 362	1 859
Hickory Grove division	3 870	...
Mayfield division	14 391	...
Mayfield city[41]	10 705	10 724
Sedalia division	2 831	2 764
Symsonia division	4 771	4 015
Wingo–Water Valley division	3 889	3 378
Water Valley city[41]	395	285
Wingo city	606	593
Grayson County[42]	20 854	16 445
Caneyville division	3 675	...
Caneyville city[42]	642	530
Clarkson division	2 874	2 392
Clarkson city	666	660
Leitchfield division	10 158	...
Leitchfield city[42]	4 533	2 983
Millerstown division	2 055	...
Short Creek division	2 092	1 739
Green County[43]	11 043	10 350
Donansburg division	2 282	2 229
Greensburg division	4 359	3 703
Greensburg city[43]	2 377	1 990
Gresham division	1 557	1 601
Summersville division	2 845	2 817
Greenup County[44]	39 132	33 192
Fullerton division	3 951	3 831
South Shore city	1 525	'1 750
Greenup division	8 045	6 458
Greenup city[44]	1 386	1 284
Russell division	17 961	...
Bellefonte city[44]	908	966
Flatwoods city[44]	8 354	7 380
Raceland city	1 970	1 857
Russell city[44]	3 824	'2 925
Worthington city (pt.)	1 699	1 364
Wurtland city (pt.)[44]	7	...
Tygarts division	3 391	3 021
Wurtland division	5 784	...
Worthington city (pt.)	249	...
Wurtland city (pt.)[44]	1 294	...
Hancock County[45]	7 742	7 080
Hawesville division	2 641	2 786
Hawesville city	1 036	1 262
Lewisport division	3 267	2 695
Lewisport city[45]	1 832	1 595
Patesville division	1 834	1 599

County Subdivisions	1980	1970
Hardin County[46]	88 917	78 421
Cecilia division	2 960	...
Elizabethtown city (pt.)[46]	15	
Elizabethtown division	28 592	...
Elizabethtown city (pt.)[46]	15 365	11 748
Radcliff division	24 794	...
Radcliff city[46]	14 519	[8] 426
Vine Grove city[46]	3 583	2 987
Sonora division	3 424	2 702
Sonora city	416	390
Upton city (pt.)[46]	417	238
Summit division	3 030	2 436
West Point division	26 117	33 509
Fort Knox (CDP) (pt.)	24 738	31 751
Muldraugh city (pt.)	–	...
West Point city	1 339	1 741
Harlan County[47]	41 889	37 370
Alva division	1 019	1 044
Cawood division	3 169	...
Cumberland division	8 594	...
Benham city	936	1 000
Cumberland city[47]	3 712	[3] 380
Lynch city[47]	1 614	[1] 517
Harlan division	20 039	...
Evarts city	1 234	1 182
Harlan city	3 024	3 318
Loyall city	1 210	1 212
Verda (CDP)	1 133	...
Pine Mountain division	1 752	1 362
Poor Fork division	1 418	...
Upper Clover division	2 333	1 941
Wallins Creek division	3 565	...
Wallins Creek city	459	369
Harrison County[48]	15 166	14 158
Berry division	2 325	...
Berry city	287	266
Berry West division	1 809	1 487
Corinth city (pt.)		...
Cynthiana division	11 032	...
Cynthiana city[48]	5 881	6 356
Hart County[49]	15 402	13 980
Bonnieville division	2 218	...
Bonnieville city	372	328
Hammonville division	1 665	...
Hardyville division	2 783	...
Horse Cave division	4 395	...
Horse Cave city	2 045	2 068
Munfordville division	4 341	...
Munfordville city	1 783	1 233
Henderson County[50]	40 849	36 031
Corydon division	7 091	...
Corydon city	874	880
Henderson city (pt.)[50]	1 084	(NA)
Hebbardsville–Robards division	3 971	...
Henderson city (pt.)[50]	236	(NA)
Henderson division	21 283	...
Henderson city (pt.)[50]	21 070	(NA)
Spottsville division	8 504	...
Henderson city (pt.)[50]	2 444	(NA)
Henry County[51]	12 740	10 910
Campbellsburg division	2 418	1 933
Campbellsburg city[51]	714	479
Eminence division	4 692	3 837
Eminence city[51]	2 260	2 225
Smithfield city	137	185
New Castle division	2 837	2 531
New Castle city[51]	832	755
Pleasureville division	2 793	2 609
Lockport city[51]	84	...
Pleasureville city (pt.)[51]	758	685
Hickman County[52]	6 065	6 264
Clinton division	5 401	...
Clinton city[52]	1 720	1 618
Columbus division	664	...
Columbus city	296	371
Hopkins County[53]	46 174	38 167
Dawson Springs division	6 909	...
Dawson Springs city	3 275	[3] 009
Hanson division	2 194	...
Hanson city	485	378
Madisonville division	29 737	...
Earlington city[53]	2 011	2 321
Madisonville city[53]	16 979	15 332
Mortons Gap city	1 201	1 169
Nebo division	2 075	...
Nebo city	269	274
Nortonville division	4 446	...
Nortonville city	1 336	699
White Plains city	859	729
St. Charles division	813	...
St. Charles city	405	373
Jackson County[54]	11 996	10 005
Jackson South division	4 194	3 380
McKee division	5 111	4 117
McKee city[54]	759	255

County Subdivisions	1980	1970
Jackson County—Con.		
Sand Gap division	2 691	2 508
Jefferson County[55]	685 004	695 055
Fisherville division	3 614	3 644
Louisville division	681 390	...
Anchorage city	1 726	1 477
Audubon Park city	1 571	1 862
Bancroft city[55]	725	...
Barbourmeade city	1 038	884
Beechwood Village city	1 462	1 788
Bellemeade city[55]	918	576
Bellewood city	307	410
Blue Ridge Manor city[55]	465	[5]77
Briarwood city[55]	374	327
Broadfields city	311	534
Brownsboro Farm city	790	823
Brownsboro Village city	410	494
Buechel (CDP)	6 912	5 359
Cambridge city	193	251
Cherrywood Village city	362	481
Creekside city[55]	419	...
Crossgate city[55]	292	[2]78
Devondale city	1 466	1 071
Douglass Hills city[55]	4 384	...
Druid Hills city	338	416
Fairdale (CDP)	7 315	...
Fairmeade city	272	317
Fern Creek (CDP)	16 866	...
Fincastle city[55]	804	...
Forest Hills city[55]	502	469
Glenview Hills city[55]	433	...
Glenview Manor city[55]	212	[1]70
Goose Creek city[55]	394	[4]50
Graymoor city[55]	1 167	1 419
Green Spring city[55]	634	...
Hickory Hill city[55]	171	...
Highview (CDP)	13 286	...
Hills and Dales city[55]	151	...
Hollow Creek city[55]	1 023	...
Hollyvilla city	476	907
Houston Acres city	608	684
Hurstbourne Acres city[55]	386	289
Indian Hills city[55]	787	600
Indian Hills Cherokee Section city[55]	585	282
Jeffersontown city[55]	15 795	9 701
Keeneland city	432	587
Kingsley city	464	504
Langdon Place city[55]	308	...
Lincolnshire city	139	222
Louisville city[55]	298 451	[3]61 706
Lyndon city[55]	1 553	460
Lynnview city[55]	1 157	[1] 488
Manor Creek city[55]	241	...
Maryhill Estates city	225	211
Meadowbrook Farm city[55]	683	...
Meadow Vale city[55]	1 008	1 231
Meadowview Estates city	212	139
Middletown city[55]	414	...
Minor Lane Heights city	1 882	2 217
Mockingbird Valley city	205	255
Moorland city	513	705
Newburg (CDP)	24 612	...
Norbourne Estates city	446	467
Northfield city[55]	906	[3]64
Norwood city[55]	254	...
Okolona (CDP)	20 039	17 643
Old Brownsboro Place city[55]	358	...
Parkway Village city	754	829
Penn Run No. 1 city[55]	75	...
Plantation city	969	895
Pleasure Ridge Park (CDP)	27 332	28 566
Plymouth Village city	231	230
Prospect city[55]	1 981	...
Richlawn city	485	578
Riverwood city[55]	435	[5]15
Robinswood city[55]	273	[3]00
Rolling Fields city	731	[7]14
Rolling Hills city	1 067	1 313
St. Matthews city[55]	13 354	13 152
St. Regis Park city[55]	1 735	1 527
Seneca Gardens city	748	822
Shively city[55]	16 819	[19] 139
South Park View city	248	287
Springlee city	498	583
Strathmoor Gardens city	292	337
Strathmoor Manor city	368	464
Strathmoor Village city	466	540
Sycamore city[55]	195	...
Ten Broeck city[55]	134	...
Thornhill city[55]	233	...
Valley Station (CDP)	24 474	24 471
Wellington city	653	727
West Buechel city	1 205	1 581
Westwood city[55]	826	777
Whipps Millgate city[55]	227	[6]12
Wildwood city	309	412
Winding Falls city[55]	454	...
Windy Hills city[55]	2 214	1 692
Woodland Hills city[55]	839	1 233
Woodlawn Park city[55]	1 052	1 237
Jessamine County[56]	26 146	17 430
Keene division	2 308	...
Nicholasville division	18 210	...
Nicholasville city[56]	10 400	5 829

County Subdivisions	1980	1970
Jessamine County—Con.		
Wilmore division	5 628	...
Wilmore city[56]	3 787	3 466
Johnson County[57]	24 432	17 539
Flatgap division	2 739	...
Nippa division	2 890	...
Oil Springs division	3 216	2 144
Paintsville division	15 587	...
Paintsville city[57]	3 815	3 868
Van Lear (CDP)	2 035	1 033
Kenton County[58]	137 058	129 440
Covington division	111 377	...
Bromley city	844	1 069
Covington city (pt.)[58]	47 822	52 535
Crescent Park city	351	598
Crescent Springs city[58]	1 951	1 662
Crestview Hills city	1 408	1 114
Edgewood city (pt.)	7 230	4 139
Elsmere city (pt.)[58]	4 716	(NA)
Erlanger city (pt.)[58]	13 107	(NA)
Fairview city (pt.)	118	(NA)
Fort Mitchell city[58]	7 297	6 982
Fort Wright city[58]	4 481	4 819
Kenton Vale city	145	178
Lakeside Park city[58]	3 038	2 511
Ludlow city	4 959	5 815
Park Hills city	3 500	3 999
Taylor Mill city[58]	4 509	r3 146
Villa Hills city[58]	4 402	1 647
Independence division	19 095	...
Covington city (pt.)[58]	1 741	...
Edgewood city (pt.)	−	(NA)
Elsmere city (pt.)[58]	2 487	(NA)
Erlanger city (pt.)[58]	1 326	(NA)
Fairview city (pt.)	80	(NA)
Independence city[58]	7 998	r1 715
Latonia Lakes city	396	428
Ridgeview Heights city	729	189
Ryland Heights city[58]	252	...
Piner—Visalia division	6 586	...
Visalia city[58]	198	...
Knott County[59]	17 940	14 698
Beaver division	3 014	...
Carr Fork division	4 512	3 955
Emmalena division	3 116	...
Hindman division	4 497	...
Hindman city	876	808
Mousie division	2 801	...
Knox County[60]	30 239	23 689
Barbourville division	13 878	...
Barbourville city[60]	3 333	3 549
Bryants division	979	...
Corbin division	5 591	4 418
Corbin city (pt.)[60]	1 336	1 179
North Corbin (CDP) (pt.)	544	...
Dewitt division	2 342	...
Girdler division	3 318	...
Gray division	2 746	1 549
Trosper division	1 385	...
Larue County[61]	11 922	10 672
Buffalo division	2 086	1 887
Hodgenville division	6 632	5 977
Hodgenville city[61]	2 531	2 562
Magnolia—Upton division	3 204	2 808
Upton city (pt.)	314	314
Laurel County[62]	38 982	27 386
Bush division	2 789	1 792
Camp Ground division	2 461	1 724
Colony division	2 771	1 823
East Bernstadt division	5 688	...
Greenmount—Langnau division	1 917	...
Keavy division	4 932	3 195
London division	12 422	...
London city	4 002	4 337
North Corbin division	6 002	...
North Corbin (CDP) (pt.)	1 171	...
Lawrence County[63]	14 121	10 726
Adams division	2 807	1 617
Blaine division	1 706	...
Blaine city[63]	358	r168
Clifford division	2 391	...
Louisa division	5 600	...
Louisa city	1 832	1 781
Webbville division	1 617	...
Lee County[64]	7 754	6 587
Beattyville division	4 040	3 479
Beattyville city[64]	1 068	923
St. Helens division	1 911	1 805
South River division	1 803	1 303
Leslie County[65]	14 882	11 623
Cutshin division	3 854	...
Hyden division	6 893	...
Hyden city	488	482
Mozelle division	4 135	...
Letcher County[66]	30 687	23 165
Blackey division	6 873	...
Colson division	1 660	...
Eolia division	2 153	1 472
Jenkins division	11 612	...
Fleming—Neon city[66]	1 195	...
Jenkins city[66]	3 271	2 552
McRoberts (CDP)	1 106	1 037
Whitesburg division	8 389	...
Whitesburg city[66]	1 525	1 137
Lewis County[67]	14 545	12 355
Garrison division	4 588	...
Laurel—Petersville division	2 081	...
Tollesboro division	3 681	...
Tollesboro city[67]	808	...
Vanceburg division	4 195	...
Vanceburg city[67]	1 939	1 773
Lincoln County[68]	19 053	16 663
Crab Orchard division	3 450	3 321
Crab Orchard city	843	861
Hustonville division	3 827	3 350
Hustonville city	339	413
Stanford division	6 739	5 400
Junction City city (pt.)[68]	−	...
Stanford city[68]	2 764	2 474
Waynesburg division	5 037	4 592
Eubank city (pt.)	9	10
Livingston County[69]	9 219	7 596
Salem division	3 398	3 400
Carrsville city	99	110
Salem city[69]	833	'593
Smithland division	5 821	4 196
Grand Rivers city	428	438
Smithland city	512	514
Logan County[70]	24 138	21 793
Adairville division	3 265	3 319
Adairville city[70]	1 105	973
Auburn division	3 742	3 541
Auburn city[70]	1 467	1 160
Lewisburg division	3 507	2 797
Lewisburg city[70]	972	651
Russellville division	13 624	...
Russellville city[70]	7 520	6 456
Lyon County[71]	6 490	5 562
Eddyville division	5 288	4 361
Eddyville city[71]	1 949	1 981
Kuttawa city[71]	560	453
Southeast Lyon division	1 202	1 191
Southwest Lyon division	−	10
McCracken County[72]	61 310	58 281
McCracken Northwest division	4 600	4 318
McCracken Southwest division	3 531	2 674
Paducah division	53 179	...
Lone Oak city[72]	443	...
Paducah city[72]	29 315	31 627
Reidland (CDP)	3 730	...
Woodlawn—Oakdale (CDP)	4 722	1 639
McCreary County[73]	15 634	12 548
Co-operative division	1 109	1 157
Parkers Lake division	2 214	1 962
Pine Knot division	5 324	...
Pine Knot (CDP)	1 389	...
Stearns—Whitley City division	6 987	...
Stearns (CDP)	1 557	...
Whitley City (CDP)	1 683	1 060
McLean County[74]	10 090	9 062
Calhoun division	3 784	...
Calhoun city[74]	1 080	901
Island division	1 253	...
Island city[74]	532	410
Livermore division	3 102	2 757
Livermore city[74]	1 672	1 594
Sacramento division	1 951	...
Sacramento city[74]	538	437
Madison County[75]	53 352	42 730
Berea division	15 687	...
Berea city[75]	8 226	6 956
Cottonburg—Valley View division	1 233	...
Madison East division	3 141	...
Madison North division	3 840	...
Madison West division	1 920	...
Richmond division	27 531	...
Richmond city[75]	21 705	16 861
Magoffin County[76]	13 515	10 443
Magoffin West division	1 657	...
Royalton division	2 519	...
Salyersville division	9 339	...
Salyersville city[76]	1 352	1 196
Marion County[77]	17 910	16 714
Bradfordsville division	1 123	...
Bradfordsville city	331	338
Gravel Switch division	1 048	...
Lebanon division	9 625	...
Lebanon city[77]	6 590	5 528
Loretto division	2 833	2 816

County Subdivisions

County Subdivisions	1980	1970
Marion County—Con.		
Loretto division—Con.		
Loretto city	954	985
New Market division	785	795
Raywick division	1 024	...
St. Mary division	1 472	...
Marshall County[78]	25 637	20 381
Benton division	9 319	...
Benton city (pt.)[78]	3 700	3 652
Hardin city	545	522
Calvert City division	11 718	9 070
Benton (pt.)[78]	—	...
Calvert City city[78]	2 388	2 104
Fairdealing division	4 600	3 199
Martin County[79]	13 925	9 377
Martin West division	7 878	...
Three Forks division	1 402	1 173
Warfield division	4 645	3 311
Mason County[80]	17 765	17 273
Mays Lick division	1 850	1 869
Sardis city	198	'175
Maysville division	15 915	...
Dover city	305	277
Germantown city (pt.)[80]	186	172
Maysville city[80]	7 983	7 411
Washington city[80]	624	439
Meade County[81]	22 854	18 796
Battletown—Payneville division	3 448	2 751
Brandenburg division	7 298	5 594
Brandenburg city[81]	1 831	1 637
Ekron city[81]	239	190
Flaherty division	12 108	10 451
Fort Knox (CDP) (pt.)	6 317	5 857
Muldraugh city (pt.)[81]	1 752	1 773
Menifee County[82]	5 117	4 050
Frenchburg division	2 935	...
Frenchburg city (pt.)[82]	461	(NA)
Menifee West division	2 182	...
Frenchburg city (pt.)[82]	89	(NA)
Mercer County[83]	19 011	15 960
Burgin division	2 930	2 320
Burgin city[83]	1 008	1 002
Harrodsburg division	12 562	10 917
Harrodsburg city[83]	7 265	6 741
Salvisa—McAfee division	3 519	2 723
Metcalfe County[84]	9 484	8 177
Center division	2 497	2 404
Edmonton division	3 985	...
Edmonton city[84]	1 401	958
Summer Shade division	3 002	...
Monroe County[85]	12 353	11 642
Fountain Run division	2 526	2 436
Fountain Run city[85]	340	128
Gamaliel city[85]	456	431
Mount Herman division	2 066	...
Tompkinsville division	7 761	...
Tompkinsville city[85]	4 366	2 207
Montgomery County[86]	20 046	15 364
Jeffersonville division[86]	5 964	4 526
Camargo city (pt.)[86]	1 301	'244
Jeffersonville city[86]	1 528	'775
Mount Sterling division	14 082	...
Camargo city (pt.)[86]	—	...
Mount Sterling city[86]	5 820	5 083
Morgan County[87]	12 103	10 019
Cannel City division	1 981	...
Grassy Creek division	2 160	1 778
Paint Creek division	2 893	2 370
West Liberty division	3 430	...
West Liberty city	1 381	1 387
Wrigley division	1 639	1 457
Muhlenberg County[88]	32 238	27 537
Bremen division	3 498	2 849
Bremen city	179	299
Central City division	9 038	...
Central City city[88]	5 214	'5 450
South Carrollton city	262	218
Drakesboro division	4 172	3 539
Drakesboro city	798	907
Greenville division	12 192	...
Greenville city[88]	4 631	3 875
Powderly city	848	631
Penrod division	1 995	...
Rosewood division	1 343	...
Nelson County[89]	27 584	23 477
Bardstown division	14 535	11 582
Bardstown city[89]	6 155	5 816
Bloomfield division	3 017	3 117
Bloomfield city	954	1 072
Boston division	2 234	2 036
Coxs Creek division	4 599	3 582
Fairfield city	169	163
New Haven division	3 199	3 160

County Subdivisions	1980	1970
Nelson County—Con.		
New Haven division—Con.		
New Haven city[89]	926	977
Nicholas County[90]	7 157	6 508
Carlisle division	5 201	...
Carlisle city[90]	1 757	1 579
Headquarters division	1 956	...
Ohio County[91]	21 765	18 790
Beaver Dam division	6 445	...
Beaver Dam city[91]	3 185	2 622
Hartford city (pt.)[91]	—	...
Centertown division	1 425	1 244
Centertown city[91]	462	323
Fordsville division	2 882	...
Fordsville city[91]	561	489
Hartford division	3 821	...
Hartford city (pt.)[91]	2 512	1 868
Heflin—Beda division	2 763	...
Horse Branch division	1 972	1 781
McHenry—Rockport division	2 457	...
McHenry city	582	420
Rockport city[91]	511	377
Oldham County[92]	27 795	14 687
La Grange division	11 950	...
La Grange city[92]	2 971	1 713
Pewee Valley division	15 845	...
Crestwood city[92]	531	...
Orchard Grass Hills city[92]	1 047	...
Pewee Valley city[92]	982	950
Owen County[93]	8 924	7 470
Monterey—New Columbus division	2 402	...
Monterey city	186	205
New Liberty division (pt.)	2 175	1 909
Sparta city (pt.)	46	45
Owenton division	4 347	...
Gratz city	124	105
Owenton city[93]	1 341	1 280
Owsley County[94]	5 709	5 023
Booneville division	3 054	...
Booneville city	191	126
Cowcreek division	874	957
Sturgeon division	1 781	...
Pendleton County[95]	10 989	9 949
Butler division	5 118	...
Butler city[95]	663	558
Falmouth division	4 261	...
Falmouth city[95]	2 482	2 593
Pendleton Southwest division	1 610	...
Perry County[96]	33 763	'26 259
Buckhorn division	1 216	1 056
Daisy division	2 348	...
Defiance—Vicco division	2 616	...
Vicco city	456	377
Dice division	2 742	...
Hazard division	17 812	...
Hazard city[96]	5 371	5 459
Krypton division	3 544	...
Viper division	3 485	...
Pike County[97]	81 123	61 059
Ashcamp division	2 425	1 441
Dorton division	4 670	...
Elkhorn division	5 137	...
Cedarville city	81	140
Elkhorn City city[97]	1 446	1 081
Fedscreek division	5 455	4 255
Hellier division	3 512	...
Long Fork division	2 652	...
McCarr division	2 443	...
Mayflower division	3 605	...
Millard division	6 589	...
Phelps division	8 895	...
Phelps city	1 126	770
Pikeville division	13 824	...
Coal Run city[97]	348	234
Pikeville city[97]	4 756	'5 205
Pleasant Valley city	342	'251
Yorktown city	155	174
Raccoon division	4 859	...
Robinson Creek division	3 589	...
Sidney division	3 948	...
South Williamson division	9 520	...
South Williamson (CDP)	1 016	...
Powell County[98]	11 101	7 704
Clay City division	5 191	...
Clay City city	1 276	983
Stanton division	5 910	...
Stanton city	2 691	2 037
Pulaski County[99]	45 803	35 234
Burnside division	4 286	2 687
Burnside city (pt.)	605	586
Eubank division	4 713	3 888
Eubank city (pt.)	198	220
Mount Victory division	1 707	...

County Subdivisions

County Subdivisions	1980	1970
Pulaski County—Con.		
Nancy division	4 138	3 563
Science Hill division	3 936	3 000
Science Hill city[99]	655	470
Shopville division	2 015	1 927
Somerset division	25 008	...
Burnside city (pt.)	170	...
Ferguson city[99]	1 009	507
Somerset city[99]	10 649	10 436
Robertson County	2 265	2 163
Mount Olivet division	2 265	2 163
Mount Olivet city	346	442
Rockcastle County[100]	13 973	12 305
Conway division	2 523	...
Livingston division	3 154	...
Livingston city	334	338
Mount Vernon division	8 296	...
Brodhead city	686	769
Mount Vernon city[100]	2 334	1 639
Rowan County[101]	19 049	17 010
Morehead division	16 146	...
Clearfield (CDP)	1 250	...
Lakeview Heights city[101]	269	...
Morehead city[101]	7 789	7 191
Pine Grove division	2 903	...
Russell County[102]	13 708	10 542
Bryan division	1 576	...
Eli division	2 606	2 018
Jamestown division	3 309	...
Jamestown city[102]	1 441	1 027
Russell Springs division	6 217	...
Russell Springs city[102]	1 831	1 641
Scott County[103]	21 813	17 948
Georgetown division	16 772	...
Georgetown city[103]	10 972	8 629
Sadieville division	1 899	...
Corinth city (pt.)[103]	9	—
Sadieville city	253	272
Stamping Ground division	3 142	...
Stamping Ground city[103]	562	411
Shelby County[104]	23 328	18 999
Christianburg division	2 114	2 069
Pleasureville city (pt.)	79	62
Harrisonville division	3 415	2 783
Shelbyville division	13 929	...
Shelbyville city[104]	5 329	4 182
Simpsonville division	3 870	2 923
Simpsonville city	642	628
Simpson County[105]	14 673	13 054
Franklin division	13 144	...
Franklin city[105]	7 738	6 553
Simpson East division	1 529	...
Spencer County[106]	5 929	5 488
Spencer West division	2 913	2 218
Taylorsville division	3 016	3 270
Taylorsville city	801	897
Taylor County[107]	21 178	17 138
Campbellsville division	16 100	...
Campbellsville city[107]	8 715	7 598
Mannsville division	2 117	1 928
Saloma division	2 961	2 205
Todd County[108]	11 874	10 823
Elkton division	4 863	...
Elkton city[108]	1 815	1 612
Guthrie division	2 813	...
Allensville city	170	266
Guthrie city[108]	1 361	1 200
Kirkmansville division	2 728	2 624
Trenton division	1 470	1 489
Trenton city	465	496
Trigg County[109]	9 384	8 620
Cadiz division	4 652	...
Cadiz city	1 661	1 987
Cadiz West division	2 940	...
Cerulean Springs division	1 792	1 812
Trigg West division	—	6
Trimble County[110]	6 253	5 349
Bedford division	3 471	2 973
Bedford city	835	780
Milton division	2 782	2 376
Milton city[110]	718	756
Union County[111]	17 821	15 882
Morganfield division	10 195	...
Breckinridge Center (CDP)	3 290	...
Morganfield city[111]	3 781	3 563
Waverly city	434	335
Sturgis division	5 461	...
Caseyville city[111]	43	'23
Sturgis city	2 293	2 210
Uniontown division	2 165	...
Uniontown city[111]	1 169	1 255

County Subdivisions

County Subdivisions	1980	1970
Warren County[112]	71 828	'57 884
Bowling Green division	52 041	...
Bowling Green city[112]	40 450	'36 705
Plum Springs city[112]	393	185
Gasper River division	2 711	...
Goshen division	3 278	...
Greencastle division	1 819	...
Smiths Grove division	5 044	...
Oakland city[112]	264	144
Smiths Grove city[112]	767	756
Warren North division	3 925	...
Woodburn division	3 010	...
Woodburn city	330	351
Washington County[113]	10 764	10 728
Springfield division	8 614	...
Mackville city[113]	229	'219
Springfield city[113]	3 179	2 961
Willisburg division	2 150	1 994
Willisburg city[113]	235	'304
Wayne County[114]	17 022	14 268
Coopersville division	1 465	...
Gregory division	1 159	...
Mill Springs division	3 161	...
Monticello division	8 416	...
Monticello city[114]	5 677	3 618
Zula–Powersburg division	2 821	...
Webster County[115]	14 832	13 282
Clay division	2 936	2 617
Clay city[115]	1 356	1 426
Wheatcroft city	325	229
Dixon division	2 292	1 910
Dixon city	533	572
Providence division	5 367	5 040
Providence city	4 434	4 270
Sebree division	4 237	3 715
Sebree city[115]	1 516	1 092
Slaughters city[115]	269	276
Whitley County[116]	33 396	24 145
Corbin division	11 282	...
Corbin city (pt.)[116]	6 739	'6 295
Cumberland Falls division	3 345	...
Pearl division	254	341
Saxton division	5 108	...
Siler division	2 415	1 788
Williamsburg division	10 992	...
Williamsburg city[116]	5 560	3 687
Wolfe County[117]	6 698	5 669
Campton division	3 528	...
Campton city[117]	486	419
Hazel Green division	2 104	1 871
Malaga division	1 066	...
Woodford County[118]	17 778	14 434
Midway division	2 452	2 650
Midway city[118]	1 445	1 278
Versailles division	12 760	...
Versailles city[118]	6 427	5 679
Woodford South division	2 566	...

LOUISIANA

The name Louisiana was given to the entire Mississippi Valley by La Salle, in honor of Louis XIV of France.

The discoverers of the region constituting the present state of Louisiana were Spaniards. In 1519 De Pineda sailed along the coast and in 1543 De Soto's expedition returning from the interior of the country reached the Gulf by way of the Mississippi. Spain, however, set up no claim to this region, and in 1682 the French explorer, La Salle, completed his descent of the Mississippi River and took possession of the whole country drained by it in the name of France. The first permanent settlement within the present limits of Louisiana was made at Natchitoches, where the French established a trading post in 1715. Three years later New Orleans was founded.

The Louisiana region west of the Mississippi was ceded by France to Spain in 1762, retroceded to France in 1800, and purchased by the United States in 1803. At the time of the purchase it comprised the area of the present state of Louisiana west of the Mississippi and the Isle of Orleans east of the river. In addition, it included practically all the western watershed of the Mississippi. In 1804 the region was divided by the thirty-third parallel, which forms the present northern boundary of Louisiana, into the territory of Orleans on the south and the district of Louisiana on the north.

All of the present state of Louisiana lying east of the Mississippi, except the Isle of Orleans, was ceded to Great Britain in 1763, together with the rest of the French possessions east of the Mississippi, and in the same year the Floridas were transferred to Great Britain by Spain. Shortly afterwards the southern part of the French cession was made a part of West Florida. In 1783 the Floridas were retroceded to Spain, and in 1819 were purchased by the United States. This eastern section of Louisiana, which had been claimed by both France and Spain, was in dispute between the latter country and the United States from 1803 to 1819. In 1810, however, the inhabitants declared their independence of Spain and the United States assumed control.

In January, 1812, under authority of an enabling act passed by Congress in the preceding year, the territory of Orleans adopted a state constitution, and on April 30 of the same year it was admitted to the Union as the state of Louisiana. At this time the Baton Rouge district was not included as a part of the new state, but it was added very shortly thereafter, thus giving Louisiana its present extent.

PARISH LOCATION INDEX

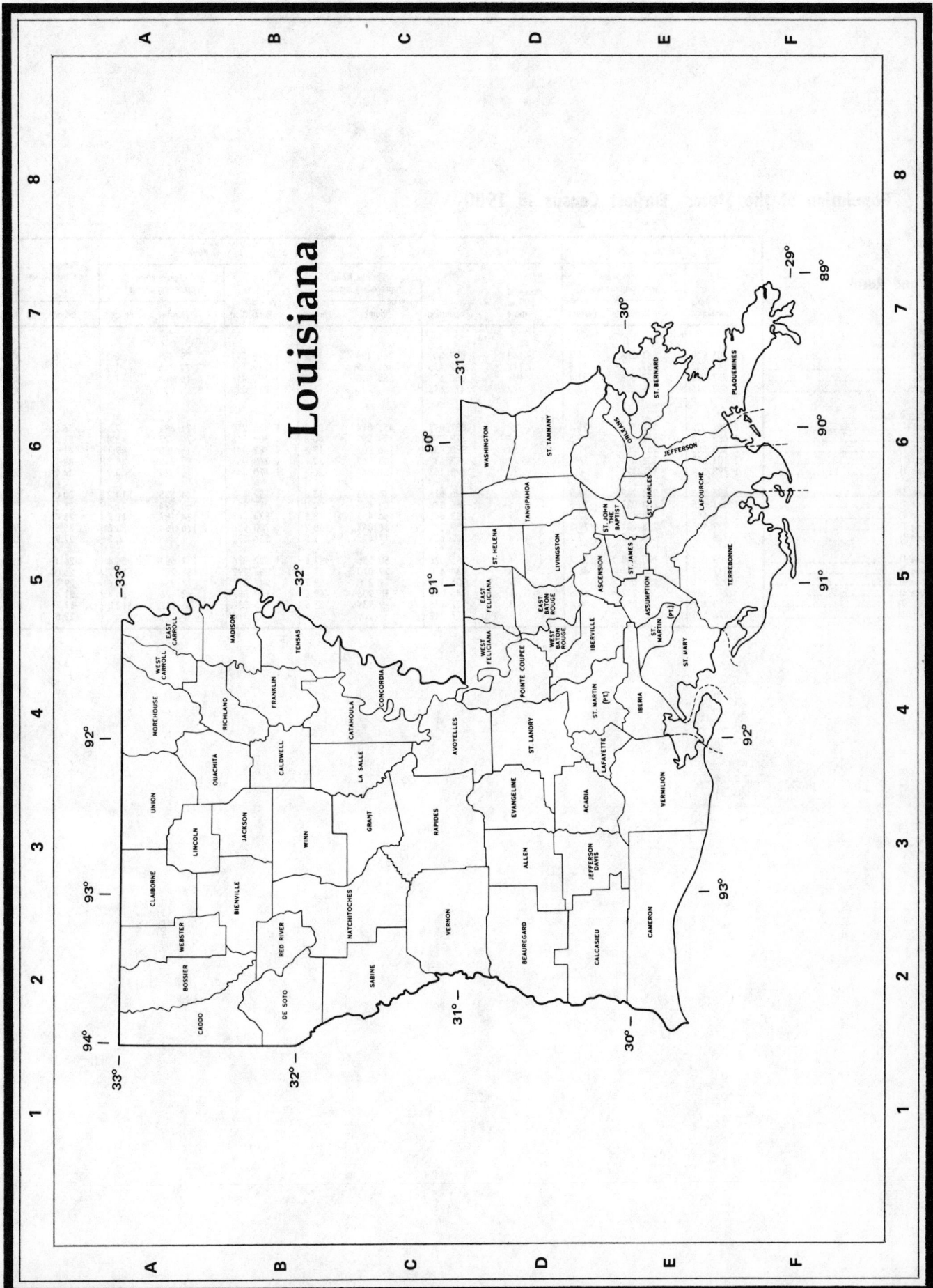

Louisiana

315

Population of the State: Earliest Census to 1980

Urban and Rural

	The State			Urban				Rural				Percent of total population	
	Total population	Change from preceding census		Places of 2,500 or more	Population	Change from preceding census		Population	Change from preceding census			Urban	Rural
		Number	Percent			Number	Percent		Number	Percent			
Current urban definition:													
1980 (Apr. 1)	4 205 900	561 263	15.4	143	2 887 309	465 134	19.2	1 318 591	99 460	8.2		68.6	31.4
1970 (Apr. 1)	3 644 637	387 615	11.9	112	2 422 175	361 569	17.5	1 219 131	22 715	1.9		66.5	33.5
1960 (Apr. 1)	3 257 022	573 506	21.4	101	2 060 606	588 910	40.0	1 196 416	−15 404	−1.3		63.3	36.7
1950 (Apr. 1)	2 683 516	319 636	13.5	72	1 471 696	...	...	1 211 820	...	...		54.8	45.2
Previous urban definition:													
1960 (Apr. 1)	3 257 022	573 506	21.4	87	1 831 812	451 814	32.7	1 425 210	121 692	9.3		56.2	43.8
1950 (Apr. 1)	2 683 516	319 636	13.5	67	1 379 998	399 559	40.8	1 303 518	−79 923	−5.8		51.4	48.6
1940 (Apr. 1)	2 363 880	262 287	12.5	54	980 439	146 907	17.6	1 383 441	115 380	9.1		41.5	58.5
1930 (Apr. 1)	2 101 593	303 084	16.9	48	833 532	205 369	32.7	1 268 061	97 715	8.3		39.7	60.3
1920 (Jan. 1)	1 798 509	142 121	8.6	38	628 163	131 647	26.5	1 170 346	10 474	0.9		34.9	65.1
1910 (Apr. 15)	1 656 388	274 763	19.9	26	496 516	130 228	35.6	1 159 872	144 535	14.2		30.0	70.0
1900 (June 1)	1 381 625	263 037	23.5	15	366 288	82 443	29.0	1 015 337	180 594	21.6		26.5	73.5
1890 (June 1)	1 118 588	178 642	19.0	9	283 845	44 455	18.6	834 743	134 187	19.2		25.4	74.6
1880 (June 1)	939 946	213 031	29.3	6	239 390	36 867	18.2	700 556	176 164	33.6		25.5	74.5
1870 (June 1)	726 915	18 913	2.7	3	202 523	17 497	*9.5	524 392	1 416	0.3		27.9	72.1
1860 (June 1)	708 002	190 240	36.7	4	185 026	50 556	37.6	522 976	139 684	36.4		26.1	73.9
1850 (June 1)	517 762	165 351	46.9	3	134 470	29 070	27.6	383 292	136 281	55.2		26.0	74.0
1840 (June 1)	352 411	136 672	63.4	2	105 400	59 318	128.7	247 011	77 354	45.6		29.9	70.1
1830 (June 1)	215 739	62 332	40.6	1	46 082	18 906	69.6	169 657	43 426	34.4		21.4	78.6
1820 (Aug. 7)	153 407	76 851	100.4	1	27 176	9 934	57.6	126 231	66 917	112.8		17.7	82.3
1810 (Aug. 6)	76 556	...	...	1	17 242	...	...	59 314	...	...		22.5	77.5

ACADIA

1890	13,231
1900	23,483
1910	31,847
1920	34,820
1930	29,326
1940	46,260
1950	47,050
1960	49,931
1970	52,109
1980	56,427

ALLEN

1920	19,382
1930	15,261
1940	17,540
1950	18,835
1960	19,867
1970	20,794
1980	21,390

ASCENSION

1810	2,219
1820	3,768
1830	5,426
1840	6,951
1850	10,752
1860	11,484
1870	11,577
1880	16,895
1890	19,545
1900	24,142
1910	23,887
1920	22,155
1930	18,438
1940	21,215
1950	22,387
1960	27,927
1970	37,086
1980	50,068

ASSUMPTION

1810	2,472
1820	3,576
1830	5,669
1840	7,141
1850	10,538
1860	15,379
1870	13,234
1880	17,010
1890	19,629
1900	21,620
1910	24,128
1920	17,192
1930	15,990
1940	18,541
1950	17,278
1960	17,991
1970	19,654
1980	22,084

AVOYELLES

1810	1,209
1820	2,245
1830	3,484
1840	6,616
1850	9,326
1860	13,167
1870	12,926
1880	16,747
1890	25,112
1900	29,701

1910	34,102
1920	35,300
1930	34,926
1940	29,256
1950	38,031
1960	37,606
1970	37,751
1980	41,393

BEAUREGARD

1920	20,767
1930	14,569
1940	14,847
1950	17,766
1960	19,191
1970	22,888
1980	29,692

BIENVILLE

1850	5,539
1860	11,000
1870	10,636
1880	10,442
1890	14,108
1900	17,588
1910	21,776
1920	20,977
1930	23,789
1940	23,933
1950	19,105
1960	16,726
1970	16,024
1980	16,387

BOSSIER

1850	6,962
1860	11,348
1870	12,675
1880	16,042
1890	20,330
1900	24,153
1910	21,738
1920	22,266
1930	28,388
1940	33,162
1950	40,139
1960	57,622
1970	65,877
1980	80,721

CADDO

1840	5,282
1850	8,884
1860	12,140
1870	21,714
1880	26,296
1890	31,555
1900	44,499
1910	58,200
1920	83,265
1930	124,670
1940	150,203
1950	176,547
1960	223,859
1970	230,184
1980	252,358

CALCASIEU

1840	2,057
1850	3,914
1860	5,928

1870	6,733
1880	12,484
1890	20,176
1900	30,428
1910	62,767
1920	32,807
1930	41,963
1940	56,503
1950	89,635
1960	145,475
1970	145,415
1980	167,223

CALDWELL

1840	2,017
1850	2,815
1860	4,833
1870	4,820
1880	5,767
1890	5,814
1900	6,917
1910	8,593
1920	9,514
1930	10,430
1940	12,046
1950	10,293
1960	9,004
1970	9,354
1980	10,761

CAMERON

1870	1,591
1880	2,416
1890	2,828
1900	3,952
1910	4,288
1920	3,952
1930	6,054
1940	7,203
1950	6,244
1960	6,909
1970	8,194
1980	9,336

CARROLL

1840	4,237
1850	8,789
1860	18,052
1870	10,110

CATAHOULA

1810	1,164
1820	2,287
1830	2,581
1840	4,955
1850	7,132
1860	11,651
1870	8,475
1880	10,277
1890	12,002
1900	16,351
1910	10,415
1920	11,074
1930	12,451
1940	14,618
1950	11,834
1960	11,421
1970	11,769
1980	12,287

CLAIBORNE

1830	1,764
1840	6,185
1850	7,471
1860	16,848
1870	20,240
1880	18,837
1890	23,312
1900	23,029
1910	25,050
1920	27,855
1930	32,285
1940	29,855
1950	25,063
1960	19,407
1970	17,024
1980	17,095

CONCORDIA

1810	2,895
1820	2,626
1830	4,662
1840	9,414
1850	7,758
1860	13,805
1870	9,977
1880	14,914
1890	14,871
1900	13,559
1910	14,278
1920	12,466
1930	12,778
1940	14,562
1950	14,398
1960	20,467
1970	22,578
1980	22,981

DE SOTO

1850	8,023
1860	13,298
1870	14,962
1880	15,603
1890	19,860
1900	25,063
1910	27,689
1920	29,376
1930	31,016
1940	31,803
1950	24,398
1960	24,248
1970	22,764
1980	25,727

EAST BATON ROUGE

1810	1,463
1820	5,220
1830	6,698
1840	8,138
1850	11,977
1860	16,046
1870	17,816
1880	19,966
1890	25,922
1900	31,153
1910	34,580
1920	44,513
1930	68,208
1940	88,415
1950	158,236
1960	230,058
1970	285,167
1980	366,191

EAST CARROLL

1880	12,134
1890	12,362
1900	11,373
1910	11,637
1920	11,231
1930	15,815
1940	19,023
1950	16,302
1960	14,433
1970	12,884
1980	11,772

EAST FELICIANA

1820	12,732
1830	8,247
1840	11,893
1850	13,598
1860	14,697
1870	13,499
1880	15,132
1890	17,903
1900	20,443
1910	20,055
1920	17,487
1930	17,449
1940	18,039
1950	19,133
1960	20,198
1970	17,657
1980	19,015

EVANGELINE

1920	23,485
1930	25,483
1940	30,497
1950	31,629
1960	31,639
1970	31,932
1980	33,343

FRANKLIN

1850	3,251
1860	6,162
1870	5,078
1880	6,495
1890	6,900
1900	8,890
1910	11,989
1920	24,100
1930	20,530
1940	32,382
1950	29,376
1960	26,088
1970	23,946
1980	24,141

GRANT

1870	4,517
1880	6,188
1890	8,270
1900	12,902
1910	15,958
1920	14,403
1930	15,709
1940	15,933
1950	14,263
1960	13,330
1970	13,671
1980	16,703

IBERIA

1870	9,042
1880	16,676
1890	20,997
1900	29,015
1910	31,262
1920	26,885
1930	28,192
1940	37,183
1950	40,059
1960	51,657
1970	57,397
1980	63,752

IBERVILLE

1810	2,697
1820	4,414
1830	7,049
1840	8,495
1850	12,278
1860	14,661
1870	12,347
1880	17,554
1890	21,848
1900	27,066
1910	30,954
1920	26,806
1930	24,638
1940	27,721
1950	26,750
1960	29,939
1970	30,746
1980	32,159

JACKSON

1850	5,566
1860	9,465
1870	7,646
1880	5,328
1890	7,453
1900	9,119
1910	13,818
1920	14,486
1930	13,808
1940	17,807
1950	15,434
1960	15,828
1970	15,963
1980	17,321

JEFFERSON

1830	6,846
1840	10,470
1850	25,093
1860	15,372
1870	17,767
1880	12,166
1890	13,221
1900	15,321
1910	18,247
1920	21,563
1930	40,032
1940	50,427
1950	103,873
1960	208,769
1970	338,229
1980	454,592

JEFFERSON DAVIS

1920	18,999
1930	19,765
1940	24,191
1950	26,298
1960	29,825
1970	29,554
1980	32,168

LAFAYETTE

1830	5,653
1840	7,841
1850	6,720
1860	9,003
1870	10,388
1880	13,235
1890	15,966
1900	22,825
1910	28,733
1920	30,841
1930	39,827
1940	43,941
1950	57,743
1960	84,656
1970	111,643
1980	150,017

LAFOURCHE

1810	1,995
1820	3,775
1830	5,503
1840	7,303
1850	9,532
1860	14,044
1870	14,719
1880	19,113
1890	22,095
1900	28,882
1910	33,111
1920	30,344
1930	32,419
1940	38,615
1950	42,209
1960	55,381
1970	68,941
1980	82,483

LA SALLE

1910	9,402
1920	9,856
1930	11,668
1940	10,959
1950	12,717
1960	13,011
1970	13,295
1980	17,004

LINCOLN

1880	11,075
1890	14,753
1900	15,898
1910	18,485
1920	16,962
1930	22,822
1940	24,790
1950	25,782
1960	28,535
1970	33,800
1980	39,763

LIVINGSTON

1840	2,315
1850	3,385
1860	4,431
1870	4,026
1880	5,258
1890	5,769
1900	8,100
1910	10,627
1920	11,643
1930	18,206
1940	17,790
1950	20,054
1960	26,974
1970	36,511
1980	58,806

MADISON

1840	5,142
1850	8,773
1860	14,133
1870	8,600
1880	13,906
1890	14,135
1900	12,322
1910	10,676
1920	10,829
1930	14,829
1940	18,443
1950	17,451
1960	16,444
1970	15,065
1980	15,975

MOREHOUSE

1850	3,913
1860	10,357
1870	9,387
1880	14,206
1890	16,786
1900	16,634
1910	18,786
1920	19,311
1930	23,689
1940	27,571
1950	32,038
1960	33,709
1970	32,463
1980	34,803

NATCHITOCHES

1810	2,870
1820	7,486
1830	7,905
1840	14,350
1850	14,228
1860	16,699
1870	18,265
1880	19,707
1890	25,836
1900	33,216
1910	36,455
1920	38,602
1930	38,477
1940	40,997
1950	38,144
1960	35,653
1970	35,219
1980	39,863

ORLEANS

1810	24,552
1820	41,351
1830	49,826
1840	102,193
1850	119,460
1860	174,491
1870	191,418
1880	216,090
1890	242,039
1900	287,104
1910	339,075
1920	387,219
1930	458,762
1940	494,537
1950	570,445
1960	627,525
1970	593,471
1980	557,515

OUACHITA

1810	1,077
1820	2,896
1830	5,140
1840	4,640
1850	5,008
1860	4,727
1870	11,582
1880	14,685
1890	17,985
1900	20,947
1910	25,830
1920	30,319
1930	54,337
1940	59,168
1950	74,713
1960	101,663
1970	115,387
1980	139,241

PLAQUEMINES

1810	1,549
1820	2,354
1830	4,489
1840	5,060
1850	7,390
1860	8,494
1870	10,552
1880	11,575
1890	12,541
1900	13,039
1910	12,524
1920	10,194
1930	9,608
1940	12,318
1950	14,239
1960	22,545
1970	25,225
1980	26,049

POINTE COUPEE

1810	4,539
1820	4,912
1830	5,936
1840	7,898
1850	11,339
1860	17,718
1870	12,981
1880	17,785
1890	19,613
1900	25,777
1910	25,289
1920	24,697
1930	21,007
1940	24,004
1950	21,841
1960	22,488
1970	22,002
1980	24,045

RAPIDES

1810	2,200
1820	6,065
1830	7,575
1840	14,132
1850	16,561
1860	25,360
1870	18,015
1880	23,563
1890	27,642
1900	39,578
1910	44,545
1920	59,444
1930	65,455
1940	73,370
1950	90,648
1960	111,351
1970	118,078
1980	135,282

RED RIVER

1880	8,573
1890	11,318
1900	11,548
1910	11,402
1920	15,301
1930	16,078
1940	15,881
1950	12,113
1960	9,978
1970	9,226
1980	10,433

RICHLAND

1870	5,110
1880	8,440
1890	10,230
1900	11,116
1910	15,769
1920	20,860
1930	26,374
1940	28,829
1950	26,672
1960	23,824
1970	21,774
1980	22,187

SABINE

1850	4,515
1860	5,828
1870	6,456
1880	7,344
1890	9,390
1900	15,421
1910	19,874
1920	20,713
1930	24,110
1940	23,586
1950	20,880
1960	18,564
1970	18,638
1980	25,280

SAINT BERNARD

1810	1,020
1820	2,635
1830	3,356
1840	3,237
1850	3,802
1860	4,076
1870	3,553

1880	4,405
1890	4,326
1900	5,031
1910	5,277
1920	4,968
1930	6,512
1940	7,280
1950	11,087
1960	32,186
1970	51,185
1980	64,097

SAINT CHARLES

1810	3,291
1820	3,862
1830	5,147
1840	4,700
1850	5,120
1860	5,297
1870	4,867
1880	7,167
1890	7,737
1900	9,072
1910	11,207
1920	8,586
1930	12,111
1940	12,321
1950	13,363
1960	21,219
1970	29,550
1980	37,259

SAINT HELENA

1820	3,026
1830	4,028
1840	3,525
1850	4,561
1860	7,130
1870	5,423
1880	7,504
1890	8,062
1900	8,479
1910	9,172
1920	8,427
1930	9,492
1940	9,542
1950	9,013
1960	9,162
1970	9,937
1980	9,827

SAINT JAMES

1810	3,955
1820	5,660
1830	7,646
1840	8,548
1850	11,098
1860	11,499
1870	10,152
1880	14,714
1890	15,715
1900	20,197
1910	23,009
1920	21,228
1930	15,338
1940	16,596
1950	15,334
1960	18,369
1970	19,733
1980	21,495

SAINT JOHN THE BAPTIST

1810	2,990
1820	3,854
1830	5,677
1840	5,776
1850	7,317
1860	7,390
1870	6,762
1880	9,686
1890	11,359
1900	12,330
1910	14,338
1920	11,896
1930	14,078
1940	14,766
1950	14,861
1960	18,439
1970	23,813
1980	31,924

SAINT LANDRY

1810	5,048
1820	10,085
1830	12,591
1840	15,233
1850	22,253
1860	23,104
1870	25,553
1880	40,004
1890	40,250
1900	52,906
1910	66,661
1920	51,697
1930	60,074
1940	71,481
1950	78,476
1960	81,493
1970	80,364
1980	84,128

SAINT MARTIN

1810	7,369
1820	12,063
1830	7,205
1840	8,674
1850	11,761
1860	12,674
1870	9,370
1880	12,663
1890	14,884
1900	18,940
1910	23,070
1920	21,990
1930	21,767
1940	26,394
1950	26,353
1960	29,063
1970	32,453
1980	40,214

SAINT MARY

1830	6,442
1840	8,950
1850	13,697
1860	16,816
1870	13,860
1880	19,891
1890	22,461
1900	34,145
1910	39,368
1920	30,754
1930	29,397
1940	31,458
1950	35,848
1960	49,833
1970	60,752
1980	64,253

SAINT TAMMANY

1820	1,733
1830	2,864
1840	4,598
1850	6,364
1860	5,406
1870	5,586
1880	6,887
1890	10,160
1900	13,335
1910	18,917
1920	20,645
1930	20,929
1940	23,624
1950	26,988
1960	38,643
1970	63,585
1980	110,869

TANGIPAHOA

1870	7,928
1880	9,638
1890	12,655
1900	17,625
1910	29,160
1920	31,440
1930	46,227
1940	45,519
1950	53,218
1960	59,434
1970	65,875
1980	80,698

TENSAS

1850	9,040
1860	16,078
1870	12,419
1880	17,185
1890	16,647
1900	19,070
1910	17,060
1920	12,085
1930	15,096
1940	15,940
1950	13,209
1960	11,796
1970	9,732
1980	8,525

TERREBONNE

1830	2,121
1840	4,410
1850	7,724
1860	12,091
1870	12,451
1880	17,957
1890	20,167
1900	24,464
1910	28,320
1920	26,974
1930	29,816
1940	35,880
1950	43,328
1960	60,771
1970	76,049
1980	94,393

UNION

1840	1,838
1850	8,203
1860	10,389
1870	11,685
1880	13,526
1890	17,304
1900	18,520
1910	20,451
1920	19,621
1930	20,731
1940	20,943
1950	19,141
1960	17,624
1970	18,447
1980	21,167

VERMILION

1850	3,409
1860	4,324
1870	4,528
1880	8,728
1890	14,234
1900	20,705
1910	26,390
1920	26,482
1930	33,684
1940	37,750
1950	36,929
1960	38,855
1970	43,071
1980	48,458

VERNON

1880	5,160
1890	5,903
1900	10,327
1910	17,324
1920	20,493
1930	20,047
1940	19,142
1950	18,974
1960	18,301
1970	53,794
1980	53,475

WASHINGTON

1820	2,517
1830	2,286
1840	2,649
1850	3,408
1860	4,708
1870	3,330
1880	5,190
1890	6,700
1900	9,628
1910	18,886
1920	24,164
1930	29,904
1940	34,443
1950	38,371
1960	44,015
1970	41,987
1980	44,207

WEBSTER

1880	10,005
1890	12,446
1900	15,125
1910	19,186
1920	24,707
1930	29,458
1940	33,676
1950	35,704
1960	39,701
1970	39,939
1980	43,631

WEST BATON ROUGE

1820	2,335
1830	3,084
1840	4,638
1850	6,270
1860	7,312
1870	5,114
1880	7,667
1890	8,363
1900	10,285
1910	12,636
1920	11,092
1930	9,716
1940	11,263
1950	11,738
1960	14,796
1970	16,864
1980	19,086

WEST CARROLL

1880	2,776
1890	3,748
1900	3,685
1910	6,249
1920	8,857
1930	13,895
1940	19,252
1950	17,248
1960	14,177
1970	13,028
1980	12,922

WEST FELICIANA

1830	8,629
1840	10,910
1850	13,245
1860	11,671
1870	10,499
1880	12,809
1890	15,062
1900	15,994
1910	13,449
1920	12,303
1930	10,924
1940	11,720
1950	10,169
1960	12,395
1970	10,761
1980	12,186

WINN

1860	6,876
1870	4,954
1880	5,846
1890	7,082
1900	9,648
1910	18,357
1920	16,119
1930	14,766
1940	16,923
1950	16,119
1960	16,034
1970	16,369
1980	17,253

NOTE

CARROLL

Taken to form East and West Carroll in 1877.

ABBEVILLE

1870	545
1880	255
1890	637
1900	1,536
1910	2,907
1920	3,461
1930	4,356
1940	6,672
1950	9,338
1960	10,414
1970	10,996
1980	12,391

ALEXANDRIA

1840	672
1850	1,461
1860	1,218
1870	1,800
1880	2,861
1890	5,648
1900	5,648
1910	11,213
1920	17,510
1930	23,025
1940	27,066
1950	34,913
1960	40,279
1970	41,811
1980	51,565

BAKER

1950	762
1960	4,823
1970	8,281
1980	12,865

BASTROP

1860	481
1870	521
1880	822
1890	(NA)
1900	787
1910	854
1920	1,216
1930	5,121
1940	6,626
1950	12,769
1960	15,193
1970	14,713
1980	15,527

BATON ROUGE

1840	2,269
1850	3,905
1860	5,428
1870	6,498
1880	7,197
1890	10,478
1900	11,269
1910	14,897
1920	21,782
1930	30,729
1940	34,719
1950	125,629
1960	152,419
1970	165,921
1980	219,419

BOGALUSA

1920	8,245
1930	14,029
1940	14,604
1950	17,798
1960	21,423
1970	18,412
1980	16,976

BOSSIER CITY

1890	202
1910	775
1920	1,094
1930	4,003
1940	5,786
1950	15,470
1960	32,776
1970	43,769
1980	50,817

CROWLEY

1890	420
1900	4,214
1910	5,099
1920	6,108
1930	7,656
1940	9,523
1950	12,784
1960	15,617
1970	16,104
1980	16,036

DE RIDDER

1910	2,100
1920	3,535
1930	3,747
1940	3,750
1950	5,799
1960	(NA)
1970	8,030
1980	11,057

EUNICE

1900	316
1910	1,684
1920	3,272
1930	3,597
1940	5,242
1950	8,184
1960	11,326
1970	11,390
1980	12,479

GRETNA

1920	7,197
1930	9,584
1940	10,879
1950	13,813
1960	21,967
1970	24,875
1980	20,615

HAMMOND

1880	277
1890	692
1900	1,511
1910	2,942
1920	3,855

1930	6,072
1940	6,033
1950	8,010
1960	10,563
1970	12,487
1980	15,043

HARAHAN

1930	892
1940	1,082
1950	3,394
1960	9,275
1970	13,037
1980	11,384

HOUMA

1860	429
1870	593
1880	1,084
1890	1,280
1900	3,212
1910	5,024
1920	5,160
1930	6,531
1940	9,052
1950	11,505
1960	22,561
1970	30,922
1980	32,602

JENNINGS

1890	412
1900	1,539
1910	3,925
1920	3,824
1930	4,036
1940	7,343
1950	9,663
1960	11,887
1970	11,783
1980	12,401

KENNER

1920	1,882
1930	2,440
1940	2,375
1950	5,535
1960	17,037
1970	29,858
1980	66,382

LAFAYETTE

1890	2,106
1900	3,314
1910	6,392
1920	7,855
1930	14,635
1940	19,210
1950	33,541
1960	40,400
1970	68,908
1980	81,961

LAKE CHARLES

1880	838
1890	3,442
1900	6,680
1910	11,449
1920	13,088

1930	15,791
1940	21,207
1950	41,272
1960	63,392
1970	77,998
1980	75,226

MINDEN

1880	1,113
1890	1,298
1900	1,561
1910	3,002
1920	6,105
1930	5,623
1940	6,677
1950	9,787
1960	12,785
1970	13,996
1980	15,084

MONROE

1850	435
1860	(NA)
1870	1,949
1880	2,070
1890	3,256
1900	5,428
1910	10,209
1920	12,675
1930	26,028
1940	28,309
1950	38,572
1960	52,219
1970	56,374
1980	57,597

MORGAN CITY

1880	2,015
1890	2,291
1900	2,332
1910	5,477
1920	5,429
1930	5,985
1940	6,969
1950	9,759
1960	13,540
1970	16,586
1980	16,114

NATCHITOCHES

1850	1,261
1860	(NA)
1870	1,401
1880	2,785
1890	1,820
1900	2,388
1910	2,532
1920	3,388
1930	4,547
1940	6,812
1950	9,914
1960	13,924
1970	15,974
1980	16,664

NEW IBERIA

1870	1,472
1880	2,709
1890	3,447
1900	6,815
1910	7,499

1920	6,278
1930	8,003
1940	13,747
1950	16,467
1960	29,062
1970	30,147
1980	32,766

NEW ORLEANS

1810	17,242
1820	27,176
1830	46,082
1840	102,193
1850	116,375
1860	168,675
1870	191,418
1880	216,090
1890	242,039
1900	287,104
1910	339,075
1920	387,219
1930	458,762
1940	494,537
1950	570,445
1960	627,525
1970	593,471
1980	557,515

OPELOUSAS

1870	786
1880	1,546
1880	1,676
1890	1,572
1900	2,951
1910	4,623
1920	4,437
1930	6,299
1940	8,890
1950	11,659
1960	17,417
1970	20,387
1980	18,903

PINEVILLE

1860	393
1870	414
1880	763
1890	540
1900	617
1910	1,212
1920	2,188
1930	3,612
1940	4,297
1950	6,423
1960	8,636
1970	8,951
1980	12,034

RUSTON

1890	767
1900	1,324
1910	3,377
1920	3,389
1930	4,400
1940	7,107
1950	10,372
1960	13,991
1970	17,365
1980	20,585

SHREVEPORT

1850	1,728
1860	2,190
1870	4,607
1880	8,004
1890	11,979
1900	16,013
1910	28,015
1920	43,874
1930	76,655
1940	98,167
1950	127,206
1960	164,372
1970	182,064
1980	205,820

SLIDELL

1890	364
1900	1,129
1910	2,188
1920	2,958
1930	2,807
1940	2,864
1950	3,464
1960	6,356
1970	16,101
1980	26,718

SULPHUR

1940	3,504
1950	5,996
1960	11,429
1970	13,551
1980	19,709

TALLULAH

1910	847
1920	1,316
1930	3,332
1940	5,712
1950	7,758
1960	9,413
1970	9,643
1980	11,634

THIBODAUX

1850	1,242
1860	1,380
1870	1,922
1880	1,515
1890	2,078
1900	3,253
1910	3,824
1920	3,526
1930	4,442
1940	5,851
1950	7,730
1960	13,403
1970	15,028
1980	15,810

WEST MONROE

1890	447
1900	775
1910	1,127
1920	2,240
1930	6,566
1940	8,560
1950	10,302
1960	15,215
1970	14,868
1980	14,993

WESTWEGO

1930	3,987
1940	4,992
1950	8,328
1960	9,815
1970	11,402
1980	12,663

CORRECTION NOTE

The official 1980 census counts of total population shown in
this report supersede counts issued previously. Corrections
to the figures were made after the counts were provided to
the State for redistricting purposes and released in Advance
Report PHC80-V for this State.

Shown below are corrections to the 1980 census counts of the
total population made after the tabulations for this report
were completed. Any additional corrections made after this
report is printed are available by writing to Data User
Services Division, Customer Services (Corrections), Bureau of
the Census, Washington, D.C. 20233

The 1980 figures shown in this publication are subject to
change pending the outcome of the various lawsuits dealing
with the census counts.

	1980 population	
	As shown in the tables	Corrected
The State...................	4 205 900	4 206 312
La Salle Parish:		
Ward 4.........................	1 310	1 344
Jena town (pt.)...............	251	302
Ward 5.........................	2 676	2 655
Jena town (pt.)..............	2 676	2 655
Ward 9.........................	2 009	1 996
Jena town (pt.)...............	---	13
Madison Parish:		
Ward 1.........................	1 737	1 865
Tallulah city (pt.)...........	(1)	128
Ward 5.........................	2 198	2 070
Tallulah city (pt.)...........	2 198	2 070
Orleans Parish....................	557 515	557 927
New Orleans city................	557 515	557 927
Vernon Parish:		
Ward 2:		
Anacoco village...............	90	820
Jena town (total)	4 332	4 375
Tallulah city (total)	11 634	(2)

(1) Not shown
(2) No change

Parish Subdivisions	1980	1970
The State	4 205 900	r3 644 637
Acadia Parish[1]	56 427	52 109
Ward 1	12 211	11 499
Rayne city[1]	9 066	9 510
Ward 2	3 440	2 763
Ward 3	8 170	7 332
Church Point town[1]	4 599	3 865
Ward 4	5 953	5 338
Iota town	1 326	1 271
Ward 5	3 828	3 559
Estherwood village	691	661
Mermentau village	771	756
Morse village	835	759
Ward 6	19 763	19 333
Crowley city[1]	16 036	16 104
Ward 7	3 062	2 285
Eunice city (pt.)	221	112
Allen Parish[2]	21 390	20 794
Ward 1	2 914	3 267
Oberlin town	1 764	1 857
Ward 2	5 242	4 804
Kinder town[2]	2 603	2 307
Ward 3	1 292	939
Reeves village	199	214
Ward 4	1 575	1 411
Ward 5	10 367	10 373
Elizabeth town	454	504
Oakdale city[2]	7 155	7 301
Ascension Parish[3]	50 068	37 086
Ward 1	3 382	3 384
Donaldsonville city (pt.)[3]	2 323	2 073
Ward 2	1 672	1 440
Donaldsonville city (pt.)[3]	559	491
Ward 3	3 568	3 932
Donaldsonville city (pt.)	3 568	3 932
Ward 4	2 820	2 070
Donaldsonville city (pt.)[3]	1 451	871
Ward 5	1 796	1 626
Gonzales city (pt.)[3]	—	...
Ward 6	293	356
Ward 7	13 602	10 349
Gonzales city (pt.)[3]	7 287	4 512
Ward 8	8 450	5 367
Ward 9	6 188	3 216
Ward 10	8 297	5 346
Sorrento town	1 197	1 182
Assumption Parish[4]	22 084	19 654
Ward 1	2 282	...
Paincourtville (CDP) (pt.)	758	...
Ward 2	2 064	...
Ward 3	4 321	...
Labadieville (CDP)	2 138	...
Ward 4	1 785	...
Ward 5	1 914	...
Napoleonville town	829	1 008
Ward 6	2 363	...
Paincourtville (CDP) (pt.)	1 055	...
Ward 7	1 943	...
Paincourtville (CDP) (pt.)	191	...
Ward 8	2 049	...
Pierre Part (CDP) (pt.)	669	...
Ward 9	3 363	...
Pierre Part (CDP) (pt.)	2 484	...
Avoyelles Parish[5]	41 393	37 751
Ward 1	2 495	1 940
Ward 2	9 707	8 645
Marksville town[5]	5 113	4 519
Ward 3	4 207	3 366
Mansura town[5]	2 074	1 699
Ward 4	3 297	2 556
Hessmer village	743	454
Ward 5	1 562	1 302
Ward 6	1 721	1 612
Ward 7	3 104	2 812
Simmesport town	2 293	2 027
Ward 8	2 597	r2 572
Cottonport town (pt.)	98	r75
Plaucheville village	196	224
Ward 9	4 066	r4 010
Cottonport town (pt.)	1 795	r1 769
Evergreen town	272	307
Ward 10	6 386	6 654
Bunkie town[5]	5 364	5 395
Ward 11	2 251	r2 282
Cottonport town (pt.)	18	r18
Moreauville village	853	807
Beauregard Parish[6]	29 692	22 888
Ward 1	651	447
Ward 2	3 228	2 579
Merryville town	1 286	1 286
Ward 3[6]	16 474	...
De Ridder city (pt.)[6]	11 057	8 030
Ward 4	1 192	708
Ward 5	2 240	1 586
Ward 6	2 927	1 502
Ward 7[6]	1 928	...

Parish Subdivisions	1980	1970
Beauregard Parish—Con.		
Ward 8[6]	1 052	...
Bienville Parish[7]	16 387	16 024
Ward 1	2 261	...
Arcadia town (pt.)[7]	1 401	(NA)
Ward 2	2 610	...
Arcadia town (pt.)[7]	2 002	(NA)
Bryceland village[7]	94	65
Ward 3	2 232	...
Gibsland town	1 354	1 380
Mount Lebanon town	105	102
Ward 4	2 285	...
Jamestown village	131	153
Ringgold town (pt.)[7]	809	(NA)
Ward 5	1 999	...
Ringgold town (pt.)[7]	846	(NA)
Ward 6	2 474	...
Bienville village	249	287
Castor village	195	r183
Ward 7	2 526	...
Lucky village[7]	370	...
Saline village	293	307
Bossier Parish[8]	80 721	r65 877
Ward 1	11 884	...
Bossier City city (pt.)[8]	11 243	(NA)
Shreveport city (pt.)[8]	635	250
Ward 2	43 120	...
Benton town[8]	1 864	1 493
Bossier City city (pt.)[8]	36 277	(NA)
Shreveport city (pt.)[8]	237	—
Ward 3	5 602	...
Plain Dealing town	1 213	r1 300
Ward 4	20 115	...
Bossier City city (pt.)[8]	3 297	(NA)
Haughton town[8]	1 510	885
Caddo Parish[9]	252 358	230 184
Ward 1	1 924	2 642
Belcher village[9]	436	r482
Gilliam village	244	211
Ward 2	7 848	7 266
Oil City town[9]	1 323	907
Vivian town[9]	4 146	4 046
Ward 3[9]	15 412	...
Blanchard village[9]	1 128	806
Mooringsport town[9]	911	830
Shreveport city (pt.)[9]	2 662	(NA)
Ward 4[9]	172 319	...
Shreveport city (pt.)[9]	169 888	(NA)
Ward 5[9]	15 914	...
Greenwood village[9]	1 043	212
Shreveport city (pt.)[9]	10 156	(NA)
Ward 6	4 597	2 755
Ward 7[9]	27 545	...
Shreveport city (pt.)[9]	21 407	(NA)
Ward 8[9]	3 965	...
Shreveport city (pt.)[9]	835	(NA)
Ward 9	2 834	2 882
Hosston village	480	428
Ida village[9]	306	370
Rodessa village	337	273
Calcasieu Parish[10]	167 223	145 415
Ward 1	10 126	4 180
Moss Bluff (CDP)	7 004	...
Ward 2	1 769	1 745
Ward 3	92 307	88 929
Lake Charles city[10]	75 226	77 998
Prien (CDP)	6 224	...
Ward 4	40 344	32 632
Carlyss (CDP)	1 806	...
Sulphur city[10]	19 709	14 959
Westlake town[10]	5 246	4 082
Ward 5	2 713	2 165
Ward 6	8 118	6 615
De Quincy town	3 966	3 448
Ward 7	6 129	5 471
Vinton town	3 631	3 454
Ward 8	5 717	3 678
Iowa town	2 437	1 944
Caldwell Parish[11]	10 761	9 354
Ward 1	985	...
Ward 2	965	...
Ward 3	1 589	...
Ward 4	687	...
Columbia town	687	1 000
Ward 5	977	...
Ward 6	1 192	...
Ward 7	1 125	...
Grayson village (pt.)	551	516
Ward 8	868	...
Ward 9	1 034	...
Clarks village	931	889
Ward 10	1 339	...
Grayson village (pt.)	13	...

Parish Subdivisions	1980	1970
Cameron Parish	9 336	8 194
Ward 1, Cow Island	532	566
Ward 2, Grand Chenier	1 256	1 166
Ward 3, Cameron	3 609	3 205
Cameron (CDP)	1 736	...
Ward 4, Grand Lake	1 522	1 218
Ward 5, Johnsons Bayou	816	704
Ward 6, Hackberry	1 601	1 335
Catahoula Parish[12]	12 287	11 769
Ward 1	1 263	...
Sicily Island village (pt.)[12]	131	(NA)
Ward 2	1 469	...
Sicily Island village (pt.)	560	(NA)
Ward 3	1 363	...
Ward 4	1 337	...
Harrisonburg village	610	626
Ward 5	1 499	...
Ward 6	1 838	...
Jonesville town (pt.)[12]	656	(NA)
Ward 7	965	...
Jonesville town (pt.)	965	(NA)
Ward 8	1 207	...
Jonesville town (pt.)	1 207	(NA)
Ward 9	1 346	...
Claiborne Parish[13]	17 095	17 024
Ward 1	1 075	1 059
Ward 2	1 009	877
Haynesville town (pt.)[13]	61	...
Ward 3	4 524	4 387
Haynesville town (pt.)[13]	3 393	3 055
Ward 4	615	594
Ward 5	1 264	1 255
Athens village	419	387
Ward 6	1 050	884
Ward 7	6 262	6 464
Homer town[13]	4 307	4 483
Ward 8	892	1 073
Lisbon village	138	151
Ward 9	404	431
Junction City village (pt.)	119	159
Concordia Parish[14]	22 981	22 578
Ward 1	3 642	...
Ferriday town (pt.)	2 679	(NA)
Ward 2	2 808	...
Ferriday town (pt.)[14]	1 793	(NA)
West Ferriday (CDP) (pt.)	975	...
Ward 3	4 721	...
Vidalia town (pt.)	4 721	(NA)
Ward 4	6 312	...
Ridgecrest town	895	1 076
Vidalia town (pt.)[14]	1 215	(NA)
West Ferriday (CDP) (pt.)	375	...
Ward 5	5 498	...
Clayton village	1 204	1 103
West Ferriday (CDP) (pt.)	49	...
De Soto Parish[15]	25 727	22 764
Ward 1	1 694	1 359
Keatchie town	342	328
Longstreet village	281	182
Ward 2	3 798	2 781
Stonewall town[15]	1 175	...
Ward 3	1 609	1 688
Stanley village	151	145
Ward 4	11 001	9 776
Mansfield city	6 485	6 432
South Mansfield village[15]	1 463	439
Ward 5	1 315	1 220
Ward 6	1 637	1 611
Grand Cane village	252	284
Ward 7	1 306	1 458
Ward 8	3 367	2 871
Logansport town	1 565	1 330
East Baton Rouge Parish[16]	366 191	285 167
Ward 1	219 419	...
Baton Rouge city[16]	219 419	'165 921
Ward 2	71 366	...
Baker city[16]	12 865	8 281
Scotlandville (CDP)	15 113	'22 599
Zachary city[16]	7 297	4 964
Ward 3	75 406	...
East Carroll Parish	11 772	12 884
Ward 1	775	875
Ward 2	1 314	1 656
Ward 3	8 278	8 228
Lake Providence town	6 361	6 183
Ward 4	91	197
Ward 5	422	642
Ward 6	305	514
Ward 7	587	772
East Feliciana Parish[17]	19 015	17 657
Ward 1	2 709	1 136
Slaughter town	729	580
Ward 2	2 194	1 704
Ward 3	6 215	7 364
Jackson town	3 133	4 697

Parish Subdivisions	1980	1970
East Feliciana Parish—Con.		
Ward 4	1 423	1 370
Norwood village[17]	421	348
Wilson village	656	606
Ward 5	3 544	3 316
Clinton town[17]	1 919	1 884
Ward 6	1 235	1 007
Ward 7	764	699
Ward 8	931	1 061
Evangeline Parish[18]	33 343	31 932
Ward 1	17 470	17 164
Chataignier village[18]	431	...
Ville Platte town[18]	9 201	9 692
Ward 2	3 705	3 359
Basile town	2 635	1 779
Ward 3	6 435	6 585
Mamou town[18]	3 194	3 275
Ward 4	2 573	2 217
Pine Prairie village	734	515
Ward 5	3 160	2 607
Turkey Creek village	366	280
Franklin Parish[19]	24 141	23 946
Ward 1	3 129	2 910
Wisner town	1 424	1 339
Ward 2	2 291	2 333
Gilbert village	800	746
Ward 3	1 811	1 906
Ward 4	1 634	1 764
Ward 5	915	1 182
Ward 6	1 782	1 682
Baskin village[19]	286	177
Ward 7	10 182	9 471
Winnsboro town[19]	5 921	5 349
Ward 8	1 212	1 124
Ward 9	1 185	1 574
Grant Parish[20]	16 703	13 671
Ward 1	2 999	2 976
Colfax town[20]	1 680	1 892
Ward 2	3 400	2 476
Ward 3	2 110	1 566
Dry Prong village	526	352
Pollock town (pt.)[20]	4	...
Ward 4	533	341
Ward 5	1 092	842
Georgetown village[20]	381	306
Ward 6	1 111	907
Ward 7	2 598	2 258
Montgomery town	843	923
Ward 8	2 860	2 305
Pollock town (pt.)[20]	395	341
Iberia Parish[21]	63 752	57 397
Ward 1	13 597	...
Delcambre town (pt.)	678	775
New Iberia city (pt.)[21]	4 971	(NA)
Ward 2	12 552	...
New Iberia city (pt.)[21]	6 369	(NA)
Ward 3	7 677	...
Jeanerette city[21]	6 511	6 322
Ward 4	11 066	...
Loreauville village[21]	860	728
New Iberia city (pt.)[21]	2 566	(NA)
Ward 5	18 860	...
New Iberia city (pt.)[21]	18 860	(NA)
Iberville Parish[22]	32 159	30 746
Ward 1	5 815	'5 447
White Castle town[22]	2 160	2 206
Ward 2	8 878	'8 287
Plaquemine city (pt.)[22]	3 612	3 175
Plaquemine Southwest (CDP) (pt.)	1 407	1 224
Seymourville (CDP)	2 891	2 506
Ward 3	2 261	2 775
Plaquemine city (pt.)	2 261	2 775
Ward 4	2 592	1 597
Ward 5	1 590	1 618
Carville (CDP)	1 037	...
Ward 6	2 676	2 809
Plaquemine city (pt.)	1 106	1 226
Ward 7	2 111	'2 077
Grosse Tete village	749	710
Rosedale village[22]	658	621
Ward 8	3 884	3 480
Plaquemine city (pt.)	542	563
Plaquemine Southwest (CDP) (pt.)	60	...
Ward 9	2 352	'2 656
Maringouin town	1 291	1 365
Jackson Parish[23]	17 321	15 963
Ward 1	2 138	...
Quitman village	231	169
Ward 2	1 707	...
Eros village	158	164
Ward 3	1 517	...
Chatham town	714	827
Ward 4	1 883	...
Ward 5	2 248	...
Jonesboro town (pt.)	1 914	(NA)
Ward 6	1 520	...

Parish Subdivisions

Parish Subdivisions	1980	1970
Jackson Parish—Con.		
Ward 6—Con.		
Jonesboro town (pt.)	1 102	(NA)
Ward 7	1 595	...
Jonesboro town (pt.)	978	(NA)
Ward 8	1 637	...
Hodge village	708	818
Jonesboro town (pt.)	201	(NA)
North Hodge village[23]	573	640
Ward 9	1 617	...
East Hodge village[23]	439	'363
Jonesboro town (pt.)	426	(NA)
Ward 10	1 459	...
Jonesboro town (pt.)[23]	440	(NA)
Jefferson Parish[24]	454 592	'338 229
Ward 1	32 013	24 732
Gretna city (pt.)	8 465	(NA)
Terrytown (CDP)	23 548	13 832
Ward 2[24]	16 675	...
Gretna city (pt.)	5 096	(NA)
Timberlane (CDP)	11 579	...
Ward 3[24]	27 075	...
Gretna city (pt.)	7 054	(NA)
Harvey (CDP) (pt.)	19 858	3 153
Ward 4	73 844	51 064
Estelle (CDP)	12 724	...
Harvey (CDP) (pt.)	2 851	3 194
Marrero (CDP)	36 548	29 015
Westwego city	12 663	11 402
Ward 5	23 890	14 297
Avondale (CDP)	6 699	...
Waggaman (CDP)	9 004	...
Ward 6	4 480	4 403
Barataria (CDP)	1 123	...
Jean Lafitte town[24]	936	...
Lafitte (CDP)	1 312	1 223
Ward 7	15 550	17 347
Jefferson (CDP)	15 550	16 489
Ward 8[24]	72 079	...
Metairie (CDP) (pt.)	72 079	(NA)
Ward 9	114 258	78 339
Harahan city	11 384	13 037
Kenner city[24]	66 382	29 858
Metairie (CDP) (pt.)	19 346	(NA)
River Ridge (CDP)	17 146	15 713
Ward 10[24]	72 735	...
Metairie (CDP) (pt.)	72 735	(NA)
Ward 11	1 993	2 244
Grand Isle town	1 982	2 236
Jefferson Davis Parish[25]	32 168	29 554
Ward 1	5 023	4 781
Lake Arthur town	3 615	3 551
Ward 2	13 788	12 826
Jennings city[25]	12 401	11 783
Ward 3	1 281	1 073
Ward 4	2 267	2 400
Elton town	1 450	1 598
Ward 5	1 222	1 167
Fenton village	491	404
Ward 6	4 956	4 477
Welsh town	3 515	3 203
Ward 7	881	723
Ward 8	1 925	1 642
Ward 9	825	465
Lafayette Parish[26]	150 017	'111 643
Ward 1	29 473	...
Carencro town[26]	3 712	2 302
Duson town (pt.)	1 007	(NA)
Lafayette city (pt.)[26]	11 633	(NA)
Scott town (pt.)[26]	1 191	(NA)
Ward 2	34 276	...
Lafayette city (pt.)[26]	26 221	(NA)
Ward 3	18 058	...
Lafayette city (pt.)	18 058	(NA)
Ward 4	29 856	...
Broussard town[26]	2 923	1 707
Lafayette city (pt.)[26]	9 174	(NA)
Youngsville village	1 053	1 002
Ward 5	38 354	...
Broadmoor (CDP)	7 051	...
Duson town (pt.)	246	(NA)
Lafayette city (pt.)[26]	16 875	(NA)
Scott town (pt.)[26]	1 048	(NA)
Lafourche Parish[27]	82 483	68 941
Ward 1	7 754	4 104
Thibodaux city (pt.)[27]	1 208	'47
Ward 2	16 174	'16 055
Thibodaux city (pt.)[27]	14 011	'14 981
Ward 3	10 414	7 561
Raceland (CDP) (pt.)	5 537	4 227
Ward 4	8 238	7 112
Larose (CDP) (pt.)	1 281	1 155
Lockport town[27]	2 424	'2 398
Ward 5	2 262	'1 762
Thibodaux city (pt.)[27]	591	...
Ward 6	5 323	4 323

Parish Subdivisions

Parish Subdivisions	1980	1970
Lafourche Parish—Con.		
Ward 7	3 576	3 603
Des Allemands (CDP) (pt.)	377	225
Raceland (CDP) (pt.)	765	653
Ward 8	795	849
Ward 9	2 175	1 708
Larose (CDP) (pt.)	663	244
Ward 10	21 328	18 831
Cut Off (CDP)	5 049	...
Galliano (CDP)	5 159	...
Golden Meadow town	2 282	2 681
Larose (CDP) (pt.)	3 290	2 868
Ward 11	4 444	3 033
Bayou Blue (CDP) (pt.)	2 333	...
La Salle Parish[28]	17 004	13 295
Ward 1	1 543	...
Ward 2	2 020	...
Olla town[28]	1 603	1 387
Ward 3	1 788	...
Tullos town (pt.)[28]	776	600
Urania town[28]	849	'874
Ward 4	1 310	...
Jena town (pt.)	251	(NA)
Ward 5	2 676	...
Jena town (pt.)[28]	2 676	(NA)
Ward 6	2 283	...
Jena town (pt.)	1 405	(NA)
Trout–Good Pine (CDP) (pt.)	302	...
Ward 7	1 598	...
Trout–Good Pine (CDP) (pt.)	731	...
Ward 8	1 777	...
Ward 9	2 009	...
Jena town (pt.)	–	(NA)
Lincoln Parish[29]	39 763	33 800
Ward 1	23 065	...
Ruston city (pt.)[29]	20 562	(NA)
Ward 2	5 713	...
Grambling town[29]	4 226	4 407
Ward 3	3 138	...
Simsboro village	553	412
Ward 4	3 578	...
Dubach town	1 161	1 096
Vienna town[29]	519	'59
Ward 5	4 269	...
Choudrant village	809	555
Downsville village (pt.)[29]	56	...
Ruston city (pt.)[29]	23	(NA)
Livingston Parish[30]	58 806	36 511
Ward 1[30]	15 751	...
Walker town[30]	2 957	1 363
Ward 2[30]	23 581	...
Denham Springs city[30]	8 563	6 752
Port Vincent village	450	387
Ward 3[30]	5 807	...
French Settlement village[30]	761	'670
Livingston town[30]	1 260	1 398
Ward 4[30]	13 667	...
Albany village	857	700
Killian village[30]	611	'293
Springfield town	424	423
Madison Parish[31]	15 975	15 065
Ward 1	1 737	...
Delta village	295	153
Mound village	40	78
Richmond village (pt.)[31]	–	...
Ward 2	1 733	...
Richmond village (pt.)	505	...
Tallulah city (pt.)[31]	451	(NA)
Ward 3	2 300	...
Tallulah city (pt.)[31]	978	(NA)
Ward 4	1 984	...
Tallulah city (pt.)[31]	1 984	(NA)
Ward 5	2 198	...
Tallulah city (pt.)	2 198	(NA)
Ward 6	1 936	...
Tallulah city (pt.)	1 936	(NA)
Ward 7	2 075	...
Tallulah city (pt.)	2 075	(NA)
Ward 8	2 012	...
Tallulah city (pt.)	2 012	(NA)
Morehouse Parish[32]	34 803	32 463
Ward 1	972	620
Ward 2	1 183	943
Ward 3	2 220	1 800
Bastrop city (pt.)[32]	–	...
Ward 4	21 434	18 774
Bastrop city (pt.)[32]	15 527	14 713
Ward 5	1 235	1 690
Oak Ridge village[32]	257	276
Ward 6	3 561	3 633
Mer Rouge village	802	819
Ward 7	893	796
Ward 8	1 275	1 519
Collinston village	439	397
Ward 9	182	154
Ward 10	1 848	2 534
Bonita village	503	533

Parish Subdivisions	1980	1970
Natchitoches Parish[33]	39 863	35 219
Ward 1	22 057	19 611
Natchitoches city[33]	16 664	15 974
Ward 2	7 111	5 701
Ashland village[33]	307	211
Campti town[33]	1 069	1 078
Clarence village	612	448
Goldonna village[33]	526	337
Ward 3	5 679	5 053
Powhatan village	279	277
Provencal village	695	530
Robeline village	238	274
Ward 4	5 016	4 854
Natchez village[33]	527	...
Orleans Parish	557 515	593 471
New Orleans city	557 515	593 471
Ouachita Parish[34]	139 241	115 387
Ward 1	7 214	4 691
Sterlington town	1 400	1 118
Ward 2	9 857	2 931
Monroe city (pt.)	—	—
Ward 3	33 554	28 034
Monroe city (pt.)[34]	22 823	21 277
Richwood town[34]	1 223	...
Ward 4	2 328	1 437
Ward 5	35 790	33 147
Brownsville–Bawcomville (CDP)	7 252	...
Claiborne (CDP)	6 278	...
West Monroe city[34]	14 993	14 868
Ward 6	3 611	2 364
Ward 7	2 088	1 206
Ward 8	3 517	1 867
Ward 9	1 057	615
Ward 10	40 225	39 095
Monroe city (pt.)[34]	34 774	35 097
Plaquemines Parish	26 049	25 225
Ward 1	1 561	1 839
Ward 2	1 281	1 276
Ward 3	7 220	6 414
Buras–Triumph (CDP)	4 137	4 113
Ward 4	5 656	7 084
Port Sulphur (CDP)	3 318	3 022
Ward 5	10 331	8 612
Belle Chasse (CDP)	5 412	...
Pointe Coupee Parish[35]	24 045	22 002
Ward 1	1 273	1 289
Ward 2	1 317	1 633
Ward 3	987	994
Ward 4	1 711	1 683
Morganza village[35]	846	836
Ward 5	1 957	1 508
Ward 6	1 106	926
Ward 7	2 127	1 856
Ward 8	2 389	1 980
Ward 9	6 748	6 603
New Roads town	3 924	3 945
Ward 10	4 430	3 530
Fordoche village	676	488
Livonia village[35]	980	611
Rapides Parish[36]	135 282	118 078
Ward 1, Alexandria	55 898	53 910
Alexandria city (pt.)[36]	50 795	41 631
Ward 2, Lamourie	3 954	3 574
Lecompte town (pt.)[36]	1	...
Woodworth village	412	409
Ward 3, Cheneyville	4 046	4 004
Cheneyville town	865	1 082
Lecompte town (pt.)[36]	1 660	1 518
Ward 4, Spring Hill	5 303	4 671
Forest Hill village[36]	494	370
Glenmora town	1 479	1 651
McNary village[36]	240	220
Ward 5, Hineston	2 954	2 115
Ward 6, Calcasieu	2 057	1 644
Ward 7, Cotile	4 886	4 121
Boyce town	1 198	1 240
Ward 8, Rapides	12 228	10 739
Alexandria city (pt.)[36]	770	180
Ward 9, Pineville	15 783	14 746
Pineville city (pt.)[36]	10 636	8 884
Ward 10, Rigolette	20 654	14 117
Ball town[36]	3 405	...
Pineville city (pt.)[36]	1 398	67
Ward 11, Buckeye	7 519	4 437
Red River Parish[37]	10 433	9 226
Ward 1	1 828	...
Ward 2	1 501	...
Martin village[37]	584	...
Ward 3	1 395	...
Hall Summit village[37]	276	190
Ward 4	1 426	...
Ward 5	517	...
Coushatta town (pt.)[37]	—	(NA)
Ward 6	989	...
Ward 7	1 426	...

Parish Subdivisions	1980	1970
Red River Parish—Con.		
Ward 7—Con.		
Coushatta town (pt.)[37]	733	(NA)
Edgefield village	312	201
Ward 8	1 351	...
Coushatta town (pt.)	1 351	(NA)
Richland Parish[38]	22 187	21 774
Ward 1	6 039	5 876
Delhi town[38]	3 290	2 887
Ward 2	9 219	9 238
Rayville town[38]	4 610	3 962
Ward 3	2 081	1 787
Ward 4	2 128	2 058
Ward 5	1 883	1 863
Mangham town	867	544
Ward 6	316	451
Ward 7	521	501
Sabine Parish[39]	25 280	18 638
Ward 1	3 003	2 158
Florien village (pt.)[39]	953	639
Ward 2	1 153	681
Ward 3	1 955	1 141
Ward 4	8 576	6 317
Fisher village[39]	325	...
Florien village (pt.)[39]	11	...
Many town[39]	3 988	3 112
Ward 5	3 317	2 385
Zwolle town (pt.)	475	432
Ward 6	1 710	1 187
Converse village (pt.)	404	341
Noble village	194	209
Ward 7	1 434	1 473
Pleasant Hill village	776	826
Ward 8	2 801	2 160
Zwolle town (pt.)	2 127	1 737
Ward 9	787	632
Ward 10	544	504
Converse village (pt.)	45	34
St. Bernard Parish[40]	64 097	51 185
Ward A	4 809	...
Arabi (CDP) (pt.)	4 809	...
Ward B	4 906	...
Arabi (CDP) (pt.)	4 392	...
Chalmette (CDP) (pt.)	514	...
Ward C	5 218	...
Arabi (CDP) (pt.)	1 047	...
Chalmette (CDP) (pt.)	4 171	...
Ward D	6 221	...
Chalmette (CDP) (pt.)	6 221	...
Ward E	6 368	...
Chalmette (CDP) (pt.)	6 349	...
Ward F	5 550	...
Chalmette (CDP) (pt.)	5 550	...
Ward G	6 563	...
Chalmette (CDP) (pt.)	6 563	...
Ward H	7 332	...
Chalmette (CDP) (pt.)	4 479	...
Violet (CDP) (pt.)	2 853	...
Ward I	6 886	...
Violet (CDP) (pt.)	6 886	...
Ward J	6 259	...
Poydras (CDP) (pt.)	4 320	...
Violet (CDP) (pt.)	1 939	...
Ward K	3 985	...
Poydras (CDP) (pt.)	1 402	...
St. Charles Parish[41]	37 259	29 550
Ward 1	5 629	...
Hahnville (CDP)	2 947	2 522
Luling (CDP) (pt.)	1 672	(NA)
Ward 2	6 919	...
Lone Star (CDP) (pt.)	1 593	...
Luling (CDP) (pt.)	2 334	(NA)
Ward 3	5 561	...
Destrehan (CDP)	2 382	...
New Sarpy (CDP) (pt.)	2 249	1 643
Norco (CDP) (pt.)	361	(NA)
Ward 4	4 966	...
Des Allemands (CDP) (pt.)	2 543	2 093
Ward 5	4 589	...
Ward 6	4 710	...
New Sarpy (CDP) (pt.)	—	...
Norco (CDP) (pt.)	4 055	(NA)
Ward 7	4 885	...
Lone Star (CDP) (pt.)	—	(NA)
Luling (CDP) (pt.)	—	(NA)
Mimosa Park (CDP)	3 737	1 624
St. Helena Parish[42]	9 827	9 937
Ward 1	716	745
Ward 2	2 170	2 585
Greensburg town (pt.)[42]	348	562
Ward 3	1 730	1 649
Greensburg town (pt.)[42]	314	90
Ward 4	1 955	1 969
Montpelier village	219	211
Ward 5	2 232	2 068
Ward 6	1 024	921

Parish Subdivisions	1980	1970
St. James Parish[43]	21 495	19 733
Ward 1	2 947	...
Gramercy town (pt.)[43]	2 947	(NA)
Ward 2	4 994	...
Gramercy town (pt.)	264	...
Lutcher town (pt.)[43]	4 730	(NA)
Ward 3	1 982	...
Lutcher town (pt.)[43]	–	(NA)
Ward 4	2 676	...
Ward 5	2 651	...
Ward 6	2 971	...
Lower Vacherie (CDP) (pt.)	150	...
Vacherie (CDP)	2 169	2 145
Ward 7	3 274	...
Lower Vacherie (CDP) (pt.)	3 039	...
St. John the Baptist Parish	31 924	23 813
Ward 1	2 424	1 716
Ward 2	366	1 563
Ward 3	1 252	1 368
Ward 4	17 032	9 286
Laplace (CDP) (pt.)	16 112	5 953
Reserve (CDP) (pt.)	3	...
Ward 5	7 369	6 667
Laplace (CDP) (pt.)	–	...
Reserve (CDP) (pt.)	7 285	6 381
Ward 6	3 481	3 213
Garyville (CDP)	2 856	2 474
St. Landry Parish[44]	84 128	80 364
Ward 1	31 839	...
Opelousas city[44]	18 903	'20 387
Port Barre town (pt.)[44]	142	77
Ward 2	7 339	...
Cankton village	303	260
Grand Coteau town[44]	1 165	1 301
Sunset town	2 300	1 675
Ward 3	6 879	...
Arnaudville town (pt.)[44]	1 530	1 550
Leonville village[44]	1,143	512
Ward 4	11 644	...
Krotz Springs town	1 374	1 435
Melville town	1 764	'1 987
Palmetto village	327	312
Port Barre town (pt.)[44]	2 483	2 056
Ward 5	5 403	...
Washington town	1 266	1 473
Ward 6[44]	21 024	18 719
Eunice city (pt.)[44]	12 258	11 278
Lawtell (CDP)	1 014	...
St. Martin Parish[45]	40 214	32 453
Ward 1	8 198	...
St. Martinville city (pt.)[45]	4 079	(NA)
Ward 2	4 567	...
St. Martinville city (pt.)[45]	3 023	(NA)
Ward 3	5 040	...
Parks village	545	491
St. Martinville city (pt.)[45]	863	(NA)
Ward 4	13 414	...
Breaux Bridge city[45]	5 922	4 942
Ward 5	8 995	...
Arnaudville town (pt.)	149	123
Henderson town[45]	1 560	...
St. Mary Parish[46]	64 253	60 752
Ward 1	3 449	2 938
Ward 2	907	957
Ward 3	13 093	13 210
Franklin city[46]	9 584	9 325
Ward 4	2 558	2 711
Ward 5	7 997	7 213
Bayou Vista (CDP) (pt.)	1 900	1 816
Patterson town[46]	4 693	4 409
Ward 6	18 625	18 870
Morgan City city[46]	16 114	16 586
Ward 7	1 641	1 555
Ward 8	8 379	7 736
Bayou Vista (CDP) (pt.)	3 905	3 305
Berwick town[46]	4 466	4 168
Ward 9	3 728	2 408
Amelia (CDP)	3 617	2 292
Ward 10	3 876	3 154
Baldwin town	2 644	2 117
St. Tammany Parish[47]	110 869	63 585
Ward 1	4 419	2 929
Madisonville town	799	801
Ward 2	6 303	4 126
Folsom village[47]	319	249
Ward 3	14 447	11 313
Covington city[47]	7 892	7 170
Ward 4	13 852	6 126
Lacombe (CDP) (pt.)	78	...
Mandeville town[47]	6 076	'2 571
Ward 5	2 064	1 500
Sun village[47]	404	288
Ward 6	4 225	2 345
Ward 7	5 012	3 031
Lacombe (CDP) (pt.)	4 763	...
Ward 8	31 018	11 730
Pearl River town	1 693	1 361
St. Tammany Parish—Con.		
Ward 8—Con.		
Slidell city (pt.)[47]	12 122	4 351
Ward 9	26 767	18 736
Lacombe (CDP) (pt.)	305	...
Slidell city (pt.)[47]	14 596	11 750
Ward 10	2 762	1 749
Abita Springs town[47]	1 072	839
Tangipahoa Parish[48]	80 698	65 875
Ward 1	4 857	4 652
Kentwood town	2 667	2 736
Tangipahoa village	493	469
Ward 2	2 023	1 624
Ward 3	10 634	9 330
Amite City town[48]	4 301	3 593
Roseland town	1 346	1 273
Ward 4[48]	4 329	...
Ward 5[48]	4 198	...
Ward 6	13 542	10 377
East Hammond (CDP) (pt.)	162	...
Hammond city (pt.)[48]	392	442
Independence town	1 684	1 770
Tickfaw village[48]	571	370
Ward 7	38 498	31 575
East Hammond (CDP) (pt.)	1 775	1 342
Hammond city (pt.)[48]	14 651	12 045
Ponchatoula city[48]	5 469	4 545
Ward 8	2 617	1 717
Tensas Parish[49]	8 525	9 732
Ward 1	1 249	...
Ward 2	1 726	...
Newellton town[49]	1 726	1 403
Ward 3	681	...
Ward 4	655	...
Ward 5	1 687	...
St. Joseph town	1 687	1 864
Ward 6	1 188	...
Ward 7	1 339	...
Waterproof town[49]	1 339	1 438
Terrebonne Parish[50]	94 393	76 049
Ward 1	14 124	9 635
Bayou Cane (CDP) (pt.)	3 272	10
Ward 2	2 802	1 345
Bayou Cane (CDP) (pt.)	383	...
Houma city (pt.)[50]	1 311	160
Ward 3	48 033	41 243
Bayou Blue (CDP) (pt.)	396	...
Bayou Cane (CDP) (pt.)	12 068	9 067
Houma city (pt.)	30 169	30 576
Ward 4	3 851	4 739
Houma city (pt.)[50]	48	186
Ward 5	3 706	2 053
Bourg (CDP)	2 073	...
Houma city (pt.)[50]	–	–
Ward 6	4 116	3 139
Ward 7	7 134	6 573
Chauvin (CDP)	3 338	...
Houma city (pt.)[50]	–	–
Ward 8	3 512	2 390
Ward 9	3 168	1 934
Houma city (pt.)[50]	1 074	...
Ward 10	3 947	2 998
Crozier (CDP)	1 150	...
Union Parish[51]	21 167	18 447
Ward 1	2 628	...
Farmerville town (pt.)	2 628	(NA)
Ward 2	2 207	...
Marion village (pt.)[51]	887	(NA)
Ward 3	2 234	...
Spearsville village	181	197
Ward 4	2 239	...
Bernice town (pt.)[51]	944	(NA)
Ward 5	2 700	...
Downsville village (pt.)[51]	157	...
Ward 6	1 899	...
Marion village (pt.)[51]	102	(NA)
Ward 7	2 386	...
Farmerville town (pt.)	1 140	(NA)
Ward 8	2 530	...
Ward 9	2 344	...
Bernice town (pt.)[51]	1 012	(NA)
Junction City village (pt.)	608	574
Lillie village	172	160
Vermilion Parish[52]	48 458	43 071
Ward 1	7 504	5 124
Delcambre town (pt.)	1 538	1 200
Erath town[52]	2 133	2 024
Ward 2	1 453	1 226
Ward 3	18 041	16 595
Abbeville city[52]	12 391	10 996
Ward 4	2 676	2 175
Maurice village	478	476
Ward 5	1 686	1 587
Ward 6	2 518	2 149
Ward 7	2 334	1 985
Ward 8	3 689	3 950

Parish Subdivisions

	1980	1970
Vermilion Parish—Con.		
Ward 8—Con.		
Gueydan town[52]	1 695	1 984
Ward 9	8 557	8 280
Kaplan city[52]	5 016	5 540
Vernon Parish[53]	53 475	53 794
Ward 1	17 596	21 767
Fort Polk North (CDP)	1 644	7 955
Leesville city[53]	9 054	8 928
Newllano village[53]	2 213	1 800
Ward 2	5 728	3 929
Anacoco village[53]	90	...
Hornbeck town	470	525
Ward 3	2 144	1 796
Ward 4	18 098	18 751
Fort Polk South (CDP)	12 498	15 600
Ward 5	2 308	2 260
Ward 6	1 380	1 102
Simpson village[53]	534	491
Ward 7	4 520	2 897
De Ridder city (pt.)[53]	—	...
Rosepine village	953	587
Ward 8	1 701	1 292
Washington Parish[54]	44 207	41 987
Ward 1	1 489	1 207
Ward 2	1 698	1 554
Ward 3	5 941	5 287
Franklinton town[54]	4 119	3 562
Ward 4	21 772	22 371
Bogalusa city	16 976	18 412
Ward 5	2 733	2 289
Varnado village	249	320
Ward 6	2 228	1 834
Ward 7	3 734	3 510
Angie village	311	317
Ward 8	3 077	2 581
Ward 9	1 535	1 354
Webster Parish[55]	43 631	39 939
Ward 1[55]	27 834	...
Dixie Inn village[55]	453	456
Doyline village	801	716
Dubberly village	421	212
Heflin village	279	314
Minden city[55]	15 084	13 996
Sibley village[55]	1 211	869
Ward 2[55]	15 797	...
Cotton Valley town[55]	1 445	1 261
Cullen town	1 869	1 956
Sarepta village	831	882
Shongaloo village	163	173
Springhill city[55]	6 516	6 496
West Baton Rouge Parish[56]	19 086	16 864
Ward 1	1 753	1 523
Addis town (pt.)[56]	1 307	696
Ward 2	3 563	2 955
Addis town (pt.)	13	28
Brusly town	1 762	1 282
Ward 3	7 877	6 983
Port Allen city[56]	6 114	5 728
Ward 4	1 964	1 889
Ward 5	1 096	1 301
Ward 6	427	614
Ward 7	2 406	1 599
West Carroll Parish[57]	12 922	13 028
Ward 1	1 849	1 872
Epps village[57]	672	448
Ward 2	1 807	1 965
Pioneer village	221	188
Ward 3	2 827	2 718
Forest village	299	221
Ward 4	4 511	4 441
Oak Grove town[57]	2 214	1 980
Ward 5	1 928	2 032
Kilbourne village	286	370
West Feliciana Parish	12 186	'10 761
Ward 1	1 289	1 505
St. Francisville town (pt.)	1 284	1 452
Ward 2	837	740
Ward 3	1 361	1 330
St. Francisville town (pt.)	187	151
Ward 4	540	408
Ward 5	385	373
Ward 7	5 746	'4 682
Ward 8	482	556
Ward 9	964	627
Ward 10	582	540
Winn Parish[58]	17 253	16 369
Ward 1	8 961	8 393
Winnfield city[58]	7 311	7 142
Ward 2	1 135	1 376
Tullos town (pt.)	—	...
Ward 3	800	701
Sikes village	226	237
Ward 4	741	630
Ward 5	1 213	1 235

Parish Subdivisions

	1980	1970
Winn Parish—Con.		
Ward 6	708	696
Atlanta village[58]	127	'197
Ward 7	1 458	1 297
Dodson village	469	457
Ward 8	1 268	1 145
Calvin village[58]	263	286
Ward 9	491	443
Ward 10	478	453

MAINE

The name "Mayne" was applied by early explorers to the mainland of the territory now occupied by the state of Maine, as distinguished from the numerous islands along the coast.

About the close of the fifteenth century the Cabots, exploring in the service of England, discovered Newfoundland and the mainland of North America. On the basis of their discoveries England claimed a large part of North America, including all the region lying along the North Atlantic coast claimed by the French as a part of New France. The territory embraced within the present limits of Maine was included, either wholly or in part, both in the French grants to the Sieur de Monts in 1603 and to the Company of New France in 1628, and in the English grants to the Plymouth Company in 1606 and to the council of Plymouth in 1620. These conflicting claims were in part responsible for the controversy and bloodshed which, for a century and a half, occurred from time to time between the two powers.

A number of temporary settlements were made in this territory during the early years of the seventeenth century, but the first permanent settlement was probably that established at Pemaquid by the English about 1623 or 1624.

In 1622 the tract between the Merrimac and Kennebec Rivers was granted by the council of Plymouth to Capt. John Mason and Sir Ferdinando Gorges. In 1629 the proprietors divided their grant, and Gorges retained the part east of the Piscataqua River, which now forms the extreme southwestern boundary of Maine. In 1639 he received a royal charter for this territory, under the name of "The Province or Countie of Mayne." In 1677 the Province of Maine was sold by the heirs of Gorges to the colony of Massachusetts Bay, which had for some time claimed this territory under a conflicting grant.

In 1663 Charles II granted to the Duke of York the territory between the St. Croix and the Kennebec Rivers, and in 1691, in the provincial charter, William and Mary granted the same territory to the Massachusetts Bay colony.

In 1763 France relinquished her claims to Maine territory to England; and in 1783, at the close of the Revolution, the British claims were ceded to the United States.

Up to March 15, 1820, Maine formed a part of the state of Massachusetts. On the date named it was admitted to the Union as a separate state, having substantially its present limits.

COUNTY LOCATION INDEX

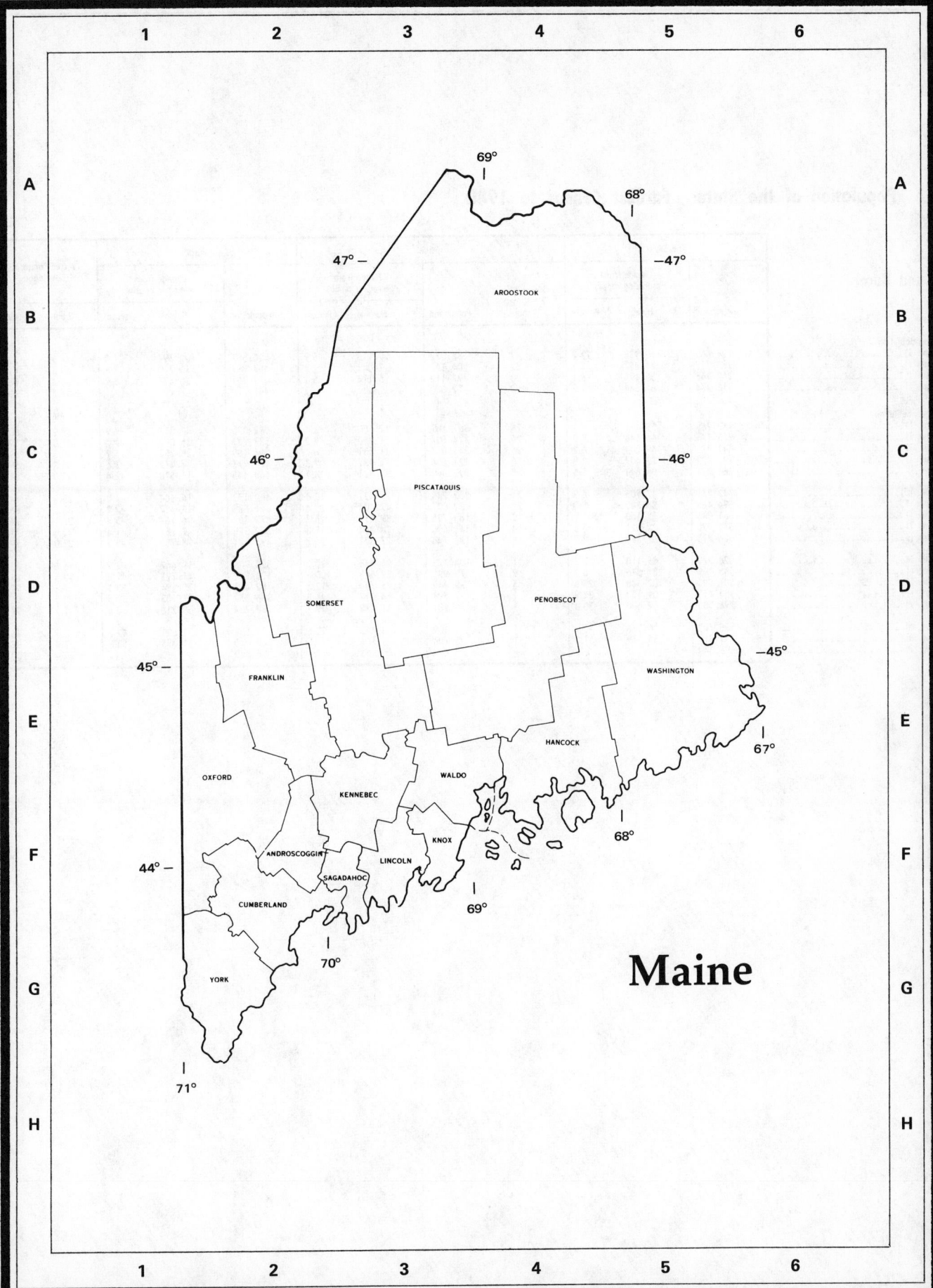

1   2   3   4   5   6

A

B

C

D

E

F

G

H

69°

68°

47° —

—47°

AROOSTOOK

46° —

—46°

PISCATAQUIS

—45°

SOMERSET

PENOBSCOT

WASHINGTON

45° —

FRANKLIN

67°

OXFORD

KENNEBEC

WALDO

HANCOCK

68°

KNOX

44° —

ANDROSCOGGIN

LINCOLN

SAGADAHOC

69°

CUMBERLAND

70°

YORK

Maine

71°

Population of the State: Earliest Census to 1980

Urban and Rural

	The State			Urban				Rural			Percent of total population	
	Total population	Change from preceding census		Places of 2,500 or more	Population	Change from preceding census		Population	Change from preceding census		Urban	Rural
		Number	Percent			Number	Percent		Number	Percent		
Current urban definition:												
1980 (Apr. 1)	1 124 660	130 938	13.2	57	534 072	29 915	5.9	590 588	102 697	21.0	47.5	52.5
1970 (Apr. 1)	'993 722	24 457	2.5	52	504 157	7 043	1.4	487 891	15 740	3.3	50.8	49.2
1960 (Apr. 1)	969 265	55 491	6.1	50	497 114	25 114	5.3	472 151	30 377	6.9	51.3	48.7
1950 (Apr. 1)	913 774	66 548	7.9	50	472 000	...	...	441 774	...	...	51.7	48.3
Previous urban definition:												
1960 (Apr. 1)	969 265	55 491	6.1	26	387 187	12 680	3.4	582 078	42 811	7.9	39.9	60.1
1950 (Apr. 1)	913 774	66 548	7.9	26	374 507	31 450	9.2	539 267	35 098	7.0	41.0	59.0
1940 (Apr. 1)	847 226	49 803	6.2	26	343 057	21 551	6.7	504 169	28 252	5.9	40.5	59.5
1930 (Apr. 1)	797 423	29 409	3.8	26	321 506	21 937	7.3	475 917	7 472	1.6	40.3	59.7
1920 (Jan. 1)	768 014	25 643	3.5	25	299 569	37 321	14.2	468 445	−11 678	−2.4	39.0	61.0
1910 (Apr. 15)	742 371	47 905	6.9	24	262 248	29 421	12.6	480 123	18 484	4.0	35.3	64.7
1900 (June 1)	694 466	33 380	5.0	22	232 827	47 102	25.4	461 639	−13 722	−2.9	33.5	66.5
1890 (June 1)	661 086	12 150	1.9	18	185 725	39 117	26.7	475 361	−26 967	−5.4	28.1	71.9
1880 (June 1)	648 936	22 021	3.5	14	146 608	14 864	11.3	502 328	7 157	1.4	22.6	77.4
1870 (June 1)	626 915	−1 364	−0.2	14	131 744	27 371	26.2	495 171	−28 735	−5.5	21.0	79.0
1860 (June 1)	628 279	45 110	7.7	11	104 373	25 448	32.2	523 906	19 662	3.9	16.6	83.4
1850 (June 1)	583 169	81 376	16.2	9	78 925	39 583	100.6	504 244	41 793	9.0	13.5	86.5
1840 (June 1)	501 793	102 338	25.6	5	39 342	26 744	212.3	462 451	75 594	19.5	7.8	92.2
1830 (June 1)	399 455	101 120	33.9	1	12 598	4 017	46.8	386 857	97 103	33.5	3.2	96.8
1820 (Aug. 7)	298 335	69 630	30.4	1	8 581	1 412	19.7	289 754	68 218	30.8	2.9	97.1
1810 (Aug. 6)	228 705	76 986	50.7	1	7 169	3 465	93.5	221 536	73 521	49.7	3.1	96.9
1800 (Aug. 4)	151 719	55 179	57.2	1	3 704	3 704	...	148 015	51 475	53.3	2.4	97.6
1790 (Aug. 2)	96 540	...	...	—	—	...	...	96 540	...	...	—	100.0

ANDROSCOGGIN

Year	Population
1860	29,726
1870	35,866
1880	45,042
1890	48,969
1900	54,242
1910	59,882
1920	65,796
1930	71,214
1940	76,679
1950	83,594
1960	86,312
1970	91,279
1980	99,657

AROOSTOOK

Year	Population
1840	9,413
1850	12,529
1860	22,479
1870	29,609
1880	41,700
1890	49,589
1900	60,744
1910	74,644
1920	81,728
1930	87,843
1940	94,436
1950	96,039
1960	106,064
1970	94,078
1980	91,331

CUMBERLAND

Year	Population
1790	25,450
1800	38,208
1810	49,445
1820	49,445
1830	60,102
1840	68,658
1850	79,538
1860	75,591
1870	82,021
1880	86,359
1890	90,949
1900	100,689
1910	112,014
1920	124,376
1930	134,645
1940	146,000
1950	169,201
1960	182,751
1970	192,528
1980	215,789

FRANKLIN

Year	Population
1840	20,801
1850	20,027
1860	20,403
1870	18,807
1880	18,180
1890	17,053
1900	18,444
1910	19,119
1920	19,825
1930	19,941
1940	19,896
1950	20,682
1960	20,069
1970	22,444
1980	27,098

HANCOCK

Year	Population
1790	9,549
1800	16,358
1810	30,031
1820	31,290
1830	24,336
1840	28,605
1850	34,372
1860	37,757
1870	36,495
1880	38,129
1890	27,312
1900	37,241
1910	35,575
1920	30,361
1930	30,721
1940	32,422
1950	32,105
1960	32,293
1970	34,590
1980	41,781

KENNEBEC

Year	Population
1800	24,571
1810	32,564
1820	42,623
1830	52,485
1840	55,823
1850	62,521
1860	55,655
1870	53,203
1880	53,058
1890	57,012
1900	59,117
1910	62,863
1920	63,844
1930	70,691
1940	77,231
1950	83,881
1960	89,150
1970	95,306
1980	109,889

KNOX

Year	Population
1860	32,716
1870	30,823
1880	32,863
1890	31,473
1900	30,406
1910	38,981
1920	26,245
1930	27,693
1940	27,191
1950	28,121
1960	28,575
1970	29,013
1980	32,941

LINCOLN

Year	Population
1790	19,962
1800	30,225
1810	42,992
1820	53,189
1830	57,192
1840	63,517
1850	74,875
1860	27,860
1870	25,597
1880	24,821
1890	21,996
1900	19,669
1910	18,216
1920	15,967

Year	Population
1930	15,498
1940	16,294
1950	18,004
1960	18,497
1970	20,537
1980	25,691

OXFORD

Year	Population
1810	17,630
1820	27,104
1830	35,219
1840	38,351
1850	39,763
1860	36,698
1870	33,488
1880	32,627
1890	30,586
1900	32,238
1910	36,256
1920	37,700
1930	41,483
1940	42,662
1950	44,221
1960	44,345
1970	43,457
1980	48,968

PENOBSCOT

Year	Population
1820	13,870
1830	31,530
1840	45,705
1850	63,089
1860	72,731
1870	75,150
1880	70,476
1890	72,865
1900	76,246
1910	85,285
1920	87,684
1930	92,379
1940	97,104
1950	108,198
1960	126,346
1970	125,393
1980	137,015

PISCATAQUIS

Year	Population
1840	13,138
1850	14,735
1860	15,032
1870	14,403
1880	14,872
1890	16,134
1900	16,949
1910	19,887
1920	20,554
1930	18,231
1940	18,467
1950	18,617
1960	17,379
1970	16,285
1980	17,634

SAGADAHOC

Year	Population
1860	21,790
1870	18,803
1880	19,272
1890	19,452
1900	20,330
1910	18,574
1920	23,021
1930	16,927

Year	Population
1940	19,123
1950	20,911
1960	22,793
1970	23,452
1980	28,795

SOMERSET

Year	Population
1810	12,910
1820	21,787
1830	35,787
1840	33,912
1850	35,581
1860	36,753
1870	34,611
1880	32,333
1890	32,627
1900	33,849
1910	36,301
1920	37,171
1930	39,111
1940	38,245
1950	39,785
1960	39,749
1970	40,597
1980	45,028

WALDO

Year	Population
1830	29,788
1840	41,509
1850	47,230
1860	38,447
1870	34,522
1880	32,463
1890	27,759
1900	24,185
1910	23,383
1920	21,383
1930	20,286
1940	21,159
1950	21,687
1960	22,632
1970	23,328
1980	28,414

WASHINGTON

Year	Population
1790	2,758
1800	4,461
1810	7,870
1820	12,744
1830	21,294
1840	28,327
1850	38,811
1860	42,534
1870	43,343
1880	44,484
1890	44,482
1900	45,232
1910	42,905
1920	41,709
1930	37,826
1940	37,767
1950	35,187
1960	32,908
1970	29,859
1980	34,963

YORK

Year	Population
1790	28,821
1800	37,896
1810	41,877
1820	46,283
1830	51,722

Year	Population
1840	54,034
1850	60,098
1860	62,107
1870	60,174
1880	62,257
1890	62,829
1900	64,885
1910	68,526
1920	70,696
1930	72,934
1940	82,550
1950	93,541
1960	99,402
1970	111,576
1980	139,666

AUBURN

1850	2,840
1860	4,022
1870	6,169
1880	9,555
1890	11,250
1900	12,951
1910	15,064
1920	16,985
1930	18,571
1940	19,817
1950	23,134
1960	24,449
1970	24,151
1980	23,128

AUGUSTA

1800	1,216
1810	1,805
1820	2,457
1830	3,980
1840	5,314
1850	8,225
1860	7,609
1870	7,808
1880	8,665
1890	10,527
1900	11,683
1910	13,211
1920	14,114
1930	17,198
1940	19,360
1950	20,913
1960	21,680
1970	21,945
1980	21,819

BANGOR

1800	277
1810	850
1820	1,221
1830	2,867
1840	8,627
1850	14,432
1860	16,407
1870	18,289
1880	16,856
1890	19,103
1900	21,850
1910	24,803
1920	25,978
1930	28,749
1940	29,822
1950	31,558
1960	38,912
1970	33,168
1980	31,643

BATH

1790	949
1800	1,225
1810	2,491
1820	3,026
1830	3,773
1840	5,141
1850	8,020
1860	8,076
1870	7,371
1880	7,874
1890	8,723
1900	10,477
1910	9,396
1920	14,731
1930	9,110

1940	10,235
1950	10,644
1960	10,717
1970	9,679
1980	10,246

BIDDEFORD

1790	1,018
1800	1,303
1810	1,563
1820	1,738
1830	1,995
1840	2,574
1850	6,095
1860	9,349
1870	10,282
1880	12,651
1890	14,443
1900	16,145
1910	17,079
1920	18,008
1930	17,633
1940	19,790
1950	20,836
1960	19,225
1970	19,983
1980	19,638

LEWISTON

1800	948
1810	1,033
1820	1,312
1830	1,549
1840	1,801
1850	3,584
1860	7,424
1870	13,600
1880	19,083
1890	27,701
1900	23,761
1910	26,247
1920	31,791
1930	34,948
1940	38,598
1950	40,974
1960	40,804
1970	41,779
1980	40,481

PORTLAND

1790	2,233
1800	3,704
1810	7,169
1820	8,581
1830	12,598
1840	15,218
1850	20,815
1860	26,341
1870	31,413
1880	33,810
1890	36,425
1900	50,145
1910	58,571
1920	69,272
1930	70,810
1940	73,643
1950	77,634
1960	72,566
1970	65,116
1980	61,572

PRESQUE ISLE

1880	523
1890	1,262
1900	1,256
1910	2,938
1920	3,452
1930	4,662
1940	7,939
1950	9,954
1960	12,886
1970	11,452
1980	11,172

SACO

1810	2,492
1820	2,532
1830	3,219
1840	4,408
1850	5,798
1860	6,223
1870	5,755
1880	6,389
1890	6,075
1900	6,122
1910	6,583
1920	6,817
1930	7,233
1940	8,631
1950	10,324
1960	10,515
1970	11,678
1980	12,921

SOUTH PORTLAND

1900	6,287
1910	7,471
1920	9,254
1930	13,840
1940	15,781
1950	21,866
1960	22,788
1970	23,367
1980	22,712

WATERVILLE

1810	1,314
1820	1,719
1830	2,216
1840	2,971
1850	3,964
1860	4,390
1870	4,852
1880	4,672
1890	7,107
1900	9,477
1910	11,458
1920	13,351
1930	15,454
1940	16,688
1950	18,287
1960	19,001
1970	18,192
1980	17,779

WESTBROOK

1820	2,502
1830	3,238
1840	4,116
1850	4,852
1860	5,113
1870	6,583
1880	3,981
1890	6,632
1900	7,283
1910	8,281
1920	9,453
1930	10,807
1940	11,087
1950	12,284
1960	13,820
1970	14,444
1980	14,976

CORRECTION NOTE

Shown below are corrections to the 1980 census counts of
the total population made after the tabulations for this
report were completed. Any additional corrections made
after this report is printed are available by writing to
Data User Services Division, Customer Services (Corrections),
Bureau of the Census, Washington, D.C. 20233.

The 1980 figures shown in this publication are subject to
change pending the outcome of the various lawsuits dealing
with the census counts.

	1980 population	
	As shown in the tables	Corrected
The State..................	1 124 660	1 125 027
Franklin County..................	27 098	27 447
East Central Franklin (unorg.)..	2	351
Somerset County..................	45 028	45 046
The Forks plantation............	72	90

County Subdivisions	1980	1970
The State	1 124 660	'993 722
Androscoggin County[1]	99 657	91 279
Auburn city	23 128	24 151
Durham town	2 074	1 264
Greene town	3 037	1 772
Leeds town	1 463	1 031
Lewiston city	40 481	41 779
Lisbon town	8 769	6 544
Lisbon Falls (CDP)	4 370	3 257
Lisbon–Lisbon Center (CDP)	1 865	1 475
Livermore town	1 826	1 610
Livermore Falls town	3 572	3 450
Livermore Falls (CDP)	2 441	2 378
Mechanic Falls town	2 616	2 193
Mechanic Falls (CDP)	2 198	1 872
Minot town	1 631	919
Poland town	3 578	2 015
Sabattus town[1]	3 081	1 681
Sabattus (CDP)	1 234	...
Turner town	3 539	2 246
Wales town	862	624
Aroostook County[2]	91 331	'94 078
Allagash town	448	456
Amity town	168	156
Ashland town	1 865	1 761
Bancroft town	61	53
Benedicta town	225	177
Blaine town	922	903
Mars Hill–Blaine (CDP) (pt.)	501	470
Bridgewater town	742	895
Caribou city	9 916	10 419
Cary plantation	229	184
Castle Hill town	509	519
Caswell plantation	586	693
Central Aroostook (unorg.)	16	82
Chapman town	406	328
Connor (unorg.)	574	575
Crystal town	349	281
Cyr plantation	147	155
Dyer Brook town	275	165
E plantation	55	18
Eagle Lake town	1 019	908
Easton town	1 305	1 305
Fort Fairfield town	4 376	4 859
Fort Fairfield (CDP)	2 282	2 322
Fort Kent town	4 826	4 575
Fort Kent (CDP)	2 375	2 876
Frenchville town	1 450	1 375
Garfield plantation	107	104
Glenwood plantation	7	9
Grand Isle town	719	797
Hamlin town	340	357
Hammond plantation	73	73
Haynesville town	169	157
Hersey town	67	81
Hodgdon town	1 084	933
Houlton town	6 766	8 111
Houlton (CDP)	5 730	6 760
Island Falls town	981	913
Limestone town	8 719	'10 360
Limestone (CDP)	1 334	1 572
Loring AFB (CDP)	6 572	'7 881
Linneus town	752	608
Littleton town	1 009	958
Ludlow town	403	259
Macwahoc plantation	126	126
Madawaska town	5 282	5 585
Madawaska (CDP)	4 165	4 452
Mapleton town	1 895	1 598
Mars Hill town	1 892	1 875
Mars Hill–Blaine (CDP) (pt.)	1 420	1 384
Masardis town	328	317
Merrill town	285	271
Monticello town	950	1 072
Moro plantation	30	24
Nashville plantation	48	50
New Canada town	269	300
New Limerick town	513	427
New Sweden town	737	639
Northwest Aroostook (unorg.)[2]	101	...
Oakfield town	847	836
Orient town	97	83
Oxbow plantation	84	92
Perham town	437	436
Portage Lake town	562	477
Presque Isle city	11 172	11 452
Reed plantation	274	273
St. Agatha town	1 035	868
St. Francis plantation	839	811
St. John plantation	322	377
Sherman town	1 021	949
Smyrna town	354	318
South Aroostook (unorg.)	261	243
Square Lake (unorg.)[2]	604	...
Stockholm town	319	388
Van Buren town	3 557	3 971

County Subdivisions	1980	1970
Aroostook County—Con.		
Van Buren town—Con.		
Van Buren (CDP)	3 282	3 429
Wade town	285	255
Wallagrass plantation	653	617
Washburn town	2 028	1 914
Washburn (CDP)	1 221	1 098
Westfield town	647	517
Westmanland town	53	52
Weston town	155	162
Winterville plantation	235	164
Woodland town	1 369	1 218
Cumberland County[3]	215 789	192 528
Baldwin town	1 140	878
Bridgton town	3 528	2 967
Bridgton (CDP)	1 639	1 779
Brunswick town	17 366	16 195
Brunswick (CDP)	10 990	10 867
Brunswick Station (CDP)	1 533	1 679
Cape Elizabeth town	7 838	7 873
Casco town	2 243	1 256
Cumberland town	5 284	4 096
Cumberland Center (CDP)	2 015	...
Falmouth town	6 853	6 291
Falmouth Foreside (CDP)	1 655	1 621
Freeport town	5 863	4 781
Freeport (CDP)	1 906	1 822
Gorham town	10 101	7 839
Gorham (CDP)	4 052	3 337
Little Falls–South Windham (CDP) (pt.)	686	748
Gray town	4 344	2 939
Harpswell town	3 796	2 552
Harrison town	1 667	1 045
Naples town	1 833	956
New Gloucester town	3 180	2 811
North Yarmouth town	1 919	1 383
Portland city	61 572	65 116
Pownal town	1 189	800
Raymond town	2 251	1 328
Scarborough town	11 347	7 845
Scarborough (CDP)	2 280	...
Sebago town	974	708
South Portland city	22 712	23 267
Standish town	5 946	3 122
Westbrook city	14 976	14 444
Windham town	11 282	6 593
Little Falls–South Windham (CDP) (pt.)	680	705
North Windham (CDP)	5 492	...
Yarmouth town	6 585	4 854
Yarmouth (CDP)	2 981	2 421
Franklin County[4]	27 098	22 444
Avon town	475	495
Carrabassett Valley town[4]	107	...
Carthage town	438	354
Chesterville town	869	643
Coplin plantation	111	50
Dallas plantation	146	105
East Central Franklin (unorg.)[4]	2	...
Eustis town	582	595
Farmington town	6 730	5 657
Farmington (CDP)	3 583	3 096
Industry town	563	347
Jay town	5 080	3 954
Chisholm (CDP)	1 796	1 530
Kingfield town	1 083	877
Madrid town	178	107
New Sharon town	969	725
New Vineyard town	607	444
North Franklin (unorg.)	28	60
Phillips town	1 092	979
Rangeley plantation	69	52
Rangeley town	1 023	941
Sandy River plantation	50	73
South Franklin (unorg.)	48	33
Strong town	1 506	1 132
Temple town	518	367
Weld town	435	360
West Central Franklin (unorg.)	–	2
Wilton town	4 382	3 802
Wilton (CDP)	2 262	2 225
Wyman (unorg.)[4]	7	...
Hancock County[5]	41 781	34 590
Amherst town	203	148
Aurora town	110	72
Bar Harbor town	4 124	3 716
Bar Harbor (CDP)	2 685	2 392
Blue Hill town	1 644	1 367
Brooklin town	619	598
Brooksville town	753	673
Bucksport town	4 345	3 756
Bucksport (CDP)	2 853	2 456
Castine town	1 304	1 080
Central Hancock (unorg.)	124	110
Cranberry Isles town	198	186
Dedham town	841	522
Deer Isle town	1 492	1 211
Eastbrook town	262	188

County Subdivisions

County Subdivisions	1980	1970
Hancock County—Con.		
East Hancock (unorg.)	44	20
Ellsworth city	5 179	4 603
Franklin town	979	708
Frenchboro town[5]	43	56
Gouldsboro town[5]	1 574	1 310
Great Pond plantation	45	43
Hancock town	1 409	1 070
Lamoine town	953	615
Mariaville town	168	108
Mount Desert town	2 063	1 659
Northwest Hancock (unorg.)	–	–
Orland town	1 645	1 307
Osborn town	47	33
Otis town	307	123
Penobscot town	1 104	786
Sedgwick town	795	578
Sorrento town	276	199
Southwest Harbor town	1 855	1 657
Southwest Harbor (CDP)	1 052	...
Stonington town	1 273	1 291
Sullivan town	967	824
Surry town	894	623
Swans Island town	337	323
Tremont town	1 222	1 003
Trenton town	718	392
Verona town	559	437
Waltham town	186	167
Winter Harbor town	1 120	1 028
Kennebec County	109 889	'95 306
Albion town	1 551	1 056
Augusta city	21 819	21 945
Belgrade town	2 043	1 302
Benton town	2 188	1 729
Chelsea town	2 522	'2 154
China town	2 918	1 850
Clinton town	2 696	1 971
Clinton (CDP)	1 305	1 124
Farmingdale town	2 535	2 423
Farmingdale (CDP)	2 014	1 832
Fayette town	812	447
Gardiner city	6 485	6 685
Hallowell city	2 502	2 814
Litchfield town	1 954	1 222
Manchester town	1 949	1 331
Monmouth town	2 888	2 062
Mount Vernon town	1 021	680
Oakland town	5 162	3 535
Oakland (CDP)	3 387	2 261
Pittston town	2 267	1 617
Randolph town	1 834	1 741
Randolph (CDP)	1 834	1 548
Readfield town	1 943	1 258
Rome town	627	362
Sidney town	2 052	1 319
Unity (unorg.)	37	45
Vassalborough town	3 410	2 618
Vienna town	454	205
Waterville city	17 779	18 192
Wayne town	680	577
West Gardiner town	2 113	1 435
Windsor town	1 702	1 097
Winslow town	8 057	7 299
Winslow (CDP)	5 903	5 389
Winthrop town	5 889	4 335
Winthrop (CDP)	3 264	2 571
Knox County[6]	32 941	29 013
Appleton town	818	628
Camden town	4 584	4 115
Camden (CDP)	3 743	3 492
Criehaven (unorg.)[6]	5	–
Cushing town	795	522
Friendship town	1 000	834
Hope town	730	500
Isle Au Haut town	57	45
Matinicus Isle plantation	66	90
North Haven town	373	399
Owls Head town	1 633	1 281
Rockland city	7 919	8 505
Rockport town	2 749	2 067
St. George town	1 948	1 639
South Thomaston town	1 064	831
Thomaston town	2 900	2 646
Thomaston (CDP)	2 348	2 160
Union town	1 569	1 189
Vinalhaven town	1 211	1 135
Warren town	2 566	1 864
Washington town	954	723
Lincoln County[7]	25 691	20 537
Alna town	425	315
Boothbay town	2 308	1 814
Boothbay Harbor town	2 207	2 320
Boothbay Harbor (CDP)	2 207	2 320
Bremen town	598	454
Bristol town	2 095	1 721
Damariscotta town	1 493	1 264

County Subdivisions

County Subdivisions	1980	1970
Lincoln County—Con.		
Damariscotta town—Con.		
Damariscotta–Newcastle (CDP) (pt.)	847	717
Dresden town	998	787
Edgecomb town	841	549
Hibberts gore	2	–
Jefferson town	1 616	1 242
Monhegan plantation	109	44
Newcastle town	1 227	1 076
Damariscotta–Newcastle (CDP) (pt.)	564	471
Nobleboro town	1 154	850
Somerville town	377	215
South Bristol town	800	664
Southport town	598	473
Waldoboro town	3 985	3 146
Waldoboro (CDP)	1 195	...
Westport town[7]	420	228
Whitefield town	1 606	1 131
Wiscasset town	2 832	2 244
Oxford County[8]	48 968	43 457
Andover town	850	791
Bethel town	2 340	2 220
Brownfield town	767	478
Buckfield town	1 333	929
Byron town	114	132
Canton town	831	742
Denmark town	672	397
Dixfield town	2 389	2 188
Dixfield (CDP)	1 725	1 535
Fryeburg town	2 715	2 208
Fryeburg (CDP)	1 644	1 075
Gilead town	191	153
Greenwood town	653	610
Hanover town	256	275
Hartford town	480	312
Hebron town	665	532
Hiram town	1 067	686
Lincoln plantation	50	60
Lovell town	767	607
Magalloway plantation	79	75
Mexico town	3 698	4 309
Mexico (CDP)	3 207	3 325
Milton (unorg.)	123	138
Newry town	235	208
North Oxford (unorg.)	37	9
Norway town	4 042	3 595
Norway (CDP)	2 653	2 430
Otisfield town[8]	897	589
Oxford town	3 143	1 892
Paris town	4 168	3 739
South Paris (CDP)	2 128	2 315
Peru town	1 564	1 345
Porter town	1 222	1 115
Roxbury town	373	271
Rumford town	8 240	9 363
Rumford (CDP)	6 256	6 198
South Oxford (unorg.)	348	184
Stoneham town	204	160
Stow town	186	109
Sumner town	613	525
Sweden town	163	110
Upton town	65	54
Waterford town	951	760
West Paris town	1 390	1 171
Woodstock town	1 087	1 005
Penobscot County[9]	137 015	125 393
Alton town	468	340
Argyle (unorg.)	225	155
Bangor city	31 643	33 168
Bradford town	888	569
Bradley town	1 149	1 010
Brewer city	9 017	9 300
Burlington town	322	266
Carmel town	1 695	1 301
Carroll plantation	175	132
Charleston town	1 037	909
Chester town	434	255
Clifton town	462	233
Corinna town	1 887	1 700
Corinth town	1 711	1 212
Dexter town	4 286	3 725
Dexter (CDP)	3 118	2 732
Dixmont town	812	559
Drew plantation	57	32
East Millinocket town	2 372	2 567
East Millinocket (CDP)	2 361	2 564
Eddington town	1 769	1 358
Edinburg town	126	67
Enfield town	1 397	1 148
Etna town	758	526
Exeter town	823	663
Garland town	718	596
Glenburn town	2 319	1 196
Grand Falls plantation	1	6
Greenbush town	1 064	591
Greenfield town	194	117

County Subdivisions	1980	1970
Penobscot County—Con.		
Hampden town	5 250	4 693
Hampden (CDP)	3 538	2 207
Hermon town	3 170	2 376
Holden town	2 554	1 841
Howland town	1 602	1 468
Howland (CDP)	1 502	1 418
Hudson town	797	482
Kenduskeag town	1 210	733
Kingman (unorg.)	281	264
Lagrange town	509	393
Lakeville plantation	32	15
Lee town	688	599
Levant town	1 117	802
Lincoln town	5 066	4 759
Lincoln (CDP)	3 524	3 482
Lowell town	194	154
Mattawamkeag town	1 000	988
Maxfield town	64	24
Medway town	1 871	1 491
Milford town	2 160	1 828
Milford (CDP)	1 688	1 519
Millinocket town	7 567	7 742
Millinocket (CDP)	7 567	7 558
Mount Chase town	233	197
Newburgh town	1 228	835
Newport town	2 755	2 260
Newport (CDP)	1 748	1 588
North Penobscot (unorg.)	246	175
Old Town city	8 422	ʳ8 741
Orono town	10 578	9 989
Orono (CDP)	9 891	9 146
Orrington town	3 244	2 702
Passadumkeag town	430	326
Patten town	1 368	1 266
Patten (CDP)	1 057	1 068
Penobscot Indian Island Indian Reservation[9]	458	ʳ317
Plymouth town	811	542
Prentiss plantation	205	159
Seboeis plantation	53	63
Springfield town	443	336
Stacyville town	554	547
Stetson town	618	395
Summit (unorg.)	7	–
Twombly (unorg.)	–	–
Veazie town	1 610	1 556
Veazie (CDP)	1 610	1 174
Webster plantation	82	56
Whitney (unorg.)	–	–
Winn town	503	516
Woodville town	226	62
Piscataquis County[10]	17 634	16 285
Abbot town	576	453
Atkinson town	306	213
Barnard plantation	48	24
Beaver Cove town[10]	56	...
Blanchard plantation	64	56
Bowerbank town	27	29
Brownville town	1 545	1 490
Dover-Foxcroft town	4 323	4 178
Dover-Foxcroft (CDP)	2 974	3 102
Elliottsville plantation	26	26
Greenville town	1 839	1 894
Greenville (CDP)	1 640	1 714
Guilford town	1 793	1 694
Guilford (CDP)	1 235	1 216
Kingsbury plantation	4	7
Lake View plantation	20	16
Medford town	163	146
Milo town	2 624	2 572
Milo (CDP)	2 255	1 514
Monson town	804	669
Northeast Piscataquis (unorg.)[10]	132	...
Northwest Piscataquis (unorg.)[10]	99	...
Parkman town	621	457
Sangerville town	1 219	1 107
Sebec town	469	325
Shirley town	242	174
Southeast Piscataquis (unorg.)	183	156
Wellington town	287	232
Willimantic town	164	126
Sagadahoc County[11]	28 795	23 452
Arrowsic town	305	188
Bath city	10 246	9 679
Bowdoin town	1 629	858
Bowdoinham town	1 828	1 294
Georgetown town	735	464
Perkins (unorg.)[11]	2	...
Phippsburg town	1 527	1 229
Richmond town	2 627	2 168
Richmond (CDP)	1 578	1 449
Topsham town	6 431	5 022
Topsham (CDP)	4 657	2 700
West Bath town	1 309	836
Woolwich town	2 156	1 710

County Subdivisions	1980	1970
Somerset County[12]	45 028	40 597
Anson town	2 226	2 168
Athens town	802	592
Bingham town	1 184	1 254
Bingham (CDP)	1 074	1 184
Brighton plantation	74	58
Cambridge town	445	281
Canaan town	1 189	904
Caratunk plantation	84	96
Central Somerset (unorg.)	278	216
Cornville town	838	623
Dennistown plantation	30	48
Detroit town	744	663
Embden town	536	418
Fairfield town	6 113	5 684
Fairfield (CDP)	3 169	3 694
Harmony town	755	650
Hartland town	1 669	1 414
Hartland (CDP)	1 041	...
Highland plantation	60	23
Jackman town	1 003	848
Madison town	4 367	4 278
Madison (CDP)	2 788	2 920
Mercer town	448	313
Moose River town	252	255
Moscow town	570	586
New Portland town	651	559
Norridgewock town	2 552	1 964
Norridgewock (CDP)	1 318	1 067
Northeast Somerset (unorg.)[12]	301	...
Northwest Somerset (unorg.)[12]	15	...
Palmyra town	1 485	1 104
Pittsfield town	4 125	4 274
Pittsfield (CDP)	3 117	3 398
Pleasant Ridge plantation	99	116
Ripley town	439	297
St. Albans town	1 400	1 041
Seboomook Lake (unorg.)[12]	37	...
Skowhegan town	8 098	7 601
Skowhegan (CDP)	6 517	6 571
Smithfield town	748	527
Solon town	827	712
Starks town	440	323
The Forks plantation	72	45
West Forks plantation	72	74
Waldo County[13]	28 414	23 328
Belfast city	6 243	5 957
Belmont town	520	349
Brooks town	804	751
Burnham town	951	802
Frankfort town	783	620
Freedom town	458	373
Islesboro town[13]	521	421
Jackson town	346	217
Knox town	558	443
Liberty town	694	515
Lincolnville town	1 414	955
Monroe town	657	478
Montville town	631	430
Morrill town	506	410
Northport town	958	744
Palermo town	760	645
Prospect town	511	358
Searsmont town	782	624
Searsport town	2 309	1 951
Searsport (CDP)	1 348	1 110
Stockton Springs town	1 230	1 142
Swanville town	873	487
Thorndike town	603	439
Troy town	701	543
Unity town	1 431	1 280
Waldo town	495	431
Winterport town	2 675	1 963
Winterport (CDP)	1 126	...
Washington County[14]	34 963	29 859
Addison town	1 061	773
Alexander town	385	169
Baileyville town	2 188	2 167
Woodland (CDP)	1 363	1 534
Baring plantation[14]	308	181
Beals town	695	663
Beddington town	36	32
Calais city	4 262	4 044
Centerville town	28	19
Charlotte town	300	199
Cherryfield town	983	771
Codyville plantation	43	45
Columbia town	275	162
Columbia Falls town	517	367
Cooper town	105	88
Crawford town	86	74
Cutler town	726	588
Danforth town	826	794
Deblois town	44	20
Dennysville town	296	278
East Central Washington (unorg.)	625	498

County Subdivisions

	1980	1970
Washington County—Con.		
East Machias town	1 233	1 057
Eastport city	1 982	1 989
Grand Lake Stream plantation	198	186
Harrington town	859	553
Jonesboro town	553	448
Jonesport town	1 512	1 326
Jonesport (CDP)	1 050	1 073
Lubec town	2 045	1 949
Machias town	2 458	2 441
Machias (CDP)	1 277	1 368
Machiasport town	1 108	887
Marshfield town	416	227
Meddybemps town	110	76
Milbridge town	1 306	1 154
Northfield town	88	57
North Washington (unorg.)	393	'500
Passamaquoddy Indian Township Indian Reservation	423	'293
Passamaquoddy Pleasant Point Indian Reservation[14]	549	'307
Pembroke town	920	700
Perry town	737	'571
Plantation No. 14	52	29
Plantation No. 21	127	83
Princeton town	994	956
Robbinston town	492	396
Roque Bluffs town	244	153
Steuben town	970	697
Talmadge town	40	25
Topsfield town[14]	240	'177
Vanceboro town	256	263
Waite town	130	70
Wesley town	140	110
Whiting town	335	269
Whitneyville town	264	155
York County[15]	139 666	111 576
Acton town	1 228	697
Alfred town	1 890	1 211
Arundel town	2 150	1 322
Berwick town	4 149	3 136
Berwick (CDP)	2 378	1 765
Biddeford city	19 638	19 983
Buxton town	5 775	3 135
Cornish town	1 047	839
Dayton town	882	546
Eliot town	4 948	3 497
South Eliot (CDP)	1 681	1 635
Hollis town	2 892	1 560
Kennebunk town	6 621	5 646
Kennebunk (CDP)	3 294	2 764
Kennebunkport (CDP) (pt.)	746	361
Kennebunkport town	2 952	2 160
Kennebunkport (CDP) (pt.)	939	736
Kittery town	9 314	11 028
Kittery (CDP)	5 465	7 363
Kittery Point (CDP)	1 260	1 172
Lebanon town	3 234	1 983
Limerick town	1 356	963
Limington town	2 203	1 066
Lyman town	2 509	864
Newfield town	644	458
North Berwick town	2 878	2 224
North Berwick (CDP)	1 436	1 449
Old Orchard Beach town[15]	6 291	5 404
Old Orchard Beach (CDP)	6 023	5 273
Parsonsfield town[15]	1 089	971
Saco city[15]	12 921	11 678
Sanford town	18 020	15 812
Sanford (CDP)	10 268	10 457
Springvale (CDP)	2 940	2 914
Shapleigh town	1 370	559
South Berwick town	4 046	3 488
South Berwick (CDP)	2 120	1 863
Waterboro town	2 943	1 208
Wells town	8 211	4 448
Ogunquit village[15]	1 492	'944
York town	8 465	5 690
York Center (CDP)	4 530	2 912

MARYLAND

Maryland was named in honor of Henrietta Maria, queen consort of Charles I of England.

The first white man to explore the region now constituting Maryland was Capt. John Smith, who sailed up Chesapeake Bay in 1608.

This region was covered by the several charters of Virginia (1606-1612), but none of the land within its limits was granted to settlers by the Virginia authorities. In 1631 William Claiborne, a Virginian, established a trading post on Kent Island in Chesapeake Bay. He had no grant of land, but had been given a license by Charles I to trade in those parts of the English possessions in America for which patents had not been issued. The result of his occupation of Kent Island was a territorial quarrel between Virginia and Maryland which lasted more than 20 years.

In 1632 a charter was granted by Charles I to Cecilius Calvert, second Lord Baltimore, as a result of the endeavors of George Calvert, his father, who died just before the patent was issued. The grant conferred on the proprietor possession of the area now comprising Maryland, Delaware, and a large part of Pennsylvania and of West Virginia. On March 27, 1634, a settlement was made, under the leadership of Leonard Calvert, brother of Lord Baltimore, at St. Mary's, in the southern part of the colony, between Chesapeake Bay and the lower Potomac. The primary motive of Calvert in founding the colony was to provide an asylum for persecuted Catholics, and from the beginning religious toleration was the established custom of the colony.

The charter granted to Calvert made Maryland a palatinate and conferred practically royal power on the proprietor. It reserved to the crown only feudal supremacy. In 1638 the right to initiate legislation, which until then had been claimed by Lord Baltimore, was conceded to the people, the proprietor reserving to himself the mere veto power.

In 1649 the assembly passed the famous Act of Toleration. In 1652 the colony was seized by the commissioners of Parliament, but it was restored to Lord Baltimore in 1657.

At some time prior to 1650 a company of Puritans from Virginia settled at Providence, now Annapolis, and in that year, because of their turbulence and by way of conciliation, their settlements were organized as Anne Arundel County.

In 1689 an association of Protestants, under the leadership of John Coode, seized St. Mary's and assumed control of the government in the name of William and Mary of England. In 1691 King William approved this act and deprived Lord Baltimore (son of the original proprietor) of his political power and privileges, but not of his property rights. In 1715 the province was restored to the fifth Lord Baltimore.

The boundaries between Maryland and Pennsylvania and between Maryland and Delaware were long a subject of controversy, until, in 1760, and agreement was reached. A few years later the lines were surveyed. By the charter of 1632 the fortieth parallel was made the northern boundary of Maryland, but the line—known as Mason and Dixon's line—was finally fixed at about latitude 39°43'.

Maryland was one of the original thirteen states.

COUNTY LOCATION INDEX

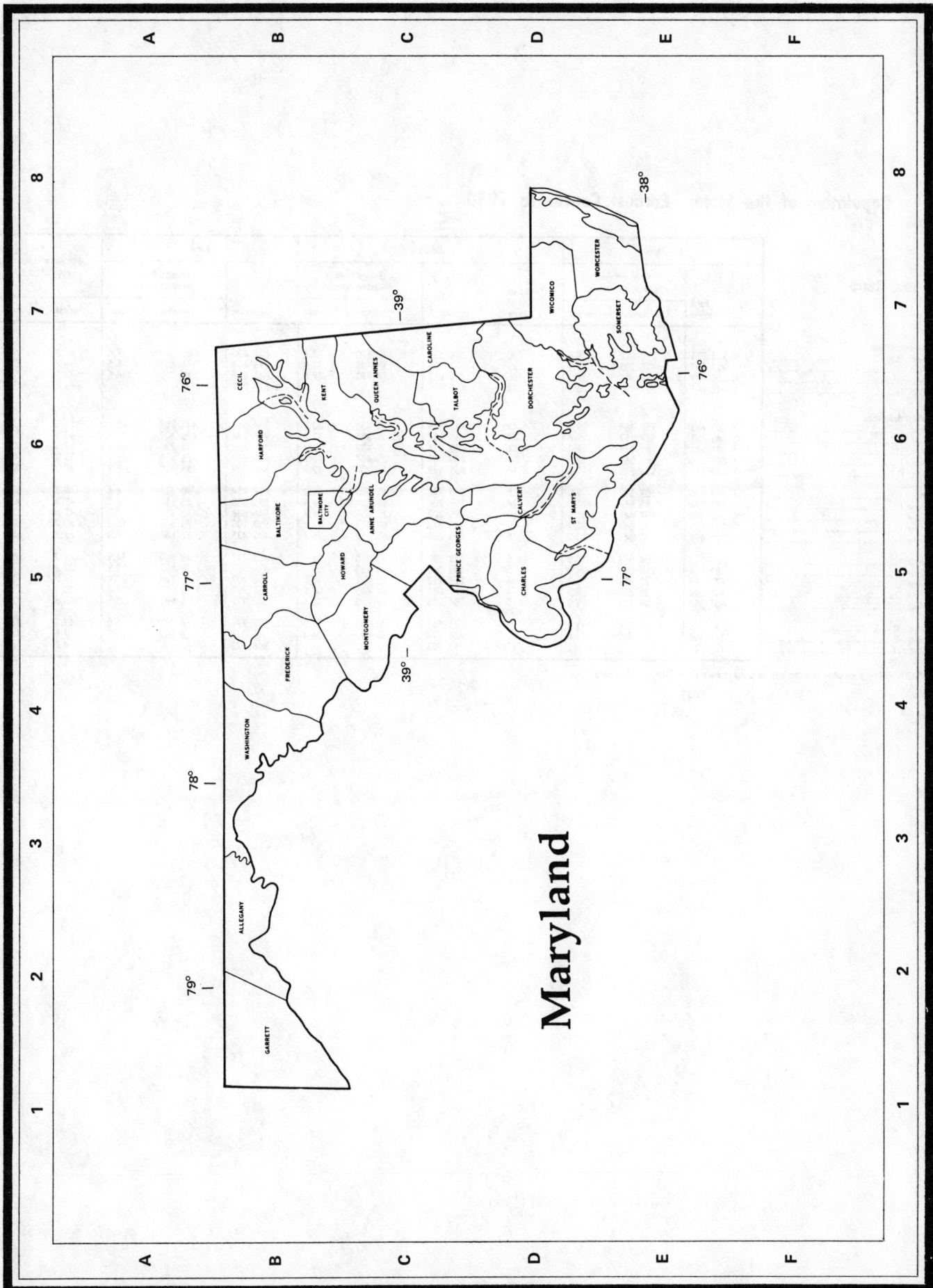

Maryland

Population of the State: Earliest Census to 1980

Urban and Rural

	The State			Urban				Rural				Percent of total population	
	Total population	Change from preceding census		Places of 2,500 or more	Population	Change from preceding census		Population	Change from preceding census			Urban	Rural
		Number	Percent			Number	Percent		Number	Percent			
Current urban definition:													
1980 (Apr. 1)	4 216 975	293 078	7.5	180	3 386 555	382 620	12.7	830 420	−88 044	−9.6		80.3	19.7
1970 (Apr. 1)	ʳ3 923 897	823 208	26.5	125	3 003 935	750 103	33.3	918 464	71 607	8.5		76.6	23.4
1960 (Apr. 1)	3 100 689	757 688	32.3	66	2 253 832	637 930	39.5	846 857	119 758	16.5		72.7	27.3
1950 (Apr. 1)	2 343 001	521 757	28.6	33	1 615 902	...	...	727 099	...	...		69.0	31.0
Previous urban definition:													
1960 (Apr. 1)	3 100 689	757 688	32.3	45	1 742 138	316 431	22.2	1 358 551	441 257	48.1		56.2	43.8
1950 (Apr. 1)	2 343 001	521 757	28.6	37	1 425 707	345 356	32.0	917 294	176 401	23.8		60.8	39.2
1940 (Apr. 1)	1 821 244	189 718	11.6	24	1 080 351	105 482	10.8	740 893	84 236	12.8		59.3	40.7
1930 (Apr. 1)	1 631 526	181 865	12.5	21	974 869	105 447	12.1	656 657	76 418	13.2		59.8	40.2
1920 (Jan. 1)	1 449 661	154 315	11.9	18	869 422	211 230	32.1	580 239	−56 915	−8.9		60.0	40.0
1910 (Apr. 15)	1 295 346	107 302	9.0	15	658 192	66 986	11.3	637 154	40 316	6.8		50.8	49.2
1900 (June 1)	1 188 044	145 654	14.0	14	591 206	95 504	19.3	596 838	50 150	9.2		49.8	50.2
1890 (June 1)	1 042 390	107 447	11.5	12	495 702	119 859	31.9	546 688	−12 412	−2.2		47.6	52.4
1880 (June 1)	934 943	154 049	19.7	9	375 843	80 384	27.2	559 100	73 665	15.2		40.2	59.8
1870 (June 1)	780 894	93 845	13.7	5	295 459	62 159	26.6	485 435	31 686	7.0		37.8	62.2
1860 (June 1)	687 049	104 015	17.8	5	233 300	45 255	24.1	453 749	58 760	14.9		34.0	66.0
1850 (June 1)	583 034	113 015	24.0	5	188 045	74 133	65.1	394 989	38 882	10.9		32.3	67.7
1840 (June 1)	470 019	22 979	5.1	4	113 912	22 871	25.1	356 107	108	−		24.2	75.8
1830 (June 1)	447 040	39 690	9.7	4	91 041	24 663	37.2	355 999	15 027	4.4		20.4	79.6
1820 (Aug. 7)	407 350	26 804	7.0	2	66 378	19 823	42.6	340 972	6 981	2.1		16.3	83.7
1810 (Aug. 6)	380 546	38 998	11.4	1	46 555	20 041	75.6	333 991	18 957	6.0		12.2	87.8
1800 (Aug. 4)	341 548	21 820	6.8	1	26 514	13 011	96.4	315 034	8 809	2.9		7.8	92.2
1790 (Aug. 2)	319 728	...	...	1	13 503	...	...	306 225	...	...		4.2	95.8

NOTE: 1790 population includes that of present area of the District of Columbia.

ALLEGANY

1790	4,809
1800	6,303
1810	6,909
1820	8,654
1830	10,609
1840	15,690
1850	22,769
1860	28,348
1870	38,536
1880	38,012
1890	41,571
1900	53,694
1910	62,411
1920	69,938
1930	79,088
1940	86,973
1950	89,556
1960	84,169
1970	84,044
1980	80,548

ANNE ARUNDEL

1790	22,598
1800	22,623
1810	26,668
1820	27,165
1830	28,295
1840	29,532
1850	32,393
1860	23,900
1870	24,457
1880	28,526
1890	34,094
1900	39,620
1910	39,553
1920	43,408
1930	55,167
1940	68,375
1950	117,392
1960	206,634
1970	298,042
1980	370,775

BALTIMORE

1790	38,937
1800	59,030
1810	75,810
1820	96,210
1830	120,870
1840	134,379
1850	210,646
1860	54,135
1870	63,387
1880	83,336
1890	72,909
1900	90,775
1910	122,349
1920	74,817
1930	124,565
1940	155,825
1950	270,273
1960	492,428
1970	620,409
1980	655,615

CALVERT

1790	8,652
1800	8,297
1810	8,005
1820	8,073
1830	8,900
1840	9,229
1850	9,646
1860	10,447
1870	9,865
1880	10,538
1890	9,860
1900	10,223
1910	10,325
1920	9,744
1930	9,525
1940	10,484
1950	12,100
1960	15,826
1970	20,682
1980	34,638

CAROLINE

1790	9,506
1800	9,226
1810	9,453
1820	10,108
1830	9,070
1840	7,806
1850	9,692
1860	11,129
1870	12,101
1880	13,766
1890	13,903
1900	16,248
1910	19,216
1920	18,652
1930	17,378
1940	17,549
1950	18,234
1960	19,462
1970	19,781
1980	23,143

CARROLL

1840	17,241
1850	20,616
1860	24,533
1870	28,619
1880	30,992
1890	32,376
1900	33,860
1910	33,934
1920	34,245
1930	35,978
1940	39,054
1950	44,907
1960	52,785
1970	69,006
1980	96,356

CECIL

1790	13,625
1800	9,018
1810	13,066
1820	16,048
1830	15,432
1840	17,232
1850	18,939
1860	23,862
1870	25,874
1880	27,108
1890	25,851
1900	24,662
1910	23,759
1920	23,612
1930	25,827
1940	26,407
1950	33,356
1960	48,408
1970	53,291
1980	60,430

CHARLES

1790	20,613
1800	19,172
1810	20,245
1820	16,500
1830	17,769
1840	16,023
1850	16,162
1860	16,517
1870	15,738
1880	18,548
1890	15,191
1900	17,662
1910	16,386
1920	17,705
1930	16,166
1940	17,162
1950	23,415
1960	32,572
1970	47,678
1980	72,751

DORCHESTER

1790	15,875
1800	16,346
1810	18,108
1820	17,759
1830	18,686
1840	18,843
1850	18,877
1860	20,461
1870	19,458
1880	23,110
1890	24,843
1900	27,962
1910	28,669
1920	27,895
1930	26,813
1940	28,006
1950	27,815
1960	29,666
1970	29,405
1980	30,623

FREDERICK

1790	30,791
1800	31,523
1810	34,437
1820	40,459
1830	45,789
1840	36,405
1850	40,987
1860	46,591
1870	47,572
1880	50,482
1890	49,512
1900	51,920
1910	52,673
1920	52,541
1930	54,440
1940	57,312
1950	62,287
1960	71,930
1970	84,927
1980	114,792

GARRETT

1880	12,175
1890	14,313
1900	17,701
1910	20,105

HARFORD

1790	14,976
1800	17,626
1810	21,258
1820	15,924
1830	16,319
1840	17,120
1850	19,356
1860	23,415
1870	22,605
1880	28,042
1890	28,993
1900	28,269
1910	27,965
1920	29,291
1930	31,603
1940	35,060
1950	51,872
1960	76,722
1970	115,378
1980	145,930

HOWARD

1860	13,338
1870	14,150
1880	16,140
1890	16,269
1900	16,715
1910	16,106
1920	15,836
1930	16,169
1940	17,175
1950	23,119
1960	36,152
1970	61,911
1980	118,572

KENT

1790	12,836
1800	11,771
1810	11,450
1820	11,453
1830	10,501
1840	10,842
1850	11,386
1860	13,267
1870	17,102
1880	17,605
1890	17,471
1900	18,786
1910	16,957
1920	15,026
1930	14,242
1940	13,465
1950	13,677
1960	15,481
1970	16,146
1980	16,695

MONTGOMERY

1790	18,003
1800	15,058
1810	17,980
1820	16,400
1830	19,816
1840	15,456
1850	15,860
1860	18,322
1870	20,563
1880	24,759
1890	27,185
1900	30,451
1910	32,089
1920	34,921
1930	49,206
1940	83,912
1950	164,401
1960	340,928
1970	522,809
1980	579,053

PRINCE GEORGES

1790	21,344
1800	21,185
1810	20,589
1820	20,216
1830	20,474
1840	19,539
1850	21,549
1860	23,327
1870	21,138
1880	26,451
1890	26,080
1900	29,898
1910	36,147
1920	43,347
1930	60,095
1940	89,490
1950	194,182
1960	357,395
1970	661,719
1980	665,071

QUEEN ANNES

1790	15,463
1800	14,857
1810	16,648
1820	14,952
1830	14,397
1840	12,633
1850	14,484
1860	15,961
1870	16,171
1880	19,257
1890	18,461
1900	18,364
1910	18,364
1920	16,001
1930	14,571
1940	14,476
1950	14,579
1960	16,569
1970	18,422
1980	25,508

SAINT MARYS

1790	15,544
1800	13,699
1810	12,794
1820	12,974
1830	13,459
1840	13,224
1850	13,698
1860	15,213
1870	14,944
1880	16,934
1890	15,819
1900	17,182
1910	17,030

1920	16,112
1930	15,189
1940	14,626
1950	29,111
1960	38,915
1970	47,388
1980	59,895

SOMERSET

1790	15,610
1800	17,358
1810	17,195
1820	19,579
1830	20,166
1840	19,508
1850	22,456
1860	24,992
1870	18,190
1880	21,668
1890	24,155
1900	25,923
1910	26,455
1920	24,602
1930	23,382
1940	20,965
1950	20,745
1960	19,623
1970	18,924
1980	19,188

TALBOT

1790	13,084
1800	13,436
1810	14,230
1820	14,389
1830	12,947
1840	12,090
1850	13,811
1860	14,795
1870	16,137
1880	19,065
1890	17,736
1900	20,342
1910	19,620
1920	18,306
1930	18,583
1940	18,784
1950	19,428
1960	21,578
1970	23,682
1980	25,604

WASHINGTON

1790	15,882
1800	18,650
1810	18,730
1820	23,075
1830	25,268
1840	28,850
1850	30,848
1860	31,417
1870	34,712
1880	38,561
1890	39,782
1900	45,133
1910	39,617
1920	59,694
1930	65,882
1940	68,838
1950	78,886
1960	92,219
1970	103,829
1980	113,086

WICOMICO

1870	15,802
1880	18,016
1890	19,930
1900	22,852
1910	26,815
1920	28,615
1930	31,229
1940	34,530
1950	39,641
1960	49,050
1970	54,236
1980	64,540

WORCESTER

1790	11,640
1800	16,370
1810	16,971
1820	17,421
1830	18,273
1840	18,377
1850	18,859
1860	20,661
1870	16,419
1880	19,539
1890	19,747
1900	20,865
1910	21,841
1920	22,309
1930	21,624
1940	21,245
1950	23,148
1960	23,733
1970	24,442
1980	30,889

ABERDEEN

1880	191
1890	448
1900	600
1910	616
1920	1,067
1930	1,240
1940	1,525
1950	2,944
1960	9,679
1970	12,375
1980	11,533

ANNAPOLIS

1820	2,260
1830	2,623
1840	2,792
1850	3,011
1860	4,529
1870	5,744
1880	6,642
1890	7,604
1900	7,657
1910	8,262
1920	8,518
1930	9,803
1940	9,812
1950	10,047
1960	23,385
1970	29,592
1980	31,740

BALTIMORE

1790	13,503
1800	26,514
1810	46,555
1820	62,738
1830	80,620
1840	102,313
1850	169,054
1860	212,418
1870	267,354
1880	332,313
1890	434,439
1900	508,957
1910	558,485
1920	733,826
1930	804,874
1940	859,100
1950	949,708
1960	939,024
1970	905,787
1980	786,775

BOWIE

1900	443
1920	677
1930	694
1940	767
1950	860
1960	1,072
1970	35,028
1980	33,695

CAMBRIDGE

1860	1,862
1870	1,642
1880	2,262
1890	4,192
1900	5,747
1910	5,407
1920	7,467

1930	8,544
1940	10,102
1950	10,351
1960	12,239
1970	11,595
1980	11,703

COLLEGE PARK

1950	11,170
1960	18,482
1970	26,156
1980	23,614

CUMBERLAND

1850	6,073
1860	4,078
1870	8,056
1880	10,693
1890	12,729
1900	17,128
1910	21,839
1920	29,837
1930	37,747
1940	39,483
1950	37,679
1960	33,415
1970	29,724
1980	25,933

FREDERICK

1820	3,640
1830	4,427
1840	5,182
1850	6,028
1860	8,143
1870	8,526
1880	8,659
1890	8,193
1900	9,296
1910	10,411
1920	11,066
1930	14,434
1940	15,802
1950	18,142
1960	21,744
1970	23,641
1980	28,086

GAITHERSBURG

1900	547
1910	825
1920	729
1930	1,068
1940	1,021
1950	1,755
1960	3,847
1970	8,344
1980	26,424

GREENBELT

1940	2,831
1950	7,074
1960	7,749
1970	18,199
1980	17,372

HAGERSTOWN

1830	3,371
1840	3,625
1850	3,879
1860	4,132
1870	5,779
1880	6,627
1890	10,118
1900	13,591
1910	16,507
1920	28,064
1930	30,861
1940	32,491
1950	36,260
1960	36,660
1970	35,862
1980	34,132

HYATTSVILLE

1880	288
1890	1,509
1900	1,222
1910	1,917
1920	2,675
1930	4,264
1940	6,565
1950	12,308
1960	15,168
1970	14,998
1980	12,709

LAUREL

1860	82
1870	1,148
1880	1,206
1890	1,984
1900	2,079
1910	2,415
1920	2,239
1930	2,532
1940	2,823
1950	4,482
1960	8,503
1970	10,525
1980	12,103

NEW CARROLLTON

1960	3,385
1970	14,870
1980	12,632

ROCKVILLE

1860	365
1870	660
1880	688
1890	1,568
1900	1,110
1910	1,181
1920	1,145
1930	1,460
1940	2,047
1950	6,934
1960	26,090
1970	42,739
1980	43,811

SALISBURY

1870	2,064
1880	2,581
1890	2,905
1900	4,277
1910	6,690
1920	7,553
1930	10,997
1940	13,313
1950	15,141
1960	16,302
1970	15,252
1980	16,429

TAKOMA PARK

1890	164
1900	756
1910	1,242
1920	3,168
1930	6,415
1940	8,938
1950	13,341
1960	16,799
1970	18,455
1980	16,231

CORRECTION NOTE

The official 1980 census counts of total population shown in this report supersede counts issued previously. Corrections to the figures were made after the counts were provided to the State for redistricting purposes and released in Advance Report PHC80-V for this State.

Shown below are corrections to the 1980 census counts of the total population made after the tabulations for this report were completed. Any additional corrections made after this report is printed are available by writing to Data User Services Division, Customer Services (Corrections), Bureau of the Census, Washington, D.C. 20233.

The 1980 figures shown in this publication are subject to change pending the outcome of the various lawsuits dealing with the census counts.

	1980 population	
	As shown in the tables	Corrected
Baltimore County:		
District 9:		
Hampton (CDP)...................	5 220	6 203
Lutherville-Timonium		
(CDP)(pt.)....................	2 311	1 328
Harford County:		
District 3, Bel Air:		
Bel Air South (CDP)(pt.).......	5 428	6 107
Bel Air South (CDP)(total)........	8 461	9 140
Lutherville-Timonium (CDP)(total)..	17 854	16 871

County Subdivisions	1980	1970
The State	4 216 975	ʼ3 923 897
Allegany County[1]	80 548	84 044
District 1, Orleans	676	588
District 2, Oldtown[1]	1 163	...
District 3, Flintstone	1 402	1 260
District 4, Canal[1]	11 347	12 509
Cumberland city (pt.)	11 155	(NA)
District 5, Wills Creek[1]	4 728	...
Cumberland city (pt.)	3 550	(NA)
District 6, Potomac River[1]	7 905	7 924
Cresaptown (CDP) (pt.)	83	...
Cumberland city (pt.)	5 463	(NA)
Potomac Park—Bowling Green (CDP)	2 275	2 253
District 7, Rawlings	6 416	5 106
Cresaptown (CDP) (pt.)	4 436	1 422
District 8, Westernport	3 896	4 553
Luke town	329	424
Westernport town[1]	2 706	3 106
District 9, Barton	1 167	1 393
Barton town	617	723
District 10, Lonaconing[1]	3 148	...
Lonaconing town	1 420	1 572
District 11, Frostburg	1 044	1 293
Frostburg city (pt.)[1]	566	768
District 12, East Frostburg[1]	3 385	...
Eckhart Mines (CDP) (pt.)	13	...
Frostburg city (pt.)[1]	2 712	2 693
District 13, Mount Savage	2 512	2 320
Mount Savage (CDP) (pt.)	1 600	1 413
District 14, Central[1]	421	973
Cumberland city (pt.)	421	973
District 16, North Branch	2 069	2 181
District 17, Vale Summit	429	164
District 18, Ocean[1]	1 713	...
Midland town	601	665
District 19, Borden Shaft[1]	724	786
District 20, Ellerslie	1 989	2 047
Corriganville (CDP)	1 020	...
La Vale—Narrows Park (CDP) (pt.)	58	...
District 21, Gross[1]	836	...
District 22, Union[1]	2 628	3 118
Cumberland city (pt.)	2 178	(NA)
District 23, Decatur[1]	2 792	...
Bedford Road (CDP) (pt.)	31	...
Cumberland city (pt.)	2 761	(NA)
District 24, Eckhart	1 789	1 764
Eckhart Mines (CDP) (pt.)	1 320	...
Frostburg city (pt.)[1]	303	58
District 26, Frostburg	3 214	...
Frostburg city (pt.)	2 754	(NA)
District 28, Frostburg	1 949	...
Frostburg city (pt.)	1 380	(NA)
District 29, La Vale	7 282	7 410
Cresaptown (CDP) (pt.)	126	309
Cumberland city (pt.)	313	...
La Vale—Narrows Park (CDP) (pt.)	5 465	3 971
District 30, Zihlman	600	448
Mount Savage (CDP) (pt.)	40	...
District 31, McCoole[1]	1 132	1 264
District 34, Bedford Road[1]	2 014	...
Bedford Road (CDP) (pt.)	1 716	...
Cumberland city (pt.)	40	(NA)
District 35, East Cumberland[1]	178	...
Cumberland city (pt.)	52	(NA)
Anne Arundel County[2]	370 775	ʼ298 042
District 1	20 420	14 207
Londontowne (CDP)	6 052	3 864
Mayo (CDP)	2 795	2 154
Riva (CDP) (pt.)	1 109	...
Selby-on-the-Bay (CDP)	3 125	2 450
District 2	39 430	25 312
Arden on the Severn (CDP)	2 303	...
Bay Ridge (CDP)	1 989	...
Crofton (CDP)	12 009	4 478
Herald Harbor (CDP)	1 266	...
Highland Beach town	8	6
Hillsmere Shores (CDP)	2 972	...
Parole (CDP)	3 377	...
Riva (CDP) (pt.)	1 478	...
District 3	130 533	96 127
Arnold (CDP)	12 285	...
Cape St. Claire (CDP)	6 022	ʼ2 689
Glen Burnie (CDP) (pt.)	21 684	21 721
Green Haven (CDP)	6 577	...
Lake Shore (CDP)	10 181	...
Pasadena (CDP)	7 439	...
Riviera Beach (CDP)	8 812	7 464
Severna Park (CDP)	21 253	16 358
South Gate (CDP) (pt.)	16 892	4 749
District 4	72 432	55 098
Dorsey (CDP) (pt.)	767	...
Fort Meade (CDP)	14 083	16 699
Jessup (CDP) (pt.)	3 586	...
Maryland City (CDP)	6 949	7 102
Odenton (CDP)	13 270	5 989
Severn (CDP)	20 147	...
South Gate (CDP) (pt.)	7 293	4 607

County Subdivisions	1980	1970
Anne Arundel County—Con.		
District 5	57 527	60 868
Brooklyn Park (CDP)	11 508	13 896
Dorsey (CDP) (pt.)	196	...
Ferndale (CDP)	14 314	9 929
Glen Burnie (CDP) (pt.)	15 579	16 887
Linthicum (CDP)	7 457	ʼ9 775
Pumphrey (CDP)	5 666	ʼ6 425
District 6	37 107	ʼ35 582
Annapolis city[2]	31 740	ʼ30 095
Naval Academy (CDP)	5 367	...
District 7	6 181	5 310
Deale (CDP)	3 008	1 059
Shady Side (CDP)	2 877	1 562
District 8	7 145	5 538
Baltimore County	655 615	ʼ620 409
District 1	62 661	63 643
Catonsville (CDP)	33 208	54 812
Security (CDP)	29 453	...
District 2	65 397	55 618
Lochearn (CDP) (pt.)	15 934	...
Milford Mill (CDP)	20 354	...
Randallstown (CDP)	25 927	33 683
District 3	39 487	38 305
Lochearn (CDP) (pt.)	10 974	...
Pikesville (CDP)	22 555	24 159
District 4	37 541	ʼ29 222
Owings Mills (CDP)	9 526	7 360
Reisterstown (CDP)	19 385	ʼ12 568
District 5	3 960	3 120
District 6	3 300	2 076
District 7	5 673	4 714
District 8	47 489	38 568
Cockeysville (CDP)	17 013	...
Lutherville—Timonium (CDP) (pt.)	15 543	19 991
Mays Chapel (CDP)	5 213	...
Towson (CDP) (pt.)	2 782	(NA)
District 9	98 859	ʼ102 336
Carney (CDP) (pt.)	13 090	...
Hampton (CDP)	5 220	...
Lutherville—Timonium (CDP) (pt.)	2 311	4 064
Parkville (CDP) (pt.)	29 937	(NA)
Towson (CDP) (pt.)	48 301	(NA)
District 10	7 607	5 647
District 11	39 440	26 614
Carney (CDP) (pt.)	8 398	...
Kingsville (CDP)	2 824	...
Long Green (CDP)	1 626	...
Perry Hall (CDP)	13 455	5 446
District 12	60 718	72 261
Dundalk (CDP) (pt.)	60 467	72 261
District 13	36 922	ʼ40 647
Arbutus (CDP)	20 163	22 745
Lansdowne—Baltimore Highlands (CDP)	16 759	ʼ17 770
District 14	42 258	ʼ36 447
Overlea (CDP)	12 965	ʼ13 124
Parkville (CDP) (pt.)	5 222	(NA)
Rosedale (CDP) (pt.)	15 680	14 841
Rossville (CDP) (pt.)	8 391	...
District 15	104 303	101 191
Dundalk (CDP) (pt.)	10 826	13 116
Edgemere (CDP)	9 078	10 352
Essex (CDP)	39 614	38 193
Middle River (CDP)	26 756	19 935
Rosedale (CDP) (pt.)	4 276	4 576
Rossville (CDP) (pt.)	255	...
Calvert County	34 638	20 682
District 1, Solomons Island	9 687	6 404
Long Beach—Calvert Beach (CDP)	1 203	...
District 2, Prince Frederick	9 330	6 211
Prince Frederick (CDP)	1 805	...
District 3, Sunderland	15 621	8 067
Chesapeake Beach town	1 408	934
North Beach town	1 504	761
Caroline County[3]	23 143	19 781
District 1, Henderson	2 338	1 887
Goldsboro town	188	231
Henderson town	156	135
Marydel town	152	176
Templeville town (pt.)[3]	36	19
District 2, Greensboro	3 371	2 817
Greensboro town[3]	1 253	1 173
District 3, Denton	4 595	3 771
Denton town[3]	1 927	1 561
District 4, Preston	3 293	2 675
Preston town	498	509
District 5, Federalsburg	4 136	4 037
Federalsburg town[3]	1 952	1 917
District 6, Hillsboro	1 565	1 313
Hillsboro town	180	177
District 7, Ridgely	2 178	1 882
Ridgely town	933	822
District 8, American Corner	1 667	1 399

County Subdivisions	1980	1970
Carroll County[4]	96 356	69 006
District 1, Taneytown	5 269	4 142
Taneytown city[4]	2 618	1 731
District 2, Uniontown	3 284	2 672
District 3, Myers	4 000	2 651
District 4, Woolerys	11 296	6 532
Westminster South (CDP) (pt.)	—	…
District 5, Freedom	13 567	11 475
Eldersburg (CDP)	4 959	1 739
Oakland (CDP)	2 242	1 256
Sykesville town[4]	1 712	1 399
District 6, Manchester	8 260	5 253
Manchester town[4]	1 830	1 466
District 7, Westminster	19 116	16 304
Westminster city[4]	8 808	7 207
Westminster South (CDP) (pt.)	3 521	2 242
District 8, Hampstead	7 857	5 290
Hampstead town[4]	1 293	961
District 9, Franklin	4 942	1 925
District 10, Middleburg	1 296	1 306
District 11, New Windsor	2 664	2 414
New Windsor town[4]	799	788
District 12, Union Bridge	1 654	1 678
Union Bridge town[4]	927	904
District 13, Mount Airy	4 174	3 106
Mount Airy town (pt.)[4]	1 910	1 311
District 14, Berrett	8 977	4 258
Cecil County[5]	60 430	53 291
District 1, Cecilton	2 880	2 658
Cecilton town	508	581
District 2, Chesapeake City	3 714	3 352
Chesapeake City town	899	1 031
District 3, Elkton	15 864	13 632
Elkton town[5]	6 468	5 362
District 4, Fair Hill	6 005	3 399
District 5, North East	12 507	8 928
Charlestown town	720	721
North East town	1 469	1 818
District 6, Rising Sun	6 201	4 993
Rising Sun town[5]	1 160	956
District 7, Port Deposit	8 628	13 182
Perryville town	2 018	2 091
Port Deposit town	664	906
District 8, Oakwood	2 109	1 491
District 9, Calvert	2 522	1 656
Charles County[6]	72 751	47 678
District 1, La Plata	7 269	4 707
La Plata town (pt.)[6]	2 481	1 561
Port Tobacco Village town[6]	40	…
White Plains (CDP) (pt.)	4	…
District 2, Hill Top	1 439	1 364
District 3, Nanjemoy	2 688	2 442
District 4, Allens Fresh	3 337	2 504
Charlotte Hall (CDP) (pt.)	535	…
District 5, Tompkinsville	3 423	2 602
District 6, Waldorf	26 460	12 607
La Plata town (pt.)[6]	3	…
St. Charles (CDP)	13 921	…
Waldorf (CDP) (pt.)	4 952	6 721
White Plains (CDP) (pt.)	5 163	…
Dist. 7, Pomonkey–Potomac Heights	11 028	10 687
Bryans Road (CDP)	3 739	…
Indian Head town[6]	1 381	1 350
Indian Head Plant (CDP)	1 154	1 449
Potomac Heights (CDP)	2 456	1 983
District 8, Bryantown	11 135	5 688
Charlotte Hall (CDP) (pt.)	353	…
Hughesville (CDP) (pt.)	504	…
La Plata town (pt.)[6]	—	…
Waldorf (CDP) (pt.)	4 830	647
District 9, Hughesville	2 409	2 129
Hughesville (CDP) (pt.)	704	…
District 10, Marbury	3 563	2 948
Marbury (CDP)	1 189	…
Dorchester County[7]	30 623	29 405
District 1, Fork	1 833	1 548
Brookview town	78	95
Eldorado town	93	99
Galestown town	142	123
District 2, East New Market	1 983	1 753
East New Market town	230	251
Secretary town	487	352
District 3, Vienna	1 089	1 300
Vienna town[7]	300	358
District 4, Taylors Island	293	285
District 5, Lakes	530	606
District 6, Hoopers Island	759	712
District 7, Cambridge	14 147	13 863
Cambridge city[7]	11 703	11 595
District 8, Neck	833	806
District 9, Church Creek	635	635
Church Creek town[7]	124	130
District 10, Straits	647	754
District 11, Drawbridge	91	108
District 12, Williamsburg	1 048	1 027
District 13, Bucktown	603	592

County Subdivisions	1980	1970
Dorchester County—Con.		
District 14, Linkwood	2 106	2 086
District 15, Hurlock	3 207	2 532
Hurlock town[7]	1 690	1 056
District 16, Madison	423	357
District 17, Salem	299	325
District 18, Elliott	97	116
Frederick County[8]	114 792	84 927
District 1, Buckeystown	2 809	2 654
District 2, Frederick	30 376	25 908
Clover Hill (CDP) (pt.)	2	…
Frederick city[8]	28 086	23 641
District 3, Middletown	5 445	2 897
Braddock Heights (CDP) (pt.)	1 054	…
Middletown town[8]	1 748	1 262
District 4, Creagerstown	1 262	1 140
District 5, Emmitsburg	5 952	5 428
Emmitsburg town[8]	1 552	1 532
District 6, Catoctin	1 478	1 262
District 7, Urbana	4 639	3 014
Green Valley (CDP) (pt.)	906	…
District 8, Liberty	1 848	1 257
District 9, New Market	9 857	4 904
Green Valley (CDP) (pt.)	3 598	…
New Market town[8]	306	339
District 10, Hauvers	2 272	2 053
Cascade–Highfield (CDP) (pt.)	46	…
District 11, Woodsboro	2 399	2 127
Woodsboro town[8]	506	439
District 12, Petersville	1 725	1 592
Rosemont town	305	250
District 13, Mount Pleasant	2 115	1 556
District 14, Jefferson	2 157	1 311
Braddock Heights (CDP) (pt.)	30	…
District 15, Thurmont	5 836	4 973
Thurmont town[8]	2 934	2 359
District 16, Jackson	2 309	1 685
Myersville town	432	450
District 17, Johnsville	1 612	1 314
District 18, Woodville	3 560	1 930
Mount Airy town (pt.)[8]	540	514
District 19, Linganore	1 153	837
District 20, Lewistown	3 147	2 121
District 21, Tuscarora	4 798	3 565
Clover Hill (CDP) (pt.)	1 722	…
District 22, Burkittsville	1 274	1 076
Burkittsville town	202	221
District 23, Ballenger	1 779	1 110
Braddock Heights (CDP) (pt.)	166	…
District 24, Braddock	4 526	3 551
Braddock Heights (CDP) (pt.)	2 973	…
District 25, Brunswick	4 572	3 566
Brunswick town	4 572	3 566
District 26, Walkersville	5 892	2 096
Discovery (CDP)	2 328	…
Walkersville town[8]	2 212	1 269
Garrett County[9]	26 498	21 476
District 1, Swanton	1 298	1 079
District 2, Friendsville[9]	1 860	1 704
Friendsville town	511	566
District 3, Grantsville	2 992	2 517
Grantsville town	498	517
District 4, Bloomington	964	895
District 5, Accident	1 321	1 071
Accident town[9]	246	237
District 6, Sang Run	1 623	974
District 7, East Oakland	2 165	1 813
Mountain Lake Park town (pt.)[9]	385	53
Oakland town (pt.)	825	885
District 8, Red House[9]	1 689	1 565
District 9, Finzel[9]	1 199	890
District 10, Deer Park	1 442	1 130
Deer Park town (pt.)	478	306
District 11, The Elbow	197	155
District 12, Bittinger	857	595
District 13, Kitzmillerville	862	911
Kitzmillerville town	387	443
District 14, West Oakland	4 509	3 443
Oakland town (pt.)	1 169	901
District 15, Avilton	398	432
District 16, Mountain Lake Park	3 122	2 302
Deer Park town (pt.)	8	4
Loch Lynn Heights town	503	507
Mountain Lake Park town (pt.)[9]	1 212	1 210
Harford County[10]	145 930	115 378
District 1, Abingdon	42 013	27 977
Bel Air South (CDP) (pt.)	3 033	…
Edgewood (CDP)	19 455	8 551
Joppatowne (CDP)	11 348	9 092
District 2, Halls Cross Roads	25 562	29 450
Aberdeen[10]	11 533	12 375
Aberdeen Proving Ground (CDP)	5 722	7 403
Perryman (CDP)	1 819	…
District 3, Bel Air	41 971	30 803
Bel Air town[10]	7 814	6 307
Bel Air North (CDP)	5 043	2 771
Bel Air South (CDP) (pt.)	5 428	3 360

County Subdivisions	1980	1970
Harford County—Con.		
District 3, Bel Air—Con.		
Fallston (CDP) (pt.)	4 948	...
Pleasant Hills (CDP)	2 790	1 754
District 4, Marshall	15 277	8 380
Fallston (CDP) (pt.)	624	...
Jarrettsville (CDP)	1 485	...
District 5, Dublin	10 558	8 977
District 6, Havre de Grace	10 549	9 791
Havre de Grace city[10]	8 763	9 791
Howard County	118 572	'62 394
District 1, Elk Ridge	8 008	9 613
Dorsey (CDP) (pt.)	223	...
Jessup (CDP) (pt.)	702	...
District 2, Ellicott City	24 274	'17 928
Ellicott City (CDP)	21 784	'9 435
District 3, West Friendship	6 053	3 667
District 4, Lisbon	6 575	4 250
District 5, Clarksville	28 798	13 536
Columbia (CDP) (pt.)	21 413	7 534
District 6, Savage	44 864	13 400
Columbia (CDP) (pt.)	31 105	1 281
North Laurel (CDP)	6 093	...
Savage–Guilford (CDP)	2 928	2 116
Kent County[11]	16 695	16 146
District 1, Masseys	2 889	2 707
Galena town	374	361
Millington town (pt.)	512	435
District 2, Kennedyville	1 796	1 840
District 3, Worton (Betterton)	2 258	1 956
Betterton town[11]	356	327
District 4, Chestertown	3 949	4 209
Chestertown town[11]	3 300	3 476
District 5, Edesville	2 861	2 889
Rock Hall town[11]	1 511	1 125
District 6, Fairlee	1 422	1 352
District 7, Pomona	1 520	1 193
Montgomery County[12]	579 053	522 809
District 1[12]	5 052	3 452
Laytonsville town	195	293
Redland (CDP) (pt.)	231	...
District 2[12]	5 278	3 980
Germantown (CDP) (pt.)	1 408	...
District 3[12]	4 987	1 993
Poolesville town	3 428	349
District 4[12]	83 646	'81 950
Aspen Hill (CDP) (pt.)	5	(NA)
Garrett Park town	1 178	'1 276
North Bethesda (CDP)	22 671	...
Potomac (CDP) (pt.)	13 209	...
Redland (CDP) (pt.)	2 078	...
Rockville city (pt.)[12]	43 811	'42 739
District 5[12]	51 923	49 605
Burtonsville (CDP)	2 046	...
Calverton (CDP) (pt.)	3 444	2 732
Cloverly (CDP)	5 153	...
Colesville (CDP)	14 359	9 455
Fairland (CDP)	5 154	...
Hillandale (CDP) (pt.)	7 251	9 529
White Oak (CDP)	13 700	...
District 6[12]	13 137	4 999
Germantown (CDP) (pt.)	1 679	...
Potomac (CDP) (pt.)	89	...
Quince Orchard (CDP) (pt.)	5 107	...
District 7[12]	86 742	'96 908
Bethesda (CDP)	62 736	71 621
Cabin John–Brookmont (CDP)	5 135	'5 122
Chevy Chase (CDP)	12 232	16 424
Chevy Chase Section Four town[12]	3 189	2 266
Chevy Chase Village town[12]	2 118	2 265
Glen Echo town[12]	229	297
Somerset town[12]	1 101	1 303
District 8[12]	24 139	12 890
Ashton–Sandy Springs (CDP)	2 659	...
Aspen Hill (CDP) (pt.)	4 025	(NA)
Brookeville town	120	136
Olney (CDP)	13 026	2 138
Redland (CDP) (pt.)	518	...
District 9[12]	67 035	23 150
Gaithersburg city[12]	26 424	8 344
Germantown (CDP) (pt.)	6 634	...
Montgomery Village (CDP)	18 725	...
Quince Orchard (CDP) (pt.)	–	...
Redland (CDP) (pt.)	7 932	...
Rockville city (pt.)	–	...
Washington Grove town	527	688
District 10[12]	27 104	'16 351
Potomac (CDP) (pt.)	27 104	...
District 11[12]	2 148	2 266
Barnesville town[12]	141	162
District 12[12]	8 486	6 372
Damascus (CDP)	4 129	2 638
District 13[12]	199 376	'218 893
Aspen Hill (CDP) (pt.)	43 425	(NA)
Kensington town	1 822	2 322
Langley Park (CDP) (pt.)	2 924	...
North Kensington (CDP)	9 039	...
Silver Spring (CDP)	72 893	'77 411

County Subdivisions	1980	1970
Montgomery County—Con.		
District 13—Con.		
South Kensington (CDP)	9 344	10 289
Takoma Park city	11 331	'12 537
Wheaton–Glenmont (CDP)	48 598	'66 280
Prince George's County[13]	665 071	'661 719
District 1, Vansville[13]	19 597	20 914
Beltsville (CDP) (pt.)	12 760	8 912
Calverton (CDP) (pt.)	4 205	3 811
College Park city (pt.)	1 230	1 320
District 2, Bladensburg[13]	36 426	'41 603
Bladensburg town[13]	7 689	'7 977
Cheverly town (pt.)[13]	5 508	'6 537
Colmar Manor town	1 286	1 715
Cottage City town	1 122	993
East Riverdale (CDP) (pt.)	4 015	—
Edmonston town (pt.)	–	(NA)
Landover (CDP)	5 374	5 597
Landover Hills town	1 428	'2 409
Woodlawn (CDP)	4 747	'6 802
District 3, Marlboro[13]	6 098	4 451
Upper Marlboro town	828	646
District 4, Nottingham[13]	2 543	2 290
District 5, Piscataway[13]	23 545	'16 495
Accokeek (CDP)	3 894	...
Friendly (CDP) (pt.)	6 159	...
Oxon Hill (CDP) (pt.)	474	...
Tantallon (CDP)	9 945	...
District 6, Spauldings[13]	92 194	'107 039
Camp Springs (CDP) (pt.)	10 312	'10 745
Coral Hills (CDP) (pt.)	4 855	'5 207
District Heights city	6 799	'7 846
Forestville (CDP) (pt.)	16 161	'16 417
Hillcrest Heights (CDP) (pt.)	10 502	20 295
Marlow Heights (CDP) (pt.)	3 465	...
Morningside town[13]	1 395	'1 659
Suitland–Silver Hill (CDP)	32 164	'30 163
Temple Hills (CDP) (pt.)	508	...
Walker Mill (CDP)	5 063	'6 902
District 7, Queen Anne[13]	26 996	21 715
Bowie city (pt.)[13]	19 786	18 749
Kettering (CDP) (pt.)	4 278	...
District 8, Aquasco	1 505	1 485
Eagle Harbor town	45	'14
District 9, Surratts[13]	36 680	'25 818
Andrews AFB (CDP)	10 064	6 418
Camp Springs (CDP) (pt.)	4 467	3 447
Clinton (CDP)	16 438	...
Friendly (CDP) (pt.)	2 689	...
District 10, Laurel[13]	38 638	31 579
Laurel city[13]	12 103	10 525
South Laurel (CDP)	18 034	13 345
District 11, Brandywine[13]	9 028	7 932
Brandywine (CDP)	1 319	...
District 12, Oxon Hill[13]	62 882	'56 175
Camp Springs (CDP) (pt.)	1 339	'7 195
Forest Heights town	2 999	'3 497
Glassmanor (CDP)	7 751	...
Hillcrest Heights (CDP) (pt.)	6 519	3 742
Marlow Heights (CDP) (pt.)	2 359	...
Oxon Hill (CDP) (pt.)	35 793	'13 642
Temple Hills (CDP) (pt.)	6 122	...
District 13, Kent[13]	41 217	30 318
Dodge Park (CDP)	5 275	...
Glenarden town (pt.)	3 173	'1 767
Glenn Dale (CDP) (pt.)	277	...
Kentland (CDP) (pt.)	8 596	9 649
Kettering (CDP) (pt.)	2 694	...
Largo (CDP)	5 557	...
Palmer Park (CDP)	7 986	8 712
District 14, Bowie[13]	26 527	29 161
Bowie city (pt.)[13]	13 909	16 279
Glenn Dale (CDP) (pt.)	4 829	...
Goddard (CDP) (pt.)	934	...
Lanham–Seabrook (CDP) (pt.)	3 153	...
District 15, Mellwood[13]	10 740	'8 774
Forestville (CDP) (pt.)	214	...
District 16, Hyattsville[13]	13 634	15 491
Bladensburg town (pt.)	2	—
East Riverdale (CDP) (pt.)	–	...
Edmonston town (pt.)	1 109	(NA)
Hyattsville city (pt.)	12 523	13 867
District 17, Chillum[13]	69 807	75 728
Adelphi (CDP) (pt.)	9 497	...
Brentwood town	2 988	3 426
Chillum (CDP)	32 775	35 656
Hillandale (CDP) (pt.)	406	5 622
Hyattsville city (pt.)	186	1 131
Langley Park (CDP) (pt.)	11 114	11 564
Mount Rainier city	7 361	8 180
North Brentwood town	580	758
Takoma Park city (pt.)	4 900	5 970
District 18, Seat Pleasant[13]	37 540	'42 482
Capitol Heights town	3 271	'3 835
Carmody Hills–Pepper Mill Village (CDP)	5 571	'6 335
Cheverly town (pt.)[13]	243	271
Coral Hills (CDP) (pt.)	6 747	'3 865
Fairmount Heights town	1 616	1 972
Forestville (CDP) (pt.)	26	...

County Subdivisions	1980	1970
Prince George's County—Con.		
District 18, Seat Pleasant—Con.		
Kentland (CDP) (pt.)	–	...
Seat Pleasant city	5 217	7 217
Walker Mill (CDP) (pt.)	5 588	...
District 19, Riverdale[13]	15 788	21 909
College Park city (pt.)	14	74
East Riverdale (CDP) (pt.)	9 747	8 941
Riverdale town (pt.)[13]	3 449	5 724
University Park town (pt.)	2 508	2 926
District 20, Lanham[13]	33 531	38 672
East Riverdale (CDP) (pt.)	355	...
Glenarden town (pt.)	1 820	2 680
Lanham–Seabrook (CDP) (pt.)	12 661	13 244
New Carrollton city[13]	12 632	14 870
Woodlawn (CDP) (pt.)	559	...
District 21, Berwyn[13]	60 155	61 688
Adelphi (CDP) (pt.)	3 033	...
Beltsville (CDP) (pt.)	–	...
Berwyn Heights town	3 135	3 934
College Park city[13]	22 370	24 762
East Riverdale (CDP) (pt.)	–	...
Goddard (CDP) (pt.)	5 213	...
Greenbelt city[13]	17 332	18 199
Hillandale (CDP) (pt.)	2 029	4 369
Riverdale town (pt.)	1 299	...
University Park town (pt.)	28	...
Queen Anne's County[14]	25 508	18 422
District 1, Dixon	2 306	2 163
Barclay town[14]	132	187
Sudlersville town[14]	443	417
Templeville town (pt.)	60	83
District 2, Church Hill	2 912	1 846
Church Hill town[14]	319	247
Kingstown (CDP)	1 192	...
District 3, Centreville	4 025	3 564
Centreville town	2 018	1 853
District 4, Kent Island	8 177	3 832
District 5, Queenstown	4 713	3 896
Grasonville (CDP)	1 910	1 182
Queenstown town	491	387
District 6, Ruthsburg	1 081	919
Queen Anne town (pt.)	131	141
District 7, Crumpton	2 294	2 202
Millington town (pt.)	34	39
St. Mary's County	59 895	47 388
District 1, St. Inigoes	5 021	4 219
District 2, Valley Lee	3 940	3 494
District 3, Leonardtown	7 671	5 811
Leonardtown town	1 448	1 406
District 4, Chaptico	3 713	2 158
District 5, Mechanicsville	7 376	3 285
Charlotte Hall (CDP) (pt.)	1 013	...
Golden Beach (CDP)	2 098	...
District 6, Patuxent	8 092	5 283
District 7, Milestown	3 194	2 976
District 8, Bay	20 562	19 837
California (CDP)	5 770	...
Lexington Park (CDP)	10 361	9 136
District 9, St. George Island	326	325
Somerset County[15]	19 188	18 924
District 1, West Princess Anne	2 470	2 181
Princess Anne town (pt.)[15]	498	537
District 2, St. Peters	577	649
District 3, Brinkleys	1 518	1 452
District 4, Dublin	1 309	1 343
District 5, Mount Vernon	843	837
District 6, Fairmount	613	788
District 7, Crisfield	3 065	3 110
Crisfield city (pt.)	2 776	3 078
Lawsonia (CDP) (pt.)	289	...
District 8, Lawsons	1 937	1 706
Crisfield city (pt.)	148	...
Lawsonia (CDP) (pt.)	240	...
District 9, Tangier	463	458
District 10, Smith Island	606	645
District 11, Dames Quarter	235	278
District 12, Asbury	1 158	1 592
Lawsonia (CDP) (pt.)	1 158	...
District 13, Westover	1 150	1 070
District 14, Deal Island	631	773
District 15, East Princess Anne	2 613	2 042
Princess Anne town (pt.)[15]	1 001	438
Talbot County[16]	25 604	23 682
District 1, Easton	12 166	11 167
Easton town[16]	7 536	6 809
District 2, St. Michaels	4 654	4 413
St. Michaels town	1 301	1 456
District 3, Trappe	3 510	3 366
Oxford town	754	750
Trappe town[16]	739	426
District 4, Chapel	3 347	2 761
Queen Anne town (pt.)	128	151
District 5, Bay Hundred	1 927	1 975

County Subdivisions	1980	1970
Washington County[17]	113 086	103 829
District 1, Sharpsburg	2 313	2 054
Sharpsburg town	721	833
District 2, Williamsport	4 718	4 057
Halfway (CDP) (pt.)	245	...
Williamsport town[17]	2 153	2 270
District 3, Hagerstown	9 250	9 257
Hagerstown city[17]	9 250	9 257
District 4, Clear Spring	2 368	2 071
Clear Spring town	477	499
District 5, Hancock	3 609	3 583
Hancock town[17]	1 887	1 881
District 6, Boonsboro	3 927	3 384
Boonsboro town[17]	1 908	1 410
District 7, Smithsburg	4 413	3 454
Cavetown (CDP) (pt.)	1 528	...
Smithsburg town[17]	833	671
District 8, Rohrersville	1 901	1 571
District 9, Leitersburg	3 070	2 267
Paramount (CDP) (pt.)	818	...
District 10, Funkstown[17]	7 801	4 761
Colonial Park (CDP) (pt.)	1 115	...
Funkstown town[17]	1 103	1 051
District 11, Sandy Hook	1 550	1 415
District 12, Fairplay	3 089	3 393
District 13, Maugansville	5 030	4 107
Maugansville (CDP)	1 707	1 069
Orchard Hills (CDP) (pt.)	16	...
District 14, Ringgold	4 155	4 481
Cascade–Highfield (CDP) (pt.)	1 050	...
Fort Ritchie	1 754	2 126
District 15, Indian Spring	1 694	1 595
District 16, Beaver Creek	2 725	2 182
District 17, Hagerstown	6 009	5 487
Hagerstown city[17]	6 009	5 487
District 18, Chewsville[17]	5 532	5 126
Bridgeport (CDP)	3 626	...
Cavetown (CDP) (pt.)	5	...
Colonial Park (CDP) (pt.)	–	...
Paramount (CDP) (pt.)	228	...
District 19, Keedysville	1 216	1 011
Keedysville town	476	431
District 20, Downsville	1 555	1 383
District 21, Hagerstown	5 456	6 111
Hagerstown city (pt.)[17]	5 456	6 111
District 22, Hagerstown	5 048	5 688
Hagerstown city (pt.)	5 048	5 688
District 23, Wilsons	2 863	2 589
District 24, Cedar Lawn	867	827
District 25, Hagerstown	8 369	9 319
Hagerstown city (pt.)	8 369	9 319
District 26, Halfway	9 489	7 346
Halfway (CDP) (pt.)	8 414	6 106
District 27, Fountain Head[17]	5 069	5 310
Fountain Head (CDP)	1 745	2 029
Orchard Hills (CDP) (pt.)	1 573	...
Paramount (CDP) (pt.)	832	...
Wicomico County[18]	64 540	54 236
District 1, Barren Creek	1 618	1 459
Mardela Springs town	320	356
District 2, Quantico	1 142	964
District 3, Tyaskin	990	1 195
District 4, Pittsburg	2 353	1 823
Pittsville town	519	477
District 5, Parsons	15 894	12 543
Salisbury city (pt.)[18]	4 629	3 759
District 6, Dennis	762	721
District 7, Trappe	1 142	1 188
District 8, Nutters[18]	4 087	2 239
Fruitland city (pt.)	–	...
Salisbury city (pt.)[18]	34	...
District 9, Salisbury	12 058	9 960
Salisbury city (pt.)	3 946	3 603
District 10, Sharptown	1 330	1 197
Sharptown town	654	660
District 11, Delmar	2 867	2 192
Delmar town	1 232	1 191
District 12, Nanticoke	954	1 103
District 13, Camden[18]	11 632	11 143
Salisbury city (pt.)[18]	7 820	7 890
District 14, Willards	1 382	1 084
Willards town	540	494
District 15, Hebron	1 954	1 558
Hebron town	714	705
District 16, Fruitland	4 375	3 867
Fruitland city (pt.)[18]	2 694	2 315
Worcester County[19]	30 889	24 442
District 1, Pocomoke	5 922	5 843
Pocomoke City city[19]	3 558	3 573
District 2, Snow Hill	4 789	4 671
Snow Hill town[19]	2 192	2 201
District 3, Berlin	8 207	6 136
Berlin town[19]	2 162	1 942
District 4, Newark	895	805
District 5, St. Martin	1 638	1 485
District 7, Atkinsons	693	525
District 8, Stockton	1 391	1 467

County Subdivisions

	1980	1970
Worcester County—Con.		
District 10, Ocean City	7 354	3 510
Ocean City town[19]	4 946	1 493
Baltimore city	786 775	r905 787

MASSACHUSETTS

Massachusetts takes its name from the Massachusetts Indians, a tribe which, at the time of the settlement of the colony, lived along the shores of Massachusetts Bay. The original significance of the word in the Indian tongue was probably "at the great hills," although other definitions have been suggested by different writers.

The region now constituting Massachusetts was included in the grants made in the patent of "Acadie" to the Sieur de Monts (French, 1603), the first charter of Virginia (English, 1606), and the charter of New England (1620). The English claim to this region was based on the discovery of the mainland of North America by the Cabots toward the close of the fifteenth century. The first permanent settlement was made by the Pilgrims, a band of about 100 Englishmen, who, landing at Plymouth in December, 1620, founded the Plymouth Colony. Between 1622 and 1628 several scattered settlements were made in and near Boston Harbor.

In 1628 the first permanent settlement in the colony of Massachusetts Bay was established, when a few settlers at Salem were found and joined by a party of English Puritans under the leadership of John Endicott, one of the proprietors of a land company which had obtained a grant extending from a line 3 miles north of the River Merrimac to a line 3 miles south of the River Charles, and from the Atlantic westward to the "South Sea." A charter for this territory was obtained from Charles I in the following year.

The charter of New England was surrendered to the Crown in 1635.

In 1684 the charter of Massachusetts Bay colony was declared forfeited, and the government was later placed in the hands of a royal governor and council. A new charter was granted in 1691, by the terms of which Massachusetts Bay, the colony of New Plymouth, the province of Maine, and the territory called Acadia or Nova Scotia were united under the name of Massachusetts Bay. This charter went into effect in the following year.

Massachusetts was one of the original thirteen states.

After the close of the Revolution (1783) Nova Scotia remained in the possession of England. In 1785 Massachusetts ceded to the United States all claims, based on its early charters, to territory west of New York. In 1820 Maine became a separate state. After these modifications the area of Massachusetts was substantially as at present, although minor changes in its boundaries have since been made.

COUNTY LOCATION INDEX

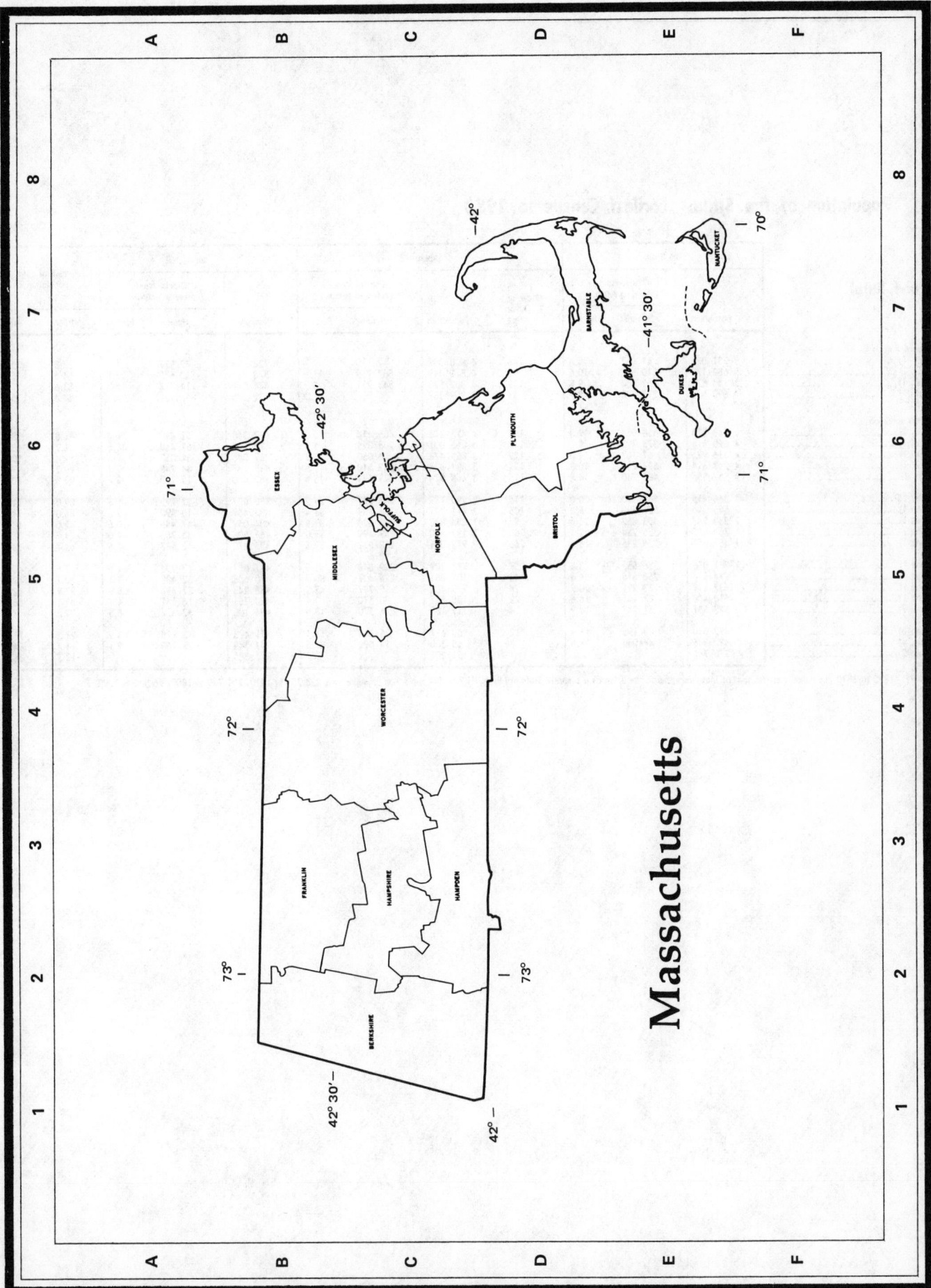

Massachusetts

Population of the State: Earliest Census to 1980

Urban and Rural

	The State			Urban				Rural			Percent of total population	
	Total population	Change from preceding census		Places of 2,500 or more	Population	Change from preceding census		Population	Change from preceding census		Urban	Rural
		Number	Percent			Number	Percent		Number	Percent		
Current urban definition:												
1980 (Apr. 1)	5 737 037	47 867	0.8	148	4 808 339	−2 110	−	928 698	49 977	5.7	83.8	16.2
1970 (Apr. 1)	5 689 170	540 592	10.5	102	4 810 449	507 919	11.8	878 721	32 673	3.9	84.6	15.4
1960 (Apr. 1)	5 148 578	458 064	9.8	119	4 302 530	343 291	8.7	846 048	114 773	15.7	83.6	16.4
1950 (Apr. 1)	4 690 514	373 793	8.7	84	3 959 239	...	...	731 275	...	...	84.4	15.6
Previous urban definition:												
1960 (Apr. 1)	5 148 578	458 064	9.8	144	4 471 215	405 414	10.0	677 363	52 650	8.4	86.8	13.2
1950 (Apr. 1)	4 690 514	373 793	8.7	119	4 065 801	206 325	5.3	624 713	167 468	36.6	86.7	13.3
1940 (Apr. 1)	4 316 721	67 107	1.6	122	3 859 476	28 050	0.7	457 245	39 057	9.3	89.4	10.6
1930 (Apr. 1)	4 249 614	397 258	10.3	122	3 831 426	362 510	10.5	418 188	34 748	9.1	90.2	9.8
1920 (Apr. 1)	3 852 356	485 940	14.4	116	3 468 916	473 177	15.8	383 440	12 763	3.4	90.0	10.0
1910 (Apr. 15)	3 366 416	561 070	20.0	115	2 995 739	583 862	24.2	370 677	−22 792	−5.8	89.0	11.0
1900 (June 1)	2 805 346	566 399	25.3	105	2 411 877	576 989	31.4	393 469	−10 590	−2.6	86.0	14.0
1890 (June 1)	2 238 947	455 862	25.6	97	1 834 888	503 308	37.8	404 059	−47 446	−10.5	82.0	18.0
1880 (June 1)	1 783 085	325 734	22.4	80	1 331 580	359 499	37.0	451 505	−33 765	−7.0	74.7	25.3
1870 (June 1)	1 457 351	226 285	18.4	65	972 081	238 872	32.6	485 270	−12 587	−2.5	66.7	33.3
1860 (June 1)	1 231 066	236 552	23.8	57	733 209	229 348	45.5	497 857	7 204	1.5	59.6	40.4
1850 (June 1)	994 514	256 815	34.8	43	503 861	224 407	80.3	490 653	32 408	7.1	50.7	49.3
1840 (June 1)	737 699	127 291	20.9	24	279 454	89 797	47.3	458 245	37 494	8.9	37.9	62.1
1830 (June 1)	610 408	87 121	16.6	22	189 657	70 470	59.1	420 751	16 651	4.1	31.1	68.9
1820 (Aug. 7)	523 287	51 247	10.9	14	119 187	18 570	18.5	404 100	32 677	8.8	22.8	77.2
1810 (Aug. 6)	472 040	49 195	11.6	12	100 617	35 317	54.1	371 423	13 878	3.9	21.3	78.7
1800 (Aug. 4)	422 845	44 058	11.6	8	65 300	14 098	27.5	357 545	29 960	9.1	15.4	84.6
1790 (Aug. 2)	378 787	...	...	7	51 202	...	...	327 585	...	...	13.5	86.5

NOTE: 1790 to 1810 population excludes that of Maine admitted to the Union as a separate State in March, 1820. The population of Maine was 228,705 in 1810; 151,719 in 1800; 96,540 in 1790.

BARNSTABLE

1790	17,354
1800	19,293
1810	22,211
1820	24,026
1830	28,514
1840	32,548
1850	35,276
1860	35,990
1870	32,774
1880	31,897
1890	29,172
1900	27,826
1910	27,542
1920	26,670
1930	32,305
1940	37,295
1950	46,805
1960	70,286
1970	96,656
1980	147,925

BERKSHIRE

1790	30,291
1800	33,885
1810	35,907
1820	35,720
1830	37,835
1840	41,745
1850	49,591
1860	55,120
1870	64,827
1880	69,032
1890	81,108
1900	95,667
1910	105,259
1920	113,033
1930	120,700
1940	122,273
1950	132,966
1960	142,135
1970	149,402
1980	145,110

BRISTOL

1790	31,709
1800	33,880
1810	37,168
1820	40,908
1830	49,592
1840	60,164
1850	76,192
1860	93,794
1870	102,886
1880	139,040
1890	186,465
1900	252,029
1910	318,573
1920	359,005
1930	364,590
1940	364,637
1950	381,569
1960	398,488
1970	444,301
1980	474,641

DUKES

1790	3,265
1800	3,118
1810	3,290
1820	3,292
1830	3,517
1840	3,958
1850	4,540
1860	4,403
1870	3,787
1880	4,300
1890	4,369
1900	4,561
1910	4,504
1920	4,372
1930	4,953
1940	5,669
1950	5,633
1960	5,829
1970	6,117
1980	8,942

ESSEX

1790	57,913
1800	61,196
1810	71,888
1820	74,655
1830	82,859
1840	94,987
1850	131,300
1860	165,611
1870	200,843
1880	244,535
1890	299,995
1900	357,030
1910	436,477
1920	482,156
1930	498,040
1940	496,313
1950	522,384
1960	568,831
1970	637,887
1980	633,632

FRANKLIN

1820	29,268
1830	29,501
1840	28,812
1850	30,870
1860	31,434
1870	32,635
1880	36,101
1890	38,610
1900	41,209
1910	43,600
1920	49,361
1930	49,612
1940	49,453
1950	52,747
1960	54,864
1970	59,210
1980	64,317

HAMPDEN

1820	28,201
1830	31,639
1840	37,366
1850	51,283
1860	57,366
1870	78,409
1880	104,142
1890	135,713
1900	175,603
1910	231,369
1920	300,305
1930	335,496
1940	332,107
1950	367,471
1960	429,353
1970	459,050
1980	443,018

HAMPSHIRE

1790	59,681
1800	72,432
1810	76,275
1820	26,487
1830	30,254
1840	30,897
1850	35,732
1860	37,823
1870	44,388
1880	47,232
1890	51,859
1900	58,820
1910	63,327
1920	69,599
1930	72,801
1940	72,461
1950	87,594
1960	103,229
1970	123,981
1980	138,813

MIDDLESEX

1790	42,737
1800	47,928
1810	52,789
1820	61,472
1830	77,961
1840	106,611
1850	161,383
1860	216,354
1870	274,353
1880	317,830
1890	431,167
1900	565,696
1910	669,915
1920	778,352
1930	934,924
1940	971,390
1950	1,064,569
1960	1,238,742
1970	1,398,397
1980	1,367,034

NANTUCKET

1790	4,620
1800	5,617
1810	6,807
1820	7,266
1830	7,202
1840	9,012
1850	8,452
1860	6,094
1870	4,123
1880	3,727
1890	3,268
1900	3,006
1910	2,962
1920	2,797
1930	3,678
1940	3,401
1950	3,484
1960	3,559
1970	3,774
1980	5,087

NORFOLK

1800	27,216
1810	31,245
1820	36,471
1830	41,972
1840	53,140
1850	78,892
1860	109,950
1870	89,443
1880	96,507
1890	118,950
1900	151,539
1910	187,506
1920	219,081
1930	299,426
1940	325,180
1950	392,308
1960	510,256
1970	604,854
1980	606,587

PLYMOUTH

1790	29,535
1800	30,073
1810	35,169
1820	38,136
1830	43,044
1840	47,373
1850	55,697
1860	64,768
1870	65,365
1880	74,018
1890	92,700
1900	113,985
1910	144,337
1920	156,968
1930	162,311
1940	168,824
1950	189,468
1960	248,449
1970	333,314
1980	405,437

SUFFOLK

1790	44,875
1800	28,015
1810	34,381
1820	43,940
1830	62,163
1840	95,773
1850	144,517
1860	192,700
1870	270,802
1880	387,927
1890	484,780
1900	611,417
1910	731,388
1920	835,522
1930	879,536
1940	863,248
1950	896,615
1960	791,329
1970	735,190
1980	650,142

WORCESTER

1790	56,807
1800	61,192
1810	64,910
1820	73,625
1830	84,355
1840	95,313
1850	130,789
1860	159,659
1870	192,716
1880	226,897
1890	280,787
1900	346,958
1910	399,657
1920	455,135
1930	491,242
1940	504,470
1950	546,401
1960	583,228
1970	637,037
1980	646,352

ATTLEBORO

1790	2,166
1800	2,480
1810	2,716
1820	3,055
1830	3,215
1840	3,585
1850	4,200
1860	6,066
1870	6,769
1880	11,111
1890	7,577
1900	11,335
1910	16,215
1920	19,731
1930	21,769
1940	22,071
1950	23,908
1960	27,118
1970	32,907
1980	34,196

BEVERLY

1790	3,290
1800	3,881
1810	4,608
1820	4,283
1830	4,073
1840	4,689
1850	5,376
1860	6,154
1870	6,507
1880	8,456
1890	10,821
1900	13,884
1910	18,650
1920	22,561
1930	25,086
1940	25,537
1950	28,884
1960	36,108
1970	38,348
1980	37,655

BOSTON

1790	18,320
1800	24,937
1810	33,787
1820	43,298
1830	61,392
1840	93,385
1850	136,881
1860	177,850
1870	250,526
1880	362,839
1890	448,477
1900	560,892
1910	670,585
1920	748,060
1930	781,188
1940	770,816
1950	801,444
1960	697,197
1970	641,071
1980	562,944

BROCKTON

1830	1,953
1840	2,616
1850	3,939
1860	6,584
1870	8,007
1880	13,608
1890	27,294
1900	40,063
1910	56,878
1920	66,254
1930	63,797
1940	62,343
1950	62,860
1960	72,813
1970	89,040
1980	95,172

CAMBRIDGE

1790	2,115
1800	2,453
1810	2,323
1820	3,295
1830	6,072
1840	8,409
1850	15,215
1860	26,060
1870	39,634
1880	52,669
1890	70,028
1900	91,886
1910	104,839
1920	109,694
1930	113,643
1940	110,879
1950	120,740
1960	107,716
1970	100,361
1980	95,322

CHELSEA

1790	472
1800	849
1810	594
1820	642
1830	771
1840	2,390
1850	6,701
1860	13,395
1870	18,547
1880	21,782
1890	21,909
1900	34,072
1910	32,452
1920	43,184
1930	45,816
1940	41,259
1950	38,912
1960	33,749
1970	30,625
1980	25,431

CHICOPEE

1850	8,291
1860	7,261
1870	9,607
1880	11,286
1890	14,050
1900	19,167
1910	25,401
1920	36,214
1930	43,930
1940	41,664
1950	49,211
1960	61,553
1970	66,616
1980	55,112

EVERETT

1860	2,220
1870	4,159
1880	11,068
1890	24,336
1900	24,336
1910	33,484
1920	40,120
1930	48,424
1940	46,784
1950	45,982
1960	43,544
1970	42,485
1980	37,195

FALL RIVER

1810	1,296
1820	1,594
1830	4,158
1840	6,738
1850	11,524
1860	14,026
1870	26,766
1880	48,961
1890	74,398
1900	104,863
1910	119,295
1920	120,485
1930	115,274
1940	115,428
1950	111,963
1960	99,942
1970	96,898
1980	92,574

FITCHBURG

1790	1,151
1800	1,390
1810	1,566
1820	1,736
1830	2,169
1840	2,604
1850	5,120
1860	7,805
1870	11,260
1880	12,429
1890	22,037
1900	31,531
1910	37,826
1920	41,029
1930	40,692
1940	41,824
1950	42,691
1960	43,021
1970	43,343
1980	39,580

GARDNER

1790	531
1800	667
1810	815
1820	911
1830	1,023
1840	1,260
1850	1,533
1860	2,646
1870	3,333
1880	4,988
1890	8,424
1900	10,813
1910	14,699
1920	16,971
1930	19,399

1940	20,206
1950	19,581
1960	19,038
1970	19,748
1980	17,900

GLOUCESTER

1790	5,317
1800	5,313
1810	5,943
1820	6,384
1830	7,510
1840	6,350
1850	7,786
1860	10,904
1870	15,389
1880	19,329
1890	24,651
1900	26,121
1910	24,398
1920	22,947
1930	24,204
1940	24,046
1950	25,167
1960	25,789
1970	27,941
1980	27,768

HAVERHILL

1790	2,408
1800	2,730
1810	2,682
1820	3,070
1830	3,896
1840	4,336
1850	5,877
1860	9,995
1870	13,092
1880	18,472
1890	27,412
1900	37,715
1910	44,115
1920	53,884
1930	48,710
1940	46,752
1950	46,280
1960	46,346
1970	46,120
1980	46,865

HOLYOKE

1850	3,245
1860	4,997
1870	10,733
1880	21,915
1890	35,637
1900	45,712
1910	57,730
1920	60,203
1930	56,537
1940	53,750
1950	54,661
1960	52,689
1970	50,112
1980	44,678

LAWRENCE

1850	8,282
1860	17,639
1870	28,921
1880	39,151
1890	44,654
1900	62,559

1910	85,892
1920	94,270
1930	85,068
1940	84,323
1950	80,536
1960	70,933
1970	66,915
1980	63,175

LEOMINSTER

1790	1,189
1800	1,486
1810	1,584
1820	1,790
1830	1,861
1840	1,069
1850	3,121
1860	3,522
1870	3,894
1880	5,772
1890	7,269
1900	12,392
1910	17,580
1920	19,744
1930	21,810
1940	22,236
1950	24,074
1960	27,929
1970	32,939
1980	34,508

LOWELL

1830	6,474
1840	20,796
1850	33,383
1860	36,827
1870	40,928
1880	59,475
1890	77,696
1900	94,969
1910	106,294
1920	112,759
1930	100,234
1940	101,389
1950	97,249
1960	92,107
1970	94,239
1980	92,418

LYNN

1790	2,291
1800	2,837
1810	4,087
1820	4,515
1830	6,138
1840	9,367
1850	14,257
1860	19,083
1870	28,233
1880	38,274
1890	55,727
1900	68,513
1910	89,336
1920	99,148
1930	102,320
1940	98,123
1950	99,738
1960	94,478
1970	90,294
1980	78,471

MALDEN

Year	Population
1790	1,033
1800	1,059
1810	1,384
1820	1,731
1830	2,010
1840	2,514
1850	3,520
1860	5,865
1870	7,367
1880	12,017
1890	23,031
1900	33,664
1910	44,404
1920	49,103
1930	58,036
1940	58,010
1950	59,804
1960	57,676
1970	56,127
1980	53,386

MARLBOROUGH

Year	Population
1790	1,554
1800	1,735
1810	1,674
1820	1,952
1830	2,077
1840	2,101
1850	2,141
1860	5,911
1870	8,474
1880	10,127
1890	13,805
1900	13,609
1910	14,579
1920	15,028
1930	15,587
1940	15,154
1950	15,736
1960	18,819
1970	27,936
1980	30,617

MEDFORD

Year	Population
1790	1,029
1800	1,114
1810	1,443
1820	1,474
1830	1,755
1840	2,478
1850	3,749
1860	4,842
1870	5,717
1880	7,573
1890	11,079
1900	18,244
1910	23,150
1920	39,038
1930	59,714
1940	63,083
1950	66,113
1960	64,971
1970	64,397
1980	58,076

MELROSE

Year	Population
1850	1,260
1860	2,532
1870	3,414
1880	4,560
1890	8,519
1900	12,962
1910	15,715
1920	18,204
1930	23,170
1940	25,333
1950	26,988
1960	29,619
1970	33,180
1980	30,055

NEW BEDFORD

Year	Population
1790	3,313
1800	4,361
1810	5,651
1820	3,947
1830	7,592
1840	12,087
1850	16,443
1860	22,300
1870	21,320
1880	26,845
1890	40,733
1900	62,442
1910	96,652
1920	121,217
1930	112,597
1940	110,341
1950	109,189
1960	102,477
1970	101,777
1980	98,478

NEWBURYPORT

Year	Population
1790	4,837
1800	5,946
1810	7,634
1820	6,852
1830	6,375
1840	7,161
1850	9,572
1860	13,401
1870	12,595
1880	13,538
1890	13,947
1900	14,478
1910	14,949
1920	15,618
1930	15,084
1940	13,916
1950	14,111
1960	14,004
1970	15,807
1980	15,900

NEWTON

Year	Population
1790	1,360
1800	1,491
1810	1,709
1820	1,850
1830	2,376
1840	3,351
1850	5,258
1860	8,382
1870	12,285
1880	16,955
1890	24,379
1900	33,587
1910	39,806
1920	46,054
1930	65,276
1940	69,873
1950	81,994
1960	92,384
1970	91,263
1980	83,622

NORTH ADAMS

Year	Population
1880	10,191
1890	16,074
1900	24,200
1910	22,019
1920	22,282
1930	21,621
1940	22,213
1950	21,567
1960	19,905
1970	19,195
1980	18,063

NORTHAMPTON

Year	Population
1790	1,628
1800	2,190
1810	2,631
1820	2,854
1830	3,613
1840	3,750
1850	5,278
1860	6,788
1870	10,160
1880	12,172
1890	14,990
1900	18,643
1910	19,431
1920	21,951
1930	24,381
1940	24,794
1950	29,063
1960	30,058
1970	29,664
1980	29,286

PEABODY

Year	Population
1860	6,549
1870	7,343
1880	9,028
1890	10,158
1900	11,523
1910	15,721
1920	19,552
1930	21,345
1940	21,711
1950	22,645
1960	32,202
1970	48,080
1980	45,976

PITTSFIELD

Year	Population
1790	1,992
1800	2,261
1810	2,665
1820	2,768
1830	3,559
1840	3,747
1850	5,872
1860	8,045
1870	11,112
1880	13,364
1890	17,281
1900	21,766
1910	32,121
1920	41,763
1930	49,677
1940	49,684
1950	53,348
1960	57,879
1970	57,020
1980	51,974

QUINCY

Year	Population
1800	1,081
1810	1,281
1820	1,623
1830	2,201
1840	3,486
1850	5,017
1860	6,778
1870	7,442
1880	10,570
1890	16,723
1900	23,899
1910	32,642
1920	47,876
1930	72,983
1940	75,810
1950	83,835
1960	87,409
1970	87,966
1980	84,743

REVERE

Year	Population
1850	935
1860	921
1870	1,197
1880	2,263
1890	5,668
1900	10,395
1910	18,219
1920	28,823
1930	35,680
1940	34,405
1950	36,763
1960	40,080
1970	43,159
1980	42,423

SALEM

Year	Population
1790	7,921
1800	9,457
1810	12,613
1820	12,731
1830	13,895
1840	15,082
1850	20,264
1860	22,252
1870	24,117
1880	27,563
1890	30,801
1900	35,956
1910	43,697
1920	42,529
1930	43,353
1940	41,213
1950	41,880
1960	39,211
1970	40,556
1980	38,220

SOMERVILLE

Year	Population
1850	3,540
1860	8,025
1870	14,685
1880	24,933
1890	40,152
1900	61,643
1910	77,236
1920	93,091
1930	103,908
1940	102,177
1950	102,351
1960	94,697
1970	88,779
1980	77,372

SPRINGFIELD

Year	Population
1790	1,574
1800	2,312
1810	2,767
1820	3,914
1830	6,784
1840	10,985
1850	11,766
1860	15,199
1870	26,703
1880	33,340
1890	44,179
1900	62,059
1910	88,926
1920	129,614
1930	149,900
1940	149,554
1950	162,399
1960	174,463
1970	163,905
1980	152,319

TAUNTON

Year	Population
1790	3,804
1800	3,860
1810	3,907
1820	4,520
1830	6,402
1840	7,645
1850	10,441
1860	15,376
1870	18,629
1880	21,213
1890	25,448
1900	31,036
1910	34,259
1920	37,137
1930	37,355
1940	37,395
1950	40,109
1960	41,132
1970	43,756
1980	45,001

WALTHAM

Year	Population
1790	882
1800	903
1810	1,014
1820	1,677
1830	1,857
1840	2,504
1850	4,464
1860	6,397
1870	9,065
1880	11,712
1890	18,707
1900	23,481
1910	27,834
1920	30,915
1930	39,247
1940	40,020
1950	47,187
1960	55,413
1970	61,582
1980	58,200

WESTFIELD

1790	2,204
1800	2,185
1810	2,130
1820	2,668
1830	2,940
1840	3,526
1850	4,180
1860	5,550
1870	6,519
1880	7,587
1890	9,805
1900	12,310
1910	16,044
1920	18,604
1930	19,775
1940	18,793
1950	20,962
1960	26,302
1970	31,433
1980	36,465

WOBURN

1790	1,727
1800	1,228
1810	1,219
1820	1,519
1830	1,977
1840	2,993
1850	3,956
1860	6,287
1870	8,560
1880	10,931
1890	13,499
1900	14,254
1910	15,308
1920	16,574
1930	19,434
1940	19,751
1950	20,492
1960	31,214
1970	37,406
1980	36,626

WORCESTER

1790	2,095
1800	2,411
1810	2,577
1820	2,962
1830	4,173
1840	7,497
1850	17,049
1860	24,960
1870	41,105
1880	58,291
1890	84,655
1900	118,421
1910	145,986
1920	179,754
1930	195,311
1940	193,694
1950	203,486
1960	186,587
1970	176,572
1980	161,799

County Subdivisions	1980	1970
The State	5 737 037	5 689 170
Barnstable County	147 925	96 656
Barnstable town	30 898	19 842
Barnstable (CDP)	2 033	1 202
Centerville (CDP)	3 640	2 876
Hyannis (CDP)	9 118	6 847
Osterville (CDP)	1 799	1 286
Bourne town	13 874	12 636
Bourne (CDP)	2 678	1 992
Buzzards Bay (CDP)	3 375	2 422
Sagamore (CDP)	1 152	1 007
Brewster town	5 226	1 790
Brewster (CDP)	1 744	...
Chatham town	6 071	4 554
Chatham (CDP)	1 922	1 652
West Chatham (CDP)	1 398	...
Dennis town	12 360	6 454
Dennis Port (CDP)	2 570	1 410
West Dennis (CDP)	2 023	1 896
Eastham town	3 472	2 043
North Eastham (CDP)	1 318	...
Falmouth town	23 640	15 942
East Falmouth (CDP)	5 181	2 971
Falmouth (CDP)	5 720	5 806
Woods Hole (CDP)	1 080	...
Harwich town	8 971	5 892
Harwich (CDP)	4 399	3 842
Mashpee town	3 700	1 288
Orleans town	5 306	3 055
Orleans (CDP)	1 811	...
Provincetown town	3 536	2 911
Provincetown (CDP)	3 372	2 836
Sandwich town	8 727	5 239
Sandwich (CDP)	1 784	1 305
Truro town	1 486	1 234
Wellfleet town	2 209	1 743
Yarmouth town	18 449	12 033
South Yarmouth (CDP)	7 525	5 380
West Yarmouth (CDP)	3 852	3 699
Yarmouth Port (CDP)	2 490	...
Berkshire County[1]	145 110	149 402
Adams town	10 381	11 772
Adams (CDP)	6 857	11 256
Alford town	394	302
Becket town	1 339	929
Cheshire town	3 124	3 006
Clarksburg town	1 871	1 987
Dalton town[1]	6 797	7 505
Egremont town	1 311	1 138
Florida town	730	672
Great Barrington town	7 405	7 537
Great Barrington (CDP)	3 150	3 203
Housatonic (CDP)	1 314	1 344
Hancock town	643	675
Hinsdale town	1 707	1 588
Lanesborough town	3 131	2 972
Lee town	6 247	6 426
Lee (CDP)	2 140	3 389
Lenox town	6 523	5 804
Lenox (CDP)	2 668	2 208
Monterey town	818	600
Mount Washington town	93	52
New Ashford town	159	183
New Marlborough town	1 160	1 031
North Adams city	18 063	19 195
Otis town	963	820
Peru town	633	256
Pittsfield city	51 974	57 020
Richmond town	1 659	1 461
Sandisfield town	720	547
Savoy town	644	322
Sheffield town	2 743	2 374
Stockbridge town	2 328	2 312
Stockbridge (CDP)	1 109	1 147
Tyringham town	344	234
Washington town	587	406
West Stockbridge town	1 280	1 354
Williamstown town	8 741	8 454
Williamstown (CDP)	4 798	4 285
Windsor town	598	468
Bristol County	474 641	444 301
Acushnet town	8 704	7 767
Attleboro city	34 196	32 907
Berkley town	2 731	2 027
Dartmouth town	23 966	18 800
Dighton town	5 352	4 667
North Dighton (CDP)	1 174	1 264
Easton town	16 623	12 157
Fairhaven town	15 759	16 332
Fall River city	92 574	96 898
Freetown town	7 058	4 270
Mansfield town	13 453	9 939
Mansfield (CDP)	6 786	4 778
New Bedford city	98 478	101 777
North Attleborough town	21 095	18 665
Norton town	12 690	9 487

County Subdivisions	1980	1970
Bristol County—Con.		
Norton town—Con.		
Norton (CDP)	2 035	2 073
Raynham town	9 085	6 705
North Raynham (CDP)	2 124	...
Raynham Center (CDP)	3 776	2 526
Rehoboth town	7 570	6 512
Seekonk town	12 269	11 116
Somerset town	18 813	18 088
Somerset (CDP)	18 813	...
Swansea town	15 461	12 640
Taunton city	45 001	43 756
Westport town	13 763	9 791
Dukes County	8 942	6 117
Chilmark town	489	340
Edgartown town	2 204	1 481
Edgartown (CDP)	1 138	1 006
Gay Head town	220	118
Gosnold town	63	83
Oak Bluffs town	1 984	1 385
Oak Bluffs (CDP)	1 124	...
Tisbury town	2 972	2 257
Vineyard Haven (CDP)	1 704	1 599
West Tisbury town	1 010	453
Essex County[2]	633 632	637 887
Amesbury town	13 971	11 388
Amesbury (CDP)	12 236	10 088
Andover town	26 370	23 695
Andover (CDP)	8 445	...
Beverly city	37 655	38 348
Boxford town	5 374	4 032
Boxford (CDP)	1 841	2 026
Danvers town	24 100	26 151
Danvers (CDP)	24 100	...
Essex town	2 998	2 670
Essex (CDP)	1 490	1 626
Georgetown town	5 687	5 290
Gloucester city	27 768	27 941
Groveland town	5 040	5 382
Hamilton town	6 960	6 373
Haverhill city	46 865	46 120
Ipswich town	11 158	10 750
Ipswich (CDP)	4 548	5 022
Lawrence city[2]	63 175	66 915
Lynn city	78 471	90 294
Lynnfield town	11 267	10 826
Lynnfield (CDP)	11 267	...
Manchester town	5 424	5 151
Marblehead town	20 126	21 295
Marblehead (CDP)	20 126	...
Merrimac town	4 451	4 245
Methuen town	36 701	35 456
Middleton town	4 135	4 044
Nahant town	3 947	4 119
Nahant (CDP)	3 947	...
Newbury town	4 529	3 804
Newburyport city	15 900	15 807
North Andover town[2]	20 129	16 284
Peabody city	45 976	48 080
Rockport town	6 345	5 636
Rowley town	3 867	3 040
Rowley (CDP)	1 321	1 325
Salem city	38 220	40 556
Salisbury town	5 973	4 179
Salisbury (CDP)	3 265	2 439
Saugus town	24 746	25 110
Saugus (CDP)	24 746	...
Swampscott town	13 837	13 578
Swampscott (CDP)	13 837	...
Topsfield town	5 709	5 225
Topsfield (CDP)	2 647	...
Wenham town	3 897	3 849
West Newbury town	2 861	2 254
Franklin County	64 317	59 210
Ashfield town	1 458	1 274
Bernardston town	1 750	1 659
Buckland town	1 864	1 892
Shelburne Falls (CDP) (pt.)	1 017	1 085
Charlemont town	1 149	897
Colrain town	1 552	1 420
Conway town	1 213	998
Deerfield town	4 517	3 850
South Deerfield (CDP)	1 926	1 628
Erving town	1 326	1 260
Millers Falls (CDP) (pt.)	549	565
Gill town	1 259	1 100
Greenfield town	18 436	18 116
Greenfield (CDP)	14 198	14 642
Hawley town	280	224
Heath town	482	383
Leverett town	1 471	1 005
Leyden town	498	376
Monroe town	179	216
Montague town	8 011	8 451
Millers Falls (CDP) (pt.)	552	621
Turners Falls (CDP)	4 711	5 168

County Subdivisions	1980	1970
Franklin County—Con.		
New Salem town	688	474
Northfield town	2 386	2 631
Northfield (CDP)	1 182	1 191
Orange town	6 844	6 104
Orange (CDP)	3 942	3 847
Rowe town	336	277
Shelburne town	2 002	1 836
Shelburne Falls (CDP) (pt.)	1 029	1 098
Shutesbury town	1 049	489
Sunderland town	2 929	2 236
Warwick town	603	492
Wendell town	694	405
Whately town	1 341	1 145
Hampden County	443 018	459 050
Agawam town	26 271	21 717
Blandford town	1 038	863
Brimfield town	2 318	1 907
Chester town	1 123	1 025
Chicopee city	55 112	66 676
East Longmeadow town	12 905	13 029
Granville town	1 204	1 008
Hampden town	4 745	4 572
Holland town	1 589	931
Holyoke city	44 678	50 112
Longmeadow town	16 301	15 630
Longmeadow (CDP)	16 301	...
Ludlow town	18 150	17 580
Monson town	7 315	7 355
Monson (CDP)	2 167	2 310
Montgomery town	637	446
Palmer town	11 389	11 680
Bondsville (CDP) (pt.)	1 743	1 450
Palmer (CDP)	3 854	3 649
Three Rivers (CDP)	3 322	3 366
Russell town	1 570	1 382
Southwick town	7 382	6 330
Springfield city	152 319	163 905
Tolland town	235	172
Wales town	1 177	852
Westfield city	36 465	31 433
West Springfield town	27 042	28 461
West Springfield (CDP)	27 042	...
Wilbraham town	12 053	11 984
Wilbraham (CDP)	3 379	3 540
Hampshire County	138 813	123 981
Amherst town	33 229	26 331
Amherst (CDP)	17 773	17 926
North Amherst (CDP)	5 616	2 854
South Amherst (CDP)	4 861	...
Belchertown town	8 339	5 936
Belchertown (CDP)	2 531	2 636
Bondsville (CDP) (pt.)	163	207
Chesterfield town	1 000	704
Cummington town	657	562
Easthampton town	15 580	13 012
Goshen town	651	483
Granby town	5 380	5 473
Granby (CDP)	1 302	1 354
Hadley town	4 125	3 750
Hatfield town	3 045	2 825
Hatfield (CDP)	1 251	1 380
Huntington town	1 804	1 593
Middlefield town	385	288
Northampton city	29 286	29 664
Pelham town	1 112	937
Plainfield town	425	287
Southampton town	4 137	3 069
South Hadley town	16 399	17 033
Ware town	8 953	8 187
Ware (CDP)	6 806	6 509
Westhampton town	1 137	793
Williamsburg town	2 237	2 342
Worthington town	932	712
Middlesex County[3]	1 367 034	[r]1 398 397
Acton town	17 544	14 770
Arlington town	48 219	53 524
Arlington (CDP)	48 219	...
Ashby town	2 311	2 274
Ashland town	9 165	8 882
Ayer town	6 993	[r]8 325
Ayer (CDP)	3 165	3 292
Fort Devens (CDP) (pt.)	710	[r]2 462
Bedford town[3]	13 067	13 513
Belmont town	26 100	28 285
Belmont (CDP)	26 100	...
Billerica town[3]	36 727	31 648
Pinehurst (CDP)	6 588	...
Boxborough town	3 126	1 451
Burlington town[3]	23 486	21 980
Burlington (CDP)	23 486	...
Cambridge city	95 322	100 361
Carlisle town	3 306	2 871
Chelmsford town[3]	31 174	31 432
Chelmsford (CDP)	31 174	...
Concord town	16 293	16 148
West Concord (CDP)	5 331	...
Middlesex County—Con.		
Dracut town	21 249	18 214
Dunstable town	1 671	1 292
Everett city	37 195	42 485
Framingham town	65 113	64 048
Framingham (CDP)	65 113	...
Groton town	6 154	5 109
Groton (CDP)	1 264	1 314
Holliston town	12 622	12 069
Hopkinton town	7 114	5 981
Hopkinton (CDP)	2 542	1 956
Hudson town	16 408	16 084
Hudson (CDP)	14 156	14 283
Lexington town	29 479	31 886
Lexington (CDP)	29 479	...
Lincoln town	7 098	7 567
Littleton town	6 970	6 380
Littleton Common (CDP)	3 109	2 764
Lowell city	92 418	94 239
Malden city	53 386	56 127
Marlborough city	30 617	27 936
Maynard town	9 590	9 710
Maynard (CDP)	9 590	...
Medford city	58 076	64 397
Melrose city	30 055	33 180
Natick town	29 461	31 057
Cochituate (CDP) (pt.)	62	...
Newton city	83 622	[r]91 263
North Reading town	11 455	11 264
Pepperell town	8 061	5 887
East Pepperell (CDP)	2 212	...
Pepperell (CDP)	2 076	1 076
Reading town	22 678	22 539
Reading (CDP)	22 678	...
Sherborn town	4 049	3 309
Shirley town	5 124	4 909
Fort Devens (CDP) (pt.)	718	957
Shirley (CDP)	1 630	1 718
Somerville city	77 372	88 779
Stoneham town	21 424	20 725
Stoneham (CDP)	21 424	...
Stow town	5 144	3 984
Sudbury town	14 027	13 506
Tewksbury town	24 635	22 755
Townsend town	7 201	4 281
Townsend (CDP)	1 266	1 329
Tyngsborough town	5 683	4 204
Wakefield town	24 895	25 402
Wakefield (CDP)	24 895	...
Waltham city	58 200	61 582
Watertown town	34 384	39 307
Watertown (CDP)	34 384	...
Wayland town	12 170	13 461
Cochituate (CDP) (pt.)	6 064	...
Westford town[3]	13 434	10 368
Weston town	11 169	10 870
Wilmington town[3]	17 471	17 102
Wilmington (CDP)	17 471	...
Winchester town	20 701	22 269
Winchester (CDP)	20 701	...
Woburn city[3]	36 626	37 406
Nantucket County	5 087	3 774
Nantucket town	5 087	3 774
Nantucket (CDP)	3 229	2 461
Norfolk County	606 587	[r]604 854
Avon town	5 026	5 295
Bellingham town	14 300	13 967
Bellingham (CDP)	4 454	4 228
Braintree town	36 337	35 050
Braintree (CDP)	36 337	...
Brookline town	55 062	[r]58 689
Brookline (CDP)	55 062	...
Canton town	18 182	17 100
Cohasset town	7 174	6 954
Dedham town	25 298	26 938
Dedham (CDP)	25 298	...
Dover town	4 703	4 529
Dover (CDP)	2 051	1 881
Foxborough town	14 148	14 218
Foxborough (CDP)	5 697	4 090
Franklin town	18 217	17 830
Franklin (CDP)	9 296	8 863
Holbrook town	11 140	11 775
Holbrook (CDP)	11 140	...
Medfield town	10 220	9 821
Medfield (CDP)	6 108	...
Medway town	8 447	7 938
Millis town	6 908	5 686
Millis–Clicquot (CDP)	3 777	3 217
Milton town	25 860	27 190
Milton (CDP)	25 860	...
Needham town	27 901	29 748
Needham (CDP)	27 901	...
Norfolk town	6 363	4 656
Norwood town	29 711	30 815
Norwood (CDP)	29 711	...

County Subdivisions	1980	1970
Norfolk County—Con.		
Plainville town	5 857	4 953
Quincy city	84 743	87 966
Randolph town	28 218	27 035
Randolph (CDP)	28 218	...
Sharon town	13 601	12 367
Sharon (CDP)	5 976	...
Stoughton town	26 710	23 459
Walpole town	18 859	18 149
Walpole (CDP)	5 274	...
Wellesley town	27 209	28 051
Wellesley (CDP)	27 209	...
Westwood town	13 212	12 750
Weymouth town	55 601	54 610
Weymouth (CDP)	55 601	...
Wrentham town	7 580	7 315
Plymouth County	405 437	333 314
Abington town	13 517	12 334
Abington (CDP)	13 517	...
Bridgewater town	17 202	ʳ12 911
Bridgewater (CDP)	6 781	ʳ5 114
Brockton city	95 172	89 040
Carver town	6 988	2 420
Duxbury town	11 807	7 636
Duxbury (CDP)	1 685	2 477
Green Harbor—Cedar Crest (CDP) (pt.)	120	...
South Duxbury (CDP)	2 985	2 075
East Bridgewater town	9 945	8 347
Halifax town	5 513	3 537
Hanover town	11 358	10 107
Hanson town	8 617	7 148
Hanson (CDP)	2 120	...
Hingham town	20 339	18 845
Hingham (CDP)	5 742	...
Hull town	9 714	9 961
Hull (CDP)	9 714	...
Kingston town	7 362	5 999
Kingston (CDP)	4 405	3 772
Lakeville town	5 931	4 376
Lakeville (CDP)	1 948	1 432
Marion town	3 932	3 466
Marion (CDP)	1 438	1 262
Marshfield town	20 916	15 223
Green Harbor—Cedar Crest (CDP) (pt.)	1 882	...
Marshfield (CDP)	4 421	2 562
Marshfield Hills (CDP)	2 308	1 646
Ocean Bluff—Brant Rock (CDP)	4 055	...
Mattapoisett town	5 597	4 500
Mattapoisett (CDP)	3 159	2 188
Middleborough town	16 404	13 607
Middleborough (CDP)	7 012	6 259
Norwell town	9 182	7 796
Pembroke town	13 487	11 193
North Pembroke (CDP)	2 215	2 881
Plymouth town	35 913	18 606
North Plymouth (CDP)	3 250	3 434
Plymouth (CDP)	7 232	6 940
Plympton town	1 974	1 224
Rochester town	3 205	1 770
Rockland town	15 695	15 674
Scituate town	17 317	16 973
North Scituate (CDP)	5 221	5 507
Scituate (CDP)	5 351	3 738
Wareham town	18 457	11 492
Onset (CDP)	1 493	1 771
Wareham (CDP)	2 493	2 024
West Wareham (CDP)	1 837	...
West Bridgewater town	6 359	ʳ6 070
Whitman town	13 534	13 059
Suffolk County	650 142	735 190
Boston city	562 994	641 071
Chelsea city	25 431	30 625
Revere city	42 423	43 159
Winthrop town	19 294	20 335
Winthrop (CDP)	19 294	...
Worcester County	646 352	ʳ637 037
Ashburnham town	4 075	3 484
South Ashburnham (CDP)	1 123	1 181
Athol town	10 634	11 185
Athol (CDP)	8 708	9 723
Auburn town	14 845	15 347
Barre town	4 102	3 825
Barre (CDP)	1 136	1 098
Berlin town	2 215	2 099
Blackstone town	6 570	6 566
Bolton town	2 530	1 905
Boylston town	3 470	2 774
Brookfield town	2 397	2 063
Brookfield (CDP)	1 037	1 197
Charlton town	6 719	4 654
Clinton town	12 771	13 383
Clinton (CDP)	12 771	...
Douglas town	3 730	2 947
East Douglas (CDP)	1 683	1 763
Dudley town	8 717	8 087
East Brookfield town	1 955	1 800
East Brookfield (CDP)	1 443	1 392

County Subdivisions	1980	1970
Worcester County—Con.		
Fitchburg city	39 580	43 343
Gardner city	17 900	19 748
Grafton town	11 238	11 659
Hardwick town	2 272	2 379
Gilbertville (CDP)	1 029	1 247
Harvard town	12 170	ʳ12 494
Fort Devens (CDP) (pt.)	8 118	ʳ9 532
Holden town	13 336	12 564
Hopedale town	3 905	4 292
Hopedale (CDP)	2 810	3 089
Hubbardston town	1 797	1 437
Lancaster town	6 334	6 095
South Lancaster (CDP)	2 329	2 679
Leicester town	9 446	9 140
Rochdale (CDP)	1 105	1 320
Leominster city	34 508	32 939
Lunenburg town	8 405	7 419
Lunenburg (CDP)	1 789	...
Mendon town	3 108	2 524
Milford town	23 390	19 352
Milford (CDP)	21 730	13 740
Millbury town	11 808	11 987
Millville town	1 693	1 764
New Braintree town	671	631
Northborough town	10 568	9 218
Northborough (CDP)	5 670	...
Northbridge town	12 246	11 795
Whitinsville (CDP)	5 379	5 210
North Brookfield town	4 150	3 967
North Brookfield (CDP)	2 543	2 677
Oakham town	994	730
Oxford town	11 680	10 345
Oxford (CDP)	6 369	6 109
Paxton town	3 762	3 731
Petersham town	1 024	1 014
Phillipston town	953	872
Princeton town	2 425	1 681
Royalston town	955	809
Rutland town	4 334	3 198
Rutland (CDP)	2 312	1 751
Shrewsbury town	22 674	19 196
Southborough town	6 193	5 798
Cordaville (CDP)	1 384	1 457
Southbridge town	16 665	17 057
Southbridge (CDP)	12 882	14 261
Spencer town	10 774	8 779
Spencer (CDP)	6 350	5 895
Sterling town	5 440	4 247
Sturbridge town	5 976	4 878
Fiskdale (CDP)	1 859	1 612
Sturbridge (CDP)	1 891	...
Sutton town	5 855	4 590
Templeton town	6 070	5 863
Baldwinville (CDP)	1 709	1 739
Upton town	3 886	3 484
Upton—West Upton (CDP)	2 184	2 131
Uxbridge town	8 374	8 253
Warren town	3 777	3 633
Warren (CDP)	1 548	1 688
Webster town	14 480	14 917
Webster (CDP)	11 175	12 432
Westborough town	13 619	12 594
Westborough (CDP)	4 238	4 474
West Boylston town	6 204	6 369
West Brookfield town	3 026	2 653
West Brookfield (CDP)	1 423	1 536
Westminster town	5 139	4 273
Winchendon town	7 019	6 635
Winchendon (CDP)	4 030	3 997
Worcester city	161 799	176 572

MICHIGAN

Michigan derives its name from the lake which forms a part of its western boundary. The word is of Indian origin and probably signifies "great lake" or "great water," though some authorities claim that its meaning is "place for catching fish."

The first well authenticated exploration by white men within the region now constituting Michigan was in 1634, when Jean Nicollet, a French explorer, passed through the Straits of Mackinaw and discovered Lake Michigan. The first settlement by Europeans within the present limits of the state was made in 1668 at Sault Ste. Marie by Father Marquette and others, who founded a mission there. In 1701 Antoine de la Motte-Cadillac, under a commission from Louis XIV of France, founded Detroit.

In 1763, at the close of the French and Indian War, this territory was transferred to the English; and in 1783, at the close of the Revolution, it passed into the hands of the United States. The British did not immediately relinquish their hold, however, and it was not until the summer of 1796 that the United States took actual possession, at Detroit.

In 1787 the region bounded by Pennsylvania, the Ohio River, the Mississippi River, and the Great Lakes, was organized as the Northwest Territory, the claims of Massachusetts, Connecticut, and Virginia, based on their early charters, having been ceded to the United States between the years 1781-1786. In 1800, when the territory of Indiana was created, the western part of what is now the Lower Peninsula of Michigan and most of the Upper Peninsula were made a part of the territory; and two years later, when Ohio was organized as a state, the remaining portions of both peninsulas were added to Indiana. In 1805 the Lower Peninsula and that part of the Upper lying east of a line drawn due north from the northern extremity of Lake Michigan were organized as the territory of Michigan. In 1809 the region between the Mississippi River and the present western line of Indiana, prolonged northward to the Canadian boundary, was organized as the territory of Illinois. The portion of the Upper Peninsula lying between Michigan and Illinois remained a part of Indiana until 1816, when Indiana was admitted to the Union. In 1818, when Illinois, with its present boundaries, became a state, the limits of Michigan were extended westward to the Mississippi River.

In 1834 the region lying north of Missouri and extending from the Mississippi to the Missouri and White Earth Rivers was added to Michigan, making it include, in addition to the area of the present state, the territory now constituting Wisconsin, Iowa, Minnesota, and parts of North and South Dakota.

In 1835 a state constitution for Michigan was adopted; in the following year Congress passed an enabling act by which the boundary between Ohio and Michigan was established; and on January 26, 1837, Michigan, with boundaries as at present, was admitted to the Union. Meanwhile, in 1836, Wisconsin had been organized as a separate territory.

COUNTY LOCATION INDEX

Michigan

Population of the State: Earliest Census to 1980

Urban and Rural

	The State			Urban				Rural				Percent of total population	
	Total population	Change from preceding census		Places of 2,500 or more	Population	Change from preceding census		Population	Change from preceding census			Urban	Rural
		Number	Percent			Number	Percent		Number	Percent			
Current urban definition:													
1980 (Apr. 1)_____	9 262 078	380 252	4.3	253	6 551 551	−14 932	−0.2	2 710 527	401 927	17.4		70.7	29.3
1970 (Apr. 1)_____	'8 881 826	1 058 632	13.5	232	6 566 483	827 351	14.4	2 308 600	224 538	10.8		74.0	26.0
1960 (Apr. 1)_____	7 823 194	1 451 428	22.8	191	5 739 132	1 236 048	27.4	2 084 062	215 380	11.5		73.4	26.6
1950 (Apr. 1)_____	6 371 766	1 115 660	21.2	150	4 503 084	...	...	1 868 682	...	...		70.7	29.3
Previous urban definition:													
1960 (Apr. 1)_____	7 823 194	1 451 428	22.8	180	5 085 882	919 717	22.1	2 737 312	531 711	24.1		65.0	35.0
1950 (Apr. 1)_____	6 371 766	1 115 660	21.2	142	4 166 165	711 298	20.6	2 205 601	404 362	22.4		65.4	34.6
1940 (Apr. 1)_____	5 256 106	413 781	8.5	125	3 454 867	152 792	4.6	1 801 239	260 989	16.9		65.7	34.3
1930 (Apr. 1)_____	4 842 325	1 173 913	32.0	114	3 302 075	1 060 515	47.3	1 540 250	113 398	7.9		68.2	31.8
1920 (Jan. 1)_____	3 668 412	858 239	30.5	93	2 241 560	914 516	68.9	1 426 852	−56 277	−3.8		61.1	38.9
1910 (Apr. 15)_____	2 810 173	389 191	16.1	79	1 327 044	374 721	39.3	1 483 129	14 470	1.0		47.2	52.8
1900 (June 1)_____	2 420 982	327 092	15.6	71	952 323	222 029	30.4	1 468 659	105 063	7.7		39.3	60.7
1890 (June 1)_____	2 093 890	456 953	27.9	63	730 294	324 882	80.1	1 363 596	132 071	10.7		34.9	65.1
1880 (June 1)_____	1 636 937	452 878	38.2	44	405 412	167 427	70.4	1 231 525	285 451	30.2		24.8	75.2
1870 (June 1)_____	1 184 059	434 946	58.1	27	237 985	138 284	138.7	946 074	296 662	45.7		20.1	79.9
1860 (June 1)_____	749 113	351 459	88.4	13	99 701	70 676	243.5	649 412	280 783	76.2		13.3	86.7
1850 (June 1)_____	397 654	185 387	87.3	4	29 025	19 923	218.9	368 629	165 464	81.4		7.3	92.7
1840 (June 1)_____	212 267	180 628	570.9	1	9 102	9 102	...	203 165	171 526	542.1		4.3	95.7
1830 (June 1)_____	31 639	22 743	255.7	–	–	–	–	31 639	22 743	255.7		–	100.0
1820 (Aug. 7)_____	8 896	4 134	86.8	–	–	–	–	8 896	4 134	86.8		–	100.0
1810 (Aug. 6)_____	4 762	...	...	–	–	...	...	4 762	...	...		–	100.0

NOTE: 1810, 1820, and 1830 populations refer to Michigan Territory as constituted at time census was taken. Boundaries changed in 1816, 1818, 1834, and 1836.

ALCONA

1860	185
1870	696
1880	3,107
1890	5,409
1900	5,691
1910	5,703
1920	5,912
1930	4,989
1940	5,463
1950	5,856
1960	6,352
1970	7,113
1980	9,740

ALGER

1890	1,238
1900	5,868
1910	7,675
1920	9,983
1930	9,327
1940	10,167
1950	10,007
1960	9,250
1970	8,568
1980	9,225

ALLEGAN

1840	1,783
1850	5,125
1860	16,087
1870	32,105
1880	37,815
1890	38,961
1900	38,812
1910	39,819
1920	37,540
1930	38,974
1940	41,839
1950	47,493
1960	57,729
1970	66,575
1980	81,555

ALPENA

1860	290
1870	2,756
1880	9,789
1890	15,581
1900	18,254
1910	19,965
1920	17,869
1930	18,574
1940	20,766
1950	22,189
1960	28,556
1970	30,708
1980	32,315

ANTRIM

1860	179
1870	1,985
1880	5,237
1890	10,413
1900	16,568
1910	15,692
1920	11,543
1930	9,979
1940	10,964
1950	10,721
1960	10,373

1970	12,612
1980	16,194

ARENAC

1890	5,683
1900	9,821
1910	9,640
1920	9,460
1930	8,007
1940	9,233
1950	9,644
1960	9,860
1970	11,149
1980	14,706

BARAGA

1880	1,804
1890	3,036
1900	4,320
1910	6,127
1920	7,662
1930	9,168
1940	9,356
1950	8,037
1960	7,151
1970	7,789
1980	8,484

BARRY

1840	1,078
1850	5,072
1860	13,858
1870	22,199
1880	25,317
1890	23,783
1900	22,514
1910	22,633
1920	21,383
1930	20,928
1940	22,613
1950	26,183
1960	31,738
1970	38,166
1980	45,781

BAY

1860	3,164
1870	15,900
1880	38,081
1890	56,412
1900	62,378
1910	68,238
1920	69,548
1930	69,474
1940	74,981
1950	88,461
1960	107,042
1970	117,339
1980	119,881

BENZIE

1870	2,184
1880	3,433
1890	5,237
1900	9,685
1910	10,638
1920	6,947
1930	6,587
1940	7,800
1950	8,306
1960	7,834

1970	8,593
1980	11,205

BERRIEN

1830	325
1840	5,011
1850	11,417
1860	22,378
1870	35,104
1880	36,785
1890	41,285
1900	49,165
1910	53,662
1920	62,653
1930	81,066
1940	89,117
1950	115,702
1960	149,865
1970	163,940
1980	171,276

BRANCH

1840	5,715
1850	12,472
1860	20,981
1870	26,226
1880	27,981
1890	26,791
1900	27,811
1910	25,605
1920	23,997
1930	23,950
1940	25,845
1950	30,202
1960	34,903
1970	37,906
1980	40,188

BROWN

1820	952
1830	1,356

CALHOUN

1840	10,599
1850	19,162
1860	29,564
1870	36,569
1880	38,452
1890	43,501
1900	49,315
1910	56,638
1920	72,918
1930	87,043
1940	94,206
1950	120,813
1960	138,858
1970	141,963
1980	141,557

CASS

1830	919
1840	5,710
1850	10,907
1860	17,721
1870	21,094
1880	22,009
1890	20,953
1900	20,876
1910	20,624
1920	20,395
1930	20,888

1940	21,910
1950	28,185
1960	36,932
1970	43,312
1980	49,499

CHARLEVOIX

1870	1,724
1880	5,115
1890	9,686
1900	13,956
1910	19,157
1920	15,788
1930	11,981
1940	13,031
1950	13,475
1960	13,421
1970	16,541
1980	19,907

CHEBOYGAN

1860	517
1870	2,196
1880	6,524
1890	11,986
1900	15,516
1910	17,872
1920	13,991
1930	11,502
1940	13,644
1950	13,731
1960	14,550
1970	16,573
1980	20,649

CHIPPEWA

1830	626
1840	534
1850	898
1860	1,603
1870	1,689
1880	5,248
1890	12,019
1900	12,338
1910	24,472
1920	24,818
1930	25,047
1940	27,807
1950	29,206
1960	32,655
1970	32,412
1980	29,029

CLARE

1870	366
1880	4,187
1890	7,558
1900	8,360
1910	9,240
1920	8,250
1930	7,032
1940	9,163
1950	10,253
1960	11,647
1970	16,695
1980	23,822

CLINTON

1840	1,614
1850	5,102
1860	13,916

1870	22,845
1880	28,100
1890	26,509
1900	25,136
1910	23,129
1920	23,110
1930	24,174
1940	26,671
1950	31,195
1960	37,969
1970	48,492
1980	55,893

CRAWFORD

1820	492
1830	692
1880	1,159
1890	2,962
1900	2,943
1910	3,934
1920	4,049
1930	3,097
1940	3,765
1950	4,151
1960	4,971
1970	6,482
1980	9,465

DELTA

1860	1,172
1870	2,542
1880	6,812
1890	15,330
1900	23,881
1910	30,108
1920	30,909
1930	32,280
1940	34,037
1950	32,913
1960	34,298
1970	35,924
1980	38,947

DICKINSON

1900	17,890
1910	20,524
1920	19,456
1930	29,941
1940	28,731
1950	24,844
1960	23,917
1970	23,753
1980	25,341

EATON

1840	2,379
1850	7,058
1860	16,476
1870	25,171
1880	31,225
1890	32,094
1900	31,668
1910	30,499
1920	29,377
1930	31,728
1940	34,124
1950	40,023
1960	49,684
1970	68,892
1980	88,337

EMMET

1860	1,149
1870	1,211
1880	6,639
1890	8,756
1900	15,931
1910	18,561
1920	15,639
1930	15,109
1940	15,791
1950	16,534
1960	15,904
1970	18,331
1980	22,992

GENESEE

1840	4,268
1850	12,031
1860	22,498
1870	33,900
1880	39,220
1890	39,430
1900	41,804
1910	64,555
1920	125,668
1930	211,641
1940	227,944
1950	270,963
1960	374,313
1970	445,589
1980	450,449

GLADWIN

1880	1,127
1890	4,208
1900	6,564
1910	8,413
1920	8,827
1930	7,424
1940	9,385
1950	9,451
1960	10,769
1970	13,471
1980	19,957

GOGEBIC

1890	13,166
1900	16,738
1910	23,333
1920	33,225
1930	31,577
1940	31,797
1950	37,053
1960	24,370
1970	20,676
1980	19,686

GRAND TRAVERSE

1860	1,286
1870	4,443
1880	8,422
1890	13,355
1900	20,479
1910	23,784
1920	19,518
1930	20,011
1940	23,390
1950	28,598
1960	33,490
1970	39,175
1980	54,899

GRATIOT

1860	4,042
1870	11,810
1880	21,936
1890	28,668
1900	29,889
1910	28,820
1920	33,914
1930	30,252
1940	32,205
1950	33,429
1960	37,012
1970	39,246
1980	40,448

HILLSDALE

1840	7,240
1850	16,159
1860	25,675
1870	31,684
1880	32,723
1890	30,660
1900	29,865
1910	29,673
1920	28,161
1930	27,417
1940	29,092
1950	31,916
1960	34,742
1970	37,171
1980	42,071

HOUGHTON

1850	708
1860	9,234
1870	13,879
1880	22,473
1890	35,385
1900	66,063
1910	99,098
1920	71,930
1930	52,851
1940	47,631
1950	39,771
1960	35,654
1970	34,652
1980	37,872

HURON

1850	210
1860	3,165
1870	9,049
1880	20,089
1890	28,545
1900	34,162
1910	34,758
1920	32,786
1930	31,132
1940	32,584
1950	33,149
1960	34,006
1970	34,083
1980	36,459

INGHAM

1840	2,498
1850	8,631
1860	17,435
1870	25,268
1880	33,676
1890	37,666
1900	39,818
1910	53,310
1920	81,554
1930	116,587
1940	130,616
1950	172,941
1960	211,296
1970	261,039
1980	275,520

IONIA

1840	1,923
1850	7,597
1860	16,682
1870	27,681
1880	33,872
1890	32,801
1900	34,329
1910	33,550
1920	33,087
1930	35,093
1940	35,710
1950	38,158
1960	43,132
1970	45,848
1980	51,815

IOSCO

1860	175
1870	3,163
1880	6,873
1890	15,224
1900	10,246
1910	9,753
1920	8,199
1930	7,517
1940	8,560
1950	10,906
1960	16,505
1970	24,905
1980	28,349

IOWA

1830	1,587

IRON

1890	4,432
1900	8,990
1910	15,164
1920	22,107
1930	20,805
1940	20,243
1950	17,692
1960	17,184
1970	13,813
1980	13,635

ISABELLA

1860	1,443
1870	4,113
1880	12,159
1890	18,784
1900	22,784
1910	23,029
1920	22,610
1930	21,126
1940	25,982
1950	28,964
1960	35,348
1970	44,594
1980	54,110

ISLE ROYAL

1870	55
1880	135

JACKSON

1840	13,130
1850	19,431
1860	26,671
1870	36,047
1880	42,031
1890	45,031
1900	48,222
1910	53,426
1920	72,539
1930	92,304
1940	93,108
1950	107,925
1960	131,994
1970	143,274
1980	151,495

KALAMAZOO

1840	7,380
1850	13,179
1860	24,646
1870	32,054
1880	34,342
1890	39,273
1900	44,310
1910	60,427
1920	71,225
1930	91,368
1940	100,085
1950	126,707
1960	169,712
1970	201,550
1980	212,378

KALKASKA

1870	424
1880	2,937
1890	5,160
1900	7,133
1910	8,097
1920	5,577
1930	3,799
1940	5,159
1950	4,597
1960	4,382
1970	5,272
1980	10,952

KENT

1840	2,587
1850	12,016
1860	30,716
1870	50,403
1880	73,253
1890	109,922
1900	129,714
1910	159,145
1920	183,041
1930	240,511
1940	246,338
1950	288,292
1960	363,187
1970	411,044
1980	444,506

KEWEENAW

1870	4,205
1880	4,270
1890	2,894
1900	3,217
1910	7,156
1920	6,322
1930	5,076
1940	4,004
1950	2,918
1960	2,417
1970	2,262
1980	1,963

LAKE

1870	548
1880	3,233
1890	6,505
1900	4,957
1910	4,939
1920	4,437
1930	4,066
1940	4,798
1950	5,257
1960	5,338
1970	5,661
1980	7,711

LAPEER

1840	4,265
1850	7,029
1860	14,754
1870	21,345
1880	30,138
1890	29,213
1900	27,641
1910	26,033
1920	25,782
1930	28,348
1940	32,116
1950	35,794
1960	41,926
1970	52,361
1980	70,038

LEELANAU

1860	2,158
1870	4,578
1880	6,253
1890	7,944
1900	10,556
1910	10,608
1920	9,061
1930	8,206
1940	8,436
1950	8,647
1960	9,321
1970	10,872
1980	14,007

LENAWEE

1830	1,491
1840	17,889
1850	26,372
1860	38,112
1870	45,595
1880	48,393
1890	48,448
1900	48,406
1910	47,907
1920	47,767

1930	49,849	1950	184,961	1980	36,961	1890	32,637	**OCEANA**
1940	53,110	1960	405,804			1900	32,754	
1950	64,629	1970	625,309	**MENOMINEE**		1910	32,069	1840	496
1960	77,789	1980	694,600			1920	30,441	1850	300
1970	81,951			1870	1,791	1930	27,471	1860	1,816
1980	89,948	**MANISTEE**		1880	11,987	1940	28,581	1870	7,222
				1890	33,639	1950	31,013	1880	11,699
LIVINGSTON		1860	975	1900	27,046	1960	35,795	1890	15,698
		1870	6,074	1910	25,648	1970	39,660	1900	16,644
1840	7,430	1880	12,532	1920	23,778	1980	47,555	1910	18,379
1850	13,485	1890	24,230	1930	23,652			1920	15,601
1860	16,851	1900	27,856	1940	24,883	**MONTMORENCY**		1930	13,805
1870	19,336	1910	26,668	1950	25,299			1940	14,812
1880	22,251	1920	20,899	1960	24,685	1890	1,487	1950	16,105
1890	20,858	1930	17,409	1970	24,587	1900	3,234	1960	16,547
1900	19,664	1940	18,450	1980	26,201	1910	3,755	1970	17,984
1910	17,736	1950	18,254			1920	4,089	1980	22,002
1920	17,522	1960	19,042	**MIDLAND**		1930	2,814	
1930	19,274	1970	20,393			1940	3,840	**OGEMAW**
1940	20,863	1980	23,019	1850	65	1950	4,125	
1950	26,725			1860	787	1960	4,424	1870	12
1960	38,233	**MANITOU**		1870	3,285	1970	5,247	1880	1,914
1970	58,967			1880	6,893	1980	7,492	1890	5,583
1980	100,289	1860	1,042	1890	10,657			1900	7,765
		1870	891	1900	14,439	**MUSKEGON**		1910	8,907
LUCE		1880	1,334	1910	14,005			1920	7,786
		1890	860	1920	17,237	1860	3,947	1930	6,595
1890	2,455			1930	19,150	1870	14,894	1940	8,720
1900	2,983	**MARQUETTE**		1940	27,094	1880	26,586	1950	9,345
1910	4,004			1950	35,662	1890	40,013	1960	9,680
1920	6,149	1850	136	1960	51,450	1900	37,036	1970	11,903
1930	6,528	1860	2,821	1970	63,769	1910	40,577	1980	16,436
1940	7,423	1870	15,033	1980	73,578	1920	62,362	
1950	8,147	1880	25,394			1930	84,630	**ONTONAGON**
1960	7,827	1890	39,521	**MISSAUKEE**		1940	94,501	
1970	6,789	1900	41,239			1950	121,545	1850	389
1980	6,659	1910	47,739	1870	130	1960	149,943	1860	4,568
		1920	45,786	1880	1,553	1970	157,426	1870	2,845
MACKINAC		1930	44,076	1890	5,048	1980	157,589	1880	2,565
		1940	47,144	1900	9,308			1890	3,756
1800	551	1950	47,654	1910	10,606	**NEWAYGO**		1900	6,197
1810	615	1960	65,154	1920	9,004			1910	8,650
1820	819	1970	64,686	1930	6,992	1850	510	1920	12,428
1830	877	1980	74,101	1940	8,034	1860	2,760	1930	11,114
1840	923			1950	7,458	1870	7,294	1940	11,359
1850	3,598	**MASON**		1960	6,784	1880	14,688	1950	10,282
1860	1,938			1970	7,126	1890	20,476	1960	10,584
1870	1,716	1850	93	1980	10,009	1900	17,673	1970	10,548
1880	2,902	1860	831			1910	19,220	1980	9,861
1890	7,830	1870	3,263	**MONROE**		1920	17,378	
1900	7,703	1880	10,065			1930	17,029	**OSCEOLA**
1910	9,249	1890	16,385	1810	1,340	1940	19,286	
1920	8,026	1900	18,885	1820	1,831	1950	21,567	1860	27
1930	8,783	1910	21,832	1830	3,187	1960	24,160	1870	2,093
1940	9,483	1920	19,831	1840	9,922	1970	27,992	1880	10,777
1950	9,287	1930	18,756	1850	14,698	1980	34,917	1890	14,630
1960	10,853	1940	19,378	1860	21,593			1900	17,859
1970	9,660	1950	20,474	1870	27,483	**OAKLAND**		1910	17,889
1980	10,178	1960	21,929	1880	33,624			1920	15,221
		1970	22,612	1890	32,337	1820	330	1930	12,806
MACOMB		1980	26,365	1900	32,754	1830	4,911	1940	13,309
				1910	32,917	1840	23,646	1950	13,797
1810	580	**MECOSTA**		1920	37,115	1850	31,270	1960	13,595
1820	898			1930	52,485	1860	38,261	1970	14,838
1830	2,413	1860	970	1940	58,620	1870	40,867	1980	18,928
1840	9,716	1870	5,642	1950	75,666	1880	41,537	
1850	15,530	1880	13,973	1960	101,120	1890	41,245	**OSCODA**
1860	22,843	1890	19,697	1970	119,215	1900	44,792	
1870	27,616	1900	20,693	1980	134,659	1910	49,576	1870	70
1880	31,627	1910	19,466			1920	90,050	1880	467
1890	31,813	1920	17,765	**MONTCALM**		1930	211,251	1890	1,904
1900	33,244	1930	15,738			1940	254,068	1900	1,468
1910	32,606	1940	16,902	1850	891	1950	396,001	1910	2,027
1920	38,103	1950	18,968	1860	3,968	1960	690,259	1920	1,783
1930	77,146	1960	21,051	1870	13,629	1970	907,871	1930	1,728
1940	107,638	1970	27,992	1880	33,148	1980	1,011,793	1940	2,543
								1950	3,134

1960	3,447
1970	4,726
1980	6,858

OTSEGO

1880	1,974
1890	4,274
1900	6,175
1910	6,552
1920	6,043
1930	5,554
1940	5,827
1950	6,435
1960	7,545
1970	10,422
1980	14,993

OTTAWA

1840	208
1850	5,587
1860	13,215
1870	26,651
1880	33,126
1890	35,358
1900	39,667
1910	45,301
1920	47,660
1930	54,858
1940	59,660
1950	73,751
1960	98,719
1970	128,181
1980	157,174

PRESQUE ISLE

1860	26
1870	355
1880	3,113
1890	4,687
1900	8,821
1910	11,249
1920	12,131
1930	11,330
1940	12,250
1950	11,996
1960	13,117
1970	12,836
1980	14,267

ROSCOMMON

1880	1,459
1890	2,033
1900	1,787
1910	2,274
1920	2,032
1930	2,055
1940	3,668
1950	5,916
1960	7,200
1970	9,892
1980	16,374

SAGINAW

1840	892
1850	2,609
1860	12,293
1870	39,097
1880	59,095
1890	82,273
1900	81,222
1910	89,290

1920	100,286
1930	120,717
1940	130,468
1950	153,515
1960	190,752
1970	219,743
1980	228,059

SAINT CLAIR

1830	1,114
1840	4,606
1850	10,420
1860	26,604
1870	36,661
1880	46,197
1890	52,105
1900	55,228
1910	52,341
1920	58,009
1930	67,563
1940	76,222
1950	91,599
1960	107,201
1970	120,175
1980	138,802

SAINT JOSEPH

1830	1,313
1840	7,608
1850	12,725
1860	21,262
1870	26,275
1880	26,626
1890	25,356
1900	23,889
1910	25,499
1920	26,818
1930	30,618
1940	31,749
1950	35,071
1960	42,332
1970	47,392
1980	56,083

SANILAC

1850	2,112
1860	7,599
1870	14,562
1880	26,341
1890	32,589
1900	35,055
1910	33,930
1920	31,237
1930	27,751
1940	30,144
1950	30,837
1960	32,314
1970	35,181
1980	40,789

SCHOOLCRAFT

1850	16
1860	78
1880	1,575
1890	5,818
1900	7,889
1910	8,681
1920	9,977
1930	8,451
1940	9,524
1950	9,148
1960	8,953

1970	8,226
1980	8,575

SHIAWASSEE

1840	2,103
1850	5,230
1860	12,349
1870	20,858
1880	27,059
1890	30,952
1900	33,866
1910	33,246
1920	35,924
1930	39,517
1940	41,207
1950	45,967
1960	53,446
1970	63,075
1980	71,140

TUSCOLA

1850	291
1860	4,886
1870	13,714
1880	25,738
1890	32,508
1900	35,890
1910	34,913
1920	33,320
1930	32,934
1940	35,694
1950	38,258
1960	43,305
1970	48,603
1980	56,961

VAN BUREN

1830	5
1840	1,910
1850	5,800
1860	15,224
1870	28,829
1880	30,807
1890	30,541
1900	33,274
1910	33,185
1920	30,715
1930	32,637
1940	35,111
1950	39,184
1960	48,395
1970	56,173
1980	66,814

WASHTENAW

1830	4,042
1840	23,571
1850	28,567
1860	35,686
1870	41,434
1880	41,848
1890	42,210
1900	47,761
1910	44,714
1920	49,520
1930	65,530
1940	80,810
1950	134,606
1960	172,440
1970	234,103
1980	264,748

WAYNE

1810	2,227
1820	3,574
1830	6,781
1840	24,173
1850	42,756
1860	75,547
1870	119,038
1880	166,144
1890	257,114
1900	348,793
1910	531,591
1920	1,177,645
1930	1,888,946
1940	2,015,623
1950	2,435,235
1960	2,666,297
1970	2,670,368
1980	2,337,891

WEXFORD

1870	650
1880	6,815
1890	11,278
1900	16,845
1910	20,769
1920	18,207
1930	16,827
1940	17,976
1950	18,628
1960	18,466
1970	19,717
1980	25,102

NOTES

ALCONA

Name changed from Neewago in 1843.

ALPENA

Name changed from Anamickee in 1843.

ANTRIM

Name changed from Meegisee in 1843.

BROWN

Transferred to Wisconsin subsequent to the 1830 census.

CHARLEVOIX

Name changed from Reshkauko in 1843.

CLARE

Name changed from Kaykakee in 1843.

CRAWFORD (1)

Transferred to Wisconsin sometime between 1830 and 1843.

CRAWFORD (2)

Name changed from Shawano in 1843.

EMMET

Name changed from Tonedagana in 1843.

IOSCO

Name changed from Kanotin in 1843.

IOWA

Transferred to Wisconsin subsequent to the 1830 census.

ISLE ROYAL

Annexed to Keweenaw in 1897.

KALKASKA

Name changed from Wabassee in 1843.

LAKE

Name changed from Aishcum in 1843.

MACKINAC

Name changed from Michilimackinac in 1843.

MANITOU

Annexed to Charlevoix and Leelanaw in 1896.

MASON

Name changed from Notipekago in 1843.

MENOMINEE

Name changed from Bleeker in 1863.

MONTMORENCY

Name changed from Cheonoquet in 1843.

OSCEOLA

Name changed from Unwattin in 1843.

OTSEGO

Name changed from Okkuddo in 1843.

ROSCOMMON

Name changed from Mikenauk in 1843.

WEXFORD

Name changed from Kautawaubet in 1843.

ADRIAN

1860	6,213
1870	8,439
1880	7,849
1890	8,756
1900	9,654
1910	10,763
1920	11,878
1930	13,064
1940	14,230
1950	18,393
1960	20,347
1970	20,382
1980	21,186

ALBION

1880	2,716
1890	3,763
1900	4,519
1910	5,833
1920	8,354
1930	8,324
1940	8,345
1950	10,406
1960	12,749
1970	12,112
1980	11,059

ALLEN PARK

1930	944
1940	3,487
1950	12,329
1960	37,494
1970	40,747
1980	34,196

ALPENA

1880	6,153
1890	11,283
1900	11,802
1910	12,706
1920	11,101
1930	12,166
1940	12,808
1950	13,135
1960	14,682
1970	13,805
1980	12,214

ANN ARBOR

1860	5,097
1870	7,363
1880	8,061
1890	9,431
1900	14,509
1910	14,817
1920	19,516
1930	26,944
1940	29,815
1950	48,251
1960	67,340
1970	100,035
1980	107,966

BATTLE CREEK

1850	1,064
1860	na
1870	5,838
1880	7,063
1890	13,197
1900	18,563
1910	25,267
1920	36,164
1930	43,573
1940	43,453
1950	48,666
1960	44,169
1970	38,931
1980	35,724

BAY CITY

1860	1,583
1870	7,074
1880	20,693
1890	27,839
1900	27,628
1910	45,166
1920	47,554
1930	47,355
1940	47,956
1950	52,523
1960	53,604
1970	49,449
1980	41,593

BENTON HARBOR

1870	661
1880	1,230
1890	3,692
1900	6,562
1910	9,185
1920	12,233
1930	15,434
1940	16,668
1950	18,769
1960	19,136
1970	16,481
1980	14,707

BERKLEY

1930	5,571
1940	6,406
1950	17,931
1960	23,275
1970	21,879
1980	18,637

BEVERLY HILLS

1960	8,633
1970	13,598
1980	11,598

BIG RAPIDS

1870	1,237
1880	3,552
1890	5,303
1900	4,686
1910	4,519
1920	4,558
1930	5,671
1940	4,987
1950	6,736
1960	8,686
1970	11,995
1980	14,361

BIRMINGHAM

1880	773
1890	899
1900	1,170
1910	1,607
1920	3,694
1930	9,539
1940	11,196
1950	15,467
1960	25,525
1970	26,170
1980	21,689

CADILLAC

1880	2,213
1890	4,461
1900	5,997
1910	8,375
1920	9,750
1930	9,570
1940	9,855
1950	10,425
1960	10,112
1970	9,990
1980	10,199

CLAWSON

1930	3,377
1940	4,006
1950	5,196
1960	14,795
1970	17,617
1980	15,103

DEARBORN

1900	844
1910	911
1920	2,470
1930	50,358
1940	63,584
1950	94,994
1960	112,007
1970	104,199
1980	90,660

DEARBORN HEIGHTS

1970	80,069
1980	67,706

DETROIT

1820	1,422
1830	2,222
1840	9,102
1850	21,019
1860	45,619
1870	79,577
1880	116,340
1890	205,876
1900	285,704
1910	465,766
1920	993,678
1930	1,568,662
1940	1,623,452
1950	1,849,568
1960	1,670,144
1970	1,514,063
1980	1,203,339

EAST DETROIT

1930	5,955
1940	8,584
1950	21,461
1960	45,746
1970	45,920
1980	38,280

EAST GRAND RAPIDS

1900	466
1910	800
1920	1,310
1930	4,024
1940	4,899
1950	6,403
1960	10,924
1970	12,565
1980	10,914

EAST LANSING

1910	802
1920	1,889
1930	4,389
1940	5,839
1950	20,325
1960	30,198
1970	47,540
1980	51,392

ECORSE

1910	1,063
1920	4,394
1930	12,716
1940	13,209
1950	17,948
1960	17,328
1970	17,515
1980	14,447

ESCANABA

1880	3,206
1890	6,808
1900	9,549
1910	13,194
1920	13,103
1930	14,524
1940	14,830
1950	15,170
1960	15,391
1970	15,368
1980	14,355

FARMINGTON

1880	377
1890	320
1900	530
1910	564
1920	853
1930	1,243
1940	1,510
1950	2,325
1960	6,881
1970	10,329
1980	11,022

FARMINGTON HILLS

1980	58,056

FERNDALE

1920	2,640
1930	20,855
1940	22,523
1950	29,675
1960	31,347
1970	30,850
1980	26,227

FLINT

1860	2,950
1870	5,386
1880	8,409
1890	9,803
1900	13,103
1910	38,550
1920	91,599
1930	156,492
1940	151,543
1950	163,143
1960	196,940
1970	196,317
1980	159,611

FRASER

1900	252
1910	220
1920	247
1930	600
1940	747
1950	1,379
1960	7,027
1970	11,868
1980	14,560

GARDEN CITY

1930	2,081
1940	4,096
1950	9,012
1960	38,017
1970	41,864
1980	35,640

GRAND HAVEN

1850	1,829
1860	1,891
1870	3,147
1880	4,862
1890	5,023
1900	4,743
1910	5,856
1920	7,205
1930	8,345
1940	8,799
1950	9,536
1960	11,066
1970	11,844
1980	11,763

GRAND RAPIDS

1850	2,686
1860	8,085
1870	16,507
1880	32,016
1890	60,278
1900	87,565
1910	112,571
1920	137,634
1930	168,592
1940	164,292
1950	176,515
1960	177,313
1970	197,649
1980	811,843

GRANDVILLE

1900	457
1910	680
1920	799

1930	1,346
1940	1,566
1950	2,022
1960	7,975
1970	10,764
1980	12,412

GROSSE POINTE FARMS

1900	817
1910	862
1920	1,649
1930	3,533
1940	7,217
1950	9,410
1960	12,172
1970	11,701
1980	10,551

GROSSE POINTE PARK

1910	290
1920	1,355
1930	11,174
1940	12,646
1950	13,075
1960	15,457
1970	15,641
1980	13,639

GROSSE POINTE WOODS

1930	961
1940	2,805
1950	10,381
1960	18,580
1970	21,878
1980	18,886

HAMTRAMCK

1910	3,559
1920	48,615
1930	56,268
1940	49,839
1950	43,355
1960	34,137
1970	26,783
1980	21,300

HARPER WOODS

1960	19,995
1970	20,186
1980	16,361

HAZEL PARK

1950	17,770
1960	25,631
1970	23,784
1980	20,914

HIGHLAND PARK

1900	427
1910	4,120
1920	46,499
1930	52,959
1940	50,810
1950	46,393
1960	38,063
1970	35,444
1980	27,909

HOLLAND

1870	2,319
1880	2,620
1890	3,945
1900	7,790
1910	10,490
1920	12,183
1930	14,346
1940	14,616
1950	15,858
1960	24,777
1970	26,479
1980	26,281

INKSTER

1930	4,440
1940	7,044
1950	16,728
1960	39,097
1970	38,595
1980	35,190

JACKSON

1850	2,363
1860	4,799
1870	11,447
1880	16,105
1890	20,798
1900	25,180
1910	31,433
1920	48,374
1930	55,187
1940	49,656
1950	51,088
1960	50,720
1970	45,484
1980	39,739

KALAMAZOO

1850	2,507
1860	6,070
1870	9,181
1880	11,937
1890	17,853
1900	24,404
1910	39,437
1920	48,487
1930	54,786
1940	54,097
1950	57,704
1960	82,089
1970	85,555
1980	79,722

KENTWOOD

1970	20,310
1980	30,438

LANSING

1860	3,074
1870	5,241
1880	8,319
1890	13,102
1900	16,485
1910	31,229
1920	57,327
1930	78,397
1940	78,753
1950	92,129
1960	107,807
1970	131,403
1980	130,414

LINCOLN PARK

1930	12,336
1940	15,236
1950	29,310
1960	53,933
1970	52,984
1980	45,105

LIVONIA

1950	17,534
1960	66,702
1970	110,109
1980	104,814

MADISON HEIGHTS

1960	33,343
1970	38,599
1980	35,375

MARQUETTE

1870	4,000
1880	4,690
1890	9,093
1900	10,058
1910	11,503
1920	12,718
1930	14,789
1940	15,928
1950	17,202
1960	19,824
1970	21,967
1980	23,288

MELVINDALE

1930	4,053
1940	4,764
1950	9,483
1960	13,089
1970	13,862
1980	12,322

MENOMINEE

1870	1,597
1880	3,288
1890	10,630
1900	12,818
1910	10,507
1920	8,907
1930	10,320
1940	10,230
1950	11,151
1960	11,289
1970	10,748
1980	10,099

MIDLAND

1870	1,160
1880	1,529
1890	2,2 7
1900	2,363
1910	2,527
1920	5,483
1930	8,038
1940	10,329
1950	14,285
1960	27,779
1970	35,176
1980	37,250

MONROE

1840	1,703
1850	2,813
1860	3,892
1870	5,086
1880	4,930
1890	5,258
1900	5,043
1910	6,893
1920	11,573
1930	18,110
1940	18,478
1950	21,467
1960	22,968
1970	23,894
1980	23,531

MOUNT CLEMENS

1850	1,302
1860	NA
1870	1,768
1880	3,057
1890	4,748
1900	6,576
1910	7,707
1920	9,488
1930	13,497
1940	14,389
1950	17,027
1960	21,016
1970	20,476
1980	18,806

MOUNT PLEASANT

1880	1,115
1890	2,701
1900	3,662
1910	3,972
1920	4,819
1930	5,211
1940	8,413
1950	11,393
1960	14,875
1970	20,524
1980	23,746

MUSKEGON

1870	6,002
1880	11,262
1890	22,702
1900	20,818
1910	24,062
1920	36,570
1930	41,390
1940	47,697
1950	48,429
1960	46,485
1970	44,631
1980	40,823

MUSKEGON HEIGHTS

1900	1,012
1910	1,690
1920	9,514
1930	15,584
1940	16,067
1950	18,828
1960	19,552
1970	17,304
1980	14,611

NILES

1860	2,826
1870	4,630
1880	4,197
1890	4,197
1900	4,287
1910	5,156
1920	7,311
1930	11,326
1940	11,328
1950	13,145
1960	13,842
1970	12,988
1980	13,115

NORTON SHORES

1970	22,271
1980	22,025

NOVI

1960	6,390
1970	9,668
1980	22,525

OAK PARK

1930	1,079
1940	1,169
1950	5,267
1960	36,632
1970	36,762
1980	31,537

OWOSSO

1860	1,160
1870	2,065
1880	2,501
1890	6,564
1900	8,696
1910	9,639
1920	12,575
1930	14,496
1940	14,424
1950	15,948
1960	17,006
1970	17,179
1980	16,455

PONTIAC

1840	1,904
1850	1,681
1860	4,867
1870	4,509
1880	6,200
1890	9,769
1900	9,769
1910	14,532
1920	34,273
1930	64,928
1940	66,626
1950	73,681
1960	82,233
1970	85,279
1980	76,715

PORTAGE

1950	1,677
1970	33,590
1980	38,157

PORT HURON

1860	4,371
1870	5,973
1880	8,883
1890	13,543
1900	19,158
1910	18,863
1920	25,944
1930	31,361
1940	32,759
1950	35,725
1960	36,084
1970	35,794
1980	33,981

RIVER ROUGE

1900	1,748
1910	4,163
1920	9,822
1930	17,314
1940	17,008
1950	20,549
1960	18,147
1970	15,947
1980	12,912

RIVERVIEW

1930	743
1940	804
1950	1,432
1960	7,237
1970	11,342
1980	14,569

ROMULUS

1980	24,857

ROSEVILLE

1930	6,836
1940	9,023
1950	15,816
1960	50,195
1970	60,529
1980	54,311

ROYAL OAK

1900	468
1910	1,071
1920	6,007
1930	22,904
1940	25,087
1950	46,898
1960	80,612
1970	86,238
1980	70,893

SAGINAW

1860	1,699
1870	7,460
1880	10,525
1890	46,322
1900	42,345
1910	50,510
1920	61,903
1930	80,715
1940	82,794
1950	92,918
1960	98,265

1970	91,849
1980	77,508

SAINT CLAIR SHORES

1930	6,745
1940	10,405
1950	19,823
1960	76,657
1970	88,093
1980	76,210

SAULT SAINTE MARIE

1860	596
1870	na
1880	1,947
1890	5,760
1900	10,538
1910	12,615
1920	12,096
1930	13,755
1940	15,847
1950	17,912
1960	18,722
1970	15,136
1980	14,448

SOUTHFIELD

1960	31,501
1970	69,285
1980	75,568

SOUTHGATE

1960	29,404
1970	33,090
1980	32,058

STERLING HEIGHTS

1970	61,365
1980	108,999

TAYLOR

1970	70,020
1980	77,568

TRAVERSE CITY

1890	4,353
1900	9,407
1910	12,155
1920	10,925
1930	12,539
1940	14,455
1950	16,974
1960	18,432
1970	18,048
1980	15,516

TRENTON

1920	1,682
1930	4,022
1940	5,284
1950	6,222
1960	18,439
1970	24,127
1980	22,762

TROY

1960	19,382
1970	39,419
1980	67,102

WALKER

1970	11,492
1980	15,088

WARREN

1900	350
1910	297
1920	326
1930	515
1940	582
1950	727
1960	89,246
1970	179,260
1980	161,134

WAYNE

1860	304
1870	833
1880	919
1890	1,226
1900	1,361
1910	1,263
1920	1,899
1930	3,423
1940	4,223
1950	9,409
1960	16,034
1970	21,054
1980	21,159

WESTLAND

1970	86,749
1980	84,603

WOODHAVEN

1970	3,566
1980	10,902

WYANDOTTE

1870	2,731
1880	3,631
1890	3,817
1900	5,183
1910	8,287
1920	13,851
1930	28,368
1940	30,618
1950	36,846
1960	43,519
1970	41,061
1980	34,006

WYOMING

1960	45,829
1970	56,560
1980	59,616

YPSILANTI

1860	3,955
1870	5,471
1880	4,984
1890	6,129
1900	7,378
1910	6,230
1920	7,413
1930	10,143
1940	12,121
1950	18,302
1960	20,957
1970	29,538
1980	24,031

County Subdivisions	1980	1970
The State	9 262 078	'8 881 826
Alcona County	9 740	7 113
Alcona township	811	486
Caledonia township	1 065	763
Curtis township	1 082	718
Greenbush township	1 292	760
Gustin township	796	613
Lincoln village (pt.)	188	146
Harrisville city	559	541
Harrisville township	1 093	902
Hawes township	996	811
Lincoln village (pt.)	173	225
Haynes township	569	416
Mikado township	865	636
Millen township	364	270
Mitchell township	248	197
Alger County	9 225	8 568
Au Train township	928	545
Burt township	539	424
Grand Island township	23	32
Limestone township	373	302
Mathias township	680	644
Munising city	3 083	3 677
Munising township	1 963	1 614
Onota township	228	128
Rock River township	1 408	1 202
Chatham village	315	246
Allegan County[1]	81 555	66 575
Allegan city	4 576	4 516
Allegan township	3 464	2 970
Casco township	2 839	2 304
Cheshire township	1 797	1 322
Clyde township	2 099	1 575
Dorr township	5 014	3 055
Fennville city	934	811
Fillmore township[1]	2 307	2 126
Ganges township	2 009	2 061
Gunplain township[1]	4 298	3 231
Heath township	1 962	1 450
Holland city (pt.)[1]	4 514	3 346
Hopkins township	2 109	2 084
Hopkins village	536	566
Laketown township	4 332	2 175
Lee township	2 249	1 934
Leighton township[1]	2 772	2 354
Manlius township	1 458	1 202
Martin township	2 331	2 125
Martin village	447	502
Monterey township	1 320	1 148
Otsego city[1]	3 802	3 957
Otsego township[1]	4 479	3 721
Overisel township	2 248	1 881
Plainwell city[1]	3 751	3 195
Salem township	2 183	1 744
Saugatuck township	3 780	3 089
Douglas village[1]	948	813
Saugatuck village[1]	1 079	1 022
Trowbridge township	2 210	1 563
Valley township	906	590
Watson township	1 658	1 331
Wayland city[1]	2 023	2 054
Wayland township	2 131	1 661
Alpena County[2]	32 315	30 708
Alpena city[2]	12 214	13 805
Alpena township[2]	10 152	9 001
Green township	1 083	863
Long Rapids township	1 006	878
Maple Ridge township	1 572	1 091
Ossineke township	1 607	1 353
Sanborn township	2 297	1 624
Wellington township	286	269
Wilson township	2 098	1 824
Antrim County[3]	16 194	12 612
Banks township	1 515	1 231
Ellsworth village	436	362
Central Lake township	1 766	1 482
Central Lake village[3]	895	741
Chestonia township	433	368
Custer township	490	381
Echo township	723	542
Elk Rapids township	2 086	1 631
Elk Rapids village	1 504	1 249
Forest Home township	1 333	1 080
Bellaire village (pt.)	499	392
Helena township	781	515
Jordan township	410	303
Kearney township	1 241	997
Bellaire village (pt.)	564	505
Mancelona township	2 720	2 258
Mancelona village	1 432	1 255
Milton township	1 271	853
Star township	453	331
Torch Lake township	711	391
Warner township	261	249

County Subdivisions	1980	1970
Arenac County[4]	14 706	11 149
Adams township	457	329
Arenac township	892	739
Au Gres city[4]	768	564
Au Gres township[4]	907	652
Clayton township	967	709
Deep River township	1 874	1 394
Sterling village	457	507
Lincoln township[4]	1 090	838
Mason township	852	676
Twining village (pt.)	85	80
Moffatt township	657	406
Omer city	403	366
Sims township	695	330
Standish city[4]	1 264	1 184
Standish township	2 011	1 493
Turner township	791	726
Turner village	187	182
Twining village (pt.)	111	118
Whitney township	1 078	743
Baraga County	8 484	7 789
Arvon township	439	317
Baraga township	2 717	2 433
Baraga village	1 055	1 116
Covington township	734	770
L'Anse township	4 316	4 086
L'Anse village	2 500	2 538
Spurr township	278	183
Barry County[5]	45 781	38 166
Assyria township	1 714	1 649
Baltimore township	1 697	1 482
Barry township	3 146	2 488
Carlton township	1 981	1 533
Freeport village (pt.)	49	50
Castleton township	3 290	2 611
Nashville village (pt.)	1 565	1 480
Hastings city[5]	6 418	6 501
Hastings township	2 638	2 159
Hope township	2 599	1 783
Irving township	1 608	1 282
Freeport village (pt.)	430	451
Johnstown township	2 895	2 388
Maple Grove township	1 358	1 111
Nashville village (pt.)[5]	63	78
Orangeville township	2 533	1 932
Prairieville township	3 031	2 519
Rutland township[5]	2 444	2 107
Thornapple township	4 298	3 363
Middleville village[5]	1 797	1 865
Woodland township	1 880	1 776
Woodland village	431	473
Yankee Springs township	2 251	1 482
Bay County[6]	119 881	117 339
Auburn city	1 921	1 919
Bangor township[6]	17 494	15 896
Bay City city[6]	41 593	49 449
Beaver township	3 027	2 346
Essexville city	4 378	4 990
Frankenlust township	2 525	2 032
Fraser township	3 954	3 412
Garfield township	1 810	1 202
Gibson township	1 068	815
Hampton township	10 418	6 868
Kawkawlin township	5 077	4 135
Merritt township	1 676	1 902
Midland city (pt.)	234	255
Monitor township	10 143	8 743
Mount Forest township	1 444	1 094
Pinconning city[6]	1 430	1 320
Pinconning township[6]	2 984	2 577
Portsmouth township[6]	4 291	4 088
Williams township	4 414	4 296
Benzie County[7]	11 205	8 593
Almira township	1 078	468
Lake Ann village	235	172
Benzonia township	2 461	2 071
Benzonia village[7]	466	412
Beulah village	454	461
Blaine township	449	358
Colfax township	340	244
Thompsonville village (pt.)	73	68
Crystal Lake township	753	534
Frankfort city	1 603	1 660
Gilmore township	794	751
Elberta village	556	542
Homestead township	1 290	854
Honor village	281	282
Inland township	843	370
Joyfield township	573	399
Lake township	387	377
Platte township	256	190
Weldon township	378	317
Thompsonville village (pt.)	258	244

Population of County Subdivisions

County Subdivisions	1980	1970
Berrien County[8]	171 276	'163 940
Bainbridge township	2 879	2 784
Baroda township	2 666	'2 167
Baroda village[8]	627	'504
Benton township[8]	19 120	19 034
Benton Heights (CDP)	6 787	8 067
Fair Plain (CDP) (pt.)	5 057	...
Benton Harbor city[8]	14 707	16 481
Berrien township	4 302	3 905
Berrien Springs village (pt.)[8]	2	—
Eau Claire village (pt.)[8]	354	279
Bertrand township	2 369	2 259
Bridgman city[8]	2 235	1 621
Buchanan city[8]	5 142	4 645
Buchanan township[8]	3 571	3 182
Chikaming township	4 302	4 051
Shorewood–Tower Hills–Harbert (CDP) (pt.)	1 720	1 629
Union Pier (CDP) (pt.)	597	...
Coloma city	1 833	1 814
Coloma township	5 345	4 376
Paw Paw Lake (CDP) (pt.)	2 720	2 580
Galien township	1 786	1 671
Galien village[8]	692	691
Hagar township	4 943	4 088
Lake Michigan Beach (CDP)	2 001	1 201
Lake township[8]	2 212	2 146
Shorewood–Tower Hills–Harbert (CDP) (pt.)	15	...
Lincoln township	13 520	11 007
Stevensville village	1 268	1 107
New Buffalo city[8]	2 821	2 784
New Buffalo township[8]	2 878	2 583
Grand Beach village	227	165
Michiana village	333	233
Union Pier (CDP) (pt.)	442	...
Niles city	13 115	12 988
Niles township	13 165	13 414
Oronoko township	10 761	8 482
Berrien Springs village (pt.)[8]	2 040	1 951
Pipestone township	2 364	2 422
Eau Claire village (pt.)[8]	219	248
Royalton township	3 046	2 513
St. Joseph city[8]	9 622	11 042
St. Joseph township	9 961	10 271
Fair Plain (CDP) (pt.)	3 232	3 680
Shoreham village	742	666
Sodus township	2 260	2 504
Three Oaks township	3 045	2 894
Three Oaks village	1 774	1 750
Watervliet city[8]	1 867	2 059
Watervliet township[8]	3 275	2 415
Paw Paw Lake (CDP) (pt.)	1 473	1 146
Weesaw township	2 164	2 338
Branch County[9]	40 188	37 906
Algansee township	1 775	1 352
Batavia township	1 572	1 351
Bethel township	1 311	1 064
Bronson city	2 271	2 390
Bronson township	1 331	1 236
Butler township	1 060	934
California township	713	616
Coldwater city[9]	9 461	'9 155
Coldwater township[9]	4 246	'5 785
Gilead township	704	634
Girard township	1 890	1 518
Kinderhook township	1 024	655
Matteson township	1 284	1 168
Noble township	508	433
Ovid township	2 065	1 709
Quincy township	3 929	3 295
Quincy village	1 569	1 540
Sherwood township	2 126	1 695
Sherwood village	353	400
Union township	2 918	2 916
Union City village (pt.)	1 646	1 714
Calhoun County[10]	141 557	141 963
Albion city[10]	11 059	12 112
Albion township[10]	1 413	1 582
Athens township	2 272	2 136
Athens village	960	996
Battle Creek city[10]	35 724	38 931
Battle Creek township[10]	20 615	21 782
Lakeview (CDP)	13 345	11 391
Springfield Place (CDP)	4 463	4 831
Bedford township[10]	10 157	10 817
Level Park–Oak Park (CDP)	3 210	3 080
Burlington township	1 909	1 528
Burlington village	367	314
Union City village (pt.)[10]	21	26
Clarence township	1 916	1 392
Clarendon township	1 176	1 137
Convis township	1 734	1 287
Eckford township[10]	1 273	1 330
Emmett township[10]	11 155	10 881
Brownlee Park (CDP) (pt.)	2 370	2 535
Sunrise Heights (CDP)	1 436	1 626
Fredonia township[10]	1 755	1 442
Homer township	3 041	2 714

County Subdivisions	1980	1970
Calhoun County—Con.		
Homer township—Con.		
Homer village[10]	1 791	1 617
Lee township	1 186	1 104
Le Roy township	2 929	2 679
Marengo township[10]	1 811	1 861
Marshall city[10]	7 201	7 253
Marshall township[10]	2 564	2 232
Newton township	1 979	1 327
Pennfield township[10]	8 743	8 290
Brownlee Park (CDP) (pt.)	346	450
Verona Park (CDP)	2 397	2 107
Sheridan township[10]	2 257	2 469
Springfield city[10]	5 917	3 994
Tekonsha township	1 771	1 683
Tekonsha village	755	739
Cass County[11]	49 499	43 312
Calvin township	1 643	1 347
Dowagiac city[11]	6 307	6 583
Howard township	6 524	5 497
Jefferson township	1 963	1 718
La Grange township[11]	3 526	3 583
Cassopolis village	1 933	2 108
Marcellus township	2 463	2 006
Marcellus village	1 134	1 139
Mason township	2 132	1 519
Milton township	2 235	1 727
Newberg township	1 382	1 174
Ontwa township	5 787	5 224
Edwardsburg village	1 135	1 107
Penn township	2 044	1 775
Vandalia village	447	427
Pokagon township[11]	2 394	2 189
Porter township	3 857	2 765
Silver Creek township	3 361	2 886
Volinia township	1 182	986
Wayne township[11]	2 699	2 333
Charlevoix County[12]	19 907	16 541
Bay township	599	456
Boyne City city	3 348	2 969
Boyne Valley township	948	832
Boyne Falls village	378	347
Chandler township	132	89
Charlevoix city[12]	3 296	3 519
Charlevoix township[12]	993	720
East Jordan city	2 185	2 041
Evangeline township	538	440
Eveline township	1 061	837
Hayes township	1 274	706
Hudson township	343	219
Marion township	946	694
Melrose township	947	830
Norwood township	540	325
Peaine township	81	58
St. James township	240	161
South Arm township	1 237	995
Wilson township	1 199	650
Cheboygan County	20 649	16 573
Aloha township	726	530
Beaugrand township	1 023	850
Benton township	2 017	1 430
Burt township	520	212
Cheboygan city	5 106	5 553
Ellis township	298	165
Forest township	971	675
Grant township	579	431
Hebron township	188	143
Inverness township	2 179	1 675
Koehler township	755	427
Mackinaw township	550	553
Mackinaw City village (pt.)	392	480
Mentor township	462	246
Mullett township	934	719
Munro township	459	321
Nunda township	690	520
Wolverine village (pt.)	314	278
Tuscarora township	1 952	1 340
Walker township	260	227
Waverly township	456	285
Wilmot township	524	271
Wolverine village (pt.)	50	25
Chippewa County[13]	29 029	32 412
Bay Mills township	695	418
Bruce township	1 449	1 019
Chippewa township	291	344
Dafter township	1 037	942
Detour township	794	735
De Tour Village village[13]	466	494
Drummond township	746	479
Hulbert township	251	289
Kinross township	1 891	6 763
Pickford township	1 264	1 198
Raber township	543	450
Rudyard township	1 260	1 273
Sault Ste. Marie city	14 448	15 136
Soo township	2 179	1 775

County Subdivisions

County Subdivisions	1980	1970
Chippewa County—Con.		
Sugar Island township	400	237
Superior township	923	694
Trout Lake township	386	306
Whitefish township	472	354
Clare County	23 822	16 695
Arthur township	562	475
Clare city (pt.)	3 300	2 639
Franklin township	631	374
Freeman township	437	212
Frost township	852	607
Garfield township	1 416	938
Grant township	2 227	1 754
Greenwood township	649	362
Hamilton township	1 595	796
Harrison city	1 700	1 460
Hatton township	638	460
Hayes township	3 609	1 942
Lincoln township	974	645
Redding township	401	281
Sheridan township	1 033	863
Summerfield township	279	214
Surrey township	3 101	2 338
Farwell village	804	777
Winterfield township	418	335
Clinton County[14]	55 893	48 492
Bath township	5 746	4 832
Bengal township	1 067	1 005
Bingham township[14]	2 371	1 561
Dallas township	2 288	2 182
Fowler village	1 021	1 020
De Witt city	3 165	1 829
De Witt township[14]	10 038	9 909
Duplain township	2 330	2 221
Elsie village	1 022	988
Eagle township	2 060	1 594
Eagle village	155	175
Essex township	1 688	1 435
Maple Rapids village	683	683
Greenbush township	1 929	1 626
Lansing city (pt.)[14]	-	-
Lebanon township	697	673
Hubbardston village (pt.)	41	26
Olive township	2 111	1 907
Ovid township	3 241	3 017
Ovid village	1 712	1 650
Riley township	1 547	1 222
St. Johns city[14]	7 376	6 672
Victor township	2 287	1 522
Watertown township	3 602	3 146
Westphalia township	2 350	2 139
Westphalia village[14]	896	806
Crawford County[15]	9 465	6 482
Beaver Creek township	745	523
Frederic township	1 142	697
Grayling city[15]	1 792	2 143
Grayling township[15]	4 019	2 252
Lovells township	316	117
Maple Forest township	355	217
South Branch township	1 096	533
Delta County[16]	38 947	35 924
Baldwin township	769	610
Bark River township	1 571	1 299
Bay de Noc township	343	312
Brampton township	1 113	737
Cornell township	531	438
Ensign township	746	505
Escanaba city	14 355	15 368
Escanaba township[16]	3 229	1 948
Fairbanks township	358	309
Ford River township	2 136	1 762
Garden township	812	713
Garden village	296	336
Gladstone city[16]	4 533	5 237
Maple Ridge township	946	775
Masonville township	1 807	1 409
Nahma township	517	499
Wells township	5 181	4 003
Dickinson County[17]	25 341	23 753
Breen township	471	462
Breitung township[17]	4 669	3 392
Felch township	615	444
Iron Mountain city[17]	8 341	8 702
Kingsford city	5 290	5 276
Norway city	2 919	3 033
Norway township	1 257	966
Sagola township	1 146	918
Waucedah township	577	503
West Branch township	56	57
Eaton County[18]	88 337	68 892
Bellevue township	2 725	2 424
Bellevue village	1 289	1 297
Benton township[18]	2 405	1 754
Brookfield township	1 380	1 113
Carmel township[18]	2 168	1 539
Charlotte city[18]	8 251	8 244

County Subdivisions	1980	1970
Eaton County—Con.		
Chester township	1 622	1 205
Delta township	23 822	17 396
Eaton township[18]	3 315	2 104
Eaton Rapids city	4 510	4 494
Eaton Rapids township	2 823	2 066
Grand Ledge city[18]	6 920	6 032
Hamlin township	2 195	1 621
Kalamo township	1 683	1 310
Lansing city (pt.)[18]	4 440	1 192
Olivet city	1 604	1 629
Oneida township[18]	3 378	2 635
Potterville city[18]	1 502	1 280
Roxand township	1 975	1 671
Mulliken village[18]	550	454
Sunfield township	1 998	1 710
Sunfield village	591	497
Vermontville township	1 942	1 734
Vermontville village[18]	832	857
Walton township	1 601	1 256
Windsor township[18]	6 078	4 483
Dimondale village[18]	1 008	970
Emmet County	22 992	18 331
Bear Creek township	3 287	2 450
Bliss township	441	282
Carp Lake township	637	439
Center township	435	349
Cross Village township	215	185
Friendship township	467	240
Harbor Springs city	1 567	1 662
Littlefield township	1 822	1 266
Alanson village	508	362
Little Traverse township	1 574	985
McKinley township	961	835
Pellston village (pt.)	488	448
Maple River township	654	415
Pellston village (pt.)	77	21
Petoskey city	6 097	6 342
Pleasant View township	212	124
Readmond township	356	234
Resort township	1 687	1 009
Springvale township	1 073	663
Wawatam township	510	431
Mackinaw City village (pt.)	428	330
West Traverse township	997	420
Genesee County[19]	450 449	445 589
Argentine township	4 180	2 901
Argentine (CDP)	1 563	...
Atlas township	4 891	3 089
Goodrich village	795	774
Burton city[19]	29 976	...
Clayton township	7 269	5 305
Lennon village (pt.)[19]	114	...
Clio city[19]	2 669	2 357
Davison city[19]	6 087	5 259
Davison township[19]	13 708	8 260
Fenton city[19]	8 098	8 284
Fenton township[19]	11 744	8 850
Lake Fenton (CDP)	3 154	2 101
Linden village[19]	2 174	1 546
Flint city[19]	159 611	193 317
Flint township[19]	35 405	31 175
Flushing city	8 624	7 190
Flushing township	9 246	6 957
Forest township	4 255	3 316
Otisville village	682	724
Otter Lake village (pt.)	14	2
Gaines township	5 209	3 379
Gaines village	440	408
Genesee township	25 065	25 589
Beecher (CDP) (pt.)	3 907	...
Grand Blanc city	6 848	5 132
Grand Blanc township	24 413	19 229
Montrose township	7 870	6 468
Montrose village[19]	1 706	1 789
Mount Morris city[19]	3 246	3 778
Mount Morris township[19]	27 928	29 349
Beecher (CDP) (pt.)	13 271	...
Mundy township	10 786	8 029
Richfield township	6 895	5 535
Swartz Creek city	5 013	4 928
Thetford township	8 499	6 014
Vienna township[19]	12 914	9 359
Gladwin County[20]	19 957	13 471
Beaverton city[20]	1 025	954
Beaverton township[20]	1 612	1 033
Bentley township	771	599
Billings township	2 076	959
Bourret township	315	225
Buckeye township[20]	970	628
Butman township	834	455
Clement township	781	362
Gladwin city[20]	2 479	2 071
Gladwin township	743	713
Grim township	115	62
Grout township[20]	1 542	1 152

County Subdivisions	1980	1970
Gladwin County—Con.		
Hay township	1 056	595
Sage township	2 049	1 323
Secord township	850	398
Sherman township	773	503
Tobacco township[20]	1 966	1 439
Gogebic County	19 686	20 676
Bessemer city	2 553	2 805
Bessemer township	1 560	1 800
Erwin township	527	545
Ironwood city	7 741	8 711
Ironwood township	2 331	2 256
Marenisco township	824	635
Wakefield city	2 591	2 757
Wakefield township	465	456
Watersmeet township	1 094	711
Grand Traverse County[21]	54 899	39 175
Acme township	2 909	1 662
Blair township	4 613	1 677
East Bay township	6 212	3 356
Fife Lake township	1 056	638
Fife Lake village	402	274
Garfield township[21]	8 747	4 917
Grant township	676	507
Green Lake township	2 997	1 206
Long Lake township	3 823	1 584
Mayfield township	806	651
Paradise township	2 117	1 434
Kingsley village[21]	664	632
Peninsula township	3 833	2 642
Traverse City city[21]	15 516	18 048
Union township	185	57
Whitewater township	1 409	796
Gratiot County[22]	40 448	39 246
Alma city[22]	9 652	9 611
Arcada township[22]	1 784	1 751
Bethany township[22]	1 526	1 514
Elba township	1 537	1 544
Ashley village	570	521
Emerson township	1 092	1 170
Fulton township	2 165	1 904
Perrinton village	448	489
Hamilton township	530	513
Ithaca city	2 950	2 749
Lafayette township	776	849
Newark township	1 097	1 047
New Haven township	1 021	915
North Shade township	815	845
North Star township	1 171	1 243
Pine River township[22]	1 939	1 887
St. Louis city[22]	4 107	4 101
Seville township	2 091	1 893
Sumner township	1 897	1 688
Washington township	1 079	1 026
Wheeler township	3 219	2 996
Breckenridge village[22]	1 495	1 257
Hillsdale County[23]	42 071	37 171
Adams township	2 260	1 849
North Adams village	565	574
Allen township	1 501	1 371
Allen village	266	385
Amboy township	936	844
Cambria township	2 326	1 880
Camden township	1 848	1 723
Camden village	420	405
Montgomery village	408	404
Fayette township[23]	3 115	2 933
Jonesville village	2 172	2 081
Hillsdale city[23]	7 432	7 728
Hillsdale township[23]	1 873	1 608
Jefferson township	2 920	2 290
Litchfield city[23]	1 353	1 167
Litchfield township[23]	1 027	2 183
Moscow township	1 396	1 093
Pittsford township	1 550	1 548
Ransom township	949	860
Reading city	1 203	1 125
Reading township	1 653	1 194
Scipio township	1 352	1 173
Somerset township	3 142	1 886
Wheatland township	1 255	1 074
Woodbridge township	1 115	1 026
Wright township	1 865	1 783
Waldron village	570	564
Houghton County[24]	37 872	34 652
Adams township	2 461	2 599
South Range village	861	898
Calumet township	7 965	8 271
Calumet village	1 013	1 007
Copper City village	244	252
Laurium village[24]	2 678	2 868
Chassell township	1 738	1 415
Duncan township	344	398
Elm River township	184	212
Franklin township	1 303	1 180
Hancock city	5 122	4 820

County Subdivisions	1980	1970
Houghton County—Con.		
Hancock township	288	169
Houghton city[24]	7 512	6 067
Laird township	646	550
Osceola township	2 074	1 957
Hubbell (CDP) (pt.)	394	429
Portage township[24]	3 244	8 646
Quincy township	256	306
Schoolcraft township	2 071	1 939
Lake Linden village	1 181	1 214
Stanton township	1 063	973
Torch Lake township	1 601	1 217
Hubbell (CDP) (pt.)	884	822
Huron County[25]	36 459	34 083
Bad Axe city[25]	3 184	2 999
Bingham township	1 679	1 617
Ubly village	862	899
Bloomfield township	632	690
Brookfield township	998	1 063
Owendale village	308	312
Caseville township	2 067	1 235
Caseville village	851	607
Chandler township	555	580
Colfax township[25]	1 907	1 684
Dwight township	1 145	1 092
Kinde village (pt.)	364	378
Fairhaven township	1 292	1 108
Gore township	175	127
Grant township	819	703
Harbor Beach city[25]	2 000	2 134
Hume township	753	573
Huron township	433	340
Lake township	822	532
Lincoln township	1 042	972
Kinde village (pt.)	236	240
McKinley township	555	637
Meade township	789	759
Kinde village (pt.)[25]	–	...
Oliver township	1 756	1 755
Elkton village	953	973
Paris township	732	755
Pointe Aux Barques township	6	6
Port Austin township	1 570	1 588
Port Austin village	839	883
Rubicon township	892	805
Port Hope village	369	377
Sand Beach township[25]	1 399	1 330
Sebewaing township	3 259	3 160
Sebewaing village	2 046	2 053
Sheridan township	812	658
Sherman township	1 251	1 204
Sigel township	673	674
Verona township[25]	1 122	993
Winsor township	2 140	2 310
Pigeon village	1 247	1 174
Ingham County[26]	275 520	261 039
Alaiedon township[26]	2 845	2 487
Aurelius township	2 460	1 987
Bunker Hill township	1 794	1 464
Delhi township	17 144	13 795
Holt (CDP)	10 097	6 980
East Lansing city	51 392	47 540
Ingham township	1 974	1 498
Dansville village	479	486
Lansing city (pt.)[26]	125 974	130 211
Lansing township[26]	10 097	11 270
Leroy township	3 413	2 598
Webberville village	1 535	1 251
Leslie city[26]	2 110	1 894
Leslie township[26]	2 190	1 718
Locke township	1 456	1 370
Mason city[26]	6 019	5 468
Meridian township	28 292	23 817
Haslett (CDP)	7 025	...
Okemos (CDP)	8 882	7 770
Onondaga township	2 299	1 981
Stockbridge township	2 914	2 526
Stockbridge village	1 213	1 190
Vevay township[26]	3 113	1 916
Wheatfield township	1 523	1 177
White Oak township	1 096	875
Williamston city[26]	2 981	2 600
Williamston township[26]	3 972	2 847
Ionia County[27]	51 815	45 848
Belding city	5 634	5 121
Berlin township	2 660	2 213
Boston township	3 681	2 751
Saranac village	1 421	1 223
Campbell township	1 692	1 560
Clarksville village	348	346
Danby township[27]	2 082	1 621
Easton township	4 501	3 908
Ionia city[27]	5 920	6 361
Ionia township[27]	2 842	2 444
Lyons village (pt.)	34	24
Keene township	1 085	947

County Subdivisions	1980	1970
Ionia County—Con.		
Lyons township	3 126	2 882
Lyons village (pt.)	674	734
Muir village[27]	698	617
Pewamo village	488	498
North Plains township	1 345	1 165
Hubbardston village (pt.)	380	377
Odessa township	3 531	3 103
Lake Odessa village	2 171	1 924
Orange township	994	866
Orleans township	2 230	1 707
Otisco township	1 826	1 479
Portland city[27]	3 963	3 817
Portland township[27]	2 245	5 532
Ronald township	1 353	1 244
Sebewa township	1 105	944
Iosco County[28]	28 349	24 905
Alabaster township	371	280
Au Sable township	2 198	1 876
Au Sable (CDP)	1 240	...
Oscoda (CDP) (pt.)	76	...
Baldwin township	1 393	'953
Burleigh township	761	569
East Tawas city	2 584	2 372
Grant township	1 043	607
Oscoda township	11 386	11 758
Oscoda (CDP) (pt.)	2 355	...
Wurtsmith AFB (CDP)	5 166	6 932
Plainfield township	3 160	2 036
Reno township	566	294
Sherman township	465	422
Tawas township[28]	1 463	'1 253
Tawas City city[28]	1 967	1 666
Whittemore city	438	460
Wilber township	554	359
Iron County[29]	13 635	13 813
Bates township	1 003	980
Caspian city	1 038	1 165
Crystal Falls city[29]	1 965	2 000
Crystal Falls township[29]	1 648	1 499
Gaastra city	404	479
Hematite township	404	439
Iron River city	2 426	2 684
Iron River township	1 445	1 398
Mineral Hills village	257	234
Mansfield township	222	173
Mastodon township	621	591
Alpha village	229	282
Stambaugh city	1 442	1 458
Stambaugh township	1 017	947
Isabella County[30]	54 110	44 594
Broomfield township	1 246	727
Chippewa township	3 784	2 552
Clare city (pt.)[30]	−	...
Coe township	3 141	2 803
Shepherd village[30]	1 534	1 416
Coldwater township	714	531
Deerfield township	2 160	1 419
Denver township	1 059	921
Fremont township	1 215	1 010
Gilmore township	966	606
Isabella township	1 916	1 757
Rosebush village	336	439
Lincoln township	1 698	1 254
Mount Pleasant city[30]	23 746	'20 524
Nottawa township	2 042	1 758
Rolland township	1 105	927
Sherman township	1 405	819
Union township[30]	5 306	'4 611
Vernon township[30]	1 389	1 310
Wise township	1 218	1 065
Jackson County[31]	151 495	143 274
Blackman township	19 741	16 997
Columbia township	6 019	4 523
Brooklyn village[31]	1 110	1 112
Cement City village (pt.)	38	42
Concord township	2 320	2 204
Concord village[31]	900	983
Grass Lake township	3 685	2 970
Grass Lake village	962	1 061
Hanover township	3 650	2 533
Hanover village	490	513
Henrietta township	3 814	3 594
Jackson city	39 739	45 484
Leoni township	14 259	13 953
Michigan Center (CDP)	5 244	...
Liberty township	2 312	1 840
Napoleon township	6 141	5 500
Napoleon (CDP)	1 400	...
Norvell township	2 418	1 788
Parma township	2 715	2 138
Parma village (pt.)[31]	280	374
Pulaski township	1 725	1 396
Rives township	4 081	2 708
Sandstone township	3 300	2 743
Parma village (pt.)[31]	593	506

County Subdivisions	1980	1970
Jackson County—Con.		
Spring Arbor township	6 868	5 650
Spring Arbor (CDP)	2 101	1 832
Springport township	1 999	1 879
Springport village	675	723
Summit township	22 113	21 754
Vandercook Lake (CDP)	4 975	...
Tompkins township	2 152	1 832
Waterloo township	2 444	1 788
Kalamazoo County[32]	212 378	201 550
Alamo township	2 909	2 413
Brady township	3 852	3 060
Vicksburg village (pt.)	736	825
Charleston township	1 748	2 687
Augusta village (pt.)	29	20
Climax township	1 978	1 818
Climax village	619	594
Comstock township	11 162	10 465
Cooper township	8 434	7 666
Galesburg city	1 822	1 355
Kalamazoo city[32]	79 722	85 555
Kalamazoo township[32]	20 942	22 301
Eastwood (CDP)	7 186	9 682
Westwood (CDP)	8 519	9 143
Oshtemo township[32]	10 958	6 237
Parchment city	1 817	2 027
Pavilion township	4 811	3 691
Portage city	38 157	33 590
Prairie Ronde township	1 189	777
Richland township	4 677	3 728
Richland village	486	728
Ross township	4 747	4 490
Augusta village (pt.)	884	1 005
Schoolcraft township	6 435	5 289
Schoolcraft village[32]	1 359	1 277
Vicksburg village (pt.)	1 488	1 314
Texas township	5 643	3 187
Wakeshma township	1 375	1 214
Kalkaska County[33]	10 952	'5 372
Bear Lake township	433	186
Blue Lake township	300	238
Boardman township	903	310
Clearwater township	1 531	884
Cold Springs township	942	321
Excelsior township	580	232
Garfield township	366	214
Kalkaska township	3 544	1 964
Kalkaska village[33]	1 654	1 475
Oliver township	241	136
Orange township	792	'358
Rapid River township	581	249
Springfield township	739	280
Kent County[34]	444 506	411 044
Ada township	6 472	4 479
Algoma township	4 411	3 088
Alpine township	8 934	8 163
Comstock Park (CDP) (pt.)	4 515	4 653
Bowne township	1 719	1 429
Byron township	10 104	7 493
Cutlerville (CDP) (pt.)	3 091	1 334
Caledonia township	4 927	3 842
Caledonia village[34]	722	716
Cannon township	4 983	3 690
Cascade township	10 120	5 243
Cedar Springs city[34]	2 615	1 807
Courtland township	3 272	2 196
East Grand Rapids city	10 914	12 565
Gaines township	10 364	8 794
Cutlerville (CDP) (pt.)	5 165	4 933
Grand Rapids city[34]	181 843	197 649
Grand Rapids township[34]	9 294	6 823
Grandville city[34]	12 412	10 764
Grattan township	2 575	1 893
Kentwood city[34]	30 438	20 310
Lowell city[34]	3 707	3 068
Lowell township[34]	3 972	2 160
Nelson township[34]	2 641	1 938
Sand Lake village	388	380
Oakfield township	2 983	2 159
Plainfield township	20 611	16 935
Comstock Park (CDP) (pt.)	991	1 113
Northview (CDP)	11 662	...
Rockford city	3 324	2 428
Solon township[34]	2 809	2 114
Sparta township	6 934	6 466
Sparta village[34]	3 373	3 094
Spencer township	2 385	1 458
Tyrone township	3 220	2 638
Casnovia village (pt.)	167	205
Kent City village	860	686
Vergennes township	1 819	1 400
Walker city	15 088	11 492
Wyoming city[34]	59 616	56 560

County Subdivisions

County Subdivisions	1980	1970
Keweenaw County	1 963	2 264
Allouez township	1 508	1 700
Ahmeek village	210	238
Eagle Harbor township	113	199
Grant township	118	68
Houghton township	161	229
Sherman township	63	68
Lake County	7 711	5 661
Chase township	858	752
Cherry Valley township	272	172
Dover township	293	201
Eden township	174	116
Elk township	538	325
Ellsworth township	542	376
Luther village (pt.)	148	129
Lake township	516	341
Newkirk township	608	426
Luther village (pt.)	266	191
Peacock township	278	144
Pinora township	348	249
Pleasant Plains township	1 401	1 211
Baldwin village (pt.)	546	502
Sauble township	260	194
Sweetwater township	206	115
Webber township	865	614
Baldwin village (pt.)	128	110
Yates township	552	425
Lapeer County[35]	70 038	'52 361
Almont township	4 124	3 163
Almont village[35]	1 857	1 634
Arcadia township	2 347	1 666
Attica township	3 642	2 695
Brown City city (pt.)[35]	5	...
Burlington township	1 562	1 423
Clifford village	406	472
Burnside township[35]	1 772	1 506
Deerfield township	4 672	2 713
Barnes Lake–Millers Lake (CDP)	1 172	...
Dryden township	2 977	2 129
Dryden village	650	654
Elba township	4 604	5 651
Goodland township	1 534	1 261
Hadley township	3 331	2 011
Imlay township[35]	2 238	4 150
Imlay City city[35]	2 495	1 980
Lapeer city[35]	6 198	'6 314
Lapeer township[35]	4 261	2 574
Marathon township	4 336	3 513
Columbiaville village (pt.)[35]	953	935
Otter Lake village (pt.)	442	549
Mayfield township	7 098	3 645
Metamora township	3 220	1 988
Metamora village	552	468
North Branch township	2 721	2 277
North Branch village[35]	896	932
Oregon township	5 652	2 510
Columbiaville village (pt.)[35]	–	...
Rich township	1 249	1 172
Leelanau County[36]	14 007	10 872
Bingham township	1 546	916
Centerville township	709	473
Cleveland township	654	393
Elmwood township	3 004	2 240
Empire township	797	956
Empire village[36]	340	409
Glen Arbor township	578	571
Kasson township	952	676
Leelanau township	1 560	1 270
Northport village	611	594
Leland township	1 446	1 219
Solon township	987	798
Suttons Bay township	1 774	1 360
Suttons Bay village	504	522
Lenawee County[37]	89 948	'81 951
Adrian city[37]	21 186	20 382
Adrian township[37]	4 612	3 725
Blissfield township	3 744	3 475
Blissfield village[37]	3 107	2 753
Cambridge township	3 800	2 647
Onsted village	670	555
Clinton township	3 413	2 540
Clinton village	2 342	1 677
Deerfield township	1 729	1 589
Deerfield village[37]	957	834
Dover township	1 933	1 637
Clayton village (pt.)	230	312
Fairfield township	1 986	2 047
Franklin township	2 463	1 768
Hudson city[37]	2 545	2 618
Hudson township[37]	1 550	1 373
Clayton village (pt.)[37]	166	193
Macon township	1 480	1 316
Madison township[37]	5 035	5 494
Medina township	1 455	1 227
Morenci city	2 110	2 132
Ogden township	1 224	'1 553

County Subdivisions	1980	1970
Lenawee County—Con.		
Palmyra township	2 476	2 424
Raisin township[37]	5 499	4 322
Ridgeway township	1 746	1 756
Britton village[37]	693	697
Riga township	1 671	1 675
Rollin township	3 428	2 983
Addison village (pt.)	416	363
Manitou Beach–Devils Lake (CDP) (pt.)	1 633	1 560
Rome township	1 681	1 330
Seneca township	1 377	1 337
Tecumseh city[37]	7 320	7 120
Tecumseh township[37]	1 480	1 048
Woodstock township	3 005	2 433
Addison village (pt.)	239	232
Cement City village (pt.)	501	489
Manitou Beach–Devils Lake (CDP) (pt.)	521	332
Livingston County[38]	100 289	58 967
Brighton city[38]	4 268	2 457
Brighton township[38]	11 222	5 882
Cohoctah township	2 436	1 454
Conway township	1 722	1 160
Deerfield township	2 611	1 734
Genoa township	9 261	4 800
Green Oak township[38]	10 802	7 598
Whitmore Lake (CDP) (pt.)	1 590	1 269
Hamburg township	11 318	5 481
Handy township	4 681	3 556
Fowlerville village[38]	2 289	1 978
Hartland township	6 034	2 630
Howell city[38]	6 976	5 224
Howell township[38]	3 999	2 426
Iosco township	1 436	817
Marion township[38]	4 754	2 668
Oceola township	4 175	2 496
Putnam township	5 643	3 354
Pinckney village[38]	1 390	921
Tyrone township	6 077	3 437
Unadilla township	2 874	1 793
Luce County	6 659	6 789
Columbus township	293	281
Lakefield township	804	627
McMillan township	3 355	3 575
Newberry village	2 120	2 334
Pentland township	2 207	2 306
Mackinac County	10 178	9 660
Bois Blanc township	62	28
Brevort township	451	476
Clark township	1 879	1 771
Garfield township	1 206	1 013
Hendricks township	166	97
Hudson township	212	138
Mackinac Island city	479	517
Marquette township	461	471
Moran township	823	779
Newton township	354	302
Portage township	747	625
St. Ignace city	2 632	2 892
St. Ignace township	706	551
Macomb County[39]	694 600	625 309
Armada township	3 887	2 953
Armada village	1 392	1 352
Bruce township	5 756	4 350
Romeo village (pt.)[39]	1 933	2 137
Center Line city	9 293	10 379
Chesterfield township	18 276	9 378
Clinton township[39]	72 400	48 865
Clinton Township (CDP)	72 400	...
East Detroit city[39]	38 280	45 920
Fraser city	14 560	11 868
Harrison township	23 649	18 755
Harrison Township (CDP)	23 649	...
Lake township	110	135
Grosse Pointe Shores village (pt.)	110	135
Lenox township	4 899	4 724
New Haven village[39]	1 871	1 855
Macomb township	14 230	6 140
Memphis city (pt.)	817	749
Mount Clemens city[39]	18 806	20 476
New Baltimore city[39]	5 439	4 132
Ray township	3 121	2 683
Richmond city	3 536	3 234
Richmond township	2 453	1 719
Roseville city[39]	54 311	60 529
St. Clair Shores city[39]	76 210	88 093
Shelby township	38 939	29 467
Sterling Heights city	108 999	61 365
Utica city	5 282	3 504
Warren city	161 134	179 260
Washington township	10 213	7 526
Romeo village (pt.)[39]	1 576	1. 875
Manistee County[40]	23 019	'20 393
Arcadia township	641	592
Bear Lake township	1 658	1 444
Bear Lake village	388	376
Brown township	631	'689

County Subdivisions	1980	1970
Manistee County—Con.		
Cleon township	764	555
Copemish village	287	237
Dickson township	777	627
Filer township	2 143	1 921
Manistee city	7 566	7 723
Manistee township	3 209	2 875
East Lake village	514	512
Maple Grove township	1 071	750
Kaleva village[40]	445	377
Marilla township	266	213
Norman township	944	678
Onekama township	1 444	1 128
Onekama village	582	638
Pleasanton township	627	486
Springdale township	452	199
Stronach township	826	513
Marquette County[41]	74 101	64 686
Champion township	460	519
Chocolay township	5 685	3 299
Harvey (CDP)	1 341	...
Ely township	1 955	1 120
Ewing township	163	176
Forsyth township	9 679	8 290
Gwinn (CDP)	1 408	1 054
K. I. Sawyer AFB (CDP) (pt.)	4 837	5 134
Humboldt township	577	444
Ishpeming city[41]	7 538	8 245
Ishpeming township[41]	3 612	2 376
Marquette city[41]	23 288	21 967
Marquette township[41]	2 669	1 703
Trowbridge Park (CDP)	1 928	...
Michigamme township	383	436
Negaunee city	5 189	5 248
Negaunee township	2 443	1 760
Powell township	667	372
Republic township	1 390	1 442
Richmond township	1 246	1 277
Sands township	2 437	2 164
K. I. Sawyer AFB (CDP) (pt.)	982	1 545
Skandia township	999	717
Tilden township	1 044	883
Turin township	160	101
Wells township	351	277
West Branch township	2 166	1 870
K. I. Sawyer AFB (CDP) (pt.)	1 526	'1 545
Mason County[42]	26 365	22 612
Amber township	1 556	1 278
Branch township	1 021	635
Custer township[42]	1 338	1 204
Custer village	341	320
Eden township	511	414
Free Soil township	925	731
Free Soil village	212	186
Grant township	747	419
Hamlin township	2 616	1 778
Logan township	177	154
Ludington city[42]	8 937	9 021
Meade township	135	59
Pere Marquette township[42]	2 068	1 846
Riverton township	1 177	1 151
Scottville city[42]	1 241	1 202
Sheridan township	828	433
Sherman township	996	867
Fountain village	195	156
Summit township	922	557
Victory township	1 170	863
Mecosta County[43]	36 961	27 992
Aetna township	1 351	1 002
Morley village (pt.)	312	297
Austin township	898	509
Big Rapids city[43]	14 361	11 995
Big Rapids township[43]	2 471	1 687
Chippewa township	1 009	765
Colfax township	1 885	1 267
Deerfield township	1 032	817
Morley village (pt.)	195	184
Fork township	1 348	1 094
Barryton village	422	368
Grant township	642	476
Green township	2 847	1 808
Hinton township	855	725
Martiny township	1 210	756
Mecosta township	1 885	1 444
Stanwood village	209	241
Millbrook township	947	819
Morton township	1 789	998
Mecosta village	428	396
Sheridan township	1 007	616
Wheatland township	1 424	1 214
Menominee County[44]	26 201	24 587
Cedarville township	212	231
Daggett township	803	777
Daggett village	274	366
Faithorn township	227	208
Gourley township	406	380

County Subdivisions	1980	1970
Menominee County—Con.		
Harris township	1 563	1 237
Holmes township	253	336
Ingallston township	1 066	877
Lake township	622	532
Mellen township	1 159	822
Menominee city[44]	10 099	10 748
Menominee township[44]	4 026	3 212
Meyer township	1 004	1 004
Nadeau township	1 219	1 084
Spalding township	1 842	1 632
Powers village	490	560
Stephenson city[44]	967	800
Stephenson township[44]	·733	'707
Midland County[45]	73 578	63 769
Coleman city[45]	1 429	1 295
Edenville township	2 029	1 169
Geneva township	1 157	683
Greendale township	1 244	1 105
Homer township	4 477	3 959
Hope township	1 249	945
Ingersoll township	3 011	2 285
Jasper township	1 129	826
Jerome township	4 171	3 154
Sanford village	864	818
Larkin township[45]	3 303	2 509
Lee township	3 325	2 531
Lincoln township	1 643	1 417
Midland city (pt.)[45]	37 016	34 921
Midland township[45]	2 389	2 521
Mills township	1 461	1 005
Mount Haley township	1 586	1 262
Porter township	1 113	899
Warren township[45]	1 846	1 283
Missaukee County[46]	10 009	7 126
Aetna township	437	395
Bloomfield township	268	166
Butterfield township	390	272
Caldwell township	856	511
Clam Union township	797	679
Enterprise township	127	118
Forest township[46]	728	441
Holland township	159	92
Lake township	1 345	524
Lake City city[46]	843	704
McBain city	519	520
Norwich township	418	321
Pioneer township	323	235
Reeder township	647	462
Richland township	1 008	865
Riverside township	773	587
West Branch township	371	234
Monroe County[47]	134 659	'119 215
Ash township	7 688	5 803
Carleton village	2 786	1 503
Bedford township	22 902	'21 505
Lambertville (CDP)	6 341	'5 711
Berlin township	6 488	5 510
Estral Beach village	463	419
South Rockwood village	1 353	1 477
Dundee township	5 395	4 911
Dundee village[47]	2 575	2 472
Erie township	4 576	'4 494
Exeter township	3 236	2 971
Maybee village	490	485
Frenchtown township[47]	18 204	14 685
Detroit Beach (CDP)	2 112	2 053
Stony Point (CDP)	1 650	1 370
Woodland Beach (CDP)	2 383	2 249
Ida township	4 467	3 377
La Salle township	5 011	4 151
London township	3 266	2 522
Luna Pier city	1 443	1 418
Milan city (pt.)[47]	922	758
Milan township[47]	2 021	1 890
Monroe city[47]	23 531	23 894
Monroe township[47]	11 654	9 351
Patterson Gardens (CDP)	3 023	2 169
South Monroe (CDP)	4 232	3 012
Petersburg city[47]	1 222	1 227
Raisinville township	4 797	4 009
Summerfield township[47]	3 176	'2 617
Whiteford township	4 660	'4 122
Montcalm County[48]	47 555	39 660
Belvidere township	1 955	1 345
Bloomer township	1 226	1 152
Bushnell township	1 270	1 025
Sheridan village (pt.)	6	3
Carson City city	1 229	1 217
Cato township	2 441	2 205
Lakeview village	1 139	1 118
Crystal township	2 224	1 781
Day township	1 234	1 180
McBride village	252	272
Douglass township	1 787	1 118
Eureka township[48]	2 303	1 938

County Subdivisions

County Subdivisions	1980	1970
Montcalm County—Con.		
Evergreen township	2 183	1 842
Sheridan village (pt.)	473	485
Fairplain township	1 380	1 087
Sheridan village (pt.)	–	–
Ferris township	1 133	991
Greenville city[48]	8 019	7 493
Home township	2 614	2 487
Edmore village[48]	1 176	1 149
Maple Valley township	1 815	1 476
Montcalm township	2 521	1 984
Pierson township	1 701	1 261
Pierson village	216	193
Pine township	1 224	984
Reynolds township	2 362	1 830
Howard City village	1 118	1 060
Richland township	2 421	1 832
Sidney township	2 053	1 504
Sheridan village (pt.)	185	165
Stanton city	1 315	1 089
Winfield township	1 145	839
Montmorency County[49]	7 492	5 247
Albert township	1 620	1 013
Avery township	552	352
Briley township	1 699	1 215
Hillman township	1 650	1 173
Hillman village[49]	373	366
Loud township	224	193
Montmorency township	884	583
Rust township	502	433
Vienna township	361	285
Muskegon County[50]	157 589	157 426
Blue Lake township	1 101	715
Casnovia township	2 158	1 879
Casnovia village (pt.)	181	198
Cedar Creek township	2 454	1 467
Dalton township	5 897	5 361
Lakewood Club village	695	590
Egelston township	7 310	6 690
Wolf Lake (CDP)	3 876	2 258
Fruitland township	4 168	3 200
Fruitport township	10 646	10 214
Fruitport village	1 143	1 409
Holton township	2 022	1 499
Laketon township	6 327	5 440
Montague city	2 332	2 396
Montague township	1 359	1 147
Moorland township	1 521	1 488
Muskegon city[50]	40 823	44 631
Muskegon township[50]	14 557	13 754
Muskegon Heights city	14 611	17 304
North Muskegon city	4 024	4 243
Norton Shores city	22 025	22 271
Ravenna township	2 471	2 403
Ravenna village[50]	951	1 048
Roosevelt Park city	4 015	4 176
Sullivan township	2 356	2 051
Whitehall city	2 856	3 017
Whitehall township	1 341	1 064
White River township	1 215	1 016
Newaygo County[51]	34 917	27 992
Ashland township[51]	1 751	2 235
Barton township	558	482
Beaver township	443	356
Big Prairie township	1 202	698
Bridgeton township	1 562	870
Brooks township	2 349	1 330
Croton township	1 556	872
Dayton township[51]	1 938	1 910
Denver township	1 422	1 362
Hesperia village (pt.)	347	352
Ensley township	1 461	1 152
Everett township	1 360	844
Fremont city[51]	3 672	3 465
Garfield township	1 822	1 448
Goodwell township	387	374
Grant city[51]	683	772
Grant township	2 274	1 719
Home township	185	132
Lilley township	568	429
Lincoln township	885	490
Merrill township	508	376
Monroe township	263	120
Newaygo city	1 271	1 381
Norwich township	450	416
Sheridan township[51]	2 465	2 477
Sherman township	1 810	1 411
Troy township	199	80
White Cloud city	1 101	1 044
Wilcox township	772	519
Oakland County[52]	1 011 793	907 871
Addison township	4 607	2 809
Leonard village	423	378
Avon township[52]	40 779	24 513
Avon Township (CDP)	40 779	...
Berkley city	18 637	'21 879
Birmingham city[52]	21 689	26 170

County Subdivisions	1980	1970
Oakland County—Con.		
Bloomfield township[52]	42 876	42 788
Bloomfield Township (CDP)	42 876	...
Bloomfield Hills city	3 985	3 672
Brandon township	9 526	4 813
Ortonville village	1 190	983
Clawson city	15 103	17 617
Commerce township[52]	23 757	18 857
Wolverine Lake village	4 968	4 301
Farmington city	11 022	'10 329
Farmington Hills city[52]	58 056	...
Ferndale city	26 227	30 850
Groveland township	4 114	2 570
Hazel Park city	20 914	23 784
Highland township	16 958	8 372
White Lake–Seven Harbors (CDP) (pt.)	5 348	3 172
Holly township	8 486	7 396
Holly village (pt.)[52]	4 874	4 355
Huntington Woods city	6 937	8 536
Independence township	21 537	17 361
Clarkston village	968	1 034
Keego Harbor city	3 083	3 092
Lathrup Village city[52]	4 639	'4 676
Lyon township[52]	7 078	4 500
Madison Heights city	35 375	38 599
Milford township	10 187	7 256
Milford village	5 041	4 699
Northville city (pt.)	2 785	2 367
Novi city[52]	22 525	9 668
Novi township[52]	150	182
Oakland township	7 628	4 793
Oak Park city	31 537	36 762
Orchard Lake Village city	1 798	1 487
Orion township	22 473	17 110
Bunny Run (CDP)	1 840	1 391
Lake Orion village	2 907	2 921
Lake Orion Heights (CDP)	4 087	2 552
Oxford township	10 569	8 489
Oxford village	2 746	2 536
Pleasant Ridge city	3 217	3 989
Pontiac city	76 715	85 279
Pontiac township	15 598	13 219
Lake Angelus village (pt.)	210	573
Rochester city[52]	7 203	7 054
Rose township	4 465	2 502
Holly village (pt.)	–	–
Royal Oak city	70 893	'86 238
Royal Oak township	5 784	6 326
Southfield city[52]	75 568	69 285
Southfield township	15 031	17 521
Beverly Hills village[52]	11 598	13 598
Bingham Farms village	529	566
Franklin village	2 864	'3 311
South Lyon city[52]	5 214	2 675
Springfield township	8 295	4 388
Sylvan Lake city	1 949	2 219
Troy city[52]	67 102	39 419
Walled Lake city[52]	4 748	3 759
Waterford township	64 437	59 123
Lake Angelus village (pt.)	187	–
Waterford (CDP)	64 250	
West Bloomfield township	41 962	28 563
West Bloomfield Township (CDP)	41 962	...
White Lake township	21 870	14 311
White Lake–Seven Harbors (CDP) (pt.)	2 209	1 332
Wixom city	6 705	2 010
Oceana County[53]	22 002	17 984
Benona township	1 203	816
Claybanks township	733	557
Colfax township	328	222
Crystal township	602	453
Elbridge township	899	799
Ferry township	898	719
Golden township	1 358	871
Grant township	2 366	1 587
New Era village (pt.)	110	74
Rothbury village[53]	522	394
Greenwood township	815	575
Hart city[53]	1 888	2 139
Hart township[53]	1 801	1 525
Leavitt township	848	773
Walkerville village	296	319
Newfield township	1 968	1 551
Hesperia village (pt.)	529	525
Otto township	426	196
Pentwater township	1 424	1 154
Pentwater village	1 165	993
Shelby township	3 506	3 352
New Era village (pt.)	424	392
Shelby village[53]	1 624	1 703
Weare township	939	695
Ogemaw County[54]	16 436	11 903
Churchill township	1 058	702
Cumming township	675	422
Edwards township	1 036	708
Foster township	463	282
Goodar township	374	222

County Subdivisions	1980	1970
Ogemaw County--Con.		
Hill township	1 301	795
Horton township	729	479
Klacking township	386	331
Logan township	567	399
Mills township	2 624	1 370
Ogemaw township	814	636
Richland township	803	701
Prescott village	332	306
Rose township	1 085	804
Rose City city	661	530
West Branch city[54]	1 785	1 912
West Branch township[54]	2 075	1 610
Ontonagon County[55]	9 861	10 548
Bergland township	648	784
Bohemia township	116	99
Carp Lake township	1 434	1 544
White Pine (CDP)	1 142	1 218
Greenland township	1 181	1 210
Haight township	228	225
Interior township	528	601
McMillan township	688	821
Matchwood township	137	167
Ontonagon township	3 525	3 751
Ontonagon village[55]	2 182	2 432
Rockland township	448	368
Stannard township	928	978
Osceola County[56]	18 928	14 838
Burdell township	1 067	737
Tustin village	264	230
Cedar township	235	103
Evart city[56]	1 945	1 707
Evart township[56]	1 029	582
Hartwick township	420	406
Hersey township	1 229	815
Hersey village	364	276
Highland township	1 063	712
Le Roy township	858	644
Le Roy village	293	248
Lincoln township	1 173	910
Marion township	1 491	1 427
Marion village	816	891
Middle Branch township	642	541
Orient township	635	552
Osceola township	920	623
Reed City city[56]	2 221	2 286
Richmond township[56]	1 649	1 318
Rose Lake township	847	380
Sherman township	847	608
Sylvan township	657	487
Oscoda County	6 858	4 726
Big Creek township	2 392	1 663
Clinton township	442	398
Comins township	1 583	1 198
Elmer township	742	412
Greenwood township	696	315
Mentor township	1 003	740
Otsego County[57]	14 993	10 422
Bagley township[57]	4 106	2 294
Charlton township	823	573
Chester township	661	332
Corwith township	1 313	1 126
Vanderbilt village	525	522
Dover township	432	317
Elmira township	899	486
Gaylord city[57]	3 011	3 012
Hayes township	888	416
Livingston township	1 703	1 393
Otsego Lake township	1 157	473
Ottawa County[58]	157 174	128 181
Allendale township	6 080	3 554
Blendon township	3 763	2 927
Chester township	2 034	1 786
Coopersville city	2 889	2 129
Crockery township	3 536	2 861
Ferrysburg city	2 440	2 196
Georgetown township[58]	26 104	17 615
Jenison (CDP)	16 330	11 266
Grand Haven township[58]	11 763	11 844
Grand Haven city[58]	7 238	5 489
Holland city (pt.)[58]	21 767	'23 133
Holland township[58]	13 739	'10 849
Beechwood (CDP) (pt.)	2 169	2 536
Hudsonville city[58]	4 844	3 523
Jamestown township[58]	3 546	2 926
Olive township	2 449	2 072
Park township	10 354	6 639
Beechwood (CDP) (pt.)	164	178
Polkton township	2 027	1 962
Port Sheldon township	2 206	1 078
Robinson township	3 018	2 051
Spring Lake township	9 588	8 013
Spring Lake village	2 731	3 034
Tallmadge township	5 927	4 883

County Subdivisions	1980	1970
Ottawa County--Con.		
Wright township	3 387	2 983
Zeeland city	4 764	4 734
Zeeland township	3 711	2 934
Presque Isle County	14 267	12 836
Allis township	834	709
Bearinger township	217	67
Belknap township	1 026	902
Bismarck township	278	236
Case township	830	506
Millersburg village	231	200
Krakow township	570	445
Metz township	421	403
Moltke township	326	303
North Allis township	485	393
Ocqueoc township	578	414
Onaway city	1 084	1 262
Posen township	1 082	1 100
Posen village	270	339
Presque Isle township	1 334	698
Pulawski township	477	396
Rogers township	802	727
Rogers City city	3 923	4 275
Roscommon County[59]	16 374	9 892
Au Sable township	229	118
Backus township	213	96
Denton township	3 555	1 828
Houghton Lake (CDP) (pt.)	766	...
Gerrish township	1 629	984
Higgins township	1 581	1 360
Roscommon village[59]	834	810
Lake township	992	550
Lyon township	910	562
Markey township	1 335	796
Nester township	245	178
Richfield township	2 926	1 520
Roscommon township	2 759	1 900
Houghton Lake (CDP) (pt.)	1 683	1 252
Saginaw County[60]	228 059	219 743
Albee township	2 642	2 242
Birch Run township	5 488	4 618
Birch Run village[60]	1 196	932
Blumfield township	2 047	1 865
Brady township	2 498	1 951
Oakley village	412	418
Brant township	1 849	1 371
St. Charles village (pt.)[60]	20	...
Bridgeport township[60]	13 978	12 896
Buena Vista township[60]	12 768	13 687
Carrollton township	7 482	8 526
Carrollton (CDP)	7 482	7 300
Chapin township	1 054	853
Chesaning township	5 317	5 278
Chesaning village	2 656	2 876
Frankenmuth city[60]	3 753	2 834
Frankenmuth township[60]	2 389	1 965
Fremont township	2 087	1 500
James township	2 168	1 999
Jonesfield township	1 920	2 005
Merrill village[60]	851	961
Kochville township	2 828	2 426
Lakefield township	960	794
Maple Grove township	2 994	2 555
Marion township	913	679
Richland township	4 402	3 490
Hemlock (CDP)	1 362	...
Saginaw city[60]	77 508	91 849
Saginaw township[60]	38 668	27 234
St. Charles township	3 689	3 619
St. Charles village (pt.)[60]	2 068	1 921
Spaulding township	3 164	3 416
Swan Creek township	2 530	2 098
St. Charles village (pt.)	188	125
Taymouth township	4 581	3 196
Thomas township	11 184	8 585
Tittabawassee township	4 908	4 031
Freeland (CDP)	1 364	1 303
Zilwaukee city	2 201	2 072
Zilwaukee township	89	109
St. Clair County[61]	138 802	120 175
Algonac city[61]	4 412	3 684
Berlin township	2 160	1 595
Brockway township	1 586	998
Burtchville township	3 069	2 037
Casco township	4 331	2 065
China township	2 466	2 106
Clay township[61]	8 518	6 372
Pearl Beach (CDP)	3 430	1 744
Clyde township	4 632	2 980
Columbus township	3 097	1 937
Cottrellville township[61]	3 075	2 194
East China township	3 122	2 139
Emmett township	1 698	1 297
Emmett village	285	297
Fort Gratiot township	8 476	7 075
Grant township	1 119	832

Population of County Subdivisions

County Subdivisions	1980	1970
St. Clair County—Con.		
Greenwood township	1 046	889
Ira township	4 316	3 612
Kenockee township	1 730	1 250
Kimball township	7 180	6 152
Sparlingville (CDP)	1 718	1 845
Lynn township	999	767
Marine City city[61]	4 414	4 567
Marysville city	7 345	5 610
Memphis city (pt.)	354	372
Mussey township	2 768	2 449
Capac village	1 377	1 279
Port Huron city[61]	33 981	35 794
Port Huron township[61]	7 886	7 635
Riley township	2 075	1 536
St. Clair city	4 780	4 770
St. Clair township	3 965	3 091
Wales township	2 368	1 970
Yale city	1 814	1 505
St. Joseph County[62]	56 083	47 392
Burr Oak township[62]	2 502	2 189
Burr Oak village	853	873
Colon township	3 033	2 580
Colon village[62]	1 190	1 172
Constantine township	3 647	3 096
Constantine village[62]	1 680	1 733
Fabius township[62]	3 153	2 080
Fawn River township	1 639	1 471
Florence township	1 403	1 125
Flowerfield township	1 290	850
Leonidas township	1 249	935
Lockport township[62]	3 048	1 889
Centreville village (pt.)[62]	100	19
Mendon township	2 820	2 065
Mendon village[62]	951	949
Mottville township	1 490	1 288
Nottawa township	3 324	2 421
Centreville village (pt.)[62]	1 102	1 025
Park township	2 772	2 208
Sherman township[62]	2 756	2 101
Sturgis city[62]	9 468	9 295
Sturgis township[62]	1 871	1 449
Three Rivers city[62]	7 015	7 355
White Pigeon township	3 603	2 995
White Pigeon village[62]	1 478	1 455
Sanilac County[63]	40 789	35 181
Argyle township	912	750
Austin township	802	730
Bridgehampton township	974	951
Carsonville village (pt.)	176	180
Brown City city (pt.)[63]	1 158	1 142
Buel township	890	691
Croswell city[63]	2 073	1 954
Custer township	1 122	959
Delaware township	1 071	967
Forestville village	159	110
Elk township	1 535	1 449
Peck village	606	580
Elmer township	829	755
Evergreen township	1 042	775
Flynn township	963	828
Forester township	958	648
Fremont township	847	564
Greenleaf township	746	667
Lamotte township	1 065	924
Lexington township[63]	2 958	2 494
Lexington village	765	834
Maple Valley township[63]	1 009	895
Marion township	1 741	1 556
Deckerville village[63]	887	817
Marlette township	3 790	3 564
Marlette village[63]	1 761	1 706
Minden township	710	685
Minden City village	284	327
Moore township	1 318	1 120
Sandusky city[63]	2 216	2 071
Sanilac township	2 284	1 652
Port Sanilac village	598	493
Speaker township	1 265	1 039
Melvin village	171	202
Washington township	1 525	1 406
Applegate village	257	301
Carsonville village (pt.)[63]	446	441
Watertown township[63]	1 346	1 192
Wheatland township	582	597
Worth township	3 058	2 156
Schoolcraft County	8 575	8 226
Doyle township	629	615
Germfask township	607	529
Hiawatha township	1 096	802
Inwood township	592	482
Manistique city	3 962	4 324
Manistique township	862	716
Mueller township	255	263
Seney township	174	178
Thompson township	398	317

County Subdivisions	1980	1970
Shiawassee County[64]	71 140	63 075
Antrim township	1 752	1 277
Bennington township	2 758	1 973
Burns township	3 273	2 127
Byron village	689	655
Caledonia township[64]	4 785	4 292
Corunna city[64]	3 206	2 829
Durand city[64]	4 241	3 678
Fairfield township	904	964
Hazelton township	2 411	2 132
New Lothrop village	646	596
Laingsburg city[64]	1 145	1 159
Middlebury township	1 574	1 362
New Haven township	1 425	1 328
Owosso city[64]	16 455	17 179
Owosso township[64]	4 530	4 002
Perry city[64]	2 051	1 531
Perry township[64]	3 467	2 598
Morrice village	733	734
Rush township	1 500	1 494
Sciota township[64]	1 527	1 054
Shiawassee township	2 709	2 549
Bancroft village	618	724
Venice township	3 063	2 516
Lennon village (pt.)[64]	486	...
Vernon township[64]	5 003	4 422
Vernon village[64]	1 008	818
Woodhull township	3 361	2 609
Tuscola County[65]	56 961	48 603
Akron township	1 811	1 865
Akron village (pt.)	340	352
Almer township	2 720	2 394
Caro village (pt.)[65]	551	...
Arbela township	3 192	2 560
Columbia township	1 428	1 598
Unionville village	578	647
Dayton township	1 728	1 138
Denmark township	3 615	2 693
Reese village[65]	1 645	1 050
Elkland township	3 449	3 171
Cass City village[65]	2 258	1 974
Ellington township	1 214	853
Elmwood township	1 337	1 246
Gagetown village	428	408
Fairgrove township	1 946	1 832
Akron village (pt.)	198	173
Fairgrove village	691	629
Fremont township	2 871	2 200
Mayville village[65]	958	872
Gilford township	915	1 065
Indianfields township	7 037	7 088
Caro village (pt.)[65]	3 766	3 701
Juniata township	1 619	1 309
Kingston township	1 539	1 307
Kingston village (pt.)	344	368
Koylton township	1 399	991
Kingston village (pt.)	73	96
Millington township	4 429	3 471
Millington village[65]	1 237	1 099
Novesta township	1 482	1 098
Tuscola township[65]	2 255	1 960
Vassar city[65]	2 727	2 802
Vassar township	3 709	2 406
Watertown township	2 122	1 626
Wells township	1 501	1 002
Wisner township	916	928
Van Buren County[66]	66 814	56 173
Almena township	2 956	1 845
Antwerp township	7 744	5 346
Lawton village	1 558	1 358
Mattawan village[66]	2 143	1 569
Paw Paw village (pt.)	133	107
Arlington township	1 884	1 645
Bangor city	2 001	2 050
Bangor township	1 993	1 708
Bloomingdale township	2 490	1 989
Bloomingdale village	537	496
Columbia township	2 248	1 866
Breedsville village	244	209
Covert township	2 706	2 659
Decatur township	3 599	3 367
Decatur village[66]	1 915	1 764
Geneva township	2 984	2 392
Gobles city	816	801
Hamilton township	1 586	1 167
Hartford city[66]	2 493	2 508
Hartford township[66]	2 707	2 211
Keeler township	2 638	2 234
Lawrence township	3 017	2 345
Lawrence village	903	790
Paw Paw township	6 285	5 645
Paw Paw village (pt.)[66]	3 078	3 053
Pine Grove township	2 379	1 835
Porter township	2 041	1 360
South Haven city[66]	5 943	6 471
South Haven township[66]	4 174	3 416
Waverly township	2 130	1 313

County Subdivisions

County Subdivisions	1980	1970
Washtenaw County[67]	264 748	234 103
Ann Arbor city[67]	107 966	'100 035
Ann Arbor township[67]	3 090	'3 488
Barton Hills village[67]	357	...
Augusta township	4 643	4 378
Bridgewater township	1 371	1 204
Dexter township	3 872	2 238
Freedom township	1 436	1 267
Lima township	2 544	1 695
Chelsea village (pt.)[67]	420	414
Lodi township[67]	2 773	1 934
Lyndon township	2 057	1 373
Manchester township	3 226	2 856
Manchester village[67]	1 686	1 650
Milan city (pt.)[67]	3 260	'3 239
Northfield township	4 672	3 975
Whitmore Lake (CDP) (pt.)	1 330	1 494
Pittsfield township[67]	12 997	'8 073
Salem township	3 342	3 001
Saline city[67]	6 483	4 811
Saline township[67]	1 221	922
Scio township[67]	8 029	'7 205
Dexter village (pt.)	1 524	1 729
Sharon township	1 363	831
Superior township	8 060	5 562
Sylvan township	5 524	5 086
Chelsea village (pt.)[67]	3 396	3 444
Webster township	2 760	1 981
Dexter village (pt.)[67]	-	...
York township[67]	5 517	'6 217
Ypsilanti city	24 031	29 538
Ypsilanti township	44 511	33 194
Wayne County[68]	2 337 891	'2 670 368
Allen Park city	34 196	40 747
Belleville city[68]	3 366	2 406
Brownstown township	18 302	'7 088
Canton township	48 616	11 026
Dearborn city	90 660	104 199
Dearborn Heights city	67 706	80 069
Detroit city	1 203 339	'1 514 063
Ecorse city	14 447	17 515
Flat Rock city	6 853	5 643
Garden City city	35 640	41 864
Gibraltar city	4 458	'3 842
Grosse Ile township	9 320	'8 306
Grosse Ile (CDP)	9 320	'8 306
Grosse Pointe city	5 901	6 637
Grosse Pointe township	3 012	2 907
Grosse Pointe Shores village (pt.)	3 012	2 907
Grosse Pointe Farms city	10 551	11 701
Grosse Pointe Park city	13 639	'15 641
Grosse Pointe Woods city	18 886	21 878
Hamtramck city	21 300	'26 783
Harper Woods city	16 361	20 186
Highland Park city	27 909	35 444
Huron township	9 849	8 030
New Boston (CDP)	1 200	...
Inkster city	35 190	38 595
Lincoln Park city	45 105	52 984
Livonia city	104 814	110 109
Melvindale city	12 322	13 862
Northville city (pt.)[68]	2 913	3 033
Northville township[68]	12 987	9 522
Plymouth city	9 986	11 758
Plymouth township	23 028	17 497
Redford township	58 441	71 901
Redford Township (CDP)	58 441	...
River Rouge city	12 912	15 947
Riverview city	14 569	1i 342
Rockwood city	3 346	'3 225
Romulus city[68]	24 857	...
Southgate city	32 058	33 909
Sumpter township	11 112	8 091
Taylor city	77 568	70 020
Trenton city	22 762	24 127
Van Buren township[68]	18 940	13 162
Wayne city	21 159	21 054
Westland city	84 603	86 749
Woodhaven city	10 902	'3 566
Wyandotte city	34 006	41 061
Wexford County[69]	25 102	19 717
Antioch township	618	395
Boon township	500	457
Harrietta village (pt.)	128	126
Cadillac city[69]	10 199	9 990
Cedar Creek township	1 010	692
Cherry Grove township	1 517	835
Clam Lake township[69]	1 658	1 084
Colfax township	602	374
Greenwood township	297	155
Hanover township	665	373
Buckley village	357	244
Haring township[69]	2 523	1 387
Henderson township	140	120
Liberty township	542	334
Manton city	1 212	1 107

County Subdivisions

County Subdivisions	1980	1970
Wexford County—Con.		
Selma township	1 289	749
Slagle township	406	286
Harrietta village (pt.)	11	6
South Branch township	276	210
Springville township	1 191	799
Mesick village	374	376
Wexford township	457	370

MINNESOTA

Minnesota is named from the river which crosses the southern part of the state in an easterly direction. The name is of Indian origin and signifies "sky-colored (cloudy or hazy) water."

Explorations in the region now constituting Minnesota were made by the French as early as 1659-60, when Groselliers and Radisson visited the Mille Lacs region. In 1686 Nicolas Perrot took formal possession of the country in the name of the King of France. Although fur traders had been in the Minnesota region for more than a century, the first permanent settlement appears to have been that made near Fort Snelling in 1826 by Swiss refugees from Lord Selkirk's colony at Pembina, now in North Dakota. The fort itself, at first called Fort St. Anthony, had been established in 1819.

In 1762 the French possessions west of the Mississippi, then known as Louisiana, were ceded to Spain, in 1800 Louisiana was retroceded to France, and in 1803 it was purchased by the United States. The French possessions east of the Mississippi were ceded to England in 1763, and at the close of the Revolution all of the present area of Minnesota lying northeast of the Mississippi became a part of the United States.

The section of the Minnesota country included in the Louisiana Purchase belonged successively to the district of Louisiana, organized in 1804, to Louisiana territory, organized in 1805, and to Missouri territory, organized in 1812. In 1834 it was added to Michigan territory, in 1836 it was made a part of Wisconsin territory, and in 1838 it was included in the territory of Iowa. That part of Minnesota northeast of the Mississippi was embraced within the Northwest Territory from the organization of that territory in 1787 until 1800, when it was made a part of the territory of Indiana. In 1809 it was attached to Illinois territory; in 1819 it was added to the territory of Michigan; and in 1836 it was included in the territory of Wisconsin. Upon the admission of Iowa and Wisconsin as states of the Union, in 1846 and 1848, respectively, the Minnesota country was left without an organized government. In 1849 the territory of Minnesota was formed, with northern, eastern, and southern limits as at present, but bounded on the southwest and west by the Missouri and White Earth Rivers, thus including more than half the area of the present states of North and South Dakota. In May, 1858, Minnesota, with boundaries as at present, became a state of the Union.

COUNTY LOCATION INDEX

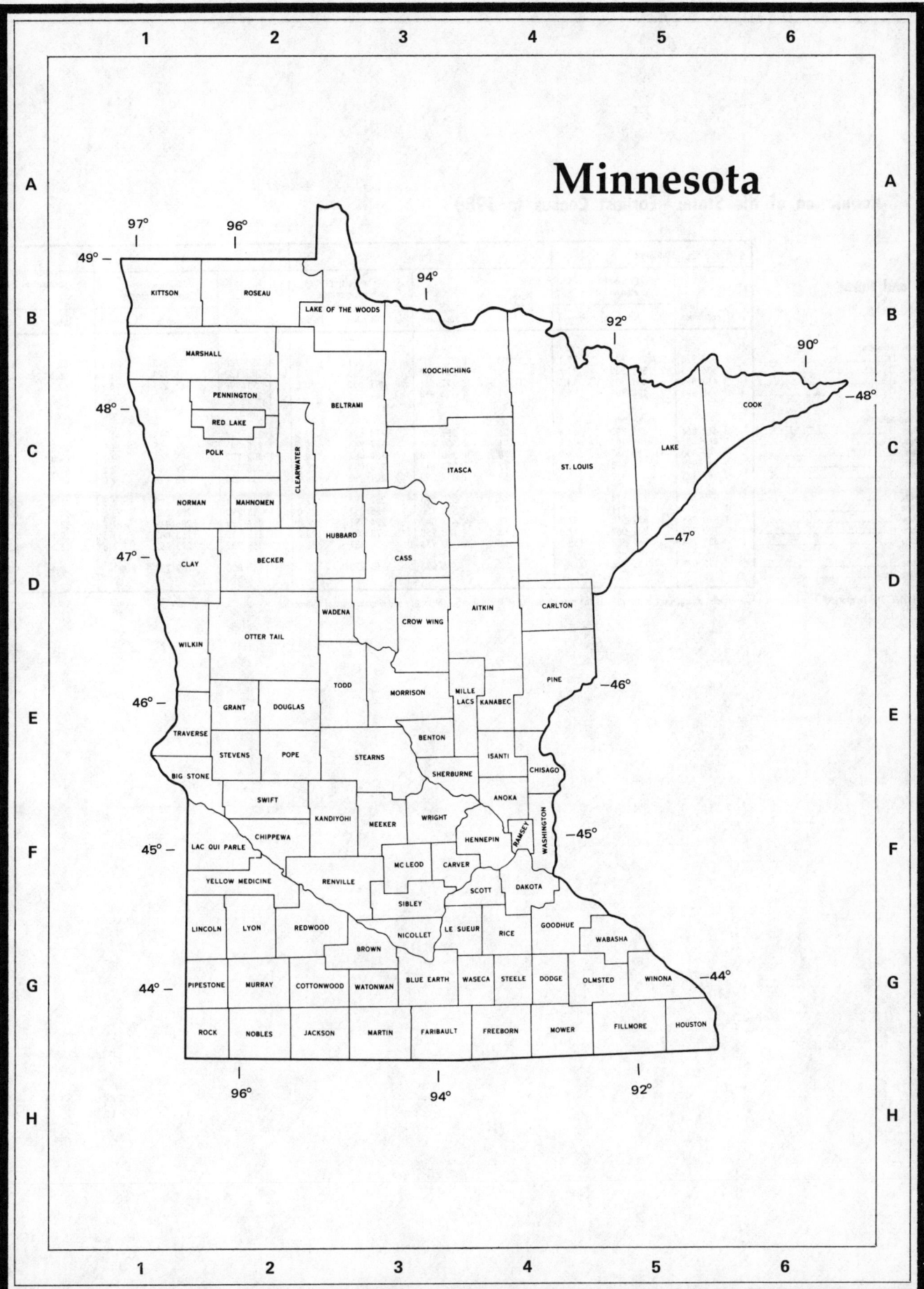

Minnesota

KITTSON
ROSEAU
LAKE OF THE WOODS
MARSHALL
PENNINGTON
RED LAKE
POLK
CLEARWATER
KOOCHICHING
BELTRAMI
COOK
NORMAN
MAHNOMEN
HUBBARD
ITASCA
LAKE
ST. LOUIS
CLAY
BECKER
CASS
WADENA
CROW WING
AITKIN
CARLTON
WILKIN
OTTER TAIL
TODD
MORRISON
MILLE LACS
KANABEC
PINE
GRANT
DOUGLAS
TRAVERSE
BENTON
STEVENS
POPE
STEARNS
ISANTI
BIG STONE
SHERBURNE
CHISAGO
ANOKA
SWIFT
KANDIYOHI
MEEKER
WRIGHT
WASHINGTON
LAC QUI PARLE
CHIPPEWA
HENNEPIN
RAMSEY
YELLOW MEDICINE
RENVILLE
MC LEOD
CARVER
SCOTT
DAKOTA
SIBLEY
LINCOLN
LYON
REDWOOD
NICOLLET
LE SUEUR
RICE
GOODHUE
BROWN
WABASHA
PIPESTONE
MURRAY
COTTONWOOD
WATONWAN
BLUE EARTH
WASECA
STEELE
DODGE
OLMSTED
WINONA
ROCK
NOBLES
JACKSON
MARTIN
FARIBAULT
FREEBORN
MOWER
FILLMORE
HOUSTON

97° 96° 94° 92° 90°
49° 48° 47° 46° 45° 44°
96° 94° 92°

Population of the State: Earliest Census to 1980

Urban and Rural

	The State			Urban				Rural				Percent of total population	
	Total population	Change from preceding census		Places of 2,500 or more	Population	Change from preceding census		Population	Change from preceding census			Urban	Rural
		Number	Percent			Number	Percent		Number	Percent			
Current urban definition:													
1980 (Apr. 1)	4 075 970	269 867	7.1	180	2 725 202	193 401	7.6	1 350 768	77 598	6.1		66.9	33.1
1970 (Apr. 1)	3 806 103	392 239	11.5	152	2 531 801	409 235	19.3	1 273 170	−18 128	−1.4		66.5	33.5
1960 (Apr. 1)	3 413 864	431 381	14.5	126	2 122 566	497 652	30.6	1 291 298	−66 271	−4.9		62.2	37.8
1950 (Apr. 1)	2 982 483	190 183	6.8	91	1 624 914	...	...	1 357 569	...	...		54.5	45.5
Previous urban definition:													
1960 (Apr. 1)	3 413 864	431 381	14.5	126	2 081 140	473 694	29.5	1 332 724	−42 313	−3.1		61.0	39.0
1950 (Apr. 1)	2 982 483	190 183	6.8	91	1 607 446	217 348	15.6	1 375 037	−27 165	−1.9		53.9	46.1
1940 (Apr. 1)	2 792 300	228 347	8.9	78	1 390 098	132 482	10.5	1 402 202	95 865	7.3		49.8	50.2
1930 (Apr. 1)	2 563 953	176 828	7.4	73	1 257 616	206 023	19.6	1 306 337	−29 195	−2.2		49.0	51.0
1920 (Jan. 1)	2 387 125	311 417	15.0	59	1 051 593	201 299	23.7	1 335 532	110 118	9.0		44.1	55.9
1910 (Apr. 15)	2 075 708	324 314	18.5	48	850 294	252 194	42.2	1 225 414	72 120	6.3		41.0	59.0
1900 (June 1)	1 751 394	441 111	33.7	37	598 100	155 051	35.0	1 153 294	286 060	33.0		34.1	65.9
1890 (June 1)	1 310 283	529 510	67.8	23	443 049	294 291	197.8	867 234	235 219	37.2		33.8	66.2
1880 (June 1)	780 773	341 067	77.6	14	148 758	78 004	110.2	632 015	263 063	71.3		19.1	80.9
1870 (June 1)	439 706	267 683	155.6	11	70 754	54 531	336.1	368 952	213 152	136.8		16.1	83.9
1860 (June 1)	172 023	165 946	1000+	3	16 223	16 223	...	155 800	149 723	1000+		9.4	90.6
1850 (June 1)	6 077	...	...	−	−	...	...	6 077	...	...		−	100.0

NOTE: The Territory of Minnesota in 1850 included a large part of the area of the present States of North and South Dakota and a small part of Nebraska.

AITKIN

1860	2
1870	178
1880	366
1890	2,462
1900	6,743
1910	10,371
1920	15,043
1930	15,009
1940	17,865
1950	14,327
1960	12,162
1970	11,403
1980	13,404

ANOKA

1860	2,106
1870	3,940
1880	7,108
1890	9,884
1900	11,313
1910	12,496
1920	15,626
1930	18,415
1940	22,443
1950	35,579
1960	85,916
1970	154,172
1980	195,998

BECKER

1860	386
1870	308
1880	5,218
1890	9,401
1900	14,375
1910	18,840
1920	22,851
1930	22,503
1940	26,562
1950	24,836
1960	23,959
1970	24,372
1980	29,336

BELTRAMI

1870	80
1880	10
1890	312
1900	11,030
1910	19,337
1920	27,079
1930	20,707
1940	26,107
1950	24,962
1960	23,425
1970	26,373
1980	30,982

BENTON

1850	418
1860	627
1870	1,558
1880	3,012
1890	6,284
1900	9,912
1910	11,615
1920	14,073
1930	15,056
1940	16,106
1950	15,911

1960	17,287
1970	20,841
1980	25,187

BIG STONE

1870	24
1880	3,688
1890	5,722
1900	8,731
1910	9,367
1920	9,766
1930	9,838
1940	10,477
1950	9,607
1960	8,954
1970	7,941
1980	7,716

BLUE EARTH

1860	4,803
1870	17,302
1880	22,889
1890	29,210
1900	32,263
1910	29,337
1920	31,477
1930	33,847
1940	36,203
1950	38,327
1960	44,385
1970	52,322
1980	52,314

BRECKINRIDGE

1860	79

BROWN

1860	2,339
1870	6,396
1880	12,018
1890	15,817
1900	19,787
1910	20,134
1920	22,421
1930	23,428
1940	25,544
1950	25,895
1960	27,676
1970	28,887
1980	28,645

BUCHANAN

1860	26

CARLTON

1860	51
1870	286
1880	1,230
1890	5,272
1900	10,017
1910	17,559
1920	19,391
1930	21,232
1940	24,212
1950	24,584
1960	27,932
1970	28,072
1980	29,936

CARVER

1860	5,106
1870	11,586
1880	14,140
1890	16,532
1900	17,544
1910	17,455
1920	16,946
1930	16,936
1940	17,606
1950	18,155
1960	21,358
1970	28,331
1980	37,046

CASS

1860	150
1870	380
1880	486
1890	1,247
1900	7,777
1910	11,620
1920	15,897
1930	15,591
1940	20,646
1950	19,468
1960	16,720
1970	17,323
1980	21,050

CHIPPEWA

1870	1,467
1880	5,408
1890	8,555
1900	12,499
1910	13,458
1920	15,720
1930	15,762
1940	16,972
1950	16,739
1960	16,320
1970	15,109
1980	14,941

CHISAGO

1860	1,743
1870	4,358
1880	7,982
1890	10,359
1900	13,248
1910	13,537
1920	14,445
1930	13,189
1940	13,124
1950	12,669
1960	13,419
1970	17,492
1980	25,717

CLAY

1870	92
1880	5,887
1890	11,517
1900	17,942
1910	19,640
1920	21,780
1930	23,120
1940	25,337
1950	30,363
1960	39,080
1970	46,608
1980	49,327

CLEARWATER

1910	6,870
1920	8,569
1930	9,546
1940	11,153
1950	10,204
1960	8,864
1970	8,013
1980	8,761

COOK

1880	65
1890	98
1900	810
1910	1,336
1920	1,841
1930	2,435
1940	3,030
1950	2,900
1960	3,377
1970	3,423
1980	4,092

COTTONWOOD

1860	12
1870	534
1880	5,533
1890	7,412
1900	12,069
1910	12.651
1920	14,570
1930	14,482
1940	16,143
1950	15,763
1960	16,166
1970	14,887
1980	14,854

CROW WING

1860	269
1870	200
1880	2,319
1890	8,852
1900	14,250
1910	16,861
1920	24,566
1930	25,627
1940	30,226
1950	30,875
1960	32,134
1970	34,826
1980	41,722

DAKOTA

1850	584
1860	9,093
1870	16,312
1880	17,391
1890	20,240
1900	21,733
1910	25,171
1920	28,967
1930	34,592
1940	39,660
1950	49,019
1960	78,303
1970	139,808
1980	194,279

DODGE

1860	3,797
1870	8,598
1880	11,344
1890	10,864
1900	13,340
1910	12,094
1920	12,552
1930	12,127
1940	12,931
1950	12,624
1960	13,259
1970	13,037
1980	14,773

DOUGLAS

1860	195
1870	4,239
1880	9,130
1890	14,606
1900	17,964
1910	17,699
1920	19,039
1930	18,813
1940	20,369
1950	21,304
1960	21,313
1970	22,910
1980	27,839

FARIBAULT

1860	1,335
1870	9,940
1880	13,016
1890	16,708
1900	22,055
1910	19,949
1920	20,998
1930	21,642
1940	23,941
1950	23,879
1960	23,685
1970	20,986
1980	19,714

FILLMORE

1860	13,542
1870	24,887
1880	28,162
1890	25,966
1900	28,238
1910	25,680
1920	25,330
1930	24,748
1940	25,830
1950	24,465
1960	23,768
1970	21,916
1980	21,930

FREEBORN

1860	3,367
1870	10,578
1880	16,069
1890	17,962
1900	21,838
1910	22,282
1920	24,692
1930	28,741
1940	31,780
1950	34,517

1960	37,891
1970	38,064
1980	36,329

GOODHUE

1860	8,977
1870	22,618
1880	29,651
1890	28,806
1900	31,137
1910	31,637
1920	30,799
1930	31,317
1940	31,564
1950	32,118
1960	33,035
1970	34,804
1980	38,749

GRANT

1870	340
1880	3,004
1890	6,875
1900	8,395
1910	9,144
1920	9,778
1930	9,558
1940	9,828
1950	9,542
1960	8,870
1970	7,462
1980	7,171

HENNEPIN

1860	12,849
1870	31,566
1880	67,013
1890	185,294
1900	228,340
1910	333,480
1920	415,419
1930	517,785
1940	568,899
1950	676,579
1960	842,854
1970	960,080
1980	941,411

HOUSTON

1860	6,645
1870	14,936
1880	16,332
1890	14,653
1900	15,400
1910	14,297
1920	14,013
1930	13,845
1940	14,735
1950	14,435
1960	16,588
1970	17,556
1980	18,382

HUBBARD

1890	1,412
1900	6,578
1910	9,831
1920	10,136
1930	9,596
1940	11,085
1950	11,085
1960	9,962
1970	10,583
1980	14,098

ISANTI

1860	284
1870	2,035
1880	5,063
1890	7,607
1900	11,675
1910	12,615
1920	13,278
1930	12,081
1940	12,950
1950	12,123
1960	13,530
1970	16,650
1980	23,600

ITASCA

1850	97
1860	51
1870	96
1880	124
1890	743
1900	4,573
1910	17,208
1920	23,876
1930	17,224
1940	32,996
1950	33,321
1960	38,006
1970	35,530
1980	43,069

JACKSON

1860	181
1870	1,825
1880	4,806
1890	8,924
1900	14,793
1910	14,491
1920	15,955
1930	15,863
1940	16,805
1950	16,306
1960	15,501
1970	14,352
1980	13,690

KANABEC

1860	30
1870	93
1880	505
1890	1,579
1900	4,614
1910	6,461
1920	9,086
1930	8,558
1940	9,651
1950	9,192
1960	9,007
1970	9,775
1980	12,161

KANDIYOHI

1860	76
1870	1,760
1880	10,159
1890	13,997
1900	18,416
1910	18,969
1920	22,060
1930	23,574
1940	26,524
1950	28,644
1960	29,987
1970	30,548
1980	36,763

KITTSON

1850	1,134
1860	1,612
1870	64
1880	905
1890	5,387
1900	7,889
1910	9,669
1920	10,638
1930	9,688
1940	10,717
1950	9,649
1960	8,343
1970	6,853
1980	6,672

KOOCHICHING

1910	6,431
1920	13,520
1930	14,078
1940	16,930
1950	16,910
1960	18,190
1970	17,131
1980	17,571

LAC QUI PARLE

1870	145
1880	4,891
1890	10,382
1900	14,289
1910	15,435
1920	15,554
1930	15,398
1940	15,509
1950	14,545
1960	13,330
1970	11,164
1980	10,592

LAKE

1860	248
1870	135
1880	106
1890	1,299
1900	4,654
1910	8,011
1920	8,251
1930	7,068
1940	6,956
1950	7,781
1960	13,702
1970	13,351
1980	13,043

LAKE OF THE WOODS

1930	4,194
1940	5,975
1950	4,955
1960	4,304
1970	3,987
1980	3,764

LE SUEUR

1860	5,318
1870	11,607
1880	16,103
1890	19,057
1900	20,234
1910	18,609
1920	17,870
1930	17,990
1940	19,227
1950	19,088
1960	19,906
1970	21,332
1980	23,434

LINCOLN

1880	2,945
1890	5,691
1900	8,966
1910	9,874
1920	11,268
1930	11,303
1940	10,797
1950	10,150
1960	9,651
1970	8,143
1980	8,207

LYON

1880	6,257
1890	9,501
1900	14,591
1910	15,772
1920	18,837
1930	19,326
1940	21,569
1950	22,253
1960	22,655
1970	24,273
1980	25,207

McLEOD

1860	1,286
1870	5,643
1880	12,342
1890	17,026
1900	19,595
1910	18,691
1920	20,444
1930	20,522
1940	21,380
1950	21,198
1960	24,401
1970	27,662
1980	29,657

MANKAHTA

1850	158

MANOMIN

1860	136

MAHNOMEN

1910	3,249
1920	6,197
1930	6,153
1940	8,054
1950	7,059
1960	6,341
1970	5,638
1980	5,535

MARSHALL

1880	992
1890	9,310
1900	15,698
1910	16,338
1920	19,443
1930	17,003
1940	18,364
1950	16,125
1960	14,262
1970	13,060
1980	13,027

MARTIN

1860	151
1870	3,867
1880	5,249
1890	9,403
1900	16,936
1910	17,518
1920	21,085
1930	22,401
1940	24,656
1950	25,655
1960	26,986
1970	24,316
1980	24,687

MEEKER

1860	928
1870	6,090
1880	11,739
1890	15,456
1900	17,753
1910	17,022
1920	18,103
1930	17,914
1940	19,277
1950	18,966
1960	18,887
1970	18,387
1980	20,594

MILLE LACS

1860	73
1870	1,109
1880	1,501
1890	2,845
1900	8,066
1910	10,705
1920	14,180
1930	14,076
1940	15,558
1950	15,165
1960	14,560
1970	15,703
1980	18,430

MONONGALIA

1860	350
1870	3,161

MORRISON

1860	618
1870	1,681
1880	5,875

1890	13,325	**NORMAN**
1900	22,891	
1910	24,053	1890	10,618
1920	25,841	1900	15,045
1930	25,442	1910	13,446
1940	27,473	1920	14,880
1950	25,832	1930	14,061
1960	26,641	1940	14,746
1970	26,949	1950	12,909
1980	29,311	1960	11,253

NORMAN

1890	10,618
1900	15,045
1910	13,446
1920	14,880
1930	14,061
1940	14,746
1950	12,909
1960	11,253
1970	10,008
1980	9,379

MOWER

1860	3,217
1870	10,477
1880	16,799
1890	18,019
1900	22,335
1910	22,640
1920	25,993
1930	28,065
1940	36,113
1950	42,277
1960	48,498
1970	44,919
1980	40,390

OLMSTED

1860	9,524
1870	19,793
1880	21,543
1890	19,806
1900	23,119
1910	22,497
1920	38,014
1930	35,426
1940	42,658
1950	48,228
1960	65,532
1970	84,104
1980	92,006

MURRAY

1860	29
1870	209
1880	3,604
1890	6,692
1900	11,911
1910	11,755
1920	13,631
1930	13,902
1940	15,060
1950	14,801
1960	14,743
1970	12,508
1980	11,507

OTTER TAIL

1860	240
1870	1,968
1880	18,645
1890	34,232
1900	45,375
1910	46,036
1920	50,818
1930	51,006
1940	53,192
1950	51,320
1960	48,960
1970	46,097
1980	51,937

NICOLLET

1860	3,773
1870	8,362
1880	12,333
1890	13,382
1900	14,774
1910	14,125
1920	15,036
1930	16,550
1940	18,282
1950	20,292
1960	23,196
1970	24,518
1980	26,929

PENNINGTON

1910	9,376
1920	12,091
1930	10,487
1940	12,913
1950	12,965
1960	12,468
1970	13,266
1980	15,258

PIERCE

1860	11

NOBLES

1860	35
1870	117
1880	4,435
1890	7,958
1900	14,932
1910	15,210
1920	17,917
1930	18,618
1940	21,215
1950	22,435
1960	23,365
1970	23,208
1980	21,840

PINE

1860	92
1870	648
1880	1,365
1890	4,052
1900	11,546
1910	15,878
1920	21,117
1930	20,264
1940	21,478
1950	18,223
1960	17,004
1970	16,821
1980	19,871

PIPESTONE

1880	2,092
1890	5,132
1900	9,264
1910	9,553
1920	12,050
1930	12,238
1940	13,794
1950	14,003
1960	13,605
1970	12,791
1980	11,690

POLK

1860	240
1880	11,433
1890	30,192
1900	35,429
1910	36,001
1920	37,090
1930	36,019
1940	37,734
1950	35,900
1960	36,182
1970	34,435
1980	34,844

POPE

1870	2,691
1880	5,874
1890	10,034
1900	12,577
1910	12,746
1920	13,631
1930	13,085
1940	13,544
1950	12,862
1960	11,914
1970	11,107
1980	11,657

RAMSEY

1850	2,227
1860	12,150
1870	23,085
1880	45,890
1890	139,796
1900	170,554
1910	223,675
1920	244,554
1930	286,721
1940	309,935
1950	355,332
1960	422,525
1970	476,255
1980	459,784

RED LAKE

1900	12,195
1910	6,564
1920	7,263
1930	6,887
1940	7,413
1950	6,806
1960	5,830
1970	5,388
1980	5,471

REDWOOD

1870	1,829

1880	5,375	
1890	9,386	
1900	17,261	
1910	18,425	
1920	20,908	
1930	20,620	
1940	22,290	
1950	22,127	
1960	21,718	
1970	20,024	
1980	19,341	

RENVILLE

1860	245
1870	3,219
1880	10,791
1890	17,099
1900	23,693
1910	23,123
1920	23,634
1930	23,645
1940	24,625
1950	23,954
1960	23,249
1970	21,139
1980	20,401

RICE

1860	7,543
1870	16,083
1880	22,481
1890	23,968
1900	26,080
1910	25,911
1920	28,307
1930	29,974
1940	32,160
1950	36,235
1960	38,988
1970	41,582
1980	46,087

ROCK

1860	23
1870	138
1880	3,669
1890	6,817
1900	9,668
1910	10,222
1920	10,965
1930	10,962
1940	10,933
1950	11,278
1960	11,864
1970	11,346
1980	10,703

ROSEAU

1900	6,994
1910	11,338
1920	13,305
1930	12,621
1940	15,103
1950	14,505
1960	12,154
1970	11,569
1980	12,574

SAINT LOUIS

1860	406
1870	4,561

1880	4,504	
1890	44,862	
1900	82,932	
1910	163,274	
1920	206,391	
1930	204,596	
1940	206,917	
1950	206,062	
1960	231,588	
1970	220,693	
1980	222,229	

SCOTT

1860	4,595
1870	11,042
1880	13,515
1890	13,831
1900	15,147
1910	14,888
1920	14,245
1930	14,116
1940	15,585
1950	16,486
1960	21,909
1970	32,423
1980	43,784

SHERBURNE

1860	723
1870	2,050
1880	3,855
1890	5,908
1900	7,281
1910	8,136
1920	9,851
1930	9,709
1940	10,456
1950	10,661
1960	12,861
1970	18,344
1980	29,908

SIBLEY

1860	3,609
1870	6,725
1880	10,637
1890	15,199
1900	16,862
1910	15,540
1920	15,635
1930	14,865
1940	16,625
1950	15,816
1960	16,228
1970	15,845
1980	15,448

STEARNS

1860	4,505
1870	14,206
1880	21,956
1890	34,844
1900	44,464
1910	47,733
1920	55,741
1930	62,121
1940	67,200
1950	70,681
1960	80,345
1970	95,400
1980	108,161

STEELE

1860	2,863
1870	8,271
1880	12,460
1890	13,232
1900	16,524
1910	16,146
1920	18,061
1930	18,475
1940	19,749
1950	21,155
1960	25,029
1970	26,931
1980	30,328

STEVENS

1870	174
1880	3,911
1890	5,251
1900	8,721
1910	8,293
1920	9,778
1930	10,185
1940	11,039
1950	11,106
1960	11,262
1970	11,218
1980	11,322

SWIFT

1880	7,473
1890	10,161
1900	13,503
1910	12,949
1920	16,093
1930	14,735
1940	15,469
1950	15,837
1960	14,936
1970	13,177
1980	12,920

TODD

1860	430
1870	2,036
1880	6,133
1890	12,930
1900	22,214
1910	22,407
1920	26,059
1930	26,170
1940	27,438
1950	25,420
1960	23,119
1970	22,114
1980	24,991

TRAVERSE

1870	13
1880	1,507
1890	4,516
1900	7,573
1910	8,049
1920	7,943
1930	7,938
1940	8,283
1950	8,053
1960	7,503
1970	6,254
1980	5,542

WABASHA

1850	243
1860	7,228
1870	15,859
1880	18,206
1890	16,972
1900	18,924
1910	18,554
1920	17,919
1930	17,613
1940	17,653
1950	16,878
1960	17,007
1970	17,224
1980	19,335

WADENA

1870	6
1880	2,080
1890	4,053
1900	7,921
1910	8,652
1920	10,699
1930	10,990
1940	12,772
1950	12,806
1960	12,199
1970	12,412
1980	14,192

WAHUATA

1850	160

WASECA

1860	2,601
1870	7,854
1880	12,385
1890	13,313
1900	14,760
1910	13,466
1920	14,133
1930	14,412
1940	15,186
1950	14,957
1960	16,041
1970	16,663
1980	18,448

WASHINGTON

1850	1,056
1860	6,123
1870	11,809
1880	19,563
1890	25,992
1900	27,808
1910	26,013
1920	23,761
1930	23,753
1940	26,430
1950	34,544
1960	52,432
1970	83,003
1980	113,571

WATONWAN

1870	2,426
1880	5,104
1890	7,746
1900	11,496
1910	11,382

1920	12,457
1930	12,802
1940	13,902
1950	13,881
1960	14,460
1970	13,298
1980	12,361

WILKIN

1860	40
1870	295
1880	1,906
1890	4,346
1900	8,080
1910	9,063
1920	10,187
1930	9,791
1940	10,475
1950	10,567
1960	10,650
1970	9,389
1980	8,454

WINONA

1860	9,208
1870	22,319
1880	27,197
1890	33,797
1900	35,686
1910	33,398
1920	33,653
1930	35,144
1940	37,795
1950	39,841
1960	40,937
1970	44,409
1980	46,256

WRIGHT

1860	3,729
1870	9,457
1880	18,104
1890	24,164
1900	29,157
1910	28,082
1920	28,685
1930	27,119
1940	27,550
1950	27,716
1960	29,935
1970	38,933
1980	58,681

YELLOW MEDICINE

1880	5,884
1890	9,854
1900	14,602
1910	15,406
1920	16,550
1930	16,625
1940	16,917
1950	16,279
1960	15,523
1970	14,523
1980	13,653

NOTES

BRECKENRIDGE

Part taken to form Clay in 1862 and the remainder annexed to Wilkin in 1868.

BUCHANAN

Annexed to Pine prior to 1870.

CLAY

Name changed from Breckenridge in 1862.

KITTSON

Name changed from Pembina in 1878.

MANKAHTA

No records by which to account for its disappearance subsequent to the 1850 census.

MANOMIN

Annexed to Anoka in 1870.

PIERCE

Taken to form Bigstone, Chippewa, Pope, Stevens, and Swift prior to 1870.

MONONGALIA

Annexed to Kandiyohi in 1870.

SAINT LOUIS

Name changed from Superior in 1855.

WAHUATA

No records by which to account for its disappearance subsequent to the 1850 census.

WILKIN

Name changed from Tooms to Andy Johnson in 1858; name changed again to Wilkin in 1868.

ALBERT LEA

1860	262
1870	(NA)
1880	1,966
1890	3,305
1900	4,500
1910	6,192
1920	8,056
1930	10,169
1940	12,200
1950	13,545
1960	17,108
1970	19,418
1980	19,200

ANOKA

1880	2,706
1890	4,252
1900	3,769
1910	3,972
1920	4,287
1930	4,851
1940	6,426
1950	7,396
1960	10,562
1970	13,298
1980	15,634

APPLE VALLEY

1970	8,502
1980	21,818

AUSTIN

1860	200
1870	2,039
1880	2,305
1890	3,901
1900	5,474
1910	6,960
1920	10,118
1930	12,276
1940	18,307
1950	23,100
1960	27,908
1970	26,210
1980	23,020

BEMIDJI

1900	2,183
1910	5,099
1920	7,086
1930	7,202
1940	9,427
1950	10,001
1960	9,958
1970	11,490
1980	10,949

BLAINE

1960	7,570
1970	20,573
1980	28,558

BLOOMINGTON

1960	50,498
1970	81,970
1980	81,831

BRAINERD

1890	5,703
1900	7,524
1910	8,526
1920	9,591
1930	10,221
1940	12,071
1950	12,637
1960	12,898
1970	11,667
1980	11,489

BROOKLYN CENTER

1920	788
1930	1,344
1940	1,870
1950	4,284
1960	24,356
1970	35,173
1980	31,230

BROOKLYN PARK

1960	10,197
1970	26,230
1980	43,332

BURNSVILLE

1970	19,940
1980	35,674

CLOQUET

1890	2,530
1900	3,072
1910	7,031
1920	5,127
1930	6,782
1940	7,304
1950	7,685
1960	9,013
1970	8,699
1980	11,142

COLUMBIA HEIGHTS

1900	123
1910	590
1920	2,968
1930	5,613
1940	6,035
1950	8,175
1960	17,533
1970	23,997
1980	20,029

COON RAPIDS

1960	14,931
1970	30,505
1980	35,826

COTTAGE GROVE

1970	13,419
1980	18,994

CRYSTAL

1920	814
1930	1,865
1940	2,373

1950	5,713
1960	24,283
1970	30,925
1980	25,543

DULUTH

1860	80
1870	3,131
1880	3,483
1890	33,115
1900	52,969
1910	78,466
1920	98,917
1930	101,463
1940	101,065
1950	104,511
1960	106,884
1970	100,578
1980	92,811

EAGAN

1980	20,700

EDEN PRAIRIE

1970	6,938
1980	16,263

EDINA

1890	531
1900	749
1910	1,191
1920	1,833
1930	3,138
1940	5,855
1950	9,744
1960	28,501
1970	44,046
1980	46,073

FAIRMONT

1880	541
1890	1,205
1900	3,040
1910	2,958
1920	4,630
1930	5,521
1940	6,988
1950	8,193
1960	9,745
1970	10,751
1980	11,506

FARIBAULT

1870	3,045
1880	5,415
1890	6,520
1900	7,868
1910	9,001
1920	11,089
1930	12,767
1940	14,527
1950	16,028
1960	16,926
1970	16,595
1980	16,241

FERGUS FALLS

1880	1,635
1890	3,772
1900	6,072
1910	6,887
1920	7,581
1930	9,389
1940	10,848
1950	12,917
1960	13,733
1970	12,443
1980	12,519

FRIDLEY

1950	3,796
1960	15,173
1970	29,233
1980	30,228

GOLDEN VALLEY

1890	509
1900	680
1910	692
1920	830
1930	1,326
1940	2,048
1950	5,551
1960	14,559
1970	24,246
1980	22,775

HASTINGS

1860	11
1870	3,458
1880	3,809
1890	3,705
1900	3,811
1910	3,983
1920	4,571
1930	5,086
1940	5,662
1950	6,560
1960	8,965
1970	12,195
1980	12,827

HIBBING

1900	2,481
1910	8,832
1920	15,089
1930	15,666
1940	16,385
1950	16,276
1960	17,731
1970	16,104
1980	21,193

HOPKINS

1900	1,648
1910	3,022
1920	3,055
1930	3,834
1940	4,100
1950	7,595
1960	11,370
1970	13,428
1980	15,336

INNER GROVE HEIGHTS

1970	12,148
1980	17,171

LAKEVILLE

1900	373
1910	385
1920	474
1930	522
1940	543
1950	628
1960	924
1970	7,556
1980	14,790

MANKATO

1870	3,482
1880	5,550
1890	8,838
1900	10,599
1910	10,365
1920	12,469
1930	14,038
1940	15,654
1950	18,809
1960	23,797
1970	30,895
1980	28,651

MAPLE GROVE

1960	2,213
1970	6,275
1980	20,525

MAPLEWOOD

1960	18,519
1970	25,186
1980	26,990

MARSHALL

1880	961
1890	1,203
1900	2,088
1910	2,152
1920	3,092
1930	3,250
1940	4,590
1950	5,923
1960	6,681
1970	9,886
1980	11,161

MINNEAPOLIS

1860	2,564
1870	13,066
1880	46,887
1890	164,738
1900	202,718
1910	301,408
1920	380,582
1930	464,356
1940	492,370
1950	521,718
1960	482,872
1970	434,400
1980	370,951

MINNETONKA

1960	25,037
1970	35,776
1980	38,683

MOOREHEAD

1890	2,008
1900	3,730
1910	4,840
1920	5,720
1930	7,651
1940	9,491
1950	14,870
1960	22,934
1970	29,687
1980	29,998

MOUNDS VIEW

1960	6,416
1970	10,599
1980	12,593

NEW BRIGHTON

1890	355
1900	350
1910	375
1920	368
1930	500
1940	658
1950	2,218
1960	6,448
1970	19,507
1980	23,269

NEW HOPE

1960	3,552
1970	23,180
1980	23,087

NEW ULM

1860	635
1870	1,310
1880	2,471
1890	3,741
1900	5,403
1910	5,648
1920	6,745
1930	7,308
1940	8,743
1950	9,348
1960	11,114
1970	13,051
1980	13,755

NORTHFIELD

1880	2,296
1890	2,659
1900	3,210
1910	3,265
1920	4,023
1930	4,153
1940	4,533
1950	7,487
1960	8,707
1970	10,235
1980	12,562

NORTH SAINT PAUL

1890	1,099
1900	1,110
1910	1,404
1920	1,979
1930	2,915
1940	3,135
1950	4,248
1960	8,520
1970	11,950
1980	11,921

OAKDALE

1930	1,151
1940	1,578
1950	3,296
1960	(NA)
1970	7,795
1980	12,123

OWATONNA

1870	2,070
1880	3,161
1890	3,849
1900	5,561
1910	5,658
1920	7,252
1930	7,654
1940	8,694
1950	10,191
1960	13,409
1970	15,341
1980	18,632

PLYMOUTH

1960	9,576
1970	18,077
1980	31,615

RAMSEY

1980	10,093

RED WING

1860	1,156
1870	4,260
1880	5,876
1890	6,294
1900	7,525
1910	9,048
1920	8,637
1930	9,629
1940	9,962
1950	10,645
1960	10,528
1970	10,441
1980	13,736

RICHFIELD

1910	2,673
1920	2,411
1930	1,301
1940	3,778
1950	17,502
1960	42,523
1970	47,231
1980	37,851

ROBBINSDALE

1900	520
1910	765
1920	1,369
1930	4,427
1940	6,018
1950	11,289
1960	16,381
1970	16,845
1980	14,422

ROCHESTER

1860	1,424
1870	3,953
1880	5,103
1890	5,321
1900	6,843
1910	7,844
1920	13,722
1930	20,621
1940	26,312
1950	29,885
1960	40,663
1970	53,766
1980	57,890

ROSEVILLE

1950	6,437
1960	23,997
1970	34,518
1980	35,820

SAINT CLOUD

1870	2,161
1880	2,462
1890	7,686
1900	8,663
1910	10,600
1920	15,873
1930	21,000
1940	24,173
1950	28,410
1960	33,815
1970	39,691
1980	42,566

SAINT LOUIS PARK

1890	499
1900	1,325
1910	1,743
1920	2,281
1930	4,710
1940	7,737
1950	22,644
1960	43,310
1970	48,883
1980	42,931

SAINT PAUL

1850	1,112
1860	10,401
1870	20,030
1880	41,473
1890	133,156
1900	163,065
1910	214,744
1920	234,698
1930	271,606
1940	287,736
1950	311,349
1960	313,411
1970	309,866
1980	270,320

SHOREVILLE

1960	7,157
1970	10,978
1980	17,300

SOUTH SAINT PAUL

1890	2,242
1900	2,322
1910	4,510
1920	6,860
1930	10,009
1940	11,844
1950	15,909
1960	22,032
1970	25,016
1980	21,235

STILLWATER

1860	2,380
1870	4,124
1880	9,065
1890	11,260
1900	12,318
1910	10,198
1920	7,735
1930	7,173
1940	7,013
1950	7,674
1960	8,310
1970	10,191
1980	12,290

VIRGINIA

1900	2,962
1910	10,473
1920	14,022
1930	11,963
1940	12,264
1950	12,486
1960	14,034
1970	12,450
1980	11,056

WEST SAINT PAUL

1890	1,596
1900	1,830
1910	2,660
1920	2,962
1930	4,463
1940	5,733
1950	7,955
1960	13,101
1970	18,802
1980	18,527

WHITE BEAR LAKE

1880	435
1890	1,356
1900	1,288
1910	1,505
1920	2,022
1930	2,600
1940	2,858
1950	3,646
1960	12,849
1970	23,313
1980	22,538

WILLMAR

1880	1,002
1890	1,825
1900	3,409
1910	4,135
1920	5,892
1930	6,173
1940	7,623
1950	9,410
1960	10,417
1970	12,869
1980	15,895

WINONA

1860	2,464
1870	7,192
1880	10,208
1890	18,208
1900	19,714
1910	18,583
1920	19,143
1930	20,850
1940	22,490
1950	25,031
1960	24,895
1970	26,438
1980	25,075

WOODBURY

1930	931
1940	954
1950	1,056
1960	(NA)
1970	6,184
1980	10,297

WORTHINGTON

1880	636
1890	1,164
1900	2,386
1910	2,385
1920	3,481
1930	3,878
1940	5,918
1950	7,923
1960	9,015
1970	9,916
1980	10,243

CORRECTION NOTE

The official 1980 census counts of total population shown in this report supersede counts issued previously. Corrections to the figures were made after the counts were provided to the State for redistricting purposes and released in Advance Report PHC80-V for this State.

Shown below are corrections to the 1980 census counts of the total population and total housing units made after the tabulations for this report were completed. Any additional corrections made after this report is printed are available by writing to Data User Services Division, Customer Services (Corrections), Bureau of the Census, Washington, D.C. 20233.

The 1980 figures shown in this publication are subject to change pending the outcome of the various lawsuits dealing with the census counts.

	1980 population	
	As shown in the tables	Corrected
Isanti County:		
Cambridge city......................	3 170	3 287
Cambridge township..................	2 452	2 417
Isanti township.....................	2 204	2 239
St. Louis County:		
Beatty township.....................	423	350
Owens township......................	245	318
Scott County:		
Jackson township....................	1 911	1 483
Spring Lake township................	2 142	2 570

County Subdivisions	1980	1970
The State[1]	4 075 970	r3 806 103
Aitkin County[2]	13 404	11 403
Aitkin city[2]	1 770	1 553
Aitkin township[2]	917	1 107
Ball Bluff township	335	283
Balsam township	43	29
Beaver township	61	50
Clark township	148	158
Cornish township	27	24
Davidson (unorg.)	62	42
Farm Island township	613	517
Fleming township	289	181
Glen township	343	276
Haugen township	150	116
Hazelton township	467	377
Hill City city[2]	533	357
Hill Lake township[2]	429	298
Idun township	202	162
Jevne township	261	212
Jewett (unorg.)	22	23
Kimberly township	220	203
Lakeside township	320	303
Lee township	60	39
Libby township	64	52
Logan township	246	251
McGrath city	81	70
McGregor city	447	331
McGregor township	106	106
Macville township	242	226
Malmo township	218	211
Morrison township	210	222
Nordland township	642	368
Northeast Aitkin (unorg.)	14	20
Northwest Aitkin (unorg.)	335	291
Palisade city	155	149
Pliny township	124	126
Rice River township	151	145
Salo township	126	107
Seavey township	70	60
Shamrock township	820	465
Southeast Aitkin (unorg.)	53	48
Spalding township	216	175
Spencer township	458	374
Tamarack city	83	100
Turner township	122	77
Verdon township	54	75
Wagner township	300	284
Waukenabo township	272	292
Wealthwood township	196	144
White Pine township	49	50
Williams township	126	115
Workman township	152	159
Anoka County[3]	195 998	r154 712
Andover city[3]	9 387	...
Anoka city[3]	15 634	r13 298
Bethel city	272	311
Blaine city (pt.)[3]	28 558	r20 568
Burns township	1 976	1 129
Centerville city	734	534
Circle Pines city[3]	3 321	r3 902
Columbia Heights city	20 029	23 997
Columbus township	3 232	1 999
Coon Rapids city[3]	35 826	30 505
East Bethel city	6 626	2 586
Fridley city[3]	30 228	29 233
Ham Lake city[3]	7 832	...
Hilltop city	817	1 015
Lexington city	2 150	r2 165
Lino Lakes city	4 966	3 692
Linwood township	2 839	1 004
Oak Grove township	3 926	1 674
Ramsey city[3]	10 093	...
St. Francis city	1 184	897
Spring Lake Park city (pt.)	6 368	6 319
Becker County[4]	29 336	24 372
Atlanta township	162	190
Audubon city[4]	383	297
Audubon township[4]	453	297
Burlington township[4]	1 149	706
Callaway city	238	233
Callaway township	355	315
Carsonville township	292	279
Cormorant township	688	409
Cuba township	273	280
Detroit township[4]	2 472	2 340
Detroit Lakes city[4]	7 106	5 797
Erie township	1 290	763
Evergreen township	348	311
Forest township[4]	53	...
Frazee city[4]	1 284	1 015
Green Valley township	312	311
Hamden township	274	298
Height of Land township	681	524
Holmesville township	460	296
Lake Eunice township	1 021	620
Lake Park city	716	658

County Subdivisions	1980	1970
Becker County—Con.		
Lake Park township	500	450
Lake View township[4]	1 915	1 856
Maple Grove township	425	269
Ogema city	215	236
Osage township	583	498
Pine Point township	446	459
Riceville township	143	181
Richwood township	596	476
Round Lake township[4]	169	154
Runeberg township[4]	392	335
Savannah township	121	108
Shell Lake township	300	254
Silver Leaf township	541	442
Spring Creek township	161	184
Spruce Grove township	454	410
Sugar Bush township	392	258
Toad Lake township	500	409
Two Inlets township	219	201
Walworth township	195	212
White Earth township	668	667
Wolf Lake city[4]	67	58
Wolf Lake township[4]	324	219
Beltrami County[5]	30 982	26 373
Alaska township	171	159
Battle township	67	63
Bemidji city[5]	10 949	11 490
Bemidji township[5]	2 270	1 622
Benville township	150	112
Birch township	71	46
Blackduck city	653	595
Brook Lake (unorg.)	183	145
Buzzle township	213	182
Cormant township	220	239
Durand township	158	162
Eckles township	607	352
Frohn township	918	453
Funkley city	18	19
Grant Valley township	868	515
Hagali township	256	152
Hamre township	31	36
Hines township	575	406
Hornet township	219	179
Jones township	219	131
Kelliher city	324	289
Kelliher township	160	122
Lammers township	386	279
Langor township	182	143
Lee township	54	58
Liberty township	342	263
Lower Red Lake (unorg.)	2 855	2 675
Maple Ridge township	117	96
Minnie township	15	19
Moose Lake township	167	93
Nebish township	292	272
North Beltrami (unorg.)	40	48
Northern township[5]	3 211	2 086
O'Brien township	85	73
Port Hope township	388	234
Quiring township	67	71
Roosevelt township	165	165
Shooks township	228	194
Shotley township	64	78
Shotley Brook (unorg.)[5]	18	...
Solway city	89	96
Spruce Grove township	64	82
Steenerson township	52	50
Sugar Bush township	121	53
Summit township	205	180
Taylor township[5]	92	...
Ten Lake township	496	231
Tenstrike city	159	138
Turtle Lake township	713	426
Turtle River city	60	50
Turtle River township	526	237
Upper Red Lake (unorg.)[5]	37	r101
Waskish township	133	r138
Wilton city	176	119
Woodrow township	83	82
Benton County[6]	25 187	20 841
Alberta township	757	r805
Foley city[6]	1 606	1 271
Gilman city[6]	156	111
Gilmanton township[6]	861	r867
Glendorado township	765	726
Graham township	579	543
Granite Ledge township	581	609
Langola township	714	338
Mayhew Lake township	743	715
Maywood township	817	855
Minden township[6]	1 828	1 307
Rice city	499	366
Ronneby city	56	59
St. Cloud city (pt.)[6]	4 645	4 180
St. George township	959	888
Sartell city (pt.)[6]	1 227	264

County Subdivisions

County Subdivisions	1980	1970
Benton County—Con.		
Sauk Rapids city[6]	5 793	5 051
Sauk Rapids township[6]	758	1 064
Watab township	1 843	1 086
Big Stone County[7]	7 716	7 941
Akron township	306	353
Almond township[7]	238	232
Artichoke township	137	163
Barry city	43	52
Big Stone township	395	349
Ortonville city (pt.)[7]	2	2
Browns Valley township	565	641
Beardsley city	344	366
Clinton city[7]	622	608
Correll city	83	95
Foster township	233	192
Graceville city[7]	780	735
Graceville township[7]	211	281
Malta township	145	192
Moonshine township	226	211
Johnson city	57	53
Odessa city	177	194
Odessa township	209	227
Ortonville township	2 745	2 841
Ortonville city (pt.)[7]	2 548	2 663
Otrey township	147	165
Prior township	332	264
Toqua township	122	146
Blue Earth County[8]	52 314	52 322
Amboy city[8]	606	571
Beauford township	509	534
Butternut Valley township	398—	437
Cambria township	319	278
Ceresco township	315	356
Danville township	332	350
Decoria township	864	763
Eagle Lake city[8]	1 470	839
Garden City township	788	785
Good Thunder city	560	489
Jamestown township[8]	448	282
Judson township	727	602
Lake Crystal city	2 078	1 807
Le Ray township	722	870
Lime township[8]	1 101	1 078
Lincoln township	305	376
Lyra township	405	481
McPherson township[8]	476	574
Madison Lake city[8]	592	587
Mankato city (pt.)[8]	28 642	30 895
Mankato township[8]	2 752	1 952
Mapleton city	1 516	1 307
Mapleton township	378	395
Medo township[8]	426	461
Pemberton city[8]	208	128
Pleasant Mound township	335	413
Rapidan township	1 060	872
St. Clair city[8]	655	488
Shelby township[8]	357	409
Skyline city	399	400
South Bend township[8]	1 514	1 397
Sterling township	315	368
Vernon Center city	365	347
Vernon Center township	377	404
Brown County[9]	28 645	28 887
Albin township	444	441
Bashaw township	356	390
Burnstown township	350	386
Cobden city	72	113
Comfrey city (pt.)	508	512
Cottonwood township[9]	946	922
Eden township	416	483
Evan city	90	126
Hanska city[9]	429	442
Home township[9]	792	821
Lake Hanska township[9]	474	528
Leavenworth township	509	576
Linden township	436	501
Milford township[9]	754	758
Mulligan township	369	491
New Ulm city[9]	13 755	13 051
North Star township	395	421
Prairieville township	401	487
Sigel township	527	629
Sleepy Eye city[9]	3 581	3 461
Springfield city	2 303	2 530
Stark township	462	493
Stately township	276	325
Carlton County[10]	29 936	28 072
Atkinson township	302	251
Automba township	204	166
Barnum city[10]	464	382
Barnum township[10]	756	699
Beseman township	106	97
Blackhoof township	573	548
Carlton city	862	884

County Subdivisions	1980	1970
Carlton County—Con.		
Clear Creek (unorg.)	134	83
Cloquet city[10]	11 142	8 699
Cromwell city	229	181
Holyoke city	226	149
Kalevala township	312	369
Kettle River city	174	173
Lakeview township	169	137
Mahtowa township	511	465
Moose Lake city[10]	1 408	1 400
Moose Lake township[10]	1 237	1 170
North Carlton (unorg.)	1 362	1 794
Perch Lake township[10]	730	...
Scanlon city	1 050	1 132
Silver township	411	363
Silver Brook township	511	503
Skelton township	355	300
Split Rock township	182	206
Thomson city	152	159
Thomson township	3 962	3 322
Twin Lakes township	1 595	1 171
Wrenshall city	333	147
Wrenshall township	322	250
Wright city	162	132
Carver County[11]	37 046	28 331
Benton township[11]	939	987
Camden township[11]	898	895
Carver city	642	669
Chanhassen city (pt.)[11]	6 351	4 839
Chaska city[11]	8 346	4 352
Chaska township[11]	205	119
Cologne city[11]	545	518
Dahlgren township	1 225	1 147
Hamburg city[11]	475	405
Hancock township	391	402
Hollywood township[11]	1 100	1 064
Laketown township[11]	2 424	1 750
Mayer city[11]	388	325
New Germany city[11]	347	303
Norwood city[11]	1 219	1 058
San Francisco township	650	509
Victoria city[11]	1 425	850
Waconia city[11]	2 638	2 445
Waconia township[11]	1 402	1 389
Watertown city[11]	1 818	1 390
Watertown township[11]	1 429	1 348
Young America city[11]	1 237	611
Young America township[11]	952	956
Cass County[12]	21 050	17 323
Ansel township	116	116
Backus city	255	257
Barclay township[12]	440	316
Becker township	355	217
Bena city	153	169
Beulah township	42	21
Birch Lake township[12]	388	268
Blind Lake township	75	51
Boy Lake township	117	117
Boy River city	50	44
Boy River township	111	87
Bull Moose township	90	80
Bungo township	98	118
Byron township	164	166
Cass Lake city	1 001	1 317
Chickamaw Beach city	124	87
Crooked Lake township	346	237
Deerfield township	91	69
East Cass (unorg.)	62	30
East Gull Lake city	586	440
Fairview township	311	135
Federal Dam city	192	147
Gould township	189	131
Hackensack city[12]	285	220
Hiram township	186	157
Home Brook township	168	173
Inguadona township	124	57
Kego township	321	188
Lake Shore city	583	410
Leech Lake township	264	188
Lima township	98	111
Longville city[12]	191	171
Loon Lake township	209	183
McKinley township	144	112
Maple township	251	263
May township	520	512
Meadow Brook township	155	159
Moose Lake township	123	119
Motley city (pt.)	2	...
North Cass (unorg.)	407	317
Pike Bay township	1 211	883
Pillager city	341	374
Pine Lake township	168	165
Pine River city[12]	881	803
Pine River township	637	384
Ponto Lake township	384	271
Poplar township	217	207

County Subdivisions	1980	1970
Cass County—Con.		
Powers township	542	386
Remer city	396	403
Remer township	190	148
Rogers township	57	67
Salem township	86	78
Shingobee township	1 472	1 275
Slater township	201	134
Smoky Hollow township	79	51
Sylvan township	846	465
Thunder Lake township	194	119
Torrey township	146	106
Trelipe township	144	113
Turtle Lake township	469	317
Wabedo township	273	157
Wahnena township	190	139
Walden township	374	344
Walker city	970	1 073
Wilkinson township	277	195
Wilson township	469	432
Woodrow township	449	274
Chippewa County[13]	14 941	15 109
Big Bend township	378	370
Clara City city[13]	1 574	1 491
Crate township	310	407
Grace township	257	297
Granite Falls city (pt.)[13]	785	643
Granite Falls township[13]	299	328
Havelock township	249	285
Kragero township[13]	244	229
Leenthrop township	334	334
Lone Tree township	321	358
Louriston township	278	333
Mandt township	251	314
Maynard city	428	455
Milan city[13]	417	427
Montevideo city[13]	5 845	5 661
Rheiderland township	382	495
Rosewood township	379	420
Sparta township[13]	1 060	1 063
Stoneham township[13]	360	395
Tunsberg township[13]	226	244
Watson city[13]	238	228
Woods township	326	332
Chisago County[14]	25 717	17 492
Amador township	593	562
Branch city	1 866	880
Center City city[14]	458	324
Chisago City city[14]	1 634	1 068
Chisago Lake township[14]	2 629	2 319
Fish Lake township	1 074	819
Franconia township	1 007	650
Harris city	678	559
Lent township[14]	1 380	556
Lindstrom city[14]	1 972	1 260
Nessel township	1 460	1 102
North Branch city	1 597	1 106
Rush City city[14]	1 198	1 130
Rushseba township[14]	732	722
Shafer city[14]	180	149
Shafer township[14]	768	636
Stacy city[14]	996	278
Sunrise township	1 001	828
Taylors Falls city	623	587
Wyoming city[14]	1 559	695
Wyoming township[14]	2 312	1 262
Clay County[15]	49 327	'46 608
Alliance township	308	358
Barnesville city[15]	2 207	1 782
Barnesville township[15]	203	200
Comstock city	110	135
Cromwell township	307	294
Dilworth city[15]	2 585	2 321
Eglon township	461	379
Elkton township	324	301
Elmwood township[15]	459	437
Felton city	264	232
Felton township	140	183
Flowing township	111	106
Georgetown city	124	141
Georgetown township	237	263
Glyndon city	882	674
Glyndon township	356	350
Goose Prairie township	221	283
Hagen township	225	171
Hawley city[15]	1 634	1 371
Hawley township[15]	379	243
Highland Grove township	343	348
Hitterdal city	253	'201
Holy Cross township	160	220
Humboldt township[15]	273	233
Keene township	161	178
Kragnes township	406	342
Kurtz township	318	262
Moland township	360	352
Moorhead city[15]	29 998	29 687

County Subdivisions	1980	1970
Clay County—Con.		
Moorhead township[15]	702	629
Morken township	203	226
Oakport township[15]	1 714	1 265
Parke township	368	354
Riverton township	466	258
Sabin city[15]	446	333
Skree township	174	191
Spring Prairie township	313	227
Tansem township	229	208
Ulen city	514	486
Ulen township	240	212
Viding township	149	172
Clearwater County[16]	8 761	8 013
Bagley city[16]	1 321	1 314
Bear Creek township	152	128
Clearbrook city[16]	579	599
Clover township	111	95
Copley township[16]	921	893
Dudley township	306	248
Eddy township	350	310
Falk township	323	283
Gonvick city	362	344
Greenwood township	102	105
Hangaard township	22	21
Holst township	333	261
Itasca township	159	86
La Prairie township	363	318
Leon township[16]	365	362
Leonard city	50	54
Minerva township	289	258
Moose Creek township	211	148
Nora township	407	389
North Clearwater (unorg.)	65	45
Pine Lake township	370	355
Popple township	469	399
Rice township	136	141
Shevlin city	193	185
Shevlin township	367	291
Sinclair township	204	160
South Clearwater (unorg.)	36	21
Winsor township	195	200
Cook County[17]	4 092	3 423
East Cook (unorg.)	475	480
Grand Marais city	1 289	1 301
Grand Portage (unorg.)[17]	324	...
Schroeder township[17]	325	...
Tofte township[17]	275	...
West Cook (unorg.)[17]	1 404	1 642
Cottonwood County[18]	14 854	14 887
Amboy township	296	338
Amo township	281	280
Ann township	321	374
Bingham Lake city	222	214
Carson township	437	488
Comfrey city (pt.)	40	13
Dale township	260	317
Delton township	215	272
Germantown township	344	349
Great Bend township[18]	708	1 034
Highwater township	276	288
Jeffers city	437	436
Lakeside township	372	405
Midway township[18]	395	495
Mountain Lake city[18]	2 277	1 986
Mountain Lake township[18]	284	365
Rose Hill township	277	314
Selma township	290	365
Southbrook township	177	219
Springfield township	264	305
Storden city	341	364
Storden township	343	357
Westbrook city[18]	978	990
Westbrook township[18]	353	367
Windom city[18]	4 666	3 952
Crow Wing County[19]	41 722	34 826
Baxter city	2 625	1 556
Bay Lake township	719	474
Brainerd city[19]	11 489	11 667
Breezy Point city[19]	384	233
Center township	470	317
Crosby city[19]	2 218	2 241
Crosslake city[19]	1 064	358
Crow Wing township[19]	687	560
Cuyuna city[19]	157	82
Daggett Brook township	458	407
Dean Lake township	72	83
Deerwood city	580	448
Deerwood township	952	815
Emily city	588	386
Fairfield township	267	237
Fifty Lakes city	263	143
Fort Ripley city[19]	83	54
Fort Ripley township[19]	450	336
Gail Lake township	106	82
Garrison city[19]	174	125

County Subdivisions

County Subdivisions	1980	1970
Crow Wing County—Con.		
Garrison township[19]	498	321
Ideal township[19]	760	345
Irondale township[19]	949	879
Riverton city	112	103
Ironton city[19]	537	562
Jenkins city[19]	219	148
Jenkins township[19]	317	189
Lake Edwards township	1 442	1 187
Little Pine township	103	80
Long Lake township	877	699
Manhattan Beach city	60	46
Maple Grove township	459	319
Mission township	527	319
Nisswa city	1 407	1 011
Nokay Lake township	530	507
Oak Lawn township[19]	2 093	2 201
Pelican township[19]	267	144
Pequot Lakes city[19]	681	499
Perry Lake township	186	190
Platte Lake township	277	250
Rabbit Lake township	184	151
Roosevelt township	404	296
Ross Lake township	109	72
St. Mathias township	440	398
Sibley township[19]	557	341
Timothy township	119	131
Trommald city	84	82
West Crow Wing (unorg.)[19]	3 655	2 425
Wolford township[19]	175	68
Dakota County[20]	194 279	139 808
Apple Valley city	21 818	8 502
Burnsville city	35 674	19 940
Castle Rock township[20]	1 340	1 235
Coates city	207	212
Douglas township	614	552
Eagan city[20]	20 700	...
Empire township[20]	1 224	1 136
Eureka township	1 268	860
Farmington city[20]	4 370	3 104
Greenvale township[20]	641	624
Hampton city	299	369
Hampton township	848	595
Hastings city (pt.)[20]	12 811	12 179
Inver Grove Heights city	17 171	12 148
Lakeville city[20]	14 790	7 556
Lilydale city[20]	417	322
Marshan township[20]	1 655	1 186
Mendota city	219	266
Mendota Heights city[20]	7 288	6 565
Miesville city	179	192
New Trier city	115	153
Nininger township[20]	774	554
Northfield city (pt.)[20]	13	...
Randolph city	351	350
Randolph township	385	267
Ravenna township	1 683	550
Rosemount city[20]	5 083	1 337
Sciota township	242	213
South St. Paul city	21 235	25 016
Sunfish Lake city	344	269
Vermillion city	438	359
Vermillion township	1 070	779
Waterford township[20]	486	521
West St. Paul city	18 527	18 802
Dodge County[21]	14 773	13 037
Ashland township	421	424
Canisteo township[21]	608	599
Claremont city	591	520
Claremont township	449	495
Concord township[21]	659	727
Dodge Center city[21]	1 816	1 603
Ellington township	363	468
Hayfield city[21]	1 243	939
Hayfield township[21]	380	456
Kasson city[21]	2 827	1 883
Mantorville city	705	479
Mantorville township[21]	1 013	813
Milton township	720	685
Ripley township	230	272
Vernon township	631	580
Wasioja township[21]	859	849
West Concord city[21]	762	718
Westfield township	496	527
Douglas County[22]	27 839	22 910
Alexandria city[22]	7 608	6 973
Alexandria township[22]	3 521	2 512
Belle River township	432	446
Brandon city	473	414
Brandon township	555	445
Carlos city	364	278
Carlos township	1 354	912
Evansville city[22]	571	553
Evansville township[22]	270	320
Forada city	191	158
Garfield city[22]	284	198

County Subdivisions

County Subdivisions	1980	1970
Douglas County—Con.		
Holmes City township	595	489
Hudson township	585	401
Ida township[22]	720	490
Kensington city[22]	331	308
La Grand township[22]	3 080	1 863
Lake Mary township	880	611
Leaf Valley township	541	446
Lund township	323	315
Millerville city	124	109
Millerville township	376	380
Miltona city[22]	187	172
Miltona township[22]	617	463
Moe township	495	372
Nelson city	209	175
Orange township	355	320
Osakis city (pt.)[22]	1 267	1 237
Osakis township[22]	555	520
Solem township[22]	303	325
Spruce Hill township	433	459
Urness township	240	246
Faribault County[23]	19 714	20 896
Barber township	431	513
Blue Earth city[23]	4 132	3 965
Blue Earth City township[23]	522	605
Bricelyn city[23]	487	470
Brush Creek township	297	375
Clark township[23]	510	644
Delavan city[23]	262	281
Delavan township	339	304
Dunbar township	422	493
Easton city[23]	283	352
Elmore city[23]	882	910
Elmore township	311	371
Emerald township	330	373
Foster township	373	451
Frost city[23]	293	290
Jo Daviess township	370	435
Kiester city[23]	670	681
Kiester township[23]	349	486
Lura township	302	366
Minnesota Lake city[23]	744	711
Minnesota Lake township	322	378
Pilot Grove township	246	359
Prescott township	308	369
Rome township	284	320
Seely township	297	377
Verona township	476	500
Walnut Lake township	362	431
Walters city[23]	118	152
Wells city[23]	2 777	2 791
Winnebago city	1 869	1 791
Winnebago City township	346	352
Fillmore County[24]	21 930	21 916
Amherst township	365	406
Arendahl township	366	355
Beaver township	294	318
Bloomfield township	454	489
Bristol township	455	530
Canton city[24]	386	391
Canton township[24]	581	563
Carimona township[24]	358	356
Carrolton township	377	387
Chatfield city (pt.)[24]	1 160	1 162
Chatfield township[24]	479	430
Fillmore township	561	599
Forestville township	478	476
Fountain city[24]	327	347
Fountain township	381	414
Harmony city[24]	1 133	1 130
Harmony township[24]	427	419
Holt township[24]	309	333
Jordan township	371	373
Lanesboro city[24]	923	850
Mabel city	861	888
Newburg township	502	560
Norway township	418	443
Ostrander city	293	268
Peterson city	291	269
Pilot Mound township	379	366
Preble township	311	320
Preston city[24]	1 478	1 413
Preston township[24]	340	374
Rushford city	1 478	1 318
Rushford Village city[24]	688	601
Spring Valley city[24]	2 616	2 572
Spring Valley township[24]	582	658
Sumner township	499	497
Whalan city	119	114
Wykoff city	482	450
York township	408	477
Freeborn County[25]	36 329	38 064
Albert Lea city[25]	19 200	19 418
Albert Lea township[25]	1 675	2 327
Alden city	687	713
Alden township	434	469
Bancroft township[25]	1 395	1 392

County Subdivisions

County Subdivisions	1980	1970
Freeborn County—Con.		
Bath township[25]	603	654
Carlston township	417	446
Clarks Grove city[25]	620	480
Conger city[25]	183	167
Emmons city[25]	465	412
Freeborn city[25]	323	296
Freeborn township[25]	421	489
Freeman township	588	648
Geneva city[25]	417	358
Geneva township[25]	574	609
Glenville city	851	740
Hartland city	322	331
Hartland township	333	419
Hayward city	294	261
Hayward township	491	638
Hollandale city	290	287
London township	419	511
Manchester city[25]	96	89
Manchester township[25]	510	610
Mansfield township	412	420
Moscow township	661	823
Myrtle city	86	83
Newry township	601	596
Nunda township[25]	414	502
Oakland township	490	540
Pickerel Lake township[25]	691	817
Riceland township	577	695
Shell Rock township	579	594
Twin Lakes city	210	230
Goodhue County[26]	38 749	34 804
Bellechester city (pt.)	157	130
Belle Creek township	518	628
Belvidere township	522	560
Cannon Falls city[26]	2 653	2 072
Cannon Falls township[26]	1 373	1 023
Cherry Grove township	435	459
Dennison city	176	'203
Featherstone township	800	646
Florence township[26]	1 123	796
Goodhue city[26]	657	539
Goodhue township[26]	576	554
Hay Creek township[26]	751	665
Holden township	504	466
Kenyon city	1 529	1 575
Kenyon township	472	500
Lake City city (pt.)[26]	470	...
Leon township	902	683
Minneola township[26]	684	648
Pine Island city (pt.)	1 977	1 640
Pine Island township[26]	634	559
Red Wing city[26]	13 736	10 441
Roscoe township	735	674
Stanton township	918	722
Vasa township	847	784
Wacouta township	350	252
Wanamingo city	717	574
Wanamingo township	511	498
Warsaw township	591	659
Welch township	689	529
Zumbrota city[26]	2 129	1 929
Zumbrota township[26]	613	627
Grant County[27]	7 171	7 462
Ashby city	486	415
Barrett city	388	342
Delaware township	172	212
Elbow Lake city	1 358	1 484
Elbow Lake township	198	197
Elk Lake township	302	299
Erdahl township	356	350
Gorton township	115	158
Herman city	600	619
Hoffman city[27]	631	627
Land township[27]	272	310
Lawrence township	127	146
Lien township	188	188
Logan township	174	188
Macsville township	194	219
Norcross city	124	137
North Ottawa township	118	138
Pelican Lake township	356	309
Pomme de Terre township	212	202
Roseville township	212	231
Sanford township	191	233
Stony Brook township	181	211
Wendell city	216	247
Hennepin County[28]	941 411	960 080
Bloomington city	81 831	81 970
Brooklyn Center city	31 230	35 173
Brooklyn Park city	43 332	26 230
Champlin city[28]	9 006	2 275
Chanhassen city (pt.)	8	40
Corcoran city	4 252	1 656
Crystal city	25 543	30 925
Dayton city (pt.)[28]	4 000	469
Deephaven city	3 716	3 853
Eden Prairie city	16 263	6 938

County Subdivisions	1980	1970
Hennepin County—Con.		
Edina city	46 073	44 046
Excelsior city	2 523	2 563
Fort Snelling (unorg.)[28]	223	624
Golden Valley city	22 775	24 246
Greenfield city[28]	1 391	977
Greenwood city	653	587
Hanover city (pt.)	248	96
Hassan township[28]	1 766	917
Hopkins city[28]	15 336	13 428
Independence city[28]	2 640	1 993
Long Lake city	1 747	1 506
Loretto city	297	340
Maple Grove city	20 525	6 275
Maple Plain city	1 421	1 169
Medicine Lake city	419	'446
Medina city	2 623	2 396
Minneapolis city	370 951	434 400
Minnetonka city[28]	38 683	35 776
Minnetonka Beach city	575	586
Minnetrista city	3 236	2 878
Mound city	9 280	7 572
New Hope city	23 087	23 180
Orono city[28]	6 845	6 787
Osseo city	2 974	2 908
Plymouth city[28]	31 615	'18 077
Richfield city	37 851	47 231
Robbinsdale city	14 422	16 845
Rockford city (pt.)[28]	380	162
Rogers city[28]	652	544
St. Anthony city (pt.)	5 619	6 886
St. Bonifacius city	857	685
St. Louis Park city	42 931	48 883
Shorewood city	4 646	4 223
Spring Park city	1 465	1 087
Tonka Bay city	1 354	1 397
Wayzata city[28]	3 621	3 700
Woodland city	526	544
Houston County[29]	18 382	17 556
Black Hammer township	356	323
Brownsville city	418	417
Brownsville township	362	358
Caledonia city	2 691	2 619
Caledonia township	528	585
Crooked Creek township	327	304
Eitzen city	226	208
Hokah city	686	697
Hokah township	562	356
Houston city[29]	1 057	1 090
Houston township[29]	468	407
Jefferson township	174	206
La Crescent city[29]	3 674	'3 296
La Crescent township[29]	1 441	'1 332
Mayville township	504	535
Money Creek township	525	479
Mound Prairie township	549	432
Sheldon township	307	361
Spring Grove city[29]	1 275	1 290
Spring Grove township[29]	566	539
Union township	422	403
Wilmington township	558	590
Winnebago township	355	361
Yucatan township	351	368
Hubbard County[30]	14 098	10 583
Akeley city	486	468
Akeley township	414	236
Arago township	385	286
Badoura township	98	105
Clay (unorg.)	71	46
Clover township	97	107
Crow Wing Lake township	191	130
Farden township	576	395
Fern township	152	117
Guthrie township	404	257
Hart Lake township	351	247
Helga township	767	430
Hendrickson township	198	123
Henrietta township	1 194	747
Hubbard township	600	395
Lake Alice township	91	87
Lake Emma township	550	375
Lake George township	319	226
Lake Hattie township	84	74
Lakeport township	436	281
Laporte city	160	154
Mantrap township	213	193
Nevis city	332	308
Nevis township	644	406
Park Rapids city[30]	2 976	2 772
Rockwood township	269	103
Schoolcraft township	58	39
Steamboat River township[30]	74	57
Straight River township	535	369
Thorpe township	24	27
Todd township[30]	1 070	803
White Oak township	279	220

County Subdivisions	1980	1970
Isanti County[31]	23 600	16 560
Athens township	1 793	849
Bradford township	2 370	912
Braham city	1 015	744
Cambridge city[31]	3 170	r2 720
Cambridge township[31]	2 452	r2 174
Dalbo township	665	595
Isanti city[31]	858	679
Isanti township[31]	2 204	1 647
Maple Ridge township	722	655
North Branch township	1 507	960
Oxford township	554	342
Spencer Brook township	1 146	666
Springvale township	1 046	817
Stanchfield township	1 077	951
Stanford township	1 592	922
Wyanett township	1 429	927
Itasca County[32]	43 069	35 530
Alvwood township	78	52
Arbo township	784	721
Ardenhurst township	160	132
Balsam township[32]	507	274
Bass Brook township[32]	1 871	961
Bearville township	115	99
Bigfork city	457	399
Bigfork township	308	295
Blackberry township	627	420
Bovey city	813	858
Bowstring township	283	125
Bowstring Lake (unorg.)	970	863
Carpenter township	236	252
Coleraine city	1 116	1 086
Deer Lake (unorg.)	2 733	1 317
Deer River city	907	815
Deer River township	541	437
Effie city	141	165
Effie (unorg.)[32]	279	...
Feeley township	320	296
Good Hope township	136	86
Goodland township	526	414
Grand Rapids township	11 649	10 323
Grand Rapids city[32]	7 934	7 247
La Prairie city	536	413
Grattan township	50	51
Greenway township[32]	2 382	2 207
Calumet city	469	460
Marble city	757	682
Harris township	3 007	1 883
Iron Range township	625	637
Taconite city[32]	331	352
Keewatin city	1 443	1 382
Kinghurst township	151	150
Lake Jessie township	278	229
Lawrence township	487	440
Liberty township	59	70
Little Sand Lake (unorg.)	438	317
Lone Pine township[32]	592	468
Marcell township	353	274
Max township	155	134
Moose Park township	86	80
Morse township	606	416
Nashwauk township[32]	2 231	2 139
Nashwauk city	1 419	1 341
Nore township	77	59
Northeast Itasca (unorg.)[32]	1 176	1 130
Oteneagen township	206	173
Pomroy township	54	41
Sago township	174	149
Sand Lake township	158	132
South Itasca (unorg.)	426	303
Spang township	203	139
Squaw Lake city	162	113
Stokes township	265	171
Third River township	56	43
Trout Lake township	836	636
Wabana township	354	199
Warba city	150	148
Wawina township	128	93
Wirt township	82	94
Zemple city	62	71
Jackson County[33]	13 690	14 352
Alba township	279	371
Alpha city	180	179
Belmont township	317	349
Christiania township	408	404
Delafield township	333	419
Des Moines township[33]	429	453
Enterprise township	328	358
Ewington township	366	425
Heron Lake city[33]	783	777
Heron Lake township[33]	512	483
Hunter township	363	436
Jackson city[33]	3 797	3 550
Kimball township	223	297
La Crosse township	295	350
Lakefield city[33]	1 845	1 820

County Subdivisions	1980	1970
Jackson County—Con.		
Middletown township	338	386
Minneota township	350	370
Okabena city	263	237
Petersburg township	386	446
Rost township	310	417
Round Lake township	293	361
Sioux Valley township	371	405
Weimer township[33]	288	285
West Heron Lake township	196	278
Wilder city	120	132
Wisconsin township[33]	317	364
Kanabec County[34]	12 161	9 775
Ann Lake township	226	193
Arthur township[34]	1 435	957
Brunswick township	978	765
Comfort township	756	569
Ford township	137	131
Grass Lake township	944	769
Grasston city	123	132
Hay Brook township	206	108
Hillman township	311	233
Kanabec township	656	423
Knife Lake township	727	557
Kroschel township	216	216
Mora city[34]	2 890	2 582
Ogilvie city	423	384
Peace township	485	386
Pomroy township	342	281
Quamba city[34]	122	114
South Fork township	568	526
Whited township[34]	616	449
Kandiyohi County[35]	36 763	30 548
Arctander township	422	412
Atwater city[35]	1 128	956
Blomkest city	200	172
Burbank township	406	359
Colfax township	490	378
Dovre township[35]	1 450	797
East Lake Lillian township[35]	283	368
Edwards township[35]	368	406
Fahlun township	358	398
Gennessee township[35]	430	366
Green Lake township[35]	1 287	912
Harrison township	596	537
Holland township	445	454
Irving township	699	478
Kandiyohi city[35]	447	295
Kandiyohi township[35]	702	591
Lake Andrew township	656	503
Lake Elizabeth township	320	342
Lake Lillian city[35]	329	316
Lake Lillian township	283	345
Mamre township	402	369
New London city[35]	812	736
New London township[35]	2 289	1 347
Norway Lake township	360	345
Pennock city	410	255
Prinsburg city	557	448
Raymond city[35]	723	589
Regal city	70	44
Roseland township	519	572
Roseville township	541	446
St. Johns township	499	433
Spicer city[35]	909	586
Sunburg city	130	144
Whitefield township	531	560
Willmar city[35]	15 895	12 869
Willmar township[35]	817	1 420
Kittson County[36]	6 672	6 853
Arveson township[26]	93	87
Cannon township	30	43
Caribou township	39	78
Clow township	49	104
Davis township	77	68
Deerwood township[36]	248	180
Donaldson city	84	69
East Kittson (unorg.)	15	19
Granville township	129	114
Hallock city[36]	1 405	1 477
Hallock township[36]	115	119
Halma city	97	96
Hampden township	64	84
Hazelton township[36]	111	130
Hill township	41	63
Humboldt city	111	112
Jupiter township	181	203
Karlstad city[36]	934	727
Kennedy city[36]	405	424
Lake Bronson city[36]	298	325
Lancaster city	368	382
McKinley township	36	60
North Red River township	31	51
Norway township	103	90
Pelan township	58	51
Percy township	69	54

County Subdivisions

County Subdivisions	1980	1970
Kittson County—Con.		
Poppleton township	167	136
Richardville township	171	162
St. Joseph township	90	101
St. Vincent city[36]	141	177
St. Vincent township[36]	127	192
Skane township[36]	76	88
South Red River township	33	57
Spring Brook township	117	121
Svea township	72	72
Tegner township	75	91
Teien township	183	220
Thompson township	229	226
Koochiching County[37]	17 571	17 131
Big Falls city	490	534
East Koochiching (unorg.)[37]	498	...
International Falls city[37]	5 611	6 439
Island View city	101	44
Littlefork city[37]	918	824
Mizpah city	129	118
Nett Lake (unorg.)[37]	77	...
Northome city[37]	312	351
Northome (unorg.)[37]	597	...
Northwest Koochiching (unorg.)	639	600
Rainy Lake (unorg.)[37]	4 793	...
Ranier city	237	255
South International Falls city[37]	2 806	2 116
South Koochiching (unorg.)[37]	363	900
Lac qui Parle County[38]	10 592	11 164
Agassiz township	153	228
Arena township	208	267
Augusta township[38]	177	212
Baxter township	285	314
Bellingham city[38]	290	263
Boyd city	329	311
Camp Release township	285	331
Cerro Gordo township	274	298
Dawson city[38]	1 901	1 699
Freeland township	200	252
Garfield township	210	255
Hamlin township	296	306
Hantho township	152	189
Lac qui Parle township	260	249
Lake Shore township	336	347
Louisburg city	52	75
Madison city[38]	2 212	2 242
Madison township[38]	370	427
Manfred township	174	203
Marietta city	279	264
Maxwell township	242	272
Mehurin township	164	214
Nassau city[38]	115	126
Perry township[38]	216	257
Providence township	253	312
Riverside township[38]	359	297
Ten Mile Lake township	253	279
Walter township	266	299
Yellow Bank township[38]	281	376
Lake County[39]	13 043	13 351
Beaver Bay city	283	362
Beaver Bay township	1 066	905
Crystal Bay township	760	824
East Lake (unorg.)	139	152
Fall Lake township[39]	522	328
Silver Bay city	2 917	3 504
Silver Creek township	1 175	923
Two Harbors city	4 039	4 437
Two Harbors (unorg.)[39]	1 976	...
West Lake (unorg.)[39]	166	1 916
Lake of the Woods County[40]	3 764	3 987
Baudette city	1 170	1 547
Beltrami Forest (unorg.)	74	95
Northwest Angle (unorg.)	71	89
Rainy River (unorg.)[40]	2 226	2 036
Roosevelt city (pt.)[40]	6	...
Williams city	217	220
Le Sueur County[41]	23 434	21 332
Cleveland city	699	492
Cleveland township	569	541
Cordova township	587	534
Derrynane township	664	762
Elysian city (pt.)	450	445
Elysian township	874	674
Heidelberg city	102	72
Kasota city	739	732
Kasota township	1 252	959
Kilkenny city[41]	177	182
Kilkenny township[41]	569	503
Lanesburgh township[41]	1 433	982
Le Center city[41]	1 967	1 890
Le Sueur city[41]	3 763	3 745
Lexington township[41]	766	802
Montgomery city[41]	2 349	2 288
Montgomery township[41]	737	727
New Prague city (pt.)[41]	1 054	949
Ottawa township[41]	376	327

County Subdivisions	1980	1970
Le Sueur County—Con.		
Sharon township	660	631
Tyrone township[41]	715	642
Washington township	616	289
Waterville city	1 717	1 539
Waterville township	599	632
Lincoln County[42]	8 207	8 143
Alta Vista township	289	359
Arco city	96	121
Ash Lake township[42]	294	275
Diamond Lake township	319	273
Drammen township	233	325
Hansonville township	202	200
Hendricks city[42]	737	712
Hendricks township[42]	377	366
Hope township[42]	407	511
Ivanhoe city[42]	761	738
Lake Benton city	869	759
Lake Benton township	238	262
Lake Stay township	248	206
Limestone township	233	256
Marble township	297	351
Marshfield township[42]	312	370
Royal township[42]	357	313
Shaokatan township	254	310
Tyler city[42]	1 353	1 069
Verdi township	331	367
Lyon County[43]	25 207	24 273
Amiret township	366	369
Balaton city[43]	752	649
Clifton township	334	369
Coon Creek township	306	334
Cottonwood city[43]	924	794
Custer township	340	359
Eidsvold township	312	334
Fairview township[43]	561	680
Florence city	55	58
Garvin city	172	201
Ghent city[43]	356	301
Grandview township[43]	332	381
Island Lake township	286	263
Lake Marshall township[43]	570	759
Lucas township[43]	321	335
Lynd city[43]	304	267
Lynd township[43]	458	400
Lyons township	258	310
Marshall city[43]	11 161	9 886
Minneota city	1 470	1 320
Monroe township[43]	294	376
Nordland township[43]	267	340
Rock Lake township[43]	362	300
Russell city	412	398
Shelburne township	285	324
Sodus township	345	351
Stanley township	299	360
Taunton city[43]	177	195
Tracy city[43]	2 478	2 516
Vallers township	313	363
Westerheim township	337	381
McLeod County[44]	29 657	27 662
Acoma township	881	848
Bergen township[44]	840	816
Biscay city[44]	114	105
Brownton city[44]	697	688
Collins township	518	518
Glencoe city[44]	4 396	4 217
Glencoe township[44]	661	662
Hale township[44]	1 004	962
Hassan Valley township[44]	926	854
Helen township[44]	868	767
Hutchinson city[44]	9 244	8 031
Hutchinson township[44]	1 090	965
Lester Prairie city[44]	1 229	1 162
Lynn township[44]	693	778
Penn township	393	470
Plato city[44]	390	303
Rich Valley township	817	875
Round Grove township	374	407
Silver Lake city[44]	698	694
Stewart city	616	666
Sumter township[44]	510	453
Winsted city[44]	1 522	1 266
Winsted township[44]	1 176	1 155
Mahnomen County[45]	5 535	5 638
Beaulieu township	175	211
Bejou city	109	157
Bejou township	133	171
Chief township	187	220
Clover township	123	119
Gregory township	150	166
Heier township	155	192
Island Lake township	274	251
La Garde township	189	177
Lake Grove township	251	294
Mahnomen city[45]	1 283	1 313
Marsh Creek township	168	191

County Subdivisions

County Subdivisions	1980	1970
Mahnomen County—Con.		
Oakland township	252	217
Pembina township[45]	598	625
Popple Grove township	203	229
Rosedale township	202	292
Southeast Mahnomen (unorg.)[45]	133	468
Twin Lakes township[45]	560	...
Waubun city	390	345
Marshall County[46]	13 027	13 060
Agder township	141	116
Alma township	149	188
Alvarado city[46]	385	302
Argyle city	741	739
Augsburg township	156	191
Big Woods township	157	185
Bloomer township	111	121
Boxville township	56	72
Cedar township	140	164
Como township	78	79
Comstock township	184	211
Donnelly township	30	50
Eagle Point township	112	170
East Park township	36	21
East Valley township	79	68
Eckvoll township	87	88
Espelie township	66	88
Excel township	307	229
Foldahl township	123	161
Fork township	50	71
Grand Plain township	86	98
Grygla city[46]	216	211
Holt city	119	97
Holt township	162	193
Huntly township	107	107
Lincoln township	166	176
Linsell township	60	39
McCrea township[46]	346	303
Marsh Grove township	162	181
Middle River city	349	369
Middle River township	162	187
Moose River township	61	70
Moylan township	159	158
Mud Lake (unorg.)	5	14
Nelson Park township	195	170
Newfolden city	384	390
New Folden township	252	212
New Maine township	231	169
New Solum township	349	258
Oak Park township	205	253
Oslo city	379	417
Parker township	54	72
Rollis township	212	182
Sinnott township	85	114
Spruce Valley township	326	247
Stephen city[46]	898	904
Strandquist city	136	138
Tamarac township[46]	185	166
Thief Lake township	103	85
Valley township[46]	224	237
Vega township[46]	167	228
Veldt township	67	62
Viking city	129	118
Viking township	233	274
Wanger township	170	233
Warren city[46]	2 105	1 999
Warrenton township[46]	112	119
West Valley township	180	204
Whiteford township	75	45
Wright township	223	247
Martin County[47]	24 687	24 316
Cedar township	326	355
Center Creek township[47]	358	439
Ceylon city	543	487
Dunnell city	216	237
East Chain township	425	475
Elm Creek township	290	298
Fairmont city[47]	11 506	10 751
Fairmont township[47]	312	308
Fox Lake township	334	416
Fraser township	373	451
Galena township	314	365
Granada city[47]	377	381
Jay township	341	443
Lake Belt township	362	397
Lake Fremont township	282	365
Manyaska township[47]	356	439
Nashville township	354	361
Northrop city[47]	269	188
Ormsby city (pt.)	65	62
Pleasant Prairie township	385	456
Rolling Green township[47]	405	461
Rutland township[47]	498	538
Sherburn city[47]	1 275	1 190
Silver Lake township	584	521
Tenhassen township	395	459
Trimont city	805	835
Truman city[47]	1 392	1 137

County Subdivisions	1980	1970
Martin County—Con.		
Waverly township	301	370
Welcome city[47]	855	694
Westford township[47]	389	437
Meeker County[48]	20 594	'18 387
Acton township	475	'394
Cedar Mills city	73	81
Cedar Mills township	569	602
Collinwood township	735	551
Cosmos city	571	570
Cosmos township	274	312
Danielson township	357	351
Darwin city	282	'361
Darwin township	606	'431
Dassel city	1 066	1 058
Dassel township	967	581
Eden Valley city (pt.)	472	489
Ellsworth township	632	524
Forest City township	661	597
Forest Prairie township[48]	920	745
Greenleaf township	664	509
Grove City city	596	'531
Harvey township	431	374
Kingston city	141	115
Kingston township	971	955
Litchfield city[48]	5 904	5 262
Litchfield township[48]	817	682
Manannah township	628	598
Swede Grove township	409	435
Union Grove township	616	494
Watkins city[48]	757	785
Mille Lacs County[49]	18 430	15 703
Bock city	105	105
Bogus Brook township	860	761
Borgholm township	1 042	856
Bradbury township	157	131
Dailey township	213	186
East Side township	621	516
Foreston city	283	273
Greenbush township	1 086	794
Hayland township	354	281
Isle city	573	551
Isle Harbor township	445	403
Kathio township	901	693
Lewis township	60	34
Milaca city[49]	2 104	1 940
Milaca township[49]	1 001	813
Milo township	957	920
Mudgett township	100	102
Onamia city	691	670
Onamia township	516	427
Page township	456	444
Pease city	174	187
Princeton city (pt.)[49]	3 144	2 531
Princeton township[49]	1 625	1 294
South Harbor township	691	583
Wahkon city	271	208
Morrison County[50]	29 311	26 949
Agram township	381	256
Belle Prairie township[50]	1 597	1 406
Bellevue township	793	504
Bowlus city	276	268
Buckman city	171	158
Buckman township	763	754
Buh township	604	570
Clough township	139	94
Culdrum township	528	540
Cushing township	337	297
Darling township	583	556
Elmdale city	126	116
Elmdale township	872	794
Flensburg city	256	259
Genola city	83	97
Granite township	524	529
Green Prairie township[50]	650	599
Harding city	93	119
Hillman city	51	49
Hillman township	171	147
Lakin township	408	383
Lastrup city	150	161
Leigh township	192	177
Little Falls city[50]	7 250	7 467
Little Falls township[50]	1 137	882
Morrill township	575	532
Motley city (pt.)	442	351
Motley township	159	134
Mount Morris township	103	94
Parker township	483	479
Pierz city	1 018	893
Pierz township	612	545
Pike Creek township	946	885
Platte township	351	361
Pulaski township	322	281
Rail Prairie township	130	87
Randall city	527	536
Richardson township	405	345

County Subdivisions

County Subdivisions	1980	1970
Morrison County—Con.		
Ripley township	615	562
Rosing township	103	64
Royalton city	660	534
Scandia Valley township	789	539
Sobieski city	219	189
Swan River township	856	733
Swanville city	295	300
Swanville township	566	493
Two Rivers township	600	518
Upsala city	400	312
Mower County[51]	40 390	'44 919
Adams city	797	771
Adams township	514	575
Austin city[51]	23 020	'26 210
Austin township[51]	2 386	2 777
Bennington township	209	244
Brownsdale city[51]	691	625
Clayton township	191	275
Dexter city	279	252
Dexter township	337	417
Elkton city	139	134
Frankford township[51]	359	482
Grand Meadow city[51]	965	869
Grand Meadow township	364	490
Lansing township[51]	1 558	1 828
Le Roy city[51]	930	870
Le Roy township[51]	422	446
Lodi township	309	408
Lyle city	576	522
Lyle township	500	511
Mapleview city	253	328
Marshall township	411	478
Nevada township	467	482
Pleasant Valley township	328	375
Racine city	285	197
Racine township	483	383
Red Rock township[51]	872	968
Rose Creek city[51]	371	390
Sargeant city	95	85
Sargeant township	338	402
Taopi city	96	59
Udolpho township	535	577
Waltham city	176	189
Waltham township	477	553
Windom township[51]	657	747
Murray County[52]	11 507	12 508
Avoca city	201	203
Belfast township	295	357
Bondin township	404	459
Cameron township	240	289
Chanarambie township[52]	311	342
Chandler city	344	319
Currie city[52]	359	368
Des Moines River township	293	308
Dovray city[52]	87	104
Dovray township	276	'306
Ellsborough township	274	350
Fenton township	295	391
Fulda city[52]	1 308	1 226
Hadley city	137	119
Holly township	248	290
Iona city	248	260
Iona township	294	349
Lake Sarah township	305	352
Lake Wilson city[52]	380	378
Leeds township	285	322
Lime Lake township	281	365
Lowville township	282	311
Mason township	344	384
Moulton township	312	472
Murray township[52]	295	386
Shetek township	300	338
Skandia township	244	282
Slayton city[52]	2 420	2 351
Slayton township[52]	445	527
Nicollet County[53]	26 929	24 518
Belgrade township[53]	1 118	1 052
Bernadotte township	433	475
Brighton township	197	245
Courtland city	399	300
Courtland township	751	628
Granby township	306	387
Lafayette city	507	498
Lafayette township	895	891
Lake Prairie township	717	756
Mankato city (pt.)[53]	9	...
New Sweden township	402	489
Nicollet city[53]	709	618
Nicollet township[53]	604	550
North Mankato city[53]	9 145	7 347
Oshawa township[53]	528	527
Ridgely township	174	192
St. Peter city[53]	9 056	8 339
Traverse township[53]	380	605
West Newton township	599	619
Nobles County[54]	21 840	23 208
Adrian city[54]	1 336	1 350
Bigelow city	249	262
Bigelow township	434	438
Bloom township	298	351
Brewster city[54]	559	563
Dewald township	366	464
Dundee city	129	138
Elk township	335	369
Ellsworth city	629	588
Graham Lakes township	298	381
Grand Prairie township	300	344
Hersey township[54]	281	324
Indian Lake township	314	389
Kinbrae city	40	37
Larkin township	312	387
Leota township	589	671
Lismore city	276	323
Lismore township	301	354
Little Rock township	342	401
Lorain township[54]	392	'504
Olney township[54]	304	400
Ransom township	384	441
Round Lake city	480	506
Rushmore city	387	394
Seward township	331	382
Summit Lake township	473	528
Westside township[54]	306	384
Wilmont city	380	390
Wilmont township	339	419
Worthington city[54]	10 243	'9 916
Worthington township[54]	433	'810
Norman County[55]	9 379	10 008
Ada city[55]	1 971	2 076
Anthony township	148	183
Bear Park township	312	349
Borup city	160	128
Flom township	286	312
Fossum township	216	260
Gary city	241	265
Good Hope township	95	122
Green Meadow township	159	191
Halstad city[55]	690	598
Halstad township[55]	217	255
Hegne township	101	140
Hendrum city[55]	336	311
Hendrum township[55]	162	233
Home Lake township	234	216
Lake Ida township	209	198
Lee township	203	199
Lockhart township	115	167
McDonaldsville township[55]	255	309
Mary township	148	187
Perley city	134	149
Pleasant View township	180	217
Rockwell township	124	99
Shelly city[55]	276	260
Shelly township[55]	210	261
Spring Creek township	126	141
Strand township	212	193
Sundal township	231	227
Twin Valley city[55]	907	868
Waukon township	231	281
Wild Rice township[55]	376	462
Winchester township	114	151
Olmsted County[56]	92 006	84 104
Byron city[56]	1 715	1 419
Cascade township[56]	2 384	2 442
Chatfield city (pt.)[56]	895	723
Dover city	312	321
Dover township	491	511
Elmira township[56]	408	445
Eyota city	1 244	639
Eyota township	523	585
Farmington township	626	649
Haverhill township[56]	1 295	1 019
High Forest township[56]	1 545	1 135
Kalmar township[56]	1 209	948
Marion township[56]	5 299	5 998
New Haven township	1 122	937
Orion township	602	466
Oronoco city[56]	574	564
Oronoco township	1 696	847
Pine Island city (pt.)	9	...
Pleasant Grove township	776	750
Quincy township	435	446
Rochester city[56]	57 890	53 766
Rochester township[56]	4 598	4 344
Rock Dell township	706	630
Salem township	1 153	1 040
Stewartville city[56]	3 925	2 802
Viola township	574	678

County Subdivisions	1980	1970
Otter Tail County[57]	51 937	46 097
Aastad township	263	247
Amor township	510	408
Aurdal township	1 268	795
Battle Lake city	708	772
Blowers township	401	400
Bluffton city	206	195
Bluffton township	553	517
Buse township[57]	608	485
Butler township	286	373
Candor township	375	269
Carlisle township	208	251
Clitherall city	121	131
Clitherall township	488	349
Compton township[57]	776	583
Corliss township	414	402
Dalton city	248	221
Dane Prairie township	768	562
Dead Lake township	398	316
Deer Creek city	392	287
Deer Creek township	372	321
Dent city[57]	167	156
Dora township	525	370
Dunn township	594	405
Eagle Lake township	361	277
Eastern township	341	294
Edna township[57]	624	469
Effington township	330	332
Elizabeth city	195	188
Elizabeth township	581	440
Elmo township	394	381
Erhard city	194	148
Erhards Grove township	406	392
Everts township	539	429
Fergus Falls city[57]	12 519	12 443
Fergus Falls township[57]	1 161	877
Folden township	321	288
Friberg township	667	511
Girard township	563	345
Gorman township	445	428
Henning city	832	850
Henning township	394	362
Hobart township	625	472
Homestead township	374	350
Inman township	370	353
Leaf Lake township	481	414
Leaf Mountain township	354	295
Lida township	526	361
Maine township	601	434
Maplewood township	294	312
Newton township[57]	831	691
New York Mills city[57]	972	791
Nidaros township	253	234
Norwegian Grove township	388	340
Oak Valley township	444	411
Orwell township	208	218
Oscar township	266	286
Ottertail city	239	180
Ottertail township	291	212
Otto township	503	367
Paddock township	402	312
Parkers Prairie city	917	882
Parkers Prairie township	364	296
Pelican township[57]	593	489
Pelican Rapids city[57]	1 867	1 835
Perham city[57]	2 086	1 933
Perham township[57]	656	504
Pine Lake township	385	294
Richville city	132	102
Rothsay city (pt.)[57]	198	147
Rush Lake township	638	483
St. Olaf township	345	324
Scambler township	433	323
Star Lake township	373	334
Sverdrup township	614	498
Tordenskjold township	477	411
Trondhjem township[57]	216	244
Tumuli township	387	349
Underwood city	332	278
Urbank city	95	125
Vergas city	287	281
Vining city	87	121
Wadena city (pt.)[57]	−	...
Western township	194	226
Woodside township	323	316
Pennington County[58]	15 258	13 266
Black River township	137	104
Bray township	95	98
Clover Leaf township	124	120
Deer Park township	162	181
Goodridge city	191	144
Goodridge township	74	69
Hickory township	130	96
Highlanding township	228	209
Kratka township	158	153
Mayfield township	96	69

County Subdivisions	1980	1970
Pennington County—Con.		
Norden township	388	208
North township[58]	700	652
Numedal township	129	113
Polk Centre township	87	124
Reiner township	134	101
River Falls township	222	171
Rocksbury township[58]	1 286	669
St. Hilaire city	388	337
Sanders township	356	254
Silverton township	209	203
Smiley township	539	274
Star township	193	180
Thief River Falls city[58]	9 105	8 618
Wyandotte township	127	119
Pine County[59]	19 871	16 821
Arlone township	281	232
Arna township	86	93
Askov city	350	287
Barry township	436	333
Birch Creek township	283	297
Bremen township	169	145
Brook Park city	93	113
Brook Park township	362	325
Bruno city[59]	130	130
Bruno township	134	161
Chengwatana township	557	377
Clover township	151	91
Crosby township	86	61
Danforth township	67	65
Dell Grove township	550	449
Denham city	48	56
Finlayson city	202	192
Finlayson township	441	334
Fleming township	66	50
Henriette city	61	56
Hinckley city[59]	963	885
Hinckley township[59]	628	501
Kerrick city	79	114
Kerrick township	270	272
Kettle River township	569	427
Rutledge city	185	123
Mission Creek township	411	437
Munch township	155	136
New Dosey township	88	67
Nickerson township	121	147
Norman township	197	190
Ogema township	157	104
Park township	60	51
Partridge township	503	399
Pine City city[59]	2 489	2 143
Pine City township[59]	876	797
Pine Lake township	440	356
Pokegama township[59]	1 611	1 091
Rock Creek city[59]	890	...
Royalton township	688	560
Sandstone city	1 594	1 641
Sandstone township	580	429
Sturgeon Lake township	607	470
Sturgeon Lake city	222	167
Willow River city[59]	303	331
Wilma township	124	100
Windemere township	915	511
Pipestone County[60]	11 690	12 791
Aetna township	295	357
Altona township	237	326
Burke township	329	298
Eden township	361	450
Edgerton city[60]	1 123	1 119
Elmer township	344	440
Fountain Prairie township	275	305
Grange township	309	335
Gray township[60]	300	368
Hatfield city	87	96
Holland city[60]	234	263
Ihlen city	129	132
Jasper city (pt.)	659	680
Osborne township[60]	454	450
Pipestone city[60]	4 887	5 328
Rock township[60]	261	306
Ruthton city	328	405
Sweet township[60]	420	406
Trosky city	113	109
Troy township	365	401
Woodstock city	180	217
Polk County[61]	34 844	34 435
Andover township	176	184
Angus township	141	179
Badger township	173	212
Belgium township	130	150
Beltrami city	134	171
Brandsvold township	295	318
Brandt township	96	113
Brislet township	84	104
Bygland township	317	352
Chester township	91	116
Climax city[61]	273	255

County Subdivisions	1980	1970
Polk County—Con.		
Columbia township[61]	448	405
Crookston city[61]	8 628	8 312
Crookston township[61]	532	580
East Grand Forks city[61]	8 537	7 607
Eden township	222	273
Erskine city	585	571
Esther township	201	154
Euclid township	256	233
Fairfax township	231	270
Fanny township	119	137
Farley township	87	75
Fertile city	869	955
Fisher city[61]	453	383
Fisher township	155	159
Fosston city[61]	1 599	1 684
Garden township	296	305
Garfield township	510	408
Gentilly township	441	395
Godfrey township	297	266
Grand Forks township[61]	275	357
Grove Park township	279	257
Gully city	116	96
Gully township	128	77
Hammond township	80	63
Helgeland township	94	85
Higdem township	125	124
Hill River township	252	238
Hubbard township	134	162
Huntsville township[61]	535	461
Johnson township	104	114
Kertsonville township	163	197
Keystone township	114	122
King township	219	236
Knute township	431	403
Lengby city[61]	123	140
Lessor township	209	206
Liberty township	156	150
Lowell township[61]	187	217
McIntosh city	681	753
Mentor city	219	236
Nesbit township	153	158
Nielsville city	145	156
Northland township	226	287
Onstad township	126	121
Parnell township	96	96
Queen township	265	291
Reis township	115	138
Rhinehart township[61]	98	416
Roome township	215	268
Rosebud township[61]	386	354
Russia township	71	85
Sandsville township	71	84
Scandia township	106	126
Sletten township	195	213
Sullivan township[61]	218	213
Tabor township	187	217
Tilden township	55	52
Trail city	97	99
Tynsid township	87	83
Vineland township[61]	156	150
Winger city	200	228
Winger township	264	281
Woodside township	312	297
Pope County[62]	11 657	11 107
Bangor township[62]	234	239
Barsness township	187	213
Ben Wade township	306	314
Blue Mounds township	284	247
Brooten city (pt.)[62]	–	...
Chippewa Falls township	341	312
Cyrus city[62]	334	289
Farwell city	77	102
Gilchrist township	218	219
Glenwood city[62]	2 523	2 584
Glenwood township[62]	827	732
Grove Lake township	314	268
Hoff township	241	255
Lake Johanna township	189	161
Langhei township	270	312
Leven township[62]	488	460
Long Beach city	263	219
Lowry city	283	257
Minnewaska township[62]	490	227
New Prairie township[62]	263	293
Nora township	306	309
Reno township	364	331
Rolling Forks township	207	246
Sedan city	62	55
Starbuck city[62]	1 224	1 138
Villard city	275	221
Walden township	261	251
Westport city	50	65
Westport township	300	337
White Bear Lake township[62]	476	451

County Subdivisions	1980	1970
Ramsey County[63]	459 784	476 255
Arden Hills city[63]	8 012	5 149
Blaine city (pt.)	–	5
Falcon Heights city	5 291	5 530
Gem Lake city	394	216
Lauderdale city	1 985	2 530
Little Canada city	7 102	3 481
Maplewood city[63]	26 990	25 186
Mounds View city	12 593	10 599
New Brighton city[63]	23 269	19 507
North Oaks city[63]	2 846	2 002
North St. Paul city[63]	11 921	11 950
Roseville city	35 820	34 438
St. Anthony city (pt.)	2 362	2 353
St. Paul city	270 230	309 866
Shoreview city	17 300	10 978
Spring Lake Park city (pt.)	109	98
Vadnais Heights city	5 111	3 411
White Bear township[63]	5 921	5 666
White Bear Lake city (pt.)[63]	22 528	23 290
Red Lake County[64]	5 471	5 388
Brooks city	173	163
Browns Creek township	75	78
Emardville township	292	318
Equality township	206	183
Garnes township	246	237
Gervais township	302	274
Lake Pleasant township	147	164
Lambert township[64]	226	240
Louisville township	241	239
Oklee city[64]	536	536
Plummer city	353	285
Poplar River township	206	265
Red Lake Falls city[64]	1 732	1 740
Red Lake Falls township[64]	318	232
River township	87	90
Terrebonne township	236	233
Wylie township	95	111
Redwood County[65]	19 341	20 024
Belview city	438	429
Brookville township	358	396
Charlestown township[65]	350	338
Clements city	227	252
Delhi city	96	154
Delhi township[65]	377	369
Gales township	226	268
Granite Rock township	330	423
Honner township[65]	133	99
Johnsonville township	241	289
Kintire township	258	288
Lamberton city[65]	1 032	962
Lamberton township[65]	329	329
Lucan city	262	254
Milroy city	242	247
Morgan city[65]	975	972
Morgan township[65]	417	429
New Avon township	328	451
North Hero township[65]	247	310
North Redwood city[65]	206	155
Paxton township[65]	449	483
Redwood Falls city[65]	5 210	4 774
Redwood Falls township[65]	333	383
Revere city	158	166
Sanborn city[65]	518	505
Seaforth city	90	132
Sheridan township	305	374
Sherman township	260	278
Springdale township	310	359
Sundown township	347	399
Swedes Forest township	143	190
Three Lakes township	299	361
Underwood township	237	322
Vail township[65]	353	432
Vesta city	360	330
Vesta township	272	341
Wabasso city[65]	745	738
Walnut Grove city[65]	753	756
Wanda city	118	124
Waterbury township	363	403
Westline township	288	331
Willow Lake township	358	429
Renville County[66]	20 401	21 139
Bandon township	295	393
Beaver Falls township	357	267
Birch Cooley township	338	349
Bird Island city[66]	1 372	1 309
Bird Island township[66]	345	412
Boon Lake township	452	438
Brookfield township	315	349
Buffalo Lake city[66]	782	758
Cairo township	372	403
Camp township[66]	305	321
Crooks township	311	363
Danube city	590	497
Emmet township[66]	323	424
Ericson township	349	369

County Subdivisions	1980	1970
Renville County—Con.		
Fairfax city[66]	1 405	1 432
Flora township	307	342
Franklin city	512	557
Hawk Creek township	253	311
Hector city	1 252	1 178
Hector township	355	425
Henryville township	353	430
Kingman township	354	349
Martinsburg township	275	340
Melville township	344	368
Morton city	549	591
Norfolk township	268	389
Olivia city[66]	2 802	2 553
Osceola township	265	411
Palmyra township	340	442
Preston Lake township[66]	365	466
Renville city[66]	1 493	1 252
Sacred Heart city	666	707
Sacred Heart township	336	407
Troy township[66]	373	374
Wang township	312	358
Wellington township	383	430
Winfield township	333	375
Rice County[67]	46 087	41 582
Bridgewater township[67]	1 691	1 315
Cannon City township[67]	1 099	1 062
Dundas city	422	460
Erin township	793	704
Faribault city[67]	16 241	16 595
Forest township	854	764
Lonsdale city[67]	1 160	622
Morristown city	639	659
Morristown township	693	681
Nerstrand city	255	231
Northfield city (pt.)[67]	12 549	10 235
Northfield township[67]	757	654
Richland township	496	563
Shieldsville township	850	611
Walcott township[67]	1 553	1 338
Warsaw township[67]	1 323	999
Webster township	1 397	1 096
Wells township[67]	1 563	1 398
Wheatland township[67]	1 230	1 068
Wheeling township	522	527
Rock County[68]	10 703	11 346
Battle Plain township	329	353
Beaver Creek city	260	235
Beaver Creek township	481	566
Clinton township	399	436
Denver township	287	334
Hardwick city	279	274
Hills city[68]	598	571
Jasper city (pt.)	72	74
Kanaranzi township	336	414
Kenneth city	95	89
Luverne city[68]	4 568	4 703
Luverne township[68]	581	462
Magnolia city[68]	234	233
Magnolia township[68]	270	279
Martin township[68]	504	555
Mound township	347	411
Rose Dell township	314	420
Springwater township	352	460
Steen city	153	191
Vienna township	244	286
Roseau County[69]	12 574	11 569
Badger city	320	327
Barnett township	202	214
Barto township	164	181
Beaver township	103	92
Cedarbend township	134	118
Deer township	153	153
Dewey township	144	137
Dieter township	216	209
Enstrom township	263	196
Falun township	250	207
Golden Valley township	184	165
Greenbush city	817	787
Grimstad township	211	198
Hereim township	257	245
Huss township	165	185
Jadis township[69]	544	425
Lake township[69]	738	415
Laona township	286	223
Lind township	92	83
Malung township	349	310
Mickinock township	301	345
Moose township	150	131
Moranville township	402	334
Nereson township	115	123
North Roseau (unorg.)	159	145
Northwest Roseau (unorg.)[69]	18	14
Palmville township	58	38
Pohlitz township	52	66
Polonia township	71	96
Poplar Grove township	127	125

County Subdivisions	1980	1970
Roseau County—Con.		
Reine township	89	90
Roosevelt city (pt.)	118	104
Roseau city[69]	2 272	2 552
Ross township	320	214
Skagen township	212	192
Soler township	110	116
Southeast Roseau (unorg.)	208	177
Spruce township	537	297
Stafford township	193	201
Stokes township	207	208
Strathcona city	47	31
Warroad city[69]	1 216	1 086
St. Louis County[70]	222 229	220 693
Alango township	318	254
Alborn township	314	261
Alden township[70]	161	156
Angora township	291	225
Arrowhead township	151	156
Ault township	119	42
Babbitt city	2 435	3 076
Balkan township[70]	934	732
Bassett township	40	40
Beatty township	423	316
Birch Lake (unorg.)	699	640
Biwabik city[70]	1 428	1 483
Biwabik township[70]	1 034	'773
Breitung township[70]	933	907
Brevator township	1 023	880
Brookston city[70]	124	137
Buhl city[70]	1 284	1 303
Canosia township	1 562	1 392
Pike Lake (CDP) (pt.)	640	...
Cedar Valley township	219	181
Cherry township	1 018	593
Chisholm city	5 930	5 913
Clinton township	1 434	'874
Colvin township	447	248
Cook city[70]	800	687
Cotton township	396	301
Culver township	332	'237
Duluth city	92 811	100 578
Duluth township	1 604	1 484
Ellsburg township	139	73
Elmer township	215	207
Ely city[70]	4 820	4 904
Embarrass township	1 154	1 021
Eveleth city[70]	5 042	4 721
Fairbanks township	75	79
Fayal township[70]	2 175	2 025
Ely Lake (CDP)	1 172	...
Fermory (unorg.)	79	93
Field township	430	315
Fine Lakes township	166	153
Floodwood city[70]	648	650
Floodwood township[70]	431	'414
Franklin city	27	41
Fredenberg township	628	408
French township	439	183
Gheen (unorg.)	92	100
Gilbert city[70]	2 721	2 287
Gnesen township	975	700
Grand Lake township	2 166	1 539
Pike Lake (CDP) (pt.)	364	...
Great Scott township[70]	883	'605
Kinney city[70]	447	325
Greenwood township[70]	565	...
Halden township	151	198
Hay Lake (unorg.)	115	91
Heikkila Lake (unorg.)	1 616	994
Hermantown city[70]	6 759	...
Hibbing city[70]	21 193	16 104
Hoyt Lakes city	3 186	3 634
Industrial township	617	509
Iron Junction city[70]	134	'150
Janette Lake (unorg.)	288	157
Kelsey township	228	161
Kugler township	230	176
Lake Vermilion (unorg.)[70]	175	...
Lakewood township	1 680	1 393
Lavell township	481	330
Leiding township	386	365
Leonidas city[70]	95	'157
Linden Grove township	160	115
McCormack Lake (unorg.)	178	116
McDavitt township	557	426
McKinley city	230	317
Meadowlands city[70]	135	128
Meadowlands township[70]	331	307
Midway township	1 656	1 751
Morcom township	141	137
Morse township[70]	1 123	'1 149
Mountain Iron city[70]	4 134	1 698
Ness township	96	97
Nett Lake (unorg.)	339	...
New Independence township	254	172
Normanna township	507	317
Northeast St. Louis (unorg.)[70]	162	492

County Subdivisions	1980	1970
St. Louis County—Con.		
Northland township	142	100
Northwest St. Louis (unorg.)[70]	571	798
Orr city	294	315
Owens township[70]	245	318
Payne township	55	48
Pequaywan township[70]	69	...
Pike township	600	406
Portage township	262	163
Potshot Lake (unorg.)	81	69
Prairie Lake township	77	43
Proctor city	3 180	3 123
Rice Lake township	3 861	3 359
Sand Lake (unorg.)	1 401	861
Sandy township	535	387
Solway township	1 663	1 378
Stoney Brook township	238	145
Sturgeon township	200	199
Toivola township	347	243
Tower city[70]	640	699
Van Buren township	189	203
Vermilion Lake township	379	305
Virginia city[70]	11 056	12 450
Waasa township	428	439
White township[70]	4 916	'4 385
Aurora city[70]	2 670	2 531
Whiteface Reservoir (unorg.)	170	133
Willow Valley township	133	158
Winton city	276	'294
Wouri township	750	474
Scott County[71]	43 784	32 423
Belle Plaine city	2 754	2 328
Belle Plaine township	765	805
Blakeley township[71]	515	565
Cedar Lake township	1 507	1 051
Credit River township	2 360	1 165
Elko city	274	115
Helena township[71]	1 215	1 156
Jackson township[71]	1 911	1 578
Jordan city[71]	2 663	1 836
Louisville township	813	519
New Market city[71]	286	215
New Market township[71]	1 636	'1 236
New Prague city (pt.)[71]	1 898	1 731
Prior Lake city[71]	7 284	1 114
St. Lawrence township	350	388
Sand Creek township[71]	1 516	1 250
Savage city[71]	3 954	3 611
Shakopee city[71]	9 941	6 876
Spring Lake township[71]	2 142	'2 684
Sherburne County[72]	29 908	18 344
Baldwin township[72]	2 412	1 099
Becker city[72]	601	365
Becker township[72]	1 341	799
Big Lake city[72]	2 210	1 015
Big Lake township[72]	2 679	1 708
Blue Hill township	678	495
Clear Lake city	266	280
Clear Lake township	1 048	612
Elk River city[72]	6 785	2 252
Haven township	1 603	1 049
Livonia township[72]	1 629	705
Orrock township[72]	1 140	502
Palmer township	1 362	663
Princeton city (pt.)[72]	2	...
St. Cloud city (pt.)	4 421	3 918
Santiago township	657	541
Zimmerman city[72]	1 074	495
Sibley County[73]	15 448	15 845
Alfsborg township[73]	469	541
Arlington city[73]	1 779	1 823
Arlington township[73]	677	641
Bismarck township	348	435
Cornish township	383	456
Dryden township[73]	543	567
Faxon township	389	304
Gaylord city[73]	1 933	1 720
Gibbon city[73]	787	877
Grafton township	332	458
Green Isle city[73]	357	363
Green Isle township[73]	633	638
Henderson city[73]	739	730
Henderson township[73]	632	582
Jessenland township	490	471
Kelso township	428	482
Moltke township	415	489
New Auburn city	331	274
New Auburn township	500	524
Severance township[73]	440	440
Sibley township	420	498
Transit township[73]	417	479
Washington Lake township[73]	630	662
Winthrop city[73]	1 376	1 391

County Subdivisions	1980	1970
Stearns County[74]	108 161	95 400
Albany city[74]	1 569	1 599
Albany township[74]	922	775
Ashley township	362	442
Avon city[74]	804	725
Avon township[74]	1 737	'1 157
Belgrade city	805	713
Brockway township[74]	1 915	1 281
Brooten city (pt.)[74]	647	615
Cold Spring city[74]	2 294	2 006
Collegeville township	3 075	2 371
Crow Lake township[74]	444	329
Crow River township	417	421
Eden Lake township[74]	1 227	922
Eden Valley city (pt.)[74]	291	287
Elrosa city[74]	214	203
Fair Haven township	1 102	818
Farming township	826	808
Freeport city	563	593
Getty township[74]	463	523
Greenwald city[74]	259	244
Grove township[74]	693	'620
Holding township[74]	1 133	1 079
Holdingford city[74]	635	551
Kimball Prairie city	651	567
Krain township	945	912
Lake George township[74]	479	526
Lake Henry city[74]	90	92
Lake Henry township	453	'472
Le Sauk township[74]	2 009	2 844
Luxemburg township	912	971
Lynden township	1 389	511
Maine Prairie township	1 518	1 294
Meire Grove city[74]	174	171
Melrose city[74]	2 409	2 273
Melrose township[74]	902	866
Millwood township[74]	909	'872
Munson township[74]	1 189	917
New Munich city[74]	302	307
North Fork township[74]	304	296
Oak township[74]	622	676
Paynesville city[74]	2 140	1 920
Paynesville township[74]	1 167	922
Pleasant Lake city	120	65
Raymond township	308	337
Richmond city[74]	867	866
Rockville city[74]	597	302
Rockville township[74]	1 255	'938
Roscoe city	154	195
St. Anthony city	78	66
St. Augusta township	2 169	1 584
St. Cloud city (pt.)[74]	33 500	31 593
St. Cloud township[74]	5 282	6 807
St. Joseph city[74]	2 994	1 786
St. Joseph township[74]	2 916	1 922
St. Martin city[74]	220	188
St. Martin township	584	'608
St. Rosa city[74]	77	93
St. Stephen city	453	331
St. Wendel township	1 773	1 051
Sartell city (pt.)[74]	2 200	1 059
Sauk Centre city[74]	3 709	3 750
Sauk Centre township[74]	1 106	871
Spring Hill city[74]	94	92
Spring Hill township	499	'540
Waite Park city[74]	3 496	2 824
Wakefield township[74]	2 230	1 540
Zion township	519	562
Steele County[75]	30 328	26 931
Aurora township	739	726
Berlin township	570	484
Blooming Prairie city	1 969	1 804
Blooming Prairie township	541	645
Clinton Falls township	486	483
Deerfield township	600	624
Ellendale city	555	569
Havana township	677	611
Lemond township	551	567
Medford city[75]	775	690
Medford township[75]	515	423
Meriden township	719	791
Merton township	427	475
Owatonna city[75]	18 632	15 341
Owatonna township[75]	1 087	1 054
Somerset township	905	991
Summit township	580	653
Stevens County[76]	11 322	11 218
Alberta city[76]	145	140
Baker township[76]	231	240
Chokio city[76]	559	455
Darnen township[76]	389	398
Donnelly city	317	252
Donnelly township	195	216
Eldorado township	162	176
Everglade township	160	204
Framnas township	397	319
Hancock city	877	806

County Subdivisions	1980	1970
Stevens County—Con.		
Hodges township	291	296
Horton township	267	306
Moore township	269	264
Morris city[76]	5 367	5 366
Morris township[76]	501	452
Pepperton township	214	264
Rendsville township	250	281
Scott township[76]	201	214
Stevens township	147	198
Swan Lake township	253	197
Synnes township	130	174
Swift County[77]	12 920	13 177
Appleton city[77]	1 842	1 789
Appleton township[77]	298	268
Benson city[77]	3 656	3 484
Benson township[77]	362	332
Camp Lake township	326	343
Cashel township	239	336
Clontarf city	196	147
Clontarf township	144	128
Danvers city	152	136
De Graff city	179	195
Dublin township	230	286
Edison township	225	275
Fairfield township	232	281
Hayes township	290	291
Hegbert township	189	238
Holloway city	142	146
Kerkhoven city[77]	761	641
Kerkhoven township	341	357
Kildare township	230	282
Marysland township	219	286
Moyer township	200	230
Murdock city	343	358
Pillsbury township[77]	336	337
Shible township	216	249
Six Mile Grove township	252	252
Swenoda township	231	300
Tara township	181	229
Torning township[77]	634	652
West Bank township	274	329
Todd County[78]	24 991	22 114
Bartlett township	469	442
Bertha city	510	512
Bertha township	490	451
Birchdale township	722	577
Browerville city[78]	693	665
Bruce township	482	393
Burleene township	436	407
Burnhamville township	671	519
Burtrum city	177	135
Clarissa city	663	599
Eagle Bend city	593	557
Eagle Valley township	714	636
Fawn Lake township	358	307
Germania township	508	450
Gordon township	635	522
Grey Eagle city	338	325
Grey Eagle township	571	522
Hartford township[78]	669	632
Hewitt city	299	198
Iona township	525	555
Kandota township	535	379
Leslie township	619	474
Little Elk township	357	245
Little Sauk township	642	510
Long Prairie city[78]	2 859	2 416
Long Prairie township[78]	938	937
Moran township	570	485
Osakis city (pt.)	88	69
Reynolds township	662	546
Round Prairie township	658	570
Staples city (pt.)[78]	2 623	2 657
Staples township[78]	1 011	900
Stowe Prairie township	595	497
Turtle Creek township	371	196
Villard township	466	402
Ward township	515	490
West Union city	74	71
West Union township	380	389
Wykeham township	505	477
Traverse County	5 542	6 254
Arthur township	151	179
Browns Valley city	887	906
Clifton township	133	176
Croke township	156	190
Dollymount township	131	158
Dumont city	173	204
Folsom township	162	196
Lake Valley township	332	380
Leonardsville township	179	244
Monson township	224	232
Parnell township	140	199
Redpath township	116	139
Tara township	183	209

County Subdivisions	1980	1970
Traverse County—Con.		
Taylor township	188	268
Tintah city	119	167
Tintah township	78	125
Walls township	136	173
Wheaton city	1 969	2 029
Windsor township	85	80
Wabasha County[79]	19 335	17 224
Bellechester city (pt.)	63	69
Chester township	515	560
Elgin city	667	580
Elgin township	751	487
Gillford township	536	539
Glasgow township	277	311
Greenfield township[79]	943	571
Hammond city	178	179
Highland township	447	475
Hyde Park township	274	268
Kellogg city[79]	440	403
Lake township	417	389
Lake City city (pt.)	4 035	3 594
Mazeppa city	680	498
Mazeppa township	492	343
Millville city	186	139
Minneiska city (pt.)	67	76
Minneiska township	143	119
Mount Pleasant township	451	458
Oakwood township	437	400
Pepin township	386	417
Plainview city	2 416	2 093
Plainview township	616	639
Wabasha city	2 372	2 371
Watopa township	277	280
West Albany township	462	379
Zumbro township	599	384
Zumbro Falls city	208	203
Wadena County[80]	14 192	12 412
Aldrich city	88	85
Aldrich township	559	445
Blueberry township	567	338
Bullard township	163	129
Huntersville township	89	70
Leaf River township[80]	663	748
Lyons township	185	162
Meadow township	270	240
Menahga city	980	835
Nimrod city	69	64
North Germany township	374	373
Orton township	234	187
Red Eye township	406	332
Rockwood township	491	465
Sebeka city	774	668
Shell River township	220	153
Staples city (pt.)[80]	264	'98
Thomastown township[80]	987	'650
Verndale city	504	570
Wadena city (pt.)[80]	4 699	4 640
Wadena township[80]	1 094	794
Wing River township	512	366
Waseca County[81]	18 448	16 663
Alton township	480	542
Blooming Grove township	564	440
Byron township	330	437
Elysian city (pt.)[81]	4	...
Freedom township	522	622
Iosco township	520	542
Janesville city	1 897	1 557
Janesville township[81]	629	610
New Richland city[81]	1 263	1 113
New Richland township[81]	546	541
Otisco township	672	665
St. Mary township[81]	540	565
Vivian township	389	452
Waldorf city	249	285
Waseca city[81]	8 219	6 789
Wilton township	448	507
Woodville township[81]	1 176	996
Washington County[82]	113 571	'83 003
Afton city[82]	2 550	'248
Bayport city	2 932	2 987
Baytown township[82]	851	723
Birchwood Village city[82]	1 059	926
Cottage Grove city	18 994	13 419
Dellwood city	751	'524
Denmark township	1 140	923
Forest Lake city[82]	4 596	3 207
Forest Lake township[82]	5 331	2 990
Grant township	3 083	'1 853
Grey Cloud Island township	351	389
Hastings city (pt.)	16	16
Hugo city[82]	3 771	751
Lake Elmo city[82]	5 296	'3 565
Lakeland city	1 812	962
Lakeland Shores city	171	72
Lake St. Croix Beach city	1 176	1 111
Landfall city	679	671

County Subdivisions	1980	1970
Washington County—Con.		
Mahtomedi city[82]	3 851	2 640
Marine on St. Croix city	543	513
May township	2 076	1 298
Newport city	3 323	2 922
New Scandia township	2 858	1 513
Oakdale city[82]	12 123	'7 795
Oak Park Heights city[82]	2 591	1 238
Pine Springs city	267	'138
St. Marys Point city	348	319
St. Paul Park city	4 864	5 587
Stillwater city[82]	12 290	10 191
Stillwater township[82]	1 599	1 014
West Lakeland township	1 318	772
White Bear Lake city (pt.)	10	23
Willernie city	654	697
Woodbury city	10 297	6 184
Watonwan County[83]	12 361	13 298
Adrian township	279	355
Antrim township	383	447
Butterfield city	634	619
Butterfield township	361	375
Darfur city	139	179
Fieldon township	305	402
La Salle city	115	132
Lewisville city	273	291
Long Lake township[83]	424	382
Madelia city[83]	2 130	2 316
Madelia township[83]	408	449
Nelson township	381	432
Odin city[83]	134	166
Odin township	276	325
Ormsby city (pt.)	116	137
Riverdale township	433	508
Rosendale township[83]	475	657
St. James city[83]	4 346	4 027
St. James township[83]	359	583
South Branch township	390	516
Wilkin County[84]	8 454	9 389
Akron township	162	178
Andrea township	91	99
Atherton township	211	219
Bradford township	170	183
Brandrup township[84]	214	'329
Breckenridge city[84]	3 909	4 200
Breckenridge township[84]	264	206
Campbell city	286	339
Campbell township	130	'178
Champion township[84]	115	254
Connelly township[84]	155	150
Deerhorn township	160	161
Doran city[84]	77	101
Foxhome city[84]	161	185
Foxhome township	175	'167
Kent city	121	139
McCauleyville township	85	110
Manston township	123	176
Meadows township	72	96
Mitchell township	128	171
Nashua city[84]	89	114
Nilsen township	105	130
Nordick township	152	216
Prairie View township	249	253
Roberts township	133	128
Rothsay city (pt.)	278	301
Sunnyside township	185	208
Tanberg township	109	123
Tenney city[84]	19	24
Wolverton city[84]	177	171
Wolverton township	149	'194
Winona County[85]	46 256	44 409
Altura city	354	334
Dakota city	350	369
Dresbach township	354	343
Elba city	198	158
Elba township	309	237
Fremont township	375	469
Goodview city[85]	2 567	1 829
Hart township	397	403
Hillsdale township[85]	704	333
Homer township	1 314	1 022
Lewiston city	1 226	1 000
Minneiska city (pt.)[85]	65	4
Minnesota City city	265	301
Mount Vernon township[85]	340	436
New Hartford township	738	718
Norton township	584	510
Pleasant Hill township	616	523
Richmond township	665	440
Rollingstone city[85]	528	450
Rollingstone township[85]	1 403	1 160
St. Charles city	2 184	1 942
St. Charles township	517	495
Saratoga township	530	484
Stockton city[85]	517	346
Utica city	249	240
Utica township	686	636

County Subdivisions	1980	1970
Winona County—Con.		
Warren township	623	599
Whitewater township	222	237
Wilson township[85]	1 141	966
Winona city[85]	25 075	26 438
Winona township[85]	815	657
Wiscoy township	345	330
Wright County[86]	58 681	38 933
Albertville city[86]	564	451
Albion township	1 127	969
Annandale city[86]	1 568	1 234
Buffalo city[86]	4 560	3 275
Buffalo township[86]	1 870	1 236
Chatham township	1 268	890
Clearwater city[86]	379	282
Clearwater township[86]	1 153	'585
Cokato city[86]	2 056	1 735
Cokato township[86]	947	754
Corinna township[86]	1 831	1 109
Dayton city (pt.)	70	48
Delano city[86]	2 480	1 851
Frankfort township[86]	2 170	'1 372
Franklin township[86]	2 712	1 808
French Lake township	936	824
Hanover city (pt.)	399	269
Howard Lake city	1 240	1 162
Maple Lake city	1 132	1 124
Maple Lake township	1 718	1 226
Marysville township	1 944	'1 481
Middleville township	1 093	1 016
Monticello city[86]	2 830	1 636
Monticello township[86]	3 588	2 240
Montrose city	762	379
Otsego township	4 769	1 526
Rockford city (pt.)[86]	2 028	568
Rockford township[86]	3 151	1 626
St. Michael city[86]	1 519	1 021
Silver Creek township	1 778	1 102
South Haven city	205	238
Southside township	1 475	918
Stockholm township	779	690
Victor township	1 012	839
Waverly city	470	'573
Woodland township	1 098	876
Yellow Medicine County[87]	13 653	'14 523
Burton township[87]	290	400
Canby city[87]	2 143	'2 147
Clarkfield city[87]	1 171	1 084
Echo city	334	356
Echo township	295	321
Florida township	211	259
Fortier township	178	243
Friendship township[87]	251	281
Granite Falls city (pt.)[87]	2 666	2 582
Hammer township[87]	362	392
Hanley Falls city	265	265
Hazel Run city	93	115
Hazel Run township	239	309
Lisbon township	270	325
Minnesota Falls township	412	452
Norman township[87]	348	'389
Normania township	228	263
Omro township[87]	244	395
Oshkosh township	286	340
Porter city	211	207
Posen township	295	388
St. Leo city[87]	147	'153
Sandnes township	244	245
Sioux Agency township	351	426
Stony Run township[87]	615	465
Swede Prairie township	243	283
Tyro township	292	309
Wergeland township	235	359
Wood Lake city	420	418
Wood Lake township	314	352

MISSISSIPPI

Mississippi takes its name from the river which borders it on the west. The word is of Indian origin and signified "great river" or "father of waters."

The earliest recorded exploration within the region now constituting Mississippi was made in 1540-41 by the Spaniard, De Soto, who traversed the northeastern part on his way from Florida to the Mississippi River. In 1673 the French missionaries, Marquette and Joliet, sailed down the Mississippi to the Arkansas, and in 1682 La Salle descended the Mississippi to its mouth. The first settlement within the present limits of the state was made by the French in 1699, at Old Biloxi, across the bay from the present site of Biloxi. This site was abandoned about 1702, and some 10 years later the first permanent settlement was made at Biloxi. The French claims to the Mississippi region were formally made by La Salle, who, on completing his voyage down the river, named the whole Mississippi Valley "Louisiana" in honor of Louis XIV. England also claimed this region by virtue of discoveries along the Atlantic coast, and the territory now comprising Mississippi was included wholly or in part by the Carolina charters of 1663 and 1665 and by the Georgia charter of 1732.

In 1763 all of the French possessions east of the Mississippi, except the isle of Orleans, were ceded to Great Britain. At the same time Great Britain acquired the Spanish province of Florida, and soon afterwards divided it into east and west Florida, extending the latter westward to the Mississippi and northward to the latitude of the mouth of the Yazoo. At the close of the Revolution the former British possessions east of the Mississippi and north of the thirty-first parallel were ceded to the United States, and at the same time the Floridas were transferred to Spain. The title to the area which had been added to west Florida by Great Britain was, however, in dispute between the United States and Spain until 1795, when the latter country relinquished its claims. Three years later this area, which had been claimed by Georgia, was organized as the territory of Mississippi.

In 1804 Mississippi Territory was extended northward to the southern boundary of Tennessee, thus including lands ceded to the Federal Government by South Carolina and Georgia. The tract south of the thirty-first parallel and between the Perdido River on the east and the Mississippi River on the west, was in dispute between the United States and Spain after the Louisiana Purchase in 1803. During the War of 1812 that portion of this area lying between the Perdido and Pearl Rivers was taken from Spain by the United States and added to Mississippi Territory. Spain did not, however, formally relinquish its claim until the Florida cession of 1819.

In March, 1817, the territory of Alabama was organized from a part of Mississippi territory, leaving the latter with substantially its present boundaries, and in December of the same year Mississippi became a state of the Union.

COUNTY LOCATION INDEX

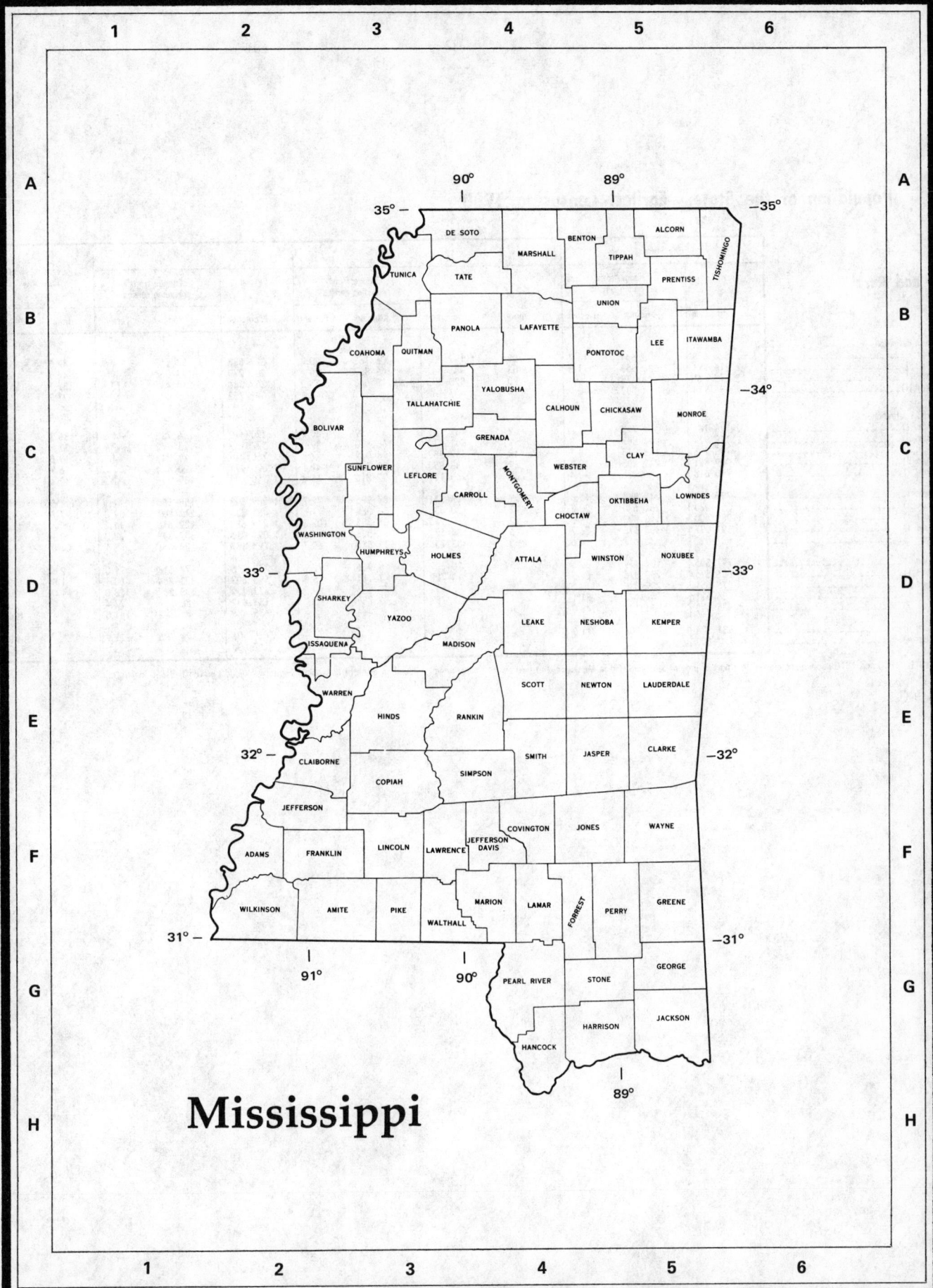

Mississippi

Population of the State: Earliest Census to 1980

Urban and Rural

	The State			Urban				Rural			Percent of total population	
	Total population	Change from preceding census		Places of 2,500 or more	Population	Change from preceding census		Population	Change from preceding census		Urban	Rural
		Number	Percent			Number	Percent		Number	Percent		
Current urban definition:												
1980 (Apr. 1)	2 520 638	303 644	13.7	98	1 192 805	206 163	20.9	1 327 833	97 563	7.9	47.3	52.7
1970 (Apr. 1)	ʳ2 216 994	38 853	1.8	83	986 642	165 837	20.2	1 230 270	-127 066	-9.4	44.5	55.5
1960 (Apr. 1)	2 178 141	-773	—	70	820 805	213 643	35.2	1 357 336	...	...	37.7	62.3
1950 (Apr. 1)	2 178 914	-4 882	-0.2	54	607 162	...	...	1 571 752	...	...	27.9	72.1
Previous urban definition:												
1960 (Apr. 1)	2 178 141	-773	—	62	787 731	185 959	30.9	1 390 410	-186 732	-11.8	36.2	63.8
1950 (Apr. 1)	2 178 914	-4 882	-0.2	53	601 772	168 890	39.0	1 577 142	-173 772	-9.9	27.6	72.4
1940 (Apr. 1)	2 183 796	173 975	8.7	48	432 882	94 032	27.8	1 750 914	79 943	4.8	19.8	80.2
1930 (Apr. 1)	2 009 821	219 203	12.2	39	338 850	98 729	41.1	1 670 971	120 474	7.8	16.9	83.1
1920 (Jan. 1)	1 790 618	-6 496	-0.4	32	240 121	32 810	15.8	1 550 497	-39 306	-2.5	13.4	86.6
1910 (Apr. 15)	1 797 114	245 844	15.8	29	207 311	87 276	72.7	1 589 803	158 568	11.1	11.5	88.5
1900 (June 1)	1 551 270	261 670	20.3	22	120 035	50 069	71.6	1 431 235	211 601	17.3	7.7	92.3
1890 (June 1)	1 289 600	158 003	14.0	12	69 966	35 385	102.3	1 219 634	122 618	11.2	5.4	94.6
1880 (June 1)	1 131 597	303 675	36.7	6	34 581	1 326	4.0	1 097 016	302 349	38.0	3.1	96.9
1870 (June 1)	827 922	36 617	4.6	5	33 255	12 566	60.7	794 667	24 051	3.1	4.0	96.0
1860 (June 1)	791 305	184 779	30.5	5	20 689	9 966	92.9	770 616	174 813	29.3	2.6	97.4
1850 (June 1)	606 526	230 875	61.5	3	10 723	7 111	196.9	595 803	223 764	60.1	1.8	98.2
1840 (June 1)	375 651	239 030	175.0	1	3 612	823	29.5	372 039	238 207	178.0	1.0	99.0
1830 (June 1)	136 621	61 173	81.1	1	2 789	2 789	...	133 832	58 384	77.4	2.0	98.0
1820 (Aug. 7)	75 448	44 142	141.0	–	–	–	–	75 448	44 142	141.0	–	100.0
1810 (Aug. 6)	31 306	23 706	311.9	–	–	–	–	31 306	23 706	311.9	–	100.0
1800 (Aug. 4)	7 600	...	...	–	–	...	...	7 600	...	...	–	100.0

NOTE: 1800 and 1810 populations are for that part of present State included in Mississippi Territory as then constituted. Population of all of Mississippi Territory: 40,352 in 1810; 8,550 in 1800.

ADAMS

1800	4,660
1810	10,002
1820	12,076
1830	14,937
1840	19,434
1850	18,601
1860	20,165
1870	19,084
1880	22,649
1890	26,031
1900	30,111
1910	35,265
1920	22,183
1930	23,564
1940	27,238
1950	32,256
1960	37,730
1970	37,293
1980	38,035

ALCORN

1870	10,431
1880	14,272
1890	13,115
1900	14,987
1910	18,159
1920	21,369
1930	23,653
1940	26,969
1950	27,158
1960	25,282
1970	27,179
1980	33,036

AMITE

1810	4,750
1820	6,853
1830	7,932
1840	9,511
1850	9,694
1860	12,336
1870	10,973
1880	14,004
1890	18,198
1900	20,708
1910	22,954
1920	18,960
1930	19,712
1940	21,892
1950	19,261
1960	15,573
1970	13,763
1980	13,369

ATTALA

1840	4,303
1850	10,991
1860	14,169
1870	14,776
1880	19,988
1890	22,213
1900	16,248
1910	28,851
1920	24,831
1930	36,035
1940	30,227
1950	26,652
1960	21,335
1970	19,570
1980	19,865

BALDWIN

1810	1,427

BENTON

1880	11,023
1890	10,585
1900	10,510
1910	10,245
1920	9,851
1930	9,813
1940	10,429
1950	8,973
1960	7,723
1970	7,505
1980	8,153

BOLIVAR

1840	1,356
1850	2,577
1860	10,471
1870	9,732
1880	18,652
1890	29,980
1900	35,427
1910	48,905
1920	57,669
1930	71,051
1940	67,574
1950	63,004
1960	54,464
1970	49,409
1980	45,965

CALHOUN

1860	9,518
1870	10,561
1880	13,492
1890	14,688
1900	16,512
1910	17,726
1920	16,823
1930	18,080
1940	20,893
1950	18,369
1960	15,941
1970	14,623
1980	15,664

CARROLL

1840	10,481
1850	18,491
1860	22,035
1870	21,047
1880	17,795
1890	18,773
1900	22,116
1910	23,139
1920	20,324
1930	19,765
1940	20,651
1950	15,499
1960	11,117
1970	9,397
1980	9,776

CHICKASAW

1840	2,995
1850	16,369
1860	16,426
1870	19,899
1880	17,905
1890	19,891
1900	19,892
1910	22,846
1920	22,212
1930	20,835
1940	21,427
1950	18,951
1960	16,891
1970	16,805
1980	17,853

CHOCTAW

1840	6,010
1850	11,402
1860	15,722
1870	16,988
1880	9,036
1890	10,847
1900	13,036
1910	14,357
1920	12,491
1930	12,339
1940	13,548
1950	11,009
1960	8,423
1970	8,440
1980	8,996

CLAIBORNE

1810	3,102
1820	5,963
1830	9,787
1840	13,078
1850	14,941
1860	15,679
1870	13,386
1880	16,768
1890	14,516
1900	20,787
1910	17,403
1920	13,019
1930	12,152
1940	12,810
1950	11,944
1960	10,845
1970	10,086
1980	12,279

CLARKE

1840	2,986
1850	5,477
1860	10,771
1870	7,505
1880	15,021
1890	15,826
1900	17,741
1910	21,630
1920	17,927
1930	19,697
1940	20,596
1950	19,362
1960	16,493
1970	15,049
1980	16,945

CLAY

1880	17,367
1890	18,607
1900	19,563
1910	20,203
1920	17,490
1930	17,931
1940	19,030
1950	17,757
1960	18,933
1970	18,840
1980	21,082

COAHOMA

1840	1,290
1850	2,780
1860	6,606
1870	7,144
1880	13,538
1890	18,342
1900	26,293
1910	34,217
1920	41,511
1930	46,327
1940	48,333
1950	49,361
1960	46,212
1970	40,447
1980	36,918

COPIAH

1830	7,001
1840	8,954
1850	11,794
1860	15,398
1870	20,608
1880	27,552
1890	30,233
1900	34,395
1910	35,914
1920	28,672
1930	31,614
1940	33,974
1950	30,493
1960	27,051
1970	24,749
1980	26,503

COVINGTON

1820	2,230
1830	2,551
1840	2,717
1850	3,338
1860	4,408
1870	4,753
1880	5,993
1890	8,299
1900	13,076
1910	16,909
1920	14,869
1930	15,028
1940	17,030
1950	16,036
1960	13,637
1970	14,002
1980	15,927

DE SOTO

1840	7,002
1850	19,042
1860	23,336
1870	32,021
1880	22,924
1890	24,183
1900	24,751
1910	23,130
1920	24,359
1930	25,438
1940	26,663

FORREST

1910	20,722
1920	21,238
1930	30,115
1940	34,901
1950	45,055
1960	52,722
1970	57,849
1980	66,018

FRANKLIN

1810	2,016
1820	3,821
1830	4,622
1840	4,775
1850	5,904
1860	8,265
1870	7,498
1880	9,729
1890	10,424
1900	13,678
1910	15,193
1920	14,156
1930	12,268
1940	12,504
1950	10,929
1960	9,286
1970	8,011
1980	8,208

GEORGE

1910	6,599
1920	5,564
1930	7,523
1940	8,704
1950	10,012
1960	11,098
1970	12,459
1980	15,297

GREENE

1820	1,445
1830	1,854
1840	1,636
1850	2,018
1860	2,232
1870	2,038
1880	3,194
1890	3,906
1900	6,795
1910	6,050
1920	10,430
1930	10,644
1940	9,512
1950	8,215
1960	8,366
1970	8,545
1980	9,827

GRENADA

1870	10,571
1880	12,071
1890	14,974
1900	14,122
1910	15,727
1920	13,607

1930	16,802
1940	19,052
1950	18,830
1960	18,409
1970	19,854
1980	21,043

HANCOCK

1820	1,594
1830	1,962
1840	3,367
1850	3,672
1860	3,139
1870	4,239
1880	6,439
1890	8,318
1900	11,886
1910	11,207
1920	10,380
1930	11,415
1940	11,328
1950	11,891
1960	14,039
1970	17,387
1980	24,537

HARRISON

1850	4,875
1860	4,819
1870	5,795
1880	7,895
1890	12,418
1900	21,002
1910	34,658
1920	32,855
1930	44,143
1940	50,799
1950	84,073
1960	119,489
1970	134,582
1980	157,665

HINDS

1830	8,645
1840	19,098
1850	25,340
1860	31,339
1870	30,488
1880	43,958
1890	39,297
1900	52,577
1910	63,726
1920	57,110
1930	85,118
1940	107,273
1950	142,164
1960	187,045
1970	214,973
1980	250,998

HOLMES

1840	9,452
1850	13,928
1860	17,791
1870	19,370
1880	27,164
1890	30,970
1900	36,828
1910	39,088
1920	34,513
1930	38,534
1940	39,710
1950	33,301

1960	27,096
1970	23,120
1980	22,970

HUMPHREYS

1920	19,192
1930	24,729
1940	26,257
1950	23,115
1960	19,093
1970	14,601
1980	13,931

ISSAQUENA

1850	4,478
1860	7,831
1870	6,887
1880	10,004
1890	12,318
1900	10,400
1910	10,560
1920	7,618
1930	5,734
1940	6,433
1950	4,966
1960	3,576
1970	2,737
1980	2,513

ITAWAMBA

1840	5,375
1850	13,528
1860	17,695
1870	7,812
1880	10,663
1890	11,708
1900	13,544
1910	14,526
1920	15,647
1930	18,225
1940	19,922
1950	17,216
1960	15,080
1970	16,847
1980	20,518

JACKSON

1820	1,682
1830	1,792
1840	1,965
1850	3,196
1860	4,122
1870	4,362
1880	7,607
1890	11,251
1900	16,513
1910	15,451
1920	19,208
1930	15,973
1940	20,601
1950	31,401
1960	55,522
1970	87,975
1980	118,015

JASPER

1840	3,958
1850	6,184
1860	11,007
1870	10,884
1880	12,126

1890	14,785
1900	15,394
1910	18,498
1920	18,508
1930	18,634
1940	19,484
1950	18,912
1960	16,909
1970	15,994
1980	17,265

JEFFERSON

1800	2,940
1810	4,001
1820	6,882
1830	9,755
1840	11,650
1850	13,193
1860	15,349
1870	13,848
1880	17,314
1890	18,947
1900	21,292
1910	18,221
1920	15,946
1930	14,291
1940	13,969
1950	11,306
1960	10,142
1970	9,295
1980	9,181

JEFFERSON DAVIS

1910	12,860
1920	12,755
1930	14,281
1940	15,869
1950	15,500
1960	13,540
1970	12,936
1980	13,846

JONES

1830	1,471
1840	1,258
1850	2,164
1860	3,323
1870	3,313
1880	3,838
1890	8,333
1900	17,846
1910	29,885
1920	23,919
1930	41,492
1940	49,227
1950	57,542
1960	59,542
1970	56,357
1980	61,912

KEMPER

1840	7,663
1850	12,517
1860	11,682
1870	12,920
1880	15,719
1890	17,961
1900	20,492
1910	20,348
1920	19,619
1930	21,881
1940	21,867
1950	15,893

1960	12,277
1970	10,233
1980	10,148

LAFAYETTE

1840	6,531
1850	14,069
1860	16,125
1870	18,802
1880	21,671
1890	20,553
1900	22,110
1910	21,883
1920	18,243
1930	19,978
1940	21,257
1950	22,798
1960	21,355
1970	24,181
1980	31,030

LAMAR

1910	11,741
1920	12,869
1930	12,848
1940	12,096
1950	13,225
1960	13,675
1970	15,209
1980	23,821

LAUDERDALE

1840	5,358
1850	8,717
1860	13,313
1870	13,462
1880	21,501
1890	29,661
1900	38,150
1910	46,919
1920	45,897
1930	52,748
1940	58,247
1950	64,171
1960	67,119
1970	67,087
1980	77,285

LAWRENCE

1820	4,916
1830	5,293
1840	5,920
1850	6,478
1860	9,213
1870	6,720
1880	9,420
1890	12,318
1900	15,103
1910	13,080
1920	12,663
1930	12,471
1940	13,983
1950	12,639
1960	10,215
1970	11,137
1980	12,518

LEAKE

1840	2,162
1850	5,533
1860	9,324

1870	8,496
1880	13,146
1890	14,803
1900	17,360
1910	18,298
1920	16,973
1930	21,803
1940	24,570
1950	21,610
1960	18,660
1970	17,085
1980	18,790

LEE

1870	15,955
1880	20,470
1890	20,040
1900	21,956
1910	28,894
1920	29,618
1930	35,313
1940	38,838
1950	38,237
1960	40,589
1970	46,148
1980	57,061

LEFLORE

1880	10,246
1890	16,869
1900	23,834
1910	36,290
1920	37,256
1930	53,560
1940	53,406
1950	51,813
1960	47,142
1970	42,111
1980	41,525

LINCOLN

1870	10,184
1880	13,547
1890	17,912
1900	21,552
1910	28,597
1920	24,652
1930	36,357
1940	27,506
1950	27,899
1960	26,759
1970	26,198
1980	30,174

LOWNDES

1830	3,173
1840	14,513
1850	19,544
1860	23,625
1870	30,502
1880	28,244
1890	27,047
1900	29,095
1910	30,703
1920	27,632
1930	29,987
1940	35,245
1950	37,852
1960	46,639
1970	49,700
1980	57,304

MADISON

1810	4,699
1830	4,973
1840	15,530
1850	18,173
1860	23,382
1870	20,948
1880	25,866
1890	27,321
1900	32,493
1910	33,505
1920	29,292
1930	35,796
1940	37,504
1950	33,860
1960	32,904
1970	29,737
1980	41,613

MARION

1820	3,116
1830	3,691
1840	3,830
1850	4,410
1860	4,686
1870	4,211
1880	6,901
1890	9,532
1900	13,510
1910	15,599
1920	17,144
1930	19,923
1940	24,085
1950	23,967
1960	23,293
1970	22,871
1980	25,708

MARSHALL

1840	17,526
1850	29,689
1860	28,823
1870	29,416
1880	29,330
1890	26,403
1900	27,674
1910	26,796
1920	26,105
1930	24,869
1940	25,522
1950	25,106
1960	24,503
1970	24,027
1980	29,296

MONROE

1820	2,721
1830	3,861
1840	9,250
1850	21,172
1860	21,283
1870	22,631
1880	28,553
1890	30,730
1900	31,216
1910	35,178
1920	32,613
1930	36,141
1940	37,648
1950	36,543
1960	33,953
1970	34,043
1980	36,404

MONTGOMERY

1880	13,348
1890	14,459
1900	16,536
1910	17,706
1920	13,805
1930	15,009
1940	15,703
1950	14,470
1960	13,320
1970	12,918
1980	13,366

NESHOBA

1840	2,437
1850	4,728
1860	8,343
1870	7,439
1880	8,741
1890	11,146
1900	12,726
1910	17,980
1920	19,303
1930	26,691
1940	27,882
1950	25,730
1960	20,927
1970	20,802
1980	23,789

NEWTON

1840	2,527
1850	4,465
1860	9,661
1870	10,067
1880	13,436
1890	16,625
1900	19,708
1910	23,085
1920	20,727
1930	22,910
1940	24,249
1950	22,681
1960	19,517
1970	18,893
1980	19,944

NOXUBEE

1840	9,975
1850	16,299
1860	20,667
1870	20,905
1880	29,874
1890	27,338
1900	30,846
1910	28,503
1920	23,710
1930	25,560
1940	25,669
1950	20,022
1960	16,826
1970	14,288
1980	13,212

OKTIBBEHA

1840	4,276
1850	9,171
1860	12,977
1870	14,891
1880	15,978
1890	17,694

1900	20,183
1910	19,696
1920	16,872
1930	19,119
1940	22,151
1950	24,569
1960	26,752
1970	28,752
1980	36,018

PANOLA

1840	4,657
1850	11,444
1860	13,794
1870	20,754
1880	28,352
1890	26,997
1900	29,027
1910	31,274
1920	47,845
1930	28,648
1940	34,421
1950	31,271
1960	28,791
1970	26,829
1980	28,164

PEARL RIVER

1890	2,957
1900	6,697
1910	10,593
1920	15,468
1930	19,405
1940	19,125
1950	20,641
1960	22,411
1970	27,802
1980	33,795

PERRY

1820	2,037
1830	2,300
1840	1,889
1850	2,438
1860	2,606
1870	2,694
1880	3,427
1890	6,494
1900	14,682
1910	7,685
1920	8,987
1930	8,197
1940	9,292
1950	9,108
1960	8,745
1970	9,065
1980	9,864

PIKE

1820	4,438
1830	5,402
1840	6,151
1850	7,360
1860	11,135
1870	11,303
1880	16,688
1890	21,203
1900	27,545
1910	37,272
1920	28,725
1930	32,201
1940	35,002

1950	35,137
1960	35,063
1970	31,813
1980	36,173

PONTOTOC

1840	4,491
1850	17,112
1860	22,113
1870	12,525
1880	13,858
1890	14,940
1900	18,274
1910	19,688
1920	19,962
1930	22,034
1940	22,904
1950	19,994
1960	17,232
1970	17,363
1980	20,918

PRENTISS

1870	9,348
1880	12,158
1890	13,679
1900	15,788
1910	16,931
1920	17,606
1930	19,265
1940	20,921
1950	19,810
1960	17,949
1970	20,133
1980	24,025

QUITMAN

1880	1,407
1890	3,286
1900	5,435
1910	11,593
1920	19,861
1930	25,304
1940	27,191
1950	25,885
1960	21,019
1970	15,888
1980	12,636

RANKIN

1830	2,083
1840	4,631
1850	7,227
1860	13,635
1870	12,977
1880	16,752
1890	17,922
1900	20,955
1910	23,944
1920	20,272
1930	20,353
1940	27,934
1950	28,881
1960	34,322
1970	43,933
1980	69,427

SCOTT

1840	1,653
1850	3,961
1860	8,139

1870	7,847
1880	10,845
1890	11,740
1900	14,316
1910	16,723
1920	16,420
1930	20,914
1940	23,144
1950	21,681
1960	21,187
1970	21,369
1980	24,556

SHARKEY

1880	6,306
1890	8,382
1900	12,178
1910	15,694
1920	14,190
1930	13,887
1940	15,433
1950	12,903
1960	10,738
1970	8,937
1980	7,964

SIMPSON

1830	2,680
1840	3,380
1850	4,734
1860	6,080
1870	5,718
1880	8,008
1890	10,138
1900	12,800
1910	17,201
1920	18,109
1930	20,897
1940	22,024
1950	21,819
1960	20,454
1970	19,947
1980	23,441

SMITH

1840	1,961
1850	4,071
1860	7,638
1870	7,126
1880	8,088
1890	10,635
1900	13,055
1910	16,603
1920	16,178
1930	18,405
1940	19,403
1950	16,740
1960	14,303
1970	13,561
1980	15,077

STONE

1920	6,528
1930	5,704
1940	6,155
1950	6,264
1960	7,013
1970	8,101
1980	9,716

SUNFLOWER

1850	1,102
1860	5,019
1870	5,015
1880	4,661
1890	9,384
1900	16,084
1910	28,787
1920	46,374
1930	66,364
1940	61,007
1950	56,031
1960	45,750
1970	37,047
1980	34,844

TALLAHATCHIE

1840	2,985
1850	4,643
1860	7,890
1870	7,852
1880	10,926
1890	14,361
1900	19,600
1910	29,078
1920	35,953
1930	25,568
1940	34,166
1950	30,486
1960	24,081
1970	19,338
1980	17,157

TATE

1880	18,721
1890	19,253
1900	20,618
1910	19,714
1920	19,636
1930	17,671
1940	19,309
1950	18,011
1960	18,138
1970	18,544
1980	20,119

TIPPAH

1840	9,444
1850	20,741
1860	22,550
1870	20,727
1880	12,867
1890	12,951
1900	12,983
1910	14,631
1920	15,419
1930	18,658
1940	19,680
1950	17,522
1960	15,093
1970	14,940
1980	18,739

TISHOMINGO

1840	6,681
1850	15,490
1860	24,129
1870	7,350
1880	8,774
1890	9,302
1900	10,124

1910	13,067
1920	15,091
1930	16,411
1940	16,974
1950	15,544
1960	13,889
1970	14,940
1980	18,434

TUNICA

1840	821
1850	1,314
1860	4,366
1870	5,358
1880	8,461
1890	12,158
1900	16,479
1910	18,646
1920	20,386
1930	21,233
1940	22,610
1950	21,664
1960	16,826
1970	11,854
1980	9,652

UNION

1880	13,030
1890	15,606
1900	16,522
1910	18,997
1920	20,044
1930	21,268
1940	21,867
1950	20,262
1960	18,904
1970	19,096
1980	21,741

WALTHALL

1920	13,455
1930	13,871
1940	17,534
1950	15,563
1960	13,512
1970	12,500
1980	13,761

WARREN

1810	1,114
1820	2,693
1830	7,861
1840	15,820
1850	18,120
1860	20,696
1870	26,769
1880	31,238
1890	33,164
1900	40,912
1910	37,488
1920	33,362
1930	35,785
1940	39,595
1950	39,616
1960	42,206
1970	44,981
1980	51,627

WASHINGTON

1800	1,250
1810	2,920

1830	1,976
1840	7,287
1850	8,389
1860	15,679
1870	14,569
1880	25,367
1890	40,414
1900	49,216
1910	48,933
1920	51,092
1930	54,310
1940	67,576
1950	70,504
1960	78,638
1970	70,581
1980	72,344

WAYNE

1810	1,253
1820	3,323
1830	2,781
1840	2,120
1850	2,892
1860	3,691
1870	4,206
1880	8,741
1890	9,817
1900	12,539
1910	14,709
1920	15,467
1930	15,295
1940	16,698
1950	17,010
1960	16,258
1970	16,650
1980	19,135

WEBSTER

1880	9,354
1890	12,060
1900	13,619
1910	14,853
1920	12,644
1930	12,128
1940	14,160
1950	11,607
1960	10,580
1970	10,047
1980	10,300

WILKINSON

1810	5,068
1820	9,718
1830	11,686
1840	14,193
1850	16,194
1860	15,933
1870	12,705
1880	17,815
1890	17,592
1900	21,453
1910	18,075
1920	15,319
1930	13,957
1940	15,955
1950	14,116
1960	13,235
1970	11,099
1980	10,021

WINSTON

1840	4,650

1850	7,956
1860	9,811
1870	8,984
1880	10,087
1890	12,089
1900	14,124
1910	17,139
1920	18,139
1930	21,239
1940	22,751
1950	22,231
1960	19,246
1970	18,406
1980	19,474

YALOBUSHA

1840	12,248
1850	17,258
1860	16,952
1870	13,254
1880	15,649
1890	16,639
1900	19,742
1910	21,519
1920	18,738
1930	17,750
1940	18,387
1950	15,191
1960	12,502
1970	11,915
1980	13,139

YAZOO

1830	6,550
1840	10,480
1850	14,418
1860	22,373
1870	17,279
1880	33,845
1890	36,394
1900	43,948
1910	46,672
1920	37,149
1930	37,262
1940	40,091
1950	35,712
1960	31,653
1970	27,314
1980	27,349

BILOXI

1870	954
1880	1,540
1890	3,234
1900	5,467
1910	8,049
1920	10,937
1930	14,850
1940	17,475
1950	37,425
1960	44,053
1970	48,486
1980	49,311

BROOKHAVEN

1870	1,614
1880	1,615
1890	2,142
1900	2,678
1910	5,293
1920	4,706
1930	5,288
1940	6,232
1950	7,801
1960	9,885
1970	10,700
1980	10,800

CANTON

1870	1,963
1880	2,083
1890	2,131
1900	3,404
1910	3,929
1920	3,252
1930	4,725
1940	6,011
1950	7,048
1960	9,707
1970	10,503
1980	11,116

CLARKSDALE

1890	781
1900	1,773
1910	4,079
1920	7,552
1930	10,043
1940	12,168
1950	16,539
1960	21,105
1970	21,673
1980	21,137

CLEVELAND

1900	479
1910	1,001
1920	1,674
1930	3,240
1940	4,189
1950	6,747
1960	10,172
1970	13,327
1980	14,524

CLINTON

1900	354
1910	767
1920	669
1930	912
1940	916
1950	2,255
1960	3,438
1970	7,289
1980	14,660

COLUMBUS

1850	2,611
1860	3,308
1870	4,812
1880	3,955
1890	4,559
1900	6,484
1910	8,988
1920	10,501
1930	10,743
1940	13,645
1950	17,172
1960	24,771
1970	25,795
1980	27,383

CORINTH

1870	1,512
1880	2,275
1890	2,111
1900	3,661
1910	5,020
1920	5,498
1930	6,220
1940	7,818
1950	9,785
1960	11,453
1970	11,581
1980	13,839

GREENVILLE

1870	890
1880	2,191
1890	6,658
1900	7,642
1910	9,610
1920	11,560
1930	14,807
1940	20,892
1950	29,936
1960	41,502
1970	39,648
1980	40,613

GREENWOOD

1880	308
1890	1,055
1900	3,026
1910	5,836
1920	7,793
1930	11,123
1940	14,767
1950	18,061
1960	20,436
1970	22,400
1980	20,115

GRENADA

1870	1,887
1880	1,914
1890	2,416
1900	2,568
1910	2,814
1920	3,402
1930	4,349
1940	5,831
1950	7,388
1960	7,914
1970	9,944
1980	12,641

GULFPORT

1900	1,060
1910	6,386
1920	8,157
1930	12,547
1940	15,195
1950	22,659
1960	30,204
1970	40,791
1980	39,676

HATTIESBURG

1890	1,172
1900	4,175
1910	11,733
1920	13,270
1930	18,601
1940	21,026
1950	29,474
1960	34,989
1970	38,277
1980	40,829

JACKSON

1850	1,881
1860	3,191
1870	4,234
1880	5,204
1890	5,920
1900	7,816
1910	21,262
1920	22,817
1930	48,282
1940	62,107
1950	98,271
1960	144,422
1970	153,968
1980	202,895

LAUREL

1900	3,193
1910	8,465
1920	13,037
1930	18,017
1940	20,598
1950	25,038
1960	27,889
1970	24,145
1980	21,897

McCOMB

1880	1,982
1890	2,383
1900	4,477
1910	6,237
1920	7,775
1930	10,057
1940	9,898
1950	10,401
1960	12,020
1970	11,969
1980	12,331

MERIDIAN

1870	2,709
1880	4,008
1890	10,624
1900	14,050
1910	23,385
1920	23,399
1930	31,954
1940	35,481
1950	41,893
1960	49,374
1970	45,083
1980	46,577

MOSS POINT

1910	3,054
1920	3,340
1930	2,453
1940	3,042
1950	3,782
1960	6,631
1970	19,321
1980	18,998

NATCHEZ

1810	1,511
1820	2,184
1830	2,789
1850	4,432
1860	6,612
1870	9,057
1880	7,058
1890	10,101
1900	12,210
1910	11,791
1920	12,608
1930	13,422
1940	15,296
1950	22,740
1960	23,791
1970	19,704
1980	22,015

OCEAN SPRINGS

1870	560
1880	849
1890	1,148
1900	1,255
1910	1,472
1920	1,732
1930	1,663
1940	1,881
1950	3,068
1960	5,025
1970	9,580
1980	14,504

PASCAGOULA

1900	708
1910	3,379
1920	6,082
1930	4,339
1940	5,900
1950	10,805
1960	17,155
1970	27,264
1980	29,318

PEARL

1980	20,778

PICAYUNE

1910	846
1920	2,479
1930	4,698
1940	5,129
1950	6,707
1960	7,834
1970	10,467
1980	10,361

STARKVILLE

1880	1,500
1890	1,725
1900	1,986
1910	2,698
1920	2,596
1930	3,612
1940	4,900
1950	7,107
1960	9,041
1970	11,369
1980	15,169

TUPELO

1870	618
1880	1,008
1890	1,477
1900	2,118
1910	3,881
1920	5,055
1930	6,361
1940	8,212
1950	11,527
1960	17,211
1970	20,471
1980	23,905

VICKSBURG

1850	3,678
1860	4,591
1870	12,443
1880	11,814
1890	13,373
1900	14,834
1910	20,814
1920	18,072
1930	22,943
1940	24,460
1950	27,948
1960	29,143
1970	25,478
1980	25,434

YAZOO CITY

1880	2,542
1890	3,286
1900	4,944
1910	6,796
1920	5,244
1930	5,579
1940	7,258
1950	9,746
1960	11,236
1970	11,688
1980	12,426

CORRECTION NOTE

Shown below are corrections to the 1980 census counts of the total population made after the tabulations for this report were completed. Any additional corrections made after this report is printed are available by writing to Data User Services Division, Customer Services (Corrections), Bureau of the Census, Washington, D.C. 20233.

The 1980 figures shown in this publication are subject to change pending the outcome of the various lawsuits dealing with the census counts.

	1980 population	
	As shown in the tables	Corrected
Choctaw County:		
District 5:		
Ackerman town...............	1 567	1 598
Coahoma County:		
District 1......................	7 491	7 122
Lyon town (pt.)................	531	162
District 3......................	6 319	6 688
Lyon town (pt.)................	(1)	266
Harrison County:		
District 1......................	29 920	22 917
Biloxi city (pt.)..............	21 924	15 170
D'Iberville CDP (pt.).........	6 240	6 236
District 2......................	25 975	27 844
Gulfport city (pt.)...........	20 097	21 966
District 3......................	35 149	34 977
Gulfport city (pt.)...........	7 427	7 255
District 4......................	30 515	31 080
Gulfport city (pt.)...........	6 924	7 489
District 5......................	36 106	40 847
Biloxi city (pt.)..............	27 387	34 141
D'Iberville CDP (pt.).........	(1)	4
Gulfport city (pt.)...........	5 228	2 966
Lafayette County:		
District 4......................	9 521	9 843
Oxford city (pt.)..............	1 813	2 135
District 5......................	8 023	7 701
Oxford city (pt.)..............	4 609	4 287
Marion County:		
District 1......................	7 522	5 470
Columbia city (pt.)...........	4 374	2 322
District 2......................	4 481	5 259
Columbia city (pt.)...........	1 509	2 287
District 3......................	4 015	4 983
Columbia city (pt.)...........	(1)	814
District 4......................	3 518	4 528
Columbia city (pt.)...........	(1)	1 085
District 5......................	6 172	5 468
Columbia city (pt.)...........	1 850	1 225
Newton County:		
District 1......................	3 395	4 114
Newton city (pt.)..............	(1)	628
District 2......................	3 858	4 049
Union town (pt.)..............	921	1 289
District 3......................	3 401	4 031
Newton city (pt.)..............	(1)	616
Union town (pt.)..............	690	322
District 4......................	6 462	4 232
Newton city (pt.)..............	3 708	1 798
District 5......................	2 828	3 518
Newton city (pt.)..............	(1)	666
Rankin County:		
District 5:		
Pearl city (pt.)...............	8 644	6 446
Wilkinson County:		
District 1......................	1 898	1 920
Woodville town (pt.)..........	131	117
District 4......................	1 854	1 885
Woodville town (pt.)..........	861	892
District 5......................	1 925	1 872
Woodville town (pt.)..........	226	209

	1980 population	
	As shown in the tables	Corrected
Yazoo County:		
District 1:		
Yazoo City city (pt.)..........	6	1 320
District 2:		
Yazoo City city (pt.)..........	2 907	1 259
Biloxi city (total)................	49 311	(2)
Columbia city (total).............	7 733	(2)
D'Iberville (CDP) (total).........	13 369	(2)
Gulfport city (total)..............	39 676	(2)
Lyon town (total).................	531	428
Newton city (total)...............	3 708	(2)
Oxford city (total)...............	9 882	(2)
Pearl city (total).................	20 778	18 580
Union town (total)................	1 931	(2)
Woodville town (total)............	1 512	(2)
Yazoo City city (total)...........	12 426	12 092

[1]Not shown separately.
[2]No change.

County Subdivisions	1980	1970
The State	2 520 638	r2 216 994
Adams County[1]	38 035	37 293
District 1	6 720	...
Natchez city (pt.)[1]	3 892	(NA)
District 2	8 357	...
Natchez city (pt.)[1]	5 922	(NA)
District 3	7 336	...
Natchez city (pt.)[1]	6 110	(NA)
District 4	6 673	...
Natchez city (pt.)[1]	3 873	(NA)
District 5	8 949	...
Morgantown (CDP)	3 445	2 008
Natchez city (pt.)[1]	2 218	(NA)
Alcorn County[2]	33 036	27 179
District 1	8 138	...
Corinth city (pt.)[2]	3 742	(NA)
District 2	6 096	...
Corinth city (pt.)[2]	1 488	(NA)
District 3	6 193	...
Corinth city (pt.)[2]	2 467	(NA)
Rienzi town	423	363
District 4	6 652	...
Corinth city (pt.)[2]	2 599	(NA)
Kossuth village	190	227
District 5	5 957	...
Corinth city (pt.)[2]	3 543	(NA)
Amite County[3]	13 369	13 763
District 1	2 463	...
Liberty town (pt.)[3]	338	(NA)
District 2	2 844	...
Centreville town (pt.)	345	323
Gloster town (pt.)[3]	710	(NA)
District 3	2 683	...
Crosby town (pt.)	119	139
Gloster town (pt.)[3]	1 016	(NA)
District 4	2 736	...
Liberty town (pt.)[3]	331	(NA)
District 5	2 643	...
Liberty town (pt.)[3]		...
Attala County[4]	19 865	19 570
District 1	12 565	12 053
Ethel town	486	560
Kosciusko city[4]	7 415	7 266
District 2	1 539	1 568
McCool town	203	225
District 3	1 217	1 273
District 4	3 299	3 446
Sallis town	211	213
District 5	1 245	1 230
Benton County[5]	8 153	7 505
District 1	1 440	...
Ashland town (pt.)	6	...
District 2	1 901	...
District 3	2 248	...
Ashland town (pt.)	526	348
District 4	1 277	...
Ashland town (pt.)[5]	–	...
District 5	1 287	...
Hickory Flat town[5]	458	354
Bolivar County[6]	45 965	49 409
District 1	7 822	...
Benoit town	499	473
Beulah town	431	443
Gunnison town	708	545
Rosedale city[6]	2 793	2 599
District 2	9 290	...
Cleveland city (pt.)	7 166	(NA)
Pace town	519	629
District 3	8 856	...
Alligator town	256	280
Duncan town	501	599
Mound Bayou city[6]	2 917	2 134
Shelby city	2 540	2 645
Winstonville village	486	536
District 4	11 160	...
Cleveland city (pt.)[6]	4 959	(NA)
Merigold town	574	772
Renova town[6]	659	...
District 5	8 837	...
Boyle town	888	861
Cleveland city (pt.)[6]	2 399	(NA)
Shaw city (pt.)[6]	2 448	2 491
Calhoun County[7]	15 664	14 623
District 1	3 010	2 772
Big Creek village	146	148
Calhoun City town (pt.)[7]	899	859
Pittsboro village	269	188
District 2	3 117	3 061
Bruce town (pt.)[7]	1 236	1 058
District 3	2 999	2 813
Bruce town (pt.)	972	975
District 4	2 762	2 926
Calhoun City town (pt.)[7]	1 134	988
Derma town (pt.)[7]	182	271
Slate Spring village	102	105

County Subdivisions	1980	1970
Calhoun County—Con.		
District 5	3 776	3 051
Derma town (pt.)	611	389
Vardaman town[7]	1 009	777
Carroll County[8]	9 776	9 397
District 1	2 262	...
Carrollton town (pt.)	254	(NA)
North Carrollton town (pt.)	859	(NA)
District 2	1 937	...
Carrollton town (pt.)[8]	8	(NA)
North Carrollton town (pt.)	–	(NA)
District 3	1 906	...
District 4	1 614	...
Carrollton town (pt.)[8]	76	(NA)
Vaiden town (pt.)[8]	19	(NA)
District 5	2 057	...
Vaiden town (pt.)[8]	905	(NA)
Chickasaw County[8]	17 853	16 805
District 1	5 676	...
Houston city[9]	3 747	2 720
District 2	3 095	...
New Houlka town[9]	710	646
District 3	4 275	...
Okolona city[9]	3 409	3 002
District 4	2 589	...
District 5	2 218	...
Woodland village	135	130
Choctaw County[10]	8 996	8 440
District 1	1 308	r1 340
District 2	1 732	1 664
Mathiston town (pt.)	95	95
District 3	1 551	1 220
French Camp village	306	174
District 4	1 683	r1 673
Weir town	553	573
District 5	2 722	r2 543
Ackerman town[10]	1 567	1 502
Claiborne County	12 279	10 086
District 1	7 195	5 793
Port Gibson city	2 371	2 589
District 2	1 760	1 279
District 3	450	446
District 4	1 710	1 528
District 5	1 164	1 040
Clarke County	16 945	15 049
District 1	3 637	3 059
Quitman city (pt.)	702	735
Stonewall town (pt.)	305	358
District 2	3 554	3 179
Pachuta town (pt.)	254	271
Shubuta town (pt.)	626	602
District 3	3 820	3 145
Enterprise town	607	458
Pachuta town (pt.)	2	–
Stonewall town (pt.)	1 040	803
District 4	3 807	2 960
Quitman city (pt.)	1 830	1 192
District 5	2 127	2 706
Quitman city (pt.)	100	775
Shubuta town (pt.)	–	–
Clay County[11]	21 082	18 840
District 1	4 601	3 698
West Point city (pt.)[11]	2 389	2 243
District 2	4 188	3 612
West Point city (pt.)[11]	1 912	1 842
District 3	3 883	3 480
West Point city (pt.)[11]	1 326	1 355
District 4	4 523	4 239
West Point city (pt.)	1 740	1 871
District 5	3 887	3 811
West Point city (pt.)	1 444	1 403
Coahoma County[12]	36 918	40 447
District 1	7 491	...
Clarksdale city (pt.)	2 487	(NA)
Lula town	394	445
Lyon town[12]	531	383
District 2	6 185	...
Clarksdale city (pt.)	2 379	(NA)
Friars Point town[12]	1 400	1 177
District 3	6 319	...
Clarksdale city (pt.)	3 043	(NA)
Jonestown town[12]	1 231	1 110
District 4	9 260	...
Clarksdale city (pt.)[12]	7 753	(NA)
District 5	7 663	...
Clarksdale city (pt.)	5 475	(NA)
Copiah County[12]	26 503	r24 764
District 1	5 811	...
Hazlehurst city (pt.)	2 663	(NA)
District 2	5 423	...
Beauregard village	185	199
Georgetown town	343	339
Wesson town	1 313	1 253
	4 872	...

County Subdivisions

County Subdivisions	1980	1970
Copiah County—Con.		
District 3—Con.		
Hazlehurst city (pt.)	1 774	(NA)
District 4	4 737	...
Crystal Springs city (pt.)[13]	2 914	(NA)
District 5	5 660	...
Crystal Springs city (pt.)[13]	1 988	(NA)
Covington County[14]	15 927	14 002
District 1	3 536	...
Collins city (pt.)	507	(NA)
Seminary town	327	269
District 2	3 420	...
Collins city (pt.)	919	(NA)
District 3	2 593	...
Collins city (pt.)	705	(NA)
District 4	3 075	...
Mount Olive town	993	923
District 5	3 303	...
De Soto County[15]	53 930	35 885
District 1	10 918	...
Olive Branch city[15]	2 067	1 513
Southaven (CDP) (pt.)	2 636	(NA)
District 2	12 187	...
Horn Lake city (pt.)	—	...
Southaven (CDP) (pt.)	9 495	(NA)
District 3	12 245	...
Horn Lake city (pt.)[15]	1 921	...
Memphis village[15]	55	...
Newport village[15]	56	...
Southaven (CDP) (pt.)	3 940	(NA)
District 4	9 428	...
Hernando city (pt.)[15]	1 500	(NA)
Horn Lake city (pt.)[15]	2 405	...
Memphis village[15]	8	...
District 5	9 152	...
Hernando city (pt.)	1 469	(NA)
Forrest County[16]	66 018	57 849
District 1	10 975	...
Hattiesburg city (pt.)	9 306	(NA)
District 2	14 008	...
Glendale (CDP)	1 329	...
Hattiesburg city (pt.)[16]	2 516	(NA)
Petal city (pt.)[16]	5 752	...
District 3	11 329	...
Hattiesburg city (pt.)	4 937	(NA)
Petal city (pt.)[16]	2 724	...
District 4	11 956	...
Hattiesburg city (pt.)	7 291	(NA)
Palmers Crossing (CDP)	2 765	2 491
District 5	17 750	...
Hattiesburg city (pt.)	15 637	(NA)
Franklin County	8 208	8 011
District 1	1 487	1 671
Roxie town	591	662
District 2	1 767	1 633
Meadville town	575	594
District 3	1 688	1 738
Bude town	1 092	1 146
District 4	1 524	1 465
District 5	1 742	1 504
George County[17]	15 297	12 459
District 1	2 877	...
District 2	2 843	...
Lucedale city (pt.)[17]	184	(NA)
District 3	3 408	...
Lucedale city (pt.)	974	(NA)
District 4	3 139	...
Lucedale city (pt.)	136	(NA)
District 5	3 030	...
Lucedale city (pt.)[17]	1 135	(NA)
Greene County[18]	9 827	8 545
District 1	1 943	...
Leakesville town (pt.)	500	(NA)
District 2	1 685	...
Leakesville town (pt.)	186	(NA)
State Line town (pt.)	282	298
District 3	2 185	...
District 4	2 127	...
Leakesville town (pt.)	434	(NA)
District 5	1 887	...
McLain town	688	632
Grenada County[19]	21 043	19 854
District 1	4 660	...
Grenada city (pt.)[19]	2 755	(NA)
District 2	3 786	...
Grenada city (pt.)	1 726	...
District 3	3 803	...
Grenada city (pt.)[19]	2 797	(NA)
District 4	4 651	...
Grenada city (pt.)[19]	2 602	(NA)
District 5	4 143	...
Grenada city (pt.)[19]	2 761	(NA)
Hancock County[20]	24 537	17 387
District 1	4 357	...
Waveland city (pt.)[20]	837	(NA)
District 2	4 190	...

County Subdivisions

County Subdivisions	1980	1970
Hancock County—Con.		
District 2—Con.		
Waveland city (pt.)[20]	2 558	(NA)
District 3	4 600	...
Bay St. Louis city (pt.)	1 941	(NA)
Diamondhead (CDP) (pt.)	385	...
District 4	5 209	...
Bay St. Louis city (pt.)	2 040	(NA)
Waveland city (pt.)[20]	791	(NA)
District 5	6 181	...
Bay St. Louis city (pt.)	3 910	(NA)
Diamondhead (CDP) (pt.)	626	...
Harrison County[21]	157 665	134 582
District 1	29 920	...
Biloxi city (pt.)[21]	21 924	18 733
D'Iberville (CDP) (pt.)	6 240	3 292
District 2	25 975	...
Gulfport city (pt.)	20 097	(NA)
Orange Grove (CDP) (pt.)	1 266	...
District 3	35 149	...
Gulfport city (pt.)	7 427	(NA)
Henderson Point (CDP)	1 114	...
Long Beach city	7 967	6 170
North Long Beach (CDP)	7 063	...
Pass Christian city	5 014	2 979
District 4	30 515	...
Gulfport city (pt.)	6 924	(NA)
North Gulfport (CDP)	6 660	6 996
Orange Grove (CDP) (pt.)	12 210	...
District 5	36 106	...
Biloxi city (pt.)[21]	27 387	29 753
Gulfport city (pt.)	5 228	(NA)
Hinds County[22]	250 998	214 973
District 1	55 212	...
Jackson city (pt.)[22]	52 418	'39 073
District 2	48 597	...
Bolton town[22]	664	787
Clinton city (pt.)	53	...
Edwards town	1 515	1 236
Jackson city (pt.)	41 345	'30 556
District 3	51 024	...
Jackson city (pt.)[22]	44 555	'36 145
Learned town	113	116
Utica town	865	1 019
District 4	56 924	...
Clinton city (pt.)[22]	14 607	'7 289
Jackson city (pt.)[22]	32 763	'21 150
Raymond town	1 967	1 620
District 5	39 241	...
Jackson city (pt.)[22]	31 812	'27 044
Terry town[22]	655	546
Holmes County[23]	22 970	23 120
District 1	3 948	...
Lexington city (pt.)	728	(NA)
District 2	4 648	...
Durant city[23]	2 889	2 752
West town	253	305
District 3	5 133	...
Goodman town	1 285	1 194
Pickens town[23]	1 386	1 012
District 4	5 056	...
Lexington city (pt.)	1 900	(NA)
District 5	4 185	...
Cruger town	540	415
Tchula town	1 931	1 729
Humphreys County	13 931	14 601
District 1	7 804	7 116
Belzoni city	2 982	'3 394
District 2	1 920	2 012
Isola town	834	458
District 3	1 325	1 981
Silver City town	378	370
District 4	612	779
District 5	2 270	2 713
Louise town	400	444
Issaquena County[24]	2 513	2 737
District 1	604	...
District 2	421	...
District 3	451	...
Mayersville town (pt.)[24]	261	...
District 4	526	...
Mayersville town (pt.)[24]	117	...
District 5	511	...
Itawamba County[25]	20 518	16 847
District 1	4 723	...
Fulton city (pt.)[25]	1 276	(NA)
District 2	3 880	...
Mantachie town[25]	732	'534
District 3	4 385	...
District 4	3 411	...
Fulton city (pt.)	623	(NA)
Tremont town[25]	379	...
District 5	4 119	...
Fulton city (pt.)	1 339	(NA)

County Subdivisions	1980	1970
Jackson County[26]	118 015	87 975
District 1	24 231	...
Escatawpa (CDP)	5 367	1 579
Moss Point city (pt.)	2 675	(NA)
Pascagoula city (pt.)	3 881	(NA)
District 2	16 987	...
Moss Point city (pt.)	16 323	(NA)
Pascagoula city (pt.)	664	(NA)
District 3	17 656	...
Pascagoula city (pt.)	17 653	(NA)
District 4	35 867	...
D'Iberville (CDP) (pt.)	7 129	3 996
Gautier (CDP) (pt.)	6 135	(NA)
Gulf Hills (CDP) (pt.)	4 495	(NA)
Ocean Springs city (pt.)[26]	12 520	(NA)
District 5	23 274	...
Gautier (CDP) (pt.)	2 782	(NA)
Gulf Hills (CDP) (pt.)	17	...
Moss Point city (pt.)	–	(NA)
Ocean Springs city (pt.)[26]	1 984	(NA)
Pascagoula city (pt.)	7 120	(NA)
Vancleave (CDP)	1 330	...
Jasper County[27]	17 265	15 994
District 1	3 436	...
Bay Springs town (pt.)	–	(NA)
District 2	3 581	...
District 3	2 828	...
Bay Springs town (pt.)[27]	864	(NA)
Louin town	338	382
Montrose town	120	160
District 4	3 865	...
Bay Springs town (pt.)[27]	1 020	(NA)
District 5	3 555	...
Heidelberg town[27]	1 098	1 112
Jefferson County[28]	9 181	9 295
District 1	858	939
District 2	1 443	1 757
District 3	4 862	4 488
Fayette town[28]	2 033	1 725
District 4	1 091	1 258
District 5	927	853
Jefferson Davis County[29]	13 846	12 936
District 1	2 878	...
Prentiss town (pt.)[29]	433	(NA)
District 2	2 170	...
District 3	3 124	...
Bassfield town	325	354
District 4	2 791	...
Prentiss town (pt.)	439	(NA)
District 5	2 883	...
Prentiss town (pt.)	593	(NA)
Jones County[30]	61 912	56 357
District 1	14 732	...
Laurel city (pt.)[30]	5 540	(NA)
Sandersville town (pt.)	337	(NA)
District 2	11 623	...
Laurel city (pt.)[30]	4 253	(NA)
Soso town[30]	434	...
District 3	11 974	...
Laurel city (pt.)[30]	2 733	(NA)
Sandersville town (pt.)	463	(NA)
District 4	13 735	...
Ellisville city (pt.)[30]	4 113	(NA)
Laurel city (pt.)	5 338	(NA)
District 5	9 848	...
Ellisville city (pt.)	539	(NA)
Laurel city (pt.)[30]	4 033	(NA)
Kemper County[31]	10 148	10 233
District 1	1 695	...
De Kalb town (pt.)	84	(NA)
Scooba town	511	626
District 2	2 302	...
De Kalb town (pt.)	401	(NA)
District 3	2 007	...
District 4	1 912	...
District 5	2 232	...
De Kalb town (pt.)	674	(NA)
Lafayette County[22]	31 030	24 181
District 1	4 475	3 701
Oxford city (pt.)[32]	1 385	'1 217
District 2	4 241	3 541
Oxford city (pt.)	1 604	'2 049
District 3	4 770	3 388
Abbeville town[32]	448	...
Oxford city (pt.)[32]	471	'553
District 4	9 521	8 100
Oxford city (pt.)[32]	1 813	'1 716
Taylor village[32]	301	92
District 5	8 023	5 451
Oxford city (pt.)[32]	4 609	'2 984
Lamar County[33]	23 821	15 209
District 1	5 092	...
Hattiesburg city (pt.)[33]	1 104	(NA)
District 2	4 399	...
Lumberton city (pt.)[33]	2 210	2 084
Purvis city (pt.)	55	(NA)

County Subdivisions	1980	1970
Lamar County—Con.		
District 3	4 535	...
Purvis city (pt.)	2 201	(NA)
District 4	4 599	...
Hattiesburg city (pt.)[33]	4	(NA)
District 5	5 196	...
Hattiesburg city (pt.)	34	(NA)
Sumrall town	1 197	955
Lauderdale County[34]	77 285	67 087
District 1	15 388	...
Marion town (pt.)[34]	641	...
Meridian city (pt.)[34]	10 668	13 584
District 2	19 886	...
Marion town (pt.)[34]	130	...
Meridian city (pt.)[34]	10 712	8 600
Meridian Station (CDP)	3 706	2 465
District 3	16 003	...
Meridian city (pt.)[34]	10 231	8 213
Nellieburg (CDP) (pt.)	723	...
District 4	12 358	...
Meridian city (pt.)[34]	7 946	9 175
Nellieburg (CDP) (pt.)	454	...
District 5	13 650	...
Meridian city (pt.)[34]	7 020	5 511
Lawrence County[35]	12 518	11 137
District 1	3 134	4 223
Monticello town (pt.)[35]	1 183	1 790
District 2	2 849	1 314
Monticello town (pt.)[35]	651	...
District 3	2 108	1 817
District 4	2 370	1 592
Newhebron village	470	456
District 5	2 057	2 191
Silver Creek town	272	257
Leake County[36]	18 790	17 085
District 1	3 573	...
Carthage city (pt.)	919	(NA)
District 2	3 802	...
Carthage city (pt.)	1 070	(NA)
District 3	3 544	...
Carthage city (pt.)	1 027	(NA)
District 4	3 941	...
Carthage city (pt.)	437	(NA)
Lena town	231	233
District 5	3 930	...
Walnut Grove town	439	398
Lee County[37]	57 061	46 148
District 1	9 936	...
Baldwyn city (pt.)[37]	1 505	1 173
Guntown town (pt.)[37]	359	(NA)
Saltillo town (pt.)	–	(NA)
Tupelo city (pt.)[37]	4 163	(NA)
District 2	9 479	...
Guntown town (pt.)	–	(NA)
Saltillo town (pt.)	1 271	(NA)
Tupelo city (pt.)[37]	4 150	(NA)
District 3	13 226	...
Tupelo city (pt.)[37]	6 350	(NA)
District 4	14 320	...
Tupelo city (pt.)[37]	6 219	(NA)
Verona town[37]	2 497	1 877
District 5	10 100	...
Nettleton town (pt.)	695	681
Plantersville town	920	910
Shannon town[37]	680	575
Tupelo city (pt.)	3 023	(NA)
Leflore County[38]	41 525	42 111
District 1	7 394	...
Greenwood city (pt.)	5 511	(NA)
District 2	7 997	...
Greenwood city (pt.)[38]	3 983	(NA)
District 3	6 582	...
Greenwood city (pt.)	4 871	(NA)
Schlater town	429	398
District 4	11 354	...
Greenwood city (pt.)	2 643	(NA)
Itta Bena city	2 904	2 489
District 5	8 198	...
Greenwood city (pt.)	3 107	(NA)
Morgan City town	319	207
Sidon town[38]	450	348
Lincoln County[39]	30 174	26 198
District 1	5 358	...
Brookhaven city (pt.)	2 561	(NA)
District 2	6 527	...
Brookhaven city (pt.)[39]	2 276	(NA)
District 3	5 594	...
Brookhaven city (pt.)	1 433	(NA)
District 4	6 095	...
Brookhaven city (pt.)[39]	2 534	(NA)
District 5	6 600	...
Brookhaven city (pt.)	1 996	(NA)
Lowndes County[40]	57 304	49 700
District 1	10 230	...
Caledonia village[40]	497	245
Columbus city (pt.)[40]	5 474	(NA)

County Subdivisions	1980	1970
Lowndes County—Con.		
District 2	16 221	...
Columbus city (pt.)[40]	5 515	(NA)
Columbus AFB (CDP)	3 650	4 074
District 3	14 045	...
Columbus city (pt.)[40]	3 988	(NA)
District 4	8 533	...
Columbus city (pt.)[40]	6 219	(NA)
Crawford town	495	391
District 5	8 275	...
Artesia town	526	444
Columbus city (pt.)[40]	6 187	(NA)
Madison County[41]	41 613	29 737
District 1	16 963	14 684
Canton city	11 116	10 503
District 2	3 823	3 393
Flora town[41]	1 507	987
District 3	14 914	6 491
Madison town[41]	2 241	853
Ridgeland city[41]	5 461	1 650
District 4	3 744	2 780
District 5	2 169	2 389
Marion County[42]	25 708	22 871
District 1	7 522	...
Columbia city (pt.)	4 374	4 244
District 2	4 481	...
Columbia city (pt.)[42]	1 509	1 150
District 3	4 015	...
District 4	3 518	...
District 5	6 172	...
Columbia city (pt.)	1 850	2 193
Marshall County[43]	29 296	24 027
District 1	5 514	...
Holly Springs city (pt.)[43]	2 525	(NA)
District 2	6 357	...
Holly Springs city (pt.)[43]	2 364	(NA)
District 3	7 229	...
Byhalia town[43]	757	702
District 4	5 648	...
Holly Springs city (pt.)[43]	462	(NA)
District 5	4 548	...
Holly Springs city (pt.)[43]	1 934	(NA)
Potts Camp town[43]	525	459
Monroe County[44]	36 404	34 043
District 1	7 020	...
Amory city (pt.)	2 633	(NA)
Hatley town[44]	497	385
Smithville town[44]	866	552
District 2	7 359	...
Amory city (pt.)	4 211	(NA)
District 3	7 188	...
Aberdeen city (pt.)	2 933	(NA)
Gattman village	151	175
District 4	7 970	...
Aberdeen city (pt.)	4 251	(NA)
District 5	6 867	...
Amory city (pt.)	463	(NA)
Nettleton town (pt.)	1 216	910
Montgomery County[45]	13 366	12 918
District 1	2 775	...
Winona city (pt.)[45]	1 742	(NA)
District 2	2 483	...
Duck Hill town	706	809
Winona city (pt.)[45]	480	(NA)
District 3	2 920	...
Winona city (pt.)[45]	2 073	(NA)
District 4	2 290	...
Kilmichael town[45]	906	543
District 5	2 898	...
Winona city (pt.)[45]	1 882	(NA)
Neshoba County[46]	23 789	20 802
District 1	6 788	...
Philadelphia city (pt.)[46]	1 886	(NA)
District 2	5 230	...
Philadelphia city (pt.)[46]	1 243	(NA)
District 3	3 758	...
Philadelphia city (pt.)[46]	1 278	(NA)
District 4	3 664	...
Philadelphia city (pt.)[46]	729	(NA)
Union town (pt.)	320	189
District 5	4 349	...
Philadelphia city (pt.)[46]	1 298	(NA)
Newton County[47]	19 944	18 983
District 1	3 395	...
Decatur town	1 148	1 311
District 2	3 858	...
Union town (pt.)[47]	921	890
District 3	3 401	...
Union town (pt.)	690	777
District 4	6 462	...
Lake town (pt.)	20	43
Newton city[47]	3 708	3 556
District 5	2 828	...
Chunky village	277	280
Hickory town	670	570

County Subdivisions	1980	1970
Noxubee County[48]	13 212	14 288
District 1	2 529	...
District 2	2 581	...
Macon city (pt.)	1 301	(NA)
District 3	3 065	...
Macon city (pt.)	1 095	(NA)
District 4	2 707	...
Shuqualak town	554	591
District 5	2 330	...
Brooksville town[48]	1 038	978
Oktibbeha County[49]	36 018	28 752
District 1	9 951	...
Starkville city (pt.)[49]	7 415	(NA)
District 2	12 696	...
Starkville city (pt.)[49]	3 818	(NA)
District 3	3 304	...
Maben town (pt.)[49]	526	469
Starkville city (pt.)[49]	389	(NA)
District 4	2 253	...
Sturgis town	269	321
District 5	7 814	...
Starkville city (pt.)[49]	3 547	(NA)
Panola County[50]	28 164	26 829
District 1	5 270	...
Como town	1 378	1 003
Sardis town (pt.)	958	(NA)
District 2	5 365	...
Crenshaw town (pt.)	760	984
Sardis town (pt.)	1 320	(NA)
District 3	5 989	...
Batesville city (pt.)[50]	106	(NA)
Courtland town	381	316
Crowder town (pt.)[50]	300	274
Pope village	208	210
District 4	4 866	...
Batesville (pt.)[50]	923	(NA)
District 5	6 674	...
Batesville (pt.)[50]	3 663	(NA)
Pearl River County[51]	33 795	27 802
District 1	6 286	...
Lumberton city (pt.)[51]	7	...
Picayune city (pt.)	968	(NA)
Poplarville city[51]	2 562	2 312
District 2	6 158	...
Picayune city (pt.)	2 217	(NA)
District 3	6 564	...
Picayune city (pt.)[51]	3 534	(NA)
District 4	6 923	...
Picayune city (pt.)[51]	2 073	(NA)
District 5	7 864	...
Picayune city (pt.)[51]	1 569	(NA)
Perry County[52]	9 864	9 065
District 1	2 100	...
Beaumont town (pt.)[52]	109	(NA)
New Augusta town[52]	589	511
Richton town (pt.)	492	(NA)
District 2	1 986	...
District 3	2 225	...
Richton town (pt.)	713	(NA)
District 4	1 843	...
Beaumont town (pt.)[52]	246	(NA)
District 5	1 710	...
Beaumont town (pt.)[52]	757	(NA)
Pike County[53]	36 173	31 813
District 1	6 618	...
McComb city (pt.)	2 126	(NA)
District 2	8 126	...
Bear Town (CDP) (pt.)	1 016	(NA)
McComb city (pt.)[53]	748	(NA)
Magnolia city[53]	2 461	1 970
District 3	6 653	...
McComb city (pt.)[53]	2 567	(NA)
Summit town (pt.)	977	(NA)
District 4	8 422	...
McComb city (pt.)[53]	4 229	(NA)
Summit town (pt.)	776	(NA)
District 5	6 354	...
Bear Town (CDP) (pt.)	261	(NA)
McComb city (pt.)[53]	2 661	(NA)
Osyka town	581	628
Pontotoc County[54]	20 918	17 363
District 1	4 155	...
Ecru town[54]	687	417
Pontotoc city (pt.)[54]	422	(NA)
Sherman town (pt.)	401	399
District 2	4 119	...
Pontotoc city (pt.)	551	(NA)
Thaxton town[54]	404	...
Toccopola town	184	175
District 3	4 850	...
Pontotoc city (pt.)	2 157	(NA)
District 4	4 198	...
Pontotoc city (pt.)[54]	320	(NA)
District 5	3 596	...
Pontotoc city (pt.)[54]	1 273	(NA)

County Subdivisions	1980	1970
Prentiss County[55]	24 025	20 133
District 1	5 874	...
Booneville city (pt.)	1 749	(NA)
District 2	4 484	...
Booneville city (pt.)	1 726	(NA)
Jumpertown town[55]	472	...
District 3	4 944	...
Baldwyn city (pt.)[55]	1 922	1 193
District 4	4 132	...
Booneville city (pt.)	1 093	(NA)
Marietta town[55]	298	'204
District 5	4 591	...
Booneville city (pt.)	1 631	(NA)
Quitman County[56]	12 636	15 888
District 1	2 553	...
Crenshaw town (pt.)	259	287
Falcon town[56]	260	...
Sledge town	699	516
District 2	2 185	...
Marks city (pt.)[56]	861	(NA)
District 3	2 744	...
Marks city (pt.)[56]	1 331	(NA)
District 4	2 234	...
Lambert town (pt.)	193	(NA)
Marks city (pt.)	68	(NA)
District 5	2 920	...
Crowder town (pt.)[56]	489	541
Lambert town (pt.)	1 431	(NA)
Rankin County[57]	69 427	43 933
District 1	14 155	...
Florence town[57]	1 111	404
Pearl city (pt.)[57]	53	...
Richland city[57]	3 955	...
District 2	15 326	...
Flowood town (pt.)[57]	775	(NA)
Jackson city (pt.)[57]	2	-
Pearl city (pt.)[57]	5 375	...
District 3	9 501	...
Flowood town (pt.)[57]	168	(NA)
Pearl city (pt.)[57]	6 706	...
District 4	15 663	...
Brandon city (pt.)[57]	8 381	(NA)
Pelahatchie town[57]	1 445	1 306
District 5	14 782	...
Brandon city (pt.)[57]	1 245	(NA)
Pearl city (pt.)[57]	8 644	(NA)
Puckett village[57]	279	333
Scott County[58]	24 556	21 369
District 1	4 820	...
Forest city (pt.)[58]	1 710	(NA)
District 2	4 590	...
Forest city (pt.)[58]	1 895	(NA)
Lake town (pt.)	504	398
District 3	4 630	...
Morton city (pt.)[58]	1 528	(NA)
District 4	4 952	...
Morton city (pt.)[58]	1 775	(NA)
District 5	5 564	...
Forest city (pt.)[58]	1 624	(NA)
Sebastopol town[58]	314	268
Sharkey County[59]	7 964	8 937
District 1	1 358	...
Rolling Fork city (pt.)[59]	880	(NA)
District 2	1 451	...
Cary town	470	517
District 3	2 046	...
Rolling Fork city (pt.)[59]	1 710	(NA)
District 4	1 750	...
Anguilla town	950	612
District 5	1 359	...
Simpson County[60]	23 441	19 947
District 1	4 624	...
Magee city (pt.)[60]	126	(NA)
Mendenhall city (pt.)	236	(NA)
District 2	4 513	...
Magee city (pt.)[60]	791	(NA)
District 3	4 749	...
Braxton village	172	180
D'Lo town[60]	463	485
Mendenhall city (pt.)	637	(NA)
District 4	4 691	...
Magee city (pt.)[60]	2 580	(NA)
District 5	4 864	...
Mendenhall city (pt.)	1 660	(NA)
Smith County[61]	15 077	13 561
District 1	3 381	...
Raleigh town (pt.)[61]	137	253
Sylvarena village (pt.)	102	(NA)
District 2	3 168	...
Taylorsville town	1 387	1 299
District 3	2 968	...
Mize town	363	372
District 4	2 771	...
Polkville village[61]	129	'166
Raleigh town (pt.)[61]	388	290

County Subdivisions	1980	1970
Smith County—Con.		
District 5	2 789	...
Raleigh town (pt.)[61]	473	475
Sylvarena village (pt.)	–	(NA)
Stone County[62]	9 716	8 101
District 1	2 039	...
Wiggins city (pt.)	1 604	...
District 2	1 691	...
Wiggins city (pt.)	–	(NA)
District 3	2 304	...
Wiggins city (pt.)	435	(NA)
District 4	1 847	...
Wiggins city (pt.)	1 121	(NA)
District 5	1 835	...
Wiggins city (pt.)	45	(NA)
Sunflower County[63]	34 844	37 047
District 1	6 697	...
Indianola city (pt.)	2 296	(NA)
Inverness town[63]	1 034	1 119
District 2	7 076	...
Indianola city (pt.)	926	(NA)
Moorhead city	2 358	2 284
Sunflower town	1 027	983
District 3	6 820	...
Indianola city (pt.)	4 999	(NA)
Shaw city (pt.)	13	22
District 4	6 337	...
Doddsville town	232	276
Ruleville city[63]	3 332	2 351
District 5	7 914	...
Drew city[63]	2 528	2 574
Tallahatchie County[64]	17 157	19 338
District 1	1 164	1 196
District 2	4 942	4 686
Charleston city	2 878	2 821
District 3	2 375	2 694
District 4	3 580	4 684
Glendora village	220	201
District 5	5 096	6 078
Sumner town[64]	452	533
Tutwiler town	1 174	1 103
Webb town[64]	782	751
Tate County[65]	20 119	18 544
District 1	3 096	...
Senatobia city (pt.)[65]	972	'1 073
District 2	4 740	...
Coldwater town (pt.)	509	(NA)
Senatobia city (pt.)[65]	1 518	'1 196
District 3	3 847	...
Coldwater town (pt.)	996	(NA)
District 4	3 492	...
Senatobia city (pt.)[65]	839	'1 593
District 5	4 944	...
Senatobia city (pt.)	1 684	'385
Tippah County[66]	18 739	15 852
District 1	3 382	...
Walnut town[66]	513	458
District 2	3 998	...
Falkner town[66]	251	'159
Ripley city (pt.)	1 301	(NA)
District 3	4 055	...
Blue Mountain town	867	677
District 4	3 788	...
Dumas town[66]	312	...
Ripley city (pt.)[66]	1 365	(NA)
District 5	3 516	...
Ripley city (pt.)	1 605	...
Tishomingo County[67]	18 434	14 940
District 1	4 387	...
Iuka city (pt.)	1 992	(NA)
District 2	3 916	...
Burnsville town[67]	889	435
Iuka city (pt.)	177	(NA)
District 3	3 403	...
Iuka city (pt.)	677	(NA)
District 4	3 585	...
Belmont town (pt.)	607	(NA)
Paden village[67]	119	97
Tishomingo town	387	410
District 5	3 143	...
Belmont town (pt.)	813	(NA)
Golden town	292	'339
Tunica County[68]	9 652	11 854
District 1	1 925	...
North Tunica (CDP) (pt.)[68]	42	(NA)
Tunica town (pt.)[68]	87	(NA)
District 2	1 762	...
Tunica town (pt.)	528	(NA)
District 3	2 651	...
North Tunica (CDP) (pt.)	–	(NA)
Tunica town (pt.)[68]	589	(NA)
District 4	1 556	...
North Tunica (CDP) (pt.)	637	(NA)
District 5	1 758	...

County Subdivisions

County Subdivisions	1980	1970
Tunica County—Con.		
District 5—Con.		
North Tunica (CDP) (pt.)	347	(NA)
Tunica town (pt.)	157	(NA)
Union County[69]	21 741	19 096
District 1	4 744	...
Myrtle town[69]	402	308
New Albany city (pt.)	1 894	(NA)
District 2	4 278	...
New Albany city (pt.)	460	(NA)
District 3	4 224	...
New Albany city (pt.)	1 274	(NA)
District 4	4 459	...
Blue Springs village	131	125
New Albany city (pt.)	1 750	(NA)
Sherman town (pt.)	98	69
District 5	4 036	...
New Albany city (pt.)	1 694	(NA)
Walthall County[70]	13 761	12 500
District 1	1 965	1 676
District 2	4 620	4 205
Tylertown town[70]	1 976	1 736
District 3	2 885	2 653
District 4	1 535	1 503
District 5	2 756	2 463
Warren County[71]	51 627	44 981
District 1	9 032	...
Kings (CDP) (pt.)	1 022	...
Vicksburg city (pt.)[71]	5 620	1 270
District 2	6 607	...
Kings (CDP) (pt.)	143	...
Vicksburg city (pt.)	4 045	7 566
District 3	15 215	...
Vicksburg city (pt.)[71]	7 420	6 217
District 4	10 247	...
Vicksburg city (pt.)[71]	4 034	7 292
District 5	10 526	...
Vicksburg city (pt.)[71]	4 315	3 133
Washington County[72]	72 344	70 581
District 1	13 477	...
Greenville city (pt.)[72]	9 862	(NA)
District 2	12 258	...
Arcola town	588	517
Greenville city (pt.)[72]	8 538	(NA)
District 3	17 434	...
Greenville city (pt.)[72]	10 303	(NA)
Metcalfe town[72]	952	...
District 4	15 469	...
Greenville city (pt.)[72]	5 105	(NA)
Leland city[72]	6 667	6 000
District 5	13 706	...
Greenville city (pt.)[72]	6 805	(NA)
Hollandale city[72]	4 336	3 260
Wayne County[73]	19 135	16 650
District 1	3 524	...
State Line town (pt.)	202	300
Waynesboro city (pt.)[73]	962	(NA)
District 2	4 002	...
Waynesboro city (pt.)[73]	743	(NA)
District 3	3 857	...
Waynesboro city (pt.)[73]	1 416	(NA)
District 4	3 928	...
Waynesboro city (pt.)[73]	1 162	(NA)
District 5	3 824	...
Waynesboro city (pt.)[73]	1 066	(NA)
Webster County[74]	10 300	10 047
District 1	2 560	...
Eupora town (pt.)[74]	1 950	(NA)
District 2	1 991	...
Walthall village	206	161
District 3	1 582	...
Eupora town (pt.)[74]	98	(NA)
District 4	2 199	...
Maben town (pt.)	329	393
Mathiston town (pt.)[74]	537	475
District 5	1 968	...
Mantee village	158	142
Wilkinson County[75]	10 021	11 099
District 1	1 898	...
Woodville town (pt.)	131	(NA)
District 2	2 282	...
Woodville town (pt.)	294	(NA)
District 3	2 062	...
Centreville town (pt.)	1 499	1 496
District 4	1 854	...
Woodville town (pt.)	861	(NA)
District 5	1 925	...
Crosby town (pt.)	230	352
Woodville town (pt.)	226	(NA)
Winston County	19 474	18 406
District 1	4 384	3 867
Louisville city (pt.)	2 913	2 468
District 2	4 433	3 954
Louisville city (pt.)	1 386	919
District 3	3 207	3 180

County Subdivisions	1980	1970
Winston County—Con.		
District 3—Con.		
Louisville city (pt.)	1 047	1 304
District 4	3 794	3 665
Louisville city (pt.)	1 329	1 248
District 5	3 656	3 740
Louisville city (pt.)	648	687
Noxapater town	516	554
Yalobusha County[76]	13 139	11 915
District 1	2 920	...
Coffeeville town (pt.)	199	(NA)
Water Valley city (pt.)[76]	657	(NA)
District 2	2 790	...
Water Valley city (pt.)[76]	1 765	(NA)
District 3	2 824	...
Water Valley city (pt.)[76]	1 725	(NA)
District 4	2 478	...
Oakland town	540	493
Tillatoba village	106	102
District 5	2 127	...
Coffeeville town (pt.)[76]	930	(NA)
Yazoo County[77]	27 349	'27 314
District 1	4 843	...
Bentonia town	518	544
Yazoo City city (pt.)	6	(NA)
District 2	5 541	...
Yazoo City city (pt.)[77]	2 907	(NA)
District 3	5 766	...
Satartia village	73	'95
Yazoo City city (pt.)	3 024	(NA)
District 4	6 491	...
Eden village	150	152
Yazoo City city (pt.)	3 741	(NA)
District 5	4 708	...
Yazoo City city (pt.)	2 748	(NA)

MISSOURI

The state of Missouri takes its name from the Missouri River, which forms a portion of its western boundary and crosses it in an easterly direction. The name of the river is derived from Indian words meaning "muddy water."

The first well authenticated visit of white men to the region now constituting Missouri occurred in 1673 when the French missionaries Marquette and Joliet descended the Mississippi as far as the mouth of the Arkansas. De Soto, a Spaniard, may, however, have ascended the Mississippi in 1541 as far as the present site of New Madrid, in the southeastern part of the state. French traders and adventurers followed the early explorers, and rumors of rich lead and silver mines led to a search for these minerals. Lead was found in abundance, and its mining was begun about the year 1720. The first permanent settlement was at Old Ste. Genevieve, which was founded by the French in the early part of the eighteenth century, probably about 1735. St. Louis was founded as a trading-post in 1764.

Missouri was formed from a portion of the vast area originally known as Louisiana. This region was claimed by the French by virtue of the discoveries of Marquette and Joliet, and of La Salle, who sailed down the Mississippi to its mouth in 1681-82.

The Louisiana region, comprising practically all of the west water-shed of the Mississippi, was ceded by France to Spain in 1762, retroceded to France in 1800, and purchased by the United States in 1803. In 1804 the region was divided by the thirth-third parallel (the present northern boundary of Louisiana) into the territory of Orleans on the south and the district of Louisiana on the north. In the following year the district of Louisiana became the territory of Louisiana, and in 1812, when the present state of Louisiana was organized, principally from the territory or Orleans, and admitted to the Union, the name "territory of Louisiana" was changed to "territory of Missouri."

A few years before the purchase of Louisiana, a steady immigration from the United States to the region now forming Missouri began. After the war of 1812 immigration became more rapid and the people were eager to be admitted to the Union. In 1820 a state constitution was adopted, under authority of Congress, and in the following year Missouri was admitted to the Union, with northern, eastern, and southern boundaries as at present. At this time the entire western boundary of the state was formed by the meridian which now constitutes its western line south of the Missouri River. It was not until 1837 that the tract lying between this line and the Missouri River and south of the parallel forming the northern boundary of the state (the Platte Purchase) was added.

COUNTY LOCATION INDEX

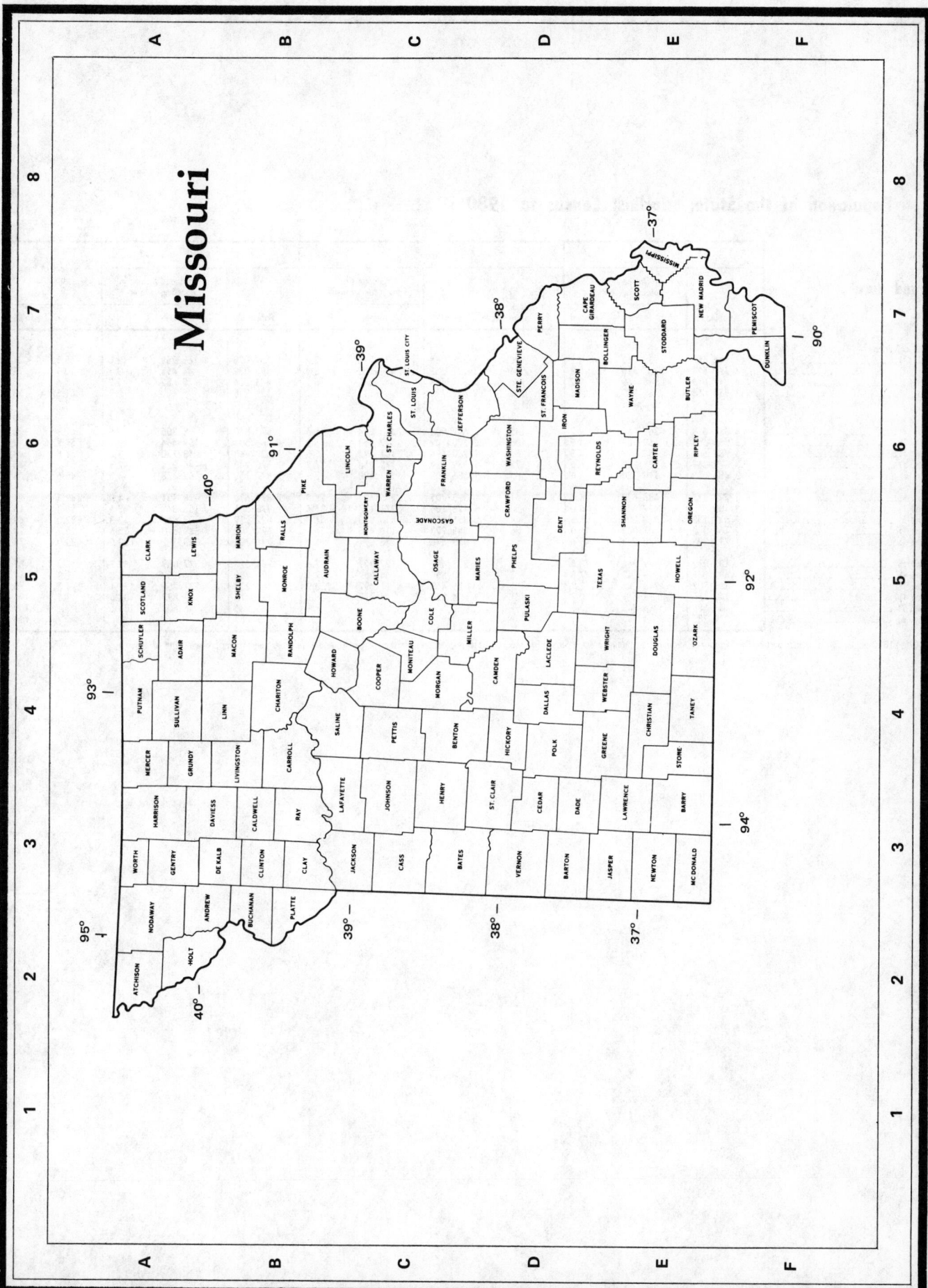

Missouri

439

Population of the State: Earliest Census to 1980

Urban and Rural

	The State			Urban				Rural				Percent of total population	
	Total population	Change from preceding census		Places of 2,500 or more	Population	Change from preceding census		Population	Change from preceding census			Urban	Rural
		Number	Percent			Number	Percent		Number	Percent			
Current urban definition:													
1980 (Apr. 1)	4 916 686	239 063	5.1	180	3 349 588	71 926	2.2	1 567 098	168 259	12.0		68.1	31.9
1970 (Apr. 1)	'4 677 623	357 810	8.3	166	3 277 662	401 105	13.9	1 398 839	−44 417	−3.1		70.1	29.9
1960 (Apr. 1)	4 319 813	365 160	9.2	145	2 876 557	443 842	18.2	1 443 256	−78 682	−5.2		66.6	33.4
1950 (Apr. 1)	3 954 653	169 989	4.5	108	2 432 715	...	...	1 521 938	...	...		61.5	38.5
Previous urban definition:													
1960 (Apr. 1)	4 319 813	365 160	9.2	145	2 647 003	356 854	15.6	1 672 810	8 306	0.5		61.3	38.7
1950 (Apr. 1)	3 954 653	169 989	4.5	108	2 290 149	329 453	16.8	1 664 504	−159 464	−8.7		57.9	42.1
1940 (Apr. 1)	3 784 664	155 297	4.3	87	1 960 696	101 577	5.5	1 823 968	53 720	3.0		51.8	48.2
1930 (Apr. 1)	3 629 367	225 312	6.6	72	1 859 119	272 216	17.2	1 770 248	−46 904	−2.6		51.2	48.8
1920 (Jan. 1)	3 404 055	110 720	3.4	63	1 586 903	193 198	13.9	1 817 152	−82 478	−4.3		46.6	53.4
1910 (Apr. 15)	3 293 335	186 670	6.0	61	1 393 705	265 601	23.5	1 899 630	−78 931	−4.0		42.3	57.7
1900 (June 1)	3 106 665	427 480	16.0	50	1 128 104	271 138	31.6	1 978 561	156 342	8.6		36.3	63.7
1890 (June 1)	2 679 185	510 805	23.6	44	856 966	310 973	57.0	1 822 219	199 832	12.3		32.0	68.0
1880 (June 1)	2 168 380	447 085	26.0	26	545 993	116 415	27.1	1 622 387	330 670	25.6		25.2	74.8
1870 (June 1)	1 721 295	539 283	45.6	19	429 578	226 091	111.1	1 291 717	313 192	32.0		25.0	75.0
1860 (June 1)	1 182 012	499 968	73.3	11	203 487	122 929	152.6	978 525	377 039	62.7		17.2	82.8
1850 (June 1)	682 044	298 342	77.8	2	80 558	64 089	389.1	601 486	234 253	63.8		11.8	88.2
1840 (June 1)	383 702	243 247	173.2	1	16 469	11 492	230.9	367 233	231 755	171.1		4.3	95.7
1830 (June 1)	140 455	73 869	110.9	1	4 977	4 977	...	135 478	68 892	103.5		3.5	96.5
1820 (Aug. 7)	66 586	46 803	236.6	−	−	−	−	66 586	46 803	236.6		−	100.0
1810 (Aug. 6)	19 783	...	...	−	−	...	...	19 783	...	...		−	100.0

NOTE: 1820 population is of that part of the Territory of Missouri constituting present State of Missouri. 1810 population is of that part of Louisiana Territory constituting present State of Missouri.

ADAIR

1850	2,342
1860	8,531
1870	11,448
1880	15,190
1890	17,417
1900	21,728
1910	22,700
1920	21,404
1930	19,436
1940	20,246
1950	19,689
1960	20,105
1970	22,472
1980	24,870

ANDREW

1850	9,433
1860	11,850
1870	15,137
1880	16,318
1890	16,000
1900	17,332
1910	15,282
1920	14,075
1930	13,469
1940	13,015
1950	11,727
1960	11,062
1970	11,913
1980	13,980

ATCHISON

1850	1,687
1860	4,649
1870	8,440
1880	14,556
1890	15,533
1900	16,501
1910	13,604
1920	13,008
1930	13,421
1940	12,897
1950	11,127
1960	9,213
1970	9,240
1980	8,605

AUDRAIN

1840	1,949
1850	3,506
1860	8,075
1870	12,307
1880	19,732
1890	22,074
1900	21,160
1910	21,687
1920	20,589
1930	22,077
1940	22,673
1950	23,829
1960	26,079
1970	25,362
1980	26,458

BARRY

1840	4,795
1850	3,467
1860	7,995
1870	10,373
1880	14,405
1890	22,943
1900	25,532
1910	23,869
1920	23,473
1930	22,803
1940	23,546
1950	21,755
1960	18,921
1970	19,597
1980	24,408

BARTON

1860	1,817
1870	5,087
1880	10,332
1890	18,504
1900	18,253
1910	16,747
1920	16,879
1930	14,560
1940	14,148
1950	12,678
1960	11,113
1970	10,431
1980	11,292

BATES

1850	3,669
1860	7,215
1870	15,960
1880	25,381
1890	32,223
1900	30,141
1910	25,869
1920	23,933
1930	22,068
1940	19,531
1950	17,534
1960	15,905
1970	15,468
1980	15,873

BENTON

1840	4,205
1850	5,015
1860	9,072
1870	11,322
1880	12,396
1890	14,973
1900	16,556
1910	14,881
1920	12,989
1930	11,708
1940	11,142
1950	9,080
1960	8,737
1970	9,695
1980	12,183

BOLLINGER

1860	7,371
1870	8,162
1880	11,130
1890	13,121
1900	14,650
1910	14,576
1920	13,909
1930	12,269
1940	12,898
1950	11,019
1960	9,167
1970	8,820
1980	10,301

BOONE

1830	8,859
1840	13,561
1850	14,979
1860	19,486
1870	20,765
1880	25,422
1890	26,043
1900	28,642
1910	30,533
1920	29,672
1930	30,995
1940	34,991
1950	48,432
1960	55,202
1970	80,935
1980	100,376

BUCHANAN

1840	6,237
1850	12,975
1860	23,861
1870	35,109
1880	49,792
1890	70,100
1900	121,838
1910	93,020
1920	93,684
1930	98,633
1940	94,067
1950	96,826
1960	90,581
1970	86,915
1980	87,888

BUTLER

1850	1,616
1860	2,891
1870	4,298
1880	6,011
1890	10,164
1900	16,769
1910	20,624
1920	24,106
1930	23,697
1940	34,276
1950	37,707
1960	34,656
1970	33,529
1980	37,693

CALDWELL

1840	1,458
1850	2,316
1860	5,034
1870	11,390
1880	13,646
1890	15,152
1900	16,656
1910	14,605
1920	13,849
1930	12,509
1940	11,629
1950	9,929
1960	8,830
1970	8,351
1980	8,660

CALLAWAY

1830	6,159
1840	11,765

1850	13,827
1860	17,449
1870	19,202
1880	23,670
1890	25,131
1900	25,984
1910	24,400
1920	23,007
1930	19,923
1940	23,094
1950	23,316
1960	23,858
1970	25,991
1980	32,252

CAMDEN

1850	2,338
1860	4,965
1870	6,108
1880	7,266
1890	10,040
1900	13,113
1910	11,582
1920	10,474
1930	9,142
1940	8,971
1950	7,861
1960	9,116
1970	13,315
1980	20,017

CAPE GIRARDEAU

1810	3,888
1820	5,968
1830	7,445
1840	9,359
1850	13,912
1860	15,547
1870	17,558
1880	20,998
1890	22,060
1900	24,315
1910	27,612
1920	29,839
1930	33,203
1940	37,775
1950	38,397
1960	42,020
1970	49,350
1980	58,837

CARROLL

1840	2,422
1850	5,441
1860	9,763
1870	17,446
1880	23,274
1890	25,742
1900	26,455
1910	23,098
1920	20,480
1930	19,940
1940	17,814
1950	15,589
1960	13,847
1970	12,565
1980	12,131

CARTER

1860	1,235
1870	1,455
1880	2,168

CASS

1850	6,090
1860	9,794
1870	19,296
1880	22,431
1890	23,301
1900	23,636
1910	22,973
1920	21,536
1930	20,962
1940	19,534
1950	19,325
1960	29,207
1970	39,448
1980	51,029

CEDAR

1850	3,361
1860	6,637
1870	9,474
1880	10,741
1890	15,620
1900	16,923
1910	16,080
1920	13,933
1930	11,136
1940	11,697
1950	10,663
1960	9,185
1970	9,424
1980	11,894

CHARITON

1830	1,780
1840	4,746
1850	7,514
1860	12,562
1870	19,136
1880	25,224
1890	26,254
1900	26,826
1910	23,503
1920	21,769
1930	19,588
1940	18,084
1950	14,944
1960	12,720
1970	11,084
1980	10,489

CHRISTIAN

1860	5,491
1870	6,707
1880	9,628
1890	14,017
1900	16,939
1910	15,832
1920	15,252
1930	13,169
1940	13,538
1950	12,412

CAMDEN

1960	12,359	COOPER		1850	5,298	1910	30,328	1930	82,929
1970	15,124			1860	9,606	1920	32,773	1940	90,541
1980	22,402	1820	6,959	1870	14,410	1930	35,799	1950	104,823
		1830	6,904	1880	19,145	1940	44,957	1960	126,276
CLARK		1840	10,484	1890	20,456	1950	45,329	1970	152,929
		1850	12,950	1900	21,325	1960	39,139	1980	185,302
1840	2,846	1860	17,356	1910	17,605	1970	33,742		
1850	5,527	1870	20,692	1920	16,641	1980	36,324	GRUNDY	
1860	11,684	1880	21,596	1930	14,424				
1870	13,667	1890	22,707	1940	13,398	FRANKLIN		1850	3,006
1880	15,031	1900	22,532	1950	11,180			1860	7,887
1890	15,126	1910	20,311	1960	9,502	1820	2,379	1870	10,567
1900	15,383	1920	19,308	1970	8,420	1830	3,484	1880	15,185
1910	12,811	1930	19,522	1980	8,905	1840	7,515	1890	17,876
1920	11,874	1940	18,075			1850	11,021	1900	17,832
1930	10,254	1950	16,608	DE KALB		1860	18,085	1910	16,744
1940	10,166	1960	15,448			1870	30,098	1920	17,554
1950	9,003	1970	14,732	1850	2,075	1880	26,534	1930	16,135
1960	8,785	1980	14,643	1860	5,224	1890	28,056	1940	15,716
1970	8,260			1870	9,858	1900	30,581	1950	13,220
1980	8,493	CRAWFORD		1880	13,334	1910	29,830	1960	12,220
				1890	14,539	1920	28,427	1970	11,819
CLAY		1830	1,712	1900	14,418	1930	30,519	1980	11,959
		1840	3,561	1910	12,531	1940	33,868		
1830	5,338	1850	6,397	1920	11,694	1950	36,046	HARRISON	
1840	8,282	1860	5,823	1930	10,270	1960	44,566		
1850	10,332	1870	7,982	1940	9,751	1970	55,116	1850	2,447
1860	13,023	1880	10,756	1950	8,047	1980	71,233	1860	10,626
1870	15,564	1890	11,961	1960	7,226			1870	14,635
1880	15,572	1900	12,959	1970	7,305	GASCONADE		1880	20,304
1890	19,856	1910	13,576	1980	8,222			1890	21,033
1900	18,903	1920	12,355			1830	1,545	1900	24,398
1910	20,302	1930	11,287	DENT		1840	5,330	1910	20,466
1920	20,455	1940	12,693			1850	4,966	1920	19,719
1930	26,811	1950	11,615	1860	5,654	1860	8,727	1930	17,233
1940	30,417	1960	12,647	1870	6,357	1870	10,093	1940	16,525
1950	45,221	1970	14,828	1880	10,646	1880	11,153	1950	14,107
1960	87,474	1980	18,300	1890	12,149	1890	11,706	1960	11,603
1970	123,702			1900	12,986	1900	12,298	1970	10,257
1980	136,488	DADE		1910	13,245	1910	12,847	1980	9,890
				1920	12,318	1920	12,381		
CLINTON		1850	4,246	1930	10,974	1930	12,172	HENRY	
		1860	7,072	1940	11,763	1940	12,414		
1840	2,724	1870	8,683	1950	10,936	1950	12,342	1840	4,726
1850	3,786	1880	12,557	1960	10,445	1960	12,195	1850	4,052
1860	7,848	1890	17,526	1970	11,457	1970	11,878	1860	9,866
1870	14,063	1900	18,125	1980	14,517	1980	13,181	1870	17,401
1880	16,073	1910	15,613					1880	23,906
1890	17,138	1920	14,173	DODGE		GENTRY		1890	28,235
1900	17,363	1930	11,764					1900	28,054
1910	15,297	1940	11,248	1850	375	1850	4,248	1910	27,242
1920	14,461	1950	9,324			1860	11,980	1920	25,116
1930	13,505	1960	7,577	DOUGLAS		1870	11,607	1930	22,931
1940	13,261	1970	6,850			1880	17,176	1940	22,313
1950	11,726	1980	7,383	1860	2,414	1890	19,018	1950	20,043
1960	11,588			1870	3,915	1900	20,554	1960	19,226
1970	12,462	DALLAS		1880	7,753	1910	16,820	1970	18,451
1980	15,916			1890	14,111	1920	15,634	1980	19,672
		1850	3,648	1900	16,802	1930	14,348		
COLE		1860	5,892	1910	16,664	1940	13,359	HICKORY	
		1870	8,383	1920	15,436	1950	11,036		
1830	3,023	1880	9,263	1930	13,959	1960	8,793	1850	2,329
1840	9,286	1890	12,647	1940	15,600	1970	8,060	1860	4,705
1850	6,696	1900	13,903	1950	12,638	1980	7,887	1870	6,452
1860	9,697	1910	13,181	1960	9,653			1880	7,837
1870	10,292	1920	12,033	1970	9,268			1890	9,453
1880	15,515	1930	10,541	1980	11,594	GREENE		1900	9,985
1890	17,281	1940	11,523					1910	8,741
1900	20,578	1950	10,392	DUNKLIN		1840	5,372	1920	7,033
1910	21,957	1960	9,314			1850	12,785	1930	6,430
1920	24,680	1970	10,054	1850	1,229	1860	13,186	1940	6,506
1930	30,848	1980	12,096	1860	5,026	1870	21,549	1950	6,387
1940	34,912			1870	5,982	1880	28,801	1960	4,516
1950	35,464	DAVIESS		1880	9,604	1890	48,616	1970	4,481
1960	40,761			1890	15,085	1900	52,713	1980	6,367
1970	46,228	1840	2,736	1900	21,706	1910	63,831		
1980	56,663					1920	68,698		

HOLT

1850	3,957
1860	6,550
1870	11,652
1880	15,509
1890	15,469
1900	17,083
1910	14,539
1920	14,084
1930	12,720
1940	12,476
1950	9,833
1960	7,885
1970	6,654
1980	6,882

HOWARD

1820	13,426
1830	10,854
1840	13,108
1850	13,969
1860	15,946
1870	17,233
1880	18,428
1890	17,317
1900	18,337
1910	15,653
1920	13,997
1930	13,490
1940	13,026
1950	11,857
1960	10,859
1970	10,561
1980	10,008

HOWELL

1860	3,169
1870	4,218
1880	8,814
1890	18,618
1900	21,834
1910	21,065
1920	21,102
1930	19,962
1940	22,270
1950	22,725
1960	22,027
1970	23,521
1980	28,807

IRON

1860	5,842
1870	6,278
1880	8,183
1890	9,119
1900	8,716
1910	8,563
1920	9,458
1930	9,642
1940	10,440
1950	9,458
1960	8,041
1970	9,529
1980	11,084

JACKSON

1830	2,823
1840	7,612
1850	14,000
1860	22,913
1870	55,041
1880	82,325
1890	160,510
1900	195,193
1910	283,552
1920	367,846
1930	470,454
1940	477,828
1950	541,035
1960	622,732
1970	654,178
1980	629,266

JASPER

1850	4,223
1860	6,883
1870	14,928
1880	32,019
1890	50,500
1900	84,018
1910	89,673
1920	75,941
1930	73,810
1940	78,705
1950	79,106
1960	78,863
1970	79,852
1980	86,958

JEFFERSON

1820	1,835
1830	2,592
1840	4,296
1850	6,928
1860	10,344
1870	15,380
1880	18,736
1890	22,484
1900	25,712
1910	27,878
1920	26,555
1930	27,563
1940	32,023
1950	38,007
1960	66,377
1970	105,248
1980	146,183

JOHNSON

1840	4,471
1850	7,464
1860	14,644
1870	24,648
1880	28,172
1890	18,132
1900	27,843
1910	26,297
1920	24,899
1930	22,413
1940	21,617
1950	20,716
1960	28,981
1970	34,172
1980	39,059

KNOX

1850	2,894
1860	8,727
1870	10,974
1880	13,047
1890	13,501
1900	13,479
1910	12,403
1920	10,783
1930	9,658
1940	8,878
1950	7,617
1960	6,558
1970	5,692
1980	5,508

LACLEDE

1850	2,498
1860	5,182
1870	9,380
1880	11,524
1890	14,701
1900	16,523
1910	17,363
1920	16,857
1930	16,320
1940	18,718
1950	19,010
1960	18,991
1970	19,944
1980	24,323

LAFAYETTE

1830	2,912
1840	6,815
1850	13,690
1860	20,098
1870	22,623
1880	25,710
1890	30,184
1900	31,679
1910	30,154
1920	30,006
1930	29,259
1940	27,856
1950	25,272
1960	25,274
1970	26,626
1980	29,925

LAWRENCE

1850	4,859
1860	8,846
1870	13,067
1880	17,583
1890	26,228
1900	31,662
1910	26,585
1920	24,211
1930	23,774
1940	24,637
1950	23,420
1960	23,260
1970	24,585
1980	28,973

LEWIS

1840	6,040
1850	6,587
1860	12,286
1870	15,114
1880	15,925
1890	15,935
1900	16,724
1910	15,514
1920	13,465
1930	12,093
1940	11,490
1950	10,733
1960	10,984
1970	10,993
1980	10,901

LINCOLN

1820	1,662
1830	4,059
1840	7,449
1850	9,421
1860	14,210
1870	15,960
1880	17,426
1890	18,346
1900	18,352
1910	17,033
1920	15,596
1930	13,929
1940	14,395
1950	13,478
1960	14,783
1970	18,041
1980	22,193

LINN

1840	2,245
1850	4,058
1860	9,112
1870	15,900
1880	20,016
1890	24,121
1900	25,503
1910	25,253
1920	24,778
1930	23,339
1940	21,416
1950	18,865
1960	16,815
1970	15,125
1980	15,495

LIVINGSTON

1840	4,325
1850	4,247
1860	7,417
1870	16,730
1880	20,196
1890	20,668
1900	22,302
1910	19,453
1920	18,857
1930	18,615
1940	18,000
1950	16,532
1960	15,771
1970	15,368
1980	15,739

McDONALD

1850	2,236
1860	4,038
1870	5,226
1880	7,816
1890	11,283
1900	13,574
1910	13,539
1920	14,690
1930	13,936
1940	15,749
1950	14,144
1960	11,798
1970	12,357
1980	14,917

MACON

1840	6,034
1850	6,565
1860	14,346
1870	23,230
1880	26,222
1890	30,575
1900	33,018
1910	30,868
1920	27,518
1930	23,070
1940	21,396
1950	18,332
1960	16,473
1970	15,432
1980	16,313

MADISON

1820	2,047
1830	2,371
1840	3,395
1850	6,003
1860	5,664
1870	5,849
1880	8,876
1890	9,268
1900	9,975
1910	11,273
1920	10,721
1930	9,418
1940	9,656
1950	10,380
1960	9,366
1970	8,461
1980	10,725

MARIES

1860	4,901
1870	5,916
1880	7,304
1890	8,600
1900	9,616
1910	10,088
1920	9,500
1930	8,368
1940	8,638
1950	7,423
1960	7,282
1970	6,851
1980	7,551

MARION

1830	4,837
1840	9,623
1850	12,230
1860	18,838
1870	23,780
1880	24,837
1890	26,233
1900	26,331
1910	30,572
1920	30,226
1930	33,493
1940	31,576
1950	29,765
1960	29,765
1970	28,121
1980	28,638

MERCER

1850	2,691
1860	9,300
1870	11,557
1880	14,673
1890	14,581
1900	14,703

1910	12,335	**1980**	**9,716**	**1980**	**40,555**	1900	12,115	1930	18,001
1920	11,281					1910	19,559	1940	18,327
1930	9,350	**MONTGOMERY**		**NODAWAY**		1920	26,634	1950	16,844
1940	8,766					1930	37,284	1960	16,706
1950	7,235	1820	3,074	1850	2,118	1940	47,857	1970	16,928
1960	5,750	1830	3,902	1860	5,252	1950	45,624	1980	17,568
1970	4,910	1840	4,371	1870	14,751	1960	38,095		
1980	4,685	1850	5,489	1880	29,544	1970	26,373	**PLATTE**	
		1860	9,178	1890	30,914	1980	24,987		
MILLER		1870	10,405	1900	32,938			1840	8,913
		1880	16,249	1910	28,833	**PERRY**		1850	16,845
1840	2,282	1890	16,850	1920	27,744			1860	18,350
1850	3,834	1900	16,571	1930	27,371	1830	3,349	1870	17,352
1860	6,812	1910	15,604	1940	25,556	1840	5,760	1880	17,366
1870	6,616	1920	15,233	1950	24,033	1850	7,215	1890	16,248
1880	9,085	1930	13,011	1960	22,215	1860	9,128	1900	16,193
1890	14,162	1940	12,442	1970	22,467	1870	9,877	1910	14,429
1900	15,187	1950	11,555	1980	21,996	1880	11,895	1920	13,996
1910	16,171	1960	11,097			1890	13,237	1930	13,819
1920	15,567	1970	11,000	**OREGON**		1900	15,134	1940	13,862
1930	16,728	1980	11,537			1910	14,898	1950	14,973
1940	14,798			1850	1,432	1920	14,434	1960	23,350
1950	13,734	**MORGAN**		1860	3,009	1930	13,707	1970	32,081
1960	13,800			1870	3,287	1940	15,358	1980	46,341
1970	15,026	1840	4,407	1880	5,791	1950	14,890		
1980	18,532	1850	4,650	1890	10,467	1960	14,642	**POLK**	
		1860	8,202	1900	13,906	1970	14,393		
MISSISSIPPI		1870	8,434	1910	14,681	1980	16,784	1840	8,449
		1880	10,132	1920	12,889			1850	6,186
1850	3,123	1890	12,311	1930	12,220	**PETTIS**		1860	9,995
1860	4,859	1900	12,175	1940	13,390			1870	12,445
1870	4,982	1910	12,863	1950	11,978	1840	2,930	1880	15,734
1880	9,270	1920	12,015	1960	9,845	1850	5,150	1890	20,339
1890	10,134	1930	10,968	1970	9,180	1860	9,392	1900	23,255
1900	11,837	1940	11,140	1980	10,238	1870	18,706	1910	21,561
1910	14,557	1950	10,207			1880	27,271	1920	20,351
1920	12,860	1960	9,476	**OSAGE**		1890	31,151	1930	17,803
1930	15,762	1970	10,083			1900	32,438	1940	17,400
1940	23,149	1980	13,807	1850	6,704	1910	33,913	1950	16,062
1950	22,551			1860	7,879	1920	25,813	1960	13,753
1960	20,695	**NEW MADRID**		1870	10,793	1930	34,664	1970	15,415
1970	16,647			1880	11,824	1940	33,336	1980	18,822
1980	15,726	1810	3,165	1890	13,080	1950	31,577		
		1820	2,296	1900	14,096	1960	35,120	**PULASKI**	
MONITEAU		1830	2,350	1910	14,283	1970	34,137		
		1840	4,554	1920	13,559	1980	36,378	1840	6,529
1850	6,004	1850	5,541	1930	12,462			1850	3,998
1860	10,124	1860	5,654	1940	12,375	**PHELPS**		1860	3,835
1870	11,375	1870	6,357	1950	11,301			1870	4,714
1880	14,346	1880	7,694	1960	10,867	1860	5,714	1880	7,250
1890	15,630	1890	9,317	1970	10,994	1870	10,506	1890	9,387
1900	15,931	1900	11,280	1980	12,014	1880	12,568	1900	10,394
1910	14,375	1910	19,488			1890	12,636	1910	11,438
1920	13,532	1920	25,180	**OZARK**		1900	14,194	1920	10,490
1930	12,173	1930	30,262			1910	15,796	1930	10,755
1940	11,775	1940	39,787	1850	2,294	1920	14,941	1940	10,775
1950	10,840	1950	39,444	1860	2,447	1930	15,308	1950	10,392
1960	10,500	1960	31,350	1870	3,363	1940	17,437	1960	46,567
1970	10,742	1970	23,420	1880	5,618	1950	21,504	1970	53,967
1980	12,068	1980	22,945	1890	9,795	1960	25,396	1980	42,011
				1900	12,145	1970	29,481		
MONROE		**NEWTON**		1910	11,926	1980	33,633	**PUTNAM**	
				1920	11,125				
1840	9,505	1840	3,790	1930	9,537	**PIKE**		1850	1,636
1850	10,541	1850	4,268	1940	10,766			1860	9,207
1860	14,785	1860	9,319	1950	8,856	1820	3,747	1870	11,217
1870	17,149	1870	12,821	1960	6,744	1830	6,129	1880	13,555
1880	19,071	1880	18,947	1970	6,266	1840	10,646	1890	15,365
1890	20,790	1890	22,108	1980	7,961	1850	13,609	1900	16,688
1900	19,716	1900	27,001			1860	18,417	1910	14,308
1910	18,304	1910	27,136	**PEMISCOT**		1870	23,076	1920	13,115
1920	16,414	1920	24,886			1880	26,715	1930	11,503
1930	13,466	1930	26,959	1860	2,962	1890	26,231	1940	11,327
1940	13,195	1940	29,039	1870	2,059	1900	25,744	1950	9,166
1950	11,314	1950	28,240	1880	4,299	1910	22,556	1960	6,999
1960	10,688	1960	30,093	1890	5,975	1920	20,345	1970	5,916
1970	9,542	1970	32,981					1980	6,092

RALLS

1830	4,375
1840	5,670
1850	6,151
1860	8,592
1870	10,510
1880	11,838
1890	12,294
1900	12,287
1910	12,913
1920	10,412
1930	10,704
1940	10,040
1950	8,868
1960	8,078
1970	7,764
1980	8,911

RANDOLPH

1830	2,942
1840	7,198
1850	9,439
1860	11,407
1870	15,908
1880	22,751
1890	24,893
1900	24,442
1910	26,182
1920	17,633
1930	26,431
1940	24,458
1950	22,918
1960	22,014
1970	22,434
1980	25,460

RAY

1830	2,657
1840	6,553
1850	10,373
1860	14,092
1870	18,700
1880	20,190
1890	24,215
1900	24,805
1910	21,451
1920	20,508
1930	19,846
1940	18,584
1950	15,932
1960	16,075
1970	17,599
1980	21,378

REYNOLDS

1850	1,849
1860	3,173
1870	3,756
1880	5,722
1890	6,803
1900	8,161
1910	9,592
1920	10,106
1930	8,923
1940	9,370
1950	6,918
1960	5,161
1970	6,106
1980	7,230

RIPLEY

1840	2,856
1850	2,830
1860	3,747
1870	3,175
1880	5,377
1890	8,512
1900	13,186
1910	13,099
1920	12,061
1930	11,176
1940	12,606
1950	11,414
1960	9,096
1970	9,803
1980	12,458

SAINT CHARLES

1810	3,505
1820	3,970
1830	4,320
1840	7,911
1850	11,454
1860	16,523
1870	21,304
1880	23,065
1890	22,977
1900	24,474
1910	24,695
1920	22,828
1930	24,354
1940	25,562
1950	29,834
1960	52,970
1970	92,954
1980	144,107

SAINT CLAIR

1850	3,556
1860	6,812
1870	6,742
1880	14,125
1890	16,747
1900	17,907
1910	16,412
1920	15,341
1930	13,289
1940	13,146
1950	10,482
1960	8,421
1970	7,667
1980	8,622

SAINT FRANCOIS

1830	2,366
1840	3,211
1850	4,964
1860	7,249
1870	9,742
1880	13,822
1890	17,347
1900	24,051
1910	35,738
1920	31,403
1930	35,832
1940	35,950
1950	35,276
1960	36,516
1970	36,875
1980	42,600

SAINT LOUIS

1810	5,667
1820	10,049
1830	14,125
1840	35,979
1850	104,978
1860	190,524
1870	351,189
1880	31,888
1890	36,307
1900	50,040
1910	82,417
1920	100,737
1930	211,593
1940	274,230
1950	406,349
1960	703,532
1970	951,671
1980	973,896

SAINTE GENEVIEVE

1810	4,620
1820	4,962
1830	2,186
1840	3,148
1850	5,313
1860	8,029
1870	8,384
1880	10,390
1890	9,883
1900	10,359
1910	10,607
1920	9,809
1930	10,097
1940	10,905
1950	11,237
1960	12,116
1970	12,867
1980	15,180

SALINE

1830	2,873
1840	5,258
1850	8,843
1860	14,699
1870	21,672
1880	29,911
1890	33,762
1900	33,703
1910	29,448
1920	28,826
1930	30,598
1940	29,416
1950	26,694
1960	25,148
1970	24,837
1980	24,919

SCHUYLER

1850	3,287
1860	6,697
1870	8,820
1880	10,470
1890	11,249
1900	10,840
1910	9,062
1920	8,383
1930	6,951
1940	6,627
1950	5,760
1960	5,052
1970	4,665
1980	4,979

SCOTLAND

1850	3,782
1860	8,873
1870	10,670
1880	12,508
1890	12,674
1900	13,232
1910	11,869
1920	10,700
1930	8,853
1940	8,557
1950	7,332
1960	6,484
1970	5,599
1980	5,415

SCOTT

1830	2,136
1840	5,974
1850	3,182
1860	5,247
1870	7,317
1880	8,587
1890	11,228
1900	13,092
1910	22,372
1920	23,409 •
1930	24,913
1940	30,377
1950	32,842
1960	32,748
1970	33,250
1980	39,647

SHANNON

1850	1,199
1860	2,284
1870	2,339
1880	3,441
1890	8,898
1900	11,247
1910	11,443
1920	11,865
1930	10,894
1940	11,831
1950	8,377
1960	7,087
1970	7,196
1980	7,885

SHELBY

1840	3,056
1850	4,253
1860	7,301
1870	10,119
1880	14,024
1890	15,642
1900	16,167
1910	14,864
1920	13,617
1930	11,983
1940	11,224
1950	9,730
1960	9,063
1970	7,906
1980	7,826

STODDARD

1840	3,153
1850	4,277
1860	7,877
1870	8,535

1880	13,431
1890	17,327
1900	24,669
1910	27,807
1920	29,755
1930	27,452
1940	33,009
1950	33,463
1960	29,490
1970	25,771
1980	29,009

STONE

1860	2,400
1870	3,253
1880	4,404
1890	7,090
1900	9,892
1910	11,559
1920	11,941
1930	11,614
1940	11,298
1950	9,748
1960	8,176
1970	9,921
1980	15,587

SULLIVAN

1850	2,983
1860	9,198
1870	11,907
1880	16,569
1890	19,000
1900	20,282
1910	18,598
1920	17,781
1930	15,212
1940	13,701
1950	11,299
1960	8,783
1970	7,572
1980	7,434

TANEY

1840	3,264
1850	4,373
1860	3,576
1870	4,407
1880	5,599
1890	7,973
1900	10,127
1910	9,134
1920	8,178
1930	8,867
1940	10,323
1950	9,863
1960	10,238
1970	13,023
1980	20,467

TEXAS

1850	2,312
1860	6,067
1870	9,618
1880	12,206
1890	19,406
1900	22,192
1910	21,458
1920	20,548
1930	18,580
1940	19,813
1950	18,992

1960	17,758		1940	12,794
1970	18,320		1950	10,514
1980	21,070		1960	8,638
			1970	8,546
VAN BUREN			1980	11,277
1840	4,698		**WEBSTER**	
VERNON			1860	7,099
			1870	10,434
1860	4,850		1880	12,175
1870	11,247		1890	15,177
1880	19,369		1900	16,640
1890	31,505		1910	17,377
1900	31,619		1920	16,609
1910	28,827		1930	16,148
1920	26,069		1940	17,226
1930	25,031		1950	15,072
1940	25,586		1960	13,753
1950	22,685		1970	15,562
1960	20,540		1980	20,414
1970	19,065			
1980	19,806		**WORTH**	
WARREN			1870	5,004
			1880	8,203
1840	4,253		1890	8,738
1850	5,860		1900	9,832
1860	8,839		1910	8,007
1870	9,673		1920	7,642
1880	10,806		1930	6,525
1890	9,913		1940	6,345
1900	9,919		1950	5,120
1910	9,123		1960	3,936
1920	8,490		1970	3,359
1930	8,082		1980	3,008
1940	7,734			
1950	7,666		**WRIGHT**	
1960	8,750			
1970	9,699		1850	3,387
1980	14,900		1860	4,508
			1870	5,684
WASHINGTON			1880	9,172
			1890	14,484
1820	2,769		1900	17,519
1830	6,784		1910	18,315
1840	7,213		1920	17,733
1850	8,811		1930	16,741
1860	9,723		1940	17,967
1870	11,719		1950	15,834
1880	12,896		1960	14,183
1890	13,153		1970	13,667
1900	14,263		1980	16,188
1910	13,378			
1920	13,803			
1930	14,450			
1940	17,492			
1950	14,689			
1960	14,346			
1970	15,086			
1980	17,983			
WAYNE				
1820	1,443			
1830	3,264			
1840	3,403			
1850	4,518			
1860	5,629			
1870	6,068			
1880	9,096			
1890	11,927			
1900	15,309			
1910	15,181			
1920	13,012			
1930	12,243			

NOTES

ATCHISON

Name changed from Allen in 1845.

CAMDEN

Name changed from Kinderhook in 1843.

CASS

Name changed from Van Buren in 1849.

DALLAS

Name changed from Niangua in 1844.

DODGE

Annexed to Putnam prior to 1860.

HENRY

Name changed from Rives in 1841.

HOLT

Name changed from Nodaway in 1841.

LAFAYETTE

Name changed from Lillard in 1825.

OZARK

Name changed to Decatur in 1843; name changed back to Ozark in 1845.

TEXAS

Name changed from Ashley in 1845.

VAN BUREN

Annexed to Bates and Cass prior to 1850.

ARNOLD

1980	19,141

BALLWIN

1960	5,710
1970	10,656
1980	12,656

BELLEFONTAINE NEIGHBORS

1960	13,650
1970	14,084
1980	12,082

BELTON

1880	552
1890	988
1900	1,005
1910	922
1920	899
1930	992
1940	971
1950	1,233
1960	4,897
1970	12,270
1980	12,708

BERKELEY

1940	2,577
1950	5,268
1960	18,676
1970	19,743
1980	16,146

BLUE SPRINGS

1900	468
1910	561
1920	551
1930	706
1940	788
1950	1,068
1960	2,555
1970	6,779
1980	25,927

BRIDGETON

1880	197
1890	237
1900	178
1910	129
1920	121
1930	152
1940	169
1950	202
1960	7,820
1970	19,992
1980	18,445

CAPE GIRARDEAU

1860	2,663
1870	3,585
1880	3,889
1890	4,297
1900	4,815
1910	8,475
1920	10,252
1930	16,227
1940	19,426

1950	21,578
1960	24,947
1970	31,282
1970	34,361

CARTHAGE

1880	4,167
1890	7,981
1900	9,416
1910	9,483
1920	10,068
1930	9,736
1940	10,585
1950	11,188
1960	11,264
1970	11,035
1980	11,104

CLAYTON

1920	3,028
1930	9,613
1940	13,069
1950	16,035
1960	15,245
1970	16,100
1980	14,219

COLUMBIA

1850	651
1860	1,414
1870	2,236
1880	3,326
1890	4,000
1900	5,651
1910	9,662
1920	10,392
1930	14,967
1940	18,399
1950	31,974
1960	36,650
1970	58,812
1980	62,061

CRESTWOOD

1950	1,645
1960	11,106
1970	15,123
1980	12,815

CREVE COEUR

1950	2,040
1960	5,122
1970	8,967
1980	11,757

EXCELSIOR SPRINGS

1890	2,034
1900	1,881
1910	3,900
1920	4,165
1930	4,565
1940	4,821
1950	5,841
1960	6,473
1970	9,411
1980	10,424

FERGUSON

1900	1,015
1910	1,658
1920	1,874
1930	3,798
1940	5,724
1950	11,573
1960	22,149
1970	28,759
1980	24,740

FLORISSANT

1900	732
1910	765
1920	682
1930	1,039
1940	1,369
1950	3,737
1960	38,166
1970	65,908
1980	55,372

FULTON

1870	1,585
1880	2,409
1890	4,314
1900	4,883
1910	5,228
1920	5,595
1930	6,105
1940	8,297
1950	10,052
1960	11,131
1970	12,148
1980	11,046

GLADSTONE

1960	14,502
1970	23,422
1980	24,990

GRANDVIEW

1920	410
1930	707
1940	596
1950	1,556
1960	6,027
1970	17,456
1980	24,502

HANNIBAL

1850	2,020
1860	6,505
1870	10,125
1880	11,074
1890	12,857
1900	12,780
1910	18,341
1920	19,306
1930	22,761
1940	20,865
1950	20,444
1960	20,028
1970	18,609
1980	18,881

HAZELWOOD

1950	336
1960	6,045
1970	14,082
1980	12,935

INDEPENDENCE

1860	3,164
1870	3,184
1880	3,146
1890	6,380
1900	6,974
1910	9,859
1920	11,686
1930	15,296
1940	16,066
1950	36,963
1960	62,328
1970	111,630
1980	111,806

JEFFERSON CITY

1860	3,082
1870	4,420
1880	5,271
1890	6,742
1900	9,664
1910	11,850
1920	14,490
1930	21,596
1940	24,268
1950	25,099
1960	28,228
1970	32,407
1980	33,619

JENNINGS

1950	15,282
1960	19,965
1970	19,379
1980	17,026

JOPLIN

1880	7,038
1890	9,943
1900	26,023
1910	32,073
1920	29,902
1930	33,454
1940	37,144
1950	38,711
1960	38,958
1970	39,256
1980	38,893

KANSAS CITY

1860	4,418
1870	32,260
1880	55,785
1890	132,716
1900	163,752
1910	248,381
1920	324,410
1930	399,746
1940	399,178
1950	456,622
1960	475,539
1970	507,330
1980	448,159

KENNETT

1880	171
1890	302
1900	1,509
1910	3,033
1920	3,622
1930	4,128
1940	6,335
1950	8,685
1960	9,098
1970	10,090
1980	10,145

KIRKSVILLE

1860	658
1870	1,471
1880	2,314
1890	3,510
1900	5,966
1910	6,347
1920	7,213
1930	8,293
1940	10,080
1950	11,110
1960	13,123
1970	15,560
1980	17,167

KIRKWOOD

1880	1,280
1890	1,777
1900	2,825
1910	4,171
1920	4,422
1930	9,169
1940	12,132
1950	18,640
1960	29,421
1970	31,679
1980	27,987

LEE'S SUMMIT

1880	693
1890	1,369
1900	1,453
1910	1,455
1920	1,467
1930	2,035
1940	2,263
1950	2,554
1960	8,267
1970	16,230
1980	28,741

LIBERTY

1850	827
1860	1,288
1870	1,700
1880	1,476
1890	2,558
1900	2,407
1910	2,980
1920	3,097
1930	3,516
1940	3,598
1950	4,709
1960	8,909
1970	13,704
1980	16,251

MAPLEWOOD

1910	4,976
1920	7,431
1930	12,657
1940	12,875
1950	13,416
1960	12,552
1970	12,785
1980	10,960

MARSHALL

1880	2,701
1890	4,297
1900	5,086
1910	4,869
1920	5,200
1930	8,103
1940	8,533
1950	8,850
1960	9,572
1970	12,051
1980	12,781

MEXICO

1860	960
1870	2,602
1880	3,835
1890	4,789
1900	5,099
1910	5,939
1920	6,013
1930	8,290
1940	9,053
1950	11,623
1960	12,889
1970	11,807
1980	12,276

MOBERLY

1870	1,514
1880	6,070
1890	8,215
1900	8,012
1910	10,923
1920	12,808
1930	13,772
1940	12,920
1950	13,115
1960	13,170
1970	12,998
1980	13,418

OVERLAND

1940	2,934
1950	11,556
1960	22,763
1970	24,819
1980	19,620

POLAR BLUFF

1880	791
1890	2,187
1900	4,321
1910	6,916
1920	8,042
1930	7,551
1940	11,163
1950	15,064
1960	15,926
1970	16,653
1980	17,139

RAYTOWN

1960	17,083
1970	33,306
1980	31,759

RICHMOND HEIGHTS

1920	2,136
1930	9,150
1940	12,802
1950	15,045
1960	15,622
1970	13,802
1980	11,516

ROLLA

1870	1,354
1880	1,582
1890	1,592
1900	1,600
1910	2,261
1920	2,077
1930	3,670
1940	5,141
1950	9,354
1960	11,132
1970	13,571
1980	13,303

SAINT ANN

1950	4,557
1960	12,155
1970	18,215
1980	15,523

SAINT CHARLES

1850	1,498
1860	3,239
1870	5,570
1880	5,014
1890	6,161
1900	7,982
1910	9,437
1920	8,503
1930	10,491
1940	10,803
1950	14,314
1960	21,189
1970	31,834
1980	37,379

SAINT JOSEPH

1860	8,932
1870	19,565
1880	32,431
1890	52,324
1900	102,979
1910	77,403
1920	77,939
1930	80,935
1940	74,711
1950	78,588
1960	79,673
1970	72,748
1980	76,691

SAINT LOUIS

1830	4,977
1840	16,469
1850	77,860
1860	160,773
1870	310,864
1880	350,518
1890	451,770
1900	575,238
1910	687,029
1920	772,897
1930	821,960
1940	816,048
1950	856,796
1960	750,026
1970	622,236
1980	453,085

SAINT PETERS

1910	269
1920	358
1930	248
1940	305
1950	377
1960	404
1970	486
1980	15,700

SEDALIA

1870	4,560
1880	9,561
1890	14,068
1900	15,231
1910	17,822
1920	21,144
1930	20,806
1940	20,428
1950	20,354
1960	23,874
1970	22,847
1980	20,927

SIKESTON

1880	191
1890	636
1900	1,077
1910	3,327
1920	3,613
1930	5,676
1940	7,944
1950	11,640
1960	13,765
1970	14,699
1980	17,431

SPRINGFIELD

1850	415
1860	na
1870	5,555
1880	6,522
1890	21,850
1900	23,267
1910	35,201
1920	39,631
1930	57,527
1940	61,238
1950	66,731
1960	95,865
1970	120,096
1980	113,116

UNIVERSITY CITY

1910	2,417
1920	6,972
1930	25,809
1940	33,023

1950	39,892
1960	51,249
1970	47,527
1980	42,738

WARRENSBURG

1850	241
1860	982
1870	2,945
1880	4,049
1890	4,706
1900	4,724
1910	4,689
1920	4,811
1930	5,146
1940	5,868
1950	6,857
1960	9,689
1970	13,125
1980	13,807

WEBSTER GROVES

1890	1,783
1900	1,895
1910	7,080
1920	9,474
1930	16,487
1940	18,934
1950	23,390
1960	28,990
1970	27,457
1980	23,097

CORRECTION NOTE

The official 1980 census counts of total population shown in
this report supersede counts issued previously. Corrections
to the figures were made after the counts were provided to
the State for redistricting purposes and released in Advance
Report PHC80-V for this State.

Shown below are corrections to the 1980 census counts of the
total population made after the tabulations for this report
were completed. Any additional corrections made after this
report is printed are available by writing to Data User
Services Division, Customer Services (Corrections), Bureau of
the Census, Washington, D.C. 20233.

The 1980 figures shown in this publication are subject to
change pending the outcome of the various lawsuits dealing
with the census counts.

	1980 population	
	As shown in the tables	Corrected
The State...................	4 916 686	4 916 759
Boone County:		
Rocky Fork township:		
Hallsville city...............	457	624
Cass County:		
West Dolan township:		
West Line village.............	91	109
Jasper County:		
Galena township:		
Joplin city (pt.).............	17 011	17 009
Morgan County:		
Osage township:		
Laurie village................	(1)	44
Newton County:		
Shoal Creek township:		
Joplin city (pt.).............	2 196	2 328
Leawood village...............	631	509
Midway village................	223	127
Sunnyvale town (pt.)...........	353	439
Ralls County.....................	8 911	8 984
Center township.................	964	1 037
Center city....................	596	669
Randolph County:		
South Sugar Creek township......	7 861	8 222
Union township.................	1 136	775
St. Charles County:		
Cave Springs township..........	10 172	9 950
St. Charles city (pt.)........	244	22
Friedens township.............	13 282	13 725
St. Charles township..........	36 308	36 087
St. Charles city (pt.)........	35 865	36 087
St. Louis County:		
Airport township:		
Berkeley city (pt.)...........	13 893	13 669
Woodson Terrace city..........	4 564	4 788
Clayton township..............	34 895	34 949
Clayton city (pt.)............	7 473	7 527
Creve Coeur township..........	56 913	56 859
Olivette city.................	8 039	7 985
Missouri River township........	72 506	72 463
Queeny township................	76 531	76 574
Berkeley city (total)............	16 146	15 922
Clayton city (total).............	14 219	14 273
Joplin city (total)..............	38 893	39 023
St. Charles city (total)..........	37 379	(2)
Sunnyvale town (total)...........	353	439

[1]Not returned separately.
[2]No change.

County Subdivisions	1980	1970
The State	4 916 686	4 677 623
Adair County[1]	24 870	22 472
Benton township	19 204	17 439
Kirksville city[1]	17 167	15 560
Clay township	657	619
Liberty township	399	375
Morrow township	393	345
Nineveh township	1 381	1 164
Novinger city	626	547
Pettis township	666	545
Millard village[1]	92	...
Polk township	519	406
Greentop village (pt.)[1]	115	...
Salt River township	970	823
Brashear city	332	316
Walnut township	218	259
Wilson township	463	497
Gibbs town	107	112
Andrew County[2]	13 980	11 913
Benton township	1 103	1 047
Bolckow town	245	225
Rosendale town	223	245
Clay township	340	340
Empire township	351	394
Jackson township	651	623
Fillmore city	265	251
Jefferson township	3 053	2 168
Country Club village[2]	1 234	943
Lincoln township	916	908
Amazonia town	314	326
Monroe township	702	699
Cosby town	148	130
Nodaway township	5 077	4 036
Savannah city[2]	4 184	3 324
Platte township	578	681
Rea town	78	54
Rochester township	1 209	1 017
Atchison County[3]	8 605	9 240
Benton township	61	93
Buchanan township	182	168
Clark township	1 283	1 381
Fairfax city	835	835
Clay township[3]	2 293	2 276
Rock Port city	1 511	1 575
Colfax township	155	207
Dale township	360	499
Lincoln township	711	801
Westboro village	188	234
Nishnabotna township[3]	290	294
Watson town	171	164
Polk township[3]	442	473
Tarkio township	2 665	2 842
Tarkio city	2 375	2 517
Templeton township[3]	163	206
Phelps City town	39	76
Audrain County[4]	26 458	25 362
Cuivre township	4 864	4 786
Farber city[4]	503	470
Vandalia city[4]	3 170	3 160
Linn township	773	844
Laddonia city (pt.)	13	9
Rush Hill town	140	151
Loutre township	991	988
Benton City town	155	121
Martinsburg town	309	318
Prairie township	1 269	1 258
Laddonia city (pt.)	713	736
Saling township	1 048	1 032
Salt River township	10 842	9 842
Mexico city (pt.)[4]	7 858	7 790
South Fork township	5 219	5 210
Mexico city (pt.)[4]	4 418	4 017
Vandiver village	88	102
Wilson township	1 452	1 402
Centralia city (pt.)[4]	-	...
Barry County[5]	24 408	19 597
Ash township	594	529
Butterfield township	594	484
Butterfield village	234	125
Capps Creek township	390	429
Corsicana township	307	264
Crane Creek township	646	529
Exeter township	1 197	993
Exeter city[5]	588	434
Flat Creek township	4 091	3 261
Cassville city[5]	2 091	1 910
Jenkins township	344	306
Kings Prairie township[5]	670	496
Liberty township	872	797
McDonald township	625	521
McDowell township	278	249
Mineral township	741	631
Monett township	5 010	4 601
Monett city (pt.)	4 367	4 225
Mountain township	183	133
Ozark township	504	391

County Subdivisions	1980	1970
Barry County—Con.		
Pioneer township	184	167
Pleasant Ridge township	344	309
Purdy township	1 590	1 172
Purdy city	928	588
Roaring River township	809	380
Chain-O-Lakes village[5]	76	...
Shell Knob township	604	230
Sugar Creek township	1 044	815
Seligman city	508	424
Washburn township	840	735
Washburn city[5]	289	257
Wheaton township	911	703
Wheaton city[5]	548	360
White River township	1 036	472
Barton County[6]	11 292	10 431
Barton City township	246	285
Central township	545	501
City township	4 053	3 760
Lamar city[6]	4 053	3 760
Doylesport township	260	267
Golden City township	1 252	1 142
Golden City city	900	810
Lamar township[6]	1 053	723
Lamar Heights village[6]	171	96
Leroy township	250	257
Milford township	292	266
Milford village[6]	67	23
Nashville township	405	363
Newport township	247	226
North Fork township	256	305
Ozark township[6]	975	998
Burgess town	98	69
Liberal city	701	644
Richland township	556	565
South West township[6]	538	438
Mindenmines city	318	279
Union township	364	335
Bates County[7]	15 873	15 468
Charlotte township	299	312
Deepwater township	294	294
Deer Creek township	1 741	1 529
Adrian city (pt.)[7]	1 316	1 083
East Boone township	407	377
Elkhart township	334	298
Grand River township	238	219
Homer township	487	492
Amoret city	238	219
Howard township	535	573
Hume town	315	350
Hudson township	268	278
Lone Oak township	279	268
Mingo township	177	169
Mound township	638	579
Adrian city (pt.)[7]	168	176
Passaic town	53	56
Mount Pleasant township	4 863	4 647
Butler city[7]	4 107	3 984
New Home township	224	259
Osage township	1 851	1 998
Rich Hill city	1 471	1 661
Pleasant Gap township	315	346
Prairie township	181	191
Rockville township	384	316
Rockville city[7]	281	203
Shawnee township	277	302
Spruce township	325	340
Summit township	278	295
Walnut township	469	493
Foster town	175	178
West Boone township	472	381
Drexel city (pt.)	127	98
Merwin town	85	64
West Point township	537	512
Amsterdam city[7]	231	120
Benton County[8]	12 183	9 695
Alexander township	274	273
Cole township	1 178	768
Fristoe township	1 601	1 132
Lindsey township	2 482	2 169
Warsaw city[8]	1 494	1 423
Tom township	894	683
Union township	1 051	593
White township	2 034	1 762
Ionia town (pt.)	131	151
Lincoln city[8]	819	574
Williams township	2 669	2 315
Cole Camp city	1 022	1 038
Bollinger County[9]	10 301	8 820
Crooked Creek township	903	807
Fillmore township	362	352
Liberty township	1 066	918
Lorance township	3 798	3 191
Glenallen town	125	134
Lutesville[9]	865	626

County Subdivisions	1980	1970
Bollinger County—Con.		
Lorance township—Con.		
Marble Hill city[9]	601	589
Scopus township	952	812
Union township	911	779
Wayne township	1 574	1 343
Zalma village	121	118
Whitewater township	735	618
Sedgewickville village	115	92
Boone County[10]	100 376	'80 935
Bourbon township	2 031	1 661
Sturgeon city	901	787
Cedar township[10]	7 797	4 534
Ashland city[10]	1 021	769
Hartsburg town	118	120
Centralia township	4 238	'4 127
Centralia city (pt.)[10]	3 537	'3 623
Columbia township	35 754	'29 066
Columbia city (pt.)[10]	28 979	'25 905
Missouri township[10]	41 834	'36 556
Columbia city (pt.)[10]	33 082	'32 907
Rocheport city	272	307
Perche township	3 199	1 550
Harrisburg town[10]	283	150
Rocky Fork township	5 523	3 441
Columbia city (pt.)[10]	–	...
Hallsville city	457	790
Buchanan County[11]	87 888	86 915
Agency township	912	563
Agency town[11]	419	141
Bloomington township	639	695
De Kalb town	245	287
Center township	2 756	2 253
St. Joseph city (pt.)	998	1 024
Crawford township	1 068	776
Jackson township	464	291
Dearborn city (pt.)[11]	–	...
Lake township	53	56
Marion township	1 217	1 023
Easton city[11]	313	183
Platte township	543	421
Gower city (pt.)	87	29
Rush township	966	1 103
Lewis and Clark Village town[11]	131	...
Rushville town	271	300
Tremont township	571	588
Washington township	77 984	78 462
St. Joseph city (pt.)[11]	75 616	'71 724
Wayne township	715	684
St. Joseph city (pt.)	77	–
Butler County[12]	37 693	33 529
Ash Hill township	4 199	4 182
Fisk city	450	503
Qulin town[12]	545	496
Beaver Dam township[12]	2 971	2 055
Black River township	846	447
Cane Creek township	353	221
Coon Island township	348	400
Epps township	1 167	567
Gillis Bluff township	826	972
Neely township	1 498	1 553
Neelyville city	474	'381
Poplar Bluff township	24 243	22 239
Poplar Bluff city[12]	17 139	16 653
St. Francois township	1 242	893
Caldwell County[13]	8 660	8 351
Breckenridge township	723	868
Breckenridge city	523	598
Davis township	1 377	1 284
Braymer city[13]	986	919
Fairview township	208	207
Gomer township	333	397
Grant township	1 019	840
Polo city[13]	583	438
Hamilton township	2 107	2 043
Hamilton city[13]	1 582	1 645
Kidder township	745	664
Kidder city	265	231
Kingston township	546	544
Kingston city	280	291
Lincoln township	513	530
Cowgill city	267	232
Mirabile township	386	358
New York township	303	273
Rockford township	400	343
Callaway County[14]	32 252	'25 991
Auxvasse township	941	637
Bourbon township	1 119	634
Caldwell township	339	158
Calwood township	747	592
Cedar township	1 571	1 087
Lake Mykee Town village[14]	188	...
New Bloomfield city	519	427
Cleveland township	499	399
Cote Sans Dessein township	565	425
East Fulton township	6 109	7 559

County Subdivisions	1980	1970
Callaway County—Con.		
East Fulton township—Con.		
Fulton city (pt.)[14]	5 183	6 904
Guthrie township	367	284
Jackson township	1 757	1 521
Auxvasse city[14]	858	808
Liberty township	550	413
McCredie township	588	'596
Kingdom City village	146	'53
Nine Mile Prairie township	620	303
Round Prairie township	500	344
St. Aubert township	1 434	1 242
Mokane town	293	398
Shamrock township	336	264
Summit township	6 037	2 853
Cedar City city	427	454
Holts Summit city[14]	2 540	...
Jefferson City city (pt.)[14]	25	...
West Fulton township	8 173	'6 680
Fulton city (pt.)	5 863	'5 344
Camden County[15]	20 017	13 315
Adair township[15]	1 676	1 334
Climax Springs village	87	104
Auglaize township	1 907	1 558
Richland city (pt.)[15]	97	8
Stoutland village (pt.)[15]	240	168
Jackson township	422	302
Jasper township[15]	2 425	1 347
Hurricane Deck village	210	169
Sunrise Beach village (pt.)	100	95
Osage township[15]	10 642	6 695
Camdenton city[15]	2 303	1 636
Lake Ozark city (pt.)	98	98
Linn Creek town	242	268
Osage Beach city (pt.)[15]	1 924	1 091
Russell township[15]	1 730	1 326
Macks Creek village	171	106
Warren township	1 215	753
Cape Girardeau County[16]	58 837	49 350
Apple Creek township	1 586	1 440
Oak Ridge town	252	181
Old Appleton town[16]	80	77
Byrd township	10 635	7 928
Jackson city (pt.)[16]	7 827	5 896
Cape Girardeau township	36 866	32 903
Cape Girardeau city[16]	34 361	31 282
Hubble township	1 420	1 188
Gordonville town[16]	267	125
Whitewater town	161	135
Kinder township	651	437
Liberty township	325	288
Randol township	2 534	1 229
Jackson city (pt.)[16]	–	...
Shawnee township[16]	2 200	1 597
Pocahontas town	130	'127
Welch township	1 471	1 438
Delta city[16]	524	462
Whitewater township	1 149	902
Carroll County[17]	12 131	12 565
Carrollton township	4 592	4 755
Carrollton city (pt.)	4 104	4 268
Cherry Valley township	84	78
Combs township	304	333
De Witt township[17]	341	390
De Witt city[17]	132	135
Egypt township	1 224	1 255
Norborne city[17]	931	950
Eugene township	313	410
Wakenda town	98	116
Fairfield township	224	244
Hill township	280	294
Hurricane township	793	772
Hale city	529	461
Leslie township	212	203
Miami township	64	61
Moss Creek township	207	246
Prairie township	237	258
Ridge township	602	596
Bosworth city	394	386
Rockford township	119	106
Stokes Mound township	458	436
Tina town	202	167
Sugartree township	52	86
Trotter township	283	303
Van Horn township	617	581
Bogard town	285	294
Wakenda township	868	884
Carrollton city (pt.)[17]	596	579
Washington township	257	274
Carter County[18]	5 428	3 878
Carter township	2 048	1 570
Van Buren town[18]	850	714
Jackson township	588	428
Johnson township	2 097	1 311
Ellsinore town[18]	362	342
Grandin city[18]	265	243
Kelly township	311	206

County Subdivisions	1980	1970
Carter County—Con.		
Pike township[18]	384	363
Cass County[19]	51 029	39 448
Austin township	1 450	1 189
Archie city[19]	753	525
Big Creek township	1 698	1 053
Lake Winnebago city[19]	681	432
Lee's Summit city (pt.)[19]	50	...
Camp Branch township	1 735	1 496
East Lynne town[19]	286	255
Garden City city (pt.)[19]	252	229
Coldwater township	1 068	941
Drexel city (pt.)	781	625
Dayton township	648	512
Garden City city (pt.)[19]	143	...
Dolan township	1 376	1 102
Freeman city[19]	485	417
Everett township	395	358
Grand River township	7 932	6 075
Harrisonville city (pt.)[19]	5 824	'4 719
Index township	1 264	968
Garden City city (pt.)[19]	626	404
Gunn City village	58	71
Mount Pleasant township	12 771	13 247
Belton city (pt.)[19]	10 341	'11 312
Peculiar township	1 680	1 107
Harrisonville city (pt.)	548	'333
Pleasant Hill township	4 022	3 931
Baldwin Park village[19]	126	...
Pleasant Hill city	3 301	3 396
Polk township	1 378	1 050
Strasburg town	170	181
Raymore township	7 332	2 471
Belton city (pt.)[19]	2 367	'958
Raymore city[19]	3 154	587
Sherman township	701	686
Creighton city	301	294
Union township	1 506	989
Cleveland town (pt.)[19]	329	254
West Dolan township	703	422
Cleveland town (pt.)[19]	156	2
West Line village	91	114
West Peculiar township	3 370	1 851
Peculiar city[19]	1 571	705
Cedar County[20]	11 894	9 424
Benton township	934	843
Jerico Springs village[20]	208	188
Box township	5 923	4 724
El Dorado Springs city[20]	3 868	3 300
Cedar township	487	445
Jefferson township	565	444
Linn township	2 679	2 010
Stockton city[20]	1 432	1 063
Umber View Heights village[20]	41	...
Madison township	572	444
Washington township	734	514
Chariton County[21]	10 489	11 084
Bee Branch township	449	494
Bowling Green township	272	384
Dalton town	76	135
Brunswick township	1 929	2 090
Brunswick city	1 272	1 370
Chariton township	451	525
Glasgow city (pt.)	52	55
Clark township	412	367
Cockrell township	238	237
Cunningham township	389	415
Sumner town	182	178
Keytesville township	1 233	1 308
Keytesville city	689	730
Mendon township	469	542
Mendon town	252	289
Missouri township	42	55
Musselfork township	353	279
Salisbury township	2 978	2 962
Salisbury city[21]	1 975	1 960
Salt Creek township	244	258
Triplett township	314	409
Triplett city	137	191
Wayland township	255	297
Yellow Creek township	461	462
Rothville village	118	131
Christian County[22]	22 402	15 124
Bruner township	519	400
Chadwick township	437	414
East Benton township	292	192
Finley township	6 260	3 852
Ozark city	2 980	2 384
Garrison township	152	124
Lead Hill township	158	127
Lincoln township	1 499	1 199
Clever city	551	430
Linden township	657	475
McCracken township	575	406
North Galloway township	1 307	905

County Subdivisions	1980	1970
Christian County—Con.		
North Linn township	301	...
Oldfield township	316	223
Polk township	2 038	1 693
Billings city	911	760
Porter township	5 391	3 119
Nixa city[22]	2 662	1 636
Seneca township	106	64
South Galloway township	767	590
South Linn township	192	...
Sparta township	1 213	867
Sparta city[22]	743	380
West Benton township	222	200
Clark County[23]	8 493	8 260
Clay township	402	420
Des Moines township	953	838
Wayland city[23]	498	467
Folker township	302	277
Grant township	192	188
Jackson township	571	575
Jefferson township	220	244
Lincoln township	2 977	2 898
Kahoka city	2 101	2 207
Madison township	524	409
Sweet Home township	463	490
Revere town	191	184
Union township	328	361
Vernon township	469	507
Alexandria city	417	453
Washington township	293	330
Wyaconda city (pt.)	10	38
Wyaconda township	799	723
Luray town	175	149
Wyaconda city (pt.)	349	318
Clay County[24]	136 488	'123 702
Chouteau township	29 923	'29 825
Birmingham village	240	266
Claycomo village (pt.)	1 667	1 837
Independence city (pt.)	—	-
Kansas City city (pt.)	27 913	'27 586
Pleasant Valley city (pt.)	12	22
Randolph village	91	106
Sugar Creek city (pt.)	—	-
Fishing River township	10 987	10 345
Excelsior Springs city (pt.)	8 809	8 399
Missouri City city	343	375
Mosby city	284	337
Prathersville village[24]	141	153
Gallatin township	61 511	'58 190
Avondale city	612	'512
Gladstone city	24 990	'23 422
Kansas City city (pt.)	30 184	'27 780
North Kansas City city	4 507	5 183
Oaks village	126	162
Oakview village	497	'494
Oakwood village	227	'201
Oakwood Manor village	137	170
Oakwood Park village	231	'266
Kearney township	4 680	2 407
Holt city (pt.)[24]	276	263
Kearney city[24]	1 433	984
Liberty township	20 895	'17 109
Claycomo village (pt.)	4	4
Glenaire village	541	505
Kansas City city (pt.)	602	238
Liberty city[24]	16 251	'13 704
Pleasant Valley city (pt.)	1 533	1 513
Platte township	4 972	3 915
Kansas City city (pt.)	1 875	764
Smithville city[24]	1 873	1 785
Washington township	3 520	1 911
Excelsior Springs city (pt.)	1 459	895
Lawson city (pt.)[24]	72	19
Clinton County[25]	15 916	12 462
Atchison township	1 659	1 117
Gower city (pt.)[25]	1 189	729
Clinton township	430	286
Concord township	2 712	2 386
Plattsburg city[25]	2 095	1 832
Hardin township	796	777
Trimble town[25]	262	206
Jackson township	1 826	665
Holt city (pt.)[25]	—	56
Lafayette township	690	671
Lathrop township	2 625	1 904
Lathrop city[25]	1 732	1 268
Turney town (pt.)	166	142
Platte township	427	485
Osborn city (pt.)	58	53
Shoal township	4 751	4 171
Cameron city (pt.)[25]	3 829	3 469
Turney town (pt.)[25]	213	...
Cole County[26]	56 663	46 228
Clark township	2 935	1 906
Eugene town[26]	220	163
Jefferson township	43 271	36 777

County Subdivisions	1980	1970
Cole County—Con.		
Jefferson township—Con.		
Jefferson City city (pt.)[26]	33 594	32 407
Liberty township	3 210	1 886
Taos city[26]	759	...
Marion township	2 851	1 975
Centertown town[26]	304	277
St. Martins city[26]	739	...
Moreau township	2 032	1 675
Lohman town[26]	168	109
Russellville city[26]	667	557
Osage township	2 364	2 009
Jefferson City city (pt.)[26]	–	...
St. Thomas town[26]	337	195
Wardsville town	535	460
Cooper County[27]	14 643	14 732
Blackwater township	533	492
Blackwater city	290	249
Boonville township	7 849	8 245
Boonville city[27]	6 959	7 514
Clark Fork township	524	506
Clear Creek township	440	506
Kelly township	771	831
Bunceton city	419	437
Lamine township	322	370
Lebanon township	364	330
North Moniteau township	159	151
Otterville township	811	763
Otterville city	472	440
Palestine township	398	414
Pilot Grove township	1 158	1 091
Pilot Grove city	745	701
Prairie Home township	553	442
Prairie Home city	279	231
Saline township	545	387
Wooldridge town	79	97
South Moniteau township	216	204
Crawford County[28]	18 300	14 828
Benton township	4 617	3 492
Cuba city[28]	2 120	2 070
Leasburg village (pt.)[28]	78	...
Boone township	4 315	3 452
Bourbon city[28]	1 259	955
St. Cloud village[28]	40	34
Sullivan city (pt.)	1 025	1 058
Courtois township	1 139	1 070
Knobview township	986	696
Liberty township	1 040	951
Leasburg village (pt.)	226	218
Meramec township	2 855	2 646
Steelville city[28]	1 470	1 392
Oak Hill township	1 260	767
Osage township	1 286	1 086
Union township	802	668
Dade County[29]	7 383	6 850
Cedar township	364	336
Center township	2 040	1 711
Greenfield city	1 394	1 172
Ernest township	118	135
Grant township	339	325
Lockwood township	1 273	1 273
Lockwood city[29]	971	887
Marion township	201	197
North township	293	271
Arcola city[29]	136	80
North Morgan township	153	136
Pilgrim township	156	160
Polk township	410	368
Rock Prairie township	812	707
Everton city	317	264
Sac township	201	171
Smith township	199	218
South township	194	195
South Morgan township	369	335
Dadeville village	216	149
Washington township	261	312
South Greenfield village[29]	110	144
Dallas County[30]	12 096	10 054
Grant township	1 088	836
Louisburg village[30]	140	152
Jackson township	1 373	1 170
Jasper township	863	701
Lincoln township	779	717
Urbana city	329	369
Miller township	393	274
North Benton township	3 223	2 421
Buffalo city (pt.)	1 767	1 267
Sheridan township	805	615
Sherman township	376	317
South Benton township	1 634	1 681
Buffalo city (pt.)	450	648
Washington township	648	632
Wilson township	914	690

County Subdivisions	1980	1970
Daviess County[31]	8 905	8 420
Benton township	761	868
Pattonsburg city	502	540
Colfax township	614	555
Winston town	246	189
Grand River township	500	543
Jameson town	172	172
Harrison township	103	129
Jackson township	728	573
Lock Springs town	85	85
Jamesport township	1 183	1 016
Jamesport city	651	614
Jefferson township	378	351
Altamont town (pt.)	–	8
Liberty township	706	528
Altamont town (pt.)	192	217
Lincoln township	192	221
Gilman City city (pt.)[31]	2	...
Marion township	249	296
Monroe township	210	194
Salem township	396	426
Coffey town	165	157
Sheridan township	316	313
Union township	2 378	2 146
Gallatin city	2 063	1 833
Washington township	191	261
De Kalb County[32]	8 222	7 305
Adams township	620	514
Weatherby town	121	91
Camden township	1 756	1 547
Amity town	74	86
Maysville city	1 187	1 045
Colfax township	660	659
Osborn city (pt.)	323	285
Dallas township	200	293
Grand River township	1 384	948
Cameron city (pt.)[32]	690	491
Grant township	279	357
Polk township	754	890
Union Star town	423	417
Sherman township	633	612
Washington township	1 936	1 485
Clarksdale town	278	248
Stewartsville city	832	634
Dent County[33]	14 517	11 457
Current township	434	373
Franklin township	933	750
Gladden township	390	319
Linn township	152	108
Meramec township	228	171
Norman township	707	401
Osage township	504	529
Short Bend township	465	352
Sinking township	436	362
Bunker city (pt.)	268	209
Spring Creek township	8 333	6 601
Salem city[33]	4 454	4 363
Texas township	702	493
Watkins township	1 233	998
Douglas County[34]	11 594	9 268
Benton township	3 837	3 177
Ava city[34]	2 761	2 504
Boone township	534	418
Brown township	194	168
Brush Creek township	315	302
Bryan township	320	258
Buchanan township	247	144
Campbell township	326	304
Cass township	285	216
Champion township	209	211
Clay township	196	138
Clinton township	247	207
Findley township	527	454
Jackson township	302	261
Lincoln township	433	288
McKinley township	179	159
McMurtrey township	315	201
Miller township	545	342
Richland township	216	211
Spencer township	263	241
Spring Creek township	567	382
Walls township	523	465
Washington township	655	482
Wood township	359	239
Dunklin County[35]	36 324	33 742
Buffalo township	1 766	1 676
Arbyrd city (pt.)	29	10
Cardwell city[35]	831	859
Clay township	2 047	2 589
Hornersville city	704	693
Cotton Hill township	7 808	6 328
Malden city[35]	6 096	5 374
Freeborn township	1 865	1 881
Clarkton city	1 228	1 177
Holcomb township	1 454	1 561
Holcomb city[35]	632	593

County Subdivisions	1980	1970
Dunklin County—Con.		
Independence township	13 284	12 459
Kennett city[35]	10 145	'10 090
Salem township	3 590	3 263
Arbyrd city (pt.)	675	565
Senath city	1 728	1 484
Union township	4 510	3 985
Campbell city[35]	2 134	1 979
Franklin County[36]	71 233	'55 127
Boeuf township	1 883	1 613
Berger city	214	226
Boles township	12 913	8 686
Pacific city (pt.)[36]	4 398	3 247
Boone township	4 260	3 379
Gerald city	921	762
Leslie village (pt.)[36]	96	81
Sullivan city (pt.)[36]	104	...
Calvey township	3 856	2 342
Central township	9 956	7 450
Parkway village	254	233
St. Clair city[36]	3 485	2 978
Union city (pt.)[36]	–	...
Lyon township	3 175	2 241
Leslie village (pt.)[36]	12	...
Meramec township	6 845	'5 791
Oak Grove village	386	340
Sullivan city (pt.)[36]	4 332	'4 053
New Haven township	1 581	1 474
New Haven city	1 581	1 474
Prairie township	2 794	1 949
St. Johns township[36]	3 919	2 882
Union township	10 800	8 821
Union city (pt.)[36]	5 506	5 183
Washington township	9 251	8 499
Washington city[36]	9 251	8 499
Gasconade County[37]	13 181	11 878
Boeuf township	851	679
Boulware township	545	536
Bourbois township	398	333
Brush Creek township	596	405
Canaan township	4 396	3 786
Owensville city[37]	2 241	2 416
Rosebud city	326	305
Clay township	1 407	1 318
Bland city (pt.)[37]	662	621
Richland township	882	952
Gasconade city[37]	250	235
Morrison city	169	234
Roark township	3 757	3 626
Hermann city[37]	2 695	2 658
Third Creek township	349	243
Gentry County[38]	7 887	8 060
Athens township	2 649	2 405
Albany city[38]	2 152	1 804
Bogle township	303	384
Gentry village	126	143
Cooper township	2 167	2 240
Darlington town[38]	131	164
Stanberry city[38]	1 387	1 479
Howard township	164	193
Huggins township	170	217
Jackson township	1 544	1 538
Ford City town	30	42
King City city	1 063	1 023
Miller township	613	781
McFall city	139	203
Wilson township	277	302
Greene County[39]	185 302	152 929
Boone No. 1 township	1 002	...
Ash Grove city (pt.)[39]	632	(NA)
Boone No. 2 township	799	...
Ash Grove city (pt.)[39]	525	(NA)
Brookline township	1 250	...
Brookline village (pt.)[39]	193	(NA)
Campbell No. 1 township	1 861	...
Campbell No. 2 township	1 880	...
Cass township	851	...
Center No. 1 township	1 885	...
Brookline village (pt.)[39]	18	(NA)
Center No. 2 township	434	...
Center No. 3 township	1 247	...
Clay township	4 437	...
East Republic township	3 257	...
Republic city (pt.)[39]	2 707	(NA)
Franklin No. 1 township	996	...
Franklin No. 2 township	2 378	...
Jackson No. 1 township	1 939	...
Fair Grove city[39]	863	431
Jackson No. 2 township	2 672	...
Strafford city[39]	1 121	491
Murray township	2 756	...
Willard city (pt.)[39]	1 799	(NA)
North Campbell No. 1 township	2 101	...
North Campbell No. 2 township	1 193	...
North Campbell No. 3 township	812	...
Pond Creek township	713	446

County Subdivisions	1980	1970
Greene County—Con.		
Robberson No. 1 township	1 545	...
Robberson No. 2 township	1 900	...
Willard city (pt.)[39]	–	(NA)
Springfield township	133 157	...
Springfield city	133 116	120 096
Taylor township	1 799	...
Walnut Grove township	1 187	...
Walnut Grove city	504	442
Washington township	1 854	1 238
Rogersville town (pt.)[39]	35	'21
West Republic township	2 113	...
Republic city (pt.)[39]	1 778	(NA)
Wilson township	7 284	...
Battlefield town[39]	1 227	...
Grundy County[40]	11 959	11 819
Franklin township	566	620
Spickard city[40]	389	408
Harrison township	189	177
Jackson township	190	190
Jefferson township	419	428
Liberty township	561	525
Galt city	323	261
Lincoln township	549	477
Tindall town	104	92
Madison township	633	422
Marion township	355	448
Myers township	202	244
Taylor township	223	222
Brimson town	104	103
Trenton township	7 317	7 309
Trenton city[40]	6 811	6 063
Washington township	145	121
Wilson township	610	636
Laredo city	340	383
Harrison County[41]	9 890	10 257
Adams township	224	281
Bethany township	3 535	3 300
Bethany city	3 095	2 914
Butler township	184	213
Clay township	160	208
Colfax township	540	566
Blythedale town	219	213
Eagleville town (pt.)	36	58
Cypress township	155	213
Dallas township	221	255
Martinsville town[41]	44	'39
Fox Creek township	158	197
Grant township	557	567
Ridgeway city (pt.)	374	331
Hamilton township	149	214
Jefferson township	235	262
Lincoln township	169	187
Madison township	727	740
Cainsville city	496	454
Marion township	517	540
Eagleville town (pt.)	114	111
Ridgeway city (pt.)	142	138
Sherman township	211	233
Sugar Creek township	621	641
Gilman City city (pt.)	412	376
Trail Creek township	328	350
Mount Moriah town	162	165
Union township	451	480
Eagleville town (pt.)	214	219
Washington township	173	183
White Oak township	575	627
New Hampton city	358	327
Henry County[42]	19 672	18 451
Bear Creek township	243	263
Bethlehem township	477	394
Big Creek township	267	277
Bogard township	502	534
Blairstown city	144	161
Urich city (pt.)	5	–
Clinton township	8 001	7 710
Clinton city (pt.)[42]	7 846	7 343
Davis township	258	333
Deepwater township	752	867
Montrose city	498	531
Deer Creek township	327	335
Fairview township	728	847
Deepwater city[42]	475	565
Fields Creek township	1 033	423
Clinton city (pt.)	520	161
Honey Creek township	228	206
Hartwell village[42]	13	...
Leesville township	663	600
Osage township	397	356
Brownington town[42]	112	95
Shawnee township	383	305
Springfield township	247	212
Tebo township	768	629
Calhoun city	427	360
Walker township	252	286
White Oak township	785	721
Urich city (pt.)	504	433

County Subdivisions	1980	1970
Henry County—Con.		
Windsor township	3 361	3 153
Windsor city (pt.)[42]	2 940	2 734
Hickory County[43]	6 367	4 481
Center township	1 154	627
Hermitage city[43]	384	284
Cross Timbers township	471	428
Cross Timbers city	217	204
Green township	1 223	691
Jordan township	190	181
Montgomery township	244	254
Stark township	701	601
Preston town	149	132
Tyler township	675	352
Weaubleau township	921	708
Weaubleau city	464	343
Wheatland township	788	639
Wheatland city[43]	364	317
Holt County[44]	6 882	6 654
Benton township	1 902	1 639
Mound City city	1 447	1 202
Bigelow township	321	256
Bigelow village	67	84
Clay township	728	608
Maitland city	415	319
Forbes township	222	271
Forest township	499	577
Forest City city (pt.)[44]	383	365
Hickory township	362	376
Lewis township	1 234	1 145
Forest City city (pt.)[44]	4	...
Oregon city[44]	901	789
Liberty township	311	388
Lincoln township	213	233
Corning town	126	134
Minton township	201	223
Fortescue town	51	63
Nodaway township	210	252
Union township	679	686
Craig city	379	369
Howard County[45]	10 008	10 561
Bonne Femme township	366	383
Boons Lick township	437	469
Burton township	131	191
Chariton township	1 879	1 862
Glasgow city (pt.)[45]	1 284	1 281
Franklin township	1 986	2 035
Franklin city	196	252
New Franklin city	1 228	1 122
Moniteau township	578	480
Prairie township	845	879
Armstrong city	360	354
Richmond township	3 786	4 262
Fayette city	2 983	3 520
Howell County[46]	28 807	23 521
Benton township	1 587	1 404
Chapel township	51?	355
Dry Creek township	1 312	940
Goldsberry township	2 858	2 459
Mountain View city[46]	1 664	1 320
Howell township	13 417	10 856
Brandsville city	133	145
West Plains city[46]	7 741	6 893
Hutton Valley township	833	647
Myatt township	473	383
Siloam Springs township	466	397
Sisson township	1 148	960
South Fork township	695	518
Spring Creek township	1 276	995
Willow Springs township	4 231	3 607
Willow Springs city[46]	2 215	2 045
Iron County[47]	11 084	9 529
Arcadia township	5 517	4 707
Arcadia city	683	627
Ironton city[47]	1 743	1 452
Pilot Knob city[47]	722	582
Dent township	1 621	1 138
Viburnum town[47]	836	520
Iron township	1 273	1 116
Kaolin township	496	489
Liberty township	466	478
Union township	1 711	1 601
Annapolis city	370	330
Des Arc village	237	222
Jackson County[48]	629 266	'654 178
Blue township[48]	165 441	'186 127
Independence city (pt.)[48]	110 327	'111 612
Kansas City city (pt.)	45 233	64 596
Sugar Creek city (pt.)[48]	4 305	4 755
Brooking township	87 265	'63 938
Kansas City city (pt.)	55 753	'30 632
Raytown city (pt.)	31 512	'33 306
Fort Osage township	5 628	4 193
Buckner city[48]	2 848	1 695
Independence city (pt.)[48]	321	18
Levasy city[48]	235	283

County Subdivisions	1980	1970
Jackson County—Con.		
Fort Osage township—Con.		
Sibley village	382	279
Kaw township	220 125	276 992
Kansas City city (pt.)	220 125	276 992
Prairie township	31 712	18 369
Blue Springs city (pt.)[48]	72	...
Greenwood city	1 315	925
Kansas City city (pt.)	21	54
Lee's Summit city (pt.)[48]	28 691	16 230
Unity Village village[48]	202	242
Sni-A-Bar township	38 534	15 244
Blue Springs city (pt.)[48]	25 855	6 779
Grain Valley city[48]	1 327	709
Independence city (pt.)[48]	1 158	...
Lake Tapawingo city[48]	925	867
Oak Grove city (pt.)[48]	4 067	2 025
Van Buren township	4 953	3 602
Lake Lotawana city	1 875	1 786
Lone Jack village	420	'199
Tarsney Lakes village	329	401
Washington township	75 608	85 713
Grandview city	24 502	17 456
Kansas City city (pt.)	50 859	68 257
Raytown city (pt.)	247	—
Jasper County[49]	86 958	79 852
Duval township	599	493
Neck City city (pt.)	40	32
Galena township	21 819	20 681
Airport Drive village (pt.)[49]	572	145
Carl Junction city (pt.)[49]	1 086	...
Iron Gates village	314	367
Joplin city (pt.)[49]	17 011	18 045
Jackson township	3 184	2 377
Carthage city (pt.)[49]	1 162	629
Fidelity town (pt.)[49]	252	173
Jasper township	589	608
Asbury city	210	201
Joplin township	32 912	30 969
Airport Drive village (pt.)	130	155
Carterville city (pt.)	1 736	1 658
Duenweg city	703	656
Duquesne village[49]	1 252	738
Joplin city (pt.)	19 666	18 973
Oakland Park village	143	156
Sunnyvale town (pt.)[49]	—	...
Webb City city (pt.)	7 133	6 811
Lincoln township	286	309
McDonald township	734	699
Avilla town	151	119
Madison township	1 630	1 222
Marion township	12 302	12 541
Brooklyn Heights village	126	128
Carthage city (pt.)	9 942	10 406
Carytown city (pt.)[49]	108	...
Mineral township	3 244	2 571
Alba city	474	365
Carterville city (pt.)[49]	237	58
Joplin city (pt.)[49]	20	22
Neck City city (pt.)	111	82
Oronogo city	525	492
Purcell city	322	325
Webb City city (pt.)[49]	176	'112
Preston township	1 418	1 274
Carytown city (pt.)[49]	42	...
Jasper city	1 012	796
Sarcoxie township	2 509	2 190
La Russell city	126	97
Reeds town	105	122
Sarcoxie city	1 381	1 175
Sheridan township	408	423
Twin Groves township	3 844	2 512
Carl Junction city (pt.)[49]	2 851	1 661
Waco town	129	108
Union township	1 480	983
Fidelity town (pt.)	22	18
Jefferson County[50]	146 183	105 248
Big River township	4 439	2 633
Cedar Hill Lakes village (pt.)[50]	12	
Central township	8 868	5 427
Hillsboro city[50]	1 508	'831
Joachim township	25 617	21 938
Crystal City city[50]	3 618	3 898
Festus city[50]	7 574	7 530
Herculaneum city[50]	2 293	'2 439
Pevely city[50]	2 732	517
Meramec township	25 396	16 117
Cedar Hill (CDP)	1 512	...
Cedar Hill Lakes village (pt.)[50]	188	...
Parksdale town[50]	270	836
Scotsdale town[50]	183	...
Plattin township	6 046	4 487
Olympian Village city	774	'399
Rock township	63 052	44 671
Arnold city[50]	19 141	...
Kimmswick city	207	268
Murphy (CDP)	8 121	...
Valle township	12 765	9 975

County Subdivisions	1980	1970
Jefferson County—Con.		
Valle township—Con.		
De Soto city[50]	5 993	5 984
Johnson County[51]	39 059	34 172
Centerview township	1 134	909
Centerview town	223	234
Chilhowee township	1 048	954
Chilhowee town	349	297
Columbus township	707	427
Grover township	489	418
Hazel Hill township	975	616
Jackson township	1 848	1 144
Jefferson township	458	440
Kingsville township	1 119	874
Kingsville city	365	284
Madison township	2 825	2 586
Holden city	2 195	2 089
Montserrat township	917	455
Whiteman AFB (CDP) (pt.)	–	
Post Oak township	1 491	1 208
Leeton city[51]	604	425
Rose Hill township	798	783
Latour town	84	83
Simpson township	472	448
Warrensburg township	16 880	14 486
Warrensburg city[51]	13 807	13 125
Washington township	7 898	8 424
Knob Noster city	2 040	2 264
Whiteman AFB (CDP) (pt.)	4 305	5 040
Knox County	5 508	5 692
Bee Ridge township	154	171
Benton township	239	180
Bourbon township	198	260
Center township	1 520	1 574
Edina city	1 520	1 574
Colony township	282	233
Fabius township	265	332
Newark town	105	114
Greensburg township	544	567
Baring city	206	206
Jeddo township	111	130
Liberty township	337	282
Lyon township	633	647
Hurdland town	227	225
Myrtle township	490	552
Knox City town	281	284
Salt River township	460	449
Novelty town	187	156
Shelton township	275	315
Laclede County[52]	24 323	19 944
Auglaize township	1 324	852
Eldridge township	468	450
Franklin township	691	754
Gasconade township	853	786
Hooker township	701	428
Lebanon township	13 676	11 521
Lebanon city[52]	9 507	8 616
Mayfield township	331	314
Richland city (pt.)	22	42
Stoutland village (pt.)[52]	46	37
Osage township	1 167	827
Phillipsburg township	863	847
Phillipsburg town	134	173
Smith township	674	461
Spring Hollow township	955	676
Union township	1 098	923
Conway city[52]	601	547
Washington township	1 522	1 105
Lafayette County[53]	29 925	26 626
Clay township	4 036	3 188
Bates City village (pt.)	145	186
Napoleon city	271	263
Odessa city (pt.)	648	668
Wellington city	780	720
Davis township	4 519	4 111
Higginsville city (pt.)[53]	3 596	3 170
Dover township	2 523	2 636
Corder city[53]	483	476
Dover town	126	133
Higginsville city (pt.)	999	1 148
Freedom township	3 255	3 050
Aullville town	92	108
Concordia city[53]	2 129	1 854
Emma city (pt.)	109	75
Lexington township	6 601	6 689
Lexington city[53]	5 063	5 388
Middleton township	1 835	1 753
Alma city	445	380
Waverly town	941	827
Sni-A-Bar township	4 802	3 358
Bates City village (pt.)	54	43
Oak Grove city (pt.)[53]	–	...
Odessa city (pt.)[53]	2 172	2 090
Washington township	2 354	1 841
Mayview city	291	330
Odessa city (pt.)[53]	268	81

County Subdivisions	1980	1970
Lawrence County[54]	28 973	24 585
Aurora township	7 631	6 413
Aurora city[54]	6 437	5 359
Buck Prairie township	3 147	2 553
Marionville city[54]	1 920	1 496
Freistatt township	458	442
Freistatt town	139	115
Green township	416	401
Hoberg township	418	325
Hoberg village	77	64
Lincoln township	1 598	1 398
Miller city	795	676
Mount Pleasant township	716	574
Mount Vernon township	5 058	4 582
Mount Vernon city[54]	3 341	2 600
Ozark township	1 196	999
Halltown town	149	106
Pierce township	4 741	3 827
Monett city (pt.)[54]	1 781	1 712
Pierce City city[54]	1 391	1 097
Red Oak township	385	384
Spring River township	1 491	1 269
Verona town[54]	592	515
Turnback township	922	644
Vineyard township	796	774
Stotts City city	232	203
Lewis County[55]	10 901	10 993
Canton township	3 141	3 326
Canton city[55]	2 435	2 680
Dickerson township	646	630
Monticello town	134	157
Highland township	1 631	1 430
Ewing city[55]	400	330
La Belle township	1 945	2 040
La Belle city[55]	845	848
Lewistown town	502	615
Lyon township	377	429
Reddish township	452	472
Salem township	392	425
Union township	2 317	2 241
La Grange city	1 217	1 237
Lincoln County[56]	22 193	18 041
Bedford township	4 194	3 775
Troy city[56]	2 624	2 538
Burr Oak township	1 724	1 134
Foley city	216	224
Clark township	2 126	1 482
Moscow Mills city	484	399
Hawk Point township	1 305	1 092
Hawk Point city	386	354
Hurricane township	3 255	3 129
Elsberry city	1 272	1 398
Millwood township	595	563
Monroe township	5 254	3 958
Old Monroe city	272	330
Winfield city	592	620
Nineveh township	415	382
Prairie township	248	219
Snow Hill township	1 247	595
Union township	1 532	1 407
Silex village	287	306
Whiteside village	97	125
Waverly township	298	305
Linn County[57]	15 495	15 125
Baker township	311	294
Benton township	719	764
Browning city (pt.)	281	320
Purdin city	243	236
Brookfield township	6 136	6 122
Brookfield city[57]	5 555	5 491
Bucklin township	1 029	980
Bucklin city	713	654
Clay township	292	365
Enterprise township	144	172
Grantsville township	267	251
Jackson township	266	334
Jefferson township	825	864
Laclede city	445	430
Locust Creek township	762	703
Linneus city	421	400
Marceline township	3 368	2 937
Marceline city	2 938	2 622
North Salem township	194	245
Parson Creek township	797	785
Meadville city	416	409
Yellow Creek township	385	309
Livingston County[58]	15 739	15 368
Blue Mound township	544	431
Chillicothe township	10 081	10 159
Chillicothe city (pt.)[58]	8 778	9 308
Cream Ridge township	638	667
Chula city	244	244
Fairview township	473	426
Grand River township	306	344
Green township	418	353

County Subdivisions	1980	1970
Livingston County—Con.		
Jackson township	431	472
Medicine township	176	185
Monroe township	438	409
Ludlow town	178	175
Mooresville township	386	408
Mooresville town	129	131
Rich Hill township	996	809
Chillicothe city (pt.)	311	211
Sampsel township	283	261
Wheeling township	569	444
Wheeling city	379	268
McDonald County[59]	14 917	12 357
Anderson East township	1 241	...
Anderson city (pt.)	682	(NA)
Anderson West township	1 387	...
Anderson city (pt.)	555	(NA)
Buffalo Hart township	319	...
Buffalo May township	404	...
Center township	431	323
Elk Horn township	863	812
Elk River East township	1 132	...
Noel city (pt.)[59]	855	(NA)
Elk River West township	978	...
Noel city (pt.)[59]	306	(NA)
Spring Valley village	67	60
Erie Goodman township	1 617	...
Goodman town[59]	1 030	565
Erie McNatt township	296	...
McMillen Coy township	724	...
McMillen Tiff township	335	...
Mountain township	630	327
Pineville Lanagan township	584	...
Lanagan town[59]	440	374
Pineville North township	1 055	...
Pineville town	504	444
Pineville South township	542	...
Prairie township	1 103	973
South West City city	516	453
Richwood township[59]	609	563
White Rock township	667	650
Macon County[60]	16 313	15 432
Bevier township	1 274	1 372
Bevier city	733	806
Callao township	567	662
Callao city	326	373
Chariton township	349	305
Drake township	79	104
Eagle township	390	315
Easley township	286	276
Elmer city (pt.)	22	20
South Gifford village	98	64
Hudson township	6 752	5 887
Macon city[60]	5 680	5 301
Independence township	202	238
Jackson township	154	182
Johnston township	79	67
La Plata township	1 833	1 673
La Plata city	1 423	1 377
Liberty township	219	245
Lingo township	649	644
New Cambria town	246	260
Lyda township	694	649
Atlanta city	441	377
Middle Fork township	227	229
Morrow township	196	163
Narrows township	363	360
Richland township	247	221
Round Grove township	371	357
Russell township	222	188
Ten Mile township	356	409
Valley township	193	201
Walnut Creek township	351	406
Elmer city (pt.)	158	173
Ethel town (pt.)	43	50
White township	260	279
Ethel town (pt.)	102	112
Madison County[61]	10 725	8 641
Big Creek township	204	197
Castor township	686	434
Central township	485	419
Liberty township	368	279
Marquand township	924	779
Marquand city	397	400
Mine La Motte township	408	240
Polk township	741	398
St. Francois township	331	268
St. Michael township	6 272	5 369
Cobalt City village	272	238
Fredericktown city[61]	4 036	3 799
Junction City village	238	166
Twelvemile township	306	258
Maries County[62]	7 551	6 851
Boone township	700	575
Dry Creek township	428	420
Jackson township	1 897	1 708

County Subdivisions	1980	1970
Maries County—Con.		
Jackson township—Con.		
Argyle town (pt.)[62]	10	...
Vienna city	514	505
Jefferson township	2 310	2 190
Belle city (pt.)	1 099	1 042
Johnson township	1 047	920
Miller township	867	805
Spring Creek township	302	233
Marion County[63]	28 638	28 121
Fabius township	1 279	1 298
Liberty township	4 099	3 842
Palmyra city	3 469	3 188
Mason township	19 074	19 205
Hannibal city (pt.)[63]	18 623	18 406
Miller township	877	803
Hannibal city (pt.)[63]	16	...
Round Grove township	833	767
South River township	350	345
Union township	748	654
Warren township	1 978	1 207
Monroe City city (pt.)	370	337
Mercer County[64]	4 685	4 910
Harrison township	299	309
Lindley township	299	341
Madison township	226	321
Marion township	1 002	863
Mercer town[64]	442	364
South Lineville town	55	52
Medicine township	248	306
Morgan township	1 697	1 774
Princeton city	1 264	1 328
Ravanna township	293	354
Somerset township	205	279
Washington township	416	363
Miller County[65]	18 532	15 026
Equality township	1 275	1 114
Tuscumbia town	241	256
Franklin township	3 544	2 138
Bagnell town	71	60
Eldon city (pt.)[65]	634	62
Lakeland town[65]	197	62
Lakeside village (pt.)	109	79
Lakeview village[65]	119	35
Glaze township	2 497	1 968
Brumley town	109	87
Lake Ozark city (pt.)	329	409
Lakeside village (pt.)	106	45
Osage Beach city (pt.)[65]	68	...
Jim Henry township	1 243	1 038
St. Elizabeth town (pt.)	298	276
Osage township	770	731
St. Elizabeth town (pt.)	14	11
Richwoods township	2 876	2 474
Iberia city	852	741
Saline township	6 327	5 563
Eldon city (pt.)[65]	3 708	3 458
Olean town	128	151
Mississippi County[66]	15 726	16 647
James Bayou township	282	593
Long Prairie township	1 300	1 144
Bertrand city[66]	688	604
Mississippi township	164	405
Ohio township	1 127	1 546
Wilson City town	309	295
Wyatt city	441	562
St. James township	6 139	5 654
Anniston town	320	515
East Prairie city[66]	3 713	3 275
Tywappity township	6 291	6 739
Charleston city[66]	5 230	5 131
Wolf Island township	423	566
Moniteau County[67]	12 068	10 742
Burris Fork township	506	424
Harrison township	572	446
Linn township[67]	1 045	967
Jamestown town	317	243
Lupus town	50	68
Moreau township	798	657
Clarksburg city	352	343
Pilot Grove township	848	797
Walker township	5 322	4 791
California city[67]	3 381	3 105
Willow Fork township	2 977	2 660
Tipton city[67]	2 155	1 914
Monroe County[68]	9 716	9 542
Clay township	367	391
Indian Creek township	193	176
Jackson township	2 913	2 668
Paris city	1 598	1 442
Jefferson township	372	540
Stoutsville village[68]	34	61
Marion township	1 460	1 315
Holliday village	168	167
Madison city	656	540

County Subdivisions	1980	1970
Monroe County—Con.		
Monroe township	2 462	2 421
Monroe City city (pt.)	2 187	2 119
South Fork township	577	598
Union township	685	690
Washington township	327	380
Woodlawn township	360	363
Montgomery County[69]	11 537	11 000
Bear Creek township	2 409	2 177
Bellflower town	403	360
High Hill town[69]	254	192
Jonesburg city[69]	614	479
Danville township	1 653	1 394
New Florence city	731	635
Loutre township	1 406	1 337
McKittrick town	87	101
Rhineland town	172	190
Montgomery township	2 965	2 995
Montgomery City city	2 101	2 187
Prairie township	974	918
Middletown town	268	235
Upper Loutre township	2 130	2 179
Wellsville city	1 546	1 565
Morgan County[70]	13 807	'10 083
Buffalo township	851	446
Haw Creek township[70]	3 216	2 266
Stover city[70]	1 041	849
Versailles city (pt.)[70]	384	'—
Mill Creek township	902	'717
Syracuse city	222	'214
Moreau township	4 519	4 057
Barnett city	203	167
Versailles city (pt.)	2 022	2 244
Osage township	3 392	1 819
Sunrise Beach village (pt.)	48	31
Richland township	927	778
New Madrid County[71]	22 945	23 420
Anderson township	1 862	1 979
Gideon city	1 240	1 112
Big Prairie township[71]	2 340	...
Matthews city	547	538
Sikeston city (pt.)[71]	664	309
Como township	3 036	3 009
Catron town	180	122
Parma city	1 081	1 051
Risco city[71]	446	412
Tallapoosa city[71]	197	'205
Hough township	54	86
La Font township	1 493	1 677
Marston city	742	666
Le Sieur township	752	742
Lewis township	2 664	2 634
Howardville city (pt.)	536	500
Lilbourn city[71]	1 463	1 152
North Lilbourn village	237	334
New Madrid township	4 131	4 361
Howardville city (pt.)[71]	-	...
New Madrid city	3 204	2 719
Portage township	4 173	4 261
Portageville city[71]	3 470	3 117
St. John township	97	181
West township[71]	2 343	...
Canalou city	369	358
Morehouse city[71]	1 220	1 332
Sikeston city (pt.)	4	...
Newton County[72]	40 555	'32 981
Benton township	420	402
Berwick township	238	257
Buffalo township	1 575	1 242
Dayton township	1 089	890
Five Mile township	2 013	1 369
Franklin township	1 405	1 368
Fairview town	282	263
Stella town	230	197
Granby township	3 367	2 893
Granby city	1 908	1 678
Marion township	2 579	'2 077
Diamond town	766	'608
Neosho township	13 780	11 409
Neosho city (pt.)[72]	9 130	7 517
Newtonia township	749	'654
Newtonia town	224	'208
Stark City town	132	122
Seneca township	2 469	2 219
Seneca city[72]	1 853	1 577
Shoal Creek township	8 341	6 190
Cliff Village village	24	39
Dennis Acres village	56	64
Joplin city (pt.)[72]	2 196	2 216
Leawood village	631	174
Midway village[72]	223	234
Redings Mill village	222	179
Saginaw village	293	'224
Shoal Creek Drive village	374	329
Shoal Creek Estates town[72]	89	...
Silver Creek village[72]	519	'381
Sunnyvale town (pt.)[72]	353	311

County Subdivisions	1980	1970
Newton County—Con.		
Van Buren township	1 287	1 070
Ritchey town	126	101
Wentworth village	138	132
West Benton township	1 243	941
Neosho city (pt.)[72]	363	...
Nodaway County[73]	21 996	22 467
Atchison township	672	621
Clearmont town	261	226
Grant township	675	672
Barnard city	234	206
Green township	375	512
Quitman town	66	95
Hopkins township	956	1 073
Hopkins city	634	656
Hughes township	666	724
Graham town	253	213
Independence township	616	700
Parnell city	223	232
Jackson township	985	937
Ravenwood town[73]	436	336
Jefferson township	945	1 131
Clyde village	61	158
Conception Junction town	252	237
Lincoln township	563	650
Elmo city	215	'204
Monroe township	738	810
Skidmore city	437	440
Nodaway township	998	1 049
Burlington Junction city	657	634
Polk township	12 237	11 871
Maryville city[73]	9 558	9 970
Union township	588	600
Pickering town	215	245
Washington township	405	501
Guilford town	87	105
White Cloud township	577	616
Arkoe town	63	49
Oregon County[74]	10 238	9 180
Big Apple township	689	568
Koshkonong town	245	216
Billmore township	105	125
Black Pond township	215	189
Cedar Bluff township	140	101
Couch township	466	438
Falling Spring township	56	62
Goebel township	251	293
Highland township	374	313
Jeff township	284	282
Jobe township	155	185
Johnson township	259	229
King township	117	80
Moore township	404	364
Myrtle township	549	475
Ozark township	84	103
Piney township	1 976	1 638
Alton city[74]	721	715
Thayer township	3 776	3 388
Thayer city[74]	2 211	1 609
Woodside township	338	347
Osage County[75]	12 014	10 994
Benton township	1 412	1 444
Chamois city	546	615
Crawford township	3 359	3 009
Linn city[75]	1 211	1 289
Jackson township	1 374	1 243
Argyle town (pt.)	36	51
Meta city	336	387
Jefferson township	1 032	969
Belle city (pt.)	134	91
Bland city (pt.)[75]	-	...
Linn township	1 903	1 669
Washington township	2 934	2 660
Argyle town (pt.)	170	211
Freeburg village	554	577
Westphalia city	285	332
Ozark County[76]	7 961	6 226
Barren Fork township	427	418
Bayou township	1 197	914
Bakersfield village	241	210
Big Creek township	661	501
Theodosia village (pt.)	121	132
Bridges township	1 922	1 464
Gainesville city	707	627
Dawt township	237	158
Jackson township	197	160
Jasper township	505	332
Sundown village[76]	39	...
Theodosia village (pt.)[76]	83	...
Lick Creek township	413	306
Longrun township	91	80
Noble township	346	302
Nottinghill township	155	121
Pine Creek township	288	218
Pontiac township	207	127
Richland township[76]	742	658

County Subdivisions	1980	1970
Ozark County—Con.		
Spring Creek township	89	77
Thornfield township	484	390
Pemiscot County[77]	24 987	26 373
Braggadocio township	1 243	1 583
Butler township	400	456
Hayward town[77]	56	...
Concord township	357	531
Cooter township	3 519	3 243
Cooter town	479	414
Steele city (pt.)[77]	2 418	2 107
Godair township	500	594
Hayti township	5 319	5 599
Hayti city[77]	3 964	3 841
Hayti Heights city[77]	1 023	...
Holland township	727	919
Holland town	295	329
Little Prairie township	9 204	8 791
Caruthersville city[77]	7 958	7 350
Little River township	1 303	1 563
Homestown city	306	273
North Wardell village[77]	184	'157
Wardell town	299	275
Pascola township	991	1 250
Bragg City town	200	210
Pascola town	211	180
Pemiscot township	571	819
Virginia township	853	1 025
Steele city (pt.)[77]	1	...
Perry County[78]	16 784	14 393
Bois Brule township	696	829
Brazeau township	1 173	1 204
Altenburg city[78]	280	277
Frohna city[78]	265	225
Wittenberg town[78]	4	9
Central township	9 582	7 814
Perryville city[78]	7 343	5 149
Cinque Hommes township	1 178	992
St. Marys township	1 017	742
Salem township	789	681
Saline township	1 305	1 055
Lithium village	81	56
Union township	1 044	1 076
Longtown town	121	113
Pettis County[79]	36 378	34 137
Blackwater township	432	395
Bowling Green township	745	498
Cedar township	614	544
Dresden township	631	504
Elk Fork township	383	343
Flat Creek township	1 291	852
Green Ridge township	1 104	865
Green Ridge town[79]	488	403
Windsor city (pt.)[79]	118	'44
Heaths Creek township	482	381
Houstonia township	552	538
Houstonia city	327	312
Hughesville township	446	430
Hughesville village	152	92
Lake Creek township	394	329
La Monte township	1 474	1 211
La Monte city[79]	1 054	814
Longwood township	364	339
Prairie township	936	581
Sedalia township	23 183	24 664
Sedalia city[79]	20 927	22 847
Smithton township	2 710	1 163
Smithton city[79]	559	402
Washington township	637	500
Ionia town (pt.)[79]	−	...
Phelps County[80]	33 633	'29 567
Arlington township	2 424	2 206
Doolittle city	701	'535
Newburg city	743	806
Cold Spring township	1 676	1 022
Dawson township	490	'388
Dillon township	5 423	3 151
Rolla city (pt.)[80]	1 005	'649
St. James city (pt.)[80]	203	'56
Liberty township	314	161
Meramec township	581	578
Miller township	2 085	1 967
Northwye village	135	138
Rolla city (pt.)[80]	215	162
Rolla township	14 698	14 740
Rolla city (pt.)[80]	12 083	'12 760
St. James township	4 263	'3 881
St. James city (pt.)[80]	3 125	'2 873
Spring Creek township	1 679	1 473
Edgar Springs city[80]	271	...
Pike County[81]	17 568	16 928
Ashley township	725	718
Buffalo township	6 018	6 040
Louisiana city	4 261	4 533
Calumet township	1 657	1 859

County Subdivisions	1980	1970
Pike County—Con.		
Calumet township—Con.		
Annada town	70	109
Clarksville city	585	668
Paynesville town[81]	85	'90
Cuivre township	4 856	4 418
Bowling Green city	3 022	2 936
Tarrants village	50	45
Hartford township	558	565
Indian township	808	693
Peno township	1 067	867
Frankford city	443	472
Prairieville township	721	578
Eolia town	401	321
Salt River township	212	226
Ashburn town	89	119
Spencer township	946	964
Curryville city	323	337
Platte County[82]	46 341	32 081
Carroll township[82]	5 649	...
Kansas City city (pt.)	290	(NA)
Platte City city (pt.)[82]	2 114	2 022
Tracy city (pt.)[82]	−	...
Weatherby Lake city (pt.)	1 445	(NA)
Fair township	725	699
Platte City city (pt.)	−	...
Tracy city (pt.)[82]	310	252
Fox township[82]	7 226	...
Houston Lake city	280	338
Kansas City city (pt.)	6 479	(NA)
Platte Woods city	467	484
Green township	1 739	1 698
Camden Point city	263	'264
Dearborn city (pt.)[82]	547	543
Kickapoo township[82]	4 147	...
Weatherby Lake city (pt.)	1	(NA)
Lee township	587	543
Farley village[82]	184	174
Marshall township	1 082	1 075
Iatan village[82]	64	'75
May township[82]	5 819	3 560
Ferrelview village	447	140
Kansas City city (pt.)	4 322	(NA)
Lake Waukomis city	1 050	1 105
Pawnee township[82]	4 503	...
Kansas City city (pt.)	4 503	(NA)
Pettis township[82]	5 318	...
Northmoor city	506	562
Riverside city	3 206	2 123
Preston township	1 427	1 150
Edgerton city	584	477
Ridgely town[82]	78	'53
Sioux township[82]	5 594	...
Parkville city[82]	1 997	1 253
Waldron township[82]	437	399
Weston township	2 088	1 787
Weston city	1 440	1 267
Polk County[83]	18 822	15 415
Campbell township	323	257
Cliquot township	304	234
East Looney township	786	...
East Madison township	577	(NA)
Fair Play city (pt.)	278	(NA)
Flemington township	243	219
Flemington village	140	126
Jackson township	661	652
Jefferson township	310	250
Johnson township	1 383	1 205
Humansville city	907	825
McKinley township	455	355
Mooney township	1 861	1 312
Pleasant Hope village[83]	354	265
North Benton township	440	...
Halfway village (pt.)[83]	101	(NA)
Northeast Marion township	2 265	...
Bolivar city (pt.)[83]	1 313	(NA)
North Green township	236	...
Northwest Marion township	1 773	...
Bolivar city (pt.)[83]	1 136	(NA)
South Benton township	714	...
Halfway village (pt.)[83]	56	(NA)
Southeast Marion township	2 075	...
Bolivar city (pt.)[83]	1 453	(NA)
South Green township	318	...
Southwest Marion township	2 540	...
Bolivar city (pt.)[83]	2 017	(NA)
Union township	321	345
Aldrich town	53	66
West Looney township	538	...
Morrisville town	331	256
West Madison township	304	...
Fair Play city (pt.)	106	(NA)
Wishart township	395	294

County Subdivisions

County Subdivisions	1980	1970
Pulaski County[84]	42 011	'53 967
Cullen township	31 050	'43 070
Fort Leonard Wood (CDP) (pt.)	21 181	32 549
St. Robert city[84]	1 735	'1 465
Waynesville city[84]	2 879	3 375
Liberty township	4 132	3 383
Richland city (pt.)[84]	1 803	1 733
Piney township	352	1 500
Fort Leonard Wood (CDP) (pt.)	81	1 250
Roubidoux township	132	146
Tavern township	2 619	2 481
Crocker city[84]	979	814
Union township	3 726	3 387
Dixon city[84]	1 402	1 387
Putnam County[85]	6 092	5 916
Elm township	762	762
Worthington town[85]	105	...
Grant township	332	309
Livonia town	162	119
Jackson township	208	198
Liberty township	344	327
Lincoln township	322	323
Medicine township	328	359
Lucerne town	130	126
Richland township	263	247
Sherman township	131	158
Union township	2 266	2 163
Unionville city (pt.)[85]	1 793	1 799
Wilson township	753	663
Unionville city (pt.)	385	276
York township	383	407
Powersville town	116	125
Ralls County[86]	8 911	7 764
Center township	964	1 032
Center city	596	588
Clay township	1 799	1 437
Hannibal city (pt.)[86]	172	203
Jasper township	767	704
Saline township	488	543
Salt River township	1 323	1 311
Perry city	836	839
Saverton township	1 645	1 153
Spencer township	1 925	1 584
New London city[86]	1 161	967
Randolph County[87]	25 460	22 434
Cairo township	959	720
Cairo village	315	248
Chariton township	378	294
Clifton township	344	352
Clifton Hill city	152	174
Jackson township	348	321
Jacksonville village	130	142
Moniteau township	1 144	905
Higbee city	817	641
North Sugar Creek township[87]	6 754	6 895
Moberly city (pt.)[87]	6 014	6 311
Prairie township	3 144	2 181
Clark city	304	271
Moberly city (pt.)	25	-
Renick town	195	188
Salt River township	267	247
Salt Springs township[87]	2 803	2 408
Huntsville city	1 657	1 442
Silver Creek township	322	334
South Sugar Creek township[87]	7 861	7 211
Moberly city (pt.)[87]	7 361	6 677
Union township	1 136	566
Moberly city (pt.)[87]	18	-
Ray County[88]	21 378	17 599
Camden township	685	774
Camden city	219	286
Fleming city	144	152
Crooked River township	1 273	1 276
Hardin city	688	683
Fishing River township	4 386	2 393
Excelsior Springs city (pt.)	156	117
Homestead village[88]	138	...
Woods Heights city[88]	747	362
Grape Grove township	991	1 021
Knoxville township	698	598
Orrick township	1 421	1 428
Orrick city[88]	922	883
Polk township	3 363	2 158
Elmira village	109	124
Lawson city (pt.)[88]	1 616	1 015
Richmond township	8 561	7 951
Henrietta city	424	466
Rayville town	197	202
Richmond city[88]	5 499	4 948
Reynolds County[89]	7 230	6 106
Black River township	728	566
Carroll township	1 738	1 277
Bunker city (pt.)[89]	405	238
Centerville city	241	209
Jackson township	415	441
Lesterville township	795	762

County Subdivisions

County Subdivisions	1980	1970
Reynolds County—Con.		
Logan township	2 898	2 651
Ellington city[89]	1 215	1 094
Webb township	656	409
Ripley County[90]	12 458	9 803
Current River township	119	121
Doniphan township	4 918	3 719
Doniphan city[90]	1 921	1 850
Flatwoods township	388	266
Gatewood township	346	290
Harris township	540	516
Johnson township	315	206
Jordan township	809	594
Kelley township	65	72
Pine township	379	'237
Poynor township	326	227
Sherley township	626	'571
Thomas township	1 043	951
Naylor city[90]	602	586
Union township	387	312
Varner township	700	655
Washington township	728	573
West Doniphan township	769	493
St. Charles County[91]	144 107	92 954
Boone township	7 164	...
Augusta city[91]	308	'195
Lake St. Louis city (pt.)[91]	10	...
New Melle village[91]	168	...
Cave Springs township	10 172	...
St. Charles city (pt.)[91]	244	...
St. Peters city (pt.)[91]	2 517	...
Dardenne township	14 971	...
Lake St. Louis city (pt.)[91]	3 828	...
O'Fallon city (pt.)[91]	1 303	(NA)
Friedens township	13 282	...
St. Charles city (pt.)[91]	-	...
O'Fallon township	10 271	...
O'Fallon city (pt.)[91]	7 374	(NA)
St. Paul village[91]	607	...
St. Peters city (pt.)[91]	-	...
Portage township	9 114	...
Portage Des Sioux city	488	509
St. Charles city (pt.)[91]	1 270	...
St. Charles township	36 308	...
St. Charles city (pt.)[91]	35 865	31 834
St. Peters township	24 130	...
St. Peters city (pt.)[91]	13 170	486
Weldon Spring township	11 532	...
Cottleville town[91]	184	'230
St. Peters city (pt.)[91]	13	...
Weldon Spring Heights town	144	'172
Wentzville township	7 163	...
Flint Hill village[91]	219	...
Foristell village[91]	119	...
Josephville village[91]	58	...
Lake St. Louis city (pt.)[91]	5	...
Wentzville city[91]	3 193	3 223
St. Clair County[92]	8 622	7 667
Appleton township	1 593	1 400
Appleton City city	1 257	1 058
Butler township	1 213	1 043
Lowry City city	676	520
Center township	335	186
Chalk Level township	278	161
Collins township	557	514
Collins town	145	150
Dallas township	330	258
Gerster town	45	42
Doyal township	547	415
Vista village	73	44
Jackson township	184	141
Monegaw township	315	365
Osage township	154	194
Osceola township	1 438	1 403
Osceola city[92]	841	874
Polk township	157	149
Roscoe township	551	539
Roscoe town[92]	91	137
Speedwell township	473	413
Taber township	240	260
Washington township	257	226
Ste. Genevieve County[93]	15 180	12 867
Beauvais township	1 801	1 649
St. Mary city[93]	565	645
Jackson township	2 355	1 705
Bloomsdale city	397	411
Ste. Genevieve township	8 602	7 851
Ste. Genevieve city[93]	4 481	4 468
Saline township	813	731
Union township	1 609	931
St. Francois County[94]	42 600	'36 875
Big River township	986	581
Iron township	2 880	2 403
Bismarck city[94]	1 625	1 387
Liberty township	1 425	1 053
Marion township	1 115	658

County Subdivisions	1980	1970
St. Francois County—Con.		
Pendleton township	2 112	1 413
Perry township	6 908	5 191
Bonne Terre city[94]	3 797	3 622
Leadwood city (pt.)	–	–
Randolph township	7 615	'7 162
Deslogge city (pt.)[94]	2 834	2 342
Elvins city (pt.)[94]	1 214	'1 337
Fairview Acres village (pt.)	14	35
Flat River city (pt.)[94]	31	...
Highley Heights village	100	119
Leadwood city (pt.)	1 371	1 397
Rivermines village (pt.)	82	68
St. Francois township	19 559	18 414
Deslogge city (pt.)[94]	647	476
Elvins city (pt.)	334	323
Esther city[94]	1 038	1 040
Fairview Acres village (pt.)	17	8
Farmington city[94]	8 270	6 590
Flat River city (pt.)[94]	4 412	4 550
Leadington city	238	299
Rivermines village (pt.)	332	334
St. Louis County[95]	973 896	'951 671
Airport township	42 212	...
Bel-Ridge village (pt.)	546	(NA)
Berkeley city (pt.)[95]	13 893	(NA)
Breckenridge Hills village (pt.)	525	739
Bridgeton city (pt.)	1 208	(NA)
Bridgeton Terrace city	334	332
Cool Valley village (pt.)	690	(NA)
Edmundson village	1 374	'2 298
Kinloch city (pt.)[95]	4 138	5 433
St. Ann city (pt.)[95]	12 856	14 742
St. John city (pt.)	1 584	1 756
Schuermann Heights village	234	290
Woodson Terrace city[95]	4 564	'5 880
Bonhomme township	37 063	...
Des Peres city (pt.)[95]	467	(NA)
Fenton city	2 417	2 275
Kirkwood city	27 987	'31 679
Sappington (CDP) (pt.)	666	632
Sunset Hills city (pt.)	3 956	'3 641
Clayton township	34 895	...
Clayton city (pt.)	7 473	(NA)
Creve Coeur city (pt.)	1 832	(NA)
Crystal Lake Park city	496	356
Des Peres city (pt.)	4 165	4 659
Frontenac city	3 654	3 920
Glendale city (pt.)	141	(NA)
Huntleigh city	428	714
Ladue city (pt.)	7 559	(NA)
Rock Hill city (pt.)	4 651	(NA)
Town and Country city (pt.)	1 272	(NA)
University City city (pt.)	–	–
Warson Woods city	2 127	2 544
Webster Groves city (pt.)	396	...
Westwood village	319	311
Concord township	59 424	'58 481
Affton (CDP) (pt.)	10 897	'8 919
Concord (CDP)	20 896	21 217
Lakeshire city	1 593	1 186
Lemay (CDP) (pt.)	1 198	'3 369
St. George city	1 545	'2 033
Sappington (CDP) (pt.)	8 536	'8 244
Sunset Hills city (pt.)	22	92
Wilbur Park village	564	'692
Creve Coeur township	56 913	...
Creve Coeur city (pt.)[95]	5 934	(NA)
Olivette city	8 039	'9 156
Overland city (pt.)	445	588
University City city (pt.)	27 184	'30 307
Ferguson township	48 187	...
Calverton Park village	1 717	2 025
Cool Valley village (pt.)	1 394	(NA)
Dellwood city[95]	6 200	7 137
Ferguson city[95]	24 740	'28 759
Florissant city (pt.)	689	(NA)
Jennings city (pt.)[95]	1 952	–
Kinloch city (pt.)	317	196
Normandy city (pt.)[95]	1 603	(NA)
Florissant township	37 386	...
Florissant city (pt.)[95]	27 085	(NA)
Hazelwood city (pt.)[95]	1 444	(NA)
Gravois township	51 883	...
Affton (CDP) (pt.)	12 284	'15 345
Crestwood city	12 815	'15 123
Grantwood town	1 002	994
Mackenzie village	186	'224
Marlborough village[95]	2 012	'1 492
Oakland city	1 728	1 609
Sappington (CDP) (pt.)	2 186	'1 727
Shrewsbury city (pt.)[95]	1 458	2 033
Sunset Hills city (pt.)	385	393
Webster Groves city (pt.)	12 396	14 882
Hadley township	42 147	...
Clayton city (pt.)	6 746	(NA)
Maplewood city	10 960	12 785
Richmond Heights city (pt.)	8 632	(NA)
University City city (pt.)	15 554	'17 220

County Subdivisions	1980	1970
St. Louis County—Con.		
Hadley township—Con.		
Wellston city (pt.)		...
Jefferson township	33 779	...
Brentwood city	8 209	11 248
Glendale city (pt.)	5 894	(NA)
Ladue city (pt.)	1 817	(NA)
Richmond Heights city (pt.)	2 884	(NA)
Rock Hill city (pt.)	1 051	(NA)
Shrewsbury city (pt.)[95]	3 619	3 863
Webster Groves city (pt.)[95]	10 305	'12 575
Lemay township	72 216	60 559
Bella Villa city	758	'1 018
Lemay (CDP) (pt.)	34 226	'37 160
Lewis and Clark township	44 114	...
Florissant city (pt.)[95]	24 315	(NA)
Hazelwood city (pt.)	4 116	(NA)
Meramec township	20 667	...
Clarkson Valley village[95]	1 435	157
Ellisville city (pt.)[95]	3 056	(NA)
Eureka city[95]	3 862	2 384
Pacific city (pt.)	12	...
Times Beach city	2 041	1 265
Midland township	42 632	...
Bel-Ridge village (pt.)	–	(NA)
Breckenridge Hills village (pt.)	5 141	6 272
Charlack city	1 537	1 872
Overland city (pt.)	19 175	'24 231
St. Ann city (pt.)[95]	2 667	3 473
St. John city (pt.)[95]	6 036	7 204
Sycamore Hills village	741	821
Vinita Park city	2 283	'2 905
Vinita Terrace village (pt.)	262	(NA)
Missouri River township[95]	72 506	...
Ballwin city (pt.)[95]	5 073	(NA)
Creve Coeur city (pt.)[95]	3 991	(NA)
Ellisville city (pt.)[95]	1 942	(NA)
Maryland Heights (CDP) (pt.)	839	(NA)
Town and Country city (pt.)	622	(NA)
Normandy township	48 299	...
Bellerive village	255	437
Bel-Nor village	2 047	'2 247
Bel-Ridge village (pt.)	3 136	(NA)
Beverly Hills city	712	846
Cool Valley village (pt.)	–	(NA)
Glen Echo Park village	249	'268
Greendale city	853	972
Hanley Hills village	2 439	'2 801
Hillsdale village	2 247	2 599
Jennings city (pt.)	–	(NA)
Normandy city (pt.)[95]	3 571	(NA)
Northwoods city[95]	5 831	'4 607
Norwood Court village	881	'358
Pagedale city	4 542	'5 044
Pasadena Hills village	1 221	'1 337
Pasadena Park village	531	760
Pine Lawn city[95]	6 662	'5 745
St. John city (pt.)[95]	234	(NA)
Uplands Park village	544	695
Velda Village city[95]	1 988	'2 112
Velda Village Hills village	1 393	'1 205
Vinita Terrace village (pt.)	87	(NA)
Wellston city (pt.)	4 495	7 050
Northwest township	47 066	...
Berkeley city (pt.)	2 253	(NA)
Bridgeton city (pt.)	17 237	(NA)
Champ village[95]	28	19
Florissant city (pt.)	737	(NA)
Hazelwood city (pt.)[95]	7 375	(NA)
Maryland Heights (CDP) (pt.)	4 837	(NA)
Queeny township	76 531	...
Ballwin city (pt.)[95]	7 583	(NA)
Country Life Acres village	77	60
Des Peres city (pt.)[95]	3 622	674
Ellisville city (pt.)	1 235	(NA)
Manchester city	6 191	5 031
Peerless Park city[95]	79	'51
Town and Country city (pt.)	1 293	(NA)
Twin Oaks village	426	41
Valley Park city[95]	3 232	3 662
Winchester city	2 237	2 329
St. Ferdinand township	51 144	...
Bellefontaine Neighbors city (pt.)[95]	12 082	'14 084
Country Club Hills city	1 315	1 644
Flordell Hills city	919	989
Jennings city (pt.)	15 074	19 379
Moline Acres city	2 774	3 722
Riverview village	3 367	3 741
Spanish Lake township	54 832	...
Bellefontaine Neighbors city (pt.)	–	...
Black Jack city[95]	5 293	...
Florissant city (pt.)[95]	2 546	(NA)
Spanish Lake (CDP)	20 632	15 647
Saline County[96]	24 919	'24 837
Arrow Rock township	878	787
Arrow Rock town	82	81
Nelson city	248	230
Blackwater township	346	389
Cambridge township	3 221	3 402
Gilliam town	227	248
Slater city[96]	2 492	2 576

County Subdivisions	1980	1970
Saline County—Con.		
Clay township	485	578
Elmwood township	1 004	1 044
Blackburn city	314	294
Mount Leonard town	131	139
Grand Pass township	743	909
Grand Pass town	71	72
Malta Bend town	292	342
Liberty township	572	523
Marshall township	14 232	[r]13 628
Marshall city[96]	12 781	[r]12 051
Miami township	778	856
Miami city	177	205
Salt Fork township	313	359
Salt Pond township	2 347	2 362
Emma city (pt.)	158	149
Sweet Springs city	1 694	1 716
Schuyler County[97]	4 979	4 665
Chariton township	174	130
Fabius township	833	825
Downing city	462	406
Glenwood township	385	382
Glenwood village	218	184
Independence township	335	316
Liberty township	1 241	1 222
Lancaster city	855	821
Prairie township	1 359	1 180
Queen City city[97]	783	588
Salt River township	652	610
Greentop village (pt.)	423	351
Scotland County	5 415	5 499
Harrison township	507	515
South Gorin town	212	220
Jefferson township	2 716	2 668
Memphis city	2 105	2 081
Johnson township	224	179
Miller township	165	260
Mount Pleasant township	201	185
Sand Hill township	326	327
Rutledge town	128	139
Thomson township	485	532
Arbela town	67	70
Granger town	91	105
Tobin township	153	145
Union township	432	471
Vest township	206	217
Scott County[98]	39 647	33 250
Commerce township	666	647
Commerce town	199	234
Kelso township	9 910	8 708
Chaffee city[98]	3 241	2 793
Illmo city	1 368	1 232
Kelso town	455	401
Scott City city[98]	3 262	2 464
Moreland township	2 417	1 867
Benton city	674	640
Lambert village	34	39
Morley township	2 120	2 051
Haywood City village[98]	425	420
Morley town[98]	745	528
Vanduser village	320	306
Richland township	20 313	16 419
Miner town (pt.)[98]	1 182	640
Sikeston city (pt.)[98]	16 763	14 390
Sandywoods township	1 371	824
Blodgett town	255	220
Miner town (pt.)[98]	–	...
Sylvania township	2 406	2 243
Oran city	1 266	1 226
Tywappity township	444	491
Diehlstadt town	170	155
Shannon County[99]	7 885	7 196
Bartlett township	388	394
Birch Tree township	1 216	1 038
Birch Tree city	622	573
Bowlan township	75	75
Buckeye township	169	189
Delaware township	103	121
Eminence township	1 649	1 572
Eminence city[99]	614	520
Jackson township	137	145
Montier township	661	483
Moore township	173	137
Newton township	220	232
Spring Creek township	338	270
Spring Valley township	921	792
Summersville city (pt.)	98	52
Winona township	1 835	1 748
Winona city	1 050	973
Shelby County	7 826	7 906
Bethel township	465	497
Bethel town	132	143
Black Creek township	1 114	1 073
Shelbyville city	645	601
Clay township	1 433	1 371

County Subdivisions	1980	1970
Shelby County—Con.		
Clay township—Con.		
Clarence city	1 147	1 050
Jackson township	677	762
Hunnewell city	235	304
Jefferson township	393	452
Lentner township	244	245
North River township	179	190
Salt River township	2 714	2 687
Shelbina city	2 169	2 060
Taylor township	390	401
Leonard town	109	107
Tiger Fork township	217	228
Stoddard County[100]	29 009	25 771
Castor township	4 647	3 578
Bloomfield city	1 795	1 584
Circle City village (pt.)[100]	7	...
Duck Creek township	3 221	2 918
Dudley city[100]	287	248
Puxico city[100]	833	759
Elk township	764	1 389
Liberty township	13 583	10 886
Bernie city[100]	1 975	1 641
Dexter city[100]	7 043	6 024
New Lisbon township	905	885
Pike township	3 869	3 780
Advance city[100]	1 054	903
Bell City city[100]	539	424
Richland township	2 020	2 335
Baker village	31	72
Circle City village (pt.)[100]	147	...
Essex city	545	493
Penermon village[100]	136	...
Stone County[101]	15 587	9 921
Alpine township	443	125
Cass township	352	233
Flat Creek A township	704	...
Flat Creek B township	369	...
Grant township	502	687
Hurley township	689	680
Hurley town	125	148
Lincoln township	742	578
McKinley township	278	232
Pierce township	1 460	1 046
Crane city[101]	1 185	1 003
Pine A township	1 055	...
Blue Eye town	94	91
Pine B township	1 077	...
Ponce de Leon township	355	362
Ruth A township	1 827	...
Lakeview village (pt.)[101]	6	...
Reeds Spring city[101]	461	286
Ruth B township	2 190	...
Kimberling City city[101]	1 285	...
Ruth C township	1 423	...
Lakeview village (pt.)[101]	52	...
Union township	312	294
Washington township	1 254	1 057
Galena city	423	391
Williams township	555	532
Sullivan County[102]	7 434	7 572
Bowman township	516	543
Humphreys town	133	140
Osgood town	93	108
Buchanan township	237	311
Clay township	524	647
Harris town	116	174
Newtown town	170	211
Duncan township	500	498
Browning city (pt.)	87	92
Jackson township	637	650
Pollock village[102]	102	...
Liberty township	229	248
Morris township	255	315
Penn township	1 328	1 237
Greencastle city	285	235
Green City city	719	[r]632
Pleasant Hill township	231	291
Polk township	2 589	2 345
Milan city	1 947	1 794
Taylor township	153	198
Union township	235	289
Taney County[103]	20 467	13 023
Beaver township	803	690
Big Creek township	382	388
Branson township	5 926	3 678
Branson city[103]	2 550	2 175
Table Rock Townsite village[103]	58	[r]16
Cedar Creek township	377	230
Jasper township	1 833	816
Rockaway Beach town[103]	292	195
Oliver township	6 131	3 990
Hollister city	1 439	906
Scott township	123	81
Swan township	4 892	3 150
Forsyth city[103]	1 010	803

County Subdivisions	1980	1970
Taney County—Con.		
Swan township—Con.		
Taneyville village[103]	300	'188
Texas County[104]	21 070	18 320
Boone township	235	193
Burdine township	3 126	2 756
Cabool city[104]	2 090	1 848
Carroll township	959	871
Summersville city (pt.)	453	383
Cass township	1 152	1 088
Clinton township	1 165	1 003
Current township[104]	353	374
Date township	507	451
Jackson township[104]	1 153	980
Raymondville town	388	284
Lynch township	1 067	836
Morris township	731	740
Ozark township	497	413
Pierce township	534	371
Piney township	4 449	3 926
Houston city[104]	2 157	2 178
Roubidoux township	1 068	894
Sargent township	275	254
Sherrill township	3 161	2 536
Licking city[104]	1 272	1 002
Upton township	638	634
Vernon County[105]	19 806	19 065
Bacon township	818	816
Harwood town	104	91
Schell City city	327	367
Badger township	370	320
Blue Mound township	290	273
Center township	9 227	8 653
Nevada city (pt.)[105]	7 594	7 786
Clear Creek township	560	443
Coal township	283	279
Deerfield village (pt.)[105]	9	'8
Deerfield township	629	598
Deerfield village (pt.)[105]	86	'104
Moundville town (pt.)	–	1
Dover township	398	418
Drywood township	1 108	1 021
Milo town	78	80
Sheldon city[105]	491	498
Harrison township	268	301
Henry township	257	295
Stotesbury town	48	35
Lake township	189	228
Metz township	346	397
Metz town	136	120
Montevallo township	304	300
Moundville township	739	686
Bronaugh town	209	203
Moundville town (pt.)	149	148
Osage township	328	360
Richland township	262	276
Richards town	117	105
Virgil township	381	358
Walker township	600	520
Walker town	325	227
Washington township	2 449	2 523
Nevada city (pt.)[105]	1 450	1 950
Warren County[106]	14 900	9 699
Bridgeport township	446	295
Camp Branch township	618	549
Charrette township	3 157	2 114
Marthasville city[106]	543	415
Hickory Grove township	3 511	2 138
Wright City city[106]	1 179	943
North Elkhorn township[106]	3 630	...
Truesdail town (pt.)[106]	208	(NA)
Warrenton city (pt.)[106]	1 836	(NA)
Pinckney township	537	385
South Elkhorn township[106]	3 001	...
Truesdail town (pt.)[106]	89	(NA)
Warrenton city (pt.)[106]	1 383	(NA)
Washington County[107]	17 983	15 086
Belgrade township[107]	969	820
Belleview township[107]	802	677
Caledonia village[107]	162	113
Breton township	7 527	6 456
Mineral Point town	358	369
Potosi city	2 528	2 761
Concord township	2 011	1 455
Irondale city	349	319
Harmony township	347	363
Johnson township	496	348
Kingston township	619	548
Liberty township	848	645
Richwoods township	1 020	812
Union township	2 451	2 265
Walton township	893	697

County Subdivisions	1980	1970
Wayne County[108]	11 277	8 546
Benton township	3 528	2 663
Piedmont city[108]	2 359	1 906
Black River township	378	264
Cedar Creek township	473	433
Cowan township	498	611
Jefferson township	341	251
Logan township	1 289	976
Lost Creek township	1 037	590
Mill Spring township	867	537
Mill Spring village[108]	257	207
St. Francois township	1 971	1 456
Greenville city[108]	393	328
Williams township	895	765
Williamsville city	418	398
Webster County[109]	20 414	15 562
East Benton township	1 581	901
Diggins village (pt.)[109]	–	–
Fordland city[109]	569	399
East Dallas township[109]	1 038	864
Diggins village (pt.)[109]	222	140
Finley township	2 373	2 135
Seymour city (pt.)[109]	1 535	1 208
Grant township	1 448	1 031
Hazelwood township	1 104	905
Diggins village (pt.)[109]	23	...
Seymour city (pt.)[109]	–	...
High Prairie township[109]	694	622
Jackson township	1 077	824
Niangua township	972	761
Niangua city	376	309
Ozark township[109]	6 457	'4 490
Marshfield city	3 871	2 961
Union township	656	611
Washington township	793	592
West Benton township	1 506	1 237
Rogersville town (pt.)	706	574
West Dallas township	715	589
Worth County	3 008	3 359
Allen township	268	387
Denver village	74	104
Fletchall township	1 309	1 367
Grant City city	1 068	1 095
Greene township	175	212
Middlefork township	353	330
Worth town	137	113
Smith township	296	358
Allendale town	95	104
Union township	607	705
Sheridan town	220	251
Wright County[110]	16 188	13 667
Boone township	886	707
Brush Creek township	440	427
Clark township	1 024	868
Norwood city (pt.)[110]	354	261
Elk Creek township	448	435
Gasconade township	1 042	861
Hartville city (pt.)	84	68
Hart township	1 107	923
Hartville city (pt.)	492	456
Montgomery township	603	612
Mountain Grove township	5 343	4 291
Mountain Grove city[110]	3 974	3 377
Norwood city (pt.)[110]	37	33
Pleasant Valley township	2 530	1 987
Mansfield city[110]	1 423	1 056
Union township	970	963
Van Buren township	515	502
Wood township	1 280	1 091
St. Louis city	453 085	622 236

MONTANA

This state derives its name from the Latin and Spanish *montana*, signifying "mountainous."

The first white men to visit the region now constituting Montana were two Frenchmen, sons of Sieur de la Verendrye, who entered the southeast corner of the state. Trading posts were established on the Yellowstone and elsewhere about 1809 and at various dates thereafter. Fort Union was built by the American Fur Company in 1829, and Fort Benton by the same company in 1846. Very few settlers came, however, until about 1862, when, attracted by discoveries of gold at Gold Creek and elsewhere, prospectors and miners began to arrive in large numbers.

The area now comprised within the boundaries of Montana, except the comparatively small section west of the Rocky Mountains, was originally a part of the Louisiana country which was ceded by France to Spain in 1763, retroceded to France in 1800, and purchased by the United States in 1803. This area belonged successively to the district of Louisiana (1804-5), the territory of Louisiana (1805-1812), the territory of Missouri (1812-1834), the "Indian country" (1834-1854), the territory of Nebraska (1854-1861), and the territory of Dakota (1861-1863).

That part of the present state lying west of the Rocky Mountains was originally included in the Oregon region, which was occupied jointly by the United States and Great Britain until 1846, when the latter nation relinquished its claims. This area belonged to the territory of Oregon from 1848 to 1853. From 1853 to 1863 it belonged to Washington territory, with the exception of a small tract lying west of the Rocky Mountains and south of the forty-sixth parallel, which was not added to Washington territory until 1859.

In 1863 the territory of Idaho, including the entire area of the present state of Montana, was organized from portions of Washington, Dakota, and Nebraska territories. In 1864 Montana, with substantially the same boundaries as the present state, was organized as a separate territory.

In 1889, under authority of an enabling act passed by Congress in the same year, Montana adopted a state constitution; and in November of that year it was admitted to the Union, with boundaries as at present.

COUNTY LOCATION INDEX

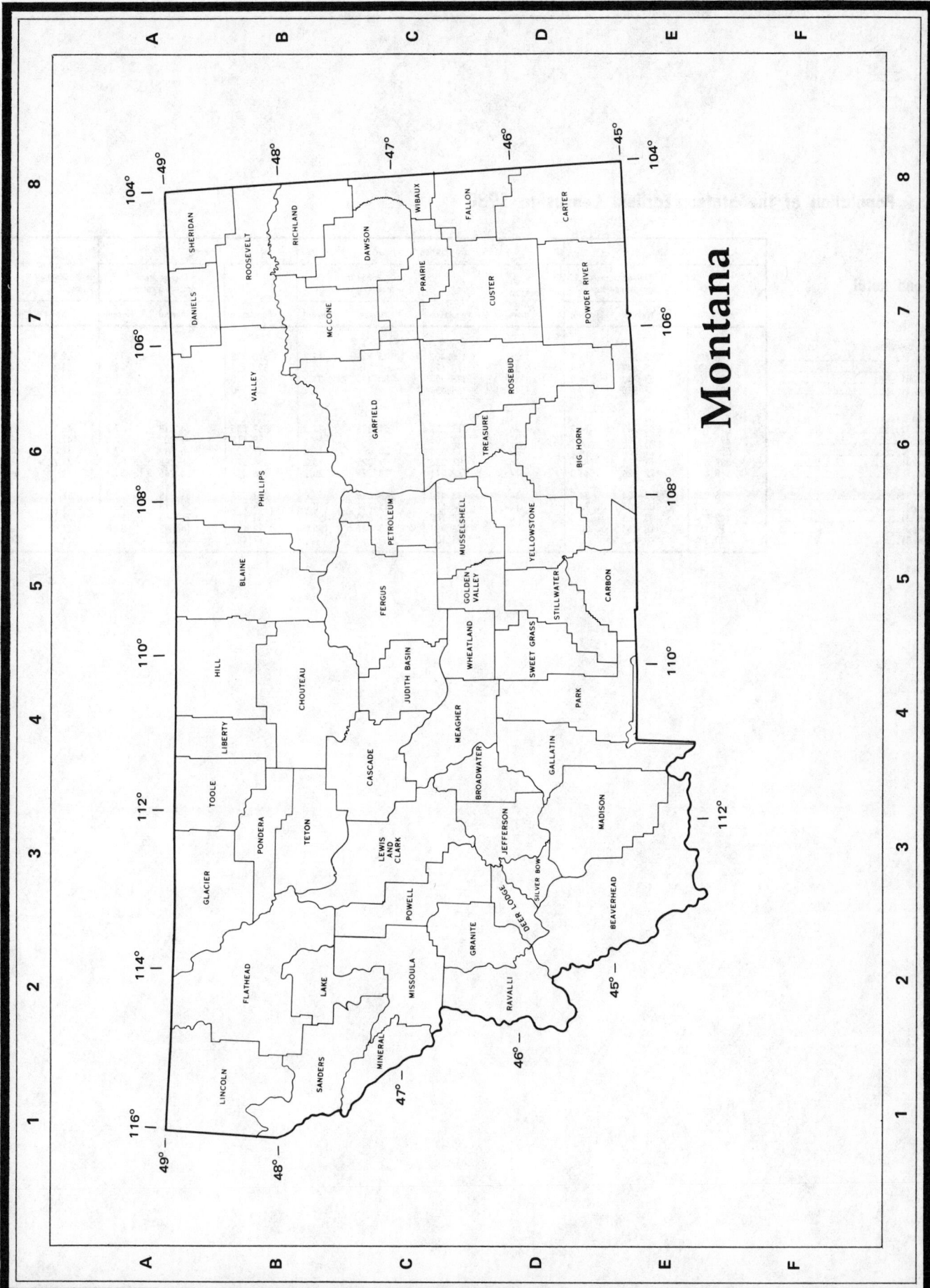

Montana

Population of the State: Earliest Census to 1980

Urban and Rural

	The State			Urban				Rural			Percent of total population	
	Total population	Change from preceding census		Places of 2,500 or more	Population	Change from preceding census		Population	Change from preceding census		Urban	Rural
		Number	Percent			Number	Percent		Number	Percent		
Current urban definition:												
1980 (Apr. 1)	786 690	92 281	13.3	35	416 402	45 726	12.3	370 288	46 555	14.4	52.9	47.1
1970 (Apr. 1)	694 409	19 642	2.9	32	370 676	32 219	9.5	323 733	−12 577	−3.7	53.4	46.6
1960 (Apr. 1)	674 767	83 743	14.2	30	338 457	80 423	31.2	336 310	3 320	1.0	50.2	49.8
1950 (Apr. 1)	591 024	31 568	5.6	26	258 034	...	...	332 990	...	...	43.7	56.3
Previous urban definition:												
1960 (Apr. 1)	674 767	83 743	14.2	26	312 232	59 326	23.5	362 535	24 417	7.2	46.3	53.7
1950 (Apr. 1)	591 024	31 568	5.6	25	252 906	41 371	19.6	338 118	−9 803	−2.8	42.8	57.2
1940 (Apr. 1)	559 456	21 850	4.1	23	211 535	30 499	16.8	347 921	−8 649	−2.4	37.8	62.2
1930 (Apr. 1)	537 606	−11 283	−2.1	18	181 036	9 025	5.2	356 570	−20 308	−5.4	33.7	66.3
1920 (Jan. 1)	548 889	172 836	46.0	17	172 011	38 591	28.9	376 878	134 245	55.3	31.3	68.7
1910 (Apr. 15)	376 053	132 724	54.5	14	133 420	48 866	57.8	242 633	83 858	52.8	35.5	64.5
1900 (June 1)	243 329	100 405	70.3	10	84 554	45 767	118.0	158 775	54 638	52.5	34.7	65.3
1890 (June 1)	142 924	103 765	265.0	6	38 787	31 800	455.1	104 137	71 965	223.7	27.1	72.9
1880 (June 1)	39 159	18 564	90.1	2	6 987	3 881	125.0	32 172	14 683	84.0	17.8	82.2
1870 (June 1)	20 595	...	...	1	3 106	...	...	17 489	...	...	15.1	84.9

BEAVERHEAD

1870	722
1880	2,712
1890	4,655
1900	5,615
1910	6,446
1920	7,369
1930	6,654
1940	6,943
1950	6,671
1960	7,194
1970	8,187
1980	8,186

BIG HORN

1920	7,015
1930	8,543
1940	10,419
1950	9,824
1960	10,007
1970	10,057
1980	11,096

BLAINE

1920	9,057
1930	9,006
1940	9,566
1950	8,516
1960	8,091
1970	6,727
1980	6,999

BROADWATER

1900	2,641
1910	3,491
1920	3,239
1930	2,738
1940	3,451
1950	2,922
1960	2,804
1970	2,526
1980	3,267

CARBON

1900	7,533
1910	13,962
1920	15,279
1930	12,571
1940	11,865
1950	10,241
1960	8,317
1970	7,080
1980	8,099

CARTER

1920	3,972
1930	4,136
1940	3,280
1950	2,798
1960	2,493
1970	1,956
1980	1,799

CASCADE

1890	8,755
1900	25,777
1910	28,833
1920	38,836
1930	41,146
1940	41,999
1950	53,027
1960	73,418
1970	81,804
1980	80,696

CHOUTEAU

1870	517
1880	3,058
1890	4,741
1900	10,966
1910	17,191
1920	11,051
1930	8,635
1940	7,316
1950	6,974
1960	7,348
1970	6,473
1980	6,092

CUSTER

1870	38
1880	2,510
1890	5,308
1900	7,891
1910	14,123
1920	12,194
1930	11,242
1940	10,422
1950	12,661
1960	13,227
1970	12,174
1980	13,109

DANIELS

1930	5,553
1940	4,563
1950	3,946
1960	3,755
1970	3,083
1980	2,835

DAWSON

1870	177
1880	180
1890	2,056
1900	2,443
1910	12,725
1920	9,239
1930	9,881
1940	8,618
1950	9,092
1960	12,314
1970	11,269
1980	11,805

DEER LODGE

1870	4,367
1880	8,876
1890	15,155
1900	17,393
1910	12,998
1920	15,323
1930	16,293
1940	13,627
1950	16,553
1960	18,640
1970	15,652
1980	12,518

FALLON

1920	4,548
1930	5,568
1940	3,719
1950	3,660
1960	3,997
1970	4,050
1980	3,763

FERGUS

1890	3,514
1900	6,937
1910	17,385
1920	28,344
1930	16,531
1940	14,040
1950	14,015
1960	14,018
1970	12,611
1980	13,076

FLATHEAD

1900	9,375
1910	18,785
1920	21,705
1930	19,200
1940	24,271
1950	31,495
1960	32,965
1970	39,460
1980	51,966

GALLATIN

1870	1,587
1880	3,643
1890	6,246
1900	9,553
1910	14,079
1920	15,864
1930	16,124
1940	18,269
1950	21,902
1960	26,045
1970	32,505
1980	42,865

GARFIELD

1920	5,368
1930	4,252
1940	2,641
1950	2,172
1960	1,981
1970	1,796
1980	1,656

GLACIER

1920	4,178
1930	5,297
1940	9,034
1950	9,645
1960	11,565
1970	10,783
1980	10,628

GOLDEN VALLEY

1930	2,126
1940	1,607
1950	1,337
1960	1,203

1970	931
1980	1,026

GRANITE

1900	4,328
1910	2,942
1920	4,167
1930	3,013
1940	3,401
1950	2,773
1960	3,014
1970	2,737
1980	2,700

HILL

1920	13,958
1930	13,775
1940	13,304
1950	14,285
1960	18,653
1970	17,358
1980	17,985

JEFFERSON

1870	1,531
1880	2,464
1890	6,026
1900	5,330
1910	5,601
1920	5,203
1930	4,133
1940	4,664
1950	4,014
1960	4,297
1970	5,238
1980	7,029

JUDITH BASIN

1930	5,238
1940	3,655
1950	3,200
1960	3,085
1970	2,667
1980	2,646

LAKE

1930	9,541
1940	13,490
1950	13,835
1960	13,104
1970	14,445
1980	19,056

LEWIS AND CLARK

1870	5,040
1880	6,521
1890	19,145
1900	19,171
1910	21,853
1920	18,660
1930	18,224
1940	22,131
1950	24,540
1960	28,006
1970	33,281
1980	43,039

LIBERTY

1920	2,416
1930	2,198
1940	2,209
1950	2,180
1960	2,624
1970	2,359
1980	2,329

LINCOLN

1910	3,638
1920	7,797
1930	7,089
1940	7,882
1950	8,693
1960	12,537
1970	18,063
1980	17,752

McCONE

1920	4,747
1930	4,790
1940	3,798
1950	3,258
1960	3,321
1970	2,875
1980	2,702

MADISON

1870	2,684
1880	3,915
1890	4,692
1900	7,695
1910	7,229
1920	7,495
1930	6,323
1940	7,294
1950	5,998
1960	5,211
1970	5,014
1980	5,448

MEAGHER

1870	1,387
1880	2,743
1890	4,749
1900	2,526
1910	4,190
1920	2,622
1930	2,272
1940	2,237
1950	2,079
1960	2,616
1970	2,122
1980	2,154

MINERAL

1920	2,327
1930	1,626
1940	2,135
1950	2,081
1960	3,037
1970	2,958
1980	3,675

MISSOULA

1870	2,554
1880	2,537
1890	14,427

1900	13,964
1910	23,596
1920	24,041
1930	21,782
1940	29,038
1950	35,493
1960	44,663
1970	58,263
1980	76,016

MUSSELSHELL

1920	12,030
1930	7,242
1940	5,717
1950	5,408
1960	4,888
1970	3,734
1980	4,428

PARK

1890	6,881
1900	7,341
1910	10,731
1920	11,330
1930	10,922
1940	11,566
1950	11,999
1960	13,168
1970	11,197
1980	12,660

PETROLEUM

1930	2,045
1940	1,083
1950	1,026
1960	894
1970	675
1980	655

PHILLIPS

1920	9,311
1930	8,208
1940	7,892
1950	6,334
1960	6,027
1970	5,386
1980	5,367

PONDERA

1920	5,741
1930	6,964
1940	6,716
1950	6,392
1960	7,653
1970	6,611
1980	6,731

POWDER RIVER

1920	3,357
1930	3,909
1940	3,159
1950	2,693
1960	2,485
1970	2,862
1980	2,520

POWELL

1910	5,904
1920	6,909

1930	6,202
1940	6,152
1950	6,301
1960	7,002
1970	6,660
1980	6,958

PRAIRIE

1920	3,684
1930	3,941
1940	2,410
1950	2,377
1960	3,318
1970	1,752
1980	1,836

RAVALLI

1900	7,822
1910	11,666
1920	10,098
1930	10,315
1940	12,978
1950	13,101
1960	12,341
1970	14,409
1980	22,493

RICHLAND

1920	8,989
1930	9,633
1940	10,209
1950	10,366
1960	10,504
1970	9,837
1980	12,243

ROOSEVELT

1920	10,347
1930	10,672
1940	9,806
1950	9,580
1960	11,731
1970	10,365
1980	10,467

ROSEBUD

1910	7,985
1920	8,002
1930	7,347
1940	6,477
1950	6,570
1960	6,187
1970	6,032
1980	9,899

SANDERS

1910	3,713
1920	4,903
1930	5,692
1940	6,926
1950	6,983
1960	6,880
1970	7,093
1980	8,675

SHERIDAN

1920	13,847
1930	9,869
1940	7,814

1950	6,674
1960	6,458
1970	5,779
1980	5,414

SILVER BOW

1890	23,744
1900	27,635
1910	56,848
1920	60,313
1930	56,969
1940	53,207
1950	48,422
1960	46,454
1970	41,981
1980	38,092

STILLWATER

1920	7,630
1930	6,253
1940	5,694
1950	5,416
1960	5,526
1970	4,632
1980	5,598

SWEET GRASS

1900	3,086
1910	4,029
1920	4,926
1930	3,944
1940	3,719
1950	3,621
1960	3,290
1970	2,980
1980	3,216

TETON

1900	5,080
1910	9,546
1920	5,870
1930	6,068
1940	6,922
1950	7,232
1960	7,295
1970	6,116
1980	6,491

TOOLE

1920	3,724
1930	6,714
1940	6,769
1950	6,867
1960	7,904
1970	5,839
1980	5,559

TREASURE

1920	1,990
1930	1,661
1940	1,499
1950	1,402
1960	1,345
1970	1,069
1980	981

VALLEY

1900	4,355
1910	13,630

1920	11,542
1930	11,181
1940	15,181
1950	11,353
1960	17,080
1970	11,471
1980	10,250

WHEATLAND

1920	5,619
1930	3,751
1940	3,286
1950	3,187
1960	3,026
1970	2,529
1980	2,359

WIBAUX

1920	3,113
1930	2,767
1940	2,161
1950	1,907
1960	1,698
1970	1,465
1980	1,476

YELLOWSTONE

1890	2,065
1900	6,212
1910	22,944
1920	29,600
1930	30,785
1940	41,182
1950	55,875
1960	79,016
1970	87,367
1980	108,035

NOTES

CUSTER

    Name changed from Big Horn in 1887.

LEWIS AND CLARK

    Name changed from Edgerton in 1868.

ANACONDA

1890	3,975
1900	9,453
1910	10,134
1920	11,668
1930	12,494
1940	11,001
1950	11,254
1960	12,054
1970	9,771
1980	12,518

BILLINGS

1890	836
1900	3,221
1910	10,031
1920	15,100
1930	16,380
1940	23,261
1950	31,834
1960	52,851
1970	61,581
1980	66,798

BOZEMAN

1870	168
1880	894
1890	2,143
1900	3,419
1910	5,107
1920	6,183
1930	6,855
1940	8,665
1950	11,235
1960	13,361
1970	18,670
1980	21,645

BUTTE

1880	3,363
1890	10,723
1900	30,470
1910	39,165
1920	41,611
1930	39,532
1940	37,081
1950	33,251
1960	27,877
1970	23,368
1980	37,205

GREAT FALLS

1890	3,979
1900	14,930
1910	13,948
1920	24,121
1930	28,822
1940	29,928
1950	39,214
1960	55,244
1970	60,091
1980	56,725

HAVRE

1900	1,033
1910	3,624
1920	5,429
1930	6,372
1940	6,427
1950	8,086
1960	10,740
1970	10,588
1980	10,891

HELENA

1870	3,106
1880	3,624
1890	13,834
1900	10,770
1910	12,515
1920	12,037
1930	11,803
1940	15,056
1950	17,581
1960	20,227
1970	22,730
1980	23,938

KALISPELL

1900	2,526
1910	5,549
1920	5,147
1930	6,094
1940	8,245
1950	9,737
1960	10,151
1970	10,526
1980	10,648

MISSOULA

1890	3,426
1900	4,366
1910	12,869
1920	12,668
1930	14,657
1940	18,449
1950	22,485
1960	27,090
1970	29,497
1980	33,388

CORRECTION NOTE

Shown below are corrections to the 1980 census counts of the total population made after the tabulations for this report were completed. Any additional corrections made after this report is printed are available by writing to Data User Services Division, Customer Services (Corrections), Bureau of the Census, Washington, D.C. 20233.

The 1980 figures shown in this publication are subject to change pending the outcome of the various lawsuits dealing with the census counts.

	1980 population	
	As shown in the tables	Corrected
Park County...........................	12 660	12 869
Gardiner-Cooke division..............	860	1 069
Yellowstone County:		
Billings division:		
Billings city (pt.)...............	66 780	66 824
Yellowstone National Park.............	275	66
Yellowstone National Park division..	275	66
Billings city (total).................	66 798	66 842

County Subdivisions	1980	1970
The State	786 690	694 409
Beaverhead County[1]	8 186	8 187
Big Hole Basin division	740	720
Clark Canyon—Horse Prairie division	426	...
Dillon division	6 567	...
Dillon city[1]	3 976	4 548
Lima—Centennial Valley division	453	...
Lima town	272	351
Big Horn County[2]	11 096	10 057
Crow Reservation division	5 645	...
Lodge Grass town	771	806
Hardin division	4 249	...
Hardin city[2]	3 300	2 733
Northern Cheyenne division	1 013	...
Tongue River division	189	...
Blaine County[3]	6 999	6 727
Chinook division	3 172	3 263
Chinook city[3]	1 660	1 813
Fort Belknap division	1 854	1 312
Harlem division	1 973	...
Harlem city[3]	1 023	1 094
Broadwater County[4]	3 267	2 526
Townsend East division	2 522	2 016
Townsend city	1 587	1 371
Townsend West division	745	510
Carbon County[5]	8 099	7 080
Carbon East division	658	...
Fromberg—Bridger division	1 753	1 613
Bridger town[5]	724	717
Fromberg town[5]	469	364
Joliet division	1 782	1 384
Joliet town[5]	580	412
Red Lodge division	3 082	...
Bearcreek town	61	31
Red Lodge city[5]	1 896	1 844
Roberts division	824	753
Carter County	1 799	1 956
Ekalaka division	1 100	1 135
Ekalaka town	620	663
Little Missouri division	699	821
Cascade County[6]	80 696	81 804
Belt division	1 626	1 406
Belt city	825	656
Cascade division	1 559	1 354
Cascade town	773	714
Eden—Stockett division	862	866
Great Falls division	70 600	...
Great Falls city (pt.)[6]	56 264	60 091
Malmstrom AFB (CDP)	6 675	8 374
Vaughn (CDP) (pt.)	344	...
Great Falls North division	2 514	...
Great Falls city (pt.)[6]	461	...
Vaughn (CDP) (pt.)	1 287	...
Monarch—Neihart division	277	260
Neihart town	91	109
Sun River Valley division	3 258	2 558
Vaughn (CDP) (pt.)	639	...
Chouteau County[7]	6 092	6 473
Big Sandy division	1 998	2 127
Big Sandy town	835	827
Fort Benton division	2 866	3 066
Fort Benton city	1 693	1 863
Geraldine division	1 228	...
Geraldine town	305	370
Custer County[8]	13 109	12 174
Miles City division	11 846	...
Miles City city[8]	9 602	9 023
Mizpah—Pumpkin division	511	...
North Custer division	383	...
Shirley—Ismay division	369	...
Ismay town	31	40
Daniels County[9]	2 835	3 083
Daniels North division	2 709	...
Flaxville town	142	185
Scobey city	1 382	1 486
Fort Peck Reservation division	126	...
Dawson County[10]	11 805	11 269
Dawson North division	1 552	...
Richey town	417	389
Glendive division	10 253	...
Glendive city[10]	5 978	6 305
Deer Lodge County[11]	12 518	15 652
Anaconda division	10 403	...
Anaconda—Deer Lodge County (pt.)[11]	10 403	9 771
Deer Lodge Valley division	2 115	3 255
Anaconda—Deer Lodge County (pt.)[11]	2 115	...
Fallon County[12]	3 763	4 050
Baker division	3 235	3 471
Baker city[12]	2 354	2 584
Plevna division	528	579
Plevna town	191	189

County Subdivisions	1980	1970
Fergus County[13]	13 076	12 611
Denton division	820	977
Denton town[13]	356	398
Grass Range division	617	721
Grass Range town[13]	139	181
Hanover division	765	899
Lewistown division	10 046	...
Lewistown city[13]	7 104	6 437
Moore town[13]	229	219
Roy division	405	437
Winifred division	423	492
Winifred town	155	190
Flathead County[14]	51 966	39 460
Bad Rock—Columbia Heights division	2 793	1 697
Columbia Falls division	6 574	...
Columbia Falls city[14]	3 112	2 652
Whitefish city (pt.)[14]	8	...
Creston—Bigfork division	4 114	2 315
Bigfork (CDP)	1 080	...
Glacier National Park division	105	153
Kalispell division	22 860	...
Evergreen (CDP)	3 746	...
Kalispell city[14]	10 648	10 526
Kalispell Northwest division	1 939	...
Kalispell Southwest division	2 700	...
Lower Valley—Somers division	1 183	...
South Fork division	2 000	1 759
Whitefish division	7 698	...
Whitefish city (pt.)[14]	3 695	3 349
Gallatin County[15]	42 865	32 505
Belgrade division	5 884	...
Belgrade town[15]	2 336	1 307
Bozeman division	28 604	...
Bozeman city[15]	21 645	18 670
Gallatin Gateway division	1 949	...
Manhattan division	3 057	2 448
Manhattan town[15]	988	816
Three Forks division	1 997	1 839
Three Forks town	1 247	1 188
West Yellowstone division	1 374	1 099
West Yellowstone town	735	756
Garfield County[16]	1 656	1 796
North Garfield division	1 204	1 309
Jordan town[16]	485	529
South Garfield division	452	487
Glacier County[17]	10 628	10 783
Blackfeet division	6 039	...
Browning town	1 226	1 700
Cut Bank division	4 540	...
Cut Bank city[17]	3 688	4 004
Glacier National Park division	49	...
Golden Valley County[18]	1 026	931
Lavina division	438	...
Lavina town	164	169
Ryegate division	588	...
Ryegate town	273	261
Granite County[19]	2 700	2 737
Drummond division	1 092	1 141
Drummond town	414	494
Philipsburg division	1 608	1 596
Philipsburg town[19]	1 138	1 128
Hill County[20]	17 985	17 358
Gildford division	910	...
Hingham town	186	262
Havre division	13 738	...
Havre city[20]	10 891	10 558
Havre North (CDP)	1 230	1 073
Rocky Boy division	1 778	...
Rudyard division	998	...
Wild Horse Lake division	561	...
Jefferson County[21]	7 029	5 238
Boulder division	4 518	3 350
Boulder town	1 441	1 342
Whitehall division	2 511	1 888
Whitehall town[21]	1 030	1 035
Judith Basin County[22]	2 646	2 667
Geyser division	542	644
Hobson division	920	960
Hobson town	261	192
Stanford division	1 184	1 063
Stanford town[22]	595	505
Lake County[23]	19 056	14 445
Big Fork—Swan River division	1 998	...
Charlo division	1 242	1 111
Polson division	7 492	...
Polson city[23]	2 798	2 464
Ronan division	4 875	...
Ronan city[23]	1 530	1 347
St. Ignatius division	3 449	2 797
St. Ignatius town[23]	877	925
Lewis and Clark County[24]	43 039	33 281
Augusta division	847	854
Helena division	38 853	...
East Helena town[24]	1 647	1 651

County Subdivisions	1980	1970
Lewis and Clark County—Con.		
Helena division—Con.		
Helena city[24]	23 938	22 730
Lincoln division	2 234	...
Wolf Creek division	1 105	
Liberty County[25]	2 329	2 359
Chester division	1 839	1 851
Chester town[25]	963	936
Joplin division	490	508
Lincoln County[26]	17 752	18 063
Eureka division	3 727	3 558
Eureka town	1 119	1 195
Rexford town	130	243
Libby division	10 960	12 045
Libby city[26]	2 748	3 286
Troy division	3 065	2 460
Troy town[26]	1 088	1 046
McCone County[27]	2 702	2 875
Circle division	1 766	...
Circle town[27]	931	964
North McCone division	936	...
Madison County[28]	5 448	5 014
Harrison division	762	800
Madison Valley division	1 466	1 179
Ennis town[28]	660	501
Sheridan division	1 525	1 337
Sheridan town	646	636
Twin Bridges division	1 387	1 437
Twin Bridges town	437	613
Virginia City division	308	261
Virginia City town	192	149
Meagher County[29]	2 154	2 122
Martinsdale–Ringling division	377	...
White Sulphur Springs division	1 777	...
White Sulphur Springs city[29]	1 302	1 200
Mineral County[30]	3 675	2 958
Alberton division	587	600
Alberton town[30]	368	363
Superior division	2 126	1 580
Superior town[30]	1 054	993
West End division	962	778
Missoula County[31]	76 016	58 263
Frenchtown–Evaro division	3 665	1 547
Lolo division	4 871	1 747
Lolo (CDP)	2 418	...
Missoula division	65 476	...
Bonner–West Riverside (CDP)	1 742	...
East Missoula (CDP)	1 707	...
Missoula city[31]	33 388	29 497
Missoula South (CDP)	5 557	4 886
Orchard Homes (CDP)	10 837	...
Rattlesnake (CDP)	3 474	1 492
Seeley Lake–Blackfoot Valley division	2 004	1 201
Musselshell County[32]	4 428	3 734
Klein division	988	411
Melstone division	656	623
Melstone town[32]	238	227
Roundup division	2 784	...
Roundup city[32]	2 119	2 116
Park County[33]	12 660	11 197
Gardiner–Cooke division	860	845
Shields Valley division	1 471	...
Clyde Park town	283	244
Upper Yellowstone Valley division	10 329	...
Livingston city[33]	6 994	6 883
Petroleum County	655	675
Winnett North division	189	457
Winnett town (pt.)	–	271
Winnett South division	466	218
Winnett town (pt.)	207	...
Phillips County[34]	5 367	5 386
Belknap division	206	...
Malta division	4 242	...
Dodson town	158	196
Malta city[34]	2 367	2 195
Saco town	252	356
Phillips South division	390	...
Whitewater division	529	...
Pondera County[35]	6 731	6 611
Blackfeet East division	148	...
Blackfeet West division	473	...
Conrad division	4 522	...
Conrad city[35]	3 074	2 770
Valier–Dupuyer division	1 588	...
Valier town	640	651
Powder River County[36]	2 520	2 862
Broadus division	1 321	1 442
Broadus town[36]	712	799
East Powder River division	725	928
Otter division	474	...

County Subdivisions	1980	1970
Powell County[37]	6 958	6 660
Avon–Elliston division	1 002	1 018
Deer Lodge division	5 473	...
Deer Lodge city	4 023	4 306
Helmville division	483	...
Prairie County	1 836	1 752
Terry North division	270	259
Terry South division	1 566	1 493
Terry city	929	870
Ravalli County[38]	22 493	14 409
Darby division	1 718	...
Darby town[38]	581	538
Hamilton division	11 467	...
Hamilton city[38]	2 661	2 499
Stevensville division	6 516	...
Stevensville town[38]	1 207	829
Sula–Edwards division	950	...
Victor division	1 842	...
Richland County[39]	12 243	9 837
Fairview division	2 267	...
Fairview city[39]	1 366	956
Lambert division	753	...
Savage–Crane division	1 341	...
Sidney division	7 882	...
Sidney city[39]	5 726	4 543
Roosevelt County[40]	10 467	10 365
East Roosevelt division	2 134	...
Bainville town	245	217
Culbertson town[40]	887	821
Froid town	323	330
Fort Peck Reservation division	8 333	...
Brockton town	374	401
Poplar town	995	1 389
Wolf Point city[40]	3 074	3 095
Rosebud County[41]	9 899	6 032
Ashland division	564	...
Forsyth division	3 516	...
Forsyth city[41]	2 553	1 873
Northern Cheyenne division	2 651	...
Rosebud division	3 168	...
Colstrip (CDP)	1 476	...
Sanders County[42]	8 675	7 093
Flathead division	1 887	1 907
Hot Springs town	601	664
Plains division	2 553	1 938
Plains town[42]	1 116	1 046
Thompson Falls–West End division	4 235	3 248
Thompson Falls town[42]	1 478	1 356
Sheridan County[43]	5 414	5 779
Fort Peck Reservation division	179	...
Medicine Lake division	1 040	...
Medicine Lake town	408	393
Plentywood division	3 562	...
Outlook town	122	153
Plentywood city[43]	2 476	2 381
Westby division	633	721
Westby town	291	287
Silver Bow County[44]	38 092	41 981
Butte division	36 817	...
Butte–Silver Bow (pt.)[44]	35 930	23 368
Walkerville city[44]	887	1 097
Silver Bow Northwest division	491	...
Butte–Silver Bow (pt.)[44]	491	...
Silver Bow South division	784	...
Butte–Silver Bow (pt.)[44]	784	...
Stillwater County[45]	5 598	4 632
Absarokee division	1 407	...
Columbus division	2 387	...
Columbus town[45]	1 439	1 173
Park City town	1 223	822
Stillwater North division	581	...
Sweet Grass County[46]	3 216	2 980
North of the Yellowstone division	675	678
South of the Yellowstone division	2 541	2 302
Big Timber city[46]	1 690	1 592
Teton County[47]	6 491	6 116
Choteau division	3 481	...
Choteau city[47]	1 798	1 586
Dutton–Power division	1 198	1 298
Dutton town[47]	359	415
Fairfield division	1 812	1 719
Fairfield town[47]	650	638
Toole County[48]	5 559	5 839
South Toole division	3 932	...
Shelby city[48]	3 142	3 111
Sunburst division	1 627	1 904
Kevin town	208	250
Sunburst town	476	604
Treasure County	981	1 069
North Treasure division	288	427
South Treasure division	693	642
Hysham town	449	373

County Subdivisions

	1980	1970
Valley County[49]	10 250	11 471
Fort Peck Reservation division	1 283	...
Glasgow division	6 636	...
Glasgow city[49]	4 455	4 700
Nashua town	495	513
Hinsdale division	786	...
Opheim division	663	...
Opheim town	210	306
South Valley division	882	917
Wheatland County[50]	2 359	2 529
Harlowton division	1 821	...
Harlowton city[50]	1 181	1 375
Judith Gap–Shawmut division	538	...
Judith Gap city	213	160
Wibaux County	1 476	1 465
Pine Hills–St. Phillips division	347	459
Wibaux division	1 129	1 006
Wibaux town	782	644
Yellowstone County[51]	108 035	87 367
Billings division	86 493	...
Billings city (pt.)[51]	66 780	61 581
Billings Heights (CDP)	8 480	...
Buffalo Creek division	191	156
Huntley Project division	2 905	2 179
Laurel division	10 086	...
Laurel city[51]	5 481	4 454
Northwest Yellowstone division	1 669	...
Billings city (pt.)[51]	18	...
Broadview town	120	123
Shepherd division	2 550	1 226
South Yellowstone division	4 141	1 320
Billings city (pt.)[51]	–	...
Yellowstone National Park	275	64
Yellowstone National Park division	275	64

NEBRASKA

This state takes its name from the Nebraska River, generally known as the Platte. The word is of Indian-origin and signifies "shallow water."

The earliest recorded exploration in the region now constituting Nebraska was made in 1739 when Frenchmen followed the Platte to its Forks. In 1804 a United States Government expedition under Lewis and Clark passed up the Missouri River, which forms the eastern and northeastern boundary of the state, returning in 1806. The first settlement was made in 1807, when Emanuel Lisa, a fur trader, built Fort Lisa near the present site of Fort Calhoun. Other trading posts as well as military posts were established from time to time, but very few settlers came to this region until about the middle of the century.

The area now known as Nebraska was originally a part of the vast Louisiana region, which was ceded by France to Spain in 1762, retroceded to France in 1800, and purchased by the United States in 1803. The area now forming the state belonged successively to the district of Louisiana (1804-5), the territory of Louisiana (1805-1812), the territory of Missouri (1812-34), and the "Indian Country" (1834-1854).

In 1854 the territory of Nebraska was organized from the section of the Indian Country lying between the fortieth and forty-ninth parallels and extending from the Rocky Mountains to the Missouri and White Earth Rivers. It thus included, in addition to the area of the present state, territory now forming portions of North and South Dakota, Montana, Wyoming, and Colorado. In 1861 the area of Nebraska was greatly reduced by the organization of Dakota territory, which extended westward to the Rocky Mountains, and of Colorado territory, in which was included what had been the southwestern corner of Nebraska. In the same year, however, territory was added to Nebraska by the extension of the western boundary to the thirty-third meridian from Washington (approximately the one hundred and tenth from Greenwich). In 1863 Idaho territory was organized with boundaries including that part of Nebraska lying west of the twenty-seventh meridian from Washington (approximately the one hundred and fourth from Greenwich) and the territory of Nebraska was left with substantially the same limits as the present state.

In March, 1867, Nebraska was admitted to the Union. In 1882 a small tract of land, formerly a part of Dakota, lying south of the forty-third parallel and between the Keyapaha and Missouri Rivers, was added to Nebraska, since which time there have been no changes in the boundaries of the state.

COUNTY LOCATION INDEX

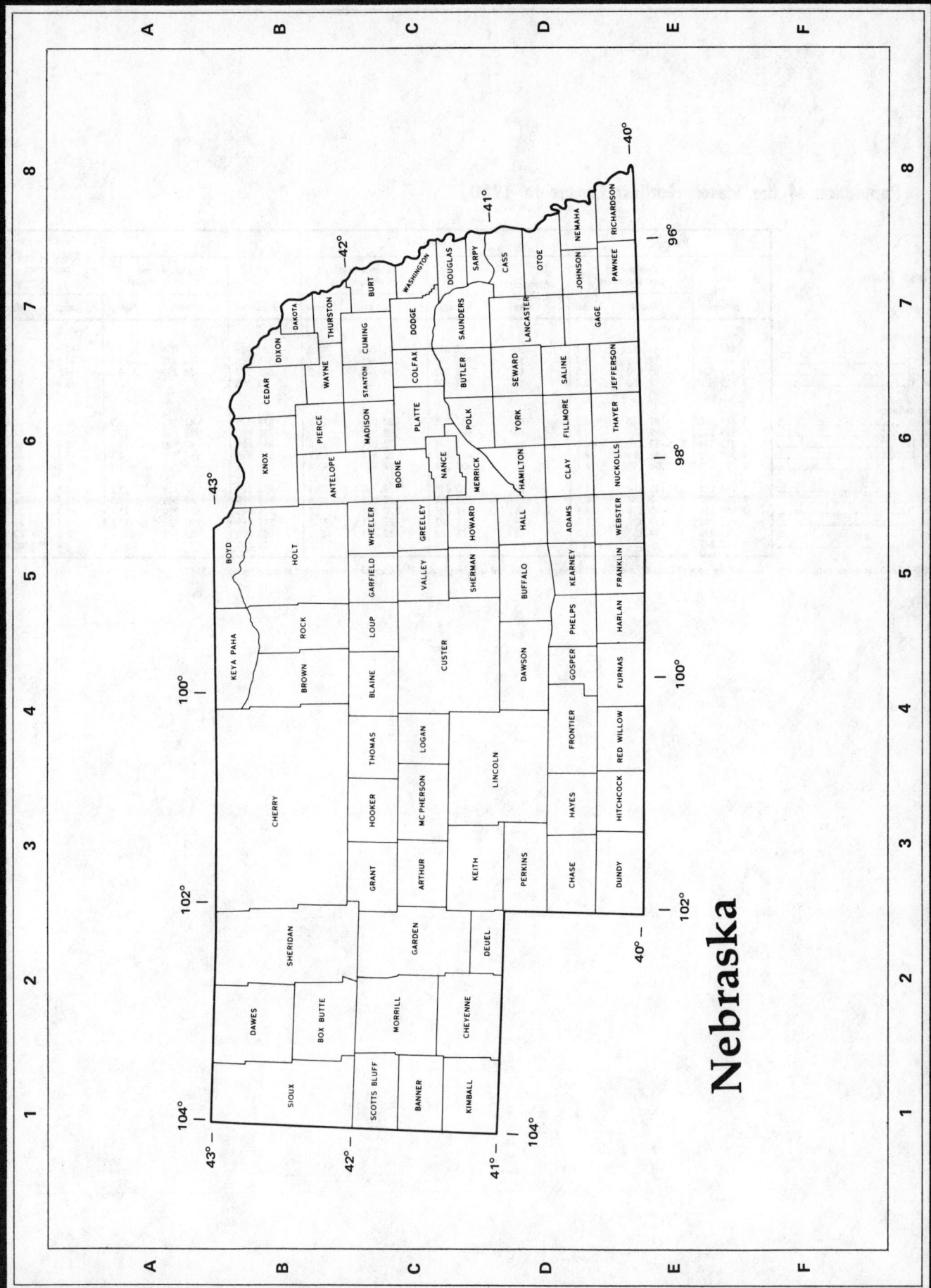

Nebraska

Population of the State: Earliest Census to 1980

Urban and Rural

	The State			Urban				Rural				Percent of total population	
	Total population	Change from preceding census		Places of 2,500 or more	Population	Change from preceding census		Population	Change from preceding census			Urban	Rural
		Number	Percent			Number	Percent		Number	Percent			
Current urban definition:													
1980 (Apr. 1)	1 569 825	84 492	5.7	50	987 859	75 261	8.2	581 966	11 071	1.9		62.9	37.1
1970 (Apr. 1)	1 485 333	74 003	5.2	50	912 598	146 545	19.1	570 895	−74 382	−11.5		61.5	38.5
1960 (Apr. 1)	1 411 330	85 820	6.5	43	766 053	144 148	23.2	645 277	−58 328	−8.3		54.3	45.7
1950 (Apr. 1)	1 325 510	9 676	0.7	41	621 905	...	...	703 605	...	...		46.9	53.1
Previous urban definition:													
1960 (Apr. 1)	1 411 330	85 820	6.5	43	733 595	127 065	20.9	677 735	−41 245	−5.7		52.0	48.0
1950 (Apr. 1)	1 325 510	9 676	0.7	40	606 530	92 382	18.0	718 980	−82 706	−10.3		45.8	54.2
1940 (Apr. 1)	1 315 834	−62 129	−4.5	36	514 148	28 041	5.8	801 686	−90 170	−10.1		39.1	60.9
1930 (Apr. 1)	1 377 963	81 591	6.3	35	486 107	80 814	19.9	891 856	777	0.1		35.3	64.7
1920 (Jan. 1)	1 296 372	104 158	8.7	31	405 293	94 441	30.4	891 079	9 717	1.1		31.3	68.7
1910 (Apr. 15)	1 192 214	125 914	11.8	27	310 852	58 150	23.0	881 362	67 764	8.3		26.1	73.9
1900 (June 1)	1 066 300	3 644	0.3	21	252 702	−38 939	−13.4	813 598	42 583	5.5		23.7	76.3
1890 (June 1)	1 062 656	610 254	134.9	16	291 641	230 334	375.7	771 015	379 920	97.1		27.4	72.6
1880 (June 1)	452 402	329 409	267.8	7	61 307	39 174	177.0	391 095	290 235	287.8		13.6	86.4
1870 (June 1)	122 993	94 152	326.5	2	22 133	22 133	...	100 860	72 019	249.7		18.0	82.0
1860 (June 1)	28 841	...	...	−	−	...	...	28 841	...	...		−	100.0

NOTE: 1860 population excludes areas taken to form parts of Colorado and Dakota Territories in 1861, but includes population of area taken to form part of Idaho Territory in 1863.

ADAMS

1870	19
1880	10,235
1890	24,303
1900	18,840
1910	20,900
1920	22,621
1930	26,275
1940	24,576
1950	28,885
1960	29,994
1970	30,553
1980	30,656

ANTELOPE

1880	3,935
1890	10,399
1900	11,344
1910	14,003
1920	15,243
1930	15,206
1940	13,289
1950	11,624
1960	10,176
1970	9,047
1980	8,675

ARTHUR

1890	91
1920	1,412
1930	1,344
1940	1,045
1950	803
1960	680
1970	606
1980	513

BANNER

1890	2,435
1900	1,114
1910	1,444
1920	1,435
1930	1,676
1940	1,403
1950	1,325
1960	1,269
1970	1,034
1980	918

BLAINE

1890	1,146
1900	603
1910	1,672
1920	1,778
1930	1,584
1940	1,538
1950	1,203
1960	1,016
1970	847
1980	867

BOONE

1880	4,170
1890	8,683
1900	11,689
1910	13,145
1920	14,146
1930	14,738
1940	12,127
1950	10,721

1960	9,134
1970	8,190
1980	7,391

BOX BUTTE

1890	5,494
1900	5,572
1910	6,131
1920	8,407
1930	11,861
1940	10,736
1950	12,279
1960	11,688
1970	10,094
1980	13,696

BOYD

1890	695
1900	7,332
1910	8,826
1920	8,243
1930	7,169
1940	6,060
1950	4,911
1960	4,513
1970	3,752
1980	3,331

BROWN

1890	4,359
1900	3,470
1910	6,083
1920	6,749
1930	5,772
1940	5,962
1950	5,164
1960	4,436
1970	4,021
1980	4,377

BUFFALO

1860	114
1870	193
1880	7,531
1890	22,162
1900	20,254
1910	21,907
1920	23,787
1930	24,388
1940	23,655
1950	25,134
1960	26,236
1970	31,222
1980	34,797

BURT

1860	388
1870	2,847
1880	6,937
1890	11,069
1900	13,040
1910	12,726
1920	12,559
1930	13,062
1940	12,546
1950	11,536
1960	10,192
1970	9,247
1980	8,813

BUTLER

1860	27
1870	1,290
1880	9,194
1890	15,454
1900	15,703
1910	15,403
1920	14,606
1930	14,410
1940	13,106
1950	11,432
1960	10,312
1970	9,461
1980	9,330

CALHOUN

1860	41

CASS

1860	3,369
1870	8,151
1880	16,683
1890	24,080
1900	21,330
1910	19,786
1920	18,029
1930	17,684
1940	16,992
1950	16,361
1960	17,821
1970	18,076
1980	20,297

CEDAR

1860	246
1870	1,032
1880	2,899
1890	7,028
1900	12,467
1910	15,191
1920	16,225
1930	16,427
1940	15,126
1950	13,843
1960	13,368
1970	12,192
1980	11,375

CHASE

1880	70
1890	4,807
1900	2,559
1910	3,613
1920	4,939
1930	5,484
1940	5,310
1950	5,176
1960	4,317
1970	4,129
1980	4,758

CHERRY

1890	6,428
1900	6,541
1910	10,414
1920	11,753
1930	10,898
1940	9,637
1950	8,397
1960	8,218

1970	6,846
1980	6,758

CHEYENNE

1870	190
1880	1,558
1890	5,693
1900	5,570
1910	4,551
1920	8,405
1930	10,187
1940	9,505
1950	12,081
1960	14,828
1970	10,778
1980	10,057

CLAY

1860	165
1870	54
1880	11,294
1890	16,310
1900	15,735
1910	15,729
1920	14,486
1930	13,571
1940	10,445
1950	8,700
1960	8,717
1970	8,266
1980	8,106

COLFAX

1870	1,414
1880	6,588
1890	10,453
1900	11,211
1910	11,610
1920	11,624
1930	11,434
1940	10,627
1950	10,010
1960	9,595
1970	9,498
1980	9,890

CUMING

1860	67
1870	2,964
1880	5,569
1890	12,265
1900	14,584
1910	13,782
1920	13,769
1930	14,327
1940	13,562
1950	12,994
1960	12,435
1970	12,034
1980	11,664

CUSTER

1880	2,211
1890	21,677
1900	19,758
1910	25,668
1920	26,407
1930	26,189
1940	22,591
1950	19,170
1960	16,517

1970	14,092
1980	13,877

DAKOTA

1860	819
1870	2,040
1880	3,213
1890	5,386
1900	6,286
1910	6,564
1920	7,694
1930	9,505
1940	9,836
1950	10,401
1960	12,168
1970	13,137
1980	16,573

DAWES

1890	9,722
1900	6,215
1910	8,254
1920	10,160
1930	11,493
1940	10,128
1950	9,708
1960	9,536
1970	9,761
1980	9,609

DAWSON

1860	16
1870	103
1880	2,909
1890	10,129
1900	12,214
1910	15,960
1920	16,004
1930	17,875
1940	17,890
1950	19,393
1960	19,405
1970	19,771
1980	22,304

DEUEL

1890	2,893
1900	2,630
1910	1,786
1920	3,282
1930	3,992
1940	3,580
1950	3,330
1960	3,125
1970	2,717
1980	2,462

DIXON

1860	247
1870	1,345
1880	4,177
1890	8,084
1900	10,535
1910	11,477
1920	11,815
1930	11,586
1940	10,413
1950	9,129
1960	8,106
1970	7,453
1980	7,137

DODGE

Year	Pop.
1860	309
1870	4,212
1880	11,263
1890	19,260
1900	22,298
1910	22,145
1920	23,197
1930	25,273
1940	23,799
1950	26,265
1960	32,471
1970	34,782
1980	35,847

DOUGLAS

Year	Pop.
1860	4,328
1870	19,982
1880	37,645
1890	158,008
1900	140,590
1910	168,546
1920	204,524
1930	232,982
1940	247,562
1950	281,020
1960	343,490
1970	389,455
1980	397,038

DUNDY

Year	Pop.
1880	37
1890	4,012
1900	2,433
1910	4,098
1920	4,869
1930	5,610
1940	5,122
1950	4,354
1960	3,570
1970	2,926
1980	2,861

FILLMORE

Year	Pop.
1870	238
1880	10,204
1890	16,022
1900	15,087
1910	14,674
1920	13,671
1930	12,971
1940	11,417
1950	9,610
1960	9,425
1970	8,137
1980	7,920

FORT RANDALL

Year	Pop.
1860	353

FRANKLIN

Year	Pop.
1870	26
1880	5,465
1890	7,693
1900	9,455
1910	10,303
1920	10,067
1930	9,094
1940	7,740
1950	7,096
1960	5,449
1970	4,566
1980	4,377

FRONTIER

Year	Pop.
1880	934
1890	8,497
1900	8,781
1910	8,572
1920	8,540
1930	8,144
1940	6,417
1950	5,282
1960	4,311
1970	3,982
1980	3,647

FURNAS

Year	Pop.
1880	6,407
1890	9,840
1900	12,373
1910	12,083
1920	11,657
1930	12,140
1940	10,098
1950	9,385
1960	7,711
1970	6,897
1980	6,486

GAGE

Year	Pop.
1860	421
1870	3,359
1880	13,164
1890	36,344
1900	30,051
1910	30,325
1920	29,721
1930	30,242
1940	29,588
1950	28,052
1960	26,818
1970	25,731
1980	24,456

GARDEN

Year	Pop.
1910	3,538
1920	4,572
1930	5,099
1940	4,680
1950	4,114
1960	3,472
1970	2,929
1980	2,802

GARFIELD

Year	Pop.
1890	1,659
1900	2,127
1910	3,417
1920	3,496
1930	3,207
1940	3,444
1950	2,912
1960	2,699
1970	2,411
1980	2,363

GOSPER

Year	Pop.
1880	1,673
1890	4,816
1900	5,301
1910	4,933
1920	4,669
1930	4,287
1940	3,687
1950	2,734
1960	2,489
1970	2,178
1980	2,140

GRANT

Year	Pop.
1870	484
1890	458
1900	763
1910	1,097
1920	1,486
1930	1,427
1940	1,327
1950	1,057
1960	1,009
1970	1,019
1980	877

GREELEY

Year	Pop.
1880	1,461
1890	4,869
1900	5,691
1910	8,047
1920	8,685
1930	8,442
1940	6,845
1950	5,575
1960	4,595
1970	4,000
1980	3,462

GREEN

Year	Pop.
1860	16

HALL

Year	Pop.
1860	116
1870	1,057
1880	8,572
1890	16,513
1900	17,206
1910	20,361
1920	23,720
1930	27,117
1940	27,523
1950	32,186
1960	35,757
1970	42,851
1980	47,690

HAMILTON

Year	Pop.
1870	130
1880	8,267
1890	14,096
1900	13,330
1910	13,459
1920	13,237
1930	12,159
1940	9,982
1950	8,778
1960	8,174
1970	8,867
1980	9,301

HARLAN

Year	Pop.
1880	6,086
1890	8,158
1900	9,370
1910	9,578
1920	8,220
1930	8,957
1940	7,120
1950	7,189
1960	5,081
1970	4,357
1980	4,292

HARRISON

Year	Pop.
1870	631

HAYES

Year	Pop.
1880	119
1890	3,953
1900	2,708
1910	3,011
1920	3,327
1930	3,603
1940	2,958
1950	2,404
1960	1,919
1970	1,530
1980	1,356

HITCHCOCK

Year	Pop.
1880	1,012
1890	5,799
1900	4,409
1910	4,415
1920	6,045
1930	7,269
1940	6,404
1950	5,867
1960	4,829
1970	4,051
1980	4,079

HOLT

Year	Pop.
1880	3,287
1890	13,672
1900	12,224
1910	15,545
1920	17,151
1930	16,509
1940	16,552
1950	14,859
1960	13,722
1970	12,933
1980	13,552

HOOKER

Year	Pop.
1890	426
1900	432
1910	981
1920	1,378
1930	1,180
1940	1,253
1950	1,061
1960	1,130
1970	939
1980	990

HOWARD

Year	Pop.
1880	4,391
1890	9,430
1900	10,343
1910	10,783
1920	10,739
1930	10,020
1940	8,422
1950	7,226
1960	6,541
1970	6,807
1980	6,773

JACKSON

Year	Pop.
1870	9

JEFFERSON

Year	Pop.
1870	2,440
1880	8,096
1890	14,850
1900	15,196
1910	16,852
1920	16,140
1930	16,409
1940	15,532
1950	13,623
1960	11,620
1970	10,436
1980	9,817

JOHNSON

Year	Pop.
1860	528
1870	3,429
1880	7,595
1890	10,333
1900	11,197
1910	10,187
1920	8,940
1930	9,157
1940	8,662
1950	7,251
1960	6,281
1970	5,743
1980	5,285

JONES

Year	Pop.
1860	122

KEARNEY

Year	Pop.
1860	474
1870	58
1880	4,072
1890	9,061
1900	9,866
1910	9,106
1920	8,583
1930	8,094
1940	6,854
1950	6,409
1960	6,580
1970	6,707
1980	7,053

KEITH

Year	Pop.
1880	194
1890	2,556
1900	1,951
1910	3,692
1920	5,294
1930	6,721
1940	8,333
1950	7,449
1960	7,958
1970	8,487
1980	9,364

KEYA PAHA

1890	3,920
1900	3,076
1910	3,452
1920	3,594
1930	3,203
1940	3,235
1950	2,160
1960	1,672
1970	1,340
1980	1,301

KIMBALL

1890	959
1900	758
1910	1,942
1920	4,498
1930	4,675
1940	3,913
1950	4,283
1960	7,975
1970	6,009
1980	4,882

KNOX

1860	152
1870	261
1880	3,666
1890	8,582
1900	14,343
1910	18,358
1920	18,894
1930	19,110
1940	16,478
1950	14,820
1960	13,300
1970	11,723
1980	11,457

LANCASTER

1860	153
1870	7,074
1880	28,090
1890	76,395
1900	64,835
1910	73,793
1920	85,902
1930	100,324
1940	100,585
1950	119,742
1960	155,272
1970	167,972
1980	192,884

LINCOLN

1870	17
1880	3,632
1890	10,441
1900	11,416
1910	15,684
1920	23,420
1930	25,627
1940	25,425
1950	27,380
1960	28,491
1970	29,538
1980	36,455

LOGAN

1890	1,378

1900	960
1910	1,521
1920	1,596
1930	2,014
1940	1,742
1950	1,357
1960	1,108
1970	991
1980	983

LOUP

1890	1,662
1900	1,305
1910	2,188
1920	1,946
1930	1,818
1940	1,777
1950	1,348
1960	1,097
1970	854
1980	859

LYON

1870	78

McPHERSON

1890	401
1900	517
1910	2,470
1920	1,692
1930	1,358
1940	1,175
1950	825
1960	725
1970	623
1980	593

MADISON

1870	1,133
1880	5,589
1890	13,669
1900	16,697
1910	19,101
1920	22,511
1930	26,037
1940	24,269
1950	24,338
1960	25,145
1970	27,402
1980	31,382

MERRICK

1860	109
1870	557
1880	5,341
1890	8,758
1900	9,255
1910	10,379
1920	10,763
1930	10,619
1940	9,354
1950	8,812
1960	8,363
1970	8,751
1980	8,945

MORRILL

1910	4,584
1920	9,151
1930	9,950

1940	9,436
1950	8,263
1960	7,057
1970	5,813
1980	6,085

MONROE

1870	235

NANCE

1870	44
1880	1,212
1890	5,773
1900	8,222
1910	8,926
1920	8,712
1930	8,718
1940	7,653
1950	6,512
1960	5,635
1970	5,142
1980	4,740

NEMAHA

1860	3,139
1870	7,593
1880	10,451
1890	12,930
1900	14,952
1910	13,095
1920	12,547
1930	12,356
1940	12,781
1950	10,973
1960	9,099
1970	8,986
1980	8,367

NUCKOLLS

1860	22
1870	8
1880	4,235
1890	11,417
1900	12,414
1910	13,019
1920	13,236
1930	12,629
1940	10,446
1950	9,609
1960	8,217
1970	7,404
1980	6,726

OTOE

1860	4,211
1870	12,345
1880	15,727
1890	25,403
1900	22,288
1910	19,323
1920	19,494
1930	19,901
1940	18,994
1950	17,056
1960	16,053
1970	15,576
1980	15,183

PAWNEE

1860	882

1870	4,171
1880	6,920
1890	10,340
1900	11,770
1910	10,582
1920	9,587
1930	9,423
1940	8,514
1950	6,744
1960	5,356
1970	4,473
1980	3,937

PERKINS

1890	4,364
1900	1,702
1910	2,570
1920	3,967
1930	5,834
1940	5,197
1950	4,809
1960	4,189
1970	3,423
1980	3,637

PHELPS

1880	2,447
1890	9,869
1900	10,772
1910	10,451
1920	9,990
1930	9,261
1940	8,452
1950	9,048
1960	9,800
1970	9,553
1980	9,769

PIERCE

1870	152
1880	1,202
1890	4,864
1900	8,445
1910	10,122
1920	10,681
1930	11,080
1940	10,211
1950	9,405
1960	8,722
1970	8,493
1980	8,481

PLATTE

1860	782
1870	1,899
1880	9,511
1890	15,437
1900	17,747
1910	19,006
1920	19,464
1930	21,181
1940	20,191
1950	19,910
1960	23,992
1970	26,544
1980	28,852

POLK

1860	19
1870	136
1880	6,846

1890	10,817
1900	10,542
1910	10,521
1920	10,714
1930	10,092
1940	8,748
1950	8,044
1960	7,210
1970	6,468
1980	6,320

RED WILLOW

1880	3,044
1890	8,837
1900	9,604
1910	11,056
1920	11,434
1930	13,859
1940	11,951
1950	12,977
1960	12,940
1970	12,191
1980	12,615

RICHARDSON

1860	2,835
1870	9,780
1880	15,031
1890	17,574
1900	19,614
1910	17,448
1920	18,968
1930	19,826
1940	19,178
1950	16,886
1960	13,903
1970	12,277
1980	11,315

ROCK

1890	3,083
1900	2,809
1910	3,627
1920	3,703
1930	3,366
1940	3,977
1950	3,026
1960	2,554
1970	2,231
1980	2,383

SALINE

1860	39
1870	3,106
1880	14,491
1890	20,097
1900	18,252
1910	17,866
1920	16,514
1930	16,356
1940	15,010
1950	14,046
1960	12,542
1970	12,809
1980	13,131

SARPY

1860	1,201
1870	2,913
1880	4,481
1890	6,875

1900	9,090	1960	5,382	1920	9,589	1940	2,170
1910	9,274	1970	4,725	1930	10,462	1950	1,526
1920	9,370	1980	4,226	1940	10,243	1960	1,297
1930	10,402			1950	8,590	1970	1,054
1940	10,835	**SHORTER**		1960	7,237	1980	1,060
1950	15,693			1970	6,942		
1960	31,281	1860	177	1980	7,186	**YORK**	
1970	66,200						
1980	86,015	**SIOUX**		**VALLEY**		1870	604

SAUNDERS

		1880	699			1880	11,170
1870	4,547	1890	2,452	1880	2,324	1890	17,279
1880	15,180	1900	2,055	1890	7,092	1900	18,205
1890	21,577	1910	5,599	1900	7,339	1910	18,721
1900	22,085	1920	4,528	1910	9,480	1920	17,146
1910	21,179	1930	4,667	1920	9,823	1930	17,239
1920	20,589	1940	4,001	1930	9,533	1940	14,874
1930	20,167	1950	3,124	1940	8,163	1950	14,346
1940	17,892	1960	2,575	1950	7,252	1960	13,724
1950	16,923	1970	2,034	1960	6,590	1970	13,685
1960	17,270	1980	1,845	1970	5,783	1980	14,798
1970	17,018			1980	5,633		
1980	18,716	**STANTON**					

SCOTTS BLUFF

		1870	636	**WASHINGTON**	
		1880	1,813		
1890	1,888	1890	4,619	1860	1,249
1900	2,552	1900	6,959	1870	4,452
1910	8,355	1910	7,542	1880	8,631
1920	20,710	1920	7,756	1890	11,869
1930	28,644	1930	7,809	1900	13,086
1940	33,917	1940	6,887	1910	12,738
1950	33,939	1950	6,387	1920	12,180
1960	33,809	1960	5,783	1930	12,095
1970	36,432	1970	5,758	1940	11,578
1980	38,344	1980	6,549	1950	11,511
				1960	12,103
		TAYLOR		1970	13,310
SEWARD				1980	15,508
		1870	97		
1870	2,953			**WAYNE**	
1880	11,147	**THAYER**			
1890	16,140			1870	182
1900	15,690			1880	813
1910	15,895	1880	6,113	1890	6,169
1920	15,867	1890	12,738	1900	9,862
1930	15,938	1900	14,325	1910	10,397
1940	14,167	1910	14,775	1920	9,725
1950	13,155	1920	13,976	1930	10,556
1960	13,581	1930	13,684	1940	9,880
1970	14,460	1940	12,262	1950	10,129
1980	15,789	1950	10,563	1960	9,959
		1960	9,118	1970	10,400
		1970	7,779	1980	9,858
SHERIDAN		1980	7,582		
				WEBSTER	
1890	8,687				
1900	6,033	**THOMAS**		1870	16
1910	7,328			1880	7,104
1920	9,625	1890	517	1890	11,210
1930	10,793	1900	628	1900	11,619
1940	9,869	1910	1,191	1910	12,008
1950	9,539	1920	1,773	1920	10,922
1960	9,049	1930	1,510	1930	10,210
1970	7,285	1940	1,553	1940	8,071
1980	7,544	1950	1,206	1950	7,395
		1960	1,078	1960	6,224
		1970	954	1970	6,477
SHERMAN		1980	973	1980	4,858
1880	2,061	**THURSTON**		**WHEELER**	
1890	6,399				
1900	6,550	1870	31	1880	644
1910	8,278	1880	109	1890	1,683
1920	8,877	1890	3,176	1900	1,362
1930	9,122	1900	6,517	1910	2,292
1940	7,764	1910	8,704	1920	2,531
1950	6,421			1930	2,335

NOTES

ARTHUR

Formed from unorganized territory in 1887; annexed to McPherson prior to 1900.

CALHOUN

Annexed to Saunders in 1862.

EMMET

Name changed from L'Eau qui Court in 1867.

FORT RANDALL

No records by which to account for its disappearance subsequent to the 1860 census.

GREEN

No records by which to account for its disappearance subsequent to the 1860 census.

HARRISON

Never had a legal existence.

HOLT

Name changed from West in 1862.

JACKSON

Never had a legal existence.

JONES

Annexed to Jefferson in 1866.

KNOX

ame changed from L'Eau qui Court in 1873.

LINCOLN

Name changed from Shorter in 1861.

LYON

Never had a legal existence.

MONROE

Never had a legal existence.

NEMAHA

Name changed from Forney in (?).

OTOE

Name changed from Pierce in (?).

SAUNDERS

Name changed from Calhoun in 1862.

SEWARD

Name changed from Greene in 1862.

STANTON

Name changed from Izard in (?).

SHORTER

Never had a legal existence.

TAYLOR

Never had a legal existence.

THAYER

Name changed from Jefferson in 1871.

THURSTON

Name changed from Blackbird in 1889.

BEATRICE

1880	2,447
1890	13,836
1900	7,875
1910	9,356
1920	9,664
1930	10,297
1940	10,883
1950	11,813
1960	12,132
1970	12,389
1980	12,891

BELLEVUE

1900	527
1910	596
1920	695
1930	1,017
1940	1,184
1950	3,858
1960	8,831
1970	21,953
1980	21,813

COLUMBUS

1870	526
1880	2,131
1890	3,134
1900	3,522
1910	5,014
1920	5,410
1930	6,898
1940	7,632
1950	8,884
1960	12,476
1970	15,471
1980	17,328

FREMONT

1870	1,195
1880	3,013
1890	6,747
1900	7,241
1910	8,718
1920	9,592
1930	11,407
1940	11,862
1950	14,762
1960	19,698
1970	22,962
1980	23,979

GRAND ISLAND

1880	2,963
1890	7,536
1900	7,554
1910	10,326
1920	13,947
1930	18,041
1940	19,130
1950	22,682
1960	25,742
1970	32,358
1980	33,180

HASTINGS

1880	2,817
1890	13,584
1900	7,188
1910	9,338

1920	11,647
1930	15,490
1940	15,145
1950	20,211
1960	21,412
1970	23,580
1980	23,045

KEARNEY

1880	1,782
1890	8,074
1900	5,634
1910	6,202
1920	7,702
1930	8,575
1940	9,643
1950	12,115
1960	14,210
1970	19,181
1980	21,158

LINCOLN

1880	13,003
1890	55,154
1900	40,169
1910	43,973
1920	54,948
1930	75,933
1940	81,984
1950	98,884
1960	128,521
1970	149,518
1980	171,932

NORFOLK

1890	3,038
1900	3,883
1910	6,025
1920	8,634
1930	10,717
1940	10,490
1950	11,335
1960	13,640
1970	16,607
1980	19,449

NORTH PLATTE

1880	363
1890	3,055
1900	3,640
1910	4,793
1920	10,466
1930	12,061
1940	12,429
1950	15,433
1960	17,184
1970	19,447
1980	24,479

OMAHA

1860	1,883
1870	16,083
1880	30,518
1890	140,452
1900	102,555
1910	124,096
1920	191,601
1930	214,006
1940	223,844
1950	251,117

1960	301,598
1970	346.929
1980	314,255

SCOTTSBLUFF

1910	1,746
1920	6,912
1930	8,465
1940	12,057
1950	12,858
1960	13,377
1970	14,507
1980	14,156

CORRECTION NOTE

The official 1980 census counts of total population shown in
this report supersede counts issued previously. Corrections
to the figures were made after the counts were provided to
the State for redistricting purposes and released in Advance
Report PHC80-V for this State.

Shown below are corrections to the 1980 census counts of the
total population made after the tabulations for this report
were completed. Any additional corrections made after this
report is printed are available by writing to Data User
Services Division, Customer Services (Corrections), Bureau of
the Census, Washington, D.C. 20233.

The 1980 figures shown in this publication are subject to
change pending the outcome of the various lawsuits dealing
with the census counts.

	1980 population	
	As shown in the tables	Corrected
Box Butte County:		
Alliance precinct..............	9 869	9 920
Alliance city................	9 869	9 920
Wright precinct...............	739	688
Douglas County:		
Benson precinct...............	969	854
Florence precinct..............	3 059	3 181
McArdle precinct..............	22 258	22 455
Millard precinct..............	26 149	26 283
Omaha city....................	314 255	313 911
Union precinct................	7 900	7 906
Lincoln County:		
East Hinman precinct..........	556	526
North Platte precinct.........	24 479	24 509
North Platte city............	24 479	24 509
Nance County:		
Genoa city....................	(1)	1 090
Genoa township	1 337	247
Genoa city..................	1 090	(2)
Sheridan County:		
North Rushville precinct:		
Clinton village..............	(1)	80

(1) Not shown
(2) Delete, Genoa city is independent of Genoa
      township.

County Subdivisions	1980	1970
The State	1 569 825	'1 485 333
Adams County[1]	30 656	30 553
Ayr township	348	314
Ayr village (pt.)	54	56
Blaine township[1]	1 089	654
Cottonwood township	384	403
Holstein village	241	231
Denver township[1]	941	1 139
Hanover township	230	189
Hastings city[1]	23 045	23 580
Highland township[1]	512	398
Juniata township	978	751
Juniata village	703	480
Kenesaw township	980	934
Kenesaw village[1]	854	728
Little Blue township	260	226
Logan township	100	123
Roseland township	517	491
Roseland village	254	212
Silver Lake township	160	178
Verona township	330	288
Prosser village	98	70
Wanda township	178	236
West Blue township	304	324
Trumbull village (pt.)	–	4
Zero township	300	325
Ayr village (pt.)	58	84
Antelope County[2]	8 675	9 047
Bazile township	189	235
Blaine township	198	204
Burnett township	225	249
Cedar township	199	294
Clearwater township	630	601
Clearwater village[2]	409	398
Crawford township	217	252
Custer township	154	175
Eden township	164	199
Elgin township	151	161
Ellsworth township	348	405
Brunswick village	190	229
Elm township	103	147
Frenchtown township	173	176
Garfield township	653	643
Orchard village[2]	482	467
Grant township	141	200
Lincoln township	126	150
Logan township[2]	1 064	1 242
Elgin city[2]	807	917
Neligh city[2]	1 893	1 764
Neligh township[2]	369	285
Oakdale township	571	492
Oakdale village	410	322
Ord township	114	138
Royal township	253	247
Royal village	86	86
Sherman township	119	127
Stanton township	147	164
Tilden city (pt.)	293	262
Verdigris township	83	92
Willow township	98	143
Arthur County[3]	513	606
Arthur precinct[3]	513	353
Arthur village	124	175
Banner County[4]	918	1 034
Long Springs precinct[4]	918	426
Blaine County[5]	867	847
Brewster precinct[5]	335	289
Brewster village	46	54
Dunning precinct[5]	296	386
Dunning village[5]	182	162
Purdum precinct[5]	236	84
Halsey village (pt.)	10	3
Boone County[6]	7 391	8 190
Albion city[6]	1 997	2 074
Ashland precinct	198	262
Beaver precinct	1 121	1 077
St. Edward city	891	853
Bonanza precinct	150	192
Boone precinct	274	266
Cedar precinct	813	969
Cedar Rapids village	447	449
Dublin precinct	337	382
Primrose village	102	88
Manchester precinct[6]	496	474
Midland precinct	198	261
North Branch precinct	185	255
Oakland precinct	882	1 027
Petersburg village[6]	381	370
Plum Creek precinct	184	204
Roselma precinct	196	262
Shell Creek precinct	184	268
Weitzel precinct	176	217

County Subdivisions	1980	1970
Box Butte County[7]	13 696	10 094
Alliance precinct	9 869	6 862
Alliance city[7]	9 869	6 862
Box Butte precinct	413	351
Dorsey precinct	1 376	1 098
Hemingford village[7]	1 023	734
Lake precinct[7]	760	595
Lawn precinct	211	285
Nonpareil precinct	328	337
Wright precinct[7]	739	566
Boyd County[8]	3 331	3 752
Basin precinct	422	505
Naper village	136	159
Bristow township	196	227
Bristow village	123	127
Bush township	122	138
Monowi village	18	16
Butte township[8]	798	878
Anoka village	24	25
Butte village	529	575
Lynch township	484	532
Lynch village	357	375
McCulley township	130	153
Morton township	221	231
Gross village	2	8
Mullen township	66	73
Spencer township[8]	892	890
Spencer village[8]	596	606
Brown County[9]	4 377	4 021
Ainsworth city[9]	2 256	2 073
Ainsworth precinct[9]	803	557
Johnstown precinct[9]	470	362
Johnstown village	78	82
Long Pine city	521	363
North Pine precinct[9]	196	...
South Pine precinct[9]	131	...
Buffalo County[10]	34 797	31 222
Armada township	259	249
Miller village	147	130
Beaver township	183	173
Cedar township	223	241
Center township[10]	629	575
Cherry Creek township[10]	130	135
Collins township[10]	1 684	909
Divide township	345	303
Riverdale village (pt.)	6	7
Elm Creek township	1 144	1 083
Elm Creek village	862	798
Gardner township[10]	158	172
Garfield township	327	294
Gibbon township	1 905	1 797
Gibbon city	1 531	1 388
Grant township	457	447
Amherst village	269	259
Harrison township	80	100
Kearney city[10]	21 158	19 181
Logan township	105	117
Loup township	518	463
Pleasanton village	349	261
Odessa township	367	326
Platte township	225	198
Ravenna city	1 296	1 356
Riverdale township[10]	1 113	547
Riverdale village (pt.)	198	148
Rusco township	178	187
Sartoria township	104	130
Schneider township	210	239
Scott township	124	131
Sharon township	212	243
Shelton township	1 337	1 289
Shelton village	1 046	1 028
Thornton township	190	200
Valley township	136	137
Burt County[11]	8 813	9 247
Arizona township[11]	353	445
Bell Creek township[11]	306	380
Craig township	677	817
Craig village[11]	237	295
Decatur township	998	989
Decatur village[11]	723	679
Everett township	1 447	1 447
Lyons city[11]	1 214	1 177
Logan township	339	379
Oakland city[11]	1 393	1 355
Oakland township[11]	225	317
Pershing township[11]	199	245
Quinnebaugh township	95	108
Riverside township	152	159
Silver Creek township	223	222
Summit township	520	536
Tekamah city[11]	1 886	1 848
Butler County[12]	9 330	9 461
Alexis township	519	381
Bone Creek township	386	416
Octavia village	127	97
Center township	291	316

County Subdivisions

County Subdivisions	1980	1970
Butler County[12]—Con.		
David City city[12]	2 514	2 380
Franklin township[12]	418	361
Linwood township	322	331
Abie village	107	78
Oak Creek township	611	601
Brainard village[12]	275	309
Olive township	261	306
Platte township	193	193
Linwood village	119	108
Plum Creek township	282	319
Read township	317	360
Surprise village	60	77
Reading township	617	608
Rising City village	392	344
Richardson township	424	481
Dwight village	221	224
Savannah township	746	738
Bellwood village[12]	407	361
Skull Creek township	399	440
Bruno village[12]	154	142
Summit township	223	261
Ulysses township	504	604
Ulysses village	270	312
Union township	303	365
Garrison village	68	60
Cass County[13]	20 297	18 076
Avoca precinct	391	382
Avoca village (pt.)	182	170
Center precinct[13]	457	486
Manley village[13]	124	150
East Rock Bluffs precinct	582	255
Eight Mile Grove precinct	662	513
Cedar Creek village[13]	311	119
Elmwood precinct	647	638
Murdock village[13]	242	262
Greenwood precinct	411	442
Alvo village (pt.)	124	134
Liberty precinct	944	622
Union village[13]	307	275
Louisville precinct	1 360	1 323
Louisville village[13]	1 022	1 036
Mount Pleasant precinct	304	327
Nehawka precinct	463	474
Nehawka village	270	298
Plattsmouth city[13]	6 295	6 371
Plattsmouth precinct[13]	1 615	1 150
Salt Creek precinct	886	749
Greenwood village	587	506
South Bend precinct	482	403
South Bend village	107	86
Stove Creek precinct	938	898
Elmwood village[13]	598	548
Tipton precinct	1 388	801
Alvo village (pt.)	20	17
Eagle village[13]	832	441
Weeping Water city[13]	1 109	1 143
Weeping Water precinct[13]	341	414
Avoca village (pt.)	60	59
West Rock Bluff precinct	1 022	685
Murray village[13]	465	286
Cedar County[14]	11 375	12 192
Hartington city[14]	1 730	1 581
Precinct 1	497	500
St. Helena village	111	102
Precinct 2	456	473
Precinct 3	398	431
Precinct 4	507	432
Fordyce village (pt.)	–	–
Precinct 5	605	702
Wynot village	222	226
Precinct 6	117	160
Precinct 7	281	309
Obert village	44	36
Precinct 8	361	419
Precinct 9[14]	334	422
Precinct 9A	194	197
Fordyce village (pt.)	148	146
Precinct 10	278	323
Precinct 11	180	268
Precinct 12	240	311
Precinct 13	271	325
Precinct 14	245	241
Precinct 15	291	342
Precinct 16	900	905
Coleridge village[14]	673	608
Precinct 17	196	266
Precinct 18	257	352
Magnet village	59	88
Precinct 19	233	335
Precinct 20	421	454
Belden village[14]	151	162
Precinct 21	1 277	1 314
Laurel city[14]	1 031	1 009
Randolph city	1 106	1 130

County Subdivisions	1980	1970
Chase County[15]	4 758	4 129
Champion precinct	320	298
Imperial East precinct[15]	873	...
Imperial city (pt.)[15]	873	(NA)
Imperial Rural precinct[15]	478	...
Imperial West precinct[15]	1 068	...
Imperial city (pt.)[15]	1 068	(NA)
Lamar precinct[15]	367	185
Lamar village	60	30
Macedonia precinct[15]	372	158
Pioneer precinct	263	269
Wauneta precinct[15]	1 017	911
Wauneta village[15]	746	738
Cherry County[16]	6 758	6 846
Barley precinct[16]	80	117
Calf Creek precinct	51	49
Cleveland precinct	164	181
Cody precinct[16]	303	366
Cody village	177	246
Crookston precinct[16]	262	207
Crookston village[16]	86	86
Gillaspie precinct	85	91
Goose Creek precinct[16]	157	118
Kennedy precinct	85	97
Kilgore precinct[16]	169	...
Kilgore village[16]	76	110
King precinct[16]	66	76
Lackey precinct[16]	110	123
Loup precinct[16]	315	312
Merriman precinct[16]	550	282
Merriman village[16]	159	172
Mother Lake precinct	124	134
Nenzel precinct	74	78
Nenzel village	28	27
Russell precinct	76	105
Valentine city[16]	2 829	2 662
Valentine precinct[16]	812	462
Wells precinct[16]	150	140
Wood Lake precinct	296	331
Wood Lake village	89	117
Cheyenne County[17]	10 057	10 778
Brownson precinct[17]	145	175
Colton precinct	267	341
Gurley precinct[17]	984	393
Gurley village	212	233
Lodgepole precinct[17]	736	720
Lodgepole village[17]	413	407
Lorenzo precinct[17]	379	146
Potter precinct[17]	677	599
Potter village	369	356
Sidney city[17]	6 010	6 403
Sidney Rural precinct[17]	291	598
Union Valley precinct[17]	568	513
Dalton village	345	354
Clay County[18]	8 106	8 266
Clay Center city[18]	962	952
Edgar township	802	821
Edgar city[18]	705	707
Eldorado township	183	201
Fairfield township	819	789
Deweese village	69	86
Fairfield city	543	487
Glenvil township	504	477
Glenvil village[18]	363	332
Harvard township	1 410	1 449
Harvard city	1 217	1 230
Inland township	107	122
Leicester township	378	385
Trumbull village (pt.)	216	216
Lewis township	200	259
Saronville village (pt.)	34	48
Logan township	235	263
Ong village	104	129
Lone Tree township[18]	132	127
Lynn township	105	123
Marshall township	79	100
School Creek township	251	258
Sheridan township	128	136
Spring Ranch township	174	204
Sutton city	1 416	1 361
Sutton township	221	239
Saronville village (pt.)	29	26
Colfax County[19]	9 890	9 498
Adams precinct	1 100	1 204
Clarkson city[19]	817	805
Colfax precinct	196	204
Grant precinct	299	265
Lincoln precinct	1 044	1 154
Howells village	677	682
Maple Creek precinct	255	277
Midland precinct	331	376
Richland precinct	472	419
Richland village	114	123
Rogers precinct	189	266
Rogers village	89	95

County Subdivisions	1980	1970
Colfax County—Con.		
Schuyler city[19]	4 151	3 597
Schuyler precinct[19]	420	256
Shell Creek precinct	287	291
Stanton precinct	857	866
Leigh village	509	501
Wilson precinct	289	323
Cuming County[20]	11 664	12 034
Bancroft township	811	876
Bancroft village	552	545
Beemer township	1 132	990
Beemer village[20]	853	699
Bismarck township	288	376
Blaine township	213	264
Cleveland township	298	345
Cuming township[20]	368	386
Elkhorn township	418	495
Garfield township	378	450
Grant township	242	291
Lincoln township	326	434
Logan township	374	423
Monterey township	440	448
Neligh township	325	349
St. Charles township	324	393
Sherman township[20]	532	528
West Point city[20]	3 609	3 385
Wisner city[20]	1 335	1 315
Wisner township[20]	251	286
Custer County[21]	13 877	14 092
Algernon township	470	525
Mason City village	196	196
Ansley township	823	841
Ansley village	644	631
Arnold township	1 134	1 097
Arnold village[21]	813	752
Berwyn township	321	328
Berwyn village	104	110
Broken Bow city[21]	3 979	3 734
Broken Bow township[21]	802	660
Cliff township	153	272
Comstock township	247	277
Comstock village	168	155
Corner township	47	53
Custer township	90	111
Delight township	798	809
Callaway village	579	523
Douglas Grove township	141	155
East Custer township	48	81
Elim township	196	234
Elk Creek township	187	229
Garfield township	122	160
Grant township	71	95
Hayes township	69	72
Kilfoil township	716	681
Merna village	389	322
Lillian township	220	232
Loup township	224	239
Milburn township	93	110
Myrtle township	149	181
Ryno township	107	116
Sargent township	1 060	997
Sargent city	828	789
Spring Creek township	31	54
Triumph township	130	145
Victoria township	496	574
Anselmo village[21]	187	180
Wayne township	188	181
Westerville township	192	242
West Union township	111	127
Wood River township	462	480
Oconto village	176	155
Dakota County[22]	16 573	13 137
Covington precinct[22]	2 095	1 056
Dakota precinct	2 132	1 631
Dakota City city	1 440	1 057
Emerson precinct[22]	625	495
Emerson village (pt.)	312	176
Hubbard precinct[22]	547	375
Hubbard village[22]	234	151
Omadi precinct[22]	1 029	893
Homer village[22]	564	457
St. Johns precinct	484	395
Jackson village[22]	287	232
South Sioux City city[22]	9 339	7 920
Summit precinct[22]	322	195
Dawes County[23]	9 609	9 761
Antelope precinct[23]	148	326
Chadron city[23]	5 933	5 921
Craig precinct[23]	141	187
East Chadron precinct	351	325
Leonard precinct	119	122
Marsland village	27	17
North Crawford precinct[23]	776	190
Crawford city (pt.)[23]	564	(NA)
North West Chadron precinct[23]	125	...
South Crawford precinct[23]	978	147

County Subdivisions	1980	1970
Dawes County—Con.		
South Crawford precinct—Con.		
Crawford city (pt.)[23]	751	(NA)
South West Chadron precinct[23]	364	...
Table precinct[23]	389	97
Whitney precinct[23]	285	243
Whitney village	72	82
Dawson County[24]	22 304	19 771
Buffalo precinct	59	75
Coyote precinct[24]	625	500
Cozad city[24]	4 453	4 225
Cozad precinct[24]	220	237
Fairview precinct[24]	313	181
Farnam precinct	338	343
Farnam village	268	270
German precinct[24]	424	251
Gillan precinct	250	292
Gothenburg city[24]	3 479	3 158
Gothenburg precinct[24]	208	180
Grant precinct[24]	693	631
Kennebec precinct	243	257
Eddyville village	121	128
Lexington city[24]	7 040	5 654
Lexington precinct[24]	917	642
Overton precinct[24]	1 244	872
Overton village[24]	633	538
Platte precinct[24]	480	259
Ringgold precinct[24]	347	295
Willow Island precinct	430	396
Wood River precinct[24]	541	484
Sumner village	254	222
Deuel County[25]	2 462	2 717
Big Springs precinct[25]	769	945
Big Springs village[25]	505	472
Chappell precinct[25]	812	1 506
Chappell city (pt.)[25]	677	1 204
Swan precinct[25]	881	266
Chappell city (pt.)	418	...
Dixon County[26]	7 137	7 453
Clark precinct	214	269
Concord township	532	615
Concord village[26]	145	180
Dixon village	127	128
Daily township	186	208
Emerson township	689	819
Emerson village (pt.)	460	558
Galena township	419	402
Martinsburg village	100	73
Hooker township	269	284
Maskell village	76	43
Logan township	314	344
Newcastle township	557	565
Newcastle village[26]	348	347
Otter Creek township	307	287
Waterbury village[26]	92	81
Ponca city	1 057	984
Ponca township	377	360
Silver Creek township	212	243
Spring Bank township	659	656
Allen village[26]	390	309
Wakefield township	1 345	1 417
Wakefield city (pt.)	991	1 064
Dodge County[27]	35 847	34 782
Cotterell township[27]	427	425
Cuming township	307	332
Elkhorn township[27]	578	395
Everett township	277	344
Fremont city[27]	23 979	22 962
Hooper township[27]	1 425	1 412
Hooper city[27]	932	895
Winslow village	143	145
Logan township	601	568
Uehling village[27]	273	249
Maple township	376	397
Nickerson township	634	568
Nickerson village	254	214
North Bend city[27]	1 368	1 350
Pebble township	673	678
Snyder village (pt.)[27]	311	274
Platte township[27]	2 172	2 015
Inglewood village[27]	257	275
Pleasant Valley township	286	361
Ridgeley township	251	354
Scribner city	1 011	1 031
Union township[27]	285	307
Webster township	1 197	1 283
Dodge village[27]	815	704
Snyder village (pt.)	76	109
Douglas County[28]	397 038	389 455
Beechwood precinct[28]	4	125
Benson precinct[28]	969	1 778
Chicago precinct[28]	6 844	2 847
Elkhorn city[28]	1 344	1 184
Douglas precinct[28]	8 129	4 911
Ralston city[28]	5 143	4 731

County Subdivisions

County Subdivisions	1980	1970
Douglas County—Con.		
Elkhorn precinct	999	664
Florence precinct	3 059	2 264
Jefferson precinct[28]	1 539	1 245
Bennington village[28]	631	683
McArdle precinct[28]	22 258	'8 187
Boys Town village[28]	622	989
Millard precinct[28]	26 149	'12 086
Omaha city[28]	314 255	'346 929
Platte Valley precinct[28]	3 029	2 596
Valley city[28]	1 716	1 595
Union precinct[28]	7 900	4 574
Waterloo precinct	1 904	1 249
Waterloo village	450	455
Dundy County[29]	2 861	2 926
Benkelman No. 1 precinct[29]	561	...
Benkelman city (pt.)[29]	412	(NA)
Benkelman No. 2 precinct[29]	711	...
Benkelman city (pt.)	565	(NA)
Benkelman No. 3 precinct[29]	334	...
Benkelman city (pt.)	258	(NA)
Haigler precinct[29]	425	417
Haigler village	225	237
Hoover precinct[29]	160	60
Max precinct[29]	226	220
Ough precinct[29]	195	102
Parks precinct[29]	249	95
Fillmore County[30]	7 920	8 137
Belle Prairie township	218	217
Strang village	59	47
Bennett township	131	131
Bryant township	617	618
Shickley village[30]	413	385
Chelsea township	167	208
Geneva city (pt.)	14	15
Exeter township	987	978
Exeter village[30]	807	759
Fairmont township	899	950
Fairmont village	767	761
Franklin township	323	385
Ohiowa village	135	156
Geneva township	1 601	'1 489
Geneva city (pt.)[30]	1 327	'1 164
Glengary township	517	498
Milligan village[30]	332	319
Grafton township	320	292
Grafton village	185	128
Hamilton township	208	269
Liberty township	171	211
Madison township	599	677
Geneva city (pt.)[30]	369	445
Momence township	136	183
Stanton township	859	'872
Geneva city (pt.)[30]	690	'651
West Blue township	167	159
Franklin County[31]	4 377	4 566
Antelope township	312	350
Upland village	192	205
Ash Grove township[31]	214	92
Bloomington township[31]	349	314
Bloomington village	138	165
Franklin city	1 167	1 193
Grant township[31]	248	201
Riverton village (pt.)	98	97
Lincoln township	150	163
Macon township	167	182
Marion township[31]	232	136
North Franklin township	521	523
Campbell village	441	447
Salem township	536	527
Hildreth village	394	352
Turkey Creek township	232	277
Naponee village	160	187
Washington township[31]	249	211
Riverton village (pt.)	114	123
Frontier County[32]	3 647	3 982
Allen precinct	103	113
Clearwater precinct	65	69
Curtis city	1 014	1 166
Curtis precinct	162	153
Earl precinct	40	73
Fairview precinct	597	556
Eustis village[32]	460	400
Garfield precinct	46	57
Grant precinct	47	56
Harrison precinct	68	83
Horrell precinct	81	82
Knowles precinct	52	81
Laird precinct	461	436
Maywood village	332	309
Laws precinct	53	58
Lincoln precinct	39	60
Logan precinct	48	67
Moorefield precinct	143	165
Moorefield village	36	56
Muddy precinct	59	67

County Subdivisions	1980	1970
Frontier County—Con.		
North Star precinct	55	60
Orafino precinct	51	56
Osborn precinct	38	35
Plum Creek precinct	62	57
Russell precinct	67	69
Sheridan precinct	69	73
Sherman precinct	38	65
Stockville precinct	103	129
Stockville village	45	61
Weaver precinct	29	34
Zimmer precinct	57	62
Furnas County[33]	6 486	6 897
Arapahoe precinct[33]	1 354	1 335
Arapahoe city[33]	1 107	1 147
Beaver City city	775	802
Beaver City precinct[33]	150	112
Cambridge precinct[33]	1 484	1 325
Cambridge city[33]	1 206	1 145
Edison precinct[33]	357	315
Edison village	210	199
Hendley precinct[33]	322	...
Hendley village	39	58
Holbrook precinct[33]	483	...
Holbrook village	297	307
Hollinger precinct[33]	174	...
New Era precinct	154	181
Oxford precinct	915	947
Oxford village (pt.)	864	878
Wilsonville precinct[33]	318	399
Wilsonville village	189	266
Gage County[34]	24 456	'25 731
Adams township	664	705
Adams village[34]	395	463
Barnston township	295	321
Barnston village (pt.)	14	14
Beatrice city[34]	12 891	12 389
Blakely township	405	429
Blue Springs township	618	'627
Blue Springs city	521	'506
Clatonia township	483	471
Clatonia village[34]	273	224
Elm township	227	246
Filley township	366	389
Filley village[34]	172	138
Glenwood township	321	366
Odell village (pt.)	99	103
Grant township	238	242
Hanover township	320	369
Highland township	669	635
Cortland village[34]	403	326
Holt township	521	432
Pickrell village[34]	184	118
Hooker township	197	204
Island Grove township	166	165
Liberty village (pt.)	22	21
Liberty township	395	456
Barnston village (pt.)	141	135
Liberty village (pt.)	83	97
Lincoln township	241	241
Logan township	316	357
Midland township[34]	1 146	2 251
Nemaha township	296	284
Paddock township	411	456
Odell village (pt.)	223	246
Riverside township[34]	452	838
Rockford township	375	405
Sherman township	261	253
Virginia village	90	83
Sicily township	233	285
Wymore township	1 949	1 915
Wymore city	1 841	1 790
Garden County[35]	2 802	2 929
Alkali precinct[35]	97	84
Blue Creek precinct[35]	729	668
Lewellen village	368	376
Kincaid precinct	50	63
Lisco precinct	241	253
Lost Creek precinct[35]	641	1 426
Oshkosh city (pt.)[35]	377	1 067
Oshkosh No. 1 precinct[35]	721	...
Oshkosh city (pt.)[35]	469	...
Oshkosh No. 3 precinct[35]	267	...
Oshkosh city (pt.)[35]	211	...
Valley precinct	56	72
Garfield County[36]	2 363	2 411
Bryan precinct	50	49
Burwell city[36]	1 383	1 341
Dry Cedar precinct	88	162
Erina precinct	45	62
Highland precinct	90	101
Kinkaid precinct	29	40
Midvale precinct	131	139
Rockford precinct[36]	290	251
Roosevelt precinct	17	21
Willow Springs precinct	240	245

County Subdivisions	1980	1970
Gosper County[37]	2 140	2 178
Bethel precinct	291	274
Brace precinct	109	111
East Muddy precinct	65	70
Elk Creek precinct	90	155
Elwood 7–22 precinct	803	682
Elwood village[37]	716	601
Elwood 7–23 precinct	78	69
Harrison precinct	246	254
Smithfield village	68	58
Highland precinct	39	65
Lincoln precinct	101	111
Robb precinct	134	163
Turkey Creek precinct	40	46
Union precinct	66	83
West Muddy precinct	78	95
Grant County	877	1 019
Ashby precinct	149	149
Hyannis precinct	490	547
Hyannis village	336	345
Whitman precinct	238	323
Greeley County[38]	3 462	4 000
Greeley precinct	911	1 012
Greeley Center village	597	580
Scotia No. 1 precinct[38]	349	354
Scotia village[38]	349	354
Scotia No. 2 precinct[38]	455	...
Spalding No. 1 precinct[38]	645	...
Spalding village[38]	645	676
Spalding No. 2 precinct[38]	567	...
Wolbach precinct	535	665
Wolbach village	301	366
Hall County[39]	47 690	42 851
Alda township	931	788
Alda village[39]	601	456
Cameron township	237	257
Center township[39]	5 432	2 625
Doniphan township	1 082	903
Doniphan village[39]	696	542
Grand Island city[39]	33 180	'32 358
Harrison township	295	327
Jackson township	564	584
Wood River city (pt.)[39]	6	'16
Lake township	439	442
Martin township	191	175
Mayfield township	578	622
Cairo village (pt.)	332	322
Prairie Creek township	287	301
South Loup township	657	594
Cairo village (pt.)[39]	405	364
South Platte township	425	232
Washington township[39]	1 687	'1 108
Wood River township	1 705	1 535
Wood River city (pt.)[39]	1 328	'1 131
Hamilton County[40]	9 301	8 867
Aurora precinct[40]	285	302
Beaver precinct	274	307
Bluff precinct	400	428
Hordville village	155	147
City precinct	3 717	3 180
Aurora city[40]	3 717	3 180
Deep Well precinct	383	285
East Otis precinct[40]	106	...
Farmers Valley precinct	238	260
Grant precinct[40]	371	354
Hamilton precinct	224	251
Monroe precinct	238	289
Orville precinct	251	277
Stockham village	68	65
Phillips precinct	586	535
Phillips village	405	341
Scovill precinct	163	200
South Platte precinct	635	587
Marquette village	303	239
Union precinct	598	615
Giltner village	400	408
Valley precinct	659	682
Hampton village[40]	419	387
West Otis precinct[40]	173	...
Harlan County[41]	4 292	4 357
Albany township	87	96
Alma city[41]	1 369	1 299
Alma township[41]	148	132
Antelope township	165	172
Ragan village (pt.)	48	38
Eldorado township	93	107
Emerson township	343	360
Oxford village (pt.)	245	238
Fairfield township	66	85
Mullally township	347	292
Republican City village	231	179
Orleans township	637	733
Orleans village	527	592
Prairie Dog township	36	29
Republican City township	101	65
Reuben township	73	132

County Subdivisions	1980	1970
Harlan County—Con.		
Sappa township	358	363
Stamford village	214	207
Scandinavia township	158	159
Ragan village (pt.)	23	22
Spring Grove township	114	112
Turkey Creek township	95	111
Huntley village (pt.)	30	29
Washington township	102	110
Huntley village (pt.)	34	38
Hayes County[42]	1 356	1 530
Antelope precinct	68	93
Blackwood precinct	69	62
Concord precinct	39	35
Deerfield precinct	46	58
Fairfield precinct	52	56
Germanville precinct	47	77
Government precinct	71	108
Hamlet precinct	274	266
Hamlet village	74	64
Harrison precinct	17	15
Hayes Center precinct	324	354
Hayes Center village[42]	231	237
Highland precinct	46	59
High Ridge precinct	40	55
Hopewell precinct	85	91
Swan Lake precinct	49	68
Thornburg precinct	89	81
Valley precinct	40	52
Hitchcock County[43]	4 079	4 051
Beverly precinct	72	84
Blackwood precinct	138	155
Cornell precinct	33	39
Culbertson precinct	960	934
Culbertson village	767	801
Driftwood precinct	42	40
Eden precinct	98	138
Freedom precinct	49	73
Grant precinct	63	61
Logan precinct	67	72
Palisade precinct	423	399
Palisade village	401	372
Pleasant Hill precinct	104	138
Pleasant View precinct	41	35
Ridnour precinct	234	194
Trenton village (pt.)	159	128
Riverside precinct	159	131
Starkey precinct	83	47
Stratton precinct	593	573
Stratton village[43]	499	481
Trenton precinct	735	736
Trenton village (pt.)[43]	637	642
Union precinct	63	56
Upper Driftwood precinct	65	77
Webster precinct	57	69
Holt County[44]	13 552	12 933
Antelope township	89	67
Atkinson township	2 127	1 933
Atkinson city[44]	1 521	1 406
Belle township	51	75
Chambers township	603	573
Chambers village	390	321
Cleveland township	99	104
Coleman township	64	61
Conley township	112	120
Deloit township	219	267
Dustin township	62	53
Emmet township	188	207
Emmet village	73	70
Ewing township	586	625
Ewing village (pt.)	479	484
Fairview township	84	85
Francis township	67	85
Golden township	202	196
Ewing village (pt.)	41	68
Grattan township[44]	1 037	652
Green Valley township	133	147
Holt Creek township	30	45
Inman township	489	447
Inman village[44]	181	160
Iowa township	86	93
Josie township	15	18
Lake township	120	137
McClure township	84	100
O'Neill city[44]	4 049	3 753
Paddock township	160	202
Pleasant View township	115	103
Rock Falls township	37	52
Sand Creek township	131	131
Saratoga township	61	66
Scott township	75	109
Shamrock township	50	64
Sheridan township	251	254
Shields township	150	168
Steel Creek township	95	105
Stuart township	1 102	1 048
Stuart village	641	561

County Subdivisions

County Subdivisions	1980	1970
Holt County—Con.		
Swan township	89	97
Verdigris township	442	472
Page village	172	177
Willowdale township	94	89
Wyoming township	104	130
Hooker County[45]	990	939
Mullen precinct[45]	990	835
Mullen village[45]	720	667
Howard County[46]	6 773	6 807
Cleveland precinct	237	216
Cotesfield precinct	192	206
Cotesfield village	82	76
Dannebrog precinct	642	654
Dannebrog village	356	384
Dannevirke precinct	140	184
Elba precinct	342	362
Elba village	218	211
Fairdale—Logan precinct	231	294
Gage Valley precinct	299	293
Kelso precinct	172	181
Loup Fork precinct	454	451
Howard City village[46]	228	182
Posen precinct	399	482
Farwell village	165	172
St. Libory precinct	795	614
St. Paul city[46]	2 094	2 026
St. Paul precinct[46]	386	387
Spring Creek precinct	240	284
Cushing village	48	43
Warsaw precinct	150	173
Jefferson County[47]	9 817	10 436
Antelope precinct	126	143
Buckley precinct	214	231
Reynolds village	125	115
Cub Creek precinct	395	426
Jansen village[47]	204	191
Endicott precinct	309	317
Endicott village	198	167
Eureka precinct	375	416
Daykin village	207	192
Fairbury city[47]	4 885	5 265
Fairbury precinct[47]	512	473
Gibson precinct	191	233
Jefferson precinct	273	277
Harbine village	50	44
Lincoln precinct	216	240
Meridian precinct	147	203
Newton precinct	327	387
Steele City village[47]	137	176
Pleasant precinct	536	512
Diller village	311	287
Plymouth precinct	754	703
Plymouth village[47]	506	424
Richland precinct	179	181
Rock Creek precinct	178	204
Washington precinct	200	225
Johnson County[48]	5 285	5 743
Helena precinct	345	375
Lincoln precinct	192	207
Maple Grove precinct	145	255
Nemaha precinct	215	297
Spring Creek precinct	639	690
Cook village[48]	341	328
Sterling precinct	976	868
Sterling village[48]	526	476
Tecumseh city	1 926	2 058
Todd Creek precinct	418	477
Elk Creek village	144	151
Vesta precinct	207	240
Western precinct	222	276
Crab Orchard village	82	96
Kearney County[49]	7 053	6 707
Blaine township	529	395
Cosmo township	115	175
Eaton township	235	258
Heartwell village	87	104
Grant township	104	135
Hayes township	1 487	1 343
Minden city (pt.)[49]	1 244	1 051
Liberty township	187	168
Lincoln township	1 884	1 847
Minden city (pt.)[49]	1 695	1 618
Logan township	167	171
Lowell township	245	203
May township	166	188
Norman village	58	52
Mirage township	1 038	1 047
Axtell village[49]	602	500
Newark township	218	171
Oneida township	558	459
Wilcox village[49]	379	280
Sherman township	120	147

County Subdivisions	1980	1970
Keith County[50]	9 364	8 487
Brule precinct[50]	958	934
Brule village	438	423
Logan precinct	376	346
Lonergan precinct	268	118
North Ogallala precinct[50]	290	...
Ogallala city[50]	5 638	4 976
Paxton precinct	964	926
Paxton village	568	503
South Ogallala precinct[50]	584	...
Whitetail precinct[50]	286	213
Keya Paha County[51]	1 301	1 340
Burton precinct	194	168
Burton village	12	23
Custer precinct	439	638
Springview village (pt.)	181	260
Garfield precinct	317	42
Springview village (pt.)	145	...
Keya Paha precinct	191	...
Norden precinct	160	...
Kimball County[52]	4 882	6 009
Antelope precinct[52]	796	4 747
Bushnell precinct[52]	439	397
Bushnell village[52]	187	211
Dix precinct[52]	527	562
Dix village	275	342
Kimball No. 1 precinct[52]	1 178	...
Kimball city (pt.)[52]	1 178	(NA)
Kimball No. 2 precinct[52]	1 942	...
Kimball city (pt.)	1 942	(NA)
Knox County[53]	11 457	11 723
Addison township	172	223
Bloomfield city[53]	1 393	1 287
Bohemia township	64	85
Central township	166	166
Cleveland township	201	258
Columbia township	231	278
Creighton city	1 341	1 461
Creighton township	327	350
Bazile Mills village	54	44
Dolphin township	286	306
Dowling township	240	313
Eastern township	1 310	1 100
Crofton village[53]	948	677
Frankfort township	229	132
Harrison township	120	136
Herrick township	54	31
Hill township	198	246
Jefferson township	136	125
Lincoln township	930	987
Wausa village[53]	647	720
Logan township	159	169
Miller township	276	317
Winnetoon village	82	84
Morton township[53]	278	358
Niobrara township	477	672
Niobrara village[53]	419	602
Peoria township	241	261
Raymond township	355	364
Verdel village	72	74
Santee township	438	101
Santee village[53]	388	...
Spade township	71	95
Sparta township	121	158
Union township	87	95
Valley township	262	269
Center village[53]	123	111
Verdigre township	830	836
Verdigre village[53]	617	570
Walnut Grove township	219	256
Washington township	153	182
Western township	92	106
Lancaster County[54]	192 884	167 972
Buda precinct	661	645
Hallam village[54]	290	280
Centerville precinct	843	642
Sprague village	168	119
Denton precinct	678	456
Denton village[54]	164	151
Elk precinct	950	503
Malcolm village[54]	355	132
Garfield precinct[54]	539	639
Grant precinct[54]	2 093	1 210
Highland precinct	433	316
Lancaster precinct[54]	421	257
Lincoln city[54]	171 932	149 518
Little Salt precinct	458	314
Middle Creek precinct[54]	715	513
Mill precinct	291	252
Nemaha precinct	892	786
Bennet village	523	489
North Bluff precinct[54]	477	413
Oak precinct[54]	1 545	679
Raymond village	179	187
Olive Branch precinct	337	334
Panama precinct	544	539
Panama village	160	153

County Subdivisions

County Subdivisions	1980	1970
Lancaster County—Con.		
Rock Creek precinct	587	518
Davey village	190	163
Saltillo precinct	1 740	942
Hickman village[54]	687	415
Roca village	130	118
South Pass precinct	1 045	790
Firth village[54]	384	328
Stevens Creek precinct	722	598
Stockton precinct	561	364
Waverly precinct	2 100	1 505
Waverly city[54]	1 726	1 152
West Lincoln precinct[54]	573	3 341
West Oak precinct	310	312
Yankee Hill precinct[54]	1 437	1 586
Lincoln County[55]	36 455	29 538
Antelope precinct[55]	145	137
Brady precinct[55]	552	
Brady village[55]	377	311
Dickens precinct[55]	153	74
Dickens village	24	22
East Hinman precinct[55]	556	590
Garfield precinct[55]	268	61
Gaslin precinct[55]	311	152
Hall precinct[55]	1 100	664
Hershey precinct[55]	1 856	949
Hershey village[55]	633	526
Hinman precinct[55]	858	1 501
Maxwell precinct[55]	866	509
Maxwell village	410	282
Medicine precinct[55]	217	181
Wellfleet village	83	51
Miller precinct	247	154
North Platte precinct	24 479	19 447
North Platte city[55]	24 479	19 447
Osgood precinct[55]	954	684
Payne precinct[55]	211	181
Peckham precinct[55]	193	154
Rosedale precinct[55]	186	167
Sellers precinct[55]	621	233
Sutherland precinct[55]	1 934	1 165
Sutherland village	1 238	840
Wallace precinct[55]	602	466
Wallace village	349	241
Well precinct[55]	146	84
Logan County[56]	983	991
Gandy precinct	165	185
Gandy village	53	50
Logan precinct	134	129
Stapleton No. 1 precinct[56]	375	...
Stapleton village (pt.)	203	(NA)
Stapleton No. 2 precinct[56]	309	...
Stapleton village (pt.)	137	(NA)
Loup County[57]	859	854
Kent precinct[57]	250	148
Madison Square precinct[57]	271	74
Taylor village (pt.)	101	...
Taylor precinct[57]	338	360
Taylor village (pt.)	177	240
McPherson County	593	623
Cottonwood precinct	53	74
Hall precinct	81	89
Lemley precinct	132	107
Tryon precinct	162	165
Whitewater precinct	77	104
Worden precinct	88	84
Madison County[58]	31 382	27 402
Battle Creek precinct	1 028	844
Battle Creek village (pt.)[58]	673	530
Emerick precinct	206	272
Enola precinct	192	219
Fairview precinct	249	349
Green Garden precinct	194	223
Grove precinct	291	283
Highland precinct[58]	686	497
Battle Creek village (pt.)[58]	239	200
Jefferson precinct[58]	155	130
Kalamazoo precinct	222	257
Madison city	1 950	1 595
Madison precinct	226	284
Meadow Grove precinct[58]	601	492
Meadow Grove village	400	372
Newman Grove city (pt.)	909	854
Norfolk city[58]	19 449	16 607
Norfolk precinct[58]	1 700	1 722
Schoolcraft precinct	195	217
Shell Creek precinct	250	267
Tilden city (pt.)[58]	719	685
Union precinct	152	146
Valley precinct	597	463
Battle Creek village (pt.)	36	38
Warnerville precinct[58]	1 411	787

County Subdivisions	1980	1970
Merrick County[59]	8 945	8 751
Central township	109	113
Central City city[59]	3 083	2 803
Chapman township	632	686
Chapman village	349	371
Clarksville township	901	973
Clarks village[59]	445	480
Lone Tree township[59]	628	703
Loup township	845	802
Palmer village[59]	487	391
Mead township	241	269
Midland township	265	284
Prairie Creek township	435	455
Prairie Island township	53	60
Silver Creek township	709	728
Silver Creek village[59]	496	483
Vieregg township	1 044	875
Morrill County[60]	6 085	5 813
Bayard city[60]	1 435	1 338
Bridgeport city[60]	1 668	1 490
Broadwater precinct[60]	459	173
Broadwater village[60]	161	141
East Bayard precinct[60]	559	...
East Camp Clarke precinct[60]	288	...
Gilchrist precinct[60]	154	84
Haynes precinct[60]	102	87
North Camp Clarke precinct[60]	577	...
Redington precinct	163	225
West Bayard precinct[60]	398	...
West Camp Clarke precinct[60]	73	...
Yockey precinct	209	213
Nance County[61]	4 740	5 142
Beaver township	196	251
Cedar township	167	227
Cottonwood township	122	150
Council Creek township	136	171
East Newman township	186	224
Fullerton city	1 506	1 444
Fullerton township	163	158
Genoa township	1 337	1 408
Genoa city[61]	1 090	1 174
Loup Ferry township	105	159
Prairie Creek township	266	295
South Branch township	89	108
Timber Creek township	345	409
Belgrade village	195	210
West Newman township	122	138
Nemaha County[62]	8 367	8 976
Auburn city[62]	3 482	3 650
Bedford precinct	252	257
Benton precinct	391	452
Brownville precinct	488	440
Brownville village	203	174
Douglas precinct[62]	443	258
First Lafayette precinct	377	438
Brock village	189	192
Glen Rock precinct	306	296
Julian village	87	80
Island precinct	23	48
Nemaha precinct	523	573
Nemaha village	209	207
Peru precinct	1 217	1 600
Peru city	998	1 380
Second Lafayette precinct	81	114
Washington precinct	784	850
Johnson village[62]	341	350
Nuckolls County[63]	6 726	7 404
Alban precinct	113	124
Beaver precinct[63]	546	434
Blaine precinct	98	125
Bostwick precinct	96	135
Elk precinct	233	288
Oak village	79	100
Garfield precinct	153	171
Hammond precinct	162	215
Hardy precinct	395	459
Hardy village[63]	232	250
Highland precinct	88	92
Liberty precinct	157	165
Nelson precinct	832	900
Nelson city[63]	733	746
Nora precinct	173	215
Nora village	24	43
St. Stephens precinct	165	211
Sherman precinct	128	170
Spring Creek precinct	380	397
Ruskin village	224	229
Superior city[63]	2 502	2 779
Victor precinct	505	524
Lawrence village	350	343
Otoe County[64]	15 183	15 576
Berlin precinct[64]	715	389
Otoe village[64]	197	204
Delaware precinct[64]	732	526
Dunbar village[64]	216	252

County Subdivisions	1980	1970
Otoe County—Con.		
Four Mile precinct[64]	441	366
Hendricks precinct	392	368
Douglas village	207	175
McWilliams precinct[64]	517	...
Lorton Village village	47	47
Talmage village	246	285
Nebraska City city[64]	7 127	7 441
North Syracuse precinct[64]	1 096	1 758
Syracuse city (pt.)[64]	959	1 559
Osage precinct	234	307
Otoe precinct	316	302
Palmyra precinct[64]	968	...
Palmyra village[64]	512	386
Rock Creek precinct	254	344
Russell precinct[64]	767	...
Unadilla village[64]	291	271
South Branch precinct	349	356
Burr village[64]	101	108
South Syracuse precinct[64]	839	130
Syracuse city (pt.)[64]	679	3
Wyoming precinct[64]	436	424
Pawnee County[65]	3 937	4 473
Pawnee City city[65]	1 156	1 267
Precinct 1, Pawnee No. 1[65]	153	...
Precinct 2, Pawnee No. 2[65]	399	...
Precinct 3, Table Rock[65]	586	...
Table Rock village	393	429
Precinct 4, Steinauer[65]	448	...
Steinauer village	108	118
Precinct 5, Burchard[65]	584	...
Burchard village	122	131
Precinct 6, South Fork[65]	375	403
Du Bois village	178	185
Precinct 7, Turkey Creek[65]	236	259
Lewiston village	102	88
Perkins County[66]	3 637	3 423
Eckery precinct	138	137
Grace precinct	354	345
Venango village[66]	230	218
Grant precinct[66]	668	...
Grant city (pt.)[66]	634	...
Liberty precinct[66]	1 033	1 366
Grant city (pt.)[66]	636	1 099
Lisbon precinct[66]	196	101
Madrid precinct	529	514
Madrid village[66]	284	234
Sawyer precinct	123	115
Woodson precinct	213	226
Yankee precinct[66]	383	266
Elsie village	133	125
Grainton village	20	20
Phelps County[67]	9 769	9 553
Anderson township	177	177
Center township	217	273
Cottonwood township	106	121
Divide township	383	370
Funk village	189	143
Garfield township	563	538
Bertrand village (pt.)	344	331
Holdrege city[67]	5 624	5 635
Industry–Rock Falls township[67]	250	232
Atlanta village	102	101
Laird township	616	533
Loomis village	447	323
Lake township	174	191
Prairie township[67]	338	160
Sheridan township[67]	209	200
Union township	536	438
Bertrand village (pt.)[67]	431	331
Westmark township	234	262
Westside township	166	186
Williamsburg township	176	198
Pierce County[68]	8 481	8 493
Allen precinct	274	317
Blaine precinct	92	113
Cleveland precinct	226	261
Clover Valley precinct	203	254
Eastern precinct	369	452
McLean village	46	67
Foster precinct	319	358
Foster village	81	79
Logan precinct	236	242
Mills precinct	78	100
North Dry Creek precinct[68]	261	309
Pierce city[68]	1 535	1 360
Pierce precinct[68]	460	387
Plainview city[68]	1 483	1 494
Plum Grove precinct	1 162	1 204
Osmond city[68]	871	883
Slough precinct	312	322
South Branch precinct	828	541
Hadar village	286	172
South Dry Creek precinct	267	288
Thompson precinct	232	316

County Subdivisions	1980	1970
Pierce County—Con.		
Willow Creek precinct	144	175
Platte County[69]	28 852	r26 544
Bismark township	471	394
Burrows township	369	426
Tarnov village	63	63
Butler township	696	568
Duncan village[69]	410	298
Columbus city[69]	17 328	15 471
Columbus township[69]	3 050	2 639
Creston township	511	511
Creston village	210	171
Grand Prairie township	455	468
Granville township	1 200	1 313
Cornlea village	40	54
Humphrey city (pt.)[69]	762	822
Humphrey township	428	482
Humphrey city (pt.)	37	40
Joliet township	226	302
Lost Creek township	636	691
Platte Center village (pt.)	313	342
Loup township	172	188
Monroe township	212	228
Newman Grove city (pt.)	21	9
Oconee township	521	r543
Monroe village[69]	294	r295
St. Bernard township	786	726
Lindsay village[69]	383	291
Shell Creek township	769	504
Platte Center village (pt.)[69]	54	42
Sherman township	372	396
Walker township	378	407
Woodville township	251	278
Polk County[70]	6 320	6 468
Canada precinct	1 055	1 046
Shelby village[70]	724	647
Clear Creek precinct	416	330
Hackberry precinct	270	386
Island precinct	170	166
Osceola city[70]	975	923
Osceola precinct[70]	347	420
Platte precinct	359	379
Pleasant Home precinct	837	865
Polk village[70]	440	413
Stromsburg city[70]	1 290	1 215
Stromsburg precinct[70]	363	417
Valley precinct	238	321
Red Willow County[71]	12 615	12 191
Alliance precinct	81	100
Beaver precinct[71]	265	...
Danbury village	143	137
Bondville precinct	88	127
Box Elder precinct[71]	95	...
Coleman precinct[71]	57	...
Danbury precinct[71]	107	...
Driftwood precinct[71]	115	...
East Valley precinct	251	255
Bartley village (pt.)	190	173
Fritsch precinct	89	96
Gerver precinct[71]	87	...
Grant precinct[71]	46	...
Indianola precinct	1 013	788
Bartley village (pt.)	152	110
Indianola city (pt.)	743	576
Lebanon precinct	159	211
Lebanon village	102	118
McCook city[71]	8 404	8 285
Missouri Ridge precinct[71]	161	...
North Valley precinct	110	102
Perry precinct[71]	315	220
Red Willow precinct	364	313
Indianola city (pt.)	113	96
Tyrone precinct	68	69
Valley Grange precinct	315	276
Willow Grove precinct[71]	425	565
Richardson County[72]	11 315	12 277
Arago precinct	249	312
Barada precinct	335	465
Barada village	36	58
East Muddy precinct	380	387
Shubert village[72]	267	240
Falls City city[72]	5 374	5 444
Falls City precinct[72]	263	417
Franklin precinct	207	268
Grant precinct	421	486
Dawson village	215	251
Humboldt city	1 176	1 194
Humboldt precinct	218	276
Jefferson precinct	268	304
Preston village	45	64
Liberty precinct	508	512
Verdon village	278	265
Nemaha precinct	131	242
Ohio precinct	301	320
Porter precinct	183	241
Rulo precinct	395	416

County Subdivisions	1980	1970
Richardson County—Con.		
Rulo precinct—Con.		
Rulo city	261	299
Salem precinct	358	416
Salem village	221	214
Speiser precinct	155	180
West Muddy precinct	393	397
Stella village	289	282
Rock County	2 383	2 231
Bassett precinct	1 366	1 163
Bassett city	1 009	983
Blaine precinct	102	139
Brinkerhoff precinct	9	7
Center precinct	83	71
Gracy precinct	40	43
Harrison precinct	102	69
Kinkaid precinct	64	55
Kirkwood precinct	91	100
Lay precinct	44	67
Long Pine precinct	35	40
Newport precinct	212	232
Newport village	141	141
Pewaukee precinct	114	132
Selden precinct	49	51
Thurman precinct	72	62
Saline County[73]	13 131	12 809
Atlanta precinct	189	198
Big Blue precinct	307	319
Brush Creek precinct	190	212
Crete city[73]	4 872	4 444
Crete precinct[73]	618	492
De Witt precinct	858	904
De Witt village[73]	642	651
Dorchester precinct	879	802
Dorchester village[73]	611	492
Friend city[73]	1 079	1 126
Friend precinct[73]	209	267
Lincoln precinct	199	238
Monroe precinct	148	176
North Fork precinct	167	205
Olive precinct	368	370
Tobias village	138	124
Pleasant Hill precinct	247	254
South Fork precinct	480	502
Western village	336	344
Swan Creek precinct	288	322
Swanton village	131	160
Turkey Creek precinct	142	188
Wilber city	1 624	1 483
Wilber precinct	267	307
Sarpy County[74]	86 015	'66 200
Bellevue precinct[74]	21 813	'21 953
Bellevue city[74]	21 813	'21 953
Bellevue No. 2 precinct[74]	13 739	9 164
Offutt AFB West (CDP)	8 787	8 445
Fairview precinct	656	396
Forest City No. 1 precinct	1 609	1 557
Gretna city[74]	1 609	1 557
Gilmore No. 1 precinct	2 446	2 129
Gilmore No. 2 precinct	3 535	3 513
Gilmore No. 3 precinct	2 152	'1 839
Good Luck precinct	1 442	1 482
Highland precinct[74]	6 117	6 042
Highland No. 3 precinct[74]	2 410	'1 655
La Platte precinct	1 243	879
La Vista precinct	9 588	'4 858
La Vista city[74]	9 588	'4 858
Melia—Forest City precinct[74]	1 639	756
Papillion precinct	6 399	5 606
Papillion city[74]	6 399	5 606
Papillion No. 2 precinct[74]	2 446	'597
Pawnee precinct	3 394	1 722
Platford—Springfield No. 2 precinct[74]	2 010	781
Richland precinct	2 595	476
Springfield No. 1 precinct	782	795
Springfield city[74]	782	795
Saunders County[75]	18 716	17 018
Ashland township	2 400	2 235
Ashland city (pt.)[75]	2 088	2 031
Bohemia township	194	224
Center township[75]	541	502
Colon village	148	109
Chapman township	623	705
Weston village[75]	286	285
Chester township	510	573
Prague village (pt.)	262	267
Clear Creek township	748	551
Ashland city (pt.)[75]	186	145
Memphis village	89	71
Douglas township	245	281
Elk township	380	413
Prague village (pt.)	23	24
Green township	276	205
Leshara township	556	301
Leshara village	133	102
Marble township	321	301

County Subdivisions	1980	1970
Saunders County—Con.		
Marietta township	846	834
Mead village[75]	506	488
Mariposa township	381	460
Malmo village	100	131
Morse Bluff township	342	381
Morse Bluff village	132	162
Newman township	250	290
North Cedar township	869	840
Cedar Bluffs village[75]	632	616
Oak Creek township	834	748
Valparaiso village	484	415
Pohocco township	740	422
Richland township	1 283	853
Ceresco village[75]	836	474
Rock Creek township	342	307
South Cedar township	264	262
Stocking township[75]	391	358
Union township	1 448	825
Yutan village[75]	631	507
Wahoo city[75]	3 555	3 835
Wahoo township	377	312
Ithaca village	156	121
Scotts Bluff County[76]	38 344	36 432
Castle Rock precinct	705	692
McGrew village	110	79
Melbeta village	151	124
Dewey precinct	508	433
East Winters Creek precinct[76]	714	861
Fanning precinct[76]	1 460	986
Ford precinct	1 874	1 723
Henry village	155	147
Morrill village[76]	1 097	937
Funston precinct	523	473
Gering city[76]	7 760	5 639
Gering precinct[76]	2 849	2 621
Terrytown village[76]	727	747
Highland precinct	597	611
Kiowa precinct	1 259	1 437
Lyman village[76]	551	561
Mitchell city[76]	1 956	1 842
Mitchell precinct	647	622
Roubadeau precinct	252	260
Scottsbluff city[76]	14 156	14 507
Tabor precinct	1 526	1 512
Minatare city	969	939
West Winters Creek precinct[76]	1 558	2 213
Seward County[77]	15 789	14 460
Precinct B	468	469
Bee village	192	156
Precinct C	645	599
Staplehurst village[77]	306	227
Precinct D	208	228
Precinct E[77]	894	842
Utica village[77]	689	602
Precinct F	399	429
Tamora village	50	93
Precinct G[77]	497	389
Precinct H[77]	822	522
Garland village[77]	257	244
Precinct I	624	598
Pleasant Dale village	259	258
Precinct J	497	406
Precinct K	451	394
Goehner village	165	113
Precinct M, Beaver Crossing[77]	900	819
Beaver Crossing village	458	400
Precinct M, Cordova[77]	268	...
Cordova village	129	141
Precinct N	308	307
Precinct O	2 650	2 440
Milford city[77]	2 108	1 846
Precinct P	445	283
Seward city[77]	5 713	5 294
Sheridan County[78]	7 544	7 285
East Gordon precinct[78]	422	345
Ellsworth precinct[78]	206	69
Gordon city[78]	2 167	2 106
Hay Springs precinct[78]	1 302	1 142
Hay Springs village	794	682
Kinkaid precinct	156	179
Mirage precinct[78]	413	...
North Rushville precinct[78]	586	...
Pine Creek precinct[78]	136	126
Reno precinct	139	132
Rushville city[78]	1 217	1 137
South Rushville precinct[78]	242	...
West Gordon precinct[78]	441	296
Wounded Knee precinct	117	163
Sherman County[79]	4 226	4 725
Ashton township	465	494
Ashton village	273	277
Bristol township	254	306
Clay township	138	179
Elm township	65	89
Harrison township	453	447

County Subdivisions	1980	1970
Sherman County—Con.		
Harrison township—Con.		
Litchfield village[79]	256	248
Hazard township	235	277
Hazard village	75	72
Logan township	154	223
Loup City township	1 698	1 781
Loup City city[79]	1 368	1 456
Oak Creek township	88	121
Rockville township	299	348
Rockville village	116	114
Scott township	119	147
Washington township	109	150
Webster township	149	163
Sioux County[80]	1 845	2 034
Bowen precinct[80]	225	478
Harrison village (pt.)	8	377
Hat Creek precinct[80]	127	68
Sheep Creek precinct[80]	724	67
Snake Creek precinct[80]	49	48
Warbonnet precinct[80]	545	46
Harrison village (pt.)[80]	353	...
Whistle Creek precinct[80]	175	77
Stanton County[81]	6 549	5 758
Butterfly precinct	193	199
Dewey precinct	238	269
Dimick precinct	164	236
Elkhorn precinct	306	257
Haymow precinct	263	360
Kingsburg precinct	165	163
Maple Creek precinct	295	372
Pilger precinct	747	802
Pilger village	400	470
Ramshorn precinct	272	359
Spring Branch precinct	1 887	971
Stanton city[81]	1 603	1 363
Stanton precinct[81]	241	233
Union Creek precinct	175	174
Thayer County[82]	7 582	7 779
Belvidere precinct	287	326
Belvidere village	158	162
Bruning precinct	513	539
Bruning village	330	315
Byron precinct	409	475
Byron village[82]	154	171
Carleton precinct	338	335
Carleton village	160	163
Chester—Stoddard precinct	702	740
Chester village	435	459
Davenport precinct	544	579
Davenport village	445	427
Deshler precinct	1 266	1 194
Deshler city	997	937
Gilead precinct	231	271
Gilead village	69	60
Hebron city[82]	1 906	1 667
Hebron precinct[82]	260	330
Highland—Alexandria precinct	521	608
Alexandria village	255	225
Hubbell—Rose Creek precinct	297	352
Hubbell village	71	83
Kiowa—Friedensau precinct	308	363
Thomas County[83]	973	954
Natick precinct	229	214
Halsey village (pt.)[83]	134	128
Seneca precinct	173	195
Seneca village	90	111
Thedford precinct	571	545
Thedford village[83]	313	303
Thurston County[84]	7 186	6 942
Anderson township	144	222
Blackbird township	1 149	953
Bryan township	157	142
Dawes township	554	616
Rosalie village	224	204
Flournoy township	364	347
Thurston village	139	117
Merry township	163	156
Omaha township	1 146	1 205
Walthill village	847	897
Pender township	1 552	1 495
Pender village[84]	1 318	1 229
Perry township	319	346
Emerson village (pt.)	102	116
Thayer township	194	220
Winnebago township	1 444	1 240
Winnebago village[84]	902	675
Valley County[85]	5 633	5 783
Arcadia township	556	612
Arcadia village	412	418
Davis Creek township	109	102
Elyria township[85]	226	295
Elyria village[85]	62	55
Enterprise township	160	184
Eureka township	114	113

County Subdivisions	1980	1970
Valley County—Con.		
Geranium township	139	167
Independent township	90	126
Liberty township	80	111
Michigan township	103	111
Noble township	130	200
North Loup township	615	657
North Loup village	405	441
Ord township[85]	2 978	2 748
Ord city[85]	2 658	2 439
Springdale township	97	103
Vinton township	127	140
Yale township	109	114
Washington County[86]	15 508	13 310
Township 1[86]	3 245	...
Fort Calhoun city[86]	641	642
Kennard village (pt.)	284	(NA)
Township 2[86]	2 054	...
Blair city (pt.)[86]	1 277	(NA)
Township 3[86]	1 808	...
Blair city (pt.)	1 808	(NA)
Township 4[86]	1 781	...
Blair city (pt.)[86]	1 781	(NA)
Township 5[86]	2 241	...
Blair city (pt.)[86]	792	(NA)
Herman village[86]	340	323
Township 6[86]	2 234	...
Blair city (pt.)[86]	760	(NA)
Township 7[86]	2 145	...
Arlington village[86]	1 117	910
Kennard village (pt.)	88	(NA)
Washington village	113	76
Wayne County[87]	9 858	10 400
Brenna precinct	261	301
Chapin precinct	526	512
Winside village (pt.)[87]	218	209
Deer Creek precinct	471	491
Carroll village[87]	246	235
Garfield precinct	212	256
Hancock precinct	456	549
Winside village (pt.)[87]	221	244
Hoskins precinct	608	593
Hoskins village	306	271
Hunter precinct	3 116	3 569
Wayne city (pt.)[87]	2 748	3 129
Leslie precinct	160	197
Logan precinct	327	273
Wakefield city (pt.)[87]	134	96
Plum Creek precinct	284	334
Sherman precinct	268	324
Sholes village	27	22
Strahan precinct	2 925	2 707
Wayne city (pt.)[87]	2 492	2 250
Wilbur precinct	244	294
Webster County[88]	4 858	5 396
Bladen precinct[88]	695	...
Bladen village[88]	298	293
Blue Hill precinct[88]	1 137	...
Blue Hill village[88]	883	784
Guide Rock No. 1 precinct[88]	644	...
Guide Rock village	344	318
Guide Rock No. 2 precinct[88]	329	...
Inavale precinct[88]	253	234
Red Cloud city	1 300	1 531
Red Cloud No. 1 precinct[88]	251	...
Cowles village	48	57
Red Cloud No. 2 precinct[88]	249	...
Wheeler County[89]	1 060	1 051
Bartlett precinct[89]	394	218
Bartlett village	144	140
Beaver precinct[89]	180	...
Clearwater precinct[89]	157	145
Ericson precinct	329	266
Ericson village[89]	132	122
York County[90]	14 798	13 685
Arborville precinct	191	273
Baker precinct[90]	509	335
Beaver precinct	274	338
Bradshaw precinct	601	625
Bradshaw village	373	347
Brown precinct	306	300
Hays precinct	375	296
McCool Junction village (pt.)	142	76
Henderson precinct	1 373	1 247
Henderson city[90]	1 072	901
Lushton village	33	34
Leroy precinct	382	414
Lockridge precinct[90]	334	296
McFadden precinct	498	427
McCool Junction village (pt.)	262	213
Morton precinct	441	433
Benedict village	228	209
New York precinct[90]	275	319
Stewart precinct	531	502
Gresham village	320	248

County Subdivisions

	1980	1970
York County—Con.		
Thayer precinct	308	336
Thayer village	70	78
Waco precinct	475	511
Waco village⁹⁰	225	214
West Blue precinct	202	255
York city⁹⁰	7 723	6 778

NEVADA

This state takes its name from the Sierra Nevada Mountains, which lie just beyond its western and southwestern borders. Nevada is a Spanish word signifying "snow clad" or "white as snow."

The first white man to enter the region now constituting Nevada was probably Francisco Garces, a Franciscan friar, who passed through the southern part in 1775 on his way from Sonora to California. Other friars followed him, but no settlements were made. In 1825 the Humboldt River was discovered by Peter S. Ogden, an employee of the Hudson Bay Company. In 1849 a trading post was founded on or near the present site of Genoa for the purpose of furnishing supplies to gold seekers on their way to California. Although many such emigrants passed through the region now included within the limits of Nevada, it had very few inhabitants until the discovery of the famous Comstock Lode in 1859, after which miners and prospectors came in large numbers.

This region formed a part of the Spanish possessions in America until the Mexican revolution in 1821, after which it became a part of Mexico. By the treaty of Guadalupe-Hidalgo, in 1848, at the close of the war with Mexico, that country ceded to the United States its claims to territory north of the Rio Grande and Gila Rivers and extending westward to the Pacific Ocean.

In 1850 the area between California and Texas was organized into the territories of Utah and New Mexico, and the greater part of what is now Nevada was included in the former territory, while that portion lying south of the thirty-seventh parallel (the northern boundary of New Mexico) was made a part of the latter. In March, 1861, that part of Utah lying west of the thirty-ninth meridian from Washington (approximately the one hundred and sixteenth from Greenwich) was organized as Nevada territory.

In 1864, under authority of an enabling act passed by Congress in the same year, a state constitution was adopted, and October of that year Nevada, with eastern boundary at longitude 38° west from Washington, was admitted to the Union. Two years later the thirty-seventh meridian from Washington was made the eastern boundary, and at the same time the area lying south of the thirty-seventh parallel and extending from California to the Colorado River and the thirty-seventh meridian from Washington was taken from the territory of Arizona and added to Nevada.

COUNTY LOCATION INDEX

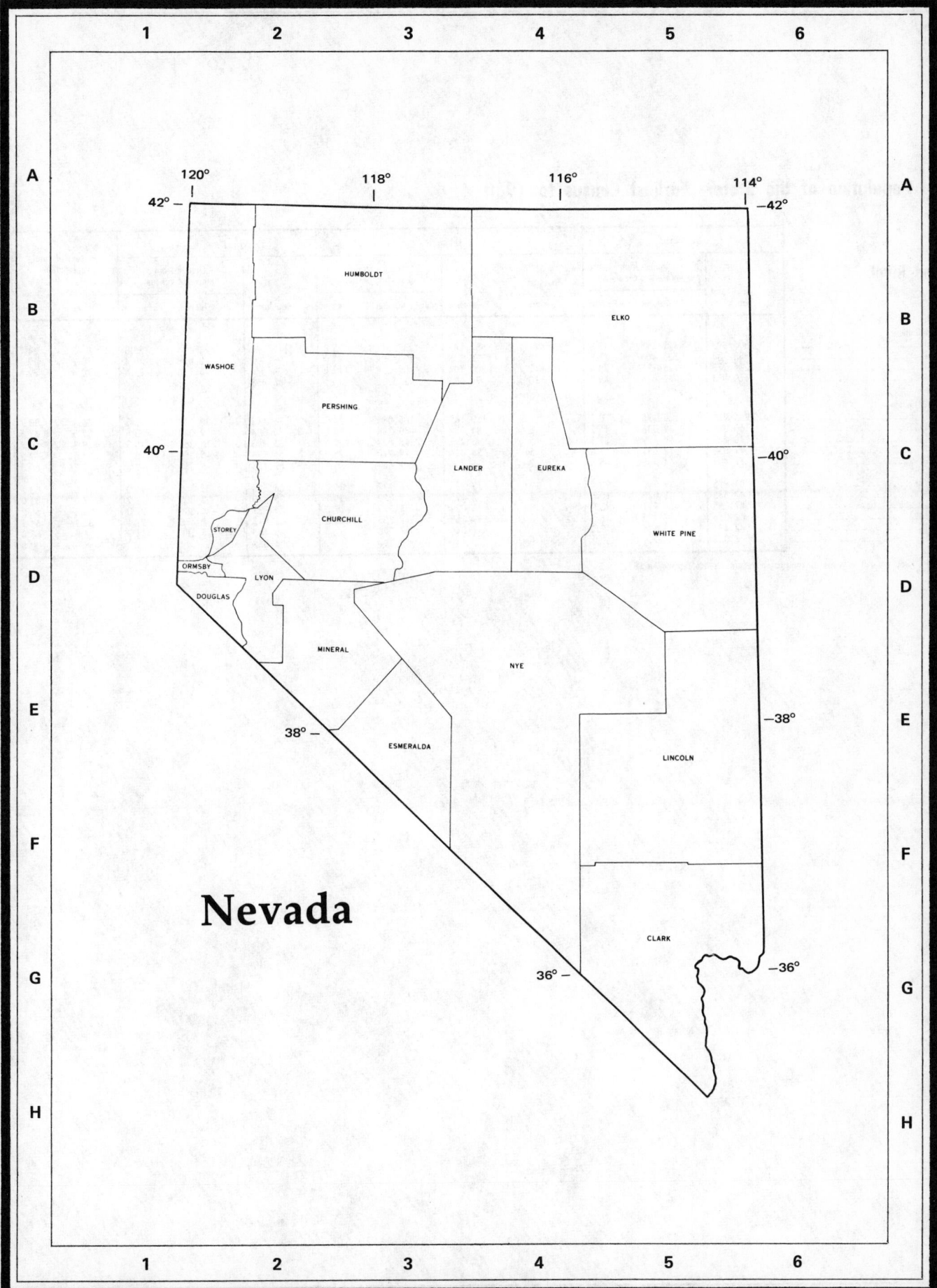

Nevada

Population of the State: Earliest Census to 1980

Urban and Rural

	The State			Urban				Rural			Percent of total population	
	Total population	Change from preceding census		Places of 2,500 or more	Population	Change from preceding census		Population	Change from preceding census		Urban	Rural
		Number	Percent			Number	Percent		Number	Percent		
Current urban definition:												
1980 (Apr. 1)	800 493	311 755	63.8	24	682 947	287 611	72.8	117 546	24 144	25.8	85.3	14.7
1970 (Apr. 1)	488 738	203 460	71.3	18	395 336	194 632	97.0	93 402	8 828	10.4	80.9	19.1
1960 (Apr. 1)	285 278	125 195	78.2	12	200 704	109 079	119.0	84 574	16 116	23.5	70.4	29.6
1950 (Apr. 1)	160 083	49 836	45.2	10	91 625	...	...	68 458	...	...	57.2	42.8
Previous urban definition:												
1960 (Apr. 1)	285 278	125 195	78.2	11	189 165	105 086	125.0	96 113	20 109	26.5	66.3	33.7
1950 (Apr. 1)	160 083	49 836	45.2	8	84 079	40 788	94.2	76 004	9 048	13.5	52.5	47.5
1940 (Apr. 1)	110 247	19 189	21.1	5	43 291	8 827	25.6	66 956	10 362	18.3	39.3	60.7
1930 (Apr. 1)	91 058	13 651	17.6	5	34 464	19 210	125.9	56 594	−5 559	−8.9	37.8	62.2
1920 (Jan. 1)	77 407	−4 468	−5.5	2	15 254	1 887	14.1	62 153	−6 355	−9.3	19.7	80.3
1910 (Apr. 15)	81 875	39 540	93.4	2	13 367	6 172	85.8	68 508	33 368	95.0	16.3	83.7
1900 (June 1)	42 335	−5 020	−10.6	2	7 195	−8 829	−55.1	35 140	3 809	12.2	17.0	83.0
1890 (June 1)	47 355	−14 911	−23.9	3	16 024	−3 329	−17.2	31 331	−11 582	−27.0	33.8	66.2
1880 (June 1)	62 266	19 775	46.5	3	19 353	12 305	174.6	42 913	7 470	21.1	31.1	68.9
1870 (June 1)	42 491	35 634	519.7	1	7 048	7 048	...	35 443	28 586	416.9	16.6	83.4
1860 (June 1)	6 857	...	...	−	−	...	...	6 857	...	...	−	100.0

NOTE: 1860 population is that of area taken to form Nevada Territory in 1861.

CARSON

1860	6,712

CHURCHHILL

1870	196
1880	479
1890	703
1900	830
1910	2,811
1920	4,649
1930	5,075
1940	5,317
1950	6,161
1960	8,452
1970	10,513
1980	13,917

CLARK

1910	3,321
1920	4,859
1930	8,532
1940	16,414
1950	48,289
1960	127,016
1970	273,288
1980	463,087

DOUGLAS

1870	1,215
1880	1,581
1890	1,551
1900	1,534
1910	1,895
1920	1,825
1930	1,840
1940	2,056
1950	2,029
1960	3,481
1970	6,882
1980	19,421

ELKO

1870	3,447
1880	5,716
1890	4,794
1900	5,688
1910	8,133
1920	8,083
1930	9,960
1940	10,912
1950	11,654
1960	12,011
1970	13,958
1980	17,269

ESMERALDA

1870	1,553
1880	3,220
1890	2,148
1900	1,972
1910	9,369
1920	2,410
1930	1,077
1940	1,554
1950	614
1960	619
1970	629
1980	777

EUREKA

1880	7,086
1890	3,275
1900	1,954
1910	1,830
1920	1,350
1930	1,333
1940	1,361
1950	896
1960	767
1970	948
1980	1,198

HUMBOLDT

1860	40
1870	1,916
1880	3,480
1890	3,434
1900	4,463
1910	6,825
1920	3,743
1930	3,795
1940	4,743
1950	4,838
1960	5,708
1970	6,375
1980	9,434

LANDER

1870	2,815
1880	3,624
1890	2,226
1900	1,534
1910	1,786
1920	1,484
1930	1,714
1940	1,745
1950	1,850
1960	1,566
1970	2,666
1980	4,076

LINCOLN

1870	2,985
1880	2,637
1890	2,466
1900	3,284
1910	3,489
1920	2,287
1930	3,601
1940	4,130
1950	3,837
1960	2,431
1970	2,557
1980	3,732

LYON

1870	1,837
1880	2,409
1890	1,987
1900	2,268
1910	3,568
1920	4,078
1930	3,810
1940	4,076
1950	3,679
1960	6,143
1970	8,221
1980	13,594

MINERAL

1920	1,848
1930	1,863
1940	2,342
1950	5,560
1960	6,329
1970	7,051
1980	6,217

NYE

1870	1,087
1880	1,875
1890	1,290
1900	1,140
1910	7,513
1920	6,504
1930	3,989
1940	3,606
1950	3,101
1960	4,374
1970	5,599
1980	9,048

ORMSBY

1870	3,668
1880	5,412
1890	4,883
1900	2,893
1910	3,415
1920	2,453
1930	2,221
1940	3,209
1950	4,172
1960	8,063

PERSHING

1920	2,803
1930	2,652
1940	2,713
1950	3,103
1960	3,199
1970	2,670
1980	3,408

ROOP

1870	133
1880	286

SAINT MARYS

1860	105

STOREY

1870	11,359
1880	16,115
1890	8,806
1900	3,637
1910	3,045
1920	1,469
1930	667
1940	1,216
1950	671
1960	568
1970	695
1980	1,503

WASHOE

1870	3,091
1880	5,644
1890	6,437
1900	9,141
1910	17,434
1920	18,627
1930	27,158
1940	32,476
1950	50,205
1960	84,743
1970	121,068
1980	193,623

WHITE PINE

1870	7,187
1880	2,682
1890	1,712
1900	1,961
1910	7,441
1920	8,935
1930	11,771
1940	12,377
1950	9,424
1960	9,808
1970	10,150
1980	8,167

NOTES

CARSON

No records by which to account for its disappearance subsequent to the 1860 census.

ORMSBY

Carson City consolidated with Ormsby County and made and independent city prior to 1970.

ROOP

Annexed to Washoe in 1883.

SAINT MARYS

No records by which to account for its disappearance subsequent to the 1860 census.

CARSON CITY

1900	2,100
1910	2,466
1920	1,685
1930	1,596
1940	2,478
1950	3,082
1960	5,163
1970	15,468
1980	32,022

HENDERSON

1960	12,525
1970	16,395
1980	24,363

LAS VEGAS

1920	2,304
1930	5,165
1940	8,422
1950	24,624
1960	64,405
1970	125,787
1980	164,674

NORTH LAS VEGAS

1950	3,875
1960	18,422
1970	36,216
1980	42,739

RENO

1870	1,035
1880	1,302
1890	3,563
1900	4,500
1910	10,867
1920	12,016
1930	18,529
1940	21,317
1950	32,497
1960	51,470
1970	72,863
1980	100,756

SPARKS

1910	2,500
1920	3,238
1930	4,508
1940	5,318
1950	8,203
1960	16,618
1970	24,187
1980	40,780

County Subdivisions

County Subdivisions	1980	1970
The State	800 493	488 738
Churchill County[1]	13 917	10 513
New River township	13 917	10 513
Fallon city[1]	4 262	2 959
Fallon Station (CDP)	1 256	1 045
Clark County[2]	463 087	273 288
Bunkerville township	492	244
Goodsprings township	1 003	314
Henderson township	24 334	16 410
Henderson city (pt.)[2]	24 291	16 395
Las Vegas township	350 511	191 260
East Las Vegas (CDP)	6 449	6 501
Henderson city (pt.)[2]	72	...
Las Vegas city[2]	164 674	125 787
Paradise (CDP)	84 818	24 477
Sunrise Manor (CDP) (pt.)	23 205	860
Winchester (CDP)	19 728	13 981
Logan township	1 087	426
Mesquite township	922	674
Moapa township	702	353
Nelson township	10 059	5 674
Boulder City city	9 590	5 223
North Las Vegas township	71 605	56 241
Nellis AFB (CDP)	7 476	6 449
North Las Vegas city[2]	42 739	46 067
Sunrise Manor (CDP) (pt.)	20 950	8 824
Overton township	1 752	1 336
Overton (CDP)	1 111	...
Searchlight township	620	356
Douglas County	19 421	6 882
East Fork township	14 053	3 867
Gardnerville–Minden (CDP)	2 638	1 320
Gardnerville Ranchos (CDP)	3 542	...
Tahoe township	5 368	3 015
Kingsbury (CDP)	2 695	...
Zephyr Cove–Round Hill Village (CDP)	1 316	...
Elko County[3]	17 269	13 958
Carlin township	1 280	1 356
Carlin city	1 232	1 313
East Line township	395	97
Elko township[3]	11 398	8 931
Elko city[3]	8 758	7 621
Jackpot township[3]	809	...
Jarbidge township[3]	33	32
Mountain City township	1 216	1 125
Tecoma township	231	221
Wells township[3]	1 907	2 196
Wells city	1 218	1 081
Esmeralda County	777	629
Esmeralda township	777	629
Eureka County	1 198	948
Beowawe township	400	401
Eureka township	798	547
Humboldt County	9 434	6 375
Gold Run township	780	238
McDermitt township	1 159	1 086
Paradise Valley township	286	257
Union township	7 209	4 794
Winnemucca city	4 140	3 587
Lander County	4 076	2 666
Argenta township	3 640	2 252
Battle Mountain (CDP)	2 749	1 856
Austin township	436	414
Lincoln County[4]	3 732	2 557
Alamo township	1 126	398
Caliente township	1 054	979
Caliente city[4]	982	916
Panaca township	758	539
Pioche township	794	641
Lyon County[5]	13 594	8 221
Canal township	3 315	1 470
Dayton township[5]	4 376	826
Mason Valley township[5]	5 050	5 187
Yerington city[5]	2 021	2 010
Smith Valley township[5]	853	738
Mineral County	6 217	7 051
Hawthorne township	5 166	5 995
Hawthorne (CDP)	3 741	3 539
Mina township	484	506
Schurz township	567	550
Nye County[6]	9 048	5 599
Beatty township[6]	3 524	1 131
Gabbs township	912	1 000
Gabbs city	811	874
Pahrump township[6]	1 358	963
Round Mountain township	574	215
Tonopah township	2 680	2 290
Tonopah (CDP)	1 952	1 716

County Subdivisions

County Subdivisions	1980	1970
Pershing County[7]	3 408	2 670
Lake township	3 408	2 670
Lovelock city[7]	1 680	1 571
Storey County[8]	1 503	695
Virginia township	1 503	695
Washoe County[9]	193 623	121 068
Gerlach township[9]	583	579
Reno township[9]	137 542	90 502
Incline Village–Crystal Bay (CDP)	6 225	...
New Washoe City (CDP)	2 543	...
Reno city (pt.)[9]	99 701	72 863
Sparks township[9]	53 230	28 702
Reno city (pt.)[9]	1 046	...
Sparks city[9]	40 780	24 187
Sun Valley (CDP)	8 822	2 414
Verdi township	1 256	716
Reno city (pt.)[9]	9	...
Wadsworth township	1 012	555
White Pine County[10]	8 167	10 150
Baker township	212	146
Ely township	7 599	9 686
Ely city[10]	4 882	4 176
McGill (CDP)	1 419	2 164
Lund township	356	318
Carson City[11]	32 022	15 468

NEW HAMPSHIRE

New Hampshire takes its name from the county of Hampshire in England, which was the home of Capt. John Mason, one of the early proprietors of what is now the eastern portion of the state.

It is not certain whether the first European to visit the territory now constituting New Hampshire was Martin Pring, who is believed by some to have sailed up the Piscataqua River in 1603 as far as what is now Dover, or Capt. John Smith, who explored the coast to some extent in his voyage to New England in 1614. This region was included in the grants made by James I of England to the Plymouth Company in 1606 and 1620. In 1622 the Council for New England, as the Plymouth Company was usually known, granted to Capt. John Mason and Sir Ferdinando Gorges all the land lying along the seacoast and for 60 miles inland between Merrimac and Kennebec Rivers with all the islands adjacent. In 1629 Mason received from the Council for New England an individual grant of that part of this territory which lay west of the Piscataqua River (the lower course of which now forms a portion of the boundary between New Hampshire and Maine), which he named New Hampshire. In the same year Mason and Gorges received the patent for Laconia, a much larger tract which may have extended to Lake Champlain.

In 1623 the first settlement was made at what is now Little Harbor in the town of Rye by David Thomson. Dover was also settled before 1628. Portsmouth was founded about 1630, Exeter in 1638, and Hampton in 1638 or 1639. At first the scattered settlements were practically independent and without much organized government, but in 1641 the towns on the Piscataqua and its branches submitted to the jurisdiction of Massachusetts Bay in 1643 Exeter petitioned to join the union. Hampton appears to have been considered from the date of its settlement as coming under the jurisdiction of Massachusetts Bay.

In 1679 New Hampshire was made a royal province. In 1690, subsequent to the fall of Andros, a number of the citizens petitioned Massachusetts to assume the government again, and accordingly the revolutionary provisional government of Massachusetts took charge of New Hampshire. In 1692, however, New Hampshire was once more made a separate province.

In 1740 the eastern and southern limits of New Hampshire were established, substantially as they now exist, by royal decree.

From 1749 the territory west of the Connecticut River (now Vermont) had been a subject of controversy between New Hampshire and New York, but in 1764 the claim of the latter colony was sustained by royal decree. Nevertheless, the "New Hampshire Grants" (as this region was then called) remained in dispute between New Hampshire and New York until 1782, when a compromise was made recognizing the independence of Vermont, which had already been proclaimed by a convention at Westminster in 1777.

New Hampshire was one of the original thirteen states.

COUNTY LOCATION INDEX

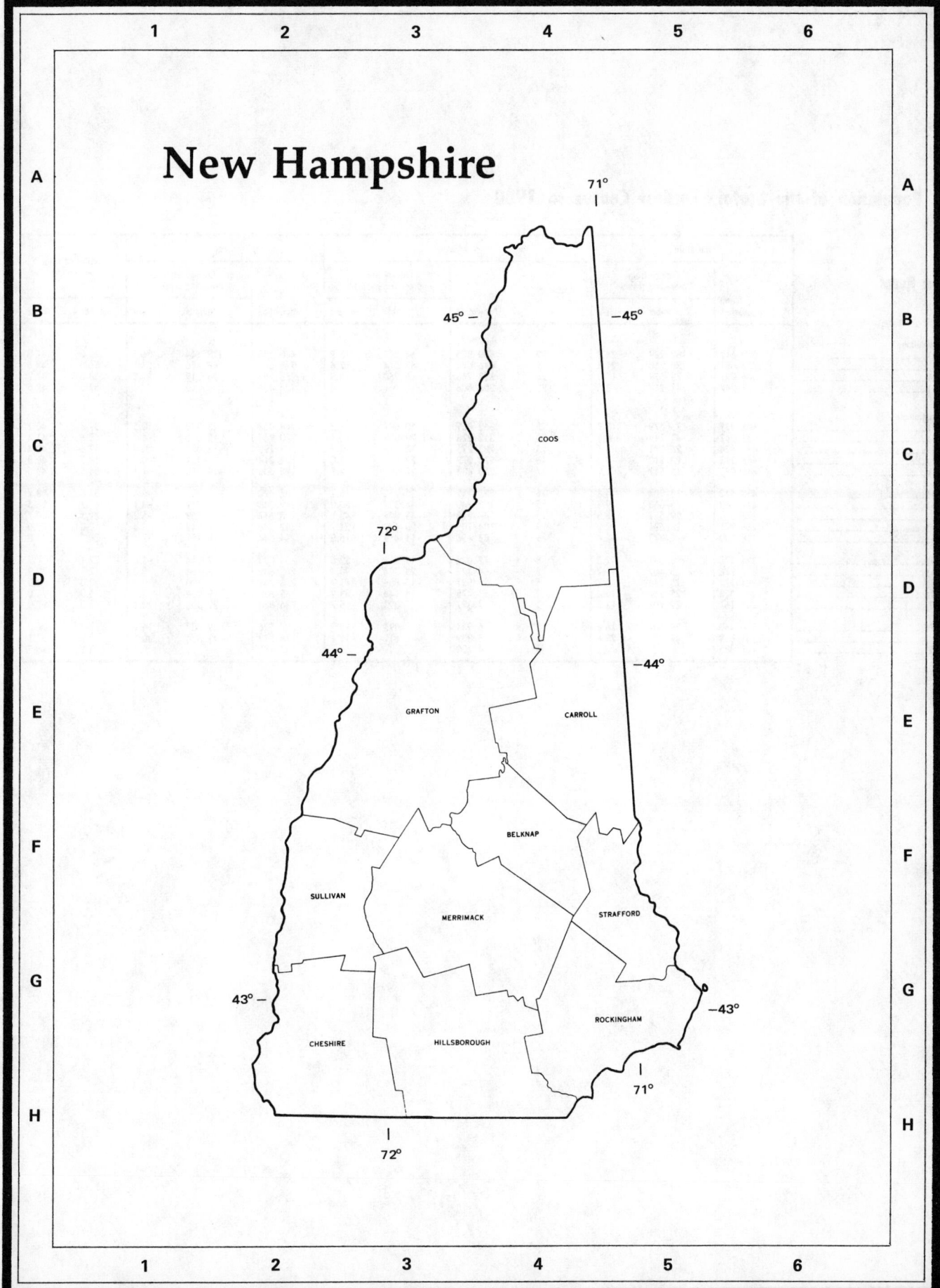

New Hampshire

Population of the State: Earliest Census to 1980

Urban and Rural

	The State			Urban				Rural			Percent of total population	
	Total population	Change from preceding census		Places of 2,500 or more	Population	Change from preceding census		Population	Change from preceding census		Urban	Rural
		Number	Percent			Number	Percent		Number	Percent		
Current urban definition:												
1980 (Apr. 1)	920 610	182 929	24.8	29	480 325	64 285	15.5	440 285	118 644	36.9	52.2	47.8
1970 (Apr. 1)	737 681	130 760	21.5	25	416 040	62 274	17.6	321 641	68 486	27.1	56.4	43.6
1960 (Apr. 1)	606 921	73 679	13.8	24	353 766	46 960	15.3	253 155	26 719	11.8	58.3	41.7
1950 (Apr. 1)	533 242	41 718	8.5	21	306 806	...	...	226 436	...	...	57.5	42.5
Previous urban definition:												
1960 (Apr. 1)	606 921	73 679	13.8	23	362 859	50 581	16.2	244 062	23 098	10.5	59.8	40.2
1950 (Apr. 1)	533 242	41 718	8.5	20	312 278	29 053	10.3	220 964	12 665	6.1	58.6	41.4
1940 (Apr. 1)	491 524	26 231	5.6	18	283 225	10 146	3.7	208 299	16 085	8.4	57.6	42.4
1930 (Apr. 1)	465 293	22 210	5.0	18	273 079	22 641	9.0	192 214	−431	−0.2	58.7	41.3
1920 (Jan. 1)	443 083	12 511	2.9	17	250 438	27 286	12.2	192 645	−14 775	−7.1	56.5	43.5
1910 (Apr. 15)	430 572	18 984	4.6	16	223 152	30 912	16.1	207 420	−11 928	−5.4	51.8	48.2
1900 (June 1)	411 588	35 058	9.3	15	192 240	44 327	30.0	219 348	−9 269	−4.1	46.7	53.3
1890 (June 1)	376 530	29 539	8.5	13	147 913	43 808	42.1	228 617	−14 269	−5.9	39.3	60.7
1880 (June 1)	346 991	28 691	9.0	9	104 105	20 649	24.7	242 886	8 042	3.4	30.0	70.0
1870 (June 1)	318 300	−7 773	−2.4	9	83 456	11 418	15.8	234 844	−19 191	−7.6	26.2	73.8
1860 (June 1)	326 073	8 097	2.5	8	72 038	17 711	32.6	254 035	−9 614	−3.6	22.1	77.9
1850 (June 1)	317 976	33 402	11.7	7	54 327	25 796	90.4	263 649	7 606	3.0	17.1	82.9
1840 (June 1)	284 574	15 246	5.7	5	28 531	15 056	111.7	256 043	190	0.1	10.0	90.0
1830 (June 1)	269 328	25 167	10.3	2	13 475	6 148	83.9	255 853	19 019	8.0	5.0	95.0
1820 (Aug. 7)	244 161	29 701	13.8	1	7 327	393	5.7	236 834	29 308	14.1	3.0	97.0
1810 (Aug. 6)	214 460	30 602	16.6	1	6 934	1 595	29.9	207 526	29 007	16.2	3.2	96.8
1800 (Aug. 4)	183 858	41 973	29.6	1	5 339	619	13.1	178 519	41 354	30.1	2.9	97.1
1790 (Aug. 2)	141 885	...	...	1	4 720	...	...	137 165	...	...	3.3	96.7

BELKNAP

1850	17,721
1860	18,549
1870	17,681
1880	17,948
1890	20,321
1900	19,526
1910	21,309
1920	21,178
1930	22,623
1940	24,328
1950	26,632
1960	28,912
1970	32,367
1980	42,884

CARROLL

1850	20,157
1860	20,465
1870	17,332
1880	18,124
1890	18,124
1900	16,895
1910	16,316
1920	15,017
1930	14,277
1940	15,589
1950	15,868
1960	15,829
1970	18,548
1980	27,931

CHESHIRE

1790	28,772
1800	29,825
1810	40,988
1820	45,376
1830	27,016
1840	26,429
1850	30,144
1860	27,434
1870	27,265
1880	28,734
1890	29,579
1900	31,321
1910	30,659
1920	30,975
1930	33,685
1940	34,953
1950	38,811
1960	43,342
1970	52,364
1980	62,116

COOS

1810	3,991
1820	5,549
1830	8,388
1840	9,849
1850	11,853
1860	13,161
1870	14,932
1880	18,580
1890	23,211
1900	29,468
1910	30,753
1920	36,093
1930	37,959
1940	39,274
1950	35,932
1960	37,140
1970	34,291
1980	35,147

GRAFTON

1790	13,472
1800	23,093
1810	28,462
1820	32,989
1830	38,682
1840	42,311
1850	42,343
1860	42,260
1870	39,103
1880	38,788
1890	37,217
1900	40,844
1910	41,652
1920	40,572
1930	42,816
1940	44,645
1950	47,923
1960	48,857
1970	54,914
1980	65,806

HILLSBOROUGH

1790	32,871
1800	43,899
1810	49,249
1820	53,884
1830	37,724
1840	42,494
1850	57,478
1860	62,140
1870	64,238
1880	75,634
1890	93,247
1900	112,640
1910	126,072
1920	135,512
1930	140,165
1940	144,888
1950	156,987
1960	178,161
1970	223,941
1980	276,608

MERRIMACK

1830	34,614
1840	36,253
1850	40,337
1860	41,408
1870	42,151
1880	46,300
1890	40,435
1900	52,430
1910	53,335
1920	51,770
1930	56,152
1940	60,710
1950	63,022
1960	67,785
1970	80,925
1980	98,302

ROCKINGHAM

1790	43,169
1800	45,427
1810	50,175
1820	55,246
1830	44,325
1840	45,771
1850	49,194
1860	50,122
1870	47,287
1880	49,064
1890	49,650
1900	51,118
1910	52,118
1920	52,498
1930	53,750
1940	58,142
1950	70,052
1960	99,029
1970	138,951
1980	190,345

STRAFFORD

1790	23,601
1800	32,614
1810	41,595
1820	51,117
1830	58,910
1840	61,127
1850	29,374
1860	31,493
1870	30,243
1880	35,558
1890	38,442
1900	39,337
1910	38,951
1920	38,546
1930	39,580
1940	43,553
1950	51,567
1960	59,799
1970	70,431
1980	85,408

SULLIVAN

1830	19,669
1840	20,340
1850	19,375
1860	19,041
1870	18,058
1880	18,161
1890	17,304
1900	18,009
1910	19,337
1920	20,992
1930	24,286
1940	25,442
1950	26,441
1960	28,067
1970	30,949
1980	36,063

BERLIN

1830	73
1840	116
1850	173
1860	433
1870	529
1880	1,144
1890	3,729
1900	8,886
1910	11,780
1920	16,104
1930	20,018
1940	19,084
1950	16,615
1960	17,821
1970	15,256
1980	13,084

CLAREMONT

1790	1,435
1800	1,889
1810	2,094
1820	1,702
1830	2,526
1840	3,217
1850	3,606
1860	4,026
1870	4,053
1880	4,704
1890	5,565
1900	6,498
1910	7,529
1920	9,524
1930	12,377
1940	12,144
1950	12,811
1960	13,563
1970	14,211
1980	14,557

CONCORD

1790	1,747
1800	2,052
1810	2,393
1820	2,838
1830	3,720
1840	4,897
1850	8,576
1860	10,896
1870	12,241
1880	13,843
1890	17,004
1900	19,632
1910	21,497
1920	22,167
1930	25,228
1940	27,171
1950	27,988
1960	28,991
1970	30,022
1980	30,400

DOVER

1790	1,998
1800	2,062
1810	2,228
1820	2,871
1830	5,449
1840	6,458
1850	8,196
1860	8,502
1870	9,294
1880	11,678

1890	12,790
1900	13,207
1910	13,147
1920	13,029
1930	13,573
1940	14,990
1950	15,874
1960	19,131
1970	20,850
1980	22,377

KEENE

1790	1,314
1800	1,645
1810	1,646
1820	1,895
1830	2,374
1840	2,610
1850	3,392
1860	4,320
1870	5,971
1880	6,784
1890	7,446
1900	9,165
1910	10,068
1920	11,210
1930	13,794
1940	13,832
1950	15,638
1960	17,572
1970	20,467
1980	21,449

LACONIA

1860	1,806
1870	2,309
1880	3,790
1890	6,143
1900	8,042
1910	10,183
1920	10,897
1930	12,471
1940	13,484
1950	14,745
1960	15,288
1970	14,888
1980	15,575

LEBANON

1950	4,614
1960	9,299
1970	9,725
1980	11,134

MANCHESTER

1790	362
1800	557
1810	615
1820	761
1830	887
1840	3,235
1850	13,932
1860	20,107
1870	23,536
1880	32,630
1890	44,126
1900	56,987
1910	70,063
1920	78,384
1930	76,834
1940	77,685
1950	82,732

1960	88,282
1970	87,754
1980	90,936

NASHUA

1790	632
1800	862
1810	1,049
1820	1,142
1830	2,014
1840	6,054
1850	5,820
1860	10,065
1870	10,543
1880	13,397
1890	19,311
1900	23,898
1910	26,005
1920	28,379
1930	31,463
1940	32,927
1950	34,669
1960	39,096
1970	55,820
1980	67,865

PORTSMOUTH

1790	4,720
1800	5,339
1810	6,934
1820	7,327
1830	8,026
1840	7,887
1850	9,738
1860	9,335
1870	9,211
1880	9,690
1890	9,827
1900	10,637
1910	11,269
1920	13,569
1930	14,495
1940	14,821
1950	18,830
1960	26,900
1970	25,717
1980	26,254

ROCHESTER

1790	2,857
1800	2,646
1810	2,118
1820	2,471
1830	2,155
1840	2,431
1850	3,006
1860	3,384
1870	4,103
1880	5,784
1890	7,396
1900	8,466
1910	8,868
1920	9,673
1930	10,209
1940	12,012
1950	13,776
1960	15,927
1970	17,938
1980	21,560

SOMERSWORTH

1850	4,943
1860	4,787
1870	4,504
1880	5,586
1890	6,207
1900	7,023
1910	6,704
1920	6,688
1930	5,680
1940	6,136
1950	6,927
1960	8,529
1970	9,026
1980	10,350

County Subdivisions	1980	1970
The State	920 610	737 681
Belknap County	42 884	32 367
Alton town	2 440	1 647
Barnstead town	2 292	1 119
Belmont town	4 026	2 493
Center Harbor town	808	540
Gilford town	4 841	3 219
Gilmanton town	1 941	1 010
Laconia city	15 575	14 888
Meredith town	4 646	2 904
Meredith (CDP)	1 202	1 017
New Hampton town	1 249	946
Sanbornton town	1 679	1 022
Tilton town	3 387	2 579
Tilton–Northfield (CDP) (pt.)	1 233	1 105
Carroll County	27 931	18 548
Albany town	383	259
Bartlett town	1 566	1 098
Brookfield town	385	198
Chatham town	189	134
Conway town	7 158	4 865
Conway (CDP)	1 781	1 489
North Conway (CDP)	2 104	1 723
Eaton town	256	221
Effingham town	599	360
Freedom town	720	387
Hale's location	2	–
Hart's location	27	7
Jackson town	642	404
Madison town	1 051	572
Moultonborough town	2 206	1 310
Ossipee town	2 465	1 647
Sandwich town	905	666
Tamworth town	1 672	1 054
Tuftonboro town	1 500	910
Wakefield town	2 237	1 420
Wolfeboro town	3 968	3 036
Wolfeboro (CDP)	2 271	1 718
Cheshire County	62 116	52 364
Alstead town	1 461	1 185
Chesterfield town	2 561	1 817
Dublin town	1 303	837
Fitzwilliam town	1 795	1 362
Gilsum town	652	570
Harrisville town	860	584
Hinsdale town	3 631	3 276
Hinsdale (CDP)	1 546	1 059
Jaffrey town	4 349	3 353
Jaffrey (CDP)	2 684	1 922
Keene city	21 449	20 467
Marlborough town	1 846	1 671
Marlborough (CDP)	1 184	1 231
Marlow town	542	390
Nelson town	442	304
Richmond town	518	287
Rindge town	3 375	2 175
Roxbury town	190	161
Stoddard town	482	242
Sullivan town	585	376
Surry town	656	507
Swanzey town	5 183	4 254
West Swanzey (CDP)	1 022	...
Troy town	2 131	1 713
Troy (CDP)	1 318	1 123
Walpole town	3 188	2 966
Westmoreland town	1 452	998
Winchester town	3 465	2 869
Winchester (CDP)	1 732	...
Coos County[1]	35 147	34 291
Atkinson and Gilmanton Academy grant	–	4
Beans grant	–	–
Beans purchase	–	–
Berlin city	13 084	15 256
Cambridge township	5	4
Carroll town	647	310
Chandlers purchase	–	–
Clarksville town	262	166
Colebrook town	2 459	2 094
Colebrook (CDP)	1 131	1 070
Columbia town	673	467
Crawfords purchase	–	–
Cutts grant	–	–
Dalton town	672	425
Dixs grant	–	–
Dixville township	36	18
Dummer town	390	225
Errol town	313	199
Ervings location	–	–
Gorham town	3 322	2 998
Gorham (CDP)	2 180	2 020
Greens grant	–	–
Hadleys purchase	–	–
Jefferson town	803	714
Kilkenny township	–	–
Lancaster town	3 401	3 166

County Subdivisions	1980	1970
Coos County—Con.		
Lancaster town—Con.		
Lancaster (CDP)	2 134	2 120
Low and Burbanks grant	1	–
Martins location	–	–
Milan town	1 013	713
Millsfield township	7	18
Northumberland town	2 520	2 493
Groveton (CDP)	1 389	1 597
Odell township	–	3
Pinkhams grant	30	16
Pittsburg town	780	726
Randolph town	274	169
Sargents purchase	1	–
Second College grant	2	–
Shelburne town	318	199
Stark town	470	343
Stewartstown town	943	1 008
Stratford town	989	980
Success township	–	2
Thompson and Meserves purchase	2	–
Wentworth location[1]	49	37
Whitefield town	1 681	1 538
Whitefield (CDP)	1 005	1 093
Grafton County[2]	65 806	54 914
Alexandria town	706	466
Ashland town	1 807	1 599
Ashland (CDP)	1 479	1 391
Bath town	761	607
Benton town	333	194
Bethlehem town	1 784	1 142
Bridgewater town	606	398
Bristol town	2 198	1 670
Bristol (CDP)	1 258	1 080
Campton town	1 694	1 171
Canaan town	2 456	1 923
Dorchester town	244	141
Easton town	124	92
Ellsworth town	53	13
Enfield town	3 175	2 345
Enfield (CDP)	1 581	1 408
Franconia town	743	655
Grafton town	739	370
Groton town	255	120
Hanover town	9 119	8 494
Hanover (CDP)	6 861	6 147
Haverhill town	3 445	3 090
Woodsville (CDP)	1 195	1 336
Hebron town	349	234
Holderness town	1 586	1 048
Landaff town	266	292
Lebanon city	11 134	9 725
Lincoln town	1 313	1 341
Lisbon town	1 517	1 480
Lisbon (CDP)	1 151	1 247
Littleton town	5 558	5 290
Littleton (CDP)	4 480	4 180
Livermore town[2]	–	...
Lyman town	281	213
Lyme town	1 289	1 112
Monroe town	619	385
Orange town	197	103
Orford town	928	793
Piermont town	507	462
Plymouth town	5 094	4 225
Plymouth (CDP)	3 628	3 109
Rumney town	1 212	870
Sugar Hill town	397	336
Thornton town	952	594
Warren town	650	539
Waterville Valley town	180	109
Wentworth town	527	376
Woodstock town	1 008	897
Hillsborough County	276 608	223 941
Amherst town	8 243	4 605
Antrim town	2 208	2 122
Antrim (CDP)	1 142	...
Bedford town	9 481	5 859
Bennington town	890	639
Brookline town	1 766	1 167
Deering town	1 041	578
Francestown town	830	525
Goffstown town	11 315	9 284
Greenfield town	972	1 058
Greenville town	1 988	1 587
Greenville (CDP)	1 447	1 332
Hancock town	1 193	909
Hillsborough town	3 437	2 775
Hillsborough (CDP)	1 797	1 784
Hollis town	4 679	2 616
Hudson town	14 022	10 638
Hudson (CDP)	6 248	...
Litchfield town	4 150	1 420
Lyndeborough town	1 070	789
Manchester city	90 936	87 754
Mason town	792	518

County Subdivisions

	1980	1970
Hillsborough County—Con.		
Merrimack town	15 406	8 595
East Merrimack (CDP)	2 052	...
Milford town	8 685	6 622
Milford (CDP)	6 269	4 997
Wilton (CDP) (pt.)	89	84
Mont Vernon town	1 444	906
Nashua city	67 865	55 820
New Boston town	1 928	1 390
New Ipswich town	2 433	1 803
Pelham town	8 090	5 408
Peterborough town	4 895	3 807
Peterborough (CDP)	2 568	2 078
Sharon town	184	136
Temple town	692	441
Weare town	3 232	1 851
Wilton town	2 669	2 276
Wilton (CDP) (pt.)	1 221	1 077
Windsor town	72	43
Merrimack County	98 302	80 925
Allenstown town	4 398	2 732
Suncook (CDP) (pt.)	1 931	1 756
Andover town	1 587	1 138
Boscawen town	3 435	3 162
Bow town	4 015	2 479
Bradford town	1 115	679
Canterbury town	1 410	895
Chichester town	1 492	1 083
Concord city	30 400	30 022
Danbury town	680	489
Dunbarton town	1 174	825
Epsom town	2 743	1 469
Franklin city	7 901	7 292
Henniker town	3 246	2 348
Henniker (CDP)	1 538	...
Hill town	736	450
Hooksett town	7 303	5 564
Hooksett (CDP)	1 868	1 303
Hopkinton town	3 861	3 007
Contoocook (CDP)	1 499	...
Loudon town	2 454	1 707
Newbury town	961	509
New London town	2 935	2 236
New London (CDP)	1 335	1 347
Northfield town	3 051	2 193
Tilton–Northfield (CDP) (pt.)	1 341	1 315
Pembroke town	4 861	4 261
Suncook (CDP) (pt.)	2 767	2 524
Pittsfield town	2 889	2 517
Pittsfield (CDP)	1 584	1 662
Salisbury town	781	589
Sutton town	1 091	642
Warner town	1 963	1 441
Webster town	1 095	680
Wilmot town	725	516
Rockingham County	190 345	138 951
Atkinson town	4 397	2 291
Auburn town	2 883	2 035
Brentwood town	2 004	1 468
Candia town	2 989	1 997
Chester town	2 006	1 382
Danville town	1 318	924
Deerfield town	1 979	1 178
Derry town	18 875	11 712
Derry (CDP)	12 248	6 090
East Kingston town	1 135	838
Epping town	3 460	2 356
Epping (CDP)	1 384	1 097
Exeter town	11 024	8 892
Exeter (CDP)	8 947	6 439
Fremont town	1 333	993
Greenland town	2 129	1 784
Hampstead town	3 785	2 401
Hampton town	10 493	8 011
Hampton (CDP)	6 779	5 407
Hampton Falls town	1 372	1 254
Kensington town	1 322	1 044
Kingston town	4 111	2 882
Londonderry town	13 598	5 346
New Castle town	936	975
Newfields town	817	843
Newington town	716	798
Newmarket town	4 290	3 361
Newmarket (CDP)	3 749	2 645
Newton town	3 068	1 920
North Hampton town	3 425	3 259
Northwood town	2 175	1 526
Nottingham town	1 952	952
Plaistow town	5 609	4 712
Portsmouth city	26 254	25 717
Raymond town	5 453	3 003
Raymond (CDP)	1 192	...
Rye town	4 508	4 083
Salem town	24 124	20 142
Sandown town	2 057	741
Seabrook town	5 917	3 053

County Subdivisions

	1980	1970
Rockingham County—Con.		
South Hampton town	660	558
Stratham town	2 507	1 512
Windham town	5 664	3 008
Strafford County	85 408	70 431
Barrington town	4 404	1 865
Dover city	22 377	20 850
Durham town	10 652	8 869
Durham (CDP)	8 448	7 221
Farmington town	4 630	3 588
Farmington (CDP)	3 284	2 884
Lee town	2 111	1 481
Madbury town	987	704
Middleton town	734	430
Milton town	2 438	1 859
New Durham town	1 183	583
Rochester city	21 560	17 938
Rollinsford town	2 319	2 273
Rollinsford (CDP)	1 173	...
Somersworth city	10 350	9 026
Strafford town	1 663	965
Sullivan County	36 063	30 949
Acworth town	590	459
Charlestown town	4 417	3 274
Charlestown (CDP)	1 294	1 285
Claremont city	14 557	14 221
Cornish town	1 390	1 268
Croydon town	457	396
Goshen town	549	395
Grantham town	704	366
Langdon town	437	337
Lempster town	637	360
Newport town	6 229	5 899
Newport (CDP)	4 388	3 296
Plainfield town	1 749	1 323
Springfield town	532	310
Sunapee town	2 312	1 384
Unity town	1 092	709
Washington town	411	248

NEW JERSEY

New Jersey takes its name from the island of Jersey, in the English Channel, and was so named in honor of Sir George Carteret, one of the early proprietors of the province, who had distinguished himself as governor of that island.

The region now constituting New Jersey was included in the grant conveyed by the first charter of Virginia (1606); and its northern portion was embraced in the grant to the Plymouth Company in 1620.

The English title was based on the discoveries of John Cabot, who had visited the coasts of Newfoundland and the mainland in 1497. In 1609 Henry Hudson, sailing under the Dutch flag, coasted the shores of what is now New Jersey. The Dutch claimed the region as a part of New Netherland (now New York), and in about the year 1620 made settlements along the west shore of the lower Hudson; in 1623 they built Fort Nassau, near Gloucester. Swedes also settled on the Delaware River, but were brought under the jurisdiction of the Dutch by the governor of New Netherland.

In 1664 New Netherland, including the present area of New Jersey, passed into the hands of the English and was granted by Charles II to the Duke of York. Before the latter took possession he conveyed to Lord Berkeley and Sir George Carteret the territory lying between the Hudson and the Delaware and limited on the north by a line differing somewhat, but not greatly, from the present boundary between New Jersey and New York.

The first permanent English settlement was probably that made at Elizabethtown about 1664. Not long after taking possession of the province, Berkeley and Carteret established a government which included a popular assembly.

In 1673 New York (formerland New Netherland) and New Jersey were surrendered to the Dutch, in whose possession they remained until early in the following year, when both provinces were again transferred to the English.

In 1673 Berkeley sold his interest in New Jersey to two Quakers, who in the following year sold it to William Penn and others. In July, 1676, was executed the "Quintipartite deed," by which the province was divided by a line drawn from Little Egg Harbor (about 15 miles north of Atlantic City) to the most northerly boundary point on the Delaware. Carteret retained the eastern part, known as East New Jersey, while the Quakers took the western portion, called West New Jersey. In 1682 East New Jersey was sold to William Penn (who in the preceding year had obtained a royal grant of Pennsylvania) and other Quakers. In 1702 the proprietors of both colonies ceded their right of government to the English Crown, and East and West New Jersey were united and placed under the governor of New York, New Jersey retaining its separate assembly. In 1738 the colony was given a separate governor.

The present boundary between New Jersey and New York was established in 1772 or 1773.

New Jersey was one of the original thirteen states.

COUNTY LOCATION INDEX

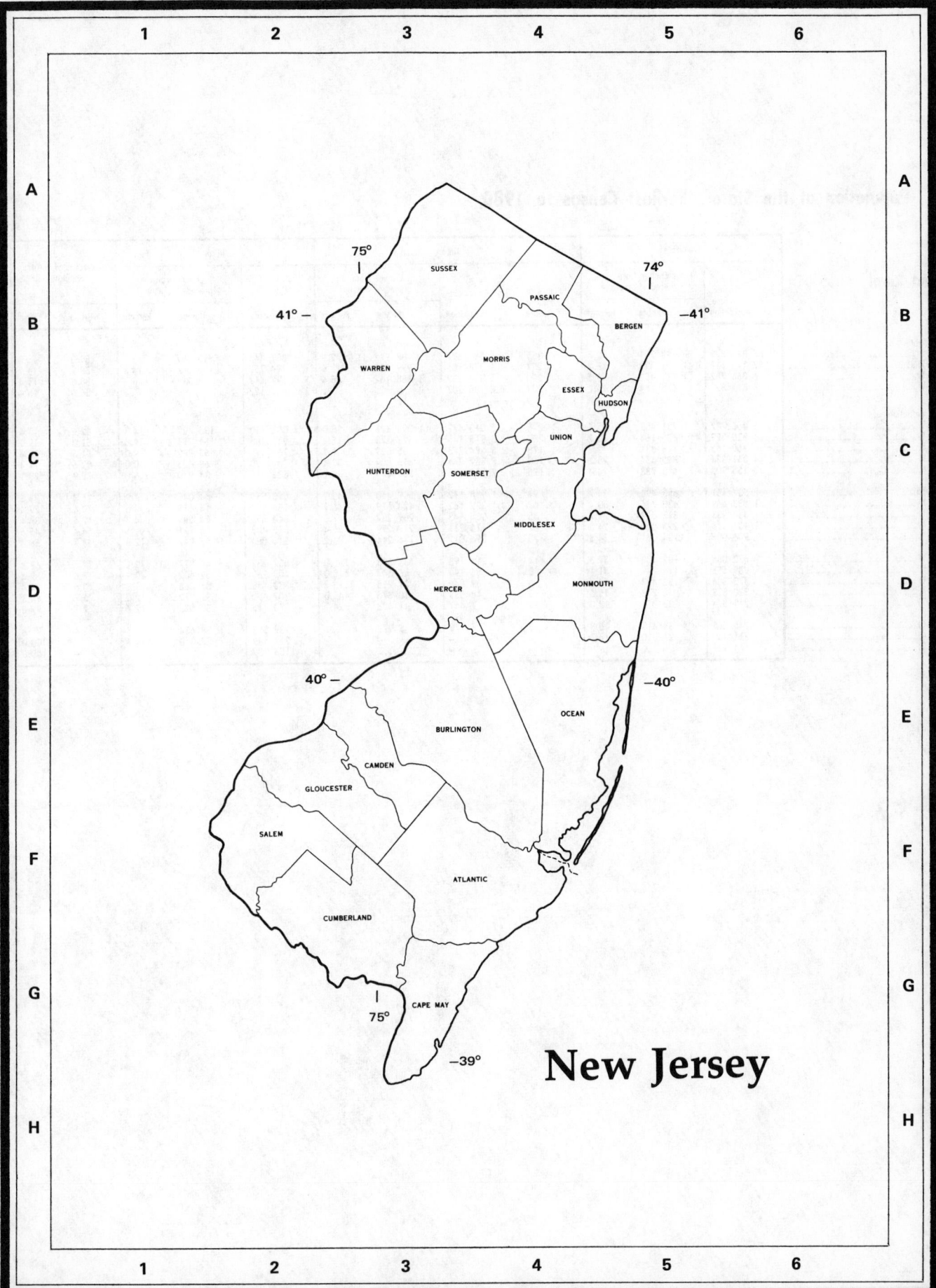

New Jersey

Population of the State: Earliest Census to 1980

Urban and Rural

	The State			Urban				Rural				Percent of total population	
	Total population	Change from preceding census		Places of 2,500 or more	Population	Change from preceding census		Population	Change from preceding census			Urban	Rural
		Number	Percent			Number	Percent		Number	Percent			
Current urban definition:													
1980 (Apr. 1)	7 364 823	193 711	2.7	355	6 557 377	183 972	2.9	807 446	12 687	1.6		89.0	11.0
1970 (Apr. 1)	ʾ7 171 112	1 104 330	18.2	287	6 373 405	999 036	18.6	794 759	102 346	14.8		88.9	11.1
1960 (Apr. 1)	6 066 782	1 231 453	25.5	290	5 374 369	1 188 162	28.4	692 413	43 291	6.7		88.6	11.4
1950 (Apr. 1)	4 835 329	675 164	16.2	209	4 186 207	...	...	649 122	...	...		86.6	13.4
Previous urban definition:													
1960 (Apr. 1)	6 066 782	1 231 453	25.5	278	5 013 472	1 095 326	28.0	1 053 310	136 127	14.8		82.6	17.4
1950 (Apr. 1)	4 835 329	675 164	16.2	209	3 918 146	523 373	15.4	917 183	151 791	19.8		81.0	19.0
1940 (Apr. 1)	4 160 165	118 831	2.9	178	3 394 773	55 529	1.7	765 392	63 302	9.0		81.6	18.4
1930 (Apr. 1)	4 041 334	885 434	28.1	169	3 339 244	816 809	32.4	702 090	68 625	10.8		82.6	17.4
1920 (Jan. 1)	3 155 900	618 733	24.4	125	2 522 435	583 823	30.1	633 465	34 910	5.8		79.9	20.1
1910 (Apr. 15)	2 537 167	653 498	34.7	91	1 938 612	609 450	45.9	598 555	44 048	7.9		76.4	23.6
1900 (June 1)	1 883 669	438 736	30.4	67	1 329 162	424 619	46.9	554 507	14 117	2.6		70.6	29.4
1890 (June 1)	1 444 933	313 817	27.7	45	904 543	289 232	47.0	540 390	24 585	4.8		62.6	37.4
1880 (June 1)	1 131 116	225 020	24.8	37	615 311	219 299	55.4	515 805	5 721	1.1		54.4	45.6
1870 (June 1)	906 096	234 061	34.8	23	396 012	176 214	80.2	510 084	57 847	12.8		43.7	56.3
1860 (June 1)	672 035	182 480	37.3	14	219 798	133 603	155.0	452 237	48 877	12.1		32.7	67.3
1850 (June 1)	489 555	116 249	31.1	8	86 195	46 647	118.0	403 360	69 602	20.9		17.6	82.4
1840 (June 1)	373 306	52 483	16.4	6	39 548	21 215	115.7	333 758	31 268	10.3		10.6	89.4
1830 (June 1)	320 823	43 248	15.6	3	18 333	10 876	145.8	302 490	32 372	12.0		5.7	94.3
1820 (Aug. 7)	277 575	32 013	13.0	2	7 457	1 478	24.7	270 118	30 535	12.7		2.7	97.3
1810 (Aug. 6)	245 562	34 413	16.3	2	5 979	5 979	...	239 583	28 434	13.5		2.4	97.6
1800 (Aug. 4)	211 149	27 010	14.7	–	–	–	–	211 149	27 010	14.7		–	100.0
1790 (Aug. 2)	184 139	...	...	–	–	...	...	184 139	...	...		–	100.0

ATLANTIC

1840	8,726
1850	8,961
1860	11,786
1870	14,093
1880	18,704
1890	28,836
1900	46,402
1910	71,894
1920	83,914
1930	124,893
1940	124,066
1950	132,399
1960	160,880
1970	175,043
1980	194,119

BERGEN

1790	12,601
1800	15,156
1810	16,603
1820	18,178
1830	22,412
1840	13,223
1850	14,725
1860	21,618
1870	30,122
1880	36,786
1890	47,266
1900	78,441
1910	138,002
1920	210,703
1930	364,977
1940	409,646
1950	539,139
1960	780,255
1970	897,148
1980	845,385

BURLINGTON

1790	18,095
1800	21,521
1810	24,979
1820	28,822
1830	31,107
1840	32,831
1850	43,203
1860	49,730
1870	53,639
1880	55,402
1890	58,528
1900	58,241
1910	66,565
1920	81,770
1930	93,541
1940	93,013
1950	135,910
1960	224,449
1970	323,132
1980	362,542

CAMDEN

1850	25,422
1860	34,457
1870	46,193
1880	62,942
1890	87,687
1900	107,643
1910	142,029
1920	190,508
1930	252,312
1940	255,727
1950	300,743

1960	392,035
1970	456,291
1980	471,650

CAPE MAY

1790	2,571
1800	3,066
1810	3,632
1820	4,265
1830	4,936
1840	5,324
1850	6,433
1860	7,130
1870	8,349
1880	9,765
1890	11,268
1900	13,201
1910	19,745
1920	19,460
1930	29,486
1940	28,919
1950	37,131
1960	48,555
1970	59,554
1980	82,266

CUMBERLAND

1790	8,248
1800	9,529
1810	12,670
1820	12,668
1830	14,093
1840	14,374
1850	17,189
1860	22,605
1870	34,665
1880	37,687
1890	45,438
1900	51,193
1910	55,153
1920	61,348
1930	69,895
1940	73,184
1950	88,597
1960	106,850
1970	121,374
1980	132,866

ESSEX

1790	17,785
1800	22,269
1810	25,984
1820	30,793
1830	41,911
1840	44,621
1850	73,950
1860	98,877
1870	143,839
1880	189,929
1890	256,098
1900	359,053
1910	512,886
1920	652,089
1930	833,513
1940	837,340
1950	905,949
1960	923,545
1970	932,526
1980	851,116

GLOUCESTER

1790	13,363

1800	16,115
1810	19,744
1820	23,089
1830	28,431
1840	25,438
1850	14,655
1860	18,444
1870	21,562
1880	25,886
1890	28,649
1900	31,905
1910	37,368
1920	48,224
1930	70,802
1940	72,219
1950	91,727
1960	134,840
1970	172,681
1980	199,917

HUDSON

1840	9,483
1850	21,822
1860	62,717
1870	129,067
1880	187,944
1890	275,126
1900	386,048
1910	537,231
1920	629,154
1930	690,730
1940	652,040
1950	647,437
1960	610,734
1970	607,839
1980	556,972

HUNTERDON

1790	20,153
1800	21,261
1810	24,556
1820	28,604
1830	31,060
1840	24,789
1850	28,990
1860	33,654
1870	36,963
1880	38,570
1890	35,335
1900	34,507
1910	33,569
1920	32,885
1930	34,728
1940	36,766
1950	42,736
1960	54,107
1970	69,718
1980	87,361

MERCER

1840	21,502
1850	27,992
1860	37,419
1870	46,386
1880	58,061
1890	79,978
1900	95,365
1910	125,657
1920	159,881
1930	187,143
1940	197,318
1950	229,781
1960	266,392
1970	304,116

1980	307,863

MIDDLESEX

1790	15,956
1800	17,890
1810	20,381
1820	21,470
1830	23,157
1840	21,893
1850	28,635
1860	34,812
1870	45,029
1880	52,286
1890	61,754
1900	79,762
1910	114,426
1920	162,334
1930	212,208
1940	217,077
1950	264,872
1960	433,856
1970	583,813
1980	595,893

MONMOUTH

1790	16,198
1800	19,872
1810	22,150
1820	25,038
1830	29,233
1840	32,909
1850	30,313
1860	39,346
1870	46,195
1880	55,538
1890	69,128
1900	82,057
1910	94,734
1920	104,925
1930	147,209
1940	161,238
1950	225,327
1960	334,401
1970	461,849
1980	503,173

MORRIS

1790	16,216
1800	17,750
1810	21,828
1820	21,368
1830	23,666
1840	25,844
1850	30,158
1860	34,677
1870	43,137
1880	50,861
1890	54,101
1900	65,156
1910	74,704
1920	82,694
1930	110,445
1940	125,732
1950	164,371
1960	261,620
1970	383,454
1980	407,630

OCEAN

1850	10,032
1860	11,176
1870	13,628

1880	14,445
1890	15,974
1900	19,747
1910	21,318
1920	22,155
1930	33,069
1940	37,706
1950	56,622
1960	108,241
1970	208,470
1980	346,038

PASSAIC

1840	16,734
1850	22,569
1860	29,013
1870	46,416
1880	68,860
1890	105,046
1900	155,202
1910	215,902
1920	259,174
1930	302,129
1940	309,353
1950	337,093
1960	408,618
1970	460,782
1980	447,585

SALEM

1790	10,437
1800	11,371
1810	12,761
1820	14,022
1830	14,155
1840	16,024
1850	19,467
1860	22,458
1870	23,940
1880	24,579
1890	25,151
1900	25,530
1910	26,999
1920	36,572
1930	36,834
1940	42,274
1950	49,508
1960	18,711
1970	60,346
1980	64,676

SOMERSET

1790	12,296
1800	12,815
1810	14,725
1820	16,605
1830	17,689
1840	17,455
1850	19,692
1860	22,057
1870	23,510
1880	27,162
1890	28,311
1900	32,948
1910	38,820
1920	47,991
1930	65,132
1940	74,390
1950	99,052
1960	143,913
1970	198,372
1980	203,129

SUSSEX

1790	19,500
1800	22,534
1810	25,549
1820	32,752
1830	20,346
1840	21,770
1850	22,989
1860	23,846
1870	23,168
1880	23,539
1890	22,259
1900	24,134
1910	26,781
1920	24,905
1930	27,830
1940	29,632
1950	34,423
1960	49,255
1970	77,528
1980	116,119

UNION

1860	27,780
1870	41,859
1880	55,571
1890	72,467
1900	99,353
1910	140,197
1920	200,157
1930	305,209
1940	328,344
1950	398,138
1960	504,255
1970	543,116
1980	504,094

WARREN

1830	18,627
1840	20,366
1850	22,358
1860	28,433
1870	34,336
1880	36,589
1890	36,553
1900	37,781
1910	43,187
1920	43,057
1930	49,319
1940	50,181
1950	54,374
1960	62,220
1970	73,879
1980	84,429

ASBURY PARK

1900	4,148
1910	10,150
1920	12,400
1930	14,981
1940	14,617
1950	17,094
1960	17,336
1970	16,533
1980	17,015

ATLANTIC CITY

1860	687
1870	1,043
1880	5,477
1890	13,055
1900	27,838
1910	46,150
1920	50,707
1930	66,198
1940	64,094
1950	61,657
1960	59,544
1970	47,859
1980	40,199

BAYONNE

1870	3,834
1880	9,372
1890	19,033
1900	32,722
1910	55,545
1920	76,754
1930	88,979
1940	79,198
1950	77,203
1960	74,215
1970	72,743
1980	65,047

BELLEVILLE

1920	15,660
1930	26,970
1940	28,167
1950	32,019
1960	35,005
1970	37,629
1980	35,367

BELLMAWR

1930	1,123
1940	1,250
1950	5,213
1960	11,853
1970	15,618
1980	13,721

BERGENFIELD

1900	729
1910	1,991
1920	3,667
1930	8,816
1940	10,275
1950	17,647
1960	27,203
1970	33,131
1980	25,568

BLOOMFIELD

1900	9,668
1910	15,070
1920	22,019
1930	38,077
1940	41,623
1950	49,307
1960	51,867
1970	52,029
1980	47,792

BRIDGETON

1870	6,380
1880	8,772
1890	11,424
1900	13,913
1910	14,209
1920	14,323
1930	15,699
1940	15,992
1950	18,378
1960	20,996
1970	20,435
1980	18,795

BURLINGTON

1850	4,536
1860	5,174
1870	5,817
1880	6,090
1890	7,264
1900	7,392
1910	8,336
1920	9,049
1930	10,844
1940	10,905
1950	12,051
1960	12,687
1970	12,010
1980	10,246

CAMDEN

1840	3,371
1850	9,479
1860	14,358
1870	20,045
1880	41,659
1890	58,313
1900	75,935
1910	94,538
1920	116,309
1930	118,700
1940	117,536
1950	124,555
1960	117,159
1970	102,551
1980	84,910

CARTERET

1910	5,786
1920	11,047
1930	13,339
1940	11,976
1950	13,030
1960	20,502
1970	23,137
1980	20,598

CLIFFSIDE PARK

1900	968
1910	3,394
1920	5,709
1930	15,267
1940	16,892
1950	17,116
1960	17,642
1970	18,891
1980	21,464

CLIFTON

1920	26,470
1930	48,875
1940	49,827
1950	64,511
1960	82,084
1970	82,437
1980	74,388

COLLINGSWOOD

1890	539
1900	1,633
1910	4,795
1920	8,714
1930	12,723
1940	12,685
1950	15,800
1960	17,370
1970	17,422
1980	15,838

DOVER

1880	2,958
1900	5,938
1910	7,468
1920	9,803
1930	10,031
1940	10,491
1950	11,174
1960	13,034
1970	15,039
1980	14,681

DUMONT

1900	643
1910	1,783
1920	2,537
1930	5,861
1940	7,556
1950	13,013
1960	18,882
1970	20,155
1980	18,334

EAST ORANGE

1890	13,282
1900	21,506
1910	34,371
1920	50,710
1930	68,020
1940	68,945
1950	79,340
1960	77,259
1970	75,471
1980	77,690

EAST PATERSON

1920	2,441
1930	4,779
1940	4,937
1950	15,386
1960	19,344
1970	22,749

EATONTOWN

1930	1,938
1940	1,758
1950	3,044
1960	10,334
1970	14,619
1980	12,703

ELIZABETH

1810	2,977
1820	3,515
1830	3,455
1840	4,184
1850	5,583
1860	11,567
1870	20,832
1880	28,229
1890	37,764
1900	52,130
1910	73,409
1920	95,783
1930	114,589
1940	109,912
1950	112,817
1960	107,698
1970	112,654
1980	106,201

ENGLEWOOD

1900	6,253
1910	9,924
1920	11,627
1930	17,805
1940	18,966
1950	23,145
1960	26,057
1970	24,985
1980	23,701

FAIR LAWN

1930	5,990
1940	9,017
1950	23,885
1960	36,421
1970	38,040
1980	32,229

FAIRVIEW

1900	1,003
1910	2,441
1920	4,882
1930	9,067
1940	8,770
1950	8,661
1960	9,399
1970	10,698
1980	10,519

FORT LEE

1880	1,424
1890	1,253

1910	4,472
1920	5,761
1930	8,759
1940	9,468
1950	11,648
1960	21,815
1970	30,631
1980	32,449

FREEHOLD

1880	2,432
1890	2,932
1900	2,934
1910	3,233
1920	4,768
1930	6,894
1940	6,952
1950	7,550
1960	9,140
1970	10,545
1980	10,020

GARFIELD

1890	1,028
1900	3,504
1910	10,213
1920	19,381
1930	29,739
1940	28,044
1950	27,550
1960	29,253
1970	30,797
1980	26,803

GLASSBORO

1930	4,799
1940	4,925
1950	5,867
1960	10,253
1970	12,938
1980	14,574

GLEN ROCK

1900	613
1910	1,055
1920	2,181
1930	4,369
1940	5,177
1950	7,145
1960	12,896
1970	13,011
1980	11,497

GLOUCESTER CITY

1870	3,682
1880	5,347
1890	6,564
1900	6,840
1910	9,462
1920	12,162
1930	13,796
1940	13,692
1950	14,357
1960	15,511
1970	14,707
1980	13,121

HACKENSACK

1880	4,248
1890	6,004
1900	9,443
1910	14,050
1920	17,667
1930	24,568
1940	26,279
1950	29,219
1960	30,521
1970	36,008
1980	36,039

HADDONFIELD

1850	944
1860	(NA)
1870	1,075
1880	1,480
1890	2,502
1900	2,776
1910	4,142
1920	5,646
1930	8,857
1940	9,742
1950	10,495
1960	13,201
1970	13,118
1980	12,337

HAMMONTON

1900	3,481
1910	5,088
1920	6,417
1930	7,656
1940	7,668
1950	8,411
1960	9,854
1970	11,464
1980	12,298

HARRISON

1870	4,129
1880	6,898
1890	8,338
1900	10,596
1910	14,498
1920	15,721
1930	15,601
1940	14,171
1950	13,490
1960	11,743
1970	11,811
1980	12,242

HASBROUCK HEIGHTS

1900	1,255
1910	2,155
1920	2,895
1930	5,658
1940	6,716
1950	9,181
1960	13,046
1970	13,651
1980	12,166

HAWTHORNE

1900	2,096
1910	3,400
1920	5,135
1930	11,868
1940	12,610
1950	14,816
1960	17,735
1970	19,173
1980	18,200

HIGHLAND PARK

1910	1,517
1920	4,866
1930	8,691
1940	9,002
1950	9,721
1960	11,049
1970	14,385
1980	13,396

HILLSDALE

1900	891
1910	1,072
1920	1,720
1930	2,959
1940	3,438
1950	4,127
1960	8,734
1970	11,768
1980	10,495

HOBOKEN

1860	9,662
1870	20,297
1880	30,999
1890	43,648
1900	59,364
1910	70,324
1920	68,166
1930	59,261
1940	50,115
1950	50,676
1960	48,441
1970	45,380
1980	43,460

HOPATCONG

1930	534
1940	660
1950	1,173
1960	3,391
1970	9,052
1980	15,531

IRVINGTON

1880	1,677
1890	(NA)
1900	5,255
1910	11,877
1920	25,480
1930	56,733
1940	55,328
1950	59,201
1960	59,379
1970	59,743
1980	61,493

JERSEY CITY

1840	3,072
1850	6,856
1860	29,226
1870	82,546
1880	120,722
1890	163,003
1900	206,433
1910	267,779
1920	298,103
1930	316,715
1940	301,173
1950	299,017
1960	276,101
1970	260,350
1980	223,532

KEANSBURG

1920	1,321
1930	2,190
1940	2,904
1950	5,559
1960	6,854
1970	9,720
1980	10,613

KEARNY

1900	10,896
1910	18,659
1920	26,724
1930	40,716
1940	39,467
1950	39,952
1960	37,472
1970	37,585
1980	35,735

LINDEN

1880	737
1890	936
1900	402
1910	610
1920	1,756
1930	21,206
1940	24,115
1950	30,644
1960	39,931
1970	41,409
1980	37,836

LINDENWOLD

1930	2,523
1940	2,552
1950	3,479
1960	7,335
1970	12,199
1980	18,196

LODI

1890	998
1900	1,917
1910	4,138
1920	8,175
1930	11,549
1940	11,552
1950	15,392
1960	23,502
1970	25,163
1980	23,956

LONG BRANCH

1880	3,833
1890	7,231
1900	8,872
1910	13,298
1920	13,521
1930	18,399
1940	17,408
1950	23,090
1960	26,228
1970	31,774
1980	29,818

MADISON

1880	1,756
1890	2,469
1900	3,754
1910	4,658
1920	5,523
1930	7,481
1940	7,944
1950	10,417
1960	15,122
1970	16,710
1980	15,357

MANVILLE

1930	5,441
1940	6,065
1950	8,597
1960	10,955
1970	13,029
1980	11,278

METUCHEN

1890	770
1900	1,786
1910	2,138
1920	3,334
1930	5,748
1940	6,557
1950	9,879
1960	14,041
1970	16,031
1980	13,762

MIDDLESEX

1920	1,852
1930	3,504
1940	3,763
1950	5,943
1960	10,520
1970	15,038
1980	13,480

MILLVILLE

1870	6,101
1880	7,660
1890	10,002
1900	10,583
1910	12,451
1920	14,691
1930	14,705
1940	14,806
1950	16,041
1960	19,096
1970	21,366
1980	24,815

MONTCLAIR

1900	13,962
1910	21,550
1920	28,810
1930	42,017
1940	39,807
1950	43,927
1960	43,129
1970	44,043
1980	38,321

MORRISTOWN

1880	5,418
1890	8,156
1900	11,267
1910	12,507
1920	12,548
1930	15,197
1940	15,270
1950	17,124
1960	17,712
1970	17,662
1980	16,614

NEWARK

1830	10,953
1840	17,290
1850	38,984
1860	71,941
1870	105,059
1880	136,508
1890	181,830
1900	246,070
1910	347,469
1920	414,524
1930	442,337
1940	429,760
1950	438,776
1960	438,776
1970	405,220
1980	329,248

NEW BRUNSWICK

1860	11,256
1870	15,058
1880	17,166
1890	18,603
1900	20,006
1910	23,388
1920	32,779
1930	34,555
1940	33,180
1950	38,811
1960	40,139
1970	41,885
1980	41,442

NEW MILFORD

1930	2,556
1940	3,215
1950	6,006
1960	18,810
1970	19,149
1980	16,876

NEW PROVIDENCE

1900	565
1910	873
1920	1,203
1930	1,918
1940	2,374
1950	3,380
1960	10,243

1970	13,796	1970	32,566			
1980	12,426	1980	31,136			

PHILLIPSBURG

1870	5,932
1880	7,181
1890	8,644
1900	10,052
1910	13,903
1920	16,923
1930	19,255
1940	18,314
1950	18,919
1960	18,502
1970	17,849
1980	16,647

RAHWAY

1860	7,103
1870	6,258
1880	6,455
1890	7,105
1900	7,935
1910	9,337
1920	11,042
1930	16,011
1940	17,498
1950	21,290
1960	27,699
1970	29,144
1980	26,723

RINGWOOD

1920	1,025
1930	1,038
1940	977
1950	1,752
1960	4,182
1970	10,393
1980	12,625

NORTH ARLINGTON

1900	290
1910	437
1920	1,767
1930	8,263
1940	9,904
1950	15,970
1960	17,477
1970	18,096
1980	16,587

PALISADES PARK

1900	644
1910	1,411
1920	2,633
1930	7,065
1940	8,141
1950	9,635
1960	11,943
1970	13,351
1980	13,732

RIVER EDGE

1900	561
1910	736
1920	1,077
1930	2,210
1940	3,287
1950	9,204
1960	13,264
1970	12,850
1980	11,111

NORTH PLAINFIELD

1900	5,009
1910	6,117
1920	6,916
1930	9,760
1940	10,586
1950	12,766
1960	16,993
1970	21,796
1980	19,108

PARAMUS

1930	2,649
1940	3,688
1950	6,268
1960	23,238
1970	28,381
1980	26,474

PLAINFIELD

1870	5,095
1880	8,125
1890	11,267
1900	15,369
1910	20,550
1920	27,700
1930	34,422
1940	37,469
1950	42,366
1960	45,330
1970	46,862
1980	45,555

RAMSEY

1910	1,667
1920	2,090
1930	3,258
1940	3,566
1950	4,670
1960	9,527
1970	12,571
1980	12,899

ROSELLE

1900	1,652
1910	2,725
1920	5,737
1930	13,021
1940	13,537
1950	17,681
1960	21,032
1970	22,585
1980	20,641

NUTLEY

1910	6,009
1920	9,421
1930	20,752
1940	21,954
1950	26,992
1960	29,513
1970	31,913
1980	28,998

PASSAIC

1880	6,532
1890	13,028
1900	27,777
1910	54,773
1920	63,841
1930	62,959
1940	61,394
1950	57,702
1960	53,963
1970	55,124
1980	52,463

PLEASANTVILLE

1900	2,182
1910	4,390
1920	5,887
1930	11,580
1940	11,050
1950	11,938
1960	15,172
1970	14,007
1980	13,435

RED BANK

1870	2,086
1890	2,648
1900	5,428
1910	7,398
1920	9,251
1930	11,622
1940	10,974
1950	12,743
1960	12,482
1970	12,847
1980	12,031

ROSELLE PARK

1910	3,138
1920	5,438
1930	8,969
1940	9,661
1950	11,537
1960	12,546
1970	14,277
1980	13,377

OAKLAND

1910	568
1920	497
1930	735
1940	932
1950	1,817
1960	9,446
1970	14,420
1980	13,443

PATERSON

1840	7,596
1850	11,334
1860	19,586
1870	33,579
1880	51,031
1890	78,347
1900	105,171
1910	125,600
1920	135,875
1930	138,153
1940	139,656
1950	139,336
1960	143,663
1970	144,824
1980	137,970

POINT PLEASANT

1930	2,058
1940	2,082
1950	4,009
1960	10,182
1970	15,968
1980	17,747

RIDGEFIELD

1900	584
1910	966
1920	1,560
1930	4,671
1940	5,271
1950	8,312
1960	10,788
1970	11,308
1980	10,294

RUTHERFORD

1890	2,293
1900	4,411
1910	7,045
1920	9,497
1930	14,915
1940	15,466
1950	17,411
1960	20,473
1970	20,802
1980	19,068

OCEAN CITY

1890	452
1900	1,307
1910	1,950
1920	2,512
1930	5,525
1940	4,672
1950	6,040
1960	7,618
1970	10,575
1980	13,949

PERTH AMBOY

1850	1,865
1860	2,302
1870	2,861
1880	4,808
1890	9,512
1900	17,699
1910	32,121
1920	41,707
1930	43,516
1940	41,242
1950	41,330
1960	38,007
1970	38,798
1980	38,951

POMPTON LAKES

1900	847
1910	1,060
1920	2,008
1930	3,104
1940	3,189
1950	4,654
1960	9,445
1970	11,397
1980	10,660

RIDGEFIELD PARK

1900	1,987
1910	4,512
1920	8,575
1930	10,764
1940	11,277
1950	11,993
1960	12,701
1970	13,990
1980	12,738

SAYREVILLE

1930	8,658
1940	8,186
1950	10,338
1960	22,553
1970	32,508
1980	29,969

ORANGE

1860	8,877
1870	9,348
1880	13,207
1890	18,844
1900	24,141
1910	29,630
1920	33,268
1930	35,399
1940	35,717
1950	38,037
1960	35,789

PRINCETON

1870	2,798
1880	3,209
1890	3,422
1900	3,899
1910	5,136
1920	5,917
1930	6,992
1940	7,719
1950	12,230
1960	11,890
1970	12,311
1980	12,035

RIDGEWOOD

1890	1,047
1900	2,685
1910	5,416
1920	7,580
1930	12,188
1940	14,948
1950	17,481
1960	25,391
1970	27,547
1980	25,268

SECAUCUS

1900	1,626
1910	4,740
1920	5,423
1930	8,950
1940	9,754
1950	9,750

1960	12,154	1950	9,651	**VINELAND**		1950	37,683
1970	13,288	1960	14,264			1960	35,547
1980	13,719	1970	14,827	1880	2,519	1970	40,627
		1980	13,552	1890	3,822	1980	39,194
				1900	4,370		
SOMERS POINT				1910	5,282		
		TOTOWA		1920	6,432	**WEST ORANGE**	
1890	191			1930	7,556		
1900	308	1900	562	1940	7,914	1900	6,889
1910	604	1910	1,130	1950	8,155	1910	10,980
1920	843	1920	1,864	1960	37,685	1920	15,573
1930	2,073	1930	4,600	1970	47,399	1930	24,327
1940	1,992	1940	5,130	1980	53,753	1940	25,662
1950	2,400	1950	6,045			1950	28,605
1960	4,504	1960	10,897	**WALDWICK**		1960	39,895
1970	7,919	1970	11,580			1970	43,715
1980	10,330	1980	11,448	1920	1,296	1980	39,510
				1930	1,728		
SOMERVILLE		**TRENTON**		1940	2,475	**WEST PATERSON**	
				1950	3,963		
1870	2,236	1810	3,002	1960	10,495	1920	1,858
1880	3,105	1820	3,942	1970	12,313	1930	3,101
1890	3,861	1830	3,925	1980	10,802	1940	3,306
1900	4,843	1840	4,035			1950	3,931
1910	5,060	1850	6,461			1960	7,602
1920	6,718	1860	17,228	**WALLINGTON**		1970	11,692
1930	8,255	1870	22,874			1980	11,293
1940	8,720	1880	29,910	1900	1,812		
1950	11,571	1890	57,458	1910	3,448		
1960	12,458	1900	73,307	1920	5,715	**WESTWOOD**	
1970	13,652	1910	96,815	1930	9,063		
1980	11,973	1920	119,289	1940	8,981	1900	828
		1930	123,356	1950	8,910	1910	1,870
		1940	124,697	1960	9,261	1920	2,597
SOUTH PLAINFIELD		1950	128,009	1970	10,284	1930	4,861
		1960	114,167	1980	10,741	1940	5,388
1930	5,047	1970	104,786			1950	6,766
1940	5,379	1980	92,124			1960	9,046
1950	8,008			**WANAQUE**		1970	11,105
1960	17,879					1980	10,714
1970	21,142	**UNION CITY**		1920	2,916		
1980	20,521			1930	3,119		
		1870	4,640	1940	3,143	**WOODBURY**	
		1880	4,849	1950	4,222		
SOUTH RIVER		1890	10,643	1960	7,126	1860	1,534
		1900	15,187	1970	8,636	1870	1,965
1890	1,796	1910	21,023	1980	10,025	1880	2,298
1900	2,792	1920	20,651			1890	3,911
1910	4,772	1930	58,659			1900	4,087
1920	6,596	1940	56,173	**WEST CALDWELL**		1910	4,642
1930	10,759	1950	55,537			1920	5,801
1940	10,714	1960	52,180	1910	494	1930	8,172
1950	11,308	1970	57,305	1920	1,085	1940	8,036
1960	13,397	1980	55,593	1930	2,911	1950	10,931
1970	15,428			1940	3,458	1960	12,453
1980	14,361			1950	4,666	1970	12,408
		VENTNOR CITY		1960	8,314	1980	10,353
				1970	11,913		
SUMMIT		1910	491	1980	11,407		
		1920	2,193				
1900	5,302	1930	6,674				
1910	7,500	1940	7,905	**WESTFIELD**			
1920	10,174	1950	8,158				
1930	14,556	1960	8,688	1910	6,420		
1940	16,165	1970	10,385	1920	9,063		
1950	17,929	1980	11,704	1930	15,801		
1960	23,677			1940	18,458		
1970	23,620			1950	21,243		
1980	21,071	**VERONA**		1960	31,447		
				1970	33,720		
		1910	1,675	1980	30,447		
TENAFLY		1920	3,039				
		1930	7,161				
1880	1,019	1940	8,957	**WEST NEW YORK**			
1890	1,046	1950	10,921				
1900	1,746	1960	13,782	1900	5,267		
1910	2,756	1970	15,067	1910	13,530		
1920	3,585	1980	14,166	1920	29,926		
1930	5,669			1930	37,107		
1940	7,413			1940	39,439		

County Subdivisions	1980	1970
The State	7 364 823	'7 171 112
Atlantic County	194 119	175 043
Absecon city	6 859	6 094
Atlantic City city	40 199	47 859
Brigantine city	8 318	6 741
Buena borough	3 642	3 283
Buena Vista township	6 959	4 239
Collings Lakes (CDP)	2 093	...
Corbin City city	254	258
Egg Harbor township	19 381	9 882
Egg Harbor City city	4 618	4 304
Estell Manor city	848	539
Folsom borough	1 892	1 767
Galloway township	12 176	8 276
Pomona (CDP)	2 358	...
Hamilton township	9 499	6 445
Mays Landing (CDP)	2 054	1 272
Hammonton town	12 298	11 464
Linwood city	6 144	6 159
Longport borough	1 249	1 225
Margate City city	9 179	10 576
Mullica township	5 243	3 391
Elwood–Magnolia (CDP)	1 538	...
Northfield city	7 795	'8 646
Pleasantville city	13 435	'14 007
Port Republic city	837	586
Somers Point city	10 330	7 919
Ventnor City city	11 704	10 385
Weymouth township	1 260	998
Bergen County[1]	845 385	'897 148
Allendale borough	5 901	6 240
Alpine borough	1 549	1 344
Bergenfield borough[1]	25 568	'29 000
Bogota borough	8 344	'8 960
Carlstadt borough	6 166	'6 724
Cliffside Park borough	21 464	'18 891
Closter borough	8 164	8 604
Cresskill borough[1]	7 609	'8 298
Demarest borough	4 963	'5 133
Dumont borough[1]	18 334	'20 155
East Rutherford borough	7 849	8 536
Edgewater borough	4 628	'4 987
Elmwood Park borough[1]	18 377	'20 511
Emerson borough	7 793	8 428
Englewood city[1]	23 701	24 985
Englewood Cliffs borough[1]	5 698	5 938
Fair Lawn borough	32 229	'38 040
Fairview borough	10 519	10 698
Fort Lee borough	32 449	30 631
Franklin Lakes borough	8 769	7 550
Garfield city	26 803	'30 797
Glen Rock borough	11 497	13 011
Hackensack city	36 039	'36 008
Harrington Park borough	4 532	4 841
Hasbrouck Heights borough	12 166	13 651
Haworth borough	3 509	3 760
Hillsdale borough	10 495	11 768
Ho–Ho–Kus borough[1]	4 129	4 348
Leonia borough	8 027	8 847
Little Ferry borough	9 399	'9 064
Lodi borough	23 956	'25 163
Lyndhurst township	20 326	22 729
Lyndhurst (CDP)	20 326	...
Mahwah township	12 127	'10 800
Maywood borough	9 895	11 087
Midland Park borough	7 381	8 159
Montvale borough	7 318	7 327
Moonachie borough	2 706	'2 951
New Milford borough	16 876	'19 149
North Arlington borough	16 587	18 096
Northvale borough	5 046	5 177
Norwood borough	4 413	4 398
Oakland borough	13 443	14 420
Old Tappan borough	4 168	3 917
Oradell borough	8 658	8 903
Palisades Park borough	13 732	13 351
Paramus borough	26 474	'28 381
Park Ridge borough	8 515	8 709
Ramsey borough	12 899	12 571
Ridgefield borough	10 294	11 308
Ridgefield Park village	12 738	'13 990
Ridgewood village[1]	25 208	27 547
River Edge borough	11 111	12 850
River Vale township	9 489	8 883
River Vale (CDP)	9 489	...
Rochelle Park township	5 603	6 380
Rochelle Park (CDP)	5 603	...
Rockleigh borough	192	308
Rutherford borough	19 068	20 802
Saddle Brook township	14 084	'15 910
Saddle Brook (CDP)	14 084	...
Saddle River borough	2 763	2 437
South Hackensack township	2 229	'2 412
Teaneck township	39 007	42 355
Teaneck (CDP)	39 007	...
Tenafly borough[1]	13 552	14 827
Teterboro borough	19	'19
Upper Saddle River borough	7 958	7 949
Waldwick borough	10 802	12 313

County Subdivisions	1980	1970
Bergen County—Con.		
Wallington borough	10 741	10 284
Washington township[1]	9 550	10 577
Washington Township (CDP)	9 550	...
Westwood borough	10 714	11 105
Woodcliff Lake borough	5 644	5 506
Wood–Ridge borough	7 929	8 311
Wyckoff township	15 500	16 039
Wyckoff (CDP)	15 500	...
Burlington County[2]	362 542	323 132
Bass River township	1 344	815
Beverly city	2 919	3 105
Bordentown city	4 441	4 490
Bordentown township	7 170	7 303
Burlington city	10 246	'12 010
Burlington township[2]	11 527	'10 621
Chesterfield township	3 867	3 190
Cinnaminson township	16 072	16 962
Cinnaminson (CDP)	16 072	...
Delanco township	3 730	4 157
Delanco (CDP)	3 730	
Delran township	14 811	'10 065
Eastampton township	3 814	2 284
Edgewater Park township	9 273	7 412
Edgewater Park (CDP)	9 273	
Evesham township	21 508	13 477
Marlton (CDP)	9 411	10 180
Fieldsboro borough	597	615
Florence township	9 084	8 560
Florence–Roebling (CDP)	7 677	7 551
Hainesport township	3 236	2 990
Lumberton township	5 236	3 945
Mansfield township	2 523	2 597
Maple Shade township	20 525	16 464
Maple Shade (CDP)	20 525	...
Medford township	17 622	8 292
Medford Lakes borough	4 958	4 792
Moorestown township	15 596	15 577
Moorestown–Lenola (CDP)	13 695	14 179
Mount Holly township	10 818	12 713
Mount Holly (CDP)	10 818	...
Mount Laurel township	17 614	11 221
Ramblewood (CDP)	6 475	5 556
New Hanover township	14 258	27 410
Fort Dix (CDP) (pt.)	11 213	23 045
McGuire AFB (CDP) (pt.)	2 538	4 109
North Hanover township	9 050	9 858
McGuire AFB (CDP) (pt.)	5 315	6 824
Palmyra borough	7 085	6 969
Pemberton borough	1 198	1 344
Pemberton township	29 720	19 754
Brown Mills (CDP)	10 568	7 144
Country Lake Estates (CDP)	3 739	...
Fort Dix (CDP) (pt.)	3 084	3 245
Pemberton Heights (CDP)	3 150	...
Presidential Lakes Estates (CDP)	2 607	...
Riverside township	7 941	'8 591
Riverside (CDP)	7 941	...
Riverton borough	3 068	3 412
Shamong township	4 537	1 318
Southampton township	8 808	4 982
Leisuretowne (CDP)	2 375	...
Springfield township	2 691	2 244
Fort Dix (CDP) (pt.)	–	...
Tabernacle township	6 236	2 103
Washington township	808	673
Westampton township[2]	3 383	2 680
Willingboro township	39 912	'43 386
Willingboro (CDP)	39 912	...
Woodland township	2 285	2 032
Wrightstown borough	3 031	2 719
Camden County[3]	471 650	456 291
Audubon borough	9 533	10 802
Audubon Park borough	1 274	1 492
Barrington borough	7 418	8 409
Bellmawr borough	13 721	15 618
Berlin borough	5 786	4 997
Berlin township	5 348	5 692
Brooklawn borough	2 133	2 870
Camden city	84 910	102 551
Cherry Hill township[3]	68 785	64 395
Cherry Hill (CDP)	68 785	...
Chesilhurst borough	1 590	801
Clementon borough	5 764	4 492
Collingswood borough	15 838	17 422
Gibbsboro borough	2 510	2 634
Gloucester township	45 156	26 511
Blackwood (CDP)	5 219	...
Glendora (CDP)	5 632	...
Gloucester City city	13 121	14 707
Haddon township	15 875	18 192
Haddonfield borough[3]	12 337	13 118
Haddon Heights borough	8 361	9 365
Hi–Nella borough	1 250	1 195
Laurel Springs borough	2 249	2 566
Lawnside borough	3 042	2 757
Lindenwold borough	18 196	12 199
Magnolia borough	4 881	5 893

County Subdivisions

County Subdivisions	1980	1970
Camden County—Con.		
Merchantville borough	3 972	4 425
Mount Ephraim borough	4 863	5 625
Oaklyn borough	4 223	4 626
Pennsauken township	33 775	36 394
Pennsauken (CDP)	33 775	...
Pine Hill borough	8 684	5 132
Pine Valley borough	23	23
Runnemede borough	9 461	10 475
Somerdale borough	5 900	6 510
Stratford borough	8 005	9 801
Tavistock borough	9	12
Voorhees township	12 919	6 214
Waterford township	8 126	4 073
Winslow township	20 034	11 202
Woodlynne borough	2 578	3 101
Cape May County[4]	82 266	59 554
Avalon borough	2 162	1 283
Cape May city	4 853	4 392
Cape May Point borough	255	204
Dennis township	3 989	2 635
Lower township[4]	17 105	10 154
Erma (CDP)	1 774	...
North Cape May (CDP)	4 029	3 812
Villas (CDP)	5 909	3 155
Middle township	11 373	8 725
Cape May Court House (CDP)	3 597	2 062
Rio Grande (CDP)	2 016	1 203
Whitesboro–Burleigh (CDP)	1 583	...
North Wildwood city	4 714	3 914
Ocean City city	13 949	10 575
Sea Isle City city	2 644	1 712
Stone Harbor borough	1 187	1 089
Upper township	6 713	3 413
West Cape May borough	1 091	1 005
West Wildwood borough	360	235
Wildwood city[4]	4 913	4 110
Wildwood Crest borough	4 149	3 483
Woodbine borough	2 809	2 625
Cumberland County	132 866	121 374
Bridgeton city	18 795	20 435
Commercial township	4 674	3 667
Port Norris (CDP)	1 730	1 955
Deerfield township	2 523	2 464
Downe township	1 803	1 777
Fairfield township	5 693	4 990
Fairton (CDP)	1 107	...
Greenwich township	973	963
Hopewell township	4 365	3 970
Lawrence township	2 116	2 329
Maurice River township	4 577	3 743
Millville city	24 815	21 366
Shiloh borough	604	573
Stow Creek township	1 365	1 050
Upper Deerfield township	6 810	6 648
Seabrook Farms (CDP)	1 411	1 569
Vineland city	53 753	47 399
Essex County[5]	851 116	932 526
Belleville town	35 367	37 629
Bloomfield town	47 792	52 029
Caldwell borough	7 624	8 677
Cedar Grove township	12 600	15 582
Cedar Grove (CDP)	12 600	...
East Orange city	77 690	75 471
Essex Fells borough	2 363	2 541
Fairfield township[5]	7 987	...
Fairfield (CDP)	7 987	...
Glen Ridge borough	7 855	8 518
Irvington town	61 493	59 743
Livingston township[5]	28 040	30 127
Livingston (CDP)	28 040	...
Maplewood township	22 950	24 932
Maplewood (CDP)	22 950	...
Millburn township	19 543	21 089
Millburn (CDP)	19 543	...
Montclair town	38 321	44 043
Newark city	329 248	381 930
North Caldwell borough	5 832	6 733
Nutley town	28 998	31 913
Orange city	31 136	32 566
Roseland borough[5]	5 330	4 453
South Orange Village township[5]	15 864	...
South Orange (CDP)	15 864	...
Verona borough	14 166	15 067
West Caldwell borough	11 407	11 913
West Orange town	39 510	43 715
Gloucester County	199 917	172 681
Clayton borough	6 013	5 193
Deptford township	23 473	24 232
East Greenwich township	4 144	3 280
Elk township	3 187	2 707
Franklin township	12 396	8 990
Glassboro borough	14 574	12 938
Greenwich township	5 404	5 676
Harrison township	3 585	2 661
Mullica Hill (CDP)	1 050	...
Logan township	3 078	1 840

County Subdivisions

County Subdivisions	1980	1970
Gloucester County—Con.		
Mantua township	9 193	9 643
Monroe township	21 639	14 071
Williamstown (CDP)	5 768	4 075
National Park borough	3 552	3 730
Newfield borough	1 563	1 487
Paulsboro borough	6 944	8 084
Pitman borough	9 744	10 257
South Harrison township	1 486	1 226
Swedesboro borough	2 031	2 287
Washington township	27 878	15 741
Wenonah borough	2 303	2 364
West Deptford township	18 002	13 928
Westville borough	4 786	5 170
Woodbury city	10 353	12 408
Woodbury Heights borough	3 460	3 621
Woolwich township	1 129	1 147
Hudson County	556 972	607 839
Bayonne city	65 047	72 743
East Newark borough	1 923	1 922
Guttenberg town	7 340	5 754
Harrison town	12 242	11 811
Hoboken city	42 460	45 380
Jersey City city	223 532	260 350
Kearny town	35 735	37 585
North Bergen township	47 019	47 751
North Bergen (CDP)	47 019	...
Secaucus town	13 719	13 228
Union City city	55 593	57 305
Weehawken township	13 168	13 383
Weehawken (CDP)	13 168	...
West New York town	39 194	40 627
Hunterdon County	87 361	69 718
Alexandria township	2 798	2 127
Bethlehem township	3 045	1 385
Bloomsbury borough	864	879
Califon borough	1 023	970
Clinton town	1 910	1 742
Clinton township	7 345	5 119
Annandale (CDP)	1 040	...
Delaware township	3 816	3 249
East Amwell township	3 468	2 568
Flemington borough	4 132	3 917
Franklin township	2 294	2 154
Frenchtown borough	1 573	1 459
Glen Gardner borough	834	874
Hampton borough	1 614	1 386
High Bridge borough	3 435	2 606
Holland township	4 593	3 587
Kingwood township	2 772	2 294
Lambertville city	4 044	4 359
Lebanon borough	820	885
Lebanon township	5 459	4 235
Milford borough	1 368	1 230
Raritan township	8 292	6 934
Readington township	10 855	7 688
Stockton borough	643	619
Tewksbury township	4 094	2 959
Union township	3 971	2 351
West Amwell township	2 299	2 142
Mercer County[6]	307 863	304 116
East Windsor township[6]	21 041	11 736
Twin Rivers (CDP)	7 742	...
Ewing township	34 842	32 831
Ewing Township (CDP)	34 842	...
Hamilton township	82 801	79 609
Mercerville–Hamilton Square (CDP)	25 446	24 465
White Horse (CDP)	10 098	18 680
Yardville–Groveville (CDP)	9 414	...
Hightstown borough[6]	4 581	5 431
Hopewell borough	2 001	2 271
Hopewell township	10 893	10 030
Lawrence township	19 724	19 567
Pennington borough	2 109	2 151
Princeton borough	12 035	12 311
Princeton township	13 683	13 651
Princeton North (CDP)	4 814	5 488
Trenton city	92 124	104 786
Washington township	3 487	3 311
West Windsor township[6]	8 542	6 431
Princeton Junction (CDP)	2 419	...
Middlesex County[7]	595 893	583 813
Carteret borough	20 598	23 137
Cranbury township	1 927	2 253
Cranbury (CDP)	1 255	1 253
Dunellen borough	6 593	7 072
East Brunswick township	37 711	34 166
East Brunswick (CDP)	37 711	...
Edison township	70 193	67 120
Edison (CDP)	70 193	...
Helmetta borough	955	955
Highland Park borough	13 396	14 385
Jamesburg borough	4 114	4 584
Metuchen borough	13 762	16 031
Middlesex borough	13 480	15 038
Milltown borough[7]	7 136	6 470

County Subdivisions

County Subdivisions	1980	1970
Middlesex County—Con.		
Monroe township	15 858	9 138
New Brunswick city	41 442	41 885
North Brunswick township[7]	22 220	16 691
Old Bridge township[7]	51 515	48 715
Laurence Harbor (CDP)	6 737	6 715
Madison Park (CDP)	7 447	...
Old Bridge (CDP)	21 815	22 240
Perth Amboy city	38 951	38 798
Piscataway township	42 223	36 418
Piscataway (CDP)	42 223	...
Plainsboro township	5 605	1 648
Sayreville borough	29 969	32 508
South Amboy city	8 322	9 338
South Brunswick township	17 127	14 058
Kendall Park (CDP)	7 419	7 412
Monmouth Junction (CDP)	2 579	...
South Plainfield borough	20 521	21 142
South River borough	14 361	15 428
Spotswood borough	7 840	7 891
Woodbridge township	90 074	98 944
Woodbridge (CDP)	90 074	...
Monmouth County[8]	503 173	461 849
Aberdeen township[8]	17 235	17 680
Aberdeen Township (CDP)	17 235	...
Allenhurst borough	912	1 012
Allentown borough	1 962	1 603
Asbury Park city	17 015	16 533
Atlantic Highlands borough	4 950	5 102
Avon-by-the-Sea borough	2 337	2 163
Belmar borough	6 771	5 782
Bradley Beach borough	4 772	4 163
Brielle borough	4 068	3 594
Colts Neck township	7 888	5 819
Clover Hill (CDP)	2 056	...
Deal borough	1 952	2 401
Eatontown borough[8]	12 703	14 619
Englishtown borough	976	1 048
Fair Haven borough	5 679	6 142
Farmingdale borough	1 348	1 148
Freehold borough	10 020	10 545
Freehold township[8]	19 202	13 185
East Freehold (CDP) (pt.)	2 984	...
West Freehold (CDP)	9 929	...
Hazlet township	23 013	22 239
Hazlet (CDP)	23 013	...
Highlands borough	5 187	3 916
Holmdel township	8 447	6 117
Howell township	25 065	21 756
Candlewood (CDP)	6 750	5 629
Interlaken borough	1 037	1 182
Keansburg borough[8]	10 613	9 720
Keyport borough	7 413	7 205
Little Silver borough	5 548	6 010
Loch Arbour village	369	395
Long Branch city	29 819	31 774
Manalapan township	18 914	14 049
Gordon's Corner (CDP)	6 320	...
Yorketown (CDP)	5 330	...
Manasquan borough	5 354	4 971
Marlboro township[8]	17 560	12 273
East Freehold (CDP) (pt.)	6	...
Robertsville (CDP)	8 461	...
Matawan borough[8]	8 837	9 136
Middletown township[8]	62 574	54 623
Middletown (CDP)	61 615	...
Millstone township	3 926	2 535
Monmouth Beach borough	3 318	2 042
Neptune township	28 366	27 863
Neptune Township (CDP)	28 366	...
Neptune City borough	5 276	5 502
Ocean township	23 570	18 643
Ocean Township (CDP)	23 570	...
Oceanport borough[8]	5 888	7 503
Red Bank borough	12 031	12 847
Roosevelt borough	835	814
Rumson borough	7 623	7 421
Sea Bright borough	1 812	1 339
Sea Girt borough	2 650	2 207
Shrewsbury borough	2 962	3 315
Shrewsbury township	995	1 164
South Belmar borough	1 566	1 490
Spring Lake borough	4 215	3 896
Spring Lake Heights borough	5 424	4 602
Tinton Falls borough[8]	7 740	8 395
Union Beach borough	6 354	6 472
Upper Freehold township	2 750	2 551
Wall township	18 952	16 498
West Long Branch borough	7 380	6 845
Morris County	407 630	383 454
Boonton town	8 620	9 261
Boonton township	3 273	3 070
Butler borough	7 616	7 051
Chatham borough	8 537	9 566
Chatham township	8 883	8 093
Chester borough	1 433	1 299
Chester township	5 198	4 265
Denville township	14 380	14 045

County Subdivisions	1980	1970
Morris County—Con.		
Dover town	14 681	15 039
East Hanover township	9 319	7 734
East Hanover (CDP)	9 319	...
Florham Park borough	9 359	9 373
Hanover township	11 846	10 700
Hanover Township (CDP)	11 846	...
Harding township	3 236	3 249
Jefferson township	16 413	14 122
Kinnelon borough	7 770	7 600
Lincoln Park borough	8 806	9 034
Madison borough	15 357	16 710
Mendham borough	4 899	3 729
Mendham township	4 488	3 697
Mine Hill township	3 325	3 557
Montville township	14 290	11 846
Morris township	18 486	18 135
Morris Plains borough	5 305	5 540
Morristown town	16 614	17 662
Mountain Lakes borough	4 153	4 739
Mount Arlington borough	4 251	3 590
Mount Olive township	18 748	10 394
Budd Lake (CDP)	6 523	3 168
Netcong borough	3 557	2 858
Parsippany–Troy Hills township	49 868	55 112
Parsippany–Troy Hills Township (CDP)	49 868	7 488
Passaic township	7 275	7 393
Pequannock township	13 776	14 350
Pequannock Township (CDP)	13 776	...
Randolph township	17 828	13 296
Riverdale borough	2 530	2 729
Rockaway borough	6 852	6 383
Rockaway township	19 850	18 955
Lake Telemark (CDP)	1 216	1 086
White Meadow Lake (CDP)	8 429	8 499
Roxbury township	18 878	15 754
Succasunna–Kenvil (CDP)	10 931	...
Victory Gardens borough	1 043	1 027
Washington township	11 402	6 962
Long Valley (CDP)	1 682	1 645
Wharton borough	5 485	5 535
Ocean County[9]	346 038	208 470
Barnegat township[9]	8 702	1 539
Barnegat (CDP)	1 012	...
Ocean Acres (CDP) (pt.)	137	...
Barnegat Light borough	619	554
Bay Head borough	1 340	1 083
Beach Haven borough	1 714	1 488
Beachwood borough	7 687	4 390
Berkeley township[9]	23 151	7 918
Holiday City–Berkeley (CDP)	9 019	...
Brick township	53 629	35 057
Brick Township (CDP)	53 629	...
Dover township[9]	64 455	43 751
Gilford Park (CDP)	6 528	4 007
Ocean Beach (CDP)	1 629	...
Silverton (CDP)	7 236	...
Toms River (CDP)	7 465	7 303
Eagleswood township	1 009	823
Harvey Cedars borough[9]	363	314
Island Heights borough	1 575	1 397
Jackson township	25 644	18 276
Lacey township	14 161	4 616
Lakehurst borough	2 908	2 641
Lakewood township	38 464	25 223
Lakewood (CDP)	22 863	17 874
Lavallette borough[9]	2 072	1 509
Little Egg Harbor township	8 483	2 972
Mystic Island (CDP)	4 929	...
Long Beach township[9]	3 488	2 910
North Beach Haven (CDP)	2 652	...
Manchester township	27 987	7 550
Cedar Glen Lakes (CDP)	1 987	...
Crestwood Village (CDP)	7 965	...
Mantoloking borough	433	319
Ocean township	3 731	2 222
Waretown (CDP)	1 175	...
Ocean Gate borough	1 385	1 081
Pine Beach borough[9]	1 796	1 395
Plumsted township	4 674	4 113
New Egypt (CDP)	2 111	1 769
Point Pleasant borough	17 747	15 968
Point Pleasant Beach borough	5 415	4 882
Seaside Heights borough	1 802	1 248
Seaside Park borough	1 795	1 432
Ship Bottom borough	1 427	1 079
South Toms River borough	3 954	3 981
Stafford township	10 385	3 684
Beach Haven West (CDP)	3 020	...
Manahawkin (CDP)	1 469	1 278
Ocean Acres (CDP) (pt.)	4 713	...
Surf City borough	1 571	1 129
Tuckerton borough	2 472	1 926
Passaic County	447 585	460 782
Bloomingdale borough	7 867	7 797
Clifton city	74 388	82 437
Haledon borough	6 607	6 767

County Subdivisions	1980	1970
Passaic County—Con.		
Hawthorne borough	18 200	19 173
Little Falls township	11 496	11 727
Little Falls (CDP)	11 496	...
North Haledon borough	8 177	7 614
Passaic city	52 463	55 124
Paterson city	137 970	144 824
Pompton Lakes borough	10 660	11 397
Prospect Park borough	5 142	5 176
Ringwood borough	12 625	10 393
Totowa borough	11 448	11 580
Wanaque borough	10 025	8 636
Wayne township	46 474	49 141
Wayne (CDP)	46 474	...
West Milford township	22 750	17 304
Upper Greenwood Lake (CDP)	2 734	1 505
West Paterson borough	11 293	11 692
Salem County[10]	64 676	60 346
Alloway township	2 680	2 550
Alloway (CDP)	1 370	...
Carneys Point township[10]	8 396	7 016
Carneys Point (CDP)	7 574	...
Elmer borough	1 569	1 592
Elsinboro township	1 290	1 204
Lower Alloways Creek township	1 547	1 400
Mannington township	1 740	1 913
Oldmans township	1 847	2 088
Penns Grove borough	5 760	5 727
Pennsville township	13 848	13 296
Pennsville (CDP)	12 467	11 014
Pilesgrove township	2 810	2 706
Pittsgrove township	6 954	4 618
Quinton township	2 887	2 567
Salem city	6 959	7 648
Upper Pittsgrove township	3 139	2 884
Woodstown borough	3 250	3 137
Somerset County[11]	203 129	198 372
Bedminster township	2 469	2 597
Bernards township	12 920	13 305
Bernardsville borough	6 715	6 652
Bound Brook borough[11]	9 710	10 450
Branchburg township	7 846	5 742
Bridgewater township[11]	29 175	30 235
Far Hills borough	677	780
Franklin township	31 358	30 389
Somerset (CDP)	21 731	...
Green Brook township	4 640	4 302
Hillsborough township	19 061	11 061
Manville borough	11 278	13 029
Millstone borough	530	630
Montgomery township	7 360	6 353
North Plainfield borough	19 108	21 796
Peapack and Gladstone borough	2 038	1 924
Raritan borough	6 128	6 691
Rocky Hill borough	717	917
Somerville borough	11 973	13 652
South Bound Brook borough	4 331	4 525
Warren township[11]	9 805	8 592
Watchung borough	5 290	4 750
Sussex County	116 119	77 528
Andover borough	892	813
Andover township	4 506	3 040
Branchville borough	870	911
Byram township	7 502	4 592
Lake Mohawk (CDP) (pt.)	668	...
Frankford township	4 654	2 777
Culvers Lake (CDP)	1 062	...
Franklin borough	4 486	4 236
Fredon township	2 281	1 372
Green township	2 450	1 343
Hamburg borough	1 832	1 820
Hampton township	3 916	2 091
Crandon Lakes (CDP) (pt.)	576	...
Hardyston township	4 553	3 499
Hopatcong borough	15 531	9 052
Lafayette township	1 614	1 202
Montague township	2 066	1 131
Newton town	7 748	7 297
Ogdensburg borough	2 737	2 222
Sandyston township	1 485	1 303
Sparta township	13 333	10 819
Lake Mohawk (CDP) (pt.)	7 830	6 262
Stanhope borough	3 638	3 040
Stillwater township	3 887	2 158
Crandon Lakes (CDP) (pt.)	507	...
Sussex borough	2 418	2 038
Vernon township	16 302	6 059
Highland Lakes (CDP)	2 888	...
Vernon Valley Lake (CDP)	1 169	...
Walpack township	150	384
Wantage township	7 268	4 329
Union County[12]	504 094	543 116
Berkeley Heights township	12 549	13 078
Berkeley Heights (CDP)	12 549	...
Clark township	16 699	18 829
Clark (CDP)	16 699	...

County Subdivisions	1980	1970
Union County—Con.		
Cranford township	24 573	27 391
Cranford (CDP)	24 573	...
Elizabeth city	106 201	112 654
Fanwood borough	7 767	8 920
Garwood borough	4 752	5 260
Hillside township	21 440	21 636
Hillside (CDP)	21 440	...
Kenilworth borough[12]	8 221	9 165
Linden city	37 836	41 409
Mountainside borough	7 118	7 520
New Providence borough	12 426	13 796
Plainfield city	45 555	46 862
Rahway city	26 723	29 114
Roselle borough	20 641	22 585
Roselle Park borough[12]	13 377	14 277
Scotch Plains township	20 774	22 279
Scotch Plains (CDP)	20 774	...
Springfield township	13 955	15 740
Springfield (CDP)	13 955	...
Summit city	21 071	23 620
Union township	50 184	53 077
Union (CDP)	50 184	...
Westfield town	30 447	33 720
Winfield township	1 785	2 184
Winfield (CDP)	1 785	...
Warren County	84 429	[1]73 960
Allamuchy township	2 560	1 138
Alpha borough	2 644	2 829
Belvidere town	2 475	[2]2 722
Blairstown township	4 360	2 189
Franklin township	2 341	1 973
Frelinghuysen township	1 435	1 118
Greenwich township	1 738	1 482
Hackettstown town	8 850	9 472
Hardwick township	947	548
Harmony township	2 592	2 195
Hope township	1 468	1 140
Independence township	2 829	2 057
Knowlton township	2 074	1 738
Liberty township	1 730	1 229
Lopatcong township	4 998	3 144
Mansfield township	5 780	3 546
Oxford township	1 659	1 742
Oxford (CDP)	1 587	1 411
Pahaquarry township	26	71
Phillipsburg town	16 647	17 849
Pohatcong township	3 856	3 924
Washington borough	6 429	5 943
Washington township	4 243	3 585
White township	2 748	2 326

NEW MEXICO

New Mexico was a part of the Mexican province of New Mexico before coming into possession of the United States, and has retained the name.

The first white men to visit the region now constituting New Mexico were Spaniards. De Vaca is believed to have entered it about the year 1536, and it was explored by Marcos de Niza in 1539 and by Coronado in 1540. In 1598 a settlement was made at or near the present site of Chamita, in Rio Arriba County. Santa Fe was founded not long afterwards.

This region formed a portion of the Spanish possessions in America until the Mexican Revolution of 1821, after which it became a part of Mexico. The section of New Mexico east of the Rio Grande was included in Texas from 1836, when that republic won its independence, until 1845, when it was annexed to the United States. This area remained a part of Texas until 1850. The region west of the Rio Grande continued in the possession of Mexico until the war between that country and the United States, ath the close of which, in February, 1848, Mexico relinquished its claims to all lands north of the present southern boundary of California, the River Gila, and a line a little north of the thirty-second parallel.

The territory of New Mexico was organized in 1850. It then included all of the present territory of New Mexico except a small section in the southwestern part, the region now constituting Arizona north of the Gila River, Nevada south of the thirty-seventh parallel, and southeastern Colorado. In December, 1853, the United States acquired from Mexico by the Gadsden Purchase the territory south of the Gila River and north of the present boundary between the two countries, and in the following year this area was added to New Mexico. In 1861 that portion of New Mexico lying north of the thiry-seventh parallel was made a part of the newly created territory of Colorado, and in 1863, upon the organization of Arizona territory, New Mexico was reduced to its present limits.

Under an enabling act passed by Congress in June, 1910, New Mexico adopted a state constitution in January, 1911, and in August of the same year this constitution received the conditional approval of the Federal Government. August 21, 1911, the territory became a state of the Union.

COUNTY LOCATION INDEX

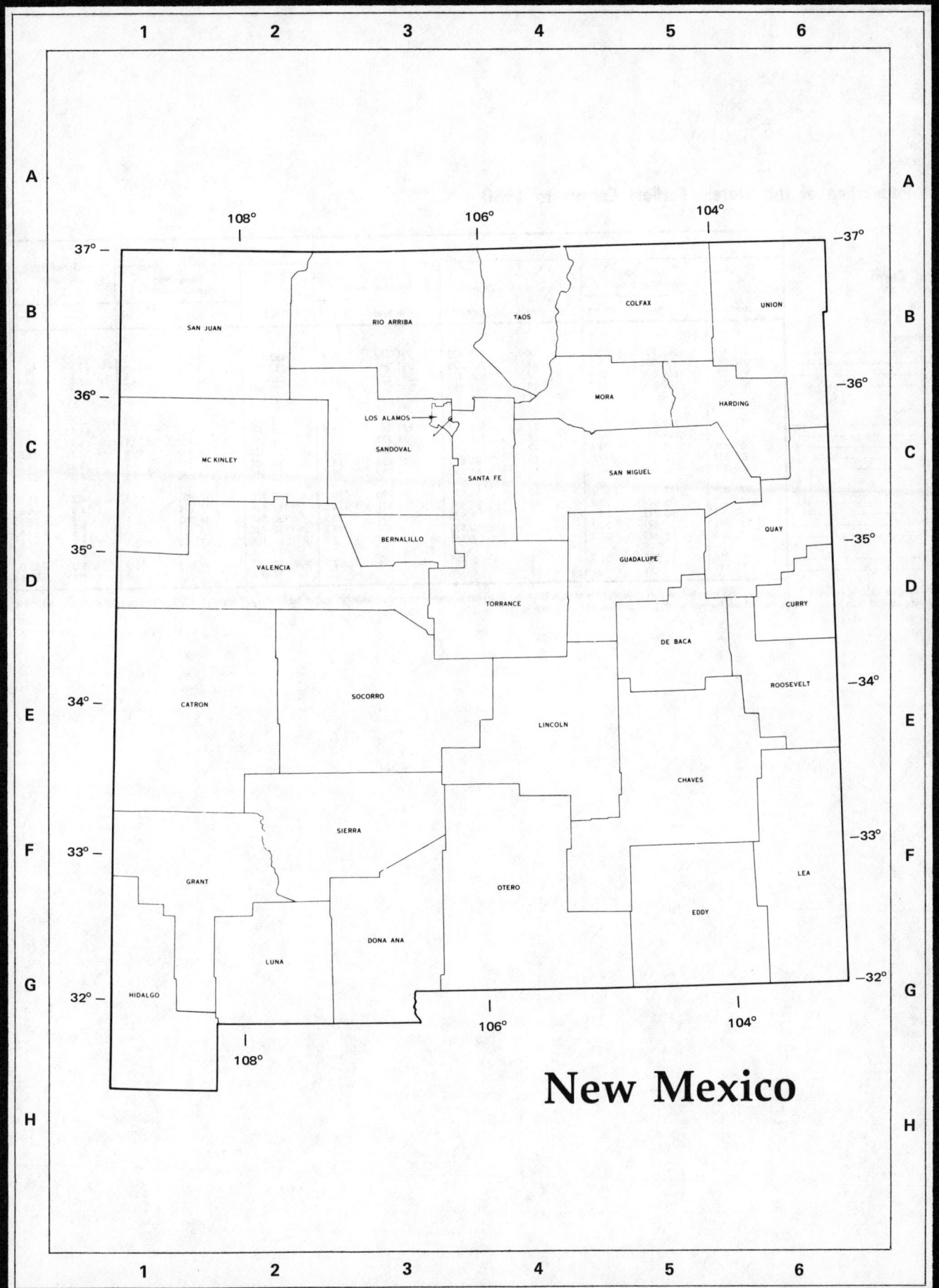

New Mexico

Population of the State: Earliest Census to 1980

Urban and Rural

	The State			Urban				Rural				Percent of total population	
	Total population	Change from preceding census		Places of 2,500 or more	Population	Change from preceding census		Population	Change from preceding census			Urban	Rural
		Number	Percent			Number	Percent		Number	Percent			
Current urban definition:													
1980 (Apr. 1)	1 302 894	285 839	28.1	54	939 963	231 188	32.6	362 931	55 706	18.1		72.1	27.9
1970 (Apr. 1)	1 017 055	66 032	6.9	41	708 775	82 296	13.1	307 225	−17 319	−5.3		69.8	30.2
1960 (Apr. 1)	951 023	269 836	39.6	34	626 479	284 590	83.2	324 544	−14 754	−4.3		65.9	34.1
1950 (Apr. 1)	681 187	149 369	28.1	29	341 889	...	...	339 298	...	...		50.2	49.8
Previous urban definition:													
1960 (Apr. 1)	951 023	269 836	39.6	32	588 177	273 541	86.9	362 846	−3 705	−1.0		61.8	38.2
1950 (Apr. 1)	681 187	149 369	28.1	24	314 636	138 235	78.4	366 551	11 134	3.1		46.2	53.8
1940 (Apr. 1)	531 818	108 501	25.6	22	176 401	69 585	65.1	355 417	38 916	12.3		33.2	66.8
1930 (Apr. 1)	423 317	62 967	17.5	16	106 816	41 856	64.4	316 501	21 111	7.1		25.2	74.8
1920 (Jan. 1)	360 350	33 049	10.1	12	64 960	18 389	39.5	295 390	14 660	5.2		18.0	82.0
1910 (Apr. 15)	327 301	131 991	67.6	10	46 571	19 190	70.1	280 730	112 801	67.2		14.2	85.8
1900 (June 1)	195 310	35 028	21.9	7	27 381	17 411	174.6	167 929	17 617	11.7		14.0	86.0
1890 (June 1)	160 282	40 717	34.1	2	9 970	3 335	50.3	150 312	37 382	33.1		6.2	93.8
1880 (June 1)	119 565	27 691	30.1	1	6 635	1 870	39.2	112 930	25 821	29.6		5.5	94.5
1870 (June 1)	91 874	−1 642	−1.8	1	4 765	130	2.8	87 109	−1 772	−2.0		5.2	94.8
1860 (June 1)	93 516	31 969	51.9	1	4 635	96	2.1	88 881	31 873	55.9		5.0	95.0
1850 (June 1)	61 547	...	...	1	4 539	...	...	57 008	...	...		7.4	92.6

NOTE: Total for 1860 is exclusive of population of area taken to form part of Colorado Territory in 1861, but it includes population of area organized as part of the Territory of Arizona in 1863. No estimate of population in 1850 is available for territory acquired from Mexico through the Gadsden Purchase in 1853 and annexed to New Mexico in 1854.

ARIZONA		
1860	6,482	

BERNALILLO		
1850	7,751	
1860	8,769	
1870	7,591	
1880	17,225	
1890	20,913	
1900	28,630	
1910	23,606	
1920	29,855	
1930	45,430	
1940	69,391	
1950	145,673	
1960	262,199	
1970	315,774	
1980	419,700	

CATRON		
1930	3,282	
1940	4,881	
1950	3,533	
1960	2,773	
1970	2,198	
1980	2,720	

CHAVES		
1900	4,773	
1910	16,850	
1920	12,075	
1930	19,549	
1940	23,980	
1950	40,605	
1960	57,649	
1970	43,335	
1980	51,103	

COLFAX		
1870	1,992	
1880	3,398	
1890	7,794	
1900	10,150	
1910	16,460	
1920	21,550	
1930	19,157	
1940	18,718	
1950	16,761	
1960	13,806	
1970	12,170	
1980	13,667	

CURRY		
1910	11,443	
1920	11,236	
1930	15,809	
1940	18,159	
1950	23,351	
1960	32,691	
1970	39,517	
1980	42,019	

DE BACA		
1920	3,196	
1930	2,893	
1940	3,725	
1950	3,464	
1960	2,991	
1970	2,547	
1980	2,454	

DONA ANA		
1860	6,239	
1870	5,864	
1880	7,612	
1890	9,191	
1900	10,187	
1910	12,893	
1920	16,548	
1930	27,445	
1940	30,411	
1950	39,557	
1960	59,948	
1970	69,773	
1980	96,340	

EDDY		
1900	3,229	
1910	12,400	
1920	9,116	
1930	15,842	
1940	24,311	
1950	40,640	
1960	50,783	
1970	41,119	
1980	47,855	

GRANT		
1870	1,143	
1880	4,539	
1890	9,657	
1900	12,883	
1910	14,813	
1920	21,939	
1930	19,050	
1940	20,050	
1950	21,649	
1960	18,700	
1970	22,030	
1980	26,204	

GUADALUPE		
1900	5,429	
1910	10,927	
1920	8,015	
1930	7,027	
1940	8,646	
1950	6,772	
1960	5,610	
1970	4,969	
1980	4,496	

HARDING		
1930	4,421	
1940	4,374	
1950	3,013	
1960	1,874	
1970	1,348	
1980	1,090	

HIDALGO		
1920	4,338	
1930	5,023	
1940	4,821	
1950	5,095	
1960	4,961	
1970	4,734	
1980	6,049	

LEA		
1920	3,545	
1930	6,144	
1940	21,154	
1950	30,717	
1960	53,429	
1970	49,554	
1980	55,993	

LINCOLN		
1870	1,803	
1880	2,513	
1890	7,081	
1900	4,953	
1910	7,822	
1920	7,823	
1930	7,198	
1940	8,557	
1950	7,409	
1960	7,744	
1970	7,560	
1980	10,997	

LOS ALAMOS		
1950	10,476	
1960	13,037	
1970	15,198	
1980	17,599	

LUNA		
1910	3,913	
1920	12,270	
1930	6,247	
1940	6,457	
1950	8,753	
1960	9,839	
1970	11,706	
1980	15,585	

McKINLEY		
1910	12,963	
1920	13,731	
1930	20,643	
1940	23,641	
1950	27,451	
1960	37,209	
1970	43,208	
1980	56,449	

MORA		
1860	5,566	
1870	8,056	
1880	9,751	
1890	10,618	
1900	10,304	
1910	12,611	
1920	13,915	
1930	10,322	
1940	10,981	
1950	8,720	
1960	6,028	
1970	4,673	
1980	4,205	

OTERO		
1900	4,791	
1910	7,069	
1920	7,902	
1930	9,779	
1940	10,522	
1950	14,909	
1960	36,976	
1970	41,097	
1980	44,665	

QUAY		
1910	14,912	
1920	10,444	
1930	10,828	
1940	12,111	
1950	13,971	
1960	12,279	
1970	10,903	
1980	10,577	

RIO ARRIBA		
1850	10,688	
1860	9,849	
1870	9,294	
1880	11,023	
1890	11,534	
1900	13,777	
1910	16,624	
1920	19,552	
1930	21,381	
1940	25,352	
1950	24,997	
1960	24,193	
1970	25,170	
1980	29,282	

ROOSEVELT		
1910	12,064	
1920	6,548	
1930	11,109	
1940	14,549	
1950	16,409	
1960	16,198	
1970	16,479	
1980	15,695	

SANDOVAL		
1910	8,579	
1920	8,863	
1930	11,144	
1940	13,898	
1950	12,438	
1960	14,201	
1970	17,492	
1980	34,799	

SAN JUAN		
1890	1,890	
1900	4,828	
1910	8,504	
1920	8,333	
1930	14,701	
1940	17,115	
1950	18,292	
1960	53,306	
1970	52,517	
1980	81,433	

SAN MIGUEL		
1850	7,074	
1860	13,714	
1870	16,058	
1880	20,638	
1890	24,204	

	1900	22,053
	1910	22,930
	1920	22,867
	1930	23,636
	1940	27,910
	1950	26,512
	1960	23,468
	1970	21,951
	1980	22,751

SANTA ANA		
1850	4,645	
1860	3,572	
1870	2,599	

SANTA FE		
1850	7,713	
1860	8,144	
1870	9,699	
1880	10,867	
1890	13,562	
1900	14,658	
1910	14,770	
1920	15,030	
1930	19,567	
1940	30,826	
1950	38,153	
1960	44,970	
1970	53,756	
1980	75,360	

SIERRA		
1890	3,630	
1900	3,158	
1910	3,536	
1920	4,619	
1930	5,184	
1940	6,962	
1950	7,186	
1960	6,409	
1970	7,189	
1980	8,454	

SOCORRO		
1860	5,787	
1870	6,603	
1880	7,875	
1890	9,595	
1900	12,195	
1910	14,761	
1920	14,061	
1930	9,611	
1940	11,422	
1950	9,670	
1960	10,168	
1970	9,763	
1980	12,566	

TAOS		
1850	9,507	
1860	14,013	
1870	12,079	
1880	11,029	
1890	9,868	
1900	10,889	
1910	12,008	
1920	12,773	
1930	14,394	
1940	18,528	
1950	17,146	
1960	15,934	

1970	17,516
1980	19,456

TORRANCE

1910	10,119
1920	9,731
1930	9,269
1940	11,026
1950	8,012
1960	6,497
1970	5,290
1980	7,491

UNION

1900	4,528
1910	11,404
1920	16,680
1930	11,036
1940	9,095
1950	7,372
1960	6,068
1970	4,925
1980	4,725

VALENCIA

1850	14,189
1860	11,321
1870	9,093
1880	13,095
1890	13,876
1900	13,895
1910	13,320
1920	13,795
1930	16,186
1940	20,245
1950	22,481
1960	39,085
1970	40,539
1980	61,115

ALAMOGORDO

1920	2,363
1930	3,096
1940	3,950
1950	6,783
1960	21,723
1970	23,035
1980	24,024

ALBUQUERQUE

1890	3,785
1900	6,238
1910	11,020
1920	15,157
1930	26,570
1940	35,449
1950	96,815
1960	201,189
1970	243,751
1980	331,767

ARTESIA

1910	1,883
1920	1,115
1930	2,427
1940	4,071
1950	8,244
1960	12,000
1970	10,315
1980	10,385

CARLSBAD

1900	963
1910	1,736
1920	2,205
1930	3,708
1940	7,116
1950	17,975
1960	25,541
1970	21,297
1980	25,496

CLOVIS

1910	3,255
1920	4,904
1930	8,027
1940	10,065
1950	17,318
1960	23,713
1970	28,495
1980	31,194

FARMINGTON

1910	785
1920	728
1930	1,350
1940	2,161
1950	3,637
1960	23,786
1970	21,979
1980	31,222

GALLUP

1900	2,946
1910	2,204
1920	3,920
1930	5,992
1940	7,041
1950	9,133

1960	14,089
1970	14,596
1980	18,161

GRANTS

1950	2,251
1960	10,274
1970	8,768
1980	11,439

HOBBS

1930	598
1940	10,619
1950	13,875
1960	26,275
1970	26,025
1980	29,153

LAS CRUCES

1910	3,836
1920	3,969
1930	5,811
1940	8,385
1950	12,325
1960	29,367
1970	37,857
1980	45,086

LAS VEGAS

1860	1,094
1890	2,385
1900	6,319
1910	6,934
1920	8,206
1930	9,097
1940	12,362
1950	13,763
1960	13,818
1970	13,835
1980	14,322

ROSWELL

1900	2,049
1910	6,172
1920	7,033
1930	11,173
1940	13,482
1950	25,738
1960	39,593
1970	33,908
1980	39,676

SANTA FE

1850	4,539
1860	4,635
1870	4,765
1880	6,635
1890	6,185
1900	5,603
1910	5,072
1920	7,236
1930	11,176
1940	20,325
1950	27,998
1960	33,394
1970	41,167
1980	48,953

CORRECTION NOTE

The official 1980 census counts of total population shown in this report supersede counts issued previously. Corrections to the figures were made after the counts were provided to the State for redistricting purposes and released in Advance Report PHC80-V for this State.

Shown below are corrections to the 1980 census counts of the total population made after the tabulations for this report were completed. Any additional corrections made after this report is printed are available by writing to Data User Services Division, Customer Services (Corrections), Bureau of the Census, Washington, D.C. 20233.

The 1980 figures shown in this publication are subject to change pending the outcome of the various lawsuits dealing with the census counts.

	1980 population	
	As shown in the tables	Corrected
The State.................	1 302 894	1 302 981
McKinley County...................	56 449	56 536
Gallup division.................	29 995	30 063
Gallup city (pt.)............	18 161	18 167
Reservation division............	8 999	9 018
Rio Arriba County:		
San Juan Pueblo division........	4 825	4 709
Espanola city (pt.)...........	712	672
South Rio Arriba division.......	5 039	5 155
Espanola city (pt.)...........	1 723	1 763
Espanola city (total).............	6 803	(1)
Gallup city (total)..............	18 161	18 167

    [1]No change.

County Subdivisions	1980	1970
The State	1 302 894	ʳ1 017 055
Bernalillo County[1]	419 700	315 774
Albuquerque division	409 589	309 681
Albuquerque city[1]	331 767	ʳ244 501
Corrales village (pt.)[1]	123	
Los Ranchos de Albuquerque village[1]	2 702	1 900
North Valley (CDP)	13 006	10 366
Paradise Hills (CDP)	5 096	
Sandia (CDP)	5 288	6 867
South Valley (CDP)	38 916	29 389
Bernalillo East division	7 360	4 055
Tijeras village[1]	311	...
Bernalillo West division	879	573
Isleta Pueblo division	1 872	1 465
Isleta Pueblo (CDP)	1 246	1 080
Catron County[2]	2 720	2 198
Quemado division	1 028	881
Reserve division	1 692	1 317
Reserve village[2]	439	...
Chaves County[3]	51 103	43 335
Dexter division	1 730	1 803
Dexter town	882	746
Hagerman division	1 951	2 121
Hagerman town	936	953
Lake Arthur town[3]	327	306
Northeast Chaves division	189	116
Northwest Chaves division	1 708	1 025
Roswell division	40 376	35 771
Roswell city (pt.)[3]	37 949	33 908
Southeast Chaves division	1 131	1 005
Southwest Chaves division	4 018	...
Roswell city (pt.)[3]	1 727	...
Colfax County[4]	13 667	12 170
Cimarron division	2 019	1 728
Cimarron village	888	927
Eagle Nest village[4]	202	...
Raton division	8 864	7 431
Maxwell village (pt.)	−	...
Raton city[4]	8 225	6 962
Springer division	2 784	3 011
Maxwell village (pt.)	316	393
Springer town	1 657	1 574
Curry County[5]	42 019	39 517
Broadview division	469	620
Grady village	122	104
Clovis division	40 455	...
Cannon AFB (CDP)	3 798	5 461
Clovis city[5]	31 194	28 495
Texico city[5]	958	772
Melrose division	1 095	1 121
Melrose village	649	636
De Baca County[6]	2 454	2 547
East De Baca division	2 247	...
Fort Sumner village[6]	1 421	1 615
West De Baca division	207	...
Dona Ana County[7]	96 340	69 773
Anthony division	9 594	4 270
Anthony (CDP)	3 285	1 728
Dona Ana–Hill division	6 811	2 274
Las Cruces city (pt.)[7]	590	...
Fairacres division	2 313	1 129
Mesilla town (pt.)[7]	35	...
Hatch division	3 235	2 902
Hatch village[7]	1 028	867
Las Cruces division	60 276	48 040
Las Cruces city (pt.)[7]	44 496	37 857
Mesilla town (pt.)[7]	1 994	1 713
San Andres–Alameda Estates (CDP)	2 024	...
University Park (CDP)	4 353	...
South Dona Ana division	10 991	...
Meadow Vista (CDP)	3 377	1 402
White Sands division	3 120	4 167
White Sands (CDP)	3 120	4 167
Eddy County[8]	47 855	41 119
Artesia division	14 077	13 331
Artesia city[8]	10 385	10 315
Hope village	111	90
Carlsbad division	31 351	...
Carlsbad city[8]	25 496	21 297
Carlsbad North (CDP)	1 271	...
Loco Hills division	443	398
Loving division	1 984	1 892
Loving village	1 355	1 192
Grant County[9]	26 204	22 030
Bayard–Santa Rita division	3 974	...
Bayard village[9]	3 036	2 908
Central division	2 968	...
Central village[9]	1 968	1 864
Hurley division	1 839	...
Hurley town[9]	1 616	1 796
Mimbres division	990	1 070
Pinos Altos division	723	...
Silver City division	13 980	...
Silver City town[9]	9 887	ʳ8 557

County Subdivisions	1980	1970
Grant County—Con.		
Tyrone division	1 730	...
Guadalupe County[10]	4 496	4 969
Dilia division	594	725
Santa Rosa division	3 060	3 221
Santa Rosa city[10]	2 469	2 485
Vaughn division	842	1 023
Vaughn town	737	867
Harding County[11]	1 090	1 348
North Harding division	916	...
Mosquero village (pt.)	197	244
Roy village	381	476
South Harding division	174	...
Hidalgo County[12]	6 049	4 734
North Hidalgo division	4 714	4 368
Lordsburg city[12]	3 195	3 429
Virden village	246	151
South Hidalgo division	1 335	366
Lea County[13]	55 993	49 554
Eunice division	3 476	...
Eunice city	2 970	2 641
Hobbs division	35 331	...
Hobbs city[13]	29 153	26 025
Jal division	3 228	...
Jal city	2 675	2 602
Lovington division	12 318	...
Lovington city[13]	9 727	8 915
Tatum division	1 640	...
Tatum town	896	982
Lincoln County[14]	10 997	7 560
Capitan division	1 749	...
Capitan village[14]	762	439
Carrizozo division	1 476	1 270
Carrizozo town[14]	1 222	1 123
Corona division	550	610
Corona village	236	262
Hondo division	846	...
Ruidoso division	6 376	3 548
Ruidoso village[14]	4 260	2 216
Ruidoso Downs village[14]	949	702
Los Alamos County[15]	17 599	15 198
Los Alamos division	11 039	...
Los Alamos (CDP)	11 039	11 310
White Rock division	6 560	...
White Rock (CDP)	6 560	3 861
Luna County[16]	15 585	11 706
Deming North division	12 796	...
Deming city[16]	9 964	8 343
Deming South division	2 789	...
Columbus village[16]	414	241
McKinley County[17]	56 449	43 208
Crownpoint division	10 598	ʳ8 506
Crownpoint (CDP)	1 134	...
Gallup city (pt.)	−	...
Thoreau (CDP) (pt.)	1 038	...
Gallup division	29 995	...
Gallup city (pt.)[17]	18 161	14 596
Thoreau (CDP) (pt.)	61	...
Reservation division	8 999	5 123
Tohatchi (CDP)	1 011	...
Zuni division	6 857	...
Zuni Pueblo (CDP)	5 551	3 958
Mora County	4 205	4 673
Mora division	3 048	3 178
Wagon Mound division	1 157	1 495
Wagon Mound village	416	630
Otero County[18]	44 665	41 097
Alamogordo division	35 369	33 834
Alamogordo city[18]	24 024	23 035
Holloman AFB (CDP)	7 245	8 001
La Luz (CDP)	1 194	...
Mescalero division	2 101	1 740
Mescalero (CDP)	1 259	...
Southeast Otero division	3 257	...
Cloudcroft village	521	525
Tularosa division	3 938	3 648
Tularosa village	2 536	2 851
Quay County[19]	10 577	10 903
House–Forrest division	488	570
House village[19]	117	119
Logan–Nara Visa division	1 024	...
Logan village[19]	735	386
San Jon division	737	802
San Jon village[19]	341	308
Tucumcari division	8 328	...
Tucumcari city[19]	6 765	7 189
Rio Arriba County[20]	29 282	25 170
Chimayo division	2 443	2 723
Chimayo (CDP) (pt.)	1 424	...
Coyote division	1 547	...
Dixon division	1 365	...
Jicarilla division	1 911	...
Dulce (CDP)	1 648	...
Rio Chama division	1 607	...

County Subdivisions	1980	1970
Rio Arriba County—Con.		
San Juan Pueblo division	4 825	...
Espanola city (pt.)	712	...
Santa Clara division	6 148	...
Espanola city (pt.)[20]	3 230	(NA)
South Rio Arriba division	5 039	...
Espanola city (pt.)[20]	1 723	(NA)
Tierra Amarilla division	3 112	...
Chama village[20]	1 090	899
Vallecitos division	562	...
Western Rio Arriba division	723	...
Roosevelt County[21]	15 695	16 479
Dora division	810	1 097
Causey village	81	150
Dora village (pt.)	168	196
Elida division	1 313	...
Elida town	202	233
Floyd village	146	248
Portales division	13 572	...
Dora village (pt.)	—	...
Portales city[21]	9 940	10 554
Sandoval County[22]	34 799	17 492
Bernalillo division	21 664	...
Bernalillo town[22]	3 012	2 016
Corrales village (pt.)[22]	2 668	...
Rio Rancho Estates (CDP)	9 985	...
Cuba division	3 877	...
Cuba village[22]	609	ʳ415
Jemez division	3 605	...
Jemez Pueblo (CDP)	1 503	1 197
Jemez Springs village	316	356
San Ysidro village[22]	199	ʳ182
Santo Domingo division	5 653	...
San Felipe Pueblo (CDP)	1 465	1 187
Santo Domingo Pueblo (CDP)	2 082	1 662
San Juan County[23]	81 433	52 517
Aztec division	11 350	5 850
Aztec city[23]	5 512	3 354
Farmington city (pt.)[23]	226	...
Bloomfield division	9 246	3 894
Bloomfield city (pt.)[23]	4 703	1 574
Burnham division	3 299	...
Farmington division	38 366	...
Farmington city (pt.)[23]	30 996	21 979
Kirtland (CDP)	2 358	...
Naschitti division	1 925	...
Shiprock—Sanostee division	14 454	...
Shiprock (CDP)	7 237	...
Simpson—Chaco division	2 793	...
Bloomfield city (pt.)[23]	178	...
Farmington city (pt.)	—	...
San Miguel County[24]	22 751	21 951
Conchas Dam division	337	261
Mosquero village (pt.)	—	...
Las Vegas division	18 087	...
Las Vegas city[24]	14 322	7 528
Pecos division	2 472	2 216
Pecos village[24]	885	598
Trementina division	299	...
Villanueva division	1 556	...
Santa Fe County[25]	75 360	ʳ54 774
Santa Fe division	52 840	...
Santa Fe city (pt.)[25]	48 953	41 167
Santa Fe North division	11 029	...
Chimayo (CDP) (pt.)	569	...
Espanola city (pt.)[25]	1 138	626
Nambe (CDP)	1 017	...
Tesuque (CDP)	1 014	...
Santa Fe South division	11 491	...
Santa Fe city (pt.)[25]	—	...
Sierra County[26]	8 454	7 189
Truth or Consequences East division	6 710	...
Truth or Consequences city[26]	5 219	4 656
Williamsburg village[26]	433	367
Truth or Consequences West division	1 744	...
Socorro County[27]	12 566	9 763
Claunch division	126	ʳ125
Magdalena division	2 524	...
Magdalena village	1 022	652
Rio Grande division	9 916	...
Socorro city[27]	7 173	ʳ5 849
Taos County[28]	19 456	17 516
Arroyo Hondo division	2 296	1 810
Penasco division	1 165	1 263
Picuris division	1 539	1 497
Questa division	3 007	3 134
Questa village[28]	1 202	1 095
Red River town[28]	332	...
Taos division	8 911	7 237
Ranchos De Taos (CDP)	1 411	...
Taos town[28]	3 369	2 475
Taos Pueblo division	2 112	2 219
Tres Piedras division	426	356

County Subdivisions	1980	1970
Torrance County[29]	7 491	5 290
Encino division	488	...
Encino village	155	250
Estancia division	5 061	...
Estancia town	830	721
Moriarty city[29]	1 276	758
Mountainair division	1 942	...
Mountainair town[29]	1 170	1 022
Willard village	166	209
Union County[30]	4 725	4 925
Clayton North division	1 011	...
Des Moines village	178	204
Folsom village	73	75
Grenville village	39	21
Clayton South division	3 714	...
Clayton city[30]	2 968	2 931
Valencia County[31]	61 115	ʳ40 576
Belen division	11 582	...
Belen city[31]	5 617	4 823
Rio Communities (CDP)	2 089	...
Fence Lake division	103	...
Grants division	24 423	...
Grants city[31]	11 439	8 768
Milan village[31]	3 747	ʳ2 222
Laguna division	4 507	...
Los Lunas division	19 131	...
Bosque Farms village[31]	3 353	...
Los Lunas village[31]	3 525	973
Zuni—Ramah Navajo division	1 369	...

NEW YORK

New York was named in honor of the Duke of York, to whom it was granted in 1664 by Charles II of England. Prior to that time it had been called New Netherland.

New York Bay was discovered in 1524 by Verrazano, a Florentine navigator in the service of France, but no important explorations in this region were made before 1609. In that year Samuel de Champlain, a Frenchman and the founder of Quebec, sailed down the lake which bears his name, and Henry Hudson, an Englishman in the service of the Dutch East India Company, explored the Hudson River as far as the present site of Albany. A trading post was established by the Dutch on Manhattan Island in 1613 and on the banks of the Hudson near the site of Albany in 1614. The real beginning of colonization in New Netherland, however, was in 1623, when settlements were made at New Amsterdam, Albany, and elsewhere.

The territory now comprising New York was included in the grants conveyed by James I of England to the Plymouth Company in 1606 and 1620.

In 1664 King Charles II of England granted to the Duke of York the region now comprising the eastern part of New York, the area included in New Jersey and Vermont, and parts of Massachusetts, Connecticut, and Maine. In the same year the duke seized New Amsterdam, which then became New York. In 1673 the Dutch regained possession of New York. but in the following year it was again transferred to the English. The settlements on the west bank of the Delaware were also surrendered by the colonists to the Duke of York and continued in his possession until 1682, when William Penn obtained from him a quit-claim to Pennsylvania and by another deed acquired Delaware.

A short time after obtaining his grant, the Duke of York had conveyed the territory now constituting New Jersey to Lord Berkeley and Sir George Carteret. In 1702 the proprietors surrendered their right of government to the English crown; and from that time until 1738 New Jersey was under the governor of New York, but had its own legislature.

In 1686 the area between the Kennebec and the St. Croix, now a part of Maine, was transferred by royal order from the jurisdiction of New York to that of the Dominion of New England, and under that charter of 1691 it became a part of the royal province of Massachusetts Bay.

The territory west of the Connecticut River which now forms parts of Massachusetts and Connecticut was, by concessions and agreements made at various times prior to the Revolution, given up by New York to those colonies.

The area now constituting Vermont was for many years in dispute between New York and New Hampshire. In 1777 the inhabitants of the disputed territory organized an independent government, and in 1790 the present boundary between New York and Vermont was established. Since that date the boundaries of New York have not been materially changed.

In 1781 New York ceded to the Federal Government its claim to lands west of its present limits.

New York was one of the original thirteen states.

COUNTY LOCATION INDEX

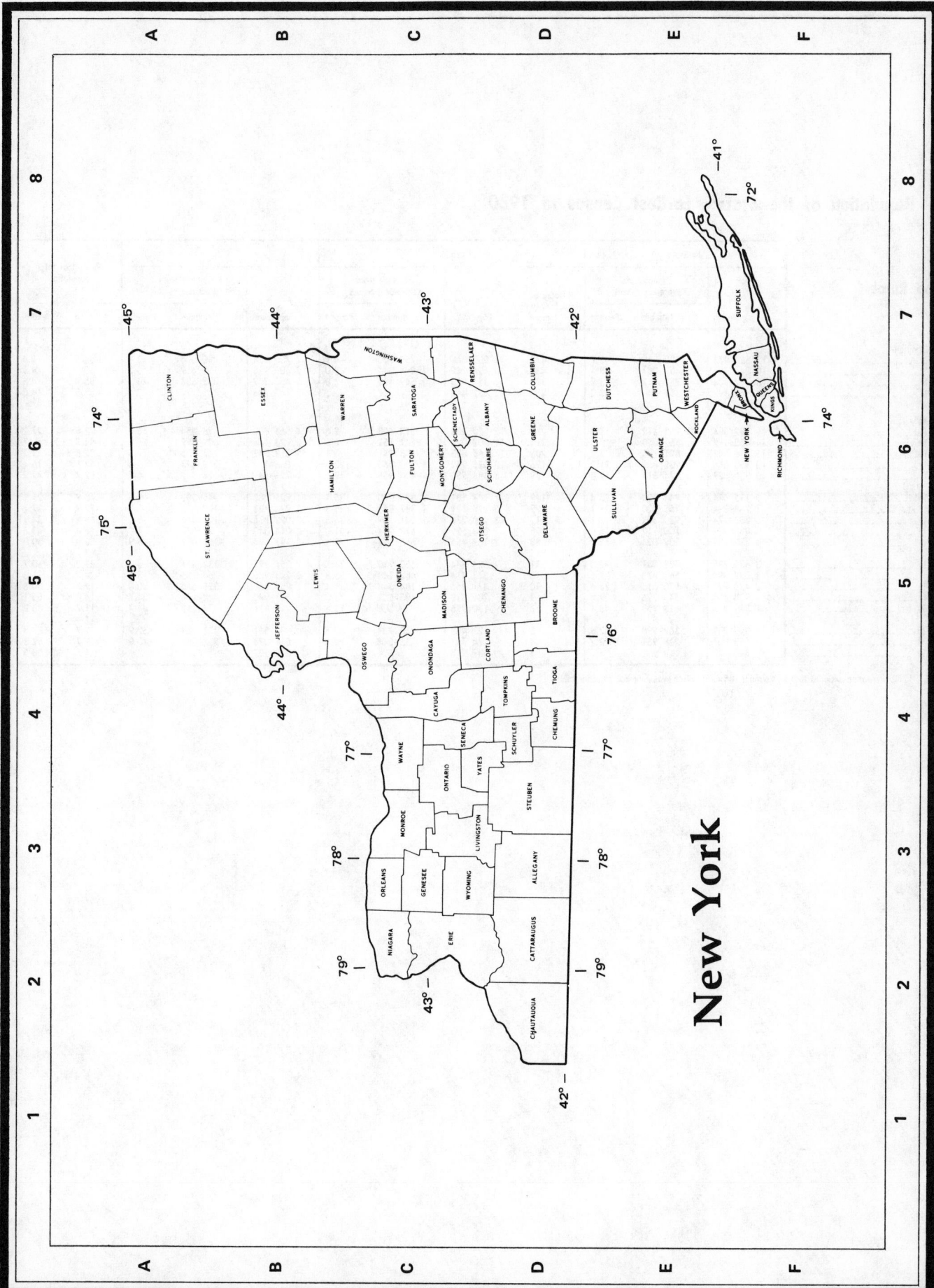

New York

Population of the State: Earliest Census to 1980

Urban and Rural

	The State			Urban				Rural				Percent of total population	
	Total population	Change from preceding census		Places of 2,500 or more	Population	Change from preceding census		Population	Change from preceding census			Urban	Rural
		Number	Percent			Number	Percent		Number	Percent			
Current urban definition:													
1980 (Apr. 1)	17 558 072	−683 319	−3.7	478	14 858 068	−768 901	−4.9	2 700 004	90 006	3.4		84.6	15.4
1970 (Apr. 1)	'18 241 391	1 459 087	8.7	431	15 626 969	1 295 044	9.0	2 609 998	159 619	6.5		85.7	14.3
1960 (Apr. 1)	16 782 304	1 952 112	13.2	326	14 331 925	1 649 479	13.0	2 450 379	302 633	14.1		85.4	14.6
1950 (Apr. 1)	14 830 192	1 351 050	10.0	230	12 682 446	...	...	2 147 746	...	...		85.5	14.5
Previous urban definition:													
1960 (Apr. 1)	16 782 304	1 952 112	13.2	251	12 220 702	313 658	2.6	4 561 602	1 638 454	56.1		72.8	27.2
1950 (Apr. 1)	14 830 192	1 351 050	10.0	214	11 907 044	741 151	6.6	2 923 148	609 899	26.4		80.3	19.7
1940 (Apr. 1)	13 479 142	891 076	7.1	203	11 165 893	643 941	6.1	2 313 249	247 135	12.0		82.8	17.2
1930 (Apr. 1)	12 588 066	2 202 839	21.2	196	10 521 952	1 933 366	22.5	2 066 114	269 473	15.0		83.6	16.4
1920 (Jan. 1)	10 385 227	1 271 613	14.0	169	8 588 586	1 400 455	19.5	1 796 641	−128 842	−6.7		82.7	17.3
1910 (Apr. 15)	9 113 614	1 844 720	25.4	149	7 188 131	1 890 020	35.7	1 925 483	−45 300	−2.3		78.9	21.1
1900 (June 1)	7 268 894	1 265 720	21.1	122	5 298 111	1 387 833	35.5	1 970 783	−122 113	−5.8		72.9	27.1
1890 (June 1)	6 003 174	920 303	18.1	117	3 910 278	1 041 749	36.3	2 092 896	−121 446	−5.5		65.1	34.9
1880 (June 1)	5 082 871	700 112	16.0	98	2 868 529	679 074	31.0	2 214 342	21 038	1.0		56.4	43.6
1870 (June 1)	4 382 759	502 024	12.9	88	2 189 455	665 111	43.6	2 193 304	−163 087	−6.9		50.0	50.0
1860 (June 1)	3 880 735	783 341	25.3	31	1 524 344	650 930	74.5	2 356 391	132 411	6.0		39.3	60.7
1850 (June 1)	3 097 394	668 473	27.5	16	873 414	402 148	85.3	2 223 980	266 325	13.6		28.2	71.8
1840 (June 1)	2 428 921	510 313	26.6	10	471 266	184 648	64.4	1 957 655	325 665	20.0		19.4	80.6
1830 (June 1)	1 918 608	545 796	39.8	9	286 618	125 622	78.0	1 631 990	420 174	34.7		14.9	85.1
1820 (Aug. 7)	1 372 812	413 763	43.1	7	160 996	39 508	32.5	1 211 816	374 255	44.7		11.7	88.3
1810 (Aug. 6)	959 049	369 998	62.8	5	121 488	46 731	62.5	837 561	323 267	62.9		12.7	87.3
1800 (Aug. 4)	589 051	248 931	73.2	4	74 757	35 544	90.6	514 294	213 387	70.9		12.7	87.3
1790 (Aug. 2)	340 120	...	...	3	39 213	...	...	300 907	...	...		11.5	88.5

NOTE: 1790 population excludes that of Vermont (85,425), which was enumerated separately.

ALBANY

1790	75,736
1800	34,103
1810	34,661
1820	38,116
1830	53,520
1840	68,593
1850	93,279
1860	113,917
1870	133,052
1880	154,890
1890	164,555
1900	165,571
1910	173,666
1920	186,106
1930	211,953
1940	221,315
1950	239,386
1960	272,926
1970	286,742
1980	285,909

ALLEGANY

1810	1,942
1820	9,330
1830	26,276
1840	40,975
1850	37,808
1860	41,881
1870	40,814
1880	41,810
1890	43,240
1900	41,501
1910	41,412
1920	36,842
1930	38,025
1940	39,681
1950	43,784
1960	43,978
1970	46,458
1980	51,742

BRONX

1920	732,016
1930	1,265,258
1940	1,394,711
1950	1,451,277
1960	1,424,815
1970	1,471,701
1980	1,168,972

BROOME

1810	8,130
1820	14,343
1830	17,759
1840	22,338
1850	30,660
1860	35,906
1870	44,103
1880	49,483
1890	62,973
1900	69,149
1910	78,809
1920	113,610
1930	147,022
1940	165,749
1950	184,698
1960	212,661
1970	221,815
1980	213,648

CATTARAUGUS

1820	4,090
1830	16,724
1840	28,872
1850	38,950
1860	43,886
1870	43,909
1880	55,806
1890	60,866
1900	65,643
1910	65,919
1920	71,323
1930	72,398
1940	72,652
1950	77,901
1960	80,187
1970	81,666
1980	85,697

CAYUGA

1800	15,907
1810	29,843
1820	38,897
1830	47,948
1840	50,338
1850	55,458
1860	55,757
1870	59,550
1880	65,081
1890	65,302
1900	66,234
1910	67,106
1920	65,221
1930	64,751
1940	65,508
1950	70,136
1960	73,942
1970	77,439
1980	79,894

CHAUTAUQUA

1820	12,568
1830	34,671
1840	47,975
1850	50,493
1860	58,422
1870	59,327
1880	65,342
1890	72,202
1900	88,314
1910	104,126
1920	115,348
1930	126,457
1940	123,580
1950	135,189
1960	145,377
1970	147,305
1980	146,925

CHEMUNG

1840	20,732
1850	38,831
1860	26,917
1870	35,281
1880	43,065
1890	48,265
1900	54,063
1910	54,662
1920	65,872
1930	74,680
1940	73,718
1950	86,827
1960	98,706
1970	101,537
1980	97,656

CHENANGO

1800	16,087
1810	21,704
1820	31,215
1830	37,238
1840	40,785
1850	40,311
1860	40,934
1870	40,564
1880	39,891
1890	37,776
1900	36,568
1910	35,575
1920	34,969
1930	34,665
1940	36,454
1950	39,138
1960	43,243
1970	46,368
1980	49,344

CLINTON

1790	1,614
1800	8,516
1810	8,002
1820	12,070
1830	19,344
1840	28,157
1850	40,047
1860	45,785
1870	47,947
1880	50,897
1890	46,437
1900	47,430
1910	48,230
1920	43,898
1930	35,687
1940	54,006
1950	53,622
1960	72,722
1970	72,934
1980	80,750

COLUMBIA

1790	27,732
1800	35,472
1810	32,390
1820	38,330
1830	39,907
1840	43,252
1850	43,073
1860	47,172
1870	47,044
1880	47,928
1890	46,172
1900	43,211
1910	43,658
1920	38,930
1930	41,617
1940	41,464
1950	43,182
1960	47,322
1970	51,519
1980	59,487

CORTLAND

1810	8,869
1820	16,507
1830	23,791

1840	24,607
1850	25,140
1860	26,294
1870	25,173
1880	25,825
1890	28,657
1900	27,576
1910	29,249
1920	29,625
1930	31,709
1940	33,668
1950	37,158
1960	41,113
1970	45,894
1980	48,820

DELAWARE

1800	10,228
1810	20,303
1820	26,587
1830	33,024
1840	35,396
1850	39,834
1860	42,465
1870	42,972
1880	42,721
1890	45,496
1900	46,413
1910	45,575
1920	42,774
1930	41,163
1940	40,989
1950	44,420
1960	43,540
1970	44,718
1980	46,824

DUTCHESS

1790	45,266
1800	47,775
1810	51,363
1820	46,615
1830	50,926
1840	52,398
1850	58,992
1860	64,941
1870	74,041
1880	79,184
1890	77,789
1900	81,670
1910	87,661
1920	91,747
1930	105,462
1940	120,542
1950	136,781
1960	176,008
1970	222,295
1980	245,055

ERIE

1830	35,719
1840	62,465
1850	100,993
1860	141,971
1870	178,699
1880	219,884
1890	322,981
1900	433,686
1910	528,985
1920	634,688
1930	762,408
1940	798,377
1950	899,238
1960	1,064,688

1970	1,113,491
1980	1,015,472

ESSEX

1810	9,477
1820	12,811
1830	19,287
1840	23,634
1850	31,148
1860	28,214
1870	29,042
1880	34,515
1890	33,052
1900	30,707
1910	33,458
1920	31,871
1930	33,959
1940	34,178
1950	35,086
1960	35,300
1970	34,631
1980	36,176

FRANKLIN

1810	2,617
1820	4,439
1830	11,312
1840	16,518
1850	25,102
1860	30,837
1870	30,217
1880	32,390
1890	38,110
1900	42,853
1910	45,717
1920	43,541
1930	45,694
1940	44,286
1950	44,830
1960	44,742
1970	43,931
1980	44,929

FULTON

1840	18,049
1850	20,171
1860	24,162
1870	27,064
1880	30,985
1890	37,650
1900	42,842
1910	44,534
1920	44,927
1930	46,560
1940	48,597
1950	51,021
1960	51,304
1970	52,637
1980	55,153

GENESEE

1810	12,588
1820	58,093
1830	52,147
1840	59,587
1850	28,488
1860	32,189
1870	31,606
1880	32,806
1890	33,265
1900	34,561
1910	37,615

1920	37,976	1830	48,493	1970	54,041	1980	1,321,582	1860	90,686
1930	44,468	1840	60,984	1980	57,006			1870	104,183
1940	44,481	1850	68,153			**NEW YORK**		1880	117,893
1950	47,584	1860	69,825	**MADISON**				1890	146,247
1960	53,994	1870	65,415			1790	33,131	1900	168,735
1970	58,722	1880	66,103	1810	25,144	1800	60,515	1910	200,298
1980	59,400	1890	68,806	1820	32,208	1810	96,373	1920	241,465
		1900	76,748	1830	39,038	1820	123,706	1930	291,606
GREENE		1910	80,382	1840	40,008	1830	202,589	1940	295,108
		1920	82,250	1850	43,072	1840	312,710	1950	341,719
1800	13,074	1930	83,574	1860	43,545	1850	515,547	1960	423,028
1810	19,536	1940	84,003	1870	43,522	1860	813,699	1970	472,835
1820	22,996	1950	85,521	1880	44,112	1870	942,292	1980	463,920
1830	29,525	1960	87,835	1890	42,892	1880	1,206,299		
1840	30,446	1970	88,508	1900	40,545	1890	1,515,301	**ONTARIO**	
1850	33,126	1980	88,151	1910	39,289	1900	2,050,600		
1860	31,930			1920	39,535	1910	2,762,522	1790	1,075
1870	31,832	**KINGS**		1930	39,790	1920	2,284,103	1800	15,218
1880	32,695			1940	39,598	1930	1,867,312	1810	42,032
1890	31,598	1790	4,495	1950	46,214	1940	1,889,924	1820	88,267
1900	31,478	1800	5,740	1960	54,635	1950	1,960,101	1830	40,288
1910	30,214	1810	8,303	1970	62,864	1960	1,698,281	1840	43,501
1920	25,796	1820	11,187	1980	65,150	1970	1,539,233	1850	43,929
1930	35,208	1830	20,535			1980	1,428,285	1860	44,563
1940	27,926	1840	47,613	**MONROE**				1870	45,108
1950	28,745	1850	138,882			**NIAGARA**		1880	49,541
1960	31,372	1860	279,122	1830	49,855			1890	48,453
1970	33,136	1870	419,921	1840	64,902	1810	8,971	1900	49,605
1980	40,861	1880	599,495	1850	87,650	1820	22,990	1910	52,286
		1890	838,547	1860	100,648	1830	18,482	1920	52,652
HAMILTON		1900	1,166,582	1870	117,868	1840	31,132	1930	54,276
		1910	1,634,351	1880	144,903	1850	42,276	1940	55,307
1820	1,251	1920	2,018,356	1890	189,586	1860	50,399	1950	60,172
1830	1,325	1930	2,560,401	1900	217,854	1870	50,437	1960	68,070
1840	1,907	1940	2,698,285	1910	283,121	1880	54,173	1970	78,849
1850	2,188	1950	2,738,175	1920	352,034	1890	62,491	1980	88,909
1860	3,024	1960	2,627,319	1930	423,881	1900	74,961		
1870	2,960	1970	2,602,012	1940	438,230	1910	92,036	**ORANGE**	
1880	3,923	1980	2,230,936	1950	487,632	1920	118,705		
1890	4,762			1960	586,387	1930	149,329	1790	18,492
1900	4,947	**LEWIS**		1970	711,917	1940	160,110	1800	29,355
1910	4,373			1980	702,238	1950	189,992	1810	34,347
1920	3,970	1810	6,433			1960	242,269	1820	41,213
1930	3,929	1820	9,277	**MONTGOMERY**		1970	235,720	1830	45,366
1940	4,188	1830	15,239			1980	227,354	1840	50,739
1950	4,105	1840	17,830	1790	28,848			1850	57,415
1960	4,267	1850	24,564	1800	22,051	**ONEIDA**		1860	63,812
1970	4,714	1860	28,580	1810	41,214			1870	80,902
1980	5,034	1870	28,699	1820	37,569	1800	22,258	1880	88,220
		1880	31,416	1830	43,715	1810	33,792	1890	97,859
HERKIMER		1890	29,806	1840	35,818	1820	50,997	1900	103,859
		1900	27,427	1850	31,992	1830	71,326	1910	116,001
1800	14,503	1910	24,849	1860	30,866	1840	85,310	1920	199,844
1810	22,046	1920	23,704	1870	34,457	1850	99,566	1930	130,383
1820	31,017	1930	23,447	1880	38,315	1860	105,202	1940	140,113
1830	35,870	1940	22,815	1890	45,699	1870	110,008	1950	152,255
1840	37,477	1950	22,521	1900	47,488	1880	115,475	1960	183,734
1850	38,244	1960	23,249	1910	57,567	1890	122,922	1970	221,657
1860	40,561	1970	23,644	1920	57,928	1900	132,800	1980	259,603
1870	39,929	1980	25,035	1930	60,076	1910	154,157		
1880	42,669			1940	59,142	1920	182,833	**ORLEANS**	
1890	45,608	**LIVINGSTON**		1950	59,594	1930	198,763		
1900	51,049			1960	57,240	1940	203,636	1830	17,732
1910	56,356	1830	27,729	1970	55,883	1950	222,855	1840	25,127
1920	64,962	1840	35,140	1980	53,439	1960	264,401	1850	28,501
1930	64,006	1850	40,875			1970	273,070	1860	28,717
1940	59,527	1860	39,546	**NASSAU**		1980	253,466	1870	27,689
1950	61,407	1870	38,309					1880	30,128
1960	66,370	1880	39,562	1900	55,448	**ONONDAGA**		1890	30,803
1970	67,407	1890	37,801	1910	83,930			1900	30,164
1980	66,714	1900	37,059	1920	126,120	1800	7,698	1910	32,000
		1910	38,037	1930	303,053	1810	25,987	1920	28,619
JEFFERSON		1920	36,830	1940	406,748	1820	41,467	1930	28,795
		1930	37,560	1950	672,765	1830	58,973	1940	27,760
1810	15,140	1940	38,510	1960	1,300,171	1840	67,911	1950	29,832
1820	32,952	1950	40,257	1970	1,428,838	1850	85,890	1960	34,159
		1960	44,053					1970	37,305

1980	38,496

OSWEGO

1820	12,374
1830	27,119
1840	43,619
1850	62,198
1860	75,958
1870	77,941
1880	77,911
1890	71,883
1900	70,881
1910	71,664
1920	71,045
1930	69,645
1940	71,275
1950	77,181
1960	86,118
1970	100,897
1980	113,901

OTSEGO

1800	21,343
1810	38,802
1820	44,856
1830	51,372
1840	49,628
1850	48,638
1860	50,157
1870	48,967
1880	51,397
1890	50,861
1900	48,939
1910	47,216
1920	46,200
1930	46,710
1940	46,082
1950	50,763
1960	51,942
1970	56,181
1980	59,075

PUTNAM

1820	11,268
1830	12,628
1840	12,825
1850	14,138
1860	14,002
1870	15,420
1880	15,181
1890	14,849
1900	13,787
1910	14,665
1920	10,802
1930	13,744
1940	16,555
1950	20,307
1960	31,722
1970	56,696
1980	77,193

QUEENS

1790	16,041
1800	16,916
1810	19,336
1820	21,519
1830	22,460
1840	30,324
1850	36,833
1860	57,391
1870	73,803
1880	90,574
1890	128,059
1900	152,999
1910	284,041
1920	469,042
1930	1,079,129
1940	1,297,634
1950	1,550,849
1960	1,809,578
1970	1,987,174
1980	1,891,325

RENSSELAER

1800	30,351
1810	36,309
1820	40,153
1830	49,424
1840	60,259
1850	73,363
1860	86,328
1870	99,549
1880	115,328
1890	124,511
1900	121,697
1910	122,276
1920	113,129
1930	119,781
1940	121,834
1950	132,607
1960	142,585
1970	152,510
1980	151,966

RICHMOND

1790	3,835
1800	4,564
1810	5,347
1820	6,135
1830	7,082
1840	10,965
1850	15,061
1860	25,492
1870	33,029
1880	38,991
1890	51,693
1900	67,021
1910	85,969
1920	116,531
1930	158,346
1940	174,441
1950	191,555
1960	221,991
1970	295,443
1980	352,121

ROCKLAND

1800	6,353
1810	7,758
1820	8,837
1830	9,388
1840	11,975
1850	16,962
1860	22,492
1870	25,213
1880	27,690
1890	35,162
1900	38,298
1910	46,873
1920	45,548
1930	59,559
1940	74,261
1950	89,276
1960	136,803
1970	229,903
1980	259,530

SAINT LAWRENCE

1810	7,885
1820	16,037
1830	36,354
1840	56,706
1850	68,617
1860	83,689
1870	84,826
1880	85,997
1890	85,048
1900	89,083
1910	89,005
1920	88,121
1930	90,960
1940	91,098
1950	98,897
1960	111,239
1970	112,309
1980	114,254

SARATOGA

1800	24,564
1810	33,147
1820	36,052
1830	38,697
1840	40,553
1850	45,646
1860	51,729
1870	51,529
1880	55,156
1890	57,663
1900	61,089
1910	61,917
1920	60,029
1930	63,314
1940	65,606
1950	74,869
1960	89,096
1970	121,764
1980	153,759

SCHENECTADY

1810	10,201
1820	13,081
1830	12,347
1840	17,387
1850	20,054
1860	20,002
1870	21,347
1880	23,538
1890	29,797
1900	46,852
1910	88,235
1920	109,363
1930	125,021
1940	122,494
1950	142,497
1960	152,896
1970	161,078
1980	149,946

SCHOHARIE

1800	9,808
1810	18,945
1820	23,154
1830	27,907
1840	32,358
1850	33,548
1860	34,469
1870	33,340
1880	32,910
1890	29,164
1900	26,854
1910	23,855
1920	21,303
1930	19,667
1940	20,812
1950	22,703
1960	22,616
1970	24,750
1980	29,710

SCHUYLER

1860	18,840
1870	18,989
1880	18,842
1890	16,711
1900	15,811
1910	14,004
1920	13,098
1930	12,909
1940	12,979
1950	14,182
1960	15,044
1970	16,737
1980	17,686

SENECA

1810	16,609
1820	23,619
1830	21,041
1840	24,874
1850	25,441
1860	28,138
1870	27,823
1880	29,278
1890	28,227
1900	28,114
1910	26,972
1920	24,735
1930	24,983
1940	25,732
1950	29,253
1960	31,984
1970	35,083
1980	33,733

STEUBEN

1800	1,788
1810	7,246
1820	21,989
1830	33,851
1840	46,138
1850	63,771
1860	66,690
1870	67,717
1880	77,586
1890	81,473
1900	82,822
1910	83,362
1920	80,627
1930	80,671
1940	84,927
1950	91,439
1960	97,691
1970	99,546
1980	99,217

SUFFOLK

1790	16,440
1800	19,735
1810	21,113
1820	24,272
1830	26,780
1840	32,469
1850	36,922
1860	43,375
1870	46,924
1880	53,888
1890	62,491
1900	77,582
1910	96,138
1920	110,246
1930	161,055
1940	197,355
1950	276,129
1960	666,784
1970	1,127,030
1980	1,284,231

SULLIVAN

1810	6,108
1820	8,900
1830	12,364
1840	15,629
1850	25,088
1860	32,385
1870	34,550
1880	32,491
1890	31,031
1900	32,306
1910	33,808
1920	33,163
1930	35,272
1940	37,901
1950	40,731
1960	45,272
1970	52,580
1980	65,155

TIOGA

1800	7,901
1810	7,899
1820	16,971
1830	27,690
1840	29,527
1850	24,880
1860	28,748
1870	30,572
1880	32,673
1890	29,935
1900	27,951
1910	25,624
1920	24,212
1930	25,480
1940	27,072
1950	30,166
1960	37,802
1970	46,513
1980	49,812

TOMPKINS

1820	20,681
1830	36,545
1840	37,948
1850	38,746
1860	31,409
1870	33,178
1880	34,445
1890	32,923
1900	33,830
1910	33,647
1920	35,285
1930	41,490
1940	42,340
1950	59,122
1960	66,164
1970	77,064
1980	87,085

ULSTER

1790	29,397
1800	24,855
1810	26,576
1820	30,934
1830	36,550
1840	45,822
1850	59,384
1860	76,381
1870	84,075
1880	85,838
1890	87,062
1900	88,422
1910	91,769
1920	74,979
1930	80,155
1940	87,017
1950	92,621
1960	118,804
1970	141,241
1980	158,158

WARREN

1820	9,453
1830	11,796
1840	13,422
1850	17,199
1860	21,434
1870	22,592
1880	25,179
1890	27,866
1900	29,943
1910	32,223
1920	31,673
1930	34,174
1940	36,035
1950	39,205
1960	44,002
1970	49,402
1980	54,854

WASHINGTON

1790	14,042
1800	35,792
1810	44,289
1820	38,831
1830	42,635
1840	41,080
1850	44,750
1860	45,904
1870	49,568
1880	47,871
1890	45,690
1900	45,624
1910	47,778
1920	44,888
1930	46,482
1940	46,726
1950	47,144
1960	48,476
1970	52,725
1980	54,795

WAYNE

1830	33,643
1840	42,057
1850	44,953
1860	47,762
1870	47,710
1880	51,700
1890	49,729
1900	48,660
1910	50,179

1920	48,827
1930	49,995
1940	52,747
1950	57,323
1960	67,989
1970	79,404
1980	84,581

WESTCHESTER

1790	24,003
1800	27,373
1810	30,272
1820	32,638
1830	36,456
1840	48,686
1850	58,263
1860	99,497
1870	131,348
1880	108,988
1890	146,772
1900	184,257
1910	283,055
1920	344,436
1930	520,947
1940	573,558
1950	625,816
1960	808,891
1970	894,406
1980	866,599

WYOMING

1850	31,981
1860	31,968
1870	29,164
1880	30,907
1890	31,193
1900	30,413
1910	31,880
1920	30,314
1930	28,764
1940	31,394
1950	32,822
1960	34,793
1970	37,688
1980	39,895

YATES

1830	19,009
1840	20,444
1850	20,590
1860	20,290
1870	19,595
1880	21,087
1890	21,001
1900	20,318
1910	18,642
1920	16,641
1930	16,848
1940	16,381
1950	17,615
1960	18,614
1970	19,831
1980	21,459

NOTES

MONTGOMERY

Name changed from Tyron in 1784.

WASHINGTON

Name changed from Charlotte in 1784.

ALBANY

1790	3,498
1800	5,349
1810	10,762
1820	12,630
1830	24,209
1840	33,721
1850	50,763
1860	62,367
1870	69,422
1880	90,753
1890	94,923
1900	94,151
1910	100,253
1920	113,344
1930	127,412
1940	130,577
1950	134,995
1960	129,726
1970	115,781
1980	101,727

AMSTERDAM

1870	5,426
1880	9,466
1890	17,336
1900	20,929
1910	31,267
1920	33,524
1930	34,817
1940	33,329
1950	32,240
1960	28,772
1970	25,524
1980	21,872

AUBURN

1840	5,626
1850	9,548
1860	10,986
1870	17,225
1880	21,924
1890	25,858
1900	30,345
1910	34,668
1920	36,192
1930	36,652
1940	35,753
1950	36,722
1960	35,249
1970	34,599
1980	32,548

BABYLON

1900	2,157
1910	2,600
1920	2,523
1930	4,342
1940	4,742
1950	6,015
1960	11,062
1970	12,897
1980	12,388

BATAVIA

1860	2,560
1870	3,890
1880	4,845
1890	7,221
1900	9,180
1910	11,613
1920	13,541

1930	17,375
1940	17,267
1950	17,799
1960	18,210
1970	17,338
1980	16,703

BEACON

1920	10,996
1930	11,933
1940	12,572
1950	14,012
1960	13,922
1970	13,255
1980	12,937

BINGHAMTON

1860	8,325
1870	12,692
1880	17,317
1890	35,005
1900	39,647
1910	48,443
1920	66,800
1930	76,662
1940	78,309
1950	80,674
1960	75,941
1970	64,123
1980	55,860

BUFFALO

1810	1,508
1820	2,095
1830	8,668
1840	18,213
1850	42,261
1860	89,124
1870	117,714
1880	155,134
1890	255,664
1900	352,387
1910	432,715
1920	506,775
1930	573,076
1940	575,901
1950	580,132
1960	532,759
1970	462,768
1980	357,870

CANANDAIGUA

1900	6,151
1910	7,217
1920	7,299
1930	7,541
1940	8,321
1950	8,332
1960	9,370
1970	10,488
1980	10,419

COHOES

1850	4,229
1860	8,800
1870	15,537
1880	19,416
1890	22,509
1900	23,910
1910	24,709
1920	22,987
1930	23,226

1940	21,955
1950	21,272
1960	20,129
1970	18,653
1980	18,144

CORNING

1870	4,018
1880	4,802
1890	8,550
1900	11,061
1910	13,730
1920	15,820
1930	15,777
1940	16,212
1950	17,684
1960	17,085
1970	15,792
1980	12,953

CORTLAND

1870	3,066
1880	4,050
1890	8,590
1900	9,014
1910	11,504
1920	13,294
1930	15,043
1940	15,881
1950	18,152
1960	19,181
1970	19,621
1980	20,138

DEPEW

1900	3,379
1910	3,921
1920	5,850
1930	6,536
1940	6,084
1950	7,217
1960	13,580
1970	22,158
1980	19,819

DOBBS FERRY

1890	2,083
1900	2,888
1910	3,455
1920	4,401
1930	5,741
1940	5,883
1950	6,268
1960	9,260
1970	10,353
1980	10,053

DUNKIRK

1870	5,231
1880	7,248
1890	9,416
1900	11,616
1910	17,221
1920	19,336
1930	17,802
1940	17,713
1950	18,007
1960	18,205
1970	16,855
1980	15,310

EAST ROCKAWAY

1900	739
1910	1,200
1920	2,005
1930	4,340
1940	5,610
1950	7,970
1960	10,721
1970	11,795
1980	10,917

ELMIRA

1870	15,863
1880	20,541
1890	30,893
1900	35,672
1910	37,176
1920	45,393
1930	47,397
1940	45,106
1950	49,716
1960	46,517
1970	39,945
1980	35,327

ENDICOTT

1910	2,408
1920	9,500
1930	16,231
1940	17,702
1950	20,050
1960	18,775
1970	16,556
1980	14,457

FLORAL PARK

1910	1,225
1920	2,097
1930	10,016
1940	12,950
1950	14,582
1960	17,499
1970	18,466
1980	16,805

FREDONIA

1880	2,692
1890	3,399
1900	4,127
1910	5,285
1920	6,051
1930	5,814
1940	5,738
1950	7,095
1960	8,477
1970	10,326
1980	11,126

FREEPORT

1900	2,612
1910	4,836
1920	8,599
1930	15,467
1940	20,410
1950	24,680
1960	34,419
1970	40,374
1980	38,272

FULTON

1870	3,507
1880	3,941
1890	4,214
1900	5,281
1910	10,480
1920	13,043
1930	12,462
1940	13,362
1950	13,922
1960	14,261
1970	14,003
1980	13,312

GARDEN CITY

1920	2,420
1930	7,810
1940	11,223
1950	14,486
1960	23,948
1970	25,373
1980	22,927

GENEVA

1870	5,521
1880	5,878
1890	7,557
1900	10,433
1910	12,446
1920	14,648
1930	16,053
1940	15,555
1950	17,144
1960	17,286
1970	16,793
1980	15,133

GLENS COVE

1920	8,664
1930	11,430
1940	12,415
1950	15,130
1960	23,817
1970	25,770
1980	24,618

GLEN FALLS

1850	2,717
1870	4,500
1880	4,900
1890	9,509
1900	12,613
1910	15,243
1920	16,638
1930	18,513
1940	18,836
1950	19 610
1960	18,580
1970	17,222
1980	15,897

GLOVERSVILLE

1870	4,518
1880	7,133
1890	13,864
1900	18,349
1910	20,642
1920	22,075
1930	23,099
1940	23,329
1950	23,634

1960	21,741
1970	19,677
1980	17,836

HAMBURG

1880	758
1890	1,331
1900	1,683
1910	2,134
1920	3,185
1930	4,731
1940	5,467
1950	6,938
1960	9,145
1970	10,215
1980	10,582

HARRISON

1980	23,046

HEMPSTEAD

1870	2,316
1880	2,521
1890	4,831
1900	3,582
1910	4,964
1920	6,382
1930	12,650
1940	20,856
1950	29,135
1960	34,641
1970	39,411
1980	40,404

HORNELL

1870	4,552
1880	8,195
1890	10,966
1900	11,918
1910	13,617
1920	15,025
1930	16,250
1940	15,649
1950	15,049
1960	13,907
1970	12,144
1980	10,234

ITHACA

1870	8,461
1880	9,105
1890	11,079
1900	13,136
1910	14,802
1920	17,004
1930	20,708
1940	19,730
1950	29,257
1960	28,799
1970	26,226
1980	28,732

JAMESTOWN

1860	3,155
1870	5,336
1880	9,357
1890	16,038
1900	22,892
1910	31,297
1920	28,917

1930	45,155
1940	42,638
1950	43,354
1960	41,818
1970	39,795
1980	35,775

JOHNSON CITY

1900	3,111
1910	3,775
1920	8,587
1930	13,567
1940	18,039
1950	19,249
1960	19,118
1970	18,025
1980	17,126

JOHNSTOWN

1870	3,282
1880	5,013
1890	7,768
1900	10,130
1910	10,447
1920	10,908
1930	10,801
1940	10,666
1950	10,023
1960	10,390
1970	10,045
1980	9,360

KENMORE

1900	318
1910	1,020
1920	3,160
1930	16,482
1940	18,612
1950	20,066
1960	21,261
1970	20,980
1976	18,474

KINGSTON

1870	6,315
1880	18,344
1890	21,261
1900	24,534
1910	25,908
1920	26,688
1930	28,088
1940	28,589
1950	28,817
1960	29,260
1970	25,544
1980	24,481

LACKAWANNA

1910	14,549
1920	17,918
1930	23,948
1940	24,058
1950	27,658
1960	29,564
1970	28,657
1980	22,701

LANCASTER

1860	1,706
1870	1,697
1880	1,602
1890	1,692
1900	3,750
1910	4,364
1920	6,059
1930	7,040
1940	7,236
1950	8,665
1960	12,254
1970	13,365
1980	13,056

LINDENHURST

1930	4,040
1940	4,756
1950	8,644
1960	20,905
1970	28,395
1980	26,919

LOCKPORT

1860	10,871
1870	12,426
1880	13,522
1890	16,038
1900	16,581
1910	17,970
1920	21,308
1930	23,160
1940	24,379
1950	25,133
1960	26,443
1970	25,399
1980	24,844

LONG BEACH

1920	282
1930	5,817
1940	9,036
1950	15,586
1960	26,473
1970	33,127
1980	34,073

LYNBROOK

1920	4,371
1930	11,993
1940	14,557
1950	17,314
1960	19,881
1970	23,776
1980	20,424

MALVERNE

1930	2,256
1940	5,153
1950	8,086
1960	9,968
1970	10,036
1980	9,262

MAMARONECK

1910	5,699
1920	6,571
1930	11,766
1940	13,034

1950	15,016
1960	17,673
1970	18,909
1980	17,616

MASSAPEQUA PARK

1940	488
1950	2,334
1960	19,904
1970	22,122
1980	19,779

MASSENA

1870	483
1880	(NA)
1890	1,049
1900	2,023
1910	2,951
1920	5,993
1930	10,637
1940	11,328
1950	13,137
1960	15,478
1970	14,042
1980	12,851

MIDDLETOWN

1870	6,049
1880	8,494
1890	11,977
1900	14,522
1910	15,313
1920	18,420
1930	21,276
1940	21,908
1950	22,586
1960	23,475
1970	22,607
1980	21,454

MINEOLA

1910	1,981
1920	3,016
1930	8,155
1940	10,064
1950	14,831
1960	20,519
1970	21,845
1980	20,757

MOUNT VERNON

1870	2,700
1880	4,586
1890	10,830
1900	21,228
1910	30,919
1920	42,726
1930	61,499
1940	67,362
1950	71,899
1960	71,010
1970	72,778
1980	66,713

NEWARK

1870	2,248
1880	2,450
1890	3,698
1900	4,578

1910	6,227
1920	6,964
1930	7,649
1940	9,646
1950	10,295
1960	12,868
1970	11,644
1980	10,017

NEWBURGH

1860	12,578
1870	17,014
1880	18,049
1890	23,087
1900	24,943
1910	27,805
1920	30,366
1930	31,275
1940	31,883
1950	31,956
1960	30,979
1970	26,219
1980	23,438

NEW ROCHELLE

1870	279
1880	(NA)
1890	8,217
1900	14,720
1910	28,867
1920	36,213
1930	54,000
1940	58,408
1950	59,725
1960	76,812
1970	75,385
1980	70,794

NEW YORK

1790	49,401
1800	79,216
1810	119,734
1820	152,056
1830	242,278
1840	391,114
1850	696,115
1860	1,174,779
1870	1,478,103
1880	1,911,698
1890	2,507,414
1900	3,437,202
1910	4,766,883
1920	5,620,048
1930	6,930,446
1940	7,454,995
1950	7,891,957
1960	7,781,984
1970	7,895,563
1980	7,071,639

BRONX BOROUGH

1790	1,781
1800	1,755
1810	2,267
1820	2,782
1830	3,023
1840	5,346
1850	8,032
1860	23,593
1870	37,393
1880	51,980
1890	88,908
1900	200,507

1910	430,980
1920	732,016
1930	1,265,258
1940	1,394,711
1950	1,451,277
1960	1,424,815
1970	1,471,701
1980	1,168,972

BROOKLYN BOROUGH

1790	4,495
1800	5,740
1810	8,303
1820	11,187
1830	20,535
1840	47,613
1850	138,882
1860	279,122
1870	419,921
1880	599,495
1890	838,547
1900	1,166,582
1910	1,634,351
1920	2,018,356
1930	2,560,401
1940	2,698,285
1950	2,738,175
1960	2,627,319
1970	2,602,012
1980	2,230,936

MANHATTEN BOROUGH

1790	33,131
1800	60,515
1810	96,373
1820	123,706
1830	202,589
1840	312,710
1850	515,547
1860	813,669
1870	942,292
1880	1,164,673
1890	1,441,216
1900	1,850,093
1910	2,331,542
1920	2,284,103
1930	1,867,312
1940	1,889,924
1950	1,960,101
1960	1,698,281
1970	1,539,233
1980	1,428,285

QUEENS BOROUGH

1790	6,159
1800	6,642
1810	7,444
1820	8,246
1830	9,049
1840	14,480
1850	18,593
1860	32,903
1870	45,468
1880	56,559
1890	87,050
1900	152,999
1910	284,041
1920	469,042
1930	1,079,129
1940	1,297,634
1950	1,550,849
1960	1,809,578
1970	1,987,174
1980	1,891,325

STATEN ISLAND BOROUGH

1790	3,835
1800	4,564
1810	5,347
1820	6,135
1830	7,082
1840	10,965
1850	15,061
1860	25,492
1870	33,029
1880	38,991
1890	51,693
1900	67,021
1910	85,969
1920	116,531
1930	158,346
1940	174,441
1950	191,555
1960	221,991
1970	295,443
1980	352,121

NIAGARA FALLS

1870	3,006
1880	3,320
1890	5,502
1900	19,457
1910	30,445
1920	50,760
1930	75,460
1940	78,029
1950	90,872
1960	102,394
1970	85,615
1980	71,384

NORTH TONAWANDA

1880	1,492
1890	4,793
1900	9,069
1910	11,955
1920	15,482
1930	19,019
1940	20,254
1950	24,731
1960	34,757
1970	36,012
1980	35,760

OGDENSBURG

1860	7,409
1870	10,076
1880	10,341
1890	11,662
1900	12,633
1910	15,933
1920	14,609
1930	16,915
1940	16,346
1950	16,166
1960	16,122
1970	14,554
1980	12,275

OLEAN

1870	1,327
1880	3,036
1890	7,358
1900	9,462
1910	14,743
1920	20,506
1930	21,790

1940	21,506
1950	22,884
1960	21,868
1970	19,169
1980	18,207

ONEIDA

1870	3,262
1880	3,934
1890	6,083
1900	6,364
1910	8,317
1920	10,541
1930	10,558
1940	10,291
1950	11,325
1960	11,677
1970	11,658
1980	10,810

ONEONTA

1870	1,016
1880	3,002
1890	6,272
1900	7,147
1910	9,491
1920	11,582
1930	12,536
1940	11,731
1950	13,564
1960	13,412
1970	16,030
1980	14,933

OSSINING

1860	5,345
1870	4,696
1880	6,578
1890	9,352
1900	7,939
1910	11,480
1920	10,739
1930	15,241
1940	15,996
1950	16,098
1960	18,662
1970	21,659
1980	20,196

OSWEGO

1850	12,205
1860	16,816
1870	20,910
1880	21,116
1890	21,842
1900	22,199
1910	23,368
1920	23,626
1930	22,652
1940	22,062
1950	22,647
1960	22,155
1970	20,913
1980	19,793

PATCHOGUE

1900	2,926
1910	3,824
1920	4,031
1930	6,860
1940	7,181

1950	7,361
1960	8,838
1970	11,582
1980	11,291

PEEKSKILL

1870	6,560
1880	6,893
1890	9,676
1900	10,358
1910	15,245
1920	15,868
1930	17,125
1940	17,311
1950	17,731
1960	18,737
1970	19,283
1980	18,236

PLATTSBURGH

1860	3,032
1870	5,139
1880	5,242
1890	7,010
1900	8,434
1910	11,138
1920	10,909
1930	13,349
1940	16,351
1950	17,738
1960	20,172
1970	18,175
1980	21,057

PORT CHESTER

1870	3,797
1880	3,254
1890	5,274
1900	7,440
1910	12,809
1920	16,573
1930	22,662
1940	23,073
1950	23,970
1960	24,960
1970	25,803
1980	23,565

POTSDAM

1840	4,476
1850	5,349
1860	6,735
1870	2,891
1880	2,762
1890	3,961
1900	3,843
1910	4,036
1920	4,039
1930	4,136
1940	4,821
1950	7,491
1960	7,765
1970	10,303
1980	10,635

POUGHKEEPSIE

1850	11,511
1860	14,726
1870	20,080
1880	20,207
1890	22,206

1900	24,029
1910	27,936
1920	35,000
1930	40,288
1940	40,478
1950	41,023
1960	38,330
1970	32,029
1980	29,757

RENSSELAER

1880	3,295
1890	7,301
1900	7,466
1910	10,711
1920	10,823
1930	11,223
1940	10,768
1950	10,856
1960	10,506
1970	10,136
1980	9,047

ROCHESTER

1830	9,207
1840	20,191
1850	36,403
1860	48,204
1870	62,386
1880	89,366
1890	133,896
1900	162,608
1910	218,149
1920	295,750
1930	328,132
1940	324,975
1950	332,488
1960	318,611
1970	295,011
1980	241,011

ROCKVILLE CENTRE

1900	1,884
1910	3,667
1920	6,262
1930	13,718
1940	18,613
1950	22,363
1960	26,355
1970	27,444
1980	25,412

ROME

1860	3,584
1870	11,000
1880	12,194
1890	14,991
1900	15,343
1910	20,497
1920	26,341
1930	32,338
1940	34,214
1950	41,682
1960	51,646
1970	50,148
1980	43,826

RYE

1910	3,964
1920	5,308
1930	8,712
1940	9,865
1950	11,721
1960	14,225
1970	15,869
1980	15,083

SARATOGA SPRINGS

1870	7,516
1880	8,421
1890	11,975
1900	12,409
1910	12,693
1920	13,181
1930	13,169
1940	13,705
1950	15,473
1960	16,630
1970	18,845
1980	23,906

SCARSDALE

1920	3,506
1930	9,690
1940	12,966
1950	13,156
1960	17,968
1970	19,299
1980	17,650

SCHENECTADY

1800	5,289
1810	5,903
1820	3,939
1830	4,268
1840	6,784
1850	8,921
1860	9,579
1870	11,026
1880	13,655
1890	19,902
1900	31,682
1910	72,826
1920	88,723
1930	95,682
1940	87,549
1950	91,785
1960	81,682
1970	77,958
1980	67,972

SPRING VALLEY

1910	2,353
1920	3,818
1930	3,948
1940	4,308
1950	4,500
1960	6,538
1970	18,112
1980	20,537

SUFFERN

1900	1,619
1910	2,663
1920	3,154
1930	3,757
1940	3,768
1950	4,010
1960	5,094
1970	8,273
1980	10,794

SYRACUSE

1850	22,271
1860	28,119
1870	43,051
1880	51,792
1890	88,143
1900	108,374
1910	137,249
1920	171,717
1930	209,326
1940	205,967
1950	220,583
1960	216,038
1970	197,297
1980	170,105

TARRYTOWN

1880	3,025
1890	3,562
1900	4,770
1910	5,600
1920	5,807
1930	6,841
1940	6,874
1950	8,851
1960	11,109
1970	11,115
1980	10,648

TONAWANDA

1870	2,812
1880	3,864
1890	7,145
1900	7,421
1910	8,290
1920	10,068
1930	12,681
1940	13,008
1950	14,617
1960	21,561
1970	21,898
1980	18,693

TROY

1820	5,264
1830	11,556
1840	19,334
1850	28,785
1860	39,235
1870	46,465
1880	56,747
1890	60,956
1900	60,651
1910	76,813
1920	71,996
1930	72,763
1940	70,034
1950	72,311
1970	62,918
1980	56,638

UTICA

1820	2,972
1830	8,323
1840	12,782
1850	17,565
1860	22,529
1870	28,804
1880	33,914
1890	44,007
1900	56,383
1910	74,419
1920	94,156
1930	101,740
1940	100,518
1950	101,531
1960	100,410
1970	91,373
1980	81,434

VALLEY STREAM

1930	11,790
1940	16,679
1950	26,854
1960	38,629
1970	40,413
1980	35,769

WATERTOWN

1870	9,336
1880	10,697
1890	14,725
1900	21,696
1910	26,730
1920	31,285
1930	32,205
1940	33,385
1950	34,350
1960	33,306
1970	30,787
1980	27,861

WATERVLIET

1850	7,564
1860	8,820
1870	10,693
1880	8,820
1890	12,967
1900	14,321
1910	15,074
1920	16,073
1930	16,083
1940	16,114
1950	15,197
1960	13,917
1970	12,404
1980	11,354

WESTBURY

1940	4,524
1950	7,112
1960	14,757
1970	15,362
1980	13,871

WHITE PLAINS

1880	2,381
1890	4,042
1900	7,889
1910	15,949
1920	21,031
1930	35,830
1940	40,327
1950	43,446
1960	50,485
1970	50,346
1980	46,999

YONKERS

1860	8,218
1870	12,733
1880	18,892
1890	32,033
1900	47,931
1910	79,803
1920	100,176
1930	134,646
1940	142,598
1960	190,634
1970	204,297
1980	195,351

County Subdivisions	1980	1970
The State	17 558 072	'18 241 391
Albany County[1]	285 909	286 742
Albany city[1]	101 727	115 781
Berne town	2 532	2 037
Bethlehem town[1]	24 296	23 427
Delmar (CDP)	8 423	...
Coeymans town	7 896	6 715
Ravena village	3 091	2 797
Cohoes city	18 144	18 653
Colonie town[1]	74 593	69 147
Colonie village	8 869	8 701
Latham (CDP)	11 182	9 661
Loudonville (CDP)	11 480	9 299
Menands village	4 012	3 449
Roessleville (CDP)	11 685	5 351
Green Island town	2 696	3 297
Green Island village	2 696	3 297
Guilderland town	26 515	21 208
Altamont village	1 292	1 561
Westmere (CDP)	6 881	6 364
Knox town	2 471	1 819
New Scotland town	8 976	8 481
Voorheesville village	3 320	2 826
Rensselaerville town	1 780	1 531
Watervliet city	11 354	12 404
Westerlo town	2 929	2 242
Allegany County[2]	51 742	46 458
Alfred town	6 191	4 875
Alfred village	4 967	3 804
Allen town	486	292
Alma town	920	839
Almond town	1 671	1 524
Almond village (pt.)	529	627
Amity town	2 272	2 150
Belmont village	1 024	1 102
Andover town	1 956	1 839
Andover village	1 120	1 214
Angelica town	1 438	1 306
Angelica village	982	948
Belfast town	1 495	1 339
Birdsall town	257	175
Bolivar town	2 496	2 391
Bolivar village	1 345	1 379
Richburg village (pt.)	139	79
Burns town	1 211	1 256
Canaseraga village	700	750
Caneadea town	2 421	2 364
Houghton (CDP)	1 604	1 620
Centerville town	696	526
Clarksville town	938	874
Cuba town	3 428	3 165
Cuba village	1 739	1 735
Friendship town[2]	2 164	2 106
Friendship (CDP)	1 461	1 285
Genesee town	1 787	1 187
Granger town	508	450
Grove town	497	415
Hume town	2 040	1 838
Fillmore village	563	537
Independence town	1 138	1 031
New Hudson town	669	579
Oil Springs Indian Reservation[2]	2	'−
Rushford town	1 125	1 021
Scio town	1 971	1 674
Ward town	362	271
Wellsville town	8 658	8 368
Stannards (CDP) (pt.)	526	...
Wellsville village[2]	5 769	5 815
West Almond town	357	213
Willing town	1 451	1 296
Stannards (CDP) (pt.)	500	...
Wirt town	1 137	1 094
Richburg village (pt.)	355	403
Bronx County	1 168 972	1 471 701
Bronx borough	1 168 972	1 471 701
New York city (pt.)	1 168 972	1 471 701
Broome County	213 648	221 815
Barker town	2 244	2 032
Binghamton city	55 860	64 123
Binghamton town	5 007	4 844
Chenango town	12 233	12 267
Colesville town	4 965	4 420
Conklin town	6 204	5 399
Dickinson town	5 594	5 687
Port Dickinson village	1 974	2 132
Fenton town	7 400	6 719
Kirkwood town	5 834	5 687
Lisle town	2 039	1 917
Lisle village	357	336
Maine town	5 262	5 842
Nanticoke town	1 425	1 020
Sanford town	2 635	2 528
Deposit village (pt.)	1 017	1 119
Triangle town	2 618	2 285
Whitney Point village	1 093	1 058

County Subdivisions	1980	1970
Broome County—Con.		
Union town	61 179	64 490
Endicott village	14 457	16 556
Endwell (CDP)	13 745	15 999
Johnson City village	17 126	18 025
Vestal town	27 238	26 909
Windsor town	5 911	5 646
Windsor village	1 155	1 098
Cattaraugus County[3]	85 697	81 666
Allegany Indian Reservation	1 243	1 113
Allegany town	8 619	7 542
Allegany village[3]	2 078	2 050
St. Bonaventure (CDP)	2 587	...
Ashford town	1 922	1 577
Carrolton town	1 566	1 507
Limestone village	466	535
Cattaraugus Indian Reservation	352	277
Coldspring town	708	638
Conewango town	1 578	1 393
East Randolph village (pt.)	248	257
Dayton town	1 981	2 004
South Dayton village	661	688
East Otto town	942	910
Ellicottville town	1 677	1 779
Ellicottville village[3]	713	955
Farmersville town	978	754
Franklinville town	3 102	2 847
Franklinville village	1 887	1 948
Freedom town	1 840	1 355
Great Valley town	2 014	1 745
Hinsdale town	2 182	1 781
Humphrey town	529	405
Ischua town	775	655
Leon town	1 055	878
Little Valley town	1 830	1 838
Little Valley village	1 203	1 340
Lyndon town	610	339
Machias town	2 058	1 749
Lime Lake—Machias (CDP)	1 191	...
Mansfield town	784	605
Napoli town	886	778
New Albion town	2 156	1 988
Cattaraugus village	1 200	1 200
Oil Springs Indian Reservation	4	5
Olean city	18 207	19 169
Olean town	2 130	2 211
Weston Mills (CDP) (pt.)	717	...
Otto town	828	731
Perrysburg town	2 180	2 236
Perrysburg village	405	433
Persia town	2 442	2 587
Gowanda village (pt.)	1 864	2 098
Portville town	4 486	4 252
Portville village	1 136	1 304
Weston Mills (CDP) (pt.)	1 120	...
Randolph town	2 593	2 621
East Randolph village (pt.)	407	379
Randolph village	1 398	1 498
Red House town	110	158
Salamanca city	6 890	7 877
Salamanca town	608	571
South Valley town	212	164
Yorkshire town	3 620	2 627
Delevan village	1 113	994
Yorkshire (CDP)	1 236	...
Cayuga County[4]	79 894	77 439
Auburn city	32 548	34 599
Aurelius town	2 920	2 851
Cayuga village	604	693
Brutus town	4 212	3 530
Weedsport village	1 952	1 900
Cato town	2 139	1 975
Cato village (pt.)	144	196
Meridian village	344	369
Conquest town	1 628	1 362
Fleming town	2 394	2 242
Melrose Park (CDP) (pt.)	−	...
Genoa town	1 921	1 744
Ira town	1 869	1 720
Cato village (pt.)	331	405
Ledyard town	1 869	1 886
Aurora village[4]	926	1 072
Locke town	1 751	1 152
Mentz town	2 441	2 338
Port Byron village	1 400	1 330
Montezuma town	1 125	857
Moravia town	2 640	2 668
Moravia village	1 582	1 642
Niles town	1 115	965
Owasco town	3 612	3 619
Melrose Park (CDP) (pt.)	2 171	2 189
Scipio town	1 471	1 290
Sempronius town	733	649
Sennett town	2 561	2 553
Springport town	2 210	1 911
Union Springs village	1 201	1 183
Sterling town	3 301	2 589

County Subdivisions	1980	1970
Cayuga County—Con.		
Sterling town—Con.		
Fair Haven village	976	859
Summerhill town	850	670
Throop town	1 797	1 757
Venice town	1 268	1 261
Victory town	1 519	1 251
Chautauqua County[5]	146 925	147 305
Arkwright town	980	833
Busti town	8 728	8 367
Lakewood village	3 941	3 864
Carroll town	3 579	3 115
Frewsburg (CDP)	1 908	1 772
Cattaraugus Indian Reservation	14	–
Charlotte town	1 494	1 400
Sinclairville village (pt.)	596	629
Chautauqua town	4 728	4 341
Mayville village	1 626	1 567
Cherry Creek town	1 227	1 140
Cherry Creek village	677	658
Clymer town	1 484	1 352
Dunkirk city	15 310	16 855
Dunkirk town	1 584	1 646
Ellery town	4 617	4 594
Bemus Point village	444	487
Ellicott town	9 979	10 233
Celoron village	1 405	1 456
Falconer village[5]	2 778	2 983
Jamestown West (CDP)	2 680	2 491
Ellington town	1 690	1 384
French Creek town	878	848
Gerry town	2 022	1 636
Sinclairville village (pt.)	176	143
Hanover town	7 876	7 829
Forestville village	804	908
Silver Creek village	3 088	3 182
Harmony town	2 121	1 922
Panama village	511	489
Jamestown city	35 775	39 795
Kiantone town	1 443	1 340
Mina town	1 245	1 129
North Harmony town	2 263	2 264
Poland town	2 639	2 318
Pomfret town	14 992	13 890
Fredonia village[5]	11 126	10 326
Portland town	4 433	3 802
Brocton village	1 416	1 370
Ripley town	3 229	2 934
Ripley (CDP)	1 205	1 173
Sheridan town	2 659	2 527
Sherman town	1 490	1 428
Sherman village	775	769
Stockton town	2 331	2 213
Cassadaga village	821	905
Villenova town	1 061	970
Westfield town	5 054	5 200
Westfield village	3 446	3 651
Chemung County[6]	97 656	101 537
Ashland town	1 967	1 726
Wellsburg village	647	779
Baldwin town	892	889
Big Flats town	7 649	6 837
Big Flats (CDP)	2 892	2 509
Catlin town	2 719	2 461
Chemung town	2 436	2 156
Elmira city	35 327	39 945
Elmira town	7 635	8 408
Elmira Heights village (pt.)	1 009	1 318
West Elmira (CDP)	5 485	5 901
Erin town	2 037	1 669
Horseheads town	20 238	20 552
Elmira Heights village (pt.)[6]	3 270	3 588
Elmira Heights North (CDP)	2 659	2 906
Horseheads village	7 348	7 989
Horseheads North (CDP)	3 081	2 753
Southport town	11 586	11 976
Southport (CDP)	8 329	8 685
Van Etten town	1 519	1 375
Van Etten village	559	522
Veteran town	3 651	3 543
Millport village	440	480
Chenango County[7]	49 344	46 368
Afton town	2 728	2 464
Afton village	982	1 064
Bainbridge town	3 331	3 370
Bainbridge village	1 603	1 674
Columbus town	802	723
Coventry town	1 271	974
German town	250	188
Greene town	5 729	5 347
Greene village	1 747	1 874
Guilford town	2 442	2 358
Lincklaen town	473	414
McDonough town	796	703
New Berlin town	3 025	2 823
New Berlin village	1 392	1 369

County Subdivisions	1980	1970
Chenango County—Con.		
North Norwich town	1 687	1 579
Norwich city[7]	8 082	8 843
Norwich town[7]	4 042	3 221
Otselic town	955	925
Oxford town	3 961	3 761
Oxford village	1 765	1 944
Pharsalia town	606	520
Pitcher town	735	627
Plymouth town	1 515	1 174
Preston town	941	714
Sherburne town	3 657	3 578
Earlville village (pt.)	363	377
Sherburne village[7]	1 561	1 613
Smithville town	1 174	956
Smyrna town	1 142	1 106
Smyrna village	225	247
Clinton County[8]	80 750	72 934
Altona town	2 077	1 852
Au Sable town	2 792	2 652
Keeseville village (pt.)	1 055	1 210
Beekmantown town	4 275	3 189
Black Brook town	1 505	1 484
Champlain town	5 889	5 633
Champlain village[8]	1 410	1 426
Rouses Point village	2 266	2 250
Chazy town	3 766	3 393
Clinton town	685	712
Dannemora town	4 717	4 719
Dannemora village (pt.)	3 327	3 260
Ellenburg town	1 751	1 775
Mooers town	2 927	2 606
Mooers village	549	536
Peru town	5 352	4 312
Peru (CDP)	1 716	1 261
Plattsburgh city[8]	21 057	18 715
Plattsburgh town[8]	16 384	15 881
Champlain Park (CDP)	1 051	1 207
Morrisonville (CDP) (pt.)	1 043	716
Plattsburgh AFB (CDP)	5 905	7 078
Plattsburgh West (CDP)	1 210	...
Saranac town	3 389	3 127
Dannemora village (pt.)	443	475
Schuyler Falls town	4 184	2 884
Morrisonville (CDP) (pt.)	678	560
Columbia County[9]	59 487	51 519
Ancram town	1 332	1 215
Austerlitz town	1 314	905
Canaan town	1 654	1 472
Chatham town	4 294	3 770
Chatham village (pt.)	889	952
Niverville (CDP) (pt.)	328	...
Claverack town	6 061	5 711
Claverack–Red Mills (CDP)	1 217	...
Philmont village[9]	1 539	1 674
Clermont town	1 269	1 120
Copake town	2 854	2 209
Gallatin town	1 292	737
Germantown town	1 922	1 782
Ghent town	4 636	3 729
Chatham village (pt.)	1 112	1 287
Greenport town	4 029	3 686
Lorenz Park (CDP)	1 720	1 995
Stottville (CDP) (pt.)	225	...
Hillsdale town	1 648	1 447
Hudson city	7 986	8 940
Kinderhook town	7 674	5 688
Kinderhook village	1 377	1 233
Niverville (CDP) (pt.)	1 528	...
Valatie village	1 492	1 288
Livingston town	3 087	2 280
New Lebanon town	2 271	2 035
Stockport town	2 847	2 324
Stottville (CDP) (pt.)	1 162	1 106
Stuyvesant town	2 216	1 665
Taghkanic town	1 101	804
Cortland County[10]	48 820	45 894
Cincinnatus town	1 151	1 080
Cortland city[10]	20 138	19 621
Cortlandville town[10]	8 299	7 469
Cortland West (CDP)	1 149	...
Homer village (pt.)	21	80
McGraw village	1 188	1 319
Munsons Corners (CDP)	2 478	2 076
Cuyler town	846	836
Freetown town	572	522
Harford town	855	748
Homer town	6 599	6 480
Homer village (pt.)[10]	3 614	4 063
Lapeer town	592	507
Marathon town	1 804	1 777
Marathon village	1 046	1 053
Preble town	1 637	1 601
Scott town	1 193	805
Solon town	865	687
Taylor town	481	493
Truxton town	988	955

County Subdivisions

County Subdivisions	1980	1970
Cortland County—Con.		
Virgil town	2 053	1 692
Willet town	747	621
Delaware County[11]	46 824	44 718
Andes town	1 312	1 193
Andes village	372	353
Bovina town	562	506
Colchester town	1 848	1 665
Davenport town	1 971	1 617
Delhi town	5 295	4 617
Delhi village[11]	3 374	3 017
Deposit town	1 610	1 656
Deposit village (pt.)	880	942
Franklin town	2 431	2 202
Franklin village	440	552
Hamden town	1 276	1 169
Hancock town	3 497	3 604
Hancock village	1 526	1 688
Harpersfield town	1 495	1 423
Stamford village (pt.)	499	521
Kortright town	1 250	1 236
Masonville town	1 156	1 140
Meredith town	1 374	1 129
Middletown town	3 555	3 466
Fleischmanns village	346	434
Margaretville village	755	816
Roxbury town	2 291	2 252
Sidney town	6 856	6 984
Sidney village[11]	4 861	4 789
Stamford town	2 038	2 072
Hobart village	473	531
Stamford village (pt.)	741	765
Tompkins town	968	905
Walton town	5 839	5 882
Walton village	3 329	3 744
Dutchess County	245 055	222 295
Amenia town	6 299	7 842
Amenia (CDP)	1 183	1 157
Dover Plains (CDP) (pt.)	511	...
Beacon city	12 937	13 255
Beekman town	7 139	5 701
Clinton town	3 394	2 604
Dover town	7 261	8 475
Dover Plains (CDP) (pt.)	1 183	...
East Fishkill town	18 091	11 092
Hillside Lake (CDP)	1 382	...
Hopewell Junction (CDP)	1 754	2 055
Sproutville (CDP)	2 303	1 871
Fishkill town	15 506	11 935
Brinckerhoff (CDP)	3 030	2 094
Brockway (CDP)	1 301	...
Fishkill village	1 555	913
Glenham (CDP)	2 832	2 720
Hyde Park town	20 768	'16 910
Fairview (CDP) (pt.)	1 930	'2 077
Haviland (CDP)	3 578	3 447
Hyde Park (CDP)	2 550	2 805
La Grange town	12 375	10 902
Red Oaks Mill (CDP) (pt.)	2 287	1 310
Milan town	1 668	1 322
North East town	2 877	2 730
Millerton village	1 013	1 042
Pawling town	5 795	4 764
Pawling village	1 996	1 914
Pine Plains town	2 199	1 792
Pine Plains (CDP)	1 303	...
Pleasant Valley town	6 892	6 021
Pleasant Valley (CDP)	1 255	1 372
Poughkeepsie city	29 757	32 029
Poughkeepsie town	39 549	'41 087
Arlington (CDP)	11 305	11 203
Cottam Hill (CDP)	1 380	...
Crown Heights (CDP)	3 225	3 292
Fairview (CDP) (pt.)	3 922	'6 440
Hillis (CDP)	2 591	2 750
Red Oaks Mill (CDP) (pt.)	2 949	2 609
Rochdale (CDP)	1 825	1 849
Spackenkill (CDP)	4 848	2 725
Wappingers Falls village (pt.)	955	1 126
Wappingers Falls North (CDP)	1 799	...
Red Hook town	8 351	7 548
Red Hook village	1 692	1 680
Tivoli village	711	739
Rhinebeck town	7 062	5 658
Rhinebeck village	2 542	2 336
Stanford town	3 319	2 479
Union Vale town	2 658	1 702
Wappinger town	26 776	22 040
Myers Corner (CDP)	5 180	2 826
New Hackensack (CDP)	1 532	1 111
Wappingers Falls village (pt.)	4 155	4 481
Wappingers Falls East (CDP)	1 818	2 017
Washington town	4 382	4 407
Dover Plains (CDP) (pt.)	59	...
Millbrook village	1 343	1 735

County Subdivisions

County Subdivisions	1980	1970
Erie County[12]	1 015 472	1 113 491
Alden town	10 093	9 787
Alden village	2 488	2 651
Town Line (CDP) (pt.)	2 720	2 240
Amherst town	108 706	93 929
Williamsville village (pt.)[12]	6 017	'6 878
Aurora town	13 872	14 426
Billington Heights (CDP) (pt.)	740	746
East Aurora village[12]	6 803	7 033
Boston town	7 687	7 158
North Boston (CDP)	2 743	1 635
Brant town	2 437	2 672
Farnham village	404	546
Buffalo city	357 870	462 768
Cattaraugus Indian Reservation	1 628	1 107
Cheektowaga town	109 442	113 844
Cheektowaga (CDP)	92 145	...
Depew village (pt.)[12]	12 768	14 392
Sloan village	4 529	5 216
Williamsville village (pt.)[12]		
Clarence town	18 146	18 168
Clarence Center (CDP)	1 300	1 332
Harris Hill (CDP)	5 087	...
Colden town	3 128	3 020
Collins town	5 037	6 400
Gowanda village (pt.)	849	1 012
Concord town	8 171	7 573
Springville village	4 285	4 350
Eden town	7 327	7 644
Eden (CDP)	3 000	2 962
Elma town	10 574	10 011
Billington Heights (CDP) (pt.)	1 042	532
Elma Center (CDP)	2 459	2 784
Evans town	17 961	14 570
Angola village	2 292	2 676
Angola on the Lake (CDP)	1 907	1 573
Lake Erie Beach (CDP)	4 625	3 467
Grand Island town	16 770	13 977
Hamburg town	53 270	47 644
Blasdell village	3 288	3 910
Hamburg village[12]	10 582	10 215
Holland town	3 446	3 140
Holland (CDP)	1 347	...
Lackawanna city	22 701	28 657
Lancaster town	30 144	30 634
Depew village (pt.)	7 051	7 766
Lancaster village	13 056	13 365
Town Line (CDP) (pt.)	197	194
Marilla town	4 861	3 250
Newstead town	7 231	6 322
Akron village[12]	2 971	2 863
North Collins town	3 791	4 090
North Collins village	1 496	1 675
Orchard Park town	24 359	19 978
Orchard Park village[12]	3 671	3 732
Sardinia town	2 792	2 505
Tonawanda city	18 693	21 898
Tonawanda Indian Reservation	12	16
Tonawanda town	91 269	107 282
Kenmore village	18 474	20 980
Tonawanda (CDP)	72 795	...
Wales town	2 844	2 617
West Seneca town	51 210	48 404
West Seneca (CDP)	51 210	...
Essex County[13]	36 176	34 631
Chesterfield town	2 398	2 010
Keeseville village (pt.)	970	912
Crown Point town	1 837	1 857
Elizabethtown town	1 267	1 284
Elizabethtown village	659	607
Essex town	880	837
Jay town	2 221	2 132
Keene town	919	763
Lewis town	922	763
Minerva town	781	733
Moriah town	5 139	5 244
Mineville–Witherbee (CDP)	1 925	1 967
Port Henry village	1 450	1 532
Newcomb town	681	957
North Elba town	6 597	5 776
Lake Placid village	2 490	2 731
Saranac Lake village (pt.)[13]	1 288	1 496
North Hudson town	179	212
St. Armand town	1 064	903
Bloomingdale (CDP)	608	536
Saranac Lake village (pt.)	174	169
Schroon town	1 606	1 403
Ticonderoga town	5 436	5 839
Ticonderoga village[13]	2 938	3 268
Westport town	1 439	1 453
Westport village	613	673
Willsboro town	1 759	1 688
Wilmington town	1 051	777
Franklin County[14]	44 929	43 931
Altamont town	6 318	6 698
Tupper Lake village[14]	4 478	4 854
Bangor town	1 960	1 909

County Subdivisions	1980	1970
Franklin County—Con.		
Bellmont town	1 045	1 055
Bombay town	1 247	1 117
Brandon town	499	333
Brighton town	1 625	1 473
Burke town	1 237	1 257
Burke village	226	237
Chateaugay town	1 863	1 948
Chateaugay village	869	976
Constable town	1 218	1 149
Dickinson town	786	832
Duane town	184	111
Fort Covington town[14]	1 804	1 963
Franklin town	926	550
Harrietstown town	5 604	5 643
Saranac Lake village (pt.)	4 116	4 421
Malone town	11 276	11 400
Malone village	7 668	8 048
Moira town	2 624	2 468
Brushton village	577	547
St. Regis Indian Reservation	1 802	1 536
Santa Clara town	310	168
Waverly town	1 110	1 022
Westville town	1 491	1 299
Fulton County[15]	55 153	52 637
Bleecker town	463	294
Broadalbin town	4 074	3 542
Broadalbin village (pt.)	1 363	1 449
Caroga town	1 177	822
Ephratah town	1 564	1 297
Gloversville city[15]	17 836	19 677
Johnstown city[15]	9 360	10 045
Johnstown town[15]	6 719	5 750
Berkshire (CDP)	1 095	...
Mayfield town	5 439	4 522
Broadalbin village (pt.)	52	3
Mayfield village	944	981
Northampton town	2 829	2 379
Northville village	1 304	1 192
Oppenheim town	1 806	1 431
Dolgeville village (pt.)	162	175
Perth town	3 261	2 383
Stratford town	625	495
Genesee County[16]	59 400	58 722
Alabama town	1 926	1 872
Alexander town	2 367	2 351
Alexander village[16]	483	474
Attica village (pt.)	16	2
Batavia city[16]	16 703	17 338
Batavia town[16]	5 565	5 440
Bergen town	2 568	2 281
Bergen village[16]	976	1 018
Bethany town	1 876	1 978
Byron town	2 242	2 020
Darien town	2 950	2 745
Elba town	2 487	2 312
Elba village	750	752
Le Roy town	8 019	7 991
Le Roy village	4 900	5 118
Oakfield town	3 213	3 364
Oakfield village	1 791	1 964
Pavilion town	2 375	2 122
Pembroke town	4 146	3 959
Corfu village	689	722
Stafford town	2 508	2 461
Tonawanda Indian Reservation	455	488
Greene County[17]	40 861	33 136
Ashland town	744	397
Athens town	3 462	3 567
Athens village	1 738	1 718
Cairo town	4 729	3 546
Cairo (CDP)	1 281	...
Catskill town	11 453	10 432
Catskill village[17]	4 718	5 317
Jefferson Heights (CDP)	1 610	...
Coxsackie town	6 018	4 236
Coxsackie village	2 786	2 399
Durham town	2 283	1 651
Greenville town	2 849	2 279
Halcott town	150	199
Hunter town	2 252	1 742
Hunter village	511	238
Tannersville village[17]	685	650
Jewett town	723	442
Lexington town	819	666
New Baltimore town	3 050	2 068
Prattsville town	666	721
Windham town	1 663	1 190
Hamilton County	5 034	4 714
Arietta town	314	350
Benson town	156	89
Hope town	311	269
Indian Lake town	1 410	1 290
Inlet town	320	287
Lake Pleasant town	859	812

County Subdivisions	1980	1970
Hamilton County—Con.		
Lake Pleasant town—Con.		
Speculator village	408	390
Long Lake town	935	900
Morehouse town	102	113
Wells town	627	604
Herkimer County[18]	66 714	'67 407
Columbia town	1 537	1 387
Danube town	1 081	1 015
Fairfield town	1 455	1 446
Middleville village (pt.)	454	562
Frankfort town	7 686	7 805
Frankfort village	2 995	3 305
German Flatts town	14 981	15 430
Ilion village[18]	9 450	9 808
Mohawk village	2 956	3 301
Herkimer town	11 027	11 451
Herkimer village[18]	8 383	8 960
Litchfield town	1 187	961
Little Falls city[18]	6 156	7 629
Little Falls town[18]	1 434	1 411
Manheim town	3 634	3 752
Dolgeville village (pt.)	2 440	2 697
Newport town	2 206	1 992
Middleville village (pt.)	193	163
Newport village	746	908
Poland village (pt.)	149	154
Norway town	662	605
Ohio town	788	468
Russia town	2 405	2 160
Cold Brook village	402	413
Poland village (pt.)	404	475
Salisbury town	1 946	1 741
Schuyler town	2 886	'2 808
Stark town	824	739
Warren town	1 065	978
Webb town	1 701	1 616
Old Forge (CDP)	1 061	...
Winfield town	2 053	2 013
West Winfield village	979	1 018
Jefferson County	88 151	88 508
Adams town	4 390	4 381
Adams village	1 701	1 951
Adams Center (CDP)	1 519	...
Alexandria town	3 587	3 515
Alexandria Bay village	1 265	1 440
Antwerp town	1 859	1 794
Antwerp village	749	872
Brownville town	5 113	4 321
Brownville village	1 099	1 187
Dexter village	1 053	1 061
Glen Park village (pt.)	470	540
Cape Vincent town	1 823	1 748
Cape Vincent village	785	820
Champion town	4 056	4 371
West Carthage village	1 824	2 047
Clayton town	4 028	4 021
Clayton village	1 816	1 970
Ellisburg town	3 312	3 385
Ellisburg village	307	337
Mannsville village	431	494
Henderson town	1 330	1 364
Hounsfield town	2 645	2 771
Sackets Harbor village	1 017	1 202
Le Ray town	5 039	3 973
Black River village (pt.)	824	720
Evans Mills village	651	714
Lorraine town	720	628
Lyme town	1 695	1 550
Chaumont village	620	567
Orleans town	2 007	1 927
Pamelia town	2 417	1 894
Glen Park village (pt.)	34	47
Philadelphia town	1 417	1 355
Philadelphia village	855	858
Rodman town	836	772
Rutland town	2 685	2 448
Black River village (pt.)	560	587
Theresa town	1 853	1 754
Theresa village	827	985
Watertown city	27 861	30 787
Watertown town	3 098	3 026
Wilna town	6 227	6 538
Carthage village	3 643	3 889
Deferiet village	326	347
Herrings village	170	137
Worth town	153	185
Kings County	2 230 936	2 602 012
Brooklyn borough	2 230 936	2 602 012
New York city (pt.)	2 230 936	2 602 012
Lewis County[19]	25 035	23 644
Croghan town	2 824	2 559
Croghan village	383	396
Denmark town	2 448	2 359
Castorland village	277	327

County Subdivisions	1980	1970
Lewis County—Con.		
Denmark town—Con.		
Copenhagen village	656	734
Diana town	1 709	1 649
Harrisville village	937	836
Greig town	1 115	774
Harrisburg town	418	431
Lewis town	720	649
Leyden town	1 660	1 677
Port Leyden village (pt.)	539	625
Lowville town	4 575	4 754
Lowville village	3 364	3 671
Lyonsdale town	1 135	1 013
Lyons Falls village (pt.)	84	101
Port Leyden village (pt.)	201	237
Martinsburg town	1 494	1 516
	32	58
New Bremen town	2 316	2 040
Croghan village (pt.)	320	369
Osceola town	321	167
Pinckney town	305	319
Turin town	824	805
Turin village	284	293
Watson town	1 272	1 072
West Turin town[19]	1 867	1 713
Constableville village	330	347
Lyons Falls village (pt.)	671	751
Livingston County[20]	57 006	54 041
Avon town	6 185	6 117
Avon village[20]	3 006	3 260
Caledonia town	4 034	3 832
Caledonia village[20]	2 188	2 327
Conesus town	1 970	1 533
Geneseo town	8 673	7 278
Geneseo village[20]	6 746	5 714
Groveland town	2 140	3 004
Leicester town	1 888	1 799
Leicester village	462	368
Lima town	3 859	3 445
Lima village	2 025	1 686
Livonia town	5 742	5 304
Livonia village	1 238	1 278
Mount Morris town	4 478	4 579
Mount Morris village	3 039	3 417
North Dansville town	5 994	6 358
Dansville village	4 979	5 436
Nunda town	2 692	2 574
Nunda village[20]	1 169	1 254
Ossian town	667	551
Portage town	771	731
Sparta town	1 458	1 157
Springwater town	2 143	1 678
West Sparta town	1 100	935
York town	3 212	3 166
Madison County[21]	65 150	62 864
Brookfield town	2 037	2 064
Cazenovia town	5 880	6 092
Cazenovia village[21]	2 599	3 031
De Ruyter town	1 349	1 366
De Ruyter village	542	643
Eaton town	5 182	4 458
Morrisville village	2 707	2 296
Fenner town	1 580	1 321
Georgetown town	779	816
Hamilton town	6 027	5 906
Earlville village (pt.)	622	673
Hamilton village[21]	3 725	3 636
Lebanon town	1 117	969
Lenox town	8 539	8 871
Canastota village[21]	4 773	5 033
Wampsville village	569	586
Lincoln town	1 722	1 168
Madison town	2 314	2 221
Madison village	396	386
Nelson town	1 495	1 410
Oneida city	10 810	11 658
Smithfield town	1 001	864
Stockbridge town	1 947	1 711
Munnsville village	499	435
Sullivan town	13 371	11 969
Chittenango village[21]	4 290	3 605
Monroe County[22]	702 238	711 917
Brighton town[22]	35 776	35 065
Brighton (CDP)	35 776	...
Chili town	23 676	19 609
Clarkson town	4 016	3 642
Brockport village (pt.)	-	-
Gates town[22]	29 756	26 442
Gates–North Gates (CDP)	15 244	...
Greece town	81 367	75 136
Greece (CDP)	16 177	...
Hamlin town	7 675	4 167
Henrietta town	36 134	33 017
Irondequoit town	57 648	[r]64 897
Irondequoit (CDP)	57 648	...
Mendon town	5 434	4 541

County Subdivisions	1980	1970
Monroe County—Con.		
Mendon town—Con.		
Honeoye Falls village[22]	2 410	2 248
Ogden town	14 693	11 736
Spencerport village	3 424	2 929
Parma town	12 585	10 748
Hilton village[22]	4 151	2 440
Penfield town	27 201	23 782
Perinton town	41 802	31 568
East Rochester village (pt.)[22]	3 473	3 485
Fairport village	5 970	6 474
Pittsford town	26 743	25 058
East Rochester village (pt.)[22]	4 123	4 862
Pittsford village	1 568	1 755
Riga town	4 309	3 746
Churchville village	1 399	1 065
Rochester city[22]	241 741	[r]295 011
Rush town	3 001	3 287
Sweden town	14 859	11 461
Brockport village (pt.)	9 776	7 878
Webster town	28 925	24 739
Webster village	5 499	5 037
Wheatland town	4 897	4 265
Scottsville village	1 789	1 967
Montgomery County[23]	53 439	55 883
Amsterdam city[23]	21 872	25 524
Amsterdam town[23]	5 721	5 795
Fort Johnson village	646	711
Hagaman village	1 331	1 410
Tribes Hill (CDP) (pt.)	197	216
Canajoharie town	4 140	4 319
Ames village	224	198
Canajoharie village[23]	2 412	2 686
Fort Plain village (pt.)	7	6
Charleston town	1 013	658
Florida town	2 578	2 283
Glen town	1 893	1 797
Fultonville village	777	812
Minden town	4 743	4 691
Fort Plain village (pt.)	2 548	2 803
Mohawk town	3 795	3 677
Fonda village[23]	1 006	1 120
Tribes Hill (CDP) (pt.)	1 005	968
Palatine town	2 819	2 711
Nelliston village	691	716
Palatine Bridge village	604	601
Root town	1 801	1 513
St. Johnsville town	3 064	2 915
St. Johnsville village	1 974	2 089
Nassau County[24]	1 321 582	[r]1 428 838
Glen Cove city	24 618	25 770
Hempstead town	738 517	[r]801 592
Atlantic Beach village	1 775	1 640
Baldwin (CDP)	31 630	34 525
Bellerose village	1 187	[r]1 136
Bellmore (CDP)	18 106	18 431
Cedarhurst village	6 162	6 941
East Meadow (CDP)	39 317	46 290
East Rockaway village[24]	10 917	[r]11 795
Elmont (CDP)	27 592	29 363
Floral Park village (pt.)	14 478	16 527
Franklin Square (CDP)	29 051	32 156
Freeport village	38 272	40 374
Garden City village	22 927	25 373
Hempstead village[24]	40 404	39 411
Hewlett (CDP)	6 986	6 796
Hewlett Bay Park village	489	586
Hewlett Harbor village[24]	1 331	[r]1 512
Hewlett Neck village	472	529
Inwood (CDP)	8 228	8 433
Island Park village	4 847	5 396
Lakeview (CDP)	5 276	5 471
Lawrence village	6 175	6 566
Levittown (CDP)	57 045	65 440
Lynbrook village	20 424	[r]23 151
Malverne village	9 262	10 036
Merrick (CDP)	24 478	25 904
Mineola village (pt.)	52	[r]101
New Hyde Park village (pt.)	4 047	4 304
North Bellmore (CDP)	20 630	22 893
North Merrick (CDP)	12 848	13 650
North Valley Stream (CDP)	14 530	14 881
North Wantagh (CDP)	12 677	15 053
Oceanside (CDP)	33 639	35 372
Rockville Centre village	25 412	27 444
Roosevelt (CDP)	14 109	15 008
Seaford (CDP)	16 117	17 379
South Floral Park village	1 490	1 032
South Valley Stream (CDP)	5 462	6 595
South Westbury (CDP)	9 732	10 978
Stewart Manor village	2 373	2 183
Uniondale (CDP)	20 016	22 077
Valley Stream village	35 769	40 413
Wantagh (CDP)	19 817	21 873
West Hempstead (CDP)	18 536	20 375
Woodmere (CDP)	17 205	19 831
Woodsburgh village	847	817
Long Beach city	34 073	33 127
North Hempstead town	218 624	[r]235 007
Albertson (CDP)	5 561	6 825

County Subdivisions

County Subdivisions	1980	1970
Nassau County—Con.		
North Hempstead town—Con.		
Baxter Estates village	911	ʳ1 026
Carle Place (CDP)	5 470	6 326
East Hills village (pt.)	7 146	ʳ8 605
East Williston village	2 708	2 808
Floral Park village (pt.)	2 327	1 939
Flower Hill village	4 558	4 486
Garden City Park (CDP)	7 712	7 488
Great Neck village	9 168	ʳ10 798
Great Neck Estates village	2 936	3 131
Great Neck Plaza village	5 604	ʳ6 043
Herricks (CDP)	8 123	9 112
Kensington village	1 132	ʳ1 402
Kings Point village	5 234	ʳ5 614
Lake Success village	2 396	3 254
Manhasset (CDP)	8 485	8 541
Manorhaven village	5 384	ʳ5 488
Mineola village (pt.)	20 705	ʳ21 744
Munsey Park village	2 806	2 980
New Cassel (CDP)	9 635	8 721
New Hyde Park village (pt.)	5 754	5 812
North Hills village	1 587	295
North New Hyde Park (CDP)	15 114	18 154
Old Westbury village (pt.)	2 175	2 186
Plandome village	1 503	1 593
Plandome Heights village	963	1 032
Plandome Manor village	883	835
Port Washington (CDP)	14 521	15 923
Port Washington North village	3 147	ʳ2 883
Roslyn village	2 134	ʳ2 607
Roslyn Estates village	1 292	1 420
Roslyn Harbor village (pt.)	785	ʳ830
Roslyn Heights (CDP)	6 546	7 242
Russell Gardens village	1 263	ʳ1 207
Saddle Rock village	921	895
Sands Point village	2 742	2 916
Thomaston village	2 684	ʳ2 811
Westbury village	13 871	15 362
Williston Park village[24]	8 216	9 154
Oyster Bay town	305 750	ʳ333 342
Bayville village	7 034	6 147
Bethpage (CDP)	16 840	18 555
Brookville village	3 290	3 212
Centre Island village	378	374
Cove Neck village	331	344
East Hills village (pt.)	14	19
East Massapequa (CDP)	13 987	15 926
Farmingdale village	7 946	9 297
Hicksville (CDP)	43 245	ʳ49 820
Jericho (CDP)	12 739	14 010
Lattingtown village	1 749	1 773
Laurel Hollow village	1 527	1 401
Locust Grove (CDP)	9 670	11 626
Massapequa (CDP)	24 454	26 821
Massapequa Park village	19 779	22 112
Matinecock village	985	841
Mill Neck village	959	982
Muttontown village[24]	2 725	2 081
North Massapequa (CDP)	21 385	23 123
Old Bethpage (CDP)	6 215	7 084
Old Brookville village	1 574	ʳ1 785
Old Westbury village (pt.)	1 102	481
Oyster Bay (CDP)	6 497	6 822
Oyster Bay Cove village[24]	1 799	1 320
Plainedge (CDP)	9 629	10 759
Plainview (CDP)	28 037	ʳ31 695
Roslyn Harbor village (pt.)	344	ʳ295
Sea Cliff village	5 364	5 890
South Farmingdale (CDP)	16 439	20 464
Syosset (CDP)	9 818	10 084
Upper Brookville village	1 245	1 182
West Amityville (CDP)	6 623	6 424
Woodbury (CDP)	7 043	...
New York County	1 428 285	1 539 233
Manhattan borough	1 428 285	1 539 233
New York city (pt.)	1 428 285	1 539 233
Niagara County[25]	227 354	235 720
Cambria town	4 419	4 193
Hartland town	4 105	4 223
Middleport village (pt.)	163	383
Lewiston town	16 219	15 888
Lewiston village	3 326	3 292
Lockport city	24 844	25 399
Lockport town	12 942	8 177
South Lockport (CDP)	3 366	1 341
Newfane town	9 268	9 459
Newfane (CDP)	3 120	2 588
Olcott (CDP)	1 571	1 592
Niagara town	9 648	8 368
Niagara Town (CDP)	9 648	...
Niagara Falls city	71 384	85 615
North Tonawanda city	35 760	36 012
Pendleton town	4 726	4 733
Porter town	7 251	7 429
Ransomville (CDP) (pt.)	1 103	1 034
Youngstown village[25]	2 191	2 169
Royalton town	7 765	7 375
Gasport (CDP)	1 339	...
Middleport village (pt.)	1 832	ʳ1 749
Somerset town	2 701	2 677

County Subdivisions	1980	1970
Niagara County—Con.		
Somerset town—Con.		
Barker village	535	567
Tonawanda Indian Reservation	—	—
Tuscarora Indian Reservation	921	1 134
Wheatfield town	9 609	9 722
Wilson town	5 792	5 316
Ransomville (CDP) (pt.)	298	
Wilson village	1 259	1 284
Oneida County[26]	253 466	ʳ273 070
Annsville town	2 389	1 917
Augusta town	2 080	2 025
Oriskany Falls village[26]	802	927
Ava town	664	541
Boonville town	4 094	3 947
Boonville village	2 344	2 488
Bridgewater town	1 455	1 251
Bridgewater village	578	601
Camden town	4 925	4 942
Camden village	2 667	2 936
Deerfield town	3 934	4 104
Florence town	688	610
Floyd town	3 863	3 620
Forestport town	1 380	1 173
Kirkland town	10 334	9 688
Clark Mills (CDP)	1 412	1 206
Clinton village	2 107	2 271
Lee town	6 892	6 095
Marcy town	6 456	ʳ7 877
Marshall town	2 131	2 072
Waterville village (pt.)	306	295
New Hartford town	21 286	21 430
New Hartford village	2 313	2 433
New York Mills village (pt.)[26]	1 930	1 868
Paris town	4 456	4 579
Clayville village[26]	478	535
Remsen town	1 614	1 366
Remsen village (pt.)	587	574
Rome city	43 826	50 148
Sangerfield town	2 397	2 475
Waterville village (pt.)	1 366	1 513
Sherrill city	2 830	2 986
Steuben town	897	735
Trenton town	4 449	4 429
Barneveld village[26]	396	423
Holland Patent village	534	556
Prospect village	368	392
Remsen village (pt.)	34	28
Utica city	75 632	ʳ91 373
Vernon town	5 354	4 871
Oneida Castle village	751	788
Vernon village[26]	1 373	1 108
Verona town	6 681	6 290
Sylvan Beach village (pt.)[26]	—	...
Verona (CDP)	1 057	...
Vienna town	5 197	3 979
Sylvan Beach village (pt.)[26]	1 243	
Western town	1 954	2 072
Westmoreland town	5 458	5 093
Whitestown town	20 150	21 382
New York Mills village (pt.)[26]	1 619	1 937
Oriskany village[26]	1 680	1 627
Whitesboro village[26]	4 460	4 805
Yorkville village	3 115	3 425
Onondaga County[27]	463 920	ʳ472 835
Camillus town	24 333	26 841
Camillus village	1 298	1 534
Fairmount (CDP) (pt.)	11 852	13 535
Cicero town	23 689	22 539
Boysen Bay (CDP)	1 160	1 191
Brewerton (CDP) (pt.)	1 586	1 201
North Syracuse village (pt.)	2 095	2 528
Clay town	52 838	36 274
Bayberry–Lynelle Meadows (CDP) (pt.)	12 952	...
North Syracuse village (pt.)	5 875	6 159
Pitcher Hill (CDP) (pt.)	4 572	...
De Witt town	26 868	29 198
De Witt (CDP)	9 024	10 032
East Syracuse village	3 412	4 333
Lyncourt (CDP) (pt.)	492	...
Elbridge town	5 885	5 503
Elbridge village	1 099	1 040
Jordan village	1 371	1 493
Fabius town	1 811	1 607
Fabius village	367	374
Geddes town	18 528	21 032
Fairmount (CDP) (pt.)	1 563	1 782
Solvay village	7 140	8 280
Westvale (CDP)	6 169	7 253
Lafayette town	4 488	4 401
Lysander town	13 897	11 968
Baldwinsville village (pt.)[27]	3 932	3 943
Manlius town	28 489	26 071
Fayetteville village[27]	4 709	4 996
Manlius village[27]	5 241	4 295
Minoa village[27]	3 640	2 245
Marcellus town	6 180	5 744
Marcellus village[27]	1 870	2 017

County Subdivisions	1980	1970
Onondaga County—Con.		
Onondaga Indian Reservation	596	785
Onondaga town[27]	17 824	16 555
Otisco town	2 112	1 470
Pompey town	4 492	4 536
Salina town	37 400	38 281
Bayberry–Lynelle Meadows (CDP) (pt.)	1 861	...
Liverpool village	2 849	3 307
Lyncourt (CDP) (pt.)	4 637	...
Mattydale (CDP)	7 511	8 292
Pitcher Hill (CDP) (pt.)	1 491	...
Skaneateles town	7 795	7 825
Skaneateles village[27]	2 789	3 055
Spafford town	1 596	1 148
Syracuse city[27]	170 105	'197 297
Tully town	2 409	1 901
Tully village	1 049	899
Van Buren town	12 585	11 859
Baldwinsville village (pt.)[27]	2 514	2 355
Ontario County[28]	88 909	78 849
Bristol town	1 802	1 307
Canadice town	1 467	971
Canandaigua city	10 419	10 488
Canandaigua town	6 060	5 419
East Bloomfield town	3 327	3 151
East Bloomfield village	587	643
Holcomb village	952	778
Farmington town	8 933	3 565
Geneva city (pt.)[28]	15 133	16 793
Geneva town[28]	3 077	2 781
Gorham town	3 598	3 033
Rushville village (pt.)	148	194
Hopewell town	2 509	2 347
Manchester town	9 002	7 840
Clifton Springs village (pt.)	1 533	1 556
Manchester village[28]	1 698	1 305
Shortsville village[28]	1 669	1 516
Naples town	2 338	2 236
Naples village	1 225	1 324
Phelps town	6 522	6 330
Clifton Springs village (pt.)	506	502
Phelps village	2 004	1 989
Richmond town	2 703	1 925
Seneca town	2 749	2 808
South Bristol town	1 205	794
Victor town	5 784	5 071
Victor village	2 370	2 187
West Bloomfield town	2 281	1 990
Orange County[29]	259 603	221 657
Blooming Grove town	12 339	8 813
Beaverdam Lake (CDP) (pt.)	13	...
Blooming Grove (CDP)	1 151	...
Merriewold Lake (CDP)	3 661	2 564
Mountain Lodge (CDP)	1 230	...
Washingtonville village (pt.)	2 380	1 887
Chester town	6 850	4 767
Chester village	1 910	1 627
Surrey Meadows (CDP)	1 203	...
Walton Park (CDP) (pt.)	678	...
Cornwall town	10 774	9 672
Beaverdam Lake (CDP) (pt.)	475	...
Cornwall on Hudson village[29]	3 164	3 131
Firthcliffe (CDP) (pt.)	4 250	4 002
New Windsor (CDP) (pt.)	–	...
Crawford town	4 910	3 896
Pine Bush (CDP)	1 255	1 183
Deerpark town	5 633	4 370
Sparrow Bush (CDP)	1 049	...
Goshen town	10 463	8 393
Florida village (pt.)[29]	–	...
Goshen village[29]	4 874	4 342
New Hampton–Denton (CDP) (pt.)	38	...
Greenville town	2 085	1 379
Hamptonburgh town	2 945	2 204
Maybrook village (pt.)	13	36
Highlands town	14 004	14 661
Fort Montgomery (CDP)	1 396	...
Highland Falls village[29]	4 187	4 638
West Point (CDP)	8 105	...
Middletown city[29]	21 454	22 607
Minisink town	2 488	1 942
Unionville village	574	576
Monroe town	14 948	9 169
Harriman village (pt.)	781	934
Harriman South (CDP)	1 254	...
Kiryas Joel village[29]	2 088	...
Monroe village[29]	5 996	4 439
Monroe Southwest (CDP)	1 267	...
Walton Park (CDP) (pt.)	797	...
Montgomery town	16 576	13 995
Coldenham (CDP)	1 064	...
Colden Hill (CDP) (pt.)	268	...
Maybrook village[29]	1 994	1 500
Montgomery village[29]	2 316	1 533
Walden village[29]	5 659	5 277
Mount Hope town	4 398	2 966
Otisville village	953	933

County Subdivisions	1980	1970
Orange County—Con.		
Newburgh city	23 438	26 219
Newburgh town	22 747	21 593
Balmville (CDP)	2 919	3 214
Colden Hill (CDP) (pt.)	1 473	1 688
Gardnertown (CDP)	4 238	4 614
Middle Hope (CDP)	3 229	2 327
Newburgh West (CDP)	1 381	...
Orange Lake (CDP)	5 120	4 348
Stewart (CDP) (pt.)	–	–
New Windsor town	19 534	16 650
Beaverdam Lake (CDP) (pt.)	836	...
Firthcliffe (CDP) (pt.)	180	23
New Windsor (CDP) (pt.)	7 812	8 803
New Windsor West (CDP)	2 120	...
Stewart (CDP) (pt.)	2 797	1 230
Vails Gate (CDP)	3 156	...
Washingtonville village (pt.)	–	...
Port Jervis city	8 699	8 852
Tuxedo town	3 069	2 967
Tuxedo Park village[29]	809	861
Wallkill town[29]	20 481	11 518
East Middletown (CDP)	4 330	2 640
Scotchtown (CDP)	7 352	2 119
Washington Heights (CDP)	1 233	1 204
Warwick town	20 976	16 956
Florida village (pt.)[29]	1 947	1 674
Greenwood Lake village	2 809	2 262
Lake (CDP)	1 210	1 352
Warwick village[29]	4 320	3 604
Wawayanda town[29]	4 298	3 408
New Hampton–Denton (CDP) (pt.)	1 347	...
Woodbury town	6 494	4 660
Central Valley (CDP)	1 705	...
Harriman village (pt.)	15	21
Highland Mills (CDP)	2 034	...
Orleans County[30]	38 496	37 305
Albion town	6 446	6 577
Albion village (pt.)[30]	4 198	4 765
Barre town	2 164	2 135
Carlton town	2 818	2 540
Clarendon town	2 148	1 969
Gaines town	2 692	2 385
Albion village (pt.)[30]	699	357
Kendall town	2 388	2 183
Murray town	4 754	4 638
Holley village[30]	1 882	1 868
Ridgeway town	7 278	7 209
Medina village (pt.)[30]	3 766	3 831
Shelby town	5 361	5 366
Medina village (pt.)[30]	2 626	2 584
Yates town	2 447	2 303
Lyndonville village[30]	916	888
Oswego County[31]	113 901	100 897
Albion town	1 730	1 452
Altmar village	347	448
Amboy town	836	557
Boylston town	390	276
Constantia town	4 312	3 547
Cleveland village	855	821
Constantia (CDP)	1 254	...
Fulton city	13 312	14 003
Granby town	6 341	4 718
Hannibal town	4 027	3 165
Hannibal village	680	686
Hastings town	7 095	6 042
Brewerton (CDP) (pt.)	384	438
Central Square village[31]	1 418	1 298
Mexico town	4 790	4 174
Mexico village	1 621	1 555
Minetto town	1 905	1 688
Minetto (CDP)	1 629	...
New Haven town	2 421	1 845
Orwell town	1 031	836
Oswego city	19 793	'20 913
Oswego town	7 865	'6 514
Palermo town	3 253	2 321
Parish town	2 172	1 782
Parish village	535	634
Redfield town	459	386
Richland town	5 594	5 324
Pulaski village	2 415	2 480
Sandy Creek town	3 256	2 644
Lacona village	582	556
Sandy Creek village	765	731
Schroeppel town	8 016	7 153
Phoenix village[31]	2 357	2 617
Sand Ridge (CDP)	1 293	1 109
Scriba town	5 455	3 619
Volney town	5 358	4 520
West Monroe town	3 482	2 535
Brewerton (CDP) (pt.)	502	346
Williamstown town	1 008	883
Otsego County[32]	59 075	56 181
Burlington town	1 045	803
Butternuts town	1 486	1 433
Gilbertsville village[32]	455	552

County Subdivisions

County Subdivisions	1980	1970
Otsego County—Con.		
Cherry Valley town	1 205	1 122
Cherry Valley village	684	661
Decatur town	312	281
Edmeston town	1 732	1 709
Exeter town	968	996
Hartwick town	1 796	1 631
Laurens town	2 101	1 730
Laurens village	276	320
Maryland town	1 690	1 465
Schenevus village	625	540
Middlefield town	1 870	1 457
Cooperstown village (pt.)	238	172
Milford town	2 685	2 485
Milford village	514	527
Morris town	1 780	1 630
Morris village	681	675
New Lisbon town	948	823
Oneonta city[32]	14 933	16 030
Oneonta town[32]	4 655	4 185
West End (CDP)	1 715	1 692
Otego town	2 801	2 249
Otego village[32]	1 089	956
Otsego town	4 012	3 998
Cooperstown village (pt.)	2 104	2 231
Pittsfield town	1 067	968
Plainfield town	847	742
Richfield town	2 608	2 602
Richfield Springs village[32]	1 561	1 540
Roseboom town	630	483
Springfield town	1 239	1 136
Unadilla town	4 020	3 863
Unadilla village	1 367	1 489
Westford town	652	435
Worcester town	1 993	1 925
Putnam County	77 193	56 696
Carmel town	27 948	21 639
Mahopac (CDP)	7 681	5 265
Kent town	12 433	8 106
Lake Carmel (CDP) (pt.)	7 210	4 796
Patterson town	7 247	4 124
Lake Carmel (CDP) (pt.)	85	...
Philipstown town	9 155	7 717
Cold Spring village	2 161	2 083
Nelsonville village	567	583
Putnam Valley town	8 994	5 209
Southeast town	11 416	9 901
Brewster village	1 650	1 638
Brewster Heights (CDP)	1 054	1 265
Brewster Hill (CDP)	2 371	1 745
Peach Lake (CDP) (pt.)	998	...
Queens County	1 891 325	1 987 174
Queens borough	1 891 325	1 987 174
New York city (pt.)	1 891 325	1 987 174
Rensselaer County[33]	151 966	152 510
Berlin town	1 696	1 562
Brunswick town	10 974	11 193
East Greenbush town	12 913	10 679
Grafton town	1 665	1 307
Hoosick town	6 732	6 651
Hoosick Falls village	3 609	3 897
Nassau town	4 479	4 043
Nassau village (pt.)	1 206	1 363
Nassau Lake (CDP) (pt.)	395	...
North Greenbush town	10 396	10 513
Petersburg town	1 369	1 187
Pittstown town	4 901	3 905
Valley Falls village (pt.)	453	606
Poestenkill town	3 664	3 426
Poestenkill (CDP)	1 031	...
Rensselaer city	9 047	10 136
Sand Lake town	7 022	5 843
Averill Park (CDP)	1 337	1 471
West Sand Lake (CDP)	2 153	1 875
Schaghticoke town	7 094	6 220
Schaghticoke village	677	860
Valley Falls village (pt.)	101	75
Schodack town	11 345	11 196
Castleton-on-Hudson village[33]	1 627	1 730
Nassau village (pt.)	79	103
Nassau Lake (CDP) (pt.)	909	...
Stephentown town	2 031	1 731
Troy city	56 638	62 918
Richmond County[34]	352 121	295 443
Staten Island borough[34]	352 121	295 443
New York city (pt.)	352 121	295 443
Rockland County	259 530	229 903
Clarkstown town	77 091	61 653
Congers (CDP)	7 123	5 928
Nanuet (CDP)	12 578	10 447
New City (CDP)	35 859	27 344
Nyack village (pt.)	696	715
Spring Valley village (pt.)	1 970	1 772
Upper Nyack village	1 906	2 096
Valley Cottage (CDP)	8 214	6 007

County Subdivisions	1980	1970
Rockland County—Con.		
Clarkstown town—Con.		
West Nyack (CDP)	8 553	5 510
Haverstraw town	31 929	25 311
Haverstraw village	8 800	8 198
Pomona village (pt.)	1 170	762
West Haverstraw village	9 181	8 558
Orangetown town	48 612	53 533
Grand View-on-Hudson village	312	325
Nyack village (pt.)	5 732	5 944
Pearl River (CDP)	15 893	17 146
Piermont village	2 269	2 386
South Nyack village	3 602	3 435
Tappan (CDP)	8 267	7 424
Ramapo town	89 060	76 702
Hillburn village	926	1 058
Hillcrest (CDP)	5 733	5 357
Monsey (CDP)	12 380	8 797
New Square village	1 750	1 156
Pomona village (pt.)	1 251	1 030
Sloatsburg village	3 154	3 134
Spring Valley village (pt.)	18 567	16 340
Suffern village	10 794	8 273
Viola (CDP)	5 340	5 136
Stony Point town	12 838	12 704
Stony Point (CDP)	8 686	8 270
St. Lawrence County[35]	114 254	112 309
Brasher town	2 375	2 410
Brasher Falls—Winthrop (CDP) (pt.)	817	...
Canton town	11 568	10 348
Canton village[35]	7 055	6 398
Rensselaer Falls village	360	332
Clare town	121	97
Clifton town	1 005	1 207
Star Lake (CDP) (pt.)	275	...
Colton town	1 292	1 249
De Kalb town	2 130	2 062
Richville village	336	334
De Peyster town	917	769
Edwards town	1 208	1 219
Edwards village	561	576
Fine town	2 243	2 302
Star Lake (CDP) (pt.)	964	...
Fowler town	1 721	1 576
Gouverneur town	6 629	6 710
Gouverneur village[35]	4 285	4 574
Hammond town	1 090	1 015
Hammond village	271	273
Hermon town	1 083	1 087
Hermon village	490	521
Hopkinton town	1 064	884
Lawrence town	1 658	1 632
Lisbon town[35]	3 548	3 271
Louisville town	2 946	2 727
Massena village (pt.)[35]	217	160
Macomb town	816	813
Madrid town	1 852	1 635
Massena town	14 856	16 021
Massena village (pt.)[35]	12 634	13 882
Morristown town	1 921	1 823
Morristown village	461	532
Norfolk town	4 992	4 701
Norfolk (CDP)	1 599	1 379
Norwood village (pt.)	70	67
Ogdensburg city[35]	12 375	14 554
Oswegatchie town[35]	3 846	3 162
Heuvelton village	777	770
Parishville town	1 951	1 631
Piercefield town	365	422
Pierrepont town	2 207	1 726
Pitcairn town	792	676
Potsdam town	17 411	16 700
Norwood village (pt.)[35]	1 832	2 031
Potsdam village[35]	10 635	10 303
Rossie town	842	643
Russell town	1 638	1 586
Stockholm town	3 676	3 597
Brasher Falls—Winthrop (CDP) (pt.)	637	...
Waddington town	2 116	2 054
Waddington village	980	955
Saratoga County[36]	153 759	121 764
Ballston town	7 714	6 720
Ballston Spa village (pt.)	995	816
Charlton town	4 019	3 772
Clifton Park town[36]	23 989	14 867
Clifton Knolls (CDP)	5 636	5 771
Country Knolls (CDP)	2 497	2 082
Corinth town	5 216	5 442
Corinth village	2 702	3 267
Day town	656	615
Edinburg town	1 126	844
Galway town	3 018	2 506
Galway village	245	270
Greenfield town[36]	5 104	4 378
Hadley town	1 351	1 128
Lake Luzerne—Hadley (CDP) (pt.)	825	...
Halfmoon town	11 860	9 287

County Subdivisions	1980	1970
Saratoga County—Con.		
Malta town[36]	6 968	3 813
Round Lake village	791	886
Mechanicville city	5 500	6 247
Milton town	12 876	10 450
Ballston Spa village (pt.)[36]	3 716	4 152
Milton (CDP)	2 063	1 861
North Ballston Spa (CDP)	1 350	1 296
Moreau town	11 188	'10 411
Fernwood (CDP)	3 640	3 659
South Glens Falls village	3 714	4 013
Northumberland town	2 732	1 779
Providence town	1 210	'803
Saratoga town	4 595	4 206
Schuylerville village	1 256	1 402
Victory village	571	718
Saratoga Springs city[36]	23 906	18 845
Stillwater town	6 316	5 023
Stillwater village	1 572	1 428
Waterford town	7 194	'7 644
Waterford village	2 405	2 879
Wilton town	7 221	'2 984
Schenectady County	149 946	'161 078
Duanesburg town	4 729	3 800
Delanson village	448	508
Glenville town	28 519	28 969
East Glenville (CDP)	6 537	5 898
Scotia village	7 280	'7 370
Niskayuna town	17 471	17 879
Niskayuna (CDP)	5 223	6 186
Princetown town	1 804	1 405
Rotterdam town	29 451	31 067
Rotterdam (CDP)	22 933	'25 214
Rotterdam Junction (CDP)	1 010	...
Schenectady city	67 972	'77 958
Schoharie County[37]	29 710	24 750
Blenheim town	292	260
Broome town	761	551
Carlisle town	1 417	1 040
Cobleskill town	7 048	6 017
Cobleskill village	5 272	4 368
Conesville town	681	489
Esperance town	1 951	1 567
Esperance village[37]	374	408
Fulton town	1 394	1 060
Gilboa town	1 078	854
Jefferson town	1 108	840
Middleburgh town	2 980	2 486
Middleburgh village[37]	1 358	1 410
Richmondville town	2 186	1 903
Richmondville village	792	826
Schoharie town	3 107	3 088
Schoharie village	1 016	1 125
Seward town	1 587	1 271
Sharon town	1 915	1 566
Sharon Springs village	514	421
Summit town	903	690
Wright town	1 302	1 068
Schuyler County[38]	17 686	16 737
Catharine town	1 932	1 886
Odessa village (pt.)	529	568
Cayuta town	566	557
Dix town	4 138	4 201
Montour Falls village (pt.)	94	25
Watkins Glen village (pt.)	2 008	2 265
Hector town	3 793	3 671
Burdett village[38]	410	454
Montour town	2 607	2 324
Montour Falls village (pt.)	1 697	1 509
Odessa village (pt.)	84	38
Orange town	1 358	1 076
Reading town	1 813	1 768
Watkins Glen village (pt.)	432	451
Tyrone town	1 479	1 254
Seneca County[39]	33 733	35 083
Covert town	2 188	2 097
Interlaken village[39]	685	733
Fayette town	3 561	2 997
Waterloo village (pt.)	732	645
Geneva city (pt.)[39]	–	'–
Junius town	1 354	1 111
Lodi town	1 184	1 287
Lodi village	334	353
Ovid town	2 530	3 107
Ovid village (pt.)	642	748
Willard (CDP) (pt.)	506	...
Romulus town	2 464	4 284
Ovid village (pt.)	24	31
Willard (CDP) (pt.)	833	...
Seneca Falls town	9 886	9 900
Seneca Falls village[39]	7 466	7 794
Tyre town	887	837
Varick town	1 868	1 700
Waterloo town	7 811	7 763
Waterloo village (pt.)	4 571	4 773

County Subdivisions	1980	1970
Steuben County[40]	99 217	99 546
Addison town	2 734	2 698
Addison village	2 028	2 104
Avoca town	2 225	2 059
Avoca village	1 144	1 153
Bath town	12 268	11 953
Bath village[40]	6 042	6 053
Savona village	932	933
Bradford town	724	630
Cameron town	917	741
Campbell town	3 801	3 180
Canisteo town	3 991	3 777
Canisteo village	2 679	2 772
Caton town	1 847	1 747
Cohocton town	2 466	2 379
Cohocton village	902	897
Corning city	12 953	15 792
Corning town	6 846	7 523
Riverside village	684	911
South Corning village	1 195	1 414
Dansville town	1 455	1 453
Erwin town	6 445	6 275
Gang Mills (CDP)	2 300	1 258
Painted Post village	2 196	2 496
Fremont town	865	884
Greenwood town	883	845
Hartsville town	509	467
Hornby town	1 786	1 377
Hornell city	10 234	12 144
Hornellsville town	4 066	3 993
Almond village (pt.)	39	31
Arkport village	811	984
North Hornell village	813	919
Howard town	1 236	1 029
Jasper town	1 128	1 042
Lindley town	1 831	1 414
Prattsburg town[40]	1 657	1 523
Pulteney town	1 274	1 167
Rathbone town	913	873
Thurston town	986	810
Troupsburg town	1 005	1 004
Tuscarora town	1 338	1 071
Urbana town	2 982	2 694
Hammondsport village	1 065	1 066
Wayland town	3 881	3 546
Wayland village	1 846	2 022
Wayne town	1 066	902
West Union town	431	426
Wheeler town	1 014	858
Woodhull town	1 460	1 270
Woodhull village	315	313
Suffolk County[41]	1 284 231	'1 127 030
Babylon town	203 483	203 570
Amityville village	9 076	9 794
Babylon village	12 388	12 897
Copiague (CDP)	20 132	19 632
Deer Park (CDP)	30 394	'32 274
East Farmingdale (CDP)	5 522	...
Lindenhurst village	26 919	28 359
North Amityville (CDP)	13 140	11 936
North Babylon (CDP)	19 019	'39 526
North Lindenhurst (CDP)	11 511	11 117
West Babylon (CDP)	41 699	12 893
Wyandanch (CDP)	13 215	15 716
Brookhaven town	364 812	'245 135
Belle Terre village	826	678
Bellport village	2 809	3 046
Centereach (CDP)	30 136	9 427
Center Moriches (CDP)	5 703	3 802
Coram (CDP)	24 752	...
East Patchogue (CDP)	18 139	8 092
Farmingville (CDP)	13 398	...
Holbrook (CDP) (pt.)	4 899	...
Holtsville (CDP) (pt.)	11 003	...
Lake Grove village	9 692	8 133
Lake Ronkonkoma (CDP) (pt.)	14 305	...
Mastic (CDP)	10 413	...
Mastic Beach (CDP)	8 318	4 870
Medford (CDP)	20 418	...
Middle Island (CDP)	5 703	...
Miller Place (CDP)	7 877	...
Mount Sinai (CDP)	6 591	...
North Bellport (CDP)	7 432	5 903
North Patchogue (CDP)	7 126	5 232
Old Field village	829	812
Patchogue village	11 291	11 582
Poquott village	588	427
Port Jefferson village[41]	6 731	5 515
Port Jefferson Station (CDP)	17 009	7 403
Ridge (CDP)	8 977	...
Rocky Point (CDP)	7 012	...
Selden (CDP)	17 259	11 613
Setauket–East Setauket (CDP)	10 176	...
Shirley (CDP)	18 072	'6 157
Shoreham village	555	524
Sound Beach (CDP)	8 071	...
Stony Brook (CDP)	16 155	6 391
East Hampton town	14 029	10 980
Amagansett (CDP)	2 188	...

County Subdivisions

County Subdivisions	1980	1970
Suffolk County—Con.		
East Hampton town—Con.		
East Hampton village	1 886	1 753
Montauk (CDP)	2 828	...
Northwest Harbor (CDP)	2 459	...
Sag Harbor village (pt.)	895	835
Springs (CDP)	3 197	...
Huntington town	201 512	'200 172
Asharoken village	635	540
Centerport (CDP)	6 576	...
Cold Spring Harbor (CDP)	5 336	'5 450
Commack (CDP) (pt.)	13 687	'16 232
Dix Hills (CDP)	26 693	10 050
East Northport (CDP)	20 187	12 392
Eatons Neck (CDP)	1 574	...
Elwood (CDP)	11 847	15 031
Fort Salonga (CDP) (pt.)	5 760	...
Greenlawn (CDP)	13 869	'8 493
Huntington (CDP)	21 727	'12 601
Huntington Bay village	1 783	1 789
Huntington Station (CDP)	28 769	28 817
Lloyd Harbor village	3 405	3 371
Melville (CDP)	8 139	6 641
Northport village	7 651	'7 494
South Huntington (CDP)	14 854	9 115
West Hills (CDP)	6 071	...
Islip town	298 897	'278 880
Bayport (CDP)	9 282	8 232
Bay Shore (CDP)	10 784	11 119
Bohemia (CDP)	9 308	8 926
Brentwood (CDP)	44 321	'28 327
Brightwaters village	3 286	3 808
Central Islip (CDP)	19 734	36 391
East Islip (CDP)	13 852	6 861
Hauppauge (CDP) (pt.)	10 196	...
Holbrook (CDP) (pt.)	19 483	...
Holtsville (CDP) (pt.)	2 442	...
Islip (CDP)	13 438	7 692
Islip Terrace (CDP)	5 588	...
Lake Ronkonkoma (CDP) (pt.)	19 692	...
North Bay Shore (CDP)	35 020	...
North Great River (CDP)	11 416	12 080
Oakdale (CDP)	8 090	7 334
Ocean Beach village	155	109
Saltaire village	35	37
Sayville (CDP)	12 013	11 680
West Bay Shore (CDP)	5 118	...
West Islip (CDP)	29 533	17 374
West Sayville (CDP)	8 185	7 386
Poospatuck Indian Reservation[41]	203	'125
Riverhead town	20 243	18 909
Calverton–Roanoke (CDP)	4 952	...
Jamesport (CDP)	1 069	...
Northville (CDP)	2 583	...
Riverhead (CDP)	6 339	7 585
Shelter Island town	2 071	1 644
Dering Harbor village	16	24
Shelter Island (CDP)	1 115	...
Shinnecock Indian Reservation	297	174
Smithtown town	116 663	'114 657
Commack (CDP) (pt.)	21 032	7 906
Fort Salonga (CDP) (pt.)	3 790	...
Hauppauge (CDP) (pt.)	10 764	13 957
Head of the Harbor village	1 023	943
Kings Park (CDP)	16 131	5 555
Lake Ronkonkoma (CDP) (pt.)	4 339	...
Nesconset (CDP)	10 706	10 048
Nissequogue village	1 462	1 120
St. James (CDP)	12 122	'10 500
Smithtown (CDP)	30 906	...
Village of the Branch village	1 707	1 675
Southampton town	42 849	35 980
Bridgehampton (CDP)	1 941	...
East Quogue (CDP)	3 668	1 143
Hampton Bays (CDP)	7 256	1 862
Hampton Park (CDP)	1 331	...
North Haven village	738	694
North Sea (CDP)	1 171	...
Noyack (CDP)	2 657	...
Quogue village	966	865
Remsenburg–Speonk (CDP)	1 868	...
Riverside–Flanders (CDP)	5 400	...
Sag Harbor village (pt.)	1 686	1 528
Shinnecock Hills (CDP)	2 344	...
Southampton village	4 000	4 904
Westhampton (CDP)	2 774	1 156
Westhampton Beach village	1 629	1 926
Southold town	19 172	16 804
Cutchogue–New Suffolk (CDP)	2 788	...
Greenport village	2 273	2 481
Greenport West (CDP)	1 571	...
Mattituck (CDP)	3 923	1 995
Peconic (CDP)	1 056	...
Southold (CDP)	4 770	2 030
Sullivan County[42]	65 155	52 580
Bethel town	3 335	2 763
Callicoon town	2 998	2 398
Jeffersonville village	554	421
Cochecton town	1 330	1 181
Delaware town	2 783	2 260

County Subdivisions	1980	1970
Sullivan County—Con.		
Fallsburg town	9 862	7 959
South Fallsburg (CDP)	2 196	1 590
Woodridge village[42]	809	1 071
Forestburgh town	796	474
Fremont town	1 346	1 047
Highland town	1 878	1 377
Liberty town	9 879	9 329
Liberty village[42]	4 293	'4 514
Lumberland town	1 210	857
Mamakating town	7 717	4 319
Bloomingburg village	338	323
Wurtsboro village	1 128	732
Neversink town	2 840	2 055
Rockland town	4 207	3 919
Livingston Manor (CDP)	1 436	1 522
Thompson town	13 550	11 418
Monticello village[42]	6 306	5 991
Tusten town	1 424	1 224
Tioga County[43]	49 812	46 513
Barton town	8 784	8 526
Waverly village[43]	4 738	5 261
Berkshire town	1 335	1 098
Candor town	4 919	4 190
Candor village	917	939
Newark Valley town	3 765	3 323
Newark Valley village[43]	1 190	1 286
Nichols town	2 567	2 271
Nichols village	613	638
Owego town	20 471	20 336
Apalachin (CDP)	1 227	1 233
Owego village	4 364	5 152
Richford town	906	916
Spencer town	2 633	2 232
Spencer village	863	854
Tioga town	4 432	3 621
Tompkins County[44]	87 085	'77 064
Caroline town	2 754	2 536
Danby town	2 449	2 141
Dryden town	12 156	9 770
Dryden village	1 761	1 490
Freeville village	449	664
Enfield town	2 375	2 028
Groton town	5 213	4 881
Groton village[44]	2 313	2 112
Ithaca city	28 732	26 226
Ithaca town	16 022	15 620
Cayuga Heights village	3 170	3 130
East Cayuga Heights (CDP)	2 630	2 611
South Hill (CDP)	5 276	...
Lansing town	8 317	5 972
Lansing village[44]	3 039	...
Newfield town	4 401	3 390
Ulysses town	4 666	'4 500
Trumansburg village[44]	1 722	'1 803
Ulster County[45]	158 158	141 241
Denning town	474	297
Esopus town	7 605	6 974
Port Ewen (CDP)	2 813	2 882
Gardiner town	3 552	2 598
Hardenbergh town[45]	280	239
Hurley town	6 992	6 496
Hurley (CDP) (pt.)	2 935	2 416
West Hurley (CDP) (pt.)	2 344	...
Kingston city	24 481	25 544
Kingston town	924	748
Lloyd town	7 875	7 032
Clintondale (CDP) (pt.)	279	...
Highland (CDP)	3 967	2 184
Marbletown town	4 956	4 146
Marlborough town	7 055	5 657
Marlboro (CDP)	2 275	1 580
Milton (CDP)	1 253	...
New Paltz town	10 183	10 415
New Paltz village[45]	4 938	6 058
Olive town	3 924	2 857
Plattekill town	7 409	4 458
Clintondale (CDP) (pt.)	914	...
Rochester town	5 344	3 940
Kerhonkson (CDP) (pt.)	655	381
Rosendale town[45]	5 933	5 422
Bloomington–Hickory Bush (CDP)	1 002	...
Rosendale Village (CDP)	1 134	...
Tillson (CDP)	1 529	1 256
Saugerties town	17 975	16 961
Glasco (CDP)	1 179	1 169
Saugerties village[45]	3 882	4 190
Saugerties South (CDP)	2 919	3 159
Shandaken town	2 912	2 593
Pine Hill village	216	247
Shawangunk town	8 186	5 749
Wallkill (CDP)	2 064	1 849
Ulster town	12 319	11 711
Hurley (CDP) (pt.)	1 957	1 665
Lake Katrine (CDP)	2 011	1 092
Lincoln Park (CDP)	2 664	2 851
Ruby (CDP)	1 059	...

County Subdivisions	1980	1970
Ulster County—Con.		
Wawarsing town	12 956	11 690
Ellenville village	4 405	4 482
Kerhonkson (CDP) (pt.)	991	862
Napanoch (CDP)	1 260	...
Woodstock town	6 823	5 714
West Hurley (CDP) (pt.)	38	...
Woodstock (CDP)	2 280	1 073
Zena (CDP)	1 435	...
Warren County	54 854	49 402
Bolton town	1 793	1 589
Chester town	2 909	2 330
Glens Falls city	15 897	17 222
Hague town	766	910
Horicon town	1 082	890
Johnsburg town	2 173	2 377
Lake George town	3 394	2 806
Lake George village	1 047	1 046
Lake Luzerne town	2 672	2 174
Lake Luzerne–Hadley (CDP) (pt.)	1 163	...
Queensbury town	18 978	14 506
Glens Falls North (CDP)	6 956	...
West Glens Falls (CDP)	5 331	3 363
Stony Creek town	528	560
Thurman town	852	708
Warrensburg town	3 810	3 330
Warrensburg (CDP)	2 834	2 743
Washington County[46]	54 795	52 725
Argyle town	2 847	2 415
Argyle village	320	392
Cambridge town	1 848	1 702
Cambridge village (pt.)	550	493
Dresden town	559	480
Easton town	2 020	1 956
Greenwich village (pt.)	282	334
Fort Ann town	4 425	3 749
Fort Ann village	509	562
Fort Edward town	6 479	6 719
Fort Edward village[46]	3 561	3 733
South Hudson Falls (CDP)	1 955	2 097
Granville town	5 566	5 412
Granville village	2 696	2 784
Greenwich town	4 276	4 177
Greenwich village (pt.)	1 673	1 758
Hampton town	559	464
Hartford town	1 742	1 398
Hebron town	1 288	1 212
Jackson town	1 228	941
Kingsbury town	11 660	11 737
Hudson Falls village	7 419	7 917
North Hudson Falls (CDP)	2 309	...
Putnam town	506	579
Salem town	2 377	2 346
Salem village	959	1 025
White Creek town	2 988	2 644
Cambridge village (pt.)	1 270	1 276
Whitehall town	4 427	4 794
Whitehall village	3 241	3 764
Wayne County[47]	84 581	79 404
Arcadia town	14 697	15 245
Newark village[47]	10 017	11 644
Butler town	1 720	1 593
Wolcott village (pt.)	246	314
Galen town	4 480	4 619
Clyde village	2 491	2 828
Huron town	1 820	1 739
Lyons town	6 073	6 015
Lyons village[47]	4 160	4 496
Macedon town	6 508	5 488
Macedon village[47]	1 400	1 168
Marion town	4 456	3 784
Marion (CDP)	1 080	...
Ontario town	7 480	6 014
Palmyra town	7 652	7 417
Palmyra village[47]	3 729	3 776
Rose town	2 684	2 356
Savannah town[47]	1 905	1 676
Sodus town	9 485	8 754
Sodus village[47]	1 790	1 813
Sodus Point village	1 334	1 172
Walworth town	5 281	4 584
Williamson town	6 319	6 356
Williamson (CDP)	1 768	1 991
Wolcott town	4 021	3 764
Red Creek village	645	626
Wolcott village (pt.)	1 250	1 303
Westchester County[48]	866 599	r894 406
Bedford town[48]	15 137	18 329
Bedford (CDP)	1 633	...
Cortlandt town	35 705	34 393
Buchanan village	2 041	2 110
Croton-on-Hudson village	6 889	7 523
Eastchester town	32 648	36 660
Bronxville village	6 267	6 674
Eastchester (CDP)	20 305	23 750
Tuckahoe village	6 076	6 236
Greenburgh town	82 881	r85 827

County Subdivisions	1980	1970
Westchester County—Con.		
Greenburgh town—Con.		
Ardsley village	4 183	4 470
Dobbs Ferry village	10 053	10 353
Elmsford village	3 361	3 911
Greenville (CDP)	8 706	...
Hartsdale (CDP)	10 216	12 226
Hastings-on-Hudson village	8 573	9 479
Irvington village	5 774	5 878
Tarrytown village	10 648	11 115
Harrison town[48]	23 046	21 544
Harrison village[48]	23 046	...
Lewisboro town	8 871	6 610
Golden's Bridge (CDP)	1 367	1 101
Mamaroneck town	29 017	31 243
Larchmont village	6 308	7 203
Mamaroneck village (pt.)	10 281	11 038
Mount Kisco town[48]	8 025	8 172
Mount Kisco[48]	8 025	8 172
Mount Pleasant town	39 298	38 535
Briarcliff Manor village (pt.)[48]	795	629
Hawthorne (CDP)	5 010	...
North Tarrytown village	7 994	8 334
Pleasantville village	6 749	7 110
Thornwood (CDP)	7 197	6 874
Mount Vernon city	66 713	72 778
New Castle town[48]	15 425	19 837
New Rochelle city	70 794	75 385
North Castle town	9 467	9 591
Armonk (CDP)	2 238	...
North Salem town	4 569	3 828
Peach Lake (CDP) (pt.)	466	...
Ossining town	30 680	32 397
Briarcliff Manor village (pt.)	6 320	5 892
Ossining village	20 196	21 659
Peekskill city	18 236	19 283
Pelham town	12 978	13 933
Pelham village[48]	6 848	2 076
Pelham Manor village	6 130	6 673
Pound Ridge town	4 009	3 792
Rye city	15 083	15 869
Rye town	38 896	43 234
Mamaroneck village (pt.)	7 335	7 871
Port Chester village	23 565	25 803
Scarsdale town	17 650	19 229
Scarsdale village	17 650	19 229
Somers town	13 133	9 402
White Plains city	46 999	r50 346
Yonkers city	195 351	204 297
Yorktown town	31 988	28 064
Jefferson Valley–Yorktown (CDP)	13 380	9 008
Yorktown Heights (CDP)	7 696	6 805
Wyoming County[49]	39 895	37 688
Arcade town	3 714	3 048
Arcade village[49]	2 052	1 972
Attica town	5 693	6 171
Attica village (pt.)	2 643	2 909
Bennington town	2 889	2 544
Castile town	2 865	3 156
Castile village	1 135	1 330
Perry village (pt.)	317	475
Covington town	1 075	953
Eagle town	1 216	996
Gainesville town	2 133	2 177
Gainesville village	334	385
Silver Springs village	801	823
Genesee Falls town	553	397
Java town	2 273	1 949
Middlebury town	1 561	1 503
Wyoming village	507	514
Orangeville town	1 103	820
Perry town	5 437	5 367
Perry village (pt.)	3 881	4 063
Pike town	991	916
Pike village	367	373
Sheldon town	2 644	2 296
Warsaw town	5 074	4 721
Warsaw village (pt.)	3 619	3 619
Wethersfield town	674	674
Yates County[50]	21 459	19 831
Barrington town	1 091	929
Benton town	1 981	2 159
Penn Yan village (pt.)[50]	410	r335
Italy town	953	532
Jerusalem town	3 908	3 581
Keuka Park (CDP)	1 153	...
Penn Yan village (pt.)	53	r17
Middlesex town	1 127	925
Milo town	6 732	6 654
Penn Yan village (pt.)[50]	4 779	r4 941
Potter town	1 436	1 082
Rushville village (pt.)	400	374
Starkey town	2 868	2 783
Dundee village[50]	1 556	1 539
Torrey town	1 363	1 186
Dresden village	378	450

NORTH CAROLINA

The original province of Carolina was named in honor of Charles I of England.

The shores of the region now constituting North Carolina may have been seen by Cabot, an Italian in the service of England, at about the close of the fifteenth century, and by Verazzano, an Italian in the service of France, in 1524, But the first well authenticated exploration was made in 1584 when a fleet sent out by Sir Walter Raleigh anchored off the coast of this region. During the years immediately following, threee unsuccessful efforts were made under the auspices of Raleigh to establish a colony on Roanoke Island.

The present area of North Carolina was included wholly or in part in the grants made to Virginia by the charters of 1606, 1609, and 1612. In 1629 Charles I granted the territory between the thirty-first and thirty-sixth parallels, under the name Carolina, to Sir Robert Heath. No settlements were made under this grant, however, and the patent was vacated. The first permanent settlement was made by colonists from Virginia about the year 1660.

In 1663 Carolina, extending from the thirty-first to the thirty-sixth parallels and from the Atlantic to the Pacific, was granted by King Charles II to eight "lords proprietors." Two years later the northern and southern limits were placed at 36°30' and 29", respectively. The grant thus included the area now constituting North and South Carolina, Georgia, and part of Florida, and extended westward to the Pacific Ocean. Settlers were promptly sent to Carolina, and a government was organized. At first there was no formal division of the province, but the northern part gradually came to be known as North Carolina and the southern part as South Carolina, and each had its own separate government. In 1729 seven of the eight "lords proprietors" sold their shares to the English crown and Carolina was definitely and authoritatively divided into the royal provinces of North and South Carolina.

Four years later the colony of Georgia was formed from territory originally included in the Carolina grants.

In 1790 the area now constituting Tennessee was transferred to the Federal Government, leaving North Carolina with substantially its present limits. North Carolina was on of the original thirteen states. It adopted a state constitution in 1776, and in November, 1789, ratified the Federal Constitution.

COUNTY LOCATION INDEX

Alamance	C-5		Gaston	C-3		Pender	D-6
Alexander	C-3		Gates	B-7		Perquimans	B-7
Alleghany	B-3		Graham	C-1		Person	B-5
Anson	D-4		Granville	B-5		Pitt	C-7
Ashe	B-3		Greene	C-6		Polk	C-3
Avery	C-3		Guilford	C-5		Randolph	C-5
Beaufort	C-7		Halifax	B-6		Richmond	D-5
Bertie	C-7		Harnett	C-5		Robeson	D-5
Bladen	D-6		Haywood	C-2		Rockingham	B-5
Brunswick	E-6		Henderson	C-2		Rowan	C-4
Buncombe	C-2		Hertford	B-7		Rutherford	C-3
Burke	C-3		Hoke	D-5		Sampson	D-6
Cabarrus	C-4		Hyde	C-7		Scotland	D-5
Caldwell	C-3		Iredell	C-4		Stanly	C-4
Camden	B-7		Jackson	C-2		Stokes	B-4
Carteret	D-7		Johnston	C-6		Surry	B-4
Caswell	B-5		Jones	D-7		Swain	C-2
Catawba	C-3		Lee	C-5		Transylvania	C-2
Chatham	C-5		Lenoir	C-6		Tyrrell	C-7
Cherokee	C-1		Lincoln	C-3		Union	D-4
Chowan	B-7		McDowell	C-3		Vance	B-6
Clay	C-1		Macon	C-2		Wake	C-5
Cleveland	C-3		Madison	C-2		Warren	B-6
Columbus	D-5		Martin	C-7		Washington	C-7
Craven	C-7		Mecklenburg	C-4		Watauga	B-3
Cumberland	D-5		Mitchell	C-3		Wayne	C-6
Currituck	B-7		Montgomery	C-4		Wilkes	B-3
Dare	C-8		Moore	C-5		Wilson	C-6
Davidson	C-4		Nash	C-6		Yadkin	B-4
Davie	C-4		New Hanover	D-6		Yancey	C-3
Duplin	D-6		Northampton	B-6			
Durham	C-5		Onslow	D-6			
Edgecombe	C-6		Orange	C-5			
Forsyth	C-4		Pamlico	C-7			
Franklin	C-6		Pasquotank	B-7			

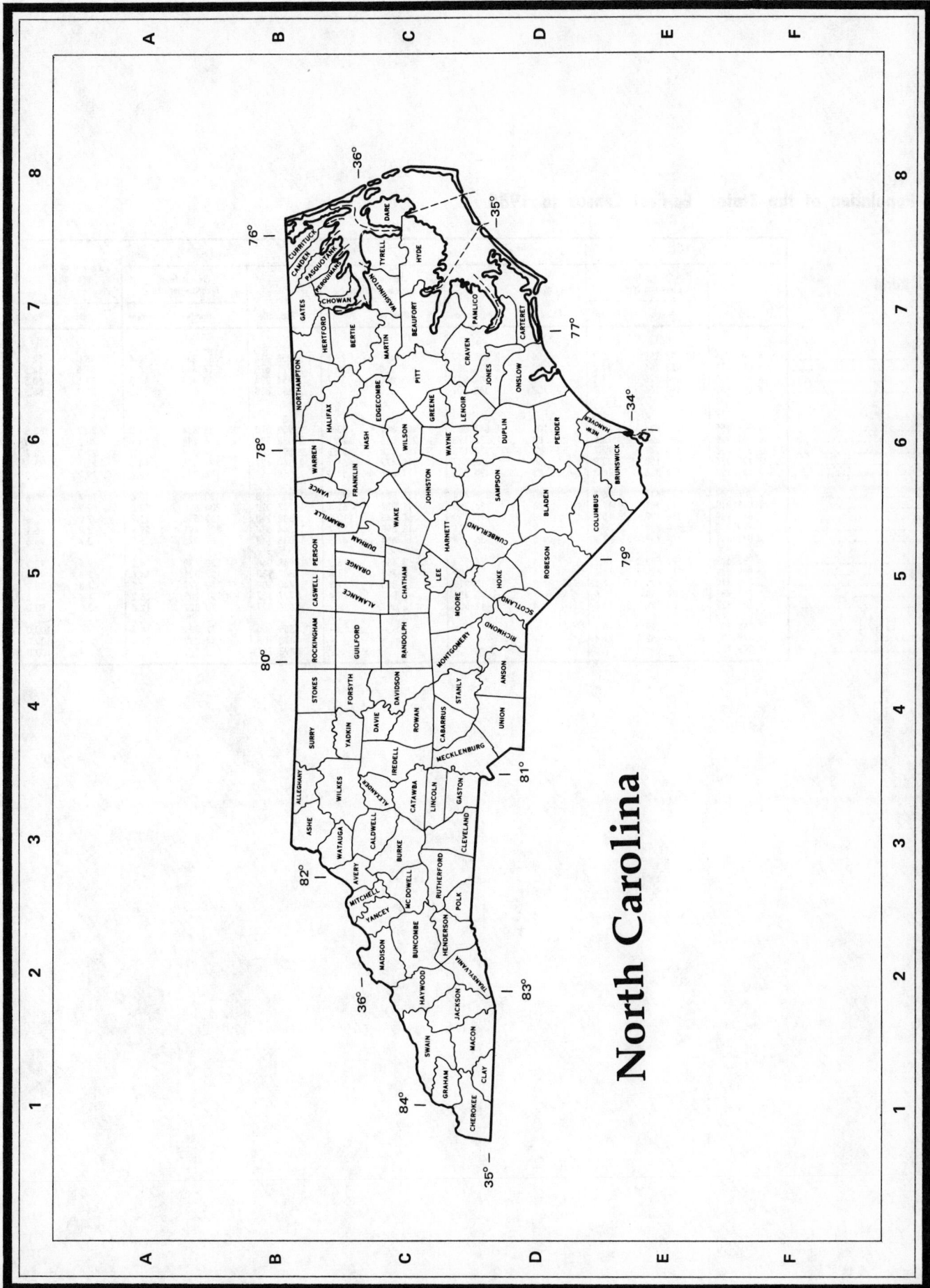

North Carolina

Population of the State: Earliest Census to 1980

Urban and Rural

	The State			Urban				Rural			Percent of total population	
	Total population	Change from preceding census		Places of 2,500 or more	Population	Change from preceding census		Population	Change from preceding census		Urban	Rural
		Number	Percent			Number	Percent		Number	Percent		
Current urban definition:												
1980 (Apr. 1)	5 881 766	797 355	15.7	188	2 822 852	512 471	22.2	3 058 914	287 236	10.4	48.0	52.0
1970 (Apr. 1)	ʹ5 084 411	528 256	11.6	138	2 310 381	508 460	28.2	2 771 678	17 444	0.6	45.5	54.5
1960 (Apr. 1)	4 556 155	494 226	12.2	125	1 801 921	433 820	31.7	2 754 234	60 406	2.2	39.5	60.5
1950 (Apr. 1)	4 061 929	490 306	13.7	107	1 368 101	...	...	2 693 828	...	...	33.7	66.3
Previous urban definition:												
1960 (Apr. 1)	4 556 155	494 226	12.2	106	1 647 085	408 892	33.0	2 909 070	85 334	3.0	36.2	63.8
1950 (Apr. 1)	4 061 929	490 306	13.7	88	1 238 193	264 018	27.1	2 823 736	226 288	8.7	30.5	69.5
1940 (Apr. 1)	3 571 623	401 347	12.7	76	974 175	164 328	20.3	2 597 448	237 019	10.0	27.3	72.7
1930 (Apr. 1)	3 170 276	611 153	23.9	68	809 847	319 477	65.2	2 360 429	291 676	14.1	25.5	74.5
1920 (Jan. 1)	2 559 123	352 836	16.0	55	490 370	171 896	54.0	2 068 753	180 940	9.6	19.2	80.8
1910 (Apr. 15)	2 206 287	312 477	16.5	40	318 474	131 684	70.5	1 887 813	180 793	10.6	14.4	85.6
1900 (June 1)	1 893 810	275 861	17.1	28	186 790	71 031	61.4	1 707 020	204 830	13.6	9.9	90.1
1890 (June 1)	1 617 949	218 199	15.6	18	115 759	60 643	110.0	1 502 190	157 556	11.7	7.2	92.8
1880 (June 1)	1 399 750	328 389	30.7	9	55 116	18 898	52.2	1 344 634	309 491	29.9	3.9	96.1
1870 (June 1)	1 071 361	78 739	7.9	5	36 218	11 664	47.5	1 035 143	67 075	6.9	3.4	96.6
1860 (June 1)	992 622	123 583	14.2	4	24 554	3 445	16.3	968 068	120 138	14.2	2.5	97.5
1850 (June 1)	869 039	115 620	15.3	4	21 109	7 799	58.6	847 930	107 821	14.6	2.4	97.6
1840 (June 1)	753 419	15 432	2.1	3	13 310	2 855	27.3	740 109	12 577	1.7	1.8	98.2
1830 (June 1)	737 987	99 158	15.5	3	10 455	-2 047	-16.4	727 532	101 205	16.2	1.4	98.6
1820 (Aug. 7)	638 829	83 329	15.0	4	12 502	12 502	...	626 327	70 827	12.8	2.0	98.0
1810 (Aug. 6)	555 500	77 397	16.2	–	–	–	–	555 500	77 397	16.2	–	100.0
1800 (Aug. 4)	478 103	84 352	21.4	–	–	–	–	478 103	84 352	21.4	–	100.0
1790 (Aug. 2)	393 751	...	...	–	–	...	...	393 751	...	...	–	100.0

ALAMANCE

1850	11,444
1860	11,852
1870	11,874
1880	14,613
1890	18,271
1900	25,665
1910	28,712
1920	32,718
1930	42,140
1940	57,427
1950	71,220
1960	85,674
1970	96,362
1980	99,319

ALEXANDER

1850	5,220
1860	6,022
1870	6,868
1880	8,355
1890	9,430
1900	10,960
1910	11,592
1920	12,212
1930	12,922
1940	13,454
1950	14,554
1960	15,625
1970	19,466
1980	24,999

ALLEGHANY

1860	3,590
1870	3,691
1880	5,486
1890	6,523
1900	7,579
1910	7,745
1920	7,403
1930	7,186
1940	8,341
1950	8,155
1960	7,734
1970	8,134
1980	9,587

ANSON

1790	5,133
1800	8,146
1810	8,831
1820	12,534
1830	14,095
1840	15,077
1850	13,489
1860	13,664
1870	12,428
1880	17,994
1890	20,027
1900	21,870
1910	25,465
1920	28,334
1930	29,349
1940	28,443
1950	26,781
1960	24,962
1970	23,488
1980	25,649

ASHE

1800	2,783
1810	3,694
1820	4,335
1830	6,987
1840	7,467
1850	8,777
1860	7,956
1870	9,573
1880	14,437
1890	15,628
1900	19,581
1910	19,074
1920	21,001
1930	21,019
1940	22,664
1950	21,878
1960	19,768
1970	19,571
1980	22,325

AVERY

1920	10,335
1930	11,803
1940	13,561
1950	13,352
1960	12,009
1970	12,655
1980	14,409

BEAUFORT

1790	5,462
1800	6,242
1810	7,203
1820	9,850
1830	10,969
1840	12,225
1850	13,816
1860	14,766
1870	13,011
1880	17,474
1890	21,072
1900	26,404
1910	30,877
1920	31,024
1930	35,026
1940	36,431
1950	37,134
1960	36,014
1970	35,980
1980	40,355

BERTIE

1790	12,606
1800	11,249
1810	11,218
1820	10,805
1830	12,262
1840	12,175
1850	12,851
1860	14,310
1870	12,950
1880	16,399
1890	19,176
1900	20,538
1910	23,039
1920	23,993
1930	25,844
1940	26,201
1950	26,439
1960	24,350
1970	20,528
1980	21,024

BLADEN

1790	5,084
1800	7,028
1810	5,671
1820	7,276
1830	7,811
1840	8,022
1850	9,767
1860	11,995
1870	12,831
1880	16,158
1890	16,763
1900	17,677
1910	18,006
1920	19,761
1930	22,389
1940	27,156
1950	29,703
1960	28,881
1970	26,477
1980	30,491

BRUNSWICK

1790	3,071
1800	4,110
1810	4,778
1820	5,480
1830	6,516
1840	5,265
1850	7,272
1860	8,406
1870	7,754
1880	9,389
1890	10,900
1900	12,657
1910	14,432
1920	14,876
1930	15,818
1940	17,125
1950	19,238
1960	20,278
1970	24,223
1980	35,777

BUNCOMBE

1800	5,812
1810	9,277
1820	10,542
1830	16,281
1840	10,084
1850	13,425
1860	12,654
1870	15,412
1880	21,909
1890	35,266
1900	44,288
1910	49,798
1920	64,148
1930	97,937
1940	108,755
1950	124,403
1960	130,074
1970	145,056
1980	160,934

BURKE

1790	8,118
1800	9,929
1810	11,007
1820	13,411
1830	17,888
1840	15,799
1850	7,772

1860	9,237
1870	9,777
1880	12,809
1890	14,939
1900	17,699
1910	21,408
1920	23,297
1930	29,410
1940	38,615
1950	45,518
1960	52,701
1970	60,364
1980	72,504

CABARRUS

1800	5,094
1810	6,158
1820	7,248
1830	8,810
1840	9,259
1850	9,747
1860	10,546
1870	11,954
1880	14,964
1890	18,142
1900	22,456
1910	26,240
1920	33,730
1930	44,331
1940	59,393
1950	63,783
1960	68,137
1970	74,629
1980	85,895

CALDWELL

1850	6,317
1860	7,497
1870	8,476
1880	10,291
1890	12,298
1900	15,694
1910	20,597
1920	19,984
1930	28,016
1940	35,795
1950	43,352
1960	49,552
1970	56,699
1980	67,746

CAMDEN

1790	4,033
1800	4,191
1810	5,347
1820	6,347
1830	6,733
1840	5,663
1850	6,049
1860	5,343
1870	5,361
1880	6,274
1890	5,667
1900	5,474
1910	5,640
1920	5,382
1930	5,461
1940	5,440
1950	5,223
1960	5,598
1970	5,453
1980	5,829

CARTERET

1790	3,732
1800	4,399
1810	4,823
1820	5,609
1830	6,597
1840	6,591
1850	6,939
1860	8,186
1870	9,010
1880	9,784
1890	10,825
1900	11,811
1910	13,776
1920	15,384
1930	16,900
1940	18,284
1950	23,059
1960	30,940
1970	31,603
1980	41,092

CASWELL

1790	10,096
1800	8,701
1810	11,757
1820	13,253
1830	15,185
1840	14,693
1850	15,269
1860	16,215
1870	16,081
1880	17,825
1890	16,028
1900	15,028
1910	14,858
1920	15,759
1930	18,214
1940	20,032
1950	20,870
1960	19,912
1970	19,055
1980	20,705

CATAWBA

1850	8,862
1860	10,729
1870	10,984
1880	14,946
1890	18,689
1900	22,133
1910	27,918
1920	33,839
1930	43,991
1940	51,653
1950	61,794
1960	73,191
1970	90,873
1980	105,208

CHATHAM

1790	9,221
1800	11,861
1810	12,977
1820	12,661
1830	15,405
1840	16,241
1850	18,449
1860	19,101
1870	19,723
1880	23,453
1890	25,413
1900	23,912

1910	22,635
1920	23,814
1930	24,177
1940	24,726
1950	25,392
1960	26,785
1970	29,554
1980	33,415

CHEROKEE

1840	3,427
1850	6,838
1860	9,166
1870	8,080
1880	8,182
1890	9,976
1900	11,860
1910	14,136
1920	15,242
1930	16,151
1940	18,813
1950	18,294
1960	16,335
1970	16,330
1980	18,933

CHOWAN

1790	5,011
1800	5,132
1810	5,297
1820	6,464
1830	6,697
1840	6,690
1850	6,721
1860	6,842
1870	6,450
1880	7,900
1890	9,167
1900	10,258
1910	11,303
1920	10,649
1930	11,282
1940	11,572
1950	12,540
1960	11,729
1970	10,764
1980	12,558

CLAY

1870	2,461
1880	3,316
1890	4,197
1900	4,532
1910	3,909
1920	4,646
1930	5,434
1940	6,405
1950	6,006
1960	5,526
1970	5,180
1980	6,619

CLEVELAND

1850	10,396
1860	12,348
1870	12,696
1880	16,571
1890	20,394
1900	25,078
1910	29,494
1920	34,272
1930	51,914

1940	58,055
1950	64,357
1960	66,048
1970	72,556
1980	83,435

COLUMBUS

1810	3,022
1820	3,912
1830	4,141
1840	3,941
1850	5,909
1860	8,597
1870	8,474
1880	14,439
1890	17,856
1900	21,274
1910	28,020
1920	30,124
1930	37,720
1940	45,663
1950	50,621
1960	48,973
1970	46,937
1980	51,037

CRAVEN

1790	10,469
1800	10,245
1810	12,676
1820	13,394
1830	13,734
1840	13,438
1850	14,709
1860	16,268
1870	20,516
1880	19,729
1890	20,533
1900	24,160
1910	25,594
1920	29,048
1930	30,685
1940	31,298
1950	48,823
1960	58,733
1970	62,554
1980	71,043

CUMBERLAND

1790	8,671
1800	9,264
1810	9,382
1820	14,446
1830	14,834
1840	15,284
1850	20,610
1860	16,369
1870	17,035
1880	23,836
1890	27,321
1900	29,249
1910	35,284
1920	35,064
1930	45,219
1940	59,320
1950	96,006
1960	148,418
1970	212,042
1980	247,160

CURRITUCK

1790	5,219

1800	6,928
1810	6,985
1820	8,098
1830	7,655
1840	6,073
1850	7,236
1860	7,415
1870	5,131
1880	6,476
1890	6,747
1900	6,529
1910	7,693
1920	7,268
1930	6,710
1940	6,709
1950	6,201
1960	6,601
1970	6,976
1980	11,089

DARE

1870	2,778
1880	3,243
1890	3,768
1900	4,757
1910	4,841
1920	5,115
1930	5,202
1940	6,041
1950	5,405
1960	5,935
1970	6,995
1980	13,377

DAVIDSON

1830	13,389
1840	14,606
1850	15,320
1860	16,601
1870	17,414
1880	20,333
1890	21,702
1900	23,403
1910	29,404
1920	35,201
1930	47,865
1940	53,377
1950	62,244
1960	79,493
1970	95,627
1980	113,162

DAVIE

1840	7,574
1850	7,866
1860	8,494
1870	9,620
1880	11,096
1890	11,621
1900	12,115
1910	13,394
1920	13,578
1930	14,386
1940	14,909
1950	15,420
1960	16,728
1970	18,855
1980	24,599

DUPLIN

1790	5,662
1800	6,796

1810	7,863
1820	9,744
1830	11,291
1840	11,182
1850	13,514
1860	15,784
1870	15,542
1880	18,773
1890	18,690
1900	22,405
1910	25,442
1920	30,223
1930	35,103
1940	39,739
1950	41,074
1960	40,270
1970	38,015
1980	40,952

DURHAM

1890	18,041
1900	26,233
1910	35,276
1920	42,219
1930	67,196
1940	80,244
1950	101,639
1960	111,995
1970	132,681
1980	152,785

EDGECOMBE

1790	10,255
1800	10,421
1810	12,423
1820	13,276
1830	14,935
1840	15,708
1850	17,189
1860	17,376
1870	22,970
1880	26,181
1890	24,113
1900	26,591
1910	32,101
1920	37,995
1930	47,894
1940	49,162
1950	51,634
1960	54,226
1970	54,226
1980	55,988

FORSYTH

1850	11,168
1860	12,692
1870	13,050
1880	18,070
1890	28,434
1900	35,261
1910	47,311
1920	77,269
1930	111,681
1940	126,475
1950	146,135
1960	189,428
1970	215,118
1980	243,683

FRANKLIN

1790	7,559
1800	8,529

1810	10,166
1820	9,741
1830	10,665
1840	10,980
1850	11,713
1860	14,107
1870	14,134
1880	29,829
1890	21,090
1900	25,116
1910	24,692
1920	26,667
1930	29,456
1940	30,382
1950	31,341
1960	28,755
1970	26,820
1980	30,055

GASTON

1850	8,073
1860	9,307
1870	12,602
1880	14,254
1890	17,674
1900	27,903
1910	37,063
1920	51,242
1930	78,093
1940	87,531
1950	110,836
1960	127,074
1970	148,415
1980	162,568

GATES

1790	5,392
1800	5,881
1810	5,965
1820	6,837
1830	7,866
1840	8,161
1850	8,426
1860	8,443
1870	7,724
1880	8,897
1890	10,254
1900	10,413
1910	10,455
1920	10,537
1930	10,551
1940	10,060
1950	9,555
1960	9,254
1970	8,524
1980	8,875

GRAHAM

1880	2,335
1890	3,313
1900	4,343
1910	4,749
1920	4,872
1930	5,841
1940	6,418
1950	6,886
1960	6,432
1970	6,562
1980	7,217

GRANVILLE

1790	10,982

1800	14,015
1810	15,476
1820	18,222
1830	19,355
1840	18,187
1850	21,249
1860	23,396
1870	24,831
1880	31,286
1890	24,484
1900	23,263
1910	25,102
1920	26,846
1930	28,723
1940	29,344
1950	31,793
1960	33,110
1970	32,762
1980	34,043

GREENE

1790	6,893
1800	4,128
1810	4,867
1820	4,533
1830	6,413
1840	6,595
1850	6,169
1860	7,925
1870	8,687
1880	10,037
1890	10,039
1900	12,038
1910	13,083
1920	16,212
1930	18,656
1940	18,548
1950	18,024
1960	16,741
1970	14,967
1980	16,117

GUILFORD

1790	7,191
1800	9,442
1810	11,420
1820	14,511
1830	18,737
1840	19,175
1850	19,754
1860	29,056
1870	21,736
1880	23,585
1890	28,052
1900	39,074
1910	60,497
1920	79,272
1930	133,010
1940	153,916
1950	191,057
1960	246,520
1970	288,645
1980	317,154

HALIFAX

1790	13,965
1800	13,945
1810	13,620
1820	17,237
1830	17,739
1840	16,865
1850	16,589
1860	19,442
1870	29,408

1880	30,300
1890	28,908
1900	30,793
1910	37,646
1920	43,766
1930	53,246
1940	56,512
1950	58,377
1960	58,956
1970	53,884
1980	55,286

HARNETT

1860	8,039
1870	8,895
1880	10,862
1890	13,700
1900	15,988
1910	22,174
1920	28,313
1930	37,911
1940	44,239
1950	47,605
1960	48,236
1970	49,667
1980	59,570

HAYWOOD

1810	2,780
1820	4,073
1830	4,578
1840	4,975
1850	7,074
1860	5,801
1870	7,921
1880	10,271
1890	13,346
1900	16,222
1910	21,020
1920	23,496
1930	28,273
1940	34,804
1950	37,631
1960	39,711
1970	41,710
1980	46,495

HENDERSON

1840	5,129
1850	6,853
1860	10,448
1870	7,706
1880	10,281
1890	12,589
1900	14,104
1910	16,262
1920	18,248
1930	23,404
1940	26,049
1950	30,921
1960	36,163
1970	42,804
1980	58,580

HERTFORD

1790	5,828
1800	6,701
1810	6,052
1820	7,712
1830	8,537
1840	7,484
1850	8,142

1860	9,504
1870	9,273
1880	11,843
1890	13,851
1900	14,294
1910	15,436
1920	16,294
1930	17,542
1940	19,352
1950	21,453
1960	22,718
1970	23,529
1980	23,368

HOKE

1920	11,722
1930	14,244
1940	14,937
1950	15,756
1960	16,356
1970	16,436
1980	20,383

HYDE

1790	4,120
1800	4,829
1810	6,029
1820	4,967
1830	6,184
1840	6,458
1850	7,636
1860	7,732
1870	6,445
1880	7,765
1890	8,903
1900	9,278
1910	8,840
1920	8,386
1930	8,550
1940	7,860
1950	6,479
1960	5,765
1970	5,571
1980	5,873

IREDELL

1790	5,435
1800	8,856
1810	10,972
1820	13,071
1830	14,918
1840	15,685
1850	14,719
1860	15,347
1870	16,931
1880	22,675
1890	25,462
1900	29,064
1910	34,315
1920	37,956
1930	46,693
1940	50,424
1950	56,303
1960	62,526
1970	72,197
1980	82,538

JACKSON

1860	5,515
1870	6,683
1880	7,343
1890	9,512

1900	11,853
1910	12,998
1920	13,396
1930	17,519
1940	19,366
1950	19,261
1960	17,780
1970	21,593
1980	25,811

JOHNSTON

1790	5,634
1800	6,301
1810	6,867
1820	9,607
1830	10,938
1840	10,599
1850	13,726
1860	15,656
1870	16,897
1880	23,461
1890	27,239
1900	32,250
1910	41,401
1920	48,998
1930	57,621
1940	63,798
1950	65,906
1960	62,936
1970	61,737
1980	70,599

JONES

1790	4,822
1800	4,339
1810	4,968
1820	5,216
1830	5,608
1840	4,945
1850	5,038
1860	5,730
1870	5,002
1880	7,491
1890	7,403
1900	8,226
1910	8,721
1920	9,912
1930	10,428
1940	10,926
1950	11,004
1960	11,005
1970	9,779
1980	9,705

LEE

1910	11,376
1920	13,400
1930	16,996
1940	18,743
1950	23,522
1960	26,561
1970	30,467
1980	36,718

LENOIR

1800	4,005
1810	5,572
1820	6,799
1830	7,723
1840	7,605
1850	7,828
1860	10,220

1870	10,434
1880	15,344
1890	14,879
1900	18,639
1910	22,769
1920	29,555
1930	35,716
1940	41,211
1950	45,953
1960	55,276
1970	55,204
1980	59,819

LINCOLN

1790	9,224
1800	12,660
1810	16,359
1820	18,147
1830	22,455
1840	25,160
1850	7,746
1860	8,195
1870	9,573
1880	11,061
1890	12,586
1900	15,498
1910	17,132
1920	17,862
1930	22,872
1940	24,187
1950	27,459
1960	28,814
1970	30,648
1980	42,372

McDOWELL

1850	6,246
1860	7,120
1870	7,592
1880	9,836
1890	10,936
1900	12,567
1910	13,538
1920	16,763
1930	20,336
1940	22,996
1950	25,720
1960	26,742
1970	30,648
1980	35,135

MACON

1830	5,333
1840	4,869
1850	6,389
1860	6,004
1870	6,615
1880	8,064
1890	10,102
1900	12,104
1910	12,191
1920	12,887
1930	13,672
1940	15,880
1950	16,174
1960	14,935
1970	15,788
1980	20,178

MADISON

1860	5,908
1870	8,192
1880	12,810

1890	17,805		
1900	29,644		
1910	20,132		
1920	20,083		
1930	20,306		
1940	22,522		
1950	20,522		
1960	17,217		
1970	16,063		
1980	16,827		

MARTIN

1790	6,080
1800	5,629
1810	5,987
1820	6,320
1830	8,539
1840	7,637
1850	8,307
1860	10,195
1870	9,647
1880	13,140
1890	15,221
1900	15,383
1910	17,797
1920	20,838
1930	23,400
1940	26,111
1950	27,938
1960	27,139
1970	24,730
1980	25,948

MECKLENBURG

1790	11,395
1800	10,439
1810	14,272
1820	16,895
1830	20,073
1840	18,273
1850	13,914
1860	17,374
1870	24,299
1880	34,175
1890	42,673
1900	55,268
1910	67,031
1920	80,695
1930	127,971
1940	151,826
1950	197,052
1960	272,111
1970	354,656
1980	404,270

MITCHELL

1870	4,705
1880	9,435
1890	12,807
1900	15,221
1910	17,245
1920	11,278
1930	13,962
1940	15,980
1950	15,143
1960	13,906
1970	13,447
1980	14,428

MONTGOMERY

1790	4,725
1800	7,677

1810	8,430
1820	8,693
1830	10,919
1840	10,780
1850	6,872
1860	7,649
1870	7,487
1880	9,374
1890	11,239
1900	14,197
1910	14,967
1920	14,607
1930	16,218
1940	16,280
1950	17,260
1960	18,408
1970	19,267
1980	22,469

MOORE

1790	3,770
1800	4,767
1810	6,367
1820	7,128
1830	7,745
1840	7,988
1850	9,342
1860	11,427
1870	12,040
1880	16,821
1890	20,479
1900	23,622
1910	17,010
1920	21,388
1930	28,215
1940	30,969
1950	33,129
1960	36,733
1970	39,048
1980	50,505

NASH

1790	7,393
1800	6,975
1810	7,268
1820	8,185
1830	8,490
1840	9,047
1850	10,657
1860	11,687
1870	11,077
1880	17,731
1890	20,707
1900	25,478
1910	33,727
1920	41,061
1930	52,782
1940	55,608
1950	59,919
1960	61,002
1970	59,122
1980	67,153

NEW HANOVER

1790	6,831
1800	7,060
1810	11,465
1820	10,866
1830	10,959
1840	13,312
1850	17,668
1860	21,715
1870	27,978
1880	21,376

1890	24,026
1900	25,785
1910	32,037
1920	40,620
1930	43,010
1940	47,935
1950	63,272
1960	71,742
1970	82,996
1980	103,471

NORTHAMPTON

1790	9,981
1800	12,353
1810	13,082
1820	13,242
1830	13,391
1840	13,369
1850	13,335
1860	13,372
1870	14,749
1880	20,032
1890	21,242
1900	21,150
1910	22,232
1920	23,184
1930	27,161
1940	28,299
1950	28,432
1960	26,811
1970	23,099
1980	22,584

ONSLOW

1790	5,387
1800	5,623
1810	6,669
1820	7,016
1830	7,814
1840	7,527
1850	8,283
1860	8,856
1870	7,569
1880	9,829
1890	10,303
1900	11,940
1910	14,125
1920	14,703
1930	15,289
1940	17,939
1950	42,047
1960	82,706
1970	103,126
1980	112,784

ORANGE

1790	12,216
1800	16,362
1810	20,135
1820	23,492
1830	23,908
1840	24,356
1850	17,055
1860	16,947
1870	17,507
1880	23,689
1890	14,948
1900	14,690
1910	15,064
1920	17,895
1930	21,171
1940	23,072
1950	34,435
1960	42,970

1970	57,567
1980	77,055

PAMLICO

1880	6,323
1890	7,146
1900	8,045
1910	9,966
1920	9,060
1930	9,299
1940	9,706
1950	9,993
1960	9,850
1970	9,467
1980	10,398

PASQUOTANK

1790	5,497
1800	5,379
1810	7,674
1820	8,008
1830	8,641
1840	8,514
1850	8,950
1860	8,940
1870	8,131
1880	10,369
1890	10,748
1900	13,660
1910	16,693
1920	17,670
1930	19,143
1940	20,568
1950	24,347
1960	25,630
1970	26,824
1980	28,462

PENDER

1880	12,468
1890	12,514
1900	13,381
1910	15,471
1920	14,788
1930	15,686
1940	17,710
1950	18,423
1960	18,508
1970	18,149
1980	22,215

PERQUIMANS

1790	5,440
1800	5,708
1810	6,052
1820	6,587
1830	7,419
1840	7,346
1850	7,332
1860	7,238
1870	7,945
1880	9,466
1890	9,293
1900	10,091
1910	11,054
1920	11,137
1930	10,668
1940	9,773
1950	9,602
1960	9,178
1970	8,351
1980	9,486

PERSON

1800	6,402
1810	6,642
1820	9,029
1830	10,027
1840	9,790
1850	10,781
1860	11,221
1870	11,170
1880	13,719
1890	15,151
1900	16,685
1910	17,356
1920	18,973
1930	22,039
1940	25,029
1950	24,361
1960	26,394
1970	25,914
1980	29,164

PITT

1790	8,275
1800	9,084
1810	9,169
1820	10,001
1830	12,093
1840	11,806
1850	13,397
1860	16,080
1870	17,376
1880	21,794
1890	25,519
1900	30,889
1910	36,340
1920	45,569
1930	54,466
1940	61,244
1950	63,789
1960	69,942
1970	73,900
1980	90,146

POLK

1860	4,043
1870	4,319
1880	5,062
1890	5,902
1900	7,004
1910	7,640
1920	8,832
1930	10,216
1940	11,874
1950	11,627
1960	11,395
1970	11,735
1980	12,984

RANDOLPH

1790	7,276
1800	9,234
1810	10,112
1820	11,331
1830	12,406
1840	12,875
1850	15,832
1860	16,793
1870	17,551
1880	20,836
1890	25,195
1900	28,232
1910	29,491
1920	30,856

1930	36,259
1940	44,554
1950	50,804
1960	61,497
1970	76,358
1980	91,728

RICHMOND

1790	5,065
1800	5,623
1810	6,695
1820	7,537
1830	9,396
1840	8,909
1850	9,818
1860	11,009
1870	12,882
1880	18,245
1890	23,948
1900	15,855
1910	19,673
1920	25,567
1930	34,016
1940	36,810
1950	39,597
1960	39,202
1970	39,889
1980	45,481

ROBESON

1790	5,326
1800	6,839
1810	7,528
1820	8,204
1830	9,433
1840	10,370
1850	12,826
1860	15,489
1870	16,262
1880	23,880
1890	31,483
1900	40,371
1910	51,945
1920	54,674
1930	66,512
1940	76,860
1950	87,769
1960	89,102
1970	84,842
1980	101,610

ROCKINGHAM

1790	6,187
1800	8,277
1810	10,316
1820	11,474
1830	12,935
1840	13,442
1850	14,495
1860	16,746
1870	15,708
1880	21,744
1890	25,363
1900	33,163
1910	36,442
1920	44,149
1930	51,083
1940	57,898
1950	64,816
1960	69,629
1970	72,402
1980	83,426

ROWAN

1790	15,828
1800	20,060
1810	21,543
1820	26,009
1830	20,786
1840	12,109
1850	13,870
1860	14,589
1870	16,810
1880	19,965
1890	24,123
1900	31,066
1910	37,521
1920	44,062
1930	56,665
1940	69,206
1950	75,410
1960	82,817
1970	90,035
1980	99,186

RUTHERFORD

1790	7,808
1800	10,753
1810	13,202
1820	15,351
1830	17,557
1840	19,202
1850	13,550
1860	11,573
1870	13,121
1880	15,198
1890	18,770
1900	25,101
1910	28,385
1920	31,426
1930	40,452
1940	45,577
1950	46,356
1960	45,091
1970	47,337
1980	53,787

SAMPSON

1790	6,065
1800	6,719
1810	6,620
1820	8,908
1830	11,634
1840	12,157
1850	14,585
1860	16,624
1870	16,436
1880	22,894
1890	25,096
1900	26,380
1910	29,982
1920	36,002
1930	40,082
1940	47,440
1950	49,780
1960	48,013
1970	44,954
1980	49,687

SCOTLAND

1900	12,553
1910	15,363
1920	15,600
1930	20,174
1940	23,232
1950	26,336

1960	25,183
1970	26,929
1980	32,273

STANLY

1850	6,922
1860	7,801
1870	8,315
1880	10,505
1890	12,136
1900	15,220
1910	19,909
1920	27,429
1930	30,216
1940	32,834
1950	37,130
1960	40,873
1970	42,822
1980	48,517

STOKES

1790	8,528
1800	11,026
1810	11,645
1820	14,033
1830	16,196
1840	16,265
1850	9,206
1860	10,402
1870	11,208
1880	15,353
1890	17,199
1900	19,866
1910	20,151
1920	20,575
1930	22,290
1940	22,656
1950	21,520
1960	22,314
1970	23,782
1980	33,086

SURRY

1790	7,191
1800	9,805
1810	10,366
1820	12,320
1830	14,504
1840	15,079
1850	18,443
1860	10,380
1870	11,252
1880	15,302
1890	19,282
1900	25,515
1910	29,705
1920	32,464
1930	39,749
1940	41,783
1950	45,593
1960	48,205
1970	51,415
1980	59,449

SWAIN

1880	3,784
1890	6,577
1900	8,401
1910	10,403
1920	13,224
1930	11,568
1940	12,177

1950	9,921
1960	8,387
1970	7,861
1980	10,283

TRANSYLVANIA

1870	3,536
1880	5,340
1890	5,881
1900	6,620
1910	7,191
1920	9,303
1930	9,589
1940	12,241
1950	15,194
1960	16,372
1970	19,713
1980	23,417

TYRRELL

1790	4,744
1800	3,395
1810	3,364
1820	4,319
1830	4,732
1840	4,657
1850	5,113
1860	4,944
1870	4,173
1880	4,545
1890	4,225
1900	4,980
1910	5,219
1920	4,849
1930	5,164
1940	5,556
1950	5,048
1960	4,520
1970	3,806
1980	3,975

UNION

1850	10,051
1860	11,202
1870	12,217
1880	18,056
1890	21,259
1900	27,156
1910	33,277
1920	36,029
1930	40,979
1940	39,097
1950	42,034
1960	44,670
1970	54,714
1980	70,380

VANCE

1890	17,581
1900	16,684
1910	19,425
1920	22,799
1930	27,294
1940	29,961
1950	32,101
1960	32,002
1970	32,691
1980	36,748

WAKE

1790	10,192

1800	13,437
1810	17,086
1820	20,102
1830	20,398
1840	21,118
1850	24,888
1860	28,627
1870	35,617
1880	47,939
1890	49,207
1900	54,626
1910	63,229
1920	75,155
1930	94,757
1940	109,544
1950	136,450
1960	169,082
1970	229,006
1980	301,327

WARREN

1790	9,297
1800	11,284
1810	11,004
1820	11,158
1830	11,887
1840	12,919
1850	13,912
1860	15,726
1870	17,768
1880	22,619
1890	19,360
1900	19,151
1910	20,266
1920	21,593
1930	23,364
1940	23,145
1950	23,539
1960	19,652
1970	15,810
1980	16,232

WASHINGTON

1800	2,422
1810	3,464
1820	3,986
1830	4,552
1840	4,525
1850	5,664
1860	6,357
1870	6,516
1880	8,928
1890	10,200
1900	10,608
1910	11,062
1920	11,429
1930	11,603
1940	12,323
1950	13,180
1960	13,488
1970	14,038
1980	14,801

WATAUGA

1850	3,400
1860	4,957
1870	5,287
1880	8,160
1890	10,611
1900	13,471
1910	13,556
1920	13,447
1930	15,165
1940	18,114

1950	18,342		1930	18,010
1960	17,529		1940	20,657
1970	23,404		1950	22,133
1980	31,666		1960	22,804
			1970	24,599
			1980	28,439

WAYNE

YANCEY

WAYNE			YANCEY	
1790	6,133			
1800	6,772			
1810	8,687		1840	5,962
1820	9,040		1850	8,205
1830	10,331		1860	8,655
1840	10,891		1870	5,909
1850	13,486		1880	7,694
1860	14,905		1890	9,490
1870	18,144		1900	11,464
1880	24,951		1910	12,072
1890	26,100		1920	15,093
1900	31,356		1930	14,486
1910	35,698		1940	17,202
1920	43,640		1950	16,306
1930	53,013		1960	14,008
1940	58,328		1970	12,629
1950	64,267		1980	14,934
1960	82,059			
1970	85,408			
1980	97,054			

WILKES

1790	8,143
1800	7,247
1810	9,054
1820	9,967
1830	11,968
1840	12,577
1850	12,099
1860	14,749
1870	15,539
1880	19,181
1890	22,675
1900	26,872
1910	30,282
1920	32,644
1930	36,162
1940	43,003
1950	45,243
1960	45,269
1970	49,524
1980	58,657

WILSON

1860	9,720
1870	12,258
1880	16,064
1890	18,644
1900	23,596
1910	28,269
1920	36,813
1930	44,914
1940	50,219
1950	54,506
1960	57,716
1970	57,486
1980	63,132

YADKIN

1860	10,714
1870	10,697
1880	12,420
1890	13,790
1900	14,083
1910	15,428
1920	16,391

NOTES

BEAUFORT

Name changed from Pamptecough in 1712.

CRAVEN

Name changed from Archdale in 1712.

HYDE

Name changed from Wickham in 1712.

ALBEMARLE

1890	248
1900	1,382
1910	2,116
1920	2,691
1930	3,493
1940	4,060
1950	11,798
1960	12,261
1970	11,126
1980	15,110

ASHEBORO

1850	176
1870	182
1880	299
1890	510
1900	992
1910	1,865
1920	2,559
1930	5,021
1940	6,981
1950	7,701
1960	9,449
1970	10,797
1980	15,252

ASHEVILLE

1870	1,400
1880	2,616
1890	10,235
1900	14,694
1910	18,762
1920	28,504
1930	50,193
1940	51,310
1950	53,000
1960	60,192
1970	57,929
1980	53,583

BOONE

1880	167
1890	144
1900	155
1910	179
1920	374
1930	1,295
1940	1,788
1950	2,973
1960	3,686
1970	8,754
1980	10,191

BURLINGTON

1880	81
1890	1,716
1900	3,692
1910	4,808
1920	5,952
1930	9,737
1940	12,198
1950	24,560
1960	33,199
1970	35,930
1980	37,266

CARY

1880	316
1890	423
1900	333
1910	383
1920	645
1930	909
1940	1,141
1950	1,446
1960	3,356
1970	7,640
1980	21,763

CHAPEL HILL

1880	831
1890	1,017
1900	1,099
1910	1,149
1920	1,483
1930	2,699
1940	3,654
1950	9,177
1960	12,573
1970	26,199
1980	32,421

CHARLOTTE

1850	1,065
1860	2,265
1870	4,473
1880	7,094
1890	11,557
1900	18,091
1910	34,014
1920	46,338
1930	82,675
1940	100,899
1950	134,042
1960	201,564
1970	241,420
1980	314,447

CONCORD

1870	878
1880	1,264
1890	4,339
1900	7,910
1910	8,715
1920	9,903
1930	11,820
1940	15,572
1950	16,486
1960	17,799
1970	18,464
1980	16,942

DURHAM

1880	2,041
1890	5,485
1900	6,679
1910	18,241
1920	21,719
1930	52,037
1940	60,195
1950	71,311
1960	78,302
1970	95,438
1980	100,831

EDEN

1970	15,871
1980	15,672

ELIZABETH CITY

1870	930
1880	2,315
1890	3,251
1900	6,348
1910	8,412
1920	8,925
1930	10,037
1940	11,564
1950	12,685
1960	14,062
1970	14,381
1980	14,004

FAYETTEVILLE

1820	3,532
1830	2,868
1840	4,285
1850	4,646
1860	4,790
1870	4,660
1880	3,485
1890	4,222
1900	4,670
1910	7,045
1920	8,877
1930	13,049
1940	17,428
1950	34,715
1960	47,106
1970	53,510
1980	59,507

GARNER

1910	284
1920	376
1930	476
1940	768
1950	1,180
1960	3,451
1970	4,923
1980	10,073

GASTONIA

1880	236
1890	1,033
1900	4,610
1910	5,759
1920	12,871
1930	17,093
1940	21,313
1950	23,069
1960	37,276
1970	47,322
1980	47,333

GOLDSBORO

1860	885
1870	1,132
1880	3,286
1890	4,017
1900	5,877
1910	6,107
1920	11,296
1930	14,985
1940	17,274
1950	21,454
1960	28,873
1970	26,810
1980	31,871

GREENSBORO

1870	497
1880	2,015
1890	3,317
1900	10,035
1910	15,895
1920	19,861
1930	53,569
1940	59,319
1950	74,389
1960	119,574
1970	144,076
1980	155,642

GREENVILLE

1850	1,893
1860	828
1870	601
1880	912
1890	1,937
1900	2,565
1910	4,101
1920	5,772
1930	9,194
1940	12,674
1950	16,724
1960	22,860
1970	29,063
1980	35,740

HAVELOCK

1960	2,433
1970	3,012
1980	17,718

HENDERSON

1860	186
1870	1,635
1880	1,421
1890	4,191
1900	3,746
1910	4,503
1920	5,222
1930	6,345
1940	7,647
1950	10,996
1960	12,740
1970	13,896
1980	13,522

HICKORY

1890	2,023
1900	2,535
1910	3,716
1920	5,076
1930	7,363
1940	13,487
1950	14,755
1960	19,328
1970	20,569
1980	20,757

HIGH POINT

1900	4,163
1910	9,525
1920	14,302
1930	36,745
1940	38,495
1950	39,973
1960	62,063

1970	63,229
1980	63,380

JACKSONVILLE

1870	60
1880	94
1890	170
1900	309
1910	505
1920	656
1930	783
1940	873
1950	3,960
1960	13,491
1970	16,289
1980	17,056

KINSTON

1850	455
1860	1,333
1870	1,103
1880	1,216
1890	1,726
1900	4,106
1910	6,995
1920	9,771
1930	11,362
1940	15,388
1950	18,336
1960	24,819
1970	23,020
1980	25,234

LAURINBURG

1900	1,334
1910	2,322
1920	2,643
1930	3,312
1940	5,685
1950	7,134
1960	8,242
1970	8,859
1980	11,480

LENOIR

1870	446
1880	442
1890	673
1900	1,296
1910	3,364
1920	3,718
1930	6,532
1940	7,598
1950	7,888
1960	10,257
1970	14,705
1980	13,748

LEXINGTON

1880	475
1890	626
1900	1,440
1910	4,163
1920	5,254
1930	9,652
1940	10,550
1950	13,571
1960	16,093
1970	17,205
1980	15,711

LUMBERTON

1870	615
1880	533
1890	584
1900	849
1910	2,230
1920	2,691
1930	4,140
1940	5,803
1950	9,186
1960	15,305
1970	16,961
1980	18,241

MONROE

1850	204
1860	239
1870	1,344
1880	1,564
1890	1,866
1900	2,427
1910	4,082
1920	4,084
1930	6,100
1940	6,475
1950	10,140
1960	10,882
1970	11,282
1980	12,639

MORGANTON

1850	558
1870	554
1880	861
1890	1,557
1900	1,938
1910	2,712
1920	2,867
1930	6,001
1940	7,670
1950	8,311
1960	9,186
1970	13,625
1980	13,763

NEW BERN

1800	2,467
1810	(NA)
1820	3,663
1830	3,796
1840	3,690
1850	4,681
1860	5,432
1870	5,849
1880	6,443
1890	7,843
1900	9,090
1910	9,961
1920	12,198
1930	11,981
1940	11,815
1950	15,812
1960	15,717
1970	14,660
1980	14,557

RALEIGH

1800	669
1810	(NA)
1820	2,674
1830	1,700
1840	2,224
1850	4,518
1870	7,790
1880	9,265
1890	12,678
1900	13,643
1910	19,218
1920	24,418
1930	37,379
1940	47,897
1950	65,679
1960	93,931
1970	122,830
1980	150,225

REIDSVILLE

1880	1,316
1890	2,969
1900	3,262
1910	4,828
1920	5,333
1930	6,851
1940	10,387
1950	11,708
1960	14,267
1970	13,636
1980	12,492

ROANOKE RAPIDS

1900	1,009
1910	1,670
1920	3,369
1930	3,404
1940	8,545
1950	8,156
1960	13,320
1970	13,508
1980	14,702

ROCKY MOUNT

1870	357
1880	552
1890	816
1900	2,937
1910	8,051
1920	12,742
1930	21,412
1940	25,568
1950	27,694
1960	32,147
1970	34,284
1980	41,283

SALISBURY

1850	1,086
1860	2,420
1880	2,723
1890	4,418
1900	6,277
1910	7,153
1920	13,884
1930	16,951
1940	19,037
1950	20,102
1960	21,297
1970	22,515
1980	22,677

SANFORD

1880	236
1890	367
1900	1,044
1910	2,282
1920	2,977
1930	4,253
1940	4,960
1950	10,013
1960	12,253
1970	11,716
1980	14,773

SHELBY

1880	990
1890	1,394
1900	1,874
1910	3,127
1920	3,609
1930	10,789
1940	14,037
1950	15,508
1960	17,698
1970	16,328
1980	15,310

STATESVILLE

1850	215
1860	320
1870	683
1880	1,062
1890	2,318
1900	3,141
1910	4,599
1920	7,895
1930	10,490
1940	11,440
1950	16,901
1960	19,844
1970	20,007
1980	18,622

THOMASVILLE

1860	308
1870	214
1880	450
1890	590
1900	751
1910	3,877
1920	5,676
1930	10,090
1940	11,041
1950	11,154
1960	15,190
1970	15,230
1980	14,144

WILMINGTON

1800	1,689
1810	(NA)
1820	2,663
1850	7,264
1860	9,552
1870	13,446
1880	17,350
1890	20,056
1900	20,976
1910	25,748
1920	33,372
1930	32,270
1940	33,407
1950	45,043
1960	44,013
1970	46,169
1980	44,000

WILSON

1860	960
1870	1,036
1880	1,475
1890	2,126
1900	3,525
1910	6,717
1920	10,612
1930	12,613
1940	19,234
1950	23,010
1960	28,753
1970	29,347
1980	34,424

WINSTON-SALEM

1870	443
1880	4,194
1890	10,729
1900	13,650
1910	22,700
1920	48,395
1930	75,274
1940	79,815
1950	87,811
1960	111,135
1970	133,683
1980	131,885

CORRECTION NOTE

The official 1980 census counts of total population shown in
this report supersede counts issued previously. Corrections
to the figures were made after the counts were provided to
the State for redistricting purposes and released in Advance
Report PHC80-V for this State.

Shown below are corrections to the 1980 census counts of the
total population made after the tabulations for this report
were completed. Any additional corrections made after this
report is printed are available by writing to Data User
Services Division, Customer Services (Corrections), Bureau of
the Census, Washington, D.C. 20233.

The 1980 figures shown in this publication are subject to
change pending the outcome of the various lawsuits dealing
with the census counts.

	1980 population	
	As shown in the tables	Corrected
The State....................	5 881 766	5 881 813
Brunswick County:		
Northwest township...........	4 657	6 143
Shallotte township...........	6 582	6 540
Town Creek township..........	8 357	6 871
Waccamaw township............	1 982	2 024
Durham County:		
Durham township..............	106 832	106 836
Durham city..................	100 831	100 538
Oak Grove township...........	12 772	12 760
Triangle township............	16 616	16 624
Forsyth County:		
Abbotts Creek township.......	11 720	11 699
Broadbay township............	6 126	6 147
Nash County:		
Nashville township:		
Nashville town............	2 678	3 033
Onslow County:		
Jacksonville township:		
Jacksonville city.........	17 056	18 237
Pender County.....................	22 215	22 262
Burgaw township:		
Burgaw town...............	1 586	1 738
Topsoil township.............	4 563	4 610
Surf City town...............	391	421
Randolph County:		
Trinity township:		
Archdale city (pt.)..........	5 606	5 187
High Point city (pt.)........	29	457
Trinity (CDP)(pt.)...........	6 880	6 871
Archdale city (total)...........	5 745	5 326
High Point city (total).........	63 380	63 808
Trinity (CDP)(total)............	6 887	6 878

County Subdivisions

County Subdivisions	1980	1970
The State	5 881 766	'5 084 411
Alamance County[1]	99 319	'96 502
Township 1, Patterson	2 847	2 555
Township 2, Coble[1]	2 909	2 893
Alamance village[1]	320	...
Township 3, Boone Station[1]	13 606	13 418
Burlington city (pt.)[1]	3 908	2 531
Elon College town[1]	2 873	2 150
Gibsonville town (pt.)[1]	889	842
Glen Raven (CDP) (pt.)	1 519	2 468
Township 4, Morton	4 300	3 151
Township 5, Faucette	2 758	2 908
Township 6, Graham	17 651	18 358
Burlington city (pt.)	6 609	6 734
Graham city (pt.)[1]	8 575	8 160
Morgantown (CDP) (pt.)	197	...
Township 7, Albright	2 061	1 522
Township 8, Newlin	2 786	2 568
Township 9, Thompson	3 053	2 878
Township 10, Melville	7 891	'6 645
Mebane town (pt.)[1]	2 403	'2 387
Township 11, Pleasant Grove	2 999	2 677
Township 12, Burlington	30 627	32 647
Burlington city (pt.)[1]	26 416	26 665
Glen Raven (CDP) (pt.)	1 236	380
Morgantown (CDP) (pt.)	1 791	3 547
Township 13, Haw River	5 831	4 282
Burlington city (pt.)[1]	333	...
Graham city (pt.)[1]	99	12
Haw River town[1]	1 858	...
Alexander County[2]	24 999	19 466
Ellendale township	2 743	2 173
Gwaltneys township	1 698	1 382
Little River township	540	537
Millers township	982	809
Sharpes township	3 627	3 092
Stony Point (CDP)	1 150	1 001
Sugar Loaf township	1 001	796
Taylorsville township	8 199	7 063
Taylorsville town[2]	1 103	1 231
Wittenberg township	6 209	3 614
Alleghany County[3]	9 587	8 134
Cherry Lane township	1 212	1 004
Cranberry township	407	441
Gap Civil township	3 640	2 862
Sparta town[3]	1 687	1 304
Glade Creek township	2 321	1 940
Piney Creek township	652	642
Prathers Creek township	762	707
Whitehead township	593	538
Anson County[4]	25 649	23 488
Ansonville township	1 900	2 019
Ansonville town[4]	794	694
Burnsville township	1 281	1 399
Gulledge township	2 184	2 140
Lanesboro township	3 129	3 142
Peachland town	506	556
Polkton town	762	845
Lilesville township	3 864	3 826
Lilesville town	588	641
Morven township	2 065	1 929
McFarlan town	133	140
Morven town	765	562
Wadesboro township	10 833	8 596
Wadesboro town[4]	4 206	3 977
White Store township	393	437
Ashe County[5]	22 325	19 571
Chestnut Hill township	442	522
Clifton township[5]	1 784	1 742
Lansing town (pt.)	12	77
Creston township	748	732
Elk township[5]	448	476
Grassy Creek township	402	468
Helton township	765	713
Horse Creek township	737	718
Lansing town (pt.)	—	—
Hurricane township	652	554
Jefferson township	3 625	2 829
Jefferson town[5]	1 086	943
Laurel township	522	491
North Fork township	881	808
Obids township	1 102	870
Oldfields township	1 412	1 090
Peak Creek township	1 118	985
Pine Swamp township	1 291	1 098
Piney Creek township	1 020	925
Lansing town (pt.)	182	206
Pond Mountain township	336	315
Walnut Hill township	1 268	1 036
West Jefferson township	3 772	3 199
West Jefferson town	822	889
Avery County[6]	14 409	12 655
Altamont township	1 420	1 261
Crossnore town	297	264
Banner Elk township	1 978	1 788

County Subdivisions	1980	1970
Avery County—Con.		
Banner Elk township—Con.		
Banner Elk town[6]	1 087	754
Beech Mountain township	750	667
Cranberry township	2 369	2 179
Elk Park town	535	503
Linville township	4 358	3 694
Linville[6]	244	(NA)
Newland town[6]	722	524
Seven Devils town (pt.)[6]	7	...
Roaring Creek township	942	935
Toe River township	2 220	1 822
Wilsons Creek township	372	309
Beaufort County[7]	40 355	35 980
Bath township	3 472	3 237
Bath town	207	231
Chocowinity township	6 241	4 661
Chocowinity town	644	566
Long Acre township[7]	7 636	6 976
Washington Park town	514	517
Pantego township	6 204	5 126
Belhaven town	2 430	2 259
Pantego town	185	218
Richland township[7]	3 898	3 626
Aurora town	698	620
Washington township	12 904	12 354
Washington city[7]	8 418	8 961
Bertie County[8]	21 024	20 528
Colerain township	3 981	4 069
Colerain town	284	373
Powellsville town (pt.)	312	223
Indian Woods township	762	874
Merry Hill township	983	630
Mitchells township	2 579	2 373
Aulander town[8]	1 214	947
Powellsville town (pt.)	8	24
Roxobel township	1 638	1 871
Kelford town	254	295
Roxobel town	278	347
Snake Bite township	1 194	1 036
Whites township	1 677	2 006
Windsor township	6 589	6 141
Askewville town	227	247
Windsor town[8]	2 126	2 199
Woodville township	1 621	1 528
Lewiston town	459	327
Woodville town	212	253
Bladen County[9]	30 491	26 477
Abbotts township	1 031	1 066
Bethel township	3 650	2 337
Dublin town	477	283
Bladenboro township	4 947	5 239
Bladenboro town[9]	1 428	783
Brown Marsh township	2 028	1 907
Clarkton town	664	662
Carvers Creek township[9]	1 999	1 780
East Arcadia town[9]	461	...
Central township	978	697
Colly township	2 320	991
White Lake town	968	232
Cypress Creek township	733	665
Elizabethtown township	5 978	5 613
Elizabethtown town[9]	3 551	1 418
Frenchs Creek township	943	925
Hollow township	1 848	1 454
Tar Heel town	118	87
Lake Creek township	675	651
Turnbull township	483	416
White Oak township	1 237	1 083
Whites Creek township	1 641	1 653
Brunswick County[10]	35 777	24 223
Lockwoods Folly township[10]	7 361	4 748
Holden Beach town[10]	232	'136
Shallotte town (pt.)[10]	475	413
Northwest township	4 657	3 356
Belville town (pt.)[10]	439	...
Navassa town[10]	...	...
Shallotte township	6 582	4 877
Calabash town[10]	128	...
Ocean Isle Beach town	143	78
Shady Forest town[o]	43	...
Shallotte town (pt.)[10]	205	184
Sunset Beach town[10]	304	108
Smithville township	6 838	4 346
Caswell Beach town[10]	110	...
Long Beach town	1 844	493
Southport city[10]	2 824	2 220
Yaupon Beach town[10]	569	334
Town Creek township[10]	8 357	5 215
Belville town (pt.)[10]	102	...
Boiling Spring Lakes city	998	245
Bolivia town	252	185
Waccamaw township	1 982	1 681

County Subdivisions

County Subdivisions	1980	1970
Buncombe County[11]	160 934	145 056
Asheville township	70 889	74 174
Asheville city (pt.)[11]	52 715	'57 700
Biltmore Forest town (pt.)[11]	876	743
Enka (CDP) (pt.)	1 236	...
Woodfin town (pt.)[11]	3 241	...
Avery Creek township	4 237	2 717
Black Mountain township	9 812	7 310
Black Mountain town[11]	4 083	3 204
Montreat town[11]	741	'581
Swannanoa (CDP) (pt.)	330	...
Broad River township	851	789
Fairview township	4 813	3 348
Flat Creek township	2 654	1 921
French Broad township	2 419	1 727
Woodfin town (pt.)[11]	19	...
Ivy township	2 572	2 705
Leicester township	9 543	7 581
Asheville city (pt.)	–	229
Limestone township	12 475	8 947
Asheville city (pt.)[11]	17	...
Biltmore Forest town (pt.)[11]	623	555
Lower Hominy township	9 011	8 302
Enka (CDP) (pt.)	4 331	...
Reems Creek township	8 610	6 182
Weaverville town[11]	1 495	1 280
Sandy Mush township	686	665
Swannanoa township	12 525	10 547
Asheville city (pt.)[11]	851	...
Swannanoa (CDP) (pt.)	5 256	1 966
Upper Hominy township	9 837	8 141
Burke County[12]	72 504	60 364
Drexel township	5 143	4 563
Drexel town[12]	1 392	1 431
Valdese town (pt.)[12]	–	–
Icard township	13 791	11 040
Hickory city (pt.)[12]	73	110
Hildebran town[12]	628	481
Icard (CDP)	2 484	...
Long View town (pt.)[12]	310	269
Penelope (CDP)	1 348	...
Rhodhiss town (pt.)	300	312
Jonas Ridge township	765	488
Linville township	1 422	1 078
Lovelady township	8 083	6 630
Rutherford College town[12]	1 108	...
Valdese town (pt.)[12]	3 364	3 182
Lower Creek township	1 957	1 389
Lower Fork township	1 896	1 722
Morganton township	24 072	22 389
Morganton city (pt.)[12]	13 507	13 625
Salem (CDP)	2 823	...
Quaker Meadow township	5 237	3 500
Morganton city (pt.)[12]	8	...
Silver Creek township	8 008	5 555
Glen Alpine town	645	797
Morganton city (pt.)[12]	248	...
Smoky Creek township	471	442
Upper Creek township	811	753
Upper Fork township	848	815
Cabarrus County[13]	85 895	74 629
Township 1, Harrisburg	5 987	3 003
Harrisburg town[13]	1 433	...
West Concord (CDP) (pt.)	–	...
Township 2, Poplar Tent	8 076	4 344
Poplar Tent (CDP) (pt.)	2 601	...
West Concord (CDP) (pt.)	771	761
Township 3, Odell	2 374	1 619
Township 4, Kannapolis	29 628	28 260
Kannapolis (CDP) (pt.)	24 962	23 952
North Concord (CDP)	2 095	2 350
Poplar Tent (CDP) (pt.)	163	...
Township 5, New Gilead[13]	2 852	1 950
Township 6, Rimertown	1 575	894
Township 7, Gold Hill	746	780
Township 8, Mount Pleasant	4 022	3 467
Mount Pleasant town[13]	1 210	1 174
Township 9, Georgeville	1 384	814
Township 10, Midland	3 503	2 782
Township 11, Central Cabarrus[13]	8 806	8 252
West Concord (CDP) (pt.)	5 088	4 586
Township 12, Concord	16 942	18 464
Concord city[13]	16 942	18 464
Caldwell County[14]	67 746	56 699
Globe township	334	292
Blowing Rock town (pt.)[14]	41	7
Hudson township	10 026	8 041
Hudson town[14]	2 888	2 820
Lenoir city (pt.)[14]	322	190
Johns River township	1 335	1 047
Kings Creek township	1 408	1 055
Lenoir township	18 750	16 979
Lenoir city (pt.)[14]	7 041	7 243
Little River township	2 782	2 337
Lovelady township	10 734	8 536
Granite Falls town[14]	2 580	2 388
Rhodhiss town (pt.)	427	472

County Subdivisions	1980	1970
Caldwell County—Con.		
Lower Creek township	12 061	10 619
Lenoir city (pt.)[14]	6 385	7 272
Mulberry township	1 111	730
North Catawba township	5 506	3 760
Patterson township[14]	2 510	2 202
Blowing Rock town (pt.)[14]	22	17
Wilson Creek township[14]	67	60
Yadkin Valley township	1 122	1 041
Camden County[15]	5 829	5 453
Court House township	2 046	1 848
Elizabeth City city (pt.)[15]	–	...
Shiloh township	1 717	1 676
South Mills township	2 066	1 929
Carteret County[16]	41 092	31 603
Atlantic township	810	814
Beaufort township	6 992	6 147
Beaufort town[16]	3 826	3 368
Cedar Island township	333	290
Davis township	492	456
Harkers Island township	1 910	1 639
Harkers Island (CDP)	1 901	1 633
Harlowe township	956	762
Marshallberg township	580	525
Merrimon township	426	330
Morehead township	15 803	11 929
Atlantic Beach town[16]	941	300
Emerald Isle town (pt.)[16]	85	8
Indian Beach town[16]	54	...
Morehead City town[16]	4 359	5 233
Pine Knoll Shores town[16]	646	...
Newport township	5 469	3 926
Newport town[16]	1 883	1 735
Portsmouth township	–	2
Sea Level township	540	347
Smyrna township	637	517
Stacy township	322	257
Straits township	1 520	1 166
White Oak township	4 302	2 496
Cape Carteret town[16]	944	616
Emerald Isle town (pt.)[16]	780	114
Caswell County	20 705	19 055
Anderson township	1 799	1 755
Dan River township	2 514	2 341
Hightowers township	1 519	1 450
Leasburg township	1 302	1 382
Locust Hill township	2 071	1 499
Milton township	2 733	2 249
Milton town	235	235
Pelham township	3 332	3 098
Stony Creek township	2 542	2 074
Yanceyville township	2 893	3 207
Yanceyville (CDP)	1 511	1 274
Catawba County[17]	105 208	90 873
Bandy's township	2 804	2 884
Caldwell township	4 771	3 625
Maiden town (pt.)[17]	430	219
Catawba township	5 429	4 143
Catawba town[17]	509	565
Clines township	13 144	8 415
Claremont city[17]	880	788
Conover city (pt.)[17]	787	283
St. Stephens (CDP) (pt.)	2 447	...
Hickory township	48 059	44 995
Brookford town[17]	467	590
Hickory city (pt.)[17]	20 684	20 459
Hickory North (CDP)	4 322	2 325
Long View town (pt.)[17]	3 277	3 091
St. Stephens (CDP) (pt.)	8 350	...
Jacobs Fork township	2 785	2 231
Mountain Creek township	3 508	2 430
Newton township	24 708	22 150
Conover city (pt.)[17]	3 458	3 072
Maiden town (pt.)[17]	2 144	2 197
Newton city[17]	7 624	7 857
Chatham County[18]	33 415	29 554
Albright township	1 921	1 664
Baldwin township	3 019	1 746
Bear Creek township	3 078	2 686
Cape Fear township	1 047	935
Center township	4 286	4 009
Pittsboro town[18]	1 332	1 447
Gulf township	3 235	2 926
Goldston town	353	364
Hadley township	945	775
Haw River township	1 034	946
Haywood town[18]	190	...
Hickory Mountain township	1 344	1 331
Matthews township	8 766	8 838
Siler City town	4 446	4 689
New Hope township	1 221	1 095
Oakland township	800	614
William township	2 719	1 989

County Subdivisions	1980	1970
Cherokee County[19]	18 933	16 330
Beaverdam township	637	555
Hot House township	864	767
Murphy township	7 835	6 723
Murphy town[19]	2 070	2 082
Notla township[19]	2 012	1 522
Shoal Creek township	1 591	1 371
Valley Town township	5 994	5 392
Andrews town	1 621	1 384
Chowan County[20]	12 558	10 764
Township 1, Edenton	7 790	6 814
Edenton town[20]	5 357	'4 956
Township 2, Middle	2 557	1 840
Township 3, Upper	1 294	1 278
Township 4, Yeopim	917	832
Clay County	6 619	5 180
Brasstown township	1 196	851
Hayesville township	2 522	2 049
Hayesville township	376	428
Hiwassee township	959	599
Shooting Creek township	957	868
Sweetwater township	550	429
Tusquittee township	435	384
Cleveland County[21]	83 435	72 556
Township 1, River	678	617
Township 2, Boiling Springs	5 773	5 193
Boiling Springs town[21]	2 381	2 284
Township 3, Rippys	7 227	4 172
Earl town[21]	206	...
Patterson Springs town[21]	731	...
Township 4, Kings Mountain	16 368	14 897
Grover town[21]	597	555
Kings Mountain city (pt.)[21]	8 430	8 323
Township 5, Warlick	5 494	3 547
Waco town	322	245
Township 6, Shelby	31 324	29 384
Shelby city[21]	15 310	16 328
Township 7, Sandy Run	5 208	3 995
Lattimore town	237	257
Mooresboro city[21]	405	...
Township 8, Polkville	2 677	2 731
Polkville city[21]	528	...
Township 9, Double Shoals	5 315	4 747
Belwood town (pt.)[21]	300	...
Fallston town[21]	614	'301
Lawndale town[21]	469	544
Township 10, Knob Creek	1 826	1 836
Belwood town (pt.)[21]	313	...
Township 11, Casar	1 545	1 437
Casar town[21]	346	'339
Columbus County[22]	51 037	46 937
Bogue township	3 135	2 896
Bolton township	1 876	1 506
Bolton town	563	534
Bug Hill township	2 129	2 111
Cerro Gordo township	2 009	1 946
Cerro Gordo town[22]	295	'322
Chadbourn township	6 202	5 460
Chadbourn town	1 975	2 213
Fair Bluff township	2 146	2 176
Fair Bluff town	1 095	1 039
Lees township	2 547	2 336
Ransom township[22]	4 157	3 611
South Williams township	5 241	4 895
Tabor City town[22]	2 710	2 400
Tatums township	3 092	2 932
Waccamaw township	1 971	1 456
Lake Waccamaw town[22]	1 133	924
Welch Creek township	1 495	1 356
Western Prong township	1 005	1 003
Whiteville township	10 387	9 799
Brunswick town	223	206
Whiteville city[22]	5 565	4 195
Williams township	3 645	3 454
Craven County[23]	71 043	62 554
Township 1	5 359	4 946
Vanceboro town	833	758
Township 2	4 414	3 257
Bridgeton town	461	520
Township 3	3 803	3 837
Cove City town	500	485
Dover town	600	585
Township 5	2 551	2 047
Township 6	21 963	20 798
Havelock city[23]	17 718	'3 012
Township 7	6 149	4 757
James City (CDP) (pt.)	2 953	2 577
Township 8	24 645	21 125
James City (CDP) (pt.)	-	...
New Bern city[23]	14 557	14 660
Trent Woods town[23]	1 177	719
Township 9	2 159	1 787
Cumberland County[24]	247 160	212 042
Beaver Dam township	1 307	1 231
Black River township	2 270	2 104
Falcon town (pt.)	339	357
Godwin town	233	129
Carvers Creek township[24]	19 723	15 400
Linden town	365	205
Cedar Creek township	8 910	7 645
Stedman town[24]	723	505
Vander (CDP) (pt.)	920	...
Cross Creek township	59 507	53 510
Fayetteville city[24]	59 507	53 510
Eastover township	7 515	6 715
Eastover (CDP)	1 075	...
Vander (CDP) (pt.)	751	...
Wade town	474	315
Grays Creek township	2 948	2 174
Manchester township	37 520	48 474
Fort Bragg (CDP) (pt.)	23 325	33 823
Spring Lake town[24]	6 273	3 968
Pearces Mill township[24]	13 547	12 929
Rockfish township	26 042	13 495
Hope Mills town[24]	5 412	'1 866
Seventy-First township[24]	67 871	48 365
Bonnie Doone (CDP)	5 950	...
Fort Bragg (CDP) (pt.)	14 509	13 172
Currituck County	11 089	6 976
Crawford township	3 974	2 487
Fruitville township	906	508
Moyock township	3 095	1 494
Poplar Branch township	3 114	2 487
Dare County[25]	13 377	6 995
Atlantic township	3 737	1 141
Kill Devil Hills town	1 796	357
Southern Shores town[25]	395	...
Croatan township	714	540
East Lake township	112	88
Hatteras township	2 783	1 333
Kennekeet township	1 060	565
Nags Head township	4 971	3 328
Manteo town[25]	902	547
Nags Head town	1 020	414
Wanchese (CDP)	1 105	...
Davidson County[26]	113 162	95 627
Abbotts Creek township	5 948	3 710
High Point city (pt.)[26]	537	...
Alleghany township	412	288
Arcadia township	4 753	2 402
Welcome (CDP) (pt.)	1	...
Boone township	2 745	1 901
Conrad Hill township	6 894	5 512
Cotton Grove township	5 618	3 878
Lexington city (pt.)[26]	16	...
Emmons township	4 745	4 471
Denton town[26]	949	1 017
Hampton township	351	255
Healing Spring township	1 303	1 000
Jackson Hill township	618	581
Lexington township	28 860	28 422
Lexington city (pt.)	15 695	17 205
Welcome (CDP) (pt.)	2 957	...
Midway township	8 392	5 984
Welcome (CDP) (pt.)	285	...
Reedy Creek township	3 043	2 163
Welcome (CDP) (pt.)	-	...
Silver Hill township	3 451	1 913
Thomasville township	30 139	28 929
Thomasville city[26]	14 144	15 230
Tyro township	5 418	3 851
Yadkin College township	472	367
Davie County[27]	24 599	18 855
Calahaln township	1 643	1 210
Clarksville township	2 127	1 634
Farmington township	6 236	3 319
Fulton township	1 713	1 307
Jerusalem township	4 275	4 220
Cooleemee (CDP)	1 448	1 115
Mocksville township	6 825	5 702
Mocksville town[27]	2 637	2 529
Shady Grove township	1 780	1 463
Duplin County[28]	40 952	38 015
Albertson township	1 351	1 292
Cypress Creek township	2 901	2 678
Faison township	3 602	3 382
Calypso town	689	462
Faison town	636	598
Mount Olive town (pt.)	7	42
Glisson township	1 108	1 098
Island Creek township	7 781	7 181
Greenevers town[28]	477	'424
Teachey town	373	219
Wallace town (pt.)[28]	2 879	2 905
Kenansville township	3 779	2 981
Kenansville town[28]	931	762
Limestone township	5 394	4 696
Beulaville town	1 060	1 156

County Subdivisions	1980	1970
Duplin County—Con.		
Magnolia township	1 744	1 632
Magnolia town[28]	592	614
Rockfish township	1 290	1 472
Harrells town (pt.)	33	6
Rose Hill township	2 846	3 203
Rose Hill town[28]	1 508	1 448
Smith township	1 749	1 678
Warsaw township	5 783	4 939
Warsaw town[28]	2 910	2 701
Wolfscrape township	1 624	1 783
Durham County[29]	152 785	132 681
Carr township	1 946	1 300
Durham township	106 832	100 630
Durham city	100 831	95 438
Lebanon township	11 903	4 795
Mangum township	2 716	2 822
Oak Grove township	12 772	10 618
Gorman (CDP)	2 662	...
Triangle township	16 616	12 516
Chapel Hill town (pt.)[29]	383	4
Parkwood (CDP)	3 420	2 267
Edgecombe County[30]	55 988	52 341
Township 1, Tarboro	15 010	13 609
Princeville town[30]	1 508	654
Tarboro town[30]	8 634	9 425
Township 2, Lower Conetoe	1 729	1 623
Conetoe town	215	160
Township 3, Upper Conetoe	953	1 463
Speed town	95	142
Township 4, Deep Creek	986	980
Township 5, Lower Fishing Creek	1 443	1 438
Leggett town[30]	99	'120
Township 6, Upper Fishing Creek	1 781	2 078
Whitakers town (pt.)	492	479
Township 7, Swift Creek	3 147	2 672
Battleboro town (pt.)	323	'277
Township 8, Sparta	1 425	1 594
Township 9, Otter Creek	1 831	1 949
Macclesfield town	504	536
Township 10, Lower Town Creek	3 253	2 839
Pinetops town	1 465	1 379
Township 11, Walnut Creek	1 244	1 260
Township 12, Rocky Mount	20 734	18 664
Rocky Mount city (pt.)[30]	17 078	15 252
Township 13, Cokey	1 267	1 167
Township 14, Upper Town Creek	1 185	1 005
Sharpsburg town (pt.)[30]	11	46
Forsyth County[31]	243 683	'215 118
Abbotts Creek township	11 720	8 170
Kernersville town (pt.)[31]	—	...
Belews Creek township	3 628	2 037
Bethania township	11 968	9 586
Rural Hall town[31]	1 336	...
Stanleyville (CDP) (pt.)	4 849	2 362
Broadbay township[31]	6 126	6 595
Clemmonsville township	7 142	3 973
Clemmons (CDP) (pt.)	5 916	...
Kernersville township	15 459	9 347
Kernersville town (pt.)[31]	6 802	4 815
Lewisville township	8 354	4 918
Clemmons (CDP) (pt.)	1 485	...
Lewisville (CDP) (pt.)	2 696	...
Middle Fork township[31]	9 011	7 057
Stanleyville (CDP) (pt.)	165	...
Old Richmond township	4 231	3 471
Old Town township[31]	7 463	6 203
Stanleyville (CDP) (pt.)	25	...
Salem Chapel township	5 740	4 954
South Fork township[31]	13 296	10 202
Vienna township	7 660	4 922
Lewisville (CDP) (pt.)	1 851	...
Winston township	131 885	'133 683
Winston-Salem city[31]	131 885	'133 683
Franklin County[32]	30 055	26 820
Township 1, Dunn	4 016	3 286
Bunn town[32]	505	284
Township 2, Harris	2 096	2 110
Township 3, Youngsville	2 318	1 774
Youngsville town	486	555
Township 4, Franklinton	6 260	5 431
Franklinton town	1 394	1 459
Township 5, Hayesville	1 557	1 504
Township 6, Sandy Creek	2 060	1 611
Township 7, Gold Mine	1 321	1 341
Centerville town	135	123
Township 8, Cedar Rock	2 165	2 184
Township 9, Cypress Creek	809	738
Township 10, Louisburg	7 453	6 841
Louisburg town[32]	3 238	2 941
Gaston County[33]	162 568	148 415
Cherryville township	12 100	11 271
Cherryville city[33]	4 844	5 258
Dellview town	7	11
Crowder Mountain township	13 403	9 759
Bessemer City city[33]	4 787	'4 991

County Subdivisions	1980	1970
Gaston County—Con.		
Crowder Mountain township—Con.		
Kings Mountain city (pt.)[33]	650	142
Dallas township	16 123	14 628
Dallas town	3 340	4 059
High Shoals city (pt.)[33]	586	...
Stanley town (pt.)	107	103
Gastonia township	70 355	64 284
Gastonia city (pt.)[33]	44 760	'45 555
Jenkins Heights (CDP)	1 156	1 316
Lowell town (pt.)[33]	167	258
Ranlo town[33]	1 774	2 092
South Gastonia (CDP)	4 767	3 718
Spencer Mountain town	169	300
Springdale (CDP)	2 443	2 370
River Bend township	17 193	14 458
Mount Holly city	4 530	5 107
North Belmont (CDP) (pt.)	860	548
Stanley town (pt.)[33]	2 234	2 233
South Point township	33 394	34 015
Belmont city[33]	4 607	'5 054
Cramerton town	1 869	2 142
Gastonia city (pt.)[33]	2 573	1 767
Lowell town (pt.)[33]	2 750	3 049
McAdenville town[33]	947	950
North Belmont (CDP) (pt.)	9 902	'10 124
South Belmont (CDP)	2 068	'2 125
Gates County[34]	8 875	8 524
Gatesville township	1 807	1 598
Gatesville town[34]	363	338
Hall township	1 098	949
Haslett township	839	767
Holly Grove township	1 336	1 367
Hunters Mill township	1 339	1 339
Mintonsville township	984	1 045
Reynoldson township	1 472	1 459
Graham County[35]	7 217	6 562
Cheoah township	5 574	5 047
Robbinsville town[35]	1 370	777
Stecoah township	907	778
Yellow Creek township	736	737
Granville County[36]	34 043	32 762
Brassfield township	2 671	2 243
Dutchville township	8 529	8 724
Butner (CDP)	4 240	3 538
Creedmoor city[36]	1 641	1 405
Fishing Creek township	6 813	2 882
Oxford city (pt.)[36]	3 161	25
Oak Hill township	1 759	1 884
Virgilina town[36]	48	...
Oxford township	6 830	9 113
Oxford city (pt.)[36]	4 442	7 153
Salem township	1 062	1 482
Sassafras Fork township	2 073	2 125
Stovall town[36]	417	405
Tally Ho township	2 504	2 252
Stem town	222	242
Walnut Grove township	1 802	2 057
Greene County[37]	16 117	14 967
Bull Head township	973	1 041
Carrs township	995	1 198
Hookerton township	3 297	2 722
Hookerton town	460	441
Jason township	1 148	955
Olds township	1 825	1 936
Ormonds township	2 404	2 069
Shine township	1 126	1 033
Snow Hill township	2 527	2 295
Snow Hill town[37]	1 374	1 359
Speights Bridge township	1 822	1 718
Walstonburg town	181	176
Guilford County[38]	317 154	'288 645
Bruce township	4 876	4 010
Summerfield (CDP) (pt.)	1 522	...
Center Grove township[38]	8 278	4 411
Summerfield (CDP) (pt.)	158	...
Clay township	4 765	2 978
Deep River township	4 144	3 701
Fentress township[38]	9 562	6 543
Pleasant Garden (CDP)	1 991	...
Friendship township[38]	11 647	7 881
Gilmer township	53 560	52 960
Greensboro city (pt.)[38]	53 560	52 960
Greene township	2 139	1 732
High Point township	66 422	'65 430
Archdale city (pt.)[38]	77	...
High Point city (pt.)[38]	62 814	'63 209
Jamestown township	10 637	'9 918
Archdale city (pt.)[38]	62	...
Jamestown town[38]	2 148	1 297
Jefferson township[38]	10 296	9 021
McLeansville (CDP)	1 176	...
Madison township	3 308	2 520
Monroe township[38]	7 354	8 398
Morehead township	102 082	91 177
Greensboro city (pt.)[38]	102 082	91 116

County Subdivisions

County Subdivisions	1980	1970
Guilford County—Con.		
Oak Ridge township	3 843	3 760
Stokesdale (CDP)	1 070	...
Rock Creek township	5 366	4 451
Gibsonville town (pt.)[38]	1 976	1 177
Sumner township[38]	6 931	7 987
Washington township	1 944	1 767
Halifax County[39]	55 286	53 884
Brinkleyville township	4 727	4 140
Butterwood township	517	588
Conoconnara township	828	1 006
Enfield township	7 271	7 616
Enfield town	2 995	3 272
Faucett township	1 983	2 089
Halifax township	2 663	2 633
Halifax town	253	335
Littleton township	3 882	3 376
Littleton town[39]	820	903
Palmyra township	1 499	1 546
Hobgood town	483	530
Roanoke Rapids township	20 340	18 505
Roanoke Rapids city (pt.)[39]	14 594	13 508
Rosemary (CDP)	1 828	...
Roseneath township	989	1 104
Scotland Neck township	4 592	5 013
Scotland Neck town[39]	2 834	2 869
Weldon township	5 995	6 268
Roanoke Rapids city (pt.)	108	-
South Weldon (CDP)	1 801	1 630
Weldon town	1 844	2 304
Harnett County[40]	59 570	49 667
Anderson Creek township	6 915	3 075
Averasboro township	13 125	11 657
Dunn city (pt.)[40]	8 962	8 302
Barbecue township	3 014	2 844
Black River township	3 827	3 699
Angier town[40]	1 709	1 431
Buckhorn township	1 103	862
Duke township	5 539	5 450
Dunn city (pt.)	-	...
Erwin town[40]	2 828	2 852
Grove township	5 716	4 494
Coats town[40]	1 385	1 051
Hectors Creek township	1 701	1 561
Johnsonville township	2 574	1 887
Lillington township	4 095	3 618
Lillington town[40]	1 948	1 155
Neills Creek township	4 456	4 072
Buies Creek (CDP)	1 939	2 024
Stewarts Creek township[40]	2 861	2 399
Upper Little River township	4 644	4 049
Haywood County[41]	46 495	41 710
Beaverdam township	11 997	11 468
Canton town[41]	4 631	5 158
Phillipsville (CDP)	1 642	1 239
Cataloochee township	56	107
Cecil township	355	418
Clyde township	4 448	3 086
Clyde town[41]	1 008	814
Crabtree township	882	794
East Fork township	1 551	1 362
Fines Creek township	764	692
Iron Duff township	668	645
Ivy Hill township	2 356	1 779
Maggie Valley town[41]	202	...
Jonathans Creek township	1 189	803
Pigeon township	3 996	3 460
Waynesville township	18 084	16 955
Hazelwood town[41]	1 811	2 057
Waynesville town[41]	6 765	6 488
White Oak township	149	141
Henderson County[42]	58 580	42 804
Blue Ridge township	5 238	3 398
East Flat Rock (CDP) (pt.)	115	...
Clear Creek township	2 711	1 726
Crab Creek township	1 771	1 096
Edneyville township	2 158	1 811
Green River township	2 749	1 877
Hendersonville township	31 525	25 018
Balfour (CDP)	1 772	2 014
Barker Heights (CDP)	1 267	2 933
East Flat Rock (CDP) (pt.)	3 250	2 627
Hendersonville city[42]	6 862	6 443
Laurel Park town[42]	764	581
Mountain Home (CDP)	1 387	...
Valley Hill (CDP)	2 396	1 558
Hoopers Creek township[42]	6 154	3 815
Mills River township	6 274	4 063
Hertford County[43]	23 368	24 439
Ahoskie township	8 707	8 535
Ahoskie town[43]	4 887	5 105
Harrellsville township	1 502	1 669
Harrellsville town	151	165
Maneys Neck township	1 451	1 385
Como town	89	211
Murfreesboro township	6 034	7 111
Murfreesboro town[43]	3 007	4 418

County Subdivisions	1980	1970
Hertford County—Con.		
St. Johns township	2 842	3 116
Winton township	2 832	2 623
Cofield village[43]	465	318
Winton town[43]	825	917
Hoke County[44]	20 383	16 436
Allendale township	427	537
Antioch township	2 455	1 514
Blue Springs township	1 373	1 113
Fort Bragg Military Reservation township	11	-
McLauchlin township	3 298	1 938
Quewhiffle township	2 536	2 607
Raeford township	8 956	7 409
Raeford city[44]	3 630	3 180
Silver City (CDP)	1 620	...
Stonewall township	1 327	1 318
Hyde County[45]	5 873	5 571
Currituck township	1 302	1 133
Fairfield township	582	541
Lake Landing township	2 217	2 377
Lake Mattamuskeet (unorg.)[45]	16	21
Ocracoke township	658	541
Swan Quarter township	1 098	958
Iredell County[46]	82 538	72 197
Barringer township	3 352	2 958
Troutman town (pt.)[46]	7	...
Bethany township	4 045	2 285
Chambersburg township	6 487	4 666
Statesville city (pt.)[46]	2	...
Coddle Creek township	14 457	13 714
Mooresville town[46]	8 575	8 808
Concord township	3 410	2 680
Cool Spring township	2 091	1 324
Davidson township	4 955	2 216
Davidson town (pt.)[46]	-	...
Eagle Mills township	1 557	1 757
Harmony town (pt.)	73	...
Fallstown township	5 151	3 568
Troutman town (pt.)[46]	1 353	797
New Hope township	1 218	1 295
Love Valley town	55	40
Olin township	1 141	1 008
Sharpesburg township	1 641	1 340
Shiloh township	4 140	3 174
Statesville township	25 167	27 079
Statesville city (pt.)[46]	18 620	20 007
Statesville West (CDP)	1 905	3 068
Turnersburg township	2 314	2 018
Harmony town (pt.)[46]	397	377
Union Grove township	1 412	1 115
Jackson County[47]	25 811	21 593
Barkers Creek township	953	730
Canada township	425	449
Caney Fork township	605	443
Cashiers township	933	610
Cashiers town	553	230
Cullowhee township	5 954	4 885
Dillsboro township	1 069	772
Dillsboro town	179	215
Sylva town (pt.)	5	-
Greens Creek township	584	525
Hamburg township	1 023	828
Mountain township	235	224
Qualla township	3 823	3 102
River township	800	618
Savannah township	908	827
Scott Creek township	1 476	1 484
Sylva township	5 433	4 800
Sylva town (pt.)[47]	1 694	1 561
Webster township	1 590	1 296
Webster town	200	181
Johnston County[48]	70 599	61 737
Banner township	5 488	4 398
Benson town[48]	2 792	2 267
Bentonsville township	1 158	1 072
Beulah township	3 773	3 628
Kenly town (pt.)[48]	1 372	1 370
Boon Hill township	4 636	4 191
Princeton town[48]	1 034	1 044
Clayton township	8 423	6 671
Clayton town[48]	4 091	3 103
Cleveland township	2 245	1 444
Elevation township	2 716	2 325
Ingrams township	4 615	3 838
Four Oaks town[48]	1 049	1 057
Meadow township	2 314	2 303
Micro township	1 561	1 384
Micro town[48]	438	300
O'Neals township	4 974	4 070
Pine Level township	2 665	2 399
Pine Level town[48]	953	983
Pleasant Grove township	2 640	2 449
Selma township	7 310	6 601
Selma town[48]	4 762	4 356
Smithfield town (pt.)[48]	188	-
Smithfield township	12 491	11 975

County Subdivisions	1980	1970
Johnston County—Con.		
Smithfield town—Con.		
Smithfield town (pt.)[48]	7 100	6 677
Wilders township	2 260	1 939
Wilson Mills township[48]	1 330	1 050
Jones County	9 705	9 779
Township 1, White Oak	1 886	1 800
Maysville town	877	912
Township 2, Pollocksville	2 452	2 576
Pollocksville town	318	456
Township 3, Trenton	1 929	1 894
Trenton town	407	539
Township 4, Cypress Creek	1 026	908
Township 5, Tuckahoe	921	846
Township 6, Chinquapin	772	879
Township 7, Beaver Creek	719	876
Lee County[49]	36 718	30 467
Township 1, Greenwood[49]	3 463	2 537
Township 2, Jonesboro	8 261	5 878
Sanford city (pt.)[49]	2 971	2 290
Township 3, Cape Fear	2 481	2 005
Broadway town[49]	908	694
Township 4, Deep River	1 795	1 318
Township 5, East Sanford	6 154	5 648
Sanford city (pt.)[49]	4 507	4 361
Township 6, West Sanford	11 479	10 656
Sanford city (pt.)[49]	7 295	5 065
Township 7, Pocket	3 085	2 425
Lenoir County[50]	59 819	55 204
Contentnea Neck township	2 981	2 806
Grifton town (pt.)	339	312
Falling Creek township	5 007	2 691
Institute township	992	1 164
Kinston township	28 046	28 563
Kinston city[50]	25 234	23 020
Moseley Hall township	5 321	4 798
La Grange town[50]	3 147	2 679
Neuse township	5 683	5 022
Pink Hill township	2 319	1 939
Pink Hill town	644	522
Sand Hill township	842	927
Southwest township	1 683	1 514
Trent township	1 998	1 788
Vance township	3 502	2 720
Woodington township	1 445	1 272
Lincoln County[51]	42 372	32 682
Catawba Springs township	6 666	3 349
Howards Creek township	4 120	3 739
Ironton township	9 061	6 092
High Shoals city (pt.)[51]	–	–
Maiden town (pt.)[51]	–	...
Lincolnton township	18 879	16 147
Boger City (CDP)	2 252	2 203
High Shoals city (pt.)[51]	–	...
Lincolnton town[51]	4 879	5 293
Maiden town (pt.)[51]	–	...
North Brook township	3 646	3 355
McDowell County[52]	35 135	30 648
Brackett township	260	135
Crooked Creek township	2 381	1 766
Dysartsville township	1 844	993
Glenwood township	1 366	1 059
Higgins township	1 837	1 522
Marion township	14 501	14 624
East Marion (CDP)	1 851	...
Garden Creek (CDP)	1 161	...
Marion city[52]	3 684	3 335
West Marion (CDP) (pt.)	1 353	3 034
Montford Cove township	2 590	1 930
West Marion (CDP) (pt.)	243	...
Nebo township	3 546	2 978
North Cove township	1 869	1 242
Old Fort township	4 941	4 399
Old Fort town	752	676
Macon County[53]	20 178	15 788
Burningtown township	664	540
Cartoogechaye township	1 370	934
Cowee township	1 152	983
Ellijay township	1 633	967
Flats township	295	247
Franklin township	8 455	7 166
Franklin town[53]	2 640	2 336
Highlands township	1 834	1 450
Highlands town	653	583
Millshoal township	1 687	920
Nantahala township	812	848
Smiths Bridge township	1 805	1 273
Sugar Fork township	471	460
Madison County[54]	16 827	16 003
Township 1, Marshall	3 408	3 471
Marshall town[54]	809	982
Township 2, Laurel	1 811	1 868
Township 3, Mars Hill	4 776	4 166
Mars Hill town[54]	2 126	1 623

County Subdivisions	1980	1970
Madison County—Con.		
Township 4, Beech Glenn	1 926	1 765
Township 5, Walnut	1 434	1 375
Township 6, Hot Springs	1 346	1 320
Hot Springs town	678	653
Township 7, Ebbs Chapel	1 201	1 053
Township 8, Spring Creek	925	985
Martin County[55]	25 948	24 730
Beargrass township	1 486	1 165
Beargrass town	82	99
Cross Roads township	1 300	965
Everetts town	213	198
Goose Nest township	1 808	2 187
Oak City town	475	559
Griffins township	1 039	1 084
Hamilton township	2 125	1 840
Hamilton town	638	579
Hassell town	109	160
Jamesville township	2 602	2 185
Jamesville town	604	533
Poplar Point township	605	601
Robersonville township[55]	4 501	4 589
Parmele town	484	373
Robersonville town[55]	1 981	1 910
Williams township	1 105	828
Williamston township	9 377	9 286
Williamston town[55]	6 159	6 570
Mecklenburg County[56]	404 270	354 656
Township 1, Charlotte	314 447	...
Charlotte city[56]	314 447	241 420
Township 2, Berryhill[56]	4 093	...
Township 3, Steel Creek[56]	4 668	...
Township 4, Sharon[56]	69	...
Township 5, Providence[56]	7 064	...
Township 6, Clear Creek[56]	11 925	...
Mint Hill town[56]	7 416	...
Township 7, Crab Orchard[56]	9 912	...
Township 8, Mallard Creek[56]	5 688	...
Township 9, Deweese	5 754	4 969
Cornelius town (pt.)[56]	1 448	1 267
Davidson town (pt.)[56]	3 241	2 931
Township 10, Lemley	3 454	1 992
Cornelius town (pt.)[56]	12	29
Township 11, Long Creek	9 735	9 059
Township 12, Paw Creek[56]	9 452	...
Township 13, Morning Star[56]	7 730	...
Matthews town[56]	1 648	783
Mint Hill town (pt.)	499	...
Township 14, Pineville[56]	6 493	...
Pineville town[56]	1 525	1 948
Township 15, Huntersville	3 786	3 334
Huntersville town[56]	1 294	1 538
Mitchell County[57]	14 428	13 447
Bakersville township	1 762	1 603
Bakersville town	373	409
Bradshaw township	556	615
Cane Creek township	729	759
Fork Mountain township	543	492
Grassy Creek No. 1 township	3 291	3 066
Spruce Pine town (pt.)[57]	1 339	1 397
Grassy Creek No. 2 township	3 729	3 331
Spruce Pine town (pt.)	943	936
Harrell township	1 128	1 094
Little Rock Creek township	307	248
Poplar township	370	311
Red Hill township	514	526
Snow Creek township	1 499	1 402
Montgomery County[58]	22 469	19 267
Biscoe township[58]	5 096	...
Biscoe town[58]	1 334	1 244
Candor town[58]	868	561
Cheek Creek township	634	643
Eldorado township	466	264
Little River township	757	437
Mount Gilead township	3 750	3 401
Mount Gilead town	1 423	1 286
Ophir township	779	371
Peedee township	750	566
Rocky Springs township	1 420	1 195
Star township[58]	2 453	...
Star town[58]	816	892
Troy township	5 491	5 225
Troy town[58]	2 702	2 429
Uwharrie township	873	452
Moore County[59]	50 505	39 048
Township 1, Carthage	5 241	4 640
Carthage town[59]	925	1 034
Township 2, Bensalem	2 725	2 903
Township 3, Sheffields	5 468	4 607
Robbins city (pt.)[59]	1 141	952
Township 4, Ritters	2 273	2 056
Robbins city (pt.)	115	107
Township 5, Deep River	348	357
Township 6, Greenwood	2 175	1 934
Cameron town	225	204

County Subdivisions

County Subdivisions	1980	1970
Moore County—Con.		
Township 7, McNeills	13 960	10 221
Pinehurst (CDP) (pt.)59	212	...
Southern Pines town (pt.)59	7 682	5 848
Vass town	828	885
Whispering Pines village59	1 160	362
Township 8, Sand Hill	9 240	6 442
Aberdeen town59	1 945	1 592
Foxfire village (pt.)59	33	...
Pinebluff town59	935	570
Pinehurst (CDP) (pt.)59	171	...
Southern Pines town (pt.)59	938	89
Township 9, Mineral Springs	8 007	5 092
Foxfire village (pt.)59	120	...
Pinehurst (CDP) (pt.)59	3 038	1 056
Township 10, Little River	1 068	796
Nash County60	67 153	59 122
Bailey township	2 547	2 707
Bailey town	685	724
Castalia township	1 328	874
Castalia town60	358	265
Coopers township	2 108	1 894
Dry Wells township	2 354	2 128
Middlesex town	837	729
Ferrells township	1 439	1 451
Griffins township	2 251	2 064
Jackson township	2 036	2 192
Mannings township	4 795	4 463
Spring Hope town60	1 254	1 334
Nashville township	6 249	4 989
Nashville town60	2 678	1 670
North Whitakers township	2 485	3 221
Whitakers town (pt.)	432	447
Oak Level township	3 049	2 578
Rocky Mount city (pt.)60	...	...
Red Oak township	1 773	1 564
Dortches town (pt.)60	3	...
Red Oak town	314	359
Rocky Mount township	18 020	17 203
Rocky Mount city (pt.)60	14 648	14 353
Sharpsburg town (pt.)60	661	447
South Whitakers township	2 513	2 399
Battleboro town (pt.)	309	285
Dortches town (pt.)60	188	...
Rocky Mount city (pt.)60	92	50
Stony Creek township	14 206	9 395
Dortches town (pt.)60	694	...
Rocky Mount city (pt.)60	9 465	4 629
New Hanover County61	103 471	82 996
Cape Fear township	10 184	6 734
Castle Hayne (CDP)	1 087	...
Kings Grant (CDP) (pt.)	1 536	...
Wrightsboro (CDP)	3 985	...
Federal Point township	8 524	5 113
Carolina Beach town61	2 000	1 663
Kure Beach town61	611	394
Myrtle Grove (CDP) (pt.)	1 381	...
Silver Lake (CDP) (pt.)	948	...
Harnett township61	26 986	17 427
Kings Grant (CDP) (pt.)	5 026	...
Masonboro (CDP) (pt.)	175	...
Ogden (CDP)	2 811	...
Seagate (CDP) (pt.)	3 421	...
Windemere (CDP)	4 115	...
Winter Park (CDP) (pt.)	4 038	...
Wrightsville Beach town	2 910	1 701
Masonboro township61	13 777	7 553
Masonboro (CDP) (pt.)	3 706	...
Myrtle Grove (CDP) (pt.)	1 171	...
Pine Valley (CDP)	3 438	...
Seagate (CDP) (pt.)	1	...
Silver Lake (CDP) (pt.)	2 730	...
Winter Park (CDP) (pt.)	466	...
Wilmington township	44 000	46 169
Wilmington city61	44 000	46 169
Northampton County62	22 584	23 099
Gaston township	4 261	3 509
Gaston town	883	1 105
Jackson township	1 131	1 224
Jackson town (pt.)	720	762
Kirby township	3 916	3 920
Conway town	678	694
Severn town	309	356
Oconeechee township	2 531	3 168
Garysburg town62	1 434	231
Pleasant Hill township	610	630
Rich Square township	4 073	4 222
Rich Square town	1 057	1 254
Woodland town	861	744
Roanoke township	2 041	2 097
Lasker town	96	114
Seaboard township	1 904	1 892
Jackson town (pt.)	-	...
Seaboard town	687	611
Wiccacanee township62	2 117	2 437

County Subdivisions	1980	1970
Onslow County63	112 784	103 126
Jacksonville township	54 111	55 737
Camp Lejeune (CDP) (pt.)	8 098	13 835
Half Moon (CDP) (pt.)	3 050	...
Jacksonville city63	17 056	16 289
Jacksonville East (CDP)	3 700	...
New River Station (CDP)	5 401	8 699
Pumpkin Center (CDP)	4 004	...
Richlands township	9 006	7 572
Half Moon (CDP) (pt.)	542	...
Richlands town	825	935
Stump Sound township	7 500	5 545
Chadwick Acres town	15	12
Holly Ridge town63	465	415
Swansboro township	23 380	20 800
Camp Lejeune (CDP) (pt.)	14 748	15 352
Swansboro town	976	1 207
White Oak township	18 787	13 472
Camp Lejeune (CDP) (pt.)	7 918	5 362
Piney Green–White Oak (CDP)	6 058	...
Orange County64	77 055	57 567
Bingham township	3 954	2 379
Cedar Grove township	3 146	3 146
Chapel Hill township	50 572	38 856
Carrboro town64	7 336	5 058
Chapel Hill town (pt.)64	32 038	26 195
Cheeks township	4 821	3 571
Fairview (CDP) (pt.)	2	...
Mebane town (pt.)64	379	186
Eno township	4 450	2 550
Hillsborough township	8 599	5 855
Fairview (CDP) (pt.)	1 120	...
Hillsborough town64	3 019	1 444
Little River township	1 493	1 210
Pamlico County65	10 398	9 467
Township 1	2 218	1 813
Township 2	1 504	1 489
Alliance town (pt.)65	6	...
Stonewall town	360	335
Township 3	2 992	2 886
Alliance town (pt.)65	610	577
Bayboro town65	759	665
Hollyville village65	100	(NA)
Mesic town65	390	...
Vandemere town	335	379
Township 4	825	922
Township 5	2 859	2 357
Arapahoe town65	467	212
Minnesott Beach town65	171	...
Oriental town	536	445
Pasquotank County66	28 462	26 824
Elizabeth City township	14 297	15 507
Elizabeth City city (pt.)66	13 148	13 652
Mount Hermon township	3 403	2 352
Elizabeth City city (pt.)	315	312
Newland township	2 059	1 923
Nixonton township	3 591	3 135
Elizabeth City city (pt.)66	454	417
Providence township	3 910	2 819
Elizabeth City city (pt.)66	87	...
Salem township	1 202	1 088
Pender County67	22 215	18 149
Burgaw township67	4 946	4 422
Burgaw town	1 586	1 744
Canetuck township67	357	256
Caswell township67	1 027	1 023
Atkinson town (pt.)	298	325
Columbia township67	1 747	1 542
Atkinson town (pt.)	-	...
Grady township67	1 372	1 264
Holly township67	1 651	1 373
Long Creek township67	1 164	886
Rocky Point township67	1 943	1 616
Topsail township67	4 563	2 860
Surf City town	391	166
Topsail Beach town	264	108
Union township67	3 445	2 907
Wallace town (pt.)67	24	...
Watha town	196	181
Perquimans County68	9 486	8 351
Belvidere township	1 301	1 265
Bethel township	1 515	851
Hertford town (pt.)68	138	14
Hertford township	2 580	2 763
Hertford town (pt.)	1 803	2 009
New Hope township	2 026	1 636
Parkville township	2 064	1 836
Hertford town (pt.)	-	...
Winfall town68	634	581
Person County69	29 164	25 914
Allensville township	1 926	1 901
Bushy Fork township	2 008	1 846
Cunningham township	1 238	967
Flat River township	2 105	1 867
Holloway township	1 315	1 480
Mount Tirzah township	1 768	1 312

County Subdivisions	1980	1970
Person County—Con.		
Olive Hill township	1 907	1 802
Roxboro township	15 154	13 372
Roxboro city[69]	7 532	5 370
Woodsdale township	1 743	1 367
Pitt County[70]	90 146	73 900
Arthur township	3 058	1 812
Ayden township	6 156	5 444
Ayden[70]	4 361	3 450
Belvoir township	4 597	2 376
Greenville city (pt.)[70]	380	172
Bethel township	3 753	3 103
Bethel town[70]	1 825	1 514
Carolina township	1 490	1 925
Chicod township	3 232	2 614
Falkland township	1 727	1 870
Falkland town	118	130
Farmville township	6 602	6 522
Farmville town[70]	4 707	4 424
Fountain township	1 369	1 443
Fountain town	424	434
Greenville township	34 557	30 486
Greenville city (pt.)[70]	31 615	27 940
Grifton township	3 358	3 552
Grifton town (pt.)[70]	1 840	1 548
Grimesland township	4 534	3 050
Grimesland town	453	394
Simpson village[70]	407	...
Pactolus township	3 451	3 215
Greenville city (pt.)[70]	−	...
Swift Creek township	1 171	1 076
Winterville township	11 091	5 412
Greenville city (pt.)[70]	3 745	951
Winterville town[70]	2 052	1 437
Polk County[71]	12 984	11 735
Columbus township	3 241	2 666
Columbus town[71]	727	731
Cooper Gap township	1 236	983
Greens Creek township	2 150	1 837
Saluda township	1 244	1 092
Saluda city	607	546
Tryon township	3 712	3 850
Tryon town	1 796	1 951
White Oak township	1 401	1 307
Randolph County[72]	91 728	76 358
Asheboro township	18 745	19 801
Asheboro city (pt.)[72]	13 757	10 797
Asheboro South (CDP) (pt.)	1 030	1 169
Asheboro West (CDP) (pt.)	537	947
Back Creek township	2 799	1 859
Asheboro city (pt.)[72]	206	−
Brower township	1 114	785
Cedar Grove township	6 058	3 534
Asheboro city (pt.)[72]	30	...
Asheboro South (CDP) (pt.)	1 374	829
Asheboro West (CDP) (pt.)	954	211
Coleridge township	1 659	1 593
Columbia township	4 600	4 295
Ramseur town[72]	1 162	1 328
Staley town	204	239
Concord township	1 279	1 093
Franklinville township	6 319	5 250
Asheboro city (pt.)[72]	936	...
Franklinville town[72]	607	794
Grant township	2 545	1 999
Asheboro South (CDP) (pt.)	41	...
Level Cross township	2 496	1 660
Liberty township	4 790	4 571
Liberty town[72]	1 997	2 167
New Hope township	849	775
New Market township	5 546	3 975
Trinity (CDP) (pt.)	7	...
Pleasant Grove township	576	484
Providence township	2 796	1 288
Randleman township	5 012	4 853
Asheboro city (pt.)[72]	323	...
Randleman city[72]	2 156	2 312
Richland township	2 413	2 472
Seagrove town	294	354
Tabernacle township	2 433	1 724
Trinity township	18 249	13 375
Archdale city (pt.)[72]	5 606	'4 874
High Point city (pt.)[72]	29	'20
Trinity (CDP) (pt.)	6 880	...
Union township	1 450	972
Richmond County[73]	45 481	39 889
Beaverdam township	2 097	1 950
Hoffman town	389	434
Black Jack township	259	247
Marks Creek township	13 319	10 730
Hamlet city (pt.)[73]	4 718	4 627
Mineral Springs township	3 892	3 663
Ellerbe town[73]	1 415	913
Norman town[73]	252	'157
Rockingham township	16 043	13 705
East Rockingham (CDP) (pt.)	12	...
Hamlet city (pt.)	2	...

County Subdivisions	1980	1970
Richmond County—Con.		
Rockingham township—Con.		
Rockingham city (pt.)[73]	8 116	5 613
West Rockingham (CDP)	2 093	...
Steeles township	754	922
Wolf Pit township	9 117	8 672
East Rockingham (CDP) (pt.)	5 178	2 858
Rockingham city (pt.)[73]	184	239
Robeson County[74]	101 610	84 842
Alfordsville township	1 391	1 511
Back Swamp township	3 063	2 641
Britts township	2 003	1 392
Burnt Swamp township	1 779	1 233
East Howellsville township	1 353	1 250
Fairmont township	5 693	5 343
Fairmont town[74]	2 658	2 827
Gaddy township	1 218	876
Lumber Bridge township	1 397	1 089
Lumber Bridge town	171	117
Lumberton township	23 301	20 318
Lumberton city[74]	18 241	16 961
Marietta township	1 713	1 273
Maxton township	6 000	4 817
Maxton town (pt.)[74]	2 585	1 885
Orrum township	1 931	1 721
Orrum town	167	162
Proctorville town	205	157
Parkton township	2 110	1 901
Parkton town	564	550
Pembroke township	8 725	5 844
Pembroke town[74]	2 698	1 982
Philadelphus township	1 959	1 908
Raft Swamp township	2 307	1 457
Red Springs township	5 712	4 952
Red Springs town[74]	3 607	3 383
Rennert township	1 433	884
Rennert town[74]	178	...
Rowland township	3 122	3 217
Rowland town	1 841	1 358
Saddletree township	2 627	1 737
St. Pauls township	6 208	5 970
St. Pauls town[74]	1 639	2 011
Shannon township	733	681
Smiths township	3 743	2 566
Smyrna township	1 132	1 167
Sterlings township	1 168	1 335
Thompson township	1 343	1 346
McDonald town	117	80
Union township	2 403	2 122
Raynham town[74]	83	...
West Howellsville township	2 390	1 922
Wishart township	3 653	2 369
Rockingham County[75]	83 426	72 402
Huntsville township	3 615	1 756
Leaksville township	22 176	20 162
Eden city[75]	15 672	15 871
Madison township	8 964	8 547
Madison town[75]	2 806	2 018
Mayodan town	2 627	2 875
Mayo township	5 519	4 458
Stoneville town	1 054	1 030
New Bethel township	3 567	3 346
Price township	1 289	1 331
Reidsville township	18 236	17 386
Reidsville city[75]	12 492	13 636
Ruffin township	5 293	6 064
Simpsonville township	4 166	2 234
Wentworth township	7 446	5 504
Williamsburg township	3 155	1 614
Rowan County[76]	99 186	90 035
Atwell township	6 580	5 408
Enochville (CDP)	2 646	...
China Grove township	20 285	20 530
China Grove town[76]	2 081	1 788
China Grove Cotton Mill Village (CDP)	1 168	1 353
Kannapolis (CDP)	9 602	10 051
Landis town[76]	2 092	2 297
Cleveland township	1 647	1 751
Cleveland town[76]	595	614
Franklin township	9 192	6 574
Salisbury city (pt.)[76]	2 423	1 769
Gold Hill township	5 675	4 442
Granite Quarry town (pt.)[76]	582	488
Rockwell town[76]	1 339	999
Litaker township	7 985	5 692
Faith town[76]	552	506
Granite Quarry town (pt.)	70	72
Salisbury city (pt.)[76]	46	...
Locke township	6 962	4 386
Salisbury city (pt.)[76]	−	...
Morgan township	2 337	1 383
Mount Ulla township	1 038	1 214
Providence township	6 195	4 201
Granite Quarry town (pt.)[76]	642	784
Salisbury township	27 389	30 937
East Spencer town[76]	2 150	2 217

County Subdivisions	1980	1970
Rowan County—Con.		
Salisbury township—Con.		
Salisbury city (pt.)[76]	20 208	20 746
Spencer town[76]	2 938	3 075
Scotch Irish township	1 220	1 295
Steele township	995	825
Unity township	1 686	1 397
Rutherford County[77]	53 787	47 337
Camp Creek township	1 054	1 084
Chimney Rock township	1 457	1 094
Lake Lure town	488	456
Colfax township	6 185	5 068
Ellenboro town[77]	560	465
Cool Spring township	15 709	13 093
Alexander Mills town	543	988
Bostic town	476	289
Forest City town[77]	7 688	7 179
Spindale town (pt.)[77]	465	...
Duncans Creek township	400	433
Gilkey township	1 154	746
Golden Valley township	721	680
Green Hill township	1 686	1 434
High Shoals township	6 270	6 351
Henrietta (CDP)	1 412	1 307
Logan Store township	2 875	2 615
Morgan township	1 005	820
Rutherfordton township	10 648	10 593
Ruth town	381	360
Rutherfordton town[77]	3 434	3 245
Spindale town (pt.)[77]	3 781	3 848
Sulphur Springs township	3 431	2 465
Union township	1 192	861
Sampson County[78]	49 687	44 954
Belvoir township	1 376	1 224
Dismal township	2 675	2 482
Franklin township	2 157	2 034
Harrells town (pt.)	222	237
Halls township	2 071	2 021
Herrings township	1 520	1 398
Honeycutts township	2 394	2 270
Salemburg town[78]	742	669
Lisbon township	1 063	901
Little Coharie township	5 863	5 339
Autryville town	228	213
Roseboro town	1 227	1 235
McDaniels township[78]	1 145	728
Mingo township	1 550	1 311
Falcon town (pt.)[78]	–	...
Newton Grove township	1 890	1 811
Newton Grove town	564	546
North Clinton township	10 054	9 597
Clinton city (pt.)[78]	5 787	5 738
Piney Grove township	1 904	1 793
Plain View township	2 524	1 925
South Clinton township	4 850	3 994
Clinton city (pt.)[78]	1 765	1 419
South River township	1 686	1 522
Garland town	885	656
Taylors Bridge township	1 480	1 429
Harrells town (pt.)	–	6
Turkey township	2 231	1 994
Turkey town[78]	417	329
Westbrooks township	1 254	1 181
Scotland County[79]	32 273	26 929
Laurel Hill township	3 222	2 539
Laurinburg city (pt.)[79]	620	204
Spring Hill township	3 651	2 949
Wagram town	617	718
Stewartsville township	19 070	16 558
East Laurinburg town	536	487
Laurinburg city (pt.)[79]	10 860	8 655
Maxton town (pt.)[79]	126	...
Williamsons township	6 330	4 883
Gibson town	533	502
Laurel Hill (CDP)	2 314	1 215
Stanly County[80]	48 517	42 822
Almond township	1 989	1 596
Big Lick township	4 361	3 552
Oakboro town[80]	587	568
Center township	5 490	4 702
Norwood town[80]	1 818	1 896
Endy township	1 280	1 124
Furr township	5 113	4 411
Locust city[80]	1 590	...
Stanfield town	463	458
Harris township	4 917	4 260
Albemarle city (pt.)[80]	52	...
Badin (CDP) (pt.)	100	67
New London town	454	285
Richfield town (pt.)[80]	234	191
North Albemarle township	13 039	12 661
Albemarle city (pt.)[80]	9 019	6 592
Badin (CDP) (pt.)	1 414	1 559
Ridenhour township	2 008	1 325
Richfield town (pt.)	139	115
South Albemarle township	8 631	7 540
Albemarle city (pt.)[80]	6 039	4 534

County Subdivisions	1980	1970
Stanly County—Con.		
Tyson township	1 689	1 651
Stokes County[81]	33 086	23 782
Beaver Island township[81]	2 725	2 024
Danbury town (pt.)[81]	–	...
Big Creek township[81]	1 868	1 725
Danbury township[81]	1 076	503
Danbury town (pt.)[81]	140	152
Meadows township[81]	3 533	2 790
Peters Creek township[81]	1 905	1 760
Danbury town (pt.)[81]	–	...
Quaker Gap township[81]	1 638	1 212
Sauratown township[81]	4 927	3 813
Walnut Cove town	1 147	1 213
Snow Creek township[81]	2 165	2 205
Yadkin township[81]	13 249	7 750
King (CDP)	8 757	1 033
Surry County[82]	59 449	51 415
Bryan township	2 244	2 051
Dobson township	6 288	5 154
Dobson town	1 222	933
Eldora township	2 243	1 722
Elkin township	5 842	5 164
Elkin town (pt.)[82]	2 804	2 899
Franklin township	1 541	1 695
Long Hill township	1 178	592
Marsh township	1 502	1 225
Mount Airy township	23 616	20 963
Bannertown (CDP)	1 028	1 138
Flat Rock (CDP)	1 922	1 688
Holly View Forest—Highland Park (CDP)	1 647	...
Mount Airy city[82]	6 862	7 325
Salem (CDP)	1 575	...
Toast (CDP)	2 339	2 635
Pilot township	3 166	3 069
Pilot Mountain town	1 090	1 309
Rockford township	1 241	1 223
Shoals township	1 198	1 049
Siloam township	879	784
South Westfield township	1 209	1 683
Stewarts Creek township	5 446	3 569
Westfield township	1 856	1 472
Swain County[83]	10 283	[8] 8 835
Charleston township	9 049	[7] 7 835
Bryson City town[83]	1 556	1 290
Forneys Creek township	21	–
Nantahala township	1 213	1 000
Transylvania County[84]	23 417	19 713
Boyd township	2 559	2 161
Pisgah Forest (CDP) (pt.)	505	...
Brevard township	10 450	9 929
Brevard city[84]	5 323	5 243
Pisgah Forest (CDP) (pt.)	1 394	...
Catheys Creek township	3 216	2 651
Rosman town (pt.)[84]	410	331
Dunns Rock township	2 129	1 022
Eastatoe township	1 714	1 352
Rosman town (pt.)[84]	102	76
Gloucester township	807	579
Hogback township	1 218	989
Little River township	1 324	1 030
Tyrrell County	3 975	3 806
Alligator township	477	482
Columbia township	2 098	1 910
Columbia town	758	902
Gum Neck township	474	523
Scuppernong township	864	838
South Fork township	62	53
Union County[85]	70 380	54 714
Buford township	6 365	5 107
Goose Creek township	7 054	5 317
Jackson township	4 507	3 276
Waxhaw town[85]	1 208	1 248
Lanes Creek township	1 266	1 388
Marshville township	6 768	5 746
Marshville town[85]	2 011	1 405
Wingate town (pt.)[85]	25	...
Monroe township	26 261	23 258
Monroe city[85]	12 639	11 282
Wingate town (pt.)[85]	2 590	2 569
New Salem township	2 025	1 746
Sandy Ridge township	4 744	2 940
Vance township	11 390	5 936
Indian Trail town[85]	811	405
Stallings town[85]	1 826	...
Vance County[86]	36 748	32 691
Dabney township	1 454	954
Henderson township	22 300	20 807
Henderson city[86]	13 522	13 896
North Henderson (CDP)	1 832	1 997
South Henderson (CDP)	2 384	1 843
Kittrell township	3 260	2 913
Kittrell town	225	427
Middleburg–Nutbush township	2 727	2 145
Middleburg town	185	149

County Subdivisions	1980	1970
Vance County—Con.		
Sandy Creek township	3 090	2 513
Townsville township	1 530	1 530
Watkins township	508	409
Williamsboro township	1 879	1 420
Williamsboro town	59	(NA)
Wake County[87]	301 327	229 006
Bartons Creek township[87]	3 989	1 788
Buckhorn township[87]	1 240	965
Cary township[87]	26 037	12 046
Cary town (pt.)[87]	21 752	7 640
Morrisville town (pt.)[87]	–	...
Raleigh city (pt.)[87]	–	95
Cedar Fork township[87]	2 056	2 533
Morrisville town (pt.)[87]	251	209
Holly Springs township[87]	3 942	3 578
Holly Springs town[87]	688	697
House Creek township[87]	21 874	22 044
Raleigh city (pt.)[87]	16 572	16 945
Leesville township[87]	5 553	1 292
Raleigh city (pt.)[87]	–	...
Little River township[87]	7 449	6 714
Zebulon town[87]	2 055	1 839
Marks Creek township[87]	7 880	5 211
Wendell town[87]	2 222	1 929
Meredith township[87]	6 268	12 579
Raleigh city (pt.)[87]	3 573	8 893
Middle Creek township[87]	9 339	9 005
Fuquay–Varina town[87]	3 110	3 576
Neuse township[87]	19 824	8 461
New Hope (CDP) (pt.)	682	...
Raleigh city (pt.)[87]	13 767	4 101
New Light township[87]	1 995	1 696
Panther Branch township[87]	4 145	2 382
Raleigh township[87]	101 909	90 208
Cary town (pt.)[87]	–	...
New Hope (CDP) (pt.)	–	...
Raleigh city (pt.)[87]	101 139	89 368
St. Marys township[87]	28 326	16 536
Garner town[87]	10 073	4 923
Raleigh city (pt.)[87]	7 720	1 441
St. Matthews township[87]	20 412	9 920
Knightdale town[87]	985	815
New Hope (CDP) (pt.)	6 063	...
Raleigh city (pt.)[87]	4 784	11
Swift Creek township[87]	11 045	8 483
Cary town (pt.)[87]	11	...
Raleigh city (pt.)[87]	2 700	1 976
Wake Forest township[87]	11 458	8 329
Rolesville town[87]	381	533
Wake Forest town[87]	3 780	3 148
White Oak township[87]	6 586	5 236
Apex town[87]	2 847	2 234
Cary town (pt.)[87]	–	46
Warren County[88]	16 232	15 810
Fishing Creek township	1 364	1 230
Fork township	556	578
Hawtree township	1 307	1 547
Judkins township	824	959
Nutbush township	1 580	1 412
River township	814	1 137
Roanoke township	269	164
Sandy Creek township	1 360	1 043
Shocco township	784	737
Sixpound township	722	706
Macon town (pt.)	153	179
Smith Creek township	2 081	2 020
Norlina town	901	969
Warrenton township	4 571	4 277
Macon town (pt.)	–	...
Warrenton town	908	1 035
Washington County[89]	14 801	14 038
Lees Mills township	3 589	3 407
Roper town	795	649
Plymouth township	7 789	7 512
Plymouth town[89]	4 571	4 774
Scuppernong township	1 540	1 733
Creswell town	426	633
Skinnersville township	1 883	1 386
Watauga County[90]	31 666	23 404
Bald Mountain township[90]	280	363
Beaverdam township	1 030	847
Blowing Rock township	2 295	1 321
Blowing Rock town (pt.)[90]	1 274	777
Blue Ridge township	1 613	898
Boone township	10 191	8 754
Boone town[90]	10 191	8 754
Brushy Fork township[90]	2 656	2 345
Cove Creek township	2 141	1 780
Elk township	260	274
Laurel Creek township	1 332	1 096
Meat Camp township	1 805	1 275
New River township[90]	3 785	1 499
North Fork township	207	231
Shawneehaw township	544	390
Stony Fork township	1 476	1 192

County Subdivisions	1980	1970
Watauga County—Con.		
Watauga township	2 051	1 139
Seven Devils town (pt.)[90]	47	...
Wayne County[91]	97 054	85 408
Brogden township	18 005	13 442
Brogden (CDP)	2 988	...
Mar–Mac (CDP)	3 366	...
Mount Olive town (pt.)[91]	4 869	4 872
Buck Swamp township[91]	2 108	...
Fork township	6 795	6 578
Rosewood (CDP) (pt.)	3 896	...
Goldsboro township	26 778	29 822
Goldsboro city (pt.)[91]	22 361	25 779
Goldsboro Northwest (CDP)	1 397	...
Rosewood (CDP) (pt.)	107	...
South Goldsboro (CDP)	2 531	2 094
Grantham township	3 086	2 872
Great Swamp township	1 239	1 286
Indian Springs township	3 552	2 242
Seven Springs town	166	188
Nahunta township	3 844	3 944
Eureka town[91]	303	263
Fremont town[91]	1 736	1 596
New Hope township	19 293	14 994
Elroy (CDP)	4 073	...
Goldsboro city (pt.)[91]	9 252	1 163
New Hope (CDP) (pt.)	3 261	...
Walnut Creek village[91]	343	...
Pikeville township[91]	1 771	...
Pikeville town[91]	662	580
Saulston township	2 659	1 858
Stony Creek township	7 924	5 166
Goldsboro city (pt.)[91]	258	18
New Hope (CDP) (pt.)	3 424	...
Wilkes County[92]	58 657	49 524
Antioch township	891	809
Beaver Creek township	477	435
Boomer township	1 840	1 402
Brushy Mountain township	481	446
Edwards township	6 385	5 786
Elkin town (pt.)[92]	54	...
Pleasant Hill (CDP)	1 278	...
Ronda town	457	465
Elk township	1 131	1 044
Jobs Cabin township	396	409
Lewis Fork township	1 194	1 162
Lovelace township	468	599
Moravian Falls township	2 220	2 004
Moravian Falls (CDP) (pt.)	921	...
Mulberry township	6 692	4 698
Fairplains (CDP) (pt.)	1 690	...
Mulberry (CDP)	2 270	...
New Castle township	1 422	1 233
North Wilkesboro township	6 387	6 650
Cricket (CDP) (pt.)	1 071	...
Fairplains (CDP) (pt.)	1 415	...
North Wilkesboro town (pt.)[92]	2 765	3 100
Wilkesboro town (pt.)[92]	6	...
Reddies River township	8 937	6 094
Cricket (CDP) (pt.)	1 236	...
Wilkesboro town (pt.)[92]	–	...
Rock Creek township	4 972	3 867
Somers township	957	846
Stanton township	408	390
Trap Hill township	2 756	2 762
Union township	1 177	1 152
Walnut Grove township	905	875
Wilkesboro township	8 561	6 861
Moravian Falls (CDP) (pt.)	631	...
North Wilkesboro town (pt.)[92]	495	257
Wilkesboro town (pt.)[92]	2 329	2 038
Wilson County[93]	63 132	57 486
Black Creek township	2 971	2 532
Black Creek town	523	449
Cross Roads township	3 075	2 640
Lucama town[93]	1 070	610
Gardner township	2 918	2 240
Old Fields township	3 359	3 188
Sims town	192	205
Saratoga township	2 192	1 923
Saratoga town	381	391
Springhill township	2 064	2 053
Kenly town (pt.)[93]	61	...
Stantonsburg township	1 620	1 770
Stantonsburg town[93]	920	869
Taylor township	2 328	2 020
Toisnot township	4 963	4 403
Elm City town[93]	1 561	1 201
Sharpsburg town (pt.)	325	296
Wilson township	37 642	34 717
Wilson city[93]	34 424	29 347
Yadkin County[94]	28 439	24 599
Boonville township	3 110	2 938
Boonville town[94]	1 028	687
Buck Shoal township	3 223	2 669
Deep Creek township	3 922	2 805
Yadkinville town (pt.)	1 137	617

County Subdivisions

County Subdivisions	1980	1970
Yadkin County—Con.		
East Bend township	2 794	2 492
East Bend town	602	485
Fall Creek township[94]	3 113	2 944
Forbush township	1 599	1 313
Knobs township	5 686	5 036
Arlington town	872	711
Jonesville town	1 752	1 659
Liberty township	4 992	4 402
Yadkinville town (pt.)[94]	1 079	1 615
Yancey County	14 934	12 629
Brush Creek township	579	422
Burnsville township	3 499	3 065
Burnsville town	1 452	1 348
Cane River township	1 362	1 426
Crabtree township	3 008	2 404
Egypt township	867	999
Green Mountain township	836	599
Jacks Creek township	1 101	692
Pensacola township	690	638
Price Creek township	1 022	768
Ramseytown township	288	326
South Toe township	1 682	1 290

NORTH DAKOTA

The name Dakota was originally that of an Indian nation which inhabited the region now comprising North Dakota and adjacent states. The word signifies "friends, allies, or confederates."

The first authentic exploration within the present limits of North Dakota was made in 1738 when the French explorers, De la Verendrye and his sons, attempted to reach the Pacific Ocean. In 1804 and 1806 the United States Government exploring expedition under Lewis and Clark passed through the Dakota country by way of the Missouri River. British subjects had trading posts in this region early in the nineteenth century, and in 1810 Lord Selkirk, considering it British territory, built a fort near Pembina. Shortly afterwards a colony was planted here under a grant from the Hudson Bay Company. In 1823 the United States discovered that this place was within its borders, and raised the American flag over it.

North Dakota was originally a part of the vast area known as Louisiana, which was ceded by France to Spain in 1763, retroceded in 1800, and purchased by the United States in 1803. It belonged successively to the district of Louisiana (1804-5), the territory of Louisiana (1805-1812), and the territory of Missouri (1812-1834). That part of the present state lying east of the Missouri and White Earth Rivers belonged to Michigan territory (1834), to Wisconsin territory (1836), to Iowa territory (1838), and to Minnesota territory (1849). The area between the Missouri and White Earth Rivers and the present western boundary of North Dakota formed a part of the "Indian Country" from 1834 to 1854, and in the latter year was included in the territory of Nebraska.

Upon the admission of the state of Minnesota in 1858, the region lying between that state and the Missouri and White Earth Rivers was left without legal name or existence, and it so remained until March, 1861, when the territory of Dakota was organized. At this time Dakota extended from the Keyapaha, Niobrara, and Missouri Rivers and the forty-third parallel to the Canadian boundary and from Minnesota to the Rocky Mountains, thus including the area now comprising most of Montana and nearly half of Wyoming. In 1863, when Idaho territory was formed, the region between the Rocky Mountains and the present western boundaries of North and South Dakota was included. Most of the present area of Wyoming was transferred from Idaho to Dakota in 1864, and continued a part of the latter territory until 1868, when Wyoming territory was organized. In 1882 a small triangular tract of land lying south of the forty-third parallel and west of the Missouri River was transferred from Dakota to Nebraska.

At the election of November, 1887, the question of the division of the Dakota territory into two states was submitted to the people and was carried at the polls. In November, 1889, North Dakota, with boundaries as at present, became a state of the Union.

COUNTY LOCATION INDEX

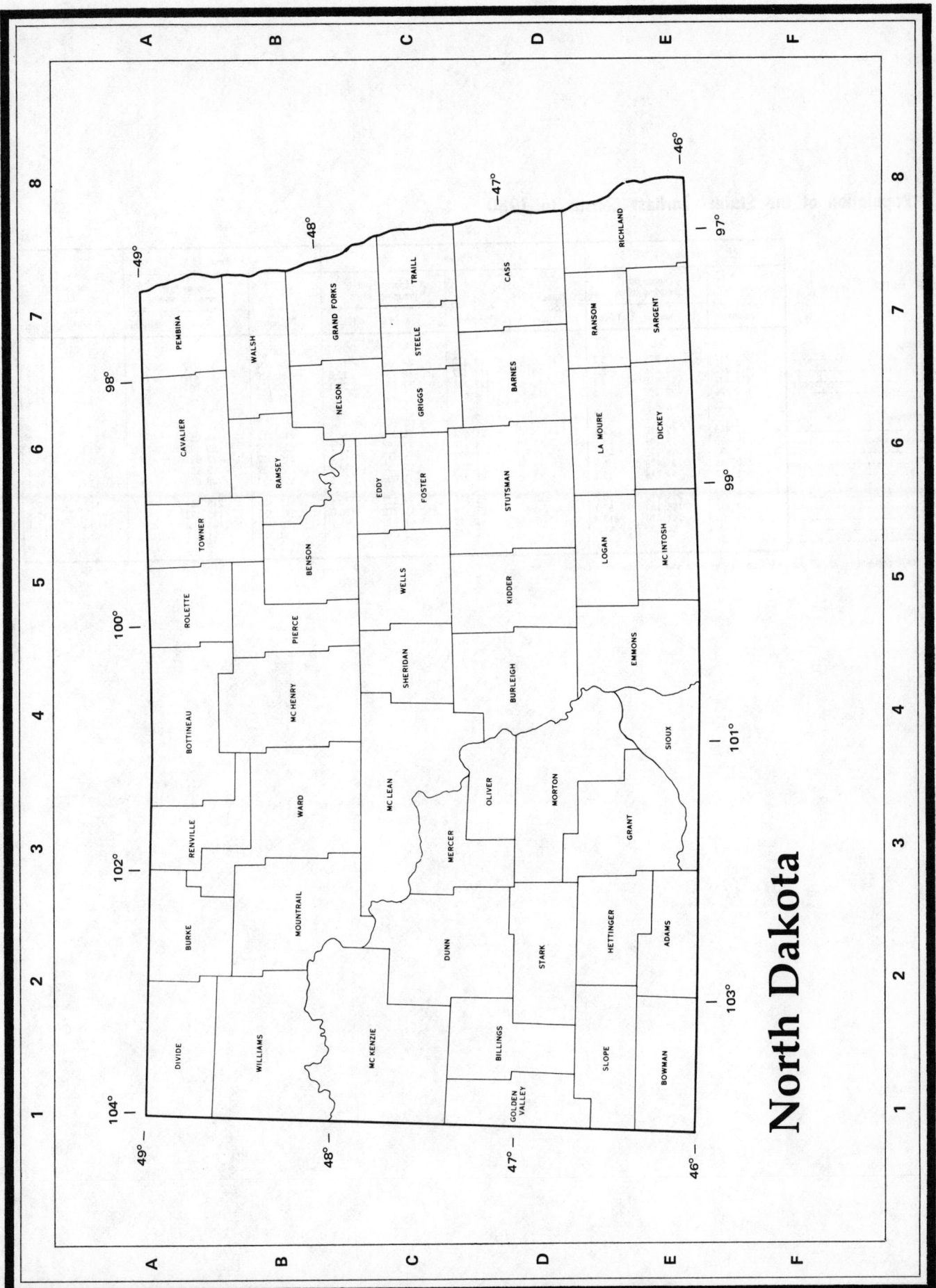

North Dakota

Population of the State: Earliest Census to 1980

Urban and Rural

	The State			Urban				Rural				Percent of total population	
	Total population	Change from preceding census		Places of 2,500 or more	Population	Change from preceding census		Population	Change from preceding census			Urban	Rural
		Number	Percent			Number	Percent		Number	Percent			
Current urban definition:													
1980 (Apr. 1)	652 717	34 925	5.7	20	318 310	44 868	16.4	334 407	−9 912	−2.9		48.8	51.2
1970 (Apr. 1)	'617 792	−14 654	−2.3	18	273 442	50 734	22.8	344 319	−65 419	−16.0		44.3	55.7
1960 (Apr. 1)	632 446	12 810	2.1	15	222 708	57 891	35.1	409 738	−45 081	−9.9		35.2	64.8
1950 (Apr. 1)	619 636	−22 299	−3.5	13	164 817			454 819	...	...		26.6	73.4
Previous urban definition:													
1960 (Apr. 1)	632 446	12 810	2.1	15	221 694	56 877	34.5	410 752	−44 067	−9.7		35.1	64.9
1950 (Apr. 1)	619 636	−22 299	−3.5	13	164 817	32 894	24.9	454 819	−55 193	−10.8		26.6	73.4
1940 (Apr. 1)	641 935	−38 910	−5.7	12	131 923	18 617	16.4	510 012	−57 527	−10.1		20.6	79.4
1930 (Apr. 1)	680 845	33 973	5.3	12	113 306	25 067	28.4	567 539	8 906	1.6		16.6	83.4
1920 (Jan. 1)	646 872	69 816	12.1	12	88 239	25 003	39.5	558 633	44 813	8.7		13.6	86.4
1910 (Apr. 15)	577 056	257 910	80.8	10	63 236	39 823	170.1	513 820	218 087	73.7		11.0	89.0
1900 (June 1)	319 146	128 163	67.1	4	23 413	12 770	120.0	295 733	115 393	64.0		7.3	92.7
1890 (June 1)	190 983	154 074	417.4	2	10 643	7 950	295.2	180 340	146 124	427.1		5.6	94.4
1880 (June 1)	36 909	34 504	1000+	1	2 693	2 693	...	34 216	31 811	1000+		7.3	92.7
1870 (June 1)	2 405	...	...	−	−	...	...	2 405	...	...		−	100.0

NOTE: 1870 population is of that part of Dakota Territory which now constitutes North Dakota.

ADAMS	
1910	5,407
1920	5,593
1930	6,343
1940	4,664
1950	4,910
1960	4,449
1970	3,832
1980	3,584

BARNES	
1880	1,585
1890	7,045
1900	13,159
1910	18,066
1920	18,678
1930	18,804
1940	17,814
1950	16,884
1960	16,718
1970	14,669
1980	13,960

BENSON	
1890	2,460
1900	8,320
1910	12,681
1920	13,095
1930	13,327
1940	12,629
1950	10,675
1960	9,435
1970	8,245
1980	7,944

BILLINGS	
1880	1,323
1890	170
1900	975
1910	10,186
1920	3,126
1930	1,168
1940	2,531
1950	1,777
1960	1,513
1970	1,198
1980	1,138

BOTTINEAU	
1890	2,893
1900	7,532
1910	17,295
1920	15,109
1930	14,853
1940	13,253
1950	12,140
1960	11,315
1970	9,496
1980	9,239

BOWMAN	
1890	6
1910	4,668
1920	4,768
1930	5,119
1940	3,860
1950	4,001
1960	4,154
1970	3,901
1980	4,229

BURKE	
1910	9,064
1920	9,511
1930	9,998
1940	7,653
1950	6,621
1960	5,886
1970	4,739
1980	3,822

BUFORD	
1890	803

BURLEIGH	
1880	3,246
1890	4,247
1900	6,081
1910	13,087
1920	15,578
1930	19,769
1940	22,736
1950	25,673
1960	34,016
1970	40,714
1980	54,811

CASS	
1880	8,998
1890	19,613
1900	28,625
1910	33,935
1920	41,477
1930	48,735
1940	52,849
1950	58,877
1960	66,947
1970	73,653
1980	88,247

CAVALIER	
1890	6,471
1900	12,580
1910	15,659
1920	15,555
1930	14,554
1940	13,923
1950	11,840
1960	10,064
1970	8,213
1980	7,636

CHURCH	
1890	74

DICKEY	
1890	5,573
1900	6,061
1910	9,839
1920	10,499
1930	10,877
1940	9,696
1950	9,121
1960	8,147
1970	6,976
1980	7,207

DIVIDE	
1910	6,015
1920	9,657
1930	9,636
1940	7,086
1950	5,967
1960	5,566
1970	4,564
1980	3,494

DUNN	
1910	5,302
1920	8,828
1930	9,566
1940	8,376
1950	7,212
1960	6,350
1970	4,895
1980	4,627

EDDY	
1890	1,377
1900	3,330
1910	4,800
1920	6,493
1930	5,346
1940	5,741
1950	5,372
1960	4,936
1970	4,103
1980	3,554

EMMONS	
1880	38
1890	1,971
1900	4,349
1910	9,796
1920	11,288
1930	12,467
1940	11,699
1950	9,715
1960	8,462
1970	7,200
1980	5,877

FLANNERY	
1890	72

FOSTER	
1880	37
1890	1,210
1900	3,770
1910	5,313
1920	6,108
1930	6,353
1940	5,824
1950	5,337
1960	5,361
1970	4,832
1980	4,611

GARFIELD	
1890	33

GOLDEN VALLEY	
1920	4,832
1930	4,122

1940	3,498
1950	3,499
1960	3,100
1970	2,611
1980	2,391

GRAND FORKS	
1880	6,248
1890	18,357
1900	24,459
1910	27,888
1920	28,795
1930	31,956
1940	34,518
1950	39,443
1960	48,677
1970	61,102
1980	66,100

GRANT	
1920	9,553
1930	10,134
1940	8,264
1950	7,114
1960	6,248
1970	5,009
1980	4,274

GRIGGS	
1890	2,817
1900	4,744
1910	6,274
1920	7,402
1930	6,889
1940	5,818
1950	5,460
1960	5,023
1970	4,184
1980	3,714

HETTINGER	
1890	81
1910	6,557
1920	7,685
1930	8,796
1940	7,457
1950	7,100
1960	6,317
1970	5,075
1980	4,275

HOWARD	
1880	12

KIDDER	
1880	89
1890	1,211
1900	1,754
1910	5,962
1920	7,798
1930	8,031
1940	6,692
1950	6,168
1960	5,386
1970	4,362
1980	3,833

LA MOURE	
1880	20
1890	3,187
1900	6,048
1910	10,724
1920	11,564
1930	11,517
1940	10,298
1950	9,498
1960	8,705
1970	7,117
1980	6,473

LOGAN	
1890	597
1900	1,625
1910	6,168
1920	7,723
1930	8,089
1940	7,561
1950	6,357
1960	5,369
1970	4,245
1980	3,493

McHENRY	
1890	1,584
1900	5,253
1910	17,627
1920	15,554
1930	15,439
1940	14,034
1950	12,556
1960	11,099
1970	8,977
1980	7,858

McINTOSH	
1890	3,248
1900	4,818
1910	7,251
1920	9,021
1930	9,621
1940	8,984
1950	7,590
1960	6,702
1970	5,545
1980	4,800

McKENZIE	
1890	3
1910	5,720
1920	9,544
1930	9,709
1940	8,426
1950	6,849
1960	7,296
1970	6,127
1980	7,132

McLEAN	
1890	860
1900	4,791
1910	14,496
1920	17,266
1930	17,991
1940	16,082
1950	18,824
1960	14,030
1970	11,251

1980	12,383

MERCER

1890	428
1900	1,778
1910	4,747
1920	8,224
1930	9,516
1940	9,611
1950	8,686
1960	6,805
1970	6,175
1980	9,404

MORTON

1880	200
1890	4,728
1900	8,069
1910	25,289
1920	18,714
1930	19,647
1940	20,184
1950	19,295
1960	20,992
1970	20,310
1980	25,177

MOUNTRAIL

1880	12
1890	122
1910	8,491
1920	12,140
1930	13,544
1940	10,482
1950	9,418
1960	10,077
1970	8,437
1980	7,679

NELSON

1890	4,293
1900	7,316
1910	10,140
1920	10,362
1930	10,203
1940	9,129
1950	8,090
1960	7,034
1970	5,806
1980	5,233

OLIVER

1890	464
1900	990
1910	3,577
1920	4,425
1930	4,262
1940	3,859
1950	3,091
1960	2,610
1970	2,322
1980	2,495

PEMBINA

1870	1,213
1880	4,862
1890	14,334
1900	17,869
1910	14,749
1920	15,177

1930	14,757
1940	15,671
1950	13,990
1960	12,946
1970	10,728
1980	10,399

PIERCE

1890	905
1900	4,765
1910	9,740
1920	9,283
1930	9,074
1940	9,208
1950	8,326
1960	7,394
1970	6,323
1980	6,166

RAMSEY

1880	281
1890	4,418
1900	9,198
1910	15,199
1920	15,427
1930	16,252
1940	15,626
1950	14,373
1960	13,443
1970	12,915
1980	13,048

RANSOM

1880	537
1890	5,393
1900	6,919
1910	10,345
1920	11,618
1930	10,983
1940	10,061
1950	8,876
1960	8,078
1970	7,102
1980	6,698

RENVILLE

1890	99
1910	7,840
1920	7,776
1930	7,263
1940	5,533
1950	5,405
1960	4,698
1970	3,828
1980	3,608

RICHLAND

1880	3,597
1890	10,751
1900	17,387
1910	19,659
1920	20,887
1930	21,008
1940	20,519
1950	19,865
1960	18,824
1970	18,089
1980	19,207

ROLETTE

1890	2,427
1900	7,795
1910	9,558
1920	10,061
1930	10,760
1940	12,583
1950	11,102
1960	10,641
1970	11,549
1980	12,177

SARGENT

1890	5,076
1900	6,039
1910	9,202
1920	9,655
1930	9,298
1940	8,693
1950	7,616
1960	6,856
1970	5,937
1980	5,512

SHERIDAN

1890	5
1910	8,103
1920	7,935
1930	7,373
1940	6,616
1950	5,253
1960	4,350
1970	3,232
1980	2,819

SIOUX

1920	3,308
1930	4,687
1940	4,419
1950	3,696
1960	3,662
1970	3,632
1980	3,620

SLOPE

1920	4,940
1930	4,150
1940	2,932
1950	2,315
1960	1,893
1970	1,484
1980	1,157

STARK

1890	2,304
1900	7,621
1910	12,504
1920	13,542
1930	15,340
1940	15,414
1950	16,137
1960	18,451
1970	19,613
1980	23,697

STEELE

1890	3,777
1900	5,888
1910	7,616

1920	7,401
1930	6,972
1940	6,193
1950	5,145
1960	4,719
1970	3,749
1980	3,106

STEVENS

1880	247
1890	16

STUTSMAN

1880	1,007
1890	5,266
1900	9,143
1910	18,189
1920	24,575
1930	26,100
1940	23,495
1950	24,158
1960	25,137
1970	23,550
1980	24,154

TOWNER

1890	1,450
1900	6,491
1910	8,963
1920	8,327
1930	8,393
1940	7,200
1950	6,360
1960	5,624
1970	4,645
1980	4,052

TRAILL

1880	4,123
1890	10,217
1900	13,107
1910	12,545
1920	12,210
1930	12,600
1940	12,300
1950	11,359
1960	10,583
1970	9,571
1980	9,624

WALLACE

1890	24

WALLETTE

1880	432

WALSH

1890	16,587
1900	20,288
1910	19,491
1920	19,078
1930	20,047
1940	20,747
1950	18,859
1960	17,997
1970	16,251
1980	15,371

WARD

1890	1,681
1900	7,961
1910	25,281
1920	28,811
1930	33,597
1940	31,981
1950	34,782
1960	47,072
1970	58,560
1980	58,392

WELLS

1890	1,212
1900	8,310
1910	11,814
1920	12,957
1930	13,285
1940	11,198
1950	10,417
1960	9,237
1970	7,847
1980	6,979

WILLIAMS[1]

1880	14
1890	109

WILLIAMS[2]

1900	1,530
1910	14,234
1920	17,980
1930	19,553
1940	16,315
1950	16,442
1960	22,051
1970	19,301
1980	22,237

NOTES

ALRED

Organized from part of Howard in 1883; part annexed to Billings in 1897, and part taken to form part of Williams prior to 1900. No population given for this county in 1890 census.

BOWMAN

Annexed to Billings in 1897.

BUFORD

Taken to form part of Williams prior to 1900.

CHURCH

Annexed to McHenry, McLean, and Pierce prior to 1900.

DESMET

Name changed from French in 1875; part taken to form part of Benson in 1883, and remainder to form Pierce in 1887. No population figures given for this county in 1870 or 1880 censuses.

FLANNERY

Taken to form part of Williams prior to 1900.

GARFIELD

Annexed to McLean in 1891.

HETTINGER

Annexed to Stark in 1897.

HOWARD

Taken to form Alred, Dunn, McKenzie, and Wallace in 1883.

MCKENZIE

Annexed to Billings in 1897.

MOUNTRAILLE

Annexed to Ward in 1891.

RENVILLE

Part taken to form part of Ward in 1885; annexed to Bottineau and Ward in 1897.

SHERIDAN

Part taken to form part of Church in 1887; annexed to McLean in 1891.

STEVENS

Parts taken to form McLean in 1883, and Garfield and part of Ward in 1885; parts annexed to McLean and Ward prior to 1900.

WALLACE

Annexed to Stark in 1897.

WALLETTE

Taken to form Buford and Flannery in 1883.

WELLS

Name changed from Gingras in 1881.

WILLIAMS[1]

Annexed to Mercer and Stark prior to 1900.

WILLIAMS[2]

Organized from Buford, Flannery and part of Alred prior to 1900.

BISMARCK

1880	1,758
1890	2,186
1900	3,319
1910	5,443
1920	7,122
1930	11,090
1940	15,496
1950	18,460
1960	27,670
1970	34,703
1980	44,485

DICKINSON

1890	987
1900	2,076
1910	3,678
1920	4,122
1930	5,025
1940	5,839
1950	7,469
1960	9,971
1970	12,405
1980	15,924

FARGO

1880	2,693
1890	5,664
1900	9,589
1910	14,331
1920	21,961
1930	28,619
1940	32,580
1950	38,256
1960	46,662
1970	53,365
1980	61,383

GRAND FORKS

1880	1,705
1890	4,979
1900	7,652
1910	12,478
1920	14,010
1930	17,112
1940	20,228
1950	26,836
1960	34,451
1970	39,008
1980	43,765

JAMESTOWN

1880	393
1890	2,296
1900	2,853
1910	4,358
1920	6,627
1930	8,187
1940	8,790
1950	10,697
1960	15,163
1970	15,385
1980	16,280

MANDAN

1880	239
1890	1,328
1900	1,673
1910	3,873
1920	4,336
1930	5,037
1940	5,685
1950	7,298
1960	10,525
1970	11,093
1980	15,513

MINOT

1890	575
1900	1,277
1910	6,188
1920	10,476
1930	16,099
1940	16,577
1950	22,032
1960	30,604
1970	32,290
1980	32,843

WEST FARGO

1940	117
1950	159
1960	3,328
1970	5,161
1980	10,099

WILLISTON

1890	295
1900	763
1910	3,124
1920	4,178
1930	5,106
1940	5,790
1950	7,378
1960	11,866
1970	11,280
1980	13,336

CORRECTION NOTE

The official 1980 census counts of total population shown in this report supersede counts issued previously. Corrections to the figures were made after the counts were provided to the State for redistricting purposes and released in Advance Report PHC80-V for this State.

Shown below are corrections to the 1980 census counts of the total population made after the tabulations for this report were completed. Any additional corrections made after this report is printed are available by writing to Data User Services Division, Customer Service (Corrections), Bureau of the Census, Washington, D.C. 20233.

The 1980 figures shown in this publication are subject to change pending the outcome of the various lawsuits dealing with the census counts.

	1980 population	
	As shown in the tables	Corrected
Bowman County:		
Adelaide township	68	48
Buena Vista township	29	42
Fischbein township	56	43
Grainbelt township	49	61
Rhame township	26	46
Talbot township	120	108

County Subdivisions	1980	1970
The State	652 717	'617 792
Adams County[1]	3 584	3 832
Beisigl township	37	44
Bucyrus city	32	42
Bucyrus township	49	60
Cedar township	30	57
Central Adams (unorg.)[1]	91	56
Chandler township	23	37
Clermont township	38	50
Darling Springs township	42	66
Duck Creek township	32	55
East Adams (unorg.)[1]	186	...
Gilstrap township	28	44
Haynes city	58	53
Hettinger city[1]	1 739	1 655
Hettinger township[1]	192	168
Holden township	43	55
Lemmon (unorg.)[1]	47	87
Lightning Creek township	27	33
Maine township	34	44
North Lemmon township	109	146
Orange township	48	53
Reeder city	355	306
Reeder township	63	90
Scott township	139	142
South Fork township	14	36
Taylor Butte township	41	40
Whetstone township	41	49
Wolf Butte township	46	60
Barnes County[2]	13 960	14 669
Alta township	116	163
Anderson township	70	107
Ashtabula township	100	130
Baldwin township	56	66
Binghampton township	118	145
Brimer township	82	68
Cuba township	93	107
Dazey city	143	128
Dazey township	76	90
Eckelson township	146	160
Edna township	100	104
Ellsbury township	77	90
Fingal city	151	166
Getchell township	75	81
Grand Prairie township	53	78
Green township	113	143
Greenland township	92	133
Hemen township	64	76
Hobart township	197	172
Kathryn city	95	109
Lake Town township	78	98
Leal city	45	41
Litchville city	251	294
Mansfield township	43	72
Marsh township	209	154
Meadow Lake township	97	115
Minnie Lake township	84	86
Nelson township	87	94
Noltimier township	117	102
Nome city	67	103
Norma township	79	120
Oakhill township	119	127
Oriska city[2]	125	128
Oriska township[2]	128	104
Pierce township	97	140
Pillsbury city	46	50
Potter township	97	83
Raritan township	138	148
Rogers city	68	96
Rogers township	70	99
Rosebud township	86	106
Sanborn city	237	255
Sibley city[2]	21	20
Sibley Trail township[2]	118	146
Skandia township	76	109
Spring Creek township	87	136
Springvale township	112	124
Stewart township	117	104
Svea township	78	84
Thordenskjold township	107	137
Tower City city (pt.)	-	2
Uxbridge township	113	118
Valley township[2]	565	...
Valley City city[2]	7 774	7 843
Weimer township	77	103
Wimbledon city	330	337
Benson County[3]	7 944	8 245
Albert township	83	109
Arne township	85	91
Aurora township	51	96
Beaver township	46	55
Brinsmade city	54	36
Broe township	89	117
Butte Valley township	143	192
East Fork township	51	76
Eldon township	74	86

County Subdivisions	1980	1970
Benson County—Con.		
Esmond city	337	416
Esmond township	114	143
Fort Totten (unorg.)[3]	1 141	...
Hesper township	110	111
Impark township	71	132
Iowa township	35	63
Irvine township	63	102
Isabel township	114	138
Knox city	69	104
Knox township	52	115
Lake Ibsen township	41	81
Lallie township	290	129
Lallie North (unorg.)[3]	21	...
Leeds city[3]	678	626
Leeds township[3]	101	85
Lohnes township	13	33
McClellan township	64	95
Maddock city	677	708
Minco township	51	45
Minnewaukan city[3]	461	496
Mission township	857	691
Normania township	74	91
North Viking township	95	103
Oberon city	150	151
Oberon township	137	153
Pleasant Lake township	104	127
Rich Valley township	93	109
Riggin township	92	111
Rock township	58	81
South Viking township	80	103
Twin Lake township	77	106
Twin Tree township	53	58
Warwick city	108	168
Warwick township	54	88
West Antelope township	60	75
West Bay township[3]	114	182
Wood Lake township	440	344
York city	69	102
York township	50	72
Billings County[4]	1 138	1 198
Medora city	94	129
North Billings (unorg.)[4]	717	...
South Billings (unorg.)[4]	327	...
Bottineau County[5]	9 239	9 496
Amity township	69	87
Antler city	101	135
Antler township	102	115
Bentinck township	85	62
Blaine township	37	61
Bottineau city[5]	2 829	2 760
Brander township	65	89
Cecil township	42	56
Chatfield township	74	90
Cordelia township	119	132
Cut Bank township	102	101
Dalen township	137	151
Eidsvold township	93	122
Elms township	74	90
Elysian township	89	82
Gardena city	66	84
Haram township	98	129
Hastings township[5]	121	96
Hoffman township	15	30
Homen township	124	141
Kane township	115	111
Kramer city	84	125
Landa city	62	61
Lansford city	294	296
Lansford township	92	77
Lewis township	50	49
Lordsburg township	53	66
Maxbass city[5]	141	174
Mount Rose township	63	81
Newborg township	74	66
Newburg city[5]	151	125
Oak Creek township	49	61
Oak Valley township	83	82
Omemee city	10	5
Ostby township	102	115
Overly city	25	28
Peabody township	33	35
Pickering township[5]	200	189
Renville township	50	67
Richburg township[5]	99	126
Roland township	433	274
Russell city	18	14
Scandia township	108	130
Scotia township	84	114
Sergius township	116	134
Sherman township	73	93
Souris city	122	151
Starbuck township	40	88
Stone Creek township	55	62
Tacoma township[5]	94	102
Wayne township	44	58
Wellington township	68	89

County Subdivisions	1980	1970
Bottineau County—Con.		
Westhope city[5]	741	705
Wheaton township	73	80
Whitby township	35	42
Whitteron township[5]	462	307
Willow City city	329	403
Willow Vale township	72	89
Bowman County[6]	4 229	3 901
Adelaide township	68	47
Amor township	35	57
Bowman city[6]	2 071	1 762
Bowman township[6]	265	113
Boyesen township	54	56
Buena Vista township	29	49
Fischbein township	56	73
Gascoyne city	23	34
Gascoyne township	30	42
Gem township	24	33
Goldfield township	56	83
Grainbelt township	49	58
Grand River township	32	34
Haley township	46	61
Hart township	42	28
Ladd township	25	29
Langberg township	26	39
Marion township	24	20
Minnehaha township	35	37
Nebo township	44	36
Rhame city	222	206
Rhame township[6]	26	59
Scranton city[6]	415	360
Scranton township[6]	107	95
Star township	44	60
Stillwater township	41	54
Sunny Slope township	13	28
Talbot township	120	82
West Bowman (unorg.)[6]	151	...
Whiting township	56	101
Burke County[7]	3 822	4 739
Battleview township	167	179
Bowbells city	587	584
Bowbells township	53	82
Carter township	31	53
Clayton township	49	64
Cleary township	53	60
Columbus city	325	465
Colville township	68	71
Dale township	59	108
Dimond township	40	20
Fay township	57	70
Flaxton city	182	286
Foothills township	58	91
Forthun township	27	39
Garness township	93	104
Harmonious township	45	78
Kandiyohi township	43	82
Keller township	27	40
Lakeview township	30	38
Larson city	21	35
Leaf Mountain township	61	80
Lignite city[7]	332	354
Lucy township	54	71
Minnesota township	43	69
North Burke (unorg.)[7]	8	...
North Star township	83	101
Portal city	238	251
Portal township	69	99
Powers Lake city	466	523
Richland township	58	89
Roseland township	31	35
Short Creek township	74	103
Soo township	50	84
Thorson township	51	56
Vale township[7]	37	69
Vanville township	55	50
Ward township	97	145
Burleigh County[8]	54 811	40 714
Apple Creek township[8]	843	270
Bismarck city[8]	44 485	34 703
Bismarck (unorg.)[8]	2 233	...
Boyd township	94	99
Canfield township	31	50
Christiania township	53	49
Clear Lake township	48	66
Crofte township	123	108
Cromwell township	43	35
Driscoll township	223	215
East Burleigh (unorg.)[8]	90	...
Ecklund township	124	142
Estherville township	63	73
Florence Lake township	41	51
Frances township	37	34
Ghylin township	54	75
Gibbs township[8]	770	302
Glenview township	160	116
Grass Lake township	65	99
Harriet township[8]	88	102

County Subdivisions	1980	1970
Burleigh County—Con.		
Hay Creek township[8]	1 658	836
Hazel Grove township	34	49
Lein township	32	48
Lincoln city[8]	656	...
Logan township	50	53
Long Lake township	144	174
Lyman (unorg.)[8]	21	...
McKenzie township	108	177
Menoken township	148	145
Missouri township	83	61
Morton township	54	48
Naughton township	110	65
Painted Woods township	115	81
Regan city	71	74
Rock Hill township	61	66
Schrunk township	34	46
Sibley Butte township	52	42
Steiber township	35	63
Sterling township	177	155
Taft township	48	50
Telfer township	94	74
Thelma township	33	45
Trygg township	57	85
West Burleigh (unorg.)[8]	628	...
Wild Rose township	54	61
Wilson township	62	75
Wilton city (pt.)	262	116
Wing city	220	223
Wing township	42	43
Cass County[9]	88 247	73 653
Addison township	103	113
Alice city	62	83
Amenia city[9]	93	80
Amenia township[9]	135	164
Argusville city	147	118
Arthur city	445	412
Arthur township	103	120
Ayr city[9]	42	48
Ayr township[9]	96	123
Barnes township[9]	490	1 221
Bell township	56	95
Berlin township	147	148
Briarwood city[9]	47	...
Buffalo city	226	241
Buffalo township	99	148
Casselton city[9]	1 661	1 485
Casselton township[9]	111	120
Clifton township	113	146
Cornell township	84	100
Davenport city	195	147
Davenport township	165	150
Dows township	93	108
Durbin township	124	128
Eldred township	124	129
Empire township	150	150
Enderlin city (pt.)[9]	11	...
Erie township	136	185
Everest township	122	142
Fargo city[9]	61 383	53 365
Fargo township	10	133
Frontier city[9]	160	...
Gardner city	94	96
Gardner township	114	146
Gill township	114	140
Grandin city (pt.)	210	187
Gunkel township	93	113
Harmony township	110	165
Harwood city[9]	326	...
Harwood township[9]	530	436
Highland township	130	123
Hill township	76	93
Horace city[9]	494	276
Howes township	98	106
Hunter city	369	362
Hunter township	117	153
Kindred city	568	495
Kinyon township	119	126
Lake township	62	78
Leonard city	289	221
Leonard township	142	124
Maple River township	155	184
Mapleton city	306	219
Mapleton township[9]	244	217
Noble township	107	129
Normanna township	331	278
North River city[9]	65	...
Page city	329	367
Page township	78	73
Pleasant township	398	326
Pontiac township[9]	140	145
Prairie Rose city[9]	76	...
Raymond township	255	199
Reed township[9]	848	655
Reile's Acres city[9]	191	...
Rich township	108	107
Riverside city[9]	465	104

County Subdivisions	1980	1970
Cass County—Con.		
Rochester township	76	84
Rush River township	141	177
Stanley township[9]	1 706	857
Tower township	69	121
Tower City city (pt.)	293	287
Walburg township	206	281
Warren township	158	160
Watson township	138	168
West Fargo city[9]	10 099	5 161
Wheatland township	183	225
Wiser township	94	97
Cavalier County[10]	7 636	8 213
Alma township	70	69
Alsen city	169	201
Banner township	70	114
Billings township	122	81
Bruce township	60	114
Byron township	74	93
Calio city	60	75
Calvin city	61	78
Cypress township	96	90
Dresden township	93	174
Easby township	96	88
East Alma township	70	62
Elgin township[10]	413	278
Fremont township	119	147
Glenila township	61	76
Gordon township	67	100
Grey township	82	98
Hannah city	90	145
Harvey township	85	81
Hay township	89	116
Henderson township[10]	109	86
Hope township	92	107
Hove Mobile Park city[10]	3	...
Huron township	79	97
Langdon city[10]	2 335	2 182
Langdon township	62	67
Linden township	65	92
Loam township	97	141
Loma city	39	'85
Manilla township	183	67
Milton city	195	198
Minto township	68	71
Montrose township	121	121
Moscow township	84	104
Mount Carmel township	164	236
Munich city[10]	300	249
Nekoma city	102	84
Nekoma township	90	80
North Loma township	33	74
North Olga township	100	156
Osford township	89	131
Osnabrock city	222	255
Osnabrock township[10]	87	115
Perry township	105	144
Sarles city (pt.)	102	138
Seivert township	53	74
South Dresden township	107	120
South Olga township	99	115
Storlie township	39	55
Trier township	119	124
Wales city	74	116
Waterloo township	65	129
West Hope township	107	120
Dickey County[11]	7 207	6 976
Ada township	101	116
Albertha township	42	53
Albion township	61	83
Bear Creek township[11]	208	234
Clement township	172	191
Divide township	108	153
Elden township	108	110
Ellendale city[11]	1 967	1 517
Ellendale township[11]	163	150
Elm township	88	97
Forbes city	84	88
Fullerton city	107	110
German township	46	89
Grand Valley township	55	99
Hamburg township	59	87
Hudson township	108	106
James River Valley township	90	87
Kent township	46	60
Kentner township	156	157
Keystone township	69	69
Lorraine township	76	94
Lovell township	66	80
Ludden city	47	44
Maple township	90	126
Merricourt city	17	22
Monango city	59	112
Northwest township	52	70
Oakes city[11]	2 112	1 742
Port Emma township	96	114

County Subdivisions	1980	1970
Dickey County—Con.		
Porter township	78	82
Potsdam township	55	76
Riverdale township	116	90
Spring Valley township	49	81
Valley township	72	81
Van Meter township	121	146
Whitestone township	46	75
Wright township	102	128
Yorktown township	69	100
Young township	46	57
Divide County[12]	3 494	4 564
Alexandria township	35	65
Ambrose city	60	109
Ambrose township	57	80
Blooming Prairie township	77	58
Blooming Valley township	55	63
Border township	55	78
Burg township	57	60
Clinton township	26	46
Coalfield township	65	98
Crosby city[12]	1 469	1 545
Daneville township	76	96
De Witt township	48	55
Elkhorn township	57	360
Fertile Valley township	43	43
Fillmore township[12]	58	68
Fortuna city	98	216
Frazier township	28	39
Frederick township	40	80
Garnet township	42	45
Gooseneck township	65	78
Hawkeye township	43	74
Hayland township	48	55
Lincoln Valley township	31	56
Long Creek township	72	69
Mentor township	43	53
Noonan city	283	403
Palmer township	32	34
Plumer township	15	30
Sioux Trail township	60	56
Smoky Butte township	44	80
Stoneview township	38	49
Troy township	81	97
Twin Butte township	38	39
Upland township	39	57
Westby township	88	93
Writing Rock township	28	37
Dunn County[13]	4 627	4 895
Dodge city	199	121
Dunn Center city[13]	170	107
Halliday city	355	413
Halliday (unorg.)[13]	1 010	...
Killdeer city[13]	790	615
Killdeer (unorg.)[13]	1 206	...
South Dunn (unorg.)[13]	897	...
Eddy County[14]	3 554	4 103
Bush township	80	81
Cherry Lake township	56	79
Columbia township	70	94
Colvin township	96	109
Eddy township	61	63
Freeborn township	142	162
Gates township[14]	103	124
Grandfield township	62	78
Hillsdale township	63	79
Lake Washington township	54	50
Munster township	88	143
New Rockford city[14]	1 791	1 969
New Rockford township[14]	141	136
Paradise township	71	93
Pleasant Prairie township	66	80
Rosefield township	58	97
Sheldon township	54	74
Sheyenne city[14]	307	362
Superior township	119	138
Tiffany township	72	92
Emmons County[15]	5 877	7 200
Braddock city	86	106
Buchanan Valley township	78	72
Campbell township	119	143
Danbury township	80	117
Hague city	127	146
Harding township	80	153
Hazelton city	266	374
Hazelton township	126	151
Linton city[15]	1 561	1 695
McCulley township	96	99
Northeast Emmons (unorg.)[15]	845	...
Prairie View township	44	91
South Emmons (unorg.)[15]	989	...
Strasburg city	623	642
Tell township	72	95
West Emmons (unorg.)[15]	616	...
Wood township	69	83

County Subdivisions	1980	1970
Foster County[16]	4 611	4 832
Birtsell township	131	164
Bordulac township	120	162
Bucephalia township	74	90
Carrington city[16]	2 641	2 491
Carrington township[16]	186	150
Eastman township	54	62
Estabrook township	89	97
Florance township	82	92
Glenfield city[16]	164	127
Glenfield township[16]	114	141
Haven township	64	91
Larrabee township	166	171
Longview township	63	108
McHenry city	113	152
McHenry township	85	158
McKinnon township	70	104
Melville township	61	89
Nordmore township	91	109
Rolling Prairie township	53	81
Rose Hill township	118	117
Wyard township	72	76
Golden Valley County[17]	2 391	2 611
Beach city[17]	1 381	1 408
Beach township[17]	218	273
Bullion township	63	53
Delhi township	33	42
East Golden Valley (unorg.)[17]	13	...
Elk Creek township	5	23
Elmwood township	16	21
Garner township	27	58
Golva city	101	104
Henry township	38	34
Lone Tree township	209	207
North Golden Valley (unorg.)[17]	55	...
Pearl township	5	14
Saddle Butte township	61	61
Sentinel township	62	107
Sentinel Butte city	86	125
South Golden Valley (unorg.)[17]	18	...
Grand Forks County[18]	66 100	61 102
Agnes township	121	144
Allendale township	261	187
Americus township	214	179
Arvilla township[18]	350	143
Avon township	128	158
Bentru township	65	66
Blooming township	786	180
Grand Forks AFB (CDP) (pt.)	527	–
Brenna township[18]	530	189
Chester township	191	215
Elkmount township	67	79
Elm Grove township	168	156
Emerado city[18]	596	515
Fairfield township	97	115
Falconer township[18]	283	159
Ferry township[18]	366	222
Gilby city[18]	283	268
Gilby township[18]	127	139
Grace township	127	105
Grand Forks city[18]	43 765	39 008
Grand Forks township[18]	789	1 083
Hegton township	182	269
Inkster city	135	198
Inkster township	127	127
Johnstown township	113	158
Lakeville township	87	88
Larimore city[18]	1 524	1 469
Larimore township[18]	202	175
Levant township	83	83
Lind township	119	125
Logan Center township	77	97
Loretta township	66	69
Manvel city[18]	308	265
Mekinock township	9 011	10 678
Grand Forks AFB (CDP) (pt.)	8 863	10 474
Michigan city[18]	198	215
Moraine township	126	96
Niagara city	76	115
Niagara township	107	115
Northwood city[18]	1 240	1 189
Northwood township[18]	204	165
Oakville township[18]	182	114
Pleasant View township	154	135
Plymouth township	121	138
Reynolds city (pt.)	115	111
Rye township	271	161
Strabane township	153	183
Thompson city[18]	785	291
Turtle River township	226	189
Union township	206	221
Walle township[18]	323	262
Washington township	171	156
Wheatfield township	94	135

County Subdivisions	1980	1970
Grant County[19]	4 274	5 009
Buckskin township	43	56
Carson city	469	466
Central Grant (unorg.)[19]	75	...
East Grant (unorg.)[19]	888	...
Elgin city[19]	930	839
Elm township	86	107
Fisher township	30	48
Freda township	23	36
Howe township	29	27
Lark township	64	93
Leipzig township	82	93
Leith city	59	92
Minnie township[19]	104	108
New Leipzig city[19]	352	354
Otter Creek township	60	57
Pretty Rock township	41	47
Raleigh township	113	150
Rock township	43	58
Schultz township	62	65
West Grant (unorg.)[19]	688	...
Winona township	33	37
Griggs County[20]	3 714	4 184
Addie township	85	88
Ball Hill township	119	113
Bartley township	48	75
Binford city	293	242
Broadview township	68	83
Bryan township	63	91
Clearfield township	94	94
Cooperstown city[20]	1 308	1 485
Cooperstown township[20]	104	109
Dover township	75	112
Greenfield township	137	181
Hannaford city	201	244
Helena township	71	152
Kingsley township	100	28
Lenora township	101	114
Mabel township	126	169
Pilot Mound township	88	107
Romness township	73	96
Rosendal township	68	68
Sverdrup township	112	139
Tyrol township	179	173
Washburn township	90	98
Willow township	111	123
Hettinger County[21]	4 275	5 075
Acme township	59	103
Alden township	38	50
Ashby township	21	30
Baer township	38	55
Berry township	37	74
Black Butte township	71	79
Brittian township	35	48
Campbell township	63	108
Cannon Ball township	95	145
Castle Rock township[21]	117	200
Chilton township	44	76
Clark township	50	67
Farina township	60	76
Havelock township	47	62
Highland township	51	50
Indian Creek township	38	41
Kennedy township	84	97
Kern township	30	34
Kunze township	93	146
Madison township	54	73
Merrill township	25	39
Mott city[21]	1 315	1 368
Mott township[21]	101	67
New England city	825	906
New England township	111	110
Odessa township	40	61
Regent city	297	344
Rifle township	68	73
St. Croix township	56	96
Solon township	44	57
Steiner township	70	89
Strehlow township	49	46
Tepee Butte township	53	50
Wagendorf township	50	74
Walker township	46	81
Kidder County[22]	3 833	4 362
Allen township	78	105
Atwood township	46	56
Baker township	87	95
Buckeye township	40	50
Bunker township	61	83
Chestina township	47	68
Clear Lake township	74	77
Crown Hill township	33	47
Crystal Springs township	48	59
Dawson city	144	131
Excelsior township	44	58
Frettim township	61	72

County Subdivisions	1980	1970
Kidder County—Con.		
Graf township	48	70
Haynes township	39	50
Kickapoo township	39	41
Lake Williams township	73	74
Manning township	98	131
Merkel township	84	101
Northwest township	35	48
Peace township	63	84
Petersville township	79	84
Pettibone city	127	173
Pettibone township	88	86
Pleasant Hill township	76	77
Quinby township	29	28
Rexine township	15	42
Robinson city[22]	129	125
Robinson township[22]	59	91
Sibley township	48	61
South Kidder (unorg.)[22]	46	...
Steele city[22]	796	696
Stewart township	37	45
Tanner township	55	57
Tappen city[22]	271	294
Tappen township[22]	83	116
Tuttle city	202	216
Tuttle township	104	118
Valley township	53	70
Vernon township	62	57
Wallace township	38	37
Weiser township	48	84
Westford township	45	73
Williams township	30	64
Woodlawn township[22]	71	108
La Moure County[23]	6 473	7 117
Adrian township	160	158
Badger township	86	101
Berlin city[23]	57	76
Black Loam township	81	95
Bluebird township	115	118
Dean township	248	203
Dickey city	74	118
Edgeley city[23]	843	888
Gladstone township	110	143
Glen township	100	163
Glenmore township	106	119
Golden Glen township[23]	162	183
Grand Rapids township	117	163
Grandview township	92	105
Greenville township	112	148
Henrietta township[23]	100	140
Jud city	118	110
Kennison township	187	210
Kulm city[23]	570	625
La Moure city	1 077	951
Litchville township	90	144
Marion city	214	215
Mikkelson township	69	80
Nora township	107	142
Norden township[23]	87	106
Ovid township	112	110
Pearl Lake township	87	105
Pomona View township	53	66
Prairie township	114	142
Raney township	60	85
Ray township	77	107
Roscoe township	118	117
Russell township	100	111
Ryan township	114	88
Saratoga township	81	93
Sheridan township	60	61
Swede township	98	127
Verona city	126	140
Wano township	65	106
Willowbank township	126	155
Logan County[24]	3 493	4 245
Bryant township[24]	90	211
Dixon township	37	72
East Logan (unorg.)[24]	719	...
Finn township[24]	53	74
Fredonia city	82	100
Gackle city[24]	456	470
Glendale township	84	99
Gutschmidt township	59	97
Haag township	55	97
Janke township	64	92
Kroeber township	57	72
Lehr city (pt.)[24]	57	72
Napoleon city[24]	1 103	1 036
Red Lake township	88	88
Sealy township	66	77
Starkey township	69	100
West Logan (unorg.)[24]	354	...
McHenry County[25]	7 858	8 977
Anamoose city	355	401
Anamoose township	109	159
Balfour city	51	93

County Subdivisions	1980	1970
McHenry County—Con.		
Balfour township	99	115
Bantry city	28	40
Bantry township	64	62
Bergen city	24	24
Berwick city	22	33
Berwick township	100	139
Bjornson township	52	104
Brown township	84	103
Cottonwood Lake township	35	39
Deep River township	79	76
Deering city[25]	85	75
Deering township[25]	135	97
Denbigh township	77	110
Drake city	479	636
East McHenry (unorg.)[25]	179	...
Egg Creek township	75	68
Falsen township	79	86
Gilmore township	15	69
Granville city	281	282
Granville township	114	133
Grilley township	84	93
Hendrickson township	81	72
Karlsruhe city	164	172
Karlsruhe township	71	115
Kief city	36	46
Kottke Valley township	61	69
Lake George township	95	117
Lake Hester township	119	141
Land township	51	89
Layton township	55	62
Lebanon township	110	111
Little Deep township	60	81
Meadow township	76	113
Mouse River township	35	36
Newport township[25]	149	182
Normal township	101	81
Northeast McHenry (unorg.)[25]	135	...
North Prairie township	112	127
Norwich township	183	142
Odin township	78	111
Olivia township	83	90
Pratt township	76	75
Riga township	71	95
Rose Hill township[25]	59	...
Round Lake township	70	99
Saline township	35	45
Schiller township	104	131
Spring Grove township	68	89
Strege township	87	96
Towner city[25]	867	870
Upham city	227	272
Velva city	1 101	1 241
Velva township	194	124
Villard township	65	100
Voltaire city	65	54
Voltaire township	53	15
Wagar township	77	81
Willow Creek township	79	101
McIntosh County[26]	4 800	5 545
Ashley city	1 192	1 236
East McIntosh (unorg.)[26]	573	...
Lehr city (pt.)[26]	197	215
Northwest McIntosh (unorg.)[26]	654	...
Roloff township	36	71
Southwest McIntosh (unorg.)[26]	510	...
Venturia city	40	77
Wishek city[26]	1 345	1 275
Zeeland city[26]	253	313
McKenzie County[27]	7 132	6 127
Alex city	51	49
Alexander city	358	208
Antelope Creek township	21	28
Arnegard city	193	141
Arnegard township	89	84
Bear Den township	61	93
Blue Butte township	98	151
Central McKenzie (unorg.)[27]	239	...
Charbon township	60	68
East McKenzie (unorg.)[27]	927	...
Elk township	26	38
Elm Tree township	71	77
Grail township	64	82
Hawkeye township[27]	67	103
Ideal township[27]	131	84
Keene township	42	94
Northfork township	65	30
North McKenzie (unorg.)[27]	225	...
Patent Gate township	14	23
Pershing (unorg.)[27]	75	...
Poe township	29	44
Randolph township	23	26
Rawson city	12	10
Red Wing township	51	35
Rhoades township	183	192
Riverview township	20	15
Schafer township[27]	223	124

County Subdivisions	1980	1970
McKenzie County—Con.		
Sioux township	174	164
Southwest McKenzie (unorg.)[27]	566	...
Timber Creek (unorg.)[27]	32	...
Twin Valley township	105	110
Watford City city[27]	2 119	1 768
Wilbur township	31	19
Yellowstone township	687	585
McLean County[28]	12 383	11 251
Amundsville township	91	110
Andrews township	76	92
Aurena township	57	82
Benedict city	68	72
Blackwater township	89	135
Blue Hill township	49	74
Butte city	157	193
Butte township	23	60
Byersville township	41	97
Coleharbor city	150	112
Cremerville township	59	88
Deepwater township	61	98
Dogden township	81	57
Douglas township	58	82
East McLean (unorg.)[28]	152	...
Economy township[28]	117	87
Garrison city[28]	1 830	1 614
Gate township	59	60
Greatstone township	62	99
Horseshoe Valley township	60	63
Lake Williams township[28]	112	89
Longfellow township	66	70
Loquemont township	76	107
McGinnis township	93	112
Malcolm township	98	123
Max city[28]	317	301
Medicine Hill township	105	97
Mercer city	134	132
Mercer township	50	66
North Central McLean (unorg.)[28]	369	...
Otis township	101	87
Poplar township	92	95
Roseglen township	77	110
Rosemont township	51	87
Ruso city	12	15
St. Mary township	116	92
Snake Creek township	58	105
Snow township	78	103
South McLean (unorg.)[28]	805	...
Turtle Lake city[28]	802	712
Turtle Lake township	75	64
Underwood city[28]	1 329	781
Underwood (unorg.)[28]	722	...
Victoria township	33	74
Washburn city[28]	1 767	804
West McLean (unorg.)[28]	752	...
Wilton city (pt.)[28]	688	579
Wise township	65	75
Mercer County[29]	9 404	6 175
Beulah city[29]	2 908	1 344
East Mercer (unorg.)[29]	1 220	...
Golden Valley city	287	235
Hazen city[29]	2 365	1 240
Pick City city	182	119
Stanton city	623	517
West Mercer (unorg.)[29]	1 308	...
Zap city[29]	511	271
Morton County[30]	25 177	20 310
Almont city	146	109
Curlew township[30]	96	90
East Morton (unorg.)[30]	2 838	...
Engelter township[30]	114	138
Flasher city	410	467
Glen Ullin city[30]	1 125	1 070
Hebron city	1 078	1 103
Mandan city[30]	15 513	11 093
Mandan (unorg.)[30]	1 408	...
New Salem city[30]	1 081	943
West Morton (unorg.)[30]	1 368	...
Mountrail County[31]	7 679	8 437
Alger township	63	60
Austin township	44	52
Banner township	41	69
Bicker township	64	58
Big Bend township	42	59
Brookbank township	40	55
Burke township	51	40
Clearwater township	53	39
Cottonwood township	54	64
Crane Creek township	62	67
Crowfoot township	38	67
Debing township	67	75
Egan township[31]	69	59
Fertile township	71	95
Howie township	38	62
Idaho township[31]	150	119
James Hill township	37	55

County Subdivisions	1980	1970
Mountrail County—Con.		
Kickapoo township	44	55
Knife River township	33	34
Liberty township	11	21
Lostwood township	64	51
Lowland township	75	113
McAlmond township	56	53
McGahan township	67	92
Manitou township	70	71
Model township	81	121
Mountrail township	64	76
Myrtle township	35	33
New Town city[31]	1 335	1 428
Oakland township	53	69
Osborn township[31]	281	250
Osloe township	62	66
Palermo city	97	146
Palermo township	30	45
Parshall city	1 059	1 246
Parshall township	73	78
Plaza city	222	291
Plaza township	66	65
Powers township	46	63
Powers Lake township	87	88
Purcell township	45	49
Rat Lake township	39	31
Redmond township	25	41
Ross city	104	125
Ross township	39	47
Shell township	46	59
Sidonia township	47	66
Sikes township	60	89
Sorkness township	36	64
Southwest Mountrail (unorg.)[31]	56	...
Spring Coulee township	86	96
Stanley city[31]	1 631	1 581
Stave township	54	57
Van Hook township	57	58
Wayzetta township	42	56
West Mountrail (unorg.)[31]	174	...
White Earth city	98	128
White Earth township	45	55
Nelson County[32]	5 233	5 807
Adler township	78	104
Aneta city	341	376
Bergen township	94	55
Central township	83	103
Clara township	75	96
Dahlen township	131	176
Dayton township	124	108
Dodds township	83	91
Enterprise township	65	81
Field township	69	105
Forde township	80	138
Hamlin township	97	118
Illinois township	63	64
Lakota city	963	964
Lakota township	65	96
Lee township	120	158
Leval township	65	76
McVille city	626	583
Melvin township	60	66
Michigan township	110	156
Michigan City city[32]	502	478
Nash township	75	87
Nesheim township	80	104
Ora township	79	82
Osago township	59	83
Pekin city	101	120
Petersburg city	230	266
Petersburg township	68	90
Rubin township	89	107
Rugh township	51	77
Sarnia township	151	184
Tolna city	241	247
Wamduska township	45	66
Williams township	70	102
Oliver County[33]	2 495	2 322
Center city[33]	900	619
East Oliver (unorg.)[33]	964	...
West Oliver (unorg.)[33]	631	...
Pembina County[34]	10 399	10 728
Advance township	222	215
Akra township	243	217
Bathgate city	67	133
Bathgate township	118	98
Beaulieu township	180	143
Canton City city[34]	68	81
Carlisle township	180	224
Cavalier city[34]	1 505	1 381
Cavalier township[34]	731	524
Crystal city	256	272
Crystal township	101	119
Drayton city[34]	1 082	1 095
Drayton township[34]	62	80

County Subdivisions	1980	1970
Pembina County—Con.		
Elora township	79	132
Felson township	118	208
Gardar township	158	211
Hamilton city	109	110
Hamilton township	100	94
Joliette township	145	135
La Moure township	156	137
Lincoln township	148	150
Lodema township	136	158
Midland township	162	172
Mountain city	156	146
Neche city	471	451
Neche township	87	136
Park township	86	103
Pembina city	673	741
Pembina township	145	176
St. Joseph township	139	188
St. Thomas city	528	508
St. Thomas township	203	266
Thingvalla township	195	165
Walhalla city[34]	1 429	1 471
Walhalla township[34]	161	288
Pierce County[35]	6 166	6 323
Alexander township	84	112
Antelope Lake township	58	80
Balta city	139	133
Balta township	89	120
Barton city	38	34
Central Pierce (unorg.)[35]	43	...
Elling township	102	140
Elverum township	100	151
Hagel township	156	210
Jefferson township	85	114
Meyer township	101	155
Ness township	105	105
North Pierce (unorg.)[35]	896	...
Reno Valley township	74	81
Rugby city[35]	3 335	2 889
Rush Lake township	63	93
South Pierce (unorg.)[35]	189	...
Torgerson township[35]	100	93
Truman township	111	116
Tuscarora township	113	128
White township	109	151
Wolford city	76	81
Ramsey County[36]	13 048	12 915
Bartlett township[36]	138	136
Brocket city	74	95
Cato township	51	78
Chain Lakes township	37	49
Churchs Ferry city	139	139
Coulee township	141	153
Crary city	139	150
Creel township[36]	1 622	1 352
De Groat township	50	52
Devils Lake city[36]	7 442	7 078
Dry Lake township	62	74
Edmore city[36]	416	398
Fancher township[36]	68	120
Freshwater township	85	96
Grand Harbor township	274	233
Hammer township[36]	74	91
Hampden city[36]	126	114
Harding township	71	84
Highland Center township	89	107
Klingstrup township	96	88
Lawton city	101	123
Lawton township	75	88
Lillehoff township	81	119
Minnewaukan township	141	137
Morris township	55	57
Newbre township	44	80
Newland township	56	76
Nixon township	28	56
Noonan township	59	89
Northfield township[36]	93	97
Odessa township	76	102
Ontario township	74	101
Overland township	39	53
Pelican township	74	66
Prospect township	72	96
Royal township	61	98
South Minnewaukan township	142	127
Starkweather city[36]	210	193
Stevens township	94	129
Sullivan township	64	74
Triumph township	59	76
Webster township	156	172
Ransom County[37]	6 698	7 102
Aliceton township	162	145
Alleghany township	87	100
Bale township	130	137
Big Bend township	156	222
Casey township	85	140
Coburn township	94	96

County Subdivisions	1980	1970
Ransom County—Con.		
Elliott city	44	50
Elliott township	119	128
Enderlin city (pt.)[37]	1 140	1 343
Fort Ransom city[37]	99	...
Fort Ransom township[37]	103	225
Greene township	192	166
Hanson township	123	177
Island Park township[37]	400	246
Isley township	69	96
Liberty township[37]	133	187
Lisbon city[37]	2 283	2 090
Moore township	133	157
Northland township	96	119
Owego township	30	49
Preston township	120	134
Rosemeade township	65	96
Sandoun township	94	93
Scoville township	33	21
Sheldon city	173	192
Shenford township	183	231
Springer township	93	143
Sydna township	88	152
Tuller township	171	167
Renville County[38]	3 608	3 828
Brandon township[38]	97	135
Callahan township	52	69
Clay township	54	67
Colquhoun township	94	139
Eden Valley township	70	89
Ensign township[38]	74	77
Fairbanks township	77	91
Glenburn city[38]	454	381
Grano city	6	4
Grassland township	62	80
Grover township	51	85
Hamerly township	56	59
Hamlet township	78	45
Hurley township	61	35
Ivanhoe township	76	103
Lockwood township	39	34
Loraine city	21	33
McKinney township	85	100
Mohall city[38]	1 049	950
Muskego township	92	98
Plain township	74	81
Prescott township	39	49
Prosperity township	72	88
Rockford township	108	103
Roosevelt township	62	65
Sherwood city	294	369
Stafford township	72	74
Tolley city	103	163
Van Buren township	72	83
White Ash township	64	79
Richland County[39]	19 207	18 089
Abercrombie city	260	262
Abercrombie township	306	384
Antelope township	148	182
Barney city	70	81
Barney township	147	174
Barrie township	133	125
Belford township	172	221
Brandenburg township	160	206
Brightwood township[39]	178	172
Center township[39]	337	332
Christine city[39]	147	...
Colfax city	101	70
Colfax township	219	235
Danton township	161	223
Devillo township	142	170
Dexter township	132	152
Duerr township	210	244
Dwight city	72	93
Dwight township[39]	240	249
Eagle township[39]	234	336
Elma township	125	202
Fairmount city	480	412
Fairmount township	177	172
Freeman township	65	167
Garborg township	123	115
Grant township[39]	202	180
Great Bend city	113	86
Greendale township	142	197
Hankinson city[39]	1 158	1 125
Helendale township	86	183
Homestead township	118	131
Ibsen township	167	182
La Mars township	118	147
Liberty Grove township	146	181
Lidgerwood city[39]	971	1 000
Mantador city	76	95
Mooreton city[39]	216	158
Mooreton township[39]	146	169
Moran township	117	144
Nansen township	118	121
Sheyenne township	62	117

County Subdivisions

County Subdivisions	1980	1970
Richland County—Con.		
Summit township	268	326
Viking township	88	116
Wahpeton city[39]	9 064	7 076
Walcott city	186	'166
Walcott township	279	250
Waldo township	112	162
West End township	54	150
Wyndmere city	550	516
Wyndmere township	111	132
Rolette County[40]	12 177	11 549
Currie township	124	163
Dunseith city	625	811
East Rolette (unorg.)[40]	586	...
Fairview township	57	102
Kohlmeier township	67	74
Leonard township	213	200
Maryville township	62	105
Mylo city	31	51
North Rolette (unorg.)[40]	2 871	...
Rolette city	667	579
Rolla city[40]	1 538	1 458
Russell township	77	107
St. John city[40]	401	367
Shell Valley township	269	136
South Rolette (unorg.)[40]	235	...
South Valley township	43	70
Turtle Mountains (unorg.)[40]	4 311	...
Belcourt (CDP)	1 803	...
Sargent County[41]	5 512	5 937
Bowen township	146	181
Brampton township	132	146
Cayuga city	75	116
Cogswell city	227	203
Denver township	111	135
Dunbar township	142	176
Forman city[41]	629	596
Forman township[41]	86	129
Gwinner city[41]	725	623
Hall township	193	234
Harlem township	61	87
Havana city[41]	148	156
Herman township	153	164
Jackson township	65	110
Kingston township	194	232
Marboe township	81	121
Milnor city	716	645
Milnor township	113	129
Ransom township	106	128
Rutland city	250	225
Rutland township	99	105
Sargent township	71	94
Shuman township	113	132
Southwest township	36	45
Taylor township	63	79
Tewaukon township	91	124
Verner township	87	89
Vivian township	198	237
Weber township[41]	137	151
Whitestone Hill township[41]	153	165
Willey township	111	180
Sheridan County[42]	2 819	3 232
Berlin township	84	106
Boone township	57	75
Central Sheridan (unorg.)[42]	357	...
Denhoff township	89	114
Edgemont township	38	35
Fairview township	34	51
Goodrich city	288	300
Goodrich township	91	122
Highland township[42]	59	...
Holmes township	52	64
Lincoln Dale township	54	79
McClusky city	658	664
McClusky township	101	96
Martin city	114	120
Martin township	94	117
Mauch township[42]	45	...
New Germantown township	87	97
North Sheridan (unorg.)[42]	215	...
Pickard township	56	60
South Sheridan (unorg.)[42]	165	...
Strassburg township	81	91
Sioux County[43]	3 620	3 632
Fort Yates city[43]	771	1 153
Fort Yates (unorg.)[43]	943	...
Menz township	70	55
North Sioux (unorg.)[43]	971	...
Selfridge city	273	346
Solen city	138	180
Southwest Sioux (unorg.)[43]	454	...
Slope County[44]	1 157	1 484
Amidon city	43	54
Bucklin township	11	19
Carroll township	34	43

County Subdivisions	1980	1970
Slope County—Con.		
Cash township	34	40
Cedar Creek township	38	55
Chalky Butte (unorg.)[44]	15	22
Connor township	61	63
Crawford township	28	43
Deep Creek (unorg.)[44]	50	...
Dovre township	18	28
E-Six (unorg.)[44]	120	...
Harper township	5	12
Hughes township	17	10
Hume township	44	64
Marmarth city	190	247
Mineral Springs township	36	42
Moord township	27	52
Mound township	25	41
Northwest Slope (unorg.)[44]	58	...
Peaceful Valley township	36	48
Rainy Butte township	63	78
Richland Center township	11	13
Sand Creek township	47	63
Sheets township	32	61
Slope Center township	11	24
Sunshine township	4	8
West Slope (unorg.)[44]	31	...
White Lake township	36	54
Woodberry township	32	37
Stark County[45]	23 697	19 613
Belfield city[45]	1 274	1 130
Dickinson city[45]	15 924	12 405
Dickinson North (unorg.)[45]	2 432	...
Dickinson South (unorg.)[45]	669	...
East Stark (unorg.)[45]	1 106	...
Gladstone city	317	222
Richardton city[45]	699	799
South Heart city[45]	294	132
Taylor city	239	162
West Stark (unorg.)[45]	743	...
Steele County	3 106	3 749
Beaver Creek township	112	147
Broadlawn township	73	98
Carpenter township	72	109
Colgate township	112	111
Easton township	118	114
Edendale township	94	97
Enger township	105	132
Finley city	718	809
Finley township	81	79
Franklin township	79	276
Golden Lake township	87	96
Greenview township	76	83
Hope city	406	364
Hugo township	71	96
Luverne city	65	84
Melrose township	91	111
Newburgh township	103	116
Primrose township	114	134
Riverside township	65	102
Sharon city	166	201
Sharon township	62	77
Sherbrooke township	85	112
Westfield township	76	90
Willow Lake township	75	111
Stutsman County[46]	24 154	23 550
Alexander township	48	75
Ashland township[46]	89	94
Bloom township[46]	347	325
Bloomfield township	53	65
Buchanan township	187	161
Chase Lake (unorg.)[46]	5	2
Chicago township	74	100
Cleveland city[46]	130	128
Conklin township	27	35
Corinne township	67	100
Corwin township	182	99
Courtenay city	110	125
Courtenay township	63	79
Cusator township	55	79
Deer Lake township	49	67
Durham township	89	107
Edmunds township	67	102
Eldridge township	204	209
Flint township	76	117
Fried township	152	113
Gerber township	28	58
Germania township	53	61
Glacier township	44	56
Gray township[46]	50	79
Griffin township	80	73
Hidden township	75	62
Homer township	309	154
Iosco township	27	37
Jamestown city[46]	16 280	15 385
Jim River Valley township	75	75
Kensal city	210	263
Kensal township	63	107

County Subdivisions	1980	1970
Stutsman County—Con.		
Lenton township	79	94
Lippert township	112	80
Lowery township	46	78
Lyon township	45	65
Manns township	98	115
Marston Moor township	55	73
Medina city	521	488
Midway township[46]	806	472
Montpelier city	96	116
Montpelier township	85	112
Moon Lake township	93	130
Newbury township	69	100
Nogosek township	49	61
Northwest Stutsman (unorg.)[46]	22	...
Paris township	76	97
Peterson township	63	80
Pingree city	88	76
Pingree township	86	76
Pipestem Valley township	75	81
Plainview township	75	77
Rose township	92	115
Round Top township	30	49
St. Paul township	83	86
Severn township	82	90
Sharlow township	61	76
Sinclair township	49	84
Spiritwood township	124	160
Spiritwood Lake city[46]	50	...
Stirton township	72	85
Streeter city	264	324
Streeter township	87	126
Strong township[46]	68	89
Sydney township	112	117
Valley Spring township	54	64
Wadsworth township	43	54
Walters township	66	100
Weld township[46]	65	89
Windsor township	80	94
Winfield township	74	87
Woodbury township[46]	264	198
Woodworth city[46]	137	139
Ypsilanti township	190	208
Towner County[47]	4 052	4 645
Armourdale township	77	103
Atkins township	50	59
Bethel township	36	70
Bisbee city	257	305
Cando city[47]	1 496	1 512
Cando township[47]	129	191
Coolin township	59	83
Crocus township	79	106
Dash township	82	97
Egeland city	112	96
Gerrard township	53	71
Grainfield township	76	95
Hansboro city	43	49
Howell township	82	99
Lansing township	34	56
Maza city	21	20
Maza township	57	56
Monroe township	47	62
Mount View township	69	62
New City township	34	55
Olson township	65	85
Paulson township	72	68
Perth city	20	44
Picton township	53	67
Rocklake city	287	270
Rock Lake township	50	67
Sarles city (pt.)	9	10
Sidney township	97	73
Smith township	56	129
Sorenson township	59	65
Springfield township	63	65
Teddy township	92	103
Twin Hill township	51	73
Victor township	52	117
Virginia township	65	81
Zion township	68	81
Traill County[48]	9 624	9 571
Belmont township	94	111
Bingham township	119	147
Blanchard township	140	144
Bloomfield township	153	152
Bohnsack township	90	122
Buxton city	336	235
Buxton township	140	128
Caledonia township	220	174
Clifford city	51	84
Eldorado township	229	242
Elm River township	73	75
Ervin township	217	228
Galesburg city	165	134
Galesburg township	143	136
Garfield township	185	193

County Subdivisions	1980	1970
Traill County—Con.		
Grandin city (pt.)[48]	–	...
Greenfield township	74	110
Hatton city	787	808
Herberg township	136	114
Hillsboro[48]	1 600	1 309
Hillsboro township[48]	151	182
Kelso township[48]	92	96
Lindaas township[48]	153	177
Mayville city[48]	2 255	2 554
Mayville township	168	196
Morgan township	126	147
Norman township	102	99
Norway township	177	198
Portland city	627	534
Reynolds city (pt.)	194	125
Roseville township	112	129
Stavanger township	135	137
Viking township[48]	213	210
Wold township	167	141
Walsh County[49]	15 371	16 251
Acton township	161	203
Adams city	303	284
Adams township	85	124
Ardoch city	78	70
Ardoch township	124	109
Cleveland township	123	138
Conway city	33	57
Dewey township	79	116
Dundee township	165	197
Eden township	64	75
Edinburg city[49]	300	315
Fairdale city	97	102
Farmington township	246	228
Fertile township	277	275
Fordville city	326	361
Forest River city	152	169
Forest River township	111	118
Glenwood township[49]	300	260
Golden township	113	104
Grafton city[49]	5 293	5 946
Grafton township[49]	327	200
Harriston township	167	167
Hoople city[49]	350	330
Kensington township[49]	258	249
Kinloss township	85	137
Lampton township[49]	209	170
Lankin city	175	221
Latona township	114	111
Martin township	135	170
Medford township	102	110
Minto city	592	636
Norton township	130	157
Oakwood township[49]	477	305
Ops township	86	123
Park River city[49]	1 844	1 680
Perth township	116	124
Pisek city	156	154
Prairie Center township	196	218
Pulaski township	150	204
Rushford township	172	170
St. Andrews township	79	95
Sauter township	82	112
Shepherd township	75	113
Silvesta township	108	136
Tiber township	124	158
Vernon township	139	176
Vesta township	60	98
Walsh Centre township	186	238
Walshville township	247	238
Ward County[50]	58 392	58 560
Afton township	575	428
Anna township	47	66
Baden township	58	93
Berthold city	485	398
Berthold township	98	89
Brillian township	56	80
Burlington city[50]	762	247
Burlington township[50]	341	428
Burt township	102	92
Cameron township	64	54
Carbondale township	98	120
Carpio city	244	215
Carpio township	89	108
Denmark township	80	110
Des Lacs city	212	197
Des Lacs township	94	121
Donnybrook city	139	163
Douglas city	112	144
Elmdale township	91	94
Eureka township	253	189
Evergreen township	9	14
Foxholm township	175	193
Freedom township	168	126
Gasman township	73	259
Greely township	50	37
Greenbush township	52	61

County Subdivisions	1980	1970
Ward County—Con.		
Harrison township	1 906	1 512
Hiddenwood township	53	87
Hilton township	50	63
Iota Flat township	99	112
Kenmare city[50]	1 456	1 515
Kenmare township[50]	110	118
Kirkelie township	288	232
Linton township	49	53
Lund township	49	58
McKinley township	157	143
Makoti city	199	159
Mandan township	67	87
Margaret township	72	115
Maryland township	76	79
Mayland township	78	82
Minot city[50]	32 843	32 290
Nedrose township[50]	1 661	1 825
Newman township	106	102
New Prairie township	234	162
Orlien township	82	109
Passport township	59	71
Ree township	57	70
Rice Lake township	56	58
Rolling Green township	97	128
Rushville township	104	114
Ryder city	158	211
Ryder township	61	87
St. Marys township	60	88
Sauk Prairie township	42	57
Sawyer city[50]	417	373
Sawyer township[50]	218	139
Shealey township	51	73
Spencer township	100	97
Spring Lake township	53	66
Sundre township	901	616
Surrey city	999	361
Surrey township	272	212
Tatman township	5 439	6 033
Minot AFB (CDP) (pt.)	5 153	(NA)
Tolgen township	28	47
Torning township	68	75
Vang township	72	81
Waterford township	4 801	12 077
Minot AFB (CDP) (pt.)	4 727	(NA)
Willis township	117	106
Wells County[51]	6 979	7 847
Berlin township	67	63
Bilodeau township	80	124
Bowdon city	220	229
Bremen township	154	175
Bull Moose township	77	78
Cathay city	66	110
Cathay township	81	124
Chaseley township	106	115
Crystal Lake township	53	71
Delger township	71	110
Fairville township	87	98
Fessenden city[51]	761	815
Forward township[51]	109	125
Fram township	110	127
Germantown township	50	74
Haaland township	79	91
Hamberg city	41	51
Hamburg township	93	118
Harvey city[51]	2 527	2 361
Hawksnest township	62	68
Heimdal township	104	149
Hillsdale township[51]	145	143
Hurdsfield city	113	139
Johnson township	78	96
Lynn township	49	78
Manfred township	106	179
Norway Lake township	98	127
Oshkosh township[51]	71	96
Pony Gulch township	96	99
Progress township	46	72
Rusland township	79	112
St. Anna township	54	99
Silver Lake township	54	89
South Cottonwood township	84	87
Speedwell township	99	143
Sykeston city	193	232
Sykeston township	75	111
Valhalla township	77	90
Wells township[51]	160	180
Western township	127	139
West Norway township	58	84
West Ontario township	57	90
Woodward township	62	86
Williams County[52]	22 237	19 301
Alamo city	122	124
Athens township	20	24
Barr Butte township	26	45
Big Meadow township	40	65
Big Stone township	50	60

County Subdivisions	1980	1970
Williams County—Con.		
Blacktail township	41	21
Blue Ridge township	69	65
Bonetraill township	35	42
Brooklyn township	38	45
Buford township	188	180
Bull Butte township	39	39
Champion township	37	55
Climax township	30	49
Cow Creek township	16	28
Dry Fork township	56	48
Dublin township	14	17
East Fork township	35	33
Ellisville township	30	35
Epping city	104	140
Equality township	70	105
Farmvale township	44	39
Golden Valley township	42	49
Good Luck township	45	49
Grenora city	362	401
Grenora township	15	22
Hanks city	10	13
Hardscrabble township	75	45
Hazel township	54	69
Hebron township	50	65
Hofflund township	32	29
Judson township	113	81
Lindahl township	42	53
Marshall township	48	39
Missouri Ridge township	550	175
Mont township	66	52
Nesson Valley (unorg.)[52]	11	...
New Home township	39	48
Oliver township	24	29
Orthell township	21	26
Pherrin township	192	89
Pleasant Valley township	157	189
Rainbow township	13	46
Ray city	766	776
Rock Island township	8	20
Round Prairie township	97	84
Sauk Valley township	134	167
Scorio township	70	94
Southeast Williams (unorg.)[52]	15	...
South Meadow township	34	47
Spring Brook city	52	27
Springbrook township	35	34
Stony Creek township[52]	394	306
Strandahl township	29	40
Tioga city[52]	1 597	1 667
Tioga township[52]	153	289
Trenton township	401	255
Truax township	72	63
Twelve Mile township	104	94
Tyrone township	59	48
View township	37	63
West Bank township	64	67
Wheelock city	34	21
Wheelock township	27	36
Wildrose city	214	235
Williston city[52]	13 336	11 280
Williston township[52]	1 384	653
Winner township	56	77

OHIO

Ohio takes its name from the river which borders it on the south and southeast. The name of the river is a contraction of the Iroquois *Ohionhiio*, "beautiful river."

The territory which now forms the state of Ohio was first explored by La Salle, a Frenchman. There are evidences that he discovered the Ohio River about 1670 and followed its course to the Louisville Rapids, but his first well-authenticated exploration was in August, 1679, when he sailed along the south shore of Lake Erie on his expedition to the Mississippi Valley. The French held possession of the territory as a trading ground until 1763, when, at the close of the French and Indian War, the French claims were relinquished in favor of the English. In 1778 the country west of the Ohio and east of the Mississippi was taken from the British by George Rogers Clark at the head of Virginia troops, and in the same year it was organized as a county of Virginia. At the close of the Revolution this territory was ceded to the United States by the British, and during the period 1781 to 1786 Massachusetts, Connecticut, New York, and Virginia ceded to the Federal Government their claims to these lands, based on their early charters. Connecticut, however, did not cede all her western lands but kept over 3,500,000 acres—the Western Reserve—in what is now northeastern Ohio, and Virginia retained rights of soil in a tract in the southwestern part of the state to be used as legal bounties for Virginia continental troops. In 1800 Connecticut transferred to the United States the jurisdiction over the Western Reserve.

The establishment, in 1787, of a territorial government for the region between the Ohio and the Mississippi, then known as the Northwest Territory, was followed by a large influx of pioneers from the older parts of the country. The first permanent settlement was made at Marietta in 1788 by a colony from Massachusetts. Later in the same year Losantiville, now Cincinnati, was founded by a party from Lexington, Ky.

In 1800 the greater part of the Northwest Territory—the area now comprising Indiana, excepting a narrow strip along the eastern boundary, Illinois, Wisconsin, western Michigan, and northeastern Minnesota—was organized as the territory of Indiana.

In November, 1802, a convention, authorized by Congress in April of the same year, met at Chillicothe and adopted a constitution for the state of Ohio; and on February 19, 1803, Congress declared the new state to be a member of the Union.

By the enabling act of 1802 the limits of Ohio were fixed as they now stand, with the exception of the northern boundary west of Lake Erie, which was established at its present location in 1836.

COUNTY LOCATION INDEX

Adams	G-3	Hamilton	F-1	Noble	E-5
Allen	C-2	Hancock	C-2	Ottawa	B-3
Ashland	C-4	Hardin	D-2	Paulding	C-1
Ashtabula	B-6	Harrison	D-6	Perry	E-4
Athens	F-4	Henry	B-2	Pickaway	E-3
Auglaize	D-1	Highland	F-2	Pike	F-3
Belmont	E-6	Hocking	F-4	Portage	C-5
Brown	G-2	Holmes	D-5	Preble	E-1
Butler	F-1	Huron	C-4	Putnam	C-2
Carroll	D-6	Jackson	G-4	Richland	C-4
Champaign	E-2	Jefferson	D-6	Ross	F-3
Clark	E-2	Knox	D-4	Sandusky	B-3
Clermont	F-2	Lake	B-5	Scioto	G-3
Clinton	F-2	Lawrence	G-4	Seneca	C-3
Columbiana	C-6	Licking	E-4	Shelby	D-1
Coshocton	D-5	Logan	D-2	Stark	C-5
Crawford	C-3	Lorain	B-4	Summit	C-5
Cuyahoga	B-5	Lucas	B-2	Trumbull	B-6
Darke	E-1	Madison	E-3	Tuscarawas	D-5
Defiance	B-1	Mahoning	C-6	Union	D-3
Delaware	D-3	Marion	D-3	Van Wert	C-1
Erie	B-4	Medina	C-5	Vinton	F-4
Fairfield	E-4	Meigs	F-4	Warren	F-2
Fayette	F-3	Mercer	D-1	Washington	F-5
Franklin	E-3	Miami	E-1	Wayne	C-5
Fulton	B-2	Monroe	E-6	Williams	B-1
Gallia	G-4	Montgomery	E-1	Wood	B-2
Geauga	B-5	Morgan	E-5	Wyandot	C-3
Greene	E-2	Morrow	D-3		
Guernsey	E-5	Muskingum	E-5		

Ohio

Population of the State: Earliest Census to 1980

Urban and Rural

	The State			Urban				Rural			Percent of total population	
	Total population	Change from preceding census		Places of 2,500 or more	Population	Change from preceding census		Population	Change from preceding census		Urban	Rural
		Number	Percent			Number	Percent		Number	Percent		
Current urban definition:												
1980 (Apr. 1)	10 797 630	140 207	1.3	382	7 918 259	−107 516	−1.3	2 879 371	253 129	9.6	73.3	26.7
1970 (Apr. 1)	'10 657 423	951 026	9.8	354	8 025 775	902 613	12.7	2 626 242	43 007	1.7	75.3	24.7
1960 (Apr. 1)	9 706 397	1 759 770	22.1	301	7 123 162	1 544 888	27.7	2 583 235	214 882	9.1	73.4	26.6
1950 (Apr. 1)	7 946 627	1 039 015	15.0	219	5 578 274	...	...	2 368 353	...	...	70.2	29.8
Previous urban definition:												
1960 (Apr. 1)	9 706 397	1 759 770	22.1	294	6 537 805	1 191 469	22.3	3 168 592	568 301	21.9	67.4	32.6
1950 (Apr. 1)	7 946 627	1 039 015	15.0	217	5 346 336	733 350	15.9	2 600 291	305 665	13.3	67.3	32.7
1940 (Apr. 1)	6 907 612	260 915	3.9	186	4 612 986	105 615	2.3	2 294 626	155 300	7.3	66.8	33.2
1930 (Apr. 1)	6 646 697	887 303	15.4	174	4 507 371	830 235	22.6	2 139 326	57 068	2.7	67.8	32.2
1920 (Jan. 1)	5 759 394	992 273	20.8	148	3 677 136	1 011 993	38.0	2 082 258	−19 720	−0.9	63.8	36.2
1910 (Apr. 15)	4 767 121	609 576	14.7	139	2 665 143	666 761	33.4	2 101 978	−57 185	−2.6	55.9	44.1
1900 (June 1)	4 157 545	485 216	13.2	126	1 998 382	488 229	32.3	2 159 163	−3 013	−0.1	48.1	51.9
1890 (June 1)	3 672 329	474 267	14.8	110	1 510 153	479 384	46.5	2 162 176	−5 117	−0.2	41.1	58.9
1880 (June 1)	3 198 062	532 802	20.0	90	1 030 769	347 847	50.9	2 167 293	184 955	9.3	32.2	67.8
1870 (June 1)	2 665 260	325 749	13.9	59	682 922	282 487	70.5	1 982 338	43 262	2.2	25.6	74.4
1860 (June 1)	2 339 511	359 182	18.1	36	400 435	158 017	65.2	1 939 076	201 165	11.6	17.1	82.9
1850 (June 1)	1 980 329	460 862	30.3	24	242 418	158 927	190.4	1 737 911	301 935	21.0	12.2	87.8
1840 (June 1)	1 519 467	581 564	62.0	9	83 491	46 833	127.8	1 435 976	534 731	59.3	5.5	94.5
1830 (June 1)	937 903	356 469	61.3	5	36 658	27 016	280.2	901 245	329 453	57.6	3.9	96.1
1820 (Aug. 7)	581 434	350 674	152.0	1	9 642	7 102	279.6	571 792	343 572	150.5	1.7	98.3
1810 (Aug. 6)	230 760	185 395	408.7	1	2 540	2 540	...	228 220	182 855	403.1	1.1	98.9
1800 (Aug. 4)	45 365	...	...	−	−	...	...	45 365	...	...	−	100.0

NOTE: 1800 population is of the Territory Northwest of the River Ohio.

ADAMS

1800	3,432
1810	9,434
1820	10,406
1830	12,281
1840	13,183
1850	18,883
1860	20,309
1870	20,750
1880	24,005
1890	26,093
1900	26,328
1910	24,755
1920	22,403
1930	20,381
1940	21,705
1950	20,499
1960	19,982
1970	18,597
1980	24,328

ALLEN

1830	578
1840	9,097
1850	12,109
1860	19,185
1870	23,623
1880	31,314
1890	40,644
1900	47,976
1910	56,580
1920	68,223
1930	69,419
1940	73,303
1950	88,183
1960	103,691
1970	111,144
1980	112,241

ASHLAND

1850	23,183
1860	22,951
1870	21,933
1880	23,883
1890	22,223
1900	21,184
1910	22,975
1920	24,627
1930	26,867
1940	29,785
1950	33,040
1960	38,771
1970	43,303
1980	46,178

ASHTABULA

1820	7,382
1830	14,584
1840	23,724
1850	28,767
1860	31,814
1870	32,517
1880	37,139
1890	43,655
1900	51,448
1910	59,547
1920	65,545
1930	68,361
1940	68,674
1950	78,695
1960	93,067
1970	98,237
1980	104,215

ATHENS

1810	2,791
1820	6,338
1830	9,787
1840	19,109
1850	18,215
1860	21,364
1870	23,768
1880	28,411
1890	35,194
1900	38,730
1910	47,798
1920	50,430
1930	44,175
1940	46,166
1950	45,839
1960	46,998
1970	55,747
1980	56,399

AUGLAIZE

1850	11,338
1860	17,187
1870	20,041
1880	25,444
1890	28,100
1900	31,192
1910	31,246
1920	29,527
1930	28,034
1940	28,037
1950	30,637
1960	36,147
1970	38,602
1980	42,554

BELMONT

1810	11,097
1820	20,329
1830	28,627
1840	30,901
1850	34,600
1860	36,398
1870	39,714
1880	49,638
1890	57,413
1900	60,875
1910	76,856
1920	93,193
1930	94,719
1940	95,614
1950	87,740
1960	83,864
1970	80,197
1980	82,569

BROWN

1820	13,356
1830	17,867
1840	22,715
1850	27,332
1860	29,958
1870	30,802
1880	32,911
1890	29,899
1900	28,237
1910	24,832
1920	22,621
1930	20,148
1940	21,638
1950	22,221
1960	25,178
1970	26,635

1980	31,920

BUTLER

1810	11,150
1820	21,746
1830	27,142
1840	28,173
1850	30,789
1860	35,840
1870	30,912
1880	42,579
1890	48,597
1900	56,870
1910	70,271
1920	87,025
1930	114,084
1940	120,249
1950	147,203
1960	199,076
1970	226,207
1980	258,787

CARROLL

1840	18,108
1850	17,685
1860	15,738
1870	14,491
1880	16,416
1890	17,566
1900	16,811
1910	15,761
1920	15,942
1930	16,057
1940	17,449
1950	19,039
1960	20,857
1970	21,597
1980	25,598

CHAMPAIGN

1810	6,303
1820	8,479
1830	12,131
1840	16,721
1850	19,782
1860	22,698
1870	24,188
1880	27,817
1890	26,980
1900	26,642
1910	26,351
1920	25,071
1930	24,103
1940	25,258
1950	26,793
1960	29,714
1970	30,491
1980	33,649

CLARK

1820	9,533
1830	13,114
1840	16,882
1850	22,178
1860	25,300
1870	32,070
1880	41,948
1890	52,277
1900	58,939
1910	66,435
1920	80,728
1930	90,936
1940	95,647

1950	111,661
1960	131,440
1970	157,115
1980	150,236

CLERMONT

1810	9,965
1820	15,820
1830	20,466
1840	23,106
1850	30,455
1860	33,034
1870	34,268
1880	36,713
1890	33,553
1900	31,610
1910	29,551
1920	28,291
1930	29,786
1940	34,109
1950	42,182
1960	80,530
1970	95,372
1980	128,483

CLINTON

1810	2,674
1820	8,085
1830	11,436
1840	15,719
1850	18,838
1860	21,461
1870	21,914
1880	24,756
1890	24,240
1900	24,202
1910	23,680
1920	23,036
1930	21,547
1940	22,574
1950	25,572
1960	30,004
1970	31,464
1980	34,603

COLUMBIANA

1810	10,878
1820	22,003
1830	35,592
1840	40,378
1850	33,621
1860	32,836
1870	38,399
1880	48,602
1890	59,029
1900	68,590
1910	76,619
1920	83,131
1930	86,484
1940	90,121
1950	98,920
1960	107,004
1970	108,310
1980	113,572

COSHOCTON

1820	7,086
1830	11,161
1840	21,590
1850	25,674
1860	25,032
1870	23,600
1880	26,642

1890	26,703
1900	29,337
1910	30,121
1920	29,595
1930	28,976
1940	30,594
1950	31,141
1960	32,224
1970	33,486
1980	36,024

CRAWFORD

1830	4,791
1840	13,152
1850	18,177
1860	23,881
1870	25,556
1880	30,583
1890	31,927
1900	33,915
1910	34,036
1920	36,054
1930	35,345
1940	35,571
1950	38,738
1960	46,775
1970	50,364
1980	50,075

CUYAHOGA

1810	1,459
1820	6,328
1830	10,373
1840	26,506
1850	48,099
1860	78,033
1870	132,010
1880	196,943
1890	309,970
1900	439,120
1910	637,425
1920	943,495
1930	1,201,455
1940	1,217,250
1950	1,389,532
1960	1,647,895
1970	1,720,835
1980	1,498,400

DARKE

1820	3,717
1830	6,204
1840	13,282
1850	20,276
1860	26,009
1870	32,278
1880	40,496
1890	42,961
1900	42,532
1910	42,933
1920	42,911
1930	38,009
1940	38,831
1950	41,799
1960	45,612
1970	49,141
1980	55,096

DEFIANCE

1850	6,966
1860	11,886
1870	15,719
1880	22,515

1890	25,769
1900	26,387
1910	24,498
1920	24,549
1930	22,714
1940	24,367
1950	25,925
1960	31,508
1970	36,949
1980	39,987

DELAWARE

1810	2,000
1820	7,639
1830	11,504
1840	22,060
1850	21,817
1860	23,902
1870	25,175
1880	27,381
1890	27,189
1900	26,401
1910	27,182
1920	26,103
1930	26,016
1940	26,780
1950	30,278
1960	36,107
1970	42,908
1980	53,840

ERIE

1840	12,599
1850	18,568
1860	24,474
1870	28,188
1880	32,640
1890	35,462
1900	37,650
1910	38,327
1920	39,789
1930	42,133
1940	43,201
1950	52,565
1960	68,000
1970	75,909
1980	79,655

FAIRFIELD

1810	11,361
1820	16,633
1830	24,786
1840	31,924
1850	30,264
1860	30,538
1870	31,138
1880	34,284
1890	33,939
1900	34,259
1910	39,201
1920	40,484
1930	44,010
1940	48,490
1950	52,130
1960	63,912
1970	73,301
1980	93,678

FAYETTE

1810	1,854
1820	6,316
1830	8,182
1840	10,984

1850	12,726
1860	15,935
1870	17,170
1880	20,364
1890	22,309
1900	21,725
1910	21,744
1920	21,518
1930	20,755
1940	21,385
1950	22,554
1960	24,775
1970	25,461
1980	27,467

FRANKLIN

1810	3,486
1820	10,292
1830	14,741
1840	25,049
1850	42,909
1860	50,361
1870	63,019
1880	86,797
1890	124,087
1900	164,460
1910	221,567
1920	283,951
1930	361,055
1940	388,712
1950	503,410
1960	682,962
1970	833,249
1980	869,132

FULTON

1850	7,781
1860	14,043
1870	17,789
1880	21,053
1890	22,023
1900	22,801
1910	23,914
1920	23,445
1930	23,447
1940	23,626
1950	25,580
1960	29,301
1970	33,071
1980	37,751

GALLIA

1810	4,181
1820	7,098
1830	9,733
1840	13,444
1850	17,063
1860	22,043
1870	25,545
1880	28,124
1890	27,005
1900	27,918
1910	25,745
1920	23,311
1930	23,050
1940	24,930
1950	24,910
1960	26,120
1970	25,239
1980	30,098

GEAUGA

1810	2,917

1820	7,791
1830	15,813
1840	16,297
1850	17,827
1860	15,817
1870	14,190
1880	14,251
1890	13,489
1900	14,744
1910	14,670
1920	15,036
1930	15,414
1940	19,430
1950	26,646
1960	47,573
1970	62,977
1980	74,474

GREENE

1810	5,870
1820	10,529
1830	14,801
1840	17,528
1850	21,946
1860	26,197
1870	28,038
1880	31,349
1890	29,820
1900	31,613
1910	29,733
1920	31,221
1930	33,259
1940	35,863
1950	58,892
1960	94,642
1970	125,057
1980	129,769

GUERNSEY

1810	3,051
1820	9,292
1830	18,036
1840	27,748
1850	30,438
1860	24,472
1870	23,838
1880	27,197
1890	28,645
1900	34,425
1910	42,716
1920	45,352
1930	41,486
1940	38,822
1950	38,452
1960	38,579
1970	37,665
1980	42,024

HAMILTON

1800	14,692
1810	15,258
1820	31,764
1830	52,317
1840	80,145
1850	156,844
1860	216,410
1870	260,370
1880	313,374
1890	374,573
1900	409,479
1910	460,732
1920	493,678
1930	589,356
1940	621,987

1950	723,952
1960	864,121
1970	925,944
1980	873,224

HANCOCK

1830	813
1840	9,986
1850	16,751
1860	22,886
1870	23,847
1880	27,784
1890	42,563
1900	41,993
1910	37,860
1920	38,394
1930	40,404
1940	40,793
1950	44,280
1960	53,686
1970	61,217
1980	64,581

HARDIN

1830	210
1840	4,598
1850	8,251
1860	13,570
1870	27,023
1880	27,023
1890	28,939
1900	31,187
1910	30,407
1920	29,167
1930	27,635
1940	27,061
1950	28,673
1960	29,633
1970	30,813
1980	32,719

HARRISON

1820	14,345
1830	20,916
1840	20,099
1850	20,157
1860	19,110
1870	18,682
1880	20,456
1890	20,830
1900	20,486
1910	19,076
1920	19,625
1930	18,884
1940	20,313
1950	19,054
1960	17,995
1970	17,013
1980	18,152

HENRY

1830	262
1840	2,503
1850	3,434
1860	8,901
1870	14,028
1880	20,585
1890	25,080
1900	27,282
1910	25,119
1920	23,362
1930	22,524
1940	22,756

1950	22,423
1960	29,633
1970	30,813
1980	28,383

HIGHLAND

1810	5,766
1820	12,308
1830	16,345
1840	22,269
1850	25,781
1860	27,773
1870	29,133
1880	30,281
1890	29,048
1900	30,982
1910	28,711
1920	27,610
1930	25,416
1940	27,099
1950	28,188
1960	29,176
1970	28,996
1980	33,477

HOCKING

1820	2,130
1830	4,008
1840	9,741
1850	14,119
1860	17,057
1870	17,925
1880	21,126
1890	22,658
1900	24,398
1910	23,650
1920	23,291
1930	20,407
1940	21,504
1950	19,520
1960	20,168
1970	20,322
1980	24,304

HOLMES

1830	9,135
1840	18,088
1850	20,452
1860	20,589
1870	18,177
1880	20,776
1890	21,139
1900	19,511
1910	17,909
1920	16,965
1930	16,726
1940	17,876
1950	18,760
1960	21,591
1970	23,024
1980	29,416

HURON

1820	6,675
1830	13,341
1840	23,933
1850	26,203
1860	29,616
1870	28,532
1880	31,609
1890	31,949
1900	32,330
1910	34,206

1920	32,424
1930	33,700
1940	34,800
1950	39,353
1960	47,326
1970	49,587
1980	54,608

JACKSON

1820	3,746
1830	5,941
1840	9,744
1850	12,719
1860	17,941
1870	21,759
1880	23,686
1890	28,408
1900	34,248
1910	30,791
1920	27,342
1930	25,040
1940	27,004
1950	27,767
1960	29,372
1970	27,174
1980	30,592

JEFFERSON

1800	8,766
1810	17,260
1820	18,531
1830	22,489
1840	25,030
1850	29,133
1860	26,115
1870	29,188
1880	33,018
1890	39,415
1900	44,357
1910	65,432
1920	77,580
1930	88,307
1940	98,129
1950	96,495
1960	99,201
1970	96,193
1980	91,564

KNOX

1810	2,149
1820	8,326
1830	17,085
1840	29,579
1850	27,872
1860	27,735
1870	26,333
1880	27,431
1890	27,600
1900	27,768
1910	30,181
1920	29,580
1930	29,338
1940	31,024
1950	35,287
1960	38,808
1970	41,795
1980	46,304

LAKE

1840	13,719
1850	14,654
1860	15,576
1870	15,935

1880	16,326
1890	18,235
1900	21,680
1910	22,927
1920	28,667
1930	41,674
1940	50,020
1950	75,979
1960	148,700
1970	197,200
1980	212,801

LAWRENCE

1820	3,499
1830	5,367
1840	9,738
1850	15,246
1860	23,249
1870	31,380
1880	39,068
1890	39,556
1900	39,534
1910	39,448
1920	39,540
1930	44,541
1940	46,705
1950	59,115
1960	15,438
1970	56,868
1980	63,849

LICKING

1810	3,852
1820	11,861
1830	20,869
1840	35,096
1850	38,846
1860	37,011
1870	35,756
1880	40,450
1890	43,279
1900	47,070
1910	55,590
1920	56,426
1930	59,962
1940	62,279
1950	70,645
1960	90,242
1970	107,799
1980	120,981

LOGAN

1820	3,181
1830	6,440
1840	14,015
1850	19,162
1860	20,996
1870	23,028
1880	26,267
1890	27,386
1900	30,420
1910	30,084
1920	30,104
1930	28,981
1940	29,624
1950	31,329
1960	34,803
1970	35,072
1980	39,155

LORAIN

1830	5,696
1840	18,467

1850	26,086
1860	29,744
1870	30,308
1880	35,526
1890	40,295
1900	54,857
1910	76,037
1920	90,612
1930	109,206
1940	112,390
1950	148,162
1960	217,500
1970	256,843
1980	274,909

LUCAS

1840	9,342
1850	12,363
1860	25,831
1870	46,722
1880	67,377
1890	102,296
1900	153,559
1910	192,728
1920	275,721
1930	347,709
1940	344,333
1950	395,551
1960	456,931
1970	483,551
1980	471,741

MADISON

1810	1,603
1820	4,799
1830	6,190
1840	9,025
1850	10,015
1860	13,015
1870	15,633
1880	20,057
1890	20,057
1900	20,590
1910	19,902
1920	19,662
1930	20,253
1940	21,811
1950	22,300
1960	26,454
1970	28,318
1980	33,004

MAHONING

1850	23,735
1860	25,894
1870	31,001
1880	42,871
1890	55,979
1900	70,134
1910	116,151
1920	186,310
1930	236,142
1940	240,251
1950	257,629
1960	300,480
1970	304,545
1980	289,487

MARION

1830	6,551
1840	14,765
1850	12,618
1860	15,490

1870	16,184
1880	20,565
1890	24,727
1900	28,678
1910	33,971
1920	42,004
1930	45,420
1940	44,898
1950	49,959
1960	60,221
1970	64,724
1980	67,974

MEDINA

1820	3,082
1830	7,560
1840	18,352
1850	24,441
1860	22,517
1870	20,092
1880	21,453
1890	21,742
1900	21,958
1910	23,598
1920	26,067
1930	29,677
1940	33,034
1950	40,417
1960	65,315
1970	82,717
1980	113,150

MEIGS

1820	4,480
1830	6,158
1840	11,452
1850	17,971
1860	26,534
1870	31,465
1880	32,325
1890	29,813
1900	28,620
1910	25,594
1920	26,189
1930	23,961
1940	24,104
1950	23,227
1960	22,159
1970	19,799
1980	23,641

MERCER

1830	1,110
1840	8,277
1850	7,712
1860	14,104
1870	17,254
1880	21,808
1890	27,220
1900	28,021
1910	27,536
1920	26,872
1930	25,096
1940	26,256
1950	28,311
1960	32,559
1970	35,558
1980	38,334

MIAMI

1810	3,941
1820	8,851
1830	12,807

1840	19,688
1850	24,999
1860	29,959
1870	32,740
1880	36,158
1890	39,754
1900	43,105
1910	45,047
1920	48,428
1930	51,301
1940	52,632
1950	61,309
1960	72,901
1970	84,342
1980	90,381

MONROE

1820	4,645
1830	8,768
1840	18,521
1850	28,351
1860	25,741
1870	25,779
1880	26,496
1890	25,175
1900	27,031
1910	24,244
1920	20,660
1930	18,426
1940	18,641
1950	15,362
1960	15,268
1970	15,739
1980	17,382

MONTGOMERY

1810	7,722
1820	15,999
1830	24,362
1840	31,938
1850	38,218
1860	52,230
1870	64,006
1880	78,550
1890	100,852
1900	130,146
1910	163,763
1920	209,532
1930	273,481
1940	295,480
1950	398,441
1960	527,080
1970	608,413
1980	571,697

MORGAN

1820	5,297
1830	11,800
1840	20,852
1850	28,585
1860	22,119
1870	20,363
1880	20,074
1890	19,143
1900	17,905
1910	16,097
1920	14,555
1930	13,583
1940	14,227
1950	12,836
1960	12,747
1970	12,375
1980	14,241

MORROW

1850	20,280
1860	20,445
1870	18,583
1880	19,072
1890	18,120
1900	17,879
1910	16,815
1920	15,570
1930	14,489
1940	15,646
1950	17,168
1960	19,405
1970	21,348
1980	26,480

MUSKINGUM

1810	10,036
1820	17,824
1830	29,334
1840	38,749
1850	45,049
1860	44,416
1870	44,886
1880	49,774
1890	51,210
1900	53,185
1910	57,980
1920	57,980
1930	67,393
1940	69,795
1950	74,535
1960	74,159
1970	77,826
1980	83,340

NOBLE

1860	20,751
1870	19,949
1880	21,138
1890	20,753
1900	19,466
1910	18,601
1920	17,849
1930	14,961
1940	14,587
1950	11,750
1960	10,982
1970	10,428
1980	11,310

OTTAWA

1840	2,248
1850	3,308
1860	7,016
1870	13,364
1880	19,762
1890	21,974
1900	22,213
1910	22,360
1920	22,193
1930	24,109
1940	24,360
1950	29,464
1960	35,323
1970	37,099
1980	40,076

PAULDING

1830	161
1840	1,034
1850	1,766

1860	4,945
1870	8,544
1880	13,485
1890	25,932
1900	27,528
1910	22,730
1920	18,736
1930	15,301
1940	15,527
1950	15,047
1960	16,792
1970	19,329
1980	21,302

PERRY

1820	8,429
1830	13,970
1840	19,344
1850	20,775
1860	19,678
1870	18,453
1880	28,218
1890	31,151
1900	31,841
1910	35,396
1920	36,098
1930	31,445
1940	31,087
1950	28,999
1960	27,864
1970	27,434
1980	31,032

PICKAWAY

1810	7,124
1820	13,149
1830	16,001
1840	19,725
1850	21,006
1860	23,469
1870	24,875
1880	27,415
1890	26,959
1900	27,016
1910	26,158
1920	27,778
1930	26,238
1940	27,889
1950	29,352
1960	35,855
1970	40,071
1980	43,662

PIKE

1820	4,253
1830	6,024
1840	7,626
1850	10,953
1860	13,643
1870	15,447
1880	17,927
1890	17,482
1900	18,172
1910	15,723
1920	14,151
1930	13,876
1940	16,113
1950	14,607
1960	19,380
1970	19,114
1980	22,802

PORTAGE

1810	2,995
1820	10,095
1830	18,826
1840	22,965
1850	24,419
1860	24,208
1870	24,584
1880	27,500
1890	27,868
1900	29,246
1910	30,307
1920	36,269
1930	42,682
1940	46,660
1950	63,954
1960	91,798
1970	125,868
1980	135,856

PREBLE

1810	3,304
1820	10,237
1830	16,291
1840	19,482
1850	21,736
1860	21,820
1870	21,809
1880	24,553
1890	23,421
1900	23,713
1910	23,834
1920	23,238
1930	22,455
1940	23,329
1950	27,081
1960	32,498
1970	34,719
1980	38,223

PUTNAM

1830	230
1840	5,189
1850	7,221
1860	12,808
1870	17,081
1880	23,713
1890	30,188
1900	32,525
1910	29,972
1920	27,751
1930	26,074
1940	25,016
1950	25,248
1960	28,331
1970	31,134
1980	32,991

RICHLAND

1820	9,169
1830	24,006
1840	44,532
1850	30,879
1860	31,158
1870	32,516
1880	36,306
1890	38,072
1900	44,289
1910	47,667
1920	55,178
1930	65,902
1940	73,853
1950	91,305

1960	117,761
1970	129,997
1980	131,205

ROSS

1800	8,540
1810	15,514
1820	20,619
1830	24,068
1840	27,460
1850	32,074
1860	35,071
1870	37,097
1880	40,307
1890	39,454
1900	40,940
1910	40,069
1920	41,556
1930	45,181
1940	52,147
1950	54,424
1960	61,125
1970	61,211
1980	65,004

SANDUSKY

1820	852
1830	2,851
1840	10,182
1850	14,305
1860	21,429
1870	25,503
1880	32,057
1890	30,617
1900	34,311
1910	35,171
1920	36,109
1930	39,731
1940	41,014
1950	46,114
1960	56,486
1970	60,983
1980	63,267

SCIOTO

1810	3,399
1820	5,750
1830	8,740
1840	11,192
1850	18,428
1860	24,297
1870	29,302
1880	33,511
1890	35,377
1900	40,981
1910	49,463
1920	62,850
1930	81,221
1940	86,565
1950	82,910
1960	84,216
1970	76,951
1980	84,545

SENECA

1830	5,159
1840	18,128
1850	27,104
1860	30,868
1870	30,827
1880	36,947
1890	40,869
1900	41,163

1910	42,421
1920	43,176
1930	47,941
1940	48,499
1950	52,978
1960	59,326
1970	60,696
1980	61,901

SHELBY

1820	2,106
1830	3,671
1840	12,154
1850	13,958
1860	17,493
1870	20,748
1880	24,137
1890	24,707
1900	24,625
1910	24,663
1920	25,923
1930	24,924
1940	26,071
1950	28,488
1960	33,586
1970	37,748
1980	43,089

STARK

1810	2,734
1820	12,406
1830	26,588
1840	34,603
1850	39,878
1860	42,978
1870	52,508
1880	64,031
1890	84,170
1900	94,747
1910	122,987
1920	177,218
1930	221,784
1940	234,887
1950	283,194
1960	340,345
1970	372,210
1980	378,823

SUMMIT

1840	22,560
1850	27,485
1860	27,344
1870	34,674
1880	43,788
1890	54,089
1900	71,715
1910	108,253
1920	286,065
1930	344,131
1940	339,405
1950	410,032
1960	513,569
1970	553,371
1980	524,472

TRUMBULL

1800	1,302
1810	8,671
1820	15,546
1830	26,153
1840	38,107
1850	30,490
1860	30,656

1870	39,659
1880	44,880
1890	42,373
1900	46,591
1910	52,776
1920	83,920
1930	123,063
1940	123,315
1950	158,915
1960	208,526
1970	232,579
1980	241,863

TUSCARAWAS

1810	3,045
1820	8,328
1830	14,298
1840	25,631
1850	31,761
1860	32,463
1870	33,840
1880	40,198
1890	46,618
1900	53,751
1910	57,035
1920	63,578
1930	68,193
1940	68,816
1950	70,320
1960	76,789
1970	77,211
1980	84,614

UNION

1820	1,996
1830	3,192
1840	8,422
1850	12,204
1860	16,507
1870	18,730
1880	22,375
1890	22,860
1900	22,342
1910	21,871
1920	20,918
1930	19,192
1940	20,012
1950	20,687
1960	22,853
1970	23,786
1980	29,536

VAN WERT

1830	49
1840	1,577
1850	4,793
1860	10,238
1870	15,823
1880	23,028
1890	29,671
1900	30,394
1910	29,119
1920	28,210
1930	26,273
1940	26,759
1950	26,971
1960	28,840
1970	29,194
1980	30,458

VINTON

1850	9,353
1860	13,631

1870	15,027
1880	17,223
1890	16,045
1900	15,330
1910	13,096
1920	12,075
1930	10,287
1940	11,573
1950	10,759
1960	10,274
1970	9,420
1980	11,584

WARREN

1810	9,925
1820	17,837
1830	21,468
1840	23,141
1850	25,560
1860	26,902
1870	26,689
1880	28,392
1890	25,468
1900	25,584
1910	24,497
1920	25,716
1930	27,348
1940	29,984
1950	38,505
1960	65,711
1970	85,505
1980	99,276

WASHINGTON

1800	5,427
1810	5,991
1820	10,425
1830	11,731
1840	20,823
1850	29,540
1860	36,268
1870	40,609
1880	43,244
1890	42,380
1900	48,245
1910	45,422
1920	43,049
1930	43,437
1940	43,537
1950	44,407
1960	51,689
1970	57,160
1980	64,266

WAYNE

1800	3,206
1820	11,933
1830	23,333
1840	35,808
1850	32,981
1860	32,483
1870	35,116
1880	40,076
1890	39,005
1900	37,870
1910	38,058
1920	41,346
1930	47,024
1940	50,520
1950	58,716
1960	75,497
1970	87,123
1980	97,408

WILLIAMS

1830	387
1840	4,465
1850	8,018
1860	16,633
1870	20,991
1880	23,821
1890	24,897
1900	24,953
1910	25,198
1920	24,627
1930	24,316
1940	25,510
1950	26,202
1960	29,968
1970	33,669
1980	36,369

WOOD

1820	733
1830	1,102
1840	5,357
1850	9,157
1860	17,886
1870	24,596
1880	34,022
1890	44,392
1900	51,555
1910	46,330
1920	44,892
1930	50,320
1940	51,796
1950	59,605
1960	72,596
1970	89,722
1980	107,372

WYANDOT

1850	11,194
1860	15,596
1870	18,553
1880	22,395
1890	21,722
1900	21,125
1910	20,760
1920	19,481
1930	19,306
1940	19,218
1950	19,786
1960	21,648
1970	21,826
1980	22,651

AKRON

1850	3,266
1860	3,477
1870	10,006
1880	16,512
1890	27,601
1900	42,728
1910	69,067
1920	208,435
1930	255,040
1940	244,791
1950	274,605
1960	290,351
1970	275,425
1980	237,177

ALLIANCE

1860	1,421
1870	4,063
1880	4,636
1890	7,607
1900	8,974
1910	15,083
1920	21,603
1930	23,047
1940	22,405
1950	26,161
1960	28,362
1970	26,527
1980	24,315

AMHERST

1910	2,106
1920	2,485
1930	2,844
1940	2,896
1950	3,542
1960	6,591
1970	9,902
1980	10,638

ASHLAND

1850	1,264
1860	1,748
1870	2,601
1880	3,004
1890	3,566
1900	4,087
1910	6,795
1920	9,249
1930	11,141
1940	12,453
1950	14,287
1960	17,419
1970	19,872
1980	20,326

ASHTABULA

1850	821
1860	1,418
1870	1,999
1880	4,445
1890	8,338
1900	12,949
1910	18,266
1920	22,082
1930	23,301
1940	21,405
1950	23,696
1960	24,559
1970	24,313
1980	23,449

ATHENS

1830	728
1840	710
1850	898
1860	1,0 2
1870	1,696
1880	2,457
1890	2,620
1900	3,066
1910	5,463
1920	6,418
1930	7,252
1940	7,696
1950	11,660
1960	16,470
1970	24,168
1980	19,743

AVON LAKE

1920	904
1930	1,610
1940	2,274
1950	4,342
1960	9,403
1970	12,261
1980	13,222

BARBERTON

1900	4,354
1910	9,410
1920	18,811
1930	23,934
1940	24,028
1950	27,820
1960	33,805
1970	33,052
1980	29,751

BAY VILLAGE

1910	450
1920	751
1930	2,294
1940	3,356
1950	6,917
1960	14,489
1970	18,163
1980	17,846

BEAVERCREEK

1980	31,589

BEDFORD

1860	859
1870	828
1880	766
1890	1,043
1900	1,486
1910	1,783
1920	2,677
1930	6,814
1940	7,390
1950	9,105
1960	15,223
1970	17,552
1980	15,056

BEDFORD HEIGHTS

1960	5,275
1970	13,063
1980	13,214

BELLEFONTAINE

1850	1,222
1860	2,599
1870	3,182
1880	3,998
1890	4,245
1900	6,649
1910	8,238
1920	9,336
1930	9,543
1940	9,808
1950	10,232
1960	11,424
1970	11,255
1980	11,888

BEREA

1870	1,628
1880	1,682
1890	2,533
1900	2,510
1910	2,609
1920	2,959
1930	5,697
1940	6,025
1950	12,051
1960	16,592
1970	22,465
1980	19,567

BEXLEY

1910	682
1920	1,342
1930	7,396
1940	8,705
1950	12,378
1960	14,319
1970	14,888
1980	13,405

BOWLING GREEN

1870	906
1880	1,539
1890	3,467
1900	5,067
1910	5,222
1920	5,788
1930	6,688
1940	7,190
1950	12,005
1960	13,574
1970	21,760
1980	25,728

BRECKSVILLE

1930	1,308
1940	1,900
1950	2,664
1960	5,435
1970	9,137
1980	10,132

BROADVIEW HEIGHTS

1930	689
1940	1,141
1950	2,279
1960	6,209
1970	11,463
1980	10,920

BROOKLYN

1930	784
1940	1,108
1950	6,317
1960	10,733
1970	13,142
1980	12,342

BROOK PARK

1920	861
1930	837
1940	1,122
1950	2,606
1960	12,856
1970	30,774
1980	26,195

BRUNSWICK

1960	11,725
1970	15,852
1980	28,104

BUCYRUS

1830	308
1840	1,634
1850	2,315
1860	2,180
1870	3,066
1880	3,835
1890	5,974
1900	6,560
1910	8,122
1920	10,425
1930	10,027
1940	9,727
1950	10,327
1960	12,276
1970	13,111
1980	13,433

CAMBRIDGE

1850	1,041
1860	1,452
1870	2,193
1880	2,883
1890	4,361
1900	8,241
1910	11,327
1920	13,104
1930	16,129
1940	15,044
1950	14,739
1960	14,562
1970	13,656
1980	13,573

CAMPBELL

1910	4,972
1920	11,237
1930	14,673
1940	13,785
1950	12,882
1960	13,406
1970	12,577
1980	11,619

CANTON

1830	1,257
1840	(NA)
1850	2,603
1860	4,041
1870	8,660
1880	12,258
1890	26,189
1900	30,667
1910	50,217
1920	87,091
1930	104,906
1940	108,401
1950	116,912
1960	113,631
1970	110,053
1980	94,730

CENTERVILLE

1960	3,490
1970	10,333
1980	18,886

CHILLICOTHE

1820	2,426
1830	2,846
1840	3,977
1850	7,100
1860	7,626
1870	8,920
1880	10,938
1890	11,288
1900	12,976
1910	14,508
1920	15,831
1930	18,340
1940	20,129
1950	20,133
1960	24,957
1970	24,842
1980	23,420

CINCINNATI

1810	2,540
1820	9,642
1830	24,831
1840	46,338
1850	115,435
1860	161,044
1870	216,239
1880	255,139
1890	296,908
1900	325,902
1910	363,591
1920	401,247
1930	451,160
1940	455,610
1950	503,998
1960	502,550
1970	453,514
1980	385,457

CIRCLEVILLE

1830	1,136
1840	2,329
1850	3,411
1860	4,383
1870	5,407
1880	6,046
1890	6,566
1900	6,991
1910	6,744

1920	7,049
1930	7,369
1940	7,982
1950	8,723
1960	11,059
1970	11,687
1980	11,700

CLEVELAND

1820	606
1830	1,076
1840	6,071
1850	17,034
1860	43,417
1870	92,829
1880	160,146
1890	261,353
1900	381,768
1910	560,663
1920	796,841
1930	900,429
1940	878,336
1950	914,808
1960	876,050
1970	750,879
1980	573,822

CLEVELAND HEIGHTS

1910	2,955
1920	15,236
1930	50,945
1940	54,992
1950	59,141
1960	61,813
1970	60,767
1980	56,438

COLUMBUS

1830	2,435
1840	6,048
1850	17,882
1860	18,554
1870	31,274
1880	51,647
1890	88,150
1900	125,560
1910	181,511
1920	237,031
1930	290,564
1940	306,087
1950	375,901
1960	471,316
1970	540,025
1980	564,871

CONNEAUT

1840	2,642
1850	818
1860	1,952
1870	1,163
1880	1,256
1890	3,241
1900	7,133
1910	8,319
1920	9,343
1930	9,691
1940	9,355
1950	10,230
1960	10,557
1970	14,552
1980	13,835

COSHOCTON

1830	330
1840	(NA)
1850	850
1840	1,151
1870	1,754
1880	3,044
1890	3,672
1 00	6,473
1910	9,603
1920	10,847
1930	10,908
1940	11,509
1950	11,675
1960	13,106
1970	13,747
1980	13,405

CUYAHOGA FALLS

1860	1,516
1870	1,861
1880	2,294
1890	2,614
1900	3,186
1910	4,020
1920	10,200
1930	19,797
1940	20,546
1950	29,195
1960	47,922
1970	49,815
1980	43,890

DAYTON

1810	383
1820	1,000
1830	2,950
1840	6,067
1850	10,977
1860	20,081
1870	30,473
1880	38,678
1890	61,220
1900	85,333
1910	116,577
1920	152,559
1930	200,982
19 0	210,718
1950	243,872
1960	262,332
1970	243,023
1980	203,371

DEFIANCE

1850	800
1860	1,399
1870	2,750
1880	5,907
1890	7,694
1900	7,579
1910	7,327
1920	8,876
1930	8,818
1940	9,744
1950	11,265
1960	14,553
1970	16,281
1980	16,810

DELAWARE

1810	200
1820	369
1830	527
1840	898
1850	2,074
1860	3,889
1870	5,641
1880	6,894
1890	8,224
1900	7,940
1910	9,076
1920	8,756
1930	8,675
1940	8,944
1950	11,804
1960	13,282
1970	15,008
1980	18,780

DOVER

1860	1,343
1870	1,593
1880	2,208
1890	3,470
1900	5,422
1910	6,621
1920	8,101
1930	9,716
1940	9,691
1950	9,852
1960	11,300
1970	11,516
1980	11,782

EAST CLEVELAND

1860	3,011
1870	(NA)
1880	2,876
1900	2,757
1910	9,159
1920	27,292
1930	39,667
1940	39,495
1950	40,047
1960	37,991
1970	39,600
1980	36,957

EASTLAKE

1950	7,486
1960	12,467
1970	19,690
1980	22,104

EAST LIVERPOOL

1870	2,105
1880	5,568
1890	10,956
1900	16,485
1910	20,387
1920	21,411
1930	23,239
1940	23,555
1950	24,217
1960	22,306
1970	20,020
1980	16,687

ELYRIA

1850	1,482
1860	1,613
1870	3,038
1880	4,777
1890	5,611
1900	8,791
1910	14,825
1920	20,474
1930	25,633
1940	25,120
1950	30,307
1960	43,782
1970	53,427
1980	57,538

ENGLEWOOD

1920	351
1930	415
1940	531
1950	678
1960	1,515
1970	7,885
1980	11,329

EUCLID

1910	1,953
1920	3,363
1930	12,751
1940	17,866
1950	41,396
1960	62,998
1970	71,552
1980	59,999

FAIRBORN

1950	7,847
1960	19,453
1970	32,267
1980	29,702

FAIRFIELD

1960	9,734
1970	14,680
1980	30,777

FAIRVIEW PARK

1920	642
1930	3,689
1940	4,700
1950	9,311
1960	14,624
1970	21,699
1980	19,311

FINDLAY

1830	52
1840	469
1850	1,256
1860	2,467
1870	3,315
1880	4,633
1890	18,553
1900	17,613
1910	14,858
1920	17,021
1930	19,363
1940	20,228
1950	23,845

1960	30,344
1970	35,800
1980	35,594

FOREST PARK

1970	15,139
1980	18,675

FOSTORIA

1860	1,027
1870	1,733
1880	3,569
1890	7,070
1900	7,730
1910	9,597
1920	9,987
1930	12,790
1940	13,453
1950	14,351
1960	15,732
1970	16,037
1980	15,743

FRANKLIN

1900	2,724
1910	2,659
1920	3,071
1930	4,491
1940	4,511
1950	5,388
1960	7,917
1970	10,075
1980	10,711

FREMONT

1850	1,464
1860	3,510
1870	5,455
1880	8,446
1890	7,141
1900	8,439
1910	9,939
1920	12,468
1930	13,422
1940	14,710
1950	16,537
1960	18,767
1970	18,490
1980	17,834

GAHANNA

1880	235
1890	207
1900	276
1910	294
1920	347
1930	417
1940	425
1950	596
1960	2,717
1970	12,400
1980	18,001

GALION

1860	1,967
1870	3,523
1880	5,635
1890	6,326
1900	7,282
1910	7,214

1920	7,374
1930	7,674
1940	8,685
1950	9,952
1960	12,650
1970	13,123
1980	12,391

GARFIELD HEIGHTS

1920	2,550
1930	15,589
1940	16,989
1950	21,662
1960	38,455
1970	41,417
1980	34,938

GIRARD

1900	2,630
1910	3,736
1920	6,556
1930	9,859
1940	9,805
1950	10,113
1960	12,997
1970	14,119
1980	12,517

GREENVILLE

1850	1,045
1860	1,650
1870	2,520
1880	3,535
1890	5,473
1900	5,501
1910	6,237
1920	7,104
1930	7,036
1940	7,745
1950	8,859
1960	10,585
1970	12,380
1980	12,999

GROVE CITY

1880	150
1890	272
1900	656
1910	837
1920	905
1930	1,546
1940	1,787
1950	2,339
1960	8,107
1970	12,911
1980	16,816

HAMILTON

1820	660
1830	1,079
1840	1,409
1850	3,210
1860	7,223
1870	11,081
1880	12,122
1890	17,565
1900	23,914
1910	35,279
1920	39,675
1930	52,176
1940	50,592
1950	57,951
1960	72,354
1970	67,865
1980	63,189

HUBER HEIGHTS

| 1980 | 35,480 |

IRONTON

1860	3,691
1870	5,686
1880	8,857
1890	10,939
1900	11,868
1910	13,147
1920	14,007
1930	16,621
1940	15,851
1950	16,333
1960	15,745
1970	15,030
1980	14,290

KENT

1880	3,309
1890	3,501
1900	4,541
1910	4,488
1920	7,070
1930	8,375
1940	8,581
1950	12,418
1960	17,836
1970	28,183
1980	26,164

KETTERING

1960	54,462
1970	71,864
1980	61,186

LAKEWOOD

1900	3,355
1910	15,181
1920	41,732
1930	70,059
1940	69,160
1950	68,071
1960	66,154
1970	70,173
1980	61,963

LANCASTER

1830	1,530
1840	3,272
1850	3,483
1860	4,303
1870	4,725
1880	6,803
1890	7,555
1900	8,991
1910	13,093
1920	14,706
1930	18,716
1940	21,940
1950	24,180
1960	29,916
1970	32,911
1980	34,953

LIMA

1850	757
1860	1,989
1870	4,500
1880	7,567
1890	15,981
1900	21,723
1910	30,508
1920	41,326
1930	42,287
1940	44,711
1950	50,142
1960	51,037
1970	53,734
1980	47,381

LORAIN

1880	1,595
1890	4,863
1900	16,028
1910	28,883
1920	37,295
1930	44,512
1940	44,125
1950	51,202
1960	68,392
1970	78,185
1980	75,416

LYNDHURST

1920	288
1930	1,922
1940	2,391
1950	7,359
1960	16,805
1970	19,749
1980	18,092

MANSFIELD

1830	840
1840	1,328
1850	3,557
1860	4,581
1870	8,029
1880	9,829
1890	13,473
1900	17,640
1910	20,768
1920	27,824
1930	33,525
1940	37,154
1950	43,564
1960	47,325
1970	55,047
1980	53,927

MAPLE HEIGHTS

1920	1,732
1930	5,950
1940	6,728
1950	15,586
1960	31,667
1970	34,093
1980	29,735

MARIETTA

1830	1,207
1840	1,814
1850	3,175
1860	4,323
1870	5,218
1880	5,444
1890	8,273
1900	13,348
1910	12,923
1920	15,140
1930	14,285
1940	14,543
1950	16,006
1960	16,847
1970	16,861
1980	16,467

MARION

1830	287
1840	570
1850	1,311
1860	1,844
1870	2,531
1880	3,899
1890	8,327
1900	11,862
1910	18,232
1920	27,891
1930	31,084
1940	30,817
1950	33,817
1960	37,079
1970	38,646
1980	37,040

MASSILLON

1860	3,819
1870	5,185
1880	6,836
1890	10,092
1900	11,944
1910	13,879
1920	17,428
1930	26,400
1940	26,644
1950	29,594
1960	31,236
1970	32,539
1980	30,557

MAUMEE

1910	2,307
1920	3,195
1930	4,588
1940	4,683
1950	5,548
1960	12,063
1970	15,937
1980	15,747

MAYFIELD HEIGHTS

1930	2,612
1940	2,696
1950	5,807
1960	13,478
1970	22,139
1980	21,550

MEDINA

1900	2,232
1910	2,734
1920	3,430
1930	4,071
1940	4,359
1950	5,097
1960	8,235
1970	10,913
1980	15,268

MENTOR

1870	416
1880	540
1890	502
1900	624
1910	732
1920	851
1930	1,589
1940	1,827
1950	2,383
1960	4,354
1970	36,912
1980	42,065

MIAMISBURG

1850	1,095
1860	1,639
1870	1,425
1880	1,936
1890	2,952
1900	3,941
1910	4,271
1920	4,383
1930	5,518
1940	5,544
1950	6,329
1960	9,893
1970	14,797
1980	15,304

MIDDLEBURG HEIGHTS

1930	874
1940	1,225
1950	2,299
1960	7,282
1970	12,367
1980	16,218

MIDDLETOWN

1850	1,087
1860	2,070
1870	3,046
1880	4,538
1890	7,681
1900	9,215
1910	13,152
1920	23,594
1930	29,992
1940	31,220
1950	33,695
1960	42,115
1970	48,767
1980	43,719

MONTGOMERY

1920	378
1930	394
1940	461
1950	579
1960	3,075
1970	5,683
1980	10,088

MOUNT VERNON

1850	3,711
1860	4,202
1870	4,876
1880	5,249
1890	6,027
1900	6,633
1910	9,087
1920	9,237
1930	9,370
1940	10,122
1950	12,185
1960	13,284
1970	13,373
1980	14,323

NEWARK

1830	999
1840	2,705
1850	3,659
1860	4,675
1870	6,698
1880	9,600
1890	14,270
1900	18,157
1910	25,404
1920	26,718
1930	30,596
1940	31,487
1950	34,275
1960	41,790
1970	41,836
1980	41,200

NEW PHILADELPHIA

1850	1,413
1860	(NA)
1870	3,143
1880	3,070
1890	4,456
1900	6,213
1910	8,542
1920	10,718
1930	12,365
1940	12,328
1950	12,948
1960	14,241
1970	15,184
1980	16,883

NILES

1880	3,879
1890	4,289
1900	7,468
1910	8,361
1920	13,080
1930	16,314
1940	16,273
1950	16,773
1960	19,545
1970	21,581
1980	23,088

NORTH CANTON

1910	865
1920	1,597
1930	2,648
1940	2,988
1950	4,032
1960	7,727
1970	15,228
1980	14,228

NORTH COLLEGE HILL

1920	1,104
1930	4,139
1940	5,231
1950	7,921
1960	12,035
1970	12,363
1980	11,114

NORTH OLMSTED

1910	1,030
1920	1,419
1930	2,624
1940	3,487
1950	6,604
1960	16,290
1970	34,861
1980	36,486

NORTH RIDGEVILLE

1960	8,057
1970	13,152
1980	21,522

NORTH ROYALTON

1930	1,397
1940	2,559
1950	3,939
1960	9,290
1970	12,807
1980	17,671

NORTON

1970	12,308
1980	12,242

NORWALK

1850	1,437
1860	2,839
1870	4,498
1880	5,704
1890	7,195
1900	7,074
1910	7,858
1920	7,379
1930	7,776
1940	8,211
1950	9,775
1960	12,900
1970	13,386
1980	14,358

NORWOOD

1900	6,480
1910	16,185
1920	24,966
1930	33,411
1940	34,010
1950	35,001
1960	34,580
1970	30,420
1980	26,342

OREGON

1960	13,319
1970	16,563
1980	18,675

OXFORD

1850	1,111
1860	1,839
1870	1,738
1880	1,743
1890	1,922
1900	2,009
1910	2,017
1920	2,146
1930	2,588
1940	2,756
1950	6,944
1960	7,828
1970	15,868
1980	17,655

PAINESVILLE

1860	2,676
1870	3,728
1880	3,841
1890	4,755
1900	5,024
1910	5,501
1920	7,272
1930	10,944
1940	12,235
1950	14,432
1950	16,116
1970	16,536
1980	16,391

PARMA

1930	13,899
1940	16,365
1950	28,897
1960	82,845
1970	100,216
1980	92,548

PARMA HEIGHTS

1920	310
1930	960
1940	1,330
1950	3,901
1960	18,100
1970	27,192
1980	23,112

PERRYSBURG

1910	541
1920	575
1930	3,182
1940	3,457
1950	4,006
1960	5,519
1970	7,693
1980	10,215

PIQUA

1850	3,277
1860	4,616
1870	5,967
1880	6,031
1890	9,090
1900	12,172
1910	13,388
1920	15,044
1930	16,009
1940	16,049
1950	17,447
1960	19,219
1970	20,741
1980	20,480

PORTSMOUTH

1820	527
1830	1,064
1840	(NA)
1850	4,011
1860	6,268
1870	10,592
1880	11,321
1890	12,394
1900	17,870
1910	23,481
1920	33,011
1930	42,560
1940	40,466
1950	36,798
1960	33,637
1970	27,633
1980	25,943

RAVENNA

1860	1,777
1870	2,188
1880	3,255
1890	3,417
1900	4,003
1910	5,310
1920	7,219
1930	8,019
1940	8,538
1950	9,857
1960	10,918
1970	11,780
1980	11,987

READING

1860	1,230
1870	1,575
1880	2,680
1890	(NA)
1900	3,076
1910	3,985
1920	4,540
1930	5,723
1940	6,079
1950	7,836
1960	12,832
1970	14,617
1980	12,843

REYNOLDSBURG

1870	457
1880	375
1890	393
1900	339
1910	431
1920	491
1930	562
1940	652
1950	724
1960	7,793
1970	13,921
1980	20,661

RICHMOND HEIGHTS

1920	265
1930	418
1940	507
1950	891
1960	5,068
1970	9,220
1980	10,095

ROCKY RIVER

1900	1,319
1910	1,174
1920	1,861
1930	5,632
1940	8,291
1950	11,237
1960	18,097
1970	22,958
1980	21,084

SALEM

1860	1,889
1870	3,700
1880	4,041
1890	5,780
1900	7,582
1910	8,943
1920	10,305
1930	10,622
1940	12,301
1950	12,754
1960	13,854
1970	14,186
1980	12,869

SANDUSKY

1850	5,087
1860	8,408
1870	13,000
1880	15,838
1890	18,471
1900	19,664
1910	19,989
1920	22,897
1930	24,662
1940	24,874
1950	29,375
1960	31,989
1970	32,674
1980	31,360

SEVEN HILLS

1930	383
1940	555
1950	1,350
1960	5,708
1970	12,700
1980	13,650

SHAKER HEIGHTS

1920	1,616
1930	17,783
1940	23,393
1950	28,222
1960	36,460
1970	36,306
1980	32,487

SHARONVILLE

1920	753
1930	1,111
1940	1,157
1950	1,318
1960	3,890
1970	11,393
1980	10,108

SHEFFIELD LAKE

1930	1,256
1940	1,099
1950	2,381
1960	6,884
1970	8,734
1980	10,484

SIDNEY

1830	240
1840	713
1850	1,302
1860	2,055
1870	2,808
1880	3,823
1890	4,850
1900	5,688
1910	6,607
1920	8,590
1930	9,301
1940	9,790
1950	11,491
1960	14,663
1970	16,332
1980	17,657

SOLON

1930	1,027
1940	1,508
1950	2,570
1960	6,333
1970	11,147
1980	14,341

SOUTH EUCLID

1920	1,605
1930	4,399
1940	6,146
1950	15,432
1960	27,569
1970	29,579
1980	25,713

SPRINGDALE

1960	3,556
1970	8,127
1980	10,111

SPRINGFIELD

1820	1,868
1830	1,080
1840	2,062
1850	5,108
1860	7,002
1870	12,652
1880	21,730
1890	31,895
1900	38,253
1910	46,921
1920	60,840
1930	68,743
1940	70,662
1950	78,508
1960	82,723
1970	81,941
1980	72,563

STEUBENVILLE

1820	2,539
1830	2,937
1840	5,203
1850	6,140
1860	6,154
1870	8,107
1880	12,093
1890	13,394
1900	14,349
1910	22,391
1920	28,508
1930	35,422
1940	37,651
1950	35,872
1960	32,495
1970	30,771
1980	26,400

STOW

1960	12,194
1970	20,061
1980	25,303

STRONGSVILLE

1930	1,349
1940	2,216
1950	3,504
1960	8,504
1970	15,182
1980	28,557

STRUTHERS

1910	3,370
1920	5,847
1930	11,249
1940	11,739
1950	11,941
1960	15,631
1970	15,343
1980	13,624

SYLVANIA

1900	617
1910	1,002
1920	1,222
1930	2,106
1940	2,199
1950	2,433
1960	5,187
1970	12,031
1980	15,527

TALLMADGE

1940	3,452
1950	5,821
1960	10,246
1970	15,274
1980	15,269

TIFFIN

1850	2,718
1860	3,992
1870	5,684
1880	7,879
1890	10,801
1900	10,989
1910	11,894
1920	14,375
1930	16,428
1940	16,102
1950	18,952
1960	21,478
1970	21,596
1980	19,549

TOLEDO

1840	1,222
1850	3,829
1860	13,768
1870	31,584
1880	50,137
1890	81,434
1900	131,822
1910	168,497
1920	243,164
1930	290,718
1940	282,349
1950	303,616
1960	318,003
1970	383,062
1980	354,635

TROY

1820	293
1830	504
1840	1,351
1850	1,956
1860	2,643
1870	3,005
1880	3,807
1890	4,497
1900	5,881
1910	6,122
1920	7,260
1930	8,675
1940	9,697
1950	10,661
1960	13,685
1970	17,186
1980	19,086

UNIVERSITY HEIGHTS

1910	221
1920	131
1930	2,237
1940	5,981
1950	11,566
1960	16,641
1970	17,055
1980	15,401

UPPER ARLINGTON

1920	620
1930	3,059
1940	5,370
1950	9,024
1960	28,486
1970	38,727
1980	35,648

URBANA

1820	644
1830	1,102
1840	1,070
1850	2,020
1860	3,429
1870	4,276
1880	6,252
1890	6,510

VANDALIA

1850	228
1870	316
1880	315
1890	265
1900	284
1910	221
1920	257
1930	331
1940	378
1950	927
1960	6,342
1970	10,796
1980	13,161

VAN WERT

1850	268
1860	1,015
1870	2,625
1880	4,079
1890	5,512
1900	6,422
1910	7,157
1920	8,100
1930	8,472
1940	9,227
1950	10,364
1960	11,323
1970	11,320
1980	11,035

VERMILION

1900	1,384
1910	1,369
1920	1,436
1930	1,464
1940	1,616
1950	2,214
1960	4,785
1970	9,872
1980	11,012

WADSWORTH

1870	949
1880	1,219
1890	1,574
1900	1,764
1910	3,073
1920	4,742
1930	5,930
1940	6,495
1950	7,966
1960	10,635
1970	13,142
1980	15,166

WARREN

1840	1,966
1850	(NA)
1860	2,402
1870	3,457
1880	4,428
1890	5,973
1900	8,529
1910	11,081
1920	27,050
1930	41,062
1940	42,837
1950	49,856
1960	59,648
1970	63,494
1980	56,629

WARRENSVILLE HEIGHTS

1930	877
1940	1,175
1950	4,126
1960	10,609
1970	18,925
1980	16,565

WASHINGTON

1850	569
1860	1,035
1870	2,117
1880	3,798
1890	5,742
1900	5,751
1910	7,277
1920	7,962
1930	8,426
1940	9,402
1950	10,560
1960	12,388
1970	12,495
1980	12,682

WEST CARROLLTON

1890	366
1900	987
1910	1,285
1920	1,430
1930	2,101
1940	2,176
1950	2,876
1960	4,749
1970	10,748
1980	13,148

WESTERVILLE

1860	668
1870	741
1880	1,148
1890	1,329
1900	1,462
1910	1,903
1920	2,480
1930	2,879
1940	3,146
1950	4,122
1960	7,011
1970	12,530
1980	23,414

WESTLAKE

1920	1,754
1930	2,453
1940	3,200
1950	4,912
1960	12,906
1970	15,689
1980	19,483

WHITEHALL

1950	4,877
1960	20,818
1970	25,263
1980	21,299

WICKLIFFE

1920	1,508
1930	2,491
1940	3,155
1950	5,002
1960	15,760
1970	20,632
1980	16,790

WILLOUGHBY

1860	589
1870	867
1880	1,001
1890	1,219
1900	1,753
1910	2,072
1920	2,656
1930	4,252
1940	4,364
1950	5,602
1960	15,058
1970	18,634
1980	19,329

WILLOWICK

1930	667
1940	915
1950	3,677
1960	18,749
1970	21,237
1980	17,834

WILMINGTON

1850	1,238
1860	915
1870	2,023
1880	2,745
1890	3,079
1900	3,613
1910	4,491
1920	5,037
1930	5,332
1940	5,971
1950	7,387
1960	8,915
1970	10,051
1980	10,431

WOOSTER

1820	467
1830	977
1840	1,913
1850	2,797
1860	3,361
1870	5,419
1880	5,840
1890	5,901
1900	6,063
1910	6,136
1920	8,204
1930	10,742

1940	11,543
1950	14,005
1960	17,046
1970	18,703
1980	19,289

WORTHINGTON

1850	494
1860	356
1880	459
1890	341
1900	443
1910	547
1920	705
1930	1,239
1940	1,569
1950	2,141
1960	9,239
1970	15,326
1980	15,016

XENIA

1850	3,024
1860	4,658
1870	6,377
1880	7,026
1890	7,301
1900	8,696
1910	8,706
1920	9,110
1930	10,507
1940	10,633
1950	12,877
1960	20,445
1970	25,373
1980	24,653

YOUNGSTOWN

1850	2,802
1860	2,759
1870	8,075
1880	15,435
1890	33,220
1900	44,885
1910	79,066
1920	132,358
1930	170,002
1940	167,720
1950	168,330
1960	166,689
1970	140,909
1980	115,436

ZANESVILLE

1820	2,052
1830	3,094
1840	4,766
1850	7,929
1860	9,229
1870	10,011
1880	18,113
1890	21,009
1900	23,538
1910	28,026
1920	29,569
1930	36,440
1940	37,500
1950	40,517
1960	39,077
1970	33,045
1980	28,655

CORRECTION NOTE

The official 1980 census counts of total population shown in
this report supersede counts issued previously. Corrections
to the figures were made after the counts were provided to
the State for redistricting purposes and released in Advance
Report PHC80-V for this State.

Shown below are corrections to the 1980 census counts of the
total population made after the tabulations for this report
were completed. Any additional corrections made after this
report is printed are available by writing to Data User
Services Division, Customer Services (Corrections), Bureau of
the Census, Washington, D.C. 20233.

The 1980 figures shown in this publication are subject to
change pending the outcome of the various lawsuits dealing
with the census counts.

	1980 population	
	As shown in the tables	Corrected
The State......................	10 797 630	10 797 624
Cuyahoga County:		
Chagrin Falls township.............	136	4 471
Chagrin Falls village............	(1)	4 335
Chagrin Falls village..............	4 335	(2)
Franklin County.....................	869 132	869 126
Blendon township...................	11 285	11 124
Columbus city (pt.).................	564 826	564 987
Perry township.....................	6 763	6 757
Greene County:		
Bath township......................	32 815	36 865
Wright-Patterson AFB (CDP)(pt.)..	(1)	4 050
Dayton city (pt.)..................	4 050	-
Highland County:		
Madison township:		
Greenfield city...................	5 034	5 150
Montgomery County:		
Dayton city (pt.)..................	199 321	193 444
Mad River township.................	26 926	32 803
Wright-Patterson AFB (CDP)(pt.)..	(1)	5 105
Stark County:		
Canton city........................	94 730	93 077
Louisville city....................	7 873	7 996
Nimishillen township...............	10 559	10 436
Plain township.....................	46 665	48 318
Columbus city (total)................	564 871	565 032
Dayton city (total)..................	203 371	193 444
Wright-Patterson AFB (CDP)(total)....	(1)	9 155

[1]Not shown.
[2]Delete, Chagrin Falls village is dependent in Chagrin
Falls township.

County Subdivisions	1980	1970
The State[1]	10 797 630	'10 657 423
Adams County[2]	24 328	18 957
Bratton township	699	514
Brush Creek township	1 278	959
Franklin township	1 002	823
Green township	795	616
Rome village	135	90
Jefferson township	981	898
Liberty township	1 247	630
West Union village (pt.)[2]	45	...
Manchester township	2 319	2 202
Manchester village[2]	2 313	2 195
Meigs township	3 473	2 863
Peebles village	1 790	1 629
Monroe township	796	652
Oliver township	715	424
Scott township	1 929	1 526
Seaman village[2]	1 039	866
Sprigg township	1 659	1 281
Tiffin township	4 549	3 448
West Union village (pt.)[2]	2 746	1 951
Wayne township	1 110	823
Cherry Fork village	210	176
Winchester township	1 776	1 298
Winchester village[2]	1 080	760
Allen County[3]	112 241	111 144
Amanda township	1 769	1 498
American township[3]	12 825	'9 977
Elida village[3]	1 349	1 211
Auglaize township	2 548	2 473
Harrod village[3]	506	533
Bath township[3]	10 443	'9 323
Jackson township	2 702	2 247
Lafayette village	488	486
Lima city[3]	47 381	'53 734
Marion township	6 718	6 945
Delphos city (pt.)[3]	3 984	4 301
Monroe township	2 217	2 077
Cairo village	596	587
Perry township[3]	3 586	'3 751
Richland township	5 357	4 975
Beaverdam village	492	525
Bluffton village (pt.)	3 237	2 935
Shawnee township[3]	12 344	'9 734
Fort Shawnee village	4 541	3 436
Spencer township	3 109	3 201
Spencerville village[3]	2 184	2 241
Sugar Creek township	1 242	1 209
Ashland County[4]	46 178	43 303
Ashland city[4]	20 326	19 872
Clear Creek township	1 702	1 639
Bailey Lakes village	397	394
Savannah village	351	361
Green township	3 867	3 368
Loudonville village (pt.)	1 440	1 184
Perrysville village[4]	836	752
Hanover township	2 383	2 438
Loudonville village (pt.)[4]	1 438	1 681
Jackson township	1 841	1 410
Polk village	351	435
Lake township	529	501
Mifflin township	1 060	932
Mifflin village	203	215
Milton township[4]	2 044	1 919
Mohican township	1 650	1 561
Jeromesville village	582	559
Montgomery township[4]	2 236	2 198
Orange township	1 968	1 843
Perry township	1 594	1 356
Ruggles township	696	666
Sullivan township	1 311	1 063
Troy township	853	749
Vermillion township	2 118	1 788
Hayesville village	518	506
Ashtabula County[5]	104 215	98 237
Andover township	2 424	2 142
Andover village[5]	1 205	1 179
Ashtabula township	25 829	27 007
Ashtabula city (pt.)[5]	18 521	19 615
Edgewood (CDP)	3 099	3 437
Austinburg township	1 869	1 487
Cherry Valley township	765	631
Colebrook township	731	731
Conneaut city[5]	13 835	14 552
Denmark township	818	773
Dorset township	952	886
Geneva township	12 017	11 099
Geneva city	6 655	6 449
Geneva-on-the-Lake village	1 634	877
Harpersfield township	2 331	1 584
Hartsgrove township	1 214	903
Jefferson township	4 987	4 140
Jefferson village[5]	2 952	2 472
Kingsville township[5]	2 162	4 181
Kingsville (CDP)	1 243	1 129

County Subdivisions	1980	1970
Ashtabula County—Con.		
Lenox township	1 291	1 182
Monroe township	2 079	1 712
Morgan township	1 359	1 501
Rock Creek village	652	731
New Lyme township	1 058	873
North Kingsville village[5]	2 939	2 458
Orwell township	2 220	1 727
Orwell village[5]	1 067	965
Pierpont township	1 074	978
Plymouth township	2 029	2 225
Richmond township	887	793
Roaming Shores village[5]	581	...
Rome township	863	707
Saybrook township	11 697	11 274
Ashtabula city (pt.)[5]	4 928	4 698
Sheffield township	1 513	1 160
Trumbull township	1 330	963
Wayne township	652	591
Williamsfield township	1 224	988
Windsor township	1 485	1 447
Athens County[6]	56 399	'55 747
Alexander township	2 096	1 368
Albany village (pt.)[6]	13	...
Ames township	1 014	922
Amesville village	247	295
Athens township	25 706	'28 668
Athens city (pt.)[6]	19 555	'23 903
The Plains (CDP) (pt.)	1 671	1 568
Bern township	538	404
Canaan township	1 430	1 157
Athens city (pt.)[6]	188	265
Carthage township	1 090	872
Dover township	3 429	3 288
Chauncey village	1 050	1 117
The Plains (CDP) (pt.)	373	...
Lee township	2 066	1 752
Albany village (pt.)[6]	892	899
Lodi township	1 112	904
Rome township	1 452	1 145
Trimble township	5 063	4 629
Glouster village	2 211	2 121
Jacksonville village	651	545
Trimble village	579	542
Troy township	2 340	1 953
Coolville village	649	672
Waterloo township	1 934	1 740
York township	7 129	6 945
Buchtel village	585	592
Nelsonville city	4 567	4 812
Auglaize County[7]	42 554	38 602
Clay township	832	889
Duchouquet township	13 371	11 294
Cridersville village	1 843	1 103
Wapakoneta city[7]	8 402	7 324
German township	3 171	2 976
New Bremen village[7]	2 393	2 185
Goshen township	517	556
Jackson township	3 298	3 130
Minster village[7]	2 557	2 405
Logan township	1 051	956
Buckland village	271	281
Moulton township	1 365	1 105
Noble township	1 081	1 047
St. Marys city (pt.)[7]	3	...
Pusheta township	1 108	964
St. Marys township	11 214	10 438
St. Marys city (pt.)[7]	8 411	7 699
Salem township	515	574
Union township	1 667	1 476
Uniopolis village	259	291
Washington township	1 706	1 740
New Knoxville village[7]	760	852
Wayne township	1 658	1 457
Waynesfield village	826	704
Belmont County[8]	82 569	80 917
Colerain township	5 316	5 266
Barton (CDP)	1 039	...
Flushing township	2 394	2 424
Flushing village	1 266	1 207
Holloway village	459	488
Goshen township	3 412	2 948
Belmont village	714	666
Bethesda village	1 429	1 157
Kirkwood township	360	513
Fairview village (pt.)	4	7
Mead township	7 038	7 524
Shadyside city (pt.)[8]	4 270	5 030
Pease township	19 471	21 511
Bridgeport village	2 642	3 001
Brookside village[8]	887	939
Martins Ferry city[8]	9 331	10 757
Wolfhurst (CDP)	1 622	...
Yorkville village (pt.)[8]	492	527
Pultney township	13 675	14 624
Bellaire city	8 241	9 655
Neffs (CDP)	1 106	...

County Subdivisions	1980	1970
Belmont County—Con.		
Pultney township—Con.		
Shadyside city (pt.)	45	40
Richland township	12 614	10 062
St. Clairsville city[8]	5 452	4 754
Smith township	1 883	1 563
Somerset township	1 062	910
Union township	2 263	1 724
Morristown village	463	385
Warren township	6 427	5 803
Barnesville village[8]	4 633	4 292
Washington township	741	606
Wayne township	677	473
Wilson village (pt.)	20	–
Wheeling township	1 823	1 747
York township	3 413	3 219
Powhatan Point village[8]	2 181	2 167
Brown County[9]	31 920	26 635
Byrd township	653	555
Clark township	2 858	2 110
Hamersville village[9]	688	567
Eagle township	941	781
Franklin township	925	632
Green township	2 415	2 197
Mount Orab village (pt.)[9]	1 070	934
Huntington township	2 534	1 779
Aberdeen village	1 566	1 165
Jackson township	747	588
Jefferson township	1 092	887
Russellville village	445	399
Lewis township	1 498	1 409
Higginsport village	343	383
Perry township	3 288	2 320
Fayetteville village	478	415
St. Martin village	126	148
Pike township	2 447	1 653
Mount Orab village (pt.)[9]	503	372
Pleasant township	4 552	4 037
Georgetown village[9]	3 467	3 087
Scott township	963	795
Sterling township	1 532	1 158
Union township	3 503	4 018
Ripley village	2 174	2 745
Washington township	1 972	1 716
Sardinia village	826	824
Butler County[10]	258 787	226 207
Fairfield township[10]	38 707	21 779
Fairfield city[10]	30 777	14 680
Hamilton city[10]	63 189	67 865
Hanover township[10]	7 290	6 175
Millville village (pt.)[10]	257	349
Lemon township[10]	12 782	11 774
Middletown South (CDP)	5 260	...
Monroe village (pt.)[10]	4 079	3 403
Liberty township	6 508	3 736
Monroe village (pt.)[10]	109	32
Madison township[10]	8 596	13 112
Middletown city[10]	43 719	48 767
Milford township	2 550	2 350
Somerville village	357	388
Morgan township	4 076	2 438
Oxford township	21 714	18 225
College Corner village (pt.)	116	125
Oxford city[10]	17 655	15 868
Reily township	2 177	1 626
Ross township[10]	5 626	3 810
Millville village (pt.)[10]	552	348
Ross (CDP)	2 767	1 661
St. Clair township[10]	8 223	7 952
New Miami village	2 980	3 273
Seven Mile village (pt.)[10]	303	233
Trenton city[10]	6 401	5 278
Union township	23 553	12 795
Pisgah (CDP)	15 660	...
Wayne township	3 676	3 803
Jacksonburg village	58	92
Seven Mile village (pt.)[10]	538	466
Carroll County[11]	25 598	21 579
Augusta township	1 394	1 281
Brown township	7 568	5 662
Malvern village	1 032	1 256
Minerva village (pt.)[11]	2 145	1 913
Center township	4 526	4 311
Carrollton village[11]	3 065	2 817
East township	742	554
Fox township	994	889
Harrison township	1 807	1 278
Lee township	1 000	999
Loudon township	976	1 107
Monroe township	1 633	1 446
Dellroy village	368	363
Sherrodsville village (pt.)	82	69
Orange township	1 171	1 075
Leesville village	233	221
Sherrodsville village (pt.)	314	331
Perry township	896	617
Rose township	1 289	1 181

County Subdivisions	1980	1970
Carroll County—Con.		
Rose township—Con.		
Magnolia village (pt.)	309	363
Union township	830	482
Washington township	772	697
Champaign County[12]	33 649	30 491
Adams township	1 146	1 077
Concord township	1 042	784
Goshen township	3 255	2 856
Mechanicsburg village[12]	1 792	1 686
Harrison township	596	590
Jackson township	2 148	2 160
Christiansburg village	593	724
St. Paris village (pt.)[12]	205	214
Johnson township	2 950	2 450
St. Paris village (pt.)[12]	1 537	1 432
Mad River township	2 203	1 680
Rush township	2 055	1 783
North Lewisburg village	1 072	840
Woodstock village[12]	292	281
Salem township	1 970	1 901
Urbana city (pt.)[12]	21	...
Union township	1 529	1 208
Mutual village	159	177
Urbana township	13 541	13 061
Urbana city (pt.)[12]	10 741	11 237
Wayne township	1 214	941
Clark County[13]	150 236	157 115
Bethel township	20 128	24 694
Crystal Lakes (CDP)	1 463	5 851
Donnelsville village[13]	219	278
New Carlisle city (pt.)[13]	6 498	6 112
Park Layne (CDP)	5 372	...
German township	7 397	5 962
Lawrenceville village	307	282
Tremont City village[13]	374	426
Green township	2 907	2 663
Clifton village (pt.)	45	66
Harmony township	3 253	2 972
South Vienna village[13]	464	545
Madison township	2 649	2 505
South Charleston village[13]	1 682	1 500
Mad River township	11 623	10 715
Enon village[13]	2 597	1 929
Green Meadows (CDP)	2 689	...
Moorefield township[13]	9 823	8 690
Northridge (CDP)	5 559	...
Pike township	3 469	2 621
New Carlisle city (pt.)[13]	–	...
North Hampton village	421	489
Pleasant township	2 760	1 791
Catawba village	317	323
Springfield city[13]	72 563	81 941
Springfield township[13]	13 664	12 561
Clermont County[14]	128 483	95 372
Batavia township	10 523	7 872
Amelia village (pt.)[14]	703	500
Batavia village[14]	1 896	1 894
Franklin township	3 191	2 368
Chilo village	173	174
Felicity village[14]	929	786
Goshen township	12 442	8 217
Jackson township	2 221	1 930
Loveland city (pt.)[14]	1 643	1 606
Miami township[14]	28 587	22 459
Milford village (pt.)[14]	5 205	4 776
Monroe township	6 133	3 180
Ohio township	5 222	4 336
New Richmond village (pt.)[14]	2 769	2 650
Pierce township	7 262	5 320
Amelia village (pt.)[14]	405	320
New Richmond village (pt.)[14]	–	...
Stonelick township	5 133	4 117
Owensville village[14]	858	707
Tate township	7 946	6 759
Bethel village[14]	2 231	2 214
Union township	28 225	20 131
Washington township	2 066	1 699
Moscow village[14]	324	348
Neville village	142	179
Wayne township	3 352	2 550
Newtonsville village	434	385
Williamsburg township	4 537	4 434
Williamsburg village[14]	1 952	2 054
Clinton County[15]	34 603	31 464
Adams township	1 371	1 009
Chester township	1 080	935
Clark township	1 672	1 518
Martinsville village	539	500
Green township	2 093	1 932
New Vienna village[15]	1 133	849
Jefferson township	1 326	1 264
Midland village	365	388
Liberty township	953	1 015
Port William village[15]	300	323

County Subdivisions	1980	1970
Clinton County—Con.		
Marion township	5 311	4 492
Blanchester village[15]	3 202	3 080
Richland township	3 735	3 139
Sabina village[15]	2 799	2 160
Union township	12 702	12 225
Wilmington city[15]	10 431	10 051
Vernon township	1 845	1 577
Clarksville village	525	574
Washington township	1 296	1 029
Wayne township	708	757
Wilson township	511	572
Columbiana County[16]	113 572	108 310
Butler township	3 228	3 001
Center township	6 549	6 222
Lisbon village[16]	3 159	3 521
East Liverpool city[16]	16 687	ʳ20 020
Elkrun township	2 288	1 836
Fairfield township	8 996	7 772
Columbiana village (pt.)[16]	4 986	4 959
Leetonia village (pt.)	116	125
Franklin township	831	782
Summitville village	146	143
Hanover township	3 288	2 609
Hanoverton village	490	483
Knox township	4 486	3 731
Liverpool township[16]	4 921	ʳ3 678
La Croft (CDP)	1 508	...
Madison township	3 387	2 438
Middleton township	3 426	2 677
Rogers village	298	310
Perry township	17 886	18 178
Salem city[16]	12 869	14 186
St. Clair township	8 080	7 428
Calcutta (CDP)	1 121	...
Glenmoor (CDP)	2 588	...
Salem township	5 365	5 109
Leetonia village (pt.)[16]	2 005	2 217
Washingtonville village (pt.)	532	500
Unity township	10 220	9 380
East Palestine city[16]	5 306	5 604
New Waterford village[16]	1 314	735
Washington township	2 618	2 540
Salineville village (pt.)[16]	1 629	1 686
Wayne township	741	567
Wellsville city	5 095	5 891
West township	3 022	2 444
Minerva village (pt.)[16]	7	...
Yellow Creek township	2 458	2 007
Coshocton County[17]	36 024	33 486
Adams township	580	581
Bedford township	405	344
Bethlehem township	1 094	797
Clark township	526	586
Coshocton city[17]	13 405	13 747
Crawford township	1 020	876
Baltic village (pt.)[17]	—	ʳ—
Franklin township	1 338	1 237
Conesville village	451	448
Jackson township[17]	1 947	2 078
Jefferson township	1 421	1 253
Nellie village	150	140
Warsaw village	765	725
Keene township	1 523	1 155
Lafayette township[17]	4 275	3 228
West Lafayette village[17]	2 225	1 719
Linton township	716	660
Plainfield village	221	183
Mill Creek township	529	433
Monroe township	381	304
Newcastle township	358	418
Oxford township	1 521	1 259
Perry township	343	324
Pike township	415	336
Tiverton township	322	300
Tuscarawas township[17]	2 010	15 490
Virginia township	516	504
Washington township	452	458
White Eyes township	927	865
Crawford County[18]	50 075	50 364
Auburn township	989	1 032
Tiro village	279	310
Bucyrus township	12 274	12 342
Bucyrus city (pt.)[18]	11 298	11 319
Chatfield township	880	905
Chatfield village	228	291
Cranberry township	1 943	2 001
New Washington village	1 213	1 251
Dallas township	482	476
Galion city[18]	12 391	13 123
Holmes township	2 551	2 495
Bucyrus city (pt.)[18]	1 094	1 086
Jackson township	5 800	6 402
Crestline city (pt.)[18]	5 392	5 947
Jefferson township	1 731	1 532
North Robinson village (pt.)	111	66

County Subdivisions	1980	1970
Crawford County—Con.		
Liberty township	1 489	1 477
Lykens township	694	744
Polk township[18]	2 770	2 617
Sandusky township	497	434
Texas township	458	404
Tod township	755	712
Vernon township	804	735
Whetstone township	3 567	2 933
Bucyrus city (pt.)[18]	1 041	706
North Robinson village (pt.)	191	211
Cuyahoga County[19]	1 498 400	ʳ1 720 835
Bay Village city	17 846	18 163
Beachwood city	9 983	9 631
Bedford city	15 056	17 552
Bedford Heights city	13 214	13 063
Bentleyville village	381	338
Berea city	19 567	ʳ22 465
Bratenahl village	1 485	1 613
Brecksville city	10 132	9 137
Broadview Heights city	10 920	11 463
Brooklyn city[19]	12 342	13 142
Brooklyn Heights village	1 653	1 527
Brook Park city	26 195	30 774
Chagrin Falls township	136	84
Chagrin Falls village	4 335	4 848
Cleveland city[19]	573 822	ʳ750 879
Cleveland Heights city	56 438	60 767
Cuyahoga Heights village	739	866
East Cleveland city	36 957	39 600
Euclid city	59 999	71 552
Fairview Park city	19 311	ʳ21 699
Garfield Heights city	34 938	41 417
Gates Mills village	2 236	2 378
Glenwillow village	492	ʳ508
Highland Heights city	5 739	5 926
Hunting Valley village (pt.)	633	673
Independence city	6 607	7 034
Lakewood city	61 963	70 173
Linndale village	129	ʳ169
Lyndhurst city	18 092	19 749
Maple Heights city	29 735	34 093
Mayfield village	3 577	3 548
Mayfield Heights city	21 550	22 139
Middleburg Heights city	16 218	12 367
Moreland Hills village	3 083	ʳ2 952
Newburgh Heights village	2 678	3 396
North Olmsted city	36 486	34 861
North Randall village[19]	1 054	1 212
North Royalton city	17 671	12 807
Oakwood village	3 786	ʳ3 499
Olmsted township	6 976	6 318
Olmsted Falls city[19]	5 868	2 504
Orange village	2 376	2 112
Parma city	92 548	100 216
Parma Heights city	23 112	27 192
Pepper Pike city	6 177	ʳ5 382
Richmond Heights city	10 095	9 220
Riveredge township	477	632
Rocky River city	21 084	22 958
Seven Hills city	13 650	12 700
Shaker Heights city	32 487	36 306
Solon city	14 341	ʳ11 147
South Euclid city	25 713	29 579
Strongsville city	28 577	15 182
University Heights city	15 401	17 055
Valley View village	1 576	1 422
Walton Hills village	2 199	2 508
Warrensville township	1 640	2 160
Warrensville Heights city[19]	16 565	18 925
Westlake city	19 483	15 689
Woodmere village	877	ʳ1 041
Darke County[20]	55 096	49 141
Adams township	3 563	3 027
Bradford village (pt.)	994	923
Gettysburg village	545	526
Allen township	1 441	1 517
Burkettsville village (pt.)	97	107
New Weston village	184	174
Rossburg village	260	275
Brown township	2 199	1 931
Ansonia village[20]	1 267	1 044
Butler township	1 842	1 623
Castine village	147	150
New Madison village (pt.)[20]	218	157
Franklin township	1 341	1 237
Greenville township	17 470	15 849
Greenville city[20]	12 999	12 380
Harrison township	2 402	2 205
Hollansburg village	339	364
New Madison village (pt.)	790	802
Jackson township	3 569	2 978
Union City village[20]	1 716	1 808
Liberty township	1 218	1 278
Palestine village	213	246
Mississinawa township	855	848
Monroe township	1 824	1 634
Pitsburg village	460	462
Neave township	2 288	1 311

County Subdivisions	1980	1970
Darke County—Con.		
Patterson township	1 434	1 448
Osgood village	306	289
Yorkshire village	146	151
Richland township	924	862
Twin township	4 063	3 623
Arcanum village[20]	2 002	1 993
Gordon village	230	232
Ithaca village	130	161
Van Buren township	1 741	1 311
Wabash township	958	1 022
North Star village	254	296
Washington township	1 390	1 074
Wayne township	4 005	3 736
Versailles village[20]	2 384	2 441
York township	569	627
Defiance County[21]	39 987	36 949
Adams township	1 038	987
Defiance township	13 613	16 729
Defiance city (pt.)[21]	11 689	14 846
Delaware township	2 100	1 912
Sherwood village[21]	915	784
Farmer township	832	884
Hicksville township	5 286	4 636
Hicksville village[21]	3 929	3 461
Highland township	2 642	2 221
Mark township	1 019	1 027
Milford township	898	778
Noble township	6 340	2 236
Defiance city (pt.)[21]	4 396	865
Richland township	2 946	2 677
Defiance city (pt.)[21]	725	570
Tiffin township	1 691	1 365
Washington township	1 582	1 497
Ney village[21]	379	378
Delaware County[22]	53 840	42 908
Ashley village[22]	1 057	1 034
Berkshire township[22]	1 630	3 108
Galena village[22]	358	361
Berlin township	1 625	1 412
Brown township	1 007	950
Concord township	3 791	2 732
Delaware city (pt.)[22]	–	...
Dublin village (pt.)[22]	595	...
Shawnee Hills village[22]	430	428
Delaware township	20 127	16 928
Delaware city (pt.)[22]	18 316	15 008
Genoa township	4 065	3 096
Westerville city (pt.)[22]	387	50
Harlem township	2 981	1 527
Kingston township	959	567
Liberty township	3 325	2 625
Powell village[22]	387	374
Marlboro township	227	219
Orange township	1 941	1 902
Oxford township[22]	723	1 742
Porter township	1 160	'743
Radnor township	1 123	966
Scioto township	1 832	1 598
Ostrander village	397	399
Sunbury village[22]	2 101	'1 820
Thompson township	566	492
Trenton township	1 722	'1 312
Troy township	1 878	989
Delaware city (pt.)[22]	464	...
Erie County	79 655	75 909
Berlin township	3 481	3 050
Berlin Heights village	756	828
Florence township	2 119	1 576
Groton township	1 235	1 122
Huron township	9 279	8 641
Huron city	7 123	6 896
Kelleys Island village	121	175
Margaretta township	6 536	5 688
Bay View village	804	798
Castalia village	973	1 045
Milan township	3 310	3 046
Milan village (pt.)	1 181	1 297
Oxford township	1 198	1 040
Perkins township	10 989	10 451
Fairview Lanes (CDP)	1 244	...
Sandusky South (CDP)	6 548	8 158
Sandusky city	31 360	32 674
Vermilion township	10 027	8 446
Vermilion city (pt.)	5 634	5 500
Fairfield County[23]	93 678	73 301
Amanda township	2 331	2 194
Amanda village	720	788
Berne township[23]	4 588	3 607
Sugar Grove village	407	469
Bloom township	5 657	3 566
Lithopolis village[23]	652	705
Clear Creek township	2 609	2 045
Stoutsville village	537	573
Greenfield township	4 322	2 929
Carroll village[23]	641	614

County Subdivisions	1980	1970
Fairfield County—Con.		
Hocking township[23]	2 864	3 270
Lancaster city[23]	34 953	32 911
Liberty township	6 221	4 406
Baltimore village[23]	2 689	2 418
Madison township	1 147	727
Pleasant township[23]	5 551	4 329
Pleasantville village (pt.)	374	372
Richland township[23]	1 616	1 280
Rushville village	299	289
West Rushville village	159	189
Rush Creek township	3 300	2 775
Bremen village	1 432	1 413
Violet township	12 613	4 387
Canal Winchester village (pt.)	37	9
Columbus city (pt.)[23]	45	–
Pickerington village (pt.)[23]	3 886	696
Reynoldsburg city (pt.)[23]	–	–
Walnut township[23]	5 906	4 875
Millersport village[23]	844	777
Pleasantville village (pt.)	406	382
Thurston village[23]	527	428
Fayette County[24]	27 467	25 461
Concord township	1 078	874
Green township	469	433
Jasper township	897	1 013
Milledgeville village	162	207
Octa village (pt.)	68	96
Jefferson township	2 712	2 372
Jeffersonville village	1 252	1 031
Octa village (pt.)	6	'6
Madison township	1 071	946
Marion township	749	670
New Holland village (pt.)[24]	116	121
Paint township	1 845	1 720
Bloomingburg village (pt.)	869	895
Perry township	904	736
Union township[24]	3 691	2 976
Bloomingburg village (pt.)	–	...
Washington city[24]	12 682	12 495
Wayne township	1 369	1 226
Franklin County[25]	869 132	833 249
Bexley city[25]	13 405	14 888
Blendon township[25]	11 285	'9 310
Huber Ridge (CDP)	5 835	...
Minerva Park village[25]	1 618	1 402
Brown township	1 538	1 084
Lake Darby (CDP) (pt.)	34	...
Clinton township[25]	5 300	8 629
Columbus city (pt.)[25]	564 826	'540 025
Franklin township[25]	14 387	'16 127
Lincoln Village (CDP) (pt.)	–	–
Marble Cliff village	630	'715
Valleyview village	730	909
Grandview Heights city	7 420	8 460
Hamilton township[25]	10 161	'12 718
Lockbourne village	373	420
Obetz village (pt.)	2 787	2 248
Rickenbacker AFB (CDP) (pt.)	1 760	5 623
Jackson township[25]	23 024	20 211
Grove City city[25]	16 816	13 911
Urbancrest village[25]	880	754
Jefferson township	4 061	4 464
Madison township[25]	20 274	17 153
Blacklick Estates (CDP) (pt.)	9 761	8 000
Canal Winchester village (pt.)	2 712	2 403
Groveport village[25]	3 286	2 490
Obetz village (pt.)[25]	308	...
Pickerington village (pt.)[25]	31	–
Rickenbacker AFB (CDP) (pt.)	3	–
Mifflin township[25]	22 832	'21 800
Gahanna city[25]	18 001	12 400
Norwich township[25]	13 258	13 468
Hilliard city (pt.)[25]	8 008	8 369
Perry township[25]	6 763	'6 761
Dublin village (pt.)[25]	1 062	17
Worthington city (pt.)[25]	350	185
Plain township[25]	4 564	3 480
New Albany village[25]	409	513
Pleasant township[25]	6 068	4 187
Darbydale village	825	743
Harrisburg village (pt.)	356	547
Prairie township[25]	16 340	'15 704
Lake Darby (CDP) (pt.)	2 270	...
Lincoln Village (CDP) (pt.)	10 548	11 215
New Rome village[25]	63	104
Sharon township[25]	17 779	'19 453
Riverlea village	528	558
Worthington city (pt.)[25]	14 666	15 141
Truro township[25]	21 551	15 775
Blacklick Estates (CDP) (pt.)	1 462	351
Brice village	93	228
Reynoldsburg city (pt.)[25]	19 668	13 912
Upper Arlington city[25]	35 648	'38 727
Washington township[25]	4 322	3 082
Dublin village (pt.)[25]	2 198	664
Hilliard city (pt.)[25]	–	...
Westerville city (pt.)[25]	23 027	'12 480

County Subdivisions	1980	1970
Franklin County—Con.		
Whitehall city	21 299	25 263
Fulton County[26]	37 751	33 071
Amboy township	1 596	1 714
Metamora village[26]	556	594
Chesterfield township	1 044	986
Clinton township	8 122	6 845
Wauseon village[26]	6 173	4 932
Dover township	1 125	1 042
Franklin township	737	740
Fulton township	3 226	2 873
Swanton village (pt.)[26]	1 716	1 527
German township	5 432	5 190
Archbold village[26]	3 318	3 047
Gorham township	2 304	2 162
Fayette village[26]	1 222	1 175
Pike township	1 436	1 100
Royalton township	1 441	1 473
Lyons village	596	630
Swan Creek township	7 307	5 241
Delta village (pt.)	282	274
Swanton village (pt.)[26]	1 708	1 400
York township	3 981	3 705
Delta village (pt.)[26]	2 549	2 270
Gallia County[27]	30 098	25 239
Addison township	2 495	1 528
Cheshire township	1 232	1 394
Cheshire village	297	315
Clay township	1 593	1 064
Gallipolis township	7 228	9 160
Gallipolis city[27]	5 576	7 490
Green township	4 907	2 601
Greenfield township	399	448
Guyan township	1 346	1 039
Crown City village	513	371
Harrison township	780	537
Huntington township	1 520	1 158
Vinton village	375	352
Morgan township	1 115	806
Ohio township	1 002	785
Perry township	946	704
Raccoon township	1 884	1 548
Centerville village	148	114
Rio Grande village[27]	864	814
Springfield township	2 792	1 707
Walnut township	859	760
Geauga County[28]	74 474	62 977
Auburn township	2 351	1 587
Bainbridge township	8 207	7 038
Burton township	4 180	3 580
Burton village[28]	1 401	1 214
Chardon township	7 907	7 171
Chardon village (pt.)[28]	4 370	3 991
Chester township	11 212	10 388
Chesterland (CDP)	2 301	...
Claridon township	2 812	2 513
Aquilla village	355	389
Hambden township	2 934	2 494
Huntsburg township	2 201	1 792
Middlefield township	5 569	4 464
Middlefield village[28]	1 997	1 726
Montville township	1 722	1 307
Munson township	5 286	3 569
Chardon village (pt.)[28]	64	...
Newbury township	5 337	4 038
Parkman township	2 638	2 084
Russell township	8 300	7 342
Hunting Valley village (pt.)	153	124
South Russell village[28]	2 784	2 673
Thompson township	2 083	1 834
Troy township	1 735	1 652
Greene County[29]	129 769	125 057
Bath township[29]	32 815	38 474
Fairborn city (pt.)[29]	29 702	32 264
Beaver Creek township[29]	33 364	26 555
Beavercreek village[29]	31 589	...
Fairborn city (pt.)[29]	–	3
Caesars Creek township	1 181	1 071
Cedarville township	3 711	3 346
Cedarville village[29]	2 799	2 342
Dayton city (pt.)[29]	4 050	...
Jefferson township	1 016	1 179
Bowersville village	329	358
Miami township	5 208	5 848
Clifton village (pt.)	137	150
Yellow Springs village	4 077	4 624
New Jasper township	2 281	1 085
Shawnee Hills (CDP) (pt.)	1 355	...
Ross township	684	895
Silver Creek township	3 326	2 907
Jamestown village[29]	1 702	1 790
Shawnee Hills (CDP) (pt.)	645	...
Spring Valley township[29]	2 492	2 136
Spring Valley village	541	667
Sugar Creek township	7 670	8 276

County Subdivisions	1980	1970
Greene County—Con.		
Sugar Creek township—Con.		
Bellbrook village[29]	5 174	1 268
Xenia city[29]	24 653	25 373
Xenia township[29]	7 318	7 912
Amlin Heights (CDP)	1 122	...
Wilberforce (CDP)	2 512	...
Guernsey County[30]	42 024	37 665
Adams township	1 759	1 224
Cambridge township	18 359	19 194
Cambridge city[30]	13 573	13 656
Center township	1 564	1 350
Lore City village (pt.)	150	96
Jackson township	5 584	4 151
Byesville village[30]	2 572	2 097
Jefferson township	51	40
Knox township	486	430
Liberty township	1 142	867
Kimbolton village	255	247
Londonderry township	689	608
Madison township	661	603
Millwood township	1 336	1 071
Quaker City village	698	510
Salesville village	139	154
Monroe township	590	424
Oxford township	632	535
Fairview village (pt.)	121	103
Richland township	1 511	1 137
Lore City village (pt.)	124	116
Senecaville village	458	497
Spencer township	1 014	910
Cumberland village	461	463
Valley township	2 567	2 332
Pleasant City village	481	494
Washington township	491	279
Westland township	1 624	948
Wheeling township	611	455
Wills township	1 353	1 107
Lore City village (pt.)	169	189
Old Washington village	279	346
Hamilton County[31]	873 224	'925 944
Amberley village	3 442	'4 761
Anderson township	34 504	'28 479
Arlington Heights village	1 082	'1 403
Blue Ash city	9 506	8 324
Cheviot city	9 888	11 135
Cincinnati city	385 457	'453 514
Colerain township	56 583	50 971
Groesbeck (CDP)	9 594	...
Northbrook (CDP)	8 357	...
White Oak (CDP) (pt.)	6 137	...
Columbia township[31]	6 428	'26 125
Fairfax village	2 222	2 705
Kenwood (CDP) (pt.)	200	4 361
Milford village (pt.)	27	52
Crosby township	2 470	1 747
Deer Park city[31]	6 745	7 415
Delhi township	29 078	25 785
Delhi Hills (CDP)	27 647	...
Elmwood Place village	2 840	3 525
Evendale village[31]	1 954	1 967
Forest Park city[31]	18 675	15 139
Glendale village	2 368	2 690
Golf Manor city[31]	4 317	5 170
Green township	50 717	49 917
Bridgetown (CDP)	11 460	13 352
Covedale (CDP)	5 830	6 639
Monfort Heights (CDP)	9 745	...
White Oak (CDP) (pt.)	3 426	...
Greenhills city[31]	4 927	6 092
Harrison township	9 310	6 226
Harrison village[31]	5 855	4 408
Lincoln Heights city	5 259	6 099
Lockland city	4 292	5 288
Loveland city (pt.)[31]	7 385	'5 476
Madeira city[31]	9 341	6 713
Mariemont village[31]	3 295	'4 204
Miami township	9 941	9 041
Addyston village	1 195	1 336
Cleves village[31]	2 094	2 044
North Bend village	546	638
Mount Healthy city[31]	7 562	7 446
Newtown village	1 817	'2 038
North College Hill city	11 114	12 363
Norwood city	26 342	30 420
Reading city	12 843	'14 617
St. Bernard city	5 396	'6 131
Sharonville city	10 108	'11 393
Silverton city[31]	6 172	6 588
Springdale city	10 111	8 127
Springfield township[31]	42 024	'49 188
Brentwood (CDP)	5 508	...
Sycamore township[31]	29 141	'31 056
Kenwood (CDP)	9 728	11 428
Montgomery city (pt.)[31]	8 383	5 683
Symmes township[31]	7 566	'10 014
Loveland Park (CDP) (pt.)	215	...
Montgomery city (pt.)[31]	1 705	...

County Subdivisions

County Subdivisions	1980	1970
Hamilton County—Con.		
Terrace Park village[31]	2 044	2 266
The Village of Indian Hill city[31]	5 521	5 651
Whitewater township	4 662	3 318
Woodlawn village	2 715	3 251
Wyoming city[31]	8 282	9 089
Hancock County[32]	64 581	61 217
Allen township[32]	1 884	1 447
Van Buren village	342	319
Amanda township	1 041	921
Vanlue village	390	539
Biglick township	1 019	840
Blanchard township	1 068	963
Benton Ridge village	343	329
Cass township	922	715
Delaware township	1 233	1 151
Mount Blanchard village	492	473
Eagle township	1 077	987
Arlington village (pt.)[32]	–	...
Findlay city[32]	35 594	35 800
Jackson township	953	883
Arlington village (pt.)[32]	10	...
Liberty township[32]	3 940	2 511
Madison township	1 872	1 716
Arlington village (pt.)[32]	1 177	1 066
Marion township[32]	2 088	2 211
Orange township	1 108	991
Bluffton village (pt.)[32]	73	...
Pleasant township	2 419	2 118
McComb village[32]	1 608	1 329
Portage township	557	494
Union township	1 808	1 638
Mount Cory village	276	302
Rawson village[32]	477	466
Van Buren township	902	917
Jenera village	302	282
Washington township	5 096	'4 914
Arcadia village	580	689
Fostoria city (pt.)[32]	3 412	'3 097
Hardin County[33]	32 719	30 813
Blanchard township	1 614	1 565
Dunkirk village[33]	954	1 036
Buck township	2 907	2 839
Kenton city (pt.)[33]	1 754	1 875
Cessna township	546	463
Dudley township	1 199	1 005
Goshen township	649	616
Hale township	1 434	1 438
Mount Victory village	667	633
Ridgeway village (pt.)	284	282
Jackson township	2 328	2 157
Forest village	1 633	1 535
Patterson village	153	201
Liberty township	7 046	6 535
Ada village[33]	5 669	5 309
Lynn township	645	597
McDonald township	958	848
Marion township	2 583	2 579
Alger village	992	1 071
McGuffey village	646	704
Pleasant township	8 648	8 037
Kenton city (pt.)[33]	6 851	6 440
Roundhead township	708	778
Taylor Creek township	559	502
Washington township	895	854
Harrison County[34]	18 152	17 013
Archer township	337	264
Athens township	605	664
New Athens village	440	450
Cadiz township	4 643	4 506
Cadiz village[34]	4 058	3 060
Franklin township	628	525
Deersville village	109	91
Freeport township	961	810
Freeport village	525	490
German township	872	749
Green township	2 062	1 987
Hopedale village	857	916
Monroe township	1 145	1 025
Bowerston village[34]	487	479
Moorefield township	563	552
North township	1 979	1 875
Scio village	1 003	1 002
Nottingham township	351	216
Rumley township	1 693	1 503
Jewett village	972	901
Short Creek township	1 337	1 323
Adena village (pt.)	153	199
Harrisville village	324	345
Stock township	441	403
Washington township	535	611
Henry County[35]	28 383	27 058
Bartlow township	2 628	2 597
Deshler village	1 870	1 938
Damascus township	1 627	1 577
McClure village	694	699

County Subdivisions	1980	1970
Henry County—Con.		
Flatrock township	1 369	1 275
Florida village	294	285
Holgate village (pt.)	56	53
Freedom township	784	810
Harrison township	1 298	1 181
Napoleon city (pt.)[35]	272	259
Liberty township	2 304	1 997
Liberty Center village (pt.)	1 023	1 007
Napoleon city (pt.)[35]	216	47
Marion township	1 443	1 396
Hamler village[35]	625	681
Monroe township	1 310	1 387
Malinta village	327	391
Napoleon township	9 656	8 885
Napoleon city (pt.)[35]	8 126	7 485
Pleasant township	2 457	2 671
Holgate village (pt.)	1 259	1 488
New Bavaria village	135	149
Richfield township	665	676
Ridgeville township	1 054	1 106
Washington township	1 788	1 500
Liberty Center village (pt.)[35]	88	...
Highland County[36]	33 477	28 996
Brush Creek township	1 033	925
Sinking Spring village	239	178
Clay township	1 200	878
Concord township	852	727
Dodson township	2 305	2 083
Lynchburg village	1 205	1 186
Fairfield township	2 473	2 216
Highland village	284	243
Leesburg village	1 019	984
Hamer township	732	712
Jackson township	639	537
Liberty township	8 806	7 562
Hillsboro city[36]	6 356	5 584
Madison township	6 982	6 758
Greenfield city[36]	5 034	4 780
Marshall township	773	499
New Market township	1 182	842
Paint township	2 362	1 575
Penn township	890	800
Salem township	561	508
Union township	827	780
Washington township	646	486
White Oak township	1 214	1 108
Mowrystown village	475	465
Hocking County[37]	24 304	20 322
Benton township	724	636
Falls township	10 984	10 041
Logan city (pt.)[37]	6 384	6 247
Good Hope township	1 337	780
Green township	2 077	1 462
Logan city (pt.)[37]	173	22
Laurel township	931	621
Marion township	1 643	1 121
Perry township	1 978	1 556
Laurelville village	591	624
Salt Creek township	961	799
Starr township	1 244	1 234
Ward township	1 706	1 525
Murray City village	579	562
Washington township	719	547
Holmes County[38]	29 416	23 024
Berlin township	2 996	2 244
Clark township	2 763	1 967
Baltic village (pt.)[38]	40	–
Hardy township	5 266	4 431
Millersburg village[38]	3 247	2 979
Killbuck township	1 941	1 694
Killbuck village[38]	937	893
Knox township	708	561
Nashville village (pt.)	39	68
Mechanic township	1 640	1 261
Monroe township	811	608
Paint township	2 325	1 710
Prairie township	2 000	1 516
Holmesville village	436	412
Richland township	936	797
Glenmont village	270	266
Ripley township	1 564	1 232
Salt Creek township	2 577	1 978
Walnut Creek township	2 629	1 954
Washington township	1 260	1 071
Loudonville village (pt.)[38]	67	–
Nashville village (pt.)	172	153
Huron County[39]	54 608	49 587
Bellevue city (pt.)[39]	3 950	4 392
Bronson township	1 591	1 042
Clarksfield township	1 289	1 116
Fairfield township	1 198	1 139
North Fairfield village	525	540
Fitchville township	938	791
Greenfield township[39]	1 144	822
Greenwich township	2 185	2 079
Greenwich village[39]	1 458	1 473

County Subdivisions	1980	1970
Huron County—Con.		
Hartland township	899	695
Lyme township[39]	954	929
New Haven township[39]	3 043	ʳ2 480
Plymouth village (pt.)	969	812
New London township	3 159	3 020
New London village[39]	2 449	2 336
Norwalk city[39]	14 358	13 386
Norwalk township[39]	3 106	15 728
Milan village (pt.)	388	ʳ565
Norwich township	892	927
Peru township	1 033	799
Richmond township[39]	1 221	ʳ1 244
Ridgefield township[39]	2 466	2 444
Monroeville village[39]	1 329	1 455
Ripley township	924	811
Sherman township	521	538
Townsend township	1 571	1 295
Wakeman township	2 446	1 786
Wakeman village	906	822
Willard city[39]	5 720	5 510
Jackson County	30 592	27 174
Bloomfield township	705	608
Coal township	2 118	1 726
Coalton village	639	550
Franklin township	1 384	1 041
Hamilton township	426	382
Jackson township	1 147	900
Jefferson township	3 475	2 909
Oak Hill village (pt.)	1 009	927
Liberty township	1 250	936
Lick township	9 054	8 844
Jackson city	6 675	6 843
Madison township	2 139	1 990
Oak Hill village (pt.)	704	715
Milton township	985	777
Scioto township	1 280	1 120
Washington township	613	531
Wellston city	6 016	5 410
Jefferson County[40]	91 564	96 193
Brush Creek township	470	362
Salineville village (pt.)[40]	–	...
Cross Creek township[40]	10 372	10 387
Brentwood (CDP)	3 636	...
New Alexandria village (pt.)	404	425
Wintersville village (pt.)	3 403	3 499
Island Creek township	12 954	12 475
Toronto city (pt.)[40]	4 102	4 651
Wintersville village (pt.)	1 321	1 422
Knox township	5 912	5 859
Empire village	484	491
Stratton village (pt.)	322	341
Toronto city (pt.)[40]	2 832	3 054
Mount Pleasant township	3 153	3 279
Dillonvale village (pt.)[40]	715	854
Mount Pleasant village[40]	616	635
Ross township	601	455
Salem township	3 569	2 856
Richmond village	624	777
Saline township	1 823	1 759
Irondale village	535	602
Stratton village (pt.)	34	45
Smithfield township	4 802	4 690
Adena village (pt.)	909	935
Dillonvale village (pt.)[40]	197	241
Smithfield village[40]	1 308	1 245
Springfield township	3 042	3 266
Amsterdam village	783	882
Bergholz village	914	914
Steubenville city[40]	26 400	30 771
Steubenville township	6 247	6 762
Mingo Junction city[40]	4 834	5 278
Warren township	5 709	6 615
Rayland village	566	617
Tiltonsville village	1 750	2 123
Yorkville village (pt.)	955	1 129
Wayne township	2 839	2 610
Bloomingdale village[40]	254	289
Wells township	3 671	4 047
Brilliant village	1 751	2 178
New Alexandria village (pt.)	6	–
Knox County[41]	46 304	41 795
Berlin township	1 452	1 192
Brown township	1 000	816
Butler township	449	373
Clay township	1 040	819
Martinsburg village	240	234
Clinton township	3 600	4 012
South Mount Vernon (CDP)	1 068	1 044
College township	2 363	1 854
Gambier village[41]	2 056	1 571
Fredericktown village[41]	2 299	1 935
Harrison township	559	529
Hilliar township	2 337	1 889
Centerburg village[41]	1 275	1 038
Howard township	1 557	947
Jackson township	674	498

County Subdivisions	1980	1970
Knox County—Con.		
Jefferson township	558	562
Liberty township	1 277	1 006
Middlebury township	950	783
Milford township	1 075	766
Miller township	722	649
Monroe township[41]	2 172	2 462
Morgan township	636	634
Utica village (pt.)[41]	17	...
Morris township[41]	1 896	1 904
Mount Vernon city[41]	14 323	13 373
Pike township	1 057	913
Pleasant township[41]	1 321	1 166
Union township	2 124	2 098
Danville village[41]	1 127	1 025
Gann village	173	172
Wayne township[41]	863	2 550
Lake County[42]	212 801	197 200
Concord township[42]	10 335	5 948
Eastlake city	22 104	19 690
Fairport Harbor village[42]	3 357	3 665
Grand River village[42]	412	613
Kirtland city	5 969	5 530
Kirtland Hills village	506	ʳ452
Lakeline village[42]	258	223
Leroy township	2 505	1 759
Madison township[42]	15 378	14 133
North Madison (CDP)	8 741	6 882
Madison village[42]	2 291	1 678
Mentor city[42]	42 065	36 912
Mentor-on-the-Lake city	7 919	ʳ6 517
North Perry village[42]	897	851
Painesville city[42]	16 391	ʳ16 536
Painesville township[42]	12 348	ʳ15 148
Perry township[42]	5 126	ʳ4 634
Perry village[42]	961	917
Timberlake village[42]	885	964
Waite Hill village	529	514
Wickliffe city	16 790	ʳ20 632
Willoughby city	19 329	18 634
Willoughby Hills city	8 612	ʳ5 969
Willowick city	17 834	21 237
Lawrence County[43]	63 849	56 868
Aid township	861	665
Decatur township	895	860
Elizabeth township	2 315	2 101
Fayette township	8 826	6 892
South Point village (pt.)	2 642	ʳ1 813
Hamilton township	2 089	2 346
Hanging Rock village	353	278
Ironton city (pt.)	1 033	1 248
Lawrence township	2 275	1 846
Mason township	1 064	873
Perry township	6 298	5 199
Coal Grove village (pt.)[43]	16	41
South Point village (pt.)	1 276	1 097
Rome township	7 496	5 758
Athalia village	367	287
Symmes township	488	462
Union township	9 695	8 192
Chesapeake village	1 370	1 364
Proctorville village	975	881
Upper township	19 089	19 504
Coal Grove village (pt.)[43]	2 586	2 718
Ironton city (pt.)[43]	13 257	13 782
Washington township	414	575
Windsor township	2 044	1 595
Licking County[44]	120 981	107 799
Bennington township	837	655
Bowling Green township	1 052	813
Burlington township	904	807
Eden township	971	627
Etna township	6 107	3 453
Reynoldsburg city (pt.)[44]	993	9
Fallsbury township	653	669
Franklin township	1 306	ʳ1 003
Granville township[44]	7 515	ʳ6 771
Granville village[44]	3 851	3 963
Hanover township	2 501	1 794
Hanover village[44]	926	626
Harrison township[44]	4 278	ʳ2 281
Kirkersville village[44]	626	578
Hartford township	1 080	1 102
Hartford village	444	455
Heath city[44]	6 969	6 768
Hopewell township	961	898
Gratiot village (pt.)	101	125
Jersey township	2 196	1 615
Liberty township	1 300	778
Licking township[44]	4 128	4 022
Lima township	4 343	ʳ3 358
McKean township	1 197	994
Madison township[44]	2 758	ʳ2 403
Mary Ann township	1 747	1 244
Monroe township	5 057	4 297
Johnstown village[44]	3 158	3 208
Newark city[44]	41 200	ʳ41 836

County Subdivisions	1980	1970
Licking County—Con.		
Newark township[44]	3 179	'2 982
Newton township[44]	3 309	3 182
St. Louisville village	375	385
Pataskala village[44]	2 284	1 831
Perry township	1 128	779
St. Albans township	1 946	1 710
Alexandria village	489	588
Union township[44]	7 054	6 316
Buckeye Lake (CDP)	2 521	2 278
Hebron village	2 035	1 699
Washington township	3 021	2 811
Utica village (pt.)[44]	2 221	1 977
Logan County[45]	39 155	35 072
Bloomfield township	403	429
Bokes Creek township	1 354	1 320
Ridgeway village (pt.)	104	97
West Mansfield village (pt.)	709	724
Harrison township	1 706	1 492
Bellefontaine city (pt.)[45]	316	359
Jefferson township	1 807	1 528
Bellefontaine city (pt.)[45]	11	...
Valley Hi village (pt.)[45]	15	'15
Zanesfield village	269	272
Lake township	12 134	11 436
Bellefontaine city (pt.)[45]	11 561	10 896
Liberty township	2 858	2 462
West Liberty village	1 653	1 580
McArthur township	1 693	1 328
Huntsville village	489	475
Miami township	2 251	2 166
De Graff village (pt.)[45]	1 142	1 007
Quincy village	633	686
Monroe township	925	678
Valley Hi village (pt.)[45]	45	'—
Perry township	872	933
West Mansfield village (pt.)	7	29
Pleasant township	887	694
De Graff village (pt.)[45]	216	110
Richland township	2 015	1 872
Belle Center village	930	985
Rushcreek township	2 075	1 588
Rushsylvania village[45]	610	526
Stokes township	4 157	3 337
Lakeview village	1 089	1 026
Union township	674	609
Washington township	2 776	2 626
Russells Point village	1 156	1 104
Zane township	568	574
Lorain County[46]	274 909	256 843
Amherst city[46]	10 638	9 902
Amherst township[46]	7 016	'16 925
South Amherst village (pt.)[46]	1 230	2 264
Avon city	7 241	7 214
Avon Lake city	13 222	12 261
Brighton township	728	591
Brownhelm township	6 705	'5 198
Vermilion city (pt.)[46]	5 378	4 372
Camden township	1 522	1 358
Kipton village	352	353
Carlisle township[46]	7 689	7 414
Columbia township	6 494	5 738
Eaton township[46]	7 803	6 839
Eaton Estates (CDP)	1 806	2 076
Grafton village (pt.)	1 170	451
Elyria city[46]	57 538	53 427
Elyria township[46]	4 576	'4 511
Grafton township	3 021	2 585
Grafton village (pt.)[46]	1 061	1 320
Henrietta township	1 864	1 543
Huntington township	1 057	784
Lagrange township	4 477	2 609
Lagrange village[46]	1 258	1 074
Lorain city[46]	75 416	'78 185
North Ridgeville city	21 522	13 152
Penfield township	1 253	802
Pittsfield township	1 436	1 159
Rochester township	627	544
Rochester village	207	210
Russia township	11 116	11 240
Oberlin city[46]	8 660	8 761
South Amherst village (pt.)[46]	618	649
Sheffield township[46]	4 170	'7 049
Sheffield village	1 886	'1 730
Sheffield Lake city	10 484	8 734
Wellington township	5 408	5 251
Wellington village[46]	4 146	4 137
Lucas County[47]	471 741	'483 551
Harbor View village	164	238
Harding township	631	719
Jerusalem township	3 327	3 405
Maumee city	15 747	15 937
Monclova township	4 285	3 340
Oregon city	18 675	16 563
Ottawa Hills village[47]	4 065	4 270
Providence township	2 702	1 856

County Subdivisions	1980	1970
Lucas County—Con.		
Richfield township	1 401	1 512
Berkey village	306	294
Spencer township	1 744	1 925
Springfield township	16 091	10 909
Holland village	1 048	1 108
Swanton township	3 379	3 026
Sylvania township[47]	33 061	'28 527
Sylvania city[47]	15 527	12 031
Toledo city[47]	354 635	'383 062
Washington township	4 000	2 146
Waterville township	7 834	6 116
Waterville village[47]	3 884	2 940
Whitehouse village[47]	2 137	1 542
Madison County[48]	33 004	28 318
Canaan township	2 210	1 065
Darby township	2 015	1 968
Plain City village (pt.)[48]	1 222	1 323
Deer Creek township[48]	1 020	1 061
Fairfield township	1 293	1 145
Jefferson township	7 055	5 747
Jefferson village[48]	4 448	3 664
London city[48]	6 958	6 481
Monroe township	1 066	634
Oak Run township	363	312
Paint township	607	738
Pike township	438	448
Pleasant township	2 768	2 779
Mount Sterling village[48]	1 623	1 536
Range township	1 085	1 081
Midway village	339	318
Somerford township	2 172	1 103
Stokes township	787	846
South Solon village	416	415
Union township[48]	3 167	9 391
Mahoning County[49]	289 487	'304 545
Alliance city (pt.)[49]	—	...
Austintown township	37 664	34 949
Austintown (CDP)	33 636	29 393
Beaver township	5 401	5 575
Columbiana village (pt.)[49]	1	...
Berlin township	2 047	1 402
Boardman township[49]	41 833	36 110
Boardman (CDP)	39 161	30 852
Campbell city[49]	11 619	'12 577
Canfield township	10 350	9 397
Canfield city[49]	5 535	4 997
Coitsville township[49]	2 105	'2 292
Ellsworth township	2 310	1 957
Goshen township	3 481	2 927
Green township	3 329	2 882
Washingtonville village (pt.)[49]	333	247
Jackson township	2 141	1 938
Milton township	4 444	4 024
Craig Beach village	1 657	1 451
New Middletown village	2 195	'1 664
Poland township	15 198	15 233
Lowellville village	1 558	1 836
Poland village	3 084	3 097
Sebring village[49]	5 078	4 954
Smith township[49]	5 321	10 375
Beloit village	1 093	921
Springfield township	5 920	'5 020
Struthers city	13 624	15 343
Youngstown city (pt.)[49]	115 427	'140 880
Marion County[50]	67 974	64 724
Big Island township	1 317	1 146
Bowling Green township	576	555
Claridon township	2 660	2 286
Caledonia village	759	792
Grand township	370	302
Grand Prairie township	1 828	1 370
Green Camp township	1 162	1 158
Green Camp village	475	537
Marion township	46 388	47 413
Marion city[50]	37 040	38 646
Montgomery township	2 466	2 109
La Rue village	861	867
New Bloomington village	303	343
Pleasant township	4 425	2 712
Prospect township	1 978	1 882
Prospect village[50]	1 159	1 031
Richland township	1 644	1 039
Salt Rock township	768	736
Morral village	454	452
Scott township	518	431
Tully township	809	704
Waldo township	1 065	881
Waldo village[50]	347	428
Medina County[51]	113 150	82 717
Brunswick city[51]	28 104	15 852
Brunswick Hills township[51]	3 324	2 293
Chatham township	1 825	1 258
Granger township	2 660	2 142
Guilford township	4 230	3 477
Rittman city (pt.)	65	47

County Subdivisions	1980	1970
Medina County—Con.		
Guilford township—Con.		
Seville village[51]	1 568	1 402
Harrisville township	4 563	3 521
Lodi village[51]	2 942	2 399
Hinckley township	5 174	4 210
Homer township	1 077	845
Lafayette township[51]	4 614	3 314
Briarwood Beach village	628	508
Chippewa-on-the-Lake village	245	341
Litchfield township	2 329	1 332
Liverpool township	3 664	2 826
Medina city[51]	15 268	10 913
Medina township[51]	3 561	2 445
Montville township[51]	2 999	2 497
Sharon township	3 398	2 764
Spencer township	1 859	1 486
Spencer village[51]	764	758
Wadsworth township	18 729	17 513
Wadsworth city[51]	15 166	13 142
Westfield township	3 242	2 300
Gloria Glens Park village	435	332
Westfield Center village[51]	791	715
York township[51]	2 530	1 729
Meigs County[52]	23 641	19 799
Bedford township	1 004	750
Chester township	2 090	1 573
Columbia township	753	619
Lebanon township	830	782
Letart township	800	854
Olive township	1 661	1 405
Orange township	898	707
Rutland township	2 434	1 874
Rutland village	635	663
Salem township	1 003	696
Salisbury township	8 037	7 303
Middleport village	2 971	2 784
Pomeroy village	2 728	2 672
Scipio township	1 026	641
Sutton township	3 105	2 595
Racine village[52]	908	583
Syracuse village	946	684
Mercer County[53]	38 334	'35 558
Black Creek township	647	604
Butler township	6 049	5 337
Coldwater village[53]	4 220	3 533
Center township	917	916
Dublin township	2 235	2 094
Rockford village[53]	1 245	1 207
Franklin township	1 790	1 606
Montezuma village	200	260
Gibson township	1 872	1 826
Fort Recovery village (pt.)[53]	916	910
Granville township	3 591	3 326
Burkettsville village (pt.)	198	172
St. Henry village[53]	1 596	1 276
Hopewell township	977	961
Jefferson township	12 151	'10 904
Celina city[53]	9 137	'8 072
Liberty township	1 014	997
Marion township	2 753	2 699
Chickasaw village[53]	381	326
Recovery township	1 447	1 531
Fort Recovery village (pt.)	454	438
Union township	1 626	1 496
Mendon village	749	672
Washington township	1 265	1 261
Miami County[54]	90 381	84 342
Bethel township	4 709	4 284
Brown township	1 515	1 621
Fletcher village	498	539
Concord township	23 392	'21 037
Troy city[54]	19 086	'17 186
Elizabeth township	1 661	1 456
Lostcreek township	1 523	1 409
Casstown village	331	380
Monroe township	11 469	9 170
Tipp City city[54]	5 595	5 090
Newberry township	6 517	6 598
Bradford village (pt.)	1 172	1 240
Covington village[54]	2 610	2 575
Newton township	3 116	2 947
Pleasant Hill village	1 051	1 025
Springcreek township	1 864	2 123
Staunton township	2 054	'1 882
Union township	10 222	9 413
Laura village	501	464
Ludlow Falls village	248	292
Potsdam village	289	311
West Milton village[54]	4 119	3 696
Washington township	22 339	22 402
Piqua city[54]	20 480	'20 741

County Subdivisions	1980	1970
Monroe County[55]	17 382	15 739
Adams township	699	540
Benton township	466	351
Bethel township	421	349
Center township	4 304	4 168
Woodsfield village[55]	3 145	3 239
Franklin township	429	442
Stafford village	98	120
Green township	400	401
Jackson township	448	452
Lee township	1 311	1 234
Malaga township	1 113	855
Jerusalem village (pt.)	149	139
Miltonsburg village	109	68
Ohio township	1 318	1 281
Perry township	600	481
Antioch village	113	112
Salem township	1 162	1 285
Clarington village[55]	558	338
Seneca township	485	366
Summit township	767	684
Lewisville village	285	294
Sunsbury township	1 804	1 370
Beallsville village	601	452
Jerusalem village (pt.)	88	66
Wilson village (pt.)	116	133
Switzerland township	575	473
Washington township	604	619
Graysville village	112	97
Wayne township	476	388
Montgomery County[56]	571 697	'608 413
Butler township[56]	9 365	'9 094
Clay township	7 959	7 438
Brookville village (pt.)[56]	3 329	3 191
Clayton village (pt.)	35	42
Phillipsburg village[56]	705	831
Verona village (pt.)	90	87
Dayton city (pt.)[56]	199 321	'243 023
German township	7 910	7 102
Germantown village[56]	5 015	4 088
Harrison township[56]	26 986	34 176
Fort McKinley (CDP) (pt.)	4 604	6 071
Northridge (CDP)	9 720	10 084
Shiloh (CDP)	11 735	11 368
Huber Heights city[56]	35 480	...
Jackson township	6 517	5 823
Farmersville village	950	865
New Lebanon village (pt.)[56]	2 920	2 579
Jefferson township[56]	9 379	11 790
Kettering city[56]	61 186	'71 864
Madison township[56]	30 586	'28 981
Fort McKinley (CDP) (pt.)	5 557	5 465
Trotwood city[56]	7 802	6 997
Mad River township[56]	26 926	'39 389
Overlook—Page Manor (CDP)	14 825	'19 869
Riverside village[56]	1 475	'1 576
Miami township[56]	33 688	43 881
Carlisle village (pt.)	308	384
Miamisburg city[56]	15 304	14 797
Moraine city[56]	5 325	4 898
Oakwood city[56]	9 372	10 095
Perry township	6 441	6 620
Brookville village (pt.)[56]	993	1 212
New Lebanon village (pt.)[56]	1 581	1 669
Randolph township	29 196	20 971
Clayton village (pt.)	717	731
Englewood city[56]	11 329	7 885
Northview (CDP)	9 973	...
Union village[56]	5 219	3 654
Vandalia city[56]	13 161	'10 796
Washington township[56]	39 751	24 497
Centerville city	18 886	10 333
Woodbourne—Hyde Park (CDP)	8 826	...
West Carrollton city[56]	13 148	10 748
Morgan County	14 241	12 375
Bloom township	1 026	612
Bristol township	216	282
Center township	615	511
Deerfield township	549	519
Homer township	683	511
Malta township	2 065	1 840
Malta village	956	1 017
Manchester township	134	185
Marion township	1 290	1 151
Chesterhill village	395	361
Meigsville township	761	614
Morgan township	2 621	2 696
McConnelsville village	2 018	2 107
Penn township	720	687
Union township	596	406
Windsor township	1 997	1 534
Stockport village	558	471
York township	968	827
Morrow County[57]	26 480	21 348
Bennington township	2 223	1 425
Marengo village	329	330
Canaan township	872	828

County Subdivisions

County Subdivisions	1980	1970
Morrow County—Con.		
Cardington township	2 574	2 451
Cardington village[57]	1 665	1 730
Chester township	1 283	992
Chesterville village	242	264
Congress township	1 200	967
Franklin township	918	730
Gilead township	5 571	5 100
Edison village[57]	504	569
Mount Gilead village[57]	2 911	2 971
Harmony township	1 338	775
Lincoln township	1 546	1 178
Fulton village	378	377
North Bloomfield township	1 861	1 454
Perry township	1 614	1 300
Peru township	921	648
South Bloomfield township	1 314	1 019
Sparta village	219	213
Troy township	1 012	633
Washington township	1 140	1 051
Westfield township	1 093	797
Muskingum County[58]	83 340	77 826
Adams township	426	298
Blue Rock township	550	425
Brush Creek township	1 256	1 095
Cass township	1 097	1 039
Dresden village (pt.)	–	–
Clay township	1 143	1 145
Roseville village (pt.)	890	862
Falls township[58]	8 733	7 653
Melody Lake (CDP)	1 000	...
North Zanesville (CDP)	2 166	3 335
Harrison township	1 418	1 372
Philo village	799	846
Highland township	761	591
Hopewell township	2 371	1 646
Gratiot village (pt.)	126	107
Jackson township	1 912	1 610
Frazeysburg village	1 025	941
Jefferson township	1 917	1 750
Dresden village (pt.)	1 646	1 516
Licking township	1 661	966
Madison township	378	363
Meigs township	208	281
Monroe township	378	429
Muskingum township	2 712	1 064
Newton township	5 230	4 344
Fultonham village	281	228
Roseville village (pt.)	6	2
South Zanesville village (pt.)	2	10
Perry township	1 959	1 546
Rich Hill township	381	449
Salem township	936	718
Adamsville village	229	174
Salt Creek township	966	876
Springfield township[58]	5 607	5 500
South Zanesville village (pt.)	1 737	1 426
Union township	3 821	3 513
New Concord village	1 860	2 318
Norwich village	170	163
Washington township[58]	4 409	3 001
Wayne township	4 455	3 107
Zanesville city[58]	28 655	33 045
Noble County[59]	11 310	10 428
Beaver township	679	654
Batesville village	129	148
Brookfield township	144	153
Buffalo township	572	456
Center township	935	797
Sarahsville village	226	181
Elk township	359	374
Enoch township	419	356
Dexter City village (pt.)	–	–
Jackson township	536	485
Dexter City village (pt.)	38	43
Jefferson township	297	281
Dexter City village (pt.)	110	112
Marion township	678	631
Summerfield village	299	306
Noble township	1 903	1 802
Belle Valley village	329	393
Olive township	3 383	3 115
Caldwell village[59]	1 935	2 082
Dexter City village (pt.)	25	23
Seneca township	368	320
Sharon township	325	357
Stock township	344	405
Wayne township	368	242
Ottawa County[60]	40 076	37 099
Allen township	3 322	2 829
Clay Center village[60]	327	370
Bay township	1 815	1 798
Port Clinton city (pt.)[60]	875	936
Benton township	2 446	2 340
Rocky Ridge village[60]	457	385
Carroll township	1 706	1 355
Catawba Island township	3 402	2 882

County Subdivisions	1980	1970
Ottawa County—Con.		
Clay township	5 359	4 918
Genoa village[60]	2 213	2 139
Danbury township	4 414	3 760
Marblehead village	679	726
Erie township	1 518	1 470
Port Clinton city (pt.)	–	3
Harris township	2 688	2 784
Elmore village[60]	1 271	1 316
Portage township	7 916	7 948
Port Clinton city (pt.)[60]	6 348	6 263
Put-in-Bay township	556	507
Put-in-Bay village	146	135
Salem township	4 934	4 508
Oak Harbor village[60]	2 678	2 807
Paulding County[61]	21 302	19 329
Auglaize township	1 427	1 115
Benton township	1 168	1 078
Payne village (pt.)	452	450
Blue Creek township	829	780
Haviland village	219	231
Scott village (pt.)	135	129
Brown township	2 594	2 253
Melrose village	315	302
Oakwood village	886	804
Carryall township	3 016	2 868
Antwerp village[61]	1 765	1 735
Crane township	1 613	1 225
Cecil village	267	295
Emerald township	852	689
Harrison township	1 720	1 699
Payne village (pt.)	947	901
Jackson township	1 952	1 639
Broughton village	171	155
Paulding village (pt.)	136	184
Latty township	1 101	1 117
Grover Hill village[61]	486	536
Paulding township	4 288	4 185
Latty village	261	269
Paulding village (pt.)[61]	2 618	2 799
Washington township	742	681
Perry County[62]	31 032	27 434
Bearfield township	1 261	1 082
Clayton township	1 038	988
Coal township	1 257	1 216
New Straitsville village	937	947
Harrison township	5 364	5 122
Crooksville village[62]	2 766	2 828
Roseville village (pt.)	1 019	903
Hopewell township	1 512	1 096
Glenford village	173	177
Jackson township	2 040	1 890
Junction City village	754	732
Madison township	774	585
Monday Creek township	567	447
Monroe township	1 628	1 717
Corning village	789	838
Rendville village	68	82
Pike township	6 697	6 048
New Lexington village	5 179	4 921
Pleasant township	817	756
Reading township	3 484	2 866
Somerset village	1 432	1 417
Salt Lick township	1 444	1 374
Hemlock village	197	199
Shawnee village	924	914
Thorn township	3 149	2 247
Thornville village	838	679
Pickaway County[63]	43 662	40 071
Circleville township	15 039	13 749
Circleville city[63]	11 700	11 687
Darby township	3 268	2 116
Harrisburg village (pt.)	7	9
Deer Creek township	1 438	1 547
Williamsport village	792	857
Harrison township	5 001	4 253
Ashville village[63]	2 046	1 772
South Bloomfield village[63]	934	610
Jackson township	839	829
Madison township	1 485	2 004
Monroe township	1 128	1 109
Muhlenberg township	734	543
Darbyville village	282	229
Perry township	1 427	1 390
New Holland village (pt.)[63]	667	675
Pickaway township	1 608	1 477
Salt Creek township	1 936	1 570
Tarlton village[63]	394	412
Scioto township	4 458	5 684
Commercial Point village[63]	316	320
Orient village	283	313
Walnut township	2 104	1 518
Washington township	2 666	1 645
Wayne township	531	637

County Subdivisions

County Subdivisions	1980	1970
Pike County[64]	22 802	19 114
Beaver township	1 115	949
Beaver village (pt.)	107	106
Benton township	1 147	934
Camp Creek township	706	602
Jackson township	1 174	1 017
Marion township	1 163	983
Beaver village (pt.)	223	211
Mifflin township	1 051	1 003
Newton township	1 476	1 083
Pebble township	1 342	910
Pee Pee township	6 986	6 367
Waverly City city[64]	4 603	4 858
Perry township	785	731
Scioto township	1 049	931
Seal township	2 754	2 063
Piketon village	1 726	1 347
Sunfish township	1 031	738
Union township	1 023	803
Portage County[65]	135 856	125 868
Atwater township	2 691	2 408
Aurora city	8 177	6 549
Brimfield township	7 868	6 721
Brimfield (CDP)	3 161	...
Kent city (pt.)	716	−
Charlestown township	1 693	864
Deerfield township	2 710	2 175
Edinburg township	1 943	1 563
Franklin township	31 206	ʳ34 472
Brady Lake village	470	450
Kent city (pt.)[65]	25 448	28 183
Freedom township	2 398	1 649
Garrettsville village	1 769	1 718
Hiram township	3 041	2 884
Hiram village	1 360	1 484
Mantua township	5 418	5 250
Mantua village	1 041	1 199
Mogadore village (pt.)[65]	1 129	ʳ1 618
Nelson township	2 424	1 839
Palmyra township	2 436	1 717
Paris township	1 629	1 358
Randolph township	5 093	4 150
Ravenna township	21 182	20 616
Ravenna city[65]	11 987	11 780
Rootstown township	6 585	6 010
Shalersville township	5 268	4 967
Aurora East (CDP)	1 218	...
Red Fox (CDP)	1 029	...
Streetsboro city	9 055	7 966
Suffield township[65]	6 211	ʳ4 832
Sugar Bush Knolls village	201	119
Windham township	5 729	4 423
Windham village	3 721	3 360
Preble County[66]	38 223	34 719
Dixon township	657	676
Eaton city[66]	6 839	ʳ6 020
Gasper township	1 114	632
Gratis township	4 140	3 782
Gratis village[66]	809	621
West Elkton village	277	291
Harrison township	4 297	4 251
Lewisburg village[66]	1 450	1 553
Verona village (pt.)	481	506
Israel township	1 404	1 452
College Corner village (pt.)[66]	248	283
Jackson township	1 314	1 211
Jefferson township	3 831	3 598
New Paris village[66]	1 709	1 692
Lanier township	3 621	3 512
West Alexandria village (pt.)[66]	801	951
Monroe township	2 496	2 272
Eldorado village[66]	509	483
West Manchester village[66]	448	469
Somers township	3 824	2 973
Camden village[66]	1 971	1 507
Twin township	2 745	2 612
West Alexandria village (pt.)[66]	512	602
Washington township[66]	1 941	ʳ1 728
Putnam County[67]	32 991	31 134
Blanchard township	1 272	1 086
Gilboa village	220	212
Greensburg township	1 116	936
Jackson township	914	847
Jennings township	1 761	1 654
Fort Jennings village	538	533
Liberty township	1 556	1 616
West Leipsic village	298	378
Monroe township	2 189	2 107
Continental village[67]	1 179	1 185
Monterey township	1 893	1 799
Ottoville village[67]	833	914
Ottawa township	7 223	6 667
Glandorf village[67]	746	732
Ottawa village[67]	3 874	3 622
Palmer township	1 266	1 282
Miller City village	168	206

County Subdivisions

County Subdivisions	1980	1970
Putnam County—Con.		
Perry township	1 216	1 178
Cloverdale village	304	253
Dupont village[67]	308	302
Pleasant township	3 873	3 785
Columbus Grove village	2 313	2 290
Riley township	1 975	1 839
Pandora village[67]	977	857
Sugar Creek township	1 126	1 099
Union township	2 368	1 956
Kalida village	1 019	900
Van Buren township	3 243	3 283
Belmore village	205	319
Leipsic village	2 171	2 072
Richland County[68]	131 205	129 997
Blooming Grove township	1 092	1 003
Butler township	899	814
Cass township	1 746	1 766
Shiloh village[68]	857	817
Franklin township	1 689	1 730
Jackson township	3 660	3 280
Shelby city (pt.)[68]	908	789
Jefferson township	4 002	3 331
Bellville village	1 714	1 685
Madison township[68]	14 624	71 206
Mansfield city[68]	53 927	55 047
Mifflin township	6 698	4 922
Monroe township	2 654	2 389
Lucas village	753	771
Perry township	1 204	824
Plymouth township	2 277	2 275
Plymouth village (pt.)	970	1 181
Shelby city (pt.)[68]	−	−
Sandusky township	1 118	902
Crestline city (pt.)[68]	14	ʳ18
Sharon township	9 967	10 589
Shelby city (pt.)[68]	8 738	9 058
Springfield township	8 596	7 960
Ontario village[68]	4 123	4 345
Troy township	5 880	4 760
Lexington village (pt.)[68]	3 823	2 972
Washington township[68]	7 150	8 583
Lexington village (pt.)[68]	−	−
Weller township	1 466	1 316
Worthington township	2 556	2 347
Butler village	991	1 052
Ross County[69]	65 004	61 211
Buckskin township	1 340	1 347
South Salem village	252	209
Colerain township	1 485	1 288
Adelphi village	472	455
Concord township	3 234	2 682
Frankfort village[69]	1 008	949
Deerfield township	1 095	1 108
Clarksburg village	483	457
Franklin township	1 588	1 230
Green township	3 380	2 884
Kingston village[69]	1 208	1 157
Harrison township	1 007	800
Huntington township	4 726	3 975
Jefferson township	1 048	916
Liberty township	1 939	1 927
Paint township	988	902
Paxton township	1 876	1 800
Bainbridge village	1 042	1 057
Scioto township	31 469	31 655
Chillicothe city[69]	23 420	24 842
Springfield township	1 805	1 446
Twin township	2 616	2 056
Union township	5 408	5 195
Sandusky County[70]	63 267	60 983
Ballville township	6 323	5 581
Ballville (CDP)	2 839	1 652
Bellevue city (pt.)[70]	4 237	4 212
Fremont city[70]	17 834	18 490
Green Creek township[70]	9 681	ʳ8 748
Clyde city[70]	5 489	5 503
Green Springs village (pt.)[70]	627	ʳ664
Jackson township	1 757	1 668
Burgoon village	244	221
Helena village (pt.)[70]	158	165
Madison township	3 662	3 849
Gibsonburg village[70]	2 479	2 585
Rice township	1 505	851
Riley township	1 633	1 381
Sandusky township[70]	4 632	4 936
Stony Prairie (CDP)	1 767	1 913
Scott township	1 539	1 279
Townsend township	1 700	1 709
Washington township	2 571	2 375
Helena village (pt.)	149	133
Lindsey village	571	652
Woodville township	3 234	3 156
Woodville village[70]	2 050	1 834
York township[70]	2 332	2 084

County Subdivisions	1980	1970
Scioto County[71]	84 545	76 951
Bloom township	3 263	2 914
South Webster village	886	825
Brush Creek township	1 102	921
Otway village	161	177
Clay township[71]	4 047	4 210
Rosemount (CDP)	1 747	1 786
Green township	3 880	2 788
Franklin Furnace (CDP)	1 093	...
Harrison township	4 288	3 533
Jefferson township	2 500	2 400
Madison township	3 325	2 381
Morgan township	1 952	1 295
New Boston village	3 188	3 325
Nile township	2 568	2 262
Porter township	9 529	7 807
Sciotodale (CDP)	1 191	...
Wheelersburg (CDP)	4 796	3 709
Portsmouth city[71]	25 943	27 633
Rarden township	853	799
Rarden village	199	232
Rush township	3 048	2 717
Union township	1 978	1 544
Valley township	4 387	2 529
Lucasville (CDP)	3 349	...
Vernon township	1 800	1 097
Washington township	6 894	6 796
West Portsmouth (CDP)	4 095	3 396
Seneca County[72]	61 901	60 696
Adams township[72]	1 338	⌐1 066
Big Spring township	1 873	1 871
New Riegel village	329	340
Bloom township	1 881	1 669
Bloomville village	1 019	884
Clinton township[72]	4 028	2 863
Eden township	2 045	1 737
Fostoria city (pt.)[72]	11 260	12 121
Green Springs village (pt.)[72]	941	⌐615
Hopewell township[72]	3 035	2 755
Jackson township[72]	1 808	1 397
Liberty township	2 350	2 218
Bettsville village	752	833
Loudon township[72]	2 507	1 983
Pleasant township	1 711	1 476
Reed township	955	952
Scipio township	1 718	1 571
Republic village	656	705
Seneca township	1 500	1 450
Thompson township	1 533	1 289
Tiffin city[72]	19 549	21 596
Venice township	1 869	2 067
Attica village[72]	865	1 005
Shelby County[73]	43 089	37 748
Clinton township	18 919	17 890
Sidney city (pt.)[73]	17 240	16 332
Cynthian township	1 808	1 431
Dinsmore township	3 179	2 614
Anna village (pt.)[73]	736	470
Botkins village[73]	1 372	1 057
Franklin township	2 142	1 242
Anna village (pt.)[73]	302	322
Sidney city (pt.)[73]	417	...
Green township	975	831
Jackson township	2 225	2 032
Jackson Center village[73]	1 310	1 119
Loramie township	2 169	1 879
Russia village[73]	438	420
McLean township	2 653	2 275
Fort Loramie village[73]	977	744
Orange township	1 167	1 010
Perry township	1 293	1 136
Sidney city (pt.)[73]	–	–
Salem township	1 888	1 534
Port Jefferson village[73]	482	416
Turtle Creek township	1 319	1 251
Van Buren township	1 709	1 482
Kettlersville village	199	252
Washington township	1 643	1 141
Lockington village	203	242
Stark County[74]	378 823	372 210
Alliance city (pt.)[74]	24 315	26 547
Bethlehem township	5 892	4 528
Navarre village	1 343	1 607
Canton city[74]	94 730	110 053
Canton township[74]	15 193	16 965
Meyers Lake village (pt.)	216	–
Jackson township	29 001	18 786
Hills and Dales village	281	280
Lake township	20 559	13 053
Hartville village[74]	1 772	1 752
Lawrence township	11 380	7 284
Canal Fulton village[74]	3 481	2 367
Lexington township[74]	6 351	5 975
Limaville village	164	303
Louisville city[74]	7 873	6 298
Marlboro township	3 748	3 552

County Subdivisions	1980	1970
Stark County—Con.		
Massillon city[74]	30 557	32 539
Nimishillen township[74]	10 559	16 560
Osnaburg township	5 867	6 067
East Canton village[74]	1 721	1 631
Paris township	6 374	6 038
Minerva village (pt.)[74]	2 397	2 446
Perry township[74]	32 675	30 443
Perry Heights (CDP)	9 206	...
Pike township	4 179	4 027
East Sparta village[74]	868	959
Plain township[74]	46 665	47 346
Meyers Lake village (pt.)	6	173
North Canton city[74]	14 228	15 228
Sandy township	3 724	4 115
Magnolia village (pt.)	677	701
Waynesburg village	1 160	1 337
Sugar Creek township	6 636	6 132
Beach City village	1 083	1 133
Brewster village[74]	2 321	2 020
Wilmot village[74]	329	378
Tuscarawas township[74]	7 369	6 894
Washington township[74]	5 176	5 306
Summit County[75]	524 472	553 371
Akron city[75]	237 177	275 425
Barberton city[75]	29 751	33 052
Bath township[75]	8 476	7 552
Boston township	2 064	⌐2 196
Peninsula village	604	⌐692
Boston Heights village	781	846
Clinton village	1 277	1 335
Copley township[75]	15 910	14 735
Fairlawn city	6 100	6 102
Coventry township[75]	11 951	13 429
Portage Lakes (CDP) (pt.)	7 312	...
Cuyahoga Falls city[75]	43 890	⌐49 815
Franklin township	16 142	15 114
Portage Lakes (CDP) (pt.)	1 919	...
Green township	17 625	13 473
Portage Lakes (CDP) (pt.)	2 079	...
Hudson township	12 645	⌐8 395
Hudson village[75]	4 615	⌐3 933
Lakemore village[75]	2 744	2 708
Macedonia city[75]	6 571	6 375
Mogadore village (pt.)[75]	3 061	3 207
Munroe Falls village	4 731	3 794
Northampton township[75]	6 636	5 662
Northfield village	3 913	⌐4 283
Northfield Center township	4 294	⌐4 364
Norton city	12 242	12 308
Reminderville village	1 960	215
Richfield township	4 941	4 943
Richfield village	3 437	3 228
Sagamore Hills township	7 189	⌐6 756
Silver Lake village	2 915	⌐3 286
Springfield township[75]	16 125	16 921
Stow city	25 303	⌐20 061
Tallmadge city	15 269	15 274
Twinsburg city[75]	7 632	⌐6 432
Twinsburg township[75]	1 257	⌐1 415
Trumbull County[76]	241 863	232 579
Bazetta township	10 107	7 008
Cortland village (pt.)[76]	4 986	2 445
Bloomfield township	1 078	1 144
Braceville township	3 132	3 098
Bristol township	3 151	2 404
Brookfield township	10 935	9 698
Brookfield (CDP)	1 527	...
Masury (CDP)	1 836	2 060
Yankee Lake village	99	43
Champion township	9 504	8 666
Farmington township	1 747	1 499
West Farmington village	563	650
Fowler township	3 066	2 544
Cortland village (pt.)[76]	25	80
Greene township	903	877
Gustavus township	1 108	1 008
Hartford township[76]	2 236	2 238
Howland township[76]	20 586	45 296
Howland (CDP)	7 441	...
Niles city (pt.)[76]	1 764	1 134
Hubbard township	16 520	16 293
Hubbard city	9 245	8 583
Johnston township	2 012	1 530
Kinsman township	2 120	1 922
Liberty township	26 827	26 679
Girard city (pt.)[76]	12 489	14 001
Lordstown village[76]	3 280	...
Mecca township	2 695	1 704
Mesopotamia township	1 966	1 496
Newton township	9 797	8 733
Newton Falls city[76]	4 960	5 378
Orangeville village[76]	223	268
Southington township	3 723	3 722
Vernon township	1 635	1 336
Vienna township	4 344	4 191

County Subdivisions	1980	1970
Trumbull County—Con.		
Warren city[76]	56 629	63 494
Warren township[76]	7 940	'46 518
Weathersfield township	34 590	30 635
Girard city (pt.)	28	118
McDonald village	3 744	3 177
Niles city (pt.)[76]	21 324	20 447
Youngstown city (pt.)	9	29
Tuscarawas County[77]	84 614	77 211
Auburn township	788	686
Bucks township	1 139	1 155
Baltic village (pt.)	523	571
Clay township	2 016	2 180
Gnadenhutten village (pt.)[77]	1 312	1 466
Dover township[77]	15 837	14 917
Dover city[77]	11 782	11 516
Parral village	259	271
Fairfield township	1 269	941
Franklin township	3 558	3 011
Strasburg village[77]	2 091	1 874
Goshen township[77]	4 551	5 103
Barnhill village	327	339
Midvale village (pt.)	636	636
Roswell village (pt.)	175	238
Jefferson township	753	794
Stone Creek village	150	171
Lawrence township	4 148	2 201
Bolivar village	989	1 084
Zoar village	264	228
Mill township	11 158	11 252
Dennison village (pt.)[77]	3 234	3 506
Midvale village (pt.)[77]	-	...
Uhrichsville city[77]	6 130	5 731
New Philadelphia city[77]	16 883	15 184
Oxford township	5 153	5 069
Newcomerstown village[77]	3 986	4 155
Perry township	362	311
Rush township	830	725
Salem township	1 629	1 357
Port Washington village	622	550
Sandy township	3 131	2 413
Mineral City village	884	860
Sugar Creek township	3 375	3 039
Sugarcreek village	1 966	1 771
Union township	1 275	890
Dennison village (pt.)[77]	164	-
Roswell village (pt.)	89	79
Warren township	980	783
Warwick township	2 714	2 511
Gnadenhutten village (pt.)[77]	8	...
Midvale village (pt.)[77]	18	...
Tuscarawas village[77]	917	830
Washington township	670	577
Wayne township	1 223	1 037
York township	1 172	1 075
Union County[78]	29 536	23 786
Allen township	1 133	616
Claibourne township	3 321	3 150
Richwood village[78]	2 181	2 072
Darby township	1 569	1 212
Unionville Center village	272	255
Dover township	1 499	954
Jackson township	690	616
Jerome township	3 290	2 509
Plain City village (pt.)	880	931
Leesburg township	1 285	1 219
Magnetic Springs village	314	349
Liberty township	1 136	1 141
Millcreek township	834	624
Paris township	10 542	7 721
Marysville city[78]	7 414	5 744
Taylor township	1 076	925
Union township	1 681	1 627
Milford Center village	764	753
Washington township	582	609
York township	898	863
Van Wert County[79]	30 458	29 194
Harrison township	992	913
Hoaglin township	598	528
Jackson township	518	481
Jennings township	749	777
Venedocia village (pt.)	58	101
Liberty township	1 789	1 619
Ohio City village	881	816
Pleasant township	12 985	12 982
Van Wert city (pt.)[79]	10 857	11 320
Ridge township	1 369	1 137
Van Wert city (pt.)[79]	178	...
Tully township	2 093	1 845
Convoy village[79]	1 140	991
Union township	976	934
Scott village (pt.)	205	200
Washington township	5 671	5 368
Delphos city (pt.)[79]	3 330	3 307
Middle Point village	709	543
Willshire township	1 874	1 839
Willshire village	564	623

County Subdivisions	1980	1970
Van Wert County—Con.		
Willshire township—Con.		
Wren village	282	282
York township	844	771
Elgin village	96	89
Venedocia village (pt.)	103	101
Vinton County	11 584	9 420
Brown township	263	277
Clinton township	1 977	1 821
Hamden village	1 010	953
Eagle township	430	341
Elk township	2 839	2 236
McArthur village	1 912	1 543
Harrison township	984	712
Jackson township	567	438
Knox township	508	304
Madison township	691	653
Zaleski village	347	304
Richland township	1 272	904
Swan township	699	545
Vinton township	516	426
Wilkesville township	838	763
Wilkesville village	189	181
Warren County[80]	99 276	'85 505
Clear Creek township	10 566	'8 576
Springboro village (pt.)[80]	4 902	2 729
Deerfield township	16 697	12 194
Landen (CDP)	2 870	...
Loveland Park (CDP) (pt.)	1 438	...
Mason city (pt.)[80]	8 571	5 554
Franklin township	28 159	25 963
Carlisle village (pt.)[80]	3 968	3 437
Franklin city[80]	10 711	10 075
Hunter (CDP)	2 270	...
Springboro village (pt.)[80]	60	70
Hamilton township[80]	5 819	5 310
Maineville village[80]	307	333
South Lebanon village (pt.)[80]	133	186
Harlan township	3 262	2 797
Butlerville village	223	204
Pleasant Plain village[80]	210	223
Lebanon city[80]	9 636	7 934
Loveland city (pt.)[80]	78	44
Massie township	802	1 072
Harveysburg village[80]	425	486
Salem township	3 812	3 931
Morrow village[80]	1 254	1 486
Turtle Creek township[80]	8 444	14 635
Mason city (pt.)	13	...
Monroe village (pt.)	68	57
Union township[80]	4 899	4 590
Mason city (pt.)[80]	108	123
South Lebanon village (pt.)[80]	2 567	2 828
Washington township	1 258	1 318
Wayne township	5 844	5 119
Corwin village	276	346
Waynesville village[80]	1 796	1 638
Washington County[81]	64 266	57 160
Adams township	1 921	1 906
Lowell village	729	852
Aurelius township	538	529
Macksburg village	295	266
Barlow township	1 981	1 557
Belpre city[81]	7 193	7 189
Belpre township[81]	4 343	9 788
Decatur township	983	776
Dunham township	2 042	1 475
Fairfield township	778	604
Fearing township[81]	917	850
Grandview township	2 119	2 036
Matamoras village[81]	1 172	940
Independence township	462	523
Lawrence township	879	787
Liberty township	540	529
Ludlow township	419	412
Marietta city[81]	16 467	16 861
Marietta New township[81]	4 333	3 378
Muskingum township	4 625	3 789
Devola (CDP)	2 708	1 989
Newport township	2 185	1 874
Palmer township	547	425
Salem township	1 085	1 003
Lower Salem village	110	106
Warren township[81]	3 635	2 534
Waterford township	3 930	3 569
Beverly village[81]	1 471	1 396
Watertown township	1 467	1 295
Wesley township	877	660
Wayne County[82]	97 408	87 123
Baughman township	4 539	4 531
Marshallville village (pt.)	665	568
Orrville city (pt.)[82]	1 405	1 671
Canaan township	4 092	3 616
Burbank village (pt.)	228	259
Creston village[82]	1 828	'1 792
Chester township	2 680	2 195
Chippewa township	9 250	7 392

County Subdivisions

County Subdivisions	1980	1970
Wayne County—Con.		
Chippewa township—Con.		
Doylestown village[82]	2 493	2 373
Marshallville village (pt.)	123	125
Rittman city (pt.)	-	-
Clinton township	2 913	2 835
Shreve village[82]	1 608	1 635
Congress township	3 724	2 779
Burbank village (pt.)	137	95
Congress village	178	205
West Salem village[82]	1 357	1 058
East Union township	5 887	6 363
Apple Creek village	741	784
Franklin township	2 815	2 225
Green township	10 980	9 476
Orrville city (pt.)	6 106	5 737
Smithville village[82]	1 467	1 278
Milton township	8 872	8 813
Rittman city (pt.)	5 998	6 261
Paint township	2 107	1 796
Mount Eaton village[82]	289	242
Plain township	2 336	2 014
Salt Creek township	2 709	2 087
Fredericksburg village[82]	511	601
Sugar Creek township	5 576	4 806
Dalton village[82]	1 357	1 177
Wayne township[82]	5 538	3 605
Wooster city[82]	19 289	18 703
Wooster township[82]	4 101	3 887
Williams County[83]	36 369	33 669
Brady township	2 528	2 407
West Unity village[83]	1 639	1 589
Bridgewater township	1 106	861
Bryan city[83]	7 879	7 008
Center township[83]	3 046	2 447
Florence township	2 133	2 013
Blakeslee village	136	163
Edon village	947	803
Jefferson township	1 857	1 667
Madison township	2 207	1 972
Pioneer village[83]	1 133	968
Mill Creek township	1 015	1 019
Alvordton village	362	351
Northwest township	1 055	914
Pulaski township[83]	2 539	2 655
St. Joseph township	2 756	3 000
Edgerton village[83]	1 813	2 126
Springfield township	2 517	2 323
Stryker village[83]	1 423	1 296
Superior township	5 731	5 383
Montpelier village[83]	4 431	4 184
Wood County[84]	107 372	89 722
Bloom township	2 665	2 602
Bairdstown village	151	138
Bloomdale village	744	727
Cygnet village	646	629
Jerry City village (pt.)	238	194
Bowling Green city[84]	25 728	'21 760
Center township[84]	1 334	'990
Fostoria city (pt.)[84]	1 071	819
Freedom township	2 536	2 365
Pemberville village[84]	1 321	1 301
Grand Rapids township	1 510	1 542
Grand Rapids village[84]	962	976
Henry township	3 835	3 797
North Baltimore village[84]	3 127	3 143
Jackson township	812	932
Hoytville village	315	403
Lake township	10 899	9 435
Millbury village[84]	955	771
Walbridge village[84]	2 900	3 208
Liberty township	1 947	1 545
Portage village (pt.)	125	137
Middleton township	2 448	2 473
Haskins village	568	549
Milton township	1 234	1 299
Custar village	254	277
Milton Center village	181	244
Weston village (pt.)	140	10
Montgomery township	4 637	4 258
Bradner village[84]	1 175	1 140
Rising Sun village[84]	698	730
Wayne village	894	921
Northwood village	5 495	4 222
Perry township[84]	1 862	1 668
West Millgrove village	205	215
Perrysburg city[84]	10 215	'7 693
Perrysburg township[84]	10 651	'5 945
Plain township[84]	2 460	'2 054
Portage township	1 690	1 654
Jerry City village (pt.)	274	276
Portage village (pt.)	354	357
Rossford city[84]	5 978	5 302
Troy township	3 558	3 221
Luckey village	895	996
Washington township	1 500	1 297
Tontogany village	367	395

County Subdivisions

County Subdivisions	1980	1970
Wood County—Con.		
Webster township	1 082	968
Weston township	2 225	1 881
Weston village (pt.)	1 568	1 259
Wyandot County[85]	22 651	21 826
Antrim township	1 414	1 354
Nevada village (pt.)	618	628
Crane township	7 064	'6 742
Upper Sandusky city[85]	5 967	'5 645
Crawford township	5 021	4 734
Carey village[85]	3 674	3 523
Eden township	1 082	1 001
Nevada village (pt.)	327	289
Jackson township	545	606
Kirby village (pt.)	75	90
Marseilles township	487	490
Marseilles village	164	155
Mifflin township	816	802
Kirby village (pt.)	83	88
Pitt township	945	941
Harpster village	239	291
Richland township	893	996
Wharton village	432	422
Ridge township	492	480
Salem township	984	858
Sycamore township	1 722	1 750
Sycamore village[85]	1 059	1 096
Tymochtee township	1 186	1 072

OKLAHOMA

The name Oklahoma is of Indian origin and signifies "Home or land of the red man."

The first white man to visit the area of the present state of Oklahoma was the Spanish explorer, De Soto, in 1541.

All but the extreme western part of the region now consituting Oklahoma was originally a portion of the vast Louisiana country, which was ceded by France to Spain in 1762, retroceded to France in 1800, and purchased by the United States in 1803.

The section of Oklahoma included in the Louisiana Purchase belonged, successively, to the district of Louisiana (1804-5), the territory of Louisiana (1805-1812), and the territory of Missouri (1812-1819). The part north of 36°30' continued in the territory of Missouri until 1834 and from 1834 to 1854 belonged to the Indian Country. The part south of 36°30', upon the organization of Arkansas territory, in 1819, was included in that territory. In 1824 the western boundary of Arkansas was place about 40 miles west of where it now stands, and in 1828 it was established at its present location; in each of these years the area west of the new line was transferred to Missouri territory and from 1834 to 1854 was a part of the Indian Country.

In 1854, by the Kansas-Nebraska act, the area of the Indian Country, or Indian Territory, as it was afterwards known, was reduced to that of the present state of Oklahoma exclusive of the three western counties. The area now constituting these three counties was a part of the Spanish possessions till 1821, of Mexico from 1821 to 1836, and of Texas from 1836 to 1850. Thereafter it remained unorganized until 1890, when Oklahoma territory was formed, but it was included in Indian Territory in 1889. Indian Territory had no organized territorial government, as had other territories of the United States, but the Five Civilized Tribes had their own forms of local self-government.

By Presidential proclamation of March 23, 1889, certain lands in the central part of Indian Territory, known as Oklahoma, were thrown open for settlement on April 22 of that year. No organized government was provided, however, until May 2, 1890, when Congress passed an act establishing the territory of Oklahoma. In September, 1893, the Cherokee Strip, was made a part of Oklahoma. The new territory was then bounded on the north by Kansas and Colorado, on the west by New Mexico and Texas, and on the south in part by Texas. The remainder of its southern and all of its eastern boundary were formed by an irregular line extending from the intersection of the ninety-eighth meridian and the Red River on the south to that of the ninety-sixth meridian and the Kansas boundary on the north. Sections of Oklahoma were thrown open for settlement at various dates, and the population of the territory rapidly increased.

In June, 1906, Congress passed an act to enable Oklahoma and Indian Territory to form a state government and in November, 1907, Oklahoma, with boundaries as at present, became a state of the Union.

COUNTY LOCATION INDEX

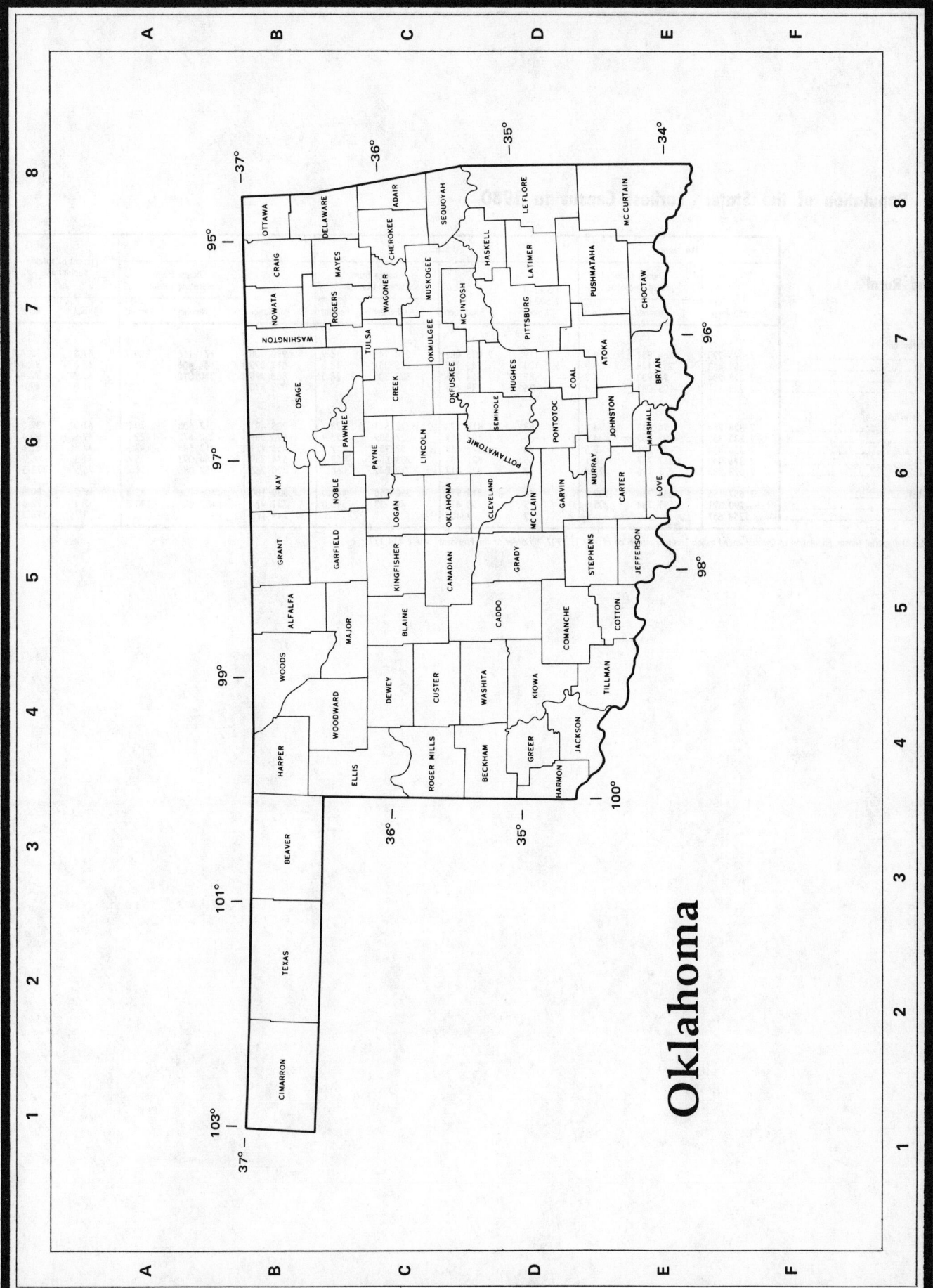

Oklahoma

Population of the State: Earliest Census to 1980

Urban and Rural

	The State			Urban				Rural			Percent of total population	
	Total population	Change from preceding census		Places of 2,500 or more	Population	Change from preceding census		Population	Change from preceding census		Urban	Rural
		Number	Percent			Number	Percent		Number	Percent		
Current urban definition:												
1980 (Apr. 1)	3 025 290	465 827	18.2	119	2 035 082	294 945	16.9	990 208	171 116	20.9	67.3	32.7
1970 (Apr. 1)	2 559 463	231 179	9.9	100	1 740 137	275 351	18.8	819 092	−44 406	−5.1	68.0	32.0
1960 (Apr. 1)	2 328 284	94 933	4.3	89	1 464 786	325 305	28.5	863 498	−230 372	−21.1	62.9	37.1
1950 (Apr. 1)	2 233 351	−103 083	−4.4	86	1 139 481	...	...	1 093 870	...	...	51.0	49.0
Previous urban definition:												
1960 (Apr. 1)	2 328 284	94 933	4.3	88	1 419 793	312 541	28.2	908 491	−217 608	−19.3	61.0	39.0
1950 (Apr. 1)	2 233 351	−103 083	−4.4	85	1 107 252	227 589	25.9	1 126 099	−330 672	−22.7	49.6	50.4
1940 (Apr. 1)	2 336 434	−59 606	−2.5	74	879 663	57 982	7.1	1 456 771	−117 588	−7.5	37.6	62.4
1930 (Apr. 1)	2 396 040	367 757	18.1	68	821 681	283 664	52.7	1 574 359	84 093	5.6	34.3	65.7
1920 (Jan. 1)	2 028 283	371 128	22.4	63	538 017	219 042	68.7	1 490 266	152 086	11.4	26.5	73.5
1910 (Apr. 15)	1 657 155	866 764	109.7	46	318 975	260 558	446.0	1 338 180	606 206	82.8	19.2	80.8
1900 (June 1)	790 391	531 734	205.6	13	58 417	48 933	516.0	731 974	482 801	193.8	7.4	92.6
1890 (June 1)	258 657	...	...	2	9 484	...	...	249 173	...	...	3.7	96.3

NOTE: The special census population of Oklahoma and Indian Territory, taken as of July 1, 1907, by order of the President, was 1,414,177.

ADAIR

1910	10,535
1920	13,703
1930	14,756
1940	15,755
1950	14,918
1960	13,122
1970	15,141
1980	18,575

ALFALFA

1910	18,138
1920	15,253
1930	15,228
1940	14,129
1950	10,699
1960	8,445
1970	7,224
1980	7,077

ATOKA

1910	13,808
1920	20,862
1930	14,533
1940	18,702
1950	14,269
1960	10,352
1970	10,972
1980	12,748

BEAVER

1890	2,674
1900	3,051
1910	13,631
1920	14,048
1930	11,452
1940	8,648
1950	7,411
1960	6,965
1970	6,282
1980	6,806

BECKHAM

1910	19,699
1920	18,898
1930	28,911
1940	22,169
1950	21,627
1960	17,782
1970	15,752
1980	19,243

BLAINE

1900	10,658
1910	17,960
1920	15,875
1930	20,452
1940	18,543
1950	15,049
1960	12,077
1970	11,794
1980	13,443

BRYAN

1910	29,854
1920	40,700
1930	32,277
1940	38,138
1950	28,999

1960	24,252
1970	25,552
1980	30,535

CADDO

1910	35,685
1920	34,207
1930	50,779
1940	41,567
1950	34,913
1960	28,621
1970	28,931
1980	30,905

CANADIAN

1890	7,158
1900	15,981
1910	23,501
1920	22,288
1930	28,115
1940	27,329
1950	25,644
1960	24,727
1970	32,245
1980	56,452

CARTER

1910	25,358
1920	40,247
1930	41,419
1940	43,292
1950	36,455
1960	39,044
1970	37,349
1980	43,610

CHEROKEE

1910	16,778
1920	19,872
1930	17,470
1940	21,030
1950	18,989
1960	17,762
1970	23,174
1980	30,684

CHOCTAW

1910	21,862
1920	32,144
1930	24,142
1940	28,358
1950	20,405
1960	15,637
1970	15,141
1980	17,203

CIMARRON

1910	4,553
1920	3,436
1930	5,408
1940	3,654
1950	4,589
1960	4,496
1970	4,145
1980	3,648

CLEVELAND

1890	6,605
1900	16,388

1910	18,843
1920	19,389
1930	24,948
1940	27,728
1950	41,443
1960	47,600
1970	81,839
1980	133,173

COAL

1910	15,817
1920	18,406
1930	11,521
1940	12,811
1950	8,056
1960	5,546
1970	5,525
1980	6,041

COMANCHE

1910	41,489
1920	26,629
1930	34,317
1940	38,998
1950	55,165
1960	90,803
1970	108,144
1980	112,456

COTTON

1920	16,679
1930	15,442
1940	12,884
1950	10,180
1960	8,031
1970	6,832
1980	7,338

CRAIG

1910	17,404
1920	19,160
1930	18,052
1940	21,083
1950	18,263
1960	16,303
1970	14,772
1980	15,014

CREEK

1910	26,223
1920	62,480
1930	64,115
1940	55,503
1950	43,143
1960	40,495
1970	45,532
1980	59,016

CUSTER

1900	12,264
1910	23,231
1920	18,736
1930	27,517
1940	23,068
1950	21,097
1960	21,040
1970	22,665
1980	25,995

DAY

1900	2,173

DELAWARE

1910	11,469
1920	13,868
1930	15,370
1940	18,592
1950	14,734
1960	13,198
1970	17,767
1980	23,946

DEWEY

1900	8,819
1910	14,132
1920	12,434
1930	13,250
1940	11,981
1950	8,789
1960	6,051
1970	5,656
1980	5,922

ELLIS

1910	15,375
1920	11,673
1930	10,541
1940	8,446
1950	7,326
1960	5,457
1970	5,129
1980	5,596

GARFIELD

1900	22,076
1910	33,050
1920	27,500
1930	45,588
1940	45,484
1950	52,820
1960	52,975
1970	56,343
1980	62,820

GARVIN

1910	26,545
1920	32,445
1930	31,401
1940	31,150
1950	29,500
1960	28,290
1970	24,874
1980	27,856

GRADY

1910	30,309
1920	33,943
1930	47,638
1940	41,116
1950	34,872
1960	29,590
1970	29,354
1980	39,490

GRANT

1900	17,273
1910	18,760

1920	16,072
1930	14,150
1940	13,128
1950	10,461
1960	8,140
1970	7,117
1980	6,518

GREER

1890	5,338
1900	17,922
1910	16,449
1920	15,836
1930	20,282
1940	14,550
1950	11,749
1960	8,877
1970	7,979
1980	7,028

HARMON

1910	11,328
1920	11,261
1930	13,834
1940	10,019
1950	8,079
1960	5,852
1970	5,136
1980	4,519

HARPER

1910	8,189
1920	7,623
1930	7,761
1940	6,454
1950	5,977
1960	5,956
1970	5,151
1980	4,715

HASKELL

1910	18,875
1920	19,397
1930	16,216
1940	17,324
1950	13,313
1960	9,121
1970	9,578
1980	11,010

HUGHES

1910	25,040
1920	26,045
1930	30,334
1940	29,189
1950	20,664
1960	15,144
1970	13,228
1980	14,338

JACKSON

1910	23,737
1920	22,141
1930	28,910
1940	22,708
1950	20,082
1960	29,736
1970	30,902
1980	30,356

JEFFERSON

Year	Population
1910	17,430
1920	17,664
1930	17,392
1940	15,107
1950	11,122
1960	8,192
1970	7,125
1980	8,183

JOHNSTON

Year	Population
1910	16,734
1920	20,125
1930	13,082
1940	15,960
1950	10,608
1960	8,517
1970	7,870
1980	10,356

KAY

Year	Population
1900	22,530
1910	26,999
1920	34,907
1930	50,186
1940	47,084
1950	48,892
1960	51,042
1970	48,791
1980	49,852

KINGFISHER

Year	Population
1890	8,332
1900	18,501
1910	18,825
1920	15,671
1930	15,960
1940	15,617
1950	12,860
1960	10,635
1970	12,857
1980	14,187

KIOWA

Year	Population
1910	27,526
1920	23,094
1930	29,630
1940	22,817
1950	18,926
1960	14,825
1970	12,532
1980	12,711

LATIMER

Year	Population
1910	11,321
1920	13,866
1930	11,184
1940	12,380
1950	9,690
1960	7,738
1970	8,601
1980	9,840

LE FLORE

Year	Population
1910	29,127
1920	42,765
1930	42,896
1940	45,866
1950	35,276
1960	29,106
1970	32,137
1980	40,698

LINCOLN

Year	Population
1900	27,007
1910	34,779
1920	33,406
1930	33,738
1940	29,529
1950	22,102
1960	18,783
1970	19,482
1980	26,601

LOGAN

Year	Population
1890	12,770
1900	26,563
1910	31,740
1920	27,550
1930	27,761
1940	25,245
1950	22,170
1960	18,662
1970	19,645
1980	26,881

LOVE

Year	Population
1910	10,236
1920	12,433
1930	9,639
1940	11,433
1950	7,721
1960	5,862
1970	5,637
1980	7,469

McCLAIN

Year	Population
1910	15,659
1920	19,326
1930	21,575
1940	19,205
1950	14,681
1960	12,740
1970	14,157
1980	20,291

McCURTAIN

Year	Population
1910	20,681
1920	37,905
1930	34,759
1940	41,318
1950	31,588
1960	25,851
1970	28,642
1980	36,151

McINTOSH

Year	Population
1910	20,961
1920	26,204
1930	24,924
1940	24,097
1950	17,829
1960	12,371
1970	12,472
1980	15,562

MAJOR

Year	Population
1910	15,248
1920	12,426
1930	12,206
1940	11,946
1950	10,279
1960	7,808
1970	7,529
1980	8,772

MARSHALL

Year	Population
1910	11,619
1920	14,674
1930	11,026
1940	12,384
1950	8,177
1960	7,263
1970	7,682
1980	10,550

MAYES

Year	Population
1910	13,596
1920	16,829
1930	17,883
1940	21,668
1950	19,743
1960	20,073
1970	23,302
1980	32,261

MURRAY

Year	Population
1910	12,744
1920	13,115
1930	12,410
1940	13,841
1950	10,775
1960	10,662
1970	10,669
1980	12,147

MUSKOGEE

Year	Population
1910	52,743
1920	61,710
1930	66,424
1940	65,914
1950	65,573
1960	61,866
1970	59,542
1980	66,939

NOBLE

Year	Population
1900	14,015
1910	14,945
1920	13,560
1930	15,139
1940	14,826
1950	12,156
1960	10,376
1970	10,043
1980	11,573

NOWATA

Year	Population
1910	14,223
1920	15,899
1930	13,611
1940	15,774
1950	12,734
1960	10,848
1970	9,773
1980	11,486

OKFUSKEE

Year	Population
1910	19,995
1920	25,051
1930	29,016
1940	26,279
1950	16,948
1960	11,706
1970	10,683
1980	11,125

OKLAHOMA

Year	Population
1890	11,742
1900	25,915
1910	85,232
1920	116,307
1930	221,738
1940	244,159
1950	325,352
1960	439,506
1970	527,717
1980	568,933

OKMULGEE

Year	Population
1910	21,115
1920	55,072
1930	56,558
1940	50,101
1950	44,561
1960	36,945
1970	25,358
1980	39,169

OSAGE

Year	Population
1910	20,101
1920	36,536
1930	47,344
1940	41,502
1950	33,071
1960	32,441
1970	29,750
1980	39,327

OTTAWA

Year	Population
1910	15,713
1920	41,108
1930	38,542
1940	35,849
1950	32,218
1960	28,301
1970	29,800
1980	32,870

PAWNEE

Year	Population
1900	12,366
1910	17,322
1920	19,126
1930	19,882
1940	17,395
1950	13,616
1960	10,884
1970	11,338
1980	15,310

PAYNE

Year	Population
1890	7,215
1900	20,909
1910	23,735
1920	30,180
1930	36,905
1940	36,057
1950	46,430
1960	44,231
1970	50,654
1980	62,435

PITTSBURG

Year	Population
1910	47,650
1920	52,570
1930	50,778
1940	48,985
1950	41,031
1960	34,360
1970	37,521
1980	40,524

PONTOTOC

Year	Population
1910	24,331
1920	30,949
1930	32,469
1940	39,972
1950	30,875
1960	28,089
1970	27,867
1980	32,598

POTTAWATOMIE

Year	Population
1900	26,412
1910	43,595
1920	46,028
1930	56,572
1940	54,377
1950	43,517
1960	41,486
1970	43,134
1980	55,239

PUSHMATAHA

Year	Population
1910	10,118
1920	17,514
1930	14,744
1940	19,466
1950	12,001
1960	9,088
1970	9,385
1980	11,773

ROGER MILLS

Year	Population
1900	6,190
1910	12,861
1920	10,638
1930	14,164
1940	10,736
1950	7,395
1960	5,090
1970	4,452
1980	4,799

ROGERS

Year	Population
1910	17,736
1920	17,605
1930	18,956
1940	21,078
1950	19,532
1960	20,614
1970	28,425
1980	46,436

SEMINOLE

1910	19,964
1920	23,808
1930	79,621
1940	61,201
1950	40,672
1960	28,066
1970	25,144
1980	27,473

SEQUOYAH

1910	25,005
1920	26,786
1930	19,505
1940	23,138
1950	19,773
1960	18,001
1970	23,370
1980	30,749

STEPHENS

1910	23,252
1920	24,692
1930	33,069
1940	31,090
1950	34,071
1960	37,990
1970	35,902
1980	43,419

TEXAS

1910	14,249
1920	13,975
1930	14,100
1940	9,896
1950	14,235
1960	14,162
1970	16,352
1980	17,727

TILLMAN

1910	18,650
1920	22,433
1930	24,390
1940	20,754
1950	17,598
1960	14,654
1970	12,901
1980	12,398

TULSA

1910	34,995
1920	109,023
1930	187,574
1940	193,363
1950	251,686
1960	346,038
1970	399,982
1980	470,593

WAGONER

1910	22,086
1920	21,371
1930	22,428
1940	21,646
1950	16,741
1960	15,673
1970	22,163
1980	41,801

WASHINGTON

1910	17,484
1920	27,002
1930	27,777
1940	30,559
1950	32,880
1960	42,347
1970	42,302
1980	48,113

WASHITA

1900	15,001
1910	25,034
1920	22,237
1930	29,435
1940	22,279
1950	17,657
1960	18,121
1970	12,141
1980	13,798

WOODS

1900	34,975
1910	17,567
1920	15,939
1930	17,005
1940	14,915
1950	14,526
1960	11,932
1970	11,920
1980	10,923

WOODWARD

1900	7,469
1910	16,592
1920	14,663
1930	15,884
1940	16,270
1950	14,383
1960	13,902
1970	15,537
1980	21,172

NOTE

DAY

Annexed to Washington in 1907.

ADA

1910	4,349
1920	8,012
1930	11,261
1940	15,143
1950	15,995
1960	14,347
1970	14,859
1980	15,902

ALTUS

1910	4,821
1920	4,522
1930	8,439
1940	8,593
1950	9,735
1960	21,225
1970	23,302
1980	23,101

ARDMORE

1900	5,681
1910	8,618
1920	14,181
1930	15,741
1940	16,886
1950	17,890
1960	20,184
1970	20,881
1980	23,689

BARTLESVILLE

1900	698
1910	6,181
1920	14,417
1930	14,763
1940	16,267
1950	19,228
1960	27,293
1970	29,683
1980	34,568

BETHANY

1920	485
1930	2,032
1940	2,590
1950	5,705
1960	12,342
1970	22,694
1980	22,130

BROKEN ARROW

1900	1,383
1910	1,576
1920	2,086
1930	1,964
1940	2,074
1950	3,262
1960	5,928
1970	11,018
1980	35,761

CHICKASHA

1900	3,209
1910	10,320
1920	10,179
1930	14,099
1940	14,111
1950	15,842

1960	14,866
1970	14,194
1980	15,828

CLAREMORE

1900	2,064
1910	2,866
1920	3,435
1930	3,720
1940	4,134
1950	5,494
1960	6,639
1970	9,084
1980	12,085

DEL CITY

1950	2,504
1960	12,934
1970	27,133
1980	28,424

DUNCAN

1900	1,164
1910	2,477
1920	3,463
1930	8,363
1940	9,207
1950	15,325
1960	20,009
1970	19,718
1980	22,517

DURANT

1900	2,969
1910	5,330
1920	7,340
1930	7,463
1940	10,027
1950	10,541
1960	10,467
1970	11,118
1980	11,972

EDMOND

1900	965
1910	2,090
1920	2,452
1930	3,576
1940	4,002
1950	6,086
1960	8,577
1970	16,663
1980	34,637

EL RENO

1890	285
1900	3,383
1910	7,782
1920	7,737
1930	9,384
1940	10,078
1950	10,991
1960	11,015
1970	14,510
1980	15,486

ENID

1900	3,444
1910	13,799
1920	16,576
1930	26,399
1940	28,081
1950	36,017
1960	38,859
1970	44,986
1980	50,363

GUTHRIE

1890	2,788
1900	11,652
1910	11,654
1920	11,757
1930	9,582
1940	10,018
1950	10,113
1960	9,502
1970	9,575
1980	10,312

LAWTON

1910	7,788
1920	8,930
1930	12,121
1940	18,055
1950	34,757
1960	61,697
1970	74,470
1980	80,054

McALESTER

1900	646
1910	11,774
1920	10,632
1930	11,804
1940	12,401
1950	17,878
1960	17,419
1970	18,802
1980	17,225

MIAMI

1900	1,527
1910	2,907
1920	6,802
1930	8,064
1940	8,345
1950	11,801
1960	12,869
1970	13,880
1980	14,237

MIDWEST CITY

1950	10,166
1960	36,058
1970	48,212
1980	49,559

MOORE

1900	129
1910	225
1920	254
1930	538
1940	499
1950	942
1960	1,783

1970	18,761
1980	35,063

MUSKOGEE

1900	4,254
1910	25,278
1920	30,277
1930	32,026
1940	32,332
1950	37,289
1960	38,059
1970	37,331
1980	40,011

NORMAN

1890	787
1900	2,225
1910	3,724
1920	5,004
1930	9,603
1940	11,429
1950	27,006
1960	33,412
1970	52,117
1980	68,020

OKLAHOMA CITY

1890	4,151
1900	10,037
1910	64,205
1920	91,295
1930	185,389
1940	204,424
1950	243,504
1960	324,253
1970	368,164
1980	403,313

OKMULGEE

1910	4,176
1920	17,430
1930	17,097
1940	16,051
1950	18,317
1960	15,951
1970	15,180
1980	16,263

PONCA CITY

1900	2,528
1910	2,521
1920	7,051
1930	16,136
1940	16,794
1950	20,180
1960	24,411
1970	25,490
1980	26,238

SAND SPRINGS

1920	4,076
1930	6,674
1940	6,137
1950	6,994
1960	7,754
1970	10,565
1980	13,246

SALPULPA

1900	891
1910	8,283
1920	11,634
1930	10,533
1940	12,249
1950	13,031
1960	14,282
1970	15,159
1980	15,853

SHAWNEE

1900	3,462
1910	12,474
1920	15,348
1930	23,283
1940	22,053
1950	22,948
1960	24,326
1970	25,075
1980	26,506

STILLWATER

1890	480
1900	2,431
1910	3,444
1920	4,701
1930	7,016
1940	10,097
1950	20,238
1960	23,965
1970	31,126
1980	38,268

THE VILLAGE

1960	12,118
1970	13,695
1980	11,049

TULSA

1900	1,390
1910	18,182
1920	72,075
1930	141,258
1940	142,157
1950	182,740
1960	261,685
1970	330,350
1980	360,919

WOODWARD

1900	2,018
1910	2,696
1920	3,849
1930	5,056
1940	5,406
1950	5,915
1960	7,747
1970	9,563
1980	13,610

YUKON

1910	1,018
1920	1,016
1930	1,455
1940	1,660
1950	1,990
1960	3,076
1970	8,411
1980	17,112

CORRECTION NOTE

The official 1980 census counts of total population shown in
this report supersede counts issued previously. Corrections
to the figures were made after the counts were provided to
the State for redistricting purposes and released in Advance
Report PHC80-V for this State.

Shown below are corrections to the 1980 census counts of the
total population made after the tabulations for this report
were completed. Any additional corrections made after this
report is printed are available by writing to Data User
Services Division, Customer Services (Corrections), Bureau of
the Census, Washington, D.C. 20233.

The 1980 figures shown in this publication are subject to
change pending the outcome of the various lawsuits dealing
with the census counts.

	1980 population	
	As shown in the tables	Corrected
Oklahoma County:		
Oklahoma City division:		
Del City city.................	28 424	28 523
Oklahoma City city (pt.).......	377 003	376 926
Smith Village town............	82	60
Springlake Park city...........	11	(1)
Osage County:		
Southeast Osage division:		
Sand Springs city (pt.)........	384	259
Rogers County:		
Catoosa division:		
Catoosa city (pt.)............	1 772	1 561
Fair Oaks town (pt.)...........	---	22
Catoosa city (total)...............	1 772	1 561
Fair Oaks town (total).............	324	346
Oklahoma City city (total).........	403 213	403 136
Sand Springs city (total)..........	13 246	13 121

(1) Delete.

County Subdivisions	1980	1970
The State	3 025 290	2 559 463
Adair County[1]	18 575	15 141
Stilwell East division	7 515	...
Stilwell city (pt.)[1]	2 365	2 134
Stilwell West division	4 233	...
Stilwell city (pt.)[1]	4	...
Watts division	2 264	1 803
Watts town[1]	316	326
Westville division	4 563	3 602
Westville town[1]	1 049	934
Alfalfa County[2]	7 077	7 224
Carmen division	1 284	1 249
Aline town	313	260
Carmen town	516	519
Cherokee division	2 537	2 617
Cherokee city[2]	2 105	2 119
Lambert town	20	16
Helena division	1 632	...
Goltry town	305	282
Helena town	710	769
North Alfalfa division	1 624	...
Amorita town	66	63
Burlington town	206	165
Byron town	67	72
Jet town[2]	352	317
Atoka County[3]	12 748	10 972
Central Atoka division	7 875	6 993
Atoka city[3]	3 409	3 346
North Atoka division	2 033	1 518
Stringtown town[3]	1 047	397
West Atoka division	2 840	2 461
Caney town[3]	147	200
Tushka town[3]	358	230
Beaver County[4]	6 806	6 282
North Beaver division	2 710	2 093
Forgan town	611	496
Gate town	146	151
Knowles town	44	52
South Beaver division	4 096	4 189
Beaver city[4]	1 939	1 853
Beckham County[5]	19 243	15 754
Carter division	748	711
Carter town[5]	367	311
Elk City division	11 779	8 772
Elk City city[5]	9 579	7 323
Erick division	2 324	2 338
Erick city[5]	1 375	1 285
Texola town	106	144
Sayre division	4 392	3 933
Sayre city[5]	3 177	2 712
Blaine County[6]	13 443	11 794
Canton division	2 333	1 992
Canton town	854	844
Longdale town	405	331
Geary division	2 437	...
Geary city (pt.)	1 557	1 315
Hydro town (pt.)	199	99
Okeene division	2 107	2 027
Okeene town[6]	1 601	1 421
Watonga division	6 566	...
Greenfield town	233	143
Hitchcock town	172	160
Watonga city[6]	4 139	3 696
Bryan County[7]	30 535	25 552
Colbert division	3 455	2 738
Colbert town	1 122	814
Durant division	20 244	...
Calera town[7]	1 390	1 063
Durant city[7]	11 972	11 118
Kenefic town[7]	140	153
Mead town[7]	143	80
Sand Point town[7]	179	...
Silo town[7]	43	...
East Bryan division	1 336	1 156
Bennington town	302	288
North Central Bryan division	3 015	...
Bokchito town[7]	628	607
Caddo town[7]	923	886
South Bryan division	1 413	1 303
Achille town[7]	480	382
Hendrix town	106	117
Kemp town	178	153
Southeast Bryan division	1 072	1 141
Caddo County[8]	30 905	28 931
Anadarko division	11 736	10 864
Anadarko city[8]	6 378	6 682
Gracemont town[8]	503	424
Apache division	2 887	2 754
Apache town[8]	1 560	1 421
Binger–Hinton division	4 810	4 451
Binger town	791	730
Bridgeport city	115	142
Hinton town[8]	1 432	889
Lookeba town	221	165
Carnegie division	4 274	3 880
Carnegie town[8]	2 016	1 723

County Subdivisions	1980	1970
Caddo County—Con.		
Cyril–Cement division	3 219	3 011
Cement town[8]	884	892
Cyril town[8]	1 220	1 302
Fort Cobb division	1 976	1 882
Fort Cobb town[8]	760	722
Hydro division	2 003	2 089
Eakly town[8]	452	228
Hydro town (pt.)	739	706
Canadian County[9]	56 452	32 245
East Canadian division	34 118	...
Mustang city	7 496	2 637
Oklahoma City city (pt.)	8 700	2 179
Piedmont town (pt.)[9]	368	(NA)
Yukon city	17 112	8 411
El Reno division	20 275	...
Calumet town (pt.)[9]	117	(NA)
El Reno city[9]	15 486	14 510
Okarche town	310	283
Oklahoma City city (pt.)	41	...
Piedmont town (pt.)[9]	1 638	(NA)
Union City town	558	306
Walnut division	497	433
West Canadian division	1 562	...
Calumet town (pt.)[9]	352	(NA)
Geary city (pt.)[9]	143	65
Carter County[10]	43 610	37 349
Ardmore division	31 194	...
Ardmore city (pt.)[10]	23 650	20 881
Dickson town[10]	996	798
Lone Grove town (pt.)	3 086	1 240
Springer town (pt.)[10]	270	...
Ardmore North division	2 993	2 990
Ardmore city (pt.)[10]	39	...
Gene Autry town	178	120
Ratliff City town (pt.)[10]	23	...
Springer town (pt.)[10]	409	256
Tatums town[10]	281	133
Healdton Central division	4 217	3 641
Healdton city[10]	3 769	2 324
Healdton North division	1 819	1 949
Ratliff City town (pt.)[10]	327	250
Wilson division[10]	3 387	2 885
Lone Grove town (pt.)	283	...
Wilson city	1 585	1 569
Cherokee County[11]	30 684	23 174
East Cherokee division	4 230	3 039
Hulbert division	3 972	3 031
Hulbert town[11]	633	505
North Cherokee division	3 586	2 621
South Cherokee division	3 277	1 989
Tahlequah division	15 619	12 494
Tahlequah city[11]	9 708	9 254
Choctaw County[12]	17 203	15 141
Fort Towson division	3 038	2 459
Fort Towson town[12]	789	430
Hugo division	10 765	9 404
Hugo city[12]	7 172	6 585
West Choctaw division	3 400	3 278
Boswell town	702	755
Soper town[12]	465	322
Cimarron County[13]	3 648	4 145
Boise City division	2 573	...
Boise City city	1 761	1 993
Keyes division	1 075	...
Keyes town	557	569
Cleveland County[14]	133 173	81 839
East Cleveland division	11 101	...
Noble town (pt.)[14]	184	...
Norman city (pt.)[14]	5 460	...
Slaughterville town (pt.)[14]	1 875	...
Lexington division	2 245	1 979
Lexington town[14]	1 731	1 516
Slaughterville town (pt.)[14]	13	...
Noble division	3 607	2 453
Noble town (pt.)[14]	3 313	2 241
Slaughterville town (pt.)[14]	65	...
Norman division	63 161	...
Hall Park town	577	163
Norman city (pt.)[14]	62 459	52 117
North Cleveland division	53 059	...
Moore city[14]	35 063	18 761
Norman city (pt.)[14]	101	...
Oklahoma City city (pt.)[14]	17 295	4 169
Ranchwood Manor town[14]	296	213
Coal County[15]	6 041	5 525
East Coal division	3 876	3 545
Coalgate city[15]	2 001	1 859
Lehigh city	284	296
Phillips town	178	106
West Coal division	2 165	1 980
Bromide town (pt.)	28	30
Centrahoma city	166	155
Tupelo city	542	485

County Subdivisions	1980	1970
Comanche County[16]	112 456	108 144
Lawton division	73 479	...
Lawton city (pt.)[16]	73 046	74 470
Northeast Comanche division	4 463	3 747
Elgin town[16]	1 003	840
Fletcher town	1 074	950
Sterling town[16]	702	675
Northwest Comanche division	3 981	2 402
Medicine Park town[16]	437	'483
Sill division	15 934	21 480
Fort Sill (CDP)	15 924	21 217
Southeast Comanche division	8 812	...
Lawton city (pt.)[16]	7 008	...
Southwest Comanche division	5 787	4 268
Cache town[16]	1 661	1 106
Chattanooga town (pt.)[16]	386	302
Faxon town	140	121
Geronimo town[16]	726	587
Indiahoma town	364	434
Lawton city (pt.)[16]	–	...
Cotton County[17]	7 338	6 832
Southwest Cotton division	1 194	...
Devol city	186	129
Randlett town	461	384
Temple division	1 847	...
Temple town[17]	1 339	1 354
Walters division	4 297	3 905
Walters city[17]	2 778	2 611
Craig County[18]	15 014	14 722
North Craig division	3 056	2 879
Bluejacket town[18]	247	234
Welch town	697	651
Vinita East division	9 450	9 630
Ketchum town[18]	326	238
Vinita city[18]	6 740	5 847
Vinita West division	2 508	2 213
Big Cabin town[18]	252	198
Creek County[19]	59 016	45 532
Bristow division	6 321	6 117
Bristow city	4 702	4 653
Bristow South division	2 638	2 235
Depew town	682	739
Drumright division	3 913	3 866
Drumright city[19]	3 162	2 740
Kellyville–Slick division[19]	2 740	1 889
Kellyville town (pt.)	942	685
Slick town	187	171
Keystone Lake division[19]	8 546	4 720
Mannford town (pt.)[19]	1 610	892
Oilton city	1 244	1 087
Sapulpa division	32 200	...
Kellyville town (pt.)	18	...
Kiefer town[19]	912	803
Mounds town	1 086	766
Sapulpa city[19]	15 853	15 159
Shamrock–Heyburn Lake division	2 658	1 378
Shamrock town	218	204
Stroud city (pt.)[19]	9	...
Custer County[20]	25 995	22 665
Butler division	1 117	1 051
Butler town	388	315
Hammon town (pt.)[20]	62	...
Clinton division	10 792	10 132
Arapaho town[20]	851	531
Clinton city[20]	8 796	8 513
Custer City division	921	950
Custer City town	530	486
Thomas division	2 078	1 851
Thomas town	1 515	1 336
Weatherford division	11 087	8 681
Weatherford city[20]	9 640	7 959
Delaware County[21]	23 946	17 767
Colcord division	3 639	...
Colcord town	530	438
West Siloam Springs town[21]	431	210
Grove division	9 642	...
Bernice town[21]	318	189
Grove town[21]	3 378	2 000
Jay division	6 897	...
Jay town[21]	2 100	1 594
Kansas division	3 768	...
Kansas town[21]	491	317
Oaks town	591	219
Dewey County[22]	5 922	5 656
Dewey South division	1 843	...
Leedey town[22]	499	465
Putnam town	74	84
Taloga town	446	363
Seiling division	2 462	2 423
Oakwood town	140	129
Seiling city[22]	1 103	1 033
Vici division	1 617	1 443
Camargo town	264	236
Vici town[22]	845	694

County Subdivisions	1980	1970
Ellis County[23]	5 596	5 129
Northeast Ellis division	1 649	...
Fargo town[23]	409	262
Gage town	667	536
Northwest Ellis division	2 299	...
Shattuck town	1 759	1 546
South Ellis division	1 648	1 730
Arnett town[23]	714	711
Garfield County[24]	62 820	'56 343
Enid division	54 327	...
Breckenridge town (pt.)[24]	223	70
Carrier town (pt.)[24]	19	...
Enid city (pt.)[24]	50 360	'44 986
Fairmont town[24]	419	154
Lahoma town[24]	537	299
North Enid town[24]	992	730
Waukomis town (pt.)[24]	6	...
North Garfield division	3 932	...
Breckenridge town (pt.)[24]	38	...
Carrier town (pt.)[24]	240	...
Enid city (pt.)[24]	3	...
Garber city	1 215	1 011
Hillsdale town	110	77
Hunter town	276	274
Kremlin town[24]	301	200
South Garfield division	4 561	...
Covington town	715	605
Douglas town	89	79
Drummond town[24]	482	326
Waukomis town (pt.)[24]	1 545	'842
Garvin County[25]	27 856	24 874
Elmore City division	3 210	2 605
Elmore City town[25]	582	653
Lindsay division	5 550	5 328
Lindsay city[25]	3 454	3 705
Maysville division	2 490	2 196
Maysville town	1 396	1 380
Pauls Valley division	13 904	12 579
Paoli town[25]	573	480
Pauls Valley city[25]	5 664	5 769
Wynnewood city[25]	2 615	2 374
Stratford division	2 702	2 166
Stratford town[25]	1 459	1 278
Grady County[26]	39 490	29 354
Amber–Pocasset division	3 651	2 132
Amber town[26]	416	...
Blanchard town (pt.)[26]	30	...
Chickasha city (pt.)	–	...
Chickasha division	19 681	...
Chickasha city (pt.)[26]	15 828	14 194
East Ninnekah town (pt.)[26]	722	...
Norge town[26]	87	...
Verden town	625	439
Minco division	2 033	1 881
Minco city[26]	1 489	1 129
Ninnekah–Alex division	3 445	2 644
Alex town[26]	769	492
Bradley town	284	247
East Ninnekah town (pt.)[26]	363	...
Rush Springs division	3 826	3 124
Rush Springs town	1 451	1 381
Tuttle division	6 854	2 608
Blanchard town (pt.)[26]	–	...
Tuttle town	3 051	1 640
Grant County[27]	6 518	7 117
Lamont division	1 145	1 190
Deer Creek town	174	203
Lamont town[27]	571	478
Medford division	2 423	2 690
Jefferson town	92	128
Medford city[27]	1 419	1 304
Renfrow town	27	39
Southwest Grant division	1 903	1 993
Nash town	301	294
Pond Creek city[27]	949	903
Wakita division	1 047	1 244
Manchester town	146	165
Wakita town	526	'545
Greer County[28]	7 028	7 979
Granite division	2 061	2 363
Granite town	1 617	1 808
Mangum division	4 638	5 161
Mangum city[28]	3 833	4 066
Northwest Greer division	329	455
Willow town[28]	162	188
Harmon County[29]	4 519	5 136
Gould division	768	...
Gould town	318	368
Hollis division	3 751	...
Hollis city[29]	2 958	3 150
Harper County[30]	4 715	5 151
Buffalo division	2 165	2 565
Buffalo town[30]	1 381	1 579
Laverne division	2 550	2 586
Laverne town[30]	1 563	1 373

County Subdivisions

County Subdivisions	1980	1970
Harper County—Con.		
Laverne division—Con.		
May town	89	91
Rosston town	66	56
Haskell County[31]	11 010	9 578
Keota division	1 822	1 836
Keota town	661	685
McCurtain division	1 353	1 284
McCurtain town[31]	549	575
Stigler division	4 893	3 976
Stigler city[31]	2 630	2 347
Tamaha town	145	83
West Haskell division	2 942	2 482
Kinta town	303	247
Whitefield town[31]	240	...
Hughes County[32]	14 338	13 228
Holdenville division	8 538	7 629
Holdenville city[32]	5 469	5 181
Lamar town	121	153
Wewoka city (pt.)[32]	–	...
Yeager town	138	107
South Hughes division	2 420	2 307
Allen town (pt.)[32]	84	67
Calvin town	315	359
Gerty town	149	139
Stuart town	235	294
Wetumka division	3 380	3 292
Dustin town	498	502
Wetumka city[32]	1 725	1 687
Jackson County[33]	30 356	30 902
Altus division	25 252	...
Altus city[33]	23 101	23 302
Blair town	1 092	1 114
Martha town	219	268
Altus South division	606	...
Elmer town	131	138
East Jackson division	1 856	...
Headrick town	223	139
West Jackson division	2 642	2 869
East Duke town[33]	484	486
Eldorado town	688	737
Olustee town	721	819
Jefferson County[34]	8 183	7 125
Ringling division	2 505	2 092
Cornish town	115	90
Ringling town[34]	1 561	1 206
South Jefferson division	2 419	2 286
Ryan town[34]	1 083	1 011
Sugden town	76	54
Terral town	604	636
Waurika division	3 259	2 747
Addington town	141	123
Hastings town	246	184
Waurika city[34]	2 258	1 833
Johnston County[35]	10 356	7 870
East Johnston division	2 854	2 239
Bromide town (pt.)	152	201
Milburn town	376	275
Wapanucka town	472	425
Tishomingo division	4 918	3 684
Tishomingo city[35]	3 212	2 663
West Johnston division	2 584	1 947
Mannsville town[35]	568	364
Mill Creek town	431	234
Ravia town	487	373
Kay County[36]	49 852	48 791
Blackwell division	9 669	10 071
Blackwell city[36]	8 400	8 645
Nardin town	98	135
Braman division	1 055	1 011
Braman town	355	295
Kaw City division	710	1 134
Kaw City city[36]	283	283
Newkirk division	3 859	3 487
Kildare town	112	79
Newkirk city[36]	2 413	2 173
Ponca City division	30 211	...
Ponca City city[36]	26 238	25 940
Tonkawa division	4 348	4 136
Tonkawa city[36]	3 524	3 337
Kingfisher County[37]	14 187	12 857
Hennessey division	4 673	4 431
Hennessey town[37]	2 287	2 181
Kingfisher division	7 437	6 696
Dover town[37]	570	...
Kingfisher city[37]	4 245	4 042
Loyal town	112	107
Okarche–Cashion division	2 077	1 730
Cashion town (pt.)[37]	491	329
Okarche town (pt.)[37]	754	543
Piedmont town (pt.)[37]	10	...
Kiowa County[38]	12 711	12 532
Hobart division	5 331	5 183
Hobart city[38]	4 735	4 638
Lone Wolf division	1 164	1 231
Lone Wolf town	613	584

County Subdivisions	1980	1970
Kiowa County—Con.		
Mountain View division	2 471	2 379
Gotebo town	457	376
Mountain View town[38]	1 189	1 110
Roosevelt division	926	1 046
Cooperton town	31	55
Roosevelt town[38]	396	353
Snyder division	2 819	2 693
Mountain Park town[38]	557	458
Snyder city	1 848	1 671
Latimer County[39]	9 840	8 601
Red Oak division	2 008	...
Fanshawe town (pt.)[39]		
Red Oak town	676	609
South Latimer division	2 154	1 740
Wilburton division	5 678	...
Wilburton city	2 996	2 504
Le Flore County[40]	40 698	32 137
Arkoma division	2 175	2 123
Arkoma town	2 175	2 098
Cameron division	2 613	...
Cameron town	365	311
Poteau city (pt.)[40]	19	...
Heavener division	6 389	5 140
Heavener city[40]	2 776	2 566
Howe town[40]	562	403
Poteau city (pt.)[40]	10	...
Panama–Bokoshe division	4 388	...
Bokoshe town[40]	556	588
Panama town[40]	1 425	1 121
Poteau city (pt.)[40]	19	...
Shady Point town[40]	235	...
Pocola division	3 484	1 972
Pocola town	3 268	1 840
Poteau division	7 363	...
Poteau city (pt.)[40]	6 971	5 500
South Le Flore division	698	641
Spiro division	6 876	...
Cowlington town	–	...
Poteau city (pt.)[40]	546	751
Spiro town[40]	2 221	2 057
Talihina division	2 757	2 588
Talihina town (pt.)[40]	1 031	1 223
Wister division	3 955	...
Fanshawe town (pt.)	416	199
Le Flore town	322	175
Poteau city (pt.)[40]	70	...
Talihina town (pt.)	356	927
Wister town	982	927
Lincoln County[41]	26 601	19 482
Chandler division	6 768	...
Chandler city[41]	2 926	2 529
Davenport town[41]	974	831
Kendrick town	132	126
Sparks town (pt.)[41]	434	183
Meeker division	4 685	2 873
Meeker town[41]	1 032	804
Sparks town (pt.)[41]	127	...
Northeast Lincoln division	4 966	...
Stroud city (pt.)[41]	3 139	2 502
Northwest Lincoln division	3 396	2 339
Agra town	354	335
Carney town[41]	622	396
Tryon town[41]	435	301
Prague division	4 025	...
Prague city[41]	2 208	1 802
Sparks town (pt.)[41]	211	...
Wellston division	2 761	...
Fallis town	22	39
Warwick town	167	146
Wellston town[41]	802	789
Logan County[42]	26 881	19 645
Crescent division	3 021	2 640
Crescent city[42]	1 651	1 568
East Logan division	2 415	...
Coyle town[42]	345	303
Langston town	443	486
Meridian town	78	104
Guthrie division	20 016	...
Cashion town (pt.)[42]	56	...
Guthrie city[42]	10 312	9 575
North Logan division	1 429	1 414
Marshall town	372	420
Mulhall town	301	250
Orlando town[42]	218	202
Love County[43]	7 469	5 637
East Love division	5 921	4 290
Marietta city[43]	2 494	2 013
Thackerville town[43]	431	257
West Love division	1 548	1 347
Leon town	120	112
McClain County[44]	20 291	14 157
Blanchard division	7 445	...
Blanchard town (pt.)	1 658	1 580
Cole town[44]	256	(NA)
Dibble town (pt.)	280	184
Newcastle town[44]	3 076	1 271

County Subdivisions	1980	1970
McClain County—Con.		
Blanchard division—Con.		
Oklahoma City city (pt.)[44]	123	249
East McClain division	1 195	828
Byars town	353	247
Rosedale town	97	98
Purcell division	11 651	
Cole town (pt.)[44]	53	(NA)
Dibble town (pt.)	68	...
Goldsby town[44]	603	298
Purcell city[44]	4 638	4 076
Washington town	477	322
Wayne town[44]	621	618
McCurtain County[45]	36 151	28 642
Broken Bow division	11 732	9 118
Broken Bow city[45]	3 965	2 980
Idabel division	10 872	...
Garvin town	162	117
Idabel city[45]	7 622	5 946
North McCurtain division	3 258	2 658
Smithville town[45]	133	144
Southeast McCurtain division	3 722	...
Harris town[45]	192	...
Haworth town[45]	341	293
Valliant division	4 329	...
Millerton town[45]	262	...
Valliant town[45]	927	840
Wright City division	2 238	1 926
Wright City town[45]	1 168	1 068
McIntosh County[46]	15 562	12 472
Checotah division	8 082	5 861
Checotah city[46]	3 454	3 074
Rentiesville town	78	96
Eufaula division	4 851	
Eufaula city[46]	3 159	2 355
Stidham town	60	53
Hanna division	1 167	
Hanna town[46]	157	181
Hitchita–Pierce division	1 462	1 202
Hitchita town	126	160
Major County[47]	8 772	7 529
East Major division	3 240	2 668
Ames town	314	227
Cleo Springs town	514	344
Meno town	171	119
Ringwood city[47]	389	241
Fairview division	5 532	4 861
Fairview city	3 370	2 894
Marshall County[48]	10 550	7 682
North Marshall division	6 336	5 112
Madill city[48]	3 173	2 875
Oakland town	485	317
South Marshall division	4 214	2 570
Kingston town[48]	1 171	710
McBride town	91	44
Woodville town[48]	94	118
Mayes County[49]	32 261	23 302
Adair division	4 049	...
Adair town	508	459
East Mayes division	7 034	4 774
Disney town	464	303
Grand Lake Towne town	36	23
Hoot Owl town[49]	3	...
Langley town[49]	582	481
Pensacola town	82	56
Salina town[49]	1 115	1 024
Spavinaw town[49]	623	470
Strang town	126	164
Locust Grove division	5 874	4 404
Locust Grove town[49]	1 179	1 090
Pryor division	15 304	...
Chouteau town[49]	1 559	1 046
Pryor Creek city[49]	8 483	7 057
Sportsmen Acres town[49]	218	...
Murray County[50]	12 147	10 669
East Murray division[50]	7 611	6 793
Hickory town	95	62
Sulphur city[50]	5 516	5 158
West Murray division	4 536	3 876
Davis city[50]	2 782	2 223
Dougherty town	210	211
Muskogee County[51]	66 939	59 542
Boynton division	1 216	1 225
Boynton town	518	522
Council Hill town	141	135
Haskell division[51]	2 989	2 916
Haskell town[51]	1 953	2 063
Muskogee division	53 721	...
Braggs town	351	325
Fort Gibson town[51]	2 477	1 418
Muskogee city[51]	40 011	37 331
Taft town[51]	489	525
Muskogee Southwest division[51]	3 161	2 098
Oktaha town[51]	376	193
Wainwright town	182	135
Porum division	2 423	1 998

County Subdivisions	1980	1970
Muskogee County—Con.		
Porum division—Con.	668	658
Porum town	2 054	1 779
Warner division	1 310	1 217
Warner town[51]	1 375	1 176
Webbers Falls division	461	485
Webbers Falls town[51]		
Noble County[52]	11 573	10 043
Billings division	1 032	1 041
Billings town[52]	632	618
East Noble division	2 718	2 059
Marland town[52]	340	236
Morrison town	671	421
Red Rock town	376	233
Perry division	7 823	6 943
Perry city[52]	5 796	5 341
Nowata County[53]	11 486	9 773
Alluwe division	803	830
New Alluwe town[53]	129	116
Lenapah–Delaware division	1 768	...
Delaware town	544	534
Lenapah town[53]	350	325
Nowata division	6 592	5 492
Nowata city[53]	4 270	3 679
South Coffeyville–Wann division	2 323	...
South Coffeyville town	873	646
Wann town[53]	156	135
Okfuskee County[54]	11 125	10 683
Boley division	1 135	...
Boley town	423	514
Okemah division	6 298	5 908
Castle town	130	212
Okemah city[54]	3 381	2 913
Paden division	1 376	...
Paden town	448	442
Weleetka division	2 316	2 389
Weleetka town	1 195	1 199
Oklahoma County[55]	568 933	r527 717
Oklahoma City division	568 933	...
Bethany city[55]	22 130	r22 694
Choctaw city	7 520	4 750
Del City city[55]	28 424	27 133
Edmond city[55]	34 637	16 633
Forest Park town[55]	1 148	835
Harrah town[55]	2 897	1 931
Jones town	2 270	1 666
Lake Aluma town	101	124
Luther town	1 159	836
Midwest City city[55]	49 559	r48 212
Nichols Hills city[55]	4 171	4 478
Nicoma Park city[55]	2 588	2 560
Oklahoma City city (pt.)[55]	377 003	r361 567
Smith Village town	82	93
Spencer city[55]	4 064	r3 714
Springlake Park city	11	14
The Village city	11 049	13 695
Valley Brook town	921	r1 197
Warr Acres city	9 940	9 887
Woodlawn Park town	167	220
Okmulgee County[56]	39 169	35 358
Beggs division	4 105	2 511
Beggs city (pt.)[56]	1 428	1 107
Winchester town[56]	150	...
Henryetta division	11 581	...
Bryant town	74	86
Dewar city[56]	1 048	933
Grayson town[56]	150	142
Henryetta city[56]	6 432	6 430
Hoffman town	407	262
Morris division[56]	2 902	2 389
Morris city[56]	1 288	1 119
Okmulgee division	20 581	...
Beggs city (pt.)[56]	–	
Okmulgee city[56]	16 263	15 180
Osage County[57]	39 327	29 750
Barnsdall division	2 876	2 988
Avant town	461	439
Barnsdall city[57]	1 501	1 579
Skiatook town (pt.)[57]	–	...
Fairfax division	2 753	2 780
Fairfax town[57]	1 949	1 889
Hominy division	5 871	4 256
Hominy city[57]	3 130	2 274
Osage town	243	170
Wynona city	780	547
McCord–Braden division	3 105	1 819
Northwest Osage division	1 926	2 175
Burbank town	161	188
Foraker town	34	52
Grainola town	67	66
Shidler town	708	717
Webb City town	157	186
Pawhuska division	8 532	7 884
Bartlesville city (pt.)	–	11
Pawhuska city[57]	4 771	4 238
Southeast Osage division	14 264	7 848
Prue town[57]	554	r271

County Subdivisions	1980	1970
Osage County—Con.		
Southeast Osage division—Con.		
Sand Springs city (pt.)[57]	384	—
Skiatook town (pt.)[57]	1 816	1 461
Tulsa city (pt.)[57]	5 475	3 167
Ottawa County[58]	32 870	29 800
Afton–Fairland division	3 645	2 918
Afton town[58]	1 174	1 022
Fairland town[58]	1 073	814
Miami division	20 634	...
Commerce city[58]	2 556	2 593
Miami city[58]	14 237	13 880
North Miami town	544	503
Picher–Peoria division	6 160	5 502
Peoria town	165	179
Picher city	2 180	2 363
Quapaw town[58]	1 097	967
Wyandotte division	2 431	2 148
Wyandotte town	336	297
Pawnee County[59]	15 310	11 338
Cleveland division[59]	9 899	5 839
Baugh town[59]	5	...
Calida town[59]	19	...
Cedar Ridge town[59]	—	...
Cleveland city[59]	2 972	2 573
Curchece town[59]	7	...
Empy town[59]	2	...
Hallett town	186	125
Jennings town	395	338
Juby's town[59]	—	...
Leander town[59]	8	...
Leroy town[59]	9	...
Mule Barn town[59]	—	...
Oak Grove town[59]	660	...
Peterman Ridge town[59]	14	...
Rabornville town[59]	12	...
Rigsby town[59]	21	...
Shady Grove town[59]	2	...
Sha-To-She town[59]	4	...
Terlton town	155	111
Timberlane town[59]	21	...
Wes town[59]	31	...
Westport town[59]	265	146
Pawnee division	5 411	5 499
Blackburn town	114	88
Maramec town	101	128
Pawnee city[59]	1 688	2 443
Quay town (pt.)	38	30
Ralston town	495	443
Skedee town	117	117
Payne County[60]	62 435	50 654
Cushing division[60]	11 644	10 584
Cushing city[60]	7 720	7 529
Ripley town	451	307
Stillwater division	48 275	...
Glencoe town[60]	490	421
Perkins town[60]	1 762	1 029
Stillwater city[60]	38 268	31 126
Yale division	2 516	2 030
Quay town (pt.)	12	11
Yale city[60]	1 652	1 239
Pittsburg County[61]	40 524	37 521
Kiowa–Pittsburg division	2 394	2 097
Ashland town	72	73
Kiowa town[61]	866	754
Pittsburg town	305	282
McAlester division	23 782	...
Alderson town	366	215
Krebs city[61]	1 754	1 515
McAlester city[61]	17 255	18 802
Savanna town	828	948
North Central Pittsburg division	3 200	2 154
Canadian town	279	304
Crowder town	431	339
Indianola town	254	205
Northwest Pittsburg division	2 453	1 603
Quinton division	3 526	2 531
Quinton town	1 228	1 262
Twin Cities division	5 169	4 757
Haileyville city	832	928
Hartshorne city[61]	2 380	2 121
Pontotoc County[62]	32 598	27 867
Ada division	20 554	...
Ada city (pt.)[62]	15 899	14 859
Northeast Pontotoc division	4 075	...
Allen town (pt.)[62]	914	907
Byng town[62]	833	...
Francis town	365	283
Northwest Pontotoc division	3 550	...
Byng town (pt.)[62]	—	...
South Central Pontotoc division	783	...
Southeast Pontotoc division	2 356	1 733
Ada city (pt.)[62]	3	...
Stonewall town[62]	672	653
Southwest Pontotoc division	1 280	1 222
Roff town	729	632

County Subdivisions	1980	1970
Pottawatomie County[63]	55 239	43 134
Maud division	1 987	...
Maud city (pt.)[63]	1 074	816
St. Louis town	109	207
Shawnee division	50 350	...
Bethel Acres town[63]	2 314	1 083
Brooksville town[63]	46	...
Earlsboro town	266	248
McLoud town	4 061	2 159
Macomb town	58	41
Oklahoma City city (pt.)	51	—
Pink town[63]	911	337
Shawnee city[63]	26 506	25 075
Tecumseh city[63]	5 123	4 451
Tribbey town (pt.)[63]	62	...
Wanette–Asher division	2 902	1 997
Asher town	659	437
Tribbey town (pt.)[63]	153	...
Wanette town[63]	473	303
Pushmataha County[64]	11 773	9 385
Antlers division	5 858	...
Antlers town[64]	2 989	2 685
Finley–Rattan division	2 593	...
Rattan town[64]	332	...
North Pushmataha division	3 322	...
Albion town	165	186
Clayton town	833	718
Roger Mills County[65]	4 799	4 452
Cheyenne division	2 789	...
Cheyenne town[65]	1 207	892
Reydon town[65]	252	215
Strong City town	56	40
East Roger Mills division	1 375	1 328
Hammon town[65]	804	677
South Roger Mills division	635	...
Rogers County[66]	46 436	28 425
Catoosa division[66]	9 324	5 230
Catoosa city (pt.)[66]	1 772	970
Collinsville city (pt.)[66]	1	...
Fair Oaks town[66]	—	—
Valley Park town[66]	16	...
Chelsea division	3 776	2 794
Chelsea city	1 754	1 622
Claremore division	25 859	...
Catoosa city (pt.)[66]		
Claremore city[66]	12 085	9 084
Foyil town	191	164
Inola division	3 812	2 260
Inola town[66]	1 550	948
Oolagah–Talala division	3 665	2 160
Jamestown town[66]	12	...
Oolagah town[66]	798	458
Talala town[66]	191	163
Seminole County[67]	27 473	25 144
Konawa division	3 173	2 988
Konawa city[67]	1 711	1 719
Seminole North division	11 948	...
Seminole city (pt.)[67]	8 551	7 878
Seminole South division	2 311	...
Bowlegs town[67]	522	...
Maud city (pt.)	370	327
Seminole city (pt.)[67]	—	...
Wewoka division	10 041	9 241
Cromwell town	337	287
Lima town[67]	256	238
Sasakwa town	335	321
Seminole city (pt.)[67]	39	...
Wewoka city (pt.)[67]	5 480	5 284
Sequoyah County[68]	30 749	23 370
Muldrow division	7 550	...
Gans town	346	238
Muldrow town[68]	2 538	1 680
Roland division	5 589	...
Moffett town	269	312
Roland town[68]	1 472	827
Sallisaw division	6 999	...
Sallisaw city[68]	6 403	4 888
Sallisaw North division	3 555	...
Marble City town	294	299
Vian division	7 056	...
Gore town[68]	445	478
Paradise Hill town[68]	154	87
Vian town[68]	1 521	1 131
Stephens County[69]	43 419	35 902
Comanche division	5 669	4 363
Comanche city[69]	1 937	1 862
Empire City city (pt.)	—	...
Loco city	215	193
Duncan division	27 128	...
Bray town (pt.)[69]	164	...
Duncan city[69]	22 517	19 718
Empire City city (pt.)	13	23
Marlow city (pt.)[69]	—	...
Marlow division	8 082	5 931
Bray town (pt.)[69]	421	...
Marlow city (pt.)[69]	5 017	3 995

County Subdivisions	1980	1970
Stephens County—Con.		
Velma–Alma division	2 540	2 141
Bray town (pt.)	6	...
Velma city[69]	831	611
Texas County[70]	17 727	16 352
Guymon division	11 955	11 136
Goodwell town	1 186	1 467
Guymon city[70]	8 492	7 674
Hardesty town	243	223
Optima town	133	103
Hooker division	4 033	3 424
Hooker city[70]	1 788	1 615
Tyrone town	928	588
West Texas division	1 739	1 792
Texhoma town[70]	785	921
Tillman County[71]	12 398	12 901
Davidson division	920	920
Davidson town	501	515
East Tillman division	2 023	2 227
Chattanooga town (pt.)[71]	17	...
Grandfield city[71]	1 445	1 524
Loveland town[71]	21	36
Frederick division	7 478	7 698
Frederick city[71]	6 153	6 132
Hollister town	82	105
Manitou town	322	308
Tipton division	1 977	2 056
Tipton town	1 475	1 206
Tulsa County[72]	470 593	r399 982
North Tulsa division	9 948	...
Collinsville city (pt.)[72]	3 555	3 009
Skiatook town (pt.)[72]	1 780	1 469
South Tulsa division	9 406	...
Bixby city (pt.)[72]	3 188	(NA)
Glenpool city[72]	2 706	770
Jenks city (pt.)[72]	8	...
Liberty town[72]	19	...
Tulsa division[72]	451 239	...
Bixby city (pt.)[72]	3 722	(NA)
Broken Arrow city (pt.)[72]	34 322	r11 009
Jenks city (pt.)[72]	5 868	r2 685
Lotsee town	7	16
Manford town (pt.)[72]	–	r–
Owasso city[72]	6 149	3 491
Sand Springs city (pt.)[72]	12 862	r10 565
Sperry town[72]	1 276	1 123
Tulsa city (pt.)[72]	355 444	r327 183
Turley (CDP)	6 336	...
Wagoner County[73]	41 801	22 163
Coweta division	25 338	...
Bixby city (pt.)[73]	59	...
Broken Arrow city (pt.)[73]	1 439	r9
Coweta city[73]	4 554	2 457
Fair Oaks town (pt.)	324	23
New Tulsa town	252	17
South Wagoner division	2 849	...
Porter town	642	624
Redbird town	199	230
Tullahassee town	145	183
Wagoner division	13 614	8 537
Okay town	554	419
Wagoner city[73]	6 191	4 959
Washington County[74]	48 113	r42 302
Bartlesville division	41 993	...
Bartlesville city (pt.)[74]	34 568	29 672
Dewey city[74]	3 545	3 958
Copan division	2 058	r1 428
Copan town[74]	960	r675
Ochelata–Ramona division	4 062	3 042
Ochelata town[74]	480	330
Ramona town[74]	567	600
Vera town[74]	182	215
Washita County[75]	13 798	12 141
Central Washita division	4 155	3 993
New Cordell city[75]	3 301	3 261
Northeast Washita division	1 411	1 367
Colony town[75]	185	r201
Corn town	542	409
Northwest Washita division	4 723	3 064
Bessie town	245	210
Burns Flat town[75]	2 431	988
Canute town[75]	676	420
Foss city[75]	188	150
Southeast Washita division	644	769
Southwest Washita division	2 865	2 948
Dill City town	649	578
Rocky town	242	260
Sentinel city[75]	1 016	984
Woods County[76]	10 923	11 920
Alva division	7 629	8 463
Alva city[76]	6 416	7 440
Capron town	54	80
South Woods division	2 633	2 780
Avard town	51	59
Dacoma town	226	226
Waynoka city[76]	1 377	1 444

County Subdivisions	1980	1970
Woods County—Con.		
West Woods division	661	677
Freedom town[76]	339	292
Woodward County[77]	21 172	15 537
Mooreland division	2 343	2 040
Mooreland town[77]	1 383	1 196
Quinlan town	64	81
Woodward division	18 829	13 497
Fort Supply town	559	550
Mutual town	135	94
Sharon town	171	155
Woodward city[77]	13 610	r9 563

OREGON

This state takes its name from the Oregon River, as the Columbia River was originally called. The derivation of the word Oregon is unknown.

The area now constituting the state of Oregon was discovered in 1543, when Ferrelo, a Spaniard, sailed up the Pacific coast as far as the southern part of the state. The first permanent settlement within the present limits of Oregon was made in 1811, when a trading post was established at Astoria by the Pacific Fur Company.

The possession of the Oregon country was at the beginning of the nineteenth century in dispute among the United States, Great Britain, Spain, and Russia, each nation basing its right to possession on discoveries and explorations. English and Spanish navigators had visited the Oregon coast from time to time during the sixteenth, seventeenth, and eighteenth centuries. In 1792 Robert Gray, captain of a merchant ship from Boston, entered the river, which he named the Columbia, and in 1805 a United States Government exploring expedition under Lewis and Clark descended the Columbia to its mouth. Russia had made settlements in Alaska in the early part of the eighteenth century and for this reason laid claim to territory as far south as the present state of California. All that remained of the Spanish claim after the cession of Louisiana to France in 1800 was relinquished at the time of the Florida Purchase in 1819, when Spain transferred to the United States "all rights, claims, and pretentions to any country north of the forty-second parallel." In 1824 Russia surrendered to the United States all claims south of 54°40'. In 1818 a treaty had been concluded between the United States and England, under which the two countries jointly occupied the Oregon region, but in 1846 this joint occupation was terminated by a treaty fixing the boundary between the territories of the two countries at its present location.

In August, 1848, the territory of Oregon was organized by act of Congress. At this time it extended from the forty-second parallel to the British possessions, from the crest of the Rocky Mountains to the Pacific Ocean, thus comprising the area which now constitutes Oregon, Washington, Idaho, and parts of western Montana and Wyoming. In 1853 that part of the territory lying north of the Columbia River and the forty-sixth parallel east of its point of intersection with that river was organized as the territory of Washington.

Four years later the people of Oregon adopted a constitution and asked for statehood; and, by act of Congress approved February 14, 1859, Oregon, with boundaries as at present, was admitted to the Union. The eastern part of the former Oregon territory was added to Washington territory, and later became a part of Idaho territory.

COUNTY LOCATION INDEX

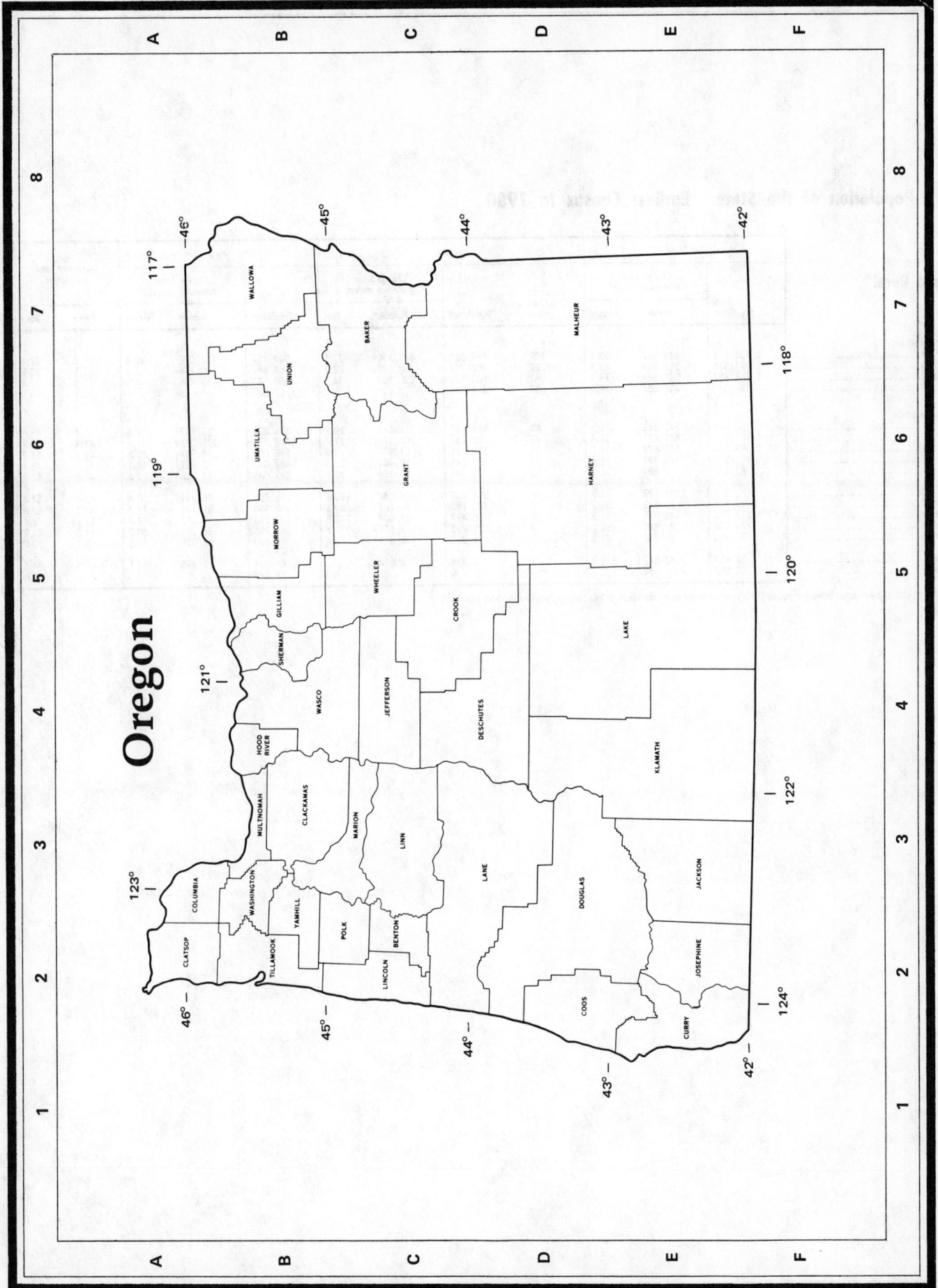

Oregon

Population of the State: Earliest Census to 1980

Urban and Rural

	The State			Urban				Rural				Percent of total population	
	Total population	Change from preceding census		Places of 2,500 or more	Population	Change from preceding census		Population	Change from preceding census			Urban	Rural
		Number	Percent			Number	Percent		Number	Percent			
Current urban definition:													
1980 (Apr. 1)	2 633 105	541 572	25.9	109	1 788 354	385 650	27.5	844 751	156 070	22.7		67.9	32.1
1970 (Apr. 1)	2 091 533	322 846	18.3	72	1 402 704	302 582	27.5	688 681	20 116	3.0		67.1	32.9
1960 (Apr. 1)	1 768 687	247 346	16.3	61	1 100 122	280 804	34.3	668 565	–33 458	–4.8		62.2	37.8
1950 (Apr. 1)	1 521 341	431 657	39.6	49	819 318		...	702 023	...	...		53.9	46.1
Previous urban definition:													
1960 (Apr. 1)	1 768 687	247 346	16.3	63	943 861	211 614	28.9	824 826	35 732	4.5		53.4	46.6
1950 (Apr. 1)	1 521 341	431 657	39.6	47	732 247	200 572	37.7	789 094	231 085	41.4		48.1	51.9
1940 (Apr. 1)	1 089 684	135 898	14.2	34	531 675	41 929	8.6	558 009	93 969	20.3		48.8	51.2
1930 (Apr. 1)	953 786	170 397	21.8	28	489 746	99 400	25.5	464 040	70 997	18.1		51.3	48.7
1920 (Jan. 1)	783 389	110 624	16.4	23	390 346	83 286	27.1	393 043	27 338	7.5		49.8	50.2
1910 (Apr. 15)	672 765	259 229	62.7	18	307 060	173 880	130.6	365 705	85 349	30.4		45.6	54.4
1900 (June 1)	413 536	95 832	30.2	11	133 180	44 689	50.5	280 356	51 143	22.3		32.2	67.8
1890 (June 1)	317 704	142 936	81.8	11	88 491	62 639	242.3	229 213	80 297	53.9		27.9	72.1
1880 (June 1)	174 768	83 845	92.2	4	25 852	17 559	211.7	148 916	66 286	80.2		14.8	85.2
1870 (June 1)	90 923	38 458	73.3	1	8 293	5 419	188.6	82 630	33 039	66.6		9.1	90.9
1860 (June 1)	52 465	40 372	333.8	1	2 874	2 874	...	49 591	37 498	310.1		5.5	94.5
1850 (June 1)	12 093	...	...	–	–	...	...	12 093	...	...		–	100.0

NOTE: 1850 population excludes population (1,201) of parts taken to form part of Washington Territory in 1853 and 1859.

BAKER

1870	2,804
1880	4,616
1890	6,764
1900	15,597
1910	18,076
1920	17,929
1930	16,754
1940	18,297
1950	16,175
1960	17,295
1970	14,919
1980	16,134

BENTON

1850	814
1860	3,074
1870	4,584
1880	6,403
1890	8,650
1900	6,706
1910	10,663
1920	13,744
1930	16,555
1940	18,629
1950	31,570
1960	39,165
1970	53,776
1980	68,211

CLACKAMAS

1850	1,859
1860	3,466
1870	5,993
1880	9,260
1890	15,233
1900	19,658
1910	29,931
1920	37,698
1930	46,205
1940	57,130
1950	86,716
1960	113,038
1970	116,088
1980	241,919

CLARKE

1850	643

CLATSOP

1850	462
1860	498
1870	1,255
1880	7,222
1890	10,016
1900	12,765
1910	16,106
1920	23,030
1930	21,124
1940	24,697
1950	30,776
1960	27,380
1970	28,473
1980	32,489

COLUMBIA

1860	532
1870	863
1880	2,042
1890	5,191
1900	6,237
1910	10,580
1920	13,960
1930	20,047
1940	20,971
1950	22,967
1960	22,379
1970	28,790
1980	35,646

COOS

1860	445
1870	1,644
1880	4,834
1890	8,874
1900	10,324
1910	17,959
1920	22,257
1930	28,373
1940	32,466
1950	42,265
1960	54,955
1970	56,515
1980	64,047

CROOK

1890	3,244
1900	3,964
1910	9,315
1920	3,424
1930	3,336
1940	5,533
1950	8,991
1960	9,430
1970	9,985
1980	13,091

CURRY

1860	393
1870	504
1880	1,208
1890	1,709
1900	1,868
1910	2,044
1920	3,025
1930	3,257
1940	4,301
1950	6,048
1960	13,983
1970	13,006
1980	16,992

DESCHUTES

1920	9,622
1930	14,749
1940	18,631
1950	21,812
1960	23,100
1970	30,442
1980	62,142

DOUGLAS

1860	3,203
1870	6,066
1880	9,596
1890	11,864
1900	14,565
1910	19,694
1920	21,332
1930	21,965
1940	25,728
1950	54,549
1960	69,458
1970	71,743
1980	93,748

GILLIAM

1890	3,600
1900	3,201
1910	3,701
1920	3,960
1930	3,467
1940	2,844
1950	2,817
1960	3,069
1970	2,342
1980	2,057

GRANT

1870	2,251
1880	4,303
1890	5,080
1900	5,948
1910	5,607
1920	5,496
1930	5,940
1940	6,380
1950	8,329
1960	7,726
1970	6,996
1980	8,210

HARNEY

1890	2,559
1900	2,598
1910	4,059
1920	3,992
1930	5,920
1940	5,374
1950	6,113
1960	6,744
1970	7,215
1980	8,314

HOOD RIVER

1910	8,016
1920	8,315
1930	8,938
1940	11,580
1950	12,740
1960	13,395
1970	13,187
1980	15,835

JACKSON

1860	3,736
1870	4,778
1880	8,154
1890	11,455
1900	13,698
1910	25,756
1920	20,405
1930	32,918
1940	36,213
1950	58,510
1960	73,962
1970	94,533
1980	132,456

JEFFERSON

1920	3,211
1930	2,291
1940	2,042
1950	5,536
1960	7,130
1970	8,548
1980	11,599

JOSEPHINE

1860	1,623
1870	1,204
1880	2,485
1890	4,878
1900	7,517
1910	9,567
1920	7,655
1930	11,498
1940	16,301
1950	26,542
1960	29,917
1970	35,746
1980	58,855

KLAMATH

1890	2,444
1900	3,970
1910	8,554
1920	11,413
1930	32,407
1940	40,497
1950	42,150
1960	47,475
1970	50,021
1980	59,117

LAKE

1880	2,804
1890	2,604
1900	2,847
1910	4,658
1920	3,991
1930	4,833
1940	6,293
1950	6,649
1960	7,158
1970	6,343
1980	7,532

LANE

1860	4,780
1870	6,426
1880	9,411
1890	15,198
1900	19,604
1910	33,783
1920	36,166
1930	54,493
1940	69,096
1950	125,776
1960	162,890
1970	215,401
1980	275,226

LEWIS

1850	558

LINCOLN

1900	3,575

LINN

1850	994
1860	6,772
1870	8,717
1880	12,676
1890	16,265
1900	18,603
1910	22,662
1920	24,550
1930	24,700
1940	30,485
1950	54,317
1960	58,867
1970	71,914
1980	89,495

MALHEUR

1890	2,601
1900	4,203
1910	8,601
1920	10,907
1930	11,269
1940	19,767
1950	23,223
1960	22,764
1970	23,169
1980	26,896

MARION

1850	2,749
1860	7,088
1870	9,965
1880	14,576
1890	22,934
1900	27,713
1910	39,780
1920	47,187
1930	60,541
1940	75,246
1950	101,401
1960	120,888
1970	151,309
1980	204,692

MORROW

1890	4,205
1900	4,151
1910	4,357
1920	5,617
1930	4,941
1940	4,337
1950	4,783
1960	4,871
1970	4,465
1980	7,519

MULTNOMAH

1860	4,150
1870	11,510
1880	25,203
1890	74,884
1900	103,167

1910	226,261	**UNION**		1860	3,245
1920	275,898			1870	5,012
1930	338,241	1870	2,552	1880	7,945
1940	355,099	1880	6,650	1890	10,692
1950	471,537	1890	12,044	1900	13,420
1960	522,813	1900	16,070	1910	18,285
1970	554,668	1910	16,191	1920	20,529
1980	562,640	1920	16,636	1930	22,036
		1930	17,492	1940	26,336
POLK		1940	17,399	1950	33,484
		1950	17,962	1960	32,478
1850	1,051	1960	18,180	1970	40,213
1860	3,625	1970	19,377	1980	55,332
1870	4,701	1980	23,921		
1880	6,601				
1890	7,858	**WALLOWA**			
1900	9,923				
1910	13,469	1890	3,661		
1920	14,181	1900	5,538		
1930	16,858	1910	8,364		
1940	19,989	1920	9,778		
1950	26,317	1930	7,814		
1960	26,523	1940	7,623		
1970	35,349	1950	7,264		
1980	45,203	1960	7,102		
		1970	6,247		
SHERMAN		1980	7,273		
1890	1,792	**WASCO**			
1900	3,477				
1910	4,242	1860	1,689		
1920	3,826	1870	2,509		
1930	2,978	1880	11,120		
1940	2,321	1890	9,183		
1950	2,271	1900	13,199		
1960	2,446	1910	16,336		
1970	2,139	1920	13,648		
1980	2,172	1930	12,646		
		1940	13,069		
TILLAMOOK		1950	15,552		
		1960	20,205		
1860	95	1970	20,133	**NOTES**	
1870	408	1980	21,732		
1880	970				
1890	2,932	**WASHINGTON**			
1900	4,471				
1910	6,266	1850	2,652	**CLARKE**	
1920	8,810	1860	2,801		
1930	11,824	1870	4,261		
1940	12,263	1880	7,802		
1950	18,606	1890	11,972		
1960	18,955	1900	14,467		
1970	18,034	1910	21,522		
1980	21,164	1920	26,376		
		1930	30,275		
UMATILLA		1940	39,194		
		1950	61,269		
1870	2,916	1960	92,237		
1880	9,607	1970	157,920		
1890	13,381	1980	245,808		
1900	18,049				
1910	20,309	**WHEELER**			
1920	25,946				
1930	24,399	1900	2,443		
1940	26,030	1910	2,484		
1950	41,703	1920	2,791		
1960	44,352	1930	2,799		
1970	44,923	1940	2,974		
1980	58,861	1950	3,313		
		1960	2,722		
UMPQUA		1970	1,849		
		1980	1,513		
1860	1,250				
		YAMHILL			
		1850	1,512		

NOTES

CLARKE

 Transferred to Washington subsequent to the 1850 census.

LEWIS

 Transferred to Washigton subsequent to the 1850 census.

MARION

 Name changed from Champoick in 1849.

UMPQUA

 Annexed to Douglas in 1862.

WASHINGTON

 Name changed from Twality in 1849.

ALBANY

1880	1,867
1890	3,079
1900	3,149
1910	4,275
1920	4,840
1930	5,325
1940	5,654
1950	10,115
1960	12,926
1970	18,181
1980	26,546

ASHLAND

1860	514
1870	(NA)
1880	824
1890	1,784
1900	2,634
1910	5,020
1920	4,283
1930	4,544
1940	4,744
1950	7,739
1960	9,119
1970	12,342
1980	14,943

BEAVERTON

1900	249
1910	386
1920	580
1930	1,138
1940	1,052
1950	2,512
1960	5,937
1970	18,577
1980	30,582

BEND

1910	536
1920	5,415
1930	8,848
1940	10,021
1950	11,409
1960	11,936
1970	13,710
1980	17,263

CITY OF THE DALLES

1860	805
1870	942
1880	2,232
1890	3,029
1900	3,542
1910	4,880
1920	5,807
1930	5,883
1940	6,266
1950	7,676
1960	10,493
1970	10,423
1980	10,820

COOS BAY

1900	1,391
1910	2,980
1920	4,034
1930	5,287
1940	5,259

1950	6,223
1960	7,084
1970	13,466
1980	14,424

CORVALLIS

1860	1,231
1870	na
1880	1,128
1890	1,527
1900	1,819
1910	4,552
1920	5,752
1930	7,585
1940	8,392
1950	16,207
1960	20,669
1970	35,056
1980	40,960

EUGENE

1870	861
1880	1,117
1890	(NA)
1900	3,236
1910	9,009
1920	10,593
1930	18,901
1940	20,838
1950	35,879
1960	50,977
1970	79,028
1980	105,624

FOREST GROVE

1870	992
1880	547
1890	668
1900	1,096
1910	1,772
1920	1,915
1930	1,859
1940	2,449
1950	4,343
1960	5,628
1970	8,725
1980	11,499

GRANTS PASS

1890	1,432
1900	2,290
1910	3,897
1920	3,151
1930	4,666
1940	6,028
1950	8,116
1960	10,118
1970	12,455
1980	15,032

GRESHAM

1910	540
1920	1,103
1930	1,635
1940	1,951
1950	3,049
1960	3,944
1970	10,030
1980	33,005

HILLSBORO

1900	980
1910	2,016
1920	2,468
1930	3,039
1940	3,747
1950	5,142
1960	8,232
1970	14,675
1980	27,664

KLAMATH FALLS

1890	364
1900	447
1910	2,758
1920	4,801
1930	16,093
1940	16,497
1950	15,875
1960	16,949
1970	15,775
1980	16,661

LA GRANDE

1890	2,583
1900	2,991
1910	4,483
1920	6,913
1930	8,050
1940	7,747
1950	8,635
1960	9,014
1970	9,645
1980	11,354

LAKE OSWEGO

1920	1,818
1930	1,285
1940	1,726
1950	3,316
1960	8,906
1970	14,573
1980	22,868

LEBANON

1890	829
1900	922
1910	1,820
1920	1,805
1930	1,851
1940	2,729
1950	5,863
1960	5,858
1970	6,636
1980	10,413

McMINNVILLE

1870	338
1880	670
1890	1,368
1900	1,420
1910	2,400
1920	2,767
1930	2,917
1940	3,706
1950	6,635
1960	7,656
1970	10,125
1980	14,080

MEDFORD

1890	967
1900	1,791
1910	8,840
1920	5,756
1930	11,007
1940	11,281
1950	17,305
1960	24,425
1970	28,973
1980	39,603

MILWAUKIE

1910	860
1920	1,172
1930	1,767
1940	1,871
1950	5,253
1960	9,099
1970	16,444
1980	17,931

NEWBERG

1890	514
1900	945
1910	2,260
1920	2,566
1930	2,951
1940	2,960
1950	3,946
1960	4,204
1970	6,507
1980	10,394

OREGON CITY

1910	2,078
1920	5,686
1930	5,761
1940	6,124
1950	7,682
1960	7,996
1970	9,176
1980	14,673

PENDLETON

1880	730
1890	2,506
1900	4,406
1910	4,460
1920	6,837
1930	6,621
1940	8,847
1950	11,774
1960	14,434
1970	13,197
1980	14,521

PORTLAND

1850	821
1860	2,874
1870	8,293
1880	17,577
1890	46,385
1900	90,426
1910	207,214
1920	258,288
1930	301,815
1940	305,394
1950	373,628

1960	372,676
1970	379,967
1980	366,383

ROSEBURG

1880	822
1890	1,472
1900	1,690
1910	4,738
1920	4,258
1930	4,362
1940	4,924
1950	8,390
1960	11,467
1970	14,461
1980	16,644

SALEM

1870	1,139
1880	2,538
1900	4,258
1910	14,094
1920	17,679
1930	26,266
1940	30,908
1950	43,140
1960	49,142
1970	68,725
1980	89,233

SPRINGFIELD

1880	160
1890	371
1900	353
1910	1,838
1920	1,855
1930	2,364
1940	3,805
1950	10,807
1960	19,616
1970	26,864
1980	41,621

TIGARD

1970	6,499
1980	14,286

WEST LINN

1920	1,628
1930	1,956
1940	2,165
1950	2,945
1960	3,933
1970	7,091
1980	12,956

WOODBURN

1890	405
1900	828
1910	1,616
1920	1,656
1930	1,675
1940	1,982
1950	2,395
1960	2,395
1970	7,495
1980	11,196

CORRECTION NOTE

The official 1980 census counts of total population shown in
this report supersede counts issued previously. Corrections
to the figures were made after the counts were provided to
the State for redistricting purposes and released in Advance
Report PHC80-V for this State.

Shown below are corrections to the 1980 census counts of the
total population made after the tabulations for this report
were completed. Any additional corrections made after this
report is printed are available by writing to Data User
Services Division, Customer Service (Corrections), Bureau of
the Census, Washington, D.C. 20233.

The 1980 figures shown in this publication are subject to
change pending the outcome of the various lawsuits dealing
with the census counts.

	1980 population	
	As shown in the tables	Corrected
The State.................	2 633 105	2 633 149
Clackamas County.................	241 919	241 911
Northwest Clackamas division...	158 773	158 765
Lake Oswego city (pt.).......	21 654	21 313
Linn County:		
Albany division:		
Albany city (pt.)............	26 540	26 672
Union County:		
Elgin division:		
Summerville town.............	132	143
Washington County.................	245 808	245 860
Beaverton-Hillsboro division...	195 857	195 909
Tualatin city (pt.)..........	7 307	7 442
Albany city (total)..............	26 546	26 678
Lake Oswego (total)..............	22 868	22 527
Tualatin city (total)............	7 348	7 483

County Subdivisions	1980	1970
The State	2 633 105	2 091 533
Baker County[1]	16 134	14 919
Baker division	10 418	...
Baker city	9 471	9 354
Eagle Valley division	995	...
Richland town	181	133
Halfway division	1 536	...
Halfway town[1]	380	317
Hereford division	875	...
Greenhorn city (pt.)[1]	–	...
Sumpter city	133	120
Unity city[1]	115	...
Huntington division	729	...
Huntington city	539	507
Wingville division	1 581	...
Haines city	341	314
Benton County[2]	68 211	53 776
Corvallis division	52 031	...
Corvallis city[2]	40 960	35 056
Philomath city[2]	2 673	1 688
North Albany division	5 976	...
Albany city (pt.)[2]	6	–
North Albany (CDP)	4 499	...
North Benton division	3 286	...
Adair Village city[2]	589	...
Southeast Benton division	3 613	...
Monroe city[2]	412	443
Southwest Benton division	3 305	...
Clackamas County[3]	241 919	166 088
Beaver Creek division	6 223	...
Canby division	9 642	...
Canby city[3]	7 659	3 813
Colton division	4 468	2 530
Estacada division	12 775	...
Estacada city[3]	1 419	1 164
Molalla division	7 009	...
Molalla city[3]	2 992	2 005
Mount Hood division	7 547	3 976
Sandy city (pt.)[3]	43	...
Mulino division	4 394	2 670
Northwest Clackamas division	158 773	...
Gladstone city[3]	9 500	6 254
Happy Valley city[3]	1 499	1 392
Johnson City city[3]	378	...
Lake Oswego city (pt.)[3]	21 654	14 597
Milwaukie city (pt.)[3]	17 931	16 444
Oak Grove (CDP)	11 640	...
Oregon City city[3]	14 673	9 176
Portland city (pt.)[3]	686	495
Rivergrove city[3]	287	...
Tualatin city (pt.)[3]	41	–
West Linn city[3]	12 956	7 091
Redland division	5 026	2 526
Sandy division	12 891	...
Sandy city (pt.)[3]	2 862	1 544
Wilsonville division	6 376	...
Barlow city	105	105
Wilsonville city (pt.)[3]	2 900	996
Yoder division	6 795	4 233
Clatsop County[4]	32 489	28 473
Astoria division	22 190	...
Astoria city[4]	9 998	10 244
Gearhart city[4]	967	829
Hammond town	516	500
Seaside city (pt.)[4]	1	...
Warrenton city[4]	2 493	1 825
Jewell division	762	...
Knappa–Brownsmead division	1 938	...
Seaside division	7 599	...
Cannon Beach city[4]	1 187	779
Seaside city (pt.)[4]	5 192	4 402
Columbia County[5]	35 646	28 790
Clatskanie division	5 223	3 825
Clatskanie city[5]	1 648	1 286
Goble division	2 055	1 490
Marshland division	711	996
Rainier division	4 202	3 469
Prescott city	73	105
Rainier city[5]	1 655	1 731
St. Helens division	14 806	...
Columbia City city[5]	678	537
McNulty (CDP)	1 805	1 017
St. Helens city[5]	7 064	6 212
Scappoose division	5 597	...
Scappoose city[5]	3 213	1 859
Vernonia division	3 052	2 636
Vernonia city[5]	1 785	1 643
Coos County[6]	64 047	56 515
Bandon division	4 932	...
Bandon city[6]	2 311	1 832
Coos Bay division	31 193	...
Barview (CDP)	1 462	1 388
Bunker Hill (CDP)	1 555	1 549
Coos Bay city[6]	14 424	13 466
North Bend city[6]	9 779	8 553

County Subdivisions	1980	1970
Coos County—Con.		
Coquille division	8 780	...
Coquille city[6]	4 481	4 437
Eastside division	6 183	4 985
Eastside city	1 601	1 331
Myrtle Point division	5 861	...
Myrtle Point city[6]	2 859	2 511
North Bayside division	6 021	...
Lakeside city[6]	1 453	...
Powers division	1 077	...
Powers city[6]	819	842
Crook County[7]	13 091	9 985
Crooked River division	1 189	...
Ochoco division	10 843	...
Prineville city[7]	5 276	4 101
Powell Butte division	1 059	...
Curry County[8]	16 992	13 006
Agness division	104	...
Brookings division	5 631	...
Brookings city[8]	3 384	2 720
Gold Beach division	4 852	...
Gold Beach city[8]	1 515	1 554
Harbor division	3 682	2 135
Harbor (CDP)	2 856	...
Port Orford division	2 723	2 607
Port Orford city[8]	1 061	1 037
Deschutes County[9]	62 142	30 442
Bend division	35 110	...
Bend city[9]	17 263	13 710
Redmond division	13 914	7 793
Redmond city[9]	6 452	3 721
Sisters–Millican division	10 223	...
Sisters city[9]	696	516
Sunriver (CDP)	1 095	...
Tumalo division	2 895	...
Douglas County[10]	93 748	71 743
Calapooia division	11 724	...
Oakland city	886	1 010
Sutherlin city[10]	4 560	3 070
Elkton–Drain division	3 124	...
Drain city	1 148	1 204
Elkton city (pt.)[10]	155	176
Kellogg–Yoncalla division	3 357	...
Elkton city (pt.)[10]	–	...
Yoncalla city[10]	805	675
Melrose division	4 644	...
Myrtle Creek–Riddle division	14 571	...
Canyonville city[10]	1 288	940
Myrtle Creek city[10]	3 365	2 733
Riddle city	1 265	1 042
Tri-City (CDP)	3 439	1 039
North Umpqua division	4 728	...
Reedsport division	7 415	...
Reedsport city[10]	4 984	4 039
Roseburg division	32 370	...
Green (CDP)	3 897	1 612
Roseburg city[10]	16 644	14 461
South Umpqua division	4 258	...
Glendale city[10]	712	709
Tenmile division	7 557	...
Winston city[10]	3 359	2 468
Gilliam County[11]	2 057	2 342
Arlington division	814	687
Arlington city[11]	521	375
Condon division	1 243	1 655
Condon city	783	973
Lonerock city	26	12
Grant County[12]	8 210	6 996
John Day division	4 976	...
Canyon City town[12]	639	600
Dayville town	199	197
John Day city[12]	2 012	1 566
Mount Vernon city	569	423
Long Creek division	1 068	962
Long Creek town	252	196
Monument city	192	161
Prairie City division	1 721	...
Granite city	17	4
Greenhorn city (pt.)[12]	–	...
Prairie City city[12]	1 106	867
Seneca division	445	541
Seneca city[12]	285	...
Harney County[13]	8 314	7 215
Burns division	6 354	5 720
Burns city	3 579	3 293
Hines city[13]	1 632	1 407
Diamond division	657	...
Drewsey division	1 303	...
Hood River County[14]	15 835	13 187
Cascade Locks division	1 033	759
Cascade Locks city[14]	838	574
Dee division	964	783
Hood River division	8 417	7 542
Hood River city[14]	4 329	3 991
Odell division	3 846	2 963

County Subdivisions	1980	1970
Hood River County—Con.		
Parkdale division	1 575	1 140
Jackson County[15]	132 456	94 533
Ashland division	20 749	...
Ashland city (pt.)[15]	14 943	12 342
Phoenix city (pt.)[15]	15	...
Talent city[15]	2 577	1 411
Butte Falls–Prospect division	2 396	...
Butte Falls town	428	358
Eagle Point division	4 707	...
Eagle Point city[15]	2 764	1 241
Medford division	79 266	...
Central Point city[15]	6 357	4 004
Jacksonville city[15]	2 030	1 611
Medford city[15]	39 603	28 973
Phoenix city (pt.)[15]	2 294	1 287
South Medford (CDP)	2 898	3 497
White City (CDP)	5 445	...
Northwest Jackson division	5 701	...
Rogue River city (pt.)[15]	1 286	841
Sams Valley division	3 799	...
Gold Hill city	904	603
Shady Cove division	4 261	...
Shady Cove city[15]	1 097	...
Southeast Jackson division	1 465	...
Southwest Jackson division	10 112	...
Ashland city (pt.)[15]	–	...
Rogue River city (pt.)[15]	22	...
Jefferson County[16]	11 599	8 548
Ashwood division	350	...
Culver division	2 744	...
Culver city[16]	514	407
Metolius city[16]	451	270
Grandview division	230	172
Madras division	6 448	...
Madras city[16]	2 235	1 689
Warm Springs division	1 827	1 324
Josephine County[17]	58 855	35 746
Cave Junction division	6 782	...
Cave Junction city[17]	1 023	415
Grants Pass division	40 947	...
Grants Pass city[17]	15 032	12 455
Harbeck–Fruitdale (CDP)	4 733	...
Redwood (CDP)	3 171	3 431
Northwest Josephine division	4 926	...
Wilderville division	3 703	...
Williams division	2 497	...
Klamath County[18]	59 117	50 021
Chiloquin division	3 691	2 437
Chiloquin city[18]	778	826
Crescent Lake division	2 202	1 689
Keno division	2 460	...
Klamath Falls division	44 606	...
Altamont (CDP)	19 805	15 746
Klamath Falls city[18]	16 661	15 775
Langell division	1 704	...
Bonanza town (pt.)	110	...
Malin division	1 341	...
Malin city[18]	539	486
Merrill division	1 942	...
Merrill city[18]	809	722
Poe Valley division	1 171	...
Bonanza town (pt.)	160	230
Lake County[19]	7 532	6 343
Lakeview division	5 356	...
Lakeview town	2 770	2 705
Silver Lake–Fort Rock division	1 227	...
Summer Lake division	655	...
Paisley city	343	260
Warner Valley division	294	...
Lane County[20]	275 226	215 401
Badger Mountain division	10 360	6 938
Veneta city	2 449	1 377
Coburg division	1 856	1 662
Coburg city[20]	699	713
Cottage Grove division	16 188	...
Cottage Grove city[20]	7 148	6 004
Creswell division	6 201	4 043
Creswell city[20]	1 770	1 199
Eugene city (pt.)[20]	237	...
Eugene–Springfield division	192 001	...
Eugene city (pt.)[20]	105 387	79 028
North Springfield (CDP)	6 140	...
River Road (CDP)	10 370	...
Santa Clara (CDP)	14 288	...
Springfield city[20]	41 621	26 874
Junction City division	10 009	7 768
Junction City city[20]	3 320	2 373
Lowell division	4 443	3 449
Lowell city	661	567
McKenzie division	5 381	3 930
Marcola division	4 169	2 959
Middle Siuslaw–Triangle Lake division	3 039	...
North Siuslaw division	7 099	4 363
Florence city[20]	4 411	2 246
Oakridge division	5 225	4 812
Oakridge city[20]	3 729	3 422

County Subdivisions	1980	1970
Lane County—Con.		
Oakridge division—Con.		
Westfir city[20]	312	...
Pleasant Hill division	5 394	4 647
South Siuslaw division	2 365	1 701
Dunes City city[20]	1 124	976
Upper Siuslaw division	1 495	1 078
Lincoln County[21]	35 264	25 755
Agate Beach division	9 947	...
Newport city[21]	7 519	5 188
De Lake division	8 733	6 228
Lincoln City city[21]	5 469	4 198
Depoe Bay division	2 529	...
Depoe Bay city[21]	723	...
Eddyville division	1 016	...
Siletz division	2 037	...
Siletz city	1 001	596
Toledo division	5 225	...
Toledo city[21]	3 151	2 818
Waldport division	5 777	...
Waldport city[21]	1 274	700
Yachats city[21]	482	441
Linn County[22]	89 495	71 914
Albany division	36 694	...
Albany city (pt.)[22]	26 540	18 181
Millersburg city[22]	562	...
Tangent city[22]	478	...
Brownsville division	3 659	...
Brownsville city[22]	1 261	1 034
Sodaville town (pt.)[22]	26	...
East Linn division	2 793	...
Harrisburg division	4 926	...
Halsey city[22]	693	467
Harrisburg city	1 881	1 311
Lebanon division	19 755	...
Lebanon city[22]	10 413	6 636
Sodaville town (pt.)[22]	145	178
South Lebanon (CDP)	1 309	2 229
Waterloo town	221	186
Mill City division	5 688	...
Gates city (pt.)[22]	38	...
Idanha city (pt.)[22]	117	102
Lyons city[22]	877	645
Mill City city (pt.)[22]	1 257	1 123
Scio–Lacomb division	5 516	...
Scio city[22]	579	447
Sweet Home division	10 464	...
Sweet Home city[22]	6 921	3 799
Malheur County[23]	26 896	23 169
Adrian division	1 156	...
Adrian city[23]	162	...
Brogan division	520	...
Dead Ox Flat division	1 630	1 520
Jordan division	1 109	...
Jordan Valley town	473	196
Juntura division	597	...
Malheur Junction division	869	...
Nyssa division	4 076	...
Nyssa town[23]	2 862	2 620
Ontario division	11 823	9 288
Ontario city[23]	8 814	6 523
Owyhee division	859	978
Vale division	3 855	...
Vale city[23]	1 558	1 448
West Vale division	402	...
Marion County[24]	204 692	151 309
Hubbard division	6 973	4 571
Aurora city[24]	523	306
Donald city[24]	267	231
Hubbard city[24]	1 640	975
Jefferson division	8 887	6 130
Aumsville city (pt.)[24]	1 432	590
Jefferson city[24]	1 702	936
Mill City division	2 424	2 201
Detroit city[24]	367	328
Gates city (pt.)	417	250
Idanha city (pt.)[24]	202	280
Mill City city (pt.)[24]	308	328
Mount Angel division	4 690	3 684
Mount Angel city[24]	2 876	1 973
St. Paul division	1 716	1 570
St. Paul city[24]	312	347
Salem division	144 286	...
Aumsville city (pt.)[24]	–	...
Four Corners (CDP)	11 331	5 823
Hayesville (CDP)	9 213	5 518
Keizer (CDP)	18 592	11 292
Salem city (pt.)[24]	78 694	63 205
Turner city[24]	1 116	846
Silverton division	10 817	...
Scotts Mills city	249	208
Silverton city[24]	5 168	4 301
Stayton division	8 520	6 343
Aumsville city (pt.)[24]	–	...
Stayton city[24]	4 396	3 170
Sublimity city[24]	1 077	634

County Subdivisions

County Subdivisions	1980	1970
Marion County—Con.		
Woodburn division	16 379	...
Gervais city[24]	799	746
Woodburn city[24]	11 196	7 495
Morrow County[25]	7 519	4 465
Boardman division	3 986	...
Boardman city[25]	1 261	192
Irrigon city[25]	700	261
Heppner division	2 278	2 107
Heppner city[25]	1 498	1 429
Ione—Lexington division	1 255	...
Ione city	345	355
Lexington town[25]	307	230
Multnomah County[26]	562 640	554 668
Corbett division	3 710	2 729
Troutdale city (pt.)[26]	77	...
Portland division	556 801	...
Centennial (CDP)	22 118	...
Cully (CDP)	10 569	...
Errol Heights (CDP)	10 487	...
Fairview[26]	1 749	1 045
Gresham city[26]	33 005	10 030
Hazelwood (CDP)	25 541	...
Lake Oswego city (pt.)	1 209	6
Maywood Park city	1 083	1 305
Milwaukie city (pt.)	–	–
Parkrose (CDP)	21 108	...
Portland city (pt.)[26]	365 027	379 416
Powellhurst (CDP)	20 132	...
Troutdale city (pt.)[26]	5 831	1 661
Wilkes—Rockwood (CDP)	23 216	...
Wood Village city[26]	2 253	1 533
Skyline division	2 129	...
Portland city (pt.)[26]	24	...
Polk County[27]	45 203	35 349
Dallas division	13 131	10 353
Dallas city[27]	8 530	6 361
Falls City division	2 574	2 293
Falls City city[27]	804	745
Monmouth—Independence division	11 964	...
Independence city[27]	4 024	2 594
Monmouth city[27]	5 594	5 237
Salem division	14 906	...
Salem city (pt.)[27]	10 539	5 520
Willamina division	2 628	2 193
Willamina city (pt.)[27]	563	478
Sherman County[28]	2 172	2 139
Moro division	984	...
Grass Valley city	164	153
Moro city	336	290
Wasco division	1 188	...
Rufus city	352	317
Wasco city	415	412
Tillamook County[29]	21 164	18 034
Bay City division	4 391	...
Bay City city[29]	986	898
Garibaldi city	999	1 083
Rockaway city[29]	906	665
Beaver division	2 068	...
Nehalem division	2 356	...
Manzanita city[29]	443	365
Nehalem town[29]	258	241
Wheeler city[29]	319	262
Neskowin division	2 259	1 831
Tillamook division	10 090	...
Tillamook city[29]	3 981	3 968
Umatilla County[30]	58 861	44 923
Athena division	1 656	1 630
Adams city	240	219
Athena city[30]	965	872
Northeast Umatilla division	8 648	...
Milton—Freewater city[30]	5 086	4 105
Northwest Umatilla division	23 319	...
Echo city	624	479
Hermiston city[30]	9 408	4 893
Stanfield city[30]	1 568	891
Umatilla city[30]	3 199	679
Pendleton division	17 731	...
Helix city	155	152
Pendleton city[30]	14 521	13 197
Pilot Rock division	2 849	...
Pilot Rock city[30]	1 630	1 612
Ukiah city[30]	249	...
Reservation division	2 619	1 800
Umapine division	909	...
Weston division	1 130	1 044
Weston city	719	660
Union County[31]	23 921	19 377
Cove division	1 801	...
Cove city[31]	451	363
Imbler city[31]	292	139
Elgin division	3 441	...
Elgin city[31]	1 701	1 375
Summerville town	132	76
La Grande division	15 314	...
Island City town[31]	477	202

County Subdivisions	1980	1970
Union County—Con.		
La Grande division—Con.		
La Grande city[31]	11 354	9 645
Starkey division	121	...
Union division	3 244	...
North Powder city[31]	430	304
Union city	2 062	1 531
Wallowa County[32]	7 273	6 247
Enterprise division	3 189	...
Enterprise city[32]	2 003	1 680
Flora division	213	217
Imnaha division	245	...
Joseph division	1 745	...
Joseph city[32]	999	839
Wallowa division	1 881	...
Lostine city[32]	250	196
Wallowa city	847	811
Wasco County[33]	21 732	20 133
Antelope division	296	...
Antelope city	39	51
Shaniko city	30	58
Dufur division	3 341	...
City of the Dalles city (pt.)[33]	–	...
Dufur town[33]	560	493
Maupin city[33]	495	428
The Dalles division	17 678	16 505
Chenoweth (CDP)	2 820	2 329
City of the Dalles city (pt.)[33]	10 820	10 423
Mosier city	340	217
Warm Springs division	417	...
Washington County[34]	245 808	157 920
Beaverton—Hillsboro division	195 857	...
Aloha (CDP)	28 353	...
Beaverton city[34]	30 582	18 577
Cedar Hills (CDP)	9 619	...
Durham city[34]	707	410
Garden Home—Whitford (CDP)	6 926	...
Hillsboro city[34]	27 664	14 675
King City city[34]	1 853	1 427
Lake Oswego city (pt.)	5	12
Metzger (CDP)	5 544	...
Portland city (pt.)[34]	646	56
Raleigh Hills (CDP)	6 517	...
Rivergrove city[34]	27	...
Sherwood city[34]	2 386	1 396
Tigard city[34]	14 286	6 499
Tualatin city (pt.)[34]	7 307	750
West Slope (CDP)	5 364	...
Wilsonville city (pt.)[34]	20	5
Chehalem Mountain division	4 994	6 239
Gaston city	471	429
Coast Range division	6 537	...
Banks city	489	430
Forest Grove—Cornelius division	21 363	16 096
Cornelius city[34]	4 462	1 903
Forest Grove city[34]	11 499	8 275
North Plains division	3 318	...
North Plains city[34]	715	690
Somerset West—Rock Creek division	13 739	...
Wheeler County[35]	1 513	1 849
Fossil division	699	1 114
Fossil town	535	511
Mitchell division	814	735
Mitchell town	183	196
Spray town	155	161
Yamhill County[36]	55 332	40 213
Carlton division	6 078	...
Carlton city	1 302	1 126
Lafayette city (pt.)	2	...
Yamhill city[36]	690	516
Dayton—Amity division	6 155	...
Amity city[36]	1 092	708
Dayton city[36]	1 409	949
McMinnville division	16 051	...
McMinnville city[36]	14 080	10 125
Newberg division	20 080	...
Dundee city[36]	1 223	588
Lafayette city (pt.)	1 213	786
Newberg city[36]	10 394	6 507
Sheridan division	6 968	...
Sheridan city	2 249	1 881
Willamina city (pt.)	1 186	715

PENNSYLVANIA

Pennsylvania was named in honor of the father of William Penn, its founder. The name was formed from *Penn* and *sylvania*, from the Latin *sylvanus*, relating to a forest.

The territory now constituting this state was included by the Virginia grant of 1606, and by the New England charter of 1620. The southern part was covered by the Maryland grant of 1632 and the northern part by the Connecticut grant of 1662. The Dutch also laid claim to this region by virtue of Henry Hudson's discovery of Delaware Bay and River in 1609. The first settlement within the present limits of Pennsylvania was made, however, by Swedish colonists in 1643, near the present site of Philadelphia. In 1655 the Swedish authority was overthrown by Gov. Stuyvesant of New Netherland. When in 1664 New Netherland was conquered by the English under the Duke of York, the settlements on the Delaware were included and, except for a brief period remained under English control.

In 1681 William Penn secured from Charles II a grant of territory lying between the "beginning of the fortieth degree of northern latitude" and the "beginning of the three and fortieth degree of northern latitude" and extending westward five degrees of longitude from the Delaware River, excluding the area, however, within a circle drawn 12 miles distant from New Castle, northward and westward, to the beginning of the fortieth degree of latitude. In 1682 the Duke of York confirmed Penn's charter and granted to him the Delaware settlements, which remained a part of Pennsylvania until the Revolution, though with a separate legislature after 1703.

The boundary between Pennsylvania and Maryland was in dispute until 1760, when a compromise was effected, as a result of which Mason and Dixon's line, the present boundary, was run a few years later. In 1779 a joint commission settled the boundary dispute between Virginia and Pennsylvania by extending Mason and Dixon's line westward through five degrees of longitude and by drawing a meridian from the western extremity of that line to the northern limit of the state. Pennsylvania and New York agreed upon the forty-second parallel as the "beginning of the three and fortieth degree of northern latitude," and in 1789 fixed this parallel as the boundary between the two states.

The small area in the extreme northwestern part of the state lying north of the forty-second parallel and bordering on Lake Erie, which had been ceded by New York and Massachusetts to the Federal Government, was purchased by Pennsylvania in 1792. No material change in boundaries has since been made.

Pennsylvania was one of the original thirteen states.

COUNTY LOCATION INDEX

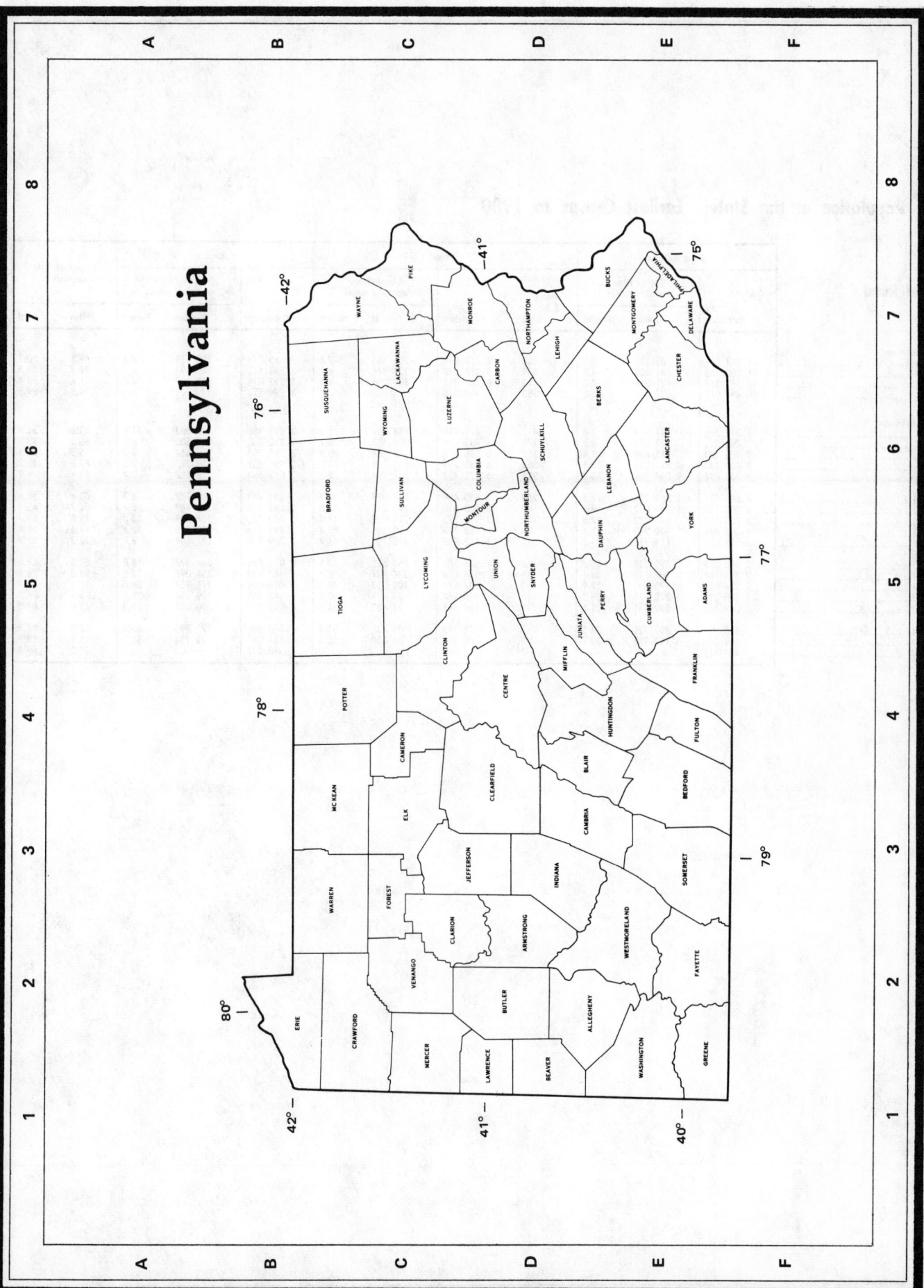

Pennsylvania

Population of the State: Earliest Census to 1980

Urban and Rural

	The State			Urban				Rural			Percent of total population	
	Total population	Change from preceding census		Places of 2,500 or more	Population	Change from preceding census		Population	Change from preceding census		Urban	Rural
		Number	Percent			Number	Percent		Number	Percent		
Current urban definition:												
1980 (Apr. 1) _____	11 863 895	63 129	0.5	483	8 220 851	−215 546	−2.6	3 643 044	285 532	8.5	69.3	30.7
1970 (Apr. 1) _____	11 800 766	481 400	4.3	449	8 436 397	334 346	4.1	3 357 512	140 197	4.4	71.5	28.5
1960 (Apr. 1) _____	11 319 366	821 354	7.8	442	8 102 051	699 015	9.4	3 217 315	122 339	4.0	71.6	28.4
1950 (Apr. 1) _____	10 498 012	597 832	6.0	383	7 403 036	...	...	3 094 976	...	...	70.5	29.5
Previous urban definition:												
1960 (Apr. 1) _____	11 319 366	821 354	7.8	412	7 419 910	434 501	6.2	3 899 456	386 853	11.0	65.6	34.4
1950 (Apr. 1) _____	10 498 012	597 832	6.0	378	6 985 409	398 532	6.1	3 512 603	199 300	6.0	66.5	33.5
1940 (Apr. 1) _____	9 900 180	268 830	2.8	355	6 586 877	53 366	0.8	3 313 303	215 464	7.0	66.5	33.5
1930 (Apr. 1) _____	9 631 350	911 333	10.5	354	6 533 511	861 058	15.2	3 097 839	50 275	1.6	67.8	32.2
1920 (Jan. 1) _____	8 720 017	1 054 906	13.8	319	5 672 453	1 041 784	22.5	3 047 564	13 122	0.4	65.1	34.9
1910 (Apr. 15) _____	7 665 111	1 362 996	21.6	263	4 630 669	1 182 059	34.3	3 034 442	180 937	6.3	60.4	39.6
1900 (June 1) _____	6 302 115	1 044 002	19.9	190	3 448 610	891 213	34.8	2 853 505	152 789	5.7	54.7	45.3
1890 (June 1) _____	5 258 113	975 222	22.8	142	2 557 397	774 019	43.4	2 700 716	201 203	8.0	48.6	51.4
1880 (June 1) _____	4 282 891	760 940	21.6	96	1 783 378	470 545	35.8	2 499 513	290 395	13.1	41.6	58.4
1870 (June 1) _____	3 521 951	615 736	21.2	75	1 312 833	418 127	46.7	2 209 118	197 609	9.8	37.3	62.7
1860 (June 1) _____	2 906 215	595 029	25.7	46	894 706	350 652	64.5	2 011 509	244 377	13.8	30.8	69.2
1850 (June 1) _____	2 311 186	587 153	34.1	35	544 054	236 077	76.7	1 767 132	351 076	24.8	23.5	76.5
1840 (June 1) _____	1 724 033	375 800	27.9	20	307 977	102 013	49.5	1 416 056	273 787	24.0	17.9	82.1
1830 (June 1) _____	1 348 233	298 775	28.5	14	205 964	69 499	50.9	1 142 269	229 276	25.1	15.3	84.7
1820 (Aug. 7) _____	1 049 458	239 367	29.5	11	136 465	32 680	31.5	912 993	206 687	29.3	13.0	87.0
1810 (Aug. 6) _____	810 091	207 726	34.5	7	103 785	35 431	51.8	706 306	172 295	32.3	12.8	87.2
1800 (Aug. 4) _____	602 365	167 992	38.7	5	68 354	24 258	55.0	534 011	143 734	36.8	11.3	88.7
1790 (Aug. 2) _____	434 373	...	...	3	44 096	...	...	390 277	...	...	10.2	89.8

ADAMS

Year	Population
1800	13,172
1810	15,152
1820	19,370
1830	21,379
1840	23,044
1850	25,981
1860	28,006
1870	30,315
1880	32,455
1890	33,486
1900	34,496
1910	34,319
1920	34,583
1930	37,128
1940	39,435
1950	44,197
1960	51,906
1970	56,937
1980	68,292

ALLEGHENY

Year	Population
1790	10,309
1800	15,087
1810	25,317
1820	34,921
1830	50,552
1840	81,235
1850	138,290
1860	178,831
1870	262,204
1880	355,869
1890	551,959
1900	775,058
1910	1,018,463
1920	1,185,808
1930	1,374,410
1940	1,411,539
1950	1,515,237
1960	1,628,587
1970	1,605,133
1980	1,450,085

ARMSTRONG

Year	Population
1800	2,399
1810	6,143
1820	10,324
1830	17,701
1840	28,365
1850	29,560
1860	35,797
1870	43,382
1880	47,641
1890	46,747
1900	52,551
1910	67,880
1920	75,568
1930	79,298
1940	81,087
1950	80,842
1960	79,524
1970	75,590
1980	77,768

BEAVER

Year	Population
1800	5,776
1810	12,168
1820	15,340
1830	24,183
1840	29,368
1850	26,689
1860	29,140
1870	36,148
1880	39,605
1890	50,077
1900	56,432
1910	78,353
1920	111,621
1930	149,062
1940	156,754
1950	175,192
1960	206,948
1970	208,418
1980	204,441

BEDFORD

Year	Population
1790	13,124
1800	12,039
1810	15,746
1820	20,248
1830	24,502
1840	29,355
1850	23,052
1860	26,736
1870	29,635
1880	34,929
1890	38,644
1900	39,468
1910	38,879
1920	38,277
1930	37,309
1940	40,809
1950	40,775
1960	42,451
1970	42,353
1980	46,784

BERKS

Year	Population
1790	30,179
1800	32,407
1810	43,146
1820	46,275
1830	53,152
1840	64,569
1850	77,129
1860	93,818
1870	106,701
1880	122,597
1890	137,327
1900	159,615
1910	183,222
1920	200,854
1930	231,717
1940	241,884
1950	255,740
1960	275,414
1970	296,382
1980	312,509

BLAIR

Year	Population
1850	21,777
1860	27,829
1870	38,051
1880	52,740
1890	70,866
1900	85,099
1910	108,858
1920	128,334
1930	139,340
1940	140,358
1950	139,514
1960	137,270
1970	135,356
1980	136,621

BRADFORD

Year	Population
1820	11,554
1830	19,746
1840	32,769
1850	42,831
1860	48,734
1870	53,204
1880	58,541
1890	59,233
1900	59,403
1910	54,526
1920	53,166
1930	49,039
1940	50,615
1950	51,722
1960	54,925
1970	57,962
1980	62,919

BUCKS

Year	Population
1790	25,401
1800	27,496
1810	32,371
1820	37,842
1830	45,745
1840	48,107
1850	56,091
1860	63,578
1870	64,336
1880	68,656
1890	70,615
1900	71,190
1910	76,530
1920	82,476
1930	96,727
1940	107,715
1950	144,620
1960	308,567
1970	416,728
1980	479,211

BUTLER

Year	Population
1800	3,916
1810	7,346
1820	10,193
1830	14,581
1840	22,378
1850	30,346
1860	35,594
1870	36,510
1880	52,536
1890	55,339
1900	56,962
1910	72,689
1920	77,270
1930	80,480
1940	87,590
1950	97,320
1960	114,639
1970	127,941
1980	147,912

CAMBRIA

Year	Population
1810	2,117
1820	3,287
1830	7,076
1840	11,256
1850	17,773
1860	29,155
1870	36,569
1880	46,811
1890	66,375
1900	104,837
1910	166,131
1920	197,839
1930	203,146
1940	213,459
1950	209,541
1960	203,283
1970	186,785
1980	183,263

CAMERON

Year	Population
1870	4,273
1880	5,159
1890	7,238
1900	7,048
1910	7,644
1920	6,297
1930	5,307
1940	6,852
1950	7,023
1960	7,586
1970	7,096
1980	6,674

CARBON

Year	Population
1850	15,686
1860	21,033
1870	28,144
1880	31,923
1890	38,624
1900	44,510
1910	52,846
1920	62,565
1930	63,380
1940	61,735
1950	57,558
1960	52,889
1970	50,573
1980	53,285

CENTRE

Year	Population
1790	7,562
1800	13,609
1810	10,681
1820	13,796
1830	18,879
1840	20,492
1850	23,355
1860	27,000
1870	34,418
1880	37,922
1890	43,269
1900	43,894
1910	43,424
1920	44,304
1930	46,294
1940	52,608
1950	65,922
1960	78,580
1970	99,267
1980	112,760

CHESTER

Year	Population
1790	27,937
1800	32,093
1810	39,596
1820	44,451
1830	50,910
1840	57,515
1850	66,438
1860	74,578
1870	77,805
1880	83,481
1890	89,377
1900	95,695
1910	109,213
1920	115,120
1930	136,629
1940	135,626
1950	159,141
1960	210,608
1970	277,746
1980	316,660

CLARION

Year	Population
1850	23,565
1860	24,988
1870	26,537
1880	40,328
1890	36,802
1900	34,283
1910	36,638
1920	36,170
1930	34,531
1940	38,410
1950	38,344
1960	37,408
1970	38,411
1980	43,362

CLEARFIELD

Year	Population
1810	875
1820	2,342
1830	4,803
1840	7,834
1850	12,586
1860	18,759
1870	25,741
1880	43,408
1890	69,565
1900	80,614
1910	93,768
1920	103,236
1930	86,727
1940	92,094
1950	85,957
1960	81,534
1970	74,619
1980	83,578

CLINTON

Year	Population
1840	8,323
1850	11,207
1860	17,723
1870	23,211
1880	26,279
1890	28,685
1900	29,197
1910	31,545
1920	33,555
1930	32,319
1940	34,557
1950	36,532
1960	37,619
1970	37,721
1980	38,971

COLUMBIA

Year	Population
1820	17,621
1830	20,059
1840	24,267
1850	17,710
1860	25,065
1870	28,766
1880	32,409

Year	Pop.
1890	36,832
1900	30,896
1910	49,467
1920	48,349
1930	48,803
1940	51,413
1950	53,460
1960	53,489
1970	55,114
1980	61,967

CRAWFORD

Year	Pop.
1800	2,346
1810	6,178
1820	9,397
1830	16,030
1840	31,724
1850	37,849
1860	48,755
1870	68,832
1880	68,607
1890	65,324
1900	63,643
1910	61,565
1920	50,667
1930	62,980
1940	71,644
1950	78,948
1960	77,956
1970	81,342
1980	88,869

CUMBERLAND

Year	Pop.
1790	18,243
1800	25,386
1810	26,757
1820	23,606
1830	29,226
1840	30,953
1850	34,327
1860	40,098
1870	43,912
1880	45,977
1890	47,271
1900	50,344
1910	54,479
1920	58,578
1930	68,236
1940	74,806
1950	94,457
1960	124,816
1970	158,177
1980	178,541

DAUPHIN

Year	Pop.
1790	18,177
1800	22,270
1810	31,883
1820	21,653
1830	25,243
1840	30,118
1850	35,754
1860	46,756
1870	60,740
1880	76,148
1890	96,977
1900	114,443
1910	136,152
1920	153,116
1930	165,231
1940	177,410
1950	197,784
1960	220,225
1970	223,713
1980	232,317

DELAWARE

Year	Pop.
1790	9,483
1800	12,809
1810	14,734
1820	14,810
1830	17,323
1840	19,791
1850	24,679
1860	30,597
1870	39,403
1880	56,101
1890	74,683
1900	94,762
1910	117,906
1920	173,084
1930	280,264
1940	310,756
1950	414,234
1960	553,154
1970	603,456
1980	555,007

ELK

Year	Pop.
1850	3,531
1860	5,915
1870	8,488
1880	12,800
1890	22,239
1900	32,903
1910	35,871
1920	34,981
1930	33,431
1940	34,443
1950	34,503
1960	37,328
1970	37,770
1980	38,338

ERIE

Year	Pop.
1800	1,468
1810	3,758
1820	8,553
1830	17,041
1840	31,344
1850	38,742
1860	49,432
1870	65,973
1880	74,688
1890	86,074
1900	98,473
1910	115,517
1920	153,536
1930	175,277
1940	180,889
1950	219,388
1960	250,682
1970	263,654
1980	279,780

FAYETTE

Year	Pop.
1790	13,325
1800	20,159
1810	24,714
1820	27,285
1830	29,172
1840	33,574
1850	39,112
1860	39,909
1870	43,284
1880	58,842
1890	80,006
1900	110,412
1910	167,449
1920	188,104
1930	198,542
1940	200,999
1950	189,899
1960	169,340
1970	154,667
1980	159,417

FOREST

Year	Pop.
1860	898
1870	4,010
1880	4,385
1890	8,482
1900	11,039
1910	9,435
1920	7,477
1930	5,180
1940	5,791
1950	4,944
1960	4,485
1970	4,926
1980	5,072

FRANKLIN

Year	Pop.
1790	15,655
1800	19,638
1810	23,083
1820	31,892
1830	35,037
1840	37,793
1850	39,904
1860	42,126
1870	45,365
1880	49,855
1890	51,433
1900	54,902
1910	59,775
1920	62,275
1930	65,010
1940	69,378
1950	75,927
1960	88,172
1970	100,833
1980	113,629

FULTON

Year	Pop.
1850	7,567
1860	9,131
1870	9,360
1880	10,149
1890	10,137
1900	9,924
1910	9,703
1920	9,617
1930	9,213
1940	10,673
1950	10,387
1960	10,597
1970	10,776
1980	12,842

GREENE

Year	Pop.
1800	8,605
1810	12,544
1820	15,554
1830	18,028
1840	19,147
1850	22,136
1860	24,343
1870	25,887
1880	28,273
1890	28,935
1900	28,281
1910	28,882
1920	30,804
1930	41,767
1940	44,671
1950	45,394
1960	49,424
1970	36,090
1980	40,476

HUNTINGDON

Year	Pop.
1790	7,565
1800	13,008
1810	14,778
1820	20,142
1830	27,145
1840	35,484
1850	24,786
1860	28,100
1870	31,251
1880	33,954
1890	35,751
1900	34,650
1910	38,304
1920	39,848
1930	39,201
1940	41,836
1950	40,872
1960	39,457
1970	39,108
1980	42,253

INDIANA

Year	Pop.
1810	6,214
1820	8,882
1830	14,252
1840	20,782
1850	27,170
1860	33,687
1870	36,138
1880	40,527
1890	42,175
1900	42,556
1910	66,210
1920	80,910
1930	75,395
1940	79,854
1950	77,106
1960	75,306
1970	79,451
1980	92,281

JEFFERSON

Year	Pop.
1810	161
1820	561
1830	2,025
1840	7,253
1850	13,518
1860	18,270
1870	21,656
1880	27,935
1890	44,005
1900	59,113
1910	63,090
1920	61,104
1930	52,114
1940	54,090
1950	49,147
1960	47,792
1970	43,695
1980	48,303

JUNIATA

Year	Pop.
1840	11,080
1850	13,029
1860	16,986
1870	17,390
1880	18,227
1890	16,655
1900	16,054
1910	15,013
1920	14,464
1930	14,325
1940	15,373
1950	15,243
1960	15,874
1970	16,172
1980	19,188

LACKAWANNA

Year	Pop.
1880	89,269
1890	142,088
1900	193,831
1910	259,570
1920	286,311
1930	310,397
1940	301,243
1950	257,396
1960	234,531
1970	234,504
1980	227,908

LANCASTER

Year	Pop.
1790	36,147
1800	43,403
1810	53,927
1820	68,336
1830	76,631
1840	84,203
1850	98,944
1860	116,314
1870	121,340
1880	139,447
1890	149,095
1900	159,241
1910	167,029
1920	173,797
1930	196,882
1940	212,504
1950	234,717
1960	278,359
1970	320,079
1980	362,346

LAWRENCE

Year	Pop.
1850	21,079
1860	22,999
1870	27,298
1880	33,312
1890	37,517
1900	57,042
1910	70,032
1920	85,545
1930	97,258
1940	96,887
1950	105,120
1960	112,965
1970	107,374
1980	107,150

LEBANON

Year	Pop.
1820	16,988
1830	20,557

1840	21,872	1960	109,367	1890	20,111	**NORTHUMBERLAND**		1910	8,033
1850	26,071	1970	113,296	1900	21,161			1920	6,818
1860	31,831	1980	118,416	1910	22,941	1790	17,161	1930	7,483
1870	34,096			1920	24,295	1800	27,797	1940	7,452
1880	38,476	**McKEAN**		1930	28,286	1810	36,327	1950	8,425
1890	48,131			1940	29,802	1820	15,424	1960	9,158
1900	53,827	1810	142	1950	33,773	1830	18,133	1970	11,818
1910	50,565	1820	728	1960	39,567	1840	20,027	1980	18,271
1920	63,152	1830	1,439	1970	45,422	1850	23,272		
1930	67,103	1840	2,975	1980	69,409	1860	28,992	**POTTER**	
1940	72,641	1850	5,254			1870	41,444		
1950	81,683	1860	8,859	**MONTGOMERY**		1880	53,123	1810	29
1960	90,853	1870	8,825			1890	74,698	1820	186
1970	99,665	1880	42,565	1790	22,929	1900	90,911	1830	1,265
1980	108,582	1890	46,863	1800	24,150	1910	111,420	1840	3,371
		1900	51,343	1810	29,703	1920	122,079	1850	6,048
LEHIGH		1910	47,868	1820	35,793	1930	128,504	1860	11,470
		1920	48,934	1830	39,406	1940	126,887	1870	11,265
1820	18,895	1930	55,167	1840	47,241	1950	117,115	1880	13,797
1830	22,256	1940	56,673	1850	58,291	1960	104,138	1890	22,778
1840	25,787	1950	56,607	1860	70,500	1970	99,190	1900	30,621
1850	32,479	1960	54,517	1870	81,612	1980	100,381	1910	29,729
1860	43,753	1970	51,915	1880	96,494			1920	21,089
1870	56,796	1980	50,635	1890	123,290	**PERRY**		1930	17,489
1880	65,969			1900	138,995			1940	18,201
1890	76,631	**MERCER**		1910	169,590	1820	1,342	1950	16,810
1900	93,893			1920	199,130	1830	14,261	1960	16,483
1910	118,832	1800	3,228	1930	265,804	1840	17,096	1970	16,393
1920	148,101	1810	8,277	1940	289,247	1850	20,088	1980	17,726
1930	172,893	1820	11,681	1950	353,068	1860	22,793		
1940	172,533	1830	19,729	1960	516,682	1870	25,477	**SCHUYLKILL**	
1950	198,207	1840	32,873	1970	624,080	1880	27,522		
1960	227,536	1850	33,172	1980	643,621	1890	26,276	1820	11,339
1970	255,304	1860	37,836			1900	26,263	1830	20,744
1980	272,349	1870	49,977	**MONTOUR**		1910	24,136	1840	29,053
		1880	56,161			1920	22,875	1850	60,713
LUZERNE		1890	55,744	1850	13,239	1930	21,744	1860	89,510
		1900	57,387	1860	13,053	1940	23,213	1870	116,428
1790	4,904	1910	77,699	1870	15,344	1950	24,782	1880	129,974
1800	12,839	192	93,788	1880	15,468	1960	26,582	1890	154,163
1810	18,109	1930	99,246	1890	15,645	1970	28,615	1900	172,927
1820	20,027	1940	101,039	1900	15,526	1980	35,718	1910	207,894
1830	27,379	1950	111,954	1910	14,868			1920	217,754
1840	44,006	1960	127,519	1920	14,080	**PHILADELPHIA**		1930	236,505
1850	56,072	1970	127,225	1930	14,517			1940	228,331
1860	90,244	1980	128,299	1940	15,466	1790	54,391	1950	200,577
1870	160,915			1950	16,001	1800	81,009	1960	173,027
1880	133,065	**MIFFLIN**		1960	16,730	1810	111,210	1970	160,089
1890	201,203			1970	16,508	1820	137,097	1980	160,630
1900	257,121	1810	12,132	1980	16,675	1830	188,797		
1910	343,186	1820	16,618			1840	258,037	**SNYDER**	
1920	390,991	1830	21,690	**NORTHAMPTON**		1850	408,762		
1930	445,109	1840	13,092			1860	565,529	1860	15,035
1940	441,518	1850	14,980	1790	24,250	1870	674,022	1870	16,606
1950	392,241	1860	16,340	1800	30,062	1880	847,170	1880	17,797
1960	346,972	1870	17,508	1810	38,145	1890	1,046,964	1890	17,651
1970	341,956	1880	19,577	1820	31,765	1900	1,293,697	1900	17,304
1980	343,079	1890	19,996	1830	39,482	1910	1,549,008	1910	16,800
		1900	23,160	1840	40,996	1920	1,823,779	1920	17,129
LYCOMING		1910	27,785	1850	40,235	1930	1,950,961	1930	18,836
		1920	31,439	1860	47,904	1940	1,931,334	1940	20,208
1800	5,414	1930	40,335	1870	61,432	1950	2,071,605	1950	22,912
1810	11,006	1940	42,933	1880	70,312	1960	2,002,512	1960	25,922
1820	13,517	1950	43,691	1890	84,220	1970	1,949,996	1970	29,269
1830	17,636	1960	44,348	1900	99,687	1980	1,688,210	1980	33,584
1840	22,649	1970	45,268	1910	127,667				
1850	26,257	1980	46,908	1920	153,506	**PIKE**		**SOMERSET**	
1860	37,399			1930	169,304				
1870	47,426	**MONROE**		1940	168,959	1820	2,894	1800	10,188
1880	57,486			1950	185,243	1830	4,843	1810	11,284
1890	70,579	1840	9,879	1960	201,412	1840	3,832	1820	13,974
1900	75,663	1850	13,270	1970	214,545	1850	5,881	1830	17,762
1910	80,813	1860	16,758	1980	225,418	1860	7,155	1840	19,650
1920	83,100	1870	18,362			1870	8,436	1850	24,416
1930	93,421	1880	20,175			1880	9,663	1860	26,778
1940	93,633					1890	9,412	1870	28,226
1950	101,249					1900	8,766	1880	33,110

Year	Pop.
1890	37,317
1900	49,416
1910	67,117
1920	82,112
1930	80,764
1940	84,957
1950	81,813
1960	77,450
1970	76,037
1980	81,243

SULLIVAN

Year	Pop.
1850	3,694
1860	5,637
1870	6,191
1880	8,073
1890	11,620
1900	12,134
1910	11,293
1920	9,520
1930	7,499
1940	7,504
1950	6,745
1960	6,251
1970	5,961
1980	6,349

SUSQUEHANNA

Year	Pop.
1820	9,960
1830	16,787
1840	21,195
1850	28,638
1860	36,267
1870	37,523
1880	40,354
1890	40,093
1900	40,043
1910	36,746
1920	34,763
1930	33,806
1940	33,893
1950	31,970
1960	33,137
1970	34,344
1980	37,876

TIOGA

Year	Pop.
1810	1,687
1820	4,021
1830	8,978
1840	15,498
1850	23,987
1860	31,044
1870	35,097
1880	45,814
1890	52,313
1900	49,086
1910	42,829
1920	37,118
1930	31,871
1940	35,004
1950	35,474
1960	36,614
1970	39,691
1980	40,973

UNION

Year	Pop.
1820	18,619
1830	20,795
1840	22,787
1850	26,083
1860	14,145

Year	Pop.
1870	15,565
1880	16,905
1890	17,820
1900	17,592
1910	16,249
1920	15,850
1930	17,468
1940	20,247
1950	23,150
1960	25,646
1970	28,603
1980	32,870

VENANGO

Year	Pop.
1800	1,130
1810	3,060
1820	4,915
1830	9,470
1840	17,900
1850	18,310
1860	25,043
1870	47,925
1880	43,670
1890	46,640
1900	49,648
1910	56,359
1920	59,184
1930	63,226
1940	63,958
1950	65,328
1960	65,295
1970	62,353
1980	64,444

WARREN

Year	Pop.
1800	233
1810	827
1820	1,976
1830	4,697
1840	9,278
1850	13,671
1860	19,190
1870	23,897
1880	27,981
1890	37,585
1900	38,946
1910	39,573
1920	40,024
1930	41,453
1940	42,789
1950	42,698
1960	45,582
1970	47,682
1980	47,449

WASHINGTON

Year	Pop.
1790	23,866
1800	28,298
1810	36,298
1820	40,038
1830	42,784
1840	41,279
1850	44,939
1860	46,805
1870	48,483
1880	55,418
1890	71,155
1900	92,181
1910	143,680
1920	188,992
1930	204,802
1940	210,852
1950	209,628
1960	217,271

Year	Pop.
1970	210,876
1980	217,074

WAYNE

Year	Pop.
1800	2,562
1810	4,125
1820	4,127
1830	7,663
1840	11,848
1850	21,890
1860	32,239
1870	33,188
1880	33,513
1890	31,010
1900	30,171
1910	29,236
1920	27,435
1930	28,420
1940	29,934
1950	28,748
1960	28,237
1970	29,581
1980	35,237

WESTMORELAND

Year	Pop.
1790	16,018
1800	22,726
1810	26,392
1820	30,540
1830	38,400
1840	42,699
1850	51,726
1860	53,736
1870	58,719
1880	78,036
1890	112,819
1900	160,175
1910	231,304
1920	273,568
1930	294,995
1940	303,441
1950	313,179
1960	352,629
1970	376,935
1980	392,294

WYOMING

Year	Pop.
1850	10,655
1860	12,540
1870	14,585
1880	15,598
1890	15,891
1900	17,152
910	15,509
1920	14,101
1930	15,517
1940	16,702
1950	16,766
1960	16,813
1970	19,082
1980	26,433

YORK

Year	Pop.
1790	37,747
1800	25,643
1810	31,958
1820	38,759
1830	42,859
1840	47,010
1850	57,450
1860	68,200
1870	76,134

Year	Pop.
1880	87,841
1890	99,489
1900	116,413
1910	136,405
1920	144,521
1930	167,135
1940	178,022
1950	202,737
1960	238,336
1970	272,603
1980	312,963

NOTES

BRADFORD

Name changed from Ontario in 1812.

ALIQUIPPA

1900	620
1910	1,743
1920	2,931
1930	27,116
1940	27,023
1950	26,132
1960	26,329
1970	22,277
1980	17,094

ALLENTOWN

1830	1,544
1840	2,493
1850	3,779
1860	8,025
1870	13,884
1880	18,063
1890	25,228
1900	35,416
1910	51,913
1920	73,502
1930	92,563
1940	96,904
1950	106,756
1960	108,347
1970	109,871
1980	103,758

ALTOONA

1860	3,591
1870	10,610
1880	19,710
1890	30,337
1900	38,973
1910	52,127
1920	60,331
1930	82,054
1940	80,214
1950	77,177
1960	69,407
1970	62,900
1980	57,078

BALDWIN

1960	24,489
1970	26,729
1980	24,598

BEAVER FALLS

1870	3,112
1880	5,104
1890	9,735
1900	10,054
1910	12,191
1920	12,802
1930	17,147
1940	17,098
1950	17,375
1960	16,240
1970	14,635
1980	12,525

BELLEVIEW

1870	384
1880	915
1890	1,418
1900	3,416
1910	6,323
1920	8,198

1930	10,252
1940	10,488
1950	11,604
1960	11,412
1970	11,586
1980	10,128

BERWICK

1870	923
1880	2,095
1890	2,701
1900	3,916
1910	5,357
1920	12,181
1930	12,660
1940	13,181
1950	14,010
1960	13,353
1970	12,274
1980	11,850

BETHEL PARK

1950	11,324
1960	23,650
1970	34,758
1980	34,755

BETHLEHEM

1850	1,516
1860	2,866
1870	4,512
1880	5,193
1890	6,762
1900	7,293
1910	12,837
1920	50,358
1930	57,892
1940	58,490
1950	66,340
1960	75,408
1970	72,686
1980	70,419

BLOOMSBURG

1820	1,626
1830	2,090
1840	1,774
1850	3,122
1860	2,668
1870	3,341
1880	3,702
1890	4,635
1900	6,170
1910	7,413
1920	7,819
1930	9,093
1940	9,799
1950	10,633
1960	10,655
1970	11,652
1980	11,717

BRADFORD

1880	9,197
1890	10,514
1900	15,029
1910	14,544
1920	15,525
1930	19,306
1940	17,691
1950	17,354

1960	15,061
1970	12,672
1980	11,211

BRENTWOOD

1920	1,695
1930	5,381
1940	7,552
1950	12,535
1960	13,706
1970	13,732
1980	11,907

BRISTOL

1800	511
1810	628
1820	908
1830	1,262
1840	1,438
1850	2,570
1860	3,314
1870	3,269
1880	5,273
1890	6,553
1900	7,104
1910	9,256
1920	10,273
1930	11,799
1940	11,895
1950	12,710
1960	12,364
1970	12,085
1980	10,867

BUTLER

1820	225
1830	580
1840	861
1850	1,148
1860	1,399
1870	1,935
1880	3,163
1890	8,734
1900	10,853
1910	20,728
1920	23,778
1930	23,568
1940	24,477
1950	23,482
1960	20,975
1970	18,691
1980	17,026

CANONSBURG

1820	440
1830	792
1840	687
1850	627
1860	650
1870	641
1880	699
1890	2,113
1900	2,714
1910	3,891
1920	10,632
1930	12,558
1940	12,599
1950	12,072
1960	11,877
1970	11,439
1980	10,459

CARBONDALE

1840	4,945
1860	6,393
1870	7,714
1880	10,833
1890	13,536
1900	13,536
1910	17,040
1920	18,640
1930	20,061
1940	19,371
1950	16,296
1960	13,595
1970	12,478
1980	11,255

CARLISLE

1820	2,908
1830	3,707
1840	4,351
1850	4,581
1860	5,664
1870	6,650
1880	6,209
1890	7,620
1900	9,626
1910	10,303
1920	10,916
1930	12,596
1940	13,984
1950	16,812
1960	16,623
1970	18,079
1980	18,314

CARNEGIE

1900	7,330
1910	10,009
1920	11,516
1930	12,497
1940	12,663
1950	12,105
1960	11,887
1970	10,864
1980	10,099

CASTLE SHANNON

1920	2,353
1930	3,810
1940	3,970
1950	5,459
1960	11,836
1970	12,036
1980	10,164

CHAMBERSBURG

1840	3,239
1850	3,335
1860	5,255
1870	6,380
1880	6,877
1890	7,863
1900	8,864
1910	11,800
1920	13,171
1930	13,788
1940	14,852
1950	17,212
1960	17,670
1970	17,315
1980	16,174

CHESTER

1820	657
1830	847
1840	(NA)
1850	1,667
1860	4,631
1870	9,485
1880	14,997
1890	20,226
1900	33,988
1910	38,357
1920	58,030
1930	59,164
1940	59,285
1950	66,039
1960	63,658
1970	56,331
1980	45,794

CLAIRTON

1910	3,326
1920	6,264
1930	15,291
1940	16,381
1950	19,652
1960	18,389
1970	15,051
1980	12,188

COATESVILLE

1870	2,025
1880	2,766
1890	3,680
1900	5,721
1910	11,084
1920	14,515
1930	14,582
1940	14,006
1950	13,826
1960	12,971
1970	12,331
1980	10,698

COLUMBIA

1820	1,891
1830	2,046
1840	2,719
1850	4,190
1860	5,007
1870	6,461
1880	8,312
1890	10,599
1900	12,316
1910	11,454
1920	10,836
1930	11,349
1940	11,547
1950	11,993
1960	12,075
1970	11,237
1980	10,466

CONNELLSVILLE

1860	996
1870	1,292
1880	3,609
1890	5,629
1900	7,160
1910	12,845
1920	13,804
1930	13,290
1940	13,608

1950	13,293
1960	12,814
1970	11,643
1980	10,319

DARBY

1860	780
1870	1,205
1880	1,779
1890	2,972
1900	3,429
1910	6,305
1920	7,922
1930	9,899
1940	10,344
1950	13,154
1960	14,059
1970	13,729
1980	11,513

DORMONT

1910	1,115
1920	6,455
1930	13,190
1940	12,974
1950	13,405
1960	13,098
1970	12,856
1980	11,275

DUNMORE

1870	4,311
1880	5,151
1890	8,315
1900	12,583
1910	17,615
1920	20,250
1930	22,627
1940	23,086
1950	20,305
1960	18,917
1970	18,168
1980	16,781

DUQUESNE

1900	9,036
1910	15,727
1920	19,011
1930	21,396
1940	20,693
1950	17,620
1960	15,019
1970	11,410
1980	10,094

EASTON

1800	1,045
1810	1,657
1820	2,370
1830	3,529
1840	4,865
1850	7,250
1860	8,944
1870	10,987
1880	11,924
1890	14,481
1900	25,238
1910	28,523
1920	33,813
1930	34,468
1940	33,589

1950	35,632
1960	31,955
1970	29,450
1980	26,027

EMMAUS

1860	381
1870	477
1880	847
1890	883
1900	1,468
1910	3,501
1920	4,370
1930	6,419
1940	6,731
1950	7,780
1960	10,262
1970	11,511
1980	11,001

EPHRATA

1900	2,451
1910	3,192
1920	3,735
1930	4,988
1940	6,199
1950	7,027
1960	7,688
1970	9,662
1980	11,095

ERIE

1800	81
1810	394
1820	635
1830	1,465
1840	3,412
1850	5,858
1860	9,419
1870	19,646
1880	27,737
1890	40,634
1900	52,733
1910	66,525
1920	93,372
1930	115,967
1940	116,955
1950	130,803
1960	138,440
1970	129,265
1980	119,123

GREENSBURG

1810	685
1820	771
1830	810
1840	800
1850	1,051
1860	1,388
1870	1,642
1880	2,500
1890	4,202
1900	6,508
1910	13,012
1920	15,033
1930	16,508
1940	16,743
1950	16,923
1960	17,383
1970	17,077
1980	17,558

HANOVER

1820	946
1830	1,006
1840	1,070
1850	1,210
1860	1,630
1870	1,839
1880	2,317
1890	3,746
1900	5,302
1910	7,057
1920	8,664
1930	11,805
1940	13,076
1950	14,048
1960	15,538
1970	15,623
1980	14,890

HARRISBURG

1800	1,472
1810	2,287
1820	2,990
1830	4,312
1840	5,980
1850	7,834
1860	13,405
1870	23,104
1880	30,762
1890	39,385
1900	50,167
1910	64,186
1920	75,917
1930	80,339
1940	83,893
1950	89,544
1960	79,697
1970	68,061
1980	53,264

HAZLETON

1850	1,707
1860	4,317
1870	6,935
1880	11,872
1890	14,230
1900	14,230
1910	25,452
1920	32,277
1930	36,765
1940	38,009
1950	35,491
1960	32,056
1970	30,426
1980	27,318

INDIANA

1850	963
1860	1,331
1870	1,605
1880	1,907
1890	1,963
1900	4,142
1910	5,749
1920	7,043
1930	9,569
1940	10,050
1950	11,743
1960	13,005
1970	16,100
1980	16,051

JEANETTE

1890	3,296
1900	5,865
1910	8,077
1920	10,627
1930	15,126
1940	16,220
1950	16,172
1960	16,565
1970	15,209
1980	13,106

JOHNSTOWN

1840	949
1850	1,269
1860	4,185
1870	6,028
1880	8,380
1890	21,805
1900	35,936
1910	55,482
1920	67,327
1930	66,993
1940	66,668
1950	63,232
1960	53,949
1970	42,476
1980	35,496

KINGSTON

1860	638
1870	1,143
1880	1,418
1890	2,381
1900	3,846
1910	6,449
1920	8,962
1930	21,600
1940	20,679
1950	21,096
1960	20,261
1970	18,325
1980	15,681

LANCASTER

1800	4,292
1810	5,405
1820	6,633
1830	7,704
1840	8,417
1850	12,369
1860	17,603
1870	20,233
1880	25,769
1890	32,011
1900	41,459
1910	47,227
1920	53,150
1930	59,949
1940	61,345
1950	63,774
1960	61,055
1970	57,690
1980	54,725

LANSDALE

1880	798
1890	1,858
1900	2,754
1910	3,551
1920	4,728
1930	8,379

1940	9,316
1950	9,762
1960	12,612
1970	18,451
1980	16,526

LANSDOWNE

1890	875
1900	2,630
1910	4,066
1920	4,797
1930	9,023
1940	10,837
1950	12,169
1960	12,601
1970	14,090
1980	11,891

LATROBE

1860	758
1870	1,127
1880	1,815
1890	3,589
1900	4,614
1910	8,777
1920	9,484
1930	10,644
1940	11,111
1950	11,811
1960	11,932
1970	11,749
1980	10,799

LEBANON

1810	1,434
1820	1,437
1830	1,826
1840	1,860
1850	2,184
1860	4,449
1870	6,727
1880	8,778
1890	14,664
1900	17,628
1910	19,240
1920	24,643
1930	25,561
1940	27,206
1950	28,156
1960	30,045
1970	28,572
1980	25,711

LOWER BURRELL

1960	11,952
1970	13,654
1980	13,200

McKEESPORT

1850	1,392
1860	2,166
1870	2,523
1880	8,212
1890	20,741
1900	34,277
1910	42,694
1920	46,781
1930	54,632
1940	55,355
1950	51,502
1960	45,489
1970	37,977
1980	31,012

MEADVILLE

1810	457
1820	649
1830	1,076
1840	1,319
1850	2,578
1860	3,702
1870	7,103
1880	8,860
1890	9,520
1900	10,291
1910	12,780
1920	14,568
1930	16,698
1940	18,919
1950	18,972
1960	16,671
1970	16,573
1980	15,544

MIDDLETOWN

1850	900
1860	2,392
1870	2,980
1880	3,351
1890	5,080
1900	5,608
1910	5,374
1920	5,920
1930	6,085
1940	7,046
1950	9,184
1960	11,182
1970	9,080
1980	10,122

MONESSEN

1900	2,197
1910	11,775
1920	18,179
1930	20,268
1940	20,257
1950	17,896
1960	18,424
1970	15,216
1980	11,928

MONROEVILLE

1960	22,446
1970	29,001
1980	30,977

MUNHALL

1910	5,185
1920	6,418
1930	12,995
1940	13,900
1950	16,437
1960	17,312
1970	16,574
1980	14,532

MURRYSVILLE

1980	16,036

NANTICOKE

1880	3,884
1890	10,044
1900	12.116

1910	18,877
1920	22,614
1930	26,043
1940	24,387
1950	20,160
1960	15,601
1970	14,632
1980	13,004

NEW CASTLE

1840	611
1850	1,614
1860	1,882
1870	6,164
1880	8,418
1890	11,600
1900	28,339
1910	36,280
1920	44,938
1930	48,674
1940	47,638
1950	48,834
1960	44,790
1970	38,559
1980	33,621

NEW KENSINGTON

1900	4,665
1910	7,707
1920	11,987
1930	16,762
1940	24,055
1950	25,146
1960	23,485
1970	20,312
1980	17,660

NORRISTOWN

1820	827
1830	1,089
1840	2,937
1850	6,024
1860	8,848
1870	10,753
1880	13,063
1890	19,791
1900	22,265
1910	27,875
1920	32,319
1930	35,853
1940	38,181
1950	38,126
1960	38,925
1970	38,169
1980	34,684

OIL CITY

1870	2,276
1880	7,315
1890	10,932
1900	13,264
1910	15,657
1920	21,274
1930	22,075
1940	20,379
1950	19,581
1960	17,692
1970	15,033
1980	13,881

PHILADELPHIA

1790	28,522
1800	41,220
1810	53,722
1820	63,802
1830	80,462
1840	93,665
1850	121,376
1860	565,529
1870	674,002
1880	847,170
1890	1,046,964
1900	1,293,697
1910	1,549,008
1920	1,823,779
1930	1,950,961
1940	1,931,334
1950	2,071,605
1960	2,002,512
1970	1,949,996
1980	1,688,210

PHOENIXVILLE

1850	2,670
1860	4,886
1870	5,292
1880	6,682
1890	8,514
1900	9,196
1910	10,743
1920	10,484
1930	12,029
1940	12,282
1950	12,932
1960	13,797
1970	14,823
1980	14,165

PITTSBURGH

1800	1,565
1810	4,768
1820	7,248
1830	15,369
1840	31,204
1850	67,863
1860	77,923
1870	139,256
1880	235,071
1890	343,904
1900	451,512
1910	533,905
1920	588,343
1930	669,817
1940	671,659
1950	676,806
1960	604,332
1970	520,089
1980	423,938

PLUM

1960	10,241
1970	21,932
1980	25,390

POTTSTOWN

1830	676
1840	721
1850	1,664
1860	2,380
1870	4,125
1880	5,305
1890	13,285

1900	13,696
1910	15,599
1920	17,431
1930	19,430
1940	20,194
1950	22,589
1960	26,144
1970	25,355
1980	22,729

POTTSVILLE

1830	2,464
1840	4,345
1850	7,515
1860	9,444
1870	12,384
1880	13,251
1890	14,117
1900	15,710
1910	20,236
1920	21,876
1930	24,300
1940	24,530
1950	23,640
1960	21,659
1970	19,715
1980	18,195

READING

1800	2,386
1820	4,332
1830	5,856
1840	8,410
1850	15,743
1860	23,162
1870	33,930
1880	43,278
1890	58,661
1900	78,961
1910	96,071
1920	107,784
1930	111,171
1940	110,568
1950	109,320
1960	98,177
1970	87,643
1980	78,686

SCRANTON

1860	9,223
1870	35,092
1880	45,850
1890	75,215
1900	102,026
1910	129,876
1920	137,783
1930	143,433
1940	140,404
1950	125,536
1960	111,443
1970	102,696
1980	88,117

SHAMOKIN

1870	4,320
1880	8,184
1890	14,403
1900	18,202
1910	19,588
1920	21,204
1930	20,274
1940	18,810
1950	16,879

1960	13,674
1970	11,719
1980	10,357

SHARON

1850	541
1860	900
1870	4,221
1880	5,684
1890	7,459
1900	8,196
1910	15,270
1920	21,747
1930	25,908
1940	25,622
1950	26,454
1960	25,267
1970	22,653
1980	19,057

STATE COLLEGE

1900	851
1910	1,425
1920	2,405
1930	4,450
1940	6,226
1950	17,227
1960	22,409
1970	32,833
1980	36,130

SUNBURY

1850	1,218
1860	1,803
1870	3,131
1880	4,077
1890	5,930
1900	9,810
1910	13,770
1920	15,721
1930	15,626
1940	15,462
1950	15,570
1960	13,687
1970	13,025
1980	12,292

SWISSVALE

1900	1,716
1910	7,381
1920	10,908
1930	16,029
1940	15,919
1950	16,488
1960	15,089
1970	13,819
1980	11,345

UNIONTOWN

1850	2,333
1860	na
1870	2,503
1880	3,265
1890	6,359
1900	7,344
1910	13,344
1920	15,692
1930	19,544
1940	21,819
1950	20,471
1960	17,942
1970	16,282
1980	14,510

WARREN

1840	737
1850	1,013
1860	1,738
1870	2,014
1880	2,810
1890	4,332
1900	8,043
1910	11,080
1920	14,272
1930	14,863
1940	14,891
1950	14,849
1960	14,505
1970	12,998
1980	12,146

WASHINGTON

1820	1,687
1830	1,816
1840	2,062
1850	2,662
1860	3,587
1870	3,571
1880	4,292
1890	7,063
1900	7,670
1910	18,778
1920	21,480
1930	24,545
1940	26,166
1950	26,280
1960	23,545
1970	19,827
1980	18,363

WEST CHESTER

1800	374
1810	471
1820	552
1830	1,258
1840	2,152
1850	3,172
1860	4,757
1870	5,630
1880	7,046
1890	8,028
1900	9,524
1910	11,767
1920	11,717
1930	12,325
1940	13,289
1950	15,168
1960	15,705
1970	19,301
1980	17,435

WEST MIFFLIN

1950	17,985
1960	27,289
1970	28,070
1980	26,279

WHITEHALL

1950	7,342
1960	16,075
1970	16,551
1980	15,206

WILKES-BARRE

1810	1,255
1820	755
1830	(NA)
1840	1,718
1850	2,723
1860	4,253
1870	10,174
1880	23,339
1890	37,718
1900	51,721
1910	67,105
1920	73,833
1930	86,626
1940	86,236
1950	76,826
1960	63,551
1970	58,856
1980	51,551

WILKINSBURG

1880	1,529
1890	4,662
1900	11,886
1910	18,924
1920	24,403
1930	29,639
1940	29,853
1950	31,418
1960	30,066
1970	26,780
1980	23,669

WILLIAMSPORT

1810	344
1820	624
1830	na
1840	1,353
1850	1,615
1860	5,664
1870	16,030
1880	18,932
1890	27,132
1900	28,757
1910	31,860
1920	36,198
1930	45,729
1940	44,355
1950	45,047
1960	41,967
1970	37,918
1980	33,401

YEADON

1900	689
1910	882
1920	1,308
1930	5,430
1940	8,524
1950	11,068
1960	11,610
1970	12,136
1980	11,727

YORK

1800	2,503
1810	2,847
1820	3,545
1830	4,216
1840	4,779
1850	6,853
1860	8,605
1870	11,003
1880	13,940
1890	20,793
1900	33,708
1910	44,750
1920	47,512
1930	55,254
1940	56,712
1950	59,953
1960	59,504
1970	50,335
1980	44,619

CORRECTION NOTE

The official 1980 census counts of total population shown
in this report supersede counts issued previously. Corrections to the figures were made after the counts were provided
to the State for redistricting purposes and released in
Advance Report PHC80-V for this State.

Shown below are corrections to the 1980 census counts of the
total population made after the tabulations for this report
were completed. Any additional corrections made after this
report is printed are available by writing to Data User
Services Division, Customer Services (Corrections), Bureau
of the Census, Washington, D.C. 20233.

The 1980 figures shown in this publication are subject to
change pending the outcome of the various lawsuits dealing
with the census counts.

	1980 population	
	As shown in the tables	Corrected
Allegheny County:		
Aleppo township:		
Aleppo (CDP)..............	(1)	1 134
Baldwin borough.............	24 598	24 712
Brentwood borough...........	11 907	11 861
Munhall borough.............	14 532	14 535
Pittsburgh city.............	423 938	423 959
Pleasant Hills borough......	9 676	9 374
West Mifflin borough........	26 279	26 552
Whitehall borough...........	15 206	15 143
Bucks County:		
Ivyland borough.............	581	661
Warminster township.........	35 543	35 463
Warminster (CDP)...........	35 543	35 463
Clarion County:		
Clarion borough.............	6 664	6 198
Clarion township............	2 847	3 313
Fulton County:		
Brush Creek township........	556	548
Valley Hi borough...........	(1)	8
Luzerne County:		
Dorrance township...........	1 829	1 815
Rice township...............	1 935	1 921
Wright township.............	4 797	4 825

[1]Not shown separately.

County Subdivisions	1980	1970
The State	11 863 895	ʳ11 800 766
Adams County[1]	68 292	56 937
Abbottstown borough	689	552
Arendtsville borough	600	589
Bendersville borough	533	528
Berwick township	1 492	1 379
Biglerville borough	991	977
Bonneauville borough	920	819
Butler township	2 166	1 757
Carroll Valley borough[1]	817	...
Conewago township	3 405	3 431
Midway (CDP)	1 599	1 636
Cumberland township[1]	4 637	3 497
East Berlin borough	1 054	1 086
Fairfield borough	591	547
Franklin township	3 692	2 744
Freedom township	650	555
Germany township	1 652	1 308
Gettysburg borough[1]	7 194	7 275
Hamilton township	1 692	1 048
Hamiltonban township[1]	1 835	1 686
Highland township	717	662
Huntington township	1 557	1 484
Latimore township	1 369	1 105
Liberty township[1]	823	1 075
Littlestown borough[1]	2 870	3 026
McSherrystown borough	2 764	2 773
Menallen township	2 354	1 937
Mount Joy township	2 564	1 795
Mount Pleasant township	3 473	1 817
New Oxford borough	1 921	1 495
Oxford township	2 302	1 808
Reading township	2 660	1 724
Straban township	4 240	3 221
Tyrone township	1 534	1 291
Union township	1 978	1 479
York Springs borough	556	467
Allegheny County[2]	1 450 085	ʳ1 605 133
Aleppo township	1 134	794
Aspinwall borough	3 284	3 541
Avalon borough	6 240	ʳ7 010
Baldwin borough[2]	24 598	26 729
Baldwin township	2 680	ʳ3 026
Baldwin Township (CDP)	2 680	...
Bell Acres borough	1 307	1 264
Bellevue borough	10 128	11 586
Ben Avon borough	2 314	2 713
Ben Avon Heights borough	398	443
Bethel Park borough	34 755	ʳ34 758
Blawnox borough	1 653	1 907
Brackenridge borough	4 297	4 796
Braddock borough	5 634	ʳ8 795
Braddock Hills borough	2 556	ʳ2 459
Bradfordwoods borough	1 264	970
Brentwood borough	11 907	13 732
Bridgeville borough	6 154	6 717
Carnegie borough	10 099	10 864
Castle Shannon borough	10 164	ʳ12 036
Chalfant borough	1 119	1 370
Cheswick borough	2 336	ʳ2 563
Churchill borough	4 285	4 690
Clairton city	12 188	15 051
Collier township	5 063	6 874
Coraopolis borough	7 308	8 435
Crafton borough	7 623	8 233
Crescent township	2 862	ʳ2 918
Crescent Township (CDP)	2 862	...
Dormont borough	11 275	12 856
Dravosburg borough	2 511	2 916
Duquesne city	10 094	11 410
East Deer township	1 658	2 081
East Deer Township (CDP)	1 658	...
East McKeesport borough	2 940	3 233
East Pittsburgh borough	2 493	3 006
Edgewood borough	4 382	ʳ5 138
Edgeworth borough	1 738	2 200
Elizabeth borough	1 892	ʳ2 273
Elizabeth township	16 269	ʳ15 525
Emsworth borough	3 074	ʳ3 345
Etna borough	4 534	5 819
Fawn township	2 899	3 167
Findlay township	4 573	4 602
Imperial—Enlow (CDP) (pt.)	1 587	1 842
Forest Hills borough	8 198	9 561
Forward township	4 335	4 496
Fox Chapel borough	5 049	4 684
Franklin Park borough[2]	6 135	5 310
Frazer township	1 509	1 887
Glassport borough	6 242	7 450
Glenfield borough	246	406
Green Tree borough	5 722	6 441
Hampton township	14 260	12 515
Harmar township	3 461	ʳ3 916
Harrison township	13 252	14 448
Haysville borough	117	154
Heidelberg borough	1 606	2 034
Homestead borough	5 092	6 309

County Subdivisions	1980	1970
Allegheny County—Con.		
Indiana township	6 080	5 621
Ingram borough	4 346	4 902
Jefferson borough	8 643	8 512
Kennedy township	7 159	6 859
Kennedy Township (CDP)	7 159	...
Kilbuck township	1 219	ʳ1 694
Kilbuck Township (CDP)	1 219	...
Leet township	1 854	1 646
Leet Township (CDP)	1 854	...
Leetsdale borough	1 604	1 862
Liberty borough	3 112	3 594
Lincoln borough	1 428	1 885
McCandless township	26 250	22 404
McCandless Township (CDP)	26 250	...
McDonald borough (pt.)	539	659
McKeesport city	31 012	37 977
McKees Rocks borough	8 742	11 901
Marshall township	2 594	2 907
Millvale borough	4 772	5 815
Monroeville borough	30 977	29 011
Moon township	20 935	18 317
Carnot—Moon (CDP)	11 102	13 093
Mount Lebanon township	34 414	ʳ39 157
Mount Lebanon (CDP)	34 414	...
Mount Oliver borough	4 576	ʳ5 509
Munhall borough	14 532	ʳ16 574
Neville township	1 416	2 017
Neville Township (CDP)	1 416	...
North Braddock borough	8 711	10 838
North Fayette township	7 351	ʳ5 626
Imperial—Enlow (CDP) (pt.)	1 620	543
Sturgeon—Noblestown (CDP) (pt.)	760	...
North Versailles township	13 294	13 416
North Versailles (CDP)	13 294	...
Oakdale borough	1 955	ʳ2 136
Oakmont borough	7 039	7 550
O'Hara township	9 233	9 209
Ohio township	2 072	ʳ2 096
Ohio Township (CDP)	2 072	...
Osborne borough	529	579
Penn Hills township	57 632	62 886
Penn Hills (CDP)	57 632	...
Pennsbury Village borough[2]	798	...
Pine township	3 908	4 259
Pitcairn borough	4 175	4 741
Pittsburgh city	423 938	ʳ520 089
Pleasant Hills borough	9 676	10 409
Plum borough	25 390	21 932
Port Vue borough	5 316	5 862
Rankin borough	2 892	ʳ3 704
Reserve township	4 306	4 151
Reserve Township (CDP)	4 306	...
Richland township	7 749	7 819
Robinson township[2]	9 416	10 158
Ross township	35 102	32 892
Ross Township (CDP)	35 102	...
Rosslyn Farms borough	521	608
Scott township	20 413	21 856
Scott Township (CDP)	20 413	...
Sewickley borough	4 778	5ʳ660
Sewickley Heights borough	899	797
Sewickley Hills borough[2]	419	270
Shaler township	33 694	33 369
Shaler Township (CDP)	33 694	...
Sharpsburg borough	4 351	ʳ5 453
South Fayette township	9 707	9 369
Sturgeon—Noblestown (CDP) (pt.)	552	...
South Park township	13 535	8 187
South Versailles township	425	558
Springdale borough	4 418	5 202
Springdale township	1 918	2 218
Stowe township	9 202	10 119
Stowe Township (CDP)	9 202	...
Swissvale borough	11 345	ʳ13 819
Tarentum borough	6 419	7 379
Thornburg borough	526	617
Trafford borough (pt.)	—	95
Turtle Creek borough	6 959	8 308
Upper St. Clair township	19 023	ʳ15 471
Upper St. Clair (CDP)	19 023	...
Verona borough	3 179	3 737
Versailles borough	2 150	2 754
Wall borough	989	1 265
West Deer township	10 897	10 074
Curtisville (CDP)	1 404	1 337
Russellton (CDP)	1 878	1 597
West Elizabeth borough	808	848
West Homestead borough	3 128	3 789
West Mifflin borough	26 279	28 070
West View borough	7 648	8 312
Whitaker borough	1 615	ʳ1 797
Whitehall borough[2]	15 206	ʳ16 450
White Oak borough	9 480	9 304
Wilkins township	8 472	8 749
Wilkins Township (CDP)	8 472	...
Wilkinsburg borough	23 669	26 780
Wilmerding borough	2 421	3 218

County Subdivisions	1980	1970
Armstrong County[3]	77 768	75 590
Apollo borough	2 212	2 308
Applewold borough	395	515
Atwood borough	107	123
Bethel township	1 349	1 128
Boggs township	953	797
Bradys Bend township	1 124	1 095
Burrell township	766	696
Cadogan township	459	563
Cowanshannock township	3 178	3 008
Dayton borough	648	715
East Franklin township	3 716	4 262
Elderton borough	420	428
Ford City borough	3 923	4 749
Ford Cliff borough	516	526
Freeport borough	2 381	2 375
Gilpin township[3]	2 967	3 086
Hovey township	103	143
Kiskiminetas township	5 875	4 657
Orchard Hills (CDP)	1 415	1 300
Kittanning borough	5 432	6 231
Kittanning township	2 160	1 809
Leechburg borough[3]	2 682	2 999
Madison township	1 030	1 012
Mahoning township	1 649	1 537
Manor township	4 819	5 030
Lenape Heights (CDP)	1 548	1 233
Manorville borough	409	445
North Apollo borough	1 487	1 618
North Buffalo township	2 827	2 521
Parker city[3]	808	843
Parks township	3 123	3 045
North Vandergrift—Pleasant View (CDP)	1 625	1 784
Perry township	396	375
Pine township	656	704
Plumcreek township	2 303	1 734
Rayburn township	1 971	1 983
Redbank township	1 161	916
Rural Valley borough	1 033	962
South Bend township	1 237	1 021
South Bethlehem borough	476	500
South Buffalo township	2 636	2 317
Sugarcreek township	1 511	1 001
Valley township	628	578
Washington township	1 008	953
Wayne township	1 020	909
West Franklin township	1 863	1 601
West Kittanning borough	1 591	956
Worthington borough	760	816
Beaver County[4]	204 441	208 418
Aliquippa borough	17 094	22 277
Ambridge borough	9 575	11 324
Baden borough	5 318	5 536
Beaver borough	5 441	6 100
Beaver Falls city	12 525	14 635
Big Beaver borough	2 815	2 739
Bridgewater borough	879	966
Brighton township	7 858	7 532
Center township	10 733	10 598
Chippewa township	7 245	6 654
Conway borough	2 747	2 822
Darlington borough	377	344
Darlington township	2 090	2 056
Daugherty township	3 605	3 719
East Rochester borough	789	920
Eastvale borough	379	453
Economy borough	9 538	7 176
Ellwood City borough (pt.)	795	1 103
Fallston borough	312	571
Frankfort Springs borough	187	144
Franklin township	3 772	3 488
Freedom borough	2 272	2 643
Georgetown borough	231	234
Glasgow borough	106	112
Greene township	2 422	1 489
Hanover township	3 443	2 154
Harmony township	3 977	5 022
Harmony Township (CDP)	3 977	...
Homewood borough	188	212
Hookstown borough	228	246
Hopewell township	14 662	14 133
Independence township	2 534	1 761
Industry borough[4]	2 417	2 442
Koppel borough	1 146	1 312
Marion township	941	1 292
Midland borough[4]	4 310	5 271
Monaca borough	7 661	7 486
New Brighton borough	7 364	7 637
New Galilee borough	596	624
New Sewickley township	7 340	5 719
North Sewickley township	6 758	6 048
Ohioville borough	4 217	3 918
Patterson township	3 288	3 442
Patterson Township (CDP)	3 288	...
Patterson Heights borough	797	777
Potter township	605	484
Pulaski township	1 998	2 126

County Subdivisions	1980	1970
Beaver County—Con.		
Pulaski township—Con.		
Pulaski Township (CDP)	1 998	...
Raccoon township	3 133	2 615
Rochester borough	4 759	4 819
Rochester township	3 427	4 089
Shippingport borough	255	328
South Beaver township	2 932	2 339
South Heights borough	765	799
Vanport township[4]	2 013	2 122
Vanport (CDP)	2 013	2 122
West Mayfield borough	1 712	2 152
White township	1 870	1 414
White Township (CDP)	1 870	...
Bedford County[5]	46 784	42 353
Bedford borough[5]	3 326	3 302
Bedford township[5]	4 692	4 253
Bloomfield township	631	506
Broad Top township	1 837	1 963
Coaldale borough	233	174
Colerain township	1 015	830
Cumberland Valley township	1 494	1 333
East Providence township	1 808	1 442
East St. Clair township	2 492	1 944
Everett borough	1 828	2 243
Harrison township	951	714
Hopewell borough	256	290
Hopewell township	1 926	1 490
Hyndman borough	1 106	1 151
Juniata township	799	684
Kimmel township[5]	1 492	1 194
King township	1 154	1 047
Liberty township	1 534	1 332
Lincoln township	349	303
Londonderry township	1 899	1 702
Mann township	455	337
Manns Choice borough	286	334
Monroe township	1 202	1 086
Napier township	1 977	1 645
New Paris borough	199	204
Pleasantville borough	275	303
Rainsburg borough	201	179
St. Clairsville borough	90	96
Saxton borough	814	858
Schellsburg borough	325	271
Snake Spring township[5]	1 498	1 252
Southampton township	825	699
South Woodbury township	1 755	1 566
Union township	215	199
West Providence township	3 361	3 132
West St. Clair township	1 251	1 209
Woodbury borough	267	298
Woodbury township	966	788
Berks County[6]	312 509	296 382
Adamstown borough (pt.)	12	4
Albany township	1 381	1 109
Alsace township	3 456	3 034
Amity township	5 883	4 718
Bally borough	1 051	1 197
Bechtelsville borough	832	728
Bern township	5 097	4 764
Bernville borough	798	848
Bethel township	3 312	2 600
Birdsboro borough	3 481	3 196
Boyertown borough	3 979	4 428
Brecknock township	2 641	1 956
Caernarvon township	1 710	1 680
Centerport borough	246	227
Centre township	2 329	1 830
Colebrookdale township	4 748	3 034
New Berlinville (CDP)	1 277	1 145
Cumru township[6]	11 474	8 367
District township	1 094	752
Douglass township	3 128	2 944
Earl township	2 607	2 290
Exeter township[6]	14 419	10 607
Fleetwood borough	3 422	3 064
Greenwich township	2 432	1 404
Hamburg borough	4 011	3 909
Heidelberg township[6]	1 561	1 263
Hereford township	2 837	1 641
Jefferson township	1 310	854
Kenhorst borough	3 187	3 482
Kutztown borough	4 040	4 166
Laureldale borough	4 047	4 519
Leesport borough	1 258	1 158
Lenhartsville borough	200	220
Longswamp township	4 627	3 727
Lower Alsace township[6]	4 906	5 091
Lower Heidelberg township	1 819	1 592
Lyons borough	579	589
Maidencreek township	2 377	2 376
Marion township	1 341	1 250
Maxatawny township	5 269	4 640
Mohnton borough	2 156	2 153
Mount Penn borough	3 187	3 465
Muhlenberg township	13 031	13 693

County Subdivisions	1980	1970
Berks County—Con.		
North Heidelberg township	953	701
Oley township	3 024	2 778
Ontelaunee township	1 408	1 568
Penn township	1 254	1 205
Perry township	2 420	2 112
Pike township	1 056	867
Reading city	78 686	87 643
Richmond township	3 204	2 745
Robeson township	4 729	3 644
Robesonia borough	1 748	1 685
Rockland township	1 911	1 452
Ruscombmanor township	2 546	1 985
St. Lawrence borough	1 376	1 256
Shillington borough⁶	5 601	6 249
Shoemakersville borough	1 391	1 427
Sinking Spring borough	2 617	2 862
South Heidelberg township	3 355	3 198
Spring township⁶	17 193	13 883
Strausstown borough	377	401
Temple borough	1 486	1 667
Tilden township	2 247	1 781
Topton borough	1 818	1 744
Tulpehocken township	2 569	1 791
Union township	2 815	2 332
Upper Bern township	1 159	930
Upper Tulpehocken township	1 154	783
Washington township	2 568	2 273
Wernersville borough	1 811	1 761
West Lawn borough	1 686	1 973
West Reading borough	4 507	4 578
Windsor township	2 199	2 108
Womelsdorf borough⁶	1 827	1 551
Wyomissing borough	6 551	7 136
Wyomissing Hills borough	2 150	1 744
Blair County⁷	136 621	135 356
Allegheny township⁷	7 463	5 943
Altoona city	57 078	⁷63 115
Antis township	6 524	5 025
Tipton (CDP)	1 348	...
Bellwood borough	2 114	2 395
Blair township⁷	3 937	⁷3 228
Catharine township	691	⁷623
Duncansville borough⁷	1 355	⁷1 427
Frankstown township	6 363	4 842
Freedom township	3 060	2 522
Greenfield township	3 758	3 543
Claysburg (CDP)	1 346	1 516
Hollidaysburg borough⁷	5 892	6 262
Huston township	1 049	873
Juniata township	1 129	879
Logan township	12 183	⁷11 281
Juniata Gap (CDP)	1 202	...
Martinsburg borough	2 231	2 088
Newry borough	353	444
North Woodbury township	1 851	1 350
Roaring Spring borough⁷	2 962	2 811
Snyder township	3 454	3 457
Taylor township⁷	2 108	2 003
Tunnelhill borough (pt.)⁷	154	–
Tyrone borough	6 346	7 072
Tyrone township	1 647	1 330
Williamsburg borough	1 400	⁷1 579
Woodbury township	1 519	1 264
Bradford County⁸	62 919	57 962
Alba borough	222	184
Albany township	853	705
Armenia township	191	62
Asylum township	1 027	843
Athens borough	3 622	4 173
Athens township	4 994	4 007
Burlington borough	162	148
Burlington township	765	585
Canton borough	1 959	2 037
Canton township	1 898	1 645
Columbia township	1 119	1 042
Franklin township	559	387
Granville township	903	761
Herrick township	601	516
Le Raysville borough	356	346
Leroy township	639	587
Litchfield township	1 203	1 002
Monroe borough	627	627
Monroe township	1 214	1 004
New Albany borough	336	382
North Towanda township	1 003	801
Orwell township	1 020	783
Overton township	239	155
Pike township	598	503
Ridgebury township	2 102	1 669
Rome borough	426	338
Rome township	938	614
Sayre borough	6 951	7 473
Sheshequin township	1 141	928
Smithfield township	1 536	1 397
South Creek township	1 345	1 114

County Subdivisions	1980	1970
Bradford County—Con.		
South Waverly borough	1 176	1 307
Springfield township	1 121	1 061
Standing Stone township	419	383
Stevens township	412	347
Sylvania borough	236	241
Terry township	823	645
Towanda borough	3 526	4 224
Towanda township	1 269	1 075
Troy borough⁸	1 381	1 315
Troy township⁸	1 666	1 545
Tuscarora township	930	779
Ulster township	1 321	1 201
Warren township	874	748
Wells township	1 080	1 004
West Burlington township	637	588
Wilmot township	995	763
Windham township	800	618
Wyalusing borough	716	723
Wyalusing township	1 192	911
Wysox township	1 796	1 666
Bucks County⁹	479 211	⁷416 728
Bedminster township	3 611	3 252
Bensalem township	52 399	⁷33 042
Bensalem Township (CDP)	52 399	...
Bridgeton township	1 242	1 092
Bristol borough	10 867	12 085
Bristol township	58 733	67 498
Bristol Township (CDP)	58 733	...
Buckingham township	8 839	5 150
Chalfont borough⁹	2 802	2 366
Doylestown borough	8 717	8 270
Doylestown township⁶	11 824	6 613
Dublin borough	1 565	657
Durham township	915	781
East Rockhill township⁹	2 971	2 866
Falls township	36 083	⁷35 850
Falls Township (CDP)	36 083	...
Haycock township	1 750	1 260
Hilltown township	9 326	7 281
Hulmeville borough	1 014	⁷906
Ivyland borough	581	600
Langhorne borough	1 697	⁷1 673
Langhorne Manor borough	1 103	⁷1 081
Lower Makefield township	17 351	14 804
Lower Southampton township	18 305	17 578
Lower Southampton Township (CDP)	18 305	...
Middletown township	34 246	⁷32 364
Milford township	6 053	4 812
Morrisville borough	9 845	11 309
New Britain borough	2 519	2 428
New Britain township⁹	7 415	5 207
New Hope borough	1 473	978
Newtown borough	2 519	2 216
Newtown township	4 527	2 002
Nockamixon township	2 787	2 095
Northampton township⁷	27 392	15 807
Richboro (CDP)	5 141	...
Penndel borough	2 703	⁷2 686
Perkasie borough⁹	5 241	5 451
Plumstead township	5 153	4 682
Quakertown borough	8 867	7 276
Richland township	6 286	4 089
Richlandtown borough	1 180	856
Riegelsville borough	993	1 050
Sellersville borough	3 143	2 829
Silverdale borough	499	545
Solebury township	4 827	3 547
Springfield township	4 817	3 702
Telford borough (pt.)	987	814
Tinicum township	3 533	2 672
Trumbauersville borough	781	831
Tullytown borough	2 277	2 194
Upper Makefield township	4 577	2 905
Upper Southampton township	15 806	13 936
Upper Southampton Township (CDP)	15 806	...
Warminster township	35 543	34 900
Warminster (CDP)	35 543	...
Warrington township	10 704	7 550
Warwick township	2 307	2 138
West Rockhill township	3 776	3 270
Wrightstown township	2 207	2 266
Yardley borough	2 533	2 616
Butler County¹⁰	147 912	127 941
Adams township¹⁰	3 816	3 352
Allegheny township	565	466
Brady township	684	598
Bruin borough	722	673
Buffalo township	6 371	5 595
Butler city	17 026	18 691
Butler township	18 651	17 422
Homeacre–Lyndora (CDP)	8 333	8 415
Meadowood (CDP)	3 320	...
Meridian (CDP)	2 513	2 234
Callery borough	415	416
Center township	6 224	5 606
Cherry township	778	643

County Subdivisions

County Subdivisions	1980	1970
Butler County—Con.		
Cherry Valley borough	91	73
Chicora borough	1 192	1 166
Clay township	2 102	1 612
Clearfield township	2 308	1 445
Clinton township	2 432	2 072
Concord township	1 367	1 071
Connoquenessing borough	539	553
Connoquenessing township	2 840	1 880
Cranberry township	11 066	4 873
Fernway (CDP)	3 843	...
Donegal township	1 540	1 189
East Butler borough	799	919
Eau Claire borough	420	428
Evans City borough[10]	2 299	2 144
Fairview borough	226	235
Fairview township	1 934	1 771
Forward township[10]	2 146	2 070
Franklin township	2 254	1 700
Harmony borough	1 334	1 207
Harrisville borough	1 033	944
Jackson township[10]	2 441	2 444
Jefferson township	3 777	2 903
Karns City borough	354	379
Lancaster township	2 300	1 430
Marion township	1 204	1 035
Mars borough[10]	1 803	1 488
Mercer township	1 103	924
Middlesex township	5 480	4 520
Muddy Creek township	1 832	1 148
Oakland township	2 767	2 548
Parker township	614	650
Penn township	5 219	4 032
Nixon (CDP)	1 196	...
Petrolia borough	472	432
Portersville borough	320	292
Prospect borough	1 016	973
Saxonburg borough	1 336	1 191
Slippery Rock borough	3 047	4 949
Slippery Rock township	4 607	1 959
Summit township	4 628	4 271
Valencia borough	340	351
Venango township	667	573
Washington township	1 287	1 226
West Liberty borough	301	224
West Sunbury borough	203	216
Winfield township	3 278	2 615
Worth township	840	752
Zelienople borough	3 502	3 602
Cambria County[11]	183 263	186 785
Adams township	7 532	5 889
St. Michael–Sidman (CDP) (pt.)	1 255	1 248
Allegheny township	1 607	1 436
Ashville borough	383	409
Barnesboro borough[11]	2 741	2 708
Barr township[11]	2 318	2 371
Blacklick township	2 364	2 029
Brownstown borough	1 077	1 035
Cambria township	7 254	6 441
Colver (CDP)	1 165	1 175
Carrolltown borough	1 395	1 507
Cassandra borough	238	250
Chest township	295	210
Chest Springs borough	198	178
Clearfield township	1 649	1 134
Conemaugh township	2 690	2 402
Cresson borough	2 184	2 446
Cresson township	2 739	2 895
Croyle township	2 550	2 384
St. Michael–Sidman (CDP) (pt.)	190	...
Daisytown borough	421	371
Dale borough	1 906	2 274
Dean township	480	530
East Carroll township[11]	2 089	1 487
East Conemaugh borough	2 128	2 710
East Taylor township	3 276	3 571
Ebensburg borough	4 096	4 318
Ehrenfeld borough	360	397
Elder township	1 272	1 293
Ferndale borough	2 204	2 482
Franklin borough	559	864
Gallitzin borough	2 315	2 496
Gallitzin township	1 250	1 041
Geistown borough	3 304	3 633
Hastings borough[11]	1 574	1 791
Jackson township	5 477	4 343
Johnstown city	35 496	42 476
Lilly borough	1 462	1 429
Lorain borough	989	972
Loretto borough	1 395	1 661
Lower Yoder township	4 026	4 099
Westwood (CDP)	2 448	...
Middle Taylor township	1 019	1 001
Munster township	675	517
Nanty–Glo borough	3 936	4 298
Patton borough[11]	2 441	2 762
Portage borough	3 510	4 151

County Subdivisions

County Subdivisions	1980	1970
Cambria County—Con.		
Portage township	4 507	3 750
Spring Hill (CDP)	1 278	1 323
Reade township	1 895	1 752
Richland township	12 899	10 195
Belmont (CDP) (pt.)	2 296	...
Sankertown borough	804	881
Scalp Level borough	1 186	1 353
South Fork borough	1 401	1 661
Southmont borough	2 683	2 653
Spangler borough[11]	2 399	3 109
Stonycreek township	4 430	4 543
Belmont (CDP) (pt.)	1 146	...
Summerhill borough	725	726
Summerhill township	2 762	2 709
Beaverdale–Lloydell (CDP)	1 187	1 579
Susquehanna township[11]	2 672	1 676
Tunnelhill borough (pt.)	359	508
Upper Yoder township	6 138	6 347
Elim (CDP)	4 669	...
Vintondale borough	697	812
Washington township	901	966
West Carroll township	1 834	1 865
Westmont borough	6 113	6 673
West Taylor township	1 150	1 193
White township	535	336
Wilmore borough	299	386
Cameron County	6 674	7 096
Driftwood borough	163	184
Emporium borough	2 837	3 074
Gibson township	214	209
Grove township	177	216
Lumber township	216	237
Portage township	304	284
Shippen township	2 763	2 892
Carbon County	53 285	50 573
Banks township	1 696	1 760
Tresckow (CDP)	1 128	1 146
Beaver Meadows borough	1 078	1 274
Bowmanstown borough	1 078	864
East Penn township	1 874	1 318
East Side borough	302	152
Franklin township	3 402	3 054
Weissport East (CDP)	1 909	2 027
Jim Thorpe borough	5 263	5 456
Kidder township	946	596
Lansford borough	4 466	5 168
Lausanne township	196	145
Lehigh township	458	577
Lehighton borough	5 826	6 095
Lower Towamensing township	2 669	2 360
Mahoning township	3 853	3 177
Nesquehoning borough	3 346	3 338
Packer township	813	646
Palmerton borough	5 455	5 620
Parryville borough	481	528
Penn Forest township	1 368	423
Summit Hill borough	3 418	3 811
Towamensing township	1 920	1 096
Weatherly borough	2 891	2 554
Weissport borough	486	561
Centre County[12]	112 760	99 267
Bellefonte borough	6 300	6 828
Benner township	3 464	2 479
Pleasant Gap (CDP) (pt.)	39	9
Boggs township	2 246	2 039
Burnside township	471	430
Centre Hall borough	1 233	1 282
College township	6 239	5 834
Lemont (CDP)	2 613	2 547
Curtin township	533	491
Ferguson township	8 105	6 531
Pine Grove Mills (CDP)	1 030	...
Gregg township	1 778	1 638
Haines township	1 217	1 147
Halfmoon township	717	543
Harris township	3 415	3 504
Boalsburg (CDP)	2 295	...
Howard borough	838	751
Howard township	931	732
Huston township	1 222	837
Liberty township	1 618	1 213
Marion township	661	447
Miles township	1 375	1 224
Milesburg borough	1 309	1 196
Millheim borough	800	871
Patton township	7 409	4 394
Penn township	853	749
Philipsburg borough[12]	3 533	3 700
Port Matilda borough	647	680
Potter township	2 643	1 878
Rush township[12]	3 434	3 167
Snow Shoe borough	852	874
Snow Shoe township	1 878	1 710
South Philipsburg borough	523	472
Spring township	5 006	4 929

County Subdivisions

County Subdivisions	1980	1970
Centre County—Con.		
Spring township—Con.		
Pleasant Gap (CDP) (pt.)	1 820	1 764
State College borough	36 130	ʳ32 833
Taylor township	657	499
Union township	1 139	809
Unionville borough	361	375
Walker township	2 655	1 706
Worth township	568	475
Chester County[13]	316 660	ʳ277 746
Atglen borough	669	740
Avondale borough	891	1 025
Birmingham township	1 584	834
Caln township	9 639	6 689
Charlestown township	2 770	3 528
Coatesville city[13]	10 698	12 331
Downingtown borough	7 650	7 437
East Bradford township	3 219	3 260
East Brandywine township	4 690	2 741
East Caln township	2 187	1 739
East Coventry township	4 085	3 284
East Fallowfield township	3 962	3 487
East Goshen township	10 021	5 138
East Marlborough township	3 953	3 031
East Nantmeal township	1 222	858
East Nottingham township	3 111	2 402
East Pikeland township	4 410	4 384
Easttown township	9 064	9 565
Devon–Berwyn (CDP)	5 246	...
East Vincent township	4 739	5 084
East Whiteland township	8 468	7 242
Elk township	750	649
Elverson borough	530	509
Franklin township	1 920	1 043
Highland township	1 244	1 248
Honey Brook borough	1 164	1 115
Honey Brook township	4 128	2 883
Kennett township	4 201	3 394
Kennett Square borough	4 715	4 876
London Britain township	1 546	963
Londonderry township	1 293	920
London Grove township	3 531	3 109
Lower Oxford township	2 836	ʳ2 804
Malvern borough	2 999	2 583
Modena borough	672	867
New Garden township	4 790	4 153
Toughkenamon (CDP)	1 111	1 233
Newlin township	725	1 464
New London township	1 312	938
North Coventry township	7 164	6 690
Kenilworth (CDP)	1 686	1 598
South Pottstown (CDP)	2 120	2 734
Oxford borough	3 633	3 658
Parkesburg borough[13]	2 578	2 701
Penn township	1 888	989
Pennsbury township	2 604	1 763
Phoenixville borough	14 165	14 823
Pocopson township	2 331	1 556
Sadsbury township[13]	2 398	2 103
Schuylkill township	5 993	5 779
South Coatesville borough	1 359	1 583
South Coventry township	1 556	1 518
Spring City borough	3 389	3 578
Thornbury township	1 323	ʳ803
Tredyffrin township	23 019	ʳ23 404
Paoli (CDP) (pt.)	2 253	1 908
Upper Oxford township	1 332	ʳ1 136
Upper Uwchlan township	1 805	996
Uwchlan township	8 364	5 473
Valley township[13]	3 598	3 791
Wallace township	1 881	1 347
Warwick township	2 350	1 667
West Bradford township	7 343	2 996
West Brandywine township	4 068	2 713
West Caln township	4 958	3 152
West Chester borough	17 435	19 301
West Fallowfield township	2 122	1 694
West Goshen township	16 164	12 858
West Goshen (CDP)	7 998	...
West Grove borough	1 820	1 870
West Marlborough township	941	917
West Nantmeal township	1 766	1 285
West Nottingham township	2 030	1 440
West Pikeland township	1 536	1 420
West Sadsbury township	1 728	1 189
Westtown township	6 774	5 069
West Vincent township	1 992	1 890
West Whiteland township	9 581	7 149
Exton (CDP)	1 853	...
Willistown township	8 284	9 128
Paoli (CDP) (pt.)	3 024	3 927
Clarion County[14]	43 362	38 414
Ashland township	1 048	872
Beaver township[14]	1 900	1 424
Brady township	94	92
Callensburg borough	248	249
Clarion borough	6 664	6 095

County Subdivisions

County Subdivisions	1980	1970
Clarion County—Con.		
Clarion township	2 847	2 287
East Brady borough	1 153	1 218
Elk township	1 615	1 295
Emlenton borough (pt.)[14]	13	...
Farmington township	1 914	1 500
Foxburg borough	289	353
Hawthorn borough[14]	547	552
Highland township	551	461
Knox borough[14]	1 364	1 306
Knox township	1 244	1 117
Licking township	585	546
Limestone township	1 558	1 179
Madison township	1 524	1 453
Millcreek township	371	297
Monroe township	1 247	1 129
New Bethlehem borough	1 441	1 406
Paint township	1 681	1 215
Perry township	1 295	1 209
Piney township	479	465
Porter township	1 657	1 436
Redbank township	1 735	1 533
Richland township[14]	541	553
Rimersburg borough	1 096	1 146
St. Petersburg borough	452	416
Salem township	906	768
Shippenville borough	558	602
Sligo borough	798	825
Strattanville borough	555	559
Toby township	1 314	1 206
Washington township	2 078	1 650
Clearfield County[15]	83 578	74 619
Beccaria township	2 102	1 877
Bell township	889	601
Bigler township	1 604	1 474
Bloom township	500	440
Boggs township	1 924	1 454
Bradford township	3 374	2 828
Brady township	1 998	1 707
Brisbin borough	387	364
Burnside borough	347	316
Burnside township	1 246	1 020
Chest township	611	469
Chester Hill borough	1 054	868
Clearfield borough	7 580	8 176
Coalport borough	739	796
Cooper township	2 819	2 585
Covington township	669	533
Curwensville borough	3 116	3 189
Decatur township	3 395	2 763
Du Bois city	9 290	10 112
Falls Creek borough (pt.)	50	70
Ferguson township	411	356
Girard township	691	588
Glen Hope borough	206	163
Goshen township	492	200
Graham township	1 211	753
Grampian borough	464	511
Greenwood township	424	737
Gulich township	1 291	1 249
Houtzdale borough	1 222	1 193
Huston township	1 390	1 268
Irvona borough	644	714
Jordan township	580	509
Karthaus township	631	774
Knox township	784	601
Lawrence township	8 563	6 094
Hyde (CDP)	1 791	1 264
Plymptonville (CDP)	1 225	1 040
Lumber City borough	117	57
Mahaffey borough	513	482
Morris township	3 006	2 915
Newburg borough	132	151
New Washington borough	103	58
Osceola Mills borough[15]	1 466	1 671
Penn township	1 378	897
Pike township	2 195	1 720
Pine township	29	34
Ramey borough	568	542
Sandy township	7 600	5 360
Sandy (CDP)	1 835	2 000
Troutville borough	204	190
Union township	807	543
Wallaceton borough	393	377
Westover borough	517	501
Woodward township	1 852	1 769
Clinton County	38 971	37 721
Allison township	237	270
Avis borough	1 718	1 749
Bald Eagle township	1 680	1 282
Beech Creek borough	760	639
Beech Creek township	951	704
Castanea township	1 204	1 279
Castanea (CDP)	1 148	...
Chapman township	1 240	981
Colebrook township	244	104
Crawford township	682	582

County Subdivisions	1980	1970
Clinton County—Con.		
Dunnstable township	982	839
East Keating township	33	28
Flemington borough	1 416	1 519
Gallagher township	194	175
Greene township	1 002	753
Grugan township	46	19
Lamar township	2 384	1 807
Leidy township	263	305
Lock Haven city	9 617	11 427
Logan township	737	636
Loganton borough	474	436
Mill Hall borough	1 744	1 838
Noyes township	631	522
Pine Creek township	3 100	2 272
Porter township	1 492	1 185
Renovo borough	1 812	2 620
South Renovo borough	663	662
Wayne township	728	602
West Keating township	43	59
Woodward township	2 894	2 427
Dunnstown (CDP)	1 486	...
Columbia County	61 967	55 114
Ashland borough (pt.)	9	–
Beaver township	718	693
Benton borough	981	1 027
Benton township	1 109	822
Berwick borough	11 850	12 274
Bloomsburg town	11 717	11 652
Briar Creek borough	637	456
Briar Creek township	3 088	2 150
Catawissa borough	1 568	1 701
Catawissa township	914	648
Centralia borough	1 017	1 165
Cleveland township	912	796
Conyngham township	1 195	1 137
Fishing Creek township	1 287	884
Franklin township	541	427
Greenwood township	1 885	1 368
Hemlock township	1 579	1 506
Jackson township	459	322
Locust township	1 152	1 046
Madison township	1 373	976
Main township	1 096	658
Mifflin township	2 192	1 781
Mifflinville (CDP)	1 341	1 074
Millville borough	975	896
Montour township	1 580	1 224
Mount Pleasant township	1 276	672
North Centre township	1 523	790
Orange township	730	453
Orangeville borough	507	431
Pine township	955	631
Roaring Creek township	469	364
Scott township	3 951	3 875
Almedia (CDP) (pt.)	711	945
Espy (CDP)	1 571	1 652
South Centre township	1 907	1 600
Almedia (CDP) (pt.)	480	212
Stillwater borough	201	208
Sugarloaf township	614	481
Crawford County[16]	88 869	81 342
Athens township	696	696
Beaver township	827	775
Bloomfield township	1 714	1 378
Blooming Valley borough	374	358
Cambridge township	1 389	1 654
Cambridge Springs borough	2 102	1 998
Centerville borough	245	246
Cochranton borough	1 240	1 229
Conneaut township	1 388	1 322
Conneaut Lake borough	767	745
Conneautville borough	971	1 032
Cussewago township	1 279	1 072
East Fairfield township	932	872
East Fallowfield township	1 259	1 130
East Mead township	1 553	1 264
Fairfield township	1 099	878
Greenwood township	1 499	1 257
Hayfield township	2 969	2 162
Hydetown borough	760	725
Linesville borough	1 198	1 265
Meadville city[16]	15 544	16 573
North Shenango township	816	621
Oil Creek township[16]	2 035	1 743
Pine township	435	392
Randolph township	1 589	1 437
Richmond township	1 228	1 023
Rockdale township	1 060	820
Rome township	1 304	1 020
Sadsbury township	2 702	2 221
Saegertown borough	942	1 348
South Shenango township	1 479	1 132
Sparta township	1 405	988
Spartansburg borough	403	464
Spring township	1 500	1 287
Springboro borough	557	584

County Subdivisions	1980	1970
Crawford County—Con.		
Steuben township	819	680
Summerhill township	1 196	963
Summit township	1 992	1 517
Titusville city[16]	6 884	7 331
Townville borough	364	349
Troy township	1 276	1 097
Union township	884	690
Venango borough	298	275
Venango township	693	528
Vernon township	6 348	5 264
Fredericksburg (CDP)	1 202	1 073
Wayne township	1 335	985
West Fallowfield township	650	647
West Mead township[16]	5 590	4 652
West Shenango township	474	424
Woodcock borough	126	108
Woodcock township	2 680	2 121
Cumberland County[17]	178 541	158 177
Camp Hill borough	8 422	9 931
Carlisle borough[17]	18 314	18 079
Cooke township	197	71
Dickinson township	3 037	2 416
East Pennsboro township	13 955	12 440
Hampden township	16 648	11 847
Hopewell township	1 411	1 026
Lemoyne borough	4 178	4 625
Lower Allen township	14 077	13 690
Lower Frankford township	1 261	813
Lower Mifflin township	1 122	746
Mechanicsburg borough	9 487	9 385
Middlesex township	4 506	2 857
Monroe township	4 836	3 326
Mount Holly Springs borough	2 068	2 009
Newburg borough	303	323
New Cumberland borough	8 051	9 803
Newville borough	1 370	1 631
North Middleton township	9 785	6 572
Carlisle Barracks (CDP)	1 032	4 358
North Newton township	1 697	1 365
Penn township	1 944	1 441
Shippensburg borough (pt.)	4 376	5 172
Shippensburg township	4 136	3 198
Shiremanstown borough	1 719	1 773
Silver Spring township	7 148	6 324
Southampton township	3 004	2 451
South Middleton township[17]	8 941	7 521
Boiling Springs (CDP)	2 323	1 521
South Newton township	972	874
Upper Allen township	10 533	7 325
Upper Frankford township	1 552	991
Upper Mifflin township	964	638
West Fairview borough	1 426	1 388
West Pennsboro township	4 329	2 937
Wormleysburg borough	2 772	3 192
Dauphin County[18]	232 317	223 713
Berrysburg borough	447	443
Conewago township	2 471	1 124
Dauphin borough	901	998
Derry township	18 115	15 452
Hershey (CDP)	13 249	6 410
East Hanover township	3 574	2 938
Elizabethville borough[18]	1 531	1 629
Gratz borough	678	675
Halifax borough	909	907
Halifax township	2 943	2 038
Harrisburg city	53 264	68 061
Highspire borough	2 959	2 947
Hummelstown borough	4 267	4 723
Jackson township	1 568	1 156
Jefferson township	340	164
Londonderry township	5 138	3 453
Lower Paxton township	34 830	26 517
Lower Swatara township	6 772	5 267
Lykens borough	2 181	2 506
Lykens township	1 138	997
Middle Paxton township	4 745	3 362
Middletown borough	10 122	9 080
Mifflin township	553	475
Millersburg borough[18]	2 770	3 074
Paxtang borough	1 649	2 039
Penbrook borough	3 006	3 379
Pillow borough	359	332
Reed township	289	259
Royalton borough	981	1 040
Rush township	212	160
South Hanover township	4 046	2 689
Steelton borough	6 484	8 556
Susquehanna township	18 034	17 008
Swatara township	18 796	17 178
Swatara Township (CDP)	18 796	...
Upper Paxton borough[18]	3 435	2 718
Washington township[18]	1 734	1 114
Wayne township	698	513
West Hanover township	6 115	4 407
Skyline View (CDP)	2 218	1 996
Wiconisco township	1 566	1 471

County Subdivisions	1980	1970
Dauphin County—Con.		
Wiconisco township—Con.		
Wiconisco (CDP)	1 321	1 236
Williams township	1 033	945
Williamstown borough	1 664	1 919
Delaware County[19]	555 007	[r]603 456
Aldan borough	4 671	5 001
Aston township	14 530	13 704
Aston Township (CDP)	14 530	...
Bethel township	2 438	2 034
Birmingham township	2 057	1 281
Brookhaven borough	7 912	7 370
Chester city	45 794	56 331
Chester township	5 687	5 708
Chester Township (CDP)	5 687	...
Chester Heights borough	1 302	[r]597
Clifton Heights borough	7 320	8 348
Collingdale borough	9 539	10 605
Colwyn borough	2 851	3 169
Concord township	6 437	4 592
Darby borough	11 513	13 729
Darby township	12 264	[r]13 603
Darby Township (CDP)	12 264	...
East Lansdowne borough	2 806	3 186
Eddystone borough	2 555	2 706
Edgmont township[19]	1 410	1 368
Folcroft borough	8 231	9 610
Glenolden borough	7 633	8 697
Haverford township	52 349	[r]56 873
Haverford Township (CDP)	52 349	...
Lansdowne borough	11 891	14 090
Lower Chichester township	3 784	4 009
Lower Chichester Township (CDP)	3 784	...
Marcus Hook borough	2 638	3 041
Marple township	23 642	25 040
Marple Township (CDP)	23 642	...
Media borough	6 119	6 444
Middletown township	12 463	12 878
Middletown Township (CDP)	12 463	...
Millbourne borough	652	637
Morton borough	2 412	2 602
Nether Providence township	12 730	[r]13 589
Nether Providence Township (CDP)	12 730	...
Newtown township	11 775	11 081
Norwood borough	6 647	7 229
Parkside borough	2 464	2 343
Prospect Park borough	6 593	7 250
Radnor township	27 676	[r]28 782
Radnor Township (CDP)	27 676	...
Ridley township	33 771	39 085
Ridley Township (CDP)	33 771	...
Ridley Park borough	7 889	9 025
Rose Valley borough	1 038	[r]876
Rutledge borough	934	1 167
Sharon Hill borough	6 221	7 464
Springfield township	25 326	29 006
Springfield (CDP)	25 326	...
Swarthmore borough	5 950	6 156
Thornbury township	3 653	[r]3 284
Tinicum township	4 291	4 906
Tinicum Township (CDP)	4 291	...
Trainer borough	2 056	2 336
Upland borough	3 458	3 930
Upper Chichester township	14 377	11 414
Upper Chichester Township (CDP)	14 377	...
Upper Darby township	84 054	95 910
Upper Darby (CDP)	84 054	...
Upper Providence township	9 477	9 234
Upper Providence Township (CDP)	9 477	...
Yeadon borough	11 727	12 136
Elk County	38 338	37 770
Benezette township	310	353
Benzinger township	8 808	7 755
Grandview Park (CDP)	2 471	...
Fox township	3 723	3 210
Highland township	672	639
Horton township	1 577	1 318
Jay township	2 166	2 115
Johnsonburg borough	3 938	4 304
Jones township	1 959	1 636
Millstone township	121	135
Ridgway borough	5 604	6 022
Ridgway township	2 777	2 578
St. Marys borough	6 417	7 470
Spring Creek township	266	235
Erie County[20]	279 780	263 654
Albion borough	1 818	1 768
Amity township	1 098	792
Concord township	1 434	1 213
Conneaut township	1 893	1 832
Corry city[20]	7 149	7 435
Cranesville borough	703	705
Edinboro borough[20]	6 324	4 871
Elgin borough	235	173
Elk Creek township	1 775	1 389
Erie city[20]	119 123	[r]129 265
Fairview borough	1 855	1 707

County Subdivisions	1980	1970
Erie County—Con.		
Fairview township	7 518	6 256
Avonia (CDP)	1 365	...
Franklin township	1 301	804
Girard borough	2 615	2 613
Girard township	4 306	3 074
Greene township	5 238	4 019
Greenfield township	1 677	1 346
Harborcreek township	14 644	12 038
Northwest Harborcreek (CDP)	7 485	...
Lake City borough	2 384	2 117
Lawrence Park township	4 584	4 517
Lawrence Park (CDP)	4 584	...
Le Boeuf township	1 500	1 043
McKean borough[20]	465	462
McKean township	4 047	2 600
Millcreek township	44 303	36 946
Mill Village borough	427	372
North East borough	4 568	3 846
North East township	5 750	4 465
Platea borough	492	354
Springfield township[20]	3 395	2 446
Summit township	5 381	4 237
Union township	1 779	[r]1 475
Union City borough	3 623	[r]3 638
Venango township	2 089	1 542
Washington township[20]	3 567	2 118
Waterford borough	1 568	1 468
Waterford township	2 874	2 119
Wattsburg borough	513	453
Wayne township[20]	1 767	1 623
Wesleyville borough	3 998	3 920
Fayette County[21]	159 417	154 667
Belle Vernon borough	1 489	1 496
Brownsville borough	4 043	4 856
Brownsville township	936	875
Bullskin township	7 008	4 923
Connellsville city[21]	10 319	11 643
Connellsville township[21]	2 761	2 554
North Connellsville (CDP)	1 282	1 226
Dawson borough	661	676
Dunbar borough	1 369	1 499
Dunbar township	7 605	7 366
Everson borough	1 032	1 143
Fairchance borough[21]	2 106	1 906
Fayette City borough	788	968
Franklin township	2 756	2 368
Georges township[21]	7 138	6 224
German township	5 900	6 808
New Salem–Buffington (CDP) (pt.)	177	...
Henry Clay township	1 663	1 420
Jefferson township	2 265	2 095
Lower Tyrone township	1 089	939
Luzerne township	5 549	[r]5 689
Hiller (CDP)	1 577	1 688
Republic–Merrittstown (CDP) (pt.)	199	...
Markleysburg borough	356	367
Masontown borough	4 909	4 226
Menallen township	5 201	4 508
New Salem–Buffington (CDP) (pt.)	1 451	1 337
Newell borough	629	650
Nicholson township	2 143	1 754
North Union township	15 340	13 561
East Uniontown (CDP) (pt.)	2 492	2 333
Hopwood (CDP) (pt.)	897	881
Oliver (CDP)	3 777	3 091
Ohiopyle borough	124	140
Perry township	3 119	2 651
Perryopolis borough	2 139	2 043
Point Marion borough	1 642	1 750
Redstone township	7 681	8 010
Republic–Merrittstown (CDP) (pt.)	2 021	2 194
Saltlick township	3 241	2 776
Seven Springs borough (pt.)	—	—
Smithfield borough	1 084	969
South Connellsville borough	2 296	2 385
South Union township	10 992	10 370
East Uniontown (CDP) (pt.)	382	...
Hopwood (CDP) (pt.)	1 523	1 309
Leith–Hatfield (CDP)	2 297	2 668
South Uniontown (CDP)	3 713	3 546
Springfield township	2 865	2 465
Springhill township	2 906	2 629
Stewart township	787	704
Uniontown city	14 510	16 282
Upper Tyrone township	1 913	2 122
Vanderbilt borough	689	755
Washington township	5 069	5 535
Fairhope–Arnold City (CDP)	2 736	3 239
Lynnwood–Pricedale (CDP) (pt.)	1 178	1 199
Wharton township	3 305	2 567
Forest County	5 072	4 926
Barnett township	333	355
Green township	400	262
Harmony township	575	631
Hickory township	560	646
Howe township	302	233
Jenks township	1 375	1 389

County Subdivisions

	1980	1970
Forest County—Con.		
Kingsley township	252	272
Tionesta borough	659	711
Tionesta township	616	427
Franklin County[22]	113 629	100 833
Antrim township[22]	9 326	7 378
State Line (CDP)	1 253	...
Chambersburg borough	16 174	17 315
Fannett township	2 016	1 640
Greencastle borough[22]	3 679	3 293
Greene township	11 470	9 504
Fayetteville (CDP) (pt.)	1 565	1 220
Guilford (CDP) (pt.)	92	...
Guilford township	10 567	9 291
Fayetteville (CDP) (pt.)	1 637	1 229
Guilford (CDP) (pt.)	1 540	...
Hamilton township	6 504	4 921
Letterkenny township	1 960	1 419
Lurgan township	1 986	1 649
Mercersburg borough	1 617	1 727
Metal township	1 576	1 205
Mont Alto borough	1 592	1 532
Montgomery township	4 252	3 221
Orrstown borough	247	262
Peters township	4 060	3 838
Quincy township	5 792	5 264
St. Thomas township	5 711	3 931
Shippensburg borough (pt.)	885	1 364
Southampton township	4 604	3 292
Warren township	269	262
Washington township[22]	9 616	8 514
Rouzerville (CDP)	1 371	1 419
Wayne Heights (CDP)	1 384	1 005
Waynesboro borough[22]	9 726	10 011
Fulton County	12 842	10 776
Ayr township	1 833	1 473
Belfast township	1 151	1 008
Bethel township	1 292	968
Brush Creek township	556	524
Dublin township	1 140	913
Licking Creek township	1 231	991
McConnellsburg borough	1 178	1 228
Taylor township	1 148	1 021
Thompson township	913	772
Todd township	1 281	929
Union township	571	438
Wells township	548	511
Greene County[23]	40 476	36 090
Aleppo township	721	659
Carmichaels borough	630	608
Center township	1 354	1 132
Clarksville borough	251	269
Cumberland township	7 053	6 204
Fairdale (CDP)	2 046	1 621
Nemacolin (CDP)	1 235	1 273
Dunkard township	2 647	2 491
Bobtown (CDP)	1 008	1 055
Franklin township[23]	4 901	4 039
Morrisville (CDP)	1 518	1 232
Freeport township	405	278
Gilmore township	356	306
Gray township	232	231
Greene township	508	428
Greensboro borough	377	439
Jackson township	539	411
Jefferson borough	413	366
Jefferson township	2 671	2 207
Monongahela township	1 920	1 852
Morgan township[23]	2 955	2 580
Morris township	870	700
Perry township	1 734	1 059
Rices Landing borough	516	473
Richhill township	1 183	1 070
Springhill township	504	439
Washington township	1 035	756
Wayne township	1 493	1 318
Waynesburg borough	4 482	5 152
Whiteley township	726	623
Huntingdon County[24]	42 253	39 108
Alexandria borough	435	495
Barree township	331	277
Birmingham borough	121	115
Brady township	967	763
Broad Top City borough	340	283
Carbon township	458	374
Cass township	892	619
Cassville borough	183	205
Clay township	903	765
Coalmont borough	128	129
Cromwell township	1 221	995
Dublin township	1 017	788
Dudley borough	282	232
Franklin township	464	457
Henderson township	854	650
Hopewell township	560	495
Huntingdon borough[24]	7 042	6 987

County Subdivisions

	1980	1970
Huntingdon County—Con.		
Jackson township	743	691
Juniata township	411	367
Lincoln township	340	406
Logan township	678	472
Mapleton borough	591	661
Marklesburg borough	188	232
Mill Creek borough	367	421
Miller township	404	285
Morris township	342	282
Mount Union borough	3 101	3 662
Oneida township[24]	1 085	1 283
Orbisonia borough	506	554
Penn township	933	719
Petersburg borough	543	555
Porter township	1 778	1 222
Rockhill Furnace borough[24]	472	480
Saltillo borough	373	341
Shade Gap borough	141	186
Shirley township	2 387	2 069
Shirleysburg borough	147	238
Smithfield township	2 495	2 488
Springfield township	498	340
Spruce Creek township	366	348
Tell township	604	571
Three Springs borough	501	495
Todd township	870	629
Union township	1 065	859
Walker township	1 390	1 212
Warriors Mark township	1 377	1 135
West township	519	439
Wood township	840	837
Indiana County[25]	92 281	79 451
Armagh borough	133	165
Armstrong township	2 786	1 867
Banks township	1 084	979
Black Lick township	1 164	917
Blairsville borough	4 166	4 411
Brush Valley township	1 815	1 343
Buffington township	1 261	909
Burrell township	4 152	3 672
Black Lick (CDP)	1 313	1 074
Canoe township	1 788	1 545
Center township	5 475	5 255
Lucerne Mines (CDP)	1 195	1 380
Cherryhill township	2 540	1 747
Cherry Tree borough	520	485
Clymer borough	1 761	2 054
Conemaugh township	2 559	2 357
Creekside borough	383	425
East Mahoning township	977	723
East Wheatfield township	2 844	2 419
Ernest borough[25]	584	...
Glen Campbell borough	352	408
Grant township	770	637
Green township	4 338	3 480
Homer City borough	2 248	2 465
Indiana borough	16 051	16 100
Jacksonville borough	121	141
Marion Center borough	494	446
Montgomery township	1 813	1 518
North Mahoning township	1 174	917
Pine township	2 152	1 984
Plumville borough	431	429
Rayne township[25]	3 207	2 782
Saltsburg borough	964	1 037
Shelocta borough	139	121
Smicksburg borough	82	79
South Mahoning township	1 608	1 128
Washington township	1 602	1 224
West Mahoning township	824	539
West Wheatfield township	2 699	2 165
White township	13 177	8 769
Chevy Chase Heights (CDP)	1 824	1 185
Young township	2 043	1 809
Jefferson County	48 303	43 695
Barnett township	262	201
Beaver township	524	526
Bell township	2 144	1 686
Big Run borough	822	826
Brockway borough	2 376	2 529
Brookville borough	4 568	4 314
Clover township	500	448
Corsica borough	381	374
Eldred township	1 111	1 056
Falls Creek borough (pt.)	1 158	1 185
Gaskill township	671	451
Heath township	138	69
Henderson township	1 287	1 006
Knox township	1 072	843
McCalmont township	1 089	978
Oliver township	1 199	955
Perry township	1 257	1 024
Pine Creek township	1 407	1 181
Polk township	216	183
Porter township	313	280

Population of County Subdivisions

County Subdivisions	1980	1970
Jefferson County—Con.		
Punxsutawney borough	7 479	7 792
Reynoldsville borough	3 016	2 771
Ringgold township	883	735
Rose township	1 157	975
Snyder township	2 626	2 280
Summerville borough	830	859
Sykesville borough	1 537	1 311
Timblin borough	197	218
Union township	721	621
Warsaw township	1 169	1 004
Washington township	1 943	1 548
Winslow township	2 586	1 996
Worthville borough	87	100
Young township	1 577	1 370
Juniata County	19 188	16 712
Beale township	578	549
Delaware township	1 408	1 082
Fayette township	2 679	2 165
Fermanagh township	2 097	1 855
Greenwood township	486	387
Lack township	616	650
Mifflin borough	648	640
Mifflintown borough	783	828
Milford township	1 452	1 160
Monroe township	1 651	1 425
Port Royal borough	835	829
Spruce Hill township	618	572
Susquehanna township	823	569
Thompsontown borough	593	677
Turbett township	793	678
Tuscarora township	1 004	879
Walker township	2 124	1 767
Lackawanna County[26]	227 908	[r]234 504
Abington township	1 487	1 316
Archbald borough	6 295	6 118
Benton township	1 670	1 141
Blakely borough	7 438	6 391
Carbondale city	11 255	[r]12 478
Carbondale township	1 032	[r]974
Clarks Green borough	1 862	1 674
Clarks Summit borough	5 272	5 376
Clifton township	855	526
Covington township	1 858	1 460
Dalton borough	1 383	1 282
Dickson City borough	6 699	7 698
Dunmore borough	16 781	[r]18 168
Elmhurst township	953	799
Fell township	2 817	[r]2 953
Glenburn township	1 257	1 113
Greenfield township	1 524	1 140
Jefferson township	3 132	1 809
Jermyn borough	2 411	2 435
Jessup borough	4 974	4 948
La Plume township	1 001	971
Lehigh township	326	167
Madison township	1 659	993
Mayfield borough	1 812	2 176
Moosic borough	6 068	[r]4 646
Moscow borough[26]	1 536	1 430
Newton township	2 521	[r]2 326
North Abington township	619	553
Old Forge borough	9 304	9 522
Olyphant borough	5 204	5 422
Ransom township	1 506	1 196
Roaring Brook township[26]	1 895	1 385
Scott township	4 624	3 803
Scranton city	88 117	[r]102 696
South Abington township	6 353	[r]3 616
Spring Brook township	2 144	1 577
Taylor borough	7 246	6 977
Throop borough	4 166	4 307
Vandling borough	557	633
West Abington township	295	309
Lancaster County[27]	362 346	[r]320 079
Adamstown borough (pt.)	1 107	1 198
Akron borough[27]	3 471	3 149
Bart township	2 235	1 838
Brecknock township	4 088	3 478
Caernarvon township	3 392	2 323
Christiana borough	1 183	1 132
Clay township	3 718	2 832
Colerain township	2 118	1 641
Columbia borough[27]	10 466	11 237
Conestoga township	3 032	2 447
Conoy township	2 309	1 977
Denver borough[27]	2 018	2 248
Drumore township	1 682	1 253
Earl township[27]	5 125	4 430
East Cocalico township	6 354	4 993
Reamstown (CDP)	1 308	1 050
East Donegal township[27]	4 063	3 003
Maytown (CDP)	1 479	...
East Drumore township	2 496	1 716
East Earl township	4 872	4 721
East Hempfield township	15 152	11 739

County Subdivisions	1980	1970
Lancaster County—Con.		
East Lampeter township	9 760	[r]8 876
East Petersburg borough	3 600	3 407
Eden township	1 498	986
Elizabeth township	2 379	1 828
Elizabethtown borough[27]	8 233	8 072
Ephrata borough[27]	11 095	9 662
Ephrata township[27]	4 789	3 532
Fulton township	2 229	1 793
Lancaster city	54 725	57 690
Lancaster township	10 833	10 329
Leacock township	4 119	3 678
Lititz borough[27]	7 590	7 072
Little Britain township	2 131	1 633
Manheim borough	5 015	5 434
Manheim township	26 042	21 539
Manor township[27]	11 474	9 769
Marietta borough[27]	2 740	2 838
Martic township	3 286	2 419
Millersville borough	7 668	6 396
Mount Joy borough[27]	5 680	5 041
Mount Joy township[27]	5 128	4 228
Rheems (CDP) (pt.)	162	...
Mountville borough[27]	1 505	1 454
New Holland borough[27]	4 147	3 971
Paradise township	4 084	3 751
Paradise (CDP)	1 107	...
Penn township	5 865	3 801
Pequea township	3 557	3 002
Providence township	4 781	2 842
Quarryville borough	1 558	1 571
Rapho township[27]	7 157	5 121
Sadsbury township	2 048	1 495
Salisbury township	7 126	5 294
Strasburg borough[27]	1 999	1 897
Strasburg township[27]	3 188	2 550
Terre Hill borough	1 217	1 129
Upper Leacock township	6 569	6 459
Warwick township[27]	8 213	6 562
Rothsville (CDP)	1 263	1 318
West Cocalico township[27]	4 948	4 247
West Donegal township	4 862	3 719
Rheems (CDP) (pt.)	1 105	...
West Earl township[27]	5 552	4 375
West Hempfield township[27]	8 239	[r]6 505
West Lampeter township	6 836	[r]6 332
Lawrence County[28]	107 150	107 374
Bessemer borough	1 293	1 427
Ellport borough	1 290	1 350
Ellwood City borough (pt.)	9 203	9 754
Enon Valley borough	408	427
Hickory township	2 456	2 236
Little Beaver township	1 060	784
Mahoning township	3 686	3 646
Neshannock township	8 662	7 982
Coaltown (CDP)	1 265	...
New Castle Northwest (CDP)	1 685	1 974
New Beaver borough	1 885	1 426
New Castle city	33 621	38 559
New Wilmington borough	2 774	2 721
North Beaver township[28]	4 367	3 475
Perry township	2 057	1 841
Plain Grove township	754	693
Pulaski township	4 189	3 187
Scott township	1 821	1 410
Shenango township	7 937	7 798
Slippery Rock township	3 234	2 541
S. N. P. J. borough[28]	16	...
South New Castle borough	879	940
Taylor township	1 519	1 152
West Pittsburg (CDP)	1 133	...
Union township	6 544	6 873
Oakland (CDP)	1 935	2 135
Oakwood (CDP)	3 090	3 094
Volant borough	203	226
Wampum borough	851	1 189
Washington township	750	547
Wayne township	3 130	3 130
Wilmington township	2 561	2 060
Lebanon County[29]	108 582	99 665
Annville township	4 493	4 704
Annville (CDP)	4 493	4 704
Bethel township	4 042	2 804
Cleona borough	2 003	2 040
Cold Spring township	89	117
Cornwall borough	2 653	2 111
East Hanover township	2 952	2 127
Heidelberg township	3 583	2 833
Jackson township	5 028	3 388
Jonestown borough	814	954
Lebanon city[29]	25 711	28 572
Millcreek township	2 564	2 544
Newmanstown (CDP)	1 417	1 532
Mount Gretna borough	280	153
Myerstown borough	3 131	3 645
North Annville township	2 421	2 180
North Cornwall township[29]	4 401	3 343

County Subdivisions	1980	1970
Lebanon County—Con.		
North Cornwall township—Con.		
Pleasant Hill (CDP) (pt.)	1 099	1 071
North Lebanon township	8 343	6 146
Avon (CDP) (pt.)	240	234
Pleasant Hill (CDP) (pt.)	17	...
Sand Hill (CDP)	1 837	...
North Londonderry township	4 749	2 752
Palmyra borough	7 228	7 615
Richland borough	1 470	1 444
South Annville township	2 792	1 403
South Lebanon township[29]	7 431	7 706
Avon (CDP) (pt.)	1 119	1 037
Lebanon South (CDP)	1 865	3 457
South Londonderry township	3 777	3 754
Campbelltown (CDP)	1 250	1 355
Swatara township	3 443	2 407
Union township	2 700	2 661
West Cornwall township	1 597	1 276
West Lebanon township	887	986
Lehigh County[30]	272 349	255 304
Alburtis borough	1 428	1 142
Allentown city	103 758	109 871
Bethlehem city (pt.)	19 865	20 621
Catasauqua borough	6 711	5 702
Coopersburg borough	2 595	2 326
Coplay borough	3 130	3 642
Emmaus borough[30]	11 001	11 511
Fountain Hill borough	4 805	5 384
Hanover township	2 223	1 217
Hanover Township (CDP)	2 223	...
Heidelberg township[30]	2 691	1 532
Lower Macungie township[30]	12 958	8 814
Lower Milford township	2 865	2 189
Lowhill township[30]	1 356	1 002
Lynn township[30]	2 733	2 047
Macungie borough	1 899	1 414
North Whitehall township[30]	8 820	6 819
Salisbury township	12 259	11 285
Slatington borough	4 277	4 687
South Whitehall township	15 919	13 971
Upper Macungie township[30]	7 446	4 390
Upper Milford township	5 013	3 992
Upper Saucon township	9 635	7 954
Washington township[30]	5 152	3 732
Weisenberg township[30]	2 272	1 737
Whitehall township	21 538	18 323
Fullerton (CDP)	8 055	7 908
Luzerne County[31]	343 079	341 956
Ashley borough	3 512	4 095
Avoca borough	3 536	3 543
Bear Creek township[31]	3 076	1 883
Black Creek township	1 927	1 745
Buck township	397	294
Butler township	5 537	3 762
Conyngham borough	2 242	1 850
Conyngham township	1 663	1 693
Courtdale borough	844	1 027
Dallas borough	2 679	2 398
Dallas township	7 287	5 747
Dennison township[31]	753	726
Dorrance township	1 829	1 209
Dupont borough	3 460	3 431
Duryea borough	5 415	5 264
Edwardsville borough	5 729	5 633
Exeter borough	5 493	4 670
Exeter township	2 355	1 869
Fairmount township	1 167	825
Fairview township	2 908	2 658
Forty Fort borough	5 590	6 114
Foster township	3 258	3 525
Woodside–Drifton (CDP) (pt.)	1 442	1 191
Franklin township	1 473	1 145
Freeland borough	4 285	4 784
Hanover township	12 601	12 102
Harveys Lake borough	2 318	1 693
Hazle township	9 495	7 619
Woodside–Drifton (CDP) (pt.)	344	104
Hazleton city	27 318	30 426
Hollenback township	1 006	663
Hughestown borough	1 783	1 407
Hunlock township	2 419	1 744
Huntington township	1 943	1 518
Jackson township	2 941	1 956
Jeddo borough	128	177
Jenkins township	4 508	3 252
Kingston borough	15 681	18 325
Kingston township[31]	6 535	6 196
Laflin borough	1 650	399
Lake township	1 783	1 332
Larksville borough	4 410	3 937
Laurel Run borough	725	327
Lehman township	3 030	2 219
Luzerne borough	3 703	4 504
Nanticoke city	13 044	14 638
Nescopeck borough	1 768	1 897
Nescopeck township	833	708

County Subdivisions	1980	1970
Luzerne County—Con.		
New Columbus borough	214	149
Newport township	4 989	6 002
Glen Lyon (CDP)	2 352	3 408
Nuangola borough	726	464
Penn Lake Park borough[31]	217	...
Pittston city	9 930	11 113
Pittston township	3 611	3 191
Plains township	11 338	11 481
Plains (CDP)	5 455	6 606
Plymouth borough	7 605	9 536
Plymouth township	2 437	2 614
Pringle borough	1 221	1 155
Rice township	1 935	941
Ross township	2 323	1 592
Salem township	4 627	3 890
East Berwick (CDP)	2 324	2 090
Shickshinny borough	1 192	1 685
Slocum township	1 015	858
Sugarloaf township	3 202	2 035
Sugar Notch borough	1 191	1 333
Swoyersville borough[31]	5 795	6 786
Union township	1 828	1 219
Warrior Run borough	784	816
West Hazleton borough	4 871	6 059
West Pittston borough	5 980	7 074
West Wyoming borough	3 288	3 659
White Haven borough	1 921	1 203
Wilkes-Barre city	51 551	58 856
Wilkes-Barre township	4 244	3 535
Wilkes-Barre Township (CDP)	4 244	...
Wright township	4 797	3 179
Wyoming borough	3 655	4 195
Yatesville borough	555	407
Lycoming County	118 416	113 296
Anthony township	730	480
Armstrong township	724	727
Bastress township	500	441
Brady township	804	255
Brown township	84	119
Cascade township	364	219
Clinton township	2 467	1 934
Cogan House township	819	521
Cummings township	369	321
Duboistown borough	1 218	1 468
Eldred township	1 771	1 066
Fairfield township	2 291	1 420
Franklin township	819	645
Gamble township	676	461
Hepburn township	2 534	1 623
Hughesville borough	2 174	2 249
Jackson township	449	352
Jersey Shore borough	4 631	5 322
Jordan township	822	663
Lewis township	1 149	750
Limestone borough	1 839	1 168
Loyalsock township	10 763	10 581
East Faxon (CDP)	3 951	4 175
Faxon (CDP)	1 635	1 946
Lycoming township	1 902	1 507
McHenry township	204	241
McIntyre township	698	720
McNett township	235	192
Mifflin township	985	688
Mill Creek township	417	265
Montgomery borough	1 653	1 902
Montoursville borough	5 403	5 985
Moreland township	868	621
Muncy borough	2 700	2 872
Muncy township	1 051	880
Muncy Creek township	3 427	2 473
Nippenose township	714	583
Old Lycoming township	5 220	4 616
Garden View (CDP)	2 777	2 662
Penn township	739	513
Piatt township	1 059	1 013
Picture Rocks borough	615	570
Pine township	312	321
Plunketts Creek township	710	692
Porter township	1 541	1 283
Salladasburg borough	273	239
Shrewsbury township	436	406
South Williamsport borough	6 581	7 153
Susquehanna township	1 099	1 046
Upper Fairfield township	1 761	1 174
Washington township	1 368	860
Watson township	530	291
Williamsport city	33 401	37 918
Wolf township	2 147	1 473
Woodward township	2 370	2 014
McKean County	50 635	51 915
Annin township	853	708
Bradford city	11 211	12 672
Bradford township	5 294	5 423
Ceres township	1 164	977
Corydon township	302	140
Eldred borough	965	1 092

County Subdivisions	1980	1970
McKean County—Con.		
Eldred township	2 146	1 846
Foster township	5 106	5 458
Hamilton township	707	828
Hamlin township	892	932
Kane borough	4 916	5 001
Keating township	3 366	3 080
Lafayette township	1 056	883
Lewis Run borough	677	756
Liberty township	1 881	1 729
Mount Jewett borough	1 053	1 060
Norwich township	599	669
Otto township	1 962	1 982
Port Allegany borough	2 593	2 703
Sergeant township	171	256
Smethport borough	1 797	1 883
Wetmore township	1 924	1 837
Mercer County[32]	128 299	'127 225
Clark borough	667	467
Coolspring township	1 984	1 518
Deer Creek township	496	398
Delaware township	2 205	1 863
East Lackawannock township[32]	1 709	'1 314
Fairview township	965	889
Farrell city	8 645	'11 000
Findley township	1 651	1 337
Fredonia borough	712	731
French Creek township	765	601
Greene township	1 292	1 099
Greenville borough	7 730	8 704
Grove City borough	8 162	8 312
Hempfield township	4 078	3 628
Greenville East (CDP)	1 523	...
Hermitage township[32]	16 365	'15 421
Hillcrest (CDP)	3 600	3 897
Sharon North (CDP)	1 401	1 328
Jackson township	1 045	'691
Jackson Center borough	265	'274
Jamestown borough	854	937
Jefferson township	2 007	1 623
Lackawannock township	2 814	1 974
Lake township	598	544
Liberty township	1 199	916
Mercer borough[32]	2 532	'2 773
Mill Creek township	587	466
New Lebanon borough	197	211
New Vernon township	476	402
Otter Creek township	605	565
Perry township	1 597	1 368
Pine township	3 762	3 514
Pymatuning township	3 880	3 073
Salem township	695	679
Sandy Creek township	847	753
Sandy Lake borough	779	772
Sandy Lake township	1 163	884
Sharon city	19 057	22 653
Sharpsville borough	5 375	6 126
Sheakleyville borough	155	141
Shenango township	4 399	3 141
South Pymatuning township	3 016	2 973
Springfield township	1 904	1 878
Stoneboro borough	1 177	1 129
Sugar Grove township	1 153	1 029
West Middlesex borough	1 064	1 293
West Salem township	3 862	3 551
Wheatland borough	1 132	1 421
Wilmington township	1 073	812
Wolf Creek township	711	610
Worth township	893	767
Mifflin County[33]	46 908	45 268
Armagh township	3 710	3 385
Milroy (CDP)	1 594	1 575
Bratton township	1 426	1 224
Brown township	3 003	2 742
Reedsville (CDP)	1 023	...
Burnham borough[33]	2 457	2 607
Decatur township	2 513	2 216
Derry township[33]	8 108	7 877
Highland Park (CDP)	1 879	1 704
Yeagertown (CDP)	1 305	1 363
Granville township	5 116	4 626
Juniata Terrace borough	631	733
Kistler borough	364	369
Lewistown borough	9 830	11 098
McVeytown borough	447	486
Menno township	1 590	1 308
Newton Hamilton borough	317	280
Oliver township	1 774	1 528
Union township	3 131	2 965
Belleville (CDP)	1 689	1 817
Wayne township	2 491	1 824
Monroe County[34]	69 409	45 422
Barrett township	3 273	2 452
Chestnuthill township	4 324	2 021
Coolbaugh township	3 993	1 626
Delaware Water Gap borough[34]	597	533

County Subdivisions	1980	1970
Monroe County—Con.		
East Stroudsburg borough	8 039	7 894
Eldred township	1 518	990
Hamilton township	5 138	2 985
Jackson township	2 315	1 212
Middle Smithfield township	3 497	1 508
Mount Pocono borough	1 237	1 019
Paradise township[34]	1 983	1 207
Pocono township[34]	5 233	1 870
Polk township	3 265	1 284
Price township	684	377
Ross township	2 267	998
Smithfield township[34]	3 466	2 285
Stroud township	9 150	7 525
Arlington Heights (CDP)	1 198	...
Stroudsburg borough	5 148	'5 451
Tobyhanna township	3 302	1 868
Tunkhannock township	980	317
Montgomery County[35]	643 621	'624 080
Abington township	59 084	'63 625
Abington Township (CDP)	59 084	'8 391
Ambler borough	6 628	7 800
Bridgeport borough	4 843	5 630
Bryn Athyn borough	947	970
Cheltenham township	35 509	'40 066
Cheltenham Township (CDP)	35 509	...
Collegeville borough	3 406	3 191
Conshohocken borough	8 475	10 195
Douglass township	5 833	4 177
Gilbertsville (CDP)	3 160	...
East Greenville borough	2 456	2 003
East Norriton township	12 711	11 837
East Norriton (CDP)	12 711	...
Franconia township	6 545	5 245
Harleysville (CDP) (pt.)	510	...
Green Lane borough	542	543
Hatboro borough	7 579	8 880
Hatfield borough	2 533	2 385
Hatfield township	13 411	8 613
Horsham township	15 959	13 888
Horsham (CDP)	9 900	...
Jenkintown borough	4 942	'5 404
Lansdale borough	16 526	18 451
Limerick township	5 298	5 556
Lower Frederick township[35]	2 379	2 515
Lower Gwynedd township	6 902	6 361
Lower Merion township	59 651	'63 594
Lower Merion Township (CDP)	59 651	...
Lower Moreland township	12 472	'11 665
Lower Moreland Township (CDP)	12 472	...
Lower Pottsgrove township	7 299	5 157
Pottsgrove (CDP)	3 199	...
Sanatoga (CDP)	3 723	...
Lower Providence township	18 945	15 169
Evansburg (CDP) (pt.)	605	...
Trooper (CDP)	7 370	'5 410
Lower Salford township	6 156	5 008
Harleysville (CDP) (pt.)	3 163	1 448
Marlborough township	2 849	2 465
Montgomery township	5 718	3 936
Narberth borough	4 496	5 151
New Hanover township	4 623	4 211
Norristown borough	34 684	38 169
North Wales borough	3 391	3 911
Pennsburg borough	2 339	2 260
Perkiomen township	3 265	'2 473
Plymouth township	17 168	'16 911
Plymouth Township (CDP)	17 168	...
Pottstown borough	22 729	25 355
Red Hill borough	1 727	1 201
Rockledge borough	2 538	2 564
Royersford borough	4 243	4 235
Salford township	1 995	1 560
Schwenksville borough[35]	1 041	809
Skippack township	5 784	'5 265
Evansburg (CDP) (pt.)	422	...
Souderton borough	6 657	6 366
Springfield township	20 344	22 394
Springfield Township (CDP)	20 344	...
Telford borough (pt.)	2 520	2 595
Towamencin township	11 112	4 738
Trappe borough	1 800	1 676
Upper Dublin township	22 348	'19 562
Upper Dublin Township (CDP)	22 348	...
Upper Frederick township	1 759	1 418
Upper Gwynedd township	9 487	6 856
Upper Hanover township	3 870	2 721
Upper Merion township	26 138	'23 743
Upper Merion (CDP)	26 138	...
Upper Moreland township	25 874	24 866
Upper Moreland Township (CDP)	25 874	...
Upper Pottsgrove township	2 873	2 477
Halfway House (CDP)	1 415	...
Upper Providence township	9 551	6 202
Upper Salford township	2 375	1 950
West Conshohocken borough	1 516	2 194
West Norriton township	14 034	12 456
West Norriton (CDP)	14 034	...

County Subdivisions

County Subdivisions	1980	1970
Montgomery County—Con.		
West Pottsgrove township	4 208	4 038
Stowe (CDP)	3 860	3 596
Whitemarsh township	15 101	15 886
Whitemarsh Township (CDP)	15 101	...
Whitpain township	11 772	9 295
Worcester township	4 661	4 243
Montour County	16 675	16 508
Anthony township	1 197	1 013
Cooper township	797	545
Danville borough	5 239	6 176
Derry township	1 061	630
Liberty township	1 308	1 070
Limestone township	755	602
Mahoning township	3 913	4 593
Mechanicsville (CDP)	2 613	2 046
Mayberry township	197	204
Valley township	1 625	1 251
Washingtonville borough	218	174
West Hemlock township	365	250
Northampton County[36]	225 418	'214 545
Allen township	2 465	1 856
Bangor borough	5 006	5 425
Bath borough	1 953	1 829
Bethlehem city (pt.)	50 554	52 065
Bethlehem township	12 094	9 071
Middletown (CDP)	5 801	...
Bushkill township	4 469	3 387
Chapman borough	255	191
East Allen township	3 605	2 737
East Bangor borough	955	905
Easton city[36]	26 027	'29 450
Forks township	4 612	'3 930
Freemansburg borough	1 879	1 681
Glendon borough	354	637
Hanover township	6 073	5 434
Hellertown borough	6 025	'6 615
Lehigh township	7 985	6 086
Lower Mount Bethel township	2 745	2 531
Lower Nazareth township	3 535	2 091
Lower Saucon township	7 372	'6 246
Moore township	7 519	3 791
Nazareth borough	5 443	5 815
Northampton borough	8 240	8 389
North Catasauqua borough	2 554	2 941
Palmer township	13 926	12 684
Highland Park (CDP)	5 922	5 500
Pen Argyl borough	3 388	3 668
Plainfield township	4 833	4 288
Portland borough	540	612
Roseto borough	1 484	1 538
Stockertown borough	661	753
Tatamy borough	910	891
Upper Mount Bethel township	4 247	3 343
Upper Nazareth township	3 407	3 605
Eastlawn Gardens (CDP)	1 771	1 613
Walnutport borough	2 007	1 942
Washington township	3 205	3 037
West Easton borough	1 033	1 123
Williams township[36]	3 843	3 282
Wilson borough	7 564	'8 406
Wind Gap borough	2 651	2 270
Northumberland County[37]	100 381	99 190
Coal township	10 984	11 781
Edgewood (CDP)	3 115	3 186
Fairview–Ferndale (CDP)	3 167	3 723
Marshallton (CDP)	1 692	1 802
Delaware township	3 640	2 619
East Cameron township	660	651
East Chillisquaque township	700	567
Herndon borough	483	507
Jackson township	859	790
Jordan township	718	698
Kulpmont borough	3 675	4 026
Lewis township	1 814	1 169
Little Mahanoy township	392	335
Lower Augusta township	983	664
Lower Mahanoy township	1 624	1 488
McEwensville borough	247	247
Marion Heights borough	921	958
Milton borough[37]	6 730	7 723
Mount Carmel borough	8 190	9 317
Mount Carmel township	2 599	2 802
Atlas (CDP)	1 162	1 527
Northumberland borough	3 636	4 102
Point township	3 338	2 308
Ralpho township	3 131	2 476
Elysburg (CDP)	1 447	1 337
Riverside borough	2 266	1 905
Rockefeller township	1 851	1 312
Rush township	1 169	995
Shamokin city	10 357	11 719
Shamokin township	2 035	1 670
Snydertown borough	358	267
Sunbury city[37]	12 292	13 025
Turbot township[37]	1 540	1 480

County Subdivisions	1980	1970
Northumberland County—Con.		
Turbotville borough	675	627
Upper Augusta township[37]	2 745	2 354
Upper Mahanoy township	648	610
Washington township	644	584
Watsontown borough	2 366	2 514
West Cameron township	476	328
West Chillisquaque township	3 384	2 376
Zerbe township	2 251	2 196
Trevorton (CDP)	2 192	2 196
Perry County[38]	35 718	28 615
Blain borough	274	287
Bloomfield borough	1 109	1 032
Buffalo township	902	599
Carroll township	3 173	1 904
Centre township	1 663	1 109
Duncannon borough	1 645	1 739
Greenwood township	947	747
Howe township	460	397
Jackson township	437	413
Juniata township	1 046	800
Landisburg borough[38]	227	269
Liverpool borough	809	847
Liverpool township	781	553
Marysville borough[38]	2 452	2 328
Miller township	660	458
Millerstown borough	550	612
New Buffalo borough	156	150
Newport borough[38]	1 600	1 747
Northeast Madison township	564	419
Oliver township[38]	1 749	1 557
Penn township	2 841	2 269
Rye township[38]	1 642	1 316
Saville township	1 622	1 200
Southwest Madison township	658	537
Spring township	1 537	1 070
Toboyne township	402	292
Tuscarora township	884	624
Tyrone township[38]	1 590	1 430
Watts township	962	613
Wheatfield township	2 376	1 297
Philadelphia County	1 688 210	'1 949 996
Philadelphia city	1 688 210	'1 949 996
Pike County	18 271	11 818
Blooming Grove township	1 176	548
Delaware township	1 492	671
Dingman township	1 855	518
Greene township	1 462	1 028
Lackawaxen township	2 111	1 363
Lehman township	1 448	624
Matamoras borough	2 111	2 244
Milford borough	1 143	1 190
Milford township	663	418
Palmyra township	1 722	1 204
Porter township	277	88
Shohola township	966	574
Westfall township	1 825	1 348
Potter County	17 726	16 395
Abbott township	240	273
Allegany township	373	287
Austin borough	740	626
Bingham township	602	558
Clara township	160	131
Coudersport borough	2 791	2 831
Eulalia township	663	509
Galeton borough	1 462	1 552
Genesee township	875	829
Harrison township	1 243	1 098
Hebron township	496	390
Hector township	343	265
Homer township	187	95
Keating township	334	235
Oswayo borough	183	195
Oswayo township	217	264
Pike township	225	272
Pleasant Valley township	99	79
Portage township	254	217
Roulette township	1 322	1 328
Sharon township	965	819
Shinglehouse borough	1 310	1 320
Stewardson township	121	119
Summit township	134	64
Sweden township	599	469
Sylvania township	89	58
Ulysses borough	654	590
Ulysses township	566	460
West Branch township	375	307
Wharton township	104	155
Schuylkill County[39]	160 630	160 089
Ashland borough (pt.)	4 226	4 737
Auburn borough[39]	999	895
Barry township	869	715
Blythe township	1 228	1 199
Branch township	1 906	1 798
Butler township	4 240	3 738
Cass township	2 414	2 508

County Subdivisions	1980	1970
Schuylkill County—Con.		
Cass township—Con.		
Primrose (CDP)	1 154	1 227
Cooldale borough	2 762	3 023
Cressona borough	1 810	1 814
Deer Lake borough	515	347
Delano township	686	643
East Brunswick township	1 554	1 165
East Norwegian township	999	1 076
East Union township	1 470	1 452
Eldred township	726	677
Foster township	289	378
Frackville borough	5 308	5 445
Frailey township	465	570
Gilberton borough	1 096	1 293
Girardville borough	2 268	2 450
Gordon borough	892	856
Hegins township	3 562	3 253
Valley View (CDP)	1 722	1 585
Hubley township	895	808
Kline township[39]	1 768	1 624
Landingville borough	170	175
McAdoo borough[39]	2 940	3 326
Mahanoy township	1 525	1 673
Mahanoy City borough	6 167	7 257
Mechanicsville borough	519	663
Middleport borough	577	609
Minersville borough[39]	5 635	6 012
Mount Carbon borough	157	184
New Castle township	718	727
New Philadelphia borough	1 341	1 528
New Ringgold borough	301	314
North Manheim township	3 574	3 312
North Union township	1 139	843
Norwegian township[39]	1 822	1 592
Orwigsburg borough	2 700	2 661
Palo Alto borough	1 321	1 428
Pine Grove borough	2 244	2 197
Pine Grove township	3 521	2 985
Port Carbon borough	2 576	2 717
Port Clinton borough	337	363
Porter township	2 593	2 525
Pottsville city	18 195	19 715
Reilly township	884	941
Ringtown borough	837	880
Rush township	3 440	2 730
Hometown (CDP)	1 346	1 013
Ryan township	1 275	1 073
St. Clair borough	4 037	4 576
Schuylkill township	1 518	1 516
Schuylkill Haven borough	5 977	6 125
Shenandoah borough	7 589	8 287
South Manheim township[39]	1 015	771
Tamaqua borough[39]	8 843	9 246
Tower City borough	1 667	1 774
Tremont borough	1 796	1 833
Tremont township	289	252
Union township	1 162	969
Upper Mahantongo township[39]	787	727
Walker township	884	730
Washington township	2 205	1 497
Wayne township	3 565	2 065
West Brunswick township	2 519	1 795
West Mahanoy township	3 934	3 968
Shenandoah Heights (CDP)	2 362	1 471
West Penn township	3 388	2 636
Snyder County	33 584	29 269
Adams township	773	664
Beaver township	470	386
Beavertown borough	853	783
Centre township	1 651	1 182
Chapman township	1 264	992
Franklin township	2 105	1 577
Freeburg borough	643	636
Jackson township	1 028	764
McClure borough	1 024	1 094
Middleburg borough	1 357	1 369
Middlecreek township	1 567	1 153
Monroe township	3 502	2 447
Hummels Wharf (CDP)	1 474	...
Penn township	3 042	3 329
Perry township	1 721	1 280
Selinsgrove borough	5 227	5 116
Shamokin Dam borough	1 622	1 562
Spring township	1 435	1 318
Union township	1 291	1 235
Washington township	1 218	866
West Beaver township	942	748
West Perry township	849	768
Somerset County[40]	81 243	76 037
Addison borough	259	370
Addison township	1 012	803
Allegheny township	596	518
Benson borough	308	297
Berlin borough	1 999	1 766
Black township	1 054	892
Boswell borough	1 480	1 529

County Subdivisions	1980	1970
Somerset County—Con.		
Brothersvalley township	2 373	2 080
Callimont borough[40]	32	...
Casselman borough	114	114
Central City borough	1 496	1 547
Conemaugh township	8 581	8 132
Davidsville (CDP)	1 155	...
Jerome (CDP)	1 196	1 158
Confluence borough	968	954
Elk Lick township	2 293	2 054
Fairhope township	155	165
Garrett borough	563	616
Greenville township	651	515
Hooversville borough	863	962
Indian Lake borough	306	129
Jefferson township	1 212	846
Jenner township	4 383	4 251
Jennerstown borough	656	621
Larimer township[40]	486	455
Lincoln township	1 718	1 547
Lower Turkeyfoot township	707	611
Meyersdale borough	2 581	2 648
Middlecreek township	838	732
Milford township	1 580	1 272
New Baltimore borough	221	214
New Centerville borough	213	253
Northampton township	433	368
Ogle township	509	280
Paint borough	1 177	1 233
Paint township	3 634	2 844
Quemahoning township	2 334	2 079
Rockwood borough	1 058	1 051
Salisbury borough	817	895
Seven Springs borough (pt.)	30	37
Shade township	3 530	3 428
Cairnbrook (CDP)	1 081	...
Shanksville borough	273	275
Somerset borough	6 474	6 269
Somerset township	8 457	7 407
Friedens (CDP)	1 065	...
Southampton township	552	516
Stonycreek township	1 997	1 813
Stoystown borough	432	446
Summit township	2 535	2 326
Upper Turkeyfoot township	1 142	995
Ursina borough	311	284
Wellersburg borough	265	266
Windber borough	5 585	6 332
Sullivan County	6 349	5 961
Cherry township	1 654	1 586
Colley township	730	613
Davidson township	649	698
Dushore borough	692	718
Eagles Mere borough	164	157
Elkland township	650	513
Forks township	342	300
Forksville borough	137	158
Fox township	295	334
Hillsgrove township	258	211
Laporte borough	230	207
Laporte township	235	136
Shrewsbury township	313	330
Susquehanna County	37 876	34 344
Apolacon township	499	319
Ararat township	356	325
Auburn township	1 390	1 222
Bridgewater township	2 284	1 876
Brooklyn township	748	807
Choconut township	735	492
Clifford township	1 704	1 351
Dimock township	1 120	983
Forest City borough	1 924	2 322
Forest Lake township	1 054	837
Franklin township	751	675
Friendsville borough	72	77
Gibson township	869	674
Great Bend borough	740	826
Great Bend township	1 936	1 441
Hallstead borough	1 280	1 447
Harford township	1 041	918
Harmony township	506	365
Herrick township	457	436
Hop Bottom borough	405	430
Jackson township	819	678
Jessup township	418	327
Lanesboro borough	465	550
Lathrop township	715	550
Lenox township	1 382	1 045
Liberty township	1 284	1 051
Little Meadows borough	375	337
Middletown township	363	261
Montrose borough	1 980	2 058
New Milford borough	1 040	1 143
New Milford township	1 637	1 266
Oakland borough	734	817
Oakland township	522	489

County Subdivisions	1980	1970
Susquehanna County—Con.		
Rush township	1 079	925
Silver Lake township	1 073	899
Springville township	1 157	919
Susquehanna Depot borough	1 994	2 319
Thompson borough	303	307
Thompson township	344	301
Union Dale borough	321	279
Tioga County	40 973	39 691
Bloss township	354	319
Blossburg borough	1 757	1 753
Brookfield township	480	502
Charleston township	2 712	2 447
Chatham township	677	507
Clymer township	654	557
Covington township	892	641
Deerfield township	619	552
Delmar township	2 732	2 249
Duncan township	268	277
Elk township	46	39
Elkland borough	1 974	1 942
Elkland township	95	57
Farmington township	722	531
Gaines township	584	457
Hamilton township	529	564
Jackson township	2 051	2 023
Knoxville borough	650	698
Lawrence township	1 522	1 192
Lawrenceville borough	327	605
Liberty borough	220	235
Liberty township	846	765
Mansfield borough	3 322	4 114
Middlebury township	1 301	1 036
Morris township	656	654
Nelson township	377	577
Osceola township	759	795
Putnam township	453	477
Richmond township	2 157	1 815
Roseville borough	211	178
Rutland township	617	476
Shippen township	455	444
Sullivan township	1 086	1 115
Tioga borough	613	624
Tioga township	1 066	1 169
Union township	915	918
Ward township	101	60
Wellsboro borough	3 805	4 003
Westfield borough	1 268	1 273
Westfield township	1 100	1 051
Union County	32 870	28 603
Buffalo township	2 562	1 789
East Buffalo township	5 111	'4 118
Linntown (CDP)	1 842	1 851
Gregg township	954	792
Hartleton borough	220	223
Hartley township	1 779	1 638
Kelly township	3 767	4 166
Lewis township	1 121	857
Lewisburg borough	5 407	'5 718
Limestone township	1 240	800
Mifflinburg borough	3 151	2 607
New Berlin borough	783	821
Union township	1 216	1 020
West Buffalo township	1 835	1 269
White Deer township	3 724	2 785
Venango County⁴¹	64 444	62 353
Allegheny township	261	210
Barkeyville borough	266	'302
Canal township	1 055	881
Cherrytree township	1 635	1 522
Clinton township	686	572
Clintonville borough	512	321
Cooperstown borough	644	478
Cornplanter township	3 038	2 391
Hasson Heights (CDP)	1 066	...
Cranberry township	7 873	6 785
Woodland Heights (CDP)	1 684	1 329
Emlenton borough (pt.)⁴¹	794	854
Franklin city	8 146	8 629
Frenchcreek township	2 076	1 383
Irwin township	1 234	'1 036
Jackson township	1 097	625
Mineral township	519	413
Oakland township	1 559	1 165
Oil City city	13 881	15 033
Oilcreek township	873	759
Pinegrove township	1 437	1 216
Pleasantville borough	1 099	1 005
Plum township	1 031	853
Polk borough	1 884	3 673
President township	534	360
Richland township⁴¹	1 055	686
Rockland township	1 310	1 255
Rouseville borough	734	877
Sandycreek township	1 948	1 844
Scrubgrass township⁴¹	719	735
Sugarcreek borough	5 954	5 944

County Subdivisions	1980	1970
Venango County—Con.		
Utica borough	255	281
Victory township	335	265
Warren County	47 449	47 682
Bear Lake borough	249	281
Brokenstraw township	1 978	1 463
Cherry Grove township	183	125
Clarendon borough	776	735
Columbus township	1 879	1 767
Conewango township	5 284	6 405
North Warren (CDP)	1 232	1 360
Deerfield township	382	232
Eldred township	655	667
Elk township	435	357
Farmington township	1 246	1 078
Freehold township	1 253	1 001
Glade township	2 512	2 711
Limestone township	315	268
Mead township	1 777	1 787
Pine Grove township	2 576	2 256
Pittsfield township	1 623	1 452
Pleasant township	2 574	2 399
Warren South (CDP)	1 855	...
Sheffield township	2 655	2 793
Sheffield (CDP)	1 471	1 564
Southwest township	609	517
Spring Creek township	755	700
Sugar Grove borough	630	701
Sugar Grove township	1 594	1 420
Tidioute borough	844	939
Triumph township	309	280
Warren borough	12 146	12 998
Watson township	204	192
Youngsville borough	2 006	2 158
Washington County⁴²	217 074	210 876
Allenport borough	735	762
Amwell township	3 563	3 030
Beallsville borough	588	434
Bentleyville borough	2 525	2 714
Blaine township	734	579
Buffalo township	2 022	1 530
Burgettstown borough	1 867	2 118
California borough	5 703	6 635
Canonsburg borough	10 459	11 439
Canton township	10 311	8 869
Carroll township	6 590	6 636
Fisher–Eldora (CDP)	2 950	3 101
Cecil township	8 923	8 362
Centerville borough	4 207	4 175
Charleroi borough	5 717	6 723
Chartiers township	7 715	7 324
Claysville borough	1 029	951
Coal Center borough	255	317
Cokeburg borough	796	845
Cross Creek township	1 704	1 667
Deemston borough	829	711
Donegal township	2 361	1 949
Donora borough	7 524	8 825
Dunlevy borough	463	405
East Bethlehem township	3 353	3 347
Fredericktown (CDP)	1 052	1 067
East Finley township	1 430	943
East Washington borough	2 241	2 198
Elco borough	417	459
Ellsworth borough	1 228	1 268
Fallowfield township	5 439	5 454
Finleyville borough	402	379
Green Hills borough⁴²	18	...
Hanover township	3 275	3 016
Hopewell township	919	816
Houston borough	1 568	1 812
Independence township	1 784	1 681
Jefferson township	1 369	1 301
Long Branch borough	610	582
McDonald borough (pt.)	2 233	2 220
Marianna borough	907	875
Midway borough	1 187	1 188
Monongahela city	5 950	7 113
Morris township	1 191	871
Mount Pleasant township	3 612	3 359
New Eagle borough	2 617	2 497
North Bethlehem township	1 897	1 736
North Charleroi borough	1 760	1 964
North Franklin township	4 648	4 444
North Strabane township	8 490	7 578
Nottingham township	2 270	1 862
Peters township	13 104	10 672
Robinson township	1 812	2 073
Roscoe borough	1 123	1 176
Smith township	5 583	5 812
Langeloth (CDP)	1 112	...
Somerset township	3 150	2 293
South Franklin township⁴²	3 548	1 730
South Strabane township	7 389	6 555
Speers borough	1 425	1 408
Stockdale borough	641	720
Twilight borough	298	272

County Subdivisions	1980	1970
Washington County—Con.		
Union township	6 692	6 071
Washington city	18 363	19 827
West Alexander borough	286	402
West Bethlehem township	1 579	1 540
West Brownsville borough	1 433	1 426
West Finley township	964	769
West Middletown borough	215	195
West Pike Run township	2 034	1 972
Wayne County	35 237	29 581
Berlin township	1 676	1 109
Bethany borough	282	267
Buckingham township	667	578
Canaan township	928	1 470
Cherry Ridge township	1 362	890
Clinton township	1 399	1 105
Damascus township	2 536	2 006
Dreher township	743	705
Dyberry township	898	706
Hawley borough	1 181	1 331
Honesdale borough	5 128	5 224
Lake township	2 453	1 755
Lebanon township	417	363
Lehigh township	884	637
Manchester township	629	494
Mount Pleasant township	1 196	967
Oregon township	518	348
Palmyra township	773	528
Paupack township	1 379	644
Preston township	1 036	946
Prompton borough	249	224
Salem township	2 538	1 581
Scott township	576	604
South Canaan township	1 345	1 106
Starrucca borough	216	292
Sterling township	730	576
Texas township	2 250	2 003
Waymart borough	1 248	1 122
Westmoreland County[43]	392 294	376 935
Adamsburg borough	236	251
Allegheny township	7 452	6 713
Arnold city	6 853	8 174
Arona borough	446	453
Avonmore borough	1 234	1 267
Bell township	2 158	1 981
Bolivar borough	706	668
Cook township	2 174	1 808
Delmont borough[43]	2 159	1 934
Derry borough	3 072	3 338
Derry township	16 193	15 902
McChesneytown–Loyalhanna (CDP)	4 108	4 283
West Derry (CDP)	1 128	1 497
Donegal borough	212	255
Donegal township	2 336	1 620
East Huntingdon township[43]	8 120	7 234
East Vandergrift borough	955	r1 151
Export borough	1 143	r1 371
Fairfield township	2 260	1 893
Greensburg city[43]	17 558	r17 077
Hempfield township[43]	43 396	r36 208
Hunker borough	359	375
Hyde Park borough	633	729
Irwin borough	4 995	4 059
Jeannette city[43]	13 106	15 209
Latrobe borough[43]	10 799	11 749
Ligonier borough[43]	1 917	2 258
Ligonier township[43]	7 513	6 278
Lower Burrell city	13 200	13 654
Loyalhanna township	2 359	1 771
Slickville (CDP) (pt.)	410	414
Madison borough	531	436
Manor borough	2 235	2 276
Monessen city	11 928	15 216
Mount Pleasant borough[43]	5 354	5 895
Mount Pleasant township[43]	11 851	10 830
Calumet–Norvelt (CDP)	2 541	2 588
Municipality of Murrysville borough[43]	16 036	...
New Alexandria borough	697	690
New Florence borough	855	929
New Kensington city	17 660	20 312
New Stanton borough[43]	2 600	r1 781
North Belle Vernon borough	2 425	2 916
North Huntingdon township	31 517	29 443
North Irwin borough	1 016	1 306
Oklahoma borough	1 078	1 084
Penn borough	619	735
Penn township[43]	16 153	r12 975
Rostraver township	11 430	10 525
Fellsburg (CDP)	1 042	1 092
Lynnwood–Pricedale (CDP) (pt.)	1 741	1 992
St. Clair township	1 668	1 507
Salem township	7 656	r6 023
Slickville (CDP) (pt.)	768	652
Scottdale borough[43]	5 833	5 818
Seward borough	675	746
Sewickley township	7 095	6 735
Smithton borough	559	552
South Greensburg borough[43]	2 605	3 288

County Subdivisions	1980	1970
Westmoreland County—Con.		
South Huntingdon township	6 366	6 071
Southwest Greensburg borough	2 898	3 186
Suterville borough	863	830
Trafford borough (pt.)	3 662	4 288
Unity township	19 976	18 419
Lawson Heights (CDP)	2 626	3 844
Upper Burrell township	2 179	1 948
Vandergrift borough	6 823	r7 889
Washington township	6 906	5 613
West Leechburg borough	1 395	1 422
West Newton borough	3 387	3 648
Youngstown borough	470	478
Youngwood borough[43]	3 749	3 057
Wyoming County	26 433	19 082
Braintrim township	396	351
Clinton township	1 099	658
Eaton township	1 636	1 163
Exeter township	640	601
Factoryville borough	924	922
Falls township	1 924	1 473
Forkston township	249	223
Laceyville borough	498	452
Lemon township	856	701
Mehoopany township	878	677
Meshoppen borough	571	482
Meshoppen township	786	452
Monroe township	1 813	1 045
Nicholson borough	945	877
Nicholson township	1 244	737
North Branch township	156	126
Northmoreland township	1 162	767
Noxen township	1 048	822
Overfield township	1 338	913
Tunkhannock borough	2 144	2 251
Tunkhannock township	4 399	2 200
Washington township	1 031	614
Windham township	696	575
York County[44]	312 963	272 603
Carroll township[44]	3 097	2 386
Chanceford township	4 584	3 119
Codorus township	3 591	2 762
Conewago township	4 979	3 719
Cross Roads borough	267	163
Dallastown borough	3 949	3 560
Delta borough	692	778
Dillsburg borough[44]	1 733	1 441
Dover borough	1 910	1 168
Dover township	12 589	8 975
Weigelstown (CDP)	5 213	...
East Hopewell township	1 450	843
East Manchester township	3 564	1 735
East Prospect borough	529	547
Fairview township[44]	11 941	9 248
Fawn township	1 671	1 309
Fawn Grove borough	516	485
Felton borough	483	425
Franklin township	2 830	1 598
Franklintown borough	280	279
Glen Rock borough	1 662	1 600
Goldsboro borough	477	576
Hallam borough	1 428	
Hanover borough	14 890	15 623
Heidelberg township	2 116	1 785
Hellam township	4 507	3 158
Hopewell township	2 600	1 728
Jackson township	5 347	3 931
Jacobus borough	1 396	1 360
Jefferson borough	685	540
Lewisberry borough[44]	309	490
Loganville borough	1 020	921
Lower Chanceford township	2 250	1 759
Lower Windsor township	5 977	3 879
Manchester borough	2 027	2 391
Manchester township	7 637	6 979
Emigsville (CDP)	2 413	...
Manheim township	2 296	1 566
Monaghan township	1 645	1 134
Mount Wolf borough	1 517	1 811
Newberry township[44]	10 047	5 978
New Freedom borough	2 205	1 495
New Salem borough	832	384
North Codorus township	6 854	4 514
North Hopewell township	1 787	1 193
North York borough	1 755	2 032
Paradise township	2 715	2 165
Peach Bottom township	2 692	1 424
Penn township	9 234	8 154
Parkville (CDP)	5 009	5 120
Pennville (CDP)	1 398	1 100
Railroad borough	272	308
Red Lion borough	5 824	5 645
Seven Valleys borough	500	688
Shrewsbury borough[44]	2 688	1 716
Shrewsbury township[44]	4 551	2 578
Springettsbury township	19 687	19 399
Pleasureville (CDP)	1 241	...

County Subdivisions

	1980	1970
York County—Con.		
Springfield township	3 506	2 221
Spring Garden township	11 127	12 443
Spring Grove borough	1 832	1 669
Stewartstown borough	1 072	1 157
Warrington township	3 586	2 494
Washington township	2 055	1 365
Wellsville borough	347	346
West Manchester township	12 728	12 257
Shiloh (CDP)	5 315	...
West Manheim township	3 688	2 246
West York borough	4 526	5 314
Windsor borough	1 205	1 298
Windsor township	8 807	6 672
Winterstown borough	491	424
Wrightsville borough	2 365	2 668
Yoe borough	990	790
York city	44 619	50 335
York township	16 893	12 702
Yorkana borough	296	262
York Haven borough	746	671

RHODE ISLAND

The full name of this state is Rhode Island and Providence Plantations, the designation employed in the charter of 1663, which remained in effect until 1843. This designation had its origin in the face that prior to the patent of 1644 the colony consisted of several independent settlements, of which those of Rhode Island and Providence were the most important.

The origin of the name "Rhode Island" is uncertain. The most usual explanation is that it is based upon a fancied resemblance of the island bearing this name to the Isle of Rhodes, although other theories have been advanced. "Providence Plantations" was the designation employed for the colony in the patent of 1644, Providence being the oldest and one of the two most important settlements.

The explorer Verrazzano, sailing under the French flag, appears to have discovered Narragansett Bay as early as 1524. Later, in 1614, it was explored by the Dutch navigator, Adrian Block. The region now covered by the state was included in the grants conveyed by the first charter of Virginia (1606) and by the charter of New England (1620). These grants appear, however, to have had no practical result so far as the territory now constituting Rhode Island was concerned.

The first English settlement in this state was made at Providence in 1636 by Roger Williams and others who had been obliged to leave the colony at Massachusetts Bay. Settlements were also made at Portsmouth in 1638, Newport in 1639, and Warwick in 1642.

In 1644 a patent was granted for the "Incorporation of Providence Plantations in the Narragansett Bay in New England." In 1663 a charter was obtained from Charles II, under which the colony and the state were successively governed until 1843, when the present state constitution went into effect. The territorial limits of Rhode Island, as defined by this charter, differed somewhat, though not greatly, from those now in existence.

The present boundary between Rhode Island and Connecticut was agreed upon in 1703 and surveyed in 1728. It was not, however, finally established until 1887. The boundary between Rhode Island and Massachusetts was in dispute for more than 200 years, and the eastern boundary of the state was not definitely established until 1861, while the northern boundary was not finally established until 1883.

Rhode Island was one of the original thirteen states.

COUNTY LOCATION INDEX

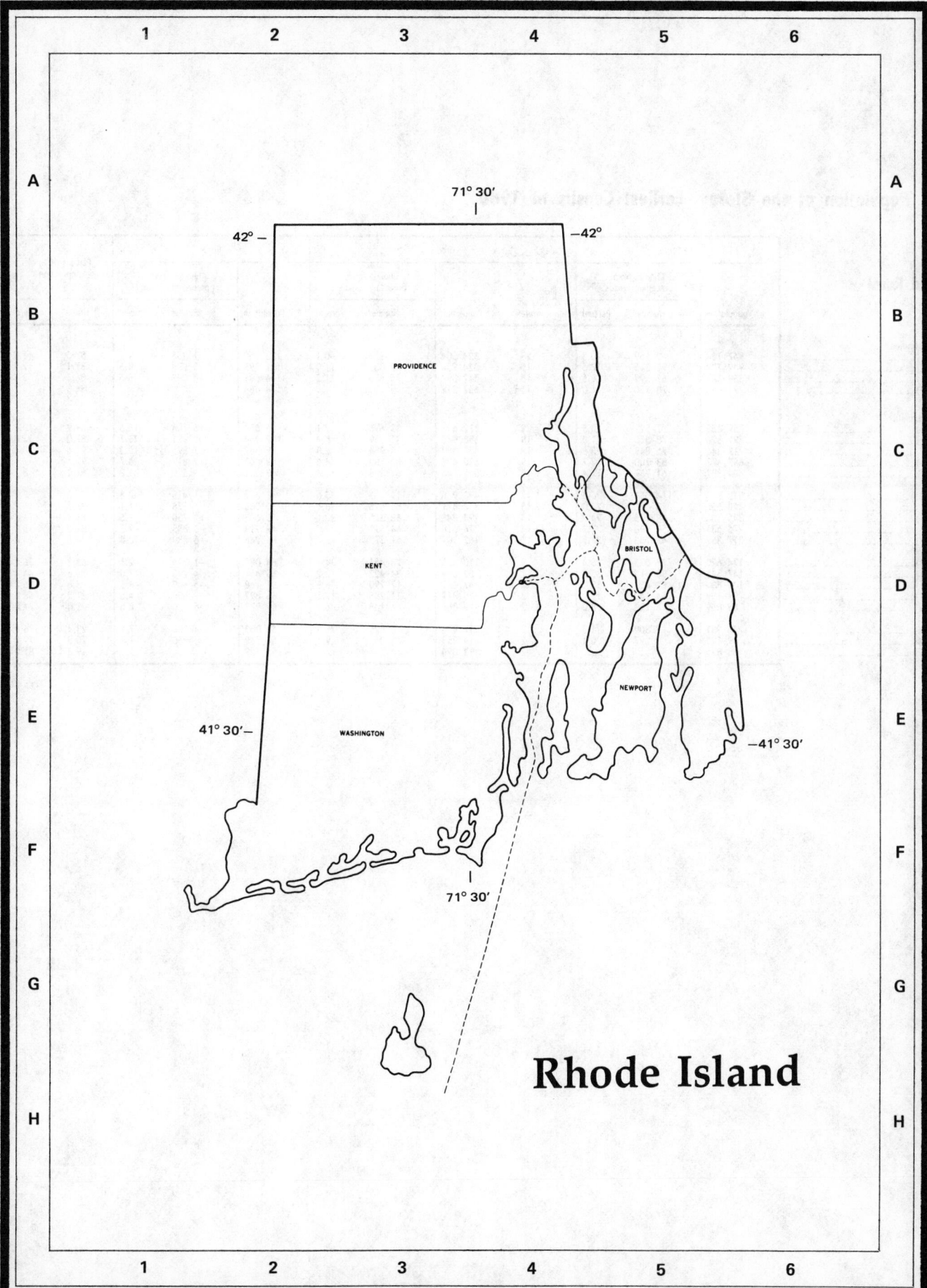

1　2　3　4　5　6

A

71° 30′

42° —　　　　—42°

B

PROVIDENCE

C

D

KENT

BRISTOL

NEWPORT

E

41° 30′—　　　　—41° 30′

WASHINGTON

F

71° 30′

G

Rhode Island

H

1　2　3　4　5　6

Population of the State: Earliest Census to 1980

Urban and Rural

	The State			Urban				Rural			Percent of total population	
	Total population	Change from preceding census		Places of 2,500 or more	Population	Change from preceding census		Population	Change from preceding census		Urban	Rural
		Number	Percent			Number	Percent		Number	Percent		
Current urban definition:												
1980 (Apr. 1)	947 154	−2 569	−0.3	23	824 004	−926	−0.1	123 150	1 355	1.1	87.0	13.0
1970 (Apr. 1)	'949 723	90 235	10.5	15	824 930	82 033	11.0	121 795	5 204	4.5	87.1	12.9
1960 (Apr. 1)	859 488	67 592	8.5	18	742 897	75 685	11.3	116 591	−8 093	−6.5	86.4	13.6
1950 (Apr. 1)	791 896	78 550	11.0	11	667 212	...	...	124 684	...	...	84.3	15.7
Previous urban definition:												
1960 (Apr. 1)	859 488	67 592	8.5	22	772 638	83 696	12.1	86 850	−16 104	−15.6	89.9	10.1
1950 (Apr. 1)	791 896	78 550	11.0	18	688 942	35 559	5.4	102 954	42 991	71.7	87.0	13.0
1940 (Apr. 1)	713 346	25 849	3.8	19	653 383	17 954	2.8	59 963	7 895	15.2	91.6	8.4
1930 (Apr. 1)	687 497	83 100	13.7	19	635 429	80 283	14.5	52 068	2 817	5.7	92.4	7.6
1920 (Jan. 1)	604 397	61 787	11.4	18	555 146	61 208	12.4	49 251	579	1.2	91.9	8.1
1910 (Apr. 15)	542 610	114 054	26.6	17	493 938	115 467	30.5	48 672	−1 413	−2.8	91.0	9.0
1900 (June 1)	428 556	83 050	24.0	15	378 471	83 628	28.4	50 085	−578	−1.1	88.3	11.7
1890 (June 1)	345 506	68 975	24.9	14	294 843	68 225	30.1	50 663	750	1.5	85.3	14.7
1880 (June 1)	276 531	59 178	27.2	14	226 618	64 511	39.8	49 913	−5 333	−9.7	82.0	18.0
1870 (June 1)	217 353	42 733	24.5	12	162 107	51 572	46.7	55 246	−8 839	−13.8	74.6	25.4
1860 (June 1)	174 620	27 075	18.4	9	110 535	28 451	34.7	64 085	−1 376	−2.1	63.3	36.7
1850 (June 1)	147 545	38 715	35.6	7	82 084	34 422	72.2	65 461	4 293	7.0	55.6	44.4
1840 (June 1)	108 830	11 631	12.0	5	47 662	17 290	56.9	61 168	−5 659	−8.5	43.8	56.2
1830 (June 1)	97 199	14 140	17.0	3	30 372	11 286	59.1	66 827	2 854	4.5	31.2	68.8
1820 (Aug. 7)	83 059	6 128	8.0	2	19 086	1 108	6.2	63 973	5 020	8.5	23.0	77.0
1810 (Aug. 6)	76 931	7 809	11.3	2	17 978	3 625	25.3	58 953	4 184	7.6	23.4	76.6
1800 (Aug. 4)	69 122	297	0.4	2	14 353	1 257	9.6	54 769	−960	−1.7	20.8	79.2
1790 (Aug. 2)	68 825	...	...	2	13 096	...	...	55 729	...	...	19.0	81.0

BRISTOL

1790	3,211
1800	3,801
1810	5,072
1820	5,637
1830	5,446
1840	6,467
1850	8,514
1860	8,907
1870	9,421
1880	11,394
1890	11,428
1900	13,144
1910	17,602
1920	23,113
1930	25,089
1940	25,548
1950	29,079
1960	37,146
1970	45,937
1980	46,942

KENT

1790	8,848
1800	8,487
1810	9,834
1820	10,228
1830	12,789
1840	13,083
1850	15,068
1860	17,303
1870	18,595
1880	20,588
1890	26,754
1900	29,976
1910	36,378
1920	28,269
1930	51,390
1940	58,311
1950	77,763
1960	112,619
1970	142,382
1980	154,163

NEWPORT

1790	14,300
1800	14,845
1810	16,294
1820	15,771
1830	16,535
1840	16,874
1850	20,007
1860	21,896
1870	20,050
1880	24,180
1890	28,552
1900	32,599
1910	39,335
1920	42,893
1930	41,668
1940	46,696
1950	61,539
1960	81,891
1970	94,228
1980	81,383

PROVIDENCE

1790	24,391
1800	25,854
1810	30,769
1820	35,736
1830	47,018
1840	58,073
1850	87,526
1860	107,799
1870	149,190
1880	197,874
1890	255,123
1900	328,683
1910	424,353
1920	475,190
1930	540,016
1940	550,298
1950	574,973
1960	568,778
1970	581,470
1980	571,349

WASHINGTON

1790	18,075
1800	16,135
1810	14,962
1820	15,687
1830	15,411
1840	14,324
1850	16,430
1860	18,715
1870	20,097
1880	22,495
1890	23,649
1900	24,154
1910	24,942
1920	24,932
1930	29,334
1940	32,493
1950	48,542
1960	59,054
1970	85,706
1980	93,317

NOTES

NEWPORT

Name changed from Rhode Island in 1729.

PROVIDENCE

Name changed from Providence Plantations in 1729.

WASHINGTON

Name changed from Kings in 1781.

CENTRAL FALLS

1900	18,167
1910	22,754
1920	24,174
1930	25,898
1940	25,248
1950	23,550
1960	19,858
1970	18,716
1980	16,995

CRANSTON

1790	1,877
1800	1,644
1810	2,261
1820	2,274
1830	2,653
1840	2,902
1850	4,311
1860	7,500
1870	4,822
1880	5,940
1890	8,099
1900	13,343
1910	21,107
1920	29,407
1930	42,911
1940	47,085
1950	55,060
1960	66,766
1970	74,287
1980	71,992

EAST PROVIDENCE

1870	2,668
1880	5,056
1890	7,116
1900	12,138
1910	15,808
1920	21,793
1930	29,995
1940	32,165
1950	35,871
1960	41,955
1970	48,207
1980	50,980

NEWPORT

1790	6,716
1800	6,739
1810	7,907
1820	7,319
1830	8,010
1840	8,333
1850	9,563
1860	10,508
1870	12,521
1880	15,693
1890	19,457
1900	22,441
1910	27,149
1920	30,255
1930	27,612
1940	30,532
1950	37,564
1960	47,049
1970	34,562
1980	29,259

PAWTUCKET

1830	1,459
1840	2,184
1850	3,753
1860	4,200
1870	6,619
1880	19,030
1890	27,633
1900	39,231
1910	51,622
1920	64,248
1930	77,149
1940	75,797
1950	81,436
1960	81,001
1970	76,984
1980	71,204

PROVIDENCE

1790	6,380
1800	7,614
1810	10,071
1820	11,767
1830	16,833
1840	23,171
1850	41,513
1860	50,666
1870	68,904
1880	104,857
1890	132,146
1900	175,597
1910	224,326
1920	237,595
1930	252,981
1940	253,504
1950	248,674
1960	207,498
1970	179,116
1980	156,804

WARWICK

1830	5,529
1840	6,726
1850	7,740
1860	8,916
1870	10,453
1880	9,440
1890	13,933
1900	21,316
1910	26,629
1920	13,481
1930	23,196
1940	28,757
1950	43,028
1960	68,504
1970	83,694
1980	87,123

WOONSOCKET

1870	11,527
1880	16,050
1890	20,830
1900	28,204
1910	38,125
1920	43,496
1930	49,376
1940	49,303
1950	50,211
1960	47,080
1970	46,820
1980	45,914

County Subdivisions

	1980	1970
The State ----------------------------------	947 154	'949 723
Bristol County ----------------------------	46 942	45 937
Barrington town --------------------------	16 174	17 554
Barrington (CDP) ------------------------	16 174	...
Bristol town ------------------------------	20 128	17 860
Bristol (CDP) ----------------------------	20 128	...
Warren town------------------------------	10 640	10 523
Kent County ------------------------------	154 163	142 382
Coventry town ----------------------------	27 065	22 947
East Greenwich town--------------------	10 211	9 577
Warwick city ------------------------------	87 123	83 694
West Greenwich town --------------------	2 738	1 841
West Warwick town ----------------------	27 026	24 323
West Warwick (CDP) --------------------	27 026	...
Newport County --------------------------	81 383	'94 228
Jamestown town--------------------------	4 040	2 911
Jamestown (CDP) ------------------------	2 156	2 114
Little Compton town --------------------	3 085	2 385
Middletown town ------------------------	17 216	'29 290
Melville (CDP) (pt.) --------------------	2 001	...
Newport East (CDP) ------------------	11 030	10 285
Newport city ------------------------------	29 259	34 562
Portsmouth town --------------------------	14 257	12 521
Melville (CDP) (pt.) --------------------	787	...
Tiverton town ----------------------------	13 526	12 559
Tiverton (CDP) --------------------------	7 653	...
Providence County ----------------------	571 349	'581 470
Burrillville town --------------------------	13 164	10 087
Harrisville (CDP) ----------------------	1 224	1 053
Pascoag (CDP) --------------------------	3 807	3 132
Central Falls city ------------------------	16 995	18 716
Cranston city ------------------------------	71 992	'74 287
Cumberland town ------------------------	27 069	26 605
Cumberland Hill (CDP) ----------------	5 421	...
Valley Falls (CDP) --------------------	10 892	...
East Providence city --------------------	50 980	'48 207
Foster town ------------------------------	3 370	2 626
Glocester town --------------------------	7 550	5 160
Johnston town ----------------------------	24 907	22 037
Lincoln town ------------------------------	16 949	16 182
North Providence town ------------------	29 188	24 337
North Providence (CDP) ----------------	29 188	...
North Smithfield town ------------------	9 972	9 349
Pawtucket city --------------------------	71 204	76 984
Providence city ------------------------	156 804	'179 116
Scituate town ----------------------------	8 405	7 489
Smithfield town --------------------------	16 886	13 468
Greenville (CDP) ----------------------	7 576	...
Woonsocket city ------------------------	45 914	46 820
Washington County --------------------	93 317	'85 706
Charlestown town ----------------------	4 800	2 863
Exeter town ------------------------------	4 453	3 245
Hopkinton town --------------------------	6 406	5 392
Ashaway (CDP) ------------------------	1 747	1 559
Hope Valley (CDP) --------------------	1 414	1 326
Narragansett town----------------------	12 088	7 138
Narragansett Pier (CDP)--------------	3 342	2 686
New Shoreham town --------------------	620	489
North Kingstown town ------------------	21 938	'29 793
Richmond town --------------------------	4 018	2 625
South Kingstown town ------------------	20 414	16 913
Kingston (CDP) ------------------------	5 479	5 601
Wakefield–Peacedale (CDP) ----------	6 474	6 331
Westerly town ----------------------------	18 580	17 248
Bradford (CDP) ------------------------	1 354	1 333
Westerly (CDP) ------------------------	14 093	13 654

SOUTH CAROLINA

The original province of Carolina was named in honor of Charles I of England.

The shores of the region now constituting South Carolina may have been seen by Cabot, an Italian in the service of England, at about the close of the fifteenth century, but no explorations were made until 1521, when an expedition sent out by De Ayllon, a Spaniard of San Domingo, visited the coast region. Five years later De Ayllon made an attempt at settlement, but no permanent settlement was made within the limits of the state until nearly a century and a half later. In 1670 a settlement was made on the Ashley River by the English, and in 1680 it was moved a few miles down the river to the present site of Charleston.

The present area of South Carolina was included in part in the grants made to Virginia by the charters of 1606, 1609, and 1612. In 1629 Charles I granted the territory between the thirty-first and thirty-sixth parallels, under the name Carolina, to Sir Robert Heath. No settlements were made under this grant, however, and the patent was vacated. In 1663 Carolina, extending from the thirty-first to the thirty-sixth parallels and from the Atlantic to the Pacific, was granted by King Charles II to eight "lords proprietors." Two years later the northern and southern limits were changed to latitudes 36°30' and 29°, respectively, and settlement was begun soon afterwards. At first there was no formal division of the province, but the northern portion gradually came to be known as North Carolina and the southern part as South Carolina, and each had its own separate government. In 1729 seven of the eight lords proprietors sold their shares to the English crown, and Carolina was definitely and authoritatively divided into the royal provinces of North and South Carolina.

In 1732 the "Trustees for Establishing the Colony of Georgia in America" obtained a royal charter granting them all the lands between the Savannah and the Altamaha, and from the heads of these rivers to the Pacific Ocean.

In 1763 the St. Marys River was, by royal proclamation, made the southern boundary of Georgia, but South Carolina did not relinquished its claim to the tract between the Altamaha and St. Marys Rivers until 1787. In the same year South Carolina ceded to the United States a strip of land about 12 miles in width, extending westward to the Mississippi River, and the state was thus reduced to its present limits.

South Carolina was one of the original thirteen states.

COUNTY LOCATION INDEX

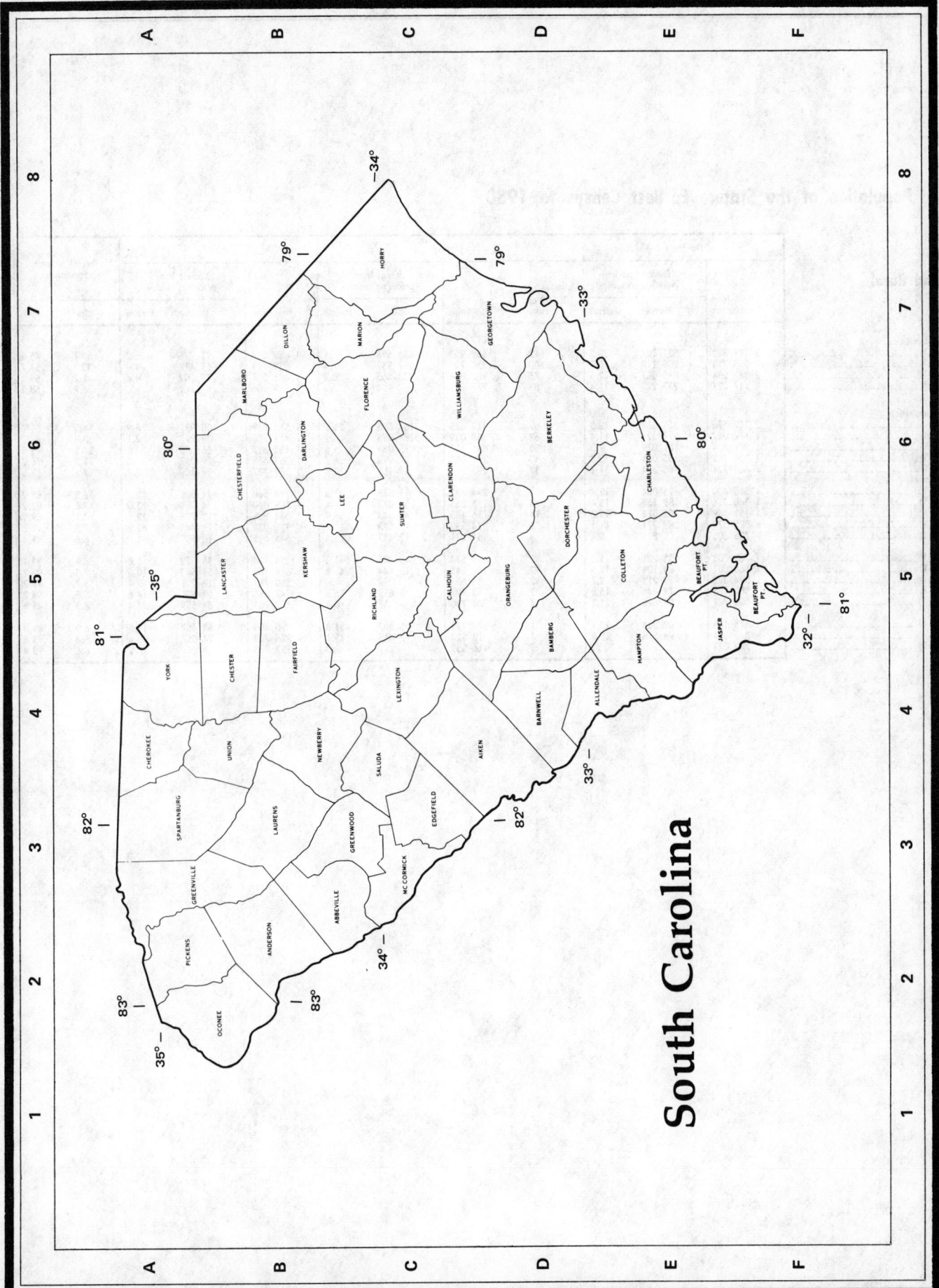

South Carolina

Population of the State: Earliest Census to 1980

Urban and Rural

	The State			Urban				Rural			Percent of total population	
	Total population	Change from preceding census		Places of 2,500 or more	Population	Change from preceding census		Population	Change from preceding census		Urban	Rural
		Number	Percent			Number	Percent		Number	Percent		
Current urban definition:												
1980 (Apr. 1)	3 121 820	531 107	20.5	142	1 689 253	438 528	35.1	1 432 567	92 776	6.9	54.1	45.9
1970 (Apr. 1)	2 590 713	208 119	8.7	100	1 250 725	269 339	27.4	1 339 791	-61 417	-4.4	48.3	51.7
1960 (Apr. 1)	2 382 594	265 567	12.5	76	981 386	203 465	26.2	1 401 208	62 102	4.6	41.2	58.8
1950 (Apr. 1)	2 117 027	217 223	11.4	83	777 921	...	...	1 339 106	...	...	36.7	63.3
Previous urban definition:												
1960 (Apr. 1)	2 382 594	265 567	12.5	69	817 675	164 636	25.2	1 564 919	100 931	6.9	34.3	65.7
1950 (Apr. 1)	2 117 027	217 223	11.4	62	653 039	186 928	40.1	1 463 988	30 295	2.1	30.8	69.2
1940 (Apr. 1)	1 899 804	161 039	9.3	50	466 111	95 031	25.6	1 433 693	66 008	4.8	24.5	75.5
1930 (Apr. 1)	1 738 765	55 041	3.3	40	371 080	77 093	26.2	1 367 685	-22 052	-1.6	21.3	78.7
1920 (Jan. 1)	1 683 724	168 324	11.1	32	293 987	69 155	30.8	1 389 737	99 169	7.7	17.5	82.5
1910 (Apr. 15)	1 515 400	175 084	13.1	25	224 832	53 576	31.3	1 290 568	121 508	10.4	14.8	85.2
1900 (June 1)	1 340 316	189 167	16.4	20	171 256	55 073	47.4	1 169 060	134 094	13.0	12.8	87.2
1890 (June 1)	1 151 149	155 572	15.6	14	116 183	41 644	55.9	1 034 966	113 928	12.4	10.1	89.9
1880 (June 1)	995 577	289 971	41.1	6	74 539	13 528	22.2	921 038	276 443	42.9	7.5	92.5
1870 (June 1)	705 606	1 898	0.3	3	61 011	12 437	25.6	644 595	-10 539	-1.6	8.6	91.4
1860 (June 1)	703 708	35 201	5.3	2	48 574	-471	-1.0	655 134	35 672	5.8	6.9	93.1
1850 (June 1)	668 507	74 109	12.5	2	49 045	15 444	46.0	619 462	58 665	10.5	7.3	92.7
1840 (June 1)	594 398	13 213	2.3	2	33 601	2	-	560 797	13 211	2.4	5.7	94.3
1830 (June 1)	581 185	78 444	15.6	2	33 599	8 819	35.6	547 586	69 625	14.6	5.8	94.2
1820 (Aug. 7)	502 741	87 626	21.1	1	24 780	69	0.3	477 961	87 557	22.4	4.9	95.1
1810 (Aug. 6)	415 115	69 524	20.1	1	24 711	5 887	31.3	390 404	63 637	19.5	6.0	94.0
1800 (Aug. 4)	345 591	96 518	38.8	1	18 824	2 465	15.1	326 767	94 053	40.4	5.4	94.6
1790 (Aug. 2)	249 073	...	...	1	16 359	...	...	232 714	...	...	6.6	93.4

ABBEVILLE

1790	9,197
1800	13,553
1810	21,156
1820	23,167
1830	28,149
1840	29,351
1850	32,318
1860	32,385
1870	31,129
1880	40,815
1890	46,856
1900	33,400
1910	34,804
1920	27,139
1930	23,323
1940	22,931
1950	22,456
1960	21,417
1970	21,112
1980	22,627

AIKEN

1880	28,112
1890	31,822
1900	39,032
1910	41,849
1920	45,574
1930	47,403
1940	49,916
1950	53,137
1960	81,038
1970	91,023
1980	105,625

ALLENDALE

1920	16,098
1930	13,294
1940	13,040
1950	11,773
1960	11,362
1970	9,692
1980	10,700

ANDERSON

1830	17,169
1840	18,493
1850	21,475
1860	22,873
1870	24,049
1880	33,612
1890	43,696
1900	55,728
1910	69,568
1920	76,349
1930	80,949
1940	88,712
1950	90,664
1960	98,478
1970	105,474
1980	133,235

BAMBERG

1900	17,296
1910	18,544
1920	20,962
1930	19,410
1940	18,643
1950	17,533
1960	16,274
1970	15,950
1980	18,118

BARNWELL

1800	7,376
1810	12,280
1820	14,750
1830	19,236
1840	21,471
1850	26,608
1860	30,743
1870	35,724
1880	39,857
1890	44,613
1900	35,504
1910	34,209
1920	23,081
1930	21,221
1940	20,138
1950	17,266
1960	17,659
1970	17,176
1980	19,868

BEAUFORT

1790	18,753
1800	20,428
1810	25,887
1820	32,199
1830	37,032
1840	35,794
1850	38,805
1860	40,053
1870	34,359
1880	30,176
1890	34,119
1900	35,495
1910	30,355
1920	22,269
1930	21,815
1940	22,037
1950	26,993
1960	44,187
1970	51,136
1980	65,364

BERKELEY

1890	55,428
1900	30,454
1910	23,487
1920	22,558
1930	22,236
1940	27,128
1950	30,251
1960	38,196
1970	56,199
1980	94,727

CALHOUN

1910	16,634
1920	18,384
1930	16,707
1940	16,229
1950	14,753
1960	12,256
1970	10,780
1980	12,206

CHARLESTON

1790	46,647
1800	57,480
1810	63,179
1820	80,212
1830	86,338
1840	82,661
1850	72,805
1860	70,100
1870	88,863
1880	102,800
1890	59,903
1900	88,006
1910	88,594
1920	108,405
1930	101,050
1940	121,105
1950	164,856
1960	216,382
1970	247,650
1980	276,974

CHEROKEE

1900	21,359
1910	26,179
1920	26,570
1930	32,201
1940	33,290
1950	34,992
1960	35,205
1970	36,791
1980	40,983

CHESTER

1790	6,866
1800	8,185
1810	11,479
1820	14,189
1830	17,182
1840	17,747
1850	18,038
1860	18,122
1870	18,805
1880	24,153
1890	26,660
1900	28,616
1910	29,425
1920	33,389
1930	31,803
1940	32,579
1950	32,597
1960	30,888
1970	29,811
1980	30,148

CHESTERFIELD

1800	5,216
1810	5,564
1820	6,645
1830	8,472
1840	8,574
1850	10,790
1860	11,834
1870	10,584
1880	16,345
1890	18,468
1900	20,401
1910	26,301
1920	31,969
1930	34,334
1940	35,963
1950	36,236
1960	33,717
1970	33,667
1980	38,161

CLARENDON

1860	13,095
1870	14,038
1880	19,190
1890	23,233
1900	28,184
1910	32,188
1920	34,878
1930	30,036
1940	31,500
1950	32,215
1960	29,490
1970	25,604
1980	27,464

COLLETON

1790	20,338
1800	24,903
1810	26,359
1820	26,404
1830	27,256
1840	25,548
1850	39,505
1860	41,916
1870	25,410
1880	36,386
1890	40,293
1900	33,452
1910	35,390
1920	29,897
1930	25,821
1940	26,268
1950	28,242
1960	27,816
1970	27,622
1980	31,776

DARLINGTON

1800	7,631
1810	9,047
1820	10,949
1830	13,728
1840	14,822
1850	16,830
1860	20,361
1870	26,243
1880	34,485
1890	29,134
1900	32,388
1910	36,027
1920	39,126
1930	41,427
1940	45,198
1950	50,016
1960	52,928
1970	53,442
1980	62,717

DILLON

1910	22,615
1920	25,278
1930	25,733
1940	29,625
1950	30,930
1960	30,584
1970	28,838
1980	31,083

DORCHESTER

1900	16,294
1910	17,891
1920	19,459
1930	18,956
1940	19,928
1950	22,601
1960	24,383
1970	32,286
1980	58,761

EDGEFIELD

1790	13,289
1800	18,130
1810	23,160
1820	25,119
1830	30,509
1840	32,852
1850	39,262
1860	39,887
1870	42,286
1880	45,844
1890	49,259
1900	25,478
1910	28,281
1920	23,928
1930	19,326
1940	17,894
1950	16,591
1960	15,735
1970	15,692
1980	17,528

FAIRFIELD

1790	7,623
1800	10,087
1810	11,857
1820	17,174
1830	21,546
1840	20,165
1850	21,404
1860	22,111
1870	19,888
1880	27,765
1890	28,599
1900	29,425
1910	29,442
1920	27,159
1930	23,287
1940	21,187
1950	21,780
1960	20,713
1970	19,999
1980	20,700

FLORENCE

1890	25,027
1900	28,474
1910	35,671
1920	50,406
1930	61,027
1940	70,582
1950	79,710
1960	84,438
1970	89,636
1980	110,163

GEORGETOWN

1790	22,122
1800	22,938
1810	15,679
1820	17,603
1830	19,943
1840	18,274
1850	20,647
1860	21,305
1870	16,161
1880	19,613

1890	20,857
1900	22,846
1910	22,270
1920	21,716
1930	21,738
1940	26,352
1950	31,762
1960	34,798
1970	33,500
1980	42,461

GREENVILLE

1790	6,503
1800	11,504
1810	13,133
1820	14,530
1830	16,476
1840	17,839
1850	20,156
1860	21,892
1870	22,262
1880	37,496
1890	44,310
1900	53,490
1910	68,377
1920	88,498
1930	117,009
1940	136,580
1950	168,152
1960	209,776
1970	240,546
1980	287,913

GREENWOOD

1900	28,343
1910	34,225
1920	35,971
1930	36,078
1940	40,083
1950	41,628
1960	44,346
1970	49,686
1980	57,847

HAMPTON

1880	18,741
1890	20,544
1900	23,738
1910	25,126
1920	19,550
1930	17,243
1940	17,465
1950	18,027
1960	17,425
1970	15,878
1980	18,159

HORRY

1810	4,349
1820	5,025
1830	5,245
1840	5,755
1850	7,646
1860	7,962
1870	10,721
1880	15,574
1890	19,256
1900	23,364
1910	26,995
1920	32,077
1930	39,376
1940	51,951

1950	59,820
1960	68,247
1970	69,992
1980	101,419

JASPER

1920	9,868
1930	9,988
1940	11,011
1950	10,995
1960	12,237
1970	11,885
1980	14,504

KERSHAW

1800	7,340
1810	9,867
1820	12,432
1830	13,545
1840	12,281
1850	14,473
1860	13,086
1870	11,754
1880	21,538
1890	22,361
1900	24,696
1910	27,094
1920	29,398
1930	32,070
1940	32,913
1950	32,287
1960	33,585
1970	34,727
1980	39,015

LANCASTER

1790	6,302
1800	6,012
1810	6,318
1820	8,716
1830	10,361
1840	9,907
1850	10,988
1860	11,797
1870	12,087
1880	16,903
1890	20,761
1900	24,311
1910	26,650
1920	28,628
1930	27,980
1940	33,542
1950	37,071
1960	39,392
1970	43,328
1980	53,361

LAURENS

1790	9,337
1800	12,809
1810	14,982
1820	17,682
1830	20,863
1840	21,584
1850	23,407
1860	23,858
1870	22,536
1880	29,444
1890	31,610
1900	37,382
1910	41,550
1920	42,560

1930	42,094
1940	44,185
1950	46,974
1960	47,609
1970	49,713
1980	52,214

LEE

1910	25,318
1920	26,827
1930	24,096
1940	24,908
1950	23,173
1960	21,832
1970	18,323
1980	18,929

LEXINGTON

1810	6,641
1820	8,083
1830	9,065
1840	12,111
1850	12,930
1860	15,579
1870	12,988
1880	18,564
1890	22,181
1900	27,264
1910	32,040
1920	35,676
1930	36,494
1940	35,994
1950	44,279
1960	60,726
1970	89,012
1980	140,353

McCORMICK

1920	16,444
1930	11,471
1940	10,367
1950	9,577
1960	8,629
1970	7,955
1980	7,797

MARION

1800	6,914
1810	8,884
1820	10,201
1830	11,208
1840	13,932
1850	17,407
1860	21,190
1870	22,160
1880	34,107
1890	29,976
1900	35,181
1910	20,596
1920	23,721
1930	27,221
1940	30,107
1950	33,110
1960	32,014
1970	30,270
1980	34,179

MARLBORO

1790	10,706
1800	5,452
1810	4,966

1820	6,425
1830	8,582
1840	8,408
1850	10,789
1860	12,434
1870	11,814
1880	20,598
1890	23,500
1900	27,639
1910	31,189
1920	33,180
1930	31,634
1940	33,281
1950	31,766
1960	28,529
1970	27,151
1980	31,634

NEWBERRY

1790	9,342
1800	12,006
1810	13,964
1820	16,104
1830	17,441
1840	18,350
1850	20,143
1860	20,879
1870	20,775
1880	26,497
1890	26,434
1900	30,182
1910	34,586
1920	35,552
1930	34,681
1940	33,577
1950	31,771
1960	29,416
1970	29,273
1980	31,242

OCONEE

1870	10,536
1880	16,256
1890	18,687
1900	23,634
1910	27,337
1920	30,117
1930	33,368
1940	36,512
1950	39,050
1960	40,204
1970	40,728
1980	48,611

ORANGEBURG

1790	18,513
1800	15,766
1810	13,229
1820	15,653
1830	18,453
1840	18,519
1850	23,582
1860	24,896
1870	16,865
1880	41,395
1890	49,393
1900	59,663
1910	55,893
1920	64,907
1930	63,864
1940	63,707
1950	68,726
1960	68,559
1970	69,789

1980	82,276

PENDLETON

1790	9,568
1800	20,052
1810	22,897
1820	27,022

PICKENS

1830	14,473
1840	14,356
1850	16,904
1860	19,639
1870	10,269
1880	14,389
1890	16,389
1900	19,375
1910	25,422
1920	28,329
1930	33,709
1940	37,111
1950	40,058
1960	46,030
1970	58,956
1980	79,292

RICHLAND

1790	3,930
1800	6,097
1810	9,027
1820	12,321
1830	14,772
1840	16,397
1850	20,243
1860	18,307
1870	23,025
1880	28,573
1890	36,821
1900	45,589
1910	55,143
1920	78,122
1930	87,667
1940	104,843
1950	142,565
1960	200,102
1970	233,868
1980	269,735

SALUDA

1900	18,966
1910	20,943
1920	22,088
1930	18,148
1940	17,192
1950	15,924
1960	14,554
1970	14,528
1980	16,150

SPARTANBURG

1790	8,800
1800	12,122
1810	14,259
1820	16,989
1830	21,150
1840	23,669
1850	26,400
1860	26,919
1870	25,784
1880	40,409
1890	55,385

1900	65,560
1910	83,465
1920	94,265
1930	116,323
1940	127,773
1950	150,349
1960	156,830
1970	173,724
1980	201,861

SUMTER

1790	6,940
1800	13,103
1810	19,054
1820	25,369
1830	28,277
1840	27,892
1850	33,220
1860	23,859
1870	25,268
1880	37,037
1890	43,605
1900	51,237
1910	38,472
1920	43,040
1930	45,902
1940	52,463
1950	57,634
1960	74,941
1970	79,425
1980	88,243

UNION

1790	7,693
1800	10,237
1810	10,995
1820	14,126
1830	17,906
1840	18,936
1850	19,852
1860	19,635
1870	19,248
1880	24,080
1890	25,363
1900	25,501
1910	29,911
1920	30,372
1930	30,920
1940	31,360
1950	31,334
1960	30,015
1970	29,230
1980	30,751

WILLIAMSBURG

1810	6,871
1820	8,716
1830	9,018
1840	10,327
1850	12,447
1860	15,489
1870	15,489
1880	24,110
1890	27,777
1900	31,685
1910	37,626
1920	38,539
1930	34,014
1940	41,011
1950	43,807
1960	40,932
1970	34,243
1980	38,226

YORK

1790	6,604
1800	10,250
1810	10,032
1820	14,936
1830	17,790
1840	18,383
1850	19,433
1860	21,502
1870	24,286
1880	30,713
1890	39,831
1900	41,684
1910	47,718
1920	50,536
1930	53,418
1940	58,663
1950	71,596
1960	78,760
1970	85,216
1980	106,720

NOTE

PENDLETON

Taken to form Anderson and Pickens in 1826.

AIKEN

1880	1,817
1890	2,362
1900	3,414
1910	3,911
1920	4,103
1930	6,033
1940	6,168
1950	7,083
1960	11,243
1970	13,436
1980	14,978

ANDERSON

1860	625
1870	1,432
1880	1,850
1890	3,018
1900	5,498
1910	9,654
1920	10,570
1930	14,383
1940	19,424
1950	19,770
1960	41,316
1970	27,556
1980	27,313

CAYCE

1920	746
1930	1,267
1940	1,476
1950	3,294
1960	8,517
1970	9,967
1980	11,701

CHARLESTON

1790	16,359
1800	18,824
1810	24,711
1820	24,780
1830	30,289
1840	29,261
1850	42,985
1860	40,522
1870	48,956
1880	49,984
1890	54,955
1900	55,807
1910	58,833
1920	67,957
1930	62,265
1940	71,275
1950	70,174
1960	65,925
1970	66,945
1980	69,510

COLUMBIA

1830	3,310
1840	4,340
1850	6,060
1860	8,052
1870	9,298
1880	10,036
1890	15,353
1900	21,108
1910	26,319
1920	37,524
1930	51,581
1940	62,396
1950	86,914
1960	97,433
1970	113,542
1980	101,208

CONWAY

1890	677
1900	705
1910	1,228
1920	1,969
1930	3,011
1940	5,066
1950	6,073
1960	8,563
1970	8,151
1980	10,240

EASLEY

1880	327
1890	421
1900	903
1910	2,983
1920	3,568
1930	4,886
1940	5,183
1950	6,316
1960	8,283
1970	11,175
1980	14,264

FLORENCE

1880	1,914
1890	3,395
1900	4,647
1910	7,057
1920	10,968
1930	14,774
1940	16,054
1950	22,513
1960	24,722
1970	25,997
1980	30,062

GAFFNEY

1880	400
1890	1,631
1900	3,937
1910	4,767
1920	5,065
1930	6,827
1940	7,636
1950	8,123
1960	10,435
1970	13,253
1980	13,453

GEORGETOWN

1850	1,628
1860	1,720
1870	2,080
1880	2,557
1890	2,895
1900	4,138
1910	5,530
1920	4,579
1930	5,082
1940	5,559
1950	6,004
1960	12,261
1970	10,449
1980	10,144

GOOSE CREEK

1970	3,825
1980	17,811

GREENVILLE

1850	1,305
1860	1,518
1870	2,757
1880	6,160
1890	8,607
1900	11,860
1910	15,741
1920	23,127
1930	29,154
1940	34,734
1950	58,161
1960	66,188
1970	61,208
1980	58,242

GREENWOOD

1870	700
1880	745
1890	1,326
1900	4,824
1910	6,614
1920	8,703
1930	11,020
1940	13,020
1950	13,806
1960	16,644
1970	21,069
1980	21,613

GREER

1900	648
1910	1,673
1920	2,292
1930	2,419
1940	2,940
1950	5,050
1960	8,967
1970	10,642
1980	10,525

HANAHAN

1980	13,224

LAURENS

1880	752
1890	2,245
1900	4,029
1910	4,818
1920	4,629
1930	5,443
1940	6,895
1950	8,658
1960	9,598
1970	10,298
1980	10,587

MOUNT PLEASANT

1910	1,346
1920	1,575
1930	1,415
1940	1,698
1950	1,857
1960	5,116
1970	6,879
1980	13,838

MYRTLE BEACH

1940	1,597
1950	3,345
1960	7,834
1970	9,035
1980	18,446

NORTH AUGUSTA

1910	1,136
1920	1,742
1930	2,003
1940	2,629
1950	3,659
1960	10,348
1970	12,883
1980	13,593

NORTH CHARLESTON

1980	62,534

ORANGEBURG

1860	997
1870	246
1880	2,140
1890	2,964
1900	4,455
1910	5,906
1920	7,290
1930	8,776
1940	10,521
1950	15,322
1960	13,852
1970	13,252
1980	14,933

ROCK HILL

1880	809
1890	2,744
1900	5,485
1910	7,216
1920	8,809
1930	11,322
1940	15,009
1950	24,502
1960	29,404
1970	33,846
1980	35,344

SPARTANBURG

1850	1,176
1860	2,216
1870	1,080
1880	3,253
1890	5,544
1900	11,395
1910	17,517
1920	22,638
1930	28,723
1940	32,249
1950	36,795
1960	44,352
1970	44,546
1980	43,968

SUMTER

1850	1,356
1860	1,119
1870	1,807
1880	2,011
1890	3,865
1900	5,673
1910	8,109
1920	9,508
1930	11,780
1940	15,874
1950	20,185
1960	23,062
1970	24,435
1980	24,890

UNION

1880	1,267
1890	1,609
1900	5,400
1910	5,623
1920	6,141
1930	7,419
1940	8,478
1950	9,730
1960	10,191
1970	10,775
1980	10,523

WEST COLUMBIA

1930	1,722
1940	1,744
1950	1,543
1960	6,410
1970	7,838
1980	10,409

CORRECTION NOTE

The official 1980 census counts of total population shown in
this report supersede counts issued previously. Corrections
to the figures were made after the counts were provided to
the State for redistricting purposes and released in Advance
Report PHC80-V for this State.

Shown below are corrections to the 1980 census counts of the
total population made after the tabulations for this report
were completed. Any additional corrections made after this
report is printed are available by writing to Data User
Services Division, Customer Service (Corrections), Bureau of
the Census, Washington, D.C. 20233.

The 1980 figures shown in this publication are subject to
change pending the outcome of the various lawsuits dealing
with the census counts.

	1980 population	
	As shown in the tables	Corrected
The State.....................	3 121 820	3 121 833
Anderson County:		
Anderson division:		
Anderson city...................	27 313	27 965
Orr Mill (CDP).................	2 416	2 478
Beaufort County:		
Sheldon division:		
Yemassee town (pt.).............	275	16
Charleston County:		
Mount Pleasant division:		
Mount Pleasant town............	13 838	14 209
Dorchester County:		
Summerville division:		
Pinehurst-Sheppard Park (CDP)...	6 956	6 936
Summerville town (pt.)..........	6 109	6 447
Florence County:		
Florence division:		
Florence city...................	30 062	29 176
Nob Hill (CDP).................	1 848	1 872
Windy Hill (CDP)...............	1 605	1 622
Greenville County:		
Greenville division:		
Mauldin city...................	8 245	8 143
Lancaster County:		
Lancaster division:		
Lancaster city.................	9 603	9 703
Lancaster Mills (CDP)...........	2 139	2 096
Richland County:		
Columbia division:		
Capitol View (CDP).............	9 962	10 741
Columbia city (pt.).............	100 792	99 969
Forest Acres city..............	6 033	6 071
Spartanburg County:		
Spartanburg division:		
Hillbrook (CDP)................	2 715	2 706
Spartanburg city...............	43 968	43 826
Union County........................	30 751	30 764
Jonesville division..............	3 514	3 527
Jonesville town................	1 188	1 201
Columbia city (total).............	101 208	100 385
Summerville town (total)...........	6 368	6 706
Yemassee town (total)..............	1 048	789

County Subdivisions	1980	1970
The State	3 121 820	r2 590 713
Abbeville County[1]	22 627	21 112
Abbeville division	10 524	9 742
Abbeville city[1]	5 833	5 515
Antreville–Lowndesville division	2 325	2 305
Lowndesville town	197	219
Calhoun Falls division	3 542	3 253
Calhoun Falls town	2 491	2 234
Donalds division	2 763	2 475
Donalds town (pt.)[1]	352	392
Honea Path town (pt.)	85	12
Ware Shoals town (pt.)	456	316
Due West division	3 473	3 337
Donalds town (pt.)[1]	14	...
Due West town	1 366	1 380
Aiken County[2]	105 625	91 023
Aiken division	38 195	...
Aiken city[2]	14 978	13 436
Aiken West (CDP)	3 083	2 689
Graniteville (CDP)	1 158	1 127
Madison (CDP)	1 150	1 337
Beech Island division	4 839	3 884
Edisto–Shaws division	2 994	2 186
Jackson division	2 650	2 929
Jackson town	1 771	1 928
Monetta division	3 138	2 460
Monetta town (pt.)[2]	84	r147
New Ellenton division	5 940	5 276
New Ellenton town	2 628	2 546
North Augusta division	40 041	...
Bath (CDP)	2 242	1 576
Belvedere (CDP)	6 859	...
Burnettown town	359	434
Clearwater (CDP)	3 967	...
Gloverville (CDP)	2 619	1 682
Langley (CDP)	1 714	...
North Augusta city[2]	13 593	12 883
Warrenville (CDP)	1 029	1 059
Salley division	2 562	2 149
Perry town	273	209
Salley town	584	450
Wagener division	3 355	2 942
Wagener town	903	723
Windsor division	1 911	1 485
Windsor town[2]	55	...
Allendale County[3]	10 700	r9 783
Allendale division	5 789	...
Allendale town	4 400	3 620
Fairfax division	2 913	r2 806
Fairfax town (pt.)	2 061	1 937
Millett division	686	552
Sycamore division	1 312	...
Sycamore town	261	229
Ulmer town	91	109
Anderson County[4]	133 235	105 474
Anderson division	64 396	...
Anderson city[4]	27 313	27 556
Appleton Mills (CDP)	2 007	...
Equinox Mill (CDP)	1 471	...
Homeland Park (CDP)	6 720	...
Orr Mill (CDP)	2 416	...
Pearman (CDP)	1 078	...
Belton division	11 977	...
Belton city[4]	5 312	5 257
Brushy Creek division	11 693	...
Piedmont (CDP) (pt.)	1 319	985
Fork division	2 050	1 687
Honea Path division	7 346	6 876
Honea Path town (pt.)	4 029	3 695
Iva division	5 029	...
Iva town[4]	1 369	1 114
Pendleton division	11 769	...
Clemson city (pt.)	46	17
Pendleton town[4]	3 154	2 615
Starr division	3 637	...
Starr town	241	190
Williamston–Pelzer division	15 338	...
Pelzer town	130	130
West Pelzer town	944	861
Williamston town	4 310	3 991
Bamberg County[5]	18 118	15 950
Bamberg division	7 119	6 244
Bamberg town[5]	3 672	3 406
Denmark division	7 399	6 205
Denmark city	4 434	3 571
Ehrhardt division	1 872	1 754
Ehrhardt town	353	478
Olar division	1 728	1 747
Govan town	109	136
Olar town	381	423
Barnwell County[6]	19 868	17 176
Barnwell division	8 340	6 962
Barnwell city[6]	5 572	4 439
Hilda town	355	331
Blackville division	4 279	3 915

County Subdivisions	1980	1970
Barnwell County—Con.		
Blackville division—Con.		
Blackville town	2 840	2 395
Kline–Snelling division	2 053	...
Kline town	315	305
Snelling town[6]	111	r150
Williston division	5 196	...
Elko town	329	202
Williston town	3 173	2 594
Beaufort County[7]	65 364	51 136
Beaufort–Port Royal division	39 258	...
Beaufort city[7]	8 634	9 434
Beaufort Station (CDP)	2 165	2 295
Burton (CDP)	3 619	...
Laurel Bay (CDP)	5 238	...
Parris Island (CDP)	7 752	8 868
Port Royal town	2 977	2 865
Shell Point (CDP)	2 475	...
Bluffton division	14 978	5 252
Bluffton town	541	529
Hilton Head Island (CDP)	11 344	...
St. Helena division	8 134	5 718
Sheldon division	2 994	2 530
Yemassee town (pt.)	275	7
Berkeley County[8]	94 727	56 199
Bonneau division	6 962	4 472
Bonneau town	401	365
Cordesville division	3 128	2 620
Jamestown town	193	190
Cross division	5 050	3 723
Goose Creek–Hanahan division	58 157	30 411
Goose Creek city[8]	17 811	r3 825
Hanahan city[8]	13 224	...
Ladson (CDP) (pt.)	10 287	...
North Charleston city (pt.)	–	...
Moncks Corner division	12 354	6 904
Moncks Corner town[8]	3 699	2 314
St. Stephen division	6 277	6 127
St. Stephen town	1 850	1 506
Wando division	2 799	1 942
Calhoun County[9]	12 206	10 780
Cameron division	2 451	2 469
Cameron town	536	476
Fort Motte–Lone Star division	1 210	...
St. Matthews division	5 568	...
St. Matthews town	2 496	2 403
Sandy Run–Staley division	2 977	2 226
Charleston County[10]	276 974	247 650
Bear Swamp division	5 000	3 472
Charleston city (pt.)[10]	345	...
Charleston–North Charleston division	187 261	...
Avondale–Moorland (CDP)	5 355	5 236
Charleston city (pt.)[10]	67 372	66 945
Dorchester Terrace–Brentwood (CDP)	7 862	...
Ladson (CDP) (pt.)	2 959	...
Lincolnville town[10]	808	504
North Charleston city (pt.)[10]	62 534	...
St. Andrews (CDP)	9 908	9 202
Summerville town (pt.)[10]	259	...
Wando Woods (CDP)	5 253	...
Edisto Island division	1 345	...
James Island division	27 719	24 197
Charleston city (pt.)[10]	1 793	...
Folly Beach city[10]	1 478	1 157
James Island (CDP)	24 124	...
Johns Island division	9 296	7 530
McClellanville division	4 199	4 094
McClellanville town[10]	436	304
Mount Pleasant division	28 764	18 440
Isle of Palms city	3 421	2 657
Mount Pleasant town[10]	13 838	r6 879
Sullivan's Island town	1 867	1 426
Ravenel division	10 950	9 235
Hollywood town[10]	729	339
Meggett town	249	180
Ravenel town	1 655	931
Wadmalaw Island division	2 440	...
Cherokee County[11]	40 983	r36 669
Blacksburg division	7 045	6 574
Blacksburg town[11]	1 873	1 977
Gaffney division	27 922	...
East Gaffney (CDP)	4 092	3 750
Gaffney city[11]	13 453	r13 131
Macedonia division	3 827	3 504
Sarratt division	2 189	1 889
Chester County[12]	30 148	29 811
Chester division	17 427	...
Chester city[12]	6 820	7 045
Eureka (CDP)	1 627	1 524
Lowrys town	225	260
Chester West division	3 398	...
Great Falls division	4 664	...
Great Falls town	2 601	2 727
Landsford division	3 103	...
Fort Lawn town	471	510
Richburg division	1 556	1 867

County Subdivisions	1980	1970
Chester County—Con.		
Richburg division—Con.		
Richburg town	269	304
Chesterfield County[13]	38 161	33 667
Cheraw division	12 920	...
Cheraw town[13]	5 654	5 627
Chesterfield division	6 503	...
Chesterfield town[13]	1 432	1 667
Jefferson division	2 787	2 739
Jefferson town	651	709
McBee division	2 090	1 572
McBee town	774	592
Mount Croghan division	2 480	2 238
Mount Croghan town	146	123
Ruby town	256	306
Pageland division	7 036	5 673
Pageland town[13]	2 720	2 122
Patrick division	4 345	3 525
Patrick town	375	421
Clarendon County[14]	27 464	25 604
Alcolu division	2 328	2 298
Manning division	9 890	...
Manning city[14]	4 746	4 025
Manning East division	2 131	...
Paxville division	2 097	1 935
Paxville town	244	261
Sardinia division	1 906	2 100
Summerton division	5 822	...
Summerton town	1 173	1 305
Turbeville division	3 290	2 966
Turbeville town[14]	549	442
Colleton County[15]	31 776	27 622
Cottageville division	2 955	2 629
Cottageville town	371	497
Green Pond division	1 812	...
Edisto Beach[15]	193	...
Hendersonville division	4 656	4 124
Lodge division	1 965	1 884
Lodge town	145	168
Smoaks division	2 016	1 898
Smoaks town[15]	165	155
Williams town	205	201
Walterboro division	18 372	...
Walterboro city[15]	6 209	6 257
Darlington County[16]	62 717	53 442
Darlington division	23 469	...
Crestview (CDP)	1 684	...
Darlington city[16]	7 989	6 990
Doneraile (CDP)	1 276	1 417
Hartsville division	19 884	...
East Hartsville (CDP)	1 149	...
Hartsville city[16]	7 631	8 017
South Hartsville (CDP)	2 385	...
Lake Swamp division	3 394	3 105
Lamar division	3 626	3 641
Lamar town[16]	1 333	1 250
North Hartsville division	8 503	6 875
North Hartsville (CDP)	2 650	1 485
Society Hill division	3 841	3 376
Society Hill town	848	806
Dillon County[17]	31 083	28 838
Dillon division	11 957	...
Dillon city[17]	7 060	'6 391
Hamer division	4 317	...
Lake View division	4 956	...
Lake View town[17]	939	949
Latta division	6 867	...
Latta town[17]	1 804	1 764
Little Rock division	2 986	2 710
Dorchester County[18]	58 761	32 276
Harleyville division	4 978	4 480
Harleyville town[18]	606	704
Reevesville division	2 483	2 257
Reevesville town (pt.)	241	247
Ridgeville division	3 334	2 797
Ridgeville town	603	563
St. George division	4 855	4 071
Reevesville town (pt.)	–	...
St. George town	2 134	1 806
Summerville division	43 111	18 671
Pinehurst–Sheppard Park (CDP)	6 956	1 711
Summerville town (pt.)[18]	6 109	3 839
Edgefield County[19]	17 528	15 692
Edgefield division	5 777	...
Edgefield town	2 713	2 750
Johnston division	4 748	4 916
Johnston town	2 624	2 552
Pleasant Lane division	1 279	1 295
Stevens Creek division	3 858	2 722
Trenton division	1 866	1 425
Trenton town[19]	404	362
Fairfield County	20 700	19 999
Monticello–Salem division	2 366	2 508
Ridgeway division	3 928	3 465
Ridgeway town	343	437

County Subdivisions	1980	1970
Fairfield County—Con.		
Winnsboro North division	3 908	3 394
Winnsboro South division	10 498	10 632
Winnsboro town	2 919	3 411
Winnsboro Mills (CDP)	1 890	2 312
Florence County[20]	110 163	89 636
Coward division	3 057	...
Coward town	428	466
Danwood division	7 991	4 732
Oakdale (CDP) (pt.)	472	...
Florence division	56 489	...
Delmae (CDP)	4 964	...
Florence city[20]	30 062	25 997
Nob Hill (CDP)	1 848	...
Oakdale (CDP) (pt.)	1 015	...
Quinby town	952	788
Windy Hill (CDP)	1 605	1 671
Johnsonville division	5 744	4 906
Johnsonville city[20]	1 421	1 267
Lake City–Scranton division	12 844	...
Lake City city[20]	6 731	6 247
Scranton town	861	732
Olanta division	3 900	...
Olanta town[20]	699	640
Pamplico division	14 020	...
Pamplico town[20]	1 213	1 068
Sardis division	2 771	2 862
Timmonsville division	3 347	3 264
Timmonsville town	2 112	2 246
Georgetown County[21]	42 461	33 500
Andrews division	6 914	...
Andrews town (pt.)	3 034	2 831
Georgetown division	19 281	...
Georgetown city[21]	10 144	10 449
Plantersville division	2 706	2 499
Pleasant Hill–Folly Grove division	3 518	...
Sampit–Santee division	3 519	...
Waccamaw division	6 523	3 153
Murrells Inlet (CDP)	2 410	...
Greenville County[22]	287 913	'240 774
Fountain Inn division	5 548	4 301
Fountain Inn town (pt.)[22]	3 391	2 800
Greenville division	197 261	...
Berea (CDP)	13 164	7 186
City View town[22]	1 662	2 497
Dunean (CDP)	5 146	...
Gantt (CDP)	13 719	11 386
Golden Grove (CDP) (pt.)	76	...
Greenville city[22]	58 242	'61 436
Mauldin city[22]	8 245	3 797
Sans Souci (CDP)	8 393	...
Taylors (CDP) (pt.)	5 451	2 027
Travelers Rest city (pt.)[22]	7	...
Wade Hampton (CDP)	20 180	17 152
Welcome (CDP)	6 922	...
Greer division	12 283	12 129
Greer city (pt.)[22]	6 594	6 611
Highland division	6 859	5 090
Piedmont division	9 271	6 989
Golden Grove (CDP) (pt.)	1 510	...
Piedmont (CDP) (pt.)	1 673	1 257
Simpsonville division	15 890	7 675
Fountain Inn town (pt.)[22]		
Simpsonville town[22]	9 037	3 308
Slater division	3 968	3 528
Slater–Marietta (CDP)	1 834	1 764
Taylors division	17 325	9 746
Taylors (CDP) (pt.)	10 350	4 804
Tigerville division	3 857	3 052
Travelers Rest division	10 832	8 038
Travelers Rest city (pt.)[22]	3 010	2 241
Woodville division	4 819	3 793
Greenwood County[23]	57 847	49 686
Greenwood division	39 624	...
Greenwood city[23]	21 613	21 069
North Greenwood (CDP)	3 739	...
West Greenwood (CDP)	2 356	...
Kirksey division	1 371	1 533
Ninety Six division	6 593	5 376
Ninety Six town	2 249	2 166
Troy division	1 159	1 669
Troy town	705	207
Ware Shoals–Hodges division	9 100	6 935
Hodges town	154	214
Ware Shoals town (pt.)[23]	1 900	2 164
Hampton County[24]	18 159	15 878
Brunson division	1 202	948
Brunson town	590	559
Fairfax town (pt.)	93	–
Estill division	4 953	4 408
Estill town	2 308	1 954
Gifford town[24]	385	
Luray town	149	72
Furman–Scotia division	2 178	1 773
Furman town	348	239
Scotia town	72	64

County Subdivisions	1980	1970
Hampton County—Con.		
Hampton–Varnville division	7 612	...
Hampton town[24]	3 143	[r]2 966
Varnville town[24]	1 948	1 555
Yemassee division	2 214	1 957
Yemassee town (pt.)	773	738
Horry County[25]	101 419	69 992
Aynor division	7 190	...
Aynor town[25]	643	536
Conway division	23 868	...
Bucksport (CDP)	1 125	...
Conway city[25]	10 240	8 151
Conway East division	8 546	3 419
Forestbrook (CDP)	1 529	...
Floyds division	3 771	3 420
Little River division	8 781	...
Atlantic Beach town	289	215
Briarcliffe Acres town[25]	338	...
North Myrtle Beach town[25]	3 960	1 957
Longs division	3 299	2 788
Loris division	11 137	...
Loris city[25]	2 193	1 741
Myrtle Beach division	34 827	...
Myrtle Beach city[25]	18 446	[r]9 035
Socastee (CDP)	1 082	...
Surfside Beach town	2 522	1 329
Jasper County[26]	14 504	11 885
Grays–Tillman division	4 202	...
Hardeeville division	4 229	...
Hardeeville town[26]	1 250	853
Ridgeland division	6 073	5 160
Ridgeland town[26]	1 143	1 165
Kershaw County[27]	39 015	34 727
Bethune division	2 378	2 158
Bethune town	481	506
Boykin division	1 902	1 492
Camden division	20 381	...
Camden city[27]	7 462	8 532
Elgin division	10 591	6 820
Elgin town[27]	595	374
Lugoff (CDP)	2 939	...
Mount Pisgah division	1 905	3 096
Westville division	1 858	...
Lancaster County[28]	53 361	43 328
Heath Springs division	4 764	...
Heath Springs town	979	955
Kershaw division	7 211	...
Kershaw town[28]	1 993	990
Spring Mills (CDP)	1 419	...
Lancaster division	34 951	...
Irwin (CDP)	1 373	1 424
Lancaster city[28]	9 603	9 186
Lancaster Mills (CDP)	2 139	2 558
Springdale (CDP)	2 570	3 193
Tradesville division	2 355	1 980
Van Wyck division	4 080	3 190
Laurens County[29]	52 214	49 713
Clinton division	16 268	16 644
Clinton city[29]	8 596	8 138
Cross Hill division	3 300	2 933
Cross Hill town	604	579
Waterloo town	200	112
Gray Court division	7 152	5 786
Fountain Inn town (pt.)	835	591
Gray Court town	988	859
Joanna division	2 485	2 853
Joanna (CDP)	1 839	1 631
Laurens division	19 150	...
Laurens city[29]	10 587	10 298
Watts Mills (CDP)	1 324	1 181
Princeton division	3 859	3 920
Ware Shoals town (pt.)[29]	14	...
Lee County[30]	18 929	18 323
Ashwood division	3 741	3 317
Bishopville division	9 327	...
Bishopville town[30]	3 429	3 404
Lynchburg division	2 266	2 434
Lynchburg town	534	546
St. Charles division	1 736	1 707
Stokes Bridge–Cypress division	1 859	2 024
Lexington County[31]	140 353	89 012
Batesburg–Leesville division	8 909	8 495
Batesburg town (pt.)[31]	3 609	3 668
Leesville town	2 296	1 907
Chapin division	4 725	2 329
Chapin town	311	342
Gilbert division	7 740	4 902
Gilbert town	211	186
Summit town	172	130
Irmo division	25 856	...
Irmo town (pt.)[31]	1 623	517
Seven Oaks (CDP)	16 604	...
Lexington division	25 820	12 297
Lexington town[31]	2 131	969
Oak Grove (CDP) (pt.)	3 915	...

County Subdivisions	1980	1970
Lexington County—Con.		
Pelion division	5 302	2 852
Pelion town[31]	213	216
Swansea division	6 419	4 651
Gaston town (pt.)[31]	809	...
Swansea town[31]	888	691
West Columbia–Cayce division	55 582	...
Cayce city[31]	11 701	9 967
Gaston town (pt.)[31]	151	...
Oak Grove (CDP) (pt.)	3 177	...
Pineridge town	1 287	633
South Congaree town	2 113	1 434
Springdale town[31]	2 985	2 638
West Columbia city[31]	10 409	7 838
McCormick County[32]	7 797	7 955
McCormick division	4 617	...
McCormick town	1 725	1 864
Mount Carmel division	1 358	...
Mount Carmel town	182	138
Parksville division	1 822	...
Parksville town	157	164
Plum Branch town	73	108
Marion County[33]	34 179	30 270
Brittons Neck division	2 205	...
Centenary division	1 670	...
Marion division	16 587	...
Marion city[33]	7 700	7 435
Sellers town	388	469
Mullins division	13 717	...
Mullins city[33]	6 068	6 006
Nichols town	606	549
Marlboro County[34]	31 634	27 151
Bennettsville division	16 731	...
Bennettsville city[34]	8 774	7 468
Bennettsville Southwest (CDP)	2 308	1 726
South Bennettsville (CDP)	1 065	...
Blenheim division	2 414	...
Blenheim town	202	236
Clio division	3 092	3 147
Clio town[34]	1 031	936
McColl division	5 881	4 996
McColl town[34]	2 677	2 524
Tatum town	101	115
Wallace division	3 516	3 258
Newberry County[35]	31 242	29 273
Chappells division	1 094	950
Chappells town	109	74
Newberry division	16 403	...
Newberry town[35]	9 866	9 218
Silverstreet town	200	156
Pomaria division	3 250	...
Pomaria town	271	264
Prosperity division	5 823	...
Little Mountain town	282	240
Peak town	82	87
Prosperity town[35]	803	762
Whitmire division	4 672	4 340
Whitmire town[35]	2 038	2 226
Oconee County[36]	48 611	40 728
Long Creek division	1 519	1 347
Mountain Rest division	1 371	1 173
Oakway division	4 587	3 701
Salem division	2 479	...
Salem town	194	301
Seneca division	17 781	...
Seneca town[36]	7 436	[r]6 573
Utica (CDP)	1 501	[r]1 198
Walhalla division	12 958	...
Walhalla town[36]	3 977	3 662
West Union town	300	388
Westminster division	7 916	6 778
Westminster town[36]	3 114	2 521
Orangeburg County[37]	82 276	69 789
Bowman division	4 339	3 565
Bowman town	1 137	1 095
Branchville division	2 338	2 116
Branchville town	1 769	1 011
Cope division	1 958	1 965
Cope town	167	202
Elloree division	3 794	3 764
Elloree town	909	940
Eutawville division	3 949	3 233
Eutawville town	615	386
Holly Hill division	4 967	4 896
Holly Hill town[37]	1 785	1 178
Neeses division	3 025	2 549
Livingston town	166	165
Neeses town[37]	557	388
North division	3 230	3 160
North town	1 304	1 076
Woodford town	206	195
Norway division	2 701	2 347
Norway town[37]	518	579
Orangeburg division	37 220	...
Brookdale (CDP)	6 123	...

County Subdivisions	1980	1970
Orangeburg County—Con.		
Orangeburg division—Con.		
North Orangeburg (CDP)	1 952	...
Orangeburg city[37]	14 933	13 252
Rowesville town	388	392
West Orangeburg (CDP)	1 558	...
Wilkinson Heights (CDP)	3 652	...
Orangeburg West division	7 763	...
Cordova town	202	205
Edisto (CDP)	3 115	...
Springfield division	2 406	2 437
Springfield town	604	724
Vance division	4 586	4 035
Santee town	612	137
Vance town	89	54
Pickens County[38]	79 292	58 956
Central division	6 267	4 838
Central town[38]	1 914	1 550
Clemson city (pt.)[38]	73	...
Norris town (pt.)	539	757
Clemson division	15 058	11 992
Clemson city (pt.)[38]	7 999	ʳ6 673
Easley division	26 029	...
Ariail (CDP)	2 419	1 150
Easley city[38]	14 264	11 175
Easley East division	4 234	2 317
Forest division	1 517	1 420
Liberty division	7 303	4 954
Liberty town[38]	3 167	2 860
Norris town (pt.)	364	...
Pickens division	12 506	...
Pickens town[38]	3 199	2 954
Six Mile division	6 378	4 878
Six Mile town	470	361
Richland County[39]	269 735	233 868
Blythewood division	5 103	3 164
Blythewood town[39]	92	...
Camp Ground division	3 665	2 460
Columbia division	195 759	...
Arcadia Lakes town	611	741
Capitol View (CDP)	9 962	...
Columbia city (pt.)[39]	100 792	113 542
Dentsville (CDP) (pt.)	10 477	...
Forest Acres city[39]	6 033	6 808
Greenview (CDP)	5 515	...
North Trenholm (CDP)	10 962	...
Valencia Heights (CDP)	5 328	...
Woodfield (CDP)	9 588	...
Dutch Fork division	30 460	12 286
Columbia city (pt.)[39]	416	...
Irmo town (pt.)[39]	2 334	...
St. Andrews (CDP)	20 245	...
Eastover division	4 724	4 740
Eastover town[39]	899	817
Hopkins division	6 035	5 250
Horrell Hill division	7 746	2 919
Pontiac division	16 243	4 482
Dentsville (CDP) (pt.)	3 102	...
Saluda County[40]	16 150	14 528
Batesburg division	3 400	2 838
Batesburg town (pt.)	414	368
Ridge Spring division	3 536	3 119
Monetta town (pt.)[40]	83	ʳ122
Ridge Spring town[40]	969	644
Ward town	98	150
Saluda division	7 429	...
Saluda town	2 752	2 442
Saluda River division	1 785	1 823
Spartanburg County[41]	201 861	173 724
Boiling Springs division	9 352	6 295
Boiling Springs (CDP)	2 095	...
Valley Falls (CDP) (pt.)	999	...
Chesnee division	4 459	3 898
Chesnee town	1 069	1 069
Cowpens division	3 991	7 334
Cowpens town[41]	2 023	2 109
Enoree division	2 997	2 989
Enoree (CDP)	1 107	...
Fairmont Mills division	3 016	2 225
Fingerville division	3 576	2 306
Gramling division	3 251	2 878
Campobello town (pt.)[41]	—	–
Greer division	11 280	8 897
Greer city (pt.)[41]	3 931	4 031
Inman division	10 402	8 161
Inman city[41]	1 554	1 661
Inman Mills (CDP)	1 885	1 811
Landrum division	5 479	5 339
Campobello town (pt.)[41]	472	530
Landrum city[41]	2 141	1 859
Mayo division	3 800	2 816
Pacolet division	5 075	...
Central Pacolet town	315	483
Pacolet town[41]	1 556	1 418
Pacolet Mills town[41]	1 051	1 504
Pauline division	4 811	4 057
Roebuck (CDP) (pt.)	228	...

County Subdivisions	1980	1970
Spartanburg County—Con.		
Reidville division	3 363	2 932
Spartanburg division	105 609	...
Arcadia (CDP)	2 088	1 887
Arkwright (CDP)	2 623	2 059
Ben Avon (CDP)	1 701	...
Camp Croft (CDP)	2 191	...
Converse (CDP)	1 173	...
Drayton (CDP)	1 443	...
Glendale (CDP)	1 049	...
Hayne (CDP)	2 226	...
Hillbrook (CDP)	2 715	...
Roebuck (CDP) (pt.)	855	...
Saxon (CDP)	4 383	4 807
Southern Shops (CDP)	3 416	2 864
Spartanburg city[41]	43 968	44 546
Springfield (CDP)	2 012	...
Una (CDP)	1 281	...
Valley Falls (CDP) (pt.)	1 848	...
Westview (CDP)	1 999	1 105
Whitney (CDP)	4 052	2 891
Woodburn Hills (CDP)	1 914	...
Wellford division	12 631	11 214
Duncan town[41]	1 259	1 266
Lyman town	1 067	1 159
Startex (CDP)	1 006	1 203
Wellford city[41]	2 143	1 298
Woodruff division	8 769	8 223
Woodruff town[41]	5 171	ʳ4 690
Sumter County[42]	88 243	79 425
Privateer division	7 163	...
Pinewood town (pt.)[42]	686	(NA)
Rembert division	2 792	2 557
Shaw—Horatio division	18 434	...
Cherryville (CDP)	2 738	...
Oakland (CDP)	1 336	...
Shaw AFB (CDP)	6 939	5 819
Shiloh division	2 997	2 751
Sumter division	45 373	...
East Sumter (CDP)	1 790	...
Millwood (CDP)	1 439	...
Mulberry (CDP)	1 688	...
South Sumter (CDP)	7 096	7 491
Sumter city[42]	24 890	ʳ24 555
Sumter Southwest (CDP)	4 075	...
Sumter North division	3 120	...
Sumter Northeast division	3 141	...
Mayesville town	663	757
Sumter Southeast division	3 735	...
Sumter Southwest division	1 515	...
Pinewood town (pt.)[42]	3	(NA)
Union County[43]	30 751	29 230
Carlisle division	1 972	1 860
Carlisle town[43]	503	670
Cross Keys division	1 322	1 306
Jonesville division	3 514	3 040
Jonesville town	1 188	1 447
Lockhart division	2 659	2 967
Lockhart town	85	103
Union division	19 571	...
Buffalo (CDP)	1 641	1 461
Monarch Mills (CDP)	2 353	1 726
Union city[43]	10 523	10 775
West Springs division	1 713	1 317
Williamsburg County[44]	38 226	34 243
Cades division	3 126	2 703
Greeleyville division	2 999	3 352
Greeleyville town[44]	593	542
Hemingway division	5 857	5 257
Hemingway town[44]	853	1 026
Stuckey town	222	193
Indian division	2 299	2 010
Kingstree division	14 093	...
Kingstree town[44]	4 147	3 381
Lane division	3 624	...
Lane town	554	517
Nesmith division	3 909	...
Trio division	2 319	2 156
Andrews town (pt.)	95	48
York County[45]	106 720	85 216
Clover division	12 902	...
Clover town[45]	3 451	3 506
Fort Mill division	12 861	8 957
Fort Mill town[45]	4 162	4 505
Riverview (CDP)	1 021	...
Tega Cay (CDP)	2 521	...
Hickory Grove division	3 298	...
Hickory Grove town	344	377
Sharon town[45]	323	268
Smyrna town	47	85
McConnells division	1 789	1 243
McConnells town	171	213
Rock Hill division	64 083	...
Lesslie (CDP)	1 102	...
North Rock Hill (CDP)	1 564	...
Rock Hill city[45]	35 344	33 846

County Subdivisions

	1980	1970
York County—Con.		
York division	11 787	...
York city[45]	6 412	5 081

SOUTH DAKOTA

The name Dakota was originally that of an Indian nation which inhabited the region now comprising North and South Dakota, Montana, and Minnesota. The word signifies friends, allies, or confederates. French explorers and traders entered the present state of South Dakota early in the eighteenth century and established a number of trading posts, but the first explorers to make an authentic and trustworthy report regarding the Dakota country were Lewis and Clark, who, at the head of a United States Government expedition, ascended the Missouri River in 1804, returning in 1806. The first permanent settlement was made at Sioux Falls in 1857.

The area now known as South Dakota was originally a part of the Louisiana region, which was ceded by France to Spain in 1762, retroceded in 1800, and purchased by the United States in 1803.

The region now constituting South Dakota belonged to the district of Louisiana from 1804 to 1805, to the territory of Louisiana from 1805 to 1812, and to the territory of Missouri from 1812 to 1834. From 1834 to 1854 the part west of the Missouri and White Earth Rivers was part of the Indian country, and from 1854 to 1861 a part of Nebraska territory. The part east of these rivers belonged successively to the territories of Michigan (1834-1836), Wisconsin (1836-1838), Iowa (1838-1849), and Minnesota (1849-1858). Upon the admission of the state of Minnesota, in 1858, the region lying between that state and the Missouri and White Earth Rivers was left without legal name or existence, and it so remained until the territory of Dakota was created.

In 1861 the region extending from the Keyapaha, Niobrara, and Missouri Rivers and the forty-third parallel to the Canadian boundary and from Minnesota to the Rocky Mountains, was organized as Dakota territory, which thus included most of the present state of Montana and nearly half of what is now Wyoming. In 1863 when Idaho territory was formed the region lying between the Rocky Mountains and the present western boundaries of North and South Dakota was included. Most of the present area of Wyoming was transferred from Idaho to Dakota in 1864, and continued as a part of the latter territory until 1868, when Wyoming territory was organized. In 1882 a small tract of land lying south of the forty-third parallel and west of the Missouri River was transferred from Dakota to Nebraska.

In October, 1889, South Dakota adopted a constitution, and in the following November, with boundaries as at present, became a state of the Union.

COUNTY LOCATION INDEX

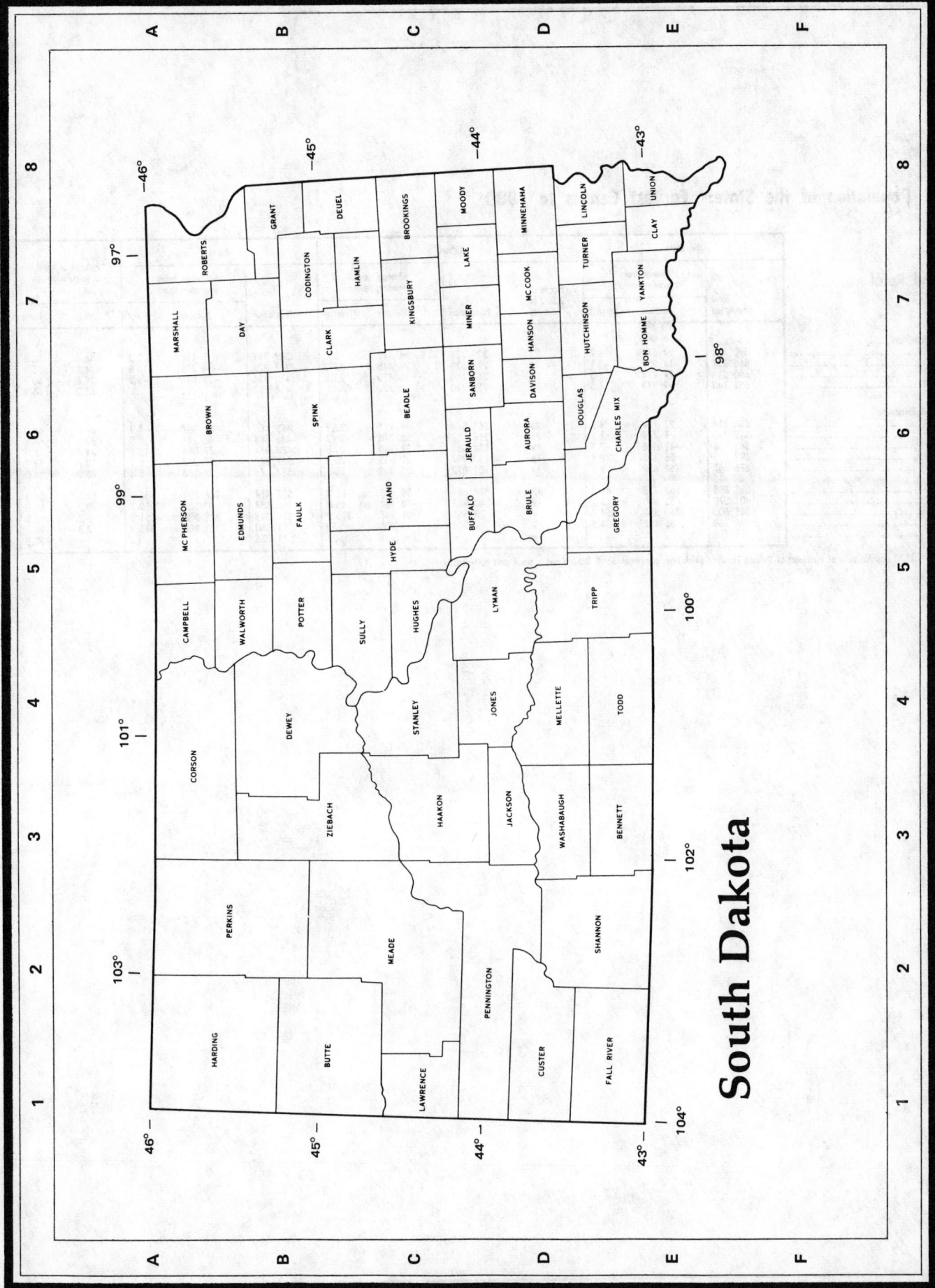

South Dakota

Population of the State: Earliest Census to 1980

Urban and Rural

	The State			Urban				Rural			Percent of total population	
	Total population	Change from preceding census		Places of 2,500 or more	Population	Change from preceding census		Population	Change from preceding census		Urban	Rural
		Number	Percent			Number	Percent		Number	Percent		
Current urban definition:												
1980 (Apr. 1)	690 768	24 511	3.7	27	320 777	24 149	8.1	369 991	1 112	0.3	46.4	53.6
1970 (Apr. 1)	'666 257	-14 257	-2.1	26	296 628	29 448	11.0	368 879	-44 455	-10.8	44.6	55.4
1960 (Apr. 1)	680 514	27 774	4.3	25	267 180	50 470	23.3	413 334	-22 696	-5.2	39.3	60.7
1950 (Apr. 1)	652 740	9 779	1.5	25	216 710	...	...	436 030	...	...	33.2	66.8
Previous urban definition:												
1960 (Apr. 1)	680 514	27 774	4.3	25	265 328	49 171	22.7	415 186	-21 397	-4.9	39.0	61.0
1950 (Apr. 1)	652 740	9 779	1.5	25	216 157	58 070	36.7	436 583	-48 291	-10.0	33.1	66.9
1940 (Apr. 1)	642 961	-49 888	-7.2	19	158 087	27 180	20.8	484 874	-77 068	-13.7	24.6	75.4
1930 (Apr. 1)	692 849	56 302	8.8	16	130 907	29 035	28.5	561 942	27 267	5.1	18.9	81.1
1920 (Jan. 1)	636 547	52 659	9.0	14	101 872	25 403	33.2	534 675	27 256	5.4	16.0	84.0
1910 (Apr. 15)	583 888	182 318	45.4	13	76 469	35 533	86.8	507 419	146 785	40.7	13.1	86.9
1900 (June 1)	401 570	52 970	15.2	9	40 936	12 381	43.4	360 634	40 589	12.7	10.2	89.8
1890 (June 1)	348 600	250 332	254.7	7	28 555	21 347	296.2	320 045	228 985	251.5	8.2	91.8
1880 (June 1)	98 268	86 492	734.5	2	7 208	7 208	...	91 060	79 284	673.3	7.3	92.7
1870 (June 1)	11 776	...	...	—	—	...	...	11 776	...	...	—	100.0

NOTE: 1870 population is of that part of Dakota Territory which now comprises South Dakota and a small part of Nebraska.

ARMSTRONG			CHARLES MIX		CUSTER			1890	4,600
								1900	5,012
1890	3		1870	152	1880	995		1910	6,400
1900	8		1880	407	1890	4,891		1920	6,993
1930	80		1890	4,178	1900	2,728		1930	7,236
1940	42		1900	8,498	1910	4,458		1940	6,348
1950	52		1910	14,899	1920	3,907		1950	5,636
			1920	16,256	1930	5,353		1960	5,113
AURORA			1930	16,703	1940	6,023		1970	4,569
			1940	13,449	1950	5,517		1980	4,181
1880	69		1950	15,558	1960	4,906			
1890	5,045		1960	11,785	1970	4,698		EDMUNDS	
1900	4,011		1970	9,944	1980	6,000			
1910	6,143		1980	9,680				1890	4,399
1920	7,246				DAVISON			1900	4,916
1930	7,139		CHOTEAU					1910	7,654
1940	5,387				1880	1,256		1920	8,336
1950	5,020		1890	8	1890	5,449		1930	8,712
1960	4,749				1900	7,483		1940	7,814
1970	4,183		CLARK		1910	11,625		1950	7,275
1980	3,628				1920	14,139		1960	6,079
			1880	114	1930	16,821		1970	5,548
BEADLE			1890	6,728	1940	15,336		1980	5,159
			1900	6,942	1950	16,522			
1880	1,290		1910	10,901	1960	16,681		EWING	
1890	9,586		1920	11,136	1970	17,319			
1900	8,081		1930	11,022	1980	17,820		1890	16
1910	15,776		1940	8,955					
1920	19,273		1950	8,369	DAY			FALL RIVER	
1930	22,917		1960	7,134					
1940	19,648		1970	5,515	1880	97		1890	4,478
1950	21,082		1980	4,894	1890	9,168		1900	3,541
1960	21,682				1900	12,254		1910	7,763
1970	20,877		CLAY		1910	14,372		1920	6,985
1980	19,195				1920	15,194		1930	8,741
			1870	2,621	1930	14,606		1940	8,089
BENNETT			1880	5,001	1940	13,565		1950	10,439
			1890	7,509	1950	12,294		1960	10,688
1910	96		1900	9,316	1960	10,516		1970	7,505
1920	1,964		1910	8,711	1970	8,173		1980	8,439
1930	4,590		1920	9,654	1980	8,133			
1940	3,983		1930	10,088				FAULK	
1950	3,396		1940	9,592	DELANO				
1960	3,053		1950	10,993				1880	4
1970	3,088		1960	10,810	1890	40		1890	4,062
1980	3,044		1970	12,923				1900	3,547
			1980	13,689	DEUEL			1910	6,716
BON HOMME								1920	6,442
			CODINGTON		1870	37		1930	6,895
1870	608				1880	2,302		1940	5,168
1880	5,468		1880	2,156	1890	4,574		1950	4,752
1890	9,057		1890	7,037	1900	6,656		1960	4,397
1900	10,379		1900	8,770	1910	7,768		1970	3,893
1910	11,061		1910	14,092	1920	8,759		1980	3,327
1920	11,940		1920	16,549	1930	8,732			
1930	11,737		1930	17,457	1940	8,450		GRANT	
1940	10,241		1940	17,014	1950	7,689			
1950	9,440		1950	18,944	1960	6,782		1880	3,010
1960	9,229		1960	20,220	1970	5,686		1890	6,814
1970	8,577		1970	19,140	1980	5,289		1900	9,103
1980	8,059		1980	20,885				1910	10,303
					DEWEY			1920	10,880
BOREMAN			CORSON					1930	10,729
					1880	46		1940	10,552
1880	534		1910	2,929	1910	1,145		1950	10,233
			1920	7,249	1920	4,802		1960	9,913
BROOKINGS			1930	9,535	1930	6,476		1970	9,055
			1940	6,755	1940	5,709		1980	9,013
1870	163		1950	6,168	1950	4,916			
1880	4,965		1960	5,798	1960	5,257		GREGORY	
1890	10,132		1970	4,994	1970	5,170			
1900	12,561		1980	5,196	1980	5,366		1890	295
1910	14,178							1900	2,211
1920	16,119				DOUGLAS			1910	13,061
1930	16,847							1920	12,700
1940	16,560				1880	6			

BROWN						
1950	17,851					
1960	20,046					
1970	22,158					
1980	24,332					
1880	353					
1890	16,855					
1900	15,286					
1910	25,867					
1920	29,509					
1930	31,458					
1940	29,676					
1950	32,617					
1960	34,106					
1970	36,920					
1980	36,962					

BRULE	
1880	238
1890	6,737
1900	5,401
1910	6,451
1920	7,141
1930	7,416
1940	6,195
1950	6,076
1960	6,319
1970	5,870
1980	5,245

BUFFALO	
1870	246
1880	63
1890	993
1900	1,790
1910	1,589
1920	1,715
1930	1,931
1940	1,853
1950	1,615
1960	1,547
1970	1,739
1980	1,795

BUTTE	
1890	1,037
1900	2,907
1910	4,993
1920	6,819
1930	8,589
1940	8,004
1950	8,161
1960	8,592
1970	7,825
1980	8,372

CAMPBELL	
1880	50
1890	3,510
1900	4,527
1910	5,244
1920	5,305
1930	5,629
1940	5,033
1950	4,046
1960	3,531
1970	2,866
1980	2,243

1930	11,420
1940	9,554
1950	8,556
1960	7,399
1970	6,710
1980	6,015

HAAKON

1920	4,596
1930	4,697
1940	3,515
1950	3,167
1960	3,303
1970	2,802
1980	2,794

HAMLIN

1880	693
1890	4,625
1900	5,945
1910	7,475
1920	8,054
1930	8,299
1940	7,562
1950	7,058
1960	6,303
1970	5,172
1980	5,261

HAND

1880	153
1890	6,546
1900	4,525
1910	7,870
1920	8,778
1930	9,485
1940	7,166
1950	7,149
1960	6,712
1970	5,883
1980	4,948

HANSON

1880	1,301
1890	4,267
1900	4,947
1910	6,237
1920	6,202
1930	6,131
1940	5,400
1950	4,896
1960	4,584
1970	3,781
1980	3,415

HARDING

1890	167
1910	4,228
1920	3,953
1930	3,589
1940	3,010
1950	2,289
1960	2,371
1970	1,855
1980	1,700

HUGHES

1880	268
1890	5,044

1900	3,684
1910	6,271
1920	5,711
1930	7,009
1940	6,624
1950	8,111
1960	12,725
1970	11,632
1980	14,220

HUTCHINSON

1870	37
1880	5,573
1890	10,469
1900	11,897
1910	12,319
1920	13,475
1930	13,904
1940	12,668
1950	11,423
1960	11,085
1970	10,379
1980	9,350

HYDE

1890	1,860
1900	1,492
1910	3,307
1920	3,315
1930	3,690
1940	3,113
1950	2,811
1960	2,602
1970	2,515
1980	2,069

JACKSON

1890	30
1920	2,472
1930	2,636
1940	1,955
1950	1,768
1960	1,985
1970	1,531
1980	3,437

JAYNE

1870	5

JERAULD

1890	3,605
1900	2,798
1910	5,120
1920	6,338
1930	5,816
1940	4,752
1950	4,476
1960	4,048
1970	3,310
1980	2,929

JONES

1920	3,004
1930	3,177
1940	2,509
1950	2,281
1960	2,066
1970	1,882
1980	1,463

KINGSBURY

1880	1,102
1890	8,562
1900	9,866
1910	12,560
1920	12,802
1930	12,805
1940	10,831
1950	9,962
1960	9,277
1970	7,657
1980	6,679

LAKE

1880	2,657
1890	7,508
1900	9,137
1910	10,711
1920	12,257
1930	12,379
1940	12,412
1950	11,792
1960	11,764
1970	11,456
1980	10,724

LAWRENCE

1880	13,248
1890	11,673
1900	17,897
1910	19,694
1920	13,029
1930	13,920
1940	19,093
1950	16,648
1960	17,075
1970	17,453
1980	18,339

LINCOLN

1870	712
1880	5,896
1890	9,143
1900	12,161
1910	12,712
1920	13,893
1930	13,918
1940	13,171
1950	12,767
1960	12,371
1970	11,761
1980	13,942

LYMAN

1880	124
1890	233
1900	2,632
1910	10,848
1920	6,591
1930	6,335
1940	5,045
1950	4,572
1960	4,428
1970	4,060
1980	3,864

McCOOK

1880	1,283
1890	6,448
1900	8,689

1910	9,589
1920	9,990
1930	10,316
1940	9,793
1950	8,828
1960	8,268
1970	7,246
1980	6,444

McPHERSON

1890	5,940
1900	6,327
1910	6,791
1920	7,705
1930	8,774
1940	8,353
1950	7,071
1960	5,821
1970	5,022
1980	4,027

MARSHALL

1890	4,544
1900	5,942
1910	8,021
1920	9,596
1930	9,540
1940	8,880
1950	7,835
1960	6,663
1970	5,965
1980	5,404

MARTIN

1890	7

MEADE

1890	4,640
1900	4,907
1910	12,640
1920	9,367
1930	11,482
1940	9,735
1950	11,516
1960	12,044
1970	16,618
1980	20,717

MELLETTE

1910	1,700
1920	3,850
1930	5,293
1940	4,107
1950	3,046
1960	2,664
1970	2,420
1980	2,249

MEYER

1880	115

MINER

1880	363
1890	5,165
1900	5,864
1910	7,661
1920	8,560
1930	8,376

1940	6,836
1950	6,268
1960	5,398
1970	4,454
1980	3,739

MINNEHAHA

1870	355
1880	8,251
1890	21,879
1900	23,926
1910	29,631
1920	42,490
1930	50,872
1940	57,697
1950	70,910
1960	86,575
1970	95,209
1980	109,435

MOODY

1880	3,915
1890	5,941
1900	8,326
1910	8,695
1920	9,742
1930	9,603
1940	9,341
1950	9,252
1960	8,810
1970	7,622
1980	6,692

NOWLIN

1890	149

PENNINGTON

1880	2,244
1890	6,540
1900	5,610
1910	12,453
1920	12,720
1930	20,079
1940	23,799
1950	34,053
1960	58,195
1970	59,349
1980	70,361

PERKINS

1910	11,348
1920	7,993
1930	8,717
1940	6,585
1950	6,776
1960	5,977
1970	4,769
1980	4,700

POTTER

1890	2,910
1900	2,988
1910	4,466
1920	4,382
1930	5,762
1940	4,614
1950	4,688
1960	4,926
1970	4,449
1980	3,674

PRATT

1890	23

PRESHO

1890	181

ROBERTS

1890	1,997
1900	12,216
1910	14,897
1920	16,514
1 30	15,782
1940	15,887
1950	14,929
1960	13,190
1970	11,678
1980	10,911

SANBORN

1890	4,610
1900	4,464
1910	6,607
1920	7,877
1930	7,326
1940	5,754
1950	5,142
1960	4,641
1970	3,697
1980	3,213

SCOBEY

1890	32

SHANNON

1880	113
1920	2,003
1930	4,058
1940	5,366
1950	5,669
1960	6,000
1970	8,198
1980	11,323

SPINK

1880	477
1890	10,581
1900	9,487
1910	15,981
1920	15,768
1930	15,304
1940	12,527
1950	12,024
1960	11,706
1970	10,595
1980	9,201

STANLEY

1880	793
1890	1,028
1900	1,341
1910	14,975
1920	2,908
1930	2,381
1940	1,959
1950	2,055
1960	4,085
1970	2,457

1980	2,533

STERLING

1890	96

SULLY

1880	296
1890	2,412
1900	1,715
1910	2,462
1920	2,831
1930	3,852
1940	2,668
1950	2,713
1960	2,607
1970	2,362
1980	1,990

TODD

1870	337
1880	203
1890	188
1910	2,164
1920	2,784
1930	5,898
1940	5,714
1950	4,758
1960	4,661
1970	6,606
1980	7,328

TRIPP

1910	8,323
1920	11,970
1930	12,712
1940	9,937
1950	9,139
1960	8,761
1970	8,171
1980	7,268

TURNER

1880	5,320
1890	10,256
1900	13,175
1910	13,840
1920	14,871
1930	14,891
1940	13,270
1950	12,100
1960	11,159
1970	9,872
1980	9,255

UNION

1870	3,507
1880	6,813
1890	9,130
1900	11,153
1910	10,676
1920	11,099
1930	11,480
1940	11,675
1950	10,792
1960	10,197
1970	9,643
1980	10,938

WALWORTH

1880	46
1890	2,153
1900	3,839
1910	6,488
1920	8,447
1930	8,791
1940	7,274
1950	7,648
1960	8,097
1970	7,842
1980	7,011

WASHABAUGH

1920	1,166
1930	2,474
1940	1,980
1950	1,551
1960	1,042
1970	1,389

WASHINGTON

1890	40
1920	1,521
1930	1,827

YANKTON

1870	2,097
1880	8,390
1890	10,444
1900	12,649
1910	13,135
1920	15,233
1930	16,589
1940	16,725
1950	16,804
1960	17,551
1970	19,039
1980	18,952

ZIEBACH

1890	510
1920	3,718
1930	4,039
1940	2,875
1950	2,606
1960	2,495
1970	2,221
1980	2,308

NOTES

ARMSTRONG

Annexed to Dewey prior to 1960.

BOREMAN

Located within the limits of Standing Rock Indian reservation.

CHOTEAU

Annexed to Butte in 1899.

DELANO

Part taken to form Scobey in 1883; annexed to Meade in 1899.

DEWEY

Name changed from Rusk in 1883.

EWING

Annexed to Butte in 1899.

HARDING

Parts taken to form Ewing and part of Butte in 1883; annexed to Butte in 1899.

JACKSON

Annexed to Stanley in 1899.

JAYNE

Annexed to Hanson, Hutchinson, McCook, and Turner prior to 1880.

LUGENBEEL

Part taken to form part of Washabaugh in 1883. Located within the limits of Pine Ridge and Rosebud Indian reservations.

MARTIN

Annexed to Butte in 1899.

MEYER

Located within the limits of Rosebud Indian reservation.

NOWLIN

Annexed to Stanley in 1899.

PRATT

Annexed to Lyman in 1899.

PRESHO

Annexed to Lyman in 1899.

SCHNASSE

Located within the limits of Cheyenne River and Standing Rock Indian reservations.

SCOBEY

Annexed to Meade in 1899.

SHANNON

Located within the limits of Pine Ridge Indian reservation.

STERLING

Annexed to Stanley in 1899.

TODD[1]

Annexed to Gregory in 1899.

TODD[2]

Established in 1909. County unorganized; attached to Tripp County for judicial purposes.

TRIPP

Located within the limits of Rosebud Indian reservation.

UNION

Name changed from Cole in 1864.

WAGNER

Annexed to Butte in 1899.

WASHABAUGH

Located within the limits of Pine Ridge and Rosebud Indian reservations.

WASHINGTON

Located both within and outside Pine Ridge Indian reservation.

ZIEBACH

Annexed to Pennington in 1899.

ABERDEEN

1890	3,182
1900	4,087
1910	10,753
1920	14,537
1930	16,465
1940	17,015
1950	21,051
1960	23,073
1970	26,476
1980	25,956

BROOKINGS

1890	1,518
1900	2,346
1910	2,971
1920	3,924
1930	4,376
1940	5,346
1950	7,764
1960	10,558
1970	13,717
1980	14,951

HURON

1880	164
1890	3,038
1900	2,793
1910	5,791
1920	8,302
1930	10,946
1940	10,843
1950	12,788
1960	14,180
1970	14,299
1980	13,000

MITCHELL

1880	320
1890	2,217
1900	4,055
1910	6,515
1920	8,478
1930	10,942
1940	10,633
1950	12,123
1960	12,555
1970	13,425
1980	13,916

PIERRE

1890	3,235
1900	2,306
1910	3,656
1920	3,209
1930	3,659
1940	4,322
1950	5,715
1960	10,088
1970	9,699
1980	11,973

RAPID CITY

1880	292
1890	2,128
1900	1,342
1910	3,854
1920	5,777
1930	10,404
1940	13,844
1950	25,310
1960	42,399
1970	43,836
1980	46,492

SIOUX FALLS

1880	2,164
1890	10,177
1900	10,266
1910	14,094
1920	25,202
1930	33,362
1940	40,832
1950	52,696
1960	65,466
1970	72,488
1980	81,343

VERMILLION

1880	714
1890	1,496
1900	2,183
1910	2,187
1920	2,590
1930	2,850
1940	3,324
1950	5,337
1960	6,102
1970	9,128
1980	10,136

WATERTOWN

1880	746
1890	2,762
1900	3,352
1910	7,010
1920	9,400
1930	10,214
1940	10,617
1950	12,699
1960	14,077
1970	13,388
1980	15,649

YANKTON

1880	3,431
1890	3,670
1900	4,125
1910	3,787
1920	5,024
1930	6,072
1940	6,798
1950	7,709
1960	9,279
1970	11,919
1980	12,011

CORRECTION NOTE

The official 1980 census counts of total population shown in this report supersede counts issued previously. Corrections to the figures were made after the counts were provided to the State for redistricting purposes and released in Advance Report PHC80-V for this State.

Shown below are corrections to the 1980 census counts of the total population made after the tabulations for this report were completed. Any additional corrections made after this report is printed are available by writing to Data User Services Division, Customer Services (Corrections), Bureau of the Census, Washington, D.C. 20233.

The 1980 figures shown in this publication are subject to change pending the outcome of the various lawsuits dealing with the census counts.

	1980 population	
	As shown in the tables	Corrected
Brown County:		
Aberdeen city...................	25 956	25 851
Aberdeen township..............	1 368	1 473

County Subdivisions	1980	1970
The State	690 768	ʳ666 257
Aurora County[1]	3 628	4 183
Aurora township	138	180
Belford township	205	295
Bristol township	81	95
Center township	177	234
Cooper township	27	38
Crystal Lake township	73	105
Dudley township[1]	106	135
Eureka township	77	83
Firesteel township	89	78
Gales township	93	127
Hopper township	103	107
Lake township	85	86
Palatine township	85	118
Patten township	61	75
Plankinton city[1]	644	613
Plankinton township	218	367
Pleasant Lake township[1]	113	102
Pleasant Valley township	58	85
Stickney town[1]	409	421
Truro township	165	184
Washington township	109	120
White Lake city	414	395
White Lake township	98	140
Beadle County[2]	19 195	20 877
Allen township	114	126
Altoona township	98	123
Banner township	59	72
Barrett township	61	105
Belle Prairie township	74	92
Bonilla township	117	137
Broadland town	49	45
Broadland township	88	103
Burr Oak township	50	68
Carlyle township	94	131
Cavour town	117	134
Cavour township	136	171
Clifton township	147	161
Clyde township[2]	617	316
Custer township	427	441
Dearborn township	155	161
Fairfield township	133	132
Foster township	78	89
Grant township	164	170
Hartland township	137	142
Hitchcock town	132	150
Huron city[2]	13 000	14 299
Iowa township	197	239
Iroquois city (pt.)	49	55
Kellogg township	84	100
Lake Byron township	182	202
Liberty township	126	142
Logan township	154	165
Milford township	107	124
Nance township	55	66
Pearl Creek township	106	155
Pleasant View township	72	90
Richland township	167	191
Sand Creek township	63	103
Theresa township[2]	264	200
Valley township[2]	233	246
Vernon township	105	113
Virgil town	37	43
Wessington city (pt.)	304	345
Wessington township	73	96
Whiteside township	77	83
Wolsey town	437	436
Wolsey township	120	167
Yale town	136	148
Bennett County[3]	3 044	3 088
East Bennett (unorg.)[3]	1 001	820
Martin city[3]	1 018	1 248
West Bennett (unorg.)	1 025	1 020
Bon Homme County[4]	8 059	8 577
Avon city	576	610
Northeast Bon Homme (unorg.)	836	...
Northwest Bon Homme (unorg.)	772	...
Scotland city	1 022	984
Southeast Bon Homme (unorg.)[4]	644	...
Southwest Bon Homme (unorg.)[4]	1 119	...
Springfield city[4]	1 377	1 566
Tabor town[4]	460	388
Tyndall city	1 253	1 245
Brookings County[5]	24 332	22 158
Afton township	224	235
Alton township	286	258
Argo township	165	211
Arlington city (pt.)[5]	3	...
Aurora town[5]	507	237
Aurora township[5]	330	290
Bangor township[5]	185	234
Brookings city[5]	14 951	13 717
Brookings township[5]	425	398
Bruce city[5]	254	217

County Subdivisions	1980	1970
Brookings County—Con.		
Bushnell town	76	65
Elkton city	632	541
Elkton township	135	148
Eureka township	208	215
Lake Hendricks township	161	185
Lake Sinai township	211	226
Laketon township	151	203
Medary township	939	508
Oak Lake township	164	233
Oakwood township	215	226
Oslo township	212	260
Parnell township	171	227
Preston township	226	239
Richland township	219	203
Sherman township	194	178
Sinai town	129	147
Sterling township[5]	341	304
Trenton township	381	273
Volga city[5]	1 221	982
Volga township[5]	328	324
White city	474	418
Winsor township	214	256
Brown County[6]	36 962	36 920
Aberdeen city[6]	25 956	26 476
Aberdeen township[6]	1 368	1 145
Allison township	28	48
Bates township	67	89
Bath township	630	518
Brainard township	149	218
Cambria township	170	194
Carlisle township	66	75
Claremont city	180	214
Claremont township	159	214
Columbia city	161	240
Columbia township	171	189
East Hanson township	141	148
East Rondell township	105	117
Franklyn township	58	71
Frederick town	307	359
Frederick township	74	92
Garden Prairie township	102	103
Garland township	90	121
Gem township	235	277
Greenfield township	88	104
Groton city[6]	1 230	1 021
Groton township[6]	128	176
Hecla city[6]	435	407
Hecla township[6]	71	88
Henry township	136	165
Highland township	95	129
Lansing township	84	121
Liberty township	123	161
Lincoln township	1 029	321
Mercier township	150	119
New Hope township	132	152
North Detroit township	87	83
Oneota township	132	168
Ordway township	387	188
Osceola township	64	90
Palmyra township	56	93
Portage township	79	88
Putney township	107	142
Ravinia township	168	124
Richland township	86	99
Riverside township	88	122
Savo township	96	142
Shelby township	155	167
South Detroit township	121	149
Stratford town	82	106
Verdon town	7	18
Warner town[6]	322	...
Warner township[6]	550	708
West Hanson township	92	124
Westport town[6]	122	...
Westport township[6]	135	310
West Rondell township	108	127
Brule County[7]	5 245	5 870
America township	76	115
Brule township[7]	81	69
Chamberlain city[7]	2 258	2 626
Chamberlain township[7]	186	165
Cleveland township	106	116
Eagle township	103	108
Grandview (unorg.)[7]	41	34
Highland township	60	83
Kimball city	752	825
Kimball township	88	102
Lyon township	73	81
Ola township	114	144
Plainfield township	56	81
Pleasant Grove township	53	77
Plummer township	45	60
Pukwana town	234	208
Pukwana township	136	136
Red Lake township	78	78

County Subdivisions

County Subdivisions	1980	1970
Brule County—Con.		
Richland township	108	123
Smith township	66	113
Torrey Lake township	159	115
Union township	78	82
Waldro township	85	89
West Point township	105	103
Wilbur township	45	66
Willow Lake township	59	71
Buffalo County[8]	1 795	1 739
Crow Creek (unorg.)[8]	1 439	...
Elvira township	96	123
North Buffalo (unorg.)[8]	176	...
Southeast Buffalo (unorg.)[8]	84	109
Butte County[9]	8 372	7 825
Belle Fourche city[9]	4 692	4 236
Cottonwood township	7	9
East Butte (unorg.)[9]	631	646
Fruitdale town	88	74
Newell city[9]	638	664
Nisland town	216	157
Union township	52	80
Vale township	315	348
West Butte (unorg.)[9]	1 733	1 611
Campbell County[10]	2 243	2 866
Artas town	43	73
Herreid city[10]	570	672
Mound City town	111	164
North Campbell (unorg.)[10]	599	822
Pollock town	355	341
South Campbell (unorg.)	565	794
Charles Mix County[11]	9 680	9 994
Bryan township[11]	257	249
Carroll township	73	97
Castalia township	99	106
Choteau Creek township	280	354
Dante town	83	88
Darlington township	167	191
Forbes township	119	151
Geddes city	303	308
Goose Lake township	268	297
Hamilton township	53	55
Highland township	387	205
Howard township	147	189
Jackson township	201	265
Kennedy township	138	174
Lake Andes city	1 029	948
Lake George township	54	60
La Roche township	239	244
Lawrence township[11]	425	267
Lone Tree township	190	211
Moore township	238	277
Plain Center township	207	173
Platte city	1 334	1 351
Platte township	264	230
Ravinia town	88	109
Ree township	183	243
Rhoda township	158	203
Rouse township	211	198
Signal township	75	106
Wagner city[11]	1 453	1 655
Wahehe township	441	390
White Swan township	516	600
Clark County[12]	4 894	5 515
Ash township	60	74
Blaine township	76	93
Bradley town	135	157
Clark city[12]	1 351	1 356
Collins township[12]	105	190
Cottonwood township	140	142
Darlington township	92	93
Day township[12]	131	155
Eden township	100	120
Elrod township	131	161
Fordham township	121	77
Foxton township	77	92
Garden City town	104	126
Garfield township	110	120
Hague township	78	120
Lake township[12]	131	165
Lincoln township	106	130
Logan township	66	105
Maydell township	50	81
Merton township	83	96
Mount Pleasant township	164	103
Naples town	45	38
Pleasant township	104	121
Raymond town	106	114
Raymond township	91	127
Richland township	105	150
Rosedale township	109	142
Spring Valley township	77	125
Thorp township	79	91
Vienna town	90	119
Warren township	77	96

County Subdivisions

County Subdivisions	1980	1970
Clark County—Con.		
Washington township	126	159
Willow Lake city[12]	375	353
Woodland township	99	124
Clay County[13]	13 689	12 923
Bethel township	239	258
Fairview township[13]	395	397
Garfield township	273	332
Glenwood township	255	250
Irene town (pt.)[13]	250	214
Meckling township	268	389
Norway township	176	214
Pleasant Valley township	221	255
Prairie Center township	220	232
Riverside township	199	227
Spirit Mound township	234	261
Star township[13]	193	273
Vermillion city[13]	10 136	9 128
Vermillion township[13]	247	203
Wakonda town	383	290
Codington County[14]	20 885	19 140
Dexter township	200	268
Eden township	131	158
Elmira township[14]	326	240
Florence town	190	175
Fuller township	278	281
Germantown township	204	216
Graceland township	149	174
Henry town[14]	217	182
Henry township[14]	125	142
Kampeska township	273	249
Kranzburg town	136	143
Kranzburg township	363	417
Lake township[14]	551	1 016
Leola township	103	121
Pelican township[14]	460	263
Phipps township	105	133
Rauville township	325	232
Richland township[14]	169	134
Sheridan township[14]	368	607
South Shore town	241	199
Wallace town	90	95
Watertown city[14]	15 649	13 388
Waverly town	232	307
Corson County[15]	5 196	4 994
Cadillac township	43	49
Central Corson (unorg.)[15]	1 399	944
Custer township	65	62
Delaney township	22	13
Fairview township	25	43
Grand Valley township	38	51
Lake township	40	65
Lincoln township	87	97
McIntosh city	418	563
McLaughlin city[15]	754	863
McLaughlin township[15]	556	339
Mahto township	36	51
Mission township	268	137
Morristown town	127	144
Northeast Corson (unorg.)	272	333
Pioneer township	76	66
Pleasant Ridge township	42	36
Prairie View township	35	45
Ridgeland township	82	81
Riverside township	22	29
Rolling Green township	39	47
Sherman township	45	40
Thunder Hawk township	103	118
Twin Butte township	36	44
Wakpala township	282	325
Walker township	38	36
Watauga township	62	86
West Corson (unorg.)[15]	184	153
Custer County[16]	6 000	4 698
Buffalo Gap town	186	155
Custer city[16]	1 830	1 597
East Custer (unorg.)	816	672
Fairburn town	41	50
Hermosa town	251	150
Pringle town	105	86
West Custer (unorg.)[16]	2 771	1 988
Davison County[17]	17 820	17 319
Badger township	166	231
Baker township	182	190
Beulah township	393	341
Blendon township	123	154
Ethan town	351	309
Lisbon township	164	168
Mitchell city[17]	13 916	13 425
Mitchell township[17]	697	656
Mount Vernon city	402	398
Mount Vernon township	186	217
Perry township[17]	198	243
Prosper township	493	290
Rome township	275	353

County Subdivisions

County Subdivisions	1980	1970
Davison County—Con.		
Tobin township	173	226
Union township	101	118
Day County[18]	8 133	8 713
Andover town	139	138
Andover township	162	199
Bristol city	445	470
Bristol township	111	135
Butler town	22	38
Butler township	91	108
Central Point township	132	185
Egeland township	128	159
Farmington township	88	98
Grenville town	119	154
Grenville township	148	232
Highland township	164	190
Homer township	91	103
Independence township	118	156
Kidder township	100	90
Kosciusko township	243	244
Liberty township	108	134
Lily town	38	62
Lynn township	85	147
Morton township	126	134
Nutley township	126	137
Oak Gulch township	54	77
Pierpont town	184	241
Racine township	122	126
Raritan township	121	142
Roslyn town	261	250
Rusk township[18]	208	298
Scotland township	60	48
Troy township	69	91
Union township	120	181
Valley township	103	116
Waubay city	675	696
Waubay township	516	467
Webster city[18]	2 417	2 252
Webster township[18]	249	176
Wheatland township	122	146
York township	68	93
Deuel County	5 289	5 686
Altamont town	58	54
Altamont township	143	160
Antelope Valley township	82	86
Astoria town	154	153
Blom township	150	213
Brandt town	129	132
Brandt township	162	194
Clear Lake city	1 310	1 157
Clear Lake township	248	243
Gary city	354	366
Glenwood township	155	187
Goodwin town	139	114
Goodwin township	219	269
Grange township	167	208
Havana township	247	290
Herrick township	162	222
Hidewood township	148	187
Lowe township	198	207
Norden township	312	370
Portland township	112	123
Rome township	143	168
Scandinavia township	261	367
Toronto town	236	216
Dewey County[19]	5 366	5 170
Eagle Butte town	435	530
Isabel city	332	394
North Dewey (unorg.)[19]	2 982	...
North Eagle Butte (CDP)	1 354	1 351
South Dewey (unorg.)[19]	957	...
Timber Lake city	660	625
Douglas County[20]	4 181	4 569
Armour city	819	925
Belmont township[20]	117	149
Chester township	164	134
Clark township	206	239
Corsica[20] city	644	615
Delmont city[20]	290	260
East Choteau township	153	128
Garfield township	104	141
Grandview township[20]	169	214
Holland township	209	243
Independence township	204	223
Iowa township	167	195
Joubert township	193	229
Lincoln township	189	235
Valley township	180	221
Walnut Grove township	201	218
Washington township	172	200
Edmunds County[21]	5 159	5 548
Adrian township	24	33
Belle township	146	57
Bowdle city	644	667
Bowdle township	89	110

County Subdivisions

County Subdivisions	1980	1970
Edmunds County—Con.		
Bryant township	65	94
Clear Lake township	66	75
Cleveland township	65	65
Cloyd Valley township	42	61
Cortlandt township	372	188
Cottonwood Lake township	77	97
Fountain township	90	138
Glen township	70	86
Glover township	60	88
Harmony (unorg.)[21]	167	...
Hillside township	65	85
Hosmer city	385	437
Hosmer township	76	112
Hudson township	67	78
Huntley township	71	67
Ipswich city[21]	1 153	1 187
Ipswich township[21]	77	84
Kent township	39	56
Liberty township	44	46
Loyalton town	6	10
Madison township	52	45
Modena township[21]	54	...
Montpelier township	77	90
North Bryant township	71	85
Odessa township	54	94
Pembrook township	67	70
Powell township	55	85
Richland township	46	64
Roscoe city	370	398
Rosette township	144	213
Sangamon township	90	126
Union township	67	81
Vermont township	52	67
Fall River County[22]	8 439	7 505
Antelope township[22]	55	'50
Ardmore town	16	14
Argentine township	25	26
Cottonwood township[22]	51	15
Dryden township	64	71
Edgemont city[22]	1 468	1 174
Harmony township	44	53
Hot Springs city	4 742	4 434
Northeast Fall River (unorg.)[22]	1 265	1 122
Oelrichs town	124	94
Provo township	139	103
Robins township	28	30
Southwest Fall River (unorg.)[22]	418	190
Faulk County[23]	3 327	3 893
Arcade township	72	132
Bryant township	67	71
Centerville township	62	72
Chelsea town	41	45
Clark township	78	96
Cresbard town	221	224
Devoe township	59	97
Ellisville township	68	52
Emerson township	50	67
Enterprise township	159	147
Fairview township	50	68
Faulkton city	981	955
Freedom township	162	179
Hillsdale township	59	96
Lafoon township	75	85
Myron township	58	88
Onaka town	70	69
O'Neil township	15	20
Orient town	87	131
Orient township	68	106
Pioneer township	58	74
Pulaski township	28	45
Rockham town	52	60
Saratoga township	24	48
Seneca town	103	118
Sherman township	53	78
Southwest Faulk (unorg.)[23]	141	155
Tamworth township	110	135
Union township	80	105
Wesley township	69	86
Zell township	107	149
Grant County[24]	9 013	9 005
Adams township[24]	242	335
Alban township[24]	624	487
Albee town	23	26
Big Stone township	285	262
Big Stone City city	672	631
Blooming Valley township	130	155
Farmington township	65	78
Georgia township[24]	140	177
Grant Center township[24]	316	289
Kilborn township	197	206
La Bolt town	94	90
Lura township	121	145
Madison township	179	217
Marvin town	52	65

County Subdivisions	1980	1970
Grant County—Con.		
Mazeppa township	136	168
Melrose township	412	434
Milbank city[24]	4 120	3 727
Osceola township	156	185
Revillo town[24]	158	142
Stockholm town[24]	95	116
Stockholm township[24]	109	149
Strandburg town[24]	79	98
Troy township[24]	92	141
Twin Brooks town	87	122
Twin Brooks township	118	169
Vernon township	311	391
Gregory County[25]	6 015	6 710
Bonesteel city	358	354
Burke city[25]	859	892
Burke Civil township[25]	105	152
Carlock township	106	136
Dallas town	199	233
Dickens township	112	159
Dixon township	132	168
East Gregory (unorg.)	26	30
Edens township	86	92
Ellston township	115	243
Fairfax town	225	199
Fairfax Civil township	145	183
Gregory city[25]	1 503	1 756
Herrick town	115	126
Jones township	96	115
Landing Creek township	50	38
Lone Star township	94	107
Northeast Gregory (unorg.)	322	413
Pleasant Valley township	224	171
Rhoades township	224	172
St. Charles township	118	150
Schriever township	75	76
Southeast Gregory (unorg.)	69	96
Spring Valley township	104	150
Star Valley township	101	144
Union township	172	170
West Gregory (unorg.)[25]	244	143
Whetstone township	36	42
Haakon County[26]	2 794	2 802
East Haakon (unorg.)[26]	616	684
Grandfield township	39	40
Mattison township	11	24
Midland town[26]	277	270
Philip city[26]	1 088	983
West Haakon (unorg.)[26]	763	801
Hamlin County[27]	5 261	5 520
Brantford township	185	242
Bryant city[27]	388	502
Castlewood city	557	523
Castlewood township	158	165
Cleveland township	195	211
Dempster township	289	330
Dixon township	96	129
Estelline city	719	624
Estelline township	292	324
Florence township	136	146
Garfield township[27]	187	179
Hamlin township	204	303
Hayti town[27]	371	393
Hayti township[27]	184	160
Hazel town	94	101
Lake Norden city	417	393
Norden township	310	300
Opdahl township	217	241
Oxford township	262	254
Hand County[28]	4 948	5 883
Alden township	52	86
Alpha township	59	75
Bates township	82	76
Burdette township	71	108
Campbell township	33	48
Carlton township	55	70
Cedar township	51	64
Como township	60	63
Fairview township	163	165
Florence township	65	76
Gilbert township	78	94
Glendale township	35	45
Grand township	94	124
Greenleaf township	35	30
Harrison township	62	68
Hiland township	47	52
Holden township	76	93
Howell township	70	89
Hulbert township	79	76
Linn township	65	80
Logan township	38	55
Midland township	37	59
Miller city[28]	1 931	2 148
Miller township[28]	164	156
Mondamin township	39	54
Ohio township	100	109

County Subdivisions	1980	1970
Hand County—Con.		
Ontario township	73	96
Park township	74	119
Pearl township	46	39
Plato township	65	84
Pleasant Valley township	48	86
Ree Heights town	88	183
Ree Heights township	41	60
Riverside township	48	47
Rockdale township	107	129
Rose Hill township	93	104
St. Lawrence town[28]	223	249
St. Lawrence township[28]	90	97
Spring township	72	99
Spring Hill township	54	75
Spring Lake township	46	62
Wessington city (pt.)	23	35
Wheaton township	62	83
York township	54	73
Hanson County	3 415	3 781
Alexandria city	588	598
Beulah township	262	251
Edgerton township	169	259
Emery city	399	452
Fairview township	152	212
Farmer town	27	58
Fulton town	108	101
Hanson township	216	189
Jasper township	157	191
Plano township	140	183
Pleasant township	172	193
Rosedale township	281	264
Spring Lake township	162	197
Taylor township	181	212
Wayne township	254	223
Worthen township	147	198
Harding County[29]	1 700	1 855
Buffalo town	453	393
Camp Crook town	100	150
North Harding (unorg.)[29]	742	716
South Harding (unorg.)	405	431
Hughes County[30]	14 220	11 632
Blunt city	424	445
Butte township	34	41
Crow Creek (unorg.)[30]	205	...
De Grey township	50	49
Harrold town	196	184
Harrold township	67	72
Logan township	30	44
North Hughes (unorg.)[30]	184	84
Pierre city[30]	11 973	9 699
Raber township	59	87
Valley township	35	54
West Hughes (unorg.)[30]	963	544
Hutchinson County[31]	9 350	10 379
Capital township	141	157
Clayton township	232	298
Cross Plains township	150	227
Dimock town	140	167
Fair township[31]	166	237
Foster township	196	166
Freeman city[31]	1 462	1 357
German township	156	216
Grandview township[31]	234	299
Kassel township	152	181
Kaylor township	269	305
Kulm township	137	185
Liberty township[31]	190	218
Menno city[31]	793	796
Milltown township	186	325
Molan township	213	263
Oak Hollow township	135	151
Olivet town	96	103
Parkston city[31]	1 545	1 611
Pleasant township	80	94
Sharon township	143	217
Silver Lake township	146	158
Starr township	188	218
Susquehanna township	262	357
Sweet township[31]	340	293
Tripp city[31]	804	851
Valley township	249	253
Wittenberg township	300	387
Wolf Creek township	245	289
Hyde County[32]	2 069	2 515
Central Hyde (unorg.)[32]	481	...
Crow Creek (unorg.)[32]	143	...
Dewey township	24	...
Highmore city	1 055	1 173
North Hyde (unorg.)[32]	291	...
Valley township	24	39
Washington township	40	36
William Hamilton township	11	27

County Subdivisions	1980	1970
Jackson County[33]	3 437	1 531
Belvidere town[33]	80	96
Cottonwood town	4	16
East Jackson (unorg.)[33]	244	101
East Washabaugh (unorg.)[33]	233	...
Grandview township	20	20
Interior town	62	81
Interior township	110	69
Jewett township	24	32
Kadoka city	832	815
Little Buffalo township	18	22
Northwest Jackson (unorg.)[33]	92	71
Wall township	27	25
West Washabaugh (unorg.)[33]	1 673	...
Weta township	18	15
Jerauld County	2 929	3 310
Alpena town	288	307
Alpena township	136	160
Anina township	76	115
Blaine township	110	133
Chery township	91	108
Crow township	162	180
Crow Lake township	73	80
Dale township	87	91
Franklin township	114	141
Harmony township	63	69
Lane town	83	94
Logan township	38	38
Marlar township	49	84
Media township	77	88
Pleasant township	100	125
Viola township	67	73
Wessington Springs city	1 203	1 300
Wessington Springs township	112	124
Jones County[34]	1 463	1 882
Banner township	5	10
Buffalo township[34]	42	81
Draper town	138	200
Draper township	44	77
Dunkel township	24	25
Grandview township	19	15
Highland township	34	31
Kolls township	30	35
Lincoln (unorg.)[34]	21	25
Morgan township	45	45
Mullen township	11	6
Murdo city[34]	723	865
Murdo township	27	61
Mussman township	15	11
Northwest Jones (unorg.)[34]	19	35
Okaton township	67	101
Richland township	8	8
Rich Valley (unorg.)[34]	7	4
Scovil township	25	38
South Creek township	26	28
Union township	13	5
Virgil township	9	23
War Creek (unorg.)[34]	22	30
Washington township	3	21
Westover township	17	11
Williams Creek township	51	70
Zickrick township	18	21
Kingsbury County[35]	6 679	7 657
Arlington city (pt.)	988	954
Badger town	99	122
Badger township	272	297
Baker township[35]	276	385
Bancroft town	41	48
Denver township	665	370
De Smet city[35]	1 237	1 336
De Smet township[35]	435	410
Erwin town	66	106
Esmond township[35]	84	159
Hartland township	202	274
Hetland town	66	81
Iroquois city (pt.)[35]	299	320
Iroquois township[35]	73	98
Lake Preston city[35]	789	812
Le Sueur township	145	236
Manchester township	131	152
Mathews township	212	317
Oldham city	222	244
Spirit Lake township	188	230
Spring Lake township	2	439
Whitewood township	187	248
Lake County[36]	10 724	11 456
Badus township	171	237
Chester township	522	530
Clarno township	202	257
Concord township	153	187
Farmington township	236	283
Franklin township	244	278
Herman township[36]	551	516
Lake View township[36]	399	388
Le Roy township	216	277
Madison city[36]	6 210	6 315

County Subdivisions	1980	1970
Lake County—Con.		
Nunda town	60	85
Nunda township	129	174
Orland township	163	204
Ramona town	241	227
Rutland township	226	258
Summit township	214	282
Wayne township	140	176
Wentworth township	226	246
Wentworth village	193	196
Winfred town	81	110
Winfred township	147	230
Lawrence County[37]	18 339	17 453
Central City city	232	188
Deadwood city	2 035	2 409
Lead city	4 330	5 420
North Lawrence (unorg.)[37]	3 582	2 149
St. Onge township	257	216
South Lawrence (unorg.)[37]	1 831	1 721
Spearfish city[37]	5 251	4 661
Whitewood city[37]	821	689
Lincoln County[38]	13 942	11 761
Beresford city (pt.)	361	319
Brooklyn township	259	293
Canton city[38]	2 886	2 665
Canton township[38]	441	426
Dayton township	484	473
Delapre township[38]	995	577
Delaware township	223	287
Eden township	220	279
Fairview town	90	72
Fairview township	155	135
Grant township	391	389
Harrisburg town[38]	558	338
Highland township	289	313
Hudson town	388	366
La Valley township[38]	443	379
Lennox city[38]	1 827	1 487
Lincoln township	230	250
Lynn township	289	342
Norway township	305	337
Perry township[38]	504	411
Pleasant township	407	493
Sioux Falls city (pt.)[38]	161	–
Springdale township[38]	919	534
Tea town[38]	729	302
Worthing town	388	294
Lyman County[39]	3 864	4 060
Annin township	20	64
Applegate township	4	7
Bailey township	53	67
Black Dog township	23	35
Brule township	17	22
Butte township	63	78
Dorman township	34	34
Earling township	50	64
Edna township	17	34
Fairland township	23	30
Grouse Creek township	19	23
Hilmoe township	37	43
Hope township	28	39
Iona township	120	133
Kennebec town[39]	334	372
Kennebec township[39]	26	44
Liberty township	30	40
Lund township	32	54
McClure township	14	14
Moore township	30	46
Morningside township	26	48
Northeast Lyman (unorg.)[39]	1 037	645
Oacoma town	289	215
Oacoma township	56	32
Pleasant township	17	19
Pratt township	15	27
Presho city	760	922
Presho township	76	66
Reliance town	190	204
Reliance township	80	50
Rex township	45	46
Rose township	48	57
Rowe township	3	4
Sioux township	30	37
South Lyman (unorg.)	7	22
Stony Butte township	18	37
Sylvia township	10	17
Tracy township	10	16
Vivian township	135	274
White River township	38	37
McCook County	6 444	7 246
Benton township	133	196
Bridgewater city	653	633
Bridgewater township	173	206
Brookfield township	192	258
Canistota city	626	636
Canistota township	194	216
Emery township	157	230

County Subdivisions	1980	1970
McCook County—Con.		
Grant township	201	282
Greenland township	182	218
Jefferson township	130	195
Montrose city	396	377
Montrose township	201	271
Pearl township	164	187
Ramsey township	148	221
Richland township	219	273
Salem city	1 486	1 391
Salem township	207	269
Spencer city	380	385
Spring Valley township	260	321
Sun Prairie township	159	229
Union township	183	252
McPherson County[40]	4 027	5 022
Carl township	63	86
Central McPherson (unorg.)[40]	922	991
Eureka city[40]	1 360	1 547
Hillsview town	9	19
Hoffman township	45	49
Leola city	645	787
Long Lake town	117	128
Wachter township	68	83
Wacker township	29	41
Weber township	113	127
West McPherson (unorg.)[40]	634	876
Wetonka town	22	31
Marshall County[41]	5 404	5 965
Britton city	1 590	1 465
Buffalo township	107	159
Dayton township	48	58
Dumarce township	71	88
Eden town[41]	142	132
Eden township[41]	129	177
Fort township	73	67
Hamilton township	65	92
Hickman township	96	123
La Belle township	110	157
Lake township	127	184
Lake City town	46	44
Langford town	307	328
Lowell township	74	100
McKinley township	75	98
Miller township	229	413
Newark township	91	103
Newport township	106	102
Nordland township	48	65
Pleasant Valley township	174	226
Red Iron Lake township	188	142
Sisseton township	100	152
Stena township	169	119
Veblen city	368	377
Veblen township	243	240
Victor township	91	96
Waverly township	94	121
Weston township	191	215
White township	206	276
Wismer township	46	46
Meade County[42]	20 717	17 020
Belle Fourche–Cheyenne Valleys (unorg.)[42]	6 451	1 071
Ellsworth AFB (CDP)	4 766	6 207
Eagle township	16	15
Faith city[42]	576	576
Howard township	13	16
Lakeside township	55	55
North Meade (unorg.)[42]	493	558
Southwest Meade (unorg.)[42]	7 861	...
Blackhawk (CDP)	1 608	...
Sturgis city[42]	5 184	4 536
Union township	28	26
Upper Red Owl township	40	40
Mellette County[43]	2 249	2 420
Bad Nation township	35	54
Blackpipe township	62	85
Butte township	8	12
Cedarbutte (unorg.)[43]	120	88
Central Mellette (unorg.)[43]	618	597
Cody township	51	60
Corn Creek township	83	82
Fairview township	47	66
Mosher township	42	79
Norris township	213	213
Pine Creek township	6	10
Prospect township	22	16
Pure Water township	23	31
Red Fish township	35	20
Ring Thunder township	17	22
Riverside township	27	41
Rocky Ford township	10	12
Rosebud township	48	76
Running Bird township	40	48
Surprise Valley township	47	30
White River city[43]	561	617
Wood town	134	132

County Subdivisions	1980	1970
Miner County	3 739	4 454
Adams township	176	242
Beaver township	108	113
Belleview township	129	152
Canova town	194	204
Canova township	106	185
Carthage city	274	362
Carthage township	61	109
Clearwater township	220	270
Clinton township	181	224
Grafton township	133	143
Green Valley township	93	138
Henden township	158	209
Howard city	1 169	1 175
Howard township	126	174
Miner township	97	128
Redstone township	50	67
Rock Creek township	172	227
Roswell town	19	32
Roswell township	88	113
Vermillion township	157	154
Vilas town	28	33
Minnehaha County[44]	109 435	95 209
Baltic town	679	364
Benton township[44]	544	679
Brandon township[44]	624	1 960
Brandon City city[44]	2 589	...
Buffalo township	260	317
Burk township	339	363
Clear Lake township	195	258
Colton city	757	601
Crooks town[44]	594	...
Dell Rapids city	2 389	1 991
Dell Rapids township	463	355
Edison township	389	352
Garretson city	963	847
Grand Meadow township	313	311
Hartford city[44]	1 207	800
Hartford township[44]	421	353
Highland township	235	238
Humboldt town[44]	487	411
Humboldt township[44]	309	284
Logan township	287	405
Lyons township	569	410
Mapleton township[44]	1 712	1 553
Palisade township	264	201
Red Rock township	323	254
Sherman town	100	82
Sioux Falls city (pt.)[44]	81 182	72 488
Sioux Falls township[44]	2 283	3 299
Split Rock township[44]	1 802	879
Sverdrup township	577	481
Taopi township	357	385
Valley Springs city[44]	801	566
Valley Springs township[44]	313	290
Wall Lake township	844	563
Wayne township[44]	3 953	2 534
Wellington township	311	335
Moody County[45]	6 692	7 622
Alliance township	141	192
Blinsmon township	276	339
Clare township	229	268
Colman city	501	456
Colman township[45]	267	272
Egan city	248	281
Egan township	211	266
Enterprise township	316	505
Flandreau city[45]	2 114	2 027
Flandreau township[45]	334	809
Fremont township	296	271
Grovena township	223	271
Jefferson township	181	202
Lone Rock township	125	159
Lynn township	320	373
Riverview township	193	242
Spring Creek township	179	202
Trent town	197	177
Union township	197	138
Ward town	43	57
Ward township	101	115
Pennington County[46]	70 361	59 349
Ash township	34	46
Badlands (unorg.)	–	–
Box Elder city[46]	3 186	607
Castle Butte township	25	57
Cedar Butte township	61	67
Central Pennington (unorg.)[46]	12 021	...
Rapid Valley (CDP)	3 265	...
Villa Ranchaero (CDP)	1 666	3 171
Cheyenne township	16	25
Conata township	13	19
Crooked Creek township	23	34
Dalzell Canyon (unorg.)	6	20
East Central Pennington (unorg.)[46]	308	308
Fairview township[46]	75	33
Flat Butte township	11	14

County Subdivisions

County Subdivisions	1980	1970
Pennington County—Con.		
Hill City town[46]	535	389
Huron township	37	49
Imlay township	6	9
Keystone town[46]	295	...
Lake Creek (unorg.)[46]	64	51
Lake Flat township[46]	40	48
Lake Hill township[46]	24	30
Mount Rushmore (unorg.)[46]	3 369	3 664
New Underwood town[46]	517	416
Northeast Pennington (unorg.)	57	69
Owanka township	42	36
Peno township	38	57
Quinn town	80	105
Quinn township	9	10
Rainy Creek township	56	51
Rapid City city[46]	46 492	43 836
Rapid City East (unorg.)[46]	800	...
Scenic township	108	143
Shyne township	11	15
Sunnyside township	14	13
Wall town[46]	770	786
Wasta town	99	127
Wasta township	27	35
West Pennington (unorg.)[46]	1 092	773
Perkins County[47]	4 700	4 769
Ada township	34	31
Anderson township	27	18
Antelope township	34	32
Barrett township	21	26
Beck township	16	26
Bison town	457	406
Bison township	37	39
Brushy township[47]	24	29
Burdick township	58	36
Cash township	34	37
Castle Butte township	23	24
Chance township	46	35
Chaudoin township	14	18
Clark township	38	43
De Witt township	81	63
Duck Creek (unorg.)	42	56
Duell township	18	22
East Perkins (unorg.)	111	139
Englewood township	17	21
Flat Creek township	172	39
Foster township	27	24
Fredlund township	42	47
Glendo township	26	26
Grand River township	34	41
Hall township	22	24
Highland township	17	27
Horse Creek township	77	100
Hudgins (unorg.)[47]	32	24
Independence township	26	27
Lemmon city[47]	1 871	1 997
Liberty township	30	25
Lincoln township[47]	156	169
Lodgepole township	51	63
Lone Tree township	51	39
Maltby township	25	18
Marshfield township	30	40
Martin township	9	3
Meadow township	60	45
Moreau township	7	9
Plateau township	24	21
Pleasant Valley township	20	19
Rainbow township	34	40
Rockford township	24	30
Scotch Cap township	29	41
Seim township	20	29
Sidney township	40	47
South Perkins (unorg.)[47]	165	84
Southwest Perkins (unorg.)	35	42
Strool township	99	104
Trail township	39	32
Vail township	18	9
Vickers township	21	35
Viking township	26	29
Vrooman township	11	14
Wells township[47]	13	...
West Central Perkins (unorg.)	27	36
West Perkins (unorg.)	21	29
White Butte township	30	32
White Hill township	22	14
Whitney township	24	30
Wilson township	42	46
Wyandotte township	19	21
Potter County[48]	3 674	4 449
Central Potter (unorg.)[48]	460	...
East Potter (unorg.)[48]	488	...
Gettysburg city[48]	1 623	1 915
Hoven town[48]	615	671
Lebanon town	129	182
Tolstoy town[48]	97	99
West Potter (unorg.)[48]	262	...

County Subdivisions	1980	1970
Roberts County[49]	10 911	11 678
Agency township	242	290
Alto township	88	102
Becker township	154	197
Bossko township	99	103
Bryant township	217	203
Claire City town	87	100
Corona town	126	133
Dry Wood Lake township	97	126
Easter township	198	162
Enterprise township	152	212
Garfield township	185	236
Geneseo township	266	303
Goodwill township	664	281
Grant township	190	205
Harmon township	295	301
Hart township	126	190
Lake township	180	242
Lawrence township	191	144
Lee township	141	188
Lien township[49]	179	266
Lockwood township	186	160
Long Hollow township	245	191
Minnesota township	203	253
New Effington town[49]	261	258
Norway township	178	214
One Road township	103	106
Ortley town	80	111
Ortley township	105	128
Peever town	232	202
Rosholt town[49]	446	456
Sisseton city[49]	2 789	3 094
Sisseton township[49]	324	338
Springdale township	173	214
Spring Grove township	248	237
Summit town[49]	290	332
Summit township[49]	78	147
Victor township[49]	268	312
White Rock town	10	35
White Rock township[49]	308	388
Wilmot city	507	518
Sanborn County	3 213	3 697
Afton township	83	100
Artesian town	227	277
Benedict township	51	79
Butler township	228	221
Diana township	81	102
Elliott township	151	182
Floyd township	121	167
Jackson township	118	127
Letcher town	221	201
Letcher township	139	167
Logan township	195	247
Oneida township	57	80
Ravenna township	79	114
Silver Creek township	135	178
Twin Lake township	141	147
Union township	96	106
Warren township	80	99
Woonsocket city	799	852
Woonsocket township	211	251
Shannon County[50]	11 323	8 198
Batesland town[50]	163	135
East Shannon (unorg.)[50]	4 652	2 899
West Shannon (unorg.)[50]	6 508	5 123
Pine Ridge (CDP)	3 059	2 768
Spink County[51]	9 201	10 595
Antelope township	93	119
Ashton city	154	137
Athol township	137	177
Belle Plaine township	96	136
Belmont township	98	122
Benton township	66	94
Beotia township	66	101
Brentford town	91	94
Buffalo township	89	107
Capitola township	254	263
Clifton township	89	140
Conde city	259	279
Conde township	32	59
Cornwall township	79	82
Crandon township	104	97
Doland city[51]	381	430
Exline township	84	91
Frankfort city[51]	209	192
Frankfort township[51]	81	122
Garfield township	65	92
Great Bend township	71	66
Groveland township	97	123
Harmony township	72	77
Harrison township	61	74
Jefferson township	89	101
Lake township	103	134
La Prairie township	93	139
Lincoln township	242	272
Lodi township	120	167
Mellette city	192	199

County Subdivisions	1980	1970
Spink County—Con.		
Mellette township	224	242
Northville town	138	119
Northville township	279	375
Olean township	66	74
Prairie Center township	54	83
Redfield city[51]	3 027	2 943
Redfield township[51]	864	1 416
Richfield township	55	68
Spring township[51]	70	74
Sumner township	46	82
Tetonka township	104	111
Three Rivers township	90	120
Tulare town	238	211
Tulare township	71	101
Turton town	101	121
Turton township	51	73
Union township	74	96
Stanley County[52]	2 533	2 457
Fort Pierre city[52]	1 789	1 448
North Stanley (unorg.)[52]	350	407
South Stanley (unorg.)[52]	394	602
Sully County	1 990	2 362
Agar town	139	156
East Sully (unorg.)	478	750
Onida city	851	785
West Sully (unorg.)	522	671
Todd County[53]	7 328	6 606
East Todd (unorg.)[53]	2 255	2 165
Mission city[53]	748	739
St. Francis town[53]	766	300
West Todd (unorg.)[53]	3 559	3 402
Tripp County[54]	7 268	8 171
Banner township	19	26
Beaver Creek township	22	47
Black township	136	135
Brunson township	65	97
Bull Creek township	43	52
Carter town	7	17
Carter township	65	66
Colome city	361	375
Colome township	104	132
Condon township	58	73
Curlew township	41	52
Dog Ear township	77	108
Elliston township	62	74
Greenwood township	29	50
Holsclaw township	34	52
Huggins township	43	68
Ideal township	223	242
Irwin township	60	57
Jordan township	50	91
Keyapaha township	43	57
King township	56	69
Lake township	89	101
Lamro township[54]	368	261
Lincoln township	61	77
Lons Star township	24	38
Lone Tree township	56	47
McNeely township	117	101
Millboro township	58	96
New Witten town	134	102
North Tripp (unorg.)	34	28
Pahapesto township	27	49
Plainview township	83	102
Pleasant Valley township	31	33
Pleasant View township	148	137
Progressive township	36	49
Rames township	57	91
Rosedale township	76	105
Roseland township	58	87
Star Prairie township	71	107
Star Valley township	37	42
Stewart township	127	171
Sully township	50	74
Taylor township	21	24
Valley township	61	79
Weaver township	76	66
Willow Creek township	62	90
Wilson township	110	131
Winner city[54]	3 472	3 789
Witten township	34	24
Wortman township	64	88
Wright township	28	42
Turner County[55]	9 255	9 872
Brothersfield township	168	198
Centerville city	892	910
Centerville township	212	273
Chancellor town	257	220
Childstown township	322	333
Daneville township[55]	230	292
Davis town	100	101
Dolton town	47	60
Dolton township	199	241
Germantown township	357	404

County Subdivisions	1980	1970
Turner County—Con.		
Home township	254	296
Hurley city	419	399
Hurley township	181	252
Irene town (pt.)[55]	268	240
Marion[55]	830	844
Marion township[55]	242	280
Middleton township	287	273
Monroe town	170	134
Monroe township	184	225
Norway township	212	280
Parker city[55]	999	1 005
Parker township[55]	326	296
Rosefield township	266	348
Salem township	264	376
Spring Valley township	255	334
Swan Lake township[55]	260	324
Turner township	242	272
Viborg city[55]	812	662
Union County[56]	10 938	9 643
Alcester city[56]	885	627
Alcester township[56]	352	531
Beresford city (pt.)	1 504	1 336
Big Sioux township[56]	403	751
Big Springs township	331	372
Brule township	271	277
Civil Bend township	358	336
Elk Point city[56]	1 661	1 372
Elk Point township[56]	338	384
Emmet township	347	354
Jefferson town[56]	592	474
Jefferson township[56]	531	445
North Sioux City city[56]	1 992	860
Prairie township	246	295
Richland (unorg.)[56]	227	...
Sioux Valley township	274	356
Spink township	328	339
Virginia township	298	314
Walworth County[57]	7 011	7 842
Akaska town	49	46
East Walworth (unorg.)[57]	705	977
Glenham town	169	178
Java city	261	305
Lowry town	22	35
Mobridge city[57]	4 174	4 545
Selby city[57]	884	957
West Walworth (unorg.)[57]	747	799
Yankton County[58]	18 952	19 039
Gayville town	407	269
Gayville township	207	239
Irene town (pt.)[58]	5	7
Jamesville township	258	331
Lesterville town[58]	156	181
Marindahl township	220	240
Mayfield township	266	343
Mission Hill town	197	161
Mission Hill township	341	290
Southeast Yankton (unorg.)	644	388
Turkey Valley township[58]	265	334
Utica town	100	89
Utica township	867	1 718
Volin town	156	157
Volin township	290	344
Walshtown township	235	281
West Yankton (unorg.)[58]	2 327	1 748
Yankton city[58]	12 011	11 919
Ziebach County[59]	2 308	2 221
Dupree city	562	523
Dupree (unorg.)[59]	150	...
North Ziebach (unorg.)[59]	442	156
South Ziebach (unorg.)[59]	1 154	...

TENNESSEE

Tennessee is named from its principal river. The meaning of the word in the original Indian tongue has been variously given, but the most generally accepted definition is "river of the big bend."

The first explorer of what is now Tennessee was De Soto, a Spaniard, who in 1541 reached the Mississippi probably at the present site of Memphis. In 1682 La Salle, a Frenchman, on his way down the Mississippi, built Fort Prud'homme where Memphis now stands. British subjects entered this region in about 1748, when Dr. Thomas Walker and other Virginians discovered and named the Cumberland River, Mountains, and Gap, but the first permanent settlement was not made until 1769, when Englishmen settled on the Wautauga River.

On the grounds of these and other explorations the arena now constituting Tennessee was claimed by the Spanish, the French, and the English. The Spanish, however, made no attempt at settlement, and the French ceded their claims to Great Britain in 1763, at the close of the French and Indian War. The Indian claims to lands in this region were ceded to the English in 1768, by the treaty of Fort Stanwix, N.Y., and at subsequent dates by other treaties.

The present area of Tennessee was included in the Virginia grants of 1609 and 1612; part of the area was included in the Carolina grant of 1663 and all was included in the extension of the grant two years later. In 1784 the Tennessee region was ceded by North Carolina to the Federal Government on condition that the cession be accepted within two years. The inhabitants indignant at this transfer organized the so-called state of Franklin, which continued in existence until 1788, although it was not recognized by Congress or the parent state.

In 1790 the Tennessee region was again ceded by North Carolina to the United States, whereupon the ceded territory, together with a strip of land about 12 miles in width, lying south of the thirty-fifth parallel and extending from the Mississippi River to the boundary of South Carolina, was organized as the Territory South of the River Ohio. Early in 1796 a state constitution was adopted for that part of the territory lying north of the thirty-fifth parallel, and, by act of Congress approved June 1 of that year, Tennessee, with boundaries as at present, was admitted to the Union.

COUNTY LOCATION INDEX

Anderson	C-6	Hardin	D-3	Putnam	C-5
Bedford	C-4	Hawkins	B-7	Rhea	C-5
Benton	C-3	Haywood	C-2	Roane	C-6
Bledsoe	C-5	Henderson	C-3	Robertson	B-4
Blount	C-6	Henry	C-3	Rutherford	C-4
Bradley	D-5	Hickman	C-3	Scott	B-6
Campbell	B-6	Houston	C-3	Sequatchie	D-5
Cannon	C-5	Humphreys	C-3	Sevier	C-7
Carroll	C-3	Jackson	C-5	Shelby	D-2
Carter	C-8	Jefferson	C-7	Smith	C-5
Cheatham	C-4	Johnson	B-8	Stewart	B-3
Chester	C-3	Knox	C-6	Sullivan	B-7
Claiborne	B-6	Lake	C-2	Sumner	B-4
Clay	B-5	Lauderdale	C-2	Tipton	C-2
Cocke	C-7	Lawrence	D-3	Trousdale	C-4
Coffee	C-5	Lewis	C-3	Unicoi	C-7
Crockett	C-2	Lincoln	D-4	Union	C-6
Cumberland	C-5	Loudon	C-6	Van Buren	C-5
Davidson	C-4	McMinn	C-6	Warren	C-5
Decatur	C-3	McNairy	D-3	Washington	C-7
De Kalb	C-5	Macon	B-5	Wayne	D-3
Dickson	C-3	Madison	C-2	Weakley	C-2
Dyer	C-2	Marion	D-5	White	C-5
Fayette	D-2	Marshall	C-4	Williamson	C-4
Fentress	C-5	Maury	C-4	Wilson	C-4
Franklin	D-5	Meigs	C-6		
Gibson	C-2	Monroe	C-6		
Giles	D-4	Montgomery	B-4		
Grainger	C-7	Moore	D-4		
Greene	C-7	Morgan	C-6		
Grundy	D-5	Obion	C-2		
Hamblen	C-7	Overton	C-5		
Hamilton	D-5	Perry	C-3		
Hancock	B-7	Pickett	B-5		
Hardeman	D-2	Polk	D-6		

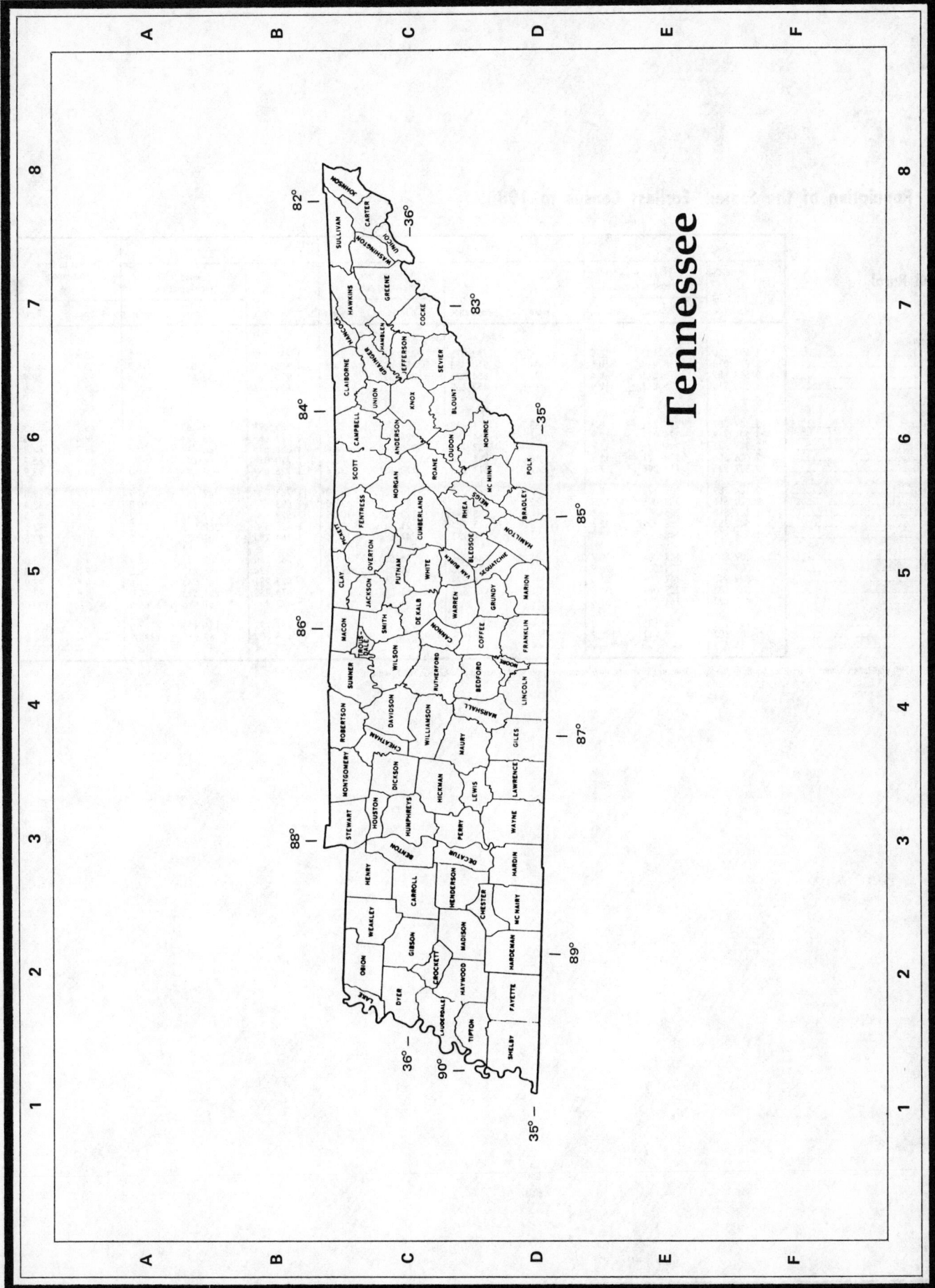

Tennessee

Table 1. **Population of the State: Earliest Census to 1980**

Urban and Rural

	The State			Urban					Rural				Percent of total population	
	Total population	Change from preceding census		Places of 2,500 or more	Population	Change from preceding census			Population	Change from preceding census			Urban	Rural
		Number	Percent			Number	Percent			Number	Percent			
Current urban definition:														
1980 (Apr. 1)	4 591 120	665 102	16.9	138	2 773 573	455 115	19.6		1 817 547	212 318	13.2		60.4	39.6
1970 (Apr. 1)	ʻ3 926 018	358 929	10.1	104	2 318 458	453 630	24.3		1 605 229	−97 032	−5.7		59.1	40.9
1960 (Apr. 1)	3 567 089	275 371	8.4	94	1 864 828	412 226	28.4		1 702 261	−136 855	−7.4		52.3	47.7
1950 (Apr. 1)	3 291 718	375 877	12.9	71	1 452 602	...	...		1 839 116	...	...		44.1	55.9
Previous urban definition:														
1960 (Apr. 1)	3 567 089	275 371	8.4	85	1 631 698	367 539	29.1		1 935 391	−92 168	−4.5		45.7	54.3
1950 (Apr. 1)	3 291 718	375 877	12.9	64	1 264 159	236 953	23.1		2 027 559	138 924	7.4		38.4	61.6
1940 (Apr. 1)	2 915 841	299 285	11.4	57	1 027 206	130 668	14.6		1 888 635	168 617	9.8		35.2	64.8
1930 (Apr. 1)	2 616 556	278 671	11.9	48	896 538	285 312	46.7		1 720 018	−6 641	−0.4		34.3	65.7
1920 (Jan. 1)	2 337 885	153 096	7.0	47	611 226	170 181	38.6		1 726 659	−17 085	−1.0		26.1	73.9
1910 (Apr. 15)	2 184 789	164 173	8.1	29	441 045	114 406	35.0		1 743 744	49 767	2.9		20.2	79.8
1900 (June 1)	2 020 616	253 098	14.3	22	326 639	88 245	37.0		1 693 977	164 853	10.8		16.2	83.8
1890 (June 1)	1 767 518	225 159	14.6	14	238 394	122 410	105.5		1 529 124	102 749	7.2		13.5	86.5
1880 (June 1)	1 542 359	283 839	22.6	8	115 984	21 747	23.1		1 426 375	262 092	22.5		7.5	92.5
1870 (June 1)	1 258 520	148 719	13.4	8	94 237	47 696	102.5		1 164 283	101 023	9.5		7.5	92.5
1860 (June 1)	1 109 801	107 084	10.7	4	46 541	24 558	111.7		1 063 260	82 526	8.4		4.2	95.8
1850 (June 1)	1 002 717	173 507	20.9	3	21 983	15 054	217.3		980 734	158 453	19.3		2.2	97.8
1840 (June 1)	829 210	147 306	21.6	1	6 929	1 363	24.5		822 281	145 943	21.6		0.8	99.2
1830 (June 1)	681 904	259 081	61.3	1	5 566	5 566	...		676 338	253 515	60.0		0.8	99.2
1820 (Aug. 7)	422 823	161 096	61.6	–	–	–	–		422 823	161 096	61.6		–	100.0
1810 (Aug. 6)	261 727	156 125	147.8	–	–	–	–		261 727	156 125	147.8		–	100.0
1800 (Aug. 4)	105 602	69 911	195.9	–	–	–	–		105 602	69 911	195.9		–	100.0
1790 (Aug. 2)	35 691	...	...	–	–	...	...		35 691	...	...		–	100.0

NOTE: 1790 population is that of Territory South of the River Ohio, including area now constituting parts of Mississippi, Alabama, and Georgia.

ANDERSON

1810	3,959
1820	4,668
1830	5,310
1840	5,658
1850	6,939
1860	7,068
1870	8,704
1880	10,820
1890	15,128
1900	17,634
1910	17,717
1920	18,298
1930	19,722
1940	26,504
1950	59,407
1960	60,032
1970	60,300
1980	67,346

BEDFORD

1810	8,242
1820	16,012
1830	30,396
1840	20,546
1850	21,511
1860	21,584
1870	24,333
1880	26,025
1890	24,739
1900	23,845
1910	22,667
1920	21,737
1930	21,077
1940	23,151
1950	23,627
1960	23,150
1970	25,039
1980	27,916

BENTON

1840	4,722
1850	6,315
1860	8,463
1870	8,234
1880	9,780
1890	11,230
1900	11,888
1910	12,452
1920	12,046
1930	11,237
1940	11,976
1950	11,495
1960	10,662
1970	12,126
1980	14,901

BLEDSOE

1810	3,259
1820	4,005
1830	4,648
1840	5,676
1850	5,959
1860	4,459
1870	4,870
1880	5,617
1890	6,134
1900	6,626
1910	6,329
1920	7,218
1930	7,128
1940	8,358
1950	8,561

1960	7,811
1970	7,643
1980	9,478

BLOUNT

1800	5,587
1810	8,839
1820	11,258
1830	11,028
1840	11,745
1850	12,424
1860	13,270
1870	14,237
1880	15,985
1890	17,589
1900	19,206
1910	20,809
1920	28,800
1930	33,989
1940	41,116
1950	54,691
1960	57,525
1970	63,744
1980	77,770

BRADLEY

1840	7,385
1850	12,259
1860	11,701
1870	11,652
1880	12,124
1890	13,607
1900	15,759
1910	16,336
1920	18,652
1930	22,870
1940	28,498
1950	32,338
1960	38,324
1970	50,686
1980	67,547

CAMPBELL

1810	2,668
1820	4,244
1830	5,110
1840	6,149
1850	6,068
1860	6,712
1870	7,445
1880	10,005
1890	13,486
1900	17,317
1910	27,387
1920	28,265
1930	26,827
1940	31,131
1950	34,369
1960	27,936
1970	26,045
1980	34,923

CANNON

1840	7,193
1850	8,982
1860	9,509
1870	10,502
1880	11,859
1890	12,197
1900	12,121
1910	10,825
1920	10,241

1930	8,935
1940	9,880
1950	9,174
1960	8,537
1970	8,467
1980	10,234

CARROLL

1830	9,397
1840	12,362
1850	15,967
1860	17,437
1870	19,447
1880	22,103
1890	23,630
1900	24,250
1910	23,971
1920	24,361
1930	26,132
1940	25,978
1950	26,553
1960	23,476
1970	25,741
1980	28,285

CARTER

1800	4,813
1810	4,190
1820	4,835
1830	6,414
1840	5,372
1850	6,296
1860	7,214
1870	7,909
1880	10,019
1890	13,389
1900	16,688
1910	19,838
1920	21,488
1930	29,233
1940	35,127
1950	42,432
1960	41,578
1970	43,259
1980	50,205

CHEATHAM

1860	7,258
1870	6,678
1880	7,956
1890	8,845
1900	10,112
1910	10,540
1920	10,039
1930	9,025
1940	9,928
1950	9,167
1960	9,428
1970	13,199
1980	21,616

CHESTER

1890	9,069
1900	9,896
1910	9,090
1920	9,669
1930	10,603
1940	11,124
1950	11,149
1960	9,569
1970	9,927
1980	12,727

CLAIBORNE

1810	4,798
1820	5,508
1830	8,470
1840	9,474
1850	9,369
1860	9,643
1870	9,321
1880	13,373
1890	15,103
1900	20,696
1910	23,504
1920	23,286
1930	24,313
1940	24,657
1950	24,788
1960	19,067
1970	19,420
1980	24,595

CLAY

1880	6,987
1890	7,260
1900	8,241
1910	9,009
1920	9,193
1930	9,577
1940	10,904
1950	8,701
1960	7,289
1970	6,624
1980	7,676

COCKE

1810	5,154
1820	4,892
1830	6,017
1840	6,992
1850	8,300
1860	10,408
1870	12,458
1880	14,808
1890	16,523
1900	19,153
1910	19,399
1920	20,782
1930	21,775
1940	24,083
1950	22,991
1960	23,390
1970	25,283
1980	28,792

COFFEE

1840	8,184
1850	8,351
1860	9,689
1870	10,237
1880	12,894
1890	13,827
1900	15,574
1910	15,625
1920	17,344
1930	16,801
1940	18,959
1950	23,049
1960	28,603
1970	32,572
1980	38,311

CROCKETT

1880	14,109
1890	15,146
1900	15,867
1910	16,076
1920	17,438
1930	17,359
1940	17,330
1950	16,624
1960	14,594
1970	14,402
1980	14,941

CUMBERLAND

1860	3,460
1870	3,461
1880	4,538
1890	5,376
1900	8,311
1910	9,327
1920	10,094
1930	11,440
1940	15,592
1950	18,877
1960	19,135
1970	20,733
1980	28,676

DAVIDSON

1790	3,459
1800	9,965
1810	15,608
1820	20,154
1830	28,122
1840	30,509
1850	38,882
1860	47,055
1870	62,897
1880	79,026
1890	108,174
1900	122,815
1910	149,478
1920	167,815
1930	222,854
1940	257,267
1950	321,758
1960	399,743
1970	447,887
1980	477,811

DECATUR

1850	6,003
1860	6,276
1870	7,772
1880	8,498
1890	8,995
1900	10,439
1910	10,093
1920	10,198
1930	10,106
1940	10,261
1950	9,442
1960	8,324
1970	9,457
1980	10,857

DE KALB

1840	5,868
1850	8,016
1860	10,573
1870	11,425

1880	14,813	1870	4,717	**GRAINGER**		**HAMILTON**		**HAWKINS**
1890	15,650	1880	5,941					
1900	16,460	1890	5,226	1800	7,367	1820	821	1790	6,970
1910	15,434	1900	6,106	1810	6,397	1830	2,276	1800	6,563
1920	15,370	1910	7,446	1820	7,651	1840	8,175	1810	7,643
1930	14,213	1920	10,435	1830	10,066	1850	10,075	1820	10,949
1940	14,588	1930	11,036	1840	10,572	1860	13,258	1830	13,683
1950	11,680	1940	14,262	1850	12,370	1870	17,241	1840	15,035
1960	10,774	1950	14,917	1860	10,962	1880	23,642	1850	13,370
1970	11,151	1960	13,288	1870	12,421	1890	53,482	1860	16,162
1980	13,589	1970	12,593	1880	12,384	1900	61,695	1870	15,837
		1980	14,826	1890	13,196	1910	89,267	1880	20,610
DICKSON				1900	15,512	1920	115,954	1890	22,246
		FRANKLIN		1910	13,888	1930	159,497	1900	24,267
1810	4,516			1920	13,369	1940	180,478	1910	23,587
1820	5,190	1810	5,730	1930	12,737	1950	208,255	1920	22,918
1830	7,265	1820	16,571	1940	14,356	1960	237,905	1930	24,117
1840	7,074	1830	15,620	1950	12,086	1970	255,077	1940	28,523
1850	8,404	1840	12,033	1960	12,506	1980	287,740	1950	30,494
1860	9,982	1850	13,768	1970	13,948			1960	30,468
1870	9,340	1860	13,848	1980	16,751	**HANCOCK**		1970	33,757
1880	12,460	1870	14,970					1980	43,751
1890	13,645	1880	17,178	**GREENE**		1850	5,660		
1900	18,635	1890	18,929			1860	7,020	**HAYWOOD**	
1910	19,955	1900	20,392	1790	7,741	1870	7,148		
1920	19,342	1910	20,491	1800	7,610	1880	9,098	1830	5,334
1930	18,491	1920	20,641	1810	9,713	1890	10,342	1840	13,870
1940	19,718	1930	21,796	1820	11,324	1900	11,147	1850	17,259
1950	18,805	1940	23,892	1830	14,410	1910	10,778	1860	19,232
1960	18,839	1950	25,431	1840	16,076	1920	10,454	1870	25,094
1970	21,977	1960	25,528	1850	17,824	1930	9,673	1880	26,053
1980	30,037	1970	27,289	1860	19,004	1940	11,231	1890	23,558
		1980	31,983	1870	21,668	1950	9,116	1900	25,189
DYER				1880	24,005	1960	7,757	1910	25,910
		GIBSON		1890	26,614	1970	6,719	1920	25,386
1830	1,904			1900	30,596	1980	6,887	1930	26,063
1840	4,484	1830	5,801	1910	31,083			1940	27,699
1850	6,361	1840	13,689	1920	32,824	**HARDEMAN**		1950	26,212
1860	10,536	1850	19,548	1930	35,119			1960	23,393
1870	13,706	1860	21,777	1940	39,405	1830	11,655	1970	19,596
1880	15,118	1870	25,666	1950	41,048	1840	14,563	1980	20,318
1890	19,878	1880	32,685	1960	42,163	1850	17,456		
1900	23,776	1890	35,859	1970	47,630	1860	17,769	**HENDERSON**	
1910	27,721	1900	39,408	1980	54,422	1870	18,074		
1920	29,893	1910	41,630			1880	22,921	1830	8,748
1930	31,405	1920	43,388	**GRUNDY**		1890	21,029	1840	11,875
1940	34,920	1930	46,528			1900	22,976	1850	13,164
1950	33,473	1940	44,835	1850	2,773	1910	23,011	1860	14,491
1960	29,537	1950	48,132	1860	3,093	1920	22,278	1870	14,217
1970	30,427	1960	44,699	1870	3,250	1930	22,193	1880	17,430
1980	34,663	1970	47,871	1880	4,592	1940	23,590	1890	16,336
		1980	49,467	1890	6,345	1950	23,311	1900	18,117
FAYETTE				1900	7,802	1960	21,517	1910	17,030
		GILES		1910	8,322	1970	22,435	1920	18,436
1830	8,652			1920	9,753	1980	23,873	1930	17,655
1840	21,501	1810	4,546	1930	9,717			1940	19,220
1850	26,719	1820	12,558	1940	11,552	**HARDIN**		1950	17,173
1860	24,327	1830	18,703	1950	12,558			1960	16,115
1870	26,145	1840	21,494	1960	11,512	1820	1,462	1970	17,291
1880	31,871	1850	25,949	1970	10,631	1830	4,868	1980	21,390
1890	28,878	1860	26,166	1980	13,787	1840	8,245		
1900	29,701	1870	32,413			1850	10,328	**HENRY**	
1910	30,257	1880	36,014	**HAMBLEN**		1860	11,214		
1920	31,499	1890	34,957			1870	11,768	1830	12,249
1930	28,891	1900	33,035	1880	10,187	1880	14,793	1840	14,906
1940	30,322	1910	32,629	1890	11,418	1890	17,698	1850	18,233
1950	27,535	1920	30,948	1900	12,728	1900	19,246	1860	19,133
1960	24,577	1930	28,016	1910	13,650	1910	17,521	1870	20,380
1970	22,692	1940	29,240	1920	15,056	1920	17,291	1880	22,142
1980	25,305	1950	26,961	1930	16,616	1930	16,213	1890	21,070
		1960	22,410	1940	18,611	1940	17,806	1900	24,208
FENTRESS		1970	22,138	1950	23,976	1950	16,908	1910	25,434
		1980	24,625	1960	33,092	1960	17,397	1920	27,151
1830	2,748			1970	38,696	1970	18,212	1930	26,432
1840	3,550			1980	49,300	1980	22,280	1940	25,877
1850	4,454							1950	23,828
1860	5,054							1960	22,275

1970	23,749	1960	9,233	1880	3,968	1880	26,960	1940	19,140
1980	28,656	1970	8,141	1890	5,304	1890	27,382	1950	20,520
		1980	9,398	1900	7,368	1900	26,304	1960	21,036
HICKMAN				1910	8,704	1910	25,908	1970	20,577
		JAMES		1920	9,075	1920	25,786	1980	24,416
1810	2,583			1930	10,486	1930	25,422		
1820	6,080	1880	5,187	1940	11,235	1940	27,214	**MARSHALL**	
1830	8,119	1890	4,903	1950	11,665	1950	25,624		
1840	8,618	1900	5,407	1960	7,952	1960	23,829	1840	14,555
1850	9,397	1910	5,210	1970	7,896	1970	24,318	1850	15,616
1860	9,312			1980	7,455	1980	26,483	1860	14,592
1870	9,856	**JEFFERSON**						1870	16,207
1880	12,095			**LAUDERDALE**		**LOUDON**		1880	19,259
1890	14,499	1800	9,017					1890	18,906
1900	16,367	1810	7,309	1840	3,435	1880	9,148	1900	18,673
1910	16,527	1820	8,953	1850	5,169	1890	9,273	1910	16,872
1920	16,216	1830	11,801	1860	7,559	1900	10,838	1920	17,375
1930	13,613	1840	12,076	1870	10,838	1910	13,612	1930	15,574
1940	14,873	1850	13,204	1880	14,918	1920	16,275	1940	16,030
1950	13,353	1860	16,043	1890	18,765	1930	17,805	1950	17,768
1960	11,862	1870	19,476	1900	21,971	1940	19,838	1960	16,859
1970	12,096	1880	15,846	1910	21,105	1950	23,182	1970	17,319
1980	15,151	1890	16,478	1920	21,494	1960	23,757	1980	19,698
		1900	18,950	1930	23,406	1970	24,266		
HOUSTON		1910	17,755	1940	24,461	1980	28,553	**MAURY**	
		1920	17,677	1950	25,047				
1880	4,295	1930	17,914	1960	21,844	**MACON**		1810	10,359
1890	5,390	1940	18,621	1970	20,271			1820	22,141
1900	6,476	1950	19,667	1980	24,555	1850	6,948	1830	27,665
1910	6,244	1960	21,493			1860	7,290	1840	28,186
1920	6,212	1970	24,940	**LAWRENCE**		1870	6,633	1850	29,520
1930	5,555	1980	31,284			1880	9,321	1860	32,498
1940	6,432			1820	3,271	1890	10,878	1870	36,289
1950	5,318	**JOHNSON**		1830	5,411	1900	12,881	1880	39,904
1960	4,794			1840	7,121	1910	14,559	1890	38,112
1970	5,845	1840	2,658	1850	9,280	1920	14,922	1900	42,703
1980	6,871	1850	3,705	1860	9,320	1930	13,872	1910	40,456
		1860	5,018	1870	7,601	1940	14,904	1920	35,403
HUMPHREYS		1870	5,852	1880	10,383	1950	13,599	1930	34,016
		1880	7,766	1890	12,286	1960	12,197	1940	40,357
1810	1,511	1890	8,858	1900	15,402	1970	12,315	1950	40,368
1820	4,067	1900	10,589	1910	17,569	1980	15,700	1960	41,699
1830	6,187	1910	13,191	1920	23,593			1970	44,028
1840	5,195	1920	12,230	1930	26,776	**MADISON**		1980	51,095
1850	6,422	1930	12,209	1940	28,726				
1860	9,096	1940	12,998	1950	28,818	1830	11,594	**McMINN**	
1870	9,326	1950	12,278	1960	28,049	1840	16,530		
1880	11,379	1960	10,765	1970	29,097	1850	21,470	1820	1,623
1890	11,720	1970	11,569	1980	34,110	1860	21,535	1830	14,460
1900	13,398	1980	13,745			1870	23,480	1840	12,719
1910	13,908			**LEWIS**		1880	30,874	1850	13,906
1920	13,482	**KNOX**				1890	30,497	1860	13,555
1930	12,039			1850	4,438	1900	36,333	1870	13,969
1940	12,421	1800	12,446	1860	2,241	1910	39,357	1880	15,064
1950	11,030	1810	10,171	1870	1,986	1920	43,824	1890	17,890
1960	11,511	1820	13,304	1880	2,181	1930	51,059	1900	19,163
1970	13,560	1830	14,498	1890	2,555	1940	54,115	1910	21,046
1980	15,957	1840	15,485	1900	4,455	1950	60,128	1920	25,133
		1850	18,807	1910	6,033	1960	60,655	1930	29,019
JACKSON		1860	22,813	1920	5,707	1970	65,774	1940	30,781
		1870	28,990	1930	5,258	1980	74,546	1950	32,024
1810	5,401	1880	39,124	1940	5,849			1960	33,662
1820	7,593	1890	59,557	1950	6,078	**MARION**		1970	35,462
1830	9,698	1900	72,302	1960	6,269			1980	41,878
1840	12,872	1910	91,187	1970	6,761	1820	3,888		
1850	15,673	1920	112,926	1980	9,700	1830	5,508	**McNAIRY**	
1860	11,725	1930	115,902			1840	6,070		
1870	12,583	1940	178,468	**LINCOLN**		1850	6,314	1830	5,697
1880	12,008	1950	223,007			1860	6,190	1840	9,385
1890	13,325	1960	250,523	1810	6,104	1870	6,841	1850	12,864
1900	15,039	1970	276,293	1820	14,761	1880	10,910	1860	14,732
1910	15,036	1980	319,694	1830	22,075	1890	15,411	1870	12,726
1920	14,955			1840	21,493	1900	17,281	1880	17,271
1930	13,589	**LAKE**		1850	23,492	1910	18,820	1890	15,510
1940	15,082			1860	22,828	1920	17,402	1900	17,760
1950	12,348	1870	2,428	1870	28,050	1930	17,549		

Year	Pop.
1910	16,356
1920	18,350
1930	19,901
1940	29,424
1950	20,390
1960	18,085
1970	18,369
1980	22,525

MEIGS

Year	Pop.
1840	4,794
1850	4,879
1860	4,667
1870	4,511
1880	7,117
1890	6,930
1900	7,491
1910	6,131
1920	6,077
1930	6,127
1940	6,393
1950	6,080
1960	5,160
1970	5,219
1980	7,431

MONROE

Year	Pop.
1820	2,529
1830	13,708
1840	12,056
1850	11,874
1860	12,607
1870	12,589
1880	14,283
1890	15,329
1900	18,585
1910	29,716
1920	22,060
1930	21,377
1940	24,275
1950	24,513
1960	23,316
1970	23,475
1980	28,700

MONTGOMERY

Year	Pop.
1790	1,387
1800	2,899
1810	8,201
1820	12,219
1830	14,349
1840	16,927
1850	21,045
1860	20,895
1870	24,747
1880	28,481
1890	29,697
1900	36,017
1910	33,672
1920	32,265
1930	30,882
1940	33,346
1950	44,186
1960	55,645
1970	62,721
1980	83,342

MOORE

Year	Pop.
1880	6,233
1890	5,975
1900	5,607
1910	4,800
1920	4,491

Year	Pop.
1930	4,037
1940	4,093
1950	3,948
1960	3,454
1970	3,568
1980	4,510

MORGAN

Year	Pop.
1820	1,676
1830	2,582
1840	2,660
1850	3,430
1860	3,353
1870	2,969
1880	5,156
1890	7,639
1900	9,587
1910	11,458
1920	13,285
1930	13,603
1940	15,242
1950	15,727
1960	14,304
1970	13,619
1980	16,604

OBION

Year	Pop.
1830	2,099
1840	4,814
1850	7,633
1860	12,817
1870	15,584
1880	22,912
1890	27,273
1900	28,286
1910	29,946
1920	28,393
1930	29,086
1940	30,978
1950	29,056
1960	26,947
1970	30,247
1980	32,781

OVERTON

Year	Pop.
1810	5,643
1820	7,128
1830	8,242
1840	9,279
1850	11,211
1860	12,637
1870	11,297
1880	12,153
1890	12,039
1900	13,353
1910	15,584
1920	17,617
1930	18,079
1940	18,883
1950	17,566
1960	14,661
1970	14,866
1980	17,575

PERRY

Year	Pop.
1820	2,384
1830	7,094
1840	7,419
1850	5,821
1860	6,042
1870	6,925
1880	7,174
1890	7,785

Year	Pop.
1900	8,800
1910	8,815
1920	7,765
1930	7,147
1940	7,535
1950	6,462
1960	5,273
1970	5,238
1980	6,111

PICKETT

Year	Pop.
1890	4,736
1900	5,366
1910	5,087
1920	5,205
1930	5,615
1940	6,213
1950	5,093
1960	4,431
1970	3,774
1980	4,358

POLK

Year	Pop.
1840	3,570
1850	6,338
1860	8,726
1870	7,369
1880	7,269
1890	8,361
1900	11,357
1910	14,116
1920	14,243
1930	15,686
1940	15,473
1950	14,074
1960	12,160
1970	11,669
1980	13,602

PUTNAM

Year	Pop.
1860	8,558
1870	8,698
1880	11,501
1890	13,683
1900	16,890
1910	20,023
1920	22,231
1930	23,759
1940	26,250
1950	29,869
1960	29,236
1970	35,487
1980	47,690

RHEA

Year	Pop.
1810	2,504
1820	4,215
1830	8,186
1840	3,985
1850	4,415
1860	4,991
1870	5,538
1880	7,073
1890	12,647
1900	14,318
1910	15,410
1920	13,812
1930	13,871
1940	16,353
1950	16,041
1960	15,863
1970	17,202
1980	24,235

ROANE

Year	Pop.
1810	5,581
1820	7,895
1830	11,341
1840	10,948
1850	12,185
1860	13,583
1870	15,622
1880	15,237
1890	17,418
1900	22,738
1910	22,860
1920	24,624
1930	24,477
1940	27,795
1950	31,665
1960	39,133
1970	38,881
1980	48,425

ROBERTSON

Year	Pop.
1800	4,280
1810	7,270
1820	9,938
1830	13,272
1840	13,801
1850	16,145
1860	15,265
1870	16,166
1880	18,861
1890	20,078
1900	25,029
1910	25,466
1920	25,621
1930	28,191
1940	29,046
1950	27,024
1960	27,335
1970	29,102
1980	37,021

RUTHERFORD

Year	Pop.
1810	10,265
1820	19,552
1830	26,134
1840	24,280
1850	29,122
1860	27,918
1870	33,289
1880	36,741
1890	35,097
1900	33,543
1910	33,199
1920	33,059
1930	32,286
1940	33,604
1950	40,696
1960	52,368
1970	59,428
1980	84,058

SCOTT

Year	Pop.
1850	1,905
1860	3,519
1870	4,054
1880	6,021
1890	9,794
1900	11,077
1910	12,947
1920	13,411
1930	14,080
1940	15,966
1950	17,362

Year	Pop.
1960	15,413
1970	14,762
1980	19,259

SEQUATCHIE

Year	Pop.
1860	2,120
1870	2,335
1880	2,565
1890	3,027
1900	3,326
1910	4,202
1920	3,632
1930	4,047
1940	5,038
1950	5,685
1960	5,915
1970	6,331
1980	8,605

SEVIER

Year	Pop.
1790	3,619
1800	3,419
1810	4,595
1820	4,772
1830	5,717
1840	6,442
1850	6,920
1860	9,122
1870	11,028
1880	15,541
1890	18,761
1900	22,021
1910	22,296
1920	22,384
1930	20,480
1940	23,291
1950	23,375
1960	24,251
1970	28,241
1980	41,418

SHELBY

Year	Pop.
1820	364
1830	5,648
1840	14,741
1850	31,157
1860	48,092
1870	76,378
1880	78,430
1890	112,740
1900	153,557
1910	191,439
1920	223,216
1930	306,482
1940	358,250
1950	482,393
1960	627,019
1970	722,111
1980	777,113

SMITH

Year	Pop.
1800	4,294
1810	11,649
1820	17,580
1830	19,906
1840	21,179
1850	18,412
1860	16,357
1870	15,994
1880	17,799
1890	18,404
1900	19,026
1910	18,548

1920	17,134	TIPTON		1970	3,758	1910	31,929
1930	15,473			1980	4,728	1920	31,053
1940	16,148	1830	5,317			1930	29,262
1950	14,098	1840	6,800			1940	29,498
1960	12,059	1850	8,887	WARREN		1950	27,962
1970	12,509	1860	10,705			1960	24,227
1980	14,935	1870	14,884	1810	5,725	1970	28,827
		1880	21,033	1820	10,348	1980	32,896
		1890	24,271	1830	15,210		
STEWART		1900	29,273	1840	10,803		
		1910	29,459	1850	10,179	WHITE	
1810	4,262	1920	30,258	1860	11,147		
1820	8,397	1930	27,498	1870	12,714	1810	4,028
1830	6,969	1940	28,036	1880	14,079	1820	8,701
1840	8,587	1950	29,782	1890	14,413	1830	9,967
1850	9,719	1960	28,564	1900	16,410	1840	10,747
1860	9,896	1970	28,001	1910	16,534	1850	11,444
1870	12,019	1980	32,930	1920	17,306	1860	9,381
1880	12,690			1930	20,209	1870	9,375
1890	12,193			1940	19,764	1880	11,176
1900	15,224	TROUSDALE		1950	22,271	1890	12,348
1910	14,860			1960	23,102	1900	14,157
1920	14,664	1880	6,646	1970	26,972	1910	15,420
1930	13,278	1890	5,850	1980	32,653	1920	15,701
1940	13,549	1900	6,004			1930	15,543
1950	9,175	1910	5,874			1940	15,983
1960	7,851	1920	5,996	WASHINGTON		1950	16,204
1970	7,319	1930	5,629			1960	15,577
1980	8,665	1940	6,113	1790	5,872	1970	17,088
		1950	5,520	1800	6,379	1980	19,567
		1960	4,914	1810	7,740		
SULLIVAN		1970	5,155	1820	9,557		
		1980	6,137	1830	10,995	WILLIAMSON	
1790	4,447			1840	11,751		
1800	10,218			1850	13,861	1800	2,868
1810	6,847	UNICOI		1860	14,849	1810	13,153
1820	7,015			1870	16,317	1820	20,640
1830	10,073	1880	3,645	1880	16,181	1830	26,638
1840	10,736	1890	4,619	1890	20,354	1840	27,006
1850	11,742	1900	5,851	1900	22,604	1850	27,201
1860	13,552	1910	7,201	1910	28,968	1860	23,827
1870	13,136	1920	10,120	1920	34,052	1870	25,328
1880	18,321	1930	12,678	1930	45,805	1880	28,313
1890	20,879	1940	14,128	1940	52,631	1890	26,321
1900	24,935	1950	15,886	1950	59,971	1900	26,429
1910	28,120	1960	15,082	1960	64,832	1910	24,213
1920	36,359	1970	15,254	1970	73,924	1920	23,409
1930	51,087	1980	16,362	1980	88,755	1930	22,845
1940	69,085					1940	25,220
1950	95,063					1950	24,307
1960	114,139	UNION		WAYNE		1960	25,267
1970	127,329					1970	34,423
1980	143,968	1860	6,117	1820	2,459	1980	58,108
		1870	7,605	1830	6,013		
		1880	10,260	1840	7,705		
SUMNER		1890	11,459	1850	8,170	WILSON	
		1900	12,894	1860	9,115		
1790	2,196	1910	11,414	1870	10,209	1800	3,261
1800	4,616	1920	11,615	1880	11,301	1810	11,952
1810	13,792	1930	11,371	1890	11,471	1820	18,730
1820	19,211	1940	9,030	1900	12,936	1830	25,472
1830	20,569	1950	8,670	1910	12,062	1840	24,460
1840	22,445	1960	8,498	1920	12,877	1850	27,443
1850	22,717	1970	9,072	1930	12,134	1860	26,072
1860	22,030	1980	11,707	1940	13,638	1870	25,881
1870	23,711			1950	13,864	1880	28,747
1880	23,625			1960	11,908	1890	27,148
1890	23,668	VAN BUREN		1970	12,365	1900	27,078
1900	26,072			1980	13,946	1910	25,394
1910	25,621	1850	2,674			1920	26,241
1920	27,708	1860	2,581			1930	23,929
1930	28,622	1870	2,725	WEAKLEY		1940	25,267
1940	32,719	1880	2,933			1950	26,318
1950	33,533	1890	2,863	1830	4,797	1960	27,668
1960	36,217	1900	3,126	1840	9,870	1970	36,999
1970	56,266	1910	2,784	1850	14,608	1980	56,064
1980	85,790	1920	2,624	1860	18,216		
		1930	3,516	1870	20,755		
		1940	4,090	1880	24,538		
		1950	3,985	1890	28,955		
		1960	3,671	1900	32,546		

NOTES

JAMES

  Annexed to Hamilton in 1919.

LOUDON

  Name changed from Christiana in 1870.

UNION

  Name changed from Cocke in 1846.

ATHENS

1860	678
1870	974
1880	1,100
1890	2,224
1900	1,849
1910	2,264
1920	2,580
1930	5,385
1940	6,930
1950	8,618
1960	12,103
1970	11,790
1980	12,080

BARTLETT

1900	200
1910	263
1920	271
1930	429
1940	400
1950	489
1960	508
1970	1,150
1980	17,170

BRISTOL

1880	1,647
1890	3,324
1900	5,271
1910	7,148
1920	8,047
1930	12,005
1940	14,004
1950	16,771
1960	17,582
1970	20,064
1980	23,986

CHATTANOOGA

1870	6,093
1880	12,892
1890	29,100
1900	30,154
1910	44,604
1920	57,895
1930	119,789
1940	128,163
1950	131,041
1960	130,009
1970	119,923
1980	169,565

CLARKSVILLE

1870	3,200
1880	3,880
1890	7,924
1900	9,431
1910	8,458
1920	8,110
1930	9,242
1940	11,831
1950	16,246
1960	22,021
1970	31,719
1980	54,777

CLEVELAND

1860	806
1870	1,658

1880	1,874
1890	2,863
1900	3,858
1910	5,549
1920	6,522
1930	9,136
1940	11,351
1950	12,605
1960	16,196
1970	20,651
1980	26,415

COLUMBIA

1850	2,977
1870	2,550
1880	3,400
1890	5,370
1900	6,052
1910	5,754
1920	5,526
1930	7,882
1940	10,579
1950	10,911
1960	17,624
1970	21,471
1980	26,372

COOKEVILLE

1910	1,848
1920	2,395
1930	3,738
1940	4,364
1950	6,924
1960	7,805
1970	14,403
1980	20,535

DYERSBURG

1870	683
1880	1,010
1890	2,009
1900	3,647
1910	4,149
1920	6,444
1930	8,733
1940	10,034
1950	10,885
1960	12,499
1970	14,523
1980	15,856

EAST RIDGE

1930	2,152
1940	2,939
1950	9,645
1960	19,570
1970	21,799
1980	21,236

ELIZABETHTON

1910	2,478
1920	2,749
1930	8,093
1940	8,516
1950	10,754
1960	10,896
1970	12,269
1980	12,431

FRANKLIN

1870	1,552
1880	1,632
1890	2,250
1900	2,180
1910	2,924
1920	3,123
1930	3,377
1940	4,120
1950	5,475
1960	6,977
1970	9,497
1980	12,407

GALLATIN

1880	1,938
1890	2,078
1900	2,409
1910	2,399
1920	2,757
1930	3,050
1940	4,829
1950	5,107
1960	7,109
1970	13,093
1980	17,191

GERMANTOWN

1910	247
1920	263
1930	322
1940	402
1950	408
1960	1,104
1970	3,474
1980	20,459

GREENEVILLE

1850	660
1860	(NA)
1870	1,039
1880	1,066
1890	1,779
1900	1,817
1910	1,920
1920	3,775
1930	5,544
1940	6,784
1950	8,721
1960	11,759
1970	13,722
1980	14,097

HENDERSONVILLE

1970	11,996
1980	26,561

HUMBOLDT

1880	1,572
1890	1,837
1900	2,866
1910	3,446
1920	3,913
1930	4,613
1940	5,160
1950	7,426
1960	8,482
1970	10,066
1980	10,209

JACKSON

1850	1,006
1860	2,407
1870	4,119
1880	5,377
1890	10,039
1900	14,511
1910	15,779
1920	18,860
1930	22,172
1940	24,332
1950	30,207
1960	34,376
1970	39,996
1980	49,131

JOHNSON CITY

1880	685
1890	4,161
1900	4,645
1910	8,502
1920	12,442
1930	25,080
1940	25,332
1950	27,864
1960	31,187
1970	33,770
1980	39,753

KINGSPORT

1920	5,692
1930	11,914
1940	14,404
1950	19,571
1960	26,314
1970	31,938
1980	32,027

KNOXVILLE

1850	2,076
1860	(NA)
1870	8,682
1880	9,693
1890	22,535
1900	32,637
1910	36,346
1920	77,818
1930	105,802
1940	111,580
1950	124,769
1960	111,827
1970	174,587
1980	175,030

LAWRENCEBURG

1870	351
1880	503
1890	618
1900	823
1910	1,687
1920	2,461
1930	3,102
1940	3,807
1950	5,442
1960	8,042
1970	8,889
1980	10,184

LEBANON

1850	1,554
1860	(NA)
1870	2,073
1880	2,296
1890	1,883
1900	1,956
1910	3,659
1920	4,084
1930	4,656
1940	5,950
1950	7,913
1960	10,512
1970	12,492
1980	11,872

McMINNVILLE

1850	420
1870	1,172
1880	1,244
1890	1,677
1900	1,980
1910	2,299
1920	2,814
1930	3,914
1940	4,649
1950	7,577
1960	9,013
1970	10,662
1980	10,683

MARYVILLE

1910	2,381
1920	3,739
1930	4,958
1940	5,609
1950	7,742
1960	10,348
1970	13,808
1980	17,480

MEMPHIS

1850	8,841
1860	22,623
1870	40,226
1880	33,592
1890	64,495
1900	102,320
1910	131,105
1920	162,351
1930	253,143
1940	292,942
1950	396,000
1960	497,524
1970	623,988
1980	646,356

MILLINGTON

1910	554
1920	657
1930	662
1940	730
1950	4,696
1960	6,059
1970	21,106
1980	20,236

MORRISTOWN

1880	1,350
1890	1,999
1900	2,973
1910	4,007
1920	5,875
1930	7,305
1940	8,050
1950	13,019
1960	21,267
1970	20,318
1980	19,683

MURFREESBORO

1850	1,917
1860	2,861
1870	3,502
1880	3,800
1890	3,739
1900	3,999
1910	4,679
1920	5,537
1930	7,993
1940	9,495
1950	13,052
1960	18,991
1970	26,360
1980	32,845

NASHVILLE

1830	5,556
1840	6,929
1850	10,165
1860	16,988
1870	25,865
1880	43,350
1890	76,168
1900	80,865
1910	110,364
1920	118,342
1930	153,866
1940	167,402
1950	174,307
1960	170,874
1970	426,029
1980	455,651

OAK RIDGE

1960	27,169
1970	28,319
1980	27,662

PARIS

1880	1,767
1890	1,917
1900	2,018
1910	3,881
1920	4,730
1930	8,164
1940	6,395
1950	8,826
1960	9,325
1970	9,892
1980	10,728

RED BANK

1960	10,777
1970	12,715
1980	13,297

SHELBYVILLE

1850	1,768
1860	776
1870	1,719
1880	1,869
1890	1,823
1900	2,236
1910	2,869
1920	2,912
1930	5,010
1940	6,537
1950	9,456
1960	10,466
1970	12,262
1980	13,530

SPRINGFIELD

1890	1,372
1900	1,732
1910	2,085
1920	3,860
1930	5,577
1940	6,668
1950	6,506
1960	9,221
1970	9,720
1980	10,814

TULLAHOMA

1860	586
1870	589
1880	1,083
1890	2,439
1900	2,684
1910	3,049
1920	3,479
1930	4,023
1940	4,549
1950	7,562
1960	12,242
1970	15,311
1980	15,800

UNION CITY

1880	1,879
1890	3,411
1900	3,407
1910	4,389
1920	4,412
1930	5,865
1940	7,256
1950	7,665
1960	8,837
1970	11,925
1980	10,436

CORRECTION NOTE

The official 1980 census counts of total population shown in
this report supersede counts issued previously. Corrections
to the figures were made after the counts were provided to
the State for redistricting purposes and released in Advance
Report PHC80-V for this State.

Shown below are corrections to the 1980 census counts of the
total population made after the tabulations for this report
were completed. Any additional corrections made after this
report is printed are available by writing to Data User
Services Division, Customer Services (Corrections), Bureau of
the Census, Washington, D.C. 20233.

The 1980 figures shown in this publication are subject to
change pending the outcome of the various lawsuits dealing
with the census counts.

	1980 population	
	As shown in the tables	Corrected
Campbell County:		
Caryville division...............	3 968	3 753
Caryville town (pt.)............	2 039	1 824
La Follette division.............	17 752	17 967
Caryville town (pt.)............	(1)	215
Hamilton County:		
Chattanooga division:		
Chattanooga city (pt.)..........	164 351	164 344
Red Bank city...................	13 297	13 299
Knox County:		
Knoxville division:		
Knoxville city	175 030	175 045
Madison County:		
Medon division:		
Medon town......................	162	169
Maury County:		
Columbia division:		
Columbia city...................	26 372	26 571
Scott County:		
Oneida division:		
Oneida town.....................	3 275	3 717
Shelby County:		
Memphis division:		
Germantown city................	20 459	21 482
Memphis city (pt.).............	646 356	646 174
Caryville town (total).............	2 039	(2)
Chattanooga city (total)...........	169 565	169 558
Memphis city (total)...............	646 356	646 174

[1]Not shown.
[2]No change.

County Subdivisions

County Subdivisions	1980	1970
The State	4 591 120	'3 926 018
Anderson County[1]	67 346	60 300
Clinton division	10 971	...
Clinton town[1]	5 245	4 794
Clinton South division	9 000	6 541
South Clinton (CDP)	1 671	1 484
Lake City East division	5 078	4 079
Lake City town[1]	2 335	1 923
Lake City West division	2 774	2 140
New River division	451	776
Norris division	7 566	5 900
Norris city[1]	1 374	1 359
Oak Ridge division	25 300	26 829
Oak Ridge city (pt.)	25 300	26 829
Walden Ridge division	6 206	5 191
Oliver Springs town (pt.)[1]	2 525	2 208
Bedford County[2]	27 916	25 039
Bedford division	1 930	...
Bell Buckle division	1 918	1 797
Bell Buckle town[2]	450	393
Flat Creek–Normandy division	2 078	...
Normandy town	118	122
Shelbyville division	17 345	...
Shelbyville city[2]	13 530	12 262
Unionville division	3 007	2 217
Wartrace division	1 638	1 636
Wartrace town	540	616
Benton County[3]	14 901	12 126
Big Sandy division	2 813	2 052
Big Sandy town	650	539
Camden division	10 814	...
Camden town[3]	3 279	3 052
Holladay division	1 274	1 180
Bledsoe County[4]	9 478	7 643
Cumberland Plateau division	2 676	2 505
Sequatchie Valley division	5 050	3 979
Pikeville town[4]	2 085	1 454
Walden Ridge division	1 752	1 159
Blount County[5]	77 770	63 744
Binfield division	4 259	3 001
Friendsville division	6 229	4 300
Friendsville city[5]	694	575
Maryville city (pt.)[5]	2	...
Lanier division	6 108	4 229
Maryville–Alcoa division	51 690	...
Alcoa city[5]	6 870	7 739
Eagleton Village (CDP)	5 331	5 345
Maryville city (pt.)[5]	17 478	13 808
Rockford city[5]	567	...
Townsend division	4 335	3 851
Townsend city[5]	351	267
Wildwood division	5 149	3 344
Bradley County[6]	67 547	50 686
Charleston division	7 994	...
Charleston town[6]	756	792
Cleveland division	46 308	...
Cleveland city[6]	26 415	'21 446
East Cleveland (CDP)	1 655	1 870
South Cleveland (CDP)	4 360	5 070
Wildwood Lake (CDP)	1 642	...
South Bradley division	3 245	...
Southeast Bradley division	3 917	...
West Bradley division	6 083	...
Campbell County[7]	34 923	26 045
Caryville division	3 968	2 800
Caryville town[7]	2 039	648
Clinchmore division	331	399
Elk Valley division	5 035	4 065
Jellico city (pt.)[7]	2 633	2 235
Fincastle division	3 771	...
Habersham division	4 066	3 351
Jellico city (pt.)[7]	165	...
La Follette division	17 752	...
Jacksboro town[7]	1 722	689
La Follette city[7]	8 198	6 902
Cannon County[8]	10 234	8 467
North Cannon division	3 013	...
Auburntown town	204	213
Woodbury town (pt.)[8]	195	...
Plateau of the Barrens division	2 370	1 912
South Cannon division	4 851	...
Woodbury town (pt.)[8]	1 965	1 725
Carroll County[9]	28 285	25 741
Bruceton division	4 527	4 144
Bruceton town[9]	1 579	1 450
Hollow Rock town[9]	955	722
Cedar Grove division	2 359	2 294
Clarksburg division	2 210	1 960
Clarksburg town[9]	400	349
Huntingdon division	7 176	...
Huntingdon town[9]	3 962	3 661
McKenzie division	7 108	6 270
McKenzie city (pt.)[9]	5 089	4 612
Trezevant division	4 905	4 771

County Subdivisions	1980	1970
Carroll County—Con.		
Trezevant division—Con.		
Atwood town[9]	1 143	937
McLemoresville town[9]	311	328
Trezevant town[9]	921	877
Carter County[10]	50 205	'43 259
Biltmore division	4 782	3 836
Biltmore (CDP)	1 962	...
Johnson City city (pt.)[10]	38	...
Watauga city[10]	376	314
Elizabethton division	28 859	...
Central (CDP)	2 630	...
Elizabethton city[10]	12 431	12 269
Johnson City city (pt.)[10]	256	...
Pine Crest (CDP)	3 992	...
Valley Forge (CDP)	2 180	...
Laurel Fork division	1 522	...
Roan Mountain division	3 469	...
Roan Mountain (CDP)	1 108	...
Stony Creek division	6 240	5 252
Hunter (CDP)	1 386	...
Tiger Valley division	5 333	...
Hampton (CDP)	2 236	1 100
Cheatham County[11]	21 616	13 199
Ashland City division	11 019	6 931
Ashland City town[11]	2 329	2 027
Kingston Springs division	4 895	3 015
Kingston Springs town[11]	1 017	312
Pegram town[11]	1 081	...
Pleasant View division	5 702	3 253
Chester County[12]	12 727	9 927
East Chester division	3 885	3 196
Enville town (pt.)[12]	234	224
Milledgeville town (pt.)	118	101
West Chester division	8 842	6 731
Henderson city[12]	4 449	3 581
Silerton town (pt.)	2	1
Claiborne County[13]	24 595	19 420
Big Barren Creek division	2 374	2 002
Clairfield division	1 425	1 262
Cumberland Gap division	4 968	3 753
Cumberland Gap town	263	231
Harrogate–Shawanee (CDP) (pt.)	2 530	...
Powell Valley division	5 367	3 758
Harrogate–Shawanee (CDP) (pt.)	–	...
Tazewell division	10 461	...
New Tazewell town[13]	1 677	1 192
Tazewell town[13]	2 090	1 860
Clay County[14]	7 676	6 624
Celina division	4 151	3 706
Celina town[14]	1 580	1 370
Fairview division	458	388
Hermitage Springs division	3 067	2 530
Cocke County[15]	28 792	25 283
Centerview division	3 015	2 584
Del Rio division	1 853	1 643
Hartford division	2 971	2 472
Newport division	17 788	...
Newport city[15]	7 580	7 328
Parrottsville division	3 165	2 777
Parrottsville town	118	115
Coffee County[16]	38 311	32 572
Beech Grove division	1 206	1 103
Hillsboro division	2 410	2 062
Manchester division	14 307	...
Manchester city[16]	7 250	6 208
Summitville division	2 880	2 008
Tullahoma division	17 508	...
Tullahoma city (pt.)[16]	15 494	14 771
Crockett County[17]	14 941	14 402
Alamo division	4 282	4 236
Alamo town	2 615	2 499
Bells division	3 297	3 155
Bells town[17]	1 571	1 474
Friendship division	2 114	1 856
Friendship town	763	441
Gadsden division	2 233	1 994
Gadsden town	683	523
Maury City division	3 015	3 161
Maury City town[17]	989	813
Cumberland County[18]	28 676	20 733
Crab Orchard division	2 994	2 941
Crab Orchard town (pt.)[18]	910	...
Crossville division	13 276	...
Crab Orchard town (pt.)[18]	155	...
Crossville city	6 394	5 381
Crossville North division	5 051	...
Lantana division	3 194	2 412
Mayland–Pleasant Hill division	4 161	3 100
Pleasant Hill town[18]	371	293
Davidson County[19]	477 811	'447 877
Metropolitan Government division	477 811	'447 877
Belle Meade city[19]	3 182	'2 933
Berry Hill city[19]	1 113	'1 517
Forest Hills city[19]	4 516	'4 255

County Subdivisions	1980	1970
Davidson County—Con.		
Metropolitan Government division—Con.		
Goodlettsville city (pt.)[19]	6 385	'6 168
Lakewood city[19]	2 325	'2 282
Nashville–Davidson[19]	455 651	'426 029
Oak Hill city[19]	4 609	'4 645
Ridgetop town (pt.)[19]	30	'48
Decatur County[20]	10 857	9 457
Decaturville division	4 638	4 295
Decaturville town	1 004	958
Scotts Hill town (pt.)[20]	246	174
Parsons division	6 219	5 162
Parsons town[20]	2 422	2 167
De Kalb County[21]	13 589	11 151
Smithville division	9 312	7 370
Smithville town[21]	3 839	2 997
Underhill division	4 277	3 781
Alexandria town	689	680
Dowelltown town	341	329
Liberty town[21]	365	332
Dickson County[22]	30 037	21 977
Burns–White Bluff division	8 560	5 340
Burns town[22]	777	'456
Dickson city (pt.)[22]	10	...
White Bluff town[22]	2 055	'1 163
Charlotte division	4 230	3 481
Charlotte town[22]	788	610
Dickson division	12 241	9 055
Dickson city (pt.)[22]	7 030	5 665
Tennessee City division	2 193	1 761
Vanleer division	2 813	2 340
Slayden town	69	95
Vanleer town[22]	401	320
Dyer County[23]	34 663	30 427
Dyersburg division	22 636	...
Dyersburg city[23]	15 856	14 523
Finley (CDP)	1 014	...
Fowlkes division	3 054	...
Mississippi–Obion division	1 320	1 724
Newbern division	5 610	4 626
Newbern town[23]	2 794	2 124
Trimble town (pt.)	719	669
Ro Ellen division	2 043	...
Fayette County[24]	25 305	22 692
Braden division	2 933	2 586
Braden city[24]	293	...
Gallaway city[24]	804	304
Fayette Corners division	1 205	1 349
Moscow–La Grange division	3 704	...
La Grange town[24]	185	213
Moscow town[24]	499	448
Oakland division	5 135	...
Oakland town[24]	472	353
Rossville division	3 736	3 567
Piperton city[24]	746	...
Rossville town	379	410
Somerville division	8 592	...
Somerville town[24]	2 264	1 816
Williston city[24]	395	...
Fentress County[25]	14 826	12 593
Clarkrange division	3 030	2 645
Jamestown division	9 221	...
Allardt city	654	610
Jamestown city	2 364	1 899
Manson–Wolf River division	2 575	...
Franklin County[26]	31 983	'27 289
Estill Springs division	6 963	...
Estill Springs town[26]	1 324	919
Tullahoma city (pt.)[26]	306	540
Harmony division	1 856	...
Huntland division	2 803	2 414
Huntland town[26]	983	849
Sewanee division	3 249	3 007
Sewanee (CDP)	2 298	1 886
Sherwood division	627	743
Winchester division	16 485	...
Cowan city[26]	1 790	1 772
Decherd town[26]	2 233	2 148
Winchester city[26]	5 821	'5 256
Gibson County[27]	49 467	47 871
Bradford division	2 796	2 719
Bradford town[27]	1 146	968
Brazil–Gibson Wells division	1 762	1 932
China Grove division	844	1 040
Dyer division	3 922	3 632
Dyer city[27]	2 419	2 501
Gibson division	1 712	1 360
Gibson town	458	302
Humboldt division	11 865	11 531
Humboldt city[27]	10 209	10 066
Medina division	1 874	1 763
Medina town	687	755
Milan division	11 592	10 838
Milan city[27]	8 083	7 313
Rutherford division	2 917	2 866
Kenton town (pt.)[27]	769	745

County Subdivisions	1980	1970
Gibson County—Con.		
Rutherford division—Con.		
Rutherford town[27]	1 378	1 385
Trenton North division	2 410	2 112
Trenton city (pt.)[27]	273	...
Trenton South division	6 395	6 430
Trenton city (pt.)[27]	4 328	4 226
Yorkville division	1 378	1 648
Yorkville town[27]	272	243
Giles County[28]	24 625	22 138
Elkton division	2 581	2 324
Ardmore city[28]	835	601
Elkton town[28]	540	341
Lynnville division	2 543	2 482
Lynnville town	383	327
Minor Hill division	2 446	'1 999
Minor Hill city[28]	564	315
Prospect division	1 403	'1 250
Pulaski division	15 652	...
Pulaski city[28]	7 184	6 989
Grainger County[29]	16 751	13 948
Bean Station division	5 450	3 992
Blaine division	3 237	2 636
Blaine city[29]	1 147	...
Rutledge division	4 696	4 167
Rutledge town	1 058	863
Thorn Hill division	1 179	1 121
Washburn division	2 189	2 032
Greene County[30]	54 422	47 630
Baileyton division	2 008	1 901
Baileyton town[30]	333	258
Greeneville division	30 231	...
Greeneville town[30]	14 097	13 722
Tusculum city[30]	1 242	'1 180
Jearoldstown division	2 495	2 239
Fall Branch (CDP) (pt.)	245	...
Mohawk division	2 747	2 446
Mosheim division	4 800	...
Mosheim town[30]	1 539	...
Rheatown–Chucky division	4 363	2 744
Southeast Nolichucky division	5 130	4 256
Southwest Nolichucky division	2 648	2 028
Grundy County[31]	13 787	10 631
Altamont division	2 518	2 151
Altamont town	679	546
Beersheba Springs town	643	560
Palmer division	4 326	2 734
Palmer town	1 027	898
Pelham division	1 808	1 528
Monteagle town (pt.)[31]	667	514
Tracy City division	5 135	4 218
Coalmont town	625	518
Monteagle town (pt.)[31]	13	...
Tracy City town[31]	1 356	1 388
Hamblen County[32]	49 300	38 696
Alpha division	7 711	...
Morristown city (pt.)[32]	–	...
Morristown division	38 059	...
Morristown city (pt.)[32]	19 683	20 318
Russellville (CDP) (pt.)	820	...
Whitesburg division	3 530	...
Russellville (CDP) (pt.)	249	...
Hamilton County[33]	287 740	'255 077
Chattanooga division	202 092	...
Chattanooga city (pt.)[33]	164 351	'119 923
Collegedale city (pt.)[33]	196	...
East Ridge city (pt.)	1 542	...
Harrison (CDP)	6 206	...
Middle Valley (CDP) (pt.)	1 051	...
Red Bank city	13 297	12 715
Ridgeside city	417	458
Signal Mountain town (pt.)[33]	41	...
Soddy–Daisy city (pt.)[33]	562	...
Summit (CDP) (pt.)	8 085	...
Walden town (pt.)[33]	–	...
East Ridge division	19 694	...
East Ridge city (pt.)	19 694	21 799
Lookout Mountain division	7 619	7 791
Chattanooga city (pt.)[33]	5 214	...
Lookout Mountain town	1 886	1 741
Middle Valley division	12 026	...
Middle Valley (CDP) (pt.)	10 369	...
Soddy–Daisy city (pt.)[33]	117	...
Ooltewah division	10 620	...
Collegedale city (pt.)[33]	4 411	3 031
Summit (CDP) (pt.)	222	...
Sale Creek division	4 522	...
Soddy–Daisy city (pt.)[33]	742	...
Signal Mountain division	10 715	...
Fairmount (CDP)	1 286	...
Signal Mountain town (pt.)[33]	5 777	4 839
Walden town (pt.)[33]	1 293	...
Snow Hill division	6 887	4 365
Soddy–Daisy division	13 565	...
Lakesite city[33]	651	...
Soddy–Daisy city (pt.)[33]	6 967	7 569

Population of County Subdivisions

County Subdivisions	1980	1970
Hancock County[34]	6 887	6 719
Big War Creek division	1 894	1 666
Kyles Ford division	1 129	1 134
Powell Valley division	1 011	907
Sneedville division	2 853	3 012
Sneedville town[34]	1 110	874
Hardeman County[35]	23 873	22 435
Bolivar division	10 303	10 082
Bolivar city[35]	6 597	6 674
Hickory Valley town (pt.)	203	180
Grand Junction division	2 695	2 526
Grand Junction city	360	427
Hickory Valley town (pt.)	49	...
Saulsbury town	156	156
Hornsby division	1 351	1 115
Hornsby town[35]	401	212
Middleton division	3 596	3 218
Middleton town	596	654
Toone division	2 628	2 336
Silerton town (pt.)	98	87
Toone town[35]	355	200
Whiteville division	3 300	3 158
Whiteville town[35]	1 270	992
Hardin County[36]	22 280	18 212
Morris Chapel division	2 651	2 028
Nixon division	4 164	3 018
Olive Hill division	2 876	2 577
Pickwick division	2 794	2 121
Saltillo division	1 240	1 157
Milledgeville town (pt.)	88	43
Saltillo town[36]	434	423
Savannah division	8 555	7 311
Savannah city[36]	6 992	5 576
Hawkins County[37]	43 751	'33 757
Beech Creek division	3 120	...
Kingsport city (pt.)[37]	−	...
Surgoinsville town (pt.)	50	...
Bulls Gap division	5 866	4 627
Bulls Gap town[37]	821	774
Church Hill division	8 529	...
Church Hill town (pt.)[37]	3 901	2 822
Eidson division	1 025	1 033
Mooresburg division	2 585	2 110
Mount Carmel division	7 820	...
Church Hill town (pt.)[37]	209	...
Kingsport city (pt.)[37]	1 340	230
Mount Carmel town[37]	3 764	2 821
Rogersville division	10 614	'8 620
Rogersville town[37]	4 368	'4 076
Surgoinsville division	4 192	...
Surgoinsville town (pt.)	1 486	1 285
Haywood County[38]	20 318	19 596
Brownsville division	11 119	9 372
Brownsville town[38]	9 307	7 011
Hillville division	985	1 007
Holly Grove–Belle Eagle division	1 552	1 843
Lebanon division	1 221	1 383
Nutbush division	1 427	1 653
Stanton division	2 455	2 657
Stanton town	540	372
Woodland division	1 559	1 681
Henderson County[39]	21 390	'17 360
Darden division	2 224	...
Lexington division	9 685	...
Lexington city[39]	5 934	'5 024
Luray division	3 510	...
Sardis division	3 317	...
Sardis town	301	350
Scotts Hill town (pt.)	422	'374
Wildersville division	2 654	...
Henry County[40]	28 656	23 749
Buchanan–Elkhorn division	2 871	1 748
Cottage Grove division	1 867	1 599
Cottage Grove town	117	119
Henry division	2 097	1 625
Henry town	295	302
McKenzie city (pt.)[40]	84	...
Paris division	17 112	15 078
Paris city[40]	10 728	9 892
Puryear division	2 672	2 234
Puryear city[40]	624	458
Springville division	2 037	1 465
Hickman County[41]	15 151	12 096
Centerville division	6 032	...
Centerville town[41]	2 824	2 592
Coble division	1 754	1 469
Littlelot division	2 769	1 976
Lyles–Wrigley division	3 284	...
Only division	1 312	706
Houston County[42]	6 871	'5 853
Erin division	4 434	...
Erin city[42]	1 614	'1 165
Tennessee Ridge division	2 437	...
Tennessee Ridge city (pt.)[42]	1 325	664

County Subdivisions	1980	1970
Humphreys County[43]	15 957	13 560
Bakerville–Bold Spring division	1 959	...
McEwen division	3 699	3 273
McEwen town[43]	1 352	1 237
Waverly division	10 299	...
New Johnsonville city[43]	1 824	970
Waverly city[43]	4 405	3 794
Jackson County[44]	9 398	8 141
Burristown division	1 491	1 327
Gainesboro town (pt.)[44]	37	...
Gainesboro division	4 272	3 474
Gainesboro town (pt.)[44]	1 082	1 101
Granville division	1 811	1 474
North of the River division	1 824	1 866
Jefferson County[45]	31 284	24 940
Chestnut Hill division	2 777	2 445
Dandridge town (pt.)[45]	5	...
Dandridge division	5 992	4 371
Dandridge town (pt.)[45]	1 378	1 270
Jefferson City division	14 196	...
Jefferson City town[45]	5 612	5 124
New Market city[45]	1 216	...
Strawberry Plains division	3 792	2 574
White Pine division	4 527	3 645
White Pine town[45]	1 900	1 532
Johnson County[46]	13 745	'11 569
Butler division	1 907	1 915
Mountain City division	8 758	...
Mountain City town	2 125	1 883
Neva division	1 941	1 748
Shady Valley division	1 139	1 083
Knox County[47]	319 694	276 293
Concord division	11 772	5 479
Concord (CDP)	8 569	...
Corryton division	1 979	1 805
Gibbs division	5 207	3 966
Halls division	20 125	12 901
Halls (CDP) (pt.)	9 955	...
Hardin Valley division	8 528	5 392
Karns (CDP) (pt.)	384	351
Karns division	6 460	4 520
Karns (CDP) (pt.)	789	754
Knoxville division	252 520	...
Cedar Bluff (CDP)	10 654	...
Halls (CDP) (pt.)	408	...
Knoxville city[47]	175 030	174 587
Powell division	9 293	6 600
Powell (CDP)	7 220	...
Skaggston division	3 810	3 613
Mascot (CDP)	2 203	...
Lake County[48]	7 455	'8 074
Ridgely division	3 119	3 409
Ridgely town[48]	1 932	1 657
Tiptonville division	4 336	'4 665
Tiptonville town[48]	2 438	'2 407
Lauderdale County[49]	24 555	20 271
Ashport–Three Point division	2 413	...
Gates division	2 685	...
Gates town	729	523
Halls town (pt.)[49]	13	...
Halls division	4 090	...
Halls town (pt.)[49]	2 431	2 323
Henning division	2 438	2 442
Henning town	638	605
Ripley division	12 929	...
Ripley town[49]	6 366	4 794
Lawrence County[50]	34 110	29 097
Deerfield division	1 909	1 786
Ethridge division	3 965	3 290
Ethridge town[50]	548	...
Five Points division	1 692	1 592
Iron City–St. Joseph division	2 640	2 570
Iron City city	482	504
St. Joseph city (pt.)[50]	796	637
Lawrenceburg division	15 423	12 651
Lawrenceburg city[50]	10 184	8 889
Leoma division	2 912	2 366
Loretto division	3 176	2 759
Loretto city[50]	1 612	1 375
St. Joseph city (pt.)[50]	101	...
Summertown division	2 393	2 083
Lewis County[51]	9 700	6 761
East Lewis division	3 645	...
Hohenwald division	6 055	...
Hohenwald city[51]	3 922	3 385
Lincoln County[52]	26 483	24 318
Belleview division	5 302	4 481
Boonshill division	1 403	1 406
Cash Point–Blanche division	2 253	2 054
Fayetteville division	10 380	9 797
Fayetteville city[52]	7 559	'7 691
Flintville division	3 634	3 198
Mulberry division	1 529	1 414
Petersburg division	1 982	1 968
Petersburg town (pt.)[52]	441	341

County Subdivisions	1980	1970
Loudon County[53]	28 553	24 266
Greenback	3 159	2 699
Greenback city[53]	546	318
Lenoir City division	15 906	13 104
Lenoir City city[53]	5 446	5 324
Loudon town (pt.)	14	...
Loudon division	7 234	6 558
Loudon town (pt.)[53]	3 929	3 728
Philadelphia division	2 254	1 905
Philadelphia city[53]	507	554
McMinn County[54]	41 878	35 462
Athens	23 308	...
Athens city[54]	12 080	11 790
Niota city[54]	765	629
Calhoun–Riceville division	4 625	3 429
Calhoun town[54]	590	624
Englewood division	3 655	...
Englewood town	1 840	1 878
Etowah division	10 290	8 716
Etowah city	3 758	3 736
McNairy County[55]	22 525	18 369
Adamsville division	3 379	...
Adamsville town[55]	1 453	1 344
Enville town (pt.)	53	4
Milledgeville town (pt.)	186	205
Bethel Springs division	2 573	...
Bethel Springs town[55]	873	781
East View–Ramer division	3 144	...
Eastview town[55]	552	423
Ramer city[55]	429	347
Finger division	1 789	1 459
Finger town[55]	245	...
Michie division	2 690	1 923
Michie town	530	377
Selmer division	7 237	...
Selmer town[55]	3 979	3 495
Stantonville division	1 713	...
Stantonville town	271	296
Macon County[56]	15 700	12 315
Lafayette division	9 287	7 009
Lafayette city[56]	3 808	2 583
Red Boiling Springs division	4 131	3 470
Red Boiling Springs city[56]	1 173	726
Siloam division	2 282	1 836
Madison County[57]	74 546	'65 774
Huntsville division	2 361	...
Denmark town	51	61
Jackson division	56 643	...
Jackson city (pt.)[57]	49 105	39 996
Medon division	3 091	...
Medon town[57]	162	136
Pinson division	3 864	2 839
Jackson city (pt.)	26	...
Pope division	2 973	...
Adair town[57]	70	'51
Spring Creek–Beech Bluff division	5 614	...
Marion County[58]	24 416	20 577
Jasper division	7 254	5 413
Jasper town[58]	2 633	'2 009
Kimball town (pt.)[58]	63	...
Monteagle–South Pittsburg division	7 711	...
Kimball town (pt.)[58]	1 157	807
Monteagle town (pt.)[58]	446	420
New Hope city[58]	681	...
Orme town	181	122
Richard City town	87	132
South Pittsburg city[58]	3 636	3 613
Whiteside division	1 499	...
Whitwell division	7 952	6 625
Powells Crossroads town[58]	918	...
Whitwell city[58]	1 783	1 669
Marshall County[59]	19 698	17 319
Chapel Hill division	2 578	2 055
Chapel Hill town[59]	861	752
Elk Ridge South division	3 207	3 036
Cornersville town	722	655
Petersburg town (pt.)[59]	240	122
Lewisburg division	10 762	9 720
Lewisburg city[59]	8 760	7 207
Rock Creek division	3 151	2 508
Maury County[60]	51 095	'44 028
Columbia division	29 311	...
Columbia city[60]	26 372	21 471
Culleoka division	1 757	1 270
Fountain Heights division	922	...
Lower Rutherford Creek division	2 534	...
Poplar Top division	2 374	'2 027
Santa Fe division	2 675	2 115
Spring Hill division	3 437	2 533
Spring Hill town (pt.)[60]	986	685
Upper Big Bigby division	8 085	7 084
Mount Pleasant town[60]	3 375	3 530
Meigs County[61]	7 431	5 219
Big Spring–East View division	2 110	1 429
Decatur division	2 878	2 221
Decatur town[61]	1 069	698
Ten Mile division	2 443	1 569
Monroe County[62]	28 700	23 475
Madisonville division	10 255	7 938
Madisonville town[62]	2 884	2 614
Sweetwater division	8 810	7 534
Sweetwater city[62]	4 725	4 340
Tellico Plains division	6 228	5 112
Tellico Plains town	698	773
Vonore division	3 407	2 891
Vonore town[62]	528	524
Montgomery County[63]	83 342	62 721
Clarksville division	53 399	...
Clarksville city (pt.)[63]	46 852	31 719
Cumberland Heights division	4 317	...
Fort Campbell division	8 340	10 069
Clarksville city (pt.)[63]	7 925	...
Lone Oak division	3 044	...
Palmyra–Shiloh division	2 084	1 692
St. Bethlehem division	8 797	4 882
Clarksville city (pt.)[63]	–	...
Woodlawn–Dotsonville division	3 361	...
Moore County[64]	4 510	3 568
Bakerstown division	2 427	...
Lynchburg division	2 083	...
Lynchburg town	668	'538
Morgan County	16 604	13 619
Coalfield division	4 343	4 114
Oliver Springs town (pt.)	59	34
Petros (CDP)	1 286	...
Lancing division	2 700	2 515
Oakdale division	3 945	2 731
Oakdale town	323	376
Sunbright division	2 904	2 462
Wartburg division	2 712	1 797
Wartburg town	761	541
Obion County[65]	32 781	'30 247
Dixie division	2 257	1 643
Elbridge–Cloverdale division	969	992
Hornbeak–Samburg division	2 856	2 539
Hornbeak town	452	418
Samburg town	465	463
Kenton–Mason Hall division	1 747	1 781
Kenton town (pt.)	782	694
Trimble town (pt.)	3	6
Obion–Troy division	4 360	3 652
Obion town	1 282	1 010
Troy town[65]	1 093	826
South Fulton division	4 845	4 061
South Fulton city[65]	2 735	3 122
Union City division	15 747	...
Rives town	386	385
Union City city[65]	10 436	11 925
Woodland Mills city[65]	526	'396
Overton County[66]	17 575	14 866
Allons division	1 627	1 396
Alpine division	1 663	1 533
Crawford division	2 090	1 835
Hilham division	1 781	1 421
Livingston division	7 083	6 243
Livingston town[66]	3 372	3 050
Rickman division	3 331	2 438
Perry County[67]	6 111	5 238
Linden division	3 919	3 533
Linden town[67]	1 087	1 062
Lobelville division	2 192	1 705
Lobelville city[67]	993	773
Pickett County[68]	4 358	3 774
Byrdstown division	2 732	2 272
Byrdstown town[68]	884	582
Midway division	594	523
Static division	1 032	979
Polk County[69]	13 602	11 669
Benton division	5 870	4 757
Benton town[69]	1 115	749
Ducktown division	3 444	3 504
Copperhill town[69]	418	563
Ducktown city[69]	583	562
Parksville division	2 584	1 837
Turtletown division	1 704	1 571
Putnam County[70]	47 690	35 487
Baxter division	4 699	...
Baxter town[70]	1 411	1 229
Buffalo Valley division	2 957	...
Cookeville division	34 781	...
Algood city[70]	2 406	1 808
Cookeville city[70]	20 535	'14 403
Monterey division	5 253	4 325
Monterey town	2 610	2 351

Population of County Subdivisions

County Subdivisions	1980	1970
Rhea County[71]	24 235	17 202
Dayton division	16 199	11 643
Dayton city[71]	5 913	4 361
Graysville town[71]	1 380	951
Spring City division[71]	8 036	5 559
Spring City town[71]	1 951	1 756
Roane County[72]	48 425	38 881
Barnard division	4 251	2 997
Harriman division	16 063	14 122
Harriman city	8 303	8 734
Kingston division	10 115	7 802
Kingston city[72]	4 441	4 142
Oak Ridge city (pt.)[72]	–	...
Oak Ridge division	7 973	5 401
Oak Ridge city (pt.)[72]	2 362	1 490
Oliver Springs town (pt.)[72]	1 075	1 163
Rockwood division	10 023	8 559
Rockwood city[72]	5 767	5 259
Robertson County[73]	37 021	29 102
Adams division	2 357	2 115
Adams town	600	458
Cedar Hill town	420	355
Barren Plains division	1 802	...
Coopertown division	2 716	...
Cross Plains division[73]	4 465	2 839
Cross Plains city[73]	655	...
White House city (pt.)[73]	1 134	...
Orlinda division	2 504	1 896
Orlinda town[73]	382	347
Springfield–Greenbrier division	23 177	...
Greenbrier town[73]	3 180	2 279
Ridgetop town[73]	1 195	810
Springfield city[73]	10 814	9 720
Rutherford County[74]	84 058	59 428
Almaville division	3 795	2 005
La Vergne city (pt.)[74]	221	...
Smyrna town (pt.)[74]	–	...
Christiana division	3 458	...
Eagleville division	2 701	2 363
Eagleville town[74]	444	437
Kittrell division	3 343	...
Lascassas division	3 727	...
Murfreesboro division	45 749	...
Murfreesboro city[74]	32 845	26 360
Smyrna division	21 285	...
La Vergne city (pt.)[74]	5 274	...
Smyrna town (pt.)[74]	8 839	5 698
Scott County[75]	19 259	14 762
Huntsville division	4 987	3 348
Huntsville town	519	337
Norma division	2 297	1 809
Oneida division	6 118	4 676
Oneida town[75]	3 275	2 602
Robbins division	2 627	2 363
Winfield division	3 230	2 566
Sequatchie County[76]	8 605	6 331
Center Point division	2 214	1 660
Dunlap division	6 391	4 671
Dunlap city[76]	3 681	1 672
Sevier County[77]	41 418	28 241
Beech Springs division	3 332	2 287
Chilhowee division	7 187	3 316
Dunn Creek division	3 352	2 444
Pittman Center town[77]	488	...
Gatlinburg division	4 455	3 646
Gatlinburg city[77]	3 210	2 329
Knob Creek division	3 477	...
Sevierville division	15 669	...
Pigeon Forge city (pt.)[77]	1 712	1 361
Sevierville city[77]	4 556	2 661
Wear Valley division	3 946	...
Pigeon Forge city (pt.)[77]	110	...
Shelby County[78]	777 113	'722 111
Arlington division	6 914	5 730
Arlington town[78]	1 778	1 349
Lakeland city[78]	612	...
Collierville division	9 715	'5 605
Collierville town[78]	7 839	'3 651
Memphis city (pt.)[78]	–	...
Fisherville division	2 310	2 517
Memphis division	722 123	...
Bartlett town[78]	17 170	1 150
Germantown city[78]	20 459	3 474
Memphis city (pt.)[78]	646 356	'623 988
Millington division	27 525	'28 170
Millington city[78]	20 236	'21 177
Rosemark division	1 679	1 838
Shelby Forest division	6 847	...
Smith County[79]	14 935	12 509
Carthage division	6 365	5 502
Carthage town	2 672	2 491
Forks of the River division	1 945	1 681
South Carthage division	6 625	5 326
Gordonsville town	893	601

County Subdivisions	1980	1970
Smith County—Con.		
South Carthage division—Con.		
South Carthage town[79]	1 004	859
Stewart County[80]	8 665	7 319
Cumberland City–Carlisle division	1 555	1 695
Cumberland City town	276	416
Tennessee Ridge city (pt.)[80]	–	...
Dover division	2 899	2 223
Dover town[80]	1 197	1 179
Indian Mound–Bumpus Mills division	4 210	3 387
Model division	1	14
Sullivan County[81]	143 968	127 329
Blountville division	12 415	...
Blountville (CDP)	2 554	...
Bluff City–Piney Flats division	15 479	...
Bluff City town	1 121	'985
Bristol division	31 047	...
Bristol city (pt.)[81]	23 983	20 064
Walnut Hill (CDP)	3 288	...
Holston Valley division	2 847	...
Bristol city (pt.)[81]	3	...
Kingsport division	82 180	...
Bloomingdale (CDP)	12 088	3 120
Bridwell Heights (CDP)	2 715	...
Colonial Heights (CDP)	6 744	3 027
Fordtown (CDP)	2 153	...
Indian Springs (CDP)	2 210	...
Kingsport city (pt.)[81]	30 687	31 708
Lynn Garden (CDP)	7 213	13 118
Morrison City (CDP)	2 032	2 178
Orebank (CDP)	1 284	1 111
Spurgeon (CDP) (pt.)	1 429	...
Sullivan Gardens (CDP)	2 513	...
Sumner County[82]	85 790	'56 266
Bethpage division	2 446	...
Gallatin city (pt.)[82]	280	...
Castalian Springs division	2 661	...
Gallatin division	20 447	...
Gallatin city (pt.)[82]	16 864	'13 253
Hendersonville division	38 513	20 979
Gallatin city (pt.)[82]	47	...
Goodlettsville city (pt.)[82]	1 942	...
Hendersonville city[82]	26 561	'412
Portland division	10 290	7 895
Mitchellville town	209	177
Portland town[82]	4 030	2 872
Westmoreland division	5 764	4 515
Westmoreland town[82]	1 754	1 423
White House division	5 669	3 528
White House city (pt.)[82]	1 091	...
Tipton County[83]	32 930	28 001
Brighton division	4 457	...
Atoka town (pt.)[83]	11	...
Brighton town[83]	976	952
Covington division	10 163	...
Covington city[83]	6 065	5 801
Drummonds division	3 033	2 019
Garland division	2 252	2 098
Burlison town	386	397
Garland town	301	292
Gilt Edge town (pt.)	–	...
Mason division	2 049	2 216
Mason town[83]	471	443
Munford–Atoka division	9 022	...
Atoka town (pt.)[83]	680	446
Gilt Edge town (pt.)	142	406
Munford town[83]	2 336	1 281
Tabernacle division	1 954	...
Trousdale County[84]	6 137	5 155
Hartsville division	6 137	5 155
Hartsville town[84]	2 674	2 243
Unicoi County[85]	16 362	15 254
Erwin division	10 146	...
Banner Hill (CDP)	2 913	2 517
Erwin city[85]	4 739	4 715
Flag Pond division	2 835	2 798
Unicoi division	3 381	...
Union County[86]	11 707	9 072
Luttrell division	4 454	3 508
Luttrell town	962	819
Maynardville division	5 934	4 392
Maynardville city	924	702
Sharps Chapel division	1 319	1 172
Van Buren County[87]	4 728	3 758
Mooneyham division	985	...
Spencer division	2 728	...
Spencer town[87]	1 126	1 179
Welchland division	1 015	...
Warren County[88]	32 653	26 972
Campaign division	2 942	1 761
Centertown division	2 188	1 575
Centertown town	300	181
Dibrell division	5 387	3 614
Irving College division	1 527	1 269
McMinnville division	16 813	15 743

County Subdivisions

	1980	1970
Warren County—Con.		
McMinnville division—Con.		
McMinnville city[88]	10 683	10 662
Morrison division	3 796	3 010
Morrison town	587	379
Viola town	149	193
Washington County[89]	88 755	73 924
Bethesda division	4 972	3 717
Johnson City division	63 372	...
Boones Creek (CDP)	1 993	...
Cherokee (CDP)	2 076	...
Gray (CDP)	1 049	...
Johnson City city (pt.)[89]	39 459	33 770
Midway (CDP)	2 754	...
Oak Grove (CDP)	3 103	...
Spurgeon (CDP) (pt.)	1 577	...
West Johnson City (CDP) (pt.)	2 178	...
Jonesboro division	6 763	4 822
Jonesboro town[89]	2 829	1 510
West Johnson City (CDP) (pt.)	4	...
Sulphur Springs division	7 112	...
Fall Branch (CDP) (pt.)	1 095	...
Telford division	6 536	5 223
Wayne County[90]	13 946	12 365
Clifton–Natural Bridge division	2 590	2 439
Clifton town[90]	773	737
Collinwood division	3 525	2 963
Collinwood city[90]	1 064	922
Lutts–Cypress Inn division	2 776	2 551
Waynesboro division	5 055	4 412
Waynesboro city[90]	2 109	1 983
Weakley County[91]	32 896	28 827
Chestnut Glade–Dukedom division	1 240	1 295
Dresden division	5 891	4 666
Dresden town[91]	2 256	1 939
Gleason division	4 052	3 911
Gleason town	1 335	1 314
McKenzie city (pt.)	232	261
Greenfield division	3 832	3 934
Greenfield town[91]	2 109	2 050
Martin division	13 777	11 246
Martin city[91]	8 898	7 781
Palmersville division	1 570	1 344
Sharon division	2 534	2 431
Sharon town[91]	1 134	1 188
White County[92]	19 567	'16 329
Bon De Croft division	2 878	2 155
Doyle division	2 705	'2 343
Doyle town	344	'446
Macedonia division	3 347	2 592
Shady Grove division	2 801	2 045
Sparta division	7 836	7 194
Sparta city[92]	4 864	4 930
Williamson County[93]	58 108	'34 423
Bethesda division	3 704	...
Boston division	3 497	...
Spring Hill town (pt.)[93]	3	–
Brentwood division	18 026	...
Berrys Chapel (CDP) (pt.)	1 098	10
Brentwood city (pt.)[93]	9 425	'4 099
Fairview division	7 343	...
Fairview city	3 648	1 630
Franklin division	20 779	...
Berrys Chapel (CDP) (pt.)	1 605	1 335
Franklin city[93]	12 407	'9 497
Nolensville division	4 759	...
Brentwood city (pt.)[93]	6	...
Wilson County[94]	56 064	36 999
Cedars division	6 662	3 192
Lebanon division	18 748	17 287
Lebanon city[94]	11 872	12 492
Martha–Laguardo division	5 764	3 215
Mount Juliet division	15 024	6 287
Mount Juliet city[94]	2 879	...
Northeast Wilson division	5 642	3 298
Watertown division	4 224	3 720
Watertown city[94]	1 300	1 061

TEXAS

Texas was named from the Tejas Indians, who once occupied part of the region now constituting this state. The meaning of the name is uncertain but it probably signifies "friends."

The first explorations of the area now constituting Texas were made by the Spaniards, Cabeza de Vaca, who wandered about in the southern part, 1528-1536, and Coronado, who crossed the northern part, 1540-1542. Other Spaniards visited the Texas country during the next hundred years, but the first attempt at settlement was made in 1685 by the French under La Salle. This attempt, though unsuccessful, incited the Spaniards to make settlements, the most important of which was begun at San Antonio in 1718. In 1728 the territory with vaguely defined limits was formed into a province of Spain.

The boundary between the Spanish possessions and the United States was in dispute during the early years of the nineteenth century, but in 1819, at the time of the Florida Purchase, the eastern and northern limits of the Spanish possessions were agreed upon and defined.

In 1821 Mexico, by revolution, became an independent nation, and three years later Texas and Coahuila were united into a single Mexican state.

Many settlers came to Texas from the United States, and their discontent with Mexican rule resulted in a successful revolution in 1835-36. In March of the latter year a constitution was adopted for the republic of Texas, which continued an independent existence until 1845, when it was annexed to the United States. Mexico's refusal to recognize the independence of Texas, together with a boundary dispute, led to war with the United States, which began early in 1846 and war brought to a close in 1848, when Mexico formally relinquished its claims to Texas, and to all lands north of the present southern boundary of California, the river Gila, and a line a little north of the thirty-second parallel.

From 1836 to 1850 Texas claimed as its southwestern and western boundaries the Rio Grande and a line drawn north from the source of that river to latitude 42°, the eastern and northern boundaries were formed by the limits of the Louisiana Purchase as defined in the Florida Purchase treaty of 1819. Texas thus included during this period, in addition to its present area, territory now constituting parts of New Mexico, Oklahoma, Kansas, Colorado, and a small part of southern Wyoming. In 1850 the state sold to the Federal Government for $10,000,000 that part lying outside its present limits.

COUNTY LOCATION INDEX

Anderson	C-6	Chambers	D-7	El Paso	C-2
Andrews	C-3	Cherokee	C-7	Erath	C-5
Angelina	C-7	Childress	B-4	Falls	C-6
Aransas	E-6	Clay	B-5	Fannin	B-6
Archer	B-5	Cochran	B-3	Fayette	D-6
Armstrong	A-4	Coke	C-4	Fisher	C-4
Atascosa	E-5	Coleman	C-5	Floyd	B-4
Austin	D-6	Collin	B-6	Foard	B-5
Bailey	B-3	Collingsworth	A-4	Fort Bend	D-6
Bandera	D-5	Colorado	D-6	Franklin	B-7
Bastrop	D-6	Comal	D-5	Freestone	C-6
Baylor	B-5	Comanche	C-5	Frio	E-5
Bee	E-6	Concho	C-4	Gaines	C-3
Bell	C-6	Cooke	B-6	Galveston	D-7
Bexar	D-5	Coryell	C-5	Garza	B-4
Blanco	D-5	Cottle	B-4	Gillespie	D-5
Borden	C-4	Crane	C-3	Glasscock	C-4
Bosque	C-5	Crockett	D-4	Goliad	E-6
Bowie	B-7	Crosby	B-4	Gonzales	D-6
Brazoria	D-7	Culberson	C-2	Gray	A-4
Brazos	D-6	Dallam	A-3	Grayson	B-6
Brewster	D-3	Dallas	C-6	Gregg	C-7
Briscoe	B-4	Dawson	C-4	Grimes	D-6
Brooks	F-5	Deaf Smith	A-3	Guadalupe	D-5
Brown	C-5	Delta	B-6	Hale	B-4
Burleson	D-6	Denton	B-6	Hall	B-4
Burnet	D-5	De Witt	D-6	Hamilton	C-5
Caldwell	D-6	Dickens	B-4	Hansford	A-4
Calhoun	E-6	Dimmit	E-5	Hardeman	B-5
Callahan	C-5	Donley	A-4	Hardin	D-7
Cameron	F-6	DuVal	E-5	Harris	D-7
Camp	B-7	Eastland	C-5	Harrison	C-7
Carson	A-4	Ector	C-3	Hartley	A-3
Cass	B-7	Edwards	D-4	Haskell	B-5
Castro	B-3	Ellis	C-6	Hays	D-5

Hamphill	A-4	Lampasas	C-5	Newton	C-7
Henderson	C-6	La Salle	E-5	Nolan	C-4
Hidalgo	F-5	Lavaca	D-6	Nueces	E-6
Hill	C-6	Lee	D-6	Ochiltree	A-4
Hockley	B-3	Leon	C-6	Oldham	A-3
Hood	C-5	Liberty	D-7	Orange	D-7
Hopkins	B-6	Limestone	C-6	Palo Pinto	C-5
Houston	C-7	Lipscomb	A-4	Panola	C-7
Howard	C-4	Live Oak	E-5	Parker	C-5
Hudspeth	C-2	Llano	D-5	Parmer	B-3
Hunt	B-6	Loving	C-3	Pecos	D-3
Hutchinson	A-4	Lubbock	B-4	Polk	D-7
Irion	C-4	Lynn	B-4	Potter	A-4
Jack	B-5	McCulloch	C-5	Presidio	D-2
Jackson	E-6	McLennan	C-6	Rains	B-6
Jasper	C-7	McMullen	E-5	Randall	A-4
Jeff Davis	D-3	Madison	C-6	Reagan	C-4
Jefferson	D-7	Marion	B-7	Real	D-5
Jim Hogg	F-5	Martin	C-4	Red River	B-7
Jim Wells	E-5	Mason	D-5	Reeves	C-3
Johnson	C-6	Matagorda	E-6	Refugio	E-6
Jones	C-4	Maverick	E-4	Roberts	A-4
Karnes	E-5	Medina	D-5	Robertson	C-6
Kaufman	C-6	Menard	D-5	Rockwall	B-6
Kendall	D-5	Midland	C-4	Runnels	C-4
Kenedy	F-6	Milam	D-6	Rusk	C-7
Kent	B-4	Mills	C-5	Sabine	C-7
Kerr	D-5	Mitchell	C-4	San Augustine	C-7
Kimble	D-5	Montague	B-5	San Jacinto	D-7
King	B-4	Montgomery	D-6	San Patricio	E-6
Kinney	D-4	Moore	A-4	San Saba	C-5
Kleberg	E-6	Morris	B-7	Schleicher	D-4
Knox	B-5	Motley	B-4	Scurry	C-4
Lamar	B-6	Nacogdoches	C-7	Shackelford	C-5
Lamb	B-3	Navarro	C-6	Shelby	C-7

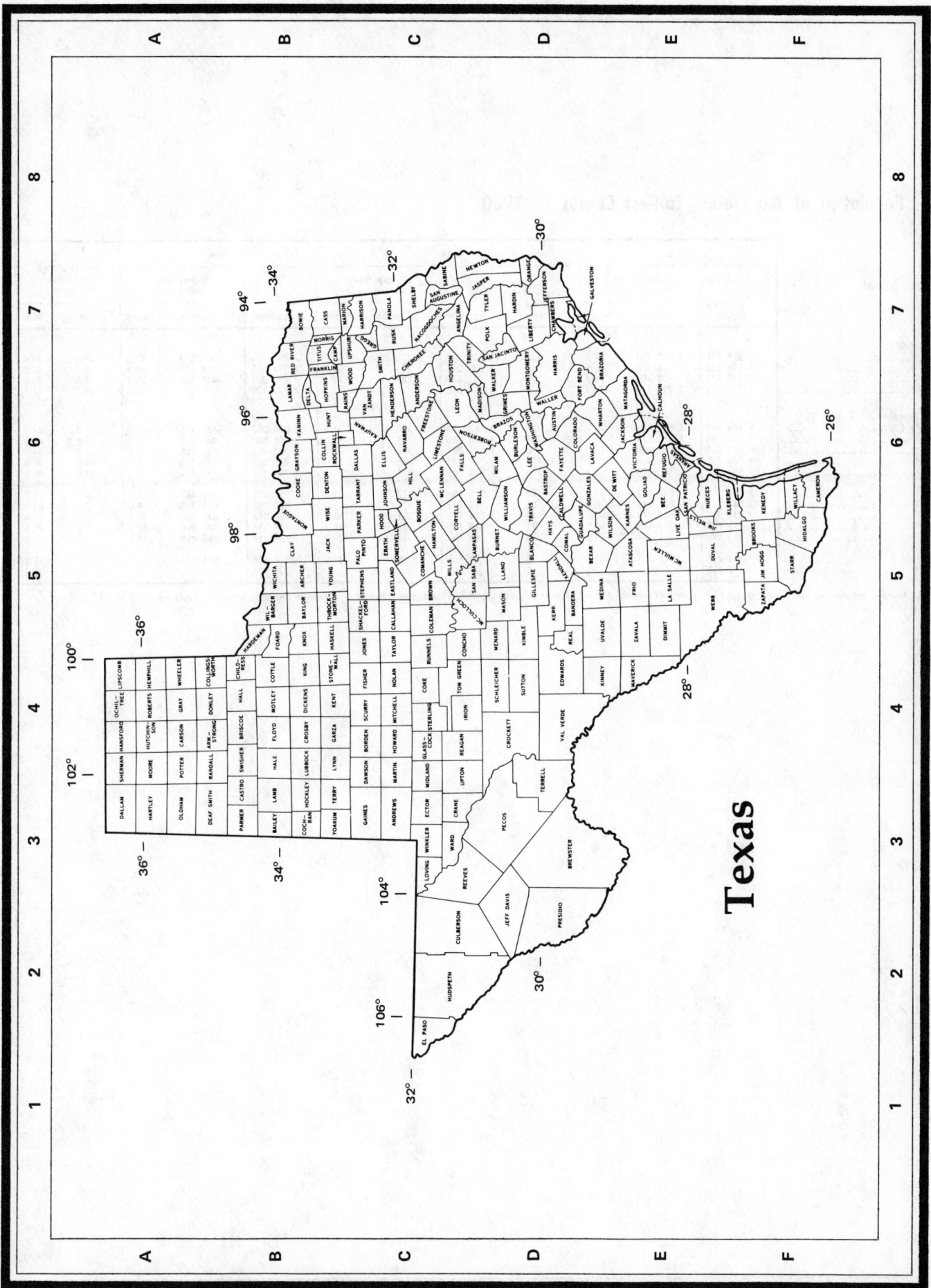

Texas

Population of the State: Earliest Census to 1980

Urban and Rural

	The State			Urban					Rural				Percent of total population	
	Total population	Change from preceding census		Places of 2,500 or more	Population	Change from preceding census		Population	Change from preceding census		Urban	Rural
		Number	Percent			Number	Percent		Number	Percent		
Current urban definition:														
1980 (Apr. 1)	14 229 191	3 030 536	27.1	434	11 333 017	2 410 806	27.0	2 896 174	621 655	27.3	79.6	20.4
1970 (Apr. 1)	'11 198 655	1 618 978	16.9	373	8 922 211	1 734 741	24.1	2 274 519	−117 688	−4.9	79.7	20.3
1960 (Apr. 1)	9 579 677	1 868 483	24.2	320	7 187 470	2 349 410	48.6	2 392 207	−480 927	−16.7	75.0	25.0
1950 (Apr. 1)	7 711 194	1 296 370	20.2	272	4 838 060	...	...	2 873 134	...	...	62.7	37.3
Previous urban definition:														
1960 (Apr. 1)	9 579 677	1 868 483	24.2	306	6 963 114	2 350 448	51.0	2 616 563	−481 965	−15.6	72.7	27.3
1950 (Apr. 1)	7 711 194	1 296 370	20.2	258	4 612 666	1 701 277	58.4	3 098 528	−404 907	−11.6	59.8	40.2
1940 (Apr. 1)	6 414 824	590 109	10.1	196	2 911 389	522 041	21.8	3 503 435	68 068	2.0	45.4	54.6
1930 (Apr. 1)	5 824 715	1 161 487	24.9	159	2 389 348	876 659	58.0	3 435 367	284 828	9.0	41.0	59.0
1920 (Jan. 1)	4 663 228	766 686	19.7	119	1 512 689	574 585	61.2	3 150 539	192 101	6.5	32.4	67.6
1910 (Apr. 15)	3 896 542	847 832	27.8	91	938 104	417 345	80.1	2 958 438	430 487	17.0	24.1	75.9
1900 (June 1)	3 048 710	813 183	36.4	56	520 759	171 248	49.0	2 527 951	641 935	34.0	17.1	82.9
1890 (June 1)	2 235 527	643 778	40.4	42	349 511	202 716	138.1	1 886 016	441 062	30.5	15.6	84.4
1880 (June 1)	1 591 749	773 170	94.5	21	146 795	92 274	169.2	1 444 954	680 896	89.1	9.2	90.8
1870 (June 1)	818 579	214 364	35.5	8	54 521	27 906	104.9	764 058	186 458	32.3	6.7	93.3
1860 (June 1)	604 215	391 623	184.2	5	26 615	18 950	247.2	577 600	372 673	181.9	4.4	95.6
1850 (June 1)	212 592	...	...	2	7 665	...	...	204 927	...	...	3.6	96.4

NOTE: Boundary between Mexico and Texas revised by the Chamizal Convention of 1963. Part of Oklahoma acquired by Texas upon settlement of a boundary dispute (U.S. Supreme Court decision of March 17, 1930).

ANDERSON

1850	2,884
1860	10,398
1870	9,229
1880	17,395
1890	20,923
1900	28,015
1910	29,650
1920	34,318
1930	34,643
1940	37,092
1950	31,875
1960	28,162
1970	27,789
1980	38,381

ANDREWS

1890	24
1900	87
1910	975
1920	350
1930	736
1940	1,277
1950	5,002
1960	13,450
1970	10,372
1980	13,323

ANGELINA

1850	1,165
1860	4,271
1870	3,985
1880	5,239
1890	6,306
1900	13,481
1910	17,705
1920	22,287
1930	27,803
1940	32,201
1950	36,032
1960	39,814
1970	49,349
1980	64,172

ARANSAS

1880	996
1890	1,824
1900	1,716
1910	2,106
1920	2,064
1930	2,219
1940	3,469
1950	4,252
1960	7,006
1970	8,902
1980	14,260

ARCHER

1880	596
1890	2,101
1900	2,508
1910	6,525
1920	5,254
1930	9,684
1940	7,599
1950	6,816
1960	6,110
1970	5,759
1980	7,266

ARMSTRONG

1880	31
1890	944
1900	1,205
1910	2,682
1920	2,816
1930	3,329
1940	2,495
1950	2,215
1960	1,966
1970	1,895
1980	1,994

ATASCOSA

1860	1,578
1870	2,915
1880	4,217
1890	6,459
1900	7,143
1910	10,004
1920	12,702
1930	15,654
1940	19,275
1950	20,048
1960	18,828
1970	18,696
1980	25,055

AUSTIN

1850	3,841
1860	10,139
1870	15,087
1880	14,429
1890	17,859
1900	20,676
1910	17,699
1920	18,874
1930	18,860
1940	17,384
1950	14,663
1960	13,777
1970	13,831
1980	17,726

BAILEY

1900	4
1910	312
1920	517
1930	5,186
1940	6,318
1950	7,592
1960	9,090
1970	8,487
1980	8,168

BANDERA

1860	399
1870	649
1880	2,158
1890	3,795
1900	5,332
1910	4,921
1920	4,001
1930	3,784
1940	4,234
1950	4,410
1960	3,892
1970	4,747
1980	7,084

BASTROP

1850	3,099
1860	7,006
1870	12,290
1880	17,215
1890	20,736
1900	26,845
1910	25,344
1920	26,469
1930	23,888
1940	21,610
1950	19,622
1960	16,295
1970	17,297
1980	24,726

BAYLOR

1880	715
1890	2,595
1900	3,052
1910	8,411
1920	7,027
1930	7,418
1940	7,755
1950	6,875
1960	5,893
1970	5,221
1980	4,919

BEE

1860	910
1870	1,082
1880	2,298
1890	3,720
1900	7,720
1910	12,090
1920	12,137
1930	15,721
1940	16,481
1950	18,174
1960	23,755
1970	22,737
1980	26,030

BELL

1860	4,799
1870	9,771
1880	20,518
1890	33,377
1900	45,535
1910	49,186
1920	46,412
1930	50,030
1940	44,863
1950	73,824
1960	94,097
1970	124,483
1980	157,889

BEXAR

1850	6,052
1860	14,454
1870	16,043
1880	30,470
1890	49,266
1900	69,422
1910	119,676
1920	202,096
1930	292,553
1940	338,176
1950	500,460
1960	687,151
1970	830,460
1980	988,800

BLANCO

1860	1,281
1870	1,187
1880	3,583
1890	4,649
1900	4,703
1910	4,311
1920	4,063
1930	3,842
1940	4,264
1950	3,780
1960	3,657
1970	3,567
1980	4,681

BORDEN

1880	35
1890	222
1900	776
1910	1,386
1920	965
1930	1,505
1940	1,396
1950	1,106
1960	1,076
1970	888
1980	859

BOSQUE

1860	2,005
1870	4,981
1880	11,217
1890	14,224
1900	17,390
1910	19,103
1920	18,032
1930	15,750
1940	15,761
1950	11,836
1960	10,809
1970	10,966
1980	13,401

BOWIE

1850	2,912
1860	5,052
1870	4,684
1880	10,965
1890	20,267
1900	26,676
1910	34,827
1920	39,472
1930	48,563
1940	50,208
1950	61,966
1960	59,971
1970	68,909
1980	75,301

BRAZORIA

1850	4,841
1860	7,143
1870	7,527
1880	9,774
1890	11,506
1900	14,861
1910	13,299
1920	20,614
1930	23,054
1940	27,069
1950	46,549
1960	76,204
1970	108,312
1980	169,587

BRAZOS

1850	614
1860	2,776
1870	9,205
1880	13,576
1890	16,650
1900	18,859
1910	18,919
1920	21,975
1930	21,835
1940	26,977
1950	38,390
1960	44,895
1970	57,978
1980	93,588

BREWSTER

1890	710
1900	2,356
1910	5,220
1920	4,822
1930	6,624
1940	6,478
1950	7,309
1960	6,434
1970	7,780
1980	7,573

BRISCOE

1880	12
1900	1,253
1910	2,162
1920	2,948
1930	5,590
1940	4,056
1950	3,528
1960	3,577
1970	2,794
1980	2,579

BROOKS

1920	4,560
1930	5,901
1940	6,362
1950	9,195
1960	8,609
1970	8,005
1980	8,428

BROWN

1860	244
1870	544
1880	8,414
1890	11,421
1900	16,019
1910	22,935
1920	21,682
1930	26,382
1940	25,924
1950	28,607
1960	24,728
1970	25,877
1980	33,057

BUCHEL

1890	298

BURLESON

1850	1,713
1860	5,683
1870	8,072
1880	9,243
1890	13,001
1900	18,367
1910	18,687
1920	16,885
1930	19,848
1940	18,334
1950	13,000
1960	11,177
1970	9,999
1980	12,313

BURNET

1860	2,487
1870	3,688
1880	6,855
1890	10,747
1900	10,528
1910	10,755
1920	9,499
1930	10,355
1940	10,771
1950	10,356
1960	9,265
1970	11,420
1980	17,803

CALDWELL

1850	1,329
1860	4,481
1870	6,572
1880	11,757
1890	15,769
1900	21,765
1910	24,237
1920	25,160
1930	31,397
1940	24,893
1950	19,350
1960	17,222
1970	21,178
1980	23,637

CALHOUN

1850	1,110
1860	2,642
1870	3,443
1880	1,739
1890	815
1900	2,395
1910	3,635
1920	4,700
1930	5,385
1940	5,911
1950	9,222
1960	16,592
1970	17,831
1980	19,574

CALLAHAN

1880	3,453
1890	5,457
1900	8,768

1910	12,973
1920	11,844
1930	12,785
1940	11,568
1950	9,087
1960	7,929
1970	8,205
1980	10,992

CAMERON

1850	8,541
1860	6,028
1870	10,999
1880	14,959
1890	14,424
1900	16,095
1910	27,158
1920	36,662
1930	77,540
1940	83,202
1950	125,170
1960	151,098
1970	140,368
1980	209,727

CAMP

1880	5,931
1890	6,624
1900	9,146
1910	9,551
1920	11,103
1930	10,063
1940	10,285
1950	8,740
1960	7,849
1970	8,005
1980	7,275

CARSON

1890	356
1900	469
1910	2,127
1920	3,078
1930	7,745
1940	6,624
1950	6,852
1960	7,781
1970	6,358
1980	6,672

CASS

1850	4,991
1860	8,411
1870	8,875
1880	16,724
1890	22,554
1900	22,841
1910	27,587
1920	30,041
1930	30,030
1940	33,496
1950	26,732
1960	23,496
1970	24,133
1980	29,430

CASTRO

1890	9
1900	400
1910	1,850
1920	1,948

1930	4,720
1940	4,631
1950	5,417
1960	8,823
1970	10,394
1980	10,556

CHAMBERS

1860	1,508
1870	1,503
1880	2,187
1890	2,241
1900	3,046
1910	4,234
1920	4,162
1930	5,710
1940	7,511
1950	7,871
1960	10,379
1970	12,187
1980	18,538

CHEROKEE

1850	6,673
1860	12,098
1870	11,079
1880	16,723
1890	22,975
1900	25,154
1910	29,038
1920	37,633
1930	43,180
1940	43,970
1950	38,694
1960	33,120
1970	32,008
1980	38,127

CHILDRESS

1880	25
1890	1,175
1900	2,138
1910	9,538
1920	10,933
1930	16,044
1940	12,149
1950	12,123
1960	8,421
1970	6,605
1980	6,950

CLAY

1860	109
1880	5,045
1890	7,503
1900	9,231
1910	17,043
1920	16,864
1930	14,545
1940	12,524
1950	9,896
1960	8,351
1970	8,079
1980	9,582

COCHRAN

1900	25
1910	65
1920	67
1930	1,963
1940	3,735

1950	5,928
1960	6,417
1970	5,326
1980	4,825

COKE

1890	2,059
1900	3,430
1910	6,412
1920	4,557
1930	5,253
1940	4,590
1950	4,045
1960	3,589
1970	3,087
1980	3,196

COLEMAN

1870	347
1880	3,603
1890	6,112
1900	10,077
1910	22,618
1920	18,805
1930	23,669
1940	20,571
1950	15,503
1960	12,458
1970	10,288
1980	10,439

COLLIN

1850	1,950
1860	9,264
1870	14,013
1880	25,983
1890	36,736
1900	50,087
1910	49,021
1920	49,609
1930	46,180
1940	47,190
1950	41,692
1960	41,247
1970	66,920
1980	144,576

COLLINGSWORTH

1880	6
1890	357
1900	1,233
1910	5,224
1920	9,154
1930	14,461
1940	10,331
1950	9,139
1960	6,276
1970	4,755
1980	4,648

COLORADO

1850	2,257
1860	7,885
1870	8,326
1880	16,673
1890	19,512
1900	22,203
1910	18,897
1920	19,013
1930	19,129
1940	17,812

1950	17,576
1960	18,463
1970	17,638
1980	18,823

COMAL

1850	1,723
1860	4,030
1870	5,283
1880	5,546
1890	6,398
1900	7,008
1910	8,434
1920	8,824
1930	11,984
1940	12,321
1950	16,357
1960	19,844
1970	24,165
1980	36,446

COMANCHE

1860	709
1870	1,001
1880	8,608
1890	15,608
1900	23,009
1910	27,186
1920	25,748
1930	18,430
1940	19,245
1950	15,516
1960	11,865
1970	11,898
1980	12,617

CONCHO

1880	800
1890	1,065
1900	1,427
1910	6,654
1920	5,847
1930	7,645
1940	6,192
1950	5,078
1960	3,672
1970	2,937
1980	2,915

COOKE

1850	220
1860	3,760
1870	5,315
1880	20,391
1890	24,696
1900	24,494
1910	26,603
1920	25,667
1930	24,136
1940	24,909
1950	22,146
1960	22,560
1970	23,471
1980	27,656

CORYELL

1860	2,666
1870	4,124
1880	10,924
1890	16,873
1900	21,308

1910	21,703
1920	20,601
1930	19,999
1940	20,226
1950	16,284
1960	23,961
1970	35,311
1980	56,767

COTTLE

1880	24
1890	240
1900	1,002
1910	4,396
1920	6,901
1930	9,395
1940	7,079
1950	6,099
1960	4,207
1970	3,204
1980	2,947

CRANE

1890	15
1900	51
1910	331
1920	37
1930	2,221
1940	2,841
1950	3,965
1960	4,699
1970	4,172
1980	4,600

CROCKETT

1880	127
1890	194
1900	1,591
1910	1,296
1920	1,500
1930	2,590
1940	2,809
1950	3,981
1960	4,209
1970	3,885
1980	4,608

CROSBY

1880	82
1890	346
1900	788
1910	1,765
1920	6,084
1930	11,023
1940	10,046
1950	9,582
1960	10,347
1970	9,085
1980	8,859

CULBERSON

1920	912
1930	1,228
1940	1,653
1950	1,825
1960	2,794
1970	3,429
1980	3,315

DALLAM

1890	112
1900	146
1910	4,001
1920	4,528
1930	7,830
1940	6,494
1950	7,640
1960	6,302
1970	6,012
1980	6,531

DALLAS

1850	2,743
1860	8,665
1870	13,314
1880	33,488
1890	67,042
1900	82,726
1910	135,748
1920	210,551
1930	325,691
1940	398,564
1950	614,799
1960	951,527
1970	1,327,695
1980	1,556,390

DAWSON

1860	281
1880	24
1890	29
1900	37
1910	2,320
1920	4,309
1930	13,573
1940	15,367
1950	19,113
1960	19,185
1970	16,604
1980	16,184

DEAF SMITH

1880	38
1890	179
1900	843
1910	3,942
1920	3,747
1930	5,979
1940	6,056
1950	9,111
1960	13,187
1970	18,999
1980	21,165

DELTA

1880	5,597
1890	9,177
1900	15,249
1910	14,566
1920	15,887
1930	13,138
1940	12,858
1950	8,964
1960	5,860
1970	4,927
1980	4,839

DENTON

1850	641

1860	5,031
1870	7,251
1880	18,143
1890	21,289
1900	28,318
1910	31,258
1920	35,355
1930	32,822
1940	33,658
1950	41,365
1960	47,432
1970	75,633
1980	143,126

DE WITT

1850	1,716
1860	5,108
1870	6,443
1880	10,082
1890	14,307
1900	21,311
1910	23,501
1920	27,971
1930	27,441
1940	24,935
1950	22,973
1960	20,683
1970	18,660
1980	18,903

DICKENS

1880	28
1890	295
1900	1,151
1910	3,092
1920	5,876
1930	8,601
1940	7,847
1950	7,177
1960	4,963
1970	3,737
1980	3,539

DIMMIT

1870	109
1880	665
1890	1,049
1900	1,106
1910	3,460
1920	5,296
1930	8,828
1940	8,542
1950	10,654
1960	10,095
1970	9,039
1980	11,367

DONLEY

1880	160
1890	1,056
1900	2,756
1910	5,284
1920	8,035
1930	10,262
1940	7,487
1950	6,216
1960	4,449
1970	3,641
1980	4,075

DUVAL

1870	1,083
1880	5,732
1890	7,598
1900	8,483
1910	8,964
1920	8,251
1930	12,191
1940	20,565
1950	15,643
1960	13,398
1970	11,722
1980	12,517

EASTLAND

1860	99
1870	88
1880	4,855
1890	10,373
1900	17,971
1910	23,421
1920	58,505
1930	34,156
1940	30,345
1950	23,942
1960	19,526
1970	18,092
1980	19,480

ECTOR

1890	244
1900	381
1910	1,178
1920	760
1930	3,958
1940	15,051
1950	42,102
1960	90,995
1970	92,660
1980	115,374

EDWARDS

1880	266
1890	1,970
1900	3,108
1910	3,768
1920	2,283
1930	2,764
1940	2,933
1950	2,908
1960	2,317
1970	2,107
1980	2,033

ELLIS

1850	989
1860	5,246
1870	7,514
1880	21,294
1890	31,774
1900	50,059
1910	53,629
1920	55,700
1930	53,936
1940	47,733
1950	45,645
1960	43,395
1970	46,638
1980	59,743

EL PASO

1860	4,051
1870	3,671
1880	3,845
1890	15,678
1900	24,886
1910	52,599
1920	101,877
1930	131,597
1940	131,067
1950	194,968
1960	314,070
1970	359,291
1980	479,899

ENCINAL

1860	43
1870	427
1880	1,902
1890	2,744

ERATH

1860	2,425
1870	1,801
1880	11,796
1890	21,594
1900	29,966
1910	32,095
1920	28,385
1930	20,804
1940	20,760
1950	18,434
1960	16,236
1970	18,141
1980	22,560

FALLS

1860	3,614
1870	9,851
1880	16,240
1890	20,706
1900	33,342
1910	35,649
1920	36,217
1930	38,771
1940	35,984
1950	26,724
1960	21,263
1970	17,300
1980	17,946

FANNIN

1850	3,788
1860	9,217
1870	13,207
1880	25,501
1890	38,709
1900	51,793
1910	44,801
1920	48,186
1930	41,163
1940	41,064
1950	31,253
1960	23,880
1970	22,705
1980	24,285

FAYETTE

1850	3,756
1860	11,604

1870	16,863
1880	27,996
1890	31,481
1900	36,542
1910	29,796
1920	29,965
1930	30,708
1940	29,246
1950	24,176
1960	20,384
1970	17,650
1980	18,832

FISHER

1880	136
1890	2,996
1900	3,708
1910	12,596
1920	11,009
1930	13,563
1940	12,932
1950	11,023
1960	7,865
1970	6,344
1980	5,891

FLOYD

1880	3
1890	529
1900	2,020
1910	4,638
1920	9,758
1930	12,409
1940	10,659
1950	10,535
1960	12,369
1970	11,044
1980	9,834

FOARD

1900	1,568
1910	5,726
1920	4,747
1930	6,315
1940	5,237
1950	4,216
1960	3,125
1970	2,211
1980	2,158

FOLEY

1890	25

FORT BEND

1850	2,533
1860	6,143
1870	7,144
1880	9,380
1890	10,586
1900	16,538
1910	18,168
1920	22,931
1930	29,718
1940	32,963
1950	31,056
1960	40,527
1970	52,314
1980	130,846

FRANKLIN

1880	5,280
1890	6,481
1900	8,674
1910	9,331
1920	9,304
1930	8,494
1940	8,378
1950	6,257
1960	5,010
1970	5,291
1980	6,893

FREESTONE

1860	6,881
1870	8,139
1880	14,921
1890	15,987
1900	18,910
1910	20,557
1920	23,264
1930	22,589
1940	21,138
1950	15,696
1960	12,525
1970	11,116
1980	14,830

FRIO

1860	42
1870	309
1880	2,130
1890	3,112
1900	4,200
1910	8,895
1920	9,296
1930	9,411
1940	9,207
1950	10,357
1960	10,112
1970	11,159
1980	13,785

GAINES

1880	8
1890	68
1900	55
1910	1,255
1920	1,018
1930	2,800
1940	8,136
1950	8,909
1960	12,267
1970	11,593
1980	13,150

GALVESTON

1850	4,529
1860	8,229
1870	15,290
1880	24,121
1890	31,476
1900	44,116
1910	44,479
1920	53,150
1930	64,401
1940	81,173
1950	113,066
1960	140,364
1970	169,812
1980	195,940

GARZA

1880	36
1890	14
1900	185
1910	1,995
1920	4,253
1930	5,586
1940	5,678
1950	6,281
1960	6,611
1970	5,289
1980	5,336

GILLESPIE

1850	1,240
1860	2,736
1870	3,566
1880	5,228
1890	7,056
1900	8,229
1910	9,447
1920	10,015
1930	11,020
1940	10,670
1950	10,520
1960	10,048
1970	10,553
1980	13,532

GLASSCOCK

1890	208
1900	286
1910	1,143
1920	555
1930	1,263
1940	1,193
1950	1,089
1960	1,118
1970	1,155
1980	1,304

GOLIAD

1850	648
1860	3,384
1870	3,628
1880	5,832
1890	5,910
1900	8,310
1910	9,909
1920	9,348
1930	10,093
1940	8,798
1950	6,219
1960	5,429
1970	4,869
1980	5,193

GONZALES

1850	1,492
1860	8,059
1870	8,951
1880	14,840
1890	18,016
1900	28,882
1910	28,055
1920	28,438
1930	28,337
1940	26,075
1950	21,164
1960	17,845
1970	16,375
1980	16,883

GRAY

1880	56
1890	203
1900	480
1910	3,405
1920	4,663
1930	22,090
1940	23,911
1950	24,728
1960	31,535
1970	26,949
1980	26,386

GRAYSON

1850	2,008
1860	8,184
1870	14,387
1880	38,108
1890	53,211
1900	63,661
1910	65,996
1920	74,165
1930	65,843
1940	69,499
1950	70,467
1960	73,043
1970	83,225
1980	89,796

GREGG

1880	8,530
1890	9,402
1900	12,343
1910	14,140
1920	16,767
1930	15,778
1940	58,027
1950	61,258
1960	69,436
1970	75,929
1980	99,487

GRIMES

1850	4,008
1860	10,307
1870	13,218
1880	18,603
1890	21,312
1900	26,106
1910	21,205
1920	23,101
1930	22,642
1940	21,960
1950	15,135
1960	12,709
1970	11,855
1980	13,580

GUADALUPE

1850	1,511
1860	5,444
1870	7,282
1880	12,202
1890	15,217
1900	21,385
1910	24,913
1920	27,719
1930	28,925
1940	25,596
1950	25,392
1960	29,107
1970	33,554

1980	46,708

HALE

1890	721
1900	1,680
1910	7,566
1920	10,104
1930	20,189
1940	18,813
1950	29,211
1960	36,798
1970	34,137
1980	37,592

HALL

1880	36
1890	703
1900	1,670
1910	8,279
1920	11,137
1930	16,966
1940	12,177
1950	10,930
1960	7,322
1970	6,015
1980	5,594

HAMILTON

1860	489
1870	733
1880	6,365
1890	9,313
1900	13,520
1910	15,315
1920	14,676
1930	13,523
1940	13,303
1950	10,660
1960	8,488
1970	7,198
1980	8,297

HANSFORD

1880	18
1890	133
1900	167
1910	935
1920	1,354
1930	3,548
1940	2,783
1950	4,202
1960	6,208
1970	6,351
1980	6,209

HARDEMAN

1880	50
1890	3,904
1900	3,634
1910	11,213
1920	12,487
1930	14,532
1940	11,073
1950	10,212
1960	8,275
1970	6,975
1980	6,368

HARDIN

1860	1,353

1870	1,460
1880	1,870
1890	3,956
1900	5,049
1910	12,947
1920	15,983
1930	13,936
1940	15,875
1950	19,535
1960	24,629
1970	29,996
1980	40,721

HARRIS

1850	4,668
1860	9,070
1870	17,375
1880	27,985
1890	37,249
1900	63,786
1910	115,693
1920	186,667
1930	359,328
1940	528,961
1950	806,701
1960	1,243,158
1970	1,741,912
1980	2,409,547

HARRISON

1850	11,822
1860	15,001
1870	13,241
1880	25,177
1890	26,721
1900	31,878
1910	37,243
1920	43,565
1930	48,937
1940	50,900
1950	47,745
1960	45,594
1970	44,841
1980	52,265

HARTLEY

1880	100
1890	252
1900	377
1910	1,298
1920	1,109
1930	2,185
1940	1,873
1950	1,913
1960	2,171
1970	2,782
1980	3,987

HASKELL

1880	48
1890	1,665
1900	2,637
1910	16,249
1920	14,193
1930	16,669
1940	14,905
1950	13,736
1960	11,174
1970	8,512
1980	7,725

HAYS

1850	387
1860	2,126
1870	4,088
1880	7,555
1890	11,352
1900	14,142
1910	15,518
1920	15,920
1930	14,915
1940	15,349
1950	17,840
1960	19,934
1970	27,642
1980	40,594

HEMPHILL

1880	149
1890	519
1900	815
1910	3,170
1920	4,280
1930	4,637
1940	31,822
1950	23,405
1960	3,185
1970	3,084
1980	5,304

HENDERSON

1850	1,237
1860	4,595
1870	6,786
1880	9,735
1890	12,285
1900	19,970
1910	20,131
1920	28,327
1930	30,583
1940	31,822
1950	23,405
1960	21,786
1970	26,466
1980	42,606

HIDALGO

1860	1,192
1870	2,387
1880	4,347
1890	6,534
1900	6,837
1910	13,728
1920	38,110
1930	77,004
1940	106,059
1950	160,446
1960	180,904
1970	181,535
1980	283,229

HILL

1860	3,653
1870	7,453
1880	16,554
1890	27,583
1900	41,355
1910	46,760
1920	43,332
1930	43,036
1940	38,355
1950	31,282
1960	23,650
1970	22,596
1980	25,024

HOCKLEY

1900	44
1910	137
1920	137
1930	9,298
1940	12,693
1950	20,407
1960	22,340
1970	20,396
1980	23,230

HOOD

1870	2,585
1880	6,125
1890	7,614
1900	9,146
1910	10,008
1920	8,759
1930	6,779
1940	6,674
1950	5,287
1960	5,443
1970	6,368
1980	17,714

HOPKINS

1850	2,623
1860	7,745
1870	12,651
1880	15,461
1890	20,572
1900	27,950
1910	31,038
1920	34,791
1930	29,410
1940	30,274
1950	23,490
1960	18,594
1970	20,710
1980	25,247

HOUSTON

1850	2,721
1860	8,058
1870	8,147
1880	16,702
1890	19,360
1900	25,452
1910	29,564
1920	28,601
1930	30,017
1940	31,137
1950	22,825
1960	19,376
1970	17,855
1980	22,299

HOWARD

1880	50
1890	1,210
1900	2,528
1910	8,881
1920	6,962
1930	22,888
1940	20,990
1950	26,722
1960	40,193
1970	37,796
1980	33,142

HUDSPETH

1920	962
1930	3,728
1940	3,149
1950	4,298
1960	3,343
1970	2,392
1980	2,728

HUNT

1850	1,520
1860	6,630
1870	10,291
1880	17,230
1890	31,885
1900	47,295
1910	48,116
1920	50,350
1930	49,016
1940	48,793
1950	42,731
1960	39,399
1970	47,948
1980	55,248

HUTCHINSON

1880	50
1890	58
1900	303
1910	892
1920	721
1930	14,848
1940	19,069
1950	31,580
1960	34,419
1970	24,443
1980	26,304

IRION

1890	870
1900	848
1910	1,283
1920	1,610
1930	2,049
1940	1,963
1950	1,590
1960	1,183
1970	1,070
1980	1,386

JACK

1860	1,000
1870	694
1880	6,626
1890	9,740
1900	10,224
1910	11,817
1920	9,683
1930	9,046
1940	10,206
1950	7,755
1960	7,418
1970	6,711
1980	7,408

JACKSON

1850	966

1860	2,612
1870	2,278
1880	2,723
1890	3,281
1900	6,094
1910	6,471
1920	11,244
1930	10,980
1940	11,720
1950	12,916
1960	14,040
1970	12,975
1980	13,352

JASPER

1850	1,767
1860	4,037
1870	4,218
1880	5,779
1890	5,592
1900	7,138
1910	14,000
1920	15,569
1930	17,064
1940	17,419
1950	20,049
1960	22,100
1970	24,692
1980	30,781

JEFF DAVIS

1890	1,394
1900	1,150
1910	1,678
1920	1,445
1930	1,800
1940	2,375
1950	2,090
1960	1,582
1970	1,527
1980	1,647

JEFFERSON

1850	1,836
1860	1,995
1870	1,906
1880	3,489
1890	5,857
1900	14,239
1910	38,182
1920	73,120
1930	133,391
1940	145,329
1950	195,083
1960	245,659
1970	246,402
1980	250,938

JIM HOGG

1920	1,914
1930	4,919
1940	5,449
1950	5,389
1960	5,022
1970	4,654
1980	5,168

JIM WELLS

1920	6,587
1930	13,456
1940	20,239

1950	27,991
1960	34,548
1970	33,032
1980	36,498

JOHNSON

1860	4,305
1870	4,923
1880	17,911
1890	22,313
1900	33,819
1910	34,460
1920	37,286
1930	33,317
1940	30,384
1950	31,390
1960	34,720
1970	45,769
1980	67,649

JONES

1880	546
1890	3,797
1900	7,053
1910	24,299
1920	22,323
1930	24,233
1940	23,378
1950	22,147
1960	19,299
1970	16,106
1980	17,268

KARNES

1860	2,171
1870	1,705
1880	3,270
1890	3,637
1900	8,681
1910	14,942
1920	19,049
1930	23,316
1940	19,248
1950	17,139
1960	14,995
1970	13,462
1980	13,593

KAUFMAN

1850	1,047
1860	3,936
1870	6,895
1880	15,448
1890	21,598
1900	33,376
1910	35,323
1920	41,276
1930	40,905
1940	38,308
1950	31,170
1960	29,931
1970	32,392
1980	39,015

KENDALL

1870	1,536
1880	2,763
1890	3,826
1900	4,103
1910	4,517
1920	4,779

1930	4,970
1940	5,080
1950	5,423
1960	5,889
1970	6,964
1980	10,635

KENEDY

1920	1,033
1930	701
1940	700
1950	632
1960	884
1970	678
1980	543

KENT

1880	92
1890	324
1900	899
1910	2,655
1920	3,335
1930	3,851
1940	3,413
1950	2,249
1960	1,727
1970	1,434
1980	1,145

KERR

1860	634
1870	1,042
1880	2,168
1890	4,462
1900	4,980
1910	5,505
1920	5,842
1930	10,151
1940	11,650
1950	14,022
1960	16,800
1970	19,454
1980	28,780

KIMBLE

1870	72
1880	1,343
1890	2,243
1900	2,503
1910	3,261
1920	3,581
1930	4,119
1940	5,064
1950	4,619
1960	3,943
1970	3,904
1980	4,063

KING

1880	40
1890	173
1900	490
1910	810
1920	655
1930	1,193
1940	1,066
1950	870
1960	640
1970	464
1980	425

KINNEY

1860	61
1870	1,204
1880	4,487
1890	3,781
1900	2,447
1910	3,401
1920	3,746
1930	3,980
1940	4,533
1950	2,668
1960	2,452
1970	2,006
1980	2,279

KLEBERG

1920	7,837
1930	12,451
1940	13,344
1950	21,991
1960	30,052
1970	33,166
1980	33,358

KNOX

1880	77
1890	1,134
1900	2,322
1910	9,625
1920	9,240
1930	11,368
1940	10,090
1950	10,082
1960	7,857
1970	5,972
1980	5,329

LAMAR

1850	3,978
1860	10,136
1870	15,790
1880	27,193
1890	37,302
1900	48,627
1910	46,544
1920	55,742
1930	48,529
1940	50,425
1950	43,033
1960	34,234
1970	36,062
1980	42,156

LAMB

1890	4
1900	31
1910	540
1920	1,175
1930	17,452
1940	17,606
1950	20,015
1960	21,896
1970	17,770
1980	18,669

LAMPASAS

1860	1,028
1870	1,344
1880	5,421
1890	7,584

1900	8,625
1910	9,532
1920	8,800
1930	8,677
1940	9,167
1950	9,929
1960	9,418
1970	9,323
1980	12,005

LA SALLE

1870	69
1880	789
1890	2,139
1900	2,303
1910	4,747
1920	4,821
1930	8,228
1940	8,003
1950	7,485
1960	5,972
1970	5,014
1980	5,514

LAVACA

1850	1,571
1860	5,945
1870	9,168
1880	13,641
1890	21,887
1900	28,121
1910	26,418
1920	28,964
1930	27,550
1940	25,485
1950	22,159
1960	20,174
1970	17,903
1980	19,004

LEE

1880	8,937
1890	11,952
1900	14,595
1910	13,132
1920	14,014
1930	13,390
1940	12,751
1950	10,144
1960	8,949
1970	8,048
1980	10,952

LEON

1850	1,946
1860	6,781
1870	6,523
1880	12,817
1890	13,841
1900	19,072
1910	16,583
1920	18,286
1930	19,898
1940	17,733
1950	12,024
1960	9,951
1970	8,738
1980	9,594

LIBERTY

1850	2,522

1860	3,189
1870	4,414
1880	4,999
1890	4,230
1900	8,102
1910	10,686
1920	14,637
1930	19,868
1940	24,541
1950	26,729
1960	31,595
1970	33,014
1980	47,088

LIMESTONE

1850	2,608
1860	4,537
1870	8,591
1880	16,246
1890	21,678
1900	32,573
1910	34,621
1920	33,283
1930	39,497
1940	33,781
1950	25,251
1960	20,413
1970	18,100
1980	20,224

LIPSCOMB

1880	69
1890	632
1900	790
1910	2,634
1920	3,684
1930	4,512
1940	3,764
1950	3,658
1960	3,406
1970	3,486
1980	3,766

LIVE OAK

1860	593
1870	852
1880	1,994
1890	2,055
1900	2,268
1910	3,442
1920	4,171
1930	8,956
1940	9,799
1950	9,054
1960	7,846
1970	6,697
1980	9,606

LLANO

1860	1,101
1870	1,379
1880	4,962
1890	6,772
1900	7,301
1910	6,520
1920	5,360
1930	5,538
1940	5,996
1950	5,377
1960	5,240
1970	6,979
1980	10,144

LOVING

1890	3
1900	33
1910	249
1920	82
1930	195
1940	285
1950	227
1960	226
1970	164
1980	91

LUBBOCK

1880	25
1890	33
1900	293
1910	3,624
1920	11,096
1930	39,104
1940	51,782
1950	101,048
1960	156,271
1970	179,295
1980	211,651

LYNN

1880	9
1890	24
1900	17
1910	1,713
1920	4,751
1930	12,372
1940	11,931
1950	11,030
1960	10,914
1970	9,107
1980	8,605

MADISON

1860	2,238
1870	4,061
1880	5,395
1890	8,512
1900	10,432
1910	10,318
1920	11,956
1930	12,227
1940	12,029
1950	7,996
1960	6,749
1970	7,693
1980	10,649

MARION

1860	3,977
1870	8,562
1880	10,983
1890	10,862
1900	10,754
1910	10,472
1920	10,886
1930	10,371
1940	11,457
1950	10,172
1960	8,049
1970	8,517
1980	10,360

MARTIN

1880	12
1890	264
1900	332
1910	1,549
1920	1,146
1930	5,785
1940	5,556
1950	5,541
1960	5,068
1970	4,774
1980	4,684

MASON

1860	630
1870	678
1880	2,655
1890	5,180
1900	5,573
1910	5,683
1920	4,824
1930	5,511
1940	5,378
1950	4,945
1960	3,780
1970	3,356
1980	3,683

MATAGORDA

1850	2,124
1860	3,454
1870	3,377
1880	3,940
1890	3,985
1900	6,097
1910	13,594
1920	16,589
1930	17,678
1940	20,066
1950	21,559
1960	25,774
1970	27,913
1980	37,828

MAVERICK

1860	726
1870	1,951
1880	2,967
1890	3,698
1900	4,066
1910	5,151
1920	7,418
1930	6,120
1940	10,071
1950	12,292
1960	14,508
1970	18,093
1980	31,398

McCULLOCH

1870	173
1880	1,533
1890	3,217
1900	3,960
1910	13,405
1920	11,020
1930	13,883
1940	13,208
1950	11,701
1960	8,815
1970	8,571
1980	8,735

McLENNAN

1860	6,206
1870	13,500
1880	26,934
1890	39,204
1900	59,772
1910	73,250
1920	82,921
1930	98,682
1940	101,898
1950	130,194
1960	150,091
1970	147,553
1980	170,755

McMULLEN

1870	230
1880	701
1890	1,038
1900	1,024
1910	1,091
1920	952
1930	1,351
1940	1,374
1950	1,187
1960	1,116
1970	1,095
1980	789

MEDINA

1850	909
1860	1,838
1870	2,078
1880	4,492
1890	5,730
1900	7,783
1910	13,415
1920	11,679
1930	13,989
1940	16,106
1950	17,013
1960	18,904
1970	20,249
1980	23,164

MENARD

1870	667
1880	1,239
1890	1,215
1900	2,011
1910	2,707
1920	3,162
1930	4,447
1940	4,521
1950	4,175
1960	2,964
1970	2,646
1980	2,346

MIDLAND

1890	1,033
1900	1,741
1910	3,464
1920	2,449
1930	8,005
1940	11,721
1950	25,785
1960	67,717
1970	65,433
1980	82,636

MILAM

1850	2,907
1860	5,175
1870	8,984
1880	18,659
1890	24,773
1900	39,666
1910	36,780
1920	38,104
1930	37,915
1940	33,120
1950	23,585
1960	22,263
1970	20,028
1980	22,732

MILLS

1890	5,493
1900	7,851
1910	9,694
1920	9,019
1930	8,293
1940	7,951
1950	5,999
1960	4,467
1970	4,212
1980	4,477

MITCHELL

1880	117
1890	2,059
1900	2,855
1910	8,956
1920	7,527
1930	14,183
1940	12,477
1950	14,357
1960	11,255
1970	9,073
1980	9,088

MONTAGUE

1860	849
1870	890
1880	11,257
1890	18,863
1900	24,800
1910	25,123
1920	22,200
1930	19,159
1940	20,442
1950	17,070
1960	14,893
1970	15,326
1980	17,410

MONTGOMERY

1850	2,384
1860	5,479
1870	6,483
1880	10,154
1890	11,765
1900	17,067
1910	15,679
1920	17,334
1930	14,588
1940	23,055
1950	24,504
1960	26,839
1970	49,479
1980	128,487

MOORE

1890	15
1900	209
1910	561
1920	571
1930	1,555
1940	4,461
1950	13,349
1960	14,773
1970	14,060
1980	16,575

MORRIS

1880	5,032
1890	6,580
1900	8,220
1910	10,439
1920	10,289
1930	10,028
1940	9,810
1950	9,433
1960	12,576
1970	12,310
1980	14,629

MOTLEY

1880	24
1890	139
1900	1,257
1910	2,396
1920	4,107
1930	6,812
1940	4,994
1950	3,963
1960	2,870
1970	2,178
1980	1,950

NACOGDOCHES

1850	5,193
1860	8,292
1870	9,614
1880	11,590
1890	15,984
1900	24,663
1910	27,406
1920	28,457
1930	30,290
1940	35,392
1950	30,326
1960	28,046
1970	36,362
1980	46,786

NAVARRO

1850	2,190
1860	5,996
1870	8,879
1880	21,702
1890	26,373
1900	43,374
1910	47,070
1920	50,624
1930	60,507
1940	51,308
1950	39,916
1960	34,423
1970	31,150
1980	35,323

NEWTON

1850	1,689
1860	3,119
1870	2,187
1880	4,359
1890	4,650
1900	7,282
1910	10,850
1920	12,196
1930	12,524
1940	13,700
1950	10,832
1960	10,372
1970	11,657
1980	13,254

NOLAN

1880	640
1890	1,573
1900	2,611
1910	11,999
1920	10,868
1930	19,323
1940	17,309
1950	19,808
1960	18,963
1970	16,220
1980	17,359

NUECES

1850	698
1860	2,906
1870	3,975
1880	7,653
1890	8,093
1900	10,439
1910	21,955
1920	22,807
1930	51,779
1940	92,681
1950	165,471
1960	221,573
1970	237,554
1980	268,215

OCHILTREE

1890	198
1900	267
1910	1,602
1920	2,331
1930	5,224
1940	4,213
1950	6,024
1960	9,380
1970	9,704
1980	9,588

OLDHAM

1880	287
1890	270
1900	349
1910	812
1920	709
1930	1,404
1940	1,385
1950	1,672
1960	1,928
1970	2,258
1980	2,283

ORANGE

1860	1,916
1870	1,255
1880	2,938
1890	4,770
1900	5,905
1910	9,528
1920	15,379
1930	15,149
1940	17,382
1950	40,567
1960	60,357
1970	71,170
1980	83,838

PALO PINTO

1860	1,524
1880	5,885
1890	8,320
1900	12,291
1910	19,506
1920	23,431
1930	17,576
1940	18,456
1950	17,154
1960	20,516
1970	28,962
1980	24,062

PANOLA

1850	3,871
1860	8,475
1870	10,119
1880	12,219
1890	14,328
1900	21,404
1910	20,424
1920	21,755
1930	24,063
1940	22,513
1950	19,250
1960	16,870
1970	15,894
1980	20,724

PARKER

1860	4,213
1870	4,186
1880	15,870
1890	21,682
1900	25,823
1910	26,311
1920	23,382
1930	18,759
1940	20,482
1950	21,528
1960	22,880
1970	33,888
1980	44,609

PARMER

1890	7
1900	34
1910	1,555
1920	1,699
1930	5,869
1940	5,890
1950	5,787
1960	9,583
1970	10,509
1980	11,038

PECOS

1880	1,807
1890	1,326
1900	2,360
1910	2,071
1920	3,857
1930	7,812
1940	8,185
1950	9,939
1960	11,957
1970	13,748
1980	14,618

POLK

1850	2,348
1860	8,300
1870	8,707
1880	7,189
1890	10,322
1900	14,447
1910	17,459
1920	16,784
1930	17,555
1940	20,635
1950	16,194
1960	13,861
1970	14,457
1980	24,407

POTTER

1880	28
1890	849
1900	1,820
1910	12,424
1920	16,710
1930	46,080
1940	54,265
1950	73,266
1960	115,580
1970	90,511
1980	98,637

PRESIDIO

1860	580
1870	1,636
1880	2,873
1890	1,698
1900	3,673
1910	5,218
1920	12,202
1930	10,154
1940	10,925
1950	7,354
1960	5,460
1970	4,842
1980	5,188

RAINS

1880	3,035
1890	3,909
1900	6,127
1910	6,787
1920	8,089
1930	7,144
1940	7,334
1950	4,266
1960	2,993
1970	3,752
1980	4,839

RANDALL

1880	3
1890	187
1900	963
1910	3,312
1920	3,675
1930	7,071
1940	7,185
1950	13,774
1960	33,913
1970	53,885
1980	75,062

REAGAN

1910	392
1920	377
1930	3,028
1940	1,997
1950	3,127
1960	3,782
1970	3,239
1980	4,135

REAL

1920	1,461
1930	2,197
1940	2,420
1950	2,479
1960	2,079
1970	2,013
1980	2,469

RED RIVER

1850	3,906
1860	8,535
1870	10,653
1880	17,194
1890	21,452
1900	29,893
1910	28,564
1920	35,829
1930	30,923
1940	29,769
1950	21,851
1960	15,682
1970	14,298
1980	16,101

REEVES

1890	1,247
1900	1,847
1910	4,392
1920	4,457
1930	6,407
1940	8,006
1950	11,745
1960	17,644
1970	16,526
1980	15,801

REFUGIO

1850	288
1860	1,600
1870	2,324
1880	1,585
1890	1,239
1900	1,641
1910	2,814
1920	4,050
1930	7,691

1940	10,383
1950	10,113
1960	10,975
1970	9,494
1980	9,289

ROBERTS

1880	32
1890	326
1900	620
1910	950
1920	1,469
1930	1,457
1940	1,289
1950	1,031
1960	1,075
1970	967
1980	1,187

ROBERTSON

1850	934
1860	4,997
1870	9,990
1880	22,383
1890	26,506
1900	31,480
1910	27,454
1920	27,933
1930	27,240
1940	25,710
1950	19,908
1960	16,157
1970	14,389
1980	14,653

ROCKWALL

1880	2,984
1890	5,972
1900	8,531
1910	8,072
1920	8,591
1930	7,658
1940	7,051
1950	6,156
1960	5,878
1970	7,046
1980	14,528

RUNNELS

1880	980
1890	3,193
1900	5,379
1910	20,858
1920	17,074
1930	21,821
1940	18,903
1950	16,771
1960	15,016
1970	12,108
1980	11,872

RUSK

1850	8,148
1860	15,803
1870	15,916
1880	18,986
1890	18,559
1900	26,099
1910	26,946
1920	31,689
1930	32,484

1940	51,023	1890	6,641	1920	1,473	1930	1,431	1970	97,853
1950	42,348	1900	7,569	1930	2,314	1940	1,404	1980	110,932
1960	36,421	1910	11,245	1940	2,026	1950	1,282		
1970	34,102	1920	10,045	1950	2,443	1960	1,177	**TERRELL**	
1980	41,382	1930	10,273	1960	2,605	1970	1,056		
		1940	11,012	1970	3,657	1980	1,206	1910	1,430
SABINE		1950	8,666	1980	3,174			1920	1,595
		1960	6,381					1930	2,660
1850	2,498	1970	5,540	**SMITH**				1940	2,952
1860	2,750	1980	6,204					1950	3,189
1870	3,356			1850	4,292	**STONEWALL**		1960	2,600
1880	4,161	**SCHLEICHER**		1860	13,392			1970	1,940
1890	4,969			1870	16,532	1880	104	1980	1,595
1900	6,394	1890	155	1880	21,863	1890	1,024		
1910	8,592	1900	515	1890	28,324	1900	2,183	**TERRY**	
1920	12,299	1910	1,893	1900	37,370	1910	5,320		
1930	11,998	1920	1,851	1910	41,746	1920	4,086	1890	21
1940	10,896	1930	3,166	1920	46,769	1930	6,667	1900	48
1950	8,568	1940	3,083	1930	53,123	1940	5,589	1910	1,474
1960	7,302	1950	2,852	1940	69,090	1950	3,679	1920	2,236
1970	7,187	1960	2,791	1950	74,701	1960	3,017	1930	8,883
1980	8,702	1970	2,277	1960	86,350	1970	2,397	1940	11,160
		1980	2,820	1970	97,096	1980	2,406	1950	13,107
SAN AUGUSTINE				1980	128,366			1960	16,286
		SCURRY				**SUTTON**		1970	14,118
1850	3,648			**SOMERVELL**				1980	14,581
1860	4,094	1880	102			1890	658		
1870	4,196	1890	1,415	1880	2,649	1900	1,727	**THROCKMORTON**	
1880	5,084	1900	4,158	1890	3,419	1910	1,569		
1890	6,668	1910	10,924	1900	3,498	1920	1,598	1860	124
1900	8,434	1920	9,003	1910	3,931	1930	2,807	1880	711
1910	11,264	1930	12,188	1920	3,563	1940	3,977	1890	902
1920	13,737	1940	11,545	1930	3,016	1950	3,746	1900	1,750
1930	12,471	1950	22,779	1940	3,071	1960	3,738	1910	4,563
1940	12,471	1960	20,369	1950	2,542	1970	3,175	1920	3,589
1950	8,837	1970	15,760	1960	2,577	1980	5,130	1930	5,253
1960	7,722	1980	18,192	1970	2,973			1940	4,275
1970	7,858			1980	4,154	**SWISHER**		1950	3,618
1980	8,785	**SHACKELFORD**						1960	2,767
				STARR		1880	4	1970	2,205
SAN JACINTO		1860	44			1890	100	1980	2,053
		1870	455	1860	2,406	1900	1,227		
1880	6,186	1880	2,037	1870	4,154	1910	4,012	**TITUS**	
1890	7,360	1890	2,012	1880	8,304	1920	4,338		
1900	10,277	1900	2,461	1890	10,749	1930	7,343	1850	3,636
1910	9,542	1910	4,201	1900	11,469	1940	6,528	1860	9,648
1920	9,867	1920	4,960	1910	13,151	1950	8,249	1870	11,339
1930	9,711	1930	6,695	1920	11,089	1960	10,607	1880	5,959
1940	9,056	1940	6,211	1930	11,409	1970	10,373	1890	8,190
1950	7,172	1950	5,001	1940	13,312	1980	9,723	1900	12,292
1960	6,153	1960	3,990	1950	13,948			1910	16,422
1970	6,072	1970	3,323	1960	17,137	**TARRANT**		1920	18,128
1980	11,434	1980	3,915	1970	17,707			1930	16,003
				1980	27,266	1850	664	1940	19,228
SAN PATRICIO		**SHELBY**				1860	6,020	1950	17,302
				STEPHENS		1870	5,788	1960	16,785
1850	200	1850	4,239			1880	24,671	1970	16,702
1860	620	1860	5,362	1860	230	1890	41,142	1980	21,442
1870	602	1870	5,732	1870	330	1900	52,376		
1880	1,010	1880	9,523	1880	4,725	1910	108,572	**TOM GREEN**	
1890	1,312	1890	14,365	1890	4,926	1920	152,800		
1900	2,372	1900	20,452	1900	6,466	1930	197,553	1880	3,615
1910	7,307	1910	26,423	1910	7,980	1940	225,521	1890	5,152
1920	11,386	1920	26,464	1920	15,403	1950	361,253	1900	6,084
1930	23,836	1930	28,627	1930	16,560	1960	538,498	1910	17,882
1940	28,871	1940	29,235	1940	12,356	1970	715,587	1920	15,210
1950	35,842	1950	23,479	1950	10,597	1980	860,880	1930	36,033
1960	45,021	1960	20,479	1960	8,885			1940	39,302
1970	47,288	1970	19,672	1970	8,414	**TAYLOR**		1950	58,929
1980	58,013	1980	23,084	1980	9,926			1960	64,630
						1880	1,736	1970	71,047
SAN SABA		**SHERMAN**		**STERLING**		1890	6,957	1980	84,784
						1900	10,499		
1860	913	1890	34	1900	1,127	1910	26,293	**TRAVIS**	
1870	1,425	1900	104	1910	1,493	1920	24,081		
1880	5,234	1910	1,376	1920	1,953	1930	41,023	1850	3,138
						1940	44,147		
						1950	63,370		
						1960	101,078		

Year	Pop.
1860	8,080
1870	13,153
1880	27,028
1890	36,322
1900	47,386
1910	55,620
1920	57,616
1930	77,777
1940	111,053
1950	160,980
1960	212,136
1970	295,516
1980	419,573

TRINITY

Year	Pop.
1860	4,392
1870	4,141
1880	4,915
1890	7,648
1900	10,976
1910	12,768
1920	13,623
1930	13,637
1940	13,705
1950	10,040
1960	7,539
1970	7,628
1980	9,450

TYLER

Year	Pop.
1850	1,894
1860	4,525
1870	5,010
1880	5,825
1890	10,887
1900	11,899
1910	10,250
1920	10,415
1930	11,448
1940	11,948
1950	11,292
1960	10,666
1970	12,417
1980	16,223

UPSHUR

Year	Pop.
1850	3,394
1860	10,645
1870	12,039
1880	10,266
1890	12,695
1900	16,266
1910	19,960
1920	22,472
1930	22,297
1940	26,178
1950	20,822
1960	19,793
1970	20,976
1980	28,595

UPTON

Year	Pop.
1890	52
1900	48
1910	501
1920	253
1930	5,968
1940	4,297
1950	5,307
1960	6,239
1970	4,697
1980	4,619

UVALDE

Year	Pop.
1860	506
1870	851
1880	2,541
1890	3,804
1900	4,647
1910	11,233
1920	10,769
1930	12,945
1940	13,246
1950	16,015
1960	16,814
1970	17,348
1980	22,441

VAL VERDE

Year	Pop.
1890	2,874
1900	5,263
1910	8,613
1920	12,706
1930	14,924
1940	15,453
1950	16,635
1960	24,461
1970	27,471
1980	35,910

VAN ZANDT

Year	Pop.
1850	1,348
1860	3,777
1870	6,494
1880	12,619
1890	16,255
1900	15,481
1910	25,651
1920	30,784
1930	32,315
1940	31,155
1950	22,593
1960	19,091
1970	22,155
1980	31,426

VICTORIA

Year	Pop.
1850	2,019
1860	4,171
1870	4,860
1880	6,289
1890	8,737
1900	13,678
1910	14,990
1920	18,271
1930	20,048
1940	23,741
1950	31,241
1960	46,475
1970	53,766
1980	68,807

WALKER

Year	Pop.
1850	3,964
1860	8,191
1870	9,776
1880	12,024
1890	12,874
1900	15,813
1910	16,061
1920	18,556
1930	18,528
1940	19,868
1950	20,163
1960	21,475
1970	27,680
1980	41,789

WALLER

Year	Pop.
1880	9,024
1890	10,888
1900	14,246
1910	12,138
1920	10,292
1930	10,014
1940	10,280
1950	11,961
1960	12,071
1970	14,285
1980	19,798

WARD

Year	Pop.
1890	77
1900	1,451
1910	2,389
1920	2,615
1930	4,599
1940	9,575
1950	13,346
1960	14,917
1970	13,019
1980	13,976

WASHINGTON

Year	Pop.
1850	5,983
1860	15,215
1870	23,104
1880	27,565
1890	29,161
1900	32,931
1910	25,561
1920	26,624
1930	25,394
1940	25,387
1950	20,542
1960	19,145
1970	18,842
1980	21,998

WEBB

Year	Pop.
1860	1,397
1870	2,615
1880	5,273
1890	14,842
1900	21,851
1910	22,503
1920	29,152
1930	42,128
1940	45,916
1950	56,141
1960	64,791
1970	72,859
1980	99,258

WHARTON

Year	Pop.
1850	1,752
1860	3,380
1870	3,426
1880	4,549
1890	7,584
1900	16,942
1910	21,123
1920	24,288
1930	29,681
1940	36,158
1950	36,077
1960	38,152
1970	36,729
1980	40,242

WHEELER

Year	Pop.
1880	512
1890	778
1900	636
1910	5,258
1920	7,397
1930	15,555
1940	12,411
1950	10,317
1960	7,947
1970	6,434
1980	7,137

WICHITA

Year	Pop.
1880	433
1890	4,831
1900	5,806
1910	16,094
1920	72,911
1930	74,416
1940	73,604
1950	98,493
1960	123,528
1970	120,563
1980	121,082

WILBARGER

Year	Pop.
1880	126
1890	7,092
1900	5,759
1910	12,000
1920	15,112
1930	24,579
1940	20,474
1950	20,552
1960	17,748
1970	15,355
1980	15,931

WILLACY

Year	Pop.
1930	10,499
1940	13,230
1950	20,920
1960	20,084
1970	15,570
1980	17,495

WILLIAMSON

Year	Pop.
1850	1,568
1860	4,529
1870	6,368
1880	15,155
1890	25,909
1900	38,072
1910	42,228
1920	42,934
1930	44,146
1940	41,698
1950	38,853
1960	35,044
1970	37,305
1980	76,521

WILSON

Year	Pop.
1870	2,556
1880	7,118
1890	10,655
1900	13,961
1910	17,066
1920	17,289
1930	17,606
1940	17,066
1950	14,672
1960	13,267
1970	13,041
1980	16,756

WINKLER

Year	Pop.
1890	10
1900	60
1910	442
1920	81
1930	6,784
1940	6,141
1950	10,064
1960	13,652
1970	9,640
1980	9,944

WISE

Year	Pop.
1860	3,160
1870	1,450
1880	16,601
1890	24,134
1900	27,116
1910	26,450
1920	23,363
1930	19,178
1940	19,074
1950	16,141
1960	17,012
1970	19,687
1980	26,575

WOOD

Year	Pop.
1860	4,968
1870	6,894
1880	11,212
1890	13,932
1900	21,048
1910	23,417
1920	27,707
1930	24,183
1940	24,360
1950	21,308
1960	17,653
1970	18,589
1980	24,697

YOAKUM

Year	Pop.
1890	4
1900	26
1910	602
1920	504
1930	1,263
1940	5,354
1950	4,339
1960	8,032
1970	7,344
1980	8,299

YOUNG

Year	Pop.
1860	592

1870	135
1880	4,726
1890	5,049
1900	6,540
1910	13,657
1920	13,379
1930	20,128
1940	19,004
1950	16,810
1960	17,254
1970	15,400
1980	19,083

ZAPATA

1860	1,248
1870	1,488
1880	3,636
1890	3,562
1900	4,760
1910	3,809
1920	2,929
1930	2,876
1940	3,916
1950	4,405
1960	4,393
1970	4,352
1980	6,628

ZAVALA

1860	26
1870	133
1880	410
1890	1,097
1900	792
1910	1,889
1920	3,108
1930	10,349
1940	11,603
1950	11,201
1960	12,696
1970	11,370
1980	11,666

NOTES

BEXAR DISTRICT

Divided into numerous counties in 1876. Returns for 1870 give 1,077.

BRAZOS

Name changed from Navasoto in 1842.

BUCHTEL

Annexed to Brewster in 1897.

CASS

Name changed to Davis in 1861; name changed back to Cass in 1871.

DAWSON

No records by which to account for its disappearance subsequent to the 1860 census.

ENCINAL

Annexed to Webb in 1899.

FOLEY

Annexed to Brewster in 1897.

HARRIS

Name changed from Harrisburg in 1839.

STEPHENS

Name changed from Buchanan in 1861.

ABILENE

1890	3,194
1900	3,411
1910	9,204
1920	10,274
1930	23,175
1940	26,612
1950	45,570
1960	90,368
1970	89,653
1980	98,315

ALICE

1910	2,136
1920	1,880
1930	4,239
1940	7,792
1950	16,449
1960	20,861
1970	20,121
1980	20,961

ALVIN

1880	676
1890	432
1900	986
1910	1,453
1920	1,519
1930	1,511
1940	3,087
1950	3,701
1960	5,643
1970	10,671
1980	16,515

AMARILLO

1890	482
1900	1,442
1910	9,957
1920	15,494
1930	43,132
1940	51,686
1950	74,246
1960	137,969
1970	127,010
1980	149,230

ANDREWS

1940	611
1950	3,294
1960	11,135
1970	8,625
1980	11,061

ANGLETON

1920	1,043
1930	1,229
1940	1,763
1950	3,399
1960	7,312
1970	9,906
1980	13,929

ARLINGTON

1880	199
1890	664
1900	1,079
1910	1,794
1920	3,031
1930	3,661
1940	4,240
1950	7,692
1960	44,775
1970	90,229
1980	160,113

ATHENS

1910	2,261
1920	3,176
1930	4,103
1940	4,765
1950	5,194
1960	7,086
1970	9,582
1980	10,197

AUSTIN

1850	629
1860	3,494
1870	4,428
1880	11,013
1890	14,575
1900	22,258
1910	29,860
1920	34,846
1930	53,120
1940	87,930
1950	132,459
1960	186,545
1970	253,539
1980	345,496

BALCH SPRINGS

1960	6,821
1970	10,464
1980	13,746

BAY CITY

1910	3,156
1920	3,454
1930	4,070
1940	6,594
1950	9,427
1960	11,656
1970	13,445
1980	17,837

BAYTOWN

1950	22,983
1960	28,159
1970	43,980
1980	56,923

BEAUMONT

1890	3,296
1900	9,427
1910	20,640
1920	40,422
1930	57,732
1940	59,061
1950	94,014
1960	119,175
1970	117,548
1980	118,102

BEDFORD

1960	2,706
1970	10,049
1980	20,821

BEEVILLE

1910	3,269
1920	3,063
1930	4,806
1940	6,789
1950	9,348
1960	13,811
1970	13,506
1980	14,574

BELLAIRE

1930	390
1940	1,124
1950	10,173
1960	19,872
1970	19,009
1980	14,950

BELTON

1870	281
1880	1,797
1890	3,000
1900	3,700
1910	4,164
1920	5,098
1930	3,779
1940	3,572
1950	5,246
1960	8,163
1970	8,696
1980	10,660

BENBROOK

1950	617
1960	3,254
1970	8,169
1980	13,579

BIG SPRING

1910	4,102
1920	4,273
1930	13,735
1940	12,604
1950	17,286
1960	31,230
1970	28,735
1980	24,804

BORGER

1930	6,532
1940	10,018
1950	18,059
1960	20,911
1970	14,195
198	15,837

BRENHAM

1860	920
1870	2,221
1880	4,101
1890	5,209
1900	5,968

1910	4,718
1920	5,066
1930	5,974
1940	6,435
1950	6,941
1960	7,740
1970	8,922
1980	10,966

BROWNFIELD

1930	1,907
1940	4,009
1950	6,161
1960	10,286
1970	9,647
1980	10,387

BROWNSVILLE

1860	2,734
1870	4,905
1880	4,938
1890	6,134
1900	6,305
1910	10,517
1920	11,791
1930	22,021
1940	22,083
1950	36,066
1960	48,040
1970	52,522
1980	84,997

BROWNWOOD

1880	725
1890	2,176
1900	3,965
1910	6,967
1920	8,223
1930	12,789
1940	13,398
1950	20,181
1960	16,974
1970	17,368
1980	19,396

BRYAN

1890	2,979
1900	3,589
1910	4,132
1920	6,307
1930	7,814
1940	11,842
1950	18,102
1960	27,542
1970	33,719
1980	44,337

BURKBURNETT

1920	5,300
1930	3,281
1940	2,814
1950	4,555
1960	7,621
1970	9,230
1980	10,668

BURLESON

1920	241
1930	591

1940	573
1950	791
1960	2,345
1970	7,713
1980	11,734

CANYON

1910	1,460
1920	1,618
1930	2,821
1940	2,622
1950	4,364
1960	5,864
1970	8,333
1980	10,724

CARROLLTON

1920	573
1930	689
1940	921
1950	1,610
1960	4,242
1970	13,855
1980	40,595

CLEBURNE

1870	686
1880	1,855
1890	3,278
1900	7,493
1910	10,364
1920	12,820
1930	11,539
1940	10,558
1950	12,905
1960	15,381
1970	16,015
1980	19,218

COLLEGE STATION

1940	2,184
1950	7,925
1960	11,396
1970	17,676
1980	37,272

CONROE

1910	1,374
1920	1,858
1930	2,457
1940	4,624
1950	7,298
1960	9,192
1970	11,969
1980	18,034

COPPERAS COVE

1920	509
1930	406
1940	356
1950	1,052
1960	4,567
1970	10,818
1980	19,469

CORPUS CHRISTI

1860	175
1870	2,140

1880	3,257
1890	4,387
1900	4,703
1910	8,222
1920	10,522
1930	27,741
1940	57,301
1950	108,287
1960	167,690
1970	204,525
1980	231,999

CORSICANA

1870	80
1880	3,373
1890	6,285
1900	9,313
1910	9,749
1920	11,356
1930	15,202
1940	15,232
1950	19,211
1960	20,344
1970	19,972
1980	21,712

DALLAS

1880	10,358
1890	38,067
1900	42,638
1910	92,104
1920	158,976
1930	260,475
1940	294,734
1950	434,462
1960	679,684
1970	844,401
1980	904,078

DE SOTO

1950	298
1960	1,969
1970	6,617
1980	15,538

DEER PARK

1950	736
1960	4,865
1970	12,773
1980	22,648

DEL RIO

1880	50
1890	1,980
1900	(NA)
1910	(NA)
1920	10,589
1930	11,693
1940	13,343
1950	14,211
1960	18,612
1970	21,330
1980	30,034

DENISON

1880	3,975
1890	10,958
1900	11,807
1910	13,632

1920	17,065
1930	13,850
1940	15,581
1950	17,504
1960	22,748
1970	24,923
1980	23,884

DENTON

1880	361
1890	2,558
1900	4,187
1910	4,732
1920	7,626
1930	9,587
1940	11,192
1950	21,372
1960	26,844
1970	39,874
1980	48,063

DUMAS

1940	2,117
1950	6,127
1960	8,477
1970	9,771
1980	12,194

DUNCANVILLE

1950	841
1960	3,744
1970	14,105
1980	27,781

EAGLE PASS

1910	3,536
1920	5,765
1930	5,059
1940	6,459
1950	7,276
1960	12,094
1970	15,364
1980	21,407

EDINBURG

1920	1,406
1930	4,821
1940	8,718
1950	12,383
1960	18,706
1970	17,163
1980	24,075

EL CAMPO

1910	1,778
1920	1,766
1930	2,034
1940	3,906
1950	6,237
1960	7,700
1970	9,332
1980	10,462

EL PASO

1880	736
1890	10,338
1900	15,906
1910	39,279

1920	77,560
1930	102,421
1940	96,810
1950	130,485
1960	276,687
1970	322,261
1980	425,259

ENNIS

1880	1,351
1890	2,171
1900	4,919
1910	5,669
1920	7,224
1930	7,069
1940	7,087
1950	7,815
1960	9,347
1970	11,046
1980	12,110

EULESS

1960	4,263
1970	19,316
1980	24,002

FARMERS BRANCH

1950	915
1960	13,441
1970	27,492
1980	24,863

FOREST HILL

1940	695
1950	1,330
1960	3,221
1970	8,236
1980	11,684

FORT WORTH

1880	6,663
1890	23,076
1900	26,688
1910	73,312
1920	106,482
1930	163,447
1940	177,662
1950	278,778
1960	356,268
1970	393,445
1980	385,164

FREEPORT

1920	1,798
1930	3,162
1940	2,579
1950	6,012
1960	11,619
1970	11,997
1980	13,444

FRIENDSWOOD

| 1970 | 5,675 |
| 1980 | 10,719 |

GAINESVILLE

1880	2,667
1890	6,594
1900	7,874
1910	7,624
1920	8,648
1930	8,915
1940	9,651
1950	11,246
1960	13,083
1970	13,830
1980	14,081

GALVESTON

1850	4,177
1860	7,307
1870	13,818
1880	22,248
1890	29,084
1900	37,789
1910	36,981
1920	44,255
1930	52,938
1940	60,862
1950	66,568
1960	67,175
1970	61,809
1980	61,902

GARLAND

1890	478
1900	819
1910	804
1920	1,421
1930	1,584
1940	2,233
1950	10,571
1960	38,501
1970	81,437
1980	138,857

GRAND PRAIRIE

1910	994
1920	1,263
1930	1,529
1940	1,595
1950	14,594
1960	30,386
1970	50,904
1980	71,462

GRAPEVINE

1910	681
1920	821
1930	936
1940	1,043
1950	1,824
1960	2,821
1970	7,049
1980	11,801

GREENVILLE

1890	4,330
1900	6,860
1910	8,850
1920	12,384
1930	12,407
1940	13,995
1950	14,727
1960	19,087
1970	22,043
1980	22,161

GROVES

1960	17,304
1970	18,067
1980	17,090

HALTOM CITY

1950	5,760
1960	23,133
1970	28,127
1980	29,014

HARLINGEN

1920	1,784
1930	12,124
1940	13,306
1950	23,229
1960	41,207
1970	33,503
1980	43,543

HENDERSON

1920	2,273
1930	2,932
1940	6,437
1950	6,833
1960	9,666
1970	10,187
1980	11,473

HEREFORD

1910	1,750
1920	1,696
1930	2,458
1940	2,584
1950	5,207
1960	7,652
1970	13,414
1980	15,853

HOUSTON

1850	2,396
1860	4,845
1870	9,382
1880	16,513
1890	27,557
1900	44,633
1910	78,800
1920	138,276
1930	292,352
1940	384,514
1950	596,163
1960	938,219
1970	1,233,535
1980	1,595,138

HUNTSVILLE

1860	939
1870	1,599
1880	2,536
1890	1,509
1900	2,485
1910	2,072
1920	4,689
1930	5,028
1940	5,108
1950	9,820
1960	11,999
1970	17,610
1980	23,936

HURST

1960	10,165
1970	27,215
1980	31,420

IRVING

1920	357
1930	731
1940	1,089
1950	2,621
1960	45,985
1970	97,260
1980	109,943

JACKSONVILLE

1880	349
1890	970
1900	2,850
1910	2,875
1920	3,723
1930	6,748
1940	7,213
1950	8,607
1960	9,590
1970	9,734
1980	12,264

KERRVILLE

1880	156
1890	1,044
1900	1,423
1910	1,843
1920	2,353
1940	4,546
1950	5,572
1960	7,961
1970	12,672
1980	15,276

KILGORE

1940	6,708
1950	9,638
1960	10,092
1970	9,495
1980	10,968

KILLEEN

1890	285
1900	780
1910	1,265
1920	1,298
1930	1,260
1940	1,263
1950	7,045
1960	23,377
1970	35,507
1980	46,296

KINGSVILLE

1920	4,770
1930	6,815
1940	7,782
1950	16,898
1960	25,297
1970	28,915
1980	28,808

LAKE JACKSON

1950	2,897
1960	9,651
1970	13,376
1980	19,102

LA MARQUE

1960	13,969
1970	16,131
1980	15,372

LA PORTE

1900	537
1910	678
1920	889
1930	1,280
1940	3,072
1950	4,429
1960	4,512
1970	7,149
1980	14,062

LAMESA

1920	1,188
1930	3,528
1940	6,038
1950	10,704
1960	12,438
1970	11,559
1980	11,790

LANCASTER

1880	497
1890	714
1900	1,045
1910	1,115
1920	1,190
1930	1,133
1940	1,151
1950	2,632
1960	7,501
1970	10,522
1980	14,807

LAREDO

1860	1,256
1870	2,046
1880	3,521
1890	11,319
1900	13,429
1910	14,855
1920	22,710
1930	32,618
1940	39,274
1950	51,910
1960	60,678
1970	69,024
1980	91,449

LEAGUE CITY

1970	10,818
1980	16,578

LEVELLAND

1930	1,661
1940	3,091
1950	8,264

1960	10,153
1970	11,445
1980	13,809

LEWISVILLE

1930	853
1940	873
1950	1,516
1960	3,956
1970	9,264
1980	24,273

LONGVIEW

1880	1,525
1890	2,034
1900	3,591
1910	5,155
1920	5,713
1930	5,036
1940	13,758
1950	24,502
1960	40,050
1970	45,547
1980	62,762

LUBBOCK

1910	1,938
1920	4,051
1930	20,520
1940	31,853
1950	71,747
1960	128,691
1970	149,101
1980	173,979

LUFKIN

1890	529
1900	1,527
1910	2,749
1920	4,878
1930	7,311
1940	9,567
1950	15,135
1960	17,641
1970	23,049
1980	28,562

MARSHALL

1870	1,970
1880	5,624
1890	7,207
1900	7,855
1910	11,452
1920	14,271
1930	16,203
1940	18,410
1950	22,327
1960	23,846
1970	22,937
1980	24,921

McALLEN

1920	5,331
1930	9,074
1940	11,877
1950	20,067
1960	32,728
1970	37,636
1980	66,281

McKINNEY

1850	315
1870	503
1880	1,479
1890	2,489
1900	4,342
1910	4,714
1920	6,677
1930	7,307
1940	8,555
1950	10,560
1960	13,763
1970	15,193
1980	16,256

MERCEDES

1910	1,209
1920	3,414
1930	6,608
1940	7,624
1950	10,081
1960	10,943
1970	9,355
1980	11,851

MESQUITE

1890	135
1900	406
1910	687
1920	674
1930	729
1940	1,045
1950	1,696
1960	27,525
1970	55,131
1980	67,053

MIDLAND

1910	2,192
1920	1,795
1930	5,484
1940	9,352
1950	21,713
1960	62,625
1970	59,463
1980	70,525

MINERAL WELLS

1890	577
1900	2,048
1910	3,950
1920	7,980
1930	5,986
1940	6,303
1950	7,801
1960	11,053
1970	18,411
1980	14,468

MISSION

1920	3,847
1930	5,120
1940	5,982
1950	10,765
1960	14,081
1970	13,043
1980	22,589

MOUNT PLEASANT

1870	275
1880	452
1890	963
1900	(NA)
1910	3,137
1920	4,099
1930	3,541
1940	4,528
1950	6,342
1960	8,027
1970	9,459
1980	11,003

NACOGDOCHES

1850	368
1860	485
1870	500
1880	333
1890	1,138
1900	1,827
1910	3,369
1920	3,546
1930	5,687
1940	7,538
1950	12,327
1960	12,674
1970	22,544
1980	27,149

NEDERLAND

1950	3,805
1960	12,036
1970	16,810
1980	16,855

NEW BRAUNFELS

1850	1,298
1860	1,740
1870	2,261
1880	1,938
1890	1,608
1900	2,097
1910	3,165
1920	3,590
1930	6,242
1940	6,976
1950	12,210
1960	15,631
1970	17,859
1980	22,402

NORTH RICHLAND HILLS

1960	8,662
1970	16,514
1980	30,592

ODESSA

1930	2,407
1940	9,573
1950	29,495
1960	80,338
1970	78,380
1980	90,027

ORANGE

1860	936
1870	(NA)

1880	(NA)
1890	3,173
1900	3,835
1910	5,527
1920	9,212
1930	7,913
1940	7,472
1950	21,174
1960	25,604
1970	24,457
1980	23,628

PALESTINE

1880	2,997
1890	5,838
1900	8,297
1910	10,482
1920	11,039
1930	11,445
1940	12,144
1950	12,503
1960	13,974
1970	14,525
1980	15,948

PAMPA

1920	987
1930	10,470
1940	12,895
1950	16,583
1960	24,664
1970	21,726
1980	21,396

PARIS

1880	3,980
1890	8,254
1900	9,358
1910	11,269
1920	15,040
1930	15,649
1940	18,678
1950	21,643
1960	20,977
1970	23,441
1980	25,498

PASADENA

1930	1,647
1940	3,436
1950	22,483
1960	58,737
1970	89,957
1980	112,560

PEARLAND

1960	1,497
1970	6,444
1980	13,248

PECOS

1890	393
1900	639
1910	1,856
1920	1,445
1930	3,304
1940	4,855
1950	8,054
1960	12,728
1970	12,662
1980	12,855

PHARR

1920	1,565
1930	3,225
1940	4,784
1950	8,690
1960	14,106
1970	15,829
1980	21,381

PLAINVIEW

1910	2,829
1920	3,989
1930	8,834
1940	8,263
1950	14,044
1960	18,735
1970	19,096
1980	22,187

PLANO

1870	155
1880	556
1890	842
1900	1,304
1910	1,258
1920	1,715
1930	1,554
1940	1,582
1950	2,126
1960	3,695
1970	17,872
1980	72,331

PORT ARTHUR

1900	900
1910	7,663
1920	22,251
1930	50,902
1940	46,140
1950	57,530
1960	66,676
1970	57,371
1980	61,251

PORT LAVACA

1910	1,699
1920	1,213
1930	1,367
1940	2,069
1950	5,599
1960	8,864
1970	10,491
1980	10,911

PORT NECHES

1930	2,327
1940	2,487
1950	5,448
1960	8,696
1970	10,894
1980	13,944

PORTLAND

1950	1,292
1960	2,538
1970	7,302
1980	12,023

RICHARDSON

1930	629
1940	720
1950	1,289
1960	16,810
1970	48,405
1980	72,496

ROBSTOWN

1920	948
1930	4,183
1940	6,780
1950	7,278
1960	10,266
1970	11,217
1980	12,100

ROSENBURG

1910	1,198
1920	1,279
1930	1,941
1940	3,457
1950	6,210
1960	9,698
1970	12,098
1980	17,995

ROUND ROCK

1920	900
1930	1,173
1940	1,240
1950	1,438
1960	1,878
1970	2,811
1980	11,812

SAN ANGELO

1910	10,321
1920	10,050
1930	25,308
1940	25,802
1950	52,093
1960	58,815
1970	63,884
1980	73,240

SAN ANTONIO

1850	3,488
1860	8,235
1870	12,256
1880	20,500
1890	37,673
1900	53,321
1910	96,614
1920	161,379
1930	231,542
1940	253,854
1950	408,442
1960	587,718
1970	654,153
1980	785,880

SAN BENITO

1920	5,070
1930	10,753
1940	9,501
1950	13,271
1960	16,422
1970	15,176
1980	17,988

SAN MARCOS

1870	742
1880	1,232
1890	2,335
1900	2,292
1910	4,071
1920	4,527
1930	5,134
1940	6,006
1950	9,980
1960	12,713
1970	18,860
1980	23,420

SEGUIN

1860	856
1870	988
1880	1,363
1890	1,716
1900	2,421
1910	3,116
1920	3,631
1930	5,225
1940	7,006
1950	9,733
1960	14,299
1970	15,934
1980	17,854

SHERMAN

1870	1,439
1880	6,093
1890	7,335
1900	10,243
1910	12,421
1920	15,031
1930	15,713
1940	17,156
1950	20,150
1960	24,988
1970	29,061
1980	30,413

SNYDER

1910	2,514
1920	2,179
1930	3,008
1940	3,815
1950	12,010
1960	13,850
1970	11,171
1980	12,705

SOUTH HOUSTON

1930	612
1940	982
1950	4,126
1960	7,532
1970	11,527
1980	13,293

STEPHENVILLE

1880	725
1890	909
1900	1,902
1910	2,561
1920	3,891
1930	3,944
1940	4,768
1950	7,155

1960	7,359
1970	9,277
1980	11,881

SULFUR SPRINGS

1860	621
1870	921
1880	1,854
1890	3,038
1900	3,635
1910	5,151
1920	5,558
1930	5,417
1940	6,742
1950	8,991
1960	9,160
1970	10,642
1980	12,804

SWEETWATER

1890	614
1900	670
1910	4,176
1920	4,307
1930	10,848
1940	10,376
1950	13,619
1960	13,914
1970	12,020
1980	12,242

TAYLOR

1890	2,584
1900	4,211
1910	5,314
1920	5,965
1930	7,463
1940	7,875
1950	9,071
1960	9,434
1970	9,616
1980	10,619

TEMPLE

1890	4,047
1900	7,065
1910	10,993
1920	11,033
1930	15,345
1940	15,344
1950	25,467
1960	30,419
1970	33,431
1980	42,483

TERRELL

1880	2,003
1890	2,988
1900	6,330
1910	7,050
1920	8,349
1930	8,795
1940	10,481
1950	11,544
1960	13,803
1970	14,182
1980	13,225

TEXARKANA

1880	1,833
1890	2,852
1900	5,256
1910	9,790
1920	11,480
1930	16,602
1940	17,019
1950	24,753
1960	30,128
1970	30,497
1980	31,271

TEXAS CITY

1920	2,509
1930	3,534
1940	5,748
1950	16,620
1960	32,065
1970	38,908
1980	41,403

THE COLONY

1980	11,586

TYLER

1880	2,423
1890	6,098
1900	8,069
1910	10,400
1920	12,085
1930	17,113
1940	28,279
1950	38,968
1960	51,230
1970	57,770
1980	70,058

UNIVERSAL CITY

1970	7,613
1980	10,720

UNIVERSITY PARK

1930	4,200
1940	14,458
1950	24,275
1960	23,202
1970	23,498
1980	22,254

UVALDE

1860	192
1870	163
1880	794
1890	1,265
1900	1,889
1910	3,998
1920	3,885
1930	5,286
1940	6,679
1950	8,674
1960	10,293
1970	10,764
1980	14,178

VERNON

1890	2,857
1900	1,993
1910	3,195
1920	5,142
1930	9,137
1940	9,277
1950	12,651
1960	12,141
1970	11,454
1980	12,695

VICTORIA

1850	806
1860	1,986
1870	2,534
1880	(NA)
1890	3,046
1900	4,010
1910	3,673
1920	5,957
1930	7,421
1940	11,566
1950	16,126
1960	33,047
1970	41,349
1980	50,695

VIDOR

1970	9,738
1980	12,117

WACO

1870	3,008
1880	7,295
1890	14,445
1900	20,686
1910	26,425
1920	38,500
1930	52,848
1940	55,982
1950	84,706
1960	97,808
1970	95,326
1980	101,261

WATAUGA

1970	3,778
1980	10,284

WAXAHACHIE

1880	1,354
1890	3,076
1900	4,215
1910	6,205
1920	7,958
1930	8,042
1940	8,655
1950	11,204
1960	12,749
1970	13,452
1980	14,624

WEATHERFORD

1880	2,046
1890	3,369
1900	4,786
1910	5,074

1920	6,203
1930	4,912
1940	5,924
1950	8,083
1960	9,759
1970	11,750
1980	12,049

WESLACO

1930	4,879
1940	6,883
1950	7,514
1960	15,649
1970	15,313
1980	19,331

WEST UNIVERSITY PLACE

1930	1,332
1940	9,221
1950	17,074
1960	14,628
1970	13,317
1980	12,010

WHITE SETTLEMENT

1950	10,827
1960	11,513
1970	13,449
1980	13,508

WICHITA FALLS

1890	1,987
1900	2,480
1910	8,200
1920	40,079
1930	43,690
1940	45,112
1950	68,042
1960	101,724
1970	96,265
1980	94,201

CORRECTION NOTE

The official 1980 census counts of total population shown in this report supersede counts issued previously. Corrections to the figures were made after the counts were provided to the State for redistricting purposes and released in Advance Report PHC80-V for this State.

Shown below are corrections to the 1980 census counts of the total population made after the tabulations for this report were completed. Any additional corrections made after this report is printed are available by writing to Data User Services Division, Customer Services (Corrections), Bureau of the Census, Washington, D.C. 20233.

The 1980 figures shown in this publication are subject to change pending the outcome of the various lawsuits dealing with the census counts.

	1980 population	
	As shown in the tables	Corrected
The State....................	14 229 191	14 229 288
Bell County.........................	157 889	157 820
Temple division.................	47 507	47 438
Temple city (pt.)..............	42 474	42 345
Bexar County........................	988 800	988 798
San Antonio division.............	970 336	970 334
Balcones Heights city..........	2 556	2 511
Converse city..................	4 907	5 150
Kirby city.....................	6 385	6 435
Leon Valley city...............	8 951	9 088
San Antonio city (pt.).........	785 861	786 004
El Paso County:		
El Paso Northwest division:		
Vinton village................	(1)	271
Gonzales County....................	16 883	16 949
Smiley division.................	988	1 054
Smiley city....................	439	505
Gregg County.......................	99 487	99 495
Sabine division.................	4 724	4 732
Kilgore city (pt.).............	104	142
Henderson County:		
Eustace-Malakoff division:		
Tool city.....................	1 591	1 464
Hidalgo County.....................	283 229	283 323
Mission division................	35 329	35 423
Mission city (pt.).............	22 589	22 653
Kaufman County.....................	39 015	39 029
Terrell division:		
Terrell city (pt.).............	13 169	13 172
Terrell South division..........	3 267	3 281
Oak Ridge town................	247	183
Post Oak Bend City town........	878	230
Terrell city (pt.).............	56	97
Orange County:		
Orange division:		
Pinehurst city................	3 055	2 928
Vidor division:		
Vidor city....................	12 117	11 834
Parker County:		
Weatherford Southeast division:		
Anneta North town.............	281	197
Anneta South town.............	115	205
Willow Park city..............	1 113	1 107

	1980 population	
	As shown in the tables	Corrected
Williamson County..................	76 521	76 507
Georgetown-Round Rock division...	39 639	39 625
Round Rock city (pt.)..........	11 812	12 740
Kilgore city (total)..............	10 968	11 006
Mission city (total)..............	22 589	22 653
Round Rock city (total)..........	11 812	12 740
San Antonio city (total)..........	785 880	786 023
Temple city (total)...............	42 483	42 354
Terrell city (total)..............	13 225	13 269

[1]Not shown separately.

County Subdivisions	1980	1970
The State	14 229 191	'11 198 655
Anderson County[1]	38 381	27 789
Cayuga division	607	682
Elkhart division	4 143	3 105
Elkhart town[1]	1 317	997
Frankston division	3 043	2 153
Frankston town[1]	1 255	1 056
Montalba–Tennessee Colony division	6 728	2 196
Palestine division	23 860	
Palestine city[1]	15 948	14 525
Andrews County[2]	13 323	10 372
Andrews North division	11 640	...
Andrews city[2]	11 061	8 625
Andrews South division	1 683	...
Angelina County[3]	64 172	49 349
Diboll division	7 654	5 133
Burke city	322	188
Diboll city[3]	5 227	3 557
Huntington division	6 446	4 416
Huntington city	1 672	1 192
Lufkin division	41 875	...
Fuller Springs town[3]	1 470	...
Hudson city (pt.)[3]	1 659	'670
Lufkin city[3]	28 562	23 049
Pollok division	6 156	4 654
Hudson city (pt.)[3]	–	...
Zavalla division	2 041	1 489
Zavalla city[3]	762	...
Aransas County[4]	14 260	8 902
Fulton division	3 311	...
Aransas Pass city (pt.)	–	...
Fulton town[4]	725	...
Port Aransas city (pt.)[4]	...	...
Rockport division	10 949	...
Aransas Pass city (pt.)	860	726
Rockport city[4]	3 686	3 879
Archer County[5]	7 266	5 759
Archer division	3 326	3 108
Archer City city[5]	1 862	1 722
Scotland city (pt.)[5]	365	'257
Windthorst town (pt.)[5]	401	'377
Holliday division	3 940	...
Holliday city[5]	1 349	1 048
Lakeside City town (pt.)[5]	515	187
Megargel town	381	373
Wichita Falls city (pt.)[5]	–	'–
Armstrong County	1 994	1 895
Claude North division	526	541
Claude South division	1 468	1 354
Claude city	1 112	992
Atascosa County[6]	25 055	18 696
Campbellton division	538	694
Charlotte division	2 060	2 040
Charlotte city	1 443	1 329
Jourdanton division	3 916	2 795
Christine city	392	289
Jourdanton city[6]	2 743	1 841
Pleasanton division	9 694	7 142
Pleasanton city[6]	6 346	5 407
Poteet division	8 847	6 025
Lytle city (pt.)	1 544	1 271
Poteet city[6]	3 086	3 013
Austin County[7]	17 726	13 831
Bellville division	5 834	4 724
Bellville city[7]	2 860	2 371
Sealy division	7 531	5 189
San Felipe town	532	422
Sealy city[7]	3 875	2 685
Wallis division	1 894	1 729
Wallis city[7]	1 138	...
West End division	2 467	2 189
Bailey County[8]	8 168	8 487
Muleshoe division	6 889	6 816
Muleshoe city[8]	4 842	4 525
South Sand Hills division	1 279	1 671
Bandera County[9]	7 084	4 747
Bandera division	5 650	3 365
Bandera city[9]	947	891
Medina division	1 434	1 382
Bastrop County[10]	24 726	17 297
Bastrop division	6 623	4 430
Bastrop city (pt.)[10]	3 603	3 112
Cedar Creek–Red Rock division	4 983	2 549
Bastrop city (pt.)[10]	186	...
Elgin division	7 752	5 927
Elgin city[10]	4 535	3 832
Smithville division	5 368	4 391
Smithville city[10]	3 470	2 959
Baylor County[11]	4 919	5 221
Seymour division	4 133	...
Seymour city[11]	3 657	3 469
Seymour Rural division	786	...

County Subdivisions	1980	1970
Bee County[12]	26 030	22 737
Beeville division	21 480	...
Beeville city[12]	14 574	13 506
Pettus–Pawnee division	2 483	2 329
Skidmore division	2 067	1 620
Bell County[13]	157 889	124 483
Belton division	13 748	...
Belton city (pt.)[13]	10 660	8 696
Temple city (pt.)	–	...
East Bell division	3 652	...
Troy town (pt.)[13]	1 316	542
Fort Hood division	19 172	...
Fort Hood (CDP) (pt.)	18 748	23 705
Killeen city (pt.)[13]	–	...
Killeen division	61 056	...
Harker Heights city[13]	7 345	4 216
Killeen city (pt.)[13]	46 296	35 507
Nolanville city[13]	1 308	902
Northwest Bell division	3 713	...
Belton city (pt.)[13]	–	...
Morgan's Point Resort city[13]	1 082	...
Temple city (pt.)[13]	9	...
Rogers division	1 941	1 627
Rogers town[13]	1 242	1 030
South Bell division	5 188	3 500
Bartlett city (pt.)[13]	696	586
Holland town	863	723
Salado (CDP)	1 035	...
Southwest Bell division	1 912	...
Temple division	47 507	...
Little River–Academy city[13]	1 155	...
Temple city (pt.)[13]	42 474	33 431
Troy town (pt.)[13]	37	...
Bexar County[14]	988 800	830 460
San Antonio division	970 336	...
Alamo Heights city	6 252	6 933
Balcones Heights city	2 556	2 504
Castle Hills city	4 773	5 311
China Grove city (pt.)	244	(NA)
Converse city[14]	4 907	1 383
Grey Forest city (pt.)	401	(NA)
Hill Country Village city[14]	972	636
Hollywood Park town[14]	3 231	2 299
Kirby city[14]	6 385	'3 238
Lackland AFB (CDP)	14 459	19 141
Leon Valley city[14]	8 951	'2 487
Live Oak city[14]	8 183	2 779
Olmos Park city	2 069	2 250
San Antonio city (pt.)[14]	785 861	654 153
Schertz city[14]	2	–
Selma city (pt.)[14]	283	207
Shavano Park town	1 448	881
Somerset city[14]	1 102	...
Terrell Hills city	4 644	5 225
Universal City city[14]	10 720	7 613
Windcrest city[14]	5 332	3 371
Southeast Bexar division	8 584	...
China Grove city (pt.)	190	(NA)
Elmendorf city[14]	492	400
San Antonio city (pt.)[14]	16	...
West Bexar division	9 880	...
Grey Forest city (pt.)[14]	41	(NA)
Lytle city (pt.)[14]	17	'27
San Antonio city (pt)[14]	3	...
Blanco County[15]	4 681	3 567
Blanco division	2 479	1 751
Blanco city[15]	1 179	1 022
Johnson City division	2 202	1 816
Johnson City city[15]	872	767
Borden County	859	888
Gail North division	384	399
Gail South division	475	489
Bosque County[16]	13 401	10 966
Clifton division	5 428	4 351
Clifton city[16]	3 063	2 578
Cranfills Gap division	753	691
Cranfills Gap city[16]	341	...
Iredell division	778	627
Iredell city[16]	407	316
Meridian division	4 738	...
Meridian city	1 330	1 162
Morgan city	485	415
Walnut Springs city	613	495
Valley Mills division	1 704	1 435
Valley Mills city (pt.)	1 226	1 002
Bowie County[17]	75 301	'68 909
Dalby Springs–Simms division	1 903	1 623
De Kalb division	5 736	6 046
De Kalb town[17]	2 217	2 197
Hooks division	5 014	5 131
Hooks city[17]	2 507	2 545
Leary city (pt.)	209	(NA)
New Boston city (pt.)[17]	–	...
Maud–Elliot Creek division	6 194	4 887
Maud city	1 059	1 107
Texarkana city (pt.)[17]	9	...

County Subdivisions

County Subdivisions	1980	1970
Bowie County—Con.		
New Boston division	6 910	ʳ6 327
New Boston town (pt.)[17]	4 628	ʳ4 034
Texarkana division	49 544	44 895
Leary city (pt.)	44	(NA)
Nash city[17]	2 022	1 961
Texarkana city (pt.)[17]	31 262	30 497
Wake Village city[17]	3 865	2 408
Brazoria County[18]	169 587	108 312
Alvin—Pearland division	57 576	...
Alvin city[18]	16 515	10 671
Brookside Village city[18]	1 453	1 507
Hillcrest village	771	ʳ650
Iowa Colony village (pt.)[18]	344	...
Liverpool village[18]	602	319
Manvel city[18]	3 549	106
Pearland city (pt.)[18]	12 461	6 444
Angleton—Rosharon division	31 942	...
Angleton city[18]	13 929	ʳ9 906
Baileys Prairie village	353	228
Bonney village[18]	94	...
Danbury city[18]	1 357	807
Iowa Colony village (pt.)[18]	241	...
Lake Jackson city (pt.)[18]	2	...
Brazoria—West Columbia division	28 036	18 339
Brazoria city[18]	3 025	1 681
Sweeny town[18]	3 538	3 191
West Columbia city[18]	4 109	3 335
Wild Peach Village (CDP)	2 385	...
Brazosport division	52 033	38 817
Clute city[18]	9 577	6 023
Freeport city[18]	13 444	11 997
Jones Creek village[18]	2 634	ʳ1 763
Lake Jackson city (pt.)[18]	19 100	13 376
Oyster Creek village[18]	1 473	...
Quintana town[18]	30	ʳ58
Richwood city[18]	2 591	1 452
Surfside Beach village[18]	577	...
Brazos County[19]	93 588	57 978
Bryan—College Station division	79 211	...
Bryan city (pt.)[19]	42 992	(NA)
College Station city (pt.)[19]	36 188	(NA)
Northeast Brazos division	4 286	...
Bryan city (pt.)[19]	686	(NA)
South Brazos division	5 477	...
Bryan city (pt.)[19]	437	(NA)
College Station city (pt.)[19]	928	(NA)
West Brazos division	4 614	...
Bryan city (pt.)[19]	222	(NA)
College Station city (pt.)[19]	156	(NA)
Brewster County[20]	7 573	7 780
Alpine division	6 859	...
Alpine city[20]	5 465	5 971
Marathon division	714	...
Briscoe County[21]	2 579	2 794
Quitaque division	971	910
Quitaque city[21]	696	601
Silverton division	1 608	1 884
Silverton city	918	1 026
Brooks County	8 428	8 005
Encino division	888	769
Falfurrias division	7 540	7 236
Falfurrias city	6 103	6 355
Brown County[22]	33 057	25 877
Bangs division	5 074	...
Bangs city[22]	1 716	1 214
Blanket division	2 028	...
Blanket town	388	346
Brownwood division	24 916	...
Brownwood city[22]	19 396	17 368
Early city[22]	2 313	1 097
May division	1 039	981
Burleson County[23]	12 313	9 999
Caldwell division	6 083	4 701
Caldwell city[23]	2 953	2 308
Cooks Point division	977	986
Old River division	2 123	2 170
Snook city[23]	408	...
Somerville division	3 130	2 142
Somerville city	1 814	1 250
Burnet County[24]	17 803	11 420
Bertram division	1 443	1 175
Bertram city[24]	824	...
Briggs division	727	626
Burnet division	7 154	5 027
Burnet town[24]	3 410	2 864
Marble Falls division	8 479	4 592
Granite Shoals city[24]	634	342
Marble Falls town[24]	3 252	2 209
Caldwell County[25]	23 637	21 178
Lockhart division	11 564	9 100
Lockhart city[25]	7 953	6 489
Luling division	6 526	6 025
Luling city[25]	5 039	4 719
Martindale division	5 547	6 053

County Subdivisions

County Subdivisions	1980	1970
Calhoun County[26]	19 574	17 831
Karney—Six Mile division	883	726
Point Comfort division	1 799	2 004
Point Comfort city[26]	1 125	1 446
Port Lavaca division	13 394	12 142
Port Lavaca city[26]	10 911	10 491
Seadrift division	3 498	2 959
Port O'Connor (CDP)	1 031	...
Seadrift city[26]	1 277	1 092
Callahan County[27]	10 992	8 205
Baird division	2 379	2 151
Baird city[27]	1 696	1 538
Putnam town	116	134
Clyde division	6 511	4 115
Clyde town[27]	2 562	1 635
Cross Plains division	2 102	1 939
Cross Plains town[27]	1 240	1 192
Cameron County[28]	209 727	140 368
Brownsville division	101 828	...
Brownsville city[28]	84 997	52 522
East Cameron division	7 994	...
Bayview town (pt.)[28]	148	(NA)
Laguna Vista village	632	287
Port Isabel city[28]	3 769	3 067
South Padre Island town[28]	791	...
Harlingen—San Benito division	89 070	...
Combes town[28]	1 488	689
Harlingen city[28]	43 543	33 503
La Feria city[28]	3 495	2 642
Primera town[28]	1 380	902
San Benito city[28]	17 988	15 176
Santa Rosa town	1 889	1 466
Los Fresnos—Laureles division	6 125	...
Bayview town (pt.)[28]	143	(NA)
Los Fresnos city[28]	2 173	1 297
Rio Hondo division	4 710	...
Rio Hondo town	1 673	1 167
Camp County[29]	9 275	8 005
Leesburg—Newsome division	1 041	869
Pittsburg division	8 234	7 136
Pittsburg city[29]	4 245	3 844
Rocky Mound town[29]	123	...
Carson County[30]	6 672	6 358
Panhandle division	3 164	...
Panhandle town[30]	2 226	2 141
White Deer—Groom division	3 508	...
Groom town	736	808
Skellytown town	899	716
White Deer town	1 210	1 092
Cass County[31]	29 430	24 133
Atlanta division	13 969	...
Atlanta city[31]	6 272	5 007
Bloomburg town	419	231
Domino town[31]	249	...
Queen City city[31]	1 748	1 227
Bivins—McLeod division	1 310	1 103
Hughes Springs—Avinger division	5 329	4 160
Avinger town	671	642
Hughes Springs city	2 196	1 701
Linden division	5 841	5 301
Linden city[31]	2 443	2 264
Marietta—Douglassville division	2 981	2 722
Douglassville town	228	282
Marietta city[31]	169	ʳ177
Castro County[32]	10 556	10 394
Dimmitt North division	7 071	...
Dimmitt city[32]	5 019	4 327
Nazareth city (pt.)[32]	272	...
Dimmitt South division	3 485	...
Hart city	1 008	ʳ905
Nazareth city (pt.)[32]	27	...
Chambers County[33]	18 538	12 187
Anahuac division[33]	5 905	4 546
Anahuac city	1 840	1 881
Seabrook city (pt.)[33]	–	...
Shoreacres city (pt.)[33]	–	...
Mont Belvieu division	7 700	3 609
Baytown city (pt.)[33]	6	...
Beach City city[33]	977	ʳ363
Cove town[33]	645	...
Mont Belvieu city[33]	1 730	1 144
Old River—Winfree city[33]	1 058	...
Winnie—Stowell division	4 933	4 032
Stowell (CDP)	1 498	...
Winnie (CDP)	2 496	1 543
Cherokee County[34]	38 127	32 008
Alto division	3 536	...
Alto town	1 203	1 045
Jacksonville division	18 091	...
Gallatin city (pt.)[34]	13	...
Jacksonville city[34]	12 264	9 734
Mount Selman division	2 098	...
Bullard town (pt.)[34]	59	27
New Summerfield division	3 100	...
New Summerfield city	319	344

Population of County Subdivisions

County Subdivisions	1980	1970
Cherokee County—Con.		
New Summerfield division—Con.		
Reklaw town (pt.)[34]	191	114
Troup city (pt.)[34]	64	62
Rusk division	9 627	...
Gallatin city (pt.)[34]	119	...
Rusk city[34]	4 681	4 914
Wells division	1 675	...
Wells town	926	671
Childress County	6 950	6 605
Childress division	6 819	6 405
Childress city	5 817	5 408
North River division	131	200
Clay County[35]	9 582	8 079
Bellevue—Joy division	1 528	1 399
Bellevue city	352	323
Scotland city (pt.)[35]	2	...
Windthorst town (pt.)[35]	8	...
Byers—Petrolia division	2 324	2 109
Byers city	556	553
Dean town (pt.)[35]	43	...
Petrolia city[35]	755	584
Henrietta division	5 730	4 571
Dean town (pt.)[35]	169	...
Henrietta city[35]	3 149	2 897
Jolly city[35]	174	...
Cochran County[36]	4 825	5 326
Morton division	4 034	4 604
Morton city[36]	2 674	2 738
Whiteface division	791	722
Whiteface town[36]	463	394
Coke County[37]	3 196	3 087
Bronte division	1 529	1 439
Blackwell town (pt.)	21	13
Bronte town[37]	983	925
Robert Lee division	1 667	1 648
Robert Lee city[37]	1 202	1 119
Coleman County[38]	10 439	10 288
Coleman division	6 802	6 710
Coleman city[38]	5 960	5 608
Novice division	630	558
Novice city	201	191
Santa Anna division	2 156	2 066
Santa Anna town	1 535	1 310
Talpa division	851	954
Talpa town	122	121
Collin County[39]	144 576	66 920
Anna division	4 213	3 180
Altoga town (pt.)[39]	128	...
Anna city	855	736
McKinney city (pt.)[39]	9	...
Melissa town[39]	604	...
New Hope town (pt.)[39]	99	...
Weston town (pt.)[39]	393	...
Blue Ridge division[39]	2 799	1 993
Altoga town (pt.)[39]	15	...
Blue Ridge town[39]	442	384
Westminster town[39]	278	257
Celina division	3 643	2 972
Celina town[39]	1 520	1 272
McKinney city (pt.)[39]	—	...
Prosper town[39]	675	501
Weston town (pt.)[39]	12	...
Farmersville division[39]	4 339	...
Farmersville city[39]	2 360	2 311
McKinney division[39]	21 232	...
Fairview town[39]	241	(NA)
Frisco city (pt.)[39]	3 414	1 845
McKinney city (pt.)[39]	16 247	15 193
Nevada division	1 901	...
Dallas city (pt.)[39]	—	...
Garland city (pt.)[39]	—	...
Josephine town[39]	416	296
Lavon town[39]	185	...
Royse City city (pt.)[39]	172	244
Plano division	101 253	...
Allen city[39]	8 314	1 940
Carrollton city (pt.)[39]	—	...
Dallas city (pt.)[39]	1 357	...
Fairview town[39]	652	(NA)
Garland city (pt.)[39]	—	...
Lowry Crossing town (pt.)[39]	106	...
Lucas town[39]	1 371	540
Murphy city[39]	1 150	261
Parker city[39]	1 098	367
Plano city (pt.)[39]	72 329	17 872
Richardson city (pt.)[39]	6 780	2 393
Sachse city (pt.)[39]	29	6
St. Paul town[39]	363	...
Wylie city[39]	3 152	2 675
Princeton division	5 196	3 276
Altoga town (pt.)[39]	126	...
Lowry Crossing town (pt.)[39]	337	...
McKinney city (pt.)[39]	—	...
New Hope town (pt.)[39]	232	...
Princeton town[39]	3 408	1 105

County Subdivisions	1980	1970
Collingsworth County[40]	4 648	4 755
Samnorwood division	433	568
Wellington division	4 215	4 187
Dodson town	185	239
Wellington city[40]	3 043	2 884
Colorado County[41]	18 823	17 638
Columbus division	7 358	...
Columbus city[41]	3 923	3 342
Eagle Lake division	5 211	...
Eagle Lake city[41]	3 921	3 587
Garwood division	2 379	2 465
Weimar division	3 875	...
Weimar city[41]	2 128	2 104
Comal County[42]	36 446	24 165
Comal North division	8 602	...
New Braunfels division	27 844	...
Garden Ridge city[42]	647	...
New Braunfels city (pt.)[42]	22 375	17 859
Schertz city (pt.)[42]	26	...
Selma city (pt.)[42]	88	...
Comanche County[43]	12 617	11 898
Comanche division	6 816	6 480
Comanche city[43]	4 075	3 933
De Leon division	4 284	3 919
De Leon city[43]	2 478	2 170
Gustine division	1 517	1 499
Gustine town	416	357
Concho County	2 915	2 937
Eden—Millersview division	1 963	1 953
Eden city	1 294	1 291
Eola—Paint Rock division	952	984
Paint Rock town	256	193
Cooke County[44]	27 656	23 471
Callisburg division	3 352	...
Callisburg town[44]	281	...
Gainesville division	15 200	...
Gainesville city (pt.)[44]	14 077	13 830
Gainesville Southeast division	2 552	...
Muenster division	4 026	...
Gainesville city (pt.)[44]	4	...
Lindsay town[44]	581	435
Muenster city[44]	1 408	1 411
Valley View division	2 526	...
Valley View town[44]	514	...
Coryell County[45]	56 767	35 311
Copperas Cove division	21 151	...
Copperas Cove city[45]	19 469	10 818
Evant division	1 021	950
Evant town (pt.)[45]	356	...
Flat division	696	702
Fort Hood division	22 478	...
Fort Hood (CDP) (pt.)	12 502	8 892
Montague Village (CDP)	1 253	1 265
Gatesville division	8 659	...
Fort Gates city[45]	777	363
Gatesville city[45]	6 260	4 683
North Coryell division	857	...
Oglesby division	1 138	1 077
Oglesby city[45]	470	440
Turnersville division	767	780
Cottle County[46]	2 947	3 204
Paducah North division	2 608	...
Paducah town	2 216	2 052
Paducah South division	339	...
Crane County[47]	4 600	4 172
Crane North division	291	...
Crane South division	4 309	...
Crane city[47]	3 622	3 427
Crockett County	4 608	3 885
East Crockett division	4 385	3 570
Ozona (CDP)	3 766	2 864
West Crockett division	223	315
Crosby County[48]	8 859	9 085
Crosbyton division	3 215	3 345
Crosbyton city[48]	2 289	2 251
Lorenzo division	2 132	2 203
Lorenzo town[48]	1 394	1 206
Ralls division	3 512	3 537
Ralls city[48]	2 422	1 962
Culberson County[49]	3 315	3 429
Van Horn division	2 851	...
Van Horn town[49]	2 772	2 889
Van Horn Rural division	464	...
Dallam County[50]	6 531	6 012
Dalhart division	5 936	5 351
Dalhart city (pt.)[50]	4 571	4 340
Texline division	595	661
Texline town	477	387
Dallas County[51]	1 556 390	1 327 695
Northeast division	993 654	...
Addison city[51]	5 553	593
Balch Springs city[51]	13 746	10 464

County Subdivisions	1980	1970
Dallas County—Con.		
Northeast division—Con.		
Buckingham town[51]	159	'218
Carrollton city (pt.)[51]	26 853	13 855
Combine city (pt.)[51]	128	'30
Dallas city (pt.)[51]	597 280	(NA)
Farmers Branch city[51]	24 863	27 492
Garland city (pt.)[51]	138 857	81 437
Highland Park town[51]	8 909	10 133
Irving city (pt.)[51]	–	–
Mesquite city[51]	67 053	55 131
Richardson city (pt.)[51]	65 716	'46 012
Rowlett city (pt.)[51]	6 348	'2 189
Sachse city[51]	1 611	771
Seagoville city (pt.)[51]	7 298	4 390
Sunnyvale town[51]	1 404	995
University Park city[51]	22 254	23 498
Southwest division	562 736	...
Carrollton city (pt.)[51]	–	...
Cedar Hill city (pt.)[51]	6 847	2 610
Cockrell Hill city	3 262	3 515
Coppell city (pt.)[51]	3 826	1 728
Dallas city (pt.)[51]	305 339	(NA)
De Soto city[51]	15 538	6 617
Duncanville city[51]	27 781	14 105
Ferris city (pt.)[51]	–	25
Glenn Heights city (pt.)[51]	1 008	'257
Grand Prairie city (pt.)[51]	65 726	47 731
Grapevine city (pt.)[51]	39	...
Hutchins city[51]	2 837	1 755
Irving city (pt.)[51]	109 943	97 260
Lancaster city[51]	14 807	10 522
Ovilla city (pt.)[51]	45	–
Wilmer city[51]	2 367	1 922
Dawson County[52]	16 184	16 604
Lamesa division	12 593	...
Lamesa city[52]	11 790	11 559
Lamesa Northeast division	651	...
O'Donnell city (pt.)	124	131
Lamesa Northwest division	963	...
Lamesa Southeast division	1 169	...
Ackerly city (pt.)	225	240
Lamesa Southwest division	808	...
Deaf Smith County[53]	21 165	18 999
Hereford East division	19 666	...
Hereford city[53]	15 853	13 414
Hereford West division	1 499	...
Delta County[54]	4 839	4 927
Cooper division	3 617	3 549
Cooper city[54]	2 338	2 258
Pecan Gap division	1 222	1 378
Pecan Gap city (pt.)[54]	234	270
Denton County[55]	143 126	75 633
Colony division	12 785	...
Eastvale town[55]	503	...
Frisco city (pt.)[55]	85	...
Lewisville city (pt.)[55]	2	...
Little Elm town (pt.)[55]	–	...
The Colony city (pt.)[55]	11 586	...
Denton division	50 354	...
Corinth town (pt.)[55]	–	...
Denton city (pt.)[55]	47 730	39 874
Krum city (pt.)[55]	19	...
Hebron division	14 376	...
Carrollton city (pt.)[55]	13 741	...
Dallas city (pt.)[55]	101	...
Hebron town[55]	385	...
Lewisville city (pt.)[55]	–	...
Plano city (pt.)[55]	2	...
The Colony city (pt.)	–	...
Justin–Roanoke division	8 763	...
Argyle city[55]	1 111	443
Bartonville city[55]	420	...
Corral City town[55]	85	...
Denton city (pt.)[55]	30	...
Double Oak town (pt.)[55]	16	...
Flower Mound town (pt.)[55]	987	(NA)
Justin city[55]	920	741
Northlake town[55]	143	20
Ponder town[55]	297	208
Roanoke city	910	817
Southlake city (pt.)	16	3
Westlake town (pt.)[55]	64	93
Lewisville division	41 820	...
Bartonville city (pt.)[55]	21	...
Carrollton city (pt.)[55]	1	–
Coppell city (pt.)[55]	–	...
Copper Canyon town[55]	465	...
Corinth town (pt.)[55]	1 264	461
Denton city (pt.)[55]	303	...
Double Oak town (pt.)[55]	820	...
Flower Mound town (pt.)[55]	3 415	(NA)
Hickory Creek town[55]	1 422	218
Highland Village city[55]	3 246	516
Lake Dallas city[55]	3 177	1 431
Lewisville city (pt.)[55]	24 271	9 264
Shady Shores town[55]	813	543
Pilot Point–Aubrey division	8 342	'5 732

County Subdivisions	1980	1970
Denton County—Con.		
Pilot Point–Aubrey division—Con.		
Aubrey town[55]	948	731
Cross Roads town[55]	302	...
Denton city (pt.)[55]	–	...
Frisco city (pt.)[55]	–	...
Krugerville city[55]	469	...
Lakewood Village city[55]	165	...
Lincoln Park town[55]	39	...
Little Elm town (pt.)[55]	926	'363
Oak Point town[55]	387	...
Pilot Point town[55]	2 211	1 663
Sanger division	6 686	3 838
Krum city (pt.)[55]	898	454
Sanger city[55]	2 574	1 603
De Witt County[56]	18 903	18 660
Cuero division	8 381	8 092
Cuero city[56]	7 124	6 956
Westhoff–Arneckville division	1 861	1 886
Yoakum division	3 950	4 029
Yoakum city (pt.)[56]	2 325	2 456
Yorktown division	4 711	4 653
Nordheim city	369	369
Yorktown city[56]	2 498	2 411
Dickens County[57]	3 539	3 737
Dickens division	1 353	1 402
Dickens city[57]	409	295
Spur division	2 186	2 335
Spur city[57]	1 690	1 747
Dimmit County[58]	11 367	9 039
Asherton division	1 989	2 065
Asherton city	1 574	1 645
Big Wells division	1 070	874
Big Wells city	939	711
Carrizo Springs division	8 308	6 100
Carrizo Springs city[58]	6 886	5 374
Donley County[59]	4 075	3 641
Clarendon division	3 172	2 668
Clarendon city	2 220	1 974
Howardwick city[59]	165	...
Hedley division	903	973
Hedley town	380	439
Duval County[60]	12 517	11 722
Benavides division	2 756	2 866
Benavides city[60]	1 978	'1 841
Freer division	3 924	3 460
Freer city[60]	3 213	...
Realitos–Concepcion division	1 225	1 297
San Diego division	4 612	4 099
San Diego city (pt.)[60]	4 331	3 759
Eastland County[61]	19 480	18 092
Cisco division	5 479	5 170
Cisco city[61]	4 517	4 160
Eastland division	5 509	4 748
Eastland city[61]	3 747	3 178
Gorman division	2 622	2 548
Carbon town	281	264
Gorman city	1 258	1 236
Ranger division	3 689	3 578
Ranger city[61]	3 142	3 094
Rising Star division	2 181	2 048
Rising Star town	1 204	1 009
Ector County[62]	115 374	'92 660
Goldsmith–Penwell division	11 430	5 055
Goldsmith city	409	387
Odessa division	103 944	...
Odessa city[62]	90 027	78 380
Edwards County	2 033	2 107
Rocksprings North division	1 491	1 445
Rocksprings town	1 317	1 221
Rocksprings South division	542	662
Ellis County[63]	59 743	46 638
Ennis division	16 236	...
Alma town[63]	171	...
Ennis city[63]	12 110	11 046
Garrett town	220	225
Rice city (pt.)[63]	7	...
Ferris division	5 781	4 585
Ferris city (pt.)[63]	2 228	2 155
Palmer town[63]	1 187	601
Italy division	3 021	2 918
Italy town[63]	1 306	1 309
Milford town	681	664
Maypearl division	1 994	1 258
Maypearl city[63]	626	462
Midlothian division	6 154	3 461
Cedar Hill city (pt.)[63]	2	...
Grand Prairie city (pt.)[63]	5	...
Midlothian city (pt.)[63]	3 202	2 322
Waxahachie division	26 557	...
Bardwell city	335	277
Glenn Heights city (pt.)[63]	25	(NA)
Midlothian city (pt.)[63]	17	...
Ovilla city (pt.)[63]	1 022	339
Red Oak city[63]	1 882	767

County Subdivisions

County Subdivisions	1980	1970
Ellis County—Con.		
Waxahachie division—Con.		
Waxahachie city[63]	14 624	13 452
El Paso County[64]	479 899	359 291
El Paso division	425 502	
El Paso city (pt.)[64]	424 114	322 261
El Paso East division	24 954	...
Clint town[64]	1 314	...
El Paso city (pt.)[64]	160	...
Fabens (CDP)	4 285	3 241
Horizon City (CDP)	1 956	...
San Elizario (CDP)	1 548	...
El Paso North Central division	16 070	...
El Paso city (pt.)[64]	—	...
Fort Bliss (CDP)	12 687	13 288
El Paso Northwest division	13 373	...
Anthony town[64]	2 640	2 154
El Paso city (pt.)[64]	985	...
Erath County[65]	22 560	18 141
Dublin division	3 963	3 896
Dublin city[65]	2 723	2 810
Morgan Mill—Bluff Dale division	1 453	1 168
Stephenville division	15 917	12 077
Stephenville city[65]	11 881	9 277
Stephenville South division	1 227	1 000
Falls County[66]	17 946	17 300
Chilton division	2 175	2 024
Bruceville—Eddy city (pt.)[66]	9	...
Golinda city (pt.)[66]	292	...
Lott division	1 955	1 786
Lott city[66]	865	799
Marlin division	8 699	8 640
Marlin city[66]	7 099	6 351
Perry division	777	798
Reagan division	881	957
Rosebud division	3 459	3 095
Rosebud city[66]	2 076	1 597
Fannin County[67]	24 285	22 705
Bonham division	9 348	9 233
Bonham city[67]	7 338	7 698
Dodd City division	1 365	1 384
Dodd City town	286	302
Windom town	276	247
Ector division	2 262	2 067
Ector town	573	549
Savoy city	855	756
Whitewright town (pt.)	—	...
Honey Grove division	2 969	2 841
Honey Grove city[67]	1 973	1 853
Ladonia division	1 040	1 122
Ladonia town[67]	761	757
Pecan Gap city (pt.)[67]	16	'21
Leonard division	4 200	3 659
Bailey city	185	197
Leonard city	1 421	1 423
Trenton town	691	599
Whitewright town (pt.)[67]	9	'3
Ravenna—Telephone division	3 101	2 399
Fayette County[68]	18 832	17 650
Fayetteville division	1 874	1 887
Fayetteville town	356	400
Flatonia division	2 809	2 969
Flatonia town[68]	1 070	1 108
La Grange division	5 793	4 793
La Grange city[68]	3 768	3 092
La Grange West division	2 596	2 106
Round Top division	1 598	1 693
Carmine city[68]	239	...
Round Top town	87	94
Schulenburg division	4 162	4 202
Schulenburg city[68]	2 469	2 294
Fisher County	5 891	6 344
McCaulley division	403	507
Hamlin city (pt.)	—	3
Roby division	2 369	2 495
Roby city	814	784
Rotan division	3 119	3 342
Rotan city	2 284	2 404
Floyd County[69]	9 834	11 044
Floydada division	5 779	6 436
Floydada city[69]	4 193	4 109
Lockney division	4 055	4 608
Lockney town	2 334	2 094
Foard County[70]	2 158	2 211
Crowell division	1 875	
Crowell city	1 509	1 399
Thalia division	283	
Fort Bend County[71]	130 846	52 314
Fulshear—Simonton division	5 268	3 587
Fulshear town[71]	594	...
Houston city (pt.)[71]	14	...
Katy city (pt.)	517	579
Simonton village[71]	603	...
Needville division	6 004	...

County Subdivisions	1980	1970
Fort Bend County—Con.		
Needville division—Con.		
Needville city[71]	1 417	1 024
Pleak village (pt.)[71]	148	...
Orchard—Kendleton division	2 983	...
Kendleton town[71]	606	...
Orchard town[71]	408	...
Richmond division	14 025	...
Richmond town[71]	9 692	5 777
Rosenberg city (pt.)[71]	1 582	...
Thompsons town[71]	240	...
Rosenberg division	20 117	...
Beasley town[71]	410	...
Pleak village (pt.)[71]	217	...
Rosenberg city (pt.)[71]	16 413	12 098
Stafford—Missouri City division	49 916	10 038
Houston city (pt.)[71]	15 399	53
Missouri City city (pt.)[71]	20 261	963
Stafford town (pt.)	3 327	2 845
Sugar Land city (pt.)[71]	—	...
Sugar Land division	32 533	...
Houston city (pt.)[71]	857	...
Missouri City city (pt.)[71]	336	...
Stafford town (pt.)	1 199	...
Sugar Land city (pt.)[71]	8 826	3 318
Franklin County[72]	6 893	5 291
Mount Vernon division	5 128	3 756
Mount Vernon town[72]	2 025	1 806
Winnsboro division	1 765	1 535
Winnsboro city (pt.)[72]	862	855
Freestone County[73]	14 830	11 116
Butler division	1 452	1 347
Fairfield division	5 524	...
Fairfield city[73]	3 505	2 074
Teague division	5 725	...
Teague city[73]	3 390	2 867
Wortham division	2 129	1 778
Kirvin town	107	65
Streetman town (pt.)[73]	396	271
Wortham town[73]	1 187	1 036
Frio County[74]	13 785	11 159
Dilley division	3 193	2 892
Dilley city[74]	2 579	2 362
Moore division	1 114	1 076
Pearsall division	9 478	7 191
Pearsall city[74]	7 383	5 545
Gaines County[75]	13 150	11 593
Seagraves division	4 106	4 157
Seagraves city	2 596	2 440
Seminole division	9 044	7 436
Seminole city[75]	6 080	5 007
Galveston County[76]	195 940	169 812
Bolivar Peninsula division	2 670	2 424
Crystal Beach city[76]	776	...
Texas City city (pt.)[76]	4	...
Galveston division	62 395	...
Galveston city[76]	61 902	61 809
Hitchcock city (pt.)[76]	—	(NA)
Jamaica Beach village[76]	365	...
La Marque—Hitchcock division	21 829	...
Highland Bayou (CDP)	1 163	...
Hitchcock city (pt.)[76]	4 987	(NA)
La Marque city (pt.)	15 207	16 131
Santa Fe city (pt.)[76]	172	...
Texas City—League City division	109 046	...
Bacliff (CDP)	4 851	...
Clear Lake Shores city[76]	755	'721
Dickinson village[76]	7 505	...
Friendswood city (pt.)[76]	10 719	5 675
Hitchcock city (pt.)[76]	1 668	(NA)
Kemah city[76]	1 304	1 144
La Marque city (pt.)	165	...
League City city[76]	16 578	10 818
San Leon (CDP)	1 745	...
Santa Fe city (pt.)[76]	6 000	...
Seabrook city (pt.)[76]	—	'_
Texas City city (pt.)[76]	41 399	38 908
Garza County[27]	5 336	5 289
Post Northwest division	1 081	1 162
Post Southeast division	4 255	4 127
Post city	3 961	3 854
Gillespie County[78]	13 532	10 553
Fredericksburg division	9 884	...
Fredericksburg town[78]	6 412	5 326
Fredericksburg East division	2 099	...
Harper division	1 549	1 107
Glasscock County	1 304	1 155
Garden City North division	581	594
Garden City South division	723	561
Goliad County[79]	5 193	4 869
Goliad North division	3 475	3 148
Goliad city[79]	1 990	1 709
Goliad South division	713	941
Weesatche—Ander division	1 005	780

County Subdivisions	1980	1970
Gonzales County[80]	16 883	16 375
Gonzales division	8 732	...
Gonzales city[80]	7 152	5 854
Gonzales Northwest division	1 629	...
Gonzales Southwest division	964	1 064
Nixon division	3 246	3 039
Nixon city (pt.)	2 008	1 925
Smiley division	988	1 108
Smiley city	439	440
Waelder division	1 324	1 605
Waelder city	942	1 138
Gray County[81]	26 386	26 949
McLean division	1 608	1 656
McLean town	1 160	1 183
Pampa division	22 981	...
Pampa city[81]	21 396	21 726
Pampa East division	1 797	...
Lefors town[81]	829	816
Grayson County[82]	89 796	83 225
East Grayson division	72 364	...
Bells town[82]	846	778
Denison city (pt.)[82]	23 813	24 923
Howe town (pt.)[82]	2 072	1 359
Luella town[82]	371	...
Sherman city (pt.)[82]	30 354	29 061
Tom Bean town[82]	811	540
Van Alstyne town[82]	1 860	1 981
Whitewright town (pt.)	1 751	1 742
Northwest Grayson division	12 562	...
Denison city (pt.)[82]	71	...
Pottsboro town[82]	895	748
Sadler city[82]	329	309
Sherman city (pt.)[82]	59	...
Southmayd town (pt.)[82]	304	222
Whitesboro city[82]	3 197	2 927
Southwest Grayson division	4 870	3 624
Collinsville town[82]	860	768
Dorchester town[82]	205	...
Gunter town	849	647
Howe town (pt.)[82]	–	...
Sherman city (pt.)[82]	–	–
Southmayd town (pt.)[32]	14	...
Tioga town[82]	511	456
Gregg County[83]	99 487	75 929
Gladewater division	7 258	...
Clarksville City city (pt.)	525	398
Gladewater city (pt.)	4 311	4 300
Warren City city (pt.)	279	146
White Oak city (pt.)[83]	1 474	2 300
Kilgore division	10 471	...
Kilgore city (pt.)[83]	8 321	7 275
Rolling Meadows city[83]	252	...
Longview division	68 917	...
Longview city (pt.)[83]	60 889	45 547
White Oak city (pt.)[83]	2 926	...
Longview Northwest division	3 439	...
Longview city (pt.)[83]	196	...
White Oak city (pt.)[83]	15	...
Longview South division	4 678	...
Easton city (pt.)	265	255
Lakeport city	835	411
Liberty City city[83]	1 121	...
Sabine division	4 724	...
Kilgore city (pt.)[83]	104	...
Grimes County[84]	13 580	11 855
Anderson–Bedias division	4 211	...
Navasota division	9 369	...
Navasota city[84]	5 971	5 111
Guadalupe County[85]	46 708	33 554
Marion division	5 366	2 633
Cibolo city (pt.)[85]	28	...
McQueeney (CDP) (pt.)	916	...
Marion city[85]	674	655
Schertz city (pt.)[85]	–	...
Schertz–Cibolo division	8 222	...
Cibolo city (pt.)[85]	521	440
Schertz city (pt.)[85]	7 234	4 061
Selma city (pt.)[85]	157	...
Seguin division	17 853	...
Seguin city (pt.)[85]	17 766	15 934
Seguin East division	3 165	...
Seguin North division	5 376	...
McQueeney (CDP) (pt.)	180	...
New Braunfels city (pt.)[85]	27	...
Seguin city (pt.)[85]	41	...
Seguin Southwest division	6 726	...
McQueeney (CDP) (pt.)	236	...
New Berlin city[85]	253	...
Seguin city (pt.)[85]	47	...
Hale County[86]	37 592	34 137
Abernathy division	3 537	3 446
Abernathy city (pt.)[86]	2 205	1 921
Hale Center division	3 719	3 667
Hale Center city	2 297	1 964
Petersburg division	2 259	2 153
Petersburg town	1 633	1 300
Plainview division	28 077	...

County Subdivisions	1980	1970
Hale County—Con.		
Plainview division—Con.		
Edmonson town	291	99
Plainview city[86]	22 187	19 096
Seth Ward (CDP)	1 186	...
Hall County[87]	5 594	6 015
Estelline division	518	663
Estelline town	258	301
Lakeview division	645	780
Lakeview town[87]	244	214
Memphis division	3 638	3 626
Memphis city	3 352	3 227
Turkey division	793	946
Turkey city[87]	644	680
Hamilton County[88]	8 297	7 198
Hamilton division	6 024	5 327
Evant town (pt.)[88]	69	...
Hamilton city[88]	3 189	2 760
Hico division	2 273	1 871
Hico city	1 375	975
Hansford County[89]	6 209	6 351
Gruver division	2 184	2 344
Gruver city[89]	1 216	1 265
Spearman division	4 025	4 007
Spearman city[89]	3 413	3 435
Hardeman County[90]	6 368	6 795
Chillicothe division	1 496	1 720
Chillicothe city	1 052	1 116
Goodlett division	300	373
Quanah division	4 572	4 702
Quanah city[90]	3 890	3 948
Hardin County[91]	40 721	29 996
Chance–Loeb division	9 808	...
Lumberton city (pt.)[91]	2 472	...
Rose Hill Acres city	460	431
Kountze division	6 844	...
Kountze city[91]	2 716	ʳ2 173
Lumberton city (pt.)[91]	8	...
Saratoga–Batson division	3 182	2 483
Silsbee division	16 832	...
Silsbee city[91]	7 684	7 271
Sour Lake division	4 055	3 230
Grayburg city[91]	194	(NA)
Sour Lake city	1 807	1 694
Harris County[92]	2 409 547	1 741 912
Baytown division	62 594	...
Baytown city (pt.)[92]	56 917	43 980
Houston city (pt.)[92]	80	...
Houston division	1 994 880	...
Aldine (CDP)	12 623	...
Bellaire city[92]	14 950	19 009
Bunker Hill Village city	3 750	3 977
Channelview (CDP)	17 471	...
Cloverleaf (CDP)	17 317	...
Friendswood city (pt.)[92]	–	...
Galena Park city	9 879	10 479
Hedwig Village city	2 506	3 255
Hilshire Village city	621	627
Houston city (pt.)[92]	1 574 602	ʳ1 233 473
Humble city[92]	6 729	ʳ3 272
Hunters Creek Village city	4 215	3 959
Jacinto City city[92]	8 953	9 563
Jersey Village city[92]	4 084	765
Katy city (pt.)[92]	4 475	2 017
Kingwood (CDP) (pt.)	16 094	...
Missouri City city (pt.)[92]	3 936	3 173
Nassau Bay city[92]	4 526	...
Pasadena city (pt.)[92]	9	...
Pearland city[92]	787	...
Piney Point Village city	2 958	2 548
Sheldon (CDP)	2 031	1 665
South Houston city	13 293	11 527
Southside Place city	1 366	1 466
Spring Valley city	3 353	3 170
Stafford town (pt.)	229	61
Webster city[92]	2 405	2 231
West University Place city	12 010	13 317
Northeast Harris division	30 179	...
Barrett (CDP)	3 183	2 750
Crosby (CDP)	1 533	1 118
Highlands (CDP)	6 467	3 462
Houston city (pt.)[92]	2 973	...
Northwest Harris division[92]	150 842	...
Champions (CDP)	14 692	...
Tomball city	3 996	2 734
Waller city (pt.)	164	131
Pasadena division	111 107	...
Houston city (pt.)[92]	1 106	...
Pasadena city (pt.)[92]	109 996	ʳ89 957
Southeast Harris division	59 945	...
Deer Park city[92]	22 648	12 773
El Lago city[92]	3 129	ʳ2 308
Houston city (pt.)[92]	88	...
La Porte city[92]	14 062	7 149
Lomax city[92]	2 991	894
Morgan's Point city	428	593
Pasadena city (pt.)[92]	2 555	...
Seabrook city (pt.)[92]	4 670	3 811

County Subdivisions

County Subdivisions	1980	1970
Harris County—Con.		
Southeast Harris division—Con.		
Shoreacres city (pt.)[92]	1 260	1 872
Taylor Lake Village city[92]	3 669	²990
Harrison County[93]	52 265	44 841
Hallsville division	11 314	...
Hallsville city	1 556	1 038
Longview city (pt.)[93]	1 677	...
Harleton division	4 110	...
Nesbitt city	129	²74
Marshall division	26 595	...
Marshall city (pt.)[93]	24 192	22 937
Waskom division	10 246	...
Marshall city (pt.)[93]	729	...
Scottsville city	245	259
Uncertain city	176	202
Waskom[93]	1 821	1 460
Hartley County[94]	3 987	2 782
Channing division	866	875
Channing city	304	336
Northwest Hartley division	3 121	1 907
Dalhart city (pt.)[94]	2 283	1 365
Haskell County[95]	7 725	8 512
Haskell division	4 549	4 598
Haskell city	3 782	3 655
Stamford city (pt.)[95]	21	130
Rochester division	1 171	1 549
O'Brien city	212	258
Rochester town	492	529
Rule division	1 269	1 415
Rule town	1 015	1 024
Sagerton division	389	503
Stamford city (pt.)[95]	24	...
Weinert division	347	447
Weinert city	253	255
Hays County[96]	40 594	27 642
Dripping Springs–Wimberly division	6 105	2 329
Kyle–Buda division	6 675	3 937
Buda city[96]	597	498
Hays city[96]	286	...
Kyle town[96]	2 093	1 629
San Marcos division	27 814	...
San Marcos city[96]	23 420	18 860
Hemphill County[97]	5 304	3 084
Canadian North division	3 896	2 393
Canadian town (pt.)[97]	3 434	2 292
Canadian South division	1 408	691
Canadian town (pt.)[97]	57	...
Henderson County[98]	42 606	26 466
Athens division	16 978	13 607
Athens city[98]	10 197	9 582
Murchison town	513	432
Brownsboro division	5 265	3 031
Brownsboro city[98]	582	474
Chandler town[98]	1 308	765
Coffee City town (pt.)[98]	—	...
Eustace–Malakoff division	16 608	...
Caney City town[98]	312	²117
Enchanted Oaks town[98]	212	...
Eustace city	541	491
Gun Barrel City town[98]	2 118	²327
Mabank town (pt.)[98]	156	...
Malakoff city[98]	2 082	2 045
Payne Springs town[98]	422	...
Seven Points town[98]	647	²186
Star Harbor town[98]	310	...
Tool city[98]	1 591	²258
Trinidad city[98]	1 130	1 079
La Rue–Poynor division	3 755	1 892
Berryville town[98]	513	...
Coffee City town (pt.)[98]	254	²157
Moore Station city[98]	335	...
Poynor town[98]	272	...
Hidalgo County[99]	283 229	181 535
Edcouch–Elsa division	15 289	12 545
Edcouch city[99]	3 092	2 656
Elsa city[99]	5 061	4 400
La Villa city[99]	1 442	1 255
Monte Alto (CDP)	1 319	...
Edinburg division	40 188	...
Edinburg city[99]	24 075	17 163
McAllen city (pt.)[99]	88	...
Hargill division	1 355	1 136
Hargill (CDP)	1 030	...
McAllen–Pharr division	120 296	...
Alamo city[99]	5 831	4 291
Hidalgo city[99]	2 288	1 289
Las Milpas–Hidalgo Park (CDP)	3 039	...
McAllen city (pt.)[99]	66 191	37 636
Mission city (pt.)[99]	—	...
Pharr city[99]	21 381	15 829
San Juan city[99]	7 608	5 070
Mission division	35 329	...
Alton city[99]	2 732	...
McAllen city (pt.)[99]	2	...
Mission city (pt.)[99]	22 589	13 043

County Subdivisions

County Subdivisions	1980	1970
Hidalgo County—Con.		
Mission division—Con.		
Palmhurst city	364	120
Palmview city (pt.)[99]	674	...
Puerto Rico–San Manuel division	1 148	1 027
Southeast Hidalgo division	62 171	...
Donna city	9 952	7 365
Mercedes city[99]	11 851	9 355
Progreso (CDP)	1 456	...
Weslaco city[99]	19 331	15 313
Sullivan division	7 453	4 790
La Joya city	2 018	1 217
Palmview city (pt.)[99]	9	...
Hill County[100]	25 024	22 596
Blum division	2 128	...
Blum town	357	382
Hillsboro division	11 080	...
Abbott city	359	375
Bynum town[100]	232	...
Hillsboro city[100]	7 397	7 224
Mertens town	133	109
Hubbard–Mount Calm division	2 618	2 413
Hubbard city[100]	1 676	1 572
Mount Calm city	393	363
Itasca division	2 921	...
Covington city[100]	259	...
Itasca city[100]	1 600	1 483
Malone–Penelope division	1 145	1 263
Malone town	315	305
Penelope town	235	212
Whitney division	5 132	3 257
Aquilla city[100]	130	²115
Whitney town[100]	1 631	1 371
Hockley County[101]	23 230	20 396
Anton division	1 662	1 565
Anton city[101]	1 180	1 034
Levelland division	18 132	15 503
Levelland city[101]	13 809	11 445
Smyer town	455	265
Ropesville division	1 556	1 713
Ropesville city	489	483
Sundown division	1 880	1 615
Sundown city[101]	1 511	1 129
Hood County[102]	17 714	6 368
Granbury East division	13 968	...
Granbury city (pt.)[102]	3 322	2 473
Granbury West division	3 746	...
Granbury city (pt.)[102]	10	...
Lipan city	435	333
Tolar city	415	312
Hopkins County[103]	25 247	20 710
Cumby division	2 629	2 344
Cumby city	647	628
North Hopkins–Sulphur Bluff division	1 707	1 461
Tira town[103]	249	...
Pickton–Pine Forest division	3 320	2 647
Como town[103]	554	474
Seymour division	2 033	1 404
Sulphur Springs division	15 558	12 854
Sulphur Springs city[103]	12 804	10 642
Houston County[104]	22 299	17 855
Crockett division	10 066	...
Crockett city[104]	7 405	6 616
Latexo city[104]	312	...
Grapeland division	4 359	...
Grapeland city[104]	1 634	1 211
Kennard–Ratcliff division	1 495	1 248
Kennard city[104]	424	²448
Lovelady division	4 964	2 861
Lovelady city[104]	509	388
Porter Springs division	1 415	1 496
Howard County[105]	33 142	37 796
Big Spring division	29 238	...
Big Spring city[105]	24 804	28 735
Forsan city[105]	239	237
Big Spring North division	1 523	...
Coahoma division	2 381	2 480
Coahoma town[105]	1 069	1 158
Hudspeth County[106]	2 728	2 392
Dell City division	1 094	943
Dell City city[106]	495	383
Fort Hancock division	857	804
Sierra Blanca division	777	645
Hunt County[107]	55 248	47 948
Caddo Mills division	2 220	1 936
Caddo Mills city[107]	1 060	935
Celeste division	1 938	1 864
Celeste city	716	736
Commerce division	9 670	10 890
Commerce city[107]	8 136	9 534
Greenville division	27 481	...
Greenville city[107]	22 161	22 043
Neylandville town[107]	168	...
Lone Oak division	2 641	2 228
Campbell town[107]	549	...
Lone Oak town	467	518

County Subdivisions	1980	1970
Hunt County—Con.		
Quinlan division	9 087	3 523
Quinlan city[107]	1 002	844
West Tawakoni town	840	465
Wolfe City division	2 211	1 908
Wolfe City city[107]	1 594	1 433
Hutchinson County[108]	26 304	24 443
Borger division	23 030	...
Borger city[108]	15 837	14 195
Fritch city (pt.)[108]	2 299	1 778
Phillips (CDP)	1 729	2 515
Sanford town	249	181
Stinnett division	3 274	3 030
Stinnett city	2 222	2 014
Irion County[109]	1 386	1 070
Mertzon North division	178	...
Mertzon South division	1 208	...
Mertzon town	687	513
Jack County[110]	7 408	6 711
Bryson division	1 103	907
Bryson city[110]	579	455
Jacksboro division	5 318	4 797
Jacksboro city[110]	4 000	3 554
Perrin division	987	1 007
Jackson County[111]	13 352	12 975
Edna–Cordele division	7 482	7 152
Edna city[111]	5 650	5 332
Ganado division	2 934	2 855
Ganado town[111]	1 770	1 640
La Ward–Lolita division	1 702	1 843
La Ward city	218	247
Vanderbilt division	1 234	1 125
Jasper County[112]	30 781	24 692
Buna division	8 980	6 769
Bessmay–Buna (CDP)	2 093	1 649
Evadale (CDP)	1 601	...
Jasper division	15 340	12 115
Browndell city[112]	228	'243
Jasper city[112]	6 959	6 251
Kirbyville division	6 461	5 808
Kirbyville city	1 972	1 869
Jeff Davis County[113]	1 647	1 527
Fort Davis division	1 212	1 187
Valentine division	435	340
Valentine town[113]	328	213
Jefferson County[114]	250 938	'246 402
Beaumont division	118 067	'117 632
Beaumont city (pt.)[114]	118 067	'117 548
East Jefferson division	118 833	
Beaumont city (pt.)[114]	-	...
Griffing Park town	1 802	2 075
Groves city	17 090	18 067
Nederland city[114]	16 855	16 810
Port Arthur city (pt.)[114]	60 562	57 371
Port Neches city[114]	13 944	10 894
Labelle city	4 663	...
Beaumont city (pt.)[114]	-	
Nome–China division	7 875	5 945
Beaumont city (pt.)[114]	35	
Bevil Oaks town	1 306	663
China city[114]	1 351	...
Nome city[114]	550	...
Sabine Pass division	1 500	...
Port Arthur city (pt.)[114]	689	...
Jim Hogg County	5 168	4 654
North Jim Hogg division	4 898	4 408
Hebbronville (CDP)	4 684	4 079
South Jim Hogg division	270	246
Jim Wells County[115]	36 498	33 032
Alice division	28 631	...
Alice city[115]	20 961	20 121
San Diego city (pt.)	894	731
Orange Grove–Sandia division	3 772	2 699
Orange Grove city	1 212	1 075
Premont division	4 095	4 514
Premont city	2 984	3 282
Johnson County[116]	67 649	45 769
Alvarado division	12 212	6 817
Alvarado city	2 701	2 129
Mansfield city (pt.)[116]	22	
Venus town	518	414
Burleson–Joshua division	22 132	...
Briaroaks city[116]	592	...
Burleson city (pt.)[116]	10 611	7 367
Joshua city[116]	1 470	924
Cleburne division	27 743	
Cleburne city (pt.)[116]	19 218	16 015
Keene city[116]	3 013	2 440
Rio Vista city	509	370
Godley division	1 959	1 413
Cleburne city (pt.)[116]	-	...
Godley town[116]	614	533
Grandview division	3 603	2 354
Grandview city	1 205	935

County Subdivisions	1980	1970
Jones County[117]	17 268	16 106
Anson division	3 994	3 779
Anson city	2 831	2 615
Hamlin division	3 783	3 990
Hamlin city (pt.)	3 248	3 322
Hawley–Noodle division	3 564	2 325
Abilene city (pt.)	503	394
Hawley city[117]	679	...
Lueders division	770	842
Lueders city (pt.)	420	511
Stamford division	5 157	5 170
Stamford city (pt.)[117]	4 497	4 428
Karnes County[118]	13 593	13 462
Falls City division	1 384	1 354
Falls City city	580	442
Gillett division	756	950
Karnes City division	4 117	...
Karnes City town[118]	3 296	2 926
Kenedy division	5 577	
Kenedy city[118]	4 356	4 156
Runge division	1 759	1 714
Runge town	1 244	1 147
Kaufman County[119]	39 015	32 392
Crandall division	3 097	'2 321
Combine city (pt.)[119]	560	'219
Crandall city (pt.)[119]	831	'774
Seagoville city (pt.)[119]		
Forney division	4 090	2 789
Crandall city (pt.)[119]	-	...
Dallas city (pt.)[119]	1	...
Forney town[119]	2 483	1 745
Heath city (pt.)[119]	5	'71
Seagoville city (pt.)[119]	6	...
Kaufman division	7 704	
Kaufman city	4 658	4 012
Oak Grove town[119]	319	
Kemp–Mabank division	4 653	3 285
Kemp town[119]	1 035	999
Mabank town (pt.)[119]	1 287	1 239
Terrell division	16 204	
Terrell city (pt.)[119]	13 169	14 182
Terrell South division	3 267	2 094
Crandall city (pt.)[119]	-	...
Oak Ridge town[119]	247	...
Post Oak Bend City town[119]	878	...
Terrell city (pt.)[119]	56	...
Kendall County[120]	10 635	6 964
Boerne division	7 649	4 784
Boerne city[120]	3 229	2 432
Comfort division	2 986	2 180
Comfort (CDP)	1 226	...
Kenedy County	543	678
Sarita division	543	678
Kent County	1 145	1 434
Jayton North division	337	447
Jayton South division	808	987
Jayton town	638	703
Kerr County[121]	28 780	19 454
Center Point division	2 162	...
Ingram division	5 191	...
Ingram (CDP)	1 921	...
Kerrville division	21 427	...
Kerrville city[121]	15 276	12 672
Kimble County	4 063	3 904
Junction Northwest division	850	631
Junction Southeast division	3 213	3 273
Junction city	2 593	2 654
King County	425	464
Guthrie division	425	464
Kinney County	2 279	2 006
Brackettville division	2 279	2 006
Brackettville city	1 676	1 539
Spofford city	77	69
Kleberg County[122]	33 358	33 166
Kingsville division	31 722	...
Corpus Christi city (pt.)[122]	-	...
Kingsville city[122]	28 808	'28 915
Riviera division	1 636	
Knox County[123]	5 329	5 972
Benjamin division	678	905
Benjamin city	257	308
Goree division	649	808
Goree city	524	538
Knox City division	1 797	1 824
Knox City city	1 546	1 536
Munday division	2 205	2 435
Munday city[123]	1 738	1 726
Lamar County[124]	42 156	36 062
Biardstown division	833	...
Blossom division	3 079	
Blossom town[124]	1 487	816
Deport division	2 033	1 787
Deport city (pt.)[124]	683	726

County Subdivisions	1980	1970
Lamar County—Con.		
Howland division	794	...
Paris division	28 671	...
Paris city[124]	25 498	23 441
Reno city[124]	1 059	487
Sun Valley town[124]	76	...
Powderly division	2 422	...
Roxton division	1 294	1 276
Roxton city[124]	735	...
Sumner division	? 030	1 998
Toco town[124]	164	...
Lamb County[125]	18 669	17 770
Earth division	2 746	2 590
Earth city[125]	1 512	1 152
Springlake town	222	209
Littlefield division	9 550	8 873
Littlefield city[125]	7 409	6 738
Olton division	3 247	3 117
Olton city[125]	2 235	1 782
Sudan—Amherst division	3 126	3 190
Amherst city[125]	971	825
Sudan city[125]	1 091	976
Lampasas County[126]	12 005	9 323
Adamsville division	750	654
Lampasas division	10 015	7 417
Lampasas city[126]	6 165	5 922
Lometa division	1 240	1 252
Lometa city[126]	666	633
La Salle County[127]	5 514	5 014
Cotulla division	4 692	4 231
Cotulla city[127]	3 912	3 415
Encinal division	822	783
Encinal city[127]	704	...
Lavaca County[128]	19 004	17 903
Hallettsville division	6 817	6 242
Hallettsville city[128]	2 865	2 712
Moulton division	2 515	2 651
Moulton town	1 009	968
Shiner division	3 712	3 722
Shiner city[128]	2 213	2 102
Yoakum division	5 960	5 288
Yoakum city (pt.)[128]	3 823	3 299
Lee County[129]	10 952	8 048
Giddings division	6 394	4 359
Giddings city[129]	3 950	2 783
Lexington division	2 432	1 679
Lexington town	1 065	719
Lincoln—Dime Box division	2 126	2 010
Leon County[130]	9 594	8 738
Buffalo division	2 214	1 885
Buffalo city	1 507	1 242
Centerville division	2 419	2 601
Centerville city	799	831
Leona town	165	96
Jewett—Marquez division	1 853	1 483
Jewett city[130]	597	447
Marquez city	231	185
Normangee division	1 908	1 609
Normangee town (pt.)	580	623
Oakwood division	1 200	1 160
Oakwood town[130]	606	547
Liberty County[131]	47 088	33 014
Cleveland division	16 068	...
Cleveland city[131]	5 977	5 627
North Cleveland city	259	404
Plum Grove city[131]	455	...
Daisetta division	4 243	3 570
Daisetta city	1 177	1 084
Devers city (pt.)[131]	500	...
Hardin town (pt.)[131]	306	...
Hardin—Rye division	3 902	2 562
Hardin town (pt.)[131]	376	...
Liberty—Dayton division	22 875	...
Ames city[131]	1 155	...
Dayton city[131]	4 908	3 804
Devers city (pt.)[131]	7	...
Hardin town (pt.)[131]	97	...
Kenefick town[131]	763	205
Liberty city[131]	7 945	5 591
Limestone County[132]	20 224	18 100
Coolidge division	1 438	1 182
Coolidge town	810	786
Groesbeck division	4 273	3 271
Groesbeck city[132]	3 373	2 396
Kosse division	773	744
Kosse town	484	471
Mexia division	11 103	10 702
Mexia city[132]	7 094	5 943
Tehuacana town	265	285
Personville division	957	722
Prairie Hill division	656	645
Thornton division	1 024	834
Thornton town	498	433

County Subdivisions	1980	1970
Lipscomb County[133]	3 766	3 486
Booker division	1 895	1 709
Booker town (pt.)[133]	1 201	904
Darrouzett town	444	396
Follett division	836	770
Follett city	547	522
Higgins division	1 035	1 007
Higgins city[133]	702	582
Live Oak County[134]	9 606	6 697
George West division	5 814	3 389
George West city[134]	2 627	2 022
Three Rivers division	3 792	3 308
Three Rivers city[134]	2 133	1 761
Llano County[135]	10 144	6 979
Llano North division	5 228	...
Kingsland (CDP)	2 241	...
Llano South division	4 916	...
Llano city[135]	3 071	2 608
Sunrise Beach Village city[135]	420	...
Loving County	91	164
Mentone division	91	164
Lubbock County[136]	211 651	179 295
Idalou division	6 019	4 780
Idalou town[136]	2 348	1 729
Lake Ransom Canyon village (pt.)[136]	483	...
Lubbock division	193 385	...
Abernathy city (pt.)[136]	699	704
Lubbock city[136]	173 979	149 101
New Deal town[136]	637	...
Reese AFB (CDP)	1 934	2 545
Wolfforth town[136]	1 701	1 090
Shallowater division	4 131	2 829
Shallowater city[136]	1 932	1 339
Slaton division	8 116	7 756
Lake Ransom Canyon village (pt.)[136]	78	...
Slaton city[136]	6 804	6 583
Lynn County[137]	8 605	9 107
O'Donnell division	1 732	1 932
O'Donnell city (pt.)	1 076	1 017
Tahoka division	5 540	5 662
New Home city[137]	274	252
Tahoka city[137]	3 262	2 956
Wilson division	1 333	1 513
Wilson city	578	433
McCulloch County[138]	8 735	8 571
Brady division	7 265	...
Brady city[138]	5 969	5 557
Melvin division	930	...
Melvin town[138]	202	290
Rochelle division	540	611
McLennan County[139]	170 755	147 553
Axtell division	2 463	1 649
Hallsburg city (pt.)[139]	45	...
Leroy city[139]	253	...
China Springs division	2 013	...
Waco city (pt.)[139]	—	...
Crawford division	2 515	...
Crawford town	610	477
Valley Mills city (pt.)	10	20
Waco city (pt.)[139]	—	...
Elm Mott division	3 004	...
Ross city (pt.)[139]	50	...
McGregor division	5 515	4 904
McGregor city[139]	4 513	4 365
Mart division	4 935	4 272
Hallsburg city (pt.)[139]	410	...
Mart city[139]	2 324	2 183
Riesel town[139]	691	...
Moody division	5 754	3 317
Bruceville—Eddy city (pt.)[139]	1 029	...
Lorena town	619	406
Moody town[139]	1 385	1 286
Waco division	138 965	...
Bellmead city[139]	7 569	7 698
Beverly Hills city	2 083	2 289
Golinda city (pt.)[139]	43	...
Hewitt city[139]	5 247	569
Lacy—Lakeview city[139]	2 752	2 558
Northcrest town	1 944	1 669
Robinson city[139]	6 074	3 807
Waco city (pt.)[139]	101 261	95 326
Woodway city[139]	7 091	4 819
West division	5 591	4 966
Gholson city[139]	263	...
Ross city (pt.)[139]	150	...
West city[139]	2 485	2 406
McMullen County	789	1 095
Tilden division	789	1 095
Madison County[140]	10 649	7 693
Madisonville division	5 385	4 204
Madisonville city[140]	3 660	2 881
Midway division	3 522	1 100
North Zulch division	1 742	2 389

County Subdivisions

County Subdivisions	1980	1970
Madison County—Con.		
North Zulch division—Con.		
Normangee town (pt.)	56	34
Marion County	10 360	8 517
Marion East division	5 213	5 154
Jefferson city	2 643	2 866
Marion West division	5 147	3 363
Martin County[141]	4 684	4 774
Stanton division	3 304	3 154
Stanton city[141]	2 314	2 117
Tarzan–Lenorah division	1 380	1 620
Ackerly city (pt.)	92	108
Mason County[142]	3 683	3 356
Mason East division	3 005	2 679
Mason city (pt.)[142]	2 153	1 806
Mason West division	678	677
Mason city (pt.)[142]	–	...
Matagorda County[143]	37 828	27 913
Bay City division	24 043	
Bay City city[143]	17 837	r13 445
Van Vleck (CDP)	1 157	1 051
Matagorda–Sargent division	3 292	...
Palacios division	5 796	4 544
Palacios town[143]	4 667	3 642
Tidehaven division	4 697	2 778
Markham (CDP)	1 554	...
Maverick County[144]	31 398	18 093
Eagle Pass division	30 047	...
Eagle Pass city[144]	21 407	15 364
Quemado division	1 351	...
Medina County[145]	23 164	20 249
Castroville–La Coste division	4 439	3 730
Castroville city	1 821	1 893
La Coste city[145]	862	r768
Devine–Natalia division	9 672	8 074
Devine city[145]	3 756	3 311
Lytle city (pt.)[145]	359	(NA)
Natalia city	1 264	1 296
D'Hanis division	1 199	...
Hondo division	7 854	...
Hondo city[145]	6 057	5 487
Menard County[146]	2 346	2 646
Menard East division	249	...
Menard West division	2 097	...
Menard city[146]	1 697	1 740
Midland County[147]	82 636	65 433
Midland division	71 011	...
Midland city (pt.)[147]	69 844	59 463
Midland Rural division	11 625	...
Midland city (pt.)[147]	681	...
Milam County[148]	22 732	20 028
Buckholts division	1 050	1 019
Buckholts town[148]	388	...
Burlington division	1 276	1 530
Cameron division	6 844	6 557
Cameron city[148]	5 721	5 546
Davilla division	907	902
Gause–Milano division	2 173	1 881
Milano town[148]	468	...
Rockdale division	8 197	6 166
Rockdale city[148]	5 611	4 655
Thorndale division	2 285	1 973
Thorndale city (pt.)[148]	1 296	1 031
Mills County[149]	4 477	4 212
Goldthwaite division	2 568	2 537
Goldthwaite city[149]	1 783	1 693
Mullin–Priddy division	1 318	1 139
Mullin town	213	203
Star division	591	536
Mitchell County	9 088	9 073
Colorado City division	6 558	6 440
Colorado City city	5 405	5 227
Loraine division	1 632	1 738
Loraine town	929	700
Westbrook division	898	895
Westbrook city	298	298
Montague County[150]	17 410	15 326
Bowie division	9 503	8 150
Bowie city[150]	5 610	5 185
Montague–Forestburg division	1 300	1 170
Nocona division	4 670	4 375
Nocona city[150]	2 992	2 871
St. Jo division	1 937	1 631
St. Jo city[150]	1 071	1 054
Montgomery County[151]	128 487	49 479
Magnolia division	12 217	...
Magnolia city[151]	867	r315
Stagecoach town[151]	349	...
Montgomery division	8 222	...
Montgomery city	258	216
Southeast Montgomery division	99 757	...
Chateau Woods village[151]	590	...

County Subdivisions	1980	1970
Montgomery County—Con.		
Southeast Montgomery division—Con.		
Conroe city[151]	18 034	11 969
Cut and Shoot town[151]	568	r451
Houston city (pt.)[151]	19	9
Kingwood (CDP)	167	...
Oak Ridge North town[151]	2 504	...
Patton village[151]	1 050	667
Porter Heights (CDP)	1 331	...
Roman Forest town[151]	929	...
Shenandoah city[151]	1 793	...
Splendora city	721	194
The Woodlands (CDP)	8 443	...
Woodbranch village[151]	720	378
Woodloch town[151]	351	...
Willis division	8 291	...
Panorama Village city[151]	1 186	...
Willis city[151]	1 674	1 577
Moore County[152]	16 575	14 060
Dumas division	14 389	11 873
Cactus city	898	644
Dumas city[152]	12 194	9 771
Fritch city (pt.)	–	...
Sunray division	2 186	2 187
Sunray city	1 952	1 854
Morris County[153]	14 629	12 310
Daingerfield division	9 762	8 009
Daingerfield town[153]	3 030	2 630
Lone Star town[153]	2 036	1 760
Naples division	4 867	4 301
Naples town[153]	1 908	1 726
Omaha city	960	898
Motley County[154]	1 950	2 178
Matador North division	385	r494
Matador South division	1 565	r1 684
Matador town[154]	1 052	r1 091
Roaring Springs town	315	r308
Nacogdoches County[155]	46 786	36 362
Chireno–Martinsville division	3 375	2 343
Chireno city[155]	371	r308
Cushing–Douglass division	3 433	2 839
Cushing city[155]	518	396
Garrison division	2 552	2 120
Garrison town	1 059	1 082
Nacogdoches division	37 426	...
Appleby city	453	280
Nacogdoches city[155]	27 149	22 544
Navarro County[156]	35 323	31 150
Blooming Grove division	2 829	2 238
Blooming Grove town[156]	823	740
Frost town	564	548
Corsicana division	25 790	...
Angus town[156]	244	...
Barry city	192	149
Corsicana city[156]	21 712	19 972
Emhouse town	197	158
Mustang town[156]	12	...
Retreat town	255	263
Dawson division	1 871	1 775
Dawson town	747	848
Kerens division	2 896	...
Goodlow city[156]	343	...
Kerens city[156]	1 582	r1 446
Powell town	111	121
Rice division	1 334	938
Rice city (pt.)[156]	432	284
Richland division	603	620
Richland town	260	309
Streetman town (pt.)	19	15
Newton County[157]	13 254	11 657
Burkeville division	1 872	...
Call division	2 913	2 460
Deweyville division	3 160	2 124
Deweyville (CDP)	1 171	...
Newton division	5 309	...
Newton city[157]	1 620	1 529
Nolan County[158]	17 359	16 220
Blackwell–Nolan division	744	798
Blackwell town (pt.)	265	266
Roscoe division	2 684	2 551
Roscoe city[158]	1 628	1 580
Sweetwater city (pt.)	10	...
Sweetwater division	13 931	...
Sweetwater city (pt.)[158]	12 232	12 020
Nueces County[159]	268 215	237 544
Bishop division	6 740	5 905
Bishop town[159]	3 706	3 466
North San Pedro (CDP) (pt.)	842	(NA)
Corpus Christi division	236 437	...
Corpus Christi city (pt.)[159]	231 875	204 525
Portland city (pt.)[159]	–	...
Corpus Christi West division	6 796	3 216
Agua Dulce city	934	742
Corpus Christi city (pt.)[159]	40	...
North San Pedro (CDP) (pt.)	1 711	(NA)
San Patricio city (pt.)[159]	31	...

County Subdivisions

County Subdivisions	1980	1970
Nueces County—Con.		
Driscoll division	1 810	2 247
Driscoll city	648	626
Port Aransas division	2 644	1 352
Aransas Pass city (pt.)[159]	5	–
Corpus Christi city (pt.)[159]	84	–
Port Aransas city (pt.)[159]	1 968	1 218
Portland city (pt.)[159]	–	–
Robstown division	13 788	16 511
Robstown city[159]	12 100	11 217
South San Pedro (CDP)	1 688	3 065
Ochiltree County[160]	9 588	9 704
Perryton East division	8 660	...
Booker town (pt.)	18	...
Perryton city[160]	7 991	7 810
Perryton West division	928	...
Oldham County[161]	2 283	2 258
Vega East division	1 952	1 885
Vega town[161]	900	839
Vega West division	331	373
Adrian city	222	228
Orange County[162]	83 838	71 170
Bridge City–Orangefield division	13 859	10 060
Bridge City city[162]	7 667	...
Mauriceville division	7 426	...
Orange division	35 411	
Orange city[162]	23 628	24 457
Pinehurst city[162]	3 055	2 198
West Orange city	4 610	4 820
Vidor division	27 142	20 331
Pine Forest town	639	512
Rose City town[162]	663	...
Vidor city[162]	12 117	9 738
Palo Pinto County[163]	24 062	28 962
Graford division	1 942	1 751
Graford city	495	613
Mineral Wells division	18 383	
Mineral Wells city (pt.)[163]	14 348	17 253
Palo Pinto–Santo division	1 869	1 643
Strawn–Gordon division	1 868	1 979
Gordon city[163]	516	457
Mingus city[163]	212	273
Strawn city	694	786
Panola County[164]	20 724	15 894
Beckville division	3 224	2 251
Beckville city[164]	945	582
Tatum city (pt.)	275	126
Carthage division	10 429	7 921
Carthage city[164]	6 447	5 392
De Berry–Deadwood division	3 712	3 148
Gary City division	1 462	1 100
Gary City town	322	202
Long Branch–Dotson division	1 897	1 474
Parker County[165]	44 609	33 888
Springtown division	13 159	7 171
Azle city (pt.)[165]	896	650
Briar city (pt.)[165]	349	...
Reno city	1 174	688
Springtown city[165]	1 658	1 194
Weatherford city (pt.)[165]	15	...
Weatherford division	19 664	
Cool city (pt.)	123	237
Millsap town[165]	439	...
Mineral Wells city (pt.)[165]	–	(NA)
Weatherford city (pt.)[165]	12 003	11 750
Weatherford Northwest division	4 824	...
Cool city (pt.)	79	...
Mineral Wells city (pt.)[165]	120	(NA)
Weatherford Southeast division	6 962	3 406
Aledo city[165]	1 027	620
Anneta town[165]	454	...
Anneta North town[165]	281	...
Anneta South town[165]	115	...
Hudson Oaks town[165]	309	...
Weatherford city (pt.)[165]	31	...
Willow Park city[165]	1 113	230
Parmer County[166]	11 038	10 509
Farwell–Bovina division	5 744	5 603
Bovina city[166]	1 499	1 428
Farwell city	1 354	1 185
Friona division	5 294	4 906
Friona city[166]	3 809	3 111
Pecos County[167]	14 618	13 748
Fort Stockton division	11 741	10 930
Fort Stockton city[167]	8 688	8 283
Imperial division	979	1 228
Iraan division	1 898	1 590
Iraan city	1 358	996
Polk County[168]	24 407	14 457
Corrigan division	4 396	
Corrigan town[168]	1 770	1 304
Livingston–New Willard division	20 011	...
Goodrich city[168]	350	...
Livingston town[168]	4 928	3 965
Onalaska city[168]	386	...
Seven Oaks city[168]	300	224

County Subdivisions	1980	1970
Potter County[169]	98 637	90 511
Amarillo division	96 211	
Amarillo city (pt.)[169]	93 019	86 477
Canadian River Breaks division	2 426	...
Presidio County[170]	5 188	4 842
Marfa division	3 078	
Marfa city	2 466	2 647
Presidio division	2 110	
Presidio (CDP)	1 723	...
Rains County[171]	4 839	3 752
Emory division	2 965	2 438
Alba town (pt.)[171]	–	(NA)
Emory city[171]	813	693
Point division	1 874	1 314
East Tawakoni city[171]	404	278
Point city	468	419
Randall County[172]	75 062	53 885
Amarillo division	57 119	
Amarillo city (pt.)[172]	56 211	40 533
Canyon division	12 785	
Canyon city (pt.)[172]	10 223	8 333
Happy town (pt.)	43	45
Lake Tanglewood village (pt.)[172]	202	...
North Randall division	5 158	...
Canyon city (pt.)[172]	501	...
Lake Tanglewood village (pt.)[172]	283	...
Reagan County[173]	4 135	3 239
Big Lake division	4 135	3 239
Big Lake city[173]	3 404	2 489
Real County[174]	2 469	2 013
Camp Wood–Leakey division	2 469	...
Camp Wood city[174]	728	660
Leakey city[174]	468	393
Red River County[175]	16 101	14 298
Annona–Avery division	3 184	3 143
Annona town[175]	471	373
Avery town[175]	520	491
Bogata division	3 071	2 788
Bogata town[175]	1 508	1 287
Deport city (pt.)[175]	41	35
Clarksville division	7 159	5 998
Clarksville city[175]	4 917	3 346
Detroit division	1 568	...
Detroit town[175]	805	668
Manchester division	1 119	...
Reeves County[176]	15 801	16 526
Balmorhea division	1 615	2 039
Balmorhea city	568	655
Pecos division	14 186	14 487
Pecos city[176]	12 855	12 682
Toyah town	165	245
Refugio County[177]	9 289	9 494
Austwell–Tivoli division	1 162	1 301
Austwell city	280	284
Refugio division	4 873	5 287
Refugio town[177]	3 898	4 340
Woodsboro division	3 254	2 906
Bayside town[177]	381	...
Woodsboro town	1 974	1 839
Roberts County	1 187	967
Miami division	1 187	967
Miami city	813	611
Robertson County[178]	14 653	14 389
Bremond division	1 854	1 974
Bremond city[178]	1 025	822
Calvert division	2 100	...
Calvert city	1 732	2 072
Franklin division	3 284	2 962
Franklin city	1 349	1 063
Hearne division	7 415	
Hearne city[178]	5 418	4 982
Rockwall County[179]	14 528	7 046
Northeast Rockwall division	2 541	1 883
Fate city	263	329
Royse City city (pt.)[179]	1 394	1 291
Northwest Rockwall division	8 281	...
Dallas city (pt.)	–	...
Garland city (pt.)[179]	–	...
Rockwall city (pt.)[179]	5 617	3 121
Rowlett city (pt.)[179]	1 174	54
South Rockwall division	3 706	...
Dallas city (pt.)[179]	–	...
Heath city (pt.)[179]	1 454	449
McLendon–Chisholm city[179]	403	...
Rockwall city (pt.)[179]	322	...
Runnels County[180]	11 872	12 108
Ballinger division	5 230	...
Ballinger city[180]	4 207	4 203
Miles division	1 022	994
Miles city	720	631
Rowena division	884	...
Winters division	4 736	4 935
Winters city[180]	3 061	2 907

County Subdivisions	1980	1970
Rusk County[181]	41 382	34 102
Carlisle–Turnertown division	1 839	1 785
Henderson division	17 421	...
Henderson city[181]	11 473	10 187
Kilgore division	6 698	5 361
Kilgore city (pt.)[181]	2 543	2 220
Laneville division	2 936	2 638
Reklaw town[181]	114	57
Mount Enterprise division	2 422	2 195
Mount Enterprise city[181]	485	...
Overton division	4 558	3 956
New London city	942	899
Overton city (pt.)	2 323	1 950
Pinehill division	1 730	1 233
Tatum division	3 778	2 503
Easton city (pt.)[181]	68	42
Tatum city (pt.)[181]	1 064	558
Sabine County[182]	8 702	7 187
Hemphill division	3 464	...
Hemphill city[182]	1 353	1 005
Milam division	1 801	1 502
Pineland division	3 437	...
Bronson city[182]	254	...
Pineland city[182]	1 111	1 127
San Augustine County[183]	8 785	7 858
Broaddus division	1 905	1 407
Broaddus town[183]	225	...
San Augustine division	6 880	6 451
San Augustine town	2 930	2 539
San Jacinto County[184]	11 434	6 702
Coldspring division	1 673	...
Coldspring city[184]	569	'488
Point Blank division	1 964	1 313
Point Blank city[184]	325	...
Shepherd–Evergreen division	7 797	...
Shepherd city	1 674	'1 037
San Patricio County[185]	58 013	47 288
Aransas Pass–Ingleside division	14 004	10 584
Aransas Pass city (pt.)	6 308	5 087
Ingleside city	5 436	3 763
Gregory–Portland division	15 742	10 589
Gregory city	2 739	2 246
Portland city (pt.)[185]	12 023	7 302
Mathis division	8 437	7 417
Corpus Christi city (pt.)[185]	–	...
Lake City town[185]	431	...
Lakeside town[185]	276	...
Mathis city	5 667	5 351
San Patricio city (pt.)[185]	210	...
Sinton–Odem division	13 196	12 145
Corpus Christi city (pt.)	–	...
Odem city[185]	2 363	2 130
Sinton city[185]	6 044	5 563
Taft division	6 634	6 553
Taft city	3 686	3 274
Taft Southwest (CDP)	2 133	2 026
San Saba County[186]	6 204	5 540
San Saba North division	1 412	...
Richland Springs town	420	425
San Saba South division	4 792	...
San Saba city[186]	2 847	2 555
Schleicher County	2 820	2 277
Eldorado East division	2 439	1 859
Eldorado town	2 061	1 446
Eldorado West division	381	418
Scurry County[187]	18 192	15 760
Fluvanna–Sharon Ridge division	1 691	1 593
Hermleigh division	1 033	910
Snyder division	15 468	...
Snyder city[187]	12 705	11 171
Shackelford County[188]	3 915	3 323
Albany division	3 377	2 765
Albany city[188]	2 450	1 978
Lueders city (pt.)[188]	–	...
Moran division	538	558
Moran city	344	335
Shelby County[189]	23 084	19 672
Aiken–Neuville division	2 305	2 000
Center division	9 721	8 280
Center city	5 827	4 989
Shelbyville division	3 008	2 433
Huxley city[189]	341	'208
Tenaha–Joaquin division	4 841	4 143
Joaquin town[189]	917	819
Tenaha town	1 005	1 094
Timpson division	3 209	2 816
Timpson city	1 164	1 254
Sherman County	3 174	3 657
Stratford East division	911	1 033
Texhoma town	358	356
Stratford West division	2 263	2 624
Stratford town	1 917	2 139

County Subdivisions	1980	1970
Smith County[190]	128 366	97 096
Bullard division	7 401	...
Bullard town (pt.)[190]	622	546
Tyler city (pt.)[190]	113	...
Lindale division	9 282	5 895
Lindale town[190]	2 180	1 631
Troup–Arp division	7 107	5 238
Arp city[190]	939	816
New Chapel Hill city (pt.)[190]	99	...
Overton city (pt.)	45	(NA)
Troup city (pt.)[190]	1 847	1 606
Tyler division	81 235	...
Tyler city (pt.)[190]	66 934	57 770
Tyler East division	10 362	...
New Chapel Hill city (pt.)[190]	519	...
Overton city (pt.)	62	(NA)
Tyler city (pt.)[190]	2 259	...
Whitehouse division	9 464	...
Tyler city (pt.)[190]	1 202	...
Whitehouse city[190]	2 172	1 245
Winona division	3 515	2 578
Winona town	443	155
Somervell County[191]	4 154	2 793
Glen Rose division	4 154	...
Glen Rose city	2 075	1 554
Starr County[192]	27 266	17 707
La Grulla division	4 280	2 678
La Grulla city	1 442	1 194
Rio Grande–San Isidro division	14 513	10 179
Rio Grande City (CDP)	8 930	5 676
Roma–Los Saenz division	8 473	4 850
Roma–Los Saenz city	3 384	2 154
Stephens County[193]	9 926	8 414
Breckenridge North division	8 777	...
Breckenridge city[193]	6 921	5 944
Breckenridge South division	1 149	...
Sterling County[194]	1 206	1 056
Sterling City division	1 206	1 056
Sterling City city[194]	915	780
Stonewall County	2 406	2 397
Aspermont North division	534	629
Aspermont town (pt.)	–	...
Aspermont South division	1 872	1 768
Aspermont town (pt.)	1 357	1 198
Sutton County[195]	5 130	3 175
Sonora division	4 702	...
Sonora city[195]	3 856	2 149
Sonora Rural division	428	...
Swisher County[196]	9 723	10 373
Happy division	1 049	1 191
Happy town (pt.)	631	627
Kress division	2 212	2 384
Kress city	783	578
Tulia division	6 462	6 798
Tulia city[196]	5 033	5 294
Tarrant County[197]	860 880	'715 587
Arlington division	187 502	...
Arlington city (pt.)[197]	160 113	'90 229
Dalworthington Gardens city	1 100	757
Fort Worth city (pt.)[197]	126	...
Grand Prairie city (pt.)[197]	5 731	3 173
Kennedale city (pt.)[197]	2 594	3 076
Mansfield city (pt.)[197]	8 080	3 658
Pantego town[197]	2 431	'1 779
Fort Worth division[197]	486 521	...
Arlington city (pt.)[197]	–	...
Azle city (pt.)[197]	4 926	3 843
Benbrook city[197]	13 579	8 169
Blue Mound city	2 169	1 283
Briar city (pt.)[197]	819	...
Burleson city (pt.)[197]	1 123	346
Crowley city[197]	5 852	2 662
Edgecliff village[197]	2 695	1 143
Everman city[197]	5 387	4 570
Forest Hill city[197]	11 684	8 236
Fort Worth city (pt.)[197]	383 131	393 455
Haslet city (pt.)	120	(NA)
Kennedale city (pt.)	–	...
Lakeside town[197]	957	988
Lake Worth city	4 394	4 958
River Oaks city	6 890	8 193
Saginaw city[197]	5 736	2 382
Sansom Park Village city	3 921	4 771
Westover Hills town[197]	671	374
Westworth village[197]	3 651	4 578
White Settlement city[197]	13 508	13 449
Northeast Tarrant division	186 857	...
Bedford city[197]	20 821	10 049
Colleyville city[197]	6 700	'3 342
Euless city[197]	24 002	19 316
Fort Worth city (pt.)[197]	1 907	...
Grapevine city[197]	11 762	'7 049
Haltom City city[197]	29 014	28 127
Haslet city (pt.)	142	(NA)
Hurst city[197]	31 420	27 215
Keller city[197]	4 156	1 474

County Subdivisions

County Subdivisions	1980	1970
Tarrant County—Con.		
Northeast Tarrant division—Con.		
North Richland Hills city[197]	30 592	16 514
Richland Hills city	7 977	8 865
Southlake city (pt.)[197]	2 792	2 028
Watauga city[197]	10 284	r3 778
Westlake town (pt.)	150	35
Taylor County[198]	110 932	97 853
Abilene division	102 942	91 749
Abilene city (pt.)[198]	97 812	89 259
Impact town	54	61
Tye town (pt.)[198]	1 392	857
Jim Ned division	3 343	2 590
Buffalo Gap town	387	320
Lawn town	390	344
Tuscola town[198]	660	497
Merkel division	4 647	3 514
Abilene city (pt.)	—	...
Merkel town[198]	2 493	2 163
Trent town	313	333
Tye town (pt.)[198]	2	...
Terrell County	1 595	1 940
East Terrell division	255	303
West Terrell division	1 340	1 637
Sanderson (CDP)	1 241	1 229
Terry County[199]	14 581	14 118
Brownfield division	13 283	12 606
Brownfield city[199]	10 387	9 647
Wellman town[199]	239	...
Meadow division	1 298	1 512
Meadow town	571	491
Throckmorton County	2 053	2 205
Throckmorton division	1 566	1 619
Throckmorton town	1 174	1 105
Woodson division	487	586
Woodson town	291	340
Titus County[200]	21 442	16 702
Cookville division	2 554	1 745
Mount Pleasant division	15 022	11 900
Mount Pleasant city[200]	11 003	r9 459
Talco division	2 008	1 794
Talco city	751	837
Winfield division	1 858	1 263
Miller's Cove town[200]	61	...
Monticello town[200]	43	...
Winfield town	349	268
Tom Green County[201]	84 784	71 047
East Tom Green division	3 274	2 338
San Angelo division	70 726	...
San Angelo city (pt.)[201]	69 148	63 884
West Tom Green division	10 784	...
San Angelo city (pt.)[201]	4 092	...
Travis County[202]	419 573	295 516
Austin division	390 838	...
Austin city (pt.)[202]	341 665	r253 539
Manor city (pt.)[202]	1 034	940
Rollingwood city[202]	1 027	780
Round Rock city (pt.)[202]	—	...
San Leanna village[202]	290	...
Sunset Valley city	773	292
West Lake Hills city[202]	2 166	1 488
Travis Northeast division	4 998	...
Austin city (pt.)[202]	3	...
Manor city (pt.)[202]	10	...
Pflugerville city[202]	745	549
Round Rock city (pt.)	—	...
Travis Northwest division	13 305	...
Austin city (pt.)[202]	3 441	...
Travis Southwest division	10 432	...
Austin city (pt.)[202]	—	...
Lakeway village[202]	790	...
Trinity County[203]	9 450	7 628
Apple Springs division	1 471	1 266
Glendale division	579	366
Groveton division	3 182	2 699
Groveton city	1 262	1 219
Trinity division	4 218	3 297
Trinity city[203]	2 620	2 512
Tyler County[204]	16 223	12 417
Colmesneil—Chester division	2 326	1 710
Chester town	305	260
Colmesneil city[204]	553	...
Spurger division	4 595	3 158
Warren division	2 240	1 549
Woodville division	7 062	6 000
Woodville town[204]	2 821	2 662
Upshur County[205]	28 595	20 976
Bettie division	2 791	2 343
Big Sandy division	2 959	2 528
Big Sandy town	1 258	1 022
Gilmer division	9 949	8 145
Gilmer city[205]	5 167	4 196
West Mountain city (pt.)[205]	5	...
Gladewater division	6 934	4 071
Clarksville City city (pt.)[205]		...

County Subdivisions	1980	1970
Upshur County—Con.		
Gladewater division—Con.		
East Mountain city[205]	855	...
Gladewater city (pt.)[205]	2 237	1 274
Union Grove city[205]	344	...
Warren city (pt.)[205]	2	4
West Mountain city (pt.)[205]	390	194
Ore City division	5 962	3 889
Ore City city[205]	1 050	830
Upton County	4 619	4 697
McCamey division	2 890	3 147
McCamey city	2 436	2 647
Rankin division	1 729	1 550
Rankin city	1 216	1 105
Uvalde County[206]	22 441	17 348
Sabinal division	3 034	2 669
Sabinal city	1 827	1 554
Uvalde division	19 407	...
Uvalde city[206]	14 178	10 764
Val Verde County[207]	35 910	27 471
Del Rio division	35 113	...
Del Rio city[207]	30 034	21 330
Laughlin AFB (CDP)	2 994	3 458
Del Rio Northeast division	266	...
Del Rio Northwest division	531	...
Van Zandt County[208]	31 426	22 155
Ben Wheeler—Edom division	3 477	2 273
Edom city	250	201
Canton division	7 140	5 065
Canton city[208]	2 845	2 283
Edgewood division	2 988	2 144
Edgewood town[208]	1 413	1 176
Grand Saline division	5 954	4 569
Fruitvale city[208]	367	206
Grand Saline city[208]	2 709	2 257
Southwest Van Zandt division	2 503	1 426
Van division	3 765	2 629
Van city[208]	1 881	1 593
Wills Point division	5 599	4 049
Wills Point city[208]	2 631	2 636
Victoria County[209]	68 807	53 766
Victoria division	56 774	...
Victoria city (pt.)[209]	50 116	41 349
Victoria South division	4 713	...
Bloomington (CDP)	1 884	1 676
Victoria West division	7 320	...
Victoria city (pt.)[209]	579	...
Walker County[210]	41 789	27 680
Huntsville division	30 333	...
Huntsville city (pt.)[210]	23 463	17 610
New Waverly town (pt.)	3	...
New Waverly division	4 535	...
Huntsville city (pt.)[210]	189	...
New Waverly town (pt.)	821	496
Riverside division	6 921	...
Huntsville city (pt.)[210]	284	...
Riverside town[210]	425	r226
Waller County[211]	19 798	14 285
Brookshire division	4 794	3 635
Brookshire city[211]	2 175	1 683
Katy city (pt.)	668	327
Pattison city[211]	318	...
Hempstead division	5 439	4 138
Hempstead city[211]	3 456	1 891
Waller division	9 565	6 512
Prairie View city[211]	3 993	r3 796
Waller city (pt.)[211]	1 077	992
Ward County[212]	13 976	13 019
Barstow—Pyote division	1 197	...
Barstow town	637	614
Pyote town	382	155
Grandfalls division	811	825
Grandfalls town[212]	635	622
Monahans division	11 968	...
Monahans city (pt.)	8 393	8 333
Thorntonville town[212]	717	r629
Wickett town[212]	689	598
Washington County[213]	21 998	18 842
Brenham division	15 057	11 931
Brenham city[213]	10 966	8 922
Burton division	2 141	2 096
Burton town[213]	325	...
Gay Hill—Independence division	2 075	2 046
Washington—Chappell Hill division	2 725	...
Webb County[214]	99 258	72 859
Bruni—Mirando division	2 436	...
Laredo division	95 882	...
Laredo city (pt.)[214]	91 449	69 024
Webb division	940	...
Laredo city (pt.)[214]	—	...
Wharton County[215]	40 242	36 729
El Campo division	15 862	14 577
El Campo city[215]	10 462	r9 332
Wharton city (pt.)[215]	—	...

County Subdivisions	1980	1970
Wharton County—Con.		
Louise division	2 281	2 407
Newgulf division	4 013	3 700
Boling–Iago (CDP)	1 348	...
Northeast Wharton division	5 897	...
East Bernard (CDP)	1 735	1 159
Wharton division	12 189	...
Wharton city (pt.)[215]	9 033	7 881
Wheeler County[216]	7 137	6 434
Shamrock division	3 673	3 580
Shamrock city[216]	2 834	2 644
Wheeler division	3 464	2 854
Mobeetie town[216]	291	...
Wheeler town[216]	1 584	1 116
Wichita County[217]	121 082	120 563
Burkburnett division	11 078	9 583
Burkburnett city[217]	10 668	9 230
Electra division	5 017	...
Electra city[217]	3 755	3 895
Iowa Park division	6 683	6 134
Iowa Park town[217]	6 173	5 796
Wichita Falls division	98 304	...
Iowa Park town (pt.)[217]	11	...
Lakeside City town (pt.)[217]	–	...
Pleasant Valley town[217]	335	323
Wichita Falls city (pt.)[217]	94 201	96 265
Wilbarger County[218]	15 931	15 355
Fargo–Odell division	933	1 080
Harrold–Oklaunion division	736	...
Lockett division	1 043	...
Vernon division	13 219	...
Vernon city[218]	12 695	11 454
Willacy County[219]	17 495	15 570
La Sara division	1 148	...
Lyford division	2 594	2 404
Lyford town	1 618	1 425
Raymondville division	10 700	...
Raymondville city[219]	9 493	7 987
San Perlita division	1 209	...
San Perlita city	475	352
Sebastian division	1 844	1 837
Williamson County[220]	76 521	37 305
Florence division	2 737	...
Florence town	744	672
Georgetown–Round Rock division	39 639	...
Austin city (pt.)[220]	364	...
Georgetown city (pt.)[220]	9 468	6 395
Round Rock city (pt.)[220]	11 812	2 811
Granger division	3 270	3 769
Bartlett city (pt.)	871	1 036
Granger city[220]	1 236	1 256
Jarrell division	2 594	1 832
Liberty Hill–Cedar Park division	11 418	...
Austin city (pt.)[220]	23	...
Cedar Park city[220]	3 474	...
Leander city[220]	2 179	...
Taylor division	16 863	...
Georgetown city (pt.)[220]	–	...
Hutto town	659	545
Taylor city[220]	10 619	9 616
Thorndale city (pt.)[220]	4	...
Thrall town	573	619
Wilson County[221]	16 756	13 041
Floresville division	8 474	...
Floresville city[221]	4 381	3 707
La Vernia division	2 899	1 387
La Vernia city[221]	632	425
Poth division	2 641	...
Poth town	1 461	1 296
Stockdale division	2 742	2 520
Nixon city (pt.)[221]	–	...
Stockdale city[221]	1 265	1 132
Winkler County[222]	9 944	9 640
Kermit division	8 647	8 564
Kermit city[222]	8 015	7 884
Wink division	1 297	1 076
Monahans city (pt.)[222]	4	(NA)
Wink city	1 182	1 023
Wise County[223]	26 575	19 687
Alvord division	1 405	1 162
Alvord town[223]	874	791
Boyd–Rhome division	6 903	4 426
Aurora town[223]	376	...
Boyd town[223]	889	695
Briar city (pt.)[223]	642	...
Fairview city[223]	180	...
Newark city[223]	466	407
Pecan Acres (CDP)	1 113	...
Rhome city[223]	478	393
Bridgeport division	10 698	8 367
Bridgeport city[223]	3 737	3 614
Chico city	890	723
Lake Bridgeport city[223]	271	...
Runaway Bay city	504	...
Decatur division	7 569	5 732
Decatur city[223]	4 104	3 240

County Subdivisions	1980	1970
Wood County[224]	24 697	18 589
Alba division	2 187	1 361
Alba town (pt.)	568	555
Hawkins division	4 174	2 912
Hawkins city	1 302	977
Mineola division	6 858	5 604
Mineola city[224]	4 346	3 926
Quitman division	5 878	4 552
Quitman city[224]	1 893	1 494
Yantis town	210	223
Winnsboro division	5 600	4 160
Winnsboro city (pt.)[224]	2 596	2 209
Yoakum County[225]	8 299	7 344
Denver City division	6 129	5 263
Denver City town[225]	4 704	4 133
Plains division	2 170	2 081
Plains town	1 457	1 087
Young County[226]	19 083	15 400
Graham division	12 711	...
Graham city[226]	9 170	7 477
Jean–Loving division	619	570
Newcastle division	1 071	...
Newcastle city	688	624
Olney division	4 682	4 169
Olney city[226]	4 060	3 624
Zapata County	6 628	4 352
San Ygnacio division	877	911
Zapata division	5 751	3 441
Zapata (CDP)	3 831	2 102
Zavala County[227]	11 666	11 370
Batesville division	1 450	1 230
Crystal City division	8 747	8 884
Crystal City city[227]	8 334	8 104
La Pryor division	1 469	1 256
La Pryor (CDP)	1 257	...

UTAH

Utah derived its name from the Ute Indians, who once occupied what is now the northeastern part of the state. The term "Ute" is equivalent to "highlander."

The first explorers of this region were Spaniards. It is probable that members of Coronado's party entered it from the south as early as 1540. In 1776 two Spanish friars, seeking a route from Santa Fe to the Pacific, discovered Utah Lake. Nearly 50 years later Great Salt Lake was discovered by James Bridger, a trapper. Other trappers followed soon afterwards and established trading posts. The first permanent settlement of the Utah country was not made, however, until July, 1847, when Salt Lake City was founded by a band o Mormons from Illinois under the leadership of Brigham Young.

The area now constituting Utah formed a portion of the Spanish possessions in America until Mexico achieved its independence in 1821, when it became a part of that country. In February, 1848, by the treaty of Guadalupe-Hidalgo, at the close of the war with Mexico, that nation ceded to the United States its claims to a large part of the region between Texas and the Pacific Ocean, which included the territory comprised within the present limits of Utah.

For two years after the founding of Salt Lake City the new colony had no secular government. In 1849 the Mormons organized the so-called state of deseret and requested admission to the Union. Congress did not grant this request, but in September, 1850, created the territory of Utah, which extended from the California boundary to the Rocky Mountains and from the thirty-seventh to the forty-second parallel. The new territory thus included the area now constituting western Colorado, southwestern Wyoming, and the greater part of Nevada. In February, 1861, when the territory of Colorado was organized, the eastern boundary of Utah, south of the forty-first parallel, was fixed at its present location. In the following month the area of Utah was further reduced by the formation of Nevada territory with its eastern boundary at longitude 39+ from Washington (approximately 116° from Greenwich). In March, 1863, that portion of Utah lying north of the forty-first parallel and east of the thirty-third meridian from Washington was made a part of the newly created territory of Idaho, which then included most of the present area of Wyoming. In October, 1864, when Nevada was admitted to the Union, the boundary between that state and Utah was moved eastward 1 degree, and two years later it was fixed at the thirty-seventh meridian from Washington. In July, 1868, the area between the forty-first and forty-second parallels and the thirty-third and thirty-fourth meridians from Washington was taken from northeastern Utah and made a part of the newly organized territory of Wyoming, leaving Utah with its present boundaries. In January, 1896, the territory became a state of the Union.

COUNTY LOCATION INDEX

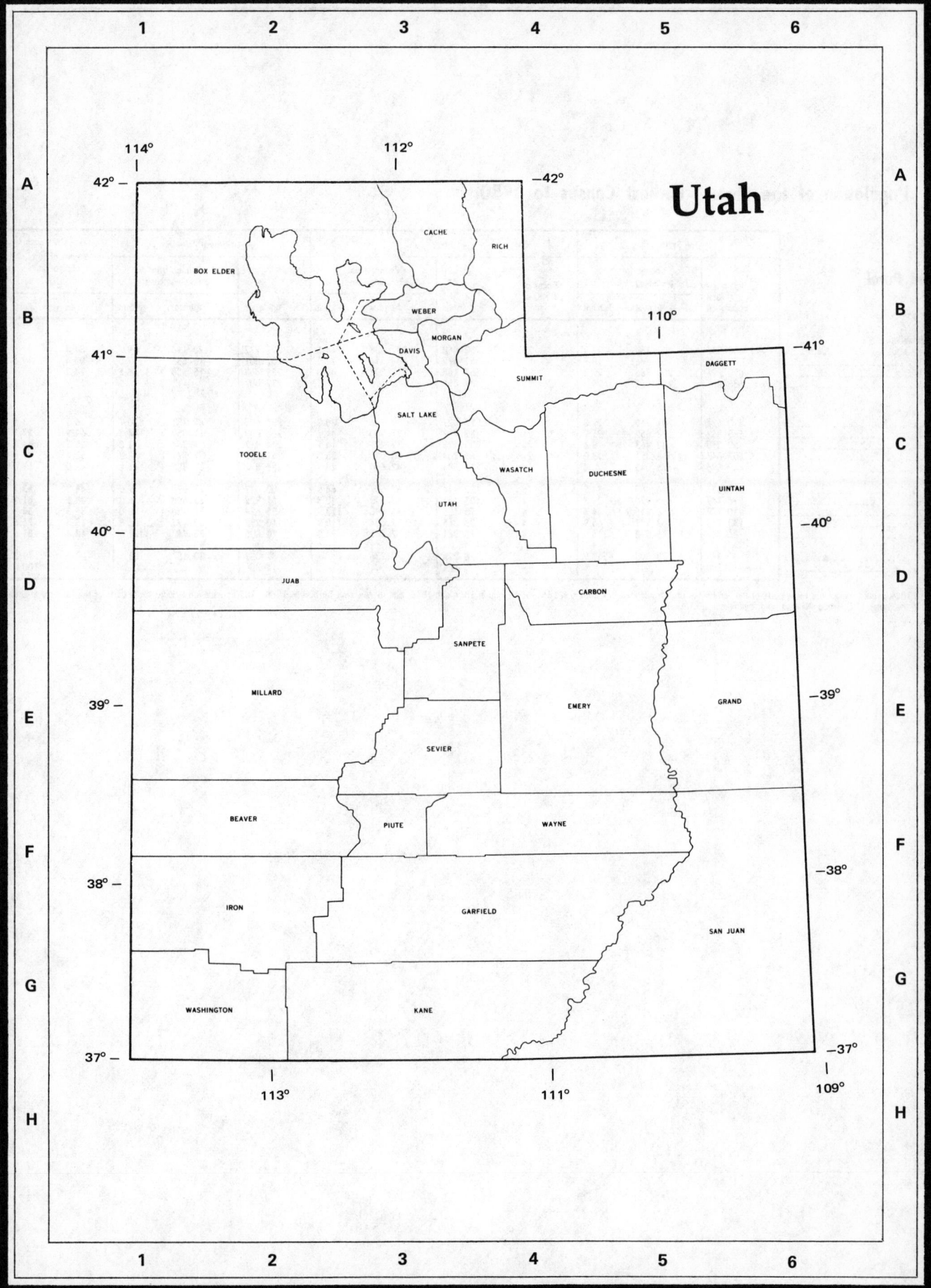

Utah

A 42° — 114° 112° —42°

CACHE

RICH

BOX ELDER

WEBER

B 41° — MORGAN 110°

DAVIS

SUMMIT DAGGETT

SALT LAKE

C TOOELE WASATCH DUCHESNE UINTAH

UTAH

D 40° — —40°

JUAB CARBON

SANPETE

E 39° — MILLARD EMERY GRAND —39°

SEVIER

F BEAVER PIUTE WAYNE

38° — —38°

IRON

GARFIELD SAN JUAN

G WASHINGTON KANE

37° — —37°

113° 111° 109°

Population of the State: Earliest Census to 1980

Urban and Rural

	The State			Urban				Rural				Percent of total population	
	Total population	Change from preceding census		Places of 2,500 or more	Population	Change from preceding census		Population	Change from preceding census			Urban	Rural
		Number	Percent			Number	Percent		Number	Percent			
Current urban definition:													
1980 (Apr. 1)_____	1 461 037	401 764	37.9	78	1 233 060	381 588	44.8	227 977	20 176	9.7		84.4	15.6
1970 (Apr. 1)_____	1 059 273	168 646	18.9	53	851 472	184 314	27.6	207 801	-15 668	-7.0		80.4	19.6
1960 (Apr. 1)_____	890 627	201 765	29.3	39	667 158	217 303	48.3	223 469	-15 538	-6.5		74.9	25.1
1950 (Apr. 1)_____	688 862	138 552	25.2	33	449 855	...	...	239 007	...	...		65.3	34.7
Previous urban definition:													
1960 (Apr. 1)_____	890 627	201 765	29.3	37	592 027	159 034	36.7	298 600	42 731	16.7		66.5	33.5
1950 (Apr. 1)_____	688 862	138 552	25.2	31	432 993	127 500	41.7	255 869	11 052	4.5		62.9	37.1
1940 (Apr. 1)_____	550 310	42 463	8.4	25	305 493	39 229	14.7	244 817	3 234	1.3		55.5	44.5
1930 (Apr. 1)_____	507 847	58 451	13.0	21	266 264	50 680	23.5	241 583	7 771	3.3		52.4	47.6
1920 (Jan. 1)_____	449 396	76 045	20.4	17	215 584	42 650	24.7	233 812	33 395	16.7		48.0	52.0
1910 (Apr. 15)_____	373 351	96 602	34.9	16	172 934	67 507	64.0	200 417	29 095	17.0		46.3	53.7
1900 (June 1)_____	276 749	65 970	31.3	12	105 427	30 272	40.3	171 322	35 698	26.3		38.1	61.9
1890 (June 1)_____	210 779	66 816	46.4	6	75 155	41 490	123.2	135 624	25 326	23.0		35.7	64.3
1880 (June 1)_____	143 963	57 177	65.9	4	33 665	17 684	110.7	110 298	39 493	55.8		23.4	76.6
1870 (June 1)_____	86 786	46 513	115.5	2	15 981	7 745	94.0	70 805	38 768	121.0		18.4	81.6
1860 (June 1)_____	40 273	28 893	253.9	1	8 236	8 236	...	32 037	20 657	181.5		20.5	79.5
1850 (June 1)_____	11 380	...	...	-	-	...	...	11 380	...	...		-	100.0

NOTE: 1860 population includes those parts of the Territory of Utah transferred to Colorado in 1861, to Nevada in 1864 and 1866, and to Wyoming Territory in 1868. 1850 population includes those parts of the Territory of Utah now included in the States of Colorado, Nevada, and Wyoming.

BEAVER

1860	785
1870	2,007
1880	3,918
1890	3,340
1900	3,613
1910	4,717
1920	5,139
1930	5,136
1940	5,014
1950	4,856
1960	4,331
1970	3,800
1980	4,378

BOX ELDER

1860	1,608
1870	4,855
1880	6,761
1890	7,642
1900	10,009
1910	13,894
1920	18,788
1930	17,810
1940	18,832
1950	19,734
1960	25,061
1970	28,129
1980	33,222

CACHE

1860	2,605
1870	8,229
1880	12,562
1890	15,509
1900	18,139
1910	23,062
1920	26,992
1930	27,424
1940	29,797
1950	33,536
1960	35,788
1970	42,311
1980	57,176

CARBON

1900	5,004
1910	8,624
1920	15,489
1930	17,798
1940	18,459
1950	24,901
1960	21,135
1970	15,647
1980	22,179

CEDAR

1860	741

DAGGETT

1920	400
1930	411
1940	564
1950	364
1960	1,164
1970	666
1980	769

DAVIS

1850	1,134
1860	2,904
1870	4,459
1880	5,279
1890	6,751
1900	7,996
1910	10,191
1920	11,450
1930	14,021
1940	15,784
1950	30,867
1960	64,760
1970	99,028
1980	146,540

DUCHESNE

1920	9,093
1930	8,263
1940	8,958
1950	8,134
1960	7,179
1970	7,299
1980	12,565

EMERY

1880	556
1890	5,076
1900	4,657
1910	6,750
1920	7,411
1930	7,042
1940	7,072
1950	6,304
1960	5,546
1970	5,137
1980	11,451

GARFIELD

1890	2,457
1900	3,400
1910	3,660
1920	4,768
1930	4,642
1940	5,253
1950	4,151
1960	3,577
1970	3,157
1980	3,673

GRAND

1890	541
1900	1,149
1910	1,598
1920	1,808
1930	1,813
1940	2,070
1950	1,903
1960	6,345
1970	6,688
1980	8,241

GREEN RIVER

1860	141

IRON

1850	360
1860	1,010
1870	2,277

1880	4,013
1890	2,683
1900	3,546
1910	3,933
1920	5,787
1930	7,227
1940	8,331
1950	9,642
1960	10,795
1970	12,177
1980	17,349

JUAB

1860	672
1870	2,034
1880	3,474
1890	5,582
1900	10,082
1910	10,702
1920	9,871
1930	8,605
1940	7,392
1950	5,981
1960	4,597
1970	4,574
1980	5,530

KANE

1870	1,513
1880	3,085
1890	1,685
1900	1,811
1910	1,652
1920	2,054
1930	2,235
1940	2,561
1950	2,299
1960	2,667
1970	2,421
1980	4,024

MILLARD

1860	715
1870	2,753
1880	3,727
1890	4,033
1900	5,678
1910	6,188
1920	8,659
1930	9,945
1940	9,613
1950	9,387
1960	7,866
1970	6,988
1980	8,970

MORGAN

1870	1,972
1880	1,783
1890	1,780
1900	2,045
1910	2,467
1920	2,542
1930	2,536
1940	2,611
1950	2,519
1960	2,837
1970	3,983
1980	4,917

PIUTE

1870	82
1880	1,651
1890	2,842
1900	1,954
1910	1,734
1920	2,770
1930	1,956
1940	2,203
1950	1,911
1960	1,436
1970	1,164
1980	1,329

RICH

1870	1,955
1880	1,263
1890	1,527
1900	1,946
1910	1,883
1920	1,890
1930	1,873
1940	2,028
1950	1,673
1960	1,685
1970	1,615
1980	2,100

RIO VIRGIN

1870	450

SALT LAKE

1850	6,157
1860	11,295
1870	19,337
1880	31,997
1890	58,457
1900	77,725
1910	131,426
1920	159,282
1930	194,102
1940	211,623
1950	274,895
1960	383,035
1970	458,607
1980	619,066

SAN JUAN

1880	204
1890	365
1900	1,023
1910	2,377
1920	3,379
1930	3,496
1940	4,712
1950	5,315
1960	9,040
1970	9,606
1980	12,253

SANPETE

1850	365
1860	3,815
1870	6,786
1880	11,557
1890	13,146
1900	16,313
1910	16,704
1920	17,505
1930	16,022

1940	16,063
1950	13,891
1960	11,053
1970	10,976
1980	14,620

SEVIER

1870	19
1880	4,457
1890	6,199
1900	8,451
1910	9,775
1920	11,281
1930	11,199
1940	12,112
1950	12,072
1960	10,565
1970	10,103
1980	14,727

SHAMBIP

1860	162

SUMMIT

1860	198
1870	2,512
1880	4,497
1890	7,733
1900	9,439
1910	8,200
1920	7,862
1930	9,527
1940	8,714
1950	6,745
1960	5,673
1970	5,879
1980	10,198

TOOELE

1850	152
1860	1,008
1870	2,177
1880	4,497
1890	3,700
1900	7,361
1910	7,924
1920	7,965
1930	9,413
1940	9,133
1950	14,636
1960	17,868
1970	21,545
1980	26,033

UINTAH

1880	799
1890	2,762
1900	6,458
1910	7,050
1920	8,470
1930	9,035
1940	9,898
1950	10,300
1960	11,582
1970	12,682
1980	20,506

UTAH

1850	2,026
1860	8,248

1870	12,203
1880	17,963
1890	23,768
1900	32,456
1910	37,942
1920	40,792
1930	49,021
1940	57,382
1950	81,912
1960	106,991
1970	137,776
1980	218,106

WASATCH

1870	1,244
1880	2,927
1890	3,595
1900	4,736
1910	8,920
1920	4,645
1930	5,636
1940	5,754
1950	5,574
1960	5,308
1970	5,863
1980	8,523

WASHINGTON

1860	691
1870	3,064
1880	4,235
1890	4,009
1900	4,612
1910	5,123
1920	6,764
1930	7,420
1940	9,269
1950	9,836
1960	10,271
1970	13,669
1980	26,065

WAYNE

1900	1,907
1910	1,749
1920	2,097
1930	2,067
1940	2,394
1950	2,205
1960	1,728
1970	1,483
1980	1,911

WEBER

1850	1,186
1860	3,675
1870	7,858
1880	12,344
1890	22,723
1900	25,239
1910	35,179
1920	43,463
1930	52,172
1940	56,714
1950	83,319
1960	110,744
1970	126,278
1980	144,616

AMERICAN FORK

1900	2,732
1910	2,797
1920	2,763
1930	3,047
1940	3,333
1950	5,126
1960	6,373
1970	7,713
1980	12,564

BOUNTIFUL

1900	1,442
1910	1,677
1920	2,063
1930	2,571
1940	3,357
1950	6,004
1960	17,039
1970	27,283
1980	32,877

BRIGHAM CITY

1860	975
1870	1,315
1880	1,877
1890	2,139
1900	2,859
1910	3,685
1920	5,282
1930	5,093
1940	5,641
1950	6,790
1960	11,728
1970	14,007
1980	15,596

CEDAR CITY

1880	691
1890	967
1900	1,425
1910	1,705
1920	2,462
1930	3,615
1940	4,695
1950	6,106
1960	7,543
1970	8,946
1980	10,972

CLEARFIELD

1930	799
1940	1,053
1950	4,723
1960	8,833
1970	13,316
1980	17,982

LAYTON

1930	597
1940	646
1950	3,456
1960	9,027
1970	13,603
1980	22,862

LOGAN

1870	1,757
1880	3,396
1890	4,565
1900	5,451
1910	7,522
1920	9,439
1930	9,979
1940	11,868
1950	16,832
1960	18,731
1970	22,333
1980	26,844

MIDVALE

1910	1,760
1920	2,209
1930	2,451
1940	2,875
1950	3,996
1960	5,802
1970	7,840
1980	10,146

MURRAY

1910	4,057
1920	4,584
1930	5,172
1940	5,740
1950	9,006
1960	16,806
1970	21,206
1980	25,750

OGDEN

1860	1,464
1870	3,127
1880	6,069
1890	14,889
1900	16,313
1910	25,580
1920	32,804
1930	40,272
1940	43,688
1950	57,112
1960	70,197
1970	69,478
1980	64,407

OREM

1930	1,915
1940	2,914
1950	8,351
1960	18,394
1970	25,729
1980	52,399

PLEASANT GROVE

1870	930
1880	1,775
1890	1,926
1900	2,460
1910	1,618
1920	1,682
1930	1,754
1940	1,941
1950	3,195
1960	4,772
1970	5,327
1980	10,833

PROVO

1860	2,030
1870	2,384
1880	3,432
1890	5,159
1900	6,185
1910	8,925
1920	10,303
1930	14,766
1940	18,071
1950	28,937
1960	36,047
1970	53,131
1980	74,108

ROY

1940	998
1950	3,723
1960	9,239
1970	14,356
1980	19,694

SAINT GEORGE

1900	1,600
1910	1,737
1920	2,215
1930	2,434
1940	3,591
1950	4,562
1960	5,130
1970	7,097
1980	11,350

SALT LAKE CITY

1860	8,236
1870	12,854
1880	20,768
1890	44,843
1900	53,531
1910	92,777
1920	118,110
1930	140,267
1940	149,934
1950	182,121
1960	189,454
1970	175,885
1980	163,033

SANDY CITY

1900	1,030
1910	1,037
1920	1,208
1930	1,436
1940	1,487
1950	2,095
1960	3,322
1970	6,438
1980	50,546

SOUTH OGDEN

1940	1,407
1950	3,763
1960	7,405
1970	9,991
1980	11,366

SOUTH SALT LAKE

1940	5,701
1950	7,704
1960	9,520
1970	7,810
1980	10,561

SPRINGVILLE

1860	1,357
1870	1,661
1880	2,312
1890	2,849
1900	3,422
1910	3,356
1920	3,010
1930	3,748
1940	4,796
1950	6,475
1960	7,913
1970	8,790
1980	12,101

TOOELE

1900	1,200
1910	2,753
1920	3,602
1930	5,135
1940	5,001
1950	7,269
1960	9,133
1970	12,539
1980	14,335

WEST JORDAN

1950	2,107
1960	3,009
1970	4,221
1980	27,192

CORRECTION NOTE

The official 1980 census counts of total population shown in
this report supersede counts issued previously. Corrections
to the figures were made after the counts were provided to
the State for redistricting purposes and released in Advance
Report PHC80-V for this State.

Shown below are corrections to the 1980 census counts of the
total population made after the tabulations for this report
were completed. Any additional corrections made after this
report is printed are available by writing to Data User
Services Division, Customer Services (Corrections), Bureau of
the Census, Washington, D.C. 20233.

The 1980 figures shown in this publication are subject to
change pending the outcome of the various lawsuits dealing
with the census counts.

	1980 population	
	As shown in the tables	Corrected
Salt Lake County:		
Salt Lake City division:		
Salt Lake City city (pt.).......	163 033	163 697
Sandy City city (pt.)...........	50 546	52 210
South Salt Lake city............	10 561	9 884
Utah County:		
American Fork-Pleasant Grove division:		
American Fork city (pt.)..........	12 148	12 277
American Fork city (total)..........	12 564	12 693
Salt Lake City city (total)........	163 033	163 697
Sandy City city (total).............	50 546	52 210

County Subdivisions	1980	1970
The State	1 461 037	1 059 273
Beaver County[1]	4 378	3 800
Beaver division	2 298	...
Beaver city[1]	1 792	1 453
Milford–Minersville division	2 080	...
Milford city[1]	1 293	1 304
Minersville town[1]	552	448
Box Elder County[2]	33 222	28 129
Brigham City division	19 533	...
Brigham City city[2]	15 596	14 007
Mantua town	484	413
Perry city[2]	1 084	909
Willard city	1 241	1 045
Howell–Snowville division	1 283	...
Howell town	176	146
Plymouth town	238	203
Portage town	196	144
Snowville town	237	174
Tremonton division	11 976	...
Bear River City town[2]	540	445
Corinne city	512	471
Deweyville town	311	248
Elwood town[2]	481	294
Fielding town	325	254
Garland city[2]	1 405	1 187
Honeyville town[2]	915	640
Tremonton city[2]	3 464	2 794
West Box Elder division	430	394
Yost town	67	51
Cache County[3]	57 176	42 331
Hyrum division	5 099	...
Hyrum city (pt.)[3]	3 952	2 340
Paradise town	542	399
Lewiston division	4 280	...
Clarkston town[3]	562	420
Cornish town[3]	181	173
Lewiston city[3]	1 438	1 244
Richmond city[3]	1 705	1 000
Logan division	37 683	...
Hyde Park city (pt.)[3]	1 495	(NA)
Hyrum city (pt.)[3]	–	...
Logan city (pt.)[3]	26 844	22 333
Millville town[3]	848	441
Nibley town[3]	1 036	367
North Logan city[3]	2 258	1 405
Providence city[3]	2 675	1 608
River Heights city[3]	1 211	1 008
Smithfield division	6 996	...
Amalga town[3]	323	207
Hyde Park city (pt.)[3]	–	(NA)
Newton town[3]	623	444
Smithfield city[3]	4 993	3 342
Trenton town	447	390
Wasatch division	36	...
Logan city (pt.)[3]	–	...
Wellsville division	3 082	...
Mendon city[3]	663	345
Wellsville city[3]	1 952	1 267
Carbon County[4]	22 179	15 647
East Carbon division	2 570	...
East Carbon city[4]	1 942	...
Sunnyside city	611	485
Helper division	4 620	...
Helper city[4]	2 724	1 964
Scofield town	105	71
Price division	14 989	...
Hiawatha town (pt.)	249	166
Price city[4]	9 086	6 218
Wellington city[4]	1 406	922
Daggett County	769	666
East Daggett division	221	265
West Daggett division	548	401
Manila town	272	226
Davis County[5]	146 540	99 028
North Davis division	80 246	51 489
Clearfield city[5]	17 982	13 316
Clinton city	5 777	1 768
East Layton city[5]	3 531	763
Fruit Heights city (pt.)[5]	2 724	800
Kaysville city[5]	9 811	6 192
Layton city[5]	22 862	13 603
South Weber city[5]	1 575	1 073
Sunset city	5 733	6 268
Syracuse city[5]	3 702	1 843
West Point city[5]	2 170	1 020
South Davis division	66 294	47 539
Bountiful city[5]	32 877	27 751
Centerville city[5]	8 069	3 268
Farmington city[5]	4 691	2 526
Fruit Heights city (pt.)[5]	4	...
North Salt Lake city[5]	5 548	2 143
Val Verda (CDP)	6 422	...
West Bountiful city[5]	3 556	1 246
Woods Cross city[5]	4 263	3 124

County Subdivisions	1980	1970
Duchesne County[6]	12 565	7 299
Duchesne division	2 829	...
Duchesne city[6]	1 677	1 094
Tabiona town[6]	152	125
North Duchesne division	10	...
Roosevelt division	9 714	...
Altamont town[6]	247	129
Myton city	500	322
Roosevelt city[6]	3 842	2 005
South Duchesne division	12	...
Emery County[7]	11 451	5 137
Castle Dale–Huntington division	7 836	2 961
Castle Dale city[7]	1 910	541
Cleveland town[7]	522	244
Elmo town[7]	300	141
Hiawatha town (pt.)	–	...
Huntington city[7]	2 316	857
Orangeville city[7]	1 309	511
Emery–Ferron division	2 500	1 077
Emery town[7]	372	216
Ferron city[7]	1 718	663
Green River division	1 115	1 099
Green River city (pt.)	956	969
Garfield County[8]	3 673	3 157
Escalante division	851	...
Boulder town	113	93
Escalante town[8]	652	638
Hite division	202	...
Panguitch division	1 667	...
Hatch town	121	139
Panguitch city	1 343	1 318
Tropic division	953	...
Antimony town	94	113
Cannonville town	134	113
Henrieville town[8]	167	145
Tropic town	338	329
Grand County[9]	8 241	6 688
Moab division	7 915	6 272
Moab city[9]	5 333	4 793
Thompson division	326	416
Green River city (pt.)	92	64
Uintah and Ouray division	–	...
Iron County[10]	17 349	12 177
Beryl–Newcastle division	755	557
Cedar City division	14 031	9 720
Cedar City city[10]	10 972	8 946
Enoch town[10]	678	120
Kanarraville town	255	204
Parowan division	2 563	1 900
Brian Head town[10]	77	...
Paragonah town	310	275
Parowan city[10]	1 836	1 423
Juab County[11]	5 530	4 574
Eureka division	763	884
Eureka city	670	753
Nephi division	4 648	3 554
Levan town	453	376
Mona town[11]	536	309
Nephi city[11]	3 285	2 699
West Juab division	119	136
Kane County[12]	4 024	2 421
Kanab division	3 116	1 621
Kanab city[12]	2 148	1 381
Orderville division	908	800
Alton town	75	62
Glendale town	237	200
Orderville town[12]	423	399
Millard County[13]	8 970	6 988
Delta division	4 394	...
Delta city	1 930	1 610
Hinckley town	464	400
Leamington town	113	112
Lynndyl town	90	111
Fillmore division	3 254	...
Fillmore city[13]	2 083	1 411
Kanosh town	435	319
Meadow town	265	238
Garrison–Sevier Lake division	223	...
Scipio division	1 099	912
Holden town[13]	364	351
Oak City town	389	278
Scipio town	257	264
Morgan County[14]	4 917	3 983
Morgan North division	3 911	...
Morgan City city[14]	1 896	1 586
Morgan South division	1 006	...
Piute County	1 329	1 164
Circleville division	889	806
Circleville town	445	443
Junction town	151	135
Kingston town	146	114
Marysvale division	440	358
Marysvale town	359	289

County Subdivisions	1980	1970
Rich County[15]	2 100	1 615
Garden City–Laketown division	872	...
Garden City town[15]	259	134
Laketown town[15]	271	208
Randolph–Woodruff division	1 228	...
Randolph town[15]	659	500
Woodruff town	222	173
Salt Lake County[16]	619 066	458 607
Bingham division	4 535	2 137
Bluffdale city (pt.)[16]	–	...
Riverton city (pt.)	70	...
South Jordan city (pt.)[16]	–	...
West Jordan city (pt.)[16]	2 687	...
Cottonwood division	3 012	...
Alta town[16]	381	...
Sandy City city (pt.)	–	...
Emigration division	9 142	...
Mount Olympus (CDP)	6 068	5 909
Magna division	14 050	...
Magna (CDP)	13 138	5 509
Salt Lake City city (pt.)[16]	–	...
Salt Lake City division	588 327	...
Bennion (CDP)	9 575	...
Bluffdale city (pt.)[16]	1 300	...
Cottonwood (CDP)	11 554	8 431
Cottonwood Heights (CDP)	22 665	...
Draper city[16]	5 521	...
East Millcreek (CDP)	24 150	26 579
Granite Park (CDP)	5 554	9 573
Holladay (CDP)	22 189	23 014
Kearns (CDP)	21 353	17 247
Midvale city[16]	10 146	7 840
Murray city[16]	25 750	21 206
Riverton city (pt.)[16]	7 223	2 820
Salt Lake City city (pt.)[16]	163 033	175 885
Sandy City city (pt.)[16]	50 546	6 438
South Cottonwood (CDP)	11 117	...
South Jordan city (pt.)[16]	7 492	2 942
South Salt Lake city[16]	10 561	7 810
Taylorsville (CDP)	17 448	...
Union–East Midvale (CDP)	9 665	...
West Jordan city (pt.)[16]	24 505	4 221
West Valley (CDP)	72 378	...
White City (CDP)	7 188	...
San Juan County[17]	12 253	9 606
Blanding division	4 439	...
Blanding city[17]	3 118	2 250
Monticello division	3 027	...
Monticello city[17]	1 929	1 431
Oljato division	1 680	...
Red Mesa division	3 107	...
Sanpete County[18]	14 620	10 976
Ephraim–Manti division	5 739	...
Ephraim city[18]	2 810	2 127
Manti city	2 080	1 803
Mayfield town	397	267
Sterling town	199	144
Gunnison division	2 431	...
Centerfield town	653	419
Fayette town	165	93
Gunnison city	1 255	1 073
Mount Pleasant–Moroni division	6 450	4 703
Fairview town	916	696
Fountain Green city	578	467
Moroni city	1 086	894
Mount Pleasant city	2 049	1 516
Spring City city	671	456
Wales town	153	89
Sevier County[19]	14 727	10 103
Monroe division	3 050	...
Elsinore town	612	357
Joseph town	217	125
Monroe city	1 476	918
Richfield division	8 062	...
Annabella town	463	221
Glenwood town	447	212
Koosharem town	183	141
Richfield city[19]	5 482	4 471
Sigurd town[19]	386	291
Salina division	3 615	...
Aurora town[19]	874	493
Redmond town[19]	619	409
Salina city[19]	1 992	1 494
Summit County[20]	10 198	5 879
Coalville division	2 898	2 223
Coalville city	1 031	864
Henefer town	547	446
Kamas division	2 903	2 091
Francis town[20]	371	268
Kamas city[20]	1 064	806
Oakley town[20]	470	265
Park City division	4 397	1 565
Park City city (pt.)[20]	2 823	1 193
Tooele County[21]	26 033	21 545
Dugway–Wendover division	3 041	...
Dugway (CDP)	1 646	2 357
Wendover town	1 099	781
Onaqui division	791	679

County Subdivisions	1980	1970
Tooele County—Con.		
Onaqui division—Con.		
Ophir town	42	76
Rush Valley town[21]	356	541
Vernon town[21]	181	...
Tooele–Grantsville division	22 201	...
Grantsville city[21]	4 419	2 931
Stockton town	437	469
Tooele city[21]	14 335	12 539
Uintah County[22]	20 506	12 684
Uintah and Ouray division	4 338	...
Ballard town[22]	558	...
Vernal division	16 168	...
Maeser (CDP)	2 216	1 248
Vernal city[22]	6 600	3 908
Utah County[23]	218 106	137 776
American Fork–Pleasant Grove division	35 306	...
Alpine city[23]	2 649	1 047
American Fork city (pt.)[23]	12 148	7 713
Cedar Hills town[23]	571	...
Highland town[23]	2 435	...
Lehi city (pt.)[23]	163	...
Lindon city (pt.)[23]	–	(NA)
Pleasant Grove city[23]	10 833	5 327
Provo city (pt.)[23]	10	(NA)
Goshen division	1 700	1 201
Genola town	630	424
Goshen town	582	459
Lehi division	9 186	...
American Fork city (pt.)[23]	416	...
Cedar Fort town	269	188
Lehi city (pt.)[23]	6 685	4 659
Lindon city (pt.)[23]	–	(NA)
Provo–Orem division	127 466	...
Lindon city (pt.)[23]	2	(NA)
Orem city[23]	52 399	25 729
Provo city (pt.)[23]	74 098	(NA)
Springville city (pt.)[23]	–	(NA)
Spanish Fork–Payson division	28 374	...
Elk Ridge town[23]	381	...
Payson city[23]	8 246	4 501
Provo city (pt.)[23]	–	(NA)
Salem city[23]	2 233	1 081
Santaquin city[23]	2 175	1 236
Spanish Fork city (pt.)[23]	9 778	7 284
Woodland Hills town[23]	60	...
Springville–Mapleton division	16 074	...
Mapleton city[23]	2 726	1 980
Provo city (pt.)[23]	–	(NA)
Soldier Summit town (pt.)[23]	–	...
Spanish Fork city (pt.)[23]	47	...
Springville city (pt.)[23]	12 101	8 790
Wasatch County[24]	8 523	5 863
Heber division	8 493	...
Charleston town	320	196
Heber city[24]	4 362	3 245
Midway city	1 194	804
Park City city (pt.)	–	...
Wallsburg town	239	211
Soldier Summit division	12	...
Soldier Summit town (pt.)	12	13
Uintah and Ouray division	18	...
Washington County[25]	26 065	13 669
Enterprise division	982	...
Enterprise city[25]	905	844
Hurricane division	6 329	...
Hildale town[25]	1 009	480
Hurricane city (pt.)[25]	2 361	1 408
La Verkin town[25]	1 174	463
Leeds town	218	151
New Harmony town	117	78
Springdale town	258	172
Toquerville town[25]	277	185
Virgin town[25]	169	119
St. George division	18 754	...
Hurricane city (pt.)[25]	–	...
Ivins town	600	137
St. George city[25]	11 350	7 097
Santa Clara town[25]	1 091	271
Washington city[25]	3 092	750
Wayne County[26]	1 911	1 483
Hanksville division	351	181
Loa division	1 560	1 302
Bicknell town[26]	296	264
Loa town	364	324
Torrey town	140	84
Weber County[27]	144 616	126 278
Ogden division	135 010	...
Harrisville city[27]	1 263	749
North Ogden city[27]	9 309	5 257
Ogden city (pt.)[27]	64 407	69 478
Pleasant View city	3 983	2 021
Riverdale city[27]	6 031	3 704
Roy city[27]	19 694	14 356
South Ogden city[27]	11 366	9 991
Uintah town[27]	439	400
Washington Terrace city[27]	8 212	7 241

County Subdivisions

	1980	1970
Weber County—Con.		
Ogden Valley division	3 294	2 148
Huntsville town	577	553
Ogden city (pt.)	−	...
Weber Northwest division	6 312	...
Harrisville city (pt.)[27]	108	...
Plain City city [27]	2 379	1 543

VERMONT

The name Vermont is of French origin and signifies "green mountain."

The first visit by white men to the territory now covered by this state was probably made in 1609, when the French explorer, Samuel de Champlain, discovered the lake which bears his name. The first permanent white settlement was founded in 1724, when the English built Fort Dummer near the present site of Brattleboro.

The territory now embraced within the limits of Vermont was included in the grants conveyed by the first charter of Virginia, 1606, the charter of New England, 1620, and the royal grants of 1664 and 1674 to the Duke of York. Until 1740 a considerable portion of what is now Vermont had been claimed by the Massachusetts colony, under the terms of the charter of 1629, which granted it all the lands lying "within the space of three English miles to the northward of the * * * Merrimac, or to the northward of any and every part thereof," and extending westward to the Pacific; but in 1740 the present northern boundary of Massachusetts was established by royal decree.

For some years prior to 1764 New Hampshire contested the claim of New York to the territory west of the Connecticut River, on the grounds that the charters of 1664 and 1674 were obsolete, and that, Massachusetts and Connecticut having been allowed to extend their boundaries westward to within about 20 miles of the Hudson, New Hampshire should be given the same privilege. The original grant of New Hampshire had not included the territory in dispute, and in 1764 the claim of New York was sustained by royal decree. Nevertheless, the "New Hampshire Grants," as the country west of the Connecticut was then called, remained in dispute between New Hampshire and New York until the outbreak of the Revolution.

In January, 1777, a convention at Westminster declared the Grants an independent state with the name New Connecticut. In June, at an adjourned session, the present name was adopted, and in July, at a third session, the constitution was drafted.

Vermont continued an independent republic until March, 1791. At that date it became a member of the Union, being the first state admitted after the adoption of the Constitution by the original thirteen states.

In 1781 Vermont had laid claim to territory extending westward to the Hudson and a line drawn due north from the source of that river to the international, but in 1790 its boundaries were established substantially as they now exist.

COUNTY LOCATION INDEX

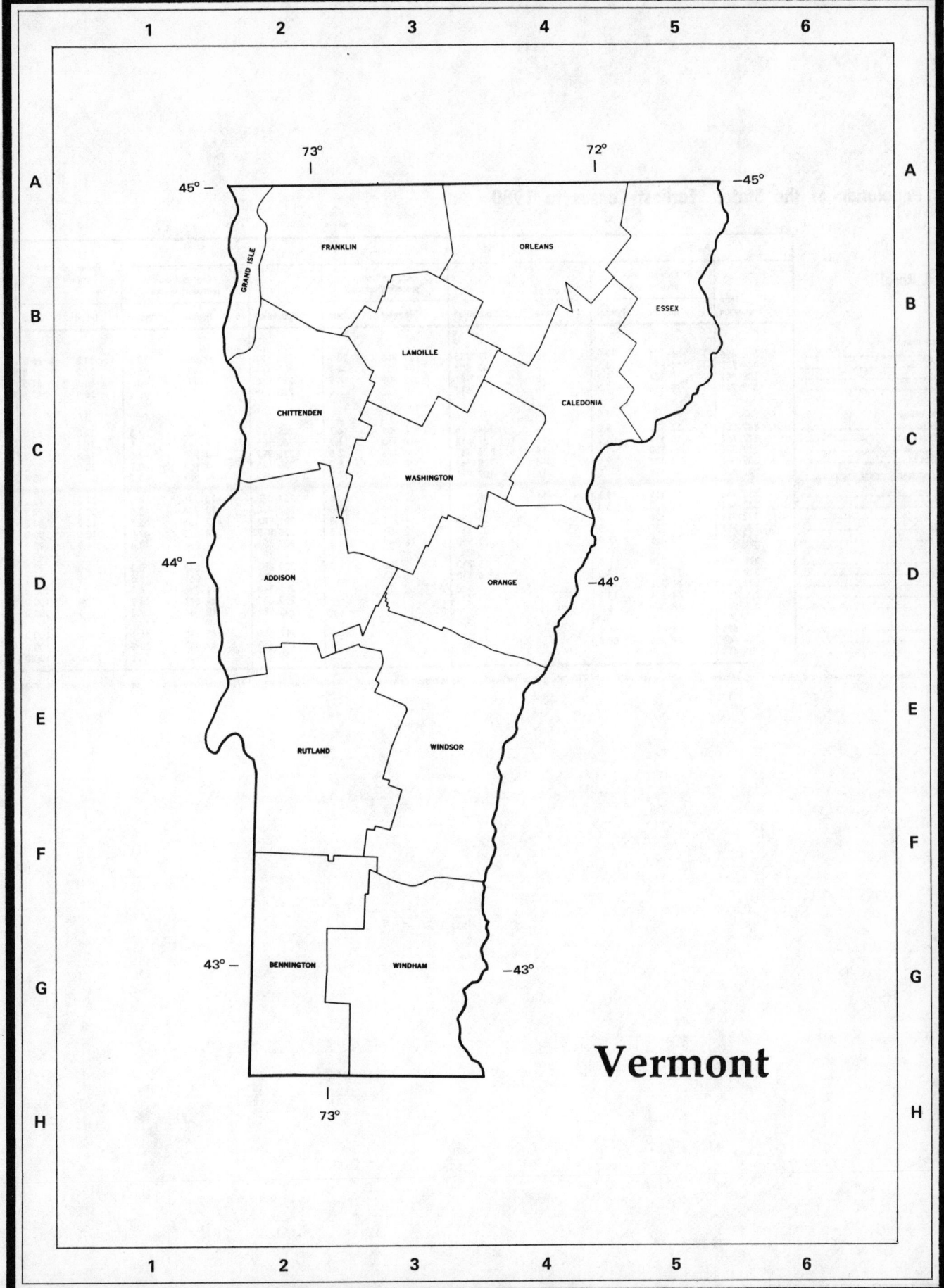

Vermont

Population of the State: Earliest Census to 1980

Urban and Rural

	The State			Urban				Rural				Percent of total population	
	Total population	Change from preceding census		Places of 2,500 or more	Population	Change from preceding census		Population	Change from preceding census			Urban	Rural
		Number	Percent			Number	Percent		Number	Percent			
Current urban definition:													
1980 (Apr. 1)_____	511 456	66 724	15.0	18	172 735	29 846	20.9	338 721	37 280	12.4		33.8	66.2
1970 (Apr. 1)_____	444 732	54 851	14.1	16	142 889	−7 032	−4.7	301 441	61 481	25.6		32.2	67.8
1960 (Apr. 1)_____	389 881	12 134	3.2	18	149 921	12 309	8.9	239 960	−175	−0.1		38.5	61.5
1950 (Apr. 1)_____	377 747	18 516	5.2	16	137 612	...	...	240 135	...	...		36.4	63.6
Previous urban definition:													
1960 (Apr. 1)_____	389 881	12 134	3.2	16	144 116	6 504	4.7	245 765	5 630	2.3		37.0	63.0
1950 (Apr. 1)_____	377 747	18 516	5.2	16	137 612	14 373	11.7	240 135	4 143	1.8		36.4	63.6
1940 (Apr. 1)_____	359 231	−380	−0.1	14	123 239	4 473	3.8	235 992	−4 853	−2.0		34.3	65.7
1930 (Apr. 1)_____	359 611	7 183	2.0	14	118 766	8 790	8.0	240 845	−1 607	−0.7		33.0	67.0
1920 (Jan. 1)_____	352 428	−3 528	−1.0	14	109 976	11 059	11.2	242 452	−14 587	−5.7		31.2	68.8
1910 (Apr. 15)_____	355 956	12 315	3.6	14	98 917	23 086	30.4	257 039	−10 771	−4.0		27.8	72.2
1900 (June 1)_____	343 641	11 219	3.4	10	75 831	25 193	49.8	267 810	−13 974	−5.0		22.1	77.9
1890 (June 1)_____	332 422	136	–	9	50 638	17 271	51.8	281 784	−17 135	−5.7		15.2	84.8
1880 (June 1)_____	332 286	1 735	0.5	6	33 367	10 407	45.3	298 919	−8 672	−2.8		10.0	90.0
1870 (June 1)_____	330 551	15 453	4.9	3	22 960	16 747	269.5	307 591	−1 294	−0.4		6.9	93.1
1860 (June 1)_____	315 098	978	0.3	1	6 213	103	1.7	308 885	875	0.3		2.0	98.0
1850 (June 1)_____	314 120	22 172	7.6	1	6 110	6 110	...	308 010	16 062	5.5		1.9	98.1
1840 (June 1)_____	291 948	11 296	4.0	–	–	–	–	291 948	11 296	4.0		–	100.0
1830 (June 1)_____	280 652	44 671	18.9	–	–	–	–	280 652	44 671	18.9		–	100.0
1820 (Aug. 7)_____	235 981	18 086	8.3	–	–	–	–	235 981	18 086	8.3		–	100.0
1810 (Aug. 6)_____	217 895	63 430	41.1	–	–	–	–	217 895	63 430	41.1		–	100.0
1800 (Aug. 4)_____	154 465	69 040	80.8	–	–	–	–	154 465	69 040	80.8		–	100.0
1790 (Aug. 2)_____	85 425	...	...	–	–	...	...	85 425	...	...		–	100.0

NOTE: Middlebury, St. Johnsbury, and Windsor villages disincorporated between 1960 and 1970; information received too late to permit delineation of unincorporated places in 1970, resulting in a major part of the decline in the urban population between 1960 and 1970.

ADDISON

1790	6,449
1800	13,417
1810	19,993
1820	20,469
1830	24,940
1840	23,583
1850	26,549
1860	24,010
1870	23,484
1880	24,173
1890	22,277
1900	21,912
1910	20,010
1920	18,666
1930	17,952
1940	17,944
1950	19,442
1960	20,076
1970	24,226
1980	29,406

BENNINGTON

1790	12,254
1800	14,617
1810	15,893
1820	16,125
1830	17,468
1840	16,872
1850	18,589
1860	19,436
1870	21,325
1880	21,950
1890	20,448
1900	21,705
1910	21,378
1920	21,577
1930	21,655
1940	22,286
1950	24,115
1960	25,088
1970	29,282
1980	33,345

CALEDONIA

1800	9,377
1810	18,730
1820	16,668
1830	20,967
1840	21,981
1850	23,595
1860	21,698
1870	22,235
1880	23,607
1890	23,436
1900	24,381
1910	26,031
1920	25,762
1930	27,253
1940	24,320
1950	24,049
1960	22,786
1970	22,789
1980	25,808

CHITTENDEN

1790	7,295
1800	12,778
1810	18,210
1820	16,272
1830	21,765
1840	22,997
1850	29,036
1860	28,171
1870	36,480
1880	32,792
1890	35,389
1900	39,600
1910	42,447
1920	43,708
1930	47,471
1940	52,098
1950	62,570
1960	74,425
1970	99,131
1980	115,534

ESSEX

1800	1,479
1810	3,087
1820	3,284
1830	3,981
1840	4,226
1850	4,650
1860	5,786
1870	6,811
1880	7,931
1890	9,511
1900	8,056
1910	7,384
1920	7,364
1930	7,067
1940	6,490
1950	6,257
1960	6,083
1970	5,416
1980	6,313

FRANKLIN

1800	8,782
1810	16,427
1820	17,192
1830	24,525
1840	24,531
1850	28,586
1860	27,231
1870	30,291
1880	30,225
1890	29,755
1900	30,198
1910	39,866
1920	30,026
1930	29,975
1940	29,601
1950	29,894
1960	29,474
1970	31,282
1980	34,788

GRAND ISLE

1810	3,445
1820	3,527
1830	3,696
1840	3,883
1850	4,145
1860	4,276
1870	4,082
1880	4,124
1890	3,843
1900	4,462
1910	3,761
1920	3,784
1930	3,944
1940	3,802
1950	3,406
1960	2,927
1970	3,574
1980	4,613

LAMOILLE

1840	10,475
1850	10,872
1860	12,311
1870	12,448
1880	12,684
1890	12,831
1900	12,289
1910	12,585
1920	11,858
1930	10,947
1940	11,028
1950	11,388
1960	11,027
1970	13,309
1980	16,767

ORANGE

1790	10,526
1800	18,238
1810	25,247
1820	24,247
1830	27,285
1840	27,283
1850	27,296
1860	25,455
1870	23,090
1880	23,525
1890	19,575
1900	19,313
1910	18,703
1920	17,279
1930	16,694
1940	17,048
1950	17,027
1960	16,014
1970	17,676
1980	22,739

ORLEANS

1800	1,439
1810	5,830
1820	6,936
1830	13,980
1840	13,634
1850	15,707
1860	18,981
1870	21,035
1880	22,083
1890	22,101
1900	22,024
1910	23,337
1920	23,913
1930	23,036
1940	21,718
1950	21,190
1960	20,143
1970	20,153
1980	23,440

RUTLAND

1790	15,591
1800	23,813
1810	29,486
1820	29,983
1830	31,294
1840	30,699
1850	33,059
1860	35,946
1870	40,651
1880	41,829
1890	45,397
1900	44,209
1910	48,139
1920	46,213
1930	48,453
1940	45,638
1950	45,905
1960	46,719
1970	52,637
1980	58,347

WASHINGTON

1820	14,113
1830	21,378
1840	23,506
1850	24,654
1860	27,622
1870	26,520
1880	25,404
1890	29,606
1900	36,607
1910	41,702
1920	38,921
1930	41,733
1940	41,546
1950	42,870
1960	42,860
1970	47,659
1980	52,393

WINDHAM

1790	17,570
1800	23,581
1810	26,760
1820	28,457
1830	28,748
1840	27,442
1850	29,062
1860	26,982
1870	26,036
1880	26,763
1890	26,547
1900	26,660
1910	26,932
1920	26,373
1930	26,015
1940	27,850
1950	28,749
1960	29,776
1970	33,476
1980	36,933

WINDSOR

1790	15,740
1800	26,944
1810	34,877
1820	38,233
1830	40,625
1840	40,356
1850	38,320
1860	37,193
1870	36,063
1880	35,196
1890	31,706
1900	32,225
1910	33,681
1920	36,984
1930	37,416
1940	37,862
1950	40,885
1960	42,483
1970	44,082
1980	51,030

NOTE

WASHINGTON

Name changed from Jefferson in 1814.

BURLINGTON

1850	6,110
1860	6,213
1870	14,387
1880	11,365
1890	14,590
1900	18,640
1910	20,468
1920	22,779
1930	24,789
1940	27,686
1950	33,155
1960	35,531
1970	38,633
1980	10,679

RUTLAND

1870	6,072
1880	7,502
1890	8,239
1900	11,499
1910	13,546
1920	14,954
1930	17,315
1940	17,082
1950	17,659
1960	18,325
1970	19,293
1980	18,436

SOUTH BURLINGTON

1980	10,679

CORRECTION NOTE

Shown below are corrections to the 1980 census counts of
the total population made after the tabulations for this
report were completed. Any additional corrections made
after this report is printed are available by writing to
Data User Services Division, Customer Services (Corrections), Bureau of the Census, Washington, D.C. 20233.

The 1980 figures shown in this publication are subject to
change pending the outcome of the various lawsuits dealing
with the census counts.

	1980 population	
	As shown in the tables	Corrected
Windsor County:		
Windsor town:		
Windsor (CDP)...................	(1)	3 478

[1]Not shown separately in the tables

County Subdivisions	1980	1970
The State	511 456	ʳ444 732
Addison County	29 406	24 266
Addison town	889	717
Bridport town	997	809
Bristol town	3 293	2 744
Bristol village	1 793	1 737
Cornwall town	993	900
Ferrisburg town	2 117	1 875
Goshen town	163	120
Granville town	288	255
Hancock town	334	283
Leicester town	803	583
Lincoln town	870	599
Middlebury town	7 574	6 532
Middlebury (CDP)	5 591	...
Monkton town	1 201	765
New Haven town	1 217	1 039
Orwell town	901	851
Panton town	537	416
Ripton town	327	187
Salisbury town	881	649
Shoreham town	972	790
Starksboro town	1 336	668
Vergennes city	2 273	2 242
Waltham town	394	265
Weybridge town	667	618
Whiting town	379	359
Bennington County[1]	33 345	29 282
Arlington town	2 184	1 934
Arlington (CDP) (pt.)	1 156	1 212
Bennington town[1]	15 815	14 586
Bennington (CDP)	9 349	...
North Bennington village	1 685	984
Old Bennington village	353	268
Dorset town	1 648	1 293
Glastenbury town[1]	3	ⁱ-
Landgrove town	121	104
Manchester town	3 261	2 919
Manchester village	563	435
Manchester Center (CDP)	1 719	1 560
Peru town	312	243
Pownal town	3 269	2 441
Readsboro town	638	638
Readsboro village	402	469
Rupert town	605	582
Sandgate town	234	127
Searsburg town	72	84
Shaftsbury town	3 001	2 411
Stamford town	773	752
Sunderland town	768	601
Arlington (CDP) (pt.)	153	...
Winhall town	327	281
Woodford town	314	286
Caledonia County[2]	25 808	22 789
Barnet town	1 338	1 342
Burke town	1 385	1 053
West Burke village	338	358
Danville town	1 705	1 405
Groton town[2]	667	666
Hardwick town	2 613	2 466
Hardwick village	1 476	1 503
Kirby town	282	224
Lyndon town[2]	4 924	3 705
Lyndonville village	1 401	1 415
Newark town	280	144
Peacham town	531	446
Ryegate town	1 000	830
St. Johnsbury town	7 938	8 409
St. Johnsbury (CDP)	7 150	...
Sheffield town	435	307
Stannard town	142	88
Sutton town	667	438
Walden town	575	442
Waterford town	882	586
Wheelock town	444	238
Chittenden County[3]	115 534	99 131
Bolton town	715	427
Buels gore	9	10
Burlington city	37 712	38 633
Charlotte town	2 561	1 802
Colchester town[3]	12 629	8 776
Essex town	14 392	10 951
Essex Junction village	7 033	6 511
Hinesburg town	2 690	1 775
Huntington town	1 161	748
Jericho town[3]	3 575	2 343
Jericho village[3]	1 340	ʳ749
Milton town	6 829	4 495
Milton village	1 411	1 164
Richmond town	3 159	2 249
Richmond village	865	935
St. George town	677	477
Shelburne town	5 000	3 728
South Burlington city[3]	10 679	...
Underhill town	2 172	1 198
Chittenden County—Con.		
Westford town	1 413	991
Williston town	3 843	3 187
Winooski city[3]	6 318	7 309
Essex County[4]	6 313	5 416
Averill town	15	8
Avery's gore	-	-
Bloomfield town	188	196
Brighton town	1 557	1 365
Island Pond (CDP)	1 216	1 123
Brunswick town	82	45
Canaan town	1 196	949
Concord town[4]	1 125	896
East Haven town	280	197
Ferdinand town	12	14
Granby town	70	52
Guildhall town	202	169
Lemington town	108	120
Lewis town	-	-
Lunenburg town	1 138	1 061
Maidstone town	100	94
Norton town	184	207
Victory town	56	42
Warner's grant	-	-
Warren's gore	-	1
Franklin County[5]	34 788	31 282
Bakersfield town	852	635
Berkshire town	1 116	931
Enosburg town	2 070	1 918
Enosburg Falls village	1 207	1 266
Fairfax town	1 805	1 366
Fairfield town	1 493	1 285
Fletcher town	626	456
Franklin town	1 006	821
Georgia town	2 818	1 711
Highgate town	2 493	1 936
Montgomery town	681	651
Richford town	2 206	2 116
Richford village	1 471	1 527
St. Albans city	7 308	8 082
St. Albans town	3 555	3 270
Sheldon town	1 618	1 481
Swanton town	5 141	4 622
Swanton village[5]	2 520	2 630
Grand Isle County	4 613	3 574
Alburg town	1 352	1 271
Alburg village	496	520
Grand Isle town	1 238	809
Isle La Motte town	393	262
North Hero town	442	364
South Hero town	1 188	868
Lamoille County[6]	16 767	13 309
Belvidere town	218	189
Cambridge town	2 019	1 528
Cambridge village	217	235
Jeffersonville village	491	382
Eden town	612	513
Elmore town	421	292
Hyde Park town	2 021	1 347
Hyde Park village[6]	475	418
Johnson town	2 581	1 927
Johnson village	1 393	1 296
Morristown town	4 448	4 052
Morrisville village	2 074	2 116
Stowe town	2 991	2 388
Stowe village	531	435
Waterville town	470	397
Wolcott town	986	676
Orange County[7]	22 739	17 676
Bradford town	2 191	1 627
Bradford village	831	709
Braintree town	1 065	751
Brookfield town	959	606
Chelsea town	1 091	983
Corinth town	904	683
Fairlee town	770	604
Newbury town	1 699	1 440
Newbury village[7]	425	ʳ344
Wells River village	396	419
Orange town	752	540
Randolph town	4 689	3 882
Randolph village	2 217	2 115
Strafford town	731	536
Thetford town	2 188	1 422
Topsham town	767	686
Tunbridge town	925	791
Vershire town	442	299
Washington town	855	667
West Fairlee town	427	337
Williamstown town	2 284	1 822
Orleans County[8]	23 440	20 153
Albany town	705	528
Albany village	174	175
Barton town	2 990	2 874
Barton village	1 062	1 051

County Subdivisions	1980	1970
Orleans County—Con.		
Barton town—Con.		
Orleans village	983	1 138
Brownington town	708	522
Charleston town	851	654
Coventry town	674	492
Craftsbury town	844	632
Derby town	4 222	3 252
Derby Center village	598	547
Derby Line village	874	834
Glover town⁸	843	649
Greensboro town	677	593
Holland town	473	383
Irasburg town	870	775
Jay town	302	182
Lowell town	573	515
Morgan town	460	286
Newport city	4 756	4 664
Newport town	1 319	1 125
Troy town	1 498	1 457
North Troy village	717	774
Westfield town	418	375
Westmore town	257	195
Rutland County	58 347	52 637
Benson town	739	583
Brandon town	4 194	3 697
Brandon (CDP)	1 925	1 720
Castleton town	3 637	2 837
Chittenden town	927	646
Clarendon town	2 372	1 537
Danby town	992	910
Fair Haven town	2 819	2 777
Fair Haven (CDP)	2 363	2 287
Hubbardton town	490	228
Ira town	354	284
Mendon town	1 056	743
Middletown Springs town	603	426
Mount Holly town	938	687
Mount Tabor town	211	184
Pawlet town	1 244	1 184
Pittsfield town	396	249
Pittsford town	2 590	2 306
Pittsford village	666	682
Poultney town	3 196	3 217
Poultney village	1 554	1 914
Proctor town	1 998	2 095
Rutland city	18 436	19 293
Rutland town	3 300	2 248
Sherburne town	891	558
Shrewsbury town	866	570
Sudbury town	380	253
Tinmouth town	406	268
Wallingford town	1 893	1 676
Wallingford (CDP)	1 141	...
Wells town	815	560
West Haven town	253	240
West Rutland town	2 351	2 381
West Rutland (CDP)	2 169	1 875
Washington County⁹	52 393	47 659
Barre city	9 824	10 209
Barre town	7 090	6 509
Graniteville—East Barre (CDP)	2 172	...
South Barre (CDP)	1 301	...
Berlin town	2 454	2 050
Cabot town	958	663
Cabot village	259	253
Calais town	1 207	749
Duxbury town	877	621
East Montpelier town	2 205	1 597
Fayston town	657	292
Marshfield town	1 267	1 033
Marshfield village	301	322
Plainfield village (pt.)	138	46
Middlesex town	1 235	857
Montpelier city	8 241	8 609
Moretown town	1 221	904
Northfield town	5 435	4 870
Northfield village	2 033	2 139
Plainfield town	1 249	1 399
Plainfield village (pt.)	461	445
Roxbury town	452	354
Waitsfield town	1 300	837
Warren town	956	588
Waterbury town	4 465	4 614
Waterbury village⁹	1 892	2 840
Woodbury town	573	399
Worcester town	727	505
Windham County¹⁰	36 933	33 476
Athens town	250	159
Brattleboro town	11 886	12 239
Brattleboro (CDP)	8 596	9 055
West Brattleboro (CDP)	2 795	...
Brookline town	310	180
Dover town	666	555
Dummerston town	1 574	1 295
Grafton town	604	465

County Subdivisions	1980	1970
Windham County—Con.		
Guilford town	1 532	1 108
Halifax town	488	295
Jamaica town	681	590
Londonderry town	1 510	1 037
Marlboro town	695	592
Newfane town	1 129	900
Newfane village	119	183
Putney town	1 850	1 727
Rockingham town	5 538	5 501
Bellows Falls village	3 456	3 505
Saxtons River village	593	581
Somerset town¹⁰	2	...
Stratton town	122	104
Townshend town¹⁰	849	668
Vernon town	1 175	1 024
Wardsboro town	505	391
Westminster town	2 493	1 875
North Westminster village	310	348
Westminster village	319	446
Whitingham town	1 043	1 011
Jacksonville village	252	251
Wilmington town¹⁰	1 808	1 586
Windham town	223	174
Windsor County	51 030	44 082
Andover town	350	239
Baltimore town	181	170
Barnard town	790	569
Bethel town	1 715	1 347
Bethel (CDP)	1 016	...
Bridgewater town	867	783
Cavendish town	1 355	1 264
Proctorsville village	481	512
Chester town	2 791	2 371
Chester—Chester Depot (CDP)	1 267	...
Hartford town	7 963	6 477
White River Junction (CDP)	2 582	2 379
Wilder (CDP)	1 461	1 328
Hartland town	2 396	1 806
Ludlow town	2 414	2 463
Ludlow village	1 352	1 508
Norwich town	2 398	1 966
Plymouth town	405	283
Pomfret town	856	620
Reading town	647	564
Rochester town	1 054	884
Royalton town	2 100	1 399
Sharon town	828	541
Springfield town	10 190	10 063
Springfield (CDP)	5 603	5 632
Stockbridge town	508	389
Weathersfield town	2 534	2 040
Perkinsville village	187	188
Weston town	627	507
West Windsor town	763	571
Windsor town	4 084	4 158
Woodstock town	3 214	2 608
Woodstock village	1 178	1 154

VIRGINIA

Virginia was named in honor of Elizabeth of England, the "Virgin Queen."

The Atlantic shore of North America was visited by John Cabot in 1497-98, and on his discovery England based its claim to a large part of the continent. In 1584 a fleet sent out by Sir Walter Raleigh anchored off the shores of what is now North Carolina, and returned with glowing accounts of the country. It was at this time that the name Virginia was given to the entire region between the Spanish claims on the south and those of France on the north.

In 1606, Virginia, extending from the thirty-fourth to the forty-fifth parallel, was divided by grants of King James I between the London Company and the Plymouth Company; and in 1607, Jamestown, on the James River, was settled by colonists sent out by the former company.

In 1609 a new charter was granted, by which the boundaries of the Virginia colony were defined as extending 200 miles north and 200 miles south of Point Comfort and "up into the land, throughout from sea to sea, west and northwest, * * *." When this charter was remodeled, some three years later, the Bermuda Islands were made a part of Virginia. In 1624 the London Company was dissolved and Virginia was erected into a crown colony.

The area of the colony was reduced in 1632 by the charter of Maryland, and in 1663 and 1665 by the charters of Carolina. Virginia, however, did not relinquish jurisdiction over a large tract at the headwaters of the Potomac within the charter boundaries of Maryland, but retained the disputed territory until it became a part of the state of West Virginia. The boundary between southwestern Pennsylvania and northern Virginia was not fixed until 1779, when it was established at its present location. In 1784 the state ceded its territory northwest of the Ohio to the Federal Government. In 1792 Kentucky, which prior to that time had formed a part of Virginia, was admitted to the Union as a separate state.

When Virginia seceded from the Union the counties northwest of the Alleghenies remained loyal to the United States, and in 1863 were admitted as the state of West Virginia. In the same year the counties of Berkeley and Jefferson were transferred from Virginia to West Virginia and in 1866 Congress recognized and approved the transfer. This left both states with substantially their present limits.

Virginia was one of the original thirteen states.

COUNTY LOCATION INDEX

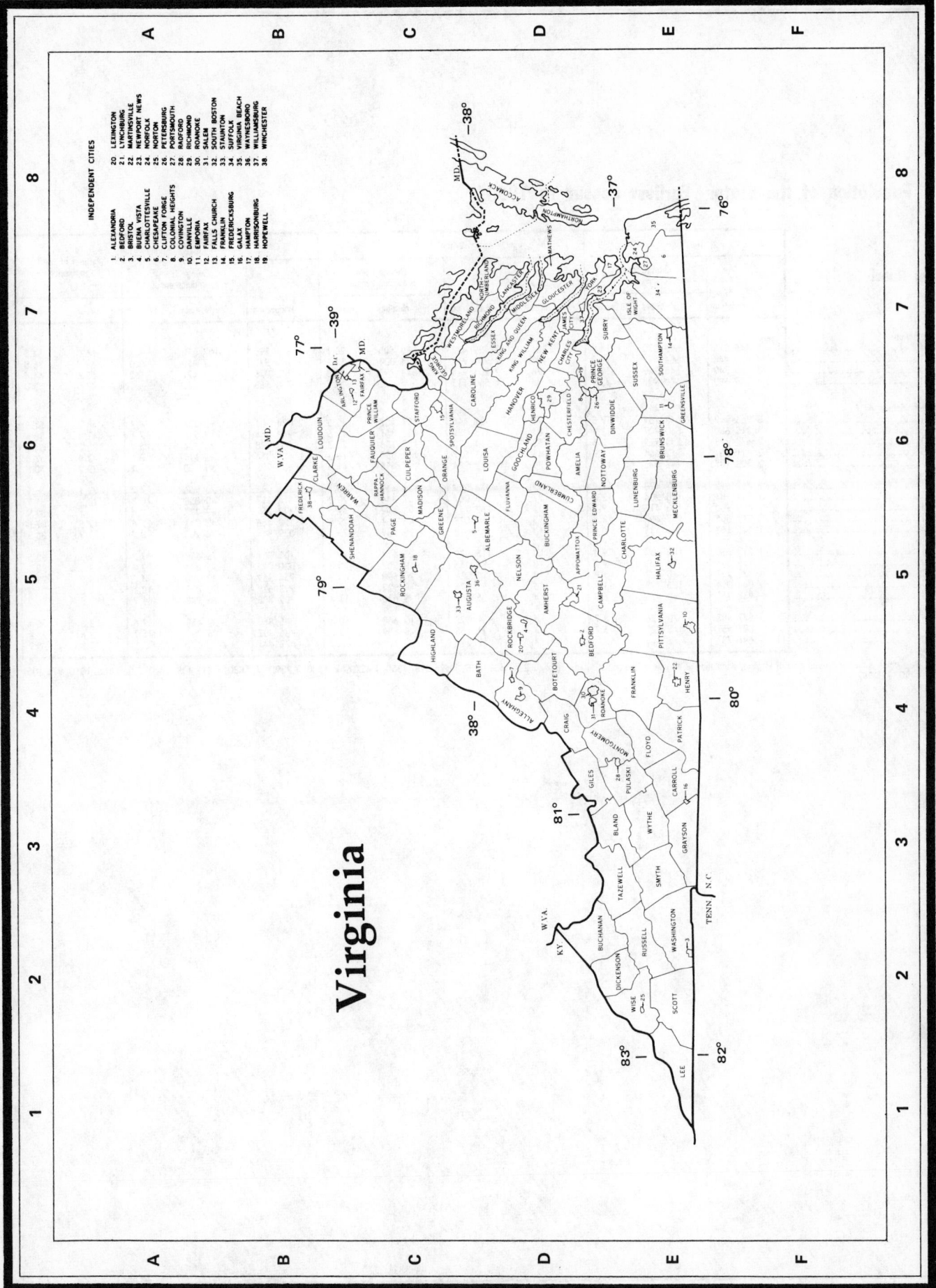

Virginia

INDEPENDENT CITIES

1 ALEXANDRIA
2 BEDFORD
3 BRISTOL
4 BUENA VISTA
5 CHARLOTTESVILLE
6 CHESAPEAKE
7 CLIFTON FORGE
8 COLONIAL HEIGHTS
9 COVINGTON
10 DANVILLE
11 EMPORIA
12 FAIRFAX
13 FALLS CHURCH
14 FRANKLIN
15 FREDERICKSBURG
16 GALAX
17 HAMPTON
18 HARRISONBURG
19 HOPEWELL
20 LEXINGTON
21 LYNCHBURG
22 MARTINSVILLE
23 NEWPORT NEWS
24 NORFOLK
25 NORTON
26 PETERSBURG
27 PORTSMOUTH
28 RADFORD
29 RICHMOND
30 ROANOKE
31 SALEM
32 SOUTH BOSTON
33 STAUNTON
34 SUFFOLK
35 VIRGINIA BEACH
36 WAYNESBORO
37 WILLIAMSBURG
38 WINCHESTER

Population of the State: Earliest Census to 1980

Urban and Rural

	The State			Urban				Rural			Percent of total population	
	Total population	Change from preceding census		Places of 2,500 or more	Population	Change from preceding census		Population	Change from preceding census		Urban	Rural
		Number	Percent			Number	Percent		Number	Percent		
Current urban definition:												
1980 (Apr. 1)	5 346 818	695 370	14.9	156	3 529 423	590 506	20.1	1 817 395	107 818	6.3	66.0	34.0
1970 (Apr. 1)	ʳ4 651 448	684 499	17.3	107	2 938 917	734 004	33.3	1 709 577	-52 459	-3.0	63.2	36.8
1960 (Apr. 1)	3 966 949	648 269	19.5	76	2 204 913	644 798	41.3	1 762 036	3 471	0.2	55.6	44.4
1950 (Apr. 1)	3 318 680	640 907	23.9	78	1 560 115	...	...	1 758 565	...	...	47.0	53.0
Previous urban definition:												
1960 (Apr. 1)	3 966 949	648 269	19.5	71	1 932 468	557 432	40.5	2 034 481	90 837	4.7	48.7	51.3
1950 (Apr. 1)	3 318 680	640 907	23.9	64	1 375 036	430 361	45.6	1 943 644	210 546	12.1	41.4	58.6
1940 (Apr. 1)	2 677 773	255 922	10.6	53	944 675	159 138	20.3	1 733 098	96 784	5.9	35.3	64.7
1930 (Apr. 1)	2 421 851	112 664	4.9	45	785 537	111 553	16.6	1 636 314	1 111	0.1	32.4	67.6
1920 (Jan. 1)	2 309 187	247 575	12.0	39	673 984	197 455	41.4	1 635 203	50 120	3.2	29.2	70.8
1910 (Apr. 15)	2 061 612	207 428	11.2	32	476 529	136 462	40.1	1 585 083	70 966	4.7	23.1	76.9
1900 (June 1)	1 854 184	198 204	12.0	27	340 067	57 346	20.3	1 514 117	140 858	10.3	18.3	81.7
1890 (June 1)	1 655 980	143 415	9.5	25	282 721	93 642	49.5	1 373 259	49 773	3.8	17.1	82.9
1880 (June 1)	1 512 565	287 402	23.5	15	189 079	43 461	29.8	1 323 486	243 941	22.6	12.5	87.5
1870 (June 1)	1 225 163	5 533	0.5	13	145 618	29 739	25.7	1 079 545	-24 206	-2.2	11.9	88.1
1860 (June 1)	1 219 630	100 282	9.0	10	115 879	26 624	29.8	1 103 751	73 658	7.2	9.5	90.5
1850 (June 1)	1 119 348	94 121	9.2	8	89 255	18 287	25.8	1 030 093	75 834	7.9	8.0	92.0
1840 (June 1)	1 025 227	-18 827	-1.8	8	70 968	20 593	40.9	954 259	-39 420	-4.0	6.9	93.1
1830 (June 1)	1 044 054	105 793	11.3	6	50 375	14 922	42.1	993 679	90 871	10.1	4.8	95.2
1820 (Aug. 7)	938 261	60 578	6.9	4	35 453	3 630	11.4	902 808	56 948	6.7	3.8	96.2
1810 (Aug. 6)	877 683	70 126	8.7	4	31 823	10 668	50.4	845 860	59 458	7.6	3.6	96.4
1800 (Aug. 4)	807 557	115 820	16.7	4	21 155	8 859	72.0	786 402	106 961	15.7	2.6	97.4
1790 (Aug. 2)	691 737	...	...	4	12 296	...	...	679 441	...	...	1.8	98.2

NOTE: Population is that of present area of Virginia; population of Virginia as then constituted: 1870, 1,225,163; 1860, 1,596,318; 1850, 1,421,661; 1840, 1,239,797; 1830, 1,211,405; 1820, 1,065,366; 1810, 974,600; 1800, 880,200; 1790, 821,287.

ACCOMACK

1790	13,959
1800	15,693
1810	15,743
1820	15,996
1830	16,656
1840	17,096
1850	17,890
1860	18,586
1870	20,409
1880	24,408
1890	27,277
1900	32,570
1910	36,650
1920	34,795
1930	35,854
1940	33,030
1950	33,832
1960	30,635
1970	29,004
1980	31,268

ALBEMARLE

1790	12,585
1800	16,439
1810	18,268
1820	19,750
1830	22,618
1840	22,924
1850	25,800
1860	26,625
1870	27,544
1880	32,618
1890	32,379
1900	28,473
1910	29,871
1920	26,005
1930	26,981
1940	24,652
1950	26,662
1960	30,969
1970	37,780
1980	55,783

ALLEGHANY

1830	2,816
1840	2,749
1850	3,515
1860	6,765
1870	3,674
1880	5,586
1890	9,283
1900	16,330
1910	14,173
1920	15,332
1930	20,188
1940	22,688
1950	23,139
1960	12,128
1970	12,461
1980	14,333

AMELIA

1790	18,097
1800	9,432
1810	10,594
1820	11,104
1830	11,036
1840	10,320
1850	9,770
1860	10,741
1870	9,878
1880	10,377

1890	9,068
1900	9,037
1910	8,720
1920	9,800
1930	8,979
1940	8,495
1950	7,908
1960	7,815
1970	7,592
1980	8,405

AMHERST

1790	13,703
1800	16,801
1810	10,548
1820	10,434
1830	12,071
1840	12,576
1850	12,699
1860	13,742
1870	14,900
1880	18,709
1890	17,551
1900	17,864
1910	18,932
1920	19,771
1930	19,020
1940	20,273
1950	20,332
1960	22,953
1970	26,072
1980	29,122

APPOMATTOX

1850	9,193
1860	8,889
1870	8,950
1880	10,080
1890	9,589
1900	9,662
1910	8,904
1920	9,255
1930	8,402
1940	9,020
1950	8,764
1960	9,148
1970	9,784
1980	11,971

ARLINGTON

1890	4,258
1900	6,430
1910	10,231
1920	16,040
1930	26,615
1940	57,040
1950	135,449
1960	163,401
1970	174,284
1980	152,599

AUGUSTA

1790	10,886
1800	11,712
1810	14,308
1820	16,742
1830	19,926
1840	19,628
1850	24,610
1860	27,749
1870	38,763
1880	35,710

1890	37,005
1900	32,370
1910	32,445
1920	34,071
1930	38,163
1940	42,772
1950	34,154
1960	37,363
1970	44,220
1980	53,732

BATH

1800	5,508
1810	4,837
1820	5,237
1830	4,002
1840	4,300
1850	3,426
1860	3,676
1870	3,795
1880	4,482
1890	4,587
1900	5,595
1910	6,538
1920	6,389
1930	8,137
1940	7,191
1950	6,296
1960	5,355
1970	5,192
1980	5,860

BEDFORD

1790	10,531
1800	14,125
1810	16,148
1820	19,305
1830	20,246
1840	20,203
1850	24,080
1860	25,068
1870	25,327
1880	31,205
1890	31,213
1900	30,356
1910	29,549
1920	30,669
1930	29,091
1940	29,687
1950	29,627
1960	31,028
1970	26,728
1980	34,927

BLAND

1870	4,000
1880	5,004
1890	5,129
1900	5,497
1910	5,154
1920	5,593
1930	6,031
1940	6,731
1950	6,436
1960	5,982
1970	5,423
1980	6,349

BOTETOURT

1790	10,524
1800	10,427
1810	13,301

1820	13,589
1830	16,354
1840	11,679
1850	14,908
1860	11,516
1870	11,329
1880	14,809
1890	14,854
1900	17,161
1910	17,727
1920	16,557
1930	15,457
1940	16,447
1950	15,766
1960	16,715
1970	18,193
1980	23,270

BRUNSWICK

1790	12,827
1800	16,339
1810	15,411
1820	16,687
1830	15,767
1840	14,346
1850	13,894
1860	14,809
1870	13,427
1880	16,707
1890	17,245
1900	18,217
1910	19,244
1920	21,025
1930	20,486
1940	19,575
1950	20,136
1960	17,779
1970	16,172
1980	15,632

BUCHANAN

1860	2,793
1870	3,777
1880	5,694
1890	5,867
1900	9,692
1910	12,334
1920	15,441
1930	16,740
1940	31,477
1950	35,748
1960	36,724
1970	32,071
1980	37,989

BUCKINGHAM

1790	9,779
1800	13,389
1810	20,059
1820	17,569
1830	18,351
1840	18,786
1850	13,837
1860	15,212
1870	13,371
1880	15,540
1890	14,383
1900	15,266
1910	15,204
1920	14,885
1930	13,315
1940	13,398
1950	12,288
1960	10,877

1970	10,597
1980	11,751

CAMPBELL

1790	7,685
1800	9,866
1810	11,001
1820	16,569
1830	20,350
1840	21,030
1850	23,245
1860	26,197
1870	28,384
1880	36,250
1890	41,087
1900	23,256
1910	23,043
1920	26,716
1930	22,885
1940	26,048
1950	28,877
1960	32,958
1970	34,248
1980	45,424

CAROLINE

1790	17,489
1800	17,438
1810	17,554
1820	18,008
1830	17,760
1840	17,813
1850	18,456
1860	18,464
1870	15,128
1880	17,243
1890	16,681
1900	16,709
1910	16,596
1920	15,954
1930	15,263
1940	13,945
1950	12,471
1960	12,725
1970	13,925
1980	17,904

CARROLL

1850	5,909
1860	8,012
1870	9,147
1880	13,323
1890	15,497
1900	19,303
1910	21,116
1920	21,283
1930	22,141
1940	25,904
1950	26,695
1960	23,187
1970	23,092
1980	27,270

CHARLES CITY

1790	5,588
1800	5,365
1810	5,186
1820	5,255
1830	5,500
1840	4,774
1850	5,200
1860	5,609

1870	4,975	**CRAIG**		**DINWIDDIE**		1880	16,025	**FRANKLIN**	
1880	5,512					1890	16,655		
1890	5,066	1860	3,553	1790	13,934	1900	18,580	1790	6,842
1900	5,040	1870	2,942	1800	15,374	1910	20,536	1800	9,302
1910	5,253	1880	3,794	1810	18,190	1920	21,943	1810	10,724
1920	4,793	1890	3,835	1820	20,482	1930	25,264	1820	12,017
1930	4,881	1900	4,293	1830	21,901	1940	40,924	1830	14,911
1940	4,275	1910	4,711	1840	22,558	1950	98,557	1840	15,832
1950	4,676	1920	4,100	1850	25,118	1960	275,002	1850	17,430
1960	5,492	1930	3,562	1860	30,198	1970	454,275	1860	20,098
1970	6,158	1940	3,769	1870	30,702	1980	596,901	1870	18,364
1980	6,692	1950	3,452	1880	32,870			1880	25,084
		1960	3,356	1890	13,515	**FAUQUIER**		1890	24,985
CHARLOTTE		1970	3,524	1900	15,374			1900	25,953
		1980	3,948	1910	15,442	1790	17,832	1910	26,480
1790	10,078			1920	17,949	1800	21,329	1920	26,283
1800	11,912	**CULPEPER**		1930	18,492	1810	22,689	1930	24,337
1810	13,161			1940	18,166	1820	23,103	1940	25,864
1820	13,290	1790	22,105	1950	18,839	1830	26,086	1950	24,560
1830	15,252	1800	18,100	1960	22,183	1840	21,897	1960	25,925
1840	14,595	1810	18,967	1970	21,668	1850	20,868	1970	28,163
1850	13,955	1820	20,944	1980	22,602	1860	21,706	1980	35,740
1860	14,471	1830	24,027			1870	19,690		
1870	14,513	1840	11,393	**ELIZABETH CITY**		1880	22,993	**FREDERICK**	
1880	16,653	1850	12,282			1890	22,590		
1890	15,077	1860	12,063	1790	3,450	1900	23,374	1790	19,681
1900	15,343	1870	12,227	1800	2,778	1910	22,526	1800	24,744
1910	15,785	1880	13,408	1810	3,608	1920	21,869	1810	22,574
1920	17,540	1890	13,233	1820	3,789	1930	21,071	1820	24,706
1930	16,061	1900	14,123	1830	5,053	1940	21,039	1830	26,046
1940	15,861	1910	13,472	1840	3,706	1950	21,248	1840	14,242
1950	14,057	1920	13,292	1850	4,586	1960	24,066	1850	15,975
1960	13,368	1930	13,306	1860	5,798	1970	26,375	1860	16,546
1970	12,366	1940	13,365	1870	8,303	1980	35,889	1870	16,596
1980	12,266	1950	13,242	1880	10,689			1880	17,553
		1960	15,088	1890	16,168	**FLOYD**		1890	17,880
CHESTERFIELD		1970	18,218	1900	19,460			1900	13,239
		1980	22,620	1910	15,720	1840	4,453	1910	12,787
1790	14,214			1920	19,111	1850	6,458	1920	12,641
1800	14,488	**CUMBERLAND**		1930	19,835	1860	8,236	1930	13,167
1810	9,979			1940	32,283	1870	9,824	1940	14,008
1820	18,003	1790	8,153	1950	55,028	1880	13,255	1950	17,537
1830	18,637	1800	9,839			1890	14,405	1960	21,941
1840	17,148	1810	9,992	**ESSEX**		1900	15,388	1970	24,107
1850	17,489	1820	11,023			1910	14,092	1980	34,150
1860	19,016	1830	11,690	1790	9,122	1920	13,115		
1870	18,470	1840	10,399	1800	9,508	1930	11,698	**GILES**	
1880	25,085	1850	9,751	1810	9,376	1940	11,967		
1890	26,211	1860	9,961	1820	9,909	1950	11,251	1810	3,745
1900	18,804	1870	8,142	1830	10,521	1960	10,462	1820	4,521
1910	21,299	1880	10,540	1840	11,309	1970	9,775	1830	5,274
1920	20,496	1890	9,482	1850	10,206	1980	11,563	1840	5,307
1930	26,049	1900	8,996	1860	10,469			1850	6,570
1940	31,183	1910	9,195	1870	9,927	**FLUVANNA**		1860	6,883
1950	40,400	1920	9,111	1880	11,032			1870	5,875
1960	71,197	1930	7,535	1890	10,047	1790	3,921	1880	8,794
1970	77,045	1940	7,505	1900	9,701	1800	4,623	1890	9,090
1980	141,372	1950	7,252	1910	9,105	1810	4,775	1900	10,793
		1960	6,360	1920	8,542	1820	6,704	1910	11,623
CLARKE		1970	6,179	1930	6,976	1830	8,221	1920	11,901
		1980	7,881	1940	7,006	1840	8,812	1930	12,804
1840	6,353			1950	6,530	1850	9,487	1940	14,635
1850	7,352	**DICKENSON**		1960	6,690	1860	10,358	1950	18,956
1860	7,146			1970	7,099	1870	9,875	1960	17,219
1870	6,670	1890	5,077	1980	8,864	1880	10,802	1970	16,741
1880	7,682	1900	7,747			1890	9,508	1980	17,810
1890	8,071	1910	9,199	**FAIRFAX**		1900	9,050		
1900	7,927	1920	13,542			1910	8,323	**GLOUCESTER**	
1910	7,468	1930	16,163	1790	12,320	1920	8,547		
1920	7,165	1940	21,266	1800	13,317	1930	7,466	1790	13,498
1930	7,167	1950	23,393	1810	13,111	1940	7,088	1800	8,181
1940	7,159	1960	20,211	1820	11,404	1950	7,121	1810	10,427
1950	7,074	1970	16,077	1830	9,204	1960	7,227	1820	9,678
1960	7,942	1980	19,806	1840	9,370	1970	7,621	1830	10,608
1970	8,102			1850	10,682	1980	10,244	1840	10,715
1980	9,965			1860	11,834			1850	10,527
				1870	12,952			1860	10,956

1870	10,211	**GREENSVILLE**		1850	43,572	**JAMES CITY**		1850	8,779

1870	10,211
1880	11,876
1890	11,653
1900	12,832
1910	12,477
1920	11,894
1930	11,019
1940	9,548
1950	10,343
1960	11,919
1970	14,059
1980	20,107

GOOCHLAND

1790	9,053
1800	9,696
1810	10,203
1820	10,007
1830	10,369
1840	9,760
1850	10,352
1860	10,656
1870	10,313
1880	10,292
1890	9,958
1900	9,519
1910	9,237
1920	8,863
1930	7,953
1940	8,454
1950	8,934
1960	9,206
1970	10,069
1980	11,761

GRAYSON

1800	3,912
1810	4,941
1820	5,598
1830	7,675
1840	9,087
1850	6,667
1860	8,252
1870	9,587
1880	13,068
1890	14,394
1900	16,853
1910	19,856
1920	19,816
1930	20,017
1940	21,916
1950	21,379
1960	17,390
1970	15,439
1980	16,579

GREENE

1840	4,232
1850	4,400
1860	5,022
1870	4,634
1880	5,830
1890	5,622
1900	6,214
1910	6,937
1920	6,369
1930	5,980
1940	5,218
1950	4,745
1960	4,715
1970	5,248
1980	7,625

GREENSVILLE

1790	6,362
1800	6,727
1810	6,853
1820	6,858
1830	7,117
1840	6,366
1850	5,639
1860	6,374
1870	6,362
1880	8,407
1890	8,230
1900	9,758
1910	11,890
1920	11,606
1930	13,388
1940	14,866
1950	16,319
1960	16,155
1970	9,604
1980	10,903

HALIFAX

1790	14,722
1800	19,377
1810	22,133
1820	19,060
1830	28,034
1840	25,936
1850	25,962
1860	26,520
1870	27,828
1880	23,588
1890	34,424
1900	37,197
1910	40,044
1920	41,374
1930	41,283
1940	41,271
1950	41,442
1960	33,637
1970	30,076
1980	30,599

HANOVER

1790	14,754
1800	14,403
1810	15,082
1820	15,267
1830	16,253
1840	14,968
1850	15,153
1860	17,222
1870	16,455
1880	18,588
1890	17,402
1900	17,618
1910	17,200
1920	18,088
1930	17,009
1940	18,500
1950	21,985
1960	27,550
1970	37,479
1980	50,398

HENRICO

1790	12,000
1800	14,836
1810	19,680
1820	23,667
1830	28,797
1840	33,076

1850	43,572
1860	61,616
1870	66,719
1880	82,703
1890	103,394
1900	30,063
1910	23,437
1920	18,972
1930	30,310
1940	41,960
1950	57,430
1960	117,339
1970	154,463
1980	180,735

HENRY

1790	8,479
1800	5,259
1810	5,611
1820	5,624
1830	7,100
1840	7,335
1850	8,872
1860	12,105
1870	12,303
1880	16,009
1890	18,208
1900	19,265
1910	18,459
1920	29,238
1930	20,088
1940	26,481
1950	31,219
1960	40,335
1970	50,901
1980	57,654

HIGHLAND

1850	4,227
1860	4,319
1870	4,151
1880	5,164
1890	5,352
1900	5,647
1910	5,317
1920	4,931
1930	4,525
1940	4,875
1950	4,069
1960	3,221
1970	2,529
1980	2,937

ISLE OF WIGHT

1790	9,028
1800	9,342
1810	9,186
1820	10,139
1830	10,517
1840	9,972
1850	9,353
1860	9,977
1870	8,320
1880	10,572
1890	11,313
1900	13,102
1910	14,929
1920	14,433
1930	13,409
1940	13,381
1950	14,906
1960	17,164
1970	18,285
1980	21,603

JAMES CITY

1790	4,070
1800	3,931
1810	4,094
1820	4,563
1830	3,838
1840	3,779
1850	4,020
1860	5,798
1870	4,425
1880	5,442
1890	5,643
1900	3,688
1910	3,624
1920	3,676
1930	3,879
1940	4,907
1950	6,317
1960	11,539
1970	17,853
1980	22,763

KING AND QUEEN

1790	9,377
1800	9,879
1810	10,988
1820	11,798
1830	11,644
1840	10,862
1850	10,319
1860	10,328
1870	9,709
1880	10,502
1890	9,669
1900	9,265
1910	9,576
1920	9,161
1930	7,618
1940	6,954
1950	6,299
1960	5,889
1970	5,491
1980	5,968

KING GEORGE

1790	7,366
1800	6,749
1810	6,454
1820	6,116
1830	6,397
1840	5,927
1850	5,971
1860	6,571
1870	5,742
1880	6,397
1890	6,641
1900	6,918
1910	6,387
1920	5,762
1930	5,297
1940	5,431
1950	6,710
1960	7,243
1970	8,039
1980	10,543

KING WILLIAM

1790	8,128
1800	9,055
1810	9,285
1820	9,697
1830	9,812
1840	9,258

1850	8,779
1860	8,530
1870	7,515
1880	8,751
1890	9,605
1900	8,380
1910	8,547
1920	8,739
1930	7,929
1940	7,855
1950	7,589
1960	7,563
1970	7,497
1980	9,334

LANCASTER

1790	5,638
1800	5,375
1810	5,592
1820	5,517
1830	4,801
1840	4,628
1850	4,708
1860	5,151
1870	5,355
1880	6,160
1890	7,191
1900	8,949
1910	9,752
1920	9,757
1930	8,896
1940	8,786
1950	8,640
1960	9,174
1970	9,126
1980	10,129

LEE

1800	3,538
1810	4,694
1820	4,256
1830	6,461
1840	8,411
1850	10,267
1860	11,032
1870	13,268
1880	15,166
1890	18,216
1900	19,856
1910	23,840
1920	25,293
1930	30,419
1940	39,296
1950	36,106
1960	25,824
1970	20,321
1980	25,956

LOUDOUN

1790	18,962
1800	20,523
1810	21,338
1820	22,702
1830	21,939
1840	20,431
1850	22,079
1860	21,774
1870	20,929
1880	23,634
1890	23,724
1900	21,948
1910	21,167
1920	20,577
1930	19,852

1940	20,291
1950	21,147
1960	24,549
1970	24,549
1980	57,427

LOUISA

1790	8,467
1800	11,892
1810	11,900
1820	13,746
1830	16,151
1840	15,433
1850	16,691
1860	16,701
1870	16,332
1880	18,942
1890	16,997
1900	16,517
1910	16,578
1920	17,089
1930	14,309
1940	13,665
1950	12,826
1960	12,959
1970	14,004
1980	17,825

LUNENBURG

1790	8,959
1800	10,381
1810	12,265
1820	10,662
1830	11,957
1840	11,055
1850	11,692
1860	11,983
1870	10,403
1880	11,535
1890	11,372
1900	11,705
1910	12,780
1920	15,260
1930	14,058
1940	13,844
1950	14,116
1960	12,523
1970	11,687
1980	12,124

MADISON

1800	8,322
1810	8,381
1820	8,490
1830	9,236
1840	8,107
1850	9,331
1860	8,854
1870	8,670
1880	10,562
1890	10,225
1900	10,216
1910	10,055
1920	9,595
1930	8,952
1940	8,465
1950	8,273
1960	8,187
1970	8,638
1980	10,232

MATHEWS

1800	5,806
1810	4,227
1820	6,920
1830	7,664
1840	7,442
1850	6,714
1860	7,091
1870	6,200
1880	7,501
1890	7,584
1900	8,239
1910	8,922
1920	8,447
1930	7,884
1940	7,149
1950	7,148
1960	7,121
1970	7,168
1980	7,995

MECKLENBURG

1790	14,733
1800	17,008
1810	18,453
1820	19,786
1830	20,477
1840	20,724
1850	20,630
1860	20,096
1870	21,318
1880	24,610
1890	25,359
1900	26,551
1910	28,956
1920	31,208
1930	32,622
1940	31,933
1950	33,497
1960	31,428
1970	29,426
1980	29,444

MIDDLESEX

1790	4,140
1800	4,203
1810	4,414
1820	4,057
1830	4,122
1840	4,392
1850	4,394
1860	4,364
1870	4,981
1880	6,252
1890	7,458
1900	8,220
1910	8,852
1920	8,157
1930	7,273
1940	6,673
1950	6,715
1960	6,319
1970	6,295
1980	7,719

MONTGOMERY

1790	13,228
1800	9,044
1810	8,409
1820	8,733
1830	12,306
1840	7,405
1850	8,359
1860	10,617
1870	12,556
1880	16,693
1890	17,742
1900	15,852
1910	17,268
1920	18,595
1930	19,605
1940	21,206
1950	29,780
1960	32,923
1970	47,157
1980	63,516

NANSEMOND

1790	9,010
1800	11,127
1810	10,324
1820	10,494
1830	11,784
1840	10,795
1850	12,283
1860	13,693
1870	11,576
1880	15,903
1890	19,692
1900	23,078
1910	26,886
1920	20,199
1930	22,530
1940	22,771
1950	25,238
1960	31,366
1970	35,166

NELSON

1810	9,684
1820	10,137
1830	11,254
1840	12,287
1850	12,758
1860	13,015
1870	13,898
1880	16,536
1890	15,366
1900	16,075
1910	16,821
1920	17,277
1930	16,345
1940	16,241
1950	14,042
1960	12,752
1970	11,702
1980	12,204

NEW KENT

1790	6,239
1800	6,363
1810	6,478
1820	6,630
1830	6,458
1840	6,230
1850	6,064
1860	5,884
1870	4,381
1880	5,515
1890	5,511
1900	4,865
1910	4,682
1920	4,541
1930	4,300
1940	4,092
1950	3,995
1960	4,504

1970	5,300
1980	8,781

NORFOLK

1790	14,524
1800	19,419
1810	22,872
1820	23,943
1830	24,806
1840	27,569
1850	33,036
1860	36,277
1870	46,702
1880	58,657
1890	77,038
1900	50,780
1910	52,744
1920	57,358
1930	30,082
1940	35,828
1950	99,937
1960	51,612

NORTHAMPTON

1790	6,889
1800	6,763
1810	7,474
1820	7,705
1830	8,641
1840	7,715
1850	7,498
1860	7,832
1870	8,046
1880	9,152
1890	10,313
1900	13,770
1910	16,672
1920	17,852
1930	18,565
1940	17,597
1950	17,300
1960	16,966
1970	14,442
1980	14,625

NORTHUMBERLAND

1790	9,163
1800	7,803
1810	8,308
1820	8,016
1830	7,953
1840	7,924
1850	7,346
1860	7,531
1870	6,863
1880	7,929
1890	7,885
1900	9,846
1910	10,777
1920	11,518
1930	11,081
1940	10,463
1950	10,012
1960	10,185
1970	9,239
1980	9,828

NOTTOWAY

1800	9,401
1810	9,278
1820	9,658
1830	10,130

1840	9,719
1850	8,437
1860	8,836
1870	9,291
1880	11,156
1890	11,582
1900	12,366
1910	13,462
1920	14,161
1930	14,866
1940	15,556
1950	15,479
1960	15,141
1970	14,260
1980	14,666

ORANGE

1790	9,921
1800	11,449
1810	12,323
1820	12,913
1830	14,637
1840	9,125
1850	10,067
1860	10,851
1870	10,396
1880	13,052
1890	12,814
1900	12,571
1910	13,486
1920	13,320
1930	12,070
1940	12,649
1950	12,755
1960	12,900
1970	13,792
1980	18,063

PAGE

1840	6,194
1850	7,600
1860	8,109
1870	8,462
1880	9,965
1890	13,092
1900	13,794
1910	14,147
1920	14,770
1930	14,852
1940	14,863
1950	15,152
1960	15,572
1970	16,581
1980	19,401

PATRICK

1800	4,331
1810	4,695
1820	5,089
1830	7,395
1840	8,032
1850	9,609
1860	9,359
1870	10,161
1880	12,833
1890	14,147
1900	15,403
1910	17,195
1920	16,850
1930	15,787
1940	16,613
1950	15,642
1960	15,282
1970	15,282

1980   17,647

PITTSYLVANIA

1790	11,579
1800	12,697
1810	17,172
1820	21,232
1830	26,034
1840	26,398
1850	28,796
1860	32,104
1870	31,343
1880	52,589
1890	50,941
1900	46,894
1910	50,709
1920	56,493
1930	61,424
1940	61,697
1950	66,096
1960	58,296
1970	58,789
1980	66,147

POWHATAN

1790	6,822
1800	7,769
1810	8,073
1820	8,292
1830	8,517
1840	7,924
1850	8,178
1860	8,392
1870	7,667
1880	7,817
1890	6,791
1900	6,824
1910	6,099
1920	6,552
1930	6,143
1940	5,671
1950	5,556
1960	6,747
1970	7,696
1980	13,062

PRINCE EDWARD

1790	8,100
1800	10,962
1810	12,409
1820	12,577
1830	14,107
1840	14,069
1850	11,857
1860	11,844
1870	12,004
1880	14,668
1890	14,694
1900	15,045
1910	14,266
1920	14,767
1930	14,520
1940	14,922
1950	15,398
1960	14,121
1970	14,379
1980	16,456

PRINCE GEORGE

1790	8,173
1800	7,425
1810	8,050
1820	8,030
1830	8,367
1840	7,175
1850	7,596
1860	8,411
1870	7,820
1880	10,054
1890	7,872
1900	7,752
1910	7,848
1920	12,915
1930	10,311
1940	12,226
1950	19,697
1960	20,270
1970	24,371
1980	25,733

PRINCE WILLIAM

1790	11,615
1800	12,733
1810	11,311
1820	9,419
1830	9,330
1840	8,144
1850	8,129
1860	8,565
1870	7,504
1880	9,180
1890	9,805
1900	11,112
1910	12,026
1920	13,660
1930	13,951
1940	17,738
1950	22,612
1960	50,164
1970	11,102
1980	144,703

PRINCESS ANNE

1790	7,795
1800	8,895
1810	9,498
1820	8,768
1830	9,102
1840	7,285
1850	7,669
1860	7,714
1870	8,273
1880	9,394
1900	11,192
1910	11,526
1920	13,626
1940	14,984
1950	42,277
1960	76,124

PULASKI

1840	3,739
1850	5,118
1860	5,416
1870	6,538
1880	8,755
1890	12,790
1900	14,609
1910	17,246
1920	17,111
1930	20,566
1940	22,767
1950	27,758
1960	27,258
1970	29,564
1980	35,229

RAPPAHANNOCK

1840	9,257
1850	9,782
1860	8,850
1870	8,261
1880	9,291
1890	8,678
1900	8,843
1910	8,044
1920	8,070
1930	7,717
1940	7,208
1950	6,112
1960	5,368
1970	5,199
1980	6,093

RICHMOND

1790	6,985
1800	13,744
1810	6,214
1820	5,706
1830	6,055
1840	5,965
1850	6,448
1860	6,856
1870	6,503
1880	7,195
1890	7,146
1900	7,088
1910	7,415
1920	7,434
1930	6,878
1940	6,634
1950	6,189
1960	6,375
1970	5,841
1980	6,952

ROANOKE

1840	5,499
1850	8,477
1860	8,048
1870	9,350
1880	13,105
1890	30,101
1900	15,837
1910	19,623
1920	22,395
1930	35,289
1940	42,897
1950	41,486
1960	61,693
1970	53,817
1980	72,945

ROCKBRIDGE

1790	6,548
1800	8,945
1810	10,318
1820	11,945
1830	14,244
1840	14,284
1850	16,045
1860	17,248
1870	16,058
1880	20,003
1890	23,062
1900	21,799
1910	21,171
1920	20,626
1930	20,902
1940	22,384
1950	23,359
1960	24,039
1970	16,637
1980	17,911

ROCKINGHAM

1790	7,449
1800	10,374
1810	12,753
1820	14,784
1830	20,683
1840	17,344
1850	20,294
1860	23,408
1870	23,668
1880	29,567
1890	31,299
1900	33,527
1910	34,903
1920	30,047
1930	29,709
1940	31,289
1950	35,079
1960	40,485
1970	47,890
1980	57,038

RUSSELL

1790	3,338
1800	4,808
1810	6,319
1820	5,536
1830	6,714
1840	7,878
1850	11,919
1860	10,280
1870	11,103
1880	13,906
1890	16,126
1900	18,031
1910	23,474
1920	26,786
1930	25,957
1940	26,627
1950	26,818
1960	26,290
1970	24,533
1980	31,761

SCOTT

1820	4,263
1830	5,724
1840	7,303
1850	9,289
1860	12,072
1870	13,036
1880	17,233
1890	21,694
1900	22,694
1910	23,814
1920	24,776
1930	24,181
1940	26,989
1950	27,640
1960	25,813
1970	24,376
1980	25,068

SHENANDOAH

1790	10,510
1800	13,823
1810	13,646
1820	18,926
1830	19,750
1840	11,618
1850	13,768
1860	13,896
1870	14,936
1880	18,204
1890	19,671
1900	20,253
1910	20,942
1920	20,808
1930	20,655
1940	20,898
1950	21,169
1960	21,825
1970	22,852
1980	27,559

SMYTH

1840	6,522
1850	8,162
1860	8,952
1870	8,898
1880	12,160
1890	13,360
1900	17,121
1910	20,326
1920	22,125
1930	25,125
1940	28,861
1950	30,187
1960	31,066
1970	31,349
1980	33,366

SOUTHAMPTON

1790	12,864
1800	13,925
1810	13,497
1820	14,170
1830	16,074
1840	14,525
1850	13,521
1860	12,915
1870	12,285
1880	18,012
1890	20,078
1900	22,848
1910	26,302
1920	27,555
1930	26,870
1940	26,442
1950	26,522
1960	27,195
1970	18,582
1980	18,731

SPOTSYLVANIA

1790	11,252
1800	13,002
1810	13,296
1820	14,254
1830	15,134
1840	15,161
1850	14,911
1860	16,076
1870	11,728
1880	14,828
1890	14,233
1900	9,239
1910	9,935
1920	10,571
1930	10,056
1940	9,905

1950	11,920	**TAZEWELL**		1940	38,197	1870	7,198
1960	13,819			1950	37,536	1880	7,349
1970	16,424	1800	2,127	1960	38,076	1890	7,596
1980	34,435	1810	3,007	1970	40,835	1900	7,482
		1820	3,916	1980	46,487	1910	7,757
		1830	5,749			1920	8,046
STAFFORD		1840	6,290	**WESTMORELAND**		1930	7,615
		1850	9,942			1940	8,857
1790	9,588	1860	9,920	1790	7,722	1950	11,750
1800	9,971	1870	10,791	1810	8,102	1960	21,583
1810	9,830	1880	12,861	1820	6,901	1970	33,203
1820	9,517	1890	19,899	1830	8,396	1980	35,463
1830	9,362	1900	23,384	1840	8,019		
1840	8,454	1910	24,946	1850	8,080		
1850	8,044	1920	27,840	1860	8,282		
1860	8,555	1930	32,477	1870	7,682		
1870	6,420	1940	41,607	1880	8,846		
1880	7,211	1950	47,512	1890	8,399		
1890	7,362	1960	44,791	1900	9,243		
1900	8,097	1970	39,816	1910	9,313		
1910	8,070	1980	50,511	1920	10,240		
1920	8,104			1930	8,497		
1930	8,050			1940	9,512		
1940	9,548	**WARREN**		1950	10,148		
1950	11,902			1960	11,042		
1960	16,876	1840	5,627	1970	12,142		
1970	24,587	1850	6,607	1980	14,041		
1980	40,470	1860	6,442				
		1870	5,716				
		1880	7,399	**WISE**			
SURRY		1890	8,280				
		1900	8,837	1860	4,508		
1790	6,227	1910	8,589	1870	4,785		
1800	6,535	1920	8,852	1880	7,772		
1810	6,885	1930	8,340	1890	9,345		
1820	6,594	1940	11,352	1900	19,653		
1830	7,109	1950	14,801	1910	34,162		
1840	6,480	1960	14,655	1920	46,500		
1850	5,679	1970	15,301	1930	51,167		
1860	6,133	1980	21,200	1940	52,458		
1870	5,585			1950	56,336		
1880	7,391			1960	43,579		
1890	8,256	**WARWICK**		1970	35,947		
1900	8,469			1980	43,863		
1910	9,715	1790	1,690				
1920	9,305	1800	1,659				
1930	7,096	1810	1,835	**WYTHE**			
1940	6,193	1820	1,608				
1950	6,220	1830	1,570	1800	6,380		
1960	6,220	1840	1,456	1810	8,356		
1970	5,882	1850	1,546	1820	9,692		
1980	6,046	1860	1,740	1830	12,163		
		1870	1,672	1840	9,375		
		1880	2,258	1850	12,024		
SUSSEX		1890	6,650	1860	12,305		
		1900	4,888	1870	11,611		
1790	10,549	1910	6,041	1880	14,318		
1800	11,062	1920	11,417	1890	18,019		
1810	11,362	1930	8,829	1900	20,437		
1820	11,884	1940	9,248	1910	20,372		
1830	12,720	1950	39,875	1920	20,217		
1840	11,229			1930	20,704		
1850	9,820			1940	22,721		
1860	10,175	**WASHINGTON**		1950	23,327		
1870	7,885			1960	21,975		
1880	10,062	1790	5,625	1970	22,139		
1890	11,100	1800	9,536	1980	25,522		
1900	12,082	1810	12,156				
1910	13,664	1820	12,444	**YORK**			
1920	12,834	1830	15,614				
1930	12,100	1840	13,001	1790	5,233		
1940	12,485	1850	14,612	1800	3,231		
1950	12,785	1860	16,892	1810	5,187		
1960	12,411	1870	16,816	1820	4,384		
1970	11,464	1880	25,203	1830	5,354		
1980	10,874	1890	29,020	1840	4,720		
		1900	28,995	1850	4,460		
		1910	32,830	1860	5,949		
		1920	32,376				
		1930	33,850				

NOTES

ARLINGTON

Name changed from Alexandria in 1920. For population prior to 1850, see District of Columbia. County retroceded to Virginia in 1846.

ELIZABETH CITY

Consolidated with Hampton, an independent city, in 1952.

NANSEMOND

Name changed from Upper Norfolk in 1642. Consolidated with Suffolk, an independent city, in 1973.

NORFOLK

Consolidated with South Norfolk and designated as Chesapeake, an independent city, in 1963.

NORTHAMPTON

Name changed from Accawmack in 1642.

PRINCESS ANNE

Consolidated with Virginia Beach, an independent city, in 1963.

SHENANDOAH

Name changed from Dunmore in 1777.

WARWICK

Consolidated with Newport News, an independent city, in 1958.

YORK

Name changed from Charles River in 1642.

ALEXANDRIA

1790	2,748
1800	4,971
1810	7,227
1820	8,218
1830	8,241
1840	8,459
1850	8,734
1860	12,652
1870	13,570
1880	13,659
1890	14,339
1900	14,528
1910	15,329
1920	18,060
1930	24,149
1940	33,523
1950	61,787
1960	91,023
1970	110,927
1980	103,217

BLACKSBURG

1900	768
1910	875
1920	1,095
1930	1,406
1940	2,133
1950	3,358
1960	7,070
1970	9,384
1980	30,638

BRISTOL

1880	1,562
1890	2,902
1900	4,579
1910	6,247
1920	6,729
1930	8,840
1940	9,768
1950	15,954
1960	17,144
1970	14,857
1980	19,042

CHARLOTTESVILLE

1870	2,838
1880	2,676
1890	5,591
1900	6,449
1910	6,765
1920	10,688
1930	15,245
1940	19,400
1950	25,969
1960	29,427
1970	38,880
1980	39,916

CHESAPEAKE

1970	89,580
1980	114,486

CHRISTIANSBURG

1900	659
1910	1,568
1920	1,641
1930	1,970
1940	2,299

1950	2,967
1960	3,653
1970	7,857
1980	10,345

COLONIAL HEIGHTS

1930	2,331
1940	3,194
1950	6,077
1960	9,587
1970	15,097
1980	16,509

DANVILLE

1850	1,514
1860	(NA)
1870	3,463
1880	7,526
1890	10,305
1900	16,520
1910	19,020
1920	21,539
1930	22,247
1940	32,749
1950	35,066
1960	46,577
1970	47,391
1980	45,642

FAIRFAX

1900	373
1910	413
1920	516
1930	640
1940	979
1950	1,946
1960	13,585
1970	22,727
1980	19,390

FREDERICKSBURG

1830	3,308
1840	3,974
1850	4,061
1860	5,022
1870	4,046
1880	5,010
1890	4,528
1900	5,068
1910	5,874
1920	5,882
1930	6,819
1940	10,066
1950	12,158
1960	13,639
1970	14,450
1980	15,322

FRONT ROYAL

1850	504
1860	807
1870	705
1880	829
1890	868
1900	1,005
1910	1,133
1920	1,404
1930	2,424
1940	3,831
1950	8,115
1960	7,949

1970	8,211
1980	11,126

HAMPTON

1890	2,513
1900	2,764
1910	5,505
1920	6,138
1930	6,382
1940	5,898
1950	5,966
1960	89,258
1970	120,779
1980	122,617

HARRISONBURG

1860	1,023
1870	2,036
1880	2,831
1890	2,792
1900	3,521
1910	4,879
1920	5,875
1930	7,232
1940	8,768
1950	10,810
1960	11,916
1970	14,605
1980	19,671

HERDON

1880	422
1890	795
1900	692
1910	802
1920	953
1930	887
1940	1,046
1950	1,461
1960	1,960
1970	4,301
1980	11,449

HOPEWELL

1920	1,397
1930	11,327
1940	8,679
1950	10,219
1960	17,895
1970	23,471
1980	23,397

LYNCHBURG

1830	4,630
1840	6,395
1850	8,071
1860	6,853
1870	6,825
1880	15,959
1890	19,709
1900	18,891
1910	28,494
1920	30,070
1930	40,661
1940	44,541
1950	47,727
1960	54,790
1970	54,083
1980	66,743

MANASSAS

1880	361
1890	530
1900	817
1910	1,217
1920	1,305
1930	1,215
1940	1,302
1950	1,804
1960	3,555
1970	9,164
1980	15,438

MARTINSVILLE

1880	289
1890	na
1900	2,384
1910	3,368
1920	4,075
1930	7,705
1940	10,080
1950	17,251
1960	18,798
1970	19,653
1980	18,149

NEWPORT NEWS

1890	4,449
1900	19,635
1910	20,205
1920	35,596
1930	34,417
1940	37,067
1950	42,358
1960	113,662
1970	138,177
1980	144,903

NORFOLK

1790	2,959
1800	6,926
1810	9,193
1820	8,478
1830	9,814
1840	10,920
1850	14,326
1860	14,620
1870	19,229
1880	21,966
1890	34,871
1900	46,624
1910	67,452
1920	115,777
1930	129,710
1940	144,332
1950	213,513
1960	304,869
1970	307,951
1980	266,979

PETERSBURG

1790	2,828
1800	3,521
1810	5,668
1820	6,690
1830	8,322
1840	11,136
1850	14,010
1860	18,226
1870	18,950
1880	21,656

1890	22,680
1900	21,810
1910	24,127
1920	31,012
1930	28,564
1940	30,631
1950	35,054
1960	36,750
1970	36,103
1980	41,055

PORTSMOUTH

1840	6,477
1850	8,122
1860	9,496
1870	10,590
1880	11,390
1890	13,268
1900	17,427
1910	33,190
1920	54,387
1930	45,704
1940	50,745
1950	80,039
1960	114,773
1970	110,963
1980	104,577

PULASKI

1890	2,112
1900	2,813
1910	4,807
1920	5,282
1930	7,168
1940	8,792
1950	9,202
1960	10,469
1970	10,279
1980	10,106

RADFORD

1900	3,344
1910	4,202
1920	4,627
1930	6,227
1940	6,990
1950	9,026
1960	9,371
1970	11,596
1980	13,225

RICHMOND

1790	3,761
1800	5,737
1810	9,735
1820	12,067
1830	16,060
1840	20,153
1850	27,570
1860	37,910
1870	51,038
1880	63,600
1890	81,388
1900	85,050
1910	127,628
1920	171,667
1930	182,929
1940	193,042
1950	230,310
1960	219,958
1970	249,332
1980	219,214

ROANOKE

1880	669
1890	16,159
1900	21,495
1910	34,874
1920	50,842
1930	69,206
1940	69,287
1950	91,921
1960	97,110
1970	92,115
1980	100,220

SALEM

1860	612
1870	1,355
1880	1,759
1890	3,279
1900	3,412
1910	3,849
1920	4,159
1930	4,833
1940	5,737
1950	6,823
1960	16,058
1970	21,982
1980	23,958

STAUNTON

1860	3,875
1870	5,120
1880	6,664
1890	6,975
1900	7,289
1910	10,604
1920	10,623
1930	11,990
1940	13,337
1950	19,927
1960	22,232
1970	24,504
1980	21,857

SUFFOLK

1860	1,395
1870	930
1880	1,963
1890	3,354
1900	3,827
1910	7,008
1920	9,123
1930	10,271
1940	11,343
1950	12,339
1960	12,609
1970	9,858
1980	47,621

VIENNA

1900	317
1910	578
1920	773
1930	903
1940	1,237
1950	2,029
1960	11,440
1970	17,152
1980	15,469

VIRGINIA BEACH

1910	320
1920	846
1930	1,719
1940	2,600
1950	5,390
1960	8,091
1970	172,106
1980	262,199

WAYNESBORO

1860	457
1870	536
1880	484
1890	646
1900	856
1910	1,389
1920	1,594
1930	6,226
1940	7,373
1950	12,357
1960	15,694
1970	16,707
1980	15,329

WINCHESTER

1840	3,454
1850	3,857
1860	4,392
1870	4,477
1880	4,958
1890	5,196
1900	5,161
1910	5,864
1920	6,883
1930	10,855
1940	12,095
1950	13,841
1960	15,110
1970	14,643
1980	20,217

CORRECTION NOTE

The official 1980 census counts of total population shown in
this report supersede counts issued previously. Corrections
to the figures were made after the counts were provided to
the State for redistricting purposes and released in Advance
Report PHC80-V for this State.

Shown below are corrections to the 1980 census counts of the
total population made after the tabulations for this report
were completed. Any additional corrections made after this
report is printed are available by writing to Data User
Services Division, Customer Services (Corrections), Bureau of
the Census, Washington, D.C. 20233.

The 1980 figures shown in this publication are subject to
change pending the outcome of the various lawsuits dealing
with the census counts.

	1980 population	
	As shown in the tables	Corrected
Greensville County:		
Hicksford district..............	3 639	3 753
Zion district..................	1 686	1 572

County Subdivisions	1980	1970
The State	5 346 818	'4 651 448
Accomack County[1]	31 268	29 004
Atlantic district	6 261	6 464
Hallwood town (pt.)	198	209
Saxis town	415	451
Lee district	8 833	8 102
Accomac town[1]	522	373
Melfa town (pt.)	176	257
Onancock town	1 461	1 614
Onley town	526	464
Tangier town	771	814
Metompkin district	6 449	5 573
Bloxom town	407	391
Hallwood town (pt.)	45	45
Parksley town	979	903
Pungoteague district	6 170	5 607
Belle Haven town (pt.)	462	411
Keller town	236	235
Melfa town (pt.)	215	202
Painter town	321	363
Wachapreague town	404	399
The Islands district	3 555	3 258
Chincoteague town	1 607	1 867
Albemarle County[2]	55 783	37 780
Charlottesville district	10 915	...
Commonwealth (CDP)	3 505	...
Hessian Hills (CDP) (pt.)	2 018	...
Hollymead (CDP) (pt.)	1 384	...
Rio (CDP) (pt.)	2 837	...
Jack Jouett district[2]	9 772	...
Hessian Hills (CDP) (pt.)	2 085	...
University Heights (CDP)	6 736	...
Rivanna district	9 352	...
Hollymead (CDP) (pt.)	1 008	...
Rio (CDP) (pt.)	14	...
Samuel Miller district[2]	7 966	4 928
Scottsville district	9 398	4 679
Scottsville town (pt.)	223	239
White Hall district[2]	8 380	4 826
Crozet (CDP)	2 553	1 433
Alleghany County	14 333	12 461
Boiling Spring district	2 479	2 218
Clifton district	2 464	2 725
Iron Gate town	620	692
Covington district	3 123	3 148
Falling Spring district	3 490	2 058
Jackson River district	2 777	2 312
Amelia County	8 405	7 592
Giles district	4 449	3 912
Jackson district	1 829	1 764
Leigh district	2 127	1 916
Amherst County	29 122	26 072
Court House district	5 827	4 836
Amherst town	1 135	1 108
Elon district	11 155	8 303
Madison Heights (CDP) (pt.)	7 301	...
Madison district	7 465	8 749
Madison Heights (CDP) (pt.)	6 845	...
Pedlar district	1 535	1 403
Temperance district	3 140	2 781
Appomattox County[3]	11 971	9 784
Clover Hill district	2 759	2 522
Pamplin City town (pt.)	237	343
Southside district	5 810	4 450
Appomattox town[3]	1 345	1 400
Stonewall district	3 402	2 812
Arlington County	152 599	174 284
Arlington (CDP)	152 599	174 284
Augusta County[4]	53 732	44 220
Beverley Manor district[4]	6 603	...
Verona (CDP) (pt.)	37	...
Middle River district[4]	8 369	...
Grottoes town (pt.)	7	8
Verona (CDP) (pt.)	361	...
North River district	7 578	6 213
Verona (CDP) (pt.)	2 384	...
Pastures district[4]	7 633	...
Craigsville town	845	988
Riverheads district[4]	7 119	...
South River district	8 600	6 409
Stuarts Draft (CDP)	1 776	...
Wayne district	7 830	6 406
Dooms (CDP)	1 173	...
Bath County	5 860	5 192
Cedar Creek district	1 118	1 327
Millboro district	1 042	949
Valley Springs district	1 605	1 106
Warm Springs district	1 275	1 101
Williamsville district	820	709
Bedford County[5]	34 927	26 728
Blue Ridge district	9 085	6 577
Center district	6 244	4 798
Jefferson district[5]	6 934	5 035

County Subdivisions	1980	1970
Bedford County—Con.		
Lakes district	6 996	5 091
Peaks district	5 668	5 227
Bland County	6 349	5 423
Mechanicsburg district	2 002	1 798
Rocky Gap district	2 239	1 527
Seddon district	1 426	1 419
Sharon district	682	679
Botetourt County[6]	23 270	18 193
Amsterdam district	4 577	...
Fincastle town (pt.)	260	(NA)
Blue Ridge district	7 021	...
Blue Ridge (CDP)	2 347	...
Buchanan district	3 885	...
Buchanan town	1 205	1 326
Fincastle district	4 028	...
Fincastle town (pt.)	22	(NA)
Valley district	3 759	...
Hollins (CDP) (pt.)	108	...
Troutville town	496	522
Brunswick County	15 632	16 172
Meherrin district	3 325	3 259
Brodnax town (pt.)	399	453
Powellton district	1 548	1 671
Red Oak district	3 047	3 330
Alberta town	394	466
Sturgeon district	2 609	2 770
Totaro district	5 103	5 142
Lawrenceville town	1 484	1 636
Buchanan County	37 989	32 071
Garden district	4 521	4 087
Hurricane district	5 641	4 627
Knox district	5 130	4 456
North Grundy district	5 235	4 791
Grundy town (pt.)	1 098	1 126
Prater district	7 442	4 788
Vansant (CDP) (pt.)	1 478	...
Rock Lick district	4 997	5 023
South Grundy district	5 023	4 299
Grundy town (pt.)	601	928
Vansant (CDP) (pt.)	1 230	...
Buckingham County	11 751	10 597
Curdsville district	2 858	2 438
Dillwyn town	637	497
Francisco district	802	738
James River district	1 585	1 445
Marshall district	3 157	3 072
Maysville district	1 650	1 558
Slate River district	1 699	1 346
Campbell County[7]	45 424	43 319
College district[7]	4 762	...
Timberlake (CDP) (pt.)	4 338	...
Flat Creek district[7]	13 280	...
Timberlake (CDP) (pt.)	1 155	...
Long Mountain district[7]	8 171	7 053
Patrick Henry district	7 373	6 904
Brookneal town[7]	1 454	1 037
Tomahawk district[7]	4 204	...
Timberlake (CDP) (pt.)	4 204	...
Vista district	7 634	7 367
Altavista town[7]	3 849	2 708
Caroline County[8]	17 904	13 925
Bowling Green district	5 237	4 447
Bowling Green town	665	528
Madison district	5 894	3 802
Port Royal district	2 612	2 161
Port Royal town	291	199
Reedy Church district	4 161	3 515
Carroll County[9]	27 270	23 092
Fancy Gap district	4 542	3 789
Laurel Fork district	4 499	4 052
Hillsville town (pt.)[9]	383	131
Pine Creek district	3 550	3 162
Hillsville town (pt.)[9]	596	384
Piper Gap district	6 787	5 640
Hillsville town (pt.)[9]	280	183
Woodlawn (CDP) (pt.)	875	...
Sulphur Springs district[9]	7 892	6 449
Hillsville town (pt.)[9]	864	451
Stevens Creek (CDP) (pt.)	253	...
Woodlawn (CDP) (pt.)	814	...
Charles City County[10]	6 692	6 158
Chickahominy district	890	...
Harrison district	3 075	...
Tyler district	2 727	...
Charlotte County	12 266	'12 366
Bacon district	2 890	2 934
Central district	1 653	1 661
Drakes Branch town	617	702
Madison district	2 368	2 256
Charlotte Court House town (pt.)	233	193
Midway district	836	836
Roanoke district	2 100	2 192
Charlotte Court House town (pt.)	158	145
Phenix town	250	260
Walton district	2 419	'2 487

County Subdivisions

County Subdivisions	1980	1970
Charlotte County—Con.		
Walton district—Con.		
Charlotte Court House town (pt.)	177	201
Keysville town	704	'818
Chesterfield County[11]	141 372	'77 045
Bermuda district	23 507	...
Bellwood (CDP)	6 439	...
Bensley (CDP) (pt.)	–	...
Chester (CDP)	11 728	5 556
Clover Hill district[11]	43 191	...
Dale district[11]	28 428	...
Bensley (CDP) (pt.)	5 299	...
Matoaca district	17 298	...
Ettrick (CDP)	4 890	...
Matoaca (CDP)	1 967	'...
Midlothian district[11]	28 948	...
Bon Air (CDP)	16 224	'10 771
Clarke County	9 965	8 102
Battletown district	4 361	3 299
Berryville town (pt.)	1 503	1 289
Chapel district	1 868	1 541
Boyce town (pt.)	202	193
Greenway district	1 644	1 482
Boyce town (pt.)	199	185
Long Marsh district	2 092	1 780
Berryville town (pt.)	249	280
Craig County[12]	3 948	3 524
Alleghany district	1 301	1 145
New Castle district[12]	1 359	...
New Castle town	213	225
Simmonsville district[12]	1 288	...
Culpeper County[13]	22 620	18 218
Catalpa district	3 538	...
Culpeper town (pt.)	1 401	(NA)
Cedar Mountain district	3 148	...
East Fairfax district[13]	2 854	...
Culpeper town (pt.)	2 854	(NA)
Jefferson district	3 632	...
Salem district	4 259	...
Stevensburg district	2 823	...
West Fairfax district[13]	2 366	...
Culpeper town (pt.)	2 366	(NA)
Cumberland County[14]	7 881	6 179
Hamilton district	2 071	1 722
Madison district	2 755	1 951
Randolph district	3 055	2 506
Farmville town (pt.)[14]	388	...
Dickenson County[15]	19 806	16 077
Clintwood district	4 640	...
Clintwood town (pt.)	786	(NA)
Ervinton district	3 243	...
Kenady district	3 934	...
Sand Lick district	4 046	...
Haysi town (pt.)	343	(NA)
Willis district	3 943	...
Clintwood town (pt.)	583	(NA)
Haysi town (pt.)	28	(NA)
Dinwiddie County[16]	22 602	25 046
Darvills district	2 041	1 839
Namozine district	3 192	2 379
Rohoic district[16]	8 143	13 540
Rowanty district	6 090	4 566
Sapony district	3 136	2 722
McKenney town[16]	473	489
Essex County[17]	8 864	7 099
Central district	4 530	3 606
Tappahannock town[17]	1 821	1 111
Occupacia district	2 219	1 759
Rappahannock district	2 115	1 734
Fairfax County[18]	596 901	'454 275
Annandale district	80 183	...
Annandale (CDP) (pt.)	26 900	(NA)
Burke (CDP) (pt.)	6 005	...
North Springfield (CDP)	9 538	8 631
Springfield (CDP) (pt.)	2 834	(NA)
West Springfield (CDP) (pt.)	8 385	(NA)
Centreville district	81 446	...
Chantilly (CDP) (pt.)	523	...
Oakton (CDP) (pt.)	8 693	...
Reston (CDP) (pt.)	35 662	(NA)
Tysons Corner (CDP) (pt.)	2 829	...
Vienna town	15 469	'17 146
Wolf Trap (CDP) (pt.)	6 617	...
Dranesville district	79 401	...
Great Falls (CDP)	2 419	...
Herndon town	11 449	4 301
Idylwood (CDP) (pt.)	5	...
McLean (CDP)	35 664	'19 494
Pimmit Hills (CDP)	6 658	...
Reston (CDP) (pt.)	745	(NA)
Tysons Corner (CDP) (pt.)	5 886	...
Wolf Trap (CDP) (pt.)	3 258	...
Lee district[18]	65 552	...
Fort Belvoir (CDP) (pt.)	2 117	(NA)
Franconia (CDP)	8 476	...

County Subdivisions	1980	1970
Fairfax County—Con.		
Lee district—Con.		
Groveton (CDP) (pt.)	14 922	(NA)
Hybla Valley (CDP) (pt.)	4 884	...
Lorton (CDP) (pt.)	2 665	...
Mount Vernon (CDP) (pt.)	13 063	...
Newington (CDP) (pt.)	2 154	...
Rose Hill (CDP)	11 926	'14 492
Springfield (CDP) (pt.)	4 863	(NA)
Mason district	60 546	...
Annandale (CDP) (pt.)	13 370	(NA)
Bailey's Crossroads (CDP)	12 564	7 295
Jefferson (CDP) (pt.)	6 908	(NA)
Lake Barcroft (CDP)	8 725	11 605
Lincolnia (CDP)	10 350	'10 761
Seven Corners (CDP)	6 058	5 590
Springfield (CDP) (pt.)	2 571	(NA)
Mount Vernon district[18]	62 358	...
Belle Haven (CDP)	6 520	8 299
Fort Belvoir (CDP) (pt.)	5 609	(NA)
Fort Hunt (CDP)	14 294	10 415
Groveton (CDP) (pt.)	3 938	(NA)
Huntington (CDP)	5 813	5 559
Hybla Valley (CDP) (pt.)	10 649	...
Lorton (CDP) (pt.)	2 664	...
Mount Vernon (CDP) (pt.)	10 995	...
Occoquan town (pt.)[18]	–	...
Providence district	70 597	...
Annandale (CDP) (pt.)	9 254	(NA)
Dunn Loring (CDP)	6 077	...
Idylwood (CDP) (pt.)	11 977	...
Jefferson (CDP) (pt.)	17 434	(NA)
Mantua (CDP)	6 523	'6 154
Merrifield (CDP)	7 525	...
Oakton (CDP) (pt.)	10 457	...
Tysons Corner (CDP) (pt.)	1 350	...
Springfield district	96 818	...
Burke (CDP) (pt.)	27 830	...
Centreville (CDP)	7 473	...
Chantilly (CDP) (pt.)	11 736	...
Clifton town	170	178
Lorton (CDP) (pt.)	484	...
Newington (CDP) (pt.)	6 159	...
Springfield (CDP) (pt.)	11 167	(NA)
West Springfield (CDP) (pt.)	16 627	(NA)
Fauquier County[19]	35 889	26 375
Cedar Run district	7 660	...
Vint Hill Farms Station (CDP)	1 130	1 018
Center district	6 189	...
Warrenton town[19]	3 907	4 027
Lee district	8 325	...
Remington town	425	321
Marshall district	6 770	...
Scott district	6 945	...
The Plains town	382	418
Floyd County	11 563	9 775
Alum Ridge district	1 196	827
Burks Fork district	1 730	1 588
Court House district	3 047	2 788
Floyd town	411	474
Indian Valley district	1 718	1 569
Little River district	1 597	1 247
Locust Grove district	2 275	1 756
Fluvanna County	10 244	7 621
Columbia district	1 502	1 290
Columbia town	111	125
Cunningham district	3 213	2 119
Scottsville town (pt.)	27	51
Fork Union district	2 630	2 500
Palmyra district	2 899	1 712
Franklin County[20]	35 740	'28 163
Blackwater district	5 085	...
Blue Ridge district	4 911	...
Boone district	6 676	...
Boones Mill town	344	363
Gills Creek district	5 533	...
Rocky Mount district	4 198	...
Rocky Mount town	4 198	4 002
Snow Creek district	4 754	...
Union Hall district	4 583	...
Frederick County[21]	34 150	28 893
Back Creek district[21]	6 731	...
Gainesboro district[21]	6 653	6 269
Opequon district	8 155	...
Middletown town[21]	841	507
Stephens City town	1 179	802
Shawnee district	6 036	...
Stonewall district[21]	6 575	...
Giles County[22]	17 810	16 741
Central district	5 864	...
Pearisburg town	2 128	2 169
Eastern district	5 745	...
Pembroke town	1 302	1 095
Western district	6 201	...
Glen Lyn town[22]	235	191
Narrows town[22]	2 516	2 421
Rich Creek town	746	729

County Subdivisions	1980	1970
Gloucester County[23]	20 107	14 059
Abingdon district	4 352	...
Gloucester Point (CDP) (pt.)	2 075	...
Gloucester district[23]	4 908	...
Gloucester Point (CDP) (pt.)	3 766	...
Petsworth district	3 822	...
Ware district	3 661	...
Gloucester Courthouse (CDP)	1 545	...
York district[23]	3 364	...
Goochland County	11 761	10 069
Byrd district	2 417	2 189
Dover district	5 084	4 529
Lickinghole district	4 260	3 351
Grayson County[24]	16 579	15 439
Elk Creek district	4 087	3 722
Independence town[24]	1 112	673
Old Town district	4 609	3 960
Providence district	3 811	3 803
Fries town	758	885
Stevens Creek (CDP) (pt.)	749	...
Wilson Creek district	4 072	3 954
Troutdale town	248	209
Greene County	7 625	5 248
Monroe district	1 364	1 270
Ruckersville district	4 018	2 089
Stanardsville district	2 243	1 889
Stanardsville town	284	296
Greensville County[25]	10 903	9 604
Belfield district	4 112	3 270
Hicksford district[25]	3 639	...
Nottoway district	1 466	1 344
Jarratt town (pt.)	449	407
Zion district[25]	1 686	...
Halifax County	30 599	30 076
Banister district	7 893	6 638
Halifax town	772	899
Birch Creek district	2 353	2 527
Black Walnut district	4 484	4 364
Meadsville district	1 799	1 972
Mount Carmel district	1 718	1 704
Redbank district	2 090	2 230
Virgilina town	212	249
Roanoke district	5 563	5 571
Clover town	215	227
Scottsburg town	335	157
Staunton district	4 699	5 070
Hanover County[26]	50 398	37 479
Ashland district	6 421	...
Ashland town[26]	4 640	2 934
Beaverdam district	5 869	...
Chickahominy district	7 801	...
Mechanicsville (CDP) (pt.)	1 135	(NA)
Cold Harbor district	8 966	...
Mechanicsville (CDP) (pt.)	1 560	(NA)
Henry district	7 589	...
Mechanicsville (CDP) (pt.)	6 629	...
Mechanicsville (CDP) (pt.)	6 574	(NA)
South Anna district	7 123	...
Henrico County[27]	180 735	'154 463
Brookland district	35 127	...
Dumbarton (CDP) (pt.)	8 044	...
Glen Allen (CDP) (pt.)	5 511	...
Lakeside (CDP) (pt.)	8 350	(NA)
Laurel (CDP)	10 569	...
Fairfield district	34 746	...
Chamberlayne (CDP)	5 136	...
East Highland Park (CDP)	11 797	...
Glen Allen (CDP) (pt.)	691	...
Highland Springs (CDP) (pt.)	1 235	(NA)
Lakeside (CDP) (pt.)	3 939	(NA)
Three Chopt district	30 443	...
Dumbarton (CDP) (pt.)	105	...
Tuckahoe (CDP) (pt.)	4 534	...
Tuckahoe district	41 011	...
Tuckahoe (CDP) (pt.)	35 334	...
Varina district	39 408	...
Highland Springs (CDP) (pt.)	10 911	(NA)
Montrose (CDP)	5 349	...
Henry County	57 654	50 901
Blackberry district	9 829	8 607
Bassett (CDP) (pt.)	662	1 043
Horse Pasture district	10 958	8 964
Fieldale (CDP) (pt.)	1 120	1 227
Horse Pasture (CDP) (pt.)	3 616	...
Iriswood district	9 140	7 465
Martinsville district	10 646	8 847
Collinsville (CDP) (pt.)	7 017	4 829
Fieldale (CDP) (pt.)	70	110
Villa Heights (CDP)	1 264	...
Reed Creek district	8 496	9 547
Bassett (CDP) (pt.)	1 372	2 015
Collinsville (CDP) (pt.)	500	1 186
Stanleytown (CDP)	1 761	...
Ridgeway district	8 585	7 471

County Subdivisions	1980	1970
Henry County—Con.		
Ridgeway district—Con.		
Horse Pasture (CDP) (pt.)	34	...
Ridgeway town	858	624
Highland County	2 937	2 529
Blue Grass district	724	685
Monterey district	1 512	1 163
Monterey town	247	223
Stonewall district	701	681
Isle of Wight County[28]	21 603	18 285
Hardy district	6 088	...
Rushmere (CDP)	1 070	...
Smithfield town (pt.)[28]	374	(NA)
Newport district	10 061	...
Smithfield town (pt.)[28]	3 344	(NA)
Windsor district	5 454	...
Windsor town	985	685
James City County[29]	22 763	17 853
Berkeley district	4 712	...
Jamestown district	3 916	...
Powhatan district	4 825	...
Roberts district	4 639	2 710
Stonehouse district	4 671	...
King and Queen County	5 968	5 491
Buena Vista district	2 491	2 229
Newtown district	2 236	2 249
Stevensville district	1 241	1 013
King George County	10 543	8 039
Potomac district	4 727	3 955
Rappahannock district	3 665	2 683
Shiloh district	2 151	1 401
King William County	9 334	7 497
Acquinton district	3 154	1 963
Mangohick district	1 944	1 443
West Point district	4 236	4 091
West Point town	2 726	2 600
Lancaster County[30]	10 129	9 126
Mantua district	1 967	1 724
White Chapel district	2 212	2 031
White Stone district	5 950	5 371
Irvington town	567	504
Kilmarnock town (pt.)[30]	896	776
White Stone town	409	381
Lee County	25 956	20 321
Jonesville district	5 408	3 894
Jonesville town	874	700
Rocky Station district	9 395	7 727
Pennington Gap town	1 716	1 886
St. Charles town	241	368
Rose Hill district	4 856	3 857
White Shoals district	1 965	1 860
Yokum Station district	4 332	2 983
Loudoun County[31]	57 427	37 150
Blue Ridge district	6 922	...
Hamilton town	598	502
Hillsboro town	115	135
Purcellville town	1 567	1 775
Round Hill town	510	581
Broad Run district	8 313	...
Sterling Park (CDP) (pt.)	912	(NA)
Sugarland Run (CDP)	6 258	...
Catoctin district	7 624	...
Lovettsville town[31]	613	185
Dulles district	5 657	...
Sterling Park (CDP) (pt.)	66	(NA)
Guilford district	6 889	...
Sterling Park (CDP) (pt.)	6 889	(NA)
Leesburg district	8 505	...
Leesburg town	8 357	4 821
Mercer district	5 254	...
Middleburg town	619	833
Sterling district	8 263	...
Sterling Park (CDP) (pt.)	8 213	(NA)
Louisa County[32]	17 825	14 004
Cuckoo district	3 096	...
Green Spring district	2 752	...
Jackson district	3 971	...
Louisa district	2 871	...
Louisa town (pt.)[32]	765	(NA)
Mineral district	2 694	...
Mineral town	399	397
Patrick Henry district[32]	2 441	...
Louisa town (pt.)[32]	167	(NA)
Lunenburg County[33]	12 124	11 687
Browns Store district	3 444	3 552
Kenbridge town[33]	1 352	1 223
Columbian Grove district	964	859
Lewiston district	1 069	1 009
Loch Leven district	1 016	1 127
Pleasant Grove district	1 724	1 419
Plymouth district	2 994	2 840
Victoria town[33]	2 004	1 408
Rehoboth district	913	881

County Subdivisions	1980	1970
Madison County	10 232	8 638
Locustdale district	3 834	3 186
Rapidan district	2 770	2 358
Madison town	267	299
Robertson district	3 628	3 094
Mathews County	7 995	7 168
Chesapeake district	2 315	2 252
Piankatank district	2 976	2 387
Westville district	2 704	2 529
Mecklenburg County[34]	29 444	29 426
Bluestone district	2 339	2 230
Boydton district	3 178	3 164
Boydton town	486	541
Buckhorn district	1 900	2 269
Chase City district	5 759	5 935
Chase City town[34]	2 749	2 909
Clarksville district	4 944	4 702
Clarksville town	1 468	1 641
La Crosse district	3 603	3 692
Brodnax town (pt.)	93	116
La Crosse town	734	674
Palmer Springs district	1 024	1 168
South Hill district	6 697	6 266
South Hill town[34]	4 347	3 858
Middlesex County[35]	7 719	6 295
Jamaica district[35]	1 272	...
Pine Top district	3 627	2 547
Deltaville (CDP)	1 082	...
Saluda district[35]	2 820	...
Urbanna town	518	475
Montgomery County[36]	63 516	47 157
Mount Tabor district	11 746	9 132
Blacksburg town (pt.)[36]	8 240	5 557
Prices Fork district	26 328	17 273
Blacksburg town (pt.)[36]	22 398	3 827
Riner district[36]	12 112	10 217
Belmont (CDP)	1 697	...
Christiansburg town (pt.)[36]	3 592	2 998
Shawsville district	13 330	10 535
Christiansburg town (pt.)[36]	6 753	4 859
Elliston–Lafayette (CDP)	1 172	...
Nelson County	12 204	11 702
Lovingston district	4 766	4 590
Massies Mill district	2 627	2 612
Rockfish district	3 051	2 664
Schuyler district	1 760	1 836
New Kent County	8 781	5 300
Black Creek district	2 810	1 364
Cumberland district	2 036	1 472
St. Peters district	2 421	1 337
Weir Creek district	1 514	1 127
Northampton County[37]	14 625	14 442
Capeville district	4 073	...
Cape Charles town	1 512	1 689
Eastville district	5 734	...
Cheriton town	695	655
Eastville town	238	203
Franktown district	4 818	...
Belle Haven town (pt.)	127	93
Exmore town	1 300	1 421
Nassawadox town	630	591
Northumberland County	9 828	9 239
Fairfield district	3 345	3 132
Heathsville district	1 562	1 593
Lottsburg district	2 874	2 696
Wicomico district	2 047	1 818
Kilmarnock town (pt.)	49	65
Nottoway County[38]	14 666	14 260
Bellefonte district	6 130	5 883
Blackstone town[38]	3 624	3 412
Blendon district	1 740	2 057
Haytokah district	2 773	2 805
Burkeville town	606	703
Crewe town (pt.)[38]	26	...
Winningham district	4 023	3 515
Crewe town (pt.)[38]	2 299	1 797
Orange County[39]	18 063	13 792
Barbour district	2 471	2 040
Gordonsville town (pt.)	55	...
Gordon district	3 320	1 404
Madison district	3 078	2 425
Gordonsville town (pt.)[39]	1 366	1 244
Spotswood district	4 760	4 708
Orange town	2 631	2 768
Taylor district	4 434	3 215
Page County	19 401	16 581
Luray district	5 611	4 887
Luray town (pt.)	3 261	3 192
Marksville district	4 854	4 277
Stanley town	1 204	1 208
Shenandoah Iron Works district	5 760	5 056
Shenandoah town	1 861	1 714
Springfield district	3 176	2 361
Luray town (pt.)	323	420

County Subdivisions	1980	1970
Patrick County[40]	17 647	15 282
Blue Ridge district	3 382	...
Stuart town (pt.)	965	(NA)
Dan River district	3 304	...
Mayo River district	3 372	...
Peters Creek district	4 316	...
Stuart town (pt.)	–	(NA)
Smith River district	3 273	...
Stuart town (pt.)[40]	166	(NA)
Pittsylvania County[41]	66 147	58 789
Blairs district[41]	9 711	...
Callands Gretna district[41]	9 268	...
Gretna town	1 255	986
Chatham district[41]	7 310	...
Chatham town	1 390	1 801
Dan River district	9 885	...
Glenwood (CDP)	2 276	1 295
Staunton River district[41]	9 296	...
Hurt town	1 481	1 434
Tunstall district[41]	11 168	...
Westover district[41]	9 509	...
Westover (CDP)	3 051	...
Powhatan County	13 062	7 696
Huguenot district	5 245	2 505
Macon district	2 386	1 655
Spencer district	5 431	3 536
Prince Edward County[42]	16 456	14 379
Buffalo district	786	660
Pamplin City town (pt.)	16	36
Farmville district	7 143	6 491
Farmville town (pt.)[42]	5 679	4 331
Hampden district	3 018	2 460
Hampden Sydney (CDP)	1 011	...
Leigh district	1 121	924
Lockett district	1 956	1 658
Prospect district	2 432	2 186
Pamplin City town (pt.)	20	15
Prince George County[43]	25 733	29 092
Blackwater district	3 378	2 968
Bland district[43]	15 248	15 633
Fort Lee (CDP) (pt.)	9 711	11 448
Brandon district	854	823
Rives district[43]	4 078	7 872
Fort Lee (CDP) (pt.)	73	987
Templeton district	2 175	1 796
Prince William County[44]	144 703	111 102
Brentsville district[44]	27 248	...
Loch Lomond (CDP) (pt.)	971	...
West Gate (CDP) (pt.)	4 542	...
Yorkshire (CDP)	4 940	4 649
Coles district	22 864	...
Dale City (CDP) (pt.)	13 928	(NA)
Quantico Station (CDP) (pt.)	6 194	(NA)
Dumfries district	22 420	...
Country Club Lake (CDP)	4 098	...
Dumfries town	3 214	1 890
Quantico town	621	719
Quantico Station (CDP) (pt.)	590	(NA)
Triangle (CDP)	4 770	3 021
Woodbridge (CDP) (pt.)	4 051	(NA)
Gainesville district[44]	17 897	...
Haymarket town	230	288
Loch Lomond (CDP) (pt.)	2 637	...
Sudley (CDP)	4 674	...
West Gate (CDP) (pt.)	2 577	...
Neabsco district	19 199	...
Dale City (CDP) (pt.)	19 199	(NA)
Occoquan district	20 208	...
Lake Ridge (CDP)	11 072	...
Occoquan town (pt.)	241	975
Woodbridge (CDP) (pt.)	5 121	(NA)
Woodbridge district[44]	14 867	...
Woodbridge (CDP) (pt.)	14 832	(NA)
Pulaski County[45]	35 229	29 564
Cloyd district	8 316	...
Fairlawn (CDP)	1 794	1 767
Draper district	5 489	5 735
Pulaski town (pt.)	3 020	3 473
Ingles district	9 139	...
Dublin town	2 368	1 653
Massie district	6 311	...
Pulaski town (pt.)	4 144	3 986
Pulaski North (CDP) (pt.)	238	(NA)
Robinson district	5 974	...
Pulaski town (pt.)	2 942	2 820
Pulaski North (CDP) (pt.)	1 167	(NA)
Rappahannock County[46]	6 093	5 199
Hampton district	1 181	...
Washington town	247	189
Jackson district	1 404	...
Piedmont district	1 131	...
Stonewall–Hawthorne district[46]	1 133	...
Wakefield district	1 244	...

County Subdivisions	1980	1970
Richmond County[47]	6 952	6 504
Farnham district	1 428	1 123
Marshall district	2 314	2 270
Warsaw town[47]	771	511
Stonewall district	814	748
Washington district	2 396	2 363
Roanoke County[48]	72 945	67 339
Catawba district[48]	16 479	...
Hollins (CDP) (pt.)	1 600	...
Cave Spring district[48]	14 717	...
Cave Spring (CDP) (pt.)	11 575	...
Hollins district[48]	11 029	...
Hollins (CDP) (pt.)	10 587	...
Vinton district[48]	17 294	...
Vinton town	8 027	6 347
Windsor Hills district[48]	13 426	...
Cave Spring (CDP) (pt.)	10 107	...
Rockbridge County[49]	17 911	16 637
Buffalo district	3 509	...
Kerrs Creek district	3 642	...
Natural Bridge district	3 268	...
Glasgow town	1 259	1 304
South River district	3 416	...
Walkers Creek district	4 076	...
Goshen town	134	121
Rockingham County[50]	57 038	47 890
Ashby district	14 150	11 942
Bridgewater town	3 289	2 828
Dayton town	1 017	978
Mount Crawford town	315	276
Central district	12 160	9 812
Parkview (CDP) (pt.)	2 196	...
Linville district	5 952	5 136
Parkview (CDP) (pt.)	28	...
Plains district	10 994	9 101
Broadway town	1 234	887
Timberville town	1 510	959
Stonewall district	13 782	11 899
Elkton town[50]	1 520	1 511
Grottoes town (pt.)	1 362	1 158
Russell County[51]	31 761	24 533
Castlewood district	8 889	7 805
Castlewood (CDP)	2 420	...
Cleveland town	360	357
Dante (CDP)	1 083	1 153
St. Paul town (pt.)[51]	168	...
Lebanon district	13 031	9 165
Lebanon town	3 206	2 272
New Garden district	9 841	7 563
Honaker town	1 475	911
Raven (CDP) (pt.)	305	373
Scott County[52]	25 068	24 376
De Kalb district	2 404	2 610
Estillville district	10 339	9 666
Gate City town[52]	2 494	1 914
Weber City town[52]	1 543	1 676
Floyd district	1 417	1 310
Dungannon town	339	282
Fulkerson district	2 259	2 397
Johnson district	2 956	2 901
Nickelsville town[52]	464	338
Powell district	2 605	2 361
Taylor district	3 088	3 131
Clinchport town	89	286
Duffield town	148	63
Shenandoah County[53]	27 559	22 852
Ashby district	4 233	3 820
Mount Jackson town[53]	1 419	681
Davis district	6 658	5 582
Strasburg town	2 311	2 431
Toms Brook town (pt.)	81	...
Johnston district	3 260	2 486
Toms Brook town (pt.)	74	132
Woodstock town (pt.)	1 044	699
Lee district	3 550	3 045
New Market town[53]	1 118	718
Madison district	4 632	3 416
Edinburg town	752	766
Stonewall district	5 226	4 503
Toms Brook town (pt.)	71	126
Woodstock town (pt.)	1 583	1 639
Smyth County[54]	33 366	31 349
Atkins district	5 093	4 381
Atkins (CDP)	1 352	...
Marion town (pt.)	1 836	(NA)
Chilhowie district	5 125	...
Chilhowie town[54]	1 269	1 317
North Fork district	4 622	...
Saltville town (pt.)	65	(NA)
Park district	5 340	...
Marion town (pt.)	3 336	(NA)
Royal Oak district	4 343	...
Marion town (pt.)	1 857	(NA)
Rye Valley district	4 824	...
Adwolf (CDP)	1 254	...

County Subdivisions	1980	1970
Smyth County—Con.		
Rye Valley district—Con.		
Sugar Grove (CDP)	1 027	...
Saltville district	4 019	...
Allison Gap (CDP)	1 060	...
Saltville town (pt.)	2 008	(NA)
Southampton County	18 731	18 582
Berlin and Ivor district	2 563	2 885
Ivor town	403	444
Boykins district	2 492	2 746
Boykins town	791	742
Branchville town	174	189
Capron district	1 611	1 867
Capron town	238	314
Drewryville district	2 348	2 009
Franklin district	4 264	3 229
Jerusalem district	3 233	3 422
Courtland town	976	899
Newsoms district	2 220	2 424
Newsoms town	368	389
Spotsylvania County[55]	34 435	16 424
Berkeley district	4 203	2 447
Chancellor district	10 979	3 872
Courtland district	8 311	3 215
Lee Hill district	6 941	4 290
Livingston district	4 001	2 600
Stafford County	40 470	24 587
Aquia district	8 568	4 109
Aquia Harbor (CDP)	2 870	...
Quantico Station (CDP) (pt.)	337	–
Falmouth–Hartwood district	6 204	4 445
Falmouth (CDP) (pt.)	864	973
George Washington district	6 037	5 015
Leeland district	7 807	4 291
Falmouth (CDP) (pt.)	2 407	1 166
Rock Hill district	11 854	6 727
Surry County[56]	6 046	5 882
Blackwater district[56]	1 204	...
Dendron town	307	336
Cobham district	2 982	2 704
Surry town	237	269
Guilford district[56]	1 860	...
Claremont town	380	383
Sussex County[57]	10 874	11 464
Courthouse district	1 222	1 481
Henry district	1 698	2 143
Jarratt town (pt.)	165	184
Newville district	861	830
Stony Creek district	1 883	1 995
Stony Creek town	329	430
Wakefield district	2 114	1 906
Wakefield town	1 355	942
Waverly district	3 096	3 109
Waverly town[57]	2 284	1 717
Tazewell County[58]	50 511	39 816
Clear Fork district	15 483	14 240
Bluefield town[58]	5 946	5 286
Pocahontas town	708	891
Jeffersonville district	13 714	9 706
Tazewell town	4 468	4 168
Maiden Spring district	21 314	15 870
Cedar Bluff town	1 550	1 050
Claypool Hill (CDP)	1 295	...
Raven (CDP) (pt.)	3 695	1 446
Richlands town[58]	5 796	4 843
Warren County[59]	21 200	15 301
Fork district	3 897	2 755
Front Royal town (pt.)	2 139	1 728
Happy Creek district	3 634	3 088
Front Royal town (pt.)[59]	2 676	2 022
North River district	5 123	3 839
Front Royal town (pt.)[59]	2 109	1 194
Shenandoah district	5 019	2 760
Front Royal town (pt.)[59]	2 785	2 184
South River district	3 527	2 859
Front Royal town (pt.)[59]	1 417	1 083
Washington County[60]	46 487	40 835
Harrison district	8 703	6 382
Abingdon town (pt.)	1 983	2 061
Emory–Meadow View (CDP) (pt.)	72	...
Jefferson district	4 421	4 274
Emory–Meadow View (CDP) (pt.)	33	...
Saltville town (pt.)	303	328
Madison district	7 666	5 455
Abingdon town (pt.)	2 335	2 315
Monroe district	7 247	6 044
Emory–Meadow View (CDP) (pt.)	2 187	...
Glade Spring town	1 722	1 615
Taylor district	5 622	4 717
Damascus town	1 330	1 230
Tyler district[60]	5 766	5 444
Wilson district[60]	7 062	8 519

County Subdivisions

County Subdivisions	1980	1970
Westmoreland County	14 041	12 142
Cople district	5 189	4 790
Montross district	2 538	2 540
Montross town	456	419
Washington district	6 314	4 812
Colonial Beach town	2 474	2 058
Wise County[61]	43 863	35 947
Gladeville district[61]	13 585	10 289
Wise town	3 894	2 891
Lipps district	9 914	8 718
Coeburn town	2 625	2 362
St. Paul town (pt.)	805	948
Richmond district[61]	14 423	12 445
Appalachia town[61]	2 418	2 161
Big Stone Gap town[61]	4 748	4 153
Roberson district	5 941	4 495
Pound town	1 086	995
Wythe County[62]	25 522	22 139
Black Lick district	4 665	3 761
Rural Retreat town	1 083	872
East Wytheville district	3 976	3 610
Wytheville town (pt.)[62]	3 638	2 980
Fort Chiswell district	4 359	3 669
Wytheville town (pt.)[62]	54	15
Lead Mines district	4 088	3 606
Speedwell district	3 542	3 535
West Wytheville district	4 892	3 958
Wytheville town (pt.)[62]	3 443	3 074
York County[63]	35 463	33 203
Bethel district	10 345	6 504
Bruton district	7 741	6 665
Grafton district	9 138	6 806
Nelson district	8 239	7 787
Alexandria city[64]	103 217	110 927
Bedford city	5 991	6 011
Bristol city[65]	19 042	14 857
Buena Vista city	6 717	6 425
Charlottesville city	39 916	38 880
Chesapeake city	114 486	89 580
Clifton Forge city	5 046	5 501
Colonial Heights city	16 509	15 097
Covington city	9 063	10 060
Danville city[66]	45 642	46 391
Emporia city	4 840	5 300
Fairfax city	19 390	22 727
Falls Church city	9 515	10 772
Franklin city	7 308	6 880
Fredericksburg city	15 322	14 450
Galax city[67]	6 524	6 278
Hampton city	122 617	120 779
Harrisonburg city	19 671	14 605
Hopewell city	23 397	23 471
Lexington city	7 292	7 597
Lynchburg city[68]	66 743	54 083
Manassas city[69]	15 438	9 164
Manassas Park city[70]	6 524	6 844
Martinsville city	18 149	19 653
Newport News city	144 903	138 177
Norfolk city	266 979	307 951
Norton city[71]	4 757	4 172
Petersburg city[72]	41 055	36 103
Poquoson city[73]	8 726	5 441
Portsmouth city	104 577	110 963
Radford city[74]	13 225	11 596
Richmond city	219 214	249 332
Roanoke city[75]	100 220	92 115
Salem city[76]	23 958	21 982
South Boston city	7 093	6 889

County Subdivisions

County Subdivisions	1980	1970
Staunton city	21 857	24 504
Suffolk city[77]	47 621	9 858
Virginia Beach city	262 199	172 106
Waynesboro city	15 329	16 707
Williamsburg city	9 870	9 069
Winchester city[78]	20 217	14 643

WASHINGTON

Washington was named in honor of the first President of the United States.

The first well authenticated exploration within the present limits of the state of Washington occurred in 1774, when Juan Perez, a Spaniard, sailed up the coast as far as 54+ north latitude. The first permanent settlement within the present limits of Washington was made in 1845 at New Market, now Tumwater.

The possession of the Oregon country of which Washington originally formed a part, was, at the beginning of the nineteenth century, in dispute among the United States, Great Britain, Spain, and Russia, each nation basing its right to possession on discoveries and explorations. English and Spanish navigators had visited the Oregon coast from time to time during the sixteenth, seventeenth, and eighteenth centuries. In 1792 Robert Gray, captain of a merchant ship from Boston, entered the river which he named the Columbia, and in 1805 the United States Government exploring expedition under Lewis and Clark descended the Columbia to its mouth. Russia had made settlements in Alaska in the early part of the eighteenth century and for this reason laid claim to territory as far south as the present state of California. All that remained of the Spanish claim after the cession of Louisiana to France in 1800 was relinquished at the time of the Florida Purchase in 1819, when Spain transferred to the United States "all rights, claims, and pretensions to any country north of the forty-second parallel." In 1824 Russia surrendered to the United States all claims south of 54°40'.

In 1818 a treaty had been concluded between the United States and England, under which the two countries jointly occupied the Oregon region, but in 1846 this joint occupation was terminated by a treaty fixing the boundary between the United States and Canada at its present location.

In 1848 Congress provided a territorial government for Oregon, which then extended from the forty-second parallel to the Canadian boundary and from the Pacific Ocean to the Rocky Mountains. In 1853 that part of Oregon lying north of the Columbia River and the forty-sixth parallel east of its point of intersection with that river was organized as Washington territory. Six years later, when Oregon, with its present boundaries, became a state of the Union, that portion of the former territory lying east of the new state was added to Washington territory, so that the latter then included the area now constituting Idaho and parts of western Montana and Wyoming. In 1863 Idaho territory was organized, leaving the territory of Washington with the same boundaries as the present state.

Washington was admitted as a state in 1889.

COUNTY LOCATION INDEX

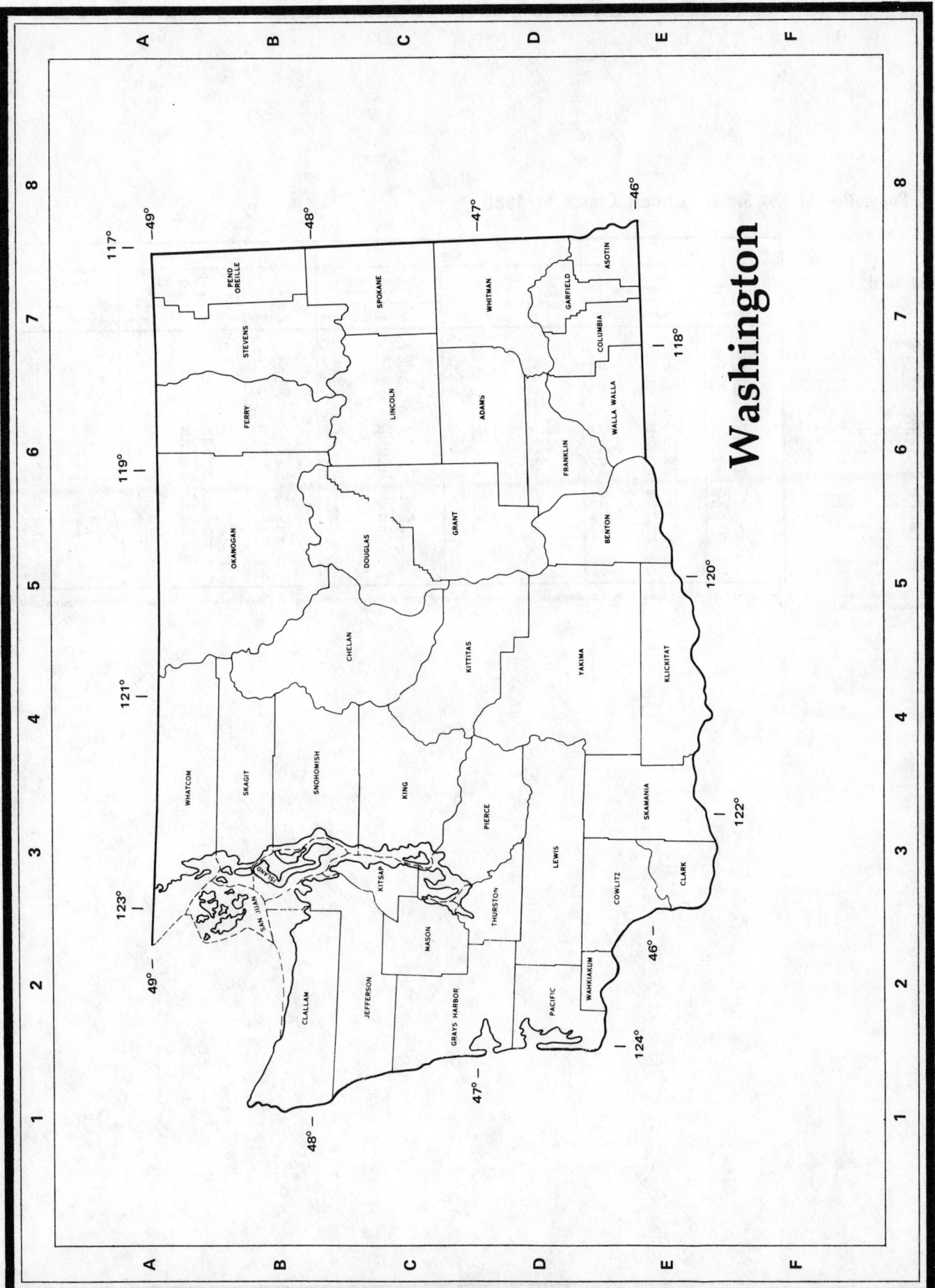

Washington

Table 1. **Population of the State: Earliest Census to 1980**

Urban and Rural

	The State			Urban					Rural				Percent of total population	
	Total population	Change from preceding census		Places of 2,500 or more	Population	Change from preceding census			Population	Change from preceding census			Urban	Rural
		Number	Percent			Number	Percent			Number	Percent			
Current urban definition:														
1980 (Apr. 1)_____	4 132 156	718 912	21.1	166	3 037 014	535 963	21.4		1 095 142	187 024	20.6		73.5	26.5
1970 (Apr. 1)_____	'3 413 244	560 030	19.6	106	2 501 051	557 802	28.7		908 118	−1 847	−0.2		73.4	26.6
1960 (Apr. 1)_____	2 853 214	474 251	19.9	84	1 943 249	440 083	29.3		909 965	34 168	3.9		68.1	31.9
1950 (Apr. 1)_____	2 378 963	642 772	37.0	66	1 503 166	...	...		875 797	...	...		63.2	36.8
Previous urban definition:														
1960 (Apr. 1)_____	2 853 214	474 251	19.9	74	1 666 500	392 348	30.8		1 186 714	81 903	7.4		58.4	41.6
1950 (Apr. 1)_____	2 378 963	642 772	37.0	55	1 274 152	352 183	38.2		1 104 811	290 589	35.7		53.6	46.4
1940 (Apr. 1)_____	1 736 191	172 795	11.1	40	921 969	37 430	4.2		814 222	135 365	19.9		53.1	46.9
1930 (Apr. 1)_____	1 563 396	206 775	15.2	38	884 539	141 738	19.1		678 857	65 037	10.6		56.6	43.4
1920 (Jan. 1)_____	1 356 621	214 631	18.8	33	742 801	137 271	22.7		613 820	77 360	14.4		54.8	45.2
1910 (Apr. 15)_____	1 141 990	623 887	120.4	27	605 530	394 053	186.3		536 460	229 834	75.0		53.0	47.0
1900 (June 1)_____	518 103	160 871	45.0	15	211 477	84 299	66.3		306 626	76 572	33.3		40.8	59.2
1890 (June 1)_____	357 232	282 116	375.6	10	127 178	120 057	1000+		230 054	162 059	238.3		35.6	64.4
1880 (June 1)_____	75 116	51 161	213.6	2	7 121	7 121	...		67 995	44 040	183.8		9.5	90.5
1870 (June 1)_____	23 955	12 361	106.6	−	−	−	−		23 955	12 361	106.6		−	100.0
1860 (June 1)_____	11 594	10 393	865.4	−	−	−	...		11 594	10 393	865.4		−	100.0
1850 (June 1)_____	1 201	...	...	−	−	...	...		1 201	...	...		−	100.0

NOTE: 1860 population is that of Washington Territory; then included present States of Washington and Idaho and parts of present States of Montana and Wyoming. 1850 population is that of those parts of Oregon Territory taken to form part of Washington Territory in 1853 and 1859.

ADAMS

1890	2,098
1900	4,840
1910	10,920
1920	9,623
1930	7,719
1940	6,209
1950	6,584
1960	9,929
1970	12,014
1980	13,267

ASOTIN

1890	1,580
1900	3,336
1910	5,831
1920	6,539
1930	8,136
1940	8,365
1950	10,878
1960	12,909
1970	13,799
1980	16,823

BENTON

1910	7,937
1920	10,903
1930	10,952
1940	12,053
1950	51,370
1960	62,070
1970	67,540
1980	109,444

CHELAN

1900	3,931
1910	15,104
1920	20,906
1930	31,634
1940	34,412
1950	39,301
1960	40,744
1970	41,355
1980	45,061

CLALLAM

1860	149
1870	408
1880	638
1890	2,771
1900	5,603
1910	6,755
1920	11,368
1930	20,449
1940	21,848
1950	26,396
1960	30,022
1970	34,770
1980	51,648

CLARK

1850	643
1860	2,384
1870	3,081
1880	5,490
1890	11,709
1900	13,419
1910	26,115
1920	32,805
1930	40,316
1940	49,852
1950	85,207
1960	93,809
1970	128,454
1980	192,227

COLUMBIA

1880	7,103
1890	6,709
1900	7,128
1910	7,042
1920	6,093
1930	5,325
1940	5,549
1950	4,860
1960	4,569
1970	4,439
1980	4,057

COWLITZ

1860	406
1870	730
1880	2,062
1890	5,917
1900	7,877
1910	12,561
1920	11,791
1930	31,906
1940	40,155
1950	53,369
1960	57,801
1970	68,616
1980	79,548

DOUGLAS

1890	3,161
1900	4,926
1910	9,227
1920	9,392
1930	7,561
1940	8,651
1950	10,817
1960	14,890
1970	16,787
1980	22,144

FERRY

1900	4,562
1910	4,800
1920	5,143
1930	4,292
1940	4,701
1950	4,096
1960	3,889
1970	3,655
1980	5,811

FRANKLIN

1890	696
1900	486
1910	5,153
1920	5,877
1930	6,137
1940	6,307
1950	13,563
1960	23,342
1970	25,816
1980	35,025

GARFIELD

1890	3,897
1900	3,918
1910	4,199
1920	3,875
1930	3,662
1940	3,383
1950	3,204
1960	2,976
1970	2,911
1980	2,468

GRANT

1910	8,698
1920	7,771
1930	5,666
1940	14,668
1950	24,346
1960	46,477
1970	41,881
1980	48,522

GRAYS HARBOR

1860	285
1870	401
1880	921
1890	9,249
1900	15,124
1910	35,590
1920	44,745
1930	59,982
1940	53,166
1950	53,644
1960	54,465
1970	59,553
1980	66,314

ISLAND

1860	294
1870	626
1880	1,087
1890	1,787
1900	1,870
1910	4,704
1920	5,489
1930	5,369
1940	6,098
1950	11,079
1960	19,638
1970	27,011
1980	44,048

JEFFERSON

1860	531
1870	1,268
1880	1,712
1890	8,368
1900	5,712
1910	8,337
1920	6,557
1930	8,346
1940	8,918
1950	11,618
1960	9,639
1970	10,661
1980	15,965

KING

1860	302
1870	2,120
1880	6,970
1890	63,989
1900	110,053
1910	284,638
1920	389,273
1930	463,517
1940	504,980
1950	732,992
1960	935,014
1970	1,159,369
1980	1,269,749

KITSAP

1860	544
1870	866
1880	1,738
1890	4,624
1900	5,767
1910	17,647
1920	33,162
1930	30,776
1940	44,387
1950	75,724
1960	84,176
1970	101,732
1980	147,152

KITTITAS

1890	8,777
1900	9,704
1910	18,561
1920	17,737
1930	18,154
1940	20,230
1950	22,235
1960	20,467
1970	25,039
1980	24,877

KLICKITAT

1860	230
1870	329
1880	4,055
1890	5,167
1900	6,407
1910	10,180
1920	9,268
1930	9,825
1940	11,357
1950	12,049
1960	13,455
1970	12,138
1980	15,822

LEWIS

1850	558
1860	384
1870	888
1880	2,600
1890	11,499
1900	15,157
1910	32,127
1920	36,840
1930	40,034
1940	41,393
1950	43,755
1960	41,858
1970	45,467
1980	56,025

LINCOLN

1890	9,312
1900	11,969
1910	17,539
1920	15,141
1930	11,876
1940	11,361
1950	10,970
1960	10,919
1970	9,572
1980	9,604

MASON

1860	162
1870	289
1880	639
1890	2,826
1900	3,810
1910	5,156
1920	4,919
1930	10,060
1940	11,603
1950	15,022
1960	16,251
1970	20,918
1980	31,184

OKANOGAN

1890	1,467
1900	4,698
1910	12,887
1920	17,094
1930	18,519
1940	24,546
1950	29,131
1960	25,520
1970	25,867
1980	30,639

PACIFIC

1860	420
1870	738
1880	1,645
1890	4,358
1900	5,983
1910	12,532
1920	14,891
1930	14,970
1940	15,928
1950	16,558
1960	14,674
1970	15,796
1980	17,237

PEND OREILLE

1920	6,363
1930	7,155
1940	7,156
1950	7,413
1960	6,914
1970	6,025
1980	8,580

PIERCE

1860	1,115
1870	1,409
1880	3,319
1890	50,940
1900	55,515
1910	120,812

1920	144,127
1930	163,842
1940	182,081
1950	275,876
1960	321,590
1970	412,344
1980	485,643

SAN JUAN

1870	554
1880	948
1890	2,072
1900	2,928
1910	3,603
1920	3,605
1930	3,097
1940	3,157
1950	3,245
1960	2,872
1970	3,856
1980	7,838

SKAGIT

1890	8,747
1900	14,272
1910	29,241
1920	33,373
1930	35,142
1940	37,650
1950	43,273
1960	51,350
1970	52,381
1980	64,138

SKAMANIA

1860	173
1870	133
1880	809
1890	774
1900	1,668
1910	2,887
1920	2,357
1930	2,891
1940	4,633
1950	4,788
1960	5,207
1970	5,845
1980	7,919

SNOHOMISH

1870	599
1880	1,387
1890	8,514
1900	23,950
1910	59,209
1920	67,690
1930	78,861
1940	88,754
1950	111,580
1960	172,199
1970	265,236
1980	337,720

SPOKANE

1880	4,262
1890	37,487
1900	57,542
1910	139,404
1920	141,289
1930	150,477
1940	164,652

1950	221,561
1960	278,333
1970	287,427
1980	341,835

STEVENS

1870	734
1880	1,245
1890	4,341
1900	10,543
1910	25,297
1920	21,605
1930	18,550
1940	19,275
1950	18,580
1960	17,884
1970	17,405
1980	28,979

THURSTON

1860	1,507
1870	2,246
1880	3,270
1890	9,675
1900	9,927
1910	17,581
1920	22,366
1930	31,351
1940	37,285
1950	44,884
1960	55,049
1970	76,894
1980	124,264

WAHKIAKUM

1860	42
1870	270
1880	1,598
1890	2,526
1900	2,819
1910	3,285
1920	3,472
1930	3,862
1940	4,286
1950	3,835
1960	3,426
1970	3,592
1980	3,832

WALLA WALLA

1860	1,318
1870	5,300
1880	8,716
1890	12,224
1900	18,860
1910	31,931
1920	27,539
1930	28,441
1940	30,547
1950	40,135
1960	42,195
1970	42,176
1980	47,435

WHATCOM

1860	352
1870	534
1880	3,137
1890	18,591
1900	24,116
1910	49,511

1920	50,600
1930	59,128
1940	60,355
1950	66,733
1960	70,317
1970	81,950
1980	106,701

WHITMAN

1880	7,014
1890	19,109
1900	25,360
1910	33,280
1920	31,323
1930	28,041
1940	27,221
1950	32,469
1960	31,263
1970	37,900
1980	40,103

YAKIMA

1870	432
1880	2,811
1890	4,429
1900	13,462
1910	41,709
1920	63,710
1930	77,402
1940	99,019
1950	135,723
1960	145,112
1970	144,971
1980	172,508

NOTES

BARRON

     Name changed from Dallas in 1869.

CLARK

     Name changed from Vancouver in 1849.

GRAYS HARBOR

     Name changed from Chehalis in 1915.

KITSAP

     Name changed from Slaughter in 1857.

MASON

     Name changed from Sawanish in 1864.

ABERDEEN

1890	1,638
1900	3,747
1910	13,660
1920	15,337
1930	21,723
1940	18,846
1950	19,653
1960	18,741
1970	18,489
1980	18,739

AUBURN

1890	740
1900	489
1910	957
1920	3,163
1930	3,906
1940	4,211
1950	6,497
1960	11,933
1970	21,653
1980	26,417

BELLEVUE

1960	12,809
1970	61,196
1980	73,903

BELLINGHAM

1910	24,298
1920	25,585
1930	30,823
1940	29,314
1950	34,112
1960	34,688
1970	39,375
1980	45,794

BREMERTON

1910	2,993
1920	8,918
1930	10,170
1940	15,134
1950	27,678
1960	28,922
1970	35,307
1980	36,208

CENTRALIA

1890	2,026
1900	1,600
1910	7,311
1920	7,549
1930	8,058
1940	7,414
1950	8,657
1960	8,586
1970	10,054
1980	11,555

EDMONDS

1900	474
1910	1,114
1920	936
1930	1,165
1940	1,288
1950	2,057
1960	8,016

1970	23,684
1980	27,679

ELLENSBURG

1890	2,768
1900	1,737
1910	4,209
1920	3,967
1930	4,621
1940	5,944
1950	8,430
1960	8,625
1970	13,568
1980	11,752

EVERETT

1900	7,838
1910	24,814
1920	27,644
1930	30,567
1940	30,244
1950	33,849
1960	40,304
1970	53,622
1980	54,413

KELSO

1900	694
1910	2,039
1920	2,228
1930	6,260
1940	6,749
1950	7,345
1960	8,379
1970	10,296
1980	11,129

KENNEWICK

1910	1,219
1920	1,684
1930	1,519
1940	1,918
1950	10,106
1960	14,244
1970	15,212
1980	34,397

KENT

1890	853
1900	755
1910	1,908
1920	2,282
1930	2,320
1940	2,586
1950	3,278
1960	9,017
1970	17,711
1980	23,152

KIRKLAND

1910	532
1920	1,354
1930	1,714
1940	2,084
1950	4,713
1960	6,025
1970	14,790
1980	18,779

LACEY

1970	9,696
1980	13,940

LONGVIEW

1930	10,652
1940	12,385
1950	20,339
1960	23,349
1970	28,373
1980	31,052

LYNNWOOD

1960	7,207
1970	17,381
1980	22,641

MERCER ISLAND

1970	19,047
1980	21,522

MOSES LAKE

1940	326
1950	2,679
1960	11,299
1970	10,310
1980	10,629

MOUNT VERNON

1890	770
1900	1,120
1910	2,381
1920	3,341
1930	3,690
1940	4,278
1950	5,230
1960	7,921
1970	8,804
1980	13,009

MOUNTLAKE TERRACE

1960	9,122
1970	16,600
1980	16,534

OAK HARBOR

1920	337
1930	362
1940	376
1950	1,193
1960	3,942
1970	9,167
1980	12,271

OLYMPIA

1870	1,203
1880	1,232
1890	4,698
1900	3,863
1910	6,996
1920	7,795
1930	11,733
1940	13,254
1950	15,819
1960	18,273
1970	23,296
1980	27,447

PASCO

1900	254
1910	2,083
1920	3,362
1930	3,496
1940	3,913
1950	10,228
1960	14,522
1970	13,920
1980	17,944

PORT ANGELES

1900	2,321
1910	2,286
1920	5,351
1930	10,188
1940	9,409
1950	11,233
1960	12,653
1970	16,367
1980	17,311

PULLMAN

1890	868
1900	1,308
1910	2,602
1920	2,440
1930	3,322
1940	4,417
1950	12,022
1960	12,957
1970	20,509
1980	23,579

PUYALLUP

1870	312
1880	297
1890	1,732
1900	1,884
1910	4,544
1920	6,323
1930	7,094
1940	7,889
1950	10,010
1960	12,063
1970	14,742
1980	18,251

REDMOND

1920	438
1930	460
1940	530
1950	573
1960	1,426
1970	11,031
1980	23,318

RENTON

1910	2,740
1920	3,301
1930	4,062
1940	4,488
1950	16,039
1960	18,453
1970	25,878
1980	30,612

RICHLAND

1960	23,548
1970	26,290
1980	33,578

SEATTLE

1870	1,107
1880	3,533
1890	42,837
1900	80,671
1910	237,194
1920	315,312
1930	365,583
1940	368,302
1950	467,591
1960	557,087
1970	430,831
1980	493,846

SPOKANE

1890	19,992
1900	36,848
1910	104,402
1920	104,437
1930	115,514
1940	122,001
1950	161,721
1960	181,608
1970	170,516
1980	171,300

TACOMA

1890	36,006
1900	37,714
1910	83,743
1920	96,965
1930	106,817
1940	109,408
1950	143,673
1960	147,979
1970	154,407
1980	158,501

VANCOUVER

1880	1,722
1890	3,545
1900	3,126
1910	9,300
1920	12,637
1930	15,766
1940	18,788
1950	41,664
1960	32,464
1970	41,859
1980	42,834

WALLA WALLA

1870	1,394
1880	3,588
1890	4,704
1900	10,049
1910	19,364
1920	15,503
1930	15,976
1940	18,109
1950	24,102
1960	24,536
1970	23,619
1980	25,618

WENATCHEE

1900	451
1910	4,050
1920	6,324
1930	11,627
1940	11,620
1950	13,072
1960	16,726
1970	16,912
1980	17,257

YAKIMA

1890	1,535
1900	3,154
1910	14,082
1920	18,539
1930	22,101
1940	27,221
1950	38,486
1960	43,284
1970	45,588
1980	49,826

CORRECTION NOTE

The official 1980 census counts of total population shown in
this report supersede counts issued previously. Corrections
to the figures were made after the counts were provided to
the State for redistricting purposes and released in Advance
Report PHC80-V for this State.

Shown below are corrections to the 1980 census counts of the
total population made after the tabulations for this report
were completed. Any additional corrections made after this
report is printed are available by writing to Data User
Services Division, Customer Services (Corrections), Bureau of
the Census, Washington, D.C. 20233.

The 1980 figures shown in this publication are subject to
change pending the outcome of the various lawsuits dealing
with the census counts.

	1980 population	
	As shown in the tables	Corrected
The State..................	4 132 156	4 132 180
Franklin County:		
Pasco division:		
Pasco city (pt.)..............	17 779	18 260
West Pasco (CDP).............	6 210	5 729
Klickitat County:		
Goldendale division:		
Goldendale city...............	3 414	3 575
Pierce County.....................	485 643	485 667
Puyallup division...............	73 736	73 760
Orting town (pt.).............	1 763	1 787
Orting town (total)...............	1 763	1 787
Pasco city (total)...............	17 944	18 425

County Subdivisions	1980	1970
The State[1]	4 132 156	3 413 244
Adams County[2]	13 267	12 014
Lind–Washtucna division	2 038	...
Hatton town	81	60
Lind town[2]	567	622
Washtucna town	266	316
Othello division	8 556	7 128
Othello city[2]	4 454	4 122
Ritzville division	2 673	...
Ritzville city[2]	1 800	1 876
Asotin County[3]	16 823	13 799
Asotin division	2 312	1 345
Asotin city	943	637
Clarkston division	14 511	...
Clarkston city[3]	6 903	6 312
West Clarkston–Highland (CDP)	3 683	3 797
Benton County[4]	109 444	67 540
Benton City division	4 168	2 158
Benton City city[4]	1 980	1 070
Federal Reservation division	73	76
Northwest Benton division	9 158	...
Prosser city[4]	3 896	2 954
Richland–Kennewick division	95 424	...
Kennewick city[4]	34 397	15 212
Richland city[4]	33 578	26 290
West Richland city[4]	2 938	1 107
South Benton division	621	242
Chelan County[5]	45 061	41 103
Cashmere division	7 885	...
Cashmere city[5]	2 240	1 976
Chelan division	4 433	...
Chelan city[5]	2 802	2 837
Entiat division	1 323	...
Entiat town[5]	445	355
Leavenworth–Lake Wenatchee division	3 591	2 639
Leavenworth city[5]	1 522	1 322
Malaga division	1 781	...
Manson division	1 861	1 615
Stehekin division	130	89
Wenatchee division	24 057	...
South Wenatchee (CDP)	1 376	...
Sunnyslope (CDP)	1 485	...
Wenatchee city[5]	17 257	16 912
West Wenatchee (CDP)	2 187	2 134
Clallam County[6]	51 648	34 770
Agnew–Carlsborg division	4 825	2 031
Clallam Bay–Neah Bay division	2 703	...
Crescent division	2 017	...
Forks division	8 015	...
Forks town[6]	3 060	1 680
Port Angeles division	25 605	...
Port Angeles city[6]	17 311	16 367
Port Angeles East (CDP)	2 786	1 523
Sequim division	8 483	...
Sequim city[6]	3 013	1 549
Clark County[7]	192 227	128 454
Battle Ground division	19 892	...
Battle Ground city[7]	2 774	1 438
Camas division	20 658	...
Camas city[7]	5 681	5 790
Washougal city[7]	3 834	3 388
La Center division	6 229	3 468
La Center town[7]	439	300
Woodland city (pt.)[7]	85	123
Orchards division	21 622	...
Orchards (CDP)	8 828	...
Ridgefield division	3 043	2 644
Ridgefield town[7]	1 062	1 004
Vancouver division	117 144	...
Hazel Dell (CDP)	15 386	...
Vancouver city[7]	42 834	41 859
Yacolt division	3 639	2 588
Yacolt town	544	488
Columbia County[8]	4 057	4 439
Dayton division	3 422	...
Dayton city	2 565	2 596
Starbuck division	635	...
Starbuck town	198	216
Cowlitz County[9]	79 548	68 616
Castle Rock division	11 565	...
Castle Rock city[9]	2 162	1 647
Cowlitz East division	1 269	...
Kalama division	3 562	...
Kalama city[9]	1 216	1 106
Longview–Kelso division	54 962	...
Beacon Hill (CDP)	1 496	1 263
Columbia Heights (CDP)	2 515	1 572
Kelso city[9]	11 129	10 296
Lexington (CDP)	1 907	...
Lone Oak (CDP)	1 121	...
Longview city[9]	31 052	28 373
Ocean Beach (CDP)	2 108	...
Rose Valley division	3 399	...
Woodland division	4 791	...
Woodland city (pt.)[9]	2 256	1 499

County Subdivisions	1980	1970
Douglas County[10]	22 144	16 787
Bridgeport division	3 971	...
Bridgeport town	1 174	952
Coulee Dam town (pt.)	234	241
Mansfield town	315	273
East Wenatchee division	16 355	11 581
East Wenatchee city[10]	1 640	913
East Wenatchee Bench (CDP)	11 410	2 446
Rock Island town[10]	491	191
Waterville division	1 818	...
Waterville town[10]	908	919
Ferry County[11]	5 811	3 655
Colville Reservation division	1 548	1 009
Curlew division	1 214	764
Orient–Sherman division	705	419
Republic division	2 344	1 463
Republic town[11]	1 018	862
Franklin County[12]	35 025	25 816
Connell division	4 708	3 556
Connell town[12]	1 981	1 161
Mesa town[12]	278	274
Kahlotus division	1 044	833
Kahlotus town	203	308
Pasco city (pt.)	–	
Pasco division	26 131	19 100
Pasco city (pt.)[12]	17 779	13 920
West Pasco (CDP)	6 210	3 809
Pasco North division	3 142	2 327
Pasco city (pt.)[12]	165	...
Garfield County[13]	2 468	2 911
Pomeroy division	2 064	...
Pomeroy city[13]	1 716	1 823
Snake River division	404	...
Grant County[14]	48 522	41 881
Coulee City division	1 204	...
Coulee City town	510	558
Hartline town	165	189
Ephrata–Soap Lake division	10 411	...
Ephrata city[14]	5 359	5 255
Soap Lake city[14]	1 196	1 064
George division	1 804	...
George town	261	273
Gloyd division	737	...
Grand Coulee division	2 531	...
Coulee Dam town (pt.)	4	7
Electric City town[14]	927	651
Grand Coulee city[14]	1 180	1 302
Moses Lake division	19 084	...
Moses Lake city[14]	10 629	10 310
Moses Lake North (CDP)	3 348	2 672
Quincy division	5 670	...
Quincy town[14]	3 525	3 237
Southern Slopes division	3 538	...
Mattawa town[14]	299	180
Royal City town[14]	676	477
Warden division	2 544	2 116
Warden town[14]	1 479	1 254
Wilson Creek division	999	...
Krupp town	83	52
Wilson Creek town	222	184
Grays Harbor County[15]	66 314	59 553
Aberdeen–Hoquiam division	35 170	...
Aberdeen city[15]	18 739	18 489
Central Park (CDP)	2 709	2 720
Cosmopolis city	1 575	1 599
Hoquiam city[15]	9 719	10 466
Elma division	5 428	...
Elma city[15]	2 720	2 227
Humptulips division	1 386	...
Lake Quinault division	1 017	907
McCleary division	2 818	...
McCleary town[15]	1 419	1 265
Malone–Porter division	1 095	...
North Beach division	4 329	3 390
Ocean Shores city[15]	1 692	...
North River division	532	...
Oakville division	1 345	...
Oakville city	537	460
Quinault Reservation division	1 116	740
South Shore division	4 337	...
Westport city[15]	1 954	1 364
Wishkah division	1 488	...
Wynoochee division	6 253	...
Montesano city[15]	3 247	2 847
Island County[16]	44 048	27 011
Camano division	5 080	2 600
Central Whidbey division	6 144	...
Coupeville town[16]	1 006	678
North Whidbey division	25 535	16 641
Ault Field (CDP)	2 553	1 478
Oak Harbor city[16]	12 271	9 167
South Whidbey division	7 289	...
Langley city[16]	650	547

County Subdivisions	1980	1970
Jefferson County[17]	15 965	10 661
Discovery Bay division	8 441	...
Port Townsend city	6 067	5 241
Oak Bay division	4 550	...
Hadlock–Irondale (CDP)	1 752	...
Quilcene Bay division	2 155	...
West End division	819	...
King County[18]	1 269 749	r1 159 369
Auburn division	90 332	...
Algona city	1 467	1 276
Auburn city (pt.)[18]	25 822	r21 653
Dumas Bay–Twin Lakes (CDP)	14 535	...
Lakeland North (CDP) (pt.)	5 236	...
Lakeland South (CDP)	5 225	...
Milton town (pt.)[18]	218	7
Pacific city	2 261	1 831
Poverty Bay (CDP)	8 353	...
West Federal Way	16 872	...
Zenith–Saltwater (CDP) (pt.)	2 464	...
East Seattle division	328 847	...
Beaux Arts Village town	328	475
Bellevue city[18]	73 903	r61 196
Bothell city[18]	7 943	r5 420
Bryn Mawr–Skyway (CDP) (pt.)	1 547	...
Cascade–Fairwood (CDP)	16 939	...
Clyde Hill town	3 229	2 987
Cottage Lake (CDP)	4 435	...
Eastgate (CDP)	8 341	...
East Renton Highlands (CDP)	12 033	...
Hunts Point town	480	578
Inglewood (CDP)	12 467	...
Issaquah city (pt.)[18]	50	...
Juanita (CDP)	17 232	...
Kenmore (CDP)	7 281	...
Kingsgate (CDP)	12 652	...
Kirkland city[18]	18 779	r14 970
Medina city	3 220	3 455
Mercer Island city[18]	21 522	19 047
Newport Hills (CDP)	12 245	...
Redmond city[18]	23 318	r11 020
Renton city (pt.)[18]	30 099	(NA)
Rose Hill (CDP)	7 616	...
Yarrow Point town	1 064	r1 101
Enumclaw Plateau division	31 081	...
Auburn city (pt.)[18]	582	...
Black Diamond city	1 170	1 160
Enumclaw city[18]	5 427	4 703
Issaquah Plateau division	19 796	...
Issaquah city (pt.)[18]	5 486	4 313
Lower Snoqualmie Valley division	5 336	...
Carnation city	913	530
Duvall city[18]	729	607
Seattle division	744 792	...
Auburn city (pt.)[18]	13	...
Boulevard Park (CDP)	8 382	...
Bryn Mawr–Skyway (CDP) (pt.)	10 207	...
Burien (CDP)	23 189	...
Des Moines city[18]	7 378	r3 951
Kent city[18]	23 152	r17 711
Lake Forest North (CDP)	7 995	...
Lake Forest Park city[18]	2 485	2 530
Lakeland North (CDP) (pt.)	6 215	...
Normandy Park city[18]	4 268	r4 202
North City–Ridgecrest (CDP)	13 551	...
North Hill (CDP)	10 170	...
Renton city (pt.)[18]	513	(NA)
Richmond Beach–Innis Arden (CDP)	6 700	...
Richmond Highlands (CDP)	24 463	...
Riverton (CDP)	14 182	...
Seattle city[18]	493 846	530 831
Sheridan Beach (CDP)	6 873	...
Tukwila city[18]	3 578	r3 509
Valley Ridge (CDP)	17 961	...
White Center–Shorewood (CDP)	19 362	...
Zenith–Saltwater (CDP) (pt.)	6 518	...
Snoqualmie National Forest division	571	...
Skykomish town	209	283
Tahoma–Maple Valley division	28 256	...
Upper Snoqualmie Valley division	13 361	...
Fall City (CDP)	1 528	...
North Bend city[18]	1 701	1 625
Snoqualmie city[18]	1 370	1 260
Vashon Island division	7 377	6 516
Kitsap County[19]	147 152	101 732
Bremerton division	71 774	...
Bremerton city (pt.)[19]	36 191	35 307
Enetai (CDP)	2 638	2 878
Erlands Point (CDP)	1 254	1 017
Kitsap Lake (CDP)	1 260	...
Navy Yard City (CDP) (pt.)	2 382	2 827
Rocky Point (CDP)	1 495	1 733
Tracyton (CDP)	2 304	1 413
Kingston division	4 574	...
Port Orchard division	37 495	...
Bremerton city (pt.)[19]	17	...
East Port Orchard (CDP)	4 631	...
Navy Yard City (CDP) (pt.)	212	...
Parkwood (CDP)	4 599	...
Port Orchard city[19]	4 787	3 904
Retsil (CDP)	1 524	...
Kitsap County—Con.		
Poulsbo division	20 995	...
Poulsbo[19]	3 453	1 856
Suquamish (CDP)	1 498	...
Winslow division	12 314	...
Winslow city[19]	2 196	1 461
Kittitas County[20]	24 877	25 039
Cle Elum division	4 067	...
Cle Elum city[20]	1 773	1 725
Roslyn city[20]	938	1 031
South Cle Elum town	449	374
Ellensburg division	13 658	...
Ellensburg city[20]	11 752	13 568
Kittitas division	2 422	...
Kittitas city[20]	782	637
Manastash division	2 544	...
Naneum division	2 186	...
Klickitat County[21]	15 822	12 138
Goldendale division	5 698	...
Goldendale city[21]	3 414	2 484
Horse Heaven division	525	...
Wahkiakus division	3 395	...
White Salmon division	5 561	...
Bingen town[21]	644	671
White Salmon city[21]	1 853	1 585
Yakima Reservation division	643	7
Lewis County[22]	56 025	45 467
Big Bottom division	3 201	...
Boistfort division	5 014	...
Pe Ell town	617	582
Winlock city[22]	1 052	890
Bunker division	2 243	...
Centralia–Chehalis division	24 695	...
Centralia city[22]	11 555	10 054
Chehalis city[22]	6 100	5 727
Fords Prairie (CDP)	2 582	2 250
Ethel division	2 140	...
Jackson Prairie division	2 935	...
Napavine city[22]	611	377
Logan Hill division	2 348	...
Mineral division	2 493	...
Morton division	3 368	...
Morton city[22]	1 264	1 134
Mossyrock division	3 334	...
Mossyrock city	463	409
Newaukum division	1 564	...
Olequa division	2 690	...
Toledo city[22]	637	654
Vader city[22]	406	387
Lincoln County[23]	9 604	9 572
Davenport division	3 314	...
Davenport city	1 559	1 363
Reardan town	498	389
Odessa division	3 358	...
Harrington town[23]	507	489
Odessa town[23]	1 009	1 074
Sprague city	473	550
Wilbur division	2 932	...
Almira town	330	376
Creston town	309	325
Wilbur town	1 122	1 074
Mason County[24]	31 184	20 918
Belfair division	3 742	...
Kamilche division	1 740	...
Olympic division	3 655	...
Shelton division	13 704	...
Shelton city[24]	7 629	6 515
Skokomish Reservation division	542	370
South Shore division	5 369	...
Tahuya division	2 432	...
Okanogan County[25]	30 639	25 867
Brewster–Wakefield division	3 056	...
Brewster town[25]	1 337	1 059
Pateros town[25]	555	472
Colville Reservation division	5 499	...
Coulee Dam town (pt.)	1 174	1 177
Elmer City town[25]	312	324
Nespelem town	284	323
Okanogan city (pt.)[25]	6	...
Omak city (pt.)[25]	736	...
Conconully–Riverside division	1 574	...
Conconully town	157	122
Riverside town	243	228
Early Winters division	102	...
Methow Valley division	3 885	...
Twisp town[25]	911	756
Winthrop town[25]	413	371
Okanogan division	3 701	...
Okanogan city (pt.)[25]	2 296	2 015
Omak division	4 927	...
Omak city (pt.)[25]	3 271	4 164
Oroville division	4 974	...
Oroville town[25]	1 483	1 555
Tonasket–Pine Creek division	2 921	...
Tonasket town[25]	985	951

County Subdivisions	1980	1970
Pacific County[26]	17 237	15 796
Naselle division	2 003	...
Peninsula division	5 426	...
Ilwaco town[26]	604	506
Long Beach town[26]	1 199	968
Raymond division	8 206	...
Raymond city[26]	2 991	3 126
South Bend city[26]	1 686	1 795
Willapa Valley division	1 602	...
Pend Oreille County[27]	8 580	6 025
Ione–Metaline Falls division	2 129	...
Ione town	594	529
Metaline town[27]	190	197
Metaline Falls town	296	307
Newport division	6 451	...
Cusick town	246	257
Newport city[27]	1 665	1 418
Pierce County[28]	485 643	412 344
Buckley division	9 806	7 240
Buckley city[28]	3 143	3 446
Carbonado town	456	394
Orting town (pt.)[28]	–	...
South Prairie town	202	206
Wilkeson town (pt.)[28]	278	317
Eatonville division	3 083	2 411
Eatonville town[28]	998	852
Fort Lewis–Dupont division	30 102	45 014
Dupont city[28]	559	384
Fort Lewis (CDP)	23 761	38 054
McChord AFB (CDP)	5 746	6 515
Gig Harbor Peninsula division	22 050	10 065
Gig Harbor town[28]	2 429	1 657
Graham–Thrift division	18 587	...
Lower Peninsula division	5 825	4 244
Mount Rainier division	1 117	771
Wilkeson town (pt.)[28]	43	...
Puyallup division	73 736	...
Bonney Lake city[28]	5 328	2 700
Orting town (pt.)[28]	1 763	1 643
Puyallup city[28]	18 251	14 742
Sumner city[28]	4 936	4 325
Roy division	5 848	2 632
Roy city	417	381
Tacoma division	315 489	...
Fife city[28]	1 823	1 458
Fircrest town[28]	5 477	5 651
Lakes District (CDP)	54 533	48 195
Milton town (pt.)[28]	2 944	2 600
Parkland (CDP)	23 355	21 012
Ruston town	612	668
Spanaway (CDP)	8 868	5 768
Steilacoom town[28]	4 886	2 850
Tacoma city[28]	158 501	154 407
University Place (CDP)	20 381	13 230
San Juan County[29]	7 838	3 856
Lopez division	1 406	737
Orcas division	2 560	1 236
San Juan division	3 872	1 883
Friday Harbor town[29]	1 200	803
Skagit County[30]	64 138	52 381
Anacortes division	11 911	...
Anacortes city	9 013	7 701
Bayview division	2 088	...
Bow division	3 763	...
Burlington division	6 312	...
Burlington city[30]	3 894	3 138
Cavanaugh division	1 177	...
Clear Lake division	1 293	...
Conway division	2 241	...
La Conner division	2 638	...
La Conner town[30]	633	639
Lyman–Hamilton division	1 778	...
Hamilton town	268	196
Lyman town	285	324
Mount Vernon division	16 237	...
Mount Vernon city[30]	13 009	8 804
Samish division	2 321	...
Sedro–Woolley division	8 346	...
Sedro–Woolley city[30]	6 110	4 598
Swinomish Reservation division	1 394	613
Upper Skagit division	2 639	...
Concrete town[30]	592	573
Skamania County[31]	7 919	5 845
Bonneville division	2 267	...
North Bonneville city[31]	394	459
Gifford Pinchot division	46	...
Stevenson division	2 010	...
Stevenson city[31]	1 172	916
Wind River division	3 596	...
Snohomish County[32]	337 720	265 236
Arlington division	10 258	...
Arlington city[32]	3 282	2 261
Cascade division	2 212	2 193
Darrington town[32]	1 064	1 094
Edmonds division	130 794	...
Alderwood Manor (CDP)	16 524	...
Brier city	2 915	3 093

County Subdivisions	1980	1970
Snohomish County—Con.		
Edmonds division—Con.		
Edmonds city[32]	27 679	23 684
Esperance (CDP)	11 120	...
Lake Stickney (CDP) (pt.)	4 057	...
Lynnwood city[32]	22 641	17 381
Martha Lake (CDP)	3 054	...
Mountlake Terrace city[32]	16 534	16 600
Woodway town[32]	832	879
Everett division	82 130	...
Everett city (pt.)[32]	54 413	53 622
Fairmont–Intercity (CDP)	6 997	...
Lake Stickney (CDP) (pt.)	2 078	...
Martha Lake (CDP) (pt.)	3 968	...
Mukilteo city	1 426	1 369
Silver Lake–Fircrest (CDP)	10 299	...
Granite Falls division	5 390	...
Granite Falls town[32]	911	813
Lake Stevens division	8 168	6 568
Lake Stevens city	1 660	1 283
Maltby division	15 624	...
Marysville division	28 316	...
Marysville city (pt.)[32]	5 080	4 343
North Marysville (CDP)	15 159	...
Monroe division	9 592	...
Monroe city[32]	2 869	2 687
Skykomish division	6 081	...
Gold Bar town[32]	794	504
Index town	147	169
Sultan town[22]	1 578	1 119
Snohomish division	20 361	...
Everett city (pt.)[32]	–	...
Marysville city (pt.)[32]	–	...
Snohomish city[32]	5 294	5 174
Stanwood division	13 748	...
Stanwood city[32]	1 646	1 347
Tulalip division	5 046	3 028
Spokane County[33]	341 835	287 487
Airway Heights division	5 060	2 317
Airway Heights city	1 730	744
Colbert division	4 995	2 940
Deer Park division	14 140	...
Deer Park city[33]	2 140	1 295
Liberty Lake division	7 488	2 303
Liberty Lake (CDP)	1 599	...
Otis Orchards–East Farms (CDP)	4 597	...
Marshall division	3 333	...
Medical Lake division	19 954	...
Cheney city (pt.)[33]	7 630	6 358
Fairchild AFB (CDP)	5 353	6 754
Medical Lake town[33]	3 600	3 529
Mount Spokane division	2 837	1 397
Rockford division	3 098	3 228
Fairfield town[33]	582	469
Latah town	155	169
Rockford town	442	327
Spangle city	276	179
Waverly town	99	48
Spokane division	277 766	...
Dishman (CDP)	10 169	9 079
Fairwood (CDP)	5 337	...
Millwood town	1 717	1 770
Opportunity (CDP)	21 241	16 604
Spokane city[33]	171 300	170 516
Town and Country (CDP)	5 578	6 484
Veradale (CDP)	7 256	...
Turnbull division	1 452	695
Cheney city (pt.)[33]	–	...
Valleyford division	1 712	953
Stevens County[34]	28 979	17 405
Chewelah division	4 201	...
Chewelah city[34]	1 888	1 365
Columbia division	1 179	...
Colville division	9 097	...
Colville city[34]	4 510	3 742
Kettle Falls division	5 481	...
Kettle Falls city[34]	1 087	893
Marcus town	174	142
Northport town	368	423
Loon Lake division	4 675	...
Spokane Reservation division	1 475	689
Springdale division	2 871	...
Springdale town	281	215
Thurston County[35]	124 264	76 894
Olympia division	84 666	...
Lacey city[35]	13 940	9 696
Olympia city[35]	27 447	23 296
Tanglewilde–Thompson Place (CDP)	5 910	...
Tumwater city (pt.)[35]	6 698	5 373
Union Mills (CDP)	4 623	...
Olympia East division	10 579	...
Yelm town[35]	1 294	628
Olympia West division	11 321	...
Tumwater city (pt.)[35]	7	...
Thurston South division	17 698	...
Bucoda town[35]	519	421

County Subdivisions	1980	1970
Thurston County—Con.		
Thurston South division—Con.		
Rainier town[35]	891	382
Tenino town[35]	1 280	962
Wahkiakum County[36]	3 832	3 592
Cathlamet–Elochoman division	1 634	...
Cathlamet town	635	647
Grays River division	924	...
Puget Island division	768	...
Skamokawa division	506	...
Walla Walla County[37]	47 435	42 176
Burbank division	3 146	...
Eureka Flat division	869	...
Prescott town	341	242
Touchet division	1 763	...
Waitsburg division	2 112	...
Waitsburg city[37]	1 035	953
Walla Walla–College Place division	39 545	...
College Place city[37]	5 771	4 510
Garrett (CDP)	1 134	1 586
Walla Walla city[37]	25 618	23 619
Walla Walla East (CDP)	3 285	2 840
Whatcom County[38]	106 701	'81 983
Bellingham division	61 024	...
Bellingham city (pt.)[38]	45 794	39 375
Ferndale city (pt.)[38]	54	...
Geneva (CDP)	1 423	...
Marietta–Alderwood (CDP)	2 324	...
Blaine division	7 854	...
Blaine city[38]	2 363	1 955
East Whatcom division	3 589	...
Ferndale division	17 910	...
Everson city (pt.)[38]	337	...
Ferndale city (pt.)[38]	3 801	2 164
Lummi Island division	538	...
Bellingham city (pt.)[38]	–	...
Lummi Reservation division	2 274	1 552
Lynden division	8 023	...
Lynden city[38]	4 022	2 808
Point Roberts division	487	662
Sumas division	5 002	...
Everson city (pt.)[38]	561	633
Nooksack city[38]	429	322
Sumas city[38]	712	'722
Whitman County[39]	40 103	37 900
Colfax–Palouse division	5 206	...
Colfax city[39]	2 780	2 664
Palouse city[39]	1 005	948
La Crosse division	1 248	...
La Crosse town	373	426
Pullman division	25 998	...
Albion town[39]	631	687
Pullman city[39]	23 579	20 509
Rock Lake division	1 949	...
Endicott town	290	333
Lamont town	101	88
St. John town[39]	529	575
Rosalia division	1 192	1 283
Malden town	200	219
Rosalia town[39]	572	569
Steptoe division	2 283	...
Farmington town[39]	176	140
Garfield town	599	610
Oakesdale town	444	447
Tekoa division	1 067	...
Tekoa city	854	808
Uniontown division	1 160	1 296
Colton town[39]	307	279
Uniontown town	286	310
Yakima County[40]	172 508	'145 212
Mabton division	2 226	1 965
Grandview city (pt.)[40]	2	...
Mabton town[40]	1 248	926
Northeast Yakima division	4 888	...
Moxee City town[40]	687	600
Northwest Yakima division	5 552	...
Naches town[40]	644	666
Southwest Yakima division	–	–
South Yakima division	3 770	...
Union Gap city (pt.)	65	...
Sunnyside division	34 333	...
Grandview city (pt.)[40]	5 613	3 605
Granger town[40]	1 812	1 567
Sunnyside city[40]	9 225	6 751
Zillah city[40]	1 599	1 138
Toppenish–Wapato division	20 953	...
Harrah town	343	305
Toppenish city[40]	6 517	5 744
Wapato city[40]	3 307	2 841
Yakima division	100 786	...
Fairview–Sumach (CDP)	2 788	2 111
Fruitvale (CDP)	3 967	3 275
North Selah (CDP)	1 901	...
Selah city[40]	4 500	'3 311
South Broadway (CDP)	3 500	3 298
Terrace Heights (CDP)	3 199	1 033
Tieton town[40]	528	415
Union Gap city (pt.)[40]	3 119	2 040

County Subdivisions	1980	1970
Yakima County—Con.		
Yakima division—Con.		
Yakima city[40]	49 826	45 588

WEST VIRGINIA

West Virginia derives its name from that of the parent state, which was called Virginia in honor of Elizabeth of England, the "Virgin Queen."

The territory now forming West Virginia was included in the grant made by the English King to the Virginia Company in 1609. It was later claimed by France by virtue of the explorations of Marquette, Joliet, La Salle, and others in the Mississippi Valley. The French claims were, however, extinguished in 1763 by the treaty of peace which concluded the French and Indian War. The Six Nations also claimed this territory by right of conquest, but in 1768 ceded their title to England by the treaty made at Fort Stanwix, N. Y.

For many years after the settlement of the eastern part of Virginia the western portion, which now constitutes West Virginia, remained unexplored. It was probably first visited by white men in 1669. In that year John Lederer, a German surgeon, in the employ of Gov. Berkeley of Virginia, made a tour of exploration westward, probably reaching the summit of the mountains which form the eastern boundary of West Virginia, and in the same year La Salle is believed to have sailed down the Ohio river, thus skirting the western boundary. Two years later Thomas Batts penetrated the state as far as the falls of the Kanawha. The date of the first settlement within the present limits of the state is uncertain, but it is known that as early as 1727 settlers from Pennsylvania had located in the northeastern part of the state at New Mecklenberg, now Shepherdstown. A few years later Scotch-Irish pioneers began to settle in western Virginia and some of them crossed the mountains into what is now West Virginia.

By the charter of Maryland granted in 1632 Virginia was deprived of the territory now constituting Maryland and nominally of a tract now in northeastern West Virginia, but notwithstanding the terms of the charter continued to retain jurisdiction over the latter region until it became a part of the state of West Virginia. The boundary dispute between Pennsylvania and Virginia was settled in 1779, when the western boundary and the western part of the southern boundary of Pennsylvania were fixed at their present location. In 1784 Virginia ceded to the United States its lands west of the Ohio River, and in 1792 the territory south of the Ohio, which up to this time had formed a part of Virginia, became the state of Kentucky. Thus the area of Virginia was reduced to the territory now comprising the states of Virginia and West Virginia.

At the outbreak of the Civil War that part of Virginia lying northwest of the Alleghenies remained loyal to the Union. A convention of delegates elected by the people of that portion of the state met at Wheeling in June, 1861, after Virginia had seceded, adopted a declaration of independence of the mother state, took measures for the establishment of a provisional government, and elected a governor. Another convention met at Wheeling in November, 1861, and framed a constitution for the state, which was ratified by popular vote in the following April. On June 20, 1863, West Virginia became a state of the Union, by act of Congress approved December, 31, 1862.

In 1863 the counties of Berkeley and Jefferson were transferred from Virginia to West Virginia and in 1866 Congress recognized and approved the transfer. This left both states with substantially their present limits.

COUNTY LOCATION INDEX

Barbour	C-5	Lewis	C-4	Raleigh	E-3
Berkeley	C-7	Lincoln	E-2	Randolph	D-5
Boone	E-3	Logan	E-3	Ritchie	C-4
Braxton	D-4	McDowell	F-3	Roane	D-3
Brooke	A-4	Marion	C-5	Summers	E-4
Cabell	D-2	Marshall	B-4	Taylor	C-5
Calhoun	C-3	Mason	D-2	Tucker	C-5
Clay	D-4	Mercer	F-3	Tyler	C-4
Doddridge	C-4	Mineral	C-6	Upshur	C-5
Fayette	E-3	Mingo	E-2	Wayne	E-2
Gilmer	C-4	Monongalia	B-5	Webster	D-4
Grant	C-6	Monroe	E-4	Wetzel	B-4
Greenbrier	E-4	Morgan	B-7	Wirt	C-3
Hampshire	C-6	Nicholas	D-4	Wood	C-3
Hancock	A-4	Ohio	B-4	Wyoming	E-3
Hardy	C-6	Pendleton	D-6		
Harrison	C-4	Pleasants	C-3		
Jackson	D-3	Pocahontas	D-5		
Jefferson	C-7	Preston	C-5		
Kanawha	D-3	Putnam	D-3		

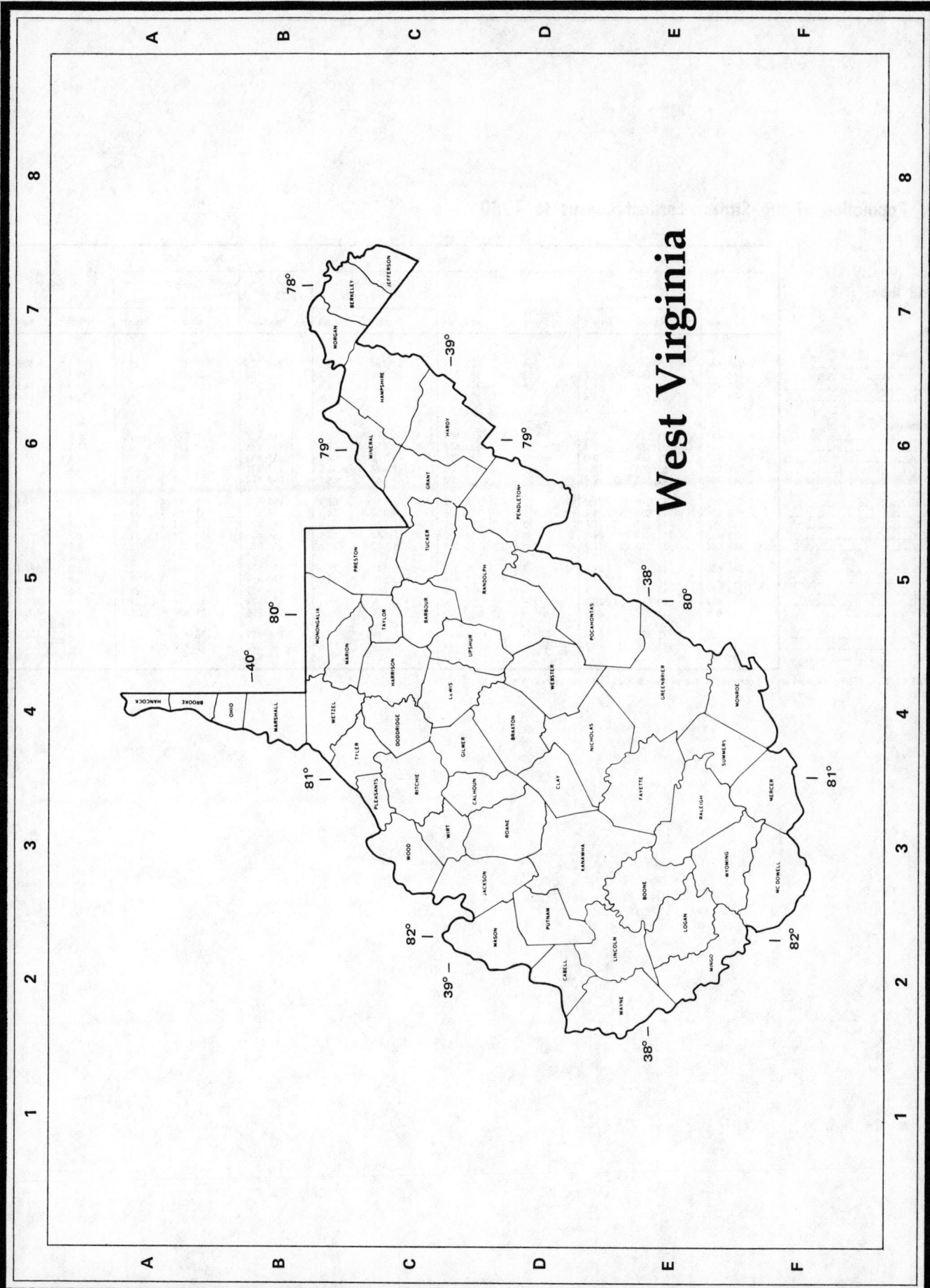

West Virginia

Population of the State: Earliest Census to 1980

Urban and Rural

	The State			Urban				Rural				Percent of total population	
	Total population	Change from preceding census		Places of 2,500 or more	Population	Change from preceding census		Population	Change from preceding census			Urban	Rural
		Number	Percent			Number	Percent		Number	Percent			
Current urban definition:													
1980 (Apr. 1)	1 949 644	205 407	11.8	64	705 319	23 764	3.5	1 244 325	181 643	17.1		36.2	63.8
1970 (Apr. 1)	1 744 237	−116 184	−6.2	53	681 555	−29 546	−4.2	1 062 682	−86 638	−7.5		39.1	60.9
1960 (Apr. 1)	1 860 421	−145 131	−7.2	56	711 101	16 614	2.4	1 149 320	−161 745	−12.3		38.2	61.8
1950 (Apr. 1)	2 005 552	103 578	5.4	61	694 487	...	...	1 311 065	...	...		34.6	65.4
Previous urban definition:													
1960 (Apr. 1)	1 860 421	−145 131	−7.2	54	665 504	24 898	3.9	1 194 917	−170 029	−12.5		35.8	64.2
1950 (Apr. 1)	2 005 552	103 578	5.4	54	640 606	106 314	19.9	1 364 946	−2 736	−0.2		31.9	68.1
1940 (Apr. 1)	1 901 974	172 769	10.0	45	534 292	42 788	8.7	1 367 682	129 981	10.5		28.1	71.9
1930 (Apr. 1)	1 729 205	265 504	18.1	39	491 504	122 497	33.2	1 237 701	143 007	13.1		28.4	71.6
1920 (Jan. 1)	1 463 701	242 582	19.9	35	369 007	140 765	61.7	1 094 694	101 817	10.3		25.2	74.8
1910 (Apr. 15)	1 221 119	262 319	27.4	25	228 242	102 777	81.9	992 877	159 542	19.1		18.7	81.3
1900 (June 1)	958 800	196 006	25.7	16	125 465	44 100	54.2	833 335	151 906	22.3		13.1	86.9
1890 (June 1)	762 794	144 337	23.3	10	81 365	27 315	50.5	681 429	117 022	20.7		10.7	89.3
1880 (June 1)	618 457	176 443	39.9	6	54 050	18 041	50.1	564 407	158 402	39.0		8.7	91.3
1870 (June 1)	442 014	65 326	17.3	5	36 009	15 932	79.4	406 005	49 394	13.9		8.1	91.9
1860 (June 1)	376 688	74 375	24.6	3	20 077	8 642	75.6	356 611	65 733	22.6		5.3	94.7
1850 (June 1)	302 313	77 776	34.6	1	11 435	3 550	45.0	290 878	74 226	34.3		3.8	96.2
1840 (June 1)	224 537	47 613	26.9	1	7 885	7 885	...	216 652	39 728	22.5		3.5	96.5
1830 (June 1)	176 924	40 116	29.3	−	−	−	−	176 924	40 116	29.3		−	100.0
1820 (Aug. 7)	136 808	31 339	29.7	−	−	−	−	136 808	31 339	29.7		−	100.0
1810 (Aug. 6)	105 469	26 877	34.2	−	−	−	−	105 469	26 877	34.2		−	100.0
1800 (Aug. 4)	78 592	22 719	40.7	−	−	−	−	78 592	22 719	40.7		−	100.0
1790 (Aug. 2)	55 873	...	...	−	−	...	...	55 873	...	...		−	100.0

NOTE: 1790 to 1860 populations are of those parts of Virginia taken in 1863 and 1866 to form West Virginia.

BARBOUR

1850	9,005
1860	8,958
1870	10,312
1880	11,870
1890	12,702
1900	14,198
1910	15,858
1920	18,028
1930	18,628
1940	19,869
1950	19,745
1960	15,474
1970	14,030
1980	16,639

BERKELEY

1790	19,713
1800	22,006
1810	11,479
1820	11,211
1830	10,518
1840	10,972
1850	11,711
1860	12,525
1870	14,900
1880	17,380
1890	18,702
1900	19,469
1910	21,999
1920	24,554
1930	28,030
1940	29,016
1950	30,359
1960	33,791
1970	36,356
1980	46,775

BOONE

1850	3,237
1860	4,840
1870	4,552
1880	5,824
1890	6,885
1900	8,194
1910	10,331
1920	15,319
1930	24,586
1940	28,556
1950	33,173
1960	28,764
1970	25,118
1980	30,447

BRAXTON

1840	2,575
1850	4,212
1860	4,992
1870	6,480
1880	9,787
1890	13,928
1900	18,904
1910	23,023
1920	23,973
1930	22,579
1940	21,658
1950	18,082
1960	15,152
1970	12,666
1980	13,894

BROOKE

1800	4,706
1810	5,843
1820	6,631
1830	7,041
1840	7,948
1850	5,054
1860	5,494
1870	5,464
1880	6,013
1890	6,660
1900	7,219
1910	11,098
1920	16,527
1930	24,663
1940	25,513
1950	26,904
1960	28,940
1970	29,685
1980	31,117

CABELL

1810	2,717
1820	4,789
1830	5,884
1840	8,163
1850	6,299
1860	8,020
1870	6,429
1880	13,774
1890	23,595
1900	29,252
1910	46,685
1920	65,746
1930	90,786
1940	97,459
1950	108,035
1960	108,202
1970	106,918
1980	106,835

CALHOUN

1860	2,502
1870	2,939
1880	6,702
1890	8,155
1900	10,266
1910	11,258
1920	10,268
1930	10,866
1940	12,455
1950	10,259
1960	7,948
1970	7,046
1980	8,250

CLAY

1860	1,787
1870	2,196
1880	3,460
1890	4,659
1900	8,248
1910	10,233
1920	11,486
1930	13,125
1940	15,206
1950	14,961
1960	11,942
1970	9,330
1980	11,265

DODDRIDGE

1850	2,750
1860	5,203
1870	7,076
1880	10,552
1890	12,183
1900	13,689
1910	12,672
1920	11,976
1930	10,488
1940	10,923
1950	9,026
1960	6,970
1970	6,389
1980	7,433

FAYETTE

1840	3,942
1850	3,955
1860	5,997
1870	6,647
1880	11,560
1890	20,542
1900	31,978
1910	51,903
1920	60,377
1930	72,050
1940	80,628
1950	82,443
1960	61,731
1970	49,332
1980	57,863

GILMER

1850	3,475
1860	3,759
1870	4,388
1880	7,108
1890	9,746
1900	11,762
1910	11,379
1920	10,668
1930	10,641
1940	12,046
1950	9,746
1960	8,050
1970	7,782
1980	8,334

GRANT

1870	4,467
1880	5,542
1890	6,802
1900	7,275
1910	7,838
1920	8,993
1930	8,441
1940	8,805
1950	8,756
1960	8,304
1970	8,607
1980	10,210

GREENBRIER

1790	6,015
1800	4,345
1810	5,914
1820	7,041
1830	9,006
1840	8,695
1850	10,022

1860	12,211
1870	11,417
1880	15,060
1890	18,034
1900	20,683
1910	24,883
1920	26,242
1930	35,878
1940	38,520
1950	39,295
1960	34,446
1970	32,090
1980	37,665

HAMPSHIRE

1790	7,346
1800	8,348
1810	9,784
1820	10,889
1830	11,279
1840	12,295
1850	14,036
1860	13,913
1870	7,643
1880	10,366
1890	11,419
1900	11,806
1910	11,694
1920	11,713
1930	11,836
1940	12,974
1950	12,577
1960	11,705
1970	11,710
1980	14,867

HANCOCK

1850	4,050
1860	4,445
1870	4,363
1880	4,882
1890	6,414
1900	6,693
1910	10,465
1920	19,975
1930	28,511
1940	31,572
1950	34,388
1960	39,615
1970	39,749
1980	40,418

HARDY

1790	7,336
1800	6,627
1810	5,525
1820	5,700
1830	6,798
1840	7,622
1850	9,543
1860	9,864
1870	5,518
1880	6,794
1890	7,567
1900	8,449
1910	9,163
1920	9,601
1930	9,816
1940	10,813
1950	10,032
1960	9,308
1970	8,855
1980	10,030

HARRISON

1790	2,080
1800	4,848
1810	9,958
1820	10,932
1830	14,722
1840	17,669
1850	11,728
1860	13,790
1870	16,714
1880	20,181
1890	21,919
1900	27,690
1910	48,381
1920	74,793
1930	78,567
1940	82,911
1950	85,296
1960	77,856
1970	73,028
1980	77,710

JACKSON

1840	4,890
1850	6,544
1860	8,306
1870	10,300
1880	16,312
1890	19,021
1900	22,987
1910	20,956
1920	18,658
1930	16,124
1940	16,598
1950	15,299
1960	18,541
1970	20,903
1980	25,794

JEFFERSON

1810	11,851
1820	13,087
1830	12,927
1840	14,082
1850	15,357
1860	14,535
1870	13,219
1880	15,005
1890	15,553
1900	15,935
1910	15,889
1920	15,729
1930	15,780
1940	16,762
1950	17,184
1960	18,665
1970	21,280
1980	30,302

KANAWHA

1800	3,239
1810	3,866
1820	6,399
1830	9,326
1840	13,567
1850	15,353
1860	16,150
1870	22,349
1880	32,466
1890	42,756
1900	54,696
1910	81,457
1920	119,650

Year	Population
1930	157,667
1940	195,619
1950	239,629
1960	252,925
1970	229,515
1980	231,414

LEWIS

Year	Population
1820	4,247
1830	6,241
1840	8,151
1850	10,031
1860	7,999
1870	10,175
1880	13,269
1890	15,895
1900	16,960
1910	18,281
1920	20,455
1930	21,794
1940	22,271
1950	21,074
1960	19,711
1970	17,847
1980	18,813

LINCOLN

Year	Population
1870	5,053
1880	8,739
1890	11,246
1900	15,434
1910	20,491
1920	19,378
1930	19,156
1940	22,886
1950	22,466
1960	20,267
1970	18,912
1980	23,675

LOGAN

Year	Population
1830	3,680
1840	4,309
1850	3,620
1860	4,938
1870	5,124
1880	7,329
1890	11,101
1900	6,955
1910	14,476
1920	41,006
1930	58,534
1940	67,768
1950	77,391
1960	61,570
1970	46,269
1980	50,679

McDOWELL

Year	Population
1860	1,535
1870	1,952
1880	3,074
1890	7,300
1900	18,747
1910	47,856
1920	68,571
1930	90,479
1940	90,354
1950	98,887
1960	71,359
1970	50,666
1980	49,899

MARION

Year	Population
1850	10,552
1860	12,722
1870	12,107
1880	17,198
1890	20,721
1900	32,430
1910	42,794
1920	54,571
1930	66,655
1940	68,683
1950	71,521
1960	63,717
1970	61,356
1980	65,789

MARSHALL

Year	Population
1840	6,937
1850	10,138
1860	12,997
1870	14,941
1880	18,840
1890	20,735
1900	26,444
1910	32,388
1920	33,681
1930	39,831
1940	40,189
1950	36,893
1960	36,041
1970	37,598
1980	41,608

MASON

Year	Population
1810	1,991
1820	4,868
1830	6,534
1840	6,777
1850	7,539
1860	9,173
1870	15,978
1880	22,293
1890	22,863
1900	24,142
1910	23,019
1920	21,459
1930	20,788
1940	22,270
1950	23,537
1960	24,459
1970	24,306
1980	27,045

MERCER

Year	Population
1840	2,233
1850	4,222
1860	6,819
1870	7,064
1880	7,467
1890	16,002
1900	23,023
1910	38,371
1920	49,588
1930	61,323
1940	68,289
1950	75,013
1960	68,206
1970	63,206
1980	73,942

MINERAL

Year	Population
1870	6,332
1880	8,630
1890	12,085
1900	12,883
1910	16,674
1920	19,849
1930	20,084
1940	22,215
1950	22,333
1960	22,354
1970	23,109
1980	27,234

MINGO

Year	Population
1900	11,359
1910	19,431
1920	26,364
1930	38,319
1940	40,802
1950	47,409
1960	39,742
1970	32,780
1980	37,336

MONONGALIA

Year	Population
1790	4,768
1800	8,540
1810	12,793
1820	11,606
1830	14,056
1840	17,368
1850	12,387
1860	13,048
1870	13,547
1880	14,985
1890	15,707
1900	19,049
1910	24,334
1920	33,618
1930	50,083
1940	51,252
1950	60,797
1960	55,617
1970	63,714
1980	75,024

MONROE

Year	Population
1800	4,188
1810	5,444
1820	6,620
1830	7,798
1840	8,422
1850	10,204
1860	10,757
1870	11,124
1880	11,501
1890	12,429
1900	13,130
1910	13,055
1920	13,141
1930	11,949
1940	13,577
1950	13,123
1960	11,584
1970	11,272
1980	12,873

MORGAN

Year	Population
1820	2,500
1830	2,694
1840	4,253
1850	3,557
1860	3,732
1870	4,315
1880	5,777
1890	6,744
1900	7,294
1910	7,848
1920	8,357
1930	8,406
1940	8,743
1950	8,276
1960	8,376
1970	8,547
1980	10,711

NICHOLAS

Year	Population
1820	1,853
1830	3,346
1840	2,515
1850	3,963
1860	4,627
1870	4,458
1880	7,223
1890	9,309
1900	11,403
1910	17,699
1920	20,717
1930	20,686
1940	24,070
1950	27,696
1960	25,414
1970	22,552
1980	28,126

OHIO

Year	Population
1790	5,121
1800	4,720
1810	8,175
1820	9,182
1830	15,584
1840	13,357
1850	18,006
1860	22,422
1870	28,831
1880	37,457
1890	41,557
1900	49,024
1910	57,572
1920	62,892
1930	72,077
1940	72,115
1950	71,672
1960	68,437
1970	64,197
1980	61,389

PENDLETON

Year	Population
1790	2,452
1800	3,962
1810	4,239
1820	4,846
1830	6,271
1840	6,940
1850	5,759
1860	6,164
1870	6,455
1880	8,022
1890	8,711
1900	9,167
1910	9,349
1920	9,652
1930	9,660
1940	10,884
1950	9,313
1960	8,093
1970	7,031
1980	7,910

PLEASANTS

Year	Population
1860	2,945
1870	3,012
1880	6,256
1890	7,539
1900	9,345
1910	8,074
1920	7,379
1930	6,545
1940	6,692
1950	6,369
1960	7,124
1970	7,274
1980	8,236

POCAHONTAS

Year	Population
1830	2,542
1840	2,922
1850	3,598
1860	3,598
1870	4,069
1880	5,591
1890	6,814
1900	8,572
1910	14,740
1920	15,002
1930	14,555
1940	13,906
1950	12,480
1960	10,136
1970	8,870
1980	9,919

PRESTON

Year	Population
1820	3,422
1830	5,144
1840	6,866
1850	11,708
1860	13,312
1870	14,555
1880	19,091
1890	20,355
1900	22,727
1910	26,341
1920	27,996
1930	29,043
1940	30,416
1950	31,399
1960	27,233
1970	25,455
1980	30,460

PUTNAM

Year	Population
1850	5,355
1860	6,301
1870	7,794
1880	11,375
1890	14,342
1900	17,330
1910	18,587
1920	17,531
1930	16,737
1940	19,511
1950	21,021
1960	23,561
1970	27,625
1980	38,181

RALEIGH		1890	13,117	1960	18,292	1830	6,429
		1900	16,265	1970	19,092	1840	7,923
1850	1,765	1910	18,420	1980	23,427	1850	9,450
1860	3,367	1920	19,092			1860	11,046
1870	3,673	1930	20,468	**WAYNE**		1870	19,000
1880	7,367	1940	20,409			1880	25,006
1890	9,597	1950	19,183	1850	4,760	1890	28,612
1900	12,436	1960	15,640	1860	6,747	1900	34,452
1910	25,633	1970	13,213	1870	7,852	1910	38,001
1920	42,482	1980	15,875	1880	14,739	1920	42,306
1930	68,072			1890	18,652	1930	56,521
1940	86,687	**TAYLOR**		1900	23,619	1940	62,399
1950	96,273			1910	24,081	1950	66,540
1960	77,286	1850	5,367	1920	26,012	1960	78,331
1970	70,080	1860	7,463	1930	31,206	1970	86,818
1980	86,821	1870	9,367	1940	35,566	1980	93,648
		1880	11,455	1950	38,696		
RANDOLPH		1890	12,147	1960	38,977	**WYOMING**	
		1900	14,978	1970	37,581		
1790	951	1910	16,554	1980	46,021	1850	1,645
1800	1,826	1920	18,742			1860	2,861
1810	2,854	1930	19,114	**WEBSTER**		1870	3,171
1820	3,357	1940	19,919			1880	4,322
1830	5,000	1950	18,422	1860	1,555	1890	6,247
1840	6,208	1960	15,010	1870	1,730	1900	8,380
1850	5,243	1970	13,878	1880	3,207	1910	10,392
1860	4,990	1980	16,584	1890	4,783	1920	15,180
1870	5,563			1900	8,862	1930	20,926
1880	8,102	**TUCKER**		1910	9,680	1940	29,774
1890	11,633			1920	11,562	1950	37,540
1900	17,670	1860	1,428	1930	14,216	1960	34,836
1910	26,028	1870	1,907	1940	18,080	1970	30,095
1920	26,804	1880	3,151	1950	17,888	1980	35,993
1930	25,049	1890	6,459	1960	13,719		
1940	30,259	1900	13,433	1970	9,809		
1950	30,558	1910	18,675	1980	12,245		
1960	26,349	1920	16,791				
1970	24,596	1930	13,374	**WETZEL**			
1980	28,734	1940	13,173				
		1950	10,600	1850	4,284		
RITCHIE		1960	7,750	1860	6,703		
		1970	7,447	1870	8,595		
1850	3,902	1980	8,675	1880	13,896		
1860	6,857			1890	16,841		
1870	9,055	**TYLER**		1900	22,880		
1880	13,474			1910	23,855		
1890	16,621	1820	2,314	1920	23,069		
1900	18,901	1830	4,104	1930	22,334		
1910	17,875	1840	6,954	1940	22,342		
1920	16,506	1850	5,498	1950	20,154		
1930	15,594	1860	6,517	1960	19,347		
1940	15,389	1870	7,832	1970	20,314		
1950	12,535	1880	11,073	1980	21,874		
1960	10,877	1890	11,962				
1970	10,145	1900	18,252	**WIRT**			
1980	11,442	1910	16,211				
		1920	14,186	1850	3,353		
ROANE		1930	12,785	1860	3,751		
		1940	12,559	1870	4,804		
1860	5,381	1950	10,535	1880	7,104		
1870	7,232	1960	10,026	1890	9,411		
1880	12,184	1970	9,929	1900	10,284		
1890	15,303	1980	11,320	1910	9,047		
1900	19,852			1920	7,536		
1910	21,543	**UPSHUR**		1930	6,358		
1920	20,129			1940	6,475		
1930	19,478	1860	7,292	1950	5,199		
1940	20,787	1870	8,023	1960	4,391		
1950	18,408	1880	10,249	1970	4,154		
1960	15,720	1890	12,714	1980	4,922		
1970	14,111	1900	14,696				
1980	15,952	1910	16,629	**WOOD**			
		1920	17,851				
SUMMERS		1930	17,944	1800	1,217		
		1940	18,360	1810	3,036		
1880	9,033	1950	19,242	1820	5,860		

BECKLEY

1880	144
1890	158
1900	342
1910	2,161
1920	4,149
1930	9,357
1940	12,852
1950	19,397
1960	18,642
1970	19,884
1980	20,492

BLUEFIELD

1890	1,775
1900	4,644
1910	11,188
1920	15,282
1930	19,339
1940	20,641
1950	21,506
1960	19,256
1970	15,291
1980	16,060

CHARLESTON

1850	1,050
1860	1,520
1870	3,162
1880	4,192
1890	6,742
1900	11,099
1910	22,996
1920	39,608
1930	60,408
1940	67,914
1950	73,501
1960	85,796
1970	71,505
1980	63,968

CLARKSBURG

1860	895
1870	(NA)
1880	2,307
1890	3,008
1900	4,050
1910	9,201
1920	27,869
1930	28,866
1940	30,579
1950	32,014
1960	28,112
1970	24,864
1980	22,371

FAIRMONT

1850	683
1860	704
1870	621
1880	900
1890	1,023
1900	5,655
1910	9,711
1920	17,851
1930	23,159
1940	23,105
1950	29,346
1960	27,477
1970	26,093
1980	23,863

HUNTINGTON

1880	3,174
1890	10,108
1900	11,923
1910	31,161
1920	50,177
1930	75,572
1940	78,836
1950	86,353
1960	83,627
1970	74,315
1980	63,684

MARTINSBURG

1850	2,190
1860	3,364
1870	4,863
1880	6,335
1890	7,226
1900	6,564
1910	10,698
1920	12,515
1930	14,857
1940	15,063
1950	15,621
1960	15,179
1970	14,626
1980	13,063

MORGANTOWN

1860	741
1870	797
1880	745
1890	1,011
1900	1,895
1910	9,150
1920	12,127
1930	16,186
1940	16,655
1950	15,525
1960	22,487
1970	29,431
1980	27,605

MOUNDSVILLE

1850	445
1860	515
1870	1,500
1880	1,744
1890	2,688
1900	5,362
1910	8,918
1920	10,669
1930	14,411
1940	14,168
1950	14,772
1960	15,163
1970	13,560
1980	12,419

PARKERSBURG

1850	1,218
1860	2,493
1870	5,546
1880	6,582
1890	8,408
1900	11,703
1910	17,842
1920	20,050
1930	29,623
1940	30,103
1950	29,684

1960	44,797
1970	44,208
1980	39,967

SAINT ALBANS

1900	816
1910	1,209
1920	2,825
1930	3,254
1940	3,558
1950	9,870
1960	15,103
1970	14,356
1980	12,402

SOUTH CHARLESTON

1920	3,650
1930	5,904
1940	10,377
1950	16,686
1960	19,180
1970	16,333
1980	15,968

VIENNA

1940	2,388
1950	6,020
1960	9,381
1970	11,549
1980	11,618

WEIRTON

1950	24,005
1960	28,201
1970	27,131
1980	24,736

WHEELING

1840	7,885
1850	11,435
1860	14,083
1870	19,280
1880	30,737
1890	34,522
1900	38,878
1910	41,641
1920	56,208
1930	61,659
1940	61,099
1950	58,891
1960	53,400
1970	48,188
1980	43,070

CORRECTION NOTE

Shown below are corrections to the 1980 census counts of the total population made after the tabulations for this report were completed. Any additional corrections made after this report is printed are available by writing to Data User Services Division, Customer Services (Corrections), Bureau of the Census, Washington, D.C. 20233.

The 1980 figures shown in this publication are subject to change pending the outcome of the various lawsuits dealing with the census counts.

	1980 population	
	As shown in the tables	Corrected
The State..................	1 949 644	1 950 279
Hancock County....................	40 418	41 053
Clay district....................	10 098	10 733
Weirton city (pt.).............	4 837	5 472
Harrison County:		
Northern district...............	14 504	14 370
Southeast district..............	13 820	13 986
Anmoore town (pt.).............	678	710
Suburban district...............	11 623	11 591
Anmore town (pt.).............	187	155
McDowell County:		
North Fork district:		
Northfork town (pt.).........	660	1 105
Ohio County:		
Richie Webster Center district:		
Bethlehem village.............	2 677	3 045
Anmoore town (total)..............	865	(1)
Northfork town (total)............	660	1 105
Weirton city (total)..............	24 736	25 371

¹No change.

County Subdivisions	1980	1970
The State	1 949 644	1 744 237
Barbour County[1]	16 639	14 030
North district	4 947	...
Philippi city (pt.)[1]	1 221	(NA)
South district	6 066	...
Belington town	2 038	1 567
Junior town	591	513
West district	5 626	...
Philippi city (pt.)[1]	1 973	(NA)
Berkeley County[2]	46 775	36 356
Arden district	11 311	8 576
Martinsburg city (pt.)[2]	1 630	1 554
Falling Waters district	3 594	2 225
Gerrardstown district	3 122	2 331
Hedgesville district	6 259	3 609
Hedgesville town	217	274
Martinsburg city (pt.)	553	260
Martinsburg district	10 485	12 453
Martinsburg city (pt.)	10 485	12 453
Mill Creek district	5 167	3 141
Inwood (CDP)	1 159	...
Opequon district	6 837	4 021
Martinsburg city (pt.)[2]	395	359
Boone County[3]	30 447	25 118
Crook district	6 586	5 366
Madison city (pt.)[3]	284	...
Peytona district	3 654	3 184
Scott district	6 772	5 666
Danville town	727	580
Madison city (pt.)[3]	2 615	2 324
Sherman district	7 318	6 134
Sylvester town	256	245
Whitesville town	689	781
Washington district	6 117	4 768
Madison city (pt.)[3]	329	18
Braxton County[4]	13 894	12 666
Birch district	2 220	1 848
Holly district	3 711	3 254
Flatwoods town (pt.)	215	176
Sutton town (pt.)[4]	980	912
Otter district	5 004	4 850
Gassaway town	1 225	1 253
Sutton town (pt.)[4]	212	119
Salt Lick district	2 959	2 714
Burnsville town	531	591
Flatwoods town (pt.)	190	44
Brooke County[5]	31 117	30 443
Buffalo district	7 224	...
Beech Bottom village	507	544
Bethany town	1 336	1 360
Cross Creek district	7 843	...
Follansbee city (pt.)[5]	–	(NA)
Hooverson Heights (CDP) (pt.)	3 111	...
Follansbee district	5 289	...
Follansbee city (pt.)[5]	3 994	(NA)
Hooverson Heights (CDP) (pt.)	–	...
Weirton district	5 982	...
Weirton city (pt.)	4 176	4 681
Wellsburg district	4 779	...
Wellsburg city	3 963	4 600
Cabell County[6]	106 835	106 918
Barboursville district	17 201	13 908
Barboursville village[6]	2 871	2 279
Gideon district	39 207	46 112
Huntington city (pt.)	39 200	46 112
Grant district	12 201	9 233
Culloden (CDP) (pt.)	2 664	1 033
Milton town[6]	2 178	1 597
Guyandotte district	13 023	11 416
Huntington city (pt.)[6]	3 814	3 840
Kyle district	15 678	18 815
Huntington city (pt.)	15 671	18 808
McComas district	5 501	4 069
Union district	4 024	3 365
Calhoun County	8 250	7 046
Center district	2 228	1 907
Grantsville town	788	795
Lee district	1 844	1 582
Sheridan district	1 053	833
Sherman district	1 528	1 389
Washington district	1 597	1 335
Clay County[7]	11 265	9 330
Buffalo district	1 570	1 302
Henry district	3 985	3 129
Clay town[7]	940	479
Otter district	988	1 192
Pleasant district	3 061	2 448
Union district	1 661	1 259
Doddridge County	7 433	6 389
Central district	983	850
Cove district	217	156
Grant district	1 185	1 016
Greenbrier district	795	674
McClellan district	1 186	957

County Subdivisions	1980	1970
Doddridge County—Con.		
New Milton district	532	313
Southwest district	282	215
West Union district	2 253	2 208
West Union town	1 090	1 141
Fayette County[8]	57 863	49 332
New Haven district	17 386	...
Ansted town	1 952	1 511
Fayetteville town[8]	2 366	1 712
Meadow Bridge town[8]	530	429
Plateau district	24 863	...
Mount Hope city[8]	1 849	1 829
Oak Hill city[8]	7 120	4 738
Pax town	274	288
Thurmond town	67	86
Valley district[8]	15 614	...
Boomer (CDP)	1 051	1 261
Gauley Bridge town[8]	1 177	...
Montgomery city (pt.)	2 218	1 786
Powellton (CDP)	1 339	...
Smithers city (pt.)	1 480	1 837
Gilmer County[9]	8 334	7 782
Center district	2 045	1 736
De Kalb district	944	844
Glenville district	4 346	4 386
Glenville town[9]	2 155	2 183
Layopolis town	280	252
Troy district	999	816
Grant County[10]	10 210	8 607
Grant district	1 814	1 522
Milroy district	5 659	4 858
Petersburg city[10]	2 084	2 177
Union district	2 737	2 227
Bayard town	540	475
Greenbrier County[11]	37 665	32 090
Anthony Creek district	1 127	563
Blue Sulphur district	2 993	2 498
Alderson town (pt.)[11]	1 118	892
Falling Spring district	1 115	915
Falling Spring town	240	255
Fort Spring district	5 365	4 299
Fairlea (CDP)	1 888	...
Ronceverte city (pt.)[11]	2 282	1 981
Frankford district	2 078	1 522
Irish Corner district	2 242	2 148
Ronceverte city (pt.)[11]	30	...
Lewisburg district	6 033	4 326
Lewisburg city[11]	3 065	2 407
Meadow Bluff district	9 741	9 346
Quinwood town[11]	460	370
Rainelle town[11]	1 983	1 826
Rupert town	1 276	1 027
White Sulphur district	5 562	5 353
White Sulphur Springs city[11]	3 371	2 869
Williamsburg district	1 409	1 120
Hampshire County	14 867	11 710
Bloomery district	1 363	1 005
Capon Bridge town (pt.)	54	68
Capon district	1 518	990
Capon Bridge town (pt.)	137	143
Gore district	2 567	1 757
Mill Creek district	712	659
Romney district	3 811	4 049
Romney city	2 094	2 364
Sherman district	2 669	1 604
Springfield district	2 227	1 646
Hancock County[12]	40 418	39 749
Butler district	15 724	...
Weirton city (pt.)	15 723	(NA)
Clay district	10 098	5 091
New Cumberland city (pt.)	751	(NA)
Weirton city (pt.)	4 837	(NA)
Grant district	14 596	...
Chester city	3 297	3 614
New Cumberland city (pt.)	1 001	(NA)
Newell (CDP)	2 032	2 300
Hardy County[13]	10 030	8 855
Capon district	1 748	1 520
Wardensville town	241	288
Lost River district	2 022	1 939
Moorefield district	3 804	3 307
Moorefield town (pt.)[13]	1 798	1 751
South Fork district	2 456	2 089
Moorefield town (pt.)	459	373
Harrison County[14]	77 710	73 028
North Clarksburg district	11 225	...
Clarksburg city (pt.)	11 225	(NA)
Northern district[14]	14 504	...
Enterprise (CDP)	1 110	...
Lumberport town	939	957
Shinnston city[14]	3 059	2 576
South Clarksburg district	11 146	...
Clarksburg city (pt.)[14]	11 146	(NA)
Southeast district	13 820	...
Anmoore town (pt.)	678	(NA)
Bridgeport city[14]	6 604	4 777
Lost Creek town	604	571

County Subdivisions

County Subdivisions	1980	1970
Harrison County—Con.		
Southeast district—Con.		
Stonewood city (pt.)[14]	–	(NA)
Southwest district	15 392	
Salem city[14]	2 706	2 597
West Milford town	510	356
Suburban district[14]	11 623	...
Anmoore town (pt.)[14]	187	(NA)
Despard (CDP)	1 434	1 400
East View (CDP)	1 222	1 618
Nutter Fort town[14]	2 078	2 379
Stonewood city (pt.)[14]	2 058	(NA)
Jackson County[15]	25 794	20 903
Grant district	1 672	1 215
Ravenswood district	8 759	7 731
Ravenswood city[15]	4 126	4 240
Ripley district	10 050	7 642
Ripley city	3 464	3 244
Union district	2 718	2 396
Washington district	2 595	1 919
Jefferson County[16]	30 302	21 280
Charles Town district	12 615	9 994
Charles Town city[16]	2 857	3 023
Ranson town[16]	2 471	2 189
Harpers Ferry district	4 937	3 572
Bolivar town	672	943
Harpers Ferry town	361	423
Kabletown district	2 657	1 739
Middleway district	4 941	2 264
Shepherdstown district	5 152	3 711
Shepherdstown town	1 791	1 688
Kanawha County[17]	231 414	229 515
District 1	48 693	...
Belle town	1 621	1 786
Cedar Grove town	1 479	1 275
Chesapeake town	2 364	2 428
Coal Fork (CDP)	2 775	...
East Bank town	1 155	1 025
Elkview (CDP) (pt.)	659	(NA)
Glasgow town	1 031	904
Handley town[17]	633	...
Marmet town	2 196	2 339
Montgomery city (pt.)	886	739
Pratt town	821	671
Smithers city (pt.)	2	183
District 2	42 692	
Charleston city (pt.)[17]	25 080	24 302
South Charleston city (pt.)[17]	7 768	8 823
District 3	48 069	
Nitro city (pt.)	6 733	6 703
St. Albans city[17]	12 402	14 356
South Charleston city (pt.)[17]	8 200	7 510
District 4	53 072	
Clendenin town	1 373	1 438
Dunbar city[17]	9 285	9 151
Elkview (CDP) (pt.)	502	(NA)
Pocatalico (CDP)	2 420	...
District 5[17]	38 888	47 203
Charleston city (pt.)[17]	38 888	47 203
Lewis County[18]	18 813	17 847
Collins Settlement district	1 909	1 452
Court House district	4 548	5 612
Weston city (pt.)[18]	2 534	3 613
Freemans Creek district	6 556	5 514
Weston city (pt.)	2 292	2 169
Hackers Creek district	5 075	4 509
Jane Lew town	406	397
Weston city (pt.)[18]	1 424	1 541
Skin Creek district	725	760
Lincoln County[19]	23 675	18 912
Carroll district	3 807	3 152
Hamlin town[19]	1 219	1 024
Duval district	3 473	2 717
Harts Creek district	4 135	2 892
Jefferson district	1 405	954
Laurel Hill district	2 651	2 400
Sheridan district	4 489	4 037
West Hamlin town	643	715
Union district	755	667
Washington district	2 960	2 093
Logan County[20]	50 679	46 269
Guyan district	15 001	12 184
Chapmanville town[20]	1 164	1 175
Mitchell Heights town	342	524
West Logan town	630	685
Island Creek district	15 146	13 523
Holden (CDP)	2 036	2 325
Mount Gay–Shamrock (CDP)	4 366	3 843
Switzer (CDP)	1 034	...
Whitman (CDP)	1 651	...
Logan district	8 444	8 944
Logan city	3 029	3 311
Triadelphia district	12 088	11 618
Amherstdale–Robinette (CDP)	1 075	1 602
Mallory (CDP)	1 330	1 240
Man town	1 333	1 201

County Subdivisions

County Subdivisions	1980	1970
McDowell County[21]	49 899	50 666
Adkin district	6 398	7 068
Anawalt town	652	801
Gary city[21]	2 233	...
Welch city (pt.)[21]	119	
Big Creek district	10 599	10 173
War city	2 158	2 004
Browns Creek district	14 851	15 686
Davy town	882	993
Keystone city	902	1 008
Kimball town	871	962
Welch city (pt.)	3 766	4 149
Elkhorn district	2 233	2 689
Northfork town (pt.)	–	...
North Fork district	3 045	3 450
Northfork town (pt.)[21]	660	737
Sandy River district	12 773	11 600
Bradshaw (CDP)	1 002	1 048
Iaeger town	833	822
Marion County[22]	65 789	61 356
District 1	19 215	20 227
Barrackville town[22]	1 815	1 545
Fairmont city (pt.)	14 499	16 460
Grant district	7 405	5 855
Fairmont city (pt.)	2 255	1 819
Monongah town (pt.)	564	642
Worthington town (pt.)	–	
Lincoln district	8 639	7 984
Farmington town	583	595
Monongah town (pt.)	568	552
Worthington town (pt.)	329	288
Mannington district	6 269	5 641
Mannington city	3 036	2 747
Paw Paw district	6 274	5 233
Fairview town	759	640
Grant Town town	987	946
Rivesville town	1 327	1 108
Union district	12 983	12 064
Fairmont city (pt.)	5 938	6 495
Winfield district	5 004	4 352
Fairmont city (pt.)	1 171	1 319
Marshall County[23]	41 608	37 598
District 1[23]	13 075	...
Benwood city	1 994	2 737
McMechen city	2 402	2 808
Wheeling city (pt.)[23]	196	...
District 2	12 419	
Moundsville city[23]	12 419	13 560
District 3	16 114	
Cameron city	1 474	1 537
Glen Dale town	1 875	2 150
Mason County	27 045	24 306
Arbuckle district	1 168	1 048
Clendenin district	4 044	3 107
Henderson town	604	496
Cologne district	1 246	1 155
Leon town	228	192
Copper district	1 718	1 270
Graham district	2 938	2 651
Hartford City town (pt.)	255	259
New Haven town	1 723	1 538
Hannan district	2 186	1 835
Lewis district	7 169	7 437
Point Pleasant city (pt.)	5 345	6 122
Robinson district	2 280	1 858
Point Pleasant city (pt.)	337	...
Union district	1 083	1 058
Waggener district	3 213	2 887
Hartford City town (pt.)	301	268
Mason town	1 432	1 319
Mercer County[24]	73 942	63 206
District No. 1	23 093	
Bluefield city[24]	16 060	15 921
Bluewell (CDP) (pt.)	2 454	...
District No. 2	26 891	
Princeton city[24]	7 493	7 253
District No. 3	23 958	
Athens town[24]	1 147	967
Bluewell (CDP) (pt.)	298	...
Bramwell town	989	1 125
Matoaka town	298	...
Montcalm (CDP)	1 544	608
Oakvale town	613	...
	208	292
Mineral County[25]	27 234	23 109
Cabin Run district	2 208	1 315
Elk district	1 510	1 313
Elk Garden town	291	291
Frankfort district	9 633	7 440
Fort Ashby (CDP)	1 205	...
Maryland Junction (CDP)	1 042	...
Ridgeley town	994	1 112
Wiley Ford (CDP)	1 224	...
New Creek district	10 611	9 806
Keyser city[25]	6 569	6 586
Piedmont district	1 792	2 158
Piedmont town	1 491	1 763
Welton district	1 480	1 077

County Subdivisions	1980	1970
Mingo County[26]	37 336	32 780
Hardee district	3 806	3 093
Harvey district	2 481	1 929
Kermit district	2 797	2 271
Kermit town	705	716
Lee district	4 327	3 374
Delbarton town	981	903
Magnolia district	7 141	6 489
Matewan town[26]	822	651
Stafford district	7 193	5 886
Gilbert town[26]	757	778
Tug River district	4 372	3 907
Chattaroy (CDP)	1 383	1 145
Williamson district	5 219	5 831
Williamson city	5 219	5 831
Monongalia County[27]	75 024	63 714
Central district	29 208	...
Morgantown city (pt.)[27]	27 374	(NA)
Star City town	1 464	1 312
Eastern district	26 401	...
Brookhaven (CDP)	1 661	...
Morgantown city (pt.)[27]	231	(NA)
Western district[27]	19 415	...
Blacksville town	248	264
Granville town	992	1 027
Osage town	285	322
Westover city[27]	4 884	5 086
Monroe County[28]	12 873	11 272
Red Sulphur district	5 031	3 912
Peterstown town[28]	648	563
Second Creek district	1 170	989
Springfield district	1 953	1 617
Sweet Springs district	1 735	1 528
Union district	1 813	1 549
Union town[28]	743	566
Wolf Creek district	1 171	1 677
Alderson town (pt.)	257	386
Morgan County	10 711	8 547
Allen district	1 768	1 243
Bath district	3 852	3 648
Bath [Berkeley Springs] town	789	944
Cacapon district	2 071	1 844
Paw Paw town	644	706
Rock Gap district	1 259	645
Sleepy Creek district	967	640
Timber Ridge district	794	527
Nicholas County[29]	28 126	22 552
Beaver district	9 369	8 089
Craigsville (CDP)	1 562	...
Richwood city	3 568	3 717
Grant district	1 480	1 129
Hamilton district	3 118	2 505
Jefferson district	2 410	2 064
Kentucky district	4 384	3 499
Summersville district	4 800	3 511
Summersville town[29]	2 972	2 429
Wilderness district	2 565	1 755
Ohio County[30]	61 389	63 439
Liberty Triadelphia district	14 756	...
Triadelphia town (pt.)[30]	1 254	(NA)
Valley Grove village	597	509
West Liberty town[30]	744	...
Wheeling city (pt.)	6 182	(NA)
Madison Union Clay Washington district	10 307	...
Wheeling city (pt.)	10 307	(NA)
Richland Washington district	14 773	...
Clearview village	740	512
Wheeling city (pt.)[30]	9 552	(NA)
Ritchie Webster Center district[30]	10 011	...
Bethlehem village[30]	2 677	2 461
Wheeling city (pt.)[30]	6 205	(NA)
Triadelphia district	11 542	...
Triadelphia town (pt.)	207	(NA)
Wheeling city (pt.)[30]	10 628	(NA)
Pendleton County	7 910	7 031
Bethel district	915	817
Circleville district	1 027	839
Franklin district	2 620	2 032
Franklin town	780	695
Mill Run district	1 219	1 156
Sugar Grove district	950	920
Union district	1 179	1 267
Pleasants County[31]	8 236	7 274
Grant district	1 707	1 526
Belmont city	887	802
Jefferson district	677	458
Lafayette district	378	311
McKim district	951	603
Union district	1 716	1 369
St. Marys city (pt.)[31]	290	109
Washington district	2 807	3 007
St. Marys city (pt.)[31]	1 929	2 239
Pocahontas County	9 919	8 870
Edray district	3 749	3 228
Marlinton town (pt.)	1 346	1 286
Greenbank district	3 084	2 894

County Subdivisions	1980	1970
Pocahontas County—Con.		
Greenbank district—Con.		
Cass town	148	173
Durbin town	379	347
Huntersville district	1 207	1 052
Marlinton town (pt.)	6	–
Little Levels district	1 879	1 696
Hillsboro village	276	267
Preston County[32]	30 460	25 455
Grant district	2 187	1 699
Brandonville town	92	82
Bruceton Mills town	296	209
Kingwood district	7 031	5 993
Kingwood city[32]	2 877	2 550
Tunnelton town	510	369
Lyon district	2 097	1 723
Newburg town	418	457
Pleasant district	2 016	1 559
Portland district	5 098	4 111
Albright town	357	319
Rowlesburg town (pt.)	133	104
Terra Alta town	1 946	1 474
Reno district	4 119	3 648
Rowlesburg town (pt.)	833	725
Union district	2 188	1 841
Rowlesburg town (pt.)	–	–
Valley district	5 724	4 881
Arthurdale (CDP)	1 063	...
Masontown town	1 052	868
Reedsville town	564	379
Putnam County	38 181	27 625
Buffalo district	3 168	2 254
Buffalo town	1 034	831
Eleanor town (pt.)	–	–
Curry district	8 423	6 268
Culloden (CDP) (pt.)	267	...
Hurricane city (pt.)	3 201	2 711
Pocatalico district	8 070	6 332
Bancroft town	528	446
Nitro city (pt.)	1 341	1 316
Poca town (pt.)	1 142	772
Scott district	9 598	5 673
Poca town (pt.)	–	–
Winfield town	329	328
Teays Valley district	3 869	2 976
Hurricane city (pt.)	550	780
Union district	5 053	4 122
Eleanor town (pt.)	1 282	1 035
Raleigh County[33]	86 821	70 080
District 1	30 229	...
Beckley city (pt.)[33]	1 702	(NA)
Coal City (CDP) (pt.)	2 099	(NA)
Crab Orchard (CDP)	3 337	1 758
Eccles (CDP)	1 162	1 105
Lester town	626	507
Mabscott town	1 668	1 254
MacArthur (CDP)	2 152	1 614
Rhodell town	472	500
Sophia town	1 216	1 303
District 2	23 964	...
Beckley city (pt.)[33]	6 566	(NA)
Bradley (CDP)	1 704	...
Prosperity (CDP)	1 298	...
District 3	32 628	...
Beaver (CDP)	1 122	...
Beckley city (pt.)[33]	12 224	(NA)
Coal City (CDP) (pt.)	225	(NA)
Daniels (CDP)	1 959	...
Piney View (CDP)	1 193	...
Shady Spring (CDP)	1 786	...
Stanaford (CDP)	2 016	...
Randolph County[34]	28 734	24 596
Beverly district	3 418	2 445
Beverly town	475	470
Dry Fork district[34]	1 753	1 693
Harman town	181	142
Huttonsville district	2 936	2 177
Huttonsville town	242	167
Mill Creek town	801	800
Leadsville district	13 979	12 662
Elkins city[34]	8 536	8 287
Middle Fork district	1 100	902
Mingo district	1 117	1 044
New Interest district	1 007	755
Montrose village	129	115
Roaring Creek district	1 702	1 508
Womelsdorf town	306	234
Valley Bend district	1 722	1 410
Ritchie County[35]	11 442	10 145
Clay district	4 108	3 665
Ellenboro town	357	267
Pennsboro city	1 652	1 614
Grant district	2 239	2 034
Cairo town	428	412
Murphy district	1 775	1 520
Union district	3 320	2 926
Auburn town	116	115

County Subdivisions

	1980	1970
Ritchie County—Con.		
Union district—Con.		
Harrisville town[35]	1 673	1 464
Pullman town	196	157
Roane County[36]	15 952	14 111
Curtis district	883	569
Geary district	2 396	1 946
Harper district	935	683
Reedy district	1 112	1 105
Reedy town	338	351
Smithfield district	1 680	1 491
Spencer district	7 007	6 573
Spencer city[36]	2 799	2 271
Walton district	1 939	1 744
Summers County[37]	15 875	13 213
Bluestone River district	3 582	...
Hinton city (pt.)	194	(NA)
Greenbrier River district	8 484	...
Hinton city (pt.)	3 301	(NA)
New River district	3 809	...
Hinton city (pt.)	1 127	(NA)
Taylor County[38]	16 584	13 878
Central district	4 448	...
Grafton city (pt.)	4 448	(NA)
Eastern district	5 524	...
Grafton city (pt.)[38]	2 397	(NA)
Western district	6 612	...
Flemington town	452	458
Grafton city (pt.)	–	(NA)
Tucker County	8 675	7 447
Black Fork district	4 362	3 899
Hambleton town	403	328
Hendricks town	390	317
Parsons city	1 937	1 784
Clover district	322	312
Davis district	1 088	983
Davis town	979	868
Dry Fork district	718	521
Fairfax district	1 111	930
Thomas city	747	713
Licking district	241	159
St. George district	833	643
Tyler County[39]	11 320	9 929
Centreville district	584	486
Ellsworth district	2 942	2 384
Middlebourne town	941	814
Lincoln district	4 712	4 559
Paden City city (pt.)	1 140	1 125
Sistersville city[39]	2 367	2 246
McElroy district	1 109	1 075
Meade district	521	412
Union district	1 452	1 013
Friendly town	242	190
Upshur County[40]	23 427	19 092
Banks district	2 451	2 059
Buckhannon district	10 113	9 733
Buckhannon city (pt.)[40]	6 233	7 013
Meade district	2 371	1 832
Union district	3 540	2 086
Buckhannon city (pt.)	587	248
Warren district	1 829	1 358
Washington district	3 123	2 024
Wayne County[41]	46 021	37 581
Butler district	5 154	4 237
Fort Gay town[41]	886	792
Ceredo district	13 346	10 387
Ceredo city (pt.)[41]	2 109	1 583
Kenova city[41]	4 454	4 860
Lincoln district	5 485	3 998
Stonewall district	3 732	2 966
Union district	10 227	6 952
Wayne town	1 495	1 385
Westmoreland district	8 077	9 041
Ceredo city (pt.)[41]	146	...
Huntington city (pt.)	4 999	5 555
Webster County	12 245	9 809
Fork Lick district	4 526	3 319
Addison town	939	1 038
Glade district	5 508	4 479
Camden-on-Gauley town	236	243
Cowen town	723	467
Hacker Valley district	800	701
Holly district	1 411	1 310
Wetzel County[42]	21 874	20 314
Center district	998	813
Church district	1 643	1 480
Hundred town	485	475
Clay district	713	734
Littleton town	335	333
Grant district	3 252	3 070
Pine Grove town[42]	767	630
Smithfield town	278	294
Green district	2 165	2 063
Magnolia district	11 800	10 894
New Martinsville city[42]	7 109	6 528
Paden City city (pt.)	2 531	2 549

County Subdivisions

	1980	1970
Wetzel County—Con.		
Proctor district	1 303	1 260
Wirt County	4 922	4 154
Burning Springs district	626	653
Clay district	408	324
Elizabeth district	1 990	1 715
Elizabeth town	856	821
Newark district	870	466
Reedy district	427	347
Spring Creek district	317	267
Tucker district	284	382
Wood County[43]	93 648	86 818
Clay district	5 730	3 944
Harris district	1 452	1 243
Lubeck district	10 621	8 757
Blennerhassett (CDP)	3 537	...
Lubeck (CDP)	1 356	...
Parkersburg city (pt.)	1 503	1 655
Parkersburg district	36 643	40 222
North Hills town	220	...
Parkersburg city (pt.)[43]	26 468	30 950
Vienna city (pt.)	6 152	5 903
Slate district	3 430	1 724
Steele district	1 206	1 044
Tygart district	15 604	14 944
Parkersburg city (pt.)	11 996	11 603
Union district	3 749	2 431
Walker district	1 280	1 085
Williams district	13 933	11 424
North Hills town (pt.)[43]	720	...
Vienna city (pt.)[43]	5 466	5 646
Williamstown city[43]	3 095	2 743
Wyoming County[44]	35 993	30 095
Baileysville district	3 051	2 061
Brenton (CDP)	1 041	...
Barkers Ridge district	3 902	3 723
Mullens city (pt.)	12	12
Center district	6 317	5 165
Pineville town[44]	1 140	1 187
Clear Fork district	2 475	2 187
Huff Creek district	2 936	2 156
Oceana district	9 190	7 242
Oceana town	2 143	1 580
Slab Fork district	8 122	7 561
Mullens city (pt.)	2 907	2 955

WISCONSIN

Wisconsin was named from its principal river. The significance of the word, which is of Indian origin, is not positively known, but among the meanings given are "wild, rushing river," "gathering of the waters," and "great stone or rocks."

The first explorers of the region now constituting Wisconsin were the French. In 1634 Jean Nicolet, sent out by the governor of New France to promote trade with the Indians, landed where the city of Green Bay now stands, and ascended the Fox River to a point about 20 miles west of Lake Winnebago. Twenty years later two fur traders, Radisson and Groseilliers, ascended the Fox and may have descended the Wisconsin to its junction with the Mississippi. In 1669 a mission was established on the Fox River a few miles above its mouth, and about this mission grew up the town of Depere, the first permanent settlement within the present limits of Wisconsin.

In 1763, at the close of the French and Indian War, the French possessions east of the Mississippi were ceded to England. At the close of the Revolution the territory northwest of the Ohio and east of the Mississippi was ceded by Great Britain to the United States. The former country, however, did not at once relinquish its hold, and, although its outposts in that region were evacuated in the summer of 1796, it was not until the close of the war of 1812 that it ceased to exercise some degree of control in the territory between Lake Michigan and the Mississippi.

In 1787 the region bounded by Pennsylvania, the Ohio River, the Mississippi River, and the Great Lakes was organized as the Northwest Territory, the claims of Massachusetts, Connecticut, and Virginia, based on their early charters, having been ceded to the United States, between 1781 and 1786. In 1800 the present area of Wisconsin was included in the newly organized territory of Indiana; in 1809 it was made a part of Illinois territory; and in 1818, when Illinois became a state, it was added to Michigan territory.

Wisconsin was organized as a separate territory in 1836. At this time it included, in addition to the area of the present state, the region now constituting Minnesota, Iowa, and those portions of North and South Dakota lying east of the Missouri and White Earth Rivers. In 1838 that part of Wisconsin territory situated west of the Mississippi River and a line drawn north from its source to the Canadian boundary was organized as the territory of Iowa. In May, 1848, Wisconsin, with boundaries as at present, became a state of the Union.

COUNTY LOCATION INDEX

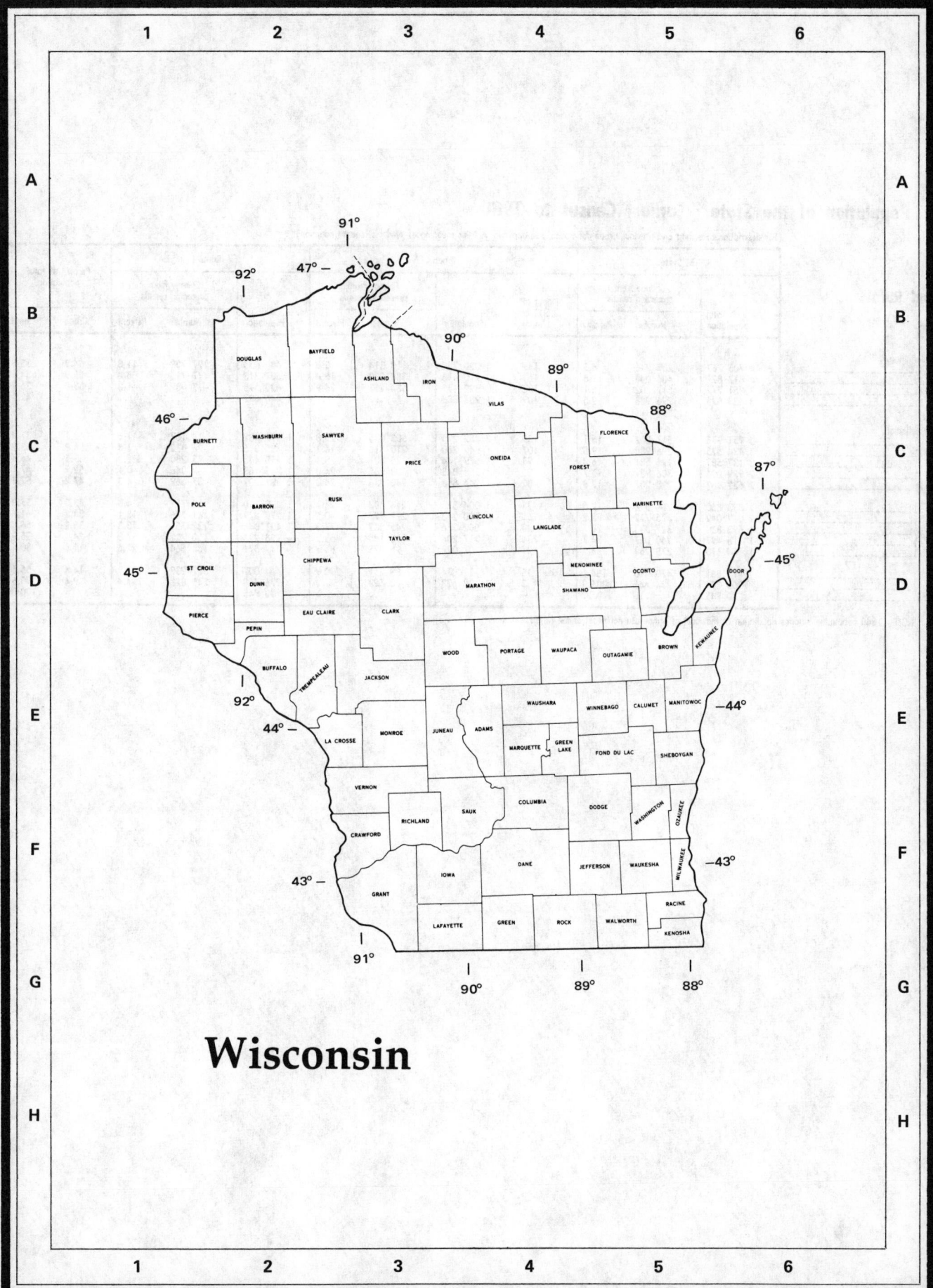

Wisconsin

Population of the State: Earliest Census to 1980

[For description of current and previous urban definitions, see appendix A. For meaning of symbols, see Introduction]

Urban and Rural

	The State			Urban				Rural				Percent of total population	
	Total population	Change from preceding census		Places of 2,500 or more	Population	Change from preceding census		Population	Change from preceding census			Urban	Rural
		Number	Percent			Number	Percent		Number	Percent			
Current urban definition:													
1980 (Apr. 1)_____	4 705 767	287 946	6.5	169	3 020 732	110 314	3.8	1 685 035	177 722	11.8		64.2	35.8
1970 (Apr. 1)_____	4 417 821	466 044	11.8	151	2 910 418	388 239	15.4	1 507 313	77 715	5.4		65.9	34.1
1960 (Apr. 1)_____	3 951 777	517 202	15.1	132	2 522 179	534 291	26.9	1 429 598	-17 089	-1.2		63.8	36.2
1950 (Apr. 1)_____	3 434 575	296 988	9.5	109	1 987 888	...	...	1 446 687	...	...		57.9	42.1
Previous urban definition:													
1960 (Apr. 1)_____	3 951 777	517 202	15.1	130	2 452 295	503 035	25.8	1 499 482	14 167	1.0		62.1	37.9
1950 (Apr. 1)_____	3 434 575	296 988	9.5	107	1 949 260	270 116	16.1	1 485 315	26 872	1.8		56.8	43.2
1940 (Apr. 1)_____	3 137 587	198 581	6.8	93	1 679 144	125 301	8.1	1 458 443	73 280	5.3		53.5	46.5
1930 (Apr. 1)_____	2 939 006	306 939	11.7	83	1 553 843	308 985	24.8	1 385 163	-2 046	-0.1		52.9	47.1
1920 (Jan. 1)_____	2 632 067	298 207	12.8	82	1 244 858	240 538	24.0	1 387 209	57 669	4.3		47.3	52.7
1910 (Apr. 15)_____	2 333 860	264 818	12.8	73	1 004 320	214 107	27.1	1 329 540	50 711	4.0		43.0	57.0
1900 (June 1)_____	2 069 042	375 712	22.2	61	790 213	227 927	40.5	1 278 829	147 785	13.1		38.2	61.8
1890 (June 1)_____	1 693 330	377 833	28.7	48	562 286	245 082	77.3	1 131 044	132 751	13.3		24.1	66.8
1880 (June 1)_____	1 315 497	260 827	24.7	34	317 204	110 105	53.2	998 293	150 722	17.8		19.6	75.9
1870 (June 1)_____	1 054 670	278 789	35.9	27	207 099	95 225	85.1	847 571	183 564	27.6		19.6	80.4
1860 (June 1)_____	775 881	470 490	154.1	15	111 874	83 251	290.9	664 007	387 239	139.9		14.4	85.6
1850 (June 1)_____	305 391	274 446	886.9	3	28 623	28 623	...	276 768	245 823	794.4		9.4	90.6
1840 (June 1)_____	30 945	...	...	-	-	...	...	30 945	...	...		-	100.0

NOTE: 1840 population includes population of that part of Minnesota northeast of the Mississippi River.

ADAMS

1850	187
1860	6,492
1870	6,601
1880	6,741
1890	6,889
1900	9,141
1910	8,604
1920	9,287
1930	8,003
1940	8,449
1950	7,906
1960	7,566
1970	9,234
1980	13,457

ASHLAND

1860	515
1870	221
1880	1,559
1890	20,063
1900	20,176
1910	21,965
1920	24,538
1930	21,054
1940	21,801
1950	19,461
1960	17,375
1970	16,743
1980	16,783

BARRON

1860	13
1870	538
1880	7,024
1890	15,416
1900	23,677
1910	29,114
1920	34,281
1930	34,301
1940	34,289
1950	34,703
1960	34,270
1970	33,955
1980	38,730

BAYFIELD

1850	489
1860	353
1870	344
1880	564
1890	7,390
1900	14,392
1910	15,987
1920	17,201
1930	15,006
1940	15,827
1950	13,760
1960	11,910
1970	11,683
1980	13,822

BROWN

1800	50
1820	952
1830	1,356
1840	2,107
1850	6,215
1860	11,795
1870	25,168
1880	34,078
1890	39,164
1900	46,359
1910	54,098
1920	61,889
1930	70,249
1940	83,109
1950	98,314
1960	125,082
1970	158,244
1980	175,280

BUFFALO

1860	3,864
1870	11,123
1880	15,528
1890	15,997
1900	16,765
1910	16,006
1920	15,615
1930	15,330
1940	16,090
1950	14,719
1960	14,202
1970	13,743
1980	14,309

BURNETT

1860	12
1870	706
1880	3,140
1890	4,393
1900	7,478
1910	9,026
1920	10,735
1930	10,233
1940	11,382
1950	10,236
1960	9,214
1970	9,276
1980	12,340

CALUMET

1840	275
1850	1,743
1860	7,895
1870	12,895
1880	16,632
1890	16,639
1900	17,078
1910	16,701
1920	17,228
1930	16,848
1940	17,618
1950	18,840
1960	22,268
1970	27,604
1980	30,867

CHIPPEWA

1850	615
1860	1,895
1870	8,311
1880	15,491
1890	25,143
1900	33,037
1910	32,103
1920	36,482
1930	37,342
1940	40,703
1950	42,839
1960	45,096
1970	47,717
1980	52,127

CLARK

1860	789
1870	3,450
1880	10,715
1890	17,708
1900	25,848
1910	30,074
1920	36,120
1930	34,165
1940	33,972
1950	32,459
1960	31,527
1970	30,361
1980	32,910

COLUMBIA

1850	9,565
1860	24,411
1870	28,802
1880	28,065
1890	38,350
1900	31,121
1910	31,129
1920	30,468
1930	30,503
1940	32,517
1950	34,023
1960	36,708
1970	40,150
1980	43,222

CRAWFORD

1800	65
1820	492
1830	692
1840	1,502
1850	2,498
1860	8,068
1870	13,075
1880	15,644
1890	15,987
1900	17,286
1910	16,288
1920	16,772
1930	16,781
1940	18,328
1950	17,652
1960	16,351
1970	15,252
1980	16,556

DANE

1840	314
1850	16,639
1860	43,922
1870	53,096
1880	53,233
1890	59,578
1900	69,435
1910	77,435
1920	89,432
1930	112,737
1940	130,660
1950	169,357
1960	222,095
1970	290,272
1980	323,545

DODGE

1840	67
1850	19,138
1860	42,818
1870	47,035
1880	45,931
1890	44,984
1900	46,631
1910	47,436
1920	49,742
1930	52,092
1940	54,280
1950	57,611
1960	63,170
1970	69,004
1980	75,064

DOOR

1860	2,948
1870	4,919
1880	11,645
1890	15,682
1900	17,583
1910	18,711
1920	19,073
1930	18,182
1940	19,095
1950	20,870
1960	20,685
1970	20,106
1980	25,029

DOUGLAS

1860	812
1870	1,122
1880	655
1890	13,468
1900	36,335
1910	47,422
1920	49,771
1930	46,583
1940	47,119
1950	46,715
1960	45,008
†1970	44,657
1980	44,421

DUNN

1860	2,074
1870	9,488
1880	16,877
1890	22,664
1900	25,043
1910	25,260
1920	26,970
1930	27,037
1940	27,375
1950	27,341
1960	26,156
1970	29,154
1980	34,314

EAU CLAIRE

1860	3,162
1870	10,769
1880	19,993
1890	30,673
1900	31,692
1910	32,721
1920	35,771
1930	41,087
1940	46,999
1950	54,187
1960	58,300
1970	67,219
1980	78,805

FLORENCE

1890	2,604
1900	3,197
1910	3,381
1920	3,602
1930	3,768
1940	4,177
1950	3,756
1960	3,437
1970	3,298
1980	4,172

FOND DU LAC

1840	139
1850	14,510
1860	34,154
1870	46,273
1880	46,859
1890	44,088
1900	47,589
1910	51,610
1920	56,119
1930	59,883
1940	62,353
1950	67,829
1960	75,085
1970	84,567
1980	88,964

FOREST

1890	1,012
1900	1,396
1910	6,782
1920	9,850
1930	11,118
1940	11,805
1950	9,437
1960	7,542
1970	7,691
1980	9,044

GRANT

1840	3,926
1850	16,169
1860	31,189
1870	37,979
1880	37,852
1890	36,651
1900	38,881
1910	39,007
1920	39,044
1930	38,469
1940	40,639
1950	41,640
1960	44,419
1970	48,398
1980	51,736

GREEN

1840	933
1850	8,566
1860	19,808
1870	23,611
1880	21,729
1890	22,732

1900	22,719
1910	21,641
1920	21,568
1930	21,870
1940	23,146
1950	24,172
1960	25,851
1970	26,714
1980	30,012

GREEN LAKE

1860	12,663
1870	13,195
1880	14,483
1890	15,163
1900	15,797
1910	15,491
1920	14,875
1930	13,913
1940	14,092
1950	14,749
1960	15,418
1970	16,878
1980	18,370

IOWA

1830	1,587
1840	3,987
1850	9,525
1860	18,967
1870	24,544
1880	23,628
1890	22,117
1900	23,114
1910	22,497
1920	21,504
1930	20,039
1940	20,595
1950	19,610
1960	19,631
1970	19,306
1980	19,802

IRON

1900	6,616
1910	8,306
1920	10,261
1930	9,933
1940	10,049
1950	8,714
1960	7,830
1970	6,533
1980	6,730

JACKSON

1860	4,170
1870	7,687
1880	13,285
1890	15,797
1900	17,466
1910	17,075
1920	17,746
1930	16,468
1940	16,599
1950	16,073
1960	15,151
1970	15,325
1980	16,831

JEFFERSON

| 1840 | 914 |

1850	15,317
1860	30,438
1870	34,040
1880	32,156
1890	33,530
1900	34,789
1910	34,306
1920	35,022
1930	36,785
1940	38,868
1950	43,069
1960	50,094
1970	60,060
1980	66,152

JUNEAU

1860	8,770
1870	12,372
1880	15,582
1890	17,121
1900	20,629
1910	19,569
1920	19,209
1930	17,264
1940	18,708
1950	18,930
1960	17,490
1970	18,455
1980	21,039

KENOSHA

1850	10,734
1860	13,900
1870	13,147
1880	13,550
1890	15,581
1900	21,707
1910	32,929
1920	51,284
1930	63,277
1940	63,505
1950	75,238
1960	100,615
1970	117,917
1980	123,137

KEWAUNEE

1860	5,530
1870	10,128
1880	15,807
1890	16,153
1900	17,212
1910	16,784
1920	16,091
1930	16,037
1940	16,680
1950	17,336
1960	18,282
1970	18,961
1980	19,539

LA CROSSE

1860	12,186
1870	20,297
1880	27,073
1890	38,801
1900	42,997
1910	43,996
1920	44,355
1930	54,455
1940	59,653
1950	67,597

1960	72,465
1970	80,468
1980	91,056

LAFAYETTE

1850	11,531
1860	18,134
1870	22,659
1880	21,279
1890	20,265
1900	20,959
1910	20,075
1920	20,002
1930	18,649
1940	18,695
1950	18,137
1960	18,142
1970	17,456
1980	17,412

LANGLADE

1880	685
1890	9,465
1900	12,553
1910	17,062
1920	21,471
1930	21,544
1940	23,227
1950	21,975
1960	19,916
1970	19,220
1980	19,978

LINCOLN

1880	2,011
1890	12,008
1900	16,269
1910	19,064
1920	21,084
1930	21,072
1940	22,536
1950	22,235
1960	22,338
1970	23,499
1980	26,555

MANITOWOC

1840	235
1850	3,702
1860	22,416
1870	33,364
1880	37,505
1890	37,831
1900	42,261
1910	44,978
1920	51,644
1930	58,674
1940	61,617
1950	67,159
1960	71,215
1970	82,294
1980	82,918

MARATHON

1850	508
1860	2,892
1870	5,885
1880	17,121
1890	30,369
1900	43,256
1910	55,054

1920	65,259
1930	70,629
1940	75,915
1950	80,337
1960	88,874
1970	97,457
1980	111,270

MARINETTE

1880	8,929
1890	20,304
1900	30,822
1910	33,812
1920	34,361
1930	33,530
1940	36,225
1950	35,748
1960	34,660
1970	35,810
1980	39,314

MARQUETTE

1840	18
1850	8,641
1860	8,233
1870	8,056
1880	8,908
1890	9,676
1900	10,509
1910	10,741
1920	10,443
1930	9,338
1940	9,097
1950	8,839
1960	8,516
1970	8,865
1980	11,672

MENOMINEE

| 1970 | 2,607 |
| 1980 | 3,373 |

MILWAUKEE

1840	5,605
1850	31,077
1860	62,518
1870	89,930
1880	138,537
1890	236,101
1900	330,017
1910	433,187
1920	539,449
1930	725,263
1940	766,885
1950	871,047
1960	1,036,041
1970	1,054,249
1980	964,988

MONROE

1860	8,410
1870	16,550
1880	21,607
1890	23,211
1900	28,103
1910	28,881
1920	28,666
1930	28,739
1940	30,080
1950	31,378
1960	31,241

| 1970 | 31,610 |
| 1980 | 35,074 |

OCONTO

1860	3,592
1870	8,321
1880	9,848
1890	15,009
1900	20,874
1910	25,657
1920	27,104
1930	26,386
1940	27,075
1950	26,238
1960	25,110
1970	25,553
1980	28,947

ONEIDA

1890	5,010
1900	8,875
1910	11,433
1920	13,996
1930	15,899
1940	18,938
1950	20,648
1960	22,112
1970	24,427
1980	31,216

OUTAGAMIE

1860	9,587
1870	18,430
1880	28,716
1890	38,690
1900	47,247
1910	49,102
1920	55,113
1930	62,790
1940	70,032
1950	81,722
1960	101,794
1970	119,398
1980	128,799

OZAUKEE

1860	15,682
1870	15,564
1880	15,461
1890	14,943
1900	16,363
1910	17,123
1920	16,335
1930	17,394
1940	18,985
1950	23,361
1960	38,441
1970	54,461
1980	66,981

PEPIN

1860	2,392
1870	4,659
1880	6,226
1890	6,932
1900	7,905
1910	7,577
1920	7,481
1930	7,450
1940	7,897
1950	7,462

1960	7,332
1970	7,319
1980	7,477

PIERCE

1860	4,672
1870	9,958
1880	17,744
1890	20,385
1900	23,943
1910	22,079
1920	21,663
1930	21,043
1940	21,471
1950	21,448
1960	22,503
1970	26,652
1980	31,149

POLK

1860	1,400
1870	3,422
1880	10,018
1890	12,968
1900	17,801
1910	21,367
1920	26,870
1930	26,567
1940	26,197
1950	24,944
1960	24,968
1970	26,666
1980	32,351

PORTAGE

1840	1,623
1850	1,250
1860	7,507
1870	10,634
1880	17,731
1890	24,798
1900	29,483
1910	30,945
1920	33,649
1930	33,827
1940	35,800
1950	34,858
1960	36,964
1970	47,541
1980	57,420

PRICE

1880	785
1890	5,258
1900	9,106
1910	13,795
1920	18,517
1930	17,284
1940	18,467
1950	16,344
1960	14,370
1970	14,520
1980	15,788

RACINE

1840	3,475
1850	14,973
1860	21,360
1870	36,740
1880	30,922
1890	36,268
1900	45,644
1910	57,424
1920	78,961
1930	90,217
1940	94,047
1950	109,585
1960	141,781
1970	170,383
1980	173,132

RICHLAND

1850	903
1860	9,732
1870	15,731
1880	18,174
1890	19,121
1900	19,483
1910	18,809
1920	19,823
1930	19,525
1940	20,381
1950	19,245
1960	17,684
1970	17,079
1980	17,476

ROCK

1840	1,701
1850	20,750
1860	36,690
1870	39,030
1880	38,823
1890	43,220
1900	51,203
1910	55,538
1920	66,150
1930	74,260
1940	80,173
1950	92,778
1960	113,913
1970	131,970
1980	139,420

RUSK

1910	11,160
1920	16,403
1930	16,081
1940	17,737
1950	16,790
1960	14,794
1970	14,238
1980	15,589

SAINT CROIX

1840	809
1850	624
1860	5,392
1870	11,035
1880	18,956
1890	23,139
1900	26,830
1910	25,910
1920	26,106
1930	25,455
1940	24,842
1950	25,905
1960	29,164
1970	34,354
1980	43,262

SAUK

1840	102
1850	4,371
1860	18,963
1870	23,860
1880	28,729
1890	30,575
1900	33,006
1910	32,869
1920	32,548
1930	32,030
1940	33,700
1950	38,120
1960	36,179
1970	39,057
1980	43,469

SAWYER

1890	1,977
1900	3,593
1910	6,227
1920	8,243
1930	8,878
1940	11,540
1950	10,323
1960	9,475
1970	9,670
1980	12,843

SHAWANO

1860	829
1870	3,166
1880	10,371
1890	19,236
1900	27,475
1910	31,884
1920	33,975
1930	33,516
1940	35,378
1950	35,249
1960	34,351
1970	32,650
1980	35,928

SHEBOYGAN

1840	133
1850	8,379
1860	26,875
1870	31,749
1880	24,206
1890	42,589
1900	50,345
1910	54,888
1920	59,913
1930	71,235
1940	76,211
1950	80,631
1960	86,484
1970	96,660
1980	100,935

TAYLOR

1880	2,311
1890	6,731
1900	11,262
1910	13,641
1920	18,045
1930	17,685
1940	20,105
1950	18,456
1960	17,843

| 1970 | 16,958 |
| 1980 | 18,817 |

TREMPEALEAU

1860	2,560
1870	10,732
1880	17,189
1890	18,920
1900	23,144
1910	22,928
1920	24,506
1930	23,910
1940	24,381
1950	23,730
1960	23,377
1970	23,344
1980	26,158

VERNON

1860	11,077
1870	18,645
1880	23,235
1890	25,111
1900	28,351
1910	28,116
1920	29,252
1930	28,537
1940	29,940
1950	27,906
1960	25,663
1970	24,557
1980	25,642

VILAS

1900	4,929
1910	6,019
1920	5,649
1930	7,294
1940	8,894
1950	9,363
1960	9,332
1970	10,958
1980	16,535

WALWORTH

1840	2,611
1850	17,862
1860	26,496
1870	25,972
1880	26,249
1890	26,860
1900	29,259
1910	29,614
1920	29,327
1930	31,058
1940	33,103
1950	41,584
1960	52,368
1970	63,444
1980	71,507

WASHBURN

1890	2,926
1900	5,521
1910	8,196
1920	11,377
1930	11,103
1940	12,496
1950	11,665
1960	10,301
1970	10,601

| 1980 | 13,174 |

WASHINGTON

1840	343
1850	19,485
1860	23,622
1870	23,919
1880	23,422
1890	22,751
1900	23,589
1910	23,784
1920	25,713
1930	26,551
1940	28,430
1950	33,902
1960	46,119
1970	63,839
1980	84,848

WAUKESHA

1850	19,258
1860	26,831
1870	28,274
1880	28,957
1890	33,270
1900	35,229
1910	37,100
1920	42,612
1930	52,358
1940	62,744
1950	85,901
1960	158,249
1970	231,335
1980	280,326

WAUPACA

1860	8,851
1870	15,539
1880	20,955
1890	26,794
1900	31,615
1910	32,782
1920	24,200
1930	33,513
1940	34,614
1950	35,056
1960	35,340
1970	37,780
1980	42,831

WAUSHARA

1860	8,770
1870	11,297
1880	12,687
1890	13,507
1900	15,972
1910	18,886
1920	16,712
1930	14,427
1940	14,268
1950	13,920
1960	13,497
1970	14,795
1980	18,526

WINNEBAGO

1840	135
1850	10,167
1860	23,770
1870	37,279
1880	42,740

1890	50,097
1900	58,225
1910	62,116
1920	63,897
1930	76,662
1940	80,507
1950	91,103
1960	107,928
1970	129,946
1980	131,703

WOOD

1860	2,425
1870	3,912
1880	8,981
1890	18,127
1900	25,865
1910	30,583
1920	34,643
1930	37,865
1940	44,465
1950	50,500
1960	59,105
1970	65,362
1980	72,799

APPLETON

1860	2,345
1870	4,518
1880	8,005
1890	11,869
1900	15,085
1910	16,773
1920	19,561
1930	25,267
1940	28,436
1950	34,010
1960	48,411
1970	56,377
1980	59,032

ASHWAUBENON

1980	14,486

BEAVER DAM

1860	2,765
1870	3,265
1880	3,416
1890	4,222
1900	5,128
1910	6,758
1920	7,992
1930	9,867
1940	10,356
1950	11,867
1960	13,118
1970	14,265
1980	14,149

BELOIT

1860	4,098
1870	4,396
1880	4,790
1890	6,315
1900	10,436
1910	15,125
1920	21,284
1930	23,611
1940	25,365
1950	29,590
1960	32,846
1970	35,729
1980	35,207

BROOKFIELD

1960	19,812
1970	31,761
1980	34,035

BROWN DEER

1960	11,280
1970	12,582
1980	12,921

CHIPPEWA FALLS

1870	2,507
1880	3,982
1890	8,670
1900	8,094
1910	8,893
1920	9,130
1930	9,539
1940	10,368
1950	11,088
1960	11,708
1970	12,351
1980	12,270

CUDAHY

1900	1,366
1910	3,691
1920	6,725
1930	10,631
1940	10,561
1950	12,182
1960	17,975
1970	22,078
1980	19,547

DE PERE

1860	508
1870	1,372
1880	1,954
1890	3,625
1900	4,038
1910	4,477
1920	5,165
1930	5,521
1940	6,373
1950	8,146
1960	10,045
1970	13,309
1980	14,892

EAU CLAIRE

1870	2,293
1880	10,119
1890	17,415
1900	17,517
1910	18,310
1920	20,906
1930	26,287
1940	30,745
1950	36,058
1960	37,987
1970	44,619
1980	51,509

FOND DU LAC

1860	5,460
1870	12,764
1880	13,094
1890	12,024
1900	15,110
1910	18,797
1920	23,427
1930	26,449
1940	27,209
1950	29,936
1960	32,719
1970	35,515
1980	35,863

FRANKLIN

1960	10,006
1970	12,247
1980	16,871

GERMANTOWN

1960	622
1970	6,974
1980	10,729

GLENDALE

1960	9,537
1970	13,426
1980	13,882

GREEN BAY

1860	2,275
1870	4,666
1880	7,464
1890	9,069
1900	18,684
1910	25,236
1920	31,017
1930	37,415
1940	46,235
1950	52,735
1960	62,888
1970	87,809
1980	87,899

GREENDALE

1940	2,527
1950	2,752
1960	6,843
1970	15,089
1980	16,928

GREENFIELD

1960	17,636
1970	24,424
1980	31,467

JANESVILLE

1860	7,703
1870	8,789
1880	9,018
1890	10,836
1900	13,185
1910	13,894
1920	18,293
1930	21,628
1940	22,992
1950	24,899
1960	35,164
1970	46,426
1980	51,071

KAUKAUNA

1880	834
1890	4,667
1900	5,115
1910	4,717
1920	5,951
1930	6,581
1940	7,382
1950	8,337
1960	10,096
1970	11,308
1980	11,310

KENOSHA

1850	3,455
1860	3,990
1870	4,309
1880	5,039
1890	6,532
1900	11,606
1910	21,371
1920	40,472
1930	50,262
1940	48,765
1950	54,368
1960	67,899
1970	78,805
1980	77,685

LA CROSSE

1860	3,860
1870	7,785
1880	14,505
1890	25,090
1900	28,895
1910	30,417
1920	30,421
1930	39,614
1940	42,707
1950	47,535
1960	47,575
1970	50,286
1980	48,347

MADISON

1850	1,525
1860	6,611
1870	9,176
1880	10,324
1890	13,426
1900	19,164
1910	25,531
1920	38,378
1930	57,899
1940	67,447
1950	96,056
1960	126,706
1970	171,809
1980	170,616

MANITOWOC

1860	3,059
1870	5,168
1880	6,376
1890	7,710
1900	11,786
1910	13,027
1920	17,563
1930	22,963
1940	24,404
1950	27,598
1960	32,275
1970	33,430
1980	32,547

MARINETTE

1890	11,523
1900	16,195
1910	14,610
1920	13,610
1930	13,734
1940	14,183
1950	14,178
1960	13,329
1970	12,696
1980	11,965

MARSHFIELD

1880	1,001
1890	3,450
1900	5,240
1910	5,783

1920	7,394
1930	8,778
1940	10,359
1950	12,394
1960	14,153
1970	15,619
1980	18,290

MENASHA

1860	1,436
1870	2,484
1880	3,144
1890	4,581
1900	5,589
1910	6,081
1920	7,214
1930	9,062
1940	10,481
1950	12,385
1960	14,647
1970	14,836
1980	14,728

MENOMONEE FALLS

1880	366
1890	422
1900	687
1910	919
1920	1,019
1930	1,291
1940	1,469
1950	2,469
1960	18,276
1970	31,697
1980	27,845

MENOMONIE

1860	955
1870	2,210
1880	2,589
1890	5,491
1900	5,655
1910	5,036
1920	5,104
1930	5,595
1940	6,582
1950	8,245
1960	8,624
1970	11,112
1980	12,769

MEQUON

1960	8,543
1970	12,150
1980	16,193

MIDDLETON

1910	679
1920	791
1930	1,064
1940	1,255
1950	1,778
1960	4,410
1970	8,246
1980	11,779

MILWUAKEE

1840	1,712
1850	20,061
1860	45,246
1870	71,440

1880	115,578
1890	204,468
1900	285,315
1910	373,857
1920	457,147
1930	578,249
1940	587,472
1950	637,392
1960	741,234
1970	717,372
1980	636,212

MONROE

1860	938
1870	3,408
1880	4,195
1890	966
1900	3,927
1910	4,410
1920	4,788
1930	5,015
1940	6,182
1950	7,037
1960	8,050
1970	8,654
1980	10,027

MUSKEGO

1960	8,888
1970	11,573
1980	15,277

NEENAH

1860	1,296
1870	2,655
1880	4,202
1890	5,083
1900	5,954
1910	5,734
1920	7,171
1930	9,151
1940	10,645
1950	12,437
1960	18,057
1970	22,902
1980	22,432

NEW BERLIN

1960	15,788
1970	26,910
1980	30,529

OAK CREEK

1960	9,372
1970	13,928
1980	16,932

OSHKOSH

1860	6,086
1870	12,663
1880	15,748
1890	22,836
1900	28,284
1910	33,062
1920	33,162
1930	40,108
1940	39,089
1950	41,084
1960	45,100
1970	53,082
1980	49,620

RACINE

1850	5,107
1860	7,822
1870	9,880
1880	16,031
1890	21,014
1900	29,102
1910	38,002
1920	58,593
1930	67,542
1940	67,195
1950	71,193
1960	89,144
1970	95,162
1980	85,725

SAINT FRANCIS

1960	10,065
1970	10,489
1980	10,066

SHEBOYGAN

1860	4,262
1870	5,310
1880	7,314
1890	16,359
1900	22,962
1910	26,398
1920	30,955
1930	39,251
1940	40,638
1950	42,365
1960	45,747
1970	48,484
1980	48,085

SHOREWOOD

1910	707
1920	2,650
1930	13,479
1940	15,184
1950	16,199
1960	15,990
1970	15,576
1980	14,320

SOUTH MILWAUKEE

1900	3,392
1910	6,092
1920	7,598
1930	10,706
1940	11,134
1950	12,855
1960	20,307
1970	23,297
1980	21,069

STEVENS POINT

1860	148
1870	1,810
1880	4,449
1890	7,896
1900	9,524
1910	8,692
1920	11,371
1930	13,623
1940	15,777
1950	16,564
1960	17,837
1970	23,479
1980	22,970

SUN PRAIRIE

1870	626
1880	923
1890	912
1900	938
1910	1,119
1920	1,236
1930	881
1940	1,007
1950	1,141
1960	4,008
1970	9,935
1980	12,931

SUPERIOR

1890	11,983
1900	31,091
1910	40,384
1920	39,671
1930	36,113
1940	35,136
1950	35,325
1960	33,563
1970	32,237
1980	29,571

TWO RIVERS

1860	1,337
1870	1,365
1880	2,052
1890	2,870
1900	3,784
1910	4,850
1920	7,305
1930	10,083
1940	10,302
1950	10,243
1960	12,393
1970	13,732
1980	13,354

WATERTOWN

1850	1,451
1860	5,302
1870	7,550
1880	7,883
1890	8,755
1900	8,437
1910	8,829
1920	9,299
1930	10,613
1940	11,301
1950	12,417
1960	13,943
1970	15,683
1980	18,113

WAUKESHA

1860	1,456
1870	2,633
1880	2,969
1890	6,321
1900	7,419
1910	8,740
1920	12,558
1930	17,176
1940	18,242
1950	21,233
1960	30,004
1970	40,258
1980	50,319

WAUSAU

1860	543
1870	1,349
1880	4,277
1890	9,253
1900	12,354
1910	16,560
1920	18,951
1930	23,758
1940	27,268
1950	30,414
1960	31,943
1970	32,806
1980	32,426

WAUWATOSA

1900	2,842
1910	3,346
1920	5,818
1930	21,914
1940	27,769
1950	33,324
1960	56,923
1970	58,676
1980	51,308

WEST ALLIS

1910	6,645
1920	13,745
1930	34,671
1940	36,364
1950	42,959
1960	68,157
1970	71,649
1980	63,982

WEST BEND

1880	1,273
1890	1,296
1900	2,119
1910	2,462
1920	3,378
1930	4,760
1940	5,452
1950	6,849
1960	9,969
1970	16,555
1980	21,484

WHITEFISH BAY

1900	512
1910	542
1920	882
1930	5,362
1940	9,651
1950	14,665
1960	18,390
1970	17,402
1980	14,930

WHITEWATER

1850	1,451
1860	5,302
1870	5,364
1880	4,519
1890	849
1900	3,405
1910	3,224
1920	3,215
1930	3,465

1940	3,689
1950	5,101
1960	6,380
1970	12,038
1980	11,520

WISCONSIN RAPIDS

1870	1,115
1880	1,350
1890	1,702
1900	4,493
1910	6,521
1920	7,243
1930	8,726
1940	11,416
1950	13,496
1960	15,042
1970	18,587
1980	17,995

CORRECTION NOTE

The official 1980 census counts of total population shown
in this report supersede counts issued previously. Corrections to the figures were made after the counts were provided
to the State for redistricting purposes and released in
Advance Report PHC80-V for this State.

Shown below are corrections to the 1980 census counts of the
total population made after the tabulations for this report
were completed. Any additional corrections made after this
report is printed are available by writing to Data User
Services Division, Customer Services (Corrections), Bureau
of the Census, Washington, D.C. 20233.

The 1980 figures shown in this publication are subject to
change pending the outcome of the various lawsuits dealing
with the census counts.

	1980 population	
	As shown in the tables	Corrected
The State.....................	4 705 767	4 705 521
Dane County:		
Middleton city...................	11 779	11 848
Middleton town...................	2 667	2 598
Milwaukee County:		
Milwaukee city (pt.).............	636 210	636 234
St. Francis city.................	10 066	10 042
Outagamie County....................	128 799	128 730
Appleton city (pt.)..............	53 531	53 424
Grand Chute town.................	9 491	9 529
St. Croix County:		
Cady town........................	719	724
River Falls city (pt.)..........	1 515	1 498
Spring Valley village (pt.)......	5	-
Troy town........................	2 309	2 326
Walworth County:		
Bloomfield town..................	3 288	3 277
Lake Geneva city.................	5 607	5 612
Linn town........................	2 053	2 064
Lyons town.......................	2 664	2 659
Waukesha County....................	280 326	280 080
Summit town......................	4 173	3 927
Waukesha city....................	50 319	50 365
Waukesha town....................	6 714	6 668
Winnebago County..................	131 703	131 722
Appleton city (pt.).............	17	5
Menasha town....................	12 226	12 307
Appleton city (total)............	59 032	58 913
Milwaukee city (total)...........	636 212	636 236
River Falls city (total).........	9 036	9 019
Spring Valley village (total).....	987	982

County Subdivisions	1980	1970
The State	4 705 767	'4 417 821
Adams County[1]	13 457	9 234
Adams city	1 744	1 440
Adams town[1]	961	692
Big Flats town	694	482
Colburn town	177	121
Dell Prairie town	856	435
Easton town	858	491
Friendship village[1]	744	641
Jackson town	640	497
Leola town	237	184
Lincoln town	289	283
Monroe town	288	252
New Chester town	1 088	420
New Haven town	522	543
Preston town	967	607
Quincy town	639	444
Richfield town	183	165
Rome town	1 110	368
Springville town	584	449
Strongs Prairie town	876	720
Ashland County[2]	16 783	16 743
Agenda town[2]	623	512
Ashland city	9 115	9 615
Ashland town	596	504
Butternut village[2]	438	453
Chippewa town	402	417
Gingles town	545	456
Gordon town	333	312
Jacobs town	907	928
La Pointe town	156	159
Marengo town	276	257
Mellen city	1 046	1 168
Morse town	469	401
Peeksville town	184	145
Sanborn town	834	662
Shanagolden town	174	148
White River town	685	606
Barron County[3]	38 730	33 955
Almena town	776	731
Almena village	526	423
Arland town	692	605
Barron city[3]	2 595	2 337
Barron town[3]	977	893
Bear Lake town	521	426
Cameron village[3]	1 115	893
Cedar Lake town	617	423
Chetek city[3]	1 931	1 630
Chetek town[3]	1 210	918
Clinton town	851	757
Crystal Lake town[3]	756	712
Cumberland city[3]	1 983	1 839
Cumberland town[3]	909	910
Dallas town	567	465
Dallas village	477	359
Dovre town[3]	526	539
Doyle town	455	426
Haugen village	251	246
Lakeland town	672	580
Maple Grove town	948	859
Maple Plain town[3]	577	493
New Auburn village (pt.)[3]	14	...
Oak Grove town	892	836
Prairie Farm town	634	594
Prairie Farm village	387	426
Prairie Lake town	1 076	923
Rice Lake city[3]	7 691	7 278
Rice Lake town[3]	2 372	1 667
Sioux Creek town	643	563
Stanfold town	721	757
Stanley town[3]	1 813	1 064
Sumner town	556	465
Turtle Lake town	587	673
Turtle Lake village (pt.)	762	637
Vance Creek town	650	608
Bayfield County[4]	13 822	11 683
Barksdale town	762	574
Barnes town	493	311
Bayfield city	778	874
Bayfield town	607	503
Bayview town	343	297
Bell town	247	205
Cable town	604	457
Cable village	227	281
Clover town	254	277
Delta town	205	150
Drummond town	442	349
Eileen town	664	599
Grand View town[4]	440	370
Hughes town	290	174
Iron River town	991	716
Kelly town	354	336
Keystone town	344	314
Lincoln town	280	206
Mason town	304	304
Mason village	102	119

County Subdivisions	1980	1970
Bayfield County—Con.		
Namakagon town	286	224
Orienta town	109	108
Oulu town	547	505
Pilsen town	222	193
Port Wing town	525	385
Russell town	791	475
Tripp town	145	138
Washburn city	2 080	1 957
Washburn town	386	282
Brown County[5]	175 280	158 244
Allouez town	14 882	13 753
Allouez (CDP)	14 882	13 753
Ashwaubenon village[5]	14 486	...
Bellevue town[5]	4 101	1 736
Denmark village[5]	1 475	1 364
De Pere city[5]	14 892	13 309
De Pere town[5]	1 535	1 365
Eaton town	1 106	1 049
Glenmore town	1 046	1 110
Green Bay city[5]	87 899	87 809
Green Bay town	1 106	958
Hobart town[5]	3 765	2 599
Holland town	1 268	1 211
Howard village[5]	8 240	4 911
Humboldt town	1 281	1 101
Lawrence town[5]	1 431	1 622
Morrison town	1 565	1 473
New Denmark town[5]	1 420	1 203
Pittsfield town[5]	2 219	1 647
Pulaski village[5]	1 875	1 717
Rockland town	882	983
Scott town[5]	1 929	1 969
Suamico town[5]	4 003	2 830
Wrightstown town	1 705	1 463
Wrightstown village	1 169	1 020
Buffalo County[6]	14 309	13 743
Alma city[6]	876	956
Alma town[6]	397	371
Belvidere town[6]	425	464
Buffalo city	894	671
Buffalo town	821	782
Canton town	359	443
Cochrane village[6]	512	506
Cross town	393	363
Dover town	455	435
Fountain City city	963	1 017
Gilmanton town	498	546
Glencoe town	558	515
Lincoln town	272	297
Maxville town	403	360
Milton town	416	370
Modena town	436	456
Mondovi city[6]	2 545	2 338
Mondovi town[6]	511	435
Montana town	337	409
Naples town	580	559
Nelson town[6]	675	870
Nelson village[6]	389	...
Waumandee town	594	580
Burnett County[7]	12 340	9 276
Anderson town	265	193
Blaine town	151	129
Daniels town	607	532
Dewey town	520	419
Grantsburg town[7]	677	501
Grantsburg village[7]	1 153	930
Jackson town	331	128
La Follette town	388	269
Lincoln town	215	119
Meenon town	838	596
Oakland town	486	311
Roosevelt town	178	177
Rusk town	349	211
Sand Lake town	422	306
Scott town	409	252
Siren town[7]	887	550
Siren village[7]	896	639
Swiss town	587	518
Trade Lake town	824	673
Union town	199	147
Webb Lake town	256	125
Webster village	610	502
West Marshland town	209	173
Wood River town	883	876
Calumet County[8]	30 867	27 604
Appleton city (pt.)[8]	5 484	3 401
Brillion city[8]	2 907	2 588
Brillion town[8]	1 191	1 324
Brothertown town	1 494	1 420
Charlestown town[8]	1 090	1 079
Chilton city[8]	2 965	3 030
Chilton town	1 120	1 116
Harrison town[8]	3 541	3 260
Hilbert village	1 176	896
Kiel city (pt.)[8]	429	298

County Subdivisions	1980	1970
Calumet County—Con.		
New Holstein city[8]	3 412	3 012
New Holstein town[8]	1 527	1 513
Rantoul town	1 184	1 243
Sherwood village[8]	372	350
Stockbridge town[8]	1 248	1 285
Stockbridge village[8]	567	582
Woodville town	1 160	1 207
Chippewa County[9]	52 127	47 717
Anson town	1 590	1 446
Arthur town	856	774
Auburn town	456	408
Birch Creek town	540	365
Bloomer city[9]	3 342	3 143
Bloomer town	930	800
Boyd village	660	574
Cadott village	1 247	977
Chippewa Falls city[9]	12 270	12 351
Cleveland town	732	607
Colburn town	760	678
Cooks Valley town	603	610
Cornell city	1 583	1 616
Delmar town	1 062	1 079
Eagle Point town[9]	2 750	2 224
Eau Claire city (pt.)[9]	1 657	957
Edson town	1 061	1 082
Estella town	483	484
Goetz town	607	613
Hallie town[9]	4 275	'3 568
Howard town	660	643
Lafayette town[9]	4 181	'4 189
Lake Wissota (CDP)	1 788	1 419
Lake Holcombe town	791	648
New Auburn village (pt.)	452	368
Ruby town	514	469
Sampson town	805	724
Sigel town	782	654
Stanley city	2 095	2 049
Tilden town	1 088	963
Wheaton town[9]	2 328	1 782
Woodmohr town[9]	967	872
Clark County[10]	32 910	30 361
Abbotsford city (pt.)[10]	1 401	1 108
Beaver town	777	718
Butler town	81	83
Colby city (pt.)[10]	1 151	885
Colby town[10]	800	812
Curtiss village	127	135
Dewhurst town	132	99
Dorchester village[10]	613	491
Eaton town	663	572
Foster town	111	51
Fremont town[10]	982	905
Grant town[10]	882	736
Granton village[10]	399	288
Green Grove town	678	663
Greenwood city	1 124	1 036
Hendren town	570	526
Hewett town	301	170
Hixon town[10]	810	791
Hoard town[10]	881	919
Levis town	433	337
Longwood town	673	728
Loyal city[10]	1 252	1 126
Loyal town[10]	882	819
Lynn town	587	555
Mayville town[10]	962	957
Mead town	303	237
Mentor town	596	584
Neillsville city[10]	2 780	2 750
Owen city[10]	998	1 031
Pine Valley town[10]	1 137	923
Reseburg town	761	742
Seif town	254	162
Sherman town	766	674
Sherwood town	173	199
Thorp city	1 635	1 469
Thorp town	743	873
Unity town	815	796
Unity village (pt.)	166	154
Warner town	668	607
Washburn town	276	325
Weston town	646	602
Withee town	859	801
Withee village[10]	509	480
Worden town	650	595
York town	903	847
Columbia County[11]	43 222	40 150
Arlington town[11]	752	701
Arlington village[11]	440	379
Caledonia town[11]	923	855
Cambria village[11]	680	631
Columbus city[11]	4 049	3 789
Columbus town[11]	704	715
Courtland town[11]	601	628
Dekorra town[11]	1 914	1 763

County Subdivisions	1980	1970
Columbia County—Con.		
Doylestown village	294	265
Fall River village[11]	850	633
Fort Winnebago town[11]	860	673
Fountain Prairie town[11]	771	816
Friesland village	267	301
Hampden town	650	704
Leeds town	845	869
Lewiston town[11]	1 122	984
Lodi city[11]	1 959	1 831
Lodi town[11]	1 855	1 357
Lowville town[11]	976	819
Marcellon town	809	759
Newport town[11]	657	562
Otsego town	767	754
Pacific town	1 215	756
Pardeeville village	1 594	1 507
Portage city[11]	7 896	7 821
Poynette village[11]	1 447	1 118
Randolph town[11]	700	729
Randolph village (pt.)[11]	485	493
Rio village[11]	785	792
Scott town	602	585
Springvale town	521	504
West Point town	1 122	873
Wisconsin Dells city (pt.)[11]	2 337	2 277
Wyocena town[11]	1 225	1 098
Wyocena village[11]	548	809
Crawford County[12]	16 556	15 252
Bell Center village	124	110
Bridgeport town	708	416
Clayton town	927	916
De Soto village (pt.)	66	79
Eastman town[12]	840	781
Eastman village	371	319
Ferryville village	227	183
Freeman town	796	677
Gays Mills village	627	623
Haney town	404	387
Lynxville village[12]	174	149
Marietta town[12]	568	601
Mount Sterling village	223	181
Prairie du Chien city	5 859	5 540
Prairie du Chien town	694	591
Scott town	472	478
Seneca town[12]	832	858
Soldiers Grove village	622	514
Steuben village[12]	175	179
Utica town	822	843
Wauzeka town	445	390
Wauzeka village	580	437
Dane County[13]	323 545	290 272
Albion town	1 918	1 926
Belleville village (pt.)[13]	1 203	972
Berry town	1 116	896
Black Earth town[13]	406	379
Black Earth village[13]	1 145	1 114
Blooming Grove town[13]	1 965	1 608
Blue Mounds town[13]	637	675
Blue Mounds village	387	261
Bristol town[13]	1 723	1 491
Brooklyn village (pt.)[13]	250	217
Burke town[13]	2 967	1 742
Cambridge village (pt.)[13]	785	672
Christiana town[13]	1 209	1 261
Cottage Grove town[13]	2 952	1 818
Cottage Grove village[13]	888	478
Cross Plains town[13]	1 003	995
Cross Plains village[13]	2 156	1 478
Dane town[13]	945	894
Dane village[13]	518	486
Deerfield town[13]	1 111	855
Deerfield village[13]	1 466	1 067
De Forest village[13]	3 367	1 911
Dunkirk town[13]	2 098	'2 139
Dunn town	4 966	3 391
Fitchburg town[13]	11 973	4 704
McFarland village	3 783	2 386
Madison city[13]	170 616	'171 809
Madison town[13]	6 162	'5 746
Maple Bluff village	1 351	1 974
Marshall village[13]	2 363	1 043
Mazomanie town[13]	1 007	789
Mazomanie village[13]	1 248	1 217
Medina town[13]	1 019	961
Middleton city[13]	11 779	'8 246
Middleton town[13]	2 667	2 028
Monona city[13]	8 809	10 420
Montrose town[13]	1 024	962
Mount Horeb village[13]	3 251	2 402
Oregon town[13]	1 798	1 115
Oregon village[13]	3 876	2 553
Perry town	632	664
Pleasant Springs town[13]	2 529	2 057
Primrose town	654	664
Rockdale village[13]	200	172
Roxbury town	1 491	1 427

County Subdivisions	1980	1970
Dane County — Con.		
Rutland town[13]	1 393	1 197
Shorewood Hills village[13]	1 837	2 206
Springdale town[13]	1 279	1 132
Springfield town[13]	2 379	1 947
Stoughton city[13]	7 589	'6 096
Sun Prairie city[13]	12 931	9 935
Sun Prairie town[13]	1 990	1 490
Vermont town[13]	634	673
Verona city[13]	3 336	2 334
Verona town[13]	2 259	2 235
Vienna town[13]	1 365	1 177
Waunakee village[13]	3 866	2 181
Westport town[13]	2 748	'2 411
Windsor town[13]	3 812	2 415
York town	714	778
Dodge County[14]	75 064	69 004
Ashippun town[14]	1 929	1 500
Beaver Dam city[14]	14 149	14 265
Beaver Dam town[14]	3 030	1 933
Brownsville village[14]	433	374
Burnett town	917	875
Calamus town	1 077	934
Chester town[14]	981	1 060
Clyman town[14]	815	889
Clyman village[14]	317	328
Elba town	1 028	960
Emmet town[14]	1 089	1 050
Fox Lake city[14]	1 373	1 242
Fox Lake town[14]	1 674	1 501
Herman town	1 131	1 215
Horicon city[14]	3 584	3 356
Hubbard town[14]	1 508	1 301
Hustisford town[14]	1 262	1 034
Hustisford village[14]	874	789
Iron Ridge village[14]	766	480
Juneau city[14]	2 045	2 043
Kekoskee village[14]	224	233
Lebanon town	1 518	1 278
Leroy town	1 110	1 146
Lomira town[14]	1 391	1 247
Lomira village[14]	1 446	1 084
Lowell town[14]	1 205	1 254
Lowell village[14]	326	322
Mayville city[14]	4 333	4 139
Neosho village[14]	575	400
Oak Grove town[14]	1 333	1 326
Portland town	976	915
Randolph village (pt.)[14]	1 206	1 089
Reeseville village[14]	649	566
Rubicon town[14]	1 759	1 564
Shields town	584	602
Theresa town[14]	1 152	1 174
Theresa village[14]	766	611
Trenton town	1 319	1 406
Watertown city (pt.)[14]	5 911	4 373
Waupun city (pt.)[14]	5 439	5 481
Westford town[14]	1 203	1 006
Williamstown town[14]	657	659
Door County[15]	25 029	20 106
Baileys Harbor town	799	615
Brussels town	1 097	1 050
Claybanks town	409	345
Egg Harbor town[15]	825	693
Egg Harbor village[15]	238	184
Ephraim village	319	236
Forestville town	1 035	902
Forestville village	455	349
Gardner town	1 084	875
Gibraltar town	742	590
Jacksonport town	707	622
Liberty Grove town[15]	1 313	1 174
Nasewaupee town[15]	1 899	1 470
Sevastopol town[15]	2 520	2 035
Sister Bay village[15]	564	483
Sturgeon Bay city[15]	8 847	6 776
Sturgeon Bay town[15]	863	641
Union town	755	620
Washington town	558	446
Douglas County	44 421	44 657
Amnicon town	916	898
Bennett town	501	333
Brule town	544	497
Cloverland town	263	255
Dairyland town	258	233
Gordon town	627	419
Hawthorne town	902	677
Highland town	190	157
Lake Nebagamon village	780	523
Lakeside town	572	514
Maple town	685	608
Oakland town	938	624
Oliver village	253	210
Parkland town	1 496	1 523
Poplar village	569	455
Solon Springs town	553	471
Solon Springs village	590	598

County Subdivisions	1980	1970
Douglas County — Con.		
Summit town	1 057	905
Superior city	29 571	32 237
Superior town	2 065	1 743
Superior village	580	476
Wascott town	511	301
Dunn County[16]	34 314	'28 991
Boyceville village	862	725
Colfax town[16]	660	499
Colfax village[16]	1 149	1 026
Downing village	242	215
Dunn town	1 294	969
Eau Galle town	944	892
Elk Mound town	668	455
Elk Mound village	737	471
Grant town	443	400
Hay River town	433	419
Knapp village	419	369
Lucas town	699	577
Menomonie village[16]	12 769	'11 112
Menomonie town[16]	2 453	1 820
New Haven town	707	645
Otter Creek town[16]	337	224
Peru town	194	245
Red Cedar town[16]	1 278	935
Ridgeland village[16]	300	266
Rock Creek town	668	632
Sand Creek town	575	579
Sheridan town	476	426
Sherman town	666	580
Spring Brook town	1 293	1 168
Stanton town	553	527
Tainter town	1 507	1 000
Tiffany town	639	485
Weston town	654	688
Wheeler village[16]	231	212
Wilson town[16]	464	430
Eau Claire County[17]	78 805	67 219
Altoona city[17]	4 393	2 842
Augusta city[17]	1 560	1 242
Bridge Creek town[17]	1 206	935
Brunswick town[17]	1 411	1 092
Clear Creek town	798	773
Drammen town	725	672
Eau Claire city (pt.)[17]	49 852	43 662
Fairchild town	278	238
Fairchild village	577	562
Fall Creek village	1 148	825
Lincoln town	1 012	962
Ludington town	969	761
Otter Creek town	497	526
Pleasant Valley town	1 908	1 223
Seymour town[17]	2 824	2 362
Union town[17]	2 689	2 355
Washington town[17]	6 489	5 757
Wilson town	469	430
Florence County	4 172	3 298
Aurora town	1 050	920
Commonwealth town	369	254
Fence town	192	191
Fern town	111	61
Florence town	1 809	1 262
Homestead town	272	258
Long Lake town	199	190
Tipler town	170	162
Fond du Lac County[18]	88 964	84 567
Alto town	1 176	1 139
Ashford town	1 596	1 470
Auburn town[18]	1 816	1 256
Brandon village	862	872
Byron town	1 681	1 300
Calumet town	1 609	1 475
Campbellsport village[18]	1 740	1 681
Eden town[18]	1 130	1 041
Eden village[18]	534	376
Eldorado town	1 502	1 302
Empire town[18]	2 359	1 730
Fairwater village	310	373
Fond du Lac city[18]	35 863	35 515
Fond du Lac town[18]	3 001	3 896
Forest town	1 098	1 106
Friendship town[18]	2 321	2 350
Lamartine town	1 749	1 416
Marshfield town	1 214	1 159
Metomen town	792	798
Mount Calvary village	585	942
North Fond du Lac village[18]	3 844	3 286
Oakfield town[18]	833	765
Oakfield village[18]	990	918
Osceola town	1 569	1 116
Ripon city[18]	7 111	7 053
Ripon town[18]	1 411	1 186
Rosendale town	763	710
Rosendale village	725	464
St. Cloud village	560	550
Springvale town	808	744
Taycheedah town	3 227	2 692

County Subdivisions	1980	1970
Fond du Lac County—Con.		
Waupun city (pt.)[18]	2 693	2 465
Waupun town[18]	1 492	1 421
Forest County	9 044	7 691
Alvin town	195	159
Argonne town	469	390
Armstrong Creek town	501	459
Blackwell town	384	418
Caswell town	85	96
Crandon city	1 969	1 582
Crandon town	569	406
Freedom town	307	276
Hiles town	327	283
Laona town	1 474	1 395
Lincoln town	577	350
Nashville town	703	519
Popple River town	59	36
Ross town	203	178
Wabeno town	1 222	1 144
Grant County[19]	51 736	48 398
Bagley village	317	271
Beetown town	933	955
Bloomington town	567	552
Bloomington village	743	719
Blue River village	412	369
Boscobel city[19]	2 662	2 510
Boscobel town[19]	494	463
Cassville town[19]	633	531
Cassville village[19]	1 270	1 343
Castle Rock town	339	393
Clifton town	404	394
Cuba City city (pt.)[19]	1 928	1 902
Dickeyville village[19]	1 156	1 057
Ellenboro town	544	517
Fennimore city[19]	2 212	1 861
Fennimore town[19]	726	676
Glen Haven town	596	679
Harrison town	600	537
Hazel Green town[19]	1 228	1 237
Hazel Green village (pt.)[19]	1 270	982
Hickory Grove town	423	444
Jamestown town	2 369	1 973
Lancaster city[19]	4 076	3 756
Liberty town	609	597
Lima town	750	667
Little Grant town	347	349
Livingston village (pt.)	626	494
Marion town	463	364
Millville town	152	170
Montfort village (pt.)	516	511
Mount Hope town	343	308
Mount Hope village	197	176
Mount Ida town	544	495
Muscoda town[19]	566	455
Muscoda village (pt.)[19]	1 331	1 099
North Lancaster town[19]	506	475
Paris town[19]	842	751
Patch Grove town[19]	421	385
Patch Grove village[19]	259	187
Platteville city[19]	9 580	9 599
Platteville town[19]	1 309	1 010
Potosi town[19]	1 104	1 037
Potosi village[19]	736	713
Smelser town[19]	970	907
South Lancaster town[19]	1 032	1 187
Tennyson village	476	402
Waterloo town	615	602
Watterstown town	348	255
Wingville town	417	388
Woodman town	216	196
Woodman village	116	102
Wyalusing town	443	396
Green County[20]	30 012	26 714
Adams town	484	484
Albany town	657	551
Albany village	1 051	875
Belleville village (pt.)	99	91
Brodhead city[20]	3 153	2 515
Brooklyn town	760	746
Brooklyn village (pt.)	377	348
Browntown village	284	253
Cadiz town	891	812
Clarno town[20]	1 069	1 072
Decatur town[20]	1 035	705
Exeter town	709	685
Jefferson town	1 204	1 123
Jordan town	585	555
Monroe city[20]	10 027	8 654
Monroe town[20]	1 054	1 145
Monticello village[20]	1 021	870
Mount Pleasant town[20]	567	597
New Glarus town[20]	510	552
New Glarus village[20]	1 763	1 454
Spring Grove town	819	798
Sylvester town	786	684

County Subdivisions	1980	1970
Green County—Con.		
Washington town	555	618
York town	552	527
Green Lake County[21]	18 370	16 878
Berlin city (pt.)	5 387	5 297
Berlin town	1 065	882
Brooklyn town[21]	1 431	1 262
Green Lake city[21]	1 208	1 109
Green Lake town[21]	1 307	1 162
Kingston town[21]	708	556
Kingston village[21]	328	343
Mackford town[21]	622	650
Manchester town	812	777
Markesan city[21]	1 446	1 285
Marquette town[21]	393	310
Marquette village[21]	204	161
Princeton city[21]	1 479	1 446
Princeton town[21]	1 287	952
St. Marie town	310	320
Seneca town	383	366
Iowa County[22]	19 802	19 306
Arena town	1 292	1 084
Arena village	451	377
Avoca village[22]	505	421
Barneveld village[22]	579	528
Blanchardville village (pt.)	139	123
Brigham town[22]	821	844
Clyde town	381	360
Cobb village	409	410
Dodgeville city[22]	3 458	3 255
Dodgeville town[22]	1 234	1 164
Eden town[22]	419	503
Highland town[22]	844	923
Highland village[22]	860	785
Hollandale village	271	256
Linden town	828	961
Linden village	395	408
Livingston village (pt.)	16	9
Mifflin town	591	664
Mineral Point city[22]	2 259	2 305
Mineral Point town[22]	792	770
Montfort village (pt.)[22]	100	7
Moscow town	568	548
Muscoda village (pt.)[22]	–	...
Pulaski town[22]	462	489
Rewey village	233	232
Ridgeway town	564	521
Ridgeway village	503	463
Waldwick town	503	598
Wyoming town	325	298
Iron County[23]	6 730	6 533
Anderson town	91	92
Carey town	179	194
Gurney town	153	135
Hurley city[23]	2 015	2 418
Kimball town[23]	499	468
Knight town	294	324
Mercer town	1 425	1 003
Montreal city	887	877
Oma town	298	265
Pence town	191	234
Saxon town	362	371
Sherman town	336	152
Jackson County[24]	16 831	15 325
Adams town[24]	1 300	980
Albion town	976	914
Alma town[24]	696	668
Alma Center village	454	495
Bear Bluff town	133	116
Black River Falls city[24]	3 434	3 273
Brockway town[24]	1 053	978
City Point town	196	180
Cleveland town	422	411
Curran town	410	360
Franklin town	417	414
Garden Valley town	421	435
Garfield town	423	369
Hixton town	646	558
Hixton village	364	300
Irving town	618	489
Knapp town	201	155
Komensky town	449	283
Manchester town	590	442
Melrose town	338	355
Melrose village	507	505
Merrillan village[24]	587	612
Millston town	202	157
North Bend town	456	498
Northfield town	652	587
Springfield town	475	469
Taylor village	411	322
Jefferson County[25]	66 152	60 060
Aztalan town[25]	1 752	1 306
Cambridge village (pt.)[25]	59	17
Cold Spring town[25]	684	1 018

County Subdivisions	1980	1970
Jefferson County—Con.		
Concord town	1 805	1 130
Farmington town[25]	1 528	1 391
Fort Atkinson city[25]	9 785	9 164
Hebron town	1 104	973
Ixonia town	2 905	2 324
Jefferson city[25]	5 647	5 429
Jefferson town[25]	2 891	3 082
Johnson Creek village[25]	1 136	790
Koshkonong town[25]	2 979	2 671
Lake Mills city[25]	3 670	3 556
Lake Mills town[25]	1 515	1 472
Milford town[25]	1 066	1 129
Oakland town[25]	2 240	1 984
Palmyra town[25]	1 069	875
Palmyra village[25]	1 515	1 341
Sullivan town	1 646	1 159
Sullivan village	434	467
Sumner town	973	954
Waterloo city	2 393	2 253
Waterloo town	811	685
Watertown city (pt.)[25]	12 202	11 310
Watertown town[25]	1 921	1 671
Whitewater city (pt.)[25]	2 422	1 909
Juneau County[26]	21 039	18 455
Armenia town	545	288
Camp Douglas village[26]	589	547
Clearfield town	538	312
Cutler town	369	294
Elroy city	1 504	1 513
Finley town	72	87
Fountain town	598	616
Germantown town	643	215
Hustler village	170	190
Kildare town	534	335
Kingston town	64	92
Lemonweir town[26]	1 327	970
Lindina town[26]	816	926
Lisbon town[26]	903	661
Lyndon town[26]	701	405
Lyndon Station village	375	533
Marion town	280	223
Mauston city[26]	3 284	3 466
Necedah town[26]	1 394	674
Necedah village[26]	773	740
New Lisbon city[26]	1 390	1 361
Orange town[26]	607	619
Plymouth town	644	647
Seven Mile Creek town	362	376
Summit town	721	566
Union Center village	216	205
Wisconsin Dells city (pt.)[26]	–	...
Wonewoc town[26]	778	759
Wonewoc village[26]	842	835
Kenosha County[27]	123 137	117 917
Brighton town	1 180	1 199
Bristol town	3 599	2 740
Kenosha city[27]	77 685	78 805
Paddock Lake village[27]	2 207	1 470
Paris town	1 612	1 744
Pleasant Prairie town[27]	12 703	12 019
Randall town[27]	2 155	1 582
Powers Lake (CDP) (pt.)	740	...
Salem town[27]	6 292	5 555
Camp Lake (CDP)	2 060	1 898
Silver Lake village[27]	1 598	1 210
Somers town[27]	7 724	7 270
Twin Lakes village[27]	3 474	2 276
Wheatland town	2 908	2 047
Powers Lake (CDP) (pt.)	102	...
Kewaunee County[28]	19 539	18 961
Ahnapee town	948	878
Algoma city	3 656	4 023
Carlton town	1 140	1 105
Casco town	1 001	979
Casco village	484	481
Franklin town	1 062	966
Kewaunee city[28]	2 801	2 901
Lincoln town	967	984
Luxemburg town[28]	1 468	1 295
Luxemburg village[28]	1 040	853
Montpelier town	1 457	1 273
Pierce town[28]	790	720
Red River town	1 431	1 308
West Kewaunee town	1 294	1 195
La Crosse County[29]	91 056	80 468
Bangor town	572	569
Bangor village	1 012	974
Barre town	901	521
Burns town[29]	988	901
Campbell town[29]	4 118	3 327
French Island (CDP)	4 118	...
Farmington town[29]	1 603	1 383
Greenfield town	1 537	1 278
Hamilton town[29]	1 472	1 229
Holland town[29]	1 776	976

County Subdivisions	1980	1970
La Crosse County—Con.		
Holmen village[29]	2 411	1 081
La Crosse city[29]	48 347	'50 286
Medary town[29]	1 794	2 333
Onalaska city[29]	9 249	4 909
Onalaska town[29]	5 386	2 973
Rockland village[29]	383	278
Shelby town[29]	5 620	'4 600
Washington town	611	670
West Salem village[29]	3 276	2 180
Lafayette County[30]	17 412	17 456
Argyle town	498	531
Argyle village	720	673
Belmont town[30]	716	626
Belmont village[30]	826	688
Benton town[30]	524	524
Benton village[30]	983	873
Blanchard town	209	233
Blanchardville village (pt.)	664	671
Cuba City city (pt.)[30]	201	91
Darlington city[30]	2 300	2 351
Darlington town[30]	842	949
Elk Grove town	522	613
Fayette town	447	444
Gratiot town[30]	706	797
Gratiot village[30]	280	249
Hazel Green village (pt.)[30]	12	...
Kendall town	432	435
Lamont town	341	387
Monticello town	202	201
New Diggings town	556	601
Seymour town	497	615
Shullsburg city[30]	1 484	1 376
Shullsburg town[30]	455	571
South Wayne village	495	436
Wayne town	559	588
White Oak Springs town	165	207
Willow Springs town	685	658
Wiota town	1 091	1 068
Langlade County[31]	19 978	19 220
Ackley town	639	681
Ainsworth town	447	348
Antigo city[31]	8 653	9 005
Antigo town[31]	1 661	1 692
Elcho town	1 078	885
Evergreen town	515	436
Langlade town	413	342
Neva town	970	819
Norwood town	866	838
Parrish town	87	60
Peck town	424	413
Polar town	827	737
Price town	243	259
Rolling town	1 236	914
Summit town	197	186
Upham town	545	486
Vilas town	264	265
White Lake village	309	309
Wolf River town	604	545
Lincoln County[32]	26 555	23 499
Birch town	689	312
Bradley town	2 235	1 753
Corning town	807	725
Harding town	261	174
Harrison town	693	607
King town	597	377
Merrill city[32]	9 578	9 502
Merrill town[32]	2 591	1 742
Pine River town[32]	1 463	1 271
Rock Falls town	434	423
Russell town	668	635
Schley town	818	811
Scott town[32]	1 149	1 046
Skanawan town	256	175
Somo town	150	113
Tomahawk city	3 527	3 419
Tomahawk town	383	256
Wilson town	256	158
Manitowoc County[33]	82 918	82 294
Cato town[33]	1 653	1 581
Centerville town[33]	796	784
Cleveland village[33]	1 270	761
Cooperstown town	1 249	1 094
Eaton town	764	741
Francis Creek village	589	492
Franklin town[33]	1 372	1 488
Gibson town	1 416	1 323
Kellnersville village[33]	369	...
Kiel city (pt.)[33]	2 654	2 550
Kossuth town[33]	2 097	1 966
Liberty town[33]	1 170	1 089
Manitowoc city[33]	32 547	33 430
Manitowoc town[33]	1 177	1 258
Manitowoc Rapids town[33]	3 186	3 552
Maple Grove town	962	910
Maribel village	363	316
Meeme town	1 535	1 480

County Subdivisions

County Subdivisions	1980	1970
Manitowoc County—Con.		
Mishicot town[33]	1 334	1 743
Mishicot village[33]	1 503	938
Newton town[33]	2 332	2 256
Reedsville village	1 134	994
Rockland town	936	971
St. Nazianz village[33]	738	718
Schleswig town[33]	1 633	1 542
Two Creeks town	489	580
Two Rivers city[33]	13 354	'13 732
Two Rivers town[33]	2 663	'2 627
Valders village[33]	984	821
Whitelaw village	649	557
Marathon County[34]	111 270	97 457
Abbotsford city (pt.)[34]	500	267
Athens village[34]	988	856
Bergen town	478	402
Berlin town	820	758
Bern town[34]	487	497
Bevent town	983	735
Brighton town	600	593
Brokaw village	298	312
Cassel town[34]	899	953
Cleveland town	958	777
Colby city (pt.)[34]	345	293
Day town	989	962
Easton town	1 046	912
Eau Pleine town	759	796
Edgar village[34]	1 194	928
Elderon town	628	506
Elderon village	191	185
Emmet town	757	850
Fenwood village	165	147
Frankfort town	743	725
Franzen town	571	535
Green Valley town	355	379
Guenther town	297	302
Halsey town	548	576
Hamburg town	749	760
Harrison town	354	422
Hatley village[34]	300	315
Hewitt town	496	486
Holton town	945	924
Hull town[34]	1 402	1 080
Johnson town[34]	933	936
Knowlton town	1 153	742
Kronenwetter town[34]	5 012	2 595
Evergreen (CDP)	1 842	...
McMillan town[34]	1 433	1 255
Maine town[34]	2 163	2 155
Marathon town[34]	1 114	918
Marathon City village[34]	1 552	1 214
Marshfield city (pt.)[34]	237	59
Mosinee city	3 015	2 395
Mosinee town	1 464	910
Norrie town	808	682
Plover town	553	405
Reid town	957	711
Rib Falls town	851	759
Rib Mountain town[34]	5 344	4 785
Wausau West–Rib Mountain (CDP) (pt.)	4 055	3 789
Rietbrock town	981	1 020
Ringle town[34]	1 097	690
Rothschild village[34]	3 338	3 141
Schofield city[34]	2 226	2 577
Spencer town[34]	989	972
Spencer village[34]	1 754	1 181
Stettin town[34]	4 436	4 199
Wausau West–Rib Mountain (CDP) (pt.)	1 950	2 610
Stratford village	1 385	1 239
Texas town[34]	1 634	1 406
Unity village (pt.)	252	209
Wausau city[34]	32 426	32 806
Wausau town[34]	2 215	2 088
Weston town[34]	11 342	6 351
Weston (CDP)	8 775	3 375
Wien town	761	824
Marinette County[35]	39 314	35 810
Amberg town	852	665
Athelstane town	364	330
Beaver town	1 042	995
Beecher town	521	279
Coleman village	852	683
Crivitz village[35]	1 041	...
Dunbar town	522	359
Goodman town	803	750
Grover town	1 709	1 575
Lake town	915	741
Marinette city[35]	11 965	12 696
Middle Inlet town	681	457
Niagara town	717	561
Niagara village	2 079	2 347
Pembine town	773	654
Peshtigo city[35]	2 807	2 836
Peshtigo town[35]	3 566	2 951
Porterfield town	1 857	1 405
Pound town	1 412	1 297

County Subdivisions

County Subdivisions	1980	1970
Marinette County—Con.		
Pound village	407	284
Silver Cliff town	267	189
Stephenson town[35]	2 137	2 202
Wagner town	624	500
Wausaukee town	753	497
Wausaukee village	648	557
Marquette County[36]	11 672	8 865
Buffalo town	745	487
Crystal Lake town	332	248
Douglas town	764	603
Endeavor village	335	328
Harris town	657	429
Mecan town	599	397
Montello city[36]	1 273	1 082
Montello town[36]	640	531
Moundville town	470	399
Neshkoro town	370	217
Neshkoro village	386	385
Newton town	460	320
Oxford town[36]	720	385
Oxford village[36]	432	453
Packwaukee town	998	668
Shields town	419	384
Springfield town	501	322
Westfield town[36]	538	343
Westfield village[36]	1 033	884
Menominee County	3 373	2 607
Menominee town	3 373	2 607
Neopit (CDP)	1 065	1 122
Milwaukee County[37]	964 988	'1 054 249
Bayside village (pt.)	4 612	4 338
Brown Deer village	12 921	'12 582
Cudahy city	19 547	22 078
Fox Point village	7 649	'7 939
Franklin city	16 871	12 247
Glendale city[37]	13 882	'13 426
Greendale village[37]	16 928	15 089
Greenfield city[37]	31 467	24 424
Hales Corners village	7 110	7 771
Milwaukee city (pt.)[37]	636 210	'717 372
Oak Creek city	16 932	'13 928
River Hills village[37]	1 642	1 561
St. Francis city	10 066	10 489
Shorewood village	14 327	15 576
South Milwaukee city	21 069	23 297
Wauwatosa city[37]	51 308	58 676
West Allis city	63 982	'71 649
West Milwaukee village	3 535	4 405
Whitefish Bay village[37]	14 930	'17 402
Monroe County[38]	35 074	31 610
Adrian town	403	405
Angelo town[38]	1 189	996
Byron town	1 162	814
Cashton village[38]	827	824
Clifton town	610	612
Glendale town	558	594
Grant town	312	218
Greenfield town	536	479
Jefferson town[38]	710	756
Kendall village	486	468
Lafayette town	256	224
La Grange town[38]	1 728	2 224
Leon town	751	641
Lincoln town[38]	644	814
Little Falls town	1 228	1 010
Melvina village	117	116
New Lyme town	123	110
Norwalk village[38]	517	432
Oakdale town	759	659
Portland town	755	695
Ridgeville town[38]	530	590
Scott town	117	78
Sheldon town	524	540
Sparta city[38]	6 934	6 258
Sparta town[38]	2 317	1 983
Tomah city[38]	7 204	5 647
Tomah town[38]	1 089	969
Warrens village[38]	300	...
Wellington town[38]	616	633
Wells town	474	423
Wilton town[38]	670	679
Wilton village[38]	465	516
Wyeville village	163	203
Oconto County[39]	28 947	25 553
Abrams town	1 181	884
Armstrong town	735	530
Bagley town	272	209
Brazeau town	1 039	924
Breed town	563	402
Chase town	1 256	1 026
Doty town	154	93
Gillett city[39]	1 356	1 288
Gillett town[39]	1 059	936
How town	592	565
Lakewood town	516	469

County Subdivisions	1980	1970
Oconto County—Con.		
Lena town	851	877
Lena village	585	569
Little River town	940	859
Little Suamico town	1 969	1 138
Maple Valley town[39]	715	679
Morgan town	726	670
Oconto city	4 505	4 667
Oconto town	937	934
Oconto Falls city[39]	2 500	2 517
Oconto Falls town[39]	1 033	895
Pensaukee town	1 000	863
Riverview town	417	321
Spruce town	805	818
Stiles town	1 261	845
Suring village[39]	581	499
Townsend town	735	463
Underhill town	664	613
Oneida County[40]	31 216	24 427
Cassian town	585	372
Crescent town[40]	1 702	1 441
Enterprise town	277	213
Hazelhurst town	780	403
Lake Tomahawk town	738	434
Little Rice town	172	99
Lynne town	185	220
Minocqua town	3 328	2 343
Monico town	291	306
Newbold town	2 171	1 234
Nokomis town	883	508
Pelican town[40]	3 387	2 576
Piehl town	94	64
Pine Lake town[40]	2 656	1 853
Rhinelander city[40]	7 873	8 218
Schoepke town	399	358
Stella town	489	299
Sugar Camp town	1 337	816
Three Lakes town	1 864	1 376
Woodboro town	547	287
Woodruff town	1 458	1 007
Outagamie County[41]	128 799	119 398
Appleton city (pt.)[41]	53 531	52 976
Bear Creek village	454	520
Black Creek town[41]	1 149	968
Black Creek village[41]	1 097	921
Bovina town[41]	822	837
Buchanan town[41]	1 742	1 987
Center town	2 570	1 853
Cicero town	1 062	1 079
Combined Locks village	2 573	2 771
Dale town	1 620	1 405
Deer Creek town	826	855
Ellington town[41]	1 865	1 696
Freedom town	3 746	2 926
Grand Chute town[41]	9 491	7 089
Greenville town	3 310	2 675
Hortonia town[41]	869	804
Hortonville village[41]	2 016	1 524
Kaukauna city[41]	11 310	11 308
Kaukauna town[41]	998	961
Kimberly village[41]	5 881	6 131
Liberty town	609	544
Little Chute village[41]	7 907	5 522
Maine town	816	725
Maple Creek town	652	586
New London city (pt.)[41]	1 269	1 368
Nichols village	267	207
Oneida town	3 499	2 624
Osborn town[41]	786	724
Seymour city[41]	2 530	2 194
Seymour town[41]	1 189	1 135
Shiocton village[41]	805	830
Vandenbroek town[41]	1 538	1 653
Ozaukee County[42]	66 981	54 461
Bayside village (pt.)	112	123
Belgium town	1 424	1 625
Belgium village	892	809
Cedarburg city[42]	9 005	7 697
Cedarburg town[42]	5 244	3 774
Fredonia town[42]	2 144	1 746
Fredonia village[42]	1 437	1 045
Grafton town[42]	3 588	3 127
Grafton village[42]	8 381	5 998
Mequon city	16 193	12 150
Newburg village (pt.)[42]	95	...
Port Washington city[42]	8 612	8 752
Port Washington town[42]	1 436	1 528
Saukville town[42]	1 583	1 516
Saukville village[42]	3 494	1 389
Thiensville village	3 341	3 182
Pepin County	7 477	7 319
Albany town	586	565
Durand city	2 047	2 103
Durand town	591	501
Frankfort town	397	409

County Subdivisions	1980	1970
Pepin County—Con.		
Lima town	631	679
Pepin town	749	740
Pepin village	890	747
Stockholm town	168	211
Stockholm village	104	99
Waterville town	1 075	1 048
Waubeek town	239	217
Pierce County[43]	31 149	26 652
Bay City village	543	317
Clifton town	975	612
Diamond Bluff town	458	355
Ellsworth town[43]	1 408	1 260
Ellsworth village[43]	2 143	1 983
Elmwood village	885	737
El Paso town	689	686
Gilman town	914	842
Hartland town	821	771
Isabelle town	190	168
Maiden Rock town	641	563
Maiden Rock village	172	172
Martell town	864	733
Oak Grove town	936	783
Plum City village	505	451
Prescott city	2 654	2 331
River Falls city (pt.)[43]	7 521	6 247
River Falls town[43]	2 168	1 642
Rock Elm town	654	638
Salem town	616	498
Spring Lake town	613	611
Spring Valley village (pt.)	982	995
Trenton town	1 624	1 286
Trimbelle town	1 420	1 225
Union town	753	746
Polk County[44]	32 351	26 666
Alden town	1 862	1 406
Amery city[44]	2 404	2 126
Apple River town	819	544
Balsam Lake town	960	631
Balsam Lake village	749	648
Beaver town[44]	755	641
Black Brook town[44]	949	775
Bone Lake town	466	416
Centuria village[44]	711	632
Clam Falls town	614	522
Clayton town[44]	789	713
Clayton village[44]	425	306
Clear Lake town	777	793
Clear Lake village	899	721
Dresser village[44]	670	533
Eureka town	1 135	1 043
Farmington town[44]	1 195	1 156
Frederic village[44]	1 039	908
Garfield town[44]	1 010	768
Georgetown town	746	526
Johnstown town	401	328
Laketown town	909	725
Lincoln town[44]	1 683	1 198
Lorain town	280	275
Luck town[44]	863	663
Luck village	997	848
McKinley town	337	297
Milltown town	943	691
Milltown village	732	634
Osceola town[44]	1 066	769
Osceola village[44]	1 581	1 152
St. Croix Falls city[44]	1 497	1 425
St. Croix Falls town[44]	873	783
Sterling town	497	379
Turtle Lake village (pt.)[44]	...	...
West Sweden town[44]	718	691
Portage County[45]	57 420	47 541
Alban town[45]	768	606
Almond town	624	529
Almond village	477	440
Amherst town	1 215	936
Amherst village	701	585
Amherst Junction village	225	141
Belmont town	496	387
Buena Vista town	1 023	827
Carson town[45]	1 441	1 295
Dewey town	803	575
Eau Pleine town[45]	963	784
Grant town	1 593	1 195
Hull town[45]	5 122	3 124
Junction City village[45]	523	396
Lanark town	1 043	578
Linwood town[45]	1 082	773
Milladore village (pt.)[45]	10	...
Nelsonville village	199	152
New Hope town	625	492
Park Ridge village	643	817
Pine Grove town	762	649
Plover town[45]	2 330	3 692
Plover village[45]	5 310	...
Rosholt village[45]	520	466

County Subdivisions	1980	1970
Portage County—Con.		
Sharon town	1 694	1 304
Stevens Point city[45]	22 970	23 479
Stockton town	2 208	1 537
Whiting village[45]	2 050	1 782
Price County[46]	15 788	14 520
Catawba town	319	338
Catawba village	205	215
Eisenstein town[46]	728	653
Elk town[46]	996	636
Emery town	308	288
Fifield town	805	763
Flambeau town	389	299
Georgetown town	166	183
Hackett town	179	190
Harmony town	268	235
Hill town	349	293
Kennan town	387	426
Kennan village	194	167
Knox town	542	539
Lake town[46]	1 369	1 473
Ogema town	850	821
Park Falls city[46]	3 192	2 953
Phillips city[46]	1 522	1 511
Prentice town[46]	547	463
Prentice village[46]	605	519
Spirit town	379	342
Worcester town[46]	1 489	1 213
Racine County[47]	173 132	170 838
Burlington city (pt.)[47]	8 385	7 479
Burlington town[47]	5 629	4 963
Bohners Lake (CDP)	1 507	1 417
Browns Lake (CDP)	1 648	1 669
Caledonia town[47]	20 940	16 748
Dover town	3 419	3 780
Elmwood Park village	483	456
Mount Pleasant town[47]	19 340	16 368
North Bay village	219	263
Norway town	4 619	4 620
Racine city[47]	85 725	95 162
Raymond town	3 610	3 735
Rochester town[47]	1 478	1 019
Rochester village[47]	746	436
Sturtevant village[47]	4 130	3 376
Union Grove village[47]	3 517	2 703
Waterford town[47]	3 984	3 483
Tichigan Lake (CDP)	1 066	...
Waterford village[47]	2 051	1 922
Wind Point village	1 695	1 251
Yorkville town[47]	3 162	3 074
Richland County[48]	17 476	17 079
Akan town	483	489
Bloom town	565	567
Boaz village	161	126
Buena Vista town[48]	1 369	1 095
Cazenovia village (pt.)	245	321
Dayton town	709	577
Eagle town	634	652
Forest town	351	391
Henrietta town	606	578
Ithaca town	702	750
Lone Rock village[48]	577	506
Marshall town	558	550
Orion town	644	619
Richland town[48]	1 442	1 283
Richland Center city[48]	4 997	5 086
Richwood town	654	640
Rockbridge town	662	654
Sylvan town	487	486
Viola village (pt.)	473	444
Westford town	558	658
Willow town	527	528
Yuba village	72	79
Rock County[49]	139 420	131 970
Avon town	555	614
Beloit city[49]	35 207	35 729
Beloit town[49]	8 382	9 182
Beloit North (CDP)	5 457	...
Bradford town	1 100	1 071
Center town	908	942
Clinton town[49]	925	1 090
Clinton village[49]	1 751	1 333
Edgerton city[49]	4 335	4 118
Evansville city[49]	2 835	2 992
Footville village[49]	794	698
Fulton town[49]	2 866	2 126
Harmony town[49]	2 090	1 364
Janesville city[49]	51 071	46 426
Janesville town[49]	3 068	2 700
Johnstown town	844	914
La Prairie town	1 099	1 086
Lima town	1 179	1 063
Magnolia town	746	736
Milton city[49]	4 092	3 699
Milton town[49]	2 306	1 977
Newark town	1 574	1 456

County Subdivisions	1980	1970
Rock County—Con.		
Orfordville village[49]	1 143	888
Plymouth town[49]	1 267	1 246
Porter town	940	884
Rock town[49]	3 399	3 050
Spring Valley town	912	852
Turtle town[49]	2 703	2 532
Union town[49]	1 329	1 202
Rusk County[50]	15 589	14 238
Atlanta town	586	489
Big Bend town	398	324
Big Falls town	122	130
Bruce village[50]	905	799
Cedar Rapids town	30	9
Conrath village	86	114
Dewey town	399	363
Flambeau town[50]	1 086	931
Glen Flora village	83	69
Grant town[50]	998	931
Grow town	560	548
Hawkins town	184	230
Hawkins village	407	385
Hubbard town	185	112
Ingram village	61	109
Ladysmith city[50]	3 826	3 674
Lawrence town	240	167
Marshall town	697	679
Murry town	301	253
Richland town	217	196
Rusk town	422	372
Sheldon village	292	218
South Fork town	146	204
Strickland town	281	262
Stubbs town[50]	612	633
Thornapple town	740	543
Tony village	146	144
True town	332	360
Washington town	318	206
Weyerhaeuser village[50]	313	285
Wilkinson town	63	44
Willard town	481	380
Wilson town	72	75
St. Croix County[51]	43 262	34 354
Baldwin town[51]	943	890
Baldwin village[51]	1 620	1 399
Cady town[51]	719	670
Cylon town[51]	717	620
Deer Park village[51]	232	217
Eau Galle town	897	720
Emerald town	638	588
Erin Prairie town	661	516
Forest town	631	649
Glenwood town	715	764
Glenwood City city	950	822
Hammond town[51]	822	764
Hammond village[51]	991	768
Hudson city[51]	5 434	5 049
Hudson town[51]	2 012	925
Kinnickinnic town[51]	1 051	755
New Richmond city[51]	4 306	3 707
North Hudson village[51]	2 218	1 547
Pleasant Valley town	360	330
Richmond town[51]	1 338	1 091
River Falls city (pt.)[51]	1 515	991
Roberts village[51]	833	484
Rush River town	476	439
St. Joseph town	2 180	1 357
Somerset town[51]	1 833	1 185
Somerset village[51]	860	778
Springfield town	816	811
Spring Valley village (pt.)[51]	5	...
Stanton town	1 083	975
Star Prairie town[51]	1 900	1 390
Star Prairie village[51]	420	362
Troy town[51]	2 309	1 517
Warren town[51]	897	622
Wilson village	155	130
Woodville village	725	522
Sauk County[52]	43 469	39 057
Baraboo city[52]	8 081	7 931
Baraboo town[52]	1 545	1 158
Bear Creek town	537	522
Cazenovia village (pt.)	14	14
Dellona town[52]	705	472
Delton town[52]	1 426	846
Excelsior town	1 266	786
Fairfield town	819	658
Franklin town	747	798
Freedom town[52]	405	371
Greenfield town	719	741
Honey Creek town	774	793
Ironton town	643	658
Ironton village	206	195
Lake Delton village[52]	1 158	1 059
La Valle town	929	693
La Valle village	412	411

County Subdivisions	1980	1970
Sauk County—Con.		
Lime Ridge village	191	203
Loganville village[52]	239	199
Merrimac town	661	435
Merrimac village	365	376
North Freedom village[52]	616	596
Plain village	676	688
Prairie du Sac town[52]	1 010	723
Prairie du Sac village[52]	2 145	1 902
Reedsburg city[52]	5 038	4 585
Reedsburg town[52]	1 468	1 442
Rock Springs village	426	432
Sauk City village	2 703	2 385
Spring Green town[52]	1 139	862
Spring Green village[52]	1 265	1 199
Sumpter town	720	883
Troy town	799	723
Washington town	741	756
West Baraboo village	846	563
Westfield town[52]	633	650
Winfield town	624	608
Wisconsin Dells city (pt.)[52]	184	124
Woodland town	594	617
Sawyer County[53]	12 843	9 670
Bass Lake town	1 288	832
Couderay town	394	170
Couderay village	114	123
Draper town	242	258
Edgewater town	441	286
Exeland village	219	189
Hayward city[53]	1 698	1 457
Hayward town[53]	2 331	1 690
Hunter town	594	381
Lenroot town	926	577
Meadowbrook town	202	190
Meteor town	105	117
Ojibwa town	264	238
Radisson town	394	371
Radisson village	280	206
Round Lake town	786	557
Sand Lake town	768	598
Spider Lake town	331	259
Weirgor town	386	331
Winter town[53]	704	840
Winter village[53]	376	...
Shawano County[54]	35 928	32 650
Almon town[54]	632	505
Angelica town	1 522	1 433
Aniwa town	612	598
Aniwa village	273	233
Bartelme town	583	399
Belle Plaine town[54]	1 626	1 636
Birnamwood town	570	484
Birnamwood village	688	632
Bonduel village[54]	1 160	995
Bowler village	339	272
Cecil village[54]	445	369
Eland village	230	229
Fairbanks town	608	631
Germania town	392	389
Grant town	976	912
Green Valley town	1 054	984
Gresham village[54]	534	448
Hartland town	872	820
Herman town[54]	834	759
Hutchins town[54]	467	409
Lessor town	955	911
Maple Grove town	1 271	1 258
Mattoon village[54]	382	377
Morris town	447	411
Navarino town	456	440
Pella town	788	734
Red Springs town	524	474
Richmond town	1 543	1 397
Seneca town[54]	525	532
Shawano city[54]	7 013	6 488
Tigerton village	865	742
Washington town[54]	1 374	974
Waukechon town[54]	874	906
Wescott town[54]	2 668	2 251
Wittenberg town[54]	829	723
Wittenberg village[54]	997	895
Sheboygan County[55]	100 935	96 660
Adell village[55]	545	380
Cascade village	615	603
Cedar Grove village[55]	1 420	1 276
Elkhart Lake village[55]	1 054	787
Glenbeulah village[55]	423	496
Greenbush town[55]	1 665	1 537
Herman town[55]	2 095	2 042
Holland town[55]	2 504	2 287
Howards Grove village[55]	1 838	998
Kohler village[55]	1 651	1 738
Lima town	2 809	2 590
Lyndon town[55]	1 342	1 198
Mitchell town	900	779
Mosel town	1 035	1 127

County Subdivisions	1980	1970
Sheboygan County—Con.		
Oostburg village[55]	1 647	1 309
Plymouth city[55]	6 027	5 810
Plymouth town[55]	3 068	2 368
Random Lake village[55]	1 287	1 068
Rhine town[55]	1 910	1 386
Russell town	429	482
Scott town	1 625	1 451
Sheboygan city[55]	48 085	48 484
Sheboygan town[55]	3 962	4 246
Sheboygan Falls city[55]	5 253	4 771
Sheboygan Falls town[55]	2 281	2 280
Sherman town[55]	1 445	1 436
Waldo village[55]	416	408
Wilson town[55]	3 604	3 323
Black River (CDP)	1 046	...
Taylor County[56]	18 817	16 958
Aurora town[56]	461	466
Browning town	702	644
Chelsea town	677	554
Cleveland town	286	250
Deer Creek town[56]	747	764
Ford town	274	248
Gilman village[56]	436	328
Goodrich town	408	373
Greenwood town	705	635
Grover town	229	210
Hammel town	562	509
Holway town	903	837
Jump River town	365	355
Little Black town	1 169	1 133
Lublin village	142	143
McKinley town	416	461
Maplehurst town	345	348
Medford city[56]	4 035	3 454
Medford town[56]	1 809	1 546
Molitor town	212	199
Pershing town	276	295
Rib Lake town[56]	682	615
Rib Lake village[56]	945	782
Roosevelt town	491	518
Stetsonville village[56]	487	305
Taft town	347	355
Westboro town	706	631
Trempealeau County[57]	26 158	23 344
Albion town	605	561
Arcadia city[57]	2 109	2 159
Arcadia town[57]	1 919	1 697
Blair city	1 142	1 036
Burnside town[57]	639	693
Caledonia town	507	341
Chimney Rock town	390	345
Dodge town	399	432
Eleva village	593	574
Ettrick town[57]	1 420	1 268
Ettrick village[57]	462	463
Gale town[57]	1 553	1 255
Galesville city[57]	1 239	1 162
Hale town	983	1 041
Independence city[57]	1 180	1 036
Lincoln town[57]	935	811
Osseo city[57]	1 474	1 356
Pigeon town[57]	876	759
Pigeon Falls village[57]	338	198
Preston town	1 112	1 027
Strum village	944	738
Sumner town[57]	785	594
Trempealeau town[57]	1 504	1 082
Trempealeau village[57]	956	743
Unity town	564	487
Whitehall city[57]	1 530	1 486
Vernon County[58]	25 642	24 557
Bergen town[58]	1 117	1 002
Chaseburg village	279	224
Christiana town[58]	823	806
Clinton town	920	830
Coon town	757	697
Coon Valley village	758	596
De Soto village (pt.)[58]	252	216
Forest town	551	571
Franklin town	1 047	926
Genoa town	787	728
Genoa village	283	305
Greenwood town	546	491
Hamburg town	774	754
Harmony town	636	712
Hillsboro city	1 263	1 231
Hillsboro town	763	617
Jefferson town	919	949
Kickapoo town	523	455
La Farge village	746	748
Liberty town	171	231
Ontario village	398	392
Readstown village	396	395
Stark town	322	356
Sterling town	626	664

County Subdivisions

County Subdivisions	1980	1970
Vernon County—Con.		
Stoddard village[58]	762	750
Union town	405	442
Viola village (pt.)	223	215
Viroqua city[58]	3 716	3 739
Viroqua town[58]	1 663	1 544
Webster town	594	520
Westby city[58]	1 797	1 568
Wheatland town[58]	407	393
Whitestown town	418	490
Vilas County[59]	16 535	10 958
Arbor Vitae town	2 303	982
Boulder Junction town	934	607
Cloverland town	692	305
Conover town	826	543
Eagle River city[59]	1 326	1 326
Lac du Flambeau town[59]	2 190	1 669
Land O'Lakes town	803	617
Lincoln town[59]	2 262	1 450
Manitowish Waters town	625	509
Phelps town	1 129	876
Plum Lake town	408	356
Presque Isle town	390	294
St. Germain town	1 176	473
Washington town	1 100	711
Winchester town	371	240
Walworth County[60]	71 507	63 444
Bloomfield town[60]	3 288	2 481
Pell Lake (CDP)	1 826	1 284
Powers Lake (CDP) (pt.)	320	...
Burlington city (pt.)[60]	–	...
Darien town[60]	1 495	1 413
Darien village	1 152	839
Delavan city[60]	5 684	5 526
Delavan town[60]	4 182	3 798
Delavan Lake (CDP) (pt.)	1 936	2 124
East Troy town[60]	3 583	2 743
Potter Lake (CDP)	1 068	...
East Troy village[60]	2 385	1 711
Elkhorn city[60]	4 605	3 992
Fontana-on-Geneva Lake village[60]	1 764	1 464
Geneva town[60]	3 933	3 490
Como (CDP)	1 376	1 132
Genoa City village[60]	1 202	1 085
Lafayette town[60]	1 024	979
La Grange town	1 661	1 311
Lake Geneva city[60]	5 607	4 890
Linn town[60]	2 053	1 910
Lyons town[60]	2 664	2 143
Richmond town	1 649	1 251
Sharon town	945	1 058
Sharon village	1 280	1 216
Spring Prairie town[60]	1 777	1 197
Sugar Creek town[60]	2 599	1 811
Troy town	1 794	1 265
Walworth town[60]	1 443	1 370
Delavan Lake (CDP) (pt.)	146	...
Walworth village[60]	1 607	1 637
Whitewater city (pt.)[60]	9 098	10 129
Whitewater town[60]	1 270	1 181
Williams Bay village[60]	1 763	1 554
Washburn County[61]	13 174	10 601
Barronett town	371	366
Bashaw town[61]	724	527
Bass Lake town	252	211
Beaver Brook town	603	400
Birchwood town	252	196
Birchwood village	437	394
Brooklyn town	273	191
Casey town	404	280
Chicog town	168	156
Crystal town	276	225
Evergreen town	798	561
Frog Creek town	142	125
Gull Lake town	141	111
Long Lake town	508	422
Madge town	317	144
Minong town[61]	761	445
Minong village[61]	557	420
Sarona town	394	352
Shell Lake city	1 135	928
Spooner city[61]	2 365	2 444
Spooner town[61]	600	351
Springbrook town	441	410
Stinnett town	179	134
Stone Lake town	379	339
Trego town	697	469
Washington County[62]	84 848	63 839
Addison town	2 834	2 375
Barton town[62]	2 493	1 624
Erin town	2 455	1 641
Farmington town	2 386	1 734
Germantown town[62]	267	416
Germantown town[62]	10 729	6 974
Hartford city[62]	7 046	6 499
Hartford town[62]	3 382	2 368
Jackson town[62]	3 180	2 844

County Subdivisions

County Subdivisions	1980	1970
Washington County—Con.		
Jackson village[62]	1 817	561
Kewaskum town[62]	1 243	1 166
Kewaskum village[62]	2 381	1 926
Milwaukee city (pt.)	2	...
Newburg village (pt.)[62]	688	...
Polk town[62]	3 486	2 846
Richfield town[62]	8 390	5 923
Slinger village[62]	1 612	1 216
Trenton town[62]	3 914	3 178
Wayne town	1 471	1 214
West Bend city[62]	21 484	16 555
West Bend town[62]	3 588	2 779
Waukesha County[63]	280 326	231 335
Big Bend village	1 345	1 148
Brookfield city[63]	34 035	31 761
Brookfield town[63]	4 364	4 303
Butler village	2 059	2 261
Chenequa village	532	642
Delafield city[63]	4 083	3 182
Delafield town[63]	4 597	3 750
Dousman village[63]	1 153	451
Eagle town	1 758	1 250
Eagle village	1 008	745
Elm Grove village	6 735	7 201
Genesee town[63]	5 126	3 172
Hartland village[63]	5 559	2 763
Lac La Belle village[63]	289	227
Lannon village	987	1 056
Lisbon town[63]	8 352	4 709
Menomonee Falls village	27 845	31 697
Merton town[63]	6 025	4 424
Okauchee Lake (CDP) (pt.)	155	173
Merton village[63]	1 045	646
Mukwonago town[63]	4 979	1 930
Mukwonago village[63]	4 014	2 367
Muskego city	15 277	11 573
Nashotah village	513	410
New Berlin city	30 529	26 910
North Prairie village	938	669
Oconomowoc city[63]	9 909	8 741
Oconomowoc town[63]	7 340	6 010
Okauchee Lake (CDP) (pt.)	3 747	2 961
Oconomowoc Lake village[63]	524	599
Ottawa town[63]	2 795	1 698
Pewaukee town[63]	8 922	7 551
Pewaukee village[63]	4 637	3 271
Summit town[63]	4 173	3 809
Okauchee Lake (CDP) (pt.)	56	...
Sussex village[63]	3 482	2 758
Vernon town	6 372	2 857
Wales village[63]	1 992	691
Waukesha city[63]	50 319	39 695
Waukesha town[63]	6 714	4 408
Waupaca County[64]	42 831	37 780
Bear Creek town	820	861
Big Falls village	107	112
Caledonia town	1 040	882
Clintonville city[64]	4 567	4 600
Dayton town	1 514	979
Dupont town	615	645
Embarrass village[64]	496	472
Farmington town	2 959	2 242
Fremont town[64]	618	514
Fremont village[64]	510	598
Harrison town	450	379
Helvetia town	568	401
Iola town[64]	702	549
Iola village[64]	957	900
Larrabee town[64]	1 254	1 295
Lebanon town	1 168	906
Lind town[64]	1 038	787
Little Wolf town[64]	1 138	1 089
Manawa city[64]	1 205	1 105
Marion city	1 348	1 218
Matteson town[64]	844	737
Mukwa town	1 946	1 208
New London city (pt.)	4 941	4 433
Ogdensburg village	214	206
Royalton town[64]	1 432	1 205
St. Lawrence town	608	517
Scandinavia town[64]	772	519
Scandinavia village	292	268
Union town	784	774
Waupaca city[64]	4 472	4 342
Waupaca town[64]	1 040	830
Weyauwega city[64]	1 549	1 377
Weyauwega town[64]	559	538
Wyoming town	304	292
Waushara County[65]	18 526	14 795
Aurora town[65]	890	802
Berlin city (pt.)[65]	91	41
Bloomfield town	931	798
Coloma town	437	382
Coloma village	367	336
Dakota town[65]	994	752

County Subdivisions

	1980	1970
Waushara County—Con.		
Deerfield town	445	367
Hancock town[65]	426	346
Hancock village[65]	419	404
Leon town	844	651
Lohrville village[65]	336	'213
Marion town[65]	1 333	877
Mount Morris town	685	517
Oasis town[65]	403	346
Plainfield town	574	447
Plainfield village[65]	813	642
Poysippi town	913	823
Redgranite village[65]	976	645
Richford town	404	322
Rose town	515	319
Saxeville town	776	612
Springwater town	924	584
Warren town[65]	573	'637
Wautoma city[65]	1 629	1 624
Wautoma town[65]	1 087	723
Wild Rose village	741	585
Winnebago County[66]	131 703	'129 946
Algoma town[66]	3 249	3 158
Appleton city (pt.)[66]	17	'—
Black Wolf town	2 318	'2 127
Clayton town	2 353	1 771
Menasha city[66]	14 728	'14 836
Menasha town[66]	12 226	'8 682
Neenah city[66]	22 432	'22 902
Neenah town[66]	2 864	'2 942
Nekimi town[66]	1 516	1 193
Nepeuskun town	682	743
Omro city[66]	2 763	2 341
Omro town[66]	1 684	1 444
Oshkosh city[66]	49 620	'53 082
Oshkosh town[66]	4 420	4 943
Winnebago (CDP)	1 433	...
Poygan town	898	734
Rushford town	1 420	1 415
Utica town	1 038	1 029
Vinland town	1 632	1 472
Winchester town	1 261	1 209
Winneconne town[66]	1 595	1 408
Winneconne village[66]	1 935	'1 611
Wolf River town	1 052	904
Wood County[67]	72 799	65 362
Arpin town[67]	764	1 088
Arpin village[67]	361	...
Auburndale town	942	911
Auburndale village	641	468
Biron village	698	771
Cameron town[67]	590	503
Cary town	382	343
Cranmoor town	234	248
Dexter town	429	341
Grand Rapids town[67]	7 319	5 147
Lake Wazeecha (CDP)	2 176	1 285
Hansen town	705	712
Hewitt village[67]	470	...
Hiles town	194	189
Lincoln town[67]	1 269	1 232
Marshfield city (pt.)[67]	18 053	15 560
Marshfield town[67]	784	1 056
Milladore town	760	728
Milladore village (pt.)	240	229
Nekoosa city	2 519	2 409
Pittsville city	810	708
Port Edwards town	1 387	1 076
Port Edwards village	2 077	2 126
Remington town	299	319
Richfield town	1 235	1 054
Rock town	745	607
Rudolph town[67]	1 385	1 340
Rudolph village[67]	392	349
Saratoga town	4 363	2 978
Seneca town	1 245	1 077
Sherry town	790	742
Sigel town	1 332	1 358
Vesper village	554	355
Wisconsin Rapids city[67]	17 995	18 587
Wood town	836	751

WYOMING

The name of this state is derived from an Indian word signifying "great plains."

The first white men to visit the region now constituting Wyoming were two Frenchmen, sons of Sieur de la Verendrye, a Canadian, who made explorations in 1743. The first permanent settlement was made in 1834, when Fort Williams later called Fort Laramie, was established as a trading post.

That part of the present state lying east of the Rocky Mountains was originally included in the vast area known as Louisiana, which was ceded by France to Spain in 1762, retroceded to France in 1800, and purchased by the United States in 1803. That part lying south of the forty-second parallel and west of a line drawn due north from the source of the Arkansas River orginally belonged to Spain but became a part of Mexico in 1821, when that country achieved its independence. The eastern part of this area, about a degree of longitude in width, formed a part of Texas from 1836, when that state became independent of Mexico, to 1850, five years after it was annexed to the United States; the western part of the area was ceded to the United States by Mexico in 1848, at the close of the Mexican War. The rest of the area of the present state, comprising the tract north of the forty-second parallel and west of the Rocky Mountains, was originally included in the Oregon country, which was occupied jointly by the United States and Great Britain until 1846, when the latter nation relinquished its claim.

That part of Wyoming which was included in the Louisiana purchase belonged successively to the district of Louisiana (1804-5), the territory of Louisiana (1805-1812), the territory of Missouri (1812-1834), and the "Indian country" (1834-1854). The area west of the Rocky Mountains and south of the forty-second parallel was made a part of the territory of Utah at its organization in 1850, and in the same year the small amount of former Mexico and Texas territory which lay east of the Rocky Mountains was added to the Indian country. In 1854 the area east of the Rocky Mountains was taken with other land to form the territory of Nebraska, and in 1861 the region east of the Rocky Mountains and north of the forty-third parallel was made a part of the territory of Dakota, while the region south of this parallel, extending west from the mountains to the one hundred and tenth meridian, was added to Nebraska. The region north of the forty-second parallel and west of the Rocky Mountains belonged to Oregon territory from 1848 to 1859 and to Washington territory from 1859 to 1863, with the exception of a small area which was transferred from Washington to Nebraska territory in 1861.

In 1863 all the present area of Wyoming except a section in the southwest corner, 1° of latitude in length and 1° of longitude in width, was included with the territory then organized as Idaho, and in 1864 all the present area except a strip 1° of longitude in width, extending from the forty-second parallel northward to the Rocky Mountains, was transferred from Idaho to Dakota.

In 1868 Wyoming, with boundaries as at present, was organized as a territory, and in 1890 became a state of the Union.

COUNTY LOCATION INDEX

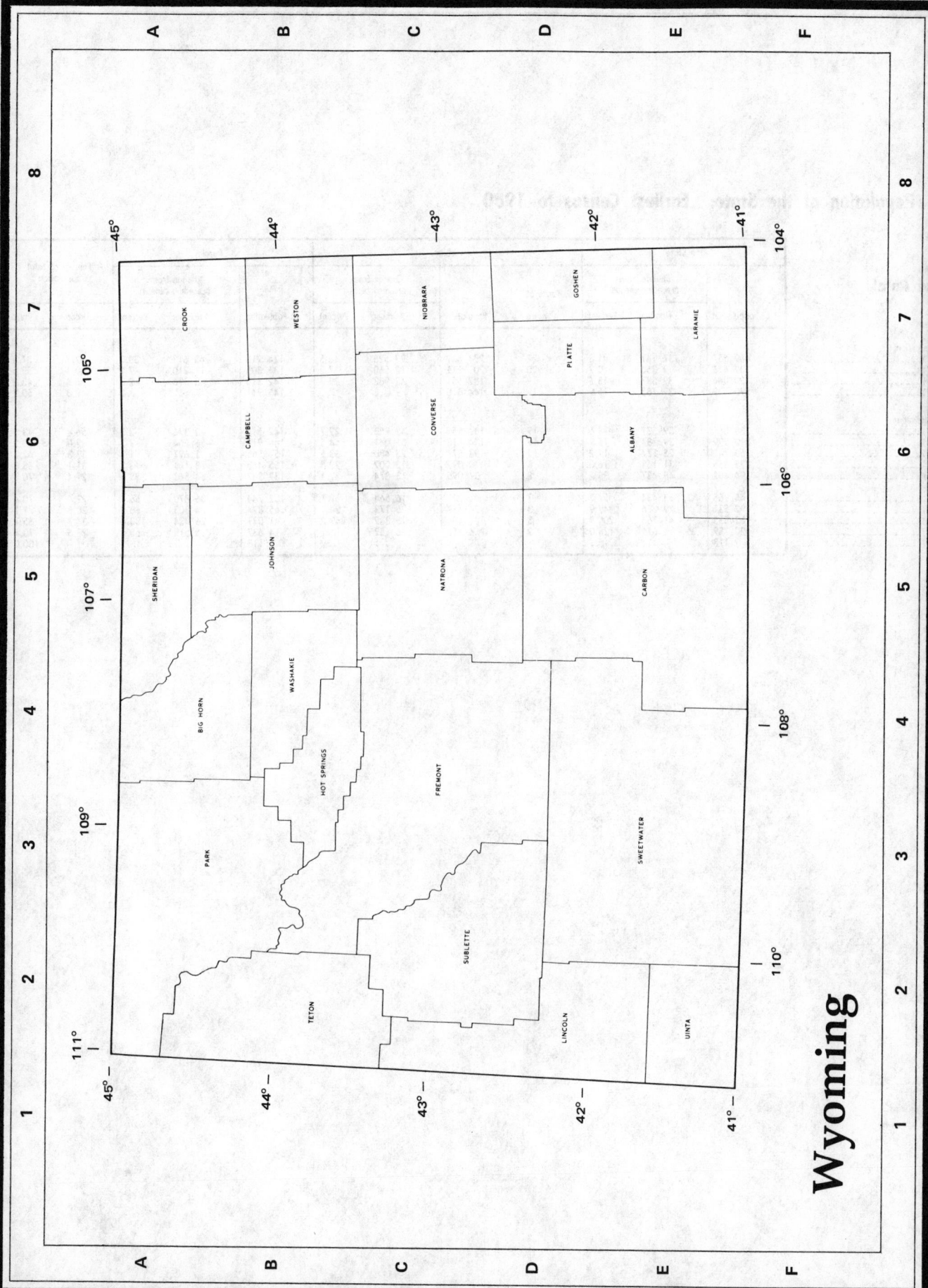

Wyoming

Population of the State: Earliest Census to 1980

Urban and Rural

	The State			Urban					Rural			Percent of total population	
	Total population	Change from preceding census		Places of 2,500 or more	Population	Change from preceding census		Population	Change from preceding census			Urban	Rural
		Number	Percent			Number	Percent		Number	Percent			
Current urban definition:													
1980 (Apr. 1)	469 557	137 141	41.3	27	294 639	93 528	46.5	174 918	43 613	33.2		62.7	37.3
1970 (Apr. 1)	332 416	2 350	0.7	20	201 111	13 560	7.2	131 305	−11 210	−7.9		60.5	39.5
1960 (Apr. 1)	330 066	39 537	13.6	19	187 551	42 933	29.7	142 515	−3 396	−2.3		56.8	43.2
1950 (Apr. 1)	290 529	39 787	15.9	19	144 618	...	...	145 911	...	...		49.8	50.2
Previous urban definition:													
1960 (Apr. 1)	330 066	39 537	13.6	19	187 551	42 933	29.7	142 515	−3 396	−2.3		56.8	43.2
1950 (Apr. 1)	290 529	39 787	15.9	19	144 618	51 041	54.5	145 911	−11 254	−7.2		49.8	50.2
1940 (Apr. 1)	250 742	25 177	11.2	12	93 577	23 480	33.5	157 165	1 697	1.1		37.3	62.7
1930 (Apr. 1)	225 565	31 163	16.0	8	70 097	13 002	22.8	155 468	18 161	13.2		31.1	68.9
1920 (Jan. 1)	194 402	48 437	33.2	8	57 095	13 874	32.1	137 307	34 563	33.6		29.4	70.6
1910 (Apr. 15)	145 965	53 434	57.7	7	43 221	16 564	62.1	102 744	36 870	56.0		29.6	70.4
1900 (June 1)	92 531	29 976	47.9	3	26 657	5 173	24.1	65 874	24 803	60.4		28.8	71.2
1890 (June 1)	62 555	41 766	200.9	3	21 484	15 332	249.2	41 071	26 434	180.6		34.3	65.7
1880 (June 1)	20 789	11 671	128.0	2	6 152	6 152	...	14 637	5 519	60.5		29.6	70.4
1870 (June 1)	9 118	...	...	−	−	...	...	9 118	...	...		−	100.0

ALBANY

1870	2,021
1880	4,626
1890	8,865
1900	13,084
1910	11,574
1920	9,283
1930	12,041
1940	13,946
1950	19,055
1960	21,290
1970	26,431
1980	29,062

BIG HORN

1900	4,328
1910	8,886
1920	12,105
1930	11,222
1940	12,911
1950	13,176
1960	11,898
1970	10,202
1980	11,896

CAMPBELL

1920	5,233
1930	6,720
1940	6,048
1950	4,839
1960	5,861
1970	12,957
1980	24,367

CARBON

1870	1,368
1880	3,438
1890	6,857
1900	9,589
1910	11,282
1920	9,525
1930	11,391
1940	12,644
1950	15,742
1960	14,937
1970	13,354
1980	21,896

CONVERSE

1890	2,738
1900	3,337
1910	6,294
1920	7,871
1930	7,145
1940	6,631
1950	5,593
1960	6,366
1970	5,938
1980	14,069

CROOK

1880	239
1890	2,338
1900	3,137
1910	6,492
1920	5,524
1930	5,333
1940	5,463
1950	4,738
1960	4,691

1970	4,535
1980	5,308

FREMONT

1890	2,463
1900	5,357
1910	11,882
1920	11,820
1930	10,490
1940	16,095
1950	19,580
1960	26,168
1970	28,352
1980	38,992

GOSHEN

1920	8,064
1930	11,754
1940	12,207
1950	12,634
1960	11,941
1970	10,885
1980	12,040

HOT SPRINGS

1920	5,164
1930	5,467
1940	4,607
1950	5,250
1960	6,365
1970	4,952
1980	5,710

JOHNSON

1880	637
1890	2,357
1900	2,361
1910	3,453
1920	4,617
1930	4,816
1940	4,980
1950	4,707
1960	5,475
1970	5,587
1980	6,700

LARAMIE

1870	2,957
1880	6,409
1890	16,777
1900	20,181
1910	26,127
1920	29,699
1930	26,845
1940	33,651
1950	47,662
1960	60,149
1970	56,360
1980	68,649

LINCOLN

1920	12,487
1930	10,894
1940	10,286
1950	9,023
1960	9,018
1970	8,640
1980	12,177

NATRONA

1890	1,094
1900	1,785
1910	4,776
1920	14,635
1930	24,272
1940	23,858
1950	31,437
1960	49,623
1970	51,264
1980	71,856

NIOBRARA

1920	6,321
1930	4,723
1940	5,988
1950	4,701
1960	3,750
1970	2,924
1980	2,924

PARK

1910	4,909
1920	7,298
1930	8,207
1940	10,976
1950	15,182
1960	16,874
1970	17,752
1980	21,639

PLATTE

1920	7,421
1930	9,695
1940	8,013
1950	9,925
1960	7,195
1970	6,486
1980	11,975

SHERIDAN

1890	1,972
1900	5,122
1910	16,324
1920	18,182
1930	16,875
1940	19,255
1950	20,185
1960	18,989
1970	17,852
1980	25,048

SUBLETTE

1930	1,944
1940	2,778
1950	2,481
1960	3,778
1970	3,775
1980	4,548

SWEETWATER

1870	1,916
1880	2,561
1890	4,941
1900	8,455
1910	11,575
1920	13,640
1930	18,165
1940	19,407

1950	22,017
1960	17,920
1970	18,391
1980	41,723

TETON

1930	2,003
1940	2,543
1950	2,593
1960	3,062
1970	4,823
1980	9,355

UINTA

1870	856
1880	2,879
1900	7,414
1910	16,982
1920	6,611
1930	6,572
1940	7,223
1950	7,331
1960	7,484
1970	7,100
1980	13,021

WASHAKIE

1920	3,106
1930	4,109
1940	5,858
1950	7,252
1960	8,883
1970	7,569
1980	9,496

WESTON

1890	2,422
1900	3,203
1910	4,960
1920	4,631
1930	4,673
1940	4,958
1950	6,733
1960	7,929
1970	6,307
1980	7,106

NOTES

JOHNSON

Name changed from Pease in 1879.

SWEETWATER

Name changed from Carter in 1869.

CASPER

1890	544
1900	883
1910	2,639
1920	11,447
1930	16,619
1940	17,964
1950	23,673
1960	38,930
1970	39,361
1980	51,016

CHEYENNE

1870	1,450
1880	3,456
1890	11,690
1900	14,087
1910	11,320
1920	13,829
1930	17,361
1940	22,474
1950	31,935
1960	43,505
1970	41,254
1980	47,283

GILLETTE

1900	151
1910	448
1920	1,157
1930	1,340
1940	2,177
1950	2,191
1960	3,580
1970	7,194
1980	12,134

GREEN RIVER

1870	106
1880	327
1890	723
1900	1,361
1910	1,313
1920	2,140
1930	2,589
1940	2,640
1950	3,187
1960	3,497
1970	4,196
1980	12,807

LARAMIE

1880	2,696
1890	6,388
1900	8,207
1910	8,237
1920	6,301
1930	8,609
1940	10,627
1950	15,581
1960	17,520
1970	23,143
1980	24,410

RAWLINS

1870	40
1880	1,451
1890	2,235
1900	2,317
1910	4,256
1920	3,969
1930	4,850
1940	5,531
1950	7,415
1960	8,968
1970	7,855
1980	11,547

ROCK SPRINGS

1870	40
1880	763
1890	3,406
1900	4,363
1910	5,778
1920	6,456
1930	8,440
1940	9,827
1950	10,857
1960	10,371
1970	11,657
1980	19,458

SHERIDAN

1890	281
1900	1,559
1910	8,408
1920	9,175
1930	8,536
1940	10,529
1950	11,500
1960	11,651
1970	10,856
1980	15,146

CORRECTION NOTE

The official 1980 census counts of total population shown in
this report supersede counts issued previously. Corrections
to the figures were made after the counts were provided to
the State for redistricting purposes and released in Advance
Report PHC80-V for this State.

Shown below are corrections to the 1980 census counts of the
total population made after the tabulations for this report
were completed. Any additional corrections made after this
report is printed are available by writing to Data User
Services Division, Customer Services (Corrections), Bureau of
the Census, Washington, D.C. 20233.

The 1980 figures shown in this publication are subject to
change pending the outcome of the various lawsuits dealing
with the census counts.

	1980 population	
	As shown in the tables	Corrected
Fremont County:		
Wind River division:		
Riverton city...................	9 588	9 247
Natrona County:		
Casper South division:		
Evansville town...............	2 652	2 335

County Subdivisions	1980	1970
The State	469 557	332 416
Albany County[1]	29 062	26 431
East Albany division	198	...
Laramie division	27 142	...
Laramie city[1]	24 410	23 143
Rock River division	692	646
Rock River town[1]	415	344
South Albany division	1 030	...
Big Horn County[2]	11 896	10 202
Big Horn Central division	3 744	...
Greybull town	2 277	1 953
Big Horn North division	5 327	4 627
Byron town	633	397
Cowley town	455	366
Deaver town	178	112
Frannie town (pt.)	121	103
Lovell town[2]	2 447	2 371
Big Horn South division	2 825	...
Basin town[2]	1 349	1 145
Manderson town	174	117
Campbell County[3]	24 367	12 957
Gillette North division	18 853	...
Gillette city[3]	12 134	7 194
Prospector-Rawhide Village (CDP)	1 100	...
Gillette South division	5 514	...
Wright (CDP)	1 117	...
Carbon County[4]	21 896	13 354
Hanna division	4 555	...
Elk Mountain town[4]	338	127
Hanna town[4]	2 288	460
Medicine Bow town	953	455
Rawlins division	13 685	9 216
Baggs town[4]	433	146
Dixon town	82	72
Rawlins city[4]	11 547	7 855
Sinclair town	586	445
Saratoga division	3 656	...
Encampment town	611	321
Riverside town	55	46
Saratoga town	2 410	1 181
Converse County[5]	14 069	5 938
Douglas division	9 364	3 995
Douglas town[5]	6 030	2 677
Lost Springs town	9	7
Glenrock division	4 705	1 943
Glenrock town[5]	2 736	1 515
Crook County[6]	5 308	4 535
Hulett division	1 225	1 143
Hulett town	291	318
Moorcroft division	1 995	1 566
Moorcroft town	1 014	981
Sundance division	2 088	1 826
Sundance town[6]	1 087	1 056
Fremont County[7]	38 992	28 352
Dubois division	1 524	1 181
Dubois town[7]	1 067	898
Lander division	10 171	...
Hudson town (pt.)[7]	412	(NA)
Lander city[7]	7 867	7 125
Shoshoni division	1 236	773
Shoshoni town[7]	879	562
Sweetwater division	3 023	...
Jeffrey City (CDP)	1 882	...
Wind River division	23 038	...
Hudson town (pt.)	102	(NA)
Pavillion town	287	181
Riverton city[7]	9 588	7 995
Goshen County[8]	12 040	10 885
Goshen Hole division	1 313	1 304
La Grange town	232	189
Yoder town	110	101
Rawhide Creek division	368	...
Torrington division	10 359	...
Fort Laramie town[8]	356	197
Lingle town[8]	475	446
Torrington town[8]	5 441	4 237
Hot Springs County[9]	5 710	4 952
Thermopolis East division	655	...
East Thermopolis town	359	316
Thermopolis West division	4 936	...
Kirby town[9]	129	75
Thermopolis town[9]	3 852	3 063
Wind River division	119	...
Johnson County[10]	6 700	5 587
Buffalo division	5 641	4 570
Buffalo city[10]	3 799	3 394
Kaycee division	1 059	1 017
Kaycee town[10]	271	272
Laramie County[11]	68 649	56 360
Cheyenne division	58 265	...
Cheyenne city (pt.)[11]	47 264	ʳ41 254
Fox Farm (CDP)	2 850	1 329
Orchard Valley (CDP)	3 327	1 015
Cheyenne East division	2 307	...
Cheyenne city (pt.)[11]	-	...
Laramie County—Con.		
Cheyenne West division	5 310	...
Cheyenne city (pt.)[11]	19	...
Warren AFB (CDP)	3 627	4 527
Pine Bluffs division	2 767	...
Albin town	128	118
Burns town	268	185
Pine Bluffs town[11]	1 077	937
Lincoln County[12]	12 177	8 640
Afton division	6 135	...
Afton town[12]	1 481	1 290
Thayne town[12]	256	195
Kemmerer East division	5 100	...
Diamondville town[12]	1 000	485
Kemmerer town[12]	3 273	2 292
La Barge town[12]	302	...
Kemmerer West division	942	...
Cokeville town[12]	515	440
Natrona County[13]	71 856	51 264
Casper division	56 333	...
Casper city (pt.)[13]	49 651	39 361
Mills town[13]	2 139	1 724
Casper North division	4 261	...
Casper city (pt.)[13]	18	...
Edgerton town	510	350
Midwest town[13]	638	...
Casper South division	6 252	...
Casper city (pt.)[13]	1 336	...
Evansville town[13]	2 652	832
Hells Half Acre division	5 010	370
Casper city (pt.)[13]	11	...
Niobrara County[14]	2 924	2 924
Niobrara East division	1 235	1 938
Lusk town (pt.)[14]	842	1 495
Van Tassell town	10	21
Niobrara West division	1 689	986
Lusk town (pt.)[14]	808	...
Manville town	94	92
Park County[15]	21 639	17 752
Cody division	11 324	...
Cody city[15]	6 790	5 161
Meeteetse division	960	...
Meeteetse town	512	459
Powell division	8 930	...
Frannie town (pt.)	17	36
Powell city[15]	5 310	4 807
Yellowstone National Park division	425	400
Platte County[16]	11 975	6 486
Chugwater division	598	531
Chugwater town[16]	282	187
Glendo division	790	497
Glendo town	367	210
Guernsey division	1 991	1 495
Guernsey town[16]	1 512	793
Hartville town	149	246
Wheatland division	8 596	3 963
Wheatland town[16]	5 816	2 498
Sheridan County[17]	25 048	17 852
Sheridan division	18 961	...
Clearmont town	191	141
Sheridan city[17]	15 146	10 856
Sheridan South division	3 851	...
Sheridan West division	2 236	...
Dayton town[17]	701	396
Ranchester town[17]	655	208
Sublette County[18]	4 548	3 755
Big Piney division	1 876	1 518
Big Piney town[18]	530	570
Marbleton town[18]	537	223
Boulder division	194	163
Pinedale division	2 478	2 074
Pinedale town[18]	1 066	948
Sweetwater County[19]	41 723	18 391
Green River North division	14 734	...
Granger town[19]	177	137
Green River city[19]	12 807	4 196
Green River South division	180	...
Rock Springs North division	25 304	...
Rock Springs city (pt.)[19]	19 454	11 657
South Superior town	586	197
Rock Springs South division	190	...
Rock Springs city (pt.)[19]	4	...
Wamsutter division	1 315	494
Wamsutter town[19]	681	139
Teton County[20]	9 355	4 823
Alta division	225	158
Jackson Hole division	9 130	4 634
Jackson town[20]	4 511	ʳ2 688
Yellowstone National Park division	-	31
Uinta County[21]	13 021	7 100
Bridger Valley division	5 642	2 136
Lyman town[21]	2 284	643
Mountain View town[21]	628	...
Evanston division	7 379	4 964
Evanston city[21]	6 421	4 462

County Subdivisions

	1980	1970
Washakie County[22]	9 496	7 569
Ten Sleep division	862	...
Ten Sleep town[22]	407	320
Worland division	8 634	...
Worland city[22]	6 391	5 055
Weston County[23]	7 106	6 307
Newcastle division	5 532	4 872
Newcastle city[23]	3 596	3 432
Upton division	1 574	1 435
Upton town[23]	1 193	987

84-00110 .